W9-CTW-420

Contemporary Authors

Contemporary Authors

A BIO-BIBLIOGRAPHICAL GUIDE TO
CURRENT AUTHORS AND THEIR WORKS

CLARE D. KINSMAN
Editor

volumes 49-52

GALE RESEARCH COMPANY • THE BOOK TOWER • DETROIT, MICHIGAN 48226

CONTEMPORARY AUTHORS

Published by
Gale Research Company, Book Tower, Detroit, Michigan 48226
Each Year's Volumes Are Cumulated and Revised About Five Years Later

Frederick G. Ruffner, *Publisher*
James M. Ethridge, *Editorial Director*

Clare D. Kinsman, *Editor*
Cynthia R. Fadool and Alexander James Roman, *Associate Editors*
Adele C. Sarkissian and Phyllis Carmel Mendelson, *Assistant Editors*
Anne Commire, *Consultant*
Eunice Bergin, *Copy Editor*
Laura Bryant, *Operations Supervisor*
Daphne Cox, *Production Manager*

WRITERS

Linda Cairo, Laurelyn Niebuhr,
Mary Reif Stevenson, Benjamin True

EDITORIAL ASSISTANTS

Norma Sawaya, Shirley Seip

ISBN 0-8103-0024-9

CONTEMPORARY AUTHORS

**Indicates that a listing has been compiled from secondary sources believed to be reliable, but has not been personally verified for this edition by the author sketched.*

AAKER, David A(llen) 1938-

PERSONAL: Born February 11, 1938, in Fargo, N.D.; married, 1963; children: two. *Education:* Massachusetts Institute of Technology, B.S., 1960; Stanford University, M.S., 1967, Ph.D., 1969. *Home:* 18 Eastwood Dr., Orinda, Calif. *Office:* School of Business Administration, University of California, Berkeley, Calif. 94720.

CAREER: Texas Instruments, Inc., Houston, Tex., cost engineer, 1960-61, sales engineer, 1961-63, product sales manager, 1963-65; Stanford University, Stanford, Calif., instructor in statistics, 1967; University of California, Berkeley, acting assistant professor, 1968-69, assistant professor, 1969-72, associate professor of marketing statistics, 1972—. *Member:* American Marketing Association, American Statistical Association, Institute of Management Sciences, Tau Beta Pi. *Awards, honors:* Special merit award from Thompson Gold Medal Competition, 1972.

WRITINGS: (Editor and contributor) *Multivariate Analysis in Marketing: Theory and Application,* Wadsworth, 1971; (editor with George S. Day) *Consumerism: Search for the Consumer Interest,* Free Press, 1971, 2nd edition, 1974; (with others) *Modern Marketing,* Random House, in press; (with John G. Myers) *Advertising Management: An Analytical Approach,* Prentice-Hall, in press.

Contributor of about twenty articles and reviews to business journals, including *Management Science, Harvard Business Review, Journal of Advertising Research, Journal of Marketing Research,* and *Journal of Marketing.* Member of editorial board of *Journal of Marketing Research,* 1969—; associate editor of *Management Science,* 1971—; member of editorial board of *Journal of Business Research,* 1973—.

* * *

AASENG, Rolf E(dward) 1923-

PERSONAL: Surname is pronounced *Aw*-sing; born November 28, 1923, in McIntosh, Minn. *Education:* Concordia College, Moorhead, Minn., B.A., 1948; Luther Theological Seminary, St. Paul, Minn., B.Th., 1950; New York Theological Seminary, S.T.M., 1958. *Home:* 2450 Cavell Ave. S., St. Louis Park, Minn. 55426.

CAREER: Pastor of Lutheran church in Park Rapids, Minn., 1951-57; *Lutheran Teacher,* Minneapolis, Minn., editor, 1958-60; *Lutheran Standard,* Minneapolis, associate editor, 1960—. President, Lutheran Church Library Association, 1966; chairman of St. Louis Park Human Rights Commission, 1972-74. *Military service:* U.S. Army, 1943-46.

WRITINGS: *Anyone Can Teach (They Said),* Augsburg, 1964; *The Sacred Sixty-Six,* Augsburg, 1966; *Blessed to Be a Blessing,* American Lutheran Church Women, 1969; *God Is Great, God Is Good,* Augsburg, 1971; *Jesus Loves Me, This I Know,* Augsburg, 1972; *Come, Lord Jesus,* Augsburg, in press.

* * *

ABDALLAH, Omar
See HUMBARACI, D(emir) Arslan

* * *

ABELL, Kathleen 1938-

PERSONAL: Born September 8, 1938, in Timmins, Ontario, Canada; daughter of Harry Robert (a teacher) and Jean (a teacher; maiden name, Millican) Jenkins; married Norman Abell (an orthopedic surgeon), July 22, 1961; children: Leslie, Robert, Caroline, Kirsten. *Education:* McGill University, B.A. (honors), 1961. *Religion:* None. *Home:* 6 Farmingdale Rd., Willowdale, Ontario M2K IZ2, Canada.

WRITINGS: *King Orville and the Bullfrogs,* Little, Brown, 1974.

* * *

ABELLA, Irving Martin 1940-

PERSONAL: Born July 2, 1940, in Toronto, Ontario, Canada; son of Louis (a merchant) and Esther (Shiff) Abella; married Rosie Silberman (a lawyer), December 8, 1968; children: Jacob Julian. *Education:* University of Toronto, B.A., 1963, M.A., 1964, Ph.D., 1969. *Home:* 375 Glengrove, Toronto, Ontario, Canada. *Office:* Glendon College, York University, Toronto 12, Ontario, Canada.

CAREER: York University, Toronto, Ontario, instructor, 1968-69, assistant professor, 1969-72, associate professor, 1972-74, professor of history in Glendon College, 1974—.

WRITINGS: *Nationalism, Communism, and Canadian Labour,* University of Toronto Press, 1973; *On Strike: Six*

Key Labour Disputes in Canadian History, James, Lewis, & Samuel, 1974.

* * *

ABRAMSON, Martin 1921-

PERSONAL: Born January 25, 1921, in New York, N.Y.; son of Jacob and Bessie (Horwitz) Abramson; married Marcia Zagon (an executive director of a social agency), May 9, 1948; children: Barry, Jill. *Education:* Attended City College (now City College of the City University of New York), 1941, Columbia University, 1942, and University of California, 1943. *Home:*827 Peninsula Blvd., Woodmere, N.Y. 11598. *Agent:* Julian Bach, 3 East 48th St., New York, N.Y. 10017. *Office:* 1 Old Country Rd., Carle Place, N.Y.

CAREER: Former feature writer and sports writer; feature writer for New York *Herald-Tribune* Sunday magazine; writer for "We the People" television show, for NBC-TV interview shows, and for Armed Forces radio. Lecturer on journalism and public relations at Long Island University. *Military service:* U.S. Army, field correspondent, 1943-45. *Member:* Overseas Press Club, Society of Magazine Writers.

WRITINGS: The Real Al Jolson, Universal Publishing, 1955; *The Barney Ross Story,* Lippincott, 1959; *The Padre of Guadalcanal Story,* Funk 1965; *Hollywood Surgeon,* Downe Publishing, 1971; *Forgotten Fortunes,* Downe Publishing, 1973; *The Trial of Chaplain Jensen,* Arbor House, 1974. Contributor to United Feature Newspaper Syndicate and to national magazines.

* * *

ABSE, David Wilfred 1915-

PERSONAL: Born March 15, 1915, in Cardiff, Wales; married Elizabeth Smith; children: Edward, Nathan. *Education:* University of Wales, B.S., 1935, M.D., 1948; Welsh National School of Medicine, B.Med. and B.Surgery, 1938; University of London, diploma in psychological medicine, 1940; postdoctoral study at London Institute of Psychoanalysis, 1948-51, and Washington Psychoanalytic Institute, 1957-60. *Home:* 1852 Winston Rd., Charlottesville, Va. 22903. *Office:* Department of Psychiatry, School of Medicine, University of Virginia, Charlottesville, Va. 22901.

CAREER: Cardiff Royal Infirmary, Cardiff, Wales, intern, 1938; University of London, Institute of Psychiatry, London, England, resident, 1939-40; West-End Hospital for Nervous Disorders, London, England, resident, 1941; Postgraduate School of Medicine, London, England, resident, 1942; Westminster Hospital, London, England, honorary clinical assistant, 1942-43; Monmouthshire Mental Hospital, Abergavenny, England, deputy medical superintendent, 1947-48; Charing Cross Hospital, School of Medicine, London, England, chief assistant psychiatrist, 1949-51; University of North Carolina, Chapel Hill, clinical assistant professor, 1952-53, associate professor, 1953-57, professor of psychiatry, 1958-62, director of postgraduate education in psychiatry, 1957-59; University of Virginia, Charlottesville, professor of psychiatry, 1962—. Lecturer at City College (London, England), 1950-51; clinical director of Dorothea Dix State Hospital, 1952-53; member of faculty of Washington Psychoanalytic Institute, 1962—, and Washington School of Psychiatry, 1971—. *Military service:* British Army, Medical Corps, 1942-46, teaching psychiatrist, 1942-45, commanding officer of mental hospital, 1945-46; served in India; became major.

MEMBER: International Psychoanalytical Association, American Medical Association, American Psychiatric Association (fellow), American Psychoanalytic Association, Royal Society of Medicine (fellow), Royal College of Psychiatrists (founding fellow), British Medical Association, British Psychological Society (fellow), Virginia Psychoanalytic Study Group (chairman).

WRITINGS: The Diagnosis of Hysteria, John Wright, 1950; (contributor) Cecily Wakely, editor, *Year Book of Treatment of 1950,* Medical Press, 1952.

(Contributor) Stephen R. Graubard and Gerald Holten, editors, *Excellence and Leadership in a Democracy,* Columbia University Press, 1962; (editor with Ethel Nash and Lucie Jessner, and contributor) *Marriage Counseling in Medical Practice,* University of North Carolina Press, 1964; (contributor) D. M. Kissen and L. L. Leshan, editors, *Psychosomatic Aspects of Neoplastic Disease,* Pitman, 1964; *Hysteria and Related Mental Disorders,* John Wright, 1966.

Speech and Reason: Language Disorder in Mental Disease, University Press of Virginia, 1971; *Clinical Notes on Group-Analytic Psychotherapy,* John Wright, 1973. Contributor to *Encyclopedia on Hysteria, Handbook of Medical Psychology,* and *American Handbook of Psychiatry.* Contributor of about forty articles to professional journals, including *Psychosomatic Medicine, Group Analysis, British Journal of Social Psychiatry, Human Sexuality, Fertility and Sterility,* and *International Journal of Social Psychiatry.*

WORK IN PROGRESS: Research on the personality and behavioral characteristics of patients with lung cancer.

* * *

ACKER, William R. B. 1910(?)-1974

1910(?)—April 20, 1974; American professor of Chinese language and culture. Obituaries: *New York Times,* April 25, 1974; *Washington Post,* April 25, 1974.

* * *

ACZEL, Tamas 1921-

PERSONAL: Born December 16, 1921, in Budapest, Hungary; son of Joseph and Cornelia (Fabian) Aczel; married Eva Kadar, 1947 (divorced, 1956); married Olga Gyarmati, 1959; children: (first marriage) Julia (Mrs. Lorant Szucs); (second marriage) Thomas George. *Education:* University of Budapest, B.A., 1948; Eotvos Lorant University, M.A., 1950. *Residence:* Amherst, Mass. *Agent:* Curtis Brown Ltd., 60 East 56th St., New York, N.Y. 10022. *Office:* Department of English, University of Massachusetts, Amherst, Mass. 01002.

CAREER: Spark Publishing House, Budapest, Hungary, editor-in-chief, 1948-50; Eotvos Lorant University, Budapest, Hungary, lecturer in modern literature, 1950-53; Hungarian Academy of Dramatic Art, Budapest, Hungary, professor of the history of drama, 1953-55; *Hungarian Literary Gazette,* London, England, editor, 1957-62; University of Massachusetts, Amherst, professor of English, 1966—. *Member:* Modern Language Association of America, American Association for the Advancement of Slavic Studies, American Association of University Professors, P.E.N. Club in Exile, Hungarian Writers Association (secretary, 1953-55). *Awards, honors:* Kossuth Prize for Poetry, 1949, for *Eberseg, huseg;* Stalin Prize for Literature, 1952, for *A szabadsag arnyekaban.*

WRITINGS: Enek a hajon (poetry; title means "A Song on the Ship"), Officina (Budapest), 1942; *A szabadsag arnyekaban* (fiction; title means "In the Shadow of Liberty"), Szikra (Budapest), 1947, 2nd edition, Athenaeum (Budapest), 1949; *Eberseg, huseg* (poetry; title means "Vigilance and Faith"), Hungaria (Budapest), 1949; *Vihar es napsutes* (novel; title means "Storm and Sunshine"), Szepirodalmi (Budapest), 1950; *Jelentes helyett* (poetry; title means "In Lieu of a Report"), Szepirodalmi, 1951; *Lang es parazs* (novel; title means "Flames and Ashes"), Szepirodalmi, 1953; *A foldrenges nyomaban* (essays; title means "In the Wake of the Tremor"), Szepirodalmi, 1955.

(With Tibor Meray) *The Revolt of the Mind: A Case History of Intellectual Resistance Behind the Iron Curtain,* Praeger, 1960; *The Ice Age* (novel), translation by John Simon and others, Simon & Schuster, 1965; (editor and contributor) *Ten Years After: A Commemoration of the Tenth Anniversary of the Hungarian Revolution,* Macgibbon & Kee, 1966, published as *Ten Years After: The Hungarian Revolution in the Perspective of History,* Holt, 1967; (translator with Laszlo Tikos) *Szabadsag a ho alatt* (poetry; title means "Freedom Under the Snow: An Anthology of Russian Underground Poetry"), Aurora Koenyvek (Munich), 1968; (translator and editor with Joseph Langland and Tikos) *Poetry from the Russian Underground: A Bilingual Anthology,* Harper, 1973. Also author of filmscript, "Two in an Apartment," 1956. Contributor to *Life, Figaro Literaire, Massachusetts Review, Forum, Saturday Review,* and other periodicals in United States and Europe. Editor-in-chief, *Star* (Budapest), 1950-53.

WORK IN PROGRESS: God's Vineyard, an autobiographical essay; an untitled novel, completion expected in 1976; *Hungary: A Cultural History.*

* * *

ADACHI, Barbara (Curtis) 1924-
(Catherine Anthony)

PERSONAL: Surname rhymes with "apache"; born July 16, 1924, in Harbin, China; daughter of John Libby (a banker) and Alice (Perkins) Curtis; married James Shogo Adachi (a lawyer), June 1, 1949; children: Catherine Anthony, Daniel Curtis. *Education:* Smith College, B.A., 1945. *Religion:* Episcopalian. *Home:* 19-3, Akasaka 6-chome, Minato-ku, Tokyo, Japan.

CAREER: Mainichi Daily News, Tokyo, Japan, writer of regular columns, "Hands of Japan" (under pseudonym Catherine Anthony) and "Something Different," 1971—. *Member:* International House, College Women's Association of Japan, Japan American Society, Asiatic Society of Japan.

WRITINGS: The Living Treasures of Japan, Kodansha International, 1973.

WORK IN PROGRESS: A cookbook with reminiscences of life in Harbin and Tokyo; research on Japanese theatre and arts; interviews of traditional craftsmen and performing artists.

SIDELIGHTS: Barbara Adachi told *CA:* "I have a great interest in the U.S.S.R. where I have traveled at length twice (once by Trans-Siberian R.R.) since I spoke Russian as a child in Harbin and followed Russian studies in college. My greatest interest, however, continues to lie in the field of traditional Japanese crafts and in Japanese theatre, particularly the puppet theatre (Bunraku). Although we both speak Japanese, my husband and I are U.S. citizens."

* * *

ADAIR, John G(lenn) 1933-

PERSONAL: Born December 19, 1933, in San Antonio, Tex.; son of Charles Glenn and Lucie (Berlon) Adair; married Carolyn Johnson, August 13, 1960; children: Leslie, Colin, Heidi, Joel. *Education:* Trinity University, B.S., 1954, M.S., 1956; University of Iowa, Ph.D., 1965. *Home:* 14 Tunis Bay, Winnipeg, Manitoba, Canada. *Office:* Department of Psychology, University of Manitoba, Winnipeg, Manitoba, Canada.

CAREER: Public school teacher of mathematics in San Antonio, Tex., 1957-59; Dakota Wesleyan University, Mitchell, assistant professor of psychology, 1959-63; University of Iowa, Iowa City, instructor in psychology, 1964-65; University of Manitoba, Winnipeg, Manitoba, assistant professor, 1965-66, associate professor, 1966-73, professor of psychology and head of department, 1973—. Visiting professor at University of Colorado, 1971-72. *Member:* Canadian Psychological Association, Canadian Association of University Professors, Manitoba Psychologocial Association (vice-president, 1968-69; president, 1969-70), American Psychological Association, Midwest Psychological Association, South Dakota Psychological Association, Sigma Xi.

WRITINGS: The Human Subject: The Social Psychology of the Psychological Experiment, Little, Brown, 1973. Contributor to proceedings and to *Psychological Reports, Canadian Psychologist, Journal of Experimental Research in Personality, Canadian Journal of Behavioral Science, Journal of Experimental Social Psychology,* and *American Psychologist.*

WORK IN PROGRESS: Editing *Social Psychology of the Experiment,* with Monte Page, for publication by University of Nebraska Press.

* * *

ADAMS, Adrienne 1906-

PERSONAL: Born February 8, 1906, in Fort Smith, Ark.; daughter of Edwin Hunt (an accountant) and Sue (Broaddus) Adams; married John Lonzo Anderson (a writer, under name Lonzo Anderson), August 17, 1935. *Education:* Stephens College, B.A., 1925; attended University of Missouri, 1927, American School of Design, New York, 1926. *Residence:* Glen Gardner, N.J.

CAREER: Artist, illustrator, author of children's books. Taught in a rural school in Oklahoma, 1927; moved to New York City in 1929, working as a free-lance designer of displays, murals, textiles, greeting cards, and other materials, 1929-45; Staples-Smith Displays, New York, N.Y., decorator of furniture and murals, and art director, 1945-52; full-time illustrator, 1952—. *Awards, honors:* Runner-up for Caldecott Medal, 1960, for illustration of *Houses from the Sea,* and 1962, for illustration of *The Day We Saw the Sun Come Up;* Rutgers Award from Rutgers University College of Library Services, 1973, for contributions to children's literature.

WRITINGS—Self-illustrated: *A Woggle of Witches,* Scribner, 1971; (compiler) *Poetry of Earth,* Scribner, 1972.

Illustrator: Lonzo Anderson, *Bag of Smoke,* Viking, 1942,

new edition, Knopf, 1968; Patricia Gordon, *The 13th Is Magic,* Lothrop, 1950; Gordon, *The Summer is Magic,* Lothrop, 1952; Elizabeth Fraser Torjesen, *Captain Ramsay's Daughter,* Lothrop, 1953; Elizabeth Rogers, *Angela of Angel Court,* Crowell, 1954; Rumer Godden, *Impunity Jane,* Viking, 1954; Mary Kennedy, *Jenny,* Lothrop, 1954; Norma Simon, *The Baby House,* Lippincott, 1955; Beth Lipkin, *The Blue Mountain,* Knopf, 1956; Godden, *The Fairy Doll,* Viking, 1956; Priscilla Friedrich, *The Easter Bunny that Overslept,* Lothrop, 1957; Gordon, *The Light in the Tower,* Lothrop, 1957; Margaret Glover Otto, *Great Aunt Victoria's House,* Holt, 1957; Godden, *Mouse House,* Viking, 1957; Rachel Lyman Field, *The Rachel Field Story Book,* Doubleday, 1958; Godden, *Die Feenpuppe,* Boje Verlag, 1958; Godden, *The Story of Holly and Ivy,* Viking, 1958; Janice Udry, *Theodore's Parents,* Lothrop, 1958; Alice E. Goudey, *Houses from the Sea,* Scribner, 1959; Paula Hendrich, *Trudy's First Day at Camp,* Lothrop, 1959; Jeanne Massey, *The Little Witch,* Knopf, 1959.

Aileen Lucia Fisher, *Going Barefoot,* Crowell, 1960; Rumer Godden, *Candy Floss,* Viking, 1960; Jakob Ludwig Karl Grimm, *The Shoemaker and the Elves,* Scribner, 1960; Hans Christian Andersen, *Thumbelina,* Scribner, 1961; Fisher, *Where Does Everyone Go?,* Crowell, 1961; Alice E. Goudey, *The Day We Saw the Sun Come Up,* Scribner, 1961; Mary Francis Shura, *Mary's Marvelous Mouse,* Knopf, 1962; Clyde Robert Bulla, *What Makes a Shadow?,* Crowell, 1962; John Lonzo Anderson, compiler, *A Fifteenth Century Cookry Boke,* Scribner, 1962; W. Saboly, *Bring a Torch, Jeannette, Isabella,* Scribner, 1963; Virginia Haviland, *Favorite Fairy Tales Told in Scotland,* Little, Brown, 1963; Shura, *The Nearsighted Knight,* Knopf, 1964; Grimm, *Snow White and Rose Red,* Scribner, 1964; Goudey, *Butterfly Time,* Scribner, 1964; Frances Carpenter, *The Mouse Palace,* McGraw, 1964; Hans Christian Andersen, *The Ugly Duckling,* Scribner, 1965; Fisher, *In the Middle of the Night,* Crowell, 1965; Jan Wahl, *Cabbage Moon,* Holt, 1965; Lonzo Anderson, *Ponies of Mykillengi,* Scribner, 1966; Andrew Lang, *The Twelve Dancing Princesses,* Holt, 1966; Barbara Schiller, *The White Rat's Tale,* Holt, 1967; Grimm, *Jorinda and Joringel,* Scribner, 1968; Lonzo Anderson, *Two Hundred Rabbits,* Viking, 1968; Leclaire Alger, *The Laird of Cockpen,* Holt, 1969.

Natalia Belting, *Summer's Coming In,* Holt, 1970; Carl Withers, *Painting the Moon,* Holt, 1970; Lonzo Anderson, *Mr. Biddle and the Bird,* Scribner, 1971; Lonzo Anderson, *Izzard,* Scribner, 1973; Irwin Shapiro, *"Twice upon a Time,"* Scribner, 1973; Lonzo Anderson, *Halloween Party,* Scribner, 1974.

SIDELIGHTS: "I love children's books," Adrienne Adams once said, "and I feel very lucky to be involved in them. As I became involved, I discovered the satisfactions of a field which can be as sweetly innocent of the rank business-and-profit taint as any I can hope for, simply because a book cannot succeed unless little children love it and wear out its cover and pages so thoroughly that librarians must reorder it for the library shelves; you can not tell a child what to like."

BIOGRAPHICAL/CRITICAL SOURCES: Horn Book, April, 1965; *American Artist,* November, 1965; Diana Klemin, *The Art of Art for Children's Books,* C. N. Potter, 1966.

ADAMS, Florence 1932-

PERSONAL: Born May 18, 1932, in New York, N.Y.; daughter of Francis Joseph and Florence M. (White) O'Neill; married Donald L. Adams, August 25, 1962 (divorced, 1966); children: David G., Sam T. *Education:* Hunter College (now Hunter College of the City University of New York), B.A., 1955. *Religion:* Roman Catholic. *Residence:* Brooklyn, N.Y. *Agent:* Raines & Raines, 244 Madison Ave., New York, N.Y. 10016. *Office:* J. K. Lasser & Co., 10 East 53rd St., New York, N.Y. 10019.

CAREER: J. K. Lasser & Co. (certified public accountants), New York, N.Y., manager of computer programming and systems department, 1965—. Has taught classes in home repair, mostly for women; producer and featured speaker, "Take a Hammer in Your Hand, Sister," WBAI, New York, N.Y., 1972-73. President of board of directors, Cobble Hill Nursery School, 1970-71. *Member:* Cobble Hill Association (former treasurer).

WRITINGS: Mushy Eggs (juvenile), Putnam, 1973; *I Took a Hammer in My Hand: The Woman's Build-It and Fix-It Handbook,* Morrow, 1973.

WORK IN PROGRESS: Research on feminist history; another book extending from *I Took a Hammer in My Hand;* a children's book; co-authoring a musical.

* * *

ADAMS, Joey 1911-

PERSONAL: Surname originally Abramowitz; legally changed, 1930; born January 6, 1911, in New York, N.Y.; son of Nathan (a tailor) and Ida (Chonin) Abramowitz; married Cindy Heller (a columnist and commentator), February 14, 1952. *Education:* Attended City College (now City College of the City University of New York), 1931. *Home:* 1050 Fifth Ave., New York, N.Y. 10028. *Office:* 160 West 46th St., Room 402A, New York, N.Y. 10036.

CAREER: Author, actor, comedian, toastmaster. Nightclub and vaudeville entertainer throughout United States, 1930—; appeared in and produced films, including "Ringside," 1945, "Singing in the Dark," 1956; appeared in stage productions, including "The Gazebo," 1959, and "Guys and Dolls," 1960; host of television and radio shows, including "Spend a Million," 1954-55, "The Joey Adams Show," 1957, "Rate Your Mate," 1958, "Back That Fact," 1958, and "Gags to Riches"; has appeared on numerous radio and television shows, including "The Ed Sullivan Show," "The Jackie Gleason Show," and "The Steve Allen Show"; host of daily radio show on WEVD, 1968—. U.S. State Department representative to entertain soldiers around the world, 1958; deputy commissioner and chairman of entertainment committee for youth of New York City Youth Board, 1959—; president of Actors Youth Fund, and Senior Citizens of America Fund; personal representative of U.S. President as entertainer to Asia and Africa, 1961; member of board of directors, Central State Bank (New York), and Theatre Authority; chairman of special events committee, March of Dimes, 1955. *Member:* American Guild of Variety Artists (president, 1959—; president of retirement foundation; chairman of youth fund), Screen Actors Guild, American Federation of Television and Radio Artists, Actors Equity Association.

AWARDS, HONORS: Doctor of Comedy, Columbia University, 1950, City College of New York, 1952, New York University, 1959; Man of the Year Award from March of Dimes, 1955, City of Hope, 1959, New York City Police

Department, 1960; honored by Israeli Government for work with United Jewish Appeal and Israel Bond drives, 1952; recipient of humanitarian awards from American Cancer Society, 1952, Crusade for Freedom, 1956, Yiddish Theatrical Alliance, 1960; recipient of Pope's Medal, 1971, and numerous other awards.

WRITINGS: From Gags to Riches, Fell, 1946; *The Curtain Never Falls,* Fell, 1949; *Joey Adams' Joke Book: A Mad, Merry Mixture of Sly Stories, Tasty Tales, and Wise Witticisms, by the Master of Mirth,* Fell, 1952; *Strictly for Laughs,* Fell, 1955; *Cindy and I: The Real Life Adventures of Mr. and Mrs. Joey Adams,* Crown, 1957; *It Takes One to Know One: The Joey Adams Do-It-Yourself Laugh Kit,* Putnam, 1959; *The Joey Adams Joke Dictionary,* Citadel Press, 1961; *On the Road for Uncle Sam,* Geis, 1963; *LBJ's Texas Laughs,* Fell, 1964; *Joey Adams' Round-the-World Joke Book,* Fell, 1965; (with Henry Tobias) *The Borscht Belt,* Bobbs-Merrill, 1966; *You Could Die Laughing: Or, I Was a Comic for the F.B.I. and the Swingers,* Bobbs-Merrill, 1968; *Encyclopedia of Humor,* Bobbs-Merrill, 1968; *Son of Encyclopedia of Humor,* Bobbs-Merrill, 1970; *Laugh Your Calories Away,* Crown, 1971; *Children's Joke Book,* Crown, 1971; *Speaker's Bible of Humor,* Doubleday, 1972; *The God Bit,* Mason and Lipscomb, 1974.

SIDELIGHTS: Adams has recorded several comedy records, including "Cindy and I" (MGM), and "Jewish Folk Songs," with Molly Picon and Sholum Secunda for Roulette Records. In 1960, the American Guild of Variety Artists created a "Joey Award" for talent in the variety field in honor of Joey Adams.

* * *

ADAMS, L(ouis) Jerold 1939-

PERSONAL: Born June 1, 1939, in Logan, Utah; son of Louis J. (a rancher) and Zada (Perry) Adams; married Tina Graves, August, 1963; children: Laura, Stephen. *Education:* Arizona State University, B.S., 1965; University of Washington, Seattle, M.A., 1968, Ph.D., 1972. *Address:* Route 5, Warrensburg, Mo. 64093. *Office:* Department of Political Science, Central Missouri State University, Warrensburg, Mo. 64093.

CAREER: Central Missouri State University, Warrensburg, assistant professor of political science, 1972—. Consultant to Treaty Research Center, University of Washington, 1972—. *Member:* International Studies Association, American Political Science Association, Midwest Political Science Association, Pi Sigma Alpha.

WRITINGS: Theory, Law, and Policy of Contemporary Japanese Treaties, Oceana, 1974.

WORK IN PROGRESS: Law and Policy in Japan's Foreign Relations.

* * *

ADAMS, Richard 1920-

PERSONAL: Born May 9, 1920, in Newbury, Berkshire, England; married Barbara Elizabeth Acland, September 26, 1949; children: Juliet, Rosamond. *Education:* Worcester College, Oxford, M.A., 1948. *Religion:* Church of England. *Home:* 26 St. Paul's Place, London N1 2QG, England. *Agent:* David Higham Associates Ltd., 5-8 Lower John St., London W1R 4HA, England.

CAREER: British Home Higher Civil Service, 1948-74, serving in Ministry of Housing and Local Government until its amalgamation as part of Department of Environment, Assistant Secretary, Department of Environment, 1968-74; full-time writer, 1974—. *Military service:* British Army, 1940-45. *Awards, honors:* Guardian Award for children's literature, and Carnegie Medal, both 1972, both for *Watership Down.*

WRITINGS: Watership Down, Rex Collings, 1972, Macmillan, 1974; *Shardik,* Rex Collings, 1974.

WORK IN PROGRESS: A fantasy novel.

SIDELIGHTS: "To the long line of antic British bestiary writers—Lewis Carroll, Edward Lear, A. A. Milne, Kenneth Grahame, J. R. R. Tolkien—must now be added Richard Adams," noted Melvin Maddocks. Adams's first novel, *Watership Down* is an adventure story, often termed "epic" or "classic," whose characters are rabbits. "[It is] an entirely absorbing and original novel," wrote a *Spectator* reviewer. "The sheer impudence of the notion takes one's breath away; but the integrity with which it is carried out provokes a deep sigh of satisfaction. The natural world is observed and rendered with wonderful precision; and the character of the wandering band of rabbit, with their language and their legends, becomes part of one's own experience.... This seems to me to be a measure of the book's excellence.... I don't know whether Mr. Adams had one or a dozen purposes in mind in creating this large-scale narrative; certainly it has many parallels—political, social, philosophic—with our own society. But these parallels are only parallels; they are not the heart of the book."

Richard Adams has denied the purposes and implications ascribed to *Watership Down,* and has been quoted as saying: "I should be very sorry if people tried to read deeper meanings into [the book]."

* * *

ADELMANN, Frederick J(oseph) 1915-

PERSONAL: Born February 18, 1915, in Norwood, Mass.; son of Fred M. and Helen (Casey) Adelmann. *Education:* Boston College, A.B., 1937, M.A., 1942; Weston College, Ph.L., 1942, S.T.L., 1948; St. Louis University, Ph.D., 1955. *Politics:* Democrat. *Home:* 140 Commonwealth Ave., Newton, Mass. 02167. *Office:* Department of Philosophy, Boston College, Chestnut Hill, Mass. 02167.

CAREER: Ordained Roman Catholic priest of the Society of Jesus (Jesuit), 1947; St. Louis University, St. Louis, Mo., teaching fellow in philosophy, 1950-54; Weston College, Weston, Mass., lecturer in philosophy, 1960-62; Boston College, Chestnut Hill, Mass., instructor in mathematics and physics in Army Specialized Training Program, 1942-44, assistant professor, 1955-68, associate professor, 1968-70, professor of philosophy, 1970—, head of department, 1955-65. *Member:* American Association of University Professors, American Philosophical Association, Jesuit Philosophical Association, Realist Society.

WRITINGS: From Dialogue to Epilogue, Nijhoff, 1967; (editor) *The Quest for the Absolute,* Nijhoff, 1968; (editor) *Demythologizing Marxism,* Nijhoff, 1970; (with J. M. Bochenski and others) *A Guide to Marxism,* Swallow Press, 1972; (editor) *Authority,* Nijhoff, 1974.

* * *

ADLER, Hans A(rnold) 1921-

PERSONAL: Born November 7, 1921, in Mayen, Germany; naturalized U.S. citizen; son of Frederik S. (a physician) and Wally (a physician; maiden name, Baum) Adler; married Mary J. Rice (a potter), 1951; children: Joan, Michael, Kenneth, Christina. *Education:* Cornell University, B.A., 1941; Harvard University, M.A., 1943, Ph.D., 1944, LL.B., 1951. *Home:* 6656 Holland St., McLean, Va. 22101. *Office:* World Bank, 1818 H St. N.W., Washington, D.C. 20433.

CAREER: Federal Reserve Bank, New York, N.Y., senior economist, 1944-46; U.S. Office of Military Government, Berlin, Germany, chief of banking section, 1946-48; U.S. Bureau of the Budget, Washington, D.C., economist, 1951-61; World Bank, Washington, D.C., director, 1961—. *Military service:* U.S. Army Air Forces, 1946. Member: American Economic Association, Royal Economic Society.

WRITINGS: (With Gary Fromm) *Transport Investment and Economic Development,* Brookings Institution, 1965; *Sector and Project Planning in Transportation,* Johns Hopkins Press, 1967; *Economic Appraisal of Transport Projects,* Indiana University Press, 1971.

* * *

ADLER, Manfred 1936-

PERSONAL: Born December 21, 1936; married, wife's name Sheila Alice; children: Steven, Laura. *Education:* Kent State University, B.S. in Ed., 1960, M.Ed., 1962, Ph.D., 1965. *Home:* 1075 Colony Dr., Highland Heights, Ohio 44143. *Office:* John Carroll University, Cleveland, Ohio 44118.

CAREER: Teacher in public schools of Cleveland, Ohio, 1961-62; intern school psychologist in public schools of South Euclid-Lyndhurst, Ohio, 1962-63; school psychologist in North Olmsted, Ohio, 1964-65; Ball State University, Muncie, Ind., assistant professor of special education, 1965-66; John Carroll University, Cleveland, Ohio, associate professor of education, 1966—. Private practice of child psychology, Cleveland, Ohio, 1966—; psychological consultant, East Cleveland Board of Education, 1967—.

MEMBER: American Psychological Association, Council for Exceptional Children, National Society for the Study of Education, Society for the Psychological Study of Social Issues, American Association of University Professors, Association for the Gifted, Ohio Psychological Association, Ohio School Psychological Association, Cuyahoga County Association for the Retarded.

WRITINGS: A Parent's Manual: Questions and Answers to Problems of Child Growth and Development, C. C Thomas, 1971; (contributor) Barbara Hauck and Maurice F. Freehill, editors, *The Gifted: Case Studies,* W. C. Brown, 1972. Contributor to *Gifted Child* and other journals. Writer of column, "Your Child," in *Cleveland Press,* 1966—.

WORK IN PROGRESS: With Walter B. Barbe, *Principal's Handbook on the Education of the Gifted;* with Patricia A. Kearney, *A Parent's Survival Guide to Education.*

* * *

ADLER, Renata 1938-

PERSONAL: Born October 19, 1938, in Milan, Italy; daughter of Frederick L. and Erna (Strauss) Adler. *Education:* Bryn Mawr College, A.B., 1959; Sorbonne, University of Paris, D.d'E.S., 1961; Harvard University, M.A., 1962. *Agent:* Lynn Nesbit, International Famous Agency, 1301 Avenue of the Americas, New York, N.Y. 10019. *Office: New Yorker,* 25 West 43rd St., New York, N.Y. 10036.

CAREER: New Yorker, New York, N.Y., writer-reporter, 1962—. Fellow of Trumbull College, Yale University, 1969-72. Judge in arts and letters for National Book Awards, 1969. Member of P.E.N. executive board, 1964-70. *Awards, honors:* Guggenheim fellow, 1973-74; first prize in O. Henry Short Story Awards, 1974.

WRITINGS: Toward a Radical Middle: Fourteen Pieces of Reporting and Criticism, Random House, 1970; *A Year in the Dark: Journal of a Film Critic, 1968-1969,* Random House, 1970. Contributor of short stories to *Harper's Bazaar* and *New Yorker.* Film critic for *New York Times,* 1968-69; member of editorial board of *American Scholar,* 1969—.

SIDELIGHTS: "Renata Adler may be taken as a sign that the war is almost over and that intellectual sexual equality comes easier than it used to," Wilfrid Sheed writes. "Not that she doesn't like to roughhouse. But she is more impulsive, and less glacially in control than the big sisters. She doesn't pull sexual rank, and she doesn't encourage you to.... As a reporter, she occasionally suffers from too much courtesy ... As a critic, she bites as hard as anyone, but always in the service of an idea ... It is good to have the whole Adler in one book ... and good to have such a gracefully phrased, ardently intelligent book from anyone."

"The radical middle according to Adler," says *Time,* "is a consciousness of 'something infinitely fragile and viable in the System, in its accommodations with radicals, rednecks, soldiers, blacks, thinkers, visionaries, lunatics, and the ordinary.' ... There is a vast no man's land between Walter Cronkite and Norman Mailer. Renata Adler is just the right woman to fill it."

Pearl K. Bell notes that "at her best, Renata Adler has perfect pitch for the high-toned slogan that is first self-righteous and within minutes of being uttered turns nasty. The consistent soundness of her judgment seems immeasurably valuable in a time when even the most sensitive liberal intellectuals seem unable to avoid the boobytraps set for them by the young."

Of herself, Renata Adler says, "I guess I am part of an age group that, through being skipped, through never having had a generational voice, was forced into the broadest possible America. Even now (and we are in our thirties), we have no journals we publish, no exile we share, no brawls, no anecdotes, no war, no solidarity, no mark.... In a way ... we are the last custodians of language ... because history, in our time, has rung so many changes on the meaning of terms, and we, having never generationally perpetrated anything, have no commitment to any distortion of them."

ADLERBLUM, Nina H. 1882-1974

August 4, 1882—July 25, 1974; Israeli-born American author and educator. Obituaries: *New York Times,* August 2, 1974.

* * *

AGOR, Weston H(arris) 1939-

PERSONAL: Born December 30, 1939, in Salamanca, N.Y.; son of Randall W. and Ruth (Barrett) Agor; married Eliana Bauer, August 20, 1963; children: Lawrence B., William B. *Education:* St. Lawrence University, B.A., 1961; University of Michigan, M.P.A., 1963; University of Wisconsin, Ph.D., 1969. *Politics:* Republican. *Religion:* Protestant. *Address:* Box 282, Lansing, Mich. 48904. *Office:* Office of Majority Leader, Michigan State Senate, Lansing, Mich.

CAREER: University of Florida, Gainesville, assistant professor of political science and Latin American studies, 1963-65; Procter & Gamble, assistant brand man, marketing, Cincinnati, Ohio, and Toronto, Ontario, 1963-65; Michigan State Senate, Lansing, executive assistant to majority leader, 1973—. Assistant director of program development for Citizens Conference on State Legislatures, 1973. Legislative consultant to several states and Latin American countries. *Member:* American Political Science Association, American Society of Public Administration, Beta Theta Pi, Pi Sigma Alpha, Psi Chi, Omicron Delta Kappa. *Awards, honors:* Fulbright scholar in Chile, 1962-63.

WRITINGS: Chilean Senate: Internal Distribution of Influence, University of Texas Press, 1971; *Latin American Legislatures: Their Role and Influence,* Praeger, 1971. Contributor to journals and periodicals, including *Inter-American Economic Affairs.*

WORK IN PROGRESS: Research on institutional management of state legislatures, and on role of legislatures to exercise policy initiative and oversight functions.

BIOGRAPHICAL/CRITICAL SOURCES: Journal of Politics, November, 1972; *American Political Science Review,* November, 1973.

* * *

AGUZZI-BARBAGLI, Danilo 1924-

PERSONAL: Born August 1, 1924, in Arezzo, Italy; son of Guglielmo and Marianna (Barbagli) Aguzzi. *Education:* University of Florence, Dottore in Lettere, 1949; Columbia University, Ph.D., 1959. *Home:* 1357 Sunnyslope Ave., Belmont, Calif. 94002. *Office:* Department of Hispanic and Italian Studies, University of British Columbia, Vancouver 8, British Columbia, Canada.

CAREER: University of Chicago, Chicago, Ill., assistant professor of Italian, 1959-63; Tulane University, New Orleans, La., associate professor of Italian, 1964-71; University of British Columbia, Vancouver, professor of Italian, 1972—. *Member:* Modern Language Association of America, Renaissance Society of America, American Association of Teachers of Italian, Accademia Petrarca, American Philosophical Society (fellow), Mediaeval Academy of America.

WRITINGS: (Editor) Francesco Patrizi da Cherso, *Della Poetica,* Instituto Nazionale di Studi sul Rinascimento (Florence), Volume I, 1969, Volume II, 1970, Volume III, 1971; (contributor) Julius A. Molinaro, editor, *Petrarch to Pirandello: Studies in Honor of B. Corrigan,* University of Toronto Press, 1973. Contributor of book reviews to *Italica, Renaissance Quarterly, Romanic Review,* and *Comparative Literature.*

WORK IN PROGRESS: A critical edition of the letters and posthumous pamphlets of Francesco Patrizi; studies in Italian Renaissance literature and culture.

AVOCATIONAL INTERESTS: Classical literatures and philosophy, history of art, science, and theatre.

AHERN, Emily M. 1944-

PERSONAL: Born November 7, 1944, in Birmingham, Ala.; daughter of Henry W. and Zoe (Martin) Godshalk; married Dennis Ahern (a professor), May 11, 1966. *Education:* University of Michigan, B.A., 1966; Cornell University, Ph.D., 1971. *Office:* Department of Anthropology, Yale University, New Haven, Conn. 06520.

CAREER: Yale University, New Haven, Conn., assistant professor of anthropology, 1972—. *Member:* American Anthropological Association, Association for Asian Studies.

WRITINGS: The Cult of the Dead in a Chinese Village, Stanford University Press, 1973.

* * *

AINSWORTH, Charles H(arold) 1935-

PERSONAL: Born April 1, 1935, in Shreveport, La.; son of Ottis W. and Fern (a genealogist; maiden name, Clark) Ainsorth; married Winnie Tew, January 20, 1964; children: Charles Lee, Winnie Marie. *Education:* Northwestern State University, Natchitoches, La., B.A., 1959, M.A. (sociology), 1964; University of Alabama, M.A. (anthropology), 1968, doctoral study, 1965—. *Religion:* Church of Jesus Christ of Latter-Day Saints (Mormon). *Home address:* P.O. Box 425, Montevallo, Ala. 35115. *Office:* Department of Social Science, University of Montevallo, Montevallo, Ala. 35115.

CAREER: Church of Jesus Christ of Latter-Day Saints, Sao Paulo, Brazil, missionary, 1959-62; elementary school teacher in New Orleans, La., 1964; University of Alabama, Birmingham, instructor in sociology and anthropology, 1965-67; Brigham Young University, Institute Program, Birmingham, Ala., part-time instructor in theology, 1965-72; University of Montevallo, Montevallo, Ala., assistant professor of sociology and anthropology, 1968—. *Military service:* U.S. Army Reserve, chaplain; became captain. *Member:* American Sociological Association, American Anthropological Association, Society for Early Historic Archaeology, Mormon History Association, Rural Sociological Society, Southern Sociological Association, Southern Anthropological Association, Alabama-Mississippi Sociological Association, Alabama Academy of Science.

WRITINGS: (Editor and contributor) *Selected Readings for Introductory Sociology,* MSS Information Corp., 1972, 2nd edition, 1974; (editor) *Selected Readings for Marriage and the Family,* MSS Information Corp., 1973; (editor) *Selected Readings for Introductory Anthropology,* MSS Information Corp., 1974; *Ute Indian Culture: From Tradition to the Reservation,* University of Montevallo, 1974; *Barriers and Stimulants to Change among the Ute Indians,* University of Montevallo, 1974. Contributor to *Journal of the Alabama Academy of Science.*

WORK IN PROGRESS: Editing *Selected Readings for Cultural Anthropology; Origins of the Native Peoples of the New World; North American Indians; Alabama Indians; Mormons and Minorities in the South;* articles on the history and contributions of the New World Archaeological Foundation, on Mormonism and the origin of indigenous New World peoples; research on Mormon dogma and Latter-Day Saint attitudes toward human evolution, and on the effects of secularism and urbanism on rural Southern Mormon racial attitudes; conducting a sample survey of Mormons in Alabama and parts of Georgia regarding their attitudes and opinions concerning current and traditional issues.

* * *

AIRD, Eileen M(argaret) 1945-

PERSONAL: Born July 26, 1945, in Halifax, Yorkshire, England; daughter of Albert (a school teacher) and Nancy (Pickles) Greenwood; married Edwin Aird (a medical physicist), July 29, 1967; children: Christopher James. *Education:* University of Durham, B.A. (honors), 1966; University of Newcastle, M.Litt., 1969. *Religion:* Quaker. *Home:* 182 Osborne Rd., Newcastle on Tyne NE2 3LE, England. *Office:* Department of English, University of Newcastle, Newcastle on Tyne NE1 199, England.

CAREER: Teacher in school for girls, 1968-72; Open University, Newcastle on Tyne, England, counsellor, 1973—; University of Newcastle, Newcastle on Tyne, tutor in English, 1973—.

WRITINGS: Sylvia Plath, Barnes & Noble, 1973.

WORK IN PROGRESS: Continued work on Sylvia Plath.

* * *

AITKEN, Dorothy 1916-

PERSONAL: Born July 19, 1916, in Colorado; daughter of Dudley Acey (a farmer) and Myrtle (Agler) Lockwood; married James Julius Aitken (a clergyman), May 27, 1939; children: Jerrold James, John Dudley, Judith Maydell Aitken Stoehr. *Education:* Student at Union College, Lincoln, Neb., 1938-40, Seventh-Day Adventists Theological Seminary, Washington, D.C., 1943-45, and Alliance Francaise, 1950. *Religion:* Seventh-Day Adventist. *Home:* 7410 Aspen Ave., Takoma Park, Md. 20012. *Office:* General Conference of Seventh-Day Adventists, 6840 Eastern Ave., Washington, D.C. 20012.

CAREER: Teacher of English and librarian in Redfield, S.D., public school, 1962-63; dental assistant in Washington, D.C., 1968-71; General Conference of Seventh-Day Adventists, Washington, D.C., editor of children's lessons, 1971-73. Free-lance writer, 1960—. Teacher of German and Spanish in Takoma Park, Md., 1969-70.

WRITINGS—All for young people: (Editor) James Julius Aitken, *In Step with Christ,* Pacific Press Publishing, 1963; *Bride in the Parsonage,* Southern Publishing, 1966; *White Wings Green Jungle,* Pacific Press Publishing, 1966; *My Love the Amazon,* Southern Publishing, 1968; *The Hard Way,* Southern Publishing, 1969; *Cherry on Top,* Review & Herald, 1973. Contributor to *Guide* and *Signs of the Times,* and other religious journals, sometimes in German, Spanish, or French.

WORK IN PROGRESS: A devotional for teen-agers.

SIDELIGHTS: The Aitkens lived in South America for eight years, and in Berne, Switzerland, for eight years. Mrs. Aitken told *CA* she has travelled most of the world gathering material and assisting her husband in his work.

* * *

ALDER, Henry (Ludwig) 1922-

PERSONAL: Born March 26, 1922, in Duisburg, Germany; naturalized U.S. citizen in 1944; son of Ludwig (a chemist) and Otti (Gottschalk) Alder; married Benne B. Daniel, April 8, 1963; children: Lawrence J. *Education:* University of California, Berkeley, A.B., 1942, Ph.D., 1947. *Home:* 724 Elmwood Dr., Davis, Calif. 95616. *Office:* Department of Mathematics, University of California, Davis, Calif. 95616.

CAREER: University of California, Berkeley, instructor in mathematics, 1947-48; University of California, Davis, instructor, 1948-49, assistant professor, 1949-55, associate professor, 1955-65, professor of mathematics, 1965—. *Military service:* U.S. Army Air Forces, 1944-45. *Member:* Mathematical Association of America (chairman of northern California section, 1956-57; national secretary, 1960-74), American Mathematical Society, Institute of Mathematical Statistics, Sigma Xi, Mu Alpha Theta (president, 1957-59), Pi Mu Epsilon. *Awards, honors:* International distinguished service award from Mu Alpha Theta, 1965; Lester R. Ford award from Mathematical Association of America, 1970.

WRITINGS: (With Edward B. Roessler) *Introduction to Probability and Statistics,* W. H. Freeman, 1960, 5th edition, 1972. Contributor to *American Mathematical Monthly, Bulletin of the American Mathematical Society, Pacific Journal of Mathematics,* and *Mathematics Magazine*. Editor of *Fibonacci Quarterly,* 1963—.

* * *

ALDRIDGE, Adele 1934-

PERSONAL: Born August 12, 1934, in Oceanside, N.Y.; daughter of John Henry and Ruth Louise (Ferris) Thompson; divorced; children: Vicki Adele, John Alan. *Education:* Studied at Parson's School of Design, 1954-56, Art Institute of Chicago, 1960, and Silvermine College of Art, 1965-68. *Home and Studio:* 31 Chapel Lane, Riverside, Conn. 06878.

CAREER: Painter and printmaker. Co-owner of Magic Circle Press. *Member:* National Organization for Women (coordinator of Women in Graphics).

WRITINGS: Notpoems, Mandala Press, limited edition, 1970, Magic Circle Press, 1972; *Changes: A Book of Prints Inspired by the I Ching,* Mandala Press, 1972; (contributor) Bill Henderson, editor, *The Publish It Yourself Hand Book,* Pushcart Press, 1973; *Once I Was a Square: And Then I Met a Circle,* Magic Circle Press, 1974; *I Ching Meditations,* Alchemist Atelier, numbers I, II, III, 1974.

WORK IN PROGRESS: The remaining sixty-one hexagrams of the *I Ching Meditations* handprinted in an edition of two hundred, with seven prints in each portfolio, a ten-year project.

SIDELIGHTS: "I have come to the book world via the visual," Adele Aldridge writes. "Consider letters in themselves beautiful. Started working with letters in paintings, then went into concrete poetry. Now incorporating my drawings and personal meditations of the *I Ching* into a unified whole. . . .Interested in elevating the role of women in this and all other societies."

* * *

ALENT, Rose Marie Bachem
See BACHEM-ALENT, Rose Marie

* * *

ALEXANDER, Jean 1926-

PERSONAL: Born April 5, 1926, in Forest Grove, Ore.; daughter of Clyde M. (a teacher) and Mildred (Carlyle) Alexander. *Education:* University of Oregon, B.A., 1947;

University of Washington, Seattle, M.A., 1955, Ph.D., 1961. *Home:* 322 First Ave., N.E., No. 504, Calgary, Alberta, Canada. *Office:* Department of English, University of Calgary, Calgary, Alberta, Canada.

CAREER: Louisiana State University, Baton Rouge, instructor in English, 1958-61; University of Calgary, Calgary, Alberta, assistant professor, 1961-68, associate professor of English, 1968—. *Member:* International Association for the Study of Anglo-Irish Literature, Canadian Association of University Teachers, Rocky Mountain Modern Language Association. *Awards, honors:* Fulbright fellow in France, 1957-58.

WRITINGS: (Compiler) *Affidavits of Genius: Edgar Allan Poe and the French Critics, 1847-1924,* Kennikat, 1971; *The Venture of Form in the Novels of Virginia Woolf,* Kennikat, 1974.

WORK IN PROGRESS: A novel.

AVOCATIONAL INTERESTS: Writing poetry, swimming, mountain climbing.

* * *

ALEXANDER, Martin 1930-

PERSONAL: Born February 4, 1930, in Newark, N.J.; son of Meyer (a haberdasher) and Sarah (Rubinstein) Alexander; married Renee R. Wulf (a lecturer), August 26, 1951; children: Miriam H., Stanley W. *Education:* Rutgers University, B.S., 1951; University of Wisconsin, M.S., 1953, Ph.D., 1955. *Home:* 301 Winthrop Dr., Ithaca, N.Y. 14850. *Office:* 708 Bradfield Hall, Cornell University, Ithaca, N.Y. 14850.

CAREER: Cornell University, Ithaca, N.Y., assistant professor, 1955-59, associate professor, 1959-64, professor of soil microbiology, 1964—. Visiting professor, Hebrew University of Jerusalem, 1961-62. *Member:* International Cell Research Organization, International Society of Soil Science, American Society for Microbiology, American Society of Agronomy, American Association for the Advancement of Science, Phi Beta Kappa. *Awards, honors:* Soil science award from American Society of Agronomy, 1966; Industrial Research-100 award, 1968.

WRITINGS: *Introduction to Soil Microbiology,* Wiley, 1961; *Microbial Ecology,* Wiley, 1971. Contributor of more than two hundred scientific articles and review to journals in his field. Consulting editor, *Soil Science,* 1965—; member of editorial board, *Journal of Bacteriology,* 1970—, and *Pesticide Biochemistry and Physiology,* 1971—.

WORK IN PROGRESS: Scientific articles.

* * *

ALLEN, Edward D(avid) 1923-

PERSONAL: Born January 29, 1923, in Perth Amboy, N.J.; married Virginia Garibaldi, 1946; children: two sons. *Education:* Montclair State Teachers College, B.A., 1943; University of Wisconsin, M.A., 1948; University of Grenoble, French Diploma, 1950; Ohio State University, Ph.D., 1954; Mexico City College, additional study, six summers. *Home:* 165 West Schreyer Pl., Columbus, Ohio 43214. *Office:* College of Education, Ohio State University, 1945 North High St., Columbus, Ohio 43210.

CAREER: High school teacher of French in Belleville, N.J., 1943-45; Ohio State University, Columbus, 1945—, assistant professor, 1955-58, associate professor, 1958-62, professor of foreign language education, 1962—, director of summer language institute at Lyon, France, 1965—. Visiting lecturer in Spanish at Ohio Wesleyan University, 1956. *Member:* American Association of Teachers of French, American Association of Teachers of Spanish and Portuguese, Modern Language Association of America, American Council on the Teaching of Foreign Languages, Association for Supervision and Curriculum Development, Ohio Modern Language Teachers Association (secretary-treasurer, 1956-59).

WRITINGS: (With Frank Otto and Leona Glenn) *The Changing Curriculum: Modern Foreign Languages,* Association for Supervision and Curriculum Development, 1968; (with Rebecca Valette) *Modern Language Classroom Techniques: A Handbook,* Harcourt, 1972. Contributor to *Encyclopedia of Education, Encyclopedia Americana,* and professional journals.

* * *

ALLEN, Leslie H. 1887(?)-1973

1887(?)—November 21, 1973; American author and former editor of the *Christian Science Monitor.* Obituaries: *AB Bookman's Weekly,* January 14, 1974.

* * *

ALLEN, Samuel 1917- (Paul Vesey)

PERSONAL: Born December 9, 1917, in Columbus, Ohio; son of Alexander Joseph (a clergyman) and Jewett (Washington) Allen; divorced; children: Marie-Christine. *Education:* Fisk University, A.B., 1938; Harvard University, J.D., 1941; graduate study at New School for Social Research, 1947-48, and Sorbonne, University of Paris, 1949-50. *Politics:* Democrat. *Religion:* African Methodist Episcopal. *Residence:* Winthrop, Mass. *Office:* Department of English, Boston University, Boston, Mass. 02215.

CAREER: Deputy assistant district attorney of City of New York, N.Y., 1946-47; civilian attorney with U.S. Armed Forces in Europe, 1951-55; private practice of law, New York, N.Y., 1956-58; Texas Southern University, Houston, Tex., associate professor of law, 1958-60; U.S. Information Agency, Washington, D.C., assistant general counsel, 1961-64; Community Relations Service, Washington, D.C., chief counsel, 1965-68; Tuskegee Institute, Tuskegee Institute, Ala., Avalon Professor of Humanities, 1968-70; Boston University, Boston, Mass., professor of English, 1971—. Member of board of directors and vice-president of Southern Education Foundation. *Military service:* U.S. Army, 1942-46; became first lieutenant. *Member:* African Studies Association, African Heritage Studies Association.

WRITINGS: (Under pseudonym Paul Vesey) *Elfenbein Zahne* (title means "Ivory Tusks"; a bilingual edition of poems), Wolfgang Rothe, 1956; (translator) Jean Paul Sartre, *Orphee Noir,* Africaine, 1960; *Ivory Tusks and Other Poems,* Poets Press, 1968; (author of introduction) Naseer Aruri and Edmund Ghareeb, editors, *Enemy of the Sun: Poetry of the Palestinian Resistance,* Drum & Spear Press, 1970; (editor and author of introduction) *Poems from Africa,* Crowell, 1973.

Poems and essays have been included in more than sixty anthologies, including *African Heritage,* edited by Jacob Drachler, Crowell, 1959, *Cavalcade,* edited by Arthur P. Davis and Saunders Redding, Houghton, 1970, *What Black Educators Are Saying,* edited by Nathan Wright, Jr., Hawthorne, 1970, *The Ideology of Blackness,* edited by Raymond F. Betts, D.C. Heath, 1971, *Background to Black American Literature,* edited by Ruth Miller, Glencoe Press, 1971.

Contributor of essays and poems to journals, including *Presence Africaine, Negro Digest, Journal of Afro-American Studies,* and *Black World.*

WORK IN PROGRESS: A collection of poems, for Paul Breman Ltd. (London).

SIDELIGHTS: A reading by Allen of his own poetry was recorded at the Library of Congress in 1972.

BIOGRAPHICAL/CRITICAL SOURCES: Rheinische Post, September 14, 1957; *Black Orpheus,* October, 1958; M. G. Cooke, editor, *Modern Black Novelists,* Prentice-Hall, 1971; Ezekiel Mphahlele, *Voices in the Whirlwind,* Hill & Wang, 1972.

* * *

ALLEN, W(illiam) Sidney 1918-

PERSONAL: Born March 18, 1918, in London, England; son of William Percy (an engineer) and Ethel (Pearce) Allen; married Aenea McCallum, August 11, 1955. *Education:* Trinity College, Cambridge, B.A., 1940, M.A., 1946, Ph.D., 1949. *Home:* 14 Applecourt, Newton Rd., Cambridge CB2 2AN, England. *Office:* Faculty Rooms, Cambridge University, Laundress Lane, Cambridge, England.

CAREER: University of London, School of Oriental and African Studies, London, England, lecturer in phonetics and comparative linguistics, 1948-55; Cambridge University, Cambridge, England, professor of comparative philology, and fellow of Trinity College, 1955—. Conducted dialect research in India, 1952; British Council visitor at University of the West Indies, 1959; Linguistic Society of America's Professor, 1961; Collitz Professor at Linguistic Institute (United States), 1962. *Military service:* British Army, Royal Tank Regiment and General Staff (intelligence), 1939-45; became captain; mentioned in dispatches.

MEMBER: British Academy (fellow), Linguistics Association of Great Britain, Philological Society (president, 1965-67), Linguistic Society of India. *Awards, honors:* Fellow of Rockefeller Foundation, 1953.

WRITINGS: Phonetics in Ancient India, Oxford University Press, 1953; *On the Linguistic Study of Languages,* Cambridge University Press, 1957, reprinted, Oxford University Press, 1966; *Sandhi,* Mouton & Co., 1962; *Vox Latina,* Cambridge University Press, 1965; *Vox Graeca,* Cambridge University Press, 1968; *Accent and Rhythm,* Cambridge University Press, 1973. Contributor of articles on linguistics, phonetics, metrics, and classical, Indian, and other languages to professional journals. Editor of *Lingua* (Amsterdam).

WORK IN PROGRESS: Indo-European Comparative Phonology; Greek and Latin Linguistics.

AVOCATIONAL INTERESTS: Travel (especially Greece).

* * *

ALLINSON, Beverley 1936-

PERSONAL: Born April 17, 1936; married Alec Allinson. *Home:* 95 Rivercrest Rd., Toronto, Ontario, Canada.

CAREER: Teacher in Australia and England, 1956-68.

WRITINGS—Children's books: *Mitzi's Magic Garden,* Garrard, 1971; (with husband, Alec Allinson, and John McInnes) *Magic Seasons,* Thomas Nelson, 1971; *Mandy's Flying Map,* Women's Educational Press, 1973; (with Alec Allinson and others) "Language Stimulus Program," Bowmar, 1970-73.

WORK IN PROGRESS: A children's novel.

* * *

ALLISON, Graham T(illett), Jr. 1940-

PERSONAL: Born March 23, 1940, in Charlotte, N.C.; son of Graham T. (a businessman) and Virginia (Wright) Allison; married Elisabeth Kovacs (a professor), September 9, 1968. *Education:* Attended Davidson College, 1958-60; Harvard University, B.A. (magna cum laude), 1962, Ph.D., 1968; Hertford College, Oxford, A.B. and A.M. (first class honors), 1964. *Home:* 35 Hamilton Rd., Belmont, Mass. 02178. *Agent:* George McCauley, P.O. Box 456, Cranbury, N.J. 08512. *Office:* Kennedy School of Government, Harvard University, Littauer Center 104, Cambridge, Mass. 02138.

CAREER: Harvard University, Kennedy School of Government, Cambridge, Mass., instructor, 1967-68, assistant professor of government, 1968-70, associate professor of politics, 1970-72, professor of politics, 1972—, research associate, Institute of Politics, 1968. Research associate, Center for International Affairs, Harvard University, 1967-68, faculty associate, 1971. Consultant to Department of Defense/International Security Affairs, RAND Corp., and Hudson Institute. *Member:* Council on Foreign Relations, Phi Beta Kappa. *Awards, honors:* International affairs fellow, Council on Foreign Relations, 1968-69.

WRITINGS: (Author of afterword, with Richard E. Neustadt) Robert F. Kennedy, *Thirteen Days,* Norton, 1971; *Essence of Decision: Explaining the Cuban Missile Crisis,* Little, Brown, 1971; (contributor) Henry Rosovsky, editor, *Discord in the Pacific: Challenges to the Japanese-American Alliance,* Columbia University, 1972; (contributor) Bernard Udis, editor, *The Economic Consequences of Reduced Military Spending,* Heath, 1973. Contributor to *The Computer Industry in Japan and Its Meaning for the U.S.,* published by National Research Council. Contributor to professional journals. Member of editorial board, *Public Policy,* 1970, *World Politics,* 1970, 1972-73.

* * *

ALLISON, Harrison C(larke) 1917-

PERSONAL: Born November 4, 1917, in West Liberty, Ky.; son of Asher Owen (a minister) and Florence (a teacher; maiden name, Davis) Allison; married Amy Lee Henry, March, 1940 (divorced December, 1946); married Jessie Hudson (a nurse), December 16, 1947; children: (first marriage) James L. Allison (deceased); (second marriage) Anita Louis (Mrs. Richard Williams), Nancy Ann, Sandra Elizabeth, Olivia Sue (Mrs. Ronney Q. Johnson). *Education:* Attended Cumberland College, 1937; Georgetown College, A.B., 1939; University of Alabama, M.S., 1950. *Politics:* Republican. *Religion:* Presbyterian. *Address:* P.O. Box 548, 701 Moore St., Marion, Ala. 36756. *Office:* Department of Science, Marion Institute, Marion, Ala. 36756.

CAREER: Fork Union Military Academy, Fork Union, Va., instructor in history and biology, 1940-41; Sylvania Electric Products, Inc., Lexington, Ky., products engineer, 1944-45; Marion Institute, Marion, Ala., instructor in law enforcement, and head of department of science, 1947-49, 1953—. City of Marion Police Department, Marion, Ala., lieutenant, 1960-64, captain in identification and training, 1964-72. Consultant in identification and criminalistics. Chairman of Perry County Republican Committee, 1962. *Military service:* U.S. Army, Chemical Warfare, 1941-44; became captain. *Member:* International Association of Chiefs of Police, International Association for Identification, American Institute of Chemists (fellow), American Association of Criminology (fellow), Alabama Peace Officers Association.

WRITINGS: Personal Identification, Holbrook, 1973. Book review editor of *Alabama Peace Officers Journal,* 1974—.

WORK IN PROGRESS: Short stories; a mystery novel involving police procedures.

* * *

ALLISON, R(ichard) Bruce 1949-

PERSONAL: Born May 10, 1949, in San Diego, Calif.; son of Harry B. (a banker) and Dorothy (Buick) Allison. *Education:* Brown University, A.B., 1971. *Home:* 107 Mineola St., Hinsdale, Ill. 60521.

CAREER: SOL Press, Hinsdale, Ill., director, 1972—.

WRITINGS: (Editor with Mildred J. Loomis) *Humanizing Our Future,* School of the Living Press, 1972; (editor) *Toward a Human Future,* School of the Living Press, 1972; *Democrats in Exile, 1968-1972: The Political Confessions of a New England Liberal,* SOL Press, 1974. Author of a syndicated college newspaper column, "Counter Culture Corner," 1973.

WORK IN PROGRESS: Travel Journals of an American Nomad; research on an anthology of decentralist writers and thinkers.

* * *

ALOYSIUS, Sister Mary
See SCHALDENBRAND, Mary

* * *

ALPER, Benedict S(olomon) 1905-

PERSONAL: Born June 28, 1905, in Revere, Mass.; son of Morris (a merchant) and Fredrika (Klatschken) Alper; married Ethel Machanic, June 14, 1935; children: Fredrika Clara. *Education:* Harvard University, A.B., 1927, graduate study in law, 1932-33. *Home:* 146 Tappan St., Brookline, Mass. 02146. *Office:* Department of Sociology, Boston College, Newton, Mass. 02167.

CAREER: Massachusetts Child Council, Boston, research director, 1934-39; Judge Baker Guidance Center, Boston, research associate, 1939-41; New York State Joint Legislative Committee on Courts, research director, 1941-42; American Parole Association, New York, N.Y., field secretary, 1942; Bureau of Prisons, Washington, D.C., chief statistician and special assistant to director, 1942-43, 1945-46; United Nations, New York, N.Y., chief of Section of Social Defence, 1946-51; treasurer for food brokerage firm in Brookline, Mass., 1951-65; Boston College, Newton, Mass., visiting professor of criminology, 1965—. Has also taught at New School for Social Research, Rutgers University, United Nations Crime Institute, Victoria University, and Australian Institute of Criminology. *Military service:* U.S. Army, 1943-45; served in North Africa, Italy, and Trieste; became major; received five battle stars. *Awards, honors:* Rockefeller Foundation grant, 1939.

WRITINGS: (With Oliver J. Keller, Jr.) *Halfway Houses: Community-Centered Correction and Treatment,* Heath, 1970; (with Jerry F. Boren) *Crime: International Agenda,* Heath, 1972; *Prisons Inside-Out,* Ballinger, 1974.

Author of reports. Contributor of articles and reviews to social sciences journals, including *Albany Law Review, Harvard Law Review, Federal Probation, Prison Journal, British Journal of Criminology,* and *Journal of Marketing.*

WORK IN PROGRESS: Compiling a textbook in criminology.

* * *

ALPEROVITZ, Gar 1936-

PERSONAL: Born May 5, 1936, in Racine, Wis. *Education:* University of Wisconsin, B.S. (with high honors), 1958; University of California, Berkeley, M.A., 1960; Cambridge University, Ph.D., 1963. *Office:* Exploratory Project for Economic Alternatives, 1519 Connecticut Ave. N.W., Washington, D.C. 20036.

CAREER: Legislative director to U.S. Senator Gaylord Nelson; special assistant to assistant secretary of state for international organization affairs, Washington, D.C.; Brookings Institution, Washington, D.C., guest scholar; Harvard University, Cambridge, Mass., fellow of John F. Kennedy School of Government's Institute of Politics; Institute for Policy Studies, Washington, D.C., fellow; Center for Community Economic Development, Washington, D.C., president; Cambridge Institute, Cambridge, Mass., president; Exploratory Project for Economic Alternatives, Washington, D.C., co-director; fellow of King's College, Cambridge University. *Member:* Phi Beta Kappa.

WRITINGS: Atomic Diplomacy: Hiroshima and Potsdam, Simon & Schuster, 1965; *Cold War Essays,* Doubleday, 1970; (with Staughton Lynd) *Strategy and Program,* Beacon Press, 1973.

* * *

ALSOP, Stewart (Johonnot Oliver) 1914-1974

May 17, 1914—May 26, 1974; American syndicated columnist and political commentator. Obituaries: *New York Times,* May 27, 1974; *Washington Post,* May 27, 1974, May 30, 1974; *AB Bookman's Weekly,* June 17, 1974; *Publishers Weekly,* June 24, 1974; *Current Biography,* July 24, 1974.

* * *

ALT, David 1933-

PERSONAL: Born September 17, 1933, in St. Louis, Mo.; son of Arthur and Louisa Alt; married second wife, Sandra Dewald, June 17, 1972; children: (first marriage) Konrad, Lisa, Sarah; stepdaughters: Debra Bestwick, Diane Bestwick. *Education:* Washington University, St. Louis, Mo., A.B., 1955; University of Minnesota, M.S., 1958; University of Texas, Ph.D., 1961. *Home:* 505 East Beckwith, Missoula, Mont. 59801. *Office:* Department of Geology, University of Montana, Missoula, Mont. 59801.

CAREER: University of Leeds, Leeds, England, research associate, 1961-62; University of Florida, Gainesville, assistant professor of geology, 1962-65; University of Montana, Missoula, assistant professor, 1965-68, associate professor, 1968-72, professor of geology, 1972—. *Member:* Geological Society of America.

WRITINGS: (With Donald Hyndman) *Roadside Geology of the Northern Rockies,* Mountain Press, 1972; (with Hyndman) *Rocks, Ice, and Water,* Mountain Press, 1973; (with Hyndman) *Roadside Geology of Northern California,* Mountain Press, 1974. Contributor to journals.

WORK IN PROGRESS: Research projects relating to the regional geography of the Pacific Northwest and the problems of petrology.

* * *

ALTER, Robert B(ernard) 1935-

PERSONAL: Born April 2, 1935, in New York, N.Y.; son of Harry (a salesman) and Tillie (Zimmerman) Alter; married Judith Berkenbilt, June 4, 1961 (divorced, December, 1972); married Carol Cosman, June 17, 1973; children: (first marriage) Miriam, Dan; (second marriage) Gabriel. *Education:* Columbia University, B.A., 1957; Harvard University, M.A., 1958, Ph.D., 1962. *Religion:* Jewish. *Home:* 123 Tamalpais Rd., Berkeley, Calif. 94708. *Agent:* Georges Borchardt, 145 East 52nd St., New York, N.Y. 10022. *Office:* Department of Comparative Literature, University of California, Berkeley, Calif. 94720.

CAREER: Columbia University, New York, N.Y., instructor, 1962-64, assistant professor of English, 1964-66; University of California, Berkeley, associate professor, 1967-69, professor of Hebrew and comparative literature, 1969—, chairman of comparative literature department, 1970-72. *Member:* American Comparative Literature Association, Association for Jewish Studies. *Awards, honors:* English Institute essay prize, 1965; Guggenheim fellow, 1966-67; National Endowment for the Humanities senior fellow, 1972-73.

WRITINGS: Rogue's Progress: Studies in the Picaresque Novel, Harvard University Press, 1965; *Fielding and the Nature of the Novel,* Harvard University Press, 1968; *After the Tradition,* Dutton, 1969; *Partial Magic: The Novel as a Self-Conscious Genre,* University of California Press, in press. Columnist for *Commentary,* 1965—; contributing editor, 1973—.

WORK IN PROGRESS: Defenses of the Imagination, a collection of essays.

* * *

ALTOMA, Salih J(awad) 1929-

PERSONAL: Surname sometimes appears as Al-Toma; born September 23, 1929, in Karbala, Iraq; son of Jawad K. (a businessman) and Muluk Altoma; married Amal A. Al Khatib, January 21, 1959; children: Tiba, Reef. *Education:* University of Baghdad, B.A., 1952; Harvard University, M.A., 1955, Ed.D., 1957. *Home:* 723 Campus View, Bloomington, Ind. 47401. *Office:* Department of Near Eastern Languages and Literatures, Indiana University, Bloomington, Ind. 47401.

CAREER: University of Baghdad, Baghdad, Iraq, instructor in Arabic, 1957-60, registrar and assistant dean, 1959-60; Embassy of Iraq, Washington, D.C., cultural attache, 1960-63; Harvard University, Cambridge, Mass., research fellow at Center for Middle East Studies, 1963-64; Indiana University, Bloomington, associate professor of Arabic, 1964—. *Member:* American Association of Teachers of Arabic, Linguistic Research Group of Pakistan, Middle East Studies Association. *Awards, honors:* National Endowment for the Humanities grant for research in Egypt.

WRITINGS: Zilal al-Ghuyum (poems), Raabita, 1950; *Al-Rabic al-Muhtadar* (poems), Zahraa, 1952; (with others) *Modern Arabic Literature* (in Arabic), Ministry of Education (Baghdad), 1959; *The Problems of Diglossia in Arabic,* Harvard University Press, 1969; *A Bibliographical Survey of Arabic Dramatic Literature,* Al-Ani (Baghdad), 1969; (co-author) *Intermediate Modern Standard Arabic,* University of Michigan, 1971; *Palestinian Themes in Modern Arabic Literature, 1917-70,* [Cairo], 1972.

WORK IN PROGRESS: A Guide to the Study of Modern Arabic Literature: 1800-1970; An Introduction to Modern Arabic Literature: 1800-1970; and *Saladin in Contemporary Arabic Poetry: A Study and Texts.*

* * *

A. M.
See MEGGED, Aharon

* * *

AMAN, Mohammed M(ohammed) 1940-

PERSONAL: Born January 3, 1940, in Alexandria, Egypt; son of Mohammed Aman (an army officer) and Fathia Ali (al-Maghrabi) Mohammed; married Mary Jo Parker (a librarian), September 15, 1972. *Education:* Cairo University, B.A., 1961; Columbia University, M.S., 1964; University of Pittsburgh, Ph.D., 1968. *Religion:* Islam. *Home:* 137-47 228th St., Laurelton, New York, N.Y. 11413. *Office:* Department of Library and Information Science, St. John's University, Jamaica, N.Y. 11439.

CAREER: Egyptian National Library, Cairo, Egypt, bibliographer and reference librarian, 1961-63; Arab Information Center, New York, N.Y., head librarian, 1963-64; Duquesne University Library, Pittsburgh, Pa., reference librarian, 1966-68; Pratt Institute, New York, N.Y., assistant professor of library science, 1968-69, head of Library Science Library, 1968-69; St. John's University, Jamaica, N.Y., assistant professor, 1969-71, associate professor, 1971-74, professor of library science, 1974—, head of department, 1973—. *Member:* American Library Association, American Society for Information Science, American Association of University Professors, Egyptian American Scholars Association, New York Library Association.

WRITINGS: Analysis of Terminology, Form, and Structure of Subject Headings in Arabic Literature and Formulation of Rules for Arabic Subject Headings, University of Pittsburgh Press, 1968; (contributor) E. J. Josey, editor, *What Black Librarians Are Saying,* Scarecrow, 1972; (contributor) Jean Lowrie, editor, *School Libraries: International Developments,* Scarecrow, 1972; *Arab States Author Headings,* St. John's University Press, 1973; (contributor) Josey, editor, *New Dimensions in Academic Librarianship,* Scarecrow, 1974. Contributor to *Encyclopedia of Library and Information Science.* Honorary contributing editor to *International Library Review,* 1969—. Book reviewer for *American Reference Books Annual,* 1974—, and *Annual Review of Library and Information Science,* 1974—.

WORK IN PROGRESS: Issues and Trends in Cataloging and Classifying Non-Western Library Material; Cataloging Notes with Exemplars.

AVOCATIONAL INTERESTS: Tennis, swimming, gardening, travel.

* * *

AMANUDDIN, Syed 1934-

PERSONAL: Born February 4, 1934, in Mysore, India; son of Syed (a businessman) and Shahzadi (Begum) Jamaluddin; married Ashraf Basith (a social worker), February 18, 1960; children: Irfan, Rizwan. *Education:* University of Mysore, B.A. (honors), 1956, M.A., 1957; Bowling Green State University, Ph.D., 1970; University of London, postdoctoral study, summer, 1973. *Address:* P.O. Box 391, Sumter, S.C. 29150. *Office:* Department of English, Morris College, Sumter, S.C. 29150.

CAREER: College of Arts, Karimnagar, India, lecturer in English, 1958-61; Osmania University, Hyderabad, India, lecturer in English, 1961-67; Morris College, Sumter, S.C., associate professor, 1970-73, professor of English, and chairman of Division of Humanities, 1973—. *Member:* Modern Language Association of America, Committee of Small Magazine Editors and Publishers.

WRITINGS: Hart Crane's Mystical Quest and Other Essays, Poetry Eastwest, 1967; *The Forbidden Fruit* (poems), Kavyalaya (Mysore, India), 1967; *Tiffin State Hospital* (poems) Poetry Eastwest, 1970; *Shoes of Tradition,* Poetry Eastwest, 1970; *The Children of Hiroshima* (poems), Poetry Eastwest, 1970; *Poems of Protest*, Poetry Eastwest, 1972; *System Shaker* (plays), Poetry Eastwest, 1972; (editor with Margaret Diesendorf) *New Poetry from Australia,* Poetry Eastwest, 1973; *Lightning and Love* (poems), Poetry Eastwest, 1973; *The Age of the Female Eunichs* (poems), Poetry Eastwest, 1974. Contributor of poems and reviews to *Books Abroad, Mahfil, Descant,* and *Poetry Australia*. Editor of *Poetry Eastwest,* 1967—, of *Creative Moment,* 1972—.

WORK IN PROGRESS: A collection of plays, *The King Who Sold His Wife; Studies in World English Poetry.*

SIDELIGHTS: Amanuddin wrote: "I love words, people, life, and nature, so I write poetry. Poetry is one thing that has not been corrupted as yet by man; it continues to have a salubrious effect on many minds....my chief contribution to literature in English will be poetry."

* * *

AMBLER, John S(teward) 1932-

PERSONAL: Born January 2, 1932, in Portland, Ore.; son of Herbert (a bank official) and Helen (Gordon) Ambler; married Joyce Hill (a social worker), June 19, 1959; children: Lorraine, Deborah, Mark. *Education:* Willamette University, B.A., 1953; Stanford University, A.M., 1954; University of Bordeaux, Certificat d'Etudes Politiques, 1955; University of California, Berkeley, Ph.D., 1964. *Politics:* Democrat. *Home:* 2242 Dryden Rd., Houston, Tex. 77025. *Office:* Department of Political Science, Rice University, Houston, Tex. 77001.

CAREER: University of California at Berkeley, instructor in political science, 1963-64; Rice University, Houston, Tex., assistant professor, 1964-67, associate professor, 1967-71; professor of political science, 1971—. *Military service:* U.S. Army, 1955-57. *Member:* American Political Science Association, Southern Political Science Association. *Awards, honors:* Fulbright scholarship, 1954-55; Social Science Research Council fellowship, 1961-62; Fulbright research scholarship, 1969.

WRITINGS: The French Army in Politics, 1945-1962, Ohio State University Press, 1966, published as *Soldiers against the State: The French Army in Politics,* Doubleday-Anchor, 1968; *The Government and Politics of France,* Houghton, 1971.

WORK IN PROGRESS: Research in attitudes toward political authorities in France.

* * *

AMBROSE, Alice 1906-

PERSONAL: Born November 25, 1906, in Lexington, Ill.; daughter of Albert Lee (a florist) and Bonnie Belle (Douglass) Ambrose; married Morris Lazerowitz (a writer and professor emeritus of philosophy), June 15, 1938. *Education:* Millikin University, A.B., 1928; University of Wisconsin, M.A., 1929, Ph.D., 1932; Cambridge University, Ph.D., 1938. *Home:* Newhall Rd., Conway, Mass. 01341. *Office:* Department of Philosophy, Smith College, Northampton, Mass. 01060.

CAREER: University of Michigan, Ann Arbor, instructor in psychology, 1935-37; Smith College, Northampton, Mass., assistant professor, 1943-51, professor, 1951-64, Sophia and Austin Smith Professor of Philosophy, 1964-72, professor emeritus, 1972—. *Member:* Mind Association, American Philosophical Association (vice-president, 1966), American Association of University Professors. *Awards, honors:* LL.D., Millikin University, 1958.

WRITINGS: (With husband, Morris Lazerowitz) *Fundamentals of Symbolic Logic* Holt, 1948, revised edition, 1962; (with Lazerowitz) *Logic: The Theory of Formal Inference,* Holt, 1961, revised edition, Scientia, 1972; *Essays in Analysis,* Allen & Unwin, 1966; (editor with Lazerowitz) *G. E. Moore: Essays in Retrospect,* Allen & Unwin, 1970; (editor with Lazerowitz) *Ludwig Wittgenstein: Philosophy and Language,* Allen & Unwin, 1972; (with Lazerowitz) *Philosophical Theories,* Mouton, in press. Editor of *Journal of Symbolic Logic,* 1953-68.

WORK IN PROGRESS; Research on philosophy of mathematics; an essay for a memorial volume on Bertrand Russell, for Allen & Unwin.

* * *

AMISHAI-MAISELS, Ziva
See MAISELS, Maxine S.

* * *

AMOS, Winsom 1921-

PERSONAL: Born May 10, 1921, in Lansing, Mich.; son of Charles and Inez Amos; married Oris Carter (a college professor), April 16, 1954; children: Patsy. *Education:* Ferris State College, B.S., 1951; Michigan State University, graduate study, 1952; Ohio State University, M.A., 1970. *Religion:* Protestant. *Home:* 698 Lawson Dr., Westerville, Ohio 43081. *Office:* Defense Construction Supply Center, 3990 East Broad St., Columbus, Ohio 43216.

CAREER: Teacher in Martinsville, Va., 1951-53; self-employed collection agent in Martinsville, Va., 1953-55; William B. Muse, Jr., Martinsville, Va., broker's assistant, 1953-55; Defense Construction Supply Center, Columbus, Ohio, supply cataloger, 1955-69, counselor, 1969-70, coordinator, 1970—. Self-employed public accountant, 1951—. President of Worthington Human Relations Council, 1971-73. *Military service:* U.S. Army, 1942-45; received Bronze Star. *Member:* Ohio Adult Education Association.

WRITINGS: Like a Dream (poems), Harlo, 1971; *Oriole to Black Mood* (poems), privately printed, 1973. Contributor of poetry to *Pittsburgh Courier, Lansing State Journal, Columbus Call and Post, Poetry Parade, Ohio Adult Education Association Newsletter, Poetry of the Year,* and *Journal of Contemporary Poetry.*

* * *

AMRINE, Michael 1919(?)-1974

1919(?)—February 17, 1974; American science and political writer. Obituaries: *Washington Post,* February 18, 1974; *New York Times,* February 19, 1974.

* * *

ANASTASIOU, Clifford (John) 1929-

PERSONAL: Born February 24, 1929, in Vancouver, British Columbia, Canada; son of John and Lydia (Stead) Anastasiou; married Joan Diane Barton (a professor), September 20, 1952; children: Melanie Jane, Karen Lea, Roger Barton. *Education:* Victoria College, student, 1947-50; University of British Columbia, B.A., 1952, M.Ed., 1957; Claremont Graduate School, Ph.D., 1963. *Home:* 3931 Southwest Marine Dr., Vancouver, British Columbia, Canada. *Office:* University of British Columbia, Vancouver, British Columbia, Canada.

CAREER: High school biology teacher in West Vancouver, British Columbia, 1955-57, and Anaheim, Calif., 1957-60; University of British Columbia, Vancouver, assistant professor, 1962-66, associate professor, 1966-71, professor of education, 1971—. Staff biologist for Education Development Corp., 1964-65.

WRITINGS: Reading about Science, Book I, Holt, 1968; *Teachers, Children, and Things,* Holt, 1971. Author of research studies in mycology.

WORK IN PROGRESS: Directing Vancouver Environment Education Project; research on children's concepts of space.

* * *

ANDERSON, Chuck 1933-

PERSONAL: Born March 25, 1933, in Queens, N.Y.; son of Charles A. (an insurance executive) and Margaret (Bassett) Anderson; married Judith Hall, August 31, 1957; children: Donald, Gordon, Edward. *Education:* Bucknell University, B.A., 1956; Adelphi University, M.A., 1970. *Politics:* Independent. *Religion:* Episcopalian. *Home:* 37 Chapel Rd., Brookhaven, N.Y. 11719. *Office:* Longwood High School, Middle Island, N.Y.

CAREER: High school teacher of English in Bellport, N.Y., 1960-63; Longwood High School, Middle Island, N.Y., teacher of English and media studies, 1963—. Instructor in philosophy and mythology at Suffolk County Community College, 1966-70; fellow, Center for Understanding Media, New York, N.Y., 1970—; artist-in-residence at St. Mary of Redman School, 1973. Member of Brookhaven Volunteer Fire Department, 1969-73. *Member:* National Educational Association, New York Teachers Association.

WRITINGS: The Electric Journalist, Praeger, 1973; *Video Power: Grass Roots Television,* Praeger, in press. Contributor of articles and reviews to *Media and Methods, Radical Software, Long Island Advance,* and *East End Independent.*

ANDERSON, James D(esmond) 1933-

PERSONAL: Born February 9, 1933, in Christiansburg, Va.; son of Walter Willard and Sarah (Hardin) Anderson; married Winifred Guthrie, June 12, 1955; children: Walter, Mark, Kent. *Education:* Northwestern University, B.A., 1955; Virginia Theological Seminary, M.Div., 1961. *Home:* 3204 Old Dominion Blvd., Alexandria, Va. 22305. *Office:* Diocese of Washington, Episcopal Church House, Mount St. Alban, Washington, D.C. 20016.

CAREER: Associate rector of Episcopal church in Kenosha, Wis., 1961-63; Bethesda-by-the-Sea, Palm Beach, Fla., director of Christian education, 1963-65; priest in charge of Episcopal church in Arlington, Va., 1965-67; Diocese of Washington, Washington, D.C., bishop's assistant for parish development, 1967—. Member of board of directors of Mid-Atlantic Training Committee, and of Metropolitan Ecumenical Training Center, Inc. *Military service:* U.S. Marine Corps, communications officer, 1955-58; became first lieutenant. *Member:* International Association of Applied Social Scientists (charter member), National Training Laboratories, Association for Creative Change.

WRITINGS: (Contributor) John Westerhoff, editor, *A Colloquy on Christian Education,* Pilgrim Press, 1972; (with Jean M. Haldane and others) *Prescription for Parishes,* Seabury, 1973; *To Come Alive!: A New Proposal for Revitalizing the Local Church,* Harper, 1973.

WORK IN PROGRESS: Research on information systems in the church, and on a behavioral scientist's view of the ministry in the local church.

* * *

ANDERSON, Mary 1939-

PERSONAL: Born January 20, 1939, in New York, N.Y.; daughter of Andrew Joseph and Nellie (DeHaan) Quirk; married Carl Anderson (a commercial artist), March 1, 1958; children: Lisa, Maja, Chersteen. *Agent:* Curtis Brown Ltd., 60 East 56th St., New York, N.Y. 10022.

CAREER: Actress in Off-Broadway productions, New York, N.Y., 1956-58; secretary in advertising and television fields, New York, N.Y., 1956-59.

WRITINGS—For young people: (With Hope Campbell, pseudonym of Geraldine Wallis) *There's a Pizza Back in Cleveland,* Four Winds, 1972; *Matilda Investigates,* Atheneum, 1973; *Emma's Search for Something,* Atheneum, 1973; *I'm Nobody! Who Are You?,* Atheneum, 1974; *The After-Christmasers,* Atheneum, in press.

SIDELIGHTS: "The main motivation behind my work is to recreate for others (and myself) the pleasure I received from reading as a child. Children's books are one of the last strongholds in literature where optimism, joy, compassion, and a sheer wonder for the world are still being portrayed successfully." *Avocational interests:* Interior decoration, biking, making miniature doll furniture, sewing.

* * *

ANDERSON, Robert H(enry) 1918-

PERSONAL: Born July 28, 1918, in Milwaukee, Wis.; son of Robert Dean (a production manager) and Eleanor (Weil) Anderson; married Mary Jane Hopkins (an educational specialist and professional harpist), July 19, 1941; children: Dean Robert, Lynn Mary (Mrs. William D. Grant), Scott William, Carol Jane. *Education:* University of Wisconsin, B.A., 1939, M.A., 1942; University of Chicago, Ph.D.,

1949. *Politics:* Democrat. *Religion:* Episcopalian. *Home:* 7703 Knoxville Dr., Lubbock, Tex. 79413. *Office:* College of Education, Texas Tech University, P. O. Box 4560, Lubbock, Tex. 79409.

CAREER: Junior high school teacher and coach in Oconomowoc, Wis., 1941-43; elementary school principal in River Forest, Ill., 1947-49; superintendent of schools, Park Forest, Ill., 1949-54; Harvard University, Graduate School of Education, Cambridge, Mass., lecturer, 1954-59, associate professor, 1959-61, professor of education, 1962-73, director of elementary school internship and apprentice-teaching program, 1954-63, director of Teaching Teams Project in Lexington, Mass., 1957-64; Texas Tech University, Lubbock, dean of College of Education, 1973—. Visiting professor, University of Iowa, 1953, University of Wisconsin, 1960, and University of Hawaii, 1962. Editorial advisor, Houghton Mifflin Co., 1968—. *Military service:* U.S. Navy Reserve, Supply Corps, 1943-46; became lieutenant. *Member:* National Society for the Study of Education, American Association of School Administrators, Association for Supervision and Curriculum Development, National Education Association, American Educational Research Association, National Association of Elementary School Principals, Phi Delta Kappa. *Awards, honors:* M.A., Harvard University, 1959; presidential citation from Illinois Association of School Administrators, 1973.

WRITINGS: (With J. I. Goodlad) *The Nongraded Elementary School,* Harcourt, 1959, revised edition, 1963; (with others) *The Healthy Child: His Physical, Psychological, and Social Development,* edited by H. C. Stuart and D. G. Prugh, Harvard University Press, 1960; *Teaching in a World of Change,* Harcourt, 1966; (editor with H. G. Shane) *As the Twig is Bent,* Houghton, 1971; (editor with M. Hiratsuka and Isao Amagi) *Current Trends in Education* (in Japanese), Dai-ichi Koki (Japan), 1971; (editor) *Education in Anticipation of Tomorrow,* Charles A. Jones Publishing, 1973; *Opting for Openness,* National Association of Elementary School Principals, 1973.

Contributor: J. T. Shaplin and H. F. Olds, Jr., editors, *Team Teaching,* Harper, 1964; Richard I. Miller, editor, *Perspectives on Educational Change,* Appleton, 1967; D. D. Bushnell and D. Allen, editors, *The Computer in American Education,* Wiley, 1967; Sidney G. Tickton, editor, *To Improve Learning: An Evaluation of Instructional Technology,* Bowker, 1971.

Author of introduction: Kaoru Yamamoto, editor, *The Child and His Image: Self-Concept in the Early Years,* Houghton, 1972; Robert D. Hess and Doreen J. Croft, *Teachers of Young Children,* Houghton, 1972; Hess and Croft, *An Activities Handbook for Teachers of Young Children,* Houghton, 1972; Richard E. Hodges and E. Hugh Rudorf, editors, *Language and Learning to Read: What Teachers Need to Know about Language,* Houghton, 1972; Kevin Ryan and James M. Cooper, *Kaleidoscope: Readings in Education,* Houghton, 1972; Ryan and Cooper, *Those Who Can, Teach,* Houghton, 1972.

Contributor to yearbooks, and to Macmillan's *Encyclopedia of Educational Research.* Contributor of about fifty articles to journals, including *NEA Journal, Educational Leadership, Architectural Record,* and *Education Digest.* Consulting editor, *Colloquy,* 1967-71.

WORK IN PROGRESS: A book on team teaching, with C. J. Gill and John Freeman, for Basil Blackwell.

SIDELIGHTS: Anderson writes that his main interests are in promoting flexible school organization patterns by implementing team teaching, open programs, open-space architecture, and flexible uses of personnel. He has both worked and traveled abroad, having made six trips around the world between 1968 and 1973.

* * *

ANDERSON, Robert Newton 1929-

PERSONAL: Born March 14, 1929, in Saskatoon, Saskatchewan, Canada; son of George W. and Bertha M. (Sloan) Anderson; married Shirley Anne Bennett, March 24, 1951; children: Janis, Ellen, Jeff, Paul, David. *Education:* University of Saskatchewan, B.A., 1949, B.Ed., 1951; University of Minnesota, M.A., 1959, Ph.D., 1963. *Religion:* United Church of Canada. *Home:* 2615 Sixth Ave. S., Lethbridge, Alberta, Canada. *Office:* Department of Comparative Education, University of Lethbridge, Lethbridge, Alberta, Canada.

CAREER: Regina Collegiate System, Regina, Saskatchewan, history teacher and head of department, 1950-58; Province of Saskatchewan Department of Education, associate director of curriculum, 1958-59; University of Calgary, Calgary, Alberta, professor of education and head of department, 1959-65; University of Saskatchewan, Regina, professor of secondary education and head of department, 1965-69; University of Lethbridge, Lethbridge, Alberta, professor of comparative education, 1969—, member of board of governors, 1970-74, dean of education, 1974—. Canadian representative to National Education Association World Conference on Education, Asilomar, Calif., 1970. Visiting professor at University of Lagos and advisor to the Government of Nigeria, 1970-71; advisor to Government of Alberta, 1974—.

Member: Comparative and International Education Society, World Council on Curriculum (founder), Philosophy of Education Society (fellow), Canadian Society for Studies in Education, Canadian Association of African Studies, Canadian Education Association, Canadian College of Teachers, Canadian Foundations of Education Association (founding president, 1962, 1970), Northwest Regional Philosophy of Education Society (president, 1965-66).

WRITINGS: Institutional Analysis of Mount Royal College, McLeod, 1964; (with others) *Foundation Disciplines and the Study of Education,* Macmillan, 1968; *Two White Oxen: A Perspective on Early Saskatoon,* Unileth Press, 1972. Contributor to education journals.

WORK IN PROGRESS: Research in international comparative studies on educational goals in Africa and North America, on Canada's involvement in international education, and on curriculum development in Nigeria.

* * *

ANDERSON, T(heodore) W(ilbur, Jr.) 1918-

PERSONAL: Born June 5, 1918, in Minneapolis, Minn.; son of Theodore Wilbur (a clergyman) and Evelyn (Johnson) Anderson; married Dorothy Fisher (a clinical social worker), July 8, 1950; children: Robert Lewis, Janet Lynn, Jeanne Elizabeth. *Education:* North Park College, A.A., 1937; Northwestern University, B.S. (with highest distinction), 1939; Princeton University, M.A., 1942, Ph.D., 1945. *Home:* 746 Santa Ynez St., Stanford, Calif. 94305. *Office:* Department of Statistics, Stanford University, Stanford, Calif. 94305.

CAREER: Princeton University, Princeton, N.J., instructor in mathematics, 1941-43, research associate for national defense research committee, 1943-45; University of Chicago, Chicago, Ill., research associate for Cowles Commission for Research in Economics, 1945-46; Columbia University, New York, N.Y., instructor, 1946-47, assistant professor, 1947-50, associate professor, 1950-56, professor of mathematical statistics, 1956-67, chairman of department, 1956-60, 1964-65; Stanford University, Stanford, Calif., professor of statistics and economics, 1967—. Visiting associate professor at Stanford University, 1954; visiting professor at Imperial College of Science and Technology (London), University of Moscow, and University of Paris, 1967-68. Fellow of Center for Advanced Study in the Behavioral Sciences, 1957-58, visiting scholar, 1972-73. Member of executive committee of Conference Board of Mathematical Sciences, 1963-64; scientific director of North Atlantic Treaty Organization (NATO) Advanced Study Institute on Discriminant Analysis and Its Applications, 1972. Member of National Academy of Sciences and National Research Council committees. Consultant to RAND Corp. and Cowles Foundation for Research in Economics.

MEMBER: International Statistical Institute, American Academy of Arts and Sciences (fellow), American Mathematical Society, American Statistical Association (fellow; vice-president, 1971-73), Institute of Mathematical Statistics (fellow; president, 1963; member of council), Econometric Society (fellow), American Association for the Advancement of Science (fellow), Biometric Society, Psychometric Society (member of council of directors), American Association of University Professors, Royal Statistical Society (fellow), Indian Statistical Institute, Phi Beta Kappa, Sigma Xi. *Awards, honors:* Guggenheim fellowship at University of Stockholm and Cambridge University, 1947-48.

WRITINGS: (Contributor) Tjalling C. Koopmans, editor, *Statistical Inference in Dynamic Economic Models,* Wiley, 1950; (contributor) Jerzy Neyman, editor, *Proceedings of the Second Berkeley Symposium on Mathematical Statistics and Probability,* University of California Press, 1951; (contributor) Paul F. Lazarsfeld, editor, *Mathematical Thinking in the Social Sciences,* Free Press, 1954; (contributor) Dwight C. Miner, editor, *History of the Faculty of Political Science,* Columbia University Press, 1955; (editor) Abraham Wald, *Selected Papers in Statistics and Probability,* McGraw, 1955; (contributor) Neyman, editor, *Proceedings of the Third Berkeley Symposium on Mathematical Statistics and Probability,* Volume V, University of California Press, 1956; *An Introduction to Multivariate Statistical Analysis,* Wiley, 1958; (contributor) Ulf Grenander, editor, *Probability and Statistics: The Harald Cramer Volume,* Almqvist & Wiksell, 1959.

(Contributor) Ingram Olkin, S. G. Ghurye, and other editors, *Contributions to Probability and Statistics: Essays in Honor of Harold Hotelling,* Stanford University Press, 1960; (contributor) Kenneth J. Arrow, Samuel Karlin, and Patrick Suppes, editors, *Mathematical Methods in the Social Sciences,* Stanford University Press, 1960; (contributor) R. Duncan Luce, Robert R. Bush, and Eugene Galanter, editors, *Readings in Mathematical Psychology,* Volume I, Wiley, 1963; (contributor) Murray Rosenblatt, editor, *Proceedings of the Symposium on Time Series Analysis,* Wiley, 1963; (contributor) *Proceedings of the IBM Scientific Computing Symposium in Statistics,* Data Processing Division, International Business Machines, 1965; (contributor) P. R. Krishnaiah, editor, *Multivariate Analysis,* Academic Press, Volume I, 1966, Volume II, 1969; (editor and contributor) S. S. Wilks, *Collected Papers: Contributions to Mathematical Statistics,* Wiley, 1967; (contributor) Lucien LeCam and Neyman, editors, *Proceedings of the Fifth Berkeley Symposium in Mathematical Statistics and Probability,* Volume I, University of California Press, 1967; (contributor) Lazarsfeld and Neil Henry, editors, *Latent Structure Analysis,* Houghton, 1968.

(Contributor) J. Malcolm Dowling and Fred Glahe, editors, *Readings in Econometric Theory,* Colorado Associated University Press, 1970; (contributor) R. C. Bose, I. M. Chakravarti, and other editors, *Essays in Probability and Statistics,* University of North Carolina Press, 1970; *The Statistical Analysis of Time Series,* Wiley, 1971; (with S. Das Gupta and G. P. H. Styan) *A Bibliography of Multivariate Statistical Analysis,* Halsted Press, 1972; (contributor) LeCam, Neyman, and Elizabeth Scott, editors, *Proceedings of the Sixth Berkeley Symposium in Mathematical Statistics and Probability,* Volume I, University of California Press, 1972; (contributor) Theophilus Cacoullos, editor, *Discriminant Analysis and Applications,* Academic Press, 1973; (with S. L. Sclove) *Introductory Statistical Analysis,* Houghton, 1974.

Contributor to *International Encyclopedia of the Social Sciences.* Contributor of about seventy articles to scientific journals, including *Journal of the American Statistical Association, Econometrica, Annals of Statistics, Biometrika, Bulletin of the International Statistical Institute,* and *Australian Journal of Statistics.* Editor of *Annals of Mathematical Statistics,* 1950-52; member of editorial board of *Psychometrika,* 1954-72.

* * *

ANDERSON, Wayne Jeremy 1908-

PERSONAL: Born August 30, 1908, in Salt Lake City, Utah; son of Parley Pratt (a plant superintendent) and Sarah Ettie (Jeremy) Anderson; married Ruth Elise Mace, June 14, 1938; children: Annette (Mrs William A. Rifley), Cherie (Mrs. Robert H. Muirbrook), James, Julie (Mrs. David Curle), Jill. *Education:* University of Utah, B.A., 1934, M.A., 1937, Ph.D., 1954; also studied at University of Minnesota. *Politics:* Independent. *Religion:* Church of Jesus Christ of Latter-day Saints (Mormon). *Home:* 4715 Girard Ave. S., Minneapolis, Minn. 55409. *Office:* University of Minnesota, 30B Nicholson Hall, Minneapolis, Minn. 55414.

CAREER: Missionary to Switzerland and Germany for Church of Jesus Christ of Latter-day Saints, 1928-31; public school teacher in Salt Lake City, Utah, 1934-41; U.S. Army, Corps of Engineers, Salt Lake City, Utah, head of expediting department, 1941-45; Utah Social Hygiene Association, Salt Lake City, Utah, executive secretary, 1945-49; University of Minnesota, Minneapolis, assistant professor, 1949-54, associate professor, 1954-65, professor of family studies, 1965—. Private marriage counselor; former human relations consultant; bishop of Mormon Church. Venereal disease educator for Utah State Health Department, 1945-49; member of Minnesota Governor's Council on Children and Youth, 1957-67; member of Planned Parenthood Speakers Bureau; member of International Advisory Committee for Parents without Partners, 1966-70.

MEMBER: American Psychological Association, American Association of Marriage and Family Counselors, Minnesota Council on Family Life (president, 1962-64).

WRITINGS: (Contributor) Horace T. Morse and Paul L. Dressel, editors, *General Education for Personal Maturity,* W. C. Brown, 1960; *Meeting the Needs of Today's Family,* Publishers Press, 1962; *Design for Family Living,* Denison, 1964; *How to Understand Sex,* Denison, 1966; *How to Discuss Sex with Teen-Agers,* Denison, 1969; (with Lindsay R. Curtis) *Living, Loving, and Marrying,* Deseret, 1969; *How to Explain Sex to Children,* Denison, 1972; *Harmon Killebrew: Baseball's Superstar,* Deseret, 1972; *Alone, But Not Lonely,* Deseret, 1973; *Challenges for Successful Family Living,* Denison, 1974. Contributor to professional journals.

* * *

ANDERSON, William H(arry) 1905-1972

PERSONAL: Born June 9, 1905, in Marinette, Wis.; son of John (a lumberman) and Anna (Olsen) Anderson; married Ione Swanson, September 2, 1936; children: William Harland. *Education:* University of Wisconsin—Madison, A.B. (cum laude), 1928, LL.B. (cum laude), 1938, Ph.D., 1945. *Religion:* Lutheran. *Home:* 539 Wesley Way, Claremont, Calif. 91711.

CAREER: High school history and social science teacher in West Chicago, Ill., 1929-36; admitted to Wisconsin Bar, 1938; Woodward & May (law office), Madison, Wis., attorney, 1938-46; University of Southern California, Los Angeles, associate professor, 1946-52, professor of economics, 1952-66, chairman of department, 1957-61; Claremont Men's College and Graduate School, Claremont, Calif., professor of economics, 1966-67, John C. Lincoln Professor of Public Finance, 1967-72, chairman of department and director of John C. Lincoln School of Public Finance, 1966-72. Assistant professor at University of Wisconsin, 1945-46; professor at Institute for Administrative Affairs (Tehran), 1956-57. *Awards, honors:* Certificate of honor from Achievement Recognition Institute, 1973, for accomplishments and contributions to American culture.

WRITINGS: *Taxation and the American Economy,* Prentice-Hall, 1951; (contributor) Arthur P. Becker, editor, *Land-Value Taxation and Contemporary Economic Thought,* Boulder Conference Committee, 1964; *Financing Modern Government,* Houghton, 1973. Contributor to *Journal of Land and Public Utility Economics.*

(Died October 6, 1972)

* * *

ANDERSSON, Theodore 1903-

PERSONAL: Surname originally Levine; name legally changed in 1931; born February 18, 1903, in New Haven, Conn.; son of Seth Samuel and Anna Erika (Johnson) Levine; married Harriet Josephine Murdock, April 8, 1930; children: Theodore Murdock, Margit (Mrs. Timothy R. Clifford). *Education:* Yale University, B.A., 1925, M.A., 1926, Ph.D., 1931. *Home:* 1006 Lund St., Austin, Tex. 78704. *Office:* Foreign Language Education Center, University of Texas, Austin, Tex. 78712.

CAREER: Yale University, New Haven, Conn., instructor, 1927-37, associate professor of French, 1946-55, director of undergraduate instruction in French, 1946-51, director of Master of Arts in Teaching program, 1951-54, associate director, 1954-55; American University, Washington, D.C., professor of Romance languages, 1937-41, head of department, 1937-41; Wells College, Aurora, N.Y., associate professor, 1941-43, professor of Romance languages, 1943-45, head of department, 1943-45; U.S. Department of State, International Exchange, Division of Cultural Cooperation and Educational Advisors, chief of Western European Section, 1945-46; Modern Language Association of America, New York, N.Y., associate secretary, 1955-56, associate director, 1955-56, director of foreign language program, 1956-57; University of Texas, Austin, professor of Romance languages, 1957—, head of department, 1959-68. Visiting professor at State University of New York at Albany, summer, 1937, Harvard University, summer, 1948, Middlebury College, summer, 1954, University of Wisconsin, summer, 1954 and 1955, Stanford University, summer, 1955, University of Washington, summer, 1958, and University of Hawaii, spring, 1959. Director of UNESCO Seminar for the Teaching of Modern Languages for World Understanding, Nuwara Eliya, Ceylon, 1953; U.S. delegate to UNESCO Institute for Education, Hamburg, Germany, 1959-62; Ford Foundation program specialist for modern languages, Santiago, Chile, 1964-65; Southwest Educational Development Laboratory, U.S. Office of Education, Austin, Tex., director of bilingual design project, 1968-69, director of bilingual section, 1969-70, resource specialist, 1970-71.

MEMBER: International Institute of Ibero-American Literature (president, 1961-63), American Council on the Teaching of Foreign Languages, Modern Language Association of America, American Association of Teachers of French, American Association of Teachers of Spanish and Portuguese (vice-president, 1972; president, 1973), National Education Association, International and Comparative Education Society, Teachers of English to Speakers of Other Languages, Phi Beta Kappa. *Awards, honors:* Decorated Chevalier of French Legion of Honor, 1954, for contributions to Franco-American educational and cultural relations.

WRITINGS: *Carlos Maria Ocantos: Argentine Novelist,* Yale University Press, 1934; (editor with Thomas G. Borgin) *French Plays,* American Book Co., 1941; *The Teaching of Foreign Languages in the Elementary School,* Heath, 1953; (with Felix Walter) *The Teaching of Modern Languages,* UNESCO, 1955; (with others) *The Education of the Secondary School Teacher,* Wesleyan University Press, 1962; *Foreign Languages in the Elementary School: A Struggle against Mediocrity,* University of Texas Press, 1969; (with Mildred Boyer) *Bilingual Schooling in the United States,* Southwest Educational Development Laboratory (Austin, Tex.), 1970; (contributor) Merrill Swain, editor, *Bilingual Schooling: Some Experiences in Canada and the United States,* Ontario Institute for Studies in Education, 1972; (editor with William F. Mackey) *Bilingualism in Early Childhood,* Newbury House Publishers, in press. Contributor to *International Review of Education, Modern Language Journal,* and other professional journals.

WORK IN PROGRESS: Research on learning of languages in early childhood, learning of reading from ages two to five, and the critical age for language learning.

* * *

ANDREAS, Thomas

See WILLIAMS, Thomas (Andrew)

* * *

ANDREWS, Allen 1913-

PERSONAL: Born April 25, 1913, in London, England;

son of Ernest Samuel and Jessie (Hammond) Andrews; married Joyce Antonietta Garbutt, January 16, 1957; children: Robert Allen. *Education:* Oxford University, M.A., 1935. *Home:* 72 Princes Ct., Brompton Rd., London SW3 1ET, England.

CAREER: Sunday Pictorial, London, England, feature writer and film critic, 1946; feature writer for *Public Opinion,* 1949, *Sunday Pictorial,* 1950, and *Illustrated,* 1952 (all in London); *Daily Herald,* London, feature writer and features editor, 1954-56; writer and free-lance journalist, 1957—. *Military service:* Royal Air Force, 1940-46; became sergeant. *Member:* Society of Authors, National Union of Journalists.

WRITINGS: Proud Fortress: The Fighting History of Gibraltar, Evans Brothers, 1958, Dutton, 1959; *Earthquake,* Angus & Robertson, 1963; *The Mad Motorists: The Great Peking-Paris Race of 1907,* Harrap, 1964, Lippincott, 1965; *Sex and Marriage,* George Newnes, 1964; *Slimming for Men and Women,* George Newnes, 1964; *Relax and Sleep Well,* George Newnes, 1965; *Those Magnificent Men in Their Flying Machines* (with drawings by Ronald Searle), Norton, 1965; *She Doubles Her Money,* Ebury Press, 1966; *The Splendid Pauper: Moreton Frewen,* Harrap, 1968, Lippincott, 1969; *The Prosecutor: Mervyn Pugh,* Harrap, 1968; *Monte Carlo or Bust: Those Daring Young Men in Their Flying Jalopies* (with drawings by Searle), Dobson, 1969; *Quotations for Speakers and Writers,* George Newnes, 1969; *The Air Marshals: The Air War in Western Europe,* Morrow, 1970; *The Royal Whore: Barbara Villiers, Countess of Castlemaine,* Chilton, 1970; *Lafayette in London,* Genevieve, 1972; *Intensive Inquiries: Britain's Best Detection Chosen by Britain's Best Detectives,* St. Martin's, 1973. Ghost writer of company histories and of several autobiographies. Contributor to London journals.

WORK IN PROGRESS: A Burning Crown, a biography of Holy Roman Emperor Frederick II; *The Man of Quality,* a biography of Horace Walpole; *Love and Death in Bloomsbury,* a novel.

SIDELIGHTS: Andrews wrote to *CA:* "My deep pleasure is to get tangled, but not drowned, in a morass of facts and to discipline them into understandable order;. . .I prefer to write creative history and biography. My additional soft spots are for crime, for show business, and for the lovely land of Italy." Andrews' books have been published in Australia, Germany, the Netherlands, Sweden, Italy, France, Spain, and Czechoslovakia. Feature-length films have been made of *The Mad Motorists, Those Magnificent Men in Their Flying Machines* and *Monte Carlo or Bust,* the latter two films having preceded the book versions.

* * *

ANDREWS, Barry Geoffrey 1943-

PERSONAL: Born February 13, 1943, in Auburn, New South Wales, Australia; son of Stanley Geoffrey William (a distributor) and Evelyn Jean (McWilliam) Andrews; married Robyn Gwladys Turner, May 10, 1968; children: Naomi Robyn, Luke Geoffrey. *Education:* University of New South Wales, B.A. (honors), 1963, M.A. (honors), 1969; University of Sydney, diploma in education, 1964. *Home:* 8 Tooms Pl., Lyons 2606, Australian Capital Territory, Australia. *Office:* Department of Language and Literature, Royal Military College, University of New South Wales, Duntroon 2606, Australian Capital Territory, Australia.

CAREER: Sydney Teachers College, Sydney, Australia, junior lecturer in English, 1965-66; English teacher in boy's school in Petersham, New South Wales, Australia, 1968-69; University of New South Wales, Royal Military College, Duntroon, Australia, lecturer in English for Faculty of Military Studies, 1970—. *Member:* Australian Society for the Study of Labour History (Australian Capital Territory branch), English Association (New South Wales branch).

WRITINGS: Tales of the Convict System: Selected Stories of Prince Warung, University of Queensland Press, 1974; *William Astley,* Twayne, in press. Contributor to *Australian Dictionary of Biography,* and to *Australian Literary Studies* and *Labour History.*

WORK IN PROGRESS: Australian Literature to 1900, for "Gale Information Guide" series, publication expected about 1976.

AVOCATIONAL INTERESTS: Cricket.

* * *

ANDREWS, Bruce 1948-

PERSONAL: Born April 1, 1948, in Chicago, Ill.; son of Thomas G. (a professor) and Vivian (Noh) Andrews; married Ellen Pennell Lukens (an educational researcher), June 7, 1969. *Education:* Johns Hopkins University, B.A., 1970, M.A., 1970; Harvard University, further graduate study, 1971—. *Home:* 15 Trowbridge St., #3, Cambridge, Mass. 02138.

CAREER: U.S. Office of Education, Washington, D.C., administrative assistant in arts and humanities program of Bureau of Research, 1969; President's Commission on International Trade and Investment Policy, Washington, D.C., assistant to the director, 1970. Consultant to planning staff for National Institute of Education, 1971.

WRITINGS: Edge (poetry and prose), Some of Us Press, 1973; *A Cappella* (poetry and prose), Ghost Dance Press, 1973; *Appalachia* (poetry), Great Outdoor Press, 1973; *Corona* (poetry), Burning Deck Press, 1973; *Vowels* (prose), O Press, 1974.

Work is represented in anthologies, including *The Young American Poets: Second Selection,* edited by Paul Carroll, Big Table Books, in press; *Living Underground: Prose,* edited by Hugh Fox, Whitson Press, in press; *Whitson Yearbook: 1974-75,* edited by Fox, Whitson Press, in press; *Essaying Essays,* edited by Richard Kostelanetz, Something Else Press, in press; *None of the Above,* edited by Michael Lally, Crossing Press, in press.

Writing has been presented at art shows, including "Words/Objects," Cambridge, Mass., 1973; "Premises Premises," Seattle, Wash., 1973; "Five Boston Conceptual Artists," Boston, Mass., 1974; "Artists' Books," Seattle, Wash., 1974; "Art and Language," Seattle, Wash., 1974.

Contributor of stories and poems to about fifty literary journals, including *Paris Review, Greenfield Review, Occident, Assembling, Black Box,* and *Alcheringa.* Co-editor of *Toothpick,* 1974.

WORK IN PROGRESS: Empire and Society: Toward an Explanation of American Policy in Vietnam; research on the relationship between domestic society and state action, on forms of explanation in the social sciences, and on roots of American imperialism.

SIDELIGHTS: Andrews writes: "Along with a group of other writers, I'm trying to explore the limits and uses of language in the arts—to use words as material, as 'self-valuable' elements, as the main event of the work, not as a transport vehicle for distracting attention away from the language and toward some prior imposed descriptive or expressivist function. Words as sensory objects with intrinsic significance, and not only as signs, representations, or mirrors. This means I've tried to use non-referential or prosodic elements as ways of organizing and not merely ornamenting the works. This allows one to attenuate the linkages of syntax, or between signifiers and signifieds. Words have connotations and associative chains but you don't need to insistently yoke these together with the aim becoming that of representation, playing with discourse or rhetoric. Language can be its own documentary, and it can do more than point outside itself to some other event or picture. It can be self-motivated, self-justifying, self-referential, and self-important. This is the lesson of modernism, of a few writers (such as Gertrude Stein, Clark Coolidge, Ron Silliman, etc.) and the major traditions in the non-language arts."

* * *

ANDREWS, Lyman 1938-

PERSONAL: Born April 2, 1938, in Denver, Colo.; son of Lyman Henry and Patricia (Yorke) Andrews. *Education:* Brandeis University, B.A., 1960; also studied at King's College, London, 1960-61, and University of California, Berkeley, 1961-63. *Politics:* Socialist. *Religion:* None. *Home:* Digby Hall, Stoughton Dr. S., Leicester LE2 2NB, England. *Office:* University of Leicester, Leicester LE1 7RH, England.

CAREER: Swansea University College, Swansea, Wales, assistant lecturer in English, 1964-65; University of Leicester, Leicester, England, lecturer in American literature, 1965—. Consultant to East Midlands Art Association, 1969-70. *Member:* International P.E.N., National Poetry Secretariat. *Awards, honors:* Fulbright fellowship, 1960-61; James Phelan fellowship in poetry, University of California, Berkeley, 1963-64.

WRITINGS: *Ash Flowers,* Contemporary Poetry, 1958; *Fugitive Visions,* White Rabbit Press, 1962; *The Death of Mayakovsky,* Calder & Boyars, 1968, Red Dust, 1970; *Kaleidoscope: New and Selected Poems,* Calder & Boyars, 1973. Author of poetry column in *Sunday Times;* associate editor of *Minnesota Review.*

WORK IN PROGRESS: A study of American culture from 1957; a long poem about Denver, Colo.

SIDELIGHTS: It is Andrews' opinion that "a writer should write, not talk about it. Anything of interest in him personally can be seen in the writings."

* * *

ANDREWS, Michael F(rank) 1916-

PERSONAL: Born March 14, 1916, in Cairnbrook, Pa.; son of Frank (a miner) and Libra (Testa) Andrews; married Helen Wilma Baker (an administrative executive), December 30, 1940; children: Judi (Mrs. Stanley Thomas III), Connee (Mrs. Larry Dolin), Michael C. *Education:* Attended Juniata College, 1935-37; University of Kansas, B.F.A., 1940, M.S., 1948; Ohio State University, Ph.D., 1952. *Home:* 6657 Woodchuck Hill Rd., Jamesville, N.Y. 13078. *Office:* Department of Synaesthetic Education, Syracuse University, Syracuse, N.Y. 13210.

CAREER: Public school teacher in Lawrence and Hays, Kan., 1940-42; University of Kansas, Lawrence, instructor in art, 1945-48; Ohio State University, Columbus, instructor in art, 1948-50; University of Southern California, Los Angeles, assistant professor of art education, 1950-52; University of Wisconsin, Madison, assistant professor of art education, 1952-55; Syracuse University, Syracuse, N.Y., professor of art, 1955-70, professor of synaesthetic education, 1970—. Visiting professor at University of Hawaii, 1963, and summer, 1967. Consultant in art therapy at Marcy State Hospital. *Military service:* U.S. Army Air Forces, 1942-45; became first lieutenant.

MEMBER: International Society for Education through Art, National Art Educators Association (president of Eastern region, 1966-68), National Education Association, Eastern Regional Art Educators Association (president, 1967-69). *Awards, honors:* First place in professional division for sculpture at Ohio State Fair, 1949; National Decorative Arts and Ceramic Exhibition honorable mention, 1949; Columbus Art League sculpture award, 1950; Sculpture House award, 1953, for metal sculpture; Wisconsin Salon of Art award, 1954; honorable mention for Hall of Education symbol for New York World's Fair, 1962.

WRITINGS: (With Maud Ellsworth) *Growing with Art,* eight books, Benjamin Sanborn, 1950; (editor and contributor) *Aesthetic Form and Education,* Syracuse University Press, 1958; (editor) *Creativity and Psychological Health,* Syracuse University Press, 1961; *Creative Printmaking,* Prentice-Hall, 1964; *Creative Education: The Liberation of Man,* Syracuse University Press, 1965; *Sculpture and Ideas,* Prentice-Hall, 1966; (with Larry Bakke, O. Charles Giordano and James Ridlon) *Synaesthetic Education,* Syracuse University Press, 1971. Co-author of educational film, "People, Purpose, Progress." Consulting editor of *Journal of Creative Behavior,* 1969—.

WORK IN PROGRESS: *Synaesthetics: Lessons in Sensory Learning.*

* * *

ANNO, Mitsumasa 1920-

PERSONAL: Born March 20, 1926, in Tokyo, Japan; son of Yojiro and Shikano Anno; married Midori Suetsugu, April 1, 1952; children: Masaichiro (son), Seiko (daughter). *Home:* 4-5-5 Midoricho, Koganei, Tokyo, Japan.

CAREER: Artist. *Member:* Illustrators Council, Nikikai (artist's club). *Awards, honors:* American Library Association Notable Book award, 1970, for *Topsy-Turvies.*

WRITINGS—Self-illustrated: *Topsy-Turvies: Pictures to Stretch the Imagination,* Weatherhill, 1970; *Upside-Downers: More Pictures to Stretch the Imagination,* Weatherhill, 1971; *Dr. Anno's Midnight Circus,* Weatherhill, 1972.

WORK IN PROGRESS: Another picture book.

* * *

ANSON, Cyril J(oseph) 1923-

PERSONAL: Born September 10, 1923, in England; married Ethel May Tomlinson, August 6, 1949; children: Nicola Jane, Paul Joseph. *Education:* University of Birmingham, B.A. (first class honors), 1949, Ph.D., 1952. *Home:* Random Ridge, Shenington, Banbury, Oxfordshire, England. *Office:* Urwick, Orr & Partners Ltd., The Rotunda, New St., Birmingham B2 4QB, England.

CAREER: Urwick, Orr & Partners Ltd. (management consultancy), Birmingham, England, partner, 1960-70, senior partner, 1970—. *Military service:* Royal Air Force, 1943-46. *Member:* Royal Statistical Society (fellow), British Computer Society, Operational Research Society, Institute of Management Consultants.

WRITINGS: (With Henry G. Cuming) *Mathematics and Statistics for Technologists,* Heywood Books, 1966, Chemical Publishing, 1967; *Quality Control as a Tool for Production,* British Productivity Council, 1959, 4th edition, 1969; *Profit from Figures: A Manager's Guide to Statistical Methods,* McGraw, 1971.

* * *

ANTHONY, Catherine
See ADACHI, Barbara (Curtis)

* * *

ANTHONY, David
See SMITH, William Dale

* * *

ANTHONY, James R. 1922-

PERSONAL: Born February 18, 1922, in Providence, R.I.; son of Howard W. (a bank teller) and Lena (Latham) Anthony; married Louise R. Macnair, May 24, 1952; children: Barbara, Janet, Stephen. *Education:* Columbia University, B.S., 1946, M.A., 1948; Sorbonne, University of Paris, Diplome, 1951; University of Southern California, Ph.D., 1964. *Home:* 800 North Wilson Ave., Tucson, Ariz. *Office:* College of Fine Arts, University of Arizona, Tucson, Ariz.

CAREER: Montana State University, Bozeman, instructor in music, 1948-50; University of Arizona, Tucson, 1952—, began as assistant professor, now professor of music. Consultant to National Endowment for the Humanities. *Military service:* U.S. Army Air Forces, 1942-45; became staff sergeant; received Air Medal and Distinguished Flying Cross. *Member:* Societe francaise de musicologie, American Council of Learned Societies, American Musicological Society, College Music Society, Music Teacher's National Association, Music Educators National Council, American Association of University Professors, Arizona State Music Teacher's Association.

WRITINGS: French Baroque Music from Beaujoyeulx to Rameau, Batsford, 1973, Norton, 1974. Contributor to *Journal of the American Musicological Society, Musical Quarterly, Notes,* and *Recherches.*

WORK IN PROGRESS: A chapter for *New Oxford History of Music,* completion expected in 1975; over thirty genre and biographical articles dealing with French seventeenth and eighteenth century composers for 6th edition of *Grove's Dictionary of Music and Musicians,* 1977.

* * *

ANTONI,
See IRANEK-OSMECKI, Kazimierz

* * *

AOKI, Haruo 1930-

PERSONAL: Born April 1, 1930, in Kunsan, Korea; son of Akira and Yae Aoki; married Mary Ann Schroeder, August 30, 1958; children: Kanna, Akemi, Mieko. *Education:* University of California, Berkeley, Ph.D., 1965. *Home:* 938 Polk St., Albany, Calif. 94706. *Office:* 102 Durant Hall, University of California, Berkeley, Calif. 94720.

CAREER: University of California, Berkeley, assistant professor, 1965-69, associate professor, 1969-72, professor of oriental languages, 1972—. *Member:* Linguistic Society of America, American Oriental Society, Linguistic Association of Great Britain, Cercle Linguistique de Copenhagne, Nihon Gengogakkai, Kokugogakkai, Kokugo Kenkyuukai, Keiryoo Kokugo Gakkai. *Awards, honors:* Fulbright fellow, 1953-54.

WRITINGS: Nez Perce Grammar, University of California Press, 1970. Associate editor of *Northwestern Anthropological Research Notes,* 1967—.

WORK IN PROGRESS: Nez Perce Myths; writing on Japanese linguistics.

* * *

APPIGNANESI, Lisa 1946-

PERSONAL: Born January 4, 1946, in Looz, Poland; daughter of Aron (a businessman) and Hana (Lipschyz) Borenstein; married Richard Appignanesi (a writer), January 3, 1967. *Education:* McGill University, B.A., 1966, M.A., 1967; Sussex University, D.Phil., 1970. *Politics:* "Reflected." *Home:* 69 Whitehall Park, London N.19, England. *Agent:* Christine Bernard, 7 Well Rd., London N.W.3, England.

CAREER: Centre for Community Research, New York, N.Y., staff writer, 1970-71; University of Essex, Colchester, Essex, England, lecturer in literature, 1971-73; New England College, Arundel, Sussex, England, lecturer in literature, 1973—.

WRITINGS: (With Douglas and Monica Holmes) *Language of Trust,* Science House, 1972; *Femininity and the Creative Imagination,* Barnes & Noble, 1973; *A History of the Literary and Political Cabaret, 1880–,* Studio Vista, in press. Contributor of articles to journals in her field.

WORK IN PROGRESS: Research on Vienna, 1900-1940.

* * *

APPS, Jerold W(illard) 1934-
(Jerry Apps)

PERSONAL: Born July 25, 1934, in Wild Rose, Wis.; son of Herman E. (a farmer) and Eleanor (Witt) Apps; married Ruth E. Olson (a home economist), May 20, 1961; children: Susan, Steven, Jeffrey. *Education:* University of Wisconsin—Madison, B.S., 1955, M.S., 1957, Ph.D., 1967. *Politics:* Independent. *Religion:* Lutheran. *Home:* 522 Togstad Glen, Madison, Wis. 53711. *Office:* Department of Continuing and Vocational Education, University of Wisconsin, 208 Agriculture Hall, Madison, Wis. 53706.

CAREER: County extension agent in Wisconsin, 1957-62; assistant state 4-H leader in Wisconsin, 1962-64; University of Wisconsin, Madison, assistant professor, 1962-67, associate professor, 1967-70, professor of adult education, 1970—. Teacher of creative writing at Rhinelander School of Arts, summers. *Military service:* U.S. Army Reserve, 1956-66, active duty in Transportation Corps, 1956; became captain. *Member:* Adult Education Association, Commission of Professors of Adult Education (president), Adult Education Association of Wisconsin (past president), Gamma Sigma Delta.

WRITINGS: (Under name Jerry Apps) *The Land Still Lives,* Wisconsin House, 1970; (under name Jerry Apps) *Cabin in the Country,* Argus, 1972; *How to Improve Adult Education in Your Church,* Augsburg, 1972; *Toward a*

Working Philosophy of Adult Education, Syracuse University, 1973; (under name Jerry Apps) *Village of Roses,* Wild Rose Historical Society, 1973; *Ideas for Better Meetings,* Augsburg, 1975; *A Man Talks with God,* Augsburg, in press. Author of "Outdoor Notebook," a weekly column in three Wisconsin newspapers. Book editor for *Journal of Adult Education,* 1967-69; editor of *Journal of Extension,* 1969-70.

WORK IN PROGRESS: Foundations of Adult and Continuing Education, with Beverly Cassara, for Adult Education Association; research on the contribution of philosophy to adult and continuing education; developing approaches for assisting rural communities with problem solving.

SIDELIGHTS: Apps writes: "I am committed to helping the university relate to the real needs of people. In doing that I'm constantly trying to combine theory and practice, and stress the importance of doing this in the classroom and the community.

"I believe that action without careful thought can be dangerous, that thought without action can be irrelevant. Thus the necessity for combining the two.

"As the population of the country grows older, I am committed to the concept of continuing education for all ages. Through education people will be able to discover latent talents, will learn to know more about themselves, and how to relate to others. Through education I believe that people can reach their highest potentials, and can learn how to work together to solve the problems they face collectively in their communities.

"I believe that religion is an important force in the lives of people, but must be viewed in ways that transcend the traditional institutional church." *Avocational interests:* Wild flower study, bird study, nature photography, hiking, camping, canoeing, fishing, farming.

* * *

APPS, Jerry
See APPS, Jerold W(illard)

* * *

ARCH, E. L.
See PAYES, Rachel C(osgrove)

* * *

ARGENTI, Philip 1891(?)-1974

1891(?)—April 7, 1974; British scholar and archaeologist. Obituaries: *AB Bookman's Weekly,* June 17, 1974.

* * *

ARIAN, Alan (Asher) 1938-

PERSONAL: Born in 1938, in Cleveland, Ohio. *Education:* Western Reserve University (now Case Western Reserve University), B.A. (cum laude), 1961; Michigan State University, M.A., 1963, Ph.D., 1965. *Office:* Department of Political Science, Tel-Aviv University, Ramat-Aviv, Israel.

CAREER: Tel-Aviv University, Ramat-Aviv, Israel, lecturer, 1966-68, senior lecturer, 1968-71, associate professor of political science, 1971—, chairman of department, 1966-70, 1971-73. Guest research associate at Israel Institute of Applied Social Research, 1967; guest lecturer at Communications Institute of Hebrew University, 1967-70; visiting associate professor at University of Minnesota, autumn, 1968; guest research associate at Center for Political Studies, University of Michigan, spring, 1971. *Awards, honors:* Naftali Award for social and economic research, 1973.

WRITINGS: (Editor with Charles Press, and contributor) *Empathy and Ideology: Aspects of Administrative Innovation,* Rand McNally, 1966; *Ideological Change in Israel,* Case Western Reserve University Press, 1968; *Consensus in Israel* (monograph), General Learning Corp., 1971; (editor and contributor) *The Elections in Israel: 1969,* Jerusalem Academic Press, 1972; (with Aaron Antonovsky) *Hopes and Fears of Israelis: Consensus in a New Society,* Jerusalem Academic Press, 1972; (with Roger W. Benjamin, Richard N. Blue, and Stephen Coleman) *Patterns of Political Development: Japan, India, Israel,* McKay, 1972; *The Choosing People: Voting Behavior in Israel,* Case Western Reserve University Press, 1973.

Contributor to political science and social science journals, including *Journal of Politics, Public Opinion Quarterly, Jewish Journal of Sociology, Western Political Quarterly, Sociological Review,* and *Journal of Human Relations.*

WORK IN PROGRESS: The Elections in Israel: 1973, for Jerusalem Academic Press; *From Party-Controlled to National Services: Political and Administrative Aspects of Institutional Change in Israel.*

* * *

ARING, Charles D(air) 1904-

PERSONAL: Born June 21, 1904, in Dent, Ohio; son of Fred (a laborer) and Alice (Dair) Aring; married Mary Shroder, October 16, 1931; children: Dair (Mrs. David C. Rausch), Charles Shroder. *Education:* University of Cincinnati, B.S. and M.D., 1929. *Politics:* Independent. *Religion:* "None; born Protestant." *Home:* 2401 Ingleside Ave., Cincinnati, Ohio 45206. *Office:* University of Cincinnati College of Medicine, 234 Goodman, Cincinnati, Ohio 45229.

CAREER: Cincinnati General Hospital, Cincinnati, Ohio, rotating intern, 1929-30, resident in psychiatry and receiving physician, 1930-31; Longview State Hospital, Cincinnati, resident physician, 1931; Boston City Hospital, Boston, Mass., house officer in neurology, 1932, resident in neurology, 1933-34; Yale University, New Haven, Conn., Sterling fellow in neurophysiology, 1934-35; Cincinnati General Hospital, assisting attending neurologist, 1935-38, attending neurologist, 1938-46, director of neurological clinic, 1941-46, and, concurrently, University of Cincinnati College of Medicine, Cincinnati, Ohio, instructor, 1936-38, assistant professor, 1938-41, associate professor of neurology, 1941-46; University of California School of Medicine, San Francisco, professor of neurology and director of neurological division of University Hospital, 1946-47; University of Cincinnati College of Medicine, professor of neurology, 1947—, and, concurrently, Cincinnati General Hospital, director of neurology service, 1947—. Voluntary assistant, Boston's Children's Hospital, 1933; Rockefeller Fellow, National Hospital, London, England, University of Madrid, and Breslau University, 1935-36. Member of committee on neurotropic virus diseases of Board for Investigation and Control of Influenza and Other Epidemic Diseases in the Army, 1941-46; member of medical advisory board, National Multiple Sclerosis Society, 1950-56; U.S. Public Health Service, member of mental health study section, 1953-57, and primate research study section, 1961-

64; member of board of directors, Foundation Fund for Research in Psychiatry, 1953-55.

MEMBER: Society for Experimental Biology and Medicine, National Research Council (member of committee on neuropsychiatry, 1947), Association for Research in Nervous and Mental Disease (vice-president, 1947, 1952), American Psychosomatic Society (member of council, 1947-48), American Psychiatric Association, American Neurological Association (member of council, 1951-53, 1961-68; president, 1962-63), American Medical Association, American League Against Epilepsy (vice-president, 1942-43; president, 1944-46), Association of British Neurologists (honorary foreign member), Cincinnati Academy of Medicine, Literary Club of Cincinnati (member of board of management, 1966-74; vice-president, 1971-72; president, 1972-73); Sigma Xi, Alpha Omega Alpha. *Awards, honors:* Rockefeller fellowship, 1935-36; Sachs Award for contributions to scholarship and intellectual climate, 1969.

WRITINGS: Writings of Charles D. Aring, University of Cincinnati Press, 1969, revised edition published as *The Understanding Physician: Writings of Charles D. Aring,* Wayne State University Press, 1971; *Man and Life,* University of Cincinnati Press, 1970.

Contributor: James C. Fox, editor, *Neurology and Psychiatry,* Volume IX, D. Appleton, 1936; Paul C. Bucy, editor, *The Precentral Motor Cortex,* University of Illinois Press, 1944, 2nd edition, 1949; A. B. Baker, editor, *Clinical Neurology,* three volumes, Hoeber, 1955, 2nd edition, 1961; Howard C. Coggeshall, editor, *Common Pain Problems,* Saunders, 1958; A. P. Friedman and H. H. Merritt, editors, *Headache: Diagnosis and Treatment,* F. A. Davis, 1959; Simeon Locke, editor, *Modern Neurology: Papers in Tribute to Derek Denny-Brown,* Little, Brown, 1969; Robert H. Moser and Erwin DiCyan, editors, *Adventures in Medical Writing,* C. C Thomas, 1970.

Contributor to *Encyclopaedia Britannica* and to journals in his field.

Member of editorial board, *Archives of Neurology and Psychiatry* (now *Archives of Neurology*), 1943-61, 1964-73, *GP,* 1950-53, *Psychosomatic Medicine,* 1961-71, *Journal of Nervous and Mental Disease,* 1962-69, *Journal of Asthma Research,* 1963—, *Journal of the American Medical Association,* 1973—; editor, *American Lectures in Neurology,* 1946-71; editor-in-chief, *Cincinnati Journal of Medicine,* 1948-49; member of advisory board, *International Journal of Neurology,* 1970—.

WORK IN PROGRESS: The Orphan, Physician, Professor.

SIDELIGHTS: Orphaned at the age of six, Aring began working as an office boy at Cincinnati General Hospital at the age of fifteen (he remains there today as director of neurology service). William B. Bean, a colleague and noted physician, has said of Aring: "My first recollections of Charles Aring date back to 1937 when I had just come to Cincinnati as a senior resident in medicine. My first service was neurology. I was immediately struck by the personality of the neurologist in charge, Dr. Charles Aring, who had theoretical as well as practical skill and know-how. Limping ever so slightly from an ancient poliomyelitis, he was full of an astonishing lore about medical history both local and general. Then and now, one of his strongest characteristics was wide reading and a fascination with books. . . .In conversation he is quizzical, presents a demeanor of one whom it would be difficult to surprise, almost impossible to upset. He is not taken in by appearance but seeks out immediately cardinal points. He has the capacity for intense concentration whether it be in reading or in conversation or in dealing with patients. One gets the impression in talking with him that his attention is undivided and fused on the person in his presence. He is courteous, with the distinguished air of a scholar and gentleman." Aring maintains a steady interest in literature and is quite active in the Literary Club of Cincinnati, where he has delivered numerous papers on subjects far removed from medical science.

BIOGRAPHICAL/CRITICAL SOURCES: International Journal of Neurology, Volume 3, number 2, 1962.

* * *

ARMBRUSTER, F(ranz) O(wen) 1929-

PERSONAL: Born April 17, 1929, in San Antonio, Tex.; son of Frank O. (a marine engineer) and Jeannette (Hansborough) Armbruster; married Mary Lou Floyd (a secretary), August 20, 1950; children: Owen, Charles. *Education:* Attended El Camino College, 1948-49; Hartnell College, A.A., 1950. *Home and office:* 19750 Drake Dr., Cupertino, Calif. 95014.

CAREER: Northrop Corp., Los Angeles, Calif., engineer and instructor, 1955-60; Craig Corp., Compton, Calif., engineer, 1960-61; chief engineer, Vought Camera Co., 1961-62; Data Technology Corp., Santa Ava, Calif., director of Instructional Systems Division, 1962-63; Nuclear Research Instruments Co., Berkeley, Calif., consultant, 1963-65; self-employed industrial consultant, 1965-68; founder and president, Products of the Behavioral Sciences, 1968-74; Lockheed Missiles & Space Co., Palo Alto, Calif., training specialist, 1974—. Lecturer in instructional and computer technology, University of Santa Clara, 1971-74; lecturer in language arts and communication skills, University of California, Santa Cruz, 1974—; consultant to various industries and institutions. *Member:* National Society of Programmed Instruction (past president of Peninsula Chapter).

WRITINGS: Think Metrics, Troubador, 1974; *Computer Crosswords,* Troubador, 1974. Author of motion picture scripts for U.S. Air Force. Co-editor of *California Mathematics Journal,* 1973; contributing editor of *Simulation/Gaming News,* 1973.

WORK IN PROGRESS: With Jean J. Pedersen and Dave Logothetti, a popular text on problem-solving; *Popular Guide to Kites & Kite Flying.*

* * *

ARMSTRONG, Martin 1882-1974

October, 1882—February 24, 1974; British poet, novelist, and short story writer. Obituaries: *AB Bookman's Weekly,* April 15, 1974.

* * *

ARMSTRONG, William M(artin) 1919-

PERSONAL: Born January 14, 1919, in Peoria, Ill.; son of Haskell R. (a newspaperman) and Lilian (Nofsinger) Armstrong; married Norma Campbell, April 17, 1943 (annulled, 1970); married Renee Isabelle Goujon, June 25, 1973; children: (first marriage) Lois Lee (Mrs. William Rockliff, Jr.), Dean, Bruce; Christine Bedel (stepdaughter). *Education:* Bradley University, A.B., 1947; Louisiana State University, A.M., 1948; Stanford University, Ph.D., 1954. *Home:* 137 Leroy St., Potsdam, N.Y. 13676. *Office:* Department of Social Sciences, Clarkson College of Technology, Potsdam, N.Y.

CAREER: Stanford University, Stanford, Calif., instructor in western civilization, 1949-50, 1951-53; Eastern Illinois University, Charleston, assistant professor of history, 1954-56; Washington College, Chestertown, Md., associate professor of history and chairman of department, 1956-59; Fairleigh Dickinson University, Rutherford, N.J., associate professor of history, 1959-60; Alma College, Alma, Mich., associate professor of history, 1961-65; Clarkson College of Technology, Potsdam, N.Y., professor of history, 1965—, chairman of department, 1973-74. Teacher at University of Delaware, Dover extension, 1959, Long Island University, summer, 1961, and Brooklyn College of the City University of New York, summers, 1963-65. Fulbright senior lecturer at Helsinki University, 1963-64. *Military service:* U.S. Army, Infantry, 1941-45; became first lieutenant; served in European and Far Eastern Theatres; received Bronze Star. *Member:* American Association of University Professors (president of local chapter, 1970-71), American Historical Association, Organization of American Historicans, American Civil Liberties Union, Phi Alpha Theta. *Awards, honors:* Research grants from American Philosophical Society, 1957-58, and National Foundation on Arts and Humanities, 1968-69.

WRITINGS: E. L. Godkin and American Foreign Policy, Bookman, 1957; (contributor) William B. Hesseltine, editor, *Civil War Prisons,* Kent State University Press, 1972; (editor) *The Gilded Age Letters of E. L. Godkin,* State University of New York Press, 1974. Contributor of articles and reviews to more than twenty professional journals.

WORK IN PROGRESS: A United States history textbook.

* * *

ARNETT, Ross H(arold), Jr. 1919-

PERSONAL: Born April 13, 1919, in Medina, N.Y.; son of Ross Harold (a veterinarian) and Hazel Dell (a musician; maiden name, Oderkirk) Arnett; married Mary Catherine Ennis (an editor's assistant), February 16, 1942; children: Ross III, Michael J., Mary Anne Arnett Held, Barbara Ellen Arnett Shephard, Francis Xavier, Joseph Anthony, Bernadette Teresa, Matthew Christopher. *Education:* Cornell University, B.S., 1942, M.S., 1946, Ph.D., 1948. *Politics:* Independent. *Religion:* Roman Catholic. *Home and office:* 57 West Glenwood Dr., Latham, N.Y. 12110.

CAREER: Cornell University, Ithaca, N.Y., instructor in biology, 1946-48; U.S. Department of Agriculture, Washington, D.C., beetle taxonomist, 1948-54; Saint John Fisher College, Rochester, N.Y., associate professor of biology, 1954-58; Catholic University of America, Washington, D.C., associate professor, 1958-61, professor of biology, 1961-66, chairman of department, 1962-66, founder and director of Institute for the Study of Natural Species, 1961-66; Purdue University, Lafayette, Ind., professor of entomology, 1966-70; Florida State University, Tallahassee, adjunct professor of biology, 1971-73; Siena College, Loudonville, N.Y., professor of biology, 1973—. Collaborator, U.S. Department of Agriculture, 1954—; research associate, Florida State Collection of Anthropods, 1964—; Bio-Rand Foundation, Inc., vice-president and member of board of directors, 1968-73; managing director, North American Beetle Fauna Project, 1971—; Biological Research Institute of America, co-founder and member of board of directors, 1973—; visiting professor, University of Oklahoma, 1969. *Military service:* U.S. Army, 1942-45; became technical sergeant.

MEMBER: International Congress of Entomology, International Congress of Systematic and Evolutionary Biology, Botanical Society of America, American Society of Information Science, Entomological Society of America (vice-president, 1967), American Society of Plant Taxonomists, American Ornithological Society, American Institute of Biological Sciences, American Association for the Advancement of Science (fellow), Coleopterists Society (president, 1971), Society of Systematic Zoology (member of council, 1960-63), Entomological Society of Washington (president, 1964), Sigma Xi, Phi Kappa Phi, Cosmos Club (Washington). *Awards, honors:* American Philosophical Society grants, 1957, 1959, 1968; National Science Foundation grant, 1958-65; McDonald Foundation grant, 1964-66; U.S. Army grant, 1966-67; Henry L. Beadel fellowship from Tall Timbers Research, Inc., 1971-73; Rockefeller grant, 1973.

WRITINGS: (With D. C. Braungart) *Introduction to Plant Science,* Mosby, 1962, 4th edition, 1974; *The Beetles of the United States,* Catholic University of America, 1963, reprinted, American Entomological Institute, 1968; (with G. Allan Samuelson) *Directory of Coleoptera Collection of North America,* Purdue University Press, 1969. Contributor to proceedings and to journals in his field. *Coleopterists' Bulletin,* founder and editor, 1947-61, member of editorial board, 1962—; editor, *Studies on Speciation,* 1962—; editor, *Entomological News,* 1967-72; editor, *Bulletin of Tall Timbers Research Station,* 1971-73; editor and publisher, *Insect World Digest,* 1973—.

WORK IN PROGRESS: New Field Book of Insects for Putnam; *North American Beetle Fauna* for Biological Research Institute of America.

SIDELIGHTS: Arnett told *CA*: "I have two major concerns: 1) teaching people to love the earth on which we live so they will treat it as if it were their own; 2) providing people with the necessary tools to help them learn about the plants and animals of the world. After years of teaching, moving, and traveling throughout much of the world during summers, I have settled in the Hudson Valley to write those books that are relevant to these interests."

* * *

ARNOLD, Corliss Richard 1926-

PERSONAL: Born November 7, 1926, in Monticello, Ark.; son of Lawrence Richard (a rural mail carrier) and Anna Marie (a legal secretary; maiden name Bennett) Arnold; married Elizabeth Wadsworth, August 5, 1961; children: Phyllis Marie, Christopher David, Kevin Richard. *Education:* Hendrix College, B.Mus. (summa cum laude), 1946; University of Michigan, M.Mus., 1948; Union Theological Seminary, S.M.D., 1954. *Politics:* Republican. *Religion:* Presbyterian. *Home:* 1114 Sunset Lane, East Lansing, Mich. 48823. *Office:* Music Bldg., Michigan State University, East Lansing, Mich. 48824.

CAREER: Hendrix College, Conway, Ark., instructor in music, 1946-47; director of music at methodist churches in El Dorado, Ark., 1948-52, and Oak Park, Ill., 1954-59; organist choirmaster in Closter, N.J., 1952-54, and Oak Park, Ill., 1957-59; Union Theological Seminary, School of Sacred Music, New York, N.Y., assistant to director, 1953-54. Michigan State University, East Lansing, associate professor of organ and church music, 1959—, director of church music workshop, 1959—. Peoples Church, East Lansing, Mich., director of music, 1959—. *Member:* American Guild of Organists (fellow, 1959; dean of Lansing chapter, 1960-62), Hymn Society of America, Alliance Francaise, Alpha Chi, Phi Mu Alpha Sinfonia, Pi Kappa Lambda. *Awards, honors:* Fulbright fellow to France, 1956-57.

WRITINGS: Organ Literature: A Comprehensive Survey, Scarecrow, 1973. Composer for organ and chorus; arranger for organ and trumpet.

AVOCATIONAL INTERESTS: Travel, languages.

* * *

ARNOLD, Peter 1943-

PERSONAL: Born January 25, 1943, in Newton, Mass.; son of Israel Isaac (a businessman) and Edith (Gordon) Arnold; married Kirsten Ellen Hannibal, July 25, 1966; children: Jeremy Gordon. *Education:* University of Michigan, B.A., 1966; University of Southern California, M.A., 1969. *Residence:* Los Angeles, Calif. *Agent:* Max Gartenberg, 331 Madison Ave., New York, N.Y. 10017. *Office:* Office of Development, Occidental College, Los Angeles, Calif. 90041.

CAREER: Writer and producer at Universal Studios, Universal City, Calif., 1967-68; free-lance film writer, Los Angeles, Calif., 1968-73; free-lance non-fiction book writer, Los Angeles, Calif., 1969—; California Institute of Technology, Development Office, Pasadena, head of writing staff, 1973-74; Occidental College, Los Angeles, Calif., director of special projects, 1974—. *Member:* Writer's Guild of America, Author's Guild.

WRITINGS: Burglar-Proof Your Home and Car, Nash Publishing, 1971; *Off the Beaten Track in Copenhagen,* Nash Publishing, 1972; *Lady Beware,* Doubleday, 1974; *Check List for Emergencies,* Doubleday, 1974. Contributor to *National Observer, Woman's Day, Coronet, Seventeen,* and *New Idea.*

WORK IN PROGRESS: Your Child and Crime, a crime-prevention book for parents; *You and Crime,* a crime-prevention book for teen-agers; editing a book on decision making, *Make Up Your Mind.*

* * *

ARNOLD, Robert E(vans) 1932-

PERSONAL: Born April 1, 1932, in Louisville, Ky.; son of Edith (Linville) Arnold; married Betty Jean Kendrick, June 12, 1954; children: Sandra, Robert, Rhonda, Elizabeth, Michelle. *Education:* University of Kentucky, B.S., 1953; University of Louisville, M.D., 1957. *Religion:* Christian and Missionary Alliance. *Home:* 13301 Seatonville Rd., Jeffersontown, Ky. 40299. *Office:* 4001 Dutchman's Lane, Suite 7-D, Louisville, Ky. 40207.

CAREER: Licensed to practice medicine in Kentucky; private practice of medicine in Louisville, Ky., 1964—; University of Louisville, Department of Surgery, Louisville, Ky., assistant professor of surgery, 1964—. *Member:* American College of Surgeons (fellow).

WRITINGS: What to Do About Bites and Stings of Venomous Animals, Macmillan, 1973.

WORK IN PROGRESS: A research program for a world-wide treatment of bites of poisonous reptiles.

* * *

ARON, Raymond (Claude Ferdinand) 1905-

PERSONAL: Born March 14, 1905, in Paris, France; son of Gustave Emile (a professor of law) and Suzanne (Levy) Aron; married Suzanne Gauchon, September 5, 1933; children: Dominique (Mme. Antoine Schnapper), Laurence. *Education:* Ecole Normale Superieure, Paris, agregation de philosophie, 1928, doctorat es lettres, 1938. *Home:* 87 boulevard Saint-Michel, Paris 75005, France. *Office:* 6 rue de Tournon, Paris 6e, France.

CAREER: University of Cologne, Cologne, Germany, lecturer, 1930-31; French Institute, Berlin, Germany, member of staff, 1931-33; Lycee du Havre, France, professor of philosophy, 1933-34; Ecole Normale Superieure, Paris, France, secretary of Center of Social Information, 1934-39; University of Toulouse, Toulouse, France, professor of sociology, 1939; *La France libre,* London, England, editor, 1940-44; Institut d'Etudes Politiques, France, professor of political science, 1945-55; University of Paris, Sorbonne, Paris, France, professor, Faculte des Lettres, 1955-68; College de France, Paris, professor of sociology, 1970—. Professor-at-large, Cornell University.

MEMBER: Academie des sciences morales et politiques, American Philosophical Society, American Academy of Arts and Sciences (honorary foreign member), British Academy. *Awards, honors:* Prix des Ambassadeurs, 1962, for *Paix et guerre entre les nations;* Prix Montaigne, 1968, for body of work; Prix des Critiques, 1973, for *Republique imperiale;* Chevalier, Legion d'Honneur, named Officier, 1974; received honorary doctorates from University of Basel, University of Brussels, Harvard University, Columbia University, University of Southampton, Hebrew University of Jerusalem, Oxford University, University of Louvain.

WRITINGS: La Sociologie allemande contemporaine, Alcan, 1935, translation by Mary Bottomore and Thomas Bottomore published as *German Sociology,* Free Press, 1957, 3rd French edition, Presses Universitaires de France, 1966; *Essai sur la theorie de l'histoire dans l'Allemagne contemporaine: La Philosophie critique de l'histoire,* Vrin, 1938, 2nd edition published as *La Philosophie critique de l'histoire: Essai sur un theorie allemande de l'histoire,* Vrin, 1950, 4th edition, 1969; *Introduction a la philosophie de l'histoire: Essai sur les limites de l'objectivite historique,* Gallimard, 1938, translation by George J. Irwin published as *Introduction to the Philosophy of History: An Essay on the Limits of Historical Objectivity,* Beacon Press, 1961, new French edition, 1967.

L'Homme contre les tyrans, Editions de la Maison Francaise (New York), 1944, 2nd edition, Gallimard, 1946; *De l'armistice a l'insurrection nationale,* Gallimard, 1945; (with F. Clairens) *Les Francais devant la constitution,* Editions Defense de la France, 1946; *L'Age des empires et l'avenir de la France,* Editions Defense de la France, 1946; *Le Grand Schisme,* Gallimard, 1948.

Les Guerres en chaine, Gallimard, 1951, translation by E. W. Dickes and O. S. Griffiths published as *The Century of Total War,* Doubleday, 1954; *L'Opium des intellectuels,* Calmann-Levy, 1955, translation by Terence Kilmartin published as *The Opium of the Intellectuals,* Doubleday, 1957, new French edition, Gallimard, 1968; *Polemiques,* Gallimard, 1955; *Le Developpement de la societe industrielle et la stratification sociale,* Centre de Documentation Universitaire (Paris), Volume I, 1956, Volume II, 1957, Volume I published as *Dix-huit lecons sur la societe industrielle,* Gallimard, 1963, translation by M. K. Bottomore published as *18 Lectures on Industrial Society,* Weidenfeld & Nicolson, 1967, Volume II published as *La Lutte des classes: Nouvelles Lecons sur les societes industrielles,* Gallimard, 1964; (editor with Daniel Lerner, and contributor) *La Querelle de la C.E.D.: Essais d'analyse sociologique,* Colin, 1956, translation published as *France Defeats E.D.C.,* edited by Aron, Praeger, 1957; *Espoir et peur du siecle: Essais non partisans,* Calmann-Levy, 1957, translation by Kilmartin of excerpted essay published as *On War: Atomic Weapons and Global Diplomacy,* Secker & Warburg, 1958, published as *On War,* Doubleday, 1959; (with August Heckscher) *Diversity of Worlds: France and the United States Look at Their Common Problems,* Reynal, 1957.

La Tragedie algerienne, Plon, 1957; (author of introduction) George Mikes, *La Revolution hongroise,* Gallimard, 1957; *L'Algerie et la Republique,* Plon, 1958; *Sociologie des societes industrielles: Equisse d'une theorie des regimes politiques,* Centre de Documentation Universitaire, 1958, reissued as *Democratie et totalitarisme,* Gallimard, 1965, translation by Valence Ionescu published as *Democracy and Totalitarianism,* Weidenfeld & Nicolson, 1968, Praeger, 1969; *War and Industrial Society,* Oxford University Press, 1958 (published in France as *La Societe Industrielle et la guerre,* Plon, 1959, 2nd edition, 1959); (contributor) Franz M. Joseph, editor, *As Others See Us: The United States through Foreign Eyes,* Princeton University Press, 1959; *Immuable et changeante: De la IVe a la Ve Republique,* Calmann-Levy, 1959, translation by J. Irwin and Luigi Einaudi published as *France Steadfast and Changing: The Fourth to the Fifth Republic,* Harvard University Press, 1960.

Les Grandes Doctrines de sociologie historique: Montesquieu, Auguste Comte, Karl Marx, Alexis de Tocqueville; Les Sociologues et la revolution de 1848, Centre de Documentation Universitaire, 1960, enlarged edition, 1961, translation of enlarged edition by Richard Howard and Helen Weaver published as *Main Currents in Sociological Thought,* Basic Books, Volume I: *Montesquieu, Comte, Marx, Tocqueville: Sociologists and the Revolution of 1848,* 1965, Volume II: *Durkheim, Pareto, Weber,* 1967, enlarged French edition reissued as *Les Etapes de la pensee sociologique: Montesquieu, Comte, Marx, Tocqueville, Durkheim, Pareto, Weber,* Gallimard, 1967; *France, the New Republic,* introduction by D. W. Brogan, Oceana, 1960; (editor) *L'Histoire et ses interpretations: Entretiens autour de Arnold Toynbee,* Mouton, 1961; *Dimensions de la conscience historique* (collected essays), Plon, 1961, 2nd edition, 1965, translation by Dorothy Pickles of excerpt, "L'Aube de l'histoire universelle," published as *The Dawn of Universal History,* Praeger, 1961; *Paix et guerre entre les nations,* Calmann-Levy, 1962, translation by Richard Howard and Annette Baker Fox published as *Peace and War: A Theory of International Relations,* Doubleday, 1966, 6th French edition, 1968.

Douze Lecons d'introduction a la strategie atomique, Institut d'Etudes Politiques, University of Paris, 1963; *Le Grand Debat: Initiation a la strategie atomique,* Calmann-Levy, 1963, translation by Ernst Pawel published as *The Great Debate: Theories of Nuclear Strategy,* Doubleday, 1965; *Trois Essais sur l'age industriel,* Plon, 1965, translation published as *The Industrial Society: Three Essays on Ideology and Development,* Praeger, 1967; (editor with Bert Hoselitz) *Le Developpement social,* Mouton, 1965, translation published as *Social Development,* Humanities, 1965; *Essai sur les libertes,* Calmann-Levy, 1965, translation by Helen Weaver published as *An Essay on Freedom,* World Publishing, 1970.

Progress and Disillusion: The Dialectics of Modern Society, Praeger, 1968 (published in France as *Les Desillusions du progres: Essai sur la dialectique de la modernite,* Calmann-Levy, 1969); *La Revolution introuvable: Reflexions sur la revolution de mai,* Fayard, 1968, translation by Gordon Clough published as *The Elusive Revolution: Anatomy of a Student Revolt,* Praeger, 1969; *DeGaulle, Israel et les juifs,* Plon, 1968, translation by John Sturrock published as *DeGaulle, Israel, and the Jews,* Praeger, 1969; *D'Une Sainte Famille a l'autre: Essais sur les marxismes imaginaires,* Gallimard, 1969, published as *Marxismes imaginaires: D'Une Sainte Famille a l'autre,* 1970; *Marxism and the Existentialists* (contains selected essays previously published in *D'Une Sainte Famille a l'autre),* Harper, 1969.

De la condition historique du sociologue, Gallimard, 1971; *Etudes politiques,* Gallimard, 1972; *Republique imperiale,* Calmann-Levy, 1973.

With others: *Bilan francais depuis la liberation,* Editions du Monde Nouveau, 1948; *The Soviet Economy: A Discussion,* Secker & Warburg, 1956; *L'Unification economique de l'Europe,* La Baconniere (Switzerland), 1957; *Colloques de Rheinfelden,* Calmann-Levy, 1960, translation by Richard Seaver published as *World Technology and Human Destiny,* edited by Aron, University of Michigan Press, 1963; *La Democratie a l'epreuve du XXe siecle,* Calmann-Levy, 1960; *Le France dans la competition economique,* Presses Universitaires de France, 1969.

Author of numerous pamphlets and bulletins, published in the United States and Europe. Contributor to journals. Cofounder, *Les Temps modernes;* member of staff, *Combat,* 1946; regular columnist, *Figaro,* 1947—.

SIDELIGHTS: "It has long been hinted that Aron is perhaps the only political scientist in France whose work De Gaulle [read] attentively," notes J. P. Nettl. Whether or not that is true, Aron does enjoy wide readership in his field in France and in America. Aron, sometimes compared to Walter Lippman, "has enjoyed in this country a reputation as a political sociologist and an engaged polemicist. A skeptic, anti-ideologue, pragmatist and 'social incrementalist,' his most distinctive quality has been that of a liberal realist." H. G. Nicholas estimates that Aron "excels amongst the intellectual analysts of our time in the dexterity and precision with which he wields the tools of his exacting trade. He is the indispensable intellectual *conferencier,* the infinitely patient unraveller of the confused and knotted argument, the typologist of the apparently untypological, the cool distiller of passion and interest into order and light. [He possesses] "an unfailing stock of cool analysis and forceful sanity, ranging over an astonishing diversity of themes with equal facility and effect."

AVOCATIONAL INTERESTS: Tennis.

* * *

ARPAD, Joseph J(ohn) 1937-

PERSONAL: Born March 9, 1937, in Randolph, Ohio; son of John A., Sr. and Pauline (Bradach) Arpad; married Sandra Sue Rose (an administration assistant), December 22, 1962. *Education:* University of California, Los Angeles, B.A., 1962; University of Iowa, M.A., 1964; Duke University, Ph.D., 1968. *Politics:* Democrat. *Home:* 10740 Ashton Ave., Los Angeles, Calif. 90024. *Office:* Department of English, University of California, Los Angeles, Calif. 90024.

CAREER: Pyron Construction, Inc., Whittier, Calif., projects manager, 1958-60; Duke University, Durham, N.C., instructor in English, 1964-68; University of California, Los Angeles, assistant professor of folklore and English, 1968—. Public lecturer; movie consultant for Twentieth Century Fox. *Member:* Modern Language Association of America, American Folklore Society, Organization of American Historians, American Studies Association, Popular Culture Association (member of advisory council; president of Western region, 1974—), American Civil Liberties Union (founding member of North Carolina unit), Philological Association of the Pacific Coast. *Awards, honors:* Humanities Institute award, University of California at Los Angeles, 1969; Faculty fellowship, University of California at Los Angeles, 1971; Regents fellowship, University of California at Los Angeles, 1974.

WRITINGS: (Editor with Kenneth Lincoln) *Buffalo Bill's Wild West,* Filter Press, 1971; (editor and author of introduction and notes) *A Narrative of the Life of David Crockett,* College & University Press, 1972; (editor with James Woodress and C. T. Ludington) *Essays Mostly on Periodical Publishing in America: A Collection in Honor of Clarence Gohdes,* Duke University Press, 1973. Contributor to *New York Folklore Quarterly, American Literature, Journal of the Folklore Institute,* and *Mississippi Quarterly.* Literature editor of *Journal of Popular Culture,* 1973—.

WORK IN PROGRESS: Between Folklore and Literature: Anomalous Traditions in American Culture (tentative title); *The Study of Popular Culture: Theory and Methods* (tentative title).

AVOCATIONAL INTERESTS: Painting, fishing, hiking, restoring old houses.

* * *

ARRIGHI, Mel 1933-

PERSONAL: Born October 5, 1933, in San Francisco, Calif.; son of Enrico (a wholesale produce merchant) and Gemma (Casentini) Arrighi; married Patricia Bosworth (a writer and magazine editor), February 15, 1966. *Education:* Attended Reed College, 1951-53; University of California, Berkeley, B.A., 1955. *Politics:* Liberal Democrat. *Home:* 344 East 79th St., New York, N.Y. 10021. *Agent:* (Literary) McIntosh & Otis, Inc., 18 East 41st St., New York, N.Y. 10017. (Dramatic) Harold Freedman, Brandt & Brandt, 101 Park Ave., New York, N.Y. 10017.

CAREER: Professional actor in New York, N.Y., 1956-62; writer, 1962—. Has acted with New York Shakespeare Festival, Shakespearwrights, and Irish Players; toured nationally with the Lunts in "The Great Sebastians."

WRITINGS—Novels: *Freak-Out,* Putnam, 1968; *An Ordinary Man,* Peter H. Wyden, 1970; *Daddy Pig,* Bobbs-Merrill, 1974.

Plays: *An Ordinary Man* (first produced on Off-Broadway at Cherry Lane Theatre, September 9, 1968), Dramatists Play Service, 1969; *The Castro Complex* (first produced in New York, N.Y., at Stairway Theatre, November 18, 1970), Dramatists Play Service, 1971. Also author of play, "The Baby Teaser."

Author of scripts for television series, including "NYPD" and "McCloud."

WORK IN PROGRESS: A novel for Bobbs-Merrill.

SIDELIGHTS: Arrighi writes: "...my impulse is to tell stories that investigate the relation of the individual to his society. I have no answers or solutions to propose. Instead, I am interested in questioning too-readily-accepted assumptions, and where possible, inspiring in the reader new lines of inquiry. In short, I am one of those who regard the creative artist as the responsive conscience of his society."

* * *

ARTEAGA, Lucio 1924-

PERSONAL: Born May 22, 1924, in Calatayuo, Spain; son of Juan and Rosa Arteaga; married Maria Navarro (a painter), October 17, 1952; children: Lucio, Jr., Robert. *Education:* University of Zaragoza, B.A., 1942; University of Madrid, Certificado De Estadistica, 1956; Dalhousie University, M.Sc., 1959; University of Saskatchewan, Ph.D., 1964. *Home:* 2712 North Terrace, Wichita, Kan. 67220. *Office:* Department of Mathematics, Wichita State University, Wichita, Kan. 67208.

CAREER: Nova Scotia Clinic, Halifax, Nova Scotia, statistician, 1956-59; University of Saskatchewan, Saskatoon, lecturer in mathematics, 1960-62; University of Windsor, Windsor, Ontario, assistant professor of mathematics, 1962-65; Dalhousie University, Halifax, Nova Scotia, assistant professor of mathematics, 1965-67; University of North Carolina at Charlotte, assistant professor of mathematics, 1967-68; Wichita State University, Wichita, Kan., associate professor, 1968-69, professor of mathematics, 1969—. Instructor at Wayne State University, summer, 1962. Member of board of directors of South Kansas Health Planning Council, 1974. *Member:* League of United Latin American Citizens (vice-president of Wichita chapter, 1974), Canadian Mathematical Congress, American Mathematical Society, American Mathematical Association, New York Academy of Sciences.

WRITINGS: (With Lloyd D. Davis) *Algorithms and Their Computer Solutions,* C. E. Merrill, 1972.

WORK IN PROGRESS: Intuitive Calculus, completion expected in 1975; with E. E. DeVun, *Topology and Its Applications,* 1975.

* * *

ARUEGO, Ariane
See DEWEY, Ariane

* * *

ASAMANI, Joseph Owusu 1934-

PERSONAL: Born June 6, 1934, in Akropong, Ghana; son of James Christian (a teacher) and Elizabeth (Mfodwo) Owusu; married Theresa Owusu (a university lecturer), December 14, 1968; children: Brenda, Karen, Kwame, Nana Afua. *Education:* University of London, B.A., 1965. *Religion:* Presbyterian. *Home address:* P.O. Box 41, Akropong-Akwapim, Ghana. *Office:* Library, University of Cape Coast, Cape Coast, Ghana.

CAREER: High school history teacher in Accra, Ghana, 1960-61; University of London, School of Oriental and African Studies, London, England, library research assistant, 1965-67; University of Cape Coast, Cape Coast, Ghana, assistant librarian, 1967—. *Member:* British Library Association, Africa Society (London).

WRITINGS: Index Africanus, Hoover Institution, 1974.

WORK IN PROGRESS: A bibliography of African history.

SIDELIGHTS: Asamani explained to *CA* that "in a comparatively new field like African studies, where scholars and facilities for publication are few, the periodical article is more often likely to remain for many years the only authority for some particular point. Some guide to published articles is therefore a great necessity; hence *Index Africanus.*"

* * *

ASH, Anthony Lee 1931-

PERSONAL: Born October 29, 1931, in Lincoln, Neb.; son of Jesse W. and Virginia (Coleman) Ash; married Barbara Bailey (a secretary), January 31, 1955. *Education:* Student at University of Oregon, 1949-51, and Florida Christian College, 1951-54; Florida State University, B.S., 1956; Abilene Christian College, M.A., 1959; University of Southern California, Ph.D., 1966. *Home:* 2959 Bear River Circle, Westlake Village, Calif. 91361. *Office:* Division of Religion, Pepperdine University, 24255 Pacific Coast Highway, Malibu, Calif. 90625.

CAREER: Minister of Church of Christ, 1951—; Pepperdine University, Malibu, Calif., assistant professor of religion and chairman of division, 1972—. *Member:* American Academy of Religion, Society of Biblical Literature.

WRITINGS: Prayer, Sweet, 1964; *The Gospel According to Luke,* Sweet, 1973; *The Word of Faith,* Biblical Research Society, 1973. Contributor to religious periodicals.

WORK IN PROGRESS: A commentary on Psalms 1-75, for Sweet.

* * *

ASKEW, William C(larence) 1910-

PERSONAL: Born November 23, 1910, in Hamilton, Ga.; son of John D. and Sallie Mae (Dean) Askew; married Alice Washburn, December 30, 1936; children: Elizabeth Anne (Mrs. Frederick William O'Brien). *Education:* Mercer University, A.B., 1931; Duke University, M.A., 1934, Ph.D., 1936. *Politics:* Democrat. *Religion:* Baptist. *Home:* 9 East Kendrick Ave., Hamilton, N.Y. 13346. *Office:* Department of History, Colgate University, Hamilton, N.Y. 13346.

CAREER: Principal of public school in Cataula, Ga., 1931-33; University of Arkansas, Fayetteville, instructor, 1936-39, assistant professor of history, 1939-43; Colgate University, Hamilton, N.Y., assistant professor, 1946-49, associate professor, 1949-55, professor of history, 1955—. Has taught at University of Texas, summer, 1949, Duke University, summer, 1962, and University of Kentucky, summer, 1965. *Military service:* U.S. Naval Reserve, active duty, 1943-46; became lieutenant commander.

MEMBER: American Historical Association, Society for Italian Historical Studies, New York State Association of European Historians (president, 1970-71), Columbia Seminar on Modern Italy (associate), Phi Beta Kappa. *Awards, honors:* Guggenheim fellowship, 1952; Fulbright grant, Italy, 1952-54.

WRITINGS: Europe and Italy's Acquisition of Libya: 1911-1912, Duke University Press, 1942; (editor with Lillian Parker Wallace, and contributor) *Power, Public Opinion, and Diplomacy,* Duke University Press, 1959; (contributor) Edward R. Tannenbaum and Emiliana P. Noether, editors, *Modern Italy: A Topical History Since 1861,* New York University Press, 1974. Contributor to scholarly journals.

WORK IN PROGRESS: Italy and the Great Powers: 1896-1914; Origins of World War One.

* * *

ASPINWALL, Dorothy B(rown) 1910-

PERSONAL: Born October 21, 1910, in Regina, Saskatchewan, Canada; daughter of Ernest T. (an architect) and Frances (a teacher; maiden name, Armstrong) Brown; married Albion N. Aspinwall, January 10, 1942 (died August 21, 1963); married Robert F. Herpick, (died December 31, 1973); children: (first marriage) Albion Lauren. *Education:* University of Alberta, B.A. (with honors), 1933, M.A., 1939; Sorbonne, University of Paris, diploma, 1938; University of Washington, Seattle, Ph.D., 1948. *Home:* 2003 Kalia Rd., Apt. 9-1, Honolulu, Hawaii 96815. *Office:* University of Hawaii, 1890 E-W Rd., Honolulu, Hawaii 96822.

CAREER: French and Latin teacher in high schools in Canada, 1933-37, 1938-40; College of Idaho, Caldwell, associate professor of French, 1941-47; University of Hawaii, Honolulu, assistant professor, 1948-52, associate professor, 1952-59, professor of French, 1959—. *Member:* Modern Language Association of America, American Association of Teachers of French (past president of Hawaii branch), Hawaii Association of Language Teachers (co-founder; past president), Alliance Francaise of Hawaii (member of board of directors). *Awards, honors:* Ford Foundation grant for research, 1954-55; Danforth Foundation grant, 1963.

WRITINGS: (Translator) Charles Peguy, *The Portico of the Mystery of the Second Virtue,* Scarecrow, 1971; (translator and editor) *French Poems in English Verse: 1850-1970,* Scarecrow, 1973. Contributor to popular magazines and literary journals, including *Atlantic Monthly, Explicator, PMLA, New Mexico Quarterly, The Husk, Poet Lore,* and *Paradise of the Pacific.*

WORK IN PROGRESS: Translating contemporary French poems into English.

* * *

ASTURIAS, Miguel Angel 1899-1974

October 19, 1899—June 9, 1974; Guatemalan poet, novelist, diplomat, and Nobel laureate. Obituaries: *Washington Post,* June 10, 1974; *Time,* June 24, 1974; *Newsweek,* June 24, 1974; *Publishers Weekly,* June 24, 1974; *Current Biography,* July, 1974; *AB Bookman's Weekly,* July 15, 1974. (*CA*-25/28).

* * *

ATCHITY, Kenneth John 1944-

PERSONAL: Born January 16, 1944, in Eunice, La.; son of Fred J. (an accountant) and Myrza (a registered nurse; maiden name, Aguillard) Atchity; married Kathleen Dillon, June 12, 1964 (divorced, 1973); married Bonnie Fraser, February 1, 1974; children: (first marriage) Vincent, Rosemary. *Education:* Georgetown University, A.B., 1965; Yale University, M.Phil., 1969, Ph.D., 1970. *Politics:* "Depends on the issue." *Religion:* "Ex-Roman Catholic." *Home:* 1600 Campus Rd., Los Angeles, Calif. 90041. *Office:* Department of English and Comparative Literature, Occidental College, Los Angeles, Calif. 90041.

CAREER: American Telephone & Telegraph (AT&T), Government Communications, Washington, D.C., communications engineer and National Aeronautics and Space

Administration headquarters account manager, 1965-66; Occidental College, Los Angeles, Calif., assistant professor of English and comparative literature, 1970—. Visiting instructor at California State College (now University), Los Angeles, 1970-71; instructor at U.S. Postal Service Management Institute, 1973; Fulbright lecturer at University of Bologna, 1974-75. Newscaster for WGTB-FM Radio, 1962-65.

MEMBER: Modern Language Association of America, American Association of Teachers of Italian, American Comparative Literature Association, Renaissance Society of America, Dante Society of America, Vergilian Society, California Educational Research Association, California State Poetry Society, Eta Sigma Phi. *Awards, honors:* Woodrow Wilson fellowship, 1966; third place in international essay contest of Dante Society of America, 1968, for "Inferno VII: The Idea of Order"; Readers' Choice award from *Bardic Echoes,* 1970, for poem "Noasis"; National Federation of State Poetry Societies Lubbe award, 1971, for poem "e e cummings i hate you," Modern Award, 1971, for poem "What Horace Meant to Say"; grant from National Endowment for the Humanities, 1972; grant from American Council of Learned Societies, 1973, for work in Florence, Italy.

WRITINGS: (Editor) *Eterne in Mutabilitie: The Unity of the Faerie Queene,* Archon, 1972. Composer of libretto *In Praise of Love* (performed by New York Philharmonic, May 13, 1974), Erik K. Marcus, 1974. Guest columnist for *Los Angeles Times,* 1971—. Contributor of more than three hundred articles, poems, and reviews to literary journals and newspapers, including *American Quarterly, Classical Philology, Comparative Literature Studies, Italian Quarterly, Kenyon Review, Western Humanities Review,* and *Washington Post.* Editor-in-chief of *Hoya* (at Georgetown University), 1962-65; features editor of *Moneysworth,* 1971; Southern California editor of *California State Poetry Society Quarterly,* 1972—; editorial consultant for Southern California Research Council, 1973—.

WORK IN PROGRESS: Homer's Iliad: The Song and Shield of Memory; Italian Literature: Roots and Branches, with Giose Rimanelli; books on Spenser and Dante; four collections of poems; a novel; research on Rabelais, Chaucer, Plato, and Euripides.

SIDELIGHTS: Atchity speaks or reads Italian, French, Latin, Greek, Spanish, Provencal, and German.

* * *

ATHERTON, James C(hristian) 1915-

PERSONAL: Born August 4, 1915, in Bolivar, La.; son of James G. (a dairy farmer) and Mary (Matthews) Atherton; married Ruth Victoria Cash (a high school mathematics teacher), November 26, 1937; children: James C., George A., Ruth Atherton Miller. *Education:* Louisiana State University, B.S., 1935, M.S., 1947; University of Illinois, Ed.M., 1949, Ed.D., 1950. *Politics:* Democrat. *Religion:* Southern Baptist. *Home:* 6099 South Pollard Pkwy., Baton Rouge, La. 70808. *Office:* Department of Agricultural Education, Louisiana State University, Baton Rouge, La. 70803.

CAREER: High school teacher and principal in Louisiana, 1935-48; University of Arkansas, Fayetteville, assistant professor, 1950-55, associate professor, 1955-60, professor of vocational education, 1960-65; Louisiana State University, Baton Rouge, professor of agricultural education, 1965—. *Military service:* U.S. Army, 1942-45. U.S. Army Reserve, 1945-64; became lieutenant colonel.

MEMBER: American Association of Teacher Educators in Agriculture, American Vocational Association, Louisiana Vocational Association, Louisiana Vocational Agricultural Teachers' Association, Louisiana Teachers Association, Phi Kappa Phi, Alpha Zeta, Gamma Sigma Delta, Phi Delta Kappa. *Awards, honors:* Distinguished Service Award in agriculture education, Southern Regional Conference in Agricultural Education, 1962; Outstanding Service Citation, National Vocational Agricultural Teachers' Association, 1968.

WRITINGS: (With Anthony Mumphrey) *Essential Aspects of Career Planning and Development,* Interstate, 1969. Contributor of more than one hundred articles to professional journals. Editor, *Arkansas Service Bulletin,* 1955-65, and *AATEA Journal* (publication of American Association of Teacher Educators in Agriculture), 1966-69; special editor, *Agricultural Education,* 1955-62, 1964—.

* * *

ATHERTON, Wallace N(ewman) 1927-

PERSONAL: Born February 11, 1927, in San Francisco, Calif.; son of Wallace (a driver's license examiner) and Marguerite (Richardson) Atherton; married Karyl Rubidge, August, 1953. *Education:* University of California, Berkeley, B.A., 1950, Ph.D., 1959. *Religion:* None. *Residence:* Long Beach, Calif. *Office:* Department of Economics, California State University at Long Beach, Long Beach, Calif. 90840.

CAREER: University of California, Davis, lecturer in economics, 1964-66; California State University at Long Beach, associate professor, 1966-70, professor of economics, 1970—, chairman of department, 1971-74. *Military service:* U.S. Army, 1945-46. *Member:* American Economic Association, Western Economic Association.

WRITINGS: Theory of Union Bargaining Goals, Princeton University Press, 1973.

* * *

ATKINSON, Hugh Craig 1933-

PERSONAL: Born November 27, 1933, in Chicago, Ill.; son of Craig Atkinson; married Mary Nugent; children: George, Mary Susan, Ann. *Education:* St. Benedict's College, Atchison, Kan., student, 1951-53; University of Chicago, B.A., 1957, M.S.L.S., 1959; U.S. National Archives, certificate in archival administration, 1958. *Home:* 520 Dunedin Rd., Columbus, Ohio 43214. *Office:* Ohio State University Libraries, 1858 Neil Ave., Columbus, Ohio 43210.

CAREER: Lawrence Scudder & Co. (certified public accountants), Chicago, Ill., junior accountant, 1951-56; University of Chicago, Library, Chicago, Ill., assistant in rare books section, 1957-58; Pennsylvania Military College, Chester, reader's services librarian, 1958-61; State University of New York at Buffalo, head of library reference department, 1961-64, assistant director of technical services libraries, 1964-67, acting assistant director of health sciences libraries, 1966-67; Ohio State University, Columbus, assistant professor, 1967-69, associate professor, 1969-74, professor of library administration, 1974—, assistant director of public services libraries, 1967-71, director of libraries, 1971—. Institutional representative of Center for Research Libraries, 1971—; member of advisory committee of Ohio Project for Research in Information Science, 1972, 1973; member of Ohio College Library Center.

MEMBER: International Federation of Documentalists, American Library Association (member of council, 1970-75), American Society for Information Science, Association of Research Libraries, American Association of University Professors, Committee on Institutional Cooperation, Ohio Library Association, Franklin County Library Association, University of Chicago Graduate Library School Alumni Association (president, 1974—).

WRITINGS: (Editor with Joseph Katz and Richard A. Ploch) *Twenty-One Letters from Hart Crane to George Bryan,* Library, Ohio State University, 1968; (compiler) *The Merrill Checklist of Theodore Dreiser,* C. E. Merrill, 1969; *Theodore Dreiser: A Checklist,* Kent State University Press, 1971; (contributor) Melvin J. Voigt, editor, *Advances in Librarianship,* Academic Press, 1974. Contributor to *The Bowker Annual of Library and Book Trade Information.* Contributor to *Library Journal* and *Library Trends.*

WORK IN PROGRESS: Research on priorities for the new librarian of Congress, on extension of new services and the role of technology in library science, and on personnel savings through computerized library systems.

BIOGRAPHICAL/CRITICAL SOURCES: Today's Education, January, 1973.

* * *

ATKINSON, Mary
See HARDWICK, Mollie

* * *

ATKYNS, Glenn C(hadwick) 1921-

PERSONAL: Born April 26, 1921, in Washington, D.C.; son of Willie Lee (a firefighter) and Marion (Van Horn) Atkyns; married Syme Vaataja (a nurse), December 9, 1945; children: Robert Lee, Suzanne Joy. *Education:* Harvard University, B.A. (cum laude), 1948, M.A.T., 1949; University of Connecticut, Ph.D., 1958. *Politics:* Republican. *Religion:* Baptist. *Home:* 83 Brookside Lane, Mansfield Center, Conn. 06250. *Office:* Department of Higher, Technical, and Adult Education, University of Connecticut, Storrs, Conn. 06268.

CAREER: High school social studies department head in West Hartford, Conn., 1949-58; University of Connecticut, Storrs, assistant professor, 1959-63, associate professor, 1963-68, professor, 1968—, head of department of higher, technical, and adult education, 1967—, assistant dean, 1959-64, 1965-66, acting dean of School of Education, 1964-65. *Military service:* U.S. Army Reserve, active service, 1941-45; became colonel; received Legion of Merit, Army Commendation Medal, Southwest Pacific Service Medal with assault arrow and three campaign stars. *Member:* American Association of Higher Education, History of Education Society, Association of American Historians, International and Comparative Education Society, Association of Professors of Higher Education, Phi Delta Kappa (chapter secretary). *Awards, honors:* Distinguished service award from Vietnam Ministry of Education for *Education Vietnam.*

WRITINGS: (With Burdette Eagon, Harold Anderson, Willard Brandt, John Furlong, and Fred E. Harris) *Education Vietnam: Proposals for Reorganization,* Agency for International Development, 1968; *National Building in Vietnam* (monograph), Asia Society, 1968; (editor) *Impact of Black Experience on Higher Education in New England,* School of Education, University of Connecticut, 1970. Contributor to *Encyclopedia of Education* and to education journals.

WORK IN PROGRESS: Research on governance models in higher education on both sides of the Iron Curtain, and on changes in the function of college student personnel officers, 1967-72.

* * *

ATTAWAY, Robert J(oseph) 1942-

PERSONAL: Born October 26, 1942, in Missouri; son of Robert H. (an optician) and Kathleen (an employee of the Internal Revenue Service; maiden name, Harrington) Attaway. *Education:* Rockhurst College, B.A., 1963; University of Missouri at Kansas City, M.A., 1969; University of Missouri at Columbia, Ph.D., 1974. *Politics:* Socialist-Democrat. *Religion:* Atheist. *Home:* 1219 West 41st St., #3E, Kansas City, Mo. 64111.

CAREER: Peace Corps, Washington, D.C., English teacher in Nigeria and Ethiopia, 1965-68; Pan American University, Edinburg, Tex., instructor in English, 1969-71; Junior College District of Kansas City, Kansas City, Mo., instructor in English, 1973—.

WRITINGS: I Think of Warri (novel), Harper, 1974.

WORK IN PROGRESS: The Magic Valley, a novel; research on Edward Albee.

* * *

ATTENBOROUGH, Bernard George (James S. Rand)

PERSONAL: Born in Moseley, England; son of George (a surveyor and architect) and Lilian Elizabeth (Oakley) Attenborough; married Eileen Osborne (a hospital executive), July 10, 1947; children: Mark Lee Quentin, Jill Alison. *Education:* Attended King Edward's School and University of Birmingham. *Politics:* "Broadly liberal. . ." *Religion:* "World Citizenship." *Home:* Green Meadows, Heads of Ayr, Scotland.

CAREER: Director of Osborne & Co. Ltd., Glasgow, and Attenborough Bros. Ltd., 1947-57; free-lance writer, 1964—. *Member:* Royal Institute of Journalists, Chartered Institute of Journalists, Society of Authors, Shark Club (Great Britain), Association de la Presse Sportive.

WRITINGS—Novels, under pseudonym James S. Rand: *The Stake,* McLellan, 1956; *Run for the Trees* (African adventure novel), Putnam, 1966; *Viva Ramirez!,* Bantam, 1970. Contributor to British and American magazines and newspapers. Contract correspondent, *News Chronicle* and *Sunday Times,* 1947-57.

WORK IN PROGRESS: Research in Africa for *The Great Sky and the Silence.*

SIDELIGHTS: "I have always been motivated by two aspects," Rand told *CA,* "physical endeavor and what some call courage and others controlled fear—as distinct from panic." Beginning in boyhood as a shooter and angler, Rand soon graduated to Scottish deerstalking ("the most delicate and difficult of all") and big-game hunting, being especially interested in the game of Africa and Central and South America. He traveled to South America to investigate the rare technique of "calling" jaguar by night ("for my money," says Rand, "the scariest big-game hunting of all"), for his book, *Viva Ramirez*.

* * *

ATTWELL, Arthur A(lbert) 1917-

PERSONAL: Born July 3, 1917, in Stevenson, Wash.; son of Walter G. (a civil engineer) and Bernice (Ginder) Attwell; married Dorothy Peterson, July 2, 1934; children: Arthur, Timothy. *Education:* Arizona State University, A.B., 1939; California State University, Los Angeles, M.A., 1955; University of Southern California, Ed.D., 1960. *Home address:* Heidi Rd., Three Rivers, Calif. 93271. *Office:* Department of Educational Psychology, California State University, Los Angeles, Calif. 90032.

CAREER: Professional trumpet player in Los Angeles, Calif., 1934-55; School District of Rosemead, Calif., psychologist, 1954-60; California State University, Los Angeles, assistant professor, 1960-64, associate professor, 1964-68, professor of educational psychology, 1968—. *Member:* American Association on Mental Deficiency (fellow), Phi Kappa Phi, Kappa Delta Pi.

WRITINGS: Counseling Parents of the Retarded, U.S. Office of Information, 1968; (with D. Ann Clabby) *The Retarded Child: Answers to Questions Parents Ask,* Western Psychological Services, 1971; *The School Psychologist's Handbook,* Western Psychological Services, 1972; *An Outline of Educational Psychology,* Burgess, 1973. Contributor of about fifty articles to professional journals.

WORK IN PROGRESS: Management of Sexual Behavior in Retarded Adolescents, for Western Psychological Services; revising *Counseling Parents of the Retarded, The Retarded Child: Answers to Questions Parents Ask,* and *The School Psychologist's Handbook.*

SIDELIGHTS: Attwell writes: "As a consultant in mental retardation and as a parent of a retarded child, I felt the need for a book on specifics, rather than philosophy. All my books and articles have been 'cookbooks,' suggesting the 'how' or 'how to' rather than the 'why.'" *Avocational interests:* Tennis.

* * *

ATWOOD, Margaret 1939-

PERSONAL: Born November 18, 1939, in Ottawa, Ontario, Canada; daughter of Carl Edmund (an entomologist) and Margaret (Killam) Atwood. *Education:* University of Toronto, B.A., 1961; Radcliffe College, A.M., 1962; Harvard University, graduate study, 1962-63, 1965-67. *Politics:* William Morrisite. *Religion:* "Pessimistic Pantheist." *Home address:* Box 1401, Alliston, Ontario, Canada. *Agent:* Phoebe Larmore, 44 Greenwich Ave., New York, N.Y. 10011.

CAREER: Worked during her early career as cashier, waitress, market research firm writer, and film script writer; University of British Columbia, Vancouver, lecturer in English literature, 1964-65; Sir George Williams University, Montreal, Quebec, lecturer in English literature, 1967-68; York University, Toronto, Ontario, assistant professor of English literature, 1971-72; University of Toronto, Toronto, Ontario, writer-in-residence, 1972-73. House of Anansi Press, Toronto, Ontario, editor and member of board of directors, 1971-73. *Member:* Canadian Civil Liberties Association (member of board of directors, 1973-75). *Awards, honors:* President's Medal from University of Western Ontario, 1965; Governor General's Award, 1966, for *The Circle Game;* first prize in Canadian Centennial Commission Poetry Competition, 1967; Union League Civic and Arts Foundation Prize from *Poetry,* 1969; D.Litt. from Trent University, 1973; LL.D. from Queen's University, 1974.

WRITINGS—Poems: *Double Persephone,* Hawkshead Press, 1961; *The Circle Game,* Contact Press, 1966; *The Animals in That Country,* Oxford University Press (Canada), 1968, Little, Brown, 1969; *The Journals of Susanna Moodie,* Oxford University Press, 1970; *Procedures for Underground,* Little, Brown, 1970; *Power Politics,* Anansi, 1971, Harper, 1973; *You Are Happy,* Harper, 1974.

Novels: *The Edible Woman,* McClelland & Stewart, 1969, Little, Brown, 1970; *Surfacing,* McClelland & Stewart, 1972, Simon & Schuster, 1973.

Nonfiction: *Survival: A Thematic Guide to Canadian Literature,* Anansi, 1972.

Poetry is represented in anthologies, including *How Do I Love Thee: Sixty Poets of Canada (and Quebec) Select and Introduce Their Favourite Poems from Their Own Work,* edited by John Robert Colombo, M. G. Hurtig (Edmonton, Alberta), 1970. Contributor of poetry to *Tamarack Review, Canadian Forum, New Yorker, Atlantic, Poetry, Kayak, Quarry, Prism,* and other magazines; contributor of short stories, reviews, and critical articles to *Harper's, Saturday Night, Ellipse,* and other periodicals.

WORK IN PROGRESS: A novel; an American edition of *Survival: A Thematic Guide to Canadian Literature.*

SIDELIGHTS: "Behind this quiet, well-taught . . . behavior," Melvin Maddocks writes, "Margaret Atwood conceals the kick of a perfume bottle converted into a Molotov cocktail. She is one of the new sisterhood . . . who seem to have sprung full-grown from condemned-property dollhouses. Hyperobservant, dangerously polite waifs, they look at the world with large, bruised eyes and gently whisper of loneliness, emptiness and casual cruelty. . . . Primeval isolation, a selfhood that is a mystery most of all to oneself, an animal sense of mortality—these are the terrors Atwood has to offer. Technology, social sophistication, are transparent pretenses behind which man is naked, with drooling fang and club at the ready."

Harriet Zinnes speaks from another point of view: ". . .the poet's sense of omnipresent death is too much even in a world threatened by total extinction. Life can do more than briefly make stones warm. People still do make love, bear children, delight in the simple (even in suburbia the driveways don't always 'neatly/sidestep hysteria'). It is simply not true that 'there's little choice between/heart and spade.' The real nightmare is that there's always the choice!"

Robert Gibbs notes that Atwood "has a way of twisting her poems in a controlled, almost deliberate fashion, to a very high pitch, then letting them fall off . . . leaving us feeling that under the strong, brilliantly painted mask that reality wears the essential is missing."

"The particular virtue of Margaret Atwood's poetry," Eric Thompson believes, "lies in the deceptive simplicity of her craft . . . the prime source for myth-making lies in the mental and emotional experiences of the writer herself, but unlike others Atwood displays a sureness of touch which enables her to clarify rather than obscure the myth-real relationships. This is not done without risks, though, and one may legitimately cavil at the limited size of her canvas."

"Her exceptional imagery and discipline survive each other," writes Michael Ondaatje. "[Her writing] displays the awesome furniture of the mind which motivates the cannibalistic speaker who demands to know everything of the people around her: those with her in train stations, and those marooned with her on islands."

BIOGRAPHICAL/CRITICAL SOURCES: Contemporary Literary Criticism, Volume II and Volume III, Gale, 1974.

* * *

AUGUST, Eugene R(obert) 1935-

PERSONAL: Born October 19, 1935, in Jersey City, N.J.; son of Joseph Lawrence (a printer) and Florence (Brown) August; married Barbara Ann Danko (a teacher), June 18, 1964; children: Robert Eugene, James Eugene. *Education:* Rutgers University, B.A., 1958; University of Connecticut, M.A., 1960; University of Pittsburgh, Ph.D., 1965. *Politics:* Democrat. *Religion:* Roman Catholic. *Home:* 801 Otterbein Ave., Dayton, Ohio 45406. *Office:* Department of English, University of Dayton, Dayton, Ohio 45469.

CAREER: Carnegie-Mellon University, Pittsburgh, Pa., instructor, 1962-64, assistant professor of English, 1964-66; University of Dayton, Dayton, Ohio, assistant professor, 1966-69, associate professor of English, 1969—. Visiting associate professor at University of Hawaii, 1974-75. *Member:* Modern Language Association of America, Tennyson Society, Hopkins Society. *Awards, honors:* Younger Humanist fellowship from National Endowment for Humanities, 1973-74, for a book-length study of the art of John Stuart Mill.

WRITINGS: (Contributor) Harry J. Cargas, editor, *The Continuous Flame: Teilhard in the Great Traditions,* B. Herder, 1970; (editor) *The Nigger Question [by Thomas Carlyle and] The Negro Question [by John Stuart Mill],* Appleton, 1971. Contributor to *PMLA, Victorian Poetry,* and *James Joyce Quarterly.*

WORK IN PROGRESS: The Philosopher's Voice: An Introduction to John Stuart Mill (tentative title).

* * *

AUSTIN, Oliver L(uther), Jr. 1903-

PERSONAL: Born May 24, 1903, in Tuckahoe, N.Y.; son of Oliver Luther (a physician) and Elizabeth (Wise) Austin; married Elizabeth Schling (an author), September 10, 1930; children: Anthony, Timothy. *Education:* Berkshire School, Sheffield, Mass., student, 1921-22; Wesleyan University, Middletown, Conn., B.S., 1926; Harvard University, Ph.D., 1931. *Home:* 205 Southeast Seventh St., Gainesville, Fla. 32601. *Office:* Florida State Museum, Seagle Building, University of Florida, Gainesville, Fla. 32601.

CAREER: U.S. Department of Agriculture, Bureau of Biological Survey, Washington, D.C., assistant biologist, 1930-35; Austin Ornithological Research Station, Wellfleet, Mass., director, 1932-57; U.S. Department of the Army, technical consultant in Tokyo, Japan, 1946-50; Air University, Maxwell Air Force Base, Ala., research and education specialist at Arctic, Desert, Tropic Information Center, Research Studies Institute, 1953-57; Florida State Museum, Gainesville, ornithological curator, 1957—. *Military service:* U.S. Naval Reserve, active duty, 1942-46; became commander. *Member:* American Ornithologists' Union (fellow), British Ornithologists' Union, Ornithological Society of Japan, Nuttall Ornithological Club, Cooper Ornithological Club, Wilson Ornithological Society, Eastern Bird-Banding Association, Explorers Club (New York). *Awards, honors:* Guggenheim fellowship, 1952-53; Distinguished Alumnus Award, Wesleyan University, 1966; co-recipient with wife, Elizabeth S. Austin, of Arthur A. Allen medal, from Cornell Laboratory of Ornithology, 1973.

WRITINGS: The Birds of Newfoundland and Labrador, Nuttall Ornithological Club, Harvard University, 1932; *The Birds of Korea,* Museum of Comparative Zoology, Harvard University, 1948; (with Nagahisa Kuroda) *The Birds of Japan,* Museum of Comparative Zoology, Harvard University, 1953; *Birds of the World: A Survey of the 27 Orders and 155 Families,* Golden Press, 1961; (editor) *Life Histories of North American Birds,* U.S. National Museum, 1968; (editor) *Antarctic Bird Studies,* American Geophysical Union, 1968; (with wife, Elizabeth S. Austin) *The Random House Book of Birds* (juvenile), Random House, 1970; *Families of Birds,* Golden Press, 1971. Contributor of about one hundred papers to ornithological journals. Editor, *Auk* (quarterly publication of American Ornithologists' Union), 1968—.

WORK IN PROGRESS: With Arthur Singer, *Field Guide to Birds of the Oceans.*

AVOCATIONAL INTERESTS: Growing orchids, gardening.

* * *

AVRICH, Paul (Henry) 1931-

PERSONAL: Born August 4, 1931, in New York, N.Y.; married, 1954. *Education:* Cornell University, A.B., 1952; Columbia University, A.M., 1959, Ph.D., 1961. *Home:* 425 Riverside Dr., New York, N.Y. 10025. *Office:* Department of History, Queens College of the City University of New York, Flushing, N.Y. 11367.

CAREER: Queens College of the City University of New York, Flushing, N.Y., instructor, 1960-65, assistant professor, 1965-66, associate professor, 1966-70, professor of history, 1970—. Visiting assistant professor, Wesleyan University, 1961-62, 1963-64. *Member:* American Historical Association, American Association for the Advancement of Slavic Studies. *Awards, honors:* Ford Foundation grant for travel in Russia, 1960; Guggenheim fellow and senior fellow at Russian Institute, Columbia University, 1967-68; National Endowment for the Humanities senior fellow, 1972-73.

WRITINGS: The Russian Anarchists, Princeton University Press, 1967; *Kronstadt 1921,* Princeton University Press, 1970; *Russian Rebels, 1600-1800,* Schocken, 1972; (editor) *The Anarchists in the Russian Revolution,* Cornell University Press, 1973.

WORK IN PROGRESS: Anarchism in America.

* * *

AZAR, Edward E. 1938-

PERSONAL: Born March 2, 1938, in Beshamoon, Lebanon. *Education:* American University of Beirut, B.A., 1960; University of the Pacific, M.A., 1965; Stanford University, Ph.D., 1969. *Home:* 51 Cedar St., Chapel Hill, N.C. 27514. *Office:* Department of Political Science, 259 Hamilton Hall, University of North Carolina, Chapel Hill, N.C. 27514.

CAREER: Arabian American Oil Co., Saudi Arabia, translator, 1960-64; San Francisco State University, San Francisco, Calif., lecturer, 1967-68; Michigan State University, East Lansing, assistant professor of political science, 1968-71; University of North Carolina, Chapel Hill, associate professor of political science, 1971—. *Member:* International Studies Association, Peace Science Society (president of Southern branch, 1971-72), Consortium on Peace Research, Teaching and Development.

WRITINGS: Probe for Peace: Small State Hostilities, Burgess, 1973; (editor with Joseph Ben-Dak) *Theory and Practice of Events Research,* Gordon & Breach, 1974. Guest editor, *Journal of Conflict Resolution,* 1972; editor, *Review of Peace Science,* 1973, and *International Interactions,* 1974—.

WORK IN PROGRESS: Research on intra-national and international tension, conflict reduction, alliance formation, and international cooperation; development of measurement instruments in international relations; building of a data bank for exploration of international behavior; a book about Lebanese foreign policy.

* * *

BABBITT, Natalie 1932-

PERSONAL: Born July 28, 1932, in Dayton, Ohio; daughter of Ralph Zane (a business administrator) and Genevieve (Converse) Moore; married Samuel Fisher Babbitt (president of Kirkland College), June 26, 1954; children: Christopher Converse, Thomas Collier II, Lucy Cullyford. *Education:* Smith College, B.A., 1954. *Politics:* Democrat. *Home:* Harding Rd., R.D. 1, Clinton, N.Y. 13323. *Agent:* Curtis Brown Ltd., 60 East 56th St., New York, N.Y. 10022.

CAREER: Majored in art at college and entered the children's book field as an illustrator. *Member:* Authors Guild of Authors League of America. *Awards, honors:* The *New York Times* listed *The Search for Delicious* as the best book of 1969 for children ages nine-twelve; *Kneeknock Rise* was an American Library Association Notable Book, 1970, a John Newbery honor book, 1971, and was on *Horn Book* honors list; *Goody Hall* was an Honor Book in the 1971 Children's Spring Book Festival sponsored by *Book World,* a Children's Book Council Showcase title, 1972, and on *School Library Journal* list.

WRITINGS—Self-illustrated: *Dick Foote and the Shark* (verse; Junior Literary Guild selection), Farrar, Straus, 1967; *Phoebe's Revolt,* Farrar, Straus, 1968; *The Search for Delicious,* Farrar, Straus, 1969; *Kneeknock Rise* (Junior Literary Guild selection), Farrar, Straus, 1970; *The Something* (Junior Literary Guild selection), Farrar, Straus, 1970; *Goody Hall,* Farrar, Straus, 1971; *The Devil's Storybook,* Farrar, Straus, 1974.

Illustrator: Samuel Fisher Babbitt, *The Forty-Ninth Magician,* Pantheon, 1966; Valerie Worth, *Small Poems,* Farrar Straus, 1972.

Contributor to *Redbook, Publishers' Weekly, Horn Book,* and *New York Times Book Review.*

WORK IN PROGRESS: An untitled children's novel about immortality and its possible miseries.

SIDELIGHTS: Mrs. Babbitt said: "As the wife of a college president and mother of three children, I have little enough time for work and none for hobbies except needlework. I write for children because I am interested in fantasy and the possibilities for experience of all kinds before the time of compromise. I believe that children are far more perceptive and wise than American books give them credit for being. I am my own best audience."

* * *

BACHEM ALENT, Rose M(arie Baake)

PERSONAL: Born in Bruehl, Germany; came to United States in 1950, naturalized in 1955; daughter of H. F. and E. C. (Beegen) Baake; married Peter J. Bachem, July 23, 1947 (divorced, 1964); married Maurice B. Alent, June 12, 1965; children: (first marriage) Yvonne Christine, Suzanne Nicole. *Education:* Attended University of Heidelberg and University of Paris; University of Berlin, Diplomdolmetscherin Staatsexamen; University of Rochester, M.A., 1953, Ph.D., 1957. *Home:* 39 Second St., Geneseo, N.Y. 14454. *Office:* State University of New York College at Geneseo, Geneseo, N.Y. 14454.

CAREER: Formerly member of faculty, Defra Language Institute and Volkshochschule, both in Berlin; State University of New York College at Geneseo, assistant professor, 1956-59, associate professor, 1960-63, professor of comparative literature, 1963—. *Member:* Modern Language Association of America, American Association of University Professors, American Association of Teachers of French, American Association of Teachers of German, American Association of University Women, New York Teachers Association, State University of New York Faculty Association, Civil Service Employees Association. *Awards, honors:* Chevalier dans l'Ordre des Palmes Academiques, 1972.

WRITINGS: The Companion to Foreign Language Composition, Volume I: *Literary Terms, German-English,* Rodopi, 1973. Contributor to journals in her field.

WORK IN PROGRESS: Second volume of *The Companion to Foreign Language Composition.*

AVOCATIONAL INTERESTS: Theatre, horticulture, gourmet food, jewelry, animals.

* * *

BADAWI, M(ohamed) M(ustafa) 1925-
(Muhammad Mustafa Badawi)

PERSONAL: Given name is sometimes listed as Muhammad; born June 10, 1925, in Alexandria, Egypt; son of Mustafa (a contractor) and Aziza (Ibrahim) Badawi; married Willemina Herderschee (a medical social worker), July 27, 1954; children: Salma, Randa, Kareema, Ramsey. *Education:* Alexandria University, B.A. (honors), 1946; University of London, B.A. (honors), 1950, Ph.D., 1954. *Office:* Department of English, St. Antony's College, Oxford University, Oxford, England.

CAREER: Alexandria University, Alexandria, Egypt, research fellow, 1947-54, lecturer, 1954-60, professor of English, 1960-64; Oxford University, Oxford, England, university lecturer in Arabic, 1964—, lecturer at Brasenose College, 1965—, fellow of St. Antony's College, 1967—. *Member:* Association of University Teachers. *Awards, honors:* M.A., Oxford University, 1964.

WRITINGS: Rasa'il min London (title means "Letters from London: A Volume of Arabic Verse"), Dar al-Talib (Alexandria), 1956; *Coleridge* (in Arabic) Dar al-Ma'arif (Cairo), 1958; *Dirasat fi'l shi'r wa'l masrah* (title means "Studies in Poetry and Drama: A Comparative Study of the Form and Language of Classical and Modern Arabic Poetry"), Dar al-Ma'rif, 1960; (editor) *Mukhtarat min al-*

shi'r al-'arabi al-hadith, Dar al-Nahar (Beirut), 1969, translation published as *An Anthology of Modern Arabic Verse,* Oxford University Press, 1970; *Coleridge: Critic of Shakespeare,* Cambridge University Press, 1973; (translator from the Arabic) Yahya Haqqi, *The Saint's Lamp and Other Stories,* E. J. Brill, 1973.

Translator into Arabic: George Santayana, *Al-Ihsas bi'l jamal* ("The Sense of Beauty"), Mu'assasat Franklin (Cairo), 1960; I. A. Richards, *Al-'Ilm wa'l shi'r* ("Science and Poetry"), Matba'at al-Anglo (Cairo), 1960; Stephen Spender, *Al-Hayat wa'l sha'ir* ("Life and the Poet"), Matba'at al-Anglo, 1960; G. Rostrevor Hamilton, *Al-Shi'r wa'l ta'ammul* ("Poetry and Contemplation"), al-Mu'assasa al-Misriyya (Cairo), 1963; Richards, *Mabadi' al-naqd al-adabi* ("Principles of Literary Criticism"), al-Mu'assasa al-Misriyya, 1963.

Contributor of essays to journals in his field. Member of the committee of correspondents for the Annual Bibliography of *Shakespeare Quarterly,* 1961—. Co-editor of *Journal of Arabic Literature,* 1970—; member of the editorial advisory board of *Cambridge History of Arabic Literature,* 1971—.

WORK IN PROGRESS: Attitudes and Assumptions in Eighteenth-Century Shakespearean Criticism; A Critical Introduction to Modern Arabic Poetry; Background to Shakespeare; Al-Malik Lir (a translation of Shakespeare's *King Lear*), to be published by the Government of Kuwait.

BIOGRAPHICAL/CRITICAL SOURCES: Bulletin of the School of Oriental and African Studies, Volume XXXI, Part I, 1968.

* * *

BADAWI, Muhammad Mustafa
See BADAWI, M(ohamed) M(ustafa)

* * *

BAENZIGER, Hans 1917-

PERSONAL: Born January 15, 1917, in Romanshorn, Switzerland; son of Emil and Lucie (Bardy) Baenziger; married Clare Sieber, July, 1943; children: Anna Barbara (Mrs. Rolf Haller), Elisabeth (Mrs. Osman Karamehmedovic), Nina. *Education:* University of Zurich, Dr.phil., 1942. *Religion:* Protestant. *Home:* 909 Montgomery Ave., Bryn Mawr, Pa. 19010. *Office:* Department of German, Bryn Mawr College, Bryn Mawr, Pa. 19010.

CAREER: Kantonsschule, Trogen, Switzerland, instructor in German, 1943-67; Hochschule fuer Wirtschafts-und Sozialwissenschaft, St. Gallen, Switzerland, dozent, 1953-67; Bryn Mawr College, Bryn Mawr, Pa., associate professor, 1967-70, professor of German, 1970—, chairman of department, 1970-72. Visiting professor at Middlebury College Summer Language School, 1963, 1965, 1968. Member of city council, Trogen, Switzerland, 1953-58. *Military service:* Swiss Army, 1937-72; became first lieutenant. *Member:* Modern Language Association of America, American Association of Teachers of German, Schweizer Schriftstellerverein, Akademische Gesellschaft schweizerischer Germahisten.

WRITINGS: Gottfried Keller und Jeremias Gotthelf, Paul Haupt, 1943; *Werner Bergengruen: Weg und Werk,* Pflugverlag, 1950, 3rd edition, Francke, 1968; *Heimat und Fremde: Ein Kapitel "Tragische Literaturgeschichte" in der Schweiz: Jakob Schaffner, Robert Walser, Albin Zollinger,* Francke, 1958; *Frisch und Duerrenmatt,* Francke, 1960, 6th edition, 1971; (contributor) *Christliche Dichter der Gegenwart,* [Heidelberg], 1955, 2nd edition, Francke, 1968. Contributor to numerous periodicals. Co-editor, *Reformatio* (Zurich), 1963-68.

WORK IN PROGRESS: Books on Max Frisch, Walser, Kafka, and others.

* * *

BAER, Curtis O. 1898-

PERSONAL: Born May 14, 1898, in Strasbourg, France; son of Salomon and Sophie (Insel) Baer; married Kathi Meyer (a musicologist), April 15, 1934; children: George Martin. *Education:* Studied at University of Strasbourg, University of Freiburg, University of Berlin, and University of Basle. *Home:* 51 French Ridge, New Rochelle, N.Y. 10801.

CAREER: Exporter of chemicals; Vassar College, Poughkeepsie, N.Y., visiting scholar, 1961—. Intermittent lecturer at Manhattanville College and New York University. *Member:* College Art Association, Morgan Library (fellow), Drawings Society (New York).

WRITINGS: Landscape Drawings, Abrams, 1973. Contributor to periodicals.

WORK IN PROGRESS: Research on Nicolas Poussin.

* * *

BAEUML, Franz H(einrich) 1926-

PERSONAL: Born June 12, 1926, in Vienna, Austria; came to United States in 1942; naturalized citizen in 1945; son of Gustav H. and Josefa (Sam) Baeuml; married Betty Jean Zeidner (a university professor), August 27, 1958; children: Carolyn, Mark, Deborah. *Education:* Armstrong College, B.S., 1950; University of California, Berkeley, B.A., 1953, M.A., 1955, Ph.D., 1957. *Home:* 12400 Marva Ave., Granada Hills, Calif. 91344. *Office:* Department of Germanic Languages, University of California, Los Angeles, Calif. 90024.

CAREER: University of California, Los Angeles, instructor, 1957-59, assistant professor, 1959-62, associate professor, 1962-65, professor of Germanic languages, 1965—. *Military service:* U.S. Army, 1944-46, 1950-51; became sergeant. *Member:* Internationaler Germanistenverein, Mediaeval Academy of America, Modern Language Association of America.

WRITINGS: Rhetorical Devices and Structure in the Ackermann aus Boehmen, University of California Press, 1960; *Medieval Civilization in Germany: 800-1273,* Praeger, 1969; *Kudrun: Die Handschrift* (title means "Kudrun: The Manuscript"), De Gruyter, 1969. Contributor to *Journal of English and Germanic Philology, Deutsche Vierteljahrsschrift,* and *Speculum.*

WORK IN PROGRESS: Concordance to the Nibelungenlied, completion expected in 1974; *Dictionary of Gestures,* 1975.

* * *

BAGNEL, Joan 1933-
(Joan Bagnel Cipolla)

PERSONAL: Surname is pronounced Bag-*nel;* born August 29, 1933, in New York, N.Y.; daughter of James Patrick (a construction engineer) and Mary J. (Powers)

Bagnel; married Thomas M. Cipolla (an audio-visual businessman), October 10, 1953 (divorced, 1974); children: Julia, Thomas. *Education:* Attended Fordham University, 1951-52, and American Theatre Wing, 1952-53. *Address:* c/o Trident Press, Simon & Schuster, Inc., 630 Fifth Ave., New York, N.Y. 10020.

CAREER: Actress in touring children's theatre groups, including Claire Tree Major's; free-lance writer of fiction and of educational films.

WRITINGS: Gone the Rainbow, Gone the Dove (novel), Trident Press, 1974. Under name Joan Bagnel Cipolla, writer (and often narrator) of about eight hundred educational films and filmstrips. Contributor to *New York Times;* contributor of short stories to magazines.

WORK IN PROGRESS: Four novels, the first three under contract: *Only of Beginnings* (tentative title), *The Seasick Camel,* an untitled book set in the world of theatre people, and *Child of Light* (working title); adaptations of fairy tales; filmstrips; writing for retarded and disturbed children.

SIDELIGHTS: "I am called sometimes a 'method writer,'" Joan Bagnel told *CA,* "as I become intensely and rather one-sidedly involved with my characters. . . .but otherwise I can usually see both sides of most questions. *Gone the Rainbow, Gone the Dove,* for example, is intensely pro-IRA (set in the period 1913-1921), but I am not involved in politics in Ireland or home, and am certainly not a 'revolutionary' in any sense of the word. I am a human being first, a woman incidentally. I only hope that my work transcends . . . 'woman's interest.' I am not 'liberated,' I am free, and that is because I have been lucky enough to be able to do what is in me to do. I wish that for all humans everywhere. I have unlimited goals for my work; I wish it to be enjoyed and remembered—not that *I* must be remembered, only what has been said through me."

AVOCATIONAL INTERESTS: Egyptology, archaeology, mythologies, cats, the occult, gardening.

* * *

BAILEY, J(ames) Martin 1929-

PERSONAL: Born July 28, 1929, in Emmetsburg, Iowa; son of Allen Ransom (a teacher) and Kathryn (a teacher and drama coach; maiden name, Ausland) Bailey; married Betty Jane Wenzel (a consultant in Christian education), June 5, 1954; children: Kristine Elizabeth, Susan Ruth. *Education:* State University of Iowa, B.A. (with certificate in journalism), 1951; Eden Theological Seminary, B.D., 1954; Northwestern University, M.S.Journalism, 1956. *Politics:* Democrat. *Home:* 45 Watchung Ave., Upper Montclair, N.J. 07043. *Office: A.D.* Magazine, 1840 Interchurch Center, 475 Riverside Dr., New York, N.Y. 10027.

CAREER: Ordained to ministry of United Church of Christ, 1954; *International Journal of Religious Education,* Chicago, Ill., and New York, N.Y., business manager, 1954-60; *United Church Herald,* St. Louis, Mo., business manager in circulation, advertising, and promotion, 1960-63, editor, 1963-73; *A.D.* (magazine), New York, N.Y., editor-in-chief, 1973—. Vice-president and member of board of directors of Associated Church Press; chairman of Interchurch Features. Member of staffs of National Council of Churches and World Council of Churches. Democratic county committeeman, 1974—.

MEMBER: National Religious Public Relations Council. *Awards, honors:* D.D. from Eden Theological Seminary, 1965, and Lakeland College, 1967; awards of merit from Associated Church Press, 1969, for series of articles, and 1972, for editorial; two Hinkhouse Awards from National Religious Public Relations Council, 1974.

WRITINGS: Windbreaks, Friendship Press, 1958; *Youth and the Town and Country Church,* Friendship Press, 1958; (with wife, Betty Jane Bailey) *Worship with Youth,* United Church Press, 1962; (with Douglas Gilbert) *Steps of Bonhoeffer,* United Church Press, 1969; *From Wrecks to Reconciliation,* Friendship Press, 1969. Correspondent for *Reformed World.* Contributor of articles to *Motive, International Journal, Presbyterian Life, Presbyterian Survey, Lutheran, Together, Lamp,* and newspapers. Editorial consultant for *Grassroots: Journal of Ecumenism* and *Lamp.*

WORK IN PROGRESS: Research for a series on the role of the church in developing countries; research on evangelism; research on the church and multinational corporations.

SIDELIGHTS: Bailey has traveled or studied in Japan, the Philippines, Vietnam, Latin America, Europe, Africa, and the Middle East.

* * *

BAILEY, Robert, Jr. 1945-

PERSONAL: Born April 27, 1945, in Kansas; son of Robert (a farmer and lawyer) and Sarah (Morgen) Bailey; married Rita Carol Burdinie (a tax auditor), June 26, 1971. *Education:* Kansas City (Kansas) Community Junior College, A.A., 1965; University of Kansas, B.A., 1967; Northwestern University, M.A., 1968, Ph.D., 1972. *Home:* 1305 Oak, Evanston, Ill. 60201. *Office:* Arthur Meyerhoff Associates, 410 North Michigan, Chicago, Ill.

CAREER: Elementary school teacher in public schools in Chicago, Ill., 1968-71; Cleveland State University, Cleveland, Ohio, assistant professor of political science, 1971-73; Arthur Meyerhoff Associates (advertising agency), Chicago, Ill., market researcher, 1973—. *Member:* American Political Science Association.

WRITINGS: Radicals in Urban Politics, University of Chicago Press, 1974. Contributor to *Journal of Voluntary Action Research, Growth and Change,* and *Planning.*

WORK IN PROGRESS: Using attitudinal research to understand consumer behavior.

* * *

BAKER, Frank 1936-

PERSONAL: Born February 28, 1936, in Dallas, Tex.; son of Dave (a cattle dealer) and Estelle (Portnoy) Baker; married Adrienne Polland, March 20, 1960; children: Steven Isaac, David Brian, Julie Suzanne. *Education:* Vanderbilt University, B.A. (cum laude), 1958; Northwestern University, M.A., 1962, Ph.D., 1964. *Home:* 14 Pythias Circle, Needham, Mass. 02192. *Office:* Laboratory of Community Psychiatry, Harvard Medical School, 58 Fenwood Rd., Boston, Mass. 02115.

CAREER: Lehigh University, Bethlehem, Pa., assistant professor of social psychology, 1963-65; Harvard University Medical School, Laboratory of Community Psychiatry, Boston, Mass., head of Program Research Unit, 1965—. *Member:* American Association for the Advancement of Science, American Public Health Association, American Psychological Association, American Sociological Association, Operations Research Society of America, Society for Applied Anthropology, Society for General Systems Research, Society for Medical Anthropology.

WRITINGS: (With P. J. McEwan and A. Sheldon) *Industrial Organizations and Health,* Tavistock, 1969; (with H. C. Schulberg and Sheldon) *Program Evaluation in the Health Fields,* Behavioral Publications, 1969; (with Sheldon and C. McLaughlin) *Systems and Medical Care,* M.I.T. Press, 1969; (with Schulberg) *Developments in Human Services,* Volume I, Behavioral Publications, 1973; *Organizational Systems: General Systems Approaches to Complex Organizations,* Irwin, 1973. Contributor to medical journals.

WORK IN PROGRESS: Book manuscripts on human service systems, program evaluation, and developments in human services.

* * *

BAKER, Jeffrey J(ohn) W(heeler) 1931-

PERSONAL: Born February 2, 1931, in Montclair, N.J.; son of Jefferson Wheeler (a stockbroker) and Monica L. (Deakin) Baker; married Barbara Bernache, August 20, 1955; children: Rebekah Monica, Deborah Ann, Jennifer Deakin, Jefferson Jonathan Farrar. *Education:* Attended University of Vermont, 1950-51; University of Virginia, B.A., 1953, M.S., 1959. *Politics:* Independent. *Religion:* None. *Home:* 13 Sunset Ter., Portland, Conn. 06480. *Office:* Wesleyan University, Middletown, Conn. 06457.

CAREER: George Washington University, Washington, D.C., associate professor, 1966-68; University of Puerto Rico, Rio Piedras, professor, 1968-69; Wesleyan University, Middletown, Conn., chairman of science program, 1969—. Editorial director and staff biologist, Commission on Undergraduate Education in the Biological Sciences (CUEBS), 1966-68. *Member:* American Institution of Biological Sciences, American Association for the Advancement of Science, National Association of Science Writers, Authors Guild. *Awards, honors: Patterns of Nature* was selected by the *New York Times* as one of the fifty best books for children, 1967.

WRITINGS: (With Rudolph E. Hafner) *The Vital Wheel: Metabolism,* American Education Publications, 1963; *In the Beginning: A Survey of Modern Embryology,* American Education Publications, 1964; *Cell,* American Education Publications, 1965; *Patterns of Nature* (juvenile), Doubleday, 1967; *The Vital Process: Photosynthesis* (young adult), Doubleday, 1969; *Strike the Tent,* Doubleday, 1970.

With Garland E. Allen: *Matter, Energy and Life: An Introduction for Biology Students,* Addison-Wesley, 1965, 2nd edition, 1970; *The Study of Biology,* Addison-Wesley, 1967, abridged edition published as *A Course in Biology,* 1968 (both original and abridged edition are accompanied by various manuals); *Hypothesis: Prediction and Implication in Biology,* Addison-Wesley, 1968; (compilers) *The Process of Biology: Primary Sources,* Addison-Wesley, 1970, 2nd edition, 1971; (and Preston Adams) *The Study of Botany,* Addison-Wesley, 1970.

Editor and contributor: *Biology in a Liberal Education,* 1966, and four other publications of Commission on Undergraduate Education in the Biological Sciences, 1967-69; *Conference on Explanation in Biology: Historical, Philosophical and Scientific Aspects* (published as special issue of *Journal of the History of Biology),* Harvard University Press, 1969.

WORK IN PROGRESS: Books in fields of science, religion, and music.

AVOCATIONAL INTERESTS: The American Civil War; playing flamenco guitar and the accordion.

BAKER, John R(andal) 1900-

PERSONAL: Born October 23, 1900, in Woodbridge, Suffolk, England; son of Julian Alleyn (a rear admiral in the Royal Navy) and Geraldine Eugenie (Alison) Baker; married Inezita Davis, 1923 (divorced, 1937); married Helen Edge, July 6, 1939; children: (first marriage) Venice Ina, Gilbert Samuel. *Education:* New College, Oxford, B.A. (first class honors), 1922, M.A., 1927, D.Phil., 1927, D.Sc., 1938. *Home:* The Mill, 26 Mill End, Kidlington, Oxford OX5 2EG, England. *Agent:* A. P. Watt & Son, 26-28 Bedford Row, London WC1R 4HL, England.

CAREER: Oxford University, Oxford, England, lecturer in zoology, reader in cytology, 1955-67, reader emeritus, 1967—, professorial fellow of New College, 1964-67. Participated in scientific expeditions to New Hebrides, 1922-23, 1927, 1933-34. *Member:* Royal Society (fellow), Royal Microscopical Society (president, 1964-65). *Awards, honors:* Oliver Bird Medal from Family Planning Association, 1958, for research on chemical contraception; honorary fellowship of Royal Microscopical Society, 1968.

WRITINGS: Sex in Man and Animals, Routledge, 1926; *Man and Animals in the New Hebrides,* Routledge, 1929; *Cytological Technique,* Methuen, 1933, 5th edition, 1963; (with J. B. S. Haldane) *Biology in Everyday Life,* Allen & Unwin, 1933; (with Julian Huxley, Bertrand Russell, and others) *Science in the Changing World,* Allen & Unwin, 1933; *The Chemical Control of Conception,* Chapman & Hall, 1935.

The Scientific Life, Allen & Unwin, 1942; *Science and the Planned State,* Allen & Unwin, 1945, Macmillan, 1946; (with C. E. K. Mees) *The Path of Science,* Wiley, 1946; *Abraham Trembley of Geneva,* E. J. Arnold, 1952; *Principles of Biological Microtechnique,* Methuen, 1958.

Race, Oxford University Press, 1974; (editor) Julian Huxley, *Evolution: The Modern Synthesis,* Allen & Unwin, 3rd edition (Baker was not associated with earlier editions), 1974. Contributor of about two hundred articles to scientific journals. Editor, *Quarterly Journal of Microscopical Society,* 1946-64.

WORK IN PROGRESS: Research for another book on race.

SIDELIGHTS: Baker writes of his expeditions to the New Hebrides: "On Espiritu Santo, the largest island of the group, we explored a large area that had not previously been entered by Europeans, and we had the opportunity to study Melanesian life while it was still scarcely affected by external influences. It was here that I first became interested in anthropology. In my opinion the interests of anthropologists tend to be centered too much on man alone. As T. H. Huxley wrote more than a century ago, 'Anthropology is a section of zoology...the problems of ethnology are simply those which are presented to the zoologist by every widely distributed animal he studies.' It is particularly important that anthropologists should be well grounded in the principles of zoological taxonomy.

"I hope to foster a less emotional outlook on racial matters. Ethical and political problems are of course involved, but for their solution one needs a solid basis of demonstrable fact. The welfare of mankind as a whole would be best served by dispassionate study of racial differences and resemblances."

BAKER, Kenneth F(rank) 1908-

PERSONAL: Born June 3, 1908, in Ashton, S.D.; son of Frank (a physician) and May (Boyer) Baker; married Katharine Cummings, June 17, 1944. *Education:* Washington State University, B.S., 1930, Ph.D., 1934; also attended University of Wisconsin, 1934-35, Cornell University, 1947-48, and University of Adelaide, 1961-62. *Home:* 999 Middlefield Rd., Berkeley, Calif. 94708. *Office:* Department of Plant Pathology, University of California, Berkeley, Calif. 94720.

CAREER: Pineapple Experiment Station, Honolulu, Hawaii, associate plant pathologist, 1936-39; University of California, Los Angeles, assistant professor, 1939-42, associate professor, 1942-48, professor of plant pathology, 1948-60, developer of research program on pathology of ornamental plants; University of California, Berkeley, professor of plant pathology, 1961—. Visiting professor, Pennsylvania State University, 1969.

MEMBER: International Society of Plant Pathologists, American Phytopathology Society (fellow), Botanical Society of America, Mycological Society of America, American Institute of Biological Sciences, American Association for the Advancement of Science, Netherlands Phytopathology Society, Australian Plant Pathology Society, British Mycological Society, Association of Applied Biology (England), British Phytopathological Society. *Awards, honors:* Research awards from California Association of Nurserymen, 1956, California Florists Association, 1966, and Federation of Australian Nurserymen's Associations, 1969; Norman J. Colman Award of American Association of Nurserymen, 1959; Fulbright fellow in Australia, 1961-62; North Atlantic Treaty Organization (NATO) fellowship, 1972.

WRITINGS: (Editor) *The U.C. System for Producing Healthy Container-Grown Plants,* Agricultural Experiment Station, University of California, 1957; (editor with W. C. Snyder) *Ecology of Soil-Borne Plant Pathogens,* University of California Press, 1965; *Wildflowers of Western Australia,* Rigby (Adelaide), 1971; (with R. J. Cook) *Biological Control of Plant Pathogens,* W. H. Freeman, 1974. Editor, monographs of American Phytopathology Society, 1963—. Editor, *Annual Review of Phytopathology,* 1963—.

WORK IN PROGRESS: Scientific papers.

AVOCATIONAL INTERESTS: Music photography, travel.

BIOGRAPHICAL/CRITICAL SOURCES: *Phytopathology,* Volume 60, number 3, 1970.

* * *

BAKULA, William J(ohn), Jr. 1936-

PERSONAL: Surname is pronounced *Back*-u-la; born January 15, 1936, in St. Louis County, Mo.; son of William John, Sr. and Eva (Dusin) Bakula; married Marilyn Eugenia Pratali (an administrator), January 9, 1960; children: Carolyn, Lisa, Ann. *Education:* St. Louis University, B.S., 1959; Georgetown University, graduate study, 1962-63; George Washington University, M.B.A., 1967. *Religion:* Roman Catholic. *Residence:* Annapolis, Md. *Office:* Department of Business Administration, Anne Arundel Community College, 101 College Pkwy., Arnold, Md. 21012.

CAREER: U.S. Navy career officer, 1959-70, leaving service as a lieutenant commander; United States Naval Academy, Annapolis, Md., instructor in accounting and finance, 1967-70; Anne Arundel Community College, Arnold, Md., associate professor of accounting and business administration, 1970—, program director, 1973—. *Member:* American Accounting Association. *Awards, honors*—Military: National Defense Medal, Navy Expeditionary Medal.

WRITINGS: *Introduction to Contemporary Business,* Harcourt, 1973.

* * *

BALDWIN, Roger E(dwin) 1929-

PERSONAL: Born October 20, 1929, in Hilo, Hawaii; son of Robert Irving and Helen (Shiras) Baldwin; married Elizabeth Mae Marcallino (a teacher), December 27, 1967; children: Anne Elizabeth. *Education:* Coalinga College, A.A., 1949; Oregon State University, B.S., 1951, M.S., 1953; University of Minnesota, Ph.D., 1964. *Religion:* Episcopalian. *Home:* 300 Lahi St., Hilo, Hawaii 96720. *Office:* Department of Biology, Hilo College, University of Hawaii, Hilo, Hawaii 96720.

CAREER: Spencer Chemical Co., Pittsburg, Kan., staff assistant, 1953-55; University of Minnesota, Minneapolis, instructor in science, 1957-64; University of Hawaii, Hilo College, Hilo, assistant professor, 1964-71, associate professor of biology, 1971—. *Member:* American Association for the Advancement of Science, National Audubon Society, Hawaii Botanical Society.

WRITINGS: *Genetics* (self-teaching guide), Wiley, 1973.

WORK IN PROGRESS: *Poisonous Plants of the Hawaiian Islands,* completion expected in 1975; *Plants Poisonous to Man,* 1976.

* * *

BALDWIN, Stan(ley C.) 1929-

PERSONAL: Born December 17, 1929, in Bend, Ore.; son of Leonard Rite (a cowboy) and Irma Mae (Brown) Baldwin; married Marjorie Antoinette Iverson, December 17, 1948; children: Kathleen (Mrs. Charles Bagley), Krystal (Mrs. Arthur W. Brown), Steven, Karen (Mrs. David Kraus), Gregory Laverne Todd. *Education:* Attended Powellhurst College, Prairie Bible Institute, and Oregon State University. *Home:* 311 Blackhawk Dr., Carol Stream, Ill. 60187. *Office:* Victor Books, 1825 College Ave., Wheaton, Ill. 60187.

CAREER: Pastor of community church in Albany, Ore., 1955-62, and of Baptist churches in Corvallis, Ore., 1962-65, and Burns, Ore., 1965-69; Scripture Press, Wheaton, Ill., editor of Victor Books and consulting editor for *Power for Living,* 1970—. Pastor of village church in Carol Stream, Ill.

WRITINGS: *Will the Real Good Guys Please Stand?,* Victor Books, 1971; *Games Satan Plays,* Victor Books, 1971; (with wife, Marjorie Baldwin) *Tough Questions Boys Ask,* Victor Books, 1972; (with Marjorie Baldwin) *Tough Questions Girls Ask,* Victor Books, 1972; (with James D. Mallory) *The Kink and I,* Victor Books, 1973; (with Hank Aaron and Jerry Jenkins) *Bad Henry,* Chilton, 1974; *What Did Jesus Say about That?,* Victor Books, in press. Contributor of articles and stories to Christian periodicals.

AVOCATIONAL INTERESTS: Sports, fishing, photography, automobile mechanics, home and yard work, boating, water skiing, travel (has visited Mexico, Israel, Asia, Africa, and Europe).

BANNER, James M(orrill), Jr. 1935-

PERSONAL: Born May 3, 1935, in New York, N.Y.; son of James M. and Dorothea (Bauer) Banner; married Lois Wendland (a historian), May 26, 1962; children: Olivia Parkes. *Education:* Yale University, B.A., 1957; Columbia University, M.A., 1961, Ph.D., 1968. *Office:* Department of History, Princeton University, Princeton, N.J. 08540.

CAREER: Princeton University, Princeton, N.J., instructor, 1966-68, assistant professor, 1968-71, associate professor of history, 1971—. Consultant to National Endowment for the Humanities and U.S. House of Representatives. *Military service:* U.S. Army, Counter-Intelligence Corps, 1957-60. *Member:* American Historical Association, Organization of American Historians, Society of American Historians, Seminar on Early American History and Culture (of Columbia University), Common Cause (chairman of New Jersey unit, 1972-74; director of national governing board, 1973-76). *Awards, honors:* Guggenheim fellowship, 1970-71; research fellowship from Charles Warren Center for Studies in American History, 1974-75.

WRITINGS: To the Hartford Convention: The Federalists and the Origins of Party Politics in Massachusetts, 1789-1815, Knopf, 1970; (with James M. McPherson, Laurence B. Holland, Nancy J. Weiss, and Michael D. Bell) *Blacks in America: Bibliographical Essays,* Doubleday, 1971.

WORK IN PROGRESS: Research on the origins of American social and humanitarian reform, 1760-1830.

* * *

BANNER, Lois W(endland) 1939-

PERSONAL: Born July 26, 1939, in Los Angeles, Calif.; daughter of Harry J. (a medical writer) and Melba (a teacher; maiden name, Parkes) Wendland; married James M. Banner, Jr. (a university professor), May 23, 1962; children: Olivia Parkes. *Education:* University of California at Los Angeles, B.A., 1960; Columbia University, M.A., 1962, Ph.D., 1970. *Politics:* Democrat. *Religion:* None. *Office:* Department of History, Douglass College, Rutgers University, New Brunswick, N.J. 08903.

CAREER: Rosemary Hall, Greenwich, Conn., teacher of history, 1962-66; Rutgers University, Douglass College, New Brunswick, N.J., instructor, 1966-71, assistant professor of history, 1971—. *Member:* Organization of American Historians, American Historical Association, Coordinating Committee for Women in the Historical Profession, Berkshire Conference of Women Historians.

WRITINGS: Women in Modern America: A Brief History, Harcourt, 1974; *Clio's Consciousness Raised: New Perspectives on the History of Women,* Harper, 1974. Contributor of articles on women and on religion in early America to professional journals.

* * *

BANZIGER, Hans
See BAENZIGER, Hans

* * *

BARBEAU, Arthur E(dward) 1936-

PERSONAL: Born February 24, 1936, in Danvers, Mass.; son of Arthur J. (a textile worker) and Addie (Howard) Barbeau; married Patricia McCord, March 1, 1957; children: Roxanne, Michael, Gabrielle. *Education:* University of Pittsburgh, A.B., 1959, M.A., 1961, Ph.D., 1970. *Politics:* Democrat. *Home:* 355A Table Rock Lane, Wheeling, W.Va. 26003. *Office:* Department of History, West Liberty State College, West Liberty, W.Va. 26074.

CAREER: Pittsburgh Coke and Chemical Co., Neville Island, Pa., laboratory technician, 1955-59; West Liberty State College, West Liberty, W.Va., assistant professor, 1965-68, associate professor, 1968-71, professor of history, 1971—, swimming coach, 1963-66, soccer coach, 1972, chairman of department, 1972—. Member of A.A.U. National Women's Swimming Committee, 1964-66. *Military service:* U.S. Naval Reserve, 1953-61. *Member:* American Historical Association, National Soccer Coaches Association, West Virginia Historical Association.

WRITINGS: (With Florette Henri) *The Unknown Soldiers,* Temple University, 1974.

WORK IN PROGRESS: A paper on eary 20th Century Black studies; research for an article on Chinese psychology.

SIDELIGHTS: Barbeau has studied Chinese. He enjoys working with foreign students and in athletics.

* * *

BARBER, Lucy L(ombardi) 1882(?)-1974

1882(?)—June 19, 1974; American author. Obituaries: *Washington Post,* June 21, 1974.

* * *

BARBOUR, Brian M(ichael) 1943-

PERSONAL: Born July 26, 1943, in Lorain, Ohio; son of William Wallace (a machinist) and Jane (Donohue) Barbour; married June Matulis, August 10, 1968; children: Abel, Stephen. *Education:* University of Notre Dame, B.A., 1965; Kent State University, M.A., 1966, Ph.D., 1969. *Politics:* Democrat. *Religion:* Roman Catholic. *Home:* 81 Lenox Ave., Providence, R.I. 02907. *Office:* Department of English, Providence College, Providence, R.I. 02918.

CAREER: Providence College, Providence, R.I., assistant professor, 1969-74, associate professor of English, 1974—.

WRITINGS: (Editor) *American Transcendentalism,* University of Notre Dame Press, 1973. Contributor to *Southern Review* and *Modern Language Quarterly.*

WORK IN PROGRESS: American Poetry from Bryant to Frost, completion expected in 1976; research on Ben Jonson and on American fiction since Clemens.

* * *

BARBOUR, Michael G(eorge) 1942-

PERSONAL: Born February 24, 1942, in Jackson, Mich.; son of George Jerome (a businessman) and Mae (a bookkeeper; maiden name, Dater) Barbour; married Norma Jean Yourist, September 26, 1963; children: Julie Ann, Alan Benjamin. *Education:* Michigan State University, B.S., 1963; Duke University, Ph.D., 1967. *Politics:* Democrat. *Religion:* Jewish. *Home:* 1418 Alice St., Davis, Calif. 95616. *Office:* Department of Botany, University of California, Davis, Calif. 95616.

CAREER: University of California, Davis, assistant professor, 1967-71, associate professor of botany, 1971-75. Consultant to Ecolabs, 1971-75. *Member:* British Ecological Society, Argentine Ecological Society, American Institute of Biological Sciences, Ecological Society of America, Sigma Xi. *Awards, honors:* Fulbright fellow in Australia, 1964; National Science Founaation research grants, 1969-71, 1971-73, 1973-75.

WRITINGS: (With T. E. Weier and C. R. Stocking) *Botany: An Introduction to Plant Biology,* 4th edition (Barbour was not associated with earlier editions), Wiley, 1970, 5th edition, 1974; (with Weier, Stocking, and J. M. Tucker) *Botany: A Laboratory Manual,* 4th edition (Barbour was not associated with earlier editions), Wiley, 1970, 5th edition, 1974; (with Robert B. Craig, F. R. Drysdale, and M. T. Ghiselin) *Coastal Ecology: Bodega Head,* University of California Press, 1973; (with R. H. Falk, S. M. Gold, J. A. Harding, and T. E. Ragland) *Biology: An Unusual Introduction,* Canfield Press, 1974.

WORK IN PROGRESS: Science fiction short stories; poetry; writing on ecology.

* * *

BARKER, Esther T(emperley) 1910-

PERSONAL: Born May 28, 1910, in Newton, Mass.; daughter of John (a printer, newspaper editor, and publisher) and Clara L. (Kellaway) Temperley; married Paul Anthony Barker (a Methodist minister), November 26, 1934; children: Martha Louise (Mrs. John Edwin Davidson), Elsie Ruth (Mrs. Jack B. Porter), Paul Anthony, Jr. *Education:* State College at Framingham (Mass.), Diploma, 1929; Hartford School of Religious Education, B.Rel.Ed., 1933; Yale University, graduate study at Divinity School, 1933-34; East Tennessee State University, B.S., 1951; University of Tennessee, M.S., 1964. *Politics:* Independent. *Religion:* Methodist. *Home:* 32 Burghard Dr., Lake Janaluska, N.C. 28745.

CAREER: Elementary teacher in Massachusetts, Tennessee, Virginia, and North Carolina prior to 1966; Haywood County Consolidated Schools, Waynesville, N.C., speech therapist, 1966—. *Member:* National Education Association, North Carolina Speech and Hearing Association, Association of Classroom Teachers, North Carolina Association of Educators.

WRITINGS: A Christmas Pantomime (children's play), Standard Press, 1947; *The Unused Cradle,* Upper Room Press, 1968; *A Book of Modern Tongue Twisters,* Interstate, 1970; *Tongue Twister Tales,* Interstate, 1974. Contributor of stories to Methodist children's magazines.

WORK IN PROGRESS: A pre-teen story, *A Longing to Be Free,* based on an aunt's life.

AVOCATIONAL INTERESTS: Cooking, hiking, reading, swimming, sewing, knitting, music.

* * *

BARKSDALE, Richard (Kenneth) 1915-

PERSONAL: Born October 31, 1915, in Winchester, Mass.; son of Simon Daniel (a jobber) and Sarah (Brooks) Barksdale; married Mildred White (a university dean), April 15, 1960; children: Adrienne B. Simkins, Richard K., Jr., James Austin, Calvin. *Education:* Bowdoin College, A.B., 1937; Syracuse University, A.M., 1938; Harvard University, Ph.D., 1951. *Religion:* Protestant. *Home:* 904 Eliot Dr., Urbana, Ill. 61801. *Office:* University of Illinois, 100 English Building, Urbana, Ill. 61801.

CAREER: Southern University, Baton Rouge, La., instructor in English, 1938-39; Tougaloo College, Tougaloo, Miss., assistant professor of English, 1939-42; North Carolina College (now North Carolina Central University), Durham, professor of English and dean of Graduate School, 1949-58; Morehouse College, Atlanta, Ga., professor of English and head of department, 1958-62; Atlanta University, Atlanta, Ga., professor of English and dean of Graduate School of Arts and Sciences, 1962-71; University of Illinois, Urbana, professor of English, 1971—. Member of board of overseers of Bowdoin College, 1974—. *Military service:* U.S. Army, field artillery, 1944-46; became second lieutenant.

MEMBER: College Language Association (president, 1972—), National Council of Teachers of English (member of board of directors), North Central Association, Phi Beta Kappa. *Awards, honors:* L.H.D. from Bowdoin College, 1972.

WRITINGS: (Editor with Keneth Kinnamon) *Black Writers of America: A Comprehensive Anthology,* Macmillan, 1972; (contributor) Donald Gibson, editor, *Modern Black Poets,* Prentice-Hall, 1973; (contributor) Louis D. Rubin, Jr., editor, *The Comic Imagination in American Literature,* Rutgers University Press, 1973; *Langston Hughes: The Poet and His Critics,* American Library Association, 1974. Contributor to literature journals, including *Western Humanities Review, Phylon, Negro American Literature Forum,* and *College Language Association Journal.*

WORK IN PROGRESS: Examining the interaction between nineteenth-century American and English writers who had mutual interests in abolitionism.

* * *

BARLOUGH, J(effrey) Ernest 1953-

PERSONAL: Born December 24, 1953, in Los Angeles, Calif.; son of Ernest Eugene and Irene (Zizda) Barlough. *Education:* Loyola Marymount University, B.S., 1973.

CAREER: Writer.

WRITINGS: (Editor) *Minor British Poetry, 1680-1800: An Anthology,* Scarecrow, 1973; (editor) *The Archaicon: A Collection of Unusual Archaic English,* Scarecrow, 1974; *Problems in Organic Synthesis,* Ryder, 1974.

WORK IN PROGRESS: The Book of Mirth: Three Centuries of Humorous British Poetry; The Bacterial Diseases of Wild and Domestic Animals; a novel of Shakespeare's day; a collection of poetry; a science fiction novel; a fantasy novel.

AVOCATIONAL INTERESTS: Veterinary medicine, paleontology, music.

* * *

BARLOW, Robert O.
See MEYER, Heinrich

* * *

BARNARD, Charles N(elson III) 1924-

PERSONAL: Born October 5, 1924, in Arlington, Mass.; son of Charles Nelson, Jr. (a horse dealer) and Mae Esther (Johnson) Barnard; married Diana Lee Pattison, August 6, 1949 (divorced August, 1970); married Karen Louise Zakrison (an editor), April 18, 1971; children: (first marriage) Jennifer Lee, Rebecca, Charles Nelson IV, Patrick. *Edu-*

cation: University of Missouri, B.J., 1949. *Politics:* Independent. *Religion:* Christian. *Home:* 225 Valley Rd., Cos Cob, Conn. 06807. *Agent:* Sterling Lord Agency, 660 Madison Ave., New York, N.Y. 10021.

CAREER: Dell Publishing Co., New York, N.Y., editor, 1949; Fawcett Publications, New York, N.Y., associate editor of *True* (magazine), 1949-54, managing editor, 1954-63; *Saturday Evening Post,* New York, N.Y., senior editor, 1964-65; Fawcett Publications, executive editor of *True,* 1965-67, editor, 1968-70; free-lance writer and editorial consultant, 1971—. War correspondent, 1943-46. *Military service:* U.S. Army, 1943-45; became sergeant.

WRITINGS: (Editor) *A Treasury of True,* A. S. Barnes, 1957; (editor) *Official Automobile Handbook,* A. S. Barnes, 1959; (editor) *Anthology of True,* A. S. Barnes, 1962; *The Winter People,* Dodd, 1973. Contributor to *Encyclopaedia Britannica;* contributor of more than fifty articles to magazines, including *Reader's Digest, Better Homes & Gardens, Signature, McCall's, Family Health,* and *TV Guide.*

WORK IN PROGRESS: A book of personal reminiscences, for Dodd.

AVOCATIONAL INTERESTS: World travel.

* * *

BARNETTE, Henlee H(ulix) 1911-

PERSONAL: Born August 14, 1911, in Taylorsville, N.C.; son of William Alexander and Winnie Helen Barnette; married Charlotte Ford (died July, 1953); married Helen Poarch (a teacher), June 9, 1956; children: (first marriage) John, Wayne; (second marriage) Martha, James. *Education:* Wake Forest University, B.A., 1940; Southern Baptist Seminary, Th.M., 1943, Th.D., 1948. *Politics:* Democrat. *Religion:* Southern Baptist. *Office:* Southern Baptist Seminary, 2825 Lexington Rd., Louisville, Ky. 40206

CAREER: Ordained to ministry, 1935; served as pastor for churches in North Carolina and Kentucky, and as superintendent of Central Baptist Mission in Louisville, Ky. Samford University, Birmingham, Ala., assistant professor of sociology, 1946-47; Stetson University, DeLand, Fla., professor of sociology, 1947-51; Southern Baptist Seminary, Louisville, Ky., professor of Christian ethics, 1951—. *Member:* American Society of Christian Ethics (member of board of directors, 1962-66), American Association for the Advancement of Science, Ethics, Society, and Life Sciences. *Awards, honors:* Carnegie Foundation research grant, 1949-50; faculty fellowship from American Association of Theological Schools, Harvard University, 1959-60; Wake Forest University distinguished alumnus award, 1970; distinguished service award from Christian Life Commission of Southern Baptist Convention, 1971.

WRITINGS: *Introducing Christian Ethics,* Broadman, 1961; *An Introduction to Communism,* Baker Book, 1964; *The New Theology and Morality,* Westminster, 1967; *Crucial Problems in Christian Perspective,* Westminster, 1970; *The Drug Crisis and the Church,* Westminster, 1971; *The Church and the Ecological Crisis,* Eerdmans, 1972.

WORK IN PROGRESS: Research on bioethics, on Christianity and revolution, and on political theology.

* * *

BARNS, John W(intour) B(aldwin) 1912-1974

May 12, 1912—January 23, 1974; British Egyptologist. Obituaries: *AB Bookman's Weekly,* April 15, 1974.

* * *

BARON, Mary (Kelley) 1944-

PERSONAL: Born November 18, 1944, in Providence, R.I.; daughter of Richard L. and Mary (Reynolds) Kelley; married Dennis E. Baron (a professor), June 5, 1965; children: Cordelia. *Education:* Brandeis University, A.B., 1969; University of Michigan, A.M., 1971; University of Illinois, Ph.D., 1973. *Home:* 151 Walden St., Cambridge, Mass. 02140. *Office:* Department of English, Tufts University, Medford, Mass. 02155.

CAREER: Tufts University, Medford, Mass., assistant professor of English, 1973—. *Member:* Modern Language Association of America, National Organization for Women, Women's Caucus. *Awards, honors:* Jule and Avery Hopwood Award for poetry, 1971.

WRITINGS: *Letters for the New England Dead* (poetry), Godine Press, 1974. Contributor to *Southern Review, Maryland Poetry Review, Back Door 5, Counter/Measures 2,* and *Folio.*

WORK IN PROGRESS: *Breaking In,* a book-length sequence of poems; *The Meaning Has a Meaning,* a critical work on the plays of Christopher Marlowe.

* * *

BARR, Alfred H(amilton), Jr. 1902-

PERSONAL: Born January 28, 1902, in Detroit, Mich.; son of Alfred Hamilton (a minister and educator) and Annie Elizabeth (Wilson) Barr; married Margaret Scolari Fitzmaurice (an art historian), May 27, 1930; children: Victoria Fitzmaurice. *Education:* Princeton University, A.B., 1922, M.A., 1923; Harvard University, Ph.D., 1946; additional study in Europe. *Religion:* Presbyterian. *Home:* 49 East 96th St., New York, N.Y. 10028. *Office:* The Museum of Modern Art, 11 West 53rd St., New York, N.Y. 10019.

CAREER: Vassar College, Poughkeepsie, N.Y., instructor in art history, 1923-24; Harvard University, Cambridge, Mass., assistant in fine arts, 1924-25; Princeton University, Princeton, N.J., instructor in art and archaeology, 1925-26; Wellesley College, Wellesley, Mass., associate professor of art, 1926-29; Museum of Modern Art, New York, N.Y., director, 1929-43, director of research, 1944-46, director of collections, 1947-67, counselor to board of trustees, 1967—, member of board of trustees, 1939—, vice president, 1939-43. Lecturer in England, Iceland, USSR, and throughout the United States; Mary Flexner lecturer, Bryn Mawr College, 1946. Harvard University, member of fine arts visiting committee, 1958-60, chairman, 1965—, overseer of Harvard College, 1964-70; member of fine arts visiting committees, Columbia University and Princeton University. Advisor to Office of Coordinator of Inter-American Affairs, 1940-43, and to art institutes and societies.

MEMBER: Association of Art Museum Directors (vice-president, 1940-41), College Art Association (director, 1943-48), American Association of Museums (councillor), American Federation of Arts (trustee, 1948-53), Society for the Arts, Religion and Contemporary Cultures (president, 1962-65; now member of board of directors), American Institute of Architects (honorary member of New York chapter).

AWARDS, HONORS: Lord & Taylor American Design award, 1947, "for bringing to a large number of Americans their first sample of modern art''; Grand Cross of the Order of Merit, Federal Republic of Germany, 1959; named chevalier of Legion of Honor, Government of France, 1959; American Federation of Arts fiftieth anniversary award, 1959; Philadelphia Museum of Art merit award, 1959; Star of Italian Solidarity from Government of Italy, 1959; annual award, *Art in America* magazine, 1962; American Institute of Architects award of merit, 1964; Special Medal from Brandeis University Creative Arts Commission, 1965, for ''notable creative achievement''; National Institute of Arts and Letters award, 1968, for distinguished service to the arts; New York State award, 1968; Art Dealers Association of America award, 1972; Skowhegan Gertrude Vanderbilt Whitney award, 1974; European Art Dealers award, 1974.

Honorary degrees: Litt.D., Princeton University, 1949; Ph.D., University of Bonn, 1958; D.F.A., University of Buffalo, 1962, Adelphi University, 1963, Yale University, 1967; L.H.D., Columbia University, 1969.

WRITINGS—All published by Museum of Modern Art, except as noted: (Author of foreword) *First Loan Exhibition: Cezanne, Gauguin, Seurat, Van Gogh,* 1929, reprinted by Arno for Museum of Modern Art, 1972.

(Author of preface) *Winslow Homer, Albert P. Ryder, Thomas Eakins: Sixth Loan Exhibition,* 1930, reprinted with *George Caleb Bingham,* by Meyric C. Rogers and others, as *Four American Painters,* Arno for Museum of Modern Art, 1969; (author of introduction and notes) *Modern German Painting and Sculpture,* 1931, reprinted by Arno for Museum of Modern Art, 1972; (with others) *American Art of the Twenties and Thirties,* 1932, reprinted by Arno for Museum of Modern Art, 1969; *A Brief Survey of Modern Painting,* 1932; (editor with Holger Cahill) *Art in America in Modern Times,* Reynal & Hitchcock, 1934, reprinted, Books for Libraries, 1969; (editor) *Vincent van Gogh,* 1935, reprinted, Greenwood Press, 1970, published under same title with bibliography by Charles Mattoon Brooks, Jr., 1942, reprinted by Arno for Museum of Modern Art, 1966; *Cubism and Abstract Art,* 1936, reprinted, 1974; (editor) Georges Hugnet, *Fantastic Art, Dada, Surrealism,* 1936, 3rd edition, 1947, reprinted by Arno for Museum of Modern Art, 1968; (editor) *Art in Our Time: An Exhibition to Celebrate the Tenth Anniversary of the Museum of Modern Art . . .,* 1939, reprinted by Arno for Museum of Modern Art, 1972; (editor) *Picasso: Forty Years of His Art,* 1939, 4th edition, 1941.

(Contributor) Margaret Miller, editor, *Paul Klee,* 1941, 2nd edition, 1945, reprinted by Arno for Museum of Modern Art, 1968; (editor) *Painting and sculpture in the Museum of Modern Art,* 1942, 4th edition, in press; *What is Modern Painting,* 1943, 10th edition, 1968; (editor with Dorothy C. Miller) *American Realists and Magic Realists,* 1943, reprinted by Arno for Museum of Modern Art, 1969; (contributor) Dorothy C. Miller, *Lyonel Feininger,* 1944, reprinted by Arno for Museum of Modern Art, 1966; *Picasso: Fifty Years of His Art,* 1946, 3rd edition, 1955, reprinted, 1974; (with James Thrall Soby) *Twentieth Century Italian Art,* 1949, reprinted by Arno for Museum of Modern Art, 1972.

(Editor) *The Museum of Modern Art; Painting and Sculpture Collection,* Les Editions Braun, 1950; (editor) *Picasso: 75th Anniversary Exhibition,* 1957; *Matisse, His Art and His Public,* 1951, reprinted, 1974; (editor) *Masters of Modern Art,* 1954; *The New American Painting as Shown in Eight European Countries, 1958-59,* 1959, reprinted by Arno for Museum of Modern Art, 1972.

De Stijl, 1917-1928 (adaptation from *Cubism and Abstract Art;* originally published as introduction to exhibition, 1952-53), 1961.

(Author of foreword) *Three Generations of Twentieth Century Art: The Sidney and Harriet Janis Collection of the Museum of Modern Art,* 1972.

Also author of numerous other exhibition catalogues. Contributor to periodicals in the United States and Europe. Member of editorial boards or committees of: *Art Bulletin,* 1939—; *Gazette des Beaux-Arts,* 1940—; *Magazine of Art,* 1942-52; *Art Quarterly,* 1953—; *Art in America,* 1957—.

SIDELIGHTS: Barr, the first director of the Museum of Modern Art, and sometimes called its ''founding father,'' was described by John Canaday in 1960 as ''the most powerful tastemaker in American art today and probably in the world.'' Barr, whose art class at Wellesley was the first college course in the United States devoted exclusively to modern art, disagreed, saying, ''The artists lead; the Museum follows. . . .''

Nonetheless, Barr's initial concept of a multidepartmental museum concerned with all the modern visual arts—architecture and industrial design, photography, film, and theater design, as well as traditional fields of art—had entered the Museum's program by 1935 and led the establishment of departments by 1941. ''The Museum of Modern Art is a laboratory,'' said Barr, in 1939. ''In its experiments the public is invited to participate.'' He has directed over one hundred exhibitions in this ''laboratory,'' including ''Matisse,'' 1931, ''Machine Art,'' 1934, ''African Negro Art,'' 1935, ''Vincent van Gogh,'' 1935-36, ''Cubism and Abstract Art,'' 1936, ''Fantastic Art, Dada, Surrealism,'' 1936, and several Picasso shows; he opened a department of architecture in 1932, with an exhibition featuring the work of Frank Lloyd Wright and introducing the ''International Style'' of Gropius, Le Corbusier, and Mies van der Rohe.

The American Federation of Arts award was presented to him in 1959 with the following comments by Lloyd Goodrich: ''To you more than to any other single person are due the foundation and flourishing of a great innovating institution. . .which introduced a new concept of a museum's function in relation to the art of its time . . . and which has had a profound and far-reaching influence on all visual aspects of American life.''

The Museum of Modern Art has set up a permanently endowed lectureship in Barr's honor.

* * *

BARRETT, Ivan J. 1910-

PERSONAL: Born April 4, 1910, in Mendon, Utah; son of Oscar J. and Elizabeth (Stumpf) Barrett; married Minnie Rogers, June 1, 1933; children: Eulene (Mrs. John Adams), Denae (Mrs. Charles S. Newton), Iva June (Mrs. Myron Walker), Annette (Mrs. Edward Bailey), Janice. *Education:* Utah State University, B.S., 1937; Brigham Young University, M.S., 1947. *Religion:* Church of Jesus Christ of Latter-Day Saints (Mormon). *Home:* 672 South 560th St. E., Orem, Utah 84057. *Office:* Brigham Young University, Provo, Utah 84601.

CAREER: Brigham Young University, Provo, Utah, instructor, 1953-56, assistant professor, 1956-66, associate professor, 1966-74, professor of religious instruction, 1974—. *Awards, honors:* Has received citations for teaching, including Karl G. Maeses Distinguished Teaching

Award from Brigham Young University Alumni Association, 1973.

WRITINGS: Life of the Master: Lectures, Brigham Young University, 1958; *Great Moments in the Life of Joseph Smith,* Brigham Young University Press, 1963; *Joseph Smith and the Restoration,* Brigham Young University Press, 1967, revised edition, Young House, 1973. Also author of *Joseph Smith the Extraordinary,* 1954; *Heroines of the Church,* 1956; *From Eden to Egypt,* 1957; *Silhouettes of Doctrine and Covenants,* 1959; *Remarkable Stories,* 1960. Contributor to magazines and newspapers.

WORK IN PROGRESS: Research in the early history of the Mormon Church and on current attitudes of youth.

* * *

BARROWS, Anita 1947-

PERSONAL: Born January 13, 1947, in Brooklyn, N.Y.; daughter of Joseph (a pharmaceutical consultant) and Sylvia (Kanfer) Barrows; married Richard Friedman (a computer scientist), October 31, 1972. *Education:* San Francisco State College (now University), B.A., 1969; Boston University, M.A., 1970; attended Camberwell School of Arts and Crafts, 1973; University of California, Berkeley, Ph.D. candidate, 1975—. *Home and office:* 546 The Alameda, Berkeley, Calif. 94707. *Agent:* Jonathan Clowes, 19 Jeffreys Place, London N.W.1, England.

CAREER: Private tutor; University of California Extension, Berkeley, instructor in English, 1972, 1974. Teacher and administrative assistant, California "Poetry in the Schools" program, 1972, 1974. *Awards, honors:* Award from *Atlantic,* 1964, for poem entered in high school contest; award from *New Magazine,* 1971, for "Upon a Time," a sequence of poems.

WRITINGS: Emigration (poems), Spindrift Press, 1972; (translator from the French) Didier Coste, *Sink Your Teeth in the Moon,* Calder & Boyars, 1974; (translator from the French) Marguerite Duras, *Abahn Sabana David,* Calder & Boyars, in press. Poetry editor for KPFA (radio), Berkeley, Calif., 1970-72.

WORK IN PROGRESS: Two translations for Calder & Boyars, Roland Dubillard's "The Beet Garden," a play, and Rene De Obaldia's *Innocentines,* a book of children's poetry; two children's books; translations; poetry.

SIDELIGHTS: "Feel I am undergoing a long apprenticeship, annexing various voices, experiences, teachings, to my own voice," Anita Barrows wrote. "Hopefully the apprenticeship will last all my life, in which sense I consider all of my work to be one piece. Am fluent in French and Italian, do translations for the discipline of it and the love of working as a craftsman with language."

* * *

BARRY, Mary J(ane) 1928-

PERSONAL: Born February 5, 1928, in Seward, Alaska; daughter of John (a lumber company owner) and Johanna (Schauer) Paulsteiner; married Melvin N. Barry (an electrician), September 24, 1951; children: Ronald Paul, Richard Earl. *Education:* University of California, Los Angeles, B.A., 1951; graduate study at University of Alaska, 1954-60, and Alaska Methodist University, 1959. *Politics:* Nonpartisan. *Religion:* Roman Catholic. *Home:* 323 West Harvard Ave., Anchorage, Alaska 99501.

CAREER: U.S. Army, Seward, Alaska, payroll clerk, 1945-46; U.S. Public Health Service Hospital, Anchorage, Alaska, personnel clerk and supervisor, 1955-57; U.S. Civil Service, Anchorage, examiner, 1958-61; Antiques and Uniques from Barry's, Anchorage, owner, 1966-73. *Member:* Alaska Historical Society, Cook Inlet Historical Society (secretary, 1967-68; member of board of directors, 1968-69).

WRITINGS: The Samovar: Its History and Use, privately printed, 1970; *The History of Mining on the Kenai Peninsula,* Alaska Northwest Publishing, 1973. Contributor to *Alaska Sportsman, Alaska Northern Lights, Alaskana,* and *Alaska Journal.*

WORK IN PROGRESS: Research on Alaskan regional gold rush histories, especially Nome and Iditarod; a compilation of Alaskan folklore; an interview history of Matanuska Valley agricultural colony.

SIDELIGHTS: Mary Barry told *CA:* "Until the 1920's, life in Alaska was much like the early American west in its isolation and lack of transportation—where the individual relied on his own courage, strength and resourcefulness to survive and improve his condition. I knew many of these pioneers personally. Their experiences compare well with any of the histories of pioneer America, and since few of their life stories have been preserved, this lore is fast disappearing." She is very interested in music, and was a professional pianist for small orchestras, for solo background music, and for singers and ballet dancers. She enjoys needlepoint, occasional painting, knitting, weaving, quilt-making, and the study of genealogy.

She has travelled throughout the western United States, northern Mexico, Denmark, Germany, Austria, Italy, and Canada. Her foreign languages include German, French, Russian, Spanish and Greek.

* * *

BASIL, Otto 1901-

PERSONAL: Born December 24, 1901, in Vienna, Austria; son of Franz and Leopoldine (Hoermann) Basil; married Christine Kuepper, April 3, 1948; children: Jutta (Mrs. Ottavio Saielli), Andreas (stepson). *Education:* Attended University of Vienna, 1921-23. *Home:* Suttingergasse 14, Vienna 19, Austria A 1190.

CAREER: Laenderbank & Marmarosh Blank Banca, Vienna, Austria, clerk, 1920-22; Bohler Steel Works, Vienna, Austria, clerk, 1924-45; Verlag Erwin Mueller (publisher), Vienna, Austria, editor and member of board of directors, 1945-48; *Neues Oesterreich* (newspaper), Vienna, Austria, theatre and movie critic and book reviewer, 1948-67; freelance writer, 1967—. *Member:* International Nestroy Society (vice-president, 1972—), P.E.N., Collegium Wiener Dramaturgie. *Awards, honors:* Literaturpreis der Stadt Wien, 1964, for his life's work in literature and journalism.

WRITINGS: Sternbild der Waage: Gedichte aus zwei Zyklen (poems; title means "Star Constellation of Scales"), Erwin Mueller (Vienna), 1945; (author of introduction) Edgar Jene, *Zeichnungen: Dessins des annees de guerre, 1939-1945* (title means "Drawings of the War Years, 1939-1945"), Erwin Mueller, 1945; *Apokalyptischer Vers* (poems; title means "Apocalyptic Poetry"), Erwin Mueller, 1947; (with Herbert Eisenreich and Iver Ivesk) *Das grosse Erbe* (title means "The Great Inheritance"), Stiasny Verlag (Vienna), 1962; *Anruf ins Ungewisse* (selected writings; title means "Call into the Uncertain"), Stiasny Verlag, 1963; *Georg Trakl in Selbstzeugnissen und*

Bilddokumenten (biography; title means "Self-Testimonies and Picture-Documents of Georg Trakl"), Rowohlt (Hamburg), 1966; *Wenn das Fuehrer wuesste* (novel), Molden, 1966, translation by Thomas Weyr published as *The Twilight Men,* Meredith, 1968; *Johann Nestroy in Selbstzeugnissen und Bilddokumenten* (biography; title means "Self-Testimonies and Picture-Documents of Johann Nestroy"), Rowohlt, 1967; *Ein wilder Garten ist dein Leib* (title means "A Wild Garden Is Your Body"), Forum Verlag (Vienna), 1970. Editor, *Plan,* 1937-38, 1945-48.

WORK IN PROGRESS: A book of poems, *Die lyrischen Kostueme* (title means "The Lyrical Costumes"); two novels.

SIDELIGHTS: Basil speaks English, French, and a little Russian.

BIOGRAPHICAL/CRITICAL SOURCES: Wort in der Zeit (Vienna), special Otto Basil issue, December 1961; Basil, *Anruf ins Ungewisse* (foreword and textual commentary by Walter Schneider), Stiasny Verlag, 1963.

* * *

BASS, Ellen 1947-

PERSONAL: Born June 16, 1947, in Philadelphia, Pa.; daughter of Martin (owner and operator of a liquor store) and Mildred (co-owner and operator of liquor store with husband; maiden name, Wolpert) Bass. *Education:* Attended Russell Sage College, 1965-66; Goucher College, A.B. (magna cum laude), 1968; Boston University, A.M., 1970; Boston Psychodrama Institute, further study, 1972-73. *Politics:* "People's." *Religion:* "Yes." *Address:* c/o Center for Studies of the Person, 1125 Torrey Pines Rd., La Jolla, Calif. 92037; or, c/o Bass, 103 South Rosborough Ave., Ventnor, N.J. 08406.

CAREER: Teacher at secondary schools in Baltimore, Md., and Washington, D.C., 1968; Project Place (social service center), Boston, Mass., administrator, 1970-71, leader of personal growth groups and trainer, 1971-74, counsellor, 1973-74. Teacher of poetry at Cambridge Center for Adult Education, 1972-73, and at Tufts Experimental College, 1973.

WRITINGS: (Editor with Florence Howe, and contributor) *No More Masks: An Anthology of Poems by Women,* Doubleday-Anchor, 1973; *I'm Not Your Laughing Daughter* (poems), University of Massachusetts Press, 1973. Author of play, "The Afternoon We Fell," first performed in Concord, Mass., at The School We Have, 1973. Poems have been included in *Ploughshares, Women: A Journal of Liberation, Second Wave, Prickly Pear, New Magazine, Moving Out, Rhode Islander, Response, Black Maria, Softball, Amazon Quarterly,* and *Ab Intra.*

WORK IN PROGRESS: A series of about one hundred poems, based on a trip to Japan in 1972.

SIDELIGHTS: Ellen Bass says that she writes "to be understood, to understand, to bridge the space between me and another, to affirm myself, to affirm you, to take the time."

* * *

BASS, Lawrence W(ade) 1898-

PERSONAL: Born June 18, 1898, in Streator, Ill.; son of John Hiram (an industrial executive) and Sara (Leek) Bass; married Edna Maria Becker (a librarian), November 23, 1935. *Education:* Tulane University, student, 1916-17; Yale University, Ph.B. (summa cum laude), 1919, Ph.D., 1922; postdoctoral studies at University of Lille, Sorbonne, University of Paris, and Pasteur Institute, France, 1923-25; attended New York University School of Law, 1927-28. *Politics:* Republican. *Religion:* Protestant. *Home:* 2000 N St. N.W., Washington, D.C. 20036. *Office:* Arthur D. Little, Inc., 1735 Eye St. N.W., Washington, D.C. 20006.

CAREER: Rockefeller Institute, New York, N.Y., member of scientific staff, 1925-29; Mellon Institute (now of Carnegie-Mellon University), Pittsburgh, Pa., executive assistant, 1929-31; Borden Co., New York, N.Y., director of research, 1931-36; Mellon Institute, assistant director, 1937-42; New England Industrial Research Foundation, Boston, Mass., director, 1942-44; Air Reduction Co., New York, N.Y., director of chemical research, 1944-48; U.S. Industrial Chemicals, New York, N.Y., technical director, 1944-48, vice-president, 1948-52; Arthur D. Little, Inc., Cambridge, Mass., member of senior technical staff, 1952-53, vice-president, 1954-64, consultant, 1964—. Member of governing board, Inveresk Research International (formerly Arthur D. Little Research Institute), Musselburgh, Scotland, 1957-73. *Military service:* U.S. Army, 1916, 1918. *Wartime service:* Consultant to Office of Scientific Research and Development, U.S. Department of Defense, 1942-48.

MEMBER: American Association for the Advancement of Science, American Institute of Chemists (honorary member), American Chemical Society (member of board, 1946-50), American Institute of Chemical Engineers (fellow; president, 1948), Society of Chemical Industry, Commercial Development Association, Institute of Food Technologists, Yale Engineering Association (president, 1950-52), Chemists' Club (New York), Tau Beta Pi (member of national council, 1950-54), Sigma Tau, Sigma Xi, Alpha Chi Sigma, Phi Lambda Upsilon, Sigma Nu, Cosmos Club (Washington, D.C.). *Awards, honors:* Presidential certificate of merit, 1947, for services to military during World War II.

WRITINGS: Inorganic Complex Compounds, Wiley, 1923; (with P. A. Levene) *Nucleic Acids,* American Chemical Society, 1931; *Management of Technical Programs,* Pregl, 1965; *Manual on the Management of Industrial Research Institutes in Developing Countries,* United Nations, 1966; (editor with B.S. Old) *Formulation of Research Policies,* American Association for the Advancement of Science, 1967; *Manual on the Use of Consultants in Developing Countries,* United Nations, 1968; *Industrial Research Institutes: Project Selection and Evaluation,* United Nations, 1970; *Industrial Research Institutes: Guidelines for Evaluation,* United Nations, 1971; *Management by Task Forces: A Manual on the Operation of Interdisciplinary Teams,* Lomond Systems, Inc. (Mt. Airy, Md.), in press.

Contributor of over 150 articles to American and foreign professional journals.

WORK IN PROGRESS: A book on the evaluation of technical programs; journal articles on technical management and economic development.

AVOCATIONAL INTERESTS: International travel, photography, ancient history.

* * *

BATES, Marston 1906-1974

July 23, 1906—April 3, 1974; American zoologist and world

authority on mosquitos. Obituaries: *Detroit Free Press,* April 5, 1974; *Detroit News,* April 5, 1974; *Current Biography,* May, 1974. (*CA*-7/8).

* * *

BATES, Scott 1923-

PERSONAL: Born June 13, 1923, in Evanston, Ill.; son of Alfred Ricker (a lawyer) and Eleanor (Fulcher) Bates; married Phoebe Strehlow (a newspaper editor), April 18, 1948; children: Robin Ricker, Jonathan Reed, David Scott, Samuel Jackson. *Education:* Carleton College, B.A., 1947; University of Wisconsin, M.A., 1948, Ph.D., 1954. *Politics:* Socialist. *Residence:* Sewanee, Tenn. *Office:* Department of French, University of the South, Sewanee, Tenn. 37375.

CAREER: University of the South, Sewanee, Tenn., assistant professor, 1954-58, associate professor, 1958-66, professor of French, 1966—. Highlander Folk School board of directors, vice-chairman, 1962-68, chairman, 1968-72, secretary-treasurer, 1972—.

WRITINGS: Guillaume Apollinaire, Twayne, 1967; *Poems of War Resistance,* Grossman, 1969; *Dictionnaire des mots libres d'Apollinaire* (title means "Dictionary of Apollinaire's Erotic Vocabulary"), Filipacchi, in press. Contributor of poems to *Furioso, Carleton Miscellany, Partisan Review, New Republic, New Yorker,* and *Sewanee Review.* Editor of *Ecology Papers.*

WORK IN PROGRESS: Poems from a Passionate Windmill, completion expected in 1975; *Poems Against Pollution,* 1976.

* * *

BATTEN, Jack 1932-

PERSONAL: Born January 23, 1932, in Toronto, Ontario, Canada; son of Jack and Kathleen (Soward) Batten; married Jane Bradshaw, June 9, 1956 (divorced, 1968); married Marjorie Harris (a magazine editor), April 20, 1968; children: (first marriage) Brad, Sarah. *Education:* University of Toronto, B.A., 1954, LL.B., 1957. *Home and office:* 199 Albany Ave., Toronto M5R 3C7, Ontario, Canada.

CAREER: McLaughlin, Macaulay, May & Soward (law firm), Toronto, Ontario, lawyer, 1959-63; staff writer at *Maclean's, Canadian Magazine,* and *Star Weekly,* and managing editor, *Saturday Night,* all 1963-68; free-lance writer, 1968—.

WRITINGS: Nancy Greene, General Publishing, 1968; *Hockey Dynasty,* General Publishing, 1969; *Champions,* New Press, 1971; *Honest Ed's Story,* Doubleday, 1973. Contributor to *Maclean's, Globe & Mail, Saturday Night, Chatelaine,* and *TV Guide.*

WORK IN PROGRESS: A detective novel.

* * *

BAUBY, Cathrina 1927-

PERSONAL: Born March 25, 1927, in Elwood, Ind.; daughter of John W. and Gretna (Hoppenrath) Bauby. *Education:* Indiana University, B.S., 1950, M.S., 1954. *Home:* 245 East 63rd St., New York, N.Y. 10021.

CAREER: Professional speaker; WMCT-TV, Memphis, Tenn., spokeswoman, 1954-59. *Member:* International Society of General Semantics, International Platform Speakers Association, National Speakers Association.

WRITINGS: O.K., Let's Talk About It, Van Nostrand, 1972; *Between Consenting Adults: Dialogue for Intimate Living,* Macmillan, 1973.

SIDELIGHTS: "In both business and personal lives. . .the most difficult thing for people to do is to understand and be understood," Cathrina Bauby wrote. "Most of the problems in our daily relations are due to a breakdown in verbal communications. We've been taught public speaking, but never to dialogue! And this is our daily form of speech. This was the motivation for both of my books, one dealing with the business world, the other with the personal lives of people."

* * *

BAUML, Franz H.
See BAEUML, Franz H(einrich)

* * *

BAYLES, Michael D(ale) 1941-

PERSONAL: Born January 21, 1941, in Charleston, Ill.; son of Dale M. (a clothier) and Elizabeth (a librarian; maiden name, Widger) Bayles; married Janice E. Morgan, January 14, 1961; children: Melanie, Michele. *Education:* University of Illinois, B.A., 1962; University of Missouri, M.A., 1963; Indiana University, Ph.D., 1967. *Home:* 3274 Maddenhurst Ct., Lexington, Ky. 40502. *Office:* Department of Philosophy, University of Kentucky, Lexington, Ky. 40506.

CAREER: University of Idaho, Moscow, instructor in philosophy, 1965-67; Brooklyn College of the City University of New York, Brooklyn, N.Y., assistant professor of philosophy, 1967-70; University of Kentucky, Lexington, associate professor, 1970-74, professor of philosophy, 1974—. *Member:* International Association for Philosophy of Law and Social Philosophy, American Philosophical Association, American Society for Political and Legal Philosophy, Society for Philosophy and Public Affairs (member of executive board, 1973). *Awards, honors:* American Council of Learned Societies study fellowship, 1974-75; Harvard Law School liberal arts fellowship, 1974-75.

WRITINGS: (Editor) *Contemporary Utilitarianism,* Doubleday, 1968; (editor) *Ethics and Population,* Schenkman, 1975.

Contributor: Ervin H. Pollack, editor, *Human Rights: Amintaphil I,* Jay Stewart, 1971; J. Roland Pennock and John W. Chapman, editors, *Coercion: Nomos XIV,* Aldine-Atherton, 1972; Norman S. Care and Thomas K. Trelogan, editors, *Issues in Law and Morality,* Press of Case Western Reserve University, 1973; Pennock and Chapman, editors, *The Limits of Law: Nomos XV,* Lieber-Atherton, 1974; James B. Wilbur and Ervin Laszlo, editors, *Human Values and the Law,* Gordon & Breach, 1974; Milton Goldinger, editor, *Punishment and Human Rights,* Schenkman, 1974; Ransom Baine Harris, editor, *Authority: A Philosophical Analysis,* University of Alabama Press, in press; Eugene Dais, editor, *Law and the Ecological Challenge: Amintaphil II,* Jay Stewart, in press.

Contributor to *Personalist, Review of Metaphysics, Analysis, Social Theory and Practice, Wayne Law Review, Journal of Value Inquiry, Metaphilosophy, Modern Schoolman,* and *Idealistic Studies.*

WORK IN PROGRESS: Editing *Medical Care of the Dying: The Moral Issues,* with Dallas High, for Schenkman; *The Uses of Political Authority.*

SIDELIGHTS: Bayles writes: "The world population crisis will be the major factor in world events to the end of this century. I intend to spend the next several years studying the value implications of this crisis and the moral acceptability of alternative policies."

* * *

BEAUMONT, George Ernest 1888-1974

July 16, 1888—April 23, 1974; British physician and author. Obituaries: *AB Bookman's Weekly,* June 17, 1974.

* * *

BEBB, Russ(ell H.), Jr. 1930-

PERSONAL: Born February 22, 1930, in Knoxville, Tenn.; son of Russell H. (a teacher) and Alice (Price) Bebb; married LaWanda Carter (a registered nurse), August 8, 1954; children: Kim, Rusty, Chris. *Education:* Attended University of Tennessee, 1950, and Carson-Newman College, 1952. *Politics:* Republican. *Religion:* Methodist. *Home:* 4720 River Oak Dr., Knoxville, Tenn. 37920. *Office: Knoxville Journal,* 210 West Church Ave., Knoxville, Tenn. 37920.

CAREER: Knoxville Journal, Knoxville, Tenn., assistant sports editor, 1953—.

WRITINGS: The Big Orange, Strode, 1973.

* * *

BEBLER, A(lex) Anton 1937-

PERSONAL: Born March 10, 1937. *Education:* University of Belgrade, B.A., 1960, M.A., 1966; University of Pennsylvania, Ph.D., 1971. *Home:* Gregorciceva lla, Apt. 20, 61000 Ljubljana, Yugoslavia. *Office:* Faculty for Sociology, Political Science, and Journalism, University of Ljubljana, 102 Titova, 61000 Ljubljana, Yugoslavia.

CAREER: Institute of International Politics and Economy, Belgrade, Yogoslavia, research fellow, 1963-70; Center of International Studies, Princeton, N.J., research associate, 1970-71; University of Ljubljana, Ljubljana, Yugoslavia, docent of faculty for sociology, political science, and journalism, 1972—.

WRITINGS: Military Rule in Africa, Praeger, 1973. Contributor of about eighty articles to periodicals.

WORK IN PROGRESS: A book, *Comparative Military Politics.*

* * *

BECHKO, Peggy Anne 1950-

PERSONAL: Surname rhymes with "echo"; born August 26, 1950, in South Haven, Mich.; daughter of Edwin Louis (a pest control operator) and Elizabeth Ann (an accountant; maiden name, Schleimer) Bechko. *Education:* Attended Manatee Junior College, 1968-69. *Residence:* Sarasota, Fla. 33581. *Agent:* George Glay, 663 5th Ave., New York, N.Y. 10022.

CAREER: Writer. Has held clerical and retail sales positions.

WRITINGS—Novels: *Night of the Flaming Guns,* Doubleday, 1974; *Gunman's Justice,* Doubleday, 1974.

WORK IN PROGRESS: A murder mystery set in the Everglades, completion expected in 1974.

SIDELIGHTS: Miss Bechko told *CA:* "Writing is a way of life for me. There is nothing I would rather do, nor has there been since I was fourteen. . . . I am especially interested in the preservation of wildlife and . . . firmly believe all national parks should be closed to *all* motorized vehicles. Special dispensation should, of course, be made to enable handicapped persons to enjoy the parks. A shuttle bus or its like could be provided." *Avocational interests:* Swimming, horseback riding, reading, travel.

* * *

BECHTOL, William M(ilton) 1931-

PERSONAL: Born November 26, 1931, in Arcanum, Ohio; son of Owen S. (an electronics repairman) and Maude (Mendenhall) Bechtol; married Mildred A. Isaacs, September 6, 1952; children: William, Jr., Susan, Robert. *Education:* Miami University, Oxford, Ohio, B.S., 1953, M.Ed., 1956, Ed.D., 1970. *Religion:* Methodist. *Home:* 902 Willow St., Marshall, Minn. 56258. *Office:* Center for Management of Education Systems, Southwest Minnesota State College, Marshall, Minn. 56258.

CAREER: Teacher in public schools of Reily, Ohio, 1953-54; Tipp City Schools, Tipp City, Ohio, teacher, 1954-56, elementary principal, 1956-66, assistant superintendent, 1967-69; Southwest Minnesota State College, Center for Management of Education Systems, Marshall, Minn., director, 1967—. *Member:* Department of Elementary School Principals, Ohio Education Association, Rotary, Phi Delta Kappa.

WRITINGS: Individualizing Instruction and Keeping Your Sanity, Follett, 1973; (contributor) Phillip and Miriam Kapfer, editors, *Learning Packages in American Education,* Educational Technology Publications, 1973; (contributor) Juanita Sorenson, editor, *The Unit Leader in the IGE School,* Addison-Wesley, 1974.

SIDELIGHTS: Bechtel, a firm believer in "individualized, personalized, humanized education," has helped over forty schools implement individualized school programs.

* * *

BECK, Clive 1939-

PERSONAL: Born January 5, 1939, in Australia; son of Lawrence Mackie (a farmer) and Sylvia (Kemble) Beck; married Julianne Galdy (a librarian), January 2, 1965; children: Paul. *Education:* University of Western Australia, B.Ed., 1959; University of Sydney, B.A., 1963; University of New England, Australia, Ph.D., 1967. *Residence:* Toronto, Ontario, Canada. *Office:* Ontario Institute for Studies in Education, 252 Bloor St. W., Toronto, Ontario, Canada.

CAREER: University of New England, Armidale, Australia, lecturer in philosophy of education, 1964-67; Ontario Institute for Studies in Education, Toronto, Ontario, assistant professor, 1967-69, associate professor, 1969-74, professor of philosophy of education, 1974—, head of department, 1969-71, co-director of Moral Education Project, 1969—. *Member:* Philosophy of Education Society, Philosophy of Education Society of Great Britain, Canadian Society for the Study of Education, American Educational Studies Association.

WRITINGS: (Editor with B. S. Crittenden and E. V. Sullivan) *Moral Education: Interdisciplinary Approaches,* University of Toronto Press, 1970; *Moral Education in the Schools,* Ontario Institute for Studies in Education, 1971; *Ethics,* McGraw, 1972; *Educational Philosophy and Theory: An Introduction,* Little, Brown, 1974.

BECKER, John E(dward) 1930-

PERSONAL: Born November 4, 1930, in Kansas City, Mo.; son of John Paul (a plumber) and Catherine (Bessenbacher) Becker; married Claire Lenore Hahn (a university professor), November 26, 1970. *Education:* St. Louis University, B.A., 1954, Licentiate in Philosophy, 1958, M.A., 1958, Licentiate in Sacred Theology (cum laude), 1963; Yale University, Ph.D., 1968. *Religion:* Roman Catholic. *Home:* 5700 Arlington Ave., 15V, Bronx, N.Y. 10471. *Office:* Department of English and Comparative Literature, Fairleigh Dickinson University, Teaneck, N.J. 07666.

CAREER: Entered Society of Jesus (Jesuit), 1948; ordained priest, 1961; resigned from Society and from active ministry, 1970. High school teacher in St. Louis, Mo., 1955-56, and in Wichita, Kan., 1956-57; Fairleigh Dickinson University, Teaneck, N.J., assistant professor of English, 1970—. *Member:* Modern Language Association of America, English Institute, Northeast Modern Language Association.

WRITINGS: *Hawthorne's Historical Allegory,* Kennikat, 1971. Assistant editor of *Review for Religious,* 1958-62; editor of *IDOC-North America* (International Documentation on the Contemporary Church), 1970-71.

WORK IN PROGRESS: A book on ritual in fiction; a monograph on Melville's Billy Budd; initiating publication of *Bible and Literature Newsletter.*

* * *

BECKETT, Lucy 1942-

PERSONAL: Born August 10, 1942, in Windsor, England; daughter of Martyn (an architect) and Priscilla (Brett) Beckett; married Adrian Whitfield, June 28, 1962 (divorced, 1969); married John Warrack (a musicologist), February 27, 1970; children: four. *Education:* Attended Sorbonne, University of Paris, 1959-60; Cambridge University, B.A. (honors), 1963. *Politics:* Liberal left. *Religion:* Roman Catholic. *Home:* Beck House, Rievaulx, Helmsley, York, England.

CAREER: Writer. Has discussed music and poetry on British Broadcasting Corp. programs.

WRITINGS: *Wallace Stevens,* Cambridge University Press, 1974; (contributor) *Wagner Companion,* Faber, in press. Contributor of articles and poems to *London Magazine, Tablet, Music and Letters,* and *Musical Times.*

WORK IN PROGRESS: *The Death of Robert Fletcher,* a novel on the Reformation, completion expected in 1976.

SIDELIGHTS: "I am classically educated (can read Latin, Greek, French, and German)," Lucy Beckett wrote, "... I read and write at home (she recently gave birth to her fourth child), being chiefly interested in modern literature, Germany, and above all the sixteenth century, theology, the importance of a Christian renewal which is not emptied of theological content or preoccupied with social ethics to the exclusion of faith."

* * *

BEDINGER, Singleton B(erry) 1907-

PERSONAL: Surname is pronounced *Bed*-in-jer; born March 22, 1907, in Terrell, Tex.; son of Singleton Berry (a school superintendent) and Nina (Terrell) Bedinger; married Thelma Showalter, August 24, 1930; children: Marion S., Celeste (Mrs. Howard Wallis Dobson). *Education:* Attended South Texas Junior College, 1947, Southern Methodist University, 1949-53, and Dallas Bible College, 1950-53; Berea School of Theology, Bachelor of Bible, 1966. *Politics:* Republican. *Home and office address:* Cardinal Hill, P.O. Box 254, Mountain View, Mo. 65548.

CAREER: Retail store manager; ordained minister of Cumberland Presbyterian Church, 1948; pastor in Texas, Louisiana, Kentucky, Illinois, and Missouri, 1958—. Moderator, Missouri Synod, 1971. *Military service:* U.S. Army, Medical Corps, 1943-45; served in Europe. Texas State Guard Reserve Corps, chaplain, 1955-61; became captain. *Member:* Sons of the American Revolution, Sons of Confederate Veterans, Lions Club, Kiwanis Club, Masons. *Awards, honors:* World War II Military Cross from United Daughters of the Confederacy, 1954; commissioned a Kentucky Colonel by Governor Edward T. Breathitt, 1964; honorary D.D. from American Divinity School, 1973.

WRITINGS: *Shields of Gold,* Royal Publishers, 1955; *Defenders in Gray,* Royal Publishers, 1962; *Kentuckians: C. S. A.,* Merchants Press, 1965; *Missouri's Confederates,* Merchants Press, 1967; *Texas and the Southern Confederacy,* Merchants Press, 1970; *Little Egypt: A Brief Historical Sketch of Southern Illinois,* Adams Press, 1973. Contributor to *Christian Economics* and other religious journals.

WORK IN PROGRESS: Research with son, Marion S. Bedinger, on a genealogy of the Bedinger family in America.

* * *

BEER, Barrett L(ynn) 1936-

PERSONAL: Born July 4, 1936, in Goshen, Ind.; son of Peter J. and Mabel Beer; married Jill Parker, 1965; children: Peter, Caroline. *Education:* DePauw University, B.A., 1958; University of Cincinnati, M.A., 1959; Northwestern University, Ph.D., 1965. *Home:* 531 Spaulding Dr., Kent, Ohio 44240. *Office:* Department of History, Kent State University, Kent, Ohio 44242.

CAREER: Kent State University, Kent, Ohio, instructor in history, 1962-65; University of New Mexico, Albuquerque, assistant professor of history, 1965-68; Kent State University, associate professor of history, 1968—. *Member:* American Historical Association, Conference on British Studies, Phi Beta Kappa.

WRITINGS: *Northumberland: The Political Career of John Dudley, Earl of Warwick and Duke of Northumberland,* Kent State University Press, 1973; (editor with S. M. Jack) *The Letters of William, Lord Paget of Beaudesert, 1547-1563, Camden Miscellany, Vol. XXV,* Royal Historical Society (London), 1974. Contributor to *Journal of British Studies, History Today,* and *Hunt Library Quarterly.*

* * *

BEERS, Dorothy Sands 1917-

PERSONAL: Born June 17, 1917, in Rye, N.Y.; daughter of Benjamin Jerome (a physician) and Josephine (Willson) Sands; married Yardley Beers (a physicist), May 12, 1945; children: G. Jerome, Deborah Yardley. *Education:* Bennington College, A.B., 1938. *Home:* 740 Willowbrook Rd., Boulder, Colo. 80302.

CAREER: Massachusetts Institute of Technology, Radiation Laboratory, Cambridge, technician, 1943, staff member, 1944-46; free-lance writer. *Member:* Women's International League for Peace and Freedom, American Pen Women, Colorado Authors League.

WRITINGS: ABC Alphabet Cookbook (juvenile), Schmitt, Hall & McCreary, 1973. Contributor of verse, fiction, and articles to children's magazines and newspapers; contributor of articles to *Denver Post* and *Christian Science Monitor.*

AVOCATIONAL INTERESTS: Violin, hiking.

* * *

BEERS, Lorna 1897-

PERSONAL: Born May 10, 1897, in Maple Plain, Minn.; daughter of John Henry (a pioneer) and Sarah (James) Beers; married Clyde Ray Chambers (an economist), December 27, 1919; children: Richard (deceased). *Education:* University of Minnesota, B.A., 1919. *Politics:* Independent. *Religion:* United Church of Christ. *Home:* 687 East Beverly, Staunton, Va. 24401.

CAREER: Teacher for two years in a prairie town. *Member:* Author's Guild, Pen and Brush, Phi Beta Kappa. *Awards, honors:* Avery Hopwood Award, 1932, for *The Mad Stone.*

WRITINGS: Prairie Fires (novel), Dutton, 1925; *A Humble Lear* (novel), Dutton, 1929; *The Mad Stone* (novel), Dutton, 1932; *The Book of Hugh Flower* (novel), Harper, 1952; *The Crystal Cornerstone* (novel), Harper, 1953; *Wild Apples and North Wind,* Norton, 1966; *My Brothers, My Country, My World,* United Church Press, 1969. Contributor of short stories and essays to *Yankee, Harper's, Christian Science Monitor,* and *New England Galaxy.*

WORK IN PROGRESS: Two books with Minnesota settings.

* * *

BEERS, V(ictor) Gilbert 1928-

PERSONAL: Born May 6, 1928, in Sidell, Ill.; son of Ernest S. (a farmer) and Jean (Bloomer) Beers; married Arlisle Felten, August 26, 1950; children: Kathleen, Douglas, Ronald, Janice, Cynthia. *Education:* Wheaton College, Wheaton, Ill., A.B., 1950; Northern Baptist Seminary, Chicago, M.R.E., 1953, M.Div., 1954, Th.M., 1955, Th.D., 1960; Northwestern University, Ph.D., 1963. *Politics:* Republican. *Home and office:* Route 1, Box 321, Elgin, Ill. 60120.

CAREER: Northern Baptist Seminary, Chicago, Ill., professor of religion, 1954-57; David C. Cook Publishing Co., Elgin, Ill., editor of senior high publications, 1957-59, executive editor, 1959-61, editorial director, 1961-67; Creative Designs, Elgin, Ill., president, 1967—. Presently member of board of directors, Summit Finance Corp., Fort Wayne, Ind., Scripture Press, and Deerfoot Lodge (boys camp), Speculator, N.Y.; member of board of directors, Wheaton Youth Symphony, Wheaton, Ill., 1962-64, president, 1963-64; trustee of David C. Cook Foundation, 1965-67. *Member:* Children's Reading Round Table (Chicago), Wheaton College Alumni Association (president, 1972-73). *Awards, honors:* Distinguished Service Award of Midland Authors, 1973, for *Cats and Bats and Things Like That* and *The ABQ Book.*

WRITINGS—Adult: *Family Bible Library,* ten volumes, Southwestern Co., 1971; *Patterns for Prayer from the Gospels,* Ravell, 1972; *Joy Is . . . ,* Revell, 1974; *The Discovery Bible Handbook,* Victor Books, 1974.

Juvenile: *A Child's Treasury of Bible Stories,* four volumes, Parent and Child Institute, 1970; *Cats and Bats and Things Like That,* Moody, 1972; *The ABQ Book,* Moody, 1972; *The House in the Hole in the Side of the Tree,* Moody, 1973; "Learning to Read from the Bible" series, four books titled *God Is My Helper, God Is My Friend, Jesus Is My Teacher,* and *Jesus Is My Guide,* Zondervan, 1973; *Coco's Candy Shop,* Moody, 1973; *Around the World with My Red Balloon,* Moody, 1973; *The Magic Merry-Go-Round,* Moody, 1973; *A Gaggle of Green Geese,* Moody, 1974; *Honeyphants and Elebees,* Moody, 1974.

* * *

BEEZLEY, William H(oward Taft) 1942-

PERSONAL: Born March 22, 1942, in Albuquerque, N.M.; son of Howard C. and Lorene (Sallee) Beezley; married Alda Reil, August 22, 1964; children: Paul Richard, John Sallee, Mark Madrid. *Education:* Chico State College, A.B., 1964; University of Nebraska, M.A., 1966, Ph.D., 1969. *Residence:* Raleigh, N.C. *Office:* Department of History, North Carolina State University, Raleigh, N.C. 27607.

CAREER: State University of New York College at Plattsburgh, assistant professor of Latin American history, 1968-72; North Carolina State University, Raleigh, assistant professor, 1972-74, associate professor of Latin American history, 1974—. *Member:* Conference on Latin American History, Latin American Studies Association, North Carolina High School Athletics Officials Association.

WRITINGS: Insurgent Governor: Abraham Gonzalez and the Mexican Revolution in Chihuahua, University of Nebraska Press, 1973. Editor of *Americas,* 1974—.

WORK IN PROGRESS: United States Consuls in Mexico; Mexican Bandits.

AVOCATIONAL INTERESTS: Sports history.

* * *

BEICHMAN, Arnold 1913-

PERSONAL: Born May 17, 1913, in New York, N.Y.; son of Solomon and Mary (Maltman) Beichman; married Doris Modry, 1936 (divorced, 1946); married Carroll Aikins (a teacher), 1950; children: (first marriage) Anthony, Janine (Mrs. Takeo Yamamoto); (second marriage) Charles, John. *Education:* Columbia University, B.A., 1934, M.A., 1967, Ph.D., 1973. *Politics:* Independent. *Religion:* None. *Home:* Rekadom, Naramata, British Columbia, Canada (temporary). *Office address:* Department of Politics, University of Massachusetts, Boston, Mass. 02125.

CAREER: Newsday, Hempstead, N.Y., reporter, feature-writer, 1939-41; *PM,* New York, N.Y., city editor, and assistant managing editor, 1944-46; *Electrical Union World,* New York, N.Y., editor, 1949-65; International Confederation of Free Trade Unions, Brussels, Belgium, press officer, 1951-62; University of Massachusetts, Boston, lecturer, 1970-73, associate professor of politics, 1973—. Visiting professor, University of British Columbia; lecturer under auspices of Canadian Institute of International Affairs, 1965, 1966, and for U.S. Information Service in Stockholm, Berlin, Hamburg, London, and Paris, 1973; lecturer at Canisius College, 1973 and 1974, National Humanities Faculty, 1973, and Georgetown University, 1973 and

1974. *Member:* American Political Science Association, National Humanities Faculty, Reform Club (London).

WRITINGS: (Contributor) Donald Robinson, editor, *The Dirty Wars: Guerilla Actions and Other Forms of Unconventional Warfare,* Delacorte, 1968; *The "Other" State Department: The U.S. Mission to the U.N.—Its Role in the Making of Foreign Policy,* Basic Books, 1968; *Nine Lies About America,* Library Press, 1972. Contributor of articles and reviews to *New York Times Magazine, New York, Columbia University Forum, New Leader, Encounter, Interplay, New Society, Newsweek, New York Herald Tribune, International Herald Tribune, London Spectator, London Daily Telegraph, AFL-CIO News, Christian Science Monitor, Boston Globe, Journal of British Studies, Art International, Lugano Review,* and *Commentary.*

* * *

BEITZ, Charles R(ichard) 1949-

PERSONAL: Born July 20, 1949, in Buffalo, N.Y.; son of Richard C. and Jean (Harris) Beitz. *Education:* Colgate University, B.A., 1970; University of Michigan, M.A., 1974; Princeton University, graduate study, 1974—. *Office:* Department of Politics, Princeton University, Princeton, N.J. 08540.

CAREER: Colgate University, Hamilton, N.Y., coordinator of Peace Studies Program, 1970-71; Institute for World Order, New York, N.Y., assistant director of University Program, 1971-72; Trenton State College, Trenton, N.J., instructor in philosophy, spring, 1974; Princeton University, Princeton, N.J., preceptor in philosophy, 1974—.

WRITINGS: (Editor with Theodore Herman) *Peace and War,* W. H. Freeman, 1973; (with Michael Washburn) *Creating the Future: A Guide to Living and Working for Social Change,* Bantam, 1974.

WORK IN PROGRESS: Dissertation research in political philosophy.

* * *

BELFIGLIO, Valentine J(ohn) 1934-

PERSONAL: Surname is pronounced Bell-*feel*-yo; born May 8, 1934, in Troy, N.Y.; son of Edmond L. (a pharmacist) and Mildred (Sherwood) Belfiglio; married Jane M. Searles, May 27, 1957 (divorced, October, 1969); children: Valentine E. *Education:* Union University, Albany, N.Y., B.S., 1956; University of Oklahoma, M.A., 1967, Ph.D., 1970. *Politics:* Republican. *Religion:* Roman Catholic. *Home:* 2707 Douglas, Apt. 107, Dallas, Tex. 75219. *Office:* Department of History and Government, Texas Woman's University, Denton, Tex. 76204.

CAREER: U.S. Air Force, hospital unit training officer, 1959-67, leaving service as captain; University of Oklahoma, Norman, instructor in political science, 1967-70; Texas Woman's University, Denton, assistant professor of history and government, 1970—. *Member:* International Studies Association, American Political Science Association, Mensa.

WRITINGS: The Essentials of American Foreign Policy, Kendall-Hunt, 1971; *The United States and World Peace,* McCutchan, 1971. Contributor to professional publications, including *Strategic Digest, Rocky Mountain Social Science Journal, Asian Survey, Asian Studies, International Studies,* and *International Problems,* and to newspapers.

WORK IN PROGRESS: "The Role of Women in Texas Politics," a chapter for *Texas Government,* edited by Richard Cramer, for West Publishing; research on relations between India and the United States.

SIDELIGHTS: Belfiglio writes: "One great advantage of the written word over the spoken word as I see it, is the ability to break-off communication whenever one desires to do so." *Avocational interests:* Gourmet cooking, bridge, golf, sailing, travel (Europe and the Orient).

* * *

BELL, Gerald D(ean) 1937-

PERSONAL: Born November 23, 1937, in Denver, Colo.; son of Louis E. and Florence I. Bell; married Christine Demeritt, June 11, 1960; children: Kathryn, Sharon. *Education:* University of Colorado, B.S., 1960, M.A. (social psychology), 1961; Yale University, M.A. (sociology), 1963, Ph.D., 1964. *Home:* 1707 Michaux Rd., Chapel Hill, N.C. 27514. *Office:* Department of Organizational Behavior, 309 Carroll Hall, University of North Carolina, Chapel Hill, N.C. 27514.

CAREER: University of North Carolina, Chapel Hill, assistant professor, 1963-66, associate professor, 1966-70, professor of sociology, 1970—, presently professor of organizational behavior. Visiting professor, Harvard University, 1965-66. *Member:* American Psychological Association, American Sociological Association, Academy of Management.

WRITINGS: Human Behavior in Organizations, Prentice-Hall, 1967; *The Achievers,* Preston-Hill, 1973.

* * *

BELL, Leland V(irgil) 1934-

PERSONAL: Born March 2, 1934, in Johnson City, N.Y.; son of Leland V. (a postal official) and Anna (Golen) Bell; married Evelyn Behnan (an artist), February 4, 1961; children: Eric, Rachel. *Education:* Wayne State University, A.B., 1958; Pennsylvania State University, A.M., 1961; University of Michigan, further graduate study, 1961-62; West Virginia University, Ph.D., 1968. *Home:* 1402 Meadow Lane, Yellow Springs, Ohio 45387. *Office:* Central State University, Wilberforce, Ohio 45384.

CAREER: Kansas City Community Junior College, Kansas City, Mo., instructor in history, 1962-64; West Liberty State College, West Liberty, W.Va., assistant professor of history, 1964-66; West Virginia University, Morgantown, instructor in history, 1966-68; Central State University, Wilberforce, Ohio, assistant professor, 1968-71, associate professor, 1971-74, professor of history, 1974—. Adjunct professor at Wittenberg University, 1970-71; adjunct associate professor at Wright State University, 1972-73; adjunct professor at Union Graduate School, 1973—. *Military service:* U.S. Army, 1953-55.

MEMBER: American Historical Association, Organization of American Historians, American Association of University Professors, Ohio Academy of History.

WRITINGS: In Hitler's Shadow, Kennikat, 1973. Contributor to *Political Science Quarterly, Journal of Human Relations,* and *Illinois Quarterly.*

WORK IN PROGRESS: The Sleep of Reason: A History of the Care and Treatment of the Mentally Ill in the United States.

SIDELIGHTS: Bell writes: "As a historian, I am interested in searching the past with the hope of gaining a better understanding of contemporary problems. Some of the subjects I have written about include political extremism, aging and death, violence and the disintegration of artistic values, and the care and treatment of the mentally ill. My purpose is informative, to arouse interest and concern in controversial topics by placing them in a historical context."

* * *

BELLAMY, James A(ndrew) 1925-

PERSONAL: Born August 12, 1925, in Evansville, Ind.; son of John Garrard and Mary (Buchanan) Bellamy. *Education:* Centre College, A.B., 1946; University of Pennsylvania, Ph.D., 1956. *Residence:* Ann Arbor, Mich. *Office:* Department of Near Eastern Studies, University of Michigan, Ann Arbor, Mich. 48104.

CAREER: U.S. State Department, Ankara, Turkey, accounting clerk, 1947-49; Wayne State University, Detroit, Mich., assistant professor of Arabic, 1958-59; University of Michigan, Ann Arbor, lecturer, 1959-60, assistant professor, 1960-65, associate professor, 1965-68, professor of Arabic literature, 1968—. *Member:* American Oriental Society, Middle East Institute, Middle East Studies Association. *Awards, honors:* Ford Foundation fellow, 1953-54; American Council of Learned Societies fellowships, 1966-67, 1973-74.

WRITINGS: (Editor and author of introduction and notes) Ibn Abi d.-Dunya, *Kitab Makarim al-Aklaq* (title means "The Noble Qualities of Character"), Franz Steiner, 1973. Associate editor of *Journal of American Oriental Society,* 1970—.

WORK IN PROGRESS: Research on medieval Arabic literature.

* * *

BELOTE, William Milton 1922-

PERSONAL: Born October 4, 1922, in Bellevue, Wash.; son of William M. (a cabinetmaker) and Adelaide (Hine) Belote; married Marilyn Pape (a teacher), February 7, 1952; children: Alan Richard. *Education:* University of Washington, Seattle, A.B., 1948, M.A., 1949; University of California, Berkeley Ph.D., 1953. *Religion:* Christian Scientist. *Home:* 324 Beach Dr., Annapolis, Md. 21403 (winter); Twanoh Falls, Belfair, Wash. (summer). *Office:* Department of History, U.S. Naval Academy, Annapolis, Md. 21402.

CAREER: Mississippi State University, State College, assistant professor, 1953-56; U.S. Naval Academy, Annapolis, Md., assistant professor, 1956-62, associate professor, 1962-68, professor of naval history, 1968—. *Military service:* U.S. Army Air Forces, 1943-46. *Member:* American Historical Association, American Military Institute, American Committee on the History of the Second World War, American Association of University Professors, U. S. Naval Institute.

WRITINGS: (Contributor) Bernard Weber, editor, *Essays in Honor of Franklin Charles Palm,* Bookman's, 1956; (contributor) E. B. Potter and C. W. Nimitz, editors, *Sea Power: A Naval History,* Prentice-Hall, 1960; (with brother, James H. Belote) *Corregidor: The Saga of a Fortress,* Harper, 1967; (with James H. Belote) *Typhoon of Steel: The Battle for Okinawa,* Harper, 1970; (with James H. Belote) *Carrier Task Forces,* Harper, in press.

AVOCATIONAL INTERESTS: Ecology of the Pacific Northwest, hiking, fishing.

BENGTSON, Vern L. 1941-

PERSONAL: Born May 2, 1941, in Lindsborg, Kan.; son of Bertil Nils (a minister) and Julia (Falk) Bengtson; married Denise Elizabeth Nordin (an early education specialist), August 15, 1964; children: Julie Linn, Christina Denise. *Education:* North Park College, B.A., 1963; University of Chicago, M.A., 1965, Ph.D., 1967. *Residence:* Pasadena, Calif. *Office:* Gerontology Center, University of Southern California, Los Angeles, Calif. 90007.

CAREER: University of Southern California, Los Angeles, assistant professor, 1967-70, associate professor of sociology, 1970—, chief of Laboratory for Social Organization and Behavior, Gerontology Center, 1972—. *Member:* American Sociological Association, American Psychological Association, Gerontological Society, Society for the Psychological Study of Social Issues, National Council on Family Relations, Pacific Sociological Association.

WRITINGS: *The Social Psychology of Aging,* Bobbs-Merrill, 1973. Contributor of twenty-four papers to sociological and psychological journals.

WORK IN PROGRESS: "Inter-generational Transmission and the 'Generation Gap'"; "Variable Solidarity: Relations between Parents and Children"; "Defining Social Problems: Tolerance for Deviance and the 'Generation Gap'."

* * *

BEN-HORAV, Naphthali
See KRAVITZ, Nathaniel

* * *

BENJAMIN, Gerald 1945-

PERSONAL: Born April 10, 1945, in Brooklyn, N.Y.; son of Rubin (a proprietor of a liquor store) and Betty Benjamin; married Helise Ilene Blutig (a speech therapist), June 23, 1968; children: Elizabeth Marianne. *Education:* St. Lawrence University, A.B. (cum laude), 1965; Columbia University, M.A., 1967, Ph.D., 1970. *Politics:* Republican. *Religion:* Jewish. *Home:* 14 Millrock Rd., New Paltz, N.Y. 12561. *Office:* 802A Faculty Tower, State University of New York College at New Paltz, New Paltz, N.Y. 12561.

CAREER: State University of New York College at New Paltz, assistant professor, 1968-72, associate professor of political science, 1972—. Research associate of Academy of Political Science; consultant to secretary of New York State Senate. *Military service:* U.S. Army, service Medical Corps, 1970-72; became captain. *Member:* American Political Science Association, Academy of Political Science, New York State Political Science Association.

WRITINGS: *Race Relations and the New York City Human Rights Commission,* Cornell University Press, 1974; (editor with Robert Connery) *Governing New York State: The Rockefeller Years,* Academy of Political Science, 1974. Contributor to *P.S.* and *Public Administration Review.*

WORK IN PROGRESS: *Rockefeller in New York,* with Robert Connery, publication expected in 1976.

SIDELIGHTS: Benjamin wrote: "I am a New York chauvinist. I am endlessly fascinated with public affairs at the city and state level. I think more needs to be done, especially on New York State, which is a relatively unexplored area for scholarship."

BENJI, Thomas
See ROBINSON, Frank M(alcolm)

* * *

BENNETT, Dennis J. 1917-

PERSONAL: Born October 28, 1917, in London, England; son of Joseph Henry and Bertha Mabel (Mills) Bennett; married Elberta Nutter, October 7, 1939; married second wife, Rita Marie Reed (a writer), October 15, 1966; children: Margaret Eleanor (Mrs. Robert Ted Jones), Stephen D., Conrad J. *Education:* San Jose State College (now California State University), student, 1935-36, 1943-44; University of Chicago, B.D., 1949. *Home:* 1921 Northwest 95th St., Seattle, Wash. 98107.

CAREER: Salesman and buyer with electronics firm in San Jose, Calif., 1937-44; pastor of Congregational churches in Illinois, 1944-49, of community church in San Diego, Calif., 1949-50; associate pastor of Congregational church in San Diego, Calif., 1950-51; vicar of Episcopal church in Lancaster, Calif., 1951-53; St. Mark's Church, Van Nuys, Calif., rector, 1953-60; St. Luke's Church, Seattle, Wash., rector, 1960—.

WRITINGS: *Nine O'Clock in the Morning,* Logos International, 1970; (with wife, Rita Marie Bennett) *The Holy Spirit and You,* Logos International, 1971.

WORK IN PROGRESS: Two books.

* * *

BENNETT, John M(ichael) 1942-

PERSONAL: Born October 12, 1942, in Chicago, Ill.; son of John William (an anthropologist) and Kathryn (Goldsmith) Bennett; married Janifer Susan Holley (a teacher), September 19, 1964. *Education:* Washington University, St. Louis, Mo., B.A. (cum laude), 1964, M.A., 1966; University of California, Los Angeles, Ph.D., 1970; also studied at Universidad de Puerto Rico, summer, 1961, Universidad Internacional, Mexico, summer, 1962, and Universidad de Guadalajara, 1962-63. *Home:* 137 Leland Ave., Columbus, Ohio 43212. *Office:* Department of Romance Languages, Ohio State University, Columbus, Ohio 43210.

CAREER: Ohio State University, Columbus, assistant professor of Hispanic literature, 1969—. Has conducted research in Santiago, Chile, and in Mexico. *Member:* Modern Language Association of America, American Association of Teachers of Spanish and Portuguese, Ohio Poets Association.

WRITINGS: *Blank Blue Side of Chevy* (pamphlet), Cuervo Press, 1970; *Found Objects* (collage poems), with supplement, *Works,* New Rivers Press, 1973; *Freeway Gas Station* (pamphlet), Frustration Press, 1973; *Seven Rituals* (pamphlet), Frustration Press, 1973; *Copy: Early Death News* (hand printed concrete poems), Luna Bisonte Prods, 1974; (with Pablo Virumbrales) *La Revolucion: A Reader in Spanish American Revolutionary Thought,* Oxford University Press, in press; *White America,* New Rivers Press, in press; (with S. G. Armistead) *Songs of the Christians in Moslem Spain: The Mozarabic Hargas,* Ohio State University Press, in press.

Work is represented in anthologies, including *The Sensuous President by K,* edited by C. W. Truesdale, New Rivers Press, 1972; *Antologia Comentada del Modernismo,* (title means "Critical Anthology of Modernism"), edited by F. E. Porrata, California State University, in press.

Author of poetry broadsides. Contributor of about 100 poems and articles to professional journals and literary magazines, including The Fault, *Revista Hispanica Moderna, Peace and Pieces Review, West Coast Poetry Review, Zebra, Assembling, Minnesota Review, Cottonwood Review,* and *Star-Web Paper.*

WORK IN PROGRESS: Poems; working with concrete and conceptual poetry; a book of poems, *Seventeen Rituals.*

* * *

BENOLIEL, Jeanne Quint 1919-
(Jeanne Quint)

PERSONAL: Surname is accented on third syllable; born December 9, 1919, in National City, Calif.; daughter of John Edwin (a machinist) and Marie Lyda (a registered nurse; maiden name, Wade) Quint; married Wilson Sherrill, September 24, 1949 (annulled, 1953); married Robert William Benoliel (a chemical engineer), February 14, 1970. *Education:* San Diego State College (now University), student, 1937-38; St. Luke's Hospital School of Nursing, R.N., 1941; University of California, Berkeley, further study, 1943; Oregon State University, B.S., 1948; University of California, Los Angeles, M.S., 1955, further graduate study, 1959-61; University of California, San Francisco, D.N.Sc., 1969. *Home address:* Route 1, Box 2515, Fall City, Wash. 98024. *Office:* School of Nursing, University of Washington, Seattle, Wash. 98195.

CAREER: Registered nurse in California, Oregon, and State of Washington. Staff nurse in hospitals in San Diego, Calif., 1941-43, Berkeley, Calif., 1943, Astoria, Ore., 1946, and Chula Vista, Calif., 1947; Fresno General Hospital School of Nursing, Fresno, Calif., instructor in medical-surgical nursing, 1948-51, educational director, 1951-53; Metropolitan State Hospital, Norwalk, Calif., staff nurse, 1953-54; San Diego County Hospital, San Diego, Calif., instructor in medical nursing, 1954; University of California, Los Angeles, instructor, 1955-57, assistant professor of surgical nursing, 1957-59, junior research statistician and junior research nurse, 1961-62; University of California, San Francisco, assistant research sociologist, 1962-67, associate professor of nursing, 1969-70; University of Washington, Seattle, professor of nursing and chairman of department of comparative nursing care systems, 1970—. Member of board of California League for Nursing, 1964-68; member of professional advisory board of Foundation of Thanatology, 1969—; member of Western Interstate Commission for Higher Education in Nursing, 1969—; member of research advisory committee of American Nurses' Foundation, 1970-74. Appointed to Washington State Board of Health, 1971—. Guest lecturer at Tel-Aviv University, 1972. Has participated in and led workshops and conferences; consultant on death-related problems and issues. *Military service:* U.S. Army, Nurse Corps, 1943-46; served in Philippines and New Guinea; became first lieutenant.

MEMBER: American Nurses Association, National League for Nursing, American Public Health Association, American Association of University Professors, Society for the Study of Social Problems, Association for Humanistic Psychology, Academy of Religion and Mental Health, American Association for the Advancement of Science, Sigma Theta Tau. *Awards, honors:* National Institute of Mental Health grant to study adjustment after mastectomy, 1961-63; National Institutes of Health grant to study hospital personnel, nursing care, and dying patients, 1962-67; professional achievement award from Alumni Association of University of California, Los Angeles, 1972; U.S. Department of Health, Education, and Welfare grant, 1973—; National Institutes of Health grant, 1973—.

WRITINGS—Under name Jeanne Quint: (Contributor) *Report of Conference on Terminal Illness and Impending Death Among the Aged,* Division of Chronic Diseases, U.S. Department of Health, Education, and Welfare, 1966; *The Nurse and the Dying Patient,* Macmillan, 1967; (contributor) Margaret Harrop and Vera M. Rubenstein, editors, *Nursing Clinics of North America,* Volume II, Saunders, 1967.

Under name Jeanne Quint Benoliel: (Contributor) Marjorie Batey, editor, *Communicating Nursing Research: Methodological Issues in Research,* Western Interstate Commission for Higher Education, 1970; (contributor) Bernard Schoenberg and others, editors, *Psychosocial Aspects of Terminal Care.* Columbia University Press, 1972; (contributor) Eliot Freidson and Judith Lorber, editors, *Medical Men and Their Work,* Aldine-Atherton, 1972; (contributor) L. H. Schwartz and J. L. Schwartz, editors, *The Psychodynamics of Patient Care,* Prentice-Hall, 1972; (contributor) Loretta Bermosk and Raymond Corsini, editors, *Critical Incidents in Nursing,* Saunders, 1973; (contributor) Richard H. Davis and Margaret Neiswender, editors, *Dealing with Death,* Ethel Percy Andrus Gerontology Center, University of Southern California, 1973; (contributor) Batey, editor, *Communicating Nursing Research: Collaboration and Competition,* Volume VI, Western Interstate Commission for Higher Education, 1973; (contributor) Stanley B. Troup, editor, *The Patient, Death, and the Family,* Scribner, in press; (contributor) Phyllis Verhonick, editor, *Research in Nursing Based on Psychosocial Data,* Little, Brown, in press; (contributor) Henry O. Heinemann and others, editors, *Medical Care of the Dying Patient,* Health Sciences Publishing, in press; (contributor) Jan Howard and Anselm Strauss, editors, *Humanizing Health Care,* Wiley, in press; (contributor) Gladys Scipien and others, editors, *The Child in the Family: Comprehensive Nursing Care,* McGraw, in press; (contributor) Ann Clark and Dyanne Affonso, editors, *Childbearing and the Nurse,* F. A. Davis, in press.

Contributor of about forty articles and reviews to health care journals, including *Imprint, Nursing Forum, Journal of Thanatology, Patient Care-Management Concepts, International Journal of Nursing Studies,* and *Nursing Research.* Member of editorial board of *Journal of Thanatology* and *Omega,* both 1970—; manuscript reviewer for *Nursing Research,* 1970—.

WORK IN PROGRESS: Research on dying in teaching hospitals, a care-cure problem.

SIDELIGHTS: Mrs. Benoliel writes: "Living close to the reality of death and dying gives zest to living. Facing up to the reality that dignity in living is the essence of dignity in dying was an important learning for me. It didn't happen suddenly but over time and by means of some difficult life experiences. The relationship between caring and human dignity underlies much of my writing."

* * *

BENSON, Lyman (David) 1909-

PERSONAL: Born May 4, 1909, in Kelseyville, Calif.; son of Charles A. (a horticulturist) and Cora (a teacher; maiden name, West) Benson; married Evelyn Linderholm, August 16, 1931; children: David, Robert Leland. *Education:* Stanford University, A.B., 1930, M.A., 1931, Ph.D., 1939. *Religion:* Protestant. *Home:* 1430 Via Zurita, Claremont, Calif. 91711. *Office:* Department of Botany, Pomona College, Claremont, Calif. 91711.

CAREER: Bakersfield Junior College (now Bakersfield College), Bakersfield, Calif., instructor in botany and zoology, 1931-38; University of Arizona, Tucson, instructor, 1938-40, assistant professor of botany, 1940-44, assistant botanist at Agricultural Experiment Station, 1938-44; Pomona College, Claremont, Calif., associate professor, 1944-49, professor of botany, 1949—, chairman of department, 1944-73, director of herbarium, 1944—; Claremont Graduate School, Claremont, Calif., associate professor, 1944-49, professor, 1949—.

MEMBER: International Organization for Succulent Plant Study, International Association for Plant Taxonomy, American Association for the Advancement of Science (fellow; member of council, 1948), Cactus and Succulent Society of America (fellow; president, 1956, 1957), American Society of Plant Taxonomists (president, 1960), Society for the Study of Evolution, American Institute of Biological Sciences, American Fern Society, Botanical Society of America (president of Pacific section, 1947), Association for Tropical Biology, Western Society of Naturalists (president, 1955), California Academy of Sciences (fellow), Southern California Academy of Sciences (fellow), Southern California Botanists (president, 1949-50), Torrey Botanical Club, Phi Beta Kappa, Sigma Xi. *Awards, honors:* Greater Linnaeus Medal from Swedish Royal Academy of Sciences, 1952; National Science Foundation grants, 1956-59, 1959-64, 1965-67.

WRITINGS: The Cacti of Arizona, University of Arizona, 1940, 3rd edition, University of Arizona Press, 1969; *A Manual of Southwestern Desert Trees and Shrubs,* University of Arizona, 1945, 2nd edition published as *The Trees and Shrubs of the Southwestern Deserts,* University of Arizona Press, 1954; *Plant Classification,* Heath, 1957; *Plant Taxonomy, Methods and Principles,* Ronald, 1962; *The Native Cacti of California,* Stanford University Press, 1969; *The Cacti of the United States and Canada,* Stanford University Press, in press.

Contributor: L. R. Abrams, editor, *Illustrated Flora of the Pacific States,* Volume II, Stanford University Press, 1944; Thomas H. Kearney and Robert H. Peebles, editors, *Arizona Flora,* University of California Press, 1951, 2nd edition, 1960; C. L. Lundell, editor, *Flora of Texas,* Texas Research Foundation, 1970; Donovan S. Correll and Marshall C. Johnston, editors, *Manual of the Vascular Plants of Texas,* Texas Research Foundation, 1970.

Contributor to reference works, including *Encyclopaedia Britannica* and *Encyclopedia Americana,* and to *Proceedings of the California Academy of Sciences.* Also contributor of about forty articles to professional journals, including *American Midland Naturalist, American Journal of Botany, Cactus and Succulent Journal, Annals of the Missouri Botanical Garden,* and *Bulletin of the Torrey Botanical Club.*

WORK IN PROGRESS: Evolution of the North American Floras, Interpreted in the Light of Geological History; Evolution of the Plant Kingdom, a general textbook; preparing a third edition of *Manual of Southwestern Desert Trees and Shrubs,* with Robert A. Darrow, to be published as *The Trees and Shrubs of the Southwestern Deserts,* by University of Arizona Press.

BIOGRAPHICAL/CRITICAL SOURCES: Madrono (journal of California Botanical Society), Volume 22.

* * *

BENSON, Mary 1919-

PERSONAL: Born December 9, 1919, in Pretoria, South Africa; daughter of Cyril (an administrator) and Lucy (Stubbs) Benson. *Education:* Attended Pretoria High School for Girls, 1932-37. *Home:* 34 Langford Ct., Abbey Rd., London N.W.8, England. *Agent:* Paul R. Reynolds, Inc., 599 Fifth Ave., New York, N.Y. 10017.

CAREER: Secretary with British High Commission in Pretoria, South Africa, 1940-41, and David Lean (film director), London, England, 1947-49; Africa Bureau, London, England, co-founder and secretary, 1950-57 (lobbied in England and at United Nations on South African issues during that period and later); writer. Active in African Development Trust and National Campaign for the Abolition of Capital Punishment. *Military service:* South African Women's Army, 1941-45; served in Cairo, Algiers, Italy, Greece, and Austria; became captain.

WRITINGS: *Tshekedi Khama,* Verry, 1960; *Chief Albert Lutuli of South Africa,* Oxford University Press, 1963; *The African Patriots,* Faber, 1963, Encyclopaedia Britannica, 1964, rewritten and enlarged edition published as *South Africa: The Struggle for a Birthright,* Penguin, 1966, Funk, 1969; (contributor) Nadine Gordimer, editor, *South African Writing Today,* Penguin, 1967; *At the Still Point* (novel), Gambit, 1970; (contributor) R. L. Markovitz, editor, *African Politics and Society,* Free Press, 1970.

Radio plays, produced by British Broadcasting Corp.: "At the Still Point" (adaptation of her novel), 1972; "Nelson Mandela and the Rivona Trial," 1972; "The Hour Is Getting Late," 1973; "The Castaways" (adaptation of novel by Sheila Fugard), 1974.

Contributor to *London Magazine, Times, Guardian, Observer, New Statesman, Spectator, New York Times,* and other publications.

WORK IN PROGRESS: Her autobiography; a documentary about Robben Island; radio plays.

SIDELIGHTS: Mary Benson says that she had the "normal prejudiced attitude of white South Africans" until she read Paton's *Cry the Beloved Country* in 1948. She has since studied, lobbied, written, and lectured about her country, testifying before United Nations committees on apartheid and human rights between 1963 and 1970, and before the United States Congressional Committee on South Africa in 1966. While reporting on political trials in South Africa she was put under house arrest and banned from all writing, finally leaving South Africa in March 1966.

* * *

BENT, Alan Edward 1939-

PERSONAL: Born June 22, 1939, in Shanghai, China; son of Walter J. and Tamara (Rocklin) Bent; separated from wife; children: Ronald Geoffrey. *Education:* San Francisco State College (now University), B.S., 1963; University of Southern California, M.A., 1968; Claremont Graduate School, M.A., 1970, Ph.D., 1971. *Home:* 1856 Vinton Ave., Memphis, Tenn. 38104. *Office:* Department of Political Science, Memphis State University, Memphis, Tenn. 38152.

CAREER: Chapman College, Orange, Calif., instructor in political science, 1969; Claremont Graduate School, Claremont, Calif., assistant director of municipal systems research, 1970-71; Memphis State University, Memphis, Tenn., assistant professor of political science, 1971—, associate director of Institute of Governmental Studies and Research, 1971—, director of Graduate Program in Public Administration, 1971—. *Military service:* U.S. Air Force, Intelligence, 1964-69; became captain. *Member:* American Political Science Association, American Society for Public Administration, Pi Sigma Alpha.

WRITINGS: *Escape from Anarchy: A Strategy for Urban Survival,* Memphis State University Press, 1972; *Behind the Blue Curtain: The Politics of Law Enforcement,* Heath, 1974. Writer of research reports. Contributor to *National Civic Review* and *Comparative Administration Group Newsletter.* Editor of *Public Affairs Forum.*

WORK IN PROGRESS: A textbook on police-community relations for Canfield Press; a book, *Industrial Relations in the Public Sector: Conflict, Power, and Politics in Urban Communities;* a reader, *Problems in Urban Administration,* with Ralph A. Rossum.

* * *

BENTON, Kenneth (Carter) 1909-

PERSONAL: Born March 4, 1909, in Sutton Coldfield, England; son of William Alfred (an engineer) and Amy Adeline (Kirton) Benton; married Peggie Pollock Lambert (an author), March 2, 1938; children: Timothy John; Alexander Pollock Lambert, Charles Mark Lambert, both stepsons. *Education:* University of London, B.A., 1936; also studied languages at University of Florence and University of Vienna. *Religion:* Church of England. *Home:* Vine House, Appledore, Ashford, Kent, England.

CAREER: British Foreign Service, London, England, 1937-68, assistant passport control officer at British Legation in Vienna, 1937-38, vice-consul in Riga, Latvia, 1938-40, third secretary of British Embassy in Madrid, 1941-42, second secretary, 1942-43, second secretary of British Embassy in Rome, 1944-46, first secretary, 1946-48, foreign office staff, 1948-50, first secretary of British Embassy in Rome, 1950-53; first secretary of British Embassy in Madrid, 1953-56, foreign office staff, 1956-62, first secretary and consul of British Embassy in Lima, Peru, 1962-63, foreign office staff, 1964-66, counsellor of British Embassy in Rio de Janeiro, 1966-68.

MEMBER: Author's Society, Crime Writers Association (vice-chairman, 1973-74; chairman, 1974-75), Detection Club, National Book League, Travellers' Club (member of committee, 1973—). *Awards, honors:* Named Companion of the Order of St. Michael and St. George (CMG), 1966.

WRITINGS: *Twenty-Fourth Level,* Dodd, 1969; *Sole Agent,* Collins, 1970, Walker & Co., 1974; *Spy in Chancery,* Collins, 1972, Walker & Co., 1973; *Craig and the Jaguar,* Macmillan (London), 1973, Walker & Co., 1974; *Craig and the Tunisian Tangle,* Macmillan (London), 1974, Walker & Co., in press; *Death on the Appian Way,* Chatto & Windus, 1974.

Contributor to *Peru's Revolution from Above,* Conflict Studies (of the Institute for the Study of Conflict), 1969.

WORK IN PROGRESS: A Craig adventure story, based in the area of the Arabian Gulf; research on subversive movements, and on political movements in southern Africa.

AVOCATIONAL INTERESTS: Carpentry.

BENTON, Peggie 1906- (Shifty Burke)

PERSONAL: Born October 19, 1906, in Valetta, Malta; daughter of Charles Edward (an army officer) and Winifred (Jay) Pollock; married Hubert Steel Lambert, February 11, 1926 (divorced March 20, 1931); married Kenneth Carter Benton (a writer), March 2, 1938; children: (first marriage) Alexander Pollock, Charles Mark; (second marriage) Timothy John. *Education:* Ecole Professionelle, Neuchatel, diploma, 1925. *Politics:* "Liberal with a small 'L'." *Religion:* Church of England. *Home:* Vine House, Appledore, Ashford, Kent TN26 2BU, England.

CAREER: British Legation, Vienna, Austria, personal assistant and press reader, 1936-38, British Consulate, Riga, Latvia, personal assistant, 1939-40, British Embassy, Madrid, Spain, research assistant, 1941-43, British Embassy, Rome, Italy, research assistant, 1944-48; writer. *Member:* Institute of Linguists (fellow), Society of Authors, National Book League. *Awards, honors:* Darmstadt Gastronomic Fair Bronze Medal, 1964, for *Meat at Any Price;* Frankfurt Book Fair Bronze Medal, 1966, for *Fish for All Seasons.*

WRITINGS: (Translator) Edouard Alexandre Pozerski, (under pseudonym Edouard de Pomiane), *Cooking in Ten Minutes,* Bruno Cassirer, 1948, 3rd edition, Faber, 1967; (self-illustrated) *Finnish Food for Your Table,* Bruno Cassirer, 1960; (editor and translator) Pozerski, (under pseudonym Edouard de Pomiane), *Cooking with Pomiane,* Bruno Cassirer, 1962, Roy, 1963; (adapter and illustrator) Ninette Lyon, *Meat at Any Price,* Faber, 1963; (adapter) Lyon, *Chicken & Game,* Faber, 1964; (with Lyon) *Fish for All Seasons,* Faber, 1966; (under pseudonym Shifty Burke) *Peterman,* Arthur Barker, 1966; (with Lyon) *Eggs, Cheese & Milk,* Faber, 1971; *One Man Against the Drylands,* Collins-Harvill, 1972.

SIDELIGHTS: Mrs. Benton speaks French, German, Italian, Portuguese, Spanish.

* * *

BERGER, Robert W(illiam) 1936-

PERSONAL: Born February 24, 1936, in New York, N.Y.; son of Kornel (a businessman) and Estelle (Alpert) Berger; married Susan Robbins (a psychologist), June 20, 1959; children: Valerie Sabrina, Pamela Stacey. *Education:* Columbia University, B.S., 1959; Harvard University, M.A., 1960, Ph.D., 1965. *Home:* 155 Sewall Ave., Brookline, Mass. 02146. *Office:* Department of Fine Arts, Brandeis University, Waltham, Mass. 02154.

CAREER: Brandeis University, Waltham, Mass., assistant professor, 1965-71, associate professor of fine arts, 1971—.

WRITINGS: *Antoine Le Pautre,* New York University Press, 1969.

* * *

BERGMAN, Floyd L(awrence) 1927-

PERSONAL: Born June 20, 1927, in Duluth, Minn.; son of Carl August (a laborer) and Ann J. (Larson) Bergman; married Virginia Bort, July 3, 1959; children: Sandra Jean Bergman McLaughlin, Carol Ann, Elizabeth Ann. *Education:* Attended University of Idaho, 1945-46; University of Minnesota, B.S., 1951, M.A., 1961; Wayne State University, Ed.D., 1966. *Home:* 2625 Antietam Ct., Ann Arbor, Mich. 48105. *Office:* 1042 School of Education, University of Michigan, Ann Arbor, Mich. 48104.

CAREER: English and social studies teacher in Floodwood, Minn., 1951-55, and Duluth, Minn., 1956-62; Wayne State University, Detroit, Mich., instructor in education, 1962-66; University of Michigan, Ann Arbor, instructor in education, 1966—. Organizer and charter member of volunteer fire department in Rice Lake Township, Minn. *Military service:* U.S. Naval Reserve, 1945-46. *Member:* National Council of Teachers of English, Michigan Council of Teachers of English (executive secretary, 1969—), University of Minnesota Alumni Association, Wayne State University Alumni Association, Phi Delta Kappa.

WRITINGS: (With William Hoth and Ray Budde) *Basic Composition Laboratory: Series III,* Science Research Associates, 1965; (with Paul O'Dea and Robert Lumsden) *Developing Ideas: An Individualized Writing Sequence,* Science Research Associates, 1966; *Reading: Who, What, When, Where, Why and How,* Campus Publishers, 1969; *Occupation: English Teacher—A Methods Laboratory Manual,* Campus Publishers, 1969; (with Glenn Knudsvig) *the Voluntutor's Handbook,* School of Education, University of Michigan, 1971; (with Mary Bradford, Harold Fine, and Hoth) *From Auditing to Editing* (writing manual), U.S. Government Printing Office, 1974; *Manuscript Diagnosis: The Text-Ray,* Campus Publishers, 1974; *The English Teacher's Ideabook: A Thousand One Teaching Tips,* Allyn & Bacon, in press.

Contributor of articles and cartoons to academic journals, including *English Journal, English Education, College Composition and Communication,* and *Journal of Reading.* Editor of *Michigan English Teacher,* 1968-69.

WORK IN PROGRESS: *Report Writing Exercises; Reading Handbook for Teachers and Tutors,* with Jacqueline Tilles and Rowena Wilhelm; editing *Teaching Each Other to Read: Programs and Procedures,* with Aaron Stander; *Looking at Visuals; Patty's Daddy's Pollution Solution,* for children.

SIDELIGHTS: Bergman writes: "My current literary thrust is to provide some practical books for teaching English, reading, and composition. I am particularly interested in expanding and refining an objective manuscript evaluation approach called Text-Ray. Most writers in education, government, and industry could improve their messages by recalling a few rhetorical principles. My approach forces writers to place key words in simple subject, verb, and complement positions, rather than in modifying phrases and clauses—a common 'doublespeak' approach." *Avocational interests:* Reading, cartooning.

* * *

BERLYE, Milton K. 1915-

PERSONAL: Born November 2, 1915, in Gloversville, N.Y.; son of Zanwell and Celia (Klauser) Berlye; married Ruth Gold, January 25, 1942; children: Jay Lynn, Sharon Kay. *Education:* State University of New York College at Oswego, B.S., 1940; New York University, M.A., 1947. *Home:* 36 York Ave., Monticello, N.Y. 12701.

CAREER: Monticello Central School, Monticello, N.Y., teacher and administrator, 1942—. Consultant to New York State Education Department. *Member:* National Education Association, American Industrial Arts Association, American Vocational Association, New York State Teachers Association, Monticello Teachers Association. *Awards, honors:* Winner of three Holy Rosary Dramatic Guild one-act play contests, Niagara Falls, N.Y.

WRITINGS: The Encyclopedia of Working with Glass, Oceana, 1968; *Selling Your Art Work: A Marketing Guide for Fine and Commercial Artists,* A. S. Barnes, 1973. Contributor to *New York State Education, School Shop, Industrial Arts and Vocational Education,* and *Camp Tips.* Author of fifteen radio stories produced on shows such as "Grand Central Station," "Stars Over Hollywood," and "Telephone Hour," as well as "soap opera" material and stories for television movies.

WORK IN PROGRESS: Your Career in the World of Work; converting an original story into a musical for a television special; a book, *The Marriage Mess.*

SIDELIGHTS: Berlye has U.S. patents on a bookbinding machine and a transporting truck.

* * *

BERMAN, Simeon M(oses) 1935-

PERSONAL: Born March 28, 1935, in Rochester, N.Y.; son of Jeremiah J. (a rabbi) and Rose (a teacher; maiden name, Rappaport) Berman; married Iona T. Grossman, December 28, 1955; children: Jeremy, Jessica, Daniel, Zachary, Migdana, Tehilah. *Education:* City College (now City College of the City University of New York), B.A., 1956; Columbia University, M.A., 1958, Ph.D., 1961. *Religion:* Jewish. *Home:* 334 Marlborough Rd., Brooklyn, N.Y. 11226. *Office:* Department of Mathematics, New York University, 251 Mercer St., New York, N.Y. 10012.

CAREER: City College (now City College of the City University of New York), New York, N.Y., lecturer in mathematics, 1957-60; Columbia University, New York, N.Y., assistant professor of mathematical statistics, 1961-65; New York University, New York, N.Y., associate professor of mathematics, 1965—. *Member:* American Mathematical Society, Institute of Mathematical Statistics, Phi Beta Kappa. *Awards, honors:* National Science Foundation grants, 1966-74, for research in mathematics.

WRITINGS: The Elements of Probability, Addison-Wesley, 1969; *Mathematical Statistics,* Intext, 1971; *Calculus for the Nonphysical Sciences,* Holt, 1974. Contributor of more than forty articles to professional mathematical journals.

WORK IN PROGRESS: Mathematics texts for college students on an elementary level.

SIDELIGHTS: Berman told *CA:* "Mathematics . . . is difficult for students who are not particularly skilled in it. I write for such students. I attempt to make the subject understandable by means of real-life examples, illustrative artwork, and conversational unpretentious writing."

* * *

BERNER, Carl Walter 1902-

PERSONAL: Born August 19, 1902; son of August George and Clara (Boekenhauer) Berner; married Myrtle Harvey, June 17, 1926; children: James, Robert, Carl, Jr. *Education:* Attended Concordia Junior College, Oakland, Calif., Concordia Seminary, St. Louis, 1922-25, and University of Southern California, 1927-34. *Home:* 5332 Bahia Blanca, Laguna Hills, Calif. 92653.

CAREER: Ordained minister of the Lutheran Church; minister of Faith Lutheran Church, Los Angeles, Calif., 1925-68. Special lecturer and faculty member at University of Southern California, Los Angeles, 1939-54. *Award, honors:* D.D. from Concordia Seminary, 1954.

WRITINGS: Spiritual Power for Your Congregation, Concordia, 1956; *Power of Pure Stewardship,* Concordia, 1970; *Why Me, Lord?,* Augsburg, 1973.

* * *

BERNSTEIN, Philip S(idney) 1901-

PERSONAL: Born June 29, 1901, in Rochester, N.Y.; son of Abraham (a manufacturer of trousers) and Sarah (Steinberg) Bernstein; married Sophy Rubin; children: Jeremy, Stephen, Alice (Mrs. Fred Perkins). *Education:* Syracuse University, A.B., 1921; Jewish Institute of Religion, M.H.L. and Rabbi, 1926; also studied at Columbia University, Cambridge University, and Hebrew University (Jerusalem). *Politics:* Liberal Democrat. *Home:* Grosvenor-East Apartments, East Ave., Rochester, N.Y. 14610. *Office:* Temple B'rith Kodesh, 2131 Elmwood Ave., Rochester, N.Y. 14618.

CAREER: Congregation B'rith Kodesh, Rochester, N.Y., rabbi, 1926-73, rabbi emeritus, 1973—. Executive director of committee on Army and Navy religious activities for National Jewish Welfare Board (directed entire Jewish religious program for armed forces), 1942-46, adviser to theater commanders in Germany and Austria, 1946-47. President of Central Conference of American Rabbis, 1950-52; former president of Rochester City Planning and Housing Council; member of Monroe County Human Relations Commission; member of board of directors of American Friends of Hebrew University. *Member:* American-Israel Public Affairs Committee (honorary member), National Rabbinic Organization for Rehabilitation Through Training Committee (honorary chairman), Rochester City Club (past president).

WRITINGS: What the Jews Believe, Farrar, Straus, 1950; *Rabbis at War,* American Jewish Historical Society, 1971. Contributor to *Life, Harper's, Nation, New Republic,* and various Jewish publications.

WORK IN PROGRESS: An autobiography.

SIDELIGHTS: During World War Two, Bernstein served as adviser on Jewish affairs to U.S. Army commanders in Europe. He was in personal contact with all the Jewish displaced persons installations in Germany and Austria. He also testified before the United Nations Special Committee on Palestine, and in the U.S. Congress.

* * *

BERRINGTON, Hugh B(ayard) 1928-

PERSONAL: Born December 12, 1928, in Surbiton, Surrey, England; son of William Majilton (an administrative assistant) and Constance (Smith) Berrington; married Catherine Llewellyn Smith, August 9, 1965; children: Andrew William, Lucy Margaret, Sarah Constance. *Education:* Kingston Technical College, B.Sc.Econ., 1954; Nuffield College, Oxford, graduate study, 1954-56. *Politics:* "originally Left, moving Right." *Religion:* Church of England. *Home:* 4 Fenwick Ter., Newcastle upon Tyne NE2 2JQ, England. *Office:* Department of Politics, University of Newcastle, Newcastle upon Tyne NE1 7RU, England.

CAREER: Barclays Bank Ltd., Merton Park, England, junior bank clerk, 1944-47; Surrey County Council, junior clerk in Divisional Health Office at Epsom, 1949-52, clerk in Education Department at Kingston upon Thames, 1952-53, administrative assistant in Divisional Health Office at Wimbledon, 1953-54; University of Keele, Keele, Staffordshire, England, assistant lecturer, 1956-59, lecturer in politics, 1959-65; University of Newcastle, Newcastle upon Tyne, England, reader, 1965-70, professor of politics, 1970—. *Military service:* Royal Air Force, 1947-49. *Member:* Political Studies Association.

WRITINGS: (With S. E. Finer and D. J. Bartholomew) *Backbench Opinion in the House of Commons: 1955-1959,* Pergamon, 1961; *How Nations Are Governed,* Pitman, 1964; *Backbench Opinion in the House of Commons: 1945-1955,* Pergamon, 1973, Contributor to scholarly journals, including *Political Quarterly, Journal of the Royal Statistical Society,* and *International Social Science Journal.*

WORK IN PROGRESS: Political Psychology: Backbench Factions in the House of Commons; research on party discipline in Parliament in the late nineteenth century.

* * *

BERTON, Ralph 1910-

PERSONAL: Born December 24, 1910, in Danville, Ill.; son of Maurice (a violinist) and Ida (a detective; maiden name, Glueck) Berton; married Shirley Maxwell; married Ann Aston Reynolds; married Sylvia Kingsley; married Joan March; married Eleanore Pekarski; married Mary-Claire Parrish; married Natalie Bowen; married Phyllis Hochhauser; married Audrey Marcus; children: (fifth marriage) Barbara (Mrs. Edwin Guerard); (eighth marriage) John, Thomas. *Education:* Attended school in Chicago and New York City. *Religion:* Atheist. *Residence:* Elizabeth, N.J.

CAREER: Has worked variously as a French tutor, artist, tennis professional, art teacher, boxer, singing waiter, bootlegger, truck driver, salesman, actor, musician, advertising copywriter, disc jockey, radio and screenwriter, editor, and free-lance writer; as an artist, has had one-man shows in New York City and Los Angeles, and group shows; has taught jazz and sociology courses at Cooper Union, Bloomfield College, Middlesex Community College, and New School for Social Research. *Wartime service:* Wrote, directed, and produced over thirty-five military instruction films, 1941-47; was civilian with officer status. *Member:* Authors Guild, Dramatists Guild of Authors League. *Awards, honors:* Recipient of best short comedy award from Film Guild Institute, 1963, for film, "The Triumph of Lester Snapwell."

WRITINGS: Remembering Bix: A Memoir of the Jazz Age, Harper, 1974; *Jewel City Inn* (novel), Harper, in press.

Plays: "Cassandra Kelly," 1937; "The Happy Marriage," 1938; "Two for Tonight," 1939; (librettist) "La Boheme Greenwich Village," 1962.

Contributor to *Harper's, Cosmopolitan, Town & Country, High Fidelity, Down Beat, FM, Jazz Review, Jazz Quarterly, World, Jazz-Hot* (Paris), *Melody Maker* (London), *Jazz Journal* (London), *Overlook.*

Classical music editor, *Status,* 1965; executive editor, *Sounds & Fury,* 1965-66.

WORK IN PROGRESS: Two books on music for Macmillan.

SIDELIGHTS: Berton told *CA:* "Though raised in show business (I was onstage at 3), child of vaudeville family, playing drums professionally at 7, I also started writing early—first published at 11. . . . As I never wasted time in school, I was free to follow varied interests in early childhood: astronomy at 6, chemistry at 8, ham radio at 11. At 12 I had a bit part in a Ziegfeld show on Broadway ("Annie Dear" with Billy Burke) and a bit in a film with Hope Hampton and James Kirkwood."

* * *

BETANCOURT, Jeanne 1941-

PERSONAL: Born October 2, 1941, in Burlington, Vt.; daughter of Henry (a certified public accountant) and Beatrice (Mario) Granger; married Jeffrey Betancourt (a city planner), July 1, 1967; *children:* Nicole. *Education:* New York University, B.A. and M.A. *Home:* 144 St. John's Pl., Brooklyn, N.Y. 11217.

CAREER: Junior and senior high school teacher of English and film studies in Vermont and in New York City, 1963—. Member of reviewing committee of film division at Brooklyn Public Library. Member of preview committee for first International Film Festival, 1972.

WRITINGS: Women in Focus, Pflaum, 1974. Contributor to *Women In Film.*

WORK IN PROGRESS: A book on her years as a nun.

SIDELIGHTS: Jeanne Betancourt served as a Catholic sister for six years.

* * *

BETTELHEIM, Frederick A(braham) 1923-

PERSONAL: Born June 3, 1923, in Gyoer, Hungary; naturalized U.S. citizen in 1963; son of Anton (an interior decorator) and Elizabeth (a manager; maiden name, Gyarfas) Bettelheim; married Annabelle Ganz (an art historian), June 8, 1947; children: Adriel. *Education:* Cornell University, B.S., 1953; University of California, Davis, M.S., 1954, Ph.D., 1956. *Politics:* Independent. *Religion:* Jewish. *Home:* 450 Garden Blvd., Garden City, N.Y. 11530. *Office:* Department of Chemistry, Adelphi University, Garden City, N.Y. 11530.

CAREER: Adelphi University, Garden City, N.Y., assistant professor, 1957-60, associate professor, 1960-64, professor of chemistry, 1964—. Director of National Science Foundation Institute for high school chemistry teachers at Adelphi University. Visiting professor at University of Uppsala, 1965, Technion, 1965, and Weizmann Institute of Science, 1973. *Military service:* Israeli Defense Army, 1947-50; became lieutenant. *Member:* American Chemistry Society, American Physical Society, American Society of Biological Chemists, Association for Research in Vision and Ophthalmology, New York Academy of Science, Sigma Xi. *Awards, honors:* Lalor award, 1958, for work on mucopolysaccarides.

WRITINGS: Experimental Physical Chemistry, Saunders, 1971; (contributor) Arthur Veis, editor, *Biological Polyelectrolytes,* Dekker, 1970; (contributor) Ward Pigman and Derek Horton, editors, *The Carbohydrates,* Academic Press, 1970; (contributor) Harry R. Elden, editor, *The Skin,* Wiley, 1972. Contributor of more than ninety articles to scientific journals.

WORK IN PROGRESS: With C. R. Nash, *Experiments in Physical Chemistry,* publication by Saunders expected in 1975; research on the molecular organization in tissues such as the cornea, lens, and vitreous of the eye, and on the aging processes of connective tissues.

SIDELIGHTS: Bettelheim has travelled and lectured at

sixty universities in the United States, Europe, Japan and Israel. He speaks, writes, and reads Hungarian, Hebrew, German, French, and Italian. During World War II he worked in the anti-Nazi underground in Hungary. After the war he worked on the illegal immigration of Jews to Palestine.

* * *

BEURDELEY, Michel 1911-

PERSONAL: Born January 17, 1911, in Paris, France; son of Jean (a mayor) and Marcelle (Elluin) Beurdeley; married Cecile Cyprien-Fabre (a writer on art), March 10, 1941; children: Gladys, Jean-Michel. *Education:* Lycee Janson-de-Sailly a Paris, diploma, 1929. *Home:* 4 rue de l'Elysee, Paris 8, France.

CAREER: Expert in Oriental art, 1947—; official expert for court of appeals, arbitrator for commercial court, and appraiser for estate administration. President of Chambre Syndicale des Experts.

WRITINGS: Porcelaine de la compagnie des Indes, Office du Livre, 1962, translation by Diana Imber published as *Chinese Trade Porcelain,* Tuttle, 1962, 2nd edition, 1963 (published in England as *Porcelain of the East India Companies,* Barrie & Rockliff, 1962); *L'Amateur chinois des Han au vingtieme siecle,* Office du Livre, 1966, translation by Imber published as *The Chinese Collector through the Centuries: From the Han to the Twentieth Century,* Tuttle, 1966; (with others) *Jeux des nuages et de la pluie,* Bibliotheque des Arts, 1969, translation by Imber published as *Chinese Erotic Art,* Tuttle, 1969 (published in England as *The Clouds and the Rain: The Art of Love in China,* Hammond, 1969).

(With wife, Cecile Beurdeley) *Castiglione, peintre jesuite a la cour de Chine,* Bibliotheque des Arts, 1971, translation by Michael Bullock published as *Giuseppe Castiglione: A Jesuit Painter at the Court of the Chinese Emperors,* Tuttle, 1972; *Chant de l'Oreiller,* Bibliotheque des Arts, 1972; *Guide de la ceramique chinoise,* Office du Livre, 1974.

* * *

BEVIS, Em Olivia 1932-

PERSONAL: Born March 20, 1932, in Graceville, Fla.; daughter of James Edison (an educator) and Willie (Bullock) Bevis. *Education:* University of Florida, student, 1950-52; Emory University, B.A., 1955; University of Chicago, M.A., 1958. *Religion:* Jewish. *Office:* Department of Nursing, California State University, San Jose, Calif. 95114.

CAREER: Emory University Hospital, Atlanta, Ga., staff nurse, 1955-56; University of North Carolina, Chapel Hill, instructor in medical-surgical nursing, 1958-62; California State University at San Jose, 1962—, now professor of nursing. *Member:* American Nurses Association, Association for Better Health, California Nurses Association, California State Employees Association, Pi Lambda Theta, Sigma Theta Tau.

WRITINGS: (With Laura Mae Douglass) *Team Leadership in Action: Principles and Application to Staff Nursing Situations,* Mosby, 1970, revised edition published as *Nursing Leadership in Action: Principles and Application to Staff Situation,* 1974; (contributor) Harriet Moidel and others, editors, *Nursing Care of the Patient with Medical-Surgical Disorders,* McGraw, 1971; *Curriculum Building in Nursing: A Process,* Mosby, 1973; (with Gwen D. Marram and Shirley Schelagle) *Primary Nursing: A Model for Individualized Care,* Mosby, 1974.

* * *

BIBERMAN, Edward 1904-

PERSONAL: Born October 23, 1904, in Philadelphia, Pa.; son of Joseph (a manufacturer) and Eva (Goldich) Biberman; married Sonja Teresa Dahl (a public relations representative), December 5, 1938; children: Sonya (Mrs. Robert Schaal). *Education:* University of Pennsylvania, B.S.E., 1924; further study at Pennsylvania Academy of Fine Arts, 1924-26. *Politics:* Democrat. *Religion:* Jewish. *Home and office:* 3332 Deronda Dr., Los Angeles, Calif. 90028.

CAREER: Painter and printmaker; has had one-man exhibitions in Paris, Berlin, and major American cities; represented by permanent exhibitions in American museums. Has painted murals for the U.S. Government. Instructor at Los Angeles Art Center School, 1938-50; lecturer at University of California at Los Angeles, at San Diego, and at Irvine. Host-narrator of television series, "Dialogues in Art," 1967-68. *Member:* National Society of Mural Painters. *Awards, honors:* Twenty awards for art work, including Lambert Fund Purchase Prize, 1930; mural awards from U.S. Section of Fine Arts, 1937, 1939, 1940; Los Angeles County Museum Award, 1955; California State Fair Award, 1956; Tupperware Award Fellowship, 1957; Los Angeles City Annual Awards, 1960, 1963.

WRITINGS—Books of the author's paintings with text: *The Best Untold,* Blue Heron Press, 1954; *Time and Circumstance,* Ritchie, 1968. Author of twenty scripts for television series, "Dialogues in Art," 1967-68.

* * *

BIBESCO, Marthe 1888-1973

January 28, 1888—November 29, 1973; French author and novelist. Obituaries: *AB Bookman's Weekly,* January 14, 1974.

* * *

BICKERSTETH, Geoffrey Langdale 1884-1974

1884—March 29, 1974; British scholar, author, and editor. Obituaries: *AB Bookman's Weekly,* June 17, 1974.

* * *

BIEGEL, John E(dward) 1925-

PERSONAL: Surname is pronounced "beagle"; born November 19, 1925, in Eau Claire, Wis.; son of Otto R. and Charlotte (McGough) Biegel; married Geraldine Lawrence (a secretary), July 22, 1955; children: Steven, N. Dale, Kurt. *Education:* Montana State University, B.S.I.E., 1948; Stanford University, M.S., 1950; Syracuse University, Ph.D., 1972. *Home:* 4878 Candy Lane, Manlius, N.Y. 13104. *Office:* College of Engineering, Syracuse University, Syracuse, N.Y. 13210.

CAREER: University of Arkansas, Fayetteville, assistant professor of engineering, 1950-52; Ford Motor Co., Claycomo, Mo., engineer, 1952-53; Sandia Corp., Albuquerque, N.M., engineer, 1953-58; Syracuse University, Syracuse, N.Y., assistant professor, 1958-62, associate professor, 1962-73, professor of industrial engineering and operations research, 1973—. Member of Town of Pompey Environmental Council, 1972-73. *Military service:* U.S. Navy, 1944-46; served in Asiatic Theater. *Member:* American Society for Engineering Education, American Institute of Industrial Engineers, Institute of Management Sciences, Society of Manufacturing Engineers, Operations Research Society of America, Alpha Pi Mu. *Awards, honors:* National Science Foundation faculty fellow at University of California, Berkeley, 1964-65.

WRITINGS: Production Control: A Quantitative Approach, Prentice-Hall, 1963, 2nd edition, 1971; (contributor) H. B. Maynard, editor, *Industrial Engineering Handbook,* McGraw, 1971. Contributor to *Encyclopedia of Science and Technology,* and to professional journals. Member of editorial board of *Current Contents, Engineering & Technology,* 1969—.

* * *

BINGHAM, M(orley) P(aul) 1918-

PERSONAL: Born March 23, 1918, in Muskegon, Mich.; son of Boyd Henry (a photographer) and Laura (McWebb) Bingham; married Leona Molnar, April 15, 1945 (died, 1971); married Lois E. Hessel (an executive secretary), August 21, 1972; children: (first marriage) Christopher, Laura. *Education:* Western Michigan University, B.S., 1947; Wayne State University, graduate study, 1949-53; Colorado State University, M.E., 1951. *Politics:* Democrat. *Religion:* Presbyterian. *Home:* 24108 East River Rd., Grosse Ile, Mich. 48138. *Office:* Theodore Roosevelt High School, 540 Eureka Rd., Wyandotte, Mich. 48192.

CAREER: High school teacher of industrial arts and driver education in Wyandotte, Mich., 1947—, chairman of industrial arts department, 1955—. President, Board of Education, Heintzen School District, Southgate, Mich., 1956—. *Military service:* U.S. Army Air Forces, 1942-45; became staff sergeant; received European African Middle Eastern ribbon, Silver Star, and three Bronze Stars. *Member:* National Education Association, American Driver and Traffic Safety Education Association, American Legion, Michigan Education Association, Wyandotte Federation of Teachers (president, 1950-52).

WRITINGS: (Editor) *The Road to Better Driving,* Cambridge Book Co., 1963; *Safe Driving Is No Accident,* Cambridge Book Co., 1973. Contributor to journals.

AVOCATIONAL INTERESTS: Boating, gardening, traveling.

* * *

BIRMINGHAM, Stephen 1932-

PERSONAL: Born May 28, 1932, in Hartford, Conn.; son of Thomas J. (a lawyer) and Editha (Gardner) Birmingham; married Janet Tillson, January 5, 1953; children: Mark, Harriet, Carey. *Education:* Williams College, B.A. (with honors), 1953. *Politics:* Democrat. *Religion:* Episcopalian. *Home:* 158 Lafayette Circle, Cincinnati, Ohio 45220. *Agent:* Carol Brandt, Brandt & Brandt, 101 Park Ave., New York, N.Y. 10017.

CAREER: Wrote advertising copy for Gimbel's, New York, briefly in the early 1950's; Needham, Harper & Steers, Inc., New York, N.Y., advertising copywriter, 1953-67; writer and novelist, 1967—. *Military service:* U.S. Army, 1953-55. *Member:* New England Society of the City of New York, Phi Beta Kappa, Coffee House (New York).

WRITINGS—Novels: *Young Mr. Keefe,* Little, Brown, 1958; *Barbara Greer,* Little, Brown, 1959; *The Towers of Love,* Little Brown, 1961; *Those Harper Women,* McGraw, 1964; *Fast Start, Fast Finish,* New American Library, 1966.

Nonfiction: *"Our Crowd": The Great Jewish Families of New York,* Harper, 1967; *The Right People: A Portrait of the American Social Establishment* (collected essays; previously published in *Holiday*), Little, Brown, 1968; *The Grandees: America's Sephardic Elite,* Harper, 1971; *The Late John Marquand: A Biography,* Lippincott, 1972; *The Right Places,* Little, Brown, 1973; *Real Lace: America's Irish Rich,* Harper, 1973.

Short fiction: *Heart Troubles,* Harper, 1968.

Contributor of numerous articles and short stories to magazines, including *Holiday, McCall's, Ladies' Home Journal,* and *Saturday Evening Post.*

WORK IN PROGRESS: Three books: "an unauthorized biography of the Duchess of Windsor," a study of the Black elite, and a study of the Hollywood establishment.

SIDELIGHTS: After publishing five novels, some of them best sellers, and for which Birmingham was frequently compared to F. Scott Fitzgerald, it was with *"Our Crowd"* and *The Right People* that Birmingham drew his most divided response, and began his nonfiction career as historian for the very rich. Writing on the high society of successful Jewish families—both Ashkenazic and Sephardic, on the WASP establishment, the Irish elite, and "The Right Places" to be, Birmingham's books have been described variously as "malicious storytelling, leavened by gossip," "harmless bunk," "fascinating reality," and almost all stops between.

Cleveland Amory comments that "underneath his apparent lightness, Mr. Birmingham is obviously in dead earnest about the snobbery of it all." That Birmingham is at the same time insider and outsider—"neither social critic nor propagandist," in one critic's words—is perhaps reflected in William F. Buckley's estimation of *The Right People:* "As it stands, Mr. Birmingham is both too unctuous and too impious; too admiring and too cynical. The book lacks an axis of true conviction. . . .[it is probable] that Mr. Birmingham is better as a raconteur than as a writer. His writing style," Buckley continues, "is better than merely serviceable. . . .he is witty and knows the journalistic imperative of briskness and anecdote."

No complete outsider to "Society" himself, Birmingham once recalled: "Sort of having gone to the 'right schools,' I was on the lists when I came to New York. . . .I know the rules and how to behave, but I wouldn't want to *live* that life; I can take it in small doses."

* * *

BIRNBAUM, Philip 1904-

PERSONAL: Born April 15, 1904, in Zarnowiec, Poland; son of Abraham Joel (a mechanic) and Roza (Rozen) Birnbaum. *Education:* Howard College, B.A., 1933; Dropsie College (now Dropsie University), Ph.D., 1939. *Home:* 41 West 86th St., New York, N.Y. 10024. *Office:* Hebrew Publishing Co., 79 Delancey St., New York, N.Y. 10002.

CAREER: Teacher; translator and editor of Jewish classical and liturgical literature. Director of Hebrew schools in Birmingham, Ala., and Camden, N.J.; directed Hebrew school in Wilmington, Del., 1943-63; currently editor and consultant, Hebrew Publishing Co., New York, N.Y.

Director of Associated Hebrew Schools and School for Advanced Jewish Studies. *Member:* National Council of Jewish Education, National Association of Professors of Hebrew, American Academy for Jewish Research, Zionist Organization of America, Histadruth Ivrith, Jewish Center, Farband.

WRITINGS: The Arabic Commentary of Yefet ben Ali, the Karaite, on the Book of Hosea, Dropsie College, 1942; (editor, translator, and annotator) *Maimonides' Mishneh Torah,* Hebrew Publishing, 1944; (translator and annotator) *The Daily Hebrew Prayer Book,* Hebrew Publishing, 1949; *Ethics of the Fathers,* Hebrew Publishing, 1949; (translator and annotator) *The High Holyday Prayer Book,* Hebrew Publishing, 1951; (translator and annotator) *Selihoth* (title means "Penitential Prayers"), Hebrew Publishing, 1952; (translator and annotator) *The Passover Haggadah,* Hebrew Publishing, 1953; (editor and translator) *A Treasury of Judaism* (anthology), Hebrew Publishing, 1957.

(Editor and Translator) *A Book of Jewish Concepts* (anthology), Hebrew Publishing, 1964; *Fluent Hebrew,* Hebrew Publishing, 1966; *Mahzor Ha-Shalem* (title means "Complete High Holyday Prayer Book"), Sephardic, 1967; *Hebrew-English Edition of Maimonides Code of Law and Ethics,* Hebrew Publishing, 1967; *Ha-Siddur Ha-Shalem* (title means "Complete Daily Prayer Book"), Sephardic, 1969; *Prayer Book for Three Festivals,* Hebrew Publishing, 1971; *Tefilloth Yisrael u-Musar ha-Yahaduth* (anthology; title means "Prayers and Ethics of Judaism"), Shulsinger, 1971; *Karaite Studies,* Herman Press, 1971; *Pletat Soferim* (collected essays; title means "Remnant of Sages"), Mossad Harav Kook, 1971; *Five Megilloth,* Hebrew Publishing, 1973. Also translated and annotated *Megillah Reading Service for Purim Evening* and *Kinnoth Reading Service for Fishah b'Av,* both 1973. Contributor to *Hadoar, Bitzaron,* and *Hatzofeh.*

* * *

BISHOP, George (Victor) 1924-

PERSONAL: Born August 28, 1924, in Montreal, Quebec, Canada; son of Victor Eugene (a railroad executive) and Zebe (Amirault) Bishop; married Patricia D. Chalut, August 14, 1948. *Education:* Sir George Williams University, B.A., 1946. *Politics:* Independent. *Religion:* No affiliation. *Residence:* Sherman Oaks, Calif. *Agent:* Vandeburg-Linkletter Associates, 8530 Wilshire Blvd., #403, Beverly Hills, Calif. 90211.

CAREER: CJAD-Radio, Montreal, Quebec, disc jockey, 1948-52; CBS (Canada), correspondent from Hollywood, Calif., 1952-58; free-lance writer, 1958—. President of Arkwood Publishers. *Member:* Writers Guild of America, West.

WRITINGS: Sex Offenders in Group Therapy, Sherbourne, 1965; *Execution: The Legal Ways of Death,* Sherbourne, 1965; *The Booze Reader,* Sherbourne, 1965; *Faith Healing: God Or Fraud?,* Sherbourne, 1967; *The Psychiatrist,* Dell, 1968; *Witness to Evil,* Dell, 1971; *Smut King,* Dell, 1974; (with Beverly Harrell) *An Orderly House,* Dell, in press; (with Richard Blackwell) *Naked Illusion: The Story of Mr. Blackwell,* Regnery, in press.

AVOCATIONAL INTERESTS: Baseball (plays second base with Hollywood No-Stars), prospecting for gold near Death Valley, watching small herds of wild burros.

BIOGRAPHICAL/CRITICAL SOURCES: Time, January 28, 1966.

BITTLINGER, Arnold 1928-

PERSONAL: Born June 13, 1928, in Edenkoben, Germany; son of Georg Friedrich (a parson) and Wilhelmine (Jung) Bittlinger; married Ilse Baumann, November 17, 1953; children: Sulamith, Andreas, Clemens, Stephan. *Education:* Studied at Universities of Mainz, Aix-en-Provence, Bethel, and Heidelberg; passed theological examination (B.D. equivalent), 1952; University of Geneva, Diploma Sc.Oec. (M.S.T. equivalent in theological ecumenical sciences), 1972; University of Birmingham, Ph.D. candidate, 1973—. *Home and office:* Schloss Craheim, D-8721 Wetzhausen, Germany.

CAREER: Lutheran clergyman, 1952—; general secretary of German Inter-School Christian Fellowship, Marburg/Lahn, Germany, 1952-55; pastor in Ludwigshafen am Rhine, 1956-59; national director of evangelism for Lutheran Church, Klingenmuenster/Pfalz, Germany, 1959-68; director of Ecumenical Academy Schloss Craheim, Wetzhausen, Germany, 1968—. Member of core team in dialogue between Vatican and Charismatic Movement, 1972—; fellow of Institute for Ecumenical and Cultural Research, Collegeville, Minn., 1972—. Member of board of directors of Student Mission in Germany, 1952-59, SCM-Postgraduate Fellowship, 1955-67, Marburger Kreis (Oxford Group), 1959-73, and Ecumenical Service, 1966—; director, Studiengemenschaft fuer Seelsorge, Bibelkunde und Mannschaftarbeit. *Member:* Verband Deutscher Schriftsteller, Lions Club. *Awards, honors:* Fellow in residence at Institute for Ecumenical and Cultural Research, 1971-72.

WRITINGS: Glossolalia: Wert und Problematik des Sprachenredens, Kuehne, 1967, 3rd edition, 1969; *Gnadengaben,* R. F. Edel, 1966, translation by Herbert Klassen published as *Gifts and Graces: A Commentary on I Corinthians 12-14,* Hodder & Stoughton, 1967, Eerdmans, 1968; *Die Ordnung der Dienste im Neuen Testament,* privately printed, 1966; *Treuhaender Gottes,* privately printed, 1967, translation by Clara K. Dyck published as *Gifts and Ministries,* Eerdmans, 1973; (editor) Carl Schneider, *Praktische Bibelkunde,* Die Rufer, 1968; *Im Kraftfeld des Heiligen Geistes,* R. F. Edel, 1968, 4th edition, 1972; *Das Abendmahl im Neuen Testament und in der fruehen Kirche,* Kuehne, 1969.

Ratschlaege fuer eine Gemeinde: Der Brief des Paulus an die Philipper, Kuehne, 1970, translation by Susan Wiesman published as *A Letter of Joy,* Bethany Fellowship, in press; (with Killian McDonnell) *The Baptism in the Holy Spirit as an Ecumenical Problem,* Charismatic Renewal Services, Inc., 1972; *Biblische Seelsorge,* Oekumenischer Schriftendienst, 1973; (contributor) Claus Heitmann and Heribert Muehlen, editors, *Erfahrung und Theologie des Heiligen Geistes,* Koesel-Verlag, 1974; (contributor) J. Elmo Agrimson, editor, *Gifts of the Spirit and the Body of Christ: Perspectives on the Charismatic Movement,* Augsburg, 1974.

Author of booklets and devotionals. Contributor to *Lexikon zur Bibel* and to *Studia Liturgica* and other journals, occasionally under a pseudonym.

WORK IN PROGRESS: A book on the ecumenical relevance of the Vatican-Pentecostal dialogue, tentatively titled *The Vatican and the Pentecostals,* completion expected in 1977; two other books, *Introduction to the Bible* and *Gifts and Sacraments.*

SIDELIGHTS: Bittlinger traveled throughout the United

States in 1962, sponsored by the Lutheran World Federation, to study evangelism, stewardship, and congregational life. That trip and his 1971-72 stay in Collegeville have been factors in his writings on the Charismatic Movement. Besides German, he speaks English and French, and reads Latin, Greek, and Hebrew.

BIOGRAPHICAL/CRITICAL SOURCES: Walter Hollenweger, *Pentecostals: The Charismatic Movement in the Churches,* Augsburg, 1972.

* * *

BIXLER, Norma 1905

PERSONAL: Born July 18, 1905, in Omaha, Neb.; daughter of Everett Ray (a plumbing contractor) and Augusta (Dorman) Hendricks; married Paul Bixler (a librarian consultant), October 6, 1926; children: Giles, Jolyon, Mark. *Education:* Ohio Wesleyan University, student, 1924-26. *Politics:* Independent. *Religion:* Ecumenical. *Home:* 1345 Rice Rd., Yellow Springs, Ohio 45387. *Office: Dayton Daily News,* Dayton, Ohio 45401.

CAREER: Cleveland News, Cleveland, Ohio, reporter and feature writer, 1926-29; *Cleveland Plain Dealer,* Cleveland, Ohio, reporter and feature writer, 1929-35; free-lance writer of magazine fiction and articles, 1935-58; Antioch College, Yellow Springs, Ohio, instructor, 1938-48, assistant professor of journalism, 1954-55, director of News Bureau, 1952-58; Burma Translation Society, Rangoon, Burma, instructor in journalism, 1959; *Cleveland Plain Dealer,* editorial columnist, 1965-67; *Dayton Daily News,* Dayton, Ohio, editorial columnist, 1967—, editorial writer, 1969—. *Member:* League of Women Voters.

WRITINGS: Burmese Journey, Antioch Press, 1967; *Burma: A Profile,* Praeger, 1971.

WORK IN PROGRESS: A book about men and women, tentatively titled *My Sisters, My Brothers.*

SIDELIGHTS: Mrs. Bixler told *CA:* "We lived two years in Rangoon, Burma, where my husband was on assignment. I learned to know and honor a country, a culture, and a religious tradition other than my own. No one can measure the profound change such an experience makes in an individual, certainly in a writer. . . . I'm convinced the peaceful viability of these [Southeast Asia] nations depends on their ability to drag their traditional villagers, kicking and screaming if need be, at least as far into the twentieth century as the life led in each capital." *Avocational interests:* Gardening.

* * *

BLACKBURN, Simon 1944-

PERSONAL: Born December 7, 1944; son of Cuthbert Walker and Edna (Walton) Blackburn; married Angela Margaret Bowles (a teacher); children: Gwendolen. *Education:* Trinity College, Cambridge, B.A., 1956; Churchill College, Cambridge, Ph.D., 1969. *Politics:* "Middle." *Religion:* None. *Home:* 219 Morrell Ave., Oxford, England. *Office:* Department of Philosophy, Pembroke College, Oxford University, Oxford, England.

CAREER: Pembroke College, Oxford University, Oxford, England, fellow in philosophy, 1969—.

WRITINGS: Reason and Prediction, Cambridge University Press, 1973.

WORK IN PROGRESS: Research in philosophical logic, the theory of meaning, and epistemology.

BLACKETT, Patrick (Maynard Stuart) 1897-1974

November 18, 1897—July 13, 1974; British nuclear physicist and Nobel laureate. Obituaries: *New York Times,* July 14, 1974; *Washington Post,* July 15, 1974.

* * *

BLAIR, Carvel Hall 1924-

PERSONAL: Born July 11, 1924, in Prince William County, Va.; son of Roswell Hadfield (a naval officer) and Julia (Hall) Blair; married Abbie Dora Ansel, July 15, 1944; children: Dennis, Sydney (Mrs. Michael Swanson), Julia (Mrs. Bruce Sanders). *Education:* U.S. Naval Academy, B.S., 1944; U.S. Naval Postgraduate School, M.S. (electrical engineering), 1953; Old Dominion University, M.S. (physical oceanography), 1973, doctoral studies, 1973—. *Religion:* Episcopalian. *Home:* 823 West 52nd St., Norfolk, Va. 23508.

CAREER: U.S. Navy, career officer, 1941-71, retiring as captain. Served in Vietnam. *Member:* U.S. Naval Institute, American Association for the Advancement of Science, Virginia Society of Ornithology. *Awards, honors*—Military: Legion of Merit, Air Medal, Dolphins (submariners).

WRITINGS: (With Willits Ansel) *A Guide to Fishing Boats and Their Gear,* Cornell Maritime, 1970; (with Ansel) *Chesapeake Bay: Notes and Sketches,* Cornell Maritime, 1972. Contributor to proceedings, and to *Journal of the Society of Naval Engineers, Journal of the Institute of Navigation,* and *Virginia Wildlife.*

WORK IN PROGRESS: Seamanship for Oceanographers, for Cornell Maritime; research on oceanography and coastal engineering.

* * *

BLAKE, Patricia 1933-

PERSONAL: Born November 29, 1933, in New York, N.Y.; daughter of Howard (a physician) and Lucille (a pianist; maiden name, Page) Blake. *Education:* Smith College, B.A. *Residence:* New York, N.Y. *Agent:* Candida Donadio, 111 West 57th St., New York, N.Y. *Office: Time,* Time & Life Building, Rockefeller Center, New York, N.Y. 10020.

CAREER: Life, New York, N.Y., correspondent, 1954-62, in Moscow, 1955, 1959, 1962; Columbia University, New York, N.Y., senior fellow at Russian Institute, 1962-65; free-lance writer, 1965-68; *Time,* New York, N.Y., contributing editor, 1968—.

WRITINGS: (Editor) Vladimir Mayakovsky, *The Bedbug and Selected Poetry,* World Publishing, 1960; (editor) *Dissonant Voices in Soviet Literature,* Pantheon, 1961; (editor) *Halfway to the Moon: New Writing from Russia,* Holt, 1963; (editor) *Antiworlds: The Poetry of Andrei Voznesensky,* Basic Books, 1966; *Solzhenitsyn: A Historical Biography,* Harcourt, in press.

WORK IN PROGRESS: Isaac Babel: A Biography, publication expected in 1976.

* * *

BLASSINGAME, John W(esley) 1940-

PERSONAL: Born March 23, 1940, in Covington, Ga. *Education:* Fort Valley State College, B.A., 1960; Howard

University, M.A., 1961; Yale University, M.Phil., 1968, Ph.D., 1971. *Office:* Department of History, Yale University, New Haven, Conn. 06520.

CAREER: Howard University, Washington, D.C., instructor in social science, 1961-65; Carnegie-Mellon University, Pittsburgh, Pa., associate of curriculum project in American history, 1965-70; Yale University, New Haven, Conn., lecturer, 1970-71, assistant professor, 1971-72, associate professor of history, 1972-73, professor, 1974—, acting chairman of Afro-American studies, 1971-72. Lecturer at University of Maryland and assistant editor of Booker T. Washington papers, 1968-69. Member of advisory board of Afro-American Bicentennial Corp., 1971—; member of board of directors of Centre Internationale de Recherches Africaines, 1971—.

MEMBER: American Historical Association (member of executive council, 1974), Organization of American Historians, Association for the Study of Afro-American Life and History (member of executive council, 1973—), Association of Behavioral and Social Sciences, Southern Historical Association, Phi Alpha Theta. *Awards, honors:* Fellowship from National Endowment for the Humanities, 1972-73.

WRITINGS: (Editor) *New Perspectives on Black Studies,* University of Illinois Press, 1971; (editor with David Fowler, Eugene Levy, and Jacqueline Haywood) *In Search of America,* Holt, 1972; (editor with Louis Harlan) *The Autobiographical Writings of Booker T. Washington,* University of Illinois Press, 1972; *The Slave Community,* Oxford University Press, 1972; *Black New Orleans: 1860-1880,* University of Chicago Press, 1973; (contributor) William H. Cartwright and Richard L. Watson, editors, *The Reinterpretation of American History,* National Council for the Social Studies, 1973.

Contributor to *Encyclopedia of Black America.* Contributor of more than twenty articles and reviews to history journals, including *Journal of Southern History, Black Scholar, Journal of Social History, Journal of Negro History, Caribbean Studies,* and *Journal of Negro Education.* Contributing editor of *Black Scholar,* 1971—; member of editorial boards of *Reviews in American History,* 1973—, and *Journal of Negro History,* 1973—. Editor of Frederick Douglass papers, jointly sponsored by National Endowment for the Humanities and National Historical Publications Commission, 1973—.

* * *

BLOCK, Allan (Forrest) 1923-

PERSONAL: Born October 6, 1923, in Oshkosh, Wis.; son of Isadore Myron (a salvager) and Valeria (Greenblatt) Block; married Jean Keller, December 23, 1947 (divorced, 1963); married Fleur Bullock (a photographer and painter), August 23, 1965 (divorced June, 1974); children: (first marriage) Mona F. Young, Aurora Valdina, Paul. *Education:* Attended University of Wisconsin, 1939-41, and Columbia University, 1945-46. *Address:* R.F.D., Francestown, N.H. 03043.

CAREER: Owner of sandal and leather-craft store in New York, N.Y., 1950-69, in Francestown, N.H., 1969—. *Wartime service:* American Field Service, ambulance driver, 1941-43. *Member:* New England Poetry Club. *Awards, honors:* Second prize for poetry from *Yankee,* 1970; Borestone Mountain poetry award, 1971, for "Through Old Farmhouse Windows."

WRITINGS—All poems: *The Swelling under the Waves,* Tigers Eye Publishing, 1948; *In Noah's Wake,* William Bauhan, 1972, 2nd edition, 1973. Represented in *Best Poems of 1970: Borestone Mountain Poetry Awards,* edited by Lionel Stevenson and others, Pacific Books, 1971. Contributor of poetry to journals.

WORK IN PROGRESS: Another book of poems.

* * *

BLODGETT, Richard 1940-

PERSONAL: Born August 24, 1940, in Bristol, Conn.; son of Harley E. and Doris (Dutton) Blodgett. *Education:* Middlebury College, B.A., 1962. *Home:* 29 Charlton St., New York, N.Y. 10014. *Agent:* A. L. Hart, Fox Chase Agency, 419 East 57th St., New York, N.Y. 10022.

CAREER: *Wall Street Journal,* New York, N.Y., writer 1962-66; *Business Week* (magazine), New York, N.Y., writer, 1966-68; Corporate Annual Reports, Inc., New York, N.Y., writer, 1968-70; free-lance writer, 1970—.

WRITINGS: *The New York Times Book of Money,* Quadrangle, 1974; *Investing in Art,* Peter H. Wyden, in press. Editor of *Corporate Communications Report,* 1969—.

* * *

BLOOM, John Porter 1924-

PERSONAL: Born December 30, 1924, in Albuquerque, N.M.; son of Lansing Bartlett and Maude (McFie) Bloom; married Louise Platt, 1954 (divorced, 1968); married Jo Tice (a college professor), July 30, 1968; children: (first marriage) Katherine Elizabeth, John Lansing, Susan Marie. *Education:* University of New Mexico, B.A., 1947; George Washington University, M.A., 1949; Emory University, Ph.D., 1956. *Politics:* Independent. *Religion:* Unitarian Universalist. *Home:* 1514 Chatham Colony Ct., Reston, Va. 22090. *Office:* Territorial Papers Office, National Archives, Washington, D.C. 20408.

CAREER: Brenau College, Gainesville, Ga., associate professor of history, 1952-56; University of Texas—El Paso, assistant professor of history, 1956-60; U.S. Department of Interior, Washington, D.C., editor and historian for National Park Service, 1960-64; National Archives, Washington, D.C., senior specialist for Western history, 1964—. *Military service:* U.S. Army Air Forces, 1943-45. *Member:* Organization of American Historians, American Association for State and Local History, Southern Historical Association, Western Literature Association, Western History Association (secretary-treasurer, 1960-66; vice-president, 1973; president, 1974).

WRITINGS: (Editor) *Territorial Papers of the United States,* Government Printing Office, Volume 27: *The Territory of Wisconsin, 1838-1848,* 1969, Volume 28: *The Territory of Wisconsin, 1838-1848,* in press; (editor) *The American Territorial System,* Ohio University Press, 1974. Book Review editor for *Arizona and the West,* 1960-63; member of editorial advisory board of *American West,* 1969—, and *Arizona and the West,* 1973—.

* * *

BLOSSOM, Frederick A. 1878(?)-1974

1878(?)—April 21, 1974; American editor, author, and educator. Obituaries: *New York Times,* April 23, 1974.

BLYTH, Alan 1929-

PERSONAL: Born July 27, 1929, in London, England; married Ursula Zumloh. *Education:* Pembroke College, Oxford, M.A., 1951. *Home:* 11 Boundary Rd., London NW8 0HE, England. *Agent:* A. M. Heath & Co., 40-2 William IV St., London WC2N 4DD, England.

CAREER: *Encyclopaedia Britannica,* London, England, sub-editor, 1951-53; Fabian Society, London, England, bookshop manager, 1953-56; feature editor and writer in London, England, 1956-63; *Times,* London, England, music critic, 1963—. Contributor to and interviewer for *Gramophone,* 1966—; associate editor of *Opera,* 1969—; music editor for *Encyclopaedia Britannica,* 1971-73. *Member:* Critics' Circle (chairman of music section, 1971-74).

WRITINGS: *The Enjoyment of Opera,* Oxford University Press, 1969; *Colin Davis: A Short Biography,* Ian Allan, 1972; *Janet Baker,* Ian Allan, 1973. Contributor to *Times* and *Musical Times.*

WORK IN PROGRESS: *Guide to Wagner's "Ring"* (tentative title), publication by David & Charles expected in 1976; a section on vocal music for a new edition of *New Companion to Music,* Gollancz, 1976; a contribution to the 6th edition of *Grove's Dictionary,* edited by Stanley Sadie, Macmillan, 1977.

AVOCATIONAL INTERESTS: History of the recorded voice, music of Verdi and Wagner, gardening, wine.

* * *

BLYTON, Carey 1932-

PERSONAL: Born March 14, 1932, in Beckenham, Kent, England; son of Hanly Harrison (a company director) and Florence Maud (Pullen) Blyton; married Patricia Eileen Joan Dennis, April 4, 1953 (divorced April 16, 1957); married Mary Josephine Mills, October 28, 1961; children: (second marriage) Matthew James, Daniel Carey. *Education:* Attended University College, London, 1950-51; Trinity College of Music, A.Mus. and L.T.C.L., 1955, F.T.C.L. and B.Mus., 1957; attended Royal Danish Academy of Music, 1957-58. *Politics:* None. *Religion:* Church of England. *Home:* 53 Cyclamen Rd., Swanley, Kent BR8 8HH, England. *Agent:* John Farquharson Ltd., 15 Red Lion Square, London WC1R 4QW, England.

CAREER: Mills Music Ltd., London, England, music editor, 1958-63; Trinity College of Music, London, England, professor of music, 1963-73; Faber Music Ltd., London, England, music editor, 1963—; Guildhall School of Music and Drama, London, England, professor of composition for films, television, and radio, 1972—; composer, author, lecturer. Music tutor, Workers' Educational Association, 1964—; music adviser, Eyre & Spottiswoode and Ballantyne publishers, 1965-67; member of executive committee, Dartford Rural District Arts Council, 1966-72; member of lecture panel, British Film Institute, 1974—. *Member:* Composers' Guild of Great Britain (member of executive committee, 1966-70), Society of Film & Television Arts, Mechanical-Copyright Protection Society, Performing Right Society. *Awards, honors:* Sir Winston Churchill Endowment Fund scholarship to Royal Danish Academy of Music, 1957.

WRITINGS: (Arranger of music) *The Faber Book of Nursery Songs,* Faber, 1968, published as *Every Child's Book of Nursery Songs,* Crown, 1969; *Bananas in Pyjamas: A Book of Nonsense Songs and Nonsense Poems for Children,* Faber, 1972, Transatlantic, 1973. Also author of musical compositions. Contributor to *Musical Times, Composer, Music in Education, Musical Opinion, Making Music, BMG, Argosy.*

WORK IN PROGRESS: *Dr. Shinfiddler's Musical Zoo,* a book of musical jokes, quodlibets, atrocious puns, and other musical nonsense.

SIDELIGHTS: Blyton told *CA:* "Although I am a professional composer, writing music for documentary films, television plays, television commercials, etc., I am intensely interested in writing words (though I haven't had much published in this way yet). My aunt, the children's writer, Enid Blyton, reckoned that 'the gift of the gab' was a Blyton trait, best put to some use like writing! Having changed horses in mid-stream (I was training to be a zoologist), I still remain deeply fascinated by natural history subjects (some of my best music scores are for natural history films), and I hope to try my hand eventually at television scripts involving pioneer naturalists and medical men, etc. I am also very involved with humour in all forms, and I hope to write more nonsense poetry in the future (which will be a lot easier than in the past)."

BIOGRAPHICAL/CRITICAL SOURCES: *Musical Times,* July, 1964; *Kent Life,* June, 1969; *Music and Musicians,* December, 1971; *Strumenti e Musica,* May, 1973; *Woodwind World,* June, 1973; *Music in Education,* March/April, 1974.

* * *

BODECKER, N. M. 1922-

PERSONAL: Born January 13, 1922, in Copenhagen, Denmark. *Education:* Attended Technical Society's Schools (Copenhagen), School of Architecture, 1939-41, School of Applied Arts, 1941-44; also attended Copenhagen School of Commerce, 1942-44. *Residence:* Hancock, N.H.

CAREER: Free-lance writer and illustrator in Copenhagen, Denmark, 1944-52, and New York, N.Y., 1952—. *Military service:* Royal Danish Artillery, 1945-47. *Awards, honors:* Citation from Society of Illustrators, 1965, for *David Copperfield; Miss Jaster's Garden* was named among the Year's Ten Best Illustrated Books by the *New York Times Book Review,* 1973; *It's Raining Said John Twaining* received a Notable Book award from the American Library Association, 1973, was named among the Best Books of the Year by the School Library Association, 1973, among the Best Children's Books of the Year by the National Book League of the United Kingdom, 1973, received a Christopher award, 1974, and has been selected by A.I.G.A. one of the twenty books to represent the United States at the Biennial of Illustration, Bratislava, 1976.

WRITINGS—Poems: *Digtervandring* (title means "Poets Ramble"), Forum, 1943; *Graa Fugle* (title means "Grey Birds"), Prior, 1946.

Juvenile: (Self-illustrated) *Miss Jaster's Garden,* Golden Press, 1972; (translator, illustrator, and editor) *It's Raining Said John Twaining* (Danish nursery rhymes), Atheneum, 1973; *The Mushroom Centre Disaster,* Atheneum, 1974; (self-illustrated) *Let's Marry Said the Cherry, and Other Nonsense Poems,* Atheneum, 1974.

Poetry represented in the anthology *Ung Dansk Lyrik* (title means "Young Danish Poetry"), edited by Niels Kaas Johansen, Hirschsprung (Copenhagen), 1949.

Illustrator: Sigfred Pedersen, *Spillebog for Hus, Hjem og Kro* (title means "Book of Games for House, Home and

Inn"), Erichsen (Copenhagen), 1948; Patric Dennis, *Oh! What a Wonderful Wedding,* Crowell, 1953; Roger Eddy, *The Bulls and the Bees,* Crowell, 1956; Russell Lynes, *Cadwallader: A Diversion,* Harper, 1959; Mark Caine, *The S-Man,* Houghton, 1960; Agnes DeMille, *The Book of the Dance,* Golden Press, 1963; Charles Dickens, *David Copperfield,* Macmillan, 1966.

Illustrator—Juvenile: Edward Eager, *Half Magic,* Harcourt, 1954; Evan Commager, *Cousins,* Harper, 1956; Eager, *Knight's Castle,* Harcourt, 1956; Anne Barrett, *Songberd's Grove,* Bobbs-Merrill, 1956; Eager, *Magic by the Lake,* Harcourt, 1957; Commanger, *Beaux,* Harper, 1958; Eager, *The Time Garden,* Harcourt, 1958; Eager, *Magic Or Not,* Harcourt, 1959; Eager, *The Well Wishers,* Harcourt, 1960; Adeline Hull, *Sylvester, The Mouse with the Musical Ear,* Golden Press, 1961; Eager, *Seven Day Magic,* Harcourt, 1962; Miriam Schlein, *The Snake in the Carpool,* Abelard, 1963; Doris Adelberg, *Lizzie's Twins,* Dial, 1964; Josephine Gibson, *Is There a Mouse in the House?,* Macmillan, 1965; Mary Francis Shura, *Shoe Full of Shamrock,* Atheneum, 1965; Michael Jennings, *Mattie Fritts and the Flying Mushroom,* Windmill Books, 1973; Robert Kraus, *Good Night Little One,* Windmill Books, 1973; Kraus, *Good Night Richard Rabbit,* Windmill Books, 1973; Kraus, *Good Night Little A.B.C.,* Windmill Books, 1973; Kraus, *The Night-Lite Calendar 1974,* Windmill Books, 1973; Kraus, *The Night-Lite Calendar 1975,* Windmill Books, 1974.

Contributor of illustrations: Celeste Andrews Seton and Clark Andrews, *Helen Gould Was My Mother-in-Law,* Crowell, 1953; Lynes, *Confessions of a Dilettante,* Harper, 1966; *Fun and Laughter: A Treasure House of Humor,* Reader's Digest, 1967; Henry F. Salerno, editor, *English Drama in Transition,* Pegasus, 1968; Helmut E. Gerber, editor, *The English Short Story in Transition,* Pegasus, 1968; John M. Munro, editor, *English Poetry in Transition,* Pegasus, 1968. Also contributor of illustrations to magazines, including *Holiday, McCall's, Saturday Evening Post, Esquire,* and *Ladies' Home Journal.*

WORK IN PROGRESS: The Day the Railroad Died (novel); *Travelling Light* (short stories); *Rook House* (autobiographical); *Good Morning, Dr. Yawning* (nonsense poems); *Pigeontoes' and Calicos'* (nursery rhymes); two novels for children, *Ben's Island* and *Colonel Crumpet's Little Journey;* and several picture books, *Who Is Mr. Giraffe?, Our House, The King with the Blooming Umbrella, Mrs. Richardson in the Chicken Coop,* and *The Story of Squilliam Squirt, and Other Stories.*

SIDELIGHTS: Bodecker writes: "I write and draw because that is what I was meant to do. I have never seriously considered any other occupation, though I have occasionally been side-tracked. I have many additional interests, but no other absolute needs. I write for children because I have retained strong emotional ties to the childhood condition and need to share my imaginings with a sympathetic audience." Bodecker's books have also been published in Canada, England, France, Sweden, Denmark, Italy, Germany, Holland, and Spain.

* * *

BOGOSLOVSKY, Christina Stael 1888(?)-1974

1888(?)—June 25, 1974; Swedish-born American educator. Obituaries: *New York Times,* July 2, 1974.

BOK, Bart J(an) 1906-

PERSONAL: Born April 28, 1906, in Hoorn, Netherlands; naturalized United States citizen in 1938; son of Jan (a Dutch soldier) and Gesina (van der Lee) Bok; married Priscilla Fairfield (a college professor and writer), September 9, 1929; children: John F., Joyce A. Bok Ambruster. *Education:* University of Leiden, candidaat, 1926; University of Groningen, Ph.D., 1932. *Politics:* Democrat. *Home:* 200 Sierra Vista Dr., Tucson, Ariz. 85719.

CAREER: Harvard University, Cambridge, Mass., Robert Wheeler Willson Fellow in Astronomy, 1929-33, assistant professor, 1933-39, associate professor of astronomy, 1939-46, Robert Wheeler Willson Professor of Astronomy, 1947-57, associate director of observatory, 1946-52; Australian National University, Canberra, Australian Capital Territory, professor of astronomy and director of Mount Stromlo Observatory, 1957-66; University of Arizona, Tucson, professor of astronomy, 1966-74, professor emeritus, 1974—, head of department and director of Steward Observatory, 1966-70. Trustee-at-large of Associated Universities, Inc., 1968-71; chairman, Gould Fund, 1969-75.

MEMBER: International Astronomical Union (vice-president, 1970-74), National Academy of Sciences, National Science Foundation, American Astronomical Society (vice-president, 1970-71; president, 1972-74), American Association for the Advancement of Science, American Academy of Arts and Sciences, Royal Astronomical Society (fellow), Institute of Physics (Australia), Royal Astronomical Society of Canada (honorary member), Royal Astronomical Society of New Zealand (honorary member), Astronomical Society of Australia (honorary member; corresponding member), Royal Netherlands Academy of Arts and Sciences (honorary member), Sigma Xi. *Awards, honors:* Dorothy Klumpke Roberts Prize from Astronomische Gesellschaft, 1934; Oranje-Nassau Medal from Government of the Netherlands, 1959; Adion Medal from the Government of France, 1971.

WRITINGS: The Distribution of the Stars in Space, University of Chicago Press, 1937; (with wife, Priscilla F. Bok) *The Milky Way,* Blakiston, 1941, 4th edition, Harvard University Press, 1974; *Navigation in Emergencies,* U.S. Coast Guard, 1942; (with F. W. Wright) *Basic Marine Navigation,* Houghton, 1944; *The Astronomer's Universe,* Melbourne University Press, 1958.

Contributor: *Vistas in Astronomy,* Pergamon, Volumes I and II, 1956, Volume VIII, 1964; *Paris Symposium on Radio Astronomy,* Stanford University; *From Nucleus to Universe,* Shakespeare Head Press, 1960; *Symposium on the Magellanic Clouds,* Mount Stromlo Observatory, Australian National University, 1965.

W. Becker and G. Contoupolos, editors, *The Spiral Structure of Our Galaxy,* D. Reidel, 1970; Hong-Yee Chiu and Amador Muriel, editors, *Galactic Astronomy,* Volume I, Gordon & Breach, 1970; B. T. Lynds, editor, *Dark Nebulae, Globules, and Protostars,* University of Arizona Press, 1971; C. de Jager, editor, *Highlights of Astronomy,* D. Reidel, 1971; M. A. Gordon and L. E. Snyder, editors, *Molecules in the Galactic Environment,* Wiley, 1973; H. Messel and S. T. Butler, editors, *Focus on the Stars,* Shakespeare Head Press, 1974.

Contributor to *Encyclopedia Americana.* Contributor of more than a hundred fifty articles and reviews to scientific journals, including *Astronomical Journal, Sky and Telescope, American Scientist, Scientific American, American*

Scholar, and *Publications of the Astronomical Society of the Pacific.*

WORK IN PROGRESS: Structure and Kinematics of Our Galaxy.

* * *

BOK, Priscilla F(airfield) 1896-

PERSONAL: Born April 14, 1896, in Spokane, Wash.; daughter of Jay (a Unitarian-Universalist minister) and Eulalie Fairfield; married Bart J. Bok (a professor of astronomy and writer), September 9, 1929; children: John F., Joyce A. Bok Ambruster. *Education:* Boston University, A.B., 1917; University of California, Berkeley, Ph.D., 1921. *Politics:* Democrat. *Religion:* Unitarian-Universalist. *Home:* 200 Sierra Vista Dr., Tucson, Ariz. 85719.

CAREER: Smith College, Northampton, Mass., assistant professor of astronomy, 1922-30; Wellesley College, Wellesley, Mass., visiting lecturer in astronomy, 1931, 1933, 1935; Connecticut College for Women (now Connecticut College), Cambridge, Mass., visiting lecturer in astronomy, 1948-49, 1952-55; Radcliffe College, Cambridge, Mass., visiting lecturer in astronomy, 1951-52; Australian National University, Canberra, research associate, 1963-66. *Member:* American Astronomical Society (life member), Phi Beta Kappa.

WRITINGS: (With husband, Bart J. Bok) *The Milky Way,* Blakiston, 1941, 4th edition, Harvard University Press, 1974; (contributor) *Science from Shipboard,* Science Service, 1943. Contributor of over twenty articles to *Astronomical Journal, Publications of the Astronomical Society of the Pacific,* and *Monthly Notices of the Royal Astronomical Society.*

* * *

BOLTON, Carole 1926-

PERSONAL: Born January 10, 1926, in Uniontown, Pa.; daughter of Harry M. and Leone (Shomo) Roberts; married John J. Bolton, February 1, 1947; children: Timothy Duke, John Christopher. *Education:* Studied at Ramsey Street School of Acting, Baltimore, Md., for three years. *Politics:* Democrat. *Religion:* "Former Catholic—now I do not go to church." *Home:* Montville, Me. (R.F.D. 2, Freedom, Me. 04941). *Office:* Thomas Nelson, Inc., 30 East 42nd St., New York, N.Y. 10017.

CAREER: Acted with little theater groups and did office work while attending dramatic school; William Morrow & Co., Inc., New York, N.Y., 1958-64, began as a secretary and became assistant editor of children's books; Meredith Press, New York, N.Y., assistant editor of children's books, 1964-67; Lothrop, Lee & Shepard Co., New York, N.Y., associate editor of children's books, 1967-70; Thomas Nelson, Inc., New York, N.Y., associate editor of children's books, 1972—. *Member:* Authors Guild.

WRITINGS: Christy, Morrow, 1960; *The Callahan Girls,* Morrow, 1961; *Reunion in December,* Morrow, 1962; *The Stage Is Set,* Morrow, 1963; *The Dark Rosaleen,* Morrow, 1964; *Never Jam Today* (Junior Literary Guild selection), Atheneum, 1971; *The Search of Mary Catherine Mulloy* (Junior Literary Guild selection), Nelson, 1974.

SIDELIGHTS: Mrs. Bolton wrote: "My husband and I moved to Maine in late summer of 1972. We had built a small cabin, which we have winterized. We are roughing it—toting our water from a spring, etc. I still go to New York once a month to report at Nelson, but I work and write at home. Someday soon my husband and I hope to raise bees."

* * *

BOND, Julian 1940-

PERSONAL: Born January 14, 1940, in Nashville, Tenn.; son of Horace Mann (a dean of education and former college president) and Julia Agnes (a college librarian; maiden name, Washington) Bond; married Alice Louise Clopton, July 28, 1961; children: Phyllis Jane, Horace Mann, Michael Julian, Jeffrey, Julia. *Education:* Morehouse College, B.A., 1971. *Home:* 361 Westview Dr. S.W., Atlanta, Ga. 30310. *Office:* House of Representatives, Georgia General Assembly, Atlanta, Ga. 30334.

CAREER: Atlanta Inquirer, Atlanta, Ga., reporter and feature writer, 1960-61, managing editor, 1963; Student Nonviolent Coordinating Committee (SNCC), Atlanta, co-founder, 1960, communications director, 1961-66; Georgia House of Representatives, Atlanta, representative from Atlanta's 111th District, 1967—, member of Education, Insurance, and State Institutions and Properties Committees. Co-chairman of Georgia Loyal National Convention. Lecturer; visiting fellow, Metropolitan Applied Research Center of New York City, 1967; research associate of Voter Education Project, 1968; honorary trustee, Institute of Applied Politics. Member of board: Delta Ministry Project of National Council of Churches, Robert F. Kennedy Memorial Fund, Martin Luther King, Jr., Center for Social Change, Center for Community Change, Highlander Research and Education Center, National Sharecroppers' Fund, Southern Regional Council, New Democratic Coalition, Voter Education Project, Voter Education Project, Southern Elections Fund (chairman).

MEMBER: Southern Correspondents Reporting Racial Equality Wars, National Association for the Advancement of Colored People, IPFU, Phi Kappa. *Awards, honors:* LL.D. from Dalhousie University, University of Bridgeport, Wesleyan University (Conn.), and University of Oregon, all in 1969, Syracuse University, 1970, and Eastern Michigan University, Tuskegee Institute, Howard University, Morgan State University, and Wilberforce University, all in 1971; D.C.L. from Lincoln University, 1970.

WRITINGS: (Contributor) James Finn, editor, *Pacifism and Politics: Some Passionate Views on War and Nonviolence,* Random House, 1968; *A Time to Speak, A Time to Act: The Movement in Politics,* Simon & Schuster, 1972.

Represented in anthologies: *American Negro Poetry,* edited by Arna Bontemps, Hill & Wang, 1963; *New Negro Poets U.S.A.,* edited by Langston Hughes, Indiana University Press, 1964; *The Book of Negro Humor,* edited by Hughes, Dodd, 1965.

Contributor of poems and articles to periodicals, including *Negro Digest, motive, Rights and Reviews, Life, Freedomways,* and *Ramparts.*

SIDELIGHTS: Bond was first elected to a seat created by reapportionment in the Georgia House of Representatives in 1965, but was prevented from taking office by members of the legislature who objected to his statements about the war in Viet Nam. After winning a second election in 1966, to fill his vacant seat, a special House Committee again voted to bar him from membership in the legislature. Bond won a third election in November, 1966; in December, 1966, the U.S. Supreme Court ruled unanimously that the

Georgia House had erred in refusing him his seat. On January 9, 1967, he officially became a member of the Georgia House of Representatives. He has since been re-elected.

Bond was the first Black man in history to have his name placed before the Democratic National Convention in nomination for the vice-presidency of the United States. At this convention, in 1968, his insurgent delegation, which charged that Negroes were excluded from significant Democratic political participation in Georgia, won half the votes that would normally have gone to the regular delegation.

Son of a prominent educator and scholar, Bond majored in English and wanted to be a writer. His early pacificism has been attributed variously to youthful years at a Quaker school, to the influence of Martin Luther King, Jr., his college philosophy professor, and to his own nonviolent nature. In his book, said *Virginia Quarterly Review,* he "present[s] his case for Black Americans with fantastic finesse. . . . he analyzes the institutions which have harmed, chained, and beaten the efforts for equality in America. The main thesis is that Blacks as a group must work toward a consolidation which can use the power of numbers to change America, to make it live up to its promises." G. L. Chamberlain believes "Bond's larger concern is to bring people together."

* * *

BONGARTZ, Heinz
See THORWALD, Juergen

* * *

BONIME, Florence 1907-
(Florence Cummings)

PERSONAL: Born May 13, 1907, in New York, N.Y.; daughter of Samuel David (in egg business) and Lena (Spieler) Levine; married Louis Cummings, May 16, 1925 (divorced, 1953); married Walter Bonime (a psychologist), September, 1954; children: (first marriage) Frank, Norma (Mrs. Alan Lovins). *Education:* Brooklyn College of the City University of New York, B.A. (summa cum laude), 1964. *Politics:* Democrat. *Religion:* None. *Home:* 37 Washington Square W., New York, N.Y. 10011. *Agent:* Paul R. Reynolds, Inc., 599 Fifth Ave., New York, N.Y. 10017. *Office:* New School for Social Research, 66 West 12th St., New York, N.Y. 10011.

CAREER: Dodd, Mead & Co., New York, N.Y., associate editor, 1950-55; Brooklyn College of the City University of New York, instructor in creative writing, 1964-65; New School for Social Research, New York, N.Y., instructor in creative writing, 1965—; free-lance writer and editor. Member of national advisory board of National Humanities Series, 1973—. *Member:* International Platform Association, Modern Language Association of America, Authors Guild, Authors League, Sigma Lambda, New York University's Graduate English Association.

WRITINGS: (Under name Florence Cummings) *The Good Mrs. Sheppard* (novel), Crown, 1950; *A Thousand Imitations* (novel), Harcourt, 1967. Contributor of short stories to magazines. Member of editorial board of *Remington Review,* 1973—, and *New Writers,* 1973—.

WORK IN PROGRESS: A novel, *Dear Ostrich.*

SIDELIGHTS: Mrs. Bonime's collected papers are at the Mungar Memorial Library of Boston University.

BONNER, John Tyler 1920-

PERSONAL: Born May 12, 1920, in New York, N.Y.; son of Paul Hyde (an author) and Lilly Marguerite (Stehli) Bonner; married Ruth Anna Graham, July 11, 1942; children: Rebecca, Jonathan Graham, Jeremy Tyndall, Andrew Duncan. *Education:* Phillips Exeter Academy, graduate, 1937; Harvard University, B.S. (magna cum laude), 1941, M.A., 1942, Ph.D., 1947. *Home:* 148 Mercer St., Princeton, N.J. 08540. *Office:* Department of Biology, Princeton University, Princeton, N.J. 08540.

CAREER: Princeton University, Princeton, N.J., assistant professor, 1947-50, associate professor, 1950-58, professor, 1958-66, George M. Moffett Professor of Biology, 1966—, chairman of department of biology, 1965—. Special lecturer at University of London, winter, 1956, and Brooklyn College of the City University of New York, spring, 1966. Trustee, *Biological Abstracts,* 1958-63; advisory editor, Dodd, Mead & Co., 1962-69; trustee and member of editorial board, Princeton University Press, 1964-68, 1971. *Military service:* U.S. Army Air Forces, 1942-46; became first lieutenant.

MEMBER: American Academy of Arts and Sciences (fellow), National Academy of Sciences, American Society of Naturalists, Society of General Physiologists, American Philosophical Society, Mycological Society of America, Phi Beta Kappa, Sigma Xi.

AWARDS, HONORS: Sheldon traveling fellow of Harvard University in Panama and Cuba, 1941; Rockefeller traveling fellow in Paris, 1953; Selman A. Waksman Award of Theobald Smith Society, 1955, for contributions to microbiology; Guggenheim fellow in Edinburgh, 1958, 1971-72; National Science Foundation senior postdoctoral fellow in Cambridge, England, 1963; D.Sc., Middlebury College, 1970.

WRITINGS: Morphogenesis: An Essay on Development, Princeton University Press, 1952; *Cells and Societies,* Princeton University Press, 1955; *The Evolution of Development,* Cambridge University Press, 1958; *The Cellular Slime Molds,* Princeton University Press, 1959, 2nd edition, 1966; (editor) D'Arcy Thompson, *Growth and Form,* abridged edition, Cambridge University Press, 1961; *The Ideas of Biology,* Harper, 1962; *Size and Cycle: An Essay on the Structure of Biology,* Princeton University Press, 1965; *The Scale of Nature,* Harper, 1969; *On Development: The Biology of Form,* Harvard University Press, 1974.

Contributor: Anton Lang, editor, *Handbuch d. Pflanzenphysiologie,* Volume XV, Springer Verlag, 1964; Eugene Bell, editor, *Molecular and Cellular Aspects of Development,* Harper, 1965; R. A. Flickinger, editor, *Developmental Biology,* W. C. Brown, 1966; I. W. Knobloch, editor, *Readings in Biological Science,* 2nd edition (Bonner did not contribute to earlier edition), Appleton, 1967; Ernest Sondheimer and J. B. Simeone, editors, *Chemical Ecology,* Academic Press, 1970; J. J. W. Baker and G. E. Allen, editors, *The Process of Biology: Primary Sources,* Addison-Wesley, 1970; Amy Kramer, editor, *Bios: Topics in the Study of Life,* Harper, 1973; Joseph Lobue and A. S. Gordon, editors, *Humoral Control of Growth and Differentiation,* Volume II, Academic Press, 1974.

Contributor of research papers, principally on the development of the cellular slime molds, to scientific journals, and popular articles to *Science Digest, Scientific American, Natural History,* and other periodicals. Member of editorial board, *Growth,* 1955—, *American Naturalist,* 1958-60, 1966-68, and *Journal of General Physiology,* 1962-69; associate editor of two sections, *Biological Abstracts,* 1957—; associate editor, *American Scientist,* 1961-69.

SIDELIGHTS: The Ideas of Biology is the most translated of Bonner's books, with editions in Italian, Danish, Portuguese, German, Arabic, and Norwegian. It also has been published in London and in paperback in the United States.

* * *

BONNER, Mary Graham 1890-1974

1890—February 12, 1974; Canadian-born American author of children's books. Obituaries: *New York Times,* February 13, 1974; *Publishers Weekly,* March 4, 1974.

* * *

BONNICE, Joseph G(regory) 1930-

PERSONAL: Born April 26, 1930, in Detroit, Mich.; son of Joseph H. and Evelyn (Andre) Bonnice; married Isabel L. Marentette, December 29, 1951; children: Lauren, Audrey, Kenneth. *Education:* University of Detroit, B.B.A., 1959; University of Michigan, M.A., 1968; New York University, graduate study, 1970—. *Home:* 77 Miller Blvd., Syosset, N.Y. 11791. *Office:* McGraw-Hill Book Co., 1221 Avenue of the Americas, New York, N.Y. 10020.

CAREER: McGraw-Hill Book Co., Gregg Division, New York, N.Y., field representative in Michigan, 1960-63, sponsoring editor, 1963-66, senior editor, 1966—. Director of Car/Puter International Corp., 1973—; member of faculty of American Institute of Banking, 1973—. *Military service:* U.S. Army, 1951-53. *Member:* American Council on Consumer Interests, American Vocational Association, National Business Teacher Association, Northeastern Business Law Association, New York Consumer Assembly, Delta Pi Epsilon.

WRITINGS: (With R. Robert Rosenberg) *Business Law/30* (with student achievement guide), McGraw, 1971. Regular columnist on consumer education for *Business Education World,* 1969—, and *Today's Secretary,* 1970—.

WORK IN PROGRESS: An extensive revision of *Business Law/30,* to be issued under a new title.

* * *

BONNY, Helen L(indquist) 1921-

PERSONAL: Born March 31, 1921, in Rockford, Ill.; daughter of G. Elmer E. (a missionary among American Indians) and Ethel (Geer) Lindquist; married Oscar E. Bonny (a minister), August 17, 1948; children: Beatrice (Mrs. Gary Starrett), Erich Lind, Francis Albert. *Education:* Oberlin College, B.Mus., 1943; University of Kansas, B.Mus.Ed., 1964, M.Mus.Ed., 1968; Union Graduate School, Antioch, Ohio, Ph.D. candidate. *Religion:* Society of Friends. *Home:* 721 St. Johns Rd., Baltimore, Md. 21210. *Agent:* Collins Associates, 225 East 57th St., New York, N.Y. 10022. *Office:* Maryland Psychiatric Research Center, Baltimore, Md. 21228.

CAREER: Registered music therapist, 1964; developer of stringed instrument department in public schools of Anthony, Kan., 1949-51; St. Mary's College, Xavier, Kan., instructor in stringed instruments, 1958-60; Kansas University Medical Center, Lawrence, music therapist in General Medical, 1962 (summer); Veterans Administration Hospital, Topeka, Kan., music therapist, 1963-64, research investigator, 1966-68; Parsons State Hospital, Parsons, Kan., music therapist, 1965; Maryland Psychiatric Research Center, Baltimore, Md., music therapist, 1969—. Coordinating secretary of National Association for Music Therapy, Lawrence, Kan., 1967-68; co-founder and president of Institute for Consciousness and Music. *Member:* National Association for Music Therapy (regional vice-president, 1968, 1972, 1973), Association for Humanistic Psychology, Association for Transpersonal Psychology (member of board of directors, 1972—), Institute for Consciousness Research (member of board of directors, 1971—), Sigma Alpha Iota, Pi Kappa Lambda.

WRITINGS: (With Louis M. Savary) *Music and Your Mind: Listening with a New Consciousness,* Harper, 1973. Contributor to *Journal of Music Therapy.*

WORK IN PROGRESS: Research in Guided Imagery and Music (GIM), a new psychotherapeutic approach; *Healing through Music,* completion expected in 1975; contributing to *Healing Approaches,* edited by Geir Vilhjalmssohn; coauthoring *Facilitators Handbook* for Institute for Consciousness and Music Press.

SIDELIGHTS: Mrs. Bonny told *CA:* "I am a professional violinist; interests in interpretive dance, mandala as an art form. Major interest lies in research in music listening techniques to enhance creativity, insight into personal problem areas, as a teaching technique, and as preparation for religious experience. Toward that end, I create listening programs, produce records, tapes, and disseminate training methods through workshops and seminars, write articles, lecture, etc."

* * *

BOROWITZ, Eugene B(ernard) 1924-

PERSONAL: Born February 20, 1924, in New York, N.Y.; son of Benjamin and Molly (Shafranik) Borowitz; married Estelle Covel, September 7, 1947; children: Lisa, Drucy, Nan. *Education:* Ohio State University, B.A., 1943; Hebrew Union College, M.H.L. and Rabbi, 1948, D.H.L., 1952; Columbia University, Ed.D., 1958. *Agent:* Arthur Pine Associates, Inc., 1780 Broadway, New York, N.Y. 10019. *Office:* Jewish Institute of Religion, Hebrew Union College, 40 West 68th St., New York, N.Y. 10023.

CAREER: Rabbi in Port Washington, N.Y., 1953-57; Union of American Hebrew Congregations, New York, N.Y., director of education, 1957-62; Hebrew Union College, Jewish Institute of Religion, New York, N.Y., professor of education and Jewish religious thought, 1962—. Visiting professor at City College of the City University of New York, Princeton University, Jewish Theological Seminary, Woodstock College, Temple University, and Columbia University. *Military service:* U.S. Naval Reserve, chaplain, active duty, 1951-53; became lieutenant junior grade. *Awards, honors:* National Jewish Book Award, 1973, for *The Mask Jews Wear.*

WRITINGS: A Layman's Introduction to Religious Existentialism, Westminster, 1965; *Toward a New Jewish Theology,* Westminster, 1967; *How Can a Jew Speak of Faith Today?,* Westminster, 1968; *Choosing a Sex Ethic,* Schocken, 1968; *The Mask Jews Wear,* Simon & Schuster, 1973. Contributor to journals. Founder and editor of *Sh'ma,* a journal of Jewish responsibility.

* * *

BOSLEY, Harold A(ugustus) 1907-

PERSONAL: Born February 19, 1907, in Burchard, Neb.;

son of Augustus Merrill (a farmer) and Effie (Sinclair) Bosley; married Margaret Marie Dahlstrom, July 21, 1928; children: Paul Shailer, Sidney (deceased), Norman Keith, Diane Marie (Mrs. Edwin R. Hazen), David Merrill. *Education:* Nebraska Wesleyan University, A.B., 1930; University of Chicago, B.D., 1932, Ph.D., 1933. *Politics:* Liberal. *Home:* 135 Elmsmere Rd., Bronxville, N.Y. 10708.

CAREER: Began Methodist ministry at age of seventeen as local preacher; ordained elder by Nebraska Conference of Methodist Church, 1933; Iowa State Teachers College (now Iowa Northern University at Cedar Falls), Ames, director of religious activities, 1934-38; minister in Baltimore, Md., 1938-47; Duke University, Durham, N.C., dean of Divinity School and university preacher, 1947-50; First Methodist Church, Evanston, Ill., senior minister, 1950-62; Christ Church, United Methodist, New York, N.Y., senior minister, 1962—. Distinguished lecturer at Pacific School of Religion, 1942, Colgate Rochester Divinity School, 1944, Tufts University, 1948, DePauw University, 1957, McMurray College, 1959. Delegate to World Council of Churches Assemblies, 1954, 1961, 1968; member of general board, National Council of Churches of Christ in the U.S.A.; member of interfaith teams to South Vietnam, 1965, Soviet Union, 1966, 1967, 1971, and Spain, 1967. Trustee of Northwestern University, Drew University, and Christian Century Foundation.

MEMBER: American Philosophical Association. *Awards, honors:* D.D. from Nebraska Wesleyan University, 1942, Northwestern University, 1950, Manchester College, 1964, Central Methodist College, 1971, and Bucknell University, 1972; S.T.D., Ripon College, 1953; L.H.D., Cornell College, 1953; Litt.D., Simpson College, 1970.

WRITINGS: The Quest for Religious Certainty, Willett, Clark, 1939.

The Philosophical Heritage of the Christian Faith, Willett, Clark, 1944; *On Final Ground,* Harper, 1946; *Main Issues Confronting Christendom* (based on conference lectures at Florida Southern College, 1946), Harper, 1948.

A Firm Faith for Today, Harper, 1950; *The Church Militant* (Carnahan lectures, 1951), Harper, 1952; *Preaching on Controversial Issues: A Free Pulpit in a Free Society,* Harper, 1953; *What Did the World Council Say to You?,* Abingdon, 1955; *Sermons on the Psalms,* Harper, 1956; *Sermons on Genesis,* Harper, 1958.

Doing What is Christian, Abingdon, 1960; *He Spoke to Them in Parables,* Harper, 1963; *The Mind of Christ,* Abingdon, 1966; *The Character of Christ,* Abingdon, 1967; *The Deeds of Christ,* Abingdon, 1969.

Men Who Build Churches, Abingdon, 1972.

WORK IN PROGRESS: Four books.

* * *

BOUDON, Raymond 1934-

PERSONAL: Born January 27, 1934, in Paris, France; son of Raymond and Helene (Millet) Boudon; married Rosemarie Reissner, April 22, 1962; children: Stephane. *Education:* Attended Ecole Normale Superieure and Sorbonne, both University of Paris, receiving Ph.D. (Doctorat D'Etat), 1967. *Home:* 51, avenue Trudaine 75009, Paris, France. *Office:* Maison des Sciences de l'Homme 54, boulevard Raspail 75006, Paris, France.

CAREER: University of Bordeaux, Bordeaux, France, associate professor of sociology, 1964-67; University of Paris, Sorbonne-Rene Descartes, Paris, France, professor of sociology, 1967—, director of Centre d'Etudes Sociologiques (CNRS), 1968-71. Ford Foundation fellow at Columbia University, 1961-62; fellow at Center for Advanced Study in the Behavioral Sciences, Stanford University, 1972-73. Visiting professor at Harvard University, 1974-75. *Military service:* French Navy, 1960-61. *Awards, honors:* Ordre National du Merite.

WRITINGS: (With Paul Lazarsfeld) *Vocabulaire des sciences sociales: Concepts et indices,* Humanities, 1965; *L'Analyse mathematique des faits sociaux* (title means "The Mathematical Analysis of Social Facts"), Plon, 1967, 2nd edition, 1970; *A quoi sert la notion de structure?: Essai sur la signification dans les sciences humaines,* Gallimard, 1968, translation by Michalina Vaughan published as *The Uses of Structuralism,* Heinemann, 1971; *Les Methodes en sociologie,* Presses Universitaires de France, 1969, 3rd edition, 1973; *Les Mathematiques en sociologie,* Presses Universitaires de France, 1971, translation by Tom Burns published as *The Logic of Sociological Explanation,* Penguin Books, 1974; *La Crise de la sociologie: Questions d'epistemologie sociologique,* Droz, 1971; *Mathematical Structures of Social Mobility,* Elsevier Publishing, 1973; *Inegalite des chances,* Colin, 1973, translation by Boudon published as *Education, Opportunity, and Social Inequality: Changing Prospects in Western Society,* Wiley, 1974. Contributor to *Social Sciences Information, Quality and Quantity, American Sociological Review, European Journal of Sociology,* and other journals in his field.

WORK IN PROGRESS: Research on social inequalities and on collective action.

* * *

BOUGHNER, Daniel C(liness) 1909-1974

April 19, 1909—May 8, 1974; American scholar and author. Obituaries: *New York Times,* May 10, 1974. (*CA*-23/24).

* * *

BOVEE, Courtland Lowell 1944-

PERSONAL: Born October 4, 1944, in Red Bluff, Calif.; son of Courtney Van (an orchardist) and Shirlee Patricia (Safford) Bovee. *Education:* Shasta College, A.A., 1965; University of North Dakota, B.S., 1967; University of Tennessee, M.S., 1968. *Politics:* Republican. *Religion:* Protestant. *Home:* 4750 70th St., Apt. 36, La Mesa, Calif. 92041. *Office:* Grossmont College, 8800 Grossmont College Dr., El Cajon, Calif. 92020.

CAREER: Grossmont College, El Cajon, Calif., instructor in business, 1968—. President of Grossmont Press, San Diego, Calif., 1969—, and Communication Dynamics, San Diego, Calif., 1970—. *Member:* International Platform Association, International Sales and Marketing Executives, American Academy of Advertising, American Business Communication Association, American Association of University Professors, National Business Education Association, Advertising Club of San Diego.

WRITINGS: Better Business Writing for Bigger Profits, Exposition, 1970; *Techniques of Writing Business Letters, Memos, and Reports,* Grossmont Press, 1974; (with Stephen G. Bottfeld and William Arens) *Advertising,* Harcourt, in press.

AVOCATIONAL INTERESTS: Travel.

BOWDEN, Henry Warner 1939-

PERSONAL: Born April 1, 1939, in Memphis, Tenn.; son of Warner Hill (a salesman) and Jeannette (Winn) Bowden; married Karin Svensson, June 9, 1962; children: Robin Warner, Annika Hillary. *Education:* Baylor University, B.A., 1961; Princeton University, Ph.D., 1966. *Home:* 12 Durst Dr., Milltown, N.J. 08850. *Office:* Department of Religion, Douglass College, Rutgers University, New Brunswick, N.J. 08903.

CAREER: Rutgers University, Douglass College, New Brunswick, N.J., instructor, 1964-67, assistant professor, 1967-71, associate professor of religion, 1971—, assistant dean, 1969-71. *Member:* American Society of Church History (member of national council, 1971-74), Organization of American Historians, American Association of University Professors.

WRITINGS: Robert Baird, Religion in America: A Critical Abridgment, Harper, 1970; *Church History in the Age of Science: Historiographical Patterns in the United States: 1876-1918,* University of North Carolina Press, 1971.

WORK IN PROGRESS: Dictionary of American Religious Biography, completion expected in 1976; research on historiography and on American Indian religions before and after contact with whites.

* * *

BOWDLE, Donald N(elson) 1935-

PERSONAL: Born February 2, 1935, in Easton, Md.; son of Nelson E. (a baker) and Katherine (Kline) Bowdle; married Nancy Lee George, August 28, 1955; children: Donald Keven, Karen Lee. *Education:* Lee College, Cleveland, Tenn., B.A., 1957; Bob Jones University, M.A., 1959, Ph.D., 1961; Princeton Theological Seminary, Th.M., 1962; Union Theological Seminary, Richmond, Va., Th.D., 1970. *Home:* 3522 Edgewood Circle N.W., Cleveland, Tenn. 37311. *Office:* Department of Religion, Lee College, Cleveland, Tenn. 37311.

CAREER: Ordained minister of Church of God, 1964; Lee College, Cleveland, Tenn., instructor, 1962-66, associate professor, 1969-71, professor of history and religion, 1971—, dean of Division of Religion, 1974—. *Member:* American Society of Church History, Society of Biblical Literature, Society for Pentecostal Studies.

WRITINGS: (Editor) *Ellicott's Bible Commentary,* Zondervan, 1971; *Redemption Accomplished and Applied,* Pathway Press, 1972. Contributor to *Church of God Evangel, Religious and Theological Abstracts,* and *Richmond Times Dispatch.*

SIDELIGHTS: Bowdle conducted a lecture tour to Israel and Greece in 1972 and to Israel and Italy in 1973.

* * *

BOWER, Muriel 1921-

PERSONAL: Born April 30, 1921, in Pomona, Calif.; daughter of Earl B. and Helen (a teacher; maiden name, Hall) Calkins; married Hayden M. Bower (a teacher), November 30, 1943; children: Hayden H., George V. *Education:* University of California, Los Angeles, B.S., 1943; University of Southern California, M.A., 1961. *Home:* 19718 Stagg St., Canoga Park, Calif. 91306. *Office:* Department of Physical Education, California State University, Northridge, Calif. 91324.

CAREER: University of Southern California, Los Angeles, lecturer in physical education, 1951-61; California State University, Northridge, assistant professor, 1961-67, associate professor of physical education, 1967—. Chairman of rules committee, National Collegiate Athletic Association; chairman of fencing committee, U.S. Collegiate Sports Council. *Member:* American Association for Health, Physical Education and Recreation, National Fencing Coaches Association of America, American Academy of Arms. *Awards, honors:* Master of Arms from National Fencing Coaches Association of America, 1970.

WRITINGS: (With Torao Mori) *Fencing,* W. C. Brown, 1966, revised edition, 1971; (contributor) Donnis Thompson and Julia Carver, editors, *Physical Activities for Women,* Prentice-Hall, 1974; (contributor) Muriel G. Bower, editor, *National Collegiate Athletic Association Fencing Rules Manual,* National Collegiate Athletic Association, 1974.

SIDELIGHTS: Muriel Bower was an official for fencing events at the 1964 Olympics in Tokyo and was manager of the women's fencing team at the 1973 World University Games in Moscow.

* * *

BOWER, Robert T(urrell) 1919-

PERSONAL: Born June 1, 1919, in Yonkers, N.Y.; son of Ernest Turrell and Katherine (Bunker) Bower; married Betty Blanchard, 1943 (divorced); married Jean Just, 1971; children: Stephen Cutler. *Education:* Yale University, A.B., 1941; Columbia University, Ph.D., 1954. *Home:* 2729 Dumbarton Ave. N.W., Washington, D.C. 20007. *Office:* Bureau of Social Science Research, 1990 M St. N.W., Washington, D.C. 20036.

CAREER: Columbia University, New York, N.Y., research associate, Bureau of Applied Social Research, 1948-50; Bureau of Social Science Research, Washington, D.C., director, 1950—. Adjunct professor at American University, 1950-56. Member of National Council on the Humanities, 1966-72; president of National Council on Public Polls, 1969—. *Military service:* U.S. Army Air Forces, 1941-45. *Member:* World Association for Public Opinion Research, American Association for Public Opinion Research (president, 1969-70), American Sociological Association, Society for International Development, Society for the Study of Social Problems.

WRITINGS: Communication of Ideas in India: A Survey in Lucknow and Three Indian Villages, three volumes, Bureau of Social Science Research, 1951; *Television and the Public,* Holt, 1973. Contributor to public opinion and other journals.

* * *

BOWLBY, John 1907-

PERSONAL: Born February 26, 1907, in London, England; son of Anthony Alfred (a surgeon) and Maria (Mostyn) Bowlby; married Ursula Longstaff, April 15, 1938; children: Mary (Mrs. Timothy Dawson), Richard, Pia (Mrs. Carlos Duran), Robert. *Education:* Trinity College, Cambridge, B.A., 1928, M.A., 1932; University College Hospital Medical School, M.D., 1939; F.R.C.Psych.; F.R.C.P. *Office:* Tavistock Institute, Belsize Lane, London N.W.3, England.

CAREER: Tavistock Institute of Human Relations, London, England, research psychiatrist and consultant psychiatrist at Tavistock Clinic, 1946—. Fellow of Center for Advanced Study in the Behavioral Sciences, Stanford, Calif., 1957-58. Consultant to World Health Organization, 1950—. Member of council, Royal College of Physicians. *Military service:* British Army, psychiatrist, 1940-45; became lieutenant colonel. *Member:* British Psychological Society (fellow), British Psychoanalytical Society. *Awards, honors:* D.Litt. from University of Leicester, 1971; named commander of the Order of the British Empire, 1972; Jame Spence Medal from British Paediatric Association, 1974; G. Stanley Hall Medal from American Psychological Association, 1974.

WRITINGS: (With E.F.M. Durbin) *Personal Aggressiveness and War,* Kegan Paul, 1938; *Personality and Mental Illness,* Kegan Paul, 1940; *Forty-Four Juvenile Thieves: Their Characters and Home Life,* Bailliere, Tindall & Cox, 1946.

Maternal Care and Mental Health (monograph), World Health Organization, 1951, Schocken, 1966, abridged version published as *Child Care and the Growth of Love,* Penguin, 1953, enlarged edition, 1965; *Attachment and Loss,* Basic Books, Volume I: *Attachment,* 1969, Volume II: *Separation: Anxiety and Anger,* 1973.

WORK IN PROGRESS: The third volume of *Attachment and Loss,* entitled *Loss,* completion expected in 1977.

SIDELIGHTS: Bowlby's books have been published in Italian, German, Spanish, French, Japanese, Yugoslav, Danish, Swedish, Finnish, Hebrew, Arabic, Greek, and Dutch.

BIOGRAPHICAL/CRITICAL SOURCES: Observer, April 20, 1969; *Guardian,* April 9, 1970; *University of Leicester Gazette,* October, 1971; *Times Educational Supplement,* January 14, 1972.

* * *

BOWMAN, Ward S(imon), Jr. 1911-

PERSONAL: Born October 29, 1911, in Everett, Wash.; son of Ward Simon (an educator) and Charity (Rice) Bowman; married Maxine Beal (a librarian), February 14, 1937; children: Gary Webster, George Thomas. *Education:* University of Washington, Seattle, A.B., 1933. *Home:* 64 Mountain View Ter., Hamden, Conn. 06517. *Office:* Yale Law School, New Haven, Conn. 06520.

CAREER: Department of Justice, Washington, D.C., economist, 1937-46; University of Chicago Law School, Chicago, Ill., research associate, 1946-56; Yale University, New Haven, Conn., associate professor, 1956-59, professor of law and economics, 1959—. Ford Foundation Professor of Law and Economics, 1974. *Member:* American Economic Association. *Awards, honors:* M.A. from Yale University, 1959.

WRITINGS: Patent and Antitrust Law, University of Chicago Press, 1973. Contributor to law and economics journals.

WORK IN PROGRESS: Research in franchising, monopoly problems, and industrial organization.

* * *

BOWNE, Ford
See BROWN, Forrest

* * *

BOWSER, Frederick P(ark) 1937-

PERSONAL: Born December 1, 1937, in Roswell, N.M.; son of Frederick P. (a merchant) and Polly (a merchant; maiden name, Pruit) Bowser; married Barbara McKnight, December 20, 1954; children: Eleanor. *Education:* University of New Mexico, B.A., 1960; University of California, Berkeley, M.A., 1961, Ph.D., 1967. *Politics:* Democrat. *Religion:* Methodist. *Home:* 922 Celia Dr., Palo Alto, Calif. 94305. *Office:* Department of History, Stanford University, Stanford, Calif. 94305.

CAREER: University of California, Los Angeles, assistant professor of history, 1966-67; Stanford University, Stanford, Calif., assistant professor of history, 1967—. *Member:* American Historical Association, Latin American Studies Association, Pacific Coast Council on Latin American Studies.

WRITINGS: (Contributor) David W. Cohen and Jack P. Greene, editors, *Neither Slave Nor Free: The Freedmen of African Descent in the Slave Societies of the New World,* Johns Hopkins Press, 1972; *The African Slave in Colonial Peru: 1524-1650,* Stanford University Press, 1974. Contributor to *Latin American Research Review.*

WORK IN PROGRESS: A book on the African contribution to Latin American civilization from the days of slavery to the present, completion expected in 1976.

* * *

BOYD, Jack 1932-

PERSONAL: Born February 9, 1932, in Indianapolis, Ind,; son of Arthur P. (a manufacturer) and Stella (Cunningham) Boyd; married Joann Orr (a teacher), May 26, 1956; children: Alan, Susan, Jeannette. *Education:* Abilene Christian College, B.S., 1955; North Texas State College (now University), M.M., 1959; University of Iowa, Ph.D., 1971. *Politics:* Republican. *Home:* 541 College Dr., Abilene, Tex. 79601. *Office:* Director of Choral Activities, Abilene Christian College, Box 8050, Abilene, Tex. 79601.

CAREER: Clergyman of Church of Christ; associate minister in Irving, Tex., 1955-57, and Paducah, Ky., 1957-63; high school choral director in Paducah, Ky., 1957-63; University of Dubuque, Dubuque, Iowa, director of choral activities, 1964-67; Abilene Christian College, Abilene, Tex., director of choral activities, 1968—, founder and conductor of Abilene Chorale, 1973—. Composer of choral works; music director of radio program, "Herald of Truth," 1968. *Member:* American Choral Directors Association (life member), Texas Choral Directors Association (life member).

WRITINGS: Rehearsal Guide for the Choral Director, Parker Publishing, 1970; *Teaching Choral Sight Reading,* Parker Publishing, in press. Contributor of articles to *Choral Journal, Music Journal, Iowa Music Educator,* and *Texas Music Educator.* Contributor of monthly column to *Choral Journal*, 1962, and *Southwestern Musician*, 1971.

WORK IN PROGRESS: The Lord's Singing; with Edwin George, *The Basics of Conducting Music.*

* * *

BOYD, James S(terling) 1917-

PERSONAL: Born March 8, 1917, in Webster, S.D.; son of Jacob (a banker) and Theresa (Hanse) Boyd; married Virginia Paul, September 11, 1942; children: Virginia Theresa, Sandra Ann Griswold, James Edwin. *Education:* South Dakota State College, B.S., 1939; Michigan State University, M.S., 1948; Iowa State University, Ph.D.,

1954. *Politics:* Republican. *Religion:* Lutheran. *Home:* 172 Orchard, East Lansing, Mich. 48823. *Office:* Department of Agricultural Engineering, Michigan State University, East Lansing, Mich. 48824.

CAREER: Michigan State University, East Lansing, assistant professor, 1946-48, associate professor, 1948-52, professor of agricultural engineering, 1954—. Instructor at University of Nigeria, 1963-65; lecturer at National College of Agricultural Engineering, Silsoe, England, University of Upsala, and Agricultural College of Norway, Oslo, all 1968, and at University of Finland, Helsinki, 1969. *Military service:* U.S. Navy, 1942-46; became lieutenant commander. *Member:* American Society of Agricultural Engineers, National Framebuilders Association (honorary member), Michigan Septic Tank Association (honorary member), Kiwanis (president of local chapter, 1967), Sigma Xi, Gamma Sigma Delta. *Awards, honors:* Metal Building Manufacturers award from American Society of Agricultural Engineers, 1961.

WRITINGS: Practical Farm Buildings, Interstate, 1973. Contributor of more than two hundred articles to bulletins and journals.

* * *

BOYER, Paul Samuel 1935-

PERSONAL: Born August 2, 1935, in Dayton, Ohio. *Education:* Harvard University, A.B. (magna cum laude), 1960, M.A., 1961, Ph.D., 1966. *Office:* Department of History, University of Massachusetts, Amherst, Mass. 01002.

CAREER: Harvard University Press, Cambridge, Mass., assistant editor, 1964-67; University of Massachusetts, Amherst, assistant professor, 1967-70, associate professor of history, 1970—. *Awards, honors:* American Philosophical Society grant, 1969; Guggenheim fellowship, 1973-74. *Member:* Phi Beta Kappa.

WRITINGS: Purity in Print: Book Censorship in America, Scribner, 1968; (editor with E. T. James and J. W. James) *Notable American Women: 1607-1950,* three volumes, Harvard University Press, 1971; (editor with Stephen Nissenbaum) *Salem Village Witchcraft: A Documentary Record of Local Conflict in Colonial New England,* Wadsworth, 1972; (with Nissenbaum) *Salem Possessed: The Social Origins of Witchcraft,* Harvard University Press, 1974.

Contributor of articles and reviews to *William and Mary Quarterly, American Quarterly, Massachusetts Alumnus, American Historical Review, Journal of American History,* and *Historian.*

WORK IN PROGRESS: A biography of U.S. Senator Bronson Cutting (1888-1935); *Urban Morality* (tentative title), for Putnam.

* * *

BRADFORD, Reed H(oward) 1912-

PERSONAL: Born April 10, 1912, in Spanish Fork, Utah; son of Pleasant Jones and Jane (Howard) Bradford; married Nora Tait, August 16, 1941 (deceased); married Shirley Aamodt, June 5, 1947; children: Mary, Sharon (Mrs. H. Michael Leigh), Ralph, Marleen, Ray, Randall, Ryan. *Education:* Brigham Young University, A.B., 1937; Louisiana State University, M.A., 1939; Harvard University, M.A., 1941, Ph.D., 1946. *Religion:* Church of Jesus Christ of Latter-Day Saints (Mormon). *Home:* 1211 Aspen Ave., Provo, Utah 84601. *Office:* Department of Sociology, Brigham Young University, Provo, Utah 84601.

CAREER: West Virginia University, Morgantown, associate professor of sociology, 1942-43, 1945-46; Brigham Young University, Provo, Utah, assistant professor, 1946-55, associate professor, 1955-62, professor of sociology, 1962—, chairman of department, 1955-61. Visiting professor, Michigan State College (now University), 1950; research specialist, University of Utah, 1963-64. President of Utah County Coordinating Council, 1965, and Utah County Community Action Agency, 1966. *Military service:* Utah National Guard, 1935; became lieutenant. U.S. Army Air Forces, 1943-45; became sergeant. *Member:* American Sociological Association, National Council on Family Relations, Rural Sociological Society, Utah Academy of Science, Sigma Xi. *Awards, honors:* Professor of the Year Award and Karl G. Maeser Award for excellence in teaching, both from Brigham Young University.

WRITINGS: (With others) *Introductory Sociology,* W. C. Brown, 1960; *And They Shall Teach Their Children,* Deseret, 1964; *The Teacher's Quest,* Brigham Young University Press, 1971. Contributor of more than 150 articles to *Instructor.*

WORK IN PROGRESS: A book on the family.

* * *

BRADFORD, Richard (Roark) 1932-

PERSONAL: Born May 1, 1932, in Chicago, Ill.; son of Roark (a writer) and Mary Rose (Sciarra) Bradford; married Julie Dollard, September 15, 1956 (divorced May 18, 1972); children: Thomas Conway. *Education:* Tulane University, B.A., 1952. *Politics:* Democrat. *Religion:* None. *Home address:* P.O. Box 1395, Santa Fe, N.M. 87501. *Agent:* McIntosh & Otis, Inc., 18 East 41st St., New York, N.Y. 10017.

CAREER: New Mexico State Tourist Bureau, Santa Fe, staff writer, 1956-59; New Orleans Chamber of Commerce, New Orleans, La., editor, 1959-61; Zia Co., Los Alamos, N.M., editor, 1962-64; New Mexico Department of Development, Santa Fe, research analyst, 1967-68; Universal Pictures, Universal City, Calif., screenwriter, 1968-70. *Military service:* U.S. Marine Corps, 1953-56; became sergeant. *Member:* Writers Guild of America, Authors Guild, Edouard Manet Society, Sigma Chi, Quien Sabe Club.

WRITINGS—Novels: *Red Sky at Morning,* Lippincott, 1968; *So Far from Heaven,* Lippincott, 1973.

WORK IN PROGRESS: A novel.

AVOCATIONAL INTERESTS: Cooking, guitar playing, amateur acting.

* * *

BRADLEY, Ritamary 1916-

PERSONAL: Born January 30, 1916, in Stuart, Iowa; daughter of James Francis (a farmer) and Alice (Muldoon) Bradley. *Education:* Marygrove College, Ph.B., 1938; St. Louis University, M.A., 1945, Ph.D., 1953. *Politics:* Democrat. *Home:* 2317 Western Ave., Davenport, Iowa 52803. *Office:* Department of English, St. Ambrose College, Davenport, Iowa 52803.

CAREER: Roman Catholic nun of Sisters for Christian Community (SFCC); Marycrest College, Davenport, Iowa, instructor, 1940-46, assistant professor of English, 1946-56, head of department, 1945-56; Ottumwa Heights College,

Ottumwa, Iowa, assistant professor of English and philosophy, 1956-61; National Catholic Educational Association, Washington, D.C., editor and administrator, 1961-64; St. Ambrose College, Davenport, Iowa, professor of English, 1965—, head of department, 1974—. Member of board of trustees, Marycrest College and Ottumwa Heights College, 1960-64; assistant executive secretary of Sister Formation Conference, National Catholic Educational Association, 1961-64. *Member:* National Catholic Educational Association, Modern Language Association of America, American Association of University Women, Religious Education Association, Mediaeval Academy of America, American Association of University Professors, Midwest Modern Language Association. *Awards, honors:* LL.D. from Marquette University, 1960; L.H.D. from Fordham University, 1960; honorary research fellow at University of Minnesota, 1964-65.

WRITINGS: (Editor) *The Mind of the Church in the Formation of Sisters,* Fordham University Press, 1956; (editor and contributor) *Spiritual and Intellectual Elements in the Formation of Sisters,* Fordham University Press, 1957; (editor and contributor) *Planning for the Formation of Sisters,* Fordham University Press, 1958; (editor and contributor) *The Juniorate in Sister Formation,* Fordham University Press, 1960; *The Challenge of Renewal to Sisters Today* (pamphlet), Liturgical Press, 1966; (contributor) Merton P. Strommen, editor, *Research on Religious Development,* Hawthorn, 1971. Co-author of "Women in Religion," a cable television script, produced by Black Hawk College, East Moline, Ill., 1973. Contributor to journals in her field. Founder and editor of *Sister Formation Bulletin,* 1954-64.

WORK IN PROGRESS: Co-authoring *Women in the Church: A Critical Evaluation of Changes in the Church;* research on mediaeval women in religion and literature, especially Juliana of Norwich.

* * *

BRANDON, (Oscar) Henry 1916-

PERSONAL: Born March 9, 1916; son of Oscar and Ida Brandon; married Mabel Hobart Wentworth (a photographer), April 4, 1970; children: Fiona. *Education:* Studied at University of Lausanne, and University of London. *Office:* 814 National Press Building, Washington, D.C. 20004.

CAREER: Sunday Times, London, England, staff member, 1939—, as war correspondent in North Africa and western Europe, 1943-45, Paris correspondent, 1945-46, roving diplomatic correspondent, 1947-49, associate editor and chief American correspondent based in Washington, D.C., 1950—. Editor-at-large, *Saturday Review. Member:* National Press Club, Overseas Writers, Federal Club. *Awards, honors:* Foreign Correspondents Award from University of California, Los Angeles, 1957; Journalism Award from Lincoln University (Jefferson City, Mo.), 1962; Hannen Swaffer Award as reporter of the year, 1964.

WRITINGS: As We Are, Doubleday, 1961; *In the Red: The Struggle for Sterling, 1964-1966,* Deutsch, 1966, Houghton, 1967; *Conversations with Henry Brandon,* Deutsch, 1966, Houghton, 1968; *The Anatomy of Error: The Inside Story of the Asian War on the Potomac, 1954-1969,* Gambit, 1969; (with others) *American Melodrama: The Presidential Campaign of 1968,* Viking, 1969; (editor) *The Retreat of American Power,* Doubleday, 1973. Contributor to *Saturday Evening Post, Harper's, Encounter,* and *New York Times Magazine.*

BRANSON, Margaret Stimmann 1922-

PERSONAL: Born August 7, 1922, in Modesto, Calif.; daughter of Georg August and Dora (Schramm) Stimmann; married Rodney B. Branson (manager of Melrose Lumber Co.), June 15, 1946; children: Rodney Thomas, Martha Elizabeth (deceased), David George. *Education:* University of the Pacific, A.B. (with high honors), 1944; University of California, Berkeley, M.A. in Ed., 1952; Holy Names College, M.A. (history), 1962. *Religion:* Lutheran. *Home:* 523 Hampton Rd., Piedmont, Calif. 94611. *Office:* Holy Names College, 3500 Mountain Blvd., Oakland, Calif. 95619.

CAREER: Oakland public schools, Oakland, Calif., teacher, counselor, and curriculum assistant, 1945-59, vice-principal, 1959-64, supervisor of secondary social sciences, 1964-69; associate professor of education at Holy Names College and instructor in teacher education at Mills College, both Oakland, Calif., 1969—. Lecturer at other colleges and universities. Consultant to Law in Free Society Project, 1969—, and to History Education Project of American Historical Association. *Member:* American Historical Association, American Academy of Political and Social Science, National Council for the Social Studies, Association for Supervision and Curriculum Development, League of Women Voters, Oakland Museum Association (member of board of directors), Pi Lambda Theta, Alpha Delta Kappa, Delta Kappa Gamma, Delta Delta Delta.

WRITINGS: American History for Today, Ginn, 1970; *Inquiry Experiences in American History,* Ginn, 1970; (with Evarts Erickson) *Urban America,* Scott, Foresman, 1970; (with Edward E. France) *The Human Side of Afro-American History,* Ginn, 1972; (with Raymond Calkins and Charles Quigley) *The Environments We Live In,* Follett, 1973; (with June Chapin) *Women: The Majority Minority,* Houghton, 1973; *Land of Promise,* Ginn, 1974. Writer of guides. Contributor to professional journals.

WORK IN PROGRESS: An elementary social studies book for Houghton; a collection of multi-ethnic folk tales adapted for young children; a collection of biographies of Afro-Asian leaders.

* * *

BRENNER, Anita 1905-

PERSONAL: Born August 13, 1905, in Aguascalientes, Mexico; daughter of Isidore and Paula (Duchan) Brenner; married David Glusker, June 18, 1929; children: Peter, Susannah (Mrs. John Page). *Education:* Attended Our Lady of the Lake, San Antonio, University of Texas, and National University of Mexico; Columbia University, Ph.D., 1929. *Religion:* Jewish. *Home:* Rancho la Barranca, Aguascalientes, Ags., Mexico. *Office:* Sierra Vertientes 335, Lomas Barrilaco, Mexico 10, D.F.

CAREER: Writer, rancher, editor. Free-lance correspondent for *New York Times Magazine* and for North American Newspaper Alliance (NANA), during 1930's, 40's, and 50's; art editor, *Brooklyn Daily Eagle,* 1935-36; special correspondent in Mexico for *Fortune* magazine, 1937; editor and publisher of *Mexico This Month,* published by Grafica de Mexico, 1955-71; currently rancher and free-lance writer. *Member:* Foreign Correspondents Club of Mexico City (founding member). *Awards, honors:* Guggenheim fellowship, 1930-32; gold medal from Boys Clubs of America, 1966, for *The Timid Ghost;* cited in *Junior Encyclopaedia Britannica* list of authors of classic children's books; decorated by National Tourist Council of Mexican Government for pioneer work in tourist development; received parchment from University of Florida for contributions to resolution of inter-American problems.

WRITINGS: Idols Behind Altars, Payson & Clarke (New York), 1929, reprinted, Beacon Press, 1970; *The Influence of Technique on the Decorative Style in the Domestic Pottery of Culhuacan,* Columbia University Press, 1931, reprinted, AMS Press, 1969; *Your Mexican Holiday: A Modern Guide,* Putnam, 1932, 4th revised edition, 1947; *The Wind that Swept Mexico: The History of the Mexican Revolution, 1910-1942,* Harper & Brothers, 1943, University of Texas Press, 1971.

Juveniles; all published by W. R. Scott, except as noted: *The Boy Who Could Do Anything, and Other Mexican Folk Tales,* 1942; *I Want to Fly,* 1943, reissued with *The Little Fireman,* by Margaret Wise Brown, E. M. Hale, 1956; *A Hero by Mistake,* 1953; *Dumb Juan and the Bandits,* 1957; *The Timid Ghost: or, What Would You Do With a Sackful of Gold?,* 1966.

Translator from the Spanish: Waldo D. Frank, *Tales from the Argentine,* Books for Libraries, 1930; Mauricio Magdaleno, *Sunburst,* Viking, 1944; Gregorio Lopez y Fuentes, *El Indio,* Ungar, 1961.

Columnist for *Mademoiselle* during 1930's; regular contributor to *Nation, New York Times, New York Post, Holiday,* and *Menorah Journal.*

WORK IN PROGRESS: Two books, one of them possibly a juvenile.

SIDELIGHTS: Anita Brenner told *CA*: "Due to having been born in Mexico, I have tended to side with the underdog and be sympathetic to rebellion and revolution whose deepest psychological, economic and social roots have always intrigued me, and into the research of which I have put much time. This is also due to the fact that I am Jewish, and although I was not an underdog on this account in Mexico, the minute we hit Texas as refugees from the Mexican Revolution (my father having been a landowner), the problem hit me full in the face when I was too small to know what it was that was hitting me. I have therefore devoted a great deal of time and research to Jewish preoccupations, history, traditions and basic commitments, which has definitely healed the scars inflicted by the roughing up when I hit Texas, and has deepened and fortified my sense of identity." Mrs. Brenner was involved with the John Dewey Committee in the 1930's, and writes that the group was among the first to attempt "to uncover and make public the 'Lie' which makes things run so brutally in the Soviet Union and which then was picked up by Hitler as a modus operandi and did the entire world an immense amount of harm. We have by now become accustomed to it as a commercial gadget and as a political way of life and it has made a climate that is as poisonous to the mind and spirit as the junk that gets dumped into the sea is to the fishes." As a result of her activities with the Committee, she earned "the honor of being attacked in *Pravda* along with many of the other members of this group which included the most vigorous writers of the time." Mrs. Brenner is the only correspondent to have interviewed Trotsky when he was in hiding outside of Paris; this interview appeared in the *New York Times.*

* * *

BRENNI, Vito J(oseph) 1923-

PERSONAL: Born March 15, 1923, in Highland, N.Y.; son of John and Marietta (Fabrizio) Brenni. *Education:* State University of New York at Albany, A.B., 1947; Columbia University, M.A., 1949, M.S., 1952; State University of New York College at New Paltz, M.A., 1970. *Home:* West Terrace Apartments, #6A, Adrian, Mich. *Office:* Siena Heights College, Adrian, Mich. 49221.

CAREER: West Virginia University, Morgantown, reference librarian, 1951-57; New York Public Library, Economics Division, part-time reference librarian, 1958-59; Villanova University, Villanova, Pa., chief reference librarian, 1960-62; Duquesne University, Pittsburgh, Pa., assistant professor of library science, 1962-65; State University of New York at Albany, assistant professor of library science, 1965-66; State University of New York College at Plattsburgh, bibliographer, 1966-68; College of Librarianship, Aberystwyth, Wales, visiting professor of library science, 1968-69; Siena Heights College, Adrian, Mich., director of libraries, 1971—. *Military service:* U.S. Army, Field Artillery, 1943-46; served in Germany. *Member:* American Library Association, Catholic Library Association.

WRITINGS: West Virginia Authors: A Bibliography, West Virginia Library Association, 1957; *American English: A Bibliography,* University of Pennsylvania Press, 1964; *Edith Wharton: A Bibliography,* West Virginia University Library, 1966; *William Dean Howells: A Bibliography,* Scarecrow, 1973. Contributor to *Bulletin of Bibliography* and *Catholic Library World.*

WORK IN PROGRESS: Editing a collection of essays on bibliography, publication expected in 1975; a guide to the literature of bibliography.

AVOCATIONAL INTERESTS: International travel, art, music, philosophy, religion.

* * *

BREYER, N(orman) L(ane) 1942-

PERSONAL: Born June 9, 1942, in Brooklyn, N.Y.; married Elaine Schwartz, July 10, 1965; children: Geniffer Michele, Joshua Aaron. *Education:* Fairleigh Dickinson University, B.A., 1964; Miami University, Miami, Ohio, M.S., 1966; Florida State University, Ph.D., 1969. *Religion:* Jewish. *Home:* Slater Rd., Tolland, Conn. 06084. *Office:* Department of Education, University of Connecticut, Box U-7, Storrs, Conn. 06268.

CAREER: University of Connecticut, Storrs, assistant professor of educational psychology, 1969—. *Member:* American Psychological Association, American Educational Research Association, Association for the Advancement of Behavior Therapy, Devereux Institute for Research and Training (fellow), Phi Delta Kappa.

WRITINGS: (Editor) *Behavior Modification in the Classroom,* MSS Educational Publishing, 1970; *Staff Development and Evaluation,* Crofts, 1971; (editor with S. Axelrod and others) *Behavior Modification: An Annotated Bibliography of Selected Behavior Modification Studies,* H & H Enterprises, 1972, (with Axelrod) revised edition, 1973. Contributor to *Journal of School Psychology* and *Psychological Reports.*

* * *

BRIDGE, Ann 1891-1974 (Lady O'Malley, Mary Dolling Sanders)

1891—March 9, 1974; British novelist. Obituaries: *AB Bookman's Weekly,* April 15, 1974.

BRIEFS, Goetz Antony 1889-1974

January 1, 1889—May 16, 1974; German-born American economist. Obituaries: *Washington Post,* May 18, 1974. (*CA*-21/22).

* * *

BRIGGS, Charlie 1927-

PERSONAL: Born July 10, 1927, in Paducah, Ky.; daughter of Frank (Kentucky agricultural commissioner) and Ora Lee (Lipford) Irwin; married Andrew Jackson Briggs (a press representative for Ringling Brothers Circus), June 7, 1948; children: Clark H., Charles A. *Education:* University of Kentucky, student, 1946-48. *Politics:* Republican. *Religion:* Christian. *Home and office:* 420 South Harbor Dr., Venice, Fla. 33595.

CAREER: Transylvania Times, Brevard, N.C., author of "Backtalk" column, 1956-60; *Tampa Tribune,* Tampa, Fla., reporter, 1963-73; writer, 1973—. Has worked as circus press agent.

WRITINGS: (With Rosemary K. Collett) *My Orphans of the Wild,* Lippincott, 1974. Work is represented in anthologies. Contributor of short stories and articles to magazines, including *American Girl, Ladies Circle, Southern Living,* and *Floridan,* and to newspapers.

WORK IN PROGRESS: Encyclopedia of the Circus, with Bill Ballantine.

AVOCATIONAL INTERESTS: People, animals, history, nostalgia.

* * *

BRIMBERG, Stanlee 1947-

PERSONAL: Born July 7, 1947, in New York. *Education:* Brooklyn College of the City University of New York, A.B., 1968. *Home:* 324 East 52nd St., New York, N.Y. 10022.

CAREER: Public School 23, Brooklyn, N.Y., teacher, 1968—.

WRITINGS: Black Stars (nonfiction children's book), Dodd, 1974.

WORK IN PROGRESS: Tarzan The Wild Man, with Laura Rader, for children.

* * *

BRIN, Herb(ert Henry) 1915-

PERSONAL: Born February 17, 1915, in Chicago, Ill.; son of Sol (in sales) and Fannie (Goroway) Brin; married Selma Stone, December 25, 1940 (divorced, 1957); married Minna Burman (an editorial assistant), September 10, 1965; children: (first marriage) Stanley R., Glen David, Daniel Jeremy. *Education:* Attended Crane Junior College, 1932, Central YMCA College (now Roosevelt University), 1933, DePaul University, 1934-36, and University of Chicago, 1939-40. *Politics:* Liberal. *Religion:* Jewish. *Home:* 18450 Clifftop Way, Malibu, Calif. 90265. *Office:* Heritage Publishing Co., 2130 South Vermont Ave., Los Angeles, Calif. 90007.

CAREER: City News Bureau, Chicago, Ill., reporter, 1942-47; *Los Angeles Times,* Los Angeles, Calif., feature writer-reporter, 1947-54; Heritage Publishing Co., Los Angeles, Calif., editor-publisher and owner, 1954—. Attended Paris Summit Conference, 1960, for *Los Angeles Times,* and Eichmann Trial in Jerusalem, Israel, 1961, for KTTV, Los Angeles, Calif; reported on Suez and Syria war scenes for McClatchey newspapers; founder and director of Westside Poetry Center, Los Angeles, Calif; founder of Pacific Southwest branches of Union of Orthodox Jewish Congregations of America, 1957. *Military service:* U.S. Army, Infantry, 1943-46; became sergeant.

MEMBER: American Jewish Committee, American Jewish Congress, Jewish War Veterans, World Federation of Jewish Journalists. *Awards, honors:* Midwest Writers Conference Award, 1944, for best non-fiction article by a serviceman; award of merit from Jewish War Veterans, 1955; Three-Bell Award from California Association for Mental Health, 1958; Torch of Hope from City of Hope, 1959; Sigma Delta Chi, San Diego, awards for best feature story (3rd place) and for best news story (2nd place), both 1968; Communications Award from Anti-Defamation League of B'nai B'rith, 1971.

WRITINGS: Wild Flowers (poems), J. David, 1966; *Justice-Justice* (poems), J. David, 1968; *Conflicts* (poems), J. David, 1971. Author of humorous articles. Contributor to *Army Times* and *Yank Magazine.*

WORK IN PROGRESS: A collection of writings; a book of poetry.

* * *

BRINDEL, June (Rachuy) 1919-

PERSONAL: Born June 5, 1919, on farm near Little Rock, Iowa; daughter of Otto (a farmer) and Mina (Balster) Rachuy; married Bernard Brindel (a composer and teacher of music), 1939; children: Paul, Jill. *Education:* University of Chicago, B.A., 1945, M.A., 1958. *Politics:* "Radical reform." *Religion:* Humanist. *Home:* 2740 Lincoln Lane, Wilmette, Ill. 60091.

CAREER: Early work ranged from dime store clerk to secretary to a poet laureate, and included factory and office jobs and free-lance writing; Chicago City College, Wright Campus, Chicago, Ill., associate professor of English, 1958—. Teacher of creative drama and children's theater at National Music Camp, Interlochen, Mich., summers, 1958-67. *Member:* College English Association, National Council of Teachers of English, Phi Beta Kappa. *Awards, honors:* First prize from Wilmette Children's Theatre, 1971, for "Automaton, King of Machines."

WRITINGS: "Automaton, King of Machines" (play for children), first produced in Interlochen, Michigan, at National Music Camp in 1967; *Luap* (Junior Literary Guild selection), Bobbs-Merrill, 1971. Collaborator with husband, Bernard Brindel, on songs and a recording for children. Contributor of poems and stories to *Carolina Quarterly, Perspective, Beloit Poetry Journal, Discourse,* and other literary magazines.

WORK IN PROGRESS: An adult novel; stories for adults and children; a collection of poems.

SIDELIGHTS: June Brindel writes: "[I] love travel, home and abroad. [Have] compulsion to verbalize experience, inability to stop writing. Find people-studying fascinating though sometimes horrifying and usually absurd. Kids are wisest."

* * *

BROKAMP, Marilyn 1920-
(Mary Lynn)

PERSONAL: Born September 9, 1920, in Covington, Ky.;

daughter of Lawrence Henry (a manager) and Elizabeth (Neuhaus) Brokamp. *Education:* Marian College, Indianapolis, Ind., B.S. in Ed., 1953; Ball State University, M.Ed., 1972. *Home:* 220 West Siebenthaler, Dayton, Ohio 45405. *Office:* Lady of Mercy School, 545 Odlin Dr., Dayton, Ohio 45405.

CAREER: Roman Catholic nun of the Sisters of Saint Francis (Franciscan; O.S.F.); primary school teacher in Indiana, Illinois, and Ohio, 1940—. Consultant to Society for Visual Education. *Member:* National Education Association, National Catholic Educational Association, Indiana Council of Teachers of English, American Association of Elementary, Kindergarten, Nursery Educators.

WRITINGS: (With Sister Marie Padua Holohan and Sister Fidelia Martini) *Primarily Yours,* Sisters of St. Francis (Oldenberg, Ind.), 1966; *Tippy-Toe and Taffy* (juvenile), McKnight, 1966; *Halfway* (juvenile), Vantage, 1970; *Skelly the Sea Horse* (juvenile), Orbis Books, 1973. Also author of *A Friend Always,* published by C. R. Gibson, three children's plays, and a television script, "Onomatopoeia," produced by WFBM-TV, Indianapolis, Ind., 1970. Contributor to education journals (occasionally under pseudonym, Mary Lynn).

WORK IN PROGRESS: Two books, *Treasures in the Meadow* and *More Ways Than One to Somewhere.*

BIOGRAPHICAL/CRITICAL SOURCES: Criterion, April 11, 1969; *Indianapolis Star,* July 16, 1970.

* * *

BROOKE, Dinah 1936-

PERSONAL: Born May 26, 1936, in Scunthorpe, England; daughter of Joseph and Christina (Herron) Brooke; married Francis Dux (a writer), 1965 (now separated); children: Felix Joseph, Emily Rachel. *Education:* St. Claire's College, Oxford, B.A. (honors), 1959; attended London Film School, 1960. *Home:* 16 Gloucester Crescent, London N.W.1, England. *Agent:* Ann McDiarmid, David Higham Associates Ltd., 5-8 Lower John St., London WIR 4HA, England.

CAREER: Samaritan Films, London, England, film production assistant, 1961-62. *Member:* Writers Guild Associates, Women's Liberation Workshop.

WRITINGS: (Translator from French) *Children of the Gods,* Lorrimer, 1967; (translator from French) *Daybreak,* Lorrimer, 1968; *Love Life of a Cheltenham Lady,* Barrie & Jenkins, 1970, Coward, 1971; *Lord Jim at Home,* Deutsch, 1973.

Plays: "Love Food" (one-act) first produced in London, England, at Almost Free Theatre, November, 1973. Contributor to *Body Politic,* 1973.

WORK IN PROGRESS: Research on war.

SIDELIGHTS: Dinah Brooke is concerned about the "relationship between war and women." She is also interested in the Middle East and Indochina.

* * *

BROOKS, Jerome 1931-

PERSONAL: Born July 17, 1931, in Chicago, Ill.; son of Samuel (a barber) and Rose (Malina) Brooks; married Marilyn Glaser, May 27, 1956 (divorced November 22, 1970); children: Eliot Mitchell, Elise Beth. *Education:* Roosevelt University, B.A., 1953; George Washington University, M.A., 1957. *Home:* 1619 Monroe, Evanston, Ill. 60202. *Office:* Department of English, Southwest College, 7500 South Pulaski, Chicago, Ill. 60652.

CAREER: Chicago City College, Chicago, Ill., Fenger Campus, instructor in English, 1958-60, Bogan Campus, assistant professor of English and chairman of department, 1960-65, acting dean of faculty, 1969, Crane Campus (now Malcolm X College), administrative assistant and assistant dean for curriculum, 1965-67, Urban Education Center, dean, and director of projects Co-op and Success, 1967-69; Southwest College, Chicago, Ill., associate professor of English, 1969—. *Military service:* U.S. Army, 1953-55.

WRITINGS: Uncle Mike's Boy (novel), Harper, 1973. Contributor to *Inditer* and *Midwest.*

* * *

BROUGHTON, James 1913-

PERSONAL: Born November 10, 1913, in Modesto, Calif.; son of Irwin (a banker) and Olga (Jungbluth) Broughton; married Suzanna Hart (an artist), December 6, 1962; children: Serena, Orion. *Education:* Stanford University, B.A., 1936. *Office address:* P. O. Box 183, Mill Valley, Calif. 94941.

CAREER: Poet, playwright, filmmaker; was involved with Art in Cinema experimental film group at the San Francisco Museum in late 1940's, and with San Francisco Renaissance poetry movement in late 1950's and early 1960's; resident playwright with Playhouse Repertory Theatre in San Francisco, 1958-64; lecturer in creative arts, San Francisco State University, 1964—, and instructor in film, San Francisco Art Institute, 1968—; playwright fellow, Eugene O'Neill Theatre Foundation, Waterford, Conn., 1969; has given public readings of his poetry. Member of board of directors, Farallone Films, 1948—, and Anthology Film Archives, 1969—. *Awards, honors:* James D. Phelan Award in Literature, 1948; Avon Foundation grant-in-aid, 1968; Guggenheim fellowships, 1970-71, 1973-74; recipient of numerous film awards, including Edinburgh Film Festival Award of Merit, 1953, Cannes Film Festival Prix du fantaisie poetique, 1954, for "The Pleasure Garden," Oberhausan Film Festival Hauptpreis der Kurzfilmtage, 1968, for "The Bed," and Bellevue Film Festival grand prize, 1970, for "The Golden Positions."

WRITINGS—Poetry: *Songs for Certain Children,* Adrian Wilson, 1947; *The Playground,* Centaur Press, 1949; *The Ballad of Mad Jenny,* Centaur Press, 1949; *Musical Chairs,* Centaur Press, 1950; *The Right Playmate,* Hart-Davis, 1952, Pterodactyl Press, 1964; *Almanac for Amorists,* Collection Merlin (Paris), 1954; *True & False Unicorn,* Grove Press, 1957; *The Water Circle,* Pterodactyl Press, 1965; *Tidings,* Pterodactyl Press, 1966; *Look In Look Out,* Toad Press, 1968; *High Kukus,* Jargon Society, 1968; *All About It,* Toad Press, 1969; *A Long Undressing: Collected Poems, 1949-1969,* Jargon Society, 1971.

Plays: "Summer Fury" (one-act; first produced in Palo Alto, Calif., at Stanford University, 1945), published in *Best One Act Plays,* edited by Margaret Mayorga, Dodd, 1957; "Burning Questions" (four-act), first produced in San Francisco at Playhouse Repertory Theatre, 1958; "The Last Word" (one-act), first produced in San Francisco at Playhouse Repertory Theatre, 1958), published in *Religious Drama 3,* edited by Marvin Halverson, Meridian Books, 1959; "The Rites of Women" (two-act), first produced at Playhouse Repertory Theatre, 1959; "Bedlam" (one-act), first produced in Waterford, Conn., by Eugene O'Neill Theatre Foundation, 1969.

Films: "The Potted Psalm," 1946; "Mother's Day," 1948; "Adventures of Jimmy," 1950; "Four in the Afternoon," 1951; "Loony Tom the Happy Lover," 1951; "The Pleasure Garden," 1953; "The Bed," 1968; "Nuptiae," 1969; "The Golden Positions," 1970; "This Is It," 1971; "Dreamwood," 1972; "High Kukus," 1973.

Work represented in anthologies, including: *Faber Book of Modern American Poetry,* edited by W. H. Auden, Faber, 1956; *Silver Treasury of Light Verse,* edited by Oscar Williams, New American Library, 1957; *A New Folder,* edited by Daisy Aldan, Folder Editions, 1959; *The New American Poetry,* edited by Donald Allen, Grove Press, 1960; *Erotic Poetry,* edited by William Cole, Random House, 1963; *America Forever New,* edited by J. E. Brewton and S. W. Brewton, Crowell, 1968; *Mark in Time,* edited by Nick Harvey, Glide Publications, 1971.

SIDELIGHTS: Broughton told *CA:* "My work in poetic cinema is a major extension of my life as a poet and dramatist." Of *Tidings,* Raymond Roseliep in *Poetry* magazine states: "Four flowing movements comprise James Broughton's *Tidings.* The first, "I Asked the Sea," is a series of quick dialogues between man and the sea; answers to questions have bite, wit, irony, riddle, humor, or meaningful charm....."The Water Circle," the last of the four movements...., [displays] uninhibited joy for all the world's waters 'that open their veins to the sea.'"

Broughton has recorded his poetry for Evergreen Records, on "San Francisco Poets," and for MEA Records on "The Bard and the Harper."

* * *

BROWN, Calvin S(mith) 1909-

PERSONAL: Born September 27, 1909, in Oxford, Miss.; son of Calvin Smith (a professor of modern languages) and I. Maud (a professor of Latin and Greek; maiden name, Morrow) Brown; married Irene M. Hughes, August 18, 1934; children: Calvin Hugh. *Education:* University of Mississippi, B.A., 1928; University of Cincinnati, M.A., 1929; Oxford University, B.A. (first-class honors), 1932; University of Wisconsin, Ph.D., 1934. *Politics:* Independent. *Religion:* None. *Home:* 145 Milledge Ter., Athens, Ga. 30601. *Office:* Department of Comparative Literature, University of Georgia, Athens, Ga. 30602.

CAREER: Phillips Exeter Academy, Exeter, N.H., instructor in English and German, 1934-35; Memphis State College (now Memphis State University), Memphis, Tenn., associate professor of English, 1935-38; University of Georgia, Athens, assistant professor, 1938-40, associate professor, 1940-46, professor of comparative literature, 1946-57, Alumni Foundation Distinguished Professor of English, 1957-64, Alumni Foundation Distinguished Professor of Comparative Literature, 1964—, head of department of comparative literature, 1968-73. Lecturer at University of Mississippi, summers, 1937-38; acting head of department of comparative literature at University of Wisconsin, 1941, 1942. *Wartime service:* Research analyst for U.S. War Department, 1942-46.

MEMBER: International Comparative Literature Association, Modern Language Association of America, American Comparative Literature Association (member of advisory board, 1968-74), American Association of Rhodes Scholars, South Atlantic Modern Language Association (member of executive committee, 1961-62). *Awards, honors:* Rhodes scholarship, Oxford University, 1930-33; American Council of Learned Societies faculty study fellowship, 1951-52.

WRITINGS: (Editor with E. M. Everett and John D. Wade) *Masterworks of World Literature,* two volumes, Dryden, 1947, 3rd edition (with Everett and R. L. Harrison), Holt, 1970; *Music and Literature: A Comparison of the Arts,* University of Georgia Press, 1948; (editor with R. E. P. King) *Goethe on Human Creativeness and Other Goethe Essays,* University of Georgia Press, 1950; *Repetition in Zola's Novels* (monograph), University of Georgia Press, 1952; *Tones into Words: Musical Compositions as Subjects of Poetry,* University of Georgia Press, 1953; (general editor) *The Reader's Companion to World Literature,* Dryden, 1956, 2nd edition, New American Library, 1973.

Author of monthly column in Athens *Banner Herald* and Athens *Daily News,* 1968—. Contributor of about a hundred articles and reviews to literature and music journals, including *American Literature, American Music Teacher, Germanic Review, Modern Language Notes, Musical Quarterly,* and *Journal of Aesthetics and Art Criticism.* Guest editor of *Comparative Literature,* 1970, and *Comparative Literature Studies,* 1973.

WORK IN PROGRESS: A Glossary of Faulkner's South; glossaries of dialect words and forms, archaic implements and processes, flora and fauna, and old slang and allusions.

SIDELIGHTS: Brown writes: "My own interest in serious music led to the attempt to interrelate music and literature....Knowing Faulkner well in my boyhood and knowing his idiom and setting led to another primary critical interest." Brown's foreign languages include French, German, Italian, Spanish, Anglo-Saxon, Old French, Latin, Old Norse, and to a lesser degree of familiarity, Greek, Russian, Dutch, and Portuguese. *Avocational interests:* The outdoors, natural history.

* * *

BROWN, Forrest (Ford Bowne, Rae Brown)

PERSONAL: Born in Chillicothe, Mo.; son of Alonzo and Isabelle Brown; married Gladys Marie Barnhart, 1918. *Education:* Missouri Wesleyan University, A.B., 1926; Boston University, S.T.B., 1929, S.T.M., 1930, Ph.D., 1942; graduate study at Harvard University, 1930; postdoctoral study at University of California, Berkeley, 1947. *Politics:* Independent. *Religion:* Protestant. *Home:* 1959 South Meyer, Springfield, Mo. 65804.

CAREER: Minister of Community church, 1926-34, and of Congregational churches in South Braintree, Mass., 1934-42, Holliston, Mass., 1946-47, Bonne Terre, Mo., 1951-59, and Springfield, Mo., 1959-62; president of Iberia Junior College, 1947-51. Communications editor, St. Joe Minerals Corp., 1950-57. *Military service:* U.S. Naval Reserve, active duty, 1942-45; became commander.

WRITINGS—All novels; under name Forrest Brown; *Danger Trail,* Loring, 1934; *Boss of Lonely Valley,* Dodge, 1935; *Guns in the Squawtooth,* Dodge, 1936; *Sheriff Wanted,* Ward, Lock, 1936; *Powdersmoke Trail,* Greenberg, 1937; *Gunman Sinister,* Ward, Lock, 1938; *Cowboy Guns,* Ward, Lock, 1940; *Professor from Texas,* Coker, 1949.

Under pseudonym Ford Bowne: *Thunderbird Mesa,* Arcadia House, 1963; *The Sagebrush Bandit,* Arcadia House,

1964; *Ride the Dark Trail,* Arcadia House, 1965; *The Ranch Stealers,* Arcadia House, 1965; *The Masked Riders,* Arcadia House, 1966; *Trail of the Golden Skull,* Arcadia House, 1967; *The Violent Men,* Arcadia House, 1967; *King of the Range,* Arcadia House, 1968; *Homestead Wagon,* Arcadia House, 1969; *Desperation Valley,* Lenox Hill, 1970; *Outlaw Spy,* Lenox Hill, 1970; *Escape from Flint Corners,* Lenox Hill, 1971; *Stagecoach to the Brazos,* Lenox Hill, 1971; *Thunderbird Range,* Lenox Hill, 1972; *Sodbuster Law,* Lenox Hill, 1972; *Rangeland Marshal,* Lenox Hill, 1972; *Drygulchers,* Lenox Hill, 1973; *Master of the Lash,* Lenox Hill, 1974.

Under pseudonym Rae Brown: *Darkness at Sunrise,* Lenox Hill, 1973.

Contributor of short stories to magazines, including *Ozark Mountaineer, Best Western, Big Book Western,* and *Modern Romances.*

SIDELIGHTS: Several of Brown's books have been published in England.

* * *

BROWN, Ivor (John Carnegie) 1891-1974

April 25, 1891—April 22, 1974; British author, critic, and editor. Obituaries: *New York Times,* April 23, 1974. (*CA*-11/12).

* * *

BROWN, John L(ackey) 1914-

PERSONAL: Born April 29, 1914, in Ilion, N.Y.; son of Leslie Beecher (a businessman) and Katherine (Lackey) Brown; married Simone-Yvette L'Evesque, August 25, 1941; children: Michel-Simon, John Halit. *Education:* Hamilton College, A.B., 1935; graduate study at Ecole des Chartes, Paris, and Sorbonne, University of Paris, 1936-38; Catholic University of America, Ph.D., 1939. *Home:* 3024 Tilden St. N.W., Washington, D.C. 20008. *Office:* Department of Comparative Literature, Catholic University of America, Washington, D.C. 20017.

CAREER: Catholic University of America, Washington, D.C., instructor in Romance languages, 1939-41; concurrently European editor for Houghton Mifflin Co., and correspondent for *New York Times* Sunday edition, both in Paris, France, 1945-48; director of information division, Marshall Plan, Paris, France, 1948-50; U.S. Embassy, Paris, chief of regional services for U.S. Information Service, 1950-54; cultural attache, U.S. Embassy in Brussels, Belgium, 1954-58, Rome, Italy, 1958-62, and Mexico City, Mexico, 1964-68; Catholic University of America, professor of comparative literature, 1968—. Barry Bingham Distinguished Professor of Humanities, University of Louisville, 1966-67; fellow, Center for Advanced Studies, Wesleyan University, Middletown, Conn., 1962-63. Member, Catholic Commission on Intellectual and Cultural Affairs, 1960—. *Wartime service:* Office of War Information, assistant chief of foreign publications, 1942-43; Office of Strategic Services, member of staff, European theatre, 1943-45.

MEMBER: Association internationale des etudes francaises, Association internationale de litterature comparee, Association internationale des critiques litteraires (vice-president, 1973—), P.E.N. Club, Dante Society of America, Medieval Academy of America, American Studies Association, American Comparative Literature Association, Modern Language Association of America, Societe d'etude du vingtieme siecle, Syndicat des critiques (Paris), Societe Paul Claudel, Les Amis de Valery Larbaud, Fondation universitaire (Brussels), University Club (Mexico), Foreign Service Association, Phi Beta Kappa, Psi Upsilon, Cosmos Club (Washington, D.C.). *Awards, honors:* Decorated Commander, Chevaliers du Tastevin (Burgundy, France), 1953; Grand Prix de la critique from Syndicat des critiques, 1954, for *Panorama de la litterature contemporaine aux Etats Unis*; named to Le Grand Ordre des Coteaux (Champagne), 1973.

WRITINGS: The Methodus ad facilem historiarum cognitionem of Jean Bodin: A Critical Study, Catholic University of America Press, 1939, reprinted as *The Methodus ad facilem historiarum cognitionem,* AMS Press, 1969; (contributor) Lester Markel, editor, *Public Opinion and Foreign Policy,* Harper, 1948; (reviser) Clara E. Laughlin, *So You're Going to Paris,* 8th edition, Houghton, 1948; *Panorama de la litterature contemporaine aux Etats Unis,* Gallimard, 1954, revised edition, 1972; (author of English adaptation) Georges Sion, *La Malle de Pamela/Key to My Heart* (five-act comedy), O. Perrin (Brussels), 1956; *Discovering Belgium,* Lumiere (Brussels), 1957; *Hemingway,* Gallimard, 1961; *Il Gigantesco Teatro: Saggi europei e americani* (title means "The Gigantic Theatre: European and American Essays"), Opere Nuove (Rome), 1963; (author of introduction) Ernest Hemingway, *Adieu aux armes (A Farewell to Arms),* Rambaldi, 1964; (contributor) *Hemingway,* Hachette, 1966. Author of book-length study, with Jerome Bruner, *Report on France,* for Rockefeller Foundation, 1946.

Poetry: *Signs,* Henneuse (Paris), 1956; *Weights and Measures,* Henneuse, 1958; *Another Language,* Il Pesce d'Oro (Milan), 1961; *Numina,* Henneuse, 1969.

Contributor to *Le Grand Larousse encyclopedique* and to *Yearbook of Comparative and General Literature.* Columnist, *New York Times Book Review,* 1945-47. Contributor to about fifty journals and popular periodicals in United States, France, Belgium, Germany, Italy, Spain, and Mexico.

WORK IN PROGRESS: Saving Grace or Scarlet Woman: Ambiguities of American Attitudes towards Europe, 1770-1970; The Exiled Heart: The Novel of Expatriation; Joel Barlow: The European Years; Shards, a book of verse.

* * *

BROWN, Louis M(orris) 1909-

PERSONAL: Born September 5, 1909, in Los Angeles, Calif.; son of Emil (a business executive) and Anna Brown; married Hermione Kopp (a lawyer), 1937; children: Lawrence David, Marshall Joseph, Harold Arthur. *Education:* University of Southern California, A.B. (cum laude), 1930; Harvard University, J.D., 1933. *Home:* 606 North Palm Dr., Beverly Hills, Calif. 90210. *Office:* School of Law, University of Southern California, Los Angeles, Calif. 90007.

CAREER: Admitted to California bar, 1933, and U.S. Supreme Court bar, 1944; attorney in Los Angeles, Calif., 1933-35; Emil Brown & Co., Los Angeles, Calif., vice-president, 1936-64; Dura Steel Products Co., Los Angeles, Calif., vice-president, 1936-41; Reconstruction Finance Corp., Washington, D.C., counsel, 1942-44; Pacht, Warne, Ross & Bernhard, Los Angeles, Calif., partner, 1944-47; Irell & Manella, Los Angeles, Calif., partner, 1947-69, counsel, 1969-72; University of Southern California, Los Angeles, lecturer, 1950-51, adjunct professor, 1960-74, professor of law, 1974—. Lecturer at Southwestern University, 1939-41, and University of California, Los Angeles, 1944-46. Member of planning committee of Tax Institute, 1948-69; member of national panel of arbitrators of American Arbitration Association, 1956-63; member of Jewish Personnel Relations Bureau and Community Relations Committee, 1950-60; founder and administrator of Emil Brown Fund for Preventive Law prize awards, 1963—, and client counseling competition, 1968—. Member of American Community Symphony Orchestra European Tour, 1968.

MEMBER: American Bar Foundation (fellow), American Bar Association, American Judicature Society, American Business Law Association, State Bar Association of California, Beverly Hills Bar Association (president, 1961), San Francisco Bar Association, Town Hall of Los Angeles, Freinds of Beverly Hills Public Library (president, 1960), Order of the Coif, Masons, B'nai B'rith.

WRITINGS: (Editor) *Major Tax Problems,* four volumes, Tax Institute, University of Southern California, 1948-51, 1962; *Preventive Law,* Prentice-Hall, 1950; *How to Negotiate a Successful Contract,* Prentice-Hall, 1955; *Planning by Lawyers,* privately printed, 1972. Author of legal course books, including *Preventive Law in the Lawyering Process,* 1963, and *Jurisprudence of the Lawyering Process,* 1964. Contributor of articles to law journals and to *Better Homes and Gardens.*

WORK IN PROGRESS: Manual for Periodic Legal Check-Up; a law student's textbook on transaction planning.

* * *

BROWN, Rae
See BROWN, Forrest

* * *

BROWN, Stanley (Branson) 1914-

PERSONAL: Born October 9, 1914, in Suva, Fiji; son of Francis Stanley (a printer) and Ruth (Branson) Brown; married Dolly Storck, December 12, 1941 (divorced, 1951); married Jean Elizabeth Dods, July 21, 1951. *Education:* Studied at a secondary school in Leicester, England, 1925-29. *Religion:* Presbyterian. *Home:* 5 Berkeley Cove, Suva, Fiji. *Office address:* Brown Marine Ltd., Box 169, Suva, Fiji.

CAREER: Mariner, ship's captain, and head of diving company, Brown Marine Ltd., Suva, Fiji. Director of Wilkins and Davies Ltd.; vice-chairman, Fiji National Trust; senior vice-president, Fiji Amateur Sports Association. *Military service:* Fiji Naval Reserve; became commander. *Member:* Royal Geographical Society (fellow), Australian Institute of Navigation (fellow). *Awards, honors:* Order of British Empire (military division).

WRITINGS: The Men from Vava Lagi, Tuttle, 1973. Contributor to *Pacific Islands Monthly.*

WORK IN PROGRESS: The Yankee Bligh, the story of Lt. Charles Wilkes, U.S.M.

BIOGRAPHICAL/CRITICAL SOURCES: Leonard Wibberley, *Islands of the Dawn,* 1964.

* * *

BROWN, Steven R(andall) 1939-

PERSONAL: Born December 22, 1939, in Kansas City, Mo.; son of Walter Yost and Maxine (Duncan) Brown; married Carolyn V. Denison (an educator), July 5, 1973; children: Robyn Denison, Lori Denison, Sheri Denison, Tom Denison (stepchildren). *Education:* University of Missouri, B.J., 1961, M.A. (journalism), 1963, M.A. (political science), 1964, Ph.D., 1968. *Politics:* Liberal Democrat. *Religion:* None. *Home:* 3096 Wayland Rd., Diamond, Ohio 44412. *Office:* Department of Political Science, Kent State University, Kent, Ohio 44242.

CAREER: Kent State University, Kent, Ohio, assistant professor, 1967-70, associate professor of political science, 1970—. Consultant to Ohio governor's work group on land use policy. *Member:* American Political Science Association, Midwest Political Science Association, Ohio Association of Economists and Political Scientists, Missouri Political Science Association. *Awards, honors:* Postdoctoral fellowship from National Institute of Mental Health, Yale University, 1970-71; fellow of Academy for Contemporary Problems, 1974.

WRITINGS: (Editor with D. J. Brenner) *Science, Psychology, and Communication,* Teachers College Press, 1972. Contributor to political science and social science journals, including *American Political Science Review, British Journal of Social and Clinical Psychology,* and *Social Science Quarterly.* Member of editorial board of *Public Opinion Quarterly.*

WORK IN PROGRESS: Editing *Number and Knowledge in the Social Sciences,* with William Stephenson, completion expected in 1976; *The Study of Political Subjectivity,* 1976; research on political psychology, subjectivity, psychoanalysis, and group dynamics, as these relate to political behavior.

* * *

BROWNE, Harry 1933-

PERSONAL: Born June 17, 1933, in New York, N.Y.; son of Bradford (a radio announcer and producer, and Christian Science practitioner) and Cecil Margaret Browne; married Gloria Maxwell, June 9, 1956 (divorced April, 1964); children: Autumn Lee. *Education:* Briefly attended Los Angeles Valley Junior College. *Politics:* None. *Religion:* None. *Home and office:* 1126 Crestline Rd., West Vancouver, British Columbia, Canada. *Agent:* Collier & Seligmann, 280 Madison Ave., New York, N.Y. 10016.

CAREER: James E. Munford Co. (advertising agency), Los Angeles, Calif., account executive and salesman, 1958-61; John Birch Society, Los Angeles, Calif., area manager, 1961-62; American Way Features, Inc. (newspaper feature service), Los Angeles, Calif., owner, writer, and editor, 1962-67; Evelyn Wood Reading Dynamics, Los Angeles, Calif., marketing manager, 1967; Economic Research Counselors (investment counselors), Los Angeles, Calif., member of sales and service staff, 1967-70; writer, 1970—. *Military service:* U.S. Army, 1953-56.

WRITINGS: How You Can Profit from the Coming Devaluation, Arlington House, 1970; *How I Found Freedom in an Unfree World,* Macmillan, 1973; *You Can Profit from a Monetary Crisis,* Macmillan, 1974, 2nd edition, in press. Author of weekly newspaper columns, "The American Way," and "Between the Bookends," published in small town weekly and daily newspapers, 1962-67. Editor of *Freedom* (magazine of Liberty Amendment Committee), 1962-66.

WORK IN PROGRESS: Why People Hate Opera (and What They're Missing).

SIDELIGHTS: Browne decided to educate himself, and found all subjects exciting except economics. About 1960, he discovered, by his own means, that economics was actually an exciting subject. In 1964, he began giving courses in economics to paying customers. He writes: "I am motivated to write about economics because the subject has been so distorted by economists and politicians—despite its simplicity. I had to be pushed into writing my first book, because I didn't think there was a market for it. . . There's a market and a need, and I've grown rich satisfying that need. I have no other affiliations because I'm a non-joiner. I went to work for the John Birch Society in 1961 to work against government intervention—but it was a mistake soon rectified."

AVOCATIONAL INTERESTS: Opera, classical music, travel, love, playing with speculative investments, making money, reading, lying on the couch ("not necessarily in that order").

* * *

BROWNING, Don (Spencer) 1934-

PERSONAL: Born January 13, 1934, in Trenton, Mo.; son of R. W. (a physician) and Nell Juanita Browning; married Carol Kohl; children: Elizabeth, Christopher. *Education:* Central Methodist College, A.B. (summa cum laude), 1956; University of Chicago, B.D., 1959, M.A., 1962, Ph.D. (with distinction), 1964. *Home:* 6927 South Constance, Chicago, Ill. 60649. *Office:* Divinity School, University of Chicago, 1025 East 58th St., Chicago, Ill. 60637.

CAREER: Minister of Christian church in Kearney, Mo., 1952-56; minister of students at University Church of Disciples of Christ, Chicago, Ill., 1957-60; chaplain at Illinois Children's Hospital School, Chicago, 1960-61; counselor at William Healy School, Chicago, 1962-63; Phillips University, Enid, Okla., assistant professor of theology and pastoral care, 1963-65; University of Chicago, Divinity School, Chicago, Ill., instructor, 1965-66, assistant professor, 1967-68, associate professor of religion and personality, 1968—. Counselor at Chicago Institute of Pastoral Care, 1970—.

MEMBER: American Association of Pastoral Counselors (fellow), American Academy of Religion, Society for the Scientific Study of Religion. *Awards, honors:* Nominated for National Book Award in philosophy and religion, 1974, for *Generative Man.*

WRITINGS: Atonement and Psychotherapy, Westminster, 1966; *Generative Man: Society and Good Man in Philip Rieff, Norman Brown, Erich Fromm, and Erik Erikson,* Westminster, 1973.

(Contributor) Peter Homans, editor, *Essays in Divinity,* University of Chicago Press, 1968; William Oglesby, editor, *Essays in Honor of Seward Hiltner,* Abingdon, 1969; Ralph James, editor, *Process Theology Reader,* Bobbs-Merrill, 1971; Howard Clinebell, editor, *Mental Health and the Church,* Abingdon, 1971; Homans, editor, *Erik Erikson and His Impact on Religious Studies,* University of Chicago Press, 1975.

Contributor of articles and reviews to theology journals, including *Criterion, Dialogue, Christian Century, Pastoral Psychology, Journal of Religion,* and *Christian Medical Society Journal.* Editor of *Pastoral Psychology,* March, 1968, and November, 1969.

WORK IN PROGRESS: Context of Care.

BRUIN, John
See BRUTUS, Dennis

* * *

BRUMBAUGH, Thomas B(rendle) 1921-

PERSONAL: Born May 23, 1921, in Chambersburg, Pa.; son of Alex Neill and Elisabeth (Brendle) Brumbaugh. *Education:* Indiana State College (now Indiana University of Pennsylvania), Indiana, Pa., B.S., 1943; State University of Iowa, M.A., 1947; Ohio State University, Ph.D., 1955. *Politics:* Democrat. *Residence:* Nashville, Tenn. *Office:* Vanderbilt University, Box 1648, Station B, Nashville, Tenn. 37235.

CAREER: Hood College, Frederick, Md., assistant professor of fine arts, 1950-53; Emory University, Atlanta, Georgia, associate professor of fine arts, 1955-61; Vanderbilt University, Nashville, Tenn., professor of fine arts, 1962—. *Military service:* U.S. Army, 1942-46. *Member:* American Institute of Archaeology, College Art Association.

WRITINGS: Architecture of Middle Tennessee, Vanderbilt University Press, 1974. Contributor to art and history journals, including *Art Journal, Art News,* and *Tennessee Historical Quarterly.*

WORK IN PROGRESS: Abbott H. Thayer: An American Painter's Life in Letters.

AVOCATIONAL INTERESTS: Collecting artists' autograph letters.

* * *

BRUNER, Richard W(allace) 1926-

PERSONAL: Born June 26, 1926, in Burlington, Iowa; son of Eugene Floyd (a salesman) and Dorothy K. (Gavin) Bruner; married Rosemary G. Holahan (a corporation planner), June 14, 1947; children: Sean H., Susan V., Richard Eugene. *Education:* University of Minnesota, B.A., 1950. *Politics:* Democrat. *Religion:* Atheist. *Home:* 172 Highland Ave., Ridgewood, N.J. 07450. *Agent:* Julian Bach, 3 East 48th St., New York, N.Y. 10017. *Office:* Bruner Productions, Ridgewood, N.J. 07450.

CAREER: Mankato Free Press, Mankato, Minn., reporter, 1950-53; United Packinghouse Workers of America, AFL-CIO, Des Moines, Iowa, editor and program coordinator, 1953-57; news and feature writer for news commentator Alex Dreier, Chicago, Ill., 1957-58; NBC Radio, New York, N.Y., news writer, 1958-66; Bruner Productions (films and filmstrips), Ridgewood, N.J., writer and producer, 1966—. Active in local Democratic Party. *Military service.:* U.S. Army Air Forces, 1944-46; served in Japan. *Member:* Writers Guild of America, Authors Guild, Dramatists Guild. *Awards, honors:* American Film Festival Blue Ribbon Award, 1968; International Film and Television Festival of New York Grand Award, 1970.

WRITINGS: Black Politicians, McKay, 1971; *Whitney M. Young, Jr.: The Pragmatic Humanist,* McKay, 1972. Contributor to *Harper's Magazine, Harvard Business Review, Rockefeller Foundation Quarterly, Saga, Look, Coronet, Progressive, Nation,* and *Challenge.*

WORK IN PROGRESS: A biography of Ralph Johnson Bunche; with Vincent Schiano, a book about his career as the chief trial lawyer and crime fighter of the New York Immigration and Naturalization Service; a book about work in America.

BRUNER, Wally 1931-

PERSONAL: Born March 4, 1931, in Woodbury County, Iowa; son of Wallace A. (a farmer) and Audrey (Scott) Bruner; married Natalie Martin (a television performer), August 3, 1968; children: Rick, Sherri, Mike, Tim, Ted, Kathy, Kevin, Kristine, Wally. *Education:* Attended Indiana University, 1952. *Politics:* Democrat. *Religion:* None. *Office:* Walnat Co., 10 North Tacoma, Indianapolis, Ind. 46201.

CAREER: American Broadcasting Co., Network News, New York, N.Y., White House correspondent, 1964-68; United Press International, New York, N.Y., congressional correspondent, 1968; Goodson-Todman, New York, N.Y., host of "What's My Line," 1968-72; producer and host of "Wally's Workshop," 1971—. President of Pan Media Productions, Inc., 1970—; owner of Walnat Co. Productions, Indianapolis, Ind., 1973—. Chairman of Indiana Cancer Crusade, 1972; board member of Salvation Army, 1972-73. *Military service:* U.S. Air Force, 1948-49.

WRITINGS: *Wally's Workshop,* Simon & Schuster, 1973. Contributor to *Family Weekly* and *Mechanix Illustrated.*

WORK IN PROGRESS: A novel, *The Chairmakers; Father and Son Workshop,* for Simon & Schuster; *Santo Domingo to Saigon,* foreign policy review.

* * *

BRUNHOUSE, Robert Levere 1908-

PERSONAL: Born September 24, 1908, in Mechanicsburg, Pa.; son of Harry F. (a pharmacist) and Hattie (Altland) Brunhouse; married Mildred Adams, 1940. *Education:* Dickinson College, A.B., 1930; University of Pennsylvania, A.M., 1936, Ph.D., 1940. *Home:* 1759 Springhill Ave., #231, Mobile, Ala. 36607. *Office:* Department of History, University of South Alabama, Mobile, Ala. 36688.

CAREER: Dickinson College, Carlisle, Pa., registrar and instructor in history, 1930-35; University of Pennsylvania, Philadelphia, assistant in history, 1935-37; Elizabethtown College, Elizabethtown, Pa., professor of history, 1940-42; Drew University, Madison, N.J., assistant professor, 1942-46, associate professor, 1946-50, professor of history, 1950-68; University of South Alabama, Mobile, professor of history, 1968—. *Member:* American Historical Association, Phi Beta Kappa.

WRITINGS: *Counter-Revolution in Pennsylvania: 1776-1790,* Pennsylvania Historical Commission, 1942; (editor with A. C. Bining and N. B. Wilkinson) *Writings on Pennsylvania History,* Pennsylvania Historical Commission, 1946; (editor) *David Ramsay, 1749-1815: Selections from His Writings,* American Philosophical Society, 1965; *Sylvanus G. Morley and the World of the Ancient Mayas,* University of Oklahoma, 1971; *In Search of the Maya: The First Archaeologists,* University of New Mexico Press, 1973; *Pursuit of the Maya,* University of New Mexico Press, in press. Contributor to professional journals.

WORK IN PROGRESS: One or two books about archaeologists in middle America.

SIDELIGHTS: Brunhouse wrote to *CA*: "On a casual visit to the Maya ruins of Yucatan and Guatemala [I] responded, like most tourists, to the amazing and intriguing nature of the ancient ruins. Soon [I] wanted to know who discovered the structures which had been hidden in the brush for centuries and who learned the facts about the forgotten civilization. [I] attempted to answer those questions in [my] recent books about archaeologists of Middle America. The biographical approach, which places a man in the context of his time, and considers the interplay of innate abilities and outside challenges, appeared to provide the most interesting way to present the subject."

* * *

BRUTUS, Dennis 1924-
(John Bruin)

PERSONAL: Born November 28, 1924, in Salisbury, Southern Rhodesia, Africa; son of Francis Henry (a teacher) and Margaret (a teacher) Brutus; married May Jaggers, May 14, 1950; eight children. *Education:* Fort Hare University College, B.A., 1946; University of the Witwatersrand, study of law, 1962-63. *Home:* 617 Haven, Evanston, Ill. 60201. *Office:* Department of English, Northwestern University, Evanston, Ill. 60201.

CAREER: High school teacher of English and Afrikaans in South Africa, 1948-62; fired from teaching post and forbidden to write by South African government as a result of anti-Apartheid activities begun in late 1950's; arrested in South Africa, 1963, for attendance at a meeting; sought refuge in Europe after being released on bail, was apprehended, and returned to South Africa where he served an eighteen-month sentence at hard labor; emigrated to London, England, 1966, working there as journalist and teacher until 1970; Northwestern University, Evanston, Ill., member of faculty of English, 1971—. Former director, World Campaign for Release of South African Political Prisoners; president of South African Non-Racial Olympic Committee; vice-president of International Defence and Aid Fund for Southern Africa; chairman of International Campaign Against Racism in Sport. *Awards, honors:* Mbari Prize from University of Ibadan, 1962, for *Sirens, Knuckles, Boots.*

WRITINGS:—All poetry: *Sirens, Knuckles, Boots,* Northwestern University Press, 1963; *Letters to Martha, and Other Poems from a South African Prison,* Heinemann, 1968; *Poems from Algiers,* African and Afro-American Research Institute, University of Texas at Austin, 1970; (under pseudonym John Bruin) *Thoughts Abroad,* Troubador, 1970; *A Simple Lust,* Hill & Wang, 1973. Poetry is represented in anthologies, including: *New Sum of Poetry from the Negro World,* Presence Africaine (Paris), 1966; *Seven South African Poets,* edited by Cosmo Pieterse, Heinemann, 1966, Humanities, 1973; *Modern Poetry from Africa,* edited by Gerald Moore and Ulli Beier, revised edition, Penguin, 1966. Contributor to journals.

WORK IN PROGRESS: Study of the poetry of Arthur Nortje, and of racism in South African sports.

SIDELIGHTS: Brutus told *CA:* "[I] have yet to find the time for serious critical (and creative) writing." His poetry has been translated into Russian and published in Moscow.

BIOGRAPHICAL/CRITICAL SOURCES: Ulli Beier, editor, *Introduction to African Literature,* Northwestern University Press, 1967; Colin Legum, editor, *The Bitter Choice,* World Publishing, 1968; *A History of Africa,* Horizon Press, 1971; Cosmo Pieterse and Dennis Duerdan, editors, *African Writers Talking,* Africana Publishing, 1972.

* * *

BRYANT, James C(ecil), Jr. 1931-

PERSONAL: Born October 21, 1931, in Lake Wales, Fla.;

son of James Cecil (a shipyard worker) and Mary Lou (McCranie) Bryant; married Marion Carnett (a school teacher), June 19, 1955; children: David, Albert. *Education:* Stetson University, B.A., 1954; Southern Baptist Theological Seminary, B.D., 1958; University of Miami, Coral Gables, Fla., M.A., 1961; University of Kentucky, Ph.D., 1967. *Politics:* Democrat. *Home:* 1470 Leafmore Pl., Decatur, Ga. 30033. *Office:* Mercer University in Atlanta, 3000 Flowers Rd. N.E., Atlanta, Ga. 30341.

CAREER: Ordained minister of Baptist Church, 1958; Arthur Murray Studio, Louisville, Ky., instructor in ballroom dance, 1955-57; pastor in Miami, Fla., 1958-63, and Corinth, Ky., 1963-67; Florida State University, Tallahassee, assistant professor of English, 1967-73, taught under auspices of Overseas Study Center in Florence, Italy, 1969-70; Mercer University in Atlanta, Atlanta, Ga., associate professor of English, 1973—, head of department, 1973—. *Military service:* U.S. Naval Reserve, 1948-52. *Member:* Modern Language Association of America, Renaissance Society of America, College English Association, American Association of University Professors, Sons of the American Revolution (treasurer and vice-president, 1971, 1972, 1973), South Atlantic Modern Language Association, Southeastern Renaissance Conference, Atlanta Writers Club (second vice-president, 1974). *Awards, honors:* Florida Heritage Award from Colonial Dames, 1972, for *Indian Springs: The Story of a Pioneer Church.*

WRITINGS: New Columbus and the Baptist Church, privately printed, 1965; *Indian Springs: The Story of a Pioneer Church,* Florida State University Press, 1972; *Smooth Runs the Water,* Broadman, 1973. Contributor to *Guideposts, Event, United Daughters of the Confederacy Magazine,* and professional journals. Literary specialist for *Youth In Action,* 1972-73.

WORK IN PROGRESS: A devotional book for Broadman; a history of the Wieuca Road Church; a group of short stories.

* * *

BRYANT, Keith L(ynn), Jr. 1937-

PERSONAL: Born November 6, 1937, in Oklahoma City, Okla.; son of Keith L. (a contractor) and Elsie Lillian (Furman) Bryant; married Margaret Anna Burum (a couturiere), August 12, 1962; children: Jennifer Lynne, Craig Warne. *Education:* University of Oklahoma, B.S., 1959, M.Ed., 1961; University of Missouri, Ph.D., 1965. *Religion:* Methodist. *Home:* 8950 North Mohawk Rd., Bayside, Wis. 53217. *Office:* Department of History, University of Wisconsin—Milwaukee, Milwaukee, Wis. 53201.

CAREER: University of Missouri, Columbia, assistant instructor in history, 1962-65; University of Wisconsin—Milwaukee, assistant professor, 1965-68, associate professor, 1968-71, professor of history, 1971—. Has given public lectures on the American Negro in the nineteenth century. *Military service:* U.S. Army Reserve, 1959-67; became first lieutenant. *Member:* Organization of American Historians, National Railway and Locomotive Historical Association, Lexington Group, Southern Historical Association. *Awards, honors:* William H. Kiekhofer Memorial Teaching Award for excellence in teaching, from University of Wisconsin, 1968; American Philosophical Society research grant, 1968.

WRITINGS: Alfalfa Bill Murray, University of Oklahoma Press, 1968; *Arthur E. Stilwell: Promoter with a Hunch,* Vanderbilt University Press, 1971; *History of the Atchison, Topeka, and Santa Fe Railway,* Macmillan, 1974. Contributor of articles and reviews to historical journals, including *Southwestern Historical Quarterly, Labor History, Journal of Southern History, Social Science Quarterly, East Texas Historical Journal,* and *Missouri Historical Review.*

WORK IN PROGRESS: Research on railway expansion and urban growth in the South and Southwest; studying the role of middle class women in the antebellum South.

* * *

BRYDEN, John Marshall 1941-

PERSONAL: Born December 18, 1941, in Perth, Scotland; son of William James and Christina (Marshall) Bryden; married Elspeth Mowat, September 2, 1967; children: Tanera Mowat, Douglas Tyrie. *Education:* University of Glasgow, B.Sc. (honors), 1965; University of the West Indies, graduate study, 1965-66; University of East Anglia, Ph.D., 1972. *Agent:* Shaw-Maclean, 2-10 St. John's Rd., London SW11 1QY, England. *Office:* Highlands-Islands Development Board, Bank St., Inverness IVI IQR, Scotland

CAREER: Ministry of Overseas Development, London, England, economic assistant, 1966-67, Caribbean regional development advisor, 1968-70; University of East Anglia, Norwich, England, lecturer in economics, 1967-72; Highlands-Islands Development Board, Inverness, Scotland, head of land development division, 1972—. *Member:* Agricultural Economics Society, Scottish Economic Society, West Indies Committee, Royal Highlands Agricultural Society, Royal Scottish Forestry Society, British Deer Society.

WRITINGS: Tourism and Development: A Case Study of the Commonwealth Caribbean, Cambridge University Press, 1973. Contributor to *Social and Economic Studies* and *Journal of Agricultural Economics.*

WORK IN PROGRESS: Research on the application of cost benefit analysis and programming techniques to public policy, especially development strategies and land use policies.

* * *

BRYSON, Bernarda 1905- (Bernarda Bryson Shahn)

PERSONAL: Born March 7, 1905, in Athens, Ohio; daughter of Charles Harvey (an editor and publisher) and Lucy (a Latin professor; maiden name, Weethee) Bryson; married Victor Luster Parks, 1927 (divorced, 1930); married Ben Shahn (the artist), 1935 (died, 1969); children: (second marriage) Jonathan, Susanna Shahn Watts (deceased), Abby Shahn Slamm; stepchildren: Judith Shahn Dugan, Ezra. *Education:* Attended Ohio University, 1922-25, Ohio State University, 1926, Western Reserve University (now Case Western Reserve University), 1927, and New School for Social Research. *Politics:* Generally Democrat. *Religion:* Protestant. *Residence:* Roosevelt, N.J.

CAREER: Illustrator for *Fortune, Harper's, Scientific American,* and other magazines. Columbus Gallery of Fine Arts School, Columbus, Ohio, instructor in etching and lithography, 1931. *Member:* Authors League, Society of Illustrators. *Awards, honors: The Twenty Miracles of Saint Nicolas* and *Gilgamesh* were chosen among the fifty books of the year by American Institute of Graphic Arts, 1962 and 1967 respectively.

WRITINGS: (Self-illustrated) *The Twenty Miracles of Saint Nicolas,* Little, Brown, 1960; (self-illustrated) *The Zoo of Zeus,* Grossman, 1964; (self-illustrated) *Gilgamesh,* Holt, 1967; *Ben Shahn,* Abrams, 1973.

Illustrator: Charlton Ogburn, *The White Falcon,* Houghton, 1955; Rutherford Platt, *The River of Life,* Simon & Schuster, 1956; *Lives in Science,* Simon & Schuster, 1957; Jane Austen, *Pride and Prejudice,* Macmillan, 1962; Natalia M. Belting, *The Sun Is a Golden Earring,* Holt, 1962; Emily Bronte, *Wuthering Heights,* Macmillan, 1963; Pauline Clarke, *The Return of the Twelves,* Coward, 1963; Belting, *Calender Moon,* Holt, 1964; Norma Keating, *Mr. Chu,* Macmillan, 1965; Frank R. Stockton, *Storyteller's Pack,* Scribner, 1968; Carl Withers, *The Grindstone of God,* Holt, 1970. Also illustrator of *Bright Hunter of the Skies* and *The Son of the Sun.*

Contributor to *Penrose Annual, Graphis,* and *Image.* Editor of *Southside Advocate,* 1929-31; art columnist for *Ohio State Journal.*

WORK IN PROGRESS: Printmaking and writing.

* * *

BUCHWALD, Emilie 1935-

PERSONAL: Born September 6, 1935, in Vienna, Austria; daughter of Norbert Norton (a lawyer) and Maryla (Knebel) Bix; married Henry Buchwald (a surgeon), June 6, 1954; children: Jane Nicole, Amy Elizabeth, Claire Gretchen, Dana Alexandra. *Education:* Barnard College, B.A. (magna cum laude), 1957; Columbia University, M.A., 1960; University of Minnesota, Ph.D., 1971. *Home:* 6808 Margaret's Lane, Edina, Minn. 55435.

CAREER: Worked summers during college as editorial assistant on New York edition of *TV Guide,* 1955, as guest fiction editor of *Mademoiselle,* 1956, and editorial secretary for *Sloane Hospital Magazine,* 1957; University of Minnesota, Minneapolis, instructor in English, 1960-68. *Member:* Modern Language Association of America, Women's National Book Association, Phi Beta Kappa. *Awards, honors: Chicago Tribune* Children's Book Festival Award in middle age group, 1973, for *Gildaen.*

WRITINGS: Gildaen: The Heroic Adventures of a Most Unusual Rabbit, Harcourt, 1973. Work is represented in anthologies, including *Prize Stories of 1959: The O. Henry Awards,* edited by Paul Engle, Doubleday, 1959; *Anthology of Magazine Verse for 1958,* edited by W.S.B. Braithwaite, Schulte, 1959; *When Women Look at Men,* edited by J. A. Kouwenhoven and J. F. Thaddeus, Harper, 1961; *Studies in Criticism and Aesthetics, 1660-1800,* edited by H. P. Anderson and J. S. Shea, University of Minnesota Press, 1968. Contributor to *Harper's, Ladies' Home Journal, Harper's Bazaar, Kenyon Review, American Quarterly,* and other periodicals.

WORK IN PROGRESS: A contemporary fantasy for children.

SIDELIGHTS: Emilie Buchwald writes: "I began writing poetry as a child and I still believe that the techniques of poetry—metaphor, allusion, compression, attention to the texture of language—are basic to any good writing. My father was a marvelous story-teller, a man who loved to talk to others and exchange ideas, ask questions; his stories, his love of books, his interest in people and joy in living had a great deal to do with my interest in writing." *Avocational interests:* Reading, playing the guitar, gardening, cooking, tennis, and most outdoor sports.

BUCKERIDGE, Anthony (Malcolm) 1912-

PERSONAL: Born June 20, 1912, in London, England; son of Ernest George (a bank official) and Gertrud (Smith) Buckeridge; married Eileen Selby, October, 1962; children: Sally, Timothy, Corin. *Education:* Studied at University College, London, 1933-35. *Politics:* Liberal. *Religion:* Church of England. *Home and office:* East Crink, Barcombe Mills, Lewes, Sussex, England. *Agent:* Hughes Massie Ltd., 69 Great Russell St., London W.C.1, England.

CAREER: Schoolmaster at boys' preparatory schools in England, with last teaching post at St. Lawrence College, Ramsgate, Kent, 1945-50; writer of series of radio plays, "Jennings at School," produced by British Broadcasting Corp., starting in 1948, and of Jennings books and other juveniles. *Member:* Society of Authors, Writers' Guild of Great Britain, British Actors' Equity Association.

WRITINGS—"Jennings" series, published in England by Collins: *Jennings Goes to School,* 1950; *Jennings Follows a Clue,* 1951; *Jennings' Little Hut,* 1951; *Jennings and Darbishire,* 1952; *Jennings' Diary,* 1953; *According to Jennings,* 1954; *Our Friend Jennings,* 1955, Penguin, 1967; *Thanks to Jennings,* 1957; *Take Jennings, for Instance,* 1958; *Jennings as Usual,* 1959; *The Trouble with Jennings,* 1960; *Just Like Jennings,* 1961; *Leave It to Jennings,* 1963; *Jennings, of Course!,* 1964; *Especially Jennings!,* 1965; *A Bookful of Jennings,* 1966; *Jennings Abounding,* 1966; *Jennings in Particular,* 1967; *Trust Jennings!,* 1968; *The Jennings Report,* 1969; *Typically Jennings,* 1970; *The Best of Jennings,* 1972; *Speaking of Jennings,* 1973.

"Rex Milligan" series, published in England by Lutterworth: *Rex Milligan's Busy Term,* 1954; *Rex Milligan Raises the Roof,* 1955; *Rex Milligan Holds Forth,* 1956; *Rex Milligan Reporting,* 1957.

Other books: *A Funny Thing Happened,* Lutterworth, 1953; (editor) *Stories for Boys,* Faber, 1956; (editor) *In and Out of School,* British Book Service, 1958; (editor) *Stories for Boys 2,* Faber, 1965; (co-author) Eric Duthie, editor, *Stirring Stories for Boys,* Odhams, 1966.

Author of radio and television plays for young people.

WORK IN PROGRESS: A new title in "Jennings" series; more television and radio plays.

SIDELIGHTS: Buckeridge said: "The humor of the Jennings stories is based upon the logical absurdities of all small boys. As an ex-schoolmaster, I enjoy writing humor set against a background with which I am familiar. If I had been an undertaker instead of a teacher I would write funny stories about funerals!

"The urge to write comedy overtook me when as a small boy I was told to write a story during an English lesson at school. My story was a tragic tale and the writing of it moved me almost to tears—but when the master read it aloud the class rocked with laughter. I was so taken aback that I decided to play for safety and write comedies in future!"

BIOGRAPHICAL/CRITICAL SOURCES: Geoffrey Trease, *Tales Out of School,* Oxford University Press, 1948; John Rowe Townsend, *Written for Children,* Garnet Miller, 1965.

* * *

BUCKEYE, Donald A(ndrew) 1930-

PERSONAL: Born March 12, 1930, in Lakewood, Ohio;

son of Andrew M. (a pattern maker) and Elizabeth (Wagner) Buckeye; married Nancy R. O'Neill, June 16, 1962; children: Pamela Jean, Karen Ann. *Education:* Ashland College, B.S.Ed., 1953; Indiana University, M.A., 1961, Ph.D., 1967. *Home:* 1823 Witmire, Ypsilanti, Mich. 48197. *Office:* Department of Mathematics, Eastern Michigan University, Ypsilanti, Mich. 48197.

CAREER: High school mathematics teacher in public schools in Lakewood, Ohio, 1957-65; Eastern Michigan University, Ypsilanti, professor of mathematics, 1967—. Teaching assistant at Ohio State University, 1962-65. *Military service:* U.S. Army, 1954-56. *Member:* National Council of Teachers of Mathematics, Michigan Council of Teachers of Mathematics, Ohio Council of Teachers of Mathematics, Cleveland Council of Teachers of Mathematics (vice-president, 1960-61; president, 1962-63), Phi Delta Kappa.

WRITINGS—All published by Midwest Publications, except where noted otherwise: *Experiments in Probability and Statistics,* 1969; (with William A. Ewbank and John L. Ginther) *Downpour of Math Lab Experiments,* 1969; *Experiments and Puzzles in Logic,* 1970; *Creative Geometry Experiments,* 1970; *Creative Experiments in Algebra,* 1971; (with Ginther) *Creative Mathematics,* Canfield Press, 1971; (with Ginther) *Creative Mathematics Laboratory Manual,* Canfield Press, 1971; (with Ewbank and Ginther) *Cloudburst of Math Lab Experiments,* five volumes, 1971; *N.R. Math Activities,* Volume I, 1972, Volume II, 1973, Volume III, 1974; *Experiments in Fractions,* 1972; *Introducing the Metric System with Activities,* 1972; *Primary Activities in Mathematics,* 1972; (with Ewbank and Ginther) *Cheap Math Lab Equipment,* 1972; *I'm OK, You're OK, Let's Go Metric,* 1974; (with others) *School Math,* eight volumes, Rand McNally, 1974.

* * *

BUCKSTEAD, Richard C(hris) 1929-

PERSONAL: Born March 17, 1929, in Viborg, S.D.; son of Lawrence J. (a farmer) and Ardath (Heddinger) Buckstead; married Geraldine Oldaker, September 8, 1957; children: Jonathan, Sarah, Chris, Brian. *Education:* Yankton College, B.A., 1950; University of South Dakota, M.A., 1956; University of Iowa, Ph.D., 1958. *Religion:* Lutheran. *Home:* 903 Highland, Northfield, Minn. 55057. *Office:* Department of English, St. Olaf College, Northfield, Minn. 55057.

CAREER: Augustana College, Sioux Falls, S.D., instructor in English, 1957-58; Southeast Missouri State College, Cape Girardeau, instructor in English, 1958-61; St. Olaf College, Northfield, Minn., assistant professor, 1961-65, associate professor of English, 1965—. Visiting professor at Chulalongkorn University, Bangkok, 1967-68. *Military service:* U.S. Army, Engineers, 1951-54; served in Korea; became master sergeant. *Member:* Modern Language Association of America, Association for Asian Studies. *Awards, honors:* Ford Foundation grant, 1957; National Endowment for the Humanities grant, 1972.

WRITINGS: A Guide to the Mechanics of the Research Paper, Sernoll, 1966; *Kawabata and the Divided Self,* China Books (Taipei), 1972. Contributor to *Tamkang Review, South Dakota Review,* and *Asian Profile* (Hong Kong).

WORK IN PROGRESS: A book on Yukio Mishima.

BUDD, William C(laude) 1923-

PERSONAL: Born February 21, 1923, in Maple Plain, Minn.; son of Claude M. (a mail carrier) and Elsie (Kuntz) Budd; married Jean Verna Dongoske, July 1, 1944; married Betty Jean Davenport (a high school teacher), May 1, 1973; children: Randall Owen, Timothy Alan. *Education:* Hamline University, B.A., 1944; University of Chicago, graduate study, 1946-47; University of Minnesota, B.S. and M.A., 1948, Ph.D., 1951. *Religion:* Congregationalist. *Home:* 735 Lake Whatcom Blvd., Bellingham, Wash. 98225. *Office:* Department of Psychology, Western Washington State College, Bellingham, Wash. 98225.

CAREER: Goucher College, Baltimore, Md., assistant professor of psychology, 1951-53; Western Washington State College, Bellingham, assistant professor, 1953-56, associate professor, 1956-65, professor of psychology, 1965—. *Military service:* U.S. Naval Reserve, active duty, 1944-46; became lieutenant junior grade. *Member:* American Psychological Association, American Educational Research Association, National Council on Measurement in Education, Council for Basic Education, Phi Delta Kappa.

WRITINGS: (With Sam Kelly) *Educational Research by Practitioners,* Harper, 1970; (with Don Blood) *Educational Measurement and Evaluation,* Harper, 1972; *Behavior Modification,* Libra, 1973. Contributor to *Northwest Salmon-Trout-Steelheader.*

WORK IN PROGRESS: Christian Behaviorism (tentative title).

AVOCATIONAL INTERESTS: Fishing (for trout), gardening (especially roses), vocal music.

* * *

BUECHNER, Thomas S(charman) 1926-

PERSONAL: Born September 25, 1926, in New York, N.Y.; son of Thomas S. (an advertising executive) and Anne (Lines) Buechner; married Mary Hawkins, September 15, 1949; children: Barbara, Thomas, Jr., Matthew. *Education:* Princeton University, B.A., 1944; attended Art Students League, 1946; L'Ecoles des Beaux Arts at Fontainebleau, 1947, and Paris, 1948; Institute Voor Pictologie, 1948. *Home:* R. D. #2, Spencer Hill, Corning, N.Y. 14830. *Office:* Corning Glass Works, Corning, N.Y. 14830.

CAREER: Metropolitan Museum of Art, New York, N.Y., assistant manager of display department, 1949-50; Corning Museum of Glass, Corning, N.Y., director, 1950-60; Brooklyn Museum, Brooklyn, N.Y., director, 1960-71; Steuben Glass, New York, N.Y., vice-president, 1971-72, president, 1972—; Corning Museum of Glass, Corning, N.Y., president, 1971—; Corning Glass Works Foundation, Corning, president, 1971—; director, Corning International Corporation, 1971—. Member of board of trustees, Brooklyn Institute of Arts and Sciences, 1971—, and Louis C. Tiffany Foundation, 1972—. *Member:* Royal Society of Art (fellow), American Association of Museums (member of council, 1969), National Collection of Fine Arts (member of advisory board, 1971). *Awards, honors:* Man of the Year award from Brooklyn College, City University of New York, 1965; Forsythia award from Brooklyn Botanic Garden, 1971; Gari Melchers Medal from American Artist Fellows, 1971.

WRITINGS: Norman Rockwell: Artist and Illustrator, Abrams, 1970. Contributor to *Encyclopaedia Britannica, Hisperia, Interiors, Life, Museum News, Antiques, Ar-*

chaeology, Art News, Connoisseur, and *Design.* Author of numerous catalogues, monographs, and histories for Corning Glass Works and Brooklyn Museums.

AVOCATIONAL INTERESTS: Portrait painter and illustrator.

BIOGRAPHICAL/CRITICAL SOURCES: New York Herald Tribune, August 4, 1960.

* * *

BUELL, Lawrence 1939-

PERSONAL: Born June 11, 1939, in Bryn Mawr, Pa.; son of C. A. (a business executive) and Marjorie (Henderson) Buell; married Phyllis Kimber (a college administrator), August 18, 1962; children: Denise, Deirdre. *Education:* Princeton University, B.A., 1961; Cornell University, M.A., 1963, Ph.D., 1966. *Office:* Department of English, Oberlin College, Oberlin, Ohio 44074.

CAREER: Tunghai University, Taichung, Taiwan, instructor in English, 1963-65; Oberlin College, Oberlin, Ohio, assistant professor, 1966-72, associate professor of English, 1972—. Chairman of board of trustees of Oberlin Shansi Memorial Association, 1972—.

WRITINGS: Design of Literature, Pendulum Press, 1973; *Literary Transcendentalism,* Cornell University Press, 1973.

AVOCATIONAL INTERESTS: Sports, reading.

* * *

BUETTNER-JANUSCH, John 1924-

PERSONAL: Surname is pronounced *Bitt*-ner-*Yah*-nush; born December 7, 1924, in Chicago, Ill.; son of Frederick William (an architect) and Gertrude (Buettner) Janusch; married Vina Mallowitz, September 22, 1950. *Education:* University of Chicago, Ph.B., 1948, S.B., 1949, A.M., 1953; University of Michigan, Ph.D., 1957. *Home:* 29 Washington Sq. W., New York, N.Y. 10011. *Office:* Department of Anthropology, New York University, New York, N.Y. 10003.

CAREER: University of Utah, Salt Lake City, instructor in anthropology for department of preventive medicine, 1953-55; Wayne State University, Detroit, Mich., instructor in sociology and anthropology, winter, 1956; University of Michigan, Ann Arbor, research assistant at Laboratory of Physical Anthropology, 1957-58; Yale University, New Haven, Conn., assistant professor, 1958-62, associate professor of anthropology, 1962-65; Duke University, Durham, N.C., associate professor, 1965-67, professor of anatomy and zoology, 1967-73, professor of sociology and anthropology, 1970-71; New York University, New York, N.Y., professor of anthropology and chairman of department, 1973—. Seminar associate, Columbia University, 1959—; research associate, Southwest Foundation for Research and Education, 1960-70; chairman of scientific advisory board, Caribbean Primate Research Center, 1971—; member, advisory panel for anthropology, National Science Foundation, 1971-74; member of Bobbs-Merrill editorial selection committee in anthropology, 1961—. Has conducted field work in Kenya and Madagascar.

MEMBER: International Society for Human Biology, American Anthropological Association (fellow), American Association of Physical Anthropologists (member of executive committee, 1971—), American Association for the Advancement of Science (fellow), New York Academy of Sciences (fellow), Sigma Xi. *Awards, honors:* National Science Foundation senior postdoctoral fellowship, 1962-63; U.S. Public Health Service research career development award, 1963-1973.

WRITINGS: (Contributor) G. E. Dole and R. L. Carneiro, editors, *Essays in the Science of Culture,* Crowell, 1960; (editor and contributor) *Evolutionary and Genetic Biology of Primates,* Academic Press, Volume I, 1963, Volume II, 1964; (contributor) H. Peeters, editor, *Protides of the Biological Fluids,* Elsevier, 1964; (contributor) Harold Vagtborg, editor, *The Baboon in Medical Research,* University of Texas Press, 1965; (contributor) Vernon Bryson and H. J. Vogel, editors, *Evolving Genes and Proteins,* Academic Press, 1965; *Origins of Man: Physical Anthropology,* Wiley, 1966.

(Contributor) E. S. E. Hafez, editor, *Comparative Reproduction of Nonhuman Primates,* C.C Thomas, 1971; *Physical Anthropology: A Perspective,* Wiley, 1973; (editor) *Yearbook of Physical Anthropology 1972,* Volume XVI, American Anthropological Association, 1973. Contributor to *International Zoo Yearbook* and *Encyclopaedia Britannica.* Contributor of about one hundred articles and reviews to scientific journals, including *American Journal of Physical Anthropology, Folia Primatologica, Annual Review of Genetics, International Journal of Biochemistry, Journal of Investigative Dermatology,* and *Science.* Associate editor, *American Journal of Physical Anthropology,* 1970—.

WORK IN PROGRESS: Research on evolution, biochemical genetics, and physical anthropology of living primates; research on the history of anthropology and history of science.

* * *

BULLINS, Ed 1935-

PERSONAL: Born July 2, 1935, in Philadelphia, Pa.; married; wife's name, Trixie. *Education:* Attended Los Angeles City College and San Francisco State College (now University). *Home:* 932 East 212th St., Bronx, N.Y. 10469. *Agent:* Whitman Mayo, The New Lafayette, 2349 Seventh Ave., New York, N.Y. 10030. *Office:* TRIXCLEV, Inc., 932 East 212th St., Bronx, N.Y. 10469.

CAREER: Left Philadelphia for Los Angeles in 1958, then moved to San Francisco in 1964; co-founder, Black Arts/West; co-founder of the Black Arts Alliance, Black House (Black Panther Party headquarters in San Francisco), cultural director until 1967, also serving briefly as Minister of Culture of the Party; joined The New Lafayette Theatre, New York, N.Y., in 1967, becoming playwright-in-residence, 1968, associate director, 1971—. Playwright-in-residence, American Place Theatre, 1973—. *Military service:* U.S. Navy, 1952-55. *Member:* Dramatists Guild. *Awards, honors:* American Place Theatre grant, 1967; Vernon Rice Drama Desk Award, 1968, for plays performed at American Place Theatre; Rockefeller Foundation grant, 1970, in support of playwriting at New Lafayette Theatre and Workshop; Obie Award for distinguished playwriting, and Black Arts Alliance award, both 1971, for "The Fabulous Miss Marie" and "In New England Winter"; Guggenheim fellowship for playwriting, 1971; grants from Rockefeller Foundation and Creative Artists Public Service Program, both 1973, in support of playwriting.

WRITINGS: (Editor and contributor) *New Plays from the Black Theatre,* Bantam, 1969; *The Hungered One* (collected short fiction), Morrow, 1971; *The Reluctant Rapist* (novel), Harper, 1973; (editor) *The New Lafayette Theatre Presents the Complete Plays and Aesthetic Comments by Six Black Playwrights* (anthology), Doubleday-Anchor, 1973.

Published plays: *How Do You Do?: A Nonsense Drama* (one-act; first produced as "How Do You Do" in San Francisco at Firehouse Repertory Theatre, August 5, 1965; produced Off-Broadway by La Mama Experimental Theatre Club at Actor's Playhouse, February, 1972), Illuminations Press, 1967; "In New England Winter" (one-act; first produced Off-Broadway at New Federal Theatre of Henry Street Playhouse, January 26, 1971), published in *New Plays from the Black Theatre,* edited by Bullins, Bantam, 1969; *Five Plays* (includes: "Goin' a Buffalo" [three-act; first produced in New York City at New Lafayette Theatre, October 24, 1969], "In the Wine Time" [three-act; first produced at New Lafayette Theatre, December 10, 1968], "A Son Come Home" [one-act; first produced Off-Broadway at American Place Theatre, February 21, 1968; originally published in Negro Digest, *April, 1968*], "The Electronic Nigger" [one-act; first produced at American Place Theatre, February 21, 1968], and "Clara's Ole Man" [one-act; first produced in San Francisco, August 5, 1965; produced at American Place Theatre, February 21, 1968]), Bobbs-Merrill, 1969 (published in England as *The Electronic Nigger, and Other Plays,* Faber, 1970).

"The Gentleman Caller" (one-act; first produced in Brooklyn, N.Y., with other plays as "A Black Quartet" by Chelsea Theatre Center at Brooklyn Academy of Music, April 25, 1969), published in *A Black Quartet,* New American Library, 1970; *The Duplex: A Black Love Fable in Four Movements* (one-act; first produced at New Lafayette Theatre, May 22, 1970; produced at Forum Theatre of Lincoln Center, New York, N.Y., March 9, 1972), Morrow, 1971.

The Theme is Blackness: The Corner, and Other Plays (includes: "The Theme Is Blackness" [first produced in San Francisco by Black Arts/West], "The Corner" [one-act; first produced in Boston; produced Off-Broadway at Public Theatre, June 22, 1972], "Dialect Determinism" [one-act; first produced in San Francisco, August 5, 1965; produced at La Mama Experimental Theatre Club, February 25, 1972], "It Has No Choice" [one-act; first produced in San Francisco by The Playwrights' Workshop; produced at La Mama Experimental Theatre Club, February 25, 1972], "The Helper" [first produced in New York by New Dramatists Workshop], "A Minor Scene" [first produced in San Francisco by Black Arts/West; produced at La Mama Experimental Theatre Club, February 25, 1972], "The Man Who Dug Fish" [first produced by New Dramatists Workshop], "Black Commercial #2," "The American Flag Ritual," "State Office Bldg. Curse," "One Minute Commercial," "A Street Play," "Street Sounds" [first produced at La Mama Experimental Theatre Club, October 14, 1970], "A Short Play for a Small Theatre," and "The Play of the Play"), Morrow, 1972.

Four Dynamite Plays (includes: "It Bees Dat Way" [one-act; first produced in London; produced in New York at ICA, October, 1970], "Death List" [one-act; first produced in New York by Theatre Black at University of the Streets, October 3, 1970], "The Pig Pen" [one-act; first produced at American Place Theatre, May 20, 1970], and "Night of the Beast" [screenplay]), Morrow, 1972.

Unpublished plays: "The Devil Catchers," first produced at New Lafayette Theatre, November 27, 1970; "The Fabulous Miss Marie" (one-act), first produced at New Lafayette Theatre, March 5, 1971; "The Psychic Pretenders" ("A Black Magic Show"), first produced at New Lafayette Theatre, December, 1971; "House Party," first produced at American Place Theatre, fall, 1973; "Home Boy," scheduled for first production at American Place Theatre; (with Shirley Tarbell) "The Game of Adam and Eve," first produced in Los Angeles at Playwrights' Theatre, later done in workshop productions in Boston and New York; "Next Time. . .," first produced in Bronx, N.Y. at Bronx Community College; "Ya Gonna Let Me Take You Out Tonight, Baby?," first produced Off-Broadway at Public Theatre.

Also author of plays, "Malcolm '71, or Publishing Blackness," and "Steve and Velma," neither as yet produced nor published.

Work is represented in *New American Plays,* Volume III, edited by William M. Hoffman, Hill & Wang, 1970. Editor of *Black Theatre,* 1968-72; editor of special black issue of *Drama Review,* summer, 1968. Contributor to *Negro Digest, New York Times,* and other periodicals.

SIDELIGHTS: Viewers of Bullins' plays are often struck by the lack of artifice in his characterizations; the actors seem to be living rather than acting on stage, and they persuade their audiences to accept their reality. "Bullins' characters are tough and funky, touching and hilarious, and they are insistently alive," Marilyn Stasio writes. Lindsay Patterson called the New Lafayette Theatre production of "In the Wine Time" "a slice of black life as it is actually lived. . . . Bullins is a superb craftsman, and he has a wonderful ear for the language of the ghetto, which is almost always cartooned by writers, and hardly ever caught correctly. His most notable achievement, however, is the lack of self-indulgence in his writing, a flaw which many young artists insist upon today with impunity. . . . He has a deep sensitivity, love and understanding for his characters that enable him to present a rare thing, a truthful presentation of ghetto dwellers."

Bullins knows the ghetto because he has always lived there. D.A.N. Jones says that "he denies being a working-class playwright: he is from the criminal class. All the other men in his family have been in prison. He is the only one who went to high school, who went to college; but he claims that working people in Harlem like his surrealist, intellectual plays." Mel Gussow observes that Bullins "wrote his autobiography at 18 and 'a ponderous novel, short stories, fantasies, dreams, poetry,' and published mostly in little Negro magazines and underground newspapers. Eventually, he made two major commitments. He turned from what had become a 'middle-class orientation' to a black self-awareness (his close friend and chief literary influence is LeRoi Jones [Imamu Amiri Baraka]), and in 1965 he began writing plays." Since then he has written over thirty, many of them regarded as classics of Black Theatre, and is now engaged in a remarkable undertaking; a 20-play cycle about the black experience in America; five of which he has completed—"In the Wine Time," "In New England Winter," "The Duplex," "The Fabulous Miss Marie," and "Home Boy."

As Clive Barnes pointed out, Bullins is so prolific that his work is predictably uneven. . . . But at his best he has a trenchancy that few American playwrights can muster." Some of his earlier plays are criticized for their "blatant" militancy. After seeing "The Gentleman Caller," Harold

Clurman remarked: "If Bullins hopes to help his cause he must do so in his own (more complex) person rather than as a private in the ranks of the committed." A critic for *Village Voice* found that "many of the play's attitudes already seem outdated (always a risk when considerations of rhetoric take precedent over those of humanity). . . . For unlike [LeRoi] Jones, Bullins isn't content to let irony make his point, and adds a rousing black power speech that brought cheers from the blacks in the audiences and a trace of white into the pink faces of the Caucasians. I couldn't help wondering why Bullins wrote a play at all if he didn't trust the form to convey his meaning." A more recent work, "Death List," drew the opposite reaction from a reviewer for *Show Business:* "Bullins is too good a playwright to write a play of rhetoric. Instead he turns out something which, it may be too impulsive to say, might become a minor classic of Black Theatre. It is a document of our times by the Minister of Culture of the Black Panther Party."

Jack Kroll once observed that Bullins "is one of the few Negro writers who, writing out of a fierce sense of black identity, refuse to accommodate their vision to white sensibilities." In a discussion of the future of Black Theatre in America, Bullins told Marvin X of *Negro Digest:* "We do not want to have a higher form of white art in black-face. We are working towards something entirely different and new that encompasses the soul and spirit and black people, which is our whole experience of being here in this oppressive land. All the things that are positive in us, our music, our very strong religion, our own life-style, [we are] incorporating into our art on a collective basis to make us individually better artists and collectively to have a uniform positive art so that 10 years from now, the things we do now will be recognized but will be far from where we have been. By then I think that we will be completely different from white Anglo-Saxon Western things, and it will be totally black."

The absence of "whitey" in Bullins' plays is especially evident in *The Duplex,* which Clurman believes is "the best thing that has been done" at the Forum Theatre of Lincoln Center. "Crazy dark laughter envelops all the proceedings, but the meaning is frightful. It is not simply a matter of revealing the horrid messiness typical of most ghettos, whatever the color of their inhabitants; there is something more damaging beyond the specifics of promiscuous fornication, smoking of pot, gambling, drunkenness, outbursts of physical brutality, irresponsibility and wrecked lives. What is really being exposed is our civilization." Catharine Hughes comments on Bullins' style: "Bullins has never paid much attention to the niceties of formal structure, choosing instead to concentrate on black life as it very likely really is—a continuing succession of encounters and dialogues, major events and non-events, small joys and ever-present sorrows. . . . *The Duplex* is virtually shapeless; it does not really end, merely stops, its central situation unresolved. It is a mixture of styles, from farce to tragedy, a play that works within its own definition of theatre (and mine), within its own definition of life. It reveals characters and situations that are, for the most part, alien to the white experience. Bullins makes you aware of why blacks have only infrequently attended white theatre. His plays grow out of black life and are written *for blacks.* The white member of the audience is in a sense almost an interloper, looking in on a culture that has a distinctly different texture."

During the 1968-69 season London playgoers had the opportunity to observe what Charles Marowitz called "America's great hopes, white and black." In his article for the *New York Times,* he sounded vaguely reminiscent of that "white interloper looking in": "Ed Bullins, out of Genet via Le Roi Jones, writes like a man trying to dislodge a big white monkey from his back. His obsession is the corruption of black integrity by white values. His plays are composed like effigies, specially designed to torture his enemies, and based on the magical assumption that if one destroys the symbol often enough, the reality will also get impaired. Like the vendettas of Le Roi Jones, they belong less to the conventions of art than they do to the world of black magic. Which is precisely why they are so fascinating in the theater. . . . Actually, what can one say about writers like Bullins and Jones? They spell out the details of the white man's corruption of their race, and remote white critics in America and England sit back and sift their perceptions as if artifacts were immune from the terrible social indictments they contain. How can you tell a man he has written a very good diagnosis of your criminality and keep a straight face?"

"Goin' a Buffalo" was filmed by the New Lafayette Theatre in 1971.

BIOGRAPHICAL/CRITICAL SOURCES: Negro Digest, April, 1969; Stanley Richards, editor, *Best Short Plays of 1970,* Chilton, 1970; Addison Gayle, editor, *The Black Aesthetic,* Doubleday, 1971; *Plays and Players,* March, 1973; *New Yorker,* June 16, 1973; *Contemporary Literary Criticism,* Volume I, Gale, 1973.*

* * *

BULLIS, Jerald 1944-

PERSONAL: Born May 5, 1944, in Sioux City, Iowa; son of L. H. (an electrician) and Hattie (Miller) Bullis; married Frances Meyers, June 1, 1968. *Education:* Central Methodist College, student, 1962-64; Washington University, St. Louis, Mo., A.B., 1966; Cornell University, M.A., 1969, Ph.D., 1970. *Home:* 600 East College Ave., Appleton, Wis. 54911. *Office:* Department of English, Lawrence University, Appleton, Wis. 54911.

CAREER: Lawrence University, Appleton, Wis., assistant professor of English, 1970-74. *Member:* Modern Language Association of America, Phi Beta Kappa. *Awards, honors:* Woodrow Wilson fellowship, 1966-67; National Endowment for the Arts research grant, 1972-73.

WRITINGS: Taking Up the Serpent: A Book of Poems, Ithaca House, 1973. Contributor to journals.

WORK IN PROGRESS: A book of poems, *Foraging.*

AVOCATIONAL INTERESTS: Hunting.

* * *

BULMAN, Oliver (Meredith Boone) 1902-1974

May 20, 1902—1974; British paleontologist and author. Obituaries: *AB Bookman's Weekly,* April 15, 1974.

* * *

BUOL, S(tanley) W(alter) 1934-

PERSONAL: Surname rhymes with "mule"; born June 14, 1934, in Madison, Wis.; son of Walter A. (a farmer) and Marie (Carteron) Buol; married Joan E. Showers, July 9, 1960; children: Gregory Stanley, Glenda Marie. *Education:* University of Wisconsin, B.S., 1956, M.S., 1958, Ph.D.,

1960. *Politics:* None. *Religion:* Protestant. *Home:* 1408 Creech Rd., Garner, N.C. 27529. *Office:* Soil Science Department, North Carolina State University, Raleigh, N.C. 27607.

CAREER: Department of Agriculture, Soil Conservation Service, Waukesha, Wis., soil scientist, 1956-57; University of Arizona, Tucson, assistant professor, 1960-64, associate professor of agriculture, 1964-66; North Carolina State University, Raleigh, associate professor, 1966-69, professor of agriculture, 1969—. Consultant to Union Camp and to Sensory Systems Laboratory. *Military service:* Wisconsin Army National Guard, 1952-60; became sergeant. *Member:* American Society of Agronomy, Soil Science Society of America, North Carolina Soil Science Society, Alpha Zeta, Sigma Xi.

WRITINGS: (With F. D. Hole and R. J. McCracken) *Soil Genesis and Classification,* Iowa State University Press, 1973. Contributor of about fifty articles to journals in his field.

WORK IN PROGRESS: Research on soil genesis and formation in the Amazon jungle, central Brazil, and Costa Rican uplands; a book about soilscapes.

SIDELIGHTS: Buol has travelled in Africa, South America, Central America, and the United States observing how people produce food.

* * *

BURCHETT, Wilfred 1911-

PERSONAL: Born September 16, 1911, in Melbourne, Australia; son of George Harold (a writer and farmer) and Mary Jane (Davy) Burchett; married Vesselina Ossikovska (a journalist and art historian), December 24, 1949; children: Peter, George, Anna. *Education:* Educated in Australia and England. *Politics:* "Ho Chi Minist." *Home:* 93, Route des Gardes, 92-Meudon, France.

CAREER: Daily Express, London, England, war correspondent in China, Burma, India, and Pacific Theatre, 1941-45, in Berlin and Central Europe, 1945-49; *Times,* London, England, foreign correspondent in Budapest, 1949-50; *Ce Soir,* Paris, France, foreign correspondent in China and Korea, 1951-53; free-lance correspondent in Hanoi, North Vietnam, 1954-57; *Daily Express,* London, foreign correspondent in Moscow, 1957-61; foreign correspondent in Moscow for *Financial Times,* London, England, and *National Guardian,* New York, N.Y., 1961-65; *Guardian,* New York, foreign correspondent in Phnom Penh, Cambodia, 1965-68, and in Paris, 1968—. *Member:* National Union of Journalists.

WRITINGS: Pacific Treasure Island, F. W. Cheshire, 1941; *Bombs Over Burma,* F. W. Cheshire, 1943; *Wingate Adventure,* F. W. Cheshire, 1944; *Democracy with a Tommygun,* F. W. Cheshire, 1946.

Cold War in Germany, World Unity Publications, 1951; *China's Feet Unbound,* World Unity Publications, 1952; *This Monstrous War,* Jo Waters, 1953; *North of the Seventeenth Parallel,* Red River Publishing House, 1955; *Mekong Upstream,* Red River Publishing House, 1957.

Gagarin: First Man into Outer Space, Panther Books, 1961; *Titov's Flight into Space,* Panther Books, 1962; *The Furtive War,* International Publishers, 1963; *Vietnam: Inside Story of the Guerilla War,* International Publishers, 1965; *Vietnam North,* International Publishers, 1966; *Again Korea?,* International Publishers, 1968; *Vietnam Will Win,* Guardian Publishing, 1968; *Passport,* Thomas Nelson, 1969.

Second Indochina War, Lorrimer, 1970; (with Prince Norodom Sihanouk) *My War with the C.I.A.,* Penguin, 1973; (with Rewi Alley) *China: The Quality of Life,* Penguin, 1974.

Author of about a dozen documentary television films on Indochina and North Korea. Contributor to *Afrique-Asie, Paris, Nation-Review,* and *Le Monde Diplomatique.*

WORK IN PROGRESS: Origins of the Korean War; The New Face of Indochina (tentative title), biographical sketches of revolutionary leaders in Southeast Asia.

SIDELIGHTS: Burchett's interests are in national liberation movements and independence struggles in Southeast Asia and throughout the rest of the world. He supports national rights and self-determination for all people. He speaks French, German, and Russian, and to a lesser degree, Chinese, Italian, and Spanish; his books have been published in thirty-one countries and in thirty-two languages.

* * *

BURCKHARDT, C(arl) J(akob) 1891-1974

September 10, 1891—March 3, 1974; Swiss historian, author, and diplomat. Obituaries: *New York Times,* March 5, 1974; *Washington Post,* March 5, 1974.

* * *

BURGWYN, Mebane Holoman 1914-

PERSONAL: Born December 10, 1914, in Rich Square, N.C.; daughter of Henry Dorsey and Pattie Vaughn (White) Holoman; married John Griffin Burgwyn (a farm owner), August 17, 1935; children: John Griffin, Jr., Josephine Mebane (Mrs. James D. Pratt), Henry Holoman, Stephen White. *Politics:* Democrat. *Religion:* Episcopalian. *Education:* University of North Carolina at Greensboro, A.B., 1935; East Carolina University, M.A., 1962. *Home:* Occoneechee Farms, Route I, Box 269, Jackson, N.C. 27845.

CAREER: Northampton County Schools, Jackson, N.C., director of guidance services, 1959-69. Member of executive committee, University of North Carolina board of trustees, 1955-71; member of board of trustees, East Carolina University, 1973—. Chairman of North Carolina Writer's Conference, 1962. *Member:* American Personnel and Guidance Association, National Education Association, North Carolina Personnel and Guidance Association (president, 1964), North Carolina Writers. Roanoke Chowan Group, Delta Kappa Gamma (honorary member). *Awards, honors:* Juvenile Award of North Carolina Division of American Association of University Women, 1954, for *Penny Rose,* and 1970, for *The Crackajack Pony;* University of North Carolina at Greensboro Service Award, 1973.

WRITINGS—All for young people: *River Treasure,* Oxford University Press, 1948; *Lucky Mischief,* Oxford University Press, 1950; *Penny Rose,* Oxford University Press, 1952; *Moonflower,* Lippincott, 1954; *True Love for Jenny,* Lippincott, 1956; *Hunter's Hideout,* Lippincott, 1959; *The Crackajack Pony,* Lippincott, 1969.

SIDELIGHTS: Mebane Burgwyn writes: "Books for children have been a result of wanting to share experiences of farm living with those who do or do not know about such activities. Teen-age books reflect experiences with teenagers and my interest in counseling young people." *Avocational interests:* Art, particularly acrylic painting.

BURKE, S(amuel) M(artin) 1906-

PERSONAL: Born July 3, 1906, in Pakistan; son of K. D. and Bashir Burke; married Queenie Louise Neville; children: four daughters. *Education:* Government College, Lahore, B.A. (honors), 1926, M.A., 1928; School of Oriental Studies, University of London, further study, 1929-31. *Home:* 1566 Coffman St., St. Paul, Minn. 55108. *Office:* 1246 Social Sciences Bldg., University of Minnesota, Minneapolis, Minn. 55455.

CAREER: Indian Civil Service, India, district officer, district and sessions judge, and chairman of first Election Petitions Commission, Punjab, 1931-47; Pakistani Foreign Service, 1948-61, ambassador, minister, or high commissioner to eleven countries, member of United Nations Committee on Contributions, 1953-55, head of special missions to Dominican Republic, Cuba, and Argentina, council representative of Pakistan in SEATO, 1956-59; University of Minnesota, Minneapolis, professor and consultant in South Asian studies, 1961—. *Member:* Royal Society for the Arts (fellow). *Awards, honors:* Hill Family Foundation research grant, 1961—; Sitara-i-Pakistan award from president of Pakistan, 1962; Ford Foundation travel and study award, 1965-69.

WRITINGS: Sir Muhammad Zafrulla Khan: The Man and His Career, privately printed, 1951; *Pakistan's Foreign Policy: An Historical Analysis,* Oxford University Press, 1973; *Mainsprings of Indian and Pakistani Foreign Policies,* University of Minnesota Press, 1974. Contributor to journals and newspapers.

WORK IN PROGRESS: The Kashmir Problem; An Historical Review of the Pakistan Movement.

SIDELIGHTS: Burke told *CA:* "I have traveled extensively in all regions of the world and have made several trips around the world. In the course of my professional duties and travels I have met almost all the contemporary world leaders."

* * *

BURKE, Shifty
See BENTON, Peggie

* * *

BURKS, Arthur W(alter) 1915-

PERSONAL: Born October 13, 1915, in Duluth, Minn.; married Alice Grace Rowe, February 27, 1943; children: Edward, Nancy, Douglas. *Education:* DePauw University, B.A., 1936; University of Michigan, M.A., 1937, Ph.D., 1941. *Office:* Department of Computer and Communication Sciences, University of Michigan, Ann Arbor, Mich. 48104.

CAREER: High school mathematics teacher in Mount Morris, Mich., 1937-38; University of Pennsylvania, Philadelphia, instructor in electrical engineering and research engineer for Moore School of Electrical Engineering, 1941-46; University of Michigan, Ann Arbor, assistant professor, 1946-48, associate professor, 1948-54, professor of philosophy, 1954—, director of Logic of Computers Group, 1956—, professor of computer and communication sciences, 1967—, chairman of department, 1967-71, member of executive committee of Computing Center, 1959-60, member of executive committee of College of Literature, Science, and the Arts, 1973-74. Instructor at Swarthmore College, 1945-46; research associate at University of Chicago, 1950-51, and at Harvard University, 1955; research professor at University of Illinois, autumn, 1960; member of committee to advise the director of research of the Atomic Energy Commission on digital computers, 1960-62; visiting professor at Indian Institute of Technology, 1965-66; fellow of Center for Advanced Study in the Behavioral Sciences, Stanford, Calif., 1971-72. Consultant to Institute for Advanced Study, Princeton, N.J., and to Burroughs Corp.

MEMBER: American Philosophical Association (member of executive committee of Western Division, 1962-65; vice-president, 1971-72; president, 1972-73), Association for Computing Machinery, Charles S. Peirce Society (president, 1954-55), University of Michigan Research Club, Phi Beta Kappa, Sigma Xi, Phi Eta Sigma, Delta Sigma Rho, Phi Kappa Phi, Eta Kappa Nu. *Awards, honors:* Guggenheim fellowship, 1953-54; Louis E. Levy gold medal from Franklin Institute, 1956, for "The Folded Tree"; American Council of Learned Societies fellowship, 1962-63; D.Sc. from DePauw University, 1972.

WRITINGS: (With John von Neumann and H. H. Goldstine) *Preliminary Discussion of the Logical Design of an Electronic Computing Instrument,* Institute for Advanced Study (Princeton, N.J.), 1946, 2nd edition, 1947.

(Editor with Max Fisch and others, and contributor) *Classic American Philosophers,* Appleton, 1951; (contributor) Morton White, editor, *Academic Freedom, Logic, and Religion,* University of Pennsylvania Press, 1953; (editor) *Collected Papers of Charles Sanders Peirce,* Harvard University Press, Volume VII (Burks was not associated with earlier volumes): *Science and Philosophy,* 1958, Volume VIII: *Reviews, Correspondence, and Bibliography,* 1958.

(Contributor) Marshall Yovits and Scott Cameron, editors, *Self-Organizing Systems,* Pergamon, 1960; (contributor) Harry Huskey and G. A. Korn, editors, *Computer Handbook,* McGraw, 1962; (contributor) Wang Hao, editor, *A Survey of Mathematical Logic,* Science Press (Peking), 1962; (contributor) Paul Braffort and Donald Hirschberg, editors, *Computer Programming and Formal Systems,* North-Holland Publishing, 1963; (contributor) A. H. Taub, editor, *John von Neumann: Collected Works,* Volume V, Pergamon, 1963; (contributor) P. A. Schilpp, editor, *The Philosophy of Rudolf Carnap,* Open Court, 1963; (contributor) Edward F. Moore, editor, *Sequential Machines: Selected Papers,* Addison-Wesley, 1964; (contributor) Robert Machol and other editors, *System Engineering Handbook,* McGraw, 1965; (editor) John von Neumann, *Theory of Self-Reproducing Automata,* University of Illinois Press, 1966; (contributor) Schilpp, editor, *The Philosophy of C. I. Lewis,* Open Court, 1968.

(Editor and contributor) *Essays on Cellular Automata,* University of Illinois Press, 1970; (contributor) C. G. Bell and Allen Newell, editors, *Computer Structures: Readings and Examples,* McGraw, 1971; (contributor) Brian Randall, editor, *The Origins of Digital Computers: Selected Papers,* Springer-Verlag, 1973; (contributor) W. D. Keidel, Wolfgang Handler, and M. Spreng, editors, *Cybernetics and Bionics: Proceedings of the Fifth Congress of the Deutsche Gesellschaft fuer Kybernetik, Nurnberg, March 28-30, 1973,* Oldenbourg, 1974; *Cause, Chance, and Reason: An Inquiry into the Nature of Scientific Evidence,* University of Chicago Press, in press.

Congributor to proceedings; contributor of about forty articles to professional journals. Consulting editor of *Synthese:*

An International Journal for Epistemology, Methodology, and Philosophy of Science, 1966—.

SIDELIGHTS: Burks is one of the principal inventors and developers of the first electronic computer. His books have been translated into Russian, German, and Japanese.

* * *

BURNETT, Janet 1915-

PERSONAL: Born August 27, 1915, in Decatur, Ill.; daughter of Herbert S. (a dentist) and Julia (Potts) Alsip; married Howard Newcomb, Jr., January 30, 1943 (divorced, 1957); married Laurence Burnett (a picture framer), October 15, 1958; children: (first marriage) Howard, David, Nancy. *Education:* James Millikin University, B.A. (cum laude), 1936. *Politics:* Democrat. *Religion:* Methodist. *Home:* 2720 Greenfield Ave., Los Angeles, Calif. 90064. *Office:* Frank's Picture Framing, 2422 West Seventh St., Los Angeles, Calif. 90057.

CAREER: Frank's Picture Framing, Los Angeles, Calif., picture framer, 1963—. *Member:* Pi Beta Phi, PEO Sisterhood.

WRITINGS: (With husband, Laurence Burnett) *Picture Framer's Handbook,* C. N. Potter, 1973.

* * *

BURNETT, Laurence 1907-

PERSONAL: Born July 9, 1907, in Eldorado, Ill.; son of Laurence Eugene (a banker) and Edna (Lincoln) Burnett; married Frances Madden, November 9, 1935 (died, 1955); married Janet Alsip Newcomb (a picture framer), October 15, 1958. *Education:* University of Southern California, student, 1927-28; University of Colorado, B.A., 1929. *Religion:* Methodist. *Home:* 2720 Greenfield Ave., Los Angeles, Calif. 90064. *Office:* Frank's Picture Framing, 2422 West Seventh St., Los Angeles, Calif. 90057.

CAREER: Frank's Picture Framing, Los Angeles, Calif., picture framer, 1963—. *Military service:* U.S. Army, 1941-45; became sergeant.

WRITINGS: (With wife, Janet Burnett) *Picture Framer's Handbook,* C. N. Potter, 1973.

* * *

BURNS, Thomas Stephen 1927-

PERSONAL: Born January 7, 1927, in Holyoke, Mass.; son of Thomas Raymond (a policeman) and Anna (Bush) Burns; married Eleanor Hartigan (a registered nurse); children: T. Brian, Erin Ann, George, Mary Beth, James, Braeden. *Education:* U.S. Naval Academy, B.S., 1951; University of Massachusetts, M.B.A., 1958; Harvard University, further graduate study, 1968. *Politics:* Democrat. *Religion:* Roman Catholic. *Home:* 3350 Valley Rd., Bonita, Calif. 92002. *Office:* National Research Resources, P.O. Box 691, Bonita, Calif. 92002.

CAREER: Registered engineer; employed in marketing, 1955-63; Simplex Co., Boston, Mass., vice-president in marketing, 1963-70; International Telephone and Telegraph, San Diego, Calif., vice-president, 1970-72; National Research Resources, Bonita, Calif., president, 1972—. Director of New Hampshire Port Authority, 1967-68; commissioner of oceanography for Maine and New Hampshire, 1966-68; director of New Hampshire Regional Planning Commission, 1966-68. *Military service:* U.S. Navy, 1951-55; served in China, Europe, and Korea; became lieutenant junior grade; received three battle stars. U.S. Naval Reserve, 1955-70. *MEMBER:* National Society of Professional Engineers, Institute of Electrical and Electronic Engineers, Engineering Society of Detroit, Army-Navy Club (Washington, D.C.), U.S. Naval Academy Alumni Association, Harvard Alumni Association, Harvard Club (Boston, Mass.), University Club of San Diego.

WRITINGS: *Tales of I.T.T.,* Houghton, 1974. Editor, *Spectator* (newspaper), 1965-67.

WORK IN PROGRESS: *I Talk and Travel* (tentative title), Volume I: *Paine,* Volume II: *Della,* Volume III: *Gilhooley,* Volume IV: *Germaine.*

* * *

BURTON, David H(enry) 1925-

PERSONAL: Born August 4, 1925, in Oil City, Pa.; son of Henry D. (a fireman) and Isabella E. (DuPlaine) Burton; married Geraldine F. Ferrari (a teacher), August 27, 1960; children: Antoinette, Monica, Victoria Regina. *Education:* University of Scranton, B.A. (magna cum laude), 1949; Georgetown University, M.A., 1950, Ph.D., 1953. *Politics:* Independent. *Religion:* Roman Catholic. *Home:* 163 Wooded Lane, Villanova, Pa. 19085. *Agent:* Shaw MacLean, 11 Rumbold Rd., London S.W.6, England. *Office:* Department of History, St. Joseph's College, Philadelphia, Pa. 19131.

CAREER: U.S. Department of Army, Washington, D.C., intelligence research specialist, 1951-52; Georgetown University, Washington, D.C., lecturer in history, 1954; Duquesne University, Pittsburgh, Pa., assistant professor, 1955-56, associate professor of history, 1956-58; St. Joseph's College, Philadelphia, Pa., professor of history, 1958—. *Military service:* U.S. Army, Infantry, 1943-45; received Bronze Star Medal and Purple Heart. *Member:* American Historical Association, Organization of American Historians, English-Speaking Union, British Association of American Studies. *Awards, honors:* Winston Churchill traveling fellowship from English-Speaking Union, 1972.

WRITINGS: *Theodore Roosevelt: Confident Imperialist,* University of Pennsylvania Press, 1968; *Theodore Roosevelt: A Biography,* Twayne, 1972; *Theodore Roosevelt and His English Correspondents,* American Philosophical Society, 1973. Contributor to *History Today, Journal of the History of Ideas, Review of Politics, Personalist,* and *History Teacher.*

WORK IN PROGRESS: *American History, British Historians; Holmes–Pollock–Laski.*

* * *

BUSCH, Noel F(airchild) 1906-

PERSONAL: Born December 27, 1906, in New York, N.Y.; son of Briton Niven (a banker) and Christine (Fairchild) Busch; married Mary Gill, June 6, 1937 (divorced); married Mary Smart, June 15, 1950; children: (second marriage) Mary Fairchild, Beatrix Akiko. *Education:* Princeton University, student, 1925-27. *Home address:* South Rd., Millbrook, N.Y. 12545. *Agent:* Julian Bach, Jr., 3 East 48th St., New York, N.Y. 10017.

CAREER: *Time* (magazine), New York, N.Y., associate editor, 1927-29, senior editor, 1931-38; *New York Daily News,* New York, N.Y., sports writer, 1929-31; *Life* (magazine), New York, N.Y., senior editor, 1938-42, war correspondent, 1942-45, senior writer, 1945-52; Asia Foundation, San Francisco, Calif., representative in Tokyo, Japan, 1952-54, and Bangkok, Thailand, 1954-58, special assistant to president, 1958-59; *Reader's Digest,* Pleasantville, N.Y., staff writer, 1959—. *Member:* American Historical Society; Racquet and Tennis Club, Century Association, and Princeton Club (all New York, N.Y.), Millbrook Golf and Tennis Club.

WRITINGS: My Unconsidered Judgment, Houghton, 1944; *What Manner of Man?,* Harper, 1944; *Lost Continent?,* Harper, 1946; *Fallen Sun: A Report on Japan,* Appleton, 1948; *Briton Hadden: A Biography of the Co-Founder of "Time,"* Farrar, Straus, 1949; *Adlai Stevenson of Illinois,* Farrar, Straus, 1952; *Thailand: An Introduction to Modern Siam,* Van Nostrand, 1959, 2nd edition, 1964.

Two Minutes to Noon, Simon & Schuster, 1962; *T. R.: The Story of Theodore Roosevelt and His Influence on Our Times,* Reynal, 1963; *The Emperor's Sword,* Funk, 1969; *The Horizon Concise History of Japan,* American Heritage Press, 1972; *Winter Quarters,* Liveright, 1974. Contributor to *New Yorker, Atlantic Monthly, Saturday Evening Post, Horizon,* and other publications.

* * *

BUSH-BROWN, Louise 1896(?)-1973

1896(?)—December 15, 1973; American author of books on horticulture. Obituaries: *AB Bookman's Weekly,* January 14, 1974.

* * *

BUSSEY, Ellen M(arion) 1926-

PERSONAL: Born 1926, in Berlin, Germany. *Education:* Bucknell University, A.B., 1948; American University, M.A., 1952, Ph.D., 1970. *Home:* 6505 Old Chesterbrook Rd., McLean, Va. 22101. *Office:* Office of Policy Evaluation and Research, Manpower Administration, U.S. Department of Labor, Washington, D.C.

CAREER: U.S. Department of State, Washington, D.C., labor affairs analyst in Benelux section of Office of Research, 1952-55; U.S. Department of Labor, Washington, D.C., had charge of Western European labor affairs in Division of Foreign Labor Conditions, 1955-60; free-lance economic consultant in Europe, 1960-64; U.S. Department of Labor, Washington, D.C., consultant to Secretary of Labor, 1965, senior labor economist in Office of the Economic Consultant, Bureau of Labor Statistics, 1965-66, senior labor economist for International Manpower Institute, 1966-67; U.S. Department of Health, Education, and Welfare, Washington, D.C., economic consultant to international staff, 1968-69; U.S. Department of Labor, Manpower Administration, Washington, D.C., senior labor economist in Office of Policy Evaluation and Research, 1970—.

MEMBER: American Economic Association, Industrial Relations Research Association, American Political Science Association.

WRITINGS: Summary of the Labor Situation in Iceland (monograph), International Cooperation Administration, 1956; *Labor in Chile* (monograph), Bureau of Labor Statistics, U.S. Department of Labor, 1956; (contributor) *Readings in Unemployment,* U.S. Government Printing Office, 1960; *Aid to Labor Surplus Areas in Great Britain, Belgium, the Federal Republic of Germany, and Sweden,* Bureau of Labor Statistics, U.S. Department of Labor, 1960; (editor) *Manpower and Employment Policies for Developing Countries: Proceedings of the Seventh International Manpower Seminar, September 28 to December 10, 1966,* Agency for International Development, U.S. Department of State, 1967; *The Flight from Rural Poverty: How Nations Cope,* Heath, 1973.

Contributor to *Labor Law, Monthly Labor Review, Industrial Relations,* and *European Demographic Information Bulletin.*

* * *

BYRNE, Gary C. 1942-

PERSONAL: Born May 1, 1942, in Upland, Calif.; son of Cecil John (a businessman) and Verda A. (an educator; maiden name, Burgess) Byrne; married Norma Elaine Elliott (an astrologer), August 19, 1967; children: Silas Elliott, Tristan Oliver. *Education:* University of Redlands, B.A. (magna cum laude), 1965; University of Bonn, graduate study, 1965-66; University of North Carolina, Ph.D., 1969. *Politics:* "Progressive Mugwump." *Home:* 909 North Carolina Ave. S.E., Washington, D.C. 20003. *Office:* Orkand Corp., 8630 Fenton St., Silver Spring, Md. 20910.

CAREER: California State University, San Diego, associate professor of political science, 1969-73; Arthur Young & Co., Washington, D.C., associate, 1973-74; Orkand Corp., Silver Spring, Md., vice-president, 1974—. *Member:* Rotary International (fellow).

WRITINGS: Politics in Western European Democracies, Wiley, 1971; *The Psychology of Youthful Dissent,* Nelson-Hall, in press; *The Great American Convention,* Pacific Books, in press. Contributor to *Journal of Politics, Summation,* and *Journalism Quarterly.*

WORK IN PROGRESS: A theoretical statement about American politics; *The Promise of American Politics.*

SIDELIGHTS: "I see the world of American politics," Bryne writes, "like a giant corporation with every potential voter a stockholder with greater or fewer shares of stock. The individuals involved are all attempting to [get] resources allocated to provide maximum benefit for themselves. The role of the government is to contain this drama within orderly bounds."

* * *

BYRNES, Eugene F. 1890(?)-1974

1890(?)—July 26, 1974; American cartoonist and writer. Obituaries: *New York Times,* July 27, 1974.

* * *

CABASSA, Victoria 1912-

PERSONAL: Born October 12, 1912, in New York, N.Y.; married H. F. Cabassa (an engineer); children: Robert, Elizabeth, David. *Home:* 700 King Rd. W., Chester, Pa. 19380.

CAREER: Newspaper columnist, free-lance poet and writer, professional artist. *Member:* National League of American Pen Women, Chester County Art Association, Philadelphia Children's Reading Round Table (Chester County branch), Wayne Art Center. *Awards, honors:* N. C. Wyeth Memorial award, first in oil painting, 1969.

WRITINGS: Trixie and the Tiger, Abelard, 1968. Author of weekly column, "Exton Events," in *Suburban Advertiser,* Wayne, Pa.

WORK IN PROGRESS: Writings from family journals: *How Can You Forget a Grandmother Who Taught a Crow to Talk; Papa, Make Me a Paper Dress; Twin Pines Farm;* verse.

* * *

CADIEUX, (Joseph Arthur) Lorenzo 1903-

PERSONAL: Born November 10, 1903, in Granby, Quebec, Canada; son of Adelard (a worker) and Claire (Dalpe) Cadieux. *Education:* Attended College Sainte-Marie, Montreal, 1918-22 and Jesuit College, Edmonton, 1922-24; University of Montreal, Ph.D. (philosophy), 1931; Laval University, Ph.D. (history), 1959; summer study at University of Paris, 1959, and Columbia University, 1961. *Home:* University of Sudbury, Ramsey Rd., Sudbury, Ontario P3E 2C6, Canada. *Office:* Department of History, Laurentian University, Sudbury, Ontario, Canada.

CAREER: Entered Roman Catholic Socicty of Jesus (Jesuits), 1924; ordained priest, 1937; University of Sudbury, Sudbury, Ontario, assistant professor, 1957-58, associate professor, 1958-59, professor of history, 1959-60, head of department, 1957-60; Laurentian University, Sudbury, Ontario, professor of history, 1960-71, professor emeritus, 1971—, head of department of history, 1960-69. Member of the Archeological and Historic Sites Advisory Board of Ontario, 1970—. *Member:* Canadian Writers Association, Canadian Catholic Historical Association (president, 1960), Institut d'Histoire de l'Amerique francaise, Northern Ontario Historical Society (La Societe historique du Nouvel-Ontario; founder; president, 1968—). *Awards, honors:* Diplome de l'Ordre du Merite scolaire franco-ontarien, 1948; award of merit from American Association for State and Local History, 1954; Prix Champlain, 1958.

WRITINGS: Fondateurs du diocese du Sault-Sainte-Marie (title means "Founders of Sault Sainte Marie Diocese"), Editions Societe historique du Nouvel-Ontario, 1944; *Un heros du lac Superieur: Frederic Baraga* (title means "Frederic Baraga, Lake Superior Hero"), Imprimerie Leclerc (Hull, Quebec), 1954; *Au royaume de Nanabozho* (title means "In the Kingdom of Nanabozho"), Editions Societe historique du Nouvel-Ontario, 1959; *De l'Aviron a L'Avion* (title means "From Paddle to Plane"), Editions Bellarmin, 1961, translation published as *Afloat and Aloft: Joseph-Marie Couture,* Brisson Printing, 1965; *Frederic Romanet du Caillaud, 'Comte' de Sudbury,* Editions Bellarmin, 1971; *Lettres des Nouvelles Missions du Canada, 1843-1852* (title means "Letters of New Missions of Canada, 1843-1852, or Jesuit Relations of the Nineteenth Century"), Editions Bellarmin, 1974.

* * *

CADWALLADER, Sharon 1936-

PERSONAL: Born January 12, 1936, in Jamestown, N.D.; daughter of Herman Julius and Mildred (Hull) Wulfsberg; married Mervyn Leland Cadwallader, July 4, 1959 (divorced, 1966); children: Leland Hull. *Education:* San Jose State College (now University), A.B., 1958. *Politics:* Democrat. *Religion:* None. *Home and office:* 174 12th Ave., Santa Cruz, Calif. 95062.

CAREER: Has taught mentally retarded children; taught English to speakers of foreign languages; medical social worker in public clinic in Santa Cruz County, Calif.; organized and operated Whole Earth Restaurant at University of California, Santa Cruz; writer, 1972—.

WRITINGS: (With Judi Ohr) *Whole Earth Cookbook,* Houghton, 1972; *In Celebration of Small Things,* Houghton, 1974; *Cooking Adventures for Kids,* Houghton, in press.

WORK IN PROGRESS: A television script about the first part of the revolution against Spain in Mexico; writing dialogues for Co-Respondents, a women's reader theater group in state of Washington.

* * *

CAFFREY, Kate (Kate Caffrey Toller)

PERSONAL: Born in Preston, Lancashire, England; daughter of Louis John and Mary (Bracher) Caffrey; married Roland Toller, January 21, 1954 (divorced, 1958); children: Owen Louis Caffrey. *Education:* University of Exeter, B.A. (honors); College of William and Mary, M.A. *Home:* 82 Castleton Ave., Wembley, Middlesex HA9 7QF, England. *Agent:* Elaine Greene Ltd., 31 Newington Green, London N16 9PJ, England.

CAREER: Teacher in London schools, 1955-67; Trent Park College of Education, Barnet, Hertfordshire, England, senior lecturer in English, 1967—. *Member:* Royal Society of Arts (fellow).

WRITINGS: The British to Southern Africa, Gentry Books, 1973; *Out In the Midday Sun: Singapore, 1941-1945,* Stein & Day, 1973; *The Mayflower,* Stein & Day, 1974.

SIDELIGHTS: Miss Caffrey told *CA:* "I cannot remember the time when I did not try to write. I took years to realize that I should never be a novelist because I can't invent plots. It never occurred to me to write histories until I became interested in the Singapore campaign. . . .My favorite period is, roughly, 1860-1945, in both history and literature." Miss Caffrey has traveled in Europe, America, and East Africa.

* * *

CAHILL, Thomas (Quinn) 1940- (Tom Cahill)

PERSONAL: Born March 29, 1940, in New York, N.Y.; son of Patrick Thomas (an insurance executive) and Margaret Mary (Buckley) Cahill; married Susan Jane Neunzig (a writer), November 4, 1966; children: Kristin Maria. *Education:* Fordham University, B.A., 1964, Ph.L., 1965; Columbia University, M.F.A., 1968. *Home:* 170-25 Highland Ave., Jamaica, N.Y. 11432. *Agent:* Marcia Higgins, William Morris Agency, 1350 Avenue of the Americas, New York, N.Y. 10019. *Office:* Center for Humanistic Studies, Seton Hall University, South Orange, N.J.

CAREER: New York Review of Books, New York, N.Y., advertising director for New York Review presentations, 1968-70; Seton Hall University, Center for Humanistic Studies, South Orange, N.J., instructor, 1968-73, assistant professor of humanistic studies, 1973—.

WRITINGS—With wife, Susan Cahill: (Editor, under name Tom Cahill) *Big City Stories by Modern American Writers,* Bantam, 1971; *A Literary Calendar: 1973,* Cahill's Literary Calendar, 1972; *A Literary Guide to Ireland,* Scribner, 1973; *A Literary Calendar: 1974* (Literary Guild selection), Universe Books, 1973. Contributor to *Horizon.*

WORK IN PROGRESS: A Literary Calendar: 1975; A Literary Guide to England.

CAHILL, Tom
See CAHILL, Thomas (Quinn)

* * *

CAHNMAN, Werner J(acob) 1902-

PERSONAL: Born September 30, 1902, in Munich, Germany; son of Sigwart (a merchant) and Hedwig (Schuelein) Cahnman; married Gisella Levi (a biophysicist), March 7, 1943. *Education:* Studied at University of Munich and University of Berlin, 1922-27; University of Munich, D.V., 1925, Dr.occ.publ., 1927; University of Chicago, postdoctoral study, 1940-43. *Religion:* Jewish. *Home:* 67-71 Yellowstone Blvd., Forest Hills, N.Y. 11375.

CAREER: Research associate of Berlin Chamber of Industry and Commerce, Berlin, Germany, 1928, and welfare inquiry committee of German Reichstag, Kiel, Germany, 1928-30; Central Union of German Jews, executive secretary of Bavarian regional office, Munich, Germany, 1930-34; prisoner in Dachau Concentration Camp, Dachau, Germany, 1938; lecturer or visiting professor at Fisk University and Vanderbilt University, Nashville, Tenn., and Atlanta University, Atlanta, Ga., 1943-45; National Jewish Welfare Board, New York, N.Y., research associate, 1946; Brooklyn College (now Brooklyn College of the City University of New York), Brooklyn, N.Y., visiting professor of sociology, 1947, 1949; Viking Fund, New York, N.Y., research fellow, 1948-50; U.S. Department of State, New York, N.Y., senior media evaluation analyst, International Broadcasting Service, 1951-53; Conference on Jewish Social Studies, New York, N.Y., executive secretary, 1954-56; lecturer in sociology at Hunter College (now Hunter College of the City University of New York), New York, N.Y., 1956-59, and Yeshiva University, New York, 1958-62; Rutgers University, New Brunswick, N.J., associate professor, 1961-66, professor of sociology, 1966-69, professor emeritus, 1969—. Member of faculty, New School for Social Research, 1963—; Fulbright professor at Sociology Institute, University of Munich, 1969-70. Presently member of board, committee on synagogue relations of Federation of Jewish Philanthropies, New York, and Jewish Information Bureau; chairman of American Committee on Dachau.

MEMBER: American Sociological Association, Society for the Study of Social Problems, American Political Science Association, Committee for Sociological History (chairman, 1968-71; member of executive committee, 1971—), Deutsche Gesellschaft fuer Sociologie, Eastern Sociological Society, B'nai B'rith. *Awards, honors:* Julius Rosenwald Fund research fellow, 1943-44; Wenner-Gren Foundation fellow, 1948-49; American Foundation for Jewish Culture grant, 1969-70.

WRITINGS: Der Oekonomische Pessimismus und das Ricardosche System, H. Meyer, 1929; *Die Deutsche Seifen-und Parfumerie Industrie,* Mittler & Son, 1931; (with Jean L. L. Comhaire) *How Cities Grew: The Historical Sociology of Cities,* Florham Park Press, 1959, 4th edition, 1971; (editor) *Intermarriage and Jewish Life,* Herzl Press, 1963; (editor with Alvin Boskoff) *Sociology and History: Theory and Research,* Free Press, 1964; *Voelker und Rassen im Urteil der Jugend,* Olzog Verlag, 1965; (editor with Rudolf Heberle and contributor) *Ferdinand Toennies on Sociology: Pure, Applied, and Empirical,* University of Chicago Press, 1971; (editor and contributor) *Ferdinand Toennies: A New Evaluation,* E. J. Brill, 1973.

Contributor to festschrift, *Encyclopaedia Judaica, Yearbook of Leo Baeck Institute,* and to journals in America and Germany. Associate editor, *Reconstructionist,* 1955—.

WORK IN PROGRESS: A book on Jews and Gentiles; a history of sociology; research for a book, *The Stigma of Obesity.*

* * *

CAIRD, Janet 1913-

PERSONAL: Born April 24, 1913, in Livingstonia, Malawi; daughter of Peter Scott (an educational missionary) and Janet (Gilmour) Kirkwood; married James Bowman Caird (in Her Majesty's Inspection Service), July 19, 1938; children: Janet (Mrs. James Ronald Burns), Elisabeth (Mrs. Michael Davenport). *Education:* Edinburgh University, M.A. (honors), 1935; graduate study at University of Grenoble and Sorbonne, University of Paris, 1935-36. *Religion:* Church of Scotland. *Home:* 1 Drummond Crescent, Inverness, Scotland. *Agent:* A. M. Heath & Co., 35 Dover St., London W1X 4EB, England.

CAREER: Teacher of English, French and Latin in Glasgow and Edinburgh, Scotland, 1937-38, 1940-43, 1958-61. *Member:* Royal Overseas League, Society of Authors, Society of Antiquarians of Scotland (fellow), British Federation of University Women (past president of Inverness Association).

WRITINGS: Angus the Tartan Partan (children's book), Nelson, 1961; *In a Glass Darkly,* M. S. Mill, 1966 (published in England as *Murder Reflected,* Bles, 1966); *Perturbing Spirit,* Doubleday, 1967; *Murder Scholastic,* Doubleday, 1968; *The Loch,* Doubleday, 1969; *Murder Remote,* Doubleday, 1973. Contributor to magazines.

WORK IN PROGRESS: Poetry; short stories.

AVOCATIONAL INTERESTS: Archaeology (especially British and Greek), travel, art.

* * *

CAMERON, Constance Carpenter 1937-

PERSONAL: Born May 13, 1937, in Des Moines, Iowa; daughter of Edwin Bernard (a lawyer) and Wilma (Willett) Carpenter; married Donald Keith Cameron (a history teacher), January 24, 1957; children: Cynthia, Wendy, Evan. *Education:* Attended Stanford University, 1955-56, and Long Beach State University. *Politics:* Republican. *Religion:* "Free Thinker." *Home:* 12152 Paseo Bonita, Los Alamitos, Calif. 90720. *Agent:* Hy Cohen, 111 West 57th St., New York, N.Y.

WRITINGS: A Different Drum, Prentice-Hall, 1973.

WORK IN PROGRESS: A novel with the theme of alienation.

SIDELIGHTS: Constance Cameron told *CA:* "I did not really want to write *A Different Drum* at all, but professionals informed me that some of my discoveries and techniques evolving from my instruction of my handicapped son should be made known. I then decided I must write the story in the hope of contributing something that would help children with similar handicaps. Most parents are afraid to trust their own instincts when they conflict with 'experts.'"

* * *

CAMP, Fred V(alterma) 1911-

PERSONAL: Born May 24, 1911, in Kenmare, N.D.; son

of Julius D. (a farmer) and Anna (Danielsen) Camp; married Bernice Nightingale, June 23, 1945; children: Julie Ann. *Education:* Attended public school in Denmark Township, N.D. *Politics:* Republican. *Religion:* Conservative Baptist. *Home:* 4142 Sylvia St., Salem, Ore. 97301.

CAREER: Fishing tackle manufacturer and retail sporting goods dealer, 1940—. *Member:* National Chin Up Club (president, 1943-44).

WRITINGS: Two Wheelchairs and a Family of Three, Tyndale, 1973.

WORK IN PROGRESS: A book of stories for children, with a Christian emphasis.

SIDELIGHTS: Both Camp and his wife are physically handicapped.

* * *

CAMPBELL, Charles Arthur 1897-1974

January 13, 1897—1974; Scottish scholar and author. Obituaries: *AB Bookman's Weekly,* June 17, 1974.

* * *

CAMPBELL, Robert C(harles) 1924-

PERSONAL: Born March 9, 1924, in Chandler, Ariz.; son of Alexander Joshua and Florence (Betzner) Campbell; married Lotus Idamae Boone; children: Robin C., Cherry Colleen. *Education:* Westmont College, A.B.; University of Southern California, M.A.; Eastern Baptist Theological Seminary, B.D., Th.M., Ph.D. *Home:* 1000 Valley Forge Circle, Apt. 607, King of Prussia, Pa. 19406. *Office:* American Baptist Churches in the United States of America, Valley Forge, Pa. 19481.

CAREER: Clergyman of American Baptist Church; Thirty-fourth Street Baptist Church, Philadelphia, Pa., pastor, 1945-49; Eastern Baptist Seminary, Philadelphia, Pa., instructor, 1949-51; Eastern Baptist College, St. Davids, Pa., assistant professor, 1951-53; American Baptist Seminary of the West, Covina, Calif., dean, 1954-72; American Baptist Churches in the United States of America, Valley Forge, Pa., general secretary, 1972—. *Member:* American Association of Theological Schools, American Academy of Religion (president of Pacific Coast section), American Baptist Churches of the Pacific Southwest. *Awards, honors:* D. Litt. and D.D. from Eastern Baptist Seminary; D.Litt., California Baptist Theological Seminary.

WRITINGS: Great Words of Faith, Judson, 1969; *The Gospel of Paul,* Judson, 1973. Contributor to handbooks and church school materials, and to journals. Former associate editor of *Foundations: A Baptist Journal of History and Theology.*

* * *

CAMPBELL, Stanley W(allace) 1926-

PERSONAL: Born October 30, 1926, in Colorado; son of George A. (a truck driver) and Cecil (Cole) Campbell; married Ella Shorthill (a dental technician), July 9, 1947; children: Elizabeth E. (Mrs. Thomas Wilson), Stanley W., Jr., Paul T. *Education:* University of Mississippi, B.A., 1957; University of North Carolina, Ph.D., 1967. *Politics:* Democrat. *Religion:* Baptist. *Home:* 328 Ivy Lane, Hewitt, Tex. 76643. *Office:* Department of History, Baylor University, Waco, Tex. 76703.

CAREER: Virginia Military Institute, Lexington, assistant professor, 1961-66, associate professor of American diplomatic and constitutional history, 1966-70; Baylor University, Waco, Tex., associate professor of American diplomatic history, Black history, and African history, 1970—. Assistant general superintendent of Horse Show Division and member of board of directors of Heart of Texas Fair. *Military service:* U.S. Navy, Ordnance, 1944-46, 1950-54. *Member:* American Association of University Professors (president of Baylor University chapter, 1974-75), Southern Historical Association, Waco Horse Show Association (member of board of directors).

WRITINGS: The Slave Catchers: Enforcement of the Fugitive Slave Law, 1850-1860, University of North Carolina Press, 1970. Contributor to *Proceedings of the Rockbridge County Historical Society.*

WORK IN PROGRESS: A comparative analysis of the slave codes of the western world; research on fugitive slaves and southern secession.

SIDELIGHTS: Campbell writes: "I am becoming increasingly interested in the social history of black folk particularly in the antebellum South; the development of a unique black culture which would sustain black nationalist movements in the twentieth century. I am also interested in African tribal religions which seem to have contributed a great deal to the black man's ability to cope with a strange and hostile world in the Western Hemisphere." *Avocational interests:* Horses (trainer and exhibitor of quarter horses and Arabians; judge of horse shows).

* * *

CAMPBELL, Stephen K(ent) 1935-

PERSONAL: Born July 2, 1935, in Oakland, Calif.; son of Donald John (a salesman) and Marr (Riley) Campbell; married Gail K. Eardley, August 25, 1960 (divorced, 1964); married Judith Prusse, June 14, 1971. *Education:* University of Utah, B.S., 1957, M.S. 1959; Columbia University, Ph.D., 1968. *Politics:* "Fed-up Republican". *Religion:* Church of Jesus Christ of Latter Day Saints. *Home:* 2372 South High, Denver, Colo. 80210. *Office:* College of Business Administration, University of Denver, 2020 South Race, Denver, Colo. 80210.

CAREER: University of Denver, Denver, Colo., assistant professor, 1963-68, associate professor of business statistics, 1968—. Free-lance consultant and speaker on statistics and economic forecasting. *Military service:* U.S. Army, 1957. *Member:* American Statistical Association, National Association of Business Economists, Beta Gamma Sigma.

WRITINGS: Flaws and Fallacies in Statistical Thinking, Prentice-Hall, 1974.

WORK IN PROGRESS: Applied Business Statistics: Text and Cases, for Prentice-Hall.

* * *

CAMPBELL, Thomas M(oody) 1936-

PERSONAL: Born May 2, 1936, in Evanston, Ill.; son of Moody (a professor) and Cora (Rolfe) Campbell; married Julia Hickson, June 18, 1960 (divorced, 1971); married Amanda Curtis (a secretary), September 13, 1973; children: (first marriage) Thomas M. III, David H., William H. *Education:* Randolph-Macon College, B.A. (cum laude), 1958; University of Virginia, M.A., 1960, Ph.D., 1964. *Religion:* Methodist. *Home:* 603 East Call St., #715, Tallahassee, Fla. 32301. *Office:* Department of History, Florida State University, Tallahassee, Fla. 32306.

CAREER: Florida State University, Tallahassee, instructor, 1963-65, assistant professor, 1965-72, associate professor of history, 1972—, assistant dean of Graduate School, 1965-67. *Member:* Organization of American Historians, Society for the History of American Foreign Relations, Phi Beta Kappa, Omicron Delta Kappa. *Awards, honors:* National Endowment for the Humanities fellowship, 1973-74.

WRITINGS: Masquerade Peace: America's U.N. Policy, 1944-1945, University Presses of Florida, 1973; (editor with George C. Herring) *The Diaries of Edward R. Stettinius, Jr., 1943-1946,* F. Watts, 1974. Contributor to *International Organization.*

WORK IN PROGRESS: A biography of Edward R. Stettinius, Jr.

* * *

CANNON, John (Ashton) 1918-

PERSONAL: Born May 10, 1918, in London, England; son of Charles Henry (a theatrical manager) and Minnieham (Clarke) Cannon; married Camilla Mary Nichol Smith, January 19, 1949; children: David Alexander, Nicola Jane. *Education:* Attended schools in England. *Politics:* "Left of centre Conservative." *Religion:* Church of England. *Home:* The Greenwood, Friary Rd., South Ascot, Berkshire, England. *Office:* British Enkalan Ltd., Lee Circle, Leicester, England.

CAREER: Link House Publications Ltd., London, England, assistant editor of *Amateur Cine World,* 1936-38, assistant editor of *The Caravan,* 1938-39, 1947, associate editor, 1949-51; County Associations Ltd., London, England, general editor of County Guide series, 1951-54; British Institute of Management, London, England, assistant editor of *The Manager,* 1954-57, editor of *Work Study and Industrial Engineering* and *Industrial Welfare,* 1957; Chemstrand Ltd., London, England, publicity manager, 1957-60; United Merchants & Manufacturers (UK) Ltd., London, England, publicity manager, 1960-63; British Enkalan Ltd., Leicester, England, publicity manager, 1963—. Consultant, J. P. Stevens (UK) Ltd., 1963. *Military service:* British Army, 1939-48; became major; mentioned in dispatches, Italy, 1944. *Member:* Incorporated Advertising Managers Association, Royal Automobile Club.

WRITINGS: The Car That Talked, Nuffield, 1951; *The Adventures of Jerry Parker,* Nuffield, 1952; *The Further Adventures of Jerry Parker,* Nuffield, 1953; *The Chartists in Bristol,* University of Bristol, 1964; *The Fox-North Coalition: Crisis of the Constitution, 1782-4,* Cambridge University Press, 1969; *Lord North: The Noble Lord in the Blue Ribbon,* Historical Association, 1970. Contributor to motoring and industrial magazines.

* * *

CANO-BALLESTA, Juan 1932-

PERSONAL: Born March 12, 1932, in Murcia, Spain; son of Jose and Marcelina (Ballesta) Cano; married Mercedes Alonso, September 12, 1969. *Education:* University of Munich, Germany, Ph.D., 1961. *Office:* Department of Modern Foreign Languages and Literatures, Boston University, 718 Commonwealth Ave., Boston, Mass. 02215.

CAREER: University of Goettingen, Goettingen, Germany, lecturer, 1962-65; Yale University, assistant professor, 1966-68, research associate, 1968-70; associate professor of Spanish, 1970-71; Boston University, Boston, Mass., associate professor of Spanish, 1971—. *Member:* Modern Language Association of America, American Association of Teachers of Spanish and Portuguese, Association Internacional de Hispanistas. *Awards, honors:* Morse research fellowship from Yale University, 1968-70.

WRITINGS: Die Dichtung des Miguel Hernandez: Eine stilistische Untersuchung (title means "The Poetry of Miguel Hernandez: A Stylistic Study"), Fernando Walter, 1962; *La poesia de Miguel Hernandez* (title means "The Poetry of Miguel Hernandez"), Editorial Gredos, 1962, revised edition, 1971; *La poesia espanola entre pureza y revolucion, 1930-1936* (title means "Spanish Lyric Between Pure Poetry and Revolution"), Editorial Gredos, 1972. Contributor to *Hispanic Review, Books Abroad, Romanische Forschungen,* and *Insula.*

WORK IN PROGRESS: Three books, *Poemas y prosas desconocidas de Miguel Hernandez* (title means "Unknown Prose and Poetry of Miguel Hernandez"), *Maestros del cuento espanol moderno* (title means "Masters of Modern Spanish Short Story"), for Scribner, and *Literary Theory in Spain between World Wars, 1920-1940.*

BIOGRAPHICAL/CRITICAL SOURCES: Alfredo Gomez Gil, *Cerebros espanoles en USA,* Plaza y Janes, 1971.

* * *

CARDEN, Karen W(ilson) 1946-

PERSONAL: Born February 7, 1946, in Knoxville, Tenn.; daughter of Ralph S. and Katherine (Pardue) Wilson; married Ray E. Carden (a salesman), December 21, 1965. *Education:* Attended University of Tennessee. *Home address:* Route 11, Loyston Rd., Knoxville, Tenn. 37918. *Agent:* Southeastern Literary Agency, Inc., P.O. Box 3007, Knoxville, Tenn. 37917. *Office:* 1212 Pierce Pkwy., Suite 200, Knoxville, Tenn.

CAREER: Realtor and writer. *Member:* American Quarter Horse Association.

WRITINGS: (With Robert W. Pelton) *Snake Handlers: God-Fearers? or Fanatics?,* Nelson, 1974; (with Pelton) *The Persecuted Prophets,* A. S. Barnes, in press; *Western Rider's Handbook,* A. S. Barnes, in press. Contributor of articles and poems to magazines, including *Grit, Babytalk, Home Life, Western Horseman, American Square Dance,* and *Caller.*

WORK IN PROGRESS: Psychic Sillies and Astro Anecdotes; Murder in the Name of Jesus, a suspense novel; *Casting Out Devils,* exorcism rituals of various faiths, completion expected in 1975; a collection of old-time recipes, *Spirit of '76 Bicentennial Cookbook,* 1975; a book of western Americana poetry; a Civil War poetry book.

SIDELIGHTS: Mrs. Carden describes her writing: "I am purging neither myself nor society—I write to sell. Writing is not a mysterious, romance-cloaked pursuit. It is a business, one I happen to love desperately, but a business, nonetheless." *Avocational interests:* Touring the American South and Midwest, horses, antiques, auctions.

* * *

CARDENAL, Ernesto 1925-

PERSONAL: Born January 20, 1925, in Granada, Nicaragua; son of Rodolfo and Esmeralda (Martinez) Cardenal. *Education:* Attended University of Mexico, 1944-48, and Columbia University, 1948-49. *Politics:* "Christian-marxist." *Residence:* Archipielago de Solentinosne, en el Lago de Nicaragua.

CAREER: Ordained Roman Catholic priest, 1965. Poet, and author.

WRITINGS: *Ansias lengua de la poesia nueva nicaraguense* (poems), [Nicaragua], 1948; *Gethsemani, Ky.* (poems), Ecuador 0°0'0", 1960, 2nd edition, with foreword by Thomas Merton, Ediciones La Tertulia (Medellin, Colombia), 1965; *Epigramas: Poemas,* Universidad Nacional Autonoma de Mexico, 1961; *Hora* (poems), Revista Mexicano de Literatura, 1960, new edition, Aqui Poesia, 1966; (translator and editor with Jorge Montoya Toro) *Literatura indigena americana: Antologia*, Editorial Universidad de Antioquia (Medellin), 1964; (translator with Jose Coronel Urtecho) *Antologia de la poesia Norteamericana,* Aguilar (Madrid), 1963; *Oracion por Marilyn Monroe, y otros poemas,* Ediciones La Tertulia, 1965; *El estrecho dudoso* (poems), Ediciones Cultura Hispanica (Madrid), 1966; *Antologia de Ernesto Cardenal* (poetry), Editora Santiago (Santiago, Chile), 1967; *Poemas de Ernesto Cardenal,* Casa de las Americas (Havana), 1967; *Mayapan* (poem), Editorial Alemana (Managua, Nicaragua), 1968; *Salmos* (poems), Institucion Gran Duque de Alba (Avila, Spain), 1967, translation by Emile G. McAnany published as *The Psalms of Struggle and Liberation,* Herder & Herder, 1971; *Homenaje a los indios americanos* (poems), Universidad Nacional Autonoma de Nicaragua, 1969, translation by Carlos and Monique Altschul published as *Homage to the American Indians,* Johns Hopkins University Press, 1974; *Vida en el amor* (meditations; with foreword by Thomas Merton), Ediciones C. Lohle (Buenos Aires), 1970, translation by Kurt Reinhardt published as *To Live Is to Love,* Herder & Herder, 1972; *In Cuba,* New Directions, 1974.

WORK IN PROGRESS: El Evangelio en Solentinosne.

* * *

CARDEW, Michael (Ambrose) 1901-

PERSONAL: Surname is accented on second syllable; born May 26, 1901, in London, England; son of Arthur (a civil servant) and Alexandra R. (Kitchin) Cardew; married Mariel Russell, December 24, 1933; children: Seth Christopher Mason, Brian Cornelius McDonough, Ennis Tuel. *Education:* Exeter College, Oxford, B.A., 1923; Leach Pottery, St. Ives, Cornwall, England, graduate study, 1923-26. *Home and office:* Wenford Bridge Pottery, St. Tudy Bodmin, Cornwall, England.

CAREER: Winchcombe Pottery, Winchcombe, Gloucestershire, founder and owner, 1926-29; Wenford Bridge Pottery, St. Tudy Bodmin, Cornwall, founder and owner, 1939-42, 1948-50; Achimota College, Accra, Ghana, ceramist, 1942-45. Volta Pottery, Vume Dugame, Accra, Ghana, founder, owner, and partner, 1945-48; Ministry of Trade and Industry, Nigeria, senior pottery officer, 1950-65; Wenford Bridge Pottery, owner, 1965—. *Member:* International Academy of Ceramics, World Crafts Council, Craftsmen Potters Association of Great Britain, British Ceramic Society. *Awards, honors:* Member of Order of the British Empire, 1964.

WRITINGS: (Contributor) Hassan and Na'ibi, editors, *A Chronicle of Abuja,* African Universities Press, 1962; *Pioneer Pottery,* Longmans, 1969; (with Sylvia Leith Ross) *Nigerian Pottery,* Ibadan University Press, 1971. Contributor to *Pottery Quarterly, Nigeria, Africa South, Craft Horizons, Ceramic Review,* and *Ceramics Monthly.*

WORK IN PROGRESS: Notes for memoirs on a potter's life, *Don't Trouble the World* (tentative title).

BIOGRAPHICAL/CRITICAL SOURCES: Apollo, May, 1943; R. G. Cooper, *The Modern Potter,* Tiranti, 1947; George Wingfield Digby, *The Work of the Modern Potter in England,* Murray, 1952; Muriel Rose, *Artist Potters in England,* Faber, 1955; *Afrique,* June, 1963; Alister Hallum, "Abuja Pottery" (film), 1971; *Craft Horizons,* February, 1972; *Ceramics,* March, 1972; Hallum, "Mud and Water Man" (film), 1973.

* * *

CARLI, Angelo 1937-

PERSONAL: Born March 7, 1937, in Brooklyn, N.Y.; son of Carlo and Amelia Carli; married Ann Laura Allenby (a teacher), June 17, 1961; children: Philip Camillo, Sabrina. *Education:* San Francisco State College (now University), B.A., 1962, M.A., 1964. *Office:* Department of English, Palomar College, San Marcos, Calif. 92069.

CAREER: Avionics Research Group, Great Neck, N.Y., designer, 1955-60; Atlas-Pacific Engineering, Emeryville, Calif., designer, 1960-62; Palomar College, San Marcos, Calif., instructor in English, 1964—. Fulbright professor at Neville's Cross College, Durham, England, 1970-71.

WRITINGS: (Editor with Theodore Kilman) *The Now Voices,* Scribner, 1971. Contributor to *Westways* and *San Diego Union.*

* * *

CARLSON, Carl Walter 1907-

PERSONAL: Born August 24, 1907, in Ashland, Wis.; son of Gustaf E. (a jeweler) and Anna (Johnson) Carlson; married Bernice Wells (a writer), September 10, 1935; children: Christine (Mrs. Paul S. Umberger), Philip Wells, Marta. *Education:* Northland College, B.S., 1929; University of Chicago, M.S., 1946; Michigan State University, Ph.D., 1956. *Home address:* Route 3, Box 332D Skillmans Lane, Somerset, N.J. 08873.

CAREER: Wisconsin Bell Telephone Co., Milwaukee, engineer, 1929-33; Michigan State University, East Lansing, instructor in chemistry, 1935-44; New Jersey College for Women (now Douglass College of Rutgers University), New Brunswick, N.J., assistant professor of chemistry, 1944-46; Heyden Chemical Co., N.J., chemist, 1945-48; Newark College of Engineering, Newark, N.J., professor of chemistry, 1948-72; tree grower. *Member:* New Jersey Association for Retarded Children, Franklin Conservation Club.

WRITINGS: (With wife, Bernice Wells Carlson) *Water Fit to Use,* John Day, 1966, revised edition, 1972.

* * *

CARLTON, Lessie 1903-

PERSONAL: Born August 4, 1903, in Etoile, Texas; daughter of David H. (a postmaster and cotton ginner) and Mollie (Mayes) Carlton. *Education:* North Texas University, B.S., and M.S.; University of Houston, Ed.D. *Religion:* Southern Baptist. *Home:* (Permanent) Melrose Acres, Route 1, Sand Flat Rd., Alto, Tex. 75925. *Office:* Reading-Study Center, Cumberland College, Williamsburg, Ky. 40769.

CAREER: High school teacher and principal in Texas, 1921-55; member of faculty in education at Stephen F.

Austin State College (now University), Nacogdoches, Tex., Nebraska State College, and Illinois State University, Normal, professor emeritus, Illinois State University, 1971—; Cumberland College, Williamsburg, Ky., professor of education, 1971—. *Member:* College Reading Association, National Education Association, Kappa Delta Pi.

WRITINGS: (With R. H. Moore) *Reading, Self-Directive Dramatization, and Self-Concept,* C. E. Merrill, 1968.

Contributor: Doris H. Crank and Floyd L. Crank, editors, *New Perspectives in Education for Business,* National Business Education Association, 1963; Virgil M. Howes, *Individualization of Instruction: A Teaching Strategy,* Macmillan, 1970. Contributor to collections of readings, to *Handbook of Texas,* and to education journals.

WORK IN PROGRESS: Collecting material for a book on her experiences with the Reading-Study Center at Cumberland College, a mountain school in the coal mining region.

* * *

CARNEY, T(homas) F(rancis) 1931-

PERSONAL: Born February 7, 1931, in Brooklyn, N.Y.; son of Felix Francis (a civil servant) and Cecelia (Burke) Carney; married Barbara Parr (a teacher), August 17, 1954; children: Michael, Judith. *Education:* University of London, B.A. (honors), 1952, Ph.D., 1957; University of South Africa, D.Litt. et Phil., 1959. *Residence:* Winnipeg, Manitoba, Canada. *Office:* Department of History and Natural Resource Institute, University of Manitoba, Winnipeg, Manitoba R3T 2N2, Canada.

CAREER: Victoria University, Wellington, New Zealand, lecturer in classics, 1953-57; University College of Rhodesia and Nyasaland, Salisbury, South Rhodesia, professor of classics, 1957-62, head of department, 1957-62; University of Sydney, Sydney, Australia, associate professor of history, 1962-66; University of Manitoba, Winnipeg, associate professor, 1966-67, professor of history, 1967—, professor of resource management, Natural Resource Institute, 1974—, head of department of history, 1968-69. Visiting research scholar at University of Vienna, 1957-58, University of Pisa, 1959-60, University of Athens and University of Thessaloniki, 1961-62, Birkbeck College, University of London, 1969-70, and Princeton University, 1972-73. *Member:* American Academy of Political and Social Science, American Philological Association, American Society for Public Administration, Classical Association of Great Britain, Classical Association of Canada, Society for the Promotion of Hellenic Studies, German Archaeological Institute (corresponding member), Society for Macedonian Studies (corresponding member), Comparative Administration Group, Canadian Council on Byzantine Studies. *Awards, honors:* Senior Fulbright scholar, Center for International Studies, Massachusetts Institute of Technology, 1965-66; Killam Award, 1969; Canada Council fellowship, 1972-73.

WRITINGS: A Biography of Caius Marius (monograph), Classical Association of Rhodesia and Nyasaland, 1961; (translator) A. P. Vacalopoulos, *History of Thessaloniki,* Institute of Balkan Studies, 1963; (editor) Terence, *Hecyra,* Classical Association of Rhodesia and Nyasaland, 1964; (translator) John the Lydian, *On the Magistracies of the Roman Constitution,* Wentworth Press, 1965; (editor and translator) *John the Lydian, De Magistratibus,* Coronado Press, 1971; *Bureaucracy in Traditional Society,* Coronado Press, 1971; *Content Analysis: A Technique for Systematic Inference from Communications,* University of Manitoba Press, 1972; *The Economies of Antiquity,* Coronado Press, 1973. Contributor of more than eighty articles and reviews to *Listener* and to classical, historical, and numismatic journals in North America and Europe.

WORK IN PROGRESS: Two books for Coronado Press, *The Shape of the Past: Models and Antiquity* and *Some of My Best Friends Are Academics;* two books for the Natural Resource Institute of the University of Manitoba, *Time-Budgeting a Thesis: The Critical Path Method* and *Constructing Simulations Games;* and the game *SIMILAK* (Simulated Interlake), with P. Nickel.

SIDELIGHTS: Carney has competence in ancient Greek and Latin, modern Greek, French, German, and Italian.

* * *

CARPELAN, Bo (Gustaf Bertelsson) 1926-

PERSONAL: Surname is pronounced *Car*-pel-an; born October 25, 1926, in Helsinki, Finland; son of Bertel Gustaf (an engineer) and Ebba (Lindahl) Carpelan; married Barbro Eriksson (a reservations clerk at Finnair), April 13, 1954; children: Anders, Johanna. *Education:* University of Helsinki, Ph.D., 1960. *Home:* Nyckelpigvaagen 2B, Tapiola, Finland.

CAREER: Poet and author; City Library, Helsinki, Finland, assistant chief librarian, 1963—. *Member:* Finnish-Swedish Authors Society, P.E.N. *Awards, honors:* Finnish State Prize and Nils Holgersson Prize, 1969, for *Baagen.*

WRITINGS—Books for children: *Anders paa oen,* Bonnier (Stockholm), 1959; *Anders i stan,* Bonnier, 1962.

Books for young people and adults: *Baagen: Beraettelsen om en sommar som var annorlunda,* Bonnier, 1968, translation by Sheila La Farge published as *Bow Island: The Story of a Summer That Was Different,* Delacorte, 1972 (translation published in England as *The Wide Wings of Summer,* Heinemann, 1972); *Paradiset,* Bonnier, 1973.

Works for adults—Collections of poems, except as noted, most published simultaneously by Bonnier in Stockholm and Holger Schildt in Helsinki: *Som en dunkel vaerme,* 1946; *Du moerka oeverlevande,* 1947; *Variationer,* 1950; *Minus sju,* 1952; *Objekt foer ord,* 1954; *Landskapets foervandlingar,* 1957; *Studier i Gunnar Bjoerlings diktning 1922-1933* (doctoral dissertation), Svenska Litteratursaellskapet i Finland, 1960; (translator into Swedish with others) Eino S. Repo and Nils B. Stormbom, compilers, *Ny finsk lyrik* (anthology), 1960; (with others) *Jag lever i republiken Finland* (essays), Suderstrom, 1961; *Den svala dagen,* 1961; (with others) *Aaret i norden* (nonfiction), Bonnier and Hasselbalch (Copenhagen), 1962; *73 dikter,* 1966; (compiler) *Finlandssvenska lyrikboken* (anthology), Forum (Stockholm), 1967; *Gaarden,* 1969; *Roesterna i den sena timmen* (novel), Bonnier, 1971; "Paluu nuoruuteen" (play), first produced in Helsinki, Finland, at Kansallisteatteri, in 1971; *Kaellan,* 1972.

Author of works for television, theater, and radio, including a radio play, "Voices at a Late Hour," produced by Canadian Broadcasting Corp.

WORK IN PROGRESS: A new collection of poems; a novel.

SIDELIGHTS: Carpelan himself made the designation that *Baagen* and *Paradiset* are books for teens *and* adults. He finds it "important to break down barrier between books for young people and books for adults." *Baagen* has been published in German, Polish, and Danish, in addition to the two editions in English. Both of the *Anders* titles have been translated into German and Polish, and *Anders paa oen* into Norwegian as well. Carpelan visited the United States in 1961.

* * *

CARPER, L. Dean 1931-

PERSONAL: Born April 10, 1931; son of George Walter and Muzzette Carper; married wife, Charlotte Darlene, November 23, 1951; children: Jeff, Cindy, Angelia. *Education:* Northwest Missouri State University, B.S.Ed., 1966; University of Nebraska at Omaha, M.S.Ed., 1971. *Politics:* Republican. *Religion:* Reorganized Church of Jesus Christ of Latter-Day Saints (Mormon). *Home:* 1101 Irene Ct., Red Oak, Iowa 51566.

CAREER: Red Oak Community School, Red Oak, Iowa, special education teacher, 1969—. Member of board of directors of National Youth Development Foundation. *Military service:* U.S. Army, 1951-53; became sergeant.

WRITINGS: A Cry in the Wind, Herald House, 1974; *The Sound of Drums,* Herald House, 1974.

WORK IN PROGRESS: A Time to Remember, of the depression in the 1930's; *Melissa of Manti,* the pioneer life of an Iowa family; a book about a man who fears his retarded son.

AVOCATIONAL INTERESTS: Reading, old cars, scouting activities.

* * *

CARR, John Dickson 1906- (Carr Dickson, Carter Dickson; John Rhode, a joint pseudonym)

PERSONAL: Born in 1906, in Uniontown, Pa.; son of Wood Nicholas (a U.S. Congressman, and later a postmaster) and Julia Carr; married Clarice Cleaves, 1931; children: three. *Education:* Haverford College. *Residence:* Mamaroneck, N.Y.

CAREER: Lived in England, 1931-48; worked as a writer for British Broadcasting Company in London during World War II; author and novelist. *Member:* Mystery Writers of America (president, 1949), London Detective Club, Baker Street Irregulars, Savage and Garrick clubs (both London).

WRITINGS—Under name John Dickson Carr: *It Walks by Night,* Harper, 1930; *Castle Skull,* Harper, 1931; *The Lost Gallows,* Harper, 1931; *The Corpse in the Waxworks,* Harper, 1932, reprinted, Collier, 1965 (published in England as *Waxworks Murder,* Hamish Hamilton, 1932, new edition, 1967); *The Mad Hatter Mystery,* Harper, 1933, reprinted, Collier, 1965; *Hag's Nook,* Harper, 1933, new edition, Collier, 1963; *Poison in Jest,* Hamish Hamilton, 1933, Harper, 1940, reprinted, Collier, 1965; *The Blind Barber,* Harper, 1934, new edition, Collier, 1962; *The Eight of Swords,* Harper, 1934, reprinted, Collier, 1962; *Death-Watch,* Harper, 1935, reprinted, Collier, 1963; *The Three Coffins* (see below), Harper, 1935 (published in England as *The Hollow Man,* Hamish Hamilton, 1935); *The Arabian Nights Murder* (also see below), Harper, 1936, reprinted, Collier, 1965; *The Burning Court* (also see below), Harper, 1937; *The Four False Weapons,* Harper, 1937; *To Wake the Dead,* Hamish Hamilton, 1937, Harper, 1938, reprinted, Collier, 1965; *The Crooked Hinge* (see below), Harper, 1938; *The Problem of the Green Capsule,* Harper, 1939 (published in England as *The Black Spectacles,* Hamish Hamilton, 1939); *The Problem of the Wire Cage* (also see below), Harper, 1939.

The Man Who Could Not Shudder, Harper, 1940; *The Case of the Constant Suicides* (see below), Harper, 1941, reprinted, Collier, 1963; *Death Turns the Tables,* Harper, 1941 (published in England as *The Seat of the Scornful,* Hamish Hamilton, 1942); *The Emperor's Snuff-Box,* Harper, 1942; *Till Death Do Us Part,* Harper, 1944; *He Who Whispers,* Harper, 1946; *Dr. Fell, Detective, and Other Stories,* edited by Ellery Queen, American Mercury, 1947; *The Sleeping Sphinx,* Harper, 1947; *Below Suspicion,* Harper, 1949.

The Bride of Newgate (historical novel), Harper, 1950; *The Devil in Velvet,* Harper, 1951; *The Nine Wrong Answers,* Harper, 1952, abridged edition, Bantam, 1962; (with Adrian Conan Doyle) *The Exploits of Sherlock Holmes,* Random House, 1954 (published in England as *More Exploits of Sherlock Holmes,* J. Murray, 1964); *The Third Bullet and Other Stories,* Harper, 1954; *Captain Cut-throat,* Harper, 1955; *Patrick Butler for the Defence,* Harper, 1956; *Fire, Burn!,* Harper, 1957; *The Dead Man's Knock,* Harper, 1958; (editor) Arthur Conan Doyle, *Great Stories,* J. Murray, 1959; *Scandal at High Chimneys,* Harper, 1959.

In Spite of Thunder, Harper, 1960; *The Witch of the Low Tide: An Edwardian Melodrama,* Harper, 1961; *The Demoniacs,* Harper, 1962; *The Men Who Explained Miracles* (short stories), Harper, 1963; *Most Secret,* Harper, 1964; *The House at Satan's Elbow,* Harper, 1965; *Panic in Box C,* Harper, 1966; *Dark of the Moon,* Harper, 1967; *Papa La-bas,* Harper, 1968.

The Ghosts' High Noon, Harper, 1970; *Deadly Hall,* Harper, 1971; *The Hungry Goblin: A Victorian Detective Novel,* Harper, 1972.

Nonfiction: *The Murder of Sir Edmund Godfrey,* Harper, 1936; *The Life of Sir Arthur Conan Doyle,* Harper, 1949, reprinted, Doubleday, 1961.

Under pseudonym Carr Dickson: *The Bowstring Murders,* Morrow, 1933, published under pseudonym Carter Dickson, Heinemann, 1966.

Under pseudonym Carter Dickson: *The Plague Court Murders,* Morrow, 1934; *The White Priory Murders,* Morrow, 1934; *The Unicorn Murders,* Morrow, 1935; *The Red Widow Murders,* Morrow, 1935; *Magic Lantern Murders,* Heinemann, 1937; *The Peacock Feather Murders,* Morrow, 1937 (published in England as *The Ten Teacups,* Heinemann, 1937); *The Punch and Judy Murders,* Morrow, 1937; *The Judas Window,* Morrow, 1938; *Death in Five Boxes,* Morrow, 1938; *The Reader Is Warned,* Morrow, 1939.

Nine—And Death Makes Ten, Morrow, 1940 (published in England as *Murder in the Submarine Zone,* Heinemann, 1940); *The Department of Queer Complaints* (short stories), Morrow, 1940; *And So to Murder,* Morrow, 1940; *Seeing Is Believing,* Morrow, 1941; *The Gilded Man,* Morrow, 1942; *She Died a Lady,* Morrow, 1943; *He Wouldn't Kill Patience,* Morrow, 1944; *The Curse of the Bronze Lamp,* Morrow, 1945 (published in England as *Lord of the Sorcerers,* Heinemann, 1946); *My Late Wives,* Morrow, 1946; *The Skeleton in the Clock,* Morrow, 1948; *A Graveyard to Let,* Morrow, 1949.

Night at the Mocking Widow, Morrow, 1950; *Behind the Crimson Blind,* Morrow, 1952; *The Cavalier's Cup,* Morrow, 1953; *Fear Is the Same,* Morrow, 1956.

Under pseudonym John Rhode; with Cecil J. C. Street: *Fatal Descent,* Dodd, 1939 (published in England as *Drop to His Death,* Heinemann, 1940).

Omnibus volumes: *A John Dickson Carr Trio* (includes *The Three Coffins, The Crooked Hinge,* and *The Case of the Constant Suicides*), Harper, 1957; *A Dr. Fell Omnibus,* Hamish Hamilton, 1959; *Three Detective Novels* (includes *The Arabian Nights, The Burning Court,* and *The Problem of the Wire Cage*), Harper, 1959.

SIDELIGHTS: Carr is a prodigious writer of detective fiction, sometimes producing as many as six novels a year. He first entered college with the intention of becoming a lawyer, but soon turned to newspaper writing. He is an acknowledged expert on the life of Sir Arthur Conan Doyle and his imperishable sleuth, Sherlock Holmes. Carr studied and wrote abroad, living in England for many years. Anthony Boucher once said that Carr wrote with "dazzling ease and inventiveness and a brilliantly unobtrusive technique." Carr now resides in New York, where his home contains one of the finest crime reference libraries in the world.

The Emperor's Snuffbox was filmed as "City After Midnight," in 1959. Carr's short stories and radio scripts have been made into films, including "Man with a Cloak," 1951, "Dangerous Crossing," 1953, and "Colonel March of Scotland Yard," 1954.

BIOGRAPHICAL/CRITICAL SOURCES: Howard Haycraft, *Murder for Pleasure: The Life and Times of the Detective Story,* Appleton, 1941; *New Yorker,* September 8, 15, 1951; C. A. Hoyt, editor, *Minor American Novelists,* Southern Illinois University Press, 1970; *Contemporary Literary Criticism,* Volume III, Gale, 1974.*

* * *

CARR, John Laurence 1916-

PERSONAL: Born August 19, 1916, in Leeds, England; son of John and Gertrude (Cropper) Carr; married Nancy Trainer (a teacher), July 29, 1944; children: John Philip, Catherine Jennifer. *Education:* University of Leeds, B.A. (first class honors), 1938; University of Paris, L. es.-l, 1944; University of Glasgow, Ph.D., 1953. *Home:* 16 Ballater Dr., Bearsden G61 1BY, Scotland. *Office:* University of Glasgow, Glasgow, Scotland.

CAREER: University of Glasgow, Glasgow, Scotland, lecturer, 1946-63, senior lecturer in French, 1963—. *Member:* Bearsden Golf Club, College Club. *Awards, honors:* Officier des Palmes Academiques (France), 1966; Silver Medal of the City of Paris, 1967.

WRITINGS: Le College des Ecossais a Paris, Suffroy, 1963; (editor and author of notes) Voltaire, *Le Philosophe ignorant,* University of London Press, 1965; *Life in France under Louis XIV* (young adult book), Batsford, 1966, Putnam, 1967, 2nd edition, Capricorn Books, 1970; *France,* Edward Arnold, 1969, 2nd edition, 1973; *Robespierre: The Force of Circumstance,* St. Martin's, 1973; (contributor) *Milestones in History,* Weidenfeld & Nicolson, in press. Contributor of about thirty articles, mainly on Franco-Scottish history, to journals.

* * *

CARTER, Dorothy Sharp 1921-

PERSONAL: Born March 22, 1921, in Chicago, Ill.; daughter of William Barnard (a professor of medicine) and Alice (Percy) Sharp; married Albert Edwin Carter (a foreign service officer), April 19, 1946; children: Robert Sharp, Janet E., Deborah C. Blank (Mrs. Jeffrey Harrison), Alice P. *Education:* Mills College, Oakland, Calif., B.A., 1942, secondary teaching certificate, 1944; University of Texas, Austin, M.L.S., 1971. *Politics:* Independent. *Religion:* Episcopalian. *Home:* 208 Gannet Cove, Austin, Tex. 78746. *Agent:* Marilyn Marlow, Curtis Brown Ltd., 60 East 56th St., New York, N.Y. 10022.

CAREER: High school English teacher, 1944-46; free-lance writer.

WRITINGS—Children's books: *The Enchanted Orchard and Other Folktales of Central America,* Harcourt, 1973; *Greedy Mariani and Other Folktales of the Antilles,* Atheneum, 1974. Contributor of short stories and articles to *Travel, Nature, Highlights for Children, Child Life,* and *Humpty Dumpty.*

WORK IN PROGRESS: Research in Latin American folktales.

AVOCATIONAL INTERESTS: Travel, foreign language study, wildlife of Texas, gardening, tennis.

* * *

CARTER, Joseph 1912-

PERSONAL: Born July 31, 1912, in Boston, Mass.; son of Joseph F. (a teacher) and Anna (a teacher) Carter; married Alison Edelman (a teacher), January 4, 1944; children: Anne, Elizabeth, Joseph J., Bryce A. *Education:* Harvard University, A.B., 1934. *Home:* 373 Main St., Westport, Conn. 06880. *Agent:* Knox Burger Associates Ltd., 33½ Washington Sq. S., New York, N.Y. 10012.

CAREER: Newsweek, New York, N.Y., associate editor, 1955-58, senior editor, 1958-60, national affairs editor, 1960-63; *New York Herald Tribune,* New York, N.Y., Sunday editor, 1963-65; *Atlas,* New York, N.Y., managing editor, 1965; free-lance writer. *Military service:* U.S. Army, 1941-46; became major; received Purple Heart and Bronze Star with oak-leaf cluster.

WRITINGS: History of the Fourteenth Armored Division, Albert Love, 1946; *Death and Four Lovers* (novel), Doubleday, 1961; *1918: Year of Crisis, Year of Change,* Prentice-Hall, 1968; *Raging Bull,* Prentice-Hall, 1970; *Nothing to Kick About,* Dodd, 1973; *Labor Lobbyist,* Bobbs-Merrill, 1973. Contributor of about three hundred short stories and articles to *Collier's, Saturday Evening Post, Saturday Review, Mademoiselle, Playboy, Twice a Year,* and other magazines.

* * *

CARTWRIGHT, Sally 1923-

PERSONAL: Born November 25, 1923, in New York, N.Y.; daughter of Henry (an engineer) and Anita (an artist; maiden name, Parkhurst) Willcox; married Roger Cartwright (a professor of education), December 25, 1943; children: Steven, Paul. *Education:* Cornell University, B.A., 1944; Harvard University, graduate study, 1970-71; Bank Street College of Education, M.S., 1971. *Politics:* Independent. *Religion:* Agnostic—no denomination. *Residence:* Cambridge, Mass. *Agent:* Evelyn Singer, P.O. Box 163, Briarcliff, N.Y. 10510. *Office:* Watertown Cooperative Nursery School, Inc., Watertown, Mass.

CAREER: Junior high school teacher in Oak Ridge, Tenn., 1945-46; American Friends Service Committee, Bengal,

India, founder and teacher of a school, 1946-49; elementary and junior high school teacher in public and private schools in New York, N.Y., at various times, 1949-70; KLH Child Development Center, Cambridge, Mass., head day care teacher, 1970-71; Watertown Cooperative Nursery School, Inc., Watertown, Mass., teacher and educational director, 1971—. *Awards, honors:* National Science Teachers Association and Children's Book Council outstanding trade book award, 1973, for *Water Is Wet*.

WRITINGS—Children's books: *The Tide,* Coward, 1970; *Why Can't You See the Wind,* Grosset, 1971; *Animal Homes,* Coward, 1973; *Water Is Wet,* Coward, 1973; *Sunlight,* Coward, 1974; *Sand,* Coward, in press. Contributor to *Young Children*. Editor of *City and Country News,* during 1950's.

WORK IN PROGRESS: More children's books; a book on the Watertown Cooperative Nursery School.

SIDELIGHTS: Sally Cartwright has sailed her own boat in the Atlantic and Pacific Oceans, Gulf of Mexico, Red Sea, and River Ganges. She also does cross-country skiing and walking, and she enjoys music and English country dancing.

* * *

CARVER, Frank G(ould) 1928-

PERSONAL: Born May 27, 1928, in Crookston, Neb.; son of Frank A. (a rancher) and Greeta (Gould) Carver; married Betty Ireland (an elementary school teacher), March 31, 1949; children: Mark Erwin, Carol Denise. *Education:* Taylor University, B.A., 1950; Nazarene Theological Seminary, B.D., 1954; Princeton Theological Seminary, M.Th., 1958; New College, Edinburgh, Ph.D., 1964. *Politics:* Republican. *Religion:* Church of the Nazarene. *Home:* 3445 Larga Circle, San Diego, Calif. 92110. *Office:* Division of Philosophy and Religion, Point Loma College, 3900 Lomaland Dr., San Diego, Calif. 92106.

CAREER: Point Loma College, San Diego, Calif. (formerly Pasadena College, Pasadena, Calif.), assistant professor, 1961-65, associate professor, 1965-68, professor of Biblical theology and Greek, 1968—, head of Division of Philosophy and Religion, 1967—. *Member:* Society of Biblical Literature, Institute for Biblical Research.

WRITINGS: (Contributor) A. F. Harper and other editors, *Beacon Bible Commentary,* Volume VIII, Beacon Hill Press, 1968; *Peter the Rock-Man,* Beacon Hill Press, 1973.

* * *

CASADO, Pablo Gil 1931-

PERSONAL: Born August 17, 1931, in Santander, Spain; came to United States in 1955, naturalized in 1963; son of Pablo (a musician) and Agueda (Casado) Gil Benet; married Carol Ann Schuman (a teacher), December 23, 1967. *Education:* Universidad Interamericana, M.A., 1960; University of Wisconsin, Ph.D., 1967. *Religion:* Unitarian Universalist. *Home:* Wolf's Pond, Route 5, Chapel Hill, N.C. 27514. *Office:* Department of Romance Languages, University of North Carolina, Chapel Hill, N.C. 27514.

CAREER: Teacher in public schools of Ashland, Wis., 1955-59, and Wauwatosa, Wis., 1959-60; University of Northern Iowa, Cedar Falls, instructor in Spanish, 1960-63; University of North Carolina, Chapel Hill, assistant professor, 1967-70, associate professor of Spanish language and literature, 1970—. *Member:* Modern Language Association of America, American Association of University Professors.

WRITINGS: Elementary Spanish, Ashland Board of Education, 1957; (with others) *Modern Foreign Languages for Iowa Schools,* Iowa State Department of Public Instruction, 1963; *La novela social espanola, 1942-1968* (title means "The Spanish Social Novel, 1942-48"), Seix Barral, 1968, corrected and enlarged edition published as *La Novela social espanola, 1920-1971,* 1973; (with Doris K. Arjona and Albert Turner) *Lengua espanola* (title means "Spanish Language"), Books I and II, Scott, Foresman, 1969. Contributor to *Cuadernos Americanos* and *Cuadernos Hispanoamericanos*. Associate editor of *Romance Notes,* 1971—.

WORK IN PROGRESS: El paralelepipedo, a novel.

* * *

CASEY, Brigid 1950-

PERSONAL: Born January 11, 1950, in New York, N.Y.; daughter of Michael T. (an educator) and Rosemary (an editor; maiden name, Christmann) Casey; *Education:* St. Francis College, Brooklyn, N.Y., B.A., 1972; New York University, M.A. candidate. *Office:* 625 East 14th St., New York, N.Y. 10009.

WRITINGS: (With Sigmund A. Lavine) *Wonders of the World of Horses,* Dodd, 1972.

WORK IN PROGRESS: Further research on horses; a study of the elderly and their forms of recreation.

* * *

CASEY, Juanita 1925-

PERSONAL: Born October 10, 1925, in England; daughter of Jobey Smith and Annie Maloney; married John Fisher (a farmer); married Sven Berlin; married Fergus Casey (died, 1971); children: William, Jasper, Sheba. *Politics:* "Life." *Religion:* "Life." *Home:* Gloragh, Sneem, County Kerry, Eire. *Address:* c/o Robert Brothers Circus, Brook Farm, Polebrook, Northamptonshire, England.

CAREER: Author of novels, poetry, short stories; painter, specializing in horses and animals. Robert Brothers Circus, Polebrook, Northamptonshire, England, horse master, 1974—. *Military service:* Women's Land Army (England), 1943. *Member:* Appaloosa Horse Club (United States), Palomino Society (Great Britain).

WRITINGS: (Self-illustrated) *Hath the Rain a Father?* (short stories), Phoenix House, 1966; (contributor) *The New Forest* (natural history), Gallery Press, 1960, revised edition, Phoenix House, 1966; (self-illustrated) *Horse by the River, and Other Poems,* Dufour, 1968; *The Horse of Selene* (novel), Dolmen Press, 1971, Grossman, 1972; *The Circus* (novel), Dolmen Press, 1974. Author of play, "30 Gnu Pence," first read in Dublin at Abbey Theatre, 1973. Author of television plays, "Fields of Praise" and "Stallion Eternity," both produced by BBC. Contributor to journals.

WORK IN PROGRESS: "All sorts of things going on if circus job leaves any spare time."

SIDELIGHTS: Juanita Casey describes herself as "horse breeder, trainer of zebras, unsuccessful domestic, yukky cook." She writes: "I travel all over and even reached Delaware (home quick)—gypsy both sides . . . great love for everything and everybody—hurray. Bliss-crystals, minerals, rocks, and fossils . . . extremely active in quarries, fields containing fauna, angels, tramps, and silence."

* * *

CASLER, Lawrence (Ray) 1932-

PERSONAL: Born January 26, 1932, in Portland, Ore.; son of David H. and Fyrne (Levinson) Casler. *Education:* Harvard University, B.A. (cum laude), 1953, M.A., 1954; Columbia University, Ph.D., 1962. *Residence:* Pittsford, N.Y. *Office:* Department of Psychology, State University of New York College at Geneseo, Geneseo, N.Y. 14454.

CAREER: Montclair Academy, Montclair, N.J., English teacher, 1954-55; Stevenson School for Veterans, New York, N.Y., teacher of English, remedial reading, and speed reading, 1956-58; Reece School, New York, N.Y., teacher and counselor of emotionally disturbed children, 1957-59; City University of New York, New York, N.Y., lecturer in psychology at City College, 1959-61, and at Brooklyn College, 1961-62; *International Encyclopedia of the Social Sciences,* New York, N.Y., staff editor for psychology, 1962-63; City College of the City University of New York, assistant professor of psychology, 1963-66; State University of New York College at Geneseo, associate professor, 1966-68, professor of psychology, 1968—. Lecturer at Long Island University, 1965; research associate for Staten Island Mental Health Society, 1965-66. *Military service:* U.S. Army, librarian, teacher, and director of education, 1955-56.

MEMBER: American Psychological Association, Parapsychological Association, American Association of University Professors. *Awards, honors:* Grant from Association for Aid of Crippled Children, 1969-71, for study of perceptual stimulation of institutionalized infants.

WRITINGS: (Contributor) Grant Newton and Seymour Levine, editors, *Early Experience and Behavior,* C. C Thomas, 1968; (contributor) R.E. Decker, editor, *Patterns of Exposition,* 2nd edition (Casler was not associated with 1st edition), Little, Brown, 1972, 3rd edition, 1974; (contributor) M. D. Curtin, editor, *Symposium on Love,* Behavioral Publications, 1973; *Is Marriage Necessary?,* Behavioral Publications, 1974.

Author of monographs. Contributor of about twenty articles and reviews to social science journals, including *Medical Aspects of Human Sexuality, Psychological Reports, Childbirth Courier, Personality, Journal of Parapsychology,* and *Hypermodern.*

WORK IN PROGRESS: An introductory psychology textbook; research on the effects of supplementary auditory and vestibular stimulation on an institutionalized population.

AVOCATIONAL INTERESTS: Travel in Europe, Mexico, India, and Egypt.

* * *

CASTLETON, Virginia 1925- (Virginia Castleton Thomas)

PERSONAL: Born December 4, 1925, in Fairbanks, La.; daughter of Pierre Ariel and Vada Al Berta (Nolan) Castleton; married Richard Thomas, 1960 (died, 1970); children: Ronald Michail. *Education:* Attended Temple University, 1951-52, New School for Social Research, 1962, and University of Paris, 1964. *Home:* Century House West, Doylestown, Pa. 18901. *Agent:* Theron Raines, 244 Madison Ave., New York, N.Y. 10016.

CAREER: MacNen's News Agency, Paris, France, correspondent, 1966-67; *Philadelphia Bulletin,* Philadelphia, Pa., feature writer, 1968-71; *Prevention,* Doylestown, Pa., beauty editor, 1970—. *Member:* Overseas Press Club (New York, N.Y. and Philadelphia, Pa.), Bucks County Writer's Guild.

WRITINGS: (Under name Virginia Castleton Thomas) *Look Younger, Look Prettier,* Rodale Press, 1972; (under name Virginia Castleton Thomas) *My Secrets of Natural Beauty,* Keats Publishing, 1972; *The Calendar Book of Natural Beauty,* Harper, 1973.

WORK IN PROGRESS: A self-help health and beauty book; research on a book for men.

AVOCATIONAL INTERESTS: Travel.

* * *

CAVALIER, Julian 1931-

PERSONAL: Born October 24, 1931, in Toronto, Ontario, Canada; son of Anthony and Helen (LaSota) Cavalier; married Dorothy Edith Theobald, June 3, 1957; children: Michael (deceased), Catherine, Linda. *Education:* Received high school education in San Francisco, Calif. *Residence:* Malton, Ontario, Canada.

CAREER: Employed by consulting engineers as draftsman in Toronto, Ontario, 1949-56, in San Francisco, Calif., 1956-61, and in Berkeley, Calif., 1961-70; full-time writer, 1970—. *Military service:* Canadian Army, Militia, 1945-50; became gunner. U.S. Army, Corps of Engineers, 1957-63.

WRITINGS: American Castles, A. S. Barnes, 1973. Contributor to magazines, including *Railroad Model Craftsman, Model Railroader, Highlights for Children,* and to newspapers.

WORK IN PROGRESS: Writing and drafting for railroad magazines.

AVOCATIONAL INTERESTS: Music, music composition, astronomy.

BIOGRAPHICAL/CRITICAL SOURCES: Railroad Model Craftsman, April, 1972.

* * *

CELESTE, Sister Marie

PERSONAL: Born in Altoona, Pa.; daughter of Frank (an electrical engineer) and Mary Ann (Dente) Cuzzolina. *Education:* Attended Seton Hill College, 1939, Western Reserve University (now Case Western Reserve University), 1940, 1943; University of Pittsburgh, B.A., 1947; Laval University, M.A. (magna cum laude), 1957, Ph.D. (cum laude), 1959; Sorbonne, University of Paris, certificate (magna cum laude), 1962; University of Madrid, certificate, 1969; University of Perugia, certificate, 1969. *Home:* Sisters of Charity, Greensburg, Pa. 15601. *Office:* Office of the Superintendent of Public Instruction, Springfield, Ill. 62706.

CAREER: Roman Catholic nun of the Sisters of Charity; high school French teacher in Pittsburgh, Pa., 1943-51; Seton Hill College, Greensburg, Pa., assistant professor of French, 1951-57; Laval University, Faculty of Letters, Quebec City, Quebec, teacher in School of English, summers, 1959-64; Loyola University, Chicago, Ill., associate professor of modern languages, 1963-67; Wisconsin State University, Eau Claire, associate professor in department of foreign languages, 1969-70; Loyola University, Chicago,

Ill., associate professor of modern languages, 1970-71; Office of the Superintendent of Public Instruction, Springfield, Ill., director of foreign languages, 1971-73. Visiting professor at University of Ottawa, 1962-63. *Member:* American Association of Teachers of French, American Association of University Professors, National Federation of Modern Language Teachers, National Council of State Supervisors for Foreign Languages, Canadian Association of University Professors of French, American Institute for Foreign Studies (advisory board, 1964-72), Central States Modern Language Association, Midwest Modern Language Association, Illinois Modern Language Association, La Societe des Amis de Georges Bernanos. *Awards, honors:* Raymond Casgrain Prize from Laval University, 1962, for *Le sens de l'agonie dans l'oeuvre de Georges Bernanos;* Chevalier dans l'Ordre des Palmes Academiques conferred by French Ministry of Education, 1965.

WRITINGS: Le sens de l'agonie dans l'oeuvre de Georges Bernanos (title means "The Meaning of Suffering in the Works of Georges Bernanos"), Lethielleux, 1962; *A Challenge to the Church,* Newman, 1965; *Etudes bernanosiennes: Bernanos et Graham Greene* (title means "Bernanos Studies: Bernanos and Graham Greene"), Minard, 1965; *Georges Bernanos et son optique de la vie chretienne* (title means "Georges Bernanos and His Vision of the Christian Life"), Nizet, 1967; (contributor) *Basic Catechetical Perspectives,* Paulist-Newman, 1970; *A Survey on Foreign Education in Illinois: A Statewide Report,* Office of the Superintendent of Public Instruction, State of Illinois, 1971; *A New Rationale for the Teaching of Foreign Languages: A Humanistic View,* Office of the Superintendent of Public Instruction, State of Illinois, 1972; *New Guidelines for Foreign Language Education in the Seventies: French, German, Latin, Spanish, Russian,* Office of the Superintendent of Public Instruction, State of Illinois, 1973; (translator) Jean Ladame, *The Church and Love,* Franciscan Publishers, 1973. Editor of *Illinois Foreign Language Directory,* 1972. Contributor to *Revue Dominicaine, Revue de l'Universite Laval, Culture,* and *Lectures.*

* * *

CHACKO, David 1942-

PERSONAL: Born January 3, 1942, in Pittsburgh, Pa.; son of Joseph W. and Evelyn (Paterline) Chacko; married Susan Myers (a systems programmer), November, 1968. *Education:* Wright State University, B.A.; University of Connecticut, M.A. *Home:* 52 Shawnee Dr., Trumbull, Conn. 06611. *Office:* Department of English, University of Bridgeport, Bridgeport, Conn. 06602.

CAREER: University of Bridgeport, Bridgeport, Conn., assistant professor of English, 1971—. *Military service:* U.S. Air Force, 1962-66. *Member:* Modern Language Association of America, American Association of University Professors, Authors Guild of Authors League of America. *Awards, honors:* Creative writing fellowship from Book-of-the-Month Club, 1968.

WRITINGS: Price (novel), St. Martin's, 1973; *Gage* (novel), St. Martin's, 1974; (editor with Dick Allen) *Crime and Compromise: An Introduction to Detective Fiction* (text), Harcourt, 1974.

WORK IN PROGRESS: Emme's Book of Miracles, a novel.

AVOCATIONAL INTERESTS: Travel.

CHADWICK, James 1891-1974

October 20, 1891—July 24, 1974; British physicist, discoverer of the neutron, and Nobel laureate. Obituaries: *New York Times,* July 25, 1974; *Washington Post,* July 26, 1974; *Time,* August 5, 1974; *Newsweek,* August 5, 1974.

* * *

CHAFE, William H(enry) 1942-

PERSONAL: Born January 28, 1942, in Boston, Mass.; son of William Robinson and Elsie (Crabtree) Chafe; married Lorna Waterhouse, July 12, 1964; children: Christopher Robert, Jennifer Elizabeth. *Education:* Harvard University, A.B. (magna cum laude), 1962; Union Theological Seminary, New York, N.Y., graduate study, 1962-63; Columbia University, M.A., 1966, Ph.D., 1971; Cornell University, summer graduate study, 1967. *Home:* 820 Tinkerbell Rd., Chapel Hill, N.C. 27514. *Office:* Department of History, Duke University, Durham, N.C. 27706.

CAREER: Columbia Grammar School, New York, N.Y., instructor in history and comparative religion, 1963-65; Vassar College, Poughkeepsie, N.Y., instructor in history, 1970-71; Duke University, Durham, NC., assistant professor of history, 1971—, associate director of Oral History Program, 1971—. *Awards, honors:* National Endowment for the Humanities summer fellowship, 1972.

WRITINGS: (Contributor) Robert C. Twombly, editor, *Blacks in White America Since 1865,* McKay, 1971; *The American Woman: Her Changing Social, Political, and Economic Roles, 1920-1970,* Oxford University Press, 1972; (contributor) James T. Patterson, editor, *The United States Since 1930,* Burgess, 1974. Contributor to *Journal of Southern History, Michigan History,* and *New England Social Studies Bulletin.*

* * *

CHAMBERLIN, M. Hope 1920-1974

December 2, 1920—March 11, 1974; American author. Obituaries: *Washington Post,* March 13, 1974; *Publishers Weekly,* April 1, 1974. (*CA*-45/48).

* * *

CHAMBERS, Howard V. See Lowenkopf, Shelly A(lan)

* * *

CHAMPLIN, Joseph M(asson) 1930-

PERSONAL: Born May 11, 1930, in Hammondsport, N.Y.; son of Francis Mulburn and Katherine (Masson) Champlin. *Education:* Attended Yale University, 1947-48; University of Notre Dame, 1948-49, St. Andrew's Seminary, 1949-50, and St. Bernard's Seminary, 1950-56. *Office:* Holy Family Church, 45 West Fourth St., Fulton, N.Y. 13069.

CAREER: Ordained Roman Catholic priest, 1956; Immaculate Conception Cathedral, Syracuse, N.Y., assistant pastor, 1956-68; Diocese of Syracuse, Syracuse, N.Y., director of vocations, 1957-60, Liturgical Commission secretary, 1961-65; Bishops' Committee on the Liturgy, Washington, D.C., associate director of secretariat, 1968-71; Holy Family Church, Fulton, N.Y., pastor, 1971—. Visiting lecturer in liturgy, Princeton Theological Seminary, winter, 1973. Chairman of board of directors, Lee Memorial Hospital, Fulton, N.Y., 1973—.

WRITINGS: Don't You Really Love Me?, Ave Maria Press, 1968; (editor and contributor) *The Priest Today and Tomorrow,* Collegeville Press, 1969; *Together For Life,* Ave Maria Press, 1970; *Christ Present and Yet to Come,* Orbis Books, 1971; *The Mass in a World of Change,* Ave Maria Press, 1973; *The Sacraments in a World of Change,* Ave Maria Press, 1973. Author of weekly column, *The Altar of God,* for Diocese of Syracuse paper, 1958-62; author of syndicated column, *Worship and the World,* 1969—.

* * *

CHANDLER, David Leon

EDUCATION: Self-educated. *Home and office:* 716 Governor Nicholls, New Orleans, La. 70116. *Agent:* Roberta Pryor, International Famous Agency, 1301 Avenue of the Americas, New York, N.Y. 10019.

CAREER: Has worked as merchant seaman and farm laborer; *Panama City News-Herald,* Panama City, Fla., reporter, 1959-61; *New Orleans States-Item,* New Orleans, La., reporter, 1961-64; *Life* (magazine), New York, N.Y., contract reporter and correspondent, 1965-71. *Member:* Dramatists Guild. *Awards, honors:* Shared Pulitzer Prize for investigative reporting, 1962; Sigma Delta Chi prize for national magazine reporting, 1970.

WRITINGS—Non-fiction: *Dragon Variation,* Dutton, 1974; *The Negro-Stealers,* Dutton, in press.

WORK IN PROGRESS: A nonfiction work for Doubleday.

* * *

CHANOVER, Hyman 1920-

PERSONAL: Born April 19, 1920, in Makow, Poland; came to United States in 1921, naturalized in 1928; son of Abraham Isaac (a roofer) and Anna (Certner) Chanover; married Alice S. Fischer (a bookkeeper), June 18, 1944; children: Leonard Joseph, David Ezra. *Education:* Yeshiva University, B.A. (summa cum laude), 1941; Jewish Theological Seminary of America, Rabbi (with merit) and M.H.L., 1945; Temple University, M.Ed., 1952; New York University, Ed.D., 1971. *Home:* 5 Sylvester Pl., Lynbrook, N.Y. 11563. *Office:* American Association for Jewish Education, 114 Fifth Ave., New York, N.Y. 10011.

CAREER: American Jewish Committee, Library of Jewish Information, New York, N.Y., research associate, 1941-42; acting rabbi of temple in Columbus, Ohio, 1945-46; rabbi of congregations in Philadelphia, Pa., 1946-52, and Albany, N.Y., 1952-54; Kew Gardens Anshe Sholom Jewish Center, Queens, New York, N.Y., principal, 1954-56; American Association for Jewish Education, New York, N.Y., director of department of personnel services and executive secretary of National Board of License, 1956-64, director of department of community service, 1964-66, director of department of community planning and studies, 1966-70, director of National Curriculum Research Institute, 1970—. Adjunct assistant professor at New York University, 1972—. Conducted workshops and seminars for school principals, teachers, and boards of Jewish education; guest lecturer at institutions of higher learning. Vice-president of National Assembly on Ethnic Studies, 1972—; National Council for Jewish Education, member of executive committee, 1956-59, 1962-65, 1972—, vice-president, 1970-72; member of executive committee, Jewish Book Council of America, 1972—; secretary-treasurer, Association for Multiethnic Programs, 1974—.

MEMBER: National Conference of Jewish Communal Workers, Rabbinical Assembly of America, American Educational Research Association. *Awards, honors:* D.D. from Jewish Theological Seminary of America, 1972.

WRITINGS: Planning for Threes to Eights in the Hebrew School, United Synagogue Commission on Jewish Education, 1954; (with wife, Alice Chanover) *Happy Hanukah Everybody,* United Synagogue Commission on Jewish Education, 1955; (with Alice Chanover) *Pesah Is Coming,* United Synagogue Commission on Jewish Education, 1956; (with Alice Chanover) *Pesah Is Here,* United Synagogue Commission on Jewish Education, 1956; *Blessed Event: A Manual for Expectant Jewish Parents,* J. David, 1956; (with Evelyn Zusman) *My Book of Prayer: Sabbath and Weekdays,* United Synagogue Commission on Jewish Education, 1959; (with Zusman) *My Book of Prayer: Holidays and Holy Days,* United Synagogue Commission on Jewish Education, 1959; (with Zusman) *A Book of Prayer for Junior Congregations,* United Synagogue Commission on Jewish Education, 1959.

(Editor) *Hebrew in the First and Second Grades of the Foundation School and Day School,* United Synagogue Commission on Jewish Education, 1960; (with Frances S. Gelbart, Leah Leshefsky, and Asenath Rosenberg) *A Curriculum Guide for the Kindergarten,* United Synagogue Commission on Jewish Education, 1960; *Intensifying the Primary Program: A Workable Syllabus for the Sixes and Sevens,* Jewish Education Committee Press, 1962; *A Haggadah for the School,* United Synagogue Commission on Jewish Education, 1964; *Teaching the Haggadah,* Jewish Education Committee Press, 1964; (contributor) Oscar I. Janowsky, editor, *The Education of American Jewish Teachers,* Beacon Press, 1967.

(With Eugene Borowitz and Harry Gersh) *When a Jew Celebrates,* Behrman, 1971; *Service for the High Holy Days: Adapted for Youth,* Behrman, 1972; (editor with Leo Blond) *The Holocaust: A Case Study of Genocide* (teaching guide), American Association for Jewish Education, 1973; (editor with Benjamin Efron) *Dilemma-Allocating the Funds of a Jewish Community* (simulation game), American Association for Jewish Education, 1973; (with Borowitz and Seymour Rossell) *When a Jew Prays,* Behrman, 1973.

Monographs: (with Zalmen Slesinger) *The Jewish School, Your Child, and You,* American Association for Jewish Education, 1956; *Directory of Scholarships and Other Student Aid Programs for Professional Training in Jewish Education,* American Association for Jewish Education, 1959; (with Evelyn Zusman) *Adults' Guide to My Book of Prayer,* United Synagogue Commission on Jewish Education, 1959; *Salary Scales for Full-Time Teaching,* American Association for Jewish Education, 1963; *Guide to a Code of Practice for Teachers and Schools,* American Association for Jewish Education, 1963; (with Azriel Eisenberg, Asenath Rosenberg, and Morris Benathen) *Unified Jewish Religious Education Curriculum for the Armed Forces,* Commission on Jewish Chaplaincy, National Jewish Welfare Board, 1964.

Editor of reports on community surveys of Jewish education and author of information bulletins. Editor of "Book Notes," a column in *Synagogue School,* 1954-61; executive editor of "Viewpoints: Major Issues Facing the State of Israel," American Association for Jewish Education, 1973. Contributor of articles and book reviews to professional journals, including *Synagogue School, Jewish Education,*

Our Age, and *Reconstructionist.* Member of editorial staff of *Contemporary Jewish Record* (now *Commentary*), 1941-42; editor of *Our Teachers,* 1958-63, *Central Intelligence,* 1965-67, *Pedagogic Reporter,* spring, 1973, and, winter, 1974; special editor of *Jewish Education,* spring, 1957; associate editor of *Synagogue School,* 1949-61.

WORK IN PROGRESS: A book on ethical behavior for a Jew, for Behrman; *Sourcebook for Teaching the Holocaust,* for American Association for Jewish Education; *Sourcebook for Teaching Jewish Civics,* American Association for Jewish Education.

SIDELIGHTS: Chanover was the initiator of a national certification system for principals of Jewish schools; he also formulated a national retirement plan for Jewish school personnel. *Avocational interests:* Music (instrumental and cantorial), travel.

* * *

CHAPMAN, Rick M. 1943-

PERSONAL: Born March 11, 1943, in Wichita, Kan.; son of Frederick Martin (a businessman) and Mara Helene (Eldredge) Chapman. *Education:* Harvard University, A.B. (cum laude), 1966; University of California, Berkeley, M.A., 1971, working toward doctoral degree. *Address:* The Agency, Box 31, Berkeley, Calif. 94701.

CAREER: Lecturer and Fulbright fellow at University of Gujarat, Gujarat, India, 1966-67; The Agency, Berkeley, Calif., consultant on drug education and research. Teacher of course on drug abuse at Berkeley Unified School District. Lecturer at Harvard University, University of California, Berkeley, and other institutions; consultant on drug education to colleges and universities.

WRITINGS: How to Choose a Guru, Harper, 1973.

SIDELIGHTS: Chapman studied and travelled in Europe and North Africa. In India he was "allowed a unique opportunity to meet with Avatar Meher Baba, the recent preeminent spiritual master who spoke out with great authority on the drug issue. Meher Baba's views on drugs have been a major influence in dissuading young people throughout the United States from indulgence in marijuana and psychedelics. Not only has he drawn attention to the physical and psychological dangers of using these drugs, but he has also made some very revealing statements about the illusory nature and 'pseudo-spirituality' of the psychedelic experience."

* * *

CHARLES, C(arol) M(organ) 1931-

PERSONAL: Born January 11, 1931, in Lorraine, Tex.; son of Joe M. and Lois (Jackson) Charles; married Ruth Kimbell (a teacher), June 3, 1951; children: Gail, Timothy. *Education:* Eastern New Mexico University, B.A., 1953, M.A., 1957; University of New Mexico, Ph.D., 1961. *Office:* School of Education, San Diego State University, San Diego, Calif. 92115.

CAREER: Teacher of English and general science in public schools in Estancia, N.M., 1953-59; University of New Mexico, Albuquerque, research assistant and visiting professor of education, 1959-61; San Diego State University, San Diego, Calif., assistant professor, 1961-63, associate professor, 1964-68, professor of education, 1969—. Associate professor at Columbia University, 1966-68. Consultant to ministries of education in Peru and Brazil.

WRITINGS: (With Madge Church) *Creative Writing Skills,* Books I and II, Denison, 1968; *Educational Psychology,* Mosby, 1972; *Teacher's Petit Piaget,* Fearon, 1974; *Individualizing Instruction,* Mosby, in press. Contributor of articles to education journals in English, Spanish, and Portuguese.

WORK IN PROGRESS: Crucial Ideas in Education.

* * *

CHARNEY, Hanna K(urz) 1931-

PERSONAL: Born January 8, 1931, in Vienna, Austria; daughter of Leopold and Frida (Wolf) Kurz; married Maurice M. Charney (a professor and author), June 20, 1954; children: Leopold J., Paul R. *Education:* Hunter College (now Hunter College of the City University of New York), B.A., 1951; Smith College, M.A., 1952; Columbia University, Ph.D., 1956. *Home:* 168 West 86th St., New York, N.Y. 10024. *Office:* Department of Romance Languages, Hunter College of the City University of New York, 695 Park Ave., New York, N.Y. 10021.

CAREER: Hunter College (now Hunter College of the City University of New York), New York, N.Y., lecturer and instructor, 1952-60, assistant professor, 1960-63, associate professor, 1963-69, professor of French, 1969—, chairman of department of Romance languages, 1967-70. Consultant to Doubleday & Co. and Rutgers University Press. Visiting professor at Rutgers University, 1968-70. *Member:* Modern Language Association of America, American Association of Teachers of French, Societe des Professeurs Francais d'Amerique, Phi Beta Kappa, Pi Delta Phi, Sigma Epsilon Phi. *Awards, honors:* Fulbright grant to France and American Association of University Women Shirley Farr fellowship, both 1960-61.

WRITINGS: Le Scepticisme de Valery (title means "Valery's Skepticism"), Didier, 1969. Contributor to *Romanic Review, Symposium,* and *French Review.*

WORK IN PROGRESS: Four books, *The Anonymous Hero in Contemporary Fiction; Film and the Novel: A Parallel Esthetic; Time and the Novel; The Detective Story and the New Novel.*

* * *

CHARY, Frederick B(arry) 1939-

PERSONAL: Born August 18, 1939, in Philadelphia, Pa.; son of Herman and Norma (a seamstress; maiden name, Silver) Chary; married Julia Grimes (a teacher), May 1, 1965; children: David Charles, Michael Alan. *Education:* University of Pennsylvania, A.B., 1962; University of Pittsburgh, M.A., 1963, Ph.D., 1968. *Politics:* Independent. *Home:* 6409 Ash Ave., Gary, Ind. 46403. *Office:* Indiana University—Northwest, 3400 Broadway, Gary, Ind. 46408.

CAREER: Indiana University—Northwest, Gary, instructor, 1967-69, assistant professor, 1969-72, associate professor of East European history, 1972—. *Member:* American Historical Association, American Association for the Advancement of Slavic Studies, American Association of South Slavic Studies, Conference of East European Historians, American Federation of Teachers (president of local union, 1955).

WRITINGS: The Bulgarian Jews and the Final Solution: 1940-1944, University of Pittsburgh, 1972. Managing editor of *Southeastern Europe.*

WORK IN PROGRESS: A Study of the Bulgarian Popular Agricultural Union: 1899-1920; a monograph.

SIDELIGHTS: Chary writes: "My interest in Balkan history has resulted in my visiting Bulgaria several times over the last fifteen years.... I became interested in the fate of the Bulgarian Jews when learning that they were saved from annihilation during the war.... I am currently interested in Bulgarian peasant movements because in the 1920's [they were] the most successful in Europe."

* * *

CHASE, Otta Louise 1909-

PERSONAL: Born July 8, 1909, in Salem, Mass.; daughter of Benjamin Franklin (a handyman) and Reta Townes (Young) Graffam; married Hunter Ellsworth Chase, February 17, 1929; children: Donald Clayton, Nancy Lee (deceased), Charles Frederick. *Education:* Attended high school in Massachusetts. *Politics:* Democrat. *Religion:* Protestant. *Home and office:* Route 93, Sweden, Me. *Mailing address:* R.F.D. #2, Harrison, Me. 04040.

CAREER: Boston Edison Co., Boston, Mass., dictaphone operator, 1927-29; Town of Sweden, Me., treasurer, 1957-58, clerk, 1959—, registrar of voters, 1968—, medical officer, 1970—. *Member:* National League of American Pen Women, American Poetry League, Poetry Fellowship of Maine (treasurer, 1964, 1965; corresponding secretary, 1966-70; member of board of review, 1971—), Poetry Society of New Hampshire (charter member), Alabama State Poetry Society (charter member), Massachusetts State Poetry Society (associate member), California Federation of Chaparral Poets (associate member), Kentucky State Poetry Society (associate member). *Awards, honors:* Freedoms Foundation George Washington Honor Medal Award, 1963 and 1967 for poetry, and 1965 for letter to editor; National Federation of State Poetry Societies award, 1973, for "The Connecticut Darn Man"; Oklahoma State Poetry Society first prize, 1974, for "Only in Oklahoma"; National League of American Pen Women (Cedar Rapids-Waterloo Branch) award for serious poetry, 1974, for "Primer."

WRITINGS: November Violets (poems), Golden Quill, 1973. Poems represented in anthologies, including *Selected Poems of the Florida State Poetry Society,* edited by Frances Clark Handler, Florida State Poetry Society, 1967-70; *Dr. Etta Josephean Murfey Memorial Book,* Florida State Poetry Society, 1968; *Alabama Sampler,* Alabama State Poetry Society, 1969-73; *Golden Quill Anthologies,* edited by Clarence E. Farrar, Golden Quill, 1969-71; *Golden Harvest,* Young Publications, 1970; *Melody of the Muse,* Young Publications, 1971; *Variation in Mulberry,* edited by Lawrence Wiggin, Poetry Society of New Hampshire, 1971; *Rock Ledge and Apple Blossoms,* edited by Ina Ladd Brown, Poetry Fellowship of Maine, 1971; *International Who's Who in Poetry Anthology,* edited by Ernest Kay, Rowman, 1972.

Contributor to State of Maine Writers Conference chapbooks nos. 4-15. Contributor of poems to newspapers and magazines.

WORK IN PROGRESS: Poetry.

AVOCATIONAL INTERESTS: Watching and feeding wild birds, button collecting, corresponding with people in foreign lands.

CHATHAM, Josiah G(eorge) 1914-

PERSONAL: Born June 20, 1914, in Vicksburg, Miss.; son of Roger Paul (a clerk) and Ethel (Griffin) Chatham. *Education:* Gregorian University of Rome, S.T.L., 1940; Catholic University of America, J.C.D., 1950. *Politics:* Democrat. *Home:* St. Dominic Hospital, 969 Lakeland Dr., Jackson, Miss. 39216.

CAREER: Ordained Roman Catholic priest, 1939; Catholic University of America, Washington, D.C., lecturer on religion, 1946-50; pastor of St. Richard's Church, Jackson, Miss., 1953-67. Lecturer on canon law, St. Michael's College, summers, 1947-49; has conducted fifty retreats for priests. *Military service:* U.S. Army Air Forces, 1943-46; chaplain. *Member:* Canon Law Society of America.

WRITINGS: Force and Fear, Catholic University of America Press, 1950; *In the Midst Stands Jesus: A Pastoral Introduction to the New Testament,* Alba, 1972. Contributor of articles and book reviews to about fifteen national publications.

WORK IN PROGRESS: Let's Discuss It: Questions on Religion; Everyman's John of the Cross: Contemplation.

SIDELIGHTS: Fr. Chatham is a victim of multiple sclerosis.

* * *

CHAVEL, Charles Ber 1906-

PERSONAL: Born July 14, 1906, in Ciechanow, Poland; son of Jacob and Feiga Rose (Zaushnitz) Chavel; married Florence Krasna, June, 1933; children: Cyrella (Mrs. Leisha A. Langer), Isaac. *Education:* Hebrew Theological College, Rabbi, 1929; University of Chicago, Ph.B., 1928; University of Louisville, M.A., 1932, LL.B., 1935. *Home:* 333 Beach 28th St., Far Rockaway, N.Y. 11691.

CAREER: Rabbi in Louisville, Ky., 1930-45; Congregation Shaare Zedek, Edgemere, N.Y., rabbi, 1946—. *Member:* Rabbinical Council of America, Mizrachi Organization of America. *Awards, honors:* Horav Kuk prize from city of Tel Aviv, 1955, for *Sefer ha-hinukh;* D.H.L., Hebrew Theological College, 1959, Yeshiva University, 1970.

WRITINGS: The Commandments, Soncino Press, 1940, 2nd edition published in two volumes, 1967; (editor) Aaron ha-Levi, *Sefer ha-hinukh,* Mosad Horav Kuk, 1952; (author of supplementary text) *The Haggadah of Passover,* Shulsinger, 1956; (editor) Moses ben Nahman, *Peirushe Ha-Torah,* two volumes, Mosad Horav Kuk, 1959; (editor) Akiba Eger, *Mishnato shel 'Akiva Eger,* [Jerusalem], 1959—; *Ramban: His Life and Teachings,* Feldheim, 1960; (editor) Nahman, *Kitve rabenu Mosheh ben Nahman,* two volumes, Mosad Horav Kuk, 1963; (editor) Nahman, *Perushe ha-RaMBaN 'al Nevi'im u-Khetuvim,* [Jerusalem], 1963; (editor) Bahya ben Asher, *Be'ur'al ha-Torah,* Mosad Horav Kuk, 1966—; *Rabbeinu Moshe ben Nahman* (biography), Mosad Horav Kuk, 1967; (editor) Rabbi Meyuchos, *Peirush Rabbeinu Meyuchos on "Job,"* Feldheim, 1970; *Ramban: Commentary on the Torah–Genesis,* Shiloh, 1971; *Ramban: Commentary on the Torah–Exodus,* Shiloh, 1973.

Contributor to Hebrew journals. Editor, *Hadorom* (Hebrew Journal of Rabbinical Council of America), 1959—.

WORK IN PROGRESS: Ramban's Commentary on Leviticus, Numbers, and Deuteronomy; The Responsa of Nahmanides.

CHEESMAN, Paul R. 1921-

PERSONAL: Born May 31, 1921, in Brigham City, Utah; married Millie Rubey Foster, June 29, 1944; children: Brian, Ross, Douglas, Larry, LuAnn, Jay. *Education:* San Diego State University, B.A., 1944; graduate study at University of California, Los Angeles, 1945, and University of Miami, Coral Gables, Fla., 1955; Brigham Young University, M.R.S., 1964, D.R.E., 1967. *Home:* 1146 Old Willow Dr., Provo, Utah 84601. *Office:* Brigham Young University, Provo, Utah 84602.

CAREER: Ordained Mormon clergyman, 1941; bishop in Linda Vista, Calif., and Provo, Utah; teacher in public schools of San Diego, Calif., 1944-49; self-employed photographer, 1949-53; corporation president in Miami, Fla., 1955-63; Brigham Young University, Provo, Utah, instructor, 1963-67, assistant professor, 1967-70, associate professor, 1970-74. Associate producer of motion pictures. *Military service:* U.S. Naval Reserve, chaplain, 1953-55; became lieutenant. *Member:* Lions Club.

WRITINGS: *Great Leaders of the Book of Mormon,* Community Press, 1970; *Early America and the Book of Mormon,* Deseret, 1972; *Keystone of Mormonism,* Deseret, 1973; *These Early Americans,* Deseret, 1974.

WORK IN PROGRESS: *The Origins of the American Indian; The Polynesians and the Book of Mormon.*

* * *

CHEN, Kan 1928-

PERSONAL: Born August 28, 1928, in Hong Kong, China; son of H. C. and S. M. Chen; married Lillian Hsieh, 1953; children: Raymond, Jeffrey, Harriet, Sloane. *Education:* Cornell University, B.E.E., 1950; Massachusetts Institute of Technology, S.M., 1951, Sc.D., 1954. *Home:* 1900 Cambridge Rd., Ann Arbor, Mich. 48104. *Office:* Department of Electrical and Computer Engineering, University of Michigan, Ann Arbor, Mich. 48104.

CAREER: Westinghouse Electric Corp., Pittsburgh, Pa., manager of systems technology research and development, 1954-65; Stanford Research Institute, Menlo Park, Calif., director of institute-wide program on urban development, 1966-70; University of Pittsburgh, Pittsburgh, Pa., professor of environmental systems engineering, 1970-71; University of Michigan, Ann Arbor, Paul G. Goebel Professor of Advanced Technology, 1971-73, professor of electrical and computer engineering, 1973—. *Member:* Institute of Electrical and Electronic Engineers (fellow), Systems, Man and Cybernetics Society.

WRITINGS: (Editor) *National Priorities,* San Francisco Press, 1970; (editor) *Urban Dynamics: Extensions and Reflections,* San Francisco Press, 1972; (with K. F. Lagler and others) *Growth Policy: Population, Environment, and Beyond,* University of Michigan Press, 1973; (editor) *Technology and Social Institutions,* Institute of Electrical and Electronic Engineers, 1974. Contributor of over forty articles to professional journals.

* * *

CHEN, Lincoln C(hih-ho) 1942-

PERSONAL: Born February 12, 1942, in China; son of Samuel S. T. (a teacher) and Winifred W. Chen; married Martha Alter, July 1, 1967; children: Gregory, Alexis. *Education:* Princeton University, B.A., 1964; Harvard University, M.D., 1968; Johns Hopkins University, M.P.H., 1973. *Politics:* None. *Religion:* None. *Address:* c/o Ford Foundation, P.O. Box 98, Ramna Dacca, Bangladesh.

CAREER: Population Council, New York, N.Y., staff associate, 1972—; Ford Foundation, New York, N.Y., program officer in Bangladesh, 1973—. *Military service:* U.S. Public Health Service, 1970-72; became lieutenant commander.

WRITINGS: (Editor) *Disaster in Bangladesh: Health Crisis in a Developing Nation,* Oxford University Press, 1973.

WORK IN PROGRESS: Population research.

* * *

CHERRY, Kelly

PERSONAL: Born in Baton Rouge, La.; daughter of J. Milton (a violinist and professor of music theory) and Mary (a violinist and writer; maiden name, Spooner) Cherry; married Jonathan Silver, December 23, 1966 (divorced, 1969). *Education:* Mary Washington College, B.A., 1961; University of Virginia, graduate study, 1961-63; University of North Carolina at Greensboro, M.F.A., 1967; also studied at New Mexico Institute of Mining and Technology, Virginia Polytechnic Institute, Richmond Professional Institute, University of Richmond, and University of Tennessee. *Residence:* Richmond, Va. *Agent:* Ellen Levine, Curtis Brown Ltd., 60 East 56th St., New York, N.Y. 10022. *Office:* Southwest Minnesota State College, Marshall, Minn.

CAREER: Behrman House, Inc. (publishers), New York, N.Y., editor and writer, 1970-71; Charles Scribner's Sons, New York, N.Y., editor, 1971-72; John Knox Press, Richmond, Va., editor, 1973; Southwest Minnesota State College, Marshall, writer-in-residence, 1974—. Has also worked as editorial assistant, copy editor, tutor, and teacher to emotionally disturbed teenagers. *Awards, honors:* Canaras Award for fiction from St. Lawrence University Writers Conference, 1974.

WRITINGS: (Contributor and author of teacher's guide) Jules Harlow, editor, *Lessons from Our Living Past,* with teacher's guide, Behrman, 1972; *Sick and Full of Burning* (novel), Viking, 1974. Work is represented in anthologies, including *Best American Short Stories,* edited by Martha Foley, Houghton, 1972; *The Girl in the Black Raincoat,* edited by George Garrett, Duell, Sloan & Pearce, 1966; *Greensboro Reader,* edited by Robert Watson and Gibbons Ruark, University of North Carolina Press, 1968; *Points of Departure,* edited by Henry Taylor, Winthrop, 1974.

Contributor of stories and poems to magazines, including *Commentary, Sou'wester, Anglican Theological Review, Southern Poetry Review, Carolina Quarterly, Descant, Fiction, Western Humanities Review,* and *Bitterroot.*

WORK IN PROGRESS: *Lovers and Agnostics,* poems; a second novel; a second collection of poems; essays, for a book to be published in 1976.

SIDELIGHTS: Kelly Cherry writes: ". . . Philosophy rightly comprehended is the becoming-aware-of abstraction in real life, since in order to abstract, you must have something to abstract from. Why, just to get from Tuesday to Thursday, you have to solve the problem of free will.

"My novels, then, deal with moral dilemmas and the shapes they create as they reveal themselves in time. My poems seek out the most suitable temporal, or kinetic, structure for a given emotion.

"I think that the crucial unit of the poem is the line; in the story, it's sentence; and in the novel, it's the scene. I know that these sentiments run counter to the American tradition, or to much of it, but I think that much of the American literary tradition is dull, anti-intellectual, and unmusical, and furthermore, easily embarrassed by emotional honesty. This of course is not to deny those American writers who are exciting, wise, and beautiful, but too many of them are dead."

AVOCATIONAL INTERESTS: Paleontology, cosmology, Russian literature from the pre-Revolutionary period, Latin, music, C. S. Peirce and Joyce Cary.

* * *

CHERRY, Sheldon H(arold) 1934-

PERSONAL: Born March 31, 1934, in New York, N.Y.; son of Nathan and Fannie (Kasofsky) Cherry; married Gloria Barry, December 18, 1955; children: Sabrina, Dana, Pamela, Cara. *Education:* Columbia University, A.B., 1954, M.D., 1958. *Religion:* Jewish. *Home:* 21 Stanton Rd., Tenafly, N.J. 07670. *Office:* 1160 Park Ave., New York, N.Y. 10028.

CAREER: Private practice in obstetrics and gynecology, New York, N.Y., 1964—. Mount Sinai School of Medicine, New York, N.Y., assistant clinical professor, 1968—. *Military service:* U.S. Air Force, 1962-64; became captain. *Member:* American College of Obstetrics and Gynecology, American Board of Obstetrics and Gynecology, American College of Surgeons (fellow), New York Obstetrical Society, Alpha Omega Alpha. *Awards, honors:* National Institutes of Health research grant, 1966.

WRITINGS: Obstetrics and Gynecology, Volume IV, Medical Examination Publishing Co., Inc., 1967; *Understanding Pregnancy and Childbirth,* Bobbs-Merrill, 1973. Contributor of sixteen research papers to medical journals.

* * *

CHESLER, Phyllis 1940-

PERSONAL: Born October 1, 1940, in Brooklyn, N.Y.; daughter of Leon and Lillian (Hammer) Chesler. *Education:* Bard College, B.A., 1962; New School for Social Research, M.A., 1967, Ph.D., 1970; New York Medical College, graduate study, 1968-69. *Religion:* Jewish. *Agent:* Cyrilly Abels, 597 Fifth Ave., New York, N.Y. 10017. *Office:* Department of Psychology, Richmond College of the City University of New York, Staten Island, N.Y. 10301.

CAREER: New York University, New York, N.Y., intern in psychotherapy at Washington Square Institute for Psychotherapy and Mental Health, 1968-69; Metropolitan Hospital, New York, N.Y., clinical research associate, 1968-69; Richmond College of the City University of New York, assistant professor of psychology, 1969—. Member of board of directors of Women's Action Alliance, 1972—, Adele Cohen Foundation, 1972—, and Center for the Study of Psychiatry, 1974—; member of New York State Council on the Arts and Women's History Research Center. *Member:* American Association for the Abolition of Involuntary Mental Hospitalization, American Association for the Advancement of Science, American Psychological Association, Association for Women in Psychology (founder), American Association of University Professors, National Organization for Women, Eastern Psychological Association, New York State Psychological Association.

WRITINGS: (Contributor) Jerome Agel, editor, *The Radical Therapist Collective Anthology,* Ballantine, 1971; (contributor) Vivian Gornick and Barbara K. Moran, editors, *Women in Sexist Society: Studies in Power and Powerlessness,* Basic Books, 1971; *Women and Madness,* Doubleday, 1972; (contributor) Philip Zimbardo and Christina Maslach, editors, *Psychology for Our Times: Readings,* Scott, Foresman, 1973; (contributor) James F. Adams, editor, *Psychology of Adjustment,* Holbrook, 1973. Contributor to *Science, Women's Studies: An Interdisciplinary Journal, New York Magazine, Ms., Journal of Marriage and the Family, Psychology Today, Radical Therapist, Aphra, Mademoiselle,* and *Village Voice.*

WORK IN PROGRESS: Male Psychology in the Twentieth Century; Memoirs: 1960-1970; Correspondences: A Selection 1969-1974; An Exploration of Money.

* * *

CHEUSE, Alan 1940-

PERSONAL: Born January 23, 1940, in Perth Amboy, N.J.; son of Philip and Henrietta (Diamond) Cheuse; married Mary Agan, October 7, 1964 (divorced, 1974); children: Joshua Todd. *Education:* Lafayette College, student, 1957-58; Rutgers University, B.A., 1961, Ph.D., 1974. *Residence:* Bennington, Vt. *Office:* Division of Literature and Languages, Bennington College, Bennington, Vt. 05201.

CAREER: New Jersey Turnpike Authority, toll taker, 1961; Fairchild Publications, reporter, 1962-63; Kirkus Review Service, member of staff, 1963-64; *Studies on the Left,* member of editorial board, 1964-65; Butler Institute, Guadalajara, Jalisco, Mexico, teacher of history and English, 1965-66; New York City Department of Welfare, New York, N.Y., case worker, 1966-67; Bennington College, Bennington, Vt., member of Division of Literature and Languages, 1970—. *Member:* Modern Language Association of America, American Comparative Literature Association.

WRITINGS: (Editor with Richard M. Koffler) *The Rarer Action: Essays in Honor of Francis Fergusson,* Rutgers University Press, 1971. Contributor of articles and reviews to *Nation, New York Times Book Review, Los Angeles Times Book Review, Los Angeles Times Calendar,* and other periodicals.

WORK IN PROGRESS: A novel based on the life of American journalist John Reed; research on Thomas Hardy, William Faulkner, and contemporary narrative.

* * *

CHICKOS, James Speros 1941-

PERSONAL: Born October 27, 1941, in Buffalo, N.Y.; son of Speros (a waiter) and Mary (Flores) Chickos; married Janet A. Hoffman, August 7, 1966 (died January, 1974); married Linda Francis Ryan, September 14, 1974; children: Mary Elizabeth, Sarah Janette. *Education:* University of Buffalo, B.A., 1963; Cornell University, Ph.D., 1966. *Home:* 2980 Clearview, Bel Nor, Mo. 63121. *Office:* Department of Chemistry, University of Missouri, St. Louis, Mo. 63121.

CAREER: Princeton University, Princeton, N.J., visiting fellow, 1966-67; University of Wisconsin, Madison, research associate, 1967-69; University of Missouri, St. Louis, assistant professor of chemistry, 1969—. *Member:* Chemistry Society (London), American Chemistry Society, Phi Beta Kappa, Sigma Psi, Phi Eta Sigma. *Awards, honors:* National Institutes of Health postdoctoral fellowships, 1967-69.

WRITINGS: (With Robert A. Rouse and David L. Garin) *Chemistry: Its Role in Society,* Heath, 1973. Contributor to *Journal of American Chemistry Society, Journal of Organic Chemistry, Journal of Chemical Education,* and *Journal of Applied Crystallography.*

WORK IN PROGRESS: Research on the role of tautomeric catalysis in organic and enzymatic systems and the mechanisms of the dimerization of ketene.

* * *

CHINMOY
See GHOSE, Sri Chinmoy Kumar

* * *

CHISHOLM, William S(herman), Jr. 1931-

PERSONAL: Born February 2, 1931, in Detroit, Mich.; married Marian Moutoux; children: Susan, James, Thomas. *Education:* Baldwin-Wallace College, A.B., 1953; Western Reserve University (now Case Western Reserve University), M.A., 1955; University of Michigan, Ph.D., 1964. *Politics:* Radical left. *Religion:* Atheist. *Office:* Department of English, Cleveland State University, Cleveland, Ohio 44115.

CAREER: University of Toledo, Toledo, Ohio, instructor, 1956-59, assistant professor of English, 1959-61; Wayne State University, Detroit, Mich., instructor in English, 1961-63; pronunciation editor, *Webster's New World Dictionary* (2nd edition), 1963-65; Western Illinois University, Macomb, associate professor of English, 1965-69; Cleveland State University, Cleveland, Ohio, associate professor, 1969-72, professor of English, 1972—. High school lecturer, 1972-74. *Member:* Linguistic Society of America, Midwest Modern Language Association.

WRITINGS: The New English, Funk, 1969; (editor with David Guralnik and others) *Webster's New World Dictionary,* 2nd edition (Chisholm was not associated with earlier edition), World Publishing, 1970; *Syllabus and Video Instruction: English 101,* Department of English, Cleveland State University, 1970; (contributor) Lance Buhl, editor, *Innovative Teaching: Issues, Strategies, and Evaluation,* Cleveland State University, 1973; (with Louis T. Milic) *The English Language: Form and Use,* McKay, 1974. Contributor to professional journals.

WORK IN PROGRESS: Essentials of English Linguistics; a massive study of college freshman writing.

SIDELIGHTS: Chisholm describes himself as a "transformationalist-integrationist linguist with emphasis on pedagogy." He writes: "The mind and how it controls language should be pursued in school. But this is impossible in a society that promotes only conformism, racism, mediocrity." He has made a sound recording "Webster's New World Phonoguide," 1970, and an audio-visual presentation, "Language Yes," 1973.

* * *

CHOATE, Ernest A(lfred) 1900-

PERSONAL: Born February 20, 1900, in Philadelphia, Pa.; son of Ernest (a bank clerk) and Eleanor (Townsend) Choate; married Mary E. Craig, May 1, 1930 (died, 1964); children: Elaine (Mrs. Charles de Marco), Shirley (Mrs. Sheldon Chaiken). *Education:* University of Pennsylvania, B.S. in Ed., 1923, M.A., 1924, Ph.D., 1930. *Residence:* Cape May Point, N.J. 08212. *Agent:* Oliver G. Swan, 599 Fifth Ave., New York, N.Y. 10017.

CAREER: Elementary, junior high school, and high school teacher and principal in the public schools of Philadelphia, Pa., 1920-65. Summer teaching at Lehigh University, 1940, University of Pennsylvania, 1941, and Temple University, 1945-56. Chairman of Cape May Point Conservation Commission, N.J., 1967—; member of board of directors of New Jersey State Environmental Commission, 1970—. *Member:* American Ornithologists Union, American Museum of Natural History, Delaware Valley Ornithological Club (president, 1958-59), Academy of Natural Sciences of Philadelphia, Cape May Geographical Society, Wilson Club.

WRITINGS: (With S. Howard Patterson and Edmund Brunner) *The School in American Society,* International Textbook, 1936; *Field List of Birds of Delaware Valley,* Delaware Valley Ornithological Club, 1959; *The Dictionary of American Bird Names,* Gambit, 1973. Contributor to *New Jersey Nature News* and *Frontiers.*

SIDELIGHTS: Choate has traveled and given illustrated bird lectures on the Galapagos Islands, Australia, East Africa, Surinam, the Caribbean, western United States, Europe, India, Nepal, and Ceylon. He has compiled the Cape May Christmas bird count for the National Audubon Society for twenty years.

* * *

CHORAO, (Ann Mc)Kay (Sproat) 1936-

PERSONAL: Surname is pronounced Shoe-*row*; born January 7, 1936, in Elkhart, Ind.; daughter of James McKay (a lawyer) and Elizabeth (Fleming) Sproat; married Ernesto A. K. Chorao (an artist), June 10, 1960; children: Jamie, Peter, Ian. *Education:* Wheaton College, Norton, Mass., B.A., 1958; graduate study at Chelsea School of Art, 1958-59. *Home:* 290 Riverside Dr., New York, N.Y. 10025.

CAREER: Artist; illustrator and writer of children's books.

WRITINGS—Self-illustrated books for children: *The Repair of Uncle Toe,* Farrar, Straus, 1972; *A Magic Eye for Ida,* Seabury, 1973; *Ralph and the Queen's Bathtub,* Farrar, Straus, 1974; *Ida Makes a Movie,* Seabury, in press.

Illustrator: Judith Viorst, *My Mama Says,* Atheneum, 1973; Madeline Edmonson, *Witch's Egg,* Seabury, 1974; Barbara Williams, *Albert's Toothache,* Dutton, in press.

WORK IN PROGRESS: Illustrations for *Kevin's Grandma,* by Barbara Williams, and *Henrietta, The Wild Woman of Borneo,* by Winifred Rosen.

* * *

CHU, Kong 1926-

PERSONAL: Born April 18, 1926, in Shanghai, China; married Yoland C. Chiang, August 1, 1952; children: Adam, Roy, Michele. *Education:* National Taiwan University, B.A., 1952; University of California, Los Angeles, M.A., 1960; Tulane University, Ph.D., 1964. *Home:* 2929 Country Squire Lane, Decatur, Ga. 30033. *Office:* College of Industrial Management, Georgia Institute of Technology, Atlanta, Ga. 30332.

CAREER: California Western University, San Diego, assistant professor, 1964-66; Georgia Institute of Technology, Atlanta, associate professor, 1966-68, professor of economics and management, 1968—. Consultant to small industry. *Member:* American Economic Association, Institute of Management Science.

WRITINGS: (With T. H. Naylor, J. L. Balintfy, and D. S. Burdick) *Computer Simulation Techniques,* Wiley, 1966; *Principles of Econometrics,* Intext, 1968, 2nd edition, 1972; *Quantitative Methods for Business and Economic Analysis,* Intext, 1969; (with H. A. Lee) *Economic Development: Theory and Strategy,* Council for International Economic Cooperation and Development (Taiwan), 1972.

WORK IN PROGRESS: Industrial Development in Nigeria, Africa; Industrial Development in Ecuador, Latin America; Industrial Development in Taiwan, Asia.

* * *

CHUN, Jinsie K(yung) S(hien) 1902- (P. M. Sung)

PERSONAL: Born December 31, 1902, in Ningpo, China; daughter of Mai-tong and Yin (Hsia) Sung; married Hong-cha Chun, October 16, 1926; children: Vung-kwan, Sze-yung. *Education:* Greensboro College, student, 1921-22; Ohio Wesleyan University, B.S., 1923; New York University, M.S., 1924. *Residence:* Los Angeles, Calif. *Agent:* Jane Browne, 9507 Santa Monica Blvd., Beverly Hills, Calif.

CAREER: National Central University, Shanghai, China, instructor in English in School of Commerce, 1932; author, novelist.

WRITINGS: I Am Heaven, Macrae, 1973. Contributor of articles and short stories, sometimes under pseudonym P. M. Sung, to *Young People, Lutheran, Citizen News,* and *National Retired Teachers Association Journal.*

WORK IN PROGRESS: Don't Poison My People, a biography of Lin Tse Hsu, a Chinese viceroy who fought against opium smuggling by the British, completion expected in 1976.

BIOGRAPHICAL/CRITICAL SOURCES: Santa Monica Evening Outlook, December 8, 1973; *San Francisco Chronicle,* February 22, 1974.

* * *

CHUNG, Joseph Sang-hoon 1929-

PERSONAL: Born October 11, 1929, in Kyong-buk, Korea; son of Anthony Do-seng and Martha Ta-yon (Cho) Chung; married Louise Carrol Guenther, August 17, 1957; children: Vincent, Sara, Melissa. *Education:* Attended Seoul National University, 1949-51; Marquette University, B.S., 1956, M.S., 1958; Wayne State University, Ph.D., 1964. *Home:* 6525 Blackhawk Trail, Indian Head Park, Ill. 60525. *Office:* Department of Economics, Illinois Institute of Technology, Chicago, Ill. 60616.

CAREER: Marquette University, Milwaukee, Wis., lecturer in economics, 1958-60; Kalamazoo College, Kalamazoo, Mich., assistant professor of economics, 1962-64; Illinois Institute of Technology, Chicago, Ill., assistant professor, 1964-68, associate professor, 1968-73, professor of economics, 1973—, chairman of department, 1973—. Fulbright Lecturer at Seoul National University, 1966-68; associate, Asia Science Research Associates, 1966—. *Member:* American Economic Association, Association for Asian Studies, Association for Comparative Economics Studies, Midwest Economic Association. *Awards, honors:* Social Science Research Council fellowship, 1962; Hoover Institution publications grant, 1964-65.

WRITINGS: (Editor and contributor) *Patterns of Economic Development: Korea,* Korea Research and Publications, Inc., 1966; *The North Korean Economy: Structure and Development,* Hoover Institution, 1974. Contributor to *Asian Forum, Journal of Korean Affairs, Asian Survey, Journal of Asiatic Studies, Studies on Asia, East-West Economy,* and *Journal of Developing Areas.*

* * *

CHUPACK, Henry 1915-

PERSONAL: Born March 10, 1915, in New York, N.Y.; son of Harry and Bessie (Golub) Chupack; married Leah Sadounick (a teacher), December 23, 1948. *Education:* Brooklyn College (now Brooklyn College of the City University of New York), B.A., 1936; New York University, Ph.D., 1952. *Home:* 5 Colgate Rd., Great Neck, N.Y. 11023. *Office:* Department of English, Kingsborough Community College, Brooklyn, N.Y. 11235.

CAREER: Santa Ana College, Santa Ana, Calif., assistant professor of English, 1955-59; C. W. Post College, Brookville, N.Y., associate professor of English, 1959-66; New York Institute of Technology, Long Island, professor of English, 1966-68; Kingsborough Community College, Brooklyn, N.Y., professor of English, 1968—. Moderator of Great Books. *Military service:* U.S. Army Air Forces, 1941-45. *Member:* American Association of University Professors, Modern Language Association of America, College English Association.

WRITINGS: Roger Williams, Twayne, 1970.

WORK IN PROGRESS: American Novel of the 1970's; James Purdy, for Twayne.

* * *

CHWAST, Jacqueline 1932-

PERSONAL: Born January 1, 1932, in Newark, N.J.; daughter of William (a cab driver) and Lillian Weiner; married Seymour Chwast, December 25, 1953 (divorced, 1971); children: Eve Raina, Pamela Ileen. *Education:* Attended Newark School of Fine and Industrial Arts, three years. *Residence:* New York, N.Y.

CAREER: Author and illustrator of children's books.

WRITINGS—Self-illustrated children's books: *When the Baby-Sitter Didn't Come,* Harcourt, 1967; *How Mr. Berry Found a Home and Happiness Forever,* Simon & Schuster, 1968.

Illustrator: Myra Cohn Livingston, *Whispers and Other Poems,* Harcourt, 1958; Livingston, *Wide Awake and Other Poems,* Harcourt, 1959; Jean L. Latham and Bee Lewi, *The Cuckoo that Couldn't Count,* Macmillan, 1961; Sandol S. Warburg, *I Like You,* Houghton, 1965; Barbara Dana, *Spencer and His Friends,* Atheneum, 1966; Mary Neville, *The First and Last Annual Pet Parade,* Pantheon, 1968; Warburg, *Hooray for Us,* Houghton, 1970; William Cole, *Aunt Bella's Umbrella,* Doubleday, 1970; Jay Williams, *A Present from a Bird,* Parents' Magazine Press, 1971; Marcia Newfield, *Iggy,* Houghton, 1962; Jean-Jacques Larrea, *Diary of a Paper Boy,* new edition, Putnam, 1972; Howard E. Smith, Jr., *Play with the Wind,* McGraw, 1972.

WORK IN PROGRESS: Writing and illustrating a book, *Riches,* for publication by Holt; *Oh Michael,* also for Holt.

CIPOLLA, Joan Bagnel
See BAGNEL, Joan

* * *

CLAPP, Margaret (Antoinette) 1910-1974

April 11, 1910—May 3, 1974; American author and educator. Obituaries: *New York Times,* May 4, 1974; *Current Biography,* June, 1974; *AB Bookman's Weekly,* June 17, 1974.

* * *

CLARK, Eugenie 1922-

PERSONAL: Born May 4, 1922, in New York, N.Y.; daughter of Charles (a barber) and Yumico (Mitomi) Clark; married Hideo Umaki (a pilot), 1942 (divorced, 1949); married Ilias Konstantinu (a physician), 1949 (divorced, 1966); married Chandler Brossard (a writer), 1966 (divorced, 1968); married Igor Klatzo (a neuropathologist), October 12, 1969 (divorced, 1974); children: (second marriage) Hera, Aya, Themistokles, Nikolas. *Education:* University of Michigan, summer study, 1940-41; Hunter College (now of the City University of New York), B.A., 1942; New York University, M.A., 1946, Ph.D., 1950; Scripps Institute of Oceanography, graduate study, 1946-47; Woods Hole Marine Biological Station, graduate summer study, 1948. *Home:* 7817 Hampden Lane, Bethesda, Md. 20014. *Agent:* Marie Rodell, 141 East 55th St., New York, N.Y. 10022. *Office:* Department of Zoology, University of Maryland, College Park, Md. 20472.

CAREER: Swimming instructor, pharmacologist; Celanese Corporation of America, Newark, N.J., chemist, 1942-46; U.S. Fish and Wildlife Service, Philippine Expedition, oceanographic chemist, 1947; Hunter College (now of the City University of New York), New York, N.Y., instructor in biology, 1953-54; Cape Haze Marine Laboratory, Sarasota, Fla., executive director of summer science training programs for high school students, 1955-67; City University of New York, New York, N.Y., associate professor of biology, 1966-67; American Museum of Natural History, New York, N.Y., research associate in animal behavior, 1954—; University of Maryland, College Park, associate professor, 1968-72, professor of zoology, 1973—. Research associate of New England Institute for Medical Research, 1956-66; leader of American delegation for Israel Red Sea Expedition to Ethiopia of International Indian Ocean Expeditions, 1962; panel member of Oceanography and Earth Science Section of National Science Foundation, 1963-68; visiting professor at New England Institute for Medical Research, 1966; research associate and member of board of directors of Mote Marine Laboratory, 1967—; founder member of international advisory committee of Hebrew University of Jerusalem, 1969—, visiting professor, 1972. Lecturer at colleges and universities in North America, Europe, the Middle East, Japan, Egypt, and Ethiopia.

MEMBER: International Association of Professional Diving Scientists (life member), CEDAM International (life member), American Association for the Advancement of Science, Academy of Underwater Arts and Sciences (honorary life member), American Institute of Biological Sciences, American Littoral Society (vice-president, 1966—), American Society of Ichthyologists and Herpetologists (life member), American Society of Mammalogists, Confederation Mondiale des Activities Subaquatiques, Society of Women Geographers, National Parks and Conservation Association (member of board of trustees, 1971—), Gesellschaft fuer Biologische Aquarien und Terrarienkund (honorary life member).

AWARDS, HONORS: Atomic Energy Commission fellowship, 1950; Fulbright fellowship to Egypt, 1951; Eugene Saxton Memorial fellowship, 1952; Breadloaf Writer's fellowship, 1952; Merit Award in Science from *Mademoiselle,* 1953; Hadassah Myrtle Wreath Award in Science, 1964; Nogi Award in Arts from Underwater Society of America, 1965; Golden Plate Award in Science from American Academy of Achievement, 1965; Dugan Award in Aquatic Sciences from American Littoral Society, 1969; fifteen research grants from National Science Foundation, Office of Naval Research, and National Geographic Society, 1955-74.

WRITINGS: Lady with a Spear (Book-of-the-Month Club selection), Harper, 1953; (contributor) P. W. Gilbert, editor, *Sharks and Survival,* Heath, 1963; *The Lady and the Sharks,* Harper, 1969. Contributor to bulletins and journals in her field.

WORK IN PROGRESS: Research in Mexican sleeping sharks and Red Sea fishes.

SIDELIGHTS: Lady with a Spear has been translated into eight languages and Braille, with twenty foreign editions and records for the blind. Eugenie Clark has made seventeen trips to the Red Sea for scientific study.

* * *

CLARKE, Austin 1896-1974

May 9, 1896—March 20, 1974; Irish poet and playwright. Obituaries: *Washington Post,* March 29, 1974; *Publishers Weekly,* April 22, 1974. (*CA*-29/32).

* * *

CLARKE, Machael
See NEWLON, Clarke

* * *

CLARKSON, Adrienne 1939-

PERSONAL: Born February 10, 1939, in Hong Kong; daughter of William G. and Ethel (Lam) Poy. *Education:* Trinity College, Toronto, B.A., 1960, M.A., 1962. *Home:* 9 Powell Ave., Toronto 5, Ontario, Canada. *Agent:* Josephine Rogers, Collins-Knowlton-Wing, 60 East 56th St., New York, N.Y. 10022.

CAREER: Canadian Broadcasting Corp., Toronto, Ontario, host and broadcaster, 1965—. Member of board of governors, York University, 1972—. *Awards, honors:* Centennial Medal, 1967.

WRITINGS—Novels: *A Lover More Condoling,* McClelland & Stewart, 1968; *Hunger Trace,* Morrow, 1970, translation by the author published as *L'Empreinte du Desir,* Presses de la Cite, 1972; *True to You in My Fashion,* New Press, 1971. Contributor to *Chatelaine, Saturday Night,* and *Canadian Forum.*

SIDELIGHTS: Adrienne Clarkson lived in France for many years.

* * *

CLAUDEL, Alice Moser 1918-

PERSONAL: Born April 5, 1918, in New Orleans, La.;

daughter of Herbert Mayberry and Jeannette McLeod (Hayes) Moser; married Enrique A. Rivera Baz, June, 1935 (divorced March, 1941); married Calvin Andre Claudel (a professor of Romance languages), February 23, 1943; children: (first marriage) William McLeod. *Education:* Attended University of North Carolina, summer, 1958, and Georgetown University, summer, 1961; Tulane University, B.A., 1964, M.A., 1968. *Home address:* P.O. Box 353, Onley, Va. 23418. *Office:* Department of English, Eastern Shore Community College, Melfa, Va. 23418.

CAREER: West Virginia Wesleyan College, Buckhannon, instructor in English, 1966-70; University of Maryland, Eastern Shore, Princess Anne, lecturer in English, 1970-71; Maryland Arts Council, Worcester County, Md., poet-in-residence, 1971-72; Eastern Shore Community College, Melfa, Va., instructor in English, 1972—. Participant in "Poet in the Schools" Program for Maryland Arts Council and National Endowment for the Arts. *Member:* Modern Language Association of America, College English Association, National Council of Teachers of English, American Folklore Society, English Speaking Union, National Federation of State Poetry Societies, Mark Twain Society, National League of American Pen Women, South Atlantic Modern Language Association, Louisiana State Poetry Society (president, 1958), Alpha Sigma Lambda.

WRITINGS: (Contributor) Alan Swallow, editor, *Three Lyric Poets,* University of New Mexico Press, 1944; (contributor) Richard P. Benton and Kenneth Cameron, editors, *New Approaches to Poe,* Transcendental, 1970; (contributor) *Papers on Poe,* Wittenberg University, 1972; *Southern Season* (poems), Pikeville College Press, 1972. Contributor of articles and poems to *Emerson Society Quarterly, Discourse, Ball State University Forum, Nimrod, SAMLA Bulletin, Experiment, Mountain Troubadour, Episcopal Churchnews, Inn Dixie, New Orleans Times Picayune, Morning Advocate, Pen Woman, Louisiana Schools, Elementary English, New Mexico Quarterly, Epos, Bitterroot, Descant, Pebble, Motive, Prairie Schooner, Furioso, Modern Verse, Quarterly Review of Literature, University Review, New York Herald Tribune, Boston Herald, Washington Post, Colorado Quarterly, Carolina Quarterly, Georgia Review, Shenandoah, Versecraft, Aerend, Crescendo, Green World, Lyric Louisiana,* and *Revue de Louisiana.* Former assistant editor of *Experiment;* guest editor of *Quarterly Review of Literature,* 1944; poetry editor, *Laurel Review,* 1966-70, and *New Laurel Review,* 1972—.

* * *

CLAUSEN, Aage R. 1932-

PERSONAL: Given name is pronounced "Augie"; born September 12, 1932, in Dannebrog, Neb.; son of Claus and Minnie (Sorensen) Clausen; married Geraldine Tate (an academician); children: Jon Morgan. *Education:* Macalester College, B.A., 1957; University of Michigan, M.A., 1958, Ph.D., 1964. *Office:* Department of Political Science, Ohio State University, Columbus, Ohio 43210.

CAREER: University of Michigan, Survey Research Center, Ann Arbor, study director, 1964-66; University of Wisconsin-Madison, assistant professor of political science, 1966-71; Ohio State University, Columbus, associate professor, 1971-73, professor of political science, 1973—. *Military service:* U.S. Army, 1953-55. *Member:* American Political Science Association, American Association for the Advancement of Science, American Association of Public Opinion Research, Midwest Political Science Association.

WRITINGS: How Congressmen Decide, St. Martin's, 1973. Contributor to *American Political Science Review, Public Opinion Quarterly, Midwest Journal of Political Science,* and other journals.

WORK IN PROGRESS: Research on congressional policy decisions, on perceptual accuracy, and on representation.

* * *

CLEAVER, Carole 1934-

PERSONAL: Born May 21, 1934, in Ridgewood, N.J.; daughter of Earl Atherton and Carroll (Amos) Cleaver; married Selden Rodman (a writer), November 7, 1962; children: Carla Pamela, Van Nostrand. *Education:* Rutgers University, student, 1952-53; other courses at Columbia University, Fairleigh Dickinson University, and University of Hawaii. *Politics:* Republican (conservative). *Religion:* Protestant. *Home:* 659 Ramapo Valley Rd., Oakland, N.J. 07436.

CAREER: Mademoiselle, New York, N.Y., assistant beauty editor, 1956-59; *Wyckoff News,* Wyckoff, N.J., editor, 1959-62; free-lance writer and editor. Member of Republican County Committee, Bergen County, N.J., 1956-62.

WRITINGS: (With husband, Selden Rodman) *Horace Pippin: The Artist as a Black American* (juvenile), Doubleday, 1972. Contributor of articles and reviews to *Harper's Bazaar, New Leader,* and other magazines.

WORK IN PROGRESS: A biography of Ben Shahn; a novel, *The Keeper of the Clocks.*

* * *

CLEEVE, Brian (Talbot) 1921-

PERSONAL: Born November 22, 1921, in Essex, England; son of Charles Edward (a businessman) and Josephine (Talbot) Cleeve; married Veronica McAdie (a business director), September 24, 1945; children: Berenice Cleeve Dezalay, Tanga. *Education:* Attended St. Edward's College, Oxford, 1935-38; University of South Africa, B.A. (honors), 1954; National University of Ireland, Ph.D., 1956. *Politics:* None. *Religion:* None. *Home:* 60 Heytesbury Lane, Ballsbridge, Dublin 4, Ireland.

CAREER: Free-lance journalist in South Africa, 1948-54, and in Ireland, 1954—. Broadcaster for Radio Telefis Eireann, 1962-72. *Wartime service:* British Merchant Navy, 1938-45. *Member:* National Union of Journalists (Ireland), Society of Authors.

WRITINGS: Dictionary of Irish Writers, Mercier Press, Volume I: *Fiction in English,* 1967, Volume II: *Non-Fiction in English and Latin,* 1969, Volume III: *All Writing in Gaelic and Latin,* 1972; (editor) *W. B. Yeats and the Designing of Ireland's Coinage,* Dolman Press, 1972.

Novels, except as noted: *The Far Hills,* Jarrolds, 1952; *Portrait of My City,* Jarrolds, 1953; *Birth of a Dark Soul,* Jarrolds, 1953, published as *The Night Winds,* Houghton, 1954; *Assignment to Vengeance,* Hammond, 1961; *Death of a Painted Lady,* Hammond, 1962, Random House, 1963; *Death of a Wicked Servant,* Hammond, 1963, Random House, 1964; *Vote X for Treason,* Collins, 1964, Random House, 1965; *Dark Blood Dark Terror,* Random House, 1965; *Vice Isn't Private,* Random House, 1966 (published in England as *The Judas Goat,* Hammond, 1966); *The Horse Thieves of Ballysaggert* (short stories), Mercier

Press, 1966; *Violent Death of a Bitter Englishman,* Random House, 1967; *You Must Never Go Back,* Random House, 1968; *Exit from Prague,* Corgi Books, 1970, published as *Escape from Prague,* Pinnacle Books, 1973; *Cry of Morning,* M. Joseph, 1971, published as *The Triumph of O'Rourke,* Doubleday, 1972; *Tread Softly in This Place,* Cassell, 1972, John Day, 1973; *The Dark Side of the Sun,* Cassell, 1973.

Contributor of short stories to magazines, including *Saturday Evening Post.*

WORK IN PROGRESS: A historical novel of nineteenth- and twentieth-century Ireland.

SIDELIGHTS: Cleeve told *CA* of his reasons for writing: "Being a sailor and having time to think. Being an historian and having something to think about. Having an idea of the flow and shape of history. I like fiction to have long perspectives." Cleeve has travelled widely. He speaks Italian, French, some German, and a smattering of Swahili.

* * *

CLEMENT, Roland C(harles) 1912-

PERSONAL: Born November 22, 1912, in Fall River, Mass.; son of Germain A. (a musician) and Angelina (DesJardins) Clement; married Muriel C. Crowly (a school nurse), December 27, 1947; children: Charles, Constance, Alison. *Education:* Attended University of Massachusetts, 1940-42; Brown University, A.B., 1949; Cornell University, M.Sc., 1950. *Home:* 71 Weed Ave., Norwalk, Conn. 06850. *Office:* National Audubon Society, 950 Third Ave., New York, N.Y. 10022.

CAREER: Businessman during early career; executive director of Audubon Society of Rhode Island, 1950-58; National Audubon Society, New York, N.Y., vice-president-biology, 1958—. Chairman of Environmental Advisory Board of U.S. Army Corps of Engineers, 1972-74; member of Norwalk, Conn. Conservation Commission, and Long Island Sound Study Commission. *Military service:* U.S. Army Air Forces, 1942-46. *Member:* International Council for Bird Preservation (chairman of U.S. section, 1972—), American Ornithologist's Union, Sigma Xi.

WRITINGS: (Editor) *A Gathering of Shore Birds,* Devin-Adair, 1960; *American Birds,* Ridge Press, 1973; *The Nature Atlas of America,* Ridge Press, 1973; *The Living World of Audubon,* Ridge Press, 1974.

WORK IN PROGRESS: Semi-technical papers in several resource conservation areas.

SIDELIGHTS: "Books are accidents," Clement wrote, "spin-off from one's interests, expertise, and contacts. They appear to be opportunities to share insights but are severely constrained by editorial exigencies. No matter, one likes to leave a trace."

* * *

CLERY, (Reginald) Val(entine) 1924- (Janus)

PERSONAL: Surname is pronounced like "Cleary"; born January 26, 1924; son of Claude Valentine (an engineer) and Dora Frances (Reilly) Clery; married Susan Salaman, October 4, 1960 (divorced, 1971); children: Emma, Daniel, Louisa. *Education:* Attended school in Ireland. *Home and office:* 40 Huntley St., Apt. 1, Toronto M4Y 1L2, Canada.

CAREER: Puppet Opera Co., Dublin, Ireland, stage manager, 1954-55; Canadian Broadcasting Corp. (CBC), London, England, producer, 1959-65, executive producer in Toronto, Ontario, 1965-70; *Books in Canada,* Toronto, Ontario, editor, 1971-73. *Military service:* British Army, Royal Artillery and Commandos, lance-bombardier, 1941-46. *Awards, honors:* Irish writing story award, 1947; story award from *Observer,* 1955.

WRITINGS: Promotion and Response: Report on Canadian Book Promotion, Canadian Book Publishers Council, 1971; *Canada in Colour,* Hounslow Press, 1972. Author of column appearing under pseudonym Janus in *Quill and Quire.* Contributor to *Globe, Globe and Mail, Toronto Star, Maclean's,* and *Weekend.*

WORK IN PROGRESS: An "inside" study of the Canadian Broadcasting Corp. and public broadcasting in Canada.

* * *

CLIFTON, Lucille 1936-

PERSONAL: Born June 27, 1936, in Depew, N.Y.; daughter of Samuel L., Sr. (a laborer) and Thelma (a laborer; maiden name, Moore) Sayles; married Fred J. Clifton (an educator, writer, and artist), May 10, 1958; children: Sidney, Fredrica, Channing, Gillian, Graham, Alexia. *Education:* Attended Howard University, 1953-55, and Fredonia State Teachers College, 1955. *Home:* 2605 Talbot Rd., Baltimore, Md. 21216. *Agent:* Curtis Brown Ltd., 60 East 56th St., New York, N.Y. 10022. *Office:* Coppin State College, 2500 West North Ave., Baltimore, Md. 21216.

CAREER: New York State Division of Employment, Buffalo, claims clerk, 1958-60; U.S. Office of Education, Washington, D.C., literature assistant for CAREL (Central Atlantic Regional Educational Laboratory), 1969-71; Coppin State College, Baltimore, Md., poet-in-residence, 1971—. *Member:* International P.E.N., Authors Guild of Authors League of America, Maryland State Committee for Black Art and Culture, Windsor Hills Association (member of board of directors, 1972). *Awards, honors:* National Endowment for the Arts awards, 1970, 1972.

WRITINGS—All for children, except as indicated: *Good Times* (poems for adults), Random House, 1969; *Some of the Days of Everett Anderson,* Holt, 1970; *The Black BC's* (alphabet poems), Dutton, 1970; *Good News About the Earth* (adult), Random House, 1972; *Everett Anderson's Christmas Coming,* Holt, 1972; *Good, Says Jerome,* Dutton, 1973; *All Us Come Cross the Water,* Holt, 1973; *Don't You Remember,* Dutton, 1973; *The Boy Who Don't Believe in Spring,* Dutton, 1973; *An Ordinary Woman* (adult), Random House, 1974; *Everett Anderson's Year,* Holt, 1974. Contributor of stories and poems to magazines, including *Redbook* and *Negro Digest.*

WORK IN PROGRESS: Generations, adult fiction; *The Land of Chimes,* a Black fairy tale, for Dutton; translating poems for an anthology; writing poems.

BIOGRAPHICAL/CRITICAL SOURCES: Redbook, November, 1969; *Black World,* July, 1970.

* * *

CLIPPER, Lawrence Jon 1930-

PERSONAL: Born December 13, 1930, in Clairton, Pa.; son of Eli and Rose (Terbovich) Clipper; married Patricia Ann Bratton (a social worker), December 10, 1955; children: Melanie Rose, Stephanie Evelyn. *Education:* Brown University, A.B. (cum laude), 1953; George Washington University, M.A., 1958; University of North Carolina, Ph.D., 1963. *Politics:* Independent. *Home:* 1114 South 26th St., South Bend, Ind. 46615. *Office:* Indiana University at South Bend, South Bend, Ind. 46615.

CAREER: Dickinson College, Carlisle, Pa., assistant professor of English, 1961-64; Ball State University, Muncie, Ind., assistant professor of English, 1964-67; Indiana University at South Bend, assistant professor, 1967-70, associate professor, 1970-74, professor of English, 1974—. *Military service:* U.S. Navy, 1953-56; served in Korea; became lieutenant junior grade. *Member:* College English Association, American Association of University Professors, Dickens Society, Midwest Modern Language Association, Phi Beta Kappa.

WRITINGS: G. K. Chesterton, Twayne, 1974. Author of study guides, all published by Bantam, for *Pride and Prejudice,* 1966, *Return of the Native,* 1966, and *Silas Marner,* 1967. Contributor of articles and reviews to magazines, including *South Atlantic Quarterly, Western Humanities Review,* and *Choice.*

WORK IN PROGRESS: Illustrations for Dickens' works; research on Malcolm Lowry's *Under the Volcano;* research on G. K. Chesterton.

* * *

COATES, Donald R(obert) 1922-

PERSONAL: Born July 23, 1922, in Grand Island, Neb.; son of Frank Jefferson and Harriet (a musician; maiden name, Ferris) Coates; married Jeanne Grandison (a psychiatric social worker), March 18, 1944; children: Cheryl (Mrs. Donn Erickson), D. Eric, Lark (Mrs. Richard Williams). *Education:* College of Wooster, B.A., 1944; Columbia University, M.A., 1948, Ph.D., 1956. *Politics:* Independent. *Religion:* Episcopalian. *Home:* 212 Edgewood Rd., Vestal, N.Y. 13850. *Office:* Department of Geological Sciences, State University of New York at Binghamton, Binghamton, N.Y. 13901.

CAREER: Earlham College, Richmond, Ind., assistant professor of geology, 1948-51; U.S. Geological Survey, Tucson, Ariz., geologist and project chief, 1951-54; State University of New York at Binghamton, assistant professor, 1954-58, associate professor, 1958-63, professor of geology, 1963—. Associate program director for National Science Foundation, 1963-64; visiting professor at Cornell University, University of Illinois, and Indiana University. Member of Broome County Environmental Management Council. Consultant to National Science Foundation, U.S. Army Corps of Engineers, N.Y. State Attorney General, American Geological Institute, and American Geophysical Union. *Military service:* U.S. Navy, 1943-46; served in South Pacific theater; became lieutenant junior grade.

MEMBER: Geological Society of America (fellow), American Geophysical Union, American Institute of Professional Geologists, National Association of Geology Teachers (president, 1962), American Association for the Advancement of Science (fellow), New York State Geological Association (president, 1963), Phi Beta Kappa. *Awards, honors:* Superior performance award from National Science Foundation, 1964; Ralph Digman Award for outstanding educational contributions, from National Association of Geology Teachers, 1972; research grants from National Science Foundation, five grants, 1968-70 and 1971-73, National Academy of Sciences, 1969, American Geological Institute, 1969, and U.S. Department of Commerce, 1971-72, 1972-73, and 1973-74.

WRITINGS—Editor: *Geology of South-Central New York,* New York State Geological Association, 1963; *Environmental Geomorphology,* State University of New York, 1971; *Environmental Science Workbook,* State University of New York, 1972; *Environmental Geomorphology and Landscape Conservation,* Dowden, Volume I: *Prior to 1900,* 1972, Volume II: *Urban Areas,* 1974, Volume III: *Nonurban Regions,* 1973; *Coastal Geomorphology,* State University of New York, 1973; *Glacial Geology of the Binghamton-Western Catskill Region,* State University of New York, 1973; *Groundwater, Soil, and Terrain Management,* State University of New York, 1973; *Glacial Geomorphology,* State University of New York, 1974; *Urban Geomorphology,* Geological Society of America, in press. Contributor of about seventy-five articles and reviews to government publications and scientific journals, including *Science, Geotimes,* and *Journal of Quaternary Research.*

WORK IN PROGRESS: Research on application of glacial models for large-scale terrain derangement; research on the glaciation of the New York region, and on coastal erosion processes of the south shore of Long Island.

SIDELIGHTS: Coates describes himself as a "geomorphologist interested in natural landscape changes." In the past fifteen years he has become especially concerned with man-made distortion of the land-water ecosystem, which he told *CA* resulted from his having grown up in the Nebraska Dust Bowl in the 1930's. In this regard he has appeared as expert witness in more than sixty court cases.

He writes: "Another special concern is with coastlines. For ten years we have had a summer home at Cape Hatteras and I am fascinated by oceans, beaches, but also with great sadness view man's degradation of this very fragile environment.

"In short I might be called a 'geomorphology missionary.' I try to spread the gospel of the importance of geomorphology in today's world. Because man lives, works, and plays on the earth's surface, nearly everything he does changes the natural processes. Since terrain is the province of the geomorphologist, it is this science discipline that has the most to offer in showing how to minimize man's destructive tendencies."

* * *

COATS, Peter 1910-

PERSONAL: Born June 26, 1910, in Sundrum, Ayr, Scotland; son of Ernest Symington (a company director) and Nora (Pountney) Coats. *Education:* Attended Eton College, 1923-27. *Religion:* Church of England. *Home:* A I Albany, Piccadilly, London W. 1., England. *Office:* Conde Nast Publications, Vogue House, Hanover Sq., London W. 1., England.

CAREER: Advertising agent in London, 1931-39; Conde Nast Publications, London, England, *House and Garden* (magazine), garden editor, 1948—, garden designer, 1958—. *Military service:* British Army, 1939-46; served in Egypt, Middle East, and India; became major. *Member:* Royal Horticulture Society (fellow), Travellers Club (London). *Awards, honors*—Military: Mentioned in dispatches.

WRITINGS: Roses, Weidenfeld & Nicolson, 1962; *Great Gardens of the Western World,* Weidenfeld & Nicolson, 1963; *Great Gardens of Britain,* Weidenfeld & Nicolson,

1968; *Flowers in History,* Weidenfeld & Nicolson, 1970; *Garden Decoration,* Conde Nast, 1971.

WORK IN PROGRESS: Plants for the Connoisseur.

* * *

COCHRAN, Leslie H(ershel) 1939-

PERSONAL: Born April 24, 1939, in Valparaiso, Ind.; son of Robert H. (a farmer) and D. Dellcena (Marquart) Cochran; married Marlene J. Brickner, August 8, 1959; children: Troy Gregory, Kirt Allen, Leslee Noelle. *Education:* Western Michigan University, B.S. (cum laude), 1961, M.A., 1962; University of Minnesota, graduate study, 1962-63; Wayne State University, Ed.D., 1968. *Home:* 1311 Crosslanes, Mount Pleasant, Mich. 48858. *Office:* School of Fine and Applied Arts, Central Michigan University, Mount Pleasant, Mich. 48859.

CAREER: High school teacher of industrial education in Detroit, Mich., 1963-67; Wayne State University, Detroit, Mich., instructor in industrial education, 1967-69; Central Michigan University, Mount Pleasant, associate professor, 1969-72, professor of industrial education, 1972—, assistant dean of School of Fine and Applied Arts, 1970-72, associate dean, 1972—. Visiting summer professor at University of Illinois and Utah State University, 1971, Iowa State University of Science and Technology, 1972, and University of New Mexico, 1973.

MEMBER: American Vocational Association, National Association of Industrial and Technical Teacher Educators (vice-president, 1971-73), American Council on Industrial Arts Teacher Education, American Conference of Academic Deans, American Industrial Arts Association, Michigan Academy of Science, Arts and Letters, Michigan Industrial Education Society, Phi Delta Kappa. *Awards, honors:* Leadership Award of Industrial Arts Division, American Vocational Association, 1971, and Service Award, 1972.

WRITINGS: Innovative Programs in Industrial Education, McKnight, 1970; (contributor) G. H. Silvius and E. H. Curry, *Managing Multiple Activities in Industrial Education,* 2nd edition (Cochran was not associated with earlier edition), McKnight, 1971; (editor) *Career Education: New Perspectives for Industrial Arts,* American Vocational Association, 1973. Contributor to other symposia and of about thirty articles to professional journals. Member of editorial staff, *Journal of Industrial Teacher Education,* 1970—.

WORK IN PROGRESS: A textbook; development and implementation of an in-service training program dealing with the use of advisory committees in Michigan's vocational education program.

AVOCATIONAL INTERESTS: Athletics and outdoor life.

* * *

COCHRANE, Eric 1928-

PERSONAL: Born May 13, 1928, in Berkeley, Calif.; son of Eric and Adelaide (Griffith) Cochrane; married Lydia Steinway (a French teacher), 1953; children: John, Nicholas. *Education:* Yale University, B.A., 1949, Ph.D., 1954. *Religion:* Roman Catholic. *Home:* 5220 South Greenwood Ave., Chicago, Ill. 60615. *Office:* Department of History, University of Chicago, 1126 East 59th St., Chicago, Ill. 60637.

CAREER: University of Chicago, Chicago, Ill., assistant professor, 1957-61, associate professor, 1961-67, professor of history, 1967—. Visiting professor at University of Perugia, 1969-70. Member of board of trustees at Newberry Library, 1966—. *Member:* American Historical Association, American Catholic Historical Association (president, 1974—), Society for Italian Historical Studies, Societa Colombaria, Renaissance Society of America, Colorado and Utah Society of Chicago (secretary, 1972—).

WRITINGS: Tradition and Enlightenment in the Tuscan Academies, University of Chicago Press, 1961; (editor) *The Late Italian Renaissance,* Harper, 1970; *Florence in the Forgotten Centuries, 1527-1800: A History of Florence and the Florentines in the Age of the Grand Dukes,* University of Chicago Press, 1973. Contributor to *Journal of Modern History, Archivio Storico Italiano, Commonweal,* and *Catholic Historical Review.*

WORK IN PROGRESS: A History of Italian Renaissance Historiography, completion expected in 1975; *Italy in the Age of the Baroque,* 1977.

SIDELIGHTS: Cochrane has organized a percussion, flute, string, and saxophone ensemble that plays at Sunday masses. He has lived in Italy for eight years.

* * *

CODE, Grant Hyde 1896-1974

PERSONAL: Born March 2, 1896, in La Crosse, Wis.; son of James Grant (a railroad employee) and Frances S. (a painter; maiden name, Cleaver) Code; married Marion Osborn Graves, June 9, 1920 (died, 1955); children: Grant Hyde, Jr. (deceased). *Education:* Harvard University, A.B., 1918; University of Toulouse, certificate of studies, 1919. *Religion:* Episcopalian. *Home:* Hotel St. France, 124 West 47th St., New York, N.Y. *Agent:* Gloria Safier, 667 Madison Ave., New York, N.Y. 10021. *Office:* Talent Exchange, 250 West 57th St., New York, N.Y.

CAREER: Instructor in English at Boston University, Boston, Mass., 1919-21, Harvard University and Radcliffe College, both Cambridge, Mass., 1921-25, and University of Delaware, 1925-27; director of research bureau in Wilmington, Del., 1927-28; Society of Arts and Crafts, Boston, Mass., director, 1928-30; American Federation of Arts, Washington, D.C., director of membership department, and circulation manager for *American Magazine of Art,* 1931-32; Works Progress Administration (WPA), Public Works of Art Project, assistant to committee for Washington, D.C., Maryland, and Virginia regions, 1932-34; Brooklyn Museum, Brooklyn, N.Y., editor of publications, including *Brooklyn Museum Quarterly* and *Children's Museum News,* 1934-39, also curator of Dance Center, conducting dance classes and recitals; editorial reader for Charles Scribner & Sons and Macmillan Co., both New York, N.Y., 1940-53; Hedgerow Theatre, Moylan, Pa., actor member, 1953-56; actor on stage, screen, and television, 1956-74. *Military service:* American Expeditionary Force in France, 1917-19; became second lieutenant. *Member:* Authors League (Authors Guild and Dramatists Guild), Actors Equity Association, Screen Actors Guild, American Federation of Television and Radio Artists, American National Theatre and Academy, Actors Fund, Institute for Advanced Studies in the Theatre Arts, United Nations Association.

WRITINGS—Poems: (Editor) *Poems by Joan Murray, 1917-1942,* Yale University Press, 1947; *This Undying*

Quest, Stanton & Lee, 1971; *Chalk Marks,* Branden Press, 1973.

Plays: *When the Fates Decree: A Play for Students of Vergil* (first produced in Pittsburgh, Pa., June, 1914; later given high school productions throughout United States), privately printed, 1914, revised edition, B. J. Brimmer Co., 1923; (translator) Moliere, "The Doctor in Spite of Himself," first produced in Pittsburgh, July, 1917; "New England Conscience"; "Moving Day"; "Hail and Farewell"; "The Naughty Princess" (musical for children); (translator) Armand Salacrou, "Oh, Elsie, Don't Run So Fast."

Also author of three novels, two biographical works, and two volumes of poetry, all unpublished. Contributor of short stories and poems to magazines. Dance critic, *Dance Observer,* 1939-40

(Died June 29, 1974)

* * *

COFFIN, Patricia 1912-1974

March 17, 1912—May 30, 1974; American author and editor. Obituaries: *New York Times,* May 31, 1974. (*CA*-33/36).

* * *

COFFMAN, Virginia (Edith) 1914- (Victor Cross, Virginia C. DuVaul)

PERSONAL: Born July 30, 1914, in San Francisco, Calif.; daughter of William M. (a corporation manager) and Edythe L. (DeuVaul) Coffman. *Education:* University of California, Berkeley, A.B., 1938. *Politics:* Republican Moderate. *Religion:* "Born Methodist-Episcopalian; no present church affiliation." *Residence:* Reno, Nev. *Agent:* Jay Garon, Jay Garon-Brooke Associates, Inc., 415 Central Park West, 17D, New York, N.Y. 10025.

CAREER: Secretary and writer in movie and television studios, including David O. Selznick, Monogram, RKO, Columbia, and Hal Roach, all in Hollywood, Calif., 1944-56; H. F. "Chick" Bennett, Inc. (realty firm), Reno, Nev., secretary and office manager, 1956-65; full-time writer, 1965—. Has also been free-lance editor, actress, lecturer, and drama teacher. *Member:* Mystery Writers Guild of America.

WRITINGS: Moura, Crown, 1959; *The Affair at Alkali,* Arcadia House, 1960 (published in England as *Nevada Gunslinger,* Gresham, 1962); *The Beckoning,* Ace Books, 1965; *Curse of the Island Pool,* Lancer Books, 1965; *Castle Barra,* Paperback Library, 1966; *Secret of Shower Tree,* Lancer Books, 1966; *Black Heather,* Lancer Books, 1966; *The High Terrace,* Lancer Books, 1966 (published in England as *To See a Dark Stranger,* R. Hale, 1969); *Castle at Witches Coven,* Lancer Books, 1966; *A Haunted Place,* Lancer Books, 1966; *The Demon Tower,* New American Library, 1966; *The Devil Vicar,* Ace Books, 1966, revised edition published as *Vicar of Moura,* 1971; *The Small Tawny Cat,* Lancer Books, 1967; *One Man Too Many,* Lancer Books, 1967; *The Shadow Box,* Lancer Books, 1967; *Richest Girl in the World,* Lancer Books, 1967; *The Chinese Door,* Lancer Books, 1967; *The Rest is Silence,* Lancer Books, 1967; *A Few Fiends to Tea,* Belmont Books, 1967; *The Hound of Hell,* Belmont Books, 1967; *The Villa Fountains,* Belmont Books, 1967; (under pseudonym Victor Cross) *Blood Sport,* Award Books, 1967; *The Mist at Darkness,* New American Library, 1968; *Call of the Flesh,* Lancer Books, 1968; *The Candidate's Wife,* Lancer Books, 1968; *Of Love and Intrigue,* New American Library, 1969; *The Dark Gondola,* Ace Books, 1969; *Lucifer Cove, Number 1: The Devil's Mistress,* Lancer Books, 1969.

(Under pseudonym Virginia C. DuVaul) *Masque by Gaslight,* Ace Books, 1970; *Isle of the Undead,* Lancer Books, 1970 (published in England as *Voodoo Widow,* R. Hale, 1970); *The Beach House,* New American Library, 1970; *The Vampyre of Moura,* Ace Books, 1970; *Lucifer Cove, Number 2: Priestess of the Damned,* Lancer Books, 1970; *Lucifer Cove, Number 3: The Devil's Virgin,* Lancer Books, 1970; *The Chinese Door,* R. Hale, 1971; *Lucifer Cove, Number 4: Masque of Satan,* Lancer Books, 1971; *Lucifer Cove, Number 5: Chalet Diabolique,* Lancer Books, 1971; *The Master of Blue Mire,* Dell, 1971; *Lucifer Cove, Number 6: From Satan, with Love,* Lancer Books, 1972; *Night at Sea Abbey,* Lancer Books, 1972; *The House on the Moat,* Lancer Books, 1972; *Mistress Devon,* Arbor House, 1972, Crest, 1973; *The Dark Palazzo,* Arbor House, 1973, Crest, 1974; *The Cliffs of Dread,* Lancer Books, 1973; *Garden of Shadows,* Lancer Books, 1973; *A Fear of Heights,* Lancer Books, 1973; *Evil at Queen's Priory,* Lancer Books, 1973; *The House at Sandalwood,* Arbor House, 1974, Crest, in press; *The Ice Forest,* Dell, 1974; *Hyde Place,* Arbor House, 1974; *The Alpine Coach,* Dell, in press.

Author of rewritten versions of scripts for movie and television studios. Contributor of movie reviews to *Oakland Tribune,* 1933-40.

WORK IN PROGRESS: The Isle of Darkness, publication by Dell expected in 1975.

SIDELIGHTS: Ms. Coffman's father founded the Shrine All-Star Football Game played in San Francisco on New Year's Day, and was its manager for forty years. She comments: "My mother was our great influence, but *she* was not famous. Only wonderful." *Avocational interests:* Travel.

* * *

COHEN, Jerome Alan 1930-

PERSONAL: Born July 1, 1930, in Elizabeth, N.J.; son of Philip and Beatrice (Kaufman) Cohen; married Joan F. Lebold, June 30, 1954; children: Peter, Seth, Ethan. *Education:* Yale University, B.A., 1951, LL.B., 1955; University of Lyon, graduate study, 1951-52. *Home:* 21 Bryant St., Cambridge, Mass. 02138. *Office:* Law School, Harvard University, Cambridge, Mass. 02138.

CAREER: Admitted to Connecticut Bar, 1955, and District of Columbia Bar, 1957; law secretary for U.S. Supreme Court, under Chief Justice Earl Warren, 1955-56, and Justice Felix Frankfurter, 1956-57; Covington & Burling (law firm), Washington, D.C., associate, 1957-58; U.S. Department of Justice, Washington, D.C., assistant U.S. attorney, 1958-59; University of California, Berkeley, associate professor, 1959-61, professor of law, 1961-64; Harvard University, Cambridge, Mass., professor of law, 1965—, and director of East Asian legal studies. Consultant to U.S. Senate Committee on Foreign Relations, 1959; visiting professor at Doshisha University, Kyoto, 1971-72. Chairman of subcommittee on Chinese law of Joint Committee on Contemporary China, American Council of Learned Societies–Social Science Research Council, 1965—.

MEMBER: American Society of International Law

(chairman of China and world order study group, 1967—), Association for Asian Studies, Phi Beta Kappa, Order of the Coif. *Awards, honors:* Rockefeller Foundation grant, 1960-64.

WRITINGS: The Criminal Process in the People's Republic of China, 1949-1963, Harvard University Press, 1968; (with Robert F. Dernberger and John R. Garson) *China Trade Prospects and U.S. Policy,* Praeger, for National Committee on United States-China Relations, 1971; (contributor) John Wilson Lewis, editor, *The City in Communist China,* Stanford University Press, 1971; (with others) *Taiwan and American Policy: The Dilemma in U.S.-China Relations,* Praeger, 1971; (with Hungdah Chiu) *People's China and International Law,* two volumes, Princeton University Press, 1974.

Editor: (With others) *Contemporary Chinese Law: Research Problems and Perspectives,* Harvard University Press, 1970; George Ginsburgs and others, *The Dynamics of China's Foreign Relations,* Harvard University Press, 1970; *China's Practice of International Law: Some Case Studies,* Harvard University Press, 1973.

Author or co-author of a number of papers published in legal journals and reprinted separately as monographs in Harvard University Law School "Studies in Chinese Law." Also contributor to popular magazines and to newspapers in United States and Japan. Member of editorial board, *American Journal of International Law,* 1972—.

WORK IN PROGRESS: Editing *China's Legal Tradition.*

* * *

COHEN, Morris L(eo) 1927-

PERSONAL: Born November 2, 1927, in New York, N.Y.; son of Emanuel (a manufacturer) and Anna (Frank) Cohen; married Gloria Weitzner (a computer programmer) February 1, 1953; children: Havi, Daniel. *Education:* University of Chicago, B.A., 1947; Columbia University, J.D., 1951; Pratt Institute, M.L.S., 1959. *Religion:* Jewish. *Home:* 336 Clark Rd., Brookline, Mass. 02146. *Office:* Law School, Harvard University, Cambridge, Mass. 02138.

CAREER: Admitted to Bar of New York State, 1951; private practice in New York, N.Y., 1951-58; assistant law librarian at Rutgers University, Law School, New Brunswick, N.J., 1958-59, and Columbia University, Law School, New York, N.Y., 1959-61; State University of New York at Buffalo, law librarian and associate professor of law, 1961-63; University of Pennsylvania, Law School, Philadelphia, Biddle Law Librarian, 1963-71, associate professor, 1963-67, professor of law, 1967-71; Harvard University, Law School, Cambridge, Mass., law librarian, and professor of law, 1971—. Lecturer at Columbia University, Library School, 1963-70, and Drexel University, Library School, 1963-71; consultant on law libraries to law schools and legal organizations.

MEMBER: International Association of Law Libraries, American Association of Law Libraries (president, 1970-71), American Library Association, American Documentation Institute, American Civil Liberties Union (member of executive board of Philadelphia chapter, 1965-71), American Bar Association, Bibliographical Society of America, American Society for Information Science, American Association of University Professors (president of University of Pennsylvania chapter, 1966-67). *Awards, honors:* National Endowment for the Humanities grant, 1968-71.

WRITINGS: Legal Bibliography Briefed, Graduate School of Library Sciences, Drexel Institute of Technology, 1965; *Legal Research in a Nutshell,* West Publishing, 1968, 2nd edition, 1971.

WORK IN PROGRESS: How to Find the Law, for West Publishing; *Bibliography of Early American Law,* completion expected in 1977.

* * *

COHEN, Roberta G. 1937-

PERSONAL: Born July 8, 1937, in Brooklyn, N.Y.; daughter of Sidney (a post office clerk) and Mae Goldberg; married Murray Cohen (a physician), November 26, 1958; children: David Aaron, Anne Rachelle. *Education:* Bellevue School of Nursing, R.N., 1957; Hunter College (now Hunter College of the City University of New York), B.S., 1960; Adelphi University, M.S., 1969. *Religion:* Hebrew. *Home:* 1695 Sutton Pl., North Merrick, N.Y. 11566. *Office:* Mercy Hospital, 1000 North Village Ave., Rockville Centre, N.Y. 11570.

CAREER: Mercy Hospital, Rockville Centre, N.Y., psychiatric nurse and clinical specialist, 1969—. *Member:* American Nurses Association, Council on Advanced Psychiatric Practice and Mental Health Nursing, Clinical Nurse Special Interest Group, Sigma Theta Tau, Bellevue Alumnae Association.

WRITINGS: (With Gladys B. Lipkin) *Effective Approaches to Patient Behavior,* Springer Publishing, 1973. Contributor to *Perspectives in Psychiatric Care, Nursing Research, American Journal of Nursing,* and *Journal of Psychiatric Nursing and Mental Health Services.*

WORK IN PROGRESS: Family Orientation Groups: Effect on Attitudes Towards Family Members Receiving Electrostimulative Therapy, completion expected in 1976.

* * *

COHEN, Stephen F(rand) 1938-

PERSONAL: Born November 25, 1938, in Indianapolis, Ind.; son of Marvin S. (a merchant) and Ruth (Frand) Cohen; married Lynn Blair (an opera singer), August 25, 1962; children: Andrew Blair, Alexandra Tucker. *Education:* Indiana University, B.S., 1960, M.A., 1962; Columbia University, Ph.D., 1969. *Politics:* "Soviet Union." *Home:* 780 West End Ave., New York, N.Y. 10025. *Office:* Department of Politics, Princeton University, Princeton, N.J. 08540.

CAREER: Princeton University, Princeton, N.J., assistant professor, 1968-72, associate professor of politics, 1973—, director of Russian studies, 1973—. Columbia University, senior fellow, Russian Institute, 1972-73, senior fellow, Research Institute on Communist Affairs, 1972—, visiting professor of history, 1973-74 and 1974-75. *Member:* American Political Science Association, American Association for the Advancement of Slavic Studies. *Awards, honors:* Nominated for National Book Award in biography, 1973, for *Bukharin and the Bolshevik Revolution.*

WRITINGS: (Editor with Robert C. Tucker) *The Great Purge Trial,* Grosset, 1965; *Bukharin and the Bolshevik Revolution: A Political Biography, 1888-1938,* Knopf, 1973. Contributor of articles and reviews to scholarly and popular journals, including *Washington Post* and *New York Times Book Review.* Associate editor of *World Politics;* member of editorial board of *Slavic Review.*

WORK IN PROGRESS: Research on the history, politics, and society of Soviet Russia, 1917-1939.

AVOCATIONAL INTERESTS: Basketball, "the world around me."

* * *

COLE, Howard C(handler) 1934-

PERSONAL: Born May 9, 1934, in Oak Park, Ill.; son of C. Chandler and Charlotte E. (Skinner) Cole; married Elizabeth Schwacke, July 8, 1961; children: Kristen Leslie, Sonja Anne. *Education:* Wheaton College, Wheaton, Ill., B.A., 1956; Yale University, M.A., 1961, Ph.D., 1963. *Politics:* Independent. *Religion:* Lutheran. *Home:* 707 Southwest Dr., Champaign, Ill. 61820. *Office:* 131 English Bldg., University of Illinois, Urbana, Ill. 61801.

CAREER: University of Illinois, Urbana, instructor, 1962-63, assistant professor, 1963-70, associate professor of English, 1970—. *Military service:* U.S. Army, 1958-59. *Member:* Modern Language Association of America, Renaissance Society of America, Midwest Modern Language Association.

WRITINGS: A Quest of Inquirie: Some Contexts of Tudor Literature, Bobbs-Merrill, 1973. Contributor of articles and book reviews to *Journal of English and Germanic Philology, Illinois English Bulletin, Quarterly Journal of Speech,* and *Seventeenth Century News.*

WORK IN PROGRESS: The "All's Well" Story from Boccaccio to Florio, completion expected in 1976.

* * *

COLEMAN, J(ohn) Winston, Jr. 1898-

PERSONAL: Born November 5, 1898, in Lexington, Ky.; son of John Winston and Mary (Payne) Coleman; married Burnetta Z. Mullen, October 15, 1930. *Education:* University of Kentucky, B.S., 1920, M.E., 1929. *Politics:* Democrat. *Religion:* Presbyterian. *Home:* 2048 Blairmore Rd., Lexington, Ky. 40502.

CAREER: Engaged in engineering work in New York and other states, 1920-23; Coleman & Davis, Inc. (general contractors and builders), Lexington, Ky., organizer and president, 1924-36; Winburn Farm, Lexington, Ky., owner and operator, 1936-66. President of board of directors, Lexington Cemetery Co., 1948—; member of board of directors, Henry Clay Memorial Foundation, 1948-73, Kentucky Civil War Round Table, 1953—, Kentucky Heritage Commission, 1961-63, Kentucky Civil War Centennial Commission, 1961-65. *Member:* Society of American Historians (fellow), American Antiquarian Society, Bibliographical Society of America, American Geographical Society, Southern Historical Association, Mississippi Valley Historical Association, Kentucky Historical Society, Cincinnati Historical Society, Kentucky Society—Sons of the Revolution (president, 1944-46), Sigma Nu, Omicron Delta Kappa, Phi Alpha Theta, Masons, Shriners, Filson Club, Rotary Club. *Awards, honors:* Litt.D., Lincoln Memorial University, 1945, University of Kentucky, 1947; University of Kentucky Distinguished Alumni Award, 1967; LL.D., Transylvania University, 1969.

WRITINGS: Masonry in the Bluegrass, Translyvania Press, 1933; *Stage-Coach Days in the Bluegrass,* Standard Press, 1935; *Lexington During the Civil War,* Commercial Printing Co., 1938, revised edition, Henry Clay Press, 1968; *Slavery Times in Kentucky,* University of North Carolina Press, 1940, reprinted, Johnson Reprint, 1970; *A Bibliography of Kentucky History,* University of Kentucky Press, 1949; *The Beauchamp-Sharp Tragedy: An Episode of Kentucky History During the Middle 1820's,* Roberts Printing Co., 1950; *Old Homes of the Blue Grass,* Kentucky Society, 1950; *Famous Kentucky Duels: The Story of the Code of Honor in the Bluegrass State,* Roberts Printing Co., 1953, reprinted, Henry Clay Press, 1969; *A Centennial History of Sayre School, 1854-1954,* Winburn Press, 1954; *An Autobiographical Sketch, with a List of Writings,* Winburn Press, 1954; *The Springs of Kentucky,* Winburn Press, 1955; *Historic Kentucky,* Henry Clay Press, 1967, 2nd edition, 1968; *The Collected Writings of J. Winston Coleman, Jr.,* Winburn Press, 1969; (editor) *Kentucky: A Pictorial History,* University of Kentucky Press, 1971; *The Squire's Sketches of Lexington,* Henry Clay Press, 1972; (editor) *Life in the Bluegrass,* Historic Records Association, 1974; *Three Kentucky Artists,* University of Kentucky Press, in press. Also author of numerous pamphlets on Kentucky history.

SIDELIGHTS: Coleman owns the largest private collection of literature by and about Kentucky.

* * *

COLEMAN, Raymond James 1923-

PERSONAL: Born January 8, 1923, in Bethel, Kan.; son of Leonard G. and Johanna (Poulsen) Coleman; married Katherine Dietrich (an interior designer), April 8, 1945; children: Katherine (Mrs. Gary J. Morehead), Jayne, Christopher. *Education:* University of Kansas, B.S., 1948; Central Missouri State University, M.A., 1963; University of Arkansas, Ph.D., 1967. *Religion:* Presbyterian. *Home:* 1924 Blue Hills Rd., Manhattan, Kan. 66502. *Office:* College of Business Administration, Kansas State University, Manhattan, Kan. 66506.

CAREER: Employed in sales by General Mills Feed Division, Kansas City, 1949-56; sales supervisor for Investors Diversified Services, Inc., Kansas City, 1957-63; University of Arkansas, Fayetteville, instructor, 1963-65; Kansas State University, Manhattan, assistant professor, 1965-69, associate professor of marketing, 1969—. Research analyst for Research Foundation of Kansas, 1965-68; management and marketing research economist for Kansas Agricultural Experiment Station, 1965—; associate of Development Planning and Research Associates, Inc., 1971—. *Military service:* U.S. Navy, pilot, 1943-46; served on U.S.S. Yorktown in Pacific theater; became lieutenant junior grade; received five air medals.

MEMBER: Sales and Marketing Executives International, American Marketing Association, Ozarks Economic Association, Kansas City Society of Financial Analysts, Delta Mu Delta, Beta Gamma Sigma.

WRITINGS: (With M. J. Riley) *Chief Executive Behavior and Corporate Growth Rate in an Agribusiness Industry,* Agricultural Experiment Station, Kansas State University, 1971; (with Riley) *MIS: Management Dimensions,* Holden-Day, 1973. Contributor to *Personnel Journal* and *Journal of Systems Management.*

WORK IN PROGRESS: A book on the concept of the organizational life cycle.

SIDELIGHTS: Coleman traveled in most of the Arab countries during the summer of 1971, while making a marketing feasibility study on the glass and ceramics industry for the Government of Jordan; he traveled in Europe and

Turkey in 1972 and 1973, while teaching in an Air Force graduate program. He is "convinced our economic system is superior to other forms. However, we seem to be on the verge of losing our vitality. Our market system must have effective competition if our economy is to be vigorous and function properly. Organizational life cycle provides the framework for understanding the operation of our economic system and the organizational subsystems." *Avocational interests:* Travel, jogging.

* * *

COLLIE, Michael (John) 1929-

PERSONAL: Born August 8, 1929, in England; son of Leslie Grant and Elizabeth (Robertson) Collie; married second wife, Joanne L'Heureux, 1960. *Education:* Cambridge University, B.A., 1952, M.A., 1956. *Home:* 914 Meadow Wood Rd., Clarkson, Ontario, Canada. *Office:* Vanier College, York University, Toronto, Ontario, Canada.

CAREER: University of Manitoba, Winnipeg, assistant professor of English, 1957-61; Exeter University, Exeter, England, staff tutor, 1961-62; Mount Allison University, Sackville, New Brunswick, assistant professor of English, 1962-65; York University, Vanier College, Toronto, Ontario, associate professor, 1965-67, professor of English literature, 1967—, dean of graduate studies, 1969-73. *Military service:* British Intelligence Corps, 1947-49. *Member:* International Association of University Professors of English, Modern Language Association of America, Modern Humanities Research Association, Association of Canadian University Teachers of English, Canadian Association of University Teachers.

WRITINGS: Poems, Ryerson, 1959; *Skirmish with Fact,* Ryerson, 1960; *Laforgue,* Oliver & Boyd, 1964; *Jules Laforgue derniers vers,* University of Toronto Press, 1965; *The House* (poems), Macmillan, 1967; *Kerdruc Notebook,* Rampant Lions Press, 1972; *New Brunswick,* Macmillan, 1974; *George Meredith: A Bibliography,* University of Toronto Press, 1974; *George Gissing: A Bibliography,* University of Toronto Press, in press.

WORK IN PROGRESS: The Life and Work of Alfred Sistey; a critical edition of Jules Laforgue's *Les Complaintes,* for Athlone Press.

* * *

COLLIER, Eugenia W(illiams) 1928-

PERSONAL: Born April 6, 1928, in Baltimore, Md.; daughter of Harry Maceo (a physician) and Eugenia (an educator; maiden name Jackson) Williams; married Charles S. Collier, July 23, 1948 (legally separated, 1968); children: Charles Maceo, Robert Nelson, Philip Gilles. *Education:* Howard University, B.A. (magna cum laude), 1948; Columbia University, M.A., 1950; University of Maryland, doctoral candidate. *Residence:* Baltimore, Md. *Office:* Community College of Baltimore, 2901 Liberty Heights Ave., Baltimore, Md. 21215.

CAREER: Baltimore Department of Public Welfare, Baltimore, Md., case worker, 1950-55; Morgan State College, Baltimore, Md., assistant instructor, 1955-56, instructor, 1956-61, assistant professor of English, 1961-66; Community College of Baltimore, Baltimore, Md., assistant professor, 1966-68, associate professor, 1968-70, professor of English, 1970—. Visiting professor at Southern Illinois University, summer, 1970, and Atlanta University, summers, 1973, 1974; lecturer, University of Maryland, Baltimore County, 1974-75. *Member:* College Language Association (member of black studies committee, 1970—). *Awards, honors:* Gwendolyn Brooks Award for Fiction, from *Negro Digest,* 1969, for story "Marigolds."

WRITINGS: (Contributor) Donald Gibson, editor, *Modern Black Poets: A Collection of Critical Essays,* Prentice-Hall, 1973; (with Ruthe T. Sheffey) *Impressions in Asphalt: Images of Urban America,* Scribner, 1969; (with Joel I. Glasser and others) *A Bridge to Saying It Well,* Norvec, 1970; (contributor) Therman O'Daniel, editor, *Langston Hughes: Black Genius,* Morrow, 1971; (with Richard A. Long) *Afro-American Writing: Poetry and Prose,* New York University Press, 1972.

Work is represented in anthologies, including *Brothers and Sisters,* edited by Arnold Adoff, Macmillan, 1970; *Accent,* edited by James B. Phillips and others, Scott, Foresman, 1972; *Oral and Written Composition: A Unit-Lesson Approach,* edited by Albert Lavin and others, Ginn, 1972. Contributor of stories, poems, and articles to *Negro Digest, Black World, TV Guide, Phylon, College Language Association Journal,* and *New York Times.*

WORK IN PROGRESS: Silver Nets, a volume of poems; a critical history of black writing of the 1960's; a critical history of black American criticism; a collection of her stories; a collection of her critical articles; "Ricky," a short story.

SIDELIGHTS: Mrs. Collier writes: "The fact of my blackness is the core and center of my creativity. After a conventional Western-type education, I discovered the richness, the diversity, the beauty of my black heritage. This discovery has meant a coalescence of personal and professional goals. It has also meant a lifetime commitment."

BIOGRAPHICAL/CRITICAL SOURCES: Ora Williams, *American Black Women in the Arts and Social Sciences: A Bibliographic Survey,* Scarecrow, 1973.

* * *

COLLINS, Christopher 1936-

PERSONAL: Born July 8, 1936, in Red Bank, N.J.; son of John (an artist) and Lily (Rasmussen) Collins; married Emily Drucker, March 9, 1968; children: Jennifer. *Education:* St. Anselm's College, B.A. (summa cum laude), 1958; University of California, Berkeley, M.A., 1959; Columbia University, Ph.D., 1964; Gonville and Caius College, Cambridge, postdoctoral study, 1970. *Politics:* "A William Blake radical." *Religion:* "Proto-Taoist." *Home:* 244 East Fifth St., New York, N.Y. 10003. *Office:* Department of English, New York University, 19 University Pl., New York, N.Y. 10003.

CAREER: State University of New York, Nassau Community College, Garden City, assistant professor of English, 1963-65; City University of New York, Borough of Manhattan Community College, New York, N.Y., associate professor of English and chairman of department, 1965-68; New York University, New York, N.Y., associate professor of English, 1968—. *Awards, honors:* Woodrow Wilson fellowship, 1958-59.

WRITINGS: The Act of Poetry, Random House, 1970; *The Uses of Observation,* Mouton & Co., 1971; (translator) Longus, *Daphnis and Chloe,* Imprint Society, 1972; (editor and translator of selections) *Brother Sun* (anthology of quotes), Sierra Club, 1974. Contributor of poems and articles to *New York Quarterly, Nation, Epoch, New York Poetry, University Review, New American Poetry,* and *Fiddlehead.*

WORK IN PROGRESS: Research on the perceptual premises of poetry.

SIDELIGHTS: "I've wanted for a long time to be a poet," Collins writes. "But telling the truth is so difficult. (Telling the truth wouldn't be so hard if one first didn't have to *admit* it.) Saying the absolutely unstrategic statement is such a scary event, while the eloquent and portentous lie is so easy to formulate. The ideal of the sooth-sayer is my ideal of the *real* poet." Collins has translated from Latin, Italian, Greek, French, and German. *Avocational interests:* Cooking, mushroom-hunting, foraging.

* * *

COLLINS, John M(artin) 1921-

PERSONAL: Born May 14, 1921, in Kansas City, Mo.; son of John M. (a newspaper editor) and Jessie F. (Wagner) Collins; married Gloria O. Demers, November 11, 1950; children: Sean K. *Education:* University of Kansas City, B.A., 1949; Clark University, Worcester, Mass., M.A., 1951; Industrial College of the Armed Forces, graduate study, 1967; National War College, graduate study, 1969. *Office:* Congressional Research Service, Library of Congress, Washington, D.C.

CAREER: U.S. Army, career officer, 1942-72; National War College, Washington, D.C., director of military strategy studies, 1968-71, first chief of Strategic Research Group, 1971-72, leaving service as colonel; Library of Congress, Congressional Research Service, Washington, D.C., senior specialist in national defense, 1972—. *Member:* International Institute for Strategic Studies, Association of the U.S. Army, National Geographic Society. *Awards, honors*—Military: Legion of Merit with oakleaf cluster.

WRITINGS: Grand Strategy: Principles and Practices, U.S. Naval Institute, 1973; *Defense Trends in the United States, 1952-1973* (monograph), Congressional Research Service, Library of Congress, 1974. Contributor to *Army, Orbis,* and publications of Congressional Research Service.

* * *

COMDEN, Betty 1919-

PERSONAL: Born May 3, 1919, in Brooklyn, N.Y.; daughter of Leo (a lawyer) and Rebecca (a school teacher; maiden name, Sadvoransky) Comden; married Steven Kyle (a designer and businessman), January 4, 1942; children: Susanna, Alan. *Education:* New York University, B.S., 1938. *Residence:* New York, N.Y. *Agent:* Ronald S. Konecky, 1 Dag Hammarskjold Plaza, New York, N.Y.

CAREER: Author of musical comedies and screenplays, collaborating with Adolph Green, 1939—. Actress, performing in night club act, "The Revuers" and in Broadway musicals, including "On the Town," and "A Party." *Member:* Writers Guild of America (East and West), American Federation of Television and Radio Artists, Screenwriters Guild, American Guild of Variety Artists, American Society of Composers, Authors, and Publishers, Dramatists Guild (member of council, 1948—). *Awards, honors:* Screenwriters Guild of America Award for "On the Town," 1949, "Singin' in the Rain," 1952, and "It's Always Fair Weather," 1955; Donaldson Award and Antoinette Perry (Tony) Award for lyrics, both 1953, for "Wonderful Town"; *Village Voice* Off-Broadway (Obie) Award, 1959, for "A Party with Betty Comden and Adolph Green"; Antoinette Perry Award for best score, 1968, for "Hallelujah, Baby"; Antoinette Perry Award for best book for musical, 1970, for "Applause."

WRITINGS—With Adolph Green: *Comden and Green on Broadway,* Drama Book, 1974.

Musicals—all with Green: (Book and lyrics) "On the Town," music by Leonard Bernstein, first produced on Broadway at Adelphi Theatre, December 28, 1944; (book and lyrics) "Billion Dollar Baby," music by Morton Gould, first produced on Broadway at Alvin Theatre, December 21, 1945; (book and lyrics) "Bonanza Bound," music by Saul Chaplin, first produced in Philadelphia at Shubert Theatre, 1947; (sketches and lyrics) "Two on the Aisle," music by Jule Styne, first produced on Broadway at Mark Hellinger Theatre, July 19, 1951; (lyrics) "Wonderful Town," music by Bernstein, first produced on Broadway at Winter Garden Theatre, February 25, 1953; (additional lyrics) "Peter Pan," music by Styne, first produced at Winter Garden Theatre, October 20, 1954; (book and lyrics) *Bells Are Ringing* (music by Styne; first produced on Broadway at Shubert Theatre, November 29, 1936), Random House, 1957; (lyrics) "Say, Darling," music by Styne, first produced on Broadway at American National Theatre and Academy, April 3, 1958; "A Party" (revue based on collection of previously written songs and sketches), first produced Off-Broadway at Cherry Lane Theatre, November 10, 1958, later expanded and produced on Broadway at Golden Theatre as "A Party with Betty Comden and Adolph Green," December 23, 1958; (lyrics) "Do Re Mi," music by Styne, first produced on Broadway at St. James Theatre, December 26, 1960; (book and lyrics) "Subways Are for Sleeping," music by Styne, first produced at St. James Theatre, December 27, 1961; (book and lyrics) *Fade Out–Fade In* (music by Styne; first produced at Mark Hellinger Theatre, May 26, 1964), Random House, 1965; (lyrics) "Hallelujah, Baby," music by Styne, first produced on Broadway at Martin Beck Theatre, April 26, 1967; (book) *Applause* (music by Charles Strouse; based on film, "All About Eve"; first produced on Broadway at Palace Theatre, March 20, 1970), Random House, 1971.

Films—all with Green: (screenplay) "Good News," 1947; (screenplay) "The Barkleys of Broadway," 1949; (screenplay and lyrics) "On the Town," 1949; (lyrics) "Take Me Out to the Ballgame," 1949; (screenplay and lyrics) *Singin' in the Rain,* 1952, Viking, 1972; (screenplay and lyrics) "The Bandwagon," 1953; (screenplay and lyrics) "It's Always Fair Weather," 1955; (screenplay) "Auntie Mame," 1958; (screenplay and lyrics) "Bells Are Ringing," 1960; (screenplay and lyrics) "What a Way to Go," 1964.

Author with Green of music, book, and lyrics for night club act, "The Revuers," 1939-43; also author with Green of musical comedy specials for ABC-TV. Contributor to *Esquire* and *Vogue.*

SIDELIGHTS: Paul Kresh said "If the names of Comden and Green were removed from the record, great blank stretches would be left in the history of the Broadway musical. We would lose some of the happiest interludes on Hollywood celluloid as well, and without the words they supplied many of the country's cleverest songs would wind up as mere fodder for Muzak." Of *Applause,* Stanley Kauffmann wrote in the *New Republic:* "Everything about it is cut to pattern: the overall shape, the shape of the individual scenes, the shape of the numbers, even the shape of the snappy-comeback dialogue exchanges. It's the biggest smash of the season—a fairly smooth bench-lathe job which Broadway buffs say is just the kind of thing ailing Broadway needs. They are evidently right." Brendan Gill wrote in the *New Yorker:* "'Applause' is a model Broadway musical—it comes on strong and coarse and bold and false and funny and eye-bedazzling and ear-deafening, and it never for a moment slackens its fierce, breakneck pace; like some merry, many-colored juggernaut, it hurls itself through two acts of songs, dances, wisecracks, and schmaltz without the least sign of tiring, or of fearing to tire us. It is a blessedly self-confident show, and there have been but few of them on Broadway recently."

The musical, "On the Town," was revived on Broadway in 1971.

BIOGRAPHICAL/CRITICAL SOURCES: Stereo Review, April, 1973.

* * *

CONLIN, Joseph R. 1940-

PERSONAL: Born January 7, 1940, in Philadelphia, Pa.; son of Joseph R. (a shipper) and Lenore (Harnage) Conlin; married wife, Mary A., September 2, 1962 (divorced, 1973); children: Eamonn J., Anna L. *Education:* Villanova University, A.B., 1961; University of Wisconsin, M.A., Ph.D., 1964. *Home:* 1406 Bidwell Ave., Chico, Calif. 95926. *Office:* Department of History, California State University, Chico, Calif. 95926.

CAREER: Teacher at various colleges in the East and Midwest, 1964-67; California State University, Chico, professor of history, 1967—. Professor at University of Warwick, 1971, and University of California, Davis, 1972-73. *Member:* American Historical Association, Organization of American Historians, Labour Historians (England), Pacific Northwest Labor History Society.

WRITINGS: American Anti-War Movements, Glencoe Press, 1968; *Big Bill Haywood and the Radical Union Movement,* Syracuse University Press, 1969; *Bread and Roses, Too: Essays on the Wobblies,* Greenwood Press, 1969; *American Radical Press: 1880-1961,* Greenwood Press, 1974. Contributor to journals.

* * *

CONNOLLY, Vivian 1925-

PERSONAL: Born August 22, 1925, in Pittsburgh, Pa.; daughter of James N. (a management consultant) and Esther (Reedy) Hauser; married Harry H. Eckstein, September, 1946 (divorced March, 1953); married John R. Connolly (a clockmaker), October, 1969. *Education:* Ohio State University, B.A., 1946, B.Sc., 1946; Manhattan State Hospital School of Nursing, diploma in nursing, 1960; University of California, San Francisco, M.S., 1967. *Residence:* Taos, N.M. *Agent:* Ray Peekner Literary Agency, 2625 North 36th St., Milwaukee, Wis. 53210.

CAREER: International Theatre Co., England and Malta, actress, 1952-53; nursing positions in New York and California, 1960-69; Visalia Day Treatment Center, Visalia, Calif., psychiatric nurse specialist, 1969-70; free-lance writer. *Member:* Phi Beta Kappa.

WRITINGS—Novels: *South Coast of Danger,* Tower, 1973; *The Velvet Prison,* Dell, in press; *The Fires of Ballymorris,* Dell, in press. Contributor to *American Mercury, American Journal of Nursing, Irish Times,* and *Irish Independent.*

WORK IN PROGRESS: Two novels, *The Final Spike* and *Five Ports to Danger.*

AVOCATIONAL INTERESTS: Traveling, making beaded Indian headbands.

* * *

CONVICT WRITER, The
See TOROK, Lou

* * *

COOK, Adrian 1940-

PERSONAL: Born May 7, 1940, in Swindon, Wiltshire, England; son of Reginald (a railwayman) and Winifred (Hopes) Cook. *Education:* Cambridge University, B.A. (first class honors), 1961, M.A., 1965, Ph.D., 1965; also studied at Johns Hopkins University, 1962-63. *Politics:* Tory Radical. *Religion:* Church of England. *Home:* 20 Nicholas Rd., Hunter's Ride, Henley-on-Thames, England. *Office:* Department of History, University of Reading, Reading, England.

CAREER: Columbia University, New York, N.Y., postdoctoral fellow in history, 1968-69; University of Virginia, Charlottesville, postdoctoral fellow in history, 1969-70; University of Wisconsin, Madison, postdoctoral fellow in history, 1970-71; University of Reading, Reading, England, lecturer in history, 1971—. *Member:* American Historical Association, Organization of American Historians, Southern Historical Association, Cambridge Film Society.

WRITINGS: The Armies of the Streets: The New York City Draft Riots of 1863, University Press of Kentucky, 1974; *The United States and Great Britain, 1865-1872: The Effect of Domestic Politics upon Foreign Policy,* Cornell University Press, in press. Editor of *Broadsheet,* 1961.

WORK IN PROGRESS: London's Black Sundays: Fascist Riots, 1936-1937; The Metropolitan Police: 1919-1939; Elsie Borders and Grass Roots Communism in Britain: 1937-1939.

AVOCATIONAL INTERESTS: Attending films, gardening, travel.

* * *

COOK, George S. 1920-

PERSONAL: Born November 26, 1920, in Chicago, Ill.; son of George Cook (a contractor) and Eva (Stenger) Cook; married Wanda Brewer (a real estate saleswoman), September 4, 1945; children: Ray E., Ronald J., Rob S., Jerry A., Elaine T. *Education:* George Washington University, B.S., 1944. *Home:* 13191 Ethelbee Way, Santa Ana, Calif. 92705. *Office:* Chemical Coatings Corp., 7300 Crider, Pico Rivera, Calif. 90660.

CAREER: Engineer Laboratories, Ft. Belvoir, Va., chemist, 1940-50; General Electric Co., Schenectady, N.Y., chemist, 1950-57; Allied Chemical Corp., Lynwood, Calif., sales representative, 1957-68; Chemical Coatings Corp., Pico Rivera, Calif., sales manager, 1968—. *Military service:* U.S. Army, Infantry, 1944-45; received Bronze Star. *Member:* American Chemical Society, Los Angeles Society for Paint Technology, Orange County Free Lance Writers (president, 1973).

WRITINGS: Paint Industry Material Man, Heckle Publishing, 1955; *Fish Heads and Fire Ants,* Young Scott Books, 1973; *Get the Man on Second,* Scholastic Magazines, 1974.

WORK IN PROGRESS: What a Person Needs to Know to be Creative, completion expected in 1974, and two novels, *On Pacific Avenue,* 1974, and *Time of Decision,* 1975.

* * *

COOK, Melvin A(lonzo) 1911-

PERSONAL: Born October 10, 1911, in Garden City, Utah; son of Alonzo Laker (a farmer) and Alice Maude (Osmond) Cook; married Wanda Garfield, June 19, 1935; children: Barbara Jean (Mrs. S. Keith Petersen), Melvin Garfield, Virginia (Mrs. Gill O. Sanders), Merrill Alonzo, Krehl Osmond. *Education:* University of Utah, B.A. (with honors), 1933, M.A., 1934; Yale University, Ph.D., 1937. *Religion:* Church of Jesus Christ of Latter-Day Saints. *Home:* 631 16th Ave., Salt Lake City, Utah 84103. *Office:* 718 Kennecott Building, Salt Lake City, Utah 84111.

CAREER: E. I. duPont de Nemours & Co., Gibbstown, N.J., research chemist, 1937-47; University of Utah, Salt Lake City, professor of metallurgy and director of Institute of Metals and Explosives Research, 1947—. President of Intermountain Research and Engineering Co. (now IRECO Chemicals), 1958-72, chairman of board, 1972—; president of Mesabi Blasting Agents, Inc., 1960—. Adviser on Minuteman to Secretary of the Air Force, 1962-64; member of advisory council, Picatinny Arsenal, 1962-65; consultant on explosives to duPont and about twenty-five other companies; expert witness in Texas City-Monsanto blast case, 1948-50. Inventor of explosive devices and boosters.

MEMBER: American Chemical Society, American Association for the Advancement of Science, American Physical Society, American Institute of Mining, Metallurgical and Petroleum Engineers, Faraday Society. *Awards, honors:* Science Award of Utah Academy of Arts, Letters and Science, 1954; Utah Award of Salt Lake City section of American Chemical Society, 1961; E. V. Murphree Award of American Chemical Society, 1968; Nitro Nobel Gold Medallion of Royal Swedish Academy of Sciences, 1968.

WRITINGS: The Science of High Explosives, Reinhold, 1958, revised edition, Krieger, 1970; *Prehistory and Earth Models,* Parrish (London), 1966, Pacific Meridian, 1967; (with son, Melvin Garfield Cook) *Science and Mormonism,* Deseret, 1967, revised edition, 1968; *Creation and Eternalism,* Deseret, 1972. Contributor of more than 180 scientific papers to journals.

WORK IN PROGRESS: The Science and Industrial Application of Modern High Explosives; and a four-volume autobiography.

SIDELIGHTS: Cook has traveled about two million miles into fifty-four countries.

* * *

COOK, Sylvia (Carol) 1938-

PERSONAL: Born November 28, 1938; daughter of Reginald Ambrose (a teacher) and Audrey Ethel (Allen) Cook; married Henry William Marrett, May, 1965 (divorced, 1971). *Education:* Attended Pitmans College, London, 1958-59. *Politics:* Liberal. *Religion:* None. *Home and office:* Flat 15, Melville Ct., Goldhawk Rd., London W12 9NY, England. *Agent:* George Greenfield, Esq., c/o John Farquharson Ltd., 15 Red Lion Sq., London W.C.1, England.

CAREER: Williams Deacon's Bank, London, England, 1953-57, became cashier; Leonard Koetser Gallery, London, England, administration and catalogue production, 1959-69.

WRITINGS: (With John Fairfax) *Oars Across the Pacific,* Norton, 1972. Contributor to *Woman's Own* and *Woman's Day* (Australia).

SIDELIGHTS: Sylvia Cook and John Fairfax took a year minus two days to row across the Pacific in the 42 foot Brittania II. Their book is a joint record, based on the separate logs they each kept, of their preparations for the voyage, and of what happened after they left San Francisco on April 26, 1971.

* * *

COOKSON, Peter W. 1913-

PERSONAL: Born May 8, 1913, in Milwaukee, Ore.; son of Gerald S. (a career officer in British Army) and Helen (a nurse; maiden name, Willis) Cookson; married Maurine Gray, June, 1938 (divorced, 1949); married Beatrice Straight (an actress), May 2, 1950; children: (first marriage) Brooksie Jane, Peter, Jr.; (second marriage) Gary, Anthony. *Education:* Attended Pasadena Playhouse School of the Theatre, 1932-33. *Residence:* New York, N.Y. *Agent:* James Oliver Brown, 20 East 60th St., New York, N.Y. 10022.

CAREER: Stage and film actor and producer of Broadway shows. *Military service:* U.S. Army, 1944. *Member:* Actors Equity Association, American Federation of Television and Radio Artists.

WRITINGS: Hender's Head (novel), Putnam, 1973. Also author of plays, "Stanley" and "Grace at Table Six."

WORK IN PROGRESS: A novel, *The Chinese Garden* (tentative title).

* * *

COOKSON, William 1939-

PERSONAL: Born May 8, 1939, in London, England; son of George H. F. (an inspector of schools and editor) and Rachel (Pelham Burn) Cookson; married Vera Lungu (a poet), December 19, 1973. *Education:* New College, Oxford, B.A., 1962. *Politics:* Socialist. *Home:* 5 Cranbourne Ct., Albert Bridge Rd., London SW11 4PE, England.

CAREER: Agenda (poetry magazine), London, England, editor and founder, 1959—.

WRITINGS: (Editor) *Selected Poems of Ezra Pound,* New Directions, 1973.

WORK IN PROGRESS: A Reader's Guide to Ezra Pound, for Thames & Hudson Ltd.

* * *

COOPER, Darien B(irla) 1937-

PERSONAL: Born September 27, 1937, in Mohawk, Tenn.; daughter of George P. (a farmer) and Mildred (Johnson) Brown; married DeWitt T. Cooper (a construction contractor), September 27, 1957; children: Craig, Brian, Ken. *Education:* Carson-Newman College, B.A., 1958. *Politics:* Republican. *Religion:* Baptist. *Home:* 2709 Rainbow Forest Dr., Decatur, Ga. 30034.

CAREER: High school teacher of mathematics in Clarkston, Ga., 1958-61; staff member of Campus Crusade for Christ, Inc., 1970-72; teacher of course on the home in metropolitan area of Atlanta, Ga., fall and spring, 1972—.

WRITINGS: You Can Be the Wife of a Happy Husband, Victor, 1974.

AVOCATIONAL INTERESTS: Painting, interior decorating, sewing, decoupage, flower arranging, tennis, swimming.

BIOGRAPHICAL/CRITICAL SOURCES: Atlanta Journal, February 10, 1974; *Christian Life,* July, 1974.

* * *

COOPER, David E. 1942-

PERSONAL: Born October 1, 1942, in England; son of Edward (a businessman) and Lilian (Turner) Cooper; married Patricia Patterson (a teacher), December 24, 1972. *Education:* Oxford University, M.A. and B.Phil. *Office:* Department of Philosophy, University of Surrey, Guildford, Surrey, England.

CAREER: Oxford University, Oxford, England, lecturer in philosophy, 1966-69; University of Miami, Coral Gables, Fla., visiting professor of philosophy, 1969-72; University of London, London, England, lecturer in philosophy, 1972-74; University of Surrey, Guildford, Surrey, England, reader in philosophy, 1974—. *Member:* Royal Institute of Philosophy, Mind Association, American Philosophical Association.

WRITINGS: Philosophy and the Nature of Language, Longmans, Green, 1973; *Presupposition,* Mouton & Co., 1974; (editor) *The Manson Murders: A Philosophical Inquiry,* Schenkman, 1974; *Knowledge of Language,* Prism, in press.

WORK IN PROGRESS: Research on philosophical anthropology.

* * *

COOPER, Emmanuel 1940- (Jonathan Sidney)

PERSONAL: Born December 12, 1940, in Derbyshire, England; son of Frederick (a butcher) and Kate Elizabeth (Cooke) Cooper. *Education:* Attended Dudley College, 1958-60, and Bournemouth Art School, 1960-61. *Home and office:* 138 Fonthill Rd., London N4 3HP, England. *Agent:* Winant Towers, 14 Cliffords Inn, London E.C.1, England.

CAREER: Potter; *Ceramic Review,* London, England, co-editor, 1969—. Part time lecturer at Hornsey College of Art, 1971—. *Military service:* Royal Air Force, 1956-58. *Member:* Craftsmen Potters Association (council member, 1969—), Federation of British Craft Society (council member, 1972—).

WRITINGS: Handbook of Pottery, Longmans, Green, 1970; *Taking Up Pottery,* Arthur Barker, 1972; *A History of Pottery,* St. Martin's, 1972; (editor with Eileen Lewenstein) *New Ceramics,* Van Nostrand, 1974; *Glazes for the Studio Potter,* Studio Vista, in press. Contributor, occasionally under pseudonym Jonathan Sidney, to *Crafts* and *Creative Crafts.*

WORK IN PROGRESS: Research in art pottery, 1870-1920.

* * *

COOPER, Paul 1926-

PERSONAL: Born May 19, 1926, in Victoria, Ill.; son of Charles Frederick and Jessie (Tullgren) Cooper; married Christiane Ebert (a poet), April 30, 1953; children: Claudia Renee, Ian Paul. *Education:* University of Southern California, A.B., 1950, M.A., 1953, D.M.A., 1956; Sorbonne, University of Paris, graduate study, 1953-54; National Conservatory, University of Paris, graduate study, 1953-54. *Home:* 4915 Valkeith Dr., Houston, Tex. 77035. *Office:* Shepherd School of Music, Rice University, Houston, Tex.

CAREER: Composer, music critic; University of Michigan, Ann Arbor, assistant professor, 1959-62, associate professor, 1962-66, professor of music theory, 1966-68; University of Cincinnati, Cincinnati, Ohio, professor of composition and theory and composer-in-residence, 1968-74; Rice University, Shepherd School of Music, Houston, Tex., professor of music and composer-in-residence, 1974—. Cultural representative for the U.S. State Department to Yugoslavia, 1965. *Military service:* U.S. Army, Infantry, 1944-46, 1950-52; became first lieutenant. *Member:* Music Teachers National Association, Sinfonia, Phi Beta Kappa, Pi Kappa Lambda. *Awards, honors:* Fulbright fellowship, 1953-54; Horace H. Rackham research grants, 1959, 1968; Guggenheim fellowships, 1965-66, 1972-73; Composer of the Year award from Music Teachers National Association, 1969.

WRITINGS: Perspectives in Music Theory, Dodd, 1973. Contributor to *Musical Quarterly* and other journals.

WORK IN PROGRESS: Workbooks for *Perspectives in Music Theory;* a book on music since 1950; original compositions.

BIOGRAPHICAL/CRITICAL SOURCES: Musical Quarterly, July, 1969, Edith Borroff, *Music in Europe and the United States,* Prentice-Hall, 1971.

* * *

COOPER, Sandi E. 1936-

PERSONAL: Born May 11, 1936, in New York, N.Y.; daughter of Irving (a decorator) and Claire (Ditzion) Cooper; married John M. Cammett (a professor and dean of faculty), December 22, 1967; children: Melani Claire. *Education:* City College (now City College of the City University of New York), B.S. (summa cum laude), 1957; New York University, M.A., 1959, Ph.D. (with honors), 1967. *Politics:* Independent. *Religion:* None. *Home:* 905 West End Ave., New York, N.Y. 10025. *Office:* Department of History, Richmond College, City University of New York, Staten Island, N.Y. 10301.

CAREER: Rutgers University, Douglass College, New Brunswick, N.J., lecturer, 1961-67; Richmond College of the City University of New York, Staten Island, N.Y., assistant professor, 1967-71, associate professor of history, 1971—. *Member:* American Historical Association, Conference on Peace Research in History (member of council, 1969-74; vice-president, 1974—), Coordinating Committee on Women in the Historical Profession (president, 1971-73), Society for French Historical Studies.

WRITINGS: (Editor, translator from the French, and author of foreward) *Peace and Civilization: Selections from the Writings of Jacques Novicon, 1849-1912,* Garland Publications, in press. Series editor, with B. W. Cook and Charles Charfield, and author of introductions for "Garland Library of War and Peace," Garland Publications, 1971—. Contributor of articles and reviews to journals.

WORK IN PROGRESS: An anthology of nineteenth-century peace ideas and movements, for Garland Publications; *A History of Internationalism in Nineteenth-Century Europe.*

COOPER, William Hurlbert 1924-

PERSONAL: Born October 19, 1924, in Philadelphia, Pa.; son of Charles M. (an industrialist) and Lois (Hurlbert) Cooper; married Joanne Coffin, February 17, 1951; children: Charles Morgan Bailey II, William Hurlbert, Jr., Arthur Stanley Coffin. *Education:* Western Reserve University (now Case Western Reserve University), B.A., 1946; George Washington University, M.D., 1949. *Politics:* Republican. *Religion:* Episcopalian. *Home:* 5024 Upton St. N.W., Washington, D.C. 20016. *Office:* 825 New Hampshire Ave. N.W., Washington, D.C. 20037.

CAREER: Physician and surgeon, specializing in obstetrics and gynecology; George Washington University, Washington, D.C., clinical instructor, 1952-60, assistant professor, 1960-67, associate professor of obstetrics and gynecology, 1967—. Member of District of Columbia Republican Central Committee, 1960—, finance chairman, 1968-74; delegate and whip, 1972 Republican National Convention. *Military service:* U.S. Army, 1942-44. *Member:* American Medical Association, Pan American Medical Association (past president), International Fertility Association, American Medical Political Action Committee (member of board of directors, 1969—; chairman of District of Columbia branch, 1959-68), Southern Medical Association (member of council, 1973-74), Kober Medical Society, District of Columbia Medical Society (president-elect, 1973-74), Academy of Medicine of Washington, D.C.

WRITINGS: *A Husband's Guide to Menopause,* Essendess, 1970. Contributor to medical journals.

* * *

COPPOCK, Joseph D(avid) 1909-

PERSONAL: Born February 10, 1909, in Peru, Ind.; son of Donald Merton and Madge (Oates) Coppock; married Esther Elizabeth McKenzie, August 1, 1940; children: David McKenzie, Jane Ann, Donald, Bruce. *Education:* Swarthmore College, A.B. (summa cum laude), 1933; Columbia University, M.A., 1934, Ph.D., 1940; also studied at University of Chicago, 1937, and University of Pennsylvania, 1938. *Religion:* Society of Friends. *Office:* Department of Economics, Pennsylvania State University, University Park, Pa. 16802.

CAREER: Instructor in economics at Hendrix College, Conway, Ark., 1934-37, Swarthmore College, Swarthmore, Pa., 1937-39, and University of California, Berkeley, 1939-40; U.S. Government, Washington, D.C., economist with Department of Agriculture, 1941, special assistant to vice-chairman, War Production Board, 1942, price executive with Office of Price Administration, 1943, and economic adviser, Office of International Trade Policy, Department of State, 1945-53; Earlham College, Richmond, Ind., professor of economics, 1953-62, research professor, 1962-65; Pennsylvania State University, University Park, professor of economics, 1965—. Visiting professor at National War College, 1951-53; with Carnegie Corp. project on education for business, 1957-58; national research professor, Brookings Institution, 1959-60; director of foreign economic advisory staff, Department of State, 1961-62; visiting professor at American University of Beirut, 1963-65, 1974-76; Rockefeller Foundation professor at Thammasat University, 1969-71. Also visiting professor at University of Oregon, University of Wisconsin, Indiana University, and University of Michigan. *Military service:* U.S. Naval Reserve, Office of Strategic Services, 1944-45.

MEMBER: American Economic Association, History of Economics Society, Midwest Economics Association (vice-president, 1956-57; president, 1962-63), Indiana Academy of Social Sciences (vice-president, 1955-56, 1959-61), Phi Beta Kappa. *Awards, honors:* Ford Foundation research grant, 1963-64, 1974.

WRITINGS: *Government Agencies of Consumer Installment Credit,* National Bureau of Economic Research, 1940; *The Food Stamp Plan: Moving Surplus Commodities with Special Purpose Money,* American Philosophical Society, 1947; *Economics of the Business Firm,* McGraw, 1959; (contributor) F. A. Pierson, editor, *The Education of American Businessmen,* McGraw, 1959; *International Economic Instability: The Experience after World War II,* McGraw, 1962; *Foreign Trade of the Middle East,* American University of Beirut, 1966; *Foreign Trade of Asia and the Far East,* Thammasat University Press (Bangkok), 1974. Contributor of articles on economics, foreign policy, and higher education to journals.

* * *

CORMIER, Ramona 1923-

PERSONAL: Born January 21, 1923, in Breaux Bridge, La.; daughter of Arthur Joseph (a principal) and Florence (a nurse; maiden name, Breaux) Cormier. *Education:* University of Southwestern Louisiana, B.A., 1943; University of Southern California, M.A., 1948; Tulane University, Ph.D., 1960. *Home:* 149 Baldwin, Bowling Green, Ohio 43402. *Office:* Department of Philosophy, Bowling Green State University, Bowling Green, Ohio 43403.

CAREER: Music teacher in Monroe, La., 1949-58; Newcomb College, New Orleans, La., instructor in philosophy, 1960-61; University of Tennessee, Knoxville, instructor, 1961-63, assistant professor of philosophy, 1963-65; Bowling Green State University, Bowling Green, Ohio, assistant professor, 1965-69, associate professor, 1969-72, professor of philosophy, 1972—, associate director of Philosophy Documentation Center, 1967-73, vice-president of Philosopher's Information Center, 1967-73. *Military service:* U.S. Navy, 1943-46. *Member:* American Philosophical Association, American Society for Aesthetics, American Association for the Advancement of Science, American Association of University Professors, British Society of Aesthetics, Southern Society for Philosophy, Ohio Philosophical Society (president, 1973-76), Delta Kappa Gamma.

WRITINGS: (Editor with Richard Lineback and Ewing Chinn) *Encounter: An Introduction to Philosophy,* Scott, Foresman, 1970; (editor with Lineback, Paul Kurtz, and Gilbert Varet) *International Directory of Philosophy and Philosophers,* Philosophy Documentation Center, Bowling Green State University, 2nd edition (Cormier was not associated with first edition), 1972, 3rd edition, 1974; (editor with Lineback and Archie Bahm) *Directory of American Philosophers,* Philosophy Documentation Center, Bowling Green State University, 6th edition (Cormier was not associated with earlier editions), 1973; (with Janis L. Pallister) *Waiting for Death: The Philosophical Significance of "En attendant Godot,"* University of Alabama Press, in press. Contributor to *Tulane Studies in Philosophy, British Journal of Aesthetics, Journal of Aesthetics and Art Criticism, L'Esprit Createur,* and *Delta Kappa Gamma Bulletin.* Editor of *Philosopher's Index,* 1967-73.

WORK IN PROGRESS: A book on the manner in which Beckett, Camus, and Sartre cope with nihilism in their literary and philosophical writings.

CORNELL, Katherine 1898(?)-1974

February 16, 1898(?)—June 9, 1974; American stage actress. Obituaries: *New York Times,* June 10, 1974; *Newsweek,* June 17, 1974; *Time,* June 24, 1974; *Current Biography,* July, 1974.

* * *

CORNWELL, Smith
See SMITH, David (Jeddie)

* * *

CORREA, Gustavo 1914-

PERSONAL: Born September 20, 1914, in Colombia, South America; son of Urbano (an engineer) and Maria (Forero) Correa; married Ines Cancino, August 20, 1947; children: Amanda, Albert, Patricia. *Education:* Johns Hopkins University, Ph.D., 1947. *Home:* 163 Hepburn Rd., Hamden, Conn. 06517. *Office:* Department of Spanish, Yale University, 493 College St., New Haven, Conn. 06520.

CAREER: Tulane University, New Orleans, La., associate professor of Spanish, 1951-54; University of Chicago, Chicago, Ill., associate professor of Spanish, 1954-56; University of Pennsylvania, Philadelphia, associate professor of Spanish, 1956-59; Yale University, New Haven, Conn., professor of Spanish, 1959—. *Member:* Modern Language Association of America, American Association of Teachers of Spanish and Portuguese. *Awards, honors:* Guggenheim fellow, 1959-60.

WRITINGS: El espiritu del mal en Guatemala, Middle American Research Institute, 1955; *La poesia mitica de Federico Garcia Lorca,* University of Oregon Press, 1957, 2nd edition, Gredos, 1971; *El simbolismo religioso en las novelas de Perez Galdos,* Gredos, 1962; *Realidad ficcion y simbolo en las novelas de Perez Galdos,* Instituto Caro y Chervo, 1967; (editor) *Poesia espanola del siglo veinte: Antologa,* Appleton, 1971.

WORK IN PROGRESS: Two books, *La mitologia en la poesia espanola del Siglo de Oro,* and *La representacion simbolica de la honra en la literatura espanola.*

* * *

CORY, Corrine
See CORY, Irene E.

* * *

CORY, Irene E. 1910-
(Corrine Cory, I. E. Corya)

PERSONAL: Born July 15, 1910, in Bloomfield, Ind.; daughter of James D. and Emma Jane (Porter) Cravens; married Thomas H. Cory, July 28, 1932 (deceased); children: Walter D. *Education:* Butler University, A.B., 1931; graduate study at University of Pittsburgh, and Southeastern Louisiana University. *Politics:* Independent ("registered Democrat"). *Religion:* Presbyterian. *Home:* 112 West Mechanic St., Bloomfield, Ind. 47424.

CAREER: Teacher of languages in the public schools of Indianapolis, Ind., 1944-67; Plano Academy of Plano University, Dallas, Tex., teacher, 1967-68; publicity writer for Blue Parrot Camping Parks, Lady Lake, Fla.; public speaker. President of Greene County (Ind.) Association for Retarded Citizens; member of board of directors of Greene County Tuberculosis Association. *Member:* Delta Kappa Gamma, Sigma Delta Pi, Delta Delta Delta.

WRITINGS: Pawdie, Vanguard, 1968. Contributor to *English Journal* and to science journals and periodicals.

WORK IN PROGRESS: Research for a book on the Doman-Delacato method for teaching brain-damaged children.

* * *

CORYA, I. E.
See CORY, Irene E.

* * *

COSGROVE, Rachel
See PAYES, Rachel C(osgrove)

* * *

COSNECK, Bernard Joseph 1912-

PERSONAL: Born January 29, 1912, in St. Louis, Mo.; son of Joseph (a hotel owner) and Fannie (Saltzman) Cosneck. *Education:* University of Illinois, B.S. in Ed., 1934; California Western University, M.A., 1964; University of Florida, Ph.D., 1966. *Religion:* Hebrew. *Home:* Hillcrest Apartments, #40, Valdosta, Ga. 31601. *Office:* Department of Sociology, Valdosta State College, Valdosta, Ga. 31601.

CAREER: Private practice as a psychotherapist and counselor in Los Angeles, Calif., 1934-63; Lamar State College (now Lamar University), Beaumont, Tex., assistant professor of sociology, 1966-67; Valdosta State College, Valdosta, Ga., associate professor, 1967-71, professor of sociology, 1971—. *Military service:* U.S. Coast Guard, 1942-44. *Member:* American Association of University Professors, Gerontological Society, American Sociological Association, Southeastern Sociological Society, Alpha Kappa Delta.

WRITINGS: Manual of Group Dynamics Workshop and Leadership Training, Afro-Asian Institute for Labor Studies, 1960; (editor and contributor) *Facets of Sociology,* Simon & Schuster, 1969; (editor and contributor) *Facets of Marriage and the Family,* Simon & Schuster, 1969; (editor and contributor) *Facets of Social Problems,* Simon & Schuster, 1970. Contributor to *Family Coordinator, Single Parent,* and *Christian Home.*

WORK IN PROGRESS: Research on the termination of long-standing marriages by divorce, remarriage of divorced persons to the original mate, attitudes of elderly people to their own death and dying, a cross-cultural study of reactions to widowhood, and the social life of police personnel.

* * *

COSTONIS, John J(oseph) 1937-

PERSONAL: Born September 2, 1937, in Boston, Mass.; son of Arthur Charles and Sylvia (Bonacorso) Costonis; married Maureen Needham (a professor of dance therapy), June 11, 1960; children: (adopted) Theresa, John. *Education:* Harvard University, A.B. (magna cum laude), 1959; Columbia University, L.L.B. (magna cum laude), 1965. *Home:* 612 West Oregon St., Urbana, Ill. 61801. *Office:* College of Law, University of Illinois, Champaign, Ill. 61820.

CAREER: University of Pennsylvania, School of Law, Philadelphia, assistant professor of law, 1965-68; University of Chicago, School of Law, Chicago, Ill., lecturer in international law, 1969; Ross, Hardies, O'Keefe, Babcock, McDugald & Parsons, Chicago, Ill., associate lawyer, 1968-70; University of Illinois, College of Law, Champaign, professor of law, 1970—. *Military service:* U.S. Army, Intelligence, 1960-62; became lieutenant. *Member:* National Trust for Historic Preservation.

WRITINGS: Space Adrift: Landmark Preservation and the Marketplace, University of Illinois Press, 1974. Contributor to *Harvard Law Review, Yale Law Review, Columbia Law Review, Michigan Law Review,* and *Architectural Forum.*

WORK IN PROGRESS: Research on environmental protection through development rights transfer.

SIDELIGHTS: Costonis would like to see law used to assist groups such as preservationists and environmentalists versus real estate developers. He also believes that American property laws unduly favor supposed "private rights" over public interests.

* * *

COTTERELL, (Francis) Peter 1930-

PERSONAL: Born May 4, 1930, in Malta; son of Leonard Charles and Edith (Stead) Cotterell; married Geraldine Brodie, June 1, 1957; children: Anne, Janet. *Education:* Brunel College (now Brunel University), B.Sc., 1955; Spurgeon's Theological College, B.D., 1960; University of London, Ph.D., 1970. *Home address:* P.O. Box 127, Addis Ababa, Ethiopia.

CAREER: Brunel College, London, England, lecturer in physics, 1955-57; Christian missionary in Ethiopia, 1957—. Visiting professor at Fuller Theological Seminary, 1973. *Member:* International African Institute, Language Study Group of East Africa, Historical Society of Ethiopia (member of board of directors).

WRITINGS: Born at Midnight, Moody, 1973. Author of more than twenty books in the Amharic language, including primers with distribution of more than one million copies. Contributor to *Journal of Ethiopian Studies.*

WORK IN PROGRESS: The Bishop Went to Bedlam, an expose of modern church problems; *Linguistics in Modern Mission.*

SIDELIGHTS: Cotterell is involved with making Christianity relevant to the younger generation, particularly through drama, radio, and in the church itself.

* * *

COULSON, Robert 1924-

PERSONAL: Born July 24, 1924, in New Rochelle, N.Y.; son of Robert Earl (a lawyer) and Abby (Stewart) Coulson; married Cynthia Cunningham, 1960; children: Cotton, Dierdre, Crocher, Robert Cromwell, Christopher. *Education:* Yale University, B.A., 1950; Harvard University, LL.B., 1953. *Home:* 211 Central Park W., New York, N.Y. 10024. *Office:* American Arbitration Association, 140 West 51st St., New York, N.Y. 10020.

CAREER: Whitman, Ransom, & Coulson (law firm), New York, N.Y., associate, 1955-61; Littlefield, Miller, & Cleaves (law firm), New York, N.Y., partner, 1961-63; American Arbitration Association, New York, N.Y., executive vice-president, 1963-71, president, 1971—. Member of boards of directors of Police Athletic League of New York, Center for Correctional Justice, Institute for Mediation and Conflict Resolution, and Federation of Protestant Welfare Agencies. *Member:* American Bar Association, New York State Bar Association, New York City Bar Association, American Society of Association Executives.

WRITINGS: Racing at Sea, Van Nostrand, 1959; *How to Stay Out of Court,* Crown, 1969; *Labor Arbitration: What You Need to Know,* American Arbitration Association, 1973. Contributor to professional journals.

* * *

COUNTS, Charles Richard 1934-

PERSONAL: Born November 13, 1934, in Lynch, Ky.; son of Arthur R. and Erma (Colley) Counts; married Rubynelle Waldrop (a teacher), June 3, 1956; children: Craig Elliott, Leila Clair. *Education:* Berea College, B.A., 1956; Southern Illinois University, M.A., 1957. *Politics:* Democrat. *Religion:* Unitarian-Universalist. *Home and office address:* Pottery Workshop, Route 2, Rising Fawn, Ga. 30738.

CAREER: Beaver Ridge Pottery, Knoxville, Tenn., owner, 1959-61; Pottery Workshop, Rising Fawn, Ga., owner, 1961—. Member of board of directors of American Crafts Council, 1967-70; chairman of Georgia Commission on the Arts, 1968, 1969. *Military service:* U.S. Army Reserve, 1959-64. *Member:* Southern Highland Handicraft Guild, Georgia Designer-Craftsmen. *Awards, honors:* Governor's Award in the Arts, 1973, from State of Georgia.

WRITINGS: Encouraging American Craftsmen, U.S. Government Printing Office, 1971; *Common Clay,* Droke, 1971; *Pottery Workshop,* Macmillan, 1973. Contributor to *Craft Horizons, Magazine of the American Crafts Council,* and *Ceramics Monthly.*

SIDELIGHTS: Counts has made two trips to West Africa, particularly Nigeria, to study local crafts. He is now aiding in a people-to-people exchange with an emphasis on craftsmen visiting from Nigeria.

* * *

COURTNEY, Robert
See ROBINSON, Frank M(alcolm)

* * *

COWIE, Peter 1939-

PERSONAL: Born December 24, 1939, in Boscombe, England; son of Donald John (an author) and Ruth Mary (Woods) Cowie; married Elisabeth von Waldow, September 22, 1962; children: Monica Anne, Felicity May. *Education:* Magdalene College, Cambridge, B.A., 1962, M.A., 1967. *Home:* 69 York Ave., London S.W. 14, England. *Office:* Tantivy Press, 108 New Bond St., London W.1. England.

CAREER: Tantivy Press, London, England, publisher, 1963—. Consultant to various international film festivals.

WRITINGS—All published by A. S. Barnes: *Antonioni-Bergman-Resnals,* 1963; *International Film Guide* (annual), 1964-74; *The Cinema of Orson Welles,* 1965, revised edition, 1973; *Swedish Cinema,* 1966, revised edition, 1970; *Seventy Years of Cinema,* 1969; (editor) *A Concise History of the Cinema,* 1971; *Fifty Major Film Makers,* in press. Contributor to periodicals in England.

COX, Joseph Mason Andrew 1923-

PERSONAL: Born July 12, 1923, in Boston, Mass.; son of Hiram and Edith (a nurse; maiden name, Henderson) Cox. *Education:* Columbia University, B.A., 1945, LL.B., 1953; World University, Hong Kong, A.Ps.D., 1972. *Politics:* Democrat. *Religion:* Unitarian-Universalist. *Home and office:* 353 West 57th St., New York, N.Y. 10019.

CAREER: New York Post, New York, N.Y., reporter and feature writer, 1958-60; Afro-Asian Purchasing Commission, New York, N.Y., president, 1961-68; New York City Board of Education, Brooklyn, N.Y., consultant, 1969-71; Manhattan Community College, New York, N.Y., lecturer, 1972-73; Medgar Evers College of the City University of New York, Brooklyn, N.Y., assistant professor of English, 1973-74; Cox & Hopewell Publishers, Inc., president, 1974—. *Member:* International Poetry Society (fellow), International Poets Shrine, United Poet Laureate International, Authors League of America, Poetry Society of America (member of executive board, 1971-72), Poetry Society of London, Centro Studi e Scambi Internazionali (Rome).

AWARDS, HONORS: International Essay Award from Daniel S. Mead Agency, 1964; "Great Society" writer's award from President Lyndon Baines Johnson, 1965; Master Poets Award from American Poet Fellowship Society, 1970; World Poets Award from World Poetry Fellowship Society, 1971; P.E.N. grant, 1972; Humanitarian Award and Gold Medal for poetry from International Poets Shrine, both 1974.

WRITINGS: The Search (novel), Freedom Press, 1963; *Ode to Dr. Martin Luther King, Jr.* (three-act play; first produced in Pittsburgh, Pa., at University of Pittsburgh, Creatadrama Theatre, 1970), published by J. Brook Dendy, 1970; *The Collected Poetry of Joseph Mason Andrew Cox,* Golden Quill, 1970; *Shore Dimly Seen* (collected poems), Cox & Hopewell Publishers, 1974. Also author of *Bouquet of Poems* and *Indestructible Monument* (novel), both published in 1974.

Work is represented in anthologies, including *Golden Quill Anthology, 1968,* edited by Paul Scott Mowrer and Clarence E. Farrar, Golden Quill, 1968; *World Poets Anthology,* edited by Frank Bensley, Lou Lu Toor, and Jerry McCarty, World of Poets Publishing, 1971; and *Poems by Blacks,* edited by Sue Scott Boyd, South and West Publishers, 1972. Columnist, *Caribbean Echo,* 1969-71. Contributor to periodicals.

WORK IN PROGRESS: A narrative poem on Haiti's independence and its impact on the United States freedom movement.

* * *

CRAIG, Robert B(ruce) 1944-

PERSONAL: Born April 22, 1944, in Washington, D.C.; son of Glenn Horace (an economist) and Evelyn May (a teacher; maiden name, Fiddler) Craig; married Judy Gail Nelson (a bank teller), April 5, 1966; children: Kimberlie, Cassandra. *Education:* Santa Monica College, A.A., 1968; University of California, Davis, B.A. (honors), 1970, M.A., 1972, doctoral candidate, 1974. *Politics:* Democrat. *Religion:* Atheist. *Home:* 1521 Oak Ave., Davis, Calif. 95616. *Office:* Department of Zoology, University of California, Davis, Calif. 95616.

CAREER: University of California, Berkeley, extension instructor in biology, 1972—; University of California, Davis, extension instructor in biology, 1972—, research associate in zoology, 1972—. *Member:* American Ornithological Union, American Society of Mammalogists, Ecological Society of America, American Society of Naturalists, American Society of Human Ecology, Cooper Ornithological Society. Alpha Gamma Sigma, Phi Kappa Phi. *Awards, honors:* National Science Foundation research fellowship, summer, 1969.

WRITINGS: (With M. G. Barbour, F. R. Drysdale, and M. T. Ghiselin) *Coastal Ecology: Bodega Head,* University of California Press, 1973; (contributor) M. A. Q. Kahn, editor, *Mechanisms for Survival in Toxic Environments,* Academic Press, 1974.

* * *

CRAM, Mildred 1889-

PERSONAL: Born October 17, 1889, in Washington, D.C.; daughter of Nathan Dow (an editor) and Mary (Queen) Cram; married Clyde S. McDowell (a naval officer), October, 1925 (deceased). *Education:* Attended Barnard School for Girls, 1905-08. *Politics:* Republican. *Home and office:* 1515 East Valley Rd., Santa Barbara, Calif. 93108.

CAREER: Author and novelist, 1917—.

WRITINGS: Old Seaport Towns of the South, Dodd, 1917, reprinted, Richard West, 1973; *Lotus Salad* (novel), Dodd, 1920; *Stanger Things* (short stories), Dodd, 1923, reprinted, Books for Libraries, 1970; *The Tide* (novel), Knopf, 1924; *Scotch Valley,* Doubleday, 1928; *Madder Music,* Little, Brown, 1930; *Forever* (novel), Knopf, 1935; *Kingdom of Innocents* (novel), Knopf, 1940; *The Promise* (novel), Knopf, 1949; *Sir,* Sunstone Press, 1973.

Filmscripts: "An Affair to Remember," "Beyond Tomorrow," "Love Affair" (received an Academy of Motion Picture Arts and Sciences nomination), "Wings Over Honolulu," and "Loves of Pandora." Contributor of over 200 short stories and articles to *Harper's Bazaar, Red Book, Cosmopolitan,* and other periodicals.

SIDELIGHTS: Several years ago Helmut Dantine reportedly offered Metro-Goldwyn-Mayer $250,000 for the film rights to *Forever,* which rights MGM has held for over thirty years.

* * *

CRAWFORD, Deborah 1922-

PERSONAL: Born January 16, 1922, in Elizabeth, N.J.; daughter of Edward Choate and Ruth (Pierce) Stonaker; married Andrew W. Crawford, Jr., 1952 (divorced, 1960). *Education:* Took night courses for six years in the 1950's at Columbia University, New York University, and New School for Social Research. *Politics:* Democrat ("usually"). *Religion:* Protestant ("lapsed"). *Home:* 54 West 16th St., New York, N.Y. 10011.

CAREER: Ruthrauff & Ryan, New York, N.Y., advertising copywriter, 1947-49; Grey Advertising, New York, N.Y., copywriter, 1952-54; Book-of-the-Month Club, New York, N.Y., reviewer, 1954—. Researcher for Willy Ley. *Member:* Authors Guild.

WRITINGS—Juvenile: *Pepper! The Story of a Parakeet,* Crown, 1966; *The King's Astronomer, William Herschel* (foreword by Willy Ley), Messner, 1968; *Lise Meitner, Atomic Pioneer,* Crown, 1969; *Four Women in a Violent Time,* Crown, 1970; *Somebody Will Miss Me,* Crown,

1971; *Franz Kafka, Man Out of Step,* Crown, 1973. Contributor to *Magazine of Fantasy and Science Fiction* and *Saint.*

WORK IN PROGRESS: A biography of the science writer, Willy Ley, who died in 1969.

AVOCATIONAL INTERESTS: Classical music, sailing, traveling to Europe and the Caribbean, walking, nature in general and birds in particular.

* * *

CRONIN, Joseph M(arr) 1935-

PERSONAL: Born August 30, 1935, in Boston, Mass.; son of Joseph Michael (an administrator) and Mary (Marr) Cronin; married Marie Whalen, 1958; children: Maureen, Kathleen, Elizabeth, Anne, Joseph, Timothy, Patricia. *Education:* Harvard University, A.B. (magna cum laude), 1956, M.A.T., 1957; Stanford University, Ed.D., 1965. *Religion:* Roman Catholic. *Home:* 49 Vaille Ave., Lexington, Mass. 02173. *Office:* Executive Office of Educational Affairs, 18 Tremont St., Boston, Mass. 02108.

CAREER: Teacher in the public schools of Braintree, Mass., 1951-58, and Palo Alto, Calif., 1958-61; principal in the public schools of Rockville, Md., 1961-64; Stanford University, Stanford, Calif., instructor in administration, 1964-65, assistant director of school board studies research for Great Cities Project, 1964-65; Harvard University, Graduate School of Education, Cambridge, Mass., assistant professor, 1965-68, associate professor of education, 1968-71, associate dean, 1971-72; Commonwealth of Massachusetts, Executive Office of Educational Affairs, Boston, secretary of educational affairs, 1972—. *Military service:* U.S. Army Reserve, 1957-63, became staff sergeant. *Member:* American Association of School Administration, American Arbitration Association, American Educational Research Association, Phi Delta Kappa. *Awards, honors:* Named Secondary School Principal of the Year by Crofts Educational Service, 1963.

WRITINGS: The Control of Urban Schools, Free Press, 1973; *Organizing an Urban School System for Diversity,* Heath, 1973. Contributor to *Phi Delta Kappan* and *American School Board Journal.*

* * *

CROSBY, Ruth 1897-

PERSONAL: Born December 9, 1897, in Arlington, Mass.; daughter of J(ohn) Howell (a market gardener) and Daisy A. (Conant) Crosby. *Education:* Mount Holyoke College, A.B., 1919; Radcliffe College, A.M., 1920, Ph.D., 1929. *Religion:* Christian. *Home:* 84 College Ave., Orono, Me. 04473; and R.F.D. 2, Bethel, Me. 04217 (summer).

CAREER: Oldfields School, Glencoe, Md., teacher of English, 1920-22; Connecticut College for Women, New London, instructor in English, 1922-25; University of Maine, Orono, 1929-62, began as assistant professor, became professor of English, professor emerita, 1962—. *Member:* Modern Language Association of America, Mediaeval Academy of America, Phi Beta Kappa.

WRITINGS: I Was a Summer Boarder (reminiscences), Christopher, 1966; *From an Old Leather Trunk* (family nostalgia), Christopher, 1974. Contributor of articles and reviews to scholarly journals, including *Publications of the Modern Language Association of America* and *Speculum.*

CROSLAND, Margaret 1920-

PERSONAL: Born June 17, 1920, in Bridgnorth, Shropshire, England; daughter of Leonard and Beatrice Masterman (Wainwright) Crosland; married Max Denis, 1950 (divorced, 1959); children: Patrick Leonard Dagobert. *Education:* University of London, B.A. (honors), 1941. *Politics:* Labour Party. *Religion:* Church of England. *Home:* The Long Croft, Upper Hartfield, Sussex, England.

CAREER: Author and translator. Literary adviser, BBC-TV film, "A Window on the War" (Colette), 1973. *Member:* P.E.N., Society of Authors.

WRITINGS: Strange Tempe (poems), Fortune Press, 1946; (compiler with Patricia Ledward) *The Happy Yes: An Anthology of Marriage Proposals, Grave and Gay,* Benn, 1949; *Madame Colette: A Provincial in Paris,* P. Owen, 1953, published as *Colette: A Provincial in Paris,* British Book Centre, 1954; *Jean Cocteau,* P. Neville, 1955, published as *Jean Cocteau: A Biography,* Knopf, 1956; *Ballet Carnival: A Companion to Ballet,* Arco, 1955, new edition, 1957; *Home Book of Opera,* Arco, 1957.

Ballet Lovers' Dictionary, Arco, 1962; *Louise of Stolberg, Countess of Albany,* Oliver & Boyd, 1962; *The Young Ballet Lover's Companion,* Souvenir Press, 1962; (adapter) Ornella Volta and Valeria Riva, compilers, *The Vampire: An Anthology,* Neville Spearman, 1963; *Philosophy Pocket Crammer,* Ken Publishing Company, 1964; (editor) Marquis de Sade, *Selected Letters,* P. Owen, 1965, October House, 1966; (editor) *A Traveller's Guide to Literary Europe,* H. Evelyn, 1965, published as *A Guide to Literary Europe,* Chilton, 1966; (editor) Jean Cocteau, *My Contemporaries,* P. Owen, 1967, Chilton, 1968; (author of introduction) Madame de Staeel, *Ten Years of Exile,* Centaur Press, 1968; (editor) *Foliejon Park: A Short History,* Mining and Chemical Products Ltd., 1970; (editor) Cocteau, *Cocteau's World: An Anthology of Major Writings by Jean Cocteau,* P. Owen, 1972, Dodd, 1973; *Colette—The Difficulty of Loving: A Biography,* Bobbs-Merrill, 1973.

Translator: Felicien Marceau, *The Flesh in the Mirror,* Vision Press, 1953; Jean Cocteau, *Paris Album, 1900-1914,* W. H. Allen, 1956; Minou Drouet, *First Poems,* Hamish Hamilton, 1956; Drouet, *Then There Was Fire,* Hamish Hamilton, 1957; (with Sinclair Road) Cocteau, *Opium,* P. Owen, 1957, Grove, 1958, new translation with introduction by translators, Icon Books, 1961; Edmund de Goncourt, *Elisa,* Neville Spearman, 1959; *The Story of Reynard,* Hamish Hamilton, 1959; Vladimir Jankelevitch, *Ravel,* Grove, 1959; Pierre Lacroix, *The Conquest of Fire,* Burke Publishing, 1959; Joseph Rovan, *Germany,* Viking, 1959; Rene Poirier, *The Fifteen Wonders of the World,* Gollancz, 1960; Emile Zola, *Earth,* New English Library, 1962; Marcel Mouloudji, *French Leave,* Neville Spearman, 1962; (and editor) Marquis de Sade, *De Sade Quartet,* P. Owen, 1963; (with Alan Daventry) Maurice Bessy, *A Pictorial History of Magic and the Supernatural,* Spring Books, 1963; (with Road) Octave Aubry, *Napoleon,* Paul Hamlyn, 1964; (and editor) *Selected Writings of de Sade,* P. Owen, 1964; Cecile Arnaud, *The Gift of Indifference,* Heinemann, 1965; Ghislain de Diesbach, *Secrets of the Gotha,* Chapman & Hall, 1967, Meredith, 1968; (with Daventry) Raymond de Becker, *The Other Face of Love,* Neville Spearman, 1967, Grove, 1969; Giorgio de Chirico, *Hebdomeros,* P. Owen, 1968; (and editor) Cesare Pavese, *A Mania for Solitude: Selected Poems, 1930-1950,* P. Owen, 1969; Minou Drouet, *Donatella,* Neville Spearman, 1969; de Chirico, *Memoirs of Giorgio de Chirico,* University of Miami Press, 1971; Colette, *The Other Woman,* P. Owen, 1971, Bobbs-Merrill, 1972; (with David Le Vay) Colette, *The Thousand and One Mornings,* Bobbs-Merrill, 1973.

Contributor to *Spectator, Observer* (London).

WORK IN PROGRESS: Books on Raymond Radiguet, modern French women writers, and the painter, Giorgio de Chirico.

SIDELIGHTS: Miss Crosland told *CA:* "I write and translate in order to support myself. I specialize in French and Italian subjects and translations. Hobbies seem to me ridiculous. I am totally absorbed by my work which takes in music and painting in addition to literature."

* * *

CROSS, Victor
See Coffman, Virginia (Edith)

* * *

CROSSMAN, R(ichard) H(oward) S(tafford) 1907-1974

December 15, 1907—April 5, 1974; British politician and author. Obituaries: *New York Times,* April 6, 1974; *Current Biography,* June, 1974.

* * *

CRUMP, (Stephen) Thomas 1929-

PERSONAL: Born September 26, 1929, in London, England; son of Norman Easedale and Kathleen Mary St. Patrick (Hodson) Crump; married Carolina Prakke, September 29, 1972; children: Maarten Thomas. *Education:* Trinity College, Cambridge, student, 1949-53, M.A., 1956, further study, 1966-68; University of Michigan, LL.M., 1954; University of London, further graduate study, 1969—. *Politics:* "Jeffersonian." *Religion:* Agnostic. *Home:* P.C. Hooftsraat 167, Amsterdam, Netherlands. *Agent:* A. D. Peters, 10 Buckingham St., London W.C.2, England. *Office:* Keizersgracht 397, Amsterdam, Netherlands.

CAREER: Director of Africa Intelligence Service, 1956-64; barrister-at-law, 1958-66; University of Amsterdam, Amsterdam, Netherlands, lecturer in cultural anthropology, 1972—. *Military service:* British Army, Royal Signal Corps, 1948-49; became second lieutenant. *Member:* Royal Geographical Society (fellow), Royal Anthropological Institute, Nederlandse Sociologische-Antropologische Vereniging.

WRITINGS: The Law for Everyman, Collins, 1963; (with G. S. A. Wheatcroft) *The Law of Income Tax, Profits Tax, and Surtax,* Sweet & Maxwell, 1963; *Man and His Kind,* Praeger, 1973.

WORK IN PROGRESS: Research on use of money in peasant communities in Southern Mexico, on micro-economic changes in Tuscany, and on traditional forces in English professional organizations.

SIDELIGHTS: Crump's interests are the ways in which people earn their livings, and the ways in which they use language. He has studied people in Europe, North and Central America, and Africa; languages he has studied include Indo-European, Semitic, Maya, and Bantu.

CULBERTSON, Manie 1927-

PERSONAL: Born December 26, 1927, in Shreveport, La.; daughter of Sam Pickles (a planter) and Mary Myrtle (Guy) Lyles; married James Forrest Culbertson (general manager of a safety equipment company), May 31, 1947; children: Kurt Douglas. *Education:* Louisiana State University, B.S., 1949; Northwestern State College, M.Ed., 1962, further graduate study, 1967. *Religion:* Methodist. *Home:* 9512 Holly Oak Dr., Shreveport, La. 71108. *Office:* Ridgewood Junior High School, 2001 Ridgewood Dr., Shreveport, La. 71108.

CAREER: High school teacher of language arts in Vinton, La., 1949-50, Winnie-Stowell, Tex., 1950-52, Blanchard, La., 1955-67, and Shreveport, La., 1967-71; Ridgewood Junior High School, Shreveport, La., language arts teacher and social studies coordinator, 1971—. *Member:* Louisiana Teachers Association, Caddo Teachers Association, Phi Kappa Phi, Alpha Delta Kappa, Phi Upsilon Omicron, Kappa Delta Pi. *Awards, honors:* Golden Apple Parent Teacher Award, 1973, for being one of ten outstanding teachers in Louisiana.

WRITINGS: May I Speak?, Pelican, 1972.

WORK IN PROGRESS: Our Louisiana Heritage, a multilevel and multi-discipline social studies textbook for eighth-graders, completion expected in 1974.

* * *

CULLEN, Joseph P(atrick) 1920-

PERSONAL: Born December 15, 1920, in New York, N.Y.; son of John and Margaret Cullen; married Virginia Herrick (a registered nurse), April 4, 1942; children: Patricia, Margaret (Mrs. James Walker), John. *Education:* Syracuse University, B.A., 1947, M.A., 1948. *Politics:* Conservative. *Home:* 1418 College Ave., Fredericksburg, Va. 22401. *Office:* National Park Service, Federal Building, Richmond, Va. 23240.

CAREER: National Park Service, Richmond, Va., historian, 1958—. *Military service:* U.S. Army Air Forces, 1942-46; B-29 pilot in the South Pacific, 1944-46; became captain. *Awards, honors:* Distinguished service award from Civil War Round Table, Chicago, Ill., 1968.

WRITINGS: The Concise Illustrated History of the American Revolution, Stackpole, 1972; *The Peninsula Campaign, 1862,* Stackpole, 1973. Contributor to historical journals.

WORK IN PROGRESS: Cold Harbor Campaign, 1864, completion expected in 1975; a history of Chimborazo Hospital, Richmond, Va., 1861-65, completion expected in 1976.

* * *

CUMMINGS, Florence
See BONIME, Florence

* * *

CUNNINGHAM, Cathy
See CUNNINGHAM, Chet

* * *

CUNNINGHAM, Chet 1928- (Cathy Cunningham)

PERSONAL: Born December 9, 1928, in Shelby, Neb.;

son of Merle Burritt and Hazel (Zedicher) Cunningham; married Rose Marie Wilhoit, January 18, 1953; children: Gregory, Scott, Christine. *Education:* Pacific University, B.A., 1950; Columbia University, M.S., 1954. *Religion:* Methodist. *Home and office:* 8431 Beaver Lake Dr., San Diego, Calif. 92119. *Agent:* Don Sheperd, 18645 Sherman Way, Suite 210, Reseda, Calif. 91335.

CAREER: *News-Times,* Forest Grove, Ore., city editor, 1954-55; Jam Handy, Detroit, Mich., writer of educational and church films, and sales training materials, 1955-59; Convair, San Diego, Calif., writer in motion picture section, 1959-60; Cunningham Press, San Diego, Calif., publisher and writer, 1960—. Free-lance writer, 1960—. Chairman of San Diego Writers Workshop, 1962—. *Military service:* U.S. Army, 1950-52; became sergeant.

WRITINGS—Fiction: *Bushwhackers at Circle K,* Avalon Books, 1969; *Killer's Range,* Avalon Books, 1970; *Gold Wagon,* Pinnacle Books, 1972; *Blood on the Strip,* Pinnacle Books, 1973; (under pseudonym Cathy Cunningham) *Demons of Highpoint House,* Popular Library, 1973; *Dead Start Scramble* (juvenile), Scholastic Press, 1973; *Fatal Friday,* Venice Publishing, 1973; *Die of Gold,* Pinnacle Books, 1973; *Hijacking Manhattan,* Pinnacle Books, 1974; *Terror in Tokyo,* Pinnacle Books, 1974; *Baja Bike* (juvenile), Putnam, 1974.

Juvenile nonfiction: *Your Wheels,* Putnam, 1973; *Your Bike,* Putnam, in press.

Author of monthly column "Truck Talk," appearing in numerous trade magazines, 1956—; author of ghost-written column "Your Car," appearing in a number of weekly and daily newspapers, 1959—.

WORK IN PROGRESS: Three novels, *One Fine Killing, Chirichaua Gold,* and *Mansions of Demons.*

* * *

CUNNINGHAM, Robert M(aris), Jr. 1909-

PERSONAL: Born May 28, 1909, in Chicago, Ill.; son of Robert Maris (a businessman) and Beda (Dickson) Cunningham; married Deborah Libby, November 24, 1934; children: Dennis, Damon, Margaret (deceased), Robert Maris III. *Education:* University of Chicago, Ph.B., 1931. *Home:* 2126 North Dayton St., Chicago, Ill. 60614. *Office:* McGraw-Hill Publications Co., 230 West Monroe St., Chicago, Ill. 60606.

CAREER: Armour Institute of Technology (now Illinois Institute of Technology), Chicago, Ill., assistant to president, 1932-34; Shell Petroleum Co., Chicago, Ill., employed in sales and promotion, 1934-37; Chicago Blue Cross, Chicago, Ill., director of public relations, 1938-41; American Medical Association, Chicago, Ill., associate editor, *Hygeia,* 1941-45; McGraw-Hill Publications Co., Chicago, Ill., managing editor of *Modern Hospital,* 1945-51, editor, 1951—, publisher, 1963-67, editorial director and publisher of *Nation's Schools,* 1963-67, publisher of *College and University Business,* 1963-67, editorial director, 1967—, editor of *Modern Nursing Home,* 1964—, publisher, 1964-67. Vice-president and member of board of directors, F. W. Dodge Corp., 1959-63. Lecturer on hospital administration at Northwestern University and University of Chicago, 1946—; consultant to American College of Surgeons, 1955-59, and to Blue Cross and U.S. Department of Health, Education, and Welfare.

MEMBER: National Association of Science Writers, Health Industries Association (member of board of directors, 1966-69; president, 1968-69), American College of Hospital Administrators (honorary fellow), American Hospital Association (honorary member), Psi Upsilon.

WRITINGS: *Hospitals, Doctors and Dollars,* F. W. Dodge, 1961; *The Third World of Medicine,* McGraw, 1968. Contributor of articles on medical and hospital topics to journals.

* * *

CURRY, Paul 1917-

PERSONAL: Born August 19, 1917, in New York, N.Y.; son of John S. (manager for New York Telephone Co.) and Anna (Delaney) Curry; married Martina Neuberg, September 30, 1937; children: Kevin, Myles. *Education:* Columbia University, student, 1935-36; University of Michigan, special degree, 1962. *Politics:* "Any party that Nixon doesn't belong to." *Home:* 201 East 28th St., New York, N.Y. 10016. *Office:* Blue Cross, 40th St. and Third Ave., New York, N.Y. 10017.

CAREER: Blue Cross (health insurance company), New York, N.Y., vice-president, 1938—.

WRITINGS: *Something Borrowed, Something New,* privately printed, 1936; *Magicians Magic,* F. Watts, 1968. Author of column in *Phoenix.*

WORK IN PROGRESS: A book on mindreading and precognition; *They,* a book on the inner workings of modern business.

* * *

CURRY-LINDAHL, Kai 1917-

PERSONAL: Born May 10, 1917, in Stockholm, Sweden; son of Kossuth (a banker) and Margit (Toernblom) Curry-Lindahl; married Anne van der Voordt, September 3, 1947; children: Brigitte (Mrs. Sven Malmberg), Edithe, Robin. *Education:* Educated at Sigtuna College, and University of Lund in Sweden, and Lycee Chateaubriand, Rome; University of Uppsala, Ph.D. *Home:* Skansen, Stockholm, Sweden; and Lyall House, Nairobi, Kenya. *Office:* Nordiska Museum and Skansen, Stockholm, Sweden; and United Nations Environment Programme, P.O. Box 30552, Nairobi, Kenya.

CAREER: Natur och Kultur Publishing House, Stockholm, Sweden, editor, 1937-44; Svensk Natur Publishing House, Stockholm, Sweden, director, 1945-53; Nordiska Museum and Skansen, Stockholm, Sweden, director of department of natural history, 1953—. United Nations, UNESCO expert in ecology and conservation, Paris, France, and Nairobi, Kenya, 1970-73, senior adviser for UN Environmental Programme, Nairobi, 1974—. Leader of Lund University Congo expedition, 1951-52, and Swedish Congo expedition, 1958-59. Member of executive board, International Union for Conservation of Nature and Natural Resources (Switzerland), 1956-63, vice-chairman of Survival Service Commission, 1963-72, and of International Commission on National Parks, 1966-72; secretary of International Council for Bird Preservation (London and Washington, D.C.), 1958—, chairman of Swedish section, 1968—; member of executive board, International Wildfowl Research Bureau (England), 1958—, and Charles Darwin Foundation for the Galapagos Isles (France), 1960—; first vice-chairman of European Committee for the Conservation of Nature and Natural Resources, Council of Europe, 1962-64; member of executive board, World Wildlife Fund, 1964-71, honorary consultant, 1971—; member of executive board of other scientific institutions, foundations, and academies in Sweden, Zaire, United States, India, Romania, South Africa, Kenya, Tanzania; visiting professor, University of California, Berkeley, 1974—. *Military service:* Swedish Army, 1939-45.

MEMBER: International Association for Ecology, International Society for Tropical Ecology, Europaeische Gesellschaft fuer Saugetierschutz, Scandinavian Herpetological Society (vice-chairman, 1947-59; member of executive board, 1959-65), Swedish Society for Conservation of Nature (member of executive board, 1957—), Ornithological Society of Sweden (member of executive board, 1945—), Ecological Society of Scandinavia, American Institute of Biological Sciences, Zoological Society of America, American Society of Mammalogists, American Ornithologists' Union, American Society of Ichthyologists and Herpetologists, British Ecological Society, British Herpetological Society, Societe Belgo-Suedoise (Stockholm; vice-chairman, 1960—), Fauna Society (Stockholm; secretary, 1943-50); member or honorary member of other ecological and zoological associations in United States, Great Britain, France, Switzerland, Germany, Belgium, Denmark, Finland, Italy, Netherlands, Norway, Sweden, India, Kenya, South Africa, Zambia, Australia.

AWARDS, HONORS: Literary Prize from Swedish Fund of Authors (government prize), 1956; Order of the Crown (Belgium), 1961; Silver Medal of Royal Swedish Academy of Science, 1962; Gold Medal Geoffroy St. Hilaire (France), 1963; Order of Leopold (Belgium), 1964; Silver Medal of Swedish Society for Conservation of Nature, 1973; Order of the Golden Ark (Netherlands), 1973; Order of the Polar Star (Sweden), 1973; and other decorations and awards bestowed in Africa, Europe, and North America.

WRITINGS: Naagra svenska Faaglar (title means "Swedish Birds"), Natur & Kultur, 1947.

Fiskarna i faerg (title means "The Fishes of Sweden"), Almqvist & Wiksell, 1953, 7th edition, 1970; *Tropiska fjaell* (title means "Tropical Mountains"), Gebers, 1953; *Djuren i faerg—daeggdjuer, kraeldjuer, groddjuer* (title means "The Mammals, Reptiles and Amphibians of Sweden"), Almqvist & Wiksell, 1955, 6th edition, 1970; *Djuren och maenniskan i svensk natur* (title means "Animals and Man in Swedish Nature"), Hoekerberg, 1955; *Ecological Studies on Mammals, Birds, Reptiles and Amphibians in the Eastern Belgian Congo,* Annales du Musee Royal d'Afrique Centrale (Tervuren, Belgium), Volume I, 1956, Volume II, 1960; *Zoogeography: Population Dynamic and Recent Faunal Changes,* Ymer, 1958; *The Vertebrate Fauna of the Sarek Mountains and the Padjelanta Plain in Swedish Lapland,* Fauna & Flora, 1958.

Sarek, Raben & Sjogren, 1960, 2nd edition, 1961; *Flyttfaaglarnas tropiska vinterhem* (title means "The Tropical Winter Quarters of the Migratory Birds"), Folket, 1961; *Skogar och djur* (title means "Forests and Animals"), Swedish Tourist Association, 1961; *Contribution a l'Etude des Vertebres Terrestres en Afrique Tropicale,* Institut des Parcs Nationaux du Congo et du Ruanda-Urundi, Volume I: *Exploration du Parc National Albert et du Parc National de la Kagera,* 1961; *Arktis och Tropik* (title means "The Arctic and the Tropics"), Bonniers, 1963; *Nordens djurvaerld* (title means "The Animal World of Scandinavia"), Forum, 1963, 3rd edition in two volumes, 1969; (with Sixten Jonsson) *Djuren paa Skansen* (title means "The Animals of Skansen"), Lts Foerlag , 1963; *Europe: A Natural History,* Random House, 1964; *Fjaell och savann: Natur och naturvaard varlden runt* (title means "Mountains and Savannas: Nature and Nature Conservation in the World"), Natur & Kultur, 1968; *Sarek, Stora Sjofallet, Padjelanta* (on three national parks in Swedish Lapland), Raben & Sjogren, 1968, 2nd edition, 1971.

Sjaunja och Kaitum (on Europe's largest nature reserve), Raben & Sjogren, 1971; *Conservation for Survival: An Ecological Strategy,* Morrow, 1972; *Let Them Live: A Worldwide Survey of Animals Threatened with Extinction,* Morrow, 1972; (with Jean-Paul Harroy) *National Parks of the World,* two volumes, Golden Press, 1972; *Aen lever jorden!* (title means "The Earth Is Still Alive!"), Natur & Kultur, 1973; *Birds Over Land and Sea: Migrations Throughout the World,* International Book Production, in press; *The Mammals of Europe,* Almqvist & Wiksell, in press; *The Amphibians and Reptiles of Europe,* Almqvist & Wiksell, in press; *The Scandanavian Lemming,* Bonniers, in press.

Editor and co-author—"Natural History" series, published by Svensk Natur: (With Bengt Pettersson) *Natur paa Gotland,* 1946; (with Bertil Hanstroem) *Natur i Skaane,* 1947; (with Erik Rosenberg) *Natur i Naerke,* 1947; (with Sven Hoerstadius) *Natur i Uppland,* 1948; (with Ragnar Arbman) *Natur i Jaemtland,* 1948; (with Carl Fries) *Natur i Oestergoetland,* 1949; (with Karl-Herman Forsslund) *Natur i Dalarna,* 1949; (with Albert Eklundh) *Natur i Smaaland,* 1950; (with Eric Persson) *Natur i Gaestrikland,* 1950; (with Per Olof Swanberg) *Natur i Vaestergoetland,* 1951; (with Tore Arnborg) *Natur i Haelsingland och Haerjedalen,* 1951; (with Sten Bergman) *Natur i Soedermanland,* 1952; (with Carl Skottsberg) *Natur i Halland,* 1952; (with Olof Elofson) *Natur i Aangermanland och Medelpad,* 1953; (with Nils-Gerhard Karvik) *Natur i Dalsland,* 1953; (with Nils H. Magnusson) *Natur i Vaermland,* 1954; (with Richard Sterner) *Natur paa Oeland,* 1955; (with Fredrik Ebeling) *Natur i Vaesterbotten och Norrbotten,* 1956; (with Hans Wachtmeister) *Natur i Blekinge,* 1957; (with Bertil Wallden) *Natur i Vaestmanland,* 1958; (with Carl Skottsberg) *Natur i Bohuslaen,* 1959. Curry-Lindahl was sole author of another volume in the series, *Natur i Lappland,* 1963.

Editor and co-author—Other books: *Vaara Faaglar i Norden* (title means "The Birds of Scandinavia"), four volumes, Natur & Kultur, 1942-47, 2nd edition, 1959-63; (with Carl Edelstam) *Foerteckning oever Sveriges faaglar* (title means "Check List of the Birds of Sweden"), Svensk Natur, 1951; (with Sven Ekmen) *Djurens Liv* (title means "The Life of Animals"), five volumes, 6th edition (Curry-Lindahl was not associated with earlier editions), Sohlman, 1955-57.

Also editor and co-author of six Swedish editions of translated books on the natural history of various continents published by Natur & Kultur, 1965-70.

Contributor: *Svenska Djurens. Faaglarna* (title means "Swedish Animals: Birds"), Norstedt, 1951, 2nd edition, 1959; *Vogels kijken in Europa,* Wetsnschappelijke Uitgeverij (Amsterdam), 1972; *Oekologie und Lebensschutz* (title means "Ecology and Bioprotection"), Rombach (Freiberg), 1973.

Writer of many monographs on natural history subjects, including one on the wilderness areas and institutions of North America, of booklets on national parks and conservation, and of ecology surveys and reports. Contributor to *Enciclopedia degli Uccelli d'Europa* and to journals. Regular reviewer for two American periodicals, *Journal of*

Wildlife Management, 1961—, and *Ecology,* 1966—; regular contributor to *Svenska Dagbladet* (Swedish newspaper), 1958—.

Editor, *Sveriges Natur* (yearbook and journal of Swedish Association for Conservation of Nature), 1943-52; co-editor, *Acta Vertebratica,* 1957-69.

WORK IN PROGRESS: Bird Migration in Africa; a section for Volume II of *Contribution a l'Etude des Vertebres Terrestres en Afrique Tropicale,* completion expected in 1976; *Herons of the World,* 1976; ecological studies on mammals, birds, reptiles and amphibians in the Eastern Zaire for Annales de Musee Royal de l'Afrique Centrale, 1976.

SIDELIGHTS: "All my books have been written on request by publishers," Curry-Lindahl says, "so I . . . regard my writing as a complementary part of my work for a better understanding of the natural environment and the ecological role animals play therein. My writing is also a sort of intellectual entertainment." His travels and expeditions cover "all continents and seas."

Europe: A Natural History, first published in America, is the mostly widely distributed of Curry-Lindahl's books, with editions in England, Germany, Switzerzerland, Netherlands, Belgium, Sweden, Finland, France, Spain, and Italy.

* * *

CUTLER, (May) Ebbitt 1923-

PERSONAL: Born September 4, 1923, in Montreal, Quebec, Canada; daughter of William Henry (a policeman) and Francis (Farrelley) Ebbitt; married Philip Cutler (an attorney), January 17, 1952; children: Keir, Michael, Adam, Roger. *Education:* McGill University, B.A. (first class honors), 1945, M.A., 1952; Columbia University, M.S., 1946. *Politics:* "Liberal; mildly socialist, mostly feminist." *Religion:* Atheist. *Home:* 3200 The Blvd., Westmount, Montreal, Quebec, Canada. *Agent:* Paul R. Reynolds, Inc., 599 Fifth Ave., New York, N.Y. 10017. *Office:* Tundra Books of Montreal, 1374 Sherbrooke St. W., Montreal, Quebec H3G 1J6, Canada.

CAREER: Canadian Press, Montreal, Quebec, and New York, N.Y., writer-editor, 1945-46; journalist on *Montreal Herald,* Montreal, 1947-48, *Standard,* Montreal, 1947-53; Tundra Books of Montreal, Montreal, founder, president, and editor-in-chief, 1967—; Tundra Books of Northern New York, Plattsburgh, N.Y., president, 1971—. *Awards, honors:* Canadian Centennial literary competitions first prize, 1967, for *The Last Noble Savage.*

WRITINGS: The Last Noble Savage, Tundra Books, 1967, reissued as *I Once Knew An Indian Woman,* Houghton, 1973. Contributor to *Canadian Art.*

WORK IN PROGRESS: Research on why Canada's literary output is so slim.

* * *

DABNEY, Joseph Earl 1929-

PERSONAL: Born January 29, 1929, in Kershaw, S.C.; son of Wade Vertell and Wincey (Hunter) Dabney; married Susanne Knight (a social caseworker), June 18, 1954; children: Geneva, Joseph Earl, Jr., Mark, Scott, Christopher. *Education:* Berry College, B.S., 1949. *Politics:* Democrat. *Religion:* Baptist. *Home:* 3966 St. Clair Ct., Atlanta, Ga. 30319. *Office:* Lockheed-Georgia Co., Marietta, Ga. 30063.

CAREER: Gainesville Daily Times, Gainesville, Ga., managing editor, 1954-56; *Florence Morning News,* Florence, S.C., managing editor, 1956-60, associate editor, 1961-62; *Atlanta Journal,* Atlanta, Ga., state news editor, 1963-64; Lockheed-Georgia Co., Marietta, Ga., public relations representative, 1965—. *Military service:* U.S. Army, 1960-62; served in Korea. *Member:* Professional Journalists Society, Southern Association of Business Communicators (vice-president, 1974; president-elect, 1975), Georgia Association of Business Communicators (president, 1969), South Carolina Associated Press Association (president, 1960), South Carolina Associated Press Association (president, 1960), Atlanta Press Club, Sigma Delta Chi. *Awards, honors:* Travel grant from Southern Association of Nieman Fellows, to Poland and the Soviet Union, 1958; Awards of Excellence for best industrial publication from Southern Association of Business Communicators, 1968, 1969, 1973; C. S. Bolen Award for outstanding chapter president from Southern Association of Business Communicators, 1969; International Association of Business Communicators Award of Merit, 1970.

WRITINGS: Mountain Spirits: A Chronicle of Corn Whiskey from King James' Ulster Plantation to America's Appalachians, Scribner, 1974. Contributor to popular magazines, including the *Atlanta Journal-Constitution Magazine, Kiwanis, Catholic Digest, Reader's Digest,* and *Atlanta.*

WORK IN PROGRESS: A book dealing with taped interviews, completion expected in 1976.

AVOCATIONAL INTERESTS: Appalachian history and folklore, folk art, reminiscences of older people.

* * *

DAHL, Gordon J. 1932-

PERSONAL: Born June 6, 1932, in Watertown, S.D.; son of William J. (a farmer) and Olga J. (Holen) Dahl; married Marlys Luedtke, June 13, 1954; children: David William, Mark Peter. *Education:* Augustana College, Sioux Falls, S.D., B.A. (with honors), 1954; Luther Theological Seminary, St. Paul, Minn., M.Th., 1960; University of Minnesota, M.A., 1967, Ph.D., 1974. *Home:* 8731 Summit Dr., Eden Prairie, Minn. 55343. *Office:* 1813 University Ave. S.E., Minneapolis, Minn. 55414.

CAREER: Ordained to Lutheran ministry, American Lutheran Church, 1961; University of Minnesota, Lutheran Campus Ministry, Minneapolis, senior pastor, 1968—; Leisure Studies, Inc., Minneapolis, Minn., executive director, 1971—; National Leisure Education Resource Center, Minneapolis, Minn., director, 1973—. *Member:* National Campus Ministry Association (member of executive committee, 1966-68), Lutheran Campus Ministry Staff Association (national chairman, 1967-68), American Association for Higher Education. *Awards, honors:* Danforth Foundation campus ministry grants, 1964, 1967.

WRITINGS: Work, Play and Worship in a Leisure-oriented Society, Augsburg, 1972; *Ministry in a Learning Society* (monograph), Lutheran Council in the U.S.A., 1973. Producer and narrator with Adele Mehta of multi-media presentation, "Introducing a Leisure Revolution," 1973. Contributor to *Christian Century, Dialog, Event, Cross-Talk, Counseling and Values,* and other periodicals.

WORK IN PROGRESS: Research on youth culture, leisure trends, post-industrial era values and institutions.

AVOCATIONAL INTERESTS: Wines (makes wine and teaches wine-making), sailing, swimming, camping.

DAHMS, Alan M(artin) 1937-

PERSONAL: Born July 2, 1937, in Council Bluffs, Iowa; son of G. M. (an investor) and Gladys (a poet; maiden name, York) Dahms; married Pollard Talton (an educator), January 26, 1973. *Education:* Gustavus Adolphus College, student, 1955-56; University of Colorado, B.A., 1960; Washington University, St. Louis, Mo., graduate study, 1958-59; University of Northern Colorado, M.A. and Ph.D. *Home:* 777 Washington St., #1102, Denver, Colo. 80203. *Office:* Department of Psychology, Metropolitan State College, 250 West 14th Ave., Denver, Colo. 80204.

CAREER: University of Colorado, Boulder, research associate in pharmacology, 1963-64; University of Northern Colorado, Greeley, counselor at counseling center, 1967-68, instructor in psychology, 1968-69; University of Florida, Gainesville, assistant professor of comprehensive logic and educational psychology, 1969-71; Metropolitan State College, Denver, associate professor, 1971-73, professor of psychology, 1973—, assistant chairman of department, 1973—, director of Center for Human Effectiveness, 1972—. Member of board of directors at Center of Man, 1970; member of executive board of Colorado Consortium of Higher Education, 1972-74, chairman of board of directors, 1974—; member of board of directors of Granfalloon Denver Educational Broadcasting, 1973—; vice-president of board of directors of Gestalt Institute of Denver, 1973—. Past member of Brush, Colorado Chamber of Commerce. Has appeared on numerous radio programs and on Canadian television. *Military service:* U.S. Navy, 1961-64.

MEMBER: American Psychological Association, Association of Humanistic Psychology, American Personnel and Guidance Association, Student Personnel Association for Teacher Education, American College Personnel Association, National Association of Student Personnel Administrators (affiliate), Association for Supervision and Curriculum Development, American Association of University Professors, American Educational Research Association, Southwestern Psychological Association, Florida Educational Research Association, Jefferson County Self-Help Association (member of board of governors, 1972—), Phi Beta Kappa, Phi Delta Kappa, Psi Chi.

WRITINGS: Emotional Intimacy: Overlooked Requirement for Survival, Shields Publishing, 1972; (contributor) G. Belkin, editor, *Foundations of Counseling,* Kendall-Hunt, 1973; (contributor) E. A. Powers and M. W. Less, editors, *The Process of Relationships,* West Publishing, 1974; *Thriving: Beyond Adjustment,* Wiley, in press. Contributor of articles and reviews to professional journals, including *Educational Leadership, Phi Delta Kappan, Journal of College Student Personnel, Human Context,* and *Journal of the Student Personnel Association for Teacher Education.*

AVOCATIONAL INTERESTS: Flying (as pilot), sculpting.

* * *

DALLMAYR, Fred R(einhard) 1928-

PERSONAL: Born October 18, 1928, in Ulm, Germany; son of Albert (a realtor) and Olga (Schnell) Dallmayr; married Ilse Balzer, August 24, 1957; children: Dominique Brigit, Philip Gregory. *Education:* Attended University of Brussels, 1953-54; University of Munich, LL.D., 1955; Southern Illinois University, M.A., 1956; Duke University, Ph.D., 1960. *Home:* 3944 Pasadena Dr., Lafayette, Ind. 47905. *Office:* Department of Political Science, Purdue University, West Lafayette, Ind. 47907.

CAREER: Milwaukee-Downer College, Milwaukee, Wis., instructor, 1961-62, assistant professor of political science, 1962-63; Purdue University, Lafayette, Ind., assistant professor, 1963-65, associate professor, 1965-68, professor of political science, 1968-71; University of Georgia, Athens, professor of political science, 1971-73; Purdue University, professor of political science, 1973—, chairman of department, 1974—. Visiting professor, University of Hamburg, 1969, 1971. *Member:* American Political Science Association, American Sociological Association, Conference for the Study of Political Thought, Society for Phenomenology and Existential Philosophy, Phi Beta Kappa.

WRITINGS: (With Robert S. Rankin) *Freedom and Emergency Powers,* Appleton, 1964; (contributor) R. Koselleck and R. Schnur, editors, *Hobbes-Forschungen* (title means "Essays on Hobbes"), Duncker & Humblot, 1969; (contributor) Carl Beck, editor, *Law and Justice,* Duke University Press, 1970; (contributor) Glen Gordon and William E. Connolly, editors, *Social Structure and Political Life,* Heath, 1973; (contributor) George Psathas, editor, *Phenomenological Sociology,* Wiley, 1973; (contributor) E. S. Casey and D. Carr, editors, *Explorations in Phenomenology,* Nijhoff, 1974; (editor and author of introduction and epilogue) *Materialienband zu Habermas' Erkenntnis und Interesse* (title means "Essays on Habermas' 'Knowledge and Human Interests'"), Suhrkamp, 1974. Contributor to *Law and Contemporary Problems, Ethics, Journal of General Education, Journal of Politics, Polity, Politics and Society, Man and World, Philosophy of the Social Sciences, Philosophische Rundschau, Human Context,* and *Inquiry.*

WORK IN PROGRESS: A book, *Equality and the Civic Culture: Rise and Decline of Public Discourse in America and France, 1750-1930; Beyond Dogma and Despair: Toward a Critical Theory of Politics.*

* * *

D'AMATO, Janet 1925-

PERSONAL: Born June 5, 1925, in Rochester, N.Y.; daughter of Earle H. and Florence (an artist; maiden name, Cowles) Potter; married Alex D'Amato (a book designer), February 28, 1949; children: Sandra (Mrs. Harry Tompkins, Jr.), Donna. *Education:* Pratt Institute, diploma, 1946. *Residence:* Bronxville, N.Y.

CAREER: Display designer; Art Studio, Mt. Vernon, N.Y., illustrator for filmstrips, 1946-47; free-lance artist, 1952—.

WRITINGS—With husband, Alex D'Amato: *U.S.A. Fun and Play,* Doubleday, 1960; *Animal Fun Time,* Doubleday, 1964; *Fun Till Christmas,* Whitman Publishing, 1965; *Cardboard Carpentry,* Lion Press, 1966; *Handicrafts for Holidays,* Lion Press, 1967; *Indian Crafts,* Lion Press, 1968; *African Crafts for You to Make,* Messner, 1968; *African Animals Through African Eyes,* Messner, 1971; *What's in the Sky,* Nutmeg Press, 1971; *Houses,* Nutmeg Press, 1971; *Animals,* Nutmeg Press, 1971; *American Indian Craft Inspirations,* M. Evans, 1972; *Gifts to Make for Love or Money,* Golden Press, 1973; *Colonial Crafts for You to Make,* Messner, in press; *Art of Quilling,* M. Evans, in press; *Weather and Weather Forecasting,* Nutmeg Press, in press.

Illustrator: Sophie Ruskay, *Discovery at Aspen,* A. S.

Barnes, 1960; Shari Lewis and Jacquelyn Reinach, *Headstart Book of Looking and Listening,* McGraw, 1960; Constantine Georgiou, *Wait and See,* Harvey House, 1962; Azriel Eisenberg, editor, *Tzedakah,* Behrman, 1963; (with husband, Alex D'Amato) Hyman Ruchlis, *Your Changing Earth,* Harvey House, 1963; (with Alex D'Amato) Mary Elting, *Water Come, Water Go,* Harvey House, 1964; (with Alex D'Amato) Elting, *Aircraft at Work,* Harvey House, 1964; (with Alex D'Amato) Norah Smaridge, *The Light Within,* Hawthorne, 1965; Joan W. Jenkins, *A Girls' World,* Hawthorne, 1967; Samm S. Baker, *Miracle Gardening Encyclopedia,* Grosset, 1967; Arthur Liebers, *50 Favorite Hobbies,* Hawthorne, 1968. Also creator, with husband, of kits and book and record cover designs.

Contributor to *Creative Crafts* and *Humpty Dumpty.*

SIDELIGHTS: Janet D'Amato wrote: "I believe. . .today's desires to establish roots with the past can be partly satisfied by understanding and actually working with old craft techniques and motifs."

* * *

DANIELOU, Jean 1905-1974

May 14, 1905—May 20, 1974; French theologian, historian, and cardinal of the Roman Catholic Church. Obituaries: *New York Times,* May 21, 1974; *Washington Post,* May 21, 1974; *Time,* June 3, 1974. (*CA*-23/24).

* * *

DANIELS, Jonathan 1902-

PERSONAL: Born April 26, 1902, in Raleigh, N.C.; son of Josephus (an editor and statesman) and Addie (Bagley) Daniels; married Elizabeth Bridgers, September 7, 1923 (died, 1929); married Lucy Billing Cathcart (an editorial researcher), April 30, 1932; children: (first marriage) Elizabeth (Mrs. C. B. Squire); (second marriage) Lucy (Mrs. Thomas Inman), Adelaide (Mrs. B. J. Key), Mary Cleves (Mrs. Steven Weber). *Education:* University of North Carolina, A.B., 1921, M.A., 1922; Columbia University, graduate study, 1923. *Politics:* Democrat. *Religion:* Episcopalian. *Agent:* Brandt & Brandt, 101 Park Ave., New York, N.Y. 10017. *Office: News and Observer,* Box 191, Raleigh, N.C. 27602.

CAREER: Louisville Times, Louisville, Ky., reporter, 1922-23; *News and Observer,* Raleigh, N.C., reporter and sports editor, 1923-25, Washington correspondent, 1925-28; *Fortune,* New York, N.Y., staff writer, 1930-31; *News and Observer,* associate editor, 1932, editor, 1933-42; associate director, Office of Civilian Defense, 1942; administrative assistant and press secretary to President Franklin D. Roosevelt, 1943-45; *News and Observer,* executive editor, 1947-48, editor, 1948-69, editor emeritus, 1969—. U.S. representative on United Nations Subcommission on Prevention of Discrimination and Protection of Minorities, 1947-53; member of Federal Hospital Council of U.S. Public Health Service, 1950-53. Democratic National committeeman from North Carolina, 1949-52; active in presidential campaigns of Harry S Truman in 1948 and Adlai Stevenson in 1952. *Awards, honors:* Guggenheim fellowship for study in France, Italy, and Switzerland, 1930.

WRITINGS: Clash of Angels (novel), Brewer & Warren, 1930; *A Southerner Discovers the South,* Macmillan, 1938; *A Southerner Discovers New England,* Macmillan, 1940; *Tar Heels: A Portrait of North Carolina,* Dodd, 1941; *Frontier on the Potomac,* Macmillan, 1946; *The Man of Independence,* Lippincott, 1950; *The End of Innocence,* Lippincott, 1954; *The Forest Is the Future,* International Paper Co., 1957; *Prince of Carpetbaggers,* Lippincott, 1958; *Mosby: Gray Ghost of the Confederacy,* Lippincott, 1959; *Stonewall Jackson,* Random House, 1959; *Robert E. Lee,* Houghton, 1960; *October Recollections,* Bostick & Thornley, 1961; *The Devil's Backbone: The Story of the Natchez Trace,* McGraw, 1962; *They Will Be Heard,* McGraw, 1964; *The Time Between the Wars,* Doubleday, 1966; *Washington Quadrille: The Dance Beside the Documents,* Doubleday, 1967; *Ordeal of Ambition,* Doubleday, 1970; *The Randolphs of Virginia,* Doubleday, 1972.

WORK IN PROGRESS: Two books, memoirs based on World War II White House days, for Doubleday, and a collection of essays, *The Gentlemanly Serpent,* for University of South Carolina Press.

* * *

DANIELS, R(obertson) Balfour 1900-

PERSONAL: Born August 6, 1900, in Princeton, N.J.; son of Winthrop More (an economist) and Joan (Robertson) Daniels; married Lola Burran, June 3, 1936; children: Penelope (Mrs. P. D. Pearson), David Winthrop. *Education:* Princeton University, A.B. (high honors), 1922; Yale University, LL.B., 1925, M.A., 1932, Ph.D., 1934. *Religion:* Episcopalian. *Home:* 20 North Wynden Dr., Houston, Tex. 77027.

CAREER: Admitted to the Bar of New York State, 1926; Hornblower, Miller & Garrison (law firm), New York, N.Y., law clerk, 1925-26; Larkin, Rathbone & Perry (law firm), New York, N.Y., law clerk, 1927-29; University of Tennessee, Knoxville, instructor in English, 1935; Edinburg College, Edinburg, Tex., head of department of English, 1935-37; Kansas State Teachers College, Pittsburg, associate professor of English, 1937-39; University of Houston, Houston, Tex., assistant professor, 1939-46, associate professor, 1946-47, professor of English, 1947-70, professor emeritus, 1970—, associate dean of College of Arts and Sciences, 1950-51, dean, 1951-58, dean of Graduate School, 1958-69. *Military service:* Student Army Training Corps., 1918. U.S. Army Air Forces, 1942-46; became major. U.S. Air Force Reserve, 1955-59; became lieutenant colonel. *Member:* Modern Language Association of America, American Name Society, Conference of College Teachers of English, American Legion, South-Central Modern Language Association, Phi Eta Sigma, Phi Delta Phi, Phi Kappa Phi, Cosmos Club (Washington, D.C.), Princeton Club of New York, Princeton Tower Club, Nassau Club (Princeton), Briar Club (Houston), Torch Club (Houston).

WRITINGS: Some Seventeenth-Century Worthies, University of North Carolina Press, 1940, 2nd edition, Russell, 1971; *To the Dark Covert* (poems), Falmouth Publishing House, 1947. Contributor of articles, essays, poems, and short stories to periodicals. Editor of *South Central Bulletin* of South Central Modern Language Association, 1966-68.

WORK IN PROGRESS: Research on Samuel Butler (1835-1902), and on George Ade.

* * *

DANN, Jack 1945-

PERSONAL: Born February 15, 1945, in Johnson City, N.Y.; son of Murray I. (an attorney) and Edith (Nash)

Dann. *Education:* State University of New York at Binghamton, B.A., 1968, graduate study, 1971—; also attended St. John's Law School, Brooklyn, N.Y., 1969-70. *Home and office address:* P.O. Box 116, Southview Station, Binghamton, N.Y. 13903.

CAREER: Broome Community College, Binghamton, N.Y., instructor in writing and science fiction, 1972, 1974. Assistant professor at Cornell University, summer, 1973; lecturer for Science Fiction Writers Speakers Bureau, 1971—; has appeared on WSKG-Television and WOR-Radio. *Member:* Science Fiction Writers of America, World Future Society. *Awards, honors:* Novella *Junction* was named finalist for Nebula Award of Science Fiction Writers of America, 1973.

WRITINGS: (Editor) *Wandering Stars of Jewish Fantasy and Science Fiction* (Science Fiction Book Club selection), Harper, 1974.

Work is represented in anthologies, including *New Worlds Two,* edited by Michael Moorcock, Berkley, 1971; *Orbit Ten,* edited by Damon Knight, Putnam, 1972; *Orbit Eleven,* edited by Knight, Putnam, 1972; *New Worlds Three,* edited by Moorcock, Berkley, 1972; *Strange Bedfellows,* edited by Thomas N. Scortia, Random House, 1972; *New Worlds Five,* edited by Moorcock, Sphere, 1973, American edition edited by Moorcock and Charles Platt, Avon, 1974; *Showcase,* edited by Roger Elwood, Harper, 1973; *New Worlds Six,* edited by Moorcock and Platt, Sphere, 1973; *Last Dangerous Visions,* edited by Harlan Ellison, Harper, in press; *New Dimensions,* edited by Robert Silverberg, Harper, in press; *Epoch,* edited by Silverberg and Elwood, Putnam, in press.

Contributor to science fiction magazines. Managing editor of *Bulletin of the Science Fiction Writers of America.*

WORK IN PROGRESS: Editing *Faster than Light,* a science fiction anthology, with George Zebrowski, for Harper; *Junction,* a novel; *Starhiker,* for Bobbs-Merrill, first in a series of six novels; *Christs and Other Poems,* for Bellevue Press; *Hospital Songs,* poems; *Going Under,* a novel; editing *Future Power,* with Gardner Dozois, for Random House; editing *Speculative Fiction Yearbook,* with David Harris.

AVOCATIONAL INTERESTS: Books, futuristics, art, film, dance.

* * *

d'ARGYRE, Gilles
See KLEIN, Gerard

See KLEIN, Gerard

* * *

DARK, Philip J(ohn) C(rosskey) 1918-

PERSONAL: Born May 15, 1918, in London, England; son of John Noel (a British civil servant) and Annie (Crosskey) Dark; married Mavis Helena Beam, March 7, 1942; children: Gail Susan, Victoria Eve. *Education:* Attended Institut du Pantheon, Paris, 1936, Middlesex Hospital Medical School, London, 1936-38, St. John's Wood Art Schools, London, 1939, and St. Martin's School of Art and Central School of Art, both London, 1939-40; University of London, diploma in fine art, 1948; Yale University, M.A., 1950, Ph.D., 1954. *Office:* Department of Anthropology, Southern Illinois University, Carbondale, Ill. 62901.

CAREER: University College, West African Institute of Social and Economic Research, Ibadan, Nigeria, assistant registrar and administrative secretary, 1954-56; University of London, University College, London, England, research assistant, 1956, Leverhulme research fellow, 1956-57; University College, Ibadan, Nigeria, senior research fellow in department of history, 1957-60; Southern Illinois University, Carbondale, professor of anthropology, 1960—, curator of anthropology in University Museum, 1961-63, chairman of department of anthropology, 1963-66. Research associate in African ethnology, Field Museum of Natural History, 1963—. Has conducted field work or research in Europe, Canada, Mexico, Africa, British Columbia, New Guinea, and New Britain. Participant in symposia and international conferences. Consultant to museums in the United States, Canada, and Australia, and to UNESCO in West Irian. Member of board of directors, Human Relations Area Files, Inc., Council of Museum Anthropology, and Society for the Anthropology of Visual Communication. *Military service:* Royal Naval Volunteer Reserve, 1940-46; became lieutenant.

MEMBER: International African Institute, American Anthropological Association (fellow), Royal Anthropological Institute of Great Britain and Northern Ireland (fellow), American Ethnological Society, American Association of University Professors, Societe des Oceanistes, Nigerian Historical Society, Hakluyt Society, Papua and New Guinea Society, Central States Anthropological Society, Royal Naval Volunteer Reserve Officers Association, Sigma Xi. *Awards, honors:* Leverhulme grant to Mexico, 1958; National Science Foundation grants, 1962-63, 1963-64, 1966-67, 1968; grants from National Institute of Mental Health and Southern Illinois University, 1964; Sigma Xi-Kaplan research award, 1968; Wenner Gren Foundation grants, 1969, 1970, 1973.

WRITINGS: Bush Negro Art: An African Art in the Americas, Tiranti, 1954, 2nd edition, 1970, Transatlantic, 1971; *Mixtec Ethnohistory: A Method of Analysis of the Codical Art,* Oxford University Press, 1958; (with W. Forman and B. Forman) *Benin Art,* Spring House Books, 1960; *The Art of Benin,* Chicago Natural History Museum, 1962; (contributor) K. P. Wachsmann, editor, *Essays on Music and History in Africa,* Northwestern University Press, 1971; *An Introduction to Benin Art and Technology,* Clarendon Press, 1973; (contributor) Anthony Forge, editor, *Primitive Art and Society,* Oxford University Press, 1973; *Kilenge Art and Life: A Look at a New Guinea People,* Academy Editions, 1974; (contributor) Daniel F. McCall and Edna G. Bay, editors, *African Images: Essays in African Iconology,* Africana Publishing, in press.

Contributor to proceedings and to *Encyclopedia universale dell'arte* and *Encyclopedia of Papua and New Guinea.* Contributor to *American Antiquity, Man, Discovery, Africa South, American Anthropologist, Africana Journal,* and other publications. Associate of *Current Anthropology.*

WORK IN PROGRESS: Dictionary of Kilenge-English, English-Kilenge; a book on animals in Benin art, with Paula Ben Amos; an illustrated ethnography of the Kilenge, West New Britain; a two-part book on man, art, and culture; writing on visual anthropology and aesthetic criteria.

SIDELIGHTS: Dark has had one-man shows of his paintings in London and New Mexico. An exhibition of his New Guinea photographs, prepared for Southern Illinois University, is a Smithsonian Institution traveling exhibit for 1972-74; duplicate versions are being sponsored by The Royal Anthropological Institute of Great Britain and Ireland and the Australian National Museum.

DARLING, Edward 1907-

PERSONAL: Born June 19, 1907, in Roxbury, Mass.; son of Charles Balfour and Effie (MacNaughton) Darling; married Dorothea Parker; children: Nancy Joan (Mrs. Carl Hard, Jr.). *Education:* Dartmouth College, A.B., 1929; Harvard University, graduate study, 1930-31. *Politics:* Independent. *Religion:* Unitarian-Universalist. *Home:* 40 Wild Hunter Rd., Dennis, Mass. 02638. *Agent:* McIntosh & Otis, Inc., 19 East 41st St., New York, N.Y. 10017.

CAREER: Held a variety of odd jobs, 1931-34; teacher of English in high school in Bass River, Mass., 1934-39, and in junior high school in Belmont, Mass., 1939-45; Beacon Press, Boston, Mass., member of staff in sales and promotion, 1945-69, director, 1967-69; Unitarian-Universalist Association, Boston, Mass., director of department of publications, 1969-72.

WRITINGS: Three Old-Timers: Sandwich, Barnstable, Yarmouth, Wayside Studio, 1936; (with Chester Howland) *Thar She Blows,* Funk, 1951; *How We Fought for Our Schools,* Norton, 1954; *Old Quotes at Home,* Beacon Press, 1958; (with Ashley Montagu) *The Prevalence of Nonsense,* Harper, 1968; (with Montagu) *The Ignorance of Certainty,* Harper, 1970; *When Sparks Fly Upward,* Washburn, 1970.

WORK IN PROGRESS: Deja Vu: So What Else Is New?; People in Trouble.

SIDELIGHTS: Darling writes: "It seems to me that mankind is in trouble, but that circumstances have never been otherwise and that most of the trouble can be traced to irrational behavior or belief. Since the bizarre so often puts human behavior under the microscope, my focus has been on popular error—particularly the error of utter certainty when the best we can hope for is the highly probable. I like to prick the pompous and expose the folly; and I claim no immunity from inaccuracy myself."

* * *

DARYUSH, Elizabeth 1887-

PERSONAL: Born December 5, 1887, in London, England; daughter of Robert Seymour (the poet) and Mary Monica (Waterhouse) Bridges; married Ali Akbar Daryush, December 29, 1923. *Education:* Privately tutored. *Home:* Stockwell, Boar's Hill, Oxford, England.

WRITINGS: Verses, Oxford University Press, 1930, Second Book, 1932, Third Book, 1933, Fourth Book, 1934; *The Last Man and Other Verses,* Oxford University Press, 1936; *Verses,* sixth Book, privately printed, 1939; (foreword by Yvor Winters) *Selected Poems,* Morrow, 1947, revised and enlarged edition, Carcanet Press, 1972; *Verses,* Seventh Book, Carcanet Press, 1971.

SIDELIGHTS: Elizabeth Daryush lived several years in Persia.

BIOGRAPHICAL/CRITICAL SOURCES: American Review, January, 1937.

* * *

DAS, Durga 1900-1974

November 23, 1900—May 17, 1974; Indian journalist and editor. Obituaries: *New York Times,* May 18, 1974; *Washington Post,* May 19, 1974. (*CA*-29/32).

DASH, Joan 1925-

PERSONAL: Born July 18, 1925, in Brooklyn, N.Y.; daughter of Samuel (a lawyer) and Louise (Sachs) Zeiger; married Jay Gregory Dash (a professor of physics), June 23, 1945; children: Michael, Elizabeth, Tony. *Education:* Barnard College, B.A. (with honors), 1946. *Religion:* Jewish. *Home:* 4529 East Laurel Dr. N.E., Seattle, Wash. 98105. *Agent:* McIntosh & Otis, Inc., 18 East 41st, New York, N.Y. 10017.

MEMBER: Hadassah, Seattle Free-Lances, Phi Beta Kappa.

WRITINGS: A Life of One's Own: Three Gifted Women and the Men They Married, Harper, 1973. Contributor of stories and articles to journals.

* * *

DATER, Henry M. 1909(?)-1974

1909(?)—June 26, 1974; American historian and author. Obituaries: *Washington Post,* June 28, 1974.

* * *

DAUGHERTY, James Henry 1889-1974

June 1, 1889—February 21, 1974; American artist and illustrator of children's books. Obituaries: *New York Times,* February 22, 1974; *Publishers Weekly,* March 18, 1974; *Current Biography,* April, 1974; *AB Bookman's Weekly,* April 15, 1974.

* * *

d'AULAIRE, Edgar Parin 1898-

PERSONAL: Surname originally Parin, took mother's maiden name as professional name; born September 30, 1898, in Munich, Germany; came to United States, 1929; naturalized, 1939; son of Gino (an artist) and Ella (an artist; maiden name d'Aulaire) Parin; married Ingri Mortenson (an artist and author of children's books), July 24, 1925; children: Per Ola, Nils Maarten. *Education:* Attended Technological Institute of Munich, 1917-19, School of Applied Arts, Munich, 1919-22, Schule Hans Hofman, 1922-24, Ecole Andre Lhote, 1924-26, Ecole Pola Gauguin, 1926-27. *Home:* Lia Farm, 74 Mather Rd., Georgetown, Conn. 06829; and Upper Lea Farms, South Royalton, Vt. 05068 (summer).

CAREER: Artist, lecturer, author and illustrator of children's books in collaboration with wife, 1929—. As an artist, d'Aulaire worked as a book illustrator in Germany, 1922-26, painted two frescoes in Norway, 1926-27, and has had exhibitions of his work in Norway, Paris, France, and in America. *Member:* Author's Guild. *Awards, honors:* American Library Association's Caldecott Medal (jointly with wife) for best illustrated children's book of 1939, *Abraham Lincoln;* Catholic Library Association Regina Medal, 1970, for "continued distinguished contribution to children's literature."

WRITINGS—All self-illustrated children's books; all with wife, Ingri d'Aulaire: *The Magic Rug,* Doubleday, 1931; *Ola,* Doubleday, 1932; *Ola and Blakken and Line, Sine, Trine,* Doubleday, 1933; *The Conquest of the Atlantic,* Viking, 1933; *The Lord's Prayer,* Doubleday, 1934; *Children of the Northlights,* Viking, 1935, new edition, 1963; *George Washington,* Doubleday, 1936; (editors) Peter Christen Asbjoernsen and J. E. Moe, *East of the Sun and West of the Moon,* Viking, 1938, reprinted, 1969; *Abraham*

Lincoln, Doubleday, 1939, new edition, 1957; *Animals Everywhere,* Doubleday, 1940; *Leif the Lucky,* Doubleday, 1941, new edition, 1951; *Star Spangled Banner,* Doubleday, 1942; *Don't Count Your Chicks,* Doubleday, 1943; *Wings for Per,* Doubleday, 1944; *Too Big,* Doubleday, 1945; *Pocahontas,* Doubleday, 1946; *Nils,* Doubleday, 1948; *Foxie,* Doubleday, 1949; *Benjamin Franklin,* Doubleday, 1950; *Buffalo Bill,* Doubleday, 1952; *The Two Cars,* Doubleday, 1955; *Columbus,* Doubleday, 1955; *The Magic Meadow,* Doubleday, 1958; *Ingri and Edgar Parin d'Aulaire's Book of Greek Myths,* Doubleday, 1962; *Norse Gods and Giants,* Doubleday, 1967; *D'Aulaire's Trolls,* Doubleday, 1972.

Illustrator: John Matheson, *Needle in the Haystack,* Morrow, 1930; Katie Seabrook, *Gao of the Ivory Coast,* Coward, 1931; Dhan Gopal Mukerji, *Rama, the Hero of India,* Dutton, 1930; Hanns H. Ewers, *Blood,* Heron Press, 1930; Florence McClurg Everson and Howard Everson, *Coming of the Dragon Ships,* Dutton, 1931; Nora Burglon, *Children of the Soil,* Doubleday, 1932.

SIDELIGHTS: d'Aulaire told *CA:* "Both my parents were artists, it never occurred to me to be anything but an artist. I grew up in the art centres of Europe—Paris, Florence, Munich, mostly Munich. I made my first picture book when I was 12—it described the adventures of my grandmother as she drove in a buggy across the prairie, pursued by Indians. It was very favorably received—by my family. As a grown-up I never thought of doing children's books. I painted frescoes and did lithographs for sophisticated limited editions. I married an art student who was very fond of children and planned to specialize in children's portraits.

"When we came to the U.S. we met the most outstanding authorities in books for children. [They] persuaded us to do books for children. Research for our books has taken us back to Europe many times, also to North Africa, and across the U.S. and to central America."

AVOCATIONAL INTERESTS: Landscaping, forestry, and working a large farm in Vermont.

* * *

d'AULAIRE, Ingri (Mortenson) 1904-

PERSONAL: Born December 27, 1904, in Kongsberg, Norway; came to United States, 1929; naturalized, 1939; daughter of Per (director of Royal Norwegian Silver Mines) and Line (Sandsmark) Mortenson; married Edgar Parin d'Aulaire (an artist and author of children's books), July 24, 1925; children: Per Ola, Nils Maarten. *Education:* Attended Kongsberg Junior College, Institute of Arts and Crafts, Oslo, Norway, Hans Hofman School of Art, Munich, Germany; also, Academie Scandinave, Academie Gauguin, and Academie Andre Lhote, Paris, France. *Home:* Lia Farm, 74 Mather Rd., Georgetown, Conn. 06829, and Upper Lea Farms, South Royalton, Vt. 05068.

CAREER: Artist, lecturer, author and illustrator of children's books in collaboration with husband, 1929—. *Member:* Authors Guild of America, Scandinavian-American Foundation. *Awards, honors:* American Library Association's Caldecott Medal (jointly with husband) for best illustrated children's book of 1939, *Abraham Lincoln;* Catholic Library Association Regina Medal, 1970, for "continued distinguished contribution to children's literature."

WRITINGS—All self-illustrated children's books, with husband, Edgar d'Aulaire: *The Magic Rug,* Doubleday, 1931; *Ola,* Doubleday, 1932; *Ola and Blakken and Line, Sine, Trine,* Doubleday, 1933; *The Conquest of the Atlantic,* Viking, 1933; *The Lord's Prayer,* Doubleday, 1934; *Children of the Northlights,* Viking, 1935, new edition, 1963; *George Washington,* Doubleday, 1936; (editors) Peter Christen Asbjoernsen and J. E. Moe, *East of the Sun and West of the Moon,* Viking, 1938, reprinted, 1969; *Abraham Lincoln,* Doubleday, 1939, new edition, 1957; *Animals Everywhere,* Doubleday, 1940; *Leif the Lucky,* Doubleday, 1941, new edition, 1951; *Star Spangled Banner,* Doubleday, 1942; *Don't Count Your Chicks,* Doubleday, 1943; *Wings for Per,* Doubleday, 1944; *Two Big,* Doubleday, 1945; *Pocahontas,* Doubleday, 1946; *Nils,* Doubleday, 1948; *Foxie,* Doubleday, 1949; *Benjamin Franklin,* Doubleday, 1950; *Buffalo Bill,* Doubleday, 1952; *The Two Cars,* Doubleday, 1955; *Columbus,* Doubleday, 1955; *The Magic Meadow,* Doubleday, 1958; *Ingri and Edgar Parin d'Aulaire's Book of Greek Myths,* Doubleday, 1962; *Norse Gods and Giants,* Doubleday, 1967; *D'Aulaire's Trolls,* Doubleday, 1972.

Illustrator: Hans Aanrud, *Sidsel Longskirt: A Girl of Norway,* Winston, 1935; Aanrud, *Solve Suntrap,* Winston, 1936; Dikken Zwilgmeyer, *Johnny Blossom,* Pilgrim Press, 1948.

SIDELIGHTS: Ingri Mortenson, a young Norwegian artist, and Edgar Parin d'Aulaire, the son of a noted Italian portrait painter, met while studying art in Munich. After a trip to Norway for approval by Ingri's family, where he was initiated into their annual thirty-mile ski trip (although Edgar had never been on skis in his life), everything was settled. They married and soon began the first of their safaris that were to give them material for a long list of distinguished children's books—commencing with Europe and North Africa. In 1929, they decided to settle in New York where *The Magic Rug,* their first book, was written and illustrated. Their books have been translated into German, French, Norwegian, Turkish, Japanese, Korean, and Burmese, and transcribed into Braille.

* * *

DAVIDSON, Clarissa Start
See START, Clarissa

* * *

DAVIDSON, David 1908-

PERSONAL: Born May 11, 1908, in New York, N.Y.; son of Hyman (a cigar manufacturer) and Jeanette (Godnick) Davidson; married Hilde Abel (a novelist), July 15, 1932; children: Carla. *Education:* City College (now City College of the City University of New York), B.A., 1928; Columbia University, B.Lit., 1930; London School of Economics and Political Science, graduate study, 1932. *Home:* 114 East 90th St., New York, N.Y. 10028; and East Boyd's Rd., R.D. 2, Carmel, N.Y. 10512. *Agent:* Ann Elmo, 52 Vanderbilt Ave., New York, N.Y. 10017.

CAREER: Newspaper reporter and foreign correspondent for *New York World,* 1929-31, Universal Service, London, England, 1932, *Baltimore News-Post,* 1932-34, and *New York Post,* 1934-39; Yale University, New Haven, Conn., writer-in-residence, 1965-66; New York University, New York, N.Y., instructor in English, 1966-67; University of Iowa, Iowa City, writer-in-residence, 1972; novelist. Visiting professor at Montana State University, 1952. *Wartime service:* U.S. Military Government, civilian specialist in Information Control Division, served in Germany, 1945-46.

Member: Writers Guild of America (president of eastern division, 1959-61; national chairman, 1961-63; chairman of pension board, 1973—), National Academy of Television Arts and Sciences (governor of New York chapter, 1960-68, 1970-72, 1973—; member of board of trustees, 1966-68, 1973—). *Awards, honors:* Pulitzer traveling scholarship, 1932; Bread Loaf Writers fellowship, 1947; recipient of television awards, including Christopher Award, 1954, Emmy Award nomination, 1955, and Silver Gavel Award, 1962; American Film Festival Award, 1968; Writers Guild Award, 1969; Atlanta International Film Festival Award, 1970.

WRITINGS—Novels: *The Steeper Cliff,* Random House, 1947; *The Hour of Truth,* Random House, 1949; *In Another Country,* Random House, 1951; *The Quest of Juror 19,* Doubleday, 1971; *We Few, We Happy Few,* Crown, 1974.

SIDELIGHTS: Davidson has lived in England, France, Germany, and Ecuador. He is interested in gardening and fishing.

* * *

DAVIDSON, Ellen Prescott

PERSONAL: Born in Los Angeles, Calif.; daughter of Herman Henry (a cotton buyer) and Maud (a teacher and social worker; maiden name, Haskell) Antholz; divorced, 1969; children: Matthew Haskell Davidson, Emily Prescott Davidson (Mrs. William Burton). *Education:* American Academy of Dramatic Arts, graduate. *Residence:* New York, N.Y.

CAREER: Actress, and union organizer for Screen Office and Professional Employees Guild in New York, N.Y., and Hollywood, Calif., 1940-50; factory worker and waitress in California and Connecticut, 1950-60; library relations work for William Morrow & Co., and Grove Press, New York, N.Y., 1960-72; Ideal Publishing Corp., New York, N.Y., editor of *Intimate Story,* 1972—. *Member:* American Library Association, Catholic Library Association.

WRITINGS: For Always Only (novel), Norton, 1973.

WORK IN PROGRESS: A novel; some short stories.

SIDELIGHTS: Ellen Davidson told *CA:* "Out of a peripatetic life: a childhood that began and ended with residence abroad, an adult life that saw coast-to-coast moves approximately every ten years and the widest variety of jobs—out of this, I think my writing represents an attempt on my part to trace my roots, to distill in fiction an essential America not bounded by region or class."

* * *

DAVIDSON, Robert F(ranklin) 1902-

PERSONAL: Born April 27, 1902, in Chester, S.C.; son of Zeb Vance and Kate (Gaston) Davidson; married Eve Carlton, July 13, 1928; children: Robert Franklin, Jr., Terrell Carlton. *Education:* Davidson College, B.A., 1923; Oxford University, M.A., 1933; Yale University, Ph.D., 1937. *Politics:* Democrat. *Religion:* Presbyterian. *Home:* 3110 South West Fourth Court, Gainesville, Fla. 32601. *Office address:* P.O. Box 871, Gainesville, Fla. 32602.

CAREER: Hiram College, Hiram, Ohio, professor of philosophy and Christian ethics, 1933-43; University of Florida, Gainesville, professor of humanities and chairman of department, 1946-62; St. Andrews Presbyterian College, Laurinburg, N.C., dean of college, 1962-71. *Wartime service:* U.S. Army Air Forces, educational consultant, 1942-43; U.S. Armed Forces Institute, consultant in philosophy, 1943-45. *Member:* Association of American Rhodes Scholars (secretary of Florida committee of selection, 1950-60), Phi Beta Kappa. *Awards, honors:* Rhodes scholar at Oxford University, 1932-33; General Education Board fellowship to University of Chicago, 1941; D.Litt., Limestone College, 1971, Davidson College, 1973.

WRITINGS: Rudolf Otto's Interpretation of Religion, Princeton University Press, 1947; (contributor) Earl McGrath, editor, *The Humanities in General Education,* W. C. Brown, 1949, 2nd edition, edited by James A. Fisher, 1960; *Philosophies Men Live By,* Holt, 1952, 2nd edition, 1974; (editor) *The Humanities in Contemporary Life,* Holt, 1955, revised edition, 1960; (editor) *The Search for Meaning in Life,* Holt, 1962. Contributor to journals.

BIOGRAPHICAL/CRITICAL SOURCES: Ronald Bayes, editor, *Humane Learning in a Changing Age: Essays in Honor of Robert F. Davidson,* St. Andrews College Press, 1971.

* * *

DAVIES, Rosemary Reeves 1925-

PERSONAL: Born December 17, 1925, in Sibley, Iowa; daughter of Fred D. (a factory owner) and Elsie (Clark) Reeves; married Phillips G. Davies (an English professor), September 3, 1949. *Education:* Cottey College, A.A., 1945; Northwestern University, B.S. (magna cum laude), 1947, M.A., 1948. *Politics:* Democrat. *Home:* 1630 Crestwood Cir., Ames, Iowa 50010. *Office:* Department of English, Iowa State University, Ames, Iowa 50010.

CAREER: Iowa State University, Ames, assistant professor of English, 1954—. *Member:* Modern Language Association of America, Phi Beta Kappa.

WRITINGS: The Rosenbluth Case: Federal Justice on Trial, Iowa State University Press, 1970. Contributor to *Philological Quarterly, American Literature,* and *Iowa English Yearbook.*

WORK IN PROGRESS: Research on the woman's suffrage movement of the 1870's.

SIDELIGHTS: Rosemary Davies told *CA:* "My book resulted from my father's connection with the case in question, and was researched principally from Justice Department records. It was a Watergate sort of affair, in which a coverup forced continuing efforts to cover up, and involved an innocent man in a murder charge."

* * *

DAVIS, Adelle 1904-1974 (Jane Dunlap)

February 25, 1904—May 31, 1974; American nutritionist and author. Obituaries: *New York Times,* June 1, 1974; *Washington Post,* June 2, 1974; *Publishers Weekly,* June 17, 1974; *Current Biography,* July, 1974. (*CA*-37/40).

* * *

DAVIS, Fitzroy 1912-

PERSONAL: Born February 27, 1912, in Evanston, Ill.; son of Frank Parker (a patent lawyer) and Edith Amanda (Kelly) Davis. *Education:* Williams College, A.B., 1933; Columbia University, M.A., 1961. *Politics:* Independent.

Religion: Protestant. *Home address:* R.F.D. 2, Putnam, Conn. 06260. *Agent:* David Stewart Hull, James E. Brown Associates, Inc., 22 East 60th St., New York, N.Y. 10022.

CAREER: Actor, 1935-62; singer, 1962-70; writer, 1970—. Has written for Metro-Goldwyn-Mayer, Columbia Pictures, United Artists, and acted for Coronet and Britannica studios; has also worked as stage manager, director, and professional lecturer. Instructor in speech at St. John's University, 1961-62.

WRITINGS: Quicksilver (novel), Harcourt, 1942; *Through the Doors of Brass,* Dodd, 1974. Author of plays, "Crossfire," and "Silver Fire," both as yet unproduced. Contributor to magazines and newspapers.

WORK IN PROGRESS: A sequel for *Through the Doors of Brass,* for Dodd; an autobiography from 1912-1927.

SIDELIGHTS: Davis has sung in concert in French, German, Italian, Spanish, Russian, and Portuguese, and speaks all of these languages except Portuguese. *Avocational interests:* Travel, stamp collecting, water color painting.

* * *

DAVIS, Harriet Eager 1892(?)-1974

1892(?)—April 24, 1974; American author and editor. Obituaries: *New York Times,* April 26, 1974.

* * *

DAVIS, Ken(neth Pickett) 1906-

PERSONAL: Born September 2, 1906, in Denver, Colo.; son of Gilbert L. (an engineer) and Charlotte (Pickett) Davis; married Mary Eliza Shope, September 10, 1929; children: Lawrence Spalding, Lenore (Mrs. William Helwig), Charlotte, Richard Shope. *Education:* University of Montana, B.S.F., 1928; University of Michigan, M.F., 1932, Ph.D., 1940. *Politics:* Republican. *Religion:* Episcopalian. *Home:* 52 Westerly Dr., Mount Carmel, Conn. 06518. *Office:* Yale University, 205 Prospect St., New Haven, Conn. 06511.

CAREER: U.S. Forest Service, Washington, D.C., worked in fire control and forest improvement in Montana, summers, 1925-27, district forest ranger in Montana, 1928-31, forest management researcher in Montana and Idaho, 1932-40, assistant chief of Division of Management Research, 1940-43, chief of division, 1943-45; University of Montana, professor of forestry and dean of School of Forestry, 1945-49; University of Michigan, Ann Arbor, professor of forest management, 1949-66, chairman of department of forestry, 1950-66, acting dean of School of Natural Resources, 1966; Yale University, New Haven, Conn., David T. Mason Professor of Forest Land Use, 1967-74; full-time writer, 1974—. Fulbright lecturer at University of Helsinki, 1963; conducted European land use study trip, 1973; president of Montana Conservation Council, 1948, 1949; member of Michigan Board of Registration for Foresters, 1956-62; chairman of wood section of Michigan Natural Resources Council, 1954-61; forestry consultant.

MEMBER: Society of American Foresters (fellow; vice-president, 1966-69; president, 1970-71), Finnish Society of Forestry (honorary member). *Awards, honors:* Medal from University of Helsinki, 1963.

WRITINGS: Forest Management: Regulation and Valuation, McGraw, 1954, 2nd edition, 1966; *Forest Fire: Control and Use,* McGraw, 1959, 2nd edition, 1973; (with A. A. Brown) *Land Use: Principles and Practice,* McGraw, in press. Author of bulletins. Contributor of about a hundred-thirty articles and reviews to education and forestry journals, and to *Choice.* Acting editor of *Forest Service,* 1957-58; consulting editor for forestry to *McGraw-Hill Encyclopedia of Science and Technology,* 1961-71.

WORK IN PROGRESS: Land use studies.

* * *

DAVIS, Martha 1942-

PERSONAL: Born July 15, 1942, in Rochester, N.Y.; daughter of Harry Irwin and Mary (Lay) Davis; married Sergio Rothstein (a clinical psychologist), November 29, 1969. *Education:* University of Rochester, A.B., 1964; Yeshiva University, M.S., 1968, Ph.D., 1973. *Office:* Department of Psychiatry, Roosevelt Hospital, 425 Ninth Ave., New York, N.Y. 10019.

CAREER: Psychiatric Day Hospital of Albert Einstein College of Medicine, New York, N.Y., research assistant in nonverbal communication project, 1962-66; Bronx State Hospital, Bronx, N.Y., psychologist, 1969-71; Hunter College of the City University of New York, New York, N.Y., assistant professor, Dance Therapy Masters Program, 1971-73; Roosevelt Hospital, New York, N.Y., research associate in department of psychiatry, 1973—; clinical psychologist in private practice, New York, 1973—.

WRITINGS: Understanding Body Movement: An Annotated Bibliography, Arno, 1972. Advisory editor of "Body Movement: Research Perspectives" (reprint collection), Arno, 1973.

WORK IN PROGRESS: Conducting a research project on the assessment of personality and interaction patterns through nonverbal communication.

* * *

DAVIS, Mary L(ee) 1935-

PERSONAL: Born March 21, 1935, in Worthington, Minn.; daughter of Homer L. (a businessman) and Minnie E. (Pearson) Davis; children: Laura Eileen. *Education:* University of Minnesota, A.A., 1954. *Politics:* "Socialist and/or Democrat." *Religion:* "No affiliation." *Home:* 316 Oak Grove St., Minneapolis, Minn. 55403.

CAREER: Staff writer for *St. Paul Dispatch,* 1958-60; political press aide in Washington, D.C., 1960; public relations representative in Minnesota, 1961-71; teacher of English in a Minnesota junior high school, 1966; free-lance writer. *Awards, honors:* Page One award from Newspaper Guild, 1959, for feature story.

WRITINGS—Juveniles; all published by Lerner: *Polly and the President,* 1967; *Careers in Baseball,* 1973; *Careers in the Bank,* 1973; *Careers in the Telephone Company,* 1973; *Careers in the Medical Center,* 1973; *Five Famous Queens,* in press. Contributor to local publications.

WORK IN PROGRESS: An adult novel set in contemporary Britain.

* * *

DAVIS, Nolan 1942-

PERSONAL: Born July 23, 1942, in Kansas City, Mo.; son of William L. (a fireman) and Frances Ann (Davis) Davis; married Carol Lorraine Christian (an artist), July 27, 1963; children: Arian Valentinian, Pelia de Valoria. *Education:*

Attended San Diego Evening College, 1964-65, and Stanford University, 1967-68. *Politics:* Democrat. *Residence:* Los Angeles, Calif.; and Trinidad, West Indies. *Agent:* Carl Brandt, Brandt & Brandt, 101 Park Ave., New York, N.Y. 10017. *Office:* SHARC Productions, Inc., 5410 Wilshire Blvd., Los Angeles, Calif. 90036.

CAREER: San Diego Evening Tribune, San Diego, Calif., staff writer, 1963-66; Economic Opportunity Commission of San Diego, San Diego, Calif., director of public relations, 1966-67; *Newsweek* (magazine), New York, N.Y., staff correspondent, 1967-70; KNXT-Television, Hollywood, Calif., producer and senior writer, 1970-71; KABC-TV, Hollywood, Calif., chief newswriter, 1971; SHARC Productions, Inc., Los Angeles, Calif., partner and vice-president, 1971—. *Military service:* U.S. Navy, journalist, 1960-63. *Member:* Authors League of America, Writers Guild, Sigma Delta Chi.

WRITINGS: Six Black Horses, Putnam, 1971; (with John O'Grady) *O'Grady,* Tarcher/Hawthorne, 1974. Author of television script, "Further Than the Pulpit," NBC, 1972. Contributor to *Newsweek, National Catholic Reporter, Reader's Digest,* and other magazines.

WORK IN PROGRESS: Empire of Eternity, a novel, completion expected in 1975; "Six Black Horses," a screenplay; "O'Grady," a pilot teleplay.

SIDELIGHTS: Davis writes of his humble beginnings: "I had a father who had eight other children by another woman. He worked at a fire station and I didn't really know him, having seen him only four times in my life. . ." At the age of fourteen Davis appeared voluntarily at juvenile court and asked to be sent to reform school, in order to escape from his nagging mother. The judge complied and he spent several years there and in a boys' home. He attended a small parochial high school, graduating with honors.

He practices transcendental meditation, and styles himself "a devastating conversationalist, a lover, father, writer, hustler, and producer, who tries ceaselessly to live by the precepts of the glorious *Bhagavad-Gita.*"

His literary concern is with the effects of the myths of society upon the individual and the myths of the individual upon society. *Avocational interests:* Reading, chess, tennis.

BIOGRAPHICAL/CRITICAL SOURCES: National Catholic Reporter, May, 1960; *Kansas City Star,* November 1, 1971; *Kansas City Call,* November 6, 1971.

* * *

DAVIS, Philip E(dward) 1927-

PERSONAL: Born November 10, 1927, in Valentine, Neb.; son of Herbert P. and Nellie (Post) Davis; married Laura Vaclavek, June 30, 1951; children: Kimberly, Katherine. *Education:* Harvard University, A.B., 1950; Yale University, M.A., 1953, Ph.D., 1955. *Home:* 20766 St. Joan Ct., Saratoga, Calif. 95070. *Office:* Department of Philosophy, San Jose State University, San Jose, Calif. 95192.

CAREER: Syracuse University, Syracuse, N.Y., instructor, 1954-56, assistant professor of philosophy, 1956-59; San Jose State University (formerly California State University), San Jose, assistant professor, 1959-61, associate professor, 1961-68, professor of philosophy, 1968—. Visiting lecturer at University of Illinois, spring, 1968. *Military service:* U.S. Navy, 1945-47. *Member:* American Philosophical Association.

WRITINGS: Moral Duty and Legal Responsibility, Appleton, 1966; *Introduction to Moral Philosophy,* C. E. Merrill, 1973.

* * *

DAWES, Nathaniel Thomas, Jr. 1937-

PERSONAL: Born December 19, 1937, in Newburgh, N.Y.; son of Nathaniel Thomas (a gravedigger) and Gertrude (a teacher; maiden name, Kopaskie) Dawes; married Helen Catherine Nedwell (a secretary), November, 1963. *Education:* Dutchess Community College of the State University of New York, A.A.S., 1966; Kent State University, B.Arch., 1971. *Politics:* "Nationalist." *Religion:* "Roman Catholic hedonist." *Home and office:* 15 Buckingham Ave., Poughkeepsie, N.Y. 12601.

CAREER: International Business Machines (IBM), Research and Development Laboratory, Poughkeepsie, N.Y., internal expediter, 1955-58; Wildwood Enterprises, Macon, Ga., partner (designer and builder of machines for forming light wire products), 1959; D. J. Magner & Associates (private investigators), Miami, Fla., photographer and surveillance operative, 1960-61; Modjeski & Masters (consulting engineers), Harrisburg, Pa., supervisory engineer of steel erection on Newburgh Beacon Bridge, 1961-62; Ross Welding Service, Rhinebeck, N.Y., welder, 1963; New York State Department of Public Works, Poughkeepsie, N.Y., highway engineer, 1963-66; self-employed general contractor in Hyde Park, N.Y., 1965-66; consultant to Wright Excavating and Power Enterprises, Akron, Ohio, 1967-71; Rudolph E. Lapar, Wappinger Falls, N.Y., architectural designer, 1973-74; Wilson Excavators, Inc., Fishkill, N.Y., construction foreman, 1974; now with Graphic Techniques, Inc., Kingston, N.Y. *Military service:* U.S. Army, 1958-60.

MEMBER: Packard International Motor Car Club (life member; president of Midwest region, 1971-72), American Association of Museums, Society of Automotive Historians, Packard Automobile Classics, Studebaker Drivers Club.

WRITINGS: The Packard: 1942-1962, A. S. Barnes, 1974.

WORK IN PROGRESS: Research for a book about the last twenty years of the Studebaker automobile; research on psychological experiences in museums as influenced by architectural design; research on alternate power sources, including electric automobiles.

SIDELIGHTS: Dawes has designed a home-size hydroelectric plant and is building a solar-heated, wind-powered greenhouse. His varied jobs, some self-employed, have included logger, mechanic, inventor, carnival shill, ditch digger, and cab driver. He writes: "You name it, I've done it. If I haven't, I'm willing to learn. If someone needs an item or something done, I have it or can do it. If I can't, I know someone who can." *Avocational interests:* Collecting early twentieth-century Americana and automobiles (especially Packards; Dawes owns more than sixty automobiles).

* * *

DAWOOD, N(essim) J(oseph) 1927-

PERSONAL: Born August 27, 1927, in Baghdad, Iraq; son of Yousef (a merchant) and Muzli (Tweg) Dawood; married Juliet Abraham, September 18, 1949; children: Richard, Norman, Andrew. *Education:* Attended schools in Baghdad; University of London, B.A. (with honors), 1949. *Office:* 296 Regent St., London W.1, England.

CAREER: Arabic Advertising and Publishing Co. Ltd., London, England, managing director, 1959—; Contemporary Translations Ltd., London, director, 1962—. Middle East consultant. *Member:* Institute of Linguists (fellow), Hurlingham Club. *Awards, honors:* Iraq State scholar in England, 1945-49.

WRITINGS: (Translator and author of introduction and notes) *The Koran,* Penguin Books, 1956, 12th edition, 1974; (translator and author of introduction) *Aladdin and Other Tales from the Thousand and One Nights,* Penguin Books, 1957; (editor) Ibn Khaldun, *The Muqaddimah: An Introduction to History,* Routledge & Kegan Paul, 1967, Princeton University Press, 1969; (translator) *Tales from the Thousand and One Nights,* Penguin Books, 1973, 2nd edition. 1974.

Translator of about fifty technical works into Arabic. Contributor to English-Arabic dictionaries. Writer and narrator of film commentaries in English and Arabic, including documentary "In the Name of Allah," with James Mason.

* * *

DAY, Richard B(ruce) 1942-

PERSONAL: Born July 22, 1942, in Toronto, Ontario, Canada; son of Raymond V. (a businessman) and Dorothy M. (Witney) Day; married Judith Sheffield, August 5, 1969. children: Tara Nicole. *Education:* University of Toronto, B.A., 1965, M.A., 1967, Dip. REES, 1967; University of London, Ph.D., 1970. *Home:* 2601 Truscott Dr., Mississauga, Ontario, Canada. *Office:* Department of Political Economy, University of Toronto, Toronto, Ontario, Canada.

CAREER: University of Toronto, Toronto, Ontario, associate professor of political economy, 1970—.

WRITINGS: Leon Trotsky and the Politics of Economic Isolation, Cambridge University Press, 1973.

WORK IN PROGRESS: The Crisis and the Crash: Evgeny Varga and the Political Economy of Capitalism.

* * *

DeCOSTER, Cyrus C(ole) 1914-

PERSONAL: Born September 21, 1914, in Leesburg, Va.; son of Cyrus C. (a businessman) and Jeanne (Brulay) DeCoster; married Barbara Krause, 1948; children: Janine, David, Kenneth, James. *Education:* Harvard University, A.B., 1937; Sorbonne, University of Paris, further study, 1937-38; University of Chicago, M.A., 1940, Ph.D., 1951. *Home:* 17 Martha Lane, Evanston, Ill. 60201. *Office:* Department of Spanish and Portuguese, Northwestern University, Evanston, Ill. 60201.

CAREER: Carleton College, Northfield, Minn., instructor, 1946-48, assistant professor, 1948-56, associate professor of Romance languages, 1956-57; University of Kansas, Lawrence, professor of Romance languages, 1957-69, head of department, 1962-65; Northwestern University, Evanston, Ill., professor of Spanish, 1969—, chairman of department of Spanish and Portuguese, 1973—. *Military service:* U.S. Naval Reserve, 1941-46; became lieutenant. *Member:* Modern Language Association of America, American Association of Teachers of Spanish and Portuguese, American Association of University Professors, Midwest Modern Language Association. *Awards, honors:* Fulbright research fellow in Madrid, 1963-64.

WRITINGS: (Editor) *Correspondencia inedita de Juan Valera,* Castalia, 1956; (editor) *Obras desconocidas de Juan Valera,* Castalia, 1965; (editor) Juan Valera, *Articulos de "El Contemporaneo,"* Castalia, 1966; (editor) Juan Valera, *Las Ilusiones del Doctor Faustino,* Castalia, 1970; *Bibliografia critica de Juan Valera,* Consejo Superior de Investigaciones Cientificas, 1970; *Juan Valera,* Twayne, 1974.

WORK IN PROGRESS: Editing Juan Valera's *Genio y figura* for "Ediciones Catedra" series; a book on Pedro Antonio de Alarcon for Twayne's "World Author" series.

* * *

de KAY, Ormonde, Jr. 1923-

PERSONAL: Born December 17, 1923, in New York, N.Y.; son of Ormonde and Margaret (McClure) de Kay; married Barbara Scott, January 20, 1967; children: Thomas. *Education:* Harvard University, A.B., 1947. *Politics:* Democrat. *Home:* 1225 Park Ave., New York, N.Y. 10028. *Agent:* Julian Bach, Jr., 3 East 48th St., New York, N.Y. 10017. *Office: Horizon,* 1221 Avenue of the Americas, New York, N.Y. 10020.

CAREER: Louis de Rochemont Associates, Inc., New York, N.Y., screenwriter, 1948-49; free-lance screenwriter in New York, Rome, Munich, and Paris, 1950-57; Central Office of Information, London, England, radio producer, 1958-60; free-lance writer in New York, N.Y., 1961-66; *Interplay,* New York, N.Y., special projects editor, 1967-69; *Horizon,* New York, N.Y., articles editor, 1970—. *Military service:* U.S. Naval Reserve, active duty, 1944-46, 1950-51. *Member:* Authors League of America, P.E.N., Coffee House, and Holland Society (all New York). *Awards, honors:* Shared with co-author M. J. Furland the Cannes Film Festival Award for Best scenerio, 1949, for "Lost Boundaries."

WRITINGS: Universal History of the World, Western Publishing, Volume V: *The East in the Middle Ages,* 1964, Volume XIII: *Imperialism and World War I,* 1964; *Meet Theodore Roosevelt* (juvenile), Random House, 1967; *Meet Andrew Jackson* (juvenile), Random House, 1967; *The Adventures of Lewis and Clark* (juvenile), Random House, 1968; (translator and author of comments) *Rimes de la Mere Oie: Mother Goose Rhymes Rendered into French* (parallel text), Little, Brown, 1971. Writer of film scripts. Contributor of poems to *Harper's, Atlantic, New Yorker,* and other magazines.

WORK IN PROGRESS: An illustrated history, for Houghton.

* * *

De KOENIGSWERTHER, Edwin Raymond 1930-

PERSONAL: Born August 20, 1930, in Bloomington, Ill. *Education:* Sorbonne, University of Paris, Doctorat d'Universite, 1965. *Religion:* Episcopalian. *Home:* Newport House, Newport, Va. 24128.

CAREER: Virginia Polytechnic Institute and University, Blacksburg, assistant professor, 1966-67, associate professor of French, 1967-71, coordinator, 1966-71; Newport House (restaurant), Newport, Va., owner, 1969—. Chairman of board of directors of Newport Enterprises, 1969—; president of Clover Hollow Crafts, 1970—. *Military service:* U.S. Army, 1952-54; became second lieutenant. *Member:* Modern Language Association of America, American Association of University Professors, American Association of Teachers of French, Association Internationale des Docteurs de l'Universite de Paris, Covered Bridge Association (chairman of board of directors), Blacksburg Art Association (treasurer).

WRITINGS: Vachel Lindsay (in French), Nizet, 1968.

* * *

DEMAS, Vida 1927-

PERSONAL: Born March 30, 1927, in Pittsburgh, Pa.; daughter of Benjamin M. (a businessman) and Cecilia (Shapiro) Kramer; married Nicholas James Demas (a university professor), March 25, 1953; children: Rebecca. *Education:* University of Pittsburgh, B.A., 1948; Radcliffe College, graduate study, 1952. *Politics:* Independent. *Home:* 1460 Graham Ave., Monessen, Pa. 15062. *Agent:* Elizabeth Otis, McIntosh & Otis, Inc., 18 East 41st St., New York, N.Y. 10017.

CAREER: Carnegie Museum, Pittsburgh, Pa., promotion assistant, 1949-50; University of Pittsburgh, Pittsburgh, Pa., special writer in public relations, 1950-52; University of Pittsburgh Press, Pittsburgh, Pa., promotion assistant, 1952-57; University of Pittsburgh, special writer in public relations, 1957-62; Chatham College, Pittsburgh, Pa., assistant director of public relations, 1963-64.

WRITINGS: First Person, Singular (novel), Putnam, 1974. Contributor to newspapers and journals.

WORK IN PROGRESS: A novel, tentatively titled *Isabella,* completion expected in 1975.

* * *

De MONTREVILLE POLAK, Doris 1904(?)-1974

1904(?)—February 19, 1974; American educator and editor. Obituaries: *Library Journal,* May 15, 1974.

* * *

de PAOLA, Thomas Anthony 1934- (Tomie de Paola)

PERSONAL: Born September 15, 1934, in Meriden, Conn.; son of Joseph N. (a union official) and Florence (Downey) de Paola. *Education:* Pratt Institute, B.F.A., 1956; California College of Arts and Crafts, M.F.A., 1969; Lone Mountain College, doctoral equivalency, 1970. *Residence:* New London, N.H. *Agent:* Florence Alexander, 50 East 42nd St., New York, N.Y. 10017. *Office:* Colby College-New Hampshire, New London, N.H. 03257.

CAREER: Professional artist and designer, 1956—; teacher of art; writer and illustrator of juvenile books. Newton College of the Sacred Heart, Newton, Mass., instructor, 1962-63, assistant professor of art, 1963-66; San Francisco College for Women (now Lone Mountain College), San Francisco, Calif., assistant professor of art, 1967-70; Chamberlayne Junior College, Boston, Mass., instructor in art, 1972-73; Colby College-New Hampshire, New London, N.H., associate professor, designer, and technical director in speech and theater department, 1973—. Painter and muralist, with many of his works done for Catholic churches and monastaries in New England; designer of theater and nightclub sets; work exhibited in eight one-man shows since 1961 and in group shows.

AWARDS, HONORS: Awards for typography and illustration, Boston Art Directors' Club, 1968; Silver Award of Franklin Typographers (New York), 1969; two books included in American Institute of Graphic Arts exhibit of outstanding children's books, *The Journey of the Kiss,* 1970, and *Who Needs Holes?,* 1973; *Andy, That's My Name* was included in *School Library Journal*'s list of best picture books of 1973 and *Charlie Needs a Cloak,* 1974; Friends of American Writers Award as best illustrator of a children's book, 1973, for *Authorized Autumn Charts of the Upper Red Canoe River Country.*

WRITINGS—All under name Tomie de Paola; all self-illustrated: *The Wonderful Dragon of Timlin,* Bobbs-Merrill, 1966; *Fight the Night,* Lippincott, 1968; *Joe and the Snow,* Hawthorn, 1968; *Parker Pig, Esquire,* Hawthorn, 1969; *The Journey of the Kiss,* Hawthorn, 1970; *The Monsters' Ball,* Hawthorn, 1970; *The Wind and the Sun,* Ginn, 1972; *Nana Upstairs, Nana Downstairs,* Putnam, 1973; *Andy, That's My Name,* Prentice-Hall, 1973; *Charlie Needs a Cloak* (Junior Literary Guild selection), Prentice-Hall, 1973; *The Unicorn and the Moon,* Ginn, 1973; *Watch Out for the Chicken Feet in Your Soup* (Junior Literary Guild selection), Prentice-Hall, 1974.

Illustrator, under name Tomie de Paola: Pura Belpre, *The Tiger and the Rabbit and Other Tales,* Lippincott, 1965; Lisa Miller, *Sound,* Coward, 1965; Miller, *Wheels,* Coward, 1965; Jeanne B. Hardendorff, editor, *Trickey Peik and Other Picture Tales,* Lippincott, 1967; Melvin L. Alexenberg, *Sound Science,* Prentice-Hall, 1968; James A. Eichner, *The Cabinet of the President of the United States,* F. Watts, 1968; Leland Blair Jacobs, compiler, *Poetry for Chuckles and Grins,* Garrard, 1968; Melvin L. Alexenberg, *Light and Sight,* Prentice-Hall, 1969; Samuel and Beryl Epstein, *Take This Hammer,* Hawthorn, 1969; Mary C. Jane, *The Rocking-Chair Ghost,* Lippincott, 1969; Nina Schneider, *Hercules, the Gentle Giant,* Hawthorn, 1969.

Eleanor Boylan, *How to Be a Puppeteer,* McCall Publishing, 1970; Samuel and Beryl Epstein, *Who Needs Holes?,* Hawthorn, 1970; Barbara Rinkoff, *Rutherford T. Finds 21 B,* Putnam, 1970; Philip Ballestrino, *Hot as an Ice Cube,* Crowell, 1971; Samuel and Beryl Epstein, *Pick It Up,* Holiday House, 1971; John Fisher, *John Fisher's Magic Book,* Prentice-Hall, 1971; William Wise, *Monsters of the Middle Ages,* Putnam, 1971; Peter Zachary Cohen, *Authorized Autumn Charts of the Upper Red Canoe River Country,* Atheneum, 1972; Sibyl Hancock, *Mario's Mystery Machine,* Putnam, 1972; Rubie Saunders, *The Franklin Watts Concise Guide to Babysitting,* F. Watts, 1972; Samuel and Beryl Epstein, *Hold Everything,* Holiday House, 1973; Katheryn F. Ernst, *Danny and His Thumb,* Prentice-Hall, 1973; Samuel and Beryl Epstein, *Look in the Mirror,* Holiday House, 1973; Alice Low, *David's Window,* Putnam, 1974; Charles Keller and Richard Baker, *The Star-Spangled Banana,* Prentice-Hall, 1974; Martha and Charles Sharp, *Lets Find Out about Houses,* F. Watts, in press.

Conceived, designed, and directed puppet ballet, "A Rainbow Christmas," at Botolph in Cambridge, Mass., 1971.

WORK IN PROGRESS: The Mermaid and the Big Sur and *Michael Bird Boy,* for Prentice-Hall; illustrating *Old Man Whickutt's Donkey,* by Mary Calhoun, and, *This Is the Ambulance Leaving the Zoo,* by Norma Farber.

SIDELIGHTS: De Paola says that from the time he started school he wanted "to be on the stage and write words and draw pictures for books. I must have been a stubborn child because I never swayed from that decision.

Although I chose teaching and books as professions, I've always been fortunate enough to be involved in theatre work including my present teaching job. I'm active in developing a Theatre for Children course at the college where I hope to expand literary and illustration ideas into 'theatre experience' for children.

"I not only enjoy doing children's books because of the freedom for my imagination but hopefully I will touch at least some children to instill in them the great love I personally have always had for books. Making children's books has literally forced me into an honesty of expression because, like the children in *The Emperor's New Clothes,* children demand honesty and recognize false performance.

"For me, my expression is always the sum total of my personal experience with people. Not that it shows consciously or conspicuously, but it is the inner support that makes the terrifying experience of starting a new project less frightening."

* * *

de PAOLA, Tomie

See de PAOLA, Thomas Anthony

* * *

DePORTE, Michael V(ital) 1939-

PERSONAL: Born April 24, 1939, in Albany, N.Y.; son of Joseph V. and Elizabeth (Parkhurst) DePorte; married Melinda A. Hitchcock, August 30, 1958; children: Catherine E., Rebecca A. *Education:* Princeton University, student, 1956-58; University of Minnesota, B.A. (magna cum laude), 1960; Stanford University, M.A. and Ph.D., 1965. *Office:* Department of English, University of New Hampshire, Durham, N.H. 03824.

CAREER: University of Chicago, Chicago, Ill., instructor, 1965-66, assistant professor of English, 1966-72; University of New Hampshire, Durham, assistant professor, 1972-73, associate professor of English, 1973—. *Member:* Modern Language Association of America. *Awards, honors:* Woodrow Wilson fellowship, 1960; Inland Steel faculty fellowship, 1968.

WRITINGS: (Editor) Henry More, *Enthusiasmus Triumphatus,* Augustan Reprint Society, 1966; (editor) Thomas Tryon, *Discourse on Madness,* Augustan Reprint Society, 1973; *Nightmares and Hobby-Horses: A Study of Swift, Sterne and the Psychopathology of the Augustan Age,* Huntington Library, 1974.

WORK IN PROGRESS: Studies on Restoration and eighteenth-century English literature.

* * *

DEPTA, Victor M(arshall) 1939-

PERSONAL: Born March 20, 1939, in Accoville, W.Va.; son of Steve (an electronics mechanic) and Opal (Waugh) Depta; married Mary Sue Allen, September 5, 1964; children: Helen. *Education:* Marshall University, B.A., 1965; San Francisco State College (now University), M.A., 1968; Ohio University, Ph.D., 1972. *Home:* 210 K St., Martin, Tenn. 38237. *Office:* University of Tennessee, Martin, Tenn. 38237.

CAREER: Morehead State University, Morehead, Ky., instructor in English, 1968-69; University of Tennessee, Martin, assistant professor of English, 1972—. *Military service:* U.S. Navy, 1956-60. *Member:* Associated Writing Programs.

WRITINGS: *The Creek* (poems), Ohio University Press, 1973. Contributor to literary magazines, including *North American Review, Southern Poetry Review, Shenandoah, Appalachian Journal, Quetzal,* and *Windless Orchard.*

WORK IN PROGRESS: Three books of poetry, *The House, The Field,* and *But Something Like.*

* * *

DERMID, Jack 1923-

PERSONAL: Born July 13, 1923, in Charlotte, N.C.; son of Eddie Franklin and Clarice (Presnell) Dermid; married Anne Johnson (a teacher technician), December 4, 1943; children: Susan. *Education:* North Carolina State University, B.S., 1949; Oregon State University, M.S., 1950. *Politics:* Democrat. *Religion:* Presbyterian. *Home:* Route 3, Box 303-D, Wilmington, N.C. 28401. *Office:* Department of Biology, University of North Carolina at Wilmington, Wilmington, N.C. 28401.

CAREER: North Carolina Wildlife Resources Commission, Raleigh, N.C., managing editor and wildlife photographer for *Wildlife in North Carolina,* 1950-62; University of North Carolina at Wilmington, assistant professor, 1962-73, associate professor of biology, 1973—; free-lance nature and biological photographer. *Military service:* U.S. Army Air Forces, 1943-45; served in European theater. *Member:* National Audubon Society, National Wildlife Federation, National Parks and Conservation Association, Wilderness Society, Conservation Council of North Carolina, North Carolina Academy of Science, Carolina Bird Club.

WRITINGS: (With F. Eugene Hester) *The World of the Wood Duck,* Lippincott, 1973; (with others) *Reptiles and Amphibians of Virginia and the Carolinas,* University of North Carolina Press, in press. Contributor of hundreds of photographs to textbooks, nature books, and magazines. Photographer of three thirty-minute motion pictures on conservation for the North Carolina Wildlife Resources Commission.

WORK IN PROGRESS: *Life of Salt Marshes,* a book or photographic study.

* * *

DESPLAND, Michel 1936-

PERSONAL: Born July 25, 1936, in Lausanne, Switzerland; son of Amy and Lisette (Vuagniaux) Despland; married Sheila McDonough (a professor); children: Emma. *Education:* Universite de Lausanne, Lic. Theol., 1958; Harvard University, Th.D., 1966. *Office:* Department of Religion, Sir George Williams University, 1455 De Maisonneuve West, Montreal, Quebec, Canada.

CAREER: Sir George Williams University, Montreal, Quebec, associate professor of religion, 1965—.

WRITINGS: *Le Choc des morales,* L'Age d'Homme, 1973; *Kant on History and Religion,* McGill-Queen's University Press, 1973.

* * *

De STEUCH, Harriet Henry 1897(?)-1974 (Harriet Henry)

1897(?)—April 19, 1974; American novelist. Obituaries: *AB Bookman's Weekly,* July 15, 1974.

DETINE, Padre
See OLSEN, Ib Spang

* * *

DEVEREUX, Frederick L(eonard), Jr. 1914-

PERSONAL: Born April 20, 1914, in New York, N.Y.; son of Frederick Leonard (an executive) and Frances (Clark) Devereux; married Ruth Wentworth Foster, June 26, 1936; children: Foster, Frances Clark, Frederick Leonard III. *Education:* University of Chicago, A.B., 1937; U.S. Army Command and General Staff College, Diploma, 1943. *Politics:* Republican. *Religion:* Episcopalian. *Home:* 24 The Green, Woodstock, Vt. 05091.

CAREER: R. H. Macy & Co., New York, N.Y., buyer, 1936-38; Young and Rubicam, Inc., New York, N.Y., merchandizing executive, 1939-40, 1946-52; Oneita Knitting Mills, Utica, N.Y., general sales manager, 1953-59; Allied Stores, Corp., New York, N.Y., marketing manager, 1960-64; Merit Stores, Inc., Middletown, N.Y., president, 1964-66. Lecturer at Graduate School of Business Administration, New York University, 1959-60; instructor for U.S. Power Squadrons classes, 1969-72. Judge at National Horse Show and other horse shows and hunter trials. *Military service:* U.S. Army, Cavalry, 1941-45; instructor in horsemanship at U.S. Military Academy, 1942-43; later assistant chief of staff, Intelligence, 86th Infantry Division; became lieutenant colonel. *Member:* Institute of Navigation, American Horse Shows Association, U.S. Power Squadrons, American Yacht Club.

WRITINGS: Practical Navigation for the Yachtsman, Norton, 1972; *Famous Horses–Past and Present* (juvenile), World Publishing, 1972; *Ride Your Pony Right* (juvenile), Dodd, 1974. Former editor, *Vermont Horse.*

WORK IN PROGRESS: Horses, A First Book and *The Backyard Pony* for Franklin Watts; *Horse Problems and Problem Horses* for Devin-Adair; *The Oxford Companion to the American Revolution* for Oxford University Press.

* * *

DEVOL, Kenneth S(towe) 1929-

PERSONAL: Born April 3, 1929, in Los Angeles, Calif.; son of Howard P. and Gladys (Harris) Devol; married Shirley Dixon (a psychiatric social worker), December 30, 1951; children: Sharon, Randall. *Education:* University of Southern California, B.A., 1951, M.S., 1954, Ph.D., 1965. *Home:* 16953 Superior St., Sepulveda, Calif. 91343. *Office:* Department of Journalism, California State University, Northridge, Calif. 91324.

CAREER: High school journalism teacher in the public schools of Van Nuys, Calif., 1953-55; Los Angeles Valley College, Los Angeles, Calif., instructor in journalism and head of department, 1955-61; California State University, Northridge (formerly San Fernando Valley State College), assistant professor, 1961-65, associate professor, 1965-69, professor of journalism and head of department, 1969—. Research writer for Andrews-Yangemann Television Productions, 1965; judge of news awards, Radio-Television News Association of Southern California, 1969; judge for National Academy of Television Arts and Sciences, 1971. *Member:* American Association of Schools and Departments of Journalism (member of executive committee, 1973-74), Association for Education in Journalism (member of executive committee, 1970-71), American Association of University Professors, American Civil Liberties Union, Society of Professional Journalists, Sigma Delta Chi, Kappa Tau Alpha. *Awards, honors:* Mott award, 1972, for research in journalism; National Endowment for the Humanities grant, 1969, for study at Stanford University.

WRITINGS: (With Esther R. Davis) *Writing Style for Journalists,* Brewster Publishers, 1962; *Mass Media and the Supreme Court: The Legacy of the Warren Years,* Hastings House, 1971. Contributor to *Journalism Quarterly.* Reporter and editor, *Valley Times* (North Hollywood, Calif.), 1957-60; member of editorial board, *College Press Review,* 1973—.

WORK IN PROGRESS: Second edition of *Mass Media and the Supreme Court: The Legacy of the Warren Years;* contributing to *For the First Amendment: Essays Honoring Justice Hugo Black.*

* * *

De WAARD, E(lliott) John 1935-

PERSONAL: Born March 30, 1935, in Sault Sainte Marie, Mich.; son of Otto (a game biologist with Michigan Department of Conservation) and Elma (Elliott) De Waard; married Nancy Jean Wisner (a teacher and writer), June 21, 1958; children: Eric, Edward. *Education:* Adrian College, B.S., 1957; Michigan State University, M.S., 1962; Ohio State University, further graduate study, 1962-63. *Residence:* 201 Creekside Dr., Palo Alto, Calif. 94306. *Office:* Addison-Wesley Publishing Co., Menlo Park, Calif. 94025.

CAREER: High school teacher of science in Napoleon, Mich., 1958-62; American Education Publications, Middletown, Conn., editor of *Current Science,* 1963-66; Silver Burdett Co., Morristown, N.J., senior editor of science textbooks, 1966-70; Addison-Wesley Publishing Co., Menlo Park, Calif., senior science editor and associate science publisher, 1970-74, executive science editor, 1974—. Special lecturer at Wesleyan University, Middletown, Conn., 1963-66. *Member:* National Science Teachers Association (life member), National Association of Biology Teachers, American Institute of Biological Sciences, National Association of Physics Teachers, School Science and Mathematics Association, American Forestry Association, New York Academy of Science.

WRITINGS: What Insect Is That?, American Education Publications, 1964; *Plants and Animals in the Air,* Doubleday, 1969; *The Shape of Living Things,* Doubleday, 1969; *The Color of Life* (Junior Literary Guild selection), Doubleday, 1971. Author with wife, Nancy De Waard, of three study guides, *The Doubleday Companion to "Through the Microscope," The Doubleday Companion to "Man and Insects,"* and *The Doubleday Companion to "Man Probes the Universe,"* all 1967. Writer of more than one hundred short feature stories for *Current Science,* 1963-66.

WORK IN PROGRESS: Two more juvenile science books.

AVOCATIONAL INTERESTS: Piloting a sailplane, woodworking, electronics, hunting, fishing, photography.

* * *

DEWEY, Ariane 1937-
(Ariane Aruego)

PERSONAL: Born August 17, 1937, in Chicago, Ill.; daughter of Charles S., Jr. and Marjorie (Goodman) Graff;

married Jose E. Aruego, Jr. (an author and illustrator), 1961 (divorced, 1973); children: Juan. *Education:* Sarah Lawrence College, B.A., 1959; studied art (woodcuts) with Antonio Frasconi. *Residence:* New York, N.Y.

CAREER: Harcourt, Brace & World, Inc., New York, N.Y., researcher and art editor for children's textbooks, 1964-65; free-lance illustrator and other work on children's books, 1969—. Member of board, Experiments in Interactive Arts, New York, 1973; performer with "Artists in Process Improvisational Dance Group," 1973-74. *Awards, honors: A Crocodile's Tale* was named to the American Institute of Graphic Arts' list of Children's Books of the Year, 1972; Brooklyn Art Books for Children citation, 1974, and Society of Illustrators citation for merit at fifteenth national exhibit, both for *Milton the Early Riser;* Society of Illustrators citation for merit at sixteenth national exhibit for a poster for the Children's Book Council.

WRITINGS: (Author and illustrator with Jose Aruego, under name Ariane Aruego) *A Crocodile's Tale,* Scribner, 1972.

Illustrator—Under name Ariane Aruego: (With Jose Aruego) Vladimir G. Suteyev, *The Chick and the Duckling,* translation by Mirra Ginsburg, Macmillan, 1972; (with Jose Aruego) Robert Kraus, *Milton the Early Riser,* Windmill Books, 1972.

Illustrator—Under name Ariane Dewey: (With Jose Aruego) Natalie Savage Carlson, *Marie Louise and Christophe,* Scribner, 1974; (with Jose Aruego) Kraus, *Herman the Helper,* Windmill Books, 1974; (with Jose Aruego) Suteyev, *Mushroom in the Rain,* adaptation by Ginsburg, Macmillan, 1974.

* * *

DIAMOND, Sander A. 1942-

PERSONAL: Born November 25, 1942, in New York, N.Y.; son of William (a window designer) and Bessie (Weltman) Diamond; married Susan Lee Dorfman (a teacher), March 20, 1966; children: Meredith Carolyn, Matthew Eric. *Education:* State University of New York College at New Paltz, B.A. (with highest honors), 1964; State University of New York at Binghamton, M.A., 1966, Ph.D., 1971. *Religion:* Jewish. *Home address:* P.O. Box 176, Keuka Park, N.Y. 14478. *Office:* Department of History, Keuka College, Keuka Park, N.Y. 14478.

CAREER: State University of New York at Binghamton, instructor in history, 1968; Keuka College, Keuka Park, N.Y., instructor, 1968-71, assistant professor, 1971-73, associate professor of history, 1973—, chairman of department, 1973—. *Member:* American Historical Association, Conference Group on German and Central European History, European Historians of New York State.

WRITINGS: The Nazi Movement in the United States: 1924-1941, Cornell University Press, 1974. Contributor of articles and reviews to journals in the United States and abroad, including *Journal of American History, American Jewish Historical Quarterly, Vierteljahrshefte fuer zeitgeschichte,* and *Yivo Annual of Jewish Social Sciences.*

WORK IN PROGRESS: A book on the formation of foreign policy between Germany and the United States in the 1920's.

AVOCATIONAL INTERESTS: Travel in Western Europe, collecting stamps, cycling, camping, fishing, handball.

DICK, Philip K(indred) 1928- (Richard Phillips)

PERSONAL: Born December 16, 1928, in Chicago, Ill.; son of Joseph Edgar (a federal employee) and Dorothy (Kindred) Dick; married fifth wife, Tessa Busby, April 18, 1973; children: (third marriage) Laura, (fourth marriage) Isolde, (fifth marriage) Christopher. *Education:* Attended University of California, Berkeley. *Politics:* "Anti-war, pro-life." *Religion:* Episcopalian. *Home and office:* 1405 Cameo Lane, #4, Fullerton, Calif. 92631. *Agent:* Scott Meredith Literary Agency, Inc., 580 Fifth Ave., New York, N.Y. 10036.

CAREER: Science fiction writer. Hosted classical music program on KSMO Radio, 1947; operated a record store, 1948-52; lectures occasionally at California State University at Fullerton; is active in drug rehabilitation and anti-abortion work. *Member:* Science Fiction Writers of America, Animal Protection Institute. *Awards, honors:* Hugo Award for best novel from World Science Fiction Convention 1962, for *The Man in the High Castle.*

WRITINGS—All science fiction: *Solar Lottery,* Ace Books, 1955; *A Handful of Darkness,* Rich & Cowan, 1955; *World of Chance,* Rich & Cowan, 1956; *The World Jones Made,* Ace Books, 1956; *The Man Who Japed,* Ace Books, 1956; *Eye in the Sky,* Ace Books, 1957; *The Cosmic Puppets,* Ace Books, 1957; *The Variable Man and Other Stories,* Ace Books, 1957; *Time Out of Joint,* Lippincott, 1959.

Doctor Futurity, Ace Books, 1960; *Vulcan's Hammer,* Ace Books, 1960; *The Man in the High Castle,* Putnam, 1962; *The Game-Players of Titan,* Ace Books, 1963; *Martian Time-Slip,* Ballantine, 1964; *The Three Stigmata of Palmer Eldritch,* Doubleday, 1964; *The Simulacra,* Ace Books, 1964; *The Penultimate Truth,* Belmont Books, 1964; *Clans of the Alphane Moon,* Ace Books, 1964; *Doctor Bloodmoney,* Ace Books, 1965; *The Crack in Space,* Ace Books, 1966; *Now Wait for Last Year,* Doubleday, 1966; *The Unteleported Man,* Ace Books, 1966; *Counter-Clock World,* Berkley Publishing, 1967; *Zap Gun,* Pyramid Publications, 1967; (with Ray Nelson) *The Ganymede Takeover,* Ace Books, 1967; *Do Androids Dream of Electric Sheep?,* Doubleday, 1968; *Ubik,* Doubleday, 1969; *Galactic Pot-Healer,* Berkley Publishing, 1969; *The Preserving Machine,* Ace Books, 1969; *A Maze of Death,* Doubleday, 1969; *Een Swibbel voor dag en nacht* (title means "A Swibbel by Day and Night"), Bruna & Zoon (Utrecht) 1969.

Our Friends from Frolix-Eight, Ace Books, 1970; *We Can Build You,* DAW Books, 1972; *The Book of Philip K. Dick,* DAW Books, 1973; *Flow My Tears, the Policeman Said,* Doubleday, 1974; *Confessions of a Crap Artist,* Hartwell-Williams (New York), in press.

Work is represented in anthologies, including *A Treasury of Great Science Fiction,* Volume I, edited by Anthony Boucher, Doubleday, 1959, and *Dangerous Visions,* edited by Harlan Ellison, Doubleday, 1967.

Author of radio scripts for Mutual Broadcasting System. Contributor of more than a hundred stories occasionally under pseudonym Richard Phillips, to science fiction and fantasy magazines.

WORK IN PROGRESS: A Scanner Darkly, a science fiction novel, for Doubleday.

SIDELIGHTS: "Of all SF writers," notes the *Times Lit-*

erary Supplement, "the prolific Mr. Dick alone has power to take all the somewhat shop-soiled props—spaceships, mutations, robots, nuclear bombs, drugs, planetary colonization—and create something of poetic significance from them. . . .the quality of his obsessions is both beautiful and alarming. Even when he disposes indifferently of superfluous characters by an outburst of shooting, as here [in *Do Androids Dream of Electric Sheep?*], the highly individual tone he has established is not entirely shattered." B. A. Young adds that with the publication of *The Penultimate Truth,* "Mr. Dick challenges Kurt Vonnegut at the top of his league."

Of his own writing, Dick told *CA:* "My major preoccupation is the question, 'What is reality?' Many of my stories and novels deal with psychotic states or drug-induced states by which I can present the concept of a multiverse rather than a universe. Music and sociology are themes in my novels, also radical political trends; in particular I've written about fascism and my fear of it."

BIOGRAPHICAL/CRITICAL SOURCES: Brian W. Aldiss, *The Shape of Future Things,* Faber, 1970; Aldiss, *The Billion Year Spree,* Doubleday, 1973.

* * *

DICKSON, Carr
See CARR, John Dickson

* * *

DICKSON, Carter
See CARR, John Dickson

* * *

DICKSON, George E(dmond) 1918-

PERSONAL: Born January 6, 1918, in Seattle, Wash.; son of Charles Edmond and Blanche Erwin (Crane) Dickson; married Dorothy O'Nita Brown, August, 1940; children: Charles, Dean. *Education:* Central Washington College of Education, B.A., 1940; Stanford University, M.A., 1948, Ed.D., 1949. *Home:* 2733 Middlesex Dr., Toledo, Ohio 43606. *Office:* College of Education, University of Toledo, Toledo, Ohio 43606.

CAREER: Teacher in public schools of Pasco, Wash., 1940-41, Toppenish, Wash., 1941-42, and Wapato, Wash., 1945, 1946-47; Central Washington College of Education (now Central Washington State College), Ellensburg, assistant professor, 1949-52, associate professor of education, 1952-53, director of student teaching, 1950-53; Ohio State University, Columbus, assistant professor, 1953-55, associate professor of education, 1955-57; University of Toledo, Toledo, Ohio, professor of education and dean of College of Education, 1957—. Member of council, National Council for Accreditation of Teacher Education, 1967-70. Member of executive committee, Ohio Department of Higher Education, 1960-62, 1966-68, president, 1961; chairman of Council of Deans of Education in State Universities of Ohio, 1972-73. *Military service:* U.S. Army Air Forces, 1942-44, 1945-46.

MEMBER: International Council on Education for Teaching, Association for Higher Education, American Educational Research Association, American Association of Colleges for Teacher Education (member of executive committee, 1968-69), Associated Organizations for Teacher Education (member of advisory council, 1964-69; chairman of council, 1968-69), Association for Supervision and Curriculum Development (member of board of directors, 1962-64), American Association of University Professors, Ohio Association for Supervision and Curriculum Development (member of board of directors, 1960-65; vice-president, 1960-62; president, 1962-64), Ohio Education Association, Kappa Delta Pi, Phi Delta Kappa, Phi Kappa Phi.

WRITINGS: (With Isabel Miller and Loren R. Tomlinson) *Guidebook for Elementary Student Teachers,* Appleton, 1958; *Planning a Prototype Teacher Center for Ohio,* College of Education, University of Toledo, 1972; (editor with Dan W. Anderson, James M. Cooper, and others) *Competency Based Teacher Education,* McCutchan, 1973; (with Richard W. Saxe) *Partners for Educational Reform and Renewal: Competency Based Teacher Education, Individually Guided Education and Multiunit Schools,* McCutchan, 1973. Project director of published reports on U.S. Office of Education research projects, including *The Characteristics of Teacher Education Students in the British Isles and the United States,* 1965, and *Educational Specifications for a Comprehensive Elementary Teacher Education Program,* two volumes, 1968. Contributor to yearbooks and journals. Member of editorial advisory board, *Journal of Teacher Education,* 1967-70.

SIDELIGHTS: Dickson made five trips to Europe and one each to Africa, Israel, and the Near East visiting educational research facilities between 1964-68. In 1965 he conducted an invitational conference on research in teacher education in London.

* * *

DILLARD, Annie 1945-

PERSONAL: Born April 30, 1945, in Pittsburgh, Pa.; daughter of Frank and Pam (Lambert) Doak; married Richard Henry Wilde Dillard (a poet and novelist), June 5, 1965. *Education:* Hollins College, B.A., 1967, M.A., 1968. *Agent:* Blanche Gregory, 2 Tudor City Place, New York, N.Y. 10017. *Office: Harper's,* 2 Park Ave., New York, N.Y. 10016.

CAREER: Harper's (Magazine), New York, N.Y., contributing editor, 1973—. *Member:* Author's Guild, P.E.N., Thoreau Society, Thoreau Lyceum, Phi Beta Kappa.

WRITINGS: Tickets for a Prayer Wheel (poems), University of Missouri Press, 1974; *Pilgrim at Tinker Creek,* Harper's Magazine Press, 1974. Contributor to *Atlantic Monthly, Sports Illustrated, Prose, Cosmopolitan, American Scholar,* and others. Columnist, *Living Wilderness,* 1973—.

SIDELIGHTS: Of *Pilgrim at Tinker Creek,* Melvin Maddocks wrote in *Time* magazine: "To an age hooked on novelty, variety and pluralism, her message is as clear as William Blake's: 'See a world in a grain of sand'—if you dare. . . . She sums up herself and perhaps her species thus: 'I am a frayed and nibbled survivor in a fallen world.' But what she has done is bear witness to her mystery as no leeched turtle (and few living writers) could—in a remarkable psalm of terror and celebration."

* * *

DIPPER, Alan 1922-

PERSONAL: Born May 1, 1922, in Sheerness, Isle of Sheppy, Kent, England; son of Cecil (a civil servant) and Dora (Warner) Dipper; married Elspeth Eliot Lloyd, March 24, 1948; children: Simon Fraser Lloyd, Frances

Anne, Nigel Harvey, Giles, Roger Martin. *Education:* Attended Royal Academy of Dramatic Art, 1937-38. *Religion:* Buddhist. *Home:* Gate House, Beckley, Rye, Sussex, England. *Agent:* Brandt & Brandt, 101 Park Ave., New York, N.Y. 10017. *Office:* Brompton Co., 58 Walton St., London S.W.3, England.

CAREER: Actor in England, 1938-40, 1945-48 (including roles in Royal Shakespeare Co. of Stratford-on-Avon); farmer near Stratford, England, 1948-63; Brompton Co. (office maintenance firm), London, England, owner, 1963—. *Military service:* Royal Air Force, air gunner, 1940-45; became flight sergeant. *Member:* Crime Writers Association.

WRITINGS: The Wave Hangs Dark, Morrow, 1968; *The Paradise Formula,* Morrow, 1970; *The Hard Trip,* M. Joseph, 1970; *The Golden Virgin* (Men's Book Club selection), Walker & Co., 1972; *The Colour of Darkness,* M. Joseph, 1974. Contributor of short stories and articles to popular magazines, including *Argosy,* and to newspapers.

WORK IN PROGRESS: Drowning Day, a novel; research for a book on Sir Richard Burton and for a book on the occult; a film play for children.

AVOCATIONAL INTERESTS: Travel, particularly in the Middle East and Europe.

* * *

DOBBS, Farrell 1907-

PERSONAL: Born July 25, 1907, in Queen City, Mo.; son of Isaac T. (a mechanic) and Ora L. (Smith) Dobbs; married Marvel S. Scholl (a writer), April 23, 1927; children: Carol Elinor (Mrs. Clifton DeBerry), Mary Lou (Mrs. Paul Montauk), Sharon Lee (Mrs. Eli Finer). *Education:* Educated in public schools of Minneapolis, Minn. *Politics:* Socialist. *Religion:* None. *Office:* Monad Press, 410 West St., New York, N.Y. 10014.

CAREER: Strutwear Knitting Co., Minneapolis, Minn., dyer, 1925; reaper and thresher in harvest fields of North Dakota, 1926; Western Electric Co., Minnesota, Iowa, and Nebraska, telephone central office equipment installer, 1926-29, foreman of installation crew, 1930-31, planning engineer, 1931-32; Pittsburgh Coal Co., Minneapolis, Minn., yardman, 1933-34; International Brotherhood of Teamsters, General Drivers local unions 574 and 544, Minneapolis, Minn., secretary-treasurer, 1934-38; Socialist Workers Party, New York, N.Y., national labor secretary, 1940-43; *Militant,* New York, N.Y., editor, 1943-48; Socialist Workers Party, national chairman, 1949-53, national secretary, 1953-72; presently in the employ of Monad Press, New York, N.Y.

WRITINGS: Teamster Rebellion, Monad, 1972; *Teamster Power,* Monad, 1973.

WORK IN PROGRESS: Teamster Bureaucracy, third of the three-volume series, for Monad.

* * *

DOBKINS, J(ames) Dwight 1943-

PERSONAL: Born November 10, 1943, in Torrance, Calif.; son of Craig Thomas and Helen (Gookins) Dobkins; married Martha Ann McCollum, June 20, 1964; children: David Duane, Lisa Rene. *Education:* Arizona State University, B.A., 1967. *Politics:* Independent. *Religion:* Southern Baptist. *Residence:* Phoenix, Ariz. *Agent:* Ann Elmo, 52 Vanderbilt Ave., New York, N.Y. 10017.

CAREER: Arizona Republic, Phoenix, Ariz., sports writer and columnist, 1961-66; Motorola Semiconductor Products, Inc., Phoenix, Ariz., administrative assistant in advertising, 1966; Arizona Public Service Co., Phoenix, Ariz., associate editor, 1967-68; A & M Associates, Inc. (advertising), Phoenix, Ariz., editor, copywriter, and public relations director, 1968-73; free-lance writer, 1973—. *Military service:* U.S. Army National Guard, 1966-72. *Member:* Authors Guild, Authors League of America.

WRITINGS: (With Robert J. Hendricks) *Winnie Ruth Judd: The Trunk Murders,* Grosset, 1973.

WORK IN PROGRESS: Two books, *Everybody's Victim* (tentative title), concerns high-level crime and bureaucracy, and *The Sledge-Hammer Diary* (tentative title), concerns corruption in major business circles and on Wall Street.

SIDELIGHTS: The movie rights to *Winnie Ruth Judd* have been acquired by Reina Productions. The movie is scheduled to be released in 1975.

* * *

"Dr. A"
See SILVERSTEIN, Alvin

* * *

DODD, Edward
See DODD, Edward Howard, Jr.

* * *

DODD, Edward Howard, Jr. 1905-
(Edward Dodd; W. M. Hill, a pseudonym)

PERSONAL: Born June 25, 1905, in New York, N.Y.; son of Edward Howard (a publisher) and Mary Elizabeth (Leggett) Dodd; married Roxana Foote Scoville, August 6, 1932 (divorced, 1950); married Camille Oberweiser Gilpatric, October, 1952; children: (first marriage) Louise Armstrong (Mrs. Desmond V. Nicholson), Roxana Foote (Mrs. Ledlie Laughlin), Edward Howard III. *Education:* Yale University, B.A. (cum laude), 1928. *Politics:* Democratic. *Religion:* None. *Home:* Windmill Hill, Putney, Vt. 05346. *Office:* Dodd, Mead & Co., 79 Madison Ave., New York, N.Y. 10016.

CAREER: After graduation sailed around the world on a small schooner with four Yale classmates, 1928-29; Dodd, Mead & Co., New York, N.Y., 1929—, became head of editorial department, 1937, member of board of directors, 1938, vice-president, 1941, president, 1953-57, chairman of editorial board, 1957-66, chairman of board of directors, 1966—; now semi-retired and spends part of the year in Polynesia. Trustee of Marlboro School of Music and Putney Grammar School. *Wartime service:* Office of Strategic Services, 1942-45; editor for Research and Analysis Branch, later Mediterranean theater officer. *Member:* Alpha Delta Phi, Century Association and Yale Club (both New York).

WRITINGS: Great Dipper to Southern Cross: The Cruise of the Schooner "Chance" through the South Seas, Dodd, 1930; *The First Hundred Years: A History of Dodd, Mead & Co.,* Dodd, 1939; *Of Nature, Time and Teale,* Dodd, 1960; (under pseudonym W. M. Hill) *Tales of Maui,* Dodd, 1964; (under name Edward Dodd) *The Ring of Fire,* Dodd, Volume I: *Polynesian Art,* 1967, Volume II: *Polynesian Seafaring,* 1972. Contributor to periodicals, including *Publishers Weekly.*

WORK IN PROGRESS: Further volumes in his series on Polynesian culture, *The Ring of Fire.*

AVOCATIONAL INTERESTS: Wildflowers, gardening, woodwork.

* * *

DODGE, Dick 1918(?)-1974

1918(?)—May 24, 1974; American artist and author of children's books. Obituaries: *AB Bookman's Weekly,* June 17, 1974.

* * *

DOERSCHUK, Anna Beatrice 1880(?)-1974

1880(?)—April 18, 1974; American educator and editor. Obituaries: *New York Times,* April 23, 1974.

* * *

DOLAN, Josephine A(loyse) 1913-

PERSONAL: Born July 27, 1913, in Cranston, R.I.; daughter of Thomas Joseph and Josephine (Tynan) Dolan. *Education:* Boston University, B.S., 1942, M.S., 1950. *Home address:* Storrs Rd., Storrs, Conn. 06268. *Office:* School of Nursing, University of Connecticut, Storrs, Conn. 06268.

CAREER: University of Connecticut, Storrs, instructor, 1944-46, assistant professor, 1946-50, associate professor, 1950-60, professor of history of nursing, 1960—. Film consultant for "A History of American Nursing," American Nursing Association-National League for Nursing Film Service, 1961; television consultant and teacher for "Nursing in Society," KTCA-Television, 1966. *Member:* National League for Nursing (member of board of directors, 1969-71), Connecticut League for Nursing (president, 1967-69), Gamma Sigma Sigma, Tau Pi Upsilon, Pi Lambda Theta, Sigma Theta Tau (president of Mu chapter, 1963-67). *Awards, honors:* Outstanding service award from Connecticut Nurses Association, 1966; distinguished service award from National League for Nursing, 1972; D.Pedagogy from Rhode Island College, 1974.

WRITINGS: Goodnow's History of Nursing, Saunders, 10th edition (Miss Dolan was not associated with earlier editions), 1958, 11th edition, 1963, 12th edition published as *History of Nursing,* 1968, 13th edition published as *Nursing in Society: A Historical Perspective,* 1973; (with Stella Goostray, Kathryn D. Drevez, and Ruth Metheney) *Three Score Years and Ten* (booklet), National League for Nursing, 1963; (with Dorothy Rogers) *The Sixth Decade: A History of the Connecticut Nurses Association* (booklet), Nursing News, 1965; *The Grace of a Great Lady* (booklet), Medical Heritage Society, 1970. Contributor of articles and reviews to nursing journals, including *Nursing Outlook, Nursing Science, Journal of Nursing Education,* and *American Journal of Nursing.* Editor of *Nursing Clinics of North America,* 1966.

WORK IN PROGRESS: Harriet Eaton: A Civil War Nurse from Maine, completion expected in 1976; *Historical Perspectives in Nursing as Depicted Through Stamps,* 1980.

* * *

DOLIBER, Earl L(awrence) 1947-

PERSONAL: Born August 18, 1947, in Marblehead, Mass.; son of Howard Franklin II (a gasoline retailer) and Gail (Greene) Doliber; married Janet Raye Ikenberry (a photographer), July 21, 1973. *Education:* Salem State College, Salem, Mass., B.S., 1969; Arizona State University, M.A., 1971. *Politics:* "Liberal independent cynic." *Religion:* Unitarian. *Residence:* Salem, Mass. *Office:* Joe Greene Insurance Agency, 121 Pleasant St., Marblehead, Mass. 01945.

CAREER: Automobile mechanic, 1964-70; Technology Guild, Salem, Mass., fiberglass technician, 1971-72; Joe Greene Insurance Agency, Marblehead, Mass., insurance agent, 1973—. *Military service:* U.S. Naval Reserve, 1965-69. *Member:* Association of American Geographers, National Hot Rod Association.

WRITINGS: Lobstering Inshore and Offshore, International Marine Publishing Co., 1973.

WORK IN PROGRESS: A photographic series on the automotive subculture; short stories.

SIDELIGHTS: Doliber feels that the "new journalism" should be more actively involved in using photographs to shape literary images, to add depth and further perception to contemporary writing. He describes himself as an "over-educated hedonist confined to an office out of the realities of greed and hunger." He has been an automobile racer and plans to participate in drag racing in the near future. He has developed a love for the Mexican way of life because "Latin countries seem to be the last frontiers of anti-puritanism.

* * *

DONALDSON, E(thelbert) Talbot 1910-

PERSONAL: Born March 18, 1910, in Bethlehem, Pa.; son of Francis (an engineer) and Anne (Talbot) Donaldson; married Christine H. Hunter, June 23, 1940 (divorced, 1966); married Jacqueline Sissa Filson, March 23, 1967 (divorced, 1969); married Judith H. Anderson (a professor), May 18, 1971; children: (first marriage) Deirdre H. *Education:* Harvard University, A.B., 1932; Yale University, Ph.D., 1943. *Home:* 2525 East Eighth St., Bloomington, Ind. 47401. *Office:* Department of English, Indiana University, Bloomington, Ind. 47401.

CAREER: Yale University, New Haven, Conn., research instructor, 1946-47, assistant professor, 1947-51, associate professor, 1951-56, professor of English, 1956-66, Bodman Professor of English, 1966-67, 1970-74; Columbia University, New York, N.Y., professor of English, 1967-70; Indiana University, Bloomington, professor of English, 1974—. Visiting professor at University College, University of London, 1951-52, Columbia University, 1966-67, 1970-71, Yale University, 1967-68, 1969-70, King's College, University of London, 1971-72, and University of Michigan, 1973-74. *Military service:* U.S. Army Air Forces, 1943-46; became captain. *Member:* International Association of University Professors of English, Modern Language Association of America, Mediaeval Academy of America (fellow), English Association, English Institute, Academy of Literary Studies, Connecticut Academy of Arts and Sciences (president, 1966-67), Phi Beta Kappa. *Awards, honors:* Guggenheim fellow, 1951-52; American Council of Learned Societies fellow, 1961.

WRITINGS: Piers Plowman: The C-Text and Its Poet, Yale University Press, 1949, 2nd edition, Archon, 1966; (editor) *Chaucer's Poetry: Anthology for the Modern Reader,* Ronald, 1958; (contributor) M. H. Abrams and others, editors *Norton Anthology of English Literature,* Norton, 1962, 3rd edition, 1974; *Speaking of Chaucer,* Norton, 1970. Medieval editor of *PMLA,* 1966-71.

WORK IN PROGRESS: Editing with George Kane the B-Text of *Piers Plowman,* for Athlone Press; writing on Chaucer.

* * *

DOOLEY, Peter C(hamberlain) 1937-

PERSONAL: Born December 27, 1937, in Washington, D.C.; son of John Warren (a stockbroker) and Helen (Harper) Dooley; married Anne Moore, August 29, 1959; children: Brigid, Kevin, Adam, Nathan. *Education:* Grinnell College, B.A., 1959; Cornell University, Ph.D., 1964. *Home:* 206 Garrison Crescent, Saskatoon, Saskatchewan, Canada. *Office:* Department of Economics and Political Science, University of Saskatchewan, Saskatoon, Saskatchewan, Canada.

CAREER: Pennsylvania State University, University Park, assistant professor of economics, 1964-66; University of Saskatchewan, Saskatoon, assistant professor, 1966-70, associate professor of economics, 1970—. *Member:* American Economic Association, Canadian Economic Association, Royal Economic Society.

WRITINGS: Elementary Price Theory, Appleton, 1967; *Introductory Principles of Macroeconomics,* Random House, in press.

* * *

DOUTY, Norman F(ranklin) 1899-

PERSONAL: Surname is pronounced *Doubt*-y; born January 14, 1899, in Rebersburg, Pa.; son of Robert Ambrose (a lumberman) and Ida A. (Beck) Douty; married Susan L. Colman, March 24, 1947 (died, 1955); married Isabel Gray, April 2, 1956. *Education:* Attended Philadelphia School of the Bible, 1919-20; Northern Baptist Theological Seminary, Th.B., 1923. *Residence:* Swengel, Pa. 17880.

CAREER: Ordained minister of the Baptist Church, 1922; pastor in Gilman, Ill., 1921-23, Philadelphia, Pa., 1923-25, and East Lansing, Mich., 1956-57; Grand Rapids Baptist Theological Seminary, Grand Rapids, Mich., president, 1944-45.

WRITINGS: Has Christ's Return Two Stages?, Pageant, 1956; *Another Look at Seventh Day Adventism,* Baker Book, 1962; *The Case of D. M. Canright,* Baker Book, 1964; *The Death of Christ,* Reiner Publications, 1972; *Union with Christ,* Reiner Publications, 1973.

WORK IN PROGRESS: The Abrahamic Covenant, for Gibbs Publishing; *The Douty-Smith and Beck-Price Families,* to be privately printed.

* * *

DOWDY, Andrew 1936-

PERSONAL: Born September 4, 1936, in Detroit, Mich.; son of Andrew H. (a physician) and Helen (Brandes) Dowdy. *Education:* Pomona College, B.A. (cum laude), 1958; University of California at Los Angeles, M.A., 1965. *Agent:* Paul R. Reynolds, 599 Fifth Ave., New York, N.Y. 10017.

CAREER: KPFK-FM, Los Angeles, Calif., literature and drama director, 1959-60; University of California at Los Angeles, English teacher, 1963-68; free-lance writer. *Military service:* U.S. Army, 1960-62. *Member:* Phi Beta Kappa.

WRITINGS: Never Take a Short Price (novel), Dodd, 1973; *"Movies Are Better Than Ever,"* Morrow, 1973.

WORK IN PROGRESS: American Crazy: Fugitive Entertainment from the Dime Museum to Disneyland; What Does Lola Want?, a novel about parapsychology.

* * *

DOWNARD, William L. 1940-

PERSONAL: Born December 28, 1940, in Cincinnati, Ohio; son of William A. (a laborer) and Mildred (Drees) Downard; married Sue E. Winblad, August 24, 1963; children: Becky, David, Mary Beth, Steven. *Education:* St. Joseph's College, Rensselaer, Ind., B.A., 1963; University of Cincinnati, M.A., 1964; Miami University, Miami, Ohio, Ph.D., 1969. *Religion:* Roman Catholic. *Home address:* Route 4, Rensselaer, Ind. 47978. *Office:* Department of History, St. Joseph's College, Rensselaer, Ind. 47978.

CAREER: Teacher of social studies in Cincinnati, Ohio, 1964-66; Mount St. Joseph's College, Cincinnati, Ohio, instructor in history, 1968-69; St. Joseph's College, Rensselaer, Ind., associate professor of history, 1969-73. *Member:* Organization of American Historians.

WRITINGS: The Cincinnati Brewing Industry: A Social and Economic History, Ohio University Press, 1973. Contributor to *Bulletin of the Cincinnati Historical Society.*

* * *

DOWNES, Randolph C(handler) 1901-

PERSONAL: Born July 26, 1901, in South Norwalk, Conn.; son of Charles Henry (a hatter) and Sarah Ruth (Gray) Downes; married Marie McKitrick, August 29, 1925; children: Philip (deceased), Paul (adopted twins). *Education:* Dartmouth College, B.S., 1923; University of Wisconsin, M.A., 1925; Ohio State University, Ph.D., 1929. *Politics:* Liberal. *Home:* 817 Ransom St., Maumee, Ohio 43437.

CAREER: Marietta College, Marietta, Ohio, instructor in history, 1925-27; University of Pittsburgh, Pittsburgh, Pa., assistant professor, 1929-32, associate professor of history, 1932-36; Centenary Junior College, Hackettstown, N.J., associate professor of social studies, 1936-37; Hartwick College, Oneonta, New York, professor of history, 1937-40; Federal Writer's Project in Akron and Columbus, Ohio, writer, 1940-43; Smith College, Northampton, Mass., visiting lecturer in history, 1943-46; University of Toledo, Toledo, Ohio, professor of history, 1946-71. *Member:* Ohio Historical Society (honorary life member), Phi Beta Kappa, Phi Kappa Phi. *Awards, honors:* Social Sciences Research fellowship for travel, 1931-32.

WRITINGS: Evolution of Ohio County Boundaries, Ohio Historical Society, 1927; *Frontier Ohio,* Ohio Historical Society, 1935; *Council Fires on the Upper Ohio,* University of Pittsburgh Press, 1940; *The Conquest,* Historical Society of Northwestern Ohio, 1949; *Canal Days,* Historical Society of Northwestern Ohio, 1949; *Lake Port,* Historical Society of Northwestern Ohio, 1951; *History of Lake Shore Ohio,* three volumes, Lewis Historical Publishing Co., 1952; *Industrial Beginnings,* Historical Society of Northwestern Ohio, 1954; (with Catherine G. Simonds) *Maumee Valley, U.S.A.,* Historical Society of Northwestern Ohio, 1955; *Rise of Warren Gamaliel Harding,*

1865-1920, Ohio State University Press, 1970. Contributor of numerous articles to historical journals. Editor, Historical Society of Northwestern Ohio (now Maumee Valley Historical Society), 1946—.

WORK IN PROGRESS: The Black Ingredient in American History (tentative title).

* * *

DOWNIE, Leonard, Jr. 1942-

PERSONAL: Born May 1, 1942, in Cleveland, Ohio; son of Leonard (a sales executive) and Pearl (Evenheimer) Downie; married second wife, Geraldine Rebach (a teacher), August 15, 1971; children: (first marriage) David, Scott. *Education:* Ohio State University, B.A., 1964, M.A., 1965. *Residence:* Washington, D.C. *Office: Washington Post,* 1150 15th St. N.W., Washington, D.C. 20005.

CAREER: Washington Post, Washington, D.C., reporter, 1965-70, day city editor, 1970-71, deputy metropolitan editor, 1972—. Instructor in communications at American University, 1972-73. *Awards, honors:* Washington-Baltimore Newspaper Guild Front Page Award for newswriting, 1967, 1968; American Bar Association gavel award, 1967; Alicia Patterson Foundation fellow, 1971-72.

WRITINGS: (Contributor) Ben W. Gilbert, editor, *Ten Blocks from the White House,* Praeger, 1968; *Justice Denied: The Case for Reform of the Courts,* Praeger, 1971; *Mortgage on America,* Praeger, 1974. Contributor to *Nation, Potomac,* and *Washington Monthly.*

SIDELIGHTS: Downie has travelled to Britain, France, Italy, Scandinavia, and Israel to study urban development. His latest book is "an expose of real estate speculation in America and its devastating effects on our communities and environment."

* * *

DOWNS, Anthony 1930-

PERSONAL: Born November 21, 1930, in Evanston, Ill.; son of James Chesterfield, Jr. (a real estate consultant) and Florence Glassbrook (Finn) Downs; married Katherine Watson, April 7, 1956; children: Kathy, Christine, Tony, Paul, Carol. *Education:* Carleton College, B.A., 1952; Stanford University, M.A., 1953, Ph.D., 1956. *Politics:* Democrat. *Religion:* Roman Catholic. *Home:* 39 Brinker Rd., Barrington, Ill. 60010. *Office:* Real Estate Research Corp., 72 West Adams St., Chicago, Ill. 60603.

CAREER: University of Chicago, Chicago, Ill., assistant professor of economics and political science, 1957-60; Real Estate Research Corp., Chicago, Ill., chairman of board of directors, 1959—. Adjunct professor at University of Illinois, Chicago Circle, 1974; member of board of directors of National Association for the Advancement of Colored People's Legal Defense Fund, Community Fund of Chicago, Rush-Presbyterian-St. Luke's Medical Center; consultant to federal agencies, local governments, private real estate developers, and corporations. *Military service:* U.S. Naval Reserve, 1956-62, active duty, 1956-59; became lieutenant junior grade. *Member:* American Finance Association, Committee on Urban Economics, Economic Club of Chicago, Commercial Club of Chicago, Lambda Alpha.

WRITINGS: An Economic Theory of Democracy, Harper, 1957; *Inside Bureaucracy,* Little, Brown, 1967; *Racism in American and How to Combat It,* U.S. Commission on Civil Rights, 1970; *Who Are the Urban Poor?,* Committee for Economic Development, 1970; *Urban Problems and Prospects,* Markham, 1970; (with Al Smith and M. Leanne Lachman) *Achieving Effective Desegregation,* Lexington Books, 1973; *Federal Housing Subsidies: How Are They Working?,* Lexington Books, 1973; *Opening Up the Suburbs,* Yale University Press, 1973. Contributor of more than a hundred articles and reviews to professional publications.

WORK IN PROGRESS: A second edition of *Urban Problems and Prospects; Analysis of Real Estate Economics and Urban Affairs.*

* * *

DRESCHER, John M(ummau) 1928-

PERSONAL: Born September 15, 1928, in Manheim, Pa.; son of John Lenhart (a builder) and Anna (Mummau) Drescher; married Betty Keener (a teacher), August 30, 1952; children: John Ronald, Sandra Kay, Rose Marie, Joseph Dean, David Carl. *Education:* Elizabethtown College, student, 1947-49; Eastern Mennonite College, A.B., 1951, Th.B., 1953; Goshen Biblical Seminary, B.D., 1954. *Home address:* Route 1, Box 157, Scottdale, Pa. 15683.

CAREER: Ordained minister of the Mennonite Church, 1954; pastor in Rittman, Ohio, 1954-62; bishop overseer of Ohio and Eastern Mennonite Conference, 1958-63; bishop of the Mennonite Church, 1958-66, assistant moderator, 1967-69, moderator, 1969-71; Scottdale Mennonite Church, Scottdale, Pa., pastor, 1973—. President of Ohio Mennonite Mission Board, 1956-62. Member of board of directors of Associated Church Press, 1970-73; member of Mennonite General Board, 1971—.

WRITINGS: (Contributor) John C. Wenger, editor, *They Met God,* Herald Press, 1964; *Meditations for the Newly Married,* Herald Press, 1969; *Now Is the Time to Love,* Herald Press, 1970; *Heartbeats,* Zondervan, 1970; *Follow Me,* Herald Press, 1971; (contributor) J. Allan Petersen, editor, *The Marriage Affair,* Tyndale, 1971; *Spirit Fruit,* Herald Press, 1974. Author of a series of ten visitation booklets for doctors, pastors, and hospital chaplains, published by Herald Press, 1969. Contributor to more than ninety magazines and journals. Editor of *Gospel Herald,* 1962-73.

WORK IN PROGRESS: A devotional book, *The Greatest Is Love; Seven Things Children Need.*

* * *

DRINKROW, John
See HARDWICK, Michael

* * *

DRISCOLL, Peter (John) 1942-

PERSONAL: Born February 4, 1942, in London, England; son of Cornelius (an engineer) and Helen (a secretary; maiden name, Ball) Driscoll; married Angela Hennessy, January 14, 1967; children: Justine Helen. *Education:* University of the Witwatersrand, B.A., 1967. *Agent:* Peter Janson-Smith, 31 Newington Green, London N16 9PU, England.

CAREER: Rand Daily Mail, Johannesburg, South Africa, reporter, 1959-67; Independent Television News, London, England, scriptwriter and sub-editor, 1969-72; writer, 1973—. *Military service:* South African Army, 1960-61. *Member:* Authors Guild of Authors League of America, Crime Writers Association (England).

WRITINGS: The White Lie Assignment, Macdonald & Co., 1971; *The Wilby Conspiracy,* Lippincott, 1972; *In Connection with Kilshaw,* Lippincott, 1974. Reviewer of books of African interest for *Washington Post.*

WORK IN PROGRESS: Research for a novel set in Africa and a novel set in Asia.

SIDELIGHTS: Driscoll writes: "I have lived for various periods in Africa, Europe, and the Far East and speak fluent Afrikaans, passable French, and execrable Greek. Until recently I have usually had at least two jobs at any one time (student and journalist, journalist and writer, and sometimes journalist and journalist) and have been too busy and nomadic to acquire a passionate interest in any pastimes—apart from travelling itself, preferably to unusual places, and, of course, reading on every conceivable subject."

* * *

DRIVING HAWK, Virginia
See SNEVE, Virginia Driving Hawk

* * *

DROWN, Harold J(ames) 1904-

PERSONAL: Born September 7, 1904, in Erie, Pa.; son of Arthur Lyle (in real estate) and Bertha (Sawtelle) Drown; married Ethel Gross, October 19, 1929; children: Nancy Ann (Mrs. Philip Wile). *Education:* University of Pittsburgh, B.A., 1944; McCormick Theological Seminary, B.D., 1946. *Politics:* Republican. *Home:* 6596 Friars Rd., San Diego, Calif. 92108. *Office:* First Presbyterian Church, 320 Date, San Diego, Calif. 92101.

CAREER: General Insurance Counselor, Erie, Pa., owner, 1924-44; Presbyterian clergyman in Iowa, New York, and California, 1946-66; marriage, family, and child counselor in Vista, Calif., and at First Presbyterian Church, San Diego, Calif., 1966—. Trustee of Parsons College, 1950-57. *Member:* California Association of Marriage and Family Counselors, Rotary International. *Awards, honors:* D.D. from Parsons College, 1953.

WRITINGS: Therefore the Family, Dorrance, 1972; *You the Graduate,* Abingdon, 1974. Also author of daily radio program, "Paths of Happiness," 1962-63.

WORK IN PROGRESS: Booster Shots, a series of uplifting vignettes; *Lydia,* historical fiction about the Holy Land, completion expected in 1976.

* * *

DRURY, Michael

PERSONAL: Born in California; daughter of Davis (in advertising) and Lucile (Rood) Drury; married John S. Calderwood, 1942 (divorced, 1961). *Education:* Stanford University, A.B., 1940. *Politics:* Independent. *Religion:* Protestant. *Residence:* Newport, R.I.

CAREER: Life, New York, N.Y., editorial assistant, 1941-43; *Harper's Monthly,* New York, N.Y., editorial assistant, 1943-44; *McCall's,* New York, N.Y., assistant fiction editor, 1946-47; free-lance writer, 1947—. Visiting instructor at University of Missouri, 1958; volunteer teacher at Women's Correctional Institution, New York, N.Y., 1959-60. *Member:* Authors' Guild (council member, 1956-74), Authors' League, Theta Sigma Phi. *Awards, honors:* Headliner award from Theta Sigma Phi, 1958; Freedoms Foundation award, 1973.

WRITINGS: (Editor with Helen Hull) *The Writers' Roundtable,* Harper, 1959; *How to Get Along with People,* Doubleday, 1965; *Advice to a Young Wife from an Old Mistress,* Doubleday, 1968; *The Inward Sea,* Doubleday, 1972; *The Everyday Miracles,* Hallmark Editions, 1972; *This Much and More,* Pocket Books, 1973. Also author of a novelette, "The Cheese Stands Alone." Contributor of more than three hundred articles, short stories, and poems to magazines, journals, and anthologies, including *Good Housekeeping, Ladies Home Journal, McCall's, Woman's Day, Family Circle, Reader's Digest, Collier's, Saturday Evening Post, Atlantic, Redbook,* and *Christian Herald.*

AVOCATIONAL INTERESTS: Theater, the outdoors, cooking, comparative religion, modern philosophers, music.

* * *

DRUXMAN, Michael Barnett 1941-

PERSONAL: Born February 23, 1941, in Seattle, Wash.; son of Harry (a jeweler) and Florence (Barnett) Druxman; married Theresa M. Lundy (a park director), March 18, 1966; children: David Michael. *Education:* University of Washington, Seattle, B.A., 1963. *Residence:* Agoura, Calif. *Office:* Michael B. Druxman & Associates, 6464 Sunset Blvd., Hollywood, Calif. 90028.

CAREER: Pope & Talbot, Inc., Seattle, Wash., real estate salesman, 1963; Retail Credit Co., Los Angeles, Calif., credit investigator, 1964-65; Michael B. Druxman & Associates (public relations firm), Hollywood, Calif., owner, 1965—.

WRITINGS: Paul Muni: His Life and His Films, A. S. Barnes, 1974; *Basil Rathbone: His Life and His Films,* A. S. Barnes, in press; *Make It Again, Sam: A Survey of Movie Remakes,* A. S. Barnes, in press. Author of "Yesterday at the Movies," a column in *Coronet,* 1973-74.

SIDELIGHTS: Druxman writes: "My interest in motion pictures stems from childhood. I appeared in and directed many plays in the Seattle area and even had two theatrical groups which I managed."

* * *

DRYANSKY, G. Y.

PERSONAL: Surname is pronounced Dree-*on*-ski; married; children: two. *Education:* Princeton University, A.B., 1959; Harvard University, A.M., 1961. *Home:* 39 rue Cambon, Paris, France 75016.

CAREER: Journalist.

WRITINGS: Other People (fiction), Dutton, 1973.

WORK IN PROGRESS: A second novel.

* * *

DUBOFSKY, Melvyn 1934-

PERSONAL: Born October 25, 1934, in Brooklyn, N.Y.; son of Harry (a projectionist) and Lillian (Schneider) Dubofsky; married Joan S. Klores (a speech pathologist), January 16, 1959; children: David Mark, Lisa Sue. *Education:* Brooklyn College (now Brooklyn College of the City University of New York), B.A., 1955; University of Rochester, Ph.D., 1960. *Home:* 23 Devon Blvd., Binghamton, N.Y. 13903. *Office:* Department of History, State University of New York at Binghamton, Binghamton, N.Y. 13903.

CAREER: Northern Illinois University, DeKalb, assistant professor of history, 1959-67; University of Massachusetts, Amherst, associate professor of history, 1967-69; University of Wisconsin, Milwaukee, professor of history, 1970-71; State University of New York, Binghamton, professor of history, 1971—. *Member:* American Historical Association, Organization of American Historians, Labor Historians Society, American Association of University Professors. *Awards, honors:* Grants from American Philosophical Society, and American Council of Learned Societies, 1965; National Endowment for the Humanities senior fellow, 1973-74.

WRITINGS: When Workers Organize, University of Massachusetts Press, 1968; *We Shall Be All: A History of the IWW,* Quadrangle, 1969; (editor) *American Labor Since the New Deal,* Quadrangle, 1971; *Industrialism and American Workers, 1865-1920,* Crowell, in press.

WORK IN PROGRESS: A biography of John L. Lewis, for Quadrangle.

* * *

DUFFY, Francis R(amon) 1915-

PERSONAL: Born March 26, 1915, in Philadelphia, Pa.; son of John J. (a police inspector) and Anna C. (Rodgers) Duffy. *Education:* Attended Holy Ghost College, 1933-35; St. Mary's College, Norwalk, Conn., B.A., 1938, B.D. (in affiliation with Yale University), 1942; Catholic University of America, M.A., 1944; University of Pittsburgh, Ph.D., 1955; Duquesne University, postdoctoral study, 1955-68. *Home and office:* St. Joseph's House, Box 4481, 16th St. and Allegheny Ave., Philadelphia, Pa. 19140.

CAREER: Roman Catholic priest; entered Order of Fathers of the Holy Ghost (C.S.Sp.), 1933. Duquesne University, Pittsburgh, Pa., began as assistant professor, 1943, professor of sociology and criminology, 1960-68, chairman of department, 1943-66, assistant to vice-president, 1966; St. Joseph's House, Philadelphia, Pa., director, 1968—. Visiting professor of psychology and social work at St. Joseph's Hospital School of Nursing, 1952-60, and St. Joseph's College, Philadelphia, Pa.; visiting lecturer at St. Vincent's College, Seton Hall College, University of Pittsburgh, University of Lagos, Steubenville College, Loyola University of Los Angeles, Wheeling College, and Marion College; in-service training instructor to Pennsylvania Board of Parole, 1949-55; instructor, Pittsburgh Police Department, 1950-60. Chaplain and counselor at Juvenile Court in Pittsburgh, 1947-67, and Pittsburgh Police Academy, 1945-68. Producer of radio series, "Exploring the Child's World," for seventy-five colleges, 1962-68. Chairman of religious affairs for High Commissioner of Germany, 1950-51, and Adoption Board, Stuttgart, 1951. Consultant to Children's Home, Allegheny County Behavior Clinic, and Medical Department of Gulf Oil Corp. *Military service:* U.S. Army, chaplain, 1950-52. U.S. Army Reserve, 1952-75; instructor in Army Chaplain School, 1965-74; received Legion of Merit and General Stewart Award; became colonel.

MEMBER: Royal Anthropological Institute (fellow), Royal College of Psychiatrists (corresponding associate), American Society of Clinical Hypnosis (fellow), American Sociological Society, American Association of University Professors.

WRITINGS: Title System in Nigeria, Catholic University of America Press, 1942; *Follow-Up Study of Delinquents,* University of Pittsburgh Press, 1955; *Exploring the Child's World,* Bradley Brothers, 1968; *Social Psychology of Growing Up,* Bradley Brothers, 1968; *Juvenile Delinquency,* St. Joseph's House, 1969; *Personality and Adjustment,* St. Joseph's House, 1969; *Accommodations for Teen-Agers,* St. Joseph's House, 1970; *Hypnosis,* St. Joseph's House, 1974.

WORK IN PROGRESS: Follow-Up Study of Smoking Intervention with Hypnosis.

* * *

DUKE, Benjamin 1931-

PERSONAL: Born February 1, 1931, in Berwick, Pa.; son of Benjamin and Adah (Bower) Duke; married June Marie Smith, January 9, 1954; children: Noriko Susan, Kimiko Anne, Christopher Kenji. *Education:* Pennsylvania State University, M.A., 1957, Ph.D., 1959; University of London, Ph.D., 1969. *Home and office:* Department of Comparative and International Education, International Christian University, Mitaka, Tokyo, Japan.

CAREER: International Christian University, Tokyo, Japan, assistant professor, 1962-65, associate professor, 1965-70, professor of comparative and international education, 1970—. *Military service:* U.S. Army, 1953-55. U.S. Army Reserve, 1955-60; became captain. *Member:* Comparative Education Society of Europe (British Section), Comparative Education Society of America, Comparative Education Society of Japan, Japan Education Society.

WRITINGS: (Editor) *Education Media Research in the Far East,* U.S. Office of Education, 1963; *Japan's Militant Teachers: A History of the Left Wing Teachers' Movement,* University Press of Hawaii, 1973. Contributor to *Saturday Review* and to education journals. English editor of *Japan Education Journal,* 1970-75.

WORK IN PROGRESS: Research on the problems of teaching and learning the native language in Japan, the United States, and England, and the educational reforms of the American Occupation of Japan.

* * *

DUKE, Will
See GAULT, William Campbell

* * *

DUNCAN, Irma 1897-

PERSONAL: Surname legally changed, 1917; born February 26, 1897, in Hamburg, Germany; became American citizen, 1934; daughter of Ernst August and Christiane (Ehrich) Grimme; adopted daughter of Isadora Duncan (a dancer); married Sherman S. Rogers (an attorney), September 19, 1935. *Education:* Attended Isadora Duncan's School of the Dance, 1905-18. *Home:* 211 East Mission St., Santa Barbara, Calif. 93101.

CAREER: Dancer, teacher of the dance, author. Teacher and associate of Isadora Duncan's School of the Dance, 1921-27, later succeeded Isadora Duncan as head of school. *Member:* Alliance Francaise de Santa Barbara, Santa Barbara Historical Society.

WRITINGS: (With Allan Ross Macdougall) *Isadora Duncan's Russian Days and Her Last Years in France,* Covici-Friede, 1929; *Duncan Dancer* (autobiography; first appeared in abridged form in *Dance Perspectives,* No. 21-22, 1965), Wesleyan University Press, 1966; *The Technique of*

Isadora Duncan, Kamin Publishers, 1937, 3rd edition, Dance Horizons, 1970.

WORK IN PROGRESS: A biography, *An American Family* (tentative title).

SIDELIGHTS: Besides speaking English, German, French, and Russian, Miss Duncan paints in oils.

* * *

DUNHAM, William Huse, Jr. 1901-

PERSONAL: Born December 31, 1901, in Evanston, Ill.; son of William Huse (a businessman) and Margaret (Little) Dunham; married Helen Suart Garrison, June 25, 1935; children: Stephanie Southgate (Mrs. Henry L. Howell), William Lee Huse. *Education:* Yale University, B.A., 1923, Ph.D., 1929. *Politics:* Independent. *Religion:* Independent. *Home:* 200 Everit St., New Haven, Conn. 06511.

CAREER: University School, Cleveland, Ohio, master in history, 1923-24; Yale University, New Haven, Conn., instructor, 1925-30, assistant professor, 1930-40, associate professor, 1940-46, professor of history, 1946-48, George Burton Adams Professor, 1948-70, professor emeritus, 1970—, chairman of department, 1948-52, fellow of Saybrook College, 1933-55, and acting master, 1955-56, master of Jonathan Edwards College, 1956-61, and former master, 1961—. Fulbright research scholar, University of London, 1952-53. *Member:* Mediaeval Academy of America (fellow), Royal Historical Society (fellow), American Historical Association, American Society of Legal Historians, Conference on British Studies (president, 1967-69; member of executive council, 1969-71, Selden Society (London; member of council, 1965—), Connecticut Academy of Arts & Sciences (president, 1959-60), Elizabethan Club (president, 1963-64), Elihu Club, Psi Upsilon. *Awards, honors:* Sterling fellowship, 1927-28; Social Science Research fellowship for study in England, 1930-31; H. E. Huntington Library Research fellowship, 1941-42; Guggenheim fellowship, 1944-46; Social Science Research Council Faculty Fellow, 1961-62; Yale University W. C. DeVane Medal, 1973.

WRITINGS: (Editor) Ralph de Hengham, *Radulphi de Hengham Summae,* Cambridge University Press, 1932; *The Fane Fragment of the 1461 Lords' Journal,* Yale University Press, 1935; (editor with Stanley M. Pargellis and author of introduction) *Complaint and Reform in England, 1436-1714,* Oxford University Press, 1938, reprinted, Octagon, 1966; (editor with W. A. Morris) *The English Government at Work, 1327-1336,* Mediaeval Academy of America, Volume III, 1950; (editor) *Casus Placitorum and Reports of Cases in the King's Courts, 1272-1278,* B. Quaritch, 1952; *Lord Hastings' Indentured Retainers, 1461-1483,* Connecticut Academy of Arts & Sciences, 1955, revised edition, Shoe String Press, 1970; (with Samuel E. Thorne, Philip B. Kurland, and Ivor Jennings) *The Great Charter,* Pantheon, 1965. Contributor to journals in his field.

WORK IN PROGRESS: The Kingdom and the Crown of Britain, 871-1971.

* * *

DUNLAP, G(eorge) D(ale) 1923-

PERSONAL: Born July 30, 1923, in Cadiz, Ohio; son of J. Harry and Alice (Moore) Dunlap; married Dorothy Wright (an artist), June 20, 1945; children: George Rion, Frank Harrison. *Education:* Attended Canton Actual Business College, 1941, and Northwestern State College of Louisiana. *Politics:* Republican. *Religion:* Southern Baptist. *Home:* 316 Halsey Rd., Annapolis, Md. 21401.

CAREER: Office of Inspector of Naval Material, Martins Ferry, Ohio, anti-aircraft gun inspector, 1942-43; Weems Organizations, Annapolis, Md., assistant manager for Weems System of Navigation, 1946-50, vice-president and technical director, 1952-64, division manager, 1964-66, vice-president and manager of Weems & Plath, Inc., 1952-66, owner, president, and program manager of thirteen professional studies, 1966-73, vice-president and manager of Aeronautical Services, Inc., 1952-64; navigational consultant in Annapolis, Md., 1973—. Licensed by Federal Aeronautics Administration as private pilot and instructor in navigation and meteorology; has invented more than seventeen navigation instruments for use in air, sea, and space. Former vice-president of Eastern region of Institute of Navigation. *Military service:* U.S. Naval Reserve, active duty, 1943-45, 1950-51.

WRITINGS: (With H. H. Shufeldt) *Dutton's Navigation and Piloting,* 12th edition (Dunlap was not associated with earlier editions), U.S. Naval Institute, 1969; (with H. H. Shufeldt) *Piloting and Dead Reckoning,* U.S. Naval Institute, 1970; *America's Cup Defenders,* American Heritage, 1970; *Book of the Sextant,* Weems & Plath, 1971; *Navigating and Finding Fish with Electronics,* International Marine Publishing, 1972.

Contributor to U.S. Naval Institute proceedings; contributor of more than twenty articles on navigation to magazines, including *Rudder, Skyways, Flying, Navigator, Aviation Age, Skipper, Ensign,* and *Canadian Aviation.*

WORK IN PROGRESS: Simplified Celestial Navigation.

* * *

DUNLAP, Jane
See DAVIS, Adelle

* * *

DUNN, Alan (Cantwell) 1900-1974

August 11, 1900—May 20, 1974; American cartoonist. Obituaries: *New York Times,* May 22, 1974; *Time,* June 3, 1974; *Newsweek,* June 3, 1974. (*CA*-33/36).

* * *

DUNN, Charles W(illiam) 1915-

PERSONAL: Born November 30, 1915, in Arbuthnott, Scotland; came to United States in 1928, naturalized in 1964; son of Peter Alexander and Alberta (Freeman) Dunn; married Patricia Campbell, June 21, 1941 (died, 1973); children: Deirdre (Mrs. Harry Strachan), Peter Arthur. *Education:* McMaster University, B.A. (with honors), 1938; Harvard University, M.A., 1939, Ph.D., 1948. *Religion:* Episcopalian. *Home:* 3 De Wolfe St., Cambridge, Mass. 02138. *Office:* Department of Celtic Languages and Literatures, Harvard University, 69 Dunster St., Cambridge, Mass. 02138.

CAREER: Stephens College, Columbia, Mo., instructor in humanities, 1941-42; Cornell University, Ithaca, N.Y., instructor in English, 1943-46; University of Toronto, Toronto, Ontario, instructor, 1946-50, assistant professor, 1950-55, associate professor of English, 1955-56; New York University, New York, N.Y., professor of English, 1956-63; Harvard University, Cambridge, Mass., professor of Celtic languages and literatures, and chairman of department, 1963—, Margaret Brooks Robinson Professor of Celtic Languages and Literatures, 1967—, master of Quincy House, 1966—. Taft Lecturer, University of Cincinnati, 1956.

MEMBER: American Academy of Arts and Sciences (fellow), Mediaeval Academy of America, American Folklore Society, Modern Language Association of America, Irish Texts Society, Early English Text Society, Royal Scottish Country Dance Society, Comunn Gaidhealach (Scotland), Celtic Union (Edinburgh; honorary president, 1963—), St. Andrews Society (New York), Odd Volumes Club (Boston), Harvard Club (New York). *Awards, honors:* Dexter fellow in Nova Scotia, 1941; Rockefeller fellow in Nova Scotia, 1942-43; Nuffield fellow in Ireland, Scotland, and Wales, 1954-55; Canada Award from Federation of Gaelic Societies, 1955; Chicago Folklore Prize, 1960, for *The Foundling and the Werewolf;* Guggenheim fellow in Scotland, Wales, and Brittany, 1962-63.

WRITINGS: Highland Settler: A Portrait of the Scottish Gael in Nova Scotia, University of Toronto Press, 1953, new edition, 1968; *The Foundling and the Werewolf: A Literary-Historical Study of Guillaume de Palerne,* University of Toronto Press, 1960; (with Edward Byrnes) *Middle English Literature,* Harcourt, 1973.

Editor: *A Chaucer Reader: Selections from the Canterbury Tales,* Harcourt, 1952, abridged edition, 1960; (and author of revised translation and introduction) Geoffrey of Monmouth, *History of the Kings of Britain,* Dutton, 1958; (and author of introduction) *The Romance of the Rose,* translated by H. W. Robbins, Dutton, 1962; (and author of introduction) *Lays of Courtly Love,* translated by Patricia Terry, Anchor Books, 1963.

Contributor: G. B. Harrison, editor, *Major British Writers,* Harcourt, 1954, revised edition, 1967; *Poems for Upper School,* Macmillan, 1956, new edition, 1962; J. B. Severs, editor, *A Manual of the Writings in Middle English, 1050-1500,* Shoe String, 1968; T. P. Cross and C. H. Slover, editors, *Ancient Irish Tales,* Barnes & Noble, 1969.

Author of introduction: (And compiler of bibliography) John Froissart, *Chronicles of England, France and Spain,* Dutton, 1961; *Poems of the Vikings: The Elder Edda,* translated by Patricia Terry, Bobbs-Merrill, 1969.

Has read in Old and Middle English, and written introductions to recordings, including "Early English Poetry," Folkways Records, 1958, and "Changing English Language" and "Changing Literary Style," both Folkways Records, 1959. Contributor to *Masterplots Cyclopedia, Encyclopedia Canadiana,* and *Encyclopedia of Poetry and Poetics.* Contributor of about forty reviews and articles to literature, philosophy, and folklore journals.

* * *

DURHAM, Marilyn 1930-

PERSONAL: Born September 8, 1930, in Evansville, Ind.; daughter of Russell (a blacksmith) and Stacy (Birdsall) Wall; married Kilburn Durham (a Social Security field worker), November 24, 1950; children: Joyce Elaine, Mary Jennifer. *Education:* Attended University of Evansville, 1949-50. *Home:* 1508 Howard St., Evansville, Ind. 47713. *Agent:* Ann Elmo Agency, 52 Vanderbilt Ave., New York, N.Y. 11017.

CAREER: Novelist and housewife. *Member:* Western Writers of America, Society of Midland Authors. *Awards, honors:* Society of Midland Authors fiction award, 1973, for *The Man Who Loved Cat Dancing.*

WRITINGS—Novels: *The Man Who Loved Cat Dancing,* Harcourt, 1972; *Dutch Uncle,* Harcourt, 1973.

SIDELIGHTS: Of *The Man Who Loved Cat Dancing,* Martin Levin has written in the *New York Times Book Review:* "If anything can be considered hot-weather literature, this is it. Mrs. Durham has staged a beautifully executed escape into the legendary past." Of the same book, Richard Werry has written in the *Detroit News:* "So when a new writer chooses a western for a first novel, that's news. And when that writer is a woman and the novel is a first rate slambanger without stereotyped descriptions and 'podner' dialog, it's even more interesting. 'The Man Who Loved Cat Dancing' is Mrs. Marilyn Durham's first published novel, and it is also the first novel she ever attempted."

BIOGRAPHICAL/CRITICAL SOURCES: Publisher's Weekly, July 31, 1972; *Time,* August 7, 1972; *Vogue,* October 1, 1972; *Woman's Day,* October, 1972; *Life,* December 8, 1972; *American Libraries,* January, 1973; *Writer's Digest,* March, 1973.

* * *

DURZAK, Manfred 1938-

PERSONAL: Born December 10, 1938, in Merkstein, Germany; son of Ludwig (a lawyer) and Helene (Grondzewski) Durzak; married Margund Klinke, November 29, 1963; children: Malte, Nike. *Education:* Attended University of Bonn, 1958-59; Free University of Berlin, D.Phil., 1961, Ph.D., 1963. *Home:* 232 Ploen, Holstein, Ulmenstrasse 86, Germany. *Office:* Department of German, Indiana University, Bloomington, Ind. 41401.

CAREER: Free University of Berlin, Berlin, Germany, university assistant in Germanistics, 1963-64; Yale University, New Haven, Conn., research scholar, 1964-65; Indiana University, Bloomington, assistant professor, 1965-68, associate professor, 1968-71, professor of German literature, 1971—; University of Kiel, Kiel, Germany, professor of German, 1969—. *Member:* Modern Language Association of America, American Association of Teachers of German, Deutsche Hochschulgermanisten, Lessing Society, Kleist-Gesellschaft, Hebbel-Gesellschaft. *Awards, honors:* Volkswagenstiftung grant, 1963; Ford Foundation grant, 1967.

WRITINGS: Der junge Stefan George: Kunsttheorie und Dichtung (title means "The Young Poet Stefan George: His Poetry and Theory of Poetry"), W. Fink, 1968; *Hermann Broch: Der Dichter und seine Zeit* (title means "Broch: The Novelist and His Contemporaries"), W. Kohlhammer, 1968; *Poesie und Ratio: Vier Lessing-Studien* (title means "Literature and Reason: Four Studies on G. E. Lessing"), Athenaeum, 1970; *Der deutsche Roman der Geganwart* (title means "The Contemporary German Novel"), W. Kohlhammer, 1971; (editor) *Die deutsche Literatur der Gegenwart* (title means "Contemporary German Literature"), Reclam, 1971; *Hermann Broch: Perspektiven du Forschung* (title means "Hermann Broch: Aspects of Broch-Scholarship Research"), W. Fink, 1972; *Duerrenmatt, Frisch, Weiss: Deutsches Drama der Gegenwart zwischen Kritik und Utopie* (title means "Duerrenmatt, Frisch, Weiss: Contemporary German Drama Between Critique and Utopian Thought"), Reclam, 1972; *Die deutsche Exilliteratur 1933-1945* (title means "German Literature of Exile 1933-1945"), Reclam, 1973; *Texte und Kontexte: Studien zur deutschen und vergleichenden Literaturwissenschaft* (title means "Texts and Contexts: Studies on German and Comparative Literature"), Francke, 1973; *Zwischen Symbolismus und Expressionismus: Stefan George* (title means "Between Symbolism and Expressionism: Stefan George"), W. Kohlhammer, 1974.

Contributor to German broadcasts and to *Die Zeit, Die Welt, Frankfurter Allgemeine Zeitung, PMLA, German Quarterly,* and *Germanic Review.*

WORK IN PROGRESS: Research in twentieth-century literature, German exile literature, and comparative literature.

* * *

DuVAUL, Virginia C.
See COFFMAN, Virginia (Edith)

* * *

DYKHUIZEN, George 1899-

PERSONAL: Born January 16, 1899, in Lafayette, Ind.; son of George (a businessman) and Gertrude (Goris) Dykhuizen; married Helen Young, December 29, 1926; children: Phyllis Dykhuizen Davis, Janice (Mrs. Kenneth Mudgett). *Education:* Indiana University, A.B., 1921; University of Chicago, A.M., 1924, Ph.D., 1934. *Politics:* Independent. *Religion:* Congregational. *Home:* 350 South Prospect St., Burlington, Vt. 05401. *Office:* Department of Philosophy, University of Vermont, Burlington, Vt. 05401.

CAREER: University of Vermont, Burlington, assistant professor, 1926-28, associate professor, 1928-45, professor of philosophy, 1945-54, James Marsh Professor of Philosophy, 1954-64, James Marsh Professor Emeritus, 1964—. Visiting professor, University of Alberta, summer, 1943; Fulbright exchange professor, University of Cairo, Egypt, 1953-54. Consultant and lecturer in social philosophy, U.S. Department of Agriculture, 1940-48, 1956; member of U.S. embassy committee for selection of Egyptian scholars, 1953-54. *Member:* American Association for the Advancement of Science, American Philosophical Association, John Dewey Society, Phi Beta Kappa, Phi Delta Kappa.

WRITINGS: The Life and Mind of John Dewey, Southern Illinois University Press, 1973. Contributor to *Journal of Religion, Educational Theory, Journal of the History of Ideas, Journal of the History of Philosophy, Journal of Philosophy,* and *Philosophical Review.*

* * *

DYMSZA, William A(lexander) 1922-

PERSONAL: Surname is pronounced Dim-za; born February 8, 1922, in Cambridge, Mass.; son of Alexander (a contractor) and Mary M. (Lucas) Dymsza; married Begona Lamana, May 20, 1957; children: Christine M., Madeline A. *Education:* Pennsylvania State University, A.B., 1943; University of Pennsylvania, M.B.A., 1948, Ph.D., 1951. *Politics:* Independent. *Religion:* Roman Catholic. *Home:* 73 Martin Rd., Livingston, N.J. 07039. *Office:* Graduate School of Business Administration, Rutgers University, 16 Washington Pl., Newark, N.J. 07102.

CAREER: Boston College, Boston, Mass., assistant professor of economics, 1948-51; Office of Price Stabilization, Boston, Mass., economist, 1951-52; U.S. Economic Mission to Vietnam, Laos, and Cambodia, program coordinating officer, 1952-55; University of Maryland, College Park, lecturer in economics, 1955-58; Rutgers University, New Brunswick, N.J., associate professor of international business, 1958-64; University of Hawaii, Honolulu, visiting professor of international economics, Economic Research Center, 1964-65; Rutgers University, Newark Campus, professor of business administration, 1965—, director of International Business Institute, 1965-70. Visiting professor at Naval War College, 1967-68. Consultant to U.S. Department of Commerce, 1962-68; member of United Nations Economic Commission to Latin America, 1970-72. *Military service:* U.S. Marine Corps, 1943-46.

MEMBER: American Economic Association, Association for Education in International Business, United Nations Association of the U.S.A., Phi Beta Kappa, Beta Gamma Sigma. *Awards, honors:* Ford Foundation fellow in international economics at Massachusetts Institute of Technology, 1959.

WRITINGS: (With Seymour Friedland and Thomas Moranian) *Financing Manufacturing Activities in New Jersey,* New Jersey Department of Economic Development, 1964; (with Chris Theodore and Fred Hung) *Hawaiian Inter-Island Ferry,* University of Hawaii, 1965; *Foreign Trade Zones and International Business,* New Jersey Department of Economic Development, 1965; *Multinational Business Strategy,* McGraw, 1972. Contributor of more than twenty articles to business and economic publications.

WORK IN PROGRESS: Further studies on multinational enterprise and its management, on foreign investment and export development in developing countries, and on East-West business arrangements.

* * *

EAGLY, Robert V(ictor) 1933-

PERSONAL: Surname is pronounced A-*glee;* born May 28, 1933, in Kalamazoo, Mich.; son of Alva Purl and F. Blanche (Gortner) Eagly; married Alice Jo Hendrickson (a professor of psychology), September 8, 1972; children: Ingrid Victoria. *Education:* University of Michigan, A.B. (with distinction), 1954; University of Stockholm, graduate study, 1954-55; University of Washington, Seattle, M.A., 1958; University of Oslo, graduate study, 1960-61; Rutgers University, Ph.D., 1962. *Office:* Federal Reserve Bank, New York, N.Y.

CAREER: Wayne State University, Detroit, Mich., assistant professor, 1962-66, associate professor of economics, 1966-67; University of Massachusetts, Amherst, associate professor of economics, 1967-72, director of graduate studies, 1968-70; State University of New York, Binghamton, visiting professor of economics, 1973—. Visiting lecturer at University of Wisconsin, summer, 1964; visiting assistant professor at University of California at Los Angeles, summer, 1965; visiting professor at University of Illinois, 1970-71, and at University of North Carolina, 1972-73. *Member:* American Economic Association, American Finance Society, American Historical Association, Economic History Association, Royal Economic Society, Southern Economic Association. *Awards, honors:* Fulbright fellowship to study in Norway, 1960-61.

WRITINGS: Events, Ideology, and Economic Theory, Wayne State University Press, 1968; *The Swedish Bullionist Controversy,* American Philosophical Society, 1971; *The Structure of Classical Economic Theory,* Oxford University Press, 1974. Contributor of about thirty articles and book reviews to journals in his field.

WORK IN PROGRESS: Research on interest rate parity.

EAKINS, David W(alter) 1923-

PERSONAL: Born February 9, 1923, in Tulare, Calif.; son of Jack M. (a rancher) and Mary Adele (Lewis) Eakins; married Anne Julia Epstein, June 17, 1951 (divorced, 1961); married Jimmie Sue Hiller, August 19, 1967; children: (first marriage) Laura, Susan; (second marriage) Benjamin Matthew. *Education:* Oregon State University, B.S., 1949; Columbia University, graduate study, 1949-51; University of Colorado, M.A., 1957; University of Wisconsin, Ph.D., 1966. *Politics:* "Variable." *Religion:* None. *Home:* 924 Roosevelt St., San Jose, Calif. 95112. *Office:* Department of History, San Jose State University, San Jose, Calif. 95192.

CAREER: Sheep butcher in Denver, Colo., 1952-56; Northwestern University, Evanston, Ill., lecturer in business history, 1961-62; San Jose State University, San Jose, Calif., assistant professor, 1962-69, associate professor, 1969-74, professor of history, 1974—. *Military service:* U.S. Army, 1943-45; became sergeant. *Member:* Organization of American Historians. *Awards, honors:* Rabinowitz Foundation grant, 1969.

WRITINGS: (Contributor) David Horowitz, editor, *Corporations and the Cold War,* Monthly Review Press, 1969; (editor with James Weinstein) *For a New America,* Random House, 1970; (contributor) Murray Rothbard and Ronald Radosh, editors, *A New History of Leviathan,* Dutton, 1972; (contributor) Jerry Israel, editor, *Building the Organizational Society,* Macmillan, 1972. Member of editorial board of *Studies on the Left,* 1958-63, and *Socialist Revolution,* 1969-74.

WORK IN PROGRESS: A book on the making of corporate liberal policy, on business liberals and the growth of national economic control in the presidency from 1885 to the present.

* * *

EARL, Paul Hunter 1945-

PERSONAL: Born August 25, 1945, in Bryn Mawr, Pa.; son of William Elias (a pharmacist) and Janet (White) Earl; married Dale Remington, July 13, 1968; children: Bradley Hunter. *Education:* Bucknell University, A.B., 1967; Georgetown University, M.A., 1971, Ph.D., 1973. *Politics:* Independent. *Religion:* Protestant. *Home:* 6019 Ninth Rd. N., Arlington, Va. 22205. *Office:* Department of Economics, Georgetown University, 36th and N Sts. N.W., Washington, D.C. 20007

CAREER: Westat, Inc., Rockville, Md., research analyst, 1967-69; Georgetown University, Washington, D.C., director of computer activities, 1968-72, assistant professor of economics, 1972—. Instructor at Foreign Service Institute, Washington, D.C., 1973-74. Consultant to Bureau of Labor Statistics, 1970-73; and Data Resources, Inc., 1973—. *Military service:* U.S. Army Reserve, 1972—; present rank, first lieutenant. *Member:* American Economic Association.

WRITINGS: *Inflation and the Structure of Industrial Prices,* Heath, 1973.

WORK IN PROGRESS: Research on industrial price behavior.

AVOCATIONAL INTERESTS: Sailing, the seashore, sports.

EARLY, Robert 1940-

PERSONAL: Born October 9, 1940, in Lincolnton, N.C.; son of Jake W. (former baseball catcher for Washington Senators) and Mildred (Sullivan) Early. *Education:* Attended St. Mary's Seminary and University, 1960-62; Belmont Abbey College, B.A., 1965; graduate study at University of North Carolina, 1967-69; Bowling Green State University, M.F.A., 1970. *Residence:* Bowling Green, Ohio. *Agent:* Elizabeth McKee, McIntosh, McKee & Dodds, Inc., 22 East 40th St., New York, N.Y. 10016. *Office:* Department of English, Bowling Green State University, Bowling Green, Ohio 43403.

CAREER: Roman Catholic monk at Belmont Abbey, Belmont, N.C., 1960-70, instructor in English and music, 1962-70; Bowling Green State University, Bowling Green, Ohio, assistant professor of English, 1970—. *Member:* Writers Guild.

WRITINGS—Novels: *The Jealous Ear,* Houghton, 1973; *Powers and Dominations,* Houghton, in press. Editor of "Itinerary," a series published by Bowling Green State University Press.

WORK IN PROGRESS: Research for a book on American imagination; a novel; a book on baseball.

AVOCATIONAL INTERESTS: Musical composition and arranging.

* * *

EASTMAN, G. Don
See OOSTERMAN, Gordon

* * *

EASTON, Allan 1916-

PERSONAL: Born September 15, 1916, in Hoboken, N.J.; married Miriam Berger (an editor of a literary journal); children: Kenneth, Barbara. *Education:* Hofstra College (now Hofstra University), B.S., 1957; Columbia University, Ph.D., 1964. *Politics:* Unaffiliated. *Religion:* Unaffiliated. *Office:* School of Business, Hofstra University, Hempstead, N.Y. 11550.

CAREER: Emerson Radio and Phonograph Corp., New York, N.Y., design engineer, 1941-46; Hazeltine Electronics, New York, design engineer, 1946-48; Teletone Radio Corp., New York, chief engineer, 1948-51; Radio Receptor Corp., New York, engineering manager, 1951-53; Granco Products, Inc., New York, vice-president and general manager, 1953-56; General Transistor Corp., New York, vice-president of marketing, 1956-60; Columbia University, New York, N.Y., instructor, 1961-64, assistant professor, 1964-65, adjunct associate professor, 1965-66, associate professor of management, 1967-73; Hofstra University, Hempstead, N.Y., professor of management, 1974—. Research associate for New York State Governor's committee on the minimum wage, 1964. *Member:* American Association of University Professors, American Institute for Decision Sciences. *Awards, honors:* Naval Ordnance Development Award, 1945.

WRITINGS: (Editor) *Managing Organization Change: Selected Case Studies,* Yearbook of Business Series, Hofstra University, 1969; (contributor) P. S. Greenlaw and R. D. Smith, editors, *Personnel Management: A Management Science Approach,* International Textbook, 1970; (contributor) J. Allison Barnhill, editor, *Sales Management: Contemporary Perspectives,* Scott, Foresman, 1970; (editor with Arnold Broser) *Current Problems in Mergers and Acquisitions,* Hofstra University Press, 1970; (editor) *Community Support of the Performing Arts: Selected Problems of Local and National Interest,* Yearbook of Business Series, Hofstra University, 1970; *Complex Managerial Decisions Involving Multiple Objectives,* with teacher's manual, Wiley, 1973; (editor) *Design of a Health Maintenance Organization,* Yearbook of Business Series, Hofstra University, 1973. Contributor of about twenty-five articles and reviews to journals and newspapers, including *Journal of Human Relations, Journal of Systems Management, Journal of Marketing, Journal of Marketing Research, Electronics,* and *New York Times.*

WORK IN PROGRESS: Productivity Analysis: A Systems View, with John Ullmann; *A Week in the Country,* a novel.

* * *

EBBESEN, Ebbe B(ruce) 1944-

PERSONAL: Born September 7, 1944, in New York, N.Y.; son of Ebbe and Minerva (Feldman) Ebbesen; married Jeanne T. Annarumma, 1966; children: Ebbe Pace. *Education:* New York University, B.A. (cum laude), 1966; Stanford University, Ph.D., 1971. *Home:* 13395 Barbados Way, Del Mar, Calif. 92014. *Office:* Department of Psychology, University of California at San Diego, P.O. Box 109, La Jolla, Calif. 92037.

CAREER: University of California at San Diego, La Jolla, assistant professor of psychology, 1970—, member of Center for Human Information Processing. Participant in conferences. *Member:* American Psychological Association, Psychonomic Society, Western Psychological Association, Phi Beta Kappa, Sigma Xi. *Awards, honors:* National Science Foundation research grant, 1973-75, for research on factors influencing the organization of response repertoires; National Institute of Mental Health research grant, 1974-77, for research on cognitive factors in learning by example.

WRITINGS: (With P. G. Zimbardo) *Influencing Attitudes and Changing Behavior,* Addison-Wesley, 1969; (contributor) H. N. Mischel and Walter Mischel, editors, *Readings in Personality,* Holt, 1973. Contributor of about twenty articles to social science journals, including *Journal of Personality and Social Psychology, Journal of Experimental Analysis of Behavior, Psychological Bulletin, Journal of Applied Social Psychology, Journal of Experimental Social Psychology,* and *Contemporary Psychology.*

WORK IN PROGRESS: Human Social Behavior: An Applied Approach, for Holt; several areas of research, including a study of decision-making and information integration in the courts with special regard to the setting of bail.

* * *

EBERHARD, Wolfram 1909-

PERSONAL: Born March 17, 1909, in Potsdam, Germany; son of Gustav (an astrophysicist) and Gertrud (Mueller) Eberhard; married Alide Roemer (a sociologist), May 19, 1934; children: Rainer, Anatol. *Education:* School for Oriental Languages, Berlin, Diploma, 1929; University of Berlin, Ph.D., 1933. *Politics:* None. *Home:* 604 Panoramic Way, Berkeley, Calif. 94704. *Office:* Department of Sociology, University of California, Berkeley, Calif. 94720.

CAREER: Museum of Anthropology, Far East Department, Berlin, Germany, assistant, 1929-34; National Peking University, Peking, China, assistant professor of German, 1934-35; Museum of Anthropology, Leipzig, Germany, chief of Far East Department, 1935-36; University of Ankara, Ankara, Turkey, professor of Chinese, 1937-48; University of California, Berkeley, lecturer, 1948-49, associate professor, 1949-52, professor of sociology, 1952—. Field research in Pakistan, 1956-58, Burma, 1958, China, Korea, and Afghanistan, 1960, and in Japan, Taiwan, and Turkey. Visiting professor in Germany, 1952, 1957, and 1969. Consultant to Orient Cultural Service (publishers), Taipei; adviser to Asia Foundation. *Member:* American Oriental Society, American Sociological Association, American Folklore Society, German Academy of Science (corresponding member), Bavarian Academy of Science (corresponding member), Turkish Historical Society (corresponding member), and other professional societies.

Awards, honors: Baessler Foundation fellowship, Berlin, 1934; Moses Mendelsohn Foundation fellowship, New York, 1937; Guggenheim fellowship, 1951-52.

WRITINGS: (Editor and translator) *Chinesische Volksmaerchen,* Insel-Buecherei, 1936, translation by Desmond Parsons published as *Chinese Fairy Tales and Folk Tales,* Kegan Paul, 1937, revised edition published as *Folktales of China,* University of Chicago Press, 1965.

Kultur und Siedlung der Randvoelker Chinas, Brill, 1942; *Lokalkulturen im alten China,* Volume I: *Die Lokalkulturen des Nordens und Westens,* Brill, 1942, Volume II: *Die Lokalkulturen des Suedens und Ostens,* Catholic University (Peking), 1943, revised translation of Volume II by Alide Eberhard published as *The Local Cultures of South and East China,* Brill, 1969; *Cin kaynaklarcna gore orta ve garbi Asya halklarin medeniyeti,* translated from the German by Mecdut Mansuroglu, [Istanbul], 1942; (with Fritz Rumpf) *China und Japan von den Anfaengen bis zur Beruehrung mit der abendlaendischen Welt,* [Berlin], 1943; *Cin: Sinoloji'ye giris,* Pulhan Matbaasi, 1946; (with wife, Alide Eberhard) *Die Mode der Han-und Chin-Zeit,* De Sikkel, 1946; *Die chinesische Novelle des 17.-19. Jahrhunderts: eine soziologische Untersuchung,* Artibus Asiae, 1948; *Chinas Geschichte,* A. Francke, 1948, translation by E. W. Dickes published as *A History of China,* University of California Press, 1950, 3rd edition, 1969; *Das Toba-Reich Nordchinas: eine soziologische Untersuchung,* Brill, 1949.

Conquerors and Rulers: Social Forces in Medieval China, Heinman, 1952, 2nd edition, 1965; *Chinese Festivals,* H. Schuman, 1952; (with Pertev Naili Boratav) *Typen tuerkischer Volksmaerchen,* F. Steiner, 1953; *Minstrel Tales from Southeastern Turkey,* University of California Press, 1955.

Social Mobility in Traditional China, Brill, 1962; (translator) Yu Li, *Die vollkommene Frau: das chinesische Schoenheitsideal,* Verlag die Waage, 1963; *Erzaehlungsgut aus Suedost-China,* W. de Gruyter, 1966; *Guilt and Sin in Traditional China,* University of California Press, 1967.

Studies in Taiwanese Folktales, Orient Cultural Service, 1970; (compiler and translator) *Wer ist schuld?* (Chinese short stories), Verlag die Waage, 1970; (with Alide Eberhard) *Geschichte Chinas,* A. Kroener, 1971.

Also author of series of collected papers: Volume I: *Settlement and Social Change in Asia,* Hong Kong University Press and Oxford University Press, 1967; Volume II: *Studies in Chinese Folklore and Related Essays,* Humanities Press for Indiana University Research Center for Language Sciences, 1970; Volume III: *Moral and Social Values of the Chinese,* Chinese Materials and Research

Aids (Taipei), 1971; Volume IV: *Sternkunde und Weltbild im alten China,* Chinese Materials and Research Aids, 1970; two additional volumes in preparation. Author of pamphlets for scholarly institutes and professional organizations.

WORK IN PROGRESS: A book in German on relations between China and Central Asia in medieval times, for Wissensch Verlagsanst; *Studies in Hakka Folktales; Climbing up a Tricky Ladder: Daily Life of Chinese Prostitutes;* a book of Chinese jokes.

SIDELIGHTS: Eberhard, who has travelled extensively in the countries about which he writes, speaks English, German, Turkish, and Chinese; he reads French, Latin, and Greek.

* * *

ECKELS, Jon

PERSONAL: Born in Indianapolis, Ind.; son of Thomas Arthur and Anna (Harris) Eckels; children: Jon David Malcolm. *Education:* Indiana Central College, B.A., 1961; Pacific School of Religion, B.D., 1966; Stanford University, Ph.D., 1975. *Politics and religion:* Christian Animist. *Home:* 1925 Miller, Indianapolis, Ind. *Agent:* Tarun Bedi, 2310 Yale St., Palo Alto, Calif. 94306. *Office address:* Firesign Press, P.O. Box 5003, Palo Alto, Calif. 94305.

CAREER: Ordained minister, 1966; pastor of United Methodist churches in Oakland and San Francisco, Calif., 1964-68; Mills College, Oakland, Calif., instructor in English, 1968; Merritt College, Oakland, Calif., instructor in English, 1969-70; Firesign Press, Palo Alto, Calif., publisher and editor, 1973—. Chairman of Anti-Poverty Commission, Oakland, Calif.; vice-president of Opportunities Industrialization Committee; chairman of Cultural Development Center, 1967-68; founder of Act III Freedom School, 1967-68; teacher and board member of Martin Luther King, Jr. In-Community School, Oakland, Calif., 1966-68, and New Community School, Berkeley, Calif., 1967-69.

WRITINGS—Poetry: *This Time Tomorrow,* Julian Richardson, 1966; *Black Dawn,* privately printed, 1966; *Home is Where the Soul Is,* Broadside Press, 1969; *Black Right On,* Julian Richardson, 1969; *Our Business in the Streets: Black Poetry,* Broadside Press, 1971; *Firesign: Poetry for the Free and Will Be,* Firesign Press, 1973.

WORK IN PROGRESS: "Black Poetry in White America," a doctoral dissertation; *Pursuing the Pursuit: The Black Plight in America,* a book of critical social essays; *Stone Spirit Space,* poetry; *One to One: Vision.*

SIDELIGHTS: Eckels told *CA:* "In my writings, both poetry and prose, I attempt to combine and reflect political radicalism and deep spirituality. I believe in personal and political freedom and responsibility. Although I feel most especially called to struggle . . . for the Third World generally and Black people specifically, I recognize my human obligation to all peoples. I believe in loving people, having faith in God, and completely working to renew and recreate. . . . I believe love is more than we know."

BIOGRAPHICAL/CRITICAL SOURCES: Time, April 4, 1970; *Phylon,* winter, 1972.

* * *

ECKER-RACZ, L. Laszlo 1906-

PERSONAL: Born November 25, 1906, in Czechoslovakia; married Cornelia B. Rose, May 17, 1934; children: Maria (Mrs. Norman Sheetz), Nicholas. *Education:* Harvard University, B.S., 1930, Ph.D., 1932; postdoctoral study at University of Budapest, 1932; and Columbia University, 1932-33. *Home:* 1318 24th St. S., Arlington, Va. 22202.

CAREER: U.S. Treasury Department, Washington, D.C., director of tax advisory staff, 1936-60; Advisory Committee on Intergovernmental Relations, Washington, D.C., assistant director, 1960-66; Virginia Military Institute, Lexington, Va., Northen Professor of Humanities, 1971. Visiting scholar at University of Hartford, 1969-70. Chairman of Board of Education, Arlington, Va., 1962-67. *Military service:* U.S. Army, 1943-45; became major. *Member:* Cosmos Club and Harvard Club (both Washington, D.C.), Army-Navy Country Club (Arlington, Va.).

WRITINGS: Politics and Economics of State-Local Finance, Prentice-Hall, 1970.

WORK IN PROGRESS: Research in financing public schools and in intergovernmental relations.

* * *

ECKLEY, Wilton Earl, Jr. 1929-

PERSONAL: Born June 25, 1929, in Alliance, Ohio; son of Wilton Earl and Louise Bert Eckley; married Grace Williamson (a professor), September 12, 1954; children: Douglas, Stephen, Timothy. *Education:* Mount Union College, A.B., 1952; Pennsylvania State University, M.A., 1955; Kent State University, further graduate study, 1958-60; Case Western Reserve University, Ph.D., 1965; also studied at DePauw University and Yale University. *Home:* 529 Waterbury Circle, Des Moines, Iowa 50312. *Office:* Department of English, Drake University, Des Moines, Iowa 50311.

CAREER: French teacher in public school in Ravenna Township, Ohio, 1952-54; high school English teacher in Euclid, Ohio, 1955-63; Hollins College, Hollins College, Va., assistant professor of English and director of teacher training, 1963-65; Drake University, Des Moines, Iowa, associate professor, 1965-68, professor of English, 1968—, chairman of department, 1967—. Visiting associate professor at University of Northern Iowa, summer, 1965; Fulbright professor at University of Ljubljana, 1972-73; has lectured at Kent State University, University of Iowa, University of Freiburg, University of Heidelberg, University of Mannheim, University of Tuebingen, Heilbronn Teacher Institute, University of Zagreb, University of Belgrade, University of Novi Sad, University of Sarajevo, University of Pristina, and Italian-American Institutes in Rome and Trieste, Italy.

WRITINGS: (Contributor) Louis Rubin, editor, *Guide to the Study of Southern Literature,* Louisiana State University Press, 1969; *Guide to e.e. cummings,* C. E. Merrill, 1970; *Checklist of e.e. cummings,* C. E. Merrill, 1970; (contributor) James Austin and Donald Kach, editors, *Popular Literature in America,* Bowling Green State University Press, 1971; *Harriette Arnow,* Twayne, 1974; (with Mirko Jurak) *Selected Lectures in English and American Literature,* Ljubljana Press, in press; *T. S. Stribling,* Twayne, in press. Contributor to journals, including *Explicator* and *Language Arts News.*

WORK IN PROGRESS: The Circus in American Culture.

* * *

ECKMAN, Lester S(amuel) 1937-

PERSONAL: Born August 7, 1937, in Poland; son of Leib

and Chaja Eckman; married Susan Molk (a school psychologist), November 22, 1964; children: Israel, Benjamin. *Education:* Boston University, A.B., 1960, M.A., 1961; Hebrew College of Boston, A.B., 1961; Jewish Theological Seminary, M.H.L., 1964; Columbia University, M.S.L.S., 1972; New York University, Ph.D., 1972. *Religion:* Jewish. *Home and office:* 747 Livingston Rd., Elizabeth, N.J. 07208.

CAREER: Upsala College, East Orange, N.J., member of faculty in history department, 1967-73; Touro College, New York, N.Y., associate professor of history and Jewish studies, 1973-74; Kean College, Union, N.J., associate professor of Jewish studies, 1974—. *Member:* American Historical Association, American Association of Slavic Studies, American Association of Jewish Studies. *Awards, honors:* Fellowships from National Foundation for Jewish Culture and Memorial Foundation, 1962-65.

WRITINGS: *Revered by All,* Shengold, 1974; *Soviet Policy toward Jews and Israel: 1917-1974,* Shengold, 1974. Contributor to *Universal Biographical Encyclopedia.*

WORK IN PROGRESS: *Ethical Movement in Eastern Europe; Eyewitness to History: World War Two; History of the Partisan Movement in World War Two.*

SIDELIGHTS: Eckman speaks Hebrew, Yiddish, German, Spanish, Russian, Latin, Aramaic, and Polish.

* * *

EDGAR, Ken 1925-

PERSONAL: Born May 23, 1925; son of Frank O. (a businessman) and Eileen (Davis) Edgar; married Aggie Sechler; children: Mike, Mark. *Education:* Pennsylvania State University, B.A., 1947; University of Pittsburgh, M.A. and Ph.D.; also studied at University of Arkansas, 1944. *Agent:* Alex Jackinson Agency, 55 West 42nd St., New York, N.Y. 10036. *Office:* Department of Psychology, Indiana University, Indiana, Pa. 15701.

CAREER: Slippery Rock State College, Slippery Rock, Pa., director of counseling center, 1961-66; Indiana University, Indiana, Pa., 1966—, now professor of psychology. Private practice in psychotherapy; clinical psychologist at Indiana County Guidance Center, part-time, 1966-71. *Military service:* U.S. Army, infantry, 1943-45. *Member:* American Psychological Association.

WRITINGS: *Starfire* (juvenile novel), Boxwood Press, 1961; *End and Beginning,* Prentice-Hall, 1972; *As If,* Prentice-Hall, 1973; (contributor) J. J. Leedy, editor, *Poetry Therapy,* Lippincott, 1969.

WORK IN PROGRESS: Four novels, three of them for Prentice-Hall; a historical novel about the Civil War.

SIDELIGHTS: Edgar writes: "I consider America's struggle with the collapse of authority, the subsequent chronic doubt and polarization to be our most critical problem in our own history." *Avocational interests:* Motorcycle riding.

* * *

EDSALL, Marian (Stickney) 1920-

PERSONAL: Born April 24, 1920, in Chicago, Ill.; daughter of Harry F. and Hazel (Dickover) Stickney; married James V. Edsall (a campus planning director), November 20, 1943; children: Sandra Lee (Mrs. Patrick O'Brien). *Education:* Wellesley College, B.A., 1941. *Home:* Deer Run Heights, Cross Plains, Wis. 53528.

CAREER: Division for Library Services, Madison, Wis., director of Co-operative Library Information Program, 1969—. *Awards, honors:* Wisconsin Library Trustee of the Year, 1971.

WRITINGS: *Our Auto Trip,* Rand McNally, 1953; *Battle on the Rosebush,* Follett, 1972. Contributor to journals and magazines. Editor, *Camping Horizons,* 1960-62, *Channel 12 Newsletter* (University of Illinois radio station), 1962-63, *Tips from CLIP,* 1970—.

* * *

EDWARDS, Elizabeth

See INDERLIED, Mary Elizabeth

* * *

EHRENSVAERD, Goesta (Carl Henrik) 1910-

PERSONAL: Born January 10, 1910, in Stockholm, Sweden; son of Count Goesta Carl Albert (an admiral) and Anna (Ensell) Ehrensvaerd; married Ingalill Rydh, March, 1934 (died, 1956); married Ursula Radbruch, April, 1957 (divorced, 1967); married Phyllis Marguerite Pearson, April, 1967; children: (first marriage) Johan A. (deceased), Ingeborg (Mrs. Christer Borgenstierna); (second marriage) Katharina, Elisabeth (twins). *Education:* University of Stockholm, B.A., 1931, M.A., 1933, Ph.D., 1942. *Politics:* "Conservative radical, and devoted anti-socialist." *Religion:* "All for God, by all means, yet no creed (so far)." *Residence:* New Orleans, La. *Office:* Department of Pharmacology, Louisiana State University Medical School, New Orleans, La.

CAREER: A. B. Astra (a pharmaceutical firm), Sweden, research chemist, 1933-39; University of Stockholm, Stockholm, Sweden, instructor, 1939-42, assistant professor, 1942-52, associate professor of biochemistry, 1952-55; University of Lund, Lund, Sweden, professor of biochemistry, 1955-75, chairman of department, 1956-74; Louisiana State University, New Orleans, visiting professor of pharmacology, 1974—. *Military service:* Swedish Army, Artillery, 1930-31, 1939-43. Swedish Army Reserve, 1947-60; became sergeant. *Member:* Royal Society of Engineers (Sweden), Royal Physiographic Society of Sweden. *Awards, honors:* Order of the North Star, knight, 1958, knight commander, 1974; Swedish Chemical Society gold medal, 1960; Swedish State Literary Award, 1965; Swedish Council of Authors award, 1974.

WRITINGS: *Ueber die Primaevorgaenge bei Chemozeptorenbeeinflussung: Eine physikalisch-chemische Uebersicht* (title means "Primary Events at the Stimulation of Chemoreceptor Systems"), P. A. Norstedt (Stockholm), 1942; *Liv: Ursprung och utformning,* Aldus/Bonniers (Stockholm), 1960, translation by Jill Aakerman published as *Life: Origin and Development,* University of Chicago Press, 1962; *Expansion: Liv i universum,* Aldus/Bonniers, 1961, translation by Lennart and Kajsa Roden published as *Man on Another World,* University of Chicago Press, 1965; (contributor) Jan Thulin, editor, *Svaerdfejare och sjaelamord: En festskrift till Malmoe Nation, 1962* (title means "Sword Sharpeners and Soul Killers: A Hommage to Malmoe Students Fraternity"), Allhem (Malmoe), 1962; *Tanke: Liv som medvetande och kaenslospel* (title means "Mind: Life as Consciousness and Emotional Display"), Bokfoerlaget Aldus, 1963; *Foere-efter* (title means "Before-After"), Aldus, 1971; *En vaer ar moejligheter* (title means

"A Web of Possibilities"), Aldus, 1972; *Levande Materia* (title means "Living Matter), Aldus, 1973. Contributor of over 200 articles to journals in his field.

WORK IN PROGRESS: A novel; some experimental contributions to the anaerobic conversion of carbohydrates to hydrocarbons.

SIDELIGHTS: Ehrensvaerd, who like his father is a count, told *CA:* "Having worked so long in science—most fields—and in specialized industry, one has gained a certain knowledge of the intricacies of matter and the conceits of Man. Three nice marriages and six grandchildren have given me some support in my attacks on problems in general."

* * *

EHRENWALD, Jan 1900-

PERSONAL: Born March 13, 1900, in Bratislava, Czechoslavakia; came to United States, 1946; son of Edward (a merchant) and Melanie (Spielmann) Ehrenwald; married Anny Stein, December 13, 1933; children: Barbara (Mrs. David Krohn). *Education:* Attended University of Vienna, 1921-22; University of Prague, M.D., 1925. *Religion:* Jewish. *Home and office:* 11 East 68th St., New York, N.Y. 10021.

CAREER: University of Prague, Prague, Czechoslovakia, clinical assistant in psychiatric clinic, 1925-27; University of Vienna, Vienna, Austria, clinical assistant in psychiatric clinic, 1927-31; psychiatrist in private practice in Bratislava, Czechoslovakia, 1931-39; Royal Western Counties Institution, Starcross, England, acting medical officer, 1942-45; Roosevelt Hospital, New York, N.Y., attending psychiatrist and chief of Adult Psychiatric Outpatient Department, 1951-69, consulting psychiatrist, 1969—. Clinical psychiatrist at various locations in England, 1940-42.

WRITINGS: *Telepathy and Medical Psychology,* Allen & Unwin, 1947, Norton, 1948; *New Dimensions of Deep Analysis,* Grune, 1954; *From Medicine Man to Freud,* Dell, 1956; *Neurosis in the Family and Patterns of Psychosocial Defense,* Hoeber, 1963; *Psychotherapy: Myth and Method,* Grune, 1966; *History of Psychotherapy: From Magic to Encounter Groups,* Science House, in press.

* * *

EICHER, Joanne B(ubolz) 1930-

PERSONAL: Born September 18, 1930, in Lansing, Mich.; daughter of George C., Sr. and Stella (Mangold) Bubolz; married Carl K. Eicher (a professor), June 8, 1952; children: Cynthia, Carolyn, Diana. *Education:* Michigan State University, B.A., 1952, M.A., 1956, Ph.D., 1959. *Politics:* Democrat. *Religion:* Lutheran. *Home:* 201 Kensington Rd., East Lansing, Mich. 48823. *Office:* Department of Human Environment and Design, College of Human Ecology, Michigan State University, East Lansing, Mich. 48824.

CAREER: Boston University, Boston, Mass., 1957-61, began as instructor, became assistant professor of social sciences; Michigan State University, East Lansing, assistant professor, 1961-69, associate professor, 1969-72, professor of human ecology, 1972—. University of Nigeria, Enugu, research associate, 1963-66. *Member:* American Home Economics Association, American Sociological Association, Association of College Professors of Textiles and Clothing, Nigeria National Museum Society, Costume Society, Founders Society of Detroit Institute of Arts, Museum of Modern Art (member of African arts committee). *Awards, honors:* Ford Foundation grant, 1973.

WRITINGS: (With Mary Ellen Roach) *Dress, Adornment, and the Social Order,* Wiley, 1965; *African Dress: A Select and Annotated Bibliography of Subsaharan Countries,* Michigan State University Press, 1970; (with Roach) *The Visible Self: Perspectives on Dress,* Prentice-Hall, 1973; (with Eleanor Kelley) *A Longitudinal Study of High School Girls' Friendship Patterns, Social Class, and Clothing,* Michigan Agricultural Experiment Station, 1973.

Contributor to journals, including *Social Forces, Journal of Home Economics, Journal of Psychology, Adolescence,* and *Kresge Art Center Bulletin.*

WORK IN PROGRESS: A book, *Nigerian Handcrafted Textiles.*

* * *

EICHORN, Dorothy H(ansen) 1924-

PERSONAL: Born November 18, 1924, in Montpelier, Vt.; daughter of George Marinus (an accountant) and Lula (Ryan) Hansen; married Herman Eichorn (a chaplain), June 28, 1947; children: Eric Hansen. *Education:* University of Vermont, B.A., 1947; Boston University, M.A., 1949; Northwestern University, Ph.D., 1951. *Address:* Box 7125, Imola Branch, Napa, Calif. 94558. *Office:* Child Study Center, Institute of Human Development, University of California, 2425 Atherton, Berkeley, Calif. 94704.

CAREER: University of California, Institute for Human Development, Berkeley, junior research psychologist, 1952-54, assistant research psychologist,1954-60, associate research psychologist, 1960-67, research psychologist, 1967—, administrator, Child Study Center, 1962—. Lecturer in physiology, University of California, Berkeley, 1952—. *Member:* Inter-American Society of Psychology, American Psychological Association (fellow; member of board of directors, 1969-72), American Association for the Advancement of Science (fellow), Society for Research in Child Development, Psychonomic Society, Society for Psychophysiological Research.

WRITINGS: (Co-editor) *Youth: Transition to Adulthood,* University of Chicago Press, 1973. Contributor of chapters to thirty-five books, and of articles to journals.

WORK IN PROGRESS: Research on two-generation similarities in developmental patterns.

* * *

EISEN, Carol G.
See RINZLER, Carol Eisen

* * *

EISENBERG, Azriel (Louis) 1903-

PERSONAL: Born August 29, 1903, in Russia; came to United States in 1914; son of Louis and Mindel (Shpetrik) Eisenberg; married Rose Leibow (a teacher), August 19, 1928; children: Sora (Mrs. Aaron Landes), Judah M. *Education:* Jewish Theological Seminary of America, student, 1922; New York University, B.S., 1926; Columbia University, Ph.D., 1935. *Politics:* Liberal. *Religion:* Jewish. *Home:* 68-52 Juno St., Forest Hills, N.Y. 11375.

CAREER: Bureau of Jewish Education, New York, N.Y., director of bureaus in Cincinnati, Ohio, 1935-40, Cleveland, Ohio, 1940-46, and Philadelphia, Pa., 1946-49; Board of

Jewish Education, New York, N.Y., executive vice-president, 1949-66; World Council of Jewish Education, New York, N.Y., director, 1966-68. American Jewish Joint Distribution Committee, organized office of Jewish education in Paris, 1956, conducted survey of Jewish education in Iran, 1969. Acting dean of Graetz College, 1946-49; chairman of United Synagogue Commission on Jewish Education, 1968-73; co-chairman of National Zionist Education Commission; organized international conferences.

MEMBER: National Council for Jewish Education (president, 1946-50), Jewish Publication Society, American Jewish Joint Distribution Committee, North Eastern Ohio Religious Education Association (past president), Jewish Teachers Association (New York; past president). *Awards, honors:* D.H.L. from Jewish Theological Seminary of America, 1959; National Jewish Book Council award, 1965, for *Worlds Lost and Found.*

WRITINGS: Children and Radio Programs, Columbia University Press, 1936; (with Leon J. Feur) *Jewish Literature Since the Bible,* two volumes, Union of American Hebrew Congregations, 1943, new edition, 1946.

Tzedakah and Federation, Jewish Education Committee of New York, 1952; *Dear Parents,* Jewish Education Committee of New York, 1952; (with Abraham Segal) *Teaching Jewish History,* Jewish Education Committee of New York, 1954; *The Great Discovery: The Dead Sea Scrolls,* Abelard, 1956; (with Segal) *Presenting Bialik: A Study of His Life and Works,* Jewish Education Committee of New York, 1956; *Teacher's Guide to Modern Jewish Life in Literature,* United Synagogue Commission on Higher Education, 1956; *Voices from the Past,* Abelard, 1958; (with Jesse B. Robinson) *My Jewish Holidays,* United Synagogue Commission on Jewish Education, 1958; *My Own J.N.F.,* Jewish National Fund, 1958; *The Story of the Jewish Calendar,* Abelard, 1959.

(With Dov Peretz Elkins) *Worlds Lost and Found,* Abelard, 1964; *Feeding the World: A Biography of David Lubin* (youth book), Abelard, 1965; *Fill a Blank Page: A Biography of Solomon Schechter* (youth book), United Synagogue Commission on Jewish Education, 1965; (with Philip Arian) *The Story of the Prayer Book,* Prayer Book Press, 1968; *Jewish Historical Treasures,* Bloch Publishing, 1969.

(With Leah Ain Globe) *Sabra Children,* J. David, 1970; (with Elkins) *Treasures from the Dust,* Abelard, 1972; *The Book of Books: Story of the Bible Text,* Soncino Press, 1974; *The Synagogue through the Ages,* Bloch Publishing, 1974.

Editor: *The Bar Mitzvah Treasury,* Behrman, 1952; *The Confirmation Reader,* Behrman, 1953; (with Abraham Segal) *Readings in the Teaching of Jewish History,* Jewish Education Committee of New York, 1956; *Modern Jewish Life in Literature,* Union of American Hebrew Congregations, Volume I, 1956, Volume II, 1968; (with Segal) *Accent on Hebrew,* Jewish Education Committee Press, 1960; (with Joseph Lukinsky) *Readings in the Teaching of Hebrew,* Jewish Education Committee Press, 1961; *Tzedakah: A Way of Life,* Behrman, 1963; *Readings in the Teaching of Prayer and Siddur,* Jewish Education Committee Press, 1964; *The Golden Land: A Literary Portrait of American Jewry, 1654 to the Present,* Yoselof, 1965; (with Leah Ain Globe) *The Bas Mitzvah Treasury,* Twayne, 1965; (and translator with Globe) *The Secret Weapon and Other Stories,* Soncino Press, 1966; (with Jacob Seegar) *World Census on Jewish Education,* World Council on Jewish Education, 1968; (with Hannah G. Goodman and Alvin I. Kass) *Eyewitness to Jewish History,* Union of American Hebrew Congregations, 1973.

In Hebrew: (Editor) *Yerushalayim,* Jewish Education Committee of New York, 1955; *Kolot mini kedem,* [Tel Aviv], 1962. Also author of *Olamot shenelinu veniglu.*

Author of over a dozen teacher's guides and manuals, and a number of other works, including textbooks. Contributor to journals and magazines.

WORK IN PROGRESS: Earth Be Not Silent: A Book on the Holocaust, for United Synagogue Commission on Jewish Education; *Eyewitness to American Jewish History,* for Union of American Hebrew Congregations.

* * *

EISENBUD, Jule 1908-

PERSONAL: Born November 20, 1908, in New York, N.Y.; son of Abraham and Sarah (Abramson) Eisenbud; married Molly Lewis, January 1, 1937; children: Joanna (Mrs. Raymond Moldow), John, Eric. *Education:* Columbia University, B.A., 1929, M.D., 1934, Med. Sci. Dr., 1939. *Religion:* Hebrew. *Home and office:* 4634 East Sixth Ave., Denver, Colo. 80220.

CAREER: Private practice of psychiatry in New York, N.Y., 1938-50, and Denver, Colo., 1950—. Columbia University, Columbia College of Physicians and Surgeons, New York, N.Y., associate in psychiatry, 1938-50; University of Colorado Medical School, Denver, associate clinical professor of psychiatry, 1950—. Lecturer at New York School of Social Work, 1938-41, and New York Psychoanalytic Institute, 1940-41. *Member:* American Psychiatric Association (fellow), American Psychoanalytic Association, Parapsychological Association.

WRITINGS: The World of Ted Serios: Thoughtographic Studies of an Extraordinary Mind, Morrow, 1967; *Psi and Psychoanalysis,* Grune, 1970. Contributor to psychiatric, psychoanalytic, and parapsychological journals.

* * *

EISENDRATH, Craig R. 1936-

PERSONAL: Born January 21, 1936; son of Ralph H. and Lucylle (Newman) Eisendrath; married Betsy Kalish, June 24, 1942; children: Aaron, Rachel. *Education:* University of Chicago, B.A. (with honors), 1954; Georgetown University, B.S. (foreign service), 1955; Harvard University, Ph.D., 1969. *Home:* 1919 19th St. N.W., Washington, D.C. 20009. *Agent:* Philip Spitzer, 111-25 76th Ave., Forest Hills, N.Y. 11375. *Office:* Graduate Program, Goddard College, Washington, D.C.

CAREER: U.S. Foreign Service, Washington, D.C., foreign service officer in Naples, 1958-65; Massachusetts Institute of Technology, Cambridge, Mass., instructor in humanities, 1969-70, instructor in writing, 1970-71; National Endowment for the Humanities, Education Division, Washington, D.C., staff member in program office, 1971-72; Goddard College, regional director of graduate program in Washington, D.C., 1972—. *Military service:* U.S. Army, 1956-58. *Member:* American Civil Liberties Union.

WRITINGS: The Unifying Moment: The Psychological Philosophy of William James and Alfred North Whitehead, Harvard University Press, 1971; (with Thomas J. Cottle) *Out of Discontent: Visions of the Contemporary University,* Schenkman, 1972.

WORK IN PROGRESS: Crisis Game, a novel about government; *After Isadora,* a novel about a painter; "Stepping Down," a political play.

* * *

ELDER, Glen(nard) H(oll), Jr. 1934-

PERSONAL: Born February 28, 1934, in Cleveland, Ohio; son of Glennard Holl (a chiropractor) and Norma (Johnson) Elder; married Karen Elwell Bixler, August 30, 1958; children: Brent, Rod, Jeffrey. *Education:* Pennsylvania State University, B.S., 1957; Kent State University, M.A., 1958; University of North Carolina, Ph.D., 1961. *Politics:* Democrat. *Religion:* Protestant. *Home address:* Hoot Owl Lane, Chapel Hill, N.C. 27514. *Office:* Department of Sociology, Hamilton Hall, University of North Carolina, Chapel Hill, N.C. 27514.

CAREER: University of California, Berkeley, assistant professor of sociology, 1962-65, assistant research sociologist at Institute of Human Development, 1962-67; University of North Carolina, Chapel Hill, associate professor, 1967-71, professor of sociology, 1971—. *Member:* International Sociological Association, American Sociological Association, Society for the Study of Social Problems, Society for the Psychological Study of Social Issues, American Association for the Advancement of Science. *Awards, honors:* Postdoctoral fellowship from National Institute of Mental Health, 1962.

WRITINGS: Adolescent Achievement and Mobility Aspirations, Institute for Research in Social Science, University of North Carolina, 1962; (contributor) Edgar Borgatta and William Lambert, editors, *The Handbook of Personality Theory and Research,* Rand McNally, 1968; *Age Groups, Status Transitions, and Socialization,* U.S. Government Printing Office, 1968; *Adolescent Socialization and Personality Development,* Rand McNally, 1971; (editor) *Linking Social Structure and Personality,* Sage Publications, 1973; *Children of the Great Depression,* University of Chicago Press, 1974; (editor with Sigmund Dragastin, and contributor) *Adolescence in the Life Cycle,* Hemisphere Press, 1975. Contributor to *Annual Review of Sociology.* Contributor of about twenty-five articles to sociology and education journals, including *American Behavioral Scientist, International Social Science Journal, Merrill-Palmer Quarterly of Behavior and Development, Youth and Society, Sociometry,* and *American Journal of Sociology.*

WORK IN PROGRESS: Families in Depression and War; a long-term study of social change in the family and life course, based upon longitudinal archives from Institute of Human Development, Berkeley, Calif.

* * *

ELDER, Mark 1935-

PERSONAL: Born May 3, 1935, in Littlefield, Tex.; son of Mark Gray and Ethel (Hill) Elder; married Wanda Roady (an artist), October 1, 1960; children: Staci. *Education:* University of Oklahoma, B.A., 1965, M.A., 1973. *Home:* 1924 Oakhurst Circle, Norman, Okla. 73069. *Agent:* Henry Morrison, Henry Morrison Inc., 311½ West 20th St., New York, N.Y. 10011. *Office:* Department of Program Development, Office of Research Administration, University of Oklahoma, 1000 Asp Ave., Norman, Okla. 73069.

CAREER: Los Alamos Scientific Laboratory, Los Alamos, N.M., technical editor, 1964-66; Martin-Marietta Corp., Orlando, Fla., technical writer and editor, 1966-67; Collins Radio Co., Dallas, Tex., technical writer and editor, 1967-68; University of Oklahoma, Norman, director of Research Institute Information Services, 1969-73, co-director of Program Development, 1973—. *Military service:* U.S. Army, 1954-56. U.S. Army Reserve, 1956-59. U.S. Air Force, 1959. U.S. Air Force Reserve, 1959-62. *Member:* National Council of University Research Administrators, Society of Research Administrators.

WRITINGS: Jedcrow, Fawcett, 1974. Author and editor of technical reports.

WORK IN PROGRESS: A novel, *Trial Run;* research on a third novel depicting the contemporary life of an American Indian family.

SIDELIGHTS: Elder wrote: "The motivation behind my work is primarily to entertain and occasionally illustrate some of the contemporary human and societal problems, especially in the American southwest. . . . In my spare time, I work with Indian tribes and individuals to help secure tribal development funds."

* * *

ELEVITCH, M(orton) D. 1925-

PERSONAL: Born July 23, 1925, in Duluth, Minn.; son of Herman and Evelyn (Blehart) Elevitch; married Carol Kageff, August 27, 1956; children: Nikolas, Ilena, Kathrin. *Education:* University of Minnesota, B.A. (summa cum laude), 1949, M.A., 1950; University of Michigan, graduate study, 1954-56. *Home:* Snedens Landing, Palisades, N.Y. 10964. *Agent:* Ellen Levine, Curtis Brown Ltd., 60 East 56th St., New York, N.Y. 10022.

CAREER: George Washington University, Washington, D.C., instructor in English, 1956-57; *Audience,* Cambridge, Mass., fiction editor, 1959-60; *First Person* (literary magazine), Boston, Mass. and New York, N.Y., founder and editor, 1960-61; Association of Literary Magazines of America, New York, N.Y., co-founder and director of information, 1961-64; Heliotrope University, San Francisco, Calif., lecturer in astrology, 1968; novelist, cartoonist, actor. *Military service:* U.S. Army, Infantry, 1943-45. *Member:* Phi Beta Kappa. *Awards, honors:* Prizes for cartoons.

WRITINGS: Grips: Or, Efforts to Revive the Host (novel), Grossman, 1972. Represented in anthologies, including *Breakthrough Fictioneers,* edited by Richard Kostelanetz, Something Else Press, 1973, and *New Departures in Fiction,* edited by Robert Bonazzi, Latitudes Press, in press. Contributor to *Audience, Trace, Chelsea, Chicago Review, Genesis West, Minnesota Quarterly, Triquarterly, Small Press Review, Lillabulero,* and *Second Assembling.*

WORK IN PROGRESS: Three novels, *West of Passion, Compass Love, Follow That Aging Bird.*

SIDELIGHTS: Of *Grips,* Sandra Hochman wrote in *Cosmopolitan:* "Mr. Elevitch is witty, in love with objects and language, and zany. His novel is whacky, too, reminding me of the Beatles' animated movie, "Yellow Submarine," hop-scotching as it does from one loony affair to the next. The author's style is charming and has a black humor all its own, making *Grips* worth reading *several* times for the puns that give you a grip on its hero, John-Juan Bascom—recorder of worldly observations, note-taker for his will—a man who wants *everything* in writing."

Elevitch has spent many years living and traveling off the beaten track—in Europe, Asia, Africa, and the Caribbean.

He now lives in a half-colonial, half-Japanese house on the Hudson River.

* * *

ELIOT, Alexander 1919-

PERSONAL: Born April 28, 1919, in Cambridge, Mass.; son of Samuel Atkins, Jr. (a professor) and Ethel (an author; maiden name, Cook) Eliot; married Jane Winslow Knapp (an author), May 3, 1952; children: May Rose, Jefferson, Winslow. *Education:* Attended Black Mountain College, 1936-38, and Boston Music School, 1938-39, and Loomis Institute. *Agent:* Owen Laster, William Morris Agency, 1350 Avenue of the Americas, New York, N.Y. 10019.

CAREER: Film writer for "March of Time" and government wartime agencies, 1940-45; *Time* (magazine), New York, N.Y., art editor, 1945-60; free-lance writer, 1960—. *Member:* Society of American Travel Writers; Century Association, Dutch Treat Club. *Awards, honors:* Guggenheim fellowship, 1960.

WRITINGS: Proud Youth, Farrar, Straus, 1953; *Three Hundred Years of American Painting,* Time, 1957; *Sight and Insight,* McDowell-Obolensky, 1959; *Earth, Air, Fire, and Water,* Simon & Schuster, 1962; *Greece,* Life World Library, 1963; *Love Play,* New World Library, 1966; *Creatures of Arcadia,* Bobbs-Merrill, 1967; *Socrates,* Crown, 1967; *Concise History of Greece,* McGraw, 1972; *The World of Myth,* McGraw, in press.

Author of "The Secret of Michelangelo: Every Man's Dream," for ABC-TV, 1968. Contributor to periodicals, including *Texas Quarterly, Furioso, Holiday, Seventeen, Greek Heritage, Horizon, Sports Illustrated, Money, Atlantic, Vogue, Saturday Evening Post, Time, Life, Panorama* (Italy), *Embros* (Greece), and *Man, Myth and Magic.* Contributing editor, *Art in America,* 1960-65.

SIDELIGHTS: Queried by *CA,* Eliot said: "Motivation? 'Travel, change, excitement!' (Isn't that how Toad of Toad Hall put it?) Seriously, we've got only one life to live this time around; and there's so much to learn and do.

* * *

ELLINGTON, Duke
See ELLINGTON, Edward Kennedy

* * *

ELLINGTON, Edward Kennedy 1899-1974 (Duke Ellington)

April 29, 1899—May 24, 1974; American jazz artist, composer and arranger, bandleader, pianist, music publisher, and author of autobiography. Obituaries: *New York Times,* May 25, 1974; *Washington Post,* May 25, 1974; *Newsweek,* June 3, 1974; *Time,* June 3, 1974; *Current Biography,* July, 1974.

* * *

ELLIOTT, Harley 1940-

PERSONAL: Born July 29, 1940, in Mitchell, S.D.; son of Alfred S. and Hazel (Moen) Elliott; married Emperatriz Arellano, May 7, 1966; children: Elaine, Dario. *Education:* Kansas Wesleyan University, B.A., 1963; New Mexico Highlands University, M.A., 1964. *Politics and religion:* Neo-pantheism. *Home:* 425 South Phillips, Salina, Kan. 67401.

CAREER: Sign painter in Salina, Kan., 1965—. Assistant production manager for Syracuse University Press, 1967-70; art teacher in Salina, Kan., 1970-72. *Awards, honors:* Lucille Medwick Award from New York Quarterly, 1973, for "The Official Indian Report."

WRITINGS—All poetry: *Dark Country,* Crossing Press, 1971; (with Kenn Kwint and Jeff Woodward) *Six Eyes Open,* Shore Press, 1972; *All Beautyfull and Foolish Souls,* Crossing Press, 1973; *The Citizen Game,* Basilisk Press, in press; *The Resident Stranger,* Juniper Books, in press.

Poems represented in anthologies, including *New American & Canadian Poetry,* edited by John Gill, Beacon Press, 1971; *Best Poems of 1972: The Borestone Mountain Poetry Awards,* edited by Lionel Stevenson, Pacific Books, 1973; *New World Issues,* Book I, Harcourt, in press.

Contributor of poems to *Carolina Quarterly, Beloit Poetry Journal, Wisconsin Review,* and others.

WORK IN PROGRESS: Two novels, *Pieman* and *Floating Heart;* editing *Kitchen Poetry,* with Jim Hawks, an anthology of poems and recipes by poets.

AVOCATIONAL INTERESTS: Archaeology, birds of prey, insects, plants, travel to Peru, oil painting, printmaking.

* * *

ELLIOTT, Thomas Joseph 1941-

PERSONAL: Born January 25, 1941, in Boston, Mass.; son of Thomas Joseph and Anne (Regan) Elliott; married Eugenia Coleman, June 18, 1966. *Education:* Boston College, A.B. (cum laude), 1963, M.A., 1967; University of Michigan, Ph.D., 1970. *Politics:* Democrat. *Religion:* Roman Catholic. *Home:* 1955 Evergreen St., La Verne, Calif. 91750. *Office:* Department of English and Modern Languages, California State Polytechnic University, Pomona, Calif. 91768.

CAREER: California State Polytechnic University, Pomona, assistant professor, 1970-74, associate professor of English, 1974—. *Member:* Modern Language Association of America, Mediaeval Academy of America, College English Association, Irish-American Cultural Institute, Mediaeval Association of the Pacific, Rocky Mountain Modern Language Association, Rocky Mountain Medieval and Renaissance Association.

WRITINGS: (Translator and editor) *A Medieval Bestiary,* David Godine, 1971; *Complaint as a Middle English Genre,* Mouton & Co., in press. Contributor to *Annuale Mediaevale,* 1973.

WORK IN PROGRESS: The Sea as Motif in Old English Literature; research on the doctrine of optimism in eighteenth-century English and French literature; research on modern Irish and Irish-American literature.

* * *

ELLIS, Ella Thorp 1928-

PERSONAL: Born July 14, 1928, in Los Angeles, Calif.; daughter of William Dunham (a film writer) and Marion (Yates) Thorp; married Leo H. Ellis (a construction engineer), December 17, 1949; children: Steven, David, Patrick. *Education:* University of California, Los Angeles, B.A., 1946. *Politics:* Democrat. *Religion:* Protestant. *Home:* 1438 Grizzly Peak, Berkeley, Calif. 94708. *Agent:* Patricia Myrer, McIntosh & Otis, Inc., 18 East 41st St., New York, N.Y. 10017.

CAREER: Writer of children's books. Teacher of English at Acalanes Adult School, 1971—. *Member:* California Writers' Club. *Awards, honors: Roam the Wild Country* was named an American Library Association honor book in 1967.

WRITINGS—Juvenile fiction; all published by Atheneum: *Roam the Wild Country,* 1967; *Riptide,* 1969; *Celebrate the Morning* (Junior Literary Guild selection), 1972; *Where the Road Ends,* 1974. Contributor of short fiction to *Mademoiselle.*

WORK IN PROGRESS: A fantasy tentatively titled *Hallelujah,* completion expected in 1975.

SIDELIGHTS: "I have always been a vagabond," Mrs. Ellis once said. "My father was a free-lance writer and during the Depression I lived up and down the coast of California . . . and in Washington, D.C., with an uncle who is a painter. But every summer I returned to Oceano, California, the small town where my mother lived and where *Riptide* and *Celebrate the Morning* take place." *Celebrate the Morning,* she continues, developed from three stories she wrote about her life with her mother, one of which appeared in *Mademoiselle.* In one of their many moves—twelve in the first five years of marriage—the Ellises lived in Argentina for two years, resulting in *Roam the Wild Country.* Attending college wherever possible while on the move, Mrs. Ellis studied at eight schools before receiving her bachelor's degree. *Avocational interests:* Reading, gardening, listening to music, attending plays, travel.

* * *

ELLIS, Howard S(ylvester) 1898-

PERSONAL: Born July 2, 1898, in Denver, Colo.; son of Sylvester Eldon (a Protestant clergyman) and Nellie Blanche (Young) Ellis; married Lilah Priscilla Whetstine, January, 1925 (divorced, 1934); married Hermine Johanna Hoerlesberger, July 6, 1945; children: (first marriage) Audrey Elinor; (second marriage) Dorothy Margaret, Martha Josephine. *Education:* State University of Iowa, A.B., 1920; University of Michigan, A.M., 1922; Harvard University, A.M., 1924, Ph.D., 1929; also studied at University of Heidelberg, 1924-25, and University of Vienna, 1933-35. *Home:* 936 Cragmont Ave., Berkeley, Calif. 94708.

CAREER: University of Michigan, Ann Arbor, instructor, 1920-22, 1925-29, assistant professor, 1929-35, associate professor, 1935-37, professor of economics, 1937-38; University of California, Berkeley, professor of economics, 1938-43; Federal Reserve System, Board of Governors, Washington, D.C., economic analyst, 1943-44, assistant director of research and statistics, 1944-45; University of California, Berkeley, Flood Professor of Economics, 1946-65, professor emeritus, 1965—. Visiting professor at Columbia University, 1944-45, 1949-50, in Tokyo, Japan, summer, 1951, in Bombay, India, 1958-59, and at Claremont Graduate School, 1969; research professor at Center of Economic Research (Athens), 1963; Knapp visiting professor at University of Wisconsin—Milwaukee, 1972. Director of Marshall Aid Research Project for Council on Foreign Relations, 1949-50; head of joint UNESCO-Economic Commission for Latin America (ECLA)—Organization of American States (OAS) Mission on Economic Education in Latin America, 1960; chief of party for U.S. Agency for International Development (U-SAID)—University of California program in Rio de Janeiro, 1965-67; member of economic policy committee of U.S. Chamber of Commerce, 1945-46; consultant to U.S. House of Representatives Committee on Postwar Planning, 1944-45, and U.S. Department of State, 1952-53.

MEMBER: International Economic Association (member of council, 1950-53, 1956-63; president, 1953-56; honorary president, 1957—), American Academy of Arts and Sciences, American Economic Association (member of executive committee, 1945-48, 1950-53; president, 1949), Royal Economic Society, Mont Pelerin Society, Phi Beta Kappa. *Awards, honors:* David A. Wells Award from Harvard University, 1930; fellowship from Social Science Research Council, 1933-35, for study in Europe; M.A., Yale University, 1946; LL.D., University of Michigan, 1951; distinguished service award from American Economic Association, 1966; LL.D., University of California, Berkeley, 1968.

WRITINGS: German Monetary Theory: 1905-1933, Harvard University Press, 1934; (with others) *Explorations in Economics,* Macmillan, 1936; *Exchange Control in Central Europe,* Harvard University Press, 1941; (with others) *Postwar Economic Problems,* McGraw, 1943; (with others) *Financing American Prosperity,* Twentieth Century Fund, 1945; (with others) *Economic Reconstruction,* McGraw, 1945; (editor) *A Survey of Contemporary Economics,* Blakeston, 1948; (editor with Lloyd A. Metzler) *Readings in the Theory of International Trade,* Blakeston, Volume I, 1949.

The Economics of Freedom: The Progress and Future of Aid to Europe, Harper, 1950; (with N. S. Buchanan) *Approaches to Economic Development,* Twentieth Century Fund, 1955; (with others) *United States Monetary Policy,* American Assembly, Columbia University, 1958, 2nd edition, 1964; (with others) *Economic Development and International Trade,* Southern Methodist University Press, 1959; (editor with Henry C. Wallich) *El Desarrollo economico y America Latina* (title means "Economic Development and Latin America"), Fondo de Cultura Economico, 1960; (with Benjamin Cornejo and Luis Escobar Cerda) *The Teaching of Economics in Latin America,* Organization of American States, 1961; (with Diomedes D. Psilos, Richard M. Westebbe, and Calliope Nicolaou) *Industrial Capital in Greek Development,* Center of Economic Development (Athens), 1964; (editor) *The Economy of Brazil,* University of California Press, 1969.

Private Enterprise and Socialism in the Middle East, American Enterprise Institute, 1970; (with others) *Ensaios Economics. Homenagema Octavio Gouvea de Bulhoes* (title means "Economic Essays in Honor of O. Gouvea de Bulhoes") APEC Editora (Rio de Janeiro), 1972. Contributor of articles on economic theory, money and banking, fiscal policy, and international finance to economic journals. Member of board of editors of American Economic Association, 1940-43; co-editor of *Kyklos: International Journal of the Social Sciences,* 1950—.

WORK IN PROGRESS: Research on multinational firms.

SIDELIGHTS: Ellis' books have been published in Japanese, Arabic, Persian, Indonesian, Bengali, and Spanish. *Avocational interests:* Music, gardening.

* * *

ELLIS, John M(artin) 1936-

PERSONAL: Born May 31, 1936, in London, England; son of John Albert (an engineer) and Emily (Silvey) Ellis; married Caroline Ayre Hails, July 3, 1959; children: Richard,

Andrew, Katherine, Jill. *Education:* University of London, B.A. (first class honors), 1959, Ph.D., 1965. *Home:* 280 Moore St., Santa Cruz, Calif. 95060. *Office:* Stevenson College, University of California, Santa Cruz, Calif. 95060.

CAREER: University of Wales, Aberystwyth, tutorial assistant in German, 1959-60; University of Leicester, Leicester, England, assistant lecturer in German, 1960-63; University of Alberta, Edmonton, assistant professor of German, 1963-66; University of California, Santa Cruz, associate professor, 1966-70, professor of German literature, 1970—. *Military service:* British Army, Royal Artillery, 1954-56.

MEMBER: Modern Language Association of America, American Association of Teachers of German, Philology Association of the Pacific Coast, Modern Humanitics Research Association, Goethe Society, American Association of University Professors (president of local chapter, 1973-74), Kleist-Gesellschaft. *Awards, honors:* Guggenheim fellowship, 1970-71.

WRITINGS: Schiller's "Kalliasbriefe" and the Study of His Aesthetic Theory, Mouton & Co., 1969; *Kleist's "Prinz Friedrich von Homburg": A Critical Study,* University of California Press, 1970; *Narration in the German Novelle: Theory and Interpretation,* Cambridge University Press, 1974; *The Theory of Literary Criticism: A Logical Analysis,* University of California Press, 1974. Contributor of about thirty articles and reviews to language journals, including *Twentieth Century, Seminar: A Journal of Germanic Studies, Modern Language Journal, Modern Language Review, Word,* and *German Quarterly.*

WORK IN PROGRESS: A book on Heinrich von Kleist; a book on the theory of language.

* * *

ELLIS, John Marion 1917-

PERSONAL: Born June 1, 1917, in Oklahoma City, Okla.; son of John M. (a physician) and Edna (Speer) Ellis; married Lucille Haenni, November 22, 1947; children: Jeffrey, Gina Ellis Baldwin, Joan Ellis Roberts, John. *Education:* Agricultural and Mechanical College of Texas (now Texas A & M University), B.S., 1939; University of Texas, Galveston, M.D., 1942. *Politics:* Democrat. *Religion:* Disciples of Christ. *Home and office:* 103 West 20th St., Mount Pleasant, Tex. 75455. *Agent:* Blanche Gregory, 2 Tudor City Pl., New York, N.Y. 10017.

CAREER: Physician in general practice; cattleman. Titus County Memorial Hospital, Mount Pleasant, Tex., member of board of managers, 1967-69, chief of medical staff, 1973. Coordinator of civil defense in Mount Pleasant and Titus County, Tex., 1956-71. *Military service:* U.S. Army, Medical Corps, 1944-46; became captain. *Member:* American Medical Association, American Brahman Breeders Association, Texas Medical Association, Texas Brahman Association (director, 1963-65).

WRITINGS: The Doctor Who Looked at Hands, Vantage, 1966; (with James Presley) *Vitamin B6: The Doctor's Report,* Harper, 1973.

WORK IN PROGRESS: Research in nutrition, particularly therapeutic uses of vitamin B6.

* * *

ELLIS, William 1918-

PERSONAL: Born August 7, 1918, in Toronto, Ontario, Canada; son of Alfred (a company director) and Edna (Henshaw) Ellis; married Margaret Paul (an artist), June 15, 1940; children: Naiad (Mrs. Hugh Herbert-Burns), Paul, Robert, Martin, William, Charles. *Education:* Attended Royal Naval College, 1932-35, and naval technical colleges, 1938-39. *Politics:* Conservative. *Religion:* Church of England. *Home:* Higher Coombe, Lustleigh, Devon TQ13 9SF, England. *Agent:* Georges Borchardt, Inc., 145 East 52nd St., New York, N.Y. 10022.

CAREER: Royal Navy, career officer, 1932-46, leaving service as lieutenant; Starch Products Ltd., Slough, England, director, 1947-68; farmer in Devon, England, breeding pedigreed Dexter cattle, 1968—. *Member:* Royal Naval Sailing Association, National Farmer's Union, Dartmoor Pony Society, Dexter Cattle Society. *Awards, honors*—Military: Mentioned in dispatches.

WRITINGS: The Knife Edge, Macmillan (London), 1972, Walker & Co., 1973.

WORK IN PROGRESS: No Will to Die, a novel.

* * *

ELLIS, William Donohue 1918-

PERSONAL: Born September 23, 1918, in Concord, Mass.; son of William Otterbein (a chemist, botanist, and entomologist) and Maude (Donohue) Ellis; married Dorothy Ann Naiden (a school library coordinator), June 13, 1942; children: William Naiden, Sarah Elizabeth. *Education:* Wesleyan University, Middletown, Conn., B.A., 1941. *Home:* 1060 Richmar Dr., Westlake, Ohio. *Office:* 1276 West 3rd St., Cleveland, Ohio 44113.

CAREER: Beaumont & Hohman, Cleveland, Ohio, writer, 1946-47; Storycraft, Inc., Cleveland, vice-president, 1947-52; Editorial Services, Inc. (script writers), Cleveland, president, 1952—. Member of advisory committee, Westlake School Board. *Military service:* U.S. Army, Infantry; served in Philippines and Guam; became captain; received Bronze Star and Purple Heart. *Awards, honors:* Ohioana Literary Award for fiction and Western Reserve Historical Society Award, both 1952, for *The Bounty Lands;* Pulitzer Prize nomination, 1954, for *Jonathan Blair;* Literature award, Cleveland Arts Prize, 1967, for *The Cuyahoga.*

WRITINGS—Novels: *The Bounty Lands* (first of a trilogy), World Publishing, 1952; *Jonathan Blair, Bounty Lands Lawyer* (second of the trilogy), World Publishing, 1954; *The Brooks Legend* (third of the trilogy), Crowell, 1958.

Nonfiction: *The Fabulous Dustpan* (business biography), World Publishing, 1953; (with Frank Siedel) *How to Win the Conference,* Prentice-Hall, 1955; *The Cuyahoga* ("Rivers of America" series), Holt, 1967; *Clarke of St. Vith: The Sergeant's General* (biography), Dillon-Liederbach, 1974.

Co-author, "The Ohio Story," a radio-TV series, 1947—. Contributor of fiction to *Saturday Evening Post,* and of nonfiction to *Reader's Digest, True, Harpers, Rotarian, Atlanta Constitution, Frontiers,* and other periodicals.

WORK IN PROGRESS: A book, tentatively titled *Great Lakes America,* for American West.

SIDELIGHTS: Ellis told *CA:* "Believe assumption of writing career carries responsibility beyond entertainment to right injustice, improve man's future, conscientious search for truth, and to abjure writing for hire in cynical causes. My present magazine work accents conservation.

Hope to get into areas of preserving personal independence in face of governmental growth and responsibilities of business toward public."

The Bounty Lands was on the *New York Times* and *New York Herald-Tribune* best-seller lists for fourteen months; *Jonathan Blair* was named in the *Saturday Review* 1954 top fiction of the year list. Edward Lasker Productions has bought the motion picture rights to *The Bounty Lands,* and television rights to *The Brooks Legend* have been sold to Alwyn Productions. The trilogy has been translated in Holland; *The Bounty Lands* has been condensed in *Omnibook.*

* * *

ELZINGA, Kenneth G(erald) 1941-

PERSONAL: Born August 11, 1941, in Coopersville, Mich.; son of Clarence Albert (an engineer) and Lettie Elizabeth (Albrecht) Elzinga; married Barbara Brunson, June 17, 1967. *Education:* Kalamazoo College, B.A., 1963; Michigan State University, M.A., 1966, Ph.D., 1967. *Religion:* Christian. *Home:* Longbrook Farm, Keswick, Va. 22947. *Office:* Department of Economics, University of Virginia, Charlottesville, Va. 22903.

CAREER: University of Virginia, Charlottesville, assistant professor, 1967-71, associate professor, 1971-74, professor of economics, 1974—, assistant dean of College of Arts and Sciences, 1971-73. Fellow in law and economics at University of Chicago, 1974. Lecturer at National Science Foundation institute for economics teachers, summer, 1970; member of Atomic Energy Commission Licensing and Safety Board Panel, 1971—; director of Summer Institute on the American Economy, 1972-73. *Awards, honors:* Woodrow Wilson fellow, 1964; Phi Beta Kappa visiting scholar, 1973-74; Sesquicentennial Associateship in Center for Advanced Studies at University of Virginia, 1973-74.

WRITINGS: (Contributor) Walter Adams, editor, *The Structure of American Industry,* 4th edition (Elzinga was not associated with earlier editions), Macmillan, 1971; (editor) *Economics: A Reader,* Harper, 1972, 2nd edition, in press; (contributor) J. A. Dalton and S. L. Levin, editors, *The Antitrust Dilemma,* Lexington, 1974. Contributor to *Social Science Quarterly, Antitrust Law and Economics Review, Journal of Law and Economics, Review of Economics and Statistics, Harvard Law Review, Antitrust Bulletin, Industrial Organization Review,* and *Journal of Economic Issues.* Advisory editor of *Social Science Quarterly,* 1969—; member of editorial board of *Industrial Organization Review,* 1972—.

WORK IN PROGRESS: A book on antitrust penalties; a mystery novel.

* * *

ENGL, Lieselotte 1918-

PERSONAL: Born April 12, 1918, in Cologne, Germany; daughter of Luitpold (an actuary) and Maria M. (Stoehr) Brigl; married Theodor Engl (an architect), July 28, 1949; children: Eva Maria. *Education:* Attended primary and secondary schools in Buenos Aires, 1925-33, and Interpreter School at University of Heidelberg, 1940-42; further study at Universities of Heidelberg, Florence, Naples, Berlin; University of Munich, Ph.D., 1954. *Religion:* Protestant. *Home:* Sappelstrasse 32, 8 Munich 70, Germany.

CAREER: Kindergarten teacher in Buenos Aires, Argentina, 1936-37, and hospital nurse, 1938; Foreign Office, Berlin, Germany, interpreter, 1943-44; American Red Cross, Munich, Germany, head clerk, 1945-46; University of Munich, Munich, Germany, lecturer in cultural and social development of Latin America, Inca tradition, and Spanish literature, 1946—. *Member:* Deutsche Gesellschaft fuer Voelkerkunde.

WRITINGS: (With husband, Theodor Engl) *Glanz und Untergang des Inkareiches: Conquistadoren, Moenche, Vizekoenige,* translation by Alisa Jaffe published as *Twilight of Ancient Peru: The Glory and Decline of the Inca Empire,* McGraw, 1969. Also author of radio play, "Der Pishtako" (title means "The Cuthroat"), broadcast by Bayerischer Fundfunk, 1971.

WORK IN PROGRESS: With Theodor Engl, *Die Entdeckung und Eroberung Perus in Augenzeugenberichten,* a translation and analysis of Spanish documents of the sixteenth and seventeenth centuries about the conquest and social history of Peru.

SIDELIGHTS: Lieselotte Engl spent her childhood and youth in Argentina, mingling with Spanish, German, and French families and the camp peoples. In addition to German and Spanish, she is competent in Italian, Portuguese, English, and Latin.

AVOCATIONAL INTERESTS: Riding, swimming, and playing the piano.

* * *

ENGL, Theodor 1925-

PERSONAL: Born September 6, 1925, in Munich, Germany; son of Manfred G. (an engineer) and Hilde (Seitz) Engl; married Lieselotte Brigl (an ethnologist), July 28, 1949; children: Eva Maria. *Education:* Technical University of Munich, Arch., 1950. *Politics:* Social Democrat. *Religion:* Protestant. *Home:* Sappelstrasse 32, 8 Munich 70, Germany. *Office:* Finanzbauamt Munich I, Deroysstrasse 22, 8 Munich 2, Germany.

CAREER: Munich Board of Works, Munich, Germany, architect, 1956—. *Member:* Board of Architects of Bavaria.

WRITINGS: (With wife, Lieselotte Engl) *Glanz und Untergang des Inkareiches: Conquistadoren, Moenche, Vizekoenige,* translation by Alisa Jaffe published as *Twilight of Ancient Peru: The Glory and Decline of the Inca Empire,* McGraw, 1969.

WORK IN PROGRESS: With Lieselotte Engl, *Die Entdeckung und Eroberung Perus in Augenzeugenberichten,* a translation and analysis of Spanish documents of the sixteenth and seventeenth centuries about the conquest and social history of Peru.

AVOCATIONAL INTERESTS: Politics, theology, cello-playing.

* * *

ENSMINGER, Marion Eugene 1908-

PERSONAL: Born May 28, 1908, in Stover, Mo.; son of Jacob and Ella (Belt) Ensminger; married Audrey Helen Watts (a nutritionist), June 11, 1941; children: John Jacob, Janet Aileen (deceased). *Education:* University of Missouri, B.S., 1931, M.S., 1932; University of Massachusetts, graduate study, 1938-40; University of Minnesota, Ph.D., 1941. *Politics:* Democrat. *Religion:* Presbyterian. *Home and office:* 3699 East Sierra Ave., Clovis, Calif. 93612.

CAREER: Missouri State University, Maryville, instructor in agriculture, summers, 1931-32; U.S. Department of Agriculture, assistant to superintendent of Soil Erosion Station, Bethany, Mo., 1933-34, soil erosion specialist in Urbana, Ill., 1934, manager of Dixon Springs Experiment Station in Robb, Ill., 1934-37; University of Massachusetts, Amherst, assistant professor of animal husbandry, 1937-40; Washington State University, Pullman, professor of animal science and chairman of department, 1941-62; Agriservices Foundation, Clovis, Calif., president, 1962—. Distinguished visiting professor at Wisconsin State University—River Falls, 1963; adjunct professor at California State University, Fresno, 1973—. President of Consultants-Agriservices and Pegus Co., both 1962—. Director of Horse Science School and Beef Cattle Stud Managers School, both 1963—. Member of technical committee of Western Cattle Breeding Laboratory and collaborator on Western Sheep Breeders Laboratory, both for U.S. Department of Agriculture. Member of national board of field advisers of U.S. Small Business Administration. Consultant to General Electric Co. and U.S. Atomic Energy Commission.

MEMBER: American Society of Agricultural Consultants (first president, 1963-64), American Society of Animal Sciences (member of executive committee; vice-president of western section, 1957-58; president, 1958-59), American Society of Range Management, American Dairy Science Association, American Genetic Association, Soil Conservation Society of America, American Association for the Advancement of Science (fellow), American Medical Writers Association, Future Farmers of America (honorary member), Indian Council for Farmers (New Delhi; honorary member), New York Academy of Sciences, Sigma Xi, Alpha Zeta, Lambda Gamma Delta. *Awards, honors:* Elected to Washington State University Animal Science Hall of Fame, 1958; distinguished teacher award from American Society of Animal Science, 1960.

WRITINGS: Animal Science, Interstate, 1950; *Beef Cattle Science,* Interstate, 1951; *Sheep and Wool Science,* Interstate, 1951; *Horses and Horsemanship,* Interstate, 1951; *Swine Science,* Interstate, 1952; *The Stockman's Handbook,* Interstate, 1955.

(Contributor) John Hammond, Ivar Johannson, and Fritz Haring, *Handbuch Der Tier-Zuechtung* (title means "Handbook of Animal Breeding"), three volumes, Verlag Paul Parey, 1961; *Horses! Horses! Horses!,* Pegus Co., 1964; *Tack! Tack! Tack!,* Pegus Co., 1965; *Dairy Cattle Science,* Interstate, 1971; *Poultry Science,* Interstate, 1971; (with wife, Audrey Ensminger) *China: The Impossible Dream* (illustrated with photographs), Agriservices Foundation, 1973.

Author of bulletins. Author of "The Stockman's Guide," a monthly syndicated column in magazines in the United States and Canada, 1956—, and "Horses, Horses, Horses!," 1962—. Contributor of more than five-hundred articles to scientific and popular magazines. Editor of *Horse Science Handbook, Beef Cattle Science Handbook,* and *Stud Managers Handbook,* annual publications of Agriservices Foundation, 1964—.

SIDELIGHTS: Ensminger has visited forty-six foreign countries, including the People's Republic of China. His books have been published in Spanish, Japanese, German, and Russian.

* * *

ENTHOVEN, Alain C(harles) 1930-

PERSONAL: Born September 10, 1930, in Seattle, Wash.; son of Richard F. and Jacqueline (Camerlynck) Enthoven; married Rosemary Fenech; children: Eleanor, Richard, Andrew, Martha, Nicholas, Daniel. *Education:* Stanford University, B.A., 1952; Oxford University, B.Phil., 1954; Massachusetts Institute of Technology, Ph.D., 1956. *Home:* One McCormick Lane, Atherton, Calif. 94025. *Office:* Graduate School of Business, Stanford University, Stanford, Calif. 94305.

CAREER: Massachusetts Institute of Technology, Cambridge, instructor in economics, 1955-56; Rand Corporation, Santa Monica, Calif., economist, 1956-60; U.S. Department of Defense, Washington, D.C., operations research analyst in Office of the Director of Defense Research and Engineering, 1960, deputy comptroller and deputy assistant secretary of defense, 1961-65, assistant secretary of defense for systems analysis, 1965-69; Litton Industries, Beverly Hills, Calif., vice-president for economic planning, 1969-71; Litton Medical Products, Beverly Hills, Calif., president, 1971-73; Stanford University, Stanford, Calif., Marriner S. Eccles Professor of Public and Private Management, 1973—, member of computer science advisory committee, 1968-73. Consultant to Brookings Institution, 1956-60, Rand Corporation, 1969—; member of board of directors, Georgetown University, 1968-73; member of board of regents, St. John's Hospital, Santa Monica, Calif., 1971-73; member of visiting committee in economics at Massachusetts Institute of Technology, 1971—, and visiting committee on environmental quality laboratory at California Institute of Technology, 1972—; visiting associate professor of economics at University of Washington, 1958. *Member:* American Economic Association, Econometric Society, Institute of Medicine of the National Academy of Sciences, Council on Foreign Relations, American Association of Rhodes Scholars, Phi Beta Kappa, Sierra Club. *Awards, honors:* President's Award for Distinguished Federal Civilian Service, 1963; Department of Defense Medal for Distinguished Public Service, 1969.

WRITINGS: (Contributor) John G. Gurley and Edward S. Shaw, *Money in a Theory of Finance,* Brookings Institution, 1960; (contributor) C. J. Hitch and R. N. McKean, *The Economics Defense in the Nuclear Age,* Harvard University Press, 1960; (with Robert S. McNamara and C. J. Hitch) *A Modern Design for Defense Decision: A McNamara-Hitch-Enthoven Anthology,* National War College, 1966; (with K. Wayne Smith) *How Much Is Enough? Shaping the Defense Program 1961-1969,* Harper, 1971. Contributor to journals in his field.

* * *

EPPS, Edgar G(ustavas) 1929-

PERSONAL: Born August 30, 1929, in Little Rock, Ark.; son of Clifford and Odelle (Hill) Epps; married Marilyn Miller, December 18, 1958; children: Carolyn Dolores, Raymond Edgar. *Education:* Talladega College, B.A., 1951; Atlanta University, M.A., 1955; Washington State University, Ph.D., 1959. *Home:* 5825 South Dorchester Ave., Chicago, Ill. 60637. *Office:* University of Chicago, 5835 South Kimbark, Chicago, Ill. 60637.

CAREER: Tennessee Agricultural and Industrial State University, Nashville, assistant professor, 1958-59, associate professor of sociology, 1959-61; Florida Agricultural and Mechanical University, Tallahassee, professor of sociology, 1961-64; University of Michigan, Ann Arbor, lecturer, 1964-65, assistant professor, 1965-66, associate professor of psychology, 1966-67, research associate at Survey Research Center of Institute for Social Research, 1964-67; Tuskegee Institute, Tuskegee Institute, Ala., professor of sociology, director of Division of Behavioral Science Research and chairman of Division of Social Sciences, 1967-70; University of Chicago, Chicago, Ill., Marshall Field IV Professor of Urban Education, 1970—. Member of Board of Education of City of Chicago, 1974-78. Member of national advisory council of Human Resources Development Center at Tuskegee Institute, 1970-73; member of board on human resources of National Research Council, 1971-73; member of panel on factors in career development of National Research Council and National Academy of Science, 1972-74; member of board of directors of National Laboratory for Higher Education, 1973-76.

MEMBER: American Sociological Association, Society for the Study of Social Problems, Society for the Psychological Study of Social Issues (member of council, 1969-72), Association of Social and Behavioral Scientists, Assembly of Behavioral and Social Sciences, American Educational Research Association, Phi Delta Kappa.

WRITINGS: Family and Achievement: A Study of the Relation of Family Background to Achievement Orientation and Performance Among Urban Negro High School Students, Survey Research Center, University of Michigan, 1969; (editor and contributor) *Black Students in White Schools,* Charles A. Jones Publishing, 1972; (editor and contributor) *Race Relations: Current Perspectives,* Winthrop, 1973; (contributor) Peter I. Rose, Stanley Rothman, and William J. Wilson, editors, *Through Different Eyes: Black and White Perspectives on American Race Relations,* Oxford University Press, 1973; (contributor) LaMar P. Miller, editor, *The Testing of Black Students,* Prentice-Hall, 1974; (contributor) Andrew Kopan and Herbert Walberg, editors, *Rethinking Educational Equality,* McCutchan, 1974; *Cultural Pluralism,* McCutchan, 1974; (contributor) James E. Blackwell and Morris Janowitz, editors, *The Black Sociologists: Historical and Contemporary Perspectives,* University of Chicago Press, 1974.

Author of research reports. Contributor of about twenty articles to sociology and education journals, including *Integrated Education, School Review, Phylon, Journal of Experimental Social Psychology, Journal of Educational Psychology,* and *Psychological Reports.* Associate editor of *American Sociological Review,* 1971-74.

WORK IN PROGRESS: Identity and Achievement in the Black College, with Patricia Gurin.

* * *

EPSTEIN, Daniel Mark 1948-

PERSONAL: Born October 25, 1948, in Washington, D.C.; son of Donald David (a businessman) and Louise (Tilman) Epstein. *Education:* Kenyon College, B.A. (with highest honors), 1970.

AWARDS, HONORS: Robert Frost Prize; Stephen Vincent Benet Prize for "Letter Concerning Yellow Fever"; Woodrow Wilson fellowship.

WRITINGS: No Vacancies in Hell (poems), Liveright, 1973. Contributor of poems to magazines, including *New Yorker, Nation, Michigan Quarterly, Virginia Quarterly, Northwest Review,* and *Modern Occasions.*

* * *

ERICKSON, W(alter) Bruce 1938-

PERSONAL: Born March 4, 1938, in Chicago, Ill.; son of Clifford Eric (a college professor) and Mildred (Brinkmeier) Erickson. *Education:* Michigan State University, B.A., 1959, M.A., 1960, Ph.D., 1965. *Home:* 2849 35th Ave. S., Minneapolis, Minn. 55406. *Office:* College of Business Administration, University of Minnesota, Minneapolis, Minn. 55455.

CAREER: U.S. Senate, Washington, D.C., staff associate of Subcommittee on Antitrust and Monopoly, 1960-61; Bowling Green University, Bowling Green, Ohio, assistant professor of business and government, 1965-66; University of Minnesota, Minneapolis, assistant professor, 1967-70, associate professor of business and government, 1971—. Consultant and expert witness in private antitrust cases. *Member:* American Economic Association, Royal Economics Society.

WRITINGS: (With William Rudelius and William J. Bakula) *An Introduction to Contemporary Business,* Harcourt, 1973. Contributor to *Antitrust Bulletin* and *Antitrust Law and Economics Review.*

WORK IN PROGRESS: The Private Antitrust Action.

AVOCATIONAL INTERESTS: Reading, travel, participatory sports.

* * *

ESMEIN, Jean 1923-

PERSONAL: Surname is pronounced Es-*meh*; born December 1, 1923, in Poitiers, France; son of Paul (a law professor and author) and Marcelle (Roux) Esmein; married Suzanne Esteve (a museum librarian), August 4, 1945; children: Pierre, Bernard. *Education:* Ecole Nationale des Langues Orientales Vivantes, diplome, 1956; Ecole Pratique des Hautes Etudes, titulaire, 1958; Tokyo University, graduate study, 1971. *Home:* 30 rue Saint Come, Luzarches, France 95270. *Office:* Credit Lyonnais, 3-2-3 Marunouchi, Tokyo, Japan 100-91.

CAREER: Marine Nationale (French Navy), career officer, 1942-58, became commander; Compagnie des Machines Bull (computers), Paris, France, manager of scientific computing center, 1959-65; French Embassy, Peking, China, press attache, 1965-68; Credit Lyonnais (bank), Tokyo, Japan, representative for the Far East, 1969—. Superior Council of the Overseas French Residents, elected representative of the French residents in China, Korea, Japan, and Philippines, 1972—. *Member:* Association for Computing Machinery, Computers Art Society, Association du Pacte d'Amitie Kyoto-Paris (secretaire general adjoint, 1958—). *Awards, honors*—Military: Croix du Combattant, Croix de Guerre, Chevalier de la Legion d'Honneur.

WRITINGS: La Revolution culturelle chinoise, Le Seuil, 1970, translation by W. J. F. Jenner published as *The Chinese Cultural Revolution,* Doubleday, 1973. Contributor to *Larousse Encyclopedique.*

WORK IN PROGRESS: Translating Ooka Shohei's *Leyte Senki* (Chroniques de la bataille de leyte); *La Politique est un vilain metier.*

* * *

ESPY, Willard R(ichardson) 1910-

PERSONAL: Born December 11, 1910, in Olympia, Wash.; son of Harry Albert and Helen (Richardson) Espy; married Hilda Cole, October 17, 1940 (divorced, 1962); married Louise Manheim (a researcher), July 10, 1962; children: (first marriage) Mona Margaret (Mrs. Eugene Schreiber), Freddy Medora (Mrs. George Ames Plimpton), Joanna Page, Cassin Richardson, Jefferson Taylor. *Education:* University of Redlands, B.A., 1930; graduate study at Sorbonne, University of Paris, 1930-31. *Politics:* Independent. *Religion:* Protestant. *Home and office:* 30 Beekman Pl., New York, N.Y. 10022.

CAREER: Reporter for California daily newspapers, 1932-33; *World Tomorrow,* New York, N.Y., promotion director, 1933-35; *Nation,* New York, N.Y., correspondent, 1935-37; *L'Agence Havas,* New York, N.Y., reporter, 1937-40; *Reader's Digest,* Pleasantville, N.Y., promotion director and public relations manager, 1941-57; free-lance writer in communications, 1957-60; Charter Publishers, New York, N.Y., president and publisher, 1960-66; free-lance writer in communications, 1966—. *Member:* Coffee House Club (New York, N.Y.).

WRITINGS: Bold New Program, Harper, 1950; *The Game of Words,* Peter Wolfe, 1971, Grosset, 1972; *The Oysterville Almanac: A Calendar of Recollections, Rhymes, and Wordplay,* C. N. Potter, in press. Contributor to magazines, including *Nation, New York Times Magazine, Atlantic, Harper's, Punch,* and *This Week.*

WORK IN PROGRESS: Omak Me Yours Tonight, a punning ballad on Washington state place names; *The Cat Word Book,* for Doubleday; a history and anthology of American dialect, completion expected in 1977.

* * *

ESSAME, Hubert 1896-

PERSONAL: Born December 2, 1896, in Exeter, England; son of Ernest Horatio and Phoebe (Salter) Essame; married Hilda Mary Kennedy, July 3, 1926 (died, 1964); married Dorothy Fox, June 6, 1964; children: (first marriage) Peter Kennedy, Robin Stephen Kennedy, Primrose Mary (Mrs. Edgar Joseph Feuchtwanger). *Education:* Army Staff College, Quetta, Pakistan, graduate, 1930. *Religion:* Anglican. *Home:* The Courtyard, West Wittering, North Chichester, England.

CAREER: British Army, career officer, 1915-49, retiring as major general; Ministry of Information, England, lecturer for army classes at University of Oxford, University of Southampton, University of Leeds, University of London, and University of Exeter, 1952-72. Chairman of Honiton Division of Conservative Party, 1952-57; chiarman of Friends of Marlpits Hospital, 1952-64; governor of Royal School for Daughters of Officers of the Army, Bath, England, 1962—. *Member:* Royal United Services Institute for Defense Studics, United Service Club. *Awards, honors*—Military: Military Cross, Distinguished Service Order, Commander of Order of the British Empire.

WRITINGS: The Forty-Third Wessex Division at War, Clowes, 1952; (with E. M. G. Belfield) *The Battle for Normandy,* Batsford, 1965; *The Battle for Germany,* Batsford, 1969; *Normandy Bridgehead,* Ballantine, 1970; *The Battle for Europe 1918,* Scribner, 1972; *Patton: A Study in Command,* Scribner, 1974. Contributor to military journals.

WORK IN PROGRESS: The Art of Command–the Human Side: Hannibal to Eisenhower, completion expected in 1975.

SIDELIGHTS: John Toland wrote of *The Battle for Germany:* "General Essame . . . writes equally well of enlisted men and generals and renders one of the most complicated campaigns in the war understandable and meaningful to the layman. Also, being a man of taste and wit with a gift for expression, he makes all this good reading.

"His portrait of Montgomery . . . is about as rich as a novelist's, yet it hews to the facts; and his detailed descriptions of the deadly mop-ups in Holland are both dramatic and militarily impeccable. His is the best account I have read of Operation Veritable, the first step in Montgomery's drive into Germany itself." *Avocational interests:* Georgian and Victorian painting, history of British India.

* * *

ETEROVICH, Adam S(lav) 1930-

PERSONAL: Born November 27, 1930, in San Francisco, Calif.; son of Ivan and Ana (Cvitanich) Eterovich; married Danica Kralj, April 15, 1957; children: Karen. *Education:* San Francisco State College (now University), B.A., 1955; University of Zagreb, graduate study, 1956-57. *Politics:* Democrat. *Religion:* Roman Catholic. *Home:* 330 King Dr., San Francisco, Calif. 94080. *Office:* 936 Industrial Ave., Palo Alto, Calif. 94303.

CAREER: Home Insurance Co., San Francisco, Calif., insurance underwriting manager, 1958-69; R & E Research Associates, San Francisco, Calif., publisher, 1970—. Member of International Hospitality House of San Francisco. *Military service:* U.S. Army, 1949-52; became sergeant first class. *Member:* California Historical Society.

WRITINGS: Dalmatians and Serbs in the West and South, 1800-1900, R & E Research, 1971; *Yugoslav Survey of California-Nevada-Arizona, 1830-1900,* R & E Research, 1971; *Yugoslavs in Nevada: 1859-1900,* R & E Research, 1973. Contributor of more than fifty articles to journals.

WORK IN PROGRESS: Yugoslavs in the West; Croatians in California; Yugoslavs in California.

* * *

ETZKORN, K(laus) Peter 1932-

PERSONAL: Born April 18, 1932, in Karlsruhe, Germany; came to United States in 1952, naturalized in 1958; son of Johannes and Luise (Schlick) Etzkorn; married Hildegard Elizabeth Garve (a lecturer), September 3, 1953; children: Kyle Peter, Lars Peter. *Education:* Ohio State University, A.B., 1955; attended Indiana University, 1955-56; Princeton University, M.A., 1958, Ph.D., 1959. *Politics:* Independent. *Home:* 8042 Gannon, St. Louis, Mo. 63130. *Office:* Department of Sociology, University of Missouri-St. Louis, St. Louis, Mo. 63121.

CAREER: University of California, Santa Barbara, assistant professor of sociology, 1959-63; American University of Beirut, Beirut, Lebanon, associate professor of sociology, 1963-64; University of Nevada, Reno, associate professor of sociology, 1964-67, head of department, 1966-67, director of Office of Institutional Research, 1965-67; University of West Florida, Pensacola, professor of sociology, 1967-68, head of department, 1967-68; California State University, Northridge, professor of sociology, 1968-69; University of Missouri, St. Louis, professor of sociology and anthropology, 1969—, head of department, 1969-72. Member of Government of Nevada Committee on Department of Correction, 1966; consultant to Bureau of Higher Education, U.S. Office of Education, 1966-71; member of Escambia County (Fla.) Juvenile Court Advisory Committee, 1967; member of Missouri Advisory Committee on Humanities. *Member:* International Studies Association, International Institute of Sociology (member of bureau),

International Political Science Association, American Anthropological Association (fellow), American Sociological Association (fellow), Society for Ethnomusicology (member of council, 1964-71; director-at-large, 1967-68), Society for the Study of Social Problems.

WRITINGS: Georg Simmel: The Conflict in Modern Culture, Teachers College Press, 1968; (contributor) Warren d'Azevedo, editor, *The Traditional Artist in West African Society,* Indiana University Press, 1973; *Music and Society,* Wiley, 1973. Contributor to about thirty journals, including *Ethnomusicology, Social Forces, American Sociological Review, Indian Sociology Bulletin,* and *Koelner Zeitschrift Soziologie.* Editor of special publications of Society for Ethnomusicology, 1968-72.

WORK IN PROGRESS: Studies on higher education problems and on music and society.

* * *

EULERT, Don 1935-

PERSONAL: Surname is pronounced *Yoo*-lert; born September 12, 1935, in Russell County, Kan.; son of Otto C. (a rancher) and Elsie (Reich) Eulert; married Jacquelyn Brock, May 12, 1957 (divorced, 1967); married Tamara Tow, April 6, 1968 (divorced, 1973); children: (first marriage) Melissa D., J. Colby, Bret R. *Education:* Fort Hays Kansas State College, B.A., 1957, M.A., 1960; University of Kansas, further graduate study, 1960-61; University of New Mexico, Ph.D., 1968. *Home address:* Star Route 1, Santa Ysabel, Calif. 92080. *Office:* U.S. International University, California Western Campus, 10455 Pomerado Rd., San Diego, Calif. 92131.

CAREER: High school teacher of English and journalism in Colby, Kan., 1957-60; University of Kansas, Lawrence, instructor in English, 1960-61; Wisconsin State University—Platteville (now University of Wisconsin—Platteville), assistant professor of English, 1961-64; Sandia Laboratories, Albuquerque, N.M., technical writer, 1964-68; U.S. International University, California Western Campus, San Diego, associate professor of English, 1968—. Senior computer programmer for Educational Research Associates, 1965-66; coordinator and member of steering committee for Bethesda Conference on Medical Uses of Technology, 1968-69; director of San Diego Council for Poetry, 1970-71; Fulbright lecturer at University of Iasi, 1971-72, 1972-73. Lecturer in the United States and abroad; has given poetry readings from his own work; has appeared on radio and television programs for WSWW-Radio (Platteville), WHA-FM Radio (Madison), KHFM-Radio, KSDS-FM Radio, Bucharest Radio, KNME-Television (New Mexico), and KCET-Television (Los Angeles).

AWARDS, HONORS: Kansas Quill Award, 1961; William Carruth Memorial Poetry Award, 1961; *Carolina Quarterly* poetry award, 1962; short story and poetry awards from Wisconsin Regional Writers, 1962.

WRITINGS: (Editor) *The Rolamite Conference* (monograph), University of New Mexico Press, 1969; *Haiku and Senryu,* Minerva Press, 1973; (editor, and translator with Stefan Avadanei) *Anthology of Modern Romanian Poetry,* Junimea Press, 1973; (translator) *Selected Poems of Lucian Blaga,* Minerva Press, in press.

Work is anthologized in *A Wisconsin Harvest,* edited by August Derleth, Hawk Press, 1966; *Poets of the Midwest,* edited by J. R. Le Master, Young Publications, 1967.

Contributor of articles, short stories, poems, and reviews to literary journals, including *American Transcendental Quarterly, New England Review, East-West Review, American Haiku, Prairie Schooner, Midwest Quarterly,* and *Coyote Journal.* Editor of *Western Poet,* 1960-62; founder and editor of *American Haiku,* 1962-64; member of editorial staff of *Abstracts of English Studies,* 1962-71, and *Lemming Review,* 1969-71.

WORK IN PROGRESS: Red and White Tram, a novel; *Critical Biography of Winfield Townley Scott; She,* a collection of poems; *The Perfect Assurance,* a collection of poems; translating *Poems of Mihia Urshaci.*

SIDELIGHTS: Eulert is especially interested in ritual, folk customs, and the primacy of mythic sources for experience and literature. He has traveled in Africa, the Balkans, Central and Western Europe, and Scandinavia.

* * *

EUSTACE, Cecil John 1903-

PERSONAL: Born June 5, 1903, in England; son of John and Edith Mary (Cutler) Eustace; married Irene Emily Agnes Van Praagh, June 3, 1930; children: Philip John, Michael Anthony, Elizabeth Mary. *Education:* Studied at Felsted College, Essex, England. *Politics:* Liberal. *Religion:* Roman Catholic. *Home:* 62 Forest Heights Blvd., Willowdale, Ontario M2L 2K6, Canada. *Agent:* Matie Molinaro, 44 Douglas Cres., Toronto, Ontario, Canada.

CAREER: Free-lance writer and journalist, 1920-30; J. M. Dent & Sons (publishers), Don Mills, Ontario, field editor, 1930-48, director, 1948-53, vice-president, 1953-61, managing director, 1961-63, president, 1963-68. Director of Cooperative Book Centre of Canada, Toronto, 1959-63, president, 1963; director of Canadian Textbook Publishers Institute, Toronto, 1961-62; president of Canadian Book Publishers Council, 1963; chairman of religion and life lectures in Toronto in the 1950's; trustee of North York Library System, 1965—, chairman of board of trustees, 1967.

MEMBER: Metropolitan Board of Trade (Toronto), York Downs Golf and Country Club, Serra Club (Toronto). *Awards, honors:* Received honorable mention in Edward O'Brien's *Best Short Stories,* 1937, and in *Prize Stories: The O. Henry Awards,* 1938; Centennial Medal from Government of Canada, 1967, in recognition of valuable service to the nation; named Knight of Equestrian Order of the Holy Sepulchre, by Pope Paul VI.

WRITINGS—Nonfiction, except where indicated: *The Scarlet Gentleman* (novel), Macmillan (Canada), 1927; *Romewards* (Catholic Book Club selection), Benziger, 1933; *Damaged Lives* (novel), Putnam, 1934; *Mind and the Mystery,* Longmans, Green, 1937; *Catholicism, Communism, and Dictatorship,* Benziger, 1938; *House of Bread,* Longmans, Green, 1943; *An Infinity of Questions,* Dobson, 1946; *A Canadian Foundress: The Life of Aurelia Caouette,* Basilian, 1947; *A Spring in the Desert* (novel), Doubleday, 1969; *Developments in Canadian Book Production and Design,* Queen's Printer, 1972; *Forgotten Music* (novel), McGraw, 1974.

Work is represented in anthologies, including: *Open House,* edited by William A. Deacon and Wilfred Reeves, Graphic Publishers (Ottawa), 1931, and *The English Review Book of Short Stories,* edited by Horace Shipp, foreword by Ford Madox Ford, Sampson, Low, & Marston, 1933.

Contributor of short stories, articles, and reviews to magazines, including *English Review, American Hebrew, Com-*

monweal, America, Catholic World, and *Culture*. Book review editor of *Catholic Register*.

WORK IN PROGRESS: A Classification of Psychic Phenomena and Mysticism (tentative title).

SIDELIGHTS: Eustace writes: "My whole life has been dominated by my interest in religion and philosophy, sometimes to the detriment, I feel, of my creative work. Most of my written work of a serious nature deals with the background of ultimate reality to be found in personal experience with God, the divine, mystical insights, biographical insights, etc."

* * *

EVANS, David Allan 1940-

PERSONAL: Born April 11, 1940, in Sioux City, Iowa; son of Arthur Clarence (an editor) and Ruth (Benson) Evans; married Janice Kaye (a secretary), July 4, 1958; children: Shelly, David, Karlin. *Education:* Augustana College, Sioux Falls, S.D., student, 1958-60; Morningside College, B.A., 1962; University of Iowa, M.A., 1964; University of Arkansas, M.F.A., 1971. *Politics:* Democrat. *Home;* 1218 Fourth, Brookings, S.D. 57006. *Office:* South Dakota State University, Brookings, S.D. 57006.

CAREER: Marshalltown Community College, Marshalltown, Iowa, instructor in English, 1964-65; Adams State College, Alamosa, Colo., assistant professor of English, 1966-68; South Dakota State University, Brookings, associate professor of English, 1968—. *Member:* Poetry Society of America. *Awards, honors:* Borestone Poetry Award, 1969; grant from National Endowment for the Arts, 1974.

WRITINGS: (Editor with Tom Kakonis) *From Language to Idea,* Holt, 1971; (editor with Kakonis) *Statement and Craft,* Prentice-Hall, 1972; *Among Athletes* (poems; pamphlet) Folder Editions, 1972; (editor) *New Voices in American Poetry,* Winthrop, 1973.

WORK IN PROGRESS: Train Windows, poems; a series of poems based on the work of artist Edward Hopper.

SIDELIGHTS: Evans told *CA:* "To me, writing poems has always meant finding the right, i.e. best-for-me, relationship between experience and words. Those experiences have been, for the most part, physical ones, hence my many poems on sports, athletes. I am a slow, usually patient writer. I take revision seriously."

* * *

EVANS, Mari

PERSONAL: Born in Toledo, Ohio; divorced. *Education:* Attended University of Toledo. *Home:* 750 West Tenth St., Indianapolis, Ind. 46202. *Office:* Afro-American Department, Memorial Hall West, Indiana University, Bloomington, Ind. 47401.

CAREER: Indiana University—Purdue University at Indianapolis, instructor in Black literature and writer-in-residence, 1970-71; Indiana University, Bloomington, assistant professor of Black literature and writer-in-residence, 1971-75. Producer, director, writer for television program, "The Black Experience," WTTV, Indianapolis, 1968-73. Visiting assistant professor, Northwestern University, 1972-73; has lectured and read at numerous colleges and universities. Consultant to Discovery Grant Program, National Endowment for the Arts, 1969-70; consultant in ethnic studies, Bobbs-Merrill Co., 1970-73. Member of literary advisory panel, Indiana State Arts Commission; chairman, Statewide Committee for Penal Reform; member of Region I Board, National Council of Young Men's Christian Association (YMCA), and of Fall Creek Parkway YMCA Board of Management. *Member:* Authors Guild, Authors League of America. *Awards, honors:* John Hay Whitney fellow, 1965-66; Woodrow Wilson Foundation grant, 1968; Indiana University Writers' Conference award, and Black Academy of Arts and Letters first annual poetry award, both 1970, for *I Am a Black Woman.*

WRITINGS: Where Is All the Music? (poems), P. Breman, 1968; *I Am a Black Woman* (poems), Morrow, 1970; *J.D.* (juvenile), Doubleday, 1973; *I Look at Me* (juvenile), Third World Press, 1974; *Rap Stories* (juvenile), Third World Press, in press. Poetry is represented in anthologies and textbooks. Writer for television program, "The Black Experience." Contributor to *Phylon, Black World* (formerly *Negro Digest*), *Dialog,* and other periodicals.

SIDELIGHTS: Mari Evans, notes a *Virginia Quarterly Review* writer, "is a powerful poet. Her craftsmanship does not interfere with the subject she treats with a fullness born of deep caring. She subtly interweaves private and public Black frustration and dignity with an infectious perception. Sparseness of speech belies a command of the language and knowledge of the Black experience.... We need to hear this authentic voice again and again, for there is strength in exquisitely revealing expressions of ghetto dynamics."

Miss Evans's poetry has been choreographed and used on record albums, filmstrips, television specials, and in two Off-Broadway productions, "A Hand Is on the Gate" and "Walk Together Children."

* * *

EVANS, Marvin R(ussell) 1915-

PERSONAL: Born October 26, 1915, in Moreland, Ga.; son of Alvin Russell (a farmer) and Julia (Haynie) Evans; married Calla Hydrick, October 7, 1944; children: Susanne (Mrs. Carey Smith), Martha Elizabeth. *Education:* Berry College, A.B., 1936; Emory University, M.A., 1941; Florida State University, Ph.D., 1968. *Politics:* Independent. *Religion:* Methodist. *Home:* 502 Brookdale Dr., Valdosta, Ga. 31601. *Office:* Department of English, Valdosta State College, Valdosta, Ga. 31601.

CAREER: Berry College, Mount Berry, Ga., instructor in French, 1936-37; high school teacher of English and Latin in Mansfield, Ga., 1937-42; Berry College, instructor in French, 1942-47; Emory-at-Valdosta, Valdosta, Ga., assistant professor of English, 1947-53; Valdosta State College, Valdosta, Ga., assistant professor, 1957-59, associate professor, 1959-68, professor of English, 1968—. Chairman of Southern Regional Library, Valdosta, 1969-70. *Member:* American Association of University Professors, Men's Garden Club (Valdosta).

WRITINGS: Poems After Midnight, Branden Press, 1973.

AVOCATIONAL INTERESTS: Collecting pewter and books by Southern authors, folklore, growing roses and camellias.

* * *

EVANS, Robert L(eonard) 1917-

PERSONAL: Born May 30, 1917, in Duluth, Minn.; son of John Leonard (a banker) and Amy (Magnusson) Evans; married Frances Bentley, December, 1941 (died, 1955); married Elsie Hardy (a teacher), January, 1957; children:

Amy Evans Levin, Thomas R., Julia (Mrs. Russell Stickle). *Education:* University of Minnesota, B. Chem., 1938, M.S., 1939, Ph.D., 1951. *Home:* 2500 St. Anthony Blvd., Minneapolis, Minn. 55418.

CAREER: Chemist, 1940-45; University of Minnesota, Minneapolis, instructor, 1945-54, assistant professor, 1954-68, associate professor, 1968-70, lecturer in biometry, 1970—. *Member:* American Association for the Advancement of Science, American Chemical Society, Minnesota Academy of Science (president, 1962-63).

WRITINGS: The Fall and Rise of Man, If . . ., Lund Press, 1973. Contributor to scientific journals.

WORK IN PROGRESS: Human Biology Quantitated.

* * *

EVANS, Rodney E(arl) 1939-

PERSONAL: Born May 15, 1939, in Pontiac, Mich.; son of Hubert and Lillian (Wilcox) Evans; married Lynn Summers, September, 1961; children: Mark, Scott, Cynthia. *Education:* Michigan State University, B.A., 1961, M.B.A., 1963, Ph.D., 1966. *Home:* 3826 Warwick Ct., Norman, Okla. 73069. *Office:* Division of Marketing, University of Oklahoma, 307 West Brooks, Norman, Okla. 73069.

CAREER: Wright State University, Dayton, Ohio, lecturer, 1967-69, associate professor of business administration, 1969-70; University of Oklahoma, Norman, associate professor of business administration, 1970—, director of Division of Marketing, 1973—. Owner of R. E. Evans & Associates (consultants), 1972—. *Military service:* U.S. Air Force, assistant professor at U.S. Air Force Institute of Technology, 1966-69; became captain. *Member:* American Marketing Association (vice-president of Oklahoma City chapter, 1973-74; president, 1974-75), Southern Marketing Association, Beta Gamma Sigma, Sigma Iota Epsilon.

WRITINGS: Fundamentals of Logistics Research, U.S. Air Force, 1968; *Marketing Strategy and Management,* Business Publications, 1975. Contributor to marketing journals.

* * *

EVARTS, Hal G. (Jr.) 1915-

PERSONAL: Born February 8, 1915, in Hutchinson, Kan.; son of Hal G. (an author) and Sylvia A. Evarts; married Dorothea Van Dusen Abbott, 1942; children: Virginia Evarts Wadsworth, William A., John V. *Education:* Stanford University, B.A., 1936. *Home:* 6625 Muirlands Dr., La Jolla, Calif. 92037.

CAREER: Set out for Europe after graduation from Stanford and continued on a knapsack trip around the world, 1936-37; worked briefly as screenwriter in Hollywood and reporter for trade journals and newspapers; in 1939 returned to Europe, where he wrote for Paris edition of *New York Herald-Tribune* until France fell to the Nazis; full-time writer of fiction, 1940—. *Military service:* U.S. Army, 1943-45; served in Europe with 89th Infantry Division. *Member:* Western Writers of America, Zeta Psi, Sigma Delta Chi.

WRITINGS—Youth books: *Jim Clyman,* Putnam, 1959; *Treasure River,* Scribner, 1964; *The Talking Mountain,* Scribner, 1966; *Smugglers' Road,* Scribner, 1968; *Mission to Tibet,* Scribner, 1970; *The Pegleg Mystery,* Scribner, 1972; *Big Foot,* Scribner, 1973.

Other fiction: *Ambush Rider,* R. Hale, 1957, Pocket Books, 1971; *Jebediah Smith, Trail Blazer of the West,* Putnam, 1959; *The Secret of the Himalayas,* Scribner, 1962; *Branded Man,* Fawcett, 1965; *Sundown Kid,* Fawcett, 1969; *Man Without a Gun,* Pocket Books, 1972; *The Night Raiders,* Pocket Books, 1972; *The Settling of the Sage,* Pocket Books, 1972; *The Long Rope,* Pocket Books, 1972; *The Man from Yuma,* Pocket Books, 1972; *Fugitive's Canyon,* Pocket Books, 1972.

Contributor of more than one hundred stories to magazines, including *Saturday Evening Post, Collier's, American, Esquire, This Week, Toronto Star Weekly, Liberty, Adventure,* and *Ellery Queen.*

SIDELIGHTS: Evarts said: "I was born in a small midwestern town in the heart of the Kansas wheat belt. My boyhood memories in this Norman Rockwell sort of town are tinged with nostalgia for the good old days.

"My father was a natural-born storyteller, and from childhood I wanted to be a writer too. I often accompanied my father on his wide travels to gather material for stories and articles on camping and hunting trips over much of the West, to Mexico, Alaska, the Florida Keys, New Guinea, and the South Pacific.

"My primary function as a writer is to entertain. I strive for realism—telling it like it is—and believe that it is possible to write about almost any subject for youngsters if the writer employs good taste, selectivity, and all his skill. My greatest challenge is to write a book that young readers find so enjoyable and meaningful they want to come back for more.

"I enjoy the reassurance of knowing that someone out there is reading my work, and derive the greatest satisfaction when I receive letters from my young readers."

* * *

EYE, Glen G(ordon) 1904-

PERSONAL: Born October 19, 1904, in Miltonvale, Kan.; son of Christopher J. and Dillie G. (Park) Eye; married Lucile Terry, June 21, 1927; children: Miriam Gale (Mrs. Fred G. Blum, Jr.), Kathryn Elaine (Mrs. Clarence Balding). *Education:* Kansas Wesleyan University, B.A., 1925; University of Wisconsin, Ph.M., 1930, Ph.D., 1942. *Home:* 913 South Whitney Way, Madison, Wis. 53711. *Office:* Department of Educational Administration, Educational Sciences Building, University of Wisconsin, Madison, Wis. 53706.

CAREER: Teacher and principal in Montana public schools, 1925-29; superintendent of elementary schools in Miles City, Mont., 1929-37; assistant principal, then principal of senior high school of Ogden, Utah, 1937-41; University of Wisconsin, Madison, principal of university high school, 1941-48, assistant professor, 1941-45, associate professor, 1945-57, professor of education, 1957-62, professor of educational administration, 1962—, chairman of department of education, 1959-62, chairman of department of educational administration, 1962-65, Avril S. Barr Distinguished Professor, 1972. Visiting summer professor at University of Oregon, 1951, and University of Southern California, 1957. Member of Wisconsin Commission on Teacher Education and Professional Standards, 1956-59, chairman, 1958-59.

MEMBER: American Association of School Administrators (co-chairman of committee on technology and instruction, 1967-69), Association for Supervision and Curriculum

Development (member of board of directors, 1967-70), American Educational Research Association, University Council for Educational Administration, Wisconsin Association of School District Administrators, Wisconsin Association for Supervision and Curriculum Development, Wisconsin Educational Research Association.

AWARDS, HONORS: L.H.D., Kansas Wesleyan University, 1957; Outstanding Educator Award, Wisconsin Association of School District Administrators, 1969; Distinguished Achievement Award, Kansas Wesleyan University, 1974.

WRITINGS: (With Milton O. Pella) "Basic Arithmetic" series, four books, U.S. Armed Forces Institute, 1946-47; (with Willard R. Lane) *The New Teacher Comes to School,* Harper, 1956; (with Lanore A. Netzer) *Supervision of Instruction: A Phase of Administration,* Harper, 1965, 2nd edition, 1971; (with Netzer) *School Administrators and Instruction,* Allyn & Bacon, 1969; (with Stephen J. Knezevich) *Instructional Technology and the School Administrator,* American Association of School District Administrators, 1970; (with Netzer, Ardelle Graef, Robert D. Krey, and J. Fred Overman) *Interdisciplinary Foundations of Supervision-Administration,* Allyn & Bacon, 1970; (with Netzer, Marshall E. Dimock, Matthew P. Dumont, Lloyd Homme, and others) *Education, Administration, and Change: The Redeployment of Resources,* Harper, 1970. Contributor of about thirty articles to educational journals. Co-editor, first *WEA Handbook of Education for Teachers,* 1954.

WORK IN PROGRESS: With Lanore A. Netzer, James C. Stoltenberg, and Dan H. McAllister, *The Art of Using Supervision and Manual for Self-Directed Analysis: Early Teaching Experiences,* publication expected in 1976; with Netzer, a new edition of *Supervision of Instruction,* 1976; with Netzer, Wayne W. Benson, and Dwight M. Stevens, *Strategies of Instructional Management,* for Allyn & Bacon.

BIOGRAPHICAL/CRITICAL SOURCES: Wisconsin Honors Professor Glen G. Eye as He Salutes the Badger State During His Golden Year (booklet), Golden Year Committee, University of Wisconsin, 1974.

* * *

FAIRFAX, John 1937-

PERSONAL: Born May 21, 1937, in Rome, Italy; son of Kenneth (a journalist) and Mara (Peneff) Fairfax. *Education:* Attended Chateaubriand College, Rome, 1943-48, San Salvador College, Buenos Aires, 1949-55, University of Buenos Aires, 1958-59. *Politics:* Right wing. *Religion:* None. *Home and office:* Flat 15, Melville Ct., Goldhawk Rd., London W12 9NY, England. *Agent:* George Greenfield, John Farquharson Ltd., 15 Red Lion Sq., London W.C.1, England.

CAREER: Big-game hunter in South America, smuggler in Central America, diver, sailor, and, Fairfax added, "whatever takes my fancy, wherever I fancy, as long as it's adventure," 1955—. *Awards, honors:* Benrus Citation award, 1969; has received keys to the cities of New York, San Francisco, and Fort Lauderdale; honorary member of Swimming Hall of Fame, Fort Lauderdale.

WRITINGS: Vagabundos bajo el sol (title means "Vagabonds under the Sun"), Stilcograf (Buenos Aires), 1957; *Britannia: Rowing Alone across the Atlantic,* Simon & Schuster, 1971; (with Sylvia Cook) *Oars across the Pacific,* Norton, 1972. Contributor to periodicals, including *True, Esquire, Match* (Paris), *Walkabout* (Australia), and *Neue Revue* (Germany).

SIDELIGHTS: Fairfax was the first man to row across the Atlantic alone in 1969, and, with Sylvia Cook, first to row the Pacific, 1971-72. Other expeditions include a 1,000-mile canoe trip along the Paraguay River in South America, treasure hunting in Guatemalan jungles ("unsuccessful"), and a six-month trip on horseback across eastern Paraguay. Fairfax is fluent in Italian, Spanish, and Bulgarian.

* * *

FALLERS, Lloyd A(shton, Jr.) 1925-1974

August 29, 1925—July 4, 1974; American anthropologist, sociologist, educator, and author of books in his field. Obituaries: *New York Times,* July 5, 1974. (*CA*-9/10).

* * *

FALORP, Nelson P.
See JONES, Stephen (Phillip)

* * *

FANG, Irving E. 1929-

PERSONAL: Born May 4, 1929, in New York, N.Y.; son of Isidor (a garment worker) and Kate (Grosin) Fang; married Shirley Campbell, September 11, 1954 (divorced December, 1972); children: Rachel, Daisy. *Education:* University of California, Los Angeles, B.A., 1951, M.S., 1960, Ph.D., 1966. *Home:* 2297 Folwell St., St. Paul, Minn. 55108. *Office:* School of Journalism and Mass Communication, University of Minnesota, Minneapolis, Minn. 55455.

CAREER: North Platte Telegraph-Bulletin, North Platte, Neb., reporter, 1952; *Florence Morning News,* Florence, S.C., reporter, 1952-53; *Montgomery Advertiser,* Montgomery, Ala., reporter, 1953-54; Reuters (news service), rewrite editor in London, England, 1954-55; *Daily Times,* Lagos, Nigeria, editorial adviser, 1955; *San Gabriel Valley Tribune,* Covina, Calif., wire editor, 1955-57; *Pasadena Independent* and *Star-News,* Pasadena, Calif., editorial writer, 1957-59; KABC-Television News, Los Angeles, Calif., writer, 1960-66; American Broadcasting Co. News, New York, N.Y., and Los Angeles, Calif., member of election unit, 1966, writer, 1966-67, assistant manager of election unit, 1967-69; University of Minnesota, Minneapolis, associate professor, 1969-73, professor of journalism and mass communication, 1973—. Lecturer at California State College (now University), Long Beach, 1965-66. *Military service:* U.S. Army, 1947-48.

MEMBER: Association for Education in Journalism, Radio-Television News Directors Association, Northwest Broadcast News Association. *Awards, honors:* Freedoms Foundation Medal, 1959, for editorial writing; International Business Machines fellowship, 1965, to use a computer in humanities research.

WRITINGS: Polls Apart (booklet), American Broadcasting Co. News, 1967; *Television News: Writing, Editing, Filming, Broadcasting,* Hastings House, 1968, 2nd edition, 1972; *Television/Radio News Workbook,* Hastings House, 1974. Contributor to periodicals and academic journals, including *Journal of Broadcasting, Saturday Review, Journalism Quarterly, Quill, Journal of Behavioral Science,* and *College and Research Libraries.*

WORK IN PROGRESS: A book on the radio commentators of the 1930's and 1940's.

FANN, William E(dwin) 1930-

PERSONAL: Born March 22, 1930, in Mobile, Ala.; son of William Zachary and Elberta (Gulledge) Fann; married Virginia Lee James, May 31, 1958; children: William E., Jr., Patricia Eileen, Alice Virginia. *Education:* Auburn University, B.S., 1955; Medical College of Alabama, M.D., 1959. *Home:* 3726 St. Marks Rd., Durham, N.C. 27707. *Office address:* Box 3812, Duke University Medical Center, Durham, N.C. 27710.

CAREER: Medical College of Alabama, Birmingham, chief resident in psychiatry, 1964-65; Vanderbilt University Medical School, Nashville, Tenn., assistant professor of psychiatry and pharmacology, 1965-71, associate director of Clinical Division of Psychopharmacology Research Center, 1971—. *Military service:* U.S. Air Force, 1947-51; became sergeant. *Member:* American Psychiatric Association, American College of Neuropsychopharmacology, American Society for Clinical Pharmacology and Therapeutics, Gerontological Society, American Association of University Professors, American Association for the Advancement of Science, New York Academy of Science.

WRITINGS: (With C. E. Goshen) *The Language of Mental Health,* Mosby, 1973; (editor with Carl Eisdorfer, and contributor) *Psychopharmacology and Aging,* Plenum, 1973; (editor with George Maddox, and contributor) *Drug Issues in Geropsychiatry,* Williams & Wilkins, 1974. Contributor to proceedings and to psychiatric and pharmacological journals.

WORK IN PROGRESS: Research in interactions of psychotropic agents with endogenous agents and xenobiotics; a study of drug-induced neurological disorders.

* * *

FANTEL, Hans 1922-

PERSONAL: Born March 1, 1922, in Vienna, Austria; married Shea Smith (a magazine editor), 1968. *Education:* Tarkio College, B.S., 1945; also studied at University of Missouri and New School for Social Research. *Home:* 187 East Broadway, New York, N.Y. 10002. *Agent:* Theron Raines, 244 Madison Ave., New York, N.Y. 10016.

CAREER: U.S. Air Force Research and Development Center, Dayton, Ohio, technical translator and editor, 1948-52; Associated Science Translators, Inc., Newark, N.J., president, 1952-54; free-lance translator in London, England, 1954-56; *Stereo Review* (magazine), New York, N.Y., associate editor, 1956-62; writer, 1962—. *Member:* National Association of Science Writers. *Awards, honors:* D.H.L. from Tarkio College, 1973.

WRITINGS: (With Renatus Hartogs) *Four-Letter Word Games,* M. Evans, 1967; (with Hope Buyukmici) *Unexpected Treasure,* M. Evans, 1968; *The Waltz Kings: Johann Strauss and His Era,* Morrow, 1972; *The True Sound of Music,* Dutton, 1973; *William Penn: Apostle of Dissent,* Morrow, 1974. Contributor of more than a hundred articles to popular magazines, including *Look, Saturday Review, Reader's Digest, Popular Science,* and to newspapers, including *New York Times.*

WORK IN PROGRESS: Translating from German a work on Marx and Weber by philosopher Karl Loewith, for Harper.

FARALLA, Dana 1909- (Dorothy W. Faralla; Dana Wilma, pseudonym)

PERSONAL: Born August 4, 1909, in Renville, Minn.; daughter of John Frederick (a merchant) and Estella (Gilger) Wein; married Dario Faralla (a film executive and producer), August 6, 1935 (died May 31, 1944). *Education:* Attended University of Minnesota, 1927-28; Williams School of Drama, Bachelor of Oral English, 1930. *Religion:* Protestant. *Agent:* Curtis Brown Ltd., 60 East 56th St., New York, N.Y. 10022.

CAREER: Has worked as a professional actress, private secretary, screen story analyst in Hollywood, Calif., and New York, N.Y., also employed in a rare book shop in New York City; *Poets Magazine,* New York, N.Y., associate editor, 1930-31; novelist and author of children's books. *Member:* Poetry Society of America.

WRITINGS—Novels: *The Magnificent Barb,* Messner, 1947; *Dream in the Stone,* Messner, 1948; *Black Renegade,* Lippincott, 1954; *A Circle of Trees,* Lippincott, 1955; *The Madstone,* Lippincott, 1958; *Children of Lucifer,* Lippincott, 1964; *The Straw Umbrella,* Gollancz, 1968.

Children's books: *The Willow in the Attic,* Lippincott, 1960; *The Singing Cupboard,* Lippincott, 1962; *Swanhilda-of-the-Swans,* Lippincott, 1964; *The Wonderful Flying-Go-Round,* World Publishing, 1965; *The Wooden Swallow,* World Publishing, 1966.

Also author, under pseudonym Dana Wilma, of original screen story for film, "El Otro Soy Yo," 1939; author of original story and collaborator on screenplay, "Papa Soltero," 1939. Contributor of travel articles to *New York Times* and *New York Herald Tribune.*

SIDELIGHTS: A reviewer for the *Young Readers Review* wrote of *The Wooden Swallow:* "The story is touching and the people are adequately developed. But it is Rhodes and the village of Lindos which are the attractions of this book. The description of the village during the winter season is so good that the reader can almost feel the wind blowing through him, and feel the all-pervading dampness during the storms which rack the island. The sunniness and warmth of spring are also pictured beautifully."

Of *Children of Lucifer,* Mary Renault wrote in the *New York Times Book Review:* "This is a humane, civilized and accomplished novel, brilliantly evocative of place and time. Corfu in the 1950's had an atmosphere so individual that one never imagined it could be captured; this book does so with effortless—seeming precision. I greatly enjoyed it."

Mrs. Faralla told *CA:* "Travel has been a motivation for my writing. More than 25 years of residence abroad: Europe, the Middle East, East Africa, Bermuda, Jamaica, Virgin Islands, Haiti, Cyprus, Malta, Madeira, Baleric Islands, Teneriffe. I have lived for long periods in Italy, Denmark, England, Switzerland, Greece, Cyprus, Lebanon. Languages in which I am most proficient are Italian and French."

* * *

FARALLA, Dorothy W. See FARALLA, Dana

* * *

FARBER, Marvin 1901-

PERSONAL: Born December 14, 1901, in Buffalo, N.Y.;

son of Simon (a businessman) and Matilda (Goldstein) Farber; married Lorraine F. Walle, December 26, 1930; children: Lawrence Alan, Roger Evan, Carol Louise (Mrs. Michael M. Reddy). *Education:* Harvard University, S.B. (summa cum laude), 1922, Ph.D., 1925. *Home:* 80 Lake Ledge Dr., Williamsville, N.Y. 14221. *Office:* Department of Philosophy, State University of New York, Buffalo, N.Y. 14226.

CAREER: Ohio State University, Columbus, instructor in philosophy, 1925; University of Buffalo, Buffalo, N.Y., instructor, 1927-28, assistant professor, 1928-30, professor of philosophy, 1930-54, distinguished professor of philosophy, 1954-61; University of Pennsylvania, Philadelphia, professor of philosophy and chairman of department, 1961-64; State University of New York at Buffalo, distinguished professor of philosophy and education, 1964—. *Member:* International Phenomenological Society (president, 1940), International Institute of Philosophy, American Philosophical Association (president, 1963-64), Symbolic Logic Association (member of executive committee, 1946-49). *Awards, honors:* Dr. honoris causa, University of Lille, 1955.

WRITINGS: Phenomenology as a Method and as a Philosophical Discipline, University of Buffalo, 1928; (editor and contributor) *Philosophical Essays in Memory of Edmund Husserl,* Harvard University Press, 1940; *The Foundation of Phenomenology: Edmund Husserl and the Quest for a Rigorous Science of Philosophy,* Harvard University Press, 1943, 3rd edition, State University of New York Press, 1967; (editor with R. W. Sellars and V. J. McGill), *Philosophy for the Future,* Macmillan, 1949; (editor and contributor) *Philosophic Thought in France and the United States,* University of Buffalo, 1950, 2nd edition, State University of New York Press, 1968; *Naturalism and Subjectivism,* C.C Thomas, 1959, 2nd edition, State University of New York Press, 1968; *The Aims of Phenomenology,* Harper, 1966; *Phenomenology and Existence: Toward a Philosophy within Nature,* Harper, 1967; *Basic Issues of Philosophy: Experience, Reality, and Human Values,* Harper, 1968; (editor) E. H. Madden and others, *Philosophical Perspectives on Punishment,* C.C Thomas, 1968; *Phenomenology and Natural Existence,* State University of New York Press, 1973. Editor of *Philosophy and Phenomenological Research: An International Quarterly Journal,* 1940—.

BIOGRAPHICAL/CRITICAL SOURCES: D. C. Mathur, *Naturalistic Philosophies of Experience,* Warren H. Green, 1971; D. M. Riepe, editor, *Phenomenology and Natural Existence: Essays in Honor of Marvin Farber,* State University of New York Press, 1972.

* * *

FARKAS, Philip 1914-

PERSONAL: Born March 5, 1914, in Chicago, Ill.; son of Emil Nelson (an advertising executive) and Anna (Cassady) Farkas; married Margaret Groves, May 11, 1939; children: Carol (Mrs. Stephen Mumma), Lynn (Mrs. Roy Weddle), Jean (Mrs. John VanMinnen), Margaret Frances. *Education:* Attended high school in Chicago, Ill. and training school for Chicago Symphony Orchestra. *Politics:* "Fluctuates." *Religion:* "Infinite Way." *Home address:* R.R. # 12, Box 323, Bloomington, Ind. 47401. *Office:* School of Music, Indiana University, Bloomington, Ind. 47401.

CAREER: Solo French horn with Kansas City Philharmonic, 1933-36, with Chicago Symphony Orchestra, 1936-41, 1947-60, with Cleveland Orchestra, 1941-45, 1946-47, with Boston Symphony Orchestra, 1945-46, and with Chicago Symphony Orchestra, 1947-60. Teacher of French horn at Kansas City Conservatory, 1933-36, Chicago Musical College, 1937-40, Cleveland Institute of Music, 1946-47, Roosevelt University, 1948-56, DePaul University, 1948-56, and Northwestern University, 1952-60; Indiana University, Bloomington, professor of music, 1960—. Member of Chicago Symphony Woodwind Quintet, 1937-60, and American Woodwind Quintet, 1960—. Performer and teacher at Aspen Music Festival, 1960—; gives lecture-performances at colleges and music conventions. *Member:* American Federation of Musicians, International Horn Society, American Navion Society, Aircraft Owners and Pilots Association, Phi Mu Alpha Sinfonia.

WRITINGS: The Art of French Horn Playing, Summy-Birchard, 1956; (editor) *French Horn Passages from Contemporary French Music,* Elkan-Vogel, 1956; *The Art of Brass Playing,* Wind Music, 1962; *A Photographic Study of Forty Virtuoso Horn Players' Embouchures,* Wind Music, 1971.

WORK IN PROGRESS: The Art of Musicianship.

SIDELIGHTS: Farkas flies his own Navion plane to most of his lecture engagements.

* * *

FARRELL, Bryan (Henry) 1923-

PERSONAL: Born April 23, 1923, in Auckland, New Zealand; son of James Patrick (a school teacher) and Eunice Ray (Jones) Farrell; married Billye Helme, March 30, 1946; children: Michael John, Anna Lee, Paddy Jane. *Education:* University of Canterbury, B.A., 1948; University of Washington, Seattle, M.A., 1949; University of Auckland, Ph.D., 1961. *Home:* 2931 Tudor Ave., Victoria, British Columbia, Canada. *Office:* Department of Geography, University of Victoria, Victoria, British Columbia, Canada.

CAREER: University of Auckland, Auckland, New Zealand, lecturer, 1954-57, senior lecturer in geography, 1957-60; University of Alberta, Edmonton, associate professor of geography, 1961-63; University of Victoria, Victoria, British Columbia, professor of geography, 1963—, head of department, 1963-69, director of Pacific studies, 1972—. Director-elect of Research Center for South Pacific Studies of University of California, Santa Cruz, 1974—. *Member:* Canadian Association of Geographers, Polynesian Society, Oceanic Society, Association of Pacific Coast Geographers (vice-president, 1969-71). *Awards, honors:* Canada Council grants, 1969, 1971, 1973.

WRITINGS: Power in New Zealand, A. H. & A. W. Reed, 1962; (contributor) J. W. Fox and K. B. Cumberland, editors, *Western Samoa,* Whitcombe and Tombes, 1962; (contributor) R. G. Ward, editor, *Man in the Pacific Islands,* Oxford University Press, 1972; (editor with M. R. C. Edgell, and contributor) *Themes on Pacific Lands,* Western Geographical Studies, 1974.

WORK IN PROGRESS: Caution: Adults at Play, a book on leisure development in Hawaii; *Changing Attitudes to Land in the Pacific Area.*

AVOCATIONAL INTERESTS: Skiing; travel in the Pacific Basin, especially islands of the South Pacific; man and nature and the philosophical relations between the two.

FARRELL, Matthew Charles 1921-

PERSONAL: Born October 30, 1921, in Pittston, Pa.; son of Peter J. (a mining engineer) and Maida (Leppert) Farrell. *Education:* Powell College of Business, Scranton, Diploma, 1941; University of Scranton, B.A. (magna cum laude), 1948, M.Sc., 1956; Fordham University, Ph.D., 1972. *Home:* 915 Albright Ave., Scranton, Pa. 18508. *Office:* Department of Education, University of Scranton, Scranton, Pa. 18510.

CAREER: Seton Hall Preparatory School, South Orange, N.J., teacher, 1954-59; Seton Hall University, South Orange, N.J., assistant professor of education at university and at University College, Newark, 1957-63, associate professor, and assistant executive dean of university, 1963-67; University of Scranton, Scranton, Pa., associate professor of education, 1967—, director of Division of Graduate Secondary Education, 1970—. Proprietor and director of Maidahurst Preserve (conservational preserve), Millerton, Pa., 1968—. Co-founder of boys' orphanage in Caserta, Italy, 1945; co-founder and director of high school for juvenile addicts at narcotic center in Newark. *Military service:* U.S. Army, research cryptanalyst, National Security Agency, 1942-45; became technical sergeant; received European, African, and Middle East campaign medals with bronze stars. U.S. Army Air Forces, research cryptanalyst, National Security Agency, 1950-53; became captain.

MEMBER: American Association of School Administrators, American Educational Research Association, National School Public Relations Association, American Academy of Political and Social Science, National Education Association, National Society for the Study of Education, National Conference of Professors of Educational Administration, Association of Elementary School Principals, American Association of University Professors, National Council of Teachers of English, National Conference on Research in English, International Reading Association, American Forestry Association, National Audubon Society, and other horticulture, wildlife, and forestry societies; Phi Delta Kappa, Knights of Columbus.

WRITINGS: (With Josephine B. Wolfe and John G. Winokur) "Merrill Phonics Skilltext: The Sound and Structure of Words," twelve-book series, C. E. Merrill, 1973.

WORK IN PROGRESS: "A Program of Language Understandings and Skills," with Josephine B. Wolfe; a program for administrative restructure of the private school system in the Diocese of Scranton.

AVOCATIONAL INTERESTS: Horticulture, woodworking; collecting art in precious medals, Americana, and paintings and sculptures of American wildlife.

BIOGRAPHICAL/CRITICAL SOURCES: *Catholic Layman,* Volume LXXX, number 2, February, 1966.

* * *

FASSETT, James 1904-

PERSONAL: Born November 27, 1904; son of Lorenzo J. (a manufacturer) and Helen (Carter) Fassett. *Education:* Dartmouth College, B.A., 1929; Harvard University, M.A., 1930. *Politics:* Independent. *Religion:* Protestant. *Home address:* Box 216, R.D. 2, Stroudsburg, Pa. 18360. *Agent:* Paul R. Reynolds, Inc., 599 Fifth Ave., New York, N.Y. 10017.

CAREER: Columbia Broadcasting System, New York, N.Y., 1936-63, supervisor of Music Division, 1946-63, commentator and producer of New York Philharmonic broadcasts, 1950-63, and European Music Festival broadcasts, 1953-63; WQXR-Radio, New York, N.Y., producer of "Lincoln Center Spotlight," 1965. *Awards, honors:* George Foster Peabody radio award, 1953; award from National Federation of Music Clubs, 1953; D.Music from Cedar Crest College, 1954; Order of the Finnish Lion, 1955.

WRITINGS: *Italian Odyssey: An Ear to the Wind,* Atheneum, 1969.

WORK IN PROGRESS: *Intermission Time: The Philharmonic Years on Radio, 1930-1963.*

* * *

FAWCETT, Claude W(eldon) 1911-

PERSONAL: Born November 4, 1911, in Fair Grove, Mo.; son of Willie Ellis (a contractor) and Laura Mietta (Smith) Fawcett; married Mary Catherine Cunningham, 1941; children: James Alan, Robert Douglas. *Education:* Southwest Missouri State College (now University), A.B., 1933; Yale University, Ph.D., 1943. *Politics:* Democrat. *Religion:* Congregationalist. *Home:* 9851 Canby Ave., Northridge, Calif. 91324. *Office:* School of Education, University of California, 405 Hilgard Ave., Los Angeles, Calif. 90024.

CAREER: Teacher in public schools of Springfield, Mo., 1934-38; Yale University, New Haven, Conn., chief supervisor of Engineering, Science and Management War Training Program, 1940-43; University of Vermont, Burlington, coordinator of student personnel, 1946-47; Grand Rapids (Mich.) public schools, superintendent, 1947-49; University of Southern California, Los Angeles, assistant dean of University College, 1949-51; National Association of Manufacturers, Western Division, San Francisco, Calif., education director, 1951-59; University of California, School of Education, Los Angeles, professor of school communications and school personnel administration, 1959—. *Military service:* U.S. Naval Reserve, active duty, 1942-46; became lieutenant.

MEMBER: National Association of School Administrators, National Society for the Study of Education, National School Public Relations Association (member of national advisory panel, 1969-70), Phi Delta Kappa, Commonwealth Club of California. *Awards, honors:* Bronze Medal of Freedoms Foundation of Valley Forge, 1957, for a public address.

WRITINGS: *School Personnel Administration,* Macmillan, 1964; (contributor) George F. Kneller, editor, *Foundations of Education,* Wiley, 1971. Contributor to *Yearbook* of National Society for the Study of Education, 1968, and to journals.

WORK IN PROGRESS: *Organizational Communication.*

* * *

FECHER, Constance 1911- (Constance Heaven)

PERSONAL: Born August 6, 1911, in London, England; daughter of Michael Joseph and Caroline (Rand) Fecher; married William Heaven (a theatrical director), May 11, 1939 (died, 1958). *Education:* Attended convent school in Woodford Green, England, 1920-28; King's College, University of London, B.A. (honors), 1932; London College of Music, Licentiate, 1931. *Politics:* Liberal. *Religion:* Roman

Catholic. *Home:* Tudor Green, 37 Teddington Park Rd., Teddington TW11 8NB, Middlesex, England. *Agent:* Carl Routledge, Charles Lavell Ltd., 176 Wardour St., London W.1, England.

CAREER: Actress, 1938-64; began writing in early 1960's; tutor in seventeenth-century history and literature and in creative writing at City Literary Institute, London, 1967—. With her husband operated a little theater at Henley-on-Thames, 1939; played with companies touring throughout England during World War II; after her husband was released from Royal Air Force they ran their own theatrical companies until his death in 1958; still gives occasional stage recitals of verse and prose. *Awards, honors:* Romantic Novelists Association major award for best romantic historical novel, 1972, for *The House of Kuragin.*

WRITINGS—Children's books: *Venture for a Crown,* Farrar, Straus, 1968; *Heir to Pendarrow,* Farrar, Straus, 1969; *Bright Star* (biography of Ellen Terry), Farrar, Straus, 1970; *The Link Boys,* Farrar, Straus, 1971; *The Last Elizabethan: A Portrait of Sir Walter Raleigh,* Farrar, Straus, 1972; *The Leopard Dagger* (Junior Literary Guild selection), Farrar, Straus, 1973.

Adult novels: Trilogy consisting of *Queen's Delight,* 1966, *Traitor's Son,* 1967, and *King's Legacy,* 1967, R. Hale; *Player Queen,* R. Hale, 1968; *Lion of Trevarrock,* R. Hale, 1969; *The Night of the Wolf,* R. Hale, 1971; (under name Constance Heaven) *The House of Kuragin,* Coward, 1972; (under name Constance Heaven) *The Astrov Legacy,* Coward, 1973; (under name Constance Heaven) *Castle of Eagles,* Coward, 1974; (under name Constance Heaven) *Place of Stones,* Heinemann, in press.

WORK IN PROGRESS: Research for a novel set in the Scottish Highlands during 1770-75; research for possible novel about the eighteenth-century actress, Peg Woffington.

* * *

FEDYSHYN, Oleh S(ylvester) 1928-

PERSONAL: Born January 1, 1928, in Ukraine, Soviet Union; son of Paul (a journalist) and Mary (Hlibovytsky) Fedyshyn; married Irene Petrenko (an artist and art teacher), August 30, 1952; children: Timothy, Vera. *Education:* Brooklyn College (now Brooklyn College of the City University of New York), B.A., 1953; Columbia University, M.A., 1955, Russian Institute, Certificate, 1955, Ph.D., 1962. *Home:* 102 Highland Ave., Montclair, N.J. 07042. *Office:* Richmond College of the City University of New York, Staten Island, N.Y. 10301.

CAREER: Michigan State University, East Lansing, instructor in Russian and German, 1956-57; University of South Carolina, Columbia, instructor in international studies, 1957-58; St. John's University, Jamaica, N.Y., assistant professor of Soviet studies, 1959-63; Rice University, Houston, Tex., assistant professor of political science, 1963-67; Richmond College of the City University of New York, Staten Island, assistant professor, 1967-69, associate professor of politics, 1969—. *Awards, honors:* Ford fellowship, 1958-59; Social Science Research Council grant, 1966-67; senior fellowship from Columbia University's Research Institute on Communist Affairs, 1974-75.

WRITINGS: Germany's Drive to the East and the Ukrainian Revolution, 1917-1918, Rutgers University Press, 1971.

WORK IN PROGRESS: A political biography of Nikita Khrushchev; a comparative study of Soviet, Yugoslav, and Chinese federalisms and nationality questions.

SIDELIGHTS: Fedyshyn is fluent in Russian, German, and Polish, as well as English and his native Ukrainian; he reads other Slavic languages and French.

* * *

FEELINGS, Thomas 1933-
(Tom Feelings)

PERSONAL: Born May 19, 1933, in Brooklyn, N.Y.; son of Samuel (a taxicab driver) and Anna (Nash) Feelings; married Muriel Grey (a school teacher), February 18, 1968 (divorced, 1974); children: Zamani, Kamili. *Education:* Attended School of Visual Art, 1951-53, 1957-60. *Home:* c/o Anna Morris, 21 St. James Pl., Brooklyn, N.Y. 11205.

CAREER: Ghana Publishing Company, Ghana, West Africa, illustrator for *African Review,* 1964-66; Government of Guyana, Guyana, South America, teacher of illustrators for Ministry of Education, 1971—; artist and illustrator. Has worked as free-lance illustrator for Ghana television programs and for newspapers and other businesses in Ghana. *Military service:* U.S. Air Force, illustrator in Graphics Division in London, England, 1953-57. *Awards, honors:* Caldecott Honor Book runner-up for best illustrated children's book, 1972, for *Mojo Means One; Black Pilgrimage* was runner-up for Coretta Scott King award, received Woodward School annual book award, and Brooklyn Museum citation, all 1973; School of Visual Art outstanding alumni achievement award, 1974.

WRITINGS—For children: *Black Pilgrimage,* Lothrop, 1972.

Illustrator: Letta Schatz, *Bola and the Oba's Drummers,* McGraw, 1967; Eleanor Heady, compiler, *When the Stones Were Soft: East African Folktales,* Funk, 1968; Julius Lester, editor, *To Be a Slave,* Dial, 1968; Osmond Molarsky, *Song of the Empty Bottles,* Walck, 1968; Robin McKown, *The Congo: River of Mystery,* McGraw, 1968; Nancy Garfield, *The Tuesday Elephant,* Crowell, 1968; Kathleen Arnot, *Tales of Temba: Traditional African Stories,* Walck, 1969; Ruskin Bond, *Panther's Moon,* Random House, 1969; Rose Blue, *A Quiet Place,* F. Watts, 1969; Lester, compiler, *Black Folktales,* Baron, 1969.

Muriel Feelings, *Zamani Goes to Market,* Seabury, 1970; Jane Kerina, *African Crafts,* Lion Press, 1970; Muriel Feelings, *Moja Means One,* Dial, 1971; Muriel Feelings, *Jambo Means Hello,* Dial, 1974.

WORK IN PROGRESS: An extensive illustrated book dealing with the history of slavery of the black man in North America; an illustrated autobiography.

SIDELIGHTS: Feelings told *CA* his "main interest has been the Black People of the world. In this connection I have traveled and drawn from life in East and West Africa and South America."

BIOGRAPHICAL/CRITICAL SOURCES: Negro Digest now *Black World*), September, 1967, August, 1971; *Sepia,* September, 1969.

* * *

FEELINGS, Tom
See FEELINGS, Thomas

FEIN, Leah Gold

PERSONAL: Born in Minsk, Russia; daughter of Jacob Lyon and Sarah Freda (Meltzer) Gold; married Alfred Gustave Fein (a sales corporation president), June 10, 1944; children: Ira Hirsch. *Education:* Attended Connecticut State Teachers College, 1925-26; Tufts University, D.H., 1927; Albertus Magnus College, B.S., 1939; Yale University, M.A., 1942, Ph.D., 1944. *Religion:* Jewish. *Home and office:* 1050 Park Ave., New York, N.Y. 10028.

CAREER: Diplomate in clinical psychology of American Board of Professional Psychology, 1964. Private practice as a psychologist in Seattle, Wash., 1948-52, Greenwich, Conn., 1952-54, Stamford, Conn., 1954-64, New Haven, Conn., 1964-67, and New York, N.Y., 1967—; Carlton College, Northfield, Minn., director of testing services, 1944-46; Connecticut State Interracial Commission, Hartford, Conn., research associate, 1946-47; University of Bridgeport, Bridgeport, Conn., assistant professor, 1946-47, professor of psychology, 1952-58; Quinnipiac College, New Haven, Conn., associate professor of psychology, 1965-66; Psychiatric Treatment Center, New York, N.Y., director of Psychology Department, 1967-68; Roosevelt Hospital, New York, N.Y., research associate, 1968-69; Greenwich Institute of Psychoanalytical Studies, Greenwich, Conn., member of faculty, 1970—. Research consultant for New York City Board of Education Bureau of Child Guidance, 1969-72; consultant on gifted children for York College of the City University of New York, 1972. Vice-president of Fein Sales Corp., 1954—.

MEMBER: International Council of Psychologists (vice-president, 1962; president-elect, 1971-73; president, 1973-75), Interamerican Psychological Association, American Psychological Association, National Association for Gifted Children (vice-president, 1958-60), American Orthopsychiatric Association, Eastern Psychological Association, New England Psychological Association, New York State Psychological Association, Connecticut Psychological Association, New York Academy of Science. *Awards, honors:* Research grant from Norwalk Hospital board of directors, 1961-63; National Institute of Mental Health Nursing Department research grant, 1964.

WRITINGS: *The Three Dimensional Personality Test,* International Universities Press, 1960; *The Changing School Scene,* Wiley, 1974. Contributor to professional journals, including *Journal of Clinical Psychology, Psychology in the Schools,* and *Gifted Child Journal.* Editor of *International Understanding,* 1974.

WORK IN PROGRESS: Boys with Problems; Five Sisters; Trials and Tribulations of a Professional Woman; J.L. the Connecticut Israelite.

* * *

FEINBERG, Hilda

PERSONAL: Born in Atlanta, Ga.; daughter of Harry (in real estate) and Emily (Domb) Warshaw; married Joseph Feinberg, June, 1940; children: Stephen, David. *Education:* University of Georgia, B.S. (summa cum laude) and M.S.; Columbia University, M.S. in L.S., and D.L.S., 1972. *Home:* 1685 Ocean Ave., Brooklyn, N.Y. 11230. *Office:* Revlon Research Center Library, 945 Zerega Ave., Bronx, N.Y. 10473.

CAREER: Chemist; Revlon Research Center Library, Bronx, N.Y., manager of library services, 1955—. Adjunct professor at Pratt Institute and Queens College, 1972-74. *Member:* American Society for Information Science, American Society of Indexers, Special Libraries Association, Medical Library Association, American Chemical Society, Society of Cosmetic Chemists, Cosmetics, Toiletry, Fragrance Association, Phi Beta Kappa, Beta Phi Mu.

WRITINGS: (With Maurice Tauber) *Book Catalogs,* Scarecrow, 1972; *Cosmetics, Perfumery Thessaurus,* Macmillan, 1972; *Title Derivative Indexing Techniques,* Scarecrow, 1973. Contributor to journals.

WORK IN PROGRESS: Technical Services in Libraries, with Maurice Tauber; a patent index.

AVOCATIONAL INTERESTS: Art, sports.

* * *

FELLMETH, Robert C(harles) 1945-

PERSONAL: Born September 21, 1945, in Lake City, Fla.; son of Robert Butler (a pilot) and Jane (Bricken) Fellmeth; married Jill D. Heiman, December 17, 1966; children: Michael Quixote, Aaron Xavier. *Education:* Stanford University, A.B. (with honors), 1967; Harvard University, J.D., 1970. *Politics:* Independent. *Religion:* Unitarian-Universalist. *Home:* 4840 49th St., San Diego, Calif. 92115. *Office:* Office of the District Attorney, 220 West Broadway, San Diego, Calif. 92101.

CAREER: Center for the Study of Responsive Law, Washington, D.C., associate, 1970-72; aide to Ralph Nader as director of Congress Project, Washington, D.C., 1972-73; Office of the District Attorney, San Diego, Calif., deputy district attorney, 1973—. *Member:* District Attorneys Association, California Bar Association.

WRITINGS: (With John Schulz and Edward Cox) *The Nader Report on the Federal Trade Commission,* Baron, 1968; *The Interstate Commerce Omission,* Grossman, 1970; (with others) *With Justice for Some,* Beacon Press, 1971; (with others) *The Voter's Guide to Environmental Politics,* Ballantine, 1971; *Politics of Land,* Grossman, 1973. Contributing editor, *Harvard Civil Rights-Civil Liberties Law Review,* 1969.

WORK IN PROGRESS: And Congress Shall Have Power Too..., with Fred Khedouri; *The Commerce Committees* and *The Revenue Rustlers,* both with others.

* * *

FELLOWS, Lawrence (Perry) 1924-

PERSONAL: Born December 24, 1924, in Detroit, Mich.; son of Perry Augustus (a civil engineer) and Gladys (Culver) Fellows; married Ruth Bell (a dance instructor and choreographer), December 27, 1952; children: Eva, Robin (daughter). *Education:* Attended American University, 1942; Ohio Wesleyan University, A.B., 1948; graduate study at University of Maryland in Bonn and Wiesbaden, Germany, 1952-53. *Politics:* Independent. *Religion:* Methodist. *Home:* 6 Stuart Dr., Bloomfield, Conn. 06002. *Office: New York Times,* New York, N.Y. 10038.

CAREER: U.S. State Department, Washington, D.C., foreign service in Berlin and Koblenz, Germany, 1948-52; *New York Times,* New York, N.Y., New York reporter and member of United Nations Bureau, 1953-59, foreign correspondent, 1959-72, chief of Connecticut Bureau, 1972—. *Military service:* U.S. Navy, 1942-45.

WRITINGS: *East Africa,* Macmillan, 1972. Contributor to *New York Times Magazine* and to other magazines.

WORK IN PROGRESS: A novel.

* * *

FENNEMA, Owen Richard 1929-

PERSONAL: Born January 23, 1929, in Hinsdale, Ill.; son of Nick (a dairy plant owner) and Fern (First) Fennema; married Ann Elizabeth Hammer (a professor), August 22, 1948; children: Linda Gail, Karen Elizabeth, Peter Scott. *Education:* Kansas State University, B.S., 1950; University of Wisconsin-Madison, M.S., 1951, Ph.D., 1960. *Religion:* Congregational. *Home:* 5010 Lake Mendota Dr., Madison, Wis. 53705. *Office:* Department of Food Science, University of Wisconsin, Madison, Wis. 53706.

CAREER: University of Wisconsin-Madison, assistant professor, 1960-64, associate professor, 1964-69, professor of food chemistry, 1969—. *Member:* Institute of Food Technologists, Society for Cryobiology, American Chemical Society, Phi Tau Sigma, Gamma Sigma Delta.

WRITINGS: Low Temperature Preservation of Foods and Living Matter, Dekker, 1973. Contributor to *Journal of Food Science* and *Journal of Agriculture and Food Chemistry.* Member of editorial board of Society for Cryobiology, 1966—, and Institute of Food Technologists, 1974—; consulting editor, *Food Science Monographs,* 1967—.

WORK IN PROGRESS: Editing three volumes of *Principles of Food Science.*

* * *

FERGUSON, Alfred R. 1915-1974

August 15, 1915—May 5, 1974; American educator, and author or editor of works on American and English literature. Obituaries: *New York Times,* May 7, 1974; *Washington Post,* May 8, 1974. (*CA*-1).

* * *

FERGUSON, M(ilton) Carr 1931-

PERSONAL: Born February 10, 1931, in Washington, D.C.; son of Milton Carr (a federal judge) and Gladys (Emery) Ferguson; married Marian Evelyn Nelson (a speech therapist), August 21, 1954; children: Laura, Sharon, Marcia, Sandra. *Education:* Cornell University, B.A., 1952, LL.B., 1954; New York University, LL.M., 1960. *Home:* 29 Washington Square W., New York, N.Y. 10011. *Office:* Wachtell, Lipton, Rosen & Katz, 299 Park Ave., New York, N.Y. 10017.

CAREER: Admitted to Bar of New York State, 1954; U.S. Department of Justice, Tax Division, Washington, D.C., trial attorney and special assistant to Attorney General, 1954-59; University of Iowa, College of Law, Iowa City, assistant professor of law, 1960-62; New York University, School of Law, New York, N.Y., 1962—, began as associate professor, currently professor of law; Wachtell, Lipton, Rosen & Katz, New York, N.Y., attorney, 1968—. Consultant to Treasurer of Puerto Rico, 1967, 1974, and to U.S. Department of Justice, 1968; visiting professor, Stanford University, 1972-73. *Awards, honors:* Ford Foundation fellowship, 1959-60.

WRITINGS: (With others) *Federal Income Taxation Legislation in Perspective,* American Law Institute, 1965; (with J. M. J. Freeland and R. B. Stevens) *Federal Income Taxation of Estates of Beneficiaries,* Little, Brown, 1970; *Federal Income Taxation of Estates and Trusts,* Little, Brown, in press. Contributor to *Iowa Law Review* and *Tax Law Review.* Author of monographs.

FERGUSON, William (Rotch) 1943-

PERSONAL: Born February 14, 1943, in Fall River, Mass.; son of William III (in insurance) and Helen (Rotch) Ferguson; married Lucy Emerson Collins, July 8, 1962 (divorced, 1968); married Raquel Halty (a professor of Hispanic language and literature), June 22, 1968. *Education:* Harvard University, B.A., 1965, M.A., 1970, doctoral candidate, 1970—. *Home:* 376 Harvard St., Cambridge, Mass. 02138. *Office:* Department of Modern Languages, Boston University, 718 Commonwealth Ave., Boston, Mass. 02215.

CAREER: Ferguson Press, Cambridge, Mass., owner, 1964—. Owner of Halty Ferguson Publishing Co. (publishers of modern poetry), 1970—; instructor at Boston University, 1971—.

WRITINGS—Poems: *Revolution Dream,* Pym-Randall, 1970; *Light of Paradise,* Penmaen Press, 1973; *Dream Reader,* Halty Ferguson Publishing, 1973.

WORK IN PROGRESS: Compiling a comprehensive anthology of Hispanic surrealism in translation; research on the versification of the sixteenth-century poet Fernando de Herrera, on anarcho-capitalism in the musical theory of Charles Ives, and on the political situation in Uruguay.

* * *

FERM, Vergilius (Ture Anselm) 1896-1974

January 6, 1896—February 4, 1974; American educator, and author or editor of books on religion, philosophy, education, and related topics. Obituaries: *Publishers Weekly,* March 18, 1974; *AB Bookman's Weekly,* April 15, 1974. (*CA*-9/10).

* * *

FERNETT, Gene 1924-

PERSONAL: Born June 16, 1924; son of J. Eugene and Carrie (Mohnk) Fernette; divorced; children: Randall E. *Education:* University of Miami, Coral Gables, Fla., B.A., 1955; Appalachian University, M.A., 1961. *Home:* Apt. 107, 122 Central Rd., Indian Harbour Beach, Fla. 32937. *Agent:* Creative Writers Agency, Satellite Beach, Fla.

CAREER: Has been a college professor and motion picture director. *Military service:* U.S. Air Force.

WRITINGS: A Thousand Golden Horns, Pendell, 1966; *Next Time Drive Off the Cliff,* Cinememories, 1969; *Starring John Wayne,* Cinememories, 1970; *Swing Out,* Pendell, 1970; *Poverty Row,* Coral Reel, 1973. Author of television documentary film, "To Worlds Beyond." Contributor to journals.

WORK IN PROGRESS: Winning Hand, completion expected in 1974.

SIDELIGHTS: Fernett has travelled extensively in Europe, Central America, and Mexico.

* * *

FERREIRA De CASTRO, Jose Maria 1898-1974

1898—June 29, 1974; Portuguese author. Obituaries: *New York Times,* July 2, 1974.

* * *

FERRITOR, Daniel Edward 1939-

PERSONAL: Born November 8, 1939, in Kansas City,

Mo.; married, wife's name Patricia Jean; children: Kimberly Ann, Kristin Marie, Sean Patrick. *Education:* Rockhurst College, B.A., 1962; Washington University, St. Louis, M.A., 1967, Ph.D., 1969. *Home:* 7107 Cornell, University City, Mo. 63130. *Office:* Southern Illinois University, Edwardsville, Ill. 62025.

CAREER: Teacher at parochial grade school in Raytown, Mo., 1962-64; University of Arkansas, Fayetteville, assistant professor of sociology, 1967-68; Southern Illinois University, Edwardsville Campus, part-time assistant professor of special education, 1969—; National Program on Early Childhood Education, part-time program associate, 1970-71, associate director, 1971—. CEMREL, Inc., St. Ann, Mo., assistant program director, 1969-70, associate director of instructional systems program, 1970-71. *Member:* American Educational Research Association, American Sociological Association, American Psychological Association.

WRITINGS: (With Robert L. Hamblin, D. Buckholdt, M. Kozloff, and L. Blackwell) *The Humanization Processes,* Wiley, 1971. Contributor to *Transaction, Psychological Record,* and other journals.

* * *

FEST, Joachim C. 1926-

PERSONAL: Born December 8, 1926, in Berlin, Germany; son of Johannes and Elisabeth (Straeter); married Ingrid Ascher, 1959; children: Alexander, Nicolaus. *Education:* Attended University of Freiburg, 1948-49, University of Frankfurt, 1949-51, University of Berlin, 1951-53. *Religion:* Roman Catholic. *Home:* Cretzschmerstrasse 73, Franfurt am Main, Germany. *Office: Frankfurter Allgemeine Zeitung,* Hellerhofstrasse 2-4, Frankfurt am Main, Germany.

CAREER: Rundfunk im amerikanischen Sektor (RIAS), Berlin, Germany, editor, 1953-61; Norddeutscher Rundfunk, Hamburg, Germany, editor, 1961-63, editor in chief, 1963-68; *Frankfurter Allgemeine Zeitung,* Frankfurt am Main, Germany, editing director, 1973—.

WRITINGS: Das Gesicht des Dritten Reiches, Piper (Munich), 1963, translation by Michael Bullock published as *The Face of the Third Reich: Portraits of the Nazi Leadership,* Pantheon, 1970; (author of foreword) Jochen van Lang, editor, *Adolf Hitler: Gesichter eines Diktators* (title means "Adolf Hitler: Faces of a Dictator"), C. Wegner, 1968; *Hitler: Eine Biographie,* Propylaeen-Verlag (Berlin), 1973, translation by Richard and Clara Winston published as *Hitler: A Biography,* Harcourt, 1974.

SIDELIGHTS: A reviewer for the *Virginia Quarterly Review* wrote of *The Face of the Third Reich:* "Joachim Fest, a West German journalist, has written a profound, absorbing, and stimulating book. It is a collection of essays, psychological studies of eighteen major figures of Nazi Germany. Each of the figures, while significant in his own right, is shown to be at the same time representative of a segment of German society seduced by National Socialism. Each biography is enlightening, and together they provide a welcome addition to the literature on the Third Reich. Fest combines the best of journalism and scholarship; his book is carefully researched, well composed, and (despite occasional lapses into ponderous prose) smoothly written."

* * *

FIELD, Walter S(herman) 1899-

PERSONAL: Born June 12, 1899, in Somers, Conn.; son of Frederick Everett and Maria E. (Johnson) Field; married Georgena Thibault, June, 1929 (divorced, 1946); married Mildred Jacobs (a teacher), June 23, 1951; children: (first marriage) Janet (Mrs. James Biestek), Judith (Mrs. Robert McCarthy), Stephen H. *Education:* University of Utah, student, 1920-21; University of Wisconsin, B.Sc., 1924. *Home:* 1425 East Ocean Blvd., #14, Long Beach, Calif. 90802. *Office:* E. F. Hutton & Co., One Oceangate, Long Beach, Calif. 90802.

CAREER: Independent petroleum geologist, Wichita, Kan., 1926-46; E. F. Hutton & Co., Long Beach, Calif., investment broker, 1958—. *Military service:* U.S. Army, Artillery, 1917-19.

WRITINGS: Achieving Order from Disorder: A Genesis of How We Know, Philosophical Library, 1973.

* * *

FIELDING, Joy 1945-

PERSONAL: Born March 18, 1945, in Toronto, Ontario, Canada; daughter of Leo H. (a jeweler) and Anne (Orenstein) Tepperman; married Warren Seyffert (a lawyer), January 11, 1974. *Education:* University of Toronto, B.A., 1966. *Residence:* Toronto, Ontario, Canada. *Agent:* Helen Barret, c/o William Morris Agency, 1350 Avenue of the Americas, New York, N.Y. 10019.

CAREER: Writer, actress, assistant social worker, substitute teacher, bank teller.

WRITINGS: The Best of Friends, Putnam, 1972. Author of two television plays, "Drifters" and "Open House," for the Canadian Broadcasting Company. Book reviewer for *Toronto Star,* 1973, *Globe & Mail* (Toronto), 1974—.

WORK IN PROGRESS: A play, a new novel, and a screenplay.

* * *

FIELDS, Arthur C. 1926(?)-1974

1926(?)—May 9, 1974; American publisher, editor, and novelist. Obituaries: *AB Bookman's Weekly,* June 17, 1974.

* * *

FIELDS, Beverly 1917-

PERSONAL: Born December 7, 1917, in Chicago, Ill.; daughter of Harry (a manufacturer) and Ann (Padorr) Frankel; married Sidney M. Fields (an attorney), September 29, 1940; children: Susan (Mrs. Daniel M. Joseph), Kathryn. *Education:* Northwestern University, B.A., 1939, M.A., 1958, Ph.D., 1965. *Home:* 1540 Lake Shore Dr., Chicago, Ill. 60610. *Office:* Department of English, University of Illinois at Chicago Circle, Chicago, Ill. 60680.

CAREER: Lake Forest College, Lake Forest, Ill., instructor in Romantic literature, 1960-62; Northwestern University, Evanston, Ill., instructor in Romantic literature, 1962-65; University of Illinois at Chicago Circle, assistant professor, 1965-69, associate professor of English, 1969—. *Member:* American Association of University Professors, Modern Language Association of America.

WRITINGS: Reality's Dark Dream: Dejection in Coleridge, Kent State University Press, 1967; (contributor) Edward Hungerford, editor, *Poets in Progress,* Northwestern University Press, 1968. Contributor of seventy-five book reviews to *Chicago Sun-Times.*

WORK IN PROGRESS: A book-length study, *Dejection: A Mode,* completion expected in 1975.

SIDELIGHTS: Beverly Fields told *CA:* "Advertising, that much-maligned activity, taught me to read when I was three years old. . . . Reading and writing are breathing, but I have also entertained myself with singing and acting. . . . Education, civil (including women's) rights, and a baroque sense of the comic are my main preoccupations."

BIOGRAPHICAL/CRITICAL SOURCES: Frank Jordan, Jr., editor, *The English Romantic Poets: A Review of Research and Criticism,* Modern Language Association of America, 1972.

* * *

FIELDS, Dorothy 1905-1974

July 15, 1905—March 28, 1974; American lyricist, librettist, and playwright. Obituaries: *New York Times,* March 29, 1974; *Washington Post,* March 30, 1974; *Newsweek,* April 8, 1974; *Time,* April 8, 1974; *Current Biography,* May, 1974.

* * *

FIELDS, Nora

PERSONAL: Born in New York, N.Y.; daughter of Alexander and Sara Soling; married Samuel B. Fields (a realtor), August 8, 1948; children: Melinda Sue, Nanette Gail. *Education:* New York University, B.S., 1942; Columbia University, M.A., 1943; further study at Art Students' League, New York, 1950-53, and at Ikenobo School of Floral Art, Kyoto, Japan. *Religion:* Congregational (United Church of Christ). *Home:* Boutonville Rd., South Salem, N.Y. 10590.

CAREER: Artist and former high school art teacher; accredited flower show judge and instructor for National Council of State Garden Clubs, and lecturer on flowers and floral arrangements. Work in watercolor, sculpture, and mosaics has been exhibited in group shows; her ecological multimedia sculpture are in the permanent collections of General Foods, International Business Machines, and in private collections. Teacher of flower arranging at Westchester Art Workshop for more than 15 years; accredited professor of Ikebana; chairman of flower arranging section of International Flower Show at New York Coliseum, 1969, 1970, district, state, and local shows.

MEMBER: Ikebana International (founder and first president of Hudson Valley Chapter, 1969-73, member of board of directors, 1969—; treasurer of Eastern Seaboard Chapter, 1967-74, member of board of directors, 1969—), Federated Garden Clubs of New York State (member of board of directors, 1965-73), Briarcliff Manor Garden Club (president, 1963-65), League of Women Voters. *Awards, honors:* Numerous flower show awards at national, local, and state level; other awards in art shows.

WRITINGS: New Ideas For Christmas Decoration, Hearthside, 1967; *Flowers and Foliage,* A. S. Barnes, 1973; *Flower Arranging For Parties,* A. S. Barnes, in press. In earlier years wrote short mystery stories for magazines; more recently contributor of articles related to art and flower arranging.

WORK IN PROGRESS: A book on recreational crafts for all ages.

* * *

FINDLAY, James F(ranklin), Jr. 1930-

PERSONAL: Born December 3, 1930, in Oklahoma City, Okla.; son of James F. (a college administrator) and Blanche (Pritchard) Findlay; married Doris Wylder (a social worker), June 10, 1955; children: James D., Eileen J., Peter F. *Education:* Drury College, A.B., 1952; Washington University, St. Louis, Mo., M.A., 1954; Northwestern University, Ph.D., 1961. *Politics:* Democrat. *Religion:* Congregationalist. *Home:* 49 Dendron Rd., Peacedale, R.I. 02879. *Office:* Department of History, University of Rhode Island, Kingston, R.I. 02879.

CAREER: DePauw University, Greencastle, Ind., 1958-71, began as instructor, became associate professor of history; University of Rhode Island, Kingston, professor of history and chairman of department, 1971—. Visiting associate professor at Northwestern University, 1964-65, and University of Wisconsin, 1969-70. *Member:* American Historical Association, Organization of American Historians, American Society of Church Historians.

WRITINGS: Dwight L. Moody: American Evangelist, 1837-1899, University of Chicago Press, 1969; (editor and contributor) *Contemporary Civilization,* Scott, Foresman, 5th edition, 1970.

WORK IN PROGRESS: Research on higher education in the American Midwest, 1830-1900.

* * *

FINE, Elsa Honig 1930-

PERSONAL: Born May 24, 1930, in Bayonne, N.J.; daughter of Samuel M. (a lawyer) and Yetta (Suskind) Honig; married Harold J. Fine (a psychologist), December 23, 1951; children: Erika Susan, Amy Minna. *Education:* Syracuse University, B.F.A., 1951; Temple University, M.Ed. in Art, 1967; University of Tennessee, Ed.D., 1971. *Home:* 7008 Sherwood Dr., Knoxville, Tenn. 37919. *Office:* Department of Art, Knoxville College, Knoxville, Tenn. 37921.

CAREER: Knoxville College, Knoxville, Tenn., assistant professor of art, 1971—. *Member:* College Art Association, Alpha Xi Alpha, Pi Lambda Theta.

WRITINGS: The Afro-American Artist: A Search for Identity, Holt, 1973. Contributor to *Art Journal.*

WORK IN PROGRESS: Research on women and art.

* * *

FITCH, Kenneth (Leonard) 1929-

PERSONAL: Born March 8, 1929, in Genoa, Neb.; son of Leonard Orson (an optometrist) and Viola (Moses) Fitch; married Jeanne Morrill Wolcott, July 3, 1950; children: David, Roger, Margaret. *Education:* University of Nebraska, B.S., 1951; University of Kansas, M.A., 1952; University of Michigan, Ph.D., 1955. *Home address:* R.R. 2, Lexington, Ill. 61753. *Office:* Department of Biological Science, Illinois State University, Normal, Ill. 61761.

CAREER: University of Missouri, Medical School, Columbia, instructor, 1956-58, assistant professor of anatomy, 1958-59; University of Nebraska, Medical School, Omaha, member of faculty, 1959-63; Illinois State University, Normal, 1963—, began as associate professor, now professor of biology. *Member:* American Association of Anatomists, American Society of Zoologists, American Association of University Professors, Sigma Xi.

WRITINGS: (With H. Chandler Elliott and Perry B. Johnson) *Life Science and Man,* Holt, 1973. Contributor to *Journal of Morphology, Journal of Cellular and Comparative Physiology,* and *Experimental Cell Research.*

WORK IN PROGRESS: A textbook, *The Biology of Physical Disability,* publication expected in 1978.

* * *

FITZ GERALD, Gregory 1923-

PERSONAL: Born April 23, 1923, in New York, N.Y.; son of Benedict J. (a composer) and Erna (a poet; maiden name, von Schueller) Fitz Gerald; married Barbara Farquhar, November 26, 1957 (divorced June 26, 1973); children: Geraldine Adare. *Education:* Boston University, A.B., 1946; Middlebury College, M.A., 1953; University of Iowa, Ph.D., 1967. *Home:* 11 Dresser Rd., Box 784, Adams Basin, N.Y. 14410. *Agent:* Elizabeth Wallace, Mary Yost Associates, 141 East 55th St., New York, N.Y. 10022. *Office:* Department of English, State University of New York College, Brockport, N.Y. 14420.

CAREER: University of Iowa, Iowa City, instructor in English, 1954-55, 1956-61; Jackson Junior College, Jackson, Mich., instructor in English, 1961-62; Indiana State University, Terre Haute, assistant professor of English, 1962-65; Ithaca College, Ithaca, N.Y., associate professor of English, 1965-67; State University of New York College at Brockport, assistant professor, 1967-69, associate professor, 1969-73, professor of English, 1973—. Has hosted or participated in numerous radio and television programs. *Member:* Authors Guild of Authors League of America, Modern Language Association of America, American Association of University Professors. *Awards, honors:* Smith-Mundt fellowship to Damascus, 1955-56; State University of New York Research Foundation grant-in-aid in satire, 1968-70, fellowship in criticism, 1969, fellowships in fiction, 1970, 1974.

WRITINGS: (Compiler) *Modern Satiric Stories: The Impropriety Principle,* Scott, Foresman, 1971; (with Jack Wolf) *Past, Present, and Future Perfect,* Fawcett, 1973; *Hunting the Yahoos,* Insight Publications, 1974. Contributor of nearly fifty stories, poems, articles, and reviews to magazines, including *Modern Poetry Studies, Fiction International, Aspect, Southwest Review,* and *Cimarron Review.*

WORK IN PROGRESS: Proxy for an Aged Swan and Other Stories; a collection of poems, *Canal Songs; Flanagan's Make,* a novel; three anthologies, *Dubious Nirvanas, The Fawcett Science Fiction Handbook,* and *Six Classic Science Fiction Novellas;* research on science fiction and on satire.

SIDELIGHTS: Fitz Gerald writes: "Though our society is doomed, I hubristically try, with infinitesimal effect, to retard its self-destruction. Science fiction is that literature which best clarifies our predicament, while satire illuminates our shortfall."

* * *

FLACKS, Richard 1938-

PERSONAL: Born April 26, 1938, in Brooklyn, N.Y.; son of David (a teacher) and Mildred (Weitz) Flacks; married Miriam Hartman (a genetics researcher), November 21, 1959; children: Charles Wright, Marc Ajay. *Education:* Brooklyn College (now Brooklyn College of the City University of New York), A.B., 1958; University of Michigan, Ph.D., 1963. *Office:* Department of Sociology, University of California, Santa Barbara, Calif. 93106.

CAREER: University of Michigan, Ann Arbor, lecturer in sociology, 1963-64; University of Chicago, Chicago, Ill., assistant professor of sociology, 1964-69; University of California, Santa Barbara, associate professor of sociology, 1969—. *Member:* American Sociological Association, Society for the Psychological Study of Social Issues (member of national council, 1970-74), Pacific Sociological Association (vice-president, 1971-72), Students for a Democratic Society (SDS; member of national executive committee), National Committee for a Sane Nuclear Policy (SANE; member of national board of directors).

WRITINGS: (With Kathryn Koenig and others) *Persistence and Change,* Wiley, 1967; *Youth and Social Change,* Markham, 1971; (editor) *Conformity, Resistance, and Self-Determination,* Little, Brown, 1973. Contributor to sociology journals, and *Playboy, New Republic, Dissent, Nation,* and *New York Review of Books.*

WORK IN PROGRESS: Making History versus Making Life; continuing research on the problems of political consciousness.

SIDELIGHTS: Flacks feels "a key problem of our time is to enhance the capabilities of people to stand against encroachments of powerful institutions." He told *CA* that while he has identified himself with the "New Left" political movement, his "interests include the full range of issues of contemporary political involvement."

* * *

FLEISSER, Marieluise
See HAINDL, Marieluise

* * *

FLENDER, Harold 1924-

PERSONAL: Born October 29, 1924, in New York, N.Y.; son of Jack (a fur trapper) and Sadie (Kasner) Flender; married Enid Rodman (a teacher), January 27, 1952; children: Nicole, Rodman. *Education:* City College (now City College of the City University of New York), B.A., 1945; Columbia University, M.A., 1950. *Politics:* Philosophical anarchist. *Religion:* None. *Home and office:* 37 Riverside Dr., New York, N.Y. 10023.

CAREER: Director and producer of films in Paris, Jerusalem, and New York, 1962—; Columbia University, New York, N.Y., instructor in film writing, 1963-65; New School of Social Research, New York, N.Y., 1963—; New York University, New York, N.Y., instructor in film writing, 1965-66; School of Visual Arts, New York, N.Y., instructor in film writing, 1969-71. Guest lecturer, Centre D'Etudes de Radio Diffusion-Television-Francaise, 1959, University of Dakar, 1960, Syracuse University, 1965. *Member:* P.E.N., Writers Guild of America—East. *Awards, honors:* National Council of Churches of Christ citation, 1954; Christopher Award, 1954, for "An Act of Faith"; Best Articles and Short Stories Award, 1958, for "Cuba Libre"; Fulbright scholarship, 1959; B'nai B'rith Human Rights Award, 1961, for "John Brown's Body"; Anti-Defamation League, grant, 1962; Writers Guild Award, 1971, for "The Bookseller".

WRITINGS: Paris Blues (novel), Ballantine, 1957; *Rescue in Denmark,* Simon & Schuster, 1963; *We Were Hooked,* Random House, 1973; *To Be* (novel), Manor Books, 1973; *The Kids Who Went to Israel,* Simon & Schuster, 1974; *Basso* (novel), Manor Books, 1974; *Troubled Summer* (novel), Avon, in press; *Two Gun Cohen* (history), Random House, in press.

Screenplays: "Alexander the Great," 1953; "Paris Blues," 1962.

Television specials: "John Brown's Body," 1962; "An Act of Faith," 1962; "The Bookseller," 1962; "The Big Sky Country," 1965; "The New South," 1965; "The Paris Collections with Lauren Bacall," 1968; "It's a Man's World," 1970; "Tony Curtis in Paris," 1970.

Television documentaries: "A Nice Place to Visit," 1953; "Answer the Call," 1953; "Wide, Wide World," 1956; "The Story of Alfred Nobel," 1959; "Heart Attack," 1965; "Honeymoon Mexican Style," 1966; "North from Mexico," 1971; "Now My Name Is," 1972; "Paintings in a Low Voice," 1973.

Also author of scripts for television shows, including "Kraft Theatre," "Four Star Playhouse," "I Spy," "The Jackie Gleason Show," "Your Show of Shows."

Educational and industrial films: "IBM," 1965; "The New Generation," 1967; "Oswego Story," 1968; "The Check-Up," 1968; "Soliciting Can Be Fun," 1968; "Thomas Jefferson," 1969; "The Rise of Big Business," 1969; "Movin' On," 1970; "Rendezvous with Destiny," 1970; "There Must Be a Catch," 1971; "The Name of the Game," 1971; "But What Do You Do If," 1971.

Contributor to *Intellectual Digest, Saturday Review, Nation, New Leader, L'Express, Variety, Boys' Life,* and other periodicals.

* * *

FLETCHER, Leon 1921-

PERSONAL: Born August 28, 1921, in San Francisco, Calif.; married: wife's name, Vivian; children: Nancy, Lorie. *Education:* College of San Mateo, A.A., 1941; San Jose State College (now California State University), B.A., 1943; Columbia University and University of California, Berkeley, graduate study; University of Southern California, M.S., 1958; University of California, Los Angeles, further graduate study, 1965. *Home:* 1110 Sinex Ave., Pacific Grove, Calif. 93950. *Office:* Monterey Peninsula College, Monterey, Calif. 93940.

CAREER: High school speech and English teacher in Monterey, Calif., 1947-50; Taft College and High School, Taft, Calif., director of public information, 1954-59, instructor in speech, radio, television, and English at college, 1959-62, director of instructional improvement at college, 1962-63; University of California, Los Angeles, research assistant in teacher education, 1963-64, communications media specialist for Nigeria project, 1964-65; Monterey Peninsula College, Monterey, Calif., coordinator of instructional services, 1965-70, instructor in speech, 1971—. Producer and director of educational television series for Columbia Broadcasting System in Bakersfield, 1958-59; consultant to more than twenty educational agencies and institutions. *Military service:* U.S. Naval Reserve, 1942-57, active duty, 1943-45, 1950-54; became lieutenant commander; received seventeen combat awards and five personal commendations.

MEMBER: Speech Association of America, National News Registry, Western Speech Association, California Teachers Association.

WRITINGS: Education Through Television, Educational Television Research Association, 1956; *Showmanship and Scholarship,* Fearon, 1958; *On the Rostrum* (booklet), Standard Oil Co., 1960; *Educational Television Review,* (booklet), Pacific Coast Publishers, 1961; *Guidelines for Teacher-Training in Educational Television,* California Council on Teacher-Training, 1963; *Basic Public Speaking,* Data-Guide, 1964; (editor) *Cases in Junior College Administration* (study book), University Council of University of California at Los Angeles, 1964; *Spotlight on Science* (booklet), California Department of Education, 1964; *Self-Enhancing Education* (training book), Sanford Press, 1966; *How to Design and Deliver a Speech,* Chandler Publishing, 1974; *Public Speaking,* United Telephone Co. of Ohio, 1974.

Filmstrips: "Public Speaking," Bailey Films, 1964; "Nigeria," Bailey Films, 1966; "Russia," Bailey Films, 1967; "Korea," Encore Visual Education, 1974. Author of educational manuals. Contributor of about a hundred seventy articles to popular magazines and to journals, including *Sail, America, TV Guide, School Executive, Junior College Journal, Audio-Visual Instruction,* and *Nigerian Television News.*

WORK IN PROGRESS: Book on contemporary dialogue; beginning publication of educational newsletter; filmstrips; articles.

AVOCATIONAL INTERESTS: Sailing and boating (owns an ocean-going yacht).

* * *

FLIEGEL, Frederick C(hristian) 1925-

PERSONAL: Born April 3, 1925, in Edmonton, Alberta, Canada; naturalized U.S. citizen, 1935; son of John Carl (a clergyman) and Ruth (Aastrup) Fliegel; married Ruth Haller, August 25, 1955; children: Frederick M., Ruth E., David C., Johanna C. *Education:* University of Wisconsin, B.A., 1949, M.A., 1952, Ph.D., 1955. *Home:* 606 West Church St., Champaign, Ill. 61820. *Office:* Department of Sociology, University of Illinois, Urbana, Ill. 61801.

CAREER: Pennsylvania State University, University Park, assistant professor, 1955-64, associate professor of agricultural economics and rural sociology, 1964-65; Michigan State University, East Lansing, associate professor of communication, 1965-67; University of Illinois, Urbana, professor of rural sociology, 1968—, head of department of sociology, 1970-73. Fulbright professor at University of Rio Grande do Sul, Brazil, 1962-63; visiting professor at University of Wisconsin, summer, 1963. *Military service:* U.S. Marine Corps Reserve, 1943-46.

MEMBER: American Sociological Association, Rural Sociological Society (council member-at-large, 1968-71; vice-president, 1973-74), American Association for the Advancement of Science, European Society for Rural Sociology, Midwest Sociological Society, Illinois Sociological Society, Alpha Kappa Delta.

WRITINGS: (Contributor) J. H. Copp, editor, *Our Changing Rural Society: Perspectives and Trends,* Iowa State University Press, 1964; (with J. E. Kivlin, Prodipto Roy, and L. K. Sen) *Communication in India: Experiments in Introducing Change,* National Institute of Community Development (Hyderabad, India), 1968; (with Roy, Kivlin, and Sen) *Agricultural Innovation among Indian Farmers,* National Institute of Community Development, 1968; (with Roy, Kivlin, and Sen) *Agricultural Innovations in Indian Villages,* National Institute of Community Development, 1968; (with Roy, Kivlin, and Sen) *Innovation in Rural India,* Bowling Green State University Press, 1971; (contributor) G. D. Hursh and Roy, editors, *Survey Research Methods in Developing Nations,* Macmillan, 1974.

Author of reports and bulletins for India's National Institute of Community Development, Brazil's Instituto de Estudos e Pesquisas Economicas, and Pennsylvania Agricultural Experiment Station. Contributor of more than thirty articles to professional journals, including *Science for the Farmer, Rural Sociology, Behavioural Sciences and Community Development, International Social Science Journal,* and *American Journal of Sociology*. Member of editorial review board of *Rural Sociology,* 1964-66, book review editor, 1965-66, editor, 1970-72; member of editorial board of *Behavioural Science and Community Development,* 1966-67.

* * *

FLINT, Cort R(ay) 1915-

PERSONAL: Born March 17, 1915, in Leedey, Okla.; son of Corties Ray (a banker) and Kathryn (an investments analyst; maiden name, Logan) Flint; married Ilene Moore (a musician), May 28, 1938; children: Cort R., Jr., Sue Ann (Mrs. Michael Douglas Glenn). *Education:* Southwestern State College, B.A., 1935; University of Oklahoma, graduate study, 1937-39; Southern Baptist Theological Seminary, Th.M., 1943, Th.D., 1952, Ph.D., 1974. *Politics:* Democrat. *Address:* Box 708, Meadows of Dan, Va. 24120. *Agent:* Guy J. Bridges, Jr., Box 30, Winston-Salem, N.C. 27101.

CAREER: Ordained Baptist minister, 1940; Baptist Theological Seminary, Louisville, Ky., vice-president, 1952-53; minister in Anderson, S.C., 1955-66; Anderson College, Anderson, S.C., president, 1957; Meadows of Dan Baptist Church, Meadows of Dan, Va., pastor, 1970—. *Military service:* Oklahoma National Guard, 1933-35. U.S. Naval Reserve, 1943-46; became lieutenant. *Member:* International Platform Association, Rotary, Kiwanis, Masons, Ruritan. *Awards, honors:* D.H., 1973.

WRITINGS: The Quotable Billy Graham, Droke, 1966; *Grief's Slow Wisdom,* Droke, 1966; *To Thine Own Self Be True,* Droke, 1968; *Better Men or Bitter Men?,* Droke, 1969; *The Purpose of Love,* Droke, 1973. Contributor to *Quotable Dr. Crane, Quote, Enterprise* (Stuart, Va.), and *Galax Gazette* (Va.).

WORK IN PROGRESS: The Best Is Yet to Come; Discoveries for Great Living; Discoveries for Greater Selling; You Were Born to Win; Living at Your Best.

* * *

FLOOD, E(dward) Thadeus 1932-

PERSONAL: Born March 15, 1932, in Seattle, Wash.; son of George Edward (a lawyer) and Virginia (Flynn) Flood; married Chadine Kanjanavanit (a college professor), September 24, 1960; children: Theresa Lynn. *Education:* Seattle University, B.S., 1958; University of Washington, Seattle, Wash., Ph.D., 1967. *Home:* 15291 Norton Rd., Saratoga, Calif. 95070. *Office:* Department of History, University of Santa Clara, Santa Clara, Calif. 95053.

CAREER: International House of Japan, Tokyo, Japan, translator and general consultant, 1963-65; University of Santa Clara, Santa Clara, Calif., assistant professor, 1966-69, associate professor of Asian history, 1970—, head of department, 1972-74. *Military service:* U.S. Marine Corps, 1951-55; served in Korea. *Member:* Association for Asian Studies, International House of Japan, Toho Gakkai, Siam Society, Committee of Concerned Asian Scholars. *Awards, honors:* Fulbright-Hayes fellowships to University of Tokyo, 1963-65, and Chulalonkorn University, 1965-66; National Endowment for the Humanities grant, 1971; special College of Humanities grants, 1969, 1970, 1971; Fulbright-Hays faculty research grant to Thailand, China, and Japan, 1974.

WRITINGS: (Editor and translator with wife, Chadine Flood) *Dynastic Chronicles, Bangkok Era, Fourth Reign,* three volumes, Center for East Asian Cultural Studies (Tokyo), 1965; (contributor) David Wurfel, editor, *Meiji Japan's Centennial: Political Thought and Action,* University Press of Kansas, 1971. Contributor to *Journal of the Siam Society* and *Journal of Southeast Asian History*.

WORK IN PROGRESS: A biography of Ho Chi Minh, 1890-1945, with special reference to French and Chinese language sources.

SIDELIGHTS: Flood is competent in Japanese, Thai, Chinese, French, German, and Latin.

* * *

FLORENTIN, Eddy 1923-

PERSONAL: Born May 27, 1923, in Paris, France; married wife, Colette, December, 1950; children: Dominique, Francoise, Thierry. *Education:* University of Paris, Licence-es-lettres, 1947. *Home:* 9 Bis Rue Casimir Pinel, Neuilly sur Seine, France 92200. *Office:* Office de Radiodiffusion Television Francaise.

CAREER: Journalist and author. *Military service:* French Army Reserve, 1950—; currently lieutenant.

WRITINGS: Stalingrad en Normandie, Presses de la Cite, 1964, translation by Mervyn Savill published as *Battle of the Falaise Gap,* Elek, 1965, Hawthorn, 1967; *Operation Paddle,* Presses de la Cite, 1969; *Der Rueckmarsch,* (title means "The German Withdrawal in August, 1944), Presses de la Cite, 1974.

WORK IN PROGRESS: Operation Astonia; Montgomery Races to Belgium.

* * *

FOLKERS, George Fulton 1929-

PERSONAL: Born August 27, 1929, in Joliet, Ill.; son of Herbert Peter (an attorney) and Leilia (Fulton) Folkers; married Jean Kendall, July 14, 1956; children: Gregory Kendall, Katherine Jean, Jonathan Kendall. *Education:* Attended University of Basel, 1949-50, 1952-53; Knox College, B.A., 1951; Princeton University, M.A., 1960, Ph.D., 1967. *Home:* 417 South 21st St., Lewisburg, Pa. 17837. *Office:* Department of German, Bucknell University, Lewisburg, Pa. 17837.

CAREER: Williams College, Williamstown, Mass., instructor in German, 1959-61; Phillips Exeter Academy, Exeter, N.H., instructor in German, 1961-64; University of Massachusetts, Amherst, assistant professor of German literature, 1964-68; Bucknell University, Lewisburg, Pa., member of faculty in department of German, and director of German program. Reader for Bucknell University Press. *Military service:* U.S. Army, 1953-58; became first lieutenant. *Member:* American Association of Teachers of German, American Council on the Teaching of Foreign Languages, American Translators Association, Modern Language Association of America.

WRITINGS: (Translator with David B. Dickens and Marion W. Sonnenfeld, and editor) *The Complete Narrative Prose of Conrad Ferdinand Meyer,* Bucknell University Press, 1974. Contributor of reviews to *German Quarterly.*

WORK IN PROGRESS: Translation of "Die schoene Seele" in Goethe's *Wilhelm Meister;* research on Franz Grillparzer's essays on the Spanish theater, and on the influences of A. Schnitzler's medical practice on his literary work.

* * *

FOLLAND, H(arold) F(reeze) 1906-

PERSONAL: Born October 1, 1906, in Salt Lake City, Utah; son of William Henry (a lawyer and judge) and Grace (Freeze) Folland; married Helen Budge (a professor), July 3, 1946. *Education:* Harvard University, A.B., 1929, M.A., 1934, Ph.D., 1940. *Office:* Department of English, University of Utah, Salt Lake City, Utah 84112.

CAREER: University of Utah, Salt Lake City, assistant professor, 1938-44, associate professor, 1944-49, professor of English and theater, 1949-74. Actor in University of Utah Theatre; narrator for Utah Symphony. *Military service:* U.S. Army, 1942-45; became second lieutenant.

WRITINGS: (With J. H. Adamson) *The Shepherd of the Ocean,* Gambit, 1969; (with Adamson) *Sir Harry Vane, 1613-1662,* Gambit, 1973. Contributor to *PMLA, Shakespeare Quarterly, Theatre Notebook,* and *Western Humanities Review.*

WORK IN PROGRESS: Research on theatrical history in Utah and on Dickens.

AVOCATIONAL INTERESTS: Music, hiking, camping, travel.

* * *

FOLLEY, Vern L(eRoy) 1936-

PERSONAL: Born October 15, 1936, in Waterloo, Iowa; son of Calvin Eugene and Carolyn (Miller) Folley; married Jorretta Longine (a teacher), July 24, 1953; children: Vern L., Jr., Stacy Lynn. *Education:* University of Arizona, B.A., 1963, M.Ed., 1964, Ed.D., 1970; Washington State University, M.A., 1965. *Home:* R.D. 1, Box 792, Shuler Dr., Etters, Pa. 17319. *Office:* Urban Development Institute, Harrisburg Area Community College, 3300 Cameron Street Rd., Harrisburg, Pa. 17110.

CAREER: Police patrolman in Tucson, Ariz., 1958-61, sergeant, 1961-62; Davis Monthan Air Force Base, Tucson, Ariz., security lieutenant, 1962-63; public school teacher in Tucson, Ariz., 1963-64; Harrisburg Area Community College, Harrisburg, Pa., associate professor, 1965-68, professor of public administration, 1968—, chairman of Division of Police and Public Administration, 1965-70, dean of Urban Development Institute, 1970—. Visiting police professor at Cochise Community College, summer, 1970, and Manatee Junior College, 1970; visiting professor at University of Arizona, 1973. Member of Southcentral Regional Council of the Governor's Justice Commission; founded Law Enforcement Educational Foundation of Greater Harrisburg; established local Criminal Justice Training Center. Consulting editor, AMS Press; manuscript reader for Prentice-Hall, McGraw, Glencoe Press, and Goodyear Publishing.

MEMBER: International Association of Chiefs of Police, Academy of Criminal Justice Sciences, Alpha Phi Sigma, Phi Kappa Phi.

WRITINGS: American Law Enforcement, Holbrook, 1973; *Police Patrol Techniques and Tactics,* C. C Thomas, 1973; *Police Organization and Administration,* Prentice-Hall, in press; *Criminal Investigation,* Holbrook, in press. Editor of criminal justice series for Holbrook, 1971—. Contributor to social science journals, including *Law and Order, Community and Junior College Journal, Police, Pennsylvanian,* and *Washington Police Journal.* Police problems editor for *Law and Order;* consulting editor for *Police.*

AVOCATIONAL INTERESTS: Riding motorcycles.

* * *

FORBES, Calvin 1945-

PERSONAL: Born May 6, 1945, in Newark, N.J.; son of Jacob and Mary (Short) Forbes. *Education:* Attended New School for Social Research and Rutgers University. *Office:* Department of English, Tufts University, Medford, Mass. 02155.

CAREER: Emerson College, Boston, Mass., assistant professor of English, 1969-73; Tufts University, Medford, Mass., assistant professor of English, 1973—. Visiting professor at University of Copenhagen, 1974-75. *Awards, honors:* Breadloaf Writers Conference fellowship in poetry, summer, 1973.

WRITINGS: Blue Mondays (poems), Wesleyan University Press, 1974; *From the Book of Shine* (poems), Wesleyan University Press, in press.

WORK IN PROGRESS: A novel.

* * *

FORD, Thomas R(obert) 1923-

PERSONAL: Born June 24, 1923, in Lake Charles, La.; son of Gervais W. (a school superintendent) and Alma (Weil) Ford; married Harriet Lowrey (a librarian), August 13, 1949; children: Margaret, Janet, Mark, Charlotte. *Education:* Louisiana State University, B.S., 1946, M.A., 1948; Vanderbilt University, Ph.D., 1951. *Home:* 1107 Eldemere Rd., Lexington, Ky. 40502. *Office:* Department of Sociology, University of Kentucky, Lexington, Ky. 40506.

CAREER: Louisiana State University, Baton Rouge, instructor in sociology, 1948-49; University of Alabama, Tuscaloosa, assistant professor of sociology, 1950-53; U.S. Air Force Personnel and Training and Research Center, Maxwell Air Force Base, Ala., statistical analyst in demography, 1953-56; Population Council, Inc., Bogota, Colombia, resident representative, 1970-72. *Military service:* U.S. Army Air Forces, 1943-45; became first lieutenant; received Air Medal with six oak leaf clusters. *Member:* American Association for the Advancement of Science, American Sociological Association, Population Association of America, Rural Sociological Society (president, 1972-73), Southern Sociological Society.

WRITINGS: Man and Land in Peru, University of Florida Press, 1955; (editor) *The Southern Appalachian Region: A Survey,* University Press of Kentucky, 1962; *Health and Demography in Kentucky,* University Press of Kentucky, 1964; (editor) *The Revolutionary Theme in Contemporary America,* University Press of Kentucky, 1966; (editor with Gordon F. DeJong) *Social Demography,* Prentice-Hall, 1970. Contributor to *Human Biology, Review of Religious Research, Social Forces, Rural Sociology,* and *Journal for the Scientific Study of Religion.*

WORK IN PROGRESS: Research on fertility of the population of Colombia and family planning; research on migration patterns for Kentucky and the southern Appalachians.

FORREST, Alfred C. 1916-

PERSONAL: Born May 24, 1916, in Mariposa, Ontario, Canada; son of Alexander (a farmer) and Jean (Greenaway) Forrest; married Esther Clipsham, January 31, 1941. *Education:* University of Toronto, B.A.; Emmanuel College, B.D. *Home:* 280 Bessborough Dr., Toronto, Ontario, M4G 3K8, Canada. *Office: United Church Observer,* 85 St. Clair Ave. E., Toronto, Ontario M4T 1M8, Canada.

CAREER: Minister of United Church of Canada, 1940—, editor of *United Church Observer,* 1955—. Lecturer and broadcaster on the Middle East. *Military service:* Royal Canadian Air Force, chaplain, 1944-46; became flight lieutenant. *Awards, honors:* D.D. from Huntington University, 1960; Canadian centennial medal, 1967.

WRITINGS: Not Tomorrow–Now, Ryerson, 1960; (with William Kilbourne and Patrick Watson) *Religion in Canada,* McClelland & Stewart, 1968; *The Unholy Land,* McClelland & Stewart, 1971, Devin-Adair, 1972. Author of weekly syndicated newspaper column "A Cleric Comments," appearing in Canadian newspapers. Contributor to religious periodicals in Canada and the United States.

WORK IN PROGRESS: Castro's Hot Little Island.

SIDELIGHTS: Forrest has traveled in Europe, Asia, and Africa and he has lived in Lebanon.

* * *

FORREST, David
See FORREST-WEBB, Robert

* * *

FORREST-WEBB, Robert 1929-
(David Forrest, Jonathan Tremayne, Forrest Webb, Robert Forrest Webb)

PERSONAL: Born April 9, 1929, in Nottingham, England; son of Cecil Frederik and Constance Ella (Wynne) Forrest-Webb; married Wendy Patricia Waterson (a secretary), December 8, 1972; children: Anne. *Education:* Attended British schools. *Politics:* "Rarely—but right." *Religion:* Agnostic. *Home and office:* Bottom Farm Cottage, Brewers Lane, West Tisted, Alresford, Hampshire, England. *Agent:* Desmond Elliot, 38 Bury St., St. James's, London SW1, England.

CAREER: Journalist and editor of magazines and of various British national newspapers; Haymarket Press, London, England, executive editor, 1965-69; writer, 1969—. Chairman of Hemarvine Productions (film company). *Awards, honors:* Salone Internazionale Umorismo award for most humorous book published in Italy, 1973, for *After Me the Deluge.*

WRITINGS—Under pseudonym David Forrest: (With David Eliades) *And to My Nephew Albert I Leave the Island What I Won off Fatty Hagan in a Poker Game* (novel), Morrow, 1969; *The Great Dinosaur Robbery,* Hodder & Stoughton, 1970; *After Me the Deluge,* Hodder & Stoughton, 1972; *The Undertaker's Dozen* (short stories), Tandem Books, 1974.

Under name Forrest Webb: *No Moss for Me* (autobiography), Transatlantic, 1958; *The Snowboys* (novel), Doubleday, 1973; *Brannington's Leopard* (novel), Hodder & Stoughton, 1973, Doubleday, in press; *The Caviar Cruise* (novel), Doubleday, in press.

Under name Robert Forrest Webb: *Motorists' Dictionary,* Arco, 1963; *You and Your Motor Scooter,* Sportshelf, 1963; *Tackle Motorcycle and Scooter Maintenance This Way,* Sportshelf, 1964, 2nd edition, 1967.

Also author of *AIKIDO,* 1968. Author (under name Robert Forrest Webb) of "A Bit of the Old Roman" (archaeological documentary film), produced for television by Peter Van Arden, 1967; (under name David Forrest) "Willie Hawk" (film about American Mid-West of 1845), in production in Spain.

WORK IN PROGRESS: A Mid-Victorian adventure series of, initially, three books, under pseudonym Johnathan Tremayne, *Pendragon, Late of Prince Albert's Own; His Highness Requests Pendragon;* and *Pendragon: Assassin,* all for Hodder & Stoughton; a novel, *Pretty Billie,* under name Forrest Webb, completion expected in 1975.

SIDELIGHTS: Forrest-Webb told *CA:* "I suppose my personal types of books are directly related to my own experiences. In the case of humourous books, I use the humour to carry messages that would otherwise be unpublishable. . .in the case of *After Me the Deluge,* it was directly aimed at archaic and hypocritical attitudes in the modern established church. *And to My Nephew Albert. . .* was a personal ending of 'cold war' techniques. *The Great Dinosaur Robbery* hoped to point out to readers how seriously a humourous situation could be viewed from the point of the establishment in a country as large as the US." He continues: "I was much influenced by Hemingway in my youth. I spent most of my twenties travelling and working abroad—some 48 countries. I lived and hunted in the jungles of India, and the forests of Africa. I shot leopard and sat in trees waiting for tiger. I regret to say I even killed an elephant (he was supposed to be a rogue, but it is hard, looking back, to decide which of us caused people the more trouble). I once drove a motorcycle both ways across the Sahara. . .quite an interesting experience as there was a war on at the time." He also writes that his family claims descent from Bonnie Prince Charlie.

Forrest-Webb has raced motorcycles in international competition. He is a sculptor when time permits, and has had an exhibition in a major London gallery. Walt Disney Productions has purchased film rights to *The Great Dinosaur Robbery.*

AVOCATIONAL INTERESTS: Rugby, kayaking (became British Canoe Champion), judo, aikido, sailing, skiing, shooting.

* * *

FORSYTHE, Irene
See HANSON, Irene (Forsythe)

* * *

FOSTER, Edward Halsey 1942-

PERSONAL: Born December 17, 1942, in Williamsburg, Mass.; son of Edward Clark (a teacher and geologist) and Edith (a school principal and teacher; maiden name, Derosia) Foster; married Elaine Dunphy (a teacher), June 22, 1968; children: Katherine Hearn, John Clark. *Education:* Columbia University, B.A., 1965, M.A., 1966, Ph.D., 1970. *Politics:* Democrat. *Religion:* Protestant. *Home:* 910 West End Ave., New York, N.Y. 10025. *Office:* Stevens Institute of Technology, Hoboken, N.J. 07030.

CAREER: Stevens Institute of Technology, Hoboken, N.J., assistant professor of American studies, 1970—.

Member: Modern Language Association of America, American Studies Association, American Association of University Professors, New York Historical Society, Constitution Island Association. *Awards, honors:* Research grant from New Jersey Historical Commission, 1974.

WRITINGS: Catharine Maria Sedgwick, Twayne, 1974; *The Civilized Wilderness,* Macmillan, in press. Contributor to journals.

WORK IN PROGRESS: Susan and Anna Warner; research on the Stevens family as patrons of the arts.

* * *

FOSTER, Joseph O'Kane 1898-
(O'Kane Foster)

PERSONAL: Born June 27, 1898, in Chicago, Ill.; son of Edward Frank (an inventor) and Allie (Vancil) Foster; married Margaret Hale, February 16, 1928 (died, 1962); married Leona Taylor (a sculptor), July 2, 1969; children: (first marriage) Paula (Mrs. Creighton Scott). *Education:* University of Wisconsin, student, 1915-1919. *Politics:* Democrat. *Religion:* Episcopalian. *Home address:* Ranches of Taos, N.M. 87557.

CAREER: Milwaukee Sentinel, Milwaukee, Wis., reporter, 1918; *Chicago Evening American,* Chicago, Ill., member of editorial staff, 1920-21. Writer and consultant for British Broadcasting Corp., London, for documentary film on D. H. Lawrence; panelist at Worldwide D. H. Lawrence Festival, Taos, N.M., 1970. Delegate to New Mexico State Democratic convention. *Military service:* U.S. Army, weather bureau man, 1919. *Awards, honors:* O. Henry Memorial Award, 1939, for "Gideon."

WRITINGS: The Great Montezuma (film play), privately printed, 1940; (under name O'Kane Foster) *In the Night Did I Sing,* Scribner, 1942; *A Cow Is Too Much Trouble in Los Angeles,* Duell, Sloan & Pearce, 1952; *Street of the Barefoot Lovers,* Little, Brown, 1953; *Time to Embrace,* Popular Library, 1955; *Stephana,* Duell, Sloan & Pearce, 1959; *D. H. Lawrence in Taos,* University of New Mexico Press, 1972. Work is represented in *O. Henry Memorial Award Prize Stories,* edited by Harry Hansen, Doubleday, 1939. Contributor to *Atlantic Monthly, Story, University of New Mexico Quarterly,* and other periodicals. Former editor of *Wisconsin Literary Magazine.*

WORK IN PROGRESS: An epic novel about the Southwest; a forthcoming movie production of "Street of the Barefoot Lovers."

SIDELIGHTS: Foster told *CA:* "The finest writing comes from our deepest most poetic self. The 'reality' of rationality is not enough. I prefer Faulkner to Hemingway, Lorca to Eliot, Lawrence to Joyce."

Foster has lived in Paris, Madrid, Rome, Vienna, Prague, and saw the beginnings of the Spanish Revolution. His handwritten manuscripts are preserved in the University of California at Los Angeles Library.

* * *

FOSTER, O'Kane
See FOSTER, Joseph O'Kane

* * *

FOUST, Paul J(ohn) 1920-

PERSONAL: Born June 16, 1920, in Hillsdale, Mich.; son of Ray A. (a farmer) and Louise (Baerlin) Foust; married Virginia Mahrley, February 2, 1945; children: Paul, Caroline (Mrs. David Jakubcin), Susan, Gretchen. *Education:* Attended Hillsdale College, 1938-39; Concordia Seminary, B.D., 1945. *Home:* 1807 Huron River Dr., Ypsilanti, Mich. 48197. *Office:* Lutheran Church-Michigan District, 3773 Geddes Rd., Ann Arbor, Mich. 48105.

CAREER: Ordained Lutheran minister, 1945; minister in Milan, Mich., 1941-54, Albion, Mich., 1954-61, Detroit, Mich., 1961-66, and Battle Creek, Mich., 1966-69; Lutheran Church-Michigan District, Ann Arbor, Mich., head of Evangelism-Stewardship Department, 1969—. Instructor in evangelism at Concordia College, 1972, and 1973-74. *Awards, honors:* Servus Ecclesiae Christi from Concordia Seminary, 1973.

WRITINGS: Reborn to Multiply, Concordia, 1973. Contributor to *Michigan Lutheran* and *Exchange.*

* * *

FOX, Ralph H(artzler) 1913-1973

1913—December 23, 1973; American mathematician and author of works on topology. Obituaries: *AB Bookman's Weekly,* January 14, 1974.

* * *

FOX, Renee C(laire) 1928-

PERSONAL: Born February 15, 1928, in New York, N.Y.; daughter of P. Fred and Henrietta (Gold) Fox. *Education:* Smith College, B.A. (summa cum laude), 1949; Harvard University, Ph.D., 1954. *Home:* 226 West Rittenhouse Sq., Philadelphia, Pa. 19103. *Office:* Department of Sociology, University of Pennsylvania, Philadelphia, Pa. 19174.

CAREER: Columbia University, New York, N.Y., research assistant, Bureau of Applied Social Research, 1953-55, research associate, 1955-58, lecturer in sociology at Barnard College, 1955-58, assistant professor at Barnard College, 1958-64, associate professor at Barnard College, 1964-66; Harvard University, Cambridge, Mass., lecturer in sociology, 1967-69, research fellow, Center for International Affairs, 1967-68, research associate, Program on Technology and Society, 1968-71; University of Pennsylvania, Philadelphia, professor of sociology in departments of psychiatry and sociology, 1969—, professor of sociology in department of medicine, 1972—, chairman of department of sociology, 1972—. Member and scientific adviser, Centre de Recherches Sociologiques, Kinshasa, Congo, 1963-67; visiting professor at Official University of the Congo, 1965; scientific adviser, Centre de Documentation et de Recherches, National School of Law and Administration, Kinshasa, Congo, 1965-66; visiting professor at Sir George Williams University, summer, 1968. Member of board of directors, Institute for Intercultural Studies, New York, 1969—, and Institute of Society, Ethics and Life Sciences, Hastings-on-Hudson, N.Y., 1969—; vice chairman of board of directors, Social Science Research Council, 1971-74. Phi Beta Kappa visiting scholar, 1973-74, 1974-75. Member of editorial advisory board, *Encyclopedia of Bioethics,* 1973—.

MEMBER: American Academy of Arts and Sciences (fellow), African Studies Association (fellow), American Academy of Psychoanalysis (scientific associate), American Sociological Association (member of council, 1973—; chairman of medical sociology section, 1974-75), American

Association for the Advancement of Science, American Psychosomatic Society, American Public Health Association, Association of American Medical Colleges, Society for Health and Human Values, Society for the Scientific Study of Religion, American Association of University Professors, American Association of University Women, Eastern Sociological Society (vice-president, 1973-74), New York Academy of Sciences.

AWARDS, HONORS: Belgian-American Educational Foundation fellow, 1960-61; Guggenheim fellow, 1962; Social Science Research Council grant, 1964-65; E. Harris Harbison Gifted Teaching Award of Danforth Foundation, 1970; M.A., University of Pennsylvania, 1971; D.Sc., Medical College of Pennsylvania, 1974.

WRITINGS: Experiment Perilous, Free Press, 1959; (with Willy De Craemer) *The Emerging Physician: A Sociological Approach to the Development of a Congolese Medical Profession,* Hoover Institution, 1968; (with Judith P. Swazey) *The Courage to Fail: A Social View of Transplantation and Dialysis,* University of Chicago Press, 1974.

Contributor: Robert K. Merton and others, editors, *The Student Physician,* Harvard University Press, 1957; Harold I. Lief and others, editors, *The Psychological Basis of Medical Practice,* Harper, 1963; Philip E. Hammond, editor, *Sociologists at Work,* Basic Books, 1964; Paul A. Freund, editor, *Experimentation with Human Subjects,* Braziller, 1970. Contributor to *International Encyclopedia of the Social Sciences* and to medical and other journals.

Associate editor, *American Sociological Review,* 1963-66; regional editor, *Social Science and Medicine,* 1968-69, associate editor, 1969—; member of editorial board, *Journal of Medical Education,* 1971-74.

WORK IN PROGRESS: With Willy De Craemer, *The Intelligence Behind the Mask: Congolese Society, 1962-1972,* for Macmillan; a section on medical evolution for a festschrift for Talcott Parsons, edited by Victor Lidz and others, for Free Press.

* * *

FOX, Col. Victor J.
See WINSTON, R(obert) A(lexander)

* * *

FOXX, Jack
See PRONZINI, Bill

* * *

FOZDAR, Jamshed K(hodadad) 1926-

PERSONAL: Born October 17, 1926, in Bombay, India; son of Khodadad M. (a physician) and Shirin (Irani) Fozdar; married Parvati Gharat, October 25, 1948; children: Vijay, Vahid (sons). *Religion:* Baha'i. *Home:* 801 Arlington Blvd., El Cerrito, Calif. 94530.

WRITINGS: The Fallacy of Ancestor Worship, privately printed, 1965; *The God of Buddha,* Asia Publishing House, 1973.

* * *

FRANCE, Harold L(eroy) 1930-

PERSONAL: Born February 6, 1930, in Sterling, Ill.; son of Joseph LeRoy and Merna A. (Oberbillig) France; married Pauline Kay Stimpson, September 8, 1951 (divorced, May 20, 1970); married Mary Helen Vaughn (a clerk and general office worker), September 12, 1970; children: (first marriage) James L., Thomas Paul; (second marriage) David Alan (adopted). *Education:* Attended high school in Dixon, Ill. *Politics:* Conservative Republican. *Religion:* Lutheran. *Home:* 621 South Spur Circle, Mesa, Ariz. 85204.

CAREER: Airesearch Manufacturing Co., Phoenix, Ariz., production machinist, 1956-58; Arizona Public Service Co., Phoenix, Ariz., general machinist, 1958-65; Motorola, Inc., Phoenix, Ariz., experimental machinist, 1965-67; Salt River Project, Tempe, Ariz., general machinist, 1967—. *Military service:* U.S. Air Force, 1948-52; became sergeant.

WRITINGS: Tomorrow's Yesterday (poems), Franklin Publishing Co., 1973.

WORK IN PROGRESS: This Way to Oblivion, a book of poems; several song lyrics; *Brady House,* a novel.

* * *

FRANK, H(ans) Eric 1921-

PERSONAL: Born July 9, 1921, in Austria; son of Emerich and Elise Frank; married Olive Mary Hunter, November 22, 1968. *Education:* University of London, B.Sc.Econ., 1946, graduate study, 1949-50. *Home:* 4 Richmond Hill, Bristol BS8 1AT, England. *Office:* School of Management, University of Bath, Bath, England.

CAREER: Educationist, 1946-55, and training director in industry, 1955-64; University of Bath, Bath, England, senior lecturer and director of studies, 1964—.

WRITINGS: (Editor) *Organization Structuring,* McGraw, 1971. Editor of McGraw-Hill "Management Manuals," 1973. Contributor to journals in the United States and Europe. Editor of *Industrial Training International,* 1969—.

* * *

FRANK, Lee
See GRIFFIN, Arthur J.

* * *

FRANKE, David 1938-

PERSONAL: Born May 4, 1938, in Houston, Tex.; son of Monroe W. (a manager of a lumber yard) and Otilie (Fick) Franke; married Holly Lambro (a writer), October 5, 1969. *Education:* Del Mar College, A.A., 1957. *Politics:* "Flat Earth Party and League of Non-Voters." *Home and office:* 51 Remington Rd., Ridgefield, Conn. 06877. *Agent:* Mrs. Henriette Neatrour, Curtis Brown Ltd., 60 East 56th St., New York, N.Y. 10022.

CAREER: Human Events (newsletter), Washington, D.C., Capitol Hill reporter, 1957-60; *National Review* (magazine), New York, N.Y., assistant to editor William F. Buckley, Jr., 1960-62; *New Guard* (magazine), Washington, D.C., editor, 1964-67; Arlington House Publishers, New Rochelle, N.Y., senior editor, 1967—. Founder of Flat Earth Party; active in young conservative movement and the Goldwater movement, 1954-64; founder and member of national board of directors of Young Americans for Freedom, 1961-62. *Military service:* U.S. Army, troop information specialist, 1962-64. *Member:* Sons of Confederate Veterans.

WRITINGS: (Compiler) *Quotations from Chairman Bill: The Best of William F. Buckley, Jr.,* Arlington House,

1970; (with wife, Holly L. Franke) *Safe Places,* Arlington House, 1972; *America's Fifty Safest Cities,* Arlington House, 1974. Contributor to magazines and newspapers in the United States and abroad, including *Esquire, American Home, National Enquirer, Travel,* and *Family Weekly*.

WORK IN PROGRESS: A biography of Senator Edward Kennedy; research for books on relocation, on travel in the United States, on outdoor recreation, amateur prospecting, and treasure hunting.

SIDELIGHTS: Franke writes: "I started out as a political journalist, combining my writing with activism. My disillusionment in 1964 and afterwards was enough to cure me of any further crusading. Present political convictions are an amalgam of anarchy, libertarianism, gut patriotism and anti-communism (Joe McCarthy was my original political hero) and the Machiavellian school of political skepticism found in Europe.

"Though I retain an intellectual interest in politics, I'd rather spend my time now looking into the history of the Old West, listening to Tom T. Hall or going to an old-time fiddler's convention, panning for gold or searching for buried treasure, and, above all, camping and traveling throughout the United States. My favorite haunts are the desert Southwest and the New England coast; paradise would be a ranch in West Texas or Arizona, and a summer house in Nantucket or Camden, Maine. I don't want much. . ."

* * *

FRANKE, Holly L(ambro) 1943-

PERSONAL: Born December 25, 1943, in Wellesley, Mass.; daughter of Pascal (a businessman) and Mary (Lapery) Lambro; married David Franke (an editor and writer), October 5, 1969; children: one. *Education:* Boston University, student, 1962-64. *Religion:* Albanian Orthodox. *Home:* 51 Remington Rd., Ridgefield, Conn. 06877.

CAREER: Congressional staff assistant in Washington, D.C., 1964-68; *London Daily Mirror,* New York, N.Y., assistant to United States bureau chief, 1968-69; writer, 1969—.

WRITINGS: (With husband, David Franke) *Safe Places,* Arlington House, 1972. Contributor to magazines and newspapers in the United States and France, including *American Home, Family Weekly,* and *International Herald Tribune*.

WORK IN PROGRESS: A gothic novel; research for several relocation and travel books.

SIDELIGHTS: The Frankes write: "*Safe Places* started out as an idea born of the crime headlines of the Sixties, and developed into an incredible four-month, twenty thousand-mile journey. . . ."

Newsweek writer Joseph Morgenstern said of *Safe Places:* "In their search for sweet wombs and snug harbors, the Frankes are onto an idea with a potentially large reactionary readership. But the search also leads to several points of convergence with middle-of-the-road emotions, liberal attitudes, and even radical left ideology. . . .Ultimately, the Frankes' twenty-thousand-mile journey of discovery and escape leads to the inescapable question of how much longer the earth itself can stay a Safe Place."

FRASCA, John (Anthony) 1916-

PERSONAL: Born May 25, 1916, in Lynn, Mass.; son of Michele Angelo (a contractor) and Maria (Gordan) Frasca; married Louise Cummings, December 20, 1948; children: Charlotte (Mrs. Eugene Krupa), Sydney (Mrs. Vincent Giovenco), Karen, Michele (Mrs. John Krentzman), John, Jr. *Education:* Holmes Junior College, student, 1936-38; Mississippi College, B.A., 1940. *Politics:* Democrat. *Religion:* Roman Catholic. *Home and office:* 4517 Vasconia St., Tampa, Fla. 33609.

CAREER: Boston Record-American, Boston, Mass., rewriter, 1948-53; *Philadelphia Daily News,* Philadelphia, Pa., rewriter, 1953-57; Pennsylvania Democratic Party, Harrisburg, publicity director, 1957-58; *Sons of Italy Times,* Philadelphia, Pa., editor, 1959-63; *Tampa Tribune,* Tampa, Fla., investigative writer and columnist, 1964-68; free-lance writer, 1968—. Press secretary to Pennsylvania Governor David L. Lawrence, 1958; publicity director for senatorial campaign of Supreme Court Justice Michael Musmano of Pennsylvania, 1964. *Military service:* U.S. Marine Corps, 1942-45; became first lieutenant. *Member:* American Newspaper Guild (chairman of *Philadelphia Daily News* unit, 1954-57).

AWARDS, HONORS: Award from Texas Associated Press, 1954, for best feature of the year; award from Philadelphia Press Association, 1956, for best writing of the year; Mental Health Bell Award from Pennsylvania Mental Health Association, 1956; second prize from Pennsylvania Newspaper Publishers Association, 1956, for "My Ten Days in a Mental Hospital"; first prize from Pennsylvania Newspaper Publishers Association, 1957, for "Children Who Walk Alone"; best feature award from Pennsylvania Newspaper Publishers Association, 1957, for "Inside Israel"; second prize for court coverage, from Pennsylvania Newspaper Publishers Association, 1957, for "Injustice for Our Kids"; Heywood Broun Memorial Award for Journalism from American Newspaper Guild, 1965, and Pulitzer Prize, 1966, for series on Robert Lamar Watson; Edgar Allan Poe Award from Mystery Writers of America, 1968, for *The Mulberry Tree*.

WRITINGS: The Mulberry Tree, Prentice-Hall, 1967; *Con Man or Saint?,* Droke House, 1969; *The Unstoppable Glenn Turner,* Marlborough House, 1970; *A Sharecropper's Best Short Stories,* Koscot, Inc., 1970.

WORK IN PROGRESS: From the Himalayas to Valley Forge (tentative title), a biography of millionaire entrepreneur Charles Woods.

SIDELIGHTS: Frasca's present concern is the "monstrous injustice perpetrated against people by prosecutors seeking headlines—with the result that the victims are found innocent and left broke." He proposes that the branch of government (Federal or state) responsible for indictments be required to reimburse people found innocent by the court or jury for the cost of their legal defense.

* * *

FRASER, Amy Stewart 1892-

PERSONAL: Born December 23, 1892, in Ballater, Scotland; daughter of James Anderson (a clergyman) and Agnes (Smart) Lowe; married Mark Stewart Fraser (a physician), July 24, 1914; children: James, Mark, Elspeth, Sheila (Mrs. Thomas Newlands), Jean (Mrs. Peter Forbes). *Education:* Attended Dunfermline College of Hygiene and Physical Education, 1911-13. *Politics:* Conservative. *Religion:*

Church of Scotland. *Home:* Hillcrest House, Harraby Grove, Carlisle, Cumbria CA1 2QN, England.

CAREER: Organizer for physical education, Perthshire Education Committee, Scotland, 1913-14; organized Woman's Voluntary Services, 1938-66; member of Carlisle City Council, 1937-46. *Member:* Electrical Association for Women (national chairman, 1961-66), Cumberland National Society for Prevention of Cruelty to Children (past president), National Council of Women (life president). *Awards, honors:* Member of Order of British Empire; award from Scottish Arts Council, 1974, for literary merit of *The Hills of Home.*

WRITINGS: The Hills of Home, Routledge & Kegan Paul, 1973.

WORK IN PROGRESS: Research on old Scottish children's games.

* * *

FRAZIER, George 1911-1974

June 10, 1911—June 13, 1974; American prose stylist, columnist, critic, and author of fiction and nonfiction. Obituaries: *New York Times,* June 15, 1974; *Washington Post,* June 15, 1974; *Newsweek,* June 24, 1974; *Time,* June 24, 1974. (*CA*-25-28).

* * *

FREDERIKSON, Edna 1904-

PERSONAL: Born January 23, 1904, in Everton, Ark.; daughter of David Walker (a hotel manager) and Britia Martia (McNair) Tutt; married Otto Frovin Frederikson (a professor of history), June 27, 1923. *Education:* Parsons College, B.A., 1925; University of Kansas, Ph.D., 1931; summer study at University of Iowa and University of Nebraska. *Politics:* Independent. *Religion:* Christian. *Home:* 130 Campbell St., Harrisonburg, Va. 22801.

CAREER: Kansas State College, Emporia, instructor in history, summer, 1931; Madison College, Harrisonburg, Va., 1932-41, began as instructor, became associate professor of English. *Member:* Phi Beta Kappa. *Awards, honors:* Bread Loaf Writers' Conference fellowship, 1940.

WRITINGS: Three Parts Earth (novel), Threshold, 1972. Also author of a biography, "John P. St. John, the Father of Constitutional Prohibition." Contributor to *Dictionary of American Biography.* Contributor of poems and short stories to little literary magazines.

WORK IN PROGRESS: Two novels and a collection of short stories.

SIDELIGHTS: Since her husband's retirement in 1957, the Frederiksons have made fourteen trips to Europe and four lengthy trips around the world, with stays in Iceland, Greenland, Russia, Siberia, and Outer Mongolia. They have visited all parts of North and South America and of Africa.

* * *

FREDRICKSON, Olive A(lta) 1901-

PERSONAL: Born July 12, 1901, in Withee, Wis.; daughter of Archie and Clara (Clark) Goodwin; married Walter Reamer, October 19, 1920 (died May, 1928); married John Fredrickson, November 22, 1941; children: (first marriage) Olive Eva Reamer Allen, Vala Beulah, Louis Elmer. *Education:* Self-educated. *Religion:* United Church of Christ. *Home and office address:* Box 123, Okanagan Falls, British Columbia, Canada.

CAREER: Housewife, farmer, and ranch-hand, 1919-60; free-lance writer, 1960—.

WRITINGS: (With Ben East) *The Silence of the North,* Crown, 1972.

SIDELIGHTS: Mrs. Fredrickson, who dislikes big cities, crowds, and noisy places, likes animals and flowers of the wild and tame variety, and to travel to far-away places, locating on quiet rivers and lakes. She says: "I also like people, good [neighbors]. Get along well with people. And I am contented with whatever I have, satisfied to face the world with what it has to give me. I thank God for everything."

* * *

FREEDMAN, Alfred M(ordecai) 1917-

PERSONAL: Born January 7, 1917, in Albany, N.Y.; son of Jacob A. and Pauline (Hoffman) Freedman; married Marcia Kohl (a labor economist), March 24, 1943; children: Paul, Daniel. *Education:* Cornell University, A.B., 1937; University of Minnesota, M.B., 1941, M.D., 1942; William Alanson White Institute for Psychoanalysis, postdoctoral study, 1955. *Office:* Department of Psychiatry, New York Medical College, Flower and Fifth Avenue Hospitals, Fifth Avenue and 106th St., New York, N.Y. 10029.

CAREER: Harlem Hospital, New York, N.Y., intern, 1941-42; Army Chemical Center, Edgewood, Md., medical psychologist, 1947-48; Bellevue Hospital, New York, N.Y., resident in psychiatry, 1948-50; New York University, New York, N.Y., clinical instructor in psychiatry, 1950-55; State University of New York, Downstate Medical Center, Brooklyn, assistant professor, 1955-57, associate professor of psychiatry, 1957-60; director of pediatric psychiatry, 1955-60; New York Medical College, New York, N.Y., professor of psychiatry and chairman of department, 1960—. Assistant pediatrician at Babies' Hospital of Presbyterian Hospital, 1953-60; senior psychiatrist in child psychiatry service of Bellevue Hospital, 1953-54; director of psychiatry at Flower and Fifth Avenue Hospitals, at Metropolitan Hospital, and at Bird S. Coler Hospital, all 1960—; chairman of dean's committee at Veterans Hospital, Montrose, N.Y., 1970—; chairman of department of psychiatry at Grasslands Hospital, 1972—; director of Metropolitan Comprehensive Community Mental Health Center, 1966-73. Diplomate in psychiatry of American Board of Psychiatry and Neurology, 1952, assistant and associate examiner, 1963—; member of New York State Board of Psychiatric Examiners, 1970—; commissioner of Temporary New York State Commission to Evaluate Drug Laws, 1970-73. Member of board of trustees and treasurer of Anthropos Academy, 1968-72. *Military service:* U.S. Army, Medical Corps, 1942-46; became major.

MEMBER: International Association for Social Psychiatry (council member of American Division, 1971—), International Association for Child Psychiatry, Collegium Internationale Neuro-Psychopharmacologicum, American Psychiatric Association (fellow; president, 1973-74), American Academy of Child Psychiatry, American College of Neuropsychopharmacology (charter fellow; president, 1972-73), American Psychopathological Association (president, 1971-72), American Orthopsychiatric Association (fellow; member of board of directors, 1962-64), American Academy of Psychoanalysis, American Association of

Chairmen of Departments of Psychiatry, American Medical Association, American Association for the Advancement of Science (fellow), American Public Health Association (fellow; chairman of subcommittee on narcotic addiction, 1961), American Arbitration Association (member of panel of arbitrators, 1973—), Turkish College of Neuropsychopharmacology (honorary member), Society for Biological Psychiatry, Society for Medical Psychoanalysts, Society for the Study of Addiction to Alcohol and Other Drugs (Great Britain), Psychiatric Research Society, New York Academy of Medicine (fellow), New York Psychiatric Society, New York Society for Clinical Psychiatry (president, 1967-68), Manhattan Society for Mental Health (member of advisory board, 1962-65), Sigma Xi. *Awards, honors:* Henry Wisner Miller Award from Manhattan Society for Mental Health, 1964; Samuel W. Hamilton Award from American Psychopathological Association, 1972.

WRITINGS: (With H. I. Kaplan) *Comprehensive Textbook of Psychiatry,* Williams & Wilkins, 1967; (with R. E. Brotman) *Perspectives on Marijuana Research,* Center for Studies in Substance Use, 1968; (editor with J. Zubin) *The Psychopathology of Adolescence,* Grune, 1970; (with Kaplan) *Diagnosing Mental Illness: Evaluation in Psychiatry and Psychology,* Atheneum, 1971; (editor with Kaplan) *Interpreting Personality: A Survey of Twentieth Century Views,* Atheneum, 1972; (editor with Kaplan) *Treating Mental Illness: Aspects of Modern Therapy,* Atheneum, 1972; (editor with Kaplan) *Human Behavior: Biological, Psychological, and Sociological,* Atheneum, 1972; (editor with Kaplan) *The Child: His Psychological and Cultural Development,* Atheneum, Volume I, *Normal Development and Psychological Assessment,* 1972, Volume II, *The Major Psychological Disorders and Their Treatment,* 1972; (with Kaplan and B. J. Sadock) *Modern Synopsis of Comprehensive Textbook of Psychiatry,* Williams & Wilkins, 1972; (editor with J. O. Cole and A. Friedhoff) *Psychopathology and Psychopharmacology,* Johns Hopkins Press, 1973; (editor with S. Fisher, and contributor) *Opiate Addiction: Origins and Treatment,* V. H. Winston, 1973.

Contributor: A. S. Marrazzi and M. H. Aprison, editors, *Festschrift to H. E. Himwich,* Galesburg State Research Hospital Press, 1960; N. W. Bell and E. F. Vogel, editors, *The Family,* Free Press, 1960; *Behavioral Approaches to Accident Research,* Association for Aid to Crippled Children, 1961; Daniel Wilner and G. G. Kassebaum, editors, *Narcotics,* McGraw, 1965; M. R. Kaufman, editor, *The Psychiatric Unit in a General Hospital,* International Universities Press, 1965; J. H. Merin, editor, *The Etiology of the Neuroses,* Science & Behavior Books, 1966; Charles Carter, editor, *Medical Aspects of Mental Retardation,* C. C Thomas, 1965; J. Zubin and F. A. Freyhan, editors, *Social Psychiatry,* Grune, 1968; R. V. Phillipson, editor, *Modern Trends in Drug Dependence and Alcoholism,* Butterworths, Bell & Bain, 1970; H. W. Kosterlitz, H. Q. J. Collier, and J. E. Villarreal, editors, *Agonist and Antagonist Actions of Narcotic Analgesic Drugs,* Macmillan, 1973.

Contributor of more than one hundred articles to journals. Member of editorial board of *Journal of American Orthopsychiatric Association,* 1964-71, *Community Mental Health Journal,* 1970, *Comprehensive Psychiatry,* 1971, and *Pharmakopsychiatrie/Neuropsychopharmacologie,* 1973—.

FREELING, Nicolas 1927- (F. R. E. Nicolas)

PERSONAL: Born March 3, 1927, in London, England; married Cornelia Termes, 1954; children: four sons, one daughter. *Education:* Attended primary and secondary schools in England, Ireland, and France, also University of Dublin. *Politics:* "Visionary." *Religion:* Roman Catholic. *Home:* Grandfontaine, 67130 Schirmeck, Bas Rhin, France. *Agent:* John Cushman Associates, Inc., 25 West 43rd St., New York, N.Y. 10036.

CAREER: Professional cook in hotels and restaurants throughout Europe, 1948-60; author and novelist, 1960—. *Military service:* Royal Air Force, 1945-47. *Member:* Authors Guild. *Awards, honors:* Crime Writers Award, 1963, and Grand Prix de Roman Policier, 1965, for *Gun Before Butter;* Mystery Writers of America Edgar Allen Poe Award, 1966, for *King of the Rainy Country.*

WRITINGS—Novels: *Love in Amsterdam,* Gollancz, 1961, Harper, 1962; *Because of the Cats,* Gollancz, 1963, Harper, 1964; *Question of Loyalty,* Harper, 1963 (published in England as *Gun Before Butter,* Gollancz, 1963); (under pseudonym F. R. E. Nicolas) *Valparaiso,* Gollancz, 1964, published under name Nicolas Freeling, Harper, 1965; *Double Barrel,* Gollancz, 1964, Harper, 1965; *Criminal Conversation,* Gollancz, 1965, Harper, 1966; *The King of the Rainy Country,* Harper, 1966; *The Dresden Green,* Gollancz, 1966, Harper, 1967; *Strike Out Where Not Applicable,* Harper, 1967; *This Is the Castle,* Harper, 1968; *The Freeling Omnibus: Comprising Love in Amsterdam, Because of the Cats, Gun Before Butter,* Gollancz, 1968; *Tsing-Boum,* Harper, 1969 (published in England as *Tsing-Boum: A Novel,* Hamish Hamilton, 1969); *The Lovely Ladies,* Harper, 1971 (published in England as *Over the High Side,* Hamish Hamilton, 1971); *Aupres de ma Blonde,* Harper, 1972 (published in England as *A Long Silence,* Hamish Hamilton, 1972); *The Second Freeling Omnibus: Comprising Double Barrel, The King of the Rainy Country, The Dresden Green,* Gollancz, 1972; *A Dressing of Diamond,* Harper, 1974.

Nonfiction: *The Kitchen: A Delicious Account of the Author's Years as a Grand Hotel Cook,* Harper, 1970 (published in England as *Kitchen Book,* Hamish Hamilton, 1970); *Cook Book,* Hamish Hamilton, 1972.

WORK IN PROGRESS: Another novel; a book to examine the relationship between the citizen and the different police forces designed to protect him, in the past, present, and future, in Europe and America; a critical work on Kipling; an autobiography.

SIDELIGHTS: Freeling told *CA:* "The crime novel is a plastic flower, an excrescence of the entertainment industry. That this must be so has been obstinately if not always ably held by most critics. I never have believed this and still don't. But it is peculiarly vulnerable to artificial convention, from the aristocrat amateur detective of the thirties to the naked raped girl (or boy) of the seventies. To attempt to match the originality of Stendhal, Dickens, Malraux or Chandler would be ridiculous, and anything less talented is a resounding crash between stools, which I have a gift for. When one looks at the admirable work done inside the convention by a writer as fine as Rex Stout it appears absurd to be dissatisfied. I am: and intend to go on being so.

"The first responsibility of the writer, perhaps, is to be a devoted and accurate witness to the thoughts and doings of his times. If, though, he is to be in any real sense creative he must make discoveries. It is sometimes valid to recall Ray Chandler's embittered remark that 'critics never discover anything: they explain it after it has become fashionable.' A writer has to do better than stay abreast of his times: he must run a little in front of them.

"Since my vocation and profession is to write novels, I have refused all offers to write screenplays, adaptations, dialogue, etc. The reason for this is that I like to be sole author, and sole judge, of what I write. Disobeying this rule may make one rich, but will certainly make one miserable."

Many of Freeling's novels have been made into films or television plays.

AVOCATIONAL INTERESTS: Planting trees.

* * *

FREIDES, Thelma K(atz) 1930-

PERSONAL: Surname is pronounced Fraydes; born February 26, 1930, in New York, N.Y.; daughter of Aaron (a dentist) and Anna (Jacobson) Katz; married David Freides (a psychologist), December 23, 1951. *Education:* Hunter College (now Hunter College of the City University of New York), B.A., 1952; Yale University, M.A., 1954; University of Michigan, M.A., 1960. *Home:* 889 Springdale Rd. N.E., Atlanta, Ga. 30306. *Office:* School of Library Science, Atlanta University, Atlanta, Ga. 30314.

CAREER: Wayne State University, Detroit, Mich., social sciences reference librarian, 1960-66; Emory University, Atlanta, Ga., government documents librarian, 1966-67; Atlanta University, School of Library Service, Atlanta, Ga., associate professor of library science, 1967—. *Member:* American Library Association, Association of American Library Schools, Special Libraries Association, American Association of University Professors.

WRITINGS: Literature and Bibliography of the Social Sciences, Melville, 1973. Contributor to *Library Journal* and *RQ*. Editor of "The Exchange" column of *RQ,* 1966-70.

WORK IN PROGRESS: Researching a bibliography of information resources relating to the public accountability of institutions.

* * *

FREUND, Gisele 1912-

PERSONAL: Born December 19, 1912, in Berlin, Germany; daughter of French citizens, Jules (an art collector) and Claire Freund; divorced. *Education:* Sorbonne, University of Paris, Docteur de l'Universite de Paris, 1936. *Home:* 12 rue Lalande, Paris, France. *Agent:* Marie Rodell, 141 East 55th St., New York, N.Y. 10022.

CAREER: Reporter-photographer for French and international newspapers and magazines, and portraitist. Photographs, particularly her collection of color portraits of internationally-known writers and artists, have been exhibited in European museums and galleries. *Member:* Association nationale des journalistes reporters photographes. *Awards, honors:* Medals and other awards in photographic exhibitions.

WRITINGS: La Photographie en France au 19e siecle, Maison des Amis des Livres, 1936; *Mexican Precolombian Art,* Ides & Calendes, 1954; (with Verna B. Carleton, author of text) *James Joyce in Paris: His Final Years* (preface by Simone de Beauvoir), Harcourt, 1966; *Le Monde et ma Camera,* Denoel, 1970, translation by June Guicharnaud published as *The World in My Camera,* Dial, 1973; *Photographie et societe,* Editions du Seuil, 1974. "Au Pays des visages," a television film directed by Frederic Rossif, was based on her photographs.

WORK IN PROGRESS: A detective story.

SIDELIGHTS: Gisele Freund has traveled all over the world on photographic assignments, including a special expedition to Tierra del Fuego.

* * *

FREUNDLICH, August L. 1924-

PERSONAL: Surname is pronounced *Froind*-lick; born May 9, 1924, in Frankfurt, Germany; son of Julius (a sales representative) and Erma (Keller) Freundlich; married Lillian Thomson, April 25, 1948; children: Mary, Jeffrey Paul, Heidi, Christopher Thomson. *Education:* Antioch College, B.A., 1949; Columbia University, M.A., 1950; New York University, Ph.D., 1960. *Home address:* Duguid Rd., Manlius, N.Y. 13104. *Office:* Lowe Art Center, Syracuse, N.Y. 13210.

CAREER: Antioch Laboratory School, Yellow Springs, Ohio, art education specialist, 1949-50; University of Arkansas, Fayetteville, instructor in art education, 1950-53; State University of New York College at New Paltz, visiting professor of art education, 1953-54; Eastern Michigan University, Ypsilanti, head of art department, 1954-58; George Peabody College for Teachers, Nashville, Tenn., chairman of Arts Division, 1958-64; University of Miami, Coral Gables, Fla., chairman of art department, 1964—, director of Joe and Emily Lowe Art Gallery, 1964—. Member of board of directors of Tennessee Fine Arts Center, 1962-64, Southeastern Museums Conference, 1967-69, and Institute to Study Art in Education; member of board of trustees of Eversen Museum. Work has been exhibited in galleries in New York, Nashville, and Woodstock, and in competitions in several states, including Ohio, Georgia, Kentucky, Michigan, New Jersey, and New Mexico. Judge of art competitions and lecturer on art and museum topics. *Military service:* U.S. Marine Corps.

MEMBER: International Council of Fine Arts Deans, American Association of Museums, College Art Association, National Art Education Association, National Council of Arts Administrators, Committee on Art Education, Committee to Rescue Italian Art (chairman of South Florida Division, 1966—), Western Arts Association (president, 1958-60; member of council, 1954-64), Southeastern Art Museum Directors, Southeastern Museums Association, Southeastern Art Association, Florida Art Museum Directors, Tennessee Museum Directors, New York State Art Education Association, New York State Association of Museums.

WRITINGS: William Gropper: Retrospective (monograph), Ritchie, 1968; *Frank Kleinholz: The Outsider,* University of Miami Press, 1969; *Karl Schrag: Graphic Works* (monograph), Syracuse University Press, 1971; (editor and translator) *Rembrandt: The Self Portrait,* University of Miami Press, 1971; *Richard Florsheim* (monograph), A. S. Barnes, 1974.

Author of exhibition catalogs and other publications of Lowe Art Center. Contributor to art journals, including *Museum News, National Art Education Association Journal, Motive, Arts, Western Arts Bulletin,* and *Christian Home.*

WORK IN PROGRESS: German Expressionist Art; Art of the Depression Years.

* * *

FRIEDRICHS, Robert W(inslow) 1923-

PERSONAL: Born February 16, 1923, in Bath, Maine; son of Hans William (a corporation executive) and Gladys (Donnelly) Friedrichs; married Pauline E. Carlson (a teacher), June 16, 1951; children: Robin, Paul, Carl. *Education:* Antioch College, student, 1941-43; Oberlin College, B.A., 1946; University of Wisconsin, M.A., 1952, Ph.D., 1957; also studied at Oxford University, 1964, Princeton University, 1970, Cambridge University, 1970, and London School of Economics and Political Science, 1971. *Politics:* "Typically Democratic." *Religion:* Protestant. *Home:* 33 Southworth St., Williamstown, Mass. 01267. *Office:* Department of Sociology, Room 320, Stetson Library, Williams College, Williamstown, Mass. 01267.

CAREER: Ming Hsien Middle School and College, Sanyuan, Shensi, and Chengtu, China, instructor in sociology, 1946-48; University of Wisconsin, Madison, laboratory instructor in statistics, 1952-53; Columbia University, New York, N.Y., instructor in sociology, 1953-56; Elmira College, Elmira, N.Y., assistant professor of sociology, 1954-57, chairman of department, 1954-57; Drew University, Madison, N.J., associate professor, 1957-65, professor of sociology, 1965-71, chairman of department, 1957-71; Williams College, Williamstown, Mass., professor of sociology and chairman of department, 1971—. Visiting professor at Brooklyn College of the City University of New York, 1962; H. Paul Douglass Lecturer for Religious Research Association, 1973. Consultant to organizations, and to Free Press and Random House.

MEMBER: International Sociological Association, Cherion: The International Society for the History of Behavioral and Social Sciences, American Sociological Association, American Association of University Professors (president of Drew University chapter, 1968-69; member of executive committee of New Jersey Conference, 1969-70), American Association for the Advancement of Science, Society for the Psychological Study of Social Issues, Society for the Scientific Study of Religion, Religious Research Association, Unified Board for Christian Higher Education in Asia (trustee), American Civil Liberties Union (New Jersey section), National Association for the Advancement of Colored People, Eastern Sociological Association, Massachusetts Sociological Association, Urban League. *Awards, honors:* Lilly postdoctoral fellow in Tokyo and at Oxford University, 1963-64; postdoctoral fellowship from Society for Religion in Higher Education, 1969—; National Science Foundation faculty fellowship in sociology of science, 1970-71; Sorokin Award from American Sociological Association, 1971.

WRITINGS: (Contributor) Jack Douglas, editor, *The Impact of the Social Sciences,* Appleton, 1970; *A Sociology of Sociology,* Free Press, 1970; (contributor) Edmund W. Gordon and Lamar P. Miller, editors, *Handbook of Research on Equality of Educational Opportunity,* AMS Press, 1973. Contributor of more than twenty articles and reviews to social science journals, including *Journal of Higher Education, American Sociologist, Journal of Negro Education, Education and Urban Society, Sociological Analysis,* and *Journal of Value Inquiry.* Member of editorial board of *American Sociological Review, American Journal of Sociology, Social Forces, Sociological Focus, Journal for the Scientific Study of Religion, Review of Religious Research.*

WORK IN PROGRESS: A book assessing the potential relationship between sociology and philosophical anthropology.

SIDELIGHTS: Friedrichs has traveled or studied in Japan, Southeast Asia, India, Europe, and the Middle East.

* * *

FROMM, Herbert 1905-

PERSONAL: Born February 23, 1905, in Kitzingen, Germany; son of Max (a merchant) and Mathilde (Maier) Fromm; married Leni Steinberg, January 22, 1942. *Education:* Attended Academy of Music, Munich, Germany, 1924-30. *Religion:* Jewish. *Home:* 94 Addington Rd., Brookline, Mass. 02146.

CAREER: Opera conductor in Wuerzburg, Germany, 1931-33; Temple Beth Zion, Buffalo, N.Y., music director and organist, 1937-41; Temple Israel, Boston, Mass., music director and organist, 1941-72, music director and organist emeritus, 1972—; composer. *Member:* American Guild of Organists. *Awards, honors:* D.H.L., Lesley College, 1966; Ernest Bloch Award for cantata, "Song of Miriam."

WRITINGS: The Key of See, Plowshare Press, 1967; (translator with Robert Lilienfeld from the German) Hans Kayser, *Akroasis: Theory of World Harmonics,* Plowshare Press, 1970. Contributor of articles and essays to *American Choral Review, Liturgical Music Society,* and *Cantors Voice.*

WORK IN PROGRESS: Seven Pockets (tentative title).

* * *

FRUTON, Joseph S(tewart) 1912-

PERSONAL: Born May 14, 1912, in Czestochowa, Poland; naturalized U.S. citizen, 1929; son of Charles (in shipping business) and Ella (a French teacher; maiden name, Eisenstadt) Fruton; married Sofia Simmonds (a biochemist), January 29, 1936. *Education:* Columbia University, B.A. (with honors), 1931, Ph.D., 1934. *Home:* 123 York St., New Haven, Conn. 06511. *Office:* Department of Biochemistry, 350 Kline Biology Tower, Yale University, New Haven, Conn. 06520.

CAREER: Rockefeller Institute for Medical Research, New York, N.Y., associate in chemistry, 1934-45; Yale University, New Haven, Conn., associate professor of physiological chemistry, 1945-50, professor of biochemistry, 1950-57, Eugene Higgins Professor of Biochemistry, 1957—, chairman of department, 1951-67, director of Division of Science, 1959-62. Harvey Lecturer, New York Academy of Medicine, 1955; Dakin Lecturer, Adelphi College, 1962; visiting professor at Rockefeller University, 1968-69; chairman or member of committees of National Research Council, 1945-64; member of International Commission on Biochemical Nomenclature, 1964-69. Consultant to American Cyanamid Co., 1951-55, and Anna Fuller Fund, 1952-72.

MEMBER: American Philosophical Society (member of council, 1972-74), National Academy of Sciences, American Academy of Arts and Sciences, American Society of Biological Chemists (member of council, 1959-62), History of Science Society (member of council, 1951-54). *Awards, honors:* Eli Lilly Award in Biological Chemistry, from American Chemical Society, 1944; M.A. from Yale University, 1950; Pfizer Award from History of Science Society, 1973, for *Molecules and Life*.

WRITINGS: (With wife, Sofia Simmonds) *General Biochemistry,* Wiley, 1953, 2nd edition, 1958; *Molecules and Life: Historical Essays on the Interplay of Chemistry and Biology,* Wiley, 1972; *Selected Bibliography of Biographical Data for the History of Biochemistry Since 1800,* Library of the American Philosophical Society, 1974. Contributor of about two hundred articles to scientific journals, including *Journal of Biological Chemistry, Biochemistry, Science, Journal of the American Chemical Society, Scientific American,* and *Proceedings of the National Academy of Sciences.* Member of editorial board of *Journal of Biological Chemistry,* 1948-58, and *Biochemistry,* 1962-72.

WORK IN PROGRESS: The Skeptical Biochemist (tentative title), essays on the history and philosophy of modern biology and chemistry, with special reference to the social and institutional factors in their development; biochemical research on enzymes.

SIDELIGHTS: Fruton's books have been published in Japanese, Spanish, Polish, and Serbo-Croatian.

* * *

FRYE, Ellen 1940-

PERSONAL: Born January 30, 1940, in Cincinnati, Ohio; daughter of John and Harriet (Bennitt) Frye; married Ken Eisler (a printer), 1968. *Education:* Columbia University, B.A., 1962. *Home:* 3400 West Second Ave., Vancouver 8, British Columbia, Canada.

CAREER: Community music teacher. Director of Community Service Program of Community Music School, Vancouver, British Columbia, 1970—; music teacher at Vancouver Indian Centre, Vancouver, 1971—; adult education teacher in New Westminster, British Columbia, 1973—.

WRITINGS: (Compiler and translator) *The Marble Threshing Floor: A Collection of Greek Folksongs,* University of Texas Press, 1973. Contributor to *Western Folklore, Satire Newsletter, Juilliard Repertory Project,* and *Music Educators Journal.*

WORK IN PROGRESS: Karagiozis in Athens, a translation of two Greek shadow plays with an introduction, for American Folklore Society Memoir Series, University of Texas Press.

* * *

FRYE, John 1910-

PERSONAL: Born September 27, 1910, in Chicago, Ill.; son of Harry C. and Lida G. (Frow) Frye; married Harriet Bennitt (an artist), August 18, 1934; children: Keith, Ann (Mrs. James W. Meyer), Ellen (Mrs. Kenneth Eisler). *Education:* Antioch College, B.A., 1934. *Address:* Route 1 Box 153, Kilmarnock, Va. 22482.

CAREER: Associated Press, reporter and editor in Columbus and Cincinnati, Ohio, 1934-48; Scripps-Howard, wire chief in Columbus, Ohio, 1949-54; advertising and free-lance public relations in Columbus, and Dayton, Ohio, 1955-62; free-lance newspaper and magazine writer in Kilmarnock, Va., 1962—.

WRITINGS: The Search for the Santa Maria, Dodd, 1973. Associate editor of *National Fisherman,* 1970—.

WORK IN PROGRESS: A history of Chesapeake Bay menhaden fishery and a history of the Conway fleet of Chesapeake Bay schooners; further research in Spanish-Portuguese discovery and colonization.

SIDELIGHTS: Frye speaks Spanish and limited French and German. He hopes to travel to Spain for further historical research on the discovery era.

* * *

FULCO, William J(ames) 1936-

PERSONAL: Born February 24, 1936, in Los Angeles, Calif.; son of Herman John (a physician) and Clelia M. (DeFeo) Fulco. *Education:* Santa Clara University, student, 1954-57, S.T.M. and S.T.L., both 1967; Gonzaga University, A.B., 1959, M.A., 1971; Yale University, Ph.D., 1971; also attended University of California, Berkeley, University of Chicago, University of Innsbruck, and Pontifical Biblical Institute. *Home and office:* 1735 LeRoy Ave., Berkeley, Calif. 94709.

CAREER: Ordained Roman Catholic priest of Society of Jesus (Jesuits; S.J.), 1966; teacher of Attic and Homeric Greek, Latin, and German in preparatory school in San Jose, Calif., 1960-63; University of Innsbruck, Innsbruck, Austria, teacher of Hebrew, 1967-68; Yale University, New Haven, Conn., instructor in Hebrew, Ugaritic, and Aramaic dialects, 1969-70; Jesuit School of Theology, Berkeley, Calif., assistant professor of Biblical studies and curator of numismatic collection, 1972—. Assistant professor at Graduate Theological Union (Berkeley), 1972—; visiting assistant professor at University of California, Berkeley, 1972—; visiting professor in Bombay, summer, 1974, and at Ecole Biblique et Archeologique (Jerusalem), 1974-75.

MEMBER: American Oriental Society, Middle East Studies Association of North America, Catholic Biblical Association, Society for Biblical Literature, American Numismatic Society, American Numismatic Association, Society for Ancient Numismatics, Numismatic Society of India. *Awards, honors:* Ph.L., Gonzaga University, 1960.

WRITINGS: Maranatha: Reflections on the Mystical Theology of John the Evangelist, Paulist-Newman, 1973. Contributor of articles and reviews to specialized journals, including *Journal of the Society for Ancient Numismatics, Bible Today, Modern Schoolman,* and *Theology.*

WORK IN PROGRESS: A book on the theology of death; three monographs on comparative Semitic phonology; research on the Canaanite god Reshep.

SIDELIGHTS: Fulco has studied and done research in most of Europe, the Soviet Union, and the Near East, and has visited Japan, Hong Kong, and Thailand.

* * *

FULDHEIM, Dorothy (Snell) 1893-

PERSONAL: Born in 1893, in Passaic, N.J.; daughter of Herman and Bertha (Wishner) Snell; children: Dorothy Fuldheim Urman. *Education:* Milwaukee Normal College, teaching degree, 1912. *Home:* 13900 Shaker Blvd., Cleveland Heights, Ohio 44118. Office: *WEWS-TV 5, 3001 Euclid Ave., Cleveland, Ohio 44115.*

CAREER: WEWS-TV, Cleveland, Ohio, news analyst, 1946—. Member of board of directors, Crippled and Disabled Children, 1948-58, Cleveland Women's Symphony, 1948—. *Member:* Theta Sigma Phi.

WRITINGS: I Laughed, I Loved, I Cried: A News Analyst's Love Affair with the World (autobiography), World

Publishing, 1966; *Where Were the Arabs?,* World Publishing, 1967; *A Thousand Friends,* Doubleday, 1974.

* * *

FUNK, Thompson 1911-
(Tom Funk)

PERSONAL: Born July 18, 1911, in Brooklyn, N.Y.; son of Merton Layton (a physician) and Marion Anna (Thompson) Funk; married Edna Eicke (an artist), December 23, 1943; children: Susan Deborah (Mrs. Robert Colburn), Victoria Greenwood, Peter. *Education:* Amherst College, B.A., 1933; studied at Art Students' League, New York, 1933-34, and Beaux-Arts Institute of Design, New York, 1934-35. *Religion:* Protestant. *Home and studio:* 7 Lincoln St., Westport, Conn. 06880. *Agent:* (Children's book art) Helen Wohlberg, Inc., 331 East 50th St., New York, N.Y. 10022.

CAREER: Lord & Taylor, New York, N.Y., display decorator, 1935-36; display designer, New York, N.Y., 1937-40; free-lance artist and illustrator, 1940—.

WRITINGS: (Under name Tom Funk; self-illustrated) *I Read Signs* (juvenile), Holiday House, 1962.

Illustrator under name Tom Funk—Books for children: *Spaniel in the Lion's Den,* Hyperion Press, 1950; Rachel Learnard, *Mrs. Roo and the Bunnies* (verse), Houghton, 1953; Ruth Crawford Seeger, *Let's Build a Railroad,* Aladdin Books, 1954; Leslie Waller, *Weather,* Holt, 1959; Margaret C. Farquhar, *Lights,* Holt, 1960; Harry Milgrom, *Adventures with a String,* Dutton, 1965; *New Math,* Birk, 1965; Edith Battles, *The Terrible Trick or Treat* (Junior Literary Guild selection), Addison-Wesley, 1970; Charlotte Herman, *String Bean,* O'Hara, 1972; Battles, *The Terrible Terrier* (Junior Literary Guild selection), Addison-Wesley, 1972; Milgrom, *Adventures with a Cardboard Tube* (Junior Literary Guild selection), Dutton, 1973; Battles, *Eddie Couldn't Find the Elephants,* Whitman, 1974.

Illustrator—Books for young people and adults: Mathurin M. Dondo, L. B. Johnson, and Morris Brenman, *French for the Modern World,* Harcourt, 1951; A. C. Moore, *How to Clean Everything,* Simon & Schuster, 1957; Pauline Arnold and Percival White, *Food: America's Biggest Business,* Holiday House, 1959; Arnold and White, *Homes: America's Building Business,* Holiday House, 1960; Hamilton Basso, *Quota of Seaweed,* Doubleday, 1960; Hoff, *Decisions about Alcohol,* Seabury Press, 1961; Arnold and White, *Money,* Holiday House, 1962; Arthur S. Gregor, *Short History of Science,* Macmillan, 1963; Gregor, *Short History of the Universe,* Macmillan, 1964; Roma Gans, *Fact and Fiction about Phonics,* Bobbs-Merrill, 1964; *The Presidency in Conflict,* Collier, 1965; Andries de Groot, *Feasts for All Seasons,* Knopf, 1966; Craig Claiborne, *Craig Claiborne's Kitchen Primer,* Knopf, 1969; Julia Dannenbaum, *Creative Cooking School,* McCall Publishing, 1971; Floss Dworkin and Stan Dworkin, *Bake Your Own Bread and Be Healthier,* Holt, 1972; Kenneth Lo, *Chinese Vegetarian Cookbook,* Pantheon, 1974.

Designer of primary level activity kits with mural posters, cut-outs, and textbooks, published by Sadlier; designer of "Playing in the Playstreet," a Headstart kit with mural posters, die-cuts, and books; also designer of other textbooks. Contributor of illustrations to *New Yorker, Harper's, Fortune, Life, Gourmet, House & Garden, Woman's Day, Cue* and other magazines. Member of staff, *Dramatists Guild Quarterly.*

SIDELIGHTS: Funk's grandfather and great-uncle founded Funk & Wagnalls Co. and an uncle, Charles E. Funk, was head lexicographer. Tom Funk has illustrated three books on word derivations written by his uncle. *Avocational interests:* Photography, playing guitar and banjo ("used to be better"), running and swimming ("practically every day"), yoga, folk dancing.

* * *

FUNK, Tom
See FUNK, Thompson

* * *

FUNKE, Lewis 1912-

PERSONAL: Born January 25, 1912, in New York, N.Y.; son of Joseph (in construction) and Rose (Keimowitz) Funke; married Blanche Bier (a teacher), July 5, 1938; children: Phyllis, Michael. *Education:* New York University, A.B., 1932. *Home:* 61 Alta Dr., Mt. Vernon, N.Y. 10552. *Agent:* Curtis Brown, Ltd., 60 East 56th St., New York, N.Y. 10022.

CAREER: New York Times, New York, N.Y., free-lance sportswriter, 1928-32, staff sportswriter, 1932-44, member of general news and movie staff, 1944, drama editor, 1945-73; Queens College of the City University of New York, lecturer, 1973—. Visiting professor, Florida State University, 1974—.

WRITINGS: (Editor with John E. Booth) *Actors Talk about Acting: Fourteen Interviews with Stars of the Theatre,* Random House, 1961 (published in England as *Actors Talk about Acting: Nine Interviews with Stars of the Theatre,* Thames & Hudson, 1962); (with Max Gordon) *Max Gordon Presents,* Geis, 1963; (with Helen Hayes) *A Gift of Joy,* M. Evans, 1965; *The Curtain Rises: The Story of Ossie Davis* (juvenile), Grosset, 1971; *Playwrights Talk about Playwriting,* Dramatic Publishing, 1974.

WORK IN PROGRESS: An oral history of the Yiddish theater, for Florida State University; a sequel to *Actors Talk about Acting,* as sole editor.

SIDELIGHTS: Funke's writing assignments abroad have included England, France, Israel, Yugoslavia, Germany, Italy, and elsewhere. *Avocational interests:* Golf, gardening.

* * *

GAATHON, A(ryeh) L(udwig) 1898-
(Ludwig Gruenbaum)

PERSONAL: Original surname was Gruenbaum; Hebrew surname, adopted in 1951, is pronounced Ga-a-*thon;* variant spelling of first name is Arie; born December 24, 1898, in Eisenach, Germany; son of Arnold (a textile merchant) and Philippine (Stettauer) Gruenbaum; married Tamar Jungerman, October 18, 1938; children: Ariel (son). *Education:* University of Berlin, Diplom-Volkswirt (with distinction), 1931, Dr.rer.pol. (summa cum laude), 1934. *Religion:* Jewish. *Home:* 45 Hehalutz St., Jerusalem 96222, Israel. *Office:* Bank of Israel, P.O.B. 780, Jerusalem, Israel.

CAREER: Jewish Agency for Palestine, Jerusalem, Palestine, research economist in Labor Department and Economic Research Institute, 1935-48; Prime Minister's Office, Jerusalem, Israel, head of economic research unit, 1948-55; Bank of Israel, Jerusalem, chief economist, 1955-75. Member of board, Maurice Falk Institute for Economic

Research in Israel, 1964-74. *Military service:* German Army, 1916-20 (prisoner of war in Egypt, 1918-20). *Member:* International Association for Research in Income and Wealth (charter member). *Awards, honors:* Bar-Eli Prize of Bank Hapoalim, 1961, for *Capital Stock, Employment and Output in Israel;* Dr.honoris causa, Hebrew University of Jerusalem, 1972; Peretz Naphtali Prize of Tel Aviv Municipality, 1973.

WRITINGS—Under name Ludwig Gruenbaum: *Arbeitsbeschaffung und Siedlung* (doctoral thesis), Emil Ebering, 1934; *National Income and Outlay in Palestine, 1936,* Economic Research Institute, Jewish Agency for Palestine, 1941; *Outlines of a Development Plan for Jewish Palestine,* Economic Research Institute, Jewish Agency for Palestine, 1946; *Four Year Development Plan of Israel 1950-1953: Summary and Conclusions* (published in Hebrew and English), Prime Minister's Office (Jerusalem), 1951; *Survey of Israel's Economy, 1951,* Central Bureau of Statistics (Jerusalem), 1959.

Under name A. L. Gaathon: *Capital Stock Employment and Output in Israel, 1950-1959,* Bank of Israel, 1961; *Economic Productivity in Israel,* Praeger, in cooperation with Bank of Israel, 1971.

Contributor under both names to symposia and journals, including *Handwoerterbuch der Sozialwissenschaften* and periodicals in England, France, Belgium, South Africa, Germany, Israel, and United States.

* * *

GADNEY, Reg 1941-

PERSONAL: Born January 20, 1941, in Cross Hills, England; son of Bernard C. (a school teacher) and Margaret A. M. (Lilley) Gadney; married Annette Kobak (a publisher's editor), July 16, 1966; children: Guy, Amy. *Education:* Attended Stowe School, Buckingham, England; St. Catharine's College, Cambridge, M.A., 1966. *Office:* Royal College of Art, London, England.

CAREER: Massachusetts Institute of Technology, Cambridge, instructor in architecture and research fellow at School of Architecture and Planning, 1966-67; National Film Theatre, London, England, deputy controller, 1967-69; Royal College of Art, London, England, tutor, 1969—. Consultant to American Arts Documentation Centre; editorial advisor to Paladin Books, Granada Publishing, and Lion and Unicorn Press. *Military service:* British Army, Coldstream Guards, assistant to naval, military, and air attache at British Embassy in Oslo, 1959-62; became lieutenant. *Member:* Marylebone Cricket Club.

WRITINGS—Novels: *Drawn Blanc,* Heinemann, 1970, Coward, 1971; *Somewhere in England,* St. Martin's, 1971; *Seduction of a Tall Man,* Heinemann, 1972; *Something Worth Fighting For,* Heinemann, 1974; *The Hours Before Dawn,* Heinemann, in press. Contributor to *Granta, Image, Broadsheet, Mosaic, Vou, Cambridge Review, London, Spectator,* and *Leonardo.* Editor of *Granta* and *Findings;* honorary editor of *Leonardo.*

WORK IN PROGRESS: A historical novel of romance and suspense; editing ten books on the history of art since 1850, for Paladin Books; a series of papers on popular culture and mass culture, for Royal College of Art.

SIDELIGHTS: Gadney spent an isolated childhood in the "wilds" of northern England; he has traveled extensively. He writes of fighting a "constant war with bureaucrats and champagne Marxists." *Avocational interests:* Cats.

GADO, Frank 1936-

PERSONAL: Born November 15, 1936, in Fairview, N.J.; son of Beniamino Eugenio and Teresa (Grimaldi) Gado; married Gunilla Stenman, October 22, 1967; children: Anna Teresa, Tobias Eugenio, Carin. *Education:* Dartmouth College, A.B., 1958; Harvard University, law study, 1958; Duke University, Ph.D., 1968. *Home:* 30 Hadel Rd., Scotia, N.Y. 12302. *Office:* Department of English, Union College, Schenectady, N.Y. 12308.

CAREER: Union College, Schenectady, N.Y., instructor, 1963-68, assistant professor, 1968-70, associate professor of American literature, 1970—, chairman of department of English, 1974—. Fulbright-Hays lecturer in American literature at University of Uppsala, 1966-67, 1969-70.

WRITINGS: First Person: Conversations with Novelists on Writers and Writing, Union College Press, 1973.

WORK IN PROGRESS: The Passion of Ingmar Bergman, for Norton.

* * *

GAFFNEY, (Merrill) Mason 1923-

PERSONAL: Born October 18, 1923, in White Plains, N.Y.; son of Matthew Page and Laura (Clarke) Gaffney; married Estelle Pao An Lau, March 8, 1952; children: Bradford Clarke, Ann Reed, Stuart Morgan. *Education:* Attended Harvard University, 1941-43, and University of Virginia, 1943-44; Reed College, B.A., 1948; University of California, Berkeley, Ph.D., 1956. *Home:* 4065 Lockehaven Dr., Victoria, B.C. V6N 156, Canada. *Office:* Economic Policy Analysis Institute of British Columbia, Box 1700, Victoria, B.C., Canada.

CAREER: University of Oregon, Eugene, instructor in economics, 1953-54; North Carolina State College (now North Carolina State University at Raleigh), Raleigh, instructor, 1954-55, assistant professor of economics, 1955-58; University of Missouri, Columbia, associate professor, 1958-61, professor of agricultural economics, 1961-62; University of Wisconsin-Milwaukee, professor of economics, 1962-71, chairman of department, 1963-65; Resources for the Future, Inc., Washington, D.C., visiting scholar, 1969-71, senior research associate, 1971-73; Economic Policy Analysis Institute of British Columbia, Victoria, director, 1973—. Visiting professor at University of California, Los Angeles, 1967-68. *Military service:* U.S. Army Air Forces, 1943-46.

MEMBER: American Economic Association, American Farm Economics Association, Regional Science Association, American Association for the Advancement of Science, American Association of University Professors, American Real Estate and Urban Economics Association, Phi Beta Kappa. *Awards, honors:* Ford Foundation faculty research fellowship, 1957-58; Jesse H. Neal Award for business journalism, 1960; grants from Lincoln Foundation, 1963-64, and Robert Schalkenbach Foundation, 1967, 1968, 1968-69.

WRITINGS: Concepts of Financial Maturity of Timber and Other Assets, Department of Agricultural Economics, North Carolina State College, 1957; (editor and contributor) *Extractive Resources and Taxation,* University of Wisconsin Press, 1967.

Contributor: Alfred Steffund, editor, *Yearbook of Agriculture,* Government Printing Office, 1958; Marion Clawson and others, editors, *Land Economics Research,* Johns

Hopkins Press, 1962; Richard Stauber, editor, *Approaches to the Study of Urbanization,* Governmental Research Center, University of Kansas, 1964; James Dixon, editor, *Air Conservation,* American Association for the Advancement of Science, 1965; Henry Jarrett, editor, *Environmental Quality in a Growing Economy,* Resources for the Future, 1966; Daniel Holland, editor, *The Assessment of Land Value,* University of Wisconsin Press, 1970; R. G. Putnam, F. J. Taylor, and P. G. Kettle, editors, *A Geography of Urban Places,* Methuen, 1970; Robert S. Ross and William C. Mitchell, editors, *Readings on Public Choice in America,* Markham, 1971; Clawson and Harvey S. Perloff, editors, *Modernizing Urban Land Policy,* Johns Hopkins Press, 1973; Robert D. Hamrin and Robert H. Haveman, editors, *The Political Economy of Federal Policy,* Harper, 1973; George Peterson, editor, *Property Tax Reform,* Urban Institute, 1973; Charles J. Meyers and Dan Tarlock, editors: *Water Resource Management,* Stanford Law School, in press. Contributor to professional journals and to *Reader's Digest, Nation, Challenge, Christian Science Monitor,* and other publications.

WORK IN PROGRESS: Full Employment on a Small Planet; Who Benefits from Military Spending?

* * *

GAGE, Nicholas
See NGAGOYEANES, Nicholas

* * *

GAINES, Richard L. 1925-

PERSONAL: Born December 2, 1925, in St. Louis, Mo.; son of Daniel Fellows (a hotel manager) and Dorothea (Haley) Gaines. *Education:* Princeton University, B.A., 1949; University of Virginia, M.A., 1952. *Home:* Church St., Edgartown, Mass. 02539. *Office:* Moses Brown School, 250 Lloyd Ave., Providence, R.I. 02906.

CAREER: High school teacher of English in Orange, Va., 1952-54, Lawrenceville, N.J., 1954-69, and Newton, Mass., 1969-70; Moses Brown School, Providence, R.I., assistant headmaster, 1971—. Tennis and wrestling coach in Orange, Va., 1952-54, and Lawrenceville, N.J. 1954-69. *Military service:* U.S. Navy, 1944-46; received Philippine Liberation medal.

WRITINGS: The Finest Education Money Can Buy, Simon & Schuster, 1972.

SIDELIGHTS: Gaines told *CA:* "My one book was written simply because I felt I had something to say about the kind of schools I had taught in, about their relationship to the larger society in which we live. I wrote only because I believed we were doing the wrong things for the wrong reasons." He is also a nationally ranked tennis player, has done a lot of hiking and camping, and has recently become interested in downhill skiing.

* * *

GAMMON, Roland 1920-

PERSONAL: Born November 18, 1920, in Caribou, Me.; son of Charles C. (a pharmacist) and Helen Fern (Irvine) Gammon; married Jean Thompson, 1947 (divorced, 1960). *Education:* Colby College, B.A., 1937; Oxford University, graduate study, 1938-39. *Politics:* Liberal Independent. *Religion:* Unitarian Universalist. *Home:* 114 East 72nd St., New York, N.Y. 10021. *Agent:* Mrs. Maxwell Aley, 145 East 35th St., New York, N.Y. 10016. *Office:* Editorial Communications, Inc., 655 Madison Ave., New York, N.Y. 10022.

CAREER: Life, New York, N.Y., reporter and editor, 1941-49; Editorial Communications, Inc., New York, N.Y., founder and president, 1960—. President of Unitarian Universalist Laymen's League, 1958-60; Universalist Church of New York City, president, 1968-72, dean of All Faith Chapel, 1972—. *Military service:* U.S. Army Air Forces, 1942-46. *Member:* World Fellowship of Faiths, Overseas Press Club of America, Temple of Understanding, United States Religious Newswriters Association, American Veterans Committee, Masons, Phi Beta Kappa.

WRITINGS: Truth Is One, Harper, 1956; *Faith Is a Star,* Dutton, 1963; *A God for Modern Man,* Sayre Ross, 1967; *All Believers Are Brothers,* Doubleday, 1970. Contributor to *Life, Look, Parade, Good Housekeeping, Redbook, Pageant, Coronet, Christian Century, Guideposts,* and *Unitarian Universalist World.*

WORK IN PROGRESS: A book on the Aquarian age and new world community.

SIDELIGHTS: Gammon has visited forty countries, led tour groups to Europe and Asia, and attended international philosophy conferences. He is interested in world religions, psychical research, the creative arts, photography, travel, and consulting on international beauty pageants such as Miss Universe, Miss World, and Miss U.S.A.

* * *

GANSS, George Edward 1905-

PERSONAL: Born September 18, 1905, in St. Louis, Mo.; son of Edward Adam and Adelaide J. (Wessels) Ganss. *Education:* St. Louis University, A.B., 1930, A.M., 1931, Ph.D., 1934; St. Mary's College, St. Marys, Kan., L.S.T., 1938. *Home and office:* Institute of Jesuit Sources, Fusz Memorial, 3700 West Pine, St. Louis, Mo. 63108.

CAREER: Entered Society of Jesus (Jesuit), 1924, ordained Roman Catholic priest, 1937; Marquette University, Milwaukee, Wis., instructor, 1939-40, assistant professor, 1940-48, associate professor, 1948-53, professor of classics and theology, 1953-62; St. Louis University, School of Divinity, St. Louis, Mo., professor of theology and classics, and director of Institute of Jesuit Sources, 1962—. Delegate to General Congregation of Society of Jesus in Rome, 1965-66. *Wartime service:* Auxiliary chaplain to servicemen attending Marquette University, 1942-46. *Member:* American Assistancy Seminar on Jesuit Spirituality (chairman, 1968—).

WRITINGS: (Translator) *St. Peter Chrysologus: Selected Sermons,* Fathers of the Church, 1953; *St. Ignatius' Idea of a Jesuit University,* Marquette University Press, 1954, 2nd edition, 1956; *The Jesuit Educational Tradition and St. Louis University,* St. Louis University Press, 1969; (translator from the Spanish and author of introduction and commentary) *St. Ignatius of Loyola: The Constitutions of the Society of Jesus,* Institute of Jesuit Sources, 1970. Contributor to *Archivum Historicum Societatis Iesu, Jesuit Educational Quarterly, Thought,* and *Review for Religious.* Editor, Institute of Jesuit Sources, 1962—.

WORK IN PROGRESS: Research in Jesuit spirituality; editing of "Studies in the Spirituality of Jesuits" series.

SIDELIGHTS: Fr. Ganss has travelled extensively in Western Europe.

GANTZ, Charlotte Orr 1909-

PERSONAL: Born July 12, 1909, in Sewickley, Pa.; daughter of John Bruce (an attorney) and Frances (Morris) Orr; married Robert J. M. Gantz, September 26, 1943; children: Jeffrey, Timothy. *Education:* Attended Bryn Mawr College, 1926-28, and American Laboratory Theatre, 1928-29; Columbia University, LL.B., 1940 (converted to J.D., 1969). *Politics:* Democrat. *Religion:* Episcopalian. *Residence:* Mechanicsville, Pa. 18934.

CAREER: An actress in Utica and New York, N.Y., 1929-32; Corporation Counsel's Office, New York, N.Y., assistant corporation counsel, 1940-43. *Member:* League of Women Voters (member of state board of Pennsylvania, 1951-53; president of New Hope chapter, 1964-66), Authors Guild.

WRITINGS: Discovering Nature, Scribner, 1958; (with Beatrice A. Warburton) *The Eupogon Iris Species in Cultivation,* Median Iris Society, 1970; *A Naturalist in Southern Florida,* University of Miami Press, 1971; *Boy with Three Names,* Houghton, 1973. Contributor to *American Iris Society Bulletin* and *Medianite.*

WORK IN PROGRESS: Research on current social problems.

SIDELIGHTS: Mrs. Gantz told *CA:* "My interest in natural history reaches back to early childhood. I collected and identified several thousand specimens of marine life, minerals, fossils, and archeological objects. The collection is now the core of the Natural History Museum in the Appalachian State University of North Carolina. Currently I'm running field trips and workshops in entomology for the Honey Hollow Nature Center in Bucks County.

"For some years I had a large iris garden with an extensive breeding program in the Median iris classes. Directed three iris robins (two of the international) providing information on iris breeding."

* * *

GANZ, Arthur (Frederick) 1928-

PERSONAL: Born May 15, 1928, in Milwaukee, Wis.; son of Jack I. (a department store executive) and Myrtle (Rickman) Ganz; married Margaret Gutwirth (a professor of English), June 12, 1962. *Education:* University of Wisconsin, B.A., 1949; University of Tennessee, M.A., 1950; Columbia University, Ph.D., 1957. *Home:* 30 East Ninth St., New York, N.Y. 10003. *Office:* Department of English, City College of the City University of New York, 138th and Convent Ave., New York, N.Y. 10031.

CAREER: Columbia University, New York, N.Y., lecturer in English, 1955-57; Rutgers University, New Brunswick, N.J., instructor, 1959-61, assistant professor of English, 1961-64; City College of the City University of New York, New York, N.Y., 1964—, began as assistant professor, became associate professor of English. *Military service:* U.S. Army, 1951-52. *Member:* Modern Language Association of America.

WRITINGS: (With Karl Beckson) *A Reader's Guide to Literary Terms,* Farrar, Straus, 1960; (editor and contributor) *Pinter: A Collection of Critical Essays,* Prentice-Hall, 1972. Contributor of articles on modern drama and dramatists to journals.

WORK IN PROGRESS: A book on modern drama.

GARDAM, Jane 1928-

PERSONAL: Born July 11, 1928, in Coatham, Yorkshire, England; daughter of William (a schoolmaster) and Kathleen (Helm) Pearson; married David Gardam (a Queen's counsel) April 20, 1952; children: Timothy, Mary, Thomas. *Education:* Bedford College, London, B.A. (honors), 1949, graduate study, 1949-52. *Politics:* Liberal. *Religion:* Anglo-Catholic. *Home:* 53 Ridgeway Pl., London SW19 4SP, England; and Fell House, Hartley Kirk by Stephen, Westmorland, England.

CAREER: Weldons Ladies Journal, London, England, sub-editor, 1952-53; *Time and Tide,* London, England, assistant literary editor, 1953-55. Organizer of hospital libraries for Red Cross, 1950.

WRITINGS: A Few Fair Days (short stories), Macmillan, 1971; *A Long Way from Verona* (novel), Macmillan, 1971; *The Summer After the Funeral* (novel), Macmillan, 1973.

WORK IN PROGRESS: A second collection of short stories.

SIDELIGHTS: Jane Gardam has travelled in the Far East, the West Indies, and Europe.

* * *

GARDNER, Anne
See SHULTZ, Gladys Denny 1895-

* * *

GARDNER, D(avid) Bruce 1924-

PERSONAL: Born December 7, 1924, in Salt Lake City, Utah; married Ila Christensen, 1945; children: Don B., Christine, Anita. *Education:* University of Utah, B.S. (with high honors), 1948, M.S., 1949; Cornell University, Ph.D., 1952. *Home:* 1820 Yorktown, Fort Collins, Colo. 80521. *Office:* Department of Child Development and Family Relationships, Colorado State University, Fort Collins, Colo. 80521.

CAREER: Utah State University, Logan, 1951-55, began as assistant professor, became associate professor of child development and psychology, head of department of child development, 1953-55; Iowa State University, Ames, 1955-67, began as assistant professor, became professor of child development and psychology, head of department of child development, 1966-67; University of Denver, Denver, Colo., professor of child psychology and director of child psychology training program, 1967-70, acting chairman of department, 1969-70; Colorado State University, Fort Collins, professor of child development and family relationships, 1970—, chairman of department, 1970—. John R. Emens Distinguished Professor at Ball State University, 1971-72; summer lecturer at University of California, Santa Barbara and Los Angeles, Colorado State University, Cornell University, Utah State University, Oregon State University, and University of Wisconsin. Postdoctoral fellow in research design at University of Wisconsin, summer, 1965. Consultant to Iowa State Department of Public Instruction, 1956-67. *Military service:* U.S. Army Air Forces, 1943-46. *Member:* Association of Aviation Psychologists, American Psychological Association, Society for Research in Child Development, American Educational Research Association, Rocky Mountain Psychological Association, Midwestern Association for the Education of Young Children (president, 1966-67), Colorado Association for the Education of Young Children (president, 1970-71).

WRITINGS: Development in Early Childhood, Harper, 1964, revised edition, 1973. Contributor to journals. Research editor for *Young Children,* 1958-62; member of editorial board of National Association for the Education of Young Children.

WORK IN PROGRESS: Research on perceptual development, and on self-evaluation processes in children.

* * *

GARIEPY, Henry 1930-

PERSONAL: Born January 17, 1930, in Meriden, Conn.; married Marjorie Ramsdell (a Salvation Army officer), January 28, 1952; children: Stephen, Priscilla, Kathryn, Elisabeth. *Education:* Attended Cortland State Teachers College, Buffalo Bible Institute, and Temple University; Cuyahoga Community College, A.A., 1971; Cleveland State University, B.A., 1972, M.S., 1973. *Home:* 3629 Strandhill Rd., Cleveland, Ohio 44122. *Office:* Salvation Army, 6000 Hough Ave., Cleveland, Ohio 44103.

CAREER: Salvation Army, commissioned, 1949, held various administrative posts throughout eastern United States, currently inner city coordinator in Cleveland, Ohio, with rank of major, 1968—. Consultant and lecturer on the subject of inner city ministry. *Member:* Cattaraugus County Ministerial Association (past president), Cortland Council of Social Agencies (past vice-president), Kiwanis Club of Cleveland (past president).

WRITINGS: Portraits of Christ, Revell, 1974. Contributor of more than a hundred articles to domestic and foreign publications of the Salvation Army.

WORK IN PROGRESS: With God in the Ghetto, about the Salvation Army's social action project in the Hough Ghetto of Cleveland, for Revell.

SIDELIGHTS: Gariepy was instrumental in inaugurating the Salvation Army's Hough Multi-Purpose Center, which serves as a model for Christian inner city work. *Avocational interests:* Outdoor activity, fishing, camping, travel.

* * *

GARSON, Paul 1946-

PERSONAL: Born March 7, 1946, in Washington, D.C. *Education:* Tulane University, B.A., 1968; Johns Hopkins University, M.A., 1970. *Home:* 223 Sunset Rd., West Palm Beach, Fla. 33401. *Agent:* Elaine Markson, 44 Greenwich Ave., New York, N.Y. 10011. *Office:* DiBacco School, Lake Worth, Fla.

CAREER: DiBacco School, Lake Worth, Fla., teacher, 1971—. *Member:* All-American Karate Federation. *Awards, honors:* First prize from *Carolina Quarterly,* 1970, for short story, "The Disguise."

WRITINGS: The Great Quill, Doubleday, 1973.

WORK IN PROGRESS: Prima Loka, a science fiction novel; *Schmeisser's Pistol,* a mystery novel; short stories and screenplays.

AVOCATIONAL INTERESTS: International travel, especially by hitchhiking, unidentified flying objects, extrasensory perception, astronomy, the art of film-making, painting, old Jaguar automobiles.

* * *

GARVIN, Richard M. 1934-

PERSONAL: Born August 4, 1934, in Hollywood, Calif.; son of John M. (a publisher's representative) and Elizabeth (Nolte) Garvin; married Carolyn Jeannine Mathis, April 21, 1961; children: Elizabeth, Jessica. *Education:* San Jose State College (now California State University), B.A., 1956. *Home address:* P. O. Box 19, Mill Valley, Calif. 94941. *Agent:* Perry Knowlton, Curtis Brown Ltd., 60 East 56th St., New York, N.Y. 10022. *Office:* Richardson, Seigle, Rolfs & McCoy, Inc., 248 Battery, San Francisco, Calif.

CAREER: Employed by Ampex Corp., 1959-61, and L. C. Cole Co., 1961-67; free lance, 1967-70; Richardson, Seigle, Rolfs & McCoy, San Francisco, Calif., creative director, 1970—. *Military service:* U.S. Army, 1957-59. *Member:* Authors Guild, Science Fiction Writers of America.

WRITINGS—Novels: (With Edmond Addeo) *The Fortec Conspiracy,* Sherbourne Press, 1967; (with Addeo) *The Talbott Agreement,* Sherbourne Press, 1968; (with Robert E. Burger) *Where They Go to Die: The Tragedy of America's Aged,* Delacorte, 1968; (with Burger) *The World of the Twilight Believers,* Sherbourne Press, 1969; (with Addeo) *The Midnight Special,* Geis, 1970; *The Crystal Skull,* Doubleday, 1972.

* * *

GASSIER, Pierre 1915-

PERSONAL: Born September 1, 1915, in Etampes, France; son of Albert (an engineer) and Louise (Chapot) Gassier; married Maria Oscoz Larralde, February 16, 1959; children: Alain, Claude, Marianne, Michel. *Education:* University of Paris, Licence es Lettres, 1935; Sorbonne, University of Paris, Doctorat es Lettres, 1972. *Home:* 4 square Moliere, Voisins, Trappes 78190, France. *Office:* French Embassy, 67 piazza Farnese, Rome, Italy.

CAREER: Art historian, diplomat. Institut Francais, Barcelona, Spain, professor of literature, 1941-51; Institut Francais, Madrid, professor of literature, 1951-57; Lycee Charlemagne, Paris, France, professor of literature, 1957-58; Consulate General, Tangier, Morocco, cultural attache, 1959-65; French Embassy, Athens, Greece, cultural attache, 1965-71; French Embassy, Rome, Italy, cultural counsel, 1971—. *Military service:* French Navy, 1936-40. *Member:* Hispanic Society of America (corresponding member). *Awards, honors:* Chevalier de l'Ordre des Palmes Academiques.

WRITINGS: (With Andre Malraux) *Les Dessins de Goya au Musee du Prado,* (title means "Drawings by Goya in the Prado Museum"), Skira, 1947; *Goya,* Skira, 1955; *Les Fresques de San Antonio de la Florida a Madrid* (title means "Frescoes of San Antonio de la Florida in Madrid"), Skira, 1955; (with Juliet Wilson) *Vie et oeuvre de Francisco Goya,* Office du Livre, 1970, translation by Christine Hauch and Juliet Wilson published as *The Life and Complete Work of Francisco Goya,* Reynal, 1971 (published in England as *Goya: His Life and His Work,* Thames & Hudson, 1971); *Les Dessins de Goya: Les Albums,* Office du Livre, 1973, translation by James Emmons and Robert Allen published as *Francisco Goya: Drawings,* Praeger, 1973.

WORK IN PROGRESS: Les Dessins de Goya: Etudes pour peintures, gravures, et divers, for Office du Livre.

SIDELIGHTS: Gassier told *CA* that he became interested in Spain and Spanish art during the sixteen years he spent teaching in Madrid and Barcelona. Of *The Life and Complete Work of Francisco Goya, Time* notes: "There was room for just one more book on Goya and this is it—the first complete edition of his works. . . . Gassier and Wilson are indispensable guides."

* * *

GATTMANN, Eric 1925-

PERSONAL: Born January 10, 1925, in Stuttgart, Germany; naturalized U.S. citizen in 1944; son of Julius and Bertha (Weinshenk) Gattmann; married Hildegard Stahl, 1947; children: Linda, Leslie. *Education:* University of California, Berkeley, B.A., 1949; San Francisco State College (now University), M.A., 1953. *Religion:* Jewish. *Home:* 2816 Monterey, San Mateo, Calif. 94403. *Office:* Department of Education, College of San Mateo, San Mateo, Calif. 94402.

CAREER: San Mateo elementary schools, San Mateo, Calif., teacher, 1950-54, school principal, 1954-66. College of San Mateo, dean of Evening College and summer session, 1966-71, instructor in education, 1971—. Consultant to Union of American Hebrew Congregations. *Military service:* U.S. Army, 1943-46; served in Europe. *Member:* California Teachers Association.

WRITINGS: (With William Henricks) *The Other Teacher Aides to Learning,* Wadsworth, 1973. Contributor to *PTA Magazine* and *Compass.*

WORK IN PROGRESS: A textbook for education classes.

* * *

GAULT, William Campbell 1910- (Will Duke)

PERSONAL: Born March 9, 1910, in Milwaukee, Wis.; son of John H. and Ella (Hovde) Gault; married Virginia Kaprelian, August 29, 1942; children: William Barry, Shelley Gault Amacher. *Education:* Attended University of Wisconsin, 1929. *Politics:* "Revolutionary Republican." *Religion:* "Faith in man." *Home and office:* 482 Vaquero Lane, Santa Barbara, Calif. 93111. *Agent:* Don Congdon, Harold Matson Co., Inc., 22 East 40th St., New York, N.Y. 10016.

CAREER: Free-lance writer, and author of mysteries and juvenile fiction. Has worked, at various times, as waiter, busboy, shoe sole cutter, hotel manager, and mailman. Secretary, Channel Cities Funeral Society. *Military service:* U.S. Army, 1943-45. *Awards, honors:* Edgar award from Mystery Writers of America, 1952, for *Don't Cry for Me*; award from Boys' Club of America, 1957, for *Speedway Challenge*; award from Southern California Council on Literature for Children and Young People, 1968.

WRITINGS—Mystery novels: *Don't Cry for Me,* Dutton, 1952; *The Bloody Bokhara,* Dutton, 1952; *The Canvas Coffin,* Dutton, 1953; *Blood on the Boards,* Dutton, 1953; *Run, Killer, Run,* Dutton, 1954; *Ring Around Rosa,* Dutton, 1955; *Day of the Ram,* Random House, 1956; *Square in the Middle,* Random House, 1956; *The Convertible Hearse,* Random House, 1957; *Night Lady,* Fawcett, 1958; *Sweet Wild Wench,* Fawcett, 1959; *The Wayward Widow,* Fawcett, 1959; *Death out of Focus,* Random House, 1959; *Come Die with Me,* Random House, 1959; *Million Dollar Tramp,* Fawcett, 1960; *Vein of Violence,* Simon & Schuster, 1961; *The Hundred Dollar Girl,* Dutton, 1961; *County Kill,* Simon & Schuster, 1962; *Dead Hero,* Dutton, 1963. Author of three additional novels published by Fawcett and Ace Books.

Under pseudonym Will Duke: *Fair Prey,* Boardman, 1958.

Juveniles; all published by Dutton: *Thunder Road,* 1952; *Mr. Fullback,* 1953; *Gallant Colt,* 1954; *Mr. Quarterback,* 1955; *Speedway Challenge,* 1956; *Bruce Benedict, Halfback,* 1957; *Rough Road to Glory,* 1958; *Dim Thunder,* 1958; *Drag Strip,* 1959.

Dirt Track Summer, 1961; *Through the Line,* 1961; *Two Wheeled Thunder,* 1962; *Road Race Rookie,* 1962; *Wheels of Fortune: Four Racing Stories,* 1963; *Little Big Foot,* 1963; *The Checkered Flag,* 1964; *The Long Green,* 1965; *The Karters,* 1965; *Sunday's Dust,* 1966; *Backfield Challenge,* 1967; *The Lonely Mound,* 1967; *The Oval Playground,* 1968; *Stubborn Sam,* 1969.

Quarterback Gamble, 1970; *The Last Lap,* 1972; *Trouble at Second,* 1973; *Gasoline Cowboy,* 1974; *Wild Willie, Wide Receiver,* 1974; *The Underground Skipper,* in press.

Contributor of about three hundred short stories to magazines, including *Grit* and *Saturday Evening Post.*

WORK IN PROGRESS: A juvenile about hockey; an adult mystery.

SIDELIGHTS: Gault's mystery novels have been translated into fourteen languages.

* * *

GAY, Carlo T(eofilo) E(berhard) 1913-

PERSONAL: Born July 12, 1913, in Villar Pellice, Torino, Italy; son of Lino Renato (a physician) and Letizia (Malan) Gay; married Claudia Boyd, July 4, 1948; children: Oliver Robin. *Education:* Institute of Oriental Languages of Naples, diploma in Amaric, 1938; University of Naples, Ph.D., 1940. *Home:* 80-71 Grenfell St., Kew Gardens, New York, N.Y. 11415.

CAREER: Dalmine (steel pipe manufacturers), Milan, Italy, executive, 1940-55, vice-president of subsidiary Dalminter, Inc., and president of Canadian subsidiary Dalminter Ltd., New York, N.Y., 1955-61. Researcher and writer on art and history of ancient Mexico. *Military service:* Italian Army, Alpine Corps, 1934-36; became lieutenant. *Member:* Society for American Archaeology, Archaeological Institute of America, Royal Anthropological Institute of Great Britain and Ireland, Institutum Canarium (Austria).

WRITINGS: Mezcala Stone Sculpture: The Human Figure, Museum of Primitive Art, 1967; *Chalcacingo,* Akademische Druck, 1971; *Xochipala: The Beginnings of Olmec Art,* Art Museum, Princeton University, 1972. Contributor to annals. Contributor to *Natural History, Archaeology, Antike Welt, Raggi,* and *Almogaren.*

WORK IN PROGRESS: Ceramic Figures of Ancient Mexico; further research on Olmec culture and related lithic traditions indigenous to the Middle Balsas River region in Guerrero, Mexico.

AVOCATIONAL INTERESTS: Mountain climbing, travel in Europe and North America, including Yukon and Alaska, exploring Mexico, photography of ancient architecture and monuments.

BIOGRAPHICAL/CRITICAL SOURCES: New York Times, April 14, 1967; *Corriere della Sera,* April 15, 1967; *Life,* May 12, 1967; *Life en Espanol,* May 22, 1967; *L'Europeo,* December, 1967; *Christian Science Monitor,* February 9, 1973.

GAZELL, James A(lbert) 1942-

PERSONAL: Surname is accented on second syllable; born March 17, 1942, in Chicago, Ill.; son of Albert James (a businessman) and Anne (Bloch) Gazell; married Monica Mary Nord (a saleswoman), August 29, 1970. *Education:* Roosevelt University, B.A. (with honors), 1963, M.A., 1966; Southern Illinois University, Ph.D., 1968. *Politics:* Independent. *Religion:* Roman Catholic. *Home:* 2960 Clairemont Dr., Apt. 23, San Diego, Calif. 92117. *Office:* School of Public Administration and Urban Studies, San Diego State University, San Diego, Calif. 92115.

CAREER: Roosevelt University, Chicago, Ill., instructor in political science, 1965, 1967; Southern Illinois University, Carbondale, instructor in government, 1968; California State University, San Diego, assistant professor, 1968-72, associate professor of public administration and urban studies, 1972—. Technical adviser to Ernst & Ernst, 1973; consultant to Human Resources Agency, 1973. *Member:* American Society for Public Administration, American Society of Criminology, American Judicature Society, Institute of Judicial Administration.

WRITINGS: (With Howard M. Rieger) *The Politics of Judicial Reform,* California Book Co., 1969; (with Rieger) *The Urban Quagmire: The Chicago Model,* California Book Co., 1971; (editor with G. Thomas Gitchoff) *Youth, Crime, and Society,* Holbrook, 1973; *Selection and Promotion in a Metropolitan Police Department,* California Book Co., 1973; *State Trial Courts as Bureaucracies: A Study in Judicial Management,* Dunellen, 1974; *Background Papers on National Trends in the Unification of State Courts,* Ernst & Ernst, 1974. Contributor of about thirty articles and reviews to professional journals.

WORK IN PROGRESS: Where Is Court Management Going? (tentative title); articles on state court unification, state court financing, state judicial personnel systems, probation and state court reform, on court reorganization in Michigan, and on O. W. Wilson's contributions to police administration.

* * *

GEDDES, Charles L(ynn) 1928-

PERSONAL: Born January 3, 1928, in Corvallis, Ore.; son of James E. II (an engineer) and Dorothy Marie (Green) Geddes; married Eloise Kelly (an editor), June 5, 1962. *Education:* University of Oregon, B.S., 1951; graduate study at University of California, Berkeley, 1952-53; University of Michigan, A.M., 1954; School of Oriental and African Studies, University of London, Ph.D., 1959. *Religion:* Protestant. *Home:* 3460 South Clermont St., Denver, Colo. 80222. *Office:* Department of History, University of Denver, Denver, Colo. 80210.

CAREER: American University of Cairo, Cairo, Egypt, assistant professor of history, 1956-61; University of Colorado, Boulder, assistant professor of history, 1961-65; University of Denver, Denver, Colo., resident director of American Institute of Islamic Studies, 1965—, assistant professor, 1967-69, associate professor of history, 1969—. Fulbright lecturer at Tribubhan University, Katmandu, Nepal, 1965-66. *Military service:* U.S. Army, 1945-47. *Member:* American Oriental Society, Middle East Studies Association, Middle East Institute (fellow).

WRITINGS: (With Florence Ljunggren) *An International Directory of Institutes and Societies Interested in the Middle East,* Djambatan (Amsterdam), 1962; *An Analytical Guide to the Bibliographies on Modern Egypt and the Sudan,* American Institute of Islamic Studies, 1972; *An Analytical Guide to the Bibliographies on Islam, Muhammed, and the Qur'an,* American Institute of Islamic Studies, 1973; *An Analytical Guide to the Bibliographies on the Arabian Peninsula,* American Institute of Islamic Studies, 1974.

WORK IN PROGRESS: Bibliographies and several historical works on Islam and the Middle East.

* * *

GELFAND, Morris Arthur 1908-

PERSONAL: Born June 1, 1908, in Bayonne, N.J.; son of Joseph Samuel (a machinist) and Sadie (Schneider) Gelfand; married Beatrice Margaret Traube (in editorial work), February 1, 1948; children: James Munn, Lisa Jay. *Education:* New York University, B.S., 1933, M.A., 1939, Ph.D., 1960; Columbia University, B.S. in L.S., 1934. *Politics:* Democrat. *Religion:* Ethical Culture. *Home:* Stone House, Post Dr., Roslyn Harbor, N.Y. 11576. *Office:* Department of Library Science, Queens College of the City University of New York, Flushing, N.Y. 11367.

CAREER: New York University, Washington Square Library, New York, N.Y., supervisor of reserve reading room, 1931-37; Queens College Library, Flushing, N.Y., library assistant, 1937-41, assistant librarian, 1941-42, librarian, 1946-70; Queens College of the City University of New York, Flushing, professor of library science and head of department, 1970—. Special examiner of library positions for New York State Civil Service Department, 1946-47; secretary of Steering Committee on Library Cooperation in Metropolitan New York, 1949; member of visitation committees, Commission on Institutions of Higher Education of Middle States Association of Colleges and Secondary Schools, 1949—; Fulbright lecturer and library consultant at University of Rangoon, 1958-59; UNESCO library expert in Thailand, 1962; American Library Association representative to United Nations, 1962-65; library consultant for Ford Foundation in Brazil, 1964, 1966, 1967, and 1969; library consultant to University of Delhi, 1966, and University of Carabobo, 1970. Member of board of trustees, New York Metropolitan Library Reference and Research Library, 1965-70, president of board of trustees, 1973—; member of board of trustees, Bryant Library, Roslyn, N.Y., 1967—. *Military service:* U.S. Army, 1942. U.S. Army Air Forces, European theater of operations and Pacific theater, 1942-46; became major; received Army Commendation Ribbon.

MEMBER: American Association of University Professors, American Library Association, Association of College and Research Libraries, Bibliographical Society of America, American Society for Information Science, Association of American Library Schools, American Association for the Advancement of Science, New York Library Club (president, 1947-48), Sigma Society of New York University, Phi Delta Kappa, Alpha Lambda Phi, Archons of Colophon, Grolier Club.

WRITINGS: University Libraries for Developing Countries, UNESCO, 1968, revised edition, 1971. Contributor to library publications.

WORK IN PROGRESS: Research in library/information networks, academic library administration, planning and design of library buildings, and international librarianship.

AVOCATIONAL INTERESTS: Foreign travel.

GELFOND, Rhoda 1946-

PERSONAL: Born May 15, 1946, in Philadelphia, Pa.; daughter of Jacob Allen and Frances (Takiff) Gelfond. *Education:* University of Pennsylvania, B.A., 1968; Johns Hopkins University, M.A., 1970; Brown University, M.A., 1972. *Religion:* Jewish. *Home:* 716 Ashbourne Rd., Philadelphia, Pa. 19117.

CAREER: Rhode Island State Arts Council, poet-in-the-schools, 1970-71; Pennsylvania Arts Council, poet-in-the-schools, 1973—. *Member:* Academy of American Poets, Pennsylvania Poetry Society. *Awards, honors:* Academy of American Poets Prize, 1971; Winfield Townley Scott Memorial Award, 1972.

WRITINGS: The First Trail (poems), Hellcoal Press of Brown University, 1972.

WORK IN PROGRESS: A collection of poems.

SIDELIGHTS: "The concern with words in my poetry," wrote Rhoda Gelfond, "is somehow connected with an attempt to work them out of tightened etymology and into present action and new meanings . . . a kind of 'raying out' of language." She has future plans of doing some French translation and learning how to bind books by hand.

* * *

GERARD, Ralph W(aldo) 1900-1974

October 7, 1900—February 17, 1974; American behavioral scientist, neurophysiologist, educator, and author. Obituaries: *New York Times,* February 19, 1974; *Current Biography,* April, 1974.

* * *

GERBER, Sanford E(dwin) 1933-

PERSONAL: Born June 16, 1933, in Chicago, Ill.; son of Leon (an executive) and Rose (Ely) Gerber; married Leila B. Greenberg, June 28, 1953 (divorced, 1965); married Louise S. Borad, October 9, 1965; children: (first marriage) Howard M., Michael B.; (second marriage) Naomi R. *Education:* Lake Forest College, B.A., 1954; University of Illinois, M.S., 1956; University of Southern California, Ph.D., 1962. *Politics:* Democratic. *Religion:* Jewish. *Home:* 10 Via Alicia, Santa Barbara, Calif. 93108. *Office:* University of California, Santa Barbara, Calif. 93106.

CAREER: East Whittier city schools, Whittier, Calif., speech therapist, 1956-58; System Development Corp., Santa Monica, Calif., senior human factors specialist, 1958-60; Hughes Aircraft Co., Fullerton, Calif., head of speech and hearing research, 1960-65; University of California, Santa Barbara, assistant professor, 1965-69, associate professor of audiology, 1969—. Consultant to U.S. Department of Defense and to Columbia Broadcasting System Laboratories.

MEMBER: International Communication Association, International Society of Audiology, International Society of Phonetic Sciences, Acoustical Society of America, American Speech and Hearing Association, Speech Communication Association, American Association of Phonetic Sciences, Western Speech Communication Association, Sigma Xi, Channel City Club.

WRITINGS: (Contributor) John A. R. Wilson, editor, *Diagnosis of Learning Difficulties,* McGraw, 1971; *Introductory Hearing Science,* Saunders, 1974. Writer of speech and hearing research reports for System Development Corp. and Hughes Aircraft Co. Contributor of more than thirty articles and reviews to journals, including *American Scientist, Space/Aeronautics,* and *Journal of the Acoustical Society of America.*

WORK IN PROGRESS: The Time-Adjustment of Speech; and *Pediatric Oto-Audiology.*

* * *

GETTENS, Rutherford John 1900(?)-1974

1900(?)—June 17, 1974; American curator, chemist, educator, and authority on the history and technology of art. Obituaries: *Washington Post,* June 20, 1974; *New York Times,* June 22, 1974.

* * *

GHIOTTO, Renato 1923-

PERSONAL: Born January 25, 1923, in Montecchio, Italy; son of Nicola and Letizia (Brendolan) Ghiotto; married Giovanna Sportiello, April 1, 1959; children: Francesca, Lucia, Agostino, Sebastiano. *Education:* Attended University of Padua. *Home:* Via Angelo Brunetti 32, Rome, Italy 00186.

CAREER: Il Veneto, Padua, Italy, journalist, 1940-43; *Il Giornale di Vicenza,* Vicenza, Italy, journalist, 1945-50; Linea Advertising Agency, Rome, Italy, general manager, 1955-70; *Il Mondo,* Rome, Italy, editor in chief, 1973—. *Member:* Accademia Olimpica (Venice). *Awards, honors:* Strega Prize runner-up, 1967, for *Check to the Queen;* Premio Selezione Campiello, 1971, for *Adios.*

WRITINGS—Novels: *Scacco alla Regina,* Rizzoli-Editore, 1967, translation by Isabel Quigley published as *Check to the Queen,* Putnam, 1969 (published in England as *The Slave,* MacDonald & Co., 1969); *Adios,* Rizzoli-Editore, 1971.

SIDELIGHTS: Check to the Queen was made into a film in 1969.

* * *

GHISELIN, Michael T(enant) 1939-

PERSONAL: Surname is pronounced *Geez*-lin; born May 13, 1939, in Salt Lake City, Utah; son of Brewster (a poet and critic) and Olive (a writer of short stories; maiden name, Franks) Ghiselin. *Education:* University of Utah, B.A. (with honors), 1960; Stanford University, Ph.D., 1965. *Residence:* Bodega Bay, Calif. *Office:* Bodega Marine Laboratory, P. O. Box 247, Bodega Bay, Calif. 94923.

CAREER: Harvard University, Cambridge, Mass., research fellow in malacology at Museum of Comparative Zoology, 1964-65; Marine Biological Laboratory, Woods Hole, Mass., fellow in systematics of Systematics-Ecology Program, 1965-67; University of California, Berkeley, assistant professor, 1967-74, associate professor of zoology at Bodega Marine Laboratory, 1974—. Participant in International Indian Ocean Expedition, 1963. Visiting investigator at Seto Marine Biological Laboratory of Kyoto University, 1963, University of Puerto Rico, 1965, Stazione Zoological di Napoli, 1968, Cambridge University, 1971, 1973, and Plymouth Laboratory of Great Britain's Marine Biological Association, 1971. Speaker at international meetings.

MEMBER: American Society of Naturalists, American Society of Zoologists, Paleontological Society, Society for the Study of Evolution, Friends of the Wagnerian Opera.

Awards, honors: Pfizer Prize from History of Science Society, 1970, for *The Triumph of the Darwinian Method;* National Science Foundation grant to study the impact of Darwinism on comparative anatomy, 1972-75.

WRITINGS: (Contributor) *Systematic Biology: Proceedings of an International Conference,* National Academy of Sciences, 1969; *The Triumph of the Darwinian Method,* University of California Press, 1969; (contributor) T. J. M. Schopf, editor, *Models in Paleobiology,* Freeman, Cooper, 1972; (with Michael G. Barbour, Robert B. Craig, and Frank R. Drysdale) *Coastal Ecology: Bodega Head,* University of California Press, 1973; *The Economy of Nature and the Evolution of Sex,* University of California Press, 1974.

Contributor of about thirty articles and reviews to science journals, including *Genetics, Journal of the History of Biology, Science, Quarterly Review of Biology, Bulletin of Marine Science,* and *Systematic Zoology.* Member of editorial board of *Systematic Zoology* and *Evolutionary Theory;* review editor of *Systematic Zoology.*

WORK IN PROGRESS: Research on high-level taxonomy and on the history of comparative anatomy.

AVOCATIONAL INTERESTS: Reading old books.

* * *

GHNASSIA, Maurice (Jean-Henri) 1920- (J. H. Morriss)

PERSONAL: Born July 23, 1920, in Paris, France; came to United States in 1955; son of Jesus and Esther (Karsenty) Ghnassia; married Luisa Facciolo (a professor of French literature), January 20, 1951; children: Barbara, Noelle. *Education:* Attended business school in France, received M.A. equivalent, 1950; Sorbonne, University of Paris, M.A. equivalent, 1951. *Residence:* New York, N.Y. *Agent:* Georges Borchardt Inc., 145 East 52nd St., New York, N.Y. 10022.

CAREER: United States and United Nations correspondent for *France Observateur,* part-time, 1956-63; Grolier, Inc., New York, N.Y., 1959-66, began as editor, became managing editor; McGraw-Hill, New York, N.Y., editing supervisor, 1967-68; free-lance editor and writer, 1968—. *Military service:* French Resistance, World War II; paratrooper attached to 101st Allied Airborne. *Member:* Society of Men of Letters of France.

WRITINGS: (Under pseudonym J. H. Morriss) *Foule aux dames* (novel), Fleuve Noir, 1952; (under pseudonym J. H. Morriss) *Un Dimanche pour pleurer* (novel), Fleuve Noir, 1954; "Les Fugitifs" (play), first produced in Paris at Comedie Francaise, 1957; *Arena* (novel), Viking, 1969. Also author of play adaptation of Albert Camus' "L'-Estranger," 1953; author of television play, "Between Midnight and Tomorrow", 1963.

WORK IN PROGRESS: Two novels, *The Temptation of the Cold* and *The Pidgeon and the 31:* a play, "Boris, My Love, is Well and Alive in the U.S.S.R."

* * *

GHOSE, Sri Chinmoy Kumar 1931- (Chinmoy)

PERSONAL: Born August 27, 1931, in Bengal, India; son of Sashi Kumar (a banker and railroad official) and Yogamaya (Biswas) Ghose. *Education:* Educated in Hindu monastery. *Politics:* "Not applicable." *Religion:* Hindu. *Home and office:* 85-45 149th St., Jamaica Hills, Queens, N.Y. 11435. *Agent:* Rudra Tamm, 80 Perry Ave., Norwalk, Conn.

CAREER: Entered Hindu spiritual community (ashram) in Southern India, 1943-63; in 1964, began traveling and lecturing throughout Europe, North America, and Far East, establishing Sri Chinmoy Meditation Centres; in 1970, began series of meditations and lectures in the Chapel of Church Center for the United Nations; in 1971, began first series of Dag Hammarskjold Lectures at United Nations.

WRITINGS: Meditations: Food for the Soul, Harper, 1971; *My Lord's Secrets Revealed,* Herder and Herder, 1971; *Songs of the Soul,* Herder and Herder, 1971; *Yoga and the Spiritual Life: The Journey of India's Soul,* Tower, 1971; *Arise! Awake! Thoughts of a Yogi,* Fell, 1971; *The Supreme and His Four Children: Five Spiritual Dictionaries,* Fleet Press, 1972; *A Commentary on the Bhagavad Gita: The Song of the Transcendental Soul,* Multimedia Publishing, 1972; *Mother World's Lighthouse,* Multimedia Publishing, 1972.

Booklets; all published by Sri Chinmoy Lighthouse: *My Ivy League Leaves,* 1970; *Father and Son,* 1971; *Man and God,* 1971; *My Yogi Friends and My Avatar Friends,* 1971; *Love Realised, Surrender Fulfilled, Oneness Manifested,* 1971; *My Rose Petals,* 1971; *Children's Conversations with God,* 1971; *My Flute,* 1972.

Author of *Garland of Nation-Souls; God's Hour; Japanese Poems; My Salutation to Japan; Sri Chinmoy Answers,* in five parts; *Eastern Light for the Western World; In Search of a Perfect Disciple* (short stories); *The Garden of Love-Light* (poems); *God's Absence and God's Presence* (poems); *A Seeker's Universe* (poems); *God's Orchestra.*

Also author of numerous pamphlets, poems, and other publications.

WORK IN PROGRESS: The Upanishad Lecture Series; parts four and five of *Sri Chinmoy Answers.*

SIDELIGHTS: Nancy E. Sands, a student of Sri Chinmoy Ghose, has written: "[His] life is one of total, dedicated surrender to the Will of the Supreme Being; of unending selfless service to sincere spiritual seekers as he guides them lovingly on their journey towards their own Self-realisation."

BIOGRAPHICAL/CRITICAL SOURCES: Madhuri, *The Life of Sri Chinmoy,* Sri Chinmoy Centre, Inc., Volume I, 1969, Volume II, 1972.

* * *

GHOUGASSIAN, Joseph P(eter) 1944-

PERSONAL: Born March 6, 1944, in Cairo, Egypt; naturalized U.S. citizen, 1972; son of Antoine (an architect) and Antoinette (Wazir) Ghougassian; married Zena S. Yasmine (an interior decorator), June 28, 1970; children: Yasmine J. *Education:* Gregorian University of Rome, B.A., 1964, M.A., 1965; Louvain University, Ph.D., 1969, graduate study, 1973-74. *Office:* Department of Philosophy, University of San Diego, San Diego, Calif. 92110.

CAREER: University of San Diego, San Diego, Calif., assistant professor, 1969-73, associate professor of philosophy, 1973—. Faculty consultant at California School of Professional Psychology, San Diego campus, 1973—. *Member:* American Philosophical Association, Society for Phenomenology and Existential Philosophy, Association for Humanistic Psychology, Phi Sigma Tau, Phi Delta Phi.

WRITINGS: Gordon W. Allport's Ontopsychology of the Person, Philosophical Library, 1972; *Kahlil Gibran: Wings of Thought: The People's Philosopher,* Philosophical Library, 1973; (contributor) Joseph Fabry and Reuven Bulka, *The Meaning of the Moment: Logotherapy,* Max Knight Books, 1974. Contributor to *Ararat.*

WORK IN PROGRESS: Research in philosophical psychology for *The Two Dimensional Man;* research in Middle East philosophy and politics for *U.S. Foreign Politics in the Middle East.*

SIDELIGHTS: Ghougassian has traveled extensively in Egypt, Lebanon, Syria, Turkey, Italy, Spain, France, Austria, Switzerland, Germany, Holland, Belgium, and England. He is competent in Arabic, Armenian, French, Italian, Spanish, and Latin.

* * *

GIBSON, Nevin H(erman) 1915-

PERSONAL: Born April 26, 1915, in Greenville, S.C.; son of Herbert David and Frossie (Ross) Gibson; married Margaret Kathleen Palmer, July 3, 1943; children: Nevin, Jr., Byron, Robert. *Education:* Attended Colorado College, Loyola University, Chicago, Ill., and Chicago Central YMCA Community College. *Politics:* Independent. *Religion:* Protestant. *Home and office:* 201 Miles Dr., Washington, D.C. 20021.

CAREER: U.S. Air Corps (now U.S. Air Force), career officer, 1936-57; served three years in Europe during World War II and a year in Korea during Korean conflict, retiring with rank of major; writer, 1957—. *Member:* Golf Writers Association of America.

WRITINGS: Encyclopedia of Golf, A. S. Barnes, 1958, revised edition, 1964; (with Charlie Bassler) *You Can Play Par Golf,* A. S. Barnes, 1966; *Pictorial History of Golf,* A. S. Barnes, 1968, revised edition, 1974; *Great Moments in Golf* (Golfers Book Club selection), A. S. Barnes, 1973. Contributor to golf magazines.

SIDELIGHTS: Gibson is himself an avid golfer, having won many amateur and professional-amateur contests. He has organized local golf tournaments, and has contributed to the present popularity of the game. He follows professional tours, taking photographs and collecting data for future books on golf. He owns one of the largest private golf libraries in the world.

* * *

GIBSON, Rosemary
See NEWELL, Rosemary

* * *

GIERE, Ronald N(elson) 1938-

PERSONAL: Surname rhymes with "Erie"; born November 29, 1938, in Cleveland, Ohio; son of Silas Irving (a mechanic) and Helen Agnes (Marusa) Giere; married Renee Grace Loeffler, June 9, 1962 (divorced, November, 1972). *Education:* Oberlin College, A.B., 1960; Cornell University, M.S., 1963, Ph.D., 1968. *Home:* 510 North Fess Ave., Bloomington, Ind. 47401. *Office:* Department of History and Philosophy of Science, 130 Goodbody Hall, Indiana University, Bloomington, Ind. 47401.

CAREER: Indiana University, Bloomington, lecturer, 1966-68, assistant professor, 1968-71, associate professor of philosophy of science, 1971—. Associate research scientist at New York University, Courant Institute of Mathematical Sciences, 1971-72; member of National Science Foundation advisory panel for history and philosophy of science, 1971-73. *Member:* American Philosophical Association, Philosophy of Science Association, American Association for the Advancement of Science, Phi Beta Kappa, Sigma Xi, Phi Kappa Phi. *Awards, honors:* Woodrow Wilson fellow, 1960-61; National Science Foundation grants, 1969-71, 1971-73.

WRITINGS: (Contributor) R. C. Buck and R. S. Cohen, editors, *Boston Studies in the Philosophy of Science,* Volume VIII, Humanities, 1971; (contributor) P. C. Suppes and others, editors, *Logic, Methodology and Philosophy of Science, IV: Proceedings of the 1971 International Congress: Bucharest,* North-Holland Publishing, 1973; (editor with Richard S. Westfall) *Foundations of Scientific Method: The Nineteenth Century,* Indiana University Press, 1973; (contributor) J. Leach and others, editors, *Science, Decision, and Value,* Reidel, 1973; (contributor) Grover Maxwell and Robert M. Anderson, Jr., editors, *Induction, Probability, and Confirmation Theory: Minnesota Studies in the Philosophy of Science,* Volume VI, University of Minnesota Press, 1974; (contributor) C. A. Hooker and W. Harper, editors, *Foundations of Probability and Statistics and Statistical Theories in Science,* Reidel, in press. Contributor to *Synthese, Philosophy of Science, British Journal for the Philosophy of Science, Science, Philosophical Review,* and *Ratio.*

WORK IN PROGRESS: A book on the foundations of statistical inference and implications for a general theory of knowledge, completion expected in 1976.

SIDELIGHTS: Giere told *CA:* "Like many others my age I am in theory a social and political radical living an outwardly 'normal' life—though ever less so. I'm into popular music (rock, some jazz), Chinese cooking, men's groups, and toying with various possibilities for communal living."

* * *

GILBERT, Amy M(argaret) 1895-

PERSONAL: Born February 23, 1895, in Chambersburg, Pa.; daughter of Daniel and Mary Margaret (Ott) Gilbert. *Education:* Cornell University, student, summer, 1914; Wilson College, A.B., 1915; University of Pennsylvania, M.A., 1919, Ph.D., 1922; postdoctoral study at Columbia University, fall, 1931, and 1940-41; summer postdoctoral study at Geneva Institute of International Relations and Geneva School of International Studies, 1926-32, University of Michigan, 1933, and University of Chicago, 1940. *Home:* Tiona Rd., Maine, N.Y. 13802.

CAREER: High school teacher of history in the public schools of Clinton, N.J., 1915-16; Wilson College, Chambersburg, Pa., instructor in history, 1916-18; Elmira College, Elmira, N.Y., professor of history, and head of department, 1922-36; Milwaukee-Downer College, Milwaukee, Wis., academic dean, 1936-41; Rhode Island State College, Kingston, dean, 1941-45; Temple University, Philadelphia, Pa., visiting professor of history, 1945-46; head of history and political science departments of the four units of Associated Colleges of Upper New York, 1946-50; State University of New York, Champlain College, Plattsburgh, dean of academic administration, 1950-52, head of the college, 1952-53; State University of New York at Binghamton, Harpur College, professor of history, 1953-65, professor emeritus, 1965—. Official historian of Associated Colleges of Upper New York; director of Broome County,

N.Y., Historical Society, 1956-71. Representative of Gannett Newspapers covering sessions of the League of Nations in Geneva, Switzerland, 1927, 1931, and 1932, and attending the Geneva Disarmament Conference and the Lausanne, Switzerland Conference, 1932; press representative of *Milwaukee Journal* at the Second Meeting of the Ministers of Foreign Affairs of the American Republics at Havana, Cuba, 1940; member of African Seminar of Comparative Educational Society, 1962.

MEMBER: American Association of University Women (life member), American Society of International Law, American Historical Association (life member), American Political Science Association, Association of European Historians of the State of New York, Phi Beta Kappa, Pi Lambda Theta, Delta Kappa Gamma, Faculty Women's Club of SUNY at Binghamton (life member). *Awards, honors:* LL.D. from Wilson College, 1939; Amy M. Gilbert Scholarship fund established at State University of New York at Binghamton, 1965.

WRITINGS: The Work of Lord Brougham for Education in England, Franklin Repository, 1922; (contributor) Alexander C. Flick, editor, *History of the State of New York,* Volume VIII, Columbia University Press, 1935; *ACUNY—The Associated Colleges of Upper New York: A Unique Response to an Emergency in Higher Education in the State of New York,* Cornell University Press, 1950; *Executive Agreements and Treaties, 1946-1973,* Thomas-Newell, 1973. Contributor to professional journals.

* * *

GILBERT, Anthony
See MALLESON, Lucy Beatrice

* * *

GILBERT, Arlene E(lsie) 1934-

PERSONAL: Born April 23, 1934, in Cleveland, Ohio; daughter of Gustav D. (an ironworker) and Helen (Hanel) Grauberger; married Walter E. Gilbert (a computer field engineer), November 21, 1956; children: Glorianne, Debra, Ralph, Bonnie. *Education:* Western Reserve University (now Case Western Reserve University), B.S., 1958. *Politics:* Independent. *Religion:* Lutheran. *Home:* 5287 Haleville Rd., Memphis, Tenn. 38116.

CAREER: Typist and secretary at White Motors, Cleveland, Ohio, 1952-53, and at Western Reserve University, Cleveland, Ohio, 1953-59. *Member:* National Multiple Sclerosis Society (member of board of Memphis chapter, 1972—).

WRITINGS: You Can Do It from a Wheelchair, Arlington House, 1974. Contributor to *Light and Life Evangel, Union Gospel Press, Lutheran Women, Fun For Middlers,* and *Accent on Living.*

SIDELIGHTS: Mrs. Gilbert, who is confined to a wheelchair with multiple sclerosis, told *CA* that she is "mostly interested in writing things that will help others."

BIOGRAPHICAL/CRITICAL SOURCES: Memphis Press-Scimitar, January 24, 1974.

* * *

GILL, Derek (Lewis Theodore) 1919-

PERSONAL: Born December 23, 1919, in Kampala, Uganda; son of William Bridson (a missionary) and Lilian (Moore) Gill; married Erica Elizabeth McPherson (an editor-in-residence), January 5, 1945; children: Diana Jane, A. Malcolm, Duncan R. *Education:* University of London, M.B. (honors), 1938; Cambridge University, graduate study, 1939-40. *Religion:* Episcopalian. *Home and office:* 421 Via Almar, Palos Verdes Estates, Calif. 90274.

CAREER: Daily Representative, Queenstown, South Africa, editor, 1948-60; *Pretoria News,* Pretoria, South Africa, city editor, 1960-63; *World* (daily newspaper), Johannesburg, South Africa, editorial director, 1963-66; *Pace* (magazine), Los Angeles, Calif., senior editor, 1966-70; researcher for author, Irving Stone, 1970—. Lecturer and broadcaster to creative writing classes and other groups; painter; exhibiting in one-man shows in Europe, the United States, and South Africa. *Military service:* British Army, 1940-44; served in Africa, Europe, and Southeast Asia; became captain. *Member:* Screen Writers Guild (West), Round Table (chairman).

WRITINGS: (With Robin Graham) *Dove,* Harper, 1972; *The Boy Who Sailed Around the World* (children's book), Western Publishing, 1973; (with Tom Sullivan) *I Can See Clearly Now,* Harper, 1974; *Adventure in the Dark* (children's book), Western Publishing, in press. Author of screenplay, "The Dove," based on own book. Contributor to journals and newspapers in the United States and abroad, including *Reader's Digest, Women's Own, London Times, New York Times, Modern Maturity,* and *Tokyo Times.*

WORK IN PROGRESS: Home Is the Sailor, a sequel to *Dove,* publication by Harper expected in 1975.

SIDELIGHTS: Gill's books have been published in German, French, Italian, Japanese, Spanish, Swedish, and Finnish. "The Dove" was produced by Gregory Peck, in 1973.

BIOGRAPHICAL/CRITICAL SOURCES: P. V. Review, May, 1973; *Star* (Johannesburg), June 15, 1973.

* * *

GILLETT, J(ohn) D(avid) 1913-

PERSONAL: Born September 8, 1913, in London, England; son of George Humphrey Gare (a silk merchant) and Beatrice (Andrews) Gillett; married Irena Charzewska, January 9, 1943; children: Richard David, Lorna Caroline. *Education:* University College, London, B.Sc. (first class honors), 1949; University of London, Ph.D., 1952, D.Sc., 1960. *Home:* 3 Owls Ears Close, Beaconsfield, Buckinghamshire HP9 1SS, England. *Office:* School of Biological Sciences, Brunel University, Uxbridge, Middlesex UB8 3PH, England.

CAREER: East African Virus Research Institute, Entebbe, Uganda, assistant director, 1957-62; Brunel University, Uxbridge, Middlesex, England, professor of biology and head of School of Biological Sciences, 1962—. Consultant to World Health Organization. *Military service:* Uganda Defence Force, 1940-45. *Member:* Royal Entomological Society of London (fellow; member of council, 1964-66), Royal Society of Tropical Medicine and Hygiene (fellow; member of council, 1973—), American Mosquito Control Association. *Awards, honors:* Rockefeller Foundation fellow in United States, 1955-56; Officer of Order of the British Empire (O.B.E.), 1962, for work on the epidemiology of yellow fever in Africa.

WRITINGS: Mosquitos, Weidenfeld & Nicolson, 1971, published as *The Mosquito: Its Life, Activities and Impact on Human Affairs,* Doubleday, 1972; *Common African*

Mosquitos and Their Medical Importance, Heinemann Medical Books, 1972. Author or co-author of more than seventy scientific papers.

WORK IN PROGRESS: Continuing research on the physiology and behavior of mosquitos in relation to the transmission of human disease.

SIDELIGHTS: Gillett has spent a total of more than twenty years in equatorial Africa. His year in the United States on a Rockefeller fellowship was followed by visits in 1963 and 1971. He also has traveled widely in Thailand, Malaysia, Japan, India, Ceylon, Australia, New Zealand, Brazil, and in most countries of Europe.

AVOCATIONAL INTERESTS: Music, airships, and growing tropical orchids.

* * *

GIRZAITIS, Loretta 1920-

PERSONAL: Surname rhymes with "bursitis"; born February 21, 1920, in Chicago, Ill.; daughter of Paul and Susan (Ignatavicius) Girzaitis. *Education:* Marywood College, Scranton, Pa., B.S. in Ed., 1953; Manhattan College, New York, N.Y., M.A., 1969; also studied at Marquette University, Notre Dame University, and University of Utah. *Politics:* Democrat. *Religion:* Roman Catholic. *Residence:* St. Paul, Minn. *Office:* Catholic Education Center, Archdiocese of St. Paul-Minneapolis, 251 Summit, St. Paul, Minn. 55102.

CAREER: Teacher of English and journalism at Catholic high school in Chicago, Ill., 1960-68; Riverdale Press, New York, N.Y., writer-photographer, 1968-69; Catholic Education Center, Archdiocese of St. Paul-Minneapolis, St. Paul, Minn., director of adult education, 1970—. Regional consultant, U.S. Catholic Conference, 1970-73. *Member:* Adult Education Association of the U.S.A., National Catholic Education Association (vice-president of Adult Education Division, 1973—), Minnesota Adult Education Association (vice-president, 1973—).

WRITINGS: Listening: A Response Ability, St. Mary's College Press (Winona, Minn.), 1972. Also author of resource books on adult education.

WORK IN PROGRESS: Developing slide-tapes on various educational subjects.

* * *

GITIN, David (Daniel) 1941-

PERSONAL: Born December 19, 1941, in Buffalo, N.Y.; son of Louis Leonard (a professor) and Miriam (Myers) Gitin; married Maria Brians (a poet and painter), March 27, 1969. *Education:* State University of New York at Buffalo, B.A., 1966; San Francisco State College (now University), M.A., 1971; University of Wisconsin, graduate study, 1972-73. *Home:* 1325 Rutledge, Apt. 1, Madison, Wis. 53703; and c/o Louis Gitin, 3063A Via Serena S., Laguna Hills, Calif. 92653.

CAREER: Poet. Lived in San Francisco's Haight-Ashbury district, 1967-70; co-founded Poets' Theatre (now defunct) at the Straight Theatre, 1968; directed series of readings and worked as counter man at I-Thou Coffeehouse, 1968; baggage clerk for Greyhound Lines, 1969-70; manager, Full Moon Bookstore, San Francisco, 1971; University of Wisconsin Extension School, Madison, teacher of English, 1972-74. Taught at Free University of San Francisco State College (now University), fall, 1968. Produced poetry programs for KDKA-FM, Berkeley, Calif., 1967-71. Has given poetry readings for Neighborhood Arts Council, and participated in Annual Arts Festival, both in San Francisco, 1967-69. Has also held jobs as postal clerk and carrier, social caseworker, record salesman, and library page. *Awards, honors:* Arx Foundation award, 1970, for four poems appearing in *Arx* magazine.

WRITINGS: Guitar against the Wall, Panjandrum, 1972; *City Air,* Ithaca House, 1974; *Vacuum Tapestries,* BB Books (England), 1974. Work is represented in anthologies, including, *Voices of Poetry, 1971,* Elman Publishing, 1971; *Mark in Time,* edited by Nick Harvey, Glide Publications, 1971. Contributor to numerous journals and little magazines, including *Arx, Red Cedar Review, Work, New: American and Canadian Poetry, Greenfield Review, Aldebaran Review, Desperado, Salt Lick, Panache, Amphora, Carolina Quarterly, Western Humanities Review, Penumbra, Rolling Stone, Juatara, Wisconsin Review, Io, Kansas Quarterly, New Dimensions, Tree,* and *Isthmus.* Editor, *Bricoleur,* 1969; guest editor, *Amphora,* October, 1971; collator, *Touch,* 1971.

WORK IN PROGRESS: Extensive study of the poetry of George Oppen, Larry Eigner, Clark Coolidge, Charles Reznikoff, and others; study of the music and writings of John Cage and Karlheinz Stockhausen; *Strobe Life,* an experimental prose autobiography; *Legwork,* collected poems; another as yet untitled collection of work, completion expected in 1974.

SIDELIGHTS: Gitin told *CA:* "Childhood exposure to music and literature, my father's library, led to interest and study of music, piano and violin lessons, the composition of plays and short stories, and by age 17, poems. The presence of LeRoi Jones in Buffalo (1964) and the friendship of John Wieners (1964 to the present) were kinetic forces, as was the presence in Buffalo of an array of composers, including Mauricio Kagel, Henri Pousseur, Lukas Foss, to finally re-stir my interests into the activity of writing poetry circa 1964. Charles Olson and Allen Ginsberg were polestars then, George Oppen and Larry Eigner and Robert Creeley and Clark Coolidge since mid-1968."

BIOGRAPHICAL/CRITICAL SOURCES: University of Wisconsin *Badger-Herald,* June 11-13, 1973.

* * *

GLANZ, Rudolf 1892-

PERSONAL: Born December 21, 1892, in Vienna, Austria; came to United States, 1938; son of David (an artisan) and Regine (Graeber) Glanz; married Rose Levi, November 29, 1921 (died, 1941); married Charlotte Brandes (a clerk), March 12, 1950; children: Ruth (Mrs. Alfred Michaels). *Education:* Attended Beth Hamidrash, 1910-14; University of Vienna, Dr. juris utriusque, 1918. *Religion:* Jewish. *Home:* 620 West 171st St., New York, N.Y. 10032.

CAREER: Admitted to bar, Vienna, Austria, 1928; Yivo Institute for Jewish Research, New York, N.Y., research historian, 1938-56, member of advisory research council, 1940, member of board of directors, 1945; author, lawyer. Vienna Jewish Community, chairman of law committee, 1924, member of executive committee, 1924, member of board of directors, 1924. *Military service:* Austrian Army, 1914-18. *Member:* American Historical Association, American Jewish Historical Society, Labor Zionist Organization of America-Poale Zion, Conference on Jewish Studies, International Mark Twain Society (honorary member).

Awards, honors: Committee for Displaced Scholars, research grant, 1940.

WRITINGS: Jews in Relation to the Cultural Milieu of Germans in America up to the Eighteen Eighties, [New York], 1947; *The Jews of California: From the Discovery of Gold until 1880,* [New York], 1960; *The Jew in the Old American Folklore,* [New York], 1961; *German Jewish Names in America,* [New York], 1961; *Jew and Mormon: Historical Group Relations and Religious Outlook,* [New York], 1963; *Jew and Irish: Historical Group Relations and Immigration,* [New York], 1966; *Geschichte des niederen Juedischen Volkes in Deutschland: Eine Studie ueber historisches Gaunertum, Bettelwesen und Vagantentum,* [New York], 1968; *The German Jew in America: An Annotated Bibliography Including Books, Pamphlets, and Articles of Special Interest,* Hebrew Union College Press, 1969; *Studies in Judaica Americana,* Ktav, 1970; *Jew and Italian: Historic Group Relations and the New Immigration (1881-1924),* [New York], 1971; *The Jew in Early American Wit and Graphic Humor,* Ktav, 1973.

Also author of *Yiddish Elements in German Thief Jargon,* 1928; *Lower Classes of German Jewry in the 18th Century,* 1932; *Immigration of German-Jews up to 1880,* 1947; *Source Material: History of Jewish Immigration to U.S.,* 1951; *Jews and Chinese in America,* 1960; *The Rothschild Legend in America,* 1960; *German Jews in New York City in the 19th Century,* 1960.

Contributor to English and Yiddish publications. Editor, *Juedische Arbeiter,* 1924.

WORK IN PROGRESS: Research on immigration, historic group relations, American social history, history of the lower classes, historic folklore, European history.

* * *

GLAZE, Eleanor 1930-

PERSONAL: Born September 25, 1930, in Columbia, Mo.; daughter of Emmette Lorraine (a builder) and Eleanor (Naulty) Sutton; married William Neal Ellis in 1963; children: Valorie Lynn Grear. *Education:* Attended public schools in Memphis, Tenn. *Politics:* Liberal. *Religion:* Buddhist. *Home:* 3561 Hanna, Memphis, Tenn. 38128. *Agent:* Ellen Levine, Curtis Brown Ltd., 60 East 56th St., New York, N.Y. 10022.

CAREER: Held various jobs in Memphis, Tenn., including those of nurse's aide, waitress; did clerical and production work; part-time teacher at Southwestern Adult Center, 1970, 1971, and 1973. *Member:* Authors Guild, Women in Communication. *Awards, honors:* Breadloaf Writers Conference fellowship, 1971.

WRITINGS: The Embrace and Stories, Bobbs-Merrill, 1970; *Fear and Tenderness,* Bobbs-Merrill, 1973. Contributor of short stories to *New Yorker, Redbook, McCall's, Atlantic,* and *Delta Review.*

WORK IN PROGRESS: A novel.

* * *

GLENDINNING, Sally
See GLENDINNING, Sara W(ilson)

* * *

GLENDINNING, Sara W(ilson) 1913- (Sally Glendinning)

PERSONAL: Born September 17, 1913, in Birmingham, Ala.; daughter of William C. (a businessman) and Marie (Harrison) Wilson; married Richard E. Glendinning (an author and historian), December 27, 1941; children: Elizabeth Ann (Mrs. Alan Burrell). *Education:* Attended Sorbonne, University of Paris, 1932; Agnes Scott College, B.A., 1933; Columbia University, B.S.J., 1934. *Residence:* Sarasota, Fla.

CAREER: Baltimore Evening Sun, Baltimore, Md., woman's page editor, 1936-45; *Herald-Tribune,* Sarasota, Fla., reporter, 1961—. *Member:* Phi Beta Kappa. *Awards, honors:* Florida School Bell Award, 1963, for news reporting on schools.

WRITINGS—Juvenile; under name Sally Glendinning: *Thomas Gainsborough: Artist of England,* Garrard, 1969; *Queen Victoria: English Empress,* Garrard, 1970; (with husband, Richard E. Glendinning) *The Ringling Brothers,* Garrard, 1972; "Jimmy and Joe" series, published by Garrard: *Jimmy and Joe Catch an Elephant,* 1969; *. . . Find a Ghost,* 1969; *. . . Get a Hen's Surprise,* 1970; *. . . Look for a Bear,* 1970; *. . . Fly a Kite,* 1970; *. . . Go to the Fair,* 1971; *. . . Meet a Halloween Witch,* 1971; *. . . See a Monster,* 1972; *. . . Save a Christmas Deer,* 1973.

SIDELIGHTS: Sally Glendinning's primary interest is in writing real adventure stories at first-grade vocabulary level to prove even to beginning readers that they can read for themselves. She is also interested in writing books at an adult level for slow readers and for other adult readers with only a sixth or seventh grade-level reading ability.

* * *

GLENN, Jacob B. 1905-1974

May 2, 1905—July 16, 1974; American physician, columnist, and author of works on health and medicine. Obituaries: *New York Times,* July 17, 1974. (*CA*-9/10).

* * *

GNAGEY, Thomas D(avid) 1938-

PERSONAL: Surname is pronounced *Na*-gee; born March 9, 1938, in Sterling, Ill.; son of Lelo Joel (a teacher) and Virginia (Thompson) Gnagey; married Patricia McCormack (a learning disability therapist), June 16, 1961; children: Robert Franklin. *Education:* Manchester College, Manchester, Ind., student, 1956-58; Illinois State University, B.S. in Ed., 1960, M.S., 1962; Bradley University, M.A., 1962; George Peabody College for Teachers, Ed.S., 1965. *Religion:* Unitarian Universalist. *Home:* 1260 Ottawa Ave., Ottawa, Ill. 61350. *Office:* Facilitation House, Box 611, Ottawa, Ill. 61350.

CAREER: State University of New York College at Geneseo, instructor in psychology, 1963-64; Livingston County schools, Pontiac, Ill., chief psychologist, special education department, 1965-69; Ottawa elementary schools, Ottawa, Ill., chief psychologist, 1969—. Private practice as clinical psychologist, 1967—; part-time instructor at Winston Churchill College, 1968-69, and National College of Education, 1970—. President of Livingston County Mental Health Association, 1968-69.

MEMBER: International Association for the Study of Perception (secretary, 1969-71; president, 1972-73), American Psychological Association, Psychologists in Private Practice, National Association of School Psychologists, Council for Exceptional Children.

WRITINGS: (With wife, Patricia Gnagey) *The Turtle and*

His Friends, Facilitation House, 1970; *How to Put Up with Parents,* Facilitation House, 1972. Writer of educational programs for children with learning disabilities, published by Facilitation House. Contributor to educational journals.

WORK IN PROGRESS: Continuing research in diagnostic testing and remediation of learning-disabled children; research on relaxation therapy.

AVOCATIONAL INTERESTS: Swimming, artistic activities.

* * *

GOCEK, Matilda A(rkenbout) 1923-

PERSONAL: Born February 18, 1923, in Hoboken, N.J.; daughter of Jacob Richard and Matilda (Meyer) Arkenbout; married H. F. Decker, May 15, 1939 (divorced, November, 1955); married John A. Gocek (an engineer), November 18, 1956; children: (first marriage) Ruth Ann (Mrs. Donald Case), Dianne Karen (Mrs. Ralph McKinstrie); (second marriage) John Jacob. *Education:* Orange County Community College, A.A., 1961; State University of New York at New Paltz, B.A. (with distinction), 1964; State University of New York at Albany, M.L.S., 1967. *Politics:* "Republican, but splits ticket." *Religion:* Presbyterian. *Home:* Dunderberg Rd., Monroe, N.Y. 10950. *Office:* Tuxedo Park Library, Orange Turnpike, Tuxedo Park, N.Y. 10987.

CAREER: Monroe Free Library, Monroe, N.Y., librarian, 1958-61; Tuxedo Park Library, Tuxedo Park, N.Y., library director, 1963—. Consultant, Tuxedo Union Free School, 1967-69; president of Orange-Sullivan Public Library Association, 1967-70; trustee, Tuxedo Park Day School, 1971—; secretary, Ramapo Catskill Library System Directors Association, 1973—. Member of South Eastern New York Library Resources Council, 1968—, and Orange County Museums and Galleries Bicentennial Committee, 1972—. Official town historian in Tuxedo, 1973—. *Member:* National Historical Society, American Library Association, Arnold Expedition Historical Society, New York Library Association, Association of Towns of New York State, Neversink Valley Area Museum-Education Committee, Orange County Historical Society. *Awards, honors:* Idiom Poetry award, 1963; honorary doctorate, Colorado State Christian College, 1973.

WRITINGS: Tuxedo Park Library: Social Aspects of Growth, 1901-1940, Library Research Associates, 1968; *Library Service for Commuting Students: Study of Four South Eastern New York Counties,* South Eastern New York Library Resources Council, 1970; (author of introduction) Thomas Benton Brooks, *The Augusta Tract,* Library Research Association, 1972. *Benedict Arnold: Readers' Guide and Bibliography,* Library Research Associates, 1973; *Orange County, New York: Readers' Guide and Bibliography,* Library Research Associates, 1973. Contributor to *Unabashed Librarian.* Editor, *Dialogue,* 1969—.

WORK IN PROGRESS: Orange County South: Collected Historical Essays, completion expected in 1974.

SIDELIGHTS: Mrs. Gocek told *CA:* "I am what is known as a 'late bloomer.' As a child raised in the depression years, I learned early to live thriftily and to do the best with what I had, taught by a mother who appreciated the finer things in life. My love of the arts came from one grandfather who was a painter, and the other who sang in the Metropolitan Opera chorus ... The love of people, books and history has brought me to a career that I accept as a public service. Perhaps to inspire some other youngster to achieve a satisfaction he thinks is unattainable, perhaps to stimulate thought in an adult who thinks life has passed her by, perhaps to open a door to life anew—these are my goals, for the world is made of people and we have only each other."

* * *

GOERNER, E(dward) A(lfred) 1929-

PERSONAL: Born December 29, 1929, in Brooklyn, N.Y.; son of Alfred (a physician) and M. Margaret (a physician; maiden name, Popp) Goerner; married Marilyn Rohrer, September 15, 1955; children: Peter, Elizabeth, Margaret, Katherine, Rebecca. *Education:* University of Notre Dame, A.B., 1952; University of Chicago, Ph.D., 1959. *Politics:* Democrat. *Religion:* Roman Catholic. *Home:* 1136 North Notre Dame Ave., South Bend, Ind. 46624. *Office:* Department of Political Science, University of Notre Dame, Notre Dame, Ind. 46556.

CAREER: Yale University, New Haven, Conn., instructor in politics, 1959-60; University of Notre Dame, Notre Dame, Ind., assistant professor, 1960-66, associate professor, 1966-70, professor of politics, 1970—. *Military service:* U.S. Navy, 1952-55; became lieutenant junior grade. *Member:* Association des Amis de l'Orgue Silbermann de l'Eglise St. Thomas de Strasbourg.

WRITINGS: Peter and Caesar, Herder, 1965; *The Constitutions of Europe,* Regnery, 1967; *Democracy in Crisis,* University of Notre Dame Press, 1971.

WORK IN PROGRESS: Gaullism and European Unification.

* * *

GOLDBECK, David M. 1942-

PERSONAL: Born September 23, 1942, in New York, N.Y.; son of Kurt L. and Ilse (Weinberger) Goldbeck; married Nikki Schulman (a writer), December 14, 1969. *Education:* Queens College of the City University of New York, B.A., 1964; Brooklyn Law School, L.L.B., 1967. *Politics:* "The Bill of Rights and the Golden Rule." *Home and office:* Old Witchtree Rd., Woodstock, N.Y. 12498. *Agent:* Georges Borchardt, Inc., 145 East 52nd St., New York, N.Y. 10022.

CAREER: Elementary school teacher in New York, N.Y., 1967-70; admitted to the Bar of New York State, 1968; South Brooklyn Legal Services, Brooklyn, N.Y., assistant attorney in charge, 1971.

WRITINGS: (With wife, Nikki Goldbeck) *The Supermarket Handbook: Access to Whole Foods,* Harper, 1973; (with Nikki Goldbeck) *The Dieter's Companion,* New American Library, in press; (with Nikki Goldbeck) *The Good Breakfast Book,* Links Books, in press.

SIDELIGHTS: Goldbeck told *CA:* "I love good hearty food and enjoy traveling to discover new food delights. Nikki and I are vegetarians and have learned much from other countries' abilities to eat well with only minimal meat. We have traveled extensively in Europe and the Mid-East and plan more in the future." He enjoys refinishing old furniture, rebuilding his house and garden, and running his four acres "like a homestead."

* * *

GOLDBECK, Nikki 1947-

PERSONAL: Born March 16, 1947, in New York, N.Y.;

daughter of Irwin and Florence (Fischer) Schulman; married David Goldbeck (a writer), December 14, 1969. *Education:* Cornell University, B.S., 1968; New School for Social Research, graduate study, 1968-69. *Home:* Old Witchtree Rd., Woodstock, N.Y. 12498. *Agent:* Georges Borchardt, Inc., 145 East 52nd St., New York, N.Y. 10022.

CAREER: Creative Food Services, Inc., New York, N.Y., freelance work in product development, 1967; D'Arcy Advertising Co., New York, N.Y., administrative assistant to account executive, 1968-69; Dudley-Anderson-Yutzy, New York, N.Y., public relations work, 1969-71; freelance writer in Woodstock, N.Y. Consultant to Rodale Press. *Member:* Omicron Nu.

WRITINGS: Cooking What Comes Naturally, Doubleday, 1972; (with husband, David Goldbeck) *The Supermarket Handbook: Access to Whole Foods,* Harper, 1973; (with David Goldbeck) *The Dieter's Companion,* New American Library, in press; (with David Goldbeck) *The Good Breakfast Book,* Links Books, in press. Contributor to *Organic Gardening and Farming* and *Fitness for Living.*

SIDELIGHTS: Mrs. Goldbeck has travelled to Europe, North Africa, and the Middle East.

* * *

GOLDBERG, Carl 1938-

PERSONAL: Born January 21, 1938, in Brooklyn, N.Y.; son of Samuel L. and Mollie (Hecht) Goldberg; married Merle Ann Cantor (a psychiatric social worker), July 3, 1959. *Education:* American International College, B.A., 1960; University of Wyoming, M.A., 1961; University of Oklahoma, Ph.D., 1966; Washington School of Psychiatry, certificate in analytic group psychotherapy, 1970. *Home:* 307 Stonington Rd., Silver Spring, Md. 20902.

CAREER: Certified psychologist by Maryland Board of Professional Examiners of Psychologists, 1970; licensed psychologist in District of Columbia, 1973. New York University, New York, N.Y., psychometrist, 1961-62; Hawthorne Cedar Knolls School, Hawthorne, N.Y., research psychologist, 1964-66; Kings County Hospital, Brooklyn, N.Y., postdoctoral clinical psychology intern, 1966-67; Saint Elizabeth's Hospital, Washington, D.C., supervisory and training clinical psychologist, 1967-71; Laurel Comprehensive Community Mental Health Center, Prince George's County, Md., director, 1971—. Instructor at University of Virginia, 1968; lecturer at Psychiatric Institute Foundation, 1971-73; member of teaching staff of Washington School of Psychiatry, 1973; guest lecturer on transatlantic voyages of "S.S. France," 1973; associate clinical professor at George Washington University, 1974. Private practice in psychotherapy in Washington, D.C., 1968. Director of Northern Prince George's County Mental Health Team, 1971—; director of Crossroads Institute (center for group psychotherapy service, training, and research), 1974. Consultant to National Drug Abuse Training Center, 1973; and to St. Elizabeth's Hospital Overholser Training Division and East Side Division.

MEMBER: American Psychological Association, American Group Psychotherapy Association, District of Columbia Psychological Association, Prince George's County Mental Health Association (professional adviser), Psi Chi.

WRITINGS: (With H. W. Polsky and D. S. Claster) *Dynamics of Residential Treatment,* University of North Carolina Press, 1968; (with Polsky and Claster) *Social System Perspectives in Residential Institutions,* Michigan State University Press, 1970; *Encounter: Group Sensitivity Training Experience* (Psychiatry and Social Science Book Club selection), Science House, 1970; *The Human Circle: An Existential Approach to the New Group Therapies,* Nelson-Hall, 1973; (contributor) D. A. Evans and W. L. Claiborn, editors, *Mental Health Issues and the Urban Poor,* Pergamon, 1974.

Author of column on mental health in *Laurel News Leader,* 1971-72. Contributor to professional journals, including *Group Psychotherapy and Psychodrama, Hospital and Community Psychiatry, Canada's Mental Health, Psychotherapy and Social Science Review, International Journal of Psychiatry,* and *Proceedings of the International Group Psychotherapy Congress.*

WORK IN PROGRESS: Contractual Psychotherapy: Beyond Technique–Ethical Concerns in the Conduct of Psychotherapy.

* * *

GOLDBERG, Gerald Jay 1929-

PERSONAL: Born December 30, 1929, in New York, N.Y.; son of Nathan and Henriette Goldberg; married Nancy Marmer (an art critic), 1954; children: Robert. *Education:* Purdue University, B.S., 1952; New York University, M.A., 1955; University of Minnesota, Ph.D., 1958. *Agent:* Georges Borchardt, Inc., 145 East 52nd St., New York, N.Y. 10022. *Office:* Department of English, University of California, Los Angeles, Calif. 90024.

CAREER: Dartmouth College, Hanover, N.H., assistant professor of English, 1958-64; University of California, Los Angeles, assistant professor, 1964-68, associate professor, 1969-73, professor of English, 1974—. Fulbright professor at University of Zaragoza, 1962-63. *Member:* Authors League of America, National Humanities Series (member of advisory committee of Western Center, 1972-73). *Awards, honors:* Fellow of Institute of Creative Arts, 1966-67, 1969; *The Lynching of Orin Newfield* was nominated for a Pulitzer Prize, 1970.

WRITINGS: Notes from the Diaspora, Atelier 21, 1962; (editor with wife, Nancy Marmer Goldberg) *The Modern Critical Spectrum,* Prentice-Hall, 1962; *The Fate of Innocence,* Prentice-Hall, 1965; *The National Standard* (novel), Holt, 1968; *The Lynching of Orin Newfield* (novel), Dial, 1970; *A Hundred Twenty-Six Days of Continuous Sunshine* (short stories), Dial, 1972. Contributor to *Harper's Bazaar, Shenandoah,* and *Lugano Review.* Editor of *Faulkner Studies* and *Critique: Studies in Modern Fiction.*

WORK IN PROGRESS: A biography of Pablo Picasso, with wife, Nancy Marmer Goldberg.

SIDELIGHTS: After writing *The National Standard,* Goldberg said: "'This time, like all times, is a very good one, if we but know what to do with it,' said Emerson, and they didn't. Witness slavery and the Mexican war. More than 100 years later there's still slavery and now it's Vietnam. Why, America, are you suffering from a foolish consistency? . . . Thus, for a writer today it's hard to decide which is the more urgent—a sense of humor or a sense of outrage. I try to keep both and cope. Non-realism is the method, for it creates an aesthetic room in which anything can happen. . . .The old ways of seeing things won't do in such a room, for now we have new relationships established and new meanings revealed. This is the ideal room for satire, and it is the one I've chosen for *The National Standard.*"

The screenplay adaptation of *The Lynching of Orin Newfield* is being written by Buck Henry.

* * *

GOLDBERG, Ray A(llan) 1926-

PERSONAL: Born October 19, 1926, in Fargo, N.D.; son of Max and Anne Libby (Paletz) Goldberg; married Thelma Ruth Englander, May 20, 1956; children: Marc Evan, Jennifer Eve, Jeffrey Lewis. *Education:* Harvard University, A.B. (cum laude), 1948, M.B.A., 1950; University of Minnesota, Ph.D., 1952. *Home:* 5 Rangeley Rd., Chestnut Hill, Mass. 02167. *Office:* Harvard Graduate School of Business Administration, Soldiers Field, Boston, Mass. 02163.

CAREER: Moorehead Seed & Grain Co., Minneapolis, Minn., chief of public relations, 1952-56, member of board of directors until 1962; Harvard University, Cambridge, Mass., lecturer, 1955-57, assistant professor, 1960-66, associate professor of business administration, 1966-70, George M. Moffett Professor of Agriculture and Business, 1970—. Officer and member of board of directors, Goldena Mills, Inc., 1952-62; secretary and member of board of directors, Experience, Inc., 1963—; member of board of directors, Red River Elevator Co., Sola Basic Industries, 1965-67, Mid-America Foods, Inc., 1969-72, International Development Foundation, 1969—, and Tri/Valley Growers, 1973—. Member of board of trustees, Roxbury Latin School, 1973—. Agribusiness consultant, Inter-University Program for Graduate Business Education of Ford Foundation, 1969; consultant, United States Dairy Association, 1965, Undersecretary of Agriculture, 1965-69, President's Food and Fiber Commission, 1966-67, Agency for International Development of U.S. Department of State, U.S. National Price Commission, 1971, National Marine Fisheries Service of U.S. Department of Agriculture, 1972, and to various agribusiness firms and cooperatives; chairman of panel on food processing for National Commission on Productivity, 1972. Chairman of Massachusetts Governor's Emergency Commission on Food.

MEMBER: American Farm Economic Association, American Marketing Association, American Dairy Science Association, Food Distribution Research Society, Agricultural Economics Association of America, Canadian Agricultural Economics Society, American Society of Animal Science, Harvard Club (Boston, New York), Oakridge Country Club. *Awards, honors:* Uhlmann Grain Award, 1952.

WRITINGS: The Soybean Industry: With Special Reference to the Competitive Position of the Minnesota Producer and Processor, University of Minnesota Press, 1952; (with John H. Davis) *A Concept of Agribusiness,* Division of Research, Graduate School of Business Administration, Harvard University, 1957; (with Henry B. Arthur and K. M. Bird) *The United States Food and Fiber System in a Changing World Environment,* National Advisory Commission on Food and Fiber, 1967; (with William Applebaum) *Brand Strategy in U.S. Food Marketing,* Division of Research, Graduate School of Business Administration, Harvard University, 1967; *Agribusiness Coordination: A Systems Approach to the Wheat, Soybean, and Florida Orange Economies,* Division of Research, Graduate School of Business Administration, Harvard University, 1968. Also author of *The Nonpartisan League in North Dakota,* 1948, (with Arthur) *Identifying Management Problems of Agribusiness Firms,* Volumes I-III, 1967, *Advanced Agribusiness Management Seminar Philippine Casebook,* 1969, (with others) *Agribusiness Management for Developing Countries: With Special Reference to the Central American Fruit and Vegetable Commodity System,* 1973, and (with Lee F. Schrader) *Federal Income Taxes and Farmers' Cooperatives,* 1973. Contributor to proceedings, symposia, and to journals in his field.

* * *

GOLDBERG, Stan J. 1939-

PERSONAL: Born March 5, 1939, in Atlanta, Ga.; son of Joseph L. (a jeweler) and Eva B. Goldberg. *Education:* Georgia Institute of Technology, B.S., 1961; graduate study at Techniche Hochschule, Hanover, Germany, 1961-62, University of Freiburg, 1963-65, and Massachusetts Institute of Technology, 1965-66. *Residence:* New York, N.Y. *Agent:* James Brown Associates, Inc., 22 East 60th St., New York, N.Y. 10022.

CAREER: Atkins & Reilly, Boston, Mass., photographic director, 1967-69; Inter-media, Inc., Boston, Mass., media specialist, 1969-70; Stan J. Goldberg Associates, Inc. (audio-visual productions), New York, N.Y., president, 1971—. Guest lecturer at Rhode Island School of Design, 1968. *Member:* Authors Guild of New York. *Awards, honors:* World Student Fund scholarship to Hanover, Germany, 1961-62.

WRITINGS: The Adventures of Stanley Kane (juvenile), Harcourt, 1973.

WORK IN PROGRESS: Six more Stanley Kane books.

SIDELIGHTS: Goldberg changed his field of interest from solid state physics to the art of photography. He was asked to design the projected sets for the Broadway production of "The Me Nobody Knows" in 1970 and "Over Here" in 1974. He began writing for children in 1972.

* * *

GOLDEMBERG, Rose Leiman (Rose Leiman Schiller, Beatrice Traven)

PERSONAL: Born in Staten Island, N.Y.; daughter of Louis I. and Esther (Friedman) Leiman; married Raymond Schiller, December, 1949 (divorced, 1969); married Robert L. Goldemberg (a cosmetic chemistry consultant), September 7, 1969; children: (first marriage) Leiman J., Lisa Hope. *Education:* Brooklyn College (now Brooklyn College of the City University of New York), B.A. (magna cum laude), 1949; Ohio State University, M.A., 1950; also studied theatre at American Theatre Wing and Columbia University. *Residence:* Teaneck, N.J. *Agent:* Robert Freedman, Brandt and Brandt, 101 Park Ave., New York, N.Y. 10017. *Office:* Department of Communication, Theatre, and Speech, Fairleigh Dickinson University, Teaneck, N.J. 07666.

CAREER: Ohio State University, Columbus, member of faculty, 1949-50; College of the City of New York (now City College of the City University of New York), New York, N.Y., member of faculty, 1953-54; University of California at Los Angeles, member of faculty, 1960-62; Valley College, Van Nuys, Calif., member of faculty, 1960-62; Fairleigh Dickinson University, Teaneck, N.J., associate professor of theatre, 1969—. Playwright, novelist, and television writer. Consultant to United Artists and Warner Brothers-Seven Arts Productions, 1966-69; special consultant, Public Broadcasting System's "Sesame Street" children's program, 1968; playwright-in-residence, Eugene O'Neill Theatre Center, summer, 1970; teacher of dramatic improvisation, Bergen Community Museum, 1973. *Member:* New Dramatists, Eugene O'Neill Playwrights, Dramatists' Guild, American Theatre Association Playwright's Unit, Phi Beta Kappa. *Awards, honors: Atlantic Monthly* Poetry Award, 1949; *Heritage* Poetry Award, 1950; American Theatre Wing Playwrighting Award, 1954-55; Ford Foundation Fund for the Republic Award, 1955, for "The Pencil Box War"; American Film Festival certificate of merit, 1959, for "You're It"; Dramatists' Guild Fund grant, 1971; Fairleigh Dickinson University Faculty Research Grant, 1971-72, 1973-74; *Earplay* Competition Award, 1973, for "Voices in My Head"; New Jersey State Council on the Arts mini-grant, 1973, for "The Merry War."

WRITINGS—Under pseudonym Beatrice Traven: *Here's Egg on Your Face,* Hewitt House, 1969; *Natural Cosmetics in Your Kitchen,* Simon & Schuster, 1974.

Plays: "Gandhiji" (full-length), first produced in Waterford, Conn., at Eugene O'Neill Playwrights Conference, July, 1970; "The Rabinowitz Gambit" (full-length), first produced in New York, N.Y., at New Theatre Workshop, April, 1971; *Marching as to War* (one-act; first produced in New York, N.Y., at East Village Theatre, May, 1971), Dramatists Play Service, 1972; "Rites of Passage" (full-length), first produced in New York, N.Y., at New Dramatists Theatre, September, 1972; "The Merry War" (full-length), first produced in New York, N.Y., at New Dramatists Theatre, April, 1973. Also author of plays as yet unpublished and unproduced: "Absolutely Everything on This Teaming Earth," and "A Little Travelling Music." Also author of several plays for series, "Plays for Living."

Television plays—All under name Rose Leiman Schiller: "The Bright Red Carpet," 1954; "Big World on My Doorstep," 1954; "The Visit," 1955; "The Pencil Box War," 1955; "Apples in Eden," 1956; "The Door of Silence," 1957; "The Story of St. Francis," 1957; "Bernadette of Lourdes," 1957; "The Brothers," 1958. Also author of 12-program pilot series for educational television, 1959.

Films—All under name Rose Leiman Schiller: "Follow Me, Girls," 1958; "Settlement House," 1959; "You're It," 1959; "The Hidden Tear," 1959; "Job," 1960; "Roundup," 1960.

Also author of novel, "The Tenafly Line."

WORK IN PROGRESS: Women in Theatre, a book on the influence of women in theatre; a play, "Love One Another"; *The Practical and Passionate Guide to Antique Jewelry,* a book on the art of collecting.

SIDELIGHTS: Mrs. Goldemberg told *CA:* "I've been a writer since I was five years old; never wanted to be anything else. I've been a female since I was born—and it's the tension between the full living out of both of these 'commitments' that has been the pith and core of my life."

* * *

GOLDMAN, Alex J. 1917-

PERSONAL: Born June 8, 1917, in Drohitin, Poland; son of Julius D. (a rabbi) and Sarah (Rubinstein) Goldman; married Edith Borovay (an artist), March 1, 1942; children: Robert, Pamela. *Education:* DePaul University, LL.B., 1939; Hebrew Theological College, Chicago, Rabbi, 1944; University of Pennsylvania, certificate in marriage counseling, 1961. *Home:* 564 Hunting Ridge Rd., Stamford, Conn. 06903. *Agent:* Bertha Klausner International Literary Agency, Inc., 71 Park Ave., New York, N.Y. 10021. *Office:* Temple Beth El, Roxbury Rd., Stamford, Conn.

CAREER: Rabbi of temple in Tallahassee, Fla., 1944-46; Florida State College for Women (now Florida State University), Tallahassee, director of Hillel Foundation, 1945-46; Temple University, Philadelphia, Pa., director of Hillel Foundation, 1946-54; Beaver College, Jenkintown, Pa., director of Hillel Foundation, 1953-54; Temple Beth El, Stamford, Conn., currently rabbi. Secretary of Zionist Youth Committee, Philadelphia, 1951-52. *Member:* Rabbinical Assembly.

WRITINGS: Handbook for the Jewish Family: Understanding and Enjoying the Sabbath and Holidays, Bloch Publishing, 1958; *Blessed Art Thou,* Hebrew Publishing, 1961; *Giants of Faith: Great American Rabbis,* Citadel, 1964; (editor) *The Quotable Kennedy,* Citadel, 1965; *A Child's Dictionary of Jewish Symbols,* Feldheim, 1967; *John Fitzgerald Kennedy: The World Remembers* (juvenile), Fleet Press, 1968; (editor) *The Truman Wit,* Citadel, 1968; *The Power of the Bible,* Fountainhead, 1972.

WORK IN PROGRESS: Three novels, *My Blood Begins to Sing, Rabbi Shirley,* and *Peniel; Judaism Confronts Contemporary Issues;* a novel-play, *My Path;* several other books on John F. Kennedy.

* * *

GOLDSMITH, Robert Hillis 1911-

PERSONAL: Born September 3, 1911, in East Lansing, Mich.; son of Robert (an author and journalist) and Edith (a lecturer; maiden name, Darrow) Goldsmith; married Mary A. Glass (a school teacher), June 1, 1942; children: Alice Darrow, Robert Glass. *Education:* Pennsylvania State University, B.A. (cum laude), 1936; Columbia University, M.A., 1943, Ph.D., 1952. *Politics:* Democrat. *Religion:* Methodist. *Home address:* P.O. Box 55, Emory, Va. 24327. *Office:* Emory and Henry College, Emory, Va. 24327.

CAREER: Temple University, Philadelphia, Pa., instructor in English, 1946-52; University of Maryland, College Park, instructor in English, 1952-55; Emory and Henry College, Emory, Va., associate professor, 1955-60, professor of English, 1960—, chairman of department, 1971—. Research fellow at Folger Shakespeare Library, summer, 1959, and at University of North Carolina, 1965, 1966-67. *Military service:* U.S. Army Air Forces, historian, 1942-46; became sergeant.

MEMBER: Modern Language Association of America, Shakespeare Association of America, American Association of University Professors (president of local chapter, 1967-69), South Atlantic Modern Language Association, Southeast Renaissance Conference (vice-president, 1972-73; president, 1973-74), Phi Kappa Phi. *Awards, honors:* Keats Memorial Award from Virginia Poetry Society, 1960, for "Anatomy of Love"; first prize in drama contest for religious plays from California Western University, 1963, for "Batter My Heart."

WRITINGS: Wise Fools in Shakespeare, Michigan State University Press, 1955; *English Literature Survey,* Volume I, Harper, in press.

Plays: "Falling Star" (blank-verse play), first performed in Emory, Va., at Emory and Henry College, April 2, 1959; "Batter My Heart," first performed in Emory, Va., at Emory and Henry College, December 7, 1962.

Also author of three-act play, "Earth Song."

Contributor of about twenty articles, poems, and reviews to literature and religious journals, including *Renaissance Papers, Interpretation: A Journal of Bible and Theology, Modern Language Review, Shakespeare Quarterly, Bulletin of Bibliography,* and *PMLA.*

* * *

GOLDSTEIN, Malcolm 1925-

PERSONAL: Born August 18, 1925, in Huntington, W. Va.; son of Jack A. (a businessman) and Lillian (Cohen) Goldstein. *Education:* Princeton University, A.B., 1949; Columbia University, M.A., 1951, Ph.D., 1956. *Residence:* New York, N.Y. *Office:* Department of English, Queens College of the City University of New York, Flushing, N.Y. 11367.

CAREER: Stanford University, Stanford, Calif., instructor, 1953-57, assistant professor of English, 1957-61; Queens College of the City University of New York, Flushing, assistant professor, 1961-65, associate professor, 1965-71, professor of English, 1971—. *Military service:* U.S. Army, Signal Corps, 1944-46; became staff sergeant. *Member:* Modern Language Association of America, American Society for Theater Research, Grolier Club, Nassau Club. *Awards, honors:* Guggenheim fellowship, 1967.

WRITINGS: Pope and the Augustan Stage, Stanford University Press, 1958; *The Art of Thornton Wilder,* University of Nebraska Press, 1965; (editor) Nicholas Rowe, *The Fair Penitent,* University of Nebraska Press, 1968; *The Political Stage: American Drama and Theater of the Great Depression,* Oxford University Press, 1974. Member of editorial board of *Theatre Research.*

WORK IN PROGRESS: A biography of George S. Kaufman; research for a biography of architect Henry Hobson Richardson.

AVOCATIONAL INTERESTS: Architectural history.

* * *

GOLDSTONE, Lawrence A. See TREAT, Lawrence

* * *

GOLDTHORPE, J(ohn) E(rnest) 1921-

PERSONAL: Born June 10, 1921, in Cleethorpes, England; son of Samuel Leonard (a businessman) and Dorothy Elizabeth (a teacher; maiden name, Cooke) Goldthorpe; married Lois Muriel Anne Slater (a college lecturer in education), March 30, 1950; children: Timothy Peter, Susan Dorothy, Joy Barbara, Jonathan Christopher. *Education:* Christ's College, Cambridge, B.A., 1942, M.A., 1946; London School of Economics and Political Science, University of London, B.Sc. (economics), 1949, Ph.D., 1961. *Home:* 17 Arncliffe Rd., Leeds LS16 5AP, England. *Office:* Department of Sociology, University of Leeds, Leeds LS2 9JT, England.

CAREER: Makerere University College, Kampala, Uganda, 1951-62, began as lecturer, became senior lecturer in sociology; University of Leeds, Leeds, England, 1962—, began as lecturer, now senior lecturer in sociology. *Military service:* Royal Navy, 1941-46. Royal Naval Volunteer Reserve; became lieutenant. *Member:* International African Institute, British Sociological Association, African Studies Association of the United Kingdom (past member of council), Society of Authors, Ramblers Association.

WRITINGS: Outlines of East African Society, Makerere University College, 1958, revised edition, 1962; (with F. B. Wilson) *Tribal Maps of East Africa,* East African Institute of Social Research, 1960; (contributor) A. W. Southall, editor, *Social Change in Modern Africa,* International African Institute, 1961; *An African Elite,* Oxford University Press (East Africa), 1965; *An Introduction to Sociology,* Cambridge University Press, 1968, 2nd edition, 1974; *The Sociology of the Third World: Disparity and Involvement,* Cambridge University Press, in press. Contributor of articles and reviews to journals, including *Journal of Glaciology, Zaire, Universities Quarterly, British Journal of Sociology, Population Studies,* and *Sociological Review,* and to newspapers.

WORK IN PROGRESS: Research on the sociology of the family.

SIDELIGHTS: Originally a student of the natural sciences, Goldthorpe told *CA* that his experiences during World War II convinced him that "the study of the social sciences was more urgent for human survival than that of physics and chemistry. . . . So after the war I enrolled again as a freshman . . . to study economics, sociology, and social anthropology." After more than a decade of teaching in Uganda, Goldthorpe said "I have tried since to broaden my horizons to include the whole of the Third World.

"A lifelong passion for mountaineering led me to participate in two scientific expeditions to the Ruwenzori Mountains in Uganda, and with my little scientific knowledge to help make a small contribution to the glaciology of the region."

* * *

GOMEZ, David F(ederico) 1940-

PERSONAL: Born November 19, 1940, in Los Angeles, Calif.; son of Federico (a garment cutter) and Jennie (Fujier) Gomez. *Education:* St. Paul's College, Washington, D.C., B.A., 1965, M.A., 1968; University of Southern California, J.D., 1974. *Politics:* La Raza Unida Party. *Office:* Legal Aid Society of San Joaquin County, 110 North San Joaquin St., Stockton, Calif. 95202.

CAREER: Entered Missionary Society of St. Paul the Apostle (Paulist Fathers; C.S.P.); ordained Roman Catholic priest, 1969; priest in Roman Catholic church in North Davis County, Utah, 1969-70; Park Street Paulist Center, Boston, Mass., priest, 1970-71; Legal Aid Society of San Joaquin County, Stockton, Calif., staff attorney, 1974—. Coordinator of legal services for El Centro Chicano, Los Angeles, 1973—; instructor in Chicano studies for Terminal Island Federal Correctional Institution, 1973—. *Military service:* U.S. Marine Corps Reserve, 1959-65. *Member:* Padres Associados Para Derechos Religiosos, Educativos y Sociales.

WRITINGS: Somos Chicanos: Strangers in Our Own Land, Beacon Press, 1973. Contributor to *Homiletic and Pastoral Review, Catholic World, Christian Century, National Catholic Reporter, Nation,* and *America.* Staff member of newspaper *Justicia O. . .!,* 1972.

WORK IN PROGRESS: A sequel to *Somos Chicanos,* with more emphasis on politics, current political activity, philosophy, and culture; a novel about the Chicano experience.

SIDELIGHTS: When Gomez began to think of himself more as a Chicano priest than a Roman Catholic priest, he left Paulist order and studied law. He writes: "I entered law school because the law was another means of ministry to poor people. At the time, I believed that the church was impotent and unable to act decisively in making a national commitment to the cause of Chicanos, Indians, blacks and other poor people. The law, I thought, might be a more effective vehicle for helping. After three years of law school, my esteem for the institutions of justice has deteriorated quite a bit. In fact, the church's inability to cope with human problems in society reflects the inability of American society at large and its institutions. . .Only in a secondary sense am I a priest; only in a secondary sense am I someone who possesses legal skills. . . .I would like to continue working with my own people in building Aztlan."

* * *

GONZALEZ LOPEZ, Emilio 1903-

PERSONAL: Born November 13, 1903, in La Coruna, Spain. *Education:* Instituto General y Tecnico de La Coruna, B.A., 1920; University of Madrid, M.Social Sciences and Law, 1926, Ph.D., 1928; University of Munich, graduate study, 1927-28. *Office:* Graduate School and University Center, City University of New York, 33 West 42nd St., New York, N.Y. 10036.

CAREER: Official of Spanish Ministry of Pardon and Justice, 1926-27, and 1928-29; Universidad de la Laguna, Canary Islands, professor of penal studies and dean of faculty, 1931; Universidad de Salamanca, Salamanca, Spain, professor of penal studies, 1932; Universidad de Oviedo, Oviedo, Spain, professor of penal studies, 1936; Universidad de Barcelona, Barcelona, Spain, professor of penal studies, 1938; Hunter College of the City University of New York, New York, N.Y., instructor, 1940-48, assistant professor, 1948-54, associate professor, 1954-59, professor of language and literature, 1959—, chairman of department of Romance languages, 1963-67, has also directed Spanish plays. Galician Republican party deputy to Spanish assembly of states (Cortes) from La Coruna, 1931; deputy for province of La Coruna, 1934; director general of Local Administration and Public Welfare, 1932; republican deputy to Cortes from La Coruna, 1936; governor of Industrial Bank of Credit, 1936; member of Permanent Commission of Cortes, 1936; secretary of Spanish delegation to League of Nations and Spanish counsul general in Switzerland, 1938. Professor of penal studies at Universidad de Panama, 1941-43; president of commission in charge of drawing up a permanent code of penal law, 1942-43; Columbia University, lecturer, 1943-56, visiting professor, 1958-64, actor with Spanish Institute Players; Middlebury College, lecturer, 1947-70, director of Spanish Summer School, 1963-70, also actor in Spanish plays, 1947-58; visiting professor at New York University, 1958-59, 1961; executive officer of doctoral program in Spanish at City University of New York, 1967—; visiting professor at University of Puerto Rico at Mayaguez, 1972. Has lectured and attended conferences all over the world.

MEMBER: American Association of Teachers of Spanish and Portuguese (vice-president of New York chapter, 1955-56, 1958-59; president, 1956-58), Royal Galician Academy (corresponding member), Hispanic Institute (Columbia University). *Awards, honors:* Certificate of merit from Spanish Office of Censorship, 1943; first prize from Centro Gallego de Buenos Aires, 1951, for *Galicia, su alma y su cultura.*

WRITINGS: El espiritu de la Universidad (title means "The Spirit of the University"), [Madrid], 1930; *La Antijuricidad* (title means "The Principles of Justice"), [Madrid], 1930; *La Teoria del delito* (title means "The Theory of Crime"), [Madrid], 1931; *Emilio-Pardo Bazan: Novelista de Galicia* (title means "Emilio Pardo Bazan: Novelist of Galicia"), Columbia University Press, 1944.

Galicia: Su alma y su culture(title means "Galicia, Its Character and Culture"), Centro Gallego (Buenos Aires), 1954; (with Vicenzo Cioffari) *Spanish Review Grammar,* Heath, 1957, 2nd edition, 1964; *Historia de la civilizacion espanola* (title means "History of Spanish Civilization"), Las Americas, 1959, 3rd edition, 1970; *Grandeza y decadencia del reino de Galicia* (title means "The Rise and Fall of the Galician Kingdom"), Editorial Citania (Buenos Aires), 1957.

La insumision gallega: Martires y rebeldes–Galicia y Portugal en la Baja Edad Media (title means "The Galician Rebellious Spirit: Martyrs and Rebels, Galicia and Portugal in the Middle Ages") Editorial Citania, 1963; (translator) Frederick W. Danforth, editor, *The Argentine Penal Code,* Fred B. Rothman, 1963; *Historia de la literatura espanola: La Edad Media y el Siglo de Oro* (title means "History of Spanish Literature: The Middle Ages and the Golden Age"), Las Americas, 1962, 2nd edition, 1972; *Historia de la literatura espanola: La Edad Moderna, Siglos XVIII y XIX* (title means "History of Spanish Literature: The Modern Age, Eighteenth and Nineteenth Centuries"), Las Americas, 1965; *El arte dramatico de Valle-Inclan* (title means "The Dramatic Art of Valle-Inclan"), Las Americas, 1967; *Los politicos gallegos en la Corte de Espana y la convivencia europa: Galicia en los reinados de Felipe III y Felipe IV* (title means "The Galician Statesmen in the Court of Spain and the European Coexistence: Galicia in the Reigns of Philip III and Philip IV"), Galaxia, 1969; (with Humberto Pinera and Solomon Lipp) *Spanish Cultural Reader,* Heath, 1969.

Bajo la doble aguila: Galicia en el reinado de Carlos V (title means "Under the Doubleheaded Eagle: Galicia in the Reign of Charles V"), Patronato da Cultura Galega, 1970; *Siempre de negro: La Contrareforma en Galicia–Galicia en el reinado de Felipe II* (title means "Always in Black: The Counter Reformation in Galicia; Galicia in the Reign of Philip II"), Galaxia, 1970; *El arte narrativo de Pio Baroja: Las Trilogias* (title means "The Narrative Art of Pio Baroja: The Trilogies"), Las Americas, 1971; *La poesia de Valle-Inclan: Del simbolismo al expresionismo* (title means "The Poetry of Valle-Inclan: From Symbolism to Expressionism"), University of Puerto Rico Press, 1973; *El aguila caida: Galicia en los reinados de Felipe IV y Carlos II* (title means "The Fallen Eagle: Galicia in the Reigns of Philip IV and Charles II), Galaxia, 1973; *El aguila gala y el buho galaico: La insurreccion gallega contra los franceses* (title means "The Gallic Eagle and the Galician Owl: The Galician Uprising against the French Army"), Vigo, Galaxia, 1974.

Author of one hundred fifty scripts for "Voice of America" radio broadcasts. Contributor to *Columbia Dictionary of Modern Western European Literature, New International Yearbook,* and *Collier's Yearbook.* Contributor of nearly one hundred articles and five hundred reviews to language journals and foreign language publications, including *Revista Interamericana de Bibliografia, Correo de Galicia, Guadernos Hispanoamericanos, Revista La Coruna, Grial,* and *Insula.*

GOODE, Erich 1938-

PERSONAL: Born September 21, 1938, in Austin, Tex.; son of William Josiah (a university professor) and Josephine (Cannizzo) Goode; married Roberta Buckingham, June 17, 1961 (divorced March 28, 1964); married Alice Neufeld (a college instructor), December 28, 1968. *Education:* Oberlin College, A.B., 1960; Columbia University, Ph.D., 1966. *Home:* 14 Shore Oaks Dr., Stony Brook, N.Y. 11790. *Office:* Department of Sociology, Social Sciences Building, State University of New York at Stony Brook, Stony Brook, N.Y. 11790.

CAREER: New York University, Washington Square College, New York, N.Y., instructor, 1965-66, assistant professor of sociology, 1966-67; State University of New York at Stony Brook, assistant professor, 1967-70, associate professor of sociology, 1970—. Consultant to National Commission on Marijuana and Drug Abuse, 1971-72. *Member:* American Sociological Association, Society for the Study of Social Problems. *Awards, honors:* National Institute of Mental Health grant, 1968-69; grant from Research Foundation of State University of New York, summers, 1968, 1969.

WRITINGS: (Editor) *Marijuana,* Atherton, 1969; *The Marijuana Smokers,* Basic Books, 1970; *Drugs in American Society,* Knopf, 1972; *The Drug Phenomenon,* Bobbs-Merrill, 1973; (editor with Harvey A. Farberman) *Social Reality,* Prentice-Hall, 1973; (editor with Richard R. Troiden) *Sexual Deviance and Sexual Deviants,* Morrow, 1974; *How Do You Know It's True?,* General Learning Press, 1974. Contributor to annals. Contributor to *Social Problems, Journal of Health and Social Behavior, American Journal of Psychiatry,* and other professional journals.

* * *

GOODE, Kenneth G. 1932-

PERSONAL: Born August 11, 1932, in New Orleans, La.; married Etsuko Yoneda; children: Georgia, Gregory. *Education:* University of Arizona, B.A., 1957, J.D., 1960; University of California, Berkeley, Ph.D. candidate. *Home:* 319 The Spiral, Berkeley, Calif. 94708. *Office:* 200 California Hall, University of California, Berkeley, Calif. 94720.

CAREER: Assistant vice-chancellor of administrative services, University of California, Berkeley. Member of Berkeley (Calif.) Community Development Council, Berkeley (Calif.) Drug Abuse Council, and Northwestern Association of Secondary Schools and Higher Education Accreditation Team; trustee of Institute of Educational Management, and Kappa Alpha Psi. *Military service:* U.S. Air Force, 1950-54. *Member:* American Academy of Social and Political Science, American Political Science Association, Association for the Study of Negro Life and History, Golden Gate College Associates, Men of Tomorrow.

WRITINGS: (Legal editor with others) *Federal Civil Practice,* Continuing Education of the Bar, University of California, 1961; (legal editor with others) *Handling Federal Tax Litigation,* Continuing Education of the Bar, University of California, 1961; (legal editor with others) *The California Family Lawyer,* two volumes, Continuing Education of the Bar, University of California, 1962-63; (legal editor with others) *California Law Office Practice Handbook,* Continuing Education of the Bar, University of California, 1962; (legal editor with others) *California's Workmen's Compensation Practice,* Continuing Education of the Bar, University of California, 1962; (legal editor with others) *Government's Contracts Practice,* Continuing Education of the Bar, University of California, 1964; *From Africa to the United States and Then* (syllabus), Locke Publishers, 1967; *From Africa to the United States and Then* (textbook), Scott, Foresman, 1969; *California's Black Pioneers,* McNally & Loftin, 1974.

Contributor: *The Rumble of California Politics,* Wiley, 1970; *The Disadvantaged Worker,* Addison-Wesley, 1971; *The Teacher's Handbook,* Scott, Foresman, 1971; *An Assessment of Educational Opportunity Programs in California Public Higher Education,* Homitz, Allen, and Associates, 1973; *Handbook on Contemporary Education,* Reference Development Corp., 1974. Contributor to *California Management Review* and *Western Museums Quarterly.*

* * *

GOODMAN, Norman 1934-

PERSONAL: Born February 19, 1934, in New York, N.Y.; son of Jack and Hannah (Hoffman) Goodman; married Marilyn Goldberg (a teacher), December 26, 1954; children: Jack, Susan Andrea, Carolyn Wendy. *Education:* Brooklyn College (of the City University of New York), B.A., 1955; New York University, M.A., 1961, Ph.D., 1963. *Home:* 4 Skylark Lane, Stony Brook, N.Y. 11790. *Office:* Department of Sociology, State University of New York at Stony Brook, Stony Brook, N.Y. 11790.

CAREER: Department of Welfare, New York, N.Y., social investigator, 1957-58; Russell Sage Foundation, New York, N.Y., research assistant, 1958-60; Association for the Aid of Crippled Children, New York, N.Y., research assistant, 1958-61; Columbia University, New York, N.Y., instructor in sociology, 1961-62; Queens College of the City University of New York, Flushing, N.Y., lecturer, 1962-63, assistant professor of sociology, 1963-64; State University of New York at Stony Brook, assistant professor, 1964-68, associate professor, 1968-73, professor of sociology and chairman of department, 1973—, assistant dean of the Graduate School, 1966-67. *Military service:* U.S. Army, 1955-56. *Member:* American Association of University Professors, American Sociological Association, National Council on Family Relations, Society for Research in Child Development, Eastern Sociological Society, Alpha Kappa Delta. *Awards, honors:* Bobbs-Merrill Award in sociology from New York University, 1963; National Institute of Mental Health special research fellowship, 1970, to London School of Economics and Political Science.

WRITINGS: An Evaluation of the Eighth World Congress of the International Society for the Rehabilitation of the Disabled, International Society for the Rehabilitation of the Disabled, 1961; (with Orville G. Brim, Jr., David C. Glass, and David E. Lavin) *Personality and Decision Processes: Studies in the Social Psychology of Thinking,* Stanford University Press, 1962; (contributor) Helmut Strasser, editor, *Fortshritte der Heilpadagogik,* Carl Marhold, 1968; (contributor) Billy J. Franklin and Frank J. Kohout, editors, *Social Psychology and Everyday Life,* McKay, 1973; (with James H. Geer) *Sexuality, Courtship and Marriage,* Prentice-Hall, in press; (contributor) Glen H. Elder, Jr. and Sigmund E. Dragastin, editors, *Adolescence in the Life Course,* Hemisphere Press, in press. Contributor to journals in his field.

WORK IN PROGRESS: Research in the effects of various educational programs in family day care, stability and change in the identities of young adults who grew up during the 1960's, and the effects of the growing "culture of permissiveness" upon college students who behave in traditional ways about premarital sex.

* * *

GOODSON, Felix E(mmett) 1922-

PERSONAL: Born November 14, 1922, in Model, Colo.; son of Felix Emmett and Stella May (Ellis) Goodson; married Juanita Allen, 1947 (divorced, 1960); married Cheryl Sorenson, June 12, 1965; children: (first marriage) Jane Ellis, James Lange, John Galen; (second marriage) Holly Vee, Felix Emmett III, Boyd McLean. *Education:* Princeton University, A.B., 1949; University of Missouri, M.A., 1952, Ph.D., 1954. *Politics:* Democrat. *Religion:* Agnostic. *Home:* R.R. 5, Greencastle, Ind. 46135. *Office:* Department of Psychology, DePauw University, Greencastle, Ind. 46135.

CAREER: University of Missouri, Columbia, instructor in psychology, 1952-54; DePauw University, Greencastle, Ind., instructor, 1954-55, assistant professor, 1955-58, associate professor, 1958-64, professor of psychology, 1964—. *Military service:* U.S. Army, 1939-45; became technical sergeant; received Purple Heart. *Member:* American Psychological Association, Psychonomic Society.

WRITINGS: The Evolutionary Foundations of Psychology, Holt, 1973. Contributor to professional journals.

WORK IN PROGRESS: A novel, *The Survivor;* coauthoring a book on contemporary theory with Melvin H. Marx, for publication by Macmillan.

* * *

GORDON, Diana R(ussell) 1938-

PERSONAL: Born July 18, 1938, in North Adams, Mass.; daughter of Hallett D. (an English professor) and Mary Elizabeth (Earl) Smith; married James D. Lorenz, August 20, 1960 (divorced, 1965); married David M. Gordon (an economist), September 7, 1967. *Education:* Attended Goucher College, 1954-56; Mills College, B.A., 1958; Radcliffe College, M.A., 1959; Harvard University, LL.B., 1964. *Politics:* Democrat. *Religion:* Protestant. *Home:* 317 East Tenth St., New York, N.Y. 10009. *Agent:* Anne Borchardt, Georges Borchardt, Inc., 145 East 52nd St., New York, N.Y. 10022. *Office:* Citizens' Inquiry on Parole and Criminal Justice, 84 Fifth Ave., Room 300, New York, N.Y. 10011.

CAREER: City of New York, New York, N.Y., program analyst, 1966-70; Harvard University, Kennedy School of Government, Cambridge, Mass., research fellow of Institute of Politics, 1970-71; consultant to Fund for the City of New York, New York, N.Y., 1971-73, and State Charter Revision Commission, New York, N.Y., 1973; Citizens' Inquiry on Parole and Criminal Justice, New York, N.Y., director, 1973—.

WRITINGS: City Limits: Barriers to Change in Urban Government, Charterhouse, 1973. Contributor to *New York Affairs* and *Ms.*

WORK IN PROGRESS: Research on parole, on probation, and on discretion in the American criminal justice system.

* * *

GORDON, Suzanne 1945-

PERSONAL: Born November 2, 1945, in New York, N.Y.; daughter of Dan M. (a physician) and Blanche Gordon; married Peter Fehler (a carpenter), August 8, 1973. *Education:* Cornell University, B.A., 1967; Johns Hopkins University, M.A., 1969. *Residence and office:* Oakland, Calif. *Agent:* David Obst, 1910 N St. N.W., Washington, D.C. 20036.

CAREER: Substitute teacher in the public schools of Baltimore, Md., 1969-70; United Press International, Baltimore, Md., reporter and photographer, 1970. Editor and translator for French journalist, Philippe DeVillers.

WRITINGS: Black Mesa: The Angel of Death, John Day, 1973. Contributor of articles, poems, and short stories to *Earth, Washington Post, Newsweek, Sundance, Ms.,* and *Ramparts.*

WORK IN PROGRESS: A book on loneliness in America, for Simon & Schuster; a novel, completion expected in 1975.

* * *

GOTTLIEB, Adolph 1903-1974

March 14, 1903—March 4, 1974; American abstract artist. Obituaries: *New York Times,* March 5, 1974; *Time,* March 18, 1974; *Newsweek,* March 18, 1974; *Current Biography,* April, 1974.

* * *

GOUDIE, Andrew Shaw 1945-

PERSONAL: Born August 21, 1945, in Cheltenham, England; son of William (a pharmacist) and Mary (Pulman) Goudie. *Education:* Trinity Hall, Cambridge, B.A., 1970, Ph.D., 1971. *Religion:* Christian. *Home:* 59 Holywell St., Oxford, England. *Office:* School of Geography, Oxford University, Mansfield Rd., Oxford, England.

CAREER: Oxford University, St. Edmund Hall and Hertford College, Oxford, England, lecturer and demonstrator in geography, 1970—. *Member:* Royal Geographical Society (fellow), Geographical Club, Institute of British Geographers.

WRITINGS: Duricrusts of Tropical and Sub-Tropical Landscapes, Clarendon Press, 1973; (editor) *Theory and Practice in Geography,* Clarendon Press, in press. Contributor to professional journals.

WORK IN PROGRESS: Research on the landforms and history of deserts; three books, *Environmental Change, Warm Deserts,* and *Landforms of the West Country,* completion expected in 1975.

SIDELIGHTS: Goudie has traveled extensively in Europe, Africa (Kenya, Ethiopia, Botswana, South West Africa) and Asia (India) with other geographers and archaeologists.

* * *

GOULD, Lilian 1920-

PERSONAL: Born April 19, 1920, in Philadelphia, Pa.; daughter of Reuben Barr (an executive) and Lilian Valentine (Scott) Seidel; married Irving Gould (owner of an advertising agency), November 16, 1944; children: Mark, Scott, Paul, John. *Education:* Charles Morris Price School of Journalism, A.A., 1938; twenty years later resumed studies in evening classes at University of Pennsylvania. *Politics:* "Mildly liberal." *Religion:* Episcopalian. *Home:* 117 Sugartown Rd., Devon, Pa. 19333. *Agent:* Lurton Blassingame, 60 East 42nd St., New York, N.Y.

MEMBER: Women's International League for Peace and Freedom, Friends' Peace Committee, Philadelphia Children's Reading Round Table.

WRITINGS: Our Living Past (juvenile), Lippincott, 1969.

WORK IN PROGRESS: A book on the evolution of behavior, tentatively titled *Hunters, Women, and War;* a juvenile nonfiction book; a juvenile novel laid in Africa, *Spear Over the Sacred Tree.*

SIDELIGHTS: Mrs. Gould says: "I am deeply concerned with the education of young people, specifically that they learn about themselves and their world: the physical and cultural development of their own species as it emerged from lower animals. This includes the origin of instinct and behavior, the causes of violence, the process of learning, sexual differences, and much more—most of which is overlooked in school. Ecology, evolution, genetics, anthropology, ethology, and related subjects could well be introduced four or five years before college, but only if it is brought within reach. This, I think, is a *writer's* job rather than a specialist's; and that is the reason why, even though I had no scientific training, I undertook to lead the young reader (and his teacher) through the maze of current theory."

* * *

GOULIANOS, Joan Rodman 1939-

PERSONAL: Born January 9, 1939, in Detroit, Mich.; daughter of Joseph David and Irene Sara (Goldberg) Rodman; married Konstantin Goulianos (a professor of physics), June 23, 1963. *Education:* Sorbonne, University of Paris, certificate, 1958; University of Michigan, B.A., 1960; Columbia University, M.A., 1962, Ph.D., 1968. *Religion:* Jewish. *Home:* 11 West 69th St., New York, N.Y. 10023. *Office:* Department of English, Ramapo College, Mahwah, N.J.

CAREER: Columbia University, New York, N.Y., lecturer in English, 1962-64; New York University, New York, N.Y., assistant professor of English, 1967-71; Ramapo College, Mahwah, N.J., associate professor of English, 1972—. *Member:* Authors Guild, Phi Beta Kappa, Alpha Lambda Delta. *Awards, honors:* Woodrow Wilson fellowship, 1960; American Academy of Poets Prize, 1963.

WRITINGS: (Editor) *by a Woman writt,* Bobbs-Merrill, 1973. Contributor to *Washington Post, Nation, Village Voice, Massachusetts Review, Virginia Quarterly, Modern Fiction Studies,* and other periodicals.

SIDELIGHTS: Mrs. Goulianos told *CA:* "I have the sense that only by writing can you find out the truth about something, or at least your true feelings about it. That is why writing is sometimes dangerous and why writers are sometimes put in prisons or yelled and shouted at and told to shut up, but they don't, thank God. Writers, I think, have the ability to put out feelers into areas that other people don't necessarily . . . care to explore; they are originals, they see and think a lot and they try to grab this cloud around them and put it on paper, and they hope that others will say yes, that is how I have seen it too." *Avocational interests:* Music, dance, swimming.

BIOGRAPHICAL/CRITICAL SOURCES: Westsider (New York, N.Y.), August 9, 1973; *Record* (New Jersey), October 21, 1973.

GRADY, Ronan Calistus, Jr. 1921- (John Murphy)

PERSONAL: Born July 14, 1921, in Boston, Mass.; son of Ronan Calistus (a naval officer) and Louise (Murphy) Grady; married Barbara Jones, June 3, 1943; children: Elizabeth Louise (Mrs. William Smith Dixon), Mary Ann. *Education:* U.S. Military Academy, B.S., 1943; Command and General Staff College, graduated, 1946; Escuela Superior del Ejercito, graduated, 1970. *Politics:* "Hamiltonian Federalist." *Religion:* Roman Catholic. *Residence:* Spain. *Agent:* Russell & Volkening, Inc., 551 Fifth Ave., New York, N.Y. 10017.

CAREER: U.S. Army, career officer, 1943-72, retiring as colonel. Served for a year or more in Turkey, Germany, France, Venezuela, Paraguay, Vietnam, and Spain. *Member:* Army and Navy Club. *Awards, honors*—Military: Silver Star, Legion of Merit with one oak leaf cluster, Bronze Star Medal, Combat Infantry Badge, Master Parachutist Badge, Organization of the Joint Chiefs of Staff Badge; from Government of Venezuela, Cross of the Land Forces third class and Parachutist Badge; from Brazil, Medal of Military Merit, grade of officer and Medal of the Peacemaker; from Paraguay, Order of Military Merit, grade of caballero, Medal of the Air Force, and Parachutist Badge; from Vietnam, Order of National Merit, fifth class, Joint Service Medal, Air Service Medal, War Service Medal, and Senior Parachutist Badge; from Spain, Cross of Military Merit, first class.

WRITINGS: The Collected Works of Ducrot Pepys, privately printed, 1944.

Under pseudonym John Murphy: *The Gunrunners* (novel), Macmillan, 1966; *The Long Reconnaissance* (novel), Doubleday, 1970; *The El Greco Puzzle* (novel), Scribner, 1974. Contributor to *Astounding Science Fiction* and *Saturday Evening Post.*

WORK IN PROGRESS: Pay on the Way Out (tentative title), a novel.

SIDELIGHTS: Grady writes: "I have always basically thought of myself as a military man (and still do, to tell the truth) but I also have done writing on the side off and on during my active service. Damned if I could give a clear reason why. Now, I'm a full time writer and I'm still hard put to say why. My ambition is to be considered a good story teller in the line of the late great Nevil Shute, and I guess that's what pushes me as much as anything.

"My hobbies are history and chess and travel. Our rich uncle has seen to it that I got plenty of the last although not always to places I would have picked on my own. As a fringe benefit I've learned fluent French and Spanish, passable Portuguese, and some Turkish and Guarani.

"*CA* asks me for my viewpoint on subjects I consider vital. Well, I don't know about that. My daughters often treat me much as they would a small dinosaur they'd trapped, tamed, and taught to do a few simple tricks—a quaint, sometimes diverting, survival from a by-gone age. They'd be mortified if they caught me showing off in public.

"As for illuminating personal data—I'm rather proud that I've earned (and I mean earned, not merely been awarded honorarily) the parachute wings of four countries. Bet there aren't too many writers who can say that."

* * *

GRAFF, S. Stewart 1908-

PERSONAL: Born May 8, 1908, in Worthington, Pa.; son

of John Francis and Martha Grier (Stewart) Graff; married Polly Anne Colver (a free-lance writer and author of children's books), March 3, 1945; children: Jeremy M. Harris (stepson); Kate G. (Mrs. Stephen L. Danielski). *Education:* Attended Taft School, Watertown, Conn., 1921-25; Williams College, student, 1925-28; Harvard University, A.B., 1930, LL.B., 1936. *Politics:* Independent. *Religion:* Lutheran. *Home:* 157 West Clinton Ave., Irvington, N.Y. 10533.

CAREER: Brown, Cross & Hamilton (law firm), New York, N.Y., associate attorney, 1936-48; Synthetic Organic Chemical Manufacturers Association, New York, N.Y., executive secretary, 1948-68; writer of children's books, 1968—. Member of board of directors of Donald R. Reed Speech Center; member of Irvington Narcotics Guidance Council and Irvington Jobs for Youth Committee. *Military service:* U.S. Army Air Forces, 1942-46; became captain. *Member:* New York County Lawyers Association, Harvard Club (New York, N.Y.), Chemists Club (New York, N.Y.).

WRITINGS—For children: *John Paul Jones,* Garrard, 1961; *George Washington,* Garrard, 1964; *Theodore Roosevelt's Boys,* Garrard, 1967; *Hernando Cortes,* Garrard, 1970.

With wife, Polly Anne (Colver) Graff: *Squanto: Indian Adventurer,* Garrard, 1965; *Helen Keller: Toward the Light,* Garrard, 1965; *The Wayfarer's Tree,* Dutton, 1973.

WORK IN PROGRESS: Editing, with wife, Polly Anne Graff, text of "Wolfert's Roost"; research on the periods of the American Revolution and World War Two.

AVOCATIONAL INTERESTS: Travel.

* * *

GRAHAM, Alistair (Dundas) 1938-

PERSONAL: Born October 25, 1938, in Kisumu, Kenya; son of Malcolm Dundas (a farmer) and Helen (Corkhill) Graham; married Jane England, May 15, 1971; children: Rebecca Louise, Daniella Ruth. *Education:* Rhodes University, B.Sc., 1960, B.Sc. (with honors), 1961; University of East Africa, M.Sc., 1968. *Politics:* None. *Religion:* Atheist. *Home and office address:* P.O. Box 44597, Nairobi, Kenya.

CAREER: Kenya Game Department, game warden, 1961-63; Wildlife Services Ltd. (firm offering wildlife research and management services to East African conservation agencies), co-owner, 1963—. Presently engaged in an ecological survey of the Okavango Delta in Botswana, for the United Nations.

WRITINGS: The Gardeners of Eden, Allen & Unwin, 1973; *Eyelids of Morning,* New York Graphic Society, 1973.

* * *

GRAHAM, Robin Lee 1949-

PERSONAL: Born March 5, 1949, in Santa Ana, Calif.; son of Lyle G. (a realtor) and Norma (Tisdel) Graham; married Patricia K. Ratterree, June 4, 1968; children: Quimby Anna. *Education:* Stanford University, student for one quarter. *Religion:* Christian. *Residence:* Kalispell, Mont. 59901.

CAREER: At the age of 16 set out from California in a 24-foot sloop and sailed solo around the world, 1965-70; after completing the 33,000-mile odyssey he settled in Montana where he has been building log cabins and farming. Member of board of directors, Flathead Innerfaith Fellowship.

WRITINGS: (With Derek T. L. Gill) *Dove* (account of his voyage), Harper, 1972; (with Gill) *The Boy Who Sailed around the World Alone* (juvenile adaptation of *Dove*), Western Publishing, 1973. Contributor to *Christian Life, Woman's World,* and *Campus Life. Awards, honors: Dove* was named to the American Library Association's list of Notable Books, 1972.

WORK IN PROGRESS: A book on the adventures of Graham and his wife in Montana and their spiritual discoveries.

AVOCATIONAL INTERESTS: Playing the violin, mountain-climbing, and snow camping.

* * *

GRAHAM, Winston (Mawdsley) 1910-

PERSONAL: Born June 30, 1910, in Victoria Park, Manchester, England; son of Albert Henry (a chemist) and Anne (Mawdsley) Graham; married Jean Mary Williamson, September 18, 1939; children: Andrew Winston, Anne Rosamund (Mrs. Douglas R. Barteau). *Home:* Abbotswood House, Buxted, Sussex, England. *Agent:* A. M. Heath & Co. Ltd., 40 William IV St., London W.C.2, England; and Christopher Mann Ltd., 140 Park Lane, London W.1, England.

CAREER: Full-time writer, 1933—. *Member:* Society of Authors (chairman, 1967-69), Royal Society of Literature (fellow), Savile Club (trustee, 1972—). *Awards, honors:* Award from Crime Writers Association, 1956, for *The Little Walls.*

WRITINGS—All novels, except as noted; all published by Ward, Lock, except as noted: *The House with Stained Glass Windows,* 1934; *Into the Fog,* 1935; *The Riddle of John Rowe,* 1935; *Without Motive,* 1936; *The Dangerous Pawn,* 1937; *The Giant's Chair,* 1938; *Strangers Meeting,* 1939; *Keys of Chance,* 1939.

No Exit: An Adventure, 1940; *Night Journey,* 1941, revised edition, Bodley Head, 1966, Doubleday, 1968; *My Turn Next,* 1942; *The Merciless Ladies,* 1944; *The Forgotten Story,* 1945, published as *The Wreck of the Grey Cat,* Doubleday Crime Club, 1958; *Ross Poldark: A Novel of Cornwall, 1783-1787,* 1945, published as *The Renegade: A Novel of Cornwall, 1783-1787,* Doubleday, 1951; *Demelza: A Novel of Cornwall, 1788-1790,* 1946, Doubleday, 1953; *Take My Life,* 1947, Doubleday, 1967; *Cordelia,* 1949, Doubleday, 1950.

Night Without Stars, Doubleday, 1950; *Jeremy Poldark: A Novel of Cornwall, 1790-1791,* 1950, published as *Venture Once More: A Novel of Cornwall, 1790-1791,* Doubleday, 1954; *Fortune Is a Woman,* Doubleday, 1953; *Warleggan: A Novel of Cornwall, 1792-1793,* 1953, published as *The Last Gamble: A Novel of Cornwall, 1792-1793,* Doubleday, 1955; *The Little Walls,* Doubleday, 1955; *The Sleeping Partner,* Doubleday, 1956; *Greek Fire,* Hodder & Stoughton, 1957, Doubleday, 1958; *The Tumbled House,* Hodder & Stoughton, 1959, Doubleday, 1960.

Marnie, Doubleday, 1961; *The Grove of Eagles,* Hodder & Stoughton, 1963, Doubleday, 1964; *After the Act,* Hodder & Stoughton, 1965, Doubleday, 1966; *The Walking Stick* (Literary Guild selection), Doubleday, 1967.

Angell, Pearl, and Little God (Literary Guild selection),

Doubleday, 1970; *The Spanish Armadas* (history), Doubleday, 1972; *The Japanese Girl* (short stories), Collins, 1971, Doubleday, 1972; *The Black Moon,* Collins, 1973, Doubleday, 1974; *Woman in the Mirror,* Doubleday, in press.

Co-author of screenplay, "Take My Life," 1947, and author of screenplay, "Night Without Stars," 1952.

SIDELIGHTS: Graham's books have been translated into fifteen languages. *Take My Life* was filmed by Eagle Lion Films in 1947; *Night Without Stars* was filmed by Rank Productions in 1951; *Fortune Is a Woman* was filmed in 1956, and released in United States as "She Played with Fire," Columbia Pictures, 1958; *The Sleeping Partner* was filmed in 1958; *Marnie* was produced by Alfred Hitchcock and released by Universal in 1964; *The Walking Stick* was filmed by MGM, 1970.

AVOCATIONAL INTERESTS: Golf, gardening, swimming.

* * *

GRANT, Eva 1907-

PERSONAL: Born November 23, 1907, in New York, N.Y.; daughter of Harry (owner of a women's clothing store) and Minnie (Cohen) Cohen; married Reuben Grant, February 5, 1927; children: Arleen (Mrs. Bud Natelson), Judith (Mrs. Kenneth Goldman). *Education:* Attended New York University, Bank Street College of Education, and New School for Social Research. *Religion:* Jewish. *Home:* 255 Kingsland Ter., South Orange, N.J. 07079. *Agent:* Ruth Cantor, 156 Fifth Ave., New York, N.Y. 10010.

AWARDS, HONORS: First prize for narrative poem from Cooper Hill Writer's Conference, 1972, for "A Bit of Cheese"; Author Award from Newark College of Engineering, 1974, for *A Cow for Jaya.*

WRITINGS: Timothy Slept On, Whitman Publishing, 1964; *Cecil Kitten,* Whitman Publishing, 1968; *A Cow for Jaya* (Junior Literary Guild selection), Coward, 1973. Also author of a series of kindergarten stories published by David C. Cook. Contributor to periodicals, including *Instructor, Highlights for Children, Young World, Humpty-Dumpty's Magazine,* Scholastic Magazines, and church publications.

WORK IN PROGRESS: A book to be illustrated with eight dolls created by Suzanne Gibson of the National Institute of American Doll Artists.

* * *

GRANT, Frederick C(lifton) 1891-1974

February 2, 1891—July 11, 1974; American clergyman, Biblical scholar, educator, and author. Obituaries: *New York Times,* July 13, 1974. (*CA*-1).

* * *

GRAUPERA, Carlos M(anuel) 1915-

PERSONAL: Born November 29, 1915, in New York, N.Y.; son of Leopoldo D. (a businessman) and Bella Maria (Coello) Graupera; married Aida de la Heria (a bilingual teacher), December 21, 1945; children: Leo, Carlos, John, George, Mary. *Education:* Havana Institute, B.Litt., 1938; University of Havana, further study, 1939-40, 1943-44; LaSalle Extension University, LL.B., 1964; University of South Dakota, M.A., 1966. *Religion:* Roman Catholic. *Home:* 325-H Eden Rd., Lancaster, Pa. 17601. *Office:* Department of Languages, Elizabethtown College, Elizabethtown, Pa. 17022.

CAREER: Teacher in Havana, Cuba, 1938-47; St. Joseph School, Havana, Cuba, founder-director, 1947-60; Mount Marty College, Yankton, S.D., instructor in Spanish, 1961-66; Elizabethtown College, Elizabethtown, Pa., associate professor of modern languages, 1966—. *Member:* American Association of Teachers of Spanish and Portuguese, Pennsylvania State Modern Language Association.

WRITINGS: Influencia arabe en la cultura espanola, Publicaciones Espanolas (Madrid), 1968; *Nuestra lengua,* Part I, Plaza Mayor Ediciones (Madrid), 1972. Contributor of articles and translations to Cuban magazines and newspapers.

WORK IN PROGRESS: Nuestra lengua, Part II.

* * *

GRAVELY, William B(ernard) 1939-

PERSONAL: Surname is pronounced *Gra*-vel-y; born August 19, 1939, in Pickens, S.C.; son of W. Marvin (a salesman) and Artie (Hughes) Gravely; married Lynn McCoy (a teacher of the educationally handicapped), June 12, 1964; children: Julia Lynn. *Education:* Wofford College, B.A. (magna cum laude), 1961; Drew Theological School, B.D. (magna cum laude), 1964; Duke University, Ph.D., 1969. *Politics:* Democrat. *Religion:* Methodist. *Home:* 2565 East Vassar Ave., Denver, Colo. 80210. *Office:* Department of Religion, University of Denver, Denver, Colo. 80210.

CAREER: Ordained Methodist deacon, 1962, elder, 1968. University of Denver, Denver, Colo., assistant professor, 1968-72, associate professor of religion, 1972—, chairman of American studies program, 1970-73. *Member:* American Studies Association, American Academy of Religion, Society for Religion in Higher Education. *Awards, honors:* Jesse Lee Prize in American Methodist History from Commission on Archives and History, United Methodist Church, 1970, for "Gilbert Haven, Racial Equalitarian"; National Endowment for the Humanities summer grant, 1970, and minority studies fellowship, 1974-75.

WRITINGS: Gilbert Haven, Methodist Abolitionist: A Study in Race, Religion, and Reform, 1850-1880, Abingdon, 1973. Contributor of articles and book reviews to religion and history journals.

WORK IN PROGRESS: Research in Afro-American religious history in the nineteenth century, in religion and reform in America, especially abolitionism, and in public rituals in American life.

SIDELIGHTS: ". . . I have been engaged for the past six years," Gravely wrote, "in uncovering the available documents of the Black religious heritage, both as it contributes to the larger perspective on American religion and as a field of study in its own right. As a native white southerner, now living in the west, I hope to make some contribution toward the nation's engagement with its own tragic past, particularly focused in the Black story, as a necessary corrective to our myths of innocence and success."

* * *

GRAY, Farnum 1940-

PERSONAL: Born July 19, 1940, in Miami, Fla.; son of Farnum (a dairy manufacturing consultant) and Mattie (Alderman) Gray; married Wanda Davis (an education writer and consultant), June 2, 1961; children: Daniel Farnum, Holly Patrice. *Education:* University of North Carolina, B.A., 1962. *Politics:* Independent Democrat. *Home:* 1475 Kay Lane, Atlanta, Ga. 30306. *Office:* Atlanta *Constitution,* Box 4689, Atlanta, Ga. 30302.

CAREER: Rocky Mount Telegram, Rocky Mount, N.C., reporter; *Winston-Salem Journal,* Winston-Salem, N.C., reporter, 1965-67; Pennsylvania Advancement School, Philadelphia, Pa., writer and chairman of editorial department, 1967-70; Aspen Community School and Teaching Center, Aspen, Colo., director, 1971-72; qresently movie and theatre critic, Atlanta *Constitution,* Atlanta Ga.; free-lance writer. *Awards, honors:* Emery A. Brownell Press Award from National Legal Aid and Defender Association, 1967.

WRITINGS: (Contributor) Beatrice Gross and Ronald Gross, editors, *Radical School Reform,* Simon & Schuster, 1970; (contributor) Vincent Rogers and Thomas Weinland, editors, *Teaching Social Studies in the Urban Classroom,* Addison-Wesley, 1972; (with George C. Mager) *Liberating Education: Psychological Learning through Improvisational Drama,* McCutchan, 1973; (contributor) Ronald Gross and Beatrice Gross, editors, *Will St Grow in a Classroom?,* Delacorte, 1974. Contributor to *Psychology Today, Nation, Colloquy, Learning and other journals.*

WORK IN PROGRESS: A second book.

* * *

GREAVES, Percy L(aurie), Jr. 1906-

PERSONAL: Born August 24, 1906, in Brooklyn, N.Y.; son of Percy Laurie (an accountant) and Grace I. (Dodge) Greaves; married Edith Leslye Platt, August 23, 1930 (divorced, 1971); married Bettina Herbert Bien (an economist), June 26, 1971; children: (first marriage) Richard Laurie, Muriel Ann (Mrs. David E. Credle), Charles Flint. *Education:* Syracuse University, B.S. (magna cum laude), 1929; Columbia University, graduate study, 1933-34. *Politics:* Libertarian. *Religion:* Episcopalian. *Home:* 19 Pine Lane, Irvington-on-Hudson, N.Y. 10533. *Office address:* P.O. Box 298, Dobbs Ferry, N.Y. 10522.

CAREER: American Trading Co., New York, N.Y., bookkeeper, 1923-25; Gillette Safety Razor Co., Boston, Mass., 1929-32, began as executive trainee, became assistant advertising manager; Young Men's Hebrew Association, New York, N.Y., instructor in economics and foreign trade, 1933-34; *U.S. News & World Report,* Washington, D.C., financial editor and research economist, 1934-36; advertising manager for European subsidiaries of Pet and Carnation Milk Cos., 1936-38; Metropolitan Life Insurance Co., New York, N.Y., advertising and public relations executive, 1938-43; Republican National Committee, Washington, D.C., associate research director, 1943-45; chief of minority staff of U.S. Joint Congressional Committee for the Investigation of Pearl Harbor Attack, 1945-46; Foundation for Freedom, Inc., Washington, D.C., executive director, 1946-48; economic consultant, writer, and lecturer, 1948—. Consulting expert, U.S. House of Representatives, Committee on Education and Labor, 1947; participant in Ludwig von Mises' Graduate Seminar at New York University, 1950-69; economic advisor, Christian Freedom Foundation, 1950-58; guest lecturer, The Freedom School, Inc., 1957-60; seminar speaker and discussion leader, Foundation for Economic Education, Inc., 1962-67; Armstrong Professor of Economics, University of Plano, Texas, 1965-71.

MEMBER: American Economic Association, American Historical Association, American Military Institute, Naval Historical Foundation, United States Naval Institute, Beta Gamma Sigma, Phi Kappa Phi.

WRITINGS: Operation Immigration, Foundation for Freedom, Inc., 1947; (contributor) H. E. Barnes, editor, *Perpetual War for Perpetual Peace,* Caxton, 1952; (contributor) Hans Sennholz, editor, *On Freedom and Free Enterprise: In Honor of Ludwig von Mises,* Van Nostrand, 1956; (contributor) *Essays on Liberty,* Foundation for Economic Education, Volume III, 1958, Volume VI, 1959, Volume XII, 1965; (with others) *Toward Liberty: Essays in Honor of Ludwig von Mises on the Occasion of His 90th Birthday, September 29, 1971,* Institute for Humane Studies, Inc., 1971; *Understanding the Dollar Crisis,* Western Islands, 1973; *Mises Made Easy: A Glossary of Mises' "Human Action",* Free Market Books, 1974. Also author of numerous articles on economics, history, and public affairs. Columnist, *Christian Economics,* 1950-58.

WORK IN PROGRESS: Editing, *Three Theoretical Studies on Inflation, Monetary Stabilization and the Trade Cycle,* by Ludwig von Mises; a book on the events leading up to the Pearl Harbor Attack and the attempts of the Roosevelt and Truman Administrations to suppress the truth; editing a collection of his own columns from *Christian Economics.*

SIDELIGHTS: Greaves has written: "I always stress, as simply as I can, that sound economics is the science which reveals that the voluntary social cooperation of a free market economy provides the greatest human satisfaction for all moral persons. Conversely, every use of force, coercion or political intervention, other than for the equal protection of life, property and free market operations, must inevitably result in a decrease in the satisfactions of all moral persons. My specialty is exploding the myth that we tried free enterprise in the twenties and that it failed in 1929, making New Deal interventions necessary."

* * *

GREEN, Hannah

PERSONAL: Daughter of Matthew Addy and Mary (Allen) Green; married John Wesley (a painter). *Education:* Wellesley College, B.A.; Stanford University, M.A. *Home:* 52 Barrow St., New York, N.Y. 10014. *Agent:* Diarmuid Russell, Russell & Volkening, Inc., 551 Fifth Ave., New York, N.Y. 10017.

CAREER: Associate professor of fiction writing, Columbia University, School of the Arts, New York, N.Y. *Member:* Authors Guild of the Authors League of America, P.E.N., MacDowell Colony Fellows (secretary, 1966—). *Awards, honors:* MacDowell Colony fellowship.

WRITINGS: The Dead of the House (novel), Doubleday, 1972.

WORK IN PROGRESS: A novel, *Dreams and Early Memories.*

SIDELIGHTS: In his review Joseph Catinella said: "The American Past, as evoked in Hannah Green's *The Dead of the House,* is never dependent on obvious literary traditions or used for surface effects. The author, who consulted records of the Cincinnati Historical Society as well as the power of her imagination, has created five generations of a family in Ohio and northern Michigan. Miss Green writes with delicacy about how the land was settled by her narrator's English and French ancestors; how European culture was transformed into an essentially American way of viewing life; and how the country's strength depended on the courage and integrity of individuals. . . . The love that pervades this book—a love of great literature, of national traditions—transcends the temporal death that awaits its characters, and celebrates a continuing life born within new generations."

BIOGRAPHICAL/CRITICAL SOURCES: Contemporary Literary Criticism, Volume III, Gale, 1974.

* * *

GREEN, Henry 1905-1974 (Henry Vincent Yorke)

British novelist. Obituaries: *AB Bookman's Weekly,* April 15, 1974. (*CLC*-2).

* * *

GREEN, Timothy (Seton) 1936-

PERSONAL: Born May 29, 1936, in Beccles, England; son of Alan Leslie (a teacher) and Phyllis (Constance) Green; married Maureen Snowball (a journalist), October, 1959; children: Miranda. *Education:* Christ's College, Cambridge, B.A. (honors), 1957; University of Western Ontario, graduate diploma in journalism, 1958. *Home:* 140 Rosendale Rd., London S.E.21, England. *Agent:* A. D. Peters, 10 Buckingham St., London W.C.2, England.

CAREER: Horizon and *American Heritage* (magazines), New York, N.Y., London correspondent, 1959-62; *Life* (magazine), New York, N.Y., London correspondent, 1962-64; *Illustrated London News,* London, England, editor, 1964-66; Consolidated Gold Fields, London, England, consultant on gold markets, 1969—.

WRITINGS: The World of Gold, Walker & Co., 1968, revised edition, Simon & Schuster, 1970; *The Smugglers,* Walker & Co., 1969; *Restless Spirit,* Walker & Co., 1970; *The Universal Eye: World Television in the Seventies,* Stein & Day, 1972; *The World of Gold Today,* Walker & Co., 1973. Contributor to *Horizon, Reader's Digest, Fortune,* and *Smithsonian.*

WORK IN PROGRESS: World of Diamonds, completion expected in 1975.

SIDELIGHTS: Green has visited nearly every country in the non-Communist world.

* * *

GREENBANK, Anthony Hunt 1933-

PERSONAL: Born December 21, 1933, in Settle, Yorkshire, England; son of Anthony and Marjorie Greenbank; married, wife's name Mary, December 10, 1958 (divorced); children: Heather Mary. *Education:* Attended schools in Yorkshire, England. *Home:* The Cottage, Walthwaite How, Great Langdale, Ambleside, Westmorland, England.

CAREER: Writer. Outward Bound instructor in Cumberland, England, 1959-60, and Marble, Colorado, summer, 1964. *Member:* London Press Club, Fell and Rock Climbing Club of the English Lake District.

WRITINGS: Instructions in Rock-Climbing, Museum Press, 1963; (with Donald Robinson) *Caving and Potholing,* Constable, 1964; *Climbing, Canoeing, Ski-ing and Caving,* Elliot Right Way Books, 1964; *Instructions in Mountaineering,* Museum Press, 1967; *The Book of Survival: How to Save Your Skin when Disaster Strikes without Warning,* Wolfe, 1967, published as *The Book of Survival: Everyman's Guide to Staying Alive and Handling Emergencies in the City, the Suburbs, and the Wild Lands Beyond,* Harper, 1968; *Mr. Tough: The Powerkit of Fitness and Strength for All Men,* Wolfe, 1969, published as *Mr. Tough,* Harper, 1970; *Survival in the City,* Harper, 1974; *The Climbers' Guide,* Harper, in press; *Survival at Sea,* William Luscombe, in press; *Survival out of Doors for Young People,* Doubleday, in press.

SIDELIGHTS: Reviewing *The Book of Survival,* William O. Douglas wrote: "[This book] covers almost every kind of an accident or episode which can maroon, engulf, injure, mutilate, immobilize, imperil, endanger or threaten anyone on this earth. There is in the book solace for any wary worry-wart, whether he ends up in an elevator that is out of control or under eight feet of avalanche snow, or facing a timber wolf, or in a hole in the ice on lake or river, or trying to start a fire in the wind, or resuscitating a person who has stopped breathing." Greenbank's suggestions, adds G. B. Weinrich, "seem to be well-conceived and practical, [although] the American reader may find some British idiomatic expressions distracting, and his spare style gives an impression of the need for breathless haste in reading."

AVOCATIONAL INTERESTS: Rock climbing, mountaineering, classical, and country and western music, soccer, cricket, and checkers.

* * *

GREENBERG, Ira A(rthur) 1924-

PERSONAL: Born June 26, 1924, in Brooklyn, N.Y.; son of Philip (a salesman) and Minnie S. Greenberg. *Education:* University of Oklahoma, B.A., 1949; University of Southern California, M.A. (English), 1962; California State University, Los Angeles, M.S. (counseling), 1963; Claremont Graduate School, Ph.D., 1967. *Politics:* Democrat. *Religion:* Jewish. *Office:* Behavioral Studies Institute, 10795 Wilshire Blvd., #6, Los Angeles, Calif. 90024; and Camarillo State Hospital, Intensive Psychiatric Intervention Program, Camarillo, Calif. 93010.

CAREER: Columbus Enquirer, Columbus, Ga., reporter, 1951-55; *Louisville Courier-Journal,* Louisville, Ky., reporter, 1955-56; *Los Angeles Times,* Los Angeles, Calif., reporter, 1956-62; Claremont Colleges, Psychological Clinic and Counseling Center, Claremont, Calif., counselor, 1964-65; Chapman College, Chapman, Calif., lecturer in psychology, 1965-66; Camarillo State Hospital, Camarillo, Calif., staff psychologist, 1967-69, supervising psychologist, 1969-72, part-time staff psychologist, 1973—, director of weekly program, "Psychodrama with Dr. Greenberg," broadcast on closed circuit television throughout the hospital, 1968—. Private practice in hypnotherapy in West Los Angeles, Calif., 1971—. Founder and director of Behavioral Studies Institute (management consultants), 1970—, and Psychodrama Center for Los Angeles, Inc. (non-profit community service institute), 1971—. Part-time instructor at California School of Professional Psychology, 1971—; part-time assistant professor at California State University, Northridge, 1967-69; member of staff of California Institute of Psychodrama, 1969-71. Member of board of directors of Topanga Center for Human Development, 1971-74. Consultant in action and fantasy techniques for organizational development and creative corporate problem-solving. *Military service:* U.S. Army, combat engineer, 1943-46. U.S. Army Reserve, active duty, 1950-51; became sergeant first class; served in European theater.

MEMBER: American Psychological Association, American Society of Group Psychotherapy and Psychodrama; American Society of Clinical Hypnosis, Society of Clinical and Experimental Hypnosis, Association for Humanistic Psychology, American Group Psychotherapy Association, American Personnel and Guidance Association, American Management Association, California Psychological Association, Southern California Society of Clinical Hypnosis (member of board of directors, 1971—; vice-president, 1973—), Group Psychotherapy Association of Southern California (member of board of directors, 1974—), Los Angeles County Psychological Association. *Awards, honors:* Medal of Valor from Alabama National Guard, 1954, for reporting on clean-up campaign of Phenix City.

WRITINGS: Psychodrama and Audience Attitude Change, Behavioral Studies Press, 1968; (editor) *Psychodrama: Theory and Therapy,* Behavioral Publications, 1974. Contributing news notes editor of *Small Group Behavior.*

WORK IN PROGRESS: Group Hypnotherapy: Theory and Techniques; Action Methods in Management Consulting; a tribute to J. L. Moreno, M.D., *Psychodrama: Old Directions and New Directions.*

* * *

GREENBERG, Martin Harry 1941-

PERSONAL: Born March 1, 1941, in Miami Beach, Fla.; son of Max Isidor (a merchant) and Mollie (Cohen) Greenberg; married Sally Shannon, June 3, 1972; children: Kari, Kathleen. *Education:* University of Miami, Coral Gables, B.B.A., 1962; University of Connecticut, M.A., 1965, Ph.D., 1969. *Politics:* "Structural anarchist." *Religion:* Jewish. *Home:* 9365 Southwest 89th St., Miami, Fla. 33156. *Agent:* Del Walker, 520 Fifth Ave., New York, N.Y. 10036. *Office:* Department of International Relations, Florida International University, Tamiami Trail, Miami, Fla. 33144.

CAREER: University of Connecticut, Storrs, lecturer in political science, summer, 1966; University of Wisconsin, Green Bay, assistant professor of political science, 1969-72, chairman of department, 1971-72; Florida International University, Miami, associate professor of political science, 1972—, chairman of department, 1972-74, chairman of department of international relations, 1974—, co-founder of H. G. Wells award for science fiction.

MEMBER: International Political Science Association, American Political Science Association, American Society for Public Administration, Latin American Development Administration Committee, Comparative Administration Group, Society for International Development, Science Fiction Research Association, Science Fiction Writers of America, Southern Political Science Association, South Florida Jewish Historical Society, Pi Sigma Alpha.

WRITINGS: Bureaucracy and Development: A Mexican Case Study, Heath, 1970.

Editor and contributor: (With Patricia Warrick) *Political Science Fiction,* Prentice-Hall, 1974; (with Warrick) *The Subliminal Man: The Social Sciences Through Science Fiction,* Dell, 1974; (with Harvey Katz and Warrick) *Psychology Through Science Fiction,* Rand McNally, 1974; (with Warrick and Joseph D. Olander) *American Government Through Science Fiction,* Rand McNally, 1974; (with Warrick and Olander) *School and Society Through Science Fiction,* Rand McNally, 1974; (with Warrick and Olander) *The Last Super Bowl Game: Sports Through Science Fiction,* Delacorte, 1974; (with Warrick and Carol Mason) *Anthropology Through Science Fiction,* St. Martin's, 1974; (with Warrick) *A New Awareness: Religion Through Science Fiction,* Dell, 1974; (with Warrick, Olander, and John Milstead) *Social Problems Through Science Fiction,* St. Martin's, 1974; (with Olander, Warrick, and Milstead) *Sociology Through Science Fiction,* St. Martin's, 1974; (with Warrick and Olander) *The Sociology of the Family Through Science Fiction,* St. Martin's, in press. Contributor to journals.

WORK IN PROGRESS: Editing *A Reader in Latin American Bureaucracy,* with James Kolka; editing *The Israeli Military Reader; International Relations Through Science Fiction,* with Joseph D. Olander; *Urban Studies Through Science Fiction,* with Olander; *The Literature of Alternatives,* with Patricia Warrick; *Political Philosophy and Science Fiction,* with Olander; a book studying the American front organizations of the former Palestinian terrorist group known as the Irgun; research on political and societal determinants of bureaucratic power in Mexico, on bureaucracy and environmental quality in a post-revolutionary system, on probable and improbable political futures (science fiction as a theoretical literature), on alternative anthropological futures (anthropological theory and science fiction), on the sociological basis of science fiction, and on a science fiction model of social problems.

SIDELIGHTS: Greenberg writes: "I have tried in my recent work to combine the insights contained in the literature of science fiction with those contained in social science research. I have found science fiction to be the most important and relevant form of literature for our time."

* * *

GREENBERG, Selig 1904-

PERSONAL: Born January 10, 1904, in Kupin, Russia; naturalized U.S. citizen in 1924; son of Abraham and Aviva (Rabinowitz) Greenberg; married Miriam Bakst, October 18, 1945; children: Ann. *Education:* Brown University, B.A., 1927. *Politics:* Democrat. *Religion:* Jewish. *Home:* 99 Oak Hill Ave., Pawtucket, R.I. 02860. *Office: Providence Journal-Bulletin,* 75 Fountain St., Providence, R.I. 02902.

CAREER: Providence Journal-Bulletin, Prividence, R.I., medical writer, 1927—. *Military service:* U.S. Army, 1942-43. *Member:* Phi Beta Kappa. *Awards, honors:* Lasker Foundation awards for excellence in medical journalism, 1951, 1955.

WRITINGS: The Troubled Calling: Crisis in the Medical Establishment, Macmillan, 1965; *The Quality of Mercy: A Report on the Critical Condition of Hospital and Medical Care in America,* Atheneum, 1971. Contributor to *Harper's, Progressive,* and *Nation.*

* * *

GREENBLATT, Edwin 1920-

PERSONAL: Born January 3, 1920, in Vineland, N.J.; son of Morris (a poultry wholesaler) and Ida (Lipman) Greenblatt; married to wife, Eunice (a photographer's representative), January 25, 1948 (separated). *Education:* New York University, B.S., 1940. *Politics:* Independent. *Religion:* Jewish. *Home:* 865 First Ave., New York, N.Y. 10017. *Agent:* Elaine Markson, 44 Greenwich Ave., New York, N.Y. 10011. *Office:* William Douglas McAdams, 110 East 59th St., New York, N.Y.

CAREER: Grey Advertising, New York, N.Y., writer, 1955-59; Sullivan, Stauffer, Colwell, & Bayles (advertising agency), New York, N.Y., creative director, 1959-71; William Douglas McAdams (advertising), New York, N.Y., copy supervisor, 1974—. *Member:* New York Advertising Club, Sierra Club.

WRITINGS: Suddenly Single: A Survival Kit for the Single Man, Quadrangle, 1973.

WORK IN PROGRESS: Articles on travels in the American West.

AVOCATIONAL INTERESTS: Bicycling, swimming, hiking, cooking, travel, backpacking.

* * *

GREENBLATT, Stephen J(ay) 1943-

PERSONAL: Born November 7, 1943, in Cambridge, Mass.; son of Harry J. (a lawyer) and Mollie (Brown) Greenblatt; married Ellen Schmidt (a teacher), April 27, 1969. *Education:* Yale University, B.A. (honors), 1964, M.Ph., 1968, Ph.D., 1969; Pembroke College, Cambridge, A.B., 1966, M.A., 1969. *Home:* 1004 Oxford St., Berkeley, Calif. 94707. *Office:* Department of English, University of California, Berkeley, Calif. 94720.

CAREER: University of California, Berkeley, assistant professor, 1969-73, associate professor of English, 1973—. *Member:* Modern Language Association of America, Berzelius, Elizabethan Club, Renaissance Society of America, Phi Beta Kappa. *Awards, honors:* Fulbright scholar, 1964-66; Lloyd Mifflin prize, 1964, for *Three Modern Satirists;* Woodrow Wilson scholar (honorary), 1966; Porter prize, 1969, for *Sir Walter Ralegh;* National Endowment for the Humanities younger humanist award, 1971-72.

WRITINGS: Three Modern Satirists: Waugh, Orwell, and Huxley, Yale University Press, 1965; *Sir Walter Ralegh: The Renaissance Man and His Roles,* Yale University Press, 1973. Contributor to *Yale Review* and *Studies in Philology.*

WORK IN PROGRESS: Self-fashioning in the English Renaissance.

BIOGRAPHICAL/CRITICAL SOURCES: New York Times Book Review, March 10, 1974.

* * *

GREENFIELD, Eloise 1929-

PERSONAL: Born May 17, 1929, in Parmele, N.C.; daughter of Weston W. and Lessie (Jones) Little; married Robert J. Greenfield (a procurement specialist), April 29, 1950; children: Steven, Monica. *Education:* Attended Miner Teachers College, 1946-49. *Home:* 830 Buchanan St. N.E., Washington, D.C. 20017. *Agent:* Curtis Brown Ltd., 60 East 56th St., New York, N.Y. 10022.

CAREER: U.S. Patent Office, Washington, D.C., clerk-typist, 1949-56, supervisory patent assistant, 1956-60; worked as a secretary, case-control technician, and an administrative assistant in Washington D.C. from 1964-68. Co-director of adult fiction of District of Columbia Black Writer's Workshop, 1971-73, director of children's literature, 1973-74; writer-in-residence with District of Columbia Commission on the Arts, 1973.

WRITINGS—Children's books: (Contributor) Alma Murray and Robert Thomas, editors, *The Journey: Scholastic Black Literature,* Scholastic Book Service, 1970; *Bubbles* (picture book), Drum & Spear Press, 1972; *Rosa Parks* (biography), Crowell, 1973; (contributor) Karen S. Kleiman and Mel Cebulash, editors, *Double Action Short Stories,* Scholastic Book Services, 1973; *Sister* (novel), Crowell, 1974; *She Come Bringing Me That Little Baby Girl* (picture book), Lippincott, 1974; *Paul Robeson* (biography), Crowell, in press. Contributor to *Black World, Ebony Jr!, Negro History Bulletin, Scholastic Scope,* and *Ms.*

SIDELIGHTS: Eloise Greenfield wrote: "I feel that it is important to give heroes and heroines of the Black liberation struggle a place of honor that will last through the generations."

* * *

GREENHALGH, P(eter) A(ndrew) L(ivsey) 1945-

PERSONAL: Surname is pronounced *Green*-halsh; born October 18, 1945, in Littleborough, Lancashire, England; son of Herbert Livsey (a draper) and Elsie (Wright) Greenhalgh; married Anna-Mary Beatrice Dixon (a solicitor), August 24, 1968. *Education:* King's College, Cambridge, B.A., 1967, M.A., 1970, Ph.D., 1971. *Home:* 16 Church Walk, Thames Ditton, Surrey, England. *Office:* Hill Samuel & Co., 100 Wood St., London E.C.2, England.

CAREER: Various business activities, 1970-72; Hill Samuel & Co., London, England, merchant banker, 1972—.

WRITINGS: Early Greek Warfare, Cambridge University Press, 1973; *The Year of the Four Emperors,* Weidenfeld & Nicolson, in press. Contributor to classical journals, including *Greece and Rome* and *Historia.*

* * *

GREENSTEIN, Fred I(rwin) 1930-

PERSONAL: Born September 1, 1930, in New York, N.Y.; son of Arthur A. and Rose Greenstein; married Barbara Elferink, 1957; children: Michael, Amy, Jessica. *Education:* Antioch College, B.A., 1953; Yale University, M.A., 1957, Ph.D., 1960; New York Psychoanalytic Institute, postdoctoral study, 1961-62. *Home:* 340 Jefferson Rd., Princeton, N.J. 08540. *Office:* Department of Politics, Princeton University, Princeton, N.J. 08540.

CAREER: Yale University, New Haven, Conn., instructor in political science, 1959-62, director of Political Science Research Library, 1960-62; Wesleyan University, Middletown, Conn., assistant professor, 1962-64, associate professor, 1964-66, professor of government, 1966-73, chairman of department, 1967-68, 1969-71; Princeton University, Princeton, N.J., Henry R. Luce Professor of Politics, Law, and Society, 1973—. Fellow at Center for Advanced Study in the Behavioral Sciences, 1964-65; visiting associate professor of Yale University, 1965-66, recurring visiting professor, 1966-70; visiting professor at University of Essex, 1968-69. Member of political science advisory panel of National Science Foundation, 1970-72. Member of council of Inter-University Political Science Research Consortium, 1969-71. *Military service:* U.S. Army, infantry, 1952-54.

MEMBER: American Political Science Association (member of council, 1969-72), Society for the Psychological Study of Social Issues. *Awards, honors:* National Science Foundation senior postdoctoral fellowship, 1968-69; Ford Foundation fellowship in political science, 1972-73.

WRITINGS: (With Robert E. Lane and James D. Barber) *An Introduction to Political Analysis,* Prentice-Hall, 1962, 2nd edition, 1967; *The American Party System and the American People,* Prentice-Hall, 1963, 2nd edition, 1970; *Children and Politics,* Yale University Press, 1965, revised edition, 1969; *Personality and Politics: Problems of Evidence, Inference, and Conceptualization,* Markham, 1969, revised edition, 1970; (with Michael Lerner) *A Source Book for the Study of Personality and Politics,* Markham, 1971.

Contributor: Nelson W. Polsby and others, editors, *Politics and Social Life,* Houghton, 1963; Bradley Greenberg and Edwin Parker, editors, *The Kennedy Assassination and the American Public,* Stanford University Press, 1965; Gilbert Kliman and Martha Wolfenstein, editors, *Children and the Death of a President: Multi-Disciplinary Studies,* Doubleday, 1965; Bradley Seasholes, editor, *Voting, Interest Groups, and Parties,* Scott-Foresman, 1966; Heinz Eulau, editor, *Political Behavior in America,* Random House, 1966; Elmer Cornwell, Jr., editor, *The American Presidency: Vital Center,* Scott-Foresman, 1966; Donald G. Herzberg and Gerald M. Pomper, editors, *American Party Politics,* Holt, 1966; Philip B. Coulter, editor, *Politics of Metropolitan Areas,* Crowell, 1967; Robert A. Dahl and Dean E. Neubauer, editors, *Readings in Modern Political Analysis,* Prentice-Hall, 1968; Seymour M. Lipset and Richard Hofstadter, editors, *Sociology and History,* Basic Books, 1968; Norman L. Zucker, editor, *The American Party Process,* Dodd, 1968; Aaron Wildavsky and Nelson W. Polsby, editors, *American Governmental Institutions,* Rand McNally, 1968; C. J. Larson and P. C. Wasburn, editors, *Power Participation and Ideology,* McKay, 1969; Leroy N. Rieselbach and George I. Balch, editors, *Psychology and Politics,* Holt, 1969; Charles F. Cnudde and Neubauer, editors, *Empirical Democratic Theory,* Markham, 1969; Wildavsky, editor, *The Presidency,* Little, Brown, 1969; Lipset, editor, *Politics and Social Change,* Oxford University Press, 1969; Alan Shank, editor, *Political Power and the Urban Crisis,* Holbrook, 1969.

Roberta Sigel, editor, *Learning About Politics: A Reader in Political Socialization,* Random House, 1970; Neil J. Smelser and William T. Smelser, editors, *Personality and Social Systems,* Wiley, 2nd edition (Greenstein was not included in first edition), 1970; (contributor) Eugene C. Lee and Willis D. Hawley, editors, *The Challenge of California,* Little, Brown, 1970; Edward S. Greenberg, editor, *Political Socialization,* Atherton, 1970; Michael McGiffert, editor, *The Character of Americans,* Dorsey, 1970; Irwin N. Gertzog, editor, *Readings on State and Local Government,* Prentice-Hall, 1970; Joseph F. Zimmerman, editor, *Subnational Politics,* Holt, 1970; Richard E. Morgan and James E. Connor, editors, *The American Political System,* Harcourt, 1971; Joseph Palamountain and Martin Shapiro, editors, *Issues and Perspectives in American Government,* Scott, Foresman, 1971; David W. Abbott and Edward T. Rogowsky, editors, *Political Parties: Leadership, Organization, Linkage,* Rand McNally, 1971; Donald C. Moe and William A. Schultze, editors, *American Government and Politics,* C. E. Merrill, 1971; Charles M. Bonjean, Terry N. Clark, and Robert L. Lineberry, editors, *Community Politics,* Free Press, 1971; Edward Keynes and David Adamany, editors, *The Borzoi Reader in American Politics,* Knopf, 1971; David R. Morgan and Samuel A. Kirkpatrick, editors, *Urban Political Analysis: A Systems Approach,* Free Press, 1972; Philip J. Briggs, editor, *Politics in America: Readings and Documents,* MSS Information Corp., 1972; Joseph R. Fiszman and Gene S. Poschman, editors, *The American Political Arena: Selected Readings,* Little, Brown, 3rd edition (Greenstein was not included in earlier editions), 1972; Samuel A. Kirkpatrick and Lawrence K. Pettit, editors, *The Social Psychology of Political Life,* Duxbury, 1972; Donald R. Reich and Paul A. Dawson, editors, *Political Images and Realities,* Duxbury, 1972; Anthony M. Orum, editor, *The Seeds of Politics: Youth and Politics in America,* Prentice-Hall, 1972; James D. Barber, editor, *Power to the Citizen,* Markham, 1972; Robert Weissberg and Mark V. Nadel, editors, *American Democracy: Theory and Reality,* Wiley, 1972; Paul Barker, editor, *One for Sorrow, Two for Joy: Ten Years of New Society,* Allen & Unwin, 1972; Richard Flacks, editor, *Conformity, Resistance, and Self Determination: The Individual and Authority,* Little, Brown, 1973; Charles G. Bell, editor, *Growth and Change: A Reader in Political Socialization,* Dickenson, 1973; Robert G. Golembiewski and others, editors, *Dilemmas of Political Participation,* Prentice-Hall, 1973; Jack Dennis, editor, *Socialization to Politics: A Reader,* Wiley, 1973; Jeanne N. Knutson, editor, *The Handbook of Political Psychology,* Jossey-Bass, 1973; James D. Barber, editor, *Choosing the President,* Prentice-Hall, 1974.

Contributor to *International Encyclopedia of the Social Sciences.* Contributor of about thirty articles and reviews to political science journals in the United States and abroad, including *Public Opinion Quarterly, World Politics, Journal of Politics, New Society, Youth and Society,* and *School Review.* Member of editorial board of *American Political Science Review,* 1968-71, *British Journal of Political Science,* 1968—, and *Journal of Youth and Adolescence,* 1970—. Member of editorial advisory board of *American Politics Quarterly,* 1972—.

WORK IN PROGRESS: Editing, with Nelson W. Polsby, and writing articles for *The Handbook of Political Science,* Volume I: *Political Science: Scope and Theory,* Volume II: *Micropolitical Theory,* Volume III: *Macropolitical Theory,* Volume IV: *Non-Governmental Politics,* Volume V: *Governmental Institutions and Processes,* Volume VI: *Policies and Policy-Making,* Volume VII: *Strategies of Inquiry,* Volume VIII: *International Politics,* for Addison-Wesley; *The Dynamics of American Politics,* with Martin Shapiro and Raymond Wolfinger, publication by Prentice-Hall expected in 1976; *Depth Studies of Comparative Political Socialization,* with Sidney Tarrow, Barbara Young, and others, Wiley, 1976; *An Annotated Bibliography of Literature on the Expansion of the Presidential Office,* with Lawrence Berman and Alvin Felzenberg; research on presidential personality, president-adviser relations, and the expansion and institutionalization of the American presidency since 1933.

* * *

GREULACH, Victor A(ugust) 1906-

PERSONAL: Surname is pronounced "groi-lak"; born December 6, 1906, in Convoy, Ohio; son of John A. (a school superintendent) and Margaret (Giessler) Greulach; married Elizabeth Dunnells, October 6, 1934; children: Dorothy (Mrs. Roger Herbert), Susan (Mrs. J. L. Scharff), Vicki (Mrs. Bruce Marsh). *Education:* DePauw University, A.B., 1929; Ohio State University, M.S., 1933, Ph.D., 1940; graduate study at Allegheny School of Natural History, summer, 1933, and University of Texas, summer, 1936; Oak Ridge Institute of Nuclear Studies, postdoctoral study, 1950. *Home:* 1815 South Lake Shore Dr., Chapel Hill, N.C. 27514.

CAREER: Muskingum College, New Concord, Ohio, instructor in biology, 1933-35; University of Houston, Houston, Tex., assistant professor, 1935-40, associate professor of biology, 1940-46, chairman of Division of Biological Sciences, 1944-46; Texas A. & M. University, College Station, associate professor of botany, 1946-49; University of North Carolina, Chapel Hill, associate professor, 1949-51, professor of botany, 1951-74, chairman of department, 1960-72. Superintendent of Natural Science Section, City of Houston Parks and Recreation Department, 1944-46. National Science Foundation, co-director of Institute for Science Teachers, 1957-61, professional assistant, summer, 1958, consultant, 1958-61. College Entrance Examination Board, member of board of examiners in biology, 1959-69, chairman, 1967-69. Executive director of Commission on Undergraduate Education in the Biological Sciences, 1964-65. Visiting professor at College of William and Mary, summer, 1948, University of Virginia, summer, 1956, and University of New Hampshire, summers, 1962, 1963.

MEMBER: Botanical Society of America, American Association for the Advancement of Science (fellow), Association of Southeastern Biologists (president, 1960-61), Texas Academy of Science (president of eastern section, 1944-45), North Carolina Academy of Science (president, 1963-64), Elisha Mitchell Science Society, Sigma Xi (president of University of North Carolina chapter, 1959-60), Phi Sigma, Phi Epsilon Phi.

WRITINGS: A Laboratory Manual for Elementary Plant Physiology, Burgess, 1952; (with J. E. Adams) *Plants: An Introduction to Modern Botany,* Wiley, 1962, 3rd edition, in press; (with Adams) *Plants: Introductory Investigations in Botany,* Wiley, 1962; *Botany Made Simple,* Doubleday, 1968; *Plant Function and Structure,* Macmillan, 1973. Contributor of about one hundred articles and reviews to magazines and professional journals, including *Reader's Digest, Scientific American, Field & Stream, Science Digest,* and *Nature.* Editor of *Association of Southeastern Biologists Bulletin,* 1954-59, *Commission on Undergraduate Education in the Biological Sciences News,* 1964-65, and *Journal of the Elisha Mitchell Scientific Society,* 1966-74.

* * *

GREY, Robert Waters 1943-

PERSONAL: Born October 12, 1943, in Sandy Spring, Md.; son of Charles Gibson and Elizabeth (Jones) Grey; married Lucinda Creswell, June 24, 1967; children: Alexander Randolph. *Education:* Brown University, B.A. (cum laude), 1965; University of Virginia, M.A., 1969. *Address:* Box 345 C, Route 12, Charlotte, N.C. 28212. *Office:* Department of English, University of North Carolina, Charlotte, N.C. 28213.

CAREER: University of North Carolina, Charlotte, instructor in English and poet-in-residence, 1969—. Member of Poetry-in-the-Schools program, 1972—. *Wartime service:* Conscientious objector, in Civilian public service with Goodwill Industries and Massachusetts General Hospital, 1966-68. *Awards, honors:* Academy of America Poets award from University of Virginia, 1969; North Carolina Poets first place award, 1972, for "The Miscellany."

WRITINGS: (Editor with Charleen Whisnant, and contributor) *Eleven Charlotte Poets,* Red Clay, 1971. Contributor of poetry to *Poem, Western Review, Southern Poetry Review, Florida Quarterly, St. Andrews Review,* and *Poet Lore.*

WORK IN PROGRESS: Cold Stone (poems).

SIDELIGHTS: Grey told *CA:* "All subjects, all things, all emotions are important to my work and emerge in the writing. I wander around a lot, and am an indiscriminate collector of 'things' which contantly surround me. I am particularly interested in natural 'things.' Have been accused of being a junkyard poet."

* * *

GRIESE, Arnold A(lfred) 1921-

PERSONAL: Surname rhymes with "rice"; born April 13, 1921, in Lakota, Iowa; son of Helmut Adam (a farmer) and Augusta (Meltz) Griese; married Jane Warren (owner of Jocyn School of Modeling, Fairbanks, Alaska), January 14, 1943; children: Warren, Cynthia (Mrs. Les Blakely). *Education:* Georgetown University, B.S., 1948; University of Miami, Coral Gables, Fla., M.Ed., 1957; University of Arizona, Ph.D., 1960. *Politics:* Independent. *Religion:* Episcopalian. *Home:* 3070 Riverview Dr., Fairbanks, Alaska 99701. *Office:* Department of Education, University of Alaska, Fairbanks, Alaska 99701.

CAREER: McGraw-Hill Publishing Co., New York, N.Y., sales representative in Colombia, South America, 1948-50; elementary school teacher in the public schools of Tanana, Alaska, 1951-56; University of Alaska, Fairbanks, assistant professor, 1960-65, associate professor, 1965-71, professor of education, 1971—. *Military service:* U.S. Army Air Forces, 1942-46; became captain. *Member:* National Council of Teachers of English, Alaska Council of Teachers of English, Delta Phi Epsilon, Phi Delta Kappa.

WRITINGS: (Contributor) Miriam Hoffman, editor, *Authors and Illustrators of Children's Books,* Bowker, 1972; *At the Mouth of the Luckiest River* (juvenile), Crowell, 1973. Contributor to *Elementary English.*

WORK IN PROGRESS: A children's book of historical fiction on the Indians of Alaska, for Crowell.

AVOCATIONAL INTERESTS: Flying (piloted his own plane), chess, swimming, travel.

* * *

GRIESON, Ronald Edward 1943-

PERSONAL: Born March 8, 1943, in New York, N.Y.; son of Hans Willhelm (a manager) and Stella Grieson; married Barbara Anne Uchal, August 29, 1970. *Education:* Queens College of the City University of New York, B.A. (cum laude), 1964; University of Rochester, M.A., 1967, Ph.D., 1971. *Politics:* Independent. *Religion:* "Protestant by birth." *Home and office:* 35 Claremont Ave., New York, N.Y. 10027.

CAREER: University of Rochester, Rochester, N.Y., instructor in economics, 1968-69; Massachusetts Institute of Technology, Cambridge, assistant professor of economics, 1969-72; Queens College and Graduate Center of the City University of New York, New York, N.Y., associate professor of economics, 1972-74; Columbia University, New York, N.Y., associate professor of economics, 1974—. Consultant to U.S. Economic Development Administration, Commonwealth of Massachusetts, and City of New York. *Member:* American Economics Association, Econometric Society.

WRITINGS: (Editor) *Urban Economics: Readings and Analysis,* Little, Brown, 1973. Contributor to *Journal of Urban Economics* and *American Economic Review.*

WORK IN PROGRESS: Research interests in transportation, juvenile crime, the effect of taxes on location, the demand and supply of heroin, rent control, and inexact proxy variables.

AVOCATIONAL INTERESTS: Fine arts, architecture, domestic and wild animals.

* * *

GRIFFIN, Arthur J. 1921- (Lee Frank)

PERSONAL: Born January 7, 1921, in Hartford, Conn.; married Jane Slattery; children: four. *Education:* Attended Hillyer College and Columbia University. *Home:* 46 Meadowood Lane, Old Saybrook, Conn. 06475. *Agent:* Chuck Neighbors, Waverly Pl., New York, N.Y.

CAREER: Worked in publishing and advertising in Mass., N.Y., and Conn.; currently employed as an advertising copywriter in Conn. *Military service:* U.S. Army Air Forces, 1942-45; became sergeant.

WRITINGS—Under pseudonym Lee Frank: *Kane,* Paperback Library, 1972; *Kane—and the Goldbar Killers,* Paperback Library, 1973. Also author of other novels under various pseudonyms.

WORK IN PROGRESS: Fiction—Westerns, Gothics, and general novels.

* * *

GRIFFIN, Susan 1943-

PERSONAL: Born January 26, 1943, in Los Angeles, Calif.; daughter of Walden and Sarah (Colvin) Griffin; married John Levy, June 11, 1966 (divorced, 1970); children: Rebecca Siobhain. *Education:* Attended University of California at Berkeley, 1960-63; San Francisco State University, B.A. (cum laude), 1965, M.A., 1972. *Politics:* Radical, feminist. *Religion:* None. *Home:* 1939 Cedar St., Berkeley, Calif. 94709. *Agent:* Julie Fallowfield, McIntosh & Otis, Inc., 18 East 41 St., New York, N.Y. 10017.

CAREER: Has worked as a waitress, switchboard and teletype operator, and housepainter; Hamilton Recreation Center, San Francisco, Calif., drama teacher, 1964-65; *Ramparts* (magazine), San Francisco, Calif., assistant editor, 1966-68; San Francisco State College (now University), San Francisco, Calif., instructor in English, 1970-71; Poetry in the Schools program, teacher of poetry in Oakland, Calif. high schools, 1972-73; University of California, Berkeley, instructor in English and women's studies in extension school, 1972—. *Awards, honors:* Ina Coolbrith Prize in Poetry, 1963; National Endowment for the Arts grant, 1974.

WRITINGS—Poetry: *Dear Sky,* Shameless Hussy Press, 1971; *Let Them Be Said,* Ma Ma Press, 1973. Work represented in anthologies, including *Women: Feminist Stories by New Fiction Authors,* Eakins, 1971; *No More Masks: An Anthology of Poems by Women,* edited by Florence Howe and Ellen Bass, Doubleday, 1973; *Rising Tides: Twentieth Century American Women Poets,* edited by Laura Chester and Sharon Barba, Washington Square Press, 1973. Contributor to *Ramparts, Scanlon's, Sundance, Shocks.*

WORK IN PROGRESS: Research on Christianity's effect as an ideology on the psychology of women; poems on the mood of fatigue of the 1970's, entitled *The Tiredness Cycle.*

GRIGSON, Jane 1928-

PERSONAL: Born March 13, 1928, in Gloucester, England; daughter of George Shipley (a town clerk) and Doris (Berkley) McIntire; children: Hester Sophia Frances. *Education:* Newnham College, Cambridge, B.A., 1949. *Home:* Broad Town Farm, Broad Town, Swindon, Wiltshire, England. *Agent:* Harold Ober Associates, Inc., 40 East 49th St., New York, N.Y. 10017; and David Higham Associates, 5-8 Lower John St., Golden Square, London W1R 3PE, England.

CAREER: Heffers Art Gallery, Cambridge, England, assistant, 1950-51; Walker's Art Gallery, London, England, assistant, 1952-53; George Rainbird Ltd. (publisher), London, England, assistant, 1953-54; Thames & Hudson Ltd. (publisher), London, England, assistant, 1954-55; editor, translator, writer. *Member:* Wine and Food Society. *Awards, honors:* John Florio Prize, 1965, for translation of *On Crimes and Punishments.*

WRITINGS: (Translator) Giovanni A. Cibotto, *Scano Boa,* Hodder & Stoughton, 1963; (translator) Cesare Beccaria, *On Crimes and Punishments,* Oxford University Press, 1964; (with Geoffrey Grigson) *Shapes and Stories,* Vanguard, 1965; (with Geoffrey Grigson) *More Shapes and Stories,* Vanguard, 1967; *Charcuterie & French Pork Cookery,* M. Joseph, 1967, published as *Art of Charcuterie,* Knopf, 1968; *Good Things,* Knopf, 1971; *Fish Cookery,* Wine and Fish Society, 1973; *The Mushroom Feast,* Knopf, in press. Cookery correspondent, *Observer Colour Magazine,* 1968—.

WORK IN PROGRESS: *English Country Cooking,* for Macmillan; *World of Food,* for Simon & Schuster.

* * *

GRILLO, Ralph David 1940-

PERSONAL: Born April 23, 1940, in Watford, England; son of Ralph (a tradesman) and Muriel May (Harries) Grillo; married Bronacha Frances Ryan, August 7, 1968; children: Claudia Serafina, Philippa Frances, Joan Benedict. *Education:* King's College, Cambridge, B.A., 1963, Ph.D., 1968. *Politics:* Labour Party. *Religion:* None. *Home:* 25 Spences Field, Lewes, Sussex, England. *Office:* School of African and Asian Studies, University of Sussex, Falmer, Brighton BN1 9QN, England.

CAREER: Queen's University, Belfast, Northern Ireland, assistant lecturer, 1967-69, lecturer in social anthropology, 1969-70; University of Sussex, Brighton, Sussex, England, lecturer in social anthropology, 1970—. *Member:* International African Institute, Association of Social Anthropologists of United Kingdom, Royal Anthropological Institute, African Studies Association of United Kingdom.

WRITINGS: *African Railwaymen: Solidarity and Opposition in an East African Labour Force,* Cambridge University Press, 1973; *Race, Class, and Militancy: An African Trade Union, 1939-1965,* Chandler Publishing, 1974. Contributor to *Africa, Man,* and other journals.

WORK IN PROGRESS: Study of ethnic and class identities among migrant workers in an industrial center in Europe, with particular reference to trade union membership and activity.

SIDELIGHTS: Grillo has done fieldwork in East Africa in 1964-65 and in the Republic of Ireland. He is interested as a spectator in films, cricket, and politics.

GRIMM, William C(arey) 1907-

PERSONAL: Born July 1, 1907, in Pittsburgh, Pa.; son of Charles and Harriet Elizabeth (Carey) Grimm; married Ruth Fahr Curtis (a school librarian), July 12, 1941. *Education:* University of Pittsburgh, B.S., 1935. *Home:* 15 Strawberry Dr., Route 9, Greenville, S.C. 29609.

CAREER: Wildlife biologist; teacher of science in Georgetown, S.C., 1951-55, Pickens, S.C., 1955-56, and Greenville, S.C., 1956-60. *Military service:* U.S. Army, 1942-45; became sergeant. *Member:* Authors Guild, National Audubon Society, American Forestry Association, National Wildlife Federation, Southern Appalachian Botanical Club, Carolina Bird Club, South Carolina Retired Educators Association.

WRITINGS: Book of Trees, Stackpole, 1957, published as *How to Recognize Trees,* Castle, 1972; *Recognizing Native Shrubs,* Stackpole, 1966, published as *How to Recognize Shrubs,* Castle, 1972; *Familiar Trees of America,* Harper, 1967; *Recognizing Flowering Wild Plants,* Stackpole, 1968, published as *How to Recognize Flowering Wild Plants,* Castle, 1972; *Home Guide to Trees, Shrubs, and Wildflowers,* Stackpole, 1970; (with M. Jean Craig) *The Wondrous World of Seedless Plants,* Bobbs-Merrill, 1973; *Indian Harvests,* McGraw, 1974.

* * *

GROH, Ed(win Charles) 1910-

PERSONAL: Born August 26, 1910, in New York, N.Y.: son of Charles J. and Margaret (Bruning) Groh; married Dorothy Thompson (a teacher), November 25, 1936; children: Frederick, Ronald, Marjorie Groh Hanak. *Education:* Occidental College, B.A., 1938; University of Southern California, M.A., 1941. *Politics:* Republican. *Home and office:* 2265 Mardavido Lane, Fallbrook, Calif. 92028. *Agent:* A. L. Fierst, 630 Ninth Ave., New York, N.Y.

CAREER: Teacher of history, coach, and year book advisor in California high schools, in Laguna Beach, 1941-45, Paramount, 1953-56, and Fallbrook, 1965-66; Taft Junior College, Taft, Calif., instructor in psychology, newspaper and yearbook advisor, coach, and counselor, 1946-48; *Santa Ana Independent* (weekly newspaper), Santa Ana, Calif., editor, 1949-52; free-lance writer, 1957-60; *Fallbrook Free Press,* Fallbrook, Calif., editor, 1961-64; *Blade Tribune,* Oceanside, Calif., reporter, 1967-69; *Vista Press,* Vista, Calif., county editor, 1967-69; writer, 1969—. *Member:* National Writers Club, International Platform Association, Phi Beta Kappa, Phi Theta Kappa, Alpha Gamma Sigma, Phi Rho Phi.

WRITINGS: Jackasses of Los Causes, Vega Books, 1964; *The Wild and the Tender,* Aero, 1973. Contributor to *Defenders of Wildlife* and *Personal Poetry.*

WORK IN PROGRESS: All the Dead Are Not Buried, a book about religious cults, their operations, and effects upon young members; *Give It Back to the Indians,* a survey of American political history; *You Can't Get Milk from a Sacred Cow,* a satire on public education; *Come Share My Electric Blanket, I Paid the Light Bill,* about marriage; *Taco: Wild Dog,* a children's book.

* * *

GROSS, Mary Anne 1943-

PERSONAL: Born August 10, 1943, in Cornwall, N.Y.; daughter of Anthony Louis (an antique dealer) and Anne M. (Buckneberg) Gross; married Angelo Ferraro, January, 1974. *Education:* State University of New York College at New Paltz, B.A. and B.S., both 1965. *Home:* Yesterday's Village, Highland Mills, N.Y. 10930.

CAREER: New York City Board of Education, New York, N.Y., teacher, 1965—. *Member:* Kappa Delta Phi.

WRITINGS: (Editor) *Mother: These Are My Friends,* City Schools Curriculum Service (Boston), 1969; (editor) *Ah, Man: You Found Me Again,* Beacon Press, 1972.

WORK IN PROGRESS: A series of readers for economically-deprived children; two novels; several picture story books.

BIOGRAPHICAL/CRITICAL SOURCES: Times Herald Record (Middleton, N.Y.), December 6, 1970, March 19, 1972, December 31, 1972; *Reading Teacher,* February, 1973.

* * *

GRUBER, Frederick C(harles) 1903-

PERSONAL: Born May 26, 1903, in Philadelphia, Pa.; son of Harry G. C. (a manufacturer) and Anna (Schussler) Gruber; married Alma Hellwege (a professor), June 30, 1936; children: Nancy (Mrs. Richard L. P. Custer). *Education:* University of Pennsylvania, B.S. in Ed., 1928, A.M., 1930, Ph.D., 1934. *Religion:* Lutheran. *Home:* 422 Dorset Rd., Devon, Pa. 19333. *Office:* Department of Education, University of Pennsylvania, Philadelphia, Pa. 19174.

CAREER: Teacher of English in the public high schools of Philadelphia, Pa., 1923-36; University of Pennsylvania, Philadelphia, assistant professor, 1939-45, associate professor, 1945-56, professor of education, 1956-73, professor emeritus, 1973—. Visiting professor at University of Amsterdam, 1954-55, Princeton Theological Seminary, 1958, Bryn Mawr College, 1960, Johns Hopkins University, 1965, American University, Beirut, 1966, and Haigazian College, Beirut, 1966. Trustee and executive secretary of Garrigues Foundation, 1956—. *Member:* American Philosophical Association, Philosophy of Education Society, John Dewey Society, History of Education Society, American Educational Studies Association, Middle States Philosophy of Education Society, Phi Delta Kappa.

WRITINGS: A Concept of Poetry, Science Press, 1936; (with T. B. Beatty) *Secondary School Activities,* McGraw, 1954; *Foundations for a Philosophy of Education,* Crowell, 1961; *Historical and Contemporary Philosophies of Education,* Crowell, 1973.

Editor; all published by University of Pennsylvania Press: *Teaching in America,* 1956; *The Good Education of Youth,* 1956; *Foundations of Education,* 1957; *Partners in Education,* 1957; *Emergence of the Modern Mind,* 1958; *Quality and Quantity in American Education,* 1958; *Aspects of Value,* 1959; *Education in Transition,* 1959; *Education and the State,* 1960; *Anthropology and Education,* 1961.

WORK IN PROGRESS: Herbert Spencer's Radical School Reform.

* * *

GRUENBAUM, Ludwig

See GAATHON, A(ryeh) L(udwig)

GRUENBERG, Sidonie Matsner 1881-1974

June 10, 1881—March 11, 1974; American authority on child care and guidance and family relationships, and author of books in her field. Obituaries: *New York Times,* March 13, 1974; *Time,* March 25, 1974; *Current Biography,* May, 1974. (*CA*-15/16).

* * *

GRUENING, Ernest (Henry) 1887-1974

PERSONAL: Born February 6, 1887, in New York, N.Y.; son of Emil (a physician) and Phebe (Fridenberg) Gruening; married Dorothy Elisabeth Smith, November 19, 1914; children: Huntington. *Education:* Harvard University, A.B., 1907, M.D., 1912. *Politics:* Democrat. *Home and office:* 7926 West Beach Dr., Washington, D.C. 20012.

CAREER: Boston Traveler, Boston, Mass., managing editor, 1914-16; *Boston Journal,* Boston, Mass., managing editor, 1916-18; *New York Herald-Tribune,* New York, N.Y., managing editor, 1918-19; *Portland Evening News,* Portland, Me., managing editor, 1927-32; U.S. Department of Interior, Washington, D.C., director of Territories and Island Possessions, 1934-39; governor of Alaska, 1939-53; U.S. senator from Alaska, 1958-69; writer and lecturer, 1969-74. *Military service:* U.S. Army, 1918. *Member:* Phi Beta Kappa, Cosmos Club (Washington, D.C.). *Awards, honors:* LL.D., University of Alberta, 1946, University of Alaska, 1955, Brandeis University, 1959; L.H.D., Wilmington College, 1968.

WRITINGS: (Editor) *These United States: A Symposium,* two volumes, Boni & Liveright, 1923-24; *Mexico and Its Heritage,* Century Co., 1928; *The Public Pays: A Study of Power Propaganda,* Vanguard, 1931, revised edition, 1964; *The State of Alaska,* Random House, 1954, revised edition, 1968; (contributor) *The Alaska Book: Story of Our Northern Treasureland,* J. G. Ferguson, 1960; (editor) *An Alaskan Reader, 1867-1967,* Meredith, 1967; (with H. W. Beaser) *Vietnam Folly,* National Press, 1968; *The Battle for Alaska Statehood,* University of Washington Press, 1967; *Many Battles* (autobiography), Liveright, 1973.

(died June 26, 1974)

* * *

GUCK, Dorothy 1913-

PERSONAL: Born May 17, 1913, in Grand Rapids, Mich.; daughter of Walter E. and Margaret (Plaat) Gray; married M. Edmund Guck (a U.S. forest ranger), December 27, 1934 (died, 1973); children: Tom, Mick, Mary (Mrs. Bobby Dan Crenshaw). *Education:* Attended University of Wisconsin, 1931-34. *Politics:* Republican. *Religion:* Roman Catholic. *Home address:* Box 515, Nogal, N.M. 88341.

CAREER: Worked as a junior high school teacher, postal clerk, forest service clerk. *Awards, honors:* U.S. Forest Service Award, 1958, for *Smokey Bear Pageant;* Zia Award from New Mexico Press Women, 1969, for *Danger Rides the Forest.*

WRITINGS: Danger Rides the Forest, Vanguard, 1969. Author of pamphlets, *Smokey Bear Pageant* and *Ranchmen's Camp Meeting.* Also author of radio scripts for WHA, Madison, Wis.

WORK IN PROGRESS: Trouble in Timberland, a juvenile book; a young adult historical novel of Revolutionary times in America.

GUERRETTE, Richard H(ector) 1930-

PERSONAL: Born June 26, 1930, in Bristol, Conn.; son of Hector (a machinist) and Leona (Marselle) Guerrette. *Education:* St. Mary's Seminary and University, Baltimore, Md., B.A., 1955; University of Notre Dame, M.A., 1971; Yale University, S.T.M., 1971. *Politics:* Democrat. *Home:* 24 Farmstead Lane, Farmington, Conn. 06032.

CAREER: Ordained Roman Catholic priest, 1959; parish priest of Roman Catholic churches in Watertown, Conn., and Bethlehem, Conn., 1959-69; principal of St. John's School, Watertown, 1959-68; minister and consultant to Emmanuel Servant Community, Watertown, 1969—. Lecturer, research associate, and conference director, Yale University Ecumenical Continuing Education Center, 1972-73.

WRITINGS: A New Identity for the Priest: Toward an Ecumenical Ministry, Paulist-Newman, 1973; (contributor) Gregory Baum and Andrew Greeley, editors, *The Church as Institution,* Stichting Concilium, 1974. Contributor to *Homiletic and Pastoral Review* and *Worship.*

WORK IN PROGRESS: From Mummification to Cosmic Burial, completion expected in 1975; *Authenticity in Church Membership: An Alternative to Infant Baptism,* 1976.

SIDELIGHTS: Guerrette is a co-founder of the Emmanuel Servant Community, an experimental parish community established in 1969. Experiences from this innovative form of Christian communal living led to the publication of his first book and to his present researches.

* * *

GUILLOT, Rene 1900-1969

PERSONAL: Born January 24, 1900, in Courcoury, Charente-Maritime, France; son of Arsene and Marie-Louise (Drouard) Guillot; married Gisele Mervaud (a writer); children: Jean Marie (son). *Education:* Studied at University of Bordeaux; Sorbonne, University of Paris, Licence es-sciences mathematiques, 1922. *Home:* 76 Avenue de Paris, Vincennes, Seine, France.

CAREER: Teacher of mathematics in French West Africa, principally in Dakar, 1923-50; professor of mathematics at Lycee Condorcet, Paris, 1950-60; writer. *Military service:* Fought with American forces as artilleryman, 1943-46; took part in campaigns in northern France and Germany; became lieutenant; received Legion d'honneur, Croix de Guerre, and Bronze Star (United States). *Member:* Societe des Gens de Lettres (Society of Men of Letters), Societe des auteurs dramatiques (Society of Dramatic Authors), Societe des ecrivains combattants (Society of Ex-Service Writers), Societe des ecrivains de la mer et de l'outre mer (Society of Writers of the Sea).

AWARDS, HONORS: Grand Prix de Litterature coloniale, 1936, for *Frontieres de Brousse* and *Ras el Gua;* Grand Prix du roman d'aventures, 1946, for *Les Equipages de Peter Hill;* Prix Jeunesse, 1950, for *Sama, prince des elephants;* Belgian Prix M. Proumen for juvenile literature, 1953, for *L'Extraordinaire aventure de Michel Santanrea;* Jugendbuchpries, 1956, for German edition of *Sirga, la lionne;* Prix Enfance du Monde, 1958, for *Grichka et son ours;* the American edition, *Grishka and the Bear,* was an American Library Association Notable Book and received a Boys' Clubs of America Junior Book Award, 1961; Hans Christian Andersen International Children's Book Medal for distinguished contribution to international literature for young people, 1964, for his complete works; two other books, *La Petite infante* and *Encyclopedia Larousse des enfants,* were cited for excellence by the French Academy.

WRITINGS—Novels, except as indicated: *Frontieres de Brousse,* Moghreb (Casablanca), 1932; *Ras el Gua, poste du Sud,* Moghreb, 1932; *Histoire d'un blanc qui s'etait fait negre,* Rieder (Paris), 1932; (compiler) *Contes de'Afrique,* published as special issue of *Bulletin de L'Enseignement de l'A.O.F.,* [Goree, West Africa], 1933; *Taillis,* Rieder, 1934; *Vent de norois,* Moghreb, 1938. *Les Equipages de Peter Hill,* Librairie des Champs-Elysees, 1946; *La Grande renaude,* Arthaud, 1946; *Atonement in the Sun,* translation from the French by P. J. Stead, Staples Press, 1947.

Books for young people: *Maraouna du Bambassou,* Amitie, 1948, published as a French reader under same title, Oxford University Press, 1956, translation by Brian Rhys published as *The White Shadow,* Oxford University Press, 1959, translation by Gwen Marsh published as *Beyond the Bambassu,* Harrap, 1961; *Chasses de brousse: Savanes et sortileges* (on hunting in Africa), Librairie des Champs-Elysees, 1948.

Les Compagnons de la fortune, Amitie, 1950, translation by Geoffrey Trease published as *Companions of Fortune,* Oxford University Press, 1952; *Sama, prince des elephants,* Delagrave, 1950, translation by Marsh published as *Sama,* Oxford University Press, 1952, Criterion, 1961; *Sirga, la lionne,* Magnard, 1951, translation by Marsh published as *Sirga, Queen of the African Bush,* Oxford University Press, 1953, Criterion, 1959; *Ouoro le chimpanze,* Magnard, 1951, translation by Marsh published as *Oworo,* Oxford University Press, 1954; *L'Extraordinaire aventure de Michel Santanrea,* Editions de l'Amitie, 1951, translation by Norman Dale published as *The Wind of Chance,* Oxford University Press, 1955, Criterion, 1958; *Betes sauvages, mes amies* (on animal habits and behavior), Magnard, 1952; *L'Aventure de Buscambille,* Magnard, 1952; *Trois bonds dans le jungle,* Magnard, 1952; *Red Kid de l'Arizona,* Hachette, 1953; *Les Cavaliers du vent,* Magnard, 1953, translation by George H. Bell published as *Riders of the Wind,* Methuen, 1960, Rand McNally, 1961, reissued in French as *Aux Quatre vents d'Afrique,* Delagrave, 1962; *La Petite infante,* Delagrave, 1953; *Plein nord,* Magnard, 1953, translation published as *A Boy and Five Huskies,* Pantheon, 1957; *Contes des mille et une betes,* Magnard, 1953; *La Legende des licornes,* Magnard, 1953, translation by Christopher Hampton published as *The Fantastic Brother,* Methuen, 1961, Rand McNally, 1963; *Luc la baleine, corsaire du roi,* Delagrave, 1953, translation by Geoffrey Trease published as *The King's Corsair,* Oxford University Press, 1954.

The 397th White Elephant (first published as "Le 397ieme elephant blanc" in *Trois bonds dans la jungle,* see above), translation by Marsh, Oxford University Press, 1954, Criterion, 1957; *Le Chevalier aux loups,* Magnard, 1954; *Shrimp, le corsaire,* Magnard, 1954, translation by Dale published as *The Sea Rover,* Oxford University Press, 1956; *De Dague et d'epee,* Delagrave, 1955; *Au Royaume de la bete,* Delagrave, 1955, translation by Marsh published as *The Animal Kingdom,* Oxford University Press, 1957; *Kpo la panthere,* Magnard, 1955, translation by Marsh published as *Kpo, the Leopard,* Oxford University Press, 1955, reprinted, 1967; *Tam-Tam de Kotokro,* Rouge et or, 1956, translation by Rhys published as *Tom-Toms in Kotokro,* Criterion, 1957; *La Biche noire,* Magnard, 1956; *Encyclopedie Larousse des enfants,* Larousse, 1956, translation and adaptation by Maurice Michael published as *The New Encyclopedia for the Younger Generation,* Spring House, 1958, and as *The Illustrated Encyclopedia: Based on an Encyclopedia of the Famous Librairie Larousse,* Grosset, 1959, also adapted by Michael for two-volume edition, *Learn About People* and *Learn About the World,* Golden Pleasure Books, 1962; *Les Elephants de Sargabal,* Delagrave, 1956, translation by Marsh published as *The Elephants of Sargabal,* Oxford University Press, 1956, Criterion, 1957; *Prince de la jungle,* Hachette, 1956, translation by Rhys published as *Prince of the Jungle,* Oxford University Press, 1958, Criterion, 1959; *Le Clan des betes sauvages,* Hachette, 1956, translation by John Marshall published as *Mokokambo, the Lost Land,* Criterion, 1961.

Bleu de cobalt, Librairie des Champs-Elysees, 1957; *La bague aux yeux de chat,* Magnard, 1958; *Grichka et son ours,* Hachette, 1958, translation by Marsh published as *Grishka and the Bear,* Oxford University Press, 1959, Criterion, 1960; *Le Chef au masque D'or,* Hachette, 1958, translation by Marshall published as *Mountain with a Secret,* Van Nostrand, 1963; *La Grande terre des elephants,* Magnard, 195?, translation by Richard Graves published as *Elephant Road,* Bodley Head, 1959, Criterion, 1960; *Le Jour bleu,* [France], 1958, translation by Marsh published as *The Blue Day,* Bodley Head, 1958, Abelard, 1959; *Le Moulin de Nicolette*, [France], 195?, translation by Marsh published as *Nicolette and the Mill,* Bodley Head, 1960, Abelard, 1961; *Crin-Blanc* (based on Albert Lamorisse's film of the same name), Hachette, 1959, translation by Marsh published as *The Wild White Stallion,* F. Watts, 1961, abridged edition edited by J. R. Watson, F. Watts, 1963; *Anne et le roi des chats,* Hachette, 1959, translation by Marshall published as *The King of the Cats,* Collins, 1962, revised translation, Lothrop, 1963.

Il Etait mille et une fois . . . : Des Contes et des histoires pour nos enfants, Magnard, 1960; *La Grande aventure des machines,* Larousse, 1960, translation published as *Man's Adventure with Machines: The Story of the Mechanical Age and How It Came About,* Odhams, 1961; *Grichka et les loups,* Hachette, 1960, translation by Joyce Emerson published as *Grichka and the Wolves,* Van Nostrand, 1965 (published in England as *Grichka and Brother Bear,* University of London Press, 1965), translation and abridgement by Christina Holyoak published as *Pascal and the Lioness,* McGraw, 1965; *Trois filles et un secret,* Hachette, 1960, translation by Joan Selby-Lowndes published as *Three Girls and a Secret,* Harrap, 1961, F. Watts, 1963; *Le Maitre des elephants,* Magnard, 1960, translation by Barbara Seccombe published as *Master of the Elephants,* Oxford University Press, 1961, and as *Fofana,* Criterion, 1962; (with A. Biancheri and P. Cousin) *Tipiti, le rouge-gorge,* Larousse, 1961, translation by Marsh published as *Tipiti, the Robin,* Bodley Head, 1962; *Marjolaine et le troubadour,* Hachette, 1961, translation by Anne Carter published as *The Troubadour,* Collins, 1965, McGraw, 1967; *Deux garcons pour un cheval,* Hachette, 1961; *Mon premier atlas: Voyage autour du monde,* Larousse, 1961, translation published as *Our Colourful World and Its Peoples,* Odhams, 1963; *L'Etranger du port,* Hachette, 1961, translation by Marsh published as *The Stranger from the Sea,* F. Watts, 1967.

(Editor) *My First English-French Dictionary/Mon premier dictionnaire anglais-francais,* Golden Pleasure Books, 1962; *La Marque de Grichka,* Hachette, 1962; *Le Voyage en ballon* (based on Albert Lamorisse's film of the same name), Hachette, 1962, translation by Carter published as *Balloon Journey,* Collins, 1964, Clark McCutcheon, 1966;

La Planete ignoree, Hachette, 1963; *L'Espace,* Hachette, 1963, translation published as *Astronomy,* Whitman Publishing, 1963; *Fonabio et le lion,* Hachette, 1963, adaptation edited by Margaret Ledesert published in French under same title, Harrap, 1966, translation by Sarah Chokla Gross published as *Fonabio and the Lion,* F. Watts, 1966; (with Biancheri and Cousin) *Rex et Mistigri,* Larousse, 196?, translation by Marsh published as *Rex and Mistigri,* Bodley Head, 1963; *Petite histoire d'un petit chien,* Hachette, 1964, translation by Selby-Lowndes published as *Little Dog Lost,* Harrap, 1968, revised translation by Selby-Lowndes published under same title, Lothrop, 1970; *Grichka et les turbans jaunes,* Hachette, 1964; *The Children of the Wind* (selections from four of Guillot's books), compiled and translated by Marsh, Oxford University Press, 1964, published as *African Folk Tales,* F. Watts, 1965; *Le Champion de'Olympie,* Hachette, 1965, translation by Carter published as *The Champion of Olympia,* Reilly & Lee, 1968; *Le Grand Marc et les aigles noirs,* Hachette, 1965; *Six destins en etoile,* Magnard, 1965.

Un Chateau en Espagne, Hachette, 1966, translation by Dorothy Ward published as *Castle in Spain,* Brockhampton Press, 1970; *Chansons de brousse* (poems), Messeiller, 1966; *Le Maison de l'oiseau,* Delagrave, 1966, translation by Marsh published as *The Castle of the Crested Bird,* F. Watts, 1968; *La Brousse et la bete,* Delagrave, 1966; *Fode Koro et les hommes-pantheres,* Hachette, 1966, translation by Selby-Lowndes published as *Fodai and the Leopard-Men,* Harrap, 1969, Funk, 1970; *King of the Reindeer and Other Animal Stories,* adapted from John Orpen's translations, Odhams, 1967; *Un Roman de Renart,* Delagrave, 1967; *La Belle au bois dore,* Hachette, 1967; *L'Equipage du grand Marc,* Hachette, 1968; *La Nuit de contrebandirs,* Hachette, 1968; *Cinq coleres de fauves,* O.D.E.G.E. (Office d'Editions Generales; distributed by Hachette), 1968; *Great Horse Stories,* adapted by Mollie Chappell, Lion Press, 1969; *Tireli, roi des rossignols,* Hachette, 1969.

Un Petit chien va dans la lune, Hachette, 1970; *Cinq tours de magiciens,* O.D.E.G.E., 1970; *Images et mots,* Larousse, 1970; *Tales of the Wild,* adapted by Chappell, Collins, 1971; *Le Chevalier sans visage,* Hachette, 1973; *L'-Extraordinaire aventure de Messieur Renart,* Delagrave, 1973. Also author of detective stories and radio scripts.

(Died March 28, 1969)

* * *

GUNN, John (Charles) 1937-

PERSONAL: Born June 6, 1937, in Hove, Sussex, England; son of Albert Charles (a grocer) and Lily (Edwards) Gunn; married Celia Ann Frances Willis, September 9, 1959; children: Richard, Frances. *Education:* University of Birmingham, M.B., Ch.B., 1961, M.D., 1969; Institute of Psychiatry, London, Academ DPM, 1966, M.R.C.Psych., 1971. *Office:* Institute of Psychiatry, De Crespigny Park, Camberwell, London SE5 8AF, England.

CAREER: University of London, London, England, senior registrar at Maudsley Hospital, 1967-71, lecturer, 1969-71, currently senior lecturer in Institute of Psychiatry and consultant to Maudsley Hospital. Member of house staff at Queen Elizabeth Hospital, Birmingham, 1961-63, and Maudsley Hospital, 1963-64; registrar at Bethlem Hospital and Dulwich Hospital, 1964-65; postgraduate fellow at National Hospital, 1965-66; registrar, Brixton Child Guidance Clinic, 1966; part-time lecturer at University of London, Extra-Mural Department, 1967-72, and Probation Training Centre, 1968—. Visiting psychiatrist to Circle Trust Club; member of executive committee, forensic section of Royal College of Psychiatrists; member of council, Royal London Aid Society.

MEMBER: World Psychiatric Association (director-advisor, 1968-71), British Society of Criminology, Howard League for Penal Reform. *Awards, honors:* Brackenbury Prize in forensic psychiatry, British Medical Association, 1969; Bronze Medal from Royal Medico-Psychological Association, 1970.

WRITINGS: (Editor with others) Aubrey Lewis, *Inquiries in Psychiatry: Clinical and Social Investigations,* Routledge & Kegan Paul, 1967; (editor with others) Aubrey Lewis, *The State of Psychiatry: Essays and Addresses,* Science House, 1967; (compiler) *A Directory of World Psychiatry,* World Psychiatric Association, 1971; *Violence,* Praeger, 1973. Contributor to *An Encyclopaedia of Psychiatry for General Practitioners,* edited by D. Leigh and J. Marks, 1972, and to professional journals. Assistant editor and book review editor, *British Journal of Psychiatry,* 1967-71.

WORK IN PROGRESS: A book on epileptics in prison, completion expected in 1975; a book on medical aspects of the English prison system, 1977.

* * *

GUNSTON, Bill
See GUNSTON, William Tudor

* * *

GUNSTON, William Tudor 1927- (Bill Gunston)

PERSONAL: Born March 1, 1927, in London, England; son of William John (a professional soldier and linguist) and Stella Hazelwood (Cooper) Gunston; married Margaret Anne Jolliff, October 10, 1964; children: Jeannette Christina, Stephanie Elaine Tracy. *Education:* University of Durham, Inter-B.Sc., 1946; attended Northampton College of Advanced Technology (now The City University), London, 1948-51. *Politics:* Conservative. *Religion:* Church of England. *Home and office:* Foxbreak, Courts Mount Rd., Haslemere, Surrey GU27-2PP, England. *Agent:* Donald Copeman, 52 Bloomsbury St., London WC1B-3QT, England.

CAREER: Iliffe & Sons, London, England, member of editorial staff of *Flight International,* 1951-54, and technical editor, 1955-64, technology editor of *Science Journal,* 1964-70; free-lance writer, 1970—. *Military service:* Royal Air Force, flying instructor, 1945-48. *Member:* Association of British Science Writers, Circle of Aviation Writers (chairman, 1956, 1961).

WRITINGS—All under name Bill Gunston: *Your Book of Light* (juvenile), Faber, 1968; *Hydrofoils and Hovercraft,* Doubleday, 1968; *Flight Handbook,* Iliffe, 1968; (with John W. R. Taylor, Kenneth Munson, and John W. Wood) *The Lore of Flight,* Time-Life, 1970; *The Jet Age,* Arthur Barker, 1972; *Transport Problems and Prospects,* Dutton, 1972; *Transport Technology,* Crowell-Collier, 1972; (contributor) Edward de Bono, editor, *Technology Today,* Routledge & Kegan Paul, 1972; (with Frank Howard) *The Conquest of the Air,* Random House, 1973; *Bombers of the West,* Scribner, 1973; *Shaping Metals* (young adult), Macdonald & Co., 1974; *Attack Aircraft of the West,* Scribner, 1974; *Philatelist's Companion,* David & Charles, 1974.

Writer of materials for industry, business, government, and education and research institutions, including Nuffield Foundation, Ford Foundation, UNESCO, British Government, Rutherford High Energy Laboratory, oil companies, British Broadcasting Corp., Hughes Aircraft, and Rolls-Royce.

Contributor to encyclopedias and yearbooks, including *National Encyclopedia, Aviation Encyclopedia, Junior Encyclopedia, Brassey's Annual and Defence Yearbook, Aircraft Annual, Jane's All the World's Aircraft* (annual), *Young Scientist's Annual,* and *Look and Learn Annual.*

Contributor to about seventy magazines, juvenile periodicals, and newspapers all over the world, including *New Scientist, Aircraft* (Australia), *Speed and Power,* and *Battle and Aeroplane Monthly.*

WORK IN PROGRESS: A large dictionary of advanced technology, especially about aerospace subjects; a book about NADGE, the European and NATO defense system; eleven other adult nonfiction books; seven juvenile books.

SIDELIGHTS: Gunston writes: "I left my old firm in 1970 . . .and cast around looking for a job (and the best offers were all outside the United Kingdom), but first I had to clear a vast backlog of free-lance work. I am still trying to clear it, but the pile is now twice as large. I have a golden rule for authors: if you are daunted at the size of the task, or the amount of research needed, just sit down and write the book. When it is finished you will wonder why you were worried."

* * *

GUTCHEON, Beth R(ichardson) 1945- (Beth Richardson)

PERSONAL: Surname rhymes with "escutcheon"; born March 18, 1945, in Sewickley, Pa.; daughter of Frank Elmer and Rosemound (Fitch) Richardson; married Jeffrey Gutcheon (an architect and piano player), March 18, 1968; children: David Stray. *Education:* Radcliffe College, B.A., 1967. *Home:* 510 Broadway, New York, N.Y. 10012. *Mailing address:* Box 461 Canal St. Station, New York, N.Y. 10013.

CAREER: Little, Brown, Inc., Boston, Mass., editorial assistant, 1967-68; Hit Factory (recording studio), New York, N.Y., manager, 1969; free-lance consultant, researcher, and writer of educational materials in the field of family planning and sex information; lecturer on making patchwork quilts. Member of Information and Education Committee of Planned Parenthood of New York, N.Y., 1971-74.

WRITINGS: The Perfect Patchwork Primer, McKay, 1973; *Abortion: A Woman's Guide,* Abelard, 1973. Contributor to *New York Magazine, New York Sunday Times,* and *Ms.*

WORK IN PROGRESS: Boy Girl Man Woman, for Harper; materials for Planned Parenthood; two children's books.

SIDELIGHTS: Beth Gutcheon wrote: "I began to write about abortion and sex education because I had an illegal abortion in 1966, with a miserable emotional aftermath; shortly after the birth of my son I had a legal abortion and rather than allow my emotions about the whole thing to come back to haunt me as they had the first time, I decided to deal with it by writing about it."

GUTMANN, Joseph 1923-

PERSONAL: Born August 17, 1923, in Wuerzburg, Germany; came to U.S. in 1936; naturalized, 1943; son of Henry (a merchant) and Selma (Eisemann) Gutmann; married Marilyn B. Tuckman (a teacher of mathematics), October 8, 1953; children: David, Sharon. *Education:* Temple University, B.S., 1949; New York University, M.A., 1952; Hebrew Union College-Jewish Institute of Religion (Cincinnati), Ph.D., 1960. *Home:* 14651 Ludlow, Oak Park, Mich. 48237. *Office:* Department of Art and Art History, Wayne State University, Detroit, Mich. 48202.

CAREER: Ordained rabbi, 1957. Hebrew Union College-Jewish Institute of Religion, Cincinnati, Ohio, assistant professor, 1960-65, associate professor of art history, 1965-69; Wayne State University, Detroit, Mich., professor of art and art history, 1969—. Adjunct professor, University of Cincinnati, 1961-68; Charles Friedman visiting lecturer, Antioch College, 1964. Member of board of advisors, Wayne State University Press, 1970—; adjunct curator, Detroit Institute of Arts; 1971—; interim associate rabbi, Temple Beth El, Detroit, 1974. *Military service:* U.S. Army Air Forces, 1943-46; interrogator and research analyst, U.S. Strategic Bombing Survey in Europe. *Member:* Society of Biblical Literature (chairman of art and bible section, 1970—), World Union of Jewish Studies, Central Conference of American Rabbis, College Art Association of America, International Center of Medieval Art, Beta Gamma Sigma. *Awards, honors:* Henry Morgenthau fellowships to Israel, 1957, 1958; Memorial Foundation for Jewish Culture grants 1959, 1972; American Philosophical Society grant to Europe, 1965; Wayne State University faculty grants, 1971, 1973; American Council of Learned Societies grant, 1973.

WRITINGS: Juedische Zeremonialkunst, Ner-Tamid-Verlag, 1963, translation by Gutmann published as *Jewish Ceremonial Art,* T. Yoseloff, 1964, revised edition, 1968; *Images of the Jewish Past: An Introduction to Medieval Hebrew Miniatures,* Society of Jewish Bibliophiles, 1965; (editor and contributor) *Beauty in Holiness: Studies in Jewish Customs and Ceremonial Art,* Ktav, 1970; (editor and contributor) *No Graven Images: Studies in Art and the Hebrew Bible,* Ktav, 1971; (with Paul Pieper) *Die Darmstaedter Pessach-Haggadah,* Propylaen Verlag, 1972; (editor and contributor) *The Dura-Europos Synagogue: A Re-Evaluation,* Council on the Study of Religion, 1973; (with Stanley Chyet) *Moses Jacob Ezekiel: Memoirs from the Baths of Diocletian,* Wayne State University Press, in press. Contributor of over one hundred articles, many reprinted separately, to scholarly journals.

WORK IN PROGRESS: Editing and contributing to *The Synagogue: Origins, Archaeology and Architecture;* publication by Ktav expected in 1975.

AVOCATIONAL INTERESTS: Travel, photography, and reading.

* * *

GUTNIK, Martin J(erome) 1942-

PERSONAL: Born December 1, 1942, in Winnipeg, Manitoba, Canada; son of Max and Sally (Kaminsky) Gutnik; married Laurel Primakow, August 28, 1966; children: Max Michael, Anne Felisha. *Education:* University of Wisconsin—Milwaukee, B.S., 1966, M.S., 1972. *Home:* 4522 West Fountain Ave., Brown Deer, Wis. 53223. *Office:* Atwater School, 2100 East Capitol Dr., Shorewood, Wis. 53211.

CAREER: Atwater School, Shorewood, Wis., elementary science teacher, 1970—. Director of Atwater Environmental Science Center; member of Wisconsin State Science Curriculum Committee. *Military service:* U.S. Army, 1966-69. *Member:* National Science Teachers Association, National Wildlife Federation, Wisconsin Elementary, Kindergarten, Nursery Education Association, Shorewood Education Association.

WRITINGS: Ecology and Pollution: Air, Childrens Press, 1973; *Ecology and Pollution: Water,* Childrens Press, 1973; *Ecology and Pollution: Land,* Childrens Press, 1973; *Photosynthesis: The Structure and Function of a Plant,* Childrens Press, in press; *Photosynthesis: Raw Materials,* Childrens Press, in press; *Photosynthesis: Products,* Childrens Press, in press; *Energy: Its Past, Present, and Future,* Childrens Press, in press.

WORK IN PROGRESS: Life Science: A Process, development of an eight-module three-year process science program; *Elsworth the First-Second-and-Third,* the life cycle of a frog.

* * *

GUTTERIDGE, Lindsay 1923-

PERSONAL: Born May 20, 1923, in Easington, Durham, England; son of Thomas (a tailor) and Alice (Lindsay) Gutteridge; married Marjorie Kathleen Carpenter; children: Susan Jane. *Education:* Attended art school in Newcastle. *Home and office:* 15 Howdale Rd., Downham Market, Norfolk, England.

CAREER: Commercial artist for companies in London, England, 1939-46, and 1950-68; King Edward School of Art, Newcastle, England, art teacher, 1941-43; stockman on Australian sheep and cattle stations, 1946-48; self-employed photographer, 1958-60; art director for Robert Sharp & Partners (advertising agency), London, England.

WRITINGS—Novels: *Cold War in a Country Garden,* Putnam, 1971; *Killer Pine,* Putnam, 1973.

WORK IN PROGRESS: Fratricide Is a Gas, a novel; research on entomology, Peru, biological warfare, espionage, and sadism.

SIDELIGHTS: Gutteridge told *CA* that he began writing "at age 46 after a life of mixed experiences," including cattle-herding in Australia and being mugged in New York's Bowery. "Started writing on a whim," he continues, "saw small insect in garden, wondered what it would feel like to be as small as that, started to write short story about tiny human being—the story just got longer. . . ." Gutteridge's novel in progress, *Fratricide is a Gas,* features the same "microman hero (Mathew Dilke, one-quarter inch tall)" as do his first two books.

* * *

GUTTMACHER, Alan F. 1898-1974

May 19, 1898—March 18, 1974; American obstetrician and gynecologist, educator, authority on family planning, and author of books on baby care, birth control, and related topics. Obituaries: *New York Times,* March 19, 1974; *Washington Post,* March 20, 1974; *Newsweek,* April 1, 1974; *Time,* April 1, 1974; *Current Biography,* May, 1974. (*CA*-4).

* * *

HAAS, LaVerne 1942-

PERSONAL: Born August 11, 1942, in Roxbury, Wis.; son of Florian Mortz (a farmer) and Loretta (Breunig) Haas; married Bertha Werth (an educator), December 14, 1968; children: Jacinta, Melanie, Bryan. *Education:* St. Francis Seminary, Milwaukee, Wis., B.A., 1964; Catholic University of America, graduate study, 1964-66. *Politics:* Democrat. *Religion:* Roman Catholic. *Home:* 343 West Madrone, Roseburg, Ore. 97470. *Office:* 823 Southeast Lane, Roseburg, Ore. 97470.

CAREER: Interparish Association, Grants Pass, Ore., adult educator, 1970-72; The Etching Tree: A Center for Religious Development, Roseburg, Ore., director and owner, 1972—. Associate counselor for Douglas County (Ore.) Family Service Clinic, 1972—; chairman of Hidden Talent Workshop, 1973-74. *Member:* Community of Religious Education Directors (regional vice-chairman, 1972—), Association of Church Teachers.

WRITINGS: Footprints: A Travelog into the World of Religion, Vantage, 1971; *Personal Pentecost,* Abbey Press, 1973.

WORK IN PROGRESS: Research on family religious education.

* * *

HACKMAN, J(ohn) Richard 1940-

PERSONAL: Born June 14, 1940, in Joliet, Ill.; son of John E. (a pipe line engineer) and Helen (Davis) Hackman; married Mary Judith Dozier (a researcher), September 1, 1962; children: Julia Beth, Laura Dianne. *Education:* MacMurray College, A.B., 1962; University of Illinois, M.A., 1965, Ph.D., 1966. *Religion:* Protestant. *Home:* Sperry Rd., Bethany, Conn. 06525. *Office:* 56 Hillhouse Ave., Yale University, New Haven, Conn. 06520.

CAREER: Yale University, New Haven, Conn., assistant professor, 1966-70, associate professor of administrative sciences and psychology, 1970—. Trustee of MacMurray College. *Member:* American Psychological Association. *Awards, honors:* Creative Talent Award of American Institute for Research in the Behavioral Sciences, 1967; James McKeen Cattell Award of American Psychological Association, 1972.

WRITINGS: (With others) *Behavior in Organizations,* McGraw, 1974; (section editor) Marvin D. Dunnette, editor, *Handbook of Industrial and Organizational Psychology,* Rand McNally, 1974. Contributor of more than twenty-five articles to journals.

WORK IN PROGRESS: A book on the quality of work life and means of redesigning work in order to facilitate both human growth and organizational effectiveness.

* * *

HAGEDORN, Robert (Bruce) 1925-

PERSONAL: Surname is pronounced Hega-dorn; born November 2, 1925, in Menlo Park, Calif.; son of Edward E. Hagedorn; married Elizabeth Masterson, November 9, 1962; children: Gerald, Richard. *Education:* San Francisco State College (now University), B.A., 1950; University of Washington, Seattle, M.A., 1953; University of Texas, Ph.D., 1963. *Office:* Department of Sociology, University of Victoria, Victoria, British Columbia, Canada.

CAREER: City College of San Francisco, San Francisco, Calif., instructor in sociology, 1954-55; Ventura College, Ventura, Calif., instructor in psychology and sociology, 1955-60; Washington State University, Pullman, assistant professor of sociology, 1963-66; California State University, Fullerton, member of faculty, 1966-69; University of Victoria, Victoria, British Columbia, Canada, associate professor of sociology, 1969—. *Military service:* U.S. Army Air Forces, 1944-46; became sergeant. *Member:* American Sociological Association, Pacific Sociological Association. *Awards, honors:* National Science Foundation research grant, 1965-66.

WRITINGS: (With Sanford Labovitz) *An Introduction to Social Research,* McGraw, 1971; (with Labovitz) *An Introduction into Sociological Orientation,* Wiley, 1973; *Introductory Sociology,* Wiley, in press. Contributor of about fifteen articles to journals in his field.

* * *

HAGOPIAN, Mark N. 1940-

PERSONAL: Born March 21, 1940, in Cambridge, Mass.; son of Jerry and Mary (Semonian) Hagopian; married Alice V. Aghababian, November 20, 1966; children: Berj Nishan. *Education:* Boston University, A.B., 1961, A.M., 1963, Ph.D., 1969. *Home:* 1167 Western Ave., Westfield, Mass. 01085. *Office:* Department of Political Science, American International College, Springfield, Mass. 01109.

CAREER: Part-time instructor in political science at Calvin Coolidge College, 1964-66; American International College, Springfield, Mass., instructor, 1966-67, assistant professor, 1967-71, associate professor of political science, 1971—. *Member:* American Political Science Association, American Association of University Professors, New England Political Science Association.

WRITINGS: *The Phenomenon of Revolution,* Dodd, 1974. Contributor to *American International College Journal.*

WORK IN PROGRESS: Translations of political writings of G. Mosca and V. Pareto.

* * *

HAHN, James (Sage) 1947-

PERSONAL: Born May 24, 1947, in Chicago, Ill.; son of James Peter (a designer and manufacturer) and Joan (Redfern) Hahn; married Mona Lynn Lowery (a writer), April 17, 1971. *Education:* Attended Wright City College, 1965-67; Northwestern University, B.A., 1970. *Politics:* Independent. *Religion:* Roman Catholic. *Home and office:* 1500 Chicago Ave., Apt. 622, Evanston, Ill. 60201.

CAREER: Free-lance writer and photographer for newspapers, magazines, and books. Lecturer. *Member:* Children's Reading Round Table.

WRITINGS—Children's books with wife, Lynn Lowery Hahn: *Recycling: Re-Using Our World's Solid Wastes,* F. Watts, 1973; *Plastics: A First Book,* F. Watts, 1974.

WORK IN PROGRESS: *Rock n' Roll Boy Is Gone,* a novel; two books of environmental science fiction for children, with wife, Lynn Lowery Hahn.

AVOCATIONAL INTERESTS: Avant garde poetry and fiction, "walking in the uncommon area of large cities."

BIOGRAPHICAL/CRITICAL SOURCES: *Evanston Review,* February 21, 1974.

* * *

HAHN, (Mona) Lynn 1949-

PERSONAL: Born July 3, 1949, in Cleveland, Ohio; daughter of James William (a boilermaker) and Mona Alice (Benjamin) Lowery; married James Hahn (a writer), April 17, 1971. *Education:* Northwestern University, B.S., 1971. *Politics:* Independent. *Religion:* United Church of Christ. *Home and office:* 1500 Chicago Ave., Apt. 622, Evanston, Ill. 60201.

CAREER: Writer for newspapers, magazines, and books. Lecturer and photographer. *Member:* Children's Reading Round Table, Kappa Tau Alpha.

WRITINGS—Children's books with husband, James Hahn: *Recycling: Re-Using Our World's Solid Wastes,* F. Watts, 1973; *Plastics: A First Book,* F. Watts, 1974. Contributor to Chicago newspapers.

WORK IN PROGRESS: *The Scrapbook from the Blue Jean Queen,* a novel; two books of environmental science fiction for children, with husband, James Hahn.

AVOCATIONAL INTERESTS: Creative photography and photographic processing, designing and sewing clothing, baking, Russian studies (has studied in the Soviet Union).

BIOGRAPHICAL/CRITICAL SOURCES: *Evanston Review,* February 21, 1974.

* * *

HAINDL, Marieluise 1901-1974 (Marieluise Fleisser)

November 23, 1901—February 2, 1974; German novelist and playwright. Obituaries: *AB Bookman's Weekly,* April 15, 1974.

* * *

HALBERSTADT, John 1941-

PERSONAL: Born September 19, 1941; son of Joseph (a chemist) and Milly (a physician; maiden name, Goldshmidt) Halberstadt. *Education:* New York University, B.A., 1963; University of California, Berkeley, M.A., 1965; Yale University, M.Ph., 1972, M.A., 1972, Ph.D., 1974. *Home:* 1627 Fairmount Ave., Wichita, Kan.; and c/o Dr. Milly Halberstadt, 49 Elm St., Malone, N.Y. 12953. *Agent:* Jane Schwenger, 245 Bennett, New York, N.Y. *Office:* Department of English, Wichita State University, Wichita, Kan. 67208.

CAREER: Thames Valley State Technical College, Norwich, Conn., instructor in English, 1969-71; Wichita State University, Wichita, Kan., instructor in English, 1973—. Instructor at Rutgers University, summer, 1969, and Mohegan Community College, 1970-71.

WRITINGS: *I'm in Love with Joanne Talsma* (poems), Goodly Co Press, 1971; *Girlfriends* (poems), Goodly Co Press, 1974. Contributor of short stories, poems, and reviews to *Mulberry, New Yale Graduate-Professional, December, Massachusetts Review, Goodly Co, Chelsea, Papertexts, Perstare, Trial Baloon, Heights Daily News, Violet, Weekend Outdoor News, Hatikvian,* and *Kansas City Star.* Editor of Psychology Textbook Division, Dushkin Publishing, 1971-72. Editor-in-chief and founder of *Bread,* 1960; associate editor of *Heights Daily News,* 1963, *Violet,* 1963, and *Perstare,* 1963; member of editorial staff of *Weekend Outdoor News,* 1965; contributing editor of *College Notes Press,* 1969, and *Papertexts,* 1969-70.

WORK IN PROGRESS: Two novels; five books of poems; a nonfiction book; some essays.

SIDELIGHTS: Halberstadt told *CA:* "If I were asked to identify myself, I'd say that I was a member of the race of the creative, a McLuhanite, a transcendental meditator, a musician as much as a writer in the sense that, as a writer, I play a primitive, roughly two-octave musical instrument such that, if you let a vowel equal a note (and let the consonants condition or stretch the vowels as their musical equivalents amplify musical notations), you'd see that any work of horizontal prose or vertical poetry can be scored—and the score is good or bad music accordingly, good writing being writing that sounds good.... I'm also interested in the physiology of literary creativity.... I'm working on something I've taught as 'mystique theory,' and would be glad to hear from anyone interested in the nature of and interrelationship of mystiques.

"I've been to Europe and Israel and at one time or another studied German, Hebrew, Russian, Latin, Spanish, French, and Middle English, but I'm no linguist. I've been influenced by poets like Barry Sheinkopf, Gary Morgan, Richard Geller, Corine Wepster, Edward Field, James Tate and so many others."

BIOGRAPHICAL/CRITICAL SOURCES: R. W. B. Lewis, *American Literature: The Makers and the Making,* St. Martin's, 1973.

* * *

HALE, Janet Campbell 1947-

PERSONAL: Born January 11, 1947, in Plummer, Idaho; daughter of Nicholas Patrick (a carpenter) and Margaret (O'Sullivan) Campbell; married Harry Arthur Dudley III, July 23, 1964 (divorced June, 1965); married Stephen Dinsmore Hale (a biology student, and baggage clerk), August 23, 1970; children: (first marriage) Aaron Nicholas; (second marriage) Jennifer Elizabeth. *Education:* Attended City College of San Francisco, 1968; University of California, Berkeley, B.A., 1972, graduate study, 1973-74. *Residence:* Richmond, Calif. 94804. *Office:* Department of Native American Studies, University of California, 3411 Dwinelle Hall, Berkeley, Calif. 94720.

CAREER: Harcourt Brace Jovanovich, Inc., San Francisco, Calif., editorial assistant, 1972; University of California, Berkeley, instructor in native American studies, 1973—. *Awards, honors:* First prize in Vincent Price Poetry Competition, 1963, and New York Poetry Day awards, 1964.

WRITINGS: (Contributor) T. D. Allen, editor, *Whispering Wind* (poems), Doubleday, 1970; *Third World Women* (poems), Third World Press, 1972; *The Owl's Song* (novel), Doubleday, 1974; (contributor) Kenneth Rosen, editor, *People of the Rainbow* (poems), Viking, in press. Contributor of short fiction to journals.

SIDELIGHTS: Janet Hale told *CA:* "Writing for me has always been a means of imposing order on experience, making sense of things. I never graduated high school and I came from a poor family. I am a member of the Coeur'd'Alene tribe of Northern Idaho and I was born and raised on the reservation. Times were very hard when I first came to the city. I wrote poetry, stories, essays because of a deep personal need."

Ms. Hale is currently studying law at the University of California at Berkeley.

* * *

HALE, William Harlan 1910-1974

July 21, 1910—June 30, 1974; American journalist, editor, and author of books on history and other topics. Obituaries: *New York Times,* July 1, 1974.

* * *

HALL, Cameron P(arker) 1898-

PERSONAL: Born August 30, 1898, in Pelham Manor, N.Y.; son of William W. (a builder) and Emily (Parker) Hall; married Margaret Conant, May 18, 1926; children: Alan C. *Education:* Williams College, B.A., 1921; graduate study at New College, Edinburgh, 1921-22, Mansfield College, Oxford, 1922-23, and Union Theological Seminary, New York, N.Y., 1923-25. *Politics:* Democratic. *Home:* 117 Kensington Rd., Garden City, N.Y. 11530.

CAREER: Ordained Presbyterian minister, 1925; pastor in New York, N.Y., 1926-35, and Madison, Wis., 1935-39; United Presbyterian Church of the U.S.A., Board of Christian Education, Philadelphia, Pa., executive director, 1939-46; International Council of Religious Education, Chicago, Ill., director of social education, 1943-46; Federal Council of Schools of Christ in America, New York, N.Y., executive secretary, 1946-50; National Council of the Churches of Christ, New York, N.Y., executive director, 1946-65, program consultant, 1965-73. Chairman of youth section of World's Sunday School Association Convention, Oslo, 1936; leader in World Conference of Christian Youth, Amsterdam, 1939. *Member:* Delta Sigma Rho, Sigma Phi. *Awards, honors:* D.D. from Yale University, 1963, Chicago Theological Seminary, 1963, and Williams College, 1964.

WRITINGS: Economic Life: A Christian Responsibility, National Council of Churches, 1947; *The Christian at His Daily Work,* National Council of Churches, 1951; *Decision Making in Business,* United Methodist Church, 1963; (contributor) Arthur E. Walmsley, editor, *The Church in a Society of Abundance,* Seabury, 1963; (contributor) Robert Spann, editor, *Social Responsibility,* Abingdon, 1963; (editor) *On the Job Ethics,* National Council of the Churches of Christ, 1963; (editor) *Human Values and Advancing Technology,* Friendship, 1967; *Technology and People,* Judson, 1969; *Lay Action: The Church's Third Force,* Friendship, 1974. Contributor to *Marriage, Lutheran Quarterly, Brethren Life and Thought,* and *Engage/Social Action.* Editor of *Social Progress,* 1939-46.

SIDELIGHTS: Hall has travelled as a church journalist. He covered the United Nations Charter Conference in San Francisco in 1945 and the World Council of Churches Assembly in New Delhi in 1956. He visited the Viking areas in Iceland and Greenland. He was also a member of the unofficial American group to attend the anniversary of the Bolivian government in 1952.

* * *

HALL, Malcolm 1945-

PERSONAL: Born June 6, 1945, in Chicago, Ill.; son of David B. (a physicist) and Jane (also a physicist; maiden name, Hamilton) Hall; married Mary J. Reneski (a teacher), June 6, 1971. *Education:* Pomona College, B.A., 1967. *Home:* 6300 Keystone St., Philadelphia, Pa. 19135.

CAREER: Has been employed as "a furniture mover, weather man, car junker, advertising writer, handyman-carpenter, thief, bookstore clerk and editor"; Media Systems, Inc., Moorestown, N.J., editor, 1973—.

WRITINGS: Headlines (Junior Literary Guild selection), Coward, 1973. Writer of more than thirty filmstrips.

WORK IN PROGRESS: The Electric Book, for publication by Coward.

* * *

HALL, R(obert) Cargill 1937-

PERSONAL: Born January 17, 1937, in Rochester, Minn.; son of Byron E. (a physician) and Elizabeth (Cargill) Hall; married Beverley Chichester, May 2, 1958; children: R. Cargill, Jr., Melanie Anne, Bradshaw Chichester. *Education:* Attended Escola Brasileira de Administracao Publica, 1957; Whitman College, B.A., 1959; San Jose State College (now University), M.A., 1966. *Politics:* Democrat. *Religion:* Roman Catholic. *Home:* 1370 Chamberlain Rd., Pasadena, Calif. 91103. *Office:* Jet Propulsion Laboratory, California Institute of Technology, 4800 Oak Grove Dr., Pasadena, Calif. 91103.

CAREER: Lockheed Missiles and Space Co., Sunnyvale, Calif., assistant historian, 1960-66, historian, 1966-67; California Institute of Technology, Pasadena, historian in Jet Propulsion Laboratory, 1967—. Member of board of directors, Linda Vista Association, 1968-71, president, 1970-71. *Member:* International Academy of Astronautics (corresponding member), American Institute of Aeronautics and Astronautics, International Institute of Space Law (member of executive committee, Association of U.S. Members of IISL), American Society of International Law. *Awards, honors:* Robert H. Goddard Historical Essay Trophy of National Space Club, 1962, 1963; named one of outstanding young men of America, U.S. Junior Chamber of Commerce, 1968.

WRITINGS: (Contributor) E. M. Emme, editor, *The History of Rocket Technology,* Wayne State University Press, 1964; *Project Ranger: A Chronology,* U.S. Government Printing Office, 1971. Contributor to *American Journal of International Law, Airpower Historian,* and other journals. Editor-coordinator, of "Chronology of International Astronautical Events," an annual feature in *Acta Astronautica.*

WORK IN PROGRESS: Lunar Impact: A History of Project Ranger (tentative title), a history of the first National Aeronautics and Space Administration unmanned lunar rough-landing project.

* * *

HALLER, William 1885-1974

May 12, 1885—April 22, 1974; American educator and author. Obituaries: *New York Times,* April 25, 1974.

* * *

HALLIDAY, William R(oss) 1926-

PERSONAL: Born May 9, 1926, in Emory University, Ga.; son of William Rose (an actuary and executive) and Jane E. (Wakefield) Halliday; married Eleanore Hartvedt, July 2, 1951; children: Marcia Lynn, Patricia Anne, William Ross III. *Education:* Swarthmore College, B.A., 1946; George Washington University, M.D., 1948. *Home:* 1117 36th Ave. E., Seattle, Wash. 98112. *Office:* Department of Labor and Industries, General Administration Bldg., Olympia, Wash. 98504.

CAREER: Private practice of thoracic surgery, Seattle, Wash., 1957-65; Department of Labor and Industries, Olympia and Seattle, Wash., medical consultant, 1965-71, chief medical consultant, 1971—. Director of Western Speleological Survey, 1955—; assistant director of International Glaciospeleological Survey, 1972—; director of speleological research for Travel Industry for the Environment, 1973—. *Military service:* U.S. Navy, Medical Corps, 1949-50, 1955-56; became lieutenant commander. *Member:* American College of Chest Physicians (fellow), National Speleological Society (fellow; trustee, 1950-72), American Spelean History Association (president, 1968), Federation of Western Outdoor Clubs (vice-president, 1959-61), North Cascades Conservation Council (vice-president, 1962-63), Explorers Club (fellow), The Mountaineers (trustee), Seattle Free Lances. *Awards, honors:* Certificate of Merit from National Speleological Society, 1960; *Desert Magazine* award, 1960, for *Adventure Is Underground;* Governor's award, 1968, for *Depths of the Earth.*

WRITINGS: Adventure Is Underground, Harper, 1959; *Depths of the Earth,* Harper, 1966; *American Caves and Caving,* Harper, 1974. Author of numerous articles and booklets. Editor of *Journal of Spelean History,* 1967-73.

WORK IN PROGRESS: Systematic research on caves and their interaction with man; research on psychosocial complications of disability programs, disability prevention, and rehabilitation.

* * *

HALLIWELL, Leslie 1929-

PERSONAL: Born February 23, 1929, in Bolton, Lancashire, England; son of James and Lily (Haslam) Halliwell; married Ruth Porter, July 11, 1958. *Education:* St. Catharine's College, Cambridge, M.A., 1955. *Politics:* Conservative. *Religion:* Church of England. *Home:* 26 Atwood Ave., Richmond, Surrey, England. *Agent:* A. M. Heath, 35 Dover St., London W.1, England; and International Famous Agency, 1301 Avenue of the Americas, New York, N.Y. 10019. *Office:* Granada TV, 36 Golden Square, London W.1, England.

CAREER: Picturegoer, London, England, columnist, 1952; Rex (specialized movie theatre), Cambridge, England, manager, 1953-56; Rank Organisation, London, England, film publicist, 1956-58; Granada TV, London, England, television film buyer, 1958—. Member of television and general selection committees, National Film Archive, 1967—.

WRITINGS: The Filmgoers Companion, with foreword by Alfred Hitchcock, MacGibbon, 1965, Hill & Wang, 1966, 4th revised edition, Hill & Wang, 1974; *The Filmgoers Book of Quotes,* Hart-Davis, 1973, Arlington House, 1974; *The Clapperboard Book of the Cinema,* Hart-Davis, 1974; *Mountain of Dreams,* Hart-Davis, 1974.

Plays: "Make Your Own Bed" (three-act), first produced in Bolton, England, at Hippodrome Theatre, 1957; "A Night on the Island" (three-act), first produced in Bristol, England at Bristol Little Theatre, 1959; "Let's Be Friends" (three-act), to be produced in 1975.

WORK IN PROGRESS: The Filmgoers Quiz Book; The Filmgoers Treasury of Talkies.

AVOCATIONAL INTERESTS: Driving in the countryside, especially in America.

* * *

HALLWARD, Michael 1889-

PERSONAL: Born October 2, 1889, in London, England; son of Reginald Francis (an artist) and Adelaide (an artist; maiden name, Bloxam) Hallward; married Jean McDougal, 1910; married second wife, Penelope Alice Bradley, October 18, 1934; children: (first marriage) Joy Hallward Mitchum, Gloria Hallward Ray (stage name Gloria Graham); (second marriage) Penelope (Mrs. Richard Gase), Peter Michael. *Education:* Attended Royal Institute of British Architects. *Home:* 14446 Valverde Ct., San Diego, Calif. 92129.

CAREER: Haslemere Craft Group, Surrey, England, owner, 1907-1910; Michael Hallward, Inc., Boston, Mass., president, 1940-54. Executive director of New Bedford Industrial Development Commission, 1954-59; founding trustee and director of American Design Institute. *Military service:* Canadian Army, 1912-16.

WRITINGS: *The Enormous Leap of Alphonse Frog* (juvenile), Nash Publishing, 1972. Also author of short stories. Contributor to magazines.

WORK IN PROGRESS: *A Nation of Usurers; The Economics of Corruption; The Small Elf Persons,* a sequel to *The Enormous Leap of Alphonse Frog;* an autobiography; revising "The Directors Meet," a play; "Before the Fall," a play.

* * *

HAMEROW, Theodore S(tephen) 1920-

PERSONAL: Born August 24, 1920, in Warsaw, Poland; emigrated to U.S. in 1930; naturalized U.S. citizen in 1930; son of Chaim Shneyer (an actor) and Bella (an actress; maiden name, Rubinlicht) Hamerow; married Marga Lotter, August 16, 1954; children: Judith, Helena. *Education:* City College (now City College of the City University of New York), B.A., 1942; Columbia University, M.A., 1947; Yale University, Ph.D., 1951. *Home:* 466 South Segoe Rd., Madison, Wis. 53711. *Office:* Department of History, University of Wisconsin, Madison, Wis. 53706.

CAREER: Wellesley College, Wellesley, Mass., instructor in history, 1950-51; University of Maryland, College Park, instructor in history, 1951-52; University of Illinois, Urbana, instructor, 1952-54, assistant professor, 1954-57, associate professor of history, 1957-58; University of Wisconsin, Madison, associate professor, 1958-61, professor of history, 1961—. Fulbright research professor at Erlangen University, Germany, 1962-63. *Military service:* U.S. Army, 1943-46. *Member:* American Historical Association, Conference Group for Central European History (secretary-treasurer, 1960-62, 1964-67). *Awards, honors:* Social Science Research Council fellow, 1962-63.

WRITINGS: *Restoration, Revolution, Reaction: Economics and Politics in Germany, 1815-1871,* Princeton University Press, 1958; (with Chester G. Starr and others) *A History of the World,* Rand McNally, 1960; *Otto Von Bismarck: A Historical Assessment,* Heath, 1962; (editor) *Otto Von Bismarck: Reflections and Reminiscences,* Harper, 1968; *The Social Foundations of German Unification,* two volumes, Princeton University Press, 1969-72; *The Age of Bismarck,* Harper, 1973. Member of board of editors of *Journal of Modern History,* 1962-64, and *Central European History,* 1966-69. Consulting editor of Dorsey Press, 1961-71.

WORK IN PROGRESS: An analytical history of the nineteenth century.

* * *

HAMMOND, Norman 1944-

PERSONAL: Born July 10, 1944, in England. *Education:* Cambridge University, B.A., 1966, diploma in classical archaeology, 1967, M.A., 1970, Ph.D., 1972. *Office:* Faculty of History, Cambridge University, West Rd., Cambridge CB3 9EF, England.

CAREER: Fitzwilliam College, Cambridge University, Cambridge, England, fellow, 1973—, Centre of Latin American Studies, research fellow, 1967-71, Leverhulme Trust Fellow in New World archaeology, 1972—. Director of television film for British Broadcasting Corp., 1970. *Member:* Royal Asiatic Society (fellow), Society for Libyan Studies, Society for Afghan Studies, American Anthropological Association (foreign fellow), Society for American Archaeology, American Association for the Advancement of Science, Prehistoric Society, Society of Antiquaries of London (fellow).

WRITINGS: *The British Museum in British Honduras: Lubaantun 1926-1970,* British Museum, 1972; (editor) *South Asian Archaeology,* Duckworth, 1973; (editor) *Mesoamerican Archaeology: New Approaches,* University of Texas Press, 1974. Contributor to *Antiquity, American Antiquity, Man and Science, Archaeology,* and *East and West.* Reviewer for British Broadcasting Corp. radio; archaeological correspondent for *Times* (London), 1967—.

WORK IN PROGRESS: Research on Maya cultures of northern Belize; a source analysis of Maya area jade sources and artifacts; an iconographic study of Lubaantun Maya figurines for the British Museum; an archaeological-ecological project.

SIDELIGHTS: Hammond has led expeditions to North Africa, Afghanistan, and Central America. He has also done archaeological work in Greece and Ecuador.

* * *

HANCOCK, Sheila 1942-

PERSONAL: Born October 8, 1942, in Hagerstown, Md.; daughter of Howard William (a purchasing agent) and Virginia (Gluck) Gibney; married Edward L. Hancock (a teacher), June 25, 1967; children: Christopher, Garth, Leslie. *Education:* Attended Lynchburg College, 1960-62, University of Nevada, 1967—. *Home:* 1420 North Virginia, Reno, Nev. 89503.

CAREER: Firestone Tire and Rubber Co., Washington, D.C., secretary, 1966-67; pre-school teacher in Reno, Nev., 1972-74; Thunderbird Records (promoters and distributors), Reno, Nev., secretarial writing and editing, 1974—.

WRITINGS: *Connections,* Harcourt, 1974.

* * *

HANCOCK, Sibyl 1940-

PERSONAL: Born November 10, 1940, in Pasadena, Tex.; daughter of Briten E. (a department manager for Shell Oil Co.) and Floreine (Fisher) Norwood; married Thomas L. Hancock (a school administrator), August 21, 1965; children: Kevin Thomas. *Education:* Attended Sam Houston State University, 1959-61, and University of Houston, 1963-65. *Religion:* Methodist. *Home:* 210 Coronation, Houston, Tex. 77034.

CAREER: Free-lance writer. Stenographer for Ellington Air Force Base, 1962. *Member:* National Writers Club, Society of Children's Book Writers (charter member), Associated Authors of Children's Literature (charter member), Pasadena Writers Club (president, 1966, 1973),

Houston Writers Workshop, Friends of the Pasadena Public Library (vice-president, 1973). *Awards, honors:* First prize for best children's book from Texas Pen Women, 1970, for *Let's Learn Hawaiian.*

WRITINGS—For children, except where noted: (With Doris Sadler) *Let's Learn Hawaiian,* Tuttle, 1969; *Mario's Mystery Machine,* Putnam, 1972; *Mosshaven* (adult gothic novel), Beagle, 1973; *The Grizzly Bear,* Steck, 1974; *The Blazing Hills,* Putnam, in press; *Theodore Roosevelt,* Putnam, in press; *Bill Pickett,* Harcourt, in press. Contributor to *Texas Star, Humpty Dumpty,* and *Kidstuff.* Juvenile book critic, *Houston Chronicle,* 1973—.

WORK IN PROGRESS: A see-and-read history book.

SIDELIGHTS: Sibyl Hancock writes: "I find writing for children challenging. It is great fun to uncover interesting stories which have been almost overlooked by history and turn them into books for young readers." *Avocational interests:* Collecting old children's books, reading, astronomy.

* * *

HANEY, Lynn 1941-

PERSONAL: Born February 12, 1941; daughter of John J. (a civil servant) and Kay (a dietician) Haney. *Education:* University of Pittsburgh, B.A., 1963; Sorbonne, University of Paris, graduate study, 1963-64. *Politics:* Independent. *Home:* 12 Trumbull St., Stonington, Conn. 06378. *Agent:* Hy Cohen, Candida Donadio Agency, 111 West 57th St., New York, N.Y. 10019. *Office:* P.O. Box 145, Stonington, Conn. 06378.

CAREER: Christian Dior (fashion design firm), Paris, France, interpreter, 1965-66; National Endowment for the Arts, Washington, D.C., member of public relations staff, 1966-68; *New York Times,* New York, N.Y., news assistant, 1969-73; writer, 1973—. *Member:* Authors Guild, Dramatists Guild, American Civil Liberties Union. *Awards, honors:* Publishers merit award from *New York Times,* for article on plastic surgery.

WRITINGS: The Lady Is a Jock, Dodd, 1973; *The Memoirs of Mason Reese: In Cahoots with Lynn Haney,* Dodd, 1974.

WORK IN PROGRESS: After Five, a lighthearted analysis of chronic marriers; *Luck Be a Lady Tonight,* a study of women gamblers.

AVOCATIONAL INTERESTS: Skiing, sailing, scuba diving.

* * *

HANKINS, John Erskine 1905-

PERSONAL: Born January 2, 1905, in Lake View, S.C.; son of James Thomas (a mailman) and Roma (McKenzie) Hankins; married Nellie E. Pottle (a teacher), August 2, 1930; children: Margaret (Mrs. A. E. van Mourik), Thomas, John David. *Education:* University of South Carolina, B.A., 1924, M.A., 1925; Yale University, Ph.D., 1929. *Religion:* Episcopalian. *Address:* R.R. 1, Oxford, Me. 04270.

CAREER: University of South Carolina, Columbia, adjunct professor of English, 1925-26; Indiana State University, Terre Haute, assistant professor of English, 1929-30; University of Kansas, Lawrence, assistant professor, 1930-37, associate professor, 1937-42, professor of English, 1942-56; University of Maine, Orono, professor of English, 1956-70, professor emeritus, 1970—, head of department, 1956-67. Fulbright lecturer at University of Leyden, 1953-54; lecturer at University of Frankfurt-am-Main, summer, 1954. Member of public library board, Lawrence, Kan., 1950-56; president of Senior Citizens, Oxford, Me., 1971—. *Member:* Modern Language Association of America, American Association of University Professors, New England Renaissance Society, Phi Beta Kappa. *Awards, honors:* Guggenheim fellowship, 1949-50.

WRITINGS: (Editor with C. K. Hyder) *Selected Nineteenth Century Essays,* Crofts, 1938; *The Life and Works of George Turberville,* University of Kansas Press, 1940; *The Character of Hamlet and Other Essays,* University of North Carolina Press, 1941, new edition, Books for Libraries, 1970; *Shakespeare's Derived Imagery,* University of Kansas, 1953, new edition, Octagon, 1967; (editor) *Romeo and Juliet,* Penguin, 1960; (with H. J. Edwards) *Lincoln the Writer,* University of Maine Press, 1962; *Poems,* University of Maine Press, 1970; *Source and Meaning in Spenser's Allegory,* Oxford University Press, 1971. Contributor of thirty-five articles to journals.

WORK IN PROGRESS: Backgrounds of Shakespeare's Thought; Literary Reminiscence in the Dream-Poem.

SIDELIGHTS: Hankins has visited Europe six times to see his Dutch grandchildren. He has attended the Shakespeare Conference at Stratford-upon-Avon twice and the International Association of University Professors of English conferences four times. His hobbies are gardening, picture-framing, collecting old books, and writing songs.

* * *

HANSEN, William F(reeman) 1941-

PERSONAL: Born June 22, 1941, in Fresno, Calif.; son of William Freeman and Helen (Jensen) Hansen; married Judith Friedman (divorced); married Marcia Jean Cebulska (a writer), August 14, 1972; children: (second marriage) Inge Margrethe. *Education:* Student at Reed College, 1959-60, and Bakersfield College, 1960-61; University of California, Berkeley, A.B., 1965, Ph.D., 1970. *Home:* 804 South Lincoln, Bloomington, Ind. 47401. *Office:* Department of Classical Studies, Indiana University, Bloomington, Ind. 47401.

CAREER: University of California, Berkeley, associate in classics, 1969-70; Indiana University, Bloomington, assistant professor of classical studies and fellow of Folklore Institute, 1970—. *Member:* American Philological Association, American Folklore Society. *Awards, honors:* Younger Humanist fellow of National Endowment for the Humanities, 1972-73, for research in Copenhagen on the legend of Hamlet.

WRITINGS: The Conference Sequence: Patterned Narration and Narrative Inconsistency in the Odyssey, University of California Classical Studies, 1972.

WORK IN PROGRESS: Hamlet in Legend: The Hero as Fool (tentative title); research on ancient folktales.

AVOCATIONAL INTERESTS: Herb gardening.

* * *

HANSON, Irene (Forsythe) 1898- (Irene Forsythe)

PERSONAL: Born August 5, 1898, in Enterprise, Ore.; daughter of Elmer Johnson (a businessman) and Amy Edna (Templeton) Forsythe; married Perry Oliver Hanson (a clergyman), August 8, 1952 (died, 1967). *Education:* Muskingum College, B.S., 1919; Moody Bible Institute, graduate, 1924; also attended Biblical Seminary, New York, N.Y., 1953, and Wheaton College, Wheaton, Ill. *Politics:* Republican. *Home:* Westminster Gardens, 1420 Santo Domingo, Duarte, Calif. 91810.

CAREER: High school teacher in Oregon, 1919-23; Presbyterian missionary in China, 1926-52.

WRITINGS: (Under name Irene Forsythe) *Cheng's Mother,* Friendship Press, 1943; (with Bernard Palmer) *The Wheelbarrow and the Comrade,* Moody, 1972.

SIDELIGHTS: Irene Hanson was the last Presbyterian missionary to leave Shantung Province where she had lived and worked for twenty-five years.

The last three years of her service in China were spent under the Communist regime. There were false accusations made against her, including that of being a "chief American spy." There were threats serious enough to put her in danger of having a public trial or of being shot.

After two plots to kill her failed, and despite the brave efforts of a Chinese man and his family to save her, she was picked up by the police in the night, put on board a freighter, and sentenced to eternal deportation from China. The next day Radio Moscow announced that the "chief American spy" was now out of China.

* * *

HANSON, James Arthur 1940-

PERSONAL: Born August 29, 1940, in Bridgeport, Conn.; son of Arthur Christian (a gasoline station operator) and Alice Elizabeth (Rohrbach) Hanson; married Barbara Anne Kennedy (a high school teacher); children: Kristina, Whitney. *Education:* Yale University, B.A., 1961, M.A., 1963, Ph.D., 1967. *Home:* 96 Lloyd Ave., Providence, R.I. 02906. *Office:* Department of Economics, Brown University, Providence, R.I. 02912.

CAREER: Brown University, Providence, R.I., assistant professor, 1965-72, associate professor of economics, 1973—. Consultant to Agency for International Development. *Member:* American Economic Association, Econometric Society. *Awards, honors:* Social Science Research Council fellowships, 1969, 1971-72.

WRITINGS: Growth in Open Economics, Springer Verlag, 1971.

WORK IN PROGRESS: Economic Development of Venezuela; Agricultural Output, Income Distribution, and Land Tenure in Latin America.

* * *

HAPGOOD, Ruth K(nott) 1920-

PERSONAL: Born May 5, 1920, in Louisville, Ky.; daughter of Richard Gillmore (a newspaperman and banker) and Ruth (a violinist under name Ruth Breton; maiden name, Jones) Knott; married Norman Hapgood, Jr. (a teacher), July 19, 1944; children: Margo Ten Eyck, Fae Breton. *Education:* Swarthmore College, B.A., 1941. *Office:* Houghton Mifflin Co., 2 Park St., Boston, Mass.

CAREER: William Morrow & Co., New York, N.Y., 1941-50, began in juvenile book department, became advertising manager; Houghton Mifflin Co., Boston, Mass., trade editor, 1962—.

WRITINGS: (With Joseph C. Aub) *Pioneer in Modern Medicine: David Linn Edsall of Harvard,* Harvard Medical Alumni Association, 1970; *First Horse: Basic Horse Care,* Chronicle Books, 1972.

* * *

HARBAUGH, John W(arvelle) 1926-

PERSONAL: Born August 6, 1926, in Madison, Wis.; son of M. Dwight and Marjorie (Warvelle) Harbaugh; married Josephine Taylor, November 25, 1951; children: Robert, Dwight, Richard. *Education:* Denison University, student, 1944-45; University of Kansas, B.S., 1948, M.S., 1950; University of Wisconsin, Ph.D., 1955. *Politics:* Republican. *Home:* 683 Salvatierra St., Stanford, Calif. 94305. *Office:* Department of Applied Earth Sciences, Stanford University, Stanford, Calif. 94305.

CAREER: Stanford University, Stanford, Calif., assistant professor, 1955-61, associate professor, 1961-66, professor of geology, 1966—.

WRITINGS: (With D. F. Merriam) *Computer Applications in Stratigraphic Analysis,* Wiley, 1968; (with Graeme Bonham-Carter) *Computer Simulation in Geology,* Wiley, 1970; *Stratigraphy and the Geologic Time Scale,* W. C. Brown, 1968, 2nd edition, 1974; *Guide to the Geology of Northern California,* W. C. Brown, 1973, new edition, 1974.

WORK IN PROGRESS: Research on exploration and exploitation of coal and oil.

* * *

HARD, Margaret (Steel) 1888(?)-1974

1888(?)—February 19, 1974; American bookseller, and author of works of fiction and nonfiction. Obituaries: *Publishers Weekly,* April 1, 1974.

* * *

HARDIN, Charles M(eyer) 1908-

PERSONAL: Born August 29, 1908, in Lander, Wyo.; son of William E. (a lawyer) and Julia (Meyer) Hardin; married Sallie Gibson, December 1, 1933; children: Julia (Mrs. John Thomas Hansen). *Education:* University of Wyoming, A.B., 1930; University of Colorado, M.A., 1938; Harvard University, Ph.D., 1942. *Politics:* Democrat. *Religion:* Protestant. *Home:* 9919 Miller Dr., Davis, Calif. 95616. *Office:* Department of Political Science, University of California, Davis, Calif. 95616.

CAREER: High school teacher of English and French in Lander, Wyo., 1934-37; Harvard University, Cambridge, Mass., instructor in government, 1940-45; University of Chicago, Chicago, Ill., assistant professor, 1945-51, associate professor, 1952-57, professor of political science, 1958-60; Rockefeller Foundation, New York, N.Y., associate director of social sciences, 1961-64; University of California, Davis, professor of political science, 1964—, director of International Agricultural Institute, 1965-70. Visiting fellow at Center for the Study of Democratic Institutions, summer, 1970. Consultant to U.S. Department of Agriculture, 1945, 1949, Tennessee Valley Authority, 1948, International Bank for Reconstruction and Development, 1959, and Ford Foundation, 1968. *Member:* American Political Science Association, American Agricultural Economic Association, Agricultural History Association, American Civil Liberties Union, Western Political Science Association. *Awards, honors:* Journal of Farm Economics best article award, 1946, for "The Bureau of Agricultural Economics Under Fire."

WRITINGS: The Politics of Agriculture, Free Press, 1952; *Freedom in Agricultural Education,* University of Chicago Press, 1955; *Food and Fiber in American Politics,* U.S. Government Printing Office, 1967; (contributor) Karl A. Fox and D. Gale Johnson, editors, *Readings in Agricultural Economics,* American Economic Association, 1969; *Presidential Power and Accountability: Toward a New Constitution,* University of Chicago Press, 1974.

WORK IN PROGRESS: Short books.

SIDELIGHTS: Charles Hardin has been around the world twice and has worked in Pakistan and India. He has traveled through Latin America three times and has worked in Colombia, Chile, Peru, Mexico, and Brazil.

* * *

HARDWICK, Michael 1924-
(John Drinkrow)

PERSONAL: Born September 10, 1924, in Leeds, England; son of George Drinkrow (a civil servant) and Katherine A. (Townend) Hardwick; married Mollie Greenhalgh (an author and playwright), October 21, 1961; children: Julian Charles Drinkrow. *Education:* Attended Leeds Grammar School. *Home:* 32 Southwood Lane, Highgate Village, London N6 5EB, England. *Agent:* London Management Ltd., 235 Regent St., London W.1, England.

CAREER: Morley Observer, Morley, Yorkshire, England, reporter, 1942-43; New Zealand National Film Unit, Wellington, writer and director, 1947-52; *Freedom* (newspaper), Wellington, New Zealand, feature writer and arts editor, 1952-54; British Broadcasting Corp. (BBC), London, England, drama script editor and director, 1955-63; free-lance author and playwright, 1963—. Has written and directed plays for television, the stage, radio, and record albums. War correspondent from Korea, 1951. *Military service:* Indian Army, Grenadiers, 1943-47; served in Japan; became captain. *Member:* Society of Authors, Writers Guild of Great Britain, Royal Society of Arts (fellow), Sherlock Holmes Society of London, Dickens Fellowship.

WRITINGS: The Royal Visit to New Zealand, A. H. & A. W. Reed, 1954; *Emigrant in Motley: Unpublished Letters of Charles Kean,* Rockliff, 1954; *Seeing New Zealand,* A. H. & A. W. Reed, 1955; *Opportunity in New Zealand,* Rockliff, 1956; (editor and contributor with Baron Birkett) *The Verdict of the Court,* Jenkins, 1961; *Doctors on Trial,* Jenkins, 1961.

The World's Greatest Air Mysteries, Odhams, 1970; *The Discovery of Japan,* Hamly, 1970; *The Osprey Guide to Gilbert and Sullivan,* Drake Publishers, 1972; *The Osprey Guide to Oscar Wilde,* Drake Publishers, 1973; *The Osprey Guide to Jane Austen,* Scribner, 1973; (under pseudonym John Drinkrow) *The Vintage Operetta Book,* Drake Publishers, 1973; *Upstairs, Downstairs: Mr. Hudson's Diaries,* Sphere, 1973; *A Literary Atlas and Gazetteer of the British Isles,* Gale, 1973; *The Osprey Guide to Anthony Trollope,* Scribner, 1974; (under pseudonym John Drinkrow) *The Vintage Musical Comedy Book,* Osprey, 1974; *The Pallisers* (abridgment of novels by Anthony Trollope), Coward, 1974; *A Christmas Carol* (a dramatized version of story by Charles Dickens), Davis-Poynter, 1974; *Upstairs, Downstairs: Mr. Bellamy's Story,* Sphere, 1974; *The Inheritors,* Mayflower, 1974.

With wife, Mollie Hardwick: *The Jolly Toper,* Jenkins, 1961; *The Sherlock Holmes Companion,* Doubleday, 1962; *Sherlock Holmes Investigates,* Lothrop, 1963; *The Man Who Was Sherlock Holmes,* Doubleday, 1964; *Four Sherlock Holmes Plays,* Samuel French, 1964; *The Charles Dickens Companion,* Holt, 1965; *The Plague and Fire of London,* Parish, 1966; *The World's Greatest Sea Mysteries,* Odhams, 1967; *Writers' Houses,* Dent, 1968, published as *A Literary Journey,* A. S. Barnes, 1968; *Alfred Deller: A Singularity of Voice,* Praeger, 1968; *Dickens's England,* A.S. Barnes, 1970; *As They Saw Him: Charles Dickens,* Harrap, 1970; *Plays from Dickens,* Samuel French, 1970; *The Game's Afoot: More Sherlock Holmes Plays,* Samuel French, 1970; *The Private Life of Sherlock Holmes,* Bantam, 1970; *The Charles Dickens Encyclopedia,* Scribner, 1973; *The Bernard Shaw Companion,* St. Martin's, 1973; *Four More Sherlock Holmes Plays,* Samuel French, 1973.

Work is represented in anthologies, including the following, all edited by John Canning: *Fifty Great Ghost Stories,* Odhams, 1966; *Living History: 1914,* Odhams, 1967; *Fifty Great Horror Stories,* Souvenir Press, 1971; *Fifty True Tales of Terror,* Souvenir Press, 1972; *Great Europeans,* Souvenir Press, 1973. Contributor to magazines and newspapers, including *Sunday Telegraph, Kent Messenger,* and *Sussex Life.*

WORK IN PROGRESS: Two sequences of novels; television plays; the formation of a company to present theatrical programs devised and directed by Hardwick and his wife.

SIDELIGHTS: Hardwick told *CA:* "I am a compulsive writer, moving without break from one commission to the next—novel to play to article to book review to novel, and so *ad infinitum.* I find it a struggle to turn down any approach . . . unless the theme is distasteful or would bore me to work on. I do not take holidays, because I can not bear professional inactivity. . . . If I were to make a fortune tomorrow I should be back at work (hangover permitting) the day after."

Of his books co-authored with his wife, Mollie Hardwick, he says: "We share an almost identical writing style and so can write a book together (and argue later as to who wrote certain passages), or take over one another's commissions, when pressure is heavy . . . but often the collaboration is largely one of discussion, and only one of us writes the book or play. We have been told that this collaboration is unique, or virtually so." *Avocational interests:* Classical music, playing piano, reading, watching good drama and comedy on television, walking, cricket, snooker.

* * *

HARDWICK, Mollie
(Mary Atkinson)

PERSONAL: Born in Manchester, England; daughter of Joseph (a manager of a textile factory) and Anne Frances (Atkinson) Greenhalgh; married Michael Hardwick (an author and playwright), October 21, 1961; children: Julian Charles Drinkrow. *Education:* Attended Manchester High School for Girls. *Home:* 32 Southwood Lane, Highgate Village, London N6 5EB, England. *Agent:* London Management Ltd., 235 Regent St., London W.L, England.

CAREER: British Broadcasting Corp. (BBC), London, England, began as radio announcer in Manchester, drama script editor and director in London, 1943-63; free-lance author and playwright, 1963—. *Member:* Society of Authors, Writers Guild of Great Britain, Royal Society of Arts (fellow), Sherlock Holmes Society of London, Dickens Fellowship.

WRITINGS: (Editor) *World of Prose: Stories from Dick-*

ens, Edward Arnold, 1968; *Emma: Lady Hamilton,* Holt, 1969; *Mrs. Dizzy: The Life of Mary Anne Disraeli,* St. Martin's, 1972; (under pseudonym Mary Atkinson) *The Thames-side Book,* Osprey, 1973; *Upstairs, Downstairs: Sarah's Story,* Sphere, 1973; *Upstairs, Downstairs: The Years of Change,* Sphere, 1974; *Alice in Wonderland* (dramatized version of Lewis Carroll's book), Davis-Poynter, 1974.

With husband, Michael Hardwick: *The Jolly Toper,* Jenkins, 1961; *The Sherlock Holmes Companion,* Doubleday, 1962; *Sherlock Holmes Investigates,* Lothrop, 1963; *The Man Who Was Sherlock Holmes,* Doubleday, 1964; *Four Sherlock Holmes Plays,* Samuel French, 1964; *The Charles Dickens Companion,* Holt, 1965; *The Plague and Fire of London,* Parish, 1966; *The World's Greatest Sea Mysteries,* Odhams, 1967; *Writers' Houses,* Dent, 1968, published as *A Literary Journey,* A. S. Barnes, 1968; *Alfred Deller: A Singularity of Voice,* Praeger, 1968; *Dickens's England,* A. S. Barnes, 1970; *As They Saw Him: Charles Dickens,* Harrap, 1970; *Plays from Dickens,* Samuel French, 1970; *The Game's Afoot: More Sherlock Holmes Plays,* Samuel French, 1970; *The Private Life of Sherlock Holmes,* Bantam, 1970; *The Charles Dickens Encyclopedia,* Scribner, 1973; *The Bernard Shaw Companion,* Scribner, 1973; *Four More Sherlock Holmes Plays,* Samuel French, 1973.

Work is represented in anthologies, including the following, all edited by John Canning: *Fifty Great Ghost Stories,* Odhams, 1966; *Living History: 1914,* Odhams, 1967; *Fifty Great Horror Stories,* Souvenir Press, 1971; *Fifty True Tales of Terror,* Souvenir Press, 1972; *Great Europeans,* Souvenir Press, 1973; *One Hundred Great Adventures,* Souvenir Press, 1973.

Writer of numerous plays for television, stage, radio, and record albums. Contributor to magazines and newspapers, including *Woman's Realm* and *Woman.*

WORK IN PROGRESS: Several novels on historical themes; projects in drama.

SIDELIGHTS: Mrs. Hardwick told *CA:* "My novels are set in period because, though I enjoy the amenities of this century, I am irresistibly drawn to the past, and find research into it the most exciting and rewarding part of a literary life. If I describe myself as a 'romantic novelist,' it is because I prefer to write about beautiful/brave/amusing people in picturesque costume and settings; for which reason I am utterly bored by current trends in fiction and the theatre (which I have always loved and still do, when it sets out to entertain me). I suppose the greatest influences on my life and work have been my father, Shakespeare, the Romantic poets, Dickens, and Emma, Lady Hamilton. I share my husband's love of Baroque music, but unlike him am a devotee of rock and country/folk. I enjoy parties, gardens, animals, whodunits of a cosy nature, and the society of actors."

* * *

HARFORD, David K(ennedy) 1947-

PERSONAL: Born May 25, 1947, in St. Marys, Pa.; son of Robert Ellsworth (a contractor) and Anne (Krchmar) Harford. *Education:* Attended Mount Union College, 1965-66, and University of Pittsburgh, 1969-71. *Politics:* None. *Religion:* "I believe in God." *Residence:* Bradford, Pa. *Office address:* P. O. Box 381, Bradford, Pa. 16701.

CAREER: Writer. Has worked as construction laborer, sawmill employee, and bartender. *Military service:* U.S. Army, military police investigator, 1967-69; served in Vietnam. *Awards, honors:* Third prize in Illinois Major Poets Contest, sponsored by Major Poets chapter of Pierson Mettler Associates, 1972.

WRITINGS: Towards Peace (poems), Branden Press, 1972.

WORK IN PROGRESS: Troubled Water, a second collection of poems; *The Great Experience,* a novel.

SIDELIGHTS: Harford writes: "Today's world and national scene is a smorgasbord of ideas for writers. We are standing in the shadows of change and once we emerge from its haze, will have to call on the thinkers to guide us. Poets, philosophers, and writers should be waiting anxiously with pen in hand. I love the mountains and the tranquility that lives there. Fly fishing is my hobby, and my pastime is sitting around wondering why I don't get a legitimate job." Harford has lived in Mexico.

* * *

HARMS, Ernest 1895-1974

September 12, 1895—July 2, 1974; German-born American clinical psychologist, editor, and author of books on child guidance and other topics. Obituaries: *New York Times,* July 7, 1974. (*CA*-13/14).

* * *

HARMS, Valerie 1940-
(Valerie Harms Sheehan)

PERSONAL: Born July 17, 1940, in Chicago, Ill.; daughter of Gunther William (a law school director) and Virginia (Jensen) Harms; married Laurence F. Sheehan (a writer and editor), December 1, 1963; children: Aurelie, Alexander. *Education:* Smith College, B.A., 1962; Silvermine School of the Arts, graduate study, 1970. *Home:* 10 Sunset Hill, Norwalk, Conn. 06851.

CAREER: Creative Communications, Chicago, Ill., scriptgirl and assistant film editor, 1962-63; free-lance editor for government film companies in Washington, D.C., 1964; The Child's Work Center (a Montessori school), Norwalk, Conn., co-founder, 1967-70; Magic Circle Press, Riverside, Conn., co-founder, 1972-74; Humanic Arts Institute/Dialogue House, New York, N.Y., associate in psychology, 1973—. Photographer. *Member:* Association Montessori Internationale, Authors Guild, National Organization of Women, Otto Rank Society, Women's Interests Centers, Connecticut Feminists in the Arts.

WRITINGS: (Contributor) Richard Kostelanetz, editor, *Assembling,* Assembling Press, 1971; (editor under name Valerie Harms Sheehan) *Unmasking: Ten Women in Metamorphosis,* Swallow Press, 1973; *Celebration with Anais Nin,* Magic Circle Press, 1973. Contributor of stories or articles to *Journal of American Montessori Society, Black Maria, Mahir,* and *New York Times.* Author of three eight-millimeter feature films, "The House," "The Grandfather," and "The Fight," and one sixteen-millimeter film, "Hands."

WORK IN PROGRESS: A study of early manuscripts of Anais Nin: a novel, *Herstory;* essays on great old women of our society.

BIOGRAPHICAL/CRITICAL SOURCES: Danbury News Times, June 5, 1973.

HARPER, Marvin Henry 1901-

PERSONAL: Born August 18, 1901, in Atlanta, Ga.; son of Henry Smith and Willie (Camp) Harper; married Emmie Ficklen (a librarian), June 30, 1926; children: Marvin Henry, Jr., Fielding Ficklen. *Education:* Emory University, B.A., 1922, Candler School of Theology, graduate study, 1923-25; Yale University, B.D., 1926; University of Chicago, Ph.D., 1935. *Home and office:* 394 Princeton Way N.E., Atlanta, Ga. 30307.

CAREER: Ordained Methodist minister, 1927; Emory University, Atlanta, Ga., instructor in physics, 1922-25; Leonard Theological College, Jabalpur, Madhya Pradesh, India, associate professor, 1927-35, professor of church history, 1935-45, president, 1945-57; Emory University, Candler School of Theology, professor of history of religions, 1957-70. *Member:* American Association of University Professors, Phi Beta Kappa, Omicron Delta Kappa.

WRITINGS: The Methodist Church in Southern Asia, Methodist Publishing House, 1936; *Gurus, Swamis, and Avataras: Spiritual Masters and Their American Disciples,* Westminster Press, 1972.

* * *

HARRIS, Barbara S(eger) 1927-

PERSONAL: Born November 15, 1927, in Earlville, Iowa; daughter of Cecil Sigsbee (a businessman) and Gladys (Bancroft) Seger; married Dale Harris (an actor and singer), February 13, 1949; children: Michael Robert. *Education:* Coe College, student, 1945-46; Goodman School of the Theatre, student, 1947-48, 1949-50. *Home:* 18858 Kilfinan St., Northridge, Calif. 91324. *Agent:* James Brown Associates, 22 East 60th St., New York, N.Y. 10022.

CAREER: Real estate property management. *Member:* Los Angeles P.E.N. Club, Soroptimist Club of San Fernando Valley, Panorama City Chamber of Commerce.

WRITINGS: Who Is Julia?, McKay, 1972.

WORK IN PROGRESS: A second novel, another physiological fantasy.

* * *

HARRIS, Errol E(ustace) 1908-

PERSONAL: Born February 19, 1908, in Kimberley, South Africa; came to United States, 1956; son of Samuel J. (a merchant) and Dora (Gross) Harris; married Sylvia Mundahl, July 11, 1946; children: Jonathan, Nigel, Hermione, Martin. *Education:* Rhodes University, B.A., 1927, M.A., 1929; Magdalen College, Oxford, B. Litt., 1933; University of the Witwatersrand, D.Litt., 1950. *Religion:* Episcopalian. *Home:* 1452 Oak Ave., Evanston, Ill. 60201. *Office:* Department of Philosophy, Northwestern University, 1830 Sheridan Rd., Evanston, Ill. 60201.

CAREER: Fort Hare University College (now University of Fort Hare), Fort Hare, South Africa, lecturer in philosophy, 1930; British Colonial Service, education officer in Basutoland and Zanzibar, 1937-42; University of the Witwatersrand, Johannesburg, South Africa, lecturer, 1946-50, senior lecturer, 1951-52, professor of philosophy, 1953-56; Connecticut College, New London, professor of philosophy, 1956-62; University of Kansas, Lawrence, Roy Roberts Distinguished Professor of Philosophy, 1962-66; Northwestern University, Evanston, Ill., professor of philosophy, 1966—, John Evans Professor of Moral and Intellectual Philosophy, 1973—. Visiting lecturer at Yale University, 1956-57, Terry lecturer, 1957; visiting professor and acting head of department of logic and metaphysics at University of Edinburgh, 1959-60. *Military service:* British Army, South African Information Service, 1942-46; became major.

MEMBER: American Philosophical Association, Metaphysical Society of America (president, 1968-69), Mind Association, Aristotelian Society. *Awards, honors:* Hugh Le May research fellow at Rhodes University, 1949; Bollingen research fellow, 1960-62; Ford Foundation research fellow, 1964.

WRITINGS: The Survival of Political Man: A Study in the Principles of International Order, Witwatersrand University Press, 1950; *"White" Civilization: How It Is Threatened and How It Can be Preserved in South Africa,* South African Institute of Race Relations, 1952; *Nature, Mind, and Modern Science,* Macmillan, 1954; *Objectivity and Reason* (inaugural lecture), Witwatersrand University Press, 1955; (editor) Harold H. Joachim, *Descartes's Rules for the Direction of the Mind* (reconstructed from notes), Allen & Unwin, 1957; *Revelation Through Reason: Religion in the Light of Science and Philosophy,* Yale University Press, 1958; *Analysis and Insight* (inaugural lecture), University of Kansas, 1962; *The Foundations of Metaphysics in Science,* Humanities, 1965; *Annihilation and Utopia: The Principles of International Politics,* Humanities, 1966; *Fundamentals of Philosophy: A Study of Classical Texts,* Holt, 1969; *Hypothesis and Perception: The Roots of Scientific Method,* Humanities, 1970; *Salvation from Despair: A Reassessment of Spinoza's Philosophy,* Nijhoff, 1973. Contributor of articles and reviews to professional journals.

* * *

HARRIS, H(arold) A(rthur) 1902-

PERSONAL: Born October 27, 1902, in Oxford, England; son of George Washington (a college servant) and Myra (Taylor) Harris; married Dorothy Nita Rees, January 5, 1946. *Education:* Jesus College, Oxford, Diploma in Education (with distinction), 1926, M.A., 1932. *Religion:* Church of England. *Home:* 42 Bickerton Rd., Headington, Oxford OX3 7LS, England.

CAREER: St. David's University College, Lampeter, Wales, lecturer in English and classics, 1926-32, professor of classics, 1932-67. Visiting lecturer at University of Illinois, 1969, and University of Western Ontario, 1973. *Military service:* Home Guard, 1940-45; became second lieutenant. *Member:* International Council of Sport and Physical Education (corresponding member) Classical Association.

WRITINGS: Greek Athletes and Athletics, Hutchinson, 1964, Indiana University Press, 1966; *Sport in Greece and Rome,* Cornell University Press, 1972; *Hatletica Havonit Jehudim* (title means "Greek Athletics and the Jews"), Am Hassefer, 1972; (contributor) Horst Ueberhorst, editor, *Geschichte der Leibesuebungen* (title means "History of Sport"), Bartels & Wernitz, 1972. Contributor to *Journal of Hellenic Studies, Classical Review,* and *Greece and Rome.*

WORK IN PROGRESS: A book, *Sport in Britain.*

* * *

HARRIS, Herbert 1914(?)-1974

1914(?)—April 18, 1974; American labor authority. Obituaries: *New York Times,* April 20, 1974.

HARRIS, Mary Imogene

PERSONAL: Born in Alabama City, Ala. *Education:* Central State University, Edmund, Okla., B.A., 1947; Northwestern University, M.A., 1949; University of Tulsa, Ed.D., 1961; also studied at University of Oklahoma. *Religion:* Methodist. *Home address:* Box 51367, Dawson Station, Tulsa, Okla. 74151. *Office:* Tulsa Public Schools, Tulsa, Okla.

CAREER: High school speech teacher in Burley, Idaho, 1948-49; Judson College, Marion, Ala., instructor in speech and English, 1949-52; Tulsa Public Schools, Tulsa, Okla., speech teacher, 1952—. *Member:* State Speech Group (vice-president), Tulsa English Club, Kappa Delta Pi (president-elect), Alpha Delta Kappa (historian), Delta Kappa Gamma. *Awards, honors:* Teachers medal from Freedoms Foundation, 1969, writing awards, 1972 and 1973; Tulsa Writers Award, 1969.

WRITINGS: *Serenity,* South and West, 1968; *Ticklers and Tinglers,* South and West, 1969; *A Handbook of Speaking and Listening Activities for the Elementary School,* Denison, 1971; *Nobody Would Believe!,* Advocate Press, 1973; *Talks with God,* Advocate Press, 1973; *They Faced the Cross,* Best Printing Corp., 1973; *A Walk in the Spirit!,* Best Printing Corp., 1973. Contributor to magazines, including *Upper Room, Instructor, Oklahoma Teacher, Today's Education, Speech Monographs,* and *Dramatics.* Author of columns appearing in *Tulsa World,* 1960-74.

WORK IN PROGRESS: A book on the Holy Land, based on four trips to the Middle East.

* * *

HARRISON, Martin 1930-

PERSONAL: Born April 19, 1930, in Bishop Auckland, England; son of Wilfred (a railway clerk) and Isabella (Armstrong) Harrison; married Wendy Hindle, April 23, 1957; children: Andrew, David, Catherine. *Education:* University of Manchester, B.A., 1952; Oxford University, Ph.D., 1956; Institut D'Etudes Politiques, Diplome, 1957. *Politics:* "No political affiliation." *Religion:* Church of England. *Home:* 20 Church Plantation, Keele, Staffordshire ST5 5AY, England. *Office:* Department of Politics, University of Keele, Keele, Staffordshire ST5 5BG, England.

CAREER: Oxford University, Nuffield College, Oxford, England, research fellow, 1957-62; University of Manchester, Manchester, England, senior lecturer in political science, 1962-66; University of Keele, Keele, England, professor of political science, 1966—. *Military service:* Royal Air Force, 1952-54; became flight lieutenant. *Member:* Radio Society of Great Britain, Political Studies Association.

WRITINGS: *Trade Unions and the Labour Party since 1945,* Allen & Unwin, 1960; (with P. M. Williams) *DeGaulle's Republic,* Longmans, Green, 1960; *French Politics,* Heath, 1969; (with Williams) *Politics and Society in DeGaulle's Republic,* Longman, 1971, Doubleday, 1972. Contributor to "Nuffield Studies of British General Elections," Macmillan. Contributor to *Political Studies, American Political Science Review, Journal of Politics,* and *Parliamentary Affairs.*

WORK IN PROGRESS: Research on trade unions and politics, on political finance, and on television in elections.

AVOCATIONAL INTERESTS: Licensed as radio amateur.

HARRISON, Roland Kenneth 1920-

PERSONAL: Born August 4, 1920, in Lancashire, England; son of William (a civil servant) and Hilda (Marsden) Harrison; married Kathleen Beattie, October 18, 1945; children: Charmian Felicity and Hermione Judith (twins), Graham Kenneth. *Education:* University of London, B.D., 1943, M.Th., 1947, Ph.D., 1952. *Politics:* Progressive Conservative. *Home:* 41 Cuthbert Crescent, Toronto, Ontario M4S 2G9, Canada. *Office:* Wycliffe College, University of Toronto, Toronto, Ontario M5S 1H7, Canada.

CAREER: Ordained Anglican priest, 1943. University of Toronto, Wycliffe College, Toronto, Ontario, professor of Old Testament, 1960—. *Member:* Worshipful Society of Apothecaries (London). *Awards, honors:* Honorary D.D. from Huron College, London, Ontario, 1963.

WRITINGS: *Teach Yourself Hebrew,* English Universities Press, 1955; *A History of Old Testament Times,* Marshall, Morgan & Scott, 1957; *The Dead Sea Scrolls,* English Universities Press, 1961; *Introduction to the Old Testament,* Eerdmans, 1969; *Jeremiah and Lamentations,* Tyndale Press, 1973; *Commentary on Book of Leviticus,* Tyndale Press, in press. Editor of *New International Commentary on the Old Testament,* 1969—.

* * *

HART, John Lewis 1931- (Johnny Hart)

PERSONAL: Born February 18, 1931, in Endicott, N.Y.; son of Irwin James (a fireman) and Grace (Brown) Hart; married Bobby Jane Hatcher, April 26, 1952; children: Patti Sue, Perri Ann. *Education:* Attended high school in New York, 1946-49. *Residence:* Endicott, N.Y. *Agent:* Publishers-Hall Syndicate, 30 East 42nd St., New York, N.Y. 10017.

CAREER: Free-lance magazine cartoonist, 1954-58; General Electric Co., Johnson City, N.Y., commercial artist, 1957-58; syndicated cartoonist, creator of "B.C." cartoon strip, 1958—, and "Wizard of Id," 1964—. Member of board of directors, Earth Awareness Foundation, 1970—. *Military service:* U.S. Air Force, 1950-53. *Member:* National Cartoonist Society, Artist and Writer's Society, National Comics Council. *Awards, honors:* "Best Humor Strip" awards, 1968 and 1971, and Reuben Award for best cartoonist, 1969, all from National Cartoonist Society; "Yellow Kid" Award for best comic strip from Congress of Luccia (Italy), 1970; "Best Humor Strip" award from French Comics Council, 1971; Public Service Award from National Aeronautics and Space Administration, 1972.

WRITINGS—All under name Johnny Hart; all published by Fawcett: *Hey B.C.,* 1958, abridged edition, 1970; *Hurray for B.C.,* 1958; *Back to B.C.,* 1959, abridged edition, 1967; *B.C. Strikes Back,* 1961, abridged edition, 1969; *What's New B.C.,* 1962; *B.C.–Big Wheel,* 1963; *B.C. Is Alive & Well,* 1964; *The Kind Is a Fink,* 1964; *Take a Bow B.C.,* 1965; (with Brant Parker) *The Wondrous Wizard of Id,* 1965; *B.C. on the Rocks,* 1966; (with Parker) *The Peasants Are Revolting,* 1966; *B.C. Right On,* 1967; *B.C. Cave In,* 1967; (with Parker) *Remember the Golden Rule,* 1967; *There's a Fly in My Swill,* 1967; (with Parker) *The Wizard's Back,* 1968; *B.C.,* 1972; *B.C. Cartoon Book,* 1973. Also author of television scripts and public service commercials.

SIDELIGHTS: Hart's books have been translated into Japanese, Finnish, Swedish, and German.

HART, Johnny
See HART, John Lewis

* * *

HARTMAN, John J(acob) 1942-

PERSONAL: Born August 13, 1942, in Detroit, Mich.; son of Manuel and Eleanor (Jacob) Hartman; married Julia Carlin, 1968; children: Michelle, Amanda. *Education:* Harvard University, A.B. (magna cum laude), 1964; University of Michigan, M.A., 1969, Ph.D., 1969. *Home:* 3689 Middleton Dr., Ann Arbor, Mich. 48105. *Office:* University of Michigan Hospital, Neuropsychiatric Institute, Ann Arbor, Mich. 48104.

CAREER: University of California, Los Angeles, assistant professor of psychology, 1969-71; University of Michigan, Neuropsychiatric Institute, Ann Arbor, assistant professor, 1971-74, associate professor of psychology in psychiatry, 1974—. *Member:* American Psychological Association, Society for the Psychological Study of Social Issues, American Group Psychotherapy Association, Michigan Psychological Association. *Awards, honors:* Woodrow Wilson fellow, 1964-65; Prytanean Distinguished Service Award for teaching from University of California at Los Angeles, 1971.

WRITINGS: (With R. D. Mann and G. S. Gibbard) *Interpersonal Styles and Group Development,* Wiley, 1967; (with M. J. Goldstein and H. S. Kant) *Pornography and Sexual Deviance,* University of California Press, 1973; (editor with Gibbard and Mann, and contributor) *Analysis of Groups: Contributions to Theory, Research, and Practice,* Jossey-Bass, 1974. Contributor to *New Directions in Teaching, American Journal of Orthopsychiatry, Contemporary Psychoanalysis, International Journal of Group Psychotherapy, Behavioral Science, Small Group Behavior,* and *Michigan Medicine.*

* * *

HARVEY, Richard B(lake) 1930-

PERSONAL: Born November 28, 1930, in Los Angeles, Calif.; son of George B. (an attorney) and Clara (Conners) Harvey; married Patricia Clougher (a teacher), August 29, 1965; children: G. Scott Floden, Timothy Patrick. *Education:* Occidental College, B.A., 1952; University of California, Los Angeles, M.A., 1954, Ph.D., 1959. *Home:* 13628 East La Cuarta St., Whittier, Calif. 90602. *Office:* Office of Academic Affairs, Whittier College, Philadelphia St., Whittier, Calif. 90608.

CAREER: California State Assembly, Sacramento, legislative intern, 1957-58; Whittier College, Whittier, Calif., instructor, 1960-62, assistant professor, 1962-65, associate professor, 1965-70, professor of political science, 1970—, assistant dean of the college, 1970-71, dean of academic affairs, 1971—. *Member:* American Political Science Association, American Association of University Professors, American Conference of Academic Deans, Western Political Science Association, Southern California Academic Deans' Group (president, 1972), Southern California Political Science Association (treasurer, 1965-67). *Awards, honors:* Haynes Foundation grants, 1961, 1968.

WRITINGS: (Contributor) Eugene P. Dvorin and Arthur J. Misner, editors, *California Politics and Policies: Original Essays,* Addison-Wesley, 1966; *Earl Warren: Governor of California,* Exposition, 1969; *The Dynamics of California Government and Politics,* Wadsworth, 1970. Contributor to *World Affairs Quarterly, Los Angeles Times,* and *California Historical Society.*

* * *

HASBROUCK, Kenneth E. 1916-

PERSONAL: Born June 30, 1916, in Gardiner, N.Y.; son of Josiah LeFevre (a farmer) and Agnes (Riley) Hasbrouck; married Alice M. Jackson, July 10, 1948; children: Kenneth E., Jr., Charles Jackson. *Education:* Teachers College at New Paltz (now State University of New York College at New Paltz), B.E., 1946; New York University, M.A., 1948, further graduate courses. *Home:* 14 Forest Glen Rd., New Paltz, N.Y. 12561. *Office:* Huguenot Historical Society, Huguenot St., New Paltz, N.Y. 12561.

CAREER: Teacher of social studies, 1941-42, 1946-72; Huguenot Historical Society (maintains, among other projects, Huguenot St. as a national historic site), New Paltz, N.Y., president, 1960—, director, 1972—. Historian, Ulster County, N.Y., 1960-72. *Military service:* U.S. Army Air Forces, 1941-46; became sergeant major. *Member:* New York Genealogical and Biographical Society, New England Genealogical Society.

WRITINGS: *Deyo Family,* Stillwagon Press, 1951; *Street of the Huguenots,* Tuttle, 1952; *History of Gardiner, N.Y.,* Stillwagon Press, 1955; *Hasbrouck Family in America,* Smith Publishing, 1961; *Bevier Family in America,* Smith Publishing, 1971. Contributor to *De Halve Maen* and *New Paltz Independent.*

WORK IN PROGRESS: Editing and compiling *Shawangunk's Hearth's.*

* * *

HASSRICK, Peter H(eyl) 1941-

PERSONAL: Born April 27, 1941, in Philadelphia, Pa.; son of Royal Brown (a writer) and Barbara (Morgan) Hassrick; married Elizabeth Drake, June 14, 1963; children: Philip Heyl, Charles Royal. *Education:* Attended Harvard University, 1962; University of Colorado, B.A., 1963; University of Denver, M.A., 1969. *Residence:* Fort Worth, Tex. *Office:* Amon Carter Museum, P. O. Box 2365, Fort Worth, Tex. 76101.

CAREER: Lone Star Ranch, Elizabeth, Colo., rancher and assistant foreman, summers, 1960-63; high school teacher of history, Spanish, and art history in Steamboat Springs, Colo., 1963-67; Amon Carter Museum, Fort Worth, Tex., curator of collections, 1969—. Rancher in Colorado, summers, 1963-65. *Member:* American Association of Museums.

WRITINGS: *Frederic Remington,* Amon Carter Museum, 1973; *Frederick Remington,* Abrams, 1973. Contributor to *American Art Review* and *Southwestern Historical Quarterly.*

* * *

HAVIGHURST, Marion Boyd (?)-1974

(?)—February 24, 1974; American educator, poet, and author. Obituaries: *Washington Post,* March 2, 1974. (*CA*-13/14).

HAWLEY, Henrietta Ripperger 1890(?)-1974 (Henrietta Ripperger)

1890(?)—April 17, 1974; American author and magazine writer. Obituaries: *New York Times,* April 18, 1974.

* * *

HAY, Thomas Robson 1888-1974

1888—May 26, 1974; American historian, editor, and author. Obituaries: *AB Bookman's Weekly,* July 15, 1974.

* * *

HAYNES, Renee (Oriana) 1906-

PERSONAL: Born July 23, 1906, in London, England; daughter of Edmund Sidney Pollock (a lawyer) and Oriane Huxley (Waller) Haynes; married Jerrard Tickell (a writer; surname pronounced Tick-*ell*), July 4, 1929 (died, 1966); children: Crispin Charles Cervantes, Patrick Jocelyn, Edmund Nicholas Thomas More. *Education:* St. Hugh's College, Oxford, B.A. (honors), 1927, and M.A. *Politics:* "Mixed." *Religion:* Roman Catholic. *Residence:* London, England. *Agent:* A.M. Heath & Co. Ltd., 35 Dover St., London W1X 4EB, England. *Office:* Society for Psychical Research, 1 Adam and Eve Mews, London 6UQ, England.

CAREER: Geoffrey Bles Ltd. (publishers), London, England, assistant, 1928-29; British Council, London, England, director of book reviews department and other posts, 1941-67; Society for Psychical Research, London, England, editor of society's journal and proceedings, 1970—. *Member:* Association for Latin Liturgy.

WRITINGS: Neapolitan Ice, Chatto & Windus, 1928, Dial, 1929; *Immortal John,* Desmond Harmsworth, 1932; *The Holy Hunger,* Hutchinson, 1935; *Pan, Caesar and God: Who Spake by the Prophets,* Heinemann, 1938; (editor, and author of introductory memoir) *The Lawyer: A Conversation Piece* (selections from the notebooks and writings of her father, Edmund Sidney Pollock Haynes), Eyre & Spottiswoode, 1951; *Hilaire Belloc* (booklet), Longmans, Green, for British Council and National Book League, 1953; (contributor) Philip Caraman, editor, *Saints and Ourselves,* 2nd series, Hollis & Carter, 1955; (contributor) Alex Natan, editor, *Sport and Society,* Bowes, 1958; (translator from the French) Reginald Omez, *Psychical Phenomena,* Hawthorn, 1958; *The Hidden Springs: An Enquiry into Extra-Sensory Perception,* Devin-Adair, 1961, revised edition, Little, Brown, 1973; *Philosopher King: The Humanist Pope Benedict XIV,* Weidenfeld & Nicolson, 1970; (author of postscript) Arthur Koestler, *Roots of Coincidence,* Hutchinson, 1970, Random House, 1972; (author of foreword) Robert Ashby, *The Guidebook for the Study of Psychical Research,* River, 1972; (contributor) Aidan Chambers, *Book of Ghosts and Hauntings,* Longmans, Green, 1973.

Contributor to *Cassell's Encyclopedia of Literature* and *Twentieth Century Catholicism.* Contributor to magazines and newspapers, including *Time and Tide, Punch, Times Literary Supplement, Catholic Herald, Blackfriars, International Journal of Parapsychology* (United States), and others in Sweden, Netherlands, and France.

WORK IN PROGRESS: A book of reminiscences; research for a book tentatively titled *The Seeing Eye the Seeing I.*

AVOCATIONAL INTERESTS: Anthropology, cooking (theoretical and practical), gardening, sailing, swimming, walking, music (seventeenth and eighteenth century), philosophy, psychical research, "and a whole rag bag of other subjects."

* * *

HAYNES, Richard F(rederick) 1935-

PERSONAL: Born January 29, 1935, in Boston, Mass.; married Carol Cook, August 23, 1961; children: Allison, Melissa. *Education:* Southeastern Louisiana University, B.A., 1961; Louisiana State University, M.A., 1963, Ph.D., 1971. *Residence:* Monroe, La. *Office:* Department of History, Northeast Louisiana University, Monroe, La. 71201.

CAREER: Northeast Louisiana University, Monroe, instructor, 1963-64, assistant professor, 1965-71, associate professor of American history, 1972—. *Military service:* U.S. Navy, 1958-60. *Member:* Organization of American Historians, Committee on the History of the Second World War, Louisiana Historical Association (member of board of directors).

WRITINGS: Awesome Power: Truman as Commander in Chief, Louisiana State University Press, 1973.

WORK IN PROGRESS: Military Powers of the American Presidency, completion expected in 1977.

AVOCATIONAL INTERESTS: Tennis, reading.

* * *

HAYWOOD, H(erbert) Carl(ton) 1931-

PERSONAL: Born July 2, 1931, in Taylor County, Ga.; married, 1951; children: Carlton, Terry, Elizabeth, Kristin. *Education:* West Georgia College, student, 1948-50; San Diego State College (now University), A.B., 1956, M.A., 1957; University of Illinois, Ph.D., 1961. *Home:* 111 Old Hickory Blvd., Apt D-140, Nashville, Tenn. 37221. *Office:* Box 40, George Peabody College for Teachers, Nashville, Tenn. 37203.

CAREER: Veterans Administration Hospital, Danville, Ill., clinical psychology trainee, 1957-61; Eastern Illinois Mental Health Unit, Danville and Watseka, Ill., clinical psychologist, 1959-61; Veterans Administration Hospital, Danville, staff psychologist, 1961-62; George Peabody College for Teachers, Nashville, Tenn., assistant professor, 1962-65, associate professor, 1965-66, Kennedy Associate Professor, 1966-69, Kennedy Professor of Psychology, 1969—, director of John F. Kennedy Center for Research on Education and Human Development, 1971—. Visiting professor at University of Toronto, 1965-66. Consultant to National Institutes of Health, President's Committee on Mental Retardation, and various institutions and government bodies; chairman of advisory board, Tennessee Association for Retarded Children and Adults, 1971—. *Military service:* U.S. Navy, 1950-54.

MEMBER: American Association on Mental Deficiency (member of council), American Psychological Association, American Association for the Advancement of Science, Psychonomic Society, Society for Research in Child Development, Institute of Medicine (National Academy of Sciences), Midwestern Psychological Association, Southeastern Psychological Association, Sigma Xi.

WRITINGS—Editor and contributor: *Brain Damage in School Children,* Council for Exceptional Children, 1968;

Social-Cultural Aspects of Mental Retardation, Appleton, 1970; *Psychometric Intelligence,* Appleton, in press.

Contributor: Joseph Zubin and George Jervis, editors, *Psychopathology of Mental Development,* Grune, 1967; H. I. Day, D. E. Berlyne, and D. E. Hunt, editors, *Intrinsic Motivation: A New Direction in Intelligence,* Holt, 1971. Contributor to *Encyclopaedia Britannica,* contributor of about thirty articles and occasional reviews to scientific journals. Co-editor, *Abstracts of Peabody Studies in Mental Retardation,* 1965, editor, 1968; consulting editor, *American Journal of Mental Deficiency,* 1966-69, editor, 1969—.

* * *

HEALD, Charles Brehmer 1882-1974

December 3, 1882—1974; British physician and author of books on medical topics. Obituaries: *AB Bookman's Weekly,* July 15, 1974.

* * *

HEALD, Timothy (Villiers) 1944-

PERSONAL: Born January 28, 1944, in Dorchester, Dorset, England; son of Villiers Archer John and Jean (Vaughan) Heald; married Alison Martina Leslie, March 30, 1968; children: Emma, Alexander, Lucy. *Education:* Balliol College, Oxford, B.A. (honors), 1965. *Home and office:* 8 Thornton Rd., London SW14 8NS, England. *Agent:* Richard Scott Simon, 36 Wellington St., London WC2E 7BD, England.

CAREER: Sunday Times, London, England, assistant diary columnist, 1965-67; *Town,* London, features editor, 1967; *Daily Express,* London, feature writer, 1967-72; free-lance journalist and writer, 1972—.

WRITINGS: It's a Dog's Life, Elm Tree Books, 1971; *Unbecoming Habits,* Stein & Day, 1973; *Blue Blood Will Out,* Stein & Day, in press. Contributor of articles and reviews to *Times, Daily Telegraph, Punch,* and British Broadcasting Corp.

WORK IN PROGRESS: A book on the effects of publicity, for Hutchinson.

SIDELIGHTS: Heald has travelled extensively as a journalist in Europe, the United States, and the Far East.

BIOGRAPHICAL/CRITICAL SOURCES: Scotsman, September 29, 1973.

* * *

HEAVEN, Constance
See FECHER, Constance

* * *

HECKELMANN, Charles N(ewman) 1913-
(Charles Lawton)

PERSONAL: Born October 24, 1913; son of Edward (a metal lithographer) and Sophia (Hodum) Heckelmann; married Anne Auer, April 17, 1937; children: Lorraine (Mrs. Richard Kane), Thomas. *Education:* University of Notre Dame, B.A. (maxima cum laude), 1934. *Religion:* Roman Catholic. *Home:* 178-19 Croydon Rd., Jamaica, N.Y. 11432. *Agent:* Scott Meredith Literary Agency, Inc., 580 Fifth Ave., New York, N.Y. 10036. *Office:* Hawthorn Books, Inc., 260 Madison Ave., New York, N.Y. 10016.

CAREER: Brooklyn Daily Eagle, Brooklyn, N.Y., sports writer, 1934-37; Cupples & Leon Co., New York, N.Y., editor and production manager, 1937-41; Popular Library, Inc., New York, N.Y., vice-president and editor-in-chief, 1941-58; Monarch Books, Inc., New York, N.Y., president and editor-in-chief, 1958-65; David McKay Co., New York, N.Y., managing editor and director of subsidiary rights, 1965-68; Cowles Book Co., New York, N.Y., senior editor, managing editor, and director of subsidiary rights, 1968-71; Hawthorn Books, Inc., New York, N.Y., vice-president and editor-in-chief, 1971—. *Member:* Catholic Writers Guild of America (president, 1949-52), Western Writers of America (vice-president, 1955-57; president, 1964-65).

WRITINGS: Vengeance Trail, Arcadia House, 1944; *Lawless Range,* Arcadia House, 1945; *Six-Gun Outcast,* Arcadia House, 1946; *Deputy Marshal,* Arcadia House, 1947; *Guns of Arizona,* Doubleday, 1949; *Outlaw Valley,* Cupples & Leon, 1950; *Danger Rides the Range,* Cupples & Leon, 1950; *Two-Bit Rancher,* Doubleday, 1950; *Let the Guns Roar,* Doubleday, 1950; *Fighting Ramrod,* Doubleday, 1951; *Hell in His Holsters,* Doubleday, 1952; *The Rawhider,* Holt, 1952; *Hard Man with a Gun,* Little, Brown, 1954; *Bullet Law,* Little, Brown, 1955; *Trumpets in the Dawn,* Doubleday, 1958; *The Big Valley,* Whitman Publishing, 1966; *The Glory Riders,* Avon, 1967; *Writing Fiction for Profit,* Coward, 1968; *Stranger from Durango,* Lancer Books, 1971.

Sports and adventure books for young adults, under pseudonym Charles Lawton: *Clarkeville's Battery,* Cupples & Leon, 1937; *Ros. Hackney: Halfback,* Cupples & Leon, 1937; *Jungle Menace: Starring Frank Buck,* Cupples & Leon, 1937; *The Winning Forward Pass,* Cupples & Leon, 1940; *Home Run Hennessey,* Cupples & Leon, 1941; *Touchdown to Victory,* Cupples & Leon, 1942.

Contributor of short fiction to magazines.

SIDELIGHTS: Heckelman has sold stories to film companies for production; "Deputy Marshal," "Stranger from Santa Fe," and "Frontier Feud," are based on his writings.

* * *

HEEZEN, Bruce C(harles) 1924-

PERSONAL: Born April 11, 1924, in Vinton, Iowa; son of Charles Christian (engaged in farming) and Esther (Schirding) Heezen. *Education:* University of Iowa, B.A., 1948; Columbia University, M.A., 1952, Ph.D., 1957. *Religion:* Unitarian Universalist. *Home:* 747 River Rd., Piermont, N.Y. 10968. *Office:* Lamont Doherty Geological Observatory, Palisades, N.Y. 10964.

CAREER: Columbia University, New York, N.Y., geologist and expedition leader at Woods Hole Oceanographic Institution, 1948, geologist at Lamont Doherty Geological Observatory, 1953-56, as research associate, 1956-58, senior research scientist, 1958-60, assistant professor of geology at observatory and in university department of geology, 1960-64, associate professor, 1964—. Explorer and mapper of ocean floors. Chairman of panel on ocean-wide survey, National Academy of Sciences, 1964-68; president of Commission for Marine Geology, International Union of Geological Sciences, 1965-70, and coordinator for Atlantic, Indian, and Pacific Oceans of Geologic Atlas of the World; secretary of International Commission on Marine Geophysics, 1969. Consultant to U.S. Naval Oceanographic

Office and Naval Research Laboratory; member of U.S. Department of State advisory committee, Law of the Sea Task Force.

MEMBER: International Association of the Physical Science of the Oceans, American Geographical Society (fellow), Geological Society of America (fellow), American Association for the Advancement of Science (fellow), Marine Biology Association (England; fellow), American Geophysical Union, American Society of Limnology and Oceanography, American Association of Petroleum Geologists, Society of Exploration Geophysicists, Sigma Xi.

AWARDS, HONORS: Henry Bryant Bigelow Gold Medal and Award from Woods Hole Oceanographic Institution, 1964, for physiographic studies of the deep ocean; *The Face of the Deep* was nominated for a National Book Award, 1972; Cullum Geographical Medal of American Geographical Society, 1973, for contributions to knowledge of the earth beneath the oceans.

WRITINGS: (With Marie Tharp and Maurice Ewing) *The Floors of the Oceans,* Geological Society of America, Volume I: *The North Atlantic* (physiographic diagram of North Atlantic and text), 1958; (with others) *Initial Reports of the Deep Sea Drilling Project,* Volume VI: *Hawaii to Guam,* National Science Foundation, 1971, Volume XX: *Japan to Fiji,* U.S. Government Printing Office, 1973; (with Charles D. Hollister) *The Face of the Deep,* Oxford University Press, 1971.

Contributor: Lewis G. Weeks, editor, *Habitat of Oil.* American Association of Petroleum Geologists, 1958; G. O. Raasch, editor, *The Geology of the Arctic,* University of Toronto Press, 1960; Mary Sears, editor, *Oceanography,* American Association for the Advancement of Science, 1961; S. K. Runcorn, editor, *Continental Drift,* Academic Press, 1962; Maurice N. Hill, editor, *The Sea,* Volume III: *The Earth Beneath the Sea,* Wiley, 1963; Askell Love and Doris Love, editors, *The North Atlantic Biota and Their History,* Pergamon, 1963; Alan E. Nairn, editor, *Problems in Paleoclimatology,* Wiley, 1964; S. W. Carey, editor, *Syntaphral Tectonics,* University of Tasmania, 1965; W. F. Whittard and R. Bradshaw, editors, *Submarine Geology and Geophysics,* Shoe String, 1965; John B. Hersey, editor, *Deep Sea Photography,* Johns Hopkins Press, 1967; A. I. Gordon, editor, *Studies in Physical Oceanography,* Volume II, Gordon & Breach, 1972.

With Marie Tharp, physiographic diagrams and maps: "Physiographic Diagram of the South Atlantic, the Caribbean, the Scotia Sea, and the Eastern Margin of the South Pacific Ocean" (with descriptive notes), Geological Society of America, 1961; "Physiographic Diagram of the Indian Ocean, the Red Sea, the South China Sea, the Sulu Sea, and the Celebes Sea," Geological Society of America, 1964; "Physiographic Diagram of the North Atlantic," Geological Society of America, 1968; "Physiographic Diagram of the Western Pacific Ocean," Geological Society of America, 1971; (with Tharp and C. R. Bentley) "Morphology of the Earth in the Antarctic and the Subantarctic," American Geographical Society, 1972. Heezen-Tharp maps of the floors of the Indian, Atlantic, Pacific, and Arctic Oceans, all painted by Henrich C. Berann, have been issued as special supplements of *National Geographic.*

Editor or convenor of six symposium volumes. Contributor to *Encyclopedia of Oceanography, International Dictionary of Geophysics,* and *Encyclopaedia Britannica.* Writer of more than two hundred scientific papers in journals and proceedings published in United States, Colombia, France, England, Canada, Germany, and other countries; also contributor of popular articles to *Saturday Review* and *Paris Match.* President of editorial committee, General Bathymetric Chart of the Oceans, 1959—; member of editorial committee, International Tectonic Map of the World, and convenor for oceans, 1965—.

WORK IN PROGRESS: With Charles D. Hollister, a book on deep sea sediments; a book on the development of the ocean floor.

SIDELIGHTS: Heezen and his associate, Marie Tharp, spend several months each year on expeditions exploring the deep sea floor. Heezen says that although they recognize the power of verbal expression, they as frequently use the economical graphic media of maps and diagrams to record their explorations. *The North Atlantic* was translated into Russian and published by Publishing House of Foreign Literature in Moscow.

* * *

HEFFRON, Dorris 1944-

PERSONAL: Born October 18, 1944, in Noranda, Quebec, Canada; daughter of William James (a salesman) and Kathleen (a teacher; maiden name, Clark) Heffron; married William Newton-Smith (a philosophy don at Balliol College, Oxford), June 29, 1968; children: Apple. *Education:* Queen's University, Kingston, Ont., B.A. (honors), 1967, M.A., 1968. *Politics:* Democratic socialist, member of Labour Party. *Religion:* Humanitarian. *Home and office:* The Critters' Patch, 92 Lonsdale Rd., Oxford, England. *Agent:* Sheila Watson, Bolt & Watson Ltd., 8 Storey's Gate, London S.W.1, England.

CAREER: Oxford University, department of extra-mural studies, Oxford, England, lecturer and tutor in literature, 1969-72. Summer lecturer at St. Francis Xavier University, Sydney, Nova Scotia, 1972. *Member:* Oxford Modern Free Dance Club. *Awards, honors:* Canada Council Arts award, 1973, to write *From Bombs to Blueberries.*

WRITINGS: A Nice Fire and Some Moonpennies, Macmillan, 1971, Atheneum, 1972.

WORK IN PROGRESS: A novel, *What Stays in Your Mind;* a novel about an evacuee from Oxford to Canada during the Second World War, *From Bombs to Blueberries.*

SIDELIGHTS: Dorris Heffron is interested in teenager's fiction and the "interaction of different cultures, hence my first two books dealt with an Indian girl in Ontario. My third book presents an Oxford girl evacuated to Canada." She has travelled through Europe, Japan, and Thailand.

* * *

HEGLAR, Mary Schnall 1934-

PERSONAL: Born November 28, 1934, in Toledo, Ohio; daughter of Blaine Allan (a pharmacist) and Dorothy (Clay) Schnall; married Rodger Heglar (a professor of physical anthropology), February 14, 1959; children: Jennifer Dorothy. *Education:* University of Michigan, B.A., 1959. *Home and office:* 15 Eastgate Dr., Daly City, Calif. 94015.

CAREER: U.S. Air Force, Wright-Patterson Air Force Base, Ohio, clerk-typist, 1954-55; National Music Camp, Interlochen, Mich., assistant publicity director, 1957; Carpenter and Harrington (attorneys), Ann Arbor, Mich., legal secretary, 1959; Bendix Systems Division, Ann Arbor,

Mich., technical editor, 1960-61. *Member:* Motor Racing Society, Women in Communications, Inc. (formerly Theta Sigma Phi).

WRITINGS: The Grand Prix Champions (novel), Bond-Parkhurst, 1973. Contributor to *Autoweek & Competition Press, San Francisco Chronicle, Literary Cavalcade,* and others.

WORK IN PROGRESS: Old Glory, a novel, completion expected in 1975; motor racing articles; research on biochronology, anti-intellectualism in the United States, individual and group tyranny, and "2,973 other interests."

SIDELIGHTS: Mary Heglar told *CA:* "I'm invariably asked: . . . How did you get into motor racing? Waaal, it's like this: I grew up in Ohio, under annual bombardments by the Indianapolis 500 hoopla. Over the years, my yearly knee-jerk attention to Indy became refined into a steady interest in grand prix. Parallel to this was my pursuit and practice of fiction writing. Quite suddenly one morning, I decided to combine the two passions of writing and racing, and *The Grand Prix Champions* was the result."

BIOGRAPHICAL/CRITICAL SOURCES: Tiffin Advertiser-Tribune, August 10, 1973; *Daly City Record,* October 17, 1973; *University of Michigan Mass Media Memo,* December, 1973.

* * *

HEIBER, Helmut 1924-

PERSONAL: Born February 22, 1924, in Leipzig, Germany; son of Otto and Emmy (Schrader) Heiber; married Ruth Matti, 1954; children: Sabine, Beatrice. *Education:* Freie Universitaet Berlin, Dr. phil., 1954. *Home:* Fontanestrasse 16, 8 Muenchen 81, Germany. *Office:* Institut fuer Zeitgeschichte, Leonrodstrasse 46b, D-8 Muenchen 19, Germany.

CAREER: Institut fuer Zeitgeschichte, Munich, Germany, research historian, 1954—. *Military service:* Wehrmacht, 1942-45, 1949.

WRITINGS: Adolf Hitler. Eine Biographie, Colloquium Verlag (Berlin), 1960, translation by Lawrence Wilson published as *Adolf Hitler: A Short Biography,* Otto Wolff (London), 1961; (editor) *Das Tagebuch von Joseph Goebbels 1925/26,* Deutsche Verlags-Anstalt (Stuttgart), 1960, translation by Oliver Watson published as *The Early Goebbels Diaries: The Journal of Joseph Goebbels from 1925-1926,* Weidenfeld & Nicolson, 1962, published as *The Early Goebbels Diaries, 1925-1926,* Praeger, 1963; *Joseph Goebbels,* Colloquium Verlag, 1962, translation by John K. Dickinson published as *Goebbels,* Hawthorn, 1972; (editor) *Hitlers Lagebesprechungen. Die Protokollfragmente seiner militaerischen Konferenzen 1942-1945* (title means "The Protocol Fragments of Hitler's Military Conferences"), Deutsche Verlags-Anstalt, 1962; (compiler) *Die Katakombe wird geschlossen* (title means "The Catacomb Is Closed"), Scherz Verlag (Munich), 1966; *Walter Frank und sein Reichsinstitut fuer Geschichte des neuen Deutschlands* (title means "Walter Frank and His Reich Institute for the History of the New Germany"), Deutsche Verlags-Anstalt, 1966; *Die Republik von Weimar,* Deutscher Taschenbuch Verlag (Munich), 1966; (editor) Heinrich Himmler, *Reichsfuehrer! Briefe an und von Himmler* (title means "Letters to and by Heinrich Himmler"), Deutsche Verlags-Anstalt, 1968; (editor with Hildegard von Kotze) *Facsimile Querschnitt durch das Schwarze Corps,* Scherz Verlag, 1968; (editor) *Goebbels-Reden,* Droste Verlag (Duesseldorf), Volume I: *1932-1939,* 1971, Volume II: *1939-1945,* 1972. Editor with Martin Brozat of series "Weltgeschichte des 20. Jahrhunderts" (title means "World History of the 20th Century"), Deutscher Taschenbuch Verlag, 1966—.

WORK IN PROGRESS: Hochschulpolitik im Dritten Reich (title means "The Universities in the Third Reich").

* * *

HEIN, Piet 1905-
(Kumbel)

PERSONAL: Born December 16, 1905, in Copenhagen, Denmark; emigrated to England in 1969; son of Hjalmar (an engineer) and Estrid (Octavius) Hein; married Gerd Ericson, 1955 (died, 1968); children: Jan, Anders, Lars, Jotun, Hugo. *Education:* Studied at Niels Bohr Institute, University of Copenhagen, and Technical University of Denmark; also attended private art schools and Royal Swedish Academy of Fine Arts. *Home:* "Heatherfield," Park Rd., Stoke Poges, Buckinghamshire, England.

CAREER: Scientist, inventor, author. Former guest playwright at Royal Theatre, Copenhagen. *Awards, honors:* Aarestrup medal from Government of Denmark, 1969, for poetry; Alexander Graham Bell Silver Bell, Boston University, 1968; named Knight of Norwegian Artists' Society, 1969; Golden Wreath from Students of Denmark, 1970; D.H.L., Yale University, 1972. *Member:* Frensham Group, International P.E.N.

WRITINGS: (Under pseudonym Kumbel) *Gruk 1-20* (poems), Politikens Forlag, 1940-63; *Vers i verdensrummet* (poems; title means "Poetry in Space"), Gyldendal, 1941; *Den tiende Muse* (poems; title means "The Loth Muse"), Gyldendal, 1941; *Man skal gaa paa jorden: Aforismer* (aphorisms; title means "You Are to Walk on Earth"), Gyldendal, 1944; *4 Digte under Sydkorset* (title means "4 Poems under the Southern Cross"), Gyldendal, 1945; *Helicopteren* (prose; title means "The Helicopter"), Gyldendal, 1947; *Vers af denne Verden* (title means "Poetry of This World"), Gyldendal, 1948; *Kumbels Foedselsdagskalender* (title means "Kumbel's Birthday Calendar"), Gyldendal, 1949.

Selv om den er gloende: Aforismer (aphorisms; title means "Although It's Glowing"), Gyldendal, 1950; *Kumbels Lyre* (selected grooks; title means "Kumbel's Lyre"), Gyldendal, 1950; (under pseudonym Kumbel) *Gruk,* Gyldendal, 1954; *Gruk, Esperanto Eldono* (title means "Grook Esperanto-Eldono"), Gyldendal, 1956.

Gruk fra alle Aarene I og II (title means "Grooks from All the Years, I and II"), Borgen, Volume I, 1960, Volume II, 1964; *Du skal plante et trae* (poems; title means "You Are to Plant a Tree"), Gyldendal, 1960; (under pseudonym Kumbel) *Gruk fra alle Aarene: et udvalg,* Gyldendal, 1960; *Husk at elske* (poems; title means "Remember to Love"), Gyldendal, 1962; *Vis Electrica* (essays), [Copenhagen], 1962; *Kilden og Krukken: Fabler og essays* (fables and essays; title means "The Well and Vessel"), Gyldendal, 1963.

Husk at leve (poems; title means "Remember to Live"), Borgen, 1966; (with Jens Arup) *Grooks,* M.I.T. Press, 1966; (with Arup) *Grooks,* Borgen, 1966, Doubleday, 1969; *Lad os blive mennesker: Udvalgte digte og gruk* (grooks and poems; title means "Let Us Become Humans"), Borgen, 1967; *Korte gruk,* Borgen, 1968; *Grooks II,* Borgen, 1968, American edition (with Arup), Doubleday, 1969; *I*

Folkemunde (short grooks; title means "To Be the Subject of Gossip"), Borgen, 1968; *Runaway Runes* (short grooks), Borgen, 1968; *Det Kraftens Ord* (short grooks; title means "A Word of Power"), Borgen, 1969.

Grooks III, Borgen, 1970, American edition (with Arup), Doubleday, 1971; (self-illustrated) *Til og af Piet Hein,* Multivers/Studenterforeningen, 1971; *Digte fra alle Aarene* (title means "Poems from All the Years"), Borgen, 1972; *Grooks IV,* Borgen, 1972, American edition (with Arup), Doubleday, 1973 (published in England as *Motes and Beams,* Basil Blackwell, 1973); *Grooks V,* Borgen, 1973, American edition (with Arup), Doubleday, 1973 (published in England as *Mist and Moonshine,* Basil Blackwell, 1973).

Author of plays for Royal Theatre in Copenhagen, including "Spirit Is to Remain," produced in 1968; writer for film, "The Industrial Country of Denmark," 1970; also writer for radio and television. Contributor to scientific journals and literary and popular periodicals.

SIDELIGHTS: Hein invented the short, aphoristic poetical form, the grook (*gruk* in Danish), during the Nazi occupation; published under a pseudonym during that time, they expressed democratic, humanistic aspects in a multimeaning form with serious perspectives behind humoristic surfaces. He has written about 7000 grooks in Danish and has translated many of them into English; he has also written grooks in English. Hein's poetry has sold about two and one-half million copies in Danish, a language spoken by scarcely five million people.

While shaping the new central point of Stockholm, Hein introduced into town planning, architecture, and designing the Super-Ellipse, a precise geometrical shape mediating between the circle and the square.

* * *

HELBLING, Robert E(ugene) 1923-

PERSONAL: Born May 6, 1923, in Lucerne, Switzerland; came to United States, 1948; naturalized citizen, 1954; son of Emil (a librarian) and Senta (Lamm) Helbling; married Suzanne O. Offinger (an assistant office manager of an insurance company), June 9, 1956. *Education:* Handelsschule, Lucerne, diplom, 1943; University of Utah, M.A., 1949; Columbia University, graduate study, 1951; Stanford University, Ph.D., 1958; University of California, Berkeley, postdoctoral study, 1961. *Politics:* Independent. *Home:* 3018 St. Mary's Circle, Salt Lake City, Utah 84108. *Office:* Department of Languages, University of Utah, Salt Lake City, Utah 84112.

CAREER: R.I. Geigy, Inc. Chemical Works, Basle, Switzerland, junior executive for foreign trade, 1945-47; University of Utah, Salt Lake City, instructor in French and German, 1950-57, assistant professor, 1958-61, associate professor, 1962-65, professor of French, German, and comparative literature, 1966—, chairman of department of languages, 1965—, coordinator of humanities program, 1958—, director of honors program, 1964-66. Occasional reader for Oxford University Press, New Directions Press, and Holt, Rinehart, Winston. Visiting associate professor, Long Island University, summer, 1962. *Military service:* Swiss Army, 1943-45. *Member:* Association of Departments of Foreign Languages (president, 1974—), Modern Language Association of America, American Association of Teachers of German, American Association of Teachers of French, American Association of University Professors (president of Salt Lake City Chapter, 1963-64), Phi Kappa Phi (president of local chapter, 1973-74), Phi Delta Phi, Phi Sigma Iota, Sigma Delta Pi, Delta Phi Alpha.

WRITINGS: (Editor with Andree M. L. Barnett) Pierre Daninos, *Les Carnets du Major Thompson* (title means "The Notebooks of Major Thompson"), Holt, 1959; (with Barnett) *Le Language de la France Moderne* (title means "The Language of Modern France"), Holt, 1961; (editor and author of essay) Friedrich Duerrenmatt, *Die Physiker,* Oxford University Press, 1965; (with Barnett) *L'Actualite Francaise* (title means "The Contemporary French Presence"), Holt, 1967; (editor and author of essay) *Heinrich von Kleist: Novellen und Aesthetische Schriften* (title means "Heinrich von Kleist: Novellas and Aesthetic Writings"), Oxford University Press, 1967; (with Morton Donner and Kenneth E. Eble) *The Intellectual Tradition of the West,* Scott, Foresman, Volume I: *From Hesiod to Calvin,* 1967, Volume II: *From Copernicus to Kafka,* 1968; (with Barnett) *Introduction au Francaise Actuel* (title means "Introduction to Contemporary French"), Holt, 1973; *Heinrich von Kleist: The Major Works,* New Directions, in press; (contributor) *Friedrich Duerrenmatt. Studien zu seinem Werk* (title means "Friedrich Duerrenmatt: Studies on His Work"), Lothar Stiehm (Heidelberg), in press.

* * *

HELLER,
See IRANEK-OSMECKI, Kazimierz

* * *

HELM, Everett 1913-

PERSONAL: Born July 17, 1913, in Minneapolis, Minn.; son of Clyde Burton (a businessman) and Alice (Stark) Helm; married Elizabeth Alber (a painter), August 31, 1955; children: Johanna (Mrs. John Pearson). *Education:* Carleton College, B.A., 1934; Harvard University, M.A., 1936, Ph.D., 1939; studied composition with F. G. Malipiero and Ralph Vaughan Williams, and musicology with Alfred Einstein. *Home:* I 31011 Asolo, Treviso, Italy.

CAREER: Longy School of Music, Cambridge, Mass., teacher of music, 1939-42; Mills College, Oakland, Calif., lecturer in music, 1942; Western College for Women, Oxford, Ohio, professor of music, 1943-44; University of Ljubliana, Ljubliana, Yugoslavia, Fulbright lecturer, 1966-68; composer, critic, and lecturer. Compositions include opera, "The Siege of Tottenburg," ballet music, and works for piano and string instruments. *Member:* American Musicological Society, P.E.N. *Awards, honors:* John Knowles Paine traveling fellowship from Harvard University, 1935.

WRITINGS: *Bela Bartok,* Rowohlt, 1965; *Composer, Performer, Public: A Study in Communication,* Olschki, 1970; *Bartok* (juvenile), Faber, 1971, Crowell, 1972; *Franz Liszt,* Rowohlt, 1972; *Tchaikowsky* (monograph), Rowohlt, in press. Contributor to *New Oxford History of Music,* to music journals, and to *Saturday Review, London Magazine, New York Times,* and other periodicals and newspapers. Editor-in-chief, *Musical America,* 1961-63.

SIDELIGHTS: Helm, who has lived in Italy since 1963, resided at other intervals in Brazil, France, England, Germany, and Yugoslavia. He says that he has been fascinated most of his life by languages (he speaks French, German, Italian, Spanish, and some Portuguese) and travel.

"If I have an avocation," he writes, "it is book collecting, and in the course of years, I have amassed a fairly formidable library that includes much practical material (reference works and the like) and a large collection of rare books and scores. I cannot explain rationally this collecting 'mania,' but since it gives me pleasure, I see no need to do so."

* * *

HELMS, Randel 1942-

PERSONAL: Born November 6, 1942, in Montgomery, Ala.; son of Loyce Virgil (a contractor) and Vernell Helms; married Penelope Palmer, August 1, 1964; children: Katherine. *Education:* University of California, Riverside, B.A. (magna cum laude), 1964; University of Washington, Seattle, Ph.D., 1968. *Home:* 19353 Bryant St., Northridge, Calif. 91324. *Office:* Department of English, University of California, Los Angeles, Calif. 90024.

CAREER: University of California, Los Angeles, assistant professor of English, 1968—. *Member:* Modern Language Association of America.

WRITINGS: *Tolkien's World,* Houghton, 1974. Contributor to literature journals.

WORK IN PROGRESS: *Tyger,* a novel based on the life of William Blake; *Intellectual Warfare,* a monograph on Blake's use of the Bible; *The Prophetic Book,* a monograph on Old Testament prophecy.

* * *

HEMPHILL, Paul 1936-

PERSONAL: Born February 18, 1936, in Birmingham, Ala.; son of Paul (a truck driver) and Velma Rebecca (an employee of the U.S. Government; maiden name, Nelson) Hemphill; married Susan Milliage Olive, September 23, 1961; children: Lisa, David, Molly. *Education:* Auburn University, B.A., 1959; Harvard University, graduate study, 1968-69. *Home address:* P. O. Box 1872, St. Simons Island, Ga. 31522. *Agent:* Sterling Lord Agency, 660 Madison Ave., New York, N.Y. 10021.

CAREER: Sports writer for newspapers in Birmingham, Ala., Augusta, Ga., and Tampa, Fla., 1958-64; *Atlanta Journal,* Atlanta, Ga., columnist, 1964-69; free-lance writer, 1969—. Visiting lecturer at University of Georgia, fall, 1973. *Military service:* Alabama Air National Guard, active duty, 1961-62; served in France. *Awards, honors:* Literary achievement award from Georgia Writers Association, 1970, for *The Nashville Sound.*

WRITINGS: *The Nashville Sound: Bright Lights and Country Music,* Simon & Schuster, 1970; (with Ivan Allen, Jr.) *Mayor: Notes on the Sixties,* Simon & Schuster, 1971; *The Good Old Boys,* Simon & Schuster, 1974. Author of columns appearing in *Sport* and *Country Music.* Contributor to *New York Times Sunday Magazine,* and to national periodicals, including *Life, Playboy, Cosmopolitan, Mademoiselle, Atlantic Monthly,* and *True.*

WORK IN PROGRESS: *Long Gone,* a novel about minor league baseball; a book about George and Cornelia Wallace.

SIDELIGHTS: Hemphill says he is "a committed 'Southern writer.' The South is all I know—my blood, my instincts, my viewpoint. I also believe a writer is giving a more honest view of the world if he lives and works Out There, going to the typewriter every day, more or less writing memos to Shakespeare and Cervantes and Dickens and the rest, telling them what went on around here yesterday. I have turned down chances to work in other places, for more money, because the South is where I belong."

* * *

HEMSCHEMEYER, Judith 1935-

PERSONAL: Born August 7, 1935, in Sheboygan, Wis.; daughter of Bernard A. and Aurelia (Miller) Hemschemeyer; married Morton S. Rosenfeld (a film teacher), August 12, 1958; children: Stephanie, David. *Education:* University of Wisconsin, B.A., 1957, M.A., 1959; University of Grenoble, graduate study, 1957-58. *Politics:* Democratic. *Home:* 803 Fourth Ave., Salt Lake City, Utah 84103. *Office:* Department of English, University of Utah, Salt Lake City, Utah 84112.

CAREER: *Time,* New York, N.Y., copy editor, 1960-62; University of Utah, Salt Lake City, associate instructor, 1972-74, adjunct associate professor of English, 1974—. *Member:* Phi Beta Kappa.

WRITINGS: *Trudie and the Milch Cow* (juvenile), Random House, 1967; *I Remember the Room Was Filled with Light,* Wesleyan University Press, 1973.

WORK IN PROGRESS: Poems; a collection of short stories.

AVOCATIONAL INTERESTS: Skiing, tennis.

* * *

HENDRICKS, William Lawrence 1929-

PERSONAL: Born March 10, 1929, in Butte, Mont.; married Lois Ann Lindsey (a teacher), June 4, 1951; children: John Lawrence. *Education:* Oklahoma Baptist University, A.B., 1951; Southwestern Baptist Theological Seminary, B.D., 1954, Th.D., 1958; University of Chicago, M.A., 1965, Ph.D., 1972. *Politics:* Democrat. *Home:* 4009 South Dr., Fort Worth, Tex. 76122. *Office:* Southwestern Baptist Theological Seminary, P.O. Box 22000, Fort Worth, Tex. 76122.

CAREER: Pastor of Southern Baptist churches in Shawnee, Okla., and Dodson, Tex., 1954-57; Southwestern Baptist Theological Seminary, Fort Worth, Tex., assistant professor, 1957-59, associate professor, 1959-68, professor of theology, 1968—. Former counselor of boys, Buckner Orphans Home, Dallas. *Member:* American Academy of Religion, Society of Biblical Literature. *Awards, honors:* American Association of Theological Schools study grant, 1964.

WRITINGS: (Contributor) H. C. Brown, editor, *Southwestern Sermons,* Broadman, 1960; *The Letters of John,* Convention Press, 1970; (contributor) Clifford Ingle, editor, *Children and Conversion,* Broadman, 1970; *Resource Unlimited,* Stewardship Commission of Southern Baptist Convention, 1972. Editor, *Southwestern Journal of Theology,* 1965, 1970.

* * *

HENDRICKSON, Robert 1933-

PERSONAL: Born August 24, 1933, in Far Rockaway, N.Y.; son of Oscar F. (a civil engineer) and Eunice (a teacher; maiden name, Tierney) Hendrickson; married Marilyn Maggio (a reading teacher), August 29, 1954; children: Robert Lawrence, Brian, Karen, Lauren, Erik. *Education:* Adelphi University, A.B. (cum laude), 1957. *Politics:* Independent. *Home:* 2417 Cornaga Ave., Far Rockaway, N.Y. 11691.

CAREER: Free-lance writer. *Military service:* U.S. Army, 1952-54; served in Korea. *Member:* Phi Alpha Theta, Pi Gamma Mu. *Awards, honors:* Ford Foundation fellowship, 1958; Macdowell Colony fellowship, 1973.

WRITINGS: Human Words, Chilton, 1972; (contributor) *The People's Almanac,* Doubleday, in press. Contributor to *New York Times Gardening Book;* contributor of about one thousand articles, stories, and poems to literary quarterlies and general magazines.

WORK IN PROGRESS: A novel and a book of poems; a book on gourmet aphrodisiac foods, for Chilton; a book on crime in America.

AVOCATIONAL INTERESTS: Gardening, philology, travel, ecology, sports.

* * *

HENDRIE, Don(ald Franz), Jr. 1942-

PERSONAL: Born May 28, 1942, in Plainfield, N.J.; son of Donald Franz (a lawyer) and Helen Marie (Pennywitt) Hendrie; married Susan Niebling (a painter), June 17, 1966; children: Nathan Zed, Arden Wing. *Education:* Tulane University, student, 1961-62; Stanford University, B.A., 1965; State University of Iowa, M.F.A., 1967. *Politics:* "Ironic socialist." *Home:* 57 Ferry St., South Hadley, Mass. 01075. *Agent:* Ellen Levine, Curtis Brown Ltd., 60 East 56th St., New York, N.Y. 10022. *Office:* Department of English, Mount Holyoke College, South Hadley, Mass. 01075.

CAREER: Nathaniel Hawthorne College, Antrim, N.H., instructor in English, 1967-69; Mount Holyoke College, South Hadley, Mass., instructor, 1970-71, assistant professor of English, 1971—. *Member:* American Association of University Professors.

WRITINGS: Boomkitchwatt (novel), John Muir, 1973. Contributor of short stories, articles, and reviews to *Lynx, Mercury Book Review, Silo 11, Iowa Review, Confluence,* and *Self-Publishing Writer.*

WORK IN PROGRESS: Blount's Anvil, a novel.

SIDELIGHTS: Hendrie presently lives in Mexico.

* * *

HENIG, Ruth B(eatrice) 1943-

PERSONAL: Born October 11, 1943, in Leicester, England; married Stanley Henig (a lecturer and writer), March 27, 1966; children: Simon Antony, Harold David. *Education:* Bedford College, London, B.A. (first class honors), 1965. *Politics:* British Labour Party. *Religion:* Jewish. *Home:* 10 Yealand Dr., Lancaster, England. *Office:* Department of History, University of Lancaster, Lancaster, England.

CAREER: University of Lancaster, Lancaster, England, lecturer in history, 1968—. *Member:* Royal Institute of International Affairs (associate member).

WRITINGS: (Editor) *League of Nations,* Barnes & Noble, 1973.

WORK IN PROGRESS: Research for books on British attitudes and policies towards the League of Nations, and on the British Foreign Office and the League of Nations; articles on British foreign policy, 1919-1939.

AVOCATIONAL INTERESTS: Politics, English football, contract and duplicate bridge.

HENRY, Harriet
See De STEUCH, Harriet Henry

* * *

HENRY, James S(helburne) 1950-

PERSONAL: Born February 26, 1950, in Minneapolis, Minn.; son of Evans James (a certified public accountant) and Evelyn (Shelburne) Henry. *Education:* Harvard University, A.B. (magna cum laude), 1972, J.D., 1975, doctoral study, 1975—. *Politics:* Conservative Socialist. *Religion:* Episcopalian. *Home address:* Route 1, Winona, Minn. 55987.

CAREER: Center for the Study of Responsive Law, Washington, D.C., writer and researcher, summers, 1970-73. *Member:* Phi Beta Kappa, Signet Society. *Awards, honors:* Danforth Foundation fellowship, 1972-77.

WRITINGS: (With Paul Starr) *The Discarded Army,* Grossman, 1974.

WORK IN PROGRESS: A film script about the Vietnam war; an essay on the origins of liberalism; a study of unemployment.

SIDELIGHTS: Henry has spent three summers as a member of "Nader's Raiders."

* * *

HERBERT, David Thomas 1935-

PERSONAL: Born December 24, 1935, in Rhondda, Wales; son of Trevor John (a traffic superintendent) and Megan (Pearce) Herbert; married Tonwen Maddock, December 30, 1967; children: David Aled, Nia Wyn. *Education:* University College of Swansea, University of Wales, B.A., 1959; University of Birmingham, Ph.D., 1964. *Home:* 119 Saundersway, Sketty, Swansea, Glamorgan, Wales. *Office:* Department of Geography, University College of Swansea, University of Wales, Swansea, Glamorgan, Wales.

CAREER: University of Wales, University College of Swansea, Swansea, Glamorgan, senior lecturer in geography, 1965—, sub-dean of faculty of economic-social studies, 1971-75. *Member:* Institute of British Geographers, Census Research Group (secretary, 1971—).

WRITINGS: Urban Geography: A Social Perspective, David & Charles, 1972, Praeger, 1973. Contributor of about thirty articles to professional journals.

WORK IN PROGRESS: Research in intra-urban residential mobility and in juvenile delinquency and urban environments.

* * *

HERBRAND, Jan(ice M.) 1931-

PERSONAL: Born October 18, 1931, in Osage, Iowa; daughter of Henry Albert and Laura Beatrice (Lonie) McRorie; married Nickolas Gayhart Herbrand (a welder), April 11, 1953; children: Susan, Randall, Shelly, Nickolas. *Education:* Attended College of Puget Sound (now University of Puget Sound), 1949-51. *Politics:* Independent. *Religion:* Methodist. *Home:* 8016 South Fawcett, Tacoma, Wash. 98408.

CAREER: Bookkeeper; Tacoma Public Library, Tacoma, Wash., part-time clerk, 1972—.

WRITINGS: Lost Heritage, Grosset, 1972; *The Altheimer Inheritance,* Warner Paperback Library, 1973.

WORK IN PROGRESS: A Gothic novel, *Dangerous House* (tentative title), for Warner Paperback Library.

* * *

HERITY, Michael 1929-

PERSONAL: Born May 29, 1929, in Donegal, Ireland. *Education:* University College, Dublin, B.A., 1957, M.A., 1960, Ph.D., 1966. *Office:* University College, National University of Ireland, Belfield, Dublin 4, Ireland.

CAREER: National University of Ireland, University College, Belfield, Dublin, lecturer in Celtic archaeology, 1961—. *Member:* Royal Society of Antiquaries of Ireland (member of council), Society of Antiquaries of London (fellow), Prehistoric Society (London; member of council).

WRITINGS: Irish Panage Graves, Barnes & Noble, 1974; (with George Eogan) *Ireland in Prehistory,* Routledge & Kegan Paul, in press. Contributor to *Journal of the Royal Society of Antiquaries of Ireland, Antiquaries Journal,* and *Ulster Journal of Archaeology.* Editor of *Journal of the Royal Society of Antiquaries of Ireland,* 1972.

WORK IN PROGRESS: The Irish Stone Age; A History of Irish Antiquarianism; Prehistoric Fields in Ireland.

* * *

HERMAN, Judith 1943-

PERSONAL: Born September 2, 1943, in Chicago, Ill.; daughter of Lewis (a writer, director, and producer) and Marguerite (a writer; maiden name, Shalett) Herman. *Education:* University of California at Los Angeles, B.A., 1966. *Home:* 10505 Hillhaven, Tujunga, Calif. 91042.

CAREER: Institute of Transportation and Traffic Engineering, University of California at Los Angeles, 1965-69, editor/librarian of Exit Ramp Project and editor of Analytical Models Project. *Awards, honors: The Cornucopia* was selected by American Institute of Graphic Arts as one of best books published in 1973.

WRITINGS: (Editor) G. R. Fisher and W. W. Mosher, Jr., *Application of Control Chart Techniques,* Institute of Transportation and Traffic Engineering, University of California at Los Angeles, 1968; (editor) *Analytical Models of Unidirectional Multi-Lane Traffic Flow: A Survey of the Literature,* System Development Corp., 1969; (with mother, Marguerite Shalett Herman) *The Cornucopia: Being a Kitchen Entertainment and Cookbook—1390-1899,* Harper, 1973. Also edited *An Extended Boltzman-type Statistical Model for Multi-level Traffic Flow,* by Juergen Pohl, 1969.

WORK IN PROGRESS: Additional research on kitchen entertainment and cooking.

AVOCATIONAL INTERESTS: History, social customs, and cooking.

* * *

HERMANN, John 1917-

PERSONAL: Born October 26, 1917, in Antigo, Wis.; son of John and Margaret (Boll) Hermann; married Margaret Freeling, July 30, 1942; children: Mary. *Education:* Carroll College, Waukesha, Wis., B.A., 1939; University of Wisconsin, M.A., 1950; University of Iowa, Ph.D., 1955. *Residence:* Long Beach, Calif. *Office:* Department of English, California State University, Long Beach, Calif. 90804.

CAREER: Springfield Junior College, Springfield, Ill., instructor in English, 1947-51; University of Iowa, Iowa City, instructor in English, 1951-55; California State University, Long Beach, assistant professor, 1955-59, associate professor, 1959-62, professor of English, 1962—. *Military service:* U.S. Army, 1942-45; served in European theatre.

WRITINGS: (Contributor) W. F. Belcher and J. W. Lee, editors, *J. D. Salinger and the Critics,* Wadsworth, 1962; (contributor) Marvin Laser and Norman Fruman, editors, *Salinger and His Critics,* Odyssey, 1963; (contributor) R. W. Royce Adams, editor, *Developing Reading Flexibility,* Holt, 1971; *An Agreement Between Us* (short stories), University of Missouri Press, 1973.

Work is anthologized in *Best American Short Stories,* edited by Martha Foley, Houghton, 1963. Contributor of short stories and articles to magazines, including *Kenyon Review, Virginia Quarterly Review, Northwest Review, Perspective, North American Review, Seneca Review,* and *Studies in Short Fiction.*

* * *

HERON, Laurence Tunstall 1902-

PERSONAL: Born July 4, 1902, in Carrollton, Ill.; son of Carl Clark (a packinghouse executive) and Marion (a teacher; maiden name, Wright) Heron; married Frances Dunlap (a writer), June 17, 1931; children: Marion Susan (Mrs. Paul A. Wollam), Alfred Tunstall, Frances E., Donald Meriwether (deceased). *Education:* University of Illinois, A.B., 1924; Washington University, St. Louis, Mo., A.M., 1925; Syracuse University, further graduate study, 1925-26. *Politics:* Democrat. *Religion:* Presbyterian. *Home:* 18520 Stewart Ave., Homewood, Ill. 60430.

CAREER: St. Louis Globe-Democrat, St. Louis, Mo., reporter, 1926-28, copy editor, 1928-33, telegraph editor, 1933; *Chicago Tribune,* Chicago, Ill., copy editor, 1933-37, section editor, 1937-43, editor of *Chicago Overseas Tribune,* 1943-46, section editor, 1946-67, author of column "Retirement River," 1967-68. *Military service:* U.S. Army Reserve, 1929-39; became second lieutenant. *Member:* American Society of Church History, Spiritual Frontiers Fellowship (member of board of directors, 1970-73), Association for Research and Enlightenment, South Suburban Genealogical and Historical Society.

WRITINGS: ESP in the Bible, Doubleday, 1974. Author of handbooks and booklets. Contributor of articles and reviews to magazines. Editor of *Classified Journal,* 1927-29; editor of *Gate Way* (of Spiritual Frontiers Fellowship), 1962-68.

WORK IN PROGRESS: Further study of psychic phenomena in the Bible.

SIDELIGHTS: The death of his son in 1959 steered Heron's interest into psychic phenomena and to investigation of prayer, spiritual healing, and evidences of immortality in the ancient Judaeo-Christian tradition.

* * *

HERRICK, Jean Mellin
See MELLIN, Jeanne

* * *

HERRICK, Neal Q(uentin) 1927-

PERSONAL: Born September 22, 1927, in Lynn, Mass.; son of Neal D. and Irma (Carr) Herrick; married Jeanne P. Morrissey, April 5, 1952 (divorced, 1972); children: Peter

F., Kenneth M., Julia A., Elizabeth K. *Education:* University of New Hampshire, B.A., 1953. *Politics:* Democrat. *Home:* 134 Preston Rd., Columbus, Ohio 43209. *Office:* Governor's Business and Employment Council, 8 East Long St., Columbus, Ohio 43215.

CAREER: Before 1953, worked as railroad lineman, salesman, construction worker, clerk, automobile worker, reporter, and since as workmen's compensation claims examiner, personnel specialist, auditor, and management analyst; W.E. Upjohn Institute for Employment Research, Washington, D.C., visiting fellow, 1970-71; U.S. Department of Labor, Washington, D.C., director of planning, 1972-73; Academy for Contemporary Problems, Columbus, Ohio, senior fellow, 1973-74; Governor's Business and Employment Council, Columbus, Ohio, consultant, 1974—. Adjunct professor at Ohio State University; director of Ohio Quality of Work Project. *Military service:* U.S. Navy, 1945-47. U.S. Army, 1953-56; became first lieutenant. *Member:* Industrial Relations Research Association, Ohio Citizens Council.

WRITINGS: (With Harold Sheppard) *Where Have All the Robots Gone?,* Free Press, 1972. Contributor to *Monthly Labor Review, Manpower, Worker Alienation,* and *Working Papers.*

WORK IN PROGRESS: A project to determine the human and economic consequences of improving the quality of work, completion expected within three to five years.

* * *

HERVE, Jean-Luc
See HUMBARACI, D(emir) Arslan

* * *

HEUVELMANS, Martin 1903-

PERSONAL: Born January 14, 1903, in Antwerp, Belgium; came to United States in 1911, naturalized in 1915; son of Antion and Marie (Noyez) Heuvelmans; married Alice Juschke, March 1, 1924; children: Cornell (deceased), Renee Heuvelmans Capas, Martha Heuvelmans Lapetina. *Education:* Attended public schools in Hoboken, N.J., and Brooklyn, N.Y. *Home address:* Box 34, 3500 South Kanner Hwy., Stuart, Fla. 33494.

CAREER: Owner of concrete materials business, Long Island, N.Y., 1924-26; built and operated Westbury Sand and Gravel Co., 1925-31; Louis Dreyfus & Co., New York, N.Y., assistant Atlantic Coast superintendent, 1932-36, Atlantic Coast superintendent, 1936-40; Army Transportation Corps, New York Port of Embarkation, Staten Island, stevedore superintendent, 1941-44; Queens Hub Realty Co., Queens, N.Y., co-owner and broker, 1946-54; Standard Waterproofing Corp., New York, N.Y., vice-president, 1955-57. Has lectured at Florida Institute of Technology, University of Florida, and Mercer University. Consultant on logistics to Pentagon during World War II.

WRITINGS: *Cargo Deadweight Distribution,* Cornell Maritime, 1942; *The River Killers,* Stackpole, 1974. Occasional contributor to *Stuart News,* Stuart, Fla.

WORK IN PROGRESS: Continued research on Civil Works Branch of U.S. Army Corps of Engineers, and efforts toward seeking its abolition.

SIDELIGHTS: Heuvelmans told *CA:* "I settled at Stuart, Florida, to enjoy a retirement way of life, which I soon discovered was systematically being destroyed by the Civil Works Branch of the Army Corps of Engineers. Inquiry grew into investigation, which soon disclosed perfidy and deceit. . . . Inquiry into other states soon disclosed the environmental destructions by the Corps were nationwide. *The River Killers* was the inevitable outcome . . . it opens new vistas for the examination of the need for the abolishment of the Corps, which is what *The River Killers* urges upon the American voter." Heuvelmans' research papers are collected at Indian River Junior College, Ft. Pierce, Fla.

AVOCATIONAL INTERESTS: Fishing, raising orchids.

* * *

HEYER, Georgette 1902-1974

August 16, 1902—July 4, 1974; British author of historical and detective novels. Obituaries: *New York Times,* July 6, 1974; *Washington Post,* July 6, 1974; *Publishers Weekly,* July 29, 1974.

* * *

HIBBS, Douglas A(lbert), Jr. 1944-

PERSONAL: Born July 17, 1944, in Miami Beach, Fla.; son of Douglas Albert and Lillian (Carter) Hibbs; married Giustina Mastrangelo (a teacher), October 31, 1965; children: Christina. *Education:* Southern Connecticut State College, B.A. (with honors), 1966; University of Wisconsin, M.A., 1968, Ph.D., 1972. *Home:* 60 Highland Ave., Cambridge, Mass. 02139. *Office:* Massachusetts Institute of Technology, E53-402, Cambridge, Mass. 02139.

CAREER: Massachusetts Institute of Technology, Cambridge, instructor, 1970-71, assistant professor of political science, 1971—. Consultant to John Wiley & Sons, Northwestern University Press, National Science Foundation. *Member:* American Political Science Association, American Sociological Association, American Statistical Association, American Economic Association, Econometric Society, American Association for the Advancement of Science. *Awards, honors:* Ford Foundation research grant for Center for International Studies, 1971; National Science Foundation research grant, 1972; National Institute of Mental Health research grant, 1974.

WRITINGS: *Mass Political Violence: A Cross-National Causal Analysis,* Wiley, 1973; (contributor) H. L. Costner, editor, *Sociological Methodology: 1973-1974,* Jossey-Bass, 1974. Consultant-reader for *Political Methodology, Journal of Conflict Resolution, Journal of Interdisciplinary History, American Journal of Political Science;* member of panel of consultants for *Comparative Political Studies.*

* * *

HIGNETT, Sean 1934-

PERSONAL: Born September 18, 1934, in Birkenhead, Cheshire, England; son of George Edward (a longshoreman) and Isabelle (Morris) Hignett; married Josephine Lewington (a social historian), September 17, 1957; children: Sara Louise, Sean Daniel Crispin. *Education:* St. Peter's College, Oxford, M.A. (honors), 1956, Diploma in Statistics, 1961. *Politics:* "Suspicious of politicians of all crews". *Religion:* None. *Home:* Brunstane House, Edinburgh 15, Scotland. *Agent:* Peter Matson, Harold Matson, Inc., 22 East 40th St., New York, N.Y. 10016. *Office:* Moray House College of Education, Edinburgh 8, Scotland.

CAREER: Assistant grammar school teacher in Oxfordshire, England, 1958-60; Moray House College, Edinburgh, Scotland, lecturer in education, 1961—. *Member:* Association of Lecturers in Colleges of Education (Scotland), Writer's Guild of Great Britain. *Awards, honors:* D. H. Lawrence fellowship from University of New Mexico, 1970.

WRITINGS—Novels: *A Picture to Hang on the Wall,* Coward, 1966; *A Cut Loaf,* M. Joseph, 1971; (contributor) Alan MacLean, editor, *Winter's Tales 16,* Macmillan (London), 1970, St. Martin's, 1971.

Plays: "Jack of Spades" (musical; three acts), first produced in Liverpool at Everyman Theatre, September, 1965; "Come Holy Ghost, Creator, Come" (one-act), first produced in Edinburgh at Traverse Theatre, October, 1972; "Allotment" (one-act), first produced in Edinburgh at Pool Theatre, July, 1973.

Also author of television and film scripts. Contributor to *Daily Telegraph Magazine* (London).

WORK IN PROGRESS: Scripts, plays, and novels on a variety of subjects.

* * *

HIGSON, James D(oran) 1925-

PERSONAL: Born June 5, 1925, in Los Angeles, Calif.; son of Alfred R. and Frances L. (Doran) Higson; married Susanne House (an interior decorator), March 21, 1953. *Education:* University of California at Los Angeles, B.A., 1950; Harvard University, graduate study, 1950-51. *Home and office:* 19 Bay Island, Newport Beach, Calif. 92661.

CAREER: Musical director and arranger; KHJ-TV, Los Angeles, Calif., executive, 1952-59; builder and real estate investor in Newport Beach, Calif., 1961—.

WRITINGS: Higson's Home Building Guide, Nash Publishing, 1972; *Higson's Home Buying Guide,* Nash Publishing, 1973.

WORK IN PROGRESS: Higson's Energy-Wise Housing Guide; foreign travel guides.

AVOCATIONAL INTERESTS: Music, including playing piano, arranging, and composing; travel.

* * *

HILL, Archibald A(nderson) 1902-

PERSONAL: Born July 5, 1902, in New York, N.Y.; son of Archibald Alexander (a social worker) and Mary Dorsey (a teacher; maiden name, Anderson) Hill; married Muriel Louise Byard, August 27, 1928. *Education:* Pomona College, A.B., 1923; Stanford University, M.A., 1924; Yale University, Ph.D., 1927. *Politics:* Liberal Democrat. *Religion:* "Not regular churchgoer." *Home:* 3403 Mount Bonnell Dr., Austin, Tex. 78731. *Office:* 513 Calhoun Hall, Box 8120, University of Texas, Austin, Tex. 78712.

CAREER: University of Michigan, Ann Arbor, instructor, 1926-29, assistant professor of English, 1929-30; University of Virginia, Charlottesville, associate professor, 1930-39, professor of English philology, 1939-50, professor of English language, 1950-53; Georgetown University, Washington, D.C., vice-director of Institute of Languages and Linguistics, 1953-55; University of Texas, Austin, professor of English and linguistics, 1955-72, professor emeritus, 1972—. *Military service:* U.S. Naval Reserve, active duty, 1942-46; became commander. *Member:* Linguistic Society of America (secretary-treasurer, 1951-68; president, 1969), Modern Language Association of America, American Anthropological Association, American Association for the Advancement of Science, Linguistic Association of the Southwest (president, 1973), Phi Beta Kappa.

WRITINGS: (Editor and contributor) *Humanistic Studies in Honor of John Calvin Metcalf,* University of Virginia, 1941; *Introduction to Linguistic Structures: From Sound to Sentence in English,* Harcourt, 1958; *Essays in Literary Analysis* (collection of essays for student use), privately printed, 1965; (editor, author of preface, and contributor) *Linguistics Today* (based on Voice of America "Forum" series), Voice of America, 1969 (distributed overseas as *Linguistics: Voice of America Forum Lectures*); (editor with E. Bagby Atwood, and contributor) *Studies in Language, Literature, and Culture of the Middle Ages and Later* (volume in honor of Rudolph Willard), University of Texas Press, 1969.

Contributor: William A. Parker, editor, *Understanding Other Cultures,* American Council of Learned Societies, 1954; William C. Doster, editor, *First Perspectives on Language,* American Book Co., 1963; J. H. Campbell and H. W. Helper, editors, *Dimensions in Communication,* Wadsworth, 1963; Harold B. Allen, editor, *Applied English Linguistics,* 2nd edition (Hill did not contribute to earlier edition), Appleton, 1964; Joseph Michel, editor, *Foreign Language Teaching* (anthology), Macmillan, 1965; Seymour Chatman and Samuel Levin, editors, *Essays on the Language of Literature,* Houghton, 1967; Arthur J. Bronstein, Claude L. Shaver, and G. J. Stevens, editors, *Essays in Honor of Claude M. Wise,* Speech Association of America, 1970; Roman Jakobson and Shigeo Kawamoto, editors, *Studies in General and Oriental Linguistics Presented to Shiro Hatori,* [Tokyo], 1970; Juanita V. Williamson and Virginia M. Burke, editors, *A Various Language: Perspectives on American Dialects,* Holt, 1971; Tristano Bolelli, editor, *Linguistica Generale: Structuralismo, Linguistica Storica,* Nistri-Lischi, 1971.

Writer of intensive course in English for adults, published in *ELEC English Course,* Part I, English Language Education Commission, [Tokyo], 1961, published in Chinese edition as *The New Linguistic Method: Drill Materials and Instructors Handbook,* edited, annotated and translated by Paul Lin and Charles Tang, University of Texas and Taiwan Normal University, 1964, published as *Oral Approach to English* (with Japanese translation), two volumes, English Language Education Commission, 1965. Writer of other course materials published by English Language Education Commission and included in *Applied Linguistics and the Teaching of English: Selected Articles from ELEC Publications,* 1970. Contributor of articles, essays, and reviews to learned journals, 1931—.

WORK IN PROGRESS: Articles for various festschrift volumes.

* * *

HILL, Pamela 1920-

PERSONAL: Born November 26, 1920, in Nairobi, Kenya; daughter of Harold John Edward (a mining engineer) and Jean Evelyn Napier (Davidson) Hill. *Education:* Glasgow School of Art, D.A., 1943; Glasgow University, B.Sc. equiv., 1952. *Religion:* Episcopalian. *Residence:* Scotland. *Agent:* Winant, Towers Ltd., 14 Cliffords Inn, London EC4A 1DA, England.

CAREER: Has worked variously as a pottery and biology

teacher in Glasgow, Edinburgh, and London, 1958-74, and as a mink farmer in Galloway, Scotland, 1965-70; novelist.

WRITINGS—Novels: *The King's Vixen,* Putnam, 1954 (published in England as *Flaming Janet: A Lady of Galloway,* Chatto & Windus, 1954); *The Crown and the Shadow: The Story of Francoise d'Aubigne, Marquise de Maintenon,* Putnam, 1955 (published in England as *Shadow of Palaces: The Story of Francoise d'Aubigne, Marquise de Maintenon,* Chatto & Windus, 1955); *Marjorie of Scotland,* Putnam, 1956; *Here Lies Margot,* Chatto & Windus, 1957, Putnam, 1958; *Maddalena,* Cassell, 1963; *Forget Not Ariadne,* Cassell, 1965, Barnes, 1967; *Julia,* Cassell, 1967; *The Devil of Aske,* St. Martin's, 1973; *The Malvie Inheritance,* St. Martin's, 1973; *The Incumbent,* St. Martin's, 1974; *Whitton's Folly,* St. Martin's, in press.

WORK IN PROGRESS: Norah Stroyan, a gothic tale; *Othello Remembers,* a fictionalized life of Prince Rupert.

* * *

HILL, W. M.
See DODD, Edward Howard, Jr.

* * *

HILLERT, Margaret 1920-

PERSONAL: Born January 22, 1920, in Saginaw, Mich.; daughter of Edward Carl (a tool and die maker) and A. Ilva (Sproull) Hillert. *Education:* Bay City Junior College, A.A., 1941; University of Michigan, R.N., 1944; Wayne University (now Wayne State University), A.B., 1948. *Residence:* Berkley, Mich. *Office:* 815 East Farnum, Royal Oak, Mich. 48067.

CAREER: Primary school teacher in public schools of Royal Oak, Mich., 1948—. Poet and writer of children's books. *Member:* International League of Children's Poets, Society of Children's Book Writers, Poetry Society of Michigan, Detroit Women Writers. *Awards, honors:* Numerous awards for poems from Poetry Society Society of Michigan.

WRITINGS—Children's Poetry: *Farther Than Far,* Follett, 1969; *I Like to Live in the City,* Golden Books, 1970; *Who Comes to Your House?,* Golden Books, 1973.

Children's books; all published by Follett: *The Birthday Car,* 1966; *The Little Runaway,* 1966; *The Yellow Boat,* 1966; *The Snow Baby,* 1969; *Circus Fun,* 1969; *A House for Little Red,* 1970; *Little Puff,* 1973.

Children's stories retold; all published by Follett: *The Funny Baby,* 1963; *The Three Little Pigs,* 1963; *The Three Bears,* 1963; *The Three Goats,* 1963; *The Magic Beans,* 1966; *Cinderella at the Ball,* 1970.

Contributor of poems to *Horn Book, Christian Science Monitor, McCall's, Saturday Evening Post, Jack and Jill, Western Humanities Review, Poet Lore, Cricket,* and others.

WORK IN PROGRESS: Five original collections of poetry for children; three juvenile books.

BIOGRAPHICAL/CRITICAL SOURCES: J. R. LeMaster, editor, *Poets of the Midwest,* Young Publications, 1966; Lee B. Hopkins, *Pass the Poetry, Please,* Citation, 1972.

* * *

HILSENRATH, Edgar 1926-

PERSONAL: Born April 2, 1926, in Leipzig, Germany; came to United States, 1951; naturalized citizen, 1958; son of David (a businessman) and Anny (Hoenigsberg) Hilsenrath. *Education:* Attended primary and secondary school in Germany. *Religion:* Jewish. *Home:* 100 Fort Washington Ave., New York, N.Y. 10032. *Agent:* Maximilian Becker, 115 East 82nd St., New York, N.Y. 10028.

CAREER: Novelist. Left Germany for Rumania in 1938, to escape Nazi persecution, was interned in Rumania and put to forced labor; later freed by the Soviet Red Army, only to be arrested; escaped internment in a Soviet forced labor camp and fled to Palestine, arriving in 1945; worked at odd jobs and on several *kibbutzim;* traveled to France in 1947 and was reunited with his family.

WRITINGS: Nacht: Roman, Kindler, 1964, translation by Michael Roloff published as *Night,* Doubleday, 1966; *The Nazi and the Barber* (translated from German manuscript by Andrew White), Doubleday, 1971.

WORK IN PROGRESS: A third novel.

SIDELIGHTS: Hilsenrath told *CA:* "At the age of 14 I was the leader of the Zionist Youth Underground movement in Siret, Rumania. I had already written a novel, several short stories and plays, all of which I carried around with me throughout the war years. Before going to Palestine, I gave them to my mother for safekeeping. When she escaped from behind the Iron Curtain in 1947, my mother was ambushed in the woods at the Hungarian frontier by bandits, and all her belongings, including my manuscripts were stolen.

"In 1944 I made an unsuccessful attempt to escape from the ghetto in Moghilev-Podolsk. I was caught and sentenced to be shot. I stood facing the firing squad for about 10 minutes. Then the order to shoot was rescinded.

"In Palestine, in 1946, I was among the first pioneers who went to the Negev desert to plant trees in that barren territory. The British arrested me in a round up of an entire district in Tel Aviv (1947) and kept me for three days in the jail at Jaffa, but released me when it was established that I was not a member of a terrorist movement."

* * *

HIMMELFARB, Gertrude 1922-

PERSONAL: Born August 8, 1922, in New York, N.Y.; daughter of Max and Bertha (Lerner) Himmelfarb; married Irving Kristol (a professor and editor), January 18, 1942; children: William, Elizabeth. *Education:* Jewish Theological Seminary, student, 1939-42; Brooklyn College (now Brooklyn College of the City University of New York), B.A., 1942; University of Chicago, M.A., 1944, Ph.D., 1950; also studied at Girton College, Cambridge, 1946-47. *Office:* City University of New York, 33 West 42nd St., New York, N.Y. 10036.

CAREER: City University of New York, New York, N.Y., professor of history at Brooklyn College and Graduate School, 1965—. Member of Presidential Advisory Commission on Economic Role of Women; member of board of overseers of Hoover Institution on War, Revolution, and Peace (Stanford University). *Member:* American Academy of Arts and Sciences (fellow), Society of American Historians, Royal Historical Society (fellow). *Awards, honors:* American Association of University Women fellowship, 1951-52; American Philosophical Society fellowship, 1953-54; Guggenheim fellowships, 1955-56, 1957-58; Rockefeller Foundation grants, 1962-63, 1963-64; National Endowment for the Humanities senior fellowship, 1968-69;

Phi Beta Kappa visiting scholarship, 1972-73; American Council of Learned Societies fellowship, 1972-73.

WRITINGS: Lord Acton: A Study in Conscience and Politics, University of Chicago Press, 1952; *Darwin and the Darwinian Revolution,* Doubleday, 1959, revised edition, Norton, 1968; *Victorian Minds,* Knopf, 1968; *On Liberty and Liberalism,* Knopf, 1974.

Editor: Lord Acton, *Essays on Freedom and Power,* Free Press, 1948; Thomas R. Malthus, *On Population,* Modern Library, 1960; John Stuart Mill, *Essays on Politics and Culture,* Doubleday, 1962; John Stuart Mill, *On Liberty,* Penguin, 1974.

Contributor: Bernard Wishy and others, editors, *Chapters in Western Civilization,* Columbia University Press, 3rd edition (Himmelfarb was not included in earlier editions), 1962; R. B. Browne, editor, *The Burke-Paine Controversy,* Harcourt, 1963; Robin Winks, editor, *British Imperialism,* Holt, 1963; Leonard M. Marsak, editor, *The Rise of Science in Relation to Society,* Macmillan, 1964; Richard Herr and Harold T. Parker, editors, *Ideas in History: Essays in Honor of Louis Gottschalk,* Duke University Press, 1965; Donald N. Baker and G. W. Fasel, editors, *Landmarks in Western Culture,* Prentice-Hall, 1967; T. W. Wallbank and other editors, *Civilization Past and Present,* Scott Foresman, 6th edition (Himmelfarb was not included in earlier editions), 1969; James B. Conacher, editor, *The Emergence of British Parliamentary Democracy in the Nineteenth Century,* Wiley, 1971; Michael Wolff and H. J. Dyos, editors, *The Victorian City: Images and Realities,* Routledge & Kegan Paul, 1973.

Contributor to journals, including *Journal of Contemporary History, Victorian Studies, Journal of British Studies, Journal of Modern History, Commentary, Encounter,* and *Twentieth Century.* Member of editorial board of *Journal of British Studies, Jewish Social Studies,* and *Reviews in European History.*

* * *

HINNELLS, John R(ussell) 1941-

PERSONAL: Born August 27, 1941, in Derby, England; son of William and Lilian (Jackson) Hinnells; married Marianne Grace Bushell (a teacher), July 24, 1965; children: Mark Julian, Duncan Keith. *Education:* King's College, London, B.D., 1964, graduate study, 1965-67. *Politics:* Moderate. *Home:* 10 St. Brannock's Rd., Chorlton-cum-Hardy, Manchester 21, England. *Office:* Department of Comparative Religion, University of Manchester, Manchester M13 9PL, England.

CAREER: Teacher of art in Ambleside, England, 1960-61, of social studies in Burton-on-Trent, Staffordshire, England, 1964-65; University of Manchester, Manchester, England, lecturer in comparative religion, 1970—. *Member:* International Association for History of Religions, Society for Mithraic Studies (treasurer, 1971—), British Institute of Persian Studies, Society for Afghan Studies, New Testament Studies, Royal Asiatic Society (fellow), Shap Working Party (vice-chairman, 1969—).

WRITINGS: (Editor) *Comparative Religion in Education,* Oriel Press, 1970; (editor with E. J. Sharpe) *Hinduism,* Oriel Press, 1972, 2nd edition, Routledge & Kegan Paul, 1973; (editor with Sharpe) *Man and His Salvation,* Manchester University Press, 1973; *Persian Mythology,* Hamlyn, 1974; (editor) *Mithraic Studies,* Manchester University Press, 1974. Editor of series "Makers of New Worlds," Scribners. Contributor to *Numen, Religion,* and *Journal of K. R. Cama Oriental Institute.* Editorial secretary of *Religion,* 1970-72.

WORK IN PROGRESS: Zoroaster, Prophet of Ancient Iran, completion expected in 1975; *Mithraism,* a book on the Iranian background to the iconography of the Roman cult, 1976; *The Parsis of Bombay,* the history and religious and social developments of Zoroastrianism, 1980.

AVOCATIONAL INTERESTS: Soccer, gardening.

* * *

HINTON, John 1926-

PERSONAL: Born March 5, 1926, in London, England; son of Albert George and Winifred (Bray) Hinton; married Patricia Watkins, August 15, 1950; children: Ruth Frances, Peter John. *Education:* King's College Hospital Medical School, London, M.B., B.S., 1949, D.P.M., 1958, M.D., 1961; F.R.C.P., 1970; F.R.C.Psych. 1971. *Office:* Middlesex Hospital Medical School, London, England.

CAREER: Middlesex Hospital Medical School, London, England, professor of psychiatry, 1966—. *Military service:* British Army, Medical Corps, 1950-52; became captain. *Member:* Royal Society of Medicine (president, psychiatry section), Association of University Teachers of Psychiatry.

WRITINGS: Dying, Penguin, 1967, 2nd edition, 1972; (with Arnold Toynbee and others) *Man's Concern with Death,* Hodder & Stoughton,1968, McGraw, 1969. Contributor to medical journals.

WORK IN PROGRESS: Continued research in terminal care.

* * *

HIRSCH, Thomas L. 1931-

PERSONAL: Born August 11, 1931, in Lake Geneva, Wis.; son of Raymon Stephen and Ruth Ann Linn (Lucas) Hirsch; married Norma Joan Primmer, June 26, 1953; children: Catharine (Mrs. Duane Alyn Wilson), Nancy Ruth. *Education:* LaCrosse State University, B.A., 1959; Stout State University, M.A., 1961; University of Minnesota, Ph.D. candidate. *Religion:* United Methodist. *Home:* 4165 West Sixth St., Winona, Minn. 55987. *Office:* Department of Art, Winona State College, Johnson and Sanborn, Winona, Minn. 55987.

CAREER: High school teacher of mathematics in the public schools of Fort Atkinson, Wis., 1962-67; Winona State College, Winona, Minn., instructor in photography, 1967—. *Military service:* U.S. Navy, 1951-55.

WRITINGS: Puzzles for Pleasure and Leisure, Abelard, 1967; *More Puzzles for Pleasure and Leisure,* Abelard, 1974.

WORK IN PROGRESS: A group of peg-solitaire puzzles.

AVOCATIONAL INTERESTS: Exercising.

* * *

HIRSH, Marilyn 1944-

PERSONAL: Born January 1, 1944, in Chicago, Ill.; daughter of Eugene (a meat-market owner) and Rose (Warshell) Hirsh; married James Harris, November 18, 1973. *Education:* Carnegie-Mellon University, B.F.A., 1965; New York University, M.A., 1974. *Religion:* Jewish. *Home:* 1580 Third Ave., Apt. 6, New York, N.Y. 10028. *Agent:* Florence Alexander, 50 East 42nd St., New York, N.Y. 10016.

CAREER: Peace Corps volunteer teaching English and art in Nasik, India, 1965-67; writer and illustrator for Children's Book Trust, New Delhi, India, 1967; writer and illustrator of children's books, New York, N.Y., 1968—. Part-time teacher of art. *Awards, honors: The Pink Suit* was named to the Child Study Association's book list, 1970.

WRITINGS—Author and illustrator: *The Elephants and the Mice: A Panchatantra Story,* Children's Book Trust (New Delhi), 1967, American edition, (Junior Literary Guild selection), World Publishing, 1970; *Where Is Yonkela?,* Crown, 1969; *The Pink Suit,* Crown, 1970; (with Maya Narayan) *Leela and the Watermelon,* Crown, 1971; *How the World Got Its Color,* Crown, 1972; *George and the Goblins,* Crown, 1972; *Ben Goes into Business,* Holiday House, 1973; *Could Anything Be Worse?,* Holiday House, 1974.

Illustrator: Florence Adams, *Mushy Eggs,* Putnam, 1973; Tillie S. Pine and Joseph Levine, *The Polynesians Knew,* McGraw, 1974.

WORK IN PROGRESS: Illustrating a poem on Jean LaFitte by Carl Carmer for Harvey House.

SIDELIGHTS: Marilyn Hirsh writes: "India is a second home to me and my career in children's books also began there." She is studying towards a doctorate in the art history of India and taking Sanskrit.

* * *

HITT, William D(ee) 1929-

PERSONAL: Born February 18, 1929, in Lexington, Ky.; son of Sellers W. and Clyde (Barnes) Hitt; married Diane Umbaugh, January 26, 1957; children: Jennifer, Jodi, Julie, Jill. *Education:* University of Kentucky, B.A., 1951; Ohio State University, M.A., 1954, Ph.D., 1956. *Home:* 223 West Southington, Worthington, Ohio 43085. *Office:* Battelle Memorial Institute, 505 King Ave., Columbus, Ohio 43201.

CAREER: Battelle Memorial Institute, Columbus, Ohio, research psychologist, 1957-59, chief of Psychological Sciences Division, 1960-63, chief of Behavioral Sciences Division, 1964-70, director of Center for Improved Education, 1970—. *Military service:* U.S. Air Force, 1951-53. *Member:* American Psychological Association, Sigma Xi.

WRITINGS: Education as a Human Enterprise, Charles A. Jones Publishing, 1973.

WORK IN PROGRESS: Designing of a humanistic educational system.

* * *

HOBART, Billie 1935-

PERSONAL: Born April 19, 1935, in Pittsburgh, Penn.; daughter of Harold James (a welder) and Rose (Sladack) Billingsley; married Cott Hobart, July 20, 1957 (divorced, 1967); children: Rawson Warner. *Education:* University of California, Berkeley, B.A., 1967; Sonoma State College (now California State College), secondary teaching credential, 1969, M.A., 1972. *Home:* 207 Kent, Kentfield, Calif. 94904. *Agent:* John Poppy, 462 Laurel, San Anselmo, Calif. 94960. *Office:* Department of Communications, College of Marin, Kentfield, Calif. 94904.

CAREER: California State College-Sonoma, Rohnert Park, instructor in psychology, 1973-74; Marin Center of Parapsychology, San Rafael, Calif., instructor in innerspace, 1973—; College of Marin, Kentfield, Calif., instructor in communications, 1969—, co-ordinator of Innerspace Series, 1973-74. Lecturer on innerspace in San Francisco, Honolulu, Las Vegas. *Military service:* Women's Army Corps (WAC), 1953-55. *Member:* Artrium (founding member).

WRITINGS: The Expanded Task, privately printed, 1971; *Expansion,* Glencoe Press, 1972; *Natural Sweet Tooth Breakfast Dessert and Candy Cookbook,* Straight Arrow, 1974. Contributor to *Woman's Day* and *Great Escape.*

WORK IN PROGRESS: Companions: Communication with Non-physical Beings; Space-Making; Creative Vocabulary; Daughter of the Universe, a psychic novel; *Healthy Yankee Cookbook; Fulcrum,* a method of writing with a humanistic approach.

* * *

HOCKER, Karla
See HOECKER, Karla

* * *

HODES, Scott 1937-

PERSONAL: Born August 14, 1937, in Chicago, Ill.; son of Barnet (an attorney) and Eleanor (Cramer) Hodes; married Barbara P. Zisook, December 19, 1961; children: Brian, Valery. *Education:* University of Chicago, A.B., 1956; University of Michigan, J.D., 1959; Northwestern University, LL.M., 1963. *Religion:* Jewish. *Home:* 1242 North Lake Shore Dr., Chicago, Ill. 60610. *Office:* Arvey, Hodes, Costello & Burman, 180 North LaSalle St., Chicago, Ill. 60601.

CAREER: Arvey, Hodes, Costello & Burman (formerly Arvey, Hodes & Mantynband), Chicago, Ill., attorney and partner, 1961—. Lecturer at Adult Education Center of University of Chicago, 1967-68; member of faculty of Practising Law Institute. Democratic State central committeeman for Ninth Congressional District of Illinois, 1970—. National chairman of Lawbooks USA (people-to-people program) of U.S. Information Agency, 1963-70; member of Civil Service Commission advisory committee for federal student interns, 1964-66; member of board of directors, Foundation of the Federal Bar Association, 1968—, Medical Research Institute Council of Michael Reese Hospital, 1966-72, United Parkinson Foundation, and Convention and Tourism Bureau of Greater Chicago, 1966-70; cochairman of Chicago's World Friendship Day, 1967; member of Illinois Arts Council, 1973—. Member of board of directors of Chicken Unlimited Enterprises, Inc., First Investors Life Insurance Co., All American Bank of Chicago, and Paul Harris Stores, Inc. *Military service:* U.S. Army, Judge Advocate Generals Corps., 1962-64; became captain.

MEMBER: Federal Bar Association (member of national council, 1967—), American Bar Association, Illinois State Bar Association, Chicago Bar Association, Judge Advocate's Association (life member), Economic Club of Chicago, Union League Club of Chicago, Standard Club of Chicago, Art Institute of Chicago (life member), Chicago Historical Society (life member), Masons. *Awards, honors:* Cassandra Foundation Award for achievement in the field of art, 1968; Federal Bar Association distinguished service award, 1971 and 1973.

WRITINGS: (With Paul Geerlings and Murray Simpson) *Conference on Mutual Funds,* Commerce Clearing House,

1966; *The Law of Art and Antiques,* Oceana, 1966; *What Every Artist and Collector Should Know about the Law,* Dutton, 1974. Contributor to law journals, including *Virginia Law Review, Boston College Industrial and Commercial Law Review, Illinois State Bar Journal, Notre Dame Law Review, Banking Law Journal, Federal Bar Journal,* and *Business Lawyer.*

* * *

HODSDON, Nicholas E(dward) 1941- (Nick Hodsdon)

PERSONAL: Born October 20, 1941, in Miami, Fla.; son of Nicholas (a civil attorney) and Mildred (a teacher; maiden name, Bachman) Hodsdon. *Education:* Tulane University, B.A., 1963; New York Theological Seminary, M.Div., 1971; Columbia University, M.A., 1972. *Home:* 334 East 105th St., #10, New York, N.Y. 10029.

CAREER: Ordained clergyman of United Church of Christ, 1974; Rochester Music Theater, Rochester, N.H., actor and singer, 1964; general science teacher in New York, N.Y., 1966-68; leader of workshops in music and movement, especially liturgically-oriented music, 1969—; writer and leader of music and liturgical drama for Roman Catholic and Episcopal churches in New York N.Y., 1970—; teacher of liturgical arts at New York Theological Seminary, 1974—. Instructor in guitar, 1970—. *Member:* New York Pinewoods Folk Music Club (of Country Dance Society).

WRITINGS—Under name Nick Hodsdon: *The Joyful Wedding,* Abingdon, 1973. Author of songs appearing in five books and several magazines. Contributor to *Liturgy* and *Catholic Mind.*

WORK IN PROGRESS: Seasons and Celebrations, a collection of songs, short plays, and suggestions for liturgical celebration of religious holidays and the seasons.

AVOCATIONAL INTERESTS: Big dogs, motorcycles.

* * *

HODSDON, Nick
See HODSDON, Nicholas E(dward)

* * *

HOECKER, Karla 1901-

PERSONAL: Born September 1, 1901, in Berlin, Germany; daughter of Paul Oskar (a writer) and Grete (Linke) Hoecker. *Education:* Attended Staatlich Akademische Hochschule fuer Musik, Berlin, 1923-27. *Religion:* Evangelical. *Home:* Andree-Zeile 27g, 1 Berlin 37, Germany.

CAREER: Writer. *Member:* Verband deutscher Schriftsteller, Neue Gesellschaft & Literatur. *Awards, honors:* Kulturbuch-Verlag Romanpreis, 1955, for *Die Mauern standen noch.*

WRITINGS: Clara Schumann, G. Bosse, 1938, revised edition, C. Bertelsmann, 1959; *Vom Trost auf Erden* (title means "Consolation of Earth"), L. Blanvalet, 1946; *Mehr als ein Leben* (novel; title means "More than One Life"), C. Bertelsmann, 1953; *Die Mauern standen noch* (novel; title means "The Walls Are Still Standing"), Kulturbuch-Verlag, 1954; *Sinfonische Reise: Konzerte, Gespraeche, Fahrten mit Wilhelm Furtwaengler und den Berliner Philharmonikern* (title means "Sinfonical Journey with Wilhelm Furtwaengler and the Berlin Philharmonic Orchestra"), C. Bertelsmann, 1955; *Begegnung mit Furtwaengler* (title means "Meeting with Furtwaengler"), C. Bertelsmann, 1956; *Ein Tag im April* (novel; title means "One Day in April"), Bechtle, 1958; *Wilhelm Furtwaengler: Begegnungen und Gespraeche* (title means "Meetings and Conversations with Wilhelm Furtwaengler"), Rembrandt Verlag, 1961; *Erna Berger, die singende Botschafterin* (title means "The Singing Messenger"), Rembrandt Verlag, 1961; *Dieses Maedchen* (novel; title means "This Girl"), Engelhornverlag, 1962; *Grosse Kammermusik* (title means "Great Chamber Music"), Rembrandt Verlag, 1962; *Gespraeche mit Berliner Kuenstlern* (title means "Conversations with Berlin Artists"), Stapp, 1964; *Die letzten und die ersten Tage: Berliner Aufzeichnungen* (title means "The Last and the First Days"), Hessling Verlag, 1966; *The Three Times Lost Dog* (juvenile; original title, *Der 3X verlorene Hund),* translated by Lynn Aubry, Atheneum, 1967; *Wilhelm Furtwaengler: Dokumente, Berichte und Bilder, Aufzeichnungen* (title means "Wilhelm Furtwaengler: Documents, Notices, Reports, and Image"), Rembrandt Verlag, 1968; *Hauskonzerte in Berlin,* Rembrandt Verlag, 1970; *Das Leben des Wolfgang Amade Mozart,* (title means "The Life of Wolfgang Amadeus Mozart") Klopp Verlag, 1973.

WORK IN PROGRESS: Das Leben von Clara Schumann, a biography.

* * *

HOEXTER, Corinne K. 1927-

PERSONAL: "O" in surname is silent; born November 3, 1927, in Scranton, Pa.; daughter of Edward D. (a manufacturer) and Aimee Helen (Rosenfelder) Katz; married Rolf Hoexter (an engineer), December 25, 1955; children: Vivien, Michael Frederic. *Education:* Wellesley College, B.A. (with high honors in English), 1949; University of Chicago, M.A., 1950. *Residence:* Englewood, N.J.

CAREER: Experiment in International Living, Putney, Vt., promotion assistant, 1950-51; *Parents' Magazine,* New York, N.Y., editorial assistant, 1951-53; Magazine Management, New York, N.Y., associate editor, 1953-54; Pines Publications, New York, N.Y., associate editor, then managing editor, 1954-57; J. J. Little & Ives, New York, N.Y., picture editor, 1957-59; *Art News Annual,* New York, N.Y., managing editor, 1959-60. Active in Englewood Social Service Federation and other civic and urban projects in the area. *Member:* Chinese Historical Society of America, League of Women Voters, National Association for the Advancement of Colored People, Englewood Nature Association, Phi Beta Kappa, Stuyvesant Yacht Club, Chatham Yacht Club (Chatham, Mass.). *Awards, honors:* Fulbright fellowship at University of Bologna, 1953; *Black Crusader* was named on the Child Study Association book list.

WRITINGS: (With Ira Peck) *A Nation Conceived and Dedicated,* Scholastic Book Services, 1970; *Black Crusader: Frederick Douglass,* Rand McNally, 1970. Contributor to *Scholastic Scope.*

WORK IN PROGRESS: A book on personalities involved in the early history of the Chinese in America.

SIDELIGHTS: Mrs. Hoexter says: "As a child . . . many of my favorite books were histories or historical novels. . . . Since history was always so real to me and threw so much light on our own world and problems, I felt it could be equally real to other young people today. I have tried to show the historical people in my books as people, after all, struggling with many of the same problems we face today, involved in the old and continuing human battle against injustice. At the same time I have tried to show individuals in relation to the great events and movements of history.

"In our small city of Englewood and the nearby metropolis, New York, my family and I have been interested in a variety of urban problems. Our chief project at the moment is preserving a beautiful piece of wild land on the west slope of the Palisades, one of the last in Englewood, and turning it into a nature center for the benefit of the whole city."

AVOCATIONAL INTERESTS: Reading, playing the piano, family singing and chamber music, walking in the city and hiking in the country, visiting places of historical and artistic interest, concerts, the theater, art museums.

* * *

HOFFMANN, Leon-Francois 1932-

PERSONAL: Born April 11, 1932, in Paris, France; naturalized U.S. citizen; son of Jean (a lawyer) and Nadia (Bloch) Hoffmann; married Anne Schmidt, February 1, 1960; children: Jacques-Henri, Philippe-Edgard. *Education:* Yale University, B.A. (magna cum laude), 1953; Princeton University, M.A., 1955, Ph.D., 1959. *Office:* Department of Romance Languages, Princeton University, Princeton, N.J. 18540.

CAREER: Princeton University, Princeton, N.J., instructor, 1957-60, assistant professor, 1960-65, associate professor, 1965-68, professor of French, 1968—. Instructor at Middlebury French Summer School, 1958, 1960; visiting professor at Institut d'Etudes francaises d'Avignon, summers, 1965, 1968, 1971, Hebrew University of Jerusalem, 1974. Lecturer at University of Paris, Syracuse University, University of Kansas, Rutgers University, and for Alliance Francaise. *Military service:* U.S. Army, 1956-57. *Member:* Modern Language Association of America, Societe des professeurs francais en Amerique, Association internationales des etudes francaises, Centre d'etudes romantiques, Phi Beta Kappa. *Awards, honors:* Bicentennial preceptor, Princeton University, 1962-65; Guggenheim fellowship, 1964.

WRITINGS: Romantique Espagne, Presses Universitaires de France, 1961; *La Peste a Barcelone,* Presses Universitaires de France, 1964; *L'Essentiel de la grammaire francaise,* Scribner, 1964, 2nd edition, 1973; *Repertoire geographique de "La Comedie humaine,"* Jose Corti, Volume I: *L'Etranger,* 1965, Volume II: *La Province,* 1968; (author of introduction and notes) Hyacinthe de Latouche and L. F. l'Heritier, *Dernieres lettres de deux amans de Barcelone,* Presses Universitaires de France, 1966; *Travaux pratiques,* Max Hueber (Munich), 1968; *Le Negre romantique: Personnage litteraire et obsession collective,* Payot, 1973; *La Pratique du francais parle,* Scribner, 1973; (author of introduction and notes) Alexander Dumas, *Georges,* Folio, 1974.

Contributor of translations to Morroe Berger's *Mme. de Stael,* Doubleday, 1963. Contributor of about twenty articles and reviews to journals in France and America.

WORK IN PROGRESS: L'Eros balzacien.

* * *

HOGARTH, Paul 1917-

PERSONAL: Born October 4, 1917, in Kendal, Westmorland, England; son of Arthur and Janet (Bownass) Hogarth; married Phyllis Daphne Pamplin; married Patricia Douthwaite, February 14, 1959; children: (first marriage) Virginia; (second marriage) Toby. *Education:* Attended Manchester College of Art, 1936-38, St. Martin's School of Art, 1938-40. *Home and office:* Can Bi Calle Es Clot, Deya, Majorca, Balearic Islands, Spain. *Agent:* Georges Borchardt, Inc., 145 East 52nd St., New York, N.Y. 10022.

CAREER: Free-lance artist and illustrator. London County Council Central School of Arts and Crafts, London, England, visiting lecturer, 1951-54; Royal College of Art, London, tutor, 1964-70, visiting lecturer in Department of Illustration, Faculty of Graphic Design, 1971—. Visiting associate professor, Philadelphia College of Art, 1968-69. *Member:* Alliance Graphique Internationale, Royal Academy of Fine Arts (associate), Society of Industrial Artists and Designers (fellow), Chelsea Art Club (London).

WRITINGS: Defiant People: Drawings of Greece Today, Lawrence & Wishart, 1953; *Looking at China,* Lawrence & Wishart, 1956; *People Like Us: Drawings of South Africa and Rhodesia,* Dobson, 1958, published as *Sons of Adam,* Thomas Nelson, 1960; (with Jean Jacques Salomon) *Prehistory: Civilizations Before Writing,* Dell, 1962; *Creative Pencil Drawing,* Watson, 1964; *Creative Ink Drawing,* Watson, 1968; *The Artist as Reporter,* Reinhold, 1967; *Drawing People,* Watson, 1971; *Artists on Horseback: The Old West in Illustrated Journalism, 1857-1900,* Watson, 1972; *Drawing Architecture,* Watson, 1973; *Paul Hogarth's American Album,* Lion Press, 1974; *Arthur Boyd Houghton: The World and Work of a Victorian Artist,* Barrie & Jenkins, in press.

Illustrator: Doris Lessing, *Going Home,* M. Joseph, 1957; Olive Schreiner, *The Story of an African Farm,* Westerham Press, 1961; Brendan Behan, *Brendan Behan's Island,* Geis, 1962; Behan, *Brendan Behan's New York,* Geis, 1964; Robert Graves, *Majorca Observed,* Doubleday, 1965; (and author of captions) Malcolm Muggeridge, *London a la Mode,* Hill & Wang, 1967; Alaric Jacob, *A Russian Journey,* Hill & Wang, 1969; James D. Atwater and R. E. Ruiz, *Out from Under,* Doubleday, 1969; Doris Whitman, *The Hand of Apollo,* Follett, 1969.

Contributor to *Penrose Annual* of Hastings House, and to *Daily Telegraph Magazine, Sports Illustrated, House & Garden,* and other periodicals. Art editor, *Contact,* 1950-51.

WORK IN PROGRESS: The Death or Glory Boys, a book about the pictorial reporting of the Victorian era; *America Observed,* with Stephen Spender, publication by Crown expected in 1976.

* * *

HOGUE, Richard 1946-

PERSONAL: Born August 16, 1946, in Lawton, Okla.; son of Coleman (a carpenter) and Eula (Johnson) Hogue; married Marilyn Billingsleá, 1966; children: Stephen Israel, John Jeremy. *Education:* Attended Oklahoma Baptist University for four years. *Office:* Richard Hogue Evangelism, Inc., 2600 Citadel Plaza, Suite 507, Houston, Tex. 77008.

CAREER: Ordained Southern Baptist minister, 1967; youth director in Chandler, Okla., 1964-65, in Ada, Okla., 1966; youth director and associate pastor in Del City, Okla., 1967-68; evangelist in Oklahoma City, Okla., 1968; Richard Hogue Evangelism, Inc., Houston, Tex., founder and evangelist, 1968—. *Member:* National Conference of

Southern Baptist Evangelists (vice-president, 1971-72; president, 1972-73).

WRITINGS: Sex and the Jesus Kids, Bridge Productions, 1971; *The Jesus Touch,* Broadman, 1972; *Sex, Satan, and Jesus,* Broadman, 1973.

* * *

HOLLISTER, Bernard C(laiborne) 1938-

PERSONAL: Born March 17, 1938, in Chicago, Ill.; son of Joseph (a newspaperman) and Mildred (Pillinger) Hollister; married Edna Rozanski, August 10, 1963; children: Suzanne. *Education:* Roosevelt University, B.A., 1962; Northern Illinois University, M.A., 1967; Illinois Institute of Technology, M.S.T., 1971; also studied at University of Chicago, summer, 1966, 1966-67, and Rutgers University, summer, 1967. *Home:* 890 Yorkshire Dr., Hanover Park, Ill. 60103. *Office:* Willowbrook High School, 1250 South Ardmore, Villa Park, Ill. 60181.

CAREER: Cook County Department of Public Aid, Chicago, Ill., caseworker, 1962-63; Willowbrook High School, Villa Park, Ill., teacher of sociology, 1963—; National College of Education, Evanston, Ill., teacher, 1972—. Has conducted workshops and clinics. *Awards, honors:* National Science Foundation grant in sociology, 1970-71.

WRITINGS: (With Deane Thompson) *Grokking the Future: Science Fiction in the Classroom,* Pflaum-Standard, 1973; (editor) *Another Tomorrow: A Science Fiction Anthology,* Pflaum-Standard, 1974; *It's Not Nice to Laugh at Martians—Or Other Folks,* with teacher's guide, Pflaum-Standard, in press; *I've Gotta Be Me!,* with teacher's guide, Pflaum-Standard, in press; *I Was Only Following Orders,* with teacher's guide, Pflaum-Standard, in press. Contributor to *Futures Conditional* and *Social Education.* Contributing editor to *Media and Methods.*

* * *

HOLLOWAY, (Rufus) Emory 1885-

PERSONAL: Born March 16, 1885, in Marshall, Mo.; son of Rufus Austin (a clergyman) and Ella (Dent) Holloway; married Ella Brooks Harris, September 7, 1915 (died, 1972); children: Robert Howard, Rita Harris Holloway Tybout. *Education:* Hendrix College, A.B., 1906; University of Texas, M.A., 1912; Columbia University, further graduate study, 1913-14. *Home:* 1013 East 26th St., Brooklyn, N.Y. 11210.

CAREER: High school teacher in Amity, Ark., 1906-08; Scarritt-Morrisville College, Morrisville, Mo., professor of English and chairman of department, 1910-11; University of Texas, Austin, instructor in English, 1912-13; Adelphi College (now Adelphi University), Garden City, N.Y., instructor, 1914-16, assistant professor, 1916-18, professor of English, 1919-37; Queens College (now Queens College of City University of New York), Flushing, N.Y., associate professor, 1937-39, professor of American literature, 1940-54, professor emeritus, 1954—, chairman of department, 1937-41. *Member:* Modern Language Association of America, American Association of University Professors, Authors Club. *Awards, honors:* Pulitzer Prize in biography, 1927, for *Whitman: An Interpretation in Narrative;* LL.D., Hendrix College, 1936; Distinguished Service Medal, Brooklyn College Library Association, 1950.

WRITINGS: (Editor and author of introduction) *The Uncollected Poetry and Prose of Walt Whitman,* two volumes, Doubleday, 1921, reprinted, Bilbo & Tannen, 1969; (editor) Walt Whitman, *Leaves of Grass,* inclusive edition, Doubleday, 1924, reprinted, 1954, editor and author of introduction of abridged edition with prose selections, Doubleday, 1926, editor of inclusive edition illustrated by Rockwell Kent, Heritage Press, 1926, editor and author of notes and introduction for comprehensive edition, Dutton, 1947; *Whitman: An Interpretation in Narrative,* Knopf, 1926, published with new preface by the author, Bilbo & Tannen, 1969; (author of introduction and notes) *Pictures: An Unpublished Poem of Walt Whitman* (booklet), June House, 1927; (author of introduction) Whitman, *Franklin Evans: Or, the Inebriate,* Random House, 1929.

(Editor with Vernolian Schwarz) *I Sit and Look Out* (selection of editorials from *Brooklyn Daily Times*), Columbia University Press, 1932; (author with Ralph Adimari of introduction and notes) *New York Dissected,* Rufus Rockwell Wilson, 1936; *Janice in Tomorrow-Land* (juvenile), American Book Co., 1936; (editor) Whitman, *Complete Poetry and Selected Prose and Letters,* Nonesuch Press, 1938, reprinted, 1964.

Whitman on the Campus (pamphlet), privately printed, 1950.

Free and Lonesome Heart: The Secret of Walt Whitman, Vantage, 1960; (associate editor) *Collected Writings of Walt Whitman,* New York University Press, 1963—; *Aspects of Immortality in Whitman,* privately printed, 1969.

Writer of other short studies on Whitman. Contributor to *Encyclopaedia Britannica* and to *Colophon* and other journals. Associate editor, *American Literature* (journal), 1940-52.

* * *

HOLLOWAY, (Percival) Geoffrey 1918-

PERSONAL: Born May 23, 1918, in Birmingham, England; widower; children: Catherine Rowan, Susan Bryony. *Education:* University of Southampton, certificate in social science, 1948. *Politics:* Liberal. *Home:* 4 Gowan Cres., Staveley near Kendal, Cumbria, England. *Office:* County Hall, Kendal, Cumbria, England.

CAREER: Cumbria County Council, Kendal, Cumbria, England, social worker, 1953—. *Military service:* British Army, Royal Army Medical Corps, 1939-45. *Member:* National Association of Local Government Officers.

WRITINGS—Poems: *To Have Eyes,* Anvil Press, 1973; *Rhine Jump* (Poetry Book Society selection), London Magazine Editions, 1974.

WORK IN PROGRESS: The Crones of Aphrodite, a book of poems.

AVOCATIONAL INTERESTS: Walking, gurning (the sport of making faces).

* * *

HOLMAN, William R(oger) 1926-

PERSONAL: Born September 7, 1926, in Oklahoma City, Okla.; married Barbara Switzer (a painter), September, 1945; children: David Kent, James Roger, Gregory Meade. *Education:* University of Oklahoma, B.A., 1949; University of Illinois, M.S. in L.S., 1951. *Politics:* Moderate Democrat. *Religion:* Protestant. *Office:* Humanities Research Center, University of Texas, Box 7219, Austin, Tex. 78712.

CAREER: Pan American College, Edinburg, Tex., head

librarian, 1951-55; Rosenberg Library, Galveston, Tex., director, 1955-57; San Antonio Public Library, San Antonio, Tex., director, 1957-60; San Francisco Public Library, San Francisco, Calif., head librarian, 1960-67; University of Texas, Humanities Research Center, Austin, professor of history and art of the book, 1967—, librarian, 1967—. Free-lance book designer and typographical consultant. *Member:* American Library Association, Book Club of California (former member of board of directors), Roxburghe Club (San Francisco). *Awards, honors:* Texas Institute of Letters award for best book produced and designed in Texas, 1973, for *This Bitterly Beautiful Land.*

WRITINGS: (Contributor) Sara Wallace, editor, *Friends of the Library,* American Library Association, 1962; *Library Publications,* Roger Beacham, 1965; (author of introduction) Edward Hampton Shickell, *Bookplates for Libraries,* Roger Beacham, 1968; (contributor) Al Lowman, editor, *Printer at the Pass: The Work of Carl Hertzog,* Institute of Texas Cultures, University of Texas, 1972. Contributor of articles and reviews to library publications, including *Library Chronicle, Library Journal, Texas Libraries,* and *Wilson Library Bulletin.*

WORK IN PROGRESS: Indians in Texas; Rivers of Texas; preparing handmarbled paper for bookmaking.

SIDELIGHTS: Holman learned the traditional method of making paper in Wookey Hole, England, and has been described as a man who"...knows more about good type and how to handle it with taste and skill than any professional printer..." One of the books he designed, *This Bitterly Beautiful Land,* compiled by Al Lowman, Roger Beacham, 1972, has received critical acclaim and is said to be a necessary addition to the library of any serious collector of materials about the state of Texas.

BIOGRAPHICAL/CRITICAL SOURCES: San Francisco Chronicle, June 21, 1967; *Dallas Morning News,* May 28, 1972.

* * *

HOLMES, Martin (Rivington) 1905-

PERSONAL: Born May 12, 1905, in London, England; son of Charles John (a landscape painter, writer on art, and gallery director) and Florence (a violinist and composer; maiden name, Hill) Rivington. *Education:* Attended Christ Church, Oxford, 1924-27, receiving second class honors in Classical Moderations, 1926. *Politics:* Conservative. *Religion:* Church of England. *Home:* Castle Bank, Appleby, Westmorland CA16 6SN, England.

CAREER: London Museum, London, England, 1932-65, member of staff at Lancaster House, at St. James's, and at Kensington Palace; writer. Member of Carl Rosa Trust, 1957—. Occasional technical advisor for BBC educational television; honorary consultant, Bankside Theatre Museum. Appleby borough councillor, 1965-74, town councillor, 1974—; Eden district councillor, 1974—. *Military service:* British Armed Forces, 1939-46; became major. *Member:* Society of Antiquaries (fellow).

WRITINGS: Medieval England, Methuen, 1934; *The Crown Jewels,* H.M.S.O., 1953, 3rd edition published as *The Crown Jewels in the Wakefield Tower of the Tower of London,* 1961; *Personalia,* Museums Association (London), 1957; *Arms and Armor in Tudor and Stuart London,* H.M.S.O., 1957, 2nd edition, 1970; *The London of Elizabeth I,* London Museums, 1959; *The London of Charles II,* H.M.S.O., 1960; *Shakespeare's Public: The Touchstone of His Genius,* Transatlantic, 1960, corrected edition, J. Murray, 1964; *Moorfields in 1559,* H.M.S.O., 1963; *The Guns of Elsinore,* Barnes & Noble, 1964; *The Parish Churches of Appleby,* privately printed, 1967; *Stage Costume and Accessories in the London Museum,* H.M.S.O., 1968; *Elizabethan London,* Praeger, 1969; *Shakespeare and His Players,* Scribner, 1972; (with H. D. W. Sitwell) *The English Regalia,* H.M.S.O., 1972; *Appleby and the Crown,* J. Whitehead & Son (Appleby), 1974.

Plays: "Crichton the Scholar," first produced in London by Playwrights' Club, 1936; *The Road to Runnymede* (three-act; first produced in London by Goodrich Players, 1946), Samuel French, 1948; "From a Fair Lady," first produced by Goodrich Players, 1948, revived as "Dragon's Deathbed" in London at Gateway Theatre, 1955; "The Waiting Lady," first produced at Gateway Theatre, 1949; "Sword of Justice," first produced at Gateway Theatre, 1949; "The Last Burgundian," first produced at Gateway Theatre, 1949; "Fotheringhay," first produced at Gateway Theatre, 1950; "The Golden Unicorn," first produced at Gateway Theatre, 1951; "The Master of the Horse," first produced at Gateway Theatre, 1951; "King's Work," first produced at Gateway Theatre, 1952, later revived as "Royal Portrait, 1666" in London at Toynbee Hall; "The Smiling Angel," first produced at Gateway Theatre, 1953; "They Call It Treason," first produced in London by Central Drama Group, 1959; "A Man Called Dante," first produced in London at Hovenden Theatre Club, 1961; "The Heavy Crown," first produced by Central Drama Group, 1961; "Duke of the English," first produced by Central Drama Group, 1966.

Contributor to *Encyclopedia Americana* and *Encyclopaedia Britannica;* contributor to journals and periodicals, including *Quarterly Review, Antiquaries Journal, Apollo, Connoisseur, Theatre Notebook, Illustrated London News, Drama, Listener,* and *Times* (London).

WORK IN PROGRESS: Proud Northern Lady, a study of Lady Anne Clifford, 1590-1676; *The Sound of Shakespeare; Appleby Castle.*

SIDELIGHTS: Holmes studied voice, and was a chorister in the last international opera season at Covent Garden in 1939; he is particularly interested in opera productions in London between 1920 and 1960. Holmes collects arms and armour, and sixteenth and seventeenth-century history and travel books.

* * *

HONIGFELD, Gilbert
See HOWARD, Gilbert

* * *

HOOD, Hugh (John Blagdon) 1928-

PERSONAL: Born April 30, 1928, in Toronto, Canada; son of Alexander (a banker) and Marguerite (Blagdon) Hood; married Ruth Noreen Mallory (a painter and printmaker), April 22, 1957; children: Sarah Barbara, Dwight Alexander, John Arthur, Alexandra Mary. *Education:* University of Toronto, B.A., 1950, M.A., 1952, Ph.D., 1955. *Politics:* Radical socialist. *Religion:* Christian. *Home and office:* 4242 Hampton Ave., Montreal, Quebec H4A 2K9, Canada.

CAREER: University of Montreal, Montreal, Quebec, professor of English, 1961—; novelist.

WRITINGS: Flying a Red Kite (short stories), Ryerson, 1962; *White Figure, White Ground* (novel), Ryerson, 1964; *Around the Mountain* (short stories), Peter Martin Associates, 1967; *The Camera Always Lies* (novel), Harcourt, 1967; *Strength Down Centre: The Jean Beliveau Story,* Prentice-Hall, 1970; *A Game of Touch* (novel), Longman, 1970; *The Fruit Man, the Meat Man and the Manager* (short stories), Oberon Press, 1971; *You Can't Get There from Here* (novel), Oberon Press, 1972; *The Governor's Bridge Is Closed* (essays), Oberon Press, 1973.

WORK IN PROGRESS: Dark Glasses, a collection of short stories; a long serial novel, *The New Age,* of which the first volume, *The Swing in the Garden,* is completed.

SIDELIGHTS: Hood told *CA:* "I consider my *roman-fleuve, The New Age/Le Nouveau Siecle* to be the great, major work of my life. It should occupy me for a generation with the final volume appearing around the year 2000. Hence the title."

* * *

HOOKER, Clifford Alan 1942-

PERSONAL: Born October 4, 1942, in Sydney, New South Wales, Australia; son of C. J. S. Hooker; married wife, Jean Barbara, 1964; children: Lyndal Claire. *Education:* University of Sydney, B.Sc. (first class honors), 1964; B.A. (first class honors equivalent), 1968, Ph.D. (physics), 1968; York University, Ph.D. (philosophy), 1970. *Office:* Department of Philosophy, University of Western Ontario, London, Ontario N6A 3K7, Canada.

CAREER: York University, Toronto, Ontario, assistant professor of natural science and special lecturer in philosophy, 1968-70; University of Western Ontario, London, associate professor, 1970-73, professor of philosophy and environmental engineering, 1973—. Consultant on environmental problems to government agencies in Canada. *Member:* Philosophy of Science Association, Canadian Association of Philosophy, Canadian Association of History and Philosophy of Science.

WRITINGS: (Editor) *Contemporary Research in the Foundations and Philosophy of Quantum Theory,* Reidel, 1973.

WORK IN PROGRESS: Books on the systematic structure of environment problems and social planning, on a materialist philosophy of man, and on the logico-algebraic approach to physics.

* * *

HOOVER, Calvin Bryce 1897-1974

April 14, 1897—June 23, 1974; American economist, educator, and author. Obituaries: *New York Times,* July 12, 1974. (*CA*-13/14).

* * *

HOOVER, Dorothy Estheryne 1918-

PERSONAL: Born July 2, 1918, in Hope, Ark.; daughter of William Matthew (a teacher) and Elizabeth Rebecca (Wilbun) McFadden; married Richard Allen Hoover, June 20, 1950 (divorced, 1959); children: Viola Clementyne Clarke (deceased), Ricardo Allen (deceased). *Education:* Arkansas Agricultural, Mechanical, and Normal College (now University of Arkansas at Pine Bluff), B.S., 1938; Atlanta University, M.S., 1943; University of Arkansas, M.A., 1954; University of Michigan, further graduate study, 1954-56. *Religion:* African Methodist Episcopal. *Home:* Wingate House, #C 1009, 4660 Martin Luther King, Jr. Ave. S.W., Washington, D.C. 20032. *Office:* Defense Communications Agency—National Military Command System Support Center, Pentagon, Washington, D.C. 20301.

CAREER: Teacher of mathematics, English, and science at schools in Newport, Ark., 1938-39, Jesup, Ga., 1939-41, Fort Valley, Ga., 1941-42, and Dayton, Tenn., 1942-43; National Advisory Committee for Aeronautics (now superseded by National Aeronautics and Space Administration), Langley Field, Va., mathematician, computer, and aeronautical research scientist, 1943-52; Fleet Weather Central, Joint Numerical Weather Prediction Unit, Suitland, Md., mathematician, 1956-59; National Aeronautics and Space Administration, mathematician in Silver Spring, Md., Greenbelt, Md., and Washington, D.C., 1959-68; Pentagon, Defense Communications Agency-National Military Command System Support Center, Washington, D.C., operations research analyst, 1968—. Member of panel on board of U.S. Civil Service Examiners for Goddard Space Flight Center and National Aeronautics and Space Administration, 1960-68.

MEMBER: Business and Professional Women's League, National Association for the Advancement of Colored People, Alumni Association of University of Arkansas (life member).

WRITINGS: (With Frank S. Malvestuto, Jr.) *Lift and Pitching Derivatives of Thin Sweptback Tapered Wings with Streamwise Tips and Subsonic Leading Edges at Supersonic Speeds,* National Advisory Committee for Aeronautics, 1951; (with Malvestuto) *Supersonic Lift and Pitching Moment of Thin Sweptback Wings Produced by Constant Vertical Acceleration,* National Advisory Committee for Aeronautics, 1951; (editor) *On Estimates of Error in Numerical Integration: Proceedings of the Arkansas Academy of Science,* Arkansas Academy of Science, 1954; (contributor) Berni Alder, Sidney Fernbach, and Manuel Rotenberg, editors, *Methods in Computational Physics,* Volume II, Academic Press, 1963; (with Franco Mariani) *A Concise Tabulation of Solar Zenithal Angles for Use in Upper Atmosphere Research,* National Aeronautics and Space Administration, 1964; *A Layman Looks with Love at Her Church,* Dorrance, 1970.

WORK IN PROGRESS: Research on past and present mission fields of African Methodist Episcopal Church.

* * *

HOPKINS, Joseph Martin 1919-

PERSONAL: Born May 10, 1919, in Pittsburgh, Pa.; son of John Howard (a civil engineer) and Grace Marie (Martin) Hopkins; married Lois Elaine McCallum (an associate professor of music), December 17, 1948; children: John, Ralph, Martin, Brooke, Elaine. *Education:* Westminster College, New Wilmington, Pa., B.Mus., 1940; Pittsburgh-Xenia Theological Seminary, B.Th., 1943; Eastman School of Music, graduate study, summer, 1948; University of Pittsburgh, M.Ed., 1950, Ph.D., 1954. *Politics:* Republican. *Home:* 530 Kathryn St., New Wilmington, Pa. 16142. *Office:* Department of Religion and Philosophy, Westminster College, New Wilmington, Pa. 16142.

CAREER: Ordained minister of United Presbyterian Church in the U.S.A., 1943; minister in Hickory, Pa., 1943-44; Westminster College, New Wilmington, Pa., instructor, 1946-52, assistant professor, 1952-55, associate professor, 1955-73, professor of religion and philosophy, 1973—. *Military service:* U.S. Naval Reserve, chaplain, 1944-46; became lieutenant; served in Philippines. *Member:* American Academy of Religion.

WRITINGS: Simple Object Lessons, Zondervan, 1970; *New Songs,* Bair Foundation, 1970; *The Armstrong Empire,* Eerdmans, 1974. Contributor to *Christian Scholar, College and University Business, Bulletin of Association of American Colleges, Pennsylvania Farmer, Christian Century, Christianity Today, Presbyterian Life, Christian Herald,* and *Monday Morning.* Contributing editor of *Presbyterian Outlook,* 1960—.

WORK IN PROGRESS: Study of American religious movements.

SIDELIGHTS: Hopkins has traveled around the world and led three tours to the Middle East. He has composed music for two stage productions and has had some fifty vocal and piano compositions published.

* * *

HOPKINS, Raymond F(rederick) 1939-

PERSONAL: Born February 15, 1939, in Cleveland, Ohio; son of William Edward (in advertising) and Ada Elizabeth (Cornwall) Hopkins; married Carol Robinson (a computer programmer), June 5, 1962; children: Mark Raymond, Kathryn Carol. *Education:* Ohio Wesleyan University, B.A., 1960; Ohio State University, M.A., 1963; Yale University, M.A., 1965, Ph.D., 1968. *Politics:* Democrat. *Home:* 308 Ogden Ave., Swarthmore, Pa. 19081. *Office:* Department of Political Science, Swarthmore College, Swarthmore, Pa. 19081.

CAREER: Assistant pastor of Methodist church, 1960-61; University College, Dar es Salaam, Tanganyika (now part of Tanzania), research associate, 1965-66; Swarthmore College, Swarthmore, Pa., instructor, 1967-68, assistant professor, 1968-73, associate professor of political science, 1973—. Visiting scholar at University of Michigan, 1968; research associate at Center for International Affairs, Harvard University, summer, 1969; visiting research associate at Indiana University and University of Nairobi, 1970-71. *Member:* American Political Science Association, African Studies Association, International Studies Association, American Association of University Professors, Inter-University Consortium for Political Research, Phi Beta Kappa. *Awards, honors:* Social Science Research Council fellow, 1969-70; American Philosophical Society grant at University of Nairobi, 1970-71; Guggenheim fellow, 1974-75.

WRITINGS: Political Roles in a New State: Tanzania's First Decade, Yale University Press, 1971; (with Richard W. Mansbach) *Structure and Process in International Politics,* Harper, 1973; *Political Legitimacy in Kenya,* International Development Research Center, Indiana University, in press.

Contributor: Marion Doro and Nowell M. Stultz, editors, *Governing in Black Africa: Perspectives on New States,* Prentice-Hall, 1970; Karl W. Deutsch, Howard R. Alker, Jr., and Antoine Stoetzel, editors, *Quantitative and Mathematical Methods in Political Science,* Elsevier, 1972; Garry Brewer, editor, *A Policy Approach to the Study of Political Development and Change,* Free Press, 1974; Barbara McLennan, *Political Opposition and Dissent,* Dunellen, 1974. Contributor to *Social Forces, World Politics,* and other journals.

HORNE, Shirley (Faith) 1919-

PERSONAL: Born October 28, 1919, in Strathalbyn, South Australia; daughter of Kenneth Bayly (a farmer) and Mina (Meyer) Kirkham; married Charles F. Horne (a mission administrator), February 16, 1944; children: Richard, Malcolm, Stephen, Margaret. *Education:* Attended Melbourne Bible Institute, 1939-41. *Religion:* Baptist. *Address:* Asia Pacific Christian Mission, Box 15, Tari 5HD, Papua, New Guinea.

CAREER: Missionary in Wasua, Papua New Guinea, 1945-55 and 1963-70, Tari, Papua New Guinea, 1955-57, Sentani, Irian Jaya, 1957-58, Bokondini, Irian Jaya, 1958-73, and Tari, Papua New Guinea, as member of Asia Pacific Christian Mission, 1973—.

WRITINGS: Out of the Dark, Oliphant, 1962; *Them Also,* Unevangelized Fields Mission Press, 1968; *An Hour to the Stone Age,* Moody, 1973. Editor of *Torch,* 1964-73, and *Onward* (which incorporated *Torch*), 1973—.

WORK IN PROGRESS: A collection of legends told by Papua New Guineans.

SIDELIGHTS: Shirley Horne, who has lived in Papua New Guinea for twenty-three years and in Irian Jaya for seven, wrote: "I have lived. . . .in a rural situation among the people of whom I have written. I have known them intimately as friends. . . .traveled by foot, by canoe, river launches with the people, lived in their homes and shared their food. As Papua New Guinea faces independence it needs the help of people who know them from the inside."

* * *

HOROWITZ, Esther 1920-

PERSONAL: Born December 17, 1920, in New York, N.Y.; daughter of Israel (a tailor) and Dora (Altschuler) Horowitz. *Education:* Brooklyn College (now Brooklyn College of the City University of New York), B.A., 1940; graduate study at Fordham University, 1944, and at Hunter College and Queens College (both now of the City University of New York), 1945; University of Wisconsin, M.A., 1949; University of London, certificate, 1950; Columbia University, Ph.D., 1959. *Office:* Department of Speech, Hofstra University, Hempstead, N.Y. 11550.

CAREER: Certified psychologist in New York State, 1958; speech clinician at Queens College of the City University of New York, 1944-46; part-time teacher of lip-reading and speech rehabilitation at City College Veterans Rehabilitation Program, New York, N.Y., 1945-49; teacher of speech improvement in New York City Schools, 1946-50; Hofstra University, Hempstead, N.Y., instructor, 1950-57, special lecturer, 1957-59, assistant professor, 1959-63, associate professor, 1963-72, professor of speech, 1972—, director of speech clinic, 1953-67. Summer instructor at Central Michigan University, 1949, and University of Syracuse, 1959. *Member:* American Association of University Professors, American Speech Correction Association, Long Island Speech Association (second vice-president, 1960), Sigma Kappa Alpha (secretary, 1965-66).

WRITINGS: (With Erwin B. Dexter) *Guidelines for Better Speech in the Schools,* W. C. Brown, 1965; (contributor) L. L. Emerick and C. E. Hamre, editors, *An Analysis of Stuttering: Selected Readings,* Interstate, 1972. Contributor to *Jefferson Encyclopedia,* and to journals in his field. Consulting editor of *Journal of the Speech Association of the Eastern States,* 1971—.

HORROCK, Nicholas (Morton) 1936-

PERSONAL: Born April 29, 1936, in New York, N.Y.; son of Erwin Norbert (a curator of classical arts) and Berta (Crone) Horrock; married Mae Seward Rennolds, May 2, 1959 (divorced, 1970); married Mary Ann Kuhn (a newspaper writer), October 16, 1971; children: (first marriage) Christopher Nicholas, Timothy Powers. *Education:* American University, B.A., 1963. *Home:* 2029 Waterside Dr. N.W., Washington, D.C. 20009. *Agent:* Philip Spitzer, 111-25 76th Ave., Forest Hills, N.Y. 11375. *Office:* 1750 Pennsylvania Ave. N.W., Room 1220, Washington, D.C. 20006.

CAREER: Baltimore Sun, Baltimore, Md., reporter, 1964, 1966; *Washington Daily News,* Washington, D.C., assistant city editor, 1966-69; Scripps-Howard Newspaper Alliance, Washington, D.C., correspondent, 1969; *Newsweek,* Washington, D.C., chief investigative correspondent, 1969—. *Military service:* U.S. Marine Corps Reserve, 1953-61. *Member:* National Press Club. *Awards, honors:* Front Page Award from Washington-Baltimore American Newspaper Guild, 1968, for expose of illegal medical experiments; American Bar Association Gavel Award, 1970, for prison expose.

WRITINGS: Contrabandista, Praeger, 1973; *Nixon's Secret Police,* Praeger, in press.

SIDELIGHTS: Horrock told *CA:* "As a working newsman I believe that the press and electronic media are protected in the Constitution solely to provide the electorate with accurate and objective information to aid the public in selecting and guiding the national leadership. I believe therefore that we have a responsibility to go beyond what we are meant to report to the public and find out what business, government, and political leaders often may not want known. This, in essence, has been the goal of my nearly fifteen years of reporting experience."

* * *

HORTON, Louise 1916-

PERSONAL: Born June 23, 1916, in Granbury, Tex.; daughter of Moten Carl (a farmer) and Willie Belle (Bryant) Walthall; married Claude Wendell Horton, Sr. (a professor of physics and geology), November 23, 1938; children: Claude Wendell, Jr., Margaret Elaine Horton Morefield. *Education:* Rice Institute (now University), B.A., 1938. *Politics:* Republican. *Religion:* Episcopalian. *Home and office:* 3213 Cherry Lane, Austin, Tex. 78703.

CAREER: Houston Chemical Commercial Laboratory, Houston, Tex., chemist, 1937-38; Church of the Good Shepherd Day School, Austin, Tex., teacher, 1947-48; Texas State Library, Archives Division, Austin, Tex., archivist, 1970-71. *Member:* Society of American Archivists, American Anthropological Association, Texas State Historical Association, Kentucky Historical Society.

WRITINGS: Samuel Bell Maxey: A Biography, University of Texas Press, 1974. Contributor to *Southwestern Historical Quarterly* and *Texana.*

WORK IN PROGRESS: A book of history, *In the Hills of the Pennyroyal* (tentative title), publication expected in 1976; an autobiographical novel.

* * *

HORTON, Rod W(illiam) 1910-

PERSONAL: Born June 28, 1910, in White Plains, N.Y.; son of Roderick G. (a banker) and Celestine (Kroeger) Horton; married Martha Karp, August 24, 1937. *Education:* New York University, B.S., 1931, M.A., 1935, Ph.D., 1945. *Home:* 6300 East 17th Ave., Denver, Colo. 80220. *Office:* Department of English, Colorado Women's College, 1800 Pontiac St., Denver, Colo. 80220.

CAREER: New York University, New York, N.Y., instructor, 1937-45, assistant professor, 1945-49, associate professor of general literature, 1949-57; United States Information Service, in Brazil and Portugal, cultural affairs officer, 1957-64; Temple Buell College (formerly Colorado Women's College), Denver, Colo., professor of English, 1964—. Visiting professor at University of Brazil, 1954-56, University of Coimbra, 1961-64. *Awards, honors:* D.Litt. from University of Coimbra, 1964.

WRITINGS: (With Herbert W. Edwards) *Backgrounds of American Literary Thought,* Appleton, 1952, 3rd edition, Prentice-Hall, 1974; (with Vincent F. Hopper) *Backgrounds of European Literature,* Appleton, 1954, 2nd edition, Prentice-Hall, in press; (translator) Gilberto Freyre, *Order and Progress,* Knopf, 1970.

* * *

HOULEHEN, Robert J. 1918-

PERSONAL: Born June 2, 1918, in Milwaukee, Wis.; son of John J. (a city health inspector) and Alvina E. (Bensel) Houlehen; married Marian E. McCurn (a preschool teacher), August 18, 1945; children: Patrick, Michael and Kathleen (twins), Barry. *Education:* University of Wisconsin, B.A., 1941. *Politics:* Democrat. *Religion:* Unaffiliated. *Home:* 5423 North Santa Monica, Milwaukee, Wis. 53217. *Office:* Allis-Chalmers Corp., Corporate Public Relations Dept., Box 512, Milwaukee, Wis. 53201.

CAREER: Milwaukee Journal, Milwaukee, Wis., reporter, 1945-54; Allis-Chalmers Corp., Milwaukee, Wis., general editor for corporate public relations, 1954—. Evening teacher at University of Wisconsin-Milwaukee, 1960-62, and Milwaukee Area Technical College, 1962—. *Military service:* U.S. Army Air Forces, 1941-45. *Member:* Authors Guild, Wisconsin Raconteurs, Wisconsin Council of Writers, Milwaukee Press Club, Milwaukee Council: Boy Scouts.

WRITINGS: Battle for Sales, Lippincott, 1973; *Jobs in Manufacturing,* Lothrop, 1973; *Jobs in Agribusiness,* Lothrop, 1974.

WORK IN PROGRESS: Patterns for Communication, a textbook.

* * *

HOURS, Madeleine 1915- (Madeleine Hours-Miedan, Magdeleine Hours-Miedan)

PERSONAL: Given name is sometimes listed as Magdeleine; born August 5, 1915, in Paris, France; daughter of Lucien (an exporter) and Suzanne (Ricard) Miedan; married Jacques Hours, January 10, 1935 (separated, 1965); children: Antoine, Emmanuel, Laurent. *Education:* Ecole du Louvre, Diploma, 1942; attended Ecole des Hautes Etudes d'Histoire et de Philologie, Sorbonne. *Home:* 98, rue de Longchamp, 75116 Paris, France. *Office:* Laboratoire de Recherche des Musees de France, 75041 Paris, France Cedex01.

CAREER: Louvre, Paris, France, member of staff, scientific laboratory, 1936-40, member of staff in department of

Oriental archaeology, 1940-44, director of research laboratory, 1946—; National Museums of France, curator, 1959-72, curator-in-chief, 1972—. Head of research, Centre National de la Recherche Scientifique (National Center of Scientific Research), 1966—; producer of regular television program, "Les Secrets des chefs d'oeuvre" ("The Secrets of Masterpieces"), O.R.T.F., 1959—; lecturer. *Member:* Societe des Gens de Lettres, International Council of Museums. *Awards, honors:* Chevalier of Legion of Honor, 1959, Officier, 1972; Officier of Arts and Letters; Silver Medal for Research, 1969.

WRITINGS—Variously listed under names Hours, or Hours-Miedan: *Carthage,* Presses universitaires de France, 1949, 2nd edition, 1959; *A la decouverte de la peinture par les methodes physiques,* Arts et metiers graphiques, 1957; *Etude photographique et radiographique de quelques tableaux de Nicolas Poussin,* Editions des musees nationaux, 1961; *Les Secrets des chefs-d'oeuvre,* R. Laffont, 1964, translation published as *Secrets of the Great Masters: A Study in Artistic Techniques,* Putnam, 1968; *Jean-Baptiste-Camille Corot,* Abrams, 1972. Author of television scripts, "Les Secrets des chefs d'oeuvre," and "Tresors de la ville." Columnist for *France-Soir* and *Figaro.* Contributor to periodicals in various countries. Editor, *Annales du Laboratoire de Recherche des Musees de France,* 1959—.

WORK IN PROGRESS: More research on scientific analysis and restoration, especially on radiography.

SIDELIGHTS: Mme. Hours commented to *CA* that the scientific study of works of art transcends both art history and scientific expertise, for it reveals the intimate relationship between the material and the process of creation.

* * *

HOURS-MIEDAN, Madeleine
See HOURS, Madeleine

* * *

HOURS-MIEDAN, Magdeleine
See HOURS, Madeleine

* * *

HOUSTON, Peyton (H.) 1910-

PERSONAL: First syllable of surname is pronounced "house"; born December 20, 1910, in Cincinnati, Ohio; son of George H. (an industrialist) and Mary S. (Hoge) Houston; married Priscilla Moore, November 26, 1942 (divorced, 1958); married Parrish Cummings Dobson, May 22, 1959; children: (stepchildren) Joseph P. Dobson, Michael Dobson, Laura Parrish Dobson. *Education:* Princeton University, A.B., 1932. *Home:* Indian Chase Dr., Greenwich, Conn. 06830. *Office:* Wheelabrator-Frye, Inc., 299 Park Ave., New York, N.Y. 10017.

CAREER: Wheelabrator-Frye, Inc., (formerly The Equity Corp.), New York, N.Y., officer and director of various subsidiaries, 1950—, corporate secretary, 1971—. *Military service:* U.S. Army, 1943-46; became sergeant. *Member:* Princeton Club of New York, Phi Beta Kappa.

WRITINGS—All poems: *Descent into the Dust,* Centaur Press, 1936; *Sonnet Variations,* Jonathan Williams, 1962; *Occasions in a World,* Jargon Society, 1969; *For the Remarkable Animals,* Burning Deck, 1970.

WORK IN PROGRESS: Points of Knowing.

BIOGRAPHICAL/CRITICAL SOURCES: Arts in Society, Volume 7, number 2, summer-fall, 1970.

* * *

HOUTS, Peter S. 1933-

PERSONAL: Born March 17, 1933, in Great Neck, N.Y.; son of Thomas C. (a banker) and Charlotte (Stevens) Houts; married Mary Davidoff (a teacher), June 6, 1960; children: Thomas, David. *Education:* Antioch College, B.A., 1955; Carnegie Institute of Technology, graduate study, 1955-57; University of Michigan, Ph.D., 1963. *Office:* Department of Behavioral Science, College of Medicine, Pennsylvania State University, Hershey, Pa. 17033.

CAREER: Goucher College, Towson, Md., assistant professor of psychology, 1963-65; Stanford University Medical School, Palo Alto, Calif., postdoctoral fellow in psychiatry, 1965-67; Pennsylvania State University, College of Medicine, Hershey, associate professor of behavioral science, 1967—. *Member:* American Psychological Association, Association for the Advancement of Behavior Therapy, Behavior Therapy and Research Society.

WRITINGS: (With Michael Serber) *After the Turn On, What?: Learning Perspectives on Humanistic Groups,* Research Press, 1972; (with Robert A. Scott) *Goal Planning in Mental Health Rehabilitation,* Mental Health Materials Center (New York), 1973; (with Scott) *What Will Therapy Do for Me?,* Mental Health Materials Center, 1973; (with Scott and Joseph P. Leaser) *Which Way Out?,* Mental Health Materials Center, 1973; (with Scott and Leaser) *Goal Planning with the Mentally Retarded,* Mental Health Materials Center, 1973; (with Scott) *Take a Small Giant Step,* Mental Health Materials Center, 1973.

* * *

HOWARD, Gilbert 1934-
(Gilbert Honigfeld)

PERSONAL: Surname originally Honigfeld; name legally changed; born September 24, 1934, in Newark, N.J.; son of Joseph (an attorney) and Regina (Plawker) Honigfeld; married Alfreda Yadman, August 28, 1955; children: Curt. *Education:* Rutgers University, A.B., 1957; Temple University, M.A., 1958, Ph.D., 1961. *Home:* 77 Lyons Pl., Westwood, N.J. 07675. *Office:* Clinical Research Department, Sandoz Pharmaceuticals, Hanover, N.J. 07936.

CAREER: Veterans Administration Hospital, Perry Point, Md., assistant chief of Central Neuropsychiatric Research Laboratory, 1961-66; Hillside Hospital, Glen Oaks, N.Y., director of treatment and evaluation program, 1966-72; Rockland State Hospital, Orangeburg, N.Y., assistant director, 1972-73; Sandoz Pharmaceuticals, Hanover, N.J., associate director of Clinical Research Department, 1973—. Visiting professor at State University of New York at Stony Brook, 1968-69, and Queens College of the City University of New York, 1970-71. Consultant to National Center for Health Services Research and Development, 1972. *Member:* American Psychological Association, Eastern Psychological Association. *Awards, honors:* National Association of Private Psychiatric Hospitals Research Award, 1972, for co-authoring paper, "Prediction of Drug Effects and Personality Disorders."

WRITINGS—All under name Gilbert Honigfeld: (with wife, Alfreda Howard) *Psychiatric Drugs: A Desk Reference,* Academic Press, 1973.

Contributor: Kurt Salzinger and Suzanne Salzinger, editors, *Research in Verbal Behavior: Some Neurophysiological Implications,* Academic Press, 1967; Karl Rickels, editor, *Non-Specific Factors in Drug Therapy,* C. C Thomas, 1968; Phillip R. A. May and J. R. Wittenborn, editors, *Psychotropic Drug Response: Advances in Prediction,* C. C Thomas, 1969; Lynn Smith, editor, *Drugs, Development and Cerebral Function,* C. C Thomas, 1972; Pierre Pichot, editor, *Modern Problems in Pharmacopsychiatry,* Karger, 1973. Contributor of more than thirty articles to about twenty scientific journals.

* * *

HOWARD, Harry Nicholas 1902-

PERSONAL: Born February 19, 1902, in Excelsior Springs, Mo.; son of Alpheus Marshall (a pharmacist) and Lois Albina (Foster) Howard; married Elizabeth Jane Polk, January 1, 1930 (died, 1931); married Virginia Faye Brubaker, August 13, 1932; children: Robert Wendell, Norman Foster, Virginia B. *Education:* William Jewell College, B.A., 1924; University of Missouri, M.A., 1927; University of California, Berkeley, Ph.D., 1930. *Politics:* Independent Democrat. *Religion:* Unitarian. *Home and office:* 6508 Greentree Rd., Bethesda, Md. 20034.

CAREER: University of Oklahoma, Norman, assistant professor of history, 1929-30; Miami University, Oxford, Ohio, assistant professor, 1930-37, associate professor, 1937-40, professor of history, 1940-42; U.S. Department of State, Washington, D.C., head of East European Unit of Division of Territorial Studies, 1942-45, chief of Near East Branch of Division of Research for Near East and Africa, 1945-47, member of U.S. Delegation of United Nations Security Council Commission for Investigation of Greek Frontier Incidents and United Nation's Special Committee on the Balkans, 1947-51, advisor to various U.S. divisions and delegations to United Nations, 1947-56, acting U.S. representative of United Nations Relief and Works Agency (UNRWA) Advisory Commission, 1956-62; United Nations, New York, N.Y., special assistant to UNRWA commissioner-general, 1962-63; American University School of International Service, Washington, D.C., professor of Middle East studies, 1963-68, adjunct professor, 1968—. Member of U.S. delegation to United Nations Conference on International Organization (UNCIO), 1945, and of U.S. mission to Wiesbaden, Germany, 1945; acting chairman, Near East and North Africa area and country studies, 1966, 1971-73; lecturer, U.S. Army War College, 1971-72; visiting professor at numerous universities. Member of board of directors, American Near East Refugee Aid (ANERA). *Member:* American Historical Association, Middle East Institute (member of board of governors), Alpha Pi Zeta, Phi Alpha Theta, Pi Kappa Delta. *Awards, honors:* Order of the Phoenix from Government of Greece, 1953.

WRITINGS: The Partition of Turkey: A Diplomatic History, 1913-1923, University of Oklahoma Press, 1931, reissued, Fertig, 1966; *Military Government in the Panama Canal Zone,* University of Oklahoma Press, 1931; (with Robert Joseph Kerner) *The Balkan Conferences and the Balkan Entente, 1930-1935: A Study in the Recent History of the Balkan and Near Eastern Peoples,* University of California Press, 1936; *The Problem of the Turkish Straits,* U.S. Government Printing Office, 1947; *The United Nations and the Problem of Greece,* United States Government Printing Office, 1947; *Greece and the United Nations, 1946-49: A Summary Record,* Office of Public Affairs, U.S. Department of State, 1949; *The King-Crane Commission: An American Inquiry in the Middle East,* Khayats (Beirut), 1963; *Turkey, the Straits, and United States Policy,* Johns Hopkins University Press, 1974.

Contributor: R. J. Kerner, editor, *Czechoslovakia: Twenty Years of Independence,* University of California, 1940; Kerner, editor, *Yugoslavia,* University of California, 1949; Tareq Y. Ismael, editor, *Government and Politics of the Contemporary Middle East,* Dorsey, 1970; Ismael, editor, *The Middle East in World Politics: A Study in Contemporary International Relations,* Syracuse University Press, 1974.

Also author of U.S. Department of State bulletins published by U.S. Government Printing Office, and other pamphlets and offprints. Book review editor, *Middle East Journal,* 1963—.

WORK IN PROGRESS: Continued research and writing on Middle Eastern problems.

SIDELIGHTS: Howard told *CA:* "I have tried to follow the philosophy embodied in William James' chapter on habit—of keeping at it in the prospect of achieving something worthwhile. My major interests . . . were stimulated by the late Professor Robert J. Kerner. I have been fortunate in my wife and family."

* * *

HOWAT, John K(eith) 1937-

PERSONAL: Born April 12, 1937, in Denver, Colo.; son of James Bowcott (an army officer) and Nancy Selden (Skinker) Howat; married Anne Hadley, January 21, 1958; children: Karen Louise, Laura Anne. *Education:* Attended Phillips Exeter Academy, 1953-55; Harvard University, B.A., 1959, M.A., 1962. *Home:* 1100 Park Ave., New York, N.Y. 10028. *Office:* Metropolitan Museum of Art, 1000 Fifth Ave., New York, N.Y. 10021.

CAREER: Hyde Collection, Glens Falls, N.Y., curator, 1962-64; Metropolitan Museum of Art, New York, N.Y., assistant curator of American paintings and sculpture, 1967-68, associate curator, 1968-70, curator, 1970—. Member of advisory committee of Smithsonian Institution Archives of American Art. *Member:* American Federation of Arts.

WRITINGS: The Hudson River and Its Painters, Viking, 1972. Author of exhibition catalogs. Contributor to *Bulletin of the Metropolitan Museum of Art, Magazine Antiques, American Art Review,* and *Journal of the Honolulu Academy of Fine Arts.* Editorial adviser to *Journal of the Archives of American Art;* editorial associate of *American Art Review.*

WORK IN PROGRESS: Landscape Painting and Topography in the United States: The Artist as Explorer, Traveller, and Tourist from the Sixteenth through the Nineteenth Centuries, completion expected in 1976.

* * *

HOWE, Doris Kathleen (Mary Munro, Kaye Stewart; Newlyn Nash, joint pseudonym)

PERSONAL: Daughter of George William and Agnes (Hepworth) Howe. *Education:* Educated in England. *Home:* Fell Cottage, Compston St., Ambleside, Cumbria, England.

CAREER: Novelist and short story writer.

WRITINGS—All published by Ward, Lock: *I Must Go Back: A Kootenay Romance,* 1946; *The Eager Heart: A Kootenay Story,* 1947; *All Vigil Ended: A Kootenay Tale,* 1947; *On Eagle's Wings: A Kootenay Incident,* 1948; *Three O'Clock,* 1949; *The Unknown Road,* 1949; *The Year of Decision,* 1951; *Second Chances,* 1951; *Deep in My Memory,* 1952; *The Happy Pilgrim,* 1953; *I Give You My Heart,* 1955; *Somewhere My Love,* 1955; *Winter Jasmine,* 1956; *Goodbye Summer,* 1957; *Trial for Love,* 1957; *The Shores of Love,* 1958; *Island Destiny,* 1958; *Forever Mine,* 1959; *Sweet Life,* 1959; *Some Other Door,* 1960; *The Waters of Time,* 1960.

Under pseudonym Mary Munro; all published by R. Hale: *The Wheel of Life,* 1958; *Moon Light,* 1958; *A Dream Came True,* 1958; *The Bargain,* 1959; *The Golden Vase,* 1959; *A Red Rose,* 1960; *Whispering Sands,* 1961; *The Honey Pot,* 1962; *Second Love,* 1962; *The Singing House,* 1974.

Under pseudonym Kaye Stewart: *The Touchstone,* Jenkins, 1945.

With sister, Muriel Howe, under joint pseudonym Newlyn Nash: all published by John Gresham: *Beach of Dreams,* 1961; *Dance of Destiny,* 1962; *Magic of Love,* 1962; *Wild Garlic,* 1962; *The Affair at Claife Manor,* 1963; *The Pearl,* 1963.

Contributor of over a hundred short stories to magazines.

WORK IN PROGRESS: A novel with a Scottish background.

* * *

HOWE, Quincy 1900-

PERSONAL: Born August 17, 1900, in Boston, Mass.; son of Mark Anthony DeWolfe (an author) and Fanny (Quincy) Howe; married Mary L. Post, May 14, 1932; children: Quincy, Jr., Tina (Mrs. Norman Levy). *Education:* Harvard University, A.B. (magna cum laude), 1921; Christ's College, Cambridge, graduate study, 1921-22. *Home:* 108 East 82nd St., New York, N.Y. 10028.

CAREER: Atlantic Monthly Co., Boston, Mass., member of staff, 1922-29; *Living Age* (monthly magazine), New York, N.Y., editor, 1929-35; Simon & Schuster, New York, N.Y., editor-in-chief, 1935-42; Station WQXR, New York, N.Y., news commentator, 1939-42; Columbia Broadcasting System, New York, N.Y., news commentator, 1942-49, for television, 1949-50; University of Illinois, Urbana, associate professor of journalism and news analyst for Station WILL, 1950-54; American Broadcasting Co., New York, N.Y., news analyst, 1954-63; *Atlas: The Magazine of the World Press,* New York, N.Y., editor, 1961-65; Radio New York Worldwide, New York, N.Y., news analyst, 1966-70; commentator over WTFM, New York, 1973-74; contributing editor, *Atlas World Press Review,* 1974—. Lecturer. *Military service:* U.S. Marine Corps, SATC, Harvard Unit, 1918. *Member:* Association of Radio-Television News Analysts, Century Association, Sigma Delta Chi. *Awards, honors:* George Foster Peabody award, 1955, and Overseas Press Club award, 1959, both for radio-television news analysis; Columbia-Catherwood award for responsible international journalism, 1962.

WRITINGS—All published by Simon & Schuster, except as noted: *World Diary: 1929-34,* McBride, 1934; *England Expects Every American to do His Duty,* 1937; *Blood is Cheaper than Water: The Prudent American's Guide to Peace and War,* 1939; (editor and author of introduction and text) David Low, *Cartoon History of Our Times,* 1949; *The News and How to Understand It, in Spite of the Newspapers, in Spite of the Magazines and in Spite of the Radio,* 1940; (editor and contributor) William Freeman, *Hear! Hear! An Informal Guide to Public Speaking,* 1941, revised edition published as *Informal Guide to Public Speaking,* 1953; *A World History of Our Own Times,* Volume I: *From the turn of the Century to the 1918 Armistice,* 1949, Volume II: *The World Between the Wars: From the 1918 Armistice to the Munich Agreement,* 1953;. *Ashes of Victory: World War II and Its Aftermath,* 1972.

SIDELIGHTS: Howe's early sardonic *England Expects Every American to do His Duty,* which provoked a furor in that country, has been attributed to Yankee rancor inherited from colonial forebears of both his mother and father (a Pulitzer prize-winner).

John Toland wrote of his latest book: "*Ashes of Victory* defies description. It is a lengthy work, concise and wordy, cerebral and showy, reasonable and inflammatory, inspiring and irritating. It is the season's most delectable sweet-and-sour pork dish, and I enjoyed it thoroughly. The author, somehow manages to be objective and subjective on the same page. . . . [His] manner of putting all the pieces together, of reappraising the war in the light of its consequences, and of making sense out of chaos, is indeed unique. He leads the reader through the maze of politics and war with the endearing arrogance of a school teacher who cares. His erudition will intimidate some; a number of his conclusions will appall even more." And Arthur Cooper commented, "The real value of this book lies in its calm, dispassionate discussion of how decisions made during the war influenced postwar policies that today find us wallowing in Vietnam."

* * *

HOWE, Russell Warren 1925-

PERSONAL: Born August 1, 1925, in London, England. *Education:* Attended Cambridge University; Sorbonne, University of Paris, D.es E.C.F., 1948. *Home:* 4000 Tunlaw Rd. N.W., Washington, D.C. 20007. *Agent:* Anita Diamant, Writer's Workshop, Inc., 51 East 42nd St., New York, N.Y. 10017.

CAREER: Foreign correspondent for Reuters Ltd., London, England, 1948-52, *Sunday Times,* London, 1955-58, *Washington Post,* Washington, D.C., 1958-65, *Christian Science Monitor,* Boston, Mass., 1968-69, and *Baltimore Sun,* Baltimore, Md., 1969-72; free-lance investigative reporter, and magazine, radio, and television correspondent, 1952-55, 1965-68, and 1972—. Special counsel to Premier Sylvanus Olympio of Togo, 1960-61, visiting professor at Dakar University, 1968-71; media consultant to Washington delegation of European Common Market, 1972—.

MEMBER: Overseas Press Club of America, Society of Authors, Aircraft Owners and Pilots Association. *Awards, honors:* Ford Foundation fellowship in advanced international reporting, Columbia University, 1965-66; guest scholar at Woodrow Wilson International Center of Smithsonian Institution, 1972.

WRITINGS: The Light and the Shadows (stories), Secker & Warburg, 1952; *Behold, the City* (novel), Secker & Warburg, 1953; *Theirs the Darkness* (African travel book), Jenkins, 1955; *Black Star Rising* (African travel and politics), Jenkins, 1958; *Black Africa,* Walker & Co., Volume I,

1966, Volume II, 1967; *The African Revolution,* Barnes & Noble, 1968; *Along the Afric Shore* (American-African diplomatic history), Barnes & Noble, in press.

WORK IN PROGRESS: The Policy Peddlers, on foreign lobbyists, with Sarah Trott.

* * *

HOWELL, Barbara 1937-

PERSONAL: Born January 26, 1937, in Chicago, Ill.; daughter of H. William (in advertising) and Margaret (Miles) Howell; divorced; children: William Leroy. *Education:* Barat College, B.A. (magna cum laude), 1957; Universite de Lille, graduate study, 1957-58; Columbia University, graduate study, 1959-60. *Home:* 55 East 87th St., New York, N.Y. 10028.

CAREER: Benton & Bowles (advertising agency), New York, N.Y., copy trainee, 1961-63; Redmond, Marcus & Shure (advertising agency), New York, N.Y., copywriter, 1963-65; Marschalk Co. (advertising agency), New York, N.Y., copy supervisor, 1965; Batten, Barton, Durstine & Osborn (advertising agency), New York, N.Y., copy supervisor, 1965-71; free-lance writer, 1971—. *Awards, honors:* Fulbright grant to France, 1957-58.

WRITINGS: Don't Bother to Come in on Monday, St. Martin's, 1973. Contributor of short stories and articles to *Cosmopolitan, True,* and *Family Weekly.*

WORK IN PROGRESS: A book on office sadism; a novel.

BIOGRAPHICAL/CRITICAL SOURCES: Chicago Daily News, July 13, 1973.

* * *

HOWSE, Ernest Marshall 1902-

PERSONAL: Born September 29, 1902, in Newfoundland, Canada; son of Charles (a clergyman) and Elfrida (Palmer) Howse; married Esther Lilian Black, September 17, 1932; children: Margery (Mrs. Raymond Dyer), David, George. *Education:* Dalhousie University, B.A., 1929; Pine Hill Divinity Hall, graduate (with honors), 1931; Union Theological Seminary, S.T.M., 1932; University of Edinburgh, Ph.D., 1934. *Home:* 29 Eastbourne Ave., Toronto, Ontario M5P 2E8, Canada.

CAREER: Ordained minister of United Church of Canada, 1931; minister in Beverly Hills, Calif., 1934-35, Winnipeg, Manitoba, 1935-48, and Toronto, Ontario, 1948-70. Co-chairman of Continuing Committee of Muslim-Christian Cooperation, Cairo, Egypt, 1955; moderator of United Church of Canada, 1964-66; Canadian delegate to First World Conference on Religion and Peace, Kyoto, Japan, 1970. *Member:* Empire Club of Canada (director, 1956-70; honorary officer, 1970—). *Awards, honors:* Received key to city and made honorary citizen of Seoul, Korea, 1965; D.D. from United College, 1948, Huntington College (now University; Sudbury, Ont.), 1964, Pine Hill Divinity Hall, 1966, and Victoria University (Toronto, Ont.), 1967; D.Litt. from University of Newfoundland, 1965.

WRITINGS: Saints in Politics, University of Toronto Press, 1952, 3rd edition, Allen & Unwin, 1971; *Spiritual Values in Shakespeare,* Abingdon, 1955; *The Lively Oracles,* Allen & Unwin, 1956; *People and Provocations,* Ryerson, 1965. Syndicated columnist in Canadian newspapers, 1956-64; columnist for *Toronto Telegram,* 1964-70, and *Toronto Star,* 1970—. Contributor to journals and newspapers.

HUBENKA, Lloyd J(ohn) 1931-

PERSONAL: Born January 1, 1931, in Omaha, Neb.; son of Lloyd J. (a dentist) and Emma (Dobrovolny) Hubenka; married Beverly Conkling, February 14, 1953; children: Elizabeth, Evan, Naomi, Sara. *Education:* Creighton University, B.A., 1952, M.A., 1959; University of Nebraska, Ph.D., 1966. *Religion:* Roman Catholic. *Home:* 4115 North Post Rd., Omaha, Neb. 68112. *Office:* Department of English, Creighton University, 24th and California, Omaha, Neb. 68112.

CAREER: Creighton University, Omaha, Neb., instructor, 1958-61, assistant professor, 1961-66, associate professor, 1966-68, professor of English, 1968—, head of department, 1966—. Director of Nebraska U.S. Office of Education Conference on Improving Higher Education, 1967; co-director of Nebraska U.S. Office of Education Conference on Modern Writers, 1970; member of secondary level inspection team of Omaha Public School System, 1970; director of Nebraska Program for the Development of Secondary Teachers, 1971. *Military service:* U.S. Army, 1952-54; served in Korea; received Commendation Medal and Bronze Star. U.S. Army Reserve, 1954—; current rank, lieutenant colonel.

MEMBER: Modern Language Association of America, American Association of University Professors (president of Nebraska State Conference, 1969-70), National Council of Teachers of English, Association of Departments of English, Victorian Periodical Society, Reserve Officers Association of the United States, Association of the United States Army. *Awards, honors:* Nebraska U.S. Office of Education Council grant, 1967, 1968; National Endowment for the Humanities fellow, 1968.

WRITINGS: (Editor) John Ruskin, *Unto This Last,* University of Nebraska Press, 1967; (with Reloy Garcia) *The Design of Drama,* McKay, 1973; (with Garcia) *The Narrative Sensibility,* McKay, in press.

WORK IN PROGRESS: Practical Politics: A Collection of Shaw's Hitherto Uncollected Essays and Lectures on Socialism, Capitalism, and Fascism; a monograph, *The Religious Philosophy of Bernard Shaw.*

* * *

HUDSON, Geoffrey Francis 1903-1974

British authority on Far Eastern affairs, editor, and author of books on Far Eastern and world affairs. Obituaries: *AB Bookman's Weekly,* July 15, 1974.

* * *

HUGHES, Arthur Montague D'Urban 1873-1974

November 3, 1873—1974; British educator and author of books on literary subjects. Obituaries: *AB Bookman's Weekly,* July 15, 1974.

* * *

HUGO, Richard 1923-

PERSONAL: Born December 21, 1923, in Seattle, Wash.; son of Herbert F. (a U.S. Navy career man) and Esther (Monk) Hugo; married Barbara Williams, August 3, 1951 (divorced February 10, 1966); married Ripley Schemm, July 12, 1974; stepchildren: Melissa Hansen, Matthew Hansen. *Education:* University of Washington, Seattle,

B.A., 1948, M.A., 1952. *Home:* 2407 Wylie, Missoula, Mont. 59801. *Office:* Department of English, University of Montana, Missoula, Mont. 59801.

CAREER: Employed in various positions at Boeing Co., Seattle, Wash., 1951-63; University of Montana, Missoula, 1964—, began as visiting lecturer, now professor of English. *Military service:* U.S. Army Air Forces, 1943-45; served in Mediterranean theater; became first lieutenant; received Distinguished Flying Cross and Air Medal. *Awards, honors:* Rockefeller Foundation creative writing grant, 1967-68.

WRITINGS: A Run of Jacks, Minnesota Press, 1961; *Death of the Kapowsin Tavern,* Harcourt, 1965; *Good Luck in Cracked Italian,* World Publishing, 1969; *The Lady in Kicking Horse Reservoir,* Norton, 1973; *What Thou Lovest Well, Remains American,* Norton, 1975.

WORK IN PROGRESS: West Marginal Way, an autobiographical work; *Thirty Letters and Thirteen Dreams,* a book of poems; more poems.

* * *

HUMBARACI, D(emir) Arslan 1923- (Omar Abdallah, Jean-Luc Herve)

PERSONAL: Surname is pronounced Houm-ba-radji; born August 21, 1923, in Istanbul, Turkey; became British citizen, 1966; son of Kazim Ziya (an Ottoman government official) and Meliha (Kazin) Humbaraci; married Melek Tansu Necla (a painter), October 29, 1941; children: Mehmet Kazim Omer. *Education:* Educated in Istanbul at Robert College, at Turco-French and Turkish lyceums, and then at Turkish Naval Academy and School, 1936-38. *Religion:* "Born Muslim—free thinker." *Home address:* 52 Tite St., London S.W.3, England. *Agent:* Patrick Seale, 2 Motcomb St., Belgravia Sq., London SW1X 8JU, England.

CAREER: Anatolia News Agency, sub-editor in Istanbul and Ankara, Turkey, 1938-41; U.S. Office of War Information, editor in Istanbul, later chief news editor in Ankara, Turkey, 1944-47; *New York Times,* correspondent in Turkey, 1947-49; newspaper reporter and correspondent in France, England, and Middle East, and co-founder and coeditor of *Mondes d'Orient,* Paris, France, 1949-58; foreign correspondent in Indonesia, 1958-60, Africa, 1960-64, and Italy, 1964-68, writing for *Economist, Observer,* and *Times* of London, and for Paris, Middle East, and Far East publications and press services; consultant to various Italian firms, and to chief of Rome Bureau of *Far Eastern Economic Review* (Hongkong), 1968-70; honorary consul general of Zambia in Rome, Italy, and director of Zambia Information and Tourist Bureau for Western Europe, 1970-71; director of external relations of United Nations for Stockholm Conference on the Human Environment, 1971-72; engaged in political activity in Southern Africa, actively supporting Movimento Popular de Libertacgo de Angola, 1972—. *Military service:* Turkish Army, Signal Corps, 1942-45.

WRITINGS: Middle East Indictment: From the Truman Doctrine, the Soviet Penetration, Britain's Downfall and the Eisenhower Doctrine, R. Hale, 1958; *Algeria: A Revolution That Failed. A Political History Since 1954,* Praeger, 1966; *Portugal's African Wars: Angola-Guinea-Bissao-Mozambique,* Third Press, 1974. Contributor to *Monde* (Paris), *Guardian* (London), *Sekai* (Tokyo), *Toronto Star, Oil and Gas Journal* (Tulsa), and other publications.

SIDELIGHTS: Humbaraci's surname derives from a French great-grandfather (the son of Count Claude de Bonneval), who turned Muslim and received the title of Humbaraci Pasha, meaning "general of artillery," for his work in reforming the artillery of the Ottoman Empire.

Humbaraci, whose pseudonyms, Omar Abdallah and Jean-Luc Herve, were used while a foreign correspondent, has been a legal resident of nine countries and traveled in more than forty others, the United States included. He is fluent in English in addition to his native Turkish, French, and Italian, and speaks some Greek, Arabic, and Malaysian.

* * *

HUMPSTONE, Charles Cheney 1931-

PERSONAL: Born January 3, 1931, in Brooklyn, N.Y.; son of John Harvey (a businessman) and Maribel (Cheney) Humpstone; married Suzanne Torchiana, 1960; children: Alessandra, Susannah. *Education:* Harvard University, A.B., 1953, LL.B., 1959. *Politics:* Democrat. *Home:* 511 Queen St., Alexandria, Va. 22134. *Office:* International Research and Technology Corp., 1501 Wilson Blvd., Arlington, Va. 22209.

CAREER: Admitted to the Bar of New York State, 1960. White & Case (attorneys), New York, N.Y., associate, 1959-64; U.S. Commission on Civil Rights, Washington, D.C., assistant general counsel, 1964-67; U.S. Department of Treasury, Washington, D.C., deputy special assistant to secretary for enforcement, 1967-69; International Research and Technology Corp., Arlington, Va., member of research staff, 1967-69, vice-president, 1969-72, president, 1972—, director, 1973—. Member of City of Alexandria Environmental Policy Commission, 1970-72. *Military service:* U.S. Marine Corps Reserve, 1953-63; active duty, 1953-55; became first lieutenant. *Awards, honors:* U.S. Department of Treasury meritorious service award, 1968.

WRITINGS: (With Theodore B. Taylor) *The Restoration of the Earth,* Harper, 1973. Author of monographs. Contributor to *Foreign Affairs* and *Church and State.*

* * *

HUNT, George Laird 1918-

PERSONAL: Born September 11, 1918, in Philadelphia, Pa. son of Henry B. (a carpenter) and Helen (Laird) Hunt; married Mary Alice Minear, August 5, 1943; children: Laurence, Bruce, Marcia Beth. *Education:* Maryville College, Maryville, Tenn., B.A., 1940; Princeton Theological Seminary, B.D., 1943. *Home:* 225 King St., Fanwood, N.J. 07023. *Office:* 74 Martine Ave., Fanwood, N.J. 07023.

CAREER: Ordained minister of the Presbyterian Church, 1943; pastor in Wilmington, Del., 1943-48, and Penn Wynne, Pa., 1960-61; Presbyterian Board of Christian Education, Philadelphia, Pa., secretary, 1948-60, 1962-63; Fanwood Presbyterian Church, Fanwood, N.J., senior minister, 1963—. Executive secretary of Consultation on Church Union, 1962-68; member of board of trustees of Bloomfield College, 1973—; editorial consultant to J. S. Paluch Co. *Awards, honors:* D.D. from Maryville College, Maryville, Tenn. 1958.

WRITINGS: Rediscovering the Church, Association Press, 1956; *A Guide to Christian Unity,* Bethany Press, 1958; (editor) *Ten Makers of Protestant Thought,* Association Press, 1958, revised edition published as *Twelve Makers of Protestant Thought,* 1971; *The Spirit Speaks to the Church: A Guide for the Study of Acts,* Board of Christian Education (Philadelphia), 1958; *Be What You Are: A*

Guide for the Study of Galatians, Board of Christian Education, 1963; (editor) *Calvinism and the Political Order,* Westminster Press, 1965; (editor) *Where We Are in Church Union,* Association Press, 1965. Contributor to religious publications. Editor of adult study materials, *Crossroads* and *Westminster Adult Leader,* published by the Board of Christian Education, 1949-59; also editor of *Today,* Presbyterian devotional magazine, 1957-59.

AVOCATIONAL INTERESTS: Family camping, modern drama and fiction, stamp collecting.

* * *

HUNT, William 1934-

PERSONAL: Born May 21, 1934; married wife, Marjorie (a poet), 1963; children: Phillip Devin. *Education:* University of Chicago, B.A., 1964. *Agent:* Wendy Weil, Julian Bach Agency, 3 East 48th St., New York, N.Y. 10017. *Office:* Department of Human Resources, 640 North LaSalle St., Chicago, Ill. 60610.

CAREER: Writer, reporter, and editor, 1960-66, 1967—. Labor organizer, 1953-58; community organizer, 1963-66; *Chicago Review,* Chicago, Ill., poetry editor, 1964-67; Department of Human Resources, Chicago, Ill., director of information, 1970—. *Awards, honors:* National Endowment for the Arts grant ($7,000), 1967-68; Langston Hughes Memorial Prize of *Poetry Magazine* for poems in February, 1970, issue.

WRITINGS: Of the Map That Changes (poems), Swallow Press, 1973.

WORK IN PROGRESS: Revising a novel; a second collection of poems.

* * *

HUNTER, Hilda 1921-

PERSONAL: Born May 11, 1921, in Liverpool, England; daughter of Frederick Newton (an engineer) and Elizabeth (Billington) Hunter. *Education:* London College of Music, A.L.C.M., 1945. *Religion:* Roman Catholic. *Home:* 44 Argyle St. S., Birkenhead L41 9BX, Cheshire, England. *Agent:* Norah Smaridge, 11 Godfrey Rd., Upper Montclair, N.J. 07043.

CAREER: Free-lance writer; pianist, appearing as soloist and accompanist at charity concerts and with local bands. *Member:* Society of Authors, Liverpool Writers Club (chairman, 1972-73).

WRITINGS: Growing Up with Music, Hewitt House, 1970; (with Norah Smaridge) *The Teen-Agers Guide to Collecting Practically Anything* (Junior Literary Guild selection), Dodd, 1972; (with Smaridge) *The Teen-Agers Guide to Hobbies for Here and Now,* Dodd, 1974. Contributor of articles on American, British, and continental silver and other subjects to *Antique Dealer, Apollo, Times* (London), trade and religious periodicals, and other journals and newspapers. Former columnist in antiques magazine, identifying silver articles and their marks.

AVOCATIONAL INTERESTS: Music (including music therapy), collecting books and antiques, visiting museums, art galleries, and historic houses.

* * *

HUNTLEY, Chester Robert 1911-1974

December 10, 1911—March 20, 1974; American newscaster and commentator. Obituaries: *Washington Post,* March 21, 1974; *Time,* April 1, 1974; *Newsweek,* April 1, 1974; *Current Biography,* May, 1974.

* * *

HUNTLEY, Chet
See HUNTLEY, Chester Robert

* * *

HURLEY, Leslie J(ohn) 1911-

PERSONAL: Born June 25, 1911, in Bangor, Me.; son of Walter James (a businessman) and Elizabeth (York) Hurley; married Pauline Mary Stetson, February 2, 1943; children: Joann (Mrs. Pasquale DiLego), John R., Robert L., Anne K. *Education:* Maine School of Commerce (now Husson College), student, 1945-46. *Religion:* Protestant. *Home:* 13 Vine St., Northfield, Vt. 05663. *Office:* Department of Physical Education, Norwich University, Northfield, Vt.

CAREER: Maine National Guard, 1935-41; U.S. Army, Infantry, 1941-61; retired as master sergeant; Norwich University, Northfield, Vt., instructor in ROTC-mountain training, 1948-61, instructor in physical education, 1961—. *Member:* National Ski Patrol, Appalachian Mountain Club, League of Vermont Writers. *Awards, honors*—Military: Bronze Star, Commendation Ribbon. Civilian: Resolution Commendation from New Hampshire State Legislature, 1959, for rescue work in the White Mountains; Humanity Award from American National Red Cross, 1972, for five-year contribution to first aid and life-saving program.

WRITINGS: (With William E. Osgood) *Ski Touring: An Introductory Guide,* Tuttle, 1969; (with Osgood) *The Snowshoe Book,* Greene, 1971; (contributor) Robert H. Chickering and Marcia S. Chickering, editors, *X-Country Skiing,* Dell, 1972.

WORK IN PROGRESS: Articles and reviews.

* * *

HUROK, Sol(omon) 1888-1974

April 9, 1888—March 5, 1974; Russian-born American impresario. Obituaries: *New York Times,* March 6, 1974; *Washington Post,* March 6, 1974, March 10, 1974; *Time,* March 18, 1974; *Newsweek,* March 18, 1974; *Current Biography,* April, 1974.

* * *

HUTCHINSON, Vernal 1922-

PERSONAL: Born July 21, 1922, in Stonington, Me.; son of Leslie Senor (a laborer) and Bessie (Richards) Hutchinson; married Shirlie Louise Eaton, January 1, 1943 (died, 1972). *Education:* Attended public schools in Stonington, Me. *Office address:* American Practical Navigators, Box 205, South Brooksville, Me. 04617.

CAREER: Laborer, employed by American Practical Navigators, South Brooksville, Me.

WRITINGS: A Maine Town in the Civil War, Wheelwright, 1965; *When Revolution Came,* Ellsworth American, 1973. Feature writer for *Ellsworth American,* 1948—.

* * *

HUVOS, Kornel 1913-

PERSONAL: Born April 25, 1913, in Budapest, Hungary;

son of Leslie (a sculptor) and Ilona (Vajda) Huvos; married Anna Maria Ledniczky (a librarian), March 25, 1945; children: Christopher L. *Education:* Attended College St. Jean, Fribourg, Switzerland, 1925-31; Royal University of Budapest, J.D., 1938; University of Cincinnati, Ph.D., 1965. *Religion:* Roman Catholic. *Home:* 615 McAlpin Ave., Cincinnati, Ohio 45220. *Office:* Department of Romance Languages and Literatures, University of Cincinnati, Cincinnati, Ohio 45221.

CAREER: Hungarian Academy of Sciences, Budapest, Hungary, head lexicographer, 1949-56; *Cincinnati Times-Star,* Cincinnati, Ohio, feature writer, 1956-57; University of Cincinnati, Ohio, instructor, 1961-63, assistant professor, 1963-68, associate professor, 1968-73, professor of Romance languages and literatures, 1973—. *Member:* American Association of University Professors, Modern Language Association of America, American Association of Teachers of French, Midwest Modern Language Association, Alliance Francaise of Cincinnati (first vice-president, 1960-70), Pi Delta Phi. *Awards, honors:* Taft research fellowship, 1968 and 1974.

WRITINGS: (Translator from the French) Bence Szabolcsi, *Bela Bartok: sa vie et son oeuvre* (title means "Bela Bartok: His Life and His Works"), Corvina, 1956; (translator from the French) Gyula Moravcsik, *Dix annees de philologie classique hongroise: 1945-1954* (title means "Ten Years of Classical Philology, 1945-1954"), Hungarian Academy of Sciences, 1955; (translator from the French) Istvan Hajnal, *L'Enseignement de l'ecriture aux universites medievales* (title means "The Teaching of Writing in Medieval Universities"), Hungarian Academy of Sciences, 1959; (editor with L. Clark Keating) *Impressions d'Amerique: Les Etats-Unis dans la litterature francaise contemporaine* (title means "American Impressions: The United States in Contemporary French Literature"), St. Martin's, 1970; *Cinq Mirages Americains: Les Etats-Unis dans l'oeuvre de Georges Duhamel, Jules Romains, Andre Maurois, Jacques Maritain, et Simone de Beauvoir* (title means "Five American Mirages: The United States in the Works of Georges Duhamel, etc."), Didier, 1972. Managing editor and head lexicographer of dictionaries published by Hungarian Academy of Sciences, 1953-56. Contributor to *French Review, Kentucky Romance Quarterly,* and *Comparative Literature Studies.*

SIDELIGHTS: Huvos has travelled extensively in Eastern and Western Europe, and Turkey.

* * *

HUYCK, Margaret Hellie 1939-

PERSONAL: Born April 14, 1939, in Waterloo, Iowa; daughter of Ole Ingeman and Elizabeth (Larsen) Hellie; married William Thomas Huyck (a lawyer), June 24, 1961; children: Elizabeth, Karen. *Education:* Vassar College, A.B., 1961; University of Chicago, M.S., 1963, Ph.D., 1970. *Religion:* Unitarian-Universalist. *Home:* 1718 East 55th St., Chicago, Ill. 60615. *Office:* Department of Psychology, Illinois Institute of Technology, Chicago, Ill. 60616.

CAREER: Illinois Institute of Technology, Chicago, Ill., assistant professor of psychology, 1969—. President of Newstyles, Inc. *Member:* American Psychological Association, American Sociological Association, Gerontological Society, Association of Women Psychologists, Society for the Study of Social Problems, American Association of University Professors, National Organization of Women, Midwest Psychological Association.

WRITINGS: Growing Older, Prentice-Hall, 1974.

WORK IN PROGRESS: Sexuality and Aging, with Jessie Potter; research on correlates of sex role ideology among adults, on age changes in self concept, body concept, sexuality, and health status, and on behavioral norms for older adults.

* * *

HYDE, Mary Morley Crapo 1912-

PERSONAL: Born July 8, 1912, in Detroit, Mich.; daughter of Stanford Tappan (an executive) and Emma Caroline (Morley) Crapo; married Donald Frizell Hyde, September 16, 1939 (died February 6, 1966). *Education:* Vassar College, A.B., 1934, Columbia University, M.A., 1936, Ph.D., 1947; Brown University, Litt.D., 1968; University of Birmingham, postdoctoral study, 1969. *Home:* Four Oaks Farm, 350 Burnt Mills Rd., Somerville, N.J. 08876. *Office:* Room 330, 1 Palmer Sq., Princeton, N.J. 08540.

CAREER: Writer. Council member of Friends of Columbia University Libraries, 1954—; member of humanities visiting committee of University of Chicago, 1956—; member of board of governors of Johnson House (London), 1963—; member of English department and library advisory councils of Princeton University, 1965—; member of English department and libraries visiting committees of Harvard University, 1966—; trustee of Yale Libraries Association, 1970—; member of Council of Friends of Folger Shakespeare Library, 1970—; trustee of Friends of Winterthur, 1971—.

MEMBER: Shakespeare Association of America (president, 1956—), Modern Language Association of America, Bibliographical Association of America, Johnsonians, Keats-Shelley Association of America (director, 1967—), Master Drawings Association, New York Horticulture Society, Johnson Society of Lichfield, England (president, 1957), Phi Beta Kappa. *Awards, honors:* D.Litt., Beaver College, 1963, Douglass College, 1964.

WRITINGS: Playwriting for Elizabethans, Columbia University Press, 1949, new edition, 1973; (editor with E. L. McAdam and husband, Donald Hyde) *Johnson's Diaries, Prayers, and Annals,* Yale University Press, 1953; *Four Oaks Farm and Its Library,* Clarke & Way, 1967; *The Impossible Friendship: Boswell and Mrs. Thrale,* Harvard University Press, 1972. Member of editorial committee of "Yale Works of Johnson," 1957, and "Private Papers of James Boswell," 1966—.

WORK IN PROGRESS: Research on Dr. Samuel Johnson and on Mrs. Thrale-Piozzi.

* * *

HYDE, Tracy Elliot
See VENNING, Corey

* * *

HYLAND, Jean Scammon 1926-

PERSONAL: Born January 12, 1926, in Minneapolis, Minn.; daughter of Richard E. (a professor) and Julia (Simms) Scammon; married Kerwin E. Hyland (a professor of zoology), May 7, 1966; children: Jeffrey; stepchildren: John, Jeanne, Janet. *Education:* MacMurray College, B.A., 1948; Western Reserve University (now Case Western Reserve University), M.A., 1953; attended University of Poitiers, 1953-54; University of Kansas, Ph.D., 1959. *Politics:* Democrat. *Religion:* Episcopal. *Home:* 967 Kingstown Rd., Peace Dale, R.I. 02879. *Office:* Department of Languages, University of Rhode Island, Kingston, R.I. 02881.

CAREER: Saint Mary's Hall, Faribault, Minn., instructor in French, 1948-52; University of Kansas, Lawrence, instructor in French, 1954-59; College of William and Mary, Williamsburg, Va., assistant professor of French, 1959-64; University of Rhode Island, Kingston, assistant professor, 1964-68, associate professor of French, 1968—. *Member:* American Association of University Professors, Modern Language Association of America, American Coucil on Teaching of Foreign Languages, New England Foreign Language Association (member of board of directors, 1973-76), Northeast Modern Language Association, Rhode Island Foreign Language Association (member of board of directors, 1969—), Virginia Foreign Language Association (president, 1962-64), Pi Delta Phi, Sigma Delta Pi. *Awards, honors:* Fulbright scholar at University of Poitiers, 1953-54.

WRITINGS: Reading Proficiency in French: Biological Sciences, Van Nostrand, 1969; *Reading Proficiency in French: Physical Sciences,* Van Nostrand, 1969; *Reading Proficiency in French: Social Sciences,* Van Nostrand, 1970; *Reading Proficiency in French: Humanities,* Van Nostrand, 1970. Editor of *Rhode Island Foreign Language Gazette,* 1964—.

WORK IN PROGRESS: Research on an intermediate reading text in French, on Victor Hugo's exile years in Belgium, and on Emile Zola.

AVOCATIONAL INTERESTS: Winter sports, gardening, travel.

* * *

HYMAN, Trina Schart 1939-

PERSONAL: Born April 8, 1939, in Philadelphia, Pa.; daughter of Albert H. and Margaret Doris (Bruck) Schart; married Harris Hyman (a mathematician and engineer), 1959 (divorced, 1968); children: Katrin. *Education:* Studied at Philadelphia Museum College of Art, 1956-59, Boston Museum School of the Arts, 1959-60, and Konstfackskolan (Swedish State Art School), Stockholm, 1960-61. *Politics:* "Royalist." *Religion:* "Druid." *Home:* Brick Hill Rd., Lyme, N.H. 03768.

CAREER: Artist and illustrator; art director of *Cricket* (magazine), LaSalle, Ill., 1972—.

WRITINGS—Self-illustrated: *How Six Found Christmas,* Little, Brown, 1969.

Illustrator: Hertha Von Gebhardt, *Toffe och den lilla Bilen,* Raben & Stoegren, 1961; Carl Memling, *Riddles, Riddles, from A to Z,* Western Publishing, 1963; Melanie Bellah, *Bow Wow! Meow!,* Western Publishing, 1963; Sandol S. Warburg, *Curl Up Small,* Houghton, 1964; Eileen O'-Faolain, *Children of the Salmon,* Little, Brown, 1965; Ruth Sawyer, *Joy to the World: Christmas Legends,* Little, Brown, 1966; Joyce Varney, *The Magic Maker,* Bobbs-Merrill, 1966; Virginia Haviland, *Favorite Fairy Tales Told in Czechoslovakia* (retold), Little, Brown, 1966; Edna Butler Trickey, *Billy Finds Out,* United Church Press, 1966; Jacob D. Townsend, *The Five Trials of the Pansy Bed,* Houghton, 1967; Elizabeth Johnson, *Stuck with Luck,* Little, Brown, 1967; Josephine Poole, *Moon Eyes,* Little, Brown, 1967; John T. Moore, *Cinnamon Seed,* Houghton, 1967; Paul Tripp, *The Little Red Flower,* Doubleday, 1968; Eve Merrian, *Epaminondas* (retold), Follett, 1968; Varney, *The Half-Time Gypsy,* Bobbs-Merrill, 1968; Johnson, *All in Free,* Little, Brown, 1968; Tom McGowen, *Dragon Stew,* Follett, 1969; Susan Meyers, *The Cabin on the Fjord,* Doubleday, 1969; Peter Hunter Blair, *The Coming of Pout,* Little, Brown, 1969; Clyde R. Bulla, *The Moon Singer,* Crowell, 1969; Ruth Nichols, *A Walk out of the World,* Harcourt, 1969; Claudia Paley, *Benjamin the True,* Little, Brown, 1969.

Paul Tripp, *The Vi-Daylin Book of Minnie the Mump,* Ross Laboratories, 1970; Donald J. Sobol, *Greta the Strong,* Follett, 1970; Blanche Luria Serwer, *Let's Steal the Moon: Jewish Tales, Ancient and Recent* (retold), Little, Brown, 1970; Maureen Mollie Hunter McIlwraith, under name Mollie Hunter, *The Walking Stones: A Story of Suspense,* Harper, 1970; Tom McGowen, *Sir Machinery,* Follett, 1970; Phyllis Krasilovsky, *The Shy Little Girl,* Houghton, 1970; Ellin Green, *The Pumpkin Giant,* Lothrop, 1970; Wylly Folk St. John, *The Ghost Next Door,* Harper, 1971; Osmond Molarsky, *The Bigger They Come,* Walck, 1971; Molarsky, *Take It or Leave It,* Walck, 1971; Carolyn Meyer, *The Bread Book: All About Bread and How to Make It,* Harcourt, 1971; Johnson, *Break a Magic Circle,* Little, Brown, 1971; Green, *Princess Rosetta and the Popcorn Man* (from *The Pot of Gold* by Mary E. Wilkins; retold), Lothrop, 1971; Eleanor Cameron, *A Room Made of Windows,* Little, Brown, 1971; Dori White, *Sarah and Katie,* Harper, 1972; Jan Wahl, *Magic Heart,* Seabury, 1972; Krasilovsky, *The Popular Girls Club,* Simon & Schuster, 1972; Paula Hendrich, *Who Says So?,* Lothrop, 1972; Howard Pyle, *King Stork* (story first published in Pyle's collection, *The Wonder Clock*), Little, Brown, 1973; Phyllis La Farge, *Joanna Runs Away,* Holt, 1973; Greene, *Clever Cooks,* Lothrop, 1973; Myra C. Livingston, editor, *Listen, Children, Listen* (anthology), Harcourt, 1973; Carol R. Brink, *The Bad Times of Irma Baumlein,* Macmillan, 1973; Brink, *Caddie Woodlawn,* Macmillan, 1973; Elizabeth Coatsworth, *The Wanderers,* 1973; Eleanor G. Vance, *The Everything Book,* Western Publishing, 1974; Dorothy S. Carter, editor, *Greedy Mariani, and Other Folktales of the Antilles,* Atheneum, 1974; Charles Causley, *Figgie Hobbin,* Walker & Co., 1974; Charlotte Herman, *You've Come a Long Way, Sybil McIntosh,* Philip J. O'Hara, 1974.

WORK IN PROGRESS: Picture books and anthologies of folk tales.

SIDELIGHTS: Trina Schart Hyman writes: "I live on a small farm in northern New Hampshire with my daughter, a friend, two dogs, nine cats, twenty-two sheep and twelve chickens. I take occasional trips to England and Scandinavia (I speak Swedish, and lived in Stockholm for two years), but mostly I stay home and work."

* * *

INALCIK, Halil 1916-

PERSONAL: Born May 26, 1916, in Istanbul, Turkey; son of Seyit Osman (a businessman) and Ayshe (Bahriye) Nuri; married wife, Sevkiye, January 18, 1945; children: Guenhan Tezgoer Ertan. *Education:* University of Ankara, M.A., 1940, Ph.D., 1942. *Religion:* Muslim. *Home:* 1648 East 50th St., Chicago, Ill. 60615. *Office:* University of Chicago, 1130 East 59th St., Chicago, Ill. 60637.

CAREER: University of Ankara, Ankara, Turkey, professor of history, 1943-72; University of Chicago, Chicago, Ill., professor of history, 1972—. *Member:* International

Association of South East European Studies, Royal Historical Society, Turkish Historical Society.

WRITINGS: The Ottoman Reforms, Tanzimat, and the Bulgarian Question (in Turkish), Turkish Historical Society, 1943; *Studies and Documents on the Reign of Mehmed the Conqueror* (in Turkish), Turkish Historical Society, 1954; *Ottoman Population and Land Survey of 1432* (in Turkish), Turkish Historical Society, 1954; *The Ottoman Empire: The Classical Age, 1300-1600,* Praeger, 1973. Editor, *Archivum Ottomanicum,* 1969—.

WORK IN PROGRESS: An Economic History of the Ottoman Empire; an enlarged version of *The Ottoman Empire,* for Praeger.

SIDELIGHTS: Inalcik told *CA*: "The Ottoman period in Turkish history is particularly interesting. It embraced the whole Middle East, and the Balkans between 1300 and 1900. There is no modern history of it, (since) the Ottoman archives, unusually rich, have not been exploited. . . . A truly scientific book on the Ottoman empire is badly needed." Inalcik does research study in French, German, Italian, Arabic, and Persian, as well as English and his native Turkish.

* * *

INDERLIED, Mary Elizabeth 1945- (Elizabeth Edwards)

PERSONAL: Third syllable of surname is pronounced "leed"; born January 12, 1945, in Flossmoor, Ill.; daughter of Tom Ellis (a businessman) and Mary (Hall) Butz; married Edward Inderlied (a minister), January 11, 1964; children: Beth, Bill. *Education:* Attended high school in Chesterland, Ohio. *Religion:* United Church of Christ. *Address:* R.R. #3, Sunman, Ind. 47041.

WRITINGS—Novels: (Under pseudonym Elizabeth Edwards) *The Proving Ground,* Zondervan, 1973; *Trappings,* Zondervan, in press.

WORK IN PROGRESS: Two novels.

* * *

INGLIS, Ruth Langdon 1927-

PERSONAL: Born December 17, 1927, in China; daughter of William Russell (U.S. consul-general) and Laura (Filer) Langdon; divorced; children: Diana Eleanor, Neil Langdon. *Education:* Barnard College, B.A., 1949. *Politics:* Democrat. *Religion:* Episcopalian. *Home and office:* 40 Winchester St., London S.W.1, England; *Agents:* A. D. Peters Ltd., 10 Buckingham St., London W.C.1, England; and Helen Brann Agency, 14 Sutton Pl. S., New York, N.Y. 10022.

CAREER: Sarah Lawrence College, Bronxville, N.Y., news bureau director, 1957-58; free-lance writer and journalist contributing especially to *Observer, Nova,* and *Daily Express,* London, England.

WRITINGS: A Time to Learn, Dial, 1973. Author of scripts for series "The Facts Are These," produced by Granada Television, London, England, 1968.

WORK IN PROGRESS: A book on parent-child relationships; group editor for *The Modern Woman's Encyclopedia,* for Elsevier.

SIDELIGHTS: Ruth Inglis wrote: "London is alive with new experiments and findings in sociology (much of it pioneered at London University) and so it is an exciting place for a London-American to be who is involved with new directions in child development and family relationships generally."

* * *

INGRAM, Thomas Henry 1924- (Tom Ingram)

PERSONAL: Born July 26, 1924, in Spaxton, England; son of John Markham (an officer in the armed forces) and Grace (Williams) Ingram; married Marie Robbins-Vona (a writer), April, 1958; children: Susanna, Patrick, Clarissa. *Education:* Corpus Christi College, Cambridge, B.A., 1948, M.A., 1957. *Home:* 38 Lyncombe Hill, Bath, England. *Agent:* Deborah Rogers, 29 Goodge St., London W.1, England.

CAREER: Teacher at Holsworthy Secondary Modern School, 1949, and Woolwich Secondary Art School, 1949-50; full-time research, writing, and work on exhibitions, 1950-58; Long Island University, Merriweather Campus (now C. W. Post Center), instructor, 1958-60, assistant professor of English, 1964-65; City of Bath Technical College, Bath, Somersetshire, England, lecturer, 1960-64, 1965-67; British Polytechnic, West of England College of Art, lecturer in English, 1967—. Lecturer in United States for Netherlands Office for Overseas Students, 1957, 1958. *Military service:* British Army, Royal Artillery, 1942-45; became lieutenant.

WRITINGS—All under name Tom Ingram: *Bells in England,* Muller, 1954; (with Douglas Newton) *Hymns as Poetry,* Constable, 1955; *Banns of Marriage* (novel), Constable, 1957; *The Hungry Cloud* (juvenile), Collins, 1971; *Garranane* (juvenile), Bradbury, 1972.

WORK IN PROGRESS: Novels for children.

AVOCATIONAL INTERESTS: The aesthetics of English horticulture, European travel.

* * *

INGRAM, Tom

See INGRAM, Thomas Henry

* * *

IORIO, John 1925-

PERSONAL: Born January 1, 1925, in Casandrino, Italy, naturalized U.S. citizen; son of Salvatore and Josephine (d'Angelo) Iorio; married Dorothy Lockett, 1950; children: Jay, Paul, Pamela. *Education:* Columbia University, B.A., 1950, M.A., 1951; further graduate study at University of Minnesota, 1954, and University of Pennsylvania, 1955. *Home:* 12905 North 52nd St., Tampa, Fla. 33617. *Agent:* McIntosh & Otis, Inc., 18 East 41st St., New York, N.Y. 10017. *Office:* Department of English, University of South Florida, Tampa, Fla. 33620.

CAREER: Dickinson College, Carlisle, Pa., instructor in English, 1952-53; Vassar College, Poughkeepsie, N.Y., instructor in English, 1953-54; Colby College, Waterville, Me., assistant professor of English, 1955-63; University of South Florida, Tampa, associate professor, 1963-73, professor of English, 1973—. *Military service:* U.S. Army, Paratroops, 1942-45; became staff sergeant; received Purple Heart. *Member:* Documentazione Internazionale (Italy). *Awards, honors:* Honorable or distinctive mention in *Best American Short Stories,* 1964, 1966, 1968.

WRITINGS: (Editor with James A. Gould) *Love, Sex and Identity,* Boyd & Fraser, 1971; (editor with Gould) *Violence in Modern Literature,* Boyd & Fraser, 1972. Contributor of short stories to *Prairie Schooner, Arizona Quarterly, Quest, Four Quarters, Southern Review,* and other literary magazines. Surburban editor and book reviewer, *Trentonian,* 1951-52; fiction editor, *Northeast,* 1960-65.

WORK IN PROGRESS: A novel, as yet untitled; a nonfiction work, *Literary Epistemology in the Contemporary Novel;* short stories.

SIDELIGHTS: "Have always wanted to write," Iorio says, "but find that teaching and writing tap the same source. My general viewpoint is that man is faced with chaos, by an absurd world. His attempts to give meaning reside in his art, in human solidarity, and in the will to create, organize, and bend the chaos to his imagination. Spent six months teaching in Florence, Italy. . . . Look forward to spending more time abroad as part of my spiritual journey."

* * *

IRANEK-OSMECKI, Kazimierz 1897- (Antoni, Heller, Makary)

PERSONAL: Born September 5, 1897, in Pstragowa, Poland; son of Jan (an engineer) and Antonina (Gokiert) Iranek; married Lidia Gwozdz, August 20, 1926; children: George. *Education:* Attended Polish Staff College, 1929-31. *Religion:* Roman Catholic. *Home:* 43a Emperors Gate, London SW7 4HJ, England. *Office:* Danina Polska Ltd., 42 Emperors Gate, London SW7 4HJ, England.

CAREER: Polish Army, 1917-48; served in secret Polish Army operation, 1917-18; served in Infantry in WW I, Polish-Soviet War, 1919-20, and in WW II; became colonel. Free-lance writer and journalist, 1948—. Director, Polish National Fund, 1952—; member of executive board, Polish Underground Movement Study Trust, 1948—, Jozef Pilsudski Institut in London, 1949—. *Member:* Polish Writers Union (member of executive board, 1968—), Polish Home Army Ex-Servicemen Association (member of executive board, 1947—). *Awards, honors*—Military: Order Virtuti Militari IV and V Class, Cross of Independence, Cross for Valour, 1919-20, and 1939-45, Silver and Gold Cross for Merit. Civilian: Polish Writers Union Literary Prize, 1959; Lanckoronski Foundation prize, 1968, and Polish Home Army Ex-Servicemen Association prize, 1973, for *Kto ratuje jedno zycie.*

WRITINGS: Wyprawa na Poryck i Torczyn (title means "Raid on Poryck and Torczyn"), Wojskowe Biuro Historyczne, 1930; (editor and contributor) *Polskie Sily Zbrojne w 2-ej wojnie swiatowej T. III, Armia Krajowa* (title means "Polish Armed Forces in the 2nd World War, Volume III: The Home Army"), Sikorski Historical Institut, 1950; (editor; and contributor under "cryptonimes" Antoni, Heller, and Makary) *Drogi Cichociemnych,* Veritas Foundation, 1954, translation by son, George Iranek-Osmecki published as *The Unseen and Silent,* Sheed, 1954; *Kto ratuje jedno zycie,* Orbis-London, 1968, translation by George Iranek-Osmecki published as *He Who Saves One Life,* Crown, 1971. Member of editorial committee of *Armia Krajowa w Dokumentach* (title means "The Home Army Through Documents"), Polish Underground Movement Study Trust, Volume I, 1970, Volume II, 1973.

WORK IN PROGRESS: Armia Krajowa w Dokumentach, Volumes III-V.

SIDELIGHTS: Iranek-Osmecki explained that the names Antoni, Heller, and Makary are "cryptonimes," which he used during the Second World War, when taking part in the conspiratory underground movement and fight in Poland against the German occupation, and these names were used in some of his publications.

* * *

IRISH, Donald P(aul) 1919-

PERSONAL: Born July 31, 1919, in Oak Park, Ill.; son of Willis Luther and Stella Bertha (Putnam) Irish; married Betty Ruth Osborn (a dietician), October 23, 1942; children: Terry Ann, Gail Lynn, Sharon Lee. *Education:* University of Colorado, B.A. (cum laude), 1941, M.A. (sociology), 1950; George Williams College, M.S. (group work education), 1944; University of Washington, Seattle, Ph.D., 1957; also studied at Centro Intercultural de Documentacion, 1972. *Religion:* Society of Friends (Quakers). *Home:* 1387 Englewood Ave., St. Paul, Minn. 55104. *Office:* Department of Sociology and Anthropology, Hamline University, St. Paul, Minn. 55104.

CAREER: Western Washington State University, Bellingham, instructor in sociology, 1947-52; Ohio Wesleyan University, Delaware, assistant professor, 1954-58, associate professor of sociology, 1958-60; University of North Carolina, Chapel Hill, research associate in sociology, 1960-63; Hamline University, St. Paul, Minn., professor of sociology, 1963—, chairman of department of sociology and anthropology, 1963-72, director of urban studies term, 1969-72. Visiting professor at Heidelberg College, Wittenberg College, University of Alberta, Millsaps College, and Xavier University. Fulbright lecturer at Universidad Pontificia, Bolivariana, Columbia, autumn, 1972.

MEMBER: American Sociological Association, Society for the Study of Social Problems, National Council on Family Relations, American Association of University Professors, Midwest Sociological Society, Southern Sociological Society, North Central Council of Latin Americanists, Minnesota Council on Family Relations, (president, 1969-71).

WRITINGS: (With Charles E. Bowerman and Hallowell Pope) *Unwed Motherhood: Personal and Social Consequences,* Institute for Research in Social Science, University of North Carolina, 1963, 2nd enlarged edition, 1965; (with Betty R. Green) *Death Education: Preparation for Living,* Schenkman, 1971. Contributor of about a dozen articles and reviews to professional journals, including *Journal of Social Issues, Marriage and Family Living, Social Forces, Journal of Chronic Diseases, Public Opinion Quarterly,* and *Research Previews.*

WORK IN PROGRESS: Research on social integration within Central America, on the stepchild, and on social change within a Mexican village.

SIDELIGHTS: Irish directed educational-community development projects in a Mexican village in 1967, 1971, and 1974; he was faculty adviser of a student group of a University of Minnesota-sponsored program in Central America in 1968.

* * *

ISBAN, Samuel

See IZBAN, Samuel

ISHMOLE, Jack 1924-

PERSONAL: Surname rhymes with "fishbowl"; born December 3, 1924, in New York, N.Y.; son of Pincus (a capmaker) and Stella (Weiss) Ishmole. *Education:* New York University, B.S., 1949. *Residence:* New York, N.Y. *Agent:* Raines & Raines, 244 Madison Ave., New York, N.Y. 10016. *Office:* Great Neck Public Schools, Great Neck, N.Y. 11023.

CAREER: U.S. Department of State, New York, N.Y., information specialist for "Voice of America" film division, 1950-52; employed in public relations work for Peerless TV Productions and Dine & Kalmus, 1952-56; teacher in the public schools of Great Neck, N.Y., 1957—. *Military service:* U.S. Army, 1942-45; served in European theatre. *Awards, honors:* Edith Busby award from Dodd, 1973, for *Walk in the Sky.*

WRITINGS: New York Portrait, Holt, 1965; *Walk in the Sky,* Dodd, 1973.

WORK IN PROGRESS: A novel, *A Taste of Ashes.*

AVOCATIONAL INTERESTS: Travel.

* * *

ISHWARAN, K(arigoudar) 1922-

PERSONAL: Born January 11, 1922, in Dharwar, Mysore State, India; son of Channappa M. (a teacher) and Basamma Patil; married wife, Wobine, May 16, 1960; children: Arundhati, Hemant, Shivakumar. *Education:* Bombay University, M.A., 1947; Karnatak University, Ph.D., 1954; Oxford University, B.Litt., 1956; International Institute, M.S.S., 1957; Leiden University, D.Litt., 1959. *Religion:* Hindu. *Home:* 374 Woodsworth Rd., Willowdale, Ontario, Canada. *Office:* Department of Sociology, York University, Toronto 12, Ontario, Canada.

CAREER: Teacher in Hubli, India, at Jagadguru Gangadhar College of Commerce, 1947-52, and S. K. Arts College, 1952-53; Sangameshwar College, Sholapur, India, principal, 1953-54; Karnatak University, Department of Graduate Studies in Social Anthropology, Dharwar, India, reader, 1959-62, professor, 1962-64, head of department, 1959-64; York University, Toronto, Ontario, professor of sociology, 1965—. Visiting professor of sociology and anthropology, Memorial University of Newfoundland, 1964-65. *Member:* Current Anthropology, Canadian Association for Sociology and Anthropology, Canadian Association for South Asian Studies (founding member, 1971), Delta Tau Kappa.

WRITINGS: Family Life in the Netherlands, Van Keulen, 1959; (with Nels Anderson) *Urban Sociology,* Asia Publishing House, 1963; *Tradition and Economy in Village India,* Routledge & Kegan Paul, 1966; *Shivapur: A South Indian Village,* Routledge & Kegan Paul, 1968; *Change and Continuity in India's Villages,* Columbia University Press, 1970; *The Canadian Family,* Holt, 1971; *A Populistic Community and Social Change in India,* Routledge & Kegan Paul, 1974; *Family Kinship and Community: A Study of Dutch Canadians,* Holt, 1974.

Series editor, with others: (And contributor) "International Studies in Sociology and Social Anthropology," E. J. Brill, 1963—; (and contributor) "Essays in Social Sciences," Asia Publishing House, 1963—; (and contributor) "Studies in Social Policy and Social Reconstruction," Allied Publishers, 1963—; "Contributions to Asian Studies," E. J. Brill, 1971—; "Monographs in Sociology and Anthropology in Honour of Nels Anderson," E. J. Brill, 1971—.

Editor of *International Journal of Comparative Sociology,* 1960—, and *Journal of Asian and African Studies,* 1966—.

WORK IN PROGRESS: Modernization in South Asia.

* * *

ISSLER, Anne Roller 1892-

PERSONAL: Born August 25, 1892, in Huntingburg, Ind.; daughter of Henry Bernhardt (a clergyman) and Mary (Katterhenry) Roller; married Clarence Hanley Issler, January 15, 1931 (divorced, 1954). *Education:* DePauw University, B.A., 1915; attended Columbia University, 1925. *Politics:* Democrat. *Religion:* Protestant. *Home and office:* 479 Seminary St., Napa, Calif. 94558. *Agent:* Lurton Blassingame, 60 East 42nd St., New York, N.Y. 10017.

CAREER: Social case worker, 1916-24, in Detroit, Mich., Louisville, Ky., and Wilkes-Barre, Pa.; free-lance writer, 1924—; *Survey Graphic,* New York, N.Y., field representative, 1928-52; curator at various times from 1954-62 of Cuyamaca State Park Museum, Vallejo Home at Sonoma, Old Courthouse at Shasta, and Robert Louis Stevenson House at Monterey. *Member:* National League of American Pen Women, American Association of University Women, Western Writers of America, Americans for Democratic Action, United Nations Association of the United States, Wilderness Society, Save-the-Redwoods League, Phi Beta Kappa.

WRITINGS: Stevenson at Silverado, Caxton, 1939, 2nd edition published as *Our Mountain Hermitage: Silverado and Robert Louis Stevenson,* Stanford University Press, 1950, 3rd edition published under original title, Valley Publishers, 1974; *Happier for His Presence: San Francisco and Robert Louis Stevenson,* Stanford University Press, 1949; *Young Red Flicker* (young adult novel), McKay, 1968; *Mystery of the Indian Cave* (young adult novel), McKay, 1970. Contributor to *Pacific Historical Review.*

WORK IN PROGRESS: Script for film strip on life of Robert Louis Stevenson.

SIDELIGHTS: Mrs. Issler, who is considered an expert on Robert Louis Stevenson's California period, has made four trips to Western Samoa, where Stevenson spent the last years of his life.

* * *

ITSE, Elizabeth M(yers) 1930-

PERSONAL: Born September 28, 1930, in Washburn, Wis.; daughter of Laurence Cooley and Frances (Drescher) Myers; married Donald Otis Itse, January 22, 1955 (divorced, 1974); children: Daniel Christofferson, Karl Laurence. *Education:* Summer study at University of Iowa, 1951; Connecticut College for Women (now Connecticut College), B.A., 1952; Boston University, graduate study, 1967-69. *Home:* 43 Greenwood St., Sherborn, Mass. 01770. *Office:* Modern Handcraft, Inc., 5 Powderhouse Lane, Sherborn, Mass. 01770.

CAREER: Modern Handcraft, Inc., Sherborn, Mass., office manager, 1971—. Secretary of Sherborn Yacht Club, Inc., 1971—.

WRITINGS: (Editor) *Hey Bug! And Other Poems about Little Things,* American Heritage Press, 1972; (illustrator) Stephen Falk, *Sailing Racing Rules the Easy Way,* St. Martin's, 1972, revised edition, 1973.

WORK IN PROGRESS: ZAT, a children's book.

AVOCATIONAL INTERESTS: Sailing, small boat racing.

IVEY, Allen E(ugene) 1933-

PERSONAL: Born November 19, 1933, in Mt. Vernon, Wash.; son of Lloyd (a grocery store owner) and Miriam (Hartson) Ivey; married Elizabeth Spencer (a professor), July 27, 1957; children: John, William. *Education:* Stanford University, A.B., 1955; Harvard University, Ed.D., 1959. *Politics:* Democrat. *Religion:* Baptist. *Home:* 72 Blackberry Lane, Amherst, Mass. 01002. *Office:* Department of Education, University of Massachusetts, Amherst, Mass. 01002.

CAREER: Fulbright scholar at University of Copenhagen, 1955-56; Boston University, Boston, Mass., instructor in guidance, 1957-59; Bucknell University, Lewisburg, Pa., director of counseling, 1959-63; Colorado State University, Fort Collins, associate professor of psychology and director of counseling, 1963-68; University of Massachusetts, Amherst, professor of education, 1968—. Has lectured at colleges and universities, including Columbia University, University of Hawaii, University of Minnesota, University of Maryland, University of Texas, and University of Puerto Rico. *Member:* American Psychological Association (fellow), American Personnel and Guidance Association, American Academy of Psychotherapists, American Board of Professional Psychology, Phi Beta Kappa, Phi Delta Kappa, Psi Chi.

WRITINGS: Microcounseling: Innovation in Interviewing Training, C.C Thomas, 1971; *Basic Attending Skills,* Microtraining Associates, 1974. Contributor of more than seventy articles to professional journals and magazines. Member of board of editors of *Journal of Counseling Psychology,* 1970—, and *Personnel and Guidance Journal,* 1971—.

WORK IN PROGRESS: Basic Influencing Skills; Beginnings: Alternatives in Human Relations.

* * *

IZARD, Carroll E(llis) 1923-

PERSONAL: Born October 8, 1923, in Georgetown, Miss.; son of Willis Lee and Willie Jane (Cliburn) Izard; married Barbara Ruth Sinquefield, December 25, 1944; children: Cal, Camille, Ashley. *Education:* Mississippi College, B.A., 1943; Yale University, B.D., 1945; Syracuse University, M.A., 1951, Ph.D., 1952. *Home:* 1701 Graybar Lane, Nashville, Tenn. 37215. *Office:* Department of Psychology, Vanderbilt University, Nashville, Tenn. 37240.

CAREER: Tulane University, New Orleans, La., research associate, 1952-54; Research Associates, Philadelphia, Pa., research associate, 1954-55; manpower development and management training specialist, General Electric, 1955-56; Vanderbilt University, Nashville, Tenn., assistant professor, 1956-61, associate professor, 1961-64, professor of psychology, 1964—. Associate, Ed Glaser & Associates (management consultants); consultant, Human Interaction Research Institute. *Military service:* U.S. Navy, 1944-47; became lieutenant junior grade.

MEMBER: American Psychological Association, American Association for the Advancement of Science, Southeastern Psychological Association, Tennessee Psychological Association, Sigma Xi. *Awards, honors:* Elliot Memorial Award from Century Psychology Series, 1969, for *The Face of Emotion;* exchange fellowship from National Academy of Sciences to Soviet Academy of Science, 1974.

WRITINGS: (Editor with S. S. Tomkins) *Affect, Cognition, and Personality,* Springer, 1965; *The Face of Emotion,* Appleton, 1971; *Patterns of Emotions: A New Analysis of Anxiety and Depression,* Academic Press, 1972. Member of board of editors, *The Subtle Languages: Nonverbal Communication in Animals and Humans.*

WORK IN PROGRESS: Personality: The Affective Domain, a textbook.

* * *

IZBAN, Samuel 1905-

PERSONAL: Surname originally Izbitsky (or Ishbitsky); adopted surname also spelled Isban; born September 26, 1905, in Gostinin, Poland; came to United States, 1938; son of Mordechai (or Mordecai; a businessman) and Leah (Laks) Izbitsky; married Sarah Epstein, June 8, 1930; children: Joseph Martin, Ruth (Mrs. Gerald Zuckerbrod), Elliot. *Education:* Attended Hebrew University of Jerusalem, 1925-26; other independent and special studies. *Home:* 2475 East 22nd St., Brooklyn, N.Y. 11235. *Office:* National Committee for Labor Israel, 33 East 67th St., New York, N.Y. 10021.

CAREER: Free-lance writer and journalist, 1925—; staff writer for *Americaner,* New York, N.Y., 1938-68, *Jewish Morning Journal,* New York, N.Y., 1942-53, *Day-Jewish Journal,* New York, N.Y., 1953-72, *Jewish Daily Forward,* New York, N.Y., 1974—. *Member:* International P.E.N., I.L. Peretz Yiddish Writers Union. *Awards, honors:* Haint-Weltspiegel Prize (Warsaw), 1936; Zukunft Literary Prize (New York), 1945; Zvi Kessel Prize (Mexico City), 1950; Literature Prize of *Yiddishe Zeitung* (Tel Aviv), 1973.

WRITINGS—In Yiddish: *Massen* (novel), Kletzkin Publishing (Vilna), 1929; *Nuchn Shturm* (short stories), Neie Kultur (Warsaw), 1929; *Kver–1914-1918* (novel), Kletzkin Publishing, 1933; *Oif Rushtovanies* (short stories), Literarishe Bleter (Warsaw), 1936; *Tzvishen Hundert Toiren* (short stories), Sklarsky (New York), 1942; *Umlegale Yidden Shpalten Yamen* (story of illegal Haganah journey), Poilishe Yidentum (Buenos Aires), 1948; *Familie Karp* (novel), Poilishe Yidentum, 1948; *Di Shpete Yorshim* (novel), Yiddish Publishing Co. (Buenos Aires), 1955; *Di shtot fun Tzorn* (short stories), Zriah Publishing Co. (Montevideo, Uruguay), 1955; *Di Kenigin Izevel* (historical novel), Yidbuch (Buenos Aires), 1959; *Jericho* (historical novel), Yidbuch, 1966.

In Hebrew—all published in Israel: *B'veth Ha-din* (short stories), Sifron, 1947; *Beth Karp* (novel), Massadah, 1956; *Misipurei New York* (short stories), Achidsaf, 1966; *Hamalka Izevel* (biblical novel), Achidsaf, 1959; *Rahav* (historical novel), Am-Hasefer, 1971.

Story included in *Yisroel: The First Jewish Omnibus,* Yoseloff, 1963. Short stories have been published in Hebrew and Yiddish magazines and newspapers in New York, Jerusalem, Warsaw, Buenos Aires, Paris, London, Mexico City, and Montreal; also reviewer of books, plays, and films. Member of editorial board, *Algemeiner Journal,* 1972-74.

WORK IN PROGRESS: A new collection of short stories, *A Whale in Jaffa;* a volume of literary essays.

SIDELIGHTS: Izban returned to Europe in 1947 as correspondent for the *Jewish Morning Journal* and covered the activities of the Jewish underground movement, Haganah, and the transport of Haganah ships with refugees to Palestine. In 1953 he covered the spy trial of Julius and Ethel Rosenberg for the Hebrew and Yiddish press. Dramatizations of his short stories were presented on radio in New York in 1948, and on stage in Buenos Aires in 1964.

BIOGRAPHICAL/CRITICAL SOURCES: A. A. Roback *Contemporary Literature,* Lincolns-Prager, 1957; Meier Waxman, *A History of Jewish Literature,* Volume V, Yoseloff, 1960; Israel C. Biletzky, *Essays on Yiddish Poetry and Prose Writers of the Twentieth Century,* Israel Press, 1970.

* * *

JABBER, Fuad 1943-

PERSONAL: Surname is accented on first syllable; born November 22, 1943, in Buenos Aires, Argentina; son of Amin R. (a businessman) and Najla (Sefa) Jabber; married Tania Leovin, July 2, 1966; children: Eve. *Education:* American University of Beirut, B.A., 1967, M.A., 1969; University of California at Los Angeles, Ph.D., 1974. *Office:* Department of Political Science, University of California at Los Angeles, Los Angeles, Calif. 90024.

CAREER: Institute for Palestine Studies, Beirut, Lebanon, research member, 1968-70; Stevenson Institute of International Affairs, Chicago, Ill., fellow, 1973-75; University of California at Los Angeles, assistant professor of political science, 1974—. *Member:* International Institute for Strategic Studies, Middle East Studies Association, Middle East Institute.

WRITINGS: (Editor) *International Documents on Palestine, 1967,* Institute for Palestine Studies (Beirut), 1970; *Israel and Nuclear Weapons,* Chatto & Windus, 1971; (with W. B. Quandt and A. M. Lesch) *The Politics of Palestinian Nationalism,* University of California Press, 1973. Contributor to Lebanese, European, and American journals and newspapers.

WORK IN PROGRESS: Books on international affairs and arms control.

* * *

JABEZ
See NICOL, Eric (Patrick)

* * *

JACK, R(obert) Ian 1935-

PERSONAL: Born March 12, 1935, in Dunfries, Scotland; son of Robert (a banker) and Janet Wilson (Swan) Jack; married Sybil Milliner Thorpe (a university lecturer), February, 1961; children: Adrian Laurence Robert, Christopher James Edmund, Antony Ronald Geoffrey. *Education:* University of Glasgow, M.A., 1957; University of London, Ph.D., 1961. *Home:* 55 Kenthurst Rd., St. Ives, New South Wales 2075, Australia. *Office:* Department of History, University of Sydney, Sydney, New South Wales 2006, Australia.

CAREER: University of London, London, England, research fellow, Institute of Historical Research, 1959-61; University of Sydney, Sydney, New South Wales, Australia, lecturer, 1961-64, senior lecturer, 1965-69, associate professor of history, 1970—, acting dean of Faculty of Arts, 1972, sub-dean, 1972-73, dean, 1974—. *Member:* Royal Historical Society (fellow), Australian Society for Historical Archaeology (president, 1972—), History Teachers Association of New South Wales (chairman, 1969-70).

WRITINGS: The Grey of Ruthin Valor, Sydney University Press, 1965; *Medieval Wales,* Cornell University Press, 1972.

General editor: "Topics in Modern History," five books, Rigby, 1973; "Monographs on Historical Archaeology," Australian Society for Historical Archaeology, 1973—.

WORK IN PROGRESS: Sections on Wales and other topics for Volume II of *Agrarian History of England and Wales,* for Cambridge University Press; *The English Nobility in the Fifteenth Century;* a monograph, *Elizabeth Farm House,* publication expected in 1976; and *Historical Archaeology,* 1976.

* * *

JACKINS, Harvey 1916-

PERSONAL: Born June 28, 1916, in Idaho; son of Harvey Wilson (a farmer) and Caroline (a teacher; maiden name, Moland) Jackins; married Dorothy Diehl (a teacher), September 2, 1939; children: Gordon, Tim, Sarah (Mrs. Don McManus), Chris. *Education:* University of Washington, Seattle, B.A., 1959. *Religion:* Methodist. *Home:* 719 2nd Ave. N., Seattle, Wash. 98109. *Office:* Personal Counselors, Inc., Seattle, Wash.

CAREER: Personal Counselors, Inc., Seattle, Wash., president, 1951—. International reference person for Re-evaluation Counseling Communities, 1971—. *Member:* American Association for the Advancement of Science, American Mathematical Society, Mathematical Association of America, American Geophysical Union, American Academy of Social and Political Science, American Academy of Political Science, Amonii Socii, Phi Beta Kappa, Phi Lambda Upsilon, Pi Mu Epsilon.

WRITINGS: The Human Side of Human Beings, Rational Island, 1965; *The Meaningful Holiday,* Rational Island, 1970; *The Human Situation,* Rational Island, 1973; *Zest Is Best,* Rational Island, 1973.

WORK IN PROGRESS: Talks on Theory from Buck Creek I; Questions and Answers on Re-evaluation Counseling; Quotations.

* * *

JACKMON, Marvin X. 1944-
(El Muhajir)

PERSONAL: Born May 29, 1944, in Fowler, Calif.; *Education:* Oakland City College (now Merritt College), A.A., 1964; San Francisco State College (now University) further study, 1964-66. *Address:* Al Kitab Sudan Publishing Co., P.O. Box 6536, San Francisco, Calif. 94101.

CAREER: Poet, playwright, and lecturer. Founder with Ed Bullins of Black Arts/West Theatre, San Francisco, Calif., 1966, and with Bullins and Eldridge Cleaver of Black House (political-cultural center), San Francisco, 1967; cofounder of Al Kitab Sudan Publishing Co., San Francisco, 1967; founder and director of Your Black Educational Theatre, Inc., San Francisco, 1971—. Teacher of black studies courses at California State University at Fresno, 1969, and University of California, Berkeley, 1972; has given lectures or poetry readings at more than twenty universities and colleges. *Awards, honors:* Writing grants totaling $8,000 from Columbia University, 1969, and National Endowment for the Arts, 1972; on-the-job training grant of $36,000 for Your Black Educational Theatre, 1971-72.

WRITINGS:—All under name El Muhajir; published by Al Kitab Sudan Publishing, except as noted: *Sudan Rajuli Samia* (poems), 1967; *Black Dialectics* (proverbs), 1967; *Fly to Allah* (poems), 1969; *Son of Man* (proverbs), 1969;

Black Man Listen (poems and proverbs), Broadside Press, 1970; *Black Bird* (parable), 1972.

Plays: "Flowers for the Trashman (one-act), first produced in San Francisco by drama department of San Francisco State College, 1965, musical version produced as "Take Care of Business," in Fresno by Your Black Educational Theatre, 1971; "The Trial," first produced in New York (Harlem) c. 1970; "Resurrection of the Dead" (dance drama), first produced in San Francisco by Your Black Educational Theatre, 1972; *Woman—Man's Best Friend* (musical dance drama; first produced in Oakland at Mills College, 1973), Al Kitab Sudan Publishing, 1973.

Poems, plays, and other writings published in eight collections, including: *Black Fire,* edited by Imamu Baraka and Larry Neal, Morrow, 1968; *New Plays from the Black Theatre,* edited by Ed Bullins, Bantam, 1969; *Vietnam and Black America,* edited by Clyde Taylor, Doubleday, 1973; *You Better Believe It,* edited by Paul Breman, Penguin, 1973. Contributor to *Soul Book, Encore, Black World,* and other magazines and newspapers. Fiction editor, *Black Dialogue,* 1965—; contributing editor, *Journal of Black Poetry,* 1965—; associate editor, *Black Theatre,* 1968—.

WORK IN PROGRESS: An elementary Arabic textbook; *Black Man in the Americas,* a series of conversations with black writers, artists, historians, musicians, and politicians, irst published in *Muhammad Speaks* (newspaper), 1970; *Handbook of Black Theatre,* a world guide; and *Bibliography for the Proper Understanding of Black People.*

* * *

JACKSON, Donald Dale 1935-

PERSONAL: Born July 18, 1935, in San Francisco, Calif.; son of Zalph Boone (an attorney) and Jean (Shuler) Jackson; married Joyce Darlene Hall, November 8, 1958; children: Dale Allen, Amy Lynn. *Education:* Northwestern University, student, 1953-54; Stanford University, A.B., 1957; Columbia University, M.A., 1958. *Home address:* Saddle Ridge Rd., Route 4, Newtown, Conn. 06470. *Agent:* John Hawkins, Paul R. Reynolds, Inc., 12 East 41st St., New York, N.Y. 10017.

CAREER: United Press International, San Francisco, Calif., reporter, 1961-63; *Life* (magazine), New York, N.Y., reporter and staff writer, 1963-72; free-lance writer, 1972—. *Military service:* U.S. Army, Counter Intelligence Corps, 1958-60. *Awards, honors:* National Headliners Club award, 1969, for an article on the trial of Dr. Benjamin Spock.

WRITINGS: Judges, Atheneum, 1974; *Sagebrush Country,* Time-Life, in press. Contributor to *Life, True,* and *Sports Illustrated.* Contributing editor of *New Times.*

SIDELIGHTS: Jackson writes: "I have been writing for pay since I was thirteen, when the local newspaper gave me five cents an inch for covering high school tennis. I have always felt most alive, most pained, and most satisfied when writing. My father, a sportswriter in his youth, inspired in me a love of writing and language which I have retained. My book on U.S. judges grew out of a long fascination with the law and our system of justice in theory and practice. I am interested in many other aspects of contemporary American life—nature, the environment, sports and politics, to name a few. More broadly, I am interested in the individual and collective components of the American character." *Avocational interests:* Travel, sports, music.

BIOGRAPHICAL/CRITICAL SOURCES: Bridgeport Sunday Post, May 5, 1974.

JACKSON, Wes 1936-

PERSONAL: Born June 15, 1936, in Topeka, Kan.; son of Howard T. (a farmer) and Nettie (Stover) Jackson; married Dana Lee Percival, December 22, 1957; children: Laura, Scott, Sara. *Education:* Kansas Wesleyan University, B.A., 1958; University of Kansas, M.A., 1960; North Carolina State University, Ph.D., 1967. *Religion:* Unitarian Universalist. *Home:* 8931 Twin Falls Dr., Sacramento, Calif. 95826. *Office:* Department of Biology, California State University, Sacramento, Calif. 95819.

CAREER: Welder, farm hand, ranch hand; high school teacher of biology in the public schools of Olathe, Kan., 1960-62; Kansas Wesleyan University, Salina, assistant professor, 1962-64, associate professor of biology, 1967-71; California State University, Sacramento, associate professor, 1971-73, professor of environmental studies, 1973—.

WRITINGS: Man and the Environment, W. C. Brown, 1971, 2nd edition, 1973. Associate editor of *International Journal of Environmental Planning and Pollution Control.*

WORK IN PROGRESS: Research toward an ecological ethic; back to the land experiments in the development of alterations of life styles and technology assessment; experimentation on solar heating equipment.

* * *

JACOBS, Francine 1935-

PERSONAL: Born May 11, 1935, in New York, N.Y.; daughter of Louis (a glove manufacturer) and Ida (Schrag) Kaufman; married Jerome L. Jacobs (a psychiatrist), June 10, 1956; children: Laurie, Larry. *Education:* Queens College (now Queens College of the City University of New York), B.A., 1956. *Home:* 93 Old Farm Rd., Pleasantville, N.Y. 10570.

CAREER: Elementary school teacher in Rye, N.Y., 1956-58, and Chappaqua, N.Y., 1967-68. *Member:* Authors Guild.

WRITINGS—Juveniles: *The Wisher's Handbook,* Funk, 1968; *The Legs of the Moon,* Coward, 1971; *The King's Ditch,* Coward, 1971; *Sea Turtles,* Morrow, 1972; *The Freshwater Eel,* Morrow, 1973; *Nature's Light: The Story of Bioluminescence,* Morrow, 1974.

WORK IN PROGRESS: A book on the sea, for Morrow.

SIDELIGHTS: Mrs. Jacobs writes: "Camping experiences with my family in shore and wilderness areas have stimulated my interest in ecology and nature science." *Avocational interests:* Travel, hiking, fishing, beachcombing, reading, cooking, gardening.

* * *

JACOBS, G(enevieve) Walker 1948-

PERSONAL: Born January 9, 1948, in Columbus, Ohio; daughter of Robert N. (a test editor) and Margherita (Leslie) Walker; married James Jacobs, November 20, 1970. *Education:* Ohio State University, A.B., 1969. *Home address:* Route 1, Staples, Minn. 56479.

CAREER: Oldstone Enterprises (gravestone rubbing materials), Marblehead, Mass., originator and owner, 1970-73.

WRITINGS: Stranger Stop and Cast An Eye, Greene, 1973.

JACOBSON, Frederick L(awrence) 1938-

PERSONAL: Born August 7, 1938, in Mt. Vernon, N.Y.; son of Ira (a textile executive) and Sylvia (Friedner) Jacobson. *Education:* Yale University, B.A., 1960. *Home:* 141 East 89th St., New York, N.Y. 10028. *Office:* Fred Jacobson Alpine Trails Ltd., 141 East 89th St., New York, N.Y. 10028; and B.E.A. Associates, Inc., 366 Madison Ave., New York, N.Y. 10017.

CAREER: Lehman Brothers (investment bankers), New York, N.Y., trainee, 1960-62; Anchor Corp. (mutual fund sponsors), Elizabeth. N.J., vice-president and director of marketing, 1962-72; B.E.A. Associates, Inc. (investment counselors), New York, N.Y., director, 1972—. Owner of Fred Jacobson Alpine Trails Ltd. (mountain guides), 1972—. *Member:* Swiss Alpine Club, Appalachian Mountaineering Club, Mount Mansfield Ski Club, Canterbury Choral Society (past president), Yale Club of New York City.

WRITINGS: The Meek Mountaineer, Liveright, 1974. Contributor to *Investment Dealers Digest, Investment Sales Monthly,* and *Appalachia.*

AVOCATIONAL INTERESTS: Mountain-climbing, hiking, skiing, ski mountaineering, tennis, swimming, ping pong, running, music (piano, choral music, operas, chamber music), reading.

* * *

JAHAN, Rounaq 1944-

PERSONAL: Born March 2, 1944, in Bangladesh; daughter of Ahmad (an employee of the government) and Razia (Begum) Ullah. *Education:* Dacca University, B.A. (honors), 1962, M.A., 1963; Harvard University, M.A., 1968, Ph.D., 1970. *Home:* 4 Elephant Rd., Dacca, Bangladesh. *Office:* Department of Political Science, Dacca University, Dacca, Bangladesh.

CAREER: Dacca University, Dacca, Bangladesh, associate professor of political science, 1970—. *Member:* American Political Science Association.

WRITINGS: Pakistan: Failure in National Integration, Columbia University Press, 1972; (contributor) Lebow and Henderson, editors, *Divided Countries in a Divided World,* McKay, 1974; (contributor) Levitt, editor, *Cross-Cultural Perspectives on Women's Status Movement,* Mouton & Co., 1974.

WORK IN PROGRESS: Research on problems of political development, and on the political system of Bangladesh.

* * *

JAHN, Joseph Michael 1943- (Mike Jahn)

PERSONAL: Born August 4, 1943, in Cincinnati, Ohio; son of Joseph C. (a newspaperman) and Anne (Loughlin) Jahn; married Catherine Knoll (a researcher), July 24, 1965; children: Evan R. *Education:* Adelphi Suffolk College of Adelphi University (now Dowling College), B.A., 1965; Adelphi University, graduate study, 1965-68. *Home and office:* 541 West 113th St., New York, N.Y. 10025. *Agent:* Theron Raines, Raines & Raines, 244 Madison Ave., New York, N.Y.

CAREER: Moriches Bay Tide (weekly newspaper), Center Moriches, N.Y., news editor, 1964-65; *Newsday* (daily newspaper), Long Island, N.Y., editorial assistant, 1965-66; *Long Island Advance* (weekly), Long Island, reporter and photographer, 1966; Columbia University, New York, N.Y., associate director for college relations, 1966-67, staff writer for Office of University Relations, 1967; free-lance writer, 1968—. Commentator over WNEW-FM, 1969-70; lecturer, New School for Social Research, 1971.

WRITINGS—All under name Mike Jahn: *The Scene* (novel), Geis, 1970; *Rock: From Elvis Presley to the Rolling Stones,* Quadrangle, 1973.

Columns: "The Pop Side," for *Ingenue,* 1968-71; "New York Current," Bell-McClure Syndicate, 1968-70; "Sounds of the Seventies," *New York Times* Syndicate, 1970-72; "New York Offbeat," *New York Times* Syndicate, 1972-73; "Jahn on Music," *Cue,* 1972—; "Music," *Gallery,* 1974—. Also rock music critic for *New York Times,* 1968-71; reviewer, *High Fidelity,* 1971—. Contributor to periodicals, including *Esquire, Vogue, Cosmopolitan,* and *Saturday Review.* Popular music editor, *Cue,* 1972—.

WORK IN PROGRESS: A suspense novel; another novel; research for a book of sea-lore.

SIDELIGHTS: Jahn told *CA:* "When I began free-lancing, I did so as a critic of rock music and a commentator on youth culture. . . . I wrote *The Scene* for fun, really. I wrote *Rock* . . . because I felt that music, being a two-billion dollar industry, deserved a straightforward, honest history of its most important factor, rock, and that one had never been done." *Avocational interests:* Yacht racing, the sea, and all nautical subjects (Jahn grew up in Sayville, Long Island); astronomy.

* * *

JAHN, Mike
See JAHN, Joseph Michael

* * *

JAMES, Leonard F(rank) 1904-

PERSONAL: Born September 3, 1904, in London, England. *Education:* University of Bristol, B.A., 1926, diploma in education, 1927; University of Michigan, M.A., 1928. *Politics:* Independent. *Religion:* Episcopalian. *Residence:* Medomak, Me. 04551.

CAREER: Phillips Academy, Andover, Mass., instructor in history, 1932-70, instructor on Cecil F. P. Bancroft Foundation, 1946-68, and Independence Foundation Teaching Endowment, 1968-70. *Member:* New England History Teachers Association (president).

WRITINGS: The Supreme Court in American Life, Scott, Foresman, 1964, 2nd edition, 1971; *American Foreign Policy,* Scott, Foresman, 1967; *Following the Frontier: American Transportation in the Nineteenth Century,* Harcourt, 1968; *How to Prepare for College Board Achievement Test in European History and World Cultures,* Barron's, 1968; *Western Man and the Modern World,* Pergamon, Volume I: *Origins of Western Civilization,* Volume II: *Rivalry, Reason, and Revolution,* Volume III: *Industrialism, Imperialism, and War,* Volume IV: *Cold War, Confrontation, and Crisis,* Volume V: *Africa, Latin America, and the East,* all volumes published in 1973.

WORK IN PROGRESS: A school text on national security affairs in co-operation with National Strategy Information Center, Inc.

JANUS
See CLERY, (Reginald) Val(entine)

* * *

JARMAN, Rosemary Hawley 1935-

PERSONAL: Born April 27, 1935, in Worcester, England; daughter of Charles (a master butcher) and Josephine (Hawley) Smith; divorced. *Education:* Until the age of eleven was educated solely by maternal grandmother, a former headmistress at British schools; attended high school in Worcester. *Residence:* Worcestershire, England. *Agent:* E.P.S. Lewin & Partners, 1 Grosvenor Court, Sloane St., London S.W.1, England.

CAREER: Worcestershire County Council, local government officer, 1960-68. Singer, specializing in lieder and oratorio work, and cellist. *Member:* Society of Authors, Richard III Society. *Awards, honors:* First Novel Award of Silver Quill (author's club), 1971, for *We Speak No Treason;* nominated Esteemed Daughter of Mark Twain by Cyril Clemens, 1973.

WRITINGS—Novels: *We Speak No Treason* (Literary Guild alternate choice), Little, Brown, 1971; *The King's Grey Mare,* Little, Brown, 1973. Contributor of short stories to *Woman* and other periodicals.

WORK IN PROGRESS: A novel about Katherine de Valois and the Valois-Tudor connections; a novel about German occupation of the Channel Islands in the 1940's.

SIDELIGHTS: Rosemary Jarman writes: "[I have] an obsession with correctitude in English history and a compulsion to challenge the Tudor-oriented propaganda in connection with the Wars of the Roses, particularly Richard III of England. Historical research immensely important in all areas."

* * *

JEANNIERE, Abel 1921-

PERSONAL: Born August 28, 1921, in Saint-Paul-en-Pareds, Vendee, France; son of Etienne and Celine (Gonnord) Jeanniere. *Education:* Sorbonne, University of Paris, licence, 1949; Gregoriana, Rome, docteur en philosophie, 1957. *Home:* 15 rue Raymond Marcheron, Vanves 92140, France.

CAREER: *Projet,* Vanves, France, assistant editor, 1970—. Professor at Institut d'Etudes Sociales, Institut Catholique, Paris, 1960—.

WRITINGS: *La pensee d'Heraclite d'Ephese,* Aubier, 1959; *Anthropologie sexuelle,* Aubier, 1964, translation by Julie Kernan published as *The Anthropology of Sex,* Harper, 1967; *Espace moble et temps incertains,* Aubier, 1970. Contributor to *Projet, Etudes, Esprit,* and other periodicals.

* * *

JENCKS, Charles 1939-

PERSONAL: Born June 21, 1939, in Baltimore, Md.; son of Gardner Platt (a composer) and Ruth (Pearl) Jencks; married Pamela Balding, June 20, 1961 (marriage ended, July, 1973); children: Ivor Cosmo, Justin Alexander. *Education:* Harvard University, B.A., 1961, M.A., 1965; University of London, Ph.D., 1970. *Office:* Architectural Association, 36 Bedford Sq., London W.C.1, England.

CAREER: Architectural Association, London, England, senior lecturer in architectural history, 1970—. *Awards, honors:* Fulbright scholarship to England, 1965-67.

WRITINGS: (Editor) *Meaning in Architecture,* Braziller, 1967; *Architecture Two Thousand: Predictions and Methods,* Praeger, 1971; (with Nathan Silver) *Adhocism,* Doubleday, 1972; *Modern Movements in Architecture,* Doubleday, 1973; *Le Corbusier and the Tragic View of Architecture,* Harvard University Press, 1973. Author of television scripts for programs on Le Corbusier and on "adhocism," for British Broadcasting Corp. (BBC).

WORK IN PROGRESS: Research on semiology and architecture; *Love in a Tub,* a farce.

* * *

JENCKS, Christopher 1936-

PERSONAL: Born October 22, 1936, in Baltimore, Md.; son of Francis Haynes (an architect) and Elizabeth (Pleasants) Jencks. *Education:* Harvard University, B.A., 1958, Ed.M., 1959; further graduate study at London School of Economics and Political Science, 1960-61. *Office:* Department of Sociology, Harvard University, Cambridge, Mass. 02138.

CAREER: *New Republic,* Washington, D.C., associate editor, 1961-63; Institute for Policy Studies, Washington, D.C., resident fellow, 1963-67, chairman of Congressional Seminar on Educational Policy, 1964-65; Harvard University, Cambridge, Mass., lecturer, 1967-69, associate professor of education, 1969-73, lecturer in sociology, 1971-73, professor of sociology, 1973—, founder and executive director of Center for Educational Policy Research, 1968-69, research associate at Center, 1968—, co-founder of Cambridge Institute, 1968, director of Carnegie project on alternative approaches to child rearing at Center for the Study of Public Policy, 1972-74. Consultant to President's Science Advisory Committee, 1966-67.

AWARDS, HONORS: Frank Knox fellowship, University of London, 1960-61; Guggenheim fellowship, 1968; award for best book on higher education from American Council on Education, 1968, for *The Academic Revolution;* LL.D. from Kalamazoo College, 1969.

WRITINGS: (Contributor) Roger Hagen, editor, *Character and Social Structure in America,* Harvard University, 1960; (contributor) Nevitt Sanford, editor, *The American College,* Wiley, 1961; (contributor) Roger Klein, editor, *Young Americans Abroad,* Harper, 1963; (contributor) *White House Conference on Education: Consultants Papers,* Volume II, U.S. Government Printing Office, 1965; (contributor) Hans Morgenthau, editor, *The Crossroad Papers,* Norton, 1965; (contributor) Irving Howe, editor, *The Radical Papers,* Doubleday, 1966; (contributor) Alvin Eurich, editor, *Campus 1980,* Delacorte, 1968.

(With David Riesman) *The Academic Revolution,* Doubleday, 1968; (with others) *Education Vouchers: A Report on Financing Education by Payments to Parents,* Center for the Study of Public Policy, 1970; (contributor) Fred Mosteller and Daniel P. Moynihan, editors, *On Equality of Educational Opportunity,* Random House, 1971; (with others) *Inequality,* Basic Books, 1972.

Contributor of about twenty articles to education journals and other scholarly periodicals, including *Dissent, Teachers College Record, Public Interest, Harvard Educational Review, Atlantic,* and *Harper's.*

JENKINS, Jerry B(ruce) 1949-

PERSONAL: Born September 23, 1949, in Kalamazoo, Mich.; son of Harry Phillip (a police chief) and Bonita Grace (Thompson) Jenkins; married Dianna Louise Whiteford (an executive secretary), January 23, 1971. *Education:* Attended Moody Bible Institute, 1967-68, Loop College, 1968, and William Rainey Harper College, 1968-70. *Politics:* Independent. *Religion:* Jesus Christ. *Home:* 218 North Morgan St., Wheaton, Ill. 60187. *Office:* Inspirational Radio-Television Guide, 30W406 Roosevelt Rd., West Chicago, Ill. 60187.

CAREER: WMBI-FM-AM-Radio, Chicago, Ill., night news editor, 1967-68; Day Publications, Mt. Prospect, Ill., assistant sports editor, 1968-69; Des Plaines Publishing Co., Des Plaines, Ill., sports editor, 1969-71; *Tri-City Herald,* Kennewick, Wash., sportswriter, 1971; Scripture Press Publications, Wheaton, Ill., associate editor, 1971-72, managing editor, 1972-73; Inspirational Radio-Television Guide, Chicago, Ill., executive editor, 1973—. *Member:* Evangelical Press Association, National Religious Broadcasters.

WRITINGS: You Can Get Thru to Teens, Victor, 1973; *Sammy Tippit: God's Love in Action,* Broadman, 1973; *VBS Unlimited,* Victor, 1974; (with Hank Aaron and Stan Baldwin) *Bad Henry,* Chilton, 1974; *The Story of the Christian Booksellers Association,* Nelson, 1974; *The Gingerbread Man: Pat Williams Then and Now,* Lippincott, 1974; *Stuff It: The Story of Dick Motta, Toughest Little Coach in the NBA,* Chilton, 1975; *The Iron Curtain Ministry of Sammy Tippit,* Whitaker House, 1975. Contributor to religious periodicals, including *Moody Monthly, Power, Contact,* and *Campus Life.* Editorial consultant to American Evangelism Association.

WORK IN PROGRESS: A book about former Olympic weightlifting champion Paul Anderson, for Victor, and one about Los Angeles Dodger's pitcher, Don Sutton, for Word Books.

AVOCATIONAL INTERESTS: Photography.

* * *

JENSEN, J(ohn) Vernon 1922-

PERSONAL: Born September 29, 1922, in Scandia, Minn.; son of James Jorgen (a buttermaker) and Verbena (Bloomquist) Jensen; married Irene Khin Khin Myint (a professor of history), June 12, 1954; children: Donald, Maythee. *Education:* Augsburg College, student, 1941-43, B.A., 1947; University of Minnesota, M.A., 1948, Ph.D., 1959. *Politics:* Democrat. *Religion:* Methodist. *Residence:* Minneapolis, Minn. *Office:* Department of Speech and Communication, 122 Klaeber Ct., University of Minnesota, Minneapolis, Minn. 55455.

CAREER: Augsburg College, Minneapolis, Minn., instructor in European history and public speaking, 1948-51; University of Minnesota, Minneapolis, instructor, 1953-59, assistant professor, 1959-64, associate professor, 1964-67, professor of communication, 1967—, director of communication program, 1970-73. Fulbright lecturer at State Training College for Teachers (Rangoon), 1961-62. *Military service:* U.S. Army, 1943-46; served in European theater.

MEMBER: International Communication Association, Speech Communication Association, National Council of Teachers of English, Conference on College Composition and Communication, Rhetoric Society of America, American Association of University Professors, American Historical Association, Association for Asian Studies, Central States Speech Association. *Awards, honors:* Danforth Foundation study grant, 1958-59.

WRITINGS: Perspectives on Oral Communication, Holbrook, 1970. Contributor of about fifteen articles to professional journals, including *ETC: A Review of General Semantics, Journal of Broadcasting, Dalhousie Review, Parliamentarian, Parliamentary Affairs,* and *British Journal for the History of Science.*

WORK IN PROGRESS: The Religious Quest: East and West, an anthology, with wife, Irene Jensen; research on fundamentals of rhetorical criticism, on the role of metaphor, on contemporary British parliamentary speaking, rhetorical practices in the British Commonwealth, and on Thomas Henry Huxley as a communicator.

AVOCATIONAL INTERESTS: International travel, reading, sports, music.

* * *

JENSEN, Jo
See PELTON, Beverly Jo

* * *

JENSEN, Michael C(ole) 1939-

PERSONAL: Born November 30, 1939, in Rochester, Minn.; son of Harold and Gertrude Jensen; married Delores A. Dvorak, August 11, 1962; children: Natalie, Stephanie. *Education:* Macalester College, A.B., 1962; University of Chicago, M.B.A., 1964, Ph.D., 1968. *Office:* Graduate School of Management, University of Rochester, Rochester, N.Y. 14627.

CAREER: Chicago Junior College System, Chicago, Ill., instructor in business administration, 1966; Northwestern University, Evanston, Ill., instructor in business administration, 1967; University of Rochester, Rochester, N.Y., assistant professor, 1967-71, associate professor of finance, 1971—. Consultant to Arthur D. Little, Inc., 1967-69. *Member:* American Economic Association, American Finance Association, Econometric Society, Beta Gamma Sigma. *Awards, honors:* Security Trust Co. fellowships, 1968-69, 1970-71, 1971-72; Ford Foundation fellowship, 1970; National Science Foundation fellowship, 1970-71.

WRITINGS: (Contributor) Henry Manne, editor, *Economic Policy and the Regulation of Corporate Securities,* American Enterprise Institute for Public Policy Research, 1969; (contributor) *Empirical Research in Accounting: Selected Studies,* Institute of Professional Accounting, University of Chicago, 1970; (contributor) E. Bruce Fredrikson, editor, *Frontiers of Investment Analysis,* International Textbook Co., 1971; (contributor) Edwin J. Elton and M. J. Gruber, editors, *Security Evaluation and Portfolio Analysis,* Prentice-Hall, 1972; (contributor) James Lorie and Richard Brealey, editors, *Modern Development in Investment Management: A Book of Readings,* Praeger, 1972; (editor and contributor) *Studies in the Theory of Capital Markets,* Praeger, 1972; (contributor) G. P. Szego, editor, *Mathematical Methods in Finance,* North-Holland Publishing, 1973.

Contributor to journals in his field. Associate editor, *Journal of Financial and Quantitative Analysis,* 1969-73; editor, *Journal of Financial Economics,* 1973—.

WORK IN PROGRESS: The Economics of Managing Computing Facilities; Corporate Objectives, Stockholder and Social Welfare, and Social Responsibility of Private Corporations; Economics, Information, Coordination Costs, and Control in Large Organizations.

* * *

JENSEN, Niels 1927-

PERSONAL: Born July 26, 1927, in Northern Schleswig, Denmark; son of Martin F. and Margretha Jensen; married Marie Raun, 1954; children: Martin, Karen, Lisbeth, Birgitte. *Education:* Ribe State Training College, graduate, 1954; Danish Post-Graduate Training College for Teachers, graduate study, 1970-71. *Home:* Vinkelvej 18, DK, 8410 Roende, Denmark.

CAREER: High school teacher in Roende, Denmark. *Awards, honors: Da landet laa oede* won Gyldendal's Anniversary Competition for the best book of fiction for children, 1970, and the Children's Book Prize from the Danish Ministry of Cultural Affairs, 1972.

WRITINGS: Da landet laa oede (title means "When the Land Lay Waste"), Gyldendal, 1971, translation by Oliver Stallybrass published as *Days of Courage,* Harcourt, 1973; *Kasper og krybskytten* (title means "Kasper and the Poacher"), Gyldendal, 1974; *Kasper og fogeden* (title means "Kasper and the Bailiff"), Gyldendal, 1974.

WORK IN PROGRESS: Further books in his fiction series for children, "Middelalderen" (title means "The Middle Ages").

* * *

JENSEN, Richard C(arl) 1936-

PERSONAL: Born February 29, 1936, in Lone Rock, Iowa; son of Ernest M. (a bank cashier) and Esther (Osher) Jensen; married Judith Snipes, August 10, 1958; children: Joseph, Mark, John. *Education:* University of Arizona, B.A., 1958; University of North Carolina, Ph.D., 1961. *Home:* 4833 East Andrew, Tucson, Ariz. 85711. *Office:* Department of Classics, University of Arizona, Tucson, Ariz. 85721.

CAREER: University of Arizona, Tucson, instructor, 1961-62, assistant professor, 1962-68, associate professor of classics, 1968—. *Member:* American Philological Association, Phi Beta Kappa, Phi Kappa Phi.

WRITINGS: (Editor, author of introduction and notes) Domenico Silvestri, *The Latin Poetry,* Wilhelm Fink Verlag, 1973.

WORK IN PROGRESS: Editing previously unpublished poetry by fourteenth-century Florentine writers, Coluccio Salutati and Zanobi da Strada.

* * *

JEPPSON, Janet O. 1926-

PERSONAL: Born August 6, 1926, in Ashland, Pa.; daughter of John Rufus (a physician) and Rae (Knudson) Jeppson; married Isaac Asimov (an author), November 30, 1973. *Education:* Attended Wellesley College, 1944-46; Stanford University, B.A., 1948; New York University, M.D., 1952; William A. White Psychoanalytic Institute, postdoctoral study, 1955-60. *Politics:* Liberal Democrat. *Religion:* None. *Home and office:* 80 Central Park West, New York, N.Y. 10023.

CAREER: Licensed to practice medicine in New York; Philadelphia General Hospital, Philadelphia, Pa., intern, 1952-53; Bellevue Hospital, New York, N.Y., psychiatric resident, 1953-56; private practice of medicine in New York, N.Y., 1953—; William A. White Psychoanalytic Institute, New York, N.Y., training and supervisory analyst, 1969—, director of training, 1974—. *Member:* American Psychiatric Association, American Academy of Psychoanalysis, William Alanson White Society, New York State Medical Society, New York County Medical Society, Phi Beta Kappa.

WRITINGS: The Second Experiment (novel), Houghton, 1974. Contributor to *Contemporary Psychoanalysis.* Associate editor of *Contemporary Psychoanalysis,* 1970—.

WORK IN PROGRESS: A novel.

SIDELIGHTS: Ms. Jeppson wrote to *CA:* "Interested in current astronomical speculation as well as research in anthropology, primate behavior, biofeedback, etc. My major interest is my husband, but I'd read science fiction and tried to write it long before I met him. We both like to read mystery stories (I even published one years ago, but he writes a lot of them nowadays). I wrote *Second Experiment* after major surgery gave me intimations of mortality." *Avocational interests:* Reading mysteries.

BIOGRAPHICAL/CRITICAL SOURCES: Albany Sunday Times-Union, July 21, 1974.

* * *

JESMER, Elaine 1939-

PERSONAL: Born March 29, 1939, in Chicago, Ill.; daughter of Julius (a lawyer) and Mary (Markin) Jesmer. *Education:* University of Illinois, B.S., 1960. *Politics:* Anarchist. *Religion:* "That's between me and Her."

CAREER: Press agent, social worker.

WRITINGS: Number One with a Bullet (novel), Farrar, Straus, 1974.

WORK IN PROGRESS: A novel, publication by Farrar, Straus expected in 1975; a third novel; short stories.

SIDELIGHTS: Elaine Jesmer told *CA:* "I write for freedom. Public and personal freedom, particularly the right to be different in a society growing increasingly intolerant of artists and other crazy people. But beyond all that, I write because it gets me off."

* * *

JOCHNOWITZ, George 1937-

PERSONAL: Born August 1, 1937, in Brooklyn, N.Y.; son of Jerome (a manufacturer) and Helen (Leiman) Jochnowitz; married Carol Fink, September 2, 1962; children: Eve, Miriam. *Education:* Columbia University, A.B., 1958, M.A., 1960, Ph.D., 1967. *Religion:* Jewish. *Home:* 54 East Eighth St., New York, N.Y. 10003. *Office:* Division of Humanities, Richmond College of the City University of New York, Staten Island, N.Y. 10301.

CAREER: Temple University, Philadelphia, Pa., instructor in French, 1961-63; New York University, New York, N.Y., instructor in French, 1963-65; Queens College of the City University of New York, Flushing, N.Y., lecturer in Romance languages, 1965-68; Richmond College of the City University of New York, Staten Island, N.Y., assistant professor, 1968-71, associate professor of linguistics, 1972—. Visiting fellow at Yale University, 1972.

WRITINGS: Dialect Boundaries and the Question of Franco-Provencal, Mouton & Co., 1973. Contributor of articles and reviews on Jewish languages and other subjects of Jewish interest to professional journals.

WORK IN PROGRESS: Research on Judeo-Italian dialects.

* * *

JOHANNES, R.
See MOSS, Rose

* * *

JOHNS, Albert Cameron 1914-

PERSONAL: Born December 28, 1914, in Rockford, Ill.; son of Robert Alexander (a contractor) and Jane Scott (Anderson) Johns; married Edna Gale (a teacher), August 23, 1941; children: Ronald Cameron, Janene Laurie, Pamela Gayle. *Education:* Los Angeles City College, A.A., 1942; Chapman College, B.A., 1948; Claremont Graduate School, M.A., 1963, Ph.D., 1965. *Religion:* Methodist. *Home:* 5433 Longridge Ave., Las Vegas, Nev. 89102. *Office:* Department of Political Science, University of Nevada, 4505 Maryland Pkwy., Las Vegas, Nev. 89109.

CAREER: Pasadena Star News, Pasadena, Calif., reporter, 1950-52; Tournament of Roses, Pasadena, Calif., director of public relations, 1952-59; *Los Angeles Times,* Los Angeles, Calif., real estate editor and columnist, 1959-62; University of Redlands, Redlands, Calif., instructor in government, 1963-64; Chapman College, Orange, Calif., assistant professor, 1964, associate professor of political science, 1965-66; University of Nevada, Las Vegas, associate professor, 1967-72, professor of political science, 1972—. Head of Al Johns Co. (public relations), in Pasadena, Calif., 1950-67, and Las Vegas, 1967—; director of public relations for Miss Universe Pageant, Long Beach, 1955-58, for political campaigns, and for organizations. Vice-president, Southern Nevada Community Concert Association. *Military service:* U.S. Army, 1942-46; became first lieutenant.

MEMBER: American Political Science Association, American Society for Public Administration, National Education Association, American Association of University Professors, Western Political Science Association, Rocky Mountain Social Science Association. *Awards, honors:* National Association of Real Estate Editors Award for Excellence, 1960; Alumnus of the Year Award, Chapman College, 1960.

WRITINGS: Rocky Mountain Urban Politics, Utah State University Press, 1971; *Nevada Government and Politics,* Kendall-Hunt, 1971; *Nevada Politics,* Kendall-Hunt, 1973. Writer of weekly column, "Down to Earth," in *Los Angeles Times,* 1959-61.

WORK IN PROGRESS: Nevada, on the legislature, budgets, and local government.

* * *

JOHNSGARD, Paul A(ustin) 1931-

PERSONAL: Born June 28, 1931, in Fargo, N.D.; son of Alfred Bernard (a sanitarian) and Yvonne (Morgan) Johnsgard; married Lois Lampe, June 24, 1956; children: Jay, Scott, Ann, Karin. *Education:* North Dakota State University, B.S., 1953; Washington State University, M.S., 1956; Cornell University, Ph.D., 1959. *Home:* 7341 Holdrege, Lincoln, Neb. 68505. *Office:* Department of Zoology, University of Nebraska, Lincoln, Neb. 68508.

CAREER: University of Nebraska, Lincoln, instructor, 1961-62, assistant professor, 1962-64, associate professor, 1964-68, professor of zoology, 1968—. *Member:* American Ornithologists Union (fellow), Wilson Ornithological Society, Cooper Ornithological Society, Sigma Xi. *Awards, honors:* National Science Foundation fellow, University of Bristol, 1959-60; U.S. Public Health Service fellow, 1960-61; National Science Foundation research grant, 1963-66; top honor book award from Chicago Book Clinic, 1969, for *Waterfowl;* Guggenheim fellowship, 1971; outstanding book publication award from Wildlife Society, 1974, for *Grouse and Quails of North America.*

WRITINGS: Handbook of Waterfowl Behavior, Cornell University Press, 1965; *Animal Behavior,* W. C. Brown, 1967, 2nd edition, 1972; *Waterfowl: Their Biology and Natural History,* University of Nebraska Press, 1968; *Grouse and Quails of North America,* University of Nebraska Press, 1973; *Song of the North Wind: A Story of the Snow Goose,* Doubleday, 1974; *American Game Birds of Upland and Shoreline,* University of Nebraska Press, in press.

WORK IN PROGRESS: A book on the ecology and behavior of the sandhill crane; a book on the waterfowl of North America.

SIDELIGHTS: Johnsgard has conducted field work in North and South America, Australia, and Europe. *Avocational interests:* Photography, art (especially line illustration).

* * *

JOHNSON, Amandus 1877-1974

1877-June 30, 1974; Swedish-born American authority on Scandinavian culture and history, linguist, and educator. Obituaries: *New York Times,* July 3, 1974.

* * *

JOHNSON, Brian Stanley 1933-1974

February 5, 1933—1974; British novelist and writer for films. Obituaries: *AB Bookman's Weekly,* July 15, 1974.

* * *

JOHNSON, Eola 1909-

PERSONAL: Born July 17, 1909, in Everett, Wash.; daughter of John Thompson (a plumber) and Dorcas (Bierce) Poindexter; married Montie Smallen, February 3, 1929 (divorced July 29, 1949); married Lloyd Johnson (a building contractor), October 17, 1954; children: (first marriage) Roberta (Mrs. Alfred Harold Schmechel), Lewis, Ralph. *Education:* Attended University of Oregon and Oceanside Junior College; additional study by correspondence courses. *Religion:* Christian. *Home address:* P.O. Box 181, Sisters, Ore. 97759.

CAREER: Bookkeeper in Portland, Ore.; saleswoman in Bible Book store, Portland; Portland Osteopathic Hospital, Portland, admitting officer and x-ray technician, 1950-51; Emanuel Hospital, Portland, member of medical records staff, 1951-52. *Member:* Oregon Association of Christian Writers (secretary, 1973), Central Oregon Gideon Camp Auxiliary (chaplain, 1973-74), Delphian Society, Opti-Mrs. Club, Toastmistress Club.

WRITINGS: Beloved Disciples, Warner Press, 1973. Contributor to religious journals.

WORK IN PROGRESS: Lower Lights: A Book on Chris-

tian Living; My Brother Speaks to Me, a book of devotional readings.

AVOCATIONAL INTERESTS: Reading, interior decorating, sewing, music, gardening, golf, travel.

* * *

JOHNSON, Howard Albert 1915-1974

October 8, 1915—June 12, 1974; American clergyman, theologian, educator, and author of books on philosophy, religion, and related topics. Obituaries: *New York Times,* June 17, 1974. (*CA*-1).

* * *

JOHNSON, Jane M(axine) 1914-

PERSONAL: Born May 26, 1914, in Driftwood, Pa.; daughter of Jesse E. and Myrtle Lola (Logue) Johnson; married William Allan McDougall (an engineer and contractor), June 21, 1945 (divorced, 1965); married Charles A. Daigle (a carpenter), September 8, 1973; children: (first marriage) Mary Jane (Mrs. John Henry), William Allan, Alexander Alden. *Education:* Attended high school in Pennsylvania. *Politics:* Conservative. *Religion:* United Church of Christ. *Home and office:* Duchess Ave., London, Ontario N6C IN6, Canada.

CAREER: Other Voices (quarterly poetry magazine), London, Ontario, editor and publisher, 1965—. Has organized poetry workshops and "Poetry in the Park" and "Poetry in the Pub" programs; free-lance writer, poet, and lecturer. *Military service:* Royal Canadian Army Medical Corps, 1939-45; served in Europe; became lieutenant. *Member:* League of Canadian Poets, Avalon Poets, Registered Nurses Association.

WRITINGS: (Editor with others) *Canadian Women Poets,* Olivant, 1967-68; *Never the Sun* (poems), Fiddlehead Books, 1971; (editor) *Showcase for the London Poets,* Alice in Wonderland Press, 1974. Poems are included in British and American anthologies. Contributor of poems to *Humanist, London Free Press.*

WORK IN PROGRESS: A narrative poem.

* * *

JOHNSTON, Mireille 1940-

PERSONAL: Born October 4, 1940, in Nice, France; daughter of Jean Philippe and Marguerite Sigard Busticaccia; married Thomas Morisson Carnegie Johnston, 1959; children: Margaret Broolle, Elizabeth. *Education:* Attended University of London, 1957-58; Aix-en-Provence University, B.A., 1961; Yale University, Ph.D., 1964. *Home:* 920 Fifth Ave., New York, N.Y. 10021.

CAREER: Yale University, New Haven, Conn., instructor in French literature, 1961-64; Barnard College, New York, N.Y., instructor in French literature, 1964-65; Sarah Lawrence College, Bronxville, N.Y., instructor in French literature, 1965-68.

WRITINGS: Central Park Country, Sierra Club, 1967; *The Sorrow and the Pity,* Outerbridge & Lazard, 1973; *La Cuisine du soleil* (title means "The Sun's Cuisine"), Random House, 1974.

* * *

JOINER, Edward Earl 1924-

PERSONAL: Born April 25, 1924, in Colquitt, Ga.; son of John B. (a farmer) and Lula (Harrison) Joiner; married Geraldine Rouse; children: Edward Earl, Jr., Paul Allen, Ann Eileen, John Andrew. *Education:* Stetson University, A.B., 1949; Southern Baptist Theological Seminary, B.D., 1953, Th.M., 1954, Th.D., 1960. *Politics:* Democrat. *Home:* 735 North Sans Souci, Deland, Fla. 32720. *Office:* Department of Religion, Stetson University, Deland, Fla. 32720.

CAREER: Pastor of Baptist church in Brownsboro, Ky., 1950-55; Stetson University, Deland, Fla., assistant professor, 1955-61, associate professor, 1961-65, professor of religion, 1965—. Member of board of directors, Volusia County Legal Services. *Military service:* U.S. Army, Infantry, 1944-46; served in European theater; received three battle stars. *Member:* American Academy of Religion, American Society of Christian Ethics.

WRITINGS: A History of Florida Baptists, Convention Press, 1972. Contributor to *Southern Baptist Encyclopedia* and to church journals.

WORK IN PROGRESS: A book on moral growth, tentatively titled *Becoming a Moral Person;* a manuscript on religion and contemporary moral issues.

* * *

JOLIAT, Eugene 1910-

PERSONAL: Born May 31, 1910, in St. Hyacinthe, Quebec, Canada; son of Henri and Adrienne (Etienne) Joliat; married Pauline Noffsinger (a professor at University of Toronto), July 19, 1935; children: Marc Louis, Suzanne Joliat Kemmsies. *Education:* McGill University, B.A. (honors), 1931; University of Paris, Docteur de l'Universite, 1935. *Home:* 64 Astley Ave., Toronto 287, Ontario, Canada. *Office:* 226 University College, University of Toronto, Toronto 181, Ontario, Canada.

CAREER: McMaster University, Hamilton, Ontario, lecturer in French, 1935-36; Wesleyan University, Middletown, Conn., instructor in Romance languages, 1936-37; University of Iowa, Iowa City, assistant professor, 1937-39, associate professor of Romance languages, 1939-42; National Council of Private Schools, Washington, D.C., assistant to director, 1942-46; University of Toronto, Toronto, Ontario, assistant professor, 1946-47, associate professor, 1947-57, professor of French, 1957—, chairman of graduate department of French, 1967-72. Visiting professor at University of British Columbia, 1959. *Member:* Modern Language Association of America, Canadian Comparative Literature Association (president, 1969-71), International Comparative Literature Association (treasurer, 1958-63), Ontario Modern Language Teachers Association (president, 1950).

WRITINGS: Smollett et la France, Honore Champion (Paris), 1935; (compiler with Robert Finch) *French Individualist Poetry,* 1686-1760 (anthology), University of Toronto Press, 1971. Contributor of articles on literary history and education to journals. Associate editor, *Canadian Modern Language Review,* 1952-72.

WORK IN PROGRESS: With Robert Finch, a critical edition of the plays of Saint-Evremond.

* * *

JOLSON, Marvin A(rnold) 1922-

PERSONAL: Born June 7, 1922, in Chicago, Ill.; son of George and Bess (Sweetow) Jolson; married Betty Harris,

July 8, 1944; children: Robert D., Nancy E. *Education:* George Washington University, B.E.E., 1949; University of Chicago, M.B.A., 1965; University of Maryland, D.B.A., 1969; also studied at University of Southern California, summer, 1967. *Home:* 7812 Ridge Ter., Pikesville, Md. 21208. *Office:* College of Business and Management, University of Maryland, Q-3114, College Park, Md. 20742.

CAREER: *Encyclopaedia Britannica,* Inc., salesman in Baltimore, Md., 1946-49, sales manager, 1950-52, district manager, 1952-58, division manager, 1959-60, Southeast zone manager in Washington, D.C., 1960-62, senior vice-president in Chicago, Ill., 1962-68; University of Maryland, College Park, lecturer, 1968-69, assistant professor of marketing, 1969—. Electrical engineer for Davies Laboratories, 1949-50. Lecturer at Roosevelt University, 1966; guest lecturer at DePaul University and University of Chicago, 1966; summer lecturer at Loyola College, Baltimore, 1971; visiting assistant professor at Johns Hopkins University, 1973. Member of board of directors of Crime Prevention Co. of America and Creative Chemical Co.; ad hoc advisor to Federal Trade Commission, 1972.

MEMBER: American Marketing Association, Association for Consumer Research, Southern Marketing Association, University of Chicago Executive Program Club, Delta Sigma Pi, Beta Gamma Sigma, Masons. *Awards, honors:* Winner of field sales management award from National Sales Executives Club, 1954.

WRITINGS: *Consumer Attitudes Toward Direct-to-Home Marketing Systems,* Dunellen, 1970; (with Richard T. Hise) *Quantitative Techniques for Marketing Decisions,* with instructor's manual, Macmillan, 1973. Contributor to proceedings. Contributor of about forty articles and reviews to business journals. Member of abstract review staff of *Journal of Marketing;* member of board of editors of *Akron Business and Economic Review.*

WORK IN PROGRESS: *Marketing Policies and Strategies: An Integration of Text and Readings; Sex-Oriented Content in General Movies: Attitudes of Moviegoers,* with Gary Ford; *The Business Executive Turned Faculty Member; A Field Study of Sales Presentation Effectiveness; Product Scarcity: A Determinant of Demand for Improved Quality.*

BIOGRAPHICAL/CRITICAL SOURCES: *New York Times,* April 25, 1965; *Baltimore Morning Sun,* February 15, 1974.

* * *

JONES, Charles Edwin 1932-

PERSONAL: Born June 1, 1932, in Kansas City, Mo.; son of Dess Dain (a streetcar and bus operator) and Dove (Barnwell) Jones; married Beverly Anne Lundy (a librarian), May 30, 1956; children: Karl Laurence. *Education:* Bethany-Peniel College, B.A., 1954; University of Oklahoma, summer graduate study, 1954; University of Michigan, M.A.L.S., 1955; University of Wisconsin, M.S., 1960, Ph.D., 1968. *Politics:* Democrat. *Religion:* Episcopalian. *Home:* 4 Barnes St., Providence, R.I. 02906. *Office:* Library, Brown University, Providence, R.I. 02912.

CAREER: Bethany Nazarene College, Bethany, Okla., reference librarian, 1955-56; Nazarene Theological Seminary, Kansas City, Mo., head librarian, 1958-59; Park College, Parkville, Mo., head librarian, 1961-63; University of Michigan, Ann Arbor, manuscript curator of Michigan Historical Collections, 1965-69; Houghton College, Houghton, N.Y., associate professor of history, 1969-71; Brown University, Providence, R.I., catalog librarian, 1971—. Visiting professor at Tuskegee Institute, 1969. *Military service:* U.S. Army, 1956-58. *Member:* Organization of American Historians, American Studies Association, American Society of Church History, Canadian Church Historical Society, Popular Culture Association, Southern Historical Association.

WRITINGS: *Perfectionist Persuasion: The Holiness Movement and American Methodism, 1867-1936,* Scarecrow, 1974; *Guide to the Study of the Holiness Movement,* Scarecrow, 1974. Contributor to *Journal of Church and State, Inland Seas, Detroit Historical Society Bulletin, Journal of the Canadian Church Historical Society, Missouri Historical Review,* and *North Dakota Quarterly.*

WORK IN PROGRESS: *Guide to the Study of the Pentecostal Movement.*

* * *

JONES, Diana Wynne 1934-

PERSONAL: Born August 16, 1934, in London, England; daughter of Richard Aneurin (an educator) and Marjorie (an educator; maiden name, Jackson) Jones; married John A. Burrow (a university professor), December 23, 1956; children: Richard, Michael, Colin. *Education:* St. Anne's College, Oxford, B.A., 1956. *Home:* 4 Herbert Close, Oxford, England. *Agent:* Laura Cecil, 10 Exeter Mansions, 106 Shaftesbury Ave., London, England.

CAREER: Writer.

WRITINGS—For children, except as noted: *Changeover* (adult novel), Macmillan, 1970; *Wilkins' Tooth,* Macmillan, 1973, published as *Witch's Business,* Dutton, 1974; *The Ogre Downstairs,* Macmillan, 1974; *Eight Days of Luke,* Macmillan, 1974.

Plays for children: "The Batterpool Business," first performed in London, England, at Arts Theatre, October, 1968; "The King's Things," first performed in London, England, at Arts Theatre, February, 1970; "The Terrible Fisk Machine," first performed in London, England, at Arts Theatre, January, 1971.

WORK IN PROGRESS: *Cart and Cwidder,* a novel for children; *Power of Three,* a novel for children; "Fred and the Bike Lamp," a play for children.

SIDELIGHTS: Diana Wynne Jones writes: "I had an eccentric and unorganized childhood. When I was not balancing along rooftops hoping to learn to fly, or hatching schemes for advancement. . . I was reading avidly. There were hardly any good books. . . So nowadays, when I write for children, my first aim is to make a story—as amusing and exciting as possible—such as I wished I could have read as a child.

"My second aim is equally important. It is to give children—without presuming to instruct them—the benefit of my greater experience. I like to explore the private terrors and troubles which beset children, because they can thereby be shown they are not unique in misery. Children create about a third of their misery themselves. The other two-thirds is caused by adults—inconsiderate, mysterious, and often downright frightening adults. I put adults like this in my stories, in some firmly contemporary situation beset with very real problems, and explore the implications by means of magic and old myths. What I am after is an exciting—and exacting—wisdom, in which contemporary life and potent myth are intricately involved and superimposed.

I would like children to discover that potent old truths are as much part of everyone's daily life as are—say—the days of the week."

* * *

JONES, Enid (Mary) Huws 1911-

PERSONAL: Middle name sounds like "Hughes"; born August 17, 1911, in Nottingham, England; married Robin Huws Jones (a consultant on social administration), December 27, 1944; children: Margaret Bronwen (Mrs. Arun Vivian Holden), Edward Mark, Mary Gwenydd. *Education:* Somerville College, Oxford, M.A., 1934. *Religion:* Quaker. *Home:* 8 Ouselea, Shipton Rd., York YO36SA, England. *Agent:* P. Corte, Hughes Massie, 69 Great Russell St., London W61, England.

CAREER: Has taught in schools, colleges of education, university extra-mural departments, and elsewhere. *Awards, honors:* First prize in *Observer* essay competition, 1951.

WRITINGS: Margery Fry: The Essential Amateur, Oxford University Press, 1966; *Mrs. Humphrey Ward,* St. Martin's, 1973. Contributor to *Guardian* and other publications. Editor, *Quaker Monthly.*

WORK IN PROGRESS: Biographical and autobiographical research.

* * *

JONES, Ken D(uane) 1930-

PERSONAL: Born July 10, 1930, in Hannibal, Mo.; son of Cliff G. (an accountant, musician, and grocer) and Clifton E. (Brown) Jones; married Nancy Johnston, December 21, 1952; children: Debra, Karen. *Education:* Hannibal LaGrange Junior College, A.A., 1950; attended Arizona State College, 1950-51; Culver-Stockton College, B.S., 1954. *Politics:* Democrat. *Religion:* Protestant. *Home:* 100 Manor Dr., Columbia, Mo. 65201. *Office:* State Farm Mutual Auto Insurance Co., Columbia, Mo. 65201.

CAREER: High school teacher of science in Wright City, Mo., 1954-56; State Farm Mutual Auto Insurance Co., Warrenton, Mo., insurance agent, 1956-57, Columbia, Mo., underwriting supervisor, 1957—. *Military service:* U.S. Army, Intelligence, 1952-54. *Member:* Tin Container Collectors Association.

WRITINGS: (With Alfred Twomey and Arthur McClure) *The Films of James Stewart,* A. S. Barnes, 1970; (with McClure) *Heroes, Heavies, and Sagebrush,* A. S. Barnes, 1972; (with McClure) *Hollywood at War,* A. S. Barnes, 1973; (with McClure) *Star Quality,* A. S. Barnes, 1974. Contributor of regular columns to *Film Collectors Registry* and *Western Film Collector.* Co-editor of *Yesteryear,* 1971—.

WORK IN PROGRESS: A book on character actors and actresses.

AVOCATIONAL INTERESTS: Collector of movie memorabilia, tobacco tins, advertising items, old toys; active in softball, basketball, golf, fishing.

* * *

JONES, Paul Davis 1940-

PERSONAL: Born February 24, 1940, in New York, N.Y.; son of John Aloysius (a lawyer) and Vera M. (Davis) Jones. *Education:* Fairfield University, A.B., 1961; Boston College, M.A., 1965; Weston College, M.Div., 1972; Syracuse University, Ph.D., 1971. *Politics:* Democrat. *Residence:* Milford, Conn. *Office:* Department of Theology, Boston College, Chestnut Hill, Mass. 02167.

CAREER: Roman Catholic priest of Society of Jesus (Jesuit); ordained, 1961; Woodstock Center for Religion and Worship, Woodstock, N.Y., assistant director, 1971-74; Boston College, Chestnut Hill, Mass., assistant professor of theology and drama, 1974—. Program developer in religious architecture and arts for International Congress, 1972—. *Member:* International Congress, Jerusalem Committee.

WRITINGS: Rediscovering Ritual, Newman, 1973. Contributor to *Kunst und Kirche, New Catholic World,* and *Faith and Form.*

WORK IN PROGRESS: The Drama of Harold Pinter; editing *The Meaning and Form of Sacred Space,* with introduction; television scripts on drama and religion; a six-part color video cassette series on ritual.

* * *

JONES, Richard 1926-

PERSONAL: Born July 25, 1926, in Aberystwyth, Wales; son of Edward Richard (a farmer) and Eunice (Silburn) Jones; married Marie Babenco, June 11, 1956; children: Katherine, Nathalie. *Education:* Attended University of Wales, 1945-46, and Sorbonne, University of Paris, 1949-51. *Politics:* Labour. *Religion:* None. *Home:* 120 Clapham Common West Side, London S.W.4, England; 12 Oak Circle, Farmington, Charlottesville, Va. 22901. *Agent:* Peter Grose, Curtis Brown Ltd., 2 Craven Hill, London W.2, England.

CAREER: Journalist, working for Reuters, 1957-50, and British Broadcasting Corp., 1960-74. Visiting lecturer at Stanford University, 1969-70, and University of Virginia, 1973, 1974-75. Member of Cardiganshire County Council, 1955-57. *Member:* International P.E.N., Welsh Academy. *Awards, honors:* Welsh Arts Council prize, 1971.

WRITINGS—Novels: *The Age of Wonder,* Macmillan (London), 1967, published as *The Three Suitors,* Little, Brown, 1968; *The Toy Crusaders,* Macmillan (London), 1968, published as *Supper with the Borgias,* Little, Brown, 1969; *A Way Out,* Macmillan (London), 1969; *The Tower Is Everywhere,* Little, Brown, 1971. Contributor of articles and reviews to magazines and newspapers, including *Atlantic Monthly, Times Literary Supplement, Guardian,* and *Listener.*

WORK IN PROGRESS: Dancing the Orange, a novel.

SIDELIGHTS: Jones writes that he has traveled in the Middle East and France; he is especially interested in modern American and Russian writing, politics, music, and art.

* * *

JONES, Richard H(utton) 1914-

PERSONAL: Born August 11, 1914, in Rye, Colo.; son of John Wiley and Jessie (Hutton) Jones; married Alyce Decker, August 15, 1935; children: Robert Charles. *Education:* Colorado State College (now University of Northern Colorado), B.A., 1934, M.A., 1937; Stanford University, Ph.D., 1947. *Politics:* Republican. *Home:* 3908 Southeast Reedway, Portland, Ore. 97202. *Office:* Department of History, Reed College, 3203 Southeast Woodstock, Portland, Ore. 97202.

CAREER: High school teacher in Fort Lupton, Colo., 1934-38; Stanford University, Stanford, Calif., instructor in history, 1940-41; Reed College, Portland, Ore., instructor, 1941-43, assistant professor, 1943-46, associate professor, 1946-48, professor of history, 1948-61, Richard F. Scholz Professor of History, 1961—. Senior fellow in law and behavioral sciences at University of Chicago, 1956-67; public member of Oregon Legislative Interim Committee on Labor, 1958-60; executive secretary of Citizens Committee for Constitutional Revision, 1963-65. Chairman of committee on European history, College Entrance Examination Board, 1960-67.

MEMBER: American Historical Association, Historical Association (England), Mediaeval Academy of America. *Awards, honors:* Social Science Research Council faculty fellow, 1951-53; Ford Foundation fellow, 1953-54.

WRITINGS: The Royal Policy of Richard II: Absolutism in the Late Middle Ages, Barnes & Noble, 1968.

WORK IN PROGRESS: Books on medieval origins of the state and on Edward I.

* * *

JONES, Robert F(rancis) 1934-

PERSONAL: Born May 26, 1934, in Milwaukee, Wis.; son of Charles F. (a banker) and Rose Mary (Pueringer) Jones; married Louise Tyor (a writer), October 21, 1956; children: Leslie Ellen, Benno Francis. *Education:* University of Michigan, B.A., 1956. *Politics:* Independent. *Religion:* None. *Home address:* Moseman Ave., R.F.D. 2, Katonah, N.Y. 10536. *Agent:* Robert D'Attilla, 225 West 49th St., New York, N.Y. *Office:* Time, Inc., 1270 Avenue of the Americas, New York, N.Y. 10020.

CAREER: Time, Inc., New York, N.Y., associate editor and writer for *Time* (magazine), 1960-68, writer for *Sports Illustrated,* 1968—. *Military service:* U.S. Navy, 1956-59; became lieutenant junior grade. *Member:* Hudson River Fishermen's Association, Kappa Tau Alpha.

WRITINGS: Blood Sport: A Journey Up the Hassayampa, Simon & Schuster, 1974. Contributor of articles and reviews to *Washington Post* and *New York Times Sunday Magazine.*

WORK IN PROGRESS: Forager, a novel.

SIDELIGHTS: Jones lists his main motivations as a boyhood spent hunting and fishing in the upper Midwest, wide travel in the Western Pacific, and further travel in Africa, Eastern Europe, Central America, and New Zealand. *Avocational interests:* Hunting, fishing, skindiving, gardening.

* * *

JONES, Stephen (Phillip) 1935- (Nelson P. Falorp; The Water Rat)

PERSONAL: Born December 29, 1935, in Hartford, Conn.; son of Edward Phillip (a carpenter) and Jessica (a painter; maiden name, Murphy) Jones; married Lois Ann Heibler (an English teacher); children: David Phillip, Geoffrey Phillip. *Education:* University of Connecticut, B.A., 1959, M.A., 1960. *Agent:* Brandt & Brandt, 101 Park Ave., New York, N.Y. 10017. *Office:* Department of English, University of Connecticut, Storrs, Conn. 06268.

CAREER: Mohican-Kelley News, West Hartford, Conn., editor, 1957-58; *Hartford Courant,* Hartford, Conn., part-time reporter (stringer), 1958; *Willimantic Chronicle,* Willimantic, Conn., reporter and sports editor, 1959; boat salesman in Mystic, Conn., 1963-64; lobsterman in Fishers Island Sound, 1964; high school English teacher in Waterford, Conn., 1964-67; University of Connecticut, Storrs, instructor, 1967-68, assistant professor, 1968-74, associate professor of English, 1974—. Member of Groton Oyster Committee, 1969-72; member of Bluff Point Advisory Council, 1973—. Navigational consultant to Museum of Natural History for Hudson River Hall of Fishes film, 1967. *Military service:* U.S. Coast Guard, worked as seaman on lifeboat station and lighthouse keeper, 1961-63. *Member:* Noank Historical Society.

WRITINGS: Turpin (novel), Macmillan, 1968; *Drifting: Being the Author's Account of His Voyages in Dooryards, Alleys, Bayous, Millraces, Swamps, Sumps, Rivers, Creeks, Canals, Lakes, Bays, and Open Sewers about the Historic Lands of New Orleans, Valley of Swans, Cape May, Yorktown, Jamestown, Mystic, Noank, and Westerly Rhode Island, with Illustrations in Pen and Ink by Richard Brown, Sometime Bow Oar* (Dolphin Watersports Book Club selection), Macmillan, 1971.

(Under pseudonym Nelson P. Falorp) *Cape May to Montauk,* Viking, 1973.

Contributing author of "Mystic Bound," a film script, Sandefjord Productions, 1973. Author, under pseudonym, "Water Rat," of a column in *Mystic Compass,* 1973-74. Co-founder of *Wormwood Review,* managing editor, 1960.

WORK IN PROGRESS: Harbor of Refuge, a novel about life in a lighthouse; *Old Men with Seagulls in Their Hair,* a novel; *Backwaters,* non-fiction "rambles and drifts"; *Foostering,* non-fiction about improvising in Ireland.

SIDELIGHTS: Of *Drifting,* R. Z. Sheppard writes: "Mostly . . . drifting gives Jones the chance to chart the indirections of his own ironic, eccentrically ballasted mind. It is the kind of mind that can easily mingle references to Henry James, Robbe-Grillet and Li-yue with equations on dam overflow, yarns about wharf characters and slices of local history . . . and, like Mark Twain in *Huckleberry Finn,* revel in naming objects for their own sake." Another reviewer feels that the book's real locus of action is not so much in the incidents that beset Jones and his companions, "but in the spirit of the book itself. This spirit, despite the comically anti-heroic tone in which the book is largely narrated, contains solid elements of those Thoreauvian virtues which we could once think of as peculiarly American. It combines with venturesome independence an affectionate regard for what is most honestly alive in American society (and a wittily sharp disregard for what is shoddy and artificial), a compellingly knowledgeable respect for our history and traditions, and a modest but unflinching love for the life of our natural environment."

Jones comes from an Irish family of carpenters and wheelwrights; he describes them as great storytellers and fair but enthusiastic musicians.

AVOCATIONAL INTERESTS: Fishing, rowing, sailing, swimming, whiffleball, trumpet, trombone, walking, book collecting, mummer's plays, pageants, mystery plays, sailboat launching speeches, wine making, apple growing, dog scratching.

BIOGRAPHICAL/CRITICAL SOURCES: New Orleans Times Picayune, March 25, 1974.

* * *

JONES, W(alton) Glyn 1928-

PERSONAL: Born October 29, 1928, in Manchester, England; son of Emrys (an engineer) and Dorothy Ada (North) Jones; married Karen Ruth Fleischer, June 12, 1953; children: Stephen Francis, Olaf Emrys Robert, Catherine Monica, Anna Elizabeth. *Education:* Pembroke College, Cambridge, B.A., 1952, M.A. and Ph.D., 1956. *Home:* 23A Douglas Rd., Harpenden, Hertfordshire AL5 2EP, England. *Office:* Department of German and Scandinavian Studies, University of Newcastle-upon-Tyne, Newcastle-upon-Tyne NE1 7RU, England.

CAREER: University of London, University College, London, England, assistant lecturer, 1956-58, lecturer, 1958-66, reader in Danish, 1966-73; University of Newcastle-upon-Tyne, Newcastle-upon-Tyne, England, professor of Scandinavian studies, 1973—. Visiting professor at University of Iceland, 1971.

WRITINGS: Johannes Joergensen's Modne Aar (title means "Johannes Joergensen's Mature Years"), Gyldendal, 1963; *Johannes Joergensen,* Twayne, 1969; *Denmark,* Praeger, 1970; *William Heinesen,* Twayne, 1974; *Faeroe og Kosmos* (title means "Faroe and Cosmos"), Gyldendal, 1974. Contributor to *Scandinavian Studies, Scandinavica, Nordisk Tidskrift, Month,* and *Times Literary Supplement.*

WORK IN PROGRESS: Research into modern Faroese literature and the work of Gunnar Gunnarsson.

AVOCATIONAL INTERESTS: Music.

* * *

JONGEWARD, Dorothy 1925-

PERSONAL: Surname sounds like *Young*-word; born November 10, 1925, in Spokane, Wash.; daughter of Joseph E. (a candy maker) and Grace (Gibbs) Kolander; married Wallace Jongeward (a sales representative), May 31, 1949; children: Mark, Jill, Sherri. *Education:* Washington State University, B.S., 1949, B.Ed., 1950, M.Ed., 1952. *Home and office:* 487 Malaga Way, Pleasant Hill, Calif. 94523.

CAREER: Licensed marriage, child, and family counselor, 1964—. Member of faculty at University of California, Berkeley, Extension Division, 1965—; interpersonal relations and communications consultant, 1968—. President of Transactional Analysis Management Institute, Inc., 1974—. Has taught at University of Idaho, Washington State University, University of Colorado, University of Richmond, University of California, California State University, Laymen's School of Religion, Cabrillo Junior College, and Diablo Valley College; has conducted workshops and seminars and given lectures; has developed programs for continuing education of women and affirmative action programs for organizations. Testified before California Advisory Committee on the Status of Women, 1966. Member of board of directors of School for Living. Has appeared on television and radio programs.

MEMBER: International Transactional Analysis Association (member of board of trustees), Southwest Institute for Transactional Analysis (honorary member of board of directors, 1974), California Marriage and Family Counseling Association (life member), Northern Virginia Association for Transactional Analysis (honorary member of board of directors, 1974), Phi Beta Kappa, Phi Kappa Phi.

WRITINGS: (With Muriel James) *Born to Win: Transactional Analysis with Gestalt Experiments,* Addison-Wesley, 1971; (with James) *Winning with People: Group Exercises in Transactional Analysis,* Addison-Wesley, 1973; (with others) *Everybody Wins: Transactional Analysis Applied to Organizations,* Addison-Wesley, 1973; (with Dru Scott) *Affirmative Action for Women: A Practical Guide,* Addison-Wesley, 1973; (with Scott) *The Trouble with Women: A Transactional Analysis,* Addison-Wesley, in press; (with James) *The People Book: Transactional Analysis for Students,* Addison-Wesley, in press. Contributor to *Marriage Counseling Quarterly, P.S. for Secretaries,* and *Transactional Analysis Journal.*

WORK IN PROGRESS: Transactional Analysis Applied to Selling, with Ed Musselwhite, completion expected in 1976; designing a compatibility profile.

SIDELIGHTS: Jongeward has been a pioneer and leader in the fields of family life education, sex education, adult education, continuing education for women, and the applications of transactional analysis to business, industry, and government. *Avocational interests:* Travel, painting, swimming, hiking, dancing.

BIOGRAPHICAL/CRITICAL SOURCES: Transactional Analysis Bulletin, July, 1970; *Bank American,* July-August, 1972; *Business Week,* January 12, 1974.

* * *

JORDAN, Gilbert John 1902-

PERSONAL: Born December 23, 1902, in Mason County, Tex.; son of Daniel (a ranchman) and Emilie (Willmann) Jordan; married Vera Tiller, 1926; children: Janice (Mrs. Thomas W. Shefelman), Terry G. *Education:* Southwestern University, Georgetown, Tex., A.B., 1924; University of Texas, M.A., 1928; University of Wisconsin, graduate study, 1930-33; Ohio State University, Ph.D., 1936. *Politics:* Independent. *Religion:* Methodist. *Home:* 3228 Milton Ave., Dallas, Tex. 75205.

CAREER: Teacher and administrator in public schools of Texas, 1924-30; Southern Methodist University, Dallas, Tex., assistant professor, 1930-38, associate professor, 1938-43, professor of German, 1943-68; Sam Houston State University, Huntsville, Tex., professor of German, 1968-73. *Member:* Modern Language Association of America, American Association of Teachers of German, American Association of University Professors, South Central Modern Language Association, Texas State Teachers Association. *Awards, honors:* Order of Merit, Federal Republic of Germany, 1960.

WRITINGS: (Editor) *Southwest Goethe Festival* (collection of papers), Southern Methodist University, 1949; (editor and author of introduction and notes) *Four German One-Act Plays,* Holt, 1951; (translator) Friedrich Von Schiller, *Wilhelm Tell* (verse translation), Bobbs-Merrill, 1964; *Ernst and Lisette Jordan: German Pioneers in Texas,* privately printed, 1971. Writer of filmstrips, "Wilhelm Tell," 1971, and "The Romantic Road," 1972, both in German and English, and both produced by Educational Film Strip Co.

WORK IN PROGRESS: Translation of W. Steinert's *North America; The Morning Is Not Far,* poems.

AVOCATIONAL INTERESTS: Photography, writing poetry, gardening.

* * *

JOUBERT, Andre J. 1924-

PERSONAL: Born July 1, 1924; son of Edmond M. and Julia (Rolland) Joubert; married Ingrid von zur Muehlen (a professor), September 2, 1968; children: Sven. *Education:* Universite de Paris, Licence es Lettres, 1946, Diplome d'Etudes Superieures, 1947; Ministere de l'Education Nationale, C.A.P.E.S. philosophie, 1956. *Office:* University of Manitoba, Winnipeg R3T 2N2, Manitoba, Canada.

CAREER: University of Manitoba, Winnipeg, professor, 1958—. *Member:* Alliance Francaise du Manitoba (president, 1964-67). *Awards, honors:* Chevalier de l'Ordre des Palmes Academiques.

WRITINGS: Colette et Cheri, A. G. Nizet, 1972.

WORK IN PROGRESS: Research on contemporary French literary criticism, on Paul Valery, and on the contemporary French novel.

* * *

JUKIC, Ilija 1901-

PERSONAL: Surname is pronounced You-kich; born April 19, 1901, in Svilaj, Yugoslavia; son of Stjepan (a farmer) and Kata (Marjancic) Jukic. *Education:* Ecole Libre des Sciences Politiques, diplome, 1924; Belgrade Faculty of Law, diplomed, 1926. *Politics:* Member of Croat Peasant Party. *Religion:* Roman Catholic. *Home:* 27 St. Mary's Grove, London W.4., England.

CAREER: Yugoslav Ministry of Foreign Affairs, Belgrade, attache, 1924-28; Yugoslav Legation, London, England, secretary, 1928-32; editor of several publications in Yugoslavia, including *Hvratski Drevnik* (Croatian daily newspaper), 1936-39; Office of Vice-Premier, Belgrade, Yugoslavia, director of cabinet, 1939-40; Yugoslav Ministry of Foreign Affairs, Belgrade, under secretary of state, 1940-43; actively engaged in politics, 1943—.

WRITINGS: Tito Between East and West, Demos Publishing Co., 1961; *Pogledi na proslost, sadasnjost i buducnost hrvatskog naroda* (title means "Views on the Past, the Present, and the Future of the Croatian People"), privately printed (Munich), 1965; *Kriza Titova rezima i Titove Jugoslavije* (title means "The Crisis of Tito's Regime and Tito's Yugoslavia"), privately printed (Munich), 1966; *The Fall of Yugoslavia,* Harcourt, 1974. Contributor to *Eastern Europe, Survey, Figaro,* and others.

WORK IN PROGRESS: A history of Yugoslavia from 1919 to the present.

* * *

JUTA, Jan 1895- (Rene Juta)

PERSONAL: Born September 1, 1895, in Capetown, South Africa; came to United States, 1926; naturalized citizen, 1940; son of Sir Henry (a judge) and Helen (Tait) Juta; married Alice Ford Huntington, 1933 (died, 1966); children: Helen Juta Scholz and Charles Marshall (both adopted). *Education:* Attended South Africa College, 1913, and Christ Church, Oxford, 1914; also attended art schools, including Slade School, London. *Religion:* Anglican. *Residence:* Mendham, N.J.

CAREER: Specialized in mural painting, executing designs for municipal buildings, Royal Institute of British Architects, the Cunard liners, "Queen Mary" and "Queen Elizabeth," and others; served with British Ministry of Information in New York and London, 1940-46; United Nations, New York, N.Y., chief of visual information, 1947-59; artist, designer, craftsman, writer. Co-producer of documentary film, "The Discoveries of Prince Henry, Navigator," 1950. *Member:* Mural Painters Society of America (president, 1947—), Architectural League (vice-president, 1950), Century Association (New York, N.Y.), Arts Club (London).

WRITINGS: Look Out for the Ostriches! Tales of South Africa, Knopf, 1949; *Background in Sunshine: Memories of South Africa,* Scribner, 1972.

Under pseudonym Rene Juta: (Self-illustrated) *Cannes and the Hills,* Small, Maynard & Company, 1924; (self-illustrated) *Concerning Corsica,* Knopf, 1926.

SIDELIGHTS: Juta told *CA:* "As a lay reader, with a permit to preach in the Episcopal Church, under the bishop of New Jersey, I preach wherever I am invited or sent. I have covered the East from Vermont to Georgia."

* * *

JUTA, Rene

See JUTA, Jan

* * *

KAESTNER, Erich 1899-1974

February 23, 1899—July 29, 1974; German editor, social critic, essayist, novelist, poet, playwright, and author of children's books. Obituaries: *New York Times,* July 30, 1974; *Washington Post,* July 30, 1974.

* * *

KAFE, Joseph Kofi Thompson 1933-

PERSONAL: Born January 20, 1933, in Likpe Avedzeme, Volta Region, Ghana; son of Thomas (a mission teacher) and Sebastiana (Akpator) Kafe; married Sussie Ablavi (a registered nurse), August 3, 1968; children: Evelyn Amesika, Michael Kosi. *Education:* Attended University of Ghana, 1957-60, and University of London, 1961-62. *Office:* Library, University of Ghana, Legon, Accra, Ghana.

CAREER: University of Ghana, Legon, Accra, junior assistant librarian, 1960-62, assistant librarian, 1962—, acting librarian, 1972—. *Member:* Ghana Library Association, Library Association (England; associate member). *Awards, honors:* Inter-University Council library training award to visit British university libraries, 1972.

WRITINGS: Ghana: An Annotated Bibliography of Academic Theses, 1920-1970, in the Commonwealth, the Republic of Ireland, and the United States of America, G. K. Hall, 1973. Contributor to *Ghana Library Journal.*

* * *

KAGAN-KANS, Eva 1928-

PERSONAL: Born December 23, 1928, in Tientsin, China; daughter of Joseph (a businessman) and Zinaida (Yanowitch) Cherniavsky; married Alexander Kagan-Kans, June 24, 1945; children: David Alan. *Education:* New York University, B.A., 1961; University of California, Berkeley, M.A., 1964, Ph.D., 1968. *Home:* 2305 East Second St., Bloomington, Ind. 47401. *Office:* Department of Slavic Languages and Literatures, Indiana University, Bloomington, Ind. 47401.

CAREER: University of Rochester, Rochester, N.Y., assistant professor of Russian literature, 1966-68; Indiana University, Bloomington, assistant professor, 1968-71, associate professor of Russian literature, 1971—, dean for women's affairs. *Member:* American Association for the Advancement of Slavic Studies, Modern Language Association of America (chairman of Slavic section, 1973),

American Association of Teachers of Slavic and East European Languages. *Awards, honors:* Exchange scholar in Soviet Union, 1973.

WRITINGS: Hamlet and Don Quixote: Ivan Turgenev's Vision, Mouton, 1973. Contributor to *Cahiers du Monde Russe et Sovietique* and *Slavic Review.*

WORK IN PROGRESS: Writing a book on the Russian short story; editing a collection of articles on Turgenev.

SIDELIGHTS: In addition to English and Russian, Eva Kagan-Kans speaks French, German, Chinese, and Czech.

* * *

KAHANE, Howard 1928-

PERSONAL: Born April 19, 1928, in Cleveland, Ohio; son of Philip (a retail merchant) and Blanche (Landesman) Kahane; married Betsy Hyman, November 23, 1955 (divorced, December, 1964); married Judith McBride Weast, June, 1967 (divorced, 1973). children: Bonny Robin. *Education:* University of California, Los Angeles, B.A., 1954, M.A., 1958; University of Pennsylvania, Ph.D., 1962. *Politics:* "Liberal conservative (or vice versa)." *Religion:* "Agnostic (ethnic Jew)." *Office:* Department of Philosophy, Bernard M. Baruch College of the City University of New York, New York, N.Y. 10010.

CAREER: Whitman College, Walla Walla, Wash., assistant professor of philosophy, 1962-64; University of Kansas, Lawrence, assistant professor, 1964-68, associate professor of philosophy, 1968-71; Bernard M. Baruch College of the City University of New York, New York, N.Y., assistant professor, 1971-73, associate professor of philosophy, 1974—, chairman of department, 1972-73. *Military service:* U.S. Army, 1954-56. *Member:* American Association of University Professors, American Philosophical Association. *Awards, honors:* Watkins summer fellowship, 1965; National Science Foundation grant, 1967-68.

WRITINGS: Logic and Philosophy, Wadsworth, 1969, 2nd edition, 1973; *Logic and Contemporary Rhetoric: The Use of Reason in Everyday Life,* Wadsworth, 1971. Contributor to *Journal of Philosophy, American Philosophical Quarterly, Review of Metaphysics, Nous, British Journal for the Philosophy of Science,* and *Philosophy of Science.*

* * *

KAHL, Virginia

PERSONAL: Born in Milwaukee, Wis.; daughter of Arthur H. and Frieda (Krause) Kahl. *Education:* Milwaukee-Downer College, B.A., 1940; University of Wisconsin, M.S.L.S., 1957. *Office:* Alexandria Public Library, Alexandria, Va.

CAREER: Milwaukee Public Library, Milwaukee, Wis., library assistant, 1942-48; U.S. Army, Special Services Section, librarian in Berlin, Germany, 1948-49, and Salzburg, Austria, 1949-55; Madison Public Schools, Madison, Wis., school librarian, 1958-61; Menomonee Falls Public Library, Menomonee Falls, Wis., library director, 1961-68; Alexandria Public Library, Alexandria, Va., branch librarian, 1971—. Teaches writing and illustrating of children's books at George Washington University. *Member:* Children's Book Guild (Washington, D.C.).

WRITINGS—All self-illustrated children's books; all published by Scribner: *Away Went Wolfgang,* 1954; *Duchess Bakes a Cake,* 1955; *Maxie,* 1956; *Plum Pudding for Christmas,* 1956; *Habits of Rabbits,* 1957; *Droopsi,* 1958; (with Edith Vacheron) *Voici Henri,* 1959; *The Perfect Pancake,* 1960; (with Vacheron) *Encore Henri,* 1961; *The Baron's Booty,* 1963; *How Do You Hide a Monster?,* 1971; *Gunhilde's Christmas Booke,* 1972; *Giants, Indeed!,* 1974.

SIDELIGHTS: Ms. Kahl has always been a compulsive reader, especially of art history, cookbooks, mysteries, travel, and biography. Her second great interest is animals—she owns seven cats and would have other creatures, if possible. She comments: "I seem to spend my life trying to take care of creatures that are perfectly capable of helping themselves—I pick up stray dogs, stop to carry turtles over busy highways, and put birds back into their nests." One cold winter she dismayed local citizens by harboring field-mice in the library.

She emphatically hates anyone who "shoots, traps, poisons, hurts or destroys wolves or eagles or prairie dogs or whales or seals, who lets oil spill onto beaches to destroy wildfowl, puts industrial wastes into streams and lakes, destroys forests, defaces mountains, or bulldozes his way across the landscape in the name of profit or progress."

* * *

KAHN, Louis I. 1901-1974

February 20, 1901—March 17, 1974; Estonian-born American architect. Obituaries: *Washington Post,* March 21, 1974; *Current Biography,* May, 1974.

* * *

KAISER, Ernest 1915-

PERSONAL: Born December 5, 1915, in Petersburg, Va., son of Ernest Bascom (a railroad car cleaner) and Elnora (Ellis) Kaiser; married Mary Orford (an office manager and proof reader), 1949; children: Eric, Joan. *Education:* City College (now City College of the City University of New York), student, 1935-38. *Home:* 31-37 95th St., East Elmhurst, N.Y. 11369. *Office:* Schomburg Center for Research in Black Culture, New York Public Library, 103 West 135th St., New York, N.Y. 10030.

CAREER: Erie Railroad, Jersey City, N.J., redcap, 1938-42; *Negro Quarterly,* New York, N.Y., member of editorial staff, 1943; Congress of Industrial Organizations, Political Action Committee, New York, N.Y., shipping clerk, 1944-45; New York Public Library, Schomburg Center for Research in Black Culture, New York, N.Y., member of staff, 1945—. Editor, reviewer, and consultant for Arno, Crowell-Collier, Beacon Press, McGraw, 1972—, Bowker, 1974—. *Member:* American Institute for Marxist Studies.

WRITINGS: In Defense of the People's Black and White History and Culture, Freedomways, 1971; (editor with Harry A. Ploski and Otto J. Lindenmeyer) *The Negro Almanac,* (also published as *Afro USA: A Reference Work on the Black Experience and Reference Library of Black America*), Bellwether, 1971; (editor with Stanton Biddle, Wendell Wray, and others) *No Crystal Stair: A Bibliography of Black Literature,* New York Public Library, 1971; (editor with Herbert Aptheker and Sidney Kaplan) *The Correspondence of W.E.B. Du Bois,* Volume I: *Selections, 1877-1934,* University of Massachusetts Press, 1973; (with Warren Halliburton) *Harlem: A History of Broken Dreams,* Doubleday, 1974; (editor with Regina Andrews) *The Black New Yorkers,* Speller, 1974; (editor with John H. Clarke, Esther Jackson, and J. H. O'Dell, and contributor) *Paul Robeson: The Great Forerunner,* Emerson Hall, 1974; (editor with Erwin A. Salk, and contributor) *A Bibliographical Guide to Black History and Culture,* Bowker, in press.

Contributor: John Henrik Clark, editor, *Harlem: A Community in Transition,* Citadel, 1964; Clarke, editor, *William Styron's "Nat Turner": Ten Black Writers Respond,* Beacon Press, 1968; Patrcia W. Romero, editor, *In Black America 1968: The Year of Awakening,* United Publishing, 1969; Addison Gayle, Jr., editor, *Black Expression: Essays by and about Black Americans in the Creative Arts,* Weybright, 1969; R. Baird Shuman, editor, *A Galaxy of Black Writing,* Moore Publishing, 1970; John M. Reilly, editor, *Twentieth Century Interpretations of "Invisible Man": A Collection of Critical Essays,* Prentice-Hall, 1970; Clarke and others, editors, *Black Titan: W.E.B. DuBois,* Beacon Press, 1970; Melvin J. Friedman and Irving Malin, editors, *William Styron's "The Confessions of Nat Turner": A Critical Handbook,* Wadsworth, 1970; Ruth Miller, editor, *Backgrounds to Blackamerican Literature,* Chandler Publishing, 1971; Werner Sollers, editor, *A Bibliographic Guide to Afro-American Studies,* John F. Kennedy Institute (Berlin), 1972; Mabel M. Smythe, editor *The American Negro Reference Book,* Prentice-Hall, 1974; Loften Mitchell, editor *Voices of Black Theatre: Told in the Words of Its Pioneers,* James T. White, 1974.

Author of introduction: George W. Williams, *History of the Negro Race in America: 1619-1880,* Arno, 1968; William J. Simmons, *Men of Mark: Eminent, Progressive, and Rising,* Arno, 1968; Sojourner Truth, *Narrative of Sojourner Truth,* Arno, 1968; W.E.B. Du Bois, *The Atlanta University Publications,* Arno, Volume I, 1968, Volume II, 1969; George Edmund Haynes, *The Negro at Work in New York City,* Arno, 1968; James Weldon Johnson, *Black Manhattan,* Arno, 1968; I. Garland Penn, *The Afro-American Press and Its Editors,* Arno, 1969; D. W. Culp, editor, *Twentieth Century Negro Literature,* Arno, 1969; *The American Negro Academy Occasional Papers 1-22,* Arno, 1969; Mary Sagarin, *John Brown Russwurm,* Lothrop, 1970.

Author of bibliography: Floyd B. Barbour, editor, *The Black Seventies,* Sargent, 1970. Also editor of reprint series in Black studies, Bobbs-Merrill, 1970.

Contributor to Black studies journals and literary publications, including *Science and Society, Black World, Journal of Negro Education, Phylon, Harlem Quarterly,* and *Masses and Mainstream.* Editor of *Dorie Miller Dispatch* (newspaper of Dorie Miller Cooperative), 1958-64; cofounder and associate editor of *Freedomways,* 1961—.

WORK IN PROGRESS: Collecting and revising his essays for publication in book form; an essay on the writings of Harold Cruse; a survey of recent books about Marcus Garvey; continued research on Marxist literary criticism.

SIDELIGHTS: Kaiser told *CA:* "I started out reading widely . . . with a view to becoming a writer. Then I focussed on trying to write literary criticism and I read as many books of literary criticism as I could find in public libraries or buy and borrow. . . . The Marxist writers, European and American, of the 1930's and 1940's seemed to place literature in a more meaningful context and perspective than the critics of any other literary school. They impressed me the most and I have been trying to write and publish Marxist social and literary criticism since the late 1940's. To agree with Kenneth Burke, it was my wide range of periodical reading over the years that shaped me. . . . I consider writing an important arm of the black liberation movement and of the struggles of all peoples for freedom."

BIOGRAPHICAL/CRITICAL SOURCES: Peter M. Bergman, *The Chronological History of the Negro in America,* Bergman, 1969; John M. Bracey, Jr., August Meier, and Elliott Rudwick, editors, *Black Nationalism in America,* Bobbs-Merrill, 1970; Addison Gayle, Jr., editor, *The Black Aesthetic,* Doubleday, 1971; George A. Panichas, editor, *The Politics of Twentieth-Century Novelists,* Hawthorn, 1971; Richard K. Barksdale and Keneth Kinnamon, editors, *Black Writers of America: A Comprehensive Anthology,* Macmillan, 1972.

* * *

KALECHOFSKY, Roberta 1931-

PERSONAL: Born May 11, 1931, in Brooklyn, N.Y.; daughter of Julius Joseph (a lawyer) and Naomi (Jacobs) Kirchik; married Robert Kalechofsky (a teacher), June 7, 1953; children: Hal Joshua, Neal Frederic. *Education:* Brooklyn College (now Brooklyn College of the City University of New York), B.A., 1952; University of Connecticut, graduate study, 1952-53; New York University, M.A., 1956, Ph.D., 1970. *Politics:* "Independent voter: mixture of socialism and democracy." *Religion:* Jewish. *Residence:* Marblehead, Mass.

CAREER: Brooklyn College of the City University of New York, Brooklyn, N.Y., instructor in literature and writing, 1956-59, 1962-63. Junior editor, Funk & Wagnalls, 1958. Tutor in remedial reading for Headstart program, 1971-72; member of Women's Israel Bond Committee, 1971—. *Member:* Modern Language Association of America, Writers' Cooperative (Montreal, Quebec), Jewish Federation, Common Cause, League of Women Voters.

WRITINGS: George Orwell, Ungar, 1973; *Justice, My Brother,* Writers' Cooperative (Montreal, Quebec), 1974. Work is anthologized in *Best American Short Stories,* edited by Martha Foley, Houghton, 1972. Contributor to *New Voices, Works, Confrontation, Western Humanities Review, Epoch, Quartet, Branching Out,* and *Ball State University Forum.* A literary editor of *Branching Out,* 1973-74.

WORK IN PROGRESS: A novel, *Orestes*; a monograph on Edmund Wilson for Ungar; *Solomon's Wisdom,* collected stories; *Priests,* a collection of short fiction dealing with the relationship of religion to the profane; compiling *Echod,* a volume of stories by and about Jews from around the world.

SIDELIGHTS: Roberta Kalechofsky has travelled through western Europe, the British Isles, Israel, and North America. She and her family enjoy jogging, biking, tennis, and dancing.

* * *

KALINA, Sigmund 1911-

PERSONAL: Born September 28, 1911, in Brooklyn, N.Y.; son of Victor and Bessie (Fram) Kalina; married Gertrude Lee Tendler (a personnel manager); children: Daniel, Susan Kalina Krenitsky. *Education:* Attended University of Arkansas, 1930-31; Long Island University, B.S., 1935; Hofstra University, M.S., 1965; State University of New York at Potsdam, graduate study, 1965-67. *Residence:* Valley Stream, N.Y. *Office:* Berner High School, Massapequa, Long Island, N.Y.

CAREER: Lifeguard at public beaches of New York, N.Y., 1930-40; high school teacher of biology in Massapequa, N.Y. Adult education instructor in Valley Stream, N.Y.; nature counselor at Shibley Camp. Science consultant to Filmstrip House, Inc. *Wartime service:* U.S. Merchant Marine, 1943-47; senior ammunition inspector in

New York and New Jersey, and supervisor at ports of embarkation.

WRITINGS: The House that Nature Built, Lothrop, 1972; *Your Bones Are Alive,* Lothrop, 1972; *About Blood,* Lothrop, 1973; *Your Nerves and Their Messages,* Lothrop, 1973; *Air: The Invisible Ocean,* Lothrop, 1973. Writer of filmstrips.

WORK IN PROGRESS: A book on pollution as it relates to flora and fauna of a developing stream.

* * *

KALINSKY, George 1936-

PERSONAL: Born April 14, 1936, in Hempstead, N.Y.; son of Samuel (a retailer) and Fay (Rosen) Kalinsky; married Ellen Wexelblatt, January 23, 1960; children: Lee, Rachelle. *Education:* Pratt Institute, B.A., 1958. *Religion:* Jewish. *Home:* 1142 Douglas Pl., Seaford, N.Y. 11783. *Office:* Madison Square Garden, 4 Pennsylvania Plaza, New York, N.Y. 10001.

CAREER: Worked two years as an art director specializing in industrial design; owner of juvenile furniture store, 1960; Madison Square Garden, New York, N.Y., art director and photographer, 1968—. Photojournalist, 1965—.

WRITINGS: Take It All, Macmillan, 1970; *From Behind the Plate,* Prentice-Hall, 1972; *A Will to Win,* Prentice-Hall, 1973.

* * *

KALLEN, Horace M(eyer) 1882-1974

August 11, 1882—February 16, 1974; American philosopher, educator, social activist, and author. Obituaries: *New York Times,* February 17, 1974; *Current Biography,* April, 1974.

* * *

KALLIR, Otto 1894-

PERSONAL: Born April 1, 1894, in Vienna, Austria; son of Jacob (a lawyer) and Clara (Engel) Kallir; married Franziska zu Loewenstein, June, 1922; children: John, Evamarie. *Education:* University of Vienna, Ph.D., 1931. *Home:* 15 West 72nd St., New York, N.Y. 10023. *Office:* 24 West 57th St., New York, N.Y. 10019.

CAREER: Neue Galerie (art gallery), Vienna, Austria, founder and owner, 1923-73. Founder and owner of Johannes Press (publishing company), 1923—, and Galerie St. Etienne (Paris), 1938-39; founder and president of Galerie St. Etienne (New York), 1939—, and Grandma Moses Properties, Inc., 1950—. President of Friends of SOS Children's Villages, Inc. *Member:* Art Dealers Association of America. *Awards, honors:* Zeppelin-Eckener Award from Aero-Philatelistenklub (Germany), 1928, for aeronautical collection; Grand Medal of Honor from Republic of Austria, 1966; Silver Medal of Honor from City of Vienna, 1968.

WRITINGS: Luftschiffahrt im alten Wien (title means "Ballooning in Old Vienna"), Oesterreichischer Flugtechnischer Verein, 1917; *Egon Schiele: Persoenlichkeit und Werk* (title means "Egon Schiele: Personality and Work"), Paul Zsolnay, 1930; *Grandma Moses: American Primitive,* Dryden, 1945; (editor) Grandma Moses, *My Life's History,* Harper, 1952; *Egon Schiele: Oeuvre Catalogue of the Paintings,* Crown, 1966; *A Sketchbook by Egon Schiele,* Johannes Press, 1967; *Egon Schiele: The Graphic Work,* Crown, 1970; *Grandma Moses,* Abrams, 1973; *Richard Gerstl: Beitraege zur Dokumentation seines Lebens und Werkes* (title means "Richard Gerstl: Contributions to the Documentation of His Life and Work"), Oesterreichische Galerie, 1974.

SIDELIGHTS: Kallir's first book concerned early aviation, and his interest in aeronautics includes an extensive personal collection of historical documents and medals.

* * *

KALNAY, Francis 1899-

PERSONAL: Surname is pronounced *Kal*-nay; born July 18, 1899, in Budapest, Hungary; came to United States, 1919; divorced; children: Elizabeth Tagora, Maria Peti, Peter. *Address:* 25005 Outlook Dr., Carmel, Calif. 93921.

CAREER: Has been farmer, journalist, actor, and done educational film work. *Military service:* U.S. Army, 1941-45. *Awards, honors: Chucaro, Wild Pony of the Pampa* received a *New York Herald Tribune* Children's Spring Book Festival Award, a Certificate of Award from the Boys' Club of America, was named a Newbery Medal Honor Book, and a Notable Children's Book by the American Library Association, all 1958.

WRITINGS: (Editor with Richard Collins) *The New America: A Handbook of Necessary Information for Aliens, Refugees, and New Citizens,* Greenberg, 1941; *Chucaro, Wild Pony of the Pampa* (juvenile), Harcourt, 1958; *The Richest Boy in the World* (autobiographical juvenile), Harcourt, 1959; *It Happened in Chichipica* (juvenile), Harcourt, 1971. Contributor of articles on gastronomy to *House Beautiful.*

WORK IN PROGRESS: A book for young children with Sierra Madre setting; short stories on adult theme.

AVOCATIONAL INTERESTS: Travel, gardening.

* * *

KANDO, Thomas M. 1941-

PERSONAL: Born April 8, 1941, in Budapest, Hungary; naturalized U.S. citizen; son of Jules (a painter) and Ata (Gorog) Kando; married Roberta Greenhauff, July, 1962 (divorced, 1967); married Anita Costa (an administrative assistant), June 30, 1973; children: (second marriage) Danielle. *Education:* University of Amsterdam, B.S., 1965; University of Minnesota, M.A., 1967, Ph.D., 1969. *Politics:* Democrat. *Home:* 8225 Cedar Crest Way, Sacramento, Calif. 95826. *Office:* Department of Sociology, California State University, Sacramento, Calif. 95819.

CAREER: University of Wisconsin—Menomonie, assistant professor of sociology, 1968-69; California State University, Sacramento, assistant professor of sociology, 1969-72; University of California, Riverside, visiting assistant professor of sociology, 1972-73; California State University, Sacramento, associate professor of sociology, 1973—. Visiting assistant professor at California State University, Hayward, 1970; consultant to California Department of Parks and Recreation. *Member:* American Sociological Association, Popular Culture Association, Pacific Sociological Association.

WRITINGS: Sex Change: The Achievement of Gender Identity among Feminized Transsexuals, C. C Thomas, 1973; *Leisure and Popular Culture in Transition,* Mosby, in press. Contributor of more than fifteen articles to social studies journals, including *Pacific Sociological Review,*

Journal of Popular Culture, Journal of Homosexuality, Psychology Today, Sociological Quarterly, and *Journal of Marriage and the Family.* Associate editor of *Pacific Sociological Review.*

WORK IN PROGRESS: Social Psychology: Knowing, Doing, and Becoming, for Mosby.

SIDELIGHTS: Kando writes: "I was born in Hungary, where I spent the first seven years of my life. The next eight years were spent in France, the next ten in the Netherlands and the last eight in the United States, of which I am now a citizen. This gives me not only fluency in five languages and familiarity with a variety of cultures (I have also traveled in the Soviet Union, Africa, and just about every country of Europe), but also a thoroughly internationalist point of view. My work reflects this, in sharp contrast with narrow specialism of any kind. I am a humanistic scientist, or a scientific humanist, if you will, integrating many contrasting influences rather than specializing in narrow fields."

BIOGRAPHICAL/CRITICAL SOURCES: Psychology Today, December, 1972; *Human Behavior,* April, 1973; *Sacramento Bee,* January, 1974.

* * *

KANE, William Everett 1943-

PERSONAL: Born August 12, 1943, in Albany, Ga.; son of Allen R. (in advertising) and Coty (an attorney; maiden name, Everett) Kane; married Sandra McMahan, June 4, 1966; children: William Everett, Jr. *Education:* University of Madrid, Certificado, 1964; Princeton University, B.A., 1966; Yale University, J.D., 1970. *Home:* Gates Garth, Sandy Way, Cobham, Surrey, England. *Office:* Continental Illinois Ltd., 40 Basinghall St., London, England.

CAREER: Caribe Mining S.A., Medellin, Colombia, executive vice-president and assistant to president, 1961-64; Graham & James (law firm), San Francisco, Calif., associate, 1970-71; Citicorp Leasing, Tokyo, Japan, legal counsel, 1971-72; Continental Illinois Ltd., London, England, vice-president and general manager, 1972—. *Member:* American Bar Association, American Association of International Law, California Bar Association, San Francisco Bar Association, Phi Beta Kappa. *Awards, honors:* Fulbright scholar, 1963-64.

WRITINGS: American Competitiveness (monograph), *Center of International Studies,* Princeton University, 1965; *Civil Strife in Latin America: A Legal History of U.S. Involvement,* Johns Hopkins Press, 1972. Editor, *Yale Law Journal,* 1969-70.

WORK IN PROGRESS: A novel on international banking; a political science fiction novel.

SIDELIGHTS: "Believing that the Renaissance is not dead to the hard-toned ego," Kane says that he has made "the alternation of advocation with vocation a career objective—hence, business man to lawyer to banker to hobby author. This frequent personal vibration has also rendered possible wide travel in Europe, Latin America and the Far East. . ."

* * *

KANTOR, Marvin 1934-

PERSONAL: Born May 9, 1934, in New York, N.Y.; son of Irving (a businessman) and Sarah (Brodsky) Kantor; married Lis Petersen, August 13, 1961; children: Michele, Robert. *Education:* Copenhagen University, Cand.Art, 1961; Fordham University, M.A., 1962; University of Michigan, Ph.D., 1966. *Politics:* Democrat. *Religion:* Jewish. *Home:* 2010 Hawthorne Lane, Evanston, Ill. 60201. *Office:* Department of Slavic Languages and Literatures, Northwestern University, 126C Centennial Hall, Evanston, Ill. 60201.

CAREER: University of Michigan, Ann Arbor, lecturer in Slavic languages, 1964-66; Brooklyn College of the City University of New York, Brooklyn, N.Y., assistant professor of Russian, 1966-67; Northwestern University, Evanston, Ill., assistant professor of Slavic languages, literatures, and linguistics, 1967—. *Military service:* U.S. Marine Corps, 1952-55. *Member:* American Society for Eighteenth-Century Studies, American Association of Teachers of Slavic and East European Languages, Modern Language Association of America. *Awards, honors:* Rackham fellow at University of Novi Sad, 1965-66.

WRITINGS: Aspectual Derivation in Contemporary Serbo-Croatian, Humanities, 1972. Contributor to *Scando-Slavica; Slavic and East European Journal,* and other journals in his field. Editor, Publications in Eighteenth-Century Russian Literature, Northwestern University Press.

WORK IN PROGRESS: A book dealing with Slavic religious writings from the ninth through thirteenth centuries, tentatively titled *Early Slavic Spirituality; Dramatic Works of D. I. Fonvizin; The Lives of Constantine and Methodius,* with Richard S. White.

SIDELIGHTS: Kantor spent more than four years in Denmark as an undergraduate and has worked as a research fellow in Finland, the Soviet Union, and Yugoslavia. Besides Russian and Danish, he is competent in Serbo-Croatian, Old Church Slavonic, and German.

* * *

KAPLAN, Bernard 1944-

PERSONAL: Born May 18, 1944, in New York, N.Y.; son of Leonard (a psychologist) and Eva (a high school department head; maiden name, Shklear) Kaplan; married Claire Savit Bacha, December 23, 1965 (divorced, 1968); married Jayne Hileman (a ceramicist), August 13, 1971 (divorced). *Education:* Antioch College, B.A., 1966; Yale University, M.A., 1970; University of Iowa, M.F.A., 1970. *Religion:* Jewish. *Agent:* Roslyn Targ, 325 East 57th St., New York, N.Y. 10022. *Office:* Department of English, Case Western Reserve University, Cleveland, Ohio 44106.

CAREER: Goddard College, Plainfield, Vt., member of faculty, 1971; Case Western Reserve University, Cleveland, Ohio, assistant professor of English, 1974—. *Member:* Authors Guild. *Awards, honors:* Woodrow Wilson fellow, 1966-67; Alan Collins fellow in prose, Bread Loaf Writers' Conference, 1970.

WRITINGS: Prisoners of This World, Grossman, 1970; *Nathanael West,* Twayne, in press. Contributor of poems to *Fiction International.* Contributing editor to *Fiction International,* 1973—.

WORK IN PROGRESS: Obituaries, fiction, completion expected in 1975.

* * *

KAPLAN, Stuart R(onald) 1932-

PERSONAL: Born April 1, 1932, in New York, N.Y.; son of William (an art dealer) and Nettie (Weiss) Kaplan; married Marilyn Reck, November 16, 1957; children: Mark Stuart, Peter John, Michael Louis, Christopher Ned, Jennifer Anne. *Education:* Sorbonne, University of Paris, certificat, 1951; University of Pennsylvania, B.S., 1955. *Religion:* Jewish. *Home:* 56 Tower Hill Dr., Port Chester, N.Y. 10573. *Office:* 486 Park Ave. S., New York, N.Y. 10016.

CAREER: Employed by Standard Industries, Inc. (conglomerate holding company), 1958-60, vice-president, 1960-73; U.S. Games Systems, Inc., New York, N.Y., president, 1968—. Vice-president of Galloway Land Co., 1963—; president of Simpson Coal & Chemical Corp., 1965—, Unit Petroleum Corp., 1972—, and Unit Resources, 1974—. *Military service:* U.S. Army, 1956-58.

WRITINGS: Mining, Minerals, and Geosciences, Wiley, 1965; *Tarot Cards for Fun and Fortune Telling,* U.S. Games Systems, 1970; *Official Rules of the Tarotrump Card Game,* U.S. Games Systems, 1972; *Tarot Classic,* Grosset, 1972; *James Bond 007 Tarot Book,* U.S. Games Systems, 1973; *The American Historical Playing Card Deck: Portraits in American History,* U.S. Games Systems, 1974.

WORK IN PROGRESS: Tarot Symbols from the Past; Pictorial History of Tarot; Encyclopedia of Tarot Cards; a book on the life of Mademoiselle LeNormand, famous sibyl to Napoleon I, completion expected in 1976.

SIDELIGHTS: Kaplan owns one of the largest private collections of original tarot fortune-telling cards, rare playing cards, and rare books from the sixteenth to the nineteenth centuries dealing with tarot symbolism; his family also owns a pre-Columbian art gallery in New York City.

BIOGRAPHICAL/CRITICAL SOURCES: New York Times, July 20, 1968; *New York Post,* July 9, 1970.

* * *

KARDISH, Laurence 1945-

PERSONAL: Born January 5, 1945, in Ottawa, Ontario, Canada; son of Samuel (a baker) and Tillie (Steinberg) Kardish; married Judith Leah Molot, August 20, 1967 (separated); children: Naomi, Francis. *Education:* Carleton University, B.A. (honors), 1966; Columbia University, M.F.A., 1968. *Home:* 165 Christopher, #2J, New York, N.Y. 10016. *Office:* Museum of Modern Art, 21 West 53rd St., New York, N.Y. 10014.

CAREER: Canadian Film Institute, Ottawa, Ontario, employed in Canadian film archives, National Film Theater, and Canadian Federation of Film Societies, 1965-66; Film-Makers Distribution Center, New York, N.Y., film distributor, 1967-68; Museum of Modern Art, New York, N.Y., assistant curator in film program, 1968—, toured Europe with museum program, 1970. *Member:* Film-Makers Co-Operative (New York), Playwrights Co-Operative (Toronto). *Awards, honors:* Award for best narrative film from Canadian artists competition at Art Gallery of Ontario, 1968.

WRITINGS: Reel Plastic Magic: A Brief History of Filmmaking in America, Little, Brown, 1972.

Plays: *Brussels Sprouts* (first performed in Toronto at Factory Lab Theatre, February, 1972), Playwrights Co-Operative, 1969; *Little Steps to Heaven,* Playwrights Co-Operative, 1973.

Also author (and producer and director) of "Slow Run," an avant garde feature film, 1968.

WORK IN PROGRESS: "Vesuvius Goes to Market," a musical play, with John Palmer; revising own screenplay "Soft Passions" for use as feature film.

* * *

KAREL, Leonard 1912-

PERSONAL: Born January 23, 1912, in Baltimore, Md.; son of Max and Fannie (Marcus) Krulevitz; married Charlotte Ruth Lockman, October 31, 1942; children: Martin Lewis, Jacqueline T., Richard Blaine. *Education:* Johns Hopkins University, A.B., 1932; University of Maryland, Ph.D., 1941. *Politics:* "Registered as Democrat; vote as independent." *Religion:* Jewish.

CAREER: National Institutes of Health, Washington, D.C., executive secretary of Division of Research Grants, 1947-51, chief of Extramural Programs Branch of National Institute of Allergy and Infectious Diseases, 1951-61; National Science Foundation, Washington, D.C., special assistant to associate director of research, 1961, associate head, 1961-63, acting head of Science Resources Planning Office, 1963-64; U.S. Public Health Service, National Library of Medicine, Washington, D.C., chief of Bibliographic Services Division, 1964-66, special assistant to associate director of library operations, 1966-74; consultant on medical information and literature evaluation, and on marketing of dried plant materials, 1974—. Lecturer in pharmacology at University of Maryland, 1947-51. Member of scientific and educational council of Allergy Foundation of America, 1956-63; member of organizing committee, Fourth International Congress of Allergology, 1959-61. Member of governmental committees, including Department of Health, Education, and Welfare committee for the inter-American workshop on mental retardation, 1956-67, and committees on information technology, Executive Office of the President, 1968, 1969-70. Member of board of directors, Common Cold Foundation, 1956-60. Consultant to Jewish National Home for Asthmatic Children, 1959; consultant to Pan American Health Organization and interim director of Regional Medical Library for South America, 1967-68. *Military service:* U.S. Army, Chemical Warfare Service, 1942-46; became captain.

MEMBER: American Society for Pharmacology and Experimental Therapeutics, American Association for the Advancement of Science (fellow), American Public Health Association, National Federation of Science Abstracting and Indexing Services.

WRITINGS: (Compiler with Elizabeth Roach) *A Dictionary of Antibiosis,* Columbia University Press, 1951; *Dried Flowers from Antiquity to the Present: A History and Practical Guide to Flower Drying,* Scarecrow, 1973. Contributor of about fifty articles to national and state medical journals. Member of editorial advisory committee, *International Nursing Index,* 1965.

WORK IN PROGRESS: Dried Grasses, Grains, Gourds, Pods, and Cones (tentative title), for Scarecrow; revising *Dried Flowers from Antiquity to the Present,* completion expected in 1976.

* * *

KARMEL-WOLFE, Henia 1923-

PERSONAL: Born May 31, 1923, in Krakow, Poland; daughter of Hirsch and Mita (Rosenbaum) Karmel; married Leon L. Wolfe (an educational director), June 17, 1941; children: John Howard, Joy Michelle. *Education:* Attended high school in Krakow, Poland. *Politics:* Democrat. *Religion:* Jewish. *Home:* 5440 Netherland Ave., Bronx, N.Y. 10471. *Agent:* Cyrilly Abels, 119 West 57th St., New York, N.Y. 10019.

CAREER: Writer.

WRITINGS: (With sister, Llona Karmel) *Spiew Za Drutami* (poems; title means "Songs from Behind the Barbed Wire"), Polish Jewish Press, 1948; *The Baders of Jacob Street,* Lippincott, 1970. Short stories are anthologized in *Best American Short Stories of 1962,* edited by Martha Foley, Houghton, 1962, and *Best American Short Stories of 1965,* edited by Foley, Houghton, 1965. Contributor of short stories to *Reporter, Madamoiselle,* and *Harper's.*

WORK IN PROGRESS: A novel, *The Story of Marek and Lisa* (tentative title); with son, John, a book of interviews.

SIDELIGHTS: Henia Karmel-Wolfe wrote *The Baders of Jacob Street* from personal experience in Krakow, Poland during World War II.

* * *

KATZ, Abraham 1926-

PERSONAL: Born December 4, 1926, in Brooklyn, N.Y.; son of Alexander (a teacher) and Zina (Rabinowitz) Katz; married Carmella Furman, June 18, 1947; children: Tamar, Jonathan, Naomi. *Educcation:* Attended Hebrew University of Jerusalem, 1946-47; Brooklyn College (now Brooklyn College of the City University of New York), A.B. (cum laude), 1948; Columbia University, M.A., 1950; Harvard University, Ph.D., 1968. *Religion:* Jewish. *Home:* 3309 Shirley Lane, Chevy Chase, Md. 20015. *Office:* U.S. Department of State, EUR/RPE, Washington, D.C. 20523.

CAREER: U.S. Department of State, Washington, D.C., foreign service officer in Merida, Yucatan, 1951-53, and Mexico City, Mexico, 1953-55, with Bureau of Intelligence, Office of the Undersecretary, 1957-59, first secretary of U.S. missions to North Atlantic Treaty Organization (NATO) and Organization for Economic Cooperation and Development (OECD) in Paris, France, 1959-64, counselor of Embassy for Economic Affairs in Moscow, Soviet Union, 1964-66, director of OECD Office of European Communities and Atlantic Political-Economic Affairs, 1967—. Fellow, Center for International Affairs, Harvard University, 1966-67. *Member:* American Foreign Service Association, American Political Science Association, American Association for the Advancement of Slavic Studies, American Society for the Study of Comparative Economic Systems. *Awards, honors:* U.S. State Department awards for commendable service, 1952, and meritorious service, 1963.

WRITINGS: The Politics of Economic Reform in the Soviet Union, Praeger, 1972. Contributor to proceedings.

* * *

KATZ, Fred(eric Phillip) 1938-

PERSONAL: Born September 23, 1938, in Rochester, N.Y.; son of Benjamin N. and Rose (Kaufman) Katz; married Elsa Szold, July 30, 1961; children: Jeffery, Stephen. *Education:* University of Michigan, B.A., 1960. *Politics:* Democrat. *Religion:* Jewish. *Home:* 5918 Briarwood Lane, Peoria, Ill. 61614. *Agent:* Don Gold, William Morris Agency, 1350 Avenue of the Americas, New York, N.Y. 10019. *Office:* Szold's, Inc., 2201 Southwest Adams, Peoria, Ill. 61602.

CAREER: Sport, New York, N.Y., member of staff, 1961-71, as managing editor, 1968-71; Szold's, Inc. (department store), Peoria, Ill., assistant vice-president, 1971—. Member of board of directors, Neighborhood House and Peoria Symphony, 1972—. *Military service:* U.S. Army Reserve, 1961-68, with active duty, 1960-61; became captain. *Member:* Society of Magazine Writers (president, 1968-70).

WRITINGS: Art Arfons: Fastest Man on Wheels, Thomas Nelson, 1965; *American Sports Heroes of Today,* Random House, 1970; (editor) *The Glory of Notre Dame,* Bartholomew House, 1971.

* * *

KATZ, Leon 1919-

PERSONAL: Born July 10, 1919, in Bronx, N.Y.; son of Bernard and Rachel (Koslov) Katz; married Sadell Kasmere (a teacher), May 9, 1942; children: Elia Jakov, Fredric Michael. *Education:* College of the City of New York (now City College of the City University of New York), B.S.S., 1940; Columbia University, M.A., 1946, Ph.D., 1962. *Politics:* None. *Religion:* Jewish. *Home:* 5742 Northumberland St., Pittsburgh, Pa. 15217. *Office:* Drama Department, Carnegie-Mellon University, Pittsburgh, Pa. 15213.

CAREER: Cornell University, Ithaca, N.Y., instructor in English, 1946-47; Hunter College (now Hunter College of the City University of New York), New York, N.Y., instructor in English, 1947-49; Vassar College, Poughkeepsie, N.Y., assistant professor of drama, 1949-58; Columbia University, New York, N.Y., lecturer in playwriting, 1958-60; Manhattanville College, Purchase, N.Y., associate professor of English, 1960-64; Stanford University, Palo Alto, Calif., visiting associate professor of drama, 1964-65; San Francisco State College (now University), San Francisco, Calif., professor of drama and English, 1965-68; Carnegie-Mellon University, Pittsburgh, Pa., professor of drama, 1968—. Theatre reviewer at station KQED, San Francisco; film reviewer for broadcasts originating in Pittsburgh, Pa. Director and actor for twenty-three years in academic and professional theater. *Military service:* U.S. Army Air Forces, 1941-45; became captain. *Member:* American Association of University Professors, American Federation of Television and Radio Artists, Actors Equity. *Awards, honors:* National Endowment for the Humanities grant, 1972.

WRITINGS: (Contributor of translation) Eric Russell Bentley, *The Classic Theatre,* Volume I: *Six Italian Plays,* Anchor, 1958; (translator with Joseph Katz) Franz Kafka, *The Trial* (Gide-Barrault adaptation), Schocken, 1962; (editor with Donald Gallup, and author of introduction) Gertrude Stein, *Fernhurst, QED and Other Early Writings,* Liveright, 1971; (editor and author of introduction) *The Major Tragedies* (critical essays), Bantam, in press; (editor and author of introduction) *Modern Dramatists* (critical essays), Bantam, in press.

Plays: "Dracula: Sabbat," first produced Off-Off-Broadway at Judson Poets' Theatre, 1970; "Toy Show," first produced Off-Off-Broadway at Cafe La Mama, 1971; "Swellfoot's Tears," scheduled for production in New York City.

Television scripts: "Confrontation," produced on NET, 1969, and "Necessity," produced on NET, 1972.

WORK IN PROGRESS: An annotated edition of *The*

Notebooks of Gertrude Stein; a critical biography of Gertrude Stein to 1911, tentatively titled *The Beginning of Gertrude Stein.*

* * *

KAUFFELD, Carl F. 1911-1974

1911—July 10, 1974; American zoological park director, herpetologist, and author of books in his field. Obituaries: *New York Times,* July 11, 1974.

* * *

KAUFFMANN, Georg (Friedrich) 1925-

PERSONAL: Born April 25, 1925, in Kiel, Germany; son of Hans K. (a university professor) and Lida (Scheder-Bieschin) Kauffmann; married Gisela Deglau, February 3, 1957; children: Hans-Eduard, Cosima, Clemens. *Education:* Sorbonne, University of Paris, Eleve titulaire de l'Ecole pratique des Hautes Etudes, 1953; University of Bonn, Dr. phil., 1954. *Religion:* Evangelical. *Home:* Hittorfstrasse 23, D 44 Muenster, Germany. *Office:* University of Muenster, Muenster, Germany.

CAREER: Kunsthistorisches Institut, Bonn, Germany, assistant, 1954-58, vice-director in Florence, Italy, 1958-60; University of Muenster, Muenster, Germany, professor of art history, 1965—. Member of Institute for Advanced Study, 1973-74; adjunct professor, Harvard University, 1962, University of Bonn, 1964. *Military service:* Wehrmacht, 1943-45; became unteroffizier.

WRITINGS: Poussin-Studien, De Gruyter, 1960; *Florenz,* Reclam Verlag (Stuttgart), 1962, translation by Edith Kuestner and J. A. Underwood published as *Florence: Art Treasures and Buildings,* Phaidon, 1971; (editor with Willibald Sauerlaender) *Walter Friedlaender zum 90. Geburtstag: Eine Festgabe seiner europaeischen Schueler, Freunde und Verehrer,* De Gruyter, 1965; (editor with Gert von der Osten) *Festschrift fuer Herbert von Einem zum 16. Februar 1965,* Mann (Berlin), 1965; *Umbrien-Marken, Emilia-Romagna,* Reclam Verlag, 1970; *Die Kunst des 16. Jahrhunderts,* Propylaeen Verlag (Berlin), 1970. Contributor of about fifty articles to periodicals. Editor, *Zeitschrift fuer Kunstgeschichte,* 1960—.

WORK IN PROGRESS: Zentraleuropaeische Kunst des 15. Jahrhunderts, for Gallimard; research on Florentine art and art theory.

AVOCATIONAL INTERESTS: Music.

* * *

KAUFMAN, Shirley 1923-

PERSONAL: Born June 5, 1923, in Seattle, Wash.; daughter of Joseph (a businessman) and Nellie (Freeman) Pincus; married Bernard Kaufman, Jr., 1946 (divorced, 1974); married Hillel Matthew Daleski (a professor of English), 1974; children: (first marriage) Sharon (Mrs. Seth Kaufman), Joan, Deborah. *Education:* University of California, Los Angeles, B.A., 1944; San Francisco State College (now University), M.A., 1967. *Religion:* Jewish. *Home:* 18 Neve Sha'anan St., Apt. 22, Jerusalem, Israel.

CAREER: Poet. Visiting lecturer, University of Massachusetts, spring, 1974. *Member:* Poetry Society of America. *Awards, honors:* International Poetry Forum United States Award, 1969, for *The Floor Keeps Turning.*

WRITINGS—All poetry: *The Floor Keeps Turning,* University of Pittsburgh Press, 1970; *Gold Country,* University of Pittsburgh Press, 1973; (translator) Abba Kovner, *A Canopy In The Desert,* University of Pittsburgh Press, 1974. Represented in numerous anthologies, including several volumes of "Borestone Mountain Poetry Awards" series, all published by Pacific Books. Contributor to *Atlantic, Harper's, Nation, New Yorker,* and other magazines.

WORK IN PROGRESS: Carbon, a book-length poem.

* * *

KAUPER, Paul Gerhardt 1907-1974

November 9, 1907—May 22, 1974; American authority on constitutional law, educator, and author of books in his field. Obituaries: *New York Times,* May 23, 1974. (*CA*-4).

* * *

KEATING, Michael (F.) 1932-

PERSONAL: Born August 28, 1932, in Montreal, Quebec, Canada; son of William James (a manufacturer) and Martha (French) Keating; married wife, Kathryn, June 24, 1955 (divorced February 25, 1974); children: Michael K., Kara A., Martha A., Neal B. *Education:* Attended St. Leo's Academy, 1951, and Loyola College, Montreal, Quebec, 1951-52; St. Francis Xavier University, B.A., 1955. *Politics:* Independent. *Religion:* None. *Home:* 924 West End Ave., New York, N.Y. 10025. *Agent:* Ellen Levine, Curtis Brown Ltd., 60 East 56th St., New York, N.Y. 10022. *Office:* Rutgers University, Newark, N.J. 07102.

CAREER: Rome Sentinel, Rome, N.Y., reporter, 1955-56; Associated Press, Albany, N.Y., legislative correspondent, 1957-62; *New York Herald Tribune,* New York, N.Y., correspondent and bureau chief, 1963-64; WCBS-Television, New York, N.Y., director of editorials, 1965-69, director of news, 1970, director of journalism apprenticeship program, 1968-70; WRVR-FM Radio, New York, N.Y., moderator and executive producer of evening news, 1971-72; Rutgers University, Newark, N.J., assistant professor of journalism, 1973—. Consultant to Public Education Association. *Military service:* Royal Canadian Navy, submarine duty, 1952-55; became lieutenant senior grade.

MEMBER: Association for Education in Journalism, New York Legislative Correspondents Alumni Association. *Awards, honors:* Page One Award from New York Newspaper Guild, 1965; gold medal from National Conference of Christians and Jews, 1969, for an editorial series; award from Citizens for Clean Air, 1965-66; New York Emmy Award, 1967; first place from Radio-Television News Directors Association, 1969.

WRITINGS: (With Jimmy Watson) *White Man/Black Man,* Praeger, 1974. Contributor to *Village Voice, Coronet, Newsday,* and *Better Homes and Gardens.*

WORK IN PROGRESS: An Ethnic Portrait of America; The War Between the Liberated Sexes, completion expected in 1976.

SIDELIGHTS: Keating writes that he is "passionately interested in cities, the people who live in them, and what goes on within them, including survival. Sinclair Lewis informs me at one end, Hermann Hesse at the other."

BIOGRAPHICAL/CRITICAL SOURCES: Newsday, October 26, 1965; *Newsweek,* November 8, 1965; *Nation,* September 4, 1967; *New York Times,* December 18, 1970, April 28, 1972; *Variety,* December 23, 1970, April 19, 1972.

KEEGAN, Marcia 1943-

PERSONAL: Born May 23, 1943, in Tulsa, Okla.; daughter of Otis Claire and Mary Elizabeth (Collar) Keegan. *Education:* University of New Mexico, B.A., 1963. *Home and office:* 140 East 46th St., New York, N.Y. 10017.

CAREER: Free-lance writer and photographer. *Member:* American Society of Magazine Photographers. *Awards, honors:* New Mexico Press Award, 1963.

WRITINGS—self-illustrated with photographs: *The Taos Indians and Their Sacred Blue Lake,* Messner, 1971; *Mother Earth, Father Sky,* Grossman, 1974; *We Can Still Hear Them Clapping,* Avon, 1974.

Illustrator: Richard Margolis, *Only the Moon and Me,* Lippincott, 1968.

* * *

KEITH, David
See STEEGMULLER, Francis

* * *

KEITH, Judith 1923-

PERSONAL: Born March 2, 1923, in Brooklyn, N.Y.; daughter of Carol J. (a lawyer) and Lottie (Weintraub) Mann; divorced; children: Jeffrey Brian, Jonathan, Elisa Bridgit Fitzgerald. *Education:* Attended American Academy of Dramatic Arts, 1942. *Politics:* Liberal Democrat. *Religion:* Jewish. *Home:* Woodstream, R. D. #1, Henryville, Pa. 18332. *Office:* Tandem Press, Inc., Tannersville, Pa. 18372.

CAREER: Free-lance actress, 1943-49; Glamorene, Inc., Clifton, N.J., advertising and publicity director, 1949-54; *Pursestrings* (women's weekly newspaper), Lakewood, N.J., editor and publisher, 1954-56; Wermen & Shore Advertising Co., Philadelphia, Pa., publicity director, 1956-59; free-lance writer and lecturer, 1959-68; Tandem Press, Inc., Tannersville, Pa., president, 1968—. Public relations consultant to organizations, including United World Federalists, Pennsylvania Ballet Co., and Professional Laundry Foundation. *Member:* Publisher's Publicity Association, Hotel Sales Management Association, American Federation of Television and Radio Artists, American Guild of Variety Artists.

WRITINGS: I Haven't a Thing to Wear, Tandem Press, 1968, revised edition, in press; (with Sandy Spring) *Candy, Chocolate, Ice Cream, and How to Lick 'Em,* Tandem Press, 1973.

WORK IN PROGRESS: We'll Pitch the Tent, Mom, a nonfiction adventure story of a cross-country camping trip, completion expected in 1975; a novel, *The Weathervane.*

SIDELIGHTS: Judith Keith told *CA:* "What motivates me most is a deeply optimistic and continually appreciative lifestyle; appreciative of being alive each day, accepting challenges, heartbreaks and joys . . . just to be alive is enough. My work reflects this optimism, this gratefulness. My major interests are close to nature and to ways and means of making living easy, physically, emotionally, and spiritually. I try to exude love in all that I do, and despite all the pessimism around me, I extol life, people and the prospects for life. My greatest competence lies in resourcefulness in that which I attempt."

KELF-COHEN, Reuben 1895-

PERSONAL: Born September 29, 1895, in Leeds, England; son of Harris and Jane Cohen; married Edith Florence Kelf, 1922 (died, 1964); children: Judith (Mrs. Peter Preece). *Education:* Wadham College, Oxford M.A. (first class honors in history), 1920; University of London, B.Sc. (first class honors in economics), 1931. *Politics:* None. *Religion:* Jewish. *Home:* 14 Harold Rd., London S.E. 19, England.

CAREER: Civil servant in London, England, 1920-55, with Board of Education, 1920-25, Board of Trade, 1925-41, Petroleum Department, 1941-42, principal assistant secretary for gas and electricity, Ministry of Fuel and Power, 1942-45, and undersecretary, Ministry of Fuel and Power, 1946-55; Radio Industry Council, London, England, director and secretary, 1960-66. Tutorial class tutor at University of London, 1924-39; lecturer at University of St. Andrews, 1970, and University College of Wales, Aberystwyth, 1971. Member of board of directors, East Indian Produce Co., 1955-59. *Military service:* British Army, Royal Field Artillery, 1915-19; wounded in action. *Member:* Royal Society of Arts (fellow). *Awards, honors:* Companion of Order of the Bath, 1950.

WRITINGS: Knights of Malta, S.P.C.K., 1920; *Nationalization in Britain: End of a Dogma,* St. Martin's, 1958, 2nd edition, Macmillan (London), 1961; *Twenty Years of Nationalization: British Experience,* St. Martin's, 1969; *British Nationalization, 1945-1973,* St. Martin's, 1974. Contributor to journals and newspapers, especially *Daily Telegraph.*

WORK IN PROGRESS: An Edwardian Boyhood.

SIDELIGHTS: Kelf-Cohen has a working knowledge of French, German, Spanish, Italian, and Russian. *Avocational interests:* Traveling worldwide, especially by sea; playing bridge.

* * *

KELLER, B(everly) L(ou)

PERSONAL: Born in San Francisco, Calif.; daughter of Wearne E. and Ruth (Burke) Harwick; married William Jon Keller, June 18, 1949 (died, 1964); children: Lisa, Kristen, Michele. *Education:* University of California, Berkeley, B.A., 1950. *Residence:* San Mateo, Calif. *Agent:* Lurton Blassingame, 60 East 42nd St., New York, N.Y. 10017.

CAREER: Author, newspaper columnist, and feature writer.

WRITINGS: The Baghdad Defections, Bobbs-Merrill, 1973. Work is anthologized in *The Best from Fantasy and Science Fiction,* edited by Edward Ferman, Doubleday, 1974. Contributor of short stories to *Atlantic Monthly* and *Cosmopolitan,* and other magazines, and of articles and reviews to *San Francisco Chronicle* and Peninsula Newspapers, Inc.

WORK IN PROGRESS: A novel.

SIDELIGHTS: Ms. Keller lived in Baghdad, Beirut, and Rome. She drove from Beirut to Athens, by way of Syria, and Turkey, and has travelled throughout Europe. *Avocational interests:* Dogs, yoga, politics.

* * *

KELLER, Charles 1942-

PERSONAL: Born March 30, 1942. *Home:* 162 19th St., Union City, N.J. 07087.

WRITINGS—For children; all published by Prentice-Hall: *Ballpoint Bananas,* 1972; *Too Funny for Words,* 1973; *Laugh Lines,* 1973.

WORK IN PROGRESS: Children's humor.

* * *

KELLOGG, Steven 1941-

PERSONAL: Born October 6, 1941, in Norwalk, Conn.; son of Robert E. and Hilma Marie (Johnson) Kellogg; married Helen Hill. *Education:* Rhode Island School of Design, B.F.A., 1963. *Home address:* Bennett's Bridge Rd., Sandy Hook, Conn. 06482. *Agent:* Sheldon Fogelman, 10 East 40th St., New York, N.Y. 10016.

CAREER: Writer and illustrator of children's books.

WRITINGS—Self-illustrated books for children: *The Wicked Kings of Bloon,* Prentice-Hall, 1970; *Can I Keep Him?,* Dial, 1971; *The Mystery Beast of Ostergeest,* Dial, 1971; *The Orchard Cat,* Dial, 1972; *Won't Somebody Play with Me?,* Dial, 1972; *The Island of the Skog,* Dial, 1973; *The Mystery of the Missing Red Mitten,* Dial, 1974; *There WAs an Old Woman.* Parents' Magazine Press, 1974.

Illustrator: Hillaire Belloc, *The yak, the Python, and the Frog.* Parents' Magazine Press, in press.

WORK IN PROGRESS: Best Friends, a self-illustrated picture book for children, for Dial.

* * *

KELLY, George E. 1887-1974

January 16, 1887—June 18, 1974; American playwright. Obituaries: *New York Times,* June 19, 1974; *Washington Post,* June 21, 1974, July 7, 1974; *Newsweek,* July 1, 1974.

* * *

KELLY, James B(urton) 1905-

PERSONAL: Born December 12, 1905, in New Castle, Pa.; son of General Jackson (a minister) and Della May (Chilcot) Kelly; married Ruby Rachel Creasy, November 22, 1946; children: Robert Jackson, Phyllis J. Kelly Lombardo, Dolores Mae Kelly Houk. *Education:* Attended Westminster College, New Wilmington, Pa., 1925-26. *Politics:* Republican. *Religion:* Protestant. *Home and office:* 7 Jacaranda Lane, Spanish Lakes, Port St. Lucie, Fla. 33452.

CAREER: U.S. Steel Corp., Pittsburgh, Pa., line supervisor, 1926-64. *Military service:* U.S. Navy, 1944-46. *Member:* Free and Accepted Masons.

WRITINGS—All novels: *The Tall Marshal,* Lenox Hill Press, 1973; *The Edge of Grass,* Lenox Hill Press, 1973; *Stage Stop,* Lenox Hill Press, 1974.

WORK IN PROGRESS: A western novel.

* * *

KELLY, Kathleen Sheridan White 1945-

PERSONAL: Born April 28, 1945, in Youngstown, Ohio; daughter of John Leonard (a supervisor for American Telephone and Telegraph) and Marjorie (Chambers) White; married John Steven Kelly (an assistant professor of marketing at Ball State University), September 4, 1966; children: Alison Colleen. *Education:* DePauw University, student, 1963-66; Ohio State University, B.A., 1967; Ohio University, M.A., 1968; Kent State University, M.L.S., 1972. *Home:* 2400 Woodbridge, Muncie, Ind. 47304.

CAREER: High school teacher of French in Marlboro, N.J., 1968-70.

WRITINGS: Jean Anouilh: An Annotated Bibliography, Scarecrow, 1973.

* * *

KEMPFER, Lester Leroy 1932-

PERSONAL: Born July 28, 1932, in Botkins, Ohio; son of Roy A. (a farmer) and Ruth (Knasel) Kempfer; married Betty Crist, February 6, 1953 (divorced, 1971); married Darlene Reimer (a teacher), June 23, 1974; children: (first marriage) Connie Jo, Mark Leroy. *Education:* High school graduate in Botkins, Ohio; International Correspondence School, student, 1969-71. *Religion:* Lutheran. *Address:* Box 317, Marysville, Ohio 43040. *Office:* 120 North Main St., Marysville, Ohio 43040.

CAREER: Has worked as a salesman, department store manager, purchasing agent, and real estate investor in Marysville, Ohio, 1954—. *Military service:* U.S. Army, 1952-54; became sergeant; served in Korea; received commendation medal, Korean service ribbon with two campaign stars, and Republic of Korea presidential unit citation. *Member:* National Writers Club, Veterans of Foreign Wars of the U.S.A., Ohio Historical Society, Union County Historical Society, Washington County Historical Society.

WRITINGS: The Salem Light Guard (nonfiction), Adams Press, 1973.

* * *

KEMPTON, Jean Welch 1914- (Jean-Louise Welch)

PERSONAL: Born April 3, 1914, in Vineland, N.J.; daughter of Howard Gow (a fund raiser) and Etta (Roat) Welch; married Donald Eugene Kempton (a psychologist), June 25, 1952. *Education:* Attended Cornell University, 1932. *Religion:* Presbyterian. *Address:* Route 2, Box 191, Horse Shoe, N.C. 28742.

CAREER: Doubleday & Co., Inc., Garden City, N.Y., correspondent, 1943-48; writer of children's educational radio and television series in Garden City, N.Y., 1948-49; director of religious education for churches in Garden City, N.Y., 1949-51, and Hagerstown, Md., 1951-52. State coordinator of Women in Community Service, 1964-70; education chairman of North Carolina Extension Homemakers, 1969. *Member:* North Carolina Mental Health Association (member of board of directors, 1968-71), Cornell Womens Club, Hendersonville Mental Health Association.

WRITINGS: (Under name Jean-Louise Welch) *The Animals Came First* (children's book), Oxford University Press, 1948, 2nd edition, Walck, 1963; *Living with Myasthenia Gravis: A Bright New Tomorrow,* C. C Thomas, 1972. Contributor to *Child Life* and *International Journal of Religious Education.*

WORK IN PROGRESS: Nutritional approach to the treatment of myasthenia gravis.

SIDELIGHTS: Jean Welch Kempton told *CA:* "While a student at Cornell I developed myasthenia gravis, a serious muscle weakness for which there is no cure. I was an invalid for a good many years during which time I did a little writing. I also worked along with my doctor on medical research and tried some nutritional therapy on myself which enabled me to become completely well. This has come to the attention of some doctors at a medical college who have asked me to help them with some research in this area."

* * *

KENNEDY, Robert Woods 1911-

PERSONAL: Born May 28, 1911, in Boston, Mass.; son of Albert Joseph (a social worker) and Edith (Knowles) Kennedy; married Gertrude Franchot; married Mary Brewster (a decorator); children: Duncan, David, Charles. *Education:* Harvard University. *Politics:* Democrat. *Religion:* None. *Home and office:* 57 Brewster St., Cambridge, Mass. 02138.

CAREER: Architect in Cambridge, Mass.; teacher at Massachusetts Institute of Technology. *Awards, honors:* Six awards for architectural design.

WRITINGS: A Classical Education (novel), Norton, 1973.

Other: (Contributor) *Sociopsychological Factors in Group Housing Design,* Harper, 1950; *The House, and the Art of Its Design,* Reinhold, 1953. Contributor to periodicals of articles on architecture, art, and planning.

WORK IN PROGRESS: Starting, a novel; a book on architect-client relationships.

SIDELIGHTS: Kennedy said he has "written since 1930 when I sent an angry letter to the Boston Sunday Transcript about public housing. They said they would publish it as a feature article and pay me for it if I would clean up its language. I did. It was almost too much of a thrill."

* * *

KERLINGER, Fred N(ichols) 1910-

PERSONAL: Born July 4, 1910, in New York, N.Y.; son of George E. and Lotte (Fisher) Kerlinger; married Betty Jane McCue, December 16, 1946; children: Paul Nichols, Stephen Charles. *Education:* New York University, B.S., 1942; University of Michigan, M.A., 1951, Ph.D., 1953. *Politics:* Democrat. *Religion:* None. *Home:* 60 Charlotte Pl., Hartsdale, N.Y. 10530. *Office:* Department of Educational Psychology, New York University, 933 Shimkin, New York, N.Y. 10003.

CAREER: U.S. Civil Service, Shikoku, Japan, regional civil education officer, 1947-50; Wayne State University, Detroit, Mich., assistant professor of educational psychology, 1953-55; New York University, New York, N.Y., associate professor, 1955-60, professor of educational psychology, 1960—, head of Division of Behavioral Sciences, 1968-71. Visiting professor at Indiana University, summer, 1953, Columbia University, summer, 1955, University of California, Berkeley, summer, 1968, University of Amsterdam, 1972-73. Member of Hartsdale Board of Education, 1960-63; chairman of Citizens Committee on Racial Disturbances, 1968-69. *Military service:* U.S. Army, 1942-46; became second lieutenant.

MEMBER: American Psychological Association (fellow), Psychometric Society, American Association for the Advancement of Science, American Association of University Professors, American Educational Research Association.

WRITINGS: Foundations of Behavioral Research, Holt, 1964, revised edition, 1973; (with Elazar J. Pedhazur) *Multiple Regression in Behavioral Research,* Holt, 1973. Contributor to journals. Review editor for *American Educational Research Journal,* 1968-70; editor of *Review of Research in Education,* 1970—.

WORK IN PROGRESS: Research on attitudes and values; a book on behavioral scientific research for laymen and teachers.

AVOCATIONAL INTERESTS: Music, especially piano.

* * *

KERNAN, Alvin B(ernard) 1923-

PERSONAL: Surname legally changed in 1943; born June 13, 1923, in Manchester, Ga.; son of Alvin Berbanks and Jimmie Katherine (Fletcher) Peters; married Suzanne Soble, December 13, 1949; children: Geoffrey, Katherine, Marjorie, Alvin. *Education:* Williams College, B.A., 1949; Oxford University, B.A., 1951; Yale University, Ph.D., 1954. *Home:* Wyman House, 50 Springdale Rd., Princeton, N.J. 08540. *Office:* 205 Nassau Hall, Princeton University, Princeton, N.J. 08540.

CAREER: Rensselaer Polytechnic Institute, Troy, N.Y., instructor in English, 1953-54; Yale University, New Haven, Conn., instructor, 1954-59, assistant professor, 1959-63, associate professor, 1963-66, professor of English, 1966-73, associate provost, 1965-68, acting provost, 1970, director of Division of Humanities, 1970-72; Princeton University, Princeton, N.J., professor of English and dean of Graduate School, 1973—. *Military service:* U.S. Navy, 1941-45; served in Pacific theatre; became aviation chief petty officer; received Navy Cross, Distinguished Flying Cross, Air Medal.

MEMBER: Phi Beta Kappa. *Awards, honors:* Morse fellowship, 1957-58; American Council of Learned Societies fellowship, 1961-62; National Endowment for the Humanities senior fellowship, 1968-69; William Clyde DeVane Medal for distinguished teaching from Yale chapter of Phi Beta Kappa, 1972.

WRITINGS: The Cankered Muse: Satire of the English Renaissance, Yale University Press, 1959; *Modern Satire,* Harcourt, 1962; *The Plot of Satire,* Yale University Press, 1965; *The Revels History of the Drama in English, Volume III: 1576-1613,* Methuen, 1974.

Editor: William Shakespeare, *Julius Caesar,* Yale University Press, 1957; Ben Jonson, *Volpone,* Yale University Press, 1962; *Character and Conflict: An Introduction to Drama,* Harcourt, 1963; Shakespeare, *Othello,* New American Library, 1964; *Classics of the Modern Theater,* Harcourt, 1965; *The Modern American Theater,* Prentice-Hall, 1967; (with J. Dennis Huston) *Classics of the Renaissance Theater,* Harcourt, 1969; *Modern Shakespearean Criticism,* Harcourt, 1970; (with Peter Brooks and Michael Holquist) *Man and His Fictions,* Harcourt, 1973; Ben Jonson, *The Alchemist,* Yale University Press, 1974.

General editor of Yale University Press series on Ben Jonson. Contributor to scholarly journals.

* * *

KERRIGAN, Anthony 1918-

PERSONAL: Born March 14, 1918, in Winchester, Mass.; son of Thomas Aloysius and Madeleine (Flood) Kerrigan; married Marjorie Burke, September 15, 1935; married Elaine Gurevitch (a musician and translator), September 1, 1951; children: Michael, Antonia, Camilo Jose, Patrick, Elie, Malachy. *Education:* Attended San Diego State College (now University), 1935-36, University of California at Berkeley, 1938-39, University of Michigan, 1941, Columbia University, 1945, University of Havana, 1945, Sorbonne,

University of Paris, 1951; also attended University of Southern California. *Home:* Dos de Mayo 33, Palma de Mallorca, Spain; and 47 Fitzwilliam Sq., Dublin, Ireland. *Agent:* Ellen Levine, Curtis Brown, 60 East 56th St., New York, N.Y. 10022.

CAREER: Author, editor, and translator; lecturer in Sino-Japanese at University of California, 1941; translator to the University of Florida, 1950-51; Bollingen Foundation/Princeton University Press, Princeton, N.J., editor, 1968—. Purser in U.S. Merchant Marine Service, 1945; visiting professor in English at State University of New York at Buffalo, 1974. *Military service:* U.S. Army, Intelligence, 1942-45; became sergeant. *Member:* P.E.N. (Ireland). *Awards, honors:* American Council of Learned Societies grants.

WRITINGS: Gaudi restaurador, o la historia de Cabrit y Bassa. [Madrid], 1959; *Gaudi en la catedral de Mallorca,* [Palma de Mallorca], 1960; *El Maestro de Santa Ursula,* [Madrid], 1960; (editor) Hiro Ishibashi, *Yeats and the Noh: Types of Japanese Beauty and Their Reflection in Yeats' Plays,* Dolmen Press, 1966; *Espousal in August* (poems), Dolmen Press, 1968; *At the Front Door of the Atlantic* (poems), Dufour, 1969.

Translator: (And editor) Andres Barcia Carballido y Zuniga, *Chronological History of Florida,* University of Florida Press, 1951; (and editor) Pedro Menendez, *Pedro Menendez* (autobiography), University of Florida Press, 1953; Jose Suarez Carreno, *Final Hours,* Knopf, 1954; Vicente Marrero Suarez, *Picasso and the Bull,* Regnery, 1956; Rodrigo Royo, *Sun and the Snow,* Regnery, 1956; (and author of introduction) Miguel de Unamuno y Jugo, *Abel Sanchez and Other Stories,* Regnery, 1956; Jose Maria Gironella, *Where the Soil Was Shallow,* Regnery, 1957; Pio Baroja y Nessi, *Restlessness of Shanti Andia and Other Writings,* University of Michigan Press, 1959.

(And editor and author of introduction) Jorge Luis Borges, *Ficciones,* Grove, 1965 (published in England as *Fictions,* J. Calder, 1965); (and author of introduction) Camilo Jose Cela y Trulock, *The Family of Pascual Duarte,* Weidenfeld & Nicolson, 1965; (and editor and author of foreword) Borges, *A Personal Anthology,* Grove, 1967; (and editor) Unamuno, *Selected Works,* Princeton University Press for the Bollingen Foundation, Volume III: *Our Lord Don Quixote: The Life of Don Quixote and Sancho, with Related Essays,* 1967, Volume IV: *The Tragic Sense of Life in Men and Nations,* 1973, Volume V: *The Agony of Christianity and Essays on Faith,* 1974; (with Alastair Reid) *Mother Goose in Spanish,* Crowell, 1968; *Con Cuba* (bilingual Cuban verse), [London], 1969; Borges, *Poems,* Dolmen, 1969; (with others) Pablo Neruda, *Selected Poems,* J. Cape, 1970, Delacorte, 1972; *A Year of Picasso Paintings: 1969,* Rafael Alberti (New York), 1972; (and author of foreword) Borges and Adolfo Bioy Casares, compilers, *Extraordinary Tales,* Souvenir Press, 1973; (adaptor into English and author of foreword and afterword) Borges, *Irish Strategies,* Dolman, 1973.

Regular contributor to *Encyclopaedia Brittanica* and *Brittanica Book of the Year.* Contributor of short stories, essays, poems, art criticism, and translations to periodicals in the United States, Spain, Ireland, Canada, and other countries.

WORK IN PROGRESS: The Hojoki: A Japanese Classic from the Year 1212, an adaptation from the Japanese, with Thomas Rowe; and an untitled book of verse.

SIDELIGHTS: Kerrigan, who says "I have lived from the typewriter since age 17," has been, with his family of 7, "in exile (from no country in particular) for 20 years without a break—in France, Spain, and Ireland." He continues: "My first 14 years were in Cuba, and intermittently in other countries. Have no 'community.'" His first writing was for the W.P.A. Writers' Project in San Diego and Los Angeles, California. He described himself to *CA* as "conservative-anarchist; anti-state Copperhead; reactionary tribalist," and as "born an Irish-Catholic; refuse to 'pass' as civilized or be traitor to my race and commitment." Beginning in Cuba, he attended eight high schools. He studied for two years in the Military Intelligence Service Language Schools of the U.S. Army.

Kerrigan writes "daily continuous verse, and daily continuous translations." He holds a private pilot's license for land and sea.

BIOGRAPHICAL/CRITICAL SOURCES: Malahat, October, 1969; *Reviste de Occidente,* January, 1973; *Parnassus,* Fall/Winter, 1973.

* * *

KERRIGAN, William J(oseph)

EDUCATION: State University of Iowa, M.A.; University of California, Los Angeles, M.A. *Politics:* Democrat. *Address:* Box 3672, Fullerton, Calif. 92634.

CAREER: United States Information Agency, Fullerton, Calif., associate, 1960—.

WRITINGS: Writing to the Point, Harcourt, 1974.

SIDELIGHTS: Kerrigan is competent in French, Italian, Spanish, German, Russian, and Latin.

* * *

KEUCHER, William F. 1918-

PERSONAL: Surname is pronounced *Koo*-cher; born June 6, 1918, in Atlantic City, N.J.; son of Otto E. R. (a newspaper columnist) and Margaret (Wilson) Keucher; married Edith Warnick Kimber (a music educator), November 28, 1940; children: Margaret Valerie (Mrs. Donald G. Savage), Louise Sherilyn Keucher Nye. *Education:* Eastern Baptist College, A.B.; Eastern Baptist Theological Seminary, Th.B. and B.D. *Politics:* Independent Republican. *Home:* 18225 Coral Gables, Lathrup Village, Mich. 48076. *Office:* Covenant Baptist Church, 18700 James Couzens, Detroit, Mich. 48235.

CAREER: Pastor of American Baptist churches in Philadelphia, Pa., 1942-48, and El Dorado, Kan., 1948-52; Kansas Baptist Convention, Topeka, executive minister, 1952-70; Covenant Baptist Church, Detroit, Mich., senior minister, 1970—. President of Kansas Baptist State Convention, 1951-52; American Baptist Convention, past associate member of general council, past member of Division of World Mission Support, past member of Division of Program Planning, president of state secretaries, 1956, member of executive committee of Council on Theological Education, 1963—, currently member of executive committee of Board of International Ministries; vice-chairman of Baptist Joint Committee on Public Affairs, 1962—. Member of Southeastern Michigan Council of Government (SEMCOG), one year. Member of summer faculty of Union Theological Seminary (Richmond, Va.), 1974. Trustee and vice-president of Central Baptist Theological Seminary; trustee of Ottawa University, 1953—. Public speaker; has appeared on television and radio programs, including American Broadcasting Corp.'s "Laymen's Hour" and WNIC-Radio's "Sounds of the New Life," 1973—; has conducted preaching missions in Europe for the military; has taught and attended conferences abroad.

MEMBER: American Academy of Religion, American Academy of Science, American Political Science Association, American Baptist Churches of the United States of America (member of general board), Fund of Renewal (national committee member), Detroit Urban League (member of board of directors and executive committee), Rotary International. *Awards, honors:* D.D. from Ottawa University, 1953, Kalamazoo College, 1971, and Eastern Michigan University, 1971.

WRITINGS: An Exodus for the Church, Judson, 1973; *Main Street and the Mind of God,* Judson, 1974. Contributor to *Christian Century, Pulpit, Foundations,* and *Baptist Leader.* Editor of *Kansas Baptist,* 1952-70.

WORK IN PROGRESS: Editing manuscripts for a book of poems written in 1972 and 1973; preparing material for his weekly radio series.

* * *

KEY, Wilson Bryan 1925-

PERSONAL: Born January 31, 1925, in Richmond, Calif.; son of Wilson Bryan and Elizabeth (Jackson) Key; married Iris Delia Ortiz, September 24, 1966; children: Lotis Melisande, Luz Clotilde, Michelle. *Education:* Mexico City College, B.A., 1952; University of California, Los Angeles, M.A., 1953; University of Denver, Ph.D., 1971. *Home:* 2289 Simos Ave., Pinole, Calif. 94564. *Agent:* American Program Bureau, 850 Boylston St., Chestnut Hill, Boston, Mass. 02167. *Office:* Department of Journalism, University of Western Ontario, London, Ontario, Canada.

CAREER: Advertising Associates, Manila, Philippines, account executive, 1947-49; University of Denver, Denver, Colo., professor of journalism and chairman of department, 1953-55; University of Kansas, Lawrence, professor of speech and journalism, 1955-56; senior writer at Northrop Corp., and Lockheed Aircraft Corp., Los Angeles, Calif., 1956-57; Boston University, Boston, Mass., professor of journalism, 1957-61; research director at Publicidad Badillo, San Juan, P.R., 1962-65, and Research and Market Development, San Juan, P.R., 1965-69; University of Western Ontario, London, Ontario, professor of journalism, 1969—. President of Mediaprobe: Center for the Study of Media, Inc., 1973—. *Military service:* U.S. Army Air Forces, 1943-47. *Member:* International Society for the Study of Symbology, International Communication Association, Association for Education in Journalism, American Sociological Association.

WRITINGS: (Contributor) *Modern Journalism,* Pitman, 1962; *Subliminal Seduction: Ad Media's Manipulation of a Not-So-Innocent America,* Prentice Hall, 1973. Contributor to *American Editor* and *Journal of Communication.* Author of more than three hundred research studies for private corporations and governments.

WORK IN PROGRESS: A book on the socio-behavioral effects of media; *Sexploitation by Media.*

SIDELIGHTS: Key has lived as a journalist in Mexico, the Philippines, Puerto Rico, North Africa, and the Far East.

KEYES, Ralph 1945-

PERSONAL: Surname rhymes with "eyes"; born January 12, 1945, in Cincinnati, Ohio; son of Scott (a regional planner) and Charlotte (a writer; maiden name, Shachmann) Keyes; married Muriel Gordon (a physical therapist), February 13, 1965. *Education:* Antioch College, B.A., 1967; London School of Economics and Political Science, graduate study, 1967-68. *Home:* 1952 Thomas Ave., San Diego, Calif. 92109. *Agent:* Donald Cutler, Sterling Lord Agency, Inc., 660 Madison Ave., New York, N.Y. 10021. *Office:* Center for Studies of the Person, 1125 Torrey Pines Rd., La Jolla, Calif. 92037.

CAREER: Newsday, Long Island, N.Y., assistant to publisher and staff writer, 1968-70; Center for Studies of the Person, La Jolla, Calif., fellow, 1970—. Visiting assistant professor at Prescott College, 1971, 1974.

WRITINGS: We, the Lonely People: Searching for Community, Harper, 1973. Contributor to *Newsweek, Nation, Playboy, Mademoiselle, Human Behavior, Popular Psychology, Car and Driver, Charge, West,* and *Parade.*

WORK IN PROGRESS: Research on the social history of bumper stickers, on political personality, on being male and proud, and on the fear of writing; possible titles for his next books include *Is There Life After High School?, How to Be a Better Person (Stop Trying),* and *Need You Be Crazy to Run for Office, or Does It Only Help?*

* * *

KILLAM, (Gordon) Douglas 1930-

PERSONAL: Born August 26, 1930, in New Westminster, British Columbia, Canada; son of Harry (a clerk) and Margaret (Currie) Killam; married Helen Shelagh Ann Anderson, August 20, 1959; children: Christopher, Sarah. *Education:* University of British Columbia, B.A. (honors), 1955; University of London, Ph.D., 1964. *Politics:* None. *Religion:* Protestant. *Home:* 60 Westwood Ave., Wolfville, Nova Scotia BOP 1XO, Canada. *Office:* Acadia University, Wolfville, Nova Scotia BOP 1XO, Canada.

CAREER: Canadian Broadcasting Corp. (CBC), Vancouver, British Columbia, television producer, 1956-60; Fourah Bay College, Freetown, Sierra Leone, lecturer in English literature, 1963-65; University of Alberta, Edmonton, assistant professor of English, 1965-66; University of Ibadan, Ibadan, Nigeria, lecturer in English, 1966-67; University of Lagos, Yaba Lagos, Nigeria, senior lecturer in English, 1967-68; York University, Downsview, Ontario, assistant professor, 1968-69, associate professor of English, 1969-73, master of Bethune College, 1971-73; Acadia University, Wolfville, Nova Scotia, professor of English and head of department, 1973—. Professor and chairman of department of literature at University of Dar Es Salaam (Tanzania), 1970-71; visiting lecturer, University of British Columbia, summer, 1965; external examiner for University of Nairobi, 1971-72.

MEMBER: Canadian Association of African Studies (vice-president, 1973-74; president, 1974-75), Canadian Association of Commonwealth Literature and Language Studies, Association of Canadian University Teachers of English, American Sociological Association, Modern Language Association of America. *Awards, honors:* Canada Council research grants, 1967, for study of J. M. Stuart-Young, and 1971, for compiling bibliography of English fiction presenting Africa; Rockefeller Foundation research and teaching fellowship, 1970-71.

WRITINGS: Africa in English Fiction: 1874-1939, Ibadan University Press, 1967; *The Novels of Chinua Achebe,* Heinemann, 1969; (contributor) B. A. King, editor, *Introductions to Nigerian Literature,* Evans Brothers, 1971; (contributor) E. D. Jones, editor, *African Literature,* Volume V, Heinemann, 1971; (editor) *African Writers on African Writing,* Heinemann, 1973; (author of introduction) Margaret Laurence, *A Jest of God,* McLelland & Stewart, 1974; (contributor) King, editor, *Ten English Literatures,* Routledge & Kegan Paul, in press; (editor) *The Literature of Eastern Africa,* Routledge & Kegan Paul, in press.

Contributor of about twenty articles and reviews to academic journals, including *Black Academy Review, Sewanee Review, Twentieth Century Literature, Black Orpheus, Insight,* and *Journal of the Historical Society of Nigeria.* Guest editor of *Journal of the Canadian Association of African Studies,* 1975.

WORK IN PROGRESS: The Writing of Margaret Laurence: The Iniquitous Coaster, a biography of John Moray Stuart-Young; *A Bibliography of English Fiction Presenting Africa: 1865-1970;* research on the theme of imperialism in nineteenth-century writing, based on *The Imperial Idea and Its Enemies,* by A. P. Thornton.

* * *

KIMMEL, Eric. A. 1946-

PERSONAL: Born October 30, 1946, in Brooklyn, N.Y.; son of Morris N. (a certified public accountant) and Anne (an elementary school teacher; maiden name, Kerker) Kimmel; married Elizabeth Marcia Sheridan (a professor of education), April 7, 1968. *Education:* Lafayette College, A.B., 1967; New York University, M.A., 1969; University of Illinois, Ph.D., 1972. *Politics:* Independent Democrat. *Religion:* Jewish. *Home:* 404 South Twyckenham Dr., South Bend, Ind. 46615. *Office:* Indiana University at South Bend, 1825 Northside Blvd., South Bend, Ind. 46615.

CAREER: Indiana University at South Bend, assistant professor of education, 1973—. *Member:* National Council of Teachers of English, American Federation of Teachers, Phi Beta Kappa, Phi Delta Kappa, Kappa Delta Pi.

WRITINGS: The Tartar's Sword, Coward, 1974. Author of children's book review column in *South Bend Tribune* and *Young Judean.* Contributor to *Horn Book, Elementary English,* and *Cricket.*

WORK IN PROGRESS: Sabbath Bride, a novel dealing with the seventeenth-century upheaval in the Jewish world caused by Shabbetai Tzvi, whom men believed to be the Messiah; *The Winds Are Laughing,* a novel set in occupied Poland during World War II.

SIDELIGHTS: Kimmel writes: "I am only just beginning to explore the marvellous artistic possibilities of the historical novel. I think the challenge of historical fiction is finding roots; not just writing about the past, but seeing the people you know, the person you are in it, meeting or succumbing to its challenges. I don't know whether I believe in reincarnation or in Jungian memories, but sometimes I find it easier to see myself on the steppes or in ghetto alleys than it is to see myself in an office in South Bend, Ind., writing this. My task, as I see it, is to find out who I really am, and from where I really come."

* * *

KIRK, Jerome (Richard) 1937-

PERSONAL: Born May 27, 1937, in Milwaukee, Wis.; son of Samuel Alexander (an educator) and Winifred (Day) Kirk; married Sara Wolff (a creative services executive), August 11, 1960. *Education:* Reed College, B.A., 1960; Johns Hopkins University, Ph.D., 1965. *Politics:* Conservative. *Home:* 1350 Dunning Dr., Laguna Beach, Calif. 92651. *Office:* School of Social Sciences, University of California, Irvine, Calif. 92664.

CAREER: Carnegie Institute of Technology (now Carnegie-Mellon University), Pittsburgh, Pa., research associate, Graduate School of Industrial Administration, 1963-66; University of California, Irvine, assistant professor of anthropology, 1966—. Adjunct associate professor of public health at University of North Carolina, 1972. Director, WLK, Inc., Los Angeles.

WRITINGS: Cultural Diversity and Character Change at Carnegie Tech, Carnegie Institute of Technology, 1965; (translator with Gia-fu Feng) Tai Chi, *A Way of Centering and I Ching,* Collier Books, 1970; *Adolescent Users of Psychedelic Drugs,* Pluto, 1971; (with P. J. Epling) *Dispersal of the Polynesian Peoples: Explorations in Phylogentic Inference from the Analysis of Taxonomy,* Institute for Research in Social Sciences, University of North Carolina, 1972.

Contributor: James A. Geschwender, editor, *The Black Revolt: The Civil Rights Movement, Ghetto Uprisings, and Separatism,* Prentice-Hall, 1971; Bernard Aronson, editor, *Workshops of the Mind,* Doubleday, in press.

Contributor to *Science, Anthropological Linguistics,* and other journals. Member of editorial board, *Study of Man.*

* * *

KIRK, John T(homas) 1933-

PERSONAL: Born May 23, 1933, in West Chester, Pa.; son of Samuel E. (a builder) and Elizabeth (Holgate) Kirk; married Elizabeth D. Hole (an associate professor), June 15, 1959. *Education:* Rochester Institute of Technology, A.A.S., 1953; attended Royal Danish Academy of Arts, 1953-55; Earlham College, B.A., 1959; Yale University, M.A., 1963. *Agent:* Ellen Neuwald, Bohan-Neuwald Agency, Inc., 905 West End Ave., New York, N.Y. 10025.

CAREER: Yale University Art Gallery, New Haven, Conn., assistant curator, 1964-67; Rhode Island Historical Society, Providence, director, 1967-70, consultant curator of John Brown House, 1970-71; Harvard University, Fogg Art Museum, Cambridge, Mass., research associate, 1971—. Consultant curator to Rhode Island School of Design, Museum of Art, Pendleton House, 1966-70; adjunct professor at Boston University, 1972—. *Awards, honors:* Fulbright fellowship in England, 1963-64, and National Endowment for the Humanities grant, 1974-75, both to study sources of American furniture design.

WRITINGS: (Contributor and author of catalog notes) *Connecticut Furniture: Seventeenth and Eighteenth Centuries,* Wadsworth Atheneum, 1967; *Early American Furniture,* Knopf, 1970; *American Chairs: Queen Anne and Chippendale,* Knopf, 1972; *The Impecunious Collector,* Knopf, in press. Contributor to *Antiques.*

WORK IN PROGRESS: American Furniture, 1630-1830, completion expected in 1976.

* * *

KIRKENDALL, Don(ald M.) 1923-

PERSONAL: Surname is accented in first syllable; born

June 17, 1923, in Parker, S.D.; son of William Ruben (a farmer) and Susan (Merritt) Kirkendall; married third wife, Mary Ann Grafton (a free-lance writer of feature stories), April 11, 1955; children: Greg, Normandie, Kip Susanne. *Education:* Attended University of Portland, Hastings Business College, and Portland Museum Art School. *Religion:* Episcopalian. *Home:* 7815 North Hudson St., Portland, Ore. 97203. *Agent:* Lenniger Literary Agency, Inc., 437 Fifth Ave., New York, N.Y. 10016.

CAREER: Owner of Carnival Games, 1942-47; KVAN-Radio, Portland, Ore., disc jockey, 1955-56; president of Don Kirkendall Agency Ltd. (collection agency), 1962-71. Disc jockey for KAST-Radio, 1942-43; owner of Photo Shop (Seaside, Ore.), 1944-45. Democratic candidate for Oregon legislature, 1966. *Member:* Rotary International (member of board of directors of North Portland Club, 1969-70).

WRITINGS: (With Mary Phraner Warren) *Bottom High to the Crowd,* Walker & Co., 1973. Former editor of *North Portland Rotary Wheelprints.*

WORK IN PROGRESS: Chicken Thief, a novel; *Out on a Limb,* non-fiction based on research of adaptation of physically disabled people to a productive life.

* * *

KIRKPATRICK, Oliver (Austin) 1911-

PERSONAL: Born June 12, 1911, in Jamaica, West Indies; son of William Henry (an accountant) and Fredericka May (Austin) Kirkpatrick; married Carol Werner (a journalist and recreation director), September 17, 1960; children: Ian, Brian. *Education:* New York University, B.Sc., 1950; Columbia University, M.L.S., 1953. *Politics:* Independent. *Religion:* Anglican. *Residence:* Brooklyn, N.Y. *Office:* Brooklyn Public Library, 3650 Nostrand Ave., Brooklyn, N.Y. 11238.

CAREER: ZQI (radio station), Jamaica, West Indies, newscaster, 1940-42; *Jamaica Standard,* Jamaica, West Indies, sports editor and columnist, 1937-42; New York Public Library, New York, N.Y., senior librarian, 1953-64; Brooklyn Public Library, New York, N.Y., supervising librarian, 1964—. *Member:* American Library Association. *Awards, honors:* Joyce Kilmer Award from New York University, 1945, for short stories.

WRITINGS: Country Cousin: A Collection of Radio Broadcasts, Gleaner (Jamaica), 1941; *Naja the Snake and Mangus the Mongoose* (juvenile), Doubleday, 1970. Contributor of articles and poems to *New Republic, Travel, Guardian,* and *Bitterroot.*

WORK IN PROGRESS: Pukka Sahib, a novel of Jamaica.

* * *

KIRKPATRICK, Ralph 1911-

PERSONAL: Born June 10, 1911, in Leominster, Mass.; son of Edwin Asbury (a psychologist) and Florence May (Clifford) Kirkpatrick. *Education:* Harvard University, A.B., 1931; studied harpsichord or music theory with Nadia Boulanger and Wanda Landowska in Paris, Arnold Dolmetsch in England, and Guenther Ramin and Heinz Tiessen in Germany. *Home:* Old Quarry, Guilford, Conn. 06437.

CAREER: Gave piano lessons and recitals as Harvard undergraduate; took up the harpsichord in 1929, made European debut as harpsichordist in Berlin, 1933, and performed in Italy and Germany before beginning U.S. concert appearances, 1934; has made annual tours as harpsichord soloist with principal orchestras in America, 1944—, and in Europe since World War II; associated with School of Music at Yale University, 1940—, as lecturer, then instructor in harpsichord, 1940-56, associate professor of music, 1956-64, professor, 1965—. Member of faculty of Mozarteum Academy, Salzburg, summers, 1933, 1934; inaugurated baroque music festivals at Governor's Palace in Historic Williamsburg, 1938, and directed the festivals, 1938-45; Ernest Bloch Professor of Music at University of California, Berkeley, spring, 1964. Recording artist in Germany and United States.

MEMBER: American Musicological Society, College Art Association, Music Library Association, American Academy of Arts and Sciences, American Philosophical Society. *Awards, honors:* John Knowles Paine traveling fellowship in Europe, Harvard University, 1931-33; Guggenheim fellowship for musical research in European libraries, 1937-38; Order of Merit of Italian Republic, 1955; Mus.D., Oberlin College, 1957.

WRITINGS: Domenico Scarlatti (biography), Princeton University Press, 1953, augmented edition, 1970.

Musical editions: Johann Sebastian Bach, "Goldberg Variations," G. Schirmer, 1938; Domenico Scarlatti, "Sixty Sonatas," G. Schirmer, 1953; Domenico Scarlatti, "Complete Keyboard Works," Johnson Reprint, 1972.

Recordings: "Bach Archive Series," twenty long-playing discs, Deutsche Grammophon Gesellschaft, 1956-67; "Sixty Sonatas," Columbia Masterworks; "Harpsichord Recital," Deutsche Grammophon Gesellschaft.

Contributor to music journals, including *Notes* and *Musical Quarterly.*

WORK IN PROGRESS: Six Approaches to Bach's "Well-Tempered Clavier."

AVOCATIONAL INTERESTS: Literature (English, French, German, Italian, and Spanish), the visual arts, including contemporary painting.

BIOGRAPHICAL/CRITICAL SOURCES: High Fidelity, September, 1965.

* * *

KIRKPATRICK, Smith 1922-

PERSONAL: Born November 28, 1922, in Roseville, Ark.; son of William Athal (a businessman) and Esther (Smith) Kirkpatrick; married Sue Wise, 1955 (divorced August 24, 1967); married Barbara Keller (a college teacher), August 5, 1968; children: (first marriage) Anna Marie. *Education:* Attended Arkansas Polytechnic College, 1941-42, 1946-48; University of Florida, B.S.J., 1953, M.A., 1955. *Home:* 1655 Northwest 10th Ave., Gainesville, Fla. 32605. *Agent:* Paul R. Reynolds, Inc., 599 Fifth Ave., New York, N.Y. 10017. *Office:* Department of English, University of Florida, Gainesville, Fla. 32601.

CAREER: U.S. Merchant Marine, ordinary seaman, 1940-41, 1942; KXRJ-Radio, Russellville, Ark., news editor, 1947; University of Florida, Gainesville, instructor, 1956-60, assistant professor, 1960-68, associate professor of English, 1968—, director of creative writing program, 1961—. Member of board of directors of Mexican land corporations; co-director, Florida Writers Conference, 1969—. *Military service:* U.S. Naval Reserve, aviator, active duty, 1942-46, 1948-50; became lieutenant junior grade. *Awards, honors: Sewanee Review* fellowship in fiction, 1958; fellowship from National Endowment for the Arts, 1973, for fiction; Order of the South, from Southern Academy of Letters, Arts, and Sciences, 1973.

WRITINGS: The Sun's Gold: A Novel of the Sea, Houghton, 1974. Contributor of articles and reviews to *Sewanee Review, Southern Review.*

WORK IN PROGRESS: A novel; short stories; a book of children's poems.

* * *

KIRSCHTEN, Ernest 1902-1974

October 21, 1902—July 26, 1974; American reporter, editorial writer, and author. Obituaries: *New York Times,* July 28, 1974. (*CA*-11/12).

* * *

KISHON, Ephraim 1924-

PERSONAL: Born August 23, 1924, in Budapest, Hungary; emigrated to Israel, 1949; son of David and Elizabeth Kishon; married Sara Lipovitz, September 10, 1959; children: Raphael, Amir, Renana. *Education:* Attended University of Budapest, 1945-48. *Home:* 48 Hamitnadev St., Afeka 69690, Israel. *Office: Maariv,* 2 Karlibach St., Tel Aviv, Israel.

CAREER: Journalist, author, humorist. *Maariv,* Tel Aviv, Israel, author of syndicated daily column, 1952—. *Member:* P.E.N. International, Israeli Writers Association, Association of Israeli Journalists, Israeli Film Producers Association (president, 1970). *Awards, honors*—Literary: Israeli Nordau Prize for literature, 1953; Sokolov Prize, 1958, for "outstanding journalistic achievement"; Israeli Herzl Prize for literature, 1970; Israeli Jabotinski Prize, 1970, for *So Sorry We Won!* and *Woe to the Victors!;* Israel Broadcasting Service prize, 1970, for radio play "The Last Angry Kick." Film: Kiner David Prize for best filmscript, 1964, Academy Award nomination for best foreign film, 1964, and Golden Globe Award for best foreign film, 1965, all for "Sallah"; Golden Globe Award nomination for best foreign film, 1969, for "The Big Dig"; Golden Globe Award and Academy Award nomination, both 1971, for "The Policeman" as best foreign-language film; various other film awards.

WRITINGS—All translated from the Hebrew by Yohanan Goldman, except as noted: *Look Back Mrs. Lot: Grins and Groans from the Holy Land,* N. Tversky (Tel Aviv), 1960, published as *Look Back, Mrs. Lot!,* Atheneum, 1961; *Noah's Ark, Tourist Class,* N. Tversky, 1961, Atheneum, 1962; *The Seasick Whale: An Israeli Abroad,* Deutsch, 1965; (with Kariel Gardosh) *Selihah shenitsahnu!,* 1967, translation published as *So Sorry We Won!,* Ma'ariv Library (Tel Aviv), 1967; *Unfair to Goliath,* Atheneum, 1968; (with Gardosh) *Oi la-menatshim,* 1969, translation published as *Woe to the Victors!,* Bloch, 1969; *Blow Softly Jericho,* Atheneum, 1970; *En-kamonim,* 1955, translation by Jacques Namiel published as *The Fox in the Chicken-Coop: A Satirical Novel,* Bronfman, 1971; *Wise Guy, Solomon,* Atheneum, 1973.

Plays: *The Licence: A Comedy in Two Acts* (first produced in 1962), [Afeka, Israel], 1969; *Shemo holekh le-fanav,* 1953, translation by Lothian Small published as *His Friend at Court: A Comedy in Two Acts* (first produced in 1953), [Afeka], 1969; *Shahor 'al gabe lavan,* 1956, translation and lyrics by Small published as *Black on White: A Comedy-Fantasy in Three Acts* (first produced in 1955), [Afeka], 1969; *Seven Columns in Carawayville: A Comedy* (first produced in 1960), translated by Yohanan Goldman, [Afeka], 1969; *Totsi et ha-shteker ha-mayim rothim,* 1965, translation published as *Pull Out the Plug, the Water's Boiling: A Satirical Farce in Six Scenes* (first produced in 1966), [Afeka], 1969. Also author of "Fifteen Light Sketches," produced in 1958, "Crooks All," 1959, "Not a Word to Morgenstern," 1960, and "The Crook," 1965.

Writer of radio plays, "The Last Angry Kick," "The Blaumilch Canal," "Ziggy and Nabooka," and "Backstage," and of filmscripts, "Sallah Shabbati," 1963, "Ervinka," 1967, "The Big Dig," 1969, and "The Policeman," 1971.

Other: *Elef gadya ve-gadya* (title means "One Thousand Lambs"), published in 1954; *Hinta-palinta: Humoresekek* (title means "See-Saw"), Kiadja Forum (Tel Aviv), 1956; *Lo nora* (title means "Never Mind"), 1957; *Ma'arkhonim* (title means "One-Acters"), 1959; *Ha-kol taluy* (title means "Everything Depends"), 1961; *Ha'ketubah* (title means "The Marriage License"), 1961; *Be-ahad ha-amashim* (title means "Once upon a Time"), 1962; *Hu ve-hi* (title means "He and She"), 1964; *Sheminiyot ba-avir* (title means "Jump!"), 1965; *Etsem ba-garon* (title means "Pain in the Neck"), 1967; *Gomzim, gomzim* (title means "Kill Them"), 1969.

SIDELIGHTS: "Nowhere in the world will the humor of Mr. Kishon seem quite alien," writes Carlyle Morgan: "Yet the reader of [*Noah's Ark, Tourist Class*] guesses that there is some charmed inner sanctum of laughter in which his stories have more overtones than these which reach us who are just outside. We are amused, or merely expectant, or perhaps delighted at times. But always we suspect there is something more here than tickles our only partly sophisticated fancy. . . . If some readers run afoul of what they consider lapses of taste, or a too-easy worldliness, they may also appreciate a general wholesomeness and an assumption on Mr. Kishon's part that behavior should be related to some sort of standard." Rinna Samuel estimates that Kishon's writing thrives on "day-to-day absurdity, commonplace pretentiousness and the hilarity of living in a country with high ideals but only average human instincts. . . . everything is grist to his sharp-bladed but essentially benign mill."

Kishon's works have been translated into French, Dutch, German, Hungarian, Spanish, Italian, Turkish, Russian, and other languages.

* * *

KLAICH, Dolores 1936-

PERSONAL: Born August 9, 1936, in Cleveland, Ohio; daughter of Jacob (an organizer for the Socialist Labor Party) and Caroline (Stampar) Klaich. *Education:* Western Reserve University (now Case Western Reserve University), B.A., 1958. *Agent:* Helen Brann Agency, 14 Sutton Pl. S., New York, N.Y. 10022. *Office: Transatlantic Review,* New York, N.Y.

CAREER: Life (magazine), New York, N.Y., reporter, 1962-67; *Transatlantic Review,* New York, N.Y., associate editor, 1968—. Reader for Sterling Lord Agency.

WRITINGS: Woman Plus Woman: Attitudes toward Lesbianism, Simon & Schuster, 1974.

WORK IN PROGRESS: A book on Yugoslavia; a biography of Natalie Clifford Barney.

SIDELIGHTS: Dolores Klaich writes: "I am a daughter of Yugoslav immigrants and grew up in an old-Left household in the Midwest. My father was an organizer for the Socialist Labor Party. I plan to devote the major portion of my future writings to exploring this . . . heritage. I am also interested in continuing to document the social history of lesbianism." Klaich has lived in Yugoslavia, France, and Spain.

* * *

KLAMKIN, Marian 1926-

PERSONAL: Born December 19, 1926, in Providence, R.I.; daughter of Abraham and Goldie (Morrisson) Spungin; married Charles Klamkin (a writer-photographer), August 22, 1948; children: Joan, Lynn, Peter. *Education:* Clark University, B.A., 1948. *Home:* Colonial Rd., Watertown, Conn. 06795. *Agent:* James Oliver Brown Associates, Inc., 22 East 60th St., New York, N.Y. 10022.

CAREER: University of Connecticut, Storrs, instructor in continuing education, 1971-73; writer. *Member:* Mattatuck Museum, Buten Museum.

WRITINGS: Flower Arrangements That Last, Macmillan, 1968; *Flower Arranging For Period Decoration,* Funk, 1968; *The Collector's Book of Boxes,* Dodd, 1970; *The Collector's Book of Art Nouveau,* Dodd, 1971; *The Collecter's Book of Wedgwood,* Dodd, 1971; *The Collector's Book of Bottles,* Dodd, 1971; *White House China,* Scribner, 1972; *Hands to Work: Shaker Folk Art and Industries,* Dodd, 1972; *American Patriotic and Political China,* Scribner, 1973; *The Collector's Guide to Depression Glass,* Hawthorn, 1973; *Picture Postcards,* Dodd, 1974; *Marine Antiques,* Dodd, 1974; *The Return of Lafayette (1824-1825),* Scribner, 1974; (with husband, Charles Klamkin) *Woodcarving: North American Folk Sculpture,* Hawthorn, 1974.

WORK IN PROGRESS: A book on antiques as an investment, for Crowell; *American Blown Glass Bottles,* Pyne; *Collector's Guide to Sheet Music,* Hawthorn.

* * *

KLAPERMAN, Gilbert 1921-

PERSONAL: Born February 25, 1921, in New York, N.Y.; son of Louis (a merchant) and Frieda (Rubinstein) Klaperman; married Libby Mindlin (a teacher and author), August 23, 1942; children: Judith Reena (Mrs. Harold Goldman), Joel Simcha, Frieda Lisa, Carol Nechama (Mrs. Ira J. Morrow). *Education:* Yeshiva University, B.A., 1940, Rabbi, 1941, D.H.L., 1955; University of Iowa, M.A., 1946. *Home:* 64 Muriel Ave., Lawrence, N.Y. 11559. *Office:* 390 Broadway, Lawrence, N.Y. 11579.

CAREER: Ordained rabbi, 1941; rabbi in Kingston, Ontario, 1942-43, West New York, N.J., 1945-47, Charleston, S.C., 1947-50; Congregation Beth Sholom, Lawrence, N.Y., rabbi, 1950—. University of Iowa, School of Religion, Iowa City, lecturer in philosophy, 1943-45; Yeshiva University, New York, N.Y., assistant professor of sociology, 1954-67. Director of B'nai B'rith Hillel Foundation at Queens University, 1942-43, University of Iowa, 1943-45, Iowa State University, 1943-45, The Citadel, 1947-50, and Clemson College, 1947-50. Member of Rabbinic Delegation to Countries Behind the Iron Curtain, 1956, and of Committee of Religious Leaders, 1967-70; chaplain of Nassau County Jail, 1955-67; director of inspection missions of ORT Schools in France, Morocco, Iran, and Israel, 1970—; founder, Hillel School, Lawrence, N.Y., 1960; chairman of New York Conference on Soviet Jewry, 1970-72. *Military service:* Canadian Army Reserve, chaplain, 1942-43. *Member:* Emet World Academy in Jerusalem (chairman of board, 1960—), American Zionist Council, Rabbinical Council of America (vice-president, 1958-60), Rabbinical Zionists of America (member of executive committee, 1960—), Jewish Book Council of America (president, 1962-66), American Organization for Rehabilitation through Training, New York Board of Rabbis (president, 1968-70). *Awards, honors:* D.D., Yeshiva University, 1971.

WRITINGS: (With wife, Libby Klaperman) *The Story of the Jewish People,* four volumes, Behrman, 1961; (with Libby Klaperman) *The Story of the Jewish People: Activity Book,* Behrman, 1961; *How and Why Wonder Book of the Old Testament,* Grosset, 1964; *The Story of Yeshiva University,* Macmillan, 1969; *Cours Programme D'Histoire Juive* (title means "Programmed Instruction Course in Jewish History"), Union Mondiale ORT, 1970. Contributor of articles and reviews to *American Educator Encyclopedia, Jewish Life, Jewish Forum, American Jewish Historical Quarterly, Jewish World, Journees Pedagogique de L'ORT, Jewish Studies in the ORT Schools, Tradition, Jewish Bookland, Chavrusa, Opinion, Horizon, Jewish Spectator,* and *American Educator.*

* * *

KLEIN, Gerard 1937- (Gilles d'Argyre)

PERSONAL: Born May 27, 1937, in Neuilly, France; son of Paul (an executive) and Antoinette (Lahure) Klein. *Education:* University of Paris, Diplome of Institut d'Etudes Politiques, 1957, Diplome of Institut de Psychologie, 1959. *Home:* 25 Rue de Jussieu, Paris, France.

CAREER: Economist specializing in the savings field; Societe d'Etudes pour le Developpement Economique et Social (Society for the Study of Economic and Social Development), Paris, France, consultant economist, 1963—. Writer, principally of science fiction. *Military service:* French Air Force, 1961-62. *Member:* Societe Francaise de Psychologie.

WRITINGS: Le Gambit des etoiles (novel), Hachette, 1958, translation by C. J. Richards published as *Starmasters' Gambit,* Daw Books, 1973; *Les Perles du Temps* (short stories), Denoel, 1958; *Le Temps n'a pas d'odeur* (novel), Denoel, 1963, translation by P. J. Sokolowski published as *The Day Before Tomorrow,* Daw Books, 1972; *Un Chant de pierre* (short stories), Losfeld, 1966; *Les Seigneures de la Guerre,* Laffont, 1970, translation by John Brunner published as *The Overlords of War,* Doubleday, 1973; *La Loi du Talion* (short stories), Laffont, 1973.

Also author of science-fiction novels under pseudonym Gilles d'Argyre: *Chirurgiens d'une planete* (title means "Surgeons of a World"); *Les Voiliers du soleil* (title means "The Sun-Sailors"); *Le Long Voyage* (title means "The Long Journey"); *Les Tueurs de temps* (title means "The Time-Killers"); *Le Sceptre du hasard* (title means "The Scepter of Chance"). Contributor of articles on economics, on utopias, on science fiction and the supernatural to periodicals. Editor of "Ailleurs et Demain" (title means "Elsewhere and Tomorrow"), Laffont, 1969—.

WORK IN PROGRESS: A novel; research on the sociology of literature, imagination, and society.

SIDELIGHTS: As an economist and as a writer, Klein finds "most important the ability of man to conceive things apparently outside his common experience and especially about his future, near or far." He has traveled widely in Europe, the United States, and North Africa. *Avocational interests:* Modern art and music.

* * *

KLEMIN, Diana

PERSONAL: Born in New York, N.Y.; daughter of Alexander (a professor and writer) and Ethel (a poet; maiden name Murton) Klemin. *Education:* Vassar College, A.B., 1944. *Office:* Doubleday & Co., Inc., 245 Park Ave., New York, N.Y. 10017.

CAREER: G. P. Putnam's Sons, New York, N.Y., book designer and production assistant, 1944-45; Doubleday & Co., Inc., New York, N.Y., book designer, 1945-52, art director, 1953—. Chairman, American Institute of Graphic Arts Young Book Designers Show, 1948, and Swiss Book Show, 1953; lecturer, Parsons School of Design, 1974. *Member:* American Institute of Graphic Arts. *Awards, honors:* Young Book Designers award, 1947; awards from Fifty Books of the Year, *Children's Books,* Society of Illustrators, and Art Director's Club of New York; Trade Book Clinic and other awards of the American Institute of Graphic Arts.

WRITINGS: Young Faces (monograph), Composing Room, 1963; *The Art of Art for Children's Books,* C. N. Potter, 1966; *The Illustrated Book: Its Art and Craft,* C. N. Potter, 1970. Contributor to *American Artist, Publishers' Weekly,* and *Book Production.*

SIDELIGHTS: Diana Klemin's work was included in a three-man show, "Exhibit of Book Design," at the American Institute of Graphic Arts, 1952.

* * *

KNIGHT, Bernard 1931- (Bernard Picton)

PERSONAL: Born May 3, 1931, in Cardiff, Wales; son of Harold Ivor (a shipbroker) and Doris (Lawes) Knight; married Jean Ogborne (a company director), February 6, 1955; children: Huw. *Education:* University of Wales, B.Surg., 1954, M.R.C. Path., 1964, Diploma in Medical Jurisprudence, 1966, M.D., 1966. *Politics:* Welsh Nationalist. *Religion:* Agnostic. *Home:* Pontsarn, Ty Gwyn Cres, Penylan, Cardiff CF2 5JL, Wales. *Office:* Welsh National School of Medicine, Cardiff CF2 1SZ, Wales.

CAREER: Forensic pathologist, specializing in legal medicine, Cardiff, Wales, barrister-at-law, and writer. Has held various medical appointments dating from qualification in 1954; University of London, London, lecturer in forensic medicine, 1959-61; Welsh National School of Medicine (independent school of University of Wales), Cardiff, 1961-65; University of Newcastle, Newcastle-upon-Tyne, England, senior lecturer in forensic pathology, 1965-68; University of Wales, Cardiff, senior lecturer in forensic pathology, 1968—. Consultant pathologist to Home Office Forensic Laboratory, Cardiff, and National Museum of Wales; honorary consultant pathologist to National Health Service, 1965—. Director, Welsh Medical Press Ltd. *Military service:* British Army, Royal Army Medical Corps, pathologist in Malaya, 1956-59; became captain. Royal Army Medical Corps Reserve, 1959-64.

MEMBER: British Academy of Forensic Sciences, British Association of Forensic Medicine, Forensic Science Society, Society of Authors, Writers Guild of Great Britain, Crime Writers' Association.

WRITINGS: Legal Aspects of Medical Practice, Churchill-Livingstone, 1972; *Lion Rampant* (historical novel), R. Hale, 1972.

Under pseudonym Bernard Picton; fiction, except as noted: *The Lately Deceased,* Jenkins, 1963; *The Thread of Evidence,* R. Hale, 1965; *Mistress Murder,* R. Hale, 1966; *Russian Roulette,* R. Hale, 1968; *Policeman's Progress,* R. Hale, 1969; *Tiger at Bay,* R. Hale, 1971; *Murder, Suicide or Accident: The Forensic Pathologist at Work* (nonfiction), St. Martin's, 1971.

Contributor: Francis E. Camps, editor, *Gradwohl's Legal Medicine,* John Wright, 1968; Camps, editor, *Recent Advances in Forensic Pathology,* Churchill, 1969, Williams & Wilkins, 1970; Cyril H. Wecht, editor, *Legal Medicine Annual,* Appleton, 1971; Cesare G. Tedeschi, editor, *Trauma & Legal Medicine,* Saunders, 1974.

Radio and television dramas produced by British Broadcasting Corp.: "Corpus Delicti" (radio drama), 1970; "Murder in Capitals" (radio drama), 1971; "Deg i Dragwyddoldeb" (title means "Ten seconds to Eternity"; seven-episode television suspense serial in Welsh), 1972-73. Also writer of three-episode documentary on forensic and archaeological study of human bones produced by BBC, 1972.

Contributor of articles on legal medicine, criminology, Welsh politics, and allied topics to scientific journals, popular periodicals, and newspapers; also has reviewed books in categories within his fields.

WORK IN PROGRESS: Prince of America, a historical novel about Madoc, a Welsh prince who discovered the American mainland (site of Mobile, Ala.), in 1170; three TV documentaries about notorious British murder cases.

SIDELIGHTS: There have been four translations of Knight's crime novels—*Mistress Murder* into French and Danish and other books into Welsh and Spanish.

* * *

KNIGHT, Damon 1922-

PERSONAL: Born September 19, 1922, in Baker, Ore.; son of Frederick Stuart and Leola (Damon) Knight; married Gertrud Werndl; married Helen Schlaz; married Kate Wilhelm (a writer), February 23, 1963; children: Valerie, Christopher, Leslie, Jonathan. *Education:* Attended high school in Hood River, Ore. *Home address:* Box 8216, Madeira Beach, Fla. 33738. *Agent:* Robert P. Mills, 156 East 52nd St., New York, N.Y. 10022.

CAREER: Science fiction writer and editor. Milford Science Fiction Writers' Conference, co-founder, 1956, director, 1956—. *Member:* Science Fiction Writers of America (founder, 1965; president, 1965-66). *Awards, honors:* Hugo award from World science Convention, 1965, for best science fiction criticism.

WRITINGS—Novels: *Hell's Pavement,* Lion Press, 1955; *Masters of Evolution,* Ace Books, 1959; *The People Maker,* Zenith Books, 1959, published as *A for Anything,* Berkley Publishing, 1965; *The Sun Saboteurs* (bound with Wallis G. McDonald, *The Light of Lilith*), Ace Books, 1961; *Beyond the Barrier,* Doubleday, 1964; *Mind Switch,* Berkley Publishing, 1965, published as *The Other Foot,*

Whiting & Wheaton, 1965, M-B Publishing, 1971; *Three Novels: Rule Golden, Natural State, [and] The Dying Man,* Doubleday, 1967; *The Rithian Terror* (originally published as "Double Meaning," in *Startling Stories,* January, 1953), Universal Publishing & Distributing, 1972.

Collections—all stories, except as noted: *In Search of Wonder: Essays on Modern Science Fiction,* Advent, 1956, 2nd edition, 1967; *Far Out: 13 Science Fiction Stories,* Simon & Schuster, 1961; *In Deep,* Berkley Publishing, 1963; *Off Center,* Ace Books, 1965; *Turning On: Thirteen Stories,* Doubleday, 1966 (published in England as *Turning On: Fourteen Stories,* Gollancz, 1967); *World without Children [and] The Earth Quarter,* Lancer Books, 1970; *The Best of Damon Knight,* Pocket Books, 1974.

Editor of anthologies: *A Century of Science Fiction,* Simon & Schuster, 1962; *First Flight,* Lancer Books, 1963, published as *Now Begins Tomorrow,* 1969; *A Century of Great Short Science Fiction Novels,* Dial, 1964; *Tomorrow X 4,* Fawcett, 1964; *The Shape of Things,* Popular Library, 1965; (and translator) *Thirteen French Science-Fiction Stories,* Bantam, 1965; *The Dark Side,* Doubleday, 1965; *Beyond Tomorrow: Ten Science Fiction Adventures,* Harper, 1965; *Cities of Wonder,* Doubleday, 1966; *Nebula Award Stories 1965,* Doubleday, 1966; *Worlds to Come: Nine Science Fiction Adventures,* Harper, 1967; *Science Fiction Inventions,* Lancer Books, 1967; *Toward Infinity: Nine Science Fiction Tales,* Simon & Schuster, 1968; *One Hundred Years of Science Fiction,* Simon & Schuster, 1968; *The Golden Road,* Simon & Schuster, 1968; *The Metal Smile,* Belmont Books, 1968.

Dimension X: Five Science Fiction Novellas, Simon & Schuster, 1970; *First Contact,* Pinnacle Books, 1971; (and contributor) *A Pocketful of Stars,* Doubleday, 1971; *Perchance to Dream,* Doubleday, 1972; *A Science Fiction Argosy,* Simon & Schuster, 1972; *Tomorrow and Tomorrow,* Simon & Schuster 1973; *Happy Endings,* Bobbs-Merrill, 1974; *Best Stories from Orbit, Volumes 1-10,* Berkley Publishing, in press. Also editor of "Orbit" series, Volumes 1-13, Putnam, 1966-73, Volumes 14-15, Harper, 1974, Volume 16, Harper, in press.

Other writing: (Translator) Rene Barjavel, *Ashes, Ashes,* Doubleday, 1967; *Charles Fort: Prophet of the Unexplained* (biography), Doubleday, 1970; *A Shocking Thing,* Pocket Books, 1974. Several of Knight's novels have appeared in revised form in periodicals.

WORK IN PROGRESS: Science Fiction of the Thirties and *Westerns of the Forties,* both for Bobbs-Merrill; *The Art of Science Fiction,* for Harper; The *Futurians.*

SIDELIGHTS: Peter J. Henniker's comment that "the editorship of Damon Knight puts a sure stamp of quality" on an anthology, explains Knight's reputation in the realm of science fiction. Theodore Sturgeon discussed his editing further: "Scheduled to publish twice a year, [*Orbit*] is its own source: the stories are all new, and written expressly for it and its erudite and tasteful editor Damon Knight. He welcomes stories which disdain convention and taboos (and does not often get them), [and] is . . . willing . . . to court the unusual, the experimental, the literate, and (although his grip has not at all slackened on sf per se) the fantastic. Best of all, he has space for the unclassifiable—the kind of stories which used never to get published at all or, if they were, were doomed to flickering appearances in little quarterlies."

KNIGHT, Douglas M(aitland) 1921-

PERSONAL: Born June 8, 1921, in Cambridge, Mass.; son of Claude R. and Fanny (Douglas) Knight; married Grace Nichols, October 31, 1942; children: Christopher, Douglas Maitland, Thomas, Stephen. *Education:* Yale University, A.B., 1942, M.A., 1944, Ph.D., 1946. *Home:* Ridge Farm, Stockton, N.J. *Office:* 59 East 54th St., New York, N.Y. 10022.

CAREER: Yale University, New Haven, Conn., assistant professor of English literature, 1947-53; Lawrence University, Appleton, Wis., president, 1953-63; Duke University, Durham, N.C., president, 1963-69; RCA Corp., New York, N.Y., vice-president of Educational Development Division, 1969-73. Member of corporation of Massachusetts Institute of Technology, 1965-70; member of educational advisory committee of ESSO Education Foundation, 1966-70; chairman of President Johnson's National Advisory Commission on Libraries, 1966-68; member of board of trustees of United Negro College Fund, 1966—; member of board of directors of Salzburg Seminar, 1969—; chairman of overseas advisory board of Gondi Shapur University, 1971—. Associate fellow of Saybrook College of Yale University, 1946—. *Member:* Council on Foreign Relations, Century Association (New York), Cosmos Club (Washington, D.C.), Elizabethan Club (New Haven).

WRITINGS: Alexander Pope and the Heroic Tradition: A Critical Study of His Iliad, Yale University Press, 1951, Archon Books, 1969; *The Federal Government and Higher Education,* Yale University Press, 1960; (editor with E. Shepley Nourse) *Medical Ventures and the University: New Values and New Validities; Report of the Thirteenth Association of American Medical Colleges Institute,* Association of American Medical Colleges, 1967; (compiler) *Libraries at Large,* Bowker, 1970; *The Dark Gate* (poems), University of Texas Press, 1971. Contributor to journals.

WORK IN PROGRESS: The Longest Journey: Brief Studies in the Epic; a book of poems, *Works and Days; Logic to Live By: A Satiric Study of Current National Attitudes.*

* * *

KNIGHT, Frida 1910-

PERSONAL: Born November 11, 1910, in Cambridge, England; daughter of Hugh Fraser and Jessie (Crum) Stewart; married B.C.J.G. Knight (a professor), December 28, 1943; children: Sophia, Frances, James, Robert. *Education:* Attended Hoch's Konservatorium, 1928-30, and Royal College of Music, 1930-33. *Home:* 28 Park Parade, Cambridge CB5 8AL, England.

CAREER: Manchester University Settlement, Manchester, England, music organizer, 1933-35; Hull University College, Hull, England, lecturer in music, 1935-37; Spanish Relief Committee, London, England, concert organizer, 1937-39; war work in London, England, 1939-40; teacher of music and English in Reading, England, 1965-68; Citizens Advice Bureau, Reading, England, employee, 1968-69.

WRITINGS: Dawn Escape, Everybody's Books, 1943; (translator) Mihail Sadoveanu, *The Mud Hut Dwellers,* [Rumania], 1952; (translator) Sadoveanu, *Mitrea Cocor,* Fore Publications, 1953; *The Strange Case of Thomas Walker,* Lawrence & Wishart, 1956; (translator) I. L. Caragiale, *The Lost Letter* (play; produced on BBC "Third Programme," 1963), Lawrence & Wishart, 1956; *University Rebel,* Gollancz, 1971; *Beethoven & the Age of Revolu-*

tion, Lawrence & Wishart, 1973. Contributor to *Daily Telegraph* (London), *New Statesman, Times Educational Supplement, Cambridge Review,* and others.

WORK IN PROGRESS: Research on war-time France, "The Resistance."

* * *

KNIGHT, Ruth Adams 1898-1974

October 5, 1898—July 4, 1974; American editor, radio script writer, and author of historical novels and books for young adults. Obituaries: *New York Times,* July 7, 1974. (*CA*-5/6).

* * *

KNOX, Warren Barr 1925-

PERSONAL: Born August 22, 1925, in Whittier, Calif.; son of Lavern V. and Bertha (Barr) Knox; married Nancy Chambers, June 20, 1945; children: Charles Warren, John Warren. *Education:* Whittier College, B.A., 1949, M.A., 1951; attended Claremont Graduate School, 1950-53. *Home:* 16200 South Pacific, Apt. 24, Lake Oswego, Ore. 97034. *Office:* Reed College, Portland, Ore. 97202.

CAREER: High school teacher of science in the public schools of Montebello, Calif., 1950-52; Pomona College, Claremont, Calif., assistant to president, 1952-59; Whitman College, Walla Walla, Wash., vice-president, 1960-64; College of Idaho, Caldwell, president, 1964-73; Reed College, Portland, Ore., vice-president, 1973—. Boy Scouts of America, honorary member of national council, 1960—, vice-chairman of Oregon-Idaho council, 1964—; chairman of Rhodes Scholarship Selection for Idaho, 1965-69; member of Idaho Higher Education Advisory Council, Idaho delegation to National Compact for Education of America, and nexus committee of Presbyterian College Union, 1970—. *Military service:* U.S. Naval Reserve, 1942-45; served in the Pacific theater. *Member:* American Alumni Council, American College Public Relations Association, American Historical Association, Association of American Colleges, Intercollegiate Knights (honorary), Wisdom Society, English-Speaking Union, Western Historical Association, Kiwanis, Boise Art Association. *Awards, honors:* LL.D. from Whittier College, 1965.

WRITINGS: Eye of the Hurricane, Oregon State University Press, 1973. Contributor to *College and University Business, Liberal Education,* and *College and University Journal.*

WORK IN PROGRESS: Poems and verse; additional essays on college presidency; research on a volume concerning responsibilities of lay boards of trustees.

* * *

KOEPPEL, Gary 1938-

PERSONAL: Born January 20, 1938, in Albany, Ore.; son of Carl M. and Barbara (Adams) Koeppel. *Education:* Portland State College (now University), B.A., 1961; University of Iowa, M.F.A., 1963. *Home and office:* Coast Gallery, Big Sur, Calif. 93921.

CAREER: University of Puerto Rico, Rio Piedras, professor of English, 1963-64; Portland State College (now Portland State University), Portland, Ore., assistant professor of English; craftsman, 1968—; Coast Gallery, Big Sur, Calif., owner, 1971—. Member of board of directors, Big Sur Chamber of Commerce. *Member:* National Audubon Society, Big Sur Grange.

WRITINGS: Sculptured Sandcast Candles, Chilton, 1972.

WORK IN PROGRESS: Big Sur: Continent's End, completion expected in 1975.

SIDELIGHTS: "Writing," Koeppel told *CA,* "should come from felt experience, from the center of one's experience. One should have something new to say, and should say it as simply, as clearly, and as directly as possible."

* * *

KOETHE, John (Louis) 1945-

PERSONAL: Surname is pronounced *Kay*-tee; born December 25, 1945, in San Diego, Calif.; son of John Louis (a naval career officer) and Sara (Mehrer) Koethe; married Susan Muench (a research immunologist), September 1, 1968. *Education:* Princeton University, A.B., 1967; Harvard University, Ph.D., 1973. *Home:* 2129 East Kenwood Blvd., Milwaukee, Wis. 53211. *Office:* Department of Philosophy, University of Wisconsin-Milwaukee, Milwaukee, Wis. 53211.

CAREER: University of Wisconsin-Milwaukee, assistant professor of philosophy, 1973—. *Awards, honors:* Poet's Foundation Award, 1969; Frank O'Hare Award, 1973, for *Domes.*

WRITINGS: Blue Vents (poems), Audit/Poetry, 1969; *Domes* (poems), Columbia University Press, 1973. Contributor of poems and articles to *Poetry, Paris Review, Quarterly Review of Literature, Parnassus,* and *Art News.*

WORK IN PROGRESS: Poems; philosophical articles.

* * *

KOHLMEIER, Louis M(artin), Jr. 1926-

PERSONAL: Born February 17, 1926, in St. Louis, Mo.; son of Louis M., Sr. and Anita (Werling) Kohlmeier; married Barbara A. Wilson, November 15, 1958; children: Daniel Kimbrell, Ann Werling. *Education:* University of Missouri, B.J., 1950. *Home:* 5902 Madawaska Rd., Washington, D.C. 20016. *Office:* 932 National Press Bldg., Washington, D.C. 20004.

CAREER: Staff writer for *Wall Street Journal* in St. Louis, Mo. and Chicago, Ill., 1952-57; *St. Louis Globe-Democrat,* St. Louis, Mo., reporter, 1957-60; *Wall Street Journal,* Washington, D.C., reporter, 1960-72; Chicago-Tribune-New York News Syndicate Inc., Washington, D.C., columnist, 1973—. *Military service:* U.S. Army, 1950-52. *Member:* White House Correspondents Association, Sigma Delta Chi. *Awards, honors:* National Headliners Club award, 1959, for national reporting; Sigma Delta Chi award, 1964, for work as a Washington correspondent; Pulitzer Prize, 1964, for national reporting on the Federal Communications Commission.

WRITINGS: The Regulators: Watchdog Agencies and the Public Interest, Harper, 1969; *God Save This Honorable Court,* Scribner, 1972.

WORK IN PROGRESS: Research on public pension funds, financed by the Twentieth Century Fund of New York.

* * *

KOLAKOWSKI, Leszek 1927-

PERSONAL: Surname is pronounced Ko-wa-kow-ski; born October 23, 1927, in Radom, Poland; son of Jerzy (a publicist) and Lucyna (Pietrusiewicz) Kolakowski; married

Tamara Dynenson (a psychiatrist), November 19, 1949; children: Agnes. *Education:* University of Lodz, M.A., 1950; University of Warsaw, Ph.D., 1953. *Politics:* Member of Communist Party in Poland, 1945-66 (expelled, 1966). *Home:* 32 Highfield Ave., Oxford, England. *Agent:* Ernst W. Geisenheyner, Gymnasiumstrasse 31B, 7 Stuttgart, West Germany. *Office:* All Souls College, Oxford University, Oxford, England.

CAREER: University of Warsaw, Warsaw, Poland, 1950-68, started as assistant, professor of philosophy, 1964-68, head of history of modern philosophy section, 1959-68 (expelled from university for political reasons, March, 1968); McGill University, Montreal, Quebec, visiting professor of philosophy, 1968-69; University of California, Berkeley, visiting professor of philosophy, 1969-70; All Souls College, Oxford University, Oxford, England, senior research fellow in philosophy, 1970—. Research professor at Institute of Philosophy, Polish Academy of Sciences, 1956-68. *Member:* International Institute of Philosophy, American Academy of Arts and Sciences (honorary member). *Awards, honors:* Jarzykowski Foundation Award (New York), 1969.

WRITINGS: Szkice o filozofi katolickiej (title means "Sketches of Catholic Philosophy"; collection of essays), Panstwowe Wydawnictwo Naukowe, 1955; *Wyklady o filozofi sredniowiecznej* (title means "Lectures on Medieval Philosophy"), Panstwowe Wydawnictwo Naukowe, 1956; *Swiatopoglad i zycie codzienne* (title means "World-View and Everyday Life"; collection of essays), Panstwowy Instytut Wydawniczy, 1957; *Jednostka i nieskonczonosc: Wolnosc i antynomie wolnosci w filozofi Spinozy* (title means "The Individual and the Infinite: Freedom and the Antinomies of Freedom in Spinoza's Philosophy"), Panstwowe Wydawnictwo Naukowe, 1958.

Notatki o wspolczesnej kontrreformacji (title means "Notes on the Contemporary Counter-Reformation"; collection of essays) Ksiazka i Wiedza, 1962; *13 bajek z krolestwa Lailonii dla duzych i malych* (title means "Thirteen Fables from the Kingdom of Lailonia for Grownups and Children"), Czytelnik, 1963; *Klucz niebieski albo opowiesci budujace z historii swietej zebrane ku pouczeniu i przestrodze* (title means "The Key to Heaven, or, Edifying Tales from Holy Scripture as a Lesson and Warning"), Panstwowy Instytut Wydawniczy, 1964, translation by Salvator Attanasio published with Celina Wieniewska's translation of *Rozmowy z diablem* as *The Key to Heaven* [and] *Conversations with the Devil,* Grove, 1973; *Rozmowy z diablem* (collection of essays), Panstwowy Instytut Wydawniczy, 1965 [supra for English translation]; *Swiadomosc religijna i wiez koscielna: Studia nad chrzescijanstwem bezwyznaniowym siedemnastego wieku* (title means "Religious Consciousness and the Ties of the Church: Studies in the Non-Denominational Christianity of the Seventeenth Century"), Panstwowe Wydawnictwo Naukowe, 1965; *Filozofia pozytywistyczna: Od Hume'a do Kola Wiedenskiego* (title means "Positivist Philosophy: From Hume to the Vienna Circle"), Panstwowe Wydawnictwo Naukowe, 1966, translation by Norbert Guterman published as *The Alienation of Reason: A History of Positivist Thought,* Doubleday, 1968, reprinted as *Positivist Philosophy,* Penguin, 1972; *Kultura i fetysze: Zbior rozpraw* (title means "Culture and Fetishes"; collection of essays), Panstwowe Wydawnictwo Naukowe, 1967.

Selections of essays and other writings, most first published in Polish, but with contents varying from any title above: *Der Mensch ohne Alternative: Von der Moeglichkeit und Unmoeglichkeit Marxist zu Sein* (German translations by Wanda Bronska-Pampuch of eleven essays), Piper, 1960, revised edition, 1967; *Filozofski eseji* (Serbo-Croation translations by Svetozar Nikolic of eight essays), Nolit, 1964; *Al ha-reshut ha-netunah: Mivhar masot* (title means "On the Possibility of Choice"; Hebrew translations by Mordecai Dekel and others of twelve essays), Sifriyat Po 'alim, 1964; *Traktat ueber die Sterblichkeit der Vernunft* (German translations by Peter Lachmann of nine essays), Piper, 1967; *Toward a Marxist Humanism: Essays on the New Left Today* (translations by Jane Zielonko Peel of eight essays), Grove, 1968 (published in England as *Marxism and Beyond: On Historical Understanding and Individual Responsibility,* Pall Mall, 1969); *Gespraeche mit dem Teufel: Acht Diskurse ueber das Boese und zwei Stuecke* (German translations by Janusz von Pilecki of *Conversations with the Devil,* "Expulsion from Paradise," and "Father Jensen's System" [q.v.]), Piper, 1968. English translations of another selection of writings were published as "A Leszek Kolakowski Reader," special (entire) issue of *TriQuarterly,* Number 22, fall, 1971.

Dramatic works: "Wygnanie z raju" (title means "Expulsion from Paradise"; scenario), first published in *Dialog,* Number 6, 1961; "System ksiedza Jensena albo wejscie i wyjscie" (title means "Father Jensen's System, or Entrance and Exit"; two-act farce), first produced in Warsaw, 1962, but withdrawn after a short run; later broadcast in English by British Broadcasting Corp.; "Zebrak i ladna dziewczyna" (title means "The Beggar and the Pretty Girl"; three scenes), first published in *Dialog,* Number 11, 1965, English translation by Nicholas Bethell published in *TriQuarterly,* Number 22, 1971.

Editor: (And author of introduction and notes) *Filozofia XVII wieku: Francja, Holandia, Niemcy* (title means "Seventeenth-Century Philosophy: France, Holland, Germany"), Panstwowe Wydawnictwo Naukowe, 1959; (with Krzysztof Pomian) *Filozofia Egzystencjalna* (title means "Existential Philosophy"), Panstwowe Wydawnictwo Naukowe, 1965. Also editor of *Z dziejow polskiej mysli filozoficznej i spolecznej* (title means "From the History of Polish Philosophical and Social Thought"), published 1956.

Contributor: *Swiatopogladowe i metodologiczne problemy abstrakcji naukowej* (title means "Problems of Scientific Abstraction from the Standpoint of World-View and Methodology"), [Warsaw], 1957; Pawel Mayewski, editor, *The Broken Mirror: A Collection of Writings from Contemporary Poland,* Random House, 1958; *Fragmenty filozoficzne: Seria druga* (title means "Philosophical Fragments: Second Series"), Panstwowe Wydawnictwo Naukowe, 1959; Paul Dibon, editor, *Pierre Bayle: Le philosophe de Rotterdam,* Vrin (Paris), 1959; K. A. Jelenski, editor, *La realta dell'ottobre polacco,* Silva (Milan), 1961; Arthur Mendel, editor, *Essential Works of Marxism,* Bantam, 1961; Leopold Labedz, editor, *Revisionism: Essays on the History of Marxist Ideas,* Praeger, 1962; Maria Kuncewicz, editor, *The Modern Polish Mind,* Little, Brown, 1962; *Filozofia i socjologia XX wieku* (title means "Twentieth-Century Philosophy and Sociology), [Warsaw], 1962; *Religie racjonalne: Studia z filozofii religii XV-XVII* (title means "Rational Religions: Studies in the Philosophy of Religion of the Fifteenth to Seventeenth Centuries"), Archive of the History of Philosophy and Social Thought (Warsaw), 1963; Frank Benseler, editor, *Festschrift zum achzigsten Geburtstag von Georg Lukacs,* Luchterhand (Berlin), 1965; Maurice Condillac, Lucien Goldmann, and Jean Piaget, editors, *Entretiens sur les notions de genese et de struc-*

ture, Mouton & Co., 1965; George Novack, editor, *Existentialism versus Marxism,* Dell, 1966; *Fragmenty filozoficzne: Seria trzecia* (title means "Philosophical Fragments: Third Series"), Panstwowe Wydawnictwo Naukowe, 1967; George Goemoeri and Charles Newman, editors, *New Writing of East Europe,* Quadrangle, 1968; Carl Oglesby, editor, *The New Left Reader,* Grove, 1969; Leonhard Reinisch, editor, *Vom Sinn der Tradition,* Beck (Munich), 1970.

Author of introductions to ten Polish editions of works of Spinoza, Bergson, Pascal, Erasmus, and other scholars, 1954-66, and translator of Spinoza's *Correspondence* and *Early Writings* into Polish.

Contributor to *Stownik filozofow* (title means "Dictionary of Philosophers"), Pantswowe Wydawnictwo Naukowe, 1966. Contributor to journals in Poland and other countries, including *Evergreen Review, Les Temps Modernes* (France), *Hid* (Yugoslavia), *Gorkaya zhatva* (Russia), *Forum* (Vienna), and *Socialist Register* (London). Member of editorial board, *Nowa Kultura* (weekly newspaper), 1956-57; editor, *Studia Filozoficzne* (journal), 1957-59.

WORK IN PROGRESS: The Presence of Myth; and a history of Marxist doctrine.

SIDELIGHTS: Kolakowski speaks, reads, and writes ("badly") in French, English, and German. He also is able to read Russian, Dutch, and Latin.

BIOGRAPHICAL/CRITICAL SOURCES: George L. Kline, editor, *European Philosophy Today,* Quadrangle, 1965; *TriQuarterly,* Number 22, fall, 1971.

* * *

KOLLER, James 1936-

PERSONAL: Born May 30, 1936, in Oak Park, Ill.; son of James and Elsie (Clark) Koller; children: Deirdre, Jessie Aldebaran, Jedediah Swift. *Education:* North Central College, B.A., 1958. *Home address:* P.O. Box 629, Brunswick, Me. 04011.

AWARDS, HONORS: National Endowment for the Arts fellowship, 1973.

WRITINGS: Two Hands, Poems 1959-61, James B. Smith, 1965; *The Dogs and Other Dark Woods* (poems), Four Seasons Foundation, 1966; *Some Cows, Poems of Civilization and Domestic Life,* Coyote, 1966; *California Poems,* Black Sparrow, 1971; *Messages,* Institute of Further Studies, 1972. Editor of *Coyote's Journal,* 1964—, and *Coyote Books,* 1964—.

WORK IN PROGRESS: Two short novels, *Shannon, Who Was Lost Before* and *If You Don't Like Me You Can Leave Me Alone.*

* * *

KOONTS, Jones Calvin 1924-

PERSONAL: Born September 19, 1924, in Lexington, N.C.; son of Harvey Hill (a lawyer) and Elsie M. (Tussey) Koonts; married Cortlandt Morper (an associate professor of music), September 6, 1953; children: Carlisle Woodson, Camille Walton. *Education:* Catawba College, A.B. (magna cum laude), 1945; George Peabody College for Teachers, M.A., 1949, Ph.D., 1958; Harvard University, postdoctoral study, 1960. *Politics:* Democrat. *Religion:* Presbyterian. *Address:* Box 163, Erskine College, Due West, S.C. 29639.

CAREER: High school teacher of English and social studies in Salisbury, N.C., 1945-48; Erskine College, Due West, S.C., professor of education and psychology, 1949-51; George Peabody College for Teachers, Nashville, Tenn., assistant to director of student teaching, 1951-52; Erskine College, professor of education and psychology, 1952—, head of department of education, 1953—. Member of South Carolina State Board of Education, 1966-71; commissioner, Piedmont Technical Education Center, 1972—. Has given poetry readings at southern colleges and in Missouri and Pennsylvania.

MEMBER: National Education Association, Association of Teacher Educators (South Carolina representative on national assembly), Academy of American Poets (fellow), Southern Council on Teacher Education, South Carolina Association for Student Teaching (founder; president, 1955-56), South Carolina State Council on Teacher Education, South Carolina College Teachers of Education, South Carolina Education Association, Sigma Pi Alpha, Kappa Delta Pi, Phi Delta Kappa. *Awards, honors:* Peabody-Harvard, 1960; Distinguished Alumnus Award, Catawba College, 1966; William Gilmore Simms Poetry Prize from Poetry Society of South Carolina, 1973.

WRITINGS—Poems: *Straws in the Wind,* State Printing Co. (Columbia, S.C.), 1968; *Under the Umbrella,* Sandlapper Press, 1971; (editor) *Green Leaves in January* (collection of student poems), Jacobs Press, 1972. Poems included in *National Poetry Anthology,* 1957, 1959, 1960, and annually, 1962-67. Also author of "I'm Living in a Dream" (song), published in 1947, and *Since Promontory,* privately printed.

WORK IN PROGRESS: A new collection of his own poems.

* * *

KOPULOS, Stella 1906-

PERSONAL: Born November 15, 1906, in Washington, D.C.; daughter of Chris (a fruit specialist) and Mary (Bolos) Sianis; married Demetrios Kopulos, January 21, 1922 (died, March 5, 1959); children: Maria Kopulos Snyder, Renee Kopulos Todd. *Education:* Privately tutored. *Religion:* Greek Orthodox. *Residence:* Washington, D.C.

CAREER: Pastry specialist, caterer, lecturer, and convention exhibitor of foods and crafts. *Member:* International Hosters for General Federation of Women's Clubs, International Platform Association, Salvation Army, Greek Women's Club, Daughters of Penelope (founder, 1931; past president), Business and Professional Women's Club, Elpiniki Pan Arcadian Federation (Washington, D.C.; founder, 1943; past president), Southeast Women's Club (Washington, D.C.; founder, 1958). *Awards, honors:* Greek Government award, 1950; Mother of the Year Award for Washington, D.C., 1962; United Nations Humanitarian Award, 1973.

WRITINGS: Adventures in Greek Cookery, World Publishing, 1966, revised edition, Crowell, 1972.

WORK IN PROGRESS: A book of original Greek recipes with folk stories.

* * *

KOSKOFF, David E(lihu) 1939-

PERSONAL: Born June 9, 1939, in New Britain, Conn.; son of Milton M. and Gertrude (Farber) Koskoff; married

Charlotte Goldstein (a teacher), April 11, 1965. *Education:* Yale University, B.A., 1961, LL.B., 1965. *Politics:* Democrat. *Religion:* Jewish. *Home:* 8 River Edge Ct., Plainville, Conn. 06062. *Agent:* Oscar Collier, 280 Madison Ave., New York, N.Y. *Office:* 73 East Main St., Plainville, Conn. 06062.

CAREER: Attorney at law in Plainville, Conn., 1965—.

WRITINGS: Joseph P. Kennedy: A Life and Times, Prentice-Hall, 1974.

* * *

KOSTYU, Frank A(lexander) 1919-

PERSONAL: Born August 3, 1919, in Lorain, Ohio; son of Frank Joseph (a steelworker) and Julia (Yager) Kostyu; married Marjorie Ann Butcher (a schoolteacher), June 11, 1944; children: Joel, Paul, Kathryn. *Education:* Heidelberg College, B.A., 1943; Eden Theological Seminary, B.D., 1945; Oberlin College, S.T.M., 1962. *Politics:* Democrat. *Office:* A. D. Publications, Inc., 475 Riverside Dr., #1840, New York, N.Y. 10027.

CAREER: Ordained United Church of Christ minister, 1945; pastor in Dayton, Ohio, 1946-50, West Alexandria, Ohio, 1950-56, Alliance, Ohio, 1956-62, and Blue Island, Ill., 1962-64; *A.D. Magazine,* New York, N.Y., senior editor, 1964—. *Awards, honors:* Freedoms Foundation awards, 1961, 1962, for sermons; several exhibition awards for photographs.

WRITINGS: Pathways to Personal Contentment, Prentice-Hall, 1960; *Power to Get What You Want out of Life,* Prentice-Hall, 1964; *Shadows in the Valley,* Doubleday, 1970; *How to Spark Your Marriage When the Kids Leave Home,* Pilgrim Press, 1972; *Sparks for Your Church Program,* Abingdon, 1974.

WORK IN PROGRESS: Fourteen Ideas to Change Your Life, Our United Church of Christ Heritage, and a photographic book on loneliness, with text, completion of all three expected in 1974.

* * *

KOTKER, Zane 1934-

PERSONAL: Born January 2, 1934, in Waterbury, Conn.; daughter of Edward S. (a clergyman) and Jean (Cadwallader) Hickcox; married Norman Richard Kotker (a writer and editor), June 7, 1965; children: David, Ariel. *Education:* Middlebury College, B.A., 1956; Columbia University, M.A., 1960. *Home:* 490 West End Ave., New York, N.Y. 10024.

CAREER: Waterbury Republican-American, Waterbury, Conn., reporter, 1957-58; *New England Review,* New Haven, Conn., co-editor and publisher, 1960-63; Silver-Burdett Co., Morristown, N.J., editor, 1963-66; Harcourt Brace Jovanovich, New York, N.Y., department head, 1966-69; writer, 1969—. *Awards, honors:* Fellowship from National Endowment for the Arts, 1974.

WRITINGS: Bodies in Motion (novel), Knopf, 1972. Contributor of short stories and articles to *Redbook, New York, Ms., Galaxy,* and *Elima.*

WORK IN PROGRESS: A second novel.

* * *

KOZER, Jose 1940-

PERSONAL: Born March 28, 1940, in Havana, Cuba; son of David (a businessman) and Ana (Katz) Kozer; married Sheila Isaac, September 1, 1962 (divorced, November, 1973); children: Mia. *Education:* Havana University, student, 1959-60; New York University, B.A., 1965; Queens College of the City University of New York, M.A., 1971. *Home:* 123-35 82nd Rd., Apt. 2G, Kew Gardens, N.Y. 11415. *Office:* Department of Romance Languages, Queens College of the City University of New York, Flushing, N.Y. 11367.

CAREER: Queens College of the City University of New York, Flushing, lecturer in Romance languages, 1965—. Free-lance translator, English into Spanish. *Member:* Phi Lambda Beta. *Awards, honors:* Gulbenkian fellow in Lisbon, summer, 1967.

WRITINGS: Padres y otras profesiones (title means "Parents and Other Professions"), Villa Miseria, 1972; *Por la libre* (title means "Moving Free"), Bayu-Menorah, 1973; *Poemas de Guadalupe* (title means "Poems by Guadalupe"), Editorial por la poesia, 1973. Contributor of poems, short stories, and essays to more than seventy literary magazines throughout the world.

WORK IN PROGRESS: Fuera de Cuba (title means "Outside Cuba"), a book of poetry on Cuban-Jewish themes; short stories; further writing in diary, now seven volumes, for projected biographical novel.

* * *

KRAGEN, Jinx
See MORGAN, Judith A(dams)

* * *

KRASNER, Jack Daniel 1921-

PERSONAL: Born June 10, 1921, in Atlanta, Ga.; son of Samuel (a merchant) and Dora (Gershman) Krasner; married Selma Levine (a travel agent), June 18, 1948; children: Stephen, Michael. *Education:* Atlanta Junior College, student, 1940-41; University of Georgia, B.S., 1945; New York University, M.A., 1950, Ph.D., 1952. *Politics:* Independent. *Religion:* Jewish. *Home and office:* 388 Lydecker St., Englewood, N.J. 07631.

CAREER: Mount Sinai Hospital, New York, N.Y., intern in psychology, 1948-50, assistant clinical psychologist, 1950-53; Postgraduate Center for Psychotherapy, New York, N.Y., fellow-in-training, 1952-55, psychologist, 1955-57, senior psychologist, 1957-61, associate supervisor, 1961-63, senior supervisor and lecturer, 1963—Fairleigh Dickinson University, Rutherford, N.J., adjunct associate professor, 1965-67, assistant professor of psychology, 1967-71; Iona College, New Rochelle, N.Y., associate professor, Graduate Division of Pastoral Counseling, 1968—. Private practice of psychoanalysis in Englewood, N.J., 1956—; attending clinical psychologist, Englewood Hospital, 1956-60; director of group psychotherapy, New Jersey Center for Psychotherapy, 1961—. *Military service:* U.S. Army Air Forces, 1942-43.

MEMBER: American Psychological Association (secretary of Division 29, 1972—), American Group Psychotherapy Association (fellow), New Jersey Psychotherapy Association (president, 1970-71), New York Society of Clinical Psychologists. *Awards, honors:* Gralnick Award of Postgraduate Center for Psychotherapy, 1957.

WRITINGS: (Contributor) P. H. Hoch and Joseph Zubin, editors, *Relationship of Psychological Tests to Psychiatry,*

Grune, 1952; (with Asya L. Kadis and others) *A Practicum of Group Psychotherapy,* Hoeber, 1963; (contributor) J. L. Moreno, editor, *The International Handbook of Group Psychotherapy,* Philosophical Library, 1966; (with Jules Barron and Benjamin Fabrikant) *Psychotherapy: A Psychological Perspective,* Selected Academic Readings, 1971. Contributor to journals. Editor, *New Jersey Psychologist.*

WORK IN PROGRESS: Psychodynamics of Dental Health and Treatment (tentative title), for C. C Thomas; *To Enjoy is to Live,* with Barron and Fabrikant, for Nelson-Hall.

* * *

KRAUSE, Herbert 1905-

PERSONAL: Born May 25, 1905, in Fergus Falls, Minn.; son of Arthur Adolph (a farmer and blacksmith) and Bertha (Peters) Krause. *Education:* St. Olaf College, B.A., 1933; University of Iowa, M.A., 1935. *Politics:* Independent. *Residence:* Sioux Falls, S.D. *Office:* Department of English, Augustana College, Sioux Falls, S.D. 57102.

CAREER: University of Iowa, Iowa City, instructor in English, 1938-39; Augustana College, Sioux Falls, S.D., professor of English, 1939—, chairman of department, 1939-45, writer-in-residence, 1945—, director of Center for Western Studies, 1970—. Fulbright lecturer at University of the Witwatersrand and University of Natal, 1961; Rockefeller visiting professor at University of the Philippines, 1966-69; lecturer at American universities, and for National Audubon Society, 1963.

MEMBER: Western History Association, Western Literature Association (member of executive council, 1971-74), Champlain Society, Hudson's Bay Record Society, South Dakota History Society, Wisconsin Historical Society, Minnesota Historical Society, South Dakota Ornithologists' Union (president, 1958-59; member of board of directors, 1960-65). *Awards, honors:* Bread Loaf Writers' Conference fellowship, 1937; Friends of American Writers Award, 1939, for *Wind Without Rain;* American Association for the Advancement of Science grant to compile the literature of South Dakota ornithology, 1958; various commissions to write commemorative poems, including one for Minnesota Statehood Centennial, 1958; Litt.D., Augustana College, Sioux Falls, 1970.

WRITINGS: Wind Without Rain (novel), Bobbs-Merrill, 1939; *Neighbor Boy* (poems), Midland House, 1939; *The Thresher* (novel), Bobbs-Merrill, 1945; *The Oxcart Trail* (novel), Bobbs-Merrill, 1954; *Myth and Reality on the High Plains,* Art Press, 1963; *Ornithology of the Great Plains,* Art Press, 1964; *The Canada Warbler,* Laboratory of Ornithology, Cornell University, 1965; (contributor) Olin Sewall Pettingill, editor, *The Bird Watcher's America,* McGraw, 1965; *The Half-Horse Alligator,* University of the Philippines Press, 1968; *The McCowan Longspur,* reprinted, Benipayo (Manila), 1968; (editor) *Fiction 151,* Benipayo, 1968; (with Gary Olson) *Prelude to Glory: Custer in the Blackhills,* Brevet Press, 1974. Contributor to "Bent's Life Histories of North American Birds"; contributor to ornithological journals. Regional editor, National Audubon Society *Field Notes,* 1958-60.

WORK IN PROGRESS: The Bald Eagle: A Vanishing Species and a Vanishing Symbol, for McGraw; editing, *Environment in Crisis;* research on a continental approach to American writing; other studies on the influence of the frontier on American writing and on American wars and American life.

SIDELIGHTS: Krause says that his most important motivation has been the "conflict between great talent or beauty (the artistic, for instance) and destructive circumstance, whether in human life or in the intrusion of thoughtless humanity upon unspoiled environments. . ." He did field research on the behavior of the Canada Warbler at the University of Michigan Biological Station, 1958-59, and has been conducting research on the bald eagle since 1966. His section of *The Bird Watcher's America* was on the Black Hills of South Dakota.

BIOGRAPHICAL/CRITICAL SOURCES: Roy W. Meyer, *The Middle Western Farm Novel in the Twentieth Century,* University of Nebraska Press, 1965.

* * *

KRAVITZ, Nathan
See KRAVITZ, Nathaniel

* * *

KRAVITZ, Nathaniel 1905-
(Naphthali Ben-Horav, Nathan Kravitz)

PERSONAL: Surname legally changed; born February 12, 1905, in Bessarabia, Romania; came to United States in 1923; became U.S. citizen; son of Moshe (a rabbi) and Lea (Ravrebe) Krivitsky; married Anna Greenberg, December 24, 1924; children: Morris A. *Education:* Studied at Odessa Academy for Higher Jewish Studies, 1919-22, and University of Bucharest, 1922-23. *Religion:* Jewish Orthodox. *Home:* 6457 North Artesian, Chicago, Ill. 60645. *Agent:* Benjamin Fain, 127 North Dearborn, Chicago, Ill. 60602.

CAREER: Jewish Daily World, Philadelphia, Pa., editor, 1924-39; *Daily Jewish Courier,* Chicago, Ill., editor, 1939-45; *Jewish Way Publication,* Chicago, publisher and editor, 1945-69. *Member:* Authors Guild, Authors League of America, Jewish Writers Union, Labor Zionist Alliance, World Jewish Bible Society, Israel Society for Biblical Research, Society for the Advancement of Hebrew (sponsor), YIVO Institute for Jewish Research (sponsor).

WRITINGS—All under name Nathan Kravitz, except as indicated: *Funem Shturem* (title means "Out of the Storm"), [Philadelphia], 1937; (under pseudonym Naphthali Ben-Horav) *Torah Lernen Bei Yidden* (title means "Studying the Torah"), [Chicago], 1943; *The People of the Book,* International Printing Co., 1945; *Zaquta the Seer,* translated from Yiddish by William Shure, Vantage, 1952; (compiler) *Sayings of the Fathers* (anthology), two volumes, Ophir, 1952, 2nd edition, 1969; *Genesis: A New Interpretation of the First Three Chapters,* Philosophical Library, 1967; *Three Thousand Years of Hebrew Literature,* Swallow Press, 1972. Contributor, sometimes under pseudonyms, to *Canader Adler, Toronto Journal, Americaner, Polisher Yid, Chicago Yom-Tov Bletter, Chicago Magazine,* and other publications.

WORK IN PROGRESS: Understanding Hassidism and Kabalah; System of Biblical Vocalization and Accentuation; King Solomon's Loves, a historical novel.

SIDELIGHTS: Kravitz is expert in Yiddish, Hebrew, Russian, Spanish, French, Arabic, Aramaic, and German.

* * *

KRETZMANN, Norman 1928-

PERSONAL: Born November 4, 1928, in Chicago, Ill.; son of Adalbert Raphael (a clergyman) and Josephine (Heidelberg) Kretzmann; married Barbara Ensign, July 22, 1957; children: Anita, Maria, Julia. *Education:* Attended Concordia Collegiate Institute, Bronxville, N.Y., 1942-48; Valparaiso University, B.A., 1949; Johns Hopkins University, Ph.D., 1953. *Home:* 117 Brandon Pl., Ithaca, N.Y. 14850. *Office:* Sage School of Philosophy, Cornell University, Ithaca, N.Y. 14850.

CAREER: Bryn Mawr College, Bryn Mawr, Pa., lecturer in philosophy, 1953-54; Ohio State University, Columbus, instructor, 1954-57, assistant professor, 1957-60; University of Illinois, Urbana, assistant professor, 1960-64, associate professor of philosophy, 1964-66; Cornell University, Ithaca, N.Y., associate professor, 1966-68, professor of philosophy, 1968—, chairman of Sage School of Philosophy, 1970—. Visiting fellow at Balliol College, Oxford, 1969-70. *Member:* American Philosophical Association, Mediaeval Academy of America. *Awards, honors:* National Endowment for the Humanities fellowship, 1969-70; faculty fellow, Society for the Humanities at Cornell, 1974.

WRITINGS: Elements of Formal Logic, Bobbs-Merrill, 1965.

Editor and translator: William Shirwood, *William of Sherwood's Introduction to Logic,* University of Minnesota Press, 1966; Shirwood, *William of Sherwood's Treatise on Syncategorematic Words,* University of Minnesota Press, 1968; (with Marilyn Adams) William Ockham, *Predestination, God's Foreknowledge, and Future Contingents,* Appleton, 1969.

Philosophical Review, co-editor, 1968-69, managing editor, 1970—; co-editor of "Synthese Historical Library," 1969—.

WORK IN PROGRESS: With wife, Barbara Ensign Kretzmann, *The Sophismata of Richard Kilmington,* completion expected in 1976.

* * *

KROCK, Arthur 1887-1974

November 16, 1887—April 11, 1974; American journalist, political commentator, editor, and author. Obituaries: *New York Times,* April 13, 1974; *Washington Post,* April 14, 1974; *Newsweek,* April 22, 1974; *Time,* April 22, 1974; *Current Biography,* June, 1974; *AB Bookman's Weekly,* July 15, 1974. (*CA*-33/36).

* * *

KROLL, Morton 1923-

PERSONAL: Born March 14, 1923, in New York, N.Y.; son of Samuel and Sarah (Silverstein) Kroll; married Florence Betty Rubinfier (a free-lance writer), March 3, 1944; children: James A. B., John J., Julie A. *Education:* University of California, Los Angeles, B.A., 1946, Ph.D., 1952. *Religion:* Jewish. *Home:* 19559 38th Ave. N.E., Seattle, Wash. 98155. *Office:* College of Arts and Sciences, University of Washington, GN-15, Seattle, Wash. 98155.

CAREER: Central Oregon Community College, Bend, assistant professor of political science, 1950-51; University of Oregon, Eugene, assistant professor of political science, 1951-54; Wayne State University, Detroit, Mich., assistant professor of political science, 1954-56; Pacific Northwest Library Association, Seattle, Wash., director of library development project, 1956-58; University of Washington, Seattle, acting associate professor, 1958-60, assistant professor, 1960-62, associate professor, 1962-68, professor of public affairs and political science, 1968—, director of Division of Correspondence Study, 1960-64, associate dean of College of Arts and Sciences, 1970—. Smith-Mundt visiting professor at University College of the West Indies, Trinidad, 1962-63; Fulbright-Hays visiting professor and acting head of department of government at University of West Indies, 1966-67. Consultant to Pennsylvania, New Jersey, Delaware Corp. (PENJERDEL), 1960-61; field research director for research project in mental health administration for National Institute of Mental Health, 1964-66. *Military service:* U.S. Army Air Forces, 1943-46; became colonel.

MEMBER: Society for International Development, American Society for Public Administration, American Political Science Association, Western Political Science Association, Northwest Political Science Association.

WRITINGS: (With James R. Donoghue and James Trump) *Fire Protection,* Haynes Foundation, 1952; (contributor) Charles P. Schleicher, editor, *Introduction to International Relations,* Prentice-Hall, 1954; (editor) *Libraries and Librarians of the Pacific Northwest,* University of Washington Press, 1960; (editor) *Elementary and Secondary School Libraries of the Pacific Northwest,* University of Washington Press, 1960; (editor) *College, University, and Special Libraries of the Pacific Northwest,* University of Washington Press, 1961; (with Robert H. Connery) *The Politics of Mental Health,* Columbia University Press, 1968; (with Fremont J. Lyden and George A. Shipman) *Policies, Decisions, and Organizations,* Appleton, 1969. Author of pamphlets. Contributor to *Social Science, Social and Economic Studies,* and *Public Administration Review.* Associate editor, *Western Political Quarterly;* senior editor, *Administration and Society;* editor, *SICA Newsletter* (of Section on International and Comparative Administration; American Society for Public Administration).

WORK IN PROGRESS: The Politics of the Policy Process; The Politics of Higher Education in Britain, completion expected in 1975; a spy novel, *London Broil,* 1975.

AVOCATIONAL INTERESTS: Travel, photography.

* * *

KROPF, Linda S(toddart) 1947-

PERSONAL: Born July 11, 1947, in Rochester, N.Y.; daughter of Gerald Robert and Luella (Knapp) Stoddart; married Daniel Michel Kropf (a banker), August 23, 1969; children: Michael David. *Education:* Stephens College, A.A., 1967; Colorado Woman's College, B.A., 1968; State University of New York College at Geneseo, M.L.S., 1970. *Home:* Seestrasse 153a, 8800 Thalwil, Switzerland; and 96 Eagle Ridge Circle, Rochester, N.Y. 14617.

CAREER: Ontario Department of Trade and Development, Toronto, Ontario, technical library assistant, 1969-70; University of Florida, Gainesville, librarian and library science instructor, 1970-72; free-lance writer. *Member:* American Library Association, La Leche League, Beta Phi Mu.

WRITINGS: Publishing in Switzerland: The Press and the Book Trade, Libraries Unlimited, 1973. Contributor to *Journal of Library History, Philosophy and Comparative Librarianship.*

WORK IN PROGRESS: Libraries and Librarianship in Switzerland, completion expected in 1976; research on publishing in multilingual nations, on comparative librarianship, and on the American abroad.

KRUEGER, Ralph R. 1927-

PERSONAL: Born March 10, 1927, in Zurich, Ontario, Canada; son of Elmer G. and Myrtle (Horner) Krueger; married B. June Hambly (a speech teacher), June 30, 1949; children: Karen, Colleen. *Education:* London Teacher's College, student, 1943-44; University of Western Ontario, B.A., 1952, M.A., 1955; Indiana University, Ph.D., 1959. *Home:* 743 Glasgow Rd., Kitchener, Ontario, Canada. *Office:* Department of Geography, University of Waterloo, Waterloo, Ontario, Canada.

CAREER: Wayne State University, Detroit, Mich., lecturer in geography, 1957-59; Waterloo Lutheran University, Waterloo, Ontario, associate professor of geography and chairman of department, 1959-62; University of Waterloo, Waterloo, Ontario, professor of geography, 1962—, chairman of department of geography and planning, 1962-70. Member of Waterloo County Area Planning Board, 1965-72. *Member:* Canadian Association of Geographers.

WRITINGS: (With Ray G. Corder) *Canada: A New Geography,* Holt, 1968; (editor with Anton deVos, Norman Pearson, and Frederic Sargent) *Regional and Resource Planning in Canada,* Holt, 1963, revised edition, 1971; (editor with Charles Bryfogle) *Urban Problems: A Canadian Reader,* Holt, 1971.

WORK IN PROGRESS: A monograph, *Regional Disparities and Regional Development in Canada,* sponsored by Canada Studies Foundation and Canadian Association of Geographers.

* * *

KRUSICH, Walter S(teve) 1922-

PERSONAL: Surname is pronounced *Kru*-sick; born February 12, 1922, in East Chicago, Ind.; son of Steve (a production engineer) and Jennie (Marta) Krusich; married Loretta M. Sells, April 22, 1947; children: Stephen, Karen, Beth, Naomi. *Education:* Indiana University, student, 1947-48; Columbia College, Chicago, Ill., B.A., 1951; Temple University, M.Ed., 1966. *Religion:* Protestant. *Home:* 315 Kimbell Ave., Elmhurst, Ill. 60126. *Office:* American Business Men's Research Foundation, 599 North York Rd., Elmhurst, Ill. 60126.

CAREER: American Business Men's Research Foundation, Elmhurst, Ill., executive director, 1967—. Has taught at Joliet Junior College, and lectured in India; attended First International Congress for the Prevention of Alcoholism and Drug Abuse in Afghanistan, 1972. *Military service:* U.S. Army Air Forces, 1942-46; became staff sergeant; received one battle star. *Member:* American Sociological Association.

WRITINGS: Straight Dope on Drugs, Creation House, 1971; (with W. Slater Hollis) *The Economic Cost of Alcoholic Beverages to Government and Taxpayers,* Moody, 1971; *Drugs: Why Unconcerned Parents Should Be Concerned,* Moody, 1973. Editor of *Report of Alcohol.*

WORK IN PROGRESS: Alcohol: The Facts and the Fables.

* * *

KUBOSE, Gyomay M(asao) 1905-

PERSONAL: Born July 7, 1905, in San Francisco, Calif.; married Minnie Taniquchi (a teacher of Japanese flower arranging and tea ceremony), January 12, 1936; children: Don, Sunnan, Joyce (Mrs. Alvin Eddie Evans). *Education:* Received primary and secondary education in Japan; University of California, Berkeley, B.A., 1935; returned to Japan to train as Buddhist minister under Haya Akegarasu, 1936-40; Otani University, M.A., 1969. *Home:* 4641 North Racine Ave., Chicago, Ill. 60640. *Office:* 1151 West Leland Ave., Chicago, Ill. 60640.

CAREER: Spent two World War II years in relocation camp at Heart Mountain, Wyo.; founder of Buddhist Temple of Chicago, Chicago, Ill., 1944, and minister, 1944-72, senior minister, 1972—. Lecturer on Buddhism and its culture. *Member:* Japanese American Association, Japanese American Citizens League, American Humanist Association, American Buddhist Association, Japan America Society, Lions Club. *Awards, honors:* Brotherhood Award of Japanese American Citizens League, 1953; Silver Beaver Award of Boy Scouts of America, 1961; Cultural Award of Japan Buddhist Mission Cultural Association, 1970.

WRITINGS: Everyday Suchness, Dharma Book, 1967, 5th edition, 1974; *Soto yori Uchi ye* (title means "Look Within Instead of Outside"), Dharma Book, 1972; *Zen Koans,* Regnery, 1973.

WORK IN PROGRESS: A translation of and commentary on *The Eternal Life Sutra.*

* * *

KUEMMERLY, Walter 1903-

PERSONAL: Born November 9, 1903, in Berne, Switzerland; son of Hermann and Magdalena (Frey) Kuemmerly; married Elisabeth Burkhardt, December 26, 1934; children: Barbara Kuemmerly Peters, Anna Kuemmerly Jeker, Franziska. *Education:* Federal Institute of Technology (ETH), Ing. forest, 1928. *Politics:* Liberal. *Religion:* Protestant. *Home:* Falkenweg 9, Berne, Switzerland 3012. *Office:* Kuemmerly & Frey AG, Hallerstrasse 10, Berne, Switzerland 3001.

CAREER: Kuemmerly & Frey (book publishers), Berne, Switzerland, manager, 1933—. *Military service:* Swiss Air Force, 1923-51; became first lieutenant. *Member:* European Association of Manufacturers and Distributors of Educational Materials (president, 1952-67), Schweizer Buchhaendler und Verlegerverein (president, 1967-68), Schweizer Kartographische Gesellschaft, Schweizer Ingenieur und Architektenverein, Schweizer Gymnasial-Lehrer Verein (honorary member), Geographical Society of Berne (honorary member), Geographical Society of Neuchatel (honorary member), Berner Wanderwege (honorary member).

WRITINGS: (Illustrator) *Malta: Insel der Mitte,* Kuemmerly & Frey, 1965, translation published as *Malta: Isle of the Middle Sea,* Harrap, 1965; (editor) *Der Wald. Welt der Baeume, Baeume der Welt,* Kuemmerly & Frey, 1966, translation by Ewald Osers published as *The Forest,* Luce, 1973. Also author of *Werdegang einer Landkarte,* a booklet.

WORK IN PROGRESS: Botanical, biological and Alpine program, "Formenreichtum der Natur" and "Unbekannte Berge."

* * *

KUETHER, Edith Lyman 1915- (Margaret Malcolm)

PERSONAL: Surname is pronounced *Kee*-ther; born May, 1915, in Columbus, Ohio; daughter of John Franklin (a university professor) and Nella (Bull) Lyman; married Carl

Albert Kuether (program administrator of National Institute of Health), June 16, 1939; children: Christian Lyman, Elizabeth Kuether Myers. *Education:* Capital University, teacher's certificate, 1934; Oberlin Conservatory of Music, B.Music, 1937; graduate study at Ohio State University, 1938-39, University of Washington, Seattle, 1949, and George Washington University, 1966. *Residence:* Chevy Chase, Md.

CAREER: Huron College, Huron, S.D., instructor in violin, ensemble, and history of music, 1938; Department of Public Welfare, Marion County, Indianapolis, Ind., child welfare visitor, 1955; violinist and violin teacher in Washington, D.C., 1962—. Teacher of violin and ensemble for Maryland Regional Center for the Arts, 1967; member of board of trustees of Washington International Music Competition. *Member:* American String Teachers Association, Arts Club of Washington, Friday Morning Music Club, Phi Beta.

WRITINGS: (under pseudonym Margaret Malcolm) *Headless Beings* (novel), Doubleday, 1973. Contributor to *American String Teacher* and *George Washington Forum*. Editor of *Tiller,* publication of Indiana Association of Congregational Women, 1958-59.

WORK IN PROGRESS: Quicken, a sequel to *Headless Beings; Shade of the Fig Tree, Fruit of the Vine,* autobiography; *The Dream Is Dear,* historical novel.

SIDELIGHTS: Mrs. Kuether told *CA:* "A career in music was curtailed because of family needs, and a later resumption was broken off because of hearing problems. Music is really not too different from writing, interest depending on repeated themes and their development—only the skills are different." In her writing, she aims "to portray women with humor, to show how a woman's intuition and experience can enlarge the awareness of humanity." *Avocational interests:* Travel.

* * *

KUHN, Harold B(arnes) 1911-

PERSONAL: Born August 21, 1911, in Belleville, Kan.; son of John William (a farmer and teacher) and Ida Alice (Morey) Kuhn; married Anne Wicker (a professor), June 11, 1934. *Education:* Malone College, Diploma, 1934; John Fletcher College, A.B. (magna cum laude), 1939; Harvard University, S.T.B., 1942, S.T.M., 1943, Ph.D., 1944, postdoctoral study 1965-67, 1970; University of Munich, postdoctoral study, 1951-52. *Politics:* Republican-Independent. *Home:* 406 Kenyon Ave., Wilmore, Ky. 40390. *Office:* Asbury Theological Seminary, 200 North Lexington Ave., Wilmore, Ky. 40390.

CAREER: Clergyman, Emmanuel Bible College, Birkenhead, England, lecturer in theology, 1936-37; pastor of Methodist church in Beacon, Iowa, 1938-39, Society of Friends (Quaker) church in Dartmouth, Mass., 1939-41, and Congregational church in Brockton, Mass., 1941-44; University of Kentucky, Lexington, research fellow in philosophy, 1944-45; Asbury Theological Seminary, Wilmore, Ky., professor of philosophy of religion, 1944—, chairman of Division of Doctrine and Philosophy of Religion, 1959—. Visiting professor at Union Biblical Seminary, Yeotmal, India, 1957. Engaged in refugee rehabilitation in western Europe, summers, 1947—; auxiliary chaplain and retreat master, U.S. Army and U.S. Air Force, summers, 1948—. Trustee of Malone College, 1967—.

MEMBER: Evangelical Theological Society, American Society for Christian Ethics, American Philosophical Association, American Association of University Professors, Wesleyan Theological Society. *Awards, honors:* Named Alumnus of the Year, Malone College, 1968; D.D., Houghton College, 1970.

WRITINGS: Examination of Liberal Theology, Asbury Press, 1943; *Colossians-Philemon,* Light & Life Press, 1966.

Contributor—All edited by Carl F. H. Henry: *Contemporary Evangelical Thought,* Channel Press, 1957; *Basic Christian Doctrines,* Holt, 1962; *Christian Faith and Modern Theology,* Channel Press, 1964; *Fundamentals of the Faith,* Zondervan, 1969. Contributor to religion journals. Editor, *Asbury Seminarian,* 1946—; contributing editor, *Christianity Today,* 1956—; consulting editor, Zondervan Publishing House, 1964—.

WORK IN PROGRESS: Christianity: Religion of the Supernatural; and *Alienation and Atonement.*

* * *

KUKLA, Robert J(ohn) 1932-

PERSONAL: Born December 1, 1932, in Chicago, Ill.; son of John (a coppersmith) and Antoinette (Habowska) Kukla; married Barbara J. Kafka, March 25, 1973. *Education:* Northwestern University, B.S., 1954, J.D., 1957. *Home and office address:* P. O. Box 398, Park Ridge, Ill., 60068.

CAREER: Attorney-at-law in Park Ridge, Ill., 1957—. *Member:* American Bar Association, American Numismatic Association, National Rifle Association (life member; member of board of directors), National Wildlife Federation, Illinois State Rifle Association, Geographic Society of Chicago, Logan Square Neighborhood Association (past president).

WRITINGS: (Contributor) Irving Goldstein, editor, *Trial Lawyer's Guide,* Callaghan, 1958; *A Study of the Administration of Chicago's Pistol Purchase Permit Law* (monograph), Illinois State Rifle Association, 1965; *Guide Booklet to the 1967 Illinois Gun Laws* (monograph), Illinois State Rifle Association, 1967; *Gun Control,* Stackpole, 1973.

* * *

KUMBEL
See HEIN, Piet

* * *

KUMMERLY, Walter
See KUEMMERLY, Walter

* * *

KURDSEN, Stephen
See NOON, Brian

* * *

KURELEK, William 1927-

PERSONAL: Surname is pronounced Coo-*reh*-lehk; born March 3, 1927, in Whitford, Alberta, Canada; son of Metro and Mary (Hululak) Kurelek; married Jean Andrews, October 8, 1962; children: Catherine, Stephen, Barbara, Thomas. *Education:* University of Manitoba, B.A., 1949. *Religion:* Roman Catholic. *Home and office:* 175 Balsam Ave., Toronto, Ontario M4E 3C2, Canada.

CAREER: Picture framer in Toronto, Ontario, 1959-71; artist in Toronto, 1960—. *Member:* Royal Canadian Academy of Art.

WRITINGS: (Self-illustrated) *A Prairie Boy's Winter*, Tundra Books, 1973; (self-illustrated) *O Toronto*, New Press, 1973; *Some One with Me* (autobiography), Cornell University Press, 1973.

WORK IN PROGRESS: Prairie Boy's Summer; Student Lumberjack.

* * *

KURTZ-PHELAN, James L(anham) 1946-

PERSONAL: Original name, James L. Phelan; name legally changed in 1973; born July 13, 1946, in El Paso, Tex.; son of John A. (a television vice-president) and Eloise (Lanham) Phelan; married Phyllis Helene Kurtz, December 9, 1973. *Education:* University of Texas, El Paso, B.B.A., 1968; Yale University, J.D., 1972. *Home:* 695 Locust St., Denver, Colo. 80220. *Office:* College of Law, University of Denver, Room 200, 209 16th St., Denver, Colo. 80202.

CAREER: Admitted to the Bar of Colorado, 1972; private law practice in Denver, Colo., 1972—; University of Denver, Denver, Colo., instructor in law, 1972—. Director of Center for Law and Research, 1972-74; organizer of Colorado Public Interest Research Group, 1972-74; director and president of Colorado Environmental Legal Services, 1974—. *Member:* Colorado Bar Association, Denver Bar Association.

WRITINGS: (With Robert C. Pozen) *The Company State: Ralph Nader's Study on DuPont in Delaware*, Grossman, 1972.

WORK IN PROGRESS: Study of legal education and the legal profession, and of the roles of lawyers in the legal process.

* * *

KWITNY, Jonathan 1941-

PERSONAL: Born March 23, 1941, in Indianapolis, Ind.; son of I. J. (a physician) and Julia (Goldberger) Kwitny; married Martha Kaplan (a lawyer), June 2, 1968; children: Carolyn, Susanna. *Education:* University of Missouri, B.J., 1962; New York University, M.A., 1964. *Office: Wall Street Journal*, 22 Cortlandt St., New York, N.Y. 10007.

CAREER: News Tribune, Perth Amboy, N.J., reporter, 1963-65, 1966-69; *New York Post*, New York, N.Y., reporter, 1969; *Wall Street Journal*, New York, N.Y., reporter, 1971—. U.S. Peace Corps volunteer in Benin City, Nigeria, 1965-66. *Awards, honors:* First prize from New Jersey Press Association, 1964, 1967, for distinguished public service.

WRITINGS—Nonfiction: *The Fountain Pen Conspiracy*, Knopf, 1973; *The Mullendore Murder Case*, Farrar, Straus, in press.

WORK IN PROGRESS: A novel, *Who Killed Thomas Jefferson?*

KYDD, Thomas
See MEYER, Thomas

* * *

KYDD, Tom
See MEYER, Thomas

* * *

KYES, Robert L(ange) 1933-

PERSONAL: Born July 8, 1933, in Allegan, Mich.; son of Walter Morris (a land appraiser) and Antoinette (Lange) Kyes; married Rose Reiman (a teacher and intern consultant), September 1, 1956 (divorced); children: Anne, Susan. *Education:* University of Michigan, B.A., 1958, Ph.D., 1964; Brown University, A.M., 1959; University of Hamburg, graduate study, 1959-60. *Home:* 1235 South Maple Rd., Apt. 102, Ann Arbor, Mich. 48103. *Office:* Department of German, University of Michigan, 3144 Modern Languages Bldg., Ann Arbor, Mich. 48104.

CAREER: University of Michigan, Ann Arbor, assistant professor, 1964-68, associate professor, 1968-74, professor of Germanic languages, 1974—. *Military service:* U.S. Navy, 1951-54. *Member:* Linguistic Society of America, American Association of Teachers of German, American Council on the Teaching of Foreign Languages, Midwest Modern Language Association.

WRITINGS: (With V. C. Hubbs) *German in Review*, Macmillan, 1966; *The Old Low Franconian Psalms and Glosses*, University of Michigan Press, 1969; (reviser with H. H. Waengler) *Contemporary German*, 2nd edition (Kyes was not associated with 1st edition), 1971. Contributor of articles and reviews to *Language*, *Lingua*, and *Modern Language Journal*.

WORK IN PROGRESS: A Glossary of Old Netherlandic, completion expected in 1977; *Old Netherlandic Phonology*, publication by Mouton & Co. expected in 1978; editing *The Old Saxon Heliand Manuscript Monacensis: Text, Notes, and Glossary*.

SIDELIGHTS: Kyes writes that his current language project is Hittite. *Avocational interests:* Travel, carpentry, nature study.

* * *

LAFFAL, Julius 1920-

PERSONAL: Born December 3, 1920, in New York, N.Y.; son of Ben (a tailor) and Rose (Heinz) Laffal; married Florence Schultz (an artist), August 24, 1943; children: Paul D., Kenneth J. *Education:* College of the City of New York (now City College of the City University of New York), B.A., 1941; New York University, M.A., 1949; University of Iowa, Ph.D., 1951. *Home:* 98 North Main St., Essex, Conn. 06426. *Office:* Connecticut Valley Hospital, Middletown, Conn. 06457.

CAREER: Yale University, New Haven, Conn., research assistant in psychiatry, 1952-53; Veterans Administration, West Haven, Conn., research psychologist, 1953-68; Yale University, New Haven, Conn., associate professor of psychology and psychiatry, 1953-68; Connecticut Valley Hospital, Middletown, Conn., director of research and psychological services, 1968—. Adjunct professor of psychology, Wesleyan University, 1973; psychology editor, Gallery Press, 1973—. *Military service:* U.S. Army, 1942-

45; became staff sergeant. *Member:* American Psychological Association, Eastern Psychological Association, Connecticut Psychological Association.

WRITINGS: Pathological and Normal Language, Atherton, 1965; *A Concept Dictionary of English,* Gallery Press, 1973.

WORK IN PROGRESS: Studies of the psychology of language; research on disturbances of language in schizophrenia; a computerized analysis of language content.

* * *

LAGERKVIST, Paer 1891-1974

May 23, 1891—July 11, 1974; Swedish novelist, poet, and playwright. Obituaries: *New York Times,* July 12, 1974; *Washington Post,* July 12, 1974; *Newsweek,* July 22, 1974; *Time,* July 22, 1974.

* * *

LAGERKVIST, Par
See LAGERKVIST, Paer

* * *

LA GUMA, (Justin) Alex(ander) 1925-

PERSONAL: Born February 20, 1925, in Cape Town, South Africa; son of Jimmy and Wilhelmina (Alexander) La Guma; married Blanche Valerie Herman (an office manager; former midwife), November 13, 1954; children: Eugene, Bartholomew. *Education:* Cape Technical College, student, 1941-42, correspondence student, 1965; London School of Journalism, correspondence student, 1964. *Home:* 36 Woodland Gardens, London N10 3UA, England. *Agent:* Hope Leresche, 11 Jubilee Pl., Chelsea, London, England.

CAREER: New Age (weekly newspaper), Cape Town, South Africa, staff journalist, 1955-62; emigrated to England, 1966; currently free-lance writer. *Member:* External Mission of African National Congress, Afro-Asian Writers Association (deputy secretary-general, 1973—). *Awards, honors:* Afro-Asian Lotus award for literature, 1969.

WRITINGS: A Walk in the Night (novelette), Mbari (Nigeria), 1962, published with stories by La Guma as *A Walk in the Night and Other Stories,* Northwestern University Press, 1967; *And a Threefold Cord* (novel), Seven Seas (Berlin), 1964; *The Stone Country* (novel), Seven Seas, 1967; *In the Fog of the Season's End* (novel), Heinemann, 1972, Third Press, 1973; (editor) *Apartheid: A Collection of Writings on South African Racism,* International Publishers, 1972.

Represented in anthologies: *Quartet: New Voices from South Africa,* edited by Richard Rive, Crown, 1963, new edition, Heinemann, 1968; *Modern African Stories,* edited by Ellis Ayitey Komey and Ezekiel Mphahlele, Faber, 1964; *African Writing Today,* edited by Mphahlele, Penguin, 1967; *Africa in Prose,* edited by O.R. Dathorne and Willfried Feuser, Penguin, 1969; *Modern African Stories,* edited by Charles R. Larson, Collins, 1971.

Contributor of short stories to magazines, including *Black Orpheus* and *Africa South.*

WORK IN PROGRESS: A novel, as yet untitled.

SIDELIGHTS: According to *The Christian Century,* "*The Stone Country* makes prison the metaphor for South Africa." And for La Guma, indeed it was. As a nonwhite, he felt fully subject to oppression outside of prison; and, as a leader against apartheid, he was actually confined to his home in Capetown under house arrest for four years, and was jailed on five different occasions between 1956 to 1966, as well. His first three books were written during those years.

Son of a former president of the South African Coloured Peoples' Congress, La Guma emigrated to London with his family in 1966. He may not be published nor quoted in South Africa.

In the Fog of the Season's End evoked the following review in the *Times Literary Supplement:* "Alex La Guma is a committed writer . . . [whose] prose is usually spare and deft. He tells it like it is, but is capable of using imagery imaginatively, and of illuminating his grim scene with wit and irony. He notes the callous signs that underline the horror of South African life: 'Drive Carefully, Natives Crossing Ahead' and 'For Children under sixteen and non-Whites.' But his ear for dialogue is even more acute, recording sensitively the idioms and peculiarities of polyglot Cape Town. . . . La Guma knows about the fog of autumn; let us hope he survives to write about the South African spring."

BIOGRAPHICAL/CRITICAL SOURCES: Ezekiel Mphahlele, *African Image,* Praeger, 1962, reissued, 1974; Dennis Duerden and Cosmo Pieterse, editors, *African Writers Talking: A Collection of Interviews,* Heinemann, 1972.

* * *

LAMB, Hugh 1946-

PERSONAL: Born February 4, 1946, in Sutton, Surrey, England; son of Charles (a plumber) and Joyce (Russell) Lamb; married Susan Tadgell, September 30, 1967; children: Richard, Andrew. *Education:* Attended county school in Sutton, England. *Politics:* "Left wing but not avidly so." *Religion:* "Never!" *Home:* 16 Thicket Crescent, Sutton, Surrey, England.

CAREER: Journalist and editor.

WRITINGS—Editor: *A Tide of Terror,* W. H. Allen, 1972, Taplinger, 1973; *A Wave of Fear,* W. H. Allen, 1973, Taplinger, 1974; *Victorian Tales of Terror,* W. H. Allen, 1974; *Sixteen Grusel Stories,* Heyne, 1974; *The Thrill of Horror,* W. H. Allen, in press. Also editor of "The Mayflower Book of Horror Stories" series, Mayflower Books, 1974, and "The Star Book of Horror Stories" series, W. H. Allen, 1974.

WORK IN PROGRESS: Researching old and new stories in the macabre vein by known and unknown authors and preparing further anthologies.

* * *

LAMM, Norman 1927-

PERSONAL: Born December 19, 1927, in Brooklyn, N.Y.; son of Samuel and Pearl (Baumol) Lamm; married Mindella Mehler, February 23, 1954; children: Chaye, Joshua, Shalom, Sara. *Education:* Yeshiva University, B.A. (summa cum laude), 1949, Rabbi, 1951, Ph.D., 1966. *Home:* 27 West 86th St., New York, N.Y. 10024. *Office:* Jewish Center, 131 West 86th St., New York, N.Y. 10024.

CAREER: Assistant (Orthodox) rabbi at Congregation Kehillath Jeshurun, New York, N.Y., 1952-53; rabbi at Congregation Kodimoh, Springfield, Mass., 1954-58;

Jewish Center, New York, N.Y., rabbi, 1958—. Jakob and Erna Michael Professor of Jewish Philosophy at Yeshiva University, 1959—. Trustee of Rabbi Isaac Elchanan Theological Seminary, 1971—. Director of Union of Orthodox Jewish Congregations of America; member of Halakhah (Jewish law) Commission of Rabbinical Council of America; former chairman of New York Conference on Soviet Jewry. Has lectured in nine countries on five continents (including India, Pakistan, South Africa, Israel, Australia, and New Zealand); has testified as an expert in Jewish law before the U.S. Senate Judiciary Committee.

MEMBER: Association of Orthodox Jewish Scientists (charter member; member of board of governors), American Zionist Youth Foundation (member of board of trustees), Yavneh (National Religious Jewish Students Association; former chairman of advisory board). *Awards, honors:* Abramowitz-Zeitlin Award for Religious Literature (Jerusalem), 1973, for *The Royal Reach* and *Faith and Doubt;* Bernard Revel Award for Religion and Religious Education from Yeshiva College Alumni Association, 1974.

WRITINGS: (Editor with Menachem M. Kasher and Leonard Rosenfeld) *The Leo Jung Jubilee Volume,* Jewish Center (New York), 1962; *A Hedge of Roses: Jewish Insights into Marriage and Married Life,* Feldheim, 1966, 2nd edition, 1970; (editor with Walter S. Wurzburger) *A Treasury of Tradition,* Hebrew Publishing, 1967; *The Royal Reach: Discourses on the Jewish Tradition and the World Today,* Feldheim, 1970; *Faith and Doubt: Studies in Traditional Jewish Thought,* Ktav, 1971; *Torah Lishmah* (title means "The Study of *Torah* for Its Own Sake"), Mossad Harav Kook (Jerusalem), 1972; *The Good Society,* Viking with B'nai B'rith, 1974. Editor of "Library of Jewish Law and Ethics," Ktav. Contributor to Hebrew and English language journals in the United States and abroad. Co-editor of *Hadarom,* 1957-60; founder and editor of *Tradition: A Journal of Orthodox Jewish Thought.*

WORK IN PROGRESS: Anthology of Hasidic Theology; The Philosophy of Character.

SIDELIGHTS: Lamm's books have been translated into Spanish, Hebrew, Portuguese, and Marathi.

* * *

LANDAU, Rom 1899-1974

October 17, 1899—1974; British-born artist, educator, critic, and author of short fiction and books on Morocco, the Near East, and other subjects. Obituaries: *AB Bookman's Weekly,* July 15, 1974. (*CA*-3).

* * *

LANDAU, Sol 1920-

PERSONAL: Born June 21, 1920, in Berlin, Germany; came to United States in 1940; naturalized U.S. citizen; son of Ezekiel (a rabbi) and Helene (Grynberg) Landau; married Gabriela Mayer (a sociologist), January 14, 1951; children: Ezra M., Tamara A. *Education:* Brooklyn College (now Brooklyn College of the City University of New York), B.A., 1949; New York University, M.A., 1958; Jewish Theological Seminary, M.H.L. and Rabbi, 1951; Florida State University, now Ph.D. candidate. *Home:* 519 Southwest 25th Rd., Miami, Fla. 33129. *Office:* Beth David Congregation, 2625 Southwest Third Ave., Miami, Fla. 33129.

CAREER: Rabbi of Jewish congregations in Whitestone, N.Y., 1952-56, Cleveland, Ohio, 1956-60 and 1963-65, and Wilmette, Ill., 1960-63; Beth David Congregation, Miami, Fla., rabbi, 1965—. National deputy chairman of Jewish War Veterans of America; member of board of directors of National Academy for Adult Jewish Studies and of Dropsie University; founding member of South Dade Mental Health Clinic. *Military service:* U.S. Army, 1942-45. *Member:* American Association of Adult Education, American Association of University Professors, Rabbinical Assembly, Rabbinical Association of Greater Miami. *Awards, honors:* Liberation Award from State of Israel, 1967.

WRITINGS: Christian-Jewish Relations, Pageant, 1958; *Length of Our Days,* Bloch Publishing, 1960; *Bridging Two Worlds* (biography of his father), J. David, 1969. Contributor to *Jewish Spectator, Adult Jewish Education, Torch, National Jewish Monthly,* and *United Synagogue Review.*

WORK IN PROGRESS: Research for a book on second careers in middle age.

* * *

LANGER, Ellen J(ane) 1947-

PERSONAL: Born March 25, 1947, in New York, N.Y.; daughter of Norman J. (a pharmacist) and Sylvia (Tobias) Langer; married Gene Most, February 3, 1967 (divorced, 1970). *Education:* New York University, B.A., 1970; Yale University, Ph.D., 1974. *Residence:* New Haven, Conn. *Office:* Graduate School and Univerity Center, City University of New York, 33 West 42nd St., New York, N.Y. 10036.

CAREER: New Century Publishing, New York, N.Y., free-lance writer, 1969-70; City University of New York, Graduate School and University Center, New York, N.Y., assistant professor of psychology, 1974—. *Member:* American Psychological Association, New England Psychological Association, Phi Beta Kappa, Psi Chi, Sigma Xi.

WRITINGS: (With Carol S. Dweck) *Personal Politics: The Psychology of Making It,* Prentice-Hall, 1973. Contributor to *Journal of Personality and Social Psychology, Journal of Consulting and Clinical Psychology,* and *Perceptual and Motor Skills.*

WORK IN PROGRESS: Three articles, "The Effects of Staring on Helping Behavior" with Phoebe Ellsworth, "Why Stigmatized Others Are Avoided: A Novel Stimulus Hypothesis" with Shelley E. Taylor and Susan Fiske, and "Pregnancy as a Social Stigma" with Taylor.

* * *

LANGHORNE, Elizabeth

PERSONAL: Born in Bryn Mawr, Pa.; daughter of Stricker (a physician) and Bertha (Lippincott) Coles; married Harry F. Langhorne, July 18, 1941 (died November, 1963); children: John Coles, Elizabeth L., Harry F., Jr. *Education:* Attended Vassar College, 1931. *Politics:* Democrat. *Religion:* Episcopal. *Address:* Box 186, Route 2, Charlottesville, Va. 22901.

CAREER: Thoroughbred horse breeder and sales stable owner in Keene, Va., 1934-42; real estate broker in Vieques, Puerto Rico, 1964—. Member of executive boards of Girl Scouts of America, Visiting Nurse Association, Prestwould Foundation; president of Virginia Center for the Creative Arts, 1971. *Member:* Farmington Hunt Club, Keswick Hunt Club, Greencroft Club.

WRITINGS: A History of Christ Church: Glendower and the Early History of St. Anne's Parish, King Lindsay, 1957;

Jean Skipwith: A Virginia Blue Stocking, Prestwould Foundation, 1966; *Nancy Astor and Her Friends,* Praeger, 1974. Contributor to *Saturday Evening Post, New Mexico Quarterly, Virginia Cavalcade,* and *Vassar Quarterly.*

WORK IN PROGRESS: Women in the Life of Thomas Jefferson; a novel dealing with race relations on an Albemarle County plantation during the Civil War and Reconstruction era.

SIDELIGHTS: Elizabeth Langhorne told *CA:* "Life seems worth living when there is a work in progress. This includes history and fiction. I write best when I can get away to a Colony, preferably the MacDowell Colony in Peterborough, N.H. People are my vital interest, individually (fiction) and in the mass (history). Horses and airplanes have long been my major sport interests, now I am declining (gracefully?) into archaeology, land use, walking, and some tennis. I speak French, and always say that one day I will 'really learn' German and Spanish. I have travelled in Europe, and [taken] one trip each to Africa and the Far East. Hopefully South America next."

* * *

LANGONE, John (Michael) 1929-

PERSONAL: Surname is pronounced Lan-*goh*-neh; born December 23, 1929, in Cambridge, Mass.; son of Joseph (a furrier) and Josephine (Consolazio) Langone; married Dolores Nobrega (a health careers counselor), September 29, 1956; children: Matthew, Gia, Lisa. *Education:* Boston University, B.S., 1953; Harvard University, special student at School of Medicine, 1969. *Politics:* Democrat. *Religion:* Roman Catholic. *Home:* 28 Jarvis Ave., Hingham, Mass. 02043. *Office: Boston Herald-American,* 300 Harrison Ave., Boston, Mass. 02106.

CAREER: Worcester Gazette, Worcester, Mass., reporter, 1954-55; United Press (UP), Boston, Mass., reporter, 1955-56; *Worcester Telegram,* Worcester, Mass., reporter, 1956-57; United Press International (UPI), Providence, R.I., bureau chief for Rhode Island, 1957-61, editor at national radio headquarters in Chicago, Ill., 1961-62; *Boston Herald-Traveler,* Boston, Mass., medical writer, 1962-66; *Psychiatric Opinion,* Framingham, Mass., editor, 1966-68; *Boston Herald-American,* Boston, Mass., editor of medical news and author of column "Medical Beat," 1968—. Member of ethics committee of Advisory Council of the Radcliffe Programs in Health Care. *Military service:* U.S. Navy, 1948-49. U.S. Air Force Reserve, 1953-62; became first lieutenant.

MEMBER: National Association of Science Writers, American Public Health Association (fellow), Harvard Medical School Alumni Association (honorary associate member). *Awards, honors:* National journalism award from American Osteopathic Association, 1966, for series on osteopathy; citation for meritorious service from U.S. Veterans Administration, 1971, for series on Veterans Administration hospitals.

WRITINGS: Death Is a Noun, Little, Brown, 1972; *Goodbye to Bedlam,* Little, Brown, 1974; *Vital Signs: The Way We Die in America,* Little, Brown, 1974. Contributor to *Saturday Review, Newsweek, Time, Woman's Day, Commonweal, Man's, Medical Tribune,* and *Medical World News.* Executive editor of *Journal of Abdominal Surgery,* 1963—; consulting science writer for Worcester Foundation for Experimental Biology, 1966-68; member of editorial board of *American Journal of Public Health,* 1971—.

WORK IN PROGRESS: Books on Antarctica; longevity studies; a novel; juvenile books on genetic manipulation, viruses, sleep and dreams, and alcoholism.

SIDELIGHTS: Langone traveled with the National Science Foundation to Antarctica and the South Pole in 1972, and to Israel in 1973, to report on twenty-five years of science and medicine.

BIOGRAPHICAL/CRITICAL SOURCES: New England Journal of Medicine, April 9, 1970.

* * *

LANSDOWNE, J(ames) F(enwick) 1937-

PERSONAL: Born August 8, 1937, in Hong Kong; son of Ernest (an engineer) and Edith (Ford) Lansdowne; married Patricia Fraser McAfee, May 15, 1964 (divorced, 1973). *Education:* Attended high school in Canada. *Home:* 681 Transit Rd., Victoria, British Columbia, Canada. *Office:* 941 Victoria Ave., Victoria, British Columbia, Canada.

CAREER: Artist; work has been exhibited at galleries in Toronto, New York, and London, England, including Royal Ontario Museum, Smithsonian Institution, and Tryon Galleries; work is also included in numerous permanent collections.

WRITINGS—Self-illustrated: *Birds of the Northern Forest,* McClelland & Stewart, 1966; *Birds of the Eastern Forest,* McClelland & Stewart, Part I, 1968, Part II, 1970; *Birds of the West Coast,* M. F. Feheley, in press.

WORK IN PROGRESS: Illustrations for *Marsh Birds of the World,* by S. Dillon Ripley to be published by the Smithsonian Institution.

* * *

LAPHAM, Arthur L(owell) 1922-

PERSONAL: Born July 2, 1922, in Houston, Tex.; son of Arthur Lowell (a civil engineer) and Lorena (Crabb) Lapham; married Alice Whitmore, February 9, 1957; children: Mary Alice, Rosanna, Justus. *Education:* Agricultural and Mechanical College of Texas (now Texas A & M University), B.A., 1948; South Texas College of Law, J.D., 1954. *Religion:* Protestant. *Home:* 102 Loma Vista, Victoria, Tex. 77901. *Office:* Hartman & Lapham, 201 South Main, Victoria, Tex. 77901.

CAREER: Admitted to Bar of State of Texas, 1954; private law practice in Victoria, Tex., 1954-71; Hartman & Lapham (attorneys), Victoria, Tex., partner, 1971—. Member of board of directors of Community Action Committee, Office of Economic Opportunity, 1970-72; chairman of advisory board of Salvation Army, 1966. *Military service:* U.S. Army Air Forces, bomber pilot, 1942-46; served in South Pacific theater; became first lieutenant. U.S. Air Force, helicopter instruction pilot, 1950-53. *Member:* American Trial Lawyers Association, National Association of Defense Lawyers, American Institute of Hypnosis, Texas Trial Lawyers, 24th-135th Judicial District Bar Association (president, 1960—), Victoria County Historical Society, Sons of Republic of Texas, Victoria Country Club.

WRITINGS: Justus (novel), Concordia, 1973. Author of three-act play, "That Book!". Contributor to *Texas Bar Journal.*

WORK IN PROGRESS: Research for a historical Biblical novel, tentatively titled *Stephen vs. Paul;* a three-act play, "The Jury"; two novels, *Tilt the Scales* and *It's Hell.*

LARRANAGA, Robert O. 1940-

PERSONAL: Born October 25, 1940, in New York; son of John O. (an insurance agent) and Eileen (Connelly) Larranaga; married Mary O'Donnell, December 29, 1962; children: Robert, James, Jeanne. *Education:* Attended St. John's University, Jamaica, N.Y., 1958-62. *Religion:* Roman Catholic. *Office:* Associates & Larranaga, 4812 I.D.S. Center, Minneapolis, Minn. 55402.

CAREER: Advertising copywriter, with Associates & Larranaga, Minneapolis, Minn.

WRITINGS: *The King's Shadow,* Carolrhoda Books, 1970; *Famous Crime Fighters,* Lerner, 1972; *Famous Pirates and Buccaneers,* Lerner, 1972; *Sniffles,* Carolrhoda Books, 1973; *Preparing for a Career in Advertising,* Dillon, 1973.

WORK IN PROGRESS: *Smokescreen,* a novel about a Congressional investigation into advertising and its practices.

SIDELIGHTS: Larranaga has made a record album, "Scrumpdillyishus" and "Sweet Tooth," for Metro-Goldwyn-Mayer.

* * *

LARSON, Calvin J. 1933-

PERSONAL: Born September 25, 1933; married wife, Edith S., February 6, 1959; children: Erik James, Adam Arthur. *Education:* University of California, Berkeley, B.A., 1956; San Jose State College (now California State University) M.S., 1960; University of Oregon, Ph.D., 1965. *Office:* Department of Sociology, University of Massachusetts, Boston, Mass. 02125.

CAREER: Member of faculty in sociology, University of Massachusetts, Boston. *Military service:* U.S. Naval Reserve, 1956-58. *Member:* American Sociological Association.

WRITINGS: (Editor with Philo Wasburn) *Power, Participation, and Ideology,* McKay, 1968; (editor with Jeffrey Hadden and Louis Massotti) *Metropolis in Crisis,* F. E. Peacock, 1971; *Major Themes in Sociological Theory,* McKay, 1973.

* * *

LASKER, Joe 1919-

PERSONAL: Born June 26, 1919, in Brooklyn, N.Y.; son of Isidore (a tailor) and Rachel (Strollowitz) Lasker; married Mildred Jaspen (a teacher), November 28, 1948; children: David, Laura, Evan. *Education:* Attended Cooper Union Art School, 1936-39. *Home and office:* 20 Dock Rd., Norwalk, Conn. 06854.

CAREER: Artist, with oil paintings in permanent collections in colleges, universities, and museums, including Whitney Museum, Philadelphia Museum, and Baltimore Museum. Art teacher at City College (now City College of the City University of New York), 1947-48, and University of Illinois, 1953-54. Illustrator of children's books. *Military service:* U.S. Army, 1941-45.

MEMBER: National Academy of Design, Authors Guild of Authors League of America, Connecticut Association for Children with Learning Disabilities (president, 1964-65). *Awards, honors:* Abbey mural painting fellowship, 1947, 1948; awards from National Academy of Design include third Hallgarten prize, 1949, first Hallgarten prize, 1955, second Altman prize, 1958, Ranger Fund purchase award, 1966, Clark prize, 1969, and Isadore medal, 1972; Prix de Rome fellowship, 1950, 1951; Guggenheim fellowship, 1954; purchase award from Springfield Art Museum, 1964; Hassam Fund purchase awards from American Academy of Arts and Letters, 1965, 1968; National Institute of Arts and Letters grant, 1968.

WRITINGS: (Self-illustrated) *Mothers Can Do Anything,* Whitman, 1972; *He's My Brother,* Whitman, 1974; *Tales of a Seadog Family,* Viking, 1974; *For Richer, for Poorer,* Viking, 1975.

Illustrator: Miriam Schlein, *The Sun, the Wind, the Sea and the Rain,* Abelard, 1960; Charlotte Zolotow, *Man with the Purple Eyes,* Abelard, 1961; Schlein, *The Way Mothers Are,* Whitman, 1963; Schlein, *Big Lion, Little Lion,* Whitman, 1964; Norma Simon, *Benjy's Bird,* Whitman, 1965; Fern Brown and Andree Grabe, *When Grandpa Wore Knickers,* Whitman, 1966; Simon, *What Do I Say?,* Whitman, 1967; Simon, *See the First Star,* Whitman, 1968; Simon, *What Do I Do?,* Whitman, 1969; Simon, *How Do I Feel?,* Whitman, 1970; Schlein, *My House,* Whitman, 1971; Joel Rothman, *Night Lights,* Whitman, 1972; Joan Fassler, *Howie Helps Himself,* Whitman, 1974; Judy Delton, *Carrot Cake,* Crown, 1975. Also illustrator of *Snow Time,* by Miriam Schlein, published by Whitman.

BIOGRAPHICAL/CRITICAL SOURCES: *Life,* March 20, 1950; Lloyd Goodrich and John Bauer, *American Art of Our Century,* Praeger, 1961; *Parade,* September 1, 1963.

SIDELIGHTS: Lasker wrote: "Painting is my first love. I illustrate and write to support my habit and family. As it must to (practically) all illustrators of children's books, I too have become an 'author.'"

* * *

LATHAM, Frank B(rown) 1910-

PERSONAL: Born October 20, 1910, in Belington, W.Va.; son of George Robert (a cabinetmaker) and Winifred (Brown) Latham; married Lucille Smith, September 4, 1937; children: Linda Jean. *Education:* West Virginia Institute of Technology, A.B., 1933; Northwestern University, B.S. (journalism), 1934. *Residence:* Carmel, N.Y. *Office:* *Reader's Digest,* 380 Madison Ave., New York, N.Y. 10017.

CAREER: Transradio Press, Chicago, Ill., news editor, 1934-35; Scholastic Magazines, New York, N.Y., 1935-45, associate editor, then managing editor; *Look,* New York, N.Y., senior editor, 1945-71; Reader's Digest Books, New York, N.Y., editorial work on *Encyclopedia of American History,* 1972—. *Member:* Authors Guild of the Authors League of America, Deadline Club of Sigma Delta Chi (New York; vice-president, 1968-70). *Awards, honors:* Named Alumnus of the Year, West Virginia Institute of Technology, 1950.

WRITINGS—All for young people except as noted: (With N. V. Carlisle) *Miracles Ahead* (adult), Macmillan, 1945; *Jed Smith, Trail Blazer,* American Book Co., 1954; *Nathaniel Greene, Fighting Quaker,* American Book Co., 1955; *The Law or the Gun: The Mormons at Far West,* American Book Co., 1956; *Abraham Lincoln,* F. Watts, 1968; *The Dred Scott Decision,* F. Watts, 1968; *Lincoln and the Emancipation Proclamation,* F. Watts, 1968; *The Trial of John Peter Zenger,* F. Watts, 1969; *The Rise and Fall of Jim Crow,* F. Watts, 1969; *The Great Dissenter: Justice John Marshall Harlan,* Cowles, 1970; *Jacob Brown and the War of 1812,* Cowles, 1971; *The Panic of 1893,* F. Watts, 1971; *F.D.R. and the Supreme Court Fight,* F. Watts, 1972; *American Justice on Trial,* F. Watts, 1972; *The Transcontinental Railroad,* F. Watts, 1973.

WORK IN PROGRESS: Serving as consultant and researcher on television program on the Constitution and the Supreme Court.

SIDELIGHTS: Latham says: "My interest in history began at seven when I saw and heard my grandfather, a Union colonel in the Civil War and member of the House during impeachment of Andrew Johnson, pacing the floor and cussing about that event; he was tossed out of the Republican party for voting against impeachment of Johnson. During school days I was greatly influenced by reading John G. Neihardt's *Song of the Indian Wars,* and Stephen Vincent Benet's *John Brown's Body*.... The most valued testimonial I ever received (unsolicitated and not influenced [I hope] by ties of blood) came from my daughter who said: 'Gee, if you had been writing history when I was in school, I'd have liked it much more!'"

* * *

LATHAM, Philip

See RICHARDSON, Robert S(hirley)

* * *

La TOURRETTE, Jacqueline 1926-

PERSONAL: Born May 5, 1926, in Denver, Colo.; daughter of Charles O. and Stella (Bobb) La Tourrette; married David Gibeson, November, 1948 (divorced, 1970); children: Noel, Shane, Brian. *Education:* Attended San Jose State College (now University), 1948-51; St. Margaret's Hospital, Epping, England, nurse's training, 1958. *Residence:* Santa Clara, Calif. *Agent:* Theron Raines, 244 Madison Ave., New York, N.Y. 10016.

CAREER: Teletype operator for Alaska Communications System, 1954-55; Massachusetts Institute of Technology, Cambridge, medical secretary, 1961-69; Kaiser-Permanente Medical Center, Santa Clara, Calif., medical secretary, 1969—.

WRITINGS—Novels: *The Joseph Stone,* Leisure Books, 1971; *A Matter of Sixpence,* Dell, 1972; *The Madonna Creek Witch,* Dell, 1973; *The Previous Lady,* Dell, 1974; *The Pompeii Scroll,* Delacorte, in press.

SIDELIGHTS: "All of my books have required research.... I try to make background material as accurate as possible, no matter how fantastic the plot of the novel. Would rather travel than anything else ... besides write. I spent five years in Alaska, one year in England and Ireland, and have been to Italy [where she researched *The Pompeii Scroll*] twice. My interest in anthropology and archaeology has never left me and I do a lot of reading in these fields, along with others."

* * *

LAURENTI, Joseph L(ucian) 1931-

PERSONAL: Born December 10, 1931, in Hesperange, Luxembourg; naturalized U.S. citizen in 1953; son of Ernest (a lawyer) and Angelina (Dal Canton) Laurenti; married A(lice) Luellen Watson, June 10, 1967. *Education:* University of Illinois, B.A. (cum laude), 1958, M.A., 1959; University of Missouri, Ph.D., 1962. *Politics:* Democrat. *Religion:* Roman Catholic. *Home:* 705 South University, Normal, Ill. 61761. *Office:* Department of Spanish and Italian, Illinois State University, Normal, Ill. 61761.

CAREER: University of Illinois, Urbana, instructor in Spanish, 1958-59; University of Missouri, Columbia, instructor in Spanish, 1959-62; Illinois State University, Normal, assistant professor, 1962-63, associate professor, 1963-66, professor of Spanish and Italian, 1966—. *Military service:* U.S. Army, Intelligence, 1952-54. *Member:* International Association of Hispanists, International Association of Philologists, Modern Language Association of America, American Association of University Professors, American Association of Teachers of Spanish and Portuguese, Midwest Modern Language Association, Illinois Association of Teachers of Modern Languages, Sigma Delta Pi (president of University of Illinois chapter, 1958-59).

WRITINGS: Lazarillo de Tormes: Estudio Critico de la Segunda parte de Juan de Luna (title means "Lazarillo de Tormes: A Critical Study of the Second Part of Juan de Luna"), Studium, 1965; *Ensayo de una bibliografia de la novela picaresca espanola* (title means "A Bibliographic Essay of the Spanish Picaresque Novel"), Consejo Superior de Investigaciones Cientificas, 1968; *Estudios sobre la novela picaresca espanola* (title means "Studies in the Spanish Picaresque Novel"), Consejo Superior de Investigaciones Cientificas, 1970; *Los Prologos en las novelas picarescas espanolas* (title means "Critical Prefaces in the Spanish Picaresque Novel"), Castalia, 1971; (with A. Porqueras Mayo) *Ensayo bibliografico del prologo en la literatura* (title means "A Bibliographic Essay of the Prologue in Literature"), Consejo Superior de Investigaciones Cientificas, 1971; (with Joseph Siracusa) *Relaciones literarias entre Espana e Italia* (title means "Literary Relations between Spain and Italy"), G. K. Hall, 1972; *A Critical Bibliography of Picaresque Literature,* G. K. Hall, 1973; (with Siracusa) *The World of Federico Garcia Lorca,* Scarecrow, 1974. Contributor of articles and reviews to journals in Spain, Italy, Germany, Mexico, and United States. Editorial consultant to *Publications of Modern Language Association,* 1972—.

SIDELIGHTS: Laurenti told *CA:* "I believe that in this world there is something that is worth more than the joys derived from material possessions, better than fortunes, better than health itself, and that is the devotion to the arts and sciences. This has always been my motivation throughout life."

* * *

LAWRENCE, Francis L(eo) 1937-

PERSONAL: Born August 25, 1937, in Woonsocket, R.I.; son of Anthony Francis and Eldora (Bachand) Lawrence; married Mary Kathryn Long, August 23, 1958; children: Elizabeth Ann, Christopher Francis, Naomi, Jennifer Marie. *Education:* St. Louis University, B.S. (honors), 1959; Tulane University, Ph.D., 1962. *Politics:* Democrat. *Religion:* Roman Catholic. *Home:* 2600 Calhoun, New Orleans, La. 70118. *Office:* Department of French and Italian, Tulane University, New Orleans, La. 70118.

CAREER: Tulane University, New Orleans, La., instructor, 1962-64, assistant professor, 1964-67, associate professor, 1967-71, professor of French, 1971—, head of department, 1969—. *Member:* Modern Language Association of America, Modern Humanities Research Association, American Association of Teachers of French, American Association of University Professors, South Central

Modern Language Association, South Central Association of Departments of Foreign Languages.

WRITINGS: Moliere: The Comedy of Unreason, Tulane Studies in Romance Languages and Literature, 1968; (contributor) George B. Daniel, editor, *Moliere Studies,* University of North Carolina Press, 1974; (contributor) Roger Johnson, Edith S. Neumann, and Guy T. Trail, editors, *Moliere and the Commonwealth of Letters: Patrimony and Posterity,* University of Southern Mississippi Press, 1974. Contributor of articles and book reviews to journals in his field. Contributing editor of *Bibliography of French Seventeenth Century Studies,* 1966-72.

WORK IN PROGRESS: A book on Moliere's middle and later work; a study on Racine.

* * *

LAWTON, Charles
See HECKELMANN, Charles N(ewman)

* * *

LAY, Norvie L(ee) 1940-

PERSONAL: Born April 17, 1940, in Cardwell, Ky.; son of Arlie H. (a farmer) and Opha (Burns) Lay; married Judith Finnell, June 12, 1960; children: Lea Anne. *Education:* University of Kentucky, B.S., 1960; University of Louisville, LL.B. (since converted to J.D.), 1963; University of Michigan, LL.M., 1964, S.J.D., 1967. *Politics:* Republican. *Religion:* Baptist. *Home:* 3501 Sorrento Ave., Louisville, Ky. 40222. *Office:* School of Law, University of Louisville, Louisville, Ky. 40208.

CAREER: University of Louisville, Louisville, Ky., assistant professor, 1964-67, associate professor, 1967-70, professor of law, 1970—, assistant dean, 1971-73, associate dean of School of Law, 1973—. Adviser, Jefferson County Bail Bond Project, 1964-68. *Member:* American Bar Association, Kentucky Bar Association, Louisville Bar Association.

WRITINGS: Tax and Estate Planning for Community Property and the Migrant Client, Estate Tax Publishing, 1970; (contributor) Marlin M. Volz, principal author, *West's Federal Practice Manual,* 2nd edition, West Publishing, 1970.

* * *

LAZARON, Hilda R(othschild) 1895-

PERSONAL: Born March 9, 1895, in Baltimore, Md.; daughter of Moses and Miriam (Moses) Rothschild; married Morris S. Lazaron; children: Lee S. Rosenblatt, Elinor Louise Thaviu. *Education:* Peabody Institute, Baltimore, Md., teacher's certificate, 1922; Johns Hopkins University, A.B., 1937, A.M., 1941; Columbia University, Ph.D., 1959. *Religion:* Jewish. *Home:* 241 West Indies Dr., Palm Beach, Fla.

CAREER: Has taught at Johns Hopkins University, and at Graham-Eckes School in Palm Beach, Fla.

WRITINGS: An Introduction to Six Centuries of French Literature, Dimension Books, 1967; *Meet Mme. de Sevigne,* Dimension Books, 1972.

* * *

LEAKE, Chauncey D(epew) 1896-

PERSONAL: Born September 5, 1896, in Elizabeth, N.J.; married, 1921; two children. *Education:* Princeton University, Litt.B., 1917; University of Wisconsin, M.S., 1920, Ph.D., 1923. *Office:* Department of Pharmacology, School of Medicine, University of California, San Francisco, Calif. 94143.

CAREER: University of Wisconsin, Madison, assistant professor, 1923-25, associate professor of pharmacology, 1925-28; University of California, San Francisco, 1928-42, serving as professor of pharmacology, professor of medical history, and librarian in School of Medicine; University of Texas, Medical Branch, Galveston, executive director, 1942-55; Ohio State University, Columbus, professor of pharmacology and lecturer in history and philosophy of medicine, 1955-62; University of California, San Francisco, senior lecturer in history and philosophy of the health professions and senior lecturer in pharmacology, 1962—, coordinator of medical student research training program, 1962-65. Visiting member of Institute for Advanced Study, Princeton, N.J., 1950, 1952, 1954; professor at Hastings College of the Law, 1962-66; member of Motorola Executive Institute, 1970—; member of board of directors of Carter-Wallace, Inc., 1970—; consultant to National Research Council and U.S. Public Health Service. *Military service:* U.S. Chemical Warfare Service, 1918-19.

MEMBER: International Academy for the History of Medicine, International Academy for the History of Science, American Medical Association, American Physiology Society, Society of Experimental History of Medicine (president, 1961-63), American Society for the History of Medicine (president, 1960), History of Science Society (president, 1936-39), American Society of Pharmacology (president, 1958-60), American Academy of Arts and Sciences, National Association of Science Writers (honorary member), Law-Science Academy of America, American Association for the Advancement of Science (fellow; vice-president, 1940; president, 1960), American College of Dentists (honorary fellow), Institute for Biomedical Research (of American Medical Association; member of scientific advisory committee, 1964-69), Hastings Institute Society (honorary fellow). *Awards, honors:* Special awards from International Anesthesia Research Society, 1928, and Western Pharmacology Society, 1965; L.H.D. from Kenyon College, 1959; S.Sc. from Medical College of Pennsylvania, 1963; LL.D. from University of California, 1965; Sc.D. from Philadelphia College of Pharmacy and Science, 1969.

WRITINGS: Personal Medical Ethics, Williams & Wilkins, 1927; (translator and annotator) *William Harvey's "De Motu Cordis,"* C.C Thomas, 1928, 5th edition, 1970; *The Opportunity for Pictorial Art in Modern Medicine: An Example in San Francisco,* privately printed, 1937; *Travelogue 1938,* privately printed, 1938; *California's Medical Story in Fresco,* privately printed, 1939.

Allegory 1945, privately printed, 1945; *Letheon: The Cadenced Story of Anesthesia,* University of Texas Press, 1947; (with Patrick Romanell) *Can We Agree?,* University of Texas Press, 1950; *Ashbel Smith and Yellow Fever in Galveston,* University of Texas Press, 1951; *The Old Egyptian Medical Papyri,* University Press of Kansas, 1952; *Tissue Culture Cadences,* privately printed, 1953; *James Blake, M.D.: On the Relation Between Chemical Constitution and Biological Action,* [Indianapolis, Ind.], 1955; *Some Founders of Physiology,* American Physiological Society, 1956; *The Amphetamines,* C.C Thomas, 1959.

(With Milton Silverman) *Alcoholic Beverages in Clinical*

Medicine, Year Book Medical Publishers, 1966; *What Are We Living For?: Practical Philosophy,* PJD Publications, Part I: *The Ethics,* 1973, Part II: *The Logics,* 1974.

Contributor of about six hundred articles to medical, scientific, philosophy, and education journals. Founder and editor of *Texas Reports on Biology and Medicine,* 1943-55. Consulting editor of *Excerpta Medica, Current Contents, Perspectives in Biology and Medicine, Archives Internationales de Pharmacodynamie,* and *Research Communications in Chemical Pathology and Pharmacology.*

* * *

LEARY, William G(ordon) 1915-

PERSONAL: Born March 26, 1915, in Minneapolis, Minn.; son of Errol W. and Lillian (Giles) Leary; married Celia Graves (a reading specialist), June 10, 1940; children: Peter C., Jan E. (Mrs. Donald M. Burland). *Education:* University of California, Los Angeles, A.B., 1936, M.A., 1938; Stanford University, Ph.D., 1953. *Politics:* Democrat. *Religion:* None. *Home:* 1333 Mountain View Ave., South Pasadena, Calif. 91030. *Office:* California State University, Los Angeles, Calif. 90032.

CAREER: California State Polytechnic University, San Luis Obispo, instructor, 1947-48, assistant professor, 1948-53; California State University, Los Angeles, associate professor, 1953-57, professor of English, 1957—, associate dean of instruction, 1953-57. Visiting professor at Stanford University, summer, 1964; fellow in humanities at Educational Testing Service, summer, 1963. *Military service:* U.S. Navy, 1942-46; became lieutenant senior grade. *Awards, honors:* James Nelson Raymond scholarship from Law School of University of Chicago, 1946, 1947.

WRITINGS: (With James Steel Smith) *Think Before You Write,* Harcourt, 1951; (with Smith) *Thought and Statement,* Harcourt, 1955, 3rd edition (with Richard Blakeslee), 1969; (with Lou LaBrant, Donald A. Bird, and Margaret Painter) *Your Language,* McGraw, Book Five (Leary was not associated with earlier volumes), 1960, Book Six, 1962; (editor with Edgar H. Knapp) *Ideas and Patterns in Literature,* four volumes, Harcourt, 1970; (with Wallace Graves) *From Word to Story,* Harcourt, 1971; *The World of Macbeth,* Harper, in press. Book reviewer and columnist for *Westwood Scene,* 1939, and *San Luis Obispo Telegram-Tribune,* 1948-50.

WORK IN PROGRESS: Shakespeare Plain, a study of Shakespeare's habitual practices as stage craftsman, dramaturgist, and prosodist.

SIDELIGHTS: Leary told *CA:* "All of my books may be described as the direct result of the teacher's itch. I have spent nearly 30 years attempting to devise strategies that will take the innocent, ignorant, unwary, and often recalcitrant student by surprise and teach him something about language and literature. When I succeed, it comes to him as both a surprise and a delight. My books are simply an effort to find a larger audience than the captive one I have in my own classrooms." Leary comments about tennis: "Coming to the game a bit late, I am like the religious convert—a helpless addict."

He adds that love of great paintings and architecture "has led to another helpless addiction—travel in Europe." He has managed to live nearly three full years in most of the countries of western Europe and says "... I stare, like Keats's explorer, with a wild surmise."

LEAS, Speed 1937-

PERSONAL: Born December 26, 1937, in Fresno, Calif.; son of Nathaniel (a contractor) and Ernestine (Burum) Leas; married Constance Stoppel; children: Jocelyn, Winston, Ellen, Nathaniel, Glenn. *Education:* University of California, Berkeley, B.A., 1960; Yale University, M.Div., 1963, M.S.T., 1964; University of California, Los Angeles, professional designation in training and development, 1973. *Office:* Institute for Advanced Pastoral Studies, P. O. Box 809, Bloomfield Hills, Mich. 48013.

CAREER: Ordained minister of United Church of Christ, 1964; University of California, Berkeley, campus minister at Plymouth House, 1959-60; minister of United Church of Christ in Los Angeles, Calif., 1964-67; Center of Metropolitan Mission In-Service Training, Los Angeles, director, 1967-73; Institute for Advanced Pastoral Studies, Bloomfield Hills, Mich., director of action research, 1973—. Interim director, Joint Metropolitan Strategy and Action Coalition, 1969-70. Has lectured at School of Theology at Claremont, American Baptist Seminary of the West, and Fuller Theological Seminary. Has served on board of directors of Family Planning Centers of Los Angeles, Mafundi Institute (cultural and arts center), Los Angeles Council of Churches, and Learning-Earning Action Program. *Member:* Association for Creative Change (professional member), Action Training Coalition.

WRITINGS: (Contributor) Malcolm Boyd, *The Underground Church,* Sheed, 1967; (with Paul Kittlaus) *Church Fights: Managing Conflict in the Local Church,* Westminster, 1973. Contributor to *Newspulse* and *Christian Ministry.*

WORK IN PROGRESS: Pastoral Care Problems and Opportunities in Social Change Ministries, for Fortress.

* * *

LEDERMANN, Walter 1911-

PERSONAL: Born March 18, 1911, in Berlin, Germany; son of William (a physician) and Charlotte (Apt) Ledermann; married Rushi Stadler (an analytical psychologist), March 15, 1946; children: Jonathan. *Education:* University of Berlin, state examination (mathematics and physics), 1933; University of St. Andrews, Ph.D., 1936; University of Edinburgh, D.Sc., 1938. *Home:* 10 Hove Park Rd., Hove, Sussex BN3 6LA, England. *Office:* Department of Mathematics, University of Sussex, Falmer, Brighton, England.

CAREER: St. Andrews University, St. Andrews, Scotland, lecturer in mathematics, 1938-46; University of Manchester, Manchester, England, lecturer, 1946-52, senior lecturer in mathematics, 1952-62; University of Sussex, Falmer, Brighton, England, reader, 1962-65, professor of mathematics, 1965—. Visiting professor of mathematics at Notre Dame University, Ohio State University, Israel Institute of Technology (Haifa), National University of Mexico, and Aarhus (Denmark). Consultant to John Wiley & Sons. *Member:* Institute of Mathematics and Its Applications (member of council, 1973—), Edinburgh Mathematical Society, Royal Society of Edinburgh, London Mathematical Society (member of council, 1967—).

WRITINGS: Introduction to the Theory of Finite Groups, Oliver & Boyd, 1949, 5th revised edition, 1964; *Complex Numbers,* Routledge & Kegan Paul, 1958; *Integral Calculus,* Routledge & Kegan Paul, 1964; *Multiple Integrals,* Routledge & Kegan Paul, 1966; *Introduction to Group

Theory, Oliver & Boyd, 1973. Editor of "Library of Mathematics," twenty-five volumes, Routledge & Kegan Paul, 1950—. Editor of *Journal of London Mathematical Society,* 1968-70, and *Bulletin of London Mathematical Society,* 1973—.

AVOCATIONAL INTERESTS: Amateur chamber music, foreign travel.

* * *

Le DUC, Don R(aymond) 1933-

PERSONAL: Born April 7, 1933, in South Milwaukee, Wis.; son of Ray J. (an engineer) and Roberta (Jones) Le Duc; married Alice M. Pranica, October 24, 1959; children: Paul, Marie. *Education:* University of Wisconsin, B.S., 1959, Ph.D., 1970; Marquette University, J.D., 1962. *Home:* 305 Cheyenne Trail, Madison, Wis. 53705. *Office:* Vilas Communications Hall, University of Wisconsin, Madison, Wis. 53705.

CAREER: Admitted to the Bar of Wisconsin, 1960, and the Bar of U.S. Supreme Court, 1969; private law practice in Green Bay, Wis., 1964-68; University of Wisconsin, Madison, assistant professor, 1970-72, associate professor, 1972-73, professor of communication arts, 1973—. Member of cable television advisory committee, Federal Communications Commission. *Military service:* U.S. Army, Counter Intelligence Corps, 1954-57. *Member:* Federal Communications Bar Association, Broadcast Education Association, Wisconsin Bar Association. *Awards, honors:* Ford Foundation fellow at University of Wisconsin, 1964; research grant from Ohio State University, 1971.

WRITINGS: Cable Television and the FCC: A Crisis in Media Control, Temple University Press, 1973; *Issues in Broadcast Regulation.* Broadcast Education Association, 1974. Contributor to *Annals, Journalism Quarterly,* and *Federal Communications Bar Journal.* Legal editor of *Journal of Broadcasting,* 1972—; editor, *Client* (broadcast regulation newsletter), 1973—.

WORK IN PROGRESS: Comparative analysis of world broadcast systems; research on censorship in national and international communication.

* * *

LEE, C(larence) P(endleton) 1913-

PERSONAL: Born May 26, 1913, in Varner, Ark.; son of C. P. (a planter) and Minnie (Daubs) Lee. *Education:* Washington and Lee University, B.A., 1932, M.A., 1933; Oxford University, B.A., 1935. *Home:* 3628 Cesery Blvd., Jacksonville, Fla. 32211. *Office:* Department of English, Jacksonville University, Jacksonville, Fla. 32211.

CAREER: Southwestern Presbyterian University (now Southwestern at Memphis), Memphis, Tenn., assistant professor of English, 1936-40; Harvard University, Cambridge, Mass., lecturer in English, 1940-45; Clark University, Worcester, Mass., assistant professor of English, 1945-46; U.S. Department of State, Brussels, Belgium, cultural attache, 1946-47; University of Tennessee, Knoxville, Tenn., assistant professor of English, 1947-55; University of Athens, Athens, Greece, Fulbright professor of English, 1955-56; Jacksonville University, Jacksonville, Fla., associate professor, 1961-70, professor of English, 1970—.

WRITINGS: The Unwilling Journey, Macmillan, 1940; *High Noon,* Macmillan, 1943; *Athenian Adventure,* Knopf, 1957; *Library Resources: How to Research and Write a Paper,* Prentice-Hall, 1971.

LEE, Essie E. 1920-

PERSONAL: Born February 9, 1920; married; children: two. *Education:* Lincoln School for Nurses, Diploma in Professional Nursing, 1940; New York University, certificate in physical therapy, 1949, B.A., 1954; Columbia University, M.A., 1956, Ed.D., 1969; City College of the City University of New York, Professional Diploma in Guidance, 1962. *Home:* 150-26 Riverside Dr. W., New York, N.Y. *Office:* Institute of Health Sciences, Hunter College of the City University of New York, New York, N.Y. 10029.

CAREER: Lincoln Hospital, Bronx, N.Y., charge nurse, 1942-44; Department of Health, New York, N.Y., public health nurse, 1944-46; Association for the Aid of Crippled Children, New York, N.Y., public health nurse and physical therapist, 1946-49; Visiting Nurse Service, New York, N.Y., consultant in orthopedic nursing, 1949-56; high school teacher of biology and guidance counselor in the public schools of New York, N.Y., 1956-64; Kingsborough Community College, Brooklyn, N.Y., assistant professor of student services, 1965-69, assistant dean of students, 1965-69, co-ordinator of College Discovery Program, 1966-69; Institute of Health Sciences, Hunter College of the City University of New York, associate professor, 1969—, director of Student Affairs, 1969—. Member of advisory board of N.Y. City Department of Mental Health-Mental Retardation Services; member of board of directors of Jewish Foundation for the Education of Girls.

MEMBER: American Nurses' Association, American Physical Therapy Association, American Personnel and Guidance Association, American Public Health Association, American School Health Association, New York State Guidance Association, New York City Guidance Association.

WRITINGS: Careers in the Health Field, Simon & Schuster, 1972. Associate editor of *Guidance News,* 1962-64; editor of *Occupational Information Newsletter,* 1963-65; reviewer of professional publications for *School Counselor,* 1972—.

WORK IN PROGRESS: A guide for teachers of the new Clara Barton High School for Health Professions; a conversational Spanish paperback; career stories for children.

* * *

LEE, Eugene (Huey) 1941-

PERSONAL: Born December 23, 1941, in Wichita, Kan.; son of Robert M. (a certified public accountant) and Katherine (Langston) Lee; married Sachiko Hattanda, September, 1970; children: Steffanie. *Education:* University of Kansas, B.A., 1963; University of Washington, Seattle, J.D., 1966, LL.M., 1968; University of Tokyo, postdoctoral study, 1968-69. *Home:* 4-2-25 Minami-Azabu, Tokyo, Japan. *Office:* Socio-Economic Institute, Sophia University, Chiyoda-ku, Tokyo, Japan.

CAREER: Sophia University, Tokyo, Japan, visiting assistant professor, 1970-72, professor of international business, 1972—. President of International Investment Consultants, Tokyo, 1973—; director of business firms. *Member:* American Bar Association, Japan Management Association, Washington State Bar Association. *Awards, honors:* Fulbright scholarship to Japan, 1968-69.

WRITINGS: (Editor with Robert J. Ballon) *Foreign Investment and Japan,* Kodansha, 1972. Contributor of articles and translations to journals. Editor, *Law in Japan: An Annual,* 1972-73.

WORK IN PROGRESS: Research on the relationship between government and business in Japan.

AVOCATIONAL INTERESTS: Travel (Korea, Taiwan, Philippines, Singapore), mountaineering.

* * *

LEE, Helen Clara 1919-

PERSONAL: Born July 13, 1919, in Lewisville, Ind.; daughter of Rex Miles (a librarian) and Gladys (Barr) Potter; married Stanley Lee (a college professor), December 22, 1951. *Education:* University of Toledo, A.B., 1940; Northwestern University, M.A., 1948; Indiana University, M.S., 1960, Ed.D., 1968. *Politics:* Democrat. *Religion:* Protestant. *Home:* 1007 Three Rivers East, Fort Wayne, Ind. 46802. *Office:* Department of English, Indiana University, 2101 Coliseum Blvd. E., Fort Wayne, Ind. 46805.

CAREER: High school teacher of English in public high schools of Fort Wayne, Ind., 1945-69; Indiana University, Fort Wayne, assistant professor, 1968-72, associate professor of English education, 1972—. Member of executive board and chairman of education task force of Fort Wayne Future Conference. *Member:* National Council of Teachers of English, Indiana Council of Teachers of English, Northeastern Indiana Council of Teachers of English.

WRITINGS: A Humanistic Approach to Teaching Secondary English, C. E. Merrill, 1973. Contributor to *English Journal, Indiana English Journal, Wisconsin English Journal,* and *Indiana Teacher.*

* * *

LEE, Raymond 1910(?)-1974

1910(?)—June 26, 1974; American actor, magazine publisher, and author of books on the film industry. Obituaries: *New York Times,* June 29, 1974.

* * *

LEECH, Alfred B. 1918(?)-1974

1918(?)—July 7, 1974; American journalist, public relations manager, and author of books on magic. Obituaries: *Washington Post,* July 10, 1974.

* * *

LEECH, Margaret 1893-1974 (Margaret Leech Pulitzer)

November 7, 1893—February 24, 1974; American historian, biographer, and novelist. Obituaries: *New York Times,* February 25, 1974; *Newsweek,* March 11, 1974; *Time,* March 11, 1974; *Current Biography,* April, 1974.

* * *

LEEMING, David Adams 1937-

PERSONAL: Born February 26, 1937, in Peekskill, N.Y.; son of Frank Clifford (an Episcopal priest) and Margaret Adams (Reeder) Leeming; married Pamela Elaine Fraser, July 2, 1967; children: Margaret Adams, Juliet Ann. *Education:* Princeton University, A.B., 1958; summer graduate study at University of Caen, 1959; New York University, M.A., 1964, Ph.D., 1970. *Religion:* Episcopalian. *Home address:* P.O. Box 72, Pomfret, Conn. 06258. *Office:* Department of English, University of Connecticut, U-25, Storrs, Conn. 06268.

CAREER: Robert College, Istanbul, Turkey, teacher of English, 1958-63, 1966-69, *lycee* English department head, 1958-63, 1966-69; University of Connecticut, Storrs, assistant professor of English, 1969—. Secretary-assistant to author James Baldwin in New York and Istanbul, 1964-67. *Member:* Modern Language Association of America, Federation of University Teachers.

WRITINGS: (Editor and author) *Mythology: The Voyage of the Hero,* Lippincott, 1973; *Flights: Readings in Magic, Mysticism, Fantasy, and Myth,* Harcourt, 1974. Contributor to *Comparative Literature, Children's Literature,* and *Revue de Litterature Comparee.*

WORK IN PROGRESS: Henry James and the French Novelists; research on religion and literature; continuing study on mythology.

* * *

LEFEVER, D(avid) Welty 1901-

PERSONAL: Born June 13, 1901, in Ephrata, Pa.; son of Elias Buckwalter (a minister) and Emma (Welty) Lefever; married Ruth Barnhizer, May 28, 1923; children: David Welty. *Education:* La Verne College, A.B., 1921; University of Southern California, M.A., 1922, Ph.D., 1927. *Politics:* Democrat. *Religion:* Church of the Brethren. *Home:* 2787 Lewis Dr., La Verne, Calif. 91750.

CAREER: La Verne College, La Verne, Calif., assistant professor of education, 1922-23; high school teacher and counselor in Compton, Calif., 1923-26; University of Southern California, Los Angeles, instructor, 1926-27, assistant professor, 1927-29, associate professor, 1929-40, professor of educational psychology, 1940-66, professor emeritus, 1966—. Research consultant to Ford Foundation Project on Teacher Education, 1954-58, to Youth Studies Center, University of Southern California, 1959-65, and to school districts. *Member:* National Society for the Study of Education, American Educational Research Association, American Association for the Advancement of Science (fellow), Psychometric Society. *Awards, honors:* D.Sc., University of Southern California, 1966.

WRITINGS: The Prognostic Values of Certain Groupings of the Test Elements of the Thorndike Intelligence Examination, University of Southern California Education Series, 1930; (with A. M. Turrell and H. I. Weitzel) *Principles and Techniques of Guidance,* Ronald, 1941, revised edition, 1950; (with Charlotte Buhler) *A Rorschach Study on the Psychological Characteristics of Alcoholics,* Laboratory of Applied Physiology, Yale University, 1948; (with C. E. Myers and Wendell E. Cannon) *The Recruitment and Training of Teacher Interns,* University of Southern California Press, 1960; (contributor) J. T. Flynn and Herbert Garber, editors, *Assessing Behavior: Readings in Educational and Psychological Measurement,* Addison-Wesley, 1967; (contributor) Ruth Cavan, editor, *Readings in Juvenile Delinquency,* 2nd edition (Lefever was not associated with earlier edition), Lippincott, 1969.

Author with Louis Thorpe and Robert Naslund of "S.R.A. Achievement Series" (comprehensive standardized tests of school achievement with manuals and guide books), Science Research Associates, 1954-58, 1964, 1972. Associate editor, *Journal of Educational Research,* 1941-66, *Journal of Experimental Education,* 1945-66, and *California Journal of Educational Research,* 1949-65.

LEFTON, Robert Eugene 1931-

PERSONAL: Born September 4, 1931, in St. Louis, Mo.; son of Henry (a businessman) and Rose (Ivster) Lefton; married Marlene Shanfeld, June 6, 1954; children: Jeffrey, Cyntheia, Bradley. *Education:* Washington University, A.B., 1953, Ph.D., 1958. *Home:* 61 Ladue Estates Dr., St. Louis, Mo. 63141. *Office:* Psychological Associates, 8220 Delmer, St. Louis, Mo. 63124.

CAREER: Psychological Associates (industrial psychologists), St. Louis, Mo., director of management services, 1958—; Washington University Medical School, St. Louis, Mo., member of faculty, 1958—. Member of board of directors, Direct Mail Corp. of America. *Member:* American Psychological Association, Missouri Psychological Association.

WRITINGS: Dimensional Management Strategies, Behavioral Science Systems, 1968; (with V. R. Buzzotta and others) *Effective Selling Through Psychology,* Wiley, 1972; *Dimensional Interviewing Strategies,* Behavioral Science Systems, 1972.

WORK IN PROGRESS: Conducting research projects on relating the concepts of the behavioral sciences to the development of mature organization and business enterprise.

* * *

LEHMAN, Celia 1928-

PERSONAL: Born April 9, 1928, in Dalton, Ohio; daughter of Grover Cleveland (a farmer) and Fairy (Amstutz) Gerber; married Calvin R. Lehman (a farmer), March 30, 1968; children: Galen, Judith, Audrey, Ethan. *Education:* Goshen College, B.S., 1957; Kent State University, M.A., 1967. *Religion:* Mennonite. *Home address:* Route 1, Dalton, Ohio 44618.

CAREER: Bookkeeper, telephone operator; elementary school teacher in the public schools of Dalton, Ohio, 1957-65; American School of Kinshesa, Democratic Republic of Zaire, teacher, 1965-67; elementary school teacher in the public schools of Kidron, Ohio, 1968—. *Member:* National Education Association, National Educators Fellowship.

WRITINGS: God Is My Best Friend, Standard Publishing, 1973. Contributor to *On the Line* and *Jet Cadets.* Coauthor of "Unto These Hills," a sesquicentennial pageant, Dalton, Ohio, 1972.

* * *

LEHMAN, Sam 1899-

PERSONAL: Born April 28, 1899, in Shawnee, Okla.; son of Glenn Edward (a hardware salesman) and Lula (Clark) Lehman; married Josephine Connor, June 20, 1923 (died, 1949); married Edith Livesay June 21, 1952; children: (first marriage) JoAnne, Jack. *Education:* Attended University of Oregon, 1917-21. *Religion:* Episcopalian. *Home:* 8226 Tenth Ave. S. W., Portland, Ore. 97219.

CAREER: Junction City State Bank, Junction City, Ore., cashier, 1921-32; Home Owner's Loan Corp., Eugene, Ore., manager, 1933-46; Veterans Administration, Portland, Ore., loan officer, 1946-63.

WRITINGS: Selected American Game Birds, Caxton, 1972.

WORK IN PROGRESS: Salmonoids of America, a book about fish.

* * *

LENARCIC, R(aymond) J(ames) 1942-

PERSONAL: Surname is pronounced Len-*are*-sick; born September 11, 1942, in Little Falls, N.Y.; son of Raymond Joseph and Vivian (Van Slyke) Lenarcic; married Faye Mertine (a teacher), August 17, 1968; children: Carrie Lynn, Jennifer Ann. *Education:* State University of New York College at Fredonia, B.A., 1965, M.S., 1966; State University of New York at Albany, further graduate study, 1973—. *Home:* 205 Willis Ave., Herkimer, N.Y. 13350. *Office:* Herkimer County Community College, Lou Ambers Dr., Herkimer, N.Y. 13350.

CAREER: Herkimer County Community College, Herkimer, N.Y., instructor, 1967-69, assistant professor, 1969-73, associate professor of history, 1974—. *Member:* American Historical Association, American Association of University Professors, Community College Social Science Association.

WRITINGS: (Editor) *Selected Readings in American Minorities: The Negro,* Simon & Schuster, 1970; *Western Civilization: A Comparative Analysis,* Selected Academic Readings, 1970; *Pre-Columbian Indians: New Perspectives,* Community College Social Science Association, 1974. Contributor to education journals, including *Eastern Business Teachers Association Journal, New York State Education Journal, Changing Education, Library-College Journal,* and *History Teacher.* Editor of *Community College Social Science Quarterly.*

WORK IN PROGRESS: A topical history of western civilization, for Prentice-Hall; research for a book on Indian wars.

AVOCATIONAL INTERESTS: Slow-pitch softball, golf, basketball, bowling, public speaking.

* * *

LEONARD, Constance (Brink) 1923-

PERSONAL: Born April 27, 1923, in Pottsville, Pa.; daughter of Harry William (an educator) and Dorothy (Jessop) Brink; married John D. Leonard (a journalist), June 21, 1949 (divorced, 1969); children: Gillian. *Education:* Wellesley College, B.A., 1944. *Residence:* Francestown, N.H. 03043.

CAREER: Writer.

WRITINGS: The Great Pumpkin Mystery, Random House, 1971; *The Other Maritha,* Dodd, 1972; *Steps to Nowhere,* Dodd, 1974. Contributor of short fiction to *Redbook* and *Woman.*

WORK IN PROGRESS: A mystery novel.

SIDELIGHTS: Constance Leonard told *CA:* "I have 'always' written—stories, verse, anything—but not for publication until the last few years when I've been settled in an old house in a tiny old village in the New Hampshire mountains. As a longtime mystery addict I thought it would be fun to try writing one, and then another, and another. Aside from writing and reading and friends and good food, I find travel the one essential and have spent quite a lot of time in Europe and Mexico, and the Caribbean. Speak some Spanish, read French better than I speak it, and have just learned my first few words of Serbo-Croatian. At home I'm involved in assorted arts and crafts, most recently pottery and crewel embroidery, and play tennis and Scrabble."

LEONARD, Frank G. 1935(?)-1974

1935(?)—March, 1974; American social worker and novelist. Obituaries: *Publishers Weekly,* April 1, 1974.

* * *

LEONTYEV, Lev Abramovich 1901-1974

Soviet educator, translator, editor, and author of books on political systems, economics, and related topics. Obituaries: *New York Times,* July 5, 1974.

* * *

LEOPOLD, Luna B(ergere) 1915-

PERSONAL: Born October 8, 1915, in Albuquerque, N.M.; son of Aldo (a professor) and Estella (Bergere) Leopold; married Carolyn Clugston, September 6, 1940 (divorced, 1973); married Barbara Beck; children: (first marriage) Madelyn Leopold Fenstermaker, Bruce Carl. *Education:* University of Wisconsin, B.S., 1936; University of California at Los Angeles, M.S., 1944; Harvard University, Ph.D., 1950. *Home:* 400 Vermont Ave., Berkeley, Calif. 94707. *Office:* Department of Geology, University of California, Berkeley, Calif. 94720.

CAREER: With U.S. Soil Conservation Service, 1938-41, U.S. Engineers Office, 1941-42, and U.S. Bureau of Reclamation, 1946; Pineapple Research Institute of Hawaii, Honolulu, head meteorologist, 1946-49; U.S. Geological Survey, hydraulic engineer, 1950—, chief hydrologist, 1957-66, senior research hydrologist, 1966-73; now in the Department of Geology at University of California, Berkeley. *Military service:* U.S. Army Air Forces, Air Weather Service, 1942-46; became captain. *Member:* American Meteorological Society, Geological Society of America (president, 1971), American Geophysical Union, American Society of Civil Engineers, American Academy of Arts and Sciences, American Philosophical Society, National Academy of Sciences, Sigma Xi, Tau Beta Pi, Phi Kappa Phi, Chi Epsilon, Cosmos Club (Washington, D.C.). *Awards, honors:* Distinguished service award from U.S. Department of Interior, 1958; Kirk Bryan award from Geological Society of America, 1958; Veth medal from Royal Netherlands Geological Society, 1963; Cullum Geographical medal from American Geographical Society, 1968; D. Geography from University of Ottawa, 1969; D.Sc. from Iowa Wesleyan College; Rockefeller public service award, 1971.

WRITINGS: (With Thomas Maddock, Jr.) *The Flood Control Controversy,* Ronald, 1954; (with W. B. Langbein) *A Primer on Water,* U.S. Government Printing Office, 1960, enlarged edition prepared by Leopold published as *Water: A Primer,* W. H. Freeman, 1974; (with M. G. Wolman and J. P. Miller) *Fluvial Processes in Geomorphology,* W. H. Freeman, 1964; (with others) *Water,* Time-Life, 1965, revised edition, 1968. Contributor of about one hundred papers to scientific journals.

* * *

LERMAN, Rhoda 1936-

PERSONAL: Born January 18, 1936, in Far Rockaway, N.Y.; daughter of Jacob (an accountant) and Gertrude (Langfur) Sniderman; married Robert Rudolph Lerman (a carpet distributor), September 15, 1957; children: Jill, Julia, Matthew. *Education:* University of Miami, Coral Gables, Fla., B.A., 1957. *Politics:* "Traditional democrat, becoming conservative." *Religion:* Jewish. *Home address:* Shore Acres, Cazenovia, N.Y. 13035. *Agent:* Helen Brann Agency, 14 Sutton Pl. S., New York, N.Y.

CAREER: Syracuse University, Syracuse, N.Y., instructor in English and parapsychology. Former manager of rock and roll band.

WRITINGS: *Call Me Ishtar,* Doubleday, 1973. Contributor to *Nickel Review* and *Syracuse New Times.*

WORK IN PROGRESS: *Kiddo,* completion expected in 1976.

* * *

LERNER, Michael G(ordon) 1943-

PERSONAL: Born January 25, 1943, in London, England; son of Henry W. and Deborah (Stollar) Lerner. *Education:* King's College, Cambridge, M.A., 1965; University of Nottingham, Ph.D., 1969. *Home:* 5 The Glade, Clayhall, Ilford, Essex, England. *Agent:* John Farquharson Ltd., 15 Red Lion Sq., London W.C.1, England. *Office:* Department of French, University of Glasgow, Glasgow W.2, Scotland.

CAREER: University of Glasgow, Glasgow, Scotland, lecturer in French, 1969—. *Member:* Society for French Studies, Oxford and Cambridge Club.

WRITINGS: *Pierre Loti,* Twayne, 1974; *Edouard Rod: A Portrait of the Novelist and His Times,* Mouton, 1974; *Maupassant,* Allen & Unwin, in press.

Author of introduction: Edouard Rod, *Le Sens de la vie,* Slatkine (Geneva), 1973; Edmond L. de Goncourt and Jules A. de Goncourt, *Germinie Lacereux,* Slatkine, in press.

Author of script for radio discussion of Loti, for British Broadcasting Corp. Contributor of more than twenty-five articles and reviews to French studies journals in Europe; contributor of travel articles to British press.

WORK IN PROGRESS: Editing correspondence of Rod and Zola for *Correspondence Generale;* translating nineteenth-century outlines; a novel; a travel book; research on Maupassant, Loti, Boris Vian, Rod, Zola, and other late nineteenth and twentieth-century writers.

SIDELIGHTS: Lerner writes: "As a great globetrotter—having visited most countries including China and worked in Europe, the United Kingdom, Australia, and Canada—I enjoyed writing on Pierre Loti who was a naval officer by profession. Having studied French, German, and Italian at Cambridge I was attracted to Edouard Rod who was Swiss and cosmopolitan in taste."

* * *

LEROUX, Etienne 1922-

PERSONAL: Born June 13, 1922, in Oudtshoorn, Cape, Republic of South Africa; son of Stephanus Petrus (a politician and farmer) and Elizabeth H. (Scholtz) Leroux; married Rene de Wet Malherbe, 1948 (divorced, 1969); married Elizabeth Joubert, November 14, 1970; children: Cherie Malherbe, Helise Scholtz, Stephanus Petrus. *Education:* University of Stellenbosch, B.A., 1942, LL.B., 1944. *Religion:* Dutch Reformed. *Home:* Janee, P. O. Box 60, Koffiefontein, Orange Free State, Republic of South Africa. *Agent:* David Higham Associates Ltd., 5-8 Lower John St., London W1R 3PE, England.

CAREER: Farmer and writer. *Member:* Suid-Afrikaanse Akademie vir Wetenskap en Kuns (South Africa), Maatschappij der Nederlandse Letterkunde (Netherlands). *Awards, honors:* Hertzog prize from South African Academy for Arts and Science, 1964, for *Seven Days at the Silbersteins;* Central News Agency prize (South Africa), 1964, for *One for the Devil.*

WRITINGS—Novels: *Die Eerste lewe van Colet* (title means "The First Life of Colet"), H.A.U.M. (Cape Town), 1955; *Hilaria,* H.A.U.M., 1957; *Die Mugu* (title means "The Square"), H.A.U.M., 1959; *Sewe dae by die Silbersteins,* Human & Rousseau (Cape Town), 1962, translation by Charles Eglington published as *Seven Days at the Silbersteins,* Houghton, 1967 (also see below); *Een vir azazel,* Human & Rousseau, 1964, translation by Eglington published as *One for the Devil,* Houghton, 1968 (also see below); *Die derde oog,* Human & Rousseau, 1966, translation by Amy Starke published as *The Third Eye,* Houghton, 1969 (also see below); *18-44,* Human & Rousseau, 1967, translation by Cassandra Perrey published under same title, Houghton, 1972; *Isis, Isis, Isis,* Human & Rousseau, 1969; *To a Dubious Salvation: A Trilogy of Fantastic Novels* (contains *Seven Days at the Silbersteins, One for the Devil,* and *The Third Eye),* Penguin, 1972; *Na'va* (title means "Beautiful"), Human & Rousseau, 1972.

Contributor of short fiction to collections: *Schrijversalmanak,* edited by Bert Voeten and M. Beck, C. P. J. van der Peet (Netherlands), 1957; *Windroos,* Afrikaanse Pers-Boekhandel, 1964; *Herinnering se wei,* Afrikaanse Pers-Boekhandel, 1966; *Son op die land,* Tafelberg-Uitgewers, 1967; *Bolder,* edited by Hennie Auchamp, Tafelberg-Uitgewers, 1973.

WORK IN PROGRESS: A novel based on the Boer War, *Magersfontein, O, Magersfontein,* completion expected in 1975.

SIDELIGHTS: Leroux told *CA:* "My novels to date consist of three trilogies [*Die Eerste lewe van colet, Hilaria,* and *Die Mugu; To a Dubious Salvation;* and *18-44, Isis, Isis, Isis,* and *Na'va*], with undercurrents of Jungian mythology. In the process I had to integrate Hebrew, Greek, Egyptian, Slavonic, and Hindu mythology at diverse levels. I do *not* write allegorical novels. I try to write *into* the symbol. A little bit of black magic is involved. I am not the best seller type and most of my readers are slightly kinky. I am seriously involved with man's estate but I am not involved with any form of social protest. As ironist, basically, I try to achieve a detachment of a clinical nature. At the same time my images occur straight from the unconscious, alive with all sorts of archetypes. In a sense, I find an affinity with someone like Herman Hesse as well as with Evelyn Waugh."

Of his novel in progress, Leroux writes: "[It is] based on a famous battle between the Boers and the English at the end of the last century. The last gentleman's war. The scene is near my farm and the novel is an experiment in irony and satire in a contemporary medium."

Leroux has traveled, mainly to gather material for his writing, to Spain, France, Greece, and Israel. He belongs to a group of writers in South Africa called the Sestigers, whose aim is complete freedom of expression.

BIOGRAPHICAL/CRITICAL SOURCES: J. C. Kannemeyer, *Op weg na welgevonden,* Human & Rousseau, 1970; F. I. J. van Rensburg, *Gesprekke met skrywers,* Tafelberg-Uitgewers, 1971.

LeROY, Douglas 1943-

PERSONAL: Born October 27, 1943, in Liberty, S.C.; son of John Thaddeus (in textiles) and Ida (Sluder) LeRoy; married Wanda Thompson, August 31, 1963; children: Dina Kay, Donald Todd, Dara Rae. *Education:* Lee College, Cleveland, Tenn., B.A., 1965. *Politics:* Republican. *Home:* 2705 Gardenia Ave. N.W., Cleveland, Tenn. 37311. *Office:* Church of God Publishing House, 1080 Montgomery Ave., Cleveland, Tenn. 37311.

CAREER: Ordained minister of the Church of God; pastor in Fargo, N.D., 1965-66; Northwest Bible College, Minot, N.D., instructor in religion, 1966-68; Church of God, Oklahoma City, Okla., youth and Christian education director, 1968-72; Church of God Publishing House, Cleveland, Tenn., administrative assistant to editor-in-chief, 1972—, managing editor, *Evangel,* 1972—. Member of executive committee of Cleveland (Tenn.) Community Service Agency, 1974—. *Member:* International Pentecostal Press Association, International Christian Camping, International Platform Association, Evangelical Press Association, National Fellowship of Christian Educators, Smithsonian Institution (associate), Upsilon Xi, Pi Delta Omicron. *Awards, honors:* Women's Christian Temperance Union Oratorical Award and American Legion Oratorical Award, both 1961; Balfour Award, 1965.

WRITINGS: I Didn't Know That, Pathway Press, 1973; *Ministering to Youth,* Pathway Press, 1973. Writer of senior high Sunday School curriculum for Church of God, 1972—. Contributor to religious publications.

WORK IN PROGRESS: We Believe (children's book); *Fruit of the Spirit,* completion expected in 1975.

AVOCATIONAL INTERESTS: Reading, tennis, softball, football, photography.

* * *

LESLIE, Anita 1914-

PERSONAL: Born November 21, 1914, in London, England; daughter of Shane (a poet and author) and Marjorie (Ide) Leslie; married William King (commander in the British Navy), 1949; children: Richard Tarka Bourke, Leonie Rose. *Education:* "Seven unfortunate governesses, five day schools, four boarding schools." *Politics and religion:* "We don't mention these in Ireland!" *Home:* Oranmore Castle, County Galway, Ireland.

CAREER: Biographer, author. Trainer of Connemara ponies and horses, 1960—. Ambulance driver attached to the British Army in the Western Desert, 1941-42, with the British Red Cross in Syria and Italy, 1943, and with the French Army in France and Germany, 1944-45.

WRITINGS: Train to Nowhere (autobiographical), Hutchinson, 1948; *Love in a Nutshell* (travel), Greenberg, 1952; *The Remarkable Mr. Jerome* (biography), Holt, 1954 (published in England as *The Fabulous Leonard Jerome,* Hutchinson, 1954); *Mrs. Fitzherbert* (biography), Scribner, 1960; *Mr. Frewen of England: A Victorian Adventurer* (biography), Hutchinson, 1966; *Jennie: The Life of Lady Randolph Churchill* (biography), Hutchinson, 1969, published as *Lady Randolph Churchill: The Story of Jennie Jerome,* Scribner, 1970; *Edwardians in Love,* Hutchinson, 1972, published as *The Marlborough House Set,* Doubleday, 1973.

SIDELIGHTS: "Miss Leslie has gracefully filled a gap in the Churchill archives," writes an *Esquire* reviewer of

Lady Randolph Churchill, "bringing into true perspective the Jerome contribution to the makeup of a character often taken to be quintessentially English." As a member of the family (she is Jennie Jerome's great-niece), Miss Leslie had access to family documents and personal reminiscences of family members, material that was not generally available (as is the case with her biographies of Leonard Jerome and Maria Fitzherbert, and the story of the Marlborough House). Often praised as a "delightful biography" and a "highly readable and sympathetic book," *Lady Randolph Churchill* is also seen as the story of a whole political and social era. V. G. Kiernan writes that "the book's real worth lies in the cumulative impression it conveys, trivial or boring as most of the detail may be, of the private life of the class by which [England] has allowed itself in modern times to be ruled."

Of her own writing, Miss Leslie once stated: "I have always been determined to keep writing a pleasure and I manage to drape the rest of my life around the job. . . . Probably few writers are lucky enough to have a secondary occupation which contrasts so nicely with their studies as I have. Horses go very well with writing. They keep me out of doors during the best hours of the day and send me indoors, mentally hungry towards sundown. After a bath I forget stable dramas and return with renewed interest to that unfinished paragraph."

* * *

LESLIE, Robert Franklin 1911-

PERSONAL: Born October 21, 1911, in Dublin, Tex.; son of Frank (a builder) and Ana May (Morison) Leslie; married Lea Rochat, September 13, 1937. *Education:* University of California, Santa Barbara, B.A., 1939; University of Southern California, M.A., 1942. *Home and office:* 4555 Longridge Ave., Sherman Oaks, Calif. 91403.

CAREER: Teacher of French and Spanish in public schools in Carpinteria, Calif., 1940-45, and Pasadena, Calif., 1949-53; Harvard School, North Hollywood, Calif., teacher of French, Spanish, and photography, 1953-70. *Wartime service:* American Red Cross, field director associated with U.S. Marine Corps, 1945-46; served in the Philippines and Japan. *Awards, honors:* Notable Book award from Southern California Council on Literature for Children and Young People, 1968, for *The Bears and I.*

WRITINGS—Nonfiction: *Green Hell,* Macfadden, 1962; *Read the Wild Water,* Dutton, 1966; *High Trails West,* Crown, 1967; *The Bears and I,* Dutton, 1968; *Wild Pets,* Crown, 1970; *Wild Burro Rescue* (juvenile), Childrens Press, 1973; *Wild Courage* (juvenile), Childrens Press, 1974; *In the Shadow of a Rainbow,* Norton, 1974. Contributor to popular magazines, including *Reader's Digest, Argosy, Westways,* and *Defenders of Wildlife.*

WORK IN PROGRESS: Two historical novels; six animal books for children.

SIDELIGHTS: Leslie, of Scottish and Cherokee Indian ancestry, has explored wilderness regions of western Canada and the United States, and Mexico, living for long periods of time in remote woodland, desert, and mountain areas. He has canoed most rivers and many back-country lakes in the western United States and Canada, hiked thousands of miles along western trail systems, and climbed mountains in North America, Japan, and Europe, including the Schwartz face of the Matterhorn.

As an amateur archaeologist, Leslie has amassed a large collection of Indian relics and lore. As an ecologist, he lectures and writes about preservation of desert, mountain, and forest wilderness areas. As a photographer, he has shown movies nationally on television and has conducted photography tours throughout Southwestern Indian reservations, Mexico, Canada, and Europe. *Avocational interests:* Leather carving, wood sculpture.

* * *

LESSER, Alexander 1902-

PERSONAL: Born October 4, 1902, in New York, N.Y.; son of Harris and Rachel (Barnett) Lesser; married Virginia M. Hirst (an artist and teacher), 1940; children: Ann (Mrs. Desmond Margetson), Stephen Alexander, Katherine Maren. *Education:* Columbia University, A.B., 1923, Ph.D., 1929; attended New School for Social Research, 1920-25. *Home:* 39 Elmtree Lane, Levittown, N.Y. 11756. *Office:* Department of Anthropology, Hofstra University, Hempstead, N.Y. 11550.

CAREER: Businessman in New York, N.Y., 1923-25; Columbia University, New York, N.Y., lecturer in anthropology, 1934-39; Brooklyn College (now Brooklyn College of the City University of New York), Brooklyn, N.Y., instructor in anthropology, 1939-46; Association on American Indian Affairs, New York, N.Y., executive director, 1947-59; Hofstra University, Hempstead, N.Y., professor of anthropology, 1960—, chairman of department, 1960-65. Visiting associate professor, University of Pennsylvania, summer, 1931, Northwestern University, 1938, and Brandeis University, 1956-59; visiting professor at University of California, Berkeley, summer, 1964, Columbia University, 1964-68, John Jay College of the City University of New York, 1968-69, and New School for Social Research, 1969; distinguished visiting professor, Brooklyn College of the City University of New York, 1974. Lecturer at institutions, organizations, and conferences, including New York University, 1935, Young Men's Hebrew Association, 1937-39, Brooklyn Academy of Arts and Sciences, 1938, and Cooper Union Institute, 1940. Field leader, Laboratory of Anthropology, Santa Fe, N.M., 1935. Social science analyst, Office of Coordinator for Inter-American Affairs, 1943-44; chief of economic studies section, Latin American Division, Office of Strategic Services, 1944-45; chief of north and northeast branch, Division of Research on American Republics, U.S. Department of State, 1945-47.

MEMBER: American Anthropological Association (fellow), American Ethnological Society (secretary-treasurer, 1933-39; vice-president, 1939-41; director, 1942-44), American Folklore Society (life member), Society for Applied Anthropology, Current Anthropology (associate), African Studies Association, Sigma Xi. *Awards, honors:* Committee on American Indian Languages research fellow, 1929, 1933-34; Social Science Research Council fellow, 1929-30; Columbia University Council for Research in the Social Sciences grant, 1930-33; American Council of Learned Societies fellow, 1931-32; certificate of merit from Office of Strategic Services, 1946; Bollingen Foundation fellow, 1960-62; American Philosophical Society grant, 1970-72.

WRITINGS: (With Paul Radin) *Social Anthropology,* McGraw, 1932; *Pawnee Ghost Dance Hand Game: A Study of Cultural Change,* Columbia University Press, 1934, reprinted, AMS Press, 1969; (editor) Franz Boas, *Race, Language, and Culture,* Macmillan, 1940; *Survey of Research in the United States on Latin America,* National

Research Council, 1946; (contributor) Morton Fried, Marvin Harris, and Robert Murphy, editors, *War: The Anthropology of Armed Conflict,* Natural History Press, 1968; *Franz Boas: His Life and Work,* Columbia University Press, in press.

Contributor to *International Encyclopedia of Social Sciences* and to professional journals. Contributing editor, *American Year Book,* 1935-38, and *New International Year Book,* 1936-39; editor and member of board of editors, American Ethnological Society, 1937-40; editor, *American Indian,* 1947-59.

WORK IN PROGRESS: Books and papers on Franz Boas.

BIOGRAPHICAL/CRITICAL SOURCES: Robert Harry Lowie, *History of Ethnological Theory,* Farrar & Rinehart, 1937.

* * *

LESSER, Eugene (Bernard) 1936-

PERSONAL: Born June 25, 1936, in New York, N.Y.; son of Sigmund (a tailor) and Beatrice (Goldman) Lesser; children: Ona. *Education:* Attended University of Connecticut, 1955-57, and San Francisco State College (now San Francisco State University), 1967-69. *Politics:* None. *Religion:* All. *Address:* Box 656, Woodacre, Calif. 94973.

CAREER: Truck driver in California, 1973—.

WRITINGS: Poems of an Acrophobic Steeplejack, Magdalene Syndrome Press, 1967; (with Janet Brown and others) *Two Births,* Bookworks, 1972. Represented in *A First Reader of Contemporary American Poetry,* edited by Patrick Gleeson, C. E. Merrill, 1969.

WORK IN PROGRESS: A book of poems; *Birthday Book,* a compilation of birthdates and birthplaces of people he knows or of whom he has heard.

AVOCATIONAL INTERESTS: Writing songs.

* * *

Le SUEUR, Meridel 1900-

PERSONAL: Born February 22, 1900, in Murray, Iowa; daughter of Arthur and Marion Le Sueur; husband deceased; children: Rachel La Sueur, Deborah Le Sueur. *Education:* "My education was to live and travel below ground and on the surface and above ground in the Midwest. I did not finish high school; was a drop out before the first world war. There have always been drop outs." *Politics:* "My politics is that of life." *Religion:* "My religion, the world." *Home:* 1635 Victoria S., St. Paul, Minn. 55118.

CAREER: Writer since the age of fifteen ("or perhaps earlier"). Instructor in writing courses at University of Minnesota. *Awards, honors:* Second prize in Work Progress Administration (WPA) writing contest in the 1940's (Richard Wright was the first-prize winner).

WRITINGS: Annunciation, limited edition, Platen Press, 1935; *Salute to Spring and Other Stories,* International Publishers, 1940; *North Star Country,* Duell, Sloan & Pearce, 1945; *Little Brother of the Wilderness: The Story of Johnny Appleseed,* Knopf, 1947; *Nancy Hanks of Wilderness Road: A Story of Abraham Lincoln's Mother,* Knopf, 1949; *Sparrow Hawk* (story of an Indian boy), Knopf, 1950; *Chanticleer of Wilderness: A Story of Davy Crockett,* Knopf, 1951; *The River Road: A Story of Abraham Lincoln,* Knopf, 1954; *Crusaders* (biography of her parents), Blue Heron, 1955; *Corn Village: A Selection,* Stanton & Lee, 1971; *The First Book of the Conquistadores,* F. Watts, in press; *The First Book of the Mound Builders,* F. Watts, in press. Work included in *American Folkways,* edited by Erskine Caldwell. Contributor to magazines and newspapers through the years.

WORK IN PROGRESS: A book of poems about Indian women, *Changing Woman;* a long narrative of Demeter and Persephone; a book on Robert Emmet, Irish patriot, researched in Dublin.

SIDELIGHTS: Ms. Le Sueur wrote: "I am very much interested in illuminating areas of history which have been in the dark. I have taken literally hundreds of tapes of Northwest farmers and workers. I love to write for the New People as I call the young of today—their minds are open, pure and alive."

Meridel Le Sueur also mentioned that she retained her maiden name after marriage, and that both daughters use her surname. "This was and is a kind of matriarchy," she notes. She lives part of the year in the Southwest, pursuing an interest in the Pueblo and Hopi Indians.

* * *

LETICHE, John M(arion) 1918-

PERSONAL: Born November 11, 1918, in Kiev, Russia; came to United States, 1941; naturalized citizen, 1949; son of Leon and Mary (Grossman) Letiche; married Emily Kuyper, November 17, 1945; children: Hugo K. *Education:* McGill University, B.A., 1940; University of Chicago, M.A., 1941, Ph.D., 1951. *Home:* 968 Grizzly Peak, Berkeley, Calif. 94708. *Office:* Department of Economics, University of California, 250 Barrows Hall, Berkeley, Calif. 94708.

CAREER: University of California, Berkeley, assistant professor, 1952-56, associate professor, 1956-60, professor of economics, 1960—. Rockefeller fellow to Council on Foreign Relations, New York, N.Y., 1945-46; special technical economic adviser, United Nations Economic Commission for Africa, 1961-62; consultant, U.S. Departments of State, Labor, and Treasury, 1962—; Smith-Mundt Visiting Professor to University of Aarhus and University of Copenhagen, 1951-52. *Member:* American Economics Association (member of nominating committee, 1968-69), Econometrica Society, Royal Economic Society, African Studies Association, American Society of International Law (member of board of directors, 1969—). *Awards, honors:* Guggenheim fellowship, 1956-57; Certificate of merit from *Encyclopaedia Britannica,* 1971, Institute of World Affairs, 1972, University of Michigan International Legal Center, 1972.

WRITINGS: Reciprocal Trade Agreements in the World Economy, King's Crown Press, 1948; *System Or Theory of the Trade of the World,* Johns Hopkins Press, 1957; *Balance of Payments and Economic Growth,* Harper, 1959, reprinted, Augustus M. Kelley, 1967; *Report on the Monetary Systems of Africa: Their Impact on Trade and Development,* United Nations Economic Commission for Africa, 1963; (editor and author of foreword) *A History of Russian Economic Thought: Ninth Through Eighteenth Centuries,* University of California Press, 1964; *Nigerian Reconstruction,* Nigerian Institute of International Affairs, 1971; *Dependent Monetary Systems and Economic Development: The Case of Sterling East Africa,* Macmillan, 1974.

Contributor to *Encyclopaedia Britannica, Encyclopedia of the Social Sciences* and to journals in his field.

LEVI, Edward H(irsch) 1911-

PERSONAL: Born June 26, 1911, in Chicago, Ill.; son of Gerson B. and Elsa B. (Hirsch) Levi; married Kate Sulzberger, June 4, 1946; children: John G., David F., Michael E. *Education:* University of Chicago, Ph.B., 1932, J.D., 1935; Yale University, J.S.D., 1938. *Home:* 5855 University Ave., Chicago, Ill. 60637. *Office:* Office of President, University of Chicago, 5801 Ellis Ave., Chicago, Ill. 60637.

CAREER: Admitted to Bar of State of Illinois, 1936; University of Chicago, Chicago, Ill., assistant professor of law, 1936-40; U.S. Department of Justice, Washington, D.C., special assistant to Attorney General, 1940-45, first assistant in War Division, 1943, chairman of Interdepartmental Committee on Monopolies and Cartels, 1944, first assistant in Antitrust Division, 1944-45; University of Chicago, professor of law, 1945—, dean, 1950-62, provost, 1962-68, president, 1968—. Counsel for Subcommittee on Monopoly Power, Judiciary Committee of U.S. Congress, 1950. Thomas Guest Professor at University of Colorado, 1960. Member of Citizens Commission of Graduate Medical Education, 1963-66, President's Task Force on Priorities in Higher Education, 1969-70, Commission on Foundations and Private Philanthropy, 1969-70, and Sloan Commission on Cable Communications, 1970-71. Member of board of trustees of International Legal Center, 1966—, University of Chicago, 1966—, Urban Institute, 1968—, Aspen Institute for Humanistic Studies, 1970, Russell Sage Foundation, 1971—, Chicago Museum of Science and Industry, 1971—, Woodrow Wilson National Fellowship Foundation, 1972—; honorary member of board of trustees, Institute of International Education, 1971—.

MEMBER: Council of American Law Institute, American Academy of Arts and Sciences (fellow), Social Science Research Council, Council on Legal Education for Professional Responsibility, American Bar Foundation (fellow), American Bar Association, American Judicature Society, Illinois Bar Association, Chicago Bar Association, Institute of Psychoanalysis (member of board of trustees), Chicago Council on Foreign Relations (director, 1973—), Phi Beta Kappa, Order of the Coif, Commercial Club, Cosmos Club, Century Club, Quadrangle Club, Columbia Yacht Club, Standard Chicago Club, Executives Club, Wayfarers Club.

AWARDS, HONORS: LL.D. from University of Michigan, 1959, Jewish Theological Seminary of America, 1968, University of Iowa, 1968, Brandeis University, 1968, University of California at Santa Cruz, 1968, Lake Forest College, 1968, University of Rochester, 1969, University of Toronto, 1971, Yale University, 1973, University of Notre Dame, 1974, Denison University, 1974; L.H.D., from Hebrew Union College, 1968, Loyola University of Chicago, 1970, DePaul University, 1973; University of California at Berkely certificate of honor, 1968; Phi Beta Kappa's distinguished service medal, 1970, Chicagoan of the Year in Education, 1970; officer of French Legion of Honor, 1973.

WRITINGS: (Editor with J. W. Moore) *Gilbert's Collier on Bankruptcy,* Mathew Bender, 1937; (editor with R. S. Steffen) *Elements of the Law, Cases and Materials on the Elements of the Law,* University of Chicago Bookstore, 1936-37, 4th edition published as University of Chicago Press, 1950; *Four Talks on Legal Education,* University of Chicago Press, 1952; (contributor) Sidney Hook, editor, *Law and Philosophy,* New York University Press, 1964; *Introduction to Legal Reasoning,* University of Chicago Press, 1949, revised edition, 1961; *Point of View,* University of Chicago Press, 1969; (contributor) George C. Christie, editor, *Jurisprudence: Text and Readings on the Philosophy of Law,* West Publishing, 1973. Contributor to journals.

* * *

LEVIN, Benjamin H.

PERSONAL: Son of Herschel (a fabric dyer) Levin; married Madeline Fuller, May, 1950; children: Bernice, Joan, Clinton. *Home:* 3190 Claridge Rd., Cornwells Heights, Bucks County, Pa. 19020.

CAREER: Illustrator, pharmacist, short story writer, and novelist.

WRITINGS: *To Spit Against the Wind* (novel), Citadel, 1971; *Black Triumvirate: A Novel of Haiti,* Citadel, 1972.

WORK IN PROGRESS: A novel.

* * *

LEVINE, Adeline 1925-

PERSONAL: Born December 12, 1925, in Geneva, New York; daughter of Benjamin and Sarah (Rosen) Gordon; married Murray Levine (professor of psychology at State University of New York at Buffalo), June 15, 1952; children: David, Zachary. *Education:* Edward J. Meyer Memorial Hospital School of Nursing, Buffalo, N.Y., R. N., 1948; Beaver College, B.A., 1962; Yale University, M.A., 1966, Ph.D., 1968. *Home:* 74 Colonial Circle, Buffalo, N.Y. 14213. *Office:* Department of Sociology, State University of New York, 4224 Ridge Lea, Buffalo, N.Y. 14226.

CAREER: Held various nursing positions, 1948-50; Delaware State Hospital, Wilmington, clinical instructor in psychiatric nursing, 1952-53; State University of New York at Buffalo, assistant professor, 1968-70, associate professor of sociology, 1970—, director of undergraduate studies, 1970-72, head of sociology department, 1972—. *Member:* American Sociological Association, American Association for the Advancement of Science, Eastern Sociological Association.

WRITINGS—All with husband, Murray Levine: *A Social History of Helping Services: Clinic, Court, School, and Community,* Appleton, 1970; (editor and author of introduction) Randolph Bourne, *The Gary Schools,* M.I.T. Press, 1970; (contributor) G.D. Goldman and D.N. Milman, editors, *Psychoanalytic Contributions to Community Psychology,* C.C Thomas, 1971; (contributor) Rollo Handy, editor, *Education and the Behavioral Sciences,* Warren H. Green, in press. Contributor to proceedings and to professional journals.

* * *

LEVINE, Faye (Iris) 1944-

PERSONAL: Born January 18, 1944, in Stamford, Conn.; daughter of Bernard Harold Shulman and Lillian (Haft) Shulman Levine. *Education:* Radcliffe College, A.B. (cum laude), 1965; Harvard University, Ed.M., 1970. *Home:* 21 West 85th St., #5A, New York, N.Y. 10024.

CAREER: Kamla Raja Girls' College, Gwalior, Madhya Pradesh, India, teacher of English, 1965-66; *New York Post,* New York, N.Y., reporter, 1968; *Herald* (weekly), New York, N.Y., assignment editor, 1971-72. *Member:* Society of Magazine Writers, Rock Writers of the World,

National Young Judaea (corresponding secretary, 1960-61), Redstockings of the Women's Liberation Movement, Bio-Feedback Research Society, Radcliffe Club of New York. *Awards, honors:* Bread Loaf Writers' Conference fellowship, 1967, for four *Atlantic Monthly* articles; Radcliffe Institute fellowship, 1973-74.

WRITINGS: The Strange World of the Hare Krishnas, Fawcett, 1974. Contributor to *New Yorker, Ms., Atlantic Monthly, Harper's, Newsday, Newsweek, Penthouse, Ramparts, Rolling Stone, Hierophant, Fusion, New York Ace, Physician's World, Boston Phoenix,* and *Harvard Graduate School of Education News.* Editor of *Harvard Crimson,* 1964, and *Redstockings Journal/Feminist Revolution,* 1974.

WORK IN PROGRESS: A nonfiction book about the arts, completion expected in 1975; a science fiction novel.

BIOGRAPHICAL/CRITICAL SOURCES: New York Times, January 24, 1965, December 6, 1965; *Fusion,* June, 1973; *Publishers Weekly,* January 21, 1974.

* * *

LEVINE, Mark Lee 1943-

PERSONAL: Born May 4, 1943, in Denver, Colo.; son of Duke (a restaurant owner) and Bee (Hellerstein) Levine; married Ellen H. Sachter (a legal secretary and real estate agent), March 9, 1972. *Education:* Colorado State University, B.A. (magna cum laude), 1965; University of Denver, J.D., 1968; Northwestern University, P.A.P., 1969; New York University, LL.M., 1969. *Religion:* Jewish. *Home:* 1818 East 7th Ave., Denver, Colo. 80218. *Office:* 1139 Delaware, Denver, Colo. 80218.

CAREER: Goldsmith & Carter (law firm), Denver, Colo., law clerk, 1966-68; state court practice and district attorney clerkship in Denver, Colo., 1967; admitted to the Bar of the State of Colorado, 1968, and the Bar of the U.S. Supreme Court, 1971; licensed as insurance broker, 1969; Arthur Young & Co. (certified public accountants), Denver, Colo., tax division lawyer, 1968; private practice of law in Denver, Colo., 1968-74; Leuwe, Potler, Wesserfeld, Denver, Colo., attorney, 1974—. Real estate broker in Denver, Colo., 1968—; president and chairman of the board, Real Estate Unlimited, Inc., 1968—; assistant professor at Metropolitan State College, 1969—; instructor at University of Colorado, 1969—, and at Real Estate Investments, 1969—; teacher at Arapahoe College, 1973, and at Community College of Denver, 1973; lecturer in real estate tax and law.

MEMBER: National Association of Realtors, American Bar Association, American Business Law Association, American Arbitration Association, Colorado Bar Association, Colorado Association of Realtors, Denver Bar Association, Denver Association of Realtors, Phi Kappa Phi, Phi Sigma Delta. *Awards, honors:* International Law Institute grant in France, 1968.

WRITINGS: Review Manual for the Colorado Real Estate Examination, Kendall/Hunt, 1972; *Real Estate Transactions, Tax and Related Consequences,* West Publishing, 1973, supplement, 1974; *Business and the Law,* W. C. Brown, 1974; *Review Manual for the Multi State and Uniform Examination,* Advantage, 1974; *Real Estate Fundamentals,* W. C. Brown, in press. Contributor to *Commercial Law Journal, Legal Economics News, Journal of Taxation, Colorado Lawyer, Colorado CPA Report,* and *New York Times.*

WORK IN PROGRESS: Future Interests in Colorado; Introduction to Business.

LEVINE, Murray 1928-

PERSONAL: Born February 24, 1928, in Brooklyn, N.Y.; son of Israel and Birdie (Cutler) Levine; married Adeline Gordon (an associate professor of sociology at State University of New York at Buffalo), June 15, 1952; children: David, Zachary. *Education:* City College (now City College of the City University of New York), B.S., 1949; University of Pennsylvania, M.A., 1951, Ph.D., 1954. *Home:* 74 Colonial Circle, Buffalo, N. Y. 14213. *Office:* Department of Psychology, State University of New York, 4230 Ridge Lea, Buffalo, N.Y. 14226.

CAREER: Veterans Administration, Philadelphia, Pa., staff psychologist, 1954-56; research clinical psychologist, Devereux Schools, 1956-63; Yale University, New Haven, Conn., assistant professor, 1963-64, associate professor of psychology and director of clinical training program, 1964-68; State University of New York at Buffalo, professor of psychology and director of graduate community psychology program, 1968—. Research consultant, Southeastern Pennsylvania Heart Association, 1957-59; associate in psychology, University of Pennsylvania, 1959; lecturer, Beaver College, 1962-63. *Member:* International Association of Applied Psychology, American Association for the Advancement of Science, American Psychological Association, American Orthopsychiatric Association, American Public Health Association, American Association of University Professors, National Society for the Study of Education, Eastern Psychological Association.

WRITINGS: (With George Spivack) *The Rorschach Index of Repressive Style,* C.C Thomas, 1964; (with S.B. Sarason, I.I. Goldenberg, D.L. Cherlin, and E.M. Bennett) *Psychology in Community Settings,* Wiley, 1966; (with wife, Adeline Levine) *A Social History of Helping Services: Clinic, Court, School, and Community,* Appleton, 1970; (editor and author of introduction with Adeline Levine) Randolph Bourne, *The Gary Schools,* M.I.T. Press, 1970.

Contributor: M.L. Hoffman and L.N. Hoffman, editors, *Review of Child Development Research,* Russell Sage, 1966; Frances Kaplan and S.B. Sarason, editors, *The Psycho-Educational Clinic Papers and Research Studies,* Massachusetts Department of Mental Health, 1969; (with wife, Adeline Levine) D.N. Milman and G.D. Goldman, editors, *Psychoanalytic Contributions to Community Psychology,* C.C Thomas, 1971; Jack Zusman and D.L. Davidson, editors, *Practical Aspects of Mental Health Consultation,* C.C Thomas, 1972; Stuart Golann and Carl Eisdorfer, editors, *Handbook of Community Mental Health,* Appleton, 1973; (with wife Adeline Levine) Rollo Handy, editor, *Education and the Behavioral Sciences,* Warren H. Green, in press; I.I. Goldenberg, editor, *Clinical Psychologists in the World of Work,* Heath, in press; H.E. Mitchell, editor, *Community Psychology Monograph Series,* Volume II, Behavioral Publications, in press.

Contributor to State University of New York at Buffalo *Studies in Psychotherapy and Behavioral Change,* and to professional journals. Member of editorial board, *American Journal of Community Psychology.*

* * *

LEVINE, Suzanne Jill 1946-

PERSONAL: Born October 21, 1946, in New York, N.Y.; daughter of Meyer and Elaine (Berger) Levine. *Education:* Vassar College, B.A., 1967; Columbia University, M.A.,

1969; New York University, Ph.D. candidate, 1972—. *Home:* 2 King St., Apt. 2A, New York, N.Y. 10012.

CAREER: Free-lance translator and writer.

WRITINGS: Latin America: Fiction and Poetry in Translation (bibliography), Center for Inter-American Relations, 1970; (contributor) Helmy F. Giacoman, editor, *Homenaje a Gabriel Garcia Marquez,* Las Americas, 1972.

Translator: (Contributor) Mark Strand, editor, *New Poetry of Mexico,* Dutton, 1970; Manuel Puig, *Betrayed by Rita Hayworth,* Dutton, 1971; G. Cabrera Infante, *Three Trapped Tigers,* Harper, 1971; Jose Donoso, Carlos Fuentes, and Severo Sarduy, *Triple Cross,* Dutton, 1972; Julio Cortazar, *All Fires the Fire,* Pantheon, 1973; Puig, *Heartbreak Tango,* Dutton, 1973; (contributor) Barbara Howes, editor, *The Eye of the Heart,* Bobbs-Merrill, 1973; (contributor) E. Rodriquez Monegal and Thomas Colchie, editors, *The Borzoi Book of Latin American Literature,* Knopf, 1974. Also translator of eight short plays produced by Miriam Colon's Puerto Rican Traveling Theatre, New York, 1972.

Contributor of articles and reviews to journals in her field.

WORK IN PROGRESS: Translating *Cobra,* by Severo Sarduy, and *Plan de evasion,* by Adolfo Bioy Casares, both for Dutton.

* * *

LEVINGER, George 1927-

PERSONAL: Born February 5, 1927, in Berlin, Germany; came to United States, 1941; son of Willy (a physician) and Charlotte (Stern) Levinger; married Ann Cotton, June 14, 1952; children: William, James, Matthew, David. *Education:* Columbia University, A.B., 1946; University of California, Berkeley, M.A., 1951; University of Michigan, Ph.D., 1955. *Religion:* Society of Friends (Quaker). *Home:* Bay Rd., Amherst, Mass. 01002. *Office:* Department of Psychology, University of Massachusetts, Amherst, Mass. 01002.

CAREER: Bunge Corp. (import-export firm), New York, N.Y., employee, 1947-48; University of Michigan, Ann Arbor, research associate at Research Center for Group Dynamics, 1954-55, and in department of psychology, 1955-57; Bryn Mawr College, Bryn Mawr, Pa., assistant professor of social work and social research, 1957-60; Western Reserve University, Cleveland, Ohio, associate professor of social work and psychology, 1960-65; University of Massachusetts, Amherst, associate professor, 1965-69, professor of psychology, 1969—. Visiting scholar at University of Konstanz, summer, 1967, and Institute for Social Research, Oslo, 1972-73; visiting fellow at Yale University, 1970-71. *Military service:* U.S. Army, 1945-47; became sergeant.

MEMBER: American Psychological Association (fellow), American Association for the Advancement of Science (fellow), Society of Experimental Social Psychology (member of executive committee, 1971-74), Eastern Psychological Association. *Awards, honors:* National Institute of Mental Health senior research fellow at Yale University, 1970-71; research grants from National Science Foundation, National Institute of Child Health and Human Development, Cleveland Foundation, and other agencies.

WRITINGS: (With J. D. Snoek) *Attraction in Relationship: A New Look at Interpersonal Attraction,* General Learning Press, 1972.

Contributor: Dorwin Cartwright, editor, *Studies in Social Power,* Institute for Social Research, University of Michigan, 1959; J. K. Hadden and M. L. Borgatta, editors, *Marriage and the Family: A Comprehensive Reader,* F. E. Peacock, 1960; R. F. Winch and L. W. Goodman, editors, *Selected Studies in Marriage and the Family,* 3rd edition (Levinger was not associated with earlier editions), Holt, 1968; P. H. Glasser and L. N. Glasser, editors, *Families in Crisis,* Harper, 1970; Alan L. Grey, editor, *Man, Woman, and Marriage,* Atherton, 1970; W. R. Scott, editor, *Social Structures and Social Processes,* Holt, 1970; Ailon Shiloh, editor, *Studies in Human Sexual Behavior: The American Scene,* C. C Thomas, 1970; T. L. Huston, editor, *Foundations of Interpersonal Attraction,* Academic Press, 1974. Contributor of articles and reviews to psychology, social work, and family life journals. Advisory editor, *Family Process,* 1968—; associate editor, *Journal of Marriage and Family,* 1969-70; consulting editor, *Sociometry,* 1970-72.

WORK IN PROGRESS: The Social Psychology of Mateship.

AVOCATIONAL INTERESTS: Chess, outdoor sports and other family recreations.

* * *

LEWIN, L(eonard) 1919-

PERSONAL: Born July 22, 1919, in Southend, England; son of Abraham (a printer) and Leza (Roth) Lewin; married Daphne Dorothy June Smith (a dental nurse), July 10, 1943; children: David Ian, Wendy Patricia (Mrs. John Collins). *Education:* Attended schools in Southend, England. *Home:* 980 McIntire, Boulder, Colo. 80303. *Office:* Department of Engineering, University of Colorado, Boulder, Colo. 80302.

CAREER: British Admiralty, engineering officer, 1940-46; Standard Telecommunication Laboratories, Harlow, England, 1946-68, becoming head of microwave department in 1950, assistant manager in 1960, and senior principal research engineer in 1968; University of Colorado, Boulder, professor of engineering, 1968—. Consultant to MEDION and to Standard Telecommunication Laboratories. Founder and president, Institute for Research on the Dissemination of Human Knowledge, 1969—. *Member:* Institution of Electrical Engineers, Institute of Electrical and Electronics Engineers. *Awards, honors:* Institute of Electrical and Electronics Engineers microwave prize, 1962; W. G. Baker award, 1962; D.Sc., University of Colorado, 1967.

WRITINGS: Advanced Theory of Waveguides, Iliffe, 1951; *Dilogarithms and Associated Functions,* Macdonald & Co., 1959; (contributor) Leo Young, editor, *Advances in Microwaves,* Academic Press, 1965; (editor) *The Diffusion of Sufi Ideas in the West: An Anthology of New Writings by and about Idries Shah,* Keysign Press, 1972; *Theory of Waveguides,* George Newnes, 1974.

WORK IN PROGRESS: Research on optical fiber communication, on antenna theory, on waveguides, and on field theory.

AVOCATIONAL INTERESTS: Entomology.

* * *

LEWIS, Harry 1942-

PERSONAL: Born November 10, 1942, in Brooklyn, N.Y.; son of Sol (a historian and publisher) and Sylvia (Pincus) Lewis. *Education:* Attended Bard College, 1960;

Brooklyn College of City University of New York, B.A. (cum laude), 1965; New York University, M.A., 1969; University of Massachusetts, further graduate study, 1972-73. *Politics:* Anarchist. *Home address:* R.D. 1, Williamsburg, Mass. 01096. *Office:* Mulch Press, P.O. Box 426, Amherst, Mass. 01002.

CAREER: Anti-Defamation League, New York, N.Y., associate editor in publishing department, 1965-66; New York University, New York, N.Y., guest lecturer, 1967-69; Mulch Press, Amherst, Mass., editor and publisher, 1970—. Instructor in American literature and remedial English at Jersey City State College, 1969-72; part-time instructor in poetry at University of Massachusetts, 1973; director of community writers project at Orchard Hill Residential College, University of Massachusetts, spring, 1974. Has taught remedial reading to high school students; has conducted readings and workshops. *Member:* Alpha Kappa Delta.

WRITINGS—Poems: *Crab Cantos,* For Now Press, 1969; *Before and After Abraham,* Loose Change Books, 1971; (translator) Vladimir Mayakovsky, *Brooklyn Bridge,* Broadway Boogie Press, 1974.

Work is represented in anthologies, including *Ten American Poets,* Euphoria Press, 1968; *Where Is Vietnam?,* edited by Walter Lowenfels, Doubleday, 1968; *Inside Outer Space,* edited by Robert Vas Dias, Doubleday, 1970.

Contributor of about sixty poems, stories, translations, and reviews to newspapers and magazines, including *Village Voice, For Now, Mulch, Boston Phoenix, Widening Circle, Promethean,* and *Nation.* Editor of *Landscapes,* of Brooklyn College of the City University of New York, 1963-64; editor of *Pogamoggan* (literary magazine), 1965-66; editor of "Planet News," poetry column in *East Village Other,* 1969; co-editor of *Mulch,* 1972—; book review editor of *Valley Advocate* (newspaper), 1973—.

WORK IN PROGRESS: A book of poems; a detective novel series; a translation of Mayakovsky's poems and journals of his American visit in 1925.

* * *

LEWIS, Hilda (Winifred) 1896-1974

British educator, and author of novels and historical works. Obituaries: *AB Bookman's Weekly,* July 15, 1974.

* * *

LEWIS, Thomas S(pottswood) W(ellford) 1942-

PERSONAL: Born May 29, 1942, in Philadelphia, Pa.; son of William Draper, Jr. (a field examiner for the National Labor Relations Board) and Belle (Wellford) Lewis; married Gillian Hollingworth (a librarian), August 29, 1964; children: Colin Geoffrey, Hilary Caroline. *Education:* University of New Brunswick, B.A., 1964; Columbia University, M.A., 1965, Ph.D., 1970. *Home:* 213 Regent St., Saratoga Springs, N.Y. 12866. *Office:* Department of English, Skidmore College, Saratoga Springs, N.Y. 12866.

CAREER: Iona College, New Rochelle, N.Y., instructor in English, summer, 1967; Skidmore College, Saratoga Springs, N.Y., instructor, 1968-70, assistant professor of English, 1970—. *Member:* Modern Language Association of America, American Association of University Professors. *Awards, honors:* Woodrow Wilson fellow, 1968; American Philosophical Association grant, 1971.

WRITINGS: (Editor) *Letters of Hart Crane and His Family,* Columbia University Press, 1974; (editor) *Virginia Woolf,* McGraw, 1974. Contributor to journals.

WORK IN PROGRESS: Books on Virginia Woolf and on the Bloomsbury Group's attitudes toward biography.

* * *

LICHTENSTEIN, Grace 1941-

PERSONAL: Born December 25, 1941, in New York, N.Y.; daughter of Alvin (a musician and civil servant) and Rose (Smith) Rosenthal; married Stephen Lichtenstein, June 9, 1962 (separated, 1970). *Education:* Brooklyn College (of City University of New York), A.B., 1962. *Home:* 16 West 74th St., New York, N.Y. 10023. *Agent:* Julian Bach Agency, 3 East 48th St., New York, N.Y. 10016. *Office: New York Times,* 229 West 43rd St., New York, N.Y. 10036.

CAREER: R. R. Bowker Co., New York, N.Y., advertising copywriter, 1964-66; *New York Times,* New York, N.Y., advertising copywriter, 1966-68, radio news scriptwriter, 1968-70, reporter, 1970—. *Member:* Newspaper Guild.

WRITINGS: A Long Way, Baby: Behind the Scenes in Women's Pro Tennis, Morrow, 1974. Contributor to *Esquire, Redbook, Seventeen, Cosmopolitan, New York Times Magazine,* and *New York.*

AVOCATIONAL INTERESTS: Skiing, tennis, watching western movies, travel, yoga, listening to rock music.

* * *

LIGHTNER, Robert P(aul) 1931-

PERSONAL: Born April 4, 1931, in Cleona, Pa.; son of Earnest A. and Edith (Miller) Lightner; married Pearl Hostetter, July 27, 1952; children: Nancy Kay, Nadine Pearl, Natalie Sue. *Education:* Baptist Bible Seminary, Johnson City, N.Y., Th.B., 1955; Dallas Theological Seminary, Th.M., 1959, Th.D., 1964; Southern Methodist University, M.L.A., 1972. *Politics:* Republican. *Home:* 2449 Wildoak Circle, Dallas, Tex. 75228. *Office:* Dallas Theological Seminary, 3909 Swiss Ave., Dallas, Tex. 75204.

CAREER: Ordained minister of the Baptist Church, 1968. Grace Baptist Church, DeQueen, Ark., pastor, 1956-57; Baptist Bible Seminary, Johnson City, N. Y., instructor, 1959-61, assistant professor, 1964-66, associate professor of systematic theology, 1967-68, head of department, 1964-66; Dallas Theological Seminary, Dallas, Tex., assistant professor of systematic theology, 1969—. *Member:* Evangelical Theological Society, Near East Archaeological Society.

WRITINGS: Neo-Liberalism, Regular Baptist Press, 1959; *Neo-Evangelicalism,* Regular Baptist Press, 1959; *The Tongues Tide,* Empire State Baptist, 1964; *Speaking in Tongues and Divine Healing,* Regular Baptist Press, 1965; *The Saviour and the Scriptures,* Presbyterian & Reformed Publishing, 1966; *The Death Christ Died: A Case for Unlimited Atonement,* Regular Baptist Press, 1967; *Triumph through Tragedy,* Baker Press, 1969; *Church Union: A Layman's Guide,* Regular Baptist Press, 1971; *The First Fundamental: God,* Thomas Nelson, 1973.

WORK IN PROGRESS: Research on salvation of infants.

* * *

LINDAUER, Lois Lyons 1933-

PERSONAL: Born February 6, 1933, in Brooklyn, N.Y.;

daughter of Kermit and Rose (Schneidman) Lyons; married William E. Seltz; children: Karen Lindauer, Amy Lindauer. *Education:* Brandeis University, B.A., 1953. *Home:* 749 Park Ln., East Meadow, N.Y. 11554. *Office:* The Diet Workshop, 1975 Hempstead Turnpike, East Meadow, N.Y. 11554.

CAREER: Copywriter in Boston advertising agency, 1956-57; designer and interior decorator in New York, N.Y., 1960-65. Founder of The Diet Workshop, first held in Boston, Mass., 1965, owner, 1965—.

WRITINGS: It's In To Be Thin . . . The Diet Workshop Way, Prentice-Hall, 1971; *The Diet Workshop Restaurant Manual,* Restaurant Business, 1972; *The Fast and Easy Teenage Diet,* Universal Publishing & Distributing, 1973. Writer of syndicated column, "It's In To Be Thin."

* * *

LINDEMANN, Albert S(hirk) 1938-

PERSONAL: Original name, Albert E. Shirk, Jr.; name legally changed in 1972; born May 19, 1938, in Santa Monica, Calif.; son of Albert Enos, Sr. and Clara (Scarth) Shirk; married Barbara K. Lindeman (a college teacher), August 31, 1964; children: Timothy William. *Education:* Pomona College, B.A., 1960; Harvard University, M.A., 1962, Ph.D., 1968. *Home:* 1470 Tunnel Rd., Santa Barbara, Calif. 93105. *Office:* Department of History, University of California, Santa Barbara, Calif. 93106.

CAREER: Stanford University, Stanford, Calif., instructor in history, 1965-66; University of California, Santa Barbara, assistant professor, 1966-73, professor of history, 1973—. Member of executive board, Tri-Counties Central Labor Council, 1972-74. *Member:* American Federation of Teachers, American Association of University Professors, American Historical Association. *Awards, honors:* Fulbright fellowship, 1960; Woodrow Wilson fellowship, 1961-62.

WRITINGS: The Red Years: European Socialism vs. Bolshevism, 1919-21, University of California Press, 1974; *History of European Socialism,* Harper, in press. Contributor to *Problems of Communism, Labor History,* and *Russian History.*

SIDELIGHTS: Lindemann has competence in French, Italian, Spanish, German, and Russian.

* * *

LINDER, Bertram L. 1931-

PERSONAL: Born June 10, 1931, in Brooklyn, N.Y.; son of Victor and Yeva (Schneidman) Linder; married Eva Feldman, July 3, 1955; children: Jeffrey, Eric, Elise. *Education:* Attended Cooper Union College, 1948-50; New York University, B.A., 1953, M.A., 1956. *Home:* 3354 Emeric Ave., Wantagh, N.Y. 11793. *Office:* Adlai E. Stevenson High School, 1980 Lafayette Ave., Bronx, N.Y. 10473.

CAREER: Assistant principal and administrator in Bronx, N.Y., and New York, N.Y., 1967-70; high school teacher of social studies and assistant principal in the public schools of Bronx, N.Y., 1970—. Adjunct assistant professor at New York University, 1963-68. *Member:* National Council for the Social Studies (president, Social Studies Supervisors Association, 1974), Association of Teachers of Social Studies (president, 1968-69), Association for Supervision and Curriculum Development, Association of Educational Communication and Technology, New York State Council for the Social Studies, New York City Social Studies Supervisors Association (president, 1968-69).

WRITINGS: Economics for Young Adults, Sadlier, 1971; *The Negro in American History* (standardized test), United States Armed Forces Institute, 1972; (with Edwin Selzer) *You the Consumer,* Sadlier, 1973; (with Selzer) *Exploring Civilizations,* Globe Book, 1974; (with Selzer) *You the Worker,* Sadlier, 1974. Contributor to *Social Education.* Multi-media editor of *Bulletin of Association of Teachers of Social Studies in New York City,* 1967—.

* * *

LINDQUIST, Emory Kempton 1908-

PERSONAL: Born February 29, 1908, in Lindsborg, Kan.; son of Harry Theodore and Augusta (Peterson) Lindquist; married Irma W. E. Lann, June 17, 1942; children: Beth, Kempton. *Education:* Bethany College, Lindsborg, Kan., A.B., 1930; Oxford University, B.A., 1930, M.A., 1933; University of Colorado, Ph.D., 1941. *Politics:* Democrat. *Religion:* Lutheran. *Home:* 3901 Pine Knot Ct., Wichita, Kan. 67208. *Office:* Clinton Hall, Wichita State University, Wichita, Kan. 67208.

CAREER: Bethany College, Lindsborg, Kan., assistant professor, 1933-38, professor of history, 1938-53, vice-president, 1938-41, acting president, 1941-43, president, 1943-53; Wichita State University, Wichita, Kan., professor of history, 1953-55, 1961-63, 1968—, dean of faculty, 1955-61, president, 1963-68. *Member:* National Education Association, American Historical Association, Kansas State Historical Society (president, 1963; member of the board of directors, 1959—), Phi Beta Kappa, Pi Kappa Delta. *Awards, honors:* Rhodes scholar at Oxford University, 1930-33; Royal Order of the North Star, from Sweden, 1952; LL.D., Augustana College, Rock Island, Ill., 1952; D.H.L., Bethany College, Lindsborg, Kan., 1964; D.Litt., Friends University, 1972.

WRITINGS: Smoky Valley People: A History of Lindsborg, Kansas, Augustana Historical Society, 1953; *Vision for a Valley: Olof Olsson and the Early History of Lindsborg,* Augustana Historical Society, 1970; *An Immigrant's Two Worlds,* Augustana Historical Society, 1972. Contributor to *Kansas Historical Quarterly, Missouri Historical Review,* and *Swedish Pioneer Historical Review.*

WORK IN PROGRESS: A biography of Ernst Skarstedt, Swedish-American journalist and author.

* * *

LINEBARGER, J(ames) M(orris) 1934-

PERSONAL: Surname is pronounced with a hard "g"; born July 6, 1934, in Abilene, Tex.; son of James Elmo (a tax assessor) and Mamie Estelle (Gaines) Linebarger; married Lillian Tillery (a professor), July 25, 1958; children: Terry Glyn, Steven Randall. *Education:* Columbia University, A.B., 1956, M.A. (with honors), 1957; Emory University, Ph.D., 1963. *Home address:* Route 1, Argyle, Tex. 76226. *Office:* Department of English, North Texas State University, Denton, Tex. 76203.

CAREER: Georgia Institute of Technology, Atlanta, instructor, 1957-59, assistant professor of English, 1960-62; North Texas State University, Denton, assistant professor, 1963-65, associate professor, 1965-70, professor of English, 1970—. *Member:* Modern Language Association of America, Conference of College Teachers of English, Poetry

Society of America, American Association of University Professors, Texas Association of College Teachers, Poetry Society of Texas.

WRITINGS: John Berryman, Twayne, 1974. Work is anthologized in *The New Breed: An Anthology of Texas Poets,* edited by Dave Oliphant, Prickly Pear Press, 1973. Contributor to literary journals, including *Concerning Poetry, Quartet, Encore, Laurel Review, Southwest Review,* and *Southern Humanities Review.*

WORK IN PROGRESS: A book of poems, for Trilobite Press.

* * *

LINOWES, David F(rancis) 1917-

PERSONAL: Born March 16, 1917, in Freehold, N.J.; married Dorothy Lee Wolf, March 24, 1946; children: Joanne Gail, Richard Gary, Susan Joyce, Jonathan Scott. *Education:* University of Illinois, B.S. (with honors), 1941. *Home:* 9 Wayside Lane, Scarsdale, N.Y. 10583. *Office:* 25th floor, 919 Third Ave., New York, N.Y. 10022.

CAREER: Leopold & Linowes, Washington, D.C., partner in certified public accounting and management consulting firm, 1946-63; L. D. Leidesdorf and Co. (certified public accountants), New York, N.Y., partner, 1963-65; Laventhol, Krekstein, Horwath & Horwath (auditors and management consultants), New York, N.Y., partner, 1965—. Chief executive officer of Mickelberry Corp., 1970-73; adjunct professor at New York University, 1966-72; Distinguished Arthur Young Visiting Professor at University of Illinois, 1973-74. Chairman of Citizens Committee to Combat Charity Rackets, 1953-58; chairman of City Affairs Committee of New York Chamber of Commerce, 1970-73; member of board of directors of Chris-Craft Industries, Horn & Hardart Corp., Piper Aircraft Corp., Saturday Review/World Magazine, Inc., University of Illinois Foundation, and Religion in American Life, Inc.; consultant to former Secretary of Health, Education, and Welfare, John W. Gardner, and to U.S. Department of State and United Nations (headed missions to Turkey, Pakistan, India, and Greece, 1967-71). *Military service:* U.S. Army, Signal Corps, 1942-46; became first lieutenant.

MEMBER: American Academy of Political Science, Committee for Economic Development, Conference Board, U.S. Chamber of Commerce, United Nations Association (director), American Institute of Certified Public Accountants (vice-president, 1962-63); District of Columbia Institute of Certified Public Accountants, (president, 1956-57), Beta Gamma Sigma (director), Phi Alpha Chi, Beta Alpha Psi. *Awards, honors:* Human Relations Award from American Jewish Committee, 1970.

WRITINGS: Managing Growth Through Acquisition, Amacom, 1968; *Strategies for Survival,* Amacom, 1973; *The Corporate Conscience,* Hawthorn, 1974.

Contributor: Alvin L. Arnold, editor, *Accounting Practice for the Seventies,* Hanover-Lamant, 1970; Maurice Moonitz, editor, *Public Accounting,* California Education and Research Foundation, 1971; D. R. Carmichael and John J. Willingham, editors, *Perspectives in Auditing,* McGraw, 1971; Ralph W. Estes, editor, *Accounting and Society,* Melville Publishing Co., 1973; K. Fred Skousen and Belverd E. Needles, Jr., editors, *Contemporary Thought in Accounting and Organizational Control,* Dickenson, 1973; John L. Livingston and Sanford C. Gunn, editors, *Accounting for Social Goals,* Harper, 1974. Contributor to business journals, including *Nation's Business, Business and Society Review, New York Times, Conference Board Record,* and *Journal of Accountancy.*

WORK IN PROGRESS: Rebirth of a Nation.

* * *

LIPKIN, Gladys B(albus) 1925-

PERSONAL: Born November 8, 1925, in New York, N.Y.; daughter of Richard Rothschild (a physician) and Sally ("a household engineer"; maiden name, Silverman) Balbus; married Nathan J. Lipkin (an orthodontist), May 28, 1953; children: Harriet, Alan, Rebecca. *Education:* Cornell University—New York Hospital School of Nursing, B.S. and R.N., 1947; Adelphi University, M.S., 1971; additional study at North Shore University Hospital, 1973—, and Rutgers University, 1973. *Politics:* Independent. *Religion:* Jewish. *Home:* 224-47 76th Rd., Bayside, N.Y. 11364. *Office:* North Shore University Hospital, Community Dr., Manhasset, N.Y. 11030.

CAREER: North Shore University Hospital, Manhasset, N.Y., clinical nurse specialist, 1971—; Adelphi University, Garden City, N.Y., assistant clinical professor, 1971—; private practioner of family and individual psychotherapy, 1973—. *Member:* American Nurses Association, Nurses Association of American College of Obstetricians and Gynecologists, American Society for Psychoprophylaxis in Obstetrics, American Society of Childbirth Educators, Sigma Theta Tau.

WRITINGS: (With Claire Hoffman and Ella Thompson) *Simplified Nursing,* 8th edition (Lipkin was not associated with earlier editions), Lippincott, 1968; (with Hoffman) *Practical Nursing Workbook,* Lippincott, 1969; (with Roberta Cohen) *Effective Approaches to Patients' Behavior,* Springer Publishing, 1973; *Psychosocial Aspects of Maternal-Child Nursing,* Mosby, 1974. Contributor to *American Journal of Nursing* and *R.N.*

WORK IN PROGRESS: A new edition of *Simplified Nursing* and a workbook, with Claire Hoffman, completion expected in 1976; longitudinal studies on parent-newborn relationships.

* * *

LIPPMAN, Leopold 1919-

PERSONAL: Born September 27, 1919, in New York, N. Y.; son of Henry J. and Fanny (Schapira) Lippman; married Eleanor Gans (a program analyst), June 17, 1942; children: Roger Henry, David Charles, Peter Jonathan, Jeremy George. *Education:* City College (now City College of the City University of New York), B.S.S., 1939; Columbia University, M.P.H., 1972. *Home:* 1162 East Laurelton Pkwy., Teaneck, N. J. 07666.

CAREER: Free-lance writer and public relations consultant in Seattle, Wash., 1949-61; Washington Association for Retarded Children, Seattle, executive director, 1952-63; State of California Mental Retardation Programs, Sacramento, coordinator, 1963-68; City of New York, Services for the Mentally and Physically Handicapped, New York, N.Y., director, 1968-72. *Member:* American Association on Mental Deficiency, Council for Exceptional Children, National Association of Social Workers, National Rehabilitation Association.

WRITINGS: Attitudes Toward the Handicapped: A Comparison Between Europe and the United States, C. C

Thomas, 1972; (with I. Ignacy Goldberg) *Right to Education: Anatomy of the Pennsylvania Case and Its Implications for Exceptional Children,* Teachers College Press, 1973.

* * *

LIPSCOMB, David M(ilton) 1935-

PERSONAL: Born August 4, 1935, in Morrill, Neb.; son of Roy Milton (a salesman) and Elsie (Schmidt) Lipscomb; married Dixie Lea Johnson, June 28, 1957; children: Scott David, Steven Roy, Shari Lea. *Education:* University of Redlands, B.A., 1957, M.A., 1959; University of Washington, Seattle, Ph.D., 1966; also studied at Purdue University, 1959-60, and University of Oregon, 1969. *Politics:* Democrat. *Religion:* Baptist. *Home:* 4524 Royalview Rd., Knoxville, Tenn. 37921. *Office:* Department of Audiology, University of Tennessee, Knoxville, Tenn. 37916.

CAREER: West Texas State University, Canyon, assistant professor of speech, 1960-62; University of Tennessee, Knoxville, assistant professor of audiology and speech pathology, 1962-64; Veterans Administration Outpatient Clinic, Seattle, Wash., audiology graduate trainee, 1964-66; University of Tennessee, assistant professor, 1966-69, associate professor, 1969-73, professor of audiology and speech pathology, 1973—, director of audiology clinical services, 1966-69, director of Noise Research Laboratory, 1970—. Clinical audiologist for Amarillo Regional Hearing and Speech Foundation, 1960-62; instructor at University of Washington, Seattle, 1965. Vice-president of Industrial Noise Consultants, Inc., 1970—; member of research advisory board of Early Auditory Research Foundation, 1972—. Member of advisory board of Tennessee Board of Hearing Aid Dispensers, 1969-70; member of scientific advisory committee of Environmental Defense Fund, 1970—; member of technical sub-committee on noise of Tennessee Environmental Council, 1971; special adviser to Environmental Protection Agency's Office of Noise Abatement and Control, 1973—. More than a hundred television and radio appearances include "First Tuesday," NBC-Television, April 1, 1969; "The Today Show"; British Broadcasting Corp., July 6, 1971; Public Broadcasting System, November, 1973; NBC-Monitor Radio, November 11, 1972. Film consultant to Public Broadcasting System; consultant to U.S. Army Medical Research Laboratory, 1971, and to industry.

MEMBER: International Audiological Society, American Association for the Advancement of Science, American Acoustical Society, American Speech and Hearing Association (fellow; member of legislative council, 1972-74), Southern Audiological Society (member of executive board, 1972-73; president, 1974-75), Tennessee Hearing Aid Society (lifetime honorary member). *Awards, honors:* University of Tennessee alumni public service award, 1973.

WRITINGS: (Contributor) William A. Thomas, editor, *Indicators of Environmental Quality,* Plenum, 1972; *Noise: The Unwanted Sounds,* Nelson-Hall, 1974; *An Introduction to Laboratory Methods for the Study of the Ear,* C.C Thomas, 1974; (contributor) Jerry Northern, editor, *Communication Problems in Hearing Loss,* Little, Brown, 1974. Contributor of more than thirty-five articles and reviews to professional journals, including *Journal of the Acoustical Society of America, Journal of Audiology Research, Journal of the Tennessee Medical Association, Hearing and Speech News, Hearing Instruments,* and *Laryngoscope.* Member of editorial board of *Clinical Pediatrics,* 1969—; member of editorial advisory board of *Hi Fi World,* 1974—.

WORK IN PROGRESS: The Ear as It Was Meant to Be Seen; research on the effects of noise on the ear and body.

BIOGRAPHICAL/CRITICAL SOURCES: National Geographic, June, 1973.

* * *

LIPSKI, Alexander 1919-

PERSONAL: Born July 29, 1919, in Berlin, Germany; naturalized U.S. citizen; son of Jack (an exporter) and Margaret (Gollust) Lipski; married Ruth-Maria Kuenkel (a school psychologist); children: Beatrice Carolyn, Irene Dorothea, Sophia Christine. *Education:* University of California, Berkeley, B.A., 1950, M.A., 1951, Ph.D., 1953. *Religion:* "Self-realization Fellowship." *Home:* 7127 Resebay St., Long Beach, Calif. 90808. *Office:* Department of History, California State University, Long Beach, Calif. 90801.

CAREER: Michigan State University, East Lansing, instructor, 1954-55, assistant professor of history, 1955-58; California State University at Long Beach, assistant professor, 1958-61, associate professor, 1961-65, professor of history, 1965—. *Member:* American Historical Association, Association for Asian Studies, American Academy of Religion, Institute of Historical Studies (Calcutta), Bengal Studies Association, Bengali Association of Southern California, Phi Beta Kappa. *Awards, honors:* American Council of Learned Societies research grant, 1960.

WRITINGS: Bengal East-West, Center for Asian Studies, Michigan State University, 1970. Contributor of articles on Indian religion to journals.

WORK IN PROGRESS: A book on the life of St. Vijay Krishna Goswami, 1841-1899, and his contribution to the religious renaissance in nineteenth-century India.

SIDELIGHTS: Besides his native German, Lipski speaks Bengali, Swedish, Russian, and French.

* * *

LISKER, Sonia O. 1933-

PERSONAL: Born March 22, 1933, in New York, N.Y.; daughter of Nat and Mrs. Olson; married Anthony Gargagliano (a commercial art studio owner), 1964; children: Shawn, Carla, Arlen, Emily, Peter. *Education:* Cooper Union, graduate, 1954. *Home and office:* 72 Cooper Lane, Larchmont, N.Y. 10538.

CAREER: Young and Rubicam, Inc. (advertising agency), New York, N.Y., television art director and writer, 1954-59; freelance illustrator, 1959—; writer. Guest teacher at College of New Rochelle, 1971—. *Member:* Authors Guild. *Awards, honors:* Art Directors awards, 1957, 1958, for television commercials.

WRITINGS—Children's books; all self-illustrated: *I Can Be,* Hastings House, 1972; *The Attic Witch,* Four Winds, 1973; *I Am,* Hastings House, 1973; *Lost,* Harcourt, in press.

Illustrator: Judy Blume, *Freckle Juice,* Four Winds, 1971; Seymour Simon, *Water on Your Street,* Holiday House, 1974.

SIDELIGHTS: Sonia O. Lisker considers herself primarily an illustrator, although she is doing an increasing amount of writing now. She describes her books as "non-sexist children's books for ages four to ten—a new look at older people—important subjects treated in an un-heavy way."

* * *

LITTLE, S. George 1903-1974

April 10, 1903—June 20, 1974; American journalist, publisher, editor, and author. Obituaries: *New York Times,* June 21, 1974.

* * *

LIVINGSTON, Dorothy Michelson 1906-

PERSONAL: Born September 1, 1906, in Chicago, Ill.; daughter of Albert Abraham (a physicist) and Edna (Stanton) Michelson; married Sheldon Dick; married John Bitter; married William D. Stevens; married Goodhue Livingston (former executive secretary to Mayor Fiorello La Guardia, and former member of New York City planning commission), June 15, 1966; children: Dorothy Dick (Mrs. James Orendurff), Ursula Bitter (Mrs. Friedrich Ulmer), Beatrice Stevens (Mrs. Michael Durkos). *Education:* University of Grenoble, student, 1925. *Politics:* Republican. *Religion:* Episcopalian. *Home:* 209 East 72nd St., New York, N.Y. 10021.

WRITINGS: The Master of Light; A Biography of Albert Michelson, Scribner, 1974.

SIDELIGHTS: Mrs. Livingston told *CA:* "I have been more interested in painting until this compulsion hit me to write about my father. Having succeeded so far I am tempted to try again." Albert Michelson won the Nobel Prize in physics in 1907, for developing optical measuring instruments, and for spectroscopic and meteorological investigations. *Avocational interests:* Travel, languages, sketching, chess, and tennis.

* * *

LIVINGSTON, Jon 1944-

PERSONAL: Born March 8, 1944, in Liberal, Kan.; son of James Lee (a member of the U.S. Air Force) and Sarah Myree (Hensley) Livingston. *Education:* Princeton University, B.A., 1967; Harvard University, M.A., 1969. *Home:* 1512 Grant, Berkeley, Calif. 94703. *Office:* Bay Area Institute, 604 Mission, San Francisco, Calif. 94105.

CAREER: Social worker, 1969-71; Bay Area Institute, San Francisco, Calif., publisher and researcher, 1970—.

WRITINGS: (With Molly Coye and Felicia Oldfather) *China!: Inside the People's Republic,* Bantam, 1972; (editor with Oldfather and Joe Moore) *The Japan Reader,* Pantheon, 1974; (editor with Coye) *China Yesterday and Today,* Bantam, 1974. Business manager and managing editor of *Bulletin of Concerned Asian Scholars.*

* * *

LIVINGSTON, Peter Van Rensselaer See TOWNSEND, James B(arclay) J(ermain)

* * *

LIVSON, Norman 1924-

PERSONAL: Born October 3, 1924, in New York, N.Y.; son of Jacob and Celia (Blumstein) Livson; married Florine Berkowitz (a psychologist), December 26, 1948; children: Paul, Katherine. *Education:* University of California, Berkeley, B.S.E., 1945, M.A., 1949, Ph.D., 1951. *Office:* Department of Psychology, California State University, Hayward, Calif. 94542.

CAREER: Worcester State Hospital and Worcester Foundation for Experimental Biology, Worcester, Mass., research psychologist, 1951-52; University of California, Berkeley, research psychologist, department of psychology, 1952-53, full-time research psychologist at Institute of Human Development, 1953-66, part-time, 1966—; California State University, Hayward, professor of psychology and chairman of department, 1966—. Lecturer at Brandeis University, spring, 1952, University of California, Berkeley, spring, 1956, and San Francisco State College (now University), fall, 1957, spring, 1965. Member of developmental behavioral sciences study section, National Institutes of Health, 1967-71.

MEMBER: American Psychological Association (fellow), American Association for the Advancement of Science (fellow), Society for Research in Child Development, Society for Life History Research in Psychopathology, International Society for the Study of Behavioral Development, American Association of University Professors, Western Psychological Association, Sigma Xi. *Awards, honors:* National Institutes of Health research fellow at Tavistock Child Development Unit (London), 1962-63; National Science Foundation travel grant, 1963; National Institute of Child Health and Human Development research grant, 1974—.

WRITINGS: Syllabus in General Psychology, University of California Press, 1959, revised edition (with M. R. Rosenzweig) published as *An Introduction to General Psychology with Special Application to Communication,* 1960; (with David Krech and R. S. Crutchfield) *Elements of Psychology,* 2nd edition (Livson was not associated with earlier edition), Knopf, 1969, 3rd edition, 1974, abridged 2nd edition published as *Elements of Psychology: A Briefer Course,* Knopf, 1970.

Contributor: M. G. Gold and Elizabeth Douvain, editors, *Adolescent Development: Readings in Research and Theory,* Allyn & Bacon, 1969; M. C. Jones and others, editors, *The Course of Human Development,* Xerox College Publishing, 1971; P. B. Baltes and K. W. Schaie, editors, *Lifespan Developmental Psychology: Personality and Socialization,* Academic Press, 1973. Contributor of more than thirty articles to journals. Consulting editor, *Child Development,* 1961-65, *Human Biology,* 1966-69, and *Merrill-Palmer Quarterly,* 1971—.

WORK IN PROGRESS: A study of stage developmental antecedents of adult psychological health.

* * *

LJOKA, Daniel J. 1935-

PERSONAL: Born August 16, 1935, in Philadelphia, Pa.; son of Marian (a longshoreman) and Marie (Leeman) Ljoka; married Jane Ryan, April 18, 1958; children: Daniel W., Linda M. *Education:* Educated in Roman Catholic schools in Philadelphia, Pa. *Home:* 23 Brandywine Dr., Marlton, N.J. 08053.

CAREER: Has worked as a longshoreman, a stockbroker, and a land developer. *Military service:* U.S. Marine Corps, 1953-56.

WRITINGS: Shelter, Manor Books, 1973.

LOBDELL, Jared C(harles) 1937-

PERSONAL: Born November 29, 1937, in New York, N.Y.; son of Charles E. (an investment analyst) and Jane (Hopkins) Lobdell. *Education:* Yale University, B.A., 1961; University of Wisconsin-Madison, M.B.A., 1966, Ph.D., 1974. *Politics:* Republican. *Religion:* Episcopalian. *Home:* 8 Cook Close, Ridgefield, Conn. 06877. *Office:* Department of Finance, Pace University, Bedford Rd., Pleasantville, N.Y. 10570.

CAREER: University of Wisconsin, Green Bay, instructor in business, 1970-72; Pace University, Graduate School, Pleasantville, N.Y., assistant professor of finance, 1972—. Member of Ridgefield Bicentennial Commission. *Member:* Mory's Association, Elizabethan Club.

WRITINGS: (Editor) *On Tolkien,* Open Court, 1974. Editor of "Pace Studies in Finance," Greenwood Press, 1974. Contributor to *Missouri Historical Review, National Review,* and *New Jersey History.* Associate editor of *Rally,* 1966-67; editor for American Enterprise Institute for Public Policy Research, 1973—.

WORK IN PROGRESS: Revolutionary War Journal and Letters of Major William Crogham, 1779-1782; Student Attitudes: A Study in Structural Change in American Society; Investor Behavior and Stock Market Profits.

* * *

LOBO, Anthony S(avio) 1937-

PERSONAL: Born May 1, 1937, in Bombay, India; son of Anthony Paul and Mariana Lobo; married Jane Anne Rehorst (an elementary school teacher), February 20, 1971; children: Robert Francis. *Education:* University of Poona, B.S., 1956, M.S. (geology), 1958; University of California, Los Angeles, M.A. (journalism), 1964. *Residence:* Los Angeles, Calif. *Office: Valley News,* 14539 Sylvan St., Van Nuys, Calif. 91401.

CAREER: El Monte Herald, El Monte, Calif., sports editor, 1964-65; high school teacher in Playa del Rey, Calif., 1965-66; Copley Newspapers, San Diego, Calif., reporter and wire editor, 1966-69; *Valley News,* Van Nuys, Calif., copy editor and wire news editor, 1970—. Free-lance correspondent on science and aerospace for Copley News Service, 1967-71; free-lance music and drama reviewer. Instructor at East Los Angeles College, 1972-73.

WRITINGS: Off the Beaten Track in Los Angeles, Nash Publishing, 1973. Author of syndicated articles on science, environment, and aerospace, which have appeared in more than one hundred newspapers.

WORK IN PROGRESS: Child Care for Fathers, non-fiction; *Travel Guide to the Moon,* non-fiction; a novel and screenplay.

SIDELIGHTS: Lobo told *CA* he is deeply interested "in the humanizing of science and technology, environmental philosophy that does not reject technological change, and a search for the meaning of Christian principles in the space age."

AVOCATIONAL INTERESTS: Opera, drama, gardening, fishing.

* * *

LOCHBILER, Don 1908-

PERSONAL: Surname is pronounced *Lock*-beeler; born January 14, 1908, in Detroit, Mich.; son of Don A. (a merchant) and Sarah Jane (Wylie) Lochbiler; married Ann Robinson, November 26, 1927 (died, 1955); married Laura Campbell, April 9, 1964; children: (first marriage) Peter. *Education:* Highland Park Junior College (now Highland Park Community College), student, 1924-26; also attended College of the City of Detroit (now Wayne State University), 1926. *Politics:* Independent. *Religion:* Nondenominational. *Home:* 20810 Randall, Farmington Hills, Mich. 48024.

CAREER: Detroit News, Detroit, Mich., reporter, 1927-29, education writer, 1929-36, feature writer, 1937-47, assistant city editor, 1947-73, author of column "Listening in on Detroit," 1945. *Member:* Detroit Historical Society. *Awards, honors:* Award of merit from Detroit Historical Society, 1972; United Press International award, 1973, for features on Detroit's history.

WRITINGS: Detroit's Coming of Age, Wayne State University Press, 1973. Also author of "Man Bites Dog" (play), first performed on Broadway at Lyceum Theatre, April 25, 1933. Contributor to *Dial.*

WORK IN PROGRESS: Detroit: City of Challenge; research on American history.

* * *

LOCK, C(lara) B(eatrice) Muriel 1914-

PERSONAL: Born April 18, 1914, in London, England; daughter of W. E. G. (an engineer and lecturer) and Clara B. (Truscott) Sillick; married Reginald Northwood Lock (a librarian and lecturer), October 25, 1941. *Education:* Bedford College, London, B.A., 1935, Ph.D., 1938. *Religion:* Church of England. *Home:* 19 Norwich Rd., Cromer, Norfolk, England.

CAREER: Croydon Reference Library, Croydon, England, librarian, 1938-46; Birmingham Polytechnic (formerly City of Birmingham School of Librarianship), Birmingham, England, lecturer in bibliography and general librarianship, 1960-70. *Member:* Royal Geographical Society, Royal Society of Arts, Schools Music Association (London), Edinburgh Festival Guild.

WRITINGS: Reference Material for Young People, Archon Books, 1967, 2nd edition, 1970; *Geography: A Reference Handbook,* Archon Books, 1968, 2nd edition, Linnet Books, 1972; *Modern Maps and Atlases,* Archon Books, 1969. Co-founder of *Library Science Abstracts,* 1950. Contributor to journals.

WORK IN PROGRESS: Third edition of *Geography: A Reference Handbook,* retitled as *Geography and Cartography: A Reference Handbook.*

* * *

LOCKE, Duane

PERSONAL: Born in Vienna, Ga.; son of J. G. and Finis (Taylor) Locke; married Frances Combee (a school teacher), June 15, 1955. *Education:* University of Tampa, B.A., 1949; University of Florida, M.A., 1955, Ph.D., 1958. *Home:* 2716 Jefferson St., Tampa, Fla. 33602. *Office:* Department of English, University of Tampa, Tampa, Fla. 33606.

CAREER: University of Tampa, Tampa, Fla., instructor, 1958-60, assistant professor, 1960-66, associate professor, 1966-72, professor of English, 1972—, poet-in-residence, 1971—. *Member:* Modern Language Association of America, Committee of Small Magazine Editors and Publishers (past member of board of directors), American Association of University Professors, North East Small Press Association, South Atlantic Modern Language Association.

WRITINGS—All poetry: *From the Bottom of the Sea,* Black Sun, 1968; *Inland Oceans,* Cornish, 1968; *Dead Cities,* Gunrunner, 1969; *Light Bulbs: Lengthened Eyelashes,* Ghost Dance, 1969; *Rainbow under Boards,* Poetry Review, 1969; *Submerged Fern,* Ann Arbor Review Press, 1972. Editor of *University of Tampa Review,* 1964, *UT Review,* 1970.

WORK IN PROGRESS: A book of poems, "in which the imagery is based on careful and direct observation as perceived by the altered consciousness in which the subject and object are fused."

SIDELIGHTS: Duane Locke is founder of the Immanentist school of poetry. He writes: "My poetry is based on altered state of consciousness that overcomes conceptualism and limited empirical observation. It is a type of psychedelic experience, self induced except for its source in the transforming experience of fused observations of herons, starfish, ferns, yuccas, and similar natural things found in Florida."

AVOCATIONAL INTERESTS: Yoga, nature photography, classical music.

* * *

LOCKRIDGE, Norman
See ROTH, Samuel

* * *

LOEB, Gerald M(artin) 1899-1974

July 24, 1899—1974; American stockbroker and author of books on investment. Obituaries: *Time,* April 29, 1974. (*CA*-15/16).

* * *

LOHNES, Walter F. W. 1925-

PERSONAL: Born February 8, 1925, in Frankfurt, Germany; naturalized U.S. citizen; son of Hans (a civil engineer) and Dina (Koch) Lohnes; married Claire Shane, February 6, 1950; children: Kristen, Peter, Claudia. *Education:* Studied at University of Frankfurt, 1945-48, Ohio Wesleyan University, 1948-49, and University of Missouri, 1949-50; Harvard University, Ph.D., 1956. *Home:* 733 Covington Rd., Los Altos, Calif. 94022. *Office:* Department of German, Stanford University, Stanford, Calif. 94305.

CAREER: University of Missouri, Columbia, instructor in German, 1949-50; Phillips Academy, Andover, Mass., head of department of German, 1951-61; Stanford University, Stanford, Calif., assistant professor, 1961-65, associate professor, 1965-69, professor of German, 1969—. Examiner for College Entrance Examination Board, Graduate Record Examination Board, and Educational Testing Service. *Member:* American Association of Teachers of German (vice-president, 1960, 1970-71), Modern Language Association of America, American Council on the Teaching of Foreign Languages.

WRITINGS: (With F. W. Strothmann) *German: A Structural Approach,* Norton, Volume I, 1967, 2nd edition, 1973. Contributor to professional journals. Editor, *Unterrichtspraxis for the Teaching of German,* 1972—.

WORK IN PROGRESS: Volume II of *German: A Structural Approach;* research in contrastive English and German syntax.

* * *

LOLLAR, Coleman Aubrey (Jr.) 1946-

PERSONAL: Born February 22, 1946, in Birmingham, Ala.; son of Coleman Aubrey and Vera (Wingard) Lollar. *Education:* University of Alabama, B.A., 1968. *Politics:* Democrat. *Home:* 124 Pacific St., New York, N.Y. 11201. *Office:* American Society of Travel Agents, *Travel News,* 488 Madison Ave., New York, N.Y. 10022.

CAREER: U.S. Peace Corps, Port Loko, Sierra Leone, volunteer, 1968-70; Metropolitan Life Corp. Communications, New York, N.Y., writer, 1970-72; Travel Communications, Inc., New York, N.Y., associate editor of *Travel News,* 1972—. Photo-journalist; has exhibited at Brooklyn Museum and Brooklyn Institute of Arts and Sciences. Press assistant to Senator John Sparkman, 1967, 1972. *Member:* Sigma Delta Chi.

WRITINGS—Self-illustrated *Islands of the Mediterranean,* Sterling, 1971; *Tunisia,* Sterling, 1972. Contributor of articles and photographs to newspapers and magazines, including *Washington Post, Chicago Tribune, Capitalist Reporter, Viva, See,* and to travel magazines.

* * *

LOMBARD, C(harles) M(orris) 1920-

PERSONAL: Born December 10, 1920, in Chicago, Ill.; son of Charles Morris and Elizabeth (Nolan) Lombard; married Louise Scherger (a pathologist), June, 1948; children: Elizabeth, Charles, Robert, James. *Education:* University of Wisconsin, Ph.D., 1953. *Politics:* Independent. *Religion:* Quaker. *Home:* 1520 North Willow, Lake Forest, Ill. 60045. *Office:* Department of French, University of Illinois, Chicago, Ill. 60680.

CAREER: Villanova University, Villanova, Pa., assistant professor of French, 1950-56; Chicago State College, Chicago, Ill., assistant professor, 1956-59, associate professor of French, 1960-62; Loyola University, Chicago, associate professor of French, 1962-66; University of Illinois at Chicago Circle, professor of French, 1966—.

WRITINGS: French Romanticism on the Frontier, Gredos, 1972; *Lamartine,* Twayne, 1973. Contributor to professional journals.

WORK IN PROGRESS: Thomas H. Chivers, for Twayne.

* * *

LONDON, H(oyt) H(obson) 1900-

PERSONAL: Born October 12, 1900, in Fannin County, Tex.; son of William H. (a farmer and construction worker) and Mary (Jones) London; married second wife, Virginia Carson, June 10, 1961; children: (first marriage) William T., Dorothy (Mrs. Edward Wagonlander), Howard K. *Education:* North Texas State Teachers College (now North Texas State University), B.S., 1924; graduate study at University of Colorado, 1926, Southern Methodist University, 1927-28, and University of Texas, 1929; University of Missouri, M.A., 1929; Ohio State University, Ph.D., 1934. *Home:* 2106 Valley View Dr., Columbia, Mo. 65201.

CAREER: North Texas Junior Agricultural, Mechanical, and Industrial College (now University of Texas at Arlington), Arlington, Tex., associate professor of industrial education, 1923-26; West Texas State Teachers College (now West Texas State University), Canyon, associate professor of industrial education, 1926-27; North Texas State Teachers College (now North Texas State University), Denton, associate professor of industrial education, 1927-28, 1929-31; South Georgia Teachers College (now Georgia Southern College), Statesboro, professor of industrial education, 1935-37; Mississippi State College (now University), Starkville, professor of industrial education, 1937-38; University of Missouri, Columbia, professor of industrial education and chairman of department, 1938-71, professor emeritus, 1971—. Education adviser of Civilian Conservation Corps, Eighth Corps area, 1935; chairman of Office of Price Administration, Missouri Price Panel, 1944; member of research team on vocational education in the Soviet Union, 1960; member of international study group on vocational education in western Nigeria, 1969; consultant on apprenticeship training to Mechanical Contractors Association, 1969—.

MEMBER: National Association of Industrial and Technical Educators (president, 1957), American Vocational Association (president, 1958-59), National Education Association, Mississippi Valley Industrial and Technical Educator Conference (chairman, 1961-71), Missouri Vocational Association (secretary-treasurer, 1953-58), Phi Delta Kappa, Rotary. *Awards, honors:* Distinguished service award from American Vocational Association, 1956; Manpower Administration research grant, 1964; inducted into Educational Exhibitors Association Hall of Fame, 1966; Faculty-Alumni award, University of Missouri, 1971; Citation of Merit, University of Missouri, 1974.

WRITINGS: Principles and Techniques of Vocational Guidance, C. E. Merrill, 1973. Contributor of articles to journals in his field.

AVOCATIONAL INTERESTS: Farming, construction, travel.

* * *

LOOMIS, Rae
See STEGER, Shelby

* * *

LORANG, Sister Mary Corde 1904-
(Ruth Mary Lorang)

PERSONAL: Secular name, Ruth Mary Lorang; born June 16, 1904, in Blue Island, Ill.; daughter of Nicholas John and Grace Cecilia (Baxter) Lorang. *Education:* Catholic University of America, A.B., 1936, M.A., 1937, Ph.D., 1945; postdoctoral study at Western Michigan University, 1959, and University of Illinois, summers, 1961-63. *Home and office:* Maryknoll Sisters, Maryknoll, N.Y. 10545. *Agent:* Curtis Brown Ltd., 60 East 56th St., New York, N.Y. 10022.

CAREER: Roman Catholic religious, member of Maryknoll Order, 1923—; Maryknoll Teachers College (later Rogers College), Maryknoll, N.Y., instructor, 1931-37, professor of science, 1937-63, head of science department, 1937-63; writer and official community photographer, Maryknoll, N.Y., 1963—. Visiting professor, St. Anne's, Kaneohe, Oahu, Hawaii, 1959-60, and Colegio Monte Maria, Guatemala City, 1962-63. *Member:* American Psychological Association, Psychologists Interested in Religious Issues.

WRITINGS: The Effect of Reading on Moral Conduct and Emotional Experience, Catholic University of America, 1945; *Footloose Scientist in Mayan America,* Scribner, 1966; *Burning Ice: The Moral and Emotional Effects of Reading,* Scribner, 1968; (with Sister Carol Cannon) *International Cookbook,* Orbis Books, 1973. Translator and abstractor of psychological articles from Spanish journals for *Psychological Abstracts.*

WORK IN PROGRESS: Mayan Tales, translated and adapted from the Spanish.

SIDELIGHTS: Although Sister Mary Corde received her Ph.D. in psychology, she was assigned to teach science for more than thirty years, and thus became interested in most scientific fields. *Footloose Scientist* was based on her archeological digging in Guatemala. While teaching at San Juan Capistrano, she visited and photographed all the Serra missions, and studied their histories. She also has supplied daily weather reports from the Maryknoll government station for Radio Station WOR in New York, since 1969.

* * *

LORANG, Ruth Mary
See LORANG, Sister Mary Corde

* * *

LOVELL, John, Jr. 1907-1974

July 25, 1907—June 6, 1974; American educator, and author of works on music and drama. Obituaries: *Washington Post,* June 10, 1974. (*CA*-33/36).

* * *

LOW, Victor N. 1931-

PERSONAL: Born August 25, 1931, in New York, N.Y.; son of Sol (a business executive) and Rosamund (Trilling) Low; married Helga L. B. Frentzel-Beyme, May 10, 1962; children: Joshua, Gideon. *Education:* University of Chicago, B.A., 1951; Columbia University, M.A., 1962; University of California, Los Angeles, Ph.D., 1967. *Politics:* Independent. *Religion:* Jewish. *Home address:* c/o Mrs. R. T. Low, 235 East 22nd St., New York, N.Y. 10010. *Office:* School of Basic Studies, Ahmadu Bello University, Zaria, Nigeria.

CAREER: Haile Selassie I University, Addis Ababa, Ethiopia, lecturer in Islamic history and institutions, 1967-69; Michigan State University, East Lansing, assistant professor of African and Middle East history, 1969-72; Hebrew University, Jerusalem, Israel, visiting senior lecturer in West African history, 1972-73; Ahmadu Bello University, Zaria, Nigeria, senior lecturer in African history, 1973—. *Military service:* U.S. Army, 1952-54. *Member:* African Studies Association, American Historical Association, Middle East Studies Association, African Studies Association (United Kingdom).

WRITINGS: Three Nigerian Emirates: A Study in Oral History, Northwestern University Press, 1972; (editor) *Africa to 1914: A Critical Survey of Relevant Books, with Special Reference to West Africa,* Cass, 1974; (editor) *From West Africa: A Political and Social Record, 1917-1973,* Cass, in press.

* * *

LOWDERMILK, W(alter) C(lay) 1888-1974

July 1, 1888—May 6, 1974; American agronomist, authority

on conservation, and author. Obituaries: *New York Times,* May 9, 1974; *Current Biography,* July, 1974.

* * *

LOWE, Gordon R(obb) 1928-

PERSONAL: Born April 19, 1928, in Glasgow, Scotland; son of Alfred (an accountant) and Ethel (Richards) Lowe; married Wilma White, September 18, 1954; children: Laura. *Education:* Glasgow University, M.A. (honors), 1952; McGill University, graduate study, 1963-64; St. Andrews University, Ph.D., 1969. *Office:* Department of Psychology, Queens University, 68 Barrie St., Kingston, Ontario, Canada.

CAREER: Clinical psychologist in private practice in Kingston, Ontario, 1956—; Montreal General Hospital, Montreal, Quebec, clinical and research psychologist, 1956-64; Liff Hospital, Dundee, Scotland, principal psychologist, 1964-69; Queens University, Kingston, Ontario, associate professor of psychology and psychiatry, 1969—; Kingston General Hospital, Kingston, Ontario, milieu director, 1969—. Student counselor, Sir George Williams University, 1956-64. *Military service:* Royal Navy, 1945-47. *Member:* British Psychological Society, American Psychological Association, American Group Psychotherapy Association, Ontario Psychological Association.

WRITINGS: Personal Relationships in Psychological Disorders, Penguin, 1969; *The Growth of Personality: From Infancy to Old Age,* Pelican, 1972. Contributor to *British Psychiatric Journal, Canadian Psychiatric Association Journal,* and *Mankind Quarterly.*

WORK IN PROGRESS: Two books, *Hallucinations and Other Mental States* and *Know Your Own Personality;* research on clinical milieus, phenomenology, psychotherapy, and diagnostics.

AVOCATIONAL INTERESTS: Music, painting, golfing, reading, fishing, sailing.

* * *

LOWENKOPF, Shelly A(lan) 1931- (Howard V. Chambers)

PERSONAL: Born September 6, 1931, in Santa Monica, Calif.; son of Jack Arthur (an auctioneer) and Anna (Engelson) Lowenkopf; married Anne Nelan (an author), August 31, 1965. *Education:* Attended Los Angeles City College, 1949-51; University of California, Los Angeles, B.A., 1954. *Politics:* "Left-of-center Democrat." *Religion:* Jewish. *Home:* 2428-C Beverley Ave., Santa Monica, Calif. 90405. *Agent:* International Literary Agents, Ltd., 9601 Wilshire Blvd., Beverly Hills, Calif. 90210. *Office:* 6399 Wilshire Blvd., Los Angeles, Calif. 90048.

CAREER: Southdown Films, Chatsworth, Calif., writer, 1954-56; J. Lesser Productions and Television Adventure Film Co., Hollywood, Calif., writer, 1956-58; free-lance writer, 1958-60; *Chase Magazine,* Los Angeles, Calif., associate editor, 1961-63; Sherbourne Press, Inc., Los Angeles, editor, 1963-68, editor-in-chief, 1968-73; Dell Publishing Co., Inc., West Coast Office, Los Angeles, editorial director, 1973—. Consulting director and production manager, Scorpion Press. *Member:* Writers Guild of America, Mystery Writers of America (regional director, 1965-66), Book Publishers of California (publicity director, 1968), Bookbuilders of Southern California (membership secretary, 1972; programs director, 1973), Bookbuilders West, American Society for Psychical Research.

WRITINGS—Editor: *Borderline Oddities,* Sherbourne, 1966, published as *Borderline Oddities for the Millions,* 1969; *Strange, Stranger, Strangest,* Paperback Library, 1970.

Under pseudonym Howard V. Chambers: (Compiler) *An Occult Dictionary for the Millions,* Sherbourne, 1966, published as *An Occult Dictionary,* 1968; *UFO's for the Millions,* Sherbourne, 1967; *The Great UFO Controversy,* Grosset, 1968; *Phrenology for the Millions,* Award Books, 1968; *Dowsing, Water Witches, Divining Rods,* Sherbourne, 1969.

Also author of *City of Hoke,* [New York], 1961; *Love of the Lion,* [New York], 1962. Columnist for *Territorial Enterprise,* Virginia City, Nev., 1965, 1970. Contributor of reviews to *Philadelphia Inquirer.*

WORK IN PROGRESS: Avatars, Messiahs, & Spirit Messengers: A Selected Guide to Mortal and Supernatural Beings, completion expected in 1975; *Madmen, Madwomen, Men with Beards: American Reformers of the 19th Century,* 1975; *The Masked Jogger* (novel), 1975.

SIDELIGHTS: Lowenkopf told *CA* he "will do or write almost anything to help attack the rationalist we've-got-to-see-it-before-we-believe-it attitude that has hampered American politics and science for too long. Put me down as one who believes that astrology, responsible, well-wrought, non-manipulative astrology is one of the break-through areas on the social sciences; it's the New Alchemy."

* * *

LOWRY, Peter 1953-

PERSONAL: Born March 6, 1953, in Berkeley, Calif.; son of Ritchie Peter (a professor) and Betty (Trishman) Lowry. *Education:* Harvard University, student, 1971-73. *Politics:* Democrat. *Religion:* None. *Home:* 79 Moore Rd., Wayland, Mass. 01778. *Office:* Porter Sargent, Inc., 11 Beacon St., Boston, Mass. 02108.

CAREER: Porter Sargent, Inc. (publisher), Boston, Mass., member of editorial staff, 1973—. *Member:* Boston Authors Club.

WRITINGS: (With Field Griffith) *Model Rocketry: Hobby of Tomorrow* (teen book), Doubleday, 1972; (Scandinavian editor) *Let's Go: A Student Guide to Europe,* Dutton, 1973. Contributor of articles, reviews, or photographs to periodicals and newspapers including *New York Times, Boston Globe, Washington Post,* and *Seventeen.*

WORK IN PROGRESS: Project assistant on book, *The Double Dealer,* financed by youth grant of National Endowment for the Humanities, completion expected in 1974.

SIDELIGHTS: Lowry has traveled in most countries of Europe and in New Zealand, Samoa, and Tahiti.

* * *

LOZIER, Herbert 1915-

PERSONAL: Born December 19, 1915, in New York, N.Y.; son of James and Celia (Reinheimer) Lozier. *Home:* 31 Fairmount St., Huntington, N.Y. *Office:* Huntington Public Library, Huntington, N.Y.

CAREER: Has worked variously since 1936 as a free-lance writer, assistant museum art director, model maker, and restorer of old and famous cars; Huntington Public Library, Huntington, N.Y., specialist and consultant on automobile, aircraft, and boats, 1970—. Chief judge at Huntington's annual "Old Car Meet." *Military service:* U.S. Army, Signal Corps, 1943; U.S. Army Air Forces, 1944; U.S. Army, Corps of Engineers, 1944-46.

WRITINGS: Auto Racing: Old and New, Fawcett, 1953; *The Car of Kings: The Mercedes "K" and "S",* Chilton, 1967; *Model Making,* Chilton, 1967; *Model Boat Building,* Sterling, 1970; *Getting Started in Model Building,* Hawthorne, 1971; *Model-Making for Young Adults,* Hawthorne, 1971. Contributor to model and science magazines. Editor of *Motor Cars Illustrated,* 1963-64.

WORK IN PROGRESS: Books about cars, as well as five model books.

* * *

LUBELL, Winifred 1914-

PERSONAL: Born June 14, 1914, in New York, N.Y.; daughter of Lester and Elsa Milius; married Cecil Lubell (a writer and editor), 1938; children: David, Stephen. *Education:* Studied at Art Students' League, New York, 1933-35, and Duncan Phillips Museum School, Washington, D.C.,, 1936. *Home:* 101 North Highland Pl., Croton-on-Hudson, N.Y. 10520.

CAREER: Artist, and designer and illustrator of children's books; has had one-woman show of drawings and prints in New York; woodcuts have been exhibited in New York, Philadelphia, Boston, and Dallas. Formerly taught art to children.

WRITINGS—Self-illustrated: *Here Comes Daddy,* W. R. Scott, 1945.

Illustrator and collaborator with husband, Cecil Lubell: *The Tall Grass Zoo,* Rand McNally, 1960; *Up a Tree* (Junior Literary Guild selection), Rand McNally, 1961; *Rosalie: The Bird Market Turtle,* Rand McNally, 1962; *Green Is for Growing* (Junior Literary Guild selection), Rand McNally, 1964; *In a Running Brook,* Rand McNally, 1968; *A Zoo for You,* Parents' Magazine Press, 1970; *Birds in the Street,* Parents' Magazine Press, 1971; *Clothes Tell a Story,* Parents' Magazine Press, 1971; *Picture Signs and Symbols,* Parents' Magazine Press, 1972; *You Will Find Seashells,* Parents' Magazine Press, 1973.

Illustrator and collaborator with others: (With I. P. Miller) *The Stitchery Book: Embroidery for Beginners,* Doubleday, 1965; (with Dorothy Sterling) *Fall Is Here* (Junior Literary Guild selection), Doubleday, 1966; (with Sterling) *The Outer Lands,* Doubleday and Natural History Press, 1967; (with Sophia A. Boyer) *Gifts from the Greeks: Alpha to Omega,* Rand McNally, 1970.

Illustrator: Millicent Selsam, *See Through the See,* Harper, 1955; Millicent Selsam, *See Through the Forest,* Harper, 1956; Dorothy Sterling, *The Story of Caves* (Junior Literary Guild selection), Doubleday, 1956; Millicent Selsam, *See Through the Jungle,* Harper, 1957; Millicent Selsam, *See Through the Lake,* Harper, 1958; Millicent Selsam, *See Up the Mountain,* Harper, 1958; Aylesa Forsee, *Louis Agassiz: Pied Piper of Science,* Viking, 1958; Millicent Selsam, *The Birth of an Island,* Harper, 1959.

Dorothy Sterling, *Creatures of the Night,* Doubleday, 1960; Mary Stuart Graham, under name Mary Stuart, *The Pirate's Bridge* (Junior Literary Guild selection), Lothrop, 1960; Dorothy Sterling, *Caterpillars,* Doubleday, 1961; Dorothy Sterling, *Ellen's Blue Jays,* Doubleday, 1961; Jay Williams, *I Wish I Had Another Name,* Atheneum, 1962; Dorothy Sterling, *Spring Is Here!,* Doubleday, 1964; Marion Garthwaite, *The Twelfth Night Santons,* Doubleday, 1965; Marguerite M. Miles and others, *Qui Est La?,* Prentice-Hall, 1966; Jean Craighead George, *The Moon of the Mountain Lion,* Crowell, 1968; William Wise, *Nanette, the Hungry Pelican,* Rand McNally, 1969.

SIDELIGHTS: Mrs. Lubell writes: "As an illustrator of nature books, the biggest challenge I face is how to make my animals or plants look alive, not pinned to a board, not stiff dead specimens. For this, photographs or 'scientific' drawings, no matter how brilliantly done, can only be supplements to careful observation of the living creature or plant."

* * *

LUKAS, J. Anthony 1933-

PERSONAL: Born April 25, 1933, in New York, N.Y.; son of Edwin Jay (a lawyer) and Elizabeth (Schamberg) Lukas. *Education:* Harvard University, B.A. (magna cum laude), 1955; graduate study at Free University of Berlin, 1955-56. *Home and office:* 25 West 76th St., New York, N.Y. 10023. *Agent:* Sterling Lord Agency, 660 Madison Ave., New York, N.Y. 10021.

CAREER: Baltimore Sun, Baltimore, Md., city hall correspondent, 1958-62; *New York Times,* New York, N.Y., member of Washington, D.C. and United Nations bureaus, 1962, correspondent in the Congo, 1962-65, and India, 1965-67, member of metropolitan staff, 1967-68, roving national correspondent, 1969-70, staff writer for Sunday magazine, 1970-71; currently free-lance writer and senior editor, (MORE) Magazine. Visiting lecturer at Yale University, 1973; member of Committee on Public Justice. *Military service:* U.S. Army, news commentator and writer of propaganda, 1956-58.

MEMBER: Phi Beta Kappa, Harvard Club (New York, N.Y.). *Awards, honors:* Pulitzer Prize for local reporting, 1968; George Polk Memorial Award from Long Island University, 1968; Mike Berger Award from Columbia University, 1968; Page One Award from New York Newspaper Guild; By-line Feature Award from Newspaper Reporters Association, 1968.

WRITINGS: The Barnyard Epithet and Other Obscenities: Notes on the Chicago Conspiracy Trial, Harper, 1970; *Don't Shoot: We Are Your Children!,* Random House, 1971. Contributor to magazines, including *Esquire, Harper's, Saturday Review, New Republic,* and *Reader's Digest.*

SIDELIGHTS: Lukas has said his journalistic specialty is domestic social unrest, especially youthful and radical. His story about Linda Fitzpatrick, a wealthy girl who was killed in Greenwich Village, won a Pulitzer Prize. Both his books were discussed with respect and enthusiasm. Critic Richard Goldstein pronounced *The Barnyard Epithet and Other Obscenities* "the only piece of reasoned reportage to come out of" the Chicago conspiracy trial. To Robert Kuttner the book is modest, remarkable for its humility, and "brilliantly evokes those weeks in Judge Julius Hoffman's courtroom," and to Gary Wills, "brilliant, short, cinematic." J. R. Walz went further, saying, "[Lukas] has a superlative ear; he is at least part poet, part playwright."

In *Don't Shoot: We Are Your Children!,* ten profiles of young Americans, Lukas "gives us, through an undistorting glass," wrote Ross MacDonald, "the dreams and hopes of children growing up, the feelings they share with their parents and the inevitable conflicts, their fears that all is not well with themselves or their world." Its central metaphor, according to Richard Goldstein, is that "young people strive to express what their parents repress."

He continued: "Lukas's skill as a reporter is evident. He is, first of all, in full possession of his faculties. That is, he has a sharply honed eye, a nimble pencil, and a refined ability to intuit the phrase-behind-the-phrases which an interview yields. These are a reporter's tools, and Lukas handles them like a carpenter. Beyond that, there is his organizational skill, his ability to balance vital and peripheral details in a way which expands and enhances our perception of an event. This talent is not to be dismissed." Yet Goldstein also faulted the consistency of Lukas' "reportorial cool," pleading that he abandon detachment for "something more spontaneous and less secure." But MacDonald concluded: "His eloquence as a writer, his tenacity in research, his respect for other human beings, have combined to give us a beautiful and important book which I think may become a classic."

BIOGRAPHICAL/CRITICAL SOURCES: Village Voice, June 24, 1971.

* * *

LUNAR, Dennis
See MUNGO, Raymond

* * *

LUNDWALL, Sam J(errie) 1941-

PERSONAL: Born February 24, 1941, in Stockholm, Sweden; married Ingrid Olofsdotter. *Education:* University of Stockholm, E.E., 1967. *Home:* Storskovsvaegen 19, S-161 39 Bromma, Sweden. *Agent:* Gunnar Dahl, Goesta Dahl & Son, Aladdinsvaegen 14, S-161 38 Bromma, Sweden. *Office:* Delta Foerlags AB, Bromma, Sweden.

CAREER: SSTA (Stockholm Technical Night-School), Stockholm, Sweden, electronics engineer, 1956-60; University of Stockholm, Stockholm, Sweden, professional photographer, 1964-67; Christer Christian Photographic School, Fox Amphoux, France, professional photographer, 1967-68; Swedish Broadcasting Corp., Stockholm, television producer, 1968-69; Askild & Kaernekull Foerlag AB (publishers), Stockholm, Sweden, editor for science fiction and the occult, 1970-73; Delta Foerlags AB (publishers), Bromma, Sweden, president, 1973—. Has directed television films; made short animated film based on his song "Waltz with Karin"; has recorded his own songs for Philips and Knaeppupp recording companies; has appeared on television, radio, and film as singer and artist throughout the Scandinavian countries. *Military service:* Swedish Air Force, 1960-61; electronics engineer. *Member:* Science Fiction Writers of America. *Awards, honors:* "Waltz with Karin" was named Sweden's best short film, by Swedish Film Institute, 1967; Alvar award as Scandinavia's leading science fiction author, from Futura (science fiction organization), 1971.

WRITINGS: Bibliografi oever Science Fiction och Fantasy (title means "Bibliography of Science Fiction and Fantasy"), Fiktiva, 1964; *Visor i Vaar Tid* (title means "Songs of Our Times"), Sonora, 1965; *Science Fiction: Fraan Begynnelsen till vaara dagar* (title means "Science Fiction: From the Beginning to Our Days"), Sveriges Radio Foerlag, 1969; *Alice's World,* Ace Books, 1971; *No Time for Heroes,* Ace Books, 1971; *Science Fiction: What It's All About,* Ace Books, 1971; *Bernhard the Conqueror,* Daw Books, 1973; *Den Fantastiska Romanen,* four volumes (textbooks on fantastic stories and novels), Gummessons Grafiska, 1973-74; *King Kong Blues,* Daw Books, 1974; *Bibliografi oever Science Fiction och Fantasy: 1741-1971,* Lindqvist Foerlag, 1974; *What is Science Fiction?,* Meulenhoff, 1974.

Editor of numerous science fiction anthologies and of collected works of Jules Verne; translator into Swedish of more than fifty novels and of poems by Francois Villon and George Brassens; author, producer, and director of television script from *The Hunting Season,* by Frank Robinson, and of other television films; author and composer of more than two hundred songs. Contributor of cartoons to Swedish edition of *Help!* and of articles to Swedish edition of *Popular Photography.* Editor of *Jules Verne–Magasinet,* 1972—.

* * *

LUNN, Arnold 1888(?)-1974

1888(?)—June 2, 1974; British authority on skiing, innovator of skiing methods, editor, and author of books on skiing, travel, mountaineering, Communism, Catholicism, and other topics. Obituaries: *New York Times,* June 3, 1974; *Time,* June 17, 1974.

* * *

LUTZ, William W(alter) 1919-

PERSONAL: Born August 26, 1919, in Detroit, Mich.; son of Walter William and Christine (Mauer) Lutz; married Eunice M. Guthrie (a teacher), February 13, 1943; children: Barbara Ann (Mrs. Donald E. Kiolbasa), Paul W. *Education:* University of Detroit, B.Ph., 1941; Michigan State University, M.A., 1971. *Politics:* Independent. *Religion:* Roman Catholic. *Home:* 6125 Westmoor Rd., Birmingham, Mich. 48010. *Agent:* Sterling Lord Agency, 660 Madison Ave., New York, N.Y. 10021. *Office:* 615 Lafayette, Detroit, Mich. 48231.

CAREER: University of Detroit, Detroit, Mich., public relations director, 1941-43; *Detroit News,* Detroit, Mich., night city editor, 1944-65, Sunday editor, 1965-68, feature editor, 1968—. Director of St. Vincent and Sarah Fisher Home for Children, 1950-55, and Guest House, Inc., 1966-71; chairman of board of trustees of Mercy College of Detroit, 1972—. *Member:* Press Club of Detroit (director, 1960-69), Twin Beach Country Club. *Awards, honors:* Michigan Probation, Prison and Parole Association award, 1953, for articles on prison reforms; American Institute of Architects award, 1958, for articles on architectural progress; Michigan Historical Commission award, 1973, for *The News of Detroit.*

WRITINGS: The News of Detroit, Little, Brown, 1973. Contributor to journals.

WORK IN PROGRESS: Research for a book concerned with "what happens after you die."

SIDELIGHTS: Lutz told *CA:* "Motivation in writing *The News of Detroit* was to discover interplay between the growth, or lack of, a city or community and its local news media, especially newspapers. This relates directly to the amount of freedom media may require in a democratic society."

BIOGRAPHICAL/CRITICAL SOURCES: Detroit News, June 25, 1973.

LYLE, Katie Letcher 1938-

PERSONAL: Born May 12, 1938, in Peking, China; daughter of John Seymour (a U.S. Marine Corps brigadier general) and Elizabeth (an artist; maiden name, Marston) Letcher; married Royster Lyle, Jr. (acting director of a research foundation), March 16, 1963; children: Royster Cochran. *Education:* Hollins College, B.A., 1959; Johns Hopkins University, M.A., 1960. *Home address:* P.O. Box 596, Lexington, Va. 24450. *Agent:* Josephine Rogers, Collins-Knowlton-Wing, Inc., 60 East 56th St., New York, N.Y. 10022. *Office:* Division of Liberal Arts, Southern Seminary Junior College, Buena Vista, Va. 24416.

CAREER: Teacher in Baltimore, Md., schools, 1960-61, and 1962-63; Vanderbilt University, Nashville, Tenn., teaching fellow, 1961-62; Southern Seminary Junior College, Buena Vista, Va., member of faculty in English, 1963—, chairman of department, 1968—, chairman of Division of Liberal Arts, 1971-73. High school teacher in Lexington, Va., summers, 1959, 1960, 1962; has also been a professional folksinger in Baltimore and Nashville, and, occasionally, an actress. *Member:* Modern Language Association of America, College English Association (North Carolina-Virginia section). *Awards, honors:* Bread Loaf fellowships, 1973, 1974.

WRITINGS: (With Maude Rubin and May Miller) *Lyrics of Three Women,* Linden Press, 1964; *On Teaching Creative Writing,* National Defense Education Act, 1968; *I Will Go Barefoot All Summer for You* (fiction), Lippincott, 1973; *Fair Day, and Another Step Begun* (fiction), Lippincott, 1974.

Work is represented in anthologies, including *Beyond the Square,* edited by Robert K. Rosenburg, Linden Press, 1972. Author of "A Foreign Flavor," weekly column on food and humor, for *Roanoke Times,* 1970—. Contributor to *Virginia Wild Rivers Study,* edited by Paul Dulaney. Contributor of poems to *Shenandoah* and other literary magazines, and of reviews and travel articles to newspapers.

WORK IN PROGRESS: Two novels; a study of lyrical themes of country songs; a collection of essays on raising a child.

AVOCATIONAL INTERESTS: European travel, mycology, foreign cooking, and archaeology, particularly Aegean.

* * *

LYNN, Mary
See BROKAMP, Marilyn

* * *

MA, John T(a-jen) 1920-

PERSONAL: Born February 22, 1920, in Wenchow, China; son of Kung-yu (an artist) and Hsiang-chuan (Huang) Ma; married May Hoo, January 19, 1959; children: Averil, Carol, Debora. *Education:* National Central University, Chungking, China, B.A., 1944; Post-Graduate School of Journalism, Chungking, Diploma, 1954; University of Wisconsin, M.A., 1948; Columbia University, M.L.S., 1958. *Home:* 943 Mears Ct., Stanford, Calif. 94305. *Office:* East Asian Collection, Hoover Institution on War, Revolution and Peace, Stanford, Calif. 94305.

CAREER: Yale University, New Haven, Conn., translator, Human Relations Area Files, 1955; University of Washington, Seattle, assistant editor of Chinese history project, 1955-56; Columbia University, New York, N.Y., associate librarian, Missionary Research Library, 1956-61; Cornell University Library, Ithaca, N.Y., Chinese bibliographer-cataloger, 1961-65; Hoover Institution on War, Revolution and Peace, Stanford, Calif., curator-librarian, East Asian Collection, 1965—. Peiping representative of Chinese Government Public Relations Office, 1945-46, and editor in international department of Chinese Ministry of Information, 1945-47. *Military service:* Chinese First Army, volunteer, 1938-39. American Volunteers Group (Flying Tigers), interpreter-codeman, 1941-42; became first lieutenant. *Member:* Association for Asian Studies, American Association of Teachers of Chinese Language and Culture (member of board of directors), Pacific Area Intercollegiate Council on Asian Studies (chairman of board of advisors; member of executive committee).

WRITINGS: (With J. J. Dresher and Elaine L. Young) *A Test of Disputed Authorship: Ch'en Tzu-chia and Chu Tzu-chia,* Douglas Advanced Research Laboratories, 1968; (with Dresher, Young, and R. E. Norton) *Power Spectral Densities of Literary Rhythms (Chinese),* Douglas Advanced Research Laboratories, 1968; *Elementary Chinese for American Librarians: A Simple Manual,* Hanover (N.H.) Oriental Society, 1968; (contributor) Winston L. Y. Yang and T. S. Y. C. Yang, editors, *Asian Resources in American Libraries,* Foreign Area Materials Center, State University of New York, and National Council for Foreign Area Materials, 1968; *East Asia: A Survey of Holdings at the Hoover Institution on War, Revolution and Peace,* Hoover Institution, 1971. Contributor to *Biographical Dictionary of Republican China* and to journals. Correspondent, *Chungking Reporter,* 1945-46.

* * *

MAASARANI, Aly Mohamed 1927-

PERSONAL: Born January 14, 1927, in Alexandria, Egypt; naturalized U.S. citizen; son of Mohamed Mohmad (an import-export businessman) and Asma Maasarani; married Shirne El-Abd, October 28, 1965; children: Nabil, Dina. *Education:* University of Alexandria, B.Comm., 1951, graduate diploma, 1954; University of Texas, M.B.A., 1959, M.A., 1961, Ph.D., 1962. *Religion:* Moslem. *Home:* 16 Shire Ct., Greenlawn, N.Y. 11740. *Office:* Department of Management, St. John's University, Jamaica, N.Y. 11439.

CAREER: Internal Revenue service, Alexandria, Egypt, 1951-57; Western State College of Colorado, Gunnison, assistant professor of management, 1961-63; Tennessee Technological University, Cookeville, associate professor of management, 1963-65; Texas A&I University, Kingsville, associate professor of management, 1965-67; St. John's University, college of Business Administration, Jamaica, N.Y., associate professor of management, 1967—, research associate, Business Research Institute, 1971. Director of research study for U.S. Office of Economic Opportunity, 1967; associate director for research, management area, Office of the Mayor, New York, N.Y., 1973-74. Guest speaker and panelist at international conferences.

MEMBER: Middle East Studies Association (fellow), American Management Association, Society for Advancement of Management, Academy of International Business, Faculty Association for Middle East Studies, Middle East Institute, Sigma Iota Epsilon, Omicron Chi Epsilon, Alpha Kappa Psi. *Awards, honors:* Faculty Seminar fellowship from American Association for Middle Eastern Studies, 1963.

WRITINGS: (Contributor) John J. Clark, editor, *The Management of Forecasting,* St. John's University Press, 1969; *American Management Consultants in the Middle East: Criteria for Success,* St. John's University Press, 1971. Contributor to *Productivity.*

WORK IN PROGRESS: Two books, *Oil in the Middle East* and *The Multinational Corporation in the Middle East.*

SIDELIGHTS: Maasarani told *CA* his motivation in research and writing is to try "to bridge the managerial gap between the United States and the Third World, especially the Middle Eastern countries," and "to show how the advanced industrial nations may help the Third World countries through the multinational corporations."

* * *

MABRY, Donald J(oseph) 1941-

PERSONAL: Born April 21, 1941, in Atlanta, Ga.; son of Jerry Leon and Eunice (Harris) Mabry; married Susan Johnston (a nursery school teacher), July 28, 1962; children: Scott Landon, Mark Robert. *Education:* Kenyon College, A.B. (cum laude), 1963; Bowling Green State University, M.Ed., 1964; University of Florida, graduate study, 1965; Syracuse University, Ph.D., 1970. *Home:* 2202 McArthur Dr., Starkville, Miss. 39759. *Office:* Department of History, Mississippi State University, Mississippi State, Miss. 39762.

CAREER: St. Johns River Junior College, Palatka, Fla., member of social science faculty, 1964-67; Mississippi State University, Mississippi State, assistant professor, 1970-74, associate professor of history, 1974—. Syracuse University, visiting lecturer, 1969-70. *Member:* Latin American Studies Association, Committee on Mexican Studies, American Historical Association.

WRITINGS: Mexico's Accion Nacional: A Catholic Alternative to Revolution, Syracuse University Press, 1973; (contributor) Harold E. Davis and others, editors, *Revolutionaries: Traditionalists and Dictators in Latin America,* Cooper Square, 1973. Contributor to *Americana Annual, Journal of Inter-American Studies and World Affairs, Western Political Quarterly, Sociology,* and *Journal of Church and State.*

WORK IN PROGRESS: Mexican elite studies, completion expected in 1975; *Mexican University Students in Revolution: 1910-1945,* 1976.

* * *

MacCRACKEN, Mary 1926-

PERSONAL: Born June 6, 1926, in Englewood, N.J.; daughter of Burnham Wilcox (an insurance broker) and Florence (Ferguson) Clifford; married Peter Thistle, 1945; married Calvin Dodd MacCracken (an inventor and engineer) June 25, 1969; children: (first marriage) Susan Lynn, Stephen Burnham, Nan Livingston. *Education:* Attended Wellesley College, 1943-45; Paterson State College, B.A., 1972, M.A., 1973. *Religion:* Presbyterian. *Home:* 92 Dwight Pl., Englewood, N.J. *Agent:* McIntosh & Otis, 18 East 41st St., New York, N.Y. 10017. *Office:* 88 West Ridgewood Ave., Ridgewood, N.J.

CAREER: Teacher of emotionally disturbed children, 1965-70; private practice as learning disabilities specialist in Ridgewood, N.J., 1973—. Supplemental teacher, 1970-73. *Member:* Junior League.

WRITINGS: A Circle of Children, Lippincott, 1974.

* * *

MACDONALD, Cynthia

PERSONAL: Born in New York, N.Y.; daughter of Leonard (a writer) and Dorothy (Kiam) Lee; married E. C. Macdonald; children: Jennifer Tim, Scott Thurston. *Education:* Bennington College, B.A., 1950; Sarah Lawrence College, M.A., 1970. *Office:* Department of English, Sarah Lawrence College, Bronxville, N.Y. 10708.

CAREER: Opera and concert singer; Sarah Lawrence College, Bronxville, N.Y., currently member of faculty in English department. *Awards, honors:* Yaddo Foundation fellowship; National Endowment for the Arts Award.

WRITINGS: Amputations (poems), Braziller, 1972. Contributor to periodicals.

WORK IN PROGRESS: A second book of poems.

* * *

MACDONALD, John (Barfoot) 1918-

PERSONAL: Born February 23, 1918, in Toronto, Ontario, Canada; son of Arthur Albert (a lawyer) and Gladys (Barfoot) Macdonald; married Beatrice Kathleen Darroch, June 5, 1942; married Liba Bocova, July 10, 1962; children: (first marriage) Kaaren (Mrs. David Ball), Grant, Scott; (second marriage) Vivian and Linda (stepchildren). *Education:* University of Toronto, D.D.S. (with honors), 1942; University of Illinois, M.S., 1948; Columbia University, Ph.D., 1953. *Home:* 39 Glenellen Dr. W., Toronto, Ontario M8Y 2H5, Canada. *Office:* Council of Ontario Universities, 130 St. George St., Toronto, Ontario, Canada.

CAREER: University of Toronto, Toronto, Ontario, lecturer, 1942-44, instructor, 1946-47, assistant professor, 1949-53, associate professor, 1953-56, professor of bacteriology, 1956, chairman of Division of Dental Research, 1953-56; Harvard University, School of Dental Medicine, Boston, Mass., professor of microbiology and director of Forsyth Dental Infirmary, 1956-62; University of British Columbia, Vancouver, president, 1962-67; University of Toronto, professor of higher education, 1968—; Council of Ontario Universities, Toronto, executive director, 1968—. Chairman of the board, Banff School for Advanced Management, 1966-67, and Donwood Institute, 1972. Consultant to Science Council of Canada and Canada Council on Support of Research in Canadian Universities, 1967-69, National Institutes of Health, 1968, Canadian International Development Agency, 1971, and other government agencies. *Military service:* Canadian Army, 1944-46; became captain.

MEMBER: International Association for Dental Research (president, 1968), International College of Dentists (honorary fellow), Canadian Mental Health Association (member of national scientific planning council, 1969), American Association for the Advancement of Science, American Society for Microbiology; honorary officer of a number of other Canadian societies. *Awards, honors:* A.M., Harvard University, 1956; LL.D. from University of Manitoba, 1962, and Simon Fraser University, 1965; D.Sc., University of British Columbia, 1967.

WRITINGS: The Motile Non-Sporulating Anaerobic Rods of the Oral Cavity, Faculty of Dentistry, University of Toronto, 1953; *A Prospectus on Dental Education for the University of British Columbia,* University of British Columbia, 1956; *Excellence and Responsibility* (inaugural address as fourth president of University of British Columbia), University of British Columbia, 1962; *Higher Education in British Columbia and a Plan for the Future,* University of British Columbia, 1962; (with others) *The Role of the Federal Government in Support of Research in Canadian Universities* (in English and French), Queen's Printer, 1969.

Contributor: Reidar F. Sognnaes, editor, *Chemistry and Prevention of Dental Caries,* C.C Thomas, 1962; *Higher Education in a Changing Canada,* University of Toronto Press, for Royal Society of Canada, 1966; J. E. Hodgetts and Robin S. Harris, editors, *Changing Patterns of Higher Education in Canada,* University of Toronto Press, 1966; Robert F. Nixon, editor, *The Guelph Papers,* Peter Marten Associates, 1970; *Towards 2000: The Future of Post-Secondary Education in Ontario,* McClelland & Stewart, 1971; E. F. Sheffield, editor, *Agencies for Higher Education,* Ontario Institute for Studies in Education, 1974.

* * *

MacKENZIE, Andrew 1911-

PERSONAL: Born May 30, 1911, in Oamaru, New Zealand; son of John Gretton (a municipal park director) and Jeannie (Carr) MacKenzie; married Kaarina Sisko Sihvonen (an agronomist), March 1, 1952; children: Annaliisa Kaarina, Elsa Helena, Donald Ensio. *Education:* Attended Wellington College, 1924-28. *Religion:* Presbyterian. *Home:* 18 Castlebar Park, London W5 1BX, England. *Agent:* Brandt & Brandt, 101 Park Ave., New York, N.Y. 10017. *Office:* United Newspapers Ltd., 23-27 Tudor St., London E.C.4, England.

CAREER: Evening Post, Wellington, New Zealand, member of editorial staff, 1928-38; United Newspapers Ltd. (formerly Kemsley Newspapers), London, England, member of editorial staff, 1946—, London news editor of *Sheffield Morning Telegraph,* 1958—, staff writer for *Yorkshire Post,* 1971—. *Military service:* British Army, 1939-45; served in Burma; became captain; mentioned in dispatches. *Member:* Society for Psychical Research (member of council, 1970—).

WRITINGS: The Unexplained, Arthur Barker, 1966, Abelard, 1970; *Frontiers of the Unknown,* Arthur Barker, 1968, Popular Library, 1970; *Apparitions and Ghosts,* Arthur Barker, 1971, Popular Library, 1972; (editor) *A Gallery of Ghosts* (anthology), Arthur Barker, 1972, Taplinger, 1973; *The Riddle of the Future: A Modern Study of Precognition,* Arthur Barker, 1974. Contributor to *Journal of the Society for Psychical Research.*

WORK IN PROGRESS: Dracula Country, a study of folk beliefs in modern Transylvania and Wallachia, for Arthur Barker.

* * *

MacKINNON, Frank 1919-

PERSONAL: Born April 24, 1919, in Charlottetown, Prince Edward Island, Canada; son of Murdoch and Perle (Taylor) MacKinnon; married Margaret Daphne Martin, April 27, 1943; children: Philip, David, Peter, Pamela. *Education:* McGill University, B.A. (honors), 1941; University of Toronto, M.A., 1942, Ph.D., 1950. *Office:* Department of Political Science, University of Calgary, Calgary, Alberta, Canada.

CAREER: Federal Department of Labor, Ottawa, Ontario, industrial relations officer, 1942-45; University of Toronto, Toronto, Ontario, instructor in political science, 1945-46; Carleton University, Ottawa, Ontario, assistant professor of political science and head of department, 1946-49; Prince of Wales College, Charlottetown, Prince Edward Island, principal, 1949-68; University of Calgary, Calgary, Alberta, professor of political science, 1968—. Member of Prince Edward Island royal commission on electoral reform, and Alberta committee of inquiry into post-secondary education; president of Fathers of Confederation Memorial Cultural Centre Project, 1957-64; representative at NATO course conference, Paris, 1958, International Public Administration Conference, Paris, 1965, and conference of Association of Commonwealth Universities, Australia, 1968. *Member:* Canada Council, Institute of Public Administration of Canada (president, 1964-65), Atlantic Provinces Economic Council (president, 1957, 1958). *Awards, honors:* LL.D. from University of New Brunswick, 1950, and Dalhousie University, 1964; Governor-General's Literary Award for non-fiction, 1951, for *The Government of Prince Edward Island;* Nuffield travel fellow, 1957; Stratford Design Award, 1964; Canada Medal, 1967; Order of Canada, 1969; Canada Council fellowship, 1972-73.

WRITINGS: The Government of Prince Edward Island, University of Toronto Press, 1951; *The Politics of Education,* University of Toronto Press, 1960; *Responsibility and Relevance in Education* (Quance lectures), Gage, 1968; *Postures and Politics: Observations on Participatory Democracy,* University of Toronto Press, 1973. Contributor of articles to professional journals.

WORK IN PROGRESS: Research on the functions of the Crown in democratic government, and relations between heads of state and heads of government.

* * *

MacPHERSON, Margaret 1908-

PERSONAL: Born June 29, 1908, in Colinton, Midlothian, Scotland; daughter of Norman (a minister) and Shina (Macaulay) Maclean; married Duncan MacPherson, June 28, 1929 (died, 1971); children: Lachlan, Alasdair, Neil, William, Allan, Andrew, Kenneth. *Education:* University of Edinburgh, M.A., 1929. *Politics:* Labour Party. *Home:* Torvaig, Portree, Isle of Skye.

CAREER: Free-lance writer. Member of Commission of Inquiry into Crofting, 1951-54, and Consultative Council of Highlands and Island Development Board, 1970—. *Member:* P.E.N. *Awards, honors: The Rough Road* was chosen among the "fifty best children's books published in the United States" in 1965.

WRITINGS—Juveniles: *The Shinty Boys,* Harcourt, 1963; *The Rough Road,* Harcourt, 1965; *Ponies for Hire,* Harcourt, 1967; *The New Tenants,* Harcourt, 1969; *The Battle of the Braes,* Collins, 1971.

WORK IN PROGRESS: The Boy on the Roof, a book on childhood in the 1920's in Edinburgh, Scotland.

* * *

MAGER, George C(lyde) 1937-

PERSONAL: Born July 6, 1937, in New York, N.Y.; son of Clyde George and Eugenia (Condos) Mager. *Education:* Franklin and Marshall College, A.B., 1959; Harvard University, Ed.M., 1970, Ed.D., 1972. *Home:* 1614 Pine Ave. W., Montreal, Quebec H3G IB4, Canada. *Office:* Department of Educational Psychology, McGill University, 3700 McTavish St., Montreal, Quebec, Canada.

CAREER: Teacher of English and drama in New York and Pennsylvania, 1959-64; Greek-American School, New York, N.Y., vice-principal, 1964-66; head of drama department in North Carolina Advancement School, Winston-Salem, 1966-68, and Pennsylvania Advancement School, Philadelphia, 1968-69; McGill University, Montreal, Quebec, assistant professor of educational psychology, 1971—. Consultant to Protestant School Board of Greater Montreal. *Military service:* Pennsylvania National Guard, 1959. *Member:* Society for Emotionally Disturbed Children, Council for Exceptional Children, Foundation for Schizophrenia, Phi Delta Kappa.

WRITINGS: (With Farnum Gray) *Liberating Education: A Psychological Approach to Improvisational Drama,* McCutchan, 1973. Contributor to journals.

WORK IN PROGRESS: Research on film and literature pertinent to adolescence, and on aesthetic development.

*   *   *

MAGUIRE, Daniel Charles 1931-

PERSONAL: Uses original spelling of surname; born April 4, 1931, in Philadelphia, Pa.; son of Bernard and Catherine (Gallagher) McGuire; married Marjorie Reiley, August 10, 1971; children: Daniel Charles, Jr. *Education:* Gregorian University of Rome, S.T.B., 1955, S.T.L., 1957, S.T.D., 1969. *Politics:* Democrat. *Religion:* Liberal Roman Catholic. *Home:* 2712 East Bradford Ave., Milwaukee, Wis. 53211. *Office:* Department of Theology, Marquette University, 1303 West Wisconsin Ave., Milwaukee, Wis. 53233.

CAREER: Roman Catholic priest, 1956-71. Villanova University, Villanova, Pa., lecturer in religious studies, 1960-64; St. Mary's University and Seminary, Baltimore, Md., extraordinary professor of ethics, 1964-66; Catholic University of America, Washington, D.C., interim assistant professor, 1966-67, assistant professor, 1967-69, associate professor of ethics, 1969-71; Marquette University, Milwaukee, Wis., associate professor of ethics, 1971—. Member of board of directors of Center for the Study of Power and Peace, 1972—. *Member:* American Society of Christian Ethics (member of board of directors, 1970-73), College Theology Society (member of board of directors, 1973-75), American Academy of Religion, Catholic Theological Society of America.

WRITINGS: The Gifts of the Holy Spirit in John of St. Thomas, Gregorian University Press, 1969; *Death by Choice,* Doubleday, 1974.

Contributor: Katherine T. Hargrove, editor, *The Paradox of Religious Secularity,* Prentice-Hall, 1968; Charles Curran, editor, *Absolutes in Moral Theology?,* Corpus Publications, 1968; Mary P. Ryan, editor, *Toward Moral Maturity: Religious Education and the Formation of Conscience,* Paulist-Newman, 1968; Thomas Quigley, editor, *American Catholics and Vietnam,* Eerdmans, 1968; Daniel Callahan, editor, *God, Jesus, Spirit,* Herder & Herder, 1969; Curran, editor, *Contraception: Authority and Dissent,* Herder & Herder, 1969; Martin Marty and Dean Peerman, editors, *New Theology,* Volume X, Macmillan, 1973.

Contributor to *Encyclopedic Dictionary of Christian Doctrine.* Contributor of articles and reviews to popular magazines and theology journals, including *Cosmopolitan, Theological Review, Humanist, Commonweal, Atlantic, Living Light,* and *Colloquy.*

WORK IN PROGRESS: A book on general ethical method applied to a wide range of subjects, including the sexual and the political.

*   *   *

MAHLENDORF, Ursula R. 1929-

PERSONAL: Born October 24, 1929, in Strehlen, Silesia; daughter of Ernst (an engineer) and Erna (Gebel) Mahlendorf. *Education:* Attended University of Tuebingen and University of Bonn, 1950-54; Brown University, M.A., 1956, Ph.D., 1958. *Home:* 399 Loma Media, Santa Barbara, Calif. 93103. *Office:* Department of German, University of California, Santa Barbara, Calif. 93107.

CAREER: University of California, Santa Barbara, assistant professor, 1957-65, associate professor of German, 1965—, associate director of education-abroad program. President of Santa Barbara Psychiatric Foundation, 1971-73, member of board of directors, 1974.

WRITINGS: (Translator) Horst Bienek, *The Cell* (novel), Unicorn Press (Santa Barbara), 1972; (editor with John L. Carleton) *Man for Man,* C.C Thomas, 1973. Contributor to professional journals, including *Monatshefte* and *Journal of Aesthetics and Art Criticism.*

WORK IN PROGRESS: Research on contemporary German literature and on psychology and literature; research on the creative process in literature, as illustrated by Gunter Grass, Thomas Mann, and Franz Kafka.

AVOCATIONAL INTERESTS: Travel, sculpting, weaving.

*   *   *

MAIOLO, Joseph 1938-

PERSONAL: Surname is pronounced Mah-ee-*o*-lo; born October 20, 1938, in Hinton, W. Va.; married Julie Ann Brown, July 18, 1964; children: Joshua, Ann. *Education:* U.S. Naval Academy, B.S., 1960; University of Virginia, M.A., 1968; further graduate study at Hollins College, 1970, and American University, 1971-73; University of North Carolina, Greensboro, M.F.A., 1974. *Home address:* R.R. 1, Box 158, Ashburn, Va. 22011. *Office:* Northern Virginia Community College, Annandale, Va.

CAREER: Northern Virginia Community College, Annandale, instructor, 1968-73, assistant professor, 1973-74, associate professor of English, 1974—. Speaker at workshops and readings; public lecturer. *Military service:* U.S. Air Force, 1960-66; became captain. *Member:* Modern Language Association of America, Associated Writing Programs. *Awards, honors:* Houghton Mifflin fiction award, 1970, for *Elverno: A Tale from a Boyhood;* writer's forum award from Virginia Commonwealth University, 1972, for story "Leather Man."

WRITINGS: Elverno: A Tale from a Boyhood (novella), Blairwood, 1972; (editor and contributor) *From Three Sides: An Anthology of Poems, Stories, and Essays,* Prentice-Hall, in press. Contributor of stories, poems, and criticism to *Magill's Literary Annual,* and to *Greensboro Review, Proteus, George Mason Review, Granite, Phoebe,* and *Inlet.*

WORK IN PROGRESS: Fall Out for Sunset, a novel; *Poems and Proems; The Fatherless,* short stories; *Josh and Gina Down on the Farm,* juvenile; *Starbright: A Christmas Story,* juvenile; editing and writing material for *New Stories from Virginia;* "Elverno," a screenplay.

MAISELS, Maxine S. 1939- (Ziva Amishai-Maisels)

PERSONAL: Born November 4, 1939, in New York, N.Y.; daughter of Misha (a writer under pseudonym M. H. Amishai) and Deborah (Wald) Maisels. *Education:* Barnard College, B.A., 1961; Columbia University, M.A., 1962; Hebrew University of Jerusalem, Ph.D., 1970. *Religion:* Jewish. *Home:* 6 Ha'Arazim St., Jerusalem, Israel. *Agent:* Barbara Boynton, 905 West End Ave., New York, N.Y. 10025. *Office:* Department of Art History, Hebrew University, Jerusalem, Israel.

CAREER: Hebrew University, Jerusalem, Israel, lecturer in art history, 1962—.

WRITINGS: (Under pseudonym Ziva Amishai-Maisels) *Marc Chagall at the Knesset,* Tudor, 1973; *Gauguin's Religious Themes,* Yale University Press, in press. Contributor to *Burlington Magazine.*

WORK IN PROGRESS: The Influence of the Holocaust on Art.

* * *

MAJOR, Jean-Louis 1937-

PERSONAL: Born July 16, 1937, in Cornwall, Ontario, Canada; son of Joseph (a businessman) and Noella (Daoust) Major; married Bibiane Landry, June 4, 1960; children: Marie-France. *Education:* University of Ottawa, B.Ph., 1959, B.A. (honors), 1960, L.Ph., 1960, M.A., 1961, Ph.D., 1965; Ecole Pratique des Hautes Etudes, postdoctoral study, 1968-69. *Home address:* Box 540, Boyer Rd., Orleans, Ontario, Canada. *Office:* Lettres francaises, University of Ottawa, Ottawa, Ontario, Canada.

CAREER: University of Ottawa, Ottawa, Ontario, lecturer, 1961-1964, assistant professor of philosophy, 1964-65, assistant professor, 1965-67, associate professor, 1967-70, professor of French Canadian literature, 1971—. Visiting professor at University of Toronto, 1970-71.

WRITINGS: (Contributor) Julien, Menard, Robidoux, Wyczynski, editors, *Le roman canadien-francais* (title means "The French Canadian Novel"), Fides, 1964; *Saint-Exupery: L'ecriture et la pensee* (title means "Saint-Exupery: Style and Logic"), Editions de l'Universite d'Ottawa, 1968; (contributor) Pierre de Grandpre, editor, *Histoire de la litterature francaise du Quebec,* Volume IV, Beauchemin, 1969; (contributor) Julien, Menard, Robidoux, Wyczynski, editors, *Poesie canadienne-francaise* (title means "French Canadian Poetry") Fides, 1969; *Anne Hebert et le miracle de la parole* (title means "Anne Hebert and the Miracle of the Word"), Presses de l'Universite de Montreal, 1974; *Edition critique de Leone de Jean Cocteau* (title means "A Critical Edition of Jean Cocteau's 'Leone' "), Editions de l'Universite d'Ottawa, 1974.

Contributor to *Canadian Author and Bookman, Citizen, Le Devoir, Dialogue, Liberte, University of Toronto Quarterly, Incidences,* and other Canadian and European journals. Literary critic, *Le Droit,* 1963-65.

WORK IN PROGRESS: Research on poetry of Quebec, theories of literature, the twentieth century novel in Quebec, and French literature of the twentieth century; "Teaching, Literature and Society," an essay.

MAKARY
See IRANEK-OSMECKI, Kazimierz

* * *

MALCOLM, Margaret
See KUETHER, Edith Lyman

* * *

MALHERBE, Abraham J(ohannes) 1930-

PERSONAL: Surname is accented on second syllable; born May 15, 1930, in Pretoria, South Africa; son of Abraham J. (an insurance agent) and Cornelia (Meyer) Malherbe; married Phyllis Melton, May 28, 1953; children: Selina, Cornelia, Abraham J. *Education:* Abilene Christian College, B.A., 1954; Harvard University, S.T.B., 1957, Th.D., 1963; also studied at University of Utrecht, 1960-61. *Home:* 71 Spring Garden St., Hamden, Conn. 06517. *Office:* Divinity School, Yale University, 409 Prospect St., New Haven, Conn. 06510.

CAREER: Minister in Churches of Christ, 1953—; Abilene Christian College, Abilene, Tex., assistant professor, 1963-64, associate professor of New Testament, 1964-69; Dartmouth College, Hanover, N.H., associate professor of New Testament, 1969-70; Yale University, New Haven, Conn., associate professor of New Testament, 1970—. *Member:* American Academy of Religion, Society of Biblical Literature, Corpus Hellenisticum Novi Testamenti, Societas Novi Testamenti Studiorum, North American Patristic Society. *Awards, honors:* Christian Research Foundation award, 1967, for translation of *De Vita Moysis.*

WRITINGS: (Editor and contributor) *The World of the New Testament,* R. B. Sweet, 1967; (contributor) Frank Magill, editor, *Current Events and Their Interpretations,* Salem Press, 1972. Also translator with W. E. Ferguson of Gregory of Nyssa, *De Vita Moysis* (title means "The Life of Moses"), in press. Contributor to honorary volumes. Contributor of articles and reviews to journals, including *Journal of Biblical Literature, Novum Testamentum, Theologische Zeitschrift, Restoration Quarterly, Journal of Ecclesiastical History,* and *Vigiliae Christianae.*

WORK IN PROGRESS: The New Testament and Cynicism, a monograph; "The New Testament and The Greek Moralists," a series of articles.

* * *

MALING, Arthur (Gordon) 1923-

PERSONAL: Born June 11, 1923, in Chicago, Ill.; son of Albert (a businessman) and Alma (Gordon) Maling; married Beatrice Goldberg, 1949 (divorced, 1958); children: Michael, Evan Beatrice. *Education:* Harvard University, B.A., 1944. *Home and office:* 860 De Witt Pl., Chicago, Ill. 60611.

CAREER: Maling Bros., Inc. (retail shoe chain), Chicago, Ill., owner, 1946-72. Member of Chicago Art Institute and Lyric Opera of Chicago. *Member:* Mystery Writers of America (regional vice-president, 1974—), Council on Foreign Relations (Chicago), Harvard Alumni Association, Authors Guild, B'nai B'rith, 210 Associates.

WRITINGS—All mystery novels; all published by Harper: *Decoy,* 1969; *Go-Between,* 1970; *Loophole,* 1971; *The Snowman,* 1973; *Dingdong,* 1974.

WORK IN PROGRESS: Another mystery novel.

MALKIEL, Burton Gordon 1932-

PERSONAL: Born August 28, 1932, in Boston, Mass.; son of Sol and Celia (Gordon) Malkiel; married Judith Atherton (an examiner for Educational Testing Service), July 16, 1954; children: Jonathan. *Education:* Harvard University, B.A., 1953, M.B.A., 1955; Princeton University, Ph.D., 1964. *Home:* 74 Wilson Rd., Princeton, N.J. 08540. *Office:* Department of Economics, Princeton University, Princeton, N.J. 08540.

CAREER: Princeton University, Princeton, N.J., assistant professor, 1964-66, associate professor, 1966-68, professor of economics, 1968—, Gordon S. Rentschler Memorial Professor of Economics, 1969—. Member of board of directors of Princeton Bank and Trust Co., 1970-72, and Prudential Insurance Company of America, 1973—; member of board of trustees, College Retirement Equities Fund, 1969-73. *Military service:* U.S. Army, 1955-58; became first lieutenant. *Member:* American Economic Association, American Finance Association (member of board of directors, 1973—). *Awards, honors:* D.H.L., University of Hartford, 1971.

WRITINGS: *The Term Structure of Interest Rates,* Princeton University Press, 1966; (with Richard E. Quandt) *Strategies and Rational Decisions in the Securities Options Market,* M.I.T. Press, 1969; *A Random Walk Down Wall Street,* Norton, 1973.

WORK IN PROGRESS: Research on securities markets.

* * *

MALKIN, Maurice L. 1900-

PERSONAL: Born November 10, 1900, in Minsk, Russia; son of Louis (a carpenter) and Hanna (Hoffman) Malkin; married Laura Dick, April 6, 1941; children: Arlene, Lana. *Education:* Educated in Manhattan and Bronx, N.Y. *Home:* 2345 Ocean Ave., Brooklyn, N.Y. 11229.

CAREER: In printing machinery business, 1945-48; U.S. Department of Justice, Washington, D.C., consultant, 1948-56; with Central Intelligence Agency (CIA), Washington, D.C., 1956-62; analyst for U.S. Foreign Service, Washington, D.C. Political organizer.

WRITINGS: *Return to My Father's House,* Arlington House, 1973.

WORK IN PROGRESS: *Schools for Treason.*

* * *

MALLESON, Lucy Beatrice 1899-1973 (Anthony Gilbert)

1899—December 9, 1973; British crime novelist. Obituaries: *AB Bookman's Weekly,* January 14, 1974.

* * *

MALLETT, Anne 1913-

PERSONAL: Born October 2, 1913, in Worcester, Mass.; daughter of Louis Edgar (an architect) and Josephine (Boyd) Vaughan; married Windsor A. Mallett (an art director), February 14, 1950; children: Christina Anne, Windsor Boyd. *Education:* Attended School of the Museum of Fine Arts, Boston, 1932-36; Fontainbleau School, France, 1937. *Home:* 21 Robinhood Rd., Natick, Mass. 01760.

CAREER: Free-lance artist in New York, N.Y., 1938-45; Worcester Art Museum School, Worcester, Mass., teacher, 1945-50; free-lance artist and writer, 1950—.

WRITINGS—All juveniles: *Whopper Whale,* Children's Press, 1950; *Who'll Mind Henry?* (Junior Literary Guild selection), Doubleday, 1965; *Here Comes Tagalong,* Parents' Magazine Press, 1971; *Secret Kitten* (self-illustrated), Parents' Magazine Press, 1972. Also illustrator of fifteen books.

* * *

MALONE, Elmer Taylor, Jr. 1943- (Ted Malone)

PERSONAL: Born December 18, 1943, in Wilson, N.C.; son of E. Taylor and Mildred (Winborne) Malone; married Lynda Cyrus, June 15, 1969. *Education:* Campbell College, B.S., 1967; University of Maryland graduate study in Europe, 1967-68; University of North Carolina, further graduate study, 1970-72, 1974. *Home:* Rt. 3, 116 Green Tree Trail, Chapel Hill, N.C. 27514. *Office:* Office of Administration, U.S. Environmental Protection Agency, Chapel Hill Blvd., Durham, N.C.

CAREER: *Raleigh Times,* Raleigh, N.C., reporter, 1969; *Dunn Dispatch,* Dunn, N.C., editor, 1970; *Harnett County News,* Lillington, N.C., editor, 1972-74; with U.S. Environmental Protection Agency, Technical Publications Division, Durham, N.C., 1974—. Member of board of directors of Lillington Chamber of Commerce; member of Lillington's Democratic precinct committee and Harnett County Democratic Executive Committee; member of board of directors of Harnett County Council on Alcohol and Drug Abuse. *Military service:* U.S. Army, 1967-68. *Member:* North Carolina Folklore Society, North Carolina Press Association, North Carolina Poetry Society, Harnett County Historical Society.

WRITINGS—Poems; under name Ted Malone: *The Cleared Place of Tara,* Pope Printing, 1970; *The Tapestry Maker,* Blair, 1972. Work is represented in *Poems of the Outer Banks,* edited by Eugene Robert Platt, Briarpatch Press, 1974. Contributor to *Journal of the American Medical Association, North Carolina Folklore Journal, Long View Journal, Crucible, Tar River Poets, Lyricist,* and *North Carolina Award Winning Poems.*

WORK IN PROGRESS: *Harnett County Historical Places; Edwin W. Fuller: His Life and Times; Pictures of Structures that Don't Exist and Other Matters of Consequence,* a book of poems, essays, and etchings.

AVOCATIONAL INTERESTS: The Irish dramatic movement, Irish history.

* * *

MALONE, Ted

See MALONE, Elmer Taylor, Jr.

* * *

MANCROFT, Stormont Mancroft Samuel 1914-

PERSONAL: Succeeded father to title of Lord Mancroft as second baron of Mancroft, 1942; born July 27, 1914, in London, England; son of Arthur Michael Samuel (1st Baron Mancroft) and Phoebe (Fletcher) Mancroft; married Diana Elizabeth Lloyd Quarry, 1951; children: Victoria, Jessica Rosetta, Benjamin Lloyd Quarry. *Education:* Christ Church, Oxford, M.A., 1937. *Home:* 80 Eaton Sq., London S.W.1, England.

CAREER: Called to Bar of Inner Temple, London, 1938, and member of Bar Council, 1947-51; member of St. Marylebone Borough Council, 1947-53; a lord in waiting to the Queen, 1952-54; British Home Office, parliamentary undersecretary of state, 1954-57; British Ministry of Defence, parliamentary secretary, 1957; minister without portfolio, 1957-58; Great Universal Stores Ltd., London, director, 1958-66; Cunard Line Ltd., London, deputy chairman, 1966-71; Cunard Steamship Co., London, member of board of directors, 1966-71. President, Institute of Marketing, 1959-63; member, Council of Industrial Design, 1960-63; president, London Tourist Board; chairman, Committee for Exports to the United States. *Military service:* Territorial Army, 1938-39, 1947-55. British Army, 1939-46; became lieutenant colonel; twice mentioned in dispatches. *Member:* Primrose League (chancellor, 1952-54), Carlton Club, Pratt's Club, West Ham Boys' Club. *Awards, honors:* Member of Order of the British Empire, 1945, Knight Commander, 1959; Croix de Guerre, 1945.

WRITINGS: Booking the Cooks, Mason Publishing, 1969; *Chinaman in My Bath,* Bachman & Turner, 1974.

* * *

MANHOFF, Bill
See MANHOFF, Wilton

* * *

MANHOFF, Wilton 1919-1974
(Bill Manhoff)

June 25, 1919—June 18, 1974; American playwright, and writer for television. Obituaries: *New York Times,* June 22, 1974.

* * *

MANN, David Douglas 1934-

PERSONAL: Born September 13, 1934, in Oklahoma City, Okla.; son of Loftin Harry and Jeannette (Kneer) Mann; married Jane McKenzie, August 12, 1962 (divorced); married Cathy Hoyser, June 18, 1972. *Education:* Oklahoma State University, B.S., 1956, M.A., 1963; Indiana University, Ph.D., 1969. *Home:* 327 East Vine St., Oxford, Ohio 45056. *Office:* Department of English, Miami University, Oxford, Ohio 45056.

CAREER: Wabash College, Crawfordsville, Ind., instructor in English, 1965-67; Miami University, Oxford, Ohio, instructor, 1968-69, assistant professor, 1969-73, associate professor of English, 1973—. *Military service:* U. S. Navy, 1956-59; became lieutenant commander. *Member:* Modern Language Association of America, National Council of Teachers of English. *Awards, honors:* Folger Shakespeare Library fellowship, 1970.

WRITINGS: (Editor) *A Concordance to the Complete Plays of William Congreve,* Cornell University Press, 1973. Contributor to *PMLA, Computers and the Humanities, Mississippi Valley Review, Wabash Review,* and *Miami Alumnus.*

WORK IN PROGRESS: Editing *A Concordance to the Complete Plays of George Etherege* and *The Complete Poems of William Congreve;* co-editing *The Complete Plays of John Gray.*

MANN, Jessica

PERSONAL: Born in London, England; daughter of Francis (a lawyer) and Eleonore (a lawyer; maiden name, Ehrlich) Mann; married A. Charles Thomas (a professor and archaeologist); children: Richard, Martin, Susanna, Lavinia. *Education:* Cambridge University, M.A.; University of Leicester, L.L.B. *Agent:* Bolt & Watson, 8 Storey's Gate, London S.W.1, England.

CAREER: Writer.

WRITINGS—All novels: *A Charitable End,* McKay, 1971; *Mrs. Knox's Profession,* McKay, 1972; *Troublecross,* McKay, 1973 (published in England as *The Only Security,* Macmillan, 1973); *The Sticking Place,* McKay, 1974.

* * *

MANN, Michael 1919-

PERSONAL: Born April 21, 1919, in Munich, Germany; son of Thomas (a writer) and Katia (Pringsheim) Mann; married Gret Moser, March 6, 1939; children: Frido, Tonio, Raju. *Education:* Duquesne University, M.M., 1957; Harvard University, Ph.D., 1961. *Residence:* Orinda, Calif. *Office:* Department of German, University of California, Berkeley, Calif. 94720.

CAREER: Member of San Francisco Symphony, 1942-49; viola soloist on concert tours, 1950-57; University of California, Berkeley, currently member of faculty in German department. *Awards, honors:* Guggenheim fellowship, 1964.

WRITINGS: Heinrich Heines Zeitungsberichte Ueber Musik und Malerei, Insel, 1964; *Die Europaeische Musik Von den Anfaengen Bis Beethoven,* Propylaen-Weltgesdridte, 1964; *Das Thomas Mann Buch,* Fischer Bucherei, 1965; *Heinrich Heines Musik Kritiken,* Campe, 1971.

WORK IN PROGRESS: Sturm und Drang Drama: Studica und Vorstudien zu Schiller's 'Rauberu'.

* * *

MANN, W(illiam) Edward 1918-

PERSONAL: Born April 4, 1918, in Toronto, Ontario, Canada; son of Charles (a transfer agent) and Laura (Wainwright) Mann; married Madeleine Helen Bear, March 16, 1951; children: Jocelyn, Gwynneth, Christopher, Allison, Andrew, Portia. *Education:* University of Toronto, B.A., 1942, M.A., 1943, Ph.D., 1953. *Politics:* "Social anarchist." *Religion:* Anglican. *Home address:* R.R. 2, Warkworth, Ontario, Canada. *Agent:* Susan Protter, 18 West 55th St., New York, N.Y. *Office:* Atkinson College, York University, 4700 Keele St., Toronto, Ontario, Canada.

CAREER: Anglican parish priest in Ontario, 1949-53; Toronto Anglican Diocesan Council for Social Service, Toronto, Ontario, executive secretary, 1953-58; Ontario Agricultural College, Guelph, Ontario, assistant professor of sociology, 1959-61; University of Western Ontario, London, Ontario, assistant professor of sociology, 1961-65; York University, Atkinson College, Toronto, Ontario, associate professor, 1965-68, professor of sociology, 1969—. Research sociologist. *Military service:* Royal Canadian Air Force, instructor in navigation and flying officer, 1943-45. *Member:* Canadian Anthropological and Sociological Association, American Sociological Association. *Awards, honors:* Canada Council fellowships and awards, 1946-47, 1958-59, 1961-62, 1968-69, 1970-71.

WRITINGS: The Rural Church in Canada, Canadian Council of Churches (Toronto), 1949; *Sect, Cult and Church in Alberta,* University of Toronto Press, 1955, reprinted, 1972; *Society behind Bars,* Social Science Publishers, 1967; *Canadian Trends in Premarital Behavior,* Anglican Church in Canada, 1967; *Canada: The Way It Is and Could Be,* Willowdale Press, 1968; *Orgone, Reich, and Eros,* Simon & Schuster, 1973. Author of a series on urbanism, for Canadian Broadcasting Corp. Contributor to *Encyclopedia Canadiana* and to periodicals, including *Canadian Review of Sociology, Continuous Learning, Christian Century, MacLean's Magazine, Toronto Star Weekly,* and *Chatelaine.*

Editor: *Canada: A Sociological Profile,* Copp Clark, 1968, 2nd edition, 1971; *Deviant Behavior in Canada,* Social Science Publishers, 1968; *The Underside of Toronto,* McClelland & Stewart, 1970; *Poverty and Social Policy in Canada,* Copp Clark, 1970; *Social and Cultural Change in Canada,* two volumes, Copp Clark, 1970; *Deviance and Social Problems in Canada,* Copp Clark, 1971.

WORK IN PROGRESS: Reich's Orgone: Fact, Fraud or Fancy; Beyond Reich, a critique; *They Were First,* on the sociology of great innovators; *Activist Sociology in Canada,* an autobiographical approach.

AVOCATIONAL INTERESTS: Travel.

BIOGRAPHICAL/CRITICAL SOURCES: Financial Post, May 1, 1974.

* * *

MANNERS, Elizabeth (Maude) 1917-

PERSONAL: Born July 20, 1917, in Newcastle-upon-Tyne, England; daughter of William George (an engineer) and Anne (Sced) Manners. *Education:* University of Durham, B.A. (honors), 1938, Diploma in Education, 1939, M.A., 1941. *Religion:* Church of England. *Home:* 18 Foxgrove Lane, Felixstowe, Suffolk IP11 7JU, England. *Agent:* Bolt and Watson Ltd., 8 Storey's Gate, London S.W.1, England. *Office:* Felixstowe College, Felixstowe, Suffolk IP11 7NQ, England.

CAREER: Assistant teacher of French in schools in England, 1939-54; Mexborough Grammar School, Yorkshire, England, deputy head, 1954-59; Central Grammar School for Girls, Manchester, England, headmistress, 1959-67; Felixstowe College, Felixstowe, England, headmistress, 1967—. Member of council of Bible Reading Fellowship, 1973—. *Military service:* Women's Royal Army Corps, Territorial Army, 1947-61; became captain; received Coronation Medal and Territorial Decoration. *Member:* Royal Society of Arts (fellow), Association of Heads of Girls' Boarding Schools, Association of Head Mistresses, Association of Independent and Direct Grant Schools, British Federation of University Women, Girl Guides' Association, Suffolk Agricultural Association, Felixstowe Celebrity Concert Society.

WRITINGS: The Vulnerable Generation, Coward, 1971. Contributor of book reviews to journals.

WORK IN PROGRESS: A novel, *Ride the White Horses,* the story of a headmistress.

AVOCATIONAL INTERESTS: Travel, fast cars, good food, wine, music, theater.

* * *

MANONI, Mary H(allahan) 1924-

PERSONAL: Born October 25, 1924, in Chicago, Ill.; daughter of John Joseph and Frances (Harris) Hallahan; married Alex Joseph Manoni, January 15, 1948 (died August 10, 1973); children: John, Joanne (Mrs. William Atwell), Melinda, Alex Joseph, Mary Kay. *Education:* DePaul University, B.S., 1967, M.A. (with distinction), 1969; Loyola University, Chicago, Ill., Ph.D., 1974. *Home:* 333 South Oak Park Ave., Oak Park, Ill. 60302. *Office:* 1345 Diversey Parkway, Chicago, Ill. 60614.

CAREER: American Bar Association, Chicago, Ill., assistant director of educational programs, 1965-70; Policy Sciences, Inc., New York, N.Y., research director, 1970-72; Singer Co., Educational Division, Chicago, Ill., educational coordinator, 1972—. Lecturer at Loyola University, Chicago, 1972—. Delegate to White House Conference on Children and Youth, 1970.

WRITINGS: Comparative Political Systems, New Orleans Public Schools, 1968; *The Black American: A Perspective Approach,* Michie Co., 1969; *Our Bill of Rights,* Scott, Foresman, 1970; *Bedford-Stuyvesant: The Anatomy of a Central City Community,* Quadrangle, 1973. Writer of a number of filmstrip series, including "Let's Talk Metric," Multi-Media Productions, 1973, "The Machinery of Justice," Walt Disney Educational Corp., 1974, and "Megalopolis: U.S.A.," 1974. Author of column in *School Weekly* of the *New York Times.* Contributor to *Focus.*

WORK IN PROGRESS: Why Don't the Media Fit the Message?; a first try at semi-fiction, *The Faces We Show;* a vocational education filmstrip.

* * *

MANUSHKIN, Fran 1942-

PERSONAL: Surname is pronounced Ma-*nush*-kin; born November 2, 1942; daughter of Meyer (a furniture salesman) and Beatrice (Kessler) Manushkin. *Education:* Attended University of Illinois and Roosevelt University; Northeastern Illinois State College, B.A. *Home:* 121 East 88th St., New York, N.Y. 10028. *Office:* Harper & Row Publishers, Inc., 10 East 53rd St., New York, N.Y. 10022.

CAREER: Elementary teacher in Chicago, Ill., 1964-65; went to New York, N.Y., and worked about six months at Doubleday Bookstore and about six months as tour guide at Lincoln Center for Performing Arts; Holt, Rinehart & Winston, Inc., New York, N.Y., secretary to college psychology editor, 1967-68; Harper & Row Publishers, Inc., New York, N.Y., 1968—, began as secretary, now associate editor of Harper Junior Books. *Member:* Sierra Club.

WRITINGS: Baby (picturebook illustrated by Ronald Himler), Harper, 1972; *Bubblebath!* (picturebook illustrated by Himler), Harper, 1974; *Shirleybird,* Harper, in press; *Swing, Swing, Swing,* Harper, in press.

AVOCATIONAL INTERESTS: Bicycling, playing guitar, cooking, daydreaming, watching children, "keeping my plants alive," going to museums and movies.

* * *

MAPLE, Terry 1946-

PERSONAL: Born September 10, 1946, in Maywood, Calif.; son of Merrill (a truck driver) and Evelyn (Hayes) Maple. *Education:* University of the Pacific, A.B., 1968; University of Stockholm, graduate study, 1971-72; University of California, Davis, M.A., 1971, Ph.D., 1974. *Office:* Department of Psychology, University of California, Davis, Calif. 95616.

CAREER: University of California, Davis, research behavioral biologist, 1973-74, lecturer in comparative psychology, 1974—. *Member:* International Communication Association, International Primatological Society, Society for the Psychological Study of Social Issues, American Association for the Advancement of Science, American Association of University Professors, American Psychological Association, American Society of Mammalogists, Animal Behavior Society, Association for the Study of Man-Environment Systems, Western Society of Naturalists, California State Psychological Association, Sigma Xi.

WRITINGS: (Editor with D. W. Matheson) *Aggression, Hostility, and Violence,* Holt, 1973. Contributor to *Primates, Archives of Sexual Behavior, Journal of Behavioural Science, International Journal of Psychobiology,* and other journals.

WORK IN PROGRESS: Classic Studies of Animal Behavior; research in interspecies social behavior, sexual behavior of macaques, human ethology, and aggression in animals and man.

AVOCATIONAL INTERESTS: Satirical cartooning, baseball, amateur drama productions.

* * *

MARCSON, Simon 1910-

PERSONAL: Born October 8, 1910, in Winnipeg, Manitoba, Canada; naturalized U.S. citizen; son of Samuel (a manager) and Fay (Breger) Marcson; married Florence Bernstein, January 31, 1936; children: Michael, Robert Anthony. *Education:* University of Chicago, A.B., 1936, A.M., 1941, Ph.D., 1950. *Politics:* Democrat. *Religion:* Jewish. *Home:* 36 Marion Rd., Princeton, N.J. 08540. *Office:* Murray Hall 214, Rutgers University, New Brunswick, N.J. 08903.

CAREER: Pennsylvania State University, University Park, assistant professor of sociology, 1942-46; Queens College (now of City University of New York), Flushing, N.Y., lecturer in anthropology and sociology, 1946-51; Brooklyn College (now of City University of New York), Brooklyn, N.Y., lecturer in anthropology and sociology, 1951-55; Rutgers University, New Brunswick, N.J., 1955—, now professor of sociology. Visiting professor at Temple University, 1949, and Wayne State University, 1950; social affairs officer of Population Division at United Nations, 1951; executive secretary and university seminar associate at Columbia University, 1954-62; research associate of industrial relations section at Princeton University, 1958-61. Consultant to United Nations, American Council of Education, and National Academy of Science. Member of New Jersey Committee on Efficiency and Economy in State Government, 1966—, and of Committee on State Aid to Education, 1966—; member of board of trustees of Mercer County Community College, 1969—.

MEMBER: International Sociological Association, American Association for the Advancement of Science (fellow), American Sociological Association (fellow), Society for Applied Anthropology (fellow), American Anthropological Association (fellow), Industrial Relations Research Association, Eastern Sociological Society. *Awards, honors:* Fulbright fellow, 1959-60; U.S. Office of Education grant, 1961-64; National Science Foundation grant, 1962-63; National Aeronautical and Space Administration grant, 1963-66.

WRITINGS: The Scientist in American Industry, Harper, 1960; *Automation, Alienation, and Anomie,* Harper, 1970. Contributor to *American Sociological Review, American Journal of Sociology, American Anthropologist, Social Science and Medicine, Social Forces,* and *Industrial Sociology.*

WORK IN PROGRESS: Sociology of Science, completion expected in 1975; research on the British government scientist, 1975.

* * *

MAREK, George R(ichard) 1902-

PERSONAL: Born July 13, 1902, in Austria; son of Martin (a physician) and Emily (Weisberger) Marek; married Muriel Hepner, August, 1925; children: Richard. *Education:* Attended Vienna College, 1916-20, and City College (now City College of the City University of New York), 1920-24. *Home:* 151 Central Park W., New York, N.Y. 10023. *Agent:* Phyllis Jackson, International Famous Agency, 1301 Avenue of the Americas, New York, N.Y. 10019.

CAREER: Good Housekeeping magazine, New York, N.Y., music editor, 1940-50; RCA Victor, New York, N.Y., vice-president and general manager, 1950-65. *Member:* Dutch Treat Club.

WRITINGS: Puccini, Simon & Schuster, 1957; *Opera as Theater,* Simon & Schuster, 1958; *R. Strauss,* Simon & Schuster, 1965; *Beethoven: The Story of a Genius,* Funk, 1970; *Mendelssohn: Gentle Genius,* Funk, 1972; *The Eagles Die,* Harper, 1974.

WORK IN PROGRESS: Toscanini, a biography.

* * *

MARIEN, Michael 1938-

PERSONAL: Born March 27, 1938, in Washington, D.C.; son of Henry Matthew (a printer) and Ida (Silver) Marien; married Mary Lou Warner (a learning counselor), January 20, 1968. *Education:* Cornell University, B.S., 1959; University of California, Berkeley, M.B.A., 1964; Syracuse University, Ph.D., 1970. *Home and office:* Webster Rd., LaFayette, N.Y. 13084.

CAREER: Educational Policy Research Center, Syracuse, N.Y., research fellow, 1968-72; World Institute Council, New York, N.Y., director of Information for Policy Design Project, 1972—.

WRITINGS: Alternative Futures for Learning: An Annotated Bibliography of Trends, Forecasts, and Proposals, Educational Policy Research Center, 1971; *Beyond the Carnegie Commission: A Policy Study Guide to Space/Time/Credit-Preference Higher Learning,* Educational Policy Research Center, 1972; (editor with Warren L. Ziegler) *The Potential of Educational Futures,* Charles A. Jones Publishing, 1972.

WORK IN PROGRESS: The World Institute Guide to Alternative Futures for Health: A Bibliocritique of Trends, Forecasts, Problems, Proposals; World Problem Handbook, North American Edition; preparing and supervising the preparation of a series of guidebooks to help researchers, teachers, students, policymakers, and citizens in general to understand the literature that describes where we are headed and/or prescribes where we ought to be headed—the policy directions that our society should take.

* * *

MARING, Joel M(arvin) 1935-

PERSONAL: Born January 17, 1935, in Waterloo, Iowa;

son of Marvyl Henry and Marjorie (Shadman) Maring; married Ester Gayo (an anthropologist), September 12, 1959; children: Lillian, Timothy, Priscilla, Mila, Geoffrey, Raymond. *Education:* Wartburg College, B.A., 1956; Indiana University, Ph.D., 1967. *Religion:* Lutheran. *Home address:* R.F.D. 1, Makanda, Ill. 62958. *Office:* Department of Anthropology, Southern Illinois University, Carbondale, Ill. 62901.

CAREER: Bonded Blueprint Co., Grants, N.M., manager, 1957-58; Indiana University, Bloomington, instructor in anthropology, 1959-63; Southern Illinois University, Carbondale, instructor, 1963-67, assistant professor, 1967-70, associate professor of anthropology, 1970—. Consultant in bilingual education to Bureau of Indian Affairs, 1972-73. *Member:* American Anthropological Association (fellow), Association for Asian Studies.

WRITINGS: *Anthropological Considerations for Evaluators, Innovators, and Implementers in American Education* (monograph), Eureka College Study Center, Illinois Department of Program Development for Gifted Children, 1969; (with wife, Ester Maring) *A Historical and Cultural Dictionary of the Philippines,* Scarecrow, 1973; (with Ester Maring) *A Historical and Cultural Dictionary of Burma,* Scarecrow, 1973; (editor) Georg Pilhofer, *The New Guinea Church: Copy or Original,* Southern Illinois University Press, in press. Member of editorial board, *Southeast Asia: An International Quarterly,* 1969—.

WORK IN PROGRESS: *Acoma Language and Culture,* for Bureau of Indian Affairs; with Ester Maring, culture-history volumes on Indonesia, Cambodia, and Laos, for Scarecrow.

SIDELIGHTS: Maring's training has been primarily in linguistics. He has analytically studied about twenty languages, written a dissertation grammar of Acoma Keresan, and carried out language studies in New Guinea, the Philippines, and West Africa.

* * *

MARKBREIT, Jerry 1935-

PERSONAL: Born March 23, 1935; son of Henry M. (a salesman) and Rena (Smith) Markbreit; married Roberta Weiner (a writer), June 17, 1956; children: Kathy, Betsy. *Education:* University of Illinois, B.Ed., 1956. *Politics:* Republican. *Religion:* Jewish. *Home:* 9739 North Keystone Ave., Skokie, Ill. 60076. *Office:* *Where,* 75 East Wacker Dr., Chicago, Ill. 60601.

CAREER: *Where* (magazine), New York, N.Y., sales manager in Chicago office, 1956—. Also serves as football referee for Big Ten games.

WRITINGS: *Armchair Referee,* Doubleday, 1973.

* * *

MARKEN, Jack W(alter) 1922-

PERSONAL: Born February 11, 1922, in Akron, Ohio; son of James W. (a laborer) and Mary (Likens) Marken; married Martha Rose McVay, July 19, 1946; children: Janice (Mrs. John Hibbard), Roger, Harold. *Education:* University of Akron, B.A., 1947; Indiana University, M.A., 1950, Ph.D., 1953; also studied at Queen Mary College, London, 1951-52. *Politics:* Liberal Democrat. *Home:* 319 20th Avenue, Brookings, S.D. 57006. *Office:* Department of English, South Dakota State University, Brookings, S.D. 57006.

CAREER: University of Kentucky, Lexington, instructor in English, 1952-54; Ohio Wesleyan University, Delaware, assistant professor of English, 1954-55; Central Michigan University, Mount Pleasant, assistant professor of English, 1955-60; Slippery Rock State College (now Pennsylvania State College), Slippery Rock, Pa., associate professor, 1960-63, professor of English, 1963-67; South Dakota State University, Brookings, professor of English and chairman of department, 1967—. Fulbright lecturer at University of Jordan, 1965-66; lectured in Finland on the American Indian, under auspices of U.S. Information Service and Finnish-American Society, 1970. *Military service:* U.S. Army Air Forces, combat cameraman, 1943-45.

MEMBER: Modern Language Association of America, National Council of Teachers of English, Keats-Shelley Society, Finnish-American Society, American Association of University Professors (vice-president of Pennsylvania Division, 1964-65), National Indian Education, Irish-American Institute, South Dakota Committee on the Humanities (chairman, 1971-74), Midwest Modern Language Association. *Awards, honors:* Fulbright grant, 1951-52.

WRITINGS: (Editor and author of introduction) *Imogen: A Pastoral Romance,* New York Public Library, 1963; (editor with Burton R. Pollin) *Uncollected Writings of William Godwin: 1785-1822,* Scholars Facsimiles & Reprints, 1968; *Bibliography of Books By and About the American Indian,* Dakota Press, 1973. Contributor to *Modern Language Notes, Georgia Historical Quarterly, Yale University Library Gazette, Bulletin of New York Public Library, Suomi-Finland U.S.A., Philological Quarterly,* and *Keats-Shelley Journal.*

WORK IN PROGRESS: Editing autobiographical writings of William Godwin; preparing a bibliography of the American Indian in language and literature.

* * *

MARKGRAF, Carl 1928-

PERSONAL: Born July 18, 1928, in Portland, Ore.; son of Carl Bertschi and Elizabeth (McNutt) Markgraf; married Mary Barbara Irene Fleming, November 13, 1952; children: Cecily B., Elinor M., Karl F., Lise M., Thomas B., Paul E., Anna D. *Education:* Attended University of California, Berkeley, 1946, and Multnomah Junior College, 1947-48; University of Portland, A.B. (cum laude), 1951; M.A., 1954; University of California, Riverside, Ph.D., 1970. *Politics:* Democrat. *Religion:* Roman Catholic. *Home:* 2224 Northeast 26th Ave., Portland, Ore. 97212. *Office:* Department of English, Portland State University, Portland, Ore. 97207.

CAREER: High school teacher of English in Hood River, Ore., 1954-57; Marylhurst College, Marylhurst, Ore., instructor, 1957-60, assistant professor of English, 1960-63, director of drama, 1957-63; Portland State University, Portland, Ore., assistant professor, 1966-70, associate professor of English, 1970—, assistant head of department, 1972-73, acting head of department, 1973-74. New Theatre, Portland, Ore., member of the board of directors, 1967-68, executive vice-president, 1968-69, president, 1969-70. *Military service:* U.S. Naval Reserve, 1946-48. U.S. Navy, 1948-49. U.S. Army Reserve, 1956-64; became first lieutenant. *Member:* American Association of University Professors, Oregon State Employees Association, Alpha Psi Omega, Delta Phi Alpha.

WRITINGS: (Contributor) Herbert M. Schueller and

Robert L. Peters, editors, *The Letters of John Addington Symonds,* Wayne State University Press, 1967; (editor) *Problems in Usage,* Teaching Research Commission, State of Oregon, 1969; (editor) *Oscar Wilde's Anonymous Criticism,* Xerox Corp., 1970; (with Alex Scharbach) *Making the Point: Challenge and Response,* Intext, in press. Contributor of book reviews to *South Atlantic Quarterly* and *Victorian Studies.*

WORK IN PROGRESS: A monograph, *An Annotated Bibliography of Writings about John Addington Symonds,* completed and awaiting publication.

* * *

MARKSON, David M(errill) 1927-

PERSONAL: Born December 20, 1927, in Albany, N.Y.; son of Samuel A. (a newspaper editor) and Florence (a school teacher; maiden name, Stone) Markson; married Elaine Kretchmar (a literary agent), September 30, 1956; children: Johanna Lowry, Jed Matthew. *Education:* Union College, Schenectady, N.Y., B.A., 1950; Columbia University, M.A., 1952. *Politics:* Liberal Democrat. *Religion:* Jewish. *Home and office:* 39½ Washington Sq. S., New York, N.Y. 10012. *Agent:* Elaine Markson, 44 Greenwich Ave., New York, N.Y. 10011.

CAREER: Albany Times-Union, Albany, N.Y., staff writer, 1944-46, 1948-50; Weyerhauser Timber Co., Molalla, Ore., rigger, 1952; Dell Publishing Co., New York, N.Y., editor, 1953-54; Lion Books, New York, N.Y., editor, 1955-56; free-lance writer, 1956-64; Long Island University, Brooklyn Center, Brooklyn, N.Y., assistant professor of English, 1964-66; free-lance writer, 1966—. *Military service:* U.S. Army, 1946-48; became staff sergeant. *Member:* Louis Norman Newsom Memorial Society (executive secretary, 1973-74). *Awards, honors:* Fellow of Centro Mexicano de Escritores, 1960-61.

WRITINGS: (Editor) *Great Tales of Old Russia* (anthology), Pyramid Publications, 1956; *Epitaph for a Tramp* (crime novel), Dell, 1959; *Epitaph for a Dead Beat* (crime novel), Dell, 1961; *Miss Doll, Go Home* (crime novel), Dell, 1965; *The Ballad of Dingus Magee* (novel), Bobbs-Merrill, 1966; *Going Down* (novel), Holt, 1970.

Author of "Face to the Wind," a screenplay, Brut Productions, 1974. Contributor to magazines and newspapers, including *Saturday Evening Post, Nation,* and *Village Voice.*

WORK IN PROGRESS: Malcolm Lowry's Volcano, a critical study; "McCoy's Last Run," a screenplay, with Leo Rost.

SIDELIGHTS: Markson lived in Mexico between 1958 and 1961, and earlier had been a close friend of author Malcolm Lowry. He has also lived in Spain, Italy, and England. He writes: "Despite the financial and critical success of *The Ballad of Dingus Magee,* an anecdotal parody, I am much more interested in the subtle, the oblique, the allusive. My next novel will contain virtually no 'action' whatsoever."

BIOGRAPHICAL/CRITICAL SOURCES: Aaron Asher and Ross Wetzsteon, editors, *Selected Letters of Malcolm Lowry,* Lippincott, 1965; Leslie A. Fiedler, *The Return of the Vanishing American,* Stein & Day, 1968; *Union College Symposium,* winter, 1970-71; Douglas Day, *Malcolm Lowry,* Oxford University Press, 1974.

MARQUESS, Harlan E(arl) 1931-

PERSONAL: Surname is pronounced *Mar*-quess; born January 23, 1931, in Sheridan, Wyo.; son of Earl D. and Fern (Kinnaman) Marquess; married Joyce Shepard (a weaver), February 1, 1958; children: Jeanette, Philip Louis, Erik Joseph. *Education:* Attended Northern Wyoming Community College, 1949; Monterey Peninsula College, A.A., 1956; University of California, Berkeley, A.B. (highest honors), 1958, M.A., 1960, Ph.D., 1966. *Home:* 913 Harrison, Madison, Wis. 53711. *Office:* Department of Slavic Languages, University of Wisconsin, Van Hise Hall, Room 720, 1220 Linden Dr., Madison, Wis. 53706.

CAREER: University of Wisconsin, Madison, instructor, 1964-66, assistant professor, 1966-71, associate professor of Slavic languages, 1971—. *Military service:* U.S. Air Force, security service, 1951-55; became staff sergeant. *Member:* International Linguistic Association, American Association of University Professors, Linguistic Society of America, American Association of Teachers of Slavic and East European Languages (president of Wisconsin chapter, 1969-70), Phi Beta Kappa, Dobro Slovo.

WRITINGS: (With Meyer Galler) *Soviet Prison Camp Speech: A Survivor's Glossary,* University of Wisconsin Press, 1972. Contributor of reviews to *Slavic and East European Journal.*

WORK IN PROGRESS: Research on all varieties of nonstandard Russian speech.

* * *

MARRIN, Albert 1936-

PERSONAL: Born July 24, 1936, in New York, N.Y.; son of Louis and Frieda (Funt) Marrin; married Yvette Rappaport (a teacher), November 22, 1959. *Education:* City College (now City College of the City University of New York), B.A., 1958; Yeshiva University, M.S.Ed., 1959; Columbia University, M.A., 1961, Ph.D., 1968. *Home:* 3419 Irwin Ave., Bronx, N.Y. 10463. *Office:* Yeshiva College, Yeshiva University, New York, N.Y. 10033.

CAREER: High school social studies teacher in New York, N.Y., 1958-68; Yeshiva University, New York, N.Y., assistant professor of history at Yeshiva College, 1968—. Visiting professor at Yeshiva University, 1967-68, and Touro College, 1972—. *Member:* American Historical Association, Phi Alpha Theta (president of Alpha Mu chapter, 1957-58).

WRITINGS: War and the Christian Conscience: Augustine to Martin Luther King, Jr., Regnery, 1971; *The Last Crusade: The Church of England in the First World War,* Duke University Press, 1973.

WORK IN PROGRESS: Nicholas Murray Butler: An Intellectual Portrait, for Twayne; editing *A Reader in War and Peace.*

AVOCATIONAL INTERESTS: Travel (Europe).

* * *

MARSHALL, Michael (Kim) 1948-

PERSONAL: Born March 11, 1948, in Oakland, Calif.; son of Randolph Laughlin and Anne (Grant) Marshall; married Rhoda Schneider, May 25, 1973. *Education:* Harvard University, B.A. (magna cum laude), 1969. *Politics:* Independent. *Home:* 80 Francis St., Brookline, Mass. 02146. *Office:* Martin Luther King School, 27 Lawrence Ave., Boston, Mass. 02121.

CAREER: Martin Luther King School, Boston, Mass., sixth grade teacher, 1969—. Lecturer, Cambridge Educational Associates, 1974—. *Member:* Boston Teachers' Union.

WRITINGS: Law and Order in Grade 6-E, Little, Brown, 1972. Contributor and consultant to *Learning.*

WORK IN PROGRESS: A book of innovative worksheets for elementary school teachers.

BIOGRAPHICAL/CRITICAL SOURCES: Christian Science Monitor, June 30, 1973.

* * *

MARSHALL, Tom 1938-

PERSONAL: Born April 9, 1938, in Niagara Falls, Ontario, Canada; son of Douglas Woodworth (a chemical engineer) and Helen (Kennedy) Marshall. *Education:* Queen's University, B.A., 1961, M.A., 1965. *Residence:* Kingston, Ontario, Canada. *Office:* Queen's University, Kingston, Ontario, Canada.

CAREER: Queen's University, Kingston, Ontario, instructor, 1964-66, lecturer, 1966-69, assistant professor, 1969-73, associate professor of English, 1973—.

WRITINGS: (With Tom Eadre and Colin Norman) *The Beast with Three Backs* (poems), Quarry Press, 1965; *The Silence of Fire* (poems), Macmillan, 1969; *The Psychic Mariner* (critical study of poems by D. H. Lawrence), Viking, 1970; *A. M. Klein* (criticism), Ryerson, 1970; *Magic Water* (poems), Quarry Press, 1971; (editor with David Helwig) *Fourteen Stories High* (anthology), Oberon, 1971; *The Earth-Book* (poems), Oberon, 1974. Former chief editor of *Quarry;* poetry editor of *Canadian Forum.*

WORK IN PROGRESS: A book about Canadian literature; a novel; a fourth book of poems; editing stories of A. M. Klein.

SIDELIGHTS: Marshall writes: "I am very concerned about Canada's national identity and the future of Canada, but more optimistic about it than some of my contemporaries seem to be. I am also interested in foreign countries and cultures, and enjoy travelling." With David Helwig, Gail Fox, and Stuart MacKinnon, he has made a sound recording of his own work, "Four Kingston Poets," Quarry Recordings, 1972.

* * *

MARTIN, Renee C(ohen) 1928-

PERSONAL: Born February 26, 1928, in Brooklyn, N.Y.; daughter of Aref Max and Eleonora (Cofino) Cohen; married Howard Martin Kessler (employed in management consulting), December 24, 1950; children: Kenneth, Laurel, Elena, Julia. *Education:* Attended Brooklyn College of the City University of New York, one year; took extension courses at City College of the City University of New York, and New York University. *Residence:* Hightstown, N.J. *Office:* Handwriting Consultants, Inc., 205 Nassau St., Princeton, N.J. 08540.

CAREER: Handwriting Consultants, Inc. (graphology, penmanship instruction, and legal document examination and testimony), Princeton, N.J., president, 1950—. *Member:* American Association of Handwriting Analysts, International Association for Identification, Psychosynthesis Foundation, International Platform Association, Mensa, National League of American Pen Women, Business and Professional Women's Club (Hightstown; vice-president, 1968-69).

WRITINGS: Your Script Is Showing, Golden Press, 1969; *Renee Martin's Secrets of Handwriting,* Bantam, 1972. Regular columnist, "Your Handwriting and You," in *Companion,* 1971.

WORK IN PROGRESS: Studies on the effect of illness on the handwriting, and on the probability of personality change through handwriting change; analysis of color selection as pertaining to personality.

* * *

MASON, Douglas R(ankine) 1918- (John Rankine)

PERSONAL: Born September 26, 1918, in Hawarden, England; son of Russell (an engineer) and Bertha (Greenwood) Mason; married Norma Eveline Cooper (a social worker), May 26, 1945; children: Keith, Patricia (Mrs. Richard Morris), John, Elaine. *Education:* University of Manchester, B.A., 1947, teacher's diploma, 1948. *Politics:* "Liberal by inclination, Conservative sometimes by observation of policies." *Religion:* Methodist. *Home:* 16 Elleray Park Rd., Wallasey, Cheshire L45 OLH, England. *Agent:* E. J. Carnell, 17 Burwash Rd., Plumstead, London SE18 7QY, England. *Office:* St. George's Primary School, Wallasey, Cheshire, England.

CAREER: Taught in primary and secondary schools in Cheshire, England, 1950-67; St. George's Primary School, Wallasey, England, headmaster, 1967—. *Military service:* British Army, Royal Signals Corps, 1939-46; served in Africa; became lieutenant. *Member:* Society of Authors, National Association of Head Teachers, Wallasey Association of Head Teachers (president, 1973-74).

WRITINGS—Science fiction: *From Carthage Then I Came,* Doubleday, 1966, published as *Eight Against Utopia,* Paperback Library, 1967; *Ring of Violence,* R. Hale, 1968, Avon, 1969; *Landfall Is a State of Mind,* R. Hale, 1968; *The Tower of Rizwan,* R. Hale, 1968; *The Janus Syndrome,* R. Hale, 1969; *Matrix,* Ballantine, 1970; *Satellite 54-0,* Ballantine, 1971; *Horizon Alpha,* Ballantine, 1971; *Dilation Effect,* Ballantine, 1971; *The Resurrection of Roger Diment,* Ballantine, 1972; *The Phaeton Condition,* Putnam, 1973; *The End Bringers,* Ballantine, 1973.

Under pseudonym John Rankine: *The Blockade of Sinitron: Four Adventures of Dag Fletcher,* Thomas Nelson, 1964; *Interstellar Two Five,* Dobson, 1966; *Never the Same Door,* Dobson, 1967; *One Is One,* Dobson, 1968; *Moons of Triopus,* Dobson, 1968, Paperback Library, 1969; *Binary Z,* Dobson, 1969; *The Weizman Experiment,* Dobson, 1969; *The Plantos Affair,* Dobson, 1971; *The Ring of Garamas,* Dobson, 1972; *Operation Umanaq,* Ace Books, 1973; *The Bromius Phenomenon,* Ace Books, 1973; *The Fingalnan Conspiracy,* Sidgwick & Jackson, 1973.

WORK IN PROGRESS: The Thorburn Enterprise, Links Over Space, The Vort Programme, Pitman's Progress, Plastic Incubus, Euphor Unfree, all science fiction novels; a historical novel of the Saxon period, working title *Sturmer.*

* * *

MASON, John Brown 1904-

PERSONAL: Born July 13, 1904, in Berlin, Germany; son of American nationals, John H. Brown and Sarah (McIntosh) Mason; married Frances J. Byrnes, February 14, 1951; adopted children: Robert E., Susan E. *Education:*

Butler University, A.B., 1926; University of Wisconsin, A.M., 1927; Ph.D., 1929; Claremont Graduate School, postdoctoral study, 1936-37. *Politics:* Democrat. *Home:* 1513 North Highland Ave., Fullerton, Calif. 92635. *Office:* Department of Political Science, California State University, Fullerton, Calif. 92634.

CAREER: University of Wisconsin, Madison, instructor in political science, 1929-30; University of Arkansas, Fayetteville, assistant professor of political science and history, 1930; Colorado Woman's College, Denver, professor of social sciences, 1934-36; U.S. Office of Education, forum leader in Orange County, Calif., and Seattle, Wash., 1936-37; Santa Ana Junior College, Santa Ana, Calif., lecturer in social sciences, 1937-38; Fresno State College (now California State University at Fresno), assistant professor, 1938-40, associate professor of political science, 1940-46; Oberlin College, Oberlin, Ohio, professor of political science, 1946-50; U.S. Department of State, High Commission for Germany, Frankfurt, chief of governmental affairs branch, 1950-51, chief of civic activities division of Office of Political Affairs, 1951-52, chief of cultural liaison branch in Bonn, 1952-54, and Berlin, 1954; U.S. Embassy, Bangkok, Thailand, cultural attache, 1954-55; Georgetown University, Washington, D.C., professor of government, 1956-60; California State University at Fullerton, professor of political science, 1960-74, professor emeritus, 1974—, chairman of department, 1961-65. Acting associate professor, Civil Affairs Training School, Stanford University, 1943-44; assistant in Special War Problems Division, U.S. Department of State, 1944; chief of Training Division, Foreign Economic Administration, 1944-46; visiting professor, University of Florida, 1955-56; visiting Chester W. Nimitz Professor at Naval War College, 1957-58. Member of Patterson Historical Mission to Germany, 1945, and Hoover Food Mission to Europe, 1946. Editorial consultant to University of California Press and University of Notre Dame Press.

MEMBER: American Society of International Law (member of executive committee, 1947-50), American Political Science Association (chairman of committee on aid to foreign universities, 1948-50). *Awards, honors:* Research grants from Social Science Research Council and American Council of Learned Societies, 1944; commendations from U.S. High Commissioner to Germany, 1953, and Secretary of State John Foster Dulles, 1954; Association for Asian Studies grant, 1957; named outstanding professor, California State University at Fullerton, 1969.

WRITINGS: Hitler's First Foes: A Study in Religion and Politics, Burgess, 1936; *The Danzig Dilemma: A Study in Peacemaking by Compromise,* Stanford University Press, 1946; (with others) Fritz M. Marx, editor, *Foreign Governments,* Prentice-Hall, 1949, 2nd edition, 1952, his two chapters on Germany reprinted as *German Government and Politics,* Duncker & Humboldt (Berlin), 1954; (contributor) A. J. Zurcher, editor, *Constitutions and Constitutional Trends Since World War II,* New York University Press, 1951, 2nd edition, 1952; (editor with H. Carroll Parish) *Thailand Bibliography,* University of Florida Libraries, 1958; *Research Resources: Annotated Guide to the Social Sciences,* ABC-Clio, Volume I: *International Relations and Recent History: Indexes, Abstracts, and Periodicals,* 1968, Volume II: *Official Publications: U.S. Government, United Nations, International Organizations, and Statistical Sources,* 1971.

Has done more than 150 abstracts in political science and economics from articles in German, French, and English journals. Contributor to *Dictionary of Political Science, Jahrbuch des Oeffentlichen Rechts,* and to about fifteen periodicals, including political science and legal journals, *American Spectator, Ecclesiastical Review,* and *Sewanee Review.* Regular reviewer for political science journals. Member of editorial board, *Western Political Quarterly,* 1961-64; member of advisory board, *ABC Pol Sci,* 1969—.

* * *

MATHES, J(ohn) C(harles) 1931-

PERSONAL: Born January 3, 1931, in Toledo, Ohio; son of John Charles (an engineer) and Cletus (Fagan) Mathes; married Rosemary Lewis, March 7, 1960; children: George Malcolm, John Craig. *Education:* University of Michigan, A.B., 1952, A.M., 1953, Ph.D., 1965. *Home:* 1400 Jorn Court, Ann Arbor, Mich. 48104. *Office:* Department of Humanities, University of Michigan, Ann Arbor, Mich. 48104.

CAREER: San Diego State College (now University), San Diego, Calif., instructor in humanities, 1961-63; University of Michigan, Ann Arbor, assistant professor, 1966-70, associate professor of humanities, 1970—. *Military service:* U.S. Army, 1954-56. *Member:* American Society for Engineering Education, Society for Technical Communication, Society for History of Technology, World Future Society, Association of Teachers of Technical Writing, Systems, Man, and Cybernetics Society of Institute of Electrical and Electronics Engineers, Midwest Modern Language Association, Phi Kappa Phi.

WRITINGS: (With H. B. Benford) *Your Future in Naval Architecture,* Rosen Press, 1968; (with Kan Chen, Karl F. Lagler, and others) *Growth Policy: Population, Environment, and Beyond,* University of Michigan Press, 1974; (with D. W. Stevenson) *The Engineer Reports: Designing Communication for Audiences in Organizational Systems,* Bobbs-Merrill, in press. Contributor to *Phi Kappa Phi Journal* and *Journal of Technical Writing and Communication.*

WORK IN PROGRESS: Research in the area of science, technology, and society.

* * *

MATHEWS, Thomas G(eorge) 1925-

PERSONAL: Born October 31, 1925, in Bloomington, Ind.; son of William Barnes (a minister) and Edith (Smith) Mathews; married Joyce L. Creque (a music supervisor), August 25, 1956; children: Dale T. *Education:* Oberlin College, B.A., 1949; Columbia University, M.A., 1953, Ph.D., 1957. *Address:* Box 39X, R.R. #3, Rio Piedras, P.R. 00928. *Office:* Department of Social Science, University of Puerto Rico, Rio Piedras, P.R. 00931.

CAREER: University of Puerto Rico, Mayaguez, lecturer, 1950-53, assistant professor, 1953-57, associate professor, 1959, and at Rio Piedras, associate professor, 1960-64, professor of social science, 1964—, chairman of department, 1957-59, director of Institute of Caribbean Studies, 1961-69. *Member:* Conference of Latin American Historians, Latin American Studies Association.

WRITINGS: Puerto Rican Politics and the New Deal, University of Florida Press, 1960; (editor with F. M. Andic, and contributor) *Politics and Economics in the Caribbean,* International Publications Service, 1966, 2nd edition, 1971; *Luis Munoz Marin: A Concise Biography,* American R.D.M., 1967. Contributor to *Hispanic Amer-*

ican Historical Review, Caribbean Historical Review, Current History, Caribbean Studies, and *Caribbean Review.* Editor of *Caribbean Studies,* 1961—, *Caribbean Education Bulletin,* 1967—.

WORK IN PROGRESS: Politics of Puerto Rico: 1938-1946; The Caribbean: Seventeenth Century.

* * *

MATHUR, Y. B. 1930-

PERSONAL: Born June 2, 1930, in Delhi, India; son of Chand Bahadur (a government official) and Krishna (Pyari) Mathur; married Uma Yaduvansh (a senior lecturer in political science), November 20, 1964; children: Rohit, Monica. *Education:* University of Delhi, B.A. (honors), 1951, M.A. (history), 1954, Ph.D., 1963; Punjab University, M.A. (politics), 1955. *Religion:* Hindu (Kayasha). *Home:* 102 Banarsi Das Estate, Timar Pur, Delhi 7, India. *Office:* School of Correspondence Courses, University of Delhi, Room 42, 5 Cavalry Lines, Delhi, India.

CAREER: National Archives, New Delhi, India, assistant archivist, 1955-68; University of Delhi, Delhi, India, lecturer in modern Indian history, 1968—. Broadcaster for All India Radio, 1968—. *Member:* Indian Council of Historical Research. *Awards, honors:* Diploma from Bhavatiy a Vidya Bhavan, 1967.

WRITINGS: Muslims and Changing India, Trimurti, 1972; *Women's Education in India: 1813-1966,* Asia Publishing House, 1973; *British Administration of Punjab,* Surjeet, 1974. Editor of *Technical Education in India,* and *A Sourcebook of Indian History and Culture.* Contributor to Indian journals.

* * *

MAVES, Mary Carolyn 1916-

PERSONAL: Born April 30, 1916, in Hooker, Okla.; daughter of H. J. (a banker) and Margaret (Pittman) Hollman; married Paul B. Maves (a clergyman and professor), September 10, 1939; children: Margaret A. (Mrs. Allan K. Hansell), David H. *Education:* University of Nebraska, B.Sc. in Ed., 1938. *Religion:* United Methodist Church. *Home:* 9607 Hardy Dr., Overland Park, Kan. 66212.

CAREER: Volunteer teacher in church schools. Member of Task Group on Religious Education and Hearing-Impaired Persons, National Council of Churches. *Member:* American Association of University Women.

WRITINGS—Children's books, with husband, Paul B. Maves: *Finding Your Way through the Bible,* Abingdon, 1971; *Learning More about the Bible,* Abingdon, 1973; *Exploring How the Bible Came to Be,* Abingdon, 1973; *Discovering How the Bible Message Spread,* Abingdon, 1973. Co-author with husband of a curriculum unit for fifth and sixth grade children of the Methodist Church, "Being a Christian," Graded Press, 1965, revised edition, 1967, 2nd revised edition published as "Followers of the Way," 1970. Contributor to *Christian Home.*

WORK IN PROGRESS: Religious education materials for deaf children.

SIDELIGHTS: Mrs. Maves and her husband are the parents of a deaf son.

* * *

MAXWELL, Edith 1923-

PERSONAL: Born March 12, 1923, in Newburgh, N.Y.; daughter of James A. (a civil engineer) and Theodora (Bowerman) Smith; married Robert W. Maxwell (a stockbroker), October 18, 1945; children: Mary Christine (Mrs. Robert Hevener), Margaret, Jeanne. *Education:* Student at Mount St. Mary's Academy, Newburgh, 1936-40, and Russell Sage College, 1940-42. *Politics:* Republican. *Religion:* Episcopalian. *Home:* 20 Redwood Dr., Hillsborough, Calif. 94010. *Agent:* Edith Margolis, Lenniger Literary Agency, Inc., 437 Fifth Ave., New York, N.Y. 10016.

CAREER: Began writing in the 1940's, selling her first short stories to pulp magazines. Has been Travelers Aid volunteer at San Francisco Airport and worked with Crippled Children's Auxiliary and Peninsula Children's Theatre. *Member:* Junior League (San Francisco).

WRITINGS: Just Dial A Number (Junior Literary Guild selection), Dodd, 1971. Author of children's plays produced by Peninsula Children's Theatre. Contributor of short stories to magazines. Editor of *The Corral,* Fort Worth, Tex., Junior League magazine, 1956-57.

WORK IN PROGRESS: Research in group encounter sessions as possible theme of juvenile novel.

* * *

MAXWELL, Neville 1926-

PERSONAL: Born June 22, 1926, in London, England; son of Francis (a mechanical engineer) and Greeta (Freeman) Maxwell. *Education:* McGill University, B.A. (honors), 1950; Cambridge University, B.A. (honors), 1952, M.A., 1958. *Home:* 1 Grove Ter., London NW5, England. *Agent:* Julian Bach, 3 East 48th St., New York, N.Y. 10017. *Office:* Institute of Commonwealth Studies, Oxford University, 21 St. Giles, Oxford, England.

CAREER: Foreign correspondent for *London Times* in Washington, D.C., 1956-59, in South Asia, 1959-67; University of London; School of Oriental and African Studies, London, England, senior fellow, 1967-70; Oxford University, Institute of Commonwealth Studies, Oxford, England, senior research officer, 1970—.

WRITINGS: India's China War, J. Cape, 1970, Pantheon, 1971.

WORK IN PROGRESS: A study of the Chinese people's communes, and of the 1965 India and Pakistan war.

* * *

MAYER, Philip 1910-

PERSONAL: Born May 21, 1910, in Berlin, Germany; son of Gustav (a university professor) and Flora (Wolff) Mayer; married Iona Simon (a research fellow), July 2, 1946; children: Jessica Ruth, Helen Gabrielle, Robert David Simon. *Education:* University of Heidelberg, Dr.Jur., 1933; Oxford University, D.Phil., 1944; also studied at University of Berlin and University of London. *Home:* 112 Woodstock Rd., Oxford, England. *Office:* Rhodes University, Grahamstown, South Africa.

CAREER: Government of Kenya, sociologist in Nairobi and Kisii, 1946-49; University of London, Birkbeck College, London, England, lecturer in anthropology, 1950-53; Rhodes University, Grahamstown, South Africa, professor of social anthropology, and head of department of African studies, 1953-62; University of the Witwatersrand, Johannesburg, South Africa, professor of anthropology and head of department, 1963-65; University of Durham, Durham, England, professor of anthropology and head of department, 1966-71; Rhodes University, professor of social anthropology and head of department, 1972—.

MEMBER: International African Institute, Sociological Association of Southern Africa, Royal Anthropological Institute, Association of Social Anthropologists of the Commonwealth, African Studies Association. *Awards, honors:* Welcome Medal from Royal Anthropological Institute, 1962; leader exchange fellowship from Carnegie Corp., 1963; Rivers Memorial Medal from Royal Anthropological Institute, 1969.

WRITINGS: Gusii Bridewealth Law and Custom, Oxford University Press, 1950; *The Lineage Principle in Gusii Society,* Oxford University Press, 1951; *Townsmen or Tribesmen,* Oxford University Press, 1961, 2nd edition, 1971; (editor) *Xhosa in Town,* three volumes, Oxford University Press, 1961-63; (editor) *Socialisation: The Approach from Social Anthropology,* Tavistock Publications, 1970; *Urban Africans and the Bantustans,* Institute of Race Relations, 1972. Contributor to anthropology and sociology journals, including *Journal of the Royal Anthropological Institute, Africa, American Anthropologist, African Affairs,* and *Man.*

WORK IN PROGRESS: Self-organisation among African Youth; The Sexual Revolution among Urban Africans; Self-categorisation among urban Africans in South Africa.

AVOCATIONAL INTERESTS: Painting, walking.

* * *

MAYER-THURMAN, Christa Charlotte 1934-

PERSONAL: Born December 12, 1934, in Darmstadt, Germany; daughter of Gottfried Ernst and Dorothee (Draudt) Mayer; married Lawrence S. Thurman (an historic sites administrator), December 18, 1971. *Education:* Finch College, B.A., 1958; New York University, M.A., 1966. *Religion:* Lutheran. *Residence:* Chicago, Ill. *Office:* Art Institute of Chicago, Chicago, Ill. 60603.

CAREER: Cooper Union Museum, New York, N.Y., assistant curator of textiles, 1961-67; Art Institute of Chicago, Chicago, Ill., associate curator, 1967-68, curator of textiles, 1968—. Part-time staff member and consultant on Nubian and Egyptian textiles at Oriental Institute Museum, University of Chicago. Lecturer on history and conservation of textiles. *Member:* International Council of Museums, American Association of Museums, American Institute for Conservation, International Institute for Conservation, Centre International d'Etude des Textiles Anciens (associate), Washington Textile Museum (associate); Needle and Bobbin Club Arts Club (Chicago), Chicago Rug Society. *Awards, honors:* American Institute of Decorators grant to study historic houses and architecture in England, summer, 1965.

WRITINGS: Masterpieces of Western Textiles, Art Institute of Chicago, 1969; (with Mildred Davison) *Coverlets,* Art Institute of Chicago, 1973. Contributor to *Grolier Encyclopedia International, Grolier Universal Encyclopedia,* museum publications, and *Antiques.*

WORK IN PROGRESS: A handbook on vestments; a catalogue of the tapestry collection at Art Institute of Chicago.

SIDELIGHTS: Christa Mayer-Thurman speaks French in addition to German, and has a reading knowledge of Flemish, Spanish, and Italian.

MAYHEW, Lenore 1924-

PERSONAL: Born May 29, 1924, in Ogden, Utah; daughter of Wayne Elijah (a certified public accountant) and Vera (Hinckley) Mayhew; married Frank Laycock (a college professor), August 16, 1946; children: Vera Lenore (Mrs. Robert D. Lethbridge), John Christopher, Deirdre Ann, Megan Elizabeth. *Education:* Mills College, B.A., 1946; Oberlin College, graduate study, 1963-64. *Home:* 172 Shipherd Cir., Oberlin, Ohio 44074.

CAREER: Piano teacher in Riverside, Calif., 1953-60; Bowling Green State University, visiting lecturer in Asian literature, 1973—. *Awards, honors:* National Translation Center grant, 1967; Asia Society Chinese poetry translations projects grant, 1971, 1973.

WRITINGS: (Contributor) William McNaughton, editor, *The Taoist Vision,* University of Michigan Press, 1971; (translator with McNaughton) *A Gold Orchid: Love Poems of Tsu-Yeh,* Tuttle, 1972; (contributor) Peter Jay, editor, *The Greek Anthology,* Allen-Lane, 1974; (with McNaughton) *As Though Dreaming: Li Ch'ing-chao's Tz'u of Pure Jade,* Grossman, 1974; (contributor) McNaughton, *Chinese Literature: An Anthology,* Tuttle, 1974.

WORK IN PROGRESS: Poem without a Hero and Other Poems: A Selection from the Works of Anna Akhmatova; a volume of translations from the Chinese poet Nalan Hsingte, 1655-1685; translations of Asian poems, mostly Japanese; a volume of original poetry.

SIDELIGHTS: Lenore Mayhew has lived in Switzerland, Japan, and Taiwan, Republic of China. She has spent considerable time in Italy. Her interests include lyric poetry, music, and Russian novelists.

* * *

MAYSON, Marina
See ROGERS, Rosemary

* * *

McBRIDE, (Mary) Angela Barron 1941-

PERSONAL: Born January 16, 1941, in Baltimore, Md.; son of John Stanley (a police lieutenant) and Mary C. (a seamstress; maiden name, Szczepanski) Barron; married William Leon McBride (a philosophy professor), June 12, 1965; children: Catherine Alexandra, Kara Angela. *Education:* Georgetown University, B.S.N., 1962; Yale University, M.S.N., 1964. *Home:* 744 Cherokee Ave., Lafayette, Ind. 47905.

CAREER: Yale University, New Haven, Conn., lecturer in psychiatric nursing, 1964-73. *Member:* American Civil Liberties Union, National Organization for Women, Yale University School of Nursing Alumnae Association (member of board of directors, 1967-69), Sigma Theta Tau. *Awards, honors: The Growth and Development of Mothers* named one of the book selections of the year by *American Journal of Nursing,* 1973.

WRITINGS: (Editor and author of preface, introduction, and epilogue) *Psychiatric Nursing and the Demand for Comprehensive Health Care* (monograph), Yale University Printing Office, 1972; *The Growth and Development of Mothers,* Harper, 1973. Contributor to *Nursing Research, Nursing Outlook, American Journal of Nursing,* and *Glamour.*

WORK IN PROGRESS: Research in the influence of role

stereotype on health problems and family dynamics; contributing to *The Principles and Practice of Nursing,* for Macmillan.

* * *

McCALL, Thomas S(creven) 1936-

PERSONAL: Born September 1, 1936, in Dallas, Tex.; son of John Dean (an attorney) and Hazel (Bradfield) McCall; married Carolyn Sue Wilson (a registered nurse), August 2, 1958; children: Thomas Kevin, Carol Kathleen. *Education:* University of Texas at Austin, B.A., 1957; Talbot Theological Seminary, B.D., 1961, Th.M., 1962; Dallas Theological Seminary, Th.D., 1965. *Home:* 6516 Aberdeen Ave., Dallas, Tex. 75230. *Office:* American Board of Mission to the Jews, Inc., 5324 West Northwest Highway, Dallas, Tex. 75220.

CAREER: Ordained Baptist minister, 1958; American Board of Missions to the Jews, Dallas, Tex., missionary-in-charge of Southwestern District, 1958—. Chaplain of Sons of American Revolution, Sons of Confederate Veterans, Civitan International.

WRITINGS: (With Zola Levitt) *Satan in the Sanctuary,* Moody, 1973; (with Levitt) *The Coming Russian Invasion of Israel,* Moody, 1974. Contributor to religious journals.

WORK IN PROGRESS: Biblical prophecy; studies in Old Testament sacrifices; archaeology.

* * *

McCAMPBELL, James M. 1924-

PERSONAL: Born May 10, 1924, in Nashville, Tenn.; son of Basil Davis (an attorney) and Louise (McCall) McCampbell; married Carolyn West (a real estate saleswoman), June 20, 1946; children: Ann, Kathryn, Nancy. *Education:* University of California, Berkeley, A.B., 1949, B.S. Engineering Physics, 1950; graduate study at University of Pittsburgh and San Jose State College (now University). *Home:* 12 Bryce Ct., Belmont, Calif. 94002. *Office:* Mechanics Research, Inc., Los Angeles, Calif.

CAREER: Physicist in research on nuclear fallout at U.S. Naval Radiological Defense Laboratory, 1950-55; scientist at Westinghouse Electric Corp., Bettis Plant, 1955-57; senior theoretical physicist at American-Standard, 1957-59; Bechtel Corp., San Francisco, Calif., 1959-70, successively, nuclear engineer, project manager, assistant manager, and staff consultant to corporate management; private technical consultant, 1970-73; Mechanics Research, Inc., Los Angeles, Calif., deputy manager of environmental protection for Alaskan pipeline, 1973—. Evening instructor at Foothill College, 1959; graduate instructor for Dale Carnegie, 1962-63. *Military service:* U.S. Army, Corps of Engineers, parachutist, 1943-46; served in Okinawa; became first lieutenant. *Member:* American Association for the Advancement of Science, American Nuclear Society (chairman for northern California).

WRITINGS: *UFOlogy: New Insights from Science and Common Sense,* Waymac-Hollmann, 1974. Author of research reports.

WORK IN PROGRESS: Research on historical and religious documentation of ancient visits to earth by people from other planets.

AVOCATIONAL INTERESTS: Ballroom dancing (teaching and performing, mainly on cruise ships), tennis.

McCANDLESS, Perry 1917-

PERSONAL: Born December 9, 1917, in Lincoln, Mo.; son of William Albert (an auctioneer) and Edith (Graves) McCandless; married Opal Braland, July 5, 1947; children: Richard Lee, Anne Christine. *Education:* Central Missouri State College, B.S., 1941; Southern Methodist University, M.A., 1948; University of Missouri, Ph.D., 1953. *Politics:* Democratic. *Religion:* Methodist. *Home:* 609 Christopher, Warrensburg, Mo. 64093. *Office:* Department of History, Central Missouri State University, Warrensburg, Mo. 64093.

CAREER: Central Missouri State University, Warrensburg, assistant professor, 1949-50 and 1953-56, associate professor, 1956-60, professor of history, 1960—. *Military service:* U.S. Army Air Forces, 1941-45; became master sergeant. *Member:* Organization of American Historians, State Historical Society of Missouri, Missouri State Teachers Association, Johnson County Historical Society.

WRITINGS: *Constitutional Government in Missouri,* Sernoll, 1971; *The Missouri Experience: A History of the State,* Sernoll, 1972; *A History of Missouri, 1820-1860,* Volume I, University of Missouri Press, 1972. Contributor to *Missouri Historical Review, Social Studies,* and *Indiana Magazine of History.*

WORK IN PROGRESS: *An Introduction to the Study of History.*

* * *

McCOMBS, Philip A(lgie) 1944-

PERSONAL: Born July 20, 1944, in Ogdensburg, N.Y.; son of Kenneth L. (an accountant) and Mary (Whalen) McCombs; married Gillian Clive, July 6, 1969; children: Heather, Willow. *Education:* Yale University, B.A., 1966; Johns Hopkins School of Advanced International Studies, M.A., 1968. *Home:* 131 Nguyen Hue., Saigon, South Vietnam. *Office:* 203 Tu Do St., Saigon, South Vietnam.

CAREER: *Washington Post,* Washington, D.C., reporter, 1970—. *Military service:* U.S. Army, 1968-70; became sergeant.

WRITINGS: (With Kevin Klose) *The Typhoon Shipments,* Norton, 1974.

* * *

McCORD, Jean 1924-

PERSONAL: Born March 21, 1924, in Hayward, Wis.; daughter of Roy N. (an electronic technician) and Marie (Helms) McCord. *Education:* College of St. Scholastica, student, 1939-42; University of California, Berkeley, B.S., 1946. *Politics:* Democrat-Liberal. *Religion:* None. *Home:* 11528 Occidental Rd., Sebastopol, Calif. 95472. *Agent:* McIntosh & Otis, Inc., 18 East 41st St., New York, N.Y. 10017.

CAREER: Has worked at forty-five different occupations. *Military service:* Women's Army Corps. *Member:* California Writer's Club.

WRITINGS: *Deep Where the Octopi Lie,* Atheneum, 1968; *Bitter Is the Hawk's Path,* Atheneum, 1971. Work published in *Best American Short Stories,* edited by Martha Foley, Houghton, 1958. Contributor to *Seventeen,* and to anthologies and textbooks.

WORK IN PROGRESS: A novel, *Black John Hump.*

McCORMACK, Mark H(ume) 1930-

PERSONAL: Born November 6, 1930, in Chicago, Ill.; son of Ned H. (a publisher) and Grace (Wolfe) McCormack; married Nancy Breckenridge, October 9, 1954; children: Breck Breckenridge, Todd Hume, Mary Leslie. *Education:* Princeton University, student, 1948; William and Mary College, B.A., 1951; Yale University, LL.B., 1954. *Home:* 2830 Lander Rd., Pepper Pike, Ohio 44124. *Office:* International Management Group, Inc., Cleveland, Ohio 44124.

CAREER: Admitted to the Bar of Ohio, 1957; Arter & Hadden (law firm), Cleveland, Ohio, associate, 1957-63, partner, 1964—; International Management Group, Inc., Cleveland, Ohio, president, 1960—. *Military service:* U.S. Army, 1954-56. *Member:* Cleveland Bar Association, Union Club, Country Club of Cleveland.

WRITINGS: *The World of Professional Golf 1967,* Cassell, 1967, subsequent annual volumes published as follows: *1968,* World Publishing, *1969, 1970,* and *1971,* International Literary Management, *1972, 1973,* and *1974,* Collins; *Arnie: The Evolution of a Legend,* Simon & Schuster, 1967 (published in England as *Arnold Palmer: The Man and the Legend,* Cassell, 1968); *The Wonderful World of Professional Golf,* Atheneum, 1973. Publisher of *Golf International* (England), 1972-74.

BIOGRAPHICAL/CRITICAL SOURCES: *True,* April, 1967; *Saturday Evening Post,* May, 1968; *Cleveland Plain Dealer,* February 2, 1969; *Fortune,* January, 1970; *Signature,* October, 1972.

SIDELIGHTS: McCormack is business manager for Arnold Palmer.

* * *

McCOY, John P(leasant) 1906(?)-1974

1906(?)—April 10, 1974; American novelist. Obituaries: *Washington Post,* April 11, 1974.

* * *

McCULLOH, William Ezra 1931-

PERSONAL: Born September 8, 1931, in McPherson, Kan.; son of Samuel Ezra (a secretary for Young Men's Christian Association) and Ruth (Stoner) McCulloh; married Patricia Nilson (an artist and teacher), August 26, 1956; children: Ann Elizabeth, Michael Bruce. *Education:* Ohio Wesleyan University, B.A. (with high honors), 1953; Oxford University, B.A., 1956; Yale University, Ph.D., 1962. *Politics:* "Eclectic." *Religion:* Christian. *Home:* 313 Woodside Dr., Gambier, Ohio 43022. *Office:* Department of Classics, Kenyon College, Gambier, Ohio 43022.

CAREER: Wesleyan University, Middletown, Conn., instructor in classics, 1956-61; Kenyon College, Gambier, Ohio, instructor, 1961-62, assistant professor, 1962-64, associate professor, 1964-68, professor of classics, 1968—. *Member:* American Philological Association, Society for Ancient Greek Philosophy, Modern Greek Studies Association, Society for Religion in Higher Education, Classical Association of the Middle West and South. *Awards, honors:* Rhodes scholarship, Oxford University, 1953-56.

WRITINGS: (Author of introduction and notes) Willis Barnstone, translator and editor, *Greek Lyric Poetry,* Bantam, 1962, revised edition, 1967; (contributor) Michael Rheta Martin, editor, *The Language of Love,* Bantam, 1964; (contributor) Barnstone, translator, *Sappho,* Anchor, 1965; *Longus,* Twayne, 1970. Contributor of articles and reviews to *Classical Journal, Choice,* and *Books for College Libraries.*

WORK IN PROGRESS: *Pseudo-Dionysius Areopagita,* for Twayne.

AVOCATIONAL INTERESTS: European languages and literatures (especially German), classical European music (piano and viola), Sanskrit.

* * *

McCULLOUGH, David (Gaub) 1933-

PERSONAL: Born July 7, 1933, in Pittsburgh, Pa.; son of Christian Hax (a businessman) and Ruth (Rankin) McCullough; married Rosalee Barnes, December 18, 1954; children: Melissa, David, Jr., William, Geoffrey, Doreen. *Education:* Yale University, B.A., 1955. *Home and office:* Music Street, West Tisbury, Mass. 02575. *Agent:* Paul R. Reynolds, Inc., 599 Fifth Ave., New York, N.Y. 10017.

CAREER: Editor and writer for Time, Inc., New York, N.Y., 1956-61, U.S. Information Agency, Washington, D.C., 1961-64, and American Heritage Publishing Co., New York, N.Y., 1964-70; now full-time writer. *Member:* Society of American Historians. *Awards, honors:* Special citation for excellence from Society of American Historians, 1973, Diamond Jubilee medal for excellence from City of New York, 1973, and certificate of merit from Municipal Art Society of New York, 1974, all for *The Great Bridge.*

WRITINGS: (Editor) *American Heritage Picture History of World War II,* American Heritage Press, 1967; (editor) *Smithsonian Library,* six volumes, Smithsonian Institution Press and American Heritage Press, 1968-70; *The Johnstown Flood* (*Reader's Digest* Condensed Book), Simon & Schuster, 1968; *The Great Bridge* (*Reader's Digest* Condensed Book), Simon & Schuster, 1972. Contributor to *Audubon Magazine, Architectural Forum, American Heritage, Smithsonian, New York Times,* and *Washington Post.*

WORK IN PROGRESS: A history of the building of the Panama Canal.

BIOGRAPHICAL/CRITICAL SOURCES: *Vineyard Gazette* (Martha's Vineyard, Mass.), September 29, 1972.

* * *

McDONAGH, Don(ald Francis) 1932-

PERSONAL: Born February 6, 1932, in New York, N.Y.; son of Francis Frederick and Winifred (Tierney) McDonagh; married Jennifer Tobutt (a performing arts manager), November 16, 1957; children: Ann, Ruth, Rachel, Amy. *Education:* Fordham University, B.S., 1953. *Politics:* Democrat. *Religion:* Roman Catholic. *Home:* 150 Claremont Ave., New York, N.Y. 10027. *Agent:* Georges Borchardt, Inc., 145 East 52nd St., New York, N.Y. 10022. *Office:* *New York Times,* 229 West 43rd St., New York, N.Y. 10036.

CAREER: Benton & Bowles, Inc. (advertising agency), New York, N.Y., market research analyst, 1957-67; *New York Times,* New York, N.Y., dance reviewer, 1967—. Consultant to Schatz Research Associates (market research firm), 1967—. *Military service:* U.S. Army, 1953-55.

WRITINGS: (Contributor) Clement Crisp and Peter Brinson, editors, *Ballet for All,* Pan Books, 1970; *The Rise and Fall of Modern Dance,* Outerbridge & Dienstfrey, 1970; *Martha Graham: A Biography,* Praeger, 1973. Contributor of art column to *Financial Times,* 1968-73. Contributor of dance articles to *Time, New Republic, Hudson Review,*

Show, Dance Magazine, and *Dance and Dancers.* Associate editor of *Ballet Review,* 1967—.

WORK IN PROGRESS: A biography of painter Florine Stettheimer, with tentative title, *Florine: Family and Friends,* publication expected in 1975; *A History of Modern Dance,* 1975.

AVOCATIONAL INTERESTS: Following New York sports teams, playing stickball.

BIOGRAPHICAL/CRITICAL SOURCES: New York Times, November 7, 1970.

* * *

McDONALD, Linda 1939-

PERSONAL: Born July 11, 1939, in Ironwood, Mich.; daughter of Earl and Gladys E. (Backlund) Maiden; married George Thomas McDonald (a lawyer), December 29, 1963; children: Joseph Michael. *Education:* Attended Los Angeles City College, 1964, and Pasadena City College, 1964-67; California State College (now University) at Los Angeles, B.A., 1969. *Home:* 227 Oaklawn Ave., South Pasadena, Calif. 91030.

CAREER: Licensed as an optician by California Board of Medical Examiners, 1964; optician specializing in contact lenses in South Pasadena, Calif., 1964—. *Member:* Optical Society of America, American Association for the Advancement of Science.

WRITINGS: Ice Cream, Sherbet, and Ices, A. S. Barnes, 1971; *Contact Lenses: How to Wear Them Successfully,* Doubleday, 1972; *Baby's Recipe Book,* A. S. Barnes, 1972. Contributor to *Optometric Weekly* and *Family Health.*

WORK IN PROGRESS: A romantic comedy; research on environmental pollution, on women's liberation, on infant nutrition, on furniture restoration, on contact lenses, on animal care and feeding, on gardening, and on machine and hand knitting.

AVOCATIONAL INTERESTS: Oil painting, gardening, sewing, knitting, cooking, handcrafts.

* * *

McELROY, Colleen J(ohnson) 1935-

PERSONAL: Born October 30, 1935, in St. Louis, Mo.; daughter of Jesse O. (an army officer) and Ruth (Long) Johnson; married second husband, David F. McElroy (a writer), November 28, 1968; children: (first marriage) Kevin, Vanessa. *Education:* University of Maryland, student, 1953-55; Harris Teachers College, A.A., 1956; Kansas State University, B.S., 1958, M.A., 1963; graduate study at University of Pittsburgh, 1958-59, and Western Washington State College, 1970-71; University of Washington, Seattle, Ph.D., 1973. *Home:* 2200 Northeast 75th St., Seattle, Wash. 98115. *Office:* Department of English, University of Washington, Seattle, Wash. 98105.

CAREER: Rehabilitation Institute, Kansas City, Mo., chief speech clinician, 1963-66; Western Washington State College, Bellingham, assistant professor of English, 1966-73; University of Washington, Seattle, assistant professor of English, 1973—. Affiliate member of speech faculty, University of Missouri at Kansas City, 1965-66; summer instructor in Project Head Start and Project New Careers; moderator of "Outlook," on KVOS-TV 1968-71. *Member:* American Speech and Hearing Association, National Council of Teachers of English, Conference on College Composition and Communication, United Black Artists Guild (Seattle).

WRITINGS: Speech and Language Development of the Preschool Child: A Survey, C. C Thomas, 1972; *The Mules Done Long Since Gone* (poems), Harrison-Madronna Press, 1973. Writer of film scripts, "Tracy Gains Language" and "Introduction to Clinical Practicum," distributed by Bureau of Faculty Research, Western Washington State College. Poems have been published in *Wormwood Review, december, Poetry Northwest, Choice, Poetry Pilot,* and other literary reviews and little magazines. Editor, *Dark Waters,* 1973-74.

* * *

McFATHER, Nelle 1936-

PERSONAL: Born October 26, 1936, in Ware County, Ga.; daughter of Angus Lamar (an antique dealer and landowner) and Erma Lee (Bennett) Strickland; married Robert Hughes (a bank vice-president), August 3, 1957; children: Rob. *Education:* Agnes Scott College, B.A., 1957. *Politics:* Republican. *Religion:* Protestant. *Home:* 1028 Lower Brow Rd., Signal Mountain, Tenn. 37377.

CAREER: High school teacher of English in Jacksonville, Fla., 1957-58, Waycross, Ga., 1958-59, and Atlanta, Ga., 1960-61; Georgia Institute of Technology, School of Nuclear Engineering, Atlanta, Ga., assistant to director, 1964-70. *Member:* Daughters of the American Revolution, United Daughters of the Confederacy, Chattanooga Little Theatre.

WRITINGS—Novels: *Whispering Island,* Ace Books, 1974; *The Red Jaguar,* Ace Books, 1974.

WORK IN PROGRESS: The Iron Woman, a contemporary Gothic novel set in Grenada, West Indies.

SIDELIGHTS: Nelle McFather says she loves travel, "find my Gothics allow me to relive joy of exploring exotic places. Ever an incurable romantic, my heroines are old-fashioned about sex, have elegant tastes, and embody the self-directed humor and independent spirit that I love to see emerging in today's 'heroine.'" *Avocational interests:* Wine and candle making, treasure-seeking, needlework, banjo and guitar playing and singing, collecting "everything collectible."

* * *

McGIFFERT, Robert C(arnahan) 1922-

PERSONAL: Born November 27, 1922, in Elizabeth, N.J.; son of Julian E. (an industrialist) and Eloise (Howe) McGiffert; married Jacquelyn Stout, October 18, 1947; children: Brian S., Sarah N. *Education:* Princeton University, A.B., 1943; Ohio State University, M.A., 1965. *Politics:* Democrat. *Home:* 432 King St., Missoula, Mont. 59801. *Office:* School of Journalism, University of Montana, Missoula, Mont. 59801.

CAREER: Easton Express, Easton, Pa., reporter, 1946-52, city editor, 1952-62; Ohio State University, Columbus, assistant professor of journalism, 1962-66; University of Montana, Missoula, associate professor, 1966-71, professor of journalism 1971—. Copy editor, *Washington Post,* summers, 1967, 1972, 1974. *Military service:* U.S. Army, 1943-46; became first lieutenant.

WRITINGS: The Art of Editing the News, Chilton, 1972. Contributor to medical, dental, and journalism publications.

* * *

McGILL, Ormond 1913-

PERSONAL: Born June 15, 1913, in Palo Alto, Calif.; son

of Harry A. (a telephone company manager) and Julia (Batelle) McGill; married Delight Olmstead, September 29, 1943. *Education:* Attended San Jose State (now California State University), 1931-32 and 1941-42. *Politics:* Republican. *Religion:* Baptist. *Home:* 331 Creekside Dr., Palo Alto, Calif. 94306. *Address:* P.O. Box 1103, Palo Alto, Calif. 94302.

CAREER: Magician and hypnotist, performing in United States, Canada, and abroad, 1930—; importer and exporter of shells and marine items in Palo Alto, Calif., 1955—, professional dealer, 1960—. *Member:* International Brotherhood of Magicians, American Society of Magicians, Pacific Coast Association of Magicians, Hawaii Malacological Society.

WRITINGS: Encyclopedia of Stage Hypnotism, Abbott Magic Co., 1947; *The Secret World of Witchcraft,* A.S. Barnes, 1973; (with Ron Ormond) *Great Religious Mysteries of the Orient,* A.S. Barnes, 1974; *How to Produce Miracles,* A.S. Barnes, in press.

WORK IN PROGRESS: A two-volume set, *Magic for Family Fun* and *Magic and Wonderful Things,* for A.S. Barnes.

AVOCATIONAL INTERESTS: Photography, motion picture filming, malacology, entomology, philately.

* * *

McGIVERN, William P(eter) 1927-

PERSONAL: Born December 6, 1927, in Chicago, Ill.; son of Peter Francis (a banker) and Julia (Costello) McGivern; married Maureen Daly (a writer), December 28, 1948; children: Megan (daughter), Patrick. *Education:* Attended University of Birmingham, 1945-46. *Politics:* Democrat. *Home and office:* 73-305 Ironwood Dr., Palm Desert, Calif. *Agent:* Marvin Moss, 9229 Sunset Blvd., Los Angeles, Calif. 90069.

CAREER: Philadelphia Evening Bulletin, Philadelphia, Pa., reporter and book reviewer, 1949-51; author and novelist. *Military service:* U.S. Army, 1943-46; became master sergeant. *Member:* Writer's Guild of America, Author's League, Players Club (New York), Garrick and Savage clubs (both London). *Awards, honors:* Mystery Writers of America's Edgar award, 1952, for *The Big Heat.*

WRITINGS—Novels; all published by Dodd: *But Death Runs Faster,* 1948; *Heaven Ran Last,* 1949; *Very Cold for May,* 1950; *Shield for Murder,* 1951; *The Crooked Frame,* 1952; *The Big Heat,* 1953; *Margin of Terror,* 1953; *Rogue Cop* (also see below), 1954; *The Darkest Hour* (also see below), 1955; *The Seven File* (also see below), 1956; *Night Extra,* 1957; *Odds against Tomorrow,* 1957; *Savage Streets,* 1959; *Seven Lies South,* 1960; *The Road to the Snail,* 1961; *Police Special: Including Rogue Cop, the Seven File* [and] *The Darkest Hour,* 1962; *A Pride of Place,* 1962; *A Choice of Assassins,* 1963; *The Caper of the Golden Bulls,* 1966; *Lie Down, I Want to Talk to You,* 1967; *Caprifoil,* 1972; *Reprisal,* 1973; *Red Alert: Central Park,* 1974.

(With wife, Maureen Daly McGivern) *Mention My Name in Mombasa: The Unscheduled Adventures of an American Family Abroad,* Dodd, 1958.

Screenplays: "Chicago 7," based on own novel *The Seven File,* 1968; "The Wrecking Crew," 1968; "The Man from Nowhere," 1968; "Lie Down, I Want to Talk to You," based on own novel, 1968; "Caprifoil," based on own novel, 1973; "Joe Battle," 1974.

Television scripts: "San Francisco International Airport," 1970; "The Young Lawyers," 1970; "Banyon," 1972.

WORK IN PROGRESS: A long novel about New York and a novel about a specific action in the Battle of the Bulge, WW II; a book on modern Mexico.

SIDELIGHTS: McGivern, who has lived in a dozen countries in the Western Hemisphere, has had nine of his novels made into major motion pictures, including *The Big Heat, Seven Lies South,* and *The Caper of the Golden Bulls.* Of *The Caper of the Golden Bulls,* a *Times Literary Supplement* reviewer wrote: "A charmingly ingenious story about a retired thief in Spain who is driven by loyalties to undertake a monstrous coup, which is bedevilled by an infinitude of complications from other oddities with counterplots of their own; lighthearted yet sufficiently involved to generate enjoyable suspense."

* * *

McGOVERN, Ann

PERSONAL: Born in New York, N.Y.; daughter of Arthur (a bacteriologist) and Kate (a teacher; maiden name, Malatsky) Weinberger; married Martin L. Scheiner (an engineer), June 6, 1970; children: Peter McGovern; Charles, Ann, and Jim Scheiner. *Education:* Attended University of New Mexico. *Politics:* "Liberty and justice for all." *Residence:* Pleasantville, N.Y. *Agent:* Curtis Brown Ltd., 60 East 56th St., New York, N.Y. 10022.

CAREER: Scholastic Book Services, New York, N.Y., associate editor of Arrow Book Club, 1958-65, editor and founder of See Saw Book Club, 1965-67, presently member of editorial board of See Saw Book Club. *Member:* International P.E.N., Authors Guild. *Awards, honors:* Named author of the year by Scholastic Book Services' Lucky Book Club.

WRITINGS—For children: *Why It's a Holiday,* Random House, 1960; *Story of Christopher Columbus,* Random House, 1962; *Aesop's Fables,* Scholastic Book Services, 1963; *If You Lived in Colonial Times,* Four Winds, 1964; *Who Has a Secret?,* Houghton, 1964; *Zoo, Where Are You?,* Harper, 1964; *Little Wolf,* Abelard, 1965; *Arrow Book of Poetry,* Scholastic Book Services, 1965; *Questions and Answers about the Human Body,* Random House, 1965; *Runaway Slave: The Story of Harriet Tubman,* Four Winds, 1965; *If You Grew Up with Abraham Lincoln,* Four Winds, 1966; *Too Much Noise,* Houghton, 1967; *Robin Hood of Sherwood Forest,* Crowell, 1968; *Stone Soup,* Scholastic Book Services, 1968; *Black Is Beautiful,* Four Winds, 1969; *Hee-Haw,* Houghton, 1969; *If You Sailed on the Mayflower,* Four Winds, 1969; *Shakespearean Sallies, Sullies, and Slanders,* Crowell, 1969.

The Defenders, Scholastic Book Services, 1970; *Ghostly Fun,* Scholastic Book Services, 1970; *If You Lived with the Circus,* Four Winds, 1971; *Ghostly Giggles,* Scholastic Book Services, 1972; *Squeals and Squiggles and Ghostly Giggles,* Four Winds, 1973; *The Pilgrims' First Thanksgiving,* Scholastic Book Services, 1973; *If You Lived with the Sioux Indians,* Four Winds, 1974; *Scram, Kid,* Viking, 1974; *Secret Soldier: The Story of Deborah Sampson,* Scholastic Book Service, in press.

Contributor to *Newsday* and *Saturday Review.* Reviewer of children's books for *New York Times,* 1960-66.

WORK IN PROGRESS: The World Beneath the Sea, a book about sharks.

SIDELIGHTS: Ms. McGovern told *CA:* "Looking backward (and forward) to my books, I realize that they reflect my life in three parts: 1) ideas I strongly believe in; 2) desire for knowledge (I never finished college); 3) exciting personal experiences—scuba diving, for example, or exploring Mayan ruins or camping out in Africa, and photographing everywhere.

"*Black is Beautiful* was written right after Martin Luther King's murder. I went to a rally in the city and heard a young man say in anger and grief: 'Black is beautiful, baby. Know it. Feel it.' I knew it and felt it but I also knew that the word 'black' had held negative images for far too long. The next two days I wrote pages of positive images about blackness and it became a kind of poem. Because I was strongly against the Vietnam war, I wrote *Little Wolf* to show how one person rejected violence even though the world around him condemned pacifism. In *Runaway Slave: The Story of Harriet Tubman,* I chose a woman in history whom black and white girls could admire. There are still too few heroines for today's society, and I have just finished a book about Deborah Sampson, a young woman who was denied adventure because of her sex and poverty during Revolutionary times. In my historical books I try to ferret out the truth, even though the truth may not be popular. I think it important to tell it like it was; to show for example, that the Pilgrims got seasick on the Mayflower and threw up, like ordinary folk.

"I emphasized the Sioux nation's peaceable nature in *If You Lived With The Sioux Indians*.

"For my future writings, I plan to concentrate on events in our history long ignored, and books that reinforce humanistic values such as love, individuality, and honesty to each other."

* * *

McGOVERN, Robert 1927-

PERSONAL: Born December 2, 1927, in Minneapolis, Minn.; son of Frank Raymond (a cook) and Mary (Weimer) McGovern; married Barbara Male (an administrator of poets-in-the-schools program), October 3, 1964; children: Nicholas Robert, Brigid Johanna, James Patrick Shannon, Tara Gwendolyn. *Education:* University of Minnesota, B.A., 1951, M.A., 1957; University of London, further graduate study, 1960; Case Western Reserve University, Ph.D., 1968. *Politics:* Liberal Democrat. *Religion:* Roman Catholic. *Home address:* R.D. 4, Box 131, Ashland, Ohio 44805. *Office:* Department of English, Ashland College, Ashland, Ohio 44805.

CAREER: Moorhead Daily News, Moorhead, Minn., editor, 1951-52; Radford College, Radford, Va., assistant professor of English, 1957-65; Ashland College, Ashland, Ohio, associate professor, 1966-68, professor of English and creative writing, 1969—. Leader of jazz band; editor of Ashland Poetry Press; president of Radford Human Relations Council, 1964. *Military service:* U.S. Army, 1951-52. *Member:* American Association of University Professors, Poets in the Schools Program, Ohio Poets Association (codirector), Society for Ashland's Preservation.

WRITINGS—All published by Ashland Poetry Press: (Editor with Richard Snyder) *Sixty on the Sixties: A Decade's History in Verse* (anthology), 1970; *A Feast of Flesh and Other Occasions,* 1971; *The Way of the Cross in Time of Revolt,* 1971; (editor with Snyder) *Our Only Hope is Humor: Some Public Poems* (anthology), 1972. Work is included in *National Poets' Anthology,* Dekalb University Press, 1974. Contributor of articles, poems, and reviews to *Nation* and to literary journals and newspapers.

WORK IN PROGRESS: The Wild World of Home, a collection of poems; a textbook for critical writing, completion expected in 1975; a libretto for an opera by Jack Johnston, 1975; *A Poetry Ritual for Grammar School.*

* * *

McGRADY, Mike 1933-

PERSONAL: Born October 4, 1933, in New York, N.Y.; son of Patrick M. and Grace (Robinson) McGrady; married Corinne Young (a designer), November 28, 1958; children: Sean, Siobhan, Liam. *Education:* Yale University, B.A., 1955; Harvard University, further study, 1968-69. *Home:* 95 Eaton's Neck Rd., Northport, N.Y. 11768. *Agent:* Sterling Lord Agency, 660 Madison Ave., New York, N.Y. 10021. *Office: Newsday,* 550 Stewart Ave., Garden City, N.Y. 11530.

CAREER: Free-lance writer, 1958-62; *Newsday,* Garden City, N.Y., columnist, 1962—. *Military service:* U.S. Army, 1956-58. *Awards, honors:* Overseas Press Club Award for best interpretive reporting, 1968, for *A Dove in Vietnam;* Nieman fellow at Harvard University, 1968-69; Headliners Award of National Headliners Club for best column in the United States, 1966.

WRITINGS—Adult: *A Dove in Vietnam,* Funk, 1968; (editor with Harvey Aronson) *Naked Came the Stranger* (twenty-five author collaboration), Lyle Stuart, 1971; *Stranger Than Naked or How to Write Dirty Books for Fun & Profit,* Peter H. Wyden, 1972.

Teen books: (With John Floherty) *Youth and the FBI* (foreword by J. Edgar Hoover), Lippincott, 1960; (with Floherty) *Whirling Wings,* Lippincott, 1960; *Crime Scientists,* Lippincott, 1961; *Jungle Doctors,* Lippincott, 1962; (with Floherty) *Skin Diving Adventures,* Lippincott, 1962.

* * *

McGUANE, Thomas (Francis III) 1939-

PERSONAL: Born December 11, 1939; son of Thomas Francis (a manufacturer) and Alice (Torphy) McGuane; married Portia Rebecca Crockett, September 8, 1962; children: Thomas Francis IV. *Education:* Michigan State University, B.A., 1962; Yale University, M.F.A., 1965. *Residence:* Key West, Fla. *Agent:* Candida Donadio, 111 West 57th St., New York, N.Y. 10019.

CAREER: Full-time writer since leaving school. *Awards, honors:* Richard and Hinda Rosenthal Foundation Award in fiction from American Academy, 1971, for *The Bushwacked Piano;* National Book Awards fiction nomination, 1974, for *Ninety Two in the Shade*.

WRITINGS—Novels: *The Sporting Club,* Simon & Schuster, 1969; *The Bushwacked Piano,* Simon & Schuster, 1971; *Ninety Two in the Shade,* Farrar, Straus, 1973. Special contributor to *Sports Illustrated*.

WORK IN PROGRESS: Writing screenplay of *Ninety Two in the Shade;* another novel.

SIDELIGHTS: Jonathan Yardley wrote: "Put simply, McGuane has a talent of Faulknerian potential. His sheer writing skill is nothing short of amazing. The preternatural force, grace and self-control of his prose recall Faulkner. He is as assured in elegantly elaborate description as in the outrageously bawdy comedy first revealed in *The Sporting Club,* an account of the rich at play in the Michigan wilds, and now come to full bloom in *The Bushwacked Piano,* the saga of a young man at large in an America wallowing in its own vulgarity. At 31, McGuane is a virtuoso.

"His intelligence is as great as his style. His persistent thematic concern is the defilement of America, land and people alike, the advent of what he calls "a declining snivelization." This is no easy bow to ecological or political fashion. In his exploration of man and nature he is solidly within American literary tradition; his depiction of man's encroachment upon the land is as eloquent in its way as Faulkner's, in *Delta Autumn* and *The Bear.*

McGuane told *CA* he is "primarily interested in art; the extent to which I have been able to practice it has always seemed a privilege."

The Sporting Club was adapted by Lorenzo Semple, Jr. for a full-length film released by Avco Embassy Pictures in 1971.

BIOGRAPHICAL/CRITICAL SOURCES: New York Times Book Review, March 14, 1971; *Contemporary Literary Criticism,* Volume III, Gale, 1974.

* * *

McKENNON, Joe
See McKENNON, Joseph W(esley)

* * *

McKENNON, Joseph W(esley) 1907-
(Joe McKennon)

PERSONAL: Born July 3, 1907, in Paris, Tenn.; son of Joseph Gideon (a farmer) and Annie (Holcomb) McKennon; married Marian Leigh (an artist), August 15, 1944; children: Leigh Cross, Ann Cross Bly (stepchildren). *Education:* Studied through extension courses at University of Texas, 1931-34, Indiana University, 1935, Pasadena Junior College, 1944-45, Hardin Simmons University, 1948, and North Carolina State College, 1951-53. *Home and office:* 139 South Washington Dr., Sarasota, Fla. 33577; and 3 D Farms, Fletcher, N.C. 28732 (summer).

CAREER: Coach builder apprentice for Sante Fe Railroad, 1923-27; circus and carnival trouper for numerous shows, including Beckman and Gerity, Dodson, Goodman, Johnny J. Jones, Mighty Sheesley and the Castle, Hagenbeck-Wallace, Sells-Floto, Ringling Brothers, Barnam & Bailey Circus, and others, 1928-40; heavy construction carpenter, 1941-42; owner of McKennon Stage Shows, 1946-50; farmer in Fletcher, N.C., 1950—; Ringling Museum of the Circus, Sarasota, Fla., curator, 1968-69. Curatorial consultant to Ringling Museum of the Circus. *Military service:* Texas National Guard, infantry, 1931-32. U.S. Army, 1942-44; became staff sergeant. *Member:* Circus Historical Society, Carnival Historical Society, Ancient and Accepted Scottish Rite Masons, Rotary, Biltmore Forest Country Club.

WRITINGS: (Under name Joe McKennon) *A Pictorial History of the American Carnival,* Carnival Publishers, 1972. Author of plays for tent dramatic shows. Contributor to *Wonderland of Knowledge Encyclopedia,* and *Billroad.*

WORK IN PROGRESS: Research on circus, carnival, minstrel, and dramatic shows; *The Horse Dung Trail,* completion expected in 1975.

SIDELIGHTS: McKennon told *CA:* "Ran away with first circus at age of twelve as there were no seats on the hoe handles in my father's cotton fields. Was sent home. Had always (from age of three) intended being a circus trouper. At fourteen, fell for a 'ball game queen' named Mable and took off with a carnival. Family came and got me. At nineteen, with a good trade to bargain with (coach and car builder), went to the circus to stay. Started as a boss, so did not have to work up from roustabout. For over thirty years have carried stories of circus I wanted to tell, but never had time to put them on paper. Now I have it." McKennon restores circus wagons and wheels, and designs and builds historically-correct detailed circus exhibits for the Ringling Museum of the Circus.

* * *

McKILLIP, Patricia A(nne) 1948-

PERSONAL: Born February 29, 1948, in Salem, Ore.; daughter of Wayne T. and Helen (Roth) McKillip. *Education:* San Jose State University, B.A., 1971, M.A., 1973. *Home:* 891 Almarida Dr., San Jose, Calif. 95008.

CAREER: Writer.

WRITINGS—Fantasy adventures: *The House on Parchment Street,* Atheneum, 1973; *The Throme of the Erril of Sherill,* Atheneum, 1973; *The Forgotten Beasts of Eld,* Atheneum, 1974.

WORK IN PROGRESS: Morgon; Raederle; The Three Stars, all volumes of a fantasy trilogy.

* * *

McKISSICK, Floyd Bixler 1922-

PERSONAL: Born March 9, 1922, in Asheville, N.C.; son of Ernest Boyce and Magnolia (Thompson) McKissick; married Evelyn Williams (in municipal government), September 1, 1942; children: Joycelyn (Mrs. Lewis H. Myers), Andree, Floyd, Jr., S. Charmaine. *Education:* Student at Morehouse College, 1949, and University of North Carolina, 1951; North Carolina Central University, A.B., 1951, LL.D., 1952. *Politics:* Republican. *Religion:* Baptist. *Home:* 2 Liberation Blvd., Soul City, N.C. 27553. *Office:* Soul City Co., P.O. Box 188, Soul City, N.C. 27553.

CAREER: McKissick & Berry, Durham, N.C., senior partner in law firm, 1957-66; Congress of Racial Equality, New York, N.Y., national director, 1966-68; Floyd B. McKissick Enterprises, Inc., Soul City, N.C., president, 1968-74; Soul City Co., Soul City, N.C., president, 1974—. Senior partner in law firm of McKissick & Burt, 1960-66. Visiting professor at State University of New York at Binghamton, 1970. Counsel for Durham Business College, East End Betterment League, and CORE (Congress of Racial Equality). *Military service:* U.S. Army, World War II; became technical sergeant; received Purple Heart.

MEMBER: National Bar Association, National Committee for a Two-Party System (chairman), Southeastern Bar Association, North Carolina Central University Alumni Association, Alpha Phi Alpha. *Awards, honors:* Ike Smalls Civil Rights Award from National Association for the Advancement of Colored People, 1962; Conference Award for Civil Rights from African Methodist Episcopal Church, 1964.

WRITINGS: Three-Fifths of a Man, Macmillan, 1969. Author of pamphlets: "A Black Manifesto," "Constructive Militancy," "Genocide," and "A New Republic." Columnist for *New York Amsterdam News.*

WORK IN PROGRESS: The Building of Soul City; an autobiography; a novel.

SIDELIGHTS: McKissick writes: "I am motivated by a

desire to see Black people participate fully in all aspects of American society. It is my desire to see a society free of all racism, to see a society where all men are free and equal. The economic and political barriers must be integrated. It is important for one to establish objectives and then develop a strategy for accomplishing those objectives.... The racial progress being made in the South as compared to progress being made in the North gives one concern. The concept of colonialism and racism continues to give grave concern."

BIOGRAPHICAL/CRITICAL SOURCES: Fortune, April, 1974.

* * *

McLEAN, Gordon R(onald) 1934-

PERSONAL: Born June 22, 1934, in Regina, Saskatchewan, Canada; naturalized U.S. citizen in 1959; son of Thomas Wilbur (a printer) and Isabel (Willows) McLean. *Residence:* San Jose, Calif. 95118. *Agent:* Vandenburg-Linkletter Associates, 8530 Wilshire Blvd., #403, Beverly Hills, Calif. 90211. *Office:* Community Youth Services/ Youth for Christ, 1190 Lincoln Ave., San Jose, Calif. 95125.

CAREER: Ordained minister of Baptist General Conference, 1951; executive director of Youth for Christ International, Youth Guidance Division, in Victoria, British Columbia, Canada, 1950-52, in Great Falls, Mont., 1952-54, in Wheaton, Ill., 1954-56, and in Tacoma, Wash., 1956-67; Youth for Christ/Campus Life, San Jose, Calif., executive director, 1967—. Member of state parole committee in Montana, 1952; associate chaplain for Santa Clara County Juvenile Probation Department, 1967—. Director of weekly radio program, "Speak Out," KLIV, 1967—. Speaker at chapel programs for major league baseball and football teams. Consultant to police departments and schools on drug abuse and youth problems. *Member:* International Juvenile Officers Association, Rotary International. *Awards, honors:* Recognition of services award from California Probation, Parole and Corrections Association, 1969, for his work with youth.

WRITINGS: Coming In on the Beam: A Look at America's Teenagers, Zondervan, 1956; *We're Holding Your Son,* Revell, 1969; (with Haskell Bowen) *High on the Campus,* Tyndale, 1970; *How to Raise Your Parents,* Tyndale, 1970; *Let God Manage Your Money,* Zondervan, 1972; *God Help Me, I'm a Parent,* Creation House, 1972; *Where the Love Is,* Word Books, 1973; *Hell Bent Kid,* Creation House, 1973. Contributing editor of *Campus Life,* 1964—.

WORK IN PROGRESS: A book on personal experiences with delinquents, *Man, I Need Help; Fear Thy Neighbor: A Look at America's Crime Problem; Devil at the Wheel.*

SIDELIGHTS: McLean toured Asia in 1972 with college students to study drug trafficking to the United States. He has also assisted in the production of a movie based on his book, *High on the Campus.*

* * *

McLEOD, Raymond, Jr. 1932-

PERSONAL: Born August 19, 1932, in Cameron, Tex.; son of Raymond Gregg (a railway clerk) and Margaret (Belcher) McLeod; married Judith Ann Pollock (a teacher), December 17, 1955; children: Michael Ray, Gregg Alan, Christopher Robert, Melinda Lee, Suzanne Elaine. *Education:* Baylor University, B.B.A., 1954; Texas Christian University, M.B.A., 1957; University of Colorado, D.B.A., 1974. *Politics:* Independent. *Religion:* Methodist. *Home:* 3729 Hilltop Rd., Fort Worth, Tex. 76109. *Office:* Department of Business Administration, Texas Christian University, Fort Worth, Tex. 76129.

CAREER: International Business Machines Corp., Dallas, Tex., marketing representative, 1957-65; Lifson, Wilson, Ferguson & Winick, Dallas, Tex., consultant, 1965-67; Recognition Equipment, Inc., Dallas, Tex., marketing manager, 1967-69; Texas Christian University, Fort Worth, assistant professor of business administration, 1973—. *Military service:* U.S. Air Force, 1954-56; became captain.

WRITINGS: Computerized Business Systems, Wiley, 1973.

WORK IN PROGRESS: A textbook, *Marketing Information Systems.*

* * *

McMAHON, Robert
See WEVERKA, Robert

* * *

McNULTY, Faith 1918-

PERSONAL: Born November 28, 1918, in New York, N.Y.; daughter of Joseph Eugene (a judge) and Faith (Robinson) Corrigan; married John McNulty, 1945 (died, 1956); married Richard H. Martin, 1957; children: (first marriage) John Joseph. *Education:* Attended Barnard College, 1937-38. *Address:* Box 370, Wakefield, R.I. 02880. *Office: New Yorker,* 25 West 43rd St., New York, N.Y. 10036.

CAREER: New Yorker, New York, N.Y., staff writer, 1953—. *Awards, honors:* Dutton Animal Book Award, 1966, for *The Whooping Crane.*

WRITINGS: (With Elisabeth Keiffer) *Wholly Cats,* Bobbs-Merrill, 1962; *The Whooping Crane: The Bird That Defies Extinction,* introduction by Stewart L. Udall, Dutton, 1966; *Must They Die? The Strange Case of the Prairie Dog and the Black-Footed Ferret,* Doubleday, 1971; *The Great Whales,* Doubleday, 1974.

For children: *The Funny Mixed-up Story,* Wonder Books, 1959; *Arty the Smarty,* Wonder Books, 1962; *When a Boy Gets Up in the Morning,* Knopf, 1962; *When a Boy Goes to Bed at Night,* Knopf, 1963; *Prairie Dog Summer,* Coward, 1972; *Woodchuck,* Harper, 1974.

* * *

McNUTT, James (Allen) 1944-

PERSONAL: Born November 10, 1944, in Alexandria, Va.; son of Marvin Jacob (a mason) and Ellena (Pagliaro) McNutt; married Marcia Fields Poncia, May 22, 1963 (divorced August 8, 1968); married Joan Fujimoto, November 2, 1969 (divorced December 1, 1971); children: (first marriage) Dennis James, Jeffery Allen. *Education:* Attended high school in San Carlos, Calif. *Politics:* No affiliation. *Religion:* "I was raised Roman Catholic and soon after reaching maturity found myself walking an Eastern path with Western eyes for perceptors." *Address:* P. O. Box 535, Belmont, Calif.

CAREER: Laborer.

WRITINGS: Along the Way (poems), privately published, 1972; *Echos* (philosophical statement), Hope & Allen, 1973.

WORK IN PROGRESS: Narrative of American rural life from 1879 to 1945.

SIDELIGHTS: McNutt told *CA:* "The things necessary for motivation to my career as a writer come daily with my perception of life. The things necessary to allow this stimulus to run its course is a minimal amount of financial stability (poverty level), peace and quiet, coffee and cigarettes, and an occasional lady to appease my madness. If any one of the conditions are lacking for any length of time, the stimulus is lost and madness increases its grip."

* * *

McREYNOLDS, Ronald W(eldon) 1934-

PERSONAL: Born January 26, 1934, in Cincinnati, Ohio; son of Weldon Robert and Eva (Rue) McReynolds; married Laura Bainbridge, June, 1957; children: Rodger Weldon, Jeffrey Carl, Lesley Ellen, Jennifer Ann. *Education:* Miami University, Oxford, Ohio, B.S., 1955, M.A., 1956; University of Texas at Austin, Ph.D., 1959. *Religion:* Reorganized Church of Jesus Christ of Latter Day Saints. *Home:* High Field, R. R. 5, Warrensburg, Mo. 64093. *Office:* Department of English, Central Missouri State University, Warrensburg, Mo. 64093.

CAREER: Teacher of English in the public schools of Belleville, Mich., 1956-57; Central Missouri State University, Warrensburg, assistant professor, 1959-64, associate professor, 1964-68, professor of English, 1968—. *Awards, honors:* Heart of America Poetry Contest winner, 1964.

WRITINGS: (Editor) *Book of Mormon,* (authorized edition), Independence Press, 1966; *A Time Between and Other Poems,* Mitre (London), 1967; (contributor) *Missouri Poets,* Eads Bridge Press, 1971; *A Poet's Poetry* (pamphlet), Central Missouri State College, 1971. Contributor of poems, articles, and book reviews to *Kansas City Star, Deep Channel Packet, Caravan, Per Se,* and *Forum.*

WORK IN PROGRESS: A volume of poetry; editing *The History of Johnson County, Mo.*

* * *

McSHERRY, James E(dward) 1920-

PERSONAL: Born January 15, 1920, in Johnston City, Ill.; son of Patrick H. and Edna E. (Spence) McSherry; married, 1948 (divorced, 1958). *Education:* Southern Illinois University, B.A., 1951, M.A., 1952; graduate study at University of Illinois, 1954, and George Washington University, 1959. *Home and office:* 4201 31st St., Apt. 848, Arlington, Va. 22206.

CAREER: Editor and writer for U.S. Department of State, U.S. Department of Defense, and U.S. Air Force, 1952-60; university press editor at Southern Illinois University, Carbondale, 1960-64, and Pennsylvania State University, University Park, 1964-69; free-lance editor and indexer in Arlington, Va., 1969—. *Military service:* U.S. Army, 1938-40, 1942-48; Canadian Army, 1940-42; twice wounded in action.

WRITINGS: *Stalin, Hitler, and Europe,* World Publishing, Volume I: *The Origins of World War II, 1933-39,* 1968, Volume II: *World War, 1939-45: Causes,* 1970; *Krushchev and Kennedy in Retrospect,* Open Door Press, 1971. Contributor to United States Naval Institute *Proceedings* and *American Historical Review.*

McWILLIAMS, John P(robasco), Jr. 1940-

PERSONAL: Born July 22, 1940, in Cleveland, Ohio; son of John P. and Brooks (Barlow) McWilliams; married Margot Helen Brown, April 15, 1967; children: Andrew, Suzannah, Kirsten, Elizabeth. *Education:* Princeton University, A.B. (summa cum laude), 1962; Harvard University, Ph.D., 1968. *Home:* 51 Beach Rd., Glencoe, Ill. 60022. *Office:* Department of English, University of Illinois at Chicago Circle, Chicago, Ill. 60680.

CAREER: University of California, Berkeley, assistant professor of English, 1968-74; University of Illinois at Chicago Circle, associate professor of English, 1974—. *Member:* Phi Beta Kappa. *Awards, honors:* Woodrow Wilson fellow, 1962-63.

WRITINGS: *Political Justice in a Republic,* University of California Press, 1972; *James Fenimore Cooper: The Critical Heritage,* Routledge & Kegan Paul, 1973.

* * *

MEADE, Marion 1934-

PERSONAL: Born January 7, 1934, in Pittsburgh, Pa.; daughter of Surain (a physicist) and Mary (Homeny) Sidhu; divorced, 1972; children: Alison Linkhorn. *Education:* Northwestern University, B.S., 1955; Columbia University, M.S., 1956. *Residence:* New York, N.Y. *Agent:* James Seligmann, 280 Madison Ave., New York, N.Y. 10016.

CAREER: Free-lance writer.

WRITINGS: *Bitching,* Prentice-Hall, 1973. Contributor to *New York Times, Village Voice, McCall's, Woman's Day, Commonweal, Cosmopolitan,* and *Aphra.*

SIDELIGHTS: Ms. Meade told *CA:* "I am a feminist and my writings reflect a feminist point of view."

* * *

MEEKER, Joseph W(arren) 1932-

PERSONAL: Born August 4, 1932, in Iowa; son of Russell E. and Annamae (Block) Meeker; married Marlene Rae Rundell, December 27, 1956; children: Benjamin, Kurt. *Education:* Occidental College, B.A., 1954, M.A., 1961, Ph.D., 1963; also studied at University of California, Berkeley, 1956, and University of Oregon, 1959. *Home:* 14304 92A Ave., Edmonton, Alberta T5R 5E2, Canada. *Office:* Athabasca University, Edmonton, Alberta, Canada.

CAREER: Deep Springs College, Deep Springs, Calif., assistant professor of languages and literature, 1962-63; University of Alaska, Fairbanks, assistant professor, 1963-65, associate professor of English, 1965-67, chairman of department, 1965-67; Hiram Scott College, Scottsbluff, Neb., professor of English and comparative literature, 1967-71, chairman of Division of Humanities, 1969-71; University of California, Santa Cruz, lecturer in environmental studies at Kresge College and fellow in comparative literature, 1971-73; Athabasca University, Edmonton, Alberta, senior tutor in humanities, 1973—. Conference coordinator of World Law Fund Workshop on Global Environment, 1972; consultant to National Park Service Academy, and to Thorne Ecological Institute. Visiting professor, University of Montana, summer, 1967. *Military service:* U.S. Army, program director of Armed Forces Radio Network, 1954-56; served in Korea.

MEMBER: International Comparative Literature Association, Modern Language Association of America, National Council of Teachers of English, American Comparative Literature Association, American Association of University Professors, American Association for the Advancement of Science. *Awards, honors:* National Endowment for the Humanities fellowship in literature, philosophy, and ecology, 1971-72; Ford Foundation fellowship in innovative education, Kresge College of University of California (Santa Cruz), 1972-73.

WRITINGS: The Comedy of Survival: Studies in Literary Ecology, Scribner, 1973; *The Spheres of Life: An Introduction to World Ecology,* Scribner, 1974. Contributor of about thirty-five articles and reviews to professional journals, including *Canadian Fiction, North American Review, Ecologist, Journal of Environmental Education, Thymos, Inquiry,* and *Not Man Apart.* Environment editor for *North American Review;* editorial consultant for U.S. Forest Service research publications, 1964-67.

WORK IN PROGRESS: The Rights of Non-Human Nature; research on environmental ethics; *Nature and Other Mothers: Sexuality and Environmental Crisis.*

* * *

MEGED, Aharon
See MEGGED, Aharon

* * *

MEGED, Aron
See MEGGED, Aharon

* * *

MEGGED, Aharon 1920-
(A. M.)

PERSONAL: Name sometimes spelled Aron Meged or Aharon Meged; born August 10, 1920, in Wloclawcek, Poland; son of Moshe (a teacher) and Leah (Reichgot) Megged; married Eda Zirlin (a writer and painter), May 11, 1944; children: Eyal, Amos. *Education:* Attended high school in Israel, 1933-37. *Politics:* Labour Party. *Religion:* Jewish. *Home:* 26 Rupin St., Tel-Aviv, Israel. *Agent:* David Higham Associates, 3-5 Lower John St., London W.1, England. *Office: Davar,* Shenkin, Tel-Aviv, Israel.

CAREER: Member of a kibbutz in Sdot-Yam, Israel, 1938-50; *Massa* (bi-weekly newspaper), Tel-Aviv, Israel, editor, 1952-55; *Lamerchav* (daily newspaper), Tel-Aviv, literary editor, 1955-68; Israeli Embassy, London, England, cultural attache, 1968-71; *Davar* (daily newspaper), Tel-Aviv, literary editor, 1971—. Israeli Writer's Association (member of central committee, 1954-60), National Arts Council (member of central committee, 1962-67), Israeli Journalist's Association, P.E.N. *Awards, honors:* Ussishkin Prize, 1955, for *Hedva and I,* and 1966, for *Living on the Dead;* Brenner Prize, 1957, for *Israel Haverim;* Shlonsky Prize, 1963, for *ha-Brikha;* Bialik Prize, 1973, for *Makhbarot Evyatar* and *Al Etzim ve-avanim.*

WRITINGS: Ru'akh Yamin (title means "Spirit of the Seas"), Ha'kibutz Hame'uchad, 1950; *Harkhek ha-Arava* (title means "Far in the Wasteland"), Sifriat Po'alim, 1951; *Israel Haverim* (title means "Israeli Folk"), Ha'kibutz Hame'uchad, 1955; *Mikreh ha-kssil,* Ha'kubutz Hame'uchad, 1960, translation by Aubrey Hodes published as *Fortunes of a Fool,* Random House, 1963; *ha-Brikha* (title means "The Escape"), Ha'kibutz Hame'chad, 1962; *ha-Hai 'al ha-met,* Am Oved, 1965, translation by Misha Louvish published as *Living on the Dead,* McCall Publishing, 1970; *ha-Yom ha-Sheni* (title means "The Second Day"), Tarmil, 1967; *ha-Khayim ha-Ktzarim* (title means "The Short Life"), Ha'kibutz Hame'uchad, 1971; *Khatzot ha-Yom* (title means "Midday"), Ha'kubitz Hame'uchad, 1973; *Makhbarot Evyatar* (title means "Evyatar's Notebooks"), Ha'kibutz Hame'uchad, 1973; *Al Etzim ve-avanim* (title means "Of Trees and Stones"), Am Oved, 1973.

Plays: "Incubator on the Rocks" (three-act), first produced in Tel-Aviv, at Ohel Theatre, 1950; *Hedvah ve-ani* (two-act; first produced in Tel-Aviv, at Habimah Theatre, 1955, Ha'kibutz Hame'uchad, 1954, translation published as *Hedva and I: A Play in Two Acts,* Youth and Hechalutz Department of the Zionist Organization [Jerusalem], 1957); "The Way to Eylat" (two-act), first produced at Habimah Theatre, 1955; "I Like Mike" (three-act), first produced at Habimah Theatre, 1960; "Tit for Tat" (two-act), first produced at Ohel Theatre, 1960; *Hanna Senesh* (two-act; first produced at Habimah Theatre, 1962), Ha'kibutz Hame'uchad, 1954; "Genesis" (three-act), first produced at Habimah Theatre, 1965; *The High Season* (two-act; first produced at Habimah Theatre, 1968), Amikam, 1968.

Contributor to journals and newspapers, often under pseudonym A. M.

SIDELIGHTS: Megged told *CA:* "Life in the country, first, in childhood, in a small village, and then in a Kibbutz, had a great effect on my work. In later years I traveled much in Europe in search of Jewish medieval mysticism, especially in Spain and France. European writers, such like Kafka, Svevo, Gogol, Chekhov, had influence on my work."

* * *

MEHDEVI, Alexander (Sinclair) 1947-

PERSONAL: Born June 9, 1947, in Mazatlan, Mexico; son of Mohamed (an Iranian diplomat) and Anne-Marie (Sinclair) Mehdevi. *Education:* Attended Amherst College, 1965-66; Diplomatic Academy of Vienna, Zertifikat (M.A. equivalent), 1970; further study at Sorbonne, University of Paris, 1970, and University of Geneva, 1971. *Religion:* None. *Home:* 357 West 84th St., New York, N.Y. 10024. *Office:* Rizzoli International Bookstore, 712 Fifth Ave., New York, N.Y.

CAREER: Rizzoli International Bookstore, New York, N.Y., manager of children's book department, 1973—. Teacher of adult language courses in English and German, Paris, 1970 and 1972; interpreter for United Nations conference, Geneva, 1971.

WRITINGS: Bungling Pedro and Other Majorcan Tales (retold), Knopf, 1970; *Tales from Underground,* Macmillan, 1974; *The Flowers of Majorca,* Macmillan, 1974. Contributor to *Children's Digest, Nuevos Horizontes,* and *Moneysworth.*

WORK IN PROGRESS: Compiling the first foreign-language catalogue of children's books for U.S. publication; writing a series of anthropomorphic tales about insects.

SIDELIGHTS: A pocketbook edition of *Bungling Pedro* is to be published in German by Fischer Taschenbuch Verlag. Some of the tales were included in condensed form earlier in a German textbook. Mehdevi speaks, writes, and reads fluently in four languages—English, Spanish, French, and German—and also speaks and reads Italian. He says that he would like to teach children's literature.

* * *

MEHTA, Gaganvihari L(allubhai) 1900-1974

April 15, 1900—April 28, 1974; Indian diplomat, economist, essayist, and author of books on political philosophy and other subjects. Obituaries: *New York Times,* April 29, 1974; *Washington Post,* April 30, 1974; *Current Biography,* June, 1974.

* * *

MEISSNER, Hans-Otto 1909- (Hans Roos)

PERSONAL: Born April 6, 1909, in Strassburg, Alsace, Germany; son of Otto D. L. (a government official) and Hildegard (Roos) Meissner; married Estelle Dittenberger, 1936; married Marianne H. Mertens (an author), July 11, 1956; children: Andrea Meissner Carrasco. *Education:* Attended Trinity College, Cambridge, 1929-30, also studied at University of Berlin, University of Heidelberg, University of Freiburg, and University of Grenoble; University of Goettingen, Referendar (Doctor of Laws), 1933. *Religion:* Roman Catholic. *Home:* 22 Widenmayerstrasse 50, 8 Munich, Germany. *Office:* OBB Haus Siebenschlaf, 8211 Unterwoessen, Germany.

CAREER: Member of German diplomatic corps, serving in embassies in London, Tokyo, and Moscow, and in German Consulate in Milan, Italy; author, lawyer. *Military service:* Wehrmacht, 11th Panzer Division; became first lieutenant. Army of the Federal Republic of Germany; became lieutenant colonel. *Member:* European Cultural Community (honorary member), Freier Deutscher Autorenverband, Explorer's Club (New York). *Awards, honors:* Knight of the Teutonic Order.

WRITINGS: So schnell schlaegt Deutschlands Herz, Bruehlscher Verlag, 1951; (under pseudonym Hans Roos with Erich Ebermayer) *Gefaehrten des Teufels: Leben und Tod der Magda Goebbels,* Hoffman und Campe, 1952, translation and adaptation by Louis Hagen published as *Evil Genius: The Story of Joseph Goebbels,* Wingate, 1953; *Ich ging allein: Auf Grosswildjagd in Afrika,* Bruehlscher Verlag, 1955, translation by Robert Noble published as *One-Man Safari,* Jenkins, 1957, Rand McNally, 1963; *Reise richtig auch im Ausland,* Bruehlscher Verlag, 1955; *The Man with Three Faces,* Evans Brothers, 1955, Rinehart, 1956; *Als die Kronen fielen,* Bruehlscher Verlag, 1956; *Man benimmt sich wieder,* Bruehlscher Verlag, 1956; *Voelker, Laender und Regenten,* Bruehlscher Verlag, 1956; (under pseudonym Hans Roos) *Polen und Europa: Studien zur polnischen Aussenpolitik, 1931-1939,* Mohr, 1957; (with Harry Wilde) *Die Machtergreifung: Eine Bericht ueber die Technik des nationalsozialistischen Staatsstreichs,* J. G. Cotta, 1958; *Fernost abseits der grossen Strassen,* Bruehlscher Verlag, 1958; *Unbekanntes Europa,* J. G. Cotta, 1959, translation by Florence and Isabel McHugh published as *Unknown Europe,* Blackie, 1963; (with Manfred Behr) *Keine Angst um wilde tiere: Fuenf Kontinente geben ihnen Heimat,* BLV Verlagsgesellschaft, 1959.

(Under pseudonym Hans Roos) *Geschichte der Polinischen Nation, 1916-1960: Von der Staatsgruendung im ersten Weltkrieg bis zur Gegenwart,* Kohlhammer, 1961; (with Isabella Burkhard) *Gute Manieren stets gefragt: Takt, Benehmen, Etikette,* Verlag Mensch und Arbeit, 1962; *Bezaubernde Wildnis: Wandern Jagen, Fliegen in Alaska,* J. G. Cotta, 1963; *Hochzeitsreise mit Ursula: Roman* (novel), Hestia, 1963; *Alatna* (novel), S. Mohn, 1964, translation by Erica Pomerains published as *Duel in the Snow,* P. Davies, 1970, Morrow, 1972; *Blasse Sonne: Roman,* (novel) Hestia, 1964; *Gemsen vor meiner Tuer,* Bruckmann, 1964; *Das fuenfte Paradies. Australien: Menschen, Tiere, Abenteuer,* J. G. Cotta, 1965; *Im Alleingang zum Mississippi: Die Abenteuer des Pierre Radisson,* J. G. Cotta, 1966; *Immer noch 1000 Meilen zum Pazifik: Die Abenteuer des Alexander Mackenzie,* J. G. Cotta, 1966; *Louisiana fuer meinen Koenig: Die Abenteuer des Robert de LaSalle,* J. G. Cotta, 1966; *Kundschafter am St. Lorenzstrom: Die Abenteuer des Samuel de Champlain,* J. G. Cotta, 1966; *Die ueberlistete Wildnis: Vom Leben und Ueberleben in der freien Natur,* S. Mohn, 1967; *Ich fand kein Gold in Arizona: Die Abenteuer des Francisco Vasquez de Coronado,* J. G. Cotta, 1967; *In Alaska bin ich Zar: Die Abenteuer des Alexander Baranow,* J. G. Cotta, 1967; *Der Kaiser schenkt mir Florida: Die Abenteuer des Hernando de Soto,* J. G. Cotta, 1967; *Durch die sengende Glut der Sahara: Die Abenteuer der Gerhard Rohlfs,* J. G. Cotta, 1967; (with Francois Debergh) *Captain zu verkaufen: Ein heiterer Roman nach traurigen Tatsachen,* Bertelsmann Sachbuchverlag, 1968; *Traumland Suedwest: Suedwest-Afrika: Tiere, Farmen, Diamanten,* J. G. Cotta, 1968; *Der Kongo gibt sein Geheimnis preis: Die Abenteuer d. Henry M. Stanley,* J. G. Cotta, 1968; *An den Quellen des Nils: Die Abenteuer des Emin Pascha,* J. G. Cotta, 1969; *Wildes rauhes Land: Reisen und Jagen in Norden Kanadas,* Bertelsmann Sachbuchverlag, 1969.

Das Wunder der Aufgehenden Sonne: Japan zwischen Tradition und Fortschritt, Bertelsmann Sachbuchverlag, 1970; *Mein Leben fuer die weisse Wildnis: Die Expedition d. Roald Amundsen,* J. G. Cotta, 1971; *Im Zauber des Nordlichts: Reisen und Abenteuer am Polarkreis,* Bertelsmann Sachbuchverlag, 1972.

WORK IN PROGRESS: Two books, one on the Southwestern United States and another on Iran.

SIDELIGHTS: Meissner told *CA:* "Having been educated for three different professions—Foreign Office, the law and the Army, I chose to become a writer, just for the pleasure it gave me." He speaks and writes German, English, French, Spanish, and Italian.

* * *

MELBO, Irving Robert 1908-

PERSONAL: Born June 20, 1908, in Gully, Minn.; son of Hans H. (a merchant) and Hilda Jeanette (Bergdahl) Melbo; married Lucile Hays, May 30, 1931; married Virginia Archer (an elementary school principal), May 15, 1970; children: (first marriage) Robert Irving. *Education:* New Mexico Western University, A.B., 1930, M.A., 1932; University of Colorado, graduate study, 1931; University of California, Berkeley, Ed.D., 1934; postdoctoral study at Columbia University, 1936-37. *Religion:* Protestant. *Home:* 918 Afton Rd., San Marino, Calif. 91108. *Office:* School of Education, University of Southern California, Los Angeles, Calif. 90007.

CAREER: Principal of public elementary schools in Minnesota, 1927-28; New Mexico State Teachers College, Silver City, research assistant to president, 1928-30, instructor in social sciences and supervisor of student teachers, 1930-33; California State Department of Education,

Sacramento, staff member of Division of Textbooks and Publications, 1934-35; Oakland Public Schools, Oakland, Calif., director of department of research and curriculum, 1936-38; Alameda County Schools, Oakland, Calif., department superintendent and director of curriculum, 1938-39; University of Southern California, Los Angeles, assistant professor, 1939-45, associate professor, 1945-48, professor of educational administration, 1948—, dean of School of Education, 1953-73, director of school surveys, 1946—. Visiting professor at University of Kansas, 1937, 1938, University of Utah, 1951, University of Wisconsin, 1953, and University of Hawaii, 1956, 1960. President of Melbo Associates, Inc.; member of California State Board of Education accreditation committee, 1953-63, chairman, 1960-61; member of advisory council of Educational Policies Commission; member of board of directors of Southwest Regional Laboratory for Educational Research. *Military service:* U.S. Naval Reserve, active duty, 1942-45; served in Atlantic, European, and Mediterranean theaters; became lieutenant.

MEMBER: American Association of School Administrators, California Association of School Administrators, Educare, Sierra Club, Phi Delta Kappa. *Awards, honors:* Special Freedom Leadership Award, from Freedoms Foundation, 1964; exceptional service medal from U.S. Air Force, 1968; Irving R. Melbo Chair endowed at University of Southern California, 1973.

WRITINGS: (With Aberdeen Orlando Bowden) *Social Psychology of Education: Applications of Social Psychology to Educational Problems,* McGraw, 1937; *Our America: A Textbook for Elementary School History and Social Studies,* Bobbs-Merrill, 1937, revised edition, 1948; *Our Country's National Parks,* Volumes I and II, Bobbs-Merrill, 1941, revised edition with son, Robert Irving Melbo, 1964, centennial edition, 1973; (with Bowden) *The American Scene,* McGraw, 1942; (with Madeline Miedema and Stella May Carlson) *Young Neighbors in South America,* Silver Burdett, 1944; (with S. R. Poole and T. F. Barton) *The World About Us,* Bobbs-Merrill, 1949. Author of more than one hundred published school survey reports. Editor of public school textbooks.

WORK IN PROGRESS: Techniques of Administrative Leadership; Our Country's National Monuments.

* * *

MELHEM, D(iana) H(elen)

PERSONAL: Surname rhymes with "vellum"; born in Brooklyn, N.Y.; daughter of Nicholas (a textile executive) and Georgette (Deyratani) Melhem; children: Dana Marie Vogel, Gregory Melhem Vogel. *Education:* New York University, B.A. (cum laude); City University of New York, M.A. from City College, 1971, candidate for Ph.D., 1971—. *Home:* 250 West 94th St., New York, N.Y. 10025.

CAREER: Active in community life of West Side New York, 1950—; has read (and sometimes sung) her poems on television and radio, at schools, libraries, theaters, coffee houses, and feminist and political gatherings. Teacher of English at City College of the City University of New York, 1971. *Member:* Modern Language Association of America, Academy of American Poets, New York Poets' Cooperative, Calliope, Phi Beta Kappa, Sigma Delta Omicron.

WRITINGS: Notes on 94th Street, Poet's Press, 1972. Poems have been published in *Nation, For Now, Gnosis, Bitterroot,* and other magazines, and included in anthologies.

WORK IN PROGRESS: Rest in Love, a poem-sequence about her late mother; "country," a long narrative poem about America; an article, "On the Poetics of Charles Olson."

* * *

MELLIN, Jeanne 1929-
(Jean Mellin Herrick)

PERSONAL: Born February 3, 1929; daughter of Kenneth B. (a restaurateur) and Marjorie (Bates) Mellin; married Frederick Herrick (a professional horseman), October 23, 1955; children: Nancy Jeanne. *Education:* Rhode Island School of Design, B.F.A., 1948. *Politics:* Republican. *Religion:* Methodist. *Home and office:* Saddleback Farm, R.D. #1, Hamilton, N.Y. 13346.

CAREER: Rides, trains, and shows horses professionally; portrait painter of horses and other animals; illustrator. *Member:* American Morgan Horse Association, New York Morgan Horse Society.

WRITINGS: Horses across America, Dutton, 1953; *Horses across the Ages,* Dutton, 1954; *Pidgy's Surprise* (juvenile), Dutton, 1955; *The Morgan Horse,* Greene, 1961; *America's Own Horse Breeds* (prints), Greene, 1962; *Ponies on Parade* (prints), Greene, 1966; *Ride a Horse,* Sterling, 1970; *The Morgan Horse Handbook,* Greene, 1973. Author of script for American Morgan Horse Association movie, 1963, narrated by James Cagney.

WORK IN PROGRESS: A book on drawing and painting horses.

* * *

MENDELSOHN, Harold 1923-

PERSONAL: Born October 30, 1923, in Jersey City, N.J.; son of Louis (a businessman) and Betty (Yulinsky) Mendelsohn; married Irene Gordon (a social worker), April 10, 1949; children: Susan Lynn. *Education:* City College of New York (now City College of the City University of New York), B.S. (with honors), 1945; Columbia University, M.A., 1946; New School for Social Research, Ph.D., 1956. *Home:* 1451 East Cornell Pl., Englewood, Colo. 80110. *Office:* Department of Mass Communications, University of Denver, Denver, Colo. 80220.

CAREER: City College (now City College of the City University of New York), research fellow, 1945-47; American Jewish Committee, Department of Scientific Research, New York, N.Y., study director, 1947-52; U.S. Department of State, International Broadcasting Service, senior survey analyst, 1951-52; American University, Bureau of Social Science Research, Washington, D.C., research associate, 1952-56; McCann-Erickson, Inc., New York, N.Y., associate manager of marketing communications research, 1956-58; Psychological Corp., New York, N.Y., associate director, 1958-62; University of Denver, Denver, Colo., professor of mass communications and director of Communication Arts Center, 1962—, university lecturer, 1967—, head of department of mass communications, 1970—. Visiting professor at Survey Research Centre, London School of Economics and Political Science, 1970. Member of the U.S. Surgeon General's Scientific Advisory Committee on Television and Social Behavior, 1969-71.

MEMBER: World Association for Public Opinion Research, Radio-Television Research Council, Continuing Conference on Mass Communication and the Public Interest, American Marketing Association, Advertising Research Foundation, National Safety Council (member of board of directors, 1963-69), American Association for Public Opinion Research (vice-president, 1973-74), American Sociological Association (fellow), American Psychological Association, National Association of Educational Broadcasters, Society for the Psychological Study of Social Issues, Association for Professional Broadcasting Education, Colorado Psychological Association, Chicago Press Club, Denver Council for Educational Television, Denver Urban Coalition, Denver Forum Center for the Cultural Arts (member of board of directors, 1971—), Omicron Delta Kappa. *Awards, honors:* Award from Television Bureau of Advertising, 1962, for research in television; National Safety Council-Metropolitan Life award, 1967, for advancing the general cause of safety; "Emmy" award from National Academy of Television Arts and Sciences, 1968, for contributions in developing and evaluating the *Cancion de la Raza* series; Gold Camera award from U.S. Industrial Film Festival, 1972, for work on the alcohol-traffic safety film, "A Snort History."

WRITINGS: Listening to Radio: A Study of Audience Characteristics, Habits, Motivations, and Tastes (monograph), Psychological Corp., 1962; *Mass Communication for Safety: A Critical Review and a Proposed Theory* (monograph), National Safety Council, 1963; (contributor) M. A. May and Leon Arons, editors, *Television and Human Behavior,* Appleton, 1963; (contributor) L. A. Dexter and D. M. White, editors, *People, Society, and Mass Communications,* Free Press, 1964; (contributor) Leslie Kindred and G. N. Fehr, editors, *Communications Research and School-Community Relations,* Temple University, 1965; *Mass Entertainment,* College & University Press, 1966; *The Dogmas of Safety: A Content Analysis of Traffic Safety Messages* (monograph), Communication Arts Center, University of Denver, 1967; *The People and Their Legislators Look at Public Education in Colorado* (monograph), Communication Arts Center, University of Denver, 1967; *Radio in Contemporary American Life,* two volumes, Communication Arts Center, University of Denver, 1968; (contributor) Alan Casty, editor, *Mass Media and Mass Man,* Holt, 1968; *Edu-Drama, A Mass Communications Technique for Mass Education: A Research Analysis of the Television Series "Cancion de la Raza"* (monograph), Communication Arts Center, University of Denver, 1969; (with David H. Bayley) *Minorities and the Police: Confrontation in America,* Free Press, 1969; (contributor) Sigmund Skard and A. N. J. den Hollander, editors, *Handbook of American Studies,* Longmans, Green, 1969.

(With Irving Crespi) *Polls, Television, and the New Politics,* Intext, 1970; (contributor) Earl J. McGrath, editor, *Prospect for Renewal,* Jossey-Bass, 1972; (contributor) Alan Wells, editor, *Mass Media and Society,* National Press, 1972; (with others) *Television and Growing Up: The Impact of Televised Violence* (monograph), National Institute of Mental Health, 1972. Co-developer of "National Driver's Test," produced on television by Columbia Broadcasting System, 1965. Contributor to *Encyclopedia of Sociology;* contributor of articles and reviews to magazines and professional journals, including *Journalism Quarterly, Journal of Broadcasting, University of Denver Magazine, Nation, Traffic Digest and Review, American Journal of Public Health, Television Quarterly, Educational Broadcasting Review, Journal of Marketing Research, American Journal of Sociology,* and *Audio-Visual Communication Review.* Member of editorial advisory board, *Denver Law Journal,* 1972—.

WORK IN PROGRESS: A book, *The People Choose a President* (tentative title), concerning the voting decision process in terms of the psychological and sociological influences.

* * *

MERCIE, Jean-Luc Henri 1939-

PERSONAL: Born March 27, 1939, in Le Mans, France; son of Claude (a pediatrician) and Odette Mercie; married wife, Francoise (a research librarian), 1963; children: Nathalie, Laurent. *Education:* University of Grenoble, Licence es Lettres, 1959, Licence d'Anglais, 1962, Diplome d'Etudes Superieures, 1963, Ph.D., 1965. *Home:* 269 Stewart St., Ottawa K1N 6K3, Ontario, Canada. *Office:* Department of French, University of Ottawa, Ottawa, Ontario, Canada.

CAREER: Lycee Champollion, Grenoble, France, assistant professor of French, 1963-64; University of Grenoble, Grenoble, France, assistant professor of French, 1964-65; 93 R.A.M. Military Headquarters, Grenoble, instructor in French, 1966-67; University of Ottawa, Ottawa, Ontario, associate professor of French, 1968—. Lecturer on Canadian television and radio, 1967-69. *Member:* Modern Language Association of America, France Canada Association.

WRITINGS: Virgule ou point final?, Gastaud, 1962; *Victor Hugo et Clara Duchastel,* Minard, 1966; (editor) *The Complete Works of Victor Hugo* (in French), Volumes I, II, XV, and XVI, Club Francais du Livre, 1966-69; *Victor Hugo et Julie Chernay,* Minard, 1967; *Anacreon-le-jeune* (title means "Anacreon the Young"), University of Ottawa Press, 1971; *Manuscrits d'ecrivains francais des 19 et 20e siecles,* University of Ottawa Press, 1972. Contributor to *Arts et lettres, revue de l'Universite d'Ottawa, Cahier d'inedits,* and *Les Nouvelles Litteraires.* Founder and literary director, *Cahiers d'inedits,* 1970—; editor and artistic director, "Art Vif Canada."

WORK IN PROGRESS: Research on Dada and surrealism in modern French literature; research on modern European art; books on Francis Picabia and Antoni Clave.

* * *

MERIDETH, Robert 1935-

PERSONAL: Born September 11, 1935, in Aurora, Ill.; son of Edgar H. (a machinist) and Helen (Wessel) Merideth; married Elizabeth Evans (a counselor), August 17, 1957; children: Jonathan, Emily, Amy, Anne. *Education:* University of Illinois, B.A. (with honors), 1957; Oklahoma State University, M.A., 1958; University of Minnesota, Ph.D., 1963. *Home:* 812 Colby Dr., Davis, Calif. 95616. *Office:* 822 Sproul Hall, University of California, Davis, Calif. 95616.

CAREER: Miami University, Oxford, Ohio, instructor, 1961-63, assistant professor, 1963-67, associate professor of English, 1967-70, director of American studies, 1963-70; University of California, Davis, associate professor of English and chairman of American studies, 1970—. Visiting associate professor at Indiana University, summer, 1969. *Member:* American Studies Association (member of executive council, 1970). *Awards, honors:* Outstanding Teacher Award, Miami University, 1967; National Endowment for the Humanities fellow, 1972-73.

WRITINGS: American Literature, three volumes, General Extension Division, University of Minnesota, 1960-61, revised edition of Volume I, 1963; (editor) Bernard Strempek, *Breathing,* Miami University, 1965; (editor) Edward Beecher, *Narrative of Riots at Alton,* Dutton, 1965; (editor) *American Studies: Essays on Theory and Method,* C. E. Merrill, 1968; *The Politics of the Universe: Edward Beecher, Orthodoxy, and Abolition,* Vanderbilt University Press, 1968; (with others) *The Gentle Revolution,* Ad Lib Press, 1969; (contributor) Betty E. Chmaj, editor, *American Women and American Studies,* Know, Inc., 1972. Contributor of articles and reviews to journals, including *New England Quarterly, Connections, Nation,* and *Journal of Popular Culture.* Assistant book review editor, *Journal of Aesthetics and Art Criticism,* 1967-70, contributor to annual bibliography, 1969—.

WORK IN PROGRESS: Culture against Nature: Paul Goodman and Adam (tentative title); and *The ABC Letters.*

* * *

MERRILL, Arch 1895(?)-1974

1895(?)—July 15, 1974; American journalist and author. Obituaries: *New York Times,* July 17, 1974.

* * *

MEYER, Carolyn 1935-

PERSONAL: Born June 8, 1935, in Lewistown, Pa.; daughter of H. Victor (a businessman) and Sara (Knepp) Meyer; married Joseph Smrcka, June 4, 1960 (divorced, 1973); children: Alan, John, Christopher. *Education:* Bucknell University, B.A., 1957. *Politics:* Liberal. *Religion:* "Questioning." *Home:* 16 Murray St., Norwalk, Conn. 06851. *Agent:* Joan Daves, 515 Madison Ave., New York, N.Y. 10022.

CAREER: Institute of Children's Literature, instructor, 1973—. Secretary of board of directors, St. Paul's Housing Corp. of Norwalk, 1970—.

WRITINGS: Miss Patch's Learn-to-Sew Book, Harcourt, 1969; *Stitch by Stitch,* Harcourt, 1971; *Bread Book,* Harcourt, 1972; *Yarn,* Harcourt, 1973; *Saw, Hammer, and Paint,* Morrow, 1973; *Milk, Butter, and Cheese,* Morrow, 1974; *Christmas Crafts,* Harper, in press; *People Who Make Things,* Atheneum, in press; *The Amish of Pennsylvania,* Atheneum, in press; *Rock Tumbling,* Morrow, in press. Author of monthly book review column, "Chiefly for Children," *McCall's,* 1968-72. Contributor to magazines.

* * *

MEYER, H. K. Houston
See MEYER, Heinrich

* * *

MEYER, Heinrich 1904-
(Robert O. Barlow, H. K. Houston Meyer)

PERSONAL: Born May 17, 1904, in Nuernberg, Germany; son of Wilhelm Karl (a principal) and Anna (Ulmer) Meyer; married Sibylle Hommel (a physical therapist), February 9, 1952; children: Margret Ann. *Education:* Studied at University of Erlangen, 1923, and University of Munich, 1923-24; University of Freiburg, Ph.D., 1928. *Home:* 1114 Frances Ave., Nashville, Tenn. 37204. *Office:* Vanderbilt University, Nashville, Tenn. 37235.

CAREER: Rice University, Houston, Tex., instructor in German, 1930-42; Muhlenberg College, Allentown, Pa., professor of German, 1945-63; Princeton University, Princeton, N.J., professor of German, 1961-62; University of Hamburg, Hamburg, Germany, professor of German, 1963-64; Vanderbilt University, Nashville, Tenn., professor of German, 1964—. Visiting professor, Indiana University, summer, 1963. *Member:* Modern Language Association of America. *Awards, honors:* Guggenheim fellowship, 1953-54; Kantgesellschaft Prize and Order of Merit, from German Bundesrepublik, 1973.

WRITINGS: Deutsches Uebungsbuch (title means "German Exercises"), Prentice-Hall, 1936; (under pseudonym H. K. Houston Meyer) *Konrad Baeumlers weiter weg: Ein Texas-deutscher roman* (novel; title means "Konrad Baeumler's Long Journey: A Novel about Germans in Texas"), Deutsche Verlags-anstalt, 1938; (under pseudonym Robert O. Barlow) *The Complete Modern Garden Herbal of Robert O. Barlow* (illustrated with drawings), Organic Gardening, 1945; *Leaves and What They Do* (illustrated), Organic Gardening, 1945; *Goethe: Das Leben im Werk* (title means "Goethe: His Life in His Works"), Stromverlag, 1950, 3rd edition, 1968; *The Age of the World: A Chapter in the History of Enlightenment,* Muhlenberg College, 1951; *Was bleibt: Bemerkungen ueber Literatur und Leben, Schein und Wirk lichkeit* (essay; title means "Lasting Values: Remarks on Life and Letters, Appearance and Reality"), Guenther Verlag, 1966; *Die Kunst des Erzaehleus* (title means "The Art of Fiction"), Fraucke, 1972. Contributor of nearly thirteen hundred articles and reviews to journals and newspapers. Editor of *German Studies in America;* editor of *Organic Gardening,* 1945-46; former associate editor of *Books Abroad.*

WORK IN PROGRESS: The Future of the Dollar.

* * *

MEYER, Nicholas 1945-

PERSONAL: Born December 24, 1945, in New York, N.Y.; son of Bernard Constant (a psychoanalyst) and Elly (a concert pianist; maiden name, Kassman) Meyer. *Education:* University of Iowa, B.A., 1968. *Politics:* "Jeffersonian." *Religion:* "Idiosyncratic." *Home and office:* 15149 Camarillo St., Sherman Oaks, Calif. 91403. *Agent:* International Famous Agency, 9255 Sunset Blvd., Hollywood, Calif. 90036.

CAREER: Screenwriter and novelist. *Member:* Authors Guild of Authors League of America (West section), Sherlock Holmes Society of Los Angeles.

WRITINGS: The Love Story Story, Avon, 1971; *Target Practice* (novel), Harcourt, 1974; *The Seven-Per-Cent Solution* (novel; Literary Guild selection), Dutton, 1974. Author of "Judge Dee," a television play, American Broadcasting Co., 1974. Contributor of about four hundred film reviews to *Daily Iowan,* 1964-68.

SIDELIGHTS: Meyer writes: "In whatever medium I am working, my primary purpose is to tell a good story well. I like serious music, horseback riding, swimming, sailing, pets, movies, reading, San Francisco, pretty women—not necessarily in that order."

MEYER, Thomas 1947- (Thomas Kydd, Tom Kydd)

PERSONAL: Born February 14, 1947, in Seattle, Washington; son of Edgar Adolph (a postman and policeman) and Bertha (Rinas) Meyer. *Education:* Bard College, A.B., 1969. *Home:* Corn Close, Dentdale, Sedbergh, Cumbria, England. *Office:* Jargon Society, Book Organization, Elm St., Millerton, N.Y. 12546.

CAREER: Jargon Society, Penland, N.C., assistant to executive director, 1969—.

WRITINGS—Poems: *The Bang Book,* Jargon Society, 1971; *Poikilos,* Finial Press, 1971; *O Nathan,* Finial Press, 1973; *The Umbrella of Aesculapius,* Jargon Society, in press. Contributor to *Caterpillar* and other magazines, occasionally under pseudonyms Thomas Kydd and Tom Kydd.

WORK IN PROGRESS: A Gift, based on the Shaker movement in America, 1774-1974, Volume I: *Ann Lee Leads the Way.*

SIDELIGHTS: Meyer writes: "The greatest field of influence on my own work lies—not in my involvement with Anglo-Saxon and Greek or in earlier skirmishes with Cabalism and Analytical Psychology—but in the art of cooking. As a result of careful and plodding study of 'neo-French' culinary techniques, there grew in me certain intimations about myself as a poet."

* * *

MICHAELS, Lynn See STRONGIN, Lynn

* * *

MICKEY, Paul A(lbert) 1937-

PERSONAL: Born May 13, 1937, in Amanda, Ohio; son of Martin E. (a clergyman) and Ellen (Koons) Mickey; married Jane E. Becker (an executive secretary), October 13, 1962; children: Bruce Jon, Sandra Lee. *Education:* Harvard University, B.A., 1963; Princeton Theological Seminary, B.D., 1966, Ph.D., 1970. *Home:* 1100 Woodburn Rd., Durham, N.C. 37705. *Office:* School of Divinity, Duke University, 315 Divinity Building, Durham, N.C. 27706.

CAREER: Pastor of United Methodist churches in Cleveland, Ohio, 1966-67, and Bay Head, N.J., 1969-70; Duke University, Durham, N.C., assistant professor of pastoral theology, 1970—. Member of board of directors of CONTACT-Teleministries, 1971—, and of United Methodist Church organization, Good News, 1973—. *Military service:* U.S. Air Force, 1955-59; became staff sergeant. *Member:* American Council on Pastoral Education, Association of Professional Educators for Ministry, Aircraft Owners and Pilots Association.

WRITINGS: (With Robert Wilson) *Conflict and Resolution,* Abingdon, 1973.

WORK IN PROGRESS: Tom and George, children's stories; *Power and Restraint in Parish; Emerging Protestant Bureaucracies.*

AVOCATIONAL INTERESTS: The out-of-doors, flying (certified instrument flight instructor), farming, conservation work.

MICKLISH, Rita 1931-

PERSONAL: Surname is accented on first syllable; born February 7, 1931, in Maywood, Calif.; daughter of Herbert W. (an artist) and Dorothy (Robbeloth) Ryan; married Donald Charles Micklish (a state tax auditor), January 28, 1950; children: David, Janice, Peter, Sharon. *Education:* High school diploma. *Religion:* Roman Catholic. *Home:* 6530 Zena Dr., San Diego, Calif. 92115.

CAREER: Certified instructor in methodology for San Diego Catholic Diocese, San Diego, Calif., 1964—, member of Board of Education, 1963-67. Member of American Red Cross Youth Advisory Board, San Diego County, Calif., 1961-67. *Member:* American Red Cross, Pro-Life League (San Diego, Calif.). *Awards, honors:* Pius X Award from Confraternity of Christian Doctrine, 1964.

WRITINGS: Sugar Bee, Delacorte, 1972. Contributor of articles and short stories to *Religion Teachers Journal, U. S. Catholic, Nursing Outlook, St. Anthony Messenger,* and *The Southern Cross.*

WORK IN PROGRESS: Cloud Queen and *Ride the Wind West,* both novels for young people.

* * *

MIGUEZ-BONINO, Jose 1924-

PERSONAL: Born March 5, 1924, in Santa Fe, Argentina; son of Jose Gandara (a worker) and Agustina (Bonino) Miguez; married Noemi F. A. Nieuwenhuize (a teacher), 1947; children: Nestor Oscar, Eduardo Jose, Daniel Pedro. *Education:* Facultad Evangelica de Teologia, (Buenos Aires), Lic. Theol., 1948; Emory University, M.A., 1953; Union Theological Seminary, New York, N.Y., Th.D., 1960. *Home:* Camacua 282, Buenos Aires, Argentina. *Office:* Facultad de Teologia, Camacua 282, Buenos Aires, Argentina.

CAREER: Ordained minister of the Methodist Church, 1948; Methodist Church in Argentina, Buenos Aires, minister, 1954-57; Instituto Superior de Estudios Teologicos, Buenos Aires, Argentina, professor of theology, 1970—, dean of graduate studies, 1970—; Facultad Evangelica de Teologia, Buenos Aires, Argentina, professor of theology, 1958—, president, 1960-69. Visiting professor at Union Theological Seminary, New York, N.Y., 1968-69, and University of Birmingham, 1974. Official observer at Vatican Council II. *Member:* World Council of Churches.

WRITINGS: (Editor) *Polemica, dialogo y mision: Catolicismo Romano y Protestantismo en la America Latina* (title means "Polemics, Dialogue and Mission: Roman Catholicism and Protestantism in Latin America"), Centro de Estudios Cristianos (Montevideo), 1966; *Concilio abierto: Una Interpretacion Protestante del Concilio Vaticano II* (title means "Open Council: A Protestant Interpretation of Vatican II Council"), Editorial La Aurora (Buenos Aires), 1967; *Integracion humana y unidad Cristiana* (title means "Christian Unity and Human Integration"), La Reforma (Puerto Rico), 1969; (editor) *Out of the Hurt and Hope,* Friendship, 1970; *Ama y haz lo que quieras* (title means "Love and Do What You Wish"), La Aurora, 1971; *Christians and Marxists: The Medieval Challenge to Revolution,* Hodder & Stoughton, in press.

Contributor: M. Searle Bates and Wilhelm Pauck, editors, *The Prospects of Christianity throughout the World,* Harper, 1964; P. M. Minus, editor, *Methodism's Destiny in an Ecumenical Age,* Abingdon, 1969; Donald Cutler, editor, *The Religious Situation, 1969,* Beacon Press, 1969.

WORK IN PROGRESS: Doing Theology in a Revolutionary Context (tentative title), for Fortress; *Introduccion al Catolicismo Romano contemporaneo* (tentative title).

* * *

MILES, T(homas) R(ichard) 1923-

PERSONAL: Born March 11, 1923, in Sheffield, England; son of Richard (an engineer) and Alice (Miller) Miles; married Elaine Armstrong (a teacher of dyslexic children), August 21, 1951; children: P. J. R. *Education:* Magdalen College, Oxford, M.A., 1945, University College of North Wales, Ph.D., 1963. *Religion:* Society of Friends (Quaker). *Home:* Llys-y-Gwynt, Llandegjan, Menai Bridge, Anglesey, Wales. *Office:* Department of Psychology, University College of North Wales, Bangor, Wales.

CAREER: University College of North Wales, Bangor, assistant lecturer, 1949-52, lecturer, 1952-63, professor of psychology, 1963—. Member of staff, Tavistock Clinic, 1954-55. *Member:* Royal Institute of Philosophy (member of council), British Psychological Society (fellow), British Dyslexia Association, Cheshire and North Wales Dyslexia Association (president).

WRITINGS: Religion and the Scientific Outlook, Allen & Unwin, 1959; *Eliminating the Unconscious,* Pergamon, 1966; *On Helping the Dyslexic Child,* Methuen, 1970; *Religious Experience,* Macmillan, 1972; *More Help for Dyslexic Children,* Methuen, in press; *The Dyslexic Child,* Priory Press, in press. Contributor to *Mind, Philosophy, British Journal of Educational Psychology, British Journal for the Philosophy of Science,* and to other professional journals.

WORK IN PROGRESS: Further research on dyslexia.

AVOCATIONAL INTERESTS: Lawn tennis (former international and Wimbledon player), golf, playing the cello.

* * *

MILHAUD, Darius 1892-1974

September 4, 1892—June 22, 1974; French composer, conductor, educator, and author of autobiography. Obituaries: *New York Times,* June 25, 1974; *Washington Post,* June 25, 1974; *Time,* July 8, 1974; *Newsweek,* July 8, 1974.

* * *

MILLER, C(harles) Leslie 1908-

PERSONAL: Born September 13, 1908, in Shamokin, Pa.; son of Charles Henry (a miner) and Mary (Haines) Miller; married Pearl E. Arbogast (an office manager), July 30, 1930; children: Marion (Mrs. Rollin Mann), Leslie, Donald, Ronald. *Education:* Mennonite Brethren in Christ Colorado Springs Seminary, B.A., 1956, Th.B., 1957. *Home and office:* 1215 Anchors Way Dr., #163, Ventura, Calif. 93003.

CAREER: Ordained Mennonite Brethren in Christ minister, 1933; Unevangelized Tribes Mission, Zaire (officially Democratic Republic of the Congo), mission director, 1935-45; Mennonite Brethren in Christ, Allentown, Pa., pastor, 1949-54; Union Gospel Press, Cleveland, Ohio, managing editor, 1954-59; Gospel Light Publications, Glendale, Calif., editorial director, 1959-65; founder and director, Evangelical Editorial Services.

WRITINGS: Expository Studies on Romans, Union Gospel Press, 1955; *With Paul in Colosse,* Union Gospel Press, 1956; *Goodbye World,* Regal Books (Glendale, Calif.), 1972; *All About Angels,* Regal Books (Glendale, Calif.), 1973. Contributor to *Beacon, Revelation, Gospel Herald, Gospel Banner, Messenger,* and *Christian Life.*

WORK IN PROGRESS: They Came from Outer Space; The Angry Lamb, completion expected in 1975.

* * *

MILLER, David L(eroy) 1936-

PERSONAL: Born February 25, 1936, in Cleveland, Ohio; son of DeWitt L. (a clergyman) and Mary (Hartsough) Miller; married Donna Zirkle (a professional singer), June 28, 1958; children: Dianna Margaret, John David. *Education:* Bridgewater College, B.A., 1957; Bethany Theological Seminary, Oak Brook, Ill., B.D., 1960; Drew University, Ph.D., 1963. *Office:* Department of Religion, Syracuse University, Syracuse, N.Y. 13210.

CAREER: Minister of Church of the Brethren, ordained 1960; Drew University, Madison, N.J., instructor in English and religion, 1962-63, assistant professor of religion, 1963-67; Syracuse University, Syracuse, N.Y., associate professor, 1967-74, professor of religion, 1974—. Lecturer at Upsala College, 1962-63; visiting assistant professor at Rutgers University, 1966-67. *Member:* American Academy of Religion, Society for the Arts, Religion, and Society (vice-president), Society for Religion in Higher Education, Danforth Associates (member of advisory council).

WRITINGS: (Editor with Stanley R. Hopper) *Interpretation: The Poetry of Meaning,* Harcourt, 1967; *Gods and Games: Toward a Theology of Play,* World Publishing, 1970; *The New Polytheism: Rebirth of the Gods and Goddesses,* Harper, 1974. Editor of "Religion and Arts," a monograph series, for American Academy of Religion. Member of editorial board, *Journal* of the American Academy of Religion.

WORK IN PROGRESS: Humor, Homecoming, and Happy Ending (tentative title), a study of the religious dimensions of fairy tales, dramatic comedy, and homecoming myths.

BIOGRAPHICAL/CRITICAL SOURCES: Time, March 18, 1974.

* * *

MILLER, David W. 1940-

PERSONAL: Born July 9, 1940, in Coudersport, Pa.; son of Arthur C. (a civil engineer) and Kathryn (Long) Miller; married Margaret Richardson, August 22, 1964; children: Roberta. *Education:* Rice University, B.A., 1962; University of Wisconsin, M.A., 1963; University of Chicago, Ph.D., 1968. *Home:* 6654 Northumberland St., Pittsburgh, Pa. 15217. *Office:* Department of History, Carnegie-Mellon University, Pittsburgh, Pa. 15213.

CAREER: Carnegie-Mellon University, Pittsburgh, Pa., instructor, 1967-68, assistant professor, 1968-73, associate professor of history and director of undergraduate studies in history, 1973—. *Member:* American Historical Association, American Committee for Irish Studies.

WRITINGS: Church, State, and Nation in Ireland: 1898-1921, University of Pittsburgh Press, 1973. Contributor to scholarly journals.

WORK IN PROGRESS: Research for a projected history of Ulster since the seventeenth century.

MILLER, Isabel
See ROUTSONG, Alma

* * *

MILLER, Jim Wayne 1936-

PERSONAL: Born October 21, 1936, in Leicester, N.C.; son of James Woodrow (a service manager) and Edith (Smith) Miller; married Mary Ellen Yates (a teacher), August 17, 1958; children: James Yates, Fred Smith, Ruth Ratcliff. *Education:* Berea College, A.B., 1958; Vanderbilt University, Ph.D., 1965. *Politics:* Left-wing Democrat. *Religion:* "Not a member of any organized church." *Home:* 1512 Eastland Dr., Bowling Green, Ky. 42101. *Office:* Department of Foreign Languages, Western Kentucky University, Bowling Green, Ky. 42101.

CAREER: Western Kentucky University, Bowling Green, assistant professor, 1963-65, associate professor, 1966-70, professor of German, 1970—. *Member:* American Association of Teachers of German, American Association of University Professors. *Awards, honors:* Alice Lloyd Memorial Prize for Appalachian Poetry from Alice Lloyd College, 1967, for poems in *Copperhead Cane.*

WRITINGS: Copperhead Cane (poems), Robert Moore Allen, 1964; *The More Things Change, the More They Stay the Same* (ballads), Whippoorwill Press, 1971; *Dialogue with a Dead Man* (poems), University of Georgia Press, 1974. Contributor of short stories to literary magazines and scholarly and critical articles to journals.

WORK IN PROGRESS: Translating contemporary German lyrics and nineteenth century treatise on rhyme; papers on Appalachian folklore and folklife.

SIDELIGHTS: "Growing up in North Carolina," Miller says, "I was often amused, along with other natives, at tourists who fished the trout streams. The pools, so perfectly clear, had a deceptive depth. Fishermen unacquainted with them were forever stepping with hip waders into pools they judged to be knee-deep and going in up to their waists or even their armpits, sometimes being floated right off their feet. I try to make poems like those pools, so simple and clear their depth is deceiving. I want the writing to be so transparent that the reader forgets he is reading and is aware only that he is having an experience. He is suddenly plunged deeper than he expected and comes up shivering."

* * *

MILLER, Nicole Puleo 1944-
(Nicole Puleo)

PERSONAL: Name is pronounced Ni-*cull* Pah-*leh*-oo; born January 8, 1944, in Cleveland, Ohio; daughter of Anthony Mario (a physician) and Herta (Wemhoener) Puleo; married Bruce Leonard Miller, August 20, 1972. *Education:* Ohio Wesleyan University, B.A., 1965; University of Minnesota, M.A., 1968. *Politics:* "Socialistic-populistic." *Religion:* None. *Home address:* Route 2, Box 221A, Menomonie, Wis. 54751. *Office:* Department of English, University of Wisconsin—Stout, Menomonie, Wis. 54751.

CAREER: Twin Citian (metropolitan magazine), Minneapolis, Minn., associate editor, 1969, editor, 1970; University of Wisconsin—Stout, Menomonie, instructor in English, 1970—. *Awards, honors:* Helene Wurlitzer Foundation grant for creative writing, 1965-66.

WRITINGS—All under name Nicole Puleo: (Contributor) Robert Rosenbaum, editor, *Growing Up in America,* Doubleday, 1969; *Drag Racing,* Lerner, 1973; *Motorcycle Racing,* Lerner, 1973; *Track Racing,* Lerner, 1973; *Snowmobile Racing,* Lerner, 1973; *Road Racing,* Lerner, 1973. Contributor of articles and reviews to journals.

WORK IN PROGRESS: A novel.

SIDELIGHTS: Puleo told *CA:* "I am interested in creating multi-dimensional characters, more than I'm interested in plot. I find human beings endlessly fascinating, and some of my major hobbies are studying them, talking with them, writing letters, reading psychological novels, essays, stories, or articles."

* * *

MILLER, William Alvin 1931-

PERSONAL: Born January 1, 1931, in Pittsburgh, Pa.; son of Christ William and Anna Ernestine (Wilhelm) Miller; married Marilyn Mae Miller, August 8, 1953; children: Mark William, Eric Michael. *Education:* Capital University, B.A., 1953; Lutheran Theological Seminary, Columbus, Ohio, M.Div., 1957; Andover Newton Theological School, M.S.T., 1958, D.Ministry, 1974. *Home:* 2005 Xanthus Lane, Wayzata, Minn. 55391. *Office:* Fairview Hospital, 2312 South Sixth St., Minneapolis, Minn. 55406.

CAREER: Pastor of Lutheran church in Baltimore, Md., 1958-66; Fairview Hospital, Minneapolis, Minn., chaplain, 1966-73, director of department of religion and health, 1973—. Instructor at Fairview School of Nursing, 1967—, and Luther Theological Seminary (St. Paul, Minn.), 1973-74. *Member:* Association for Clinical Pastoral Education (certified supervisor), American Protestant Hospital Association (fellow of College of Chaplains), Association of Mental Health Chaplains (fellow), National Council on Family Relations, Minnesota Council on Family Relations.

WRITINGS: Why Do Christians Break Down?, Augsburg, 1973. Contributor to *Lutheran Standard, Contact,* and *Covenant Companion.*

WORK IN PROGRESS: Make Friends with Your Shadow; Mother Goose Revisited.

AVOCATIONAL INTERESTS: Cabinetmaking, boating, skiing.

* * *

MILLIES, Suzanne 1943-

PERSONAL: Born April 30, 1943, in New York, N.Y.; daughter of Arpad Geza (a minister) and Palma (Franko) George; married Robert Millies (a credit manager), August 28, 1965; children: Jennifer. *Education:* Elmhurst College, B.A., 1965; Northern Illinois University, M.A., 1969. *Home:* 404 West Briarcliff, Bolingbrook, Ill. 60439. *Office:* Villa Park School District, Villa Park, Ill.

CAREER: Villa Park Middle School, Villa Park, Ill., teacher of French and English, 1965-69; Willowbrook High School, Villa Park, Ill., teacher of English, 1969—.

WRITINGS: Science Fiction Primer for Teachers, Pflaum, 1974.

* * *

MILNER, Christina 1942-

PERSONAL: Born December 7, 1942, in New York, N.Y.; daughter of A. Richard (a technical writer) and

Gerda (Christensen) Fiske; married Richard B. Milner, January 21, 1962 (divorced, 1973); children: Ivory Ebony. *Education:* Queens College of the City University of New York, student, 1960-63; University of California, Los Angeles, B.A., 1965; University of California, Berkeley, Ph.D., 1970. *Home:* 21½ Yawl St., Marina del Rey, Calif. 90291.

CAREER: Merritt College, Oakland, Calif., assistant professor of anthropology, 1970-71.

WRITINGS: (With Richard B. Milner) *Black Players: The Secret World of Black Pimps,* Little, Brown, 1973.

SIDELIGHTS: Mrs. Milner told *CA* she favors legalization of prostitution, because "it is a social institution which is an integral part of a money-based economy and a matter of personal freedom."

* * *

MILNER, Richard B(ruce) 1941-

PERSONAL: Born July 10, 1941, in Brooklyn, N.Y.; son of Irving (a moving picture projectionist) and Thelma (a high school teacher; maiden name Carr) Milner; married Christina A. Fiske (an anthropologist), January 21, 1961 (divorced, 1972); children: Ivory Ebony Gillian. *Education:* Attended Hamilton College, 1958-59; Queens College of the City University of New York, B.A., 1963; University of California, Los Angeles, M.A., 1965; University of California, Berkeley, further graduate study, 1965-68. *Religion:* "Jewish Yogi." *Home and office:* 6700 192nd St., Apt. 1402, Fresh Meadows, N.Y. 11365.

CAREER: Has worked as zookeeper, film projectionist, editor, and nightclub entertainer; instructor in cultural and biological anthropology at colleges in California: University of California, Los Angeles, Extension Division, 1965, Los Angeles Valley College, 1965-66, Urban School, San Francisco, 1970, and Merritt College, Oakland, 1971. Member of staff, Los Angeles *Free Press.*

WRITINGS: (Contributor) Noel Korn and Fred Thompson, editors, *Human Evolution,* Holt, 1967; (with Christina Milner) *Black Players: The Secret World of Black Pimps,* Little, Brown, 1972; (author of foreword) Dan O'Neill, *The Collective Unconscious of Odd Bodkins,* Glide Publications, 1973.

Work is anthologized in *The Hippie Papers: Notes from the Underground Press,* edited by Jerry Hopkins, Signet, 1968. Contributor to *Urban Life and Culture.*

WORK IN PROGRESS: Exploring Eastern philosophy, altered states of consciousness, and new directions for world culture; research on human evolution and origins of man.

SIDELIGHTS: What began for Milner as a study of social deviants (Black pimps) led him to new insights into the whole of Black culture, and, he feels, into a new understanding of American culture in general.

He discovered that the pimp is regarded as a hero in the ghetto, and compares him to the "trickster" folk type frequently found in Black folklore; that is, the man "who gets his own way while avoiding open and dangerous confrontations with his enemies among the powerful majority." He also found admiration for the defiant Black man "who asserts his masculinity and refuses to bow before authority," whether authority is Black or White.

Milner adds: "After all, when you are on the bottom of the social order, there are only two basic ways to beat the Man: you can fight him directly or you can trick him."

Milner's hope is that more and more urban ethnographers will follow their research to its reasonable conclusions, avoiding isolated studies which limit understanding and "pseudo-problem areas" which actually require a more expansive viewpoint than is generally used by social scientists.

* * *

MILSTEAD, John 1924-

PERSONAL: Born July 31, 1924, in Mishawaka, Ind.; son of Wallace L. and Pauline (Gilfillan) Milstead; married wife, Beth, September 13, 1945; children: Douglas, Matthew, Eric, Elizabeth. *Education:* University of New Mexico, B.A., 1945; University of Iowa, M.A., 1947; University of Wisconsin, Ph.D., 1955. *Politics:* Democrat. *Home:* 2222 West Eighth, Stillwater, Okla. 74074. *Office:* Department of English, Oklahoma State University, Stillwater, Okla. 74074.

CAREER: University of Nevada, Reno, instructor in English, 1948-51; University of Idaho, Moscow, instructor in English, 1955-58; Louisiana Polytechnic Institute, Ruston, associate professor of English, 1958-65; Oklahoma State University, Stillwater, associate professor of English, 1965—. *Member:* Modern Language Association of America, American Association of University Professors, South-Central Modern Language Association.

WRITINGS: (Editor with H. J. Sachs and Harry M. Brown) *Readings for College Writers,* Ronald, 1962, 2nd edition, 1967; (editor with Brown) *Patterns in Poetry* (anthology), Scott, Foresman, 1968; (with Brown) *What the Poem Means* (summaries of poems), Scott, Foresman, 1970.

WORK IN PROGRESS: Reorganization of the cultural approach to English literary history; research on Wordworth's psychological theory.

* * *

MINIFIE, James MacDonald 1900-1974

PERSONAL: Born June 8, 1900, in Burton, England; son of Philip R. and Frances Marion (a corn factor; maiden name, Eglinton) Minifie; married Helen Gordon, February 25, 1929 (divorced, 1971); married Gillian Elisabeth Wadsworth (a writer), February 24, 1972; children: (first marriage) James MacDonald, Jr. *Education:* Studied at Regina College, 1919-21, and University of Saskatchewan, 1922-23; Oxford University, B.A., 1926. *Religion:* Anglican.

CAREER: *New York Herald Tribune,* New York, N.Y., journalist, 1929-53, served in Paris, covered the Spanish Civil War, 1936-37, headed Rome bureau, 1937-40, and London bureau, 1940-41, was wounded covering London blitz, covered White House, 1941-43; Canadian Broadcasting Corp., Toronto, Washington correspondent, 1953-68. *Military service:* Canadian Army, 1916-19, serving overseas. Office of Strategic Services, psychological warfare officer, 1943-46; served in Italy; received Order of British Empire and Medal of Freedom. *Awards, honors:* LL.D. from University of Saskatchewan, 1949.

WRITINGS: *Peacemaker or Powdermonkey: Canada's Role in a Revolutionary World,* McClelland & Stewart, 1960; *Open at the Top,* McClelland & Stewart, 1963; *Who's Your Fat Friend?,* McClelland & Stewart, 1967; *Homesteader* (autobiography), Macmillan (Canada), 1972.

WORK IN PROGRESS: *Expatriate* (tentative title), a second autobiographical book.

AVOCATIONAL INTERESTS: Telling and hearing stories, botany, bird-watching, studying Greek and Latin.

(Died June 13, 1974)

* * *

MINTY, Judith 1937-

PERSONAL: Born August 5, 1937, in Detroit, Mich.; daughter of Karl J. (an electrical engineer) and Margaret (Hunt) Makinen; married Edgar S. Minty (an industrial engineer), 1957; children: Lora, Reed, Ann. *Education:* Attended Michigan State University, 1954-59; Ithaca College, B.S., 1957; graduate study at Muskegon Community College, 1970-71, and Thomas Jefferson College, 1971; Western Michigan University, M.A., 1973. *Home:* 310 West Circle Dr., North Muskegon, Mich. 49445.

CAREER: Employed briefly as speech therapist in Bel Air, Md.; has also worked as cosmetic wholesaler; free-lance writer. *Awards, honors:* International Poetry Forum United States Award, 1973; Breadloaf Writer's Conference fellowship, 1974.

WRITINGS: Lake Songs and Other Fears (poems), University of Pittsburgh Press, 1974. Work appears in *Story: The Yearbook of Discovery,* edited by Whit Burnett and Hallie Burnett, Four Winds Press, 1971. Contributor of articles and poetry to *Wonderland Magazine, Ladies' Home Journal, Atlantic Monthly, New York Quarterly, Poetry Northwest, Green River Review, Poetry, Stirer's Row,* and *Sou'wester.*

WORK IN PROGRESS: Short fiction, completion expected in 1975; *Palmistry for Blind Mariners,* a book of poetry, 1975; a translated anthology of contemporary women poets of France, 1976.

SIDELIGHTS: Judith Minty told *CA:* "Writing, particularly poetry is now my life. I speak of my region, the land, and the people who are important to me. Water is a mystic power, and certain animals, the moon and sun, take part in the ritual."

* * *

MITCHELL, B(rian) R(edman) 1929-

PERSONAL: Born September 20, 1929, in Oxenhope, Yorkshire, England; son of Irvin and Dora (Redman) Mitchell; married Barbara Helen Douglas Hay, August 26, 1952; married second wife, Ann Leslie Birney, September 11, 1968; children: (second marriage) David Charles, Peter John. *Education:* University of Aberdeen, M.A., 1952; Cambridge University, Ph.D., 1955. *Home:* 20 High St., Toft, Cambridge, England. *Office:* Faculty of Economics, Cambridge University, Sidgwick Ave., Cambridge, England.

CAREER: Cambridge University, Cambridge, England, research officer and other posts, department of applied economics, 1958-67, university lecturer, Faculty of Economics, 1967—, fellow of Trinity College, 1967—. Visiting lecturer at University of Colorado, 1963-64, and Purdue University, 1964. *Military service:* Royal Air Force, 1955-58; became flight lieutenant. *Member:* Economic History Society, Economic History Association, Association of University Teachers.

WRITINGS: (With Phyllis Deane) *Abstract of British Historical Statistics,* Cambridge University Press, 1962; (with Klaus Boehm) *British Parliamentary Election Results, 1950-1964,* Cambridge University Press, 1966; (with H. G. Jones) *Second Abstract of British Historical Statistics,* Cambridge University Press, 1971; *European Historical Statistics, 1750-1970,* Macmillan, in press. Contributor to *Fontana Economic History of Europe,* Volumes IV and VI, 1972, 1974. Contributor to economic history, business history, and statistical journals.

WORK IN PROGRESS: Economic Development of the British Coal Industry 1815-1914.

* * *

MITCHELL, John D(ietrich) 1917-

PERSONAL: Born November 3, 1917, in Rockford, Ill.; son of John D. R. (a realtor) and Dora (Schroeder) Mitchell; married Miriam Pitcairn (an actress), August 25, 1956; children: John V., Lorenzo Theodore, Barbarina Dora. *Education:* University of Illinois, student, 1935-37; Northwestern University, B.S., 1939, M.A., 1940; Columbia University, Ed.D., 1956. *Religion:* Swedenborgian. *Home address:* Creek Rd., Bryn Athyn, Pa. 19009. *Office:* Institute for Advanced Studies in the Theatre Arts, 310 West 56th St., New York, N.Y. 10019.

CAREER: University of Missouri, Columbia, production director of university theater, 1939-40; Katharine Cornell-Guthrie McClintic Company, New York, N.Y., actor and stage manager, 1942-43; American Broadcasting Co. (ABC), New York, N.Y., radio producer and director of Metropolitan Opera broadcast, 1943-46; Samuel French, Inc., New York, N.Y., assistant editor and play agent, 1946-48; Manhattan College, Bronx, N.Y., assistant professor, 1948-50, associate professor of speech, 1950-58; Institute for Advanced Study in the Theatre Arts, New York, N.Y., executive producer, president, and artistic director, 1958—. Leader of study tour of theater arts in Europe for Columbia University, 1950-51, 1954, 1956; lecturer at Postgraduate Center for Psychotherapy, 1958—, and Postgraduate Center for Mental Health, 1968—; summer professor at University of Denver, 1963, 1965, 1966. U.S. delegate to International Theater Institute, (Holland) 1953 and (Bombay) 1956. Member of board of directors of Beneficia Foundation; director of Rudolf Steiner School; member of fine arts committee at Fairleigh Dickinson University.

MEMBER: American Theatre Association, Actors Equity, Television and Radio Directors Guild, Players Club, Nippon Club.

WRITINGS: (Editor, and translator from the Chinese with Richard Strassberg, Donald Chang, and William Packard) *Red Pear Garden,* Godine, 1974; (editor with Chang) *Wild Boar Forest* (annotated text on Chinese theater), Northwood Press, in press; (translator with William Packard) Paul Verlaine, *Femmes Hombres,* Godine, in press; (with Suria St. Denis) *World Masters of Style,* (on theatre), Godine, in press.

Translator; plays: "Gladiator's Thirty Million," by Eugene Labiche, first produced in New York, N.Y., at IASTA Theatre, February 10, 1969; "House of Fools," by Joseph de Valdivielso, first produced Off-Broadway at Greenwich Mews Theatre, March 19, 1972.

WORK IN PROGRESS: Translating "The Green Bird," a play by Carlo Gozzi, for adaptation for a Broadway musical; translating two farces by Feydeau; translating Chinese plays and work of Tsao Yu; writing a revue based on poems of Paul Verlaine for Broadway production.

MITCHELL, Lee M(ark) 1943-

PERSONAL: Born April 16, 1943, in Albany, N.Y.; son of Maurice B. and Mildred R. Mitchell; married Barbara Anderson, August 27, 1966; children: Mitchell, Mark Robert. *Education:* Wesleyan University, A.B., 1965; University of Chicago, J.D., 1968. *Home:* 1674 Moorings Dr., Reston, Va. 22090. *Office:* Sidley & Austin, 1730 Pennsylvania Ave. N.W., Washington, D.C. 20005.

CAREER: Admitted to Bar of State of Illinois, 1968, Bar of District of Columbia, 1969, Bar of U.S. Court of Appeals for the District of Columbia, 1970, and Bar of U.S. Supreme Court, 1972; Leibman, Williams, Bennett, Baird & Minow (attorneys), Chicago, Ill., attorney, 1968-69; Sidley & Austin, Washington, D.C., attorney, 1969—. Co-director of Study of Political Access to Television, 1971-72; rapporteur, Task Force on Political Public Affairs Broadcasting, Twentieth Century Fund, 1974; consultant to political candidates and organizations on regulation of political broadcasting. *Member:* Federal Communications Bar Association, Federal Bar Association, American Arbitration Association, National Press Club, National Lawyers Club, Chicago Bar Association, Washington Council of Lawyers.

WRITINGS: (Contributor) William L. Rivers and Michael J. Nyan, editors, *Aspen Notebook on Government and the Media,* Praeger, 1973; (with Newton N. Minow and John Bartlow Martin) *Presidential Television,* Basic Books, 1973. Contributor to *Television Quarterly.*

* * *

MITCHELL, Stephen Arnold 1903-1974

March 3, 1903—April 23, 1974; American lawyer, politician, government administrator, and author. Obituaires: *Washington Post,* April 24, 1974.

* * *

MODELSKI, George 1926-

PERSONAL: Born January 9, 1926, in Poznan, Poland; son of Ludwik (a businessman) and Wanda (Borucka) Modelski; married Sylvia Cohen, June 9, 1951. *Education:* London School of Economics and Political Science, B.Sc. (first class honors), 1950, Ph.D., 1954. *Home:* 3925 47th Ave. N.E., Seattle, Wash. 98105. *Office:* Department of Political Science, University of Washington, Seattle, Wash. 98195.

CAREER: Australian National University, Institute of Advanced Studies, Canberra, Australian Capital Territory, research fellow in international relations, 1957-59, senior research fellow, 1959-61, senior fellow, 1961-62, professorial fellow, 1962-67, acting head of department of international relations, 1961-62, 1965-66; University of Washington, Seattle, professor of political science, 1967—. Visiting assistant professor at University of Chicago, 1959-60; Princeton University, visiting research associate, 1960, and research associate at Center of International Studies, 1964, visiting lecturer with rank of professor at Woodrow Wilson School of Public and International Affairs, 1964-65; visiting professor, Stanford University, summer, 1967; research fellow, Center for International Affairs, Harvard University, 1973-74. *Member:* American Political Science Association, International Studies Association.

WRITINGS: Atomic Energy in the Communist Bloc, Melbourne University Press, 1959; *The Communist International System,* Center of International Studies, Princeton University, 1960; *A Theory of Foreign Policy,* Praeger, 1962; (editor and contributor) *SEATO: Six Studies,* F. W. Cheshire, 1962; (editor) *Documents on the Ideology of Indonesian Foreign Policy,* Department of International Relations, Australian National University, 1963; *Principles of World Politics,* Free Press, 1972; (editor) *Multinational Corporations and World Order,* Sage Publications, 1974.

Contributor: Klaus E. Knorr and Sidney Verba, editors, *The International System: Theoretical Essays,* Princeton University Press, 1961; James Rosenau, editor, *International Aspects of Civil Strife,* Princeton University Press, 1964; C. E. Black and T. P. Thornton, editors, *Communism and Revolution,* Princeton University Press, 1964; Alastair F. Buchan, editor, *China and the Peace of Asia,* Praeger, 1965; A. M. Halpern, editor, *Policies toward China,* Council on Foreign Relations (New York), 1965; Uwe Nerlich, editor, *Krieg und Frieden in der Modernen Staatenwelt,* Volume II, Bertelmansverlag, 1966; C. E. Black and R. A. Falk, editors, *The Future of the International Legal Order,* Volume I, Princeton University Press, 1969; J. R. Friedman and others, editors, *Alliance in International Politics,* Allyn & Bacon, 1970. Contributor to *International Encyclopedia of the Social Sciences, Year Book of World Affairs,* and to journals.

WORK IN PROGRESS: A book on continuities in world politics; a monograph on world power structures.

* * *

MOGAN, Joseph J(ohn), Jr. 1924-

PERSONAL: Born January 20, 1924, in Nashville, Tenn.; son of Joseph John (an accountant) and Helen (Nenon) Mogan; married Margaret Jewel Kornegay, August 31, 1957; children: Maria, Joseph, Gavin. *Education:* St. Mary's Seminary, Baltimore, Md., A.B., 1945, S.T.B., 1948; University of Notre Dame, M.A., 1954; Louisiana State University, Ph.D., 1961. *Home:* 3430 59th St., Lubbock, Tex. 79413. *Office:* Department of English, Texas Tech University, 103 English Building, Lubbock, Tex. 79409.

CAREER: St. Norbert College, DePere, Wis., assistant professor of English, 1961-63; Southern Illinois University, Edwardsville, assistant professor of English, 1963-66; Texas Tech University, Lubbock, associate professor, 1966-70, professor of English, 1970—..

WRITINGS: Chaucer and the Theme of Mutability, Mouton & Co., 1969. Contributor to scholarly journals.

WORK IN PROGRESS: A variorum edition of Chaucer's *The Parson's Tale,* publication by University of Oklahoma Press expected in 1980.

* * *

MOHR, Nicholasa 1935-

PERSONAL: Born November 1, 1935, in New York, N.Y.; daughter of Pedro and Nicholasa (Rivera) Golpe; married Irwin Mohr (a clinical child psychologist), October 5, 1957; children: David, Jason. *Education:* Attended Art Students League, 1953-56, Brooklyn Museum Art School, 1959-66, and Pratt Center for Contemporary Printmaking, 1966-69. *Residence:* Teaneck, N.J.

CAREER: Fine arts painter in New York, California, Mexico, and Puerto Rico, 1952-62; printmaker in New York, Mexico, and Puerto Rico, 1963—. Teacher in art schools in New York and New Jersey, 1967—. *Awards, honors:* MacDowell Colony fellowship, 1972; Merit award from Society of Illustrators, 1973, for book-jacket of novel, *Nilda; New York Times* outstanding books award, 1973, for *Nilda*.

WRITINGS: (Self-illustrated) *Nilda* (novel), Harper, 1973.

WORK IN PROGRESS: A collection of short stories for Harper, completion expected in 1975.

SIDELIGHTS: Nicholasa Mohr's work has appeared in museums, galleries, colleges, and art institutions in the United States and Latin America.

* * *

MOKRES, James A(llen) 1945-

PERSONAL: Born September 20, 1945, in Minneapolis, Minn.; son of Louis Charles (a telephone company employee) and Mary (Fetzek) Mokres; married Rosemary Thompson (a librarian and writer), July 3, 1971. *Education:* University of Minnesota, B.A., 1968. *Home:* 912 East Hyman, Aspen, Colo. 81611. *Agent:* Knox Burger Associates Ltd., 39½ Washington Sq. S., New York, N.Y. 10012.

CAREER: Ski instructor in Aspen, Colo., 1969—.

WRITINGS: *Ski America Cheap,* Little, Brown, 1973. Contributor to *Student Skier*.

WORK IN PROGRESS: A ski magazine, *American Skier;* travel guides.

SIDELIGHTS: Mokres told *CA:* "My primary concern has been (and still is) to supply needed information to traveling sports enthusiasts. The purpose is to make outdooring vacations more convenient and/or less expensive. My overall aim is to generate interest in travel and personal health through sporting activities. I may spend a year in France with my wife to gather information on a new book dealing with European celebrations and festivals. Both of us speak French."

BIOGRAPHICAL/CRITICAL SOURCES: *Aspen Times,* December 6, 1973.

* * *

MOL, Johannis (Hans) J(acob) 1922-

PERSONAL: Born February 14, 1922, in Rozenburg, Netherlands; naturalized U.S. citizen; son of Johannis J. (a farmer) and Jacoba J. (de Koster) Mol; married L. Ruth McIntyre, February 14, 1953; children: Ian, David, Gillian, Margery. *Education:* United Theological Faculty, Sydney, Australia, certificate, 1951; Union Theological Seminary, New York, N.Y., B.Div., 1955; Columbia University, M.A., 1956, Ph.D., 1960. *Office:* Department of Religion, McMaster University, Hamilton, Ontario, Canada.

CAREER: Deputy administrator of Dutch sugar beet industry, 1946-48; chaplain to immigrants in Bonegilla, Australia, 1952-54; pastor of Presbyterian church in White Hall, Md., 1956-60; University of Canterbury, Christchurch, New Zealand, lecturer in sociology, 1961-63; Australian National University, Canberra, fellow in sociology at Institute of Advanced Studies, 1963-70; McMaster University, Hamilton, Ontario, professor of religion, 1970—. Visiting professor at University of Arizona, summer, 1967, University of California, Santa Barbara, autumn, 1969, and Marquette University, winter, 1970. Delegate and section chairman, Eighth World Congress of Sociology, 1970. *Member:* International Sociological Association (president of Committee on the Sociology of Religion, 1974—), Religious Research Association (chairman of board of directors, 1972-74), Conference internationale de sociologie religieuse (member of executive committee, 1971—), Sociological Association of Australia and New Zealand (secretary-treasurer, 1963-69), Canberra Sociological Society (president, 1967-68).

WRITINGS: (Contributor) Alan Davies and Solomon Encel, editors, *Australian Society*, F. W. Cheshire, 1965, 2nd edition, 1970; *Race and Religion in New Zealand: A Critical Review of the Policies and Practices of the Churches in New Zealand Relevant to Racial Integration,* National Council of Churches in New Zealand, 1966; (contributor) Ivan Southall, editor, *The Challenge,* Landsdowne Press, 1966; *The Breaking of Traditions: Theological Convictions in Colonial America,* Glendessary Press, 1968; (contributor) A. L. McLeod, editor, *The Pattern of New Zealand Culture,* Cornell University Press, 1968; *Christianity in Chains: A Sociologist's Interpretation of the Churches' Dilemma in a Secular World,* Nelson (Melbourne), 1969; *Religion in Australia: A Sociological Investigation,* Nelson, 1971; (editor) *Western Religion: A Country by Country Sociological Inquiry,* Mouton, 1972.

Monographs: *Churches and Immigrants: A Sociological Study of the Mutual Effect of Religion and Emigrant Adjustment,* Research Group for European Migration Problems, 1961; *Church Attendance in Christchurch, New Zealand,* Department of Psychology and Sociology, University of Canterbury, 1962; *Changes in Religious Behaviour of Dutch Immigrants,* Research Group for European Migration Problems, 1965.

Contributor of about thirty articles to social science journals, including *Sociological Analysis, Australian Quarterly, American Sociologist, International Migration Review, Australian and New Zealand Journal of Sociology,* and *Review of Religious Research*.

SIDELIGHTS: Mol spent the years from 1943 to 1945 in German concentration camps and prisons.

* * *

MOLZ, (Redmond) Kathleen 1928-

PERSONAL: Born March 5, 1928, in Baltimore, Md.; daughter of Joseph T. (a lawyer) and Regina (Barry) Molz. *Education:* Johns Hopkins University, B.S., 1949, M.A. (English literature), 1950; University of Michigan, M.A. (library science), 1953. *Home:* 700 Seventh St. S.W., Washington, D.C. 20024. *Office:* U.S. Office of Education, Washington, D.C. 20202.

CAREER: Enoch Pratt Free Library, Baltimore, Md., reference librarian, 1953-56; Free Library of Philadelphia, Philadelphia, Pa., television specialist, 1957-58, public relations officer, 1958-62; U.S. Office of Education, Washington, D.C., chief of library planning and development branch, Bureau of Adult, Vocational, and Library Programs, 1958-70, chief of planning staff, Bureau of Libraries and Learning Resources, 1970—. Lecturer in Graduate Library School, Pratt Institute, 1965-67; alumnus-in-residence at School of Library Science, University of Michigan, 1969. Member of board of directors, Freedom to Read Foundation. *Member:* American Library Association (chairman of intellectual freedom committee, 1973—), Alumni Association of the School of Library Science, University of Michigan (president, 1967-68). *Awards, honors:* Fund for Adult Education leadership training grant, 1956-57.

WRITINGS: (Editor with Ralph W. Conant) *The Metropolitan Library,* M.I.T. Press, 1973. Writer of television series, "Alien Ground," produced by Denver Public Library and KRMA-TV, 1956-57, and "Portraits in Print," distributed by National Educational Television, 1958. Regular reviewer for *Baltimore Evening Sun* and *Baltimore Sunday Sun,* 1953-56. Contributor to *American Scholar* and library journals. Editor, *Wilson Library Bulletin,* 1962-68.

WORK IN PROGRESS: Federal Policy and Library Planning.

* * *

MONBECK, Michael E(ugene) 1942-

PERSONAL: Born February 10, 1942, in Dayton, Ohio; son of Virgil Lloyd (a toolmaker) and Janet (Davis) Monbeck; married Diana James (a photographer), October 16, 1963. *Education:* Goddard College, M.A., 1974. *Home:* 433 West 21st St., New York, N.Y. 10011. *Office:* American Foundation for the Blind, 15 West 16th St., New York, N.Y. 10011.

CAREER: American Foundation for the Blind, New York, N.Y., 1962—, *New Outlook for the Blind,* associate editor, 1969—, senior editor, 1972—. *Member:* World Future Society, American Association of Workers for the Blind, Analytical Psychology Club of New York (member of executive committee, 1970—).

WRITINGS: The Meaning of Blindness: Attitudes toward Blindness and Blind People, Indiana University Press, 1973.

WORK IN PROGRESS: A book with the tentative title, *What the Future Requires of Us: An Inquiry into the Relationship between Present-Day Trends in Western Culture and the Evolution of Human Consciousness.*

* * *

MONTGOMERY, Herbert J. 1933-

PERSONAL: Born June 26, 1933, in Deer River, Minn.; married, wife's name, Mary A. *Home:* 1100 Upton Ave. N., Minneapolis, Minn. 55411.

CAREER: Editor for Winston Press, Minneapolis, Minn. *Awards, honors:* First prize in *Writer's Digest* contest, 1965, for article co-authored with his wife.

WRITINGS: The Apple and the Envelope, Holt, 1973; (with wife, Mary A. Montgomery) *Rodeo Road,* Scholastic Book Services, 1973.

* * *

MONTGOMERY, Thomas (Andrew) 1925-

PERSONAL: Born May 19, 1925, in Seattle, Wash.; son of Earl Francis (an architect) and Elaine (MacCuaig) Montgomery; married Ellen Bliven, August 22, 1953; children: James Andrew, Anne Elizabeth, Mary Ellen. *Education:* Washington State University, B.A., 1949; University of Wisconsin, M.A., 1950, Ph.D., 1955; graduate study, University of Madrid, 1953-54, and McGill University. *Home:* 6220 Camp St., New Orleans, La. 70118. *Office:* Department of Spanish and Portuguese, Tulane University, New Orleans, La. 70118.

CAREER: University of Wichita, Wichita, Kan., instructor in Spanish, 1954-55; Elmira College, Elmira, N.Y., assistant professor of French and Spanish, 1955-58; Tulane University, New Orleans, La., assistant professor, 1958-63, associate professor, 1963-69, professor of Spanish, 1969—. *Military service:* U.S. Army, 1943-45. *Member:* Modern Language Association of America, American Association of Teachers of Spanish and Portuguese, Phi Beta Kappa. *Awards, honors:* International Institute of Education fellow at University of Madrid, 1953-54.

WRITINGS: (Editor) *El Evangelio de San Mateo segun el Manuscrito Escurialense I.I.6,* Real Academia Espanola (Madrid), 1962; (editor with Spurgeon W. Baldwin) *El Nuevo Testamento segun el Manuscrito Escurialense I.I.6,* Real Academia Espanola, 1970. Contributor of about fifteen studies on the history of the Spanish language and on medieval Spanish literature to journals.

WORK IN PROGRESS: Research on *El Poema del Cid* as a preliterate work in form and mythic content.

AVOCATIONAL INTERESTS: Music, cabinet work.

* * *

MONTY, Jeanne R(uth) 1935-

PERSONAL: Born July 19, 1935, in Holyoke, Mass.; daughter of Ernest L. (a lawyer) and Alice (Larocque) Monty. *Education:* University of Montreal, B.A. (summa cum laude), 1954; University of Caen, graduate study, 1954-55; University of Vermont, M.A., 1957; Ohio State University, Ph.D., 1960. *Home:* 3201 rue Parc Fontaine, Apt. 3112, New Orleans, La. 70114. *Office:* Department of French and Italian, Tulane University, New Orleans, La. 70118.

CAREER: University of Illinois, Urbana, instructor, 1960-62, assistant professor of French, 1962-63; Tulane University, New Orleans, La., assistant professor, 1963-66, associate professor, 1966-70, professor of French, 1970—. *Member:* American Association of Teachers of French, American Association for Eighteenth-Century Studies, Association francaise d'etudes du 18eme siecle. *Awards, honors:* Fulbright fellowship, 1954-55; Guggenheim fellowship, 1968-69.

WRITINGS: La Critique litteraire de Melchior Grimm (title means "The Literary Criticism of Melchior Grimm"), Droz, 1961; *Etude sur le style polemique de Voltaire: le "Dictionnaire philosophique"* (title means "A Study of Voltaire's Polemical Style: The "Dictionnaire Philosophique"), Institut et Musee Voltaire, 1966; *Les Romans de l'abbe Prevost: Techniques romanesques et pensee morale* (title means "The Novels of the Abbe Prevost: Novelistic Techniques and Ethical Thought"), Institut et Musee Voltaire, 1971. Co-editor of Volumes 35-46 of "Voltaire's Complete Works," edited by Theodore Besterman and others, University of Toronto Press, 1968—.

* * *

MOODY, Joseph Nestor 1904-

PERSONAL: Born April 18, 1904, in New York, N.Y.; son of Hugh A. (an engineer) and Anne (Nolan) Moody. *Education:* St. Joseph's Seminary, Brooklyn, N.Y., A.B., 1925; Fordham University, M.A., 1931, Ph.D., 1934; Columbia University, post-doctoral study, 1946-48. *Politics:* Democrat. *Religion:* Roman Catholic. *Home and office:* Catholic University of America, Washington, D.C. 20017.

CAREER: Ordained Roman Catholic priest, 1929; College of New Rochelle, New Rochelle, N.Y., assistant professor of history, 1934-40; Notre Dame College, Staten Island, N.Y., assistant professor, 1936-46, associate professor,

1946-49, professor of history, 1949-58; Ladycliff College, Highland Falls, N.Y., professor of history, 1958-65, head of department, 1958-63; Catholic University of America, Washington, D.C., professor of French history, 1965—. *Military service:* U.S. Naval Reserve, 1940-46; became commander; received Presidential Citation. *Member:* Society for French Historical Studies (president, 1968-69; vice-president, 1950-51, 1964-65; member of executive board, 1969—), American Historical Society. *Awards, honors:* Human Rights Award from B'nai B'rith, 1938.

WRITINGS: (Editor with Edgar Alexander and others) *Church and Society: Catholic Social and Political Thought and Movements, 1789-1950,* New York Arts, 1953; (with Joseph F. X. McCarthy) *Man the Citizen: The Foundations of Civil Society,* Doubleday, 1957; (editor with Justus George Lawler) *The Challenge of Mater et Magistra,* Herder & Herder, 1963; (contributor) Evelyn M. Acomb and Marvin L. Brown, editors, *French Society and Culture since the Old Regime,* Holt, 1966; *The Church as Enemy: Anticlericalism in Nineteenth Century French Literature,* Corpus Books, 1968; (contributor) Gaetano L. Vinctiorio, editor, *Crisis in the Great Republic,* Fordham University Press, 1969. Contributor to *Review of Politics* and *Bridge.* Associate editor of *Catholic Historical Review,* 1964—.

WORK IN PROGRESS: Research on the French Press under the July Monarchy.

* * *

MOONEY, Booth 1912-

PERSONAL: Born July 3, 1912, in Decatur, Tex.; son of Harvey M. (a farmer) and Eva (Mitchell) Mooney; married Elizabeth Comstock (a free-lance writer), March 9, 1946; children: Edward C., Joan H. *Education:* Attended public schools in Texas. *Politics:* Democrat. *Home:* 5709 Overlea Rd., Washington, D.C. 20016. *Agent:* Paul R. Reynolds, Inc., 599 Fifth Ave., New York, N.Y. 10017. *Office:* 1625 Eye St. N.W., Washington, D.C. 20006.

CAREER: Texas Weekly, Dallas, Tex., associate editor, 1935-41; Mooney & Cullinan (public relations consultants), Dallas, Tex., partner, 1946-52; U.S. Senate, Washington, D.C., executive assistant to Senator Lyndon B. Johnson, 1953-58; free-lance writer in Washington, D.C., 1959—. *Military service:* U.S. Army Air Forces, 1942-45; became captain. *Member:* Metropolitan Club of Washington, Kenwood Country Club.

WRITINGS: The Lyndon Johnson Story, Farrar, Straus, 1956, revised edition, 1964; *Mr. Speaker,* Follett, 1964; *Builders for Progress,* McGraw, 1965; *The Hidden Assassins,* Follett, 1966; *The Politicians: 1945-1960,* Lippincott, 1970; *Roosevelt and Rayburn,* Lippincott, 1971.

Biographies for young people: *Sam Houston,* Follett, 1966; *Henry Clay,* Follett, 1966; *General Billy Mitchell,* Follett, 1968; *Woodrow Wilson,* Follett, 1968.

* * *

MOORE, Arthur James 1888-1974

December 26, 1888—June 30, 1974; American clergyman, evangelist, and author of works on religious topics and an autobiography. Obituaries: *New York Times,* July 2, 1974; *Washington Post,* July 2, 1974. (*CA*-7/8).

* * *

MOORE, John C(lare) 1933-

PERSONAL: Born May 17, 1933, in Wichita, Kan.; son of John Howard and Kathryn (Kirlin) Moore; married Patricia Ann Hix, September 15, 1956; children: John C., Jr., Joan Marie, Carolyn Ruth, Mary Patricia. *Education:* Rockhurst College, B.A. (magna cum laude), 1955; Catholic University of Louvain, graduate study, 1958-59; Johns Hopkins University, Ph.D., 1960. *Politics:* Democrat. *Religion:* Roman Catholic. *Residence:* Hempstead, N.Y. *Office:* Department of History, Hofstra University, Hempstead, N.Y. 11550.

CAREER: Hofstra University, Hempstead, N.Y., instructor in history, 1959-62; Parsons College, Fairfield, Iowa, assistant professor of history, 1962-63; Hofstra University, assistant professor, 1963-68, associate professor, 1968-72, professor of history, 1972—, associate dean of College of Liberal Arts and Sciences, 1971—. Visiting professor at Fordham University, summer, 1970. *Member:* American Historical Association, Mediaeval Academy of America, American Association of University Professors. *Awards, honors:* Fulbright scholar in Belgium, 1958-59; fellowship at Frank L. Weil Institute for Studies in Religion and Humanities, 1965; American Philosophical Society grant for research in Paris, 1969; first prize, Medieval Institute of Western Michigan University, 1972, for playlet, "The Abbot."

WRITINGS: Love in Twelfth-Century France, University of Pennsylvania Press, 1972; "The Abbot" (playlet) first produced in Kalamazoo at annual conference of Medieval Institute of Western Michigan University, May 1, 1972. Contributor to *Encyclopedia Americana* and *New Catholic Encyclopedia;* contributor of articles and reviews to scholarly journals and to *Commonweal* and *Saturday Review.*

WORK IN PROGRESS: A biography of Pope Innocent III, 1198-1216.

* * *

MOORE, L(ittleton) Hugh 1935-

PERSONAL: Born March 24, 1935, in Atlanta, Ga.; son of L. Hugh and Irma (Moore) Moore; married Mary Stuart Hazzard (a teacher), August 9, 1959; children: Hutch, Mimi. *Education:* Emory University, B.A., 1957, M.A., 1958, Ph.D., 1964. *Politics:* Liberal. *Religion:* Episcopalian. *Home:* 362 Glenn Circle, Decatur, Ga. 30030. *Office:* Department of English, Georgia Institute of Technology, Atlanta, Ga. 30332.

CAREER: Georgia Institute of Technology, Atlanta, instructor, 1960-63, assistant professor, 1964-67, associate professor, 1967-69, professor of English, 1969—. Director of Alfred P. Sloan Program for the Disadvantaged, Moorhouse College, 1964-65; visiting professor at Emory University, 1968-69. *Member:* Modern Language Association of America, American Studies Association, Audubon Society, Georgia Conservancy, Phi Beta Kappa, Alpha Epsilon Upsilon. *Awards, honors:* National Endowment for the Humanities research grant, 1970.

WRITINGS: (Contributor) T. D. Young and others, *The Literature of the South,* revised edition (Moore was not associated with earlier edition), Scott, Foresman, 1968; *Robert Penn Warren and History: The Big Myth We Live,* Humanities, 1971; (with Karl F. Knight) *A Concise Handbook of English Composition,* Prentice-Hall, 1972. Contributor to *Studies in Short Fiction, Georgia Review, Critique,* and other journals.

WORK IN PROGRESS: A study of Alexander Wilson, early American naturalist and the father of American ornithology.

MOORE, S(arah) E.

PERSONAL: Born in Berkeley, Calif.; daughter of John W. (in U.S. Navy) and Constance Moore. *Education:* Wellesley College, B.A.; University of Lausanne, further study. *Agent:* Paul R. Reynolds, Inc., 599 Fifth Ave., New York, N.Y. 10017.

MILITARY SERVICE: U.S. Navy Women's Reserve (WAVES), communications officer and aviation safety officer during World War II; became lieutenant junior grade; received Presidential Unit Citation.

WRITINGS: Diego (juvenile), Harcourt, 1972.

WORK IN PROGRESS: Rasgayo, a sequel to *Diego;* a book on the adventures of teaspoon-size dolls and one on two boys in Civil War days.

AVOCATIONAL INTERESTS: The sea, the theater and other arts, history, foreign languages.

* * *

MOORE, W(illiam) Glenn 1925-

PERSONAL: Born December 31, 1925, in Luverne, Ala.; son of William Manning and Georgia (Morgan) Moore; married Hazel Sanders, March 18, 1949; children: Vance G., Allan W., Sheri S. *Education:* University of Alabama, A.B., 1950, M.A., 1951, Ph.D., 1960. *Religion:* Baptist. *Home:* 1506 Maple St., Carrollton, Ga. 30117. *Office:* Department of Economics, West Georgia College, Carrollton, Ga. 30117.

CAREER: West Georgia College, Carrollton, assistant professor, 1958-60, associate professor of social sciences, 1960-64, professor of economics and history, 1964-65, professor of economics and chairman of department, 1965—. Visiting professor at University of Georgia, 1965. *Military service:* U.S. Navy, 1944-46, 1952-54. U.S. Naval Reserve, 1954—; currently commander, ready reserve. *Member:* Southern Economic Association, Navy League of the United States, Naval Reserve Association, Georgia Association of Economics Educators, Phi Alpha Theta, Pi Gamma Mu.

WRITINGS: (Editor with Robert P. Vichas, and contributor) *Coeval Economics: A Book of Readings,* McCutchan, 1970.

* * *

MOOREHEAD, Agnes 1906-1974

December 6, 1906—April 30, 1974; American film actress. Obituaries: *Washington Post,* May 1, 1974; *Time,* May 13, 1974; *Newsweek,* May 13, 1974; *Current Biography,* June, 1974.

* * *

MOOS, Rudolf H. 1934-

PERSONAL: Born September 10, 1934, in Berlin, Germany; naturalized U.S. citizen; son of Henry R. and Herta (Ehrlich) Moos; married Bernice Schradski, June 9, 1963; children: Karen, Kevin. *Education:* University of California, Berkeley, B.A., 1956, Ph.D., 1960. *Home:* 25661 Fremont Rd., Los Altos Hills, Calif. 94022. *Office:* School of Medicine, Stanford University, Stanford, Calif. 94305.

CAREER: University of California Medical School, San Francisco, U.S. Public Health Service research fellow, 1960-62; Stanford University School of Medicine, Stanford, Calif., assistant professor, 1962-67, associate professor, 1967-72, professor of psychiatry, 1972—, director of Social Ecology Laboratory, 1967—. Research fellow, Veterans Administration Hospital, Palo Alto, 1962—; visiting professor at Institute of Psychiatry, and Maudsley and Royal Bethlem Hospitals, London, 1969-70. Diplomate in clinical psychology, American Board of Professional Psychology. *Member:* American Psychological Association, American Psychosomatic Society, American Sociological Association, American Association for the Advancement of Science.

WRITINGS: (Editor with Paul M. Insel) *Issues in Social Ecology: Human Milieus,* National Press Books, 1974; *Evaluating Treatment Environments: A Social Ecological Approach,* Wiley, 1974; (editor) *Health and the Social Environment,* Heath, 1974. Contributor of about eighty articles to professional journals. Member of editorial board, *Journal of Psychiatric Research,* 1966—, and *Psychosomatic Medicine,* 1971—.

WORK IN PROGRESS: Studies on evaluating correctional and military settings and on social climate scales.

* * *

MORAES, Frank Robert 1907-1974

November 12, 1907—May 2, 1974; Indian journalist, editor, and author of books on Indian and Far Eastern affairs and other subjects. Obituaries: *New York Times,* May 4, 1974; *Current Biography,* July, 1974. (*CA*-13/14).

* * *

MORALES, Angel Luis 1919-

PERSONAL: Born January 13, 1919, in Culebra, Puerto Rico; son of Angel Pablo (a police officer) and Eulalia (Couvertier) Morales; married Maria Luisa Ortiz (an associate professor of Spanish), February 9, 1945; children: Maria de Lourdes (Mrs. Carlos Paralatici). *Education:* University of Puerto Rico, B.A. in Ed. (cum laude), 1941, M.A., 1943; University of Madrid, Ph.D., 1951. *Home:* Alda St., 1575, Urb. Caribe, Rio Piedras, P.R. 00926. *Office:* Department of Hispanic Studies, University of Puerto Rico, Rio Piedras, P.R. 00931.

CAREER: University of Puerto Rico, Rio Piedras, instructor, 1943-47, assistant professor, 1947-53, associate professor, 1953-58, professor of Spanish-American literature, 1958-74, professor emeritus, 1974—, head of department of Hispanic studies, 1970-74. *Member:* Instituto Internacional de Literatura Iberoamericana, Modern Language Association of America, Associacion de Maestros de Puerto Rico, American Association of University Professors, Sociedad Bolivariana, Ateneo Puertorriqueno, Asociacion de Profesores Universitarios (University of Puerto Rico). *Awards, honors:* Scholarship from Ministerio de Relaciones Exteriores de Espana, 1950-51.

WRITINGS: (Editor and author of introduction) *Antologia de Jesus Maria Lago* (title means "An Anthology of Jesus Maria Lago"), Ateneo Puertorriqueno, 1960; (with Jose Ferrer Canales, James Willis Robb, Luis Leal, and Alfredo Roggiano) *Homenaje a Alfonso Reyes* (title means "In Homage of Alfonso Reyes"), Editorial Cultura, 1965; *Literatura hispanoamericana: Epocas y figuras* (title means "Spanish American Literature: Epochs and Authors"), two volumes, Editorial del Departamento de Instruccion Publica, Estado Libre Asociado de Puerto Rico, 1967; *Dos ensayos rubendarianos* (title means "Two Essays on Ruben Dario"), Biblioteca de Extramuros, Universidad de

Puerto Rico, 1969; *La naturaleza venezolana en la obra de Romulo Gallegos* (title means "Venezuelan Nature in the Work of Romulo Gallegos"), Editorial del Departmento de Instruccion Publica, Estado Libre Asociado de Puerto Rico, 1969; (contributor) *El Festival Ruben Dario en Puerto Rico* (title means "Ruben Dario Festival in Puerto Rico"), Recinto Universitario de Mayaguez, 1971. Contributor to journals in his field.

WORK IN PROGRESS: Two books, *Introduccion a la literatura hispanoamericana* and *Estudios literarios hispanoamericanos;* an anthology, *El cuento hispanoamericano.*

* * *

MORENO, Jacob L. 1892-1974

May 20, 1892—May 14, 1974; Rumanian-born American psychiatrist, innovative therapist, educator, and author of books on psychodrama, sociometry, and related topics. Obituaries: *New York Times,* May 16, 1974; *Newsweek,* May 27, 1974; *Time,* May 27, 1974. (*CA*-19/20).

* * *

MORGAN, Alison Mary 1930-

PERSONAL: Born March 2, 1930, in Bexley, Kent, England; daughter of Geoffrey Taunton (an army officer) and Dorothy Wilson (Fox) Raikes; married John Morgan, April 23, 1960; children: Richard, Hugh. *Education:* Somerville College, Oxford, B.A. (second class honors), 1952; University of London, certificate in education, 1953. *Politics:* "Uncommitted." *Religion:* Anglican (Church of Wales). *Home:* Talcoed, Llanafan, Builth Wells, Breconshire, Wales. *Agent:* A. P. Watt, 26/28 Bedford Row, London WC1 R4HL, England.

CAREER: Teacher of English in Great Malven, England, 1953-54, and Newtown, England, 1954-59. Justice of the Peace, 1964—. *Awards, honors:* Arts Council for Wales literary award, 1973, for *Pete.*

WRITINGS—All children's novels: *Fish,* Chatto & Windus, 1971, Harper, 1972; *Pete,* Chatto & Windus, 1972, Harper, 1973; *Ruth Crane,* Chatto & Windus, 1973, Harper, in press; *River Song,* Harper, in press. Also author of unpublished short plays produced by various local amateur groups, including "But If You Sleep," "Act of God," "The Generations," "Aren't You Lucky?," and "A Dragon for Justice." Contributor to *Times Literary Supplement,* and other publications.

WORK IN PROGRESS: Another children's novel.

SIDELIGHTS: "Writing in any form," Mrs. Morgan told *CA,* "I have always taken for granted as a form of self-expression essential to me, and always intended to take it up professionally when the opportunity arose. I think I moved from amateur to professional level with *Fish* because writing for children imposed a discipline my work had previously lacked. The best preparation was writing plays for local groups and producing them myself; I learned to prune ruthlessly. I write Welsh countryside books because that is where I live; I am tied domestically, so travel and access to literary material is limited, but staying still in one place one gets to know about people three-dimensionally."

* * *

MORGAN, Berry 1919-

PERSONAL: Born May 20, 1919, in Port Gibson, Miss.; daughter of John Marshall and Bess Berry (Taylor) Brumfield; divorced; children: Scott Ingles Morgan, Betty Lee Morgan, Aylmer L. Morgan IV, Frances Berry Morgan. *Education:* Attended Loyola University, New Orleans, La., 1947, and Tulane University, 1948-49. *Politics:* Liberal Democrat. *Religion:* Roman Catholic. *Home:* Albena Plantation, Port Gibson, Miss. 39150. *Office:* Department of English, Northeast Louisiana University, Monroe, La. 71201.

CAREER: Worked as executive secretary, and as a real estate specialist; Northeast Louisiana University, Monroe, writer-in-residence, and instructor in English, 1972—; free-lance editor in Port Gibson, Miss. *Member:* American Association of University Professors, American Academy of Arts and Sciences. *Awards, honors:* Houghton Mifflin fellowships, 1966, 1974.

WRITINGS: Pursuit, Houghton, 1966; *The Mystic Adventures of Roxie Stoner,* Houghton, 1974. Contributor of short stories to *New Yorker.*

WORK IN PROGRESS: Fornika Creek, the third book of the trilogy covered by the Houghton Mifflin fellowship awards; short stories.

AVOCATIONAL INTERESTS: Farming.

BIOGRAPHICAL/CRITICAL SOURCES: New Orleans Courier, December 12, 1973.

* * *

MORGAN, John A(ndrew), Jr. 1935-

PERSONAL: Born May 26, 1935, in Cary, N.C.; son of John Andrew (a clergyman) and Elsie (Farthing) Morgan; married Anne Desautels, June 19, 1958; children: Vicki Anne, John Andrew III, Sarah Catherine. *Education:* Stetson University, B.A. (magna cum laude), 1957; Duke University, M.A., 1959, Ph.D., 1963. *Home:* 8802 Parliament Dr., Springfield, Va. 22151. *Office:* Department of Political Science, George Washington University, Washington, D.C. 20006.

CAREER: United States Commission on Civil Rights, Washington, D.C., social science analyst, 1959; University of Southwestern Louisiana, Lafayette, instructor in political science, 1960-62; Duke University, Durham, N.C., instructor in political science, 1962-64; George Washington University, Washington, D.C., assistant professor, 1964-68, associate professor of political science, 1968—, director of undergraduate studies in department of political science, 1970—, acting head of department, 1973. Consultant to Charles E. Merrill Publishing Co., 1966-70, and National Institute of Mental Health, 1971—; lecturer at Washington International Center, 1968—. *Member:* American Political Science Association, Academy of Political Science, Law and Society Association, Southern Political Science Association. *Awards, honors:* Woodrow Wilson fellowship, 1957.

WRITINGS: (With Robert H. Connery and others) *The Politics of Mental Health,* Columbia University Press, 1968; (contributor) Carl Beck, editor, *Law and Justice,* Duke University Press, 1970; (contributor) Stephen J. Wayne, editor, *Investigating the American Political System: Problems, Methods, and Projects,* Schenkman, 1973; (contributor) Saul Feldman, editor, *The Administration of Mental Health Services,* C. C Thomas, 1973. Contributor to *Labor Law Journal* and *University of Pittsburgh Law Review.*

MORGAN, Judith A(dams) 1939-
(Jinx Kragen)

PERSONAL: Born June 9, 1939, in Napa, Calif.; daughter of John Quincy (a builder) and Gail (King) Adams; married W. Jefferson Morgan (a writer), March 26, 1971. *Education:* Stanford University, A.B., 1961; graduate study, San Francisco State University, 1961, Harvard University, 1971-72. *Home:* 5301 Broadway Terrace, Oakland, Calif. 94618. *Agent:* (Literary) Carl Brandt, 101 Park Ave., New York, N.Y. 10017; (screen) B. Franklin Kamsler, H. N. Swanson Inc., 8523 Sunset Blvd., Los Angeles, Calif. 90069.

CAREER: Editorial assistant on University of California alumni magazine, 1962; Kragen/Carroll, Inc. (a public relations firm handling entertainers such as the Smothers Brothers and Mason Williams), Beverly Hills, Calif., secretary and copywriter, 1963-64, creative director, 1964-69; free-lance writer, 1969—.

WRITINGS—All under name Jinx Kragen: (With Judy Perry) *Saucepans and the Single Girl* (serialized in five issues of *Ladies Home Journal),* Doubleday, 1965; (with Perry) *The How to Keep Him (After You've Caught Him) Cookbook* (condensed version published in *Ladies Home Journal*), Doubleday, 1968; (with Mason Williams) *Pat Paulsen for President,* Doubleday, 1968.

Author of teleplays for "The Smothers Brothers Show," 1966, and "That Girl," 1969. Also author of scripts for television pilots, and a film script, "The Crookedest Street in the World," 1972.

WORK IN PROGRESS: The Golden Door Cookbook; two novels, *The Meeting,* and one as yet untitled.

SIDELIGHTS: Mrs. Morgan has traveled to almost all the countries of Europe, to the Caribbean, the Philippines, Asian countries, Australia, and the South Sea Islands.

* * *

MORGAN, Marabel 1937-

PERSONAL: Born June 25, 1937, in Crestline, Ohio; daughter of Howard and Delsa (Smith) Hawk; married Charles O. Morgan, Jr. (an attorney), June 25, 1964; children: Laura Lynn, Michelle Rene. *Education:* Attended Ohio State University, 1959-60. *Home:* 790 Lake Rd., Bay Pt., Miami, Fla. 33137. *Agent:* Charles O. Morgan, Jr., 1300 Northwest 167th St., Miami, Fla. 33169. *Office:* Total Woman, Inc., 1300 Northwest 167th St., Miami, Fla. 33169.

CAREER: Total Woman, Inc., Miami, Fla., president, 1970—.

WRITINGS: The Total Woman, Revell, 1973.

* * *

MORRIS, Richard B(randon) 1904-

PERSONAL: Born July 24, 1904, in New York, N.Y.; son of Jacob and Tillie (Rosenberg) Morris; married Berenice Robinson (a composer of music), 1932; children: Jeffrey Brandon, Donald Robinson. *Education:* City College (now City College of the City University of New York), A.B. (cum laude), 1924; Columbia University, M.A., 1925, Ph.D., 1930. *Home:* 151 Ridgeway St., Mount Vernon, N.Y. 10552. *Office:* Department of History, Columbia University, 605 Fayerweather, New York, N.Y. 10027.

CAREER: City College (now City College of the City University of New York), New York, N.Y., instructor, 1927-32, assistant professor, 1932-37, associate professor, 1937-47, professor of history, 1947-49; Columbia University, New York, N.Y., visiting professor, 1946-49, professor of history, 1949-59, Gouverneur Morris Professor of History, 1959-73, professor emeritus and special lecturer, 1973—, chairman of department, 1958-61. Visiting professor, Princeton University, 1947-48; member of Institute for Advanced Study, 1948; visiting professor, University of Hawaii, 1957; Bacon Lecturer, Boston University, and Anson G. Phelps Lecturer, New York University, 1965-66; Distinguished Professor, Free University of Berlin, 1969; Paley Lecturer, Hebrew University, 1969; Truman Foundation lecturer, 1970. Regional director, Survey of Federal Archives, 1936-37; chairman of New York City Task Force on Municipal Archives, 1967—; member of American Revolution Bicentennial Commission, 1967-69.

MEMBER: American Historical Association, Organization of American Historians, Society of American Archivists, American Society for Legal History, American Society for Labor History (chairman of board of directors), Phi Beta Kappa. *Awards, honors:* Joint award from Colonial Dames of America and National Society of Colonial Dames of New York, 1930, for *Studies in the History of American Law;* Guggenheim fellowships, 1947-48, 1961-62; Townsend Harris medal from College of the City of New York, 1959; Fulbright research scholar, University of Paris, 1961-62; L.H.D. from Hebrew Union College, 1963; Bancroft Prize from Columbia University, 1966, for *The Peacemakers: The Great Powers and American Independence.*

WRITINGS: (With Evarts Boutell Greene) *A Guide to the Principal Sources for Early American History (1600-1800) in the City of New York,* Columbia University Press, 1929, 2nd edition, revised by Morris, 1953.

Studies in the History of American Law, with Special Reference to the Seventeenth and Eighteenth Centuries, Columbia University Press, 1930, 2nd edition, J. M. Mitchell, 1958; *Historiography of America, 1600-1800, as Represented in the Publications of Columbia University Press,* Columbia University Press, 1933.

Early American Court Records: A Publication Program, New York University School of Law, 1941; *Government and Labor in Early America,* Columbia University Press, 1946, reissued, Octagon, 1965.

Fair Trial: Fourteen Who Stood Accused, from Anne Hutchinson to Alger Hiss, Knopf, 1952, revised edition, Harper, 1967; *The American Revolution: A Short History,* Van Nostrand, 1955.

(Author of postscript) *The Autobiography of Benjamin Franklin,* Washington Square Press, 1960; *Great Presidential Decisions: State Papers that Changed the Course of History,* Lippincott, 1960, revised edition, Harper, 1973; (author of introduction) Francis Scott Key, *The First Book Edition of the Star-Spangled Banner,* F. Watts, 1961; (with editors of *Life*) *The New World: Prehistory to 1774,* Time, 1963; (with editors of *Life*) *The Making of a Nation: 1775-1789,* Time, 1963; (author of introduction) Henry Laurens, *A Letter from Henry Laurens to His Son, John Laurens, August 14, 1776,* Columbia University Libraries, 1964; *Government and Labor in Early America,* Harper Torchbooks, 1965; *The Peacemakers: The Great Powers and American Independence,* Harper, 1965; *John Jay, the Nation, and the Court,* Boston University Press, 1967; *The American Revolution Reconsidered,* Harper, 1967; (contributor) Harold M. Hyman and Leonard W. Levy,

Freedom and Reform: Essays in Honor of Henry Steele Commager, Harper, 1967; (with William Greenleaf) *U.S.A.: The History of a Nation,* two volumes, Rand McNally, 1969.

The Emerging Nations and the American Revolution, Harper, 1970; (with William Greenleaf and Robert H. Ferrell) *America: A History of the People,* Rand McNally, 1971; *Seven Who Shaped Our Destiny: The Founding Fathers as Revolutionaries,* Harper, 1973.

Editor: *The Era of the American Revolution: Studies Inscribed to Evarts Boutell Greene,* Columbia University Press, 1939, reissued, Peter Smith, 1971.

(With Louis Leo Snyder) *A Treasury of Great Reporting: "Literature under Pressure" from the Sixteenth Century to Our Own Time,* Simon & Schuster, 1949, 2nd edition, 1962.

(With Snyder) *They Saw It Happen: Eyewitness Reports of Great Events,* Stackpole, 1951; *Encyclopedia of American History,* Harper, 1953, new edition with Henry Steele Commager and others, 1970; *Basic Documents in American History,* Van Nostrand, 1956, revised edition, 1965; *The Basic Ideas of Alexander Hamilton,* Pocket Books, 1957, reissued, Washington Square Press, 1965; *Alexander Hamilton and the Founding of the Nation,* Dial, 1957, reissued, Harper, 1969; (with Henry Steele Commager) *The Spirit of 'Seventy-Six: The Story of the American Revolution as Told by Participants,* two volumes, Bobbs-Merrill, 1958.

(With James Woodress) *Voices from America's Past* (originally published in pamphlet form by Webster Publishing, 1961-62), Dutton, 1963, Volume I: *The Colonies and the New Nation,* Volume II: *Backwoods Democracy to World Power,* Volume III: *The Twentieth Century;* (with Commager) *Four Hundred Notable Americans* (originally published as biographical section of *Encyclopedia of American History*) Harper, 1965; *The Era of the American Revolution,* Harper, 1965; (and author of introduction and notes) George Otto Tevelyan, *The American Revolution,* revised edition (Morris was not associated with original edition), McKay, 1964; *Significant Documents in United States History,* two volumes, Van Nostrand, 1969.

George Dangerfield, *Defiance to the Old World: The Story behind the Monroe Doctrine,* Putnam, 1970; Alexander DeConde, *Decisions for Peace: The Federalist Era,* Putnam, 1970; (with Graham W. Irwin) *The Harper Encyclopedia of the Modern World: A Concise Reference History, from 1760 to the Present,* Harper, 1970 (published in England as *An Encyclopaedia of the Modern World: A Concise Reference History from 1760 to the Present,* Weidenfeld & Nicolson, 1970); *The American Revolution, 1763-1783: A Bicentennial Collection,* Harper, 1970; *Basic Documents on the Confederation and Constitution,* Van Nostrand, 1970; (and author of introduction) *Labor and Management in Conflict,* Arno, 1972; *John Jay Papers Project,* Volume I, Harper, in press.

Also author of children's books published by F. Watts: *The First Book of the American Revolution,* 1956; *The First Book of the Constitution,* 1958; *. . . of the Indian Wars,* 1959; *. . . of the War of 1812,* 1961; *. . . of the Founding of the Republic,* 1968.

Editor with Henry Steele Commager of "New American Nations" series, Harper, 1954—. Contributor to journals. Member of editorial board, *American Journal of Legal History.*

SIDELIGHTS: The Peacemakers, winner of the Bancroft Prize, was called by S. F. Bemis, "a model study of diplomatic history, executed with great sophistication and a profound knowledge of the intricacies of European international politics. Morris deals skillfully and at length with the central problem of the American peace commissioners, Benjamin Franklin, John Jay, and John Adams . . . Concerned with men as well as with measures, Professor Morris provides matchless descriptions . . . superbly portraying the diplomatic personalities involved. . . ." Alexander De Conde commented: "Written in graceful and often charming prose, this book tells a great story with a sure grasp of the big issues and a sensitive appreciation of the small, essential details . . . Historians will undoubtedly dispute some of Morris's views in small matters. Yet in my judgment this is a superb narrative history . . . not only one of the finest American histories it has been my pleasure to read, but also one of the best on the general subject of peacemaking in any language or period."

"For Morris," wrote Jack P. Greene, " . . . the American Revolution is relevant to the modern world not because it was similar in process and pattern to the great European revolutions—though he does note many common characteristics between the origins of the American Revolution and those of the French Revolution—but because it 'heralded the end of parochial colonialism and the fulfillment of nationhood.' The first of many anti-imperial wars for independence, the Revolution, like its modern counterparts, 'quickly burgeoned into a broader movement of national self-determination, constitutional recreation, and social and intellectual liberation,' and what 'gives it a peculiar pertinence to our own day,' Morris contends, are the lessons it provides 'in how to achieve decolonization and how to move forward from colonial subordination to equality among states.'" According to Ramon Powers, "Morris' thesis is that the American Revolution, and not the French, has always been the great beacon of human progress . . . [and] continues to exert an influence as a living phenomenon. . . . Morris presents a concise and intelligent analysis. . . . His approach is stimulating. . . . Yet, Morris' work is far from being a Whitmanesque idealization of everything American and democratic."

Reviewers have hailed *The Harper Encyclopedia of the Modern World,* which Morris edited as "a formidable task of abbreviation, which has been done with skill, lucidity, and accuracy," and "the clarity of detail is also remarkable." "The main historical coverage of all world areas during the past 200 years, broken down into assimilable morsels, constitutes a remarkably detailed sequence of highlights and overtones, readable as narrative and . . . easy to consult."

BIOGRAPHICAL/CRITICAL SOURCES: Alden T. Vaughan and George Athan Billias, editors, *Perspectives on Early American History: Essays in Honor of Richard B. Morris,* Harper, 1973.

Virginia Quarterly Review, summer, 1967.

* * *

MORRIS, Robert A(da) 1933-

PERSONAL: Born November 15, 1933, in Charlottesville, Va.; son of Charles Everett and Amy (Ada) Morris; married Sally Ward Warburton (a secretary), October 18, 1962; children: Everett Ashley. *Education:* University of Delaware, B.A., 1958; University of Hawaii, M.S., 1966; State University of New York Veterinary College at Cornell University, candidate for D.V.M., 1970—. *Home:* 1489 Coddington Rd., Brooktondale, N.Y. 14817.

CAREER: Waikiki Aquarium, Honolulu, Hawaii, assistant director, 1963-65; Marineland of Florida, St. Augustine, curator, 1965-66; New York Aquarium, New York, N.Y., curator, 1966-70. Leader of New York Aquarium expeditions to collect white whales in Hudson Bay, 1967, and first narwhale from above Arctic Circle, 1969; underwater diver. *Military service:* U.S. Navy, 1952-54. *Member:* International Association for Aquatic Animal Medicine, Explorers Club (New York). *Awards, honors: Seahorse* was selected as a Children's Book Showcase title, 1973.

WRITINGS: Seahorse (juvenile), Harper, 1972; (author of introduction) Reginald Dutta, *Tropical Fish,* Octopus Books, 1971. Contributor of scientific and popular articles to periodicals, including *Animal Kingdom, Pacific Science, Norwegian Whaling Gazette,* and *Tropical Fish Hobbyist.*

WORK IN PROGRESS: A book on dolphins for Harper's "Science I Can Read" series; a juvenile book on sharks.

* * *

MORRISON, Eleanor S(helton) 1921-

PERSONAL: Born May 21, 1921, in Stonega, Va.; daughter of Floyd Bunyan (a clergyman) and Nelle (Hines) Shelton; married Truman Aldrich Morrison, Jr. (a clergyman), August 22, 1942; children: Truman III, Melanie, Wendy, Stephanie. *Education:* Wesleyan College, B.A., 1941; Northwestern University, M.A., 1942. *Religion:* United Church of Christ. *Home:* 120 Oakland Dr., East Lansing, Mich. 48823. *Office:* College of Human Ecology, Michigan State University, East Lansing, Mich. 48824.

CAREER: Michigan State University, College of Human Ecology, East Lansing, instructor in family studies, 1967—. Chairman of United Nations Day, 1964-66. *Member:* Young Women's Christian Association (member of board of directors of local chapter, 1960), League of Women Voters (member of board of directors of local chapter, 1955-65), Child Study Association, National Council of Family Relations, American Association of Sex Educators and Counselors, Association for Creative Change in Religion and Other Systems. *Awards, honors:* D.Litt., Chicago Theological Seminary, 1965.

WRITINGS: (With Virgil Foster) *Creative Teaching in the Church,* Prentice-Hall, 1963; (with husband, Truman Morrison) *Growing Up in the Family,* United Church Press, 1964; (editor) *Human Sexuality: Contemporary Perspectives,* National Press Books, 1973; (with Mila Price) *Values in Sexuality,* Hart Publishing, 1974.

* * *

MORRISSEY, L(eroy) J(ohn) 1935-

PERSONAL: Born April 26, 1935, in Brainard, Neb.; son of Edward James and Edith (Stuchlick) Morrissey; married Alverta Strickland, July 11, 1959; children: Timothy, Kathleen, Sean. *Education:* University of Nebraska, B.A., 1958; University of Chicago, M.A., 1959; University of Pennsylvania, Ph.D., 1964. *Home:* 328 Saskatchewan Crescent W., Saskatoon, Saskatchewan, Canada. *Office:* Department of English, University of Saskatchewan, Saskatoon, Saskatchewan, Canada.

CAREER: Pennsylvania State University, University Park, instructor in English, 1959-60; Dickinson College, Carlisle, Pa., instructor in English, 1963-65; University of Western Ontario, London, assistant professor of English, 1965-69; University of Saskatchewan, Saskatoon, associate professor of Restoration and eighteenth-century literature, 1969—. *Member:* Society for Eighteenth-Century Studies (Canada; member of executive board, 1971—), Society for Eighteenth-Century Studies (United States), Modern Language Association of America, Phi Beta Kappa.

WRITINGS: (Editor and author of notes) Henry Fielding, *Tom Thumb, or The Tragedy of Tragedies,* University of California Press, 1970; (editor and author of notes) Fielding, *Grub Street Opera,* Oliver & Boyd, 1974. Contributor to journals in his field.

* * *

MORSE, Wayne (Lyman) 1900-1974

October 20, 1900—July 22, 1974; American politician, former United States senator. Obituaries: *New York Times,* July 23, 1974; *Washington Post,* July 27, 1974; *Time,* August 5, 1974; *Newsweek,* August 5, 1974.

* * *

MORTIMORE, Olive 1890-

PERSONAL: Born August 27, 1890, in Wirt, Iowa; daughter of Orlin Bissell (a minister) and Mary Elizabeth (Moffet) Thomas; married Morris E. Mortimore, June 10, 1917; children: Thomas N., James E. *Education:* Attended Graceland College, 1909-11; State University of Iowa, B.A., 1913. *Politics:* Democrat. *Religion:* Reorganized Church of Jesus Christ of Latter Day Saints. *Residence:* Lamoni, Iowa.

CAREER: Teacher of English and German in the public schools of Lamoni, Iowa, 1913-14, 1943-45, and Reosauqua, Iowa, 1914-16; Graceland College, Lamoni, Iowa, instructor in English, 1916-17, 1946-55.

WRITINGS: Out of Abundance, Herald House, 1971.

* * *

MORTON, Miriam 1918-

PERSONAL: Born June 14, 1918, in Kishinev, Russia; daughter of Efim and Sara (Rielberg) Bidner; married Lewis Morton (an editor and writer), April 24, 1937; children: two daughters. *Education:* New York University, B.S., 1942. *Home:* 61 Stockton Rd., Kendall Park, N.J. 08824.

CAREER: Author, translator and book editor. Has worked as a social worker and nursery school teacher. *Awards, honors:* Special citation award from Children's Theater Association, 1973, for *The Arts and the Soviet Child;* Newark College of Engineering author award, 1974, for *The Moon Is Like a Silver Sickle.*

WRITINGS: (Editor and translator) Kornei Chukovsky, *From Two to Five,* University of California Press, 1963; (editor and translator) *A Harvest of Russian Children's Literature,* University of California Press, 1967; (editor, translator, and author of introduction) Mikhail Sholokhov, *Fierce and Gentle Warriors* (for young readers), Doubleday, 1967; (translator and author of introduction) Semyon Rosenfeld, *The First Song* (for young readers), Doubleday, 1968; (editor, translator, and author of introduction) Anton Chekhov, *Shadows and Light* (for young readers), Doubleday, 1969; (editor, translator, and author of afterword) *Twenty-Two Tales for Young Children by Leo Tolstoy,* Simon & Schuster, 1969.

The Arts and the Soviet Child: The Esthetic Education of Children in the U.S.S.R., Free Press, 1972; *Pleasures and Palaces: The After-School Activities of Soviet Children* (for young people), Atheneum, 1972; (editor and translator) *The Moon Is Like a Silver Sickle: A Celebration of Poetry by Soviet Children,* Simon & Schuster, 1972; (translator) Samuel Marshak, *Zoo Babies* (poems for young people), Ginn, 1973; *The Making of Champions: Sports in the Soviet Union,* Atheneum, 1974; *Said the Raccoon to the Moon* (for young people), Ginn, 1974.

Translator from the French: Colette Vivier, *The House of the Four Winds* (a documentary novel for children), Doubleday, 1969; (editor and author of introduction) *Voices from France: Ten Stories by French Nobel Laureates in Literature* (for young readers), Doubleday, 1969; (editor and author of introduction) *Fifteen by Maupassant* (stories for young people), Doubleday, 1972. Contributor to Claremont Reading Conference *Yearbook,* 1972. Contributor to magazines, including *Horn Book* and *Parent-Teacher Association.*

WORK IN PROGRESS: The Russian Woman: A Social History; Love Lyrics by Soviet Women Poets; for young readers, *The Union of Soviet Socialist Republics: A Concise History.*

SIDELIGHTS: Miriam Morton writes: "The central motivation for my work is to make available to American young readers translations from the outstanding humanistic literature published in Russia and in France. A second motivation is to reveal the basic elements in Soviet child and youth culture in my writings for young readers and for American educators."

* * *

MORTON, R(obert) S(teel) 1917-

PERSONAL: Born July 5, 1917, in Glasgow, Scotland; son of Robert Barber (a clerk) and Agnes Watt (Steel) Morton; married Hilda Megan Cogbill (a social worker), January 10, 1945; children: Robert Andrew, Colin Angus Graham. *Education:* Anderson College of Medicine, L.R.C.P., L.R.C.S., L.R.F.P.S., all 1939. *Politics:* None. *Religion:* None. *Home:* 9 Cortworth Rd., Sheffield S119LN, England. *Office:* Royal Infirmary, Sheffield, England.

CAREER: Royal College of Physicians and Surgeons, Edinburgh, Scotland, member, 1953, fellow, 1962; venereologist in Newcastle-upon-Tyne, England, 1946-50; consultant venereologist in Manchester and East Cheshire, England, 1951-60; Area Health Authority, Royal Infirmary, Sheffield, England, consultant venereologist, 1960—. Clinical lecturer and tutor at University of Sheffield, 1960—. *Military service:* British Army, Royal Medical Corps, 1940-46; member of Order of British Empire (Military). *Member:* Royal College of Physicians (fellow), British Medical Association, Medical Society for the Study of Venereal Diseases (past president).

WRITINGS: Venereal Diseases, Penguin, 1966, 2nd edition, 1972; *Sexual Freedom and Venereal Diseases,* P. Owen, 1971; (with J. R. W. Harris) *Recent Advances in Sexually Transmitted Diseases,* Churchill Livingstone, 1974; *Venereal Diseases and Diseases Transmitted Sexually,* British Medical Association, 1974. Technical adviser for "Focus on Venereal Diseases," a film for British Broadcasting Corp.; member of editorial committee of *British Journal of Venereal Diseases.*

* * *

MOSEL, Arlene (Tichy) 1921-

PERSONAL: Surname is pronounced Mo-*zel;* born August 27, 1921, in Cleveland, Ohio; daughter of Edward J. (an engraver) and Marie (Fingulin) Tichy; married Victor H. Mosel (a sales engineer), December 26, 1942; children: Nancy Mosel Farrar, Joanne, James. *Education:* Ohio Wesleyan University, B.A., 1942; Western Reserve University (now Case Western Reserve University), M.S.L.S., 1959. *Religion:* Lutheran. *Home:* 3343 Braemar Rd., Shaker Heights, Ohio 44120.

CAREER: Former assistant in children's department at Enoch Pratt Free Library, Baltimore, Md.; now associate professor of library science at Case Western Reserve University, Cleveland, Ohio. Assistant coordinator of Children's Services, Cuyahoga County Public Library. *Awards, honors: Tikki Tikki Tembo* was an American Library Association Notable Book, 1968; *The Funny Little Woman* was an Honor Book in Hans Christian Andersen International Children's Book Awards, 1974, an American Library Association Notable Book, and a Horn Book honor list selection.

WRITINGS: Tikki Tikki Tembo (retold), Holt, 1968; *The Funny Little Woman* (retold), Dutton, 1972.

* * *

MOSELEY, George (V. H. III) 1931-

PERSONAL: Born September 6, 1931, in West Point, N.Y.; son of George V. H., Jr. (a U.S. Army career soldier) and Katharine (Payne) Moseley; married Eva Steiner, February 28, 1958; children: Alice Jessica, Thomas Evan. *Education:* University of Colorado, B.A., 1954; Yale University, M.A., 1960; St. Antony's College, Oxford, D.Phil., 1970. *Office:* Department of History, George Mason University, Fairfax, Va. 22030.

CAREER: University of London, School of Oriental and African Studies, London, England, fellow, 1964-65; Goddard College, Plainfield, Vt., instructor in history, 1968-70; Tufts University, Medford, Mass., assistant professor of history, 1970-72; George Mason University, Fairfax, Va., associate professor of history, 1972—. *Military service:* U.S. Army, 1954-56; became first lieutenant.

WRITINGS: A Sino-Soviet Cultural Frontier: The Ili Kazakh Autonomous Chou, Harvard University Press, 1966; *The Party and the National Question in China,* M.I.T. Press, 1966; *China: From Empire to People's Republic,* Batsford, 1968, published as *China Since 1911,* Harper, 1969; (contributor) Jack Gray, editor, *Modern China's Search for a Political Form,* Oxford University Press, 1969; *The Consolidation of the South China Frontier,* University of California Press, 1973. Contributor to *Pacific Affairs, China Quarterly, New Leader,* and *Far Eastern Economic Review.*

WORK IN PROGRESS: Research on Japanese policies in Micronesia.

SIDELIGHTS: Moseley lived in China as a child, in Japan as a student, in Indochina as a soldier, in Macao as a welfare worker, and in Hong Kong as a researcher. He is interested in the increasing impact of China and Japan on American society and on American ideas.

* * *

MOSEY, Anne Cronin 1938-

PERSONAL: Born March 29, 1938, in Minneapolis, Minn.; daughter of Carlton R. (an investment banker) and Dorothy (Leonard) Cronin; married Jeremy Todd Mosey (a photographic editor), October 9, 1964; children: Charles. *Education:* University of Minnesota, B.S. (with high distinction), 1961; New York University, M.A., 1965, Ph.D., 1968. *Home:* 2 Washington Square Village, Apt. 15-0, New York, N.Y. 10012. *Office:* Division of Health, New York University, 101 Barney Building, Washington Sq., New York, N.Y. 10003.

CAREER: Glenwood Hills Hospital, Minneapolis, Minn., staff therapist, 1961; New York State Psychiatric Institute, New York, N.Y., staff therapist, 1961-66; Columbia University, New York, N.Y., instructor in occupational therapy, 1966-68; New York University, New York, N.Y., assistant professor, 1968-72, associate professor of occupational therapy, 1972—, director of department, 1972—. Leader of workshops and seminars. *Member:* American Occupational Therapy Association (fellow; member of council on education), New York State Occupational Therapy Association (vice-chairman of Metropolitan New York district, 1968-69; member of board of directors, 1971-73, 1974-75), Metropolitan New York Committee of Occupational Therapy Program Directors (chairman, 1974—), Pi Lambda Theta.

WRITINGS: Occupational Therapy: Theory and Practice, privately printed, 1968; *Three Frames of Reference for Mental Health,* Charles B. Slack, 1970; *Activities Therapy,* Raven Press, 1974. Contributor to *America* Journal of Occupational Therapy.

WORK IN PROGRESS: Revising *Three Frames of Reference for Mental Health.*

* * *

MOSS, Bobby Gilmer 1932-

PERSONAL: Born May 20, 1932, in Blacksburg, S.C.; son of George Gilmer and Mable (Batchelor) Moss; married Catherine Bowen (a librarian), August 7, 1954; children: Nina Marie. *Education:* Mars Hill College, A.A., 1952; Wake Forest College, B.A., 1954; Southern Baptist Theological Seminary, B.D., 1957; University of Virginia, M.A., 1965; Tulane University, graduate study, 1966. *Home address:* Route 1, Box 232C, Blacksburg, S.C. 29702. *Office address:* Department of History, Limestone College, Box 65, Gaffney, S.C. 29340.

CAREER: Ordained minister of the Baptist Church, 1957; minister in Orange, Va., 1957-60; Fork Union Military Academy, Fork Union, Va., head of social studies division, 1960-65; Limestone College, Gaffney, S.C., assistant professor, 1965-68, associate professor of history, 1968—. Cherokee Historical and Preservation Society, Gaffney, founder, 1969, trustee, 1969—. *Member:* Southern Historical Association, South Carolina Historical Society, University South Caroliniana Society.

WRITINGS: (With Ronald G. Killion) *The Journal of Michael Gaffney: From Ireland to the Backwoods of South Carolina,* Pushmahataw Press, 1971; *The Old Iron District: A Study of the Development of Cherokee County, 1750-1897,* Jacobs Press, 1972; *A Voice in the Wilderness: A History of Buffalo Baptist Church,* Pushmahataw Press, 1972. Contributor to proceedings; contributor to *Sandlapper,* and to *Names and Places in South Carolina.*

WORK IN PROGRESS: Research on the American revolution in South Carolina.

AVOCATIONAL INTERESTS: Beekeeping.

MOSS, Norman 1928-

PERSONAL: Born September 30, 1928, in London, England; son of Benjamin and Lydia Moss; married Hilary Sesta (an actress); children: Paul, Antony. *Education:* Hamilton College, Clinton, N.Y., student, 1946-47. *Home:* 21 Rylett Crescent, London W.12, England. *Agent:* Collins-Knowlton-Wing, Inc., 60 East 56th St., New York, N.Y. 10022.

CAREER: Reporter and copy editor for Reuter's, 1952-56; Associated Press, London Bureau, London, England, reporter and copy editor, 1956-59; foreign correspondent, Radio Press International, 1962-65; *Sunday Times,* London, England, reporter, 1965-66; chief European correspondent, Metromedia Radio News, 1968-72; writer and broadcaster in London, 1972—.

WRITINGS: Men Who Play God: The Story of the Hydrogen Bomb and How the World Came to Live with It, Harper, 1968; *What's the Difference?: A British-American Dictionary,* Harper, 1973. Contributor to British and American magazines.

SIDELIGHTS: The widely-reviewed *Men Who Play God,* described in *The New Yorker* as a "detailed and brilliant account of how the hydrogen bomb was made and what its presence has done to transform our lives," is, according to Donald M. Kaplan, "an extraordinarily good book, finely written with a sustained, passionate intelligence. There is no question in my mind that it will belong to that valiant (and curiously meager) literature on the Bomb. . . ."

Robert Jay Lifton commented on "the basic humanism of Moss's nuclear common sense," continuing, "He speaks, for instance, of an 'almost instinctual value judgment. . . that there are some things men must not poison for any gain; that we live on this planet not as possessors, but as tenants and trustees; that we may have obligations towards the human race that go beyond our immediate acquaintance with it or our immediate concerns; that there are things before which we should be humble.' "

BIOGRAPHICAL/CRITICAL SOURCES: Saturday Review, July 5, 1969.

* * *

MOSS, (Victor) Peter (Cannings) 1921-

PERSONAL: Born March 12, 1921, in Marlborough, England; son of Frederick James (a saddler) and Olive (Cannings) Moss; married Joan Holland, October 3, 1948; children: Melanie Joan, Peter Jonathan. *Education:* Attended schools in Marlborough, England. *Home:* Brook Cottage, Ripe, Near Lewes, Sussex, England. *Agent:* Mark Paterson, 42 Canonbury Square, London N.1., England.

CAREER: Schoolmaster and lecturer in further education; currently full-time writer. *Military service:* Royal Air Force, Technical Branch, 1940-46; became flying officer; served in Middle East and India.

WRITINGS—All for young people: *Our Own Homes through the Ages,* Harrap, 1958; *Meals through the Ages,* Harrap, 1960; *Sports and Pastimes through the Ages,* Harrap, 1962, Arco, 1963; *Tombstone Treasure* (novel), Nelson, 1965; *Hermit's Hoard* (novel), Nelson, 1965; *History Alive,* five volumes, Blond Educational, 1967-71; *Today's English,* five volumes, J. Murray, 1968; *Town Life through the Ages,* Harrap, 1972; *The Media,* Harrap, 1974; *Medicine and Morality,* Harrap, 1974; *Crime and Punishment,* Harrap, 1974; *World History since 1900,* Blond Educational, 1974. Author of scripts for BBC Overseas service.

WORK IN PROGRESS: History in the Round, a primary history series for Holmes-McDougall; *Magic and the Supernatural, Censorship and Selection,* and *Prejudice,* all for Harrap.

* * *

MOSS, Rose 1937- (R. Johannes)

PERSONAL: Born January 2, 1937, in Johannesburg, South Africa; daughter of David and Yetta (Eides) Rappoport; married Stanley Moss (a city planner), April 30, 1964; children: Duncan John. *Education:* University of the Witwatersrand, B.A., 1956; University of Natal, B.A. (honours; cum laude), 1959. *Home:* 580 Walnut St., Newtonville, Mass. 02160. *Agent:* Russell & Volkening, Inc., 551 Fifth Ave., New York, N.Y. 10017. *Office:* Department of English, Wellesley College, Wellesley, Mass. 02181.

CAREER: University College of Pius XII, Basutoland, South Africa, lecturer in English, 1957; teacher in girls' high school in Pietermaritzburg, Natal, 1958; University of Natal, Pietermaritzburg and Durban, lecturer in English, 1960; University of South Africa, Pretoria, lecturer in English, 1961-63; Cambridge Center for Adult Education, Cambridge, Mass., lecturer, 1967-69, summer, 1972; University of Massachusetts, Boston, instructor, 1968-69; Wellesley College, Wellesley, Mass., part-time lecturer in English, 1972—. Has worked as governess and librarian; editorial reader for Beacon Press, 1967-69, and for Funk & Wagnalls and Harvard University Press, 1967—. *Awards, honors:* Quill Prize for fiction from *Massachusetts Review,* 1971; work is listed in Roll of Honor, *Best American Short Stories, 1971,* published by Houghton.

WRITINGS: The Family Reunion (novel), Scribner, 1974; *The Terrorist* (novel), Scribner, 1975. Author of one-act play, "Prometheus," produced in Johannesburg, 1953. Contributor of about twenty-five poems, short stories, and articles to periodicals and journals, including *Shenandoah, Antioch Review* (including one short story under pseudonym R. Johannes), *Massachusetts Review, English Studies in Africa, Lumen,* and *New Voices.*

WORK IN PROGRESS: A third novel; short stories; a children's story.

* * *

MOST, William G(eorge) 1914-

PERSONAL: Born August 13, 1914, in Dubuque, Iowa; son of George Henry (a businessman) and Mary C. (Fay) Most. *Education:* Loras College, A.B., 1936; Sulpician Seminary, Washington, D.C., seminarian, 1936-40; Catholic University of America, M.A., 1940, Ph.D., 1946. *Home and office:* Loras College, Dubuque, Iowa 52001.

CAREER: Ordained Roman Catholic diocesan priest; Loras College, Dubuque, Iowa, member of faculty, 1940-47, associate professor, 1947-62, professor of classics, 1962—. Member of classics faculty at Catholic University of America Midwest Branch, Dubuque, summers, 1948-51, 1954-63. *Member:* American Philological Association, Catholic Biblical Association, Catholic Theological Society of America, Mariological Society of America (president, 1967-68), Pontifical International Marian Academy (Rome). *Awards, honors:* Mariological Award of Mariological Society of America, 1961; Marian Medal of Marian Library, University of Dayton, 1955, for *Mary in Our Life.*

WRITINGS: The Syntax of the Vitae Sanctorum Hiberniae (doctoral dissertation), Catholic University of America Press, 1946; (editor, and author of notes and glossary) *St. Augustine's "De Civitate Dei"* (selections as college text), Catholic Education Press, 1949, revised edition, 1956; *Mary in Our Life,* Kenedy, 1954; *Latin by the Natural Method,* Regnery, Books I-II, 1957, Book III, 1961, pattern practice tapes, 1960; *Novum Tentamen ad Solutionem de Gratia et Praedestinatione,* St. Paul Editions (Rome), 1963, translation by the author published as *New Answers to Old Questions,* St. Paul Editions (London), 1971. Contributor to *New Catholic Encyclopedia, Encyclopedia Americana, Catholic Encyclopedia for Home and School;* contributor of articles in classical area and in area of scripture and theology to journals. Writer of regular theology column, "Escape from Confusion," in *National Catholic Register.*

WORK IN PROGRESS: St. Augustine; *Catholic and Manichean Morality,* a translation of and commentary on St. Augustine's *De Moribus Ecclesiae Catholicae et de Moribus Manichaeorum; Vatican II: Marian Council,* for Alba House (Athlone, Ireland); *Covenant and Redemption,* also for Alba House; studies on the technique of "focusing" in St. Paul and on the psychology of grace.

SIDELIGHTS: Most says that his Latin textbooks were an attempt to radically change the methods of teaching. "Met with some success," he comments, "with 50,000 copies of the first-year book sold. Latin almost collapsed now." In addition to Latin, he reads Greek, Hebrew, French, German, Italian, Spanish, and Portuguese. His book, *Mary in Our Life,* has been published in Ireland, India, and England, and translated into Japanese, Chinese, Italian, Malayalam, and Tamil.

* * *

MUELLER, Klaus Andrew 1921-

PERSONAL: Born June 17, 1921, in Leipzig, Germany; came to United States in 1938; naturalized U.S. citizen, 1944; son of Hans Alexander (a professor) and Maria (Riethof) Mueller; married Beverly Winter Drew, January 8, 1944; children: Dorian, Claudia, Hilary, Drew. *Education:* Columbia University, B.A., 1948, M.A., 1949; graduate study at New York University, 1949-51, and Stanford University, 1951-52. *Home:* 1205 Upper Happy Valley Rd., Lafayette, Calif. 94549. *Office:* Department of German, University of California, Berkeley, Calif. 94720.

CAREER: Bard College, Annandale-on-Hudson, N.Y., instructor, 1943-44; instructor in German and European literature at Columbia University, New York, N.Y., 1946-49, and at Princeton University, Princeton, N.J., 1949-51; U.S. Army Language School, Monterey, Calif., professor of German and chairman of department, 1951-56, professor and director of Romance and Germanic languages, 1957-60; Associated Colleges of the Midwest, Beloit College, Beloit, Wis., coordinator of language instruction programs, 1960-64; California State Department of Education, principal investigator in foreign language research project and coordinator of foreign language programs, 1964-65; University of California, Berkeley, senior lecturer in German, 1965—. Instructor, Colby-Swarthmore Summer School of Languages, 1949, 1950; lecturer, National Defense Education Act Summer Language Institutes, 1961, 1962; visiting professor, University of Colorado, 1966, University of Montana, 1967, University of Hawaii, 1969. General editor, Random House, 1960—, D. C. Heath, 1961-66. Consultant,

U.S. Office of Education, 1957—, Modern Language Association Foreign Language Research Center, 1958—; member of advisory council, Massachusetts Council for Public Schools, 1957—, Northeast Conference on Teaching Foreign Languages, 1960-62. *Military service:* U.S. Army, 1944-46.

MEMBER: American Council of Teachers of Foreign Languages, National Education Association, Association for Higher Education, Modern Language Association of America, Linguistic Society of America, Foreign Language Association of California (member of executive council, 1960-62).

WRITINGS: (With Alexander Burz) *Basic English Grammar and Workbook for Foreign Language Students,* U.S. Army Language School, 1951; (with others) *Basic German Course,* U.S. Army Language School, 1952-56; (with others) *Spanish for Secondary Schools: A Four-Level Sequence,* Heath, 1962—; (with others) *Common Concepts Foreign Language Test,* California Test Bureau, 1962; (with others) *French for Secondary Schools,* Heath, 1964; (with Aurelio M. Espinosa and Richard L. Franklin) *Spanish for Schools and Colleges,* four volumes, Heath, 1966; (with Espinosa and Franklin) *Cultura, conversacion y repaso,* Heath, 1967, 2nd edition published as *Cultura hispanica: temas para hablar y escribir,* 1972.

Director of "Elementary Foreign Language Series," Singer, 1965—. Contributor to journals.

* * *

MUENCHEN, Al(fred) 1917-

PERSONAL: Surname is pronounced *Munch*-en; born November 23, 1917, in Cincinnati, Ohio; son of Anton J. (a chef) and Anne (Daniel) Muenchen; married Juliet Ferry, July, 1941; married second wife, Prudence Peck, December, 1970; children: (first marriage) Juliet, Anita (Mrs. Tristram Miles). *Education:* Attended Carnegie-Mellon Institute, Chicago Art Institute, and Bauhaus School. *Politics:* Democrat. *Home and office:* 1070 Ridgefield Rd., Wilton, Conn. 06897. *Agent:* Knox Burger, 39½ Washington Sq. S., New York, N.Y.

CAREER: Illustrator for advertisements, magazines, and books. *Military service:* U.S. Army, 1943-45; received Bronze Star Medal. *Member:* Society of Illustrators, Explorers Club. *Awards, honors:* Awards for illustration.

WRITINGS: (illustrator) Stanley Hendricks, *Astronauts on the Moon,* Hallmark Editions, 1969; *Flying the Midnight Sun* (self-illustrated), McKay, 1972.

WORK IN PROGRESS: A novel on the mores of the 1930's and 1940's; research on Antarctica and on World War II.

* * *

MUHAJIR, El
See JACKMON, Marvin X.

* * *

MULLEN, Edward John, Jr. 1942-

PERSONAL: Born July 12, 1942, in Hackensack, N.J.; son of Edward John (an accountant) and Elsie (Powell) Mullen; married Helen Braley (a cellular immunologist), April 3, 1971. *Education:* West Virginia Wesleyan College, B.A. (magna cum laude), 1964; Northwestern University, M.A., 1965, Ph.D., 1968. *Home:* 1205 Frances Dr., Columbia, Mo. 65201. *Office:* Department of Romance Languages, University of Missouri, Columbia, Mo. 65201.

CAREER: Purdue University, Lafayette, Ind., assistant professor of modern languages, 1967-71; University of Missouri, Columbia, associate professor of Romance languages, 1971—. *Member:* American Association of Teachers of Spanish and Portuguese, Modern Language Association of America.

WRITINGS: *La Revista contemporaneos: Seleccion y prologo,* Editorial Anaya, 1972; *Encuentro: Ensayos de la actualidad,* Holt, 1974. Contributor of articles and reviews to language and drama journals.

WORK IN PROGRESS: *Carlos Pellicer,* for Twayne.

* * *

MUNCY, Raymond Lee 1928-

PERSONAL: Born June 26, 1928, in Eunice, W.Va.; son of John Dana and Flara (Dinges) Muncy; married Kathryn Eloise Griffin, June 3, 1948; children: David, Marcus, Kandace, Zachary. *Education:* Freed-Hardeman College, student, 1946-48; Indiana University, A.B., 1960, M.A., 1963; University of Mississippi, Ph.D., 1971. *Politics:* Independent. *Home:* 1002 North Hayes, Searcy, Ark. 72143. *Office:* Department of History, Harding College, Searcy, Ark. 72143.

CAREER: Church of Christ, Bloomington, Ind., minister, 1951-64; Harding College, Searcy, Ark., assistant professor, 1964-69, associate professor, 1969-73, professor of history, 1973—, chairman of department, 1965—. *Member:* American Historical Association, Association of American Historians, International Platform Association, Phi Alpha Theta, Exchange Club, Kiwanis Club. *Awards, honors:* Distinguished Professor award, Harding College, 1971.

WRITINGS: *Sex and Marriage in Utopian Communities: 19th Century America,* Indiana University Press, 1973. Contributor to denominational publications.

WORK IN PROGRESS: *Twentieth Century Communes in America.*

* * *

MUNGO, Raymond 1946-
(Dennis Lunar)

PERSONAL: Born February 21, 1946, in Lawrence, Mass.; son of Andrew J. (a laboratory technician) and Rita (La Fontaine) Mungo; married; children: Phoenix (son). *Education:* Boston University, B.A., 1967; Harvard University, graduate study, 1967-68. *Politics:* None. *Religion:* None. *Office:* Montana Books, Inc., 1716 North 45th St., Seattle, Wash. 98103.

CAREER: Liberation News Service, Washington, D.C., editor, 1967-68; Total Loss Farm, Guilford, Vt., founder, 1968-71; Montana Books, Inc., Seattle, Wash., proprietor, 1973—.

WRITINGS: *Famous Long Ago,* Beacon Press, 1970; *Total Loss Farm,* Dutton, 1970; *Between Two Moons,* Beacon Press, 1972; (under pseudonym Dennis Lunar) *Tropical Detective Story,* Dutton, 1972; (with Peter Simon) *Moving On, Holding Still,* Grossman, 1972. Contributor to *Atlantic Monthly, New Republic, New York Times, Boston Globe, Boston University News,* and *New Music Magazine.*

WORK IN PROGRESS: A book, *Return to Sender.*

MUNRO, Leslie Knox 1901-1974

February 26, 1901—February 13, 1974; New Zealand government official, diplomat, editor, and author. Obituaries: *New York Times,* February 14, 1974; *Current Biography,* April, 1974.

* * *

MUNRO, Mary
See HOWE, Doris Kathleen

* * *

MUNROE, John A(ndrew) 1914-

PERSONAL: Born March 15, 1914, in Wilmington, Del.; son of Michael John (an iron molder) and Mary (Dettling) Munroe; married Dorothy Levis (a teacher), July 7, 1945; children: Stephen Horner, Carol Levis, John Michael. *Education:* University of Delaware, B.A., 1936, M.A., 1941; University of Pennsylvania, Ph.D., 1947. *Home:* 215 Cheltenham Rd., Newark, Del. 19711. *Office:* Department of History, University of Delaware, Newark, Del. 19711.

CAREER: Teacher of history in public high schools of Newark, Del., 1936-39; University of Delaware, Newark, instructor, 1942-47, assistant professor, 1947-49, associate professor, 1949-52, professor of history, 1952-62, H. Rodney Sharp Professor of History, 1962—, assistant dean of the College of Arts and Sciences, 1949-51, head of department, 1952-69. Visiting professor at University of Wisconsin, summer, 1960, and Bath University, summer, 1969. *Member:* American Historical Association, Organization of American Historians, American Association of University Professors, Historical Society of Pennsylvania, Historical Society of Delaware (member of board of directors, 1972), Phi Beta Kappa, Phi Kappa Phi. *Awards, honors:* Ford Foundation fellow at Foundation for the Advancement of Education, 1951-52; outstanding alumnus, University of Delaware, 1963; Governor's Gold Medal, State of Delaware, 1973.

WRITINGS: Delaware Becomes a State, University of Delaware Press, 1953; *Federalist Delaware, 1775-1815,* Rutgers University Press, 1954; (editor) *Timoleon's Biographical History of Dionysius,* University of Delaware Press, 1958; *Delaware: A Students' Guide to Localized History,* Teachers College Press, 1965; *Louis McLane: Federalist and Jacksonian,* Rutgers University Press, 1974. Editor of *Delaware History,* 1969—.

WORK IN PROGRESS: Colonial Delaware, for Scribner.

* * *

MUNSTERHJELM, Erik 1905-

PERSONAL: "J" in surname is silent; born March 28, 1905, in Lojo, Finland; son of Alarik (an artist) and Vivi (an artist; maiden name, Dahlberg) Munsterhjelm; married Anne-Marie Anderzen, November 6, 1942; children: Ky Gustav, Vivi Elisabeth. *Education:* Studied one year at a military college. *Politics:* No affiliation. *Religion:* Lutheran. *Home and office address:* R.R. 1, Mindemoya, Ontario P0P 1S0, Canada; and Sun Valley Village, Rte. 5, Box 549, Harlingen, Tex. 78550 (winter). *Agent:* Laurence Pollinger Ltd., 18 Maddox St., London W.1, England.

CAREER: Prospector and geologist in the Canadian North for many years prior to 1939; International Nickel Co., Copper Cliff, Ont., geologist, 1948-70. *Military service:* Army of Finland, 1925-27, 1939-40, 1941-44; became lieutenant.

WRITINGS: Med Kanot och Hundspann (title means "By Canoe and Dogteam"), Soederstroem & Co., 1942; *Guldfeber* (title means "Gold Fever"), Soederstroem & Co., 1943; *Pionjaerens Hemlighet* (juvenile; title means "The Pioneer's Secret"), Soederstroem & Co., 1943; *Som Vagabond till Kalifornien* (title means "As Vagabond to California"), Soederstroem & Co., 1944; *Den Underbara Dalen* (juvenile; title means "The Wonderful Valley"), Soederstroem & Co., 1944; *Gamle Bill* (title means "Old Bill"), Soederstroem & Co., 1945; *Katra,* Soederstroem & Co., 1946; *Amulettens Gaata* (juvenile; title means "Riddle of the Amulet"), Soederstroem & Co., 1947; (translator into Swedish) Mark Twain, *Slita Hund* (title means "Roughing It"), Soederstroem & Co., 1947; *The Wind and the Caribou,* Allen & Unwin, 1952; *Fool's Gold,* Allen & Unwin, 1957; *A Dog Named Wolf* (juvenile), Macmillan (Canada), 1972. Author of articles and short stories in Swedish.

WORK IN PROGRESS: A novel and a juvenile story.

AVOCATIONAL INTERESTS: Music, old books.

* * *

MURPHY, Herta A(lbrecht) 1908-

PERSONAL: Born July 26, 1908, in St. Louis, Mo.; daughter of Joseph (a master cabinetmaker) and Hedwig (Heiek) Albrecht; married William Wilson Ward, June 24, 1934 (died, 1937); married Eugene Arthur Murphy (a bank officer), September 6, 1946; children: (second marriage) Jeanette Darlene. *Education:* University of Washington, Seattle, B.B.A., 1930, M.A., 1942; graduate study at University of Southern California, summer, 1938, Armstrong College of Business Administration, summer, 1939, George Washington University, 1940-41. *Politics:* "Best candidate" of Democrats or Republicans. *Religion:* Catholic. *Home:* 422 Summit Ave. East, Seattle, Wash. 98102. *Office:* School of Business Administration, University of Washington, Seattle, Wash. 98195.

CAREER: North Pacific Export Co., Seattle, Wash., bookkeeper, 1927-28; secretary for Boeing Co., Puget Sound Power & Light, Chevrolet Zone Office, and Metropolitan Building Co. in Seattle, Wash., 1928-38; business teacher in the public high schools of Silverton, Ore., 1930-31, and Olympia, Seattle, and Bremerton, Wash., 1931-39; Office of the Quartermaster General, Washington, D.C., statistical assistant and secretary, 1940-41; California State College, Chico, registrar and instructor in commerce, 1941-43; University of Alaska, Fairbanks, assistant professor, 1943-45, associate professor of business administration, 1945-46; University of Washington, Seattle, lecturer, 1946-55, assistant professor, 1955-61, associate professor, 1961-71, professor of business communication, 1971—, American Savings and Loan Institute's School for Executive Development, associate professor, 1960-65. Chairman, Capitol Hill Community Survey Committee, Seattle, Wash., 1968; Capitol Hill Community Council, Seattle, Wash., member of human relations committee, 1968-70. *Member:* American Business Communications Association (fellow), National Business Teachers Association, National League of American Pen Women, University of Washington Faculty Center, Phi Beta Kappa, Beta Gamma Sigma, Gamma Alpha Chi, Kappa Delta.

WRITINGS: (With Charles Peck and Virgil Harder) *Building Favorable Impressions by Mail,* American Savings & Loan Inst., 1960, revised edition, 1961; (with Peck) *Savings Association Letters and Reports,* American Savings & Loan Inst., 1969; (with Peck) *Instructor's Manual for Savings Association Letters and Reports,* American Savings & Loan Inst., 1969; (with Peck) *Effective Business Communications,* McGraw, 1972; *Teacher's Manual for Effective Business Communications,* McGraw, 1972; (with Peck) *Answer Book for Tests in Business Communication,* McGraw, 1972. Contributor to professional journals.

WORK IN PROGRESS: Revised, second edition of *Effective Business Communications,* publication by McGraw expected in 1976.

* * *

MURPHY, John
See GRADY, Ronan Calistus, Jr.

* * *

MURRAY, Albert 1916-

PERSONAL: Born June 12, 1916, in Nokomis, Ala.; married Mozelle Menefee; children: Michelle. *Education:* Tuskegee Institute, B.S., 1939; New York University, M.A., 1948. *Home and office:* 45 West 132nd St., New York, N.Y. 10037.

CAREER: U.S. Air Force, 1943-62, retiring as major. Instructor at Tuskegee Institute, 1940-43, 1946-51, Columbia University, 1968; O'Connor Professor of Literature at Colgate University, 1970, 1973; visiting professor at University of Massachusetts, Boston, 1971; Paul Anthony Brick Lecturer at University of Missouri, 1972; has also lectured at New School, Brandeis University, and Peace Corps Training Center, all 1973. *Member:* International P.E.N., Authors Guild, Alpha Phi Alpha.

WRITINGS: The Omni-Americans, Outerbridge & Dientsfrey, 1970; *South to a Very Old Place,* McGraw, 1972; *The Hero and the Blues,* University of Missouri Press, 1973; *The Trainwhistle Guitar,* McGraw, 1974.

WORK IN PROGRESS: The Story Teller as Blues Singer; a novel.

SIDELIGHTS: Writing in the *New York Times,* Anatole Broyard describes Albert Murray's theory "that the majority of blacks have something most whites who write about them don't seem to have noticed. They have an instinctive sense of self and place that no amount of sociological double talk can change. . . . If he agrees with black militants that white liberals don't understand him, that's about the only time he sees eye to eye with them. Because he would say that black militants don't understand him either." As R. Z. Sheppard explains: "Murray is not blind to the indignities and hardships suffered by blacks. But he feels that generalizations abstracted from lifeless data, whatever their purpose, have made the U.S. Negro 'a victim of sociology.'" Sheppard calls *South to a Very Old Place* "a highly syncopated memoir of youth and a celebration of U.S. Negro culture."

AVOCATIONAL INTERESTS: Recordings, photography, cookbooks, and gourmet cooking.

* * *

MURRAY, Edward (James, Jr.) 1928-

PERSONAL: Born April 8, 1928, in Brooklyn, N.Y.; son of Edward James and Catherine (Henn) Murray; married Margaret DeSantis, September 4, 1954; children: Michael, Lisa, Stephen, Monica, Jeannette. *Education:* Studied at Television Workshop of New York, 1953-54; Youngstown University, B.A., 1962; University of Southern California, Ph.D., 1966. *Home:* 188 Hollybrook Rd., Brockport, N.Y. 14420. *Office:* State University of New York College at Brockport, Brockport, N.Y. 14420.

CAREER: Western Illinois University, Macomb, assistant professor, 1965-66, associate professor of English, 1967-68; State University of New York College at Brockport, assistant professor, 1968-70, associate professor, 1971-74, professor of English, 1974—. *Military service:* U.S. Army, Medical Corps, 1951-53; became sergeant. *Member:* Modern Language Association of America, American Association of University Professors, American Film Institute, University Film Association. *Awards, honors:* Woodrow Wilson fellowship, 1962.

WRITINGS: Arthur Miller: Dramatist, Ungar, 1967; *Clifford Odets: The Thirties and After,* Ungar, 1968; *The Cinematic Imagination: Writers and the Motion Pictures,* Ungar, 1972; *Nine American Film Critics: A Study of Theory and Practice,* Ungar, in press. Contributor to *Literature/Film Quarterly* and *College Language Association Journal.*

WORK IN PROGRESS: Research on the work of individual film-makers, film theory, and film criticism.

* * *

MURRAY, James 1946-

PERSONAL: Born October 16, 1946, in New York, N.Y.; son of Eddie and Helena (Banks) Murray. *Education:* Syracuse University, A.B., 1968. *Home:* 56 Dobbs Ferry Rd., White Plains, N.Y. 10607. *Agent:* Charles Neighbors, 240 Waverly Pl., New York, N.Y. 10003. *Office: New York Amsterdam News,* 2340 Eighth Ave., New York, N.Y. 10027.

CAREER: American Broadcasting Co., New York, N.Y., news trainee, 1970-71; Western Electric Co., New York, N.Y., public relations associate, 1971-72; *New York Amsterdam News,* New York, N.Y., arts and entertainment editor, 1972—. *Military service:* U.S. Army, 1968-70; became first lieutenant; served in Vietnam; received Bronze Star Medal. *Member:* New York Film Critics Circle.

WRITINGS: To Find an Image: Black Films from Uncle Tom to Superfly, Bobbs-Merrill, 1974.

* * *

MURRAY, (Judith) Michele (Freedman) 1933-1974

PERSONAL: Born April 25, 1933, in Brooklyn, N.Y.; daughter of Aaron (a government clerk) and Mollie (Giseu) Freedman; married James Murray (an administrative officer with District of Columbia government), January 29, 1955; children: David, Jonathan, Sarah, Mathew. *Education:* American University, student, 1951-53; New School for Social Research, B.A., 1954; University of Connecticut, M.A., 1956. *Home:* 9816 Parkwood Dr., Bethesda, Md. 20014.

CAREER: Instructor in English at Annhurst College, Putnam, Conn., 1956-57, Georgetown University, Washington, D.C., 1957-59, and Catholic University of America, Washington, D.C., 1959-60; Howard University, Washington, D.C., instructor in humanities, 1965-66; *National Observer,* Silver Spring, Md., book review editor, 1972-74. *Awards, honors: Nellie Cameron* was named to the Child Study Association book list, 1972. *The Crystal Nights* was a Newbery Award nominee.

WRITINGS: Nellie Cameron (Junior Literary Guild selection), Seabury, 1971; *The Crystal Nights* (young adult), Seabury, 1973; (editor) *A House of Good Proportion: Images of Women in Literature,* Simon & Schuster, 1973; *The Great Mother* (poems), Sheed & Ward, 1974. Contributor of about sixty poems to literary magazines; regular contributor to *National Catholic Reporter.*

WORK IN PROGRESS: A children's novel, *Dacia's War,* to be published by Seabury as part of a memorial volume; posthumous publication also expected for the author's sixteen journals, collections of poetry, and a collection of criticism.

SIDELIGHTS: Prior to her death Mrs. Murray wrote: "I believe in the value of the artist of integrity in a time of literary careerism and try to bring to my children's books the aesthetic quality of the best fiction for adults in depth, complexity and writing style."

Reporting her death, the *Washington Post* quoted Clifford Redley, senior editor for the arts at the *National Observer:* "What we most loved and admired about Michele . . . was her absolutely breathtaking enthusiasm for her work. In her anthology, she called herself 'a woman in love with literature,' and she certainly was all of that. . . . Her enthusiasm infused her writing; when she wrote of books and authors she truly admired . . . our readers caught her sense of joy and responded in dozens of admiring letters for both the subject and the critic."

Her criticism, the *Post* noted, was in demand by book editors of the *Washington Post,* the *New York Times* and journals like *Commonwealth* and the *National Catholic Reporter.*

Mrs. Murray died of cancer at her home in Bethesda, Md.

(Died March 14, 1974)

* * *

MUSKIE, Edmund S(ixtus) 1914-

PERSONAL: Born March 28, 1914, in Rumford, Me.; son of Stephen Oliver (a tailor) and Josephine (Czarnecki) Muskie; married Jane Frances Gray, May 29, 1948; children: Stephen, Ellen (Mrs. Ernest Allen), Melinda, Martha, Edmund Sixtus, Jr. *Education:* Bates College, B.A. (cum laude), 1936; Cornell University, LL.B., 1939. *Religion:* Roman Catholic. *Residence:* Waterville, Me.; and Washington, D.C. *Agent:* Michael Hamilburg, 1104 South Robertson Blvd., Los Angeles, Calif. 90035. *Office:* U.S. Senate, Suite 115, Washington, D.C. 20510.

CAREER: Admitted to Massachusetts Bar, 1939, Mainc Bar, 1940, and to practice before U.S. District Court, 1941; private practice of law in Waterville, Me., 1940, 1945-55 (also city solicitor, 1954-55); member of Maine House of Representatives, 1948-51, as minority (Democratic) floor leader, 1949-51; district director for Maine of Office of Price Stabilization, 1951-52; Democratic national committeeman, 1952-54; governor of State of Maine, 1955-59; U.S. Senator from Maine, 1959—, assistant majority whip of Senate, 1966—. Democratic candidate for vice-president of United States, 1968; as Democratic member of Senate has served as chairman of subcommittees on intergovernmental relations, air and water pollution, arms control and international organizations, and international finance. *Military service:* U.S. Naval Reserve, active duty, 1942-45; served on destroyer escorts in Atlantic and Pacific waters; became lieutenant junior grade; received three battle stars.

MEMBER: American Academy of Arts and Sciences, Massachusetts Bar Association, Maine Bar Association, American Legion, Veterans of Foreign Wars (life member; member of national executive committee, 1947-48), Phi Beta Kappa, Phi Alpha Delta, Delta Sigma Rho. *Awards, honors:* More than twenty honorary degrees from universities and colleges, including University of New Brunswick, College of William and Mary, University of New Hampshire, Boston University, Syracuse University, Bates College, University of Maine, University of Notre Dame, George Washington University, Cornell University, Bowdoin College, and Colby College.

WRITINGS: Journeys, Doubleday, 1972; (contributor) Harold Faber, editor, *New York Times Guide to New Voters,* Quadrangle, 1972. Writer of syndicated newspaper column, "So Goes the Nation," 1969-70.

WORK IN PROGRESS: A book on environmental pollution.

AVOCATIONAL INTERESTS: Golf, fishing, hunting, sailing, carpentry.

BIOGRAPHICAL/CRITICAL SOURCES: Theo Lippman and D. C. Hanson, *Muskie,* Norton, 1971; David Nevin, *Muskie: The Man from Maine,* Random House, 1972.

* * *

MUSURILLO, Herbert (Anthony) 1917-1974

June 13, 1917—May 27, 1974; American priest, educator, classicist, and author of books on Roman Catholic church history and writings. Obituaries: *New York Times,* May 29, 1974. (*CA*-13/14).

* * *

MYERS, Gail E(ldridge) 1923-

PERSONAL: Born March 1, 1923, in Clark, S.D.; son of Larry (a painter) and Pauline (Engen) Myers; married Catherine Bonette, March 17, 1947 (divorced September, 1967); married Michele Tolela (a communication consultant), December 20, 1968; children: (first marriage) Christopher, Kathleen Myers Simon; (second marriage) Erika. *Education:* Attended South Dakota College, 1941-42, and University of Oregon, 1942; University of Iowa, B.A., 1948, M.A., 1949; University of Denver, Ph.D., 1959. *Home:* 139 Oakmont, San Antonio, Tex. 78212. *Office:* College of Arts and Sciences, Trinity University, San Antonio, Tex. 78212.

CAREER: Iowa State Teachers College, Cedar Falls, instructor in journalism and television production, director of alumni, and director of publications, 1949-53; Colorado School of Mines, Golden, instructor in journalism, director of publications, and technical editor, 1953-59; Monticello College, Godfrey, Ill., vice-president, 1959-63; University of Denver, Denver, Colo., assistant professor of speech, 1963-66; Monticello College, president, 1966-71; Trinity University, San Antonio, Tex., professor of speech and journalism, 1971—, associate dean, 1971-72, dean of College of Arts and Sciences, 1972—. President of Lewis and Clark Community College, 1970-71. Lecturer for organizations, businesses, seminars, workshops, and Peace Corps Communication Retreat. *Military service:* U.S. Army Air Forces, 1943-46; served in Pacific theater; became sergeant major.

MEMBER: International Communication Association,

International Society for the Study of General Semantics, Speech Communication Association, Greater Alton Public Relations and Advertising Club (honorary life member), Sigma Delta Chi.

WRITINGS: (Editor with Johnnye Akin and others) *Language Behavior,* Mouton & Co., 1970; *A Miracle Every March* (novel), Naylor, 1973; (with wife, Michele Myers) *Dynamics of Human Communication,* McGraw, 1973; (with Michele Myers) *Communicating When We Speak,* McGraw, 1974. Contributor to *Journal of Applied Behavioral Science* and *Junior College Journal.*

AVOCATIONAL INTERESTS: Photography, skiing, golf, music, writing.

* * *

MYERS, Norman 1934-

PERSONAL: Born August 24, 1934, in Whitewell, Yorkshire, England; son of John and Gladys (Haworth) Myers; married Dorothy Mary Halliman, December 10, 1965; children: Malindi Elizabeth. *Education:* Oxford University, M.A., 1957, Diploma in Overseas Administration, 1958; University of California, Berkeley, Ph.D., 1973. *Address:* P.O. Box 48197, Nairobi, Kenya.

CAREER: H.M. Overseas Civil Service, Kenya, district officer, 1958-61; high school teacher in Nairobi, Kenya, 1961-65; free-lance writer, photographer, film-maker, and broadcaster on conservation of African wildlands, 1965-69; consultant in conservation ecology and land-use planning in Kenya, 1972—. Lecturer on conservation in Africa on tours in Europe and United States, 1967, 1968. *Military service:* British Army, 1953. *Member:* International Union for the Conservation of Nature, East Africa Wild Life Society, National Audubon Society, Sierra Club.

WRITINGS: *The Long African Day,* Macmillan, 1972; *Nairobi National Park: An Annotated Bibliography,* Office of Ecology, Smithsonian Institution, 1973.

Contributor: R. L. Eaton, editor, *The World's Cats, Ecology and Conservation,* Volume I, World Wildlife Safari, 1973; N. Sitwell, editor, *Cats of the World,* Tom Stacey, in press. Contributor to *International Wildlife, Animal Kingdom, Natural History, Africana,* and other journals.

WORK IN PROGRESS: Four books—*Shall Serengetti Still Survive?; The Human Ecology of Emergent Africa* (textbook); *The Leopard;* and *Common Property Resources: Conservation from the Standpoint of Endangered Species and Endangered Habitats.*

* * *

NADEAU, Maurice 1911-

PERSONAL: Born May 21, 1911, in Paris, France; son of Edouard and Zilda (Clair) Nadeau; married Marthe Forni, November 29, 1934; children: Gilles, Claire. *Education:* Ecole Normale Superieure de St. Cloud, professorat lettres, 1935. *Home:* 8 rue Malebranche, Paris 75005, France. *Office:* *La Quinzaine litteraire,* 43 rue Temple, Paris 75004, France; and *Les Lettres nouvelles,* 26 rue de Conde, Paris 75006, France.

CAREER: Professor of literature in secondary schools in Paris, France, 1936-45; *Combat,* France, literary critic, 1945-47, literary director, 1947-51; Editions Correa, Paris, director of series, "Le Chemin de la vie," 1949-54; Editions Julliard, Paris, editor of "Les Lettres Nouvelles," 1953-64; Editions Denoel, Paris, editor of "Les Lettres Nouvelles," 1965—. Member of jury for Theophraste-Renaudot prize, and of various other literary committees. *Member:* P.E.N. International. *Awards, honors:* Grand Prix de la critique litteraire, 1969, for *Gustave Flaubert, ecrivain, essai.*

WRITINGS: *Histoire du surrealisme,* two volumes, Seuil, 1946-48, translation by Richard Howard published as *The History of Surrealism,* Macmillan, 1965; *Oeuvres du Marquis de Sade,* La Jeune Parque, 1948; *Litterature presente,* Correa, 1952; *"Beatniks" et jeunes ecrivains americains,* Julliard, 1960; *Michel Leiris et la quadrature du cercle,* Julliard, 1963; *Le Roman francais depuis la guerre,* Gallimard, 1963, revised edition, 1970, translation by A. M. Sheridan Smith published as *The French Novel since the War,* Methuen, 1967, Grove, 1969; (editor) *Les Oeuvres completes de Flaubert,* Rencontre, 1965; *Gustave Flaubert, ecrivain, essai,* Denoel, 1969, translation by Barbara Bray published as *The Greatness of Flaubert,* Library Press, 1972; (editor, and author of notes and introduction) *Les Chefs d'oeuvre de Gustave Flaubert,* Edito-Service (Geneva), 1970.

Editor or author of seventy-two volumes, and author of introduction for six volumes, in the "Anthologie poesie francaise" series of Editions Rencontre, 1967—.

Editor, *Les Lettres nouvelles,* 1953—, *La Quinzaine litteraire,* 1966—. Literary critic, *Mercure de France,* 1948-53, *France-Observateur,* 1952-59, and *L'Express,* 1959-64.

* * *

NAGEL, William G(eorge) 1916-

PERSONAL: Born December 17, 1916, in Trenton, N.J.; son of William H. and Emily (Toothill) Nagel; married Ethel M. Forder-Jones, June 12, 1943; children: Jack H., Robert F., William F. *Education:* Attended Wake Forest College, 1935-37, and University of Chicago, 1939-40; University of Pennsylvania, M.S.W., 1948. *Home:* 2006 Makefield Rd., Yardley, Pa. 19067. *Office:* American Foundation, Inc., 1532 Philadelphia National Bank Building, Philadelphia, Pa. 19107.

CAREER: New Jersey Correctional Institution, Bordentown, assistant superintendent, 1949-60; National Council on Crime and Delinquency, Hackensack, N.J., consultant, 1960-64; Office of the Governor of Pennsylvania, Harrisburg, executive secretary of human services, 1964-69; American Foundation, Inc., Philadelphia, Pa., executive director, 1969—. *Military service:* U.S. Army, 1941-45; became major.

WRITINGS: *The New Red Barn: A Critical Look at the Modern American Prison,* Walker & Co., 1973. Contributor to professional journals.

* * *

NAHAS, Gabriel G(eorges) 1920-

PERSONAL: Born March 4, 1920, in Alexandria, Egypt; came to United States in 1947, naturalized citizen in 1962; son of Bishara and Gabrielle (Wolff) Nahas; married Marilyn Cashman, February 13, 1954; children: Michele, Anthony, Christiane. *Education:* University of Toulouse, B.A., 1937, M.D. (cum laude), 1944; University of Rochester, M.S., 1949; University of Minnesota, Ph.D., 1953. *Home:* 114 Chestnut St., Englewood, N.J. 07631. *Office:* 630 West 168th St., New York, N.Y. 10032.

CAREER: Hospital Marie Lannelongue, Paris, France,

chief of Laboratory of Experimental Surgery, 1954-55; University of Minnesota, Minneapolis, assistant professor of physiology, 1955-57; Walter Reed Army Institute of Research, Department of Cardiorespiratory Disease, Washington, D.C., chief of respiratory section, 1957-59; George Washington University Medical School, Washington, D.C., lecturer in physiology, 1957-59; Columbia University, College of Physicians and Surgeons, New York, N.Y., associate professor, 1959-62, professor of anesthesiology, 1962—, department director of research, 1959-62; Presbyterian Hospital, New York, N.Y., attending anesthesiologist, 1967—. Consultant to Oceanographic Institute of Monaco, 1964—; adjunct professor at Institute of Anesthesiology of University of Paris, 1968—. Member of advisory board of Council on Circulation and Basic Sciences, American Heart Association; vice-president of Foundation for Research in Biology and Medicine; active in World University Service and in Experiment in International Living; member of committee on trauma, National Research Council, 1963-66. *Military service:* French Underground, special agent, 1941-44; French Army, Medical Corps, 1944-45; became first lieutenant; received Presidential Medal of Freedom with gold palm, Legion of Honor, and Croix de Guerre with three palms.

MEMBER: International Society of Hematology, American Physiological Society, American Heart Association (fellow), American Society for Pharmacology and Experimental Therapeutics, American Society of Clinical Pharmacology, Society for Artificial Internal Organs, Associacion des Physiologists de Langue Francaise, American Association for the Advancement of Science (fellow), Undersea Medical Society, American Federation for Clinical Research, National Research Council, Harvey Society, New York Academy of Science (fellow), Sigma Xi. *Awards, honors:* Member of Order of Orange Nassau, 1947, and Order of the British Empire, 1948; Fulbright scholar, 1966; silver medal from City of Paris, 1972.

WRITINGS: (Editor) *In Vitro and In Vivo Effects of Amine Buffers,* Annals of New York Academy of Science, 1961; (editor) *Regulation of Respiration,* Annals of New York Academy of Science, 1963; (editor with D. V. Bates) *Respiratory Failure,* Annals of New York Academy of Science, 1965; (editor) *Current Concepts of Acid-Base Measurements,* Annals of New York Academy of Science, 1966; (editor with Charles Fox) *Body Fluid Replacement in the Surgical Patient,* Grune, 1970; (editor with Alan Robison and Lubos Triner) *Cyclic AMP and Cell Function,* Annals of New York Academy of Science, 1973; *Marihuana: Deceptive Weed,* Raven Press, 1973; (editor with Karl Schaeffer and Nicholas Chalazonitis) *CO2 and Metabolic Regulation,* Srpinger-Verlag, 1974.

* * *

NAKAE, Noriko 1940-
(Noriko Ueno)

PERSONAL: Born September 29, 1940, in Irima-shi, Saitama-ken, Japan; daughter of Koichi and Kimiko Ueno; married Yoshio Nakae (a graphic designer), December 4, 1966. *Education:* Nihon University, B.A., 1962. *Home:* 2B-302, Sakuradai Village, 25-1, Sakuradai, Midori-ku, Yokohama-shi, Kanagawa, Japan. *Office:* 3-3-11 Kamitakaido, Suginami-ku, Tokyo 168, Japan.

CAREER: Free-lance artist, 1962—. Exhibitor in Tokyo Biennale, 1974. *Member:* Japanese Water Color Painting League, Japanese Illustrators Council. *Awards, honors:* Japanese Water Color Painting League award, 1963; Ministry of Foreign Affairs prize, 1973, for international exhibit.

WRITINGS: All under name Noriko Ueno: *Elephant Button* (drawings), Harper, 1973.

Illustrator; all authored by husband, Yoshio Nakae, except as noted: *Pera Pera no Sekai* (title means "The Flimsy World"), Atelier Chemia, 1965; *Mayoi Konda Doubutsu-tachi* (title means "Animals that Visited Chiko"), Atelier Chemia, 1966; *Marutsushi* (title means "Magician"), Atelier Chemia, 1967; *Shouchu* (title means "Microcosm"), Atelier Chemia, 1971; *Nezumikun no Chokki* (title means "The Vest of Mr. Mouse"), Poplar Publishing (Tokyo), 1974; *Kuroboushi-chan* (title means "Little Black Hat"), Bunka, 1974; Yoshitomo Imae, *Soyokaze to Watashi* (title means "A Gentle Breeze and I"), Poplar Publishing, 1974.

WORK IN PROGRESS: Designing puppets for a television show; illustrations for television commercials and other advertisements.

* * *

NASH, Newlyn
See HOWE, Doris Kathleen

* * *

NAUHEIM, Ferd(inand Alan) 1909-

PERSONAL: Born November 3, 1909, in New York, N.Y.; son of Elias and Sadie (Rosenberger) Nauheim; married Beatrice Strasburger, August 23, 1934; children: Gail (Mrs. Carter S. Kaufmann), Stephen A. *Education:* Attended high school in New York, N.Y. *Politics:* "Variable." *Religion:* Jewish. *Home:* 4201 Cathedral Ave., Washington, D.C. 20016. *Office:* Kalb, Voorhis & Co., Woodward Bldg., Washington, D.C. 20005.

CAREER: Continental Baking Company, New York, N.Y., assistant advertising manager, 1930-36; Plymouth Printing Co., Washington, D.C., owner, 1936-49; worked as a direct mail sales consultant in Washington, D.C., 1949-56; Kalb, Voorhis & Co., Washington, D.C., general partner, 1956—. Member of advisory board, Salvation Army of Washington, 1959—; chairman of board of regents, College Financial Planning, 1971-72; member of board of trustees, Columbia Lighthouse for the Blind, 1971—, Citizens Advisory Commission of Washington, D.C. Bar Association, 1973; professorial lecturer, American University's school of business, 1952-64. *Military service:* U.S. Army, 5th Armored Division, 1944-45. *Member:* International Society of Financial Planners (member of board of directors, 1973—), Direct Mail Advertising Association (member of board of governors, 1958-61), Sales and Marketing Executives of Washington (president, 1957-58), Mail Advertising Club of Washington. *Awards, honors:* Named Man of the Year, 1958, by Sales and Marketing Executives, and by Mail Advertising Club, 1968.

WRITINGS: *Business Letters That Turn Inquiries into Sales,* Prentice-Hall, 1957; *Ferd Nauheim's Nine Day Sales Clinic,* Prentice-Hall, 1964; *Salesmen's Complete Model Letter Handbook,* Prentice-Hall, 1967; *Behold the Upright* (novel), Apollo Books, 1971; *Build Family Finances & Reduce Risk & Taxes,* Acropolis Books, 1973. Also author of business and industrial related material.

NEE, Kay Bonner

PERSONAL: Born in Plummer, Minn.; daughter of David Thomas (a teacher) and Helena (Franken) Bonner; married William J. Nee (engaged in public relations), April 19, 1947; children: Christopher, Nicole, Lisa, Rachel. *Education:* College of St. Catherine, B.A., 1941; University of Minnesota, graduate study, 1947. *Politics:* Democrat. *Religion:* Roman Catholic. *Home:* 219 Logan Park Way, Fridley, Minn. 55432. *Office:* Minnesota Association of Voluntary Social Service Agencies, 355 Marshall Ave., St. Paul, Minn. 55102.

CAREER: Dayton Co., Minneapolis, Minn., emcee of radio show, 1945-50; Manson-Gold-Miller, Inc., Minneapolis, radio-television director, 1951-53; WCCO-TV, Minneapolis, writer, director, and producer, 1954-56; White-Herzog-Nee, Inc., Minneapolis, radio and television writer and producer, 1956-65; North State Advertising Agency, Minneapolis, president, 1966-70; Minnesota Association of Voluntary Social Service Agencies, St. Paul, executive director, 1972—. Television director of McCarthy for President campaign, 1968, and director of television and radio for other political campaigns. Member of Minnesota Governor's Committee on Status of Women, 1966. *Member:* American Federation of Television and Radio Artists, Delta Phi Lambda.

WRITINGS: (With husband, William Nee) *Eugene McCarthy: United States Senator,* Gilbert Press, 1964; *Powhatan* (juvenile), Dillon, 1971.

Children's one-act plays: "Rhymes Ago-go," produced in 1967; "Land of the Moogazoos," 1969; "The Winner," 1971; "Hey Joe!," 1972. Writer of weekly radio show, "Soda Set," 1945-50, ten-episode television series, "Your Child's World," 1967-68, and eleven-episode television series, "Preparing Children for the 21st Century," 1973. Former columnist in *Catholic Miss.*

WORK IN PROGRESS: "Living Married," a twelve-episode television series; *My Mother the Mayor,* a children's book on political campaigning; editing *Proven Plays for Young Productions.*

* * *

NEF, Evelyn Stefansson 1913- (Evelyn Stefansson)

PERSONAL: Born July 24, 1913, in New York, N.Y.; daughter of Jeeno and Bella (Klein) Schwartz; married William Britton Baird, 1932 (divorced, 1938); married Vilhjalmur Stefansson (a geographer and explorer), 1941 (died, 1962); married John Ulric Nef (a professor and historian), April 21, 1964. *Education:* Studied at Traphagen School of Fashion, 1927, and Art Students League, 1931. *Religion:* Humanist. *Agent:* Patricia Myrer, McIntosh & Otis, Inc., 18 East 41st St., New York, N.Y. 10017.

CAREER: Maker and operator of marionettes in New York, N.Y., 1932-38; began as librarian and researcher for Arctic explorer Vilhjalmur Stefansson in 1939, continuing her work as special assistant to Stefansson and librarian of Stefansson Polar Library, 1941-51; Dartmouth College, Hanover, N.H., librarian of Stefansson Collection in Baker Library, 1952-63, director of Arctic seminar, 1960-61; American Sociological Association, Washington, D.C., administrative officer, 1963-64. Has also worked as commercial photographer, and worked on museum dioramas and World's Fair exhibits in New York and Chicago. Trustee, Corcoran Gallery of Art, 1974—. *Member:* Society of Woman Geographers (chairman of Washington group, 1969-72; president, 1972-75).

WRITINGS—All under name Evelyn Stefansson, except as noted: *Here Is Alaska,* Scribner, 1943, revised statehood edition, 1959, new edition, 1973; *Within the Circle: Portrait of the Arctic,* Scribner, 1945; *Here Is the Far North,* Scribner, 1957. Editor-in-chief, under name Evelyn Stefansson Nef, of Delacorte's "Great Explorer" series, 1966-72.

SIDELIGHTS: Mrs. Nef has traveled extensively in Europe, Alaska, Iceland, Greenland, Siberia, and the Arctic.

* * *

NELSON, Cary (Robert) 1946-

PERSONAL: Born May 15, 1946, in Philadelphia, Pa.; son of Aaron and Sophie (Cohen) Nelson. *Education:* Antioch College, B.A., 1967; University of Rochester, Ph.D., 1970. *Home:* 204 North Lincoln Ave., Urbana, Ill. 61801. *Office:* Department of English, University of Illinois, Urbana, Ill. 61801.

CAREER: University of Illinois, Urbana, assistant professor of English, 1970—. *Member:* Modern Language Association of America.

WRITINGS: The Incarnate Word: Literature as Verbal Space, University of Illinois Press, 1973.

WORK IN PROGRESS: A book on contemporary American poetry; a monograph on literary criticism.

AVOCATIONAL INTERESTS: Modern art, photography, film.

* * *

NELSON, James B(ruce) 1930-

PERSONAL: Born May 28, 1930, in Windom, Minn.; married Wilys Claire Coulter, January 31, 1953; children: Stephen Joseph, Mary Elizabeth. *Education:* Macalester College, B.A. (summa cum laude), 1951; Yale University, B.D. (magna cum laude), 1957, M.A., 1959, Ph.D., 1962; Oxford University, postdoctoral study, 1969-70. *Office:* United Theological Seminary of the Twin Cities, New Brighton, Minn. 55112.

CAREER: Ordained Congregational minister, 1958; minister in West Haven, Conn., 1957-59, and Vermillion, S.D., 1960-63; United Theological Seminary of the Twin Cities, New Brighton, Minn., associate professor, 1963-68, professor of Christian ethics, 1968—. Visiting lecturer at Luther Theological Seminary, fall, 1966, and Yale Divinity School, spring, 1969; visiting professor at St. John's University, fall, 1968. *Military service:* U.S. Army, 1952-54. *Member:* American Academy of Religion, American Society of Christian Ethics, Society for the Scientific Study of Religion, Society for Religion in Higher Education, Phi Gamma Mu.

WRITINGS: (Contributor) Harvey Cox, editor, *The Situation Ethics Debate,* Westminster Press, 1968; *The Responsible Christian,* United Church Press, 1969; *Moral Nexus: Ethics of Christian Identity and Community,* Westminster Press, 1971; *Human Medicine: Ethical Perspectives on New Medical Issues,* Augsburg, 1973. Contributor of articles and reviews to *McCormick Quarterly, Journal of Ecumenical Studies, Theology Digest, Colloquy, Youth, Theological Markings, Theology and Life, Review of Religious Research,* and *Religious Education.*

NELSON, John Charles 1925-

PERSONAL: Born October 9, 1925, in Rome, Italy, a U.S. citizen; son of Claud Dalton (a minister, executive, and author) and Maud (Sparks) Nelson; married Bruna Marchi (an interpreter), July 24, 1948; children: Marcella. *Education:* Columbia University, B.A., 1945, M.A., 1950, Ph.D., 1954. *Home:* 430 West 116th St., New York, N.Y. 10027. *Office:* 502 Casa Italiana, Columbia University, New York, N.Y. 10027.

CAREER: University of Rochester, Rochester, N.Y., instructor in Italian and English, 1953-56; Harvard University, Cambridge, Mass., instructor, 1957-58, assistant professor of Romance languages, 1958-62; Columbia University, New York, N.Y., associate professor, 1962-66, professor of Italian, 1966—, chairman of department, 1966-70, acting chairman, 1970-71. Visiting lecturer, Columbia University, 1956-57; lecturer to Peace Corps trainees for Somalia, 1966; teacher of reading skills, 1971—. Director of music department, War Prisoners Aid of Young Men's Christian Association, 1945-46. Founder, Reading Skills Foundation, Inc., 1972. *Member:* American Association of University Professors, Dante Society of America, American Association of Teachers of Italian, Phi Beta Kappa. *Awards, honors:* Fulbright scholarship, University of Rome, 1950-51; Guggenheim fellowship, 1960-61.

WRITINGS: (With Hiram Haydn) *A Renaissance Treasury,* Doubleday, 1953; *Renaissance Theory of Love: The Context of Giordano Bruno's "Eroici Furori,"* Columbia University Press, 1958; (editor) Francesco Patrizi, *L'Amorosa Filosofia,* Felice Le Monnier, 1963; (author of introduction) *The Autobiography of Benvenuto Cellini,* Washington Square Press, 1963; (author of introduction) Torquato Tasso, *Jerusalem Delivered,* Capricorn, 1963; (contributor) Bernard S. Levy, editor, *Developments in the Early Renaissance,* State University of New York Press, 1972; (contributor and associate editor) Edward P. Mahoney, editor, *Philosophy and Humanism: Studies in Honor of Paul Oskar Kristeller,* Columbia University Press, 1974. Contributor of articles and reviews to *Encyclopedia Americana, Grolier Encyclopedia, Encyclopedia of World Biography, Dictionary of the History of Ideas, Rinascimento, American Scholar, Renaissance News, Italica,* and *Romantic Review.*

WORK IN PROGRESS: Research on Boccaccio.

BIOGRAPHICAL/CRITICAL SOURCES: *Renaissance News,* Volume XII, number 2, summer, 1959; *Romanic Review,* Volume LIX, number 1, February, 1968.

* * *

NELSON, Mary Carroll 1929-

PERSONAL: Born April 24, 1929, in College Station, Tex.; daughter of James Vincent (an army officer) and Mary (Langton) Carroll; married Edwin Blakely (a retired Army officer; now research consultant), June 27, 1950; children: Patricia Ann, Edwin Blakely, Jr. *Education:* Barnard College, B.A., 1950; University of New Mexico, M.A., 1963, further graduate study, 1969-70. *Politics:* Republican. *Religion:* Catholic. *Home:* 1408 Georgia N.E., Albuquerque, N.M. 87110.

CAREER: Teacher most of the time since 1957, presently in first grade of Sunset Mesa School, Albuquerque, N.M. Professional artist. *Member:* National Writers Club, National League of American Pen Women (member of chapter board, 1970-74; member of state board, 1972-74), Southwestern Watercolor Society, New Mexico Watercolor Society (member of board, 1970-73). *Awards, honors:* Various exhibition awards for paintings.

WRITINGS: (With Robert E. Wood) *Watercolor Workshop,* Watson, 1974.

Author of volumes in American Indian biography series, published by Dillon: *Pablita Velarde,* 1971; *Maria Martinez,* 1972; *Annie Wauneka,* 1972; *Robert L. Bennett,* in press. Contributor to art periodicals. Correspondent to *Scene* (of Southwestern Watercolor Society), 1971-74.

WORK IN PROGRESS: Elementary readers.

* * *

NELSON, Ralph 1916-

PERSONAL: Born August 12, 1916, in New York, N.Y., son of Carl Leo (a chauffeur) and Edith (Lagergreen) Nelson; married Celeste Holm (an actress), September 16, 1936 (divorced, 1938); married third wife, Barbara Powers, February 6, 1954; children: Theodor, Ralph, Peter, Meredith (daughter). *Education:* Attended public school in New York, N.Y. *Home:* 1331 Amalfi Dr., Pacific Palisades, Calif. 90272. *Office:* Rainbow Productions, 911 Gateway West, Century City, Los Angeles, Calif.

CAREER: Actor, 1933-41; director for NBC-TV, 1948-49, and for CBS-TV, 1949-52; Rainbow Productions, Los Angeles, Calif., president, 1959—. *Military service:* U.S. Army Air Force, fighter pilot, 1941-45; became captain. *Member:* Directors Guild of America, Producers Guild, Writers Guild West, Dramatists Guild, Authors' League of America (life member), Screen Actors Guild, American Federation of Radio and Television Actors, Actors Equity Association. *Awards, honors:* John Golden prize, 1943, for *Mail Call;* National Theatre awards, 1943, for *Mail Call* and "Angels Weep," and 1944, for *The Wind is Ninety;* National Theatre fellowship, 1947; Emmy award, National Academy of Television Arts and Sciences, 1956, for direction of "Requiem for a Heavyweight;" Golden Globes Humanitarian award, 1964, for direction of "Lilies of the Field;" also received Golden Bear award of Berlin Film Festival, and Bell Ringer award.

WRITINGS—Plays: *Mail Call* (one-act; produced on Broadway, 1944), French, 1943, also anthologized in *Army Play by Play,* edited by John Golden, Random House, 1943; "Angels Weep" (three-act), first produced in Cleveland at Cleveland Playhouse, 1944; *The Wind is Ninety* (three-act; produced on Broadway, 1944), Dramatic Publishing, 1946. Also author of "Mein Camp," produced for Army Special Services.

Screenplays: "The Man in the Funny Suit," produced by Desilu Playhouse, (with Frank Gabrielson) "The Flight of the Doves," produced by Columbia, and "The Wrath of God," produced by MGM.

(Adaptor with Michael Benthal) "Hamlet," for Old Vic Company, DuPont (television) Show of the Month. Contributor to magazines, including *Yale Review, American Magazine, Theatre Arts, Argosy,* and *Action.*

SIDELIGHTS: Nelson told *CA:* "As French say 'un homme engage.' Films reflect social comment. Have traveled extensively, seeing U.S.A. from frieght cars, to 67 countries first class. Can communicate in Spanish, French, Swedish. Jailed in 18 states before 16 years of age. Now university lecturer on cinema arts. Most important legacy—4 children, all the rest is make-believe." Films directed or produced by Nelson include "Lilies of the

Field," "Father Goose," "Counterpoint," "Charley," and "Requiem for a Heavyweight."

* * *

NELSON, Rosanne E(ierdanz) 1939-

PERSONAL: Born April 22, 1939, in St. Joseph, Mo.; daughter of Carwin C. and Grace (Rice) Eierdanz; married L. C. Nelson (general manager of Rudy-Patrick Co.), March 7, 1964; children: Elliot Eierdanz; stepchildren: Sally Nelson, Grata Nelson, Clayton Nelson. *Education:* Attended School of Christian Writing, Minneapolis, Minn., 1972-73. *Home:* 5625 West 97th Terrace, Overland Park, Kan. 66207.

CAREER: Legal secretary; executive secretary. *Awards, honors:* Dwight L. Moody award from *Decision,* 1973, for *Dear Jesus . . . I'm So Human.*

WRITINGS: Dear Jesus . . . I'm So Human, Doubleday, 1973. Contributor to *Decision, Ladies' Home Journal,* and *Christian Herald.*

WORK IN PROGRESS: A devotional book on loneliness, completion expected in 1974.

* * *

NELSON, Stanley 1933-

PERSONAL: Born June 9, 1933, in Brooklyn, N.Y.; son of Charles (a textile businessman) and Celia (Prager) Nelson; married Ellen Rice Beaty, March 10, 1957 (divorced December, 1965); married Betty Jean Minton Skrefstad (a medical writer/editor), June 26, 1966; children: (first marriage) Celia, Lycette. *Education:* University of Vermont, B.A., 1957. *Politics:* "I am essentially apolitical." *Religion:* Jewish. *Home:* 372 Pacific St., Brooklyn, N.Y. 11217.

CAREER: Teacher of retarded children in early years; *Medical World News,* New York, N.Y., news editor, 1963-65; *Roche Image,* New York, N.Y., senior writer, 1965-66; *Hospital Practice,* New York, N.Y., senior editor, 1966-69; poet and playwright. Director of Generalist Association; member of board of directors, Theatre 77. *Member:* National Association of Science Writers, American Medical Writers Association, American Association for the Advancement of Science. *Awards, honors:* Thomas Wolfe Memorial Award for Poetry.

WRITINGS: Idlewild (poems), Smith, 1969; *The Brooklyn Book of the Dead* (poems), Smith, 1971; (editor with Harry Smith) *The Scene/1* (play anthology), New Egypt Publications, 1972; (editor with Smith) *The Scene/2,* New Egypt Publications, 1974.

Also author of plays, including: "Emanons," "Shuffle-Off," and "Mr. Optometrist" (all one-acts), all first produced in New York, N.Y., at Bastiano's Cellar Studio, April, 1968; "The Harrison Progressive School" (one-act), first produced at Bastiano's Cellar Studio, October, 1968; "Mrs. Peacock" (one-act), first produced Off-Off-Broadway at Old Reliable Theatre, August, 1969, a two-act version produced Off-Off-Broadway at Omni Theatre Club, May, 1972; "The Examination" (one-act), produced Off-Off-Broadway by New York Theatre Ensemble, July, 1969; "The Plan," produced by New York Theatre Ensemble, January, 1970; "Ruth and the Rabbi" (one-act), produced Off-Off-Broadway at Omni Theatre Club, October, 1970; "Tsk, Mary, Tsk" (one-act), produced in New York, N.Y., at Stagelights Theatrical Club, April, 1970, produced under title, "The Mary Show," in New York, N.Y., at Stagelights II, April, 1971; "El Exejente" (one-act), first produced Off-Off-Broadway at Playhouse Theatre, September, 1971; "The Butler Carries the Sun Away" (one-act), first produced at Playhouse Theatre, 1971; "Rite of Spring" (two-act), first produced in New York, N.Y., at WPA Theatre, June, 1972; "The Master Psychoanalyst" (three-act), first produced at New Old Reliable Theatre, October, 1972; "The Poetry Reading" (one-act), first produced Off-Off-Broadway at Cubiculo Theatre, June, 1973; "No One Writes Drawing Room Comedies Anymore" (one-act), first produced in New York, N.Y., at Joseph Jefferson Theatre, August, 1973; "Poe: From His Life and Mind" (two-act), first produced in New York, N.Y., at Theatre 77, 1974.

Plays have been published in *Red Cedar Review* and *Scene* and poetry in about fifty periodicals, including *Beloit Poetry Journal, Kansas Quarterly, Caterpillar, Tri-Quarterly,* and *Confrontation.* Also contributor of theatre and poetry criticism to literary journals.

WORK IN PROGRESS: A modern version of *Ecclesiates,* titled *The Travels of Ben Sira;* and a play, "Paul, the Apostle."

AVOCATIONAL INTERESTS: Music (especially jazz), sports (especially pro football), the ancient world.

* * *

NELSON, William 1908-

PERSONAL: Born January 18, 1908, in New York, N.Y.; son of Bendet (a physician) and Margaret (Ginsburg) Nelson; married Elsa Elizabeth Robinson (a professor emeritus), June 13, 1930; children: Susan Elizabeth (Mrs. R. David Arkush), William. *Education:* City College (now City College of the City University of New York), B.S., 1927; Columbia University, M.A., 1928, Ph.D., 1939. *Home:* 410 Riverside Dr., New York, N.Y. 10025. *Office:* Department of English, Columbia University, New York, N.Y. 10027.

CAREER: High school English teacher in public schools in New York, N.Y., 1928-42; U.S. State Department, Office of War Information, Washington, D.C., field representative in Moscow, 1942-45; editor of *Amerika* magazine, 1945-47; Library of Congress, Washington, D.C., member of staff, 1947-48; Columbia University, New York, N.Y., assistant professor, 1949-53, associate professor, 1953-56, professor of English, 1956-73, William Peterfield Trent Professor of English, 1973—. *Member:* Renaissance Society of America (executive director, 1962-70; trustee, 1970—), English Association, Modern Humanities Research Association. *Awards, honors:* Guggenheim fellowship, 1956.

WRITINGS: John Skelton: Laureate, Columbia University Press, 1939; (editor) *Out of the Crocodile's Mouth,* Public Affairs Press, 1949; (editor) *Barclay's Life of St. George,* Early English Text Society, 1955; (editor) *A Fifteenth Century School Book,* Clarendon Press, 1958; *The Poetry of Edmund Spenser,* Columbia University Press, 1963; *Fact or Fiction,* Harvard University Press, 1973.

* * *

NEMEC, David 1938-

PERSONAL: Surname is pronounced *Nemm*-ick; born December 10, 1938, in Lakewood, Ohio; son of Joseph Sylvester (a businessman) and Ann (Sigan) Nemec. *Education:* Ohio State University, B.A., 1960, M.A., 1965. *Resi-*

dence: New York, N.Y. *Agent:* Mary Yost Associates, 141 East 55th St., New York, N.Y. 10022.

CAREER: Teacher in public school in Cleveland, Ohio, 1962-64; counselor in public school in New York, N.Y., 1966-70; New York State Department of Parole, New York, N.Y., parole officer, 1970—. *Military service:* U.S. Army, 1960-61. *Awards, honors:* Special mention from *Transatlantic Review*'s novella contest, 1967, for "On the Produce Dock"; included in honor roll of *Best American Short Stories,* 1968 and 1972; Yaddo summer fellowship, 1973.

WRITINGS: Survival Prose, Bobbs-Merrill, 1971. Contributor of articles and short stories to national magazines and newspapers.

WORK IN PROGRESS: Max Out, a novel; *The Baseball Expert's Quiz Book;* a book on tennis.

SIDELIGHTS: Nemec has been a college and semi-professional baseball and tennis player. He calls himself "a self-proclaimed authority on sports trivia, especially baseball."

* * *

NEWELL, Rosemary 1922- (Rosemary Gibson)

PERSONAL: Born July 13, 1922, in Parthenon, Ark.; daughter of William Russel and Madge (Thomas) Phillips; married Thomas Newton Newell, January 1, 1940 (divorced, 1973); married Arrell Morgan Gibson (a history professor and writer), July 22, 1973; children: (first marriage) Lawrence Wayne, Thomas Phillip, Vicki Margaret (Mrs. Mont Wheeler, Jr.), Rita Suzanne (Mrs. Freddy Ray Barton, Jr.). *Education:* Attended Arkansas Polytechnical College, Tulsa University, and Oklahoma University. *Agent:* Knox Burger Literary Agency, 39½ Washington Sq. S., New York, N.Y. 10012.

CAREER: Secretary at Unit Rig and Equipment Co., Tulsa, Okla., 1941-45, Geological Enterprises, Ardmore, Okla., 1948-49, 1965, and Oklahoma University, Norman, 1967. Teacher of creative writing. *Member:* Westerners International, Penwomen, Oklahoma Writers' Federation (board member, 1972-73), Norman Historical Society (charter member), Ardmore Historical Society (charter member), Norman Writer's Galaxy (president, 1972-73).

WRITINGS: Star House, Popular Library, 1973. Contributor to journals.

WORK IN PROGRESS: Dragon Door; Ride a Golden Horse, completion expected in 1974; a book about Hopi Indians, *Kachina Ghost,* 1975.

SIDELIGHTS: Rosemary Newell told *CA:* "A visit to Surinam, South America prompted my writing of *Star House*. The beauty of the jungle and the people impregnated me with plot ideas which I longed to share. The country isn't widely known in the United States and I think it should be for there are many parallels—the mixture of races, the spirit of freedom and independence—along with some striking differences as well. They have more pride in their ethnic identities. This one small country is like a composite of many countries because of the variety of races there who have maintained their ethnic individuality."

BIOGRAPHICAL/CRITICAL SOURCES: Norman Transcript, October 12, 1972; *Tulsa World,* October 31, 1972; *Lawton Morning Press,* April 21, 1973.

NEWHALL, Nancy 1908-1974

May 9, 1908—July 7, 1974; American photography critic, conservationist, biographer, and author or editor of photographic essay books. Obituaries: *New York Times,* July 10, 1974.

* * *

NEWLIN, Margaret Rudd 1925- (Margaret Rudd)

PERSONAL: Born February 27, 1925, in New York, N.Y.; daughter of James H. and Marie (McLaughlin) Rudd; married Nicholas Newlin (a professor of English), April 2, 1956; children: James, David, Robin, Thomas. *Education:* Bryn Mawr College, B.A., 1947; University of Reading, Ph.D., 1951. *Home address:* Shipley Farm, Secane, Pa. 19018.

CAREER: Bryn Mawr College, Bryn Mawr, Pa., employed in office of admissions, 1948, instructor in English, 1953-54; Washington College, Chestertown, Md., instructor in English, 1955-56. Instructor in English at Harcum Junior College, 1953-54. *Member:* Poetry Society of America, Poetry Society (London, England). *Awards, honors:* International Greenwood Prize from London Poetry Society, 1969, 1971.

WRITINGS—Under name Margaret Rudd: *Divided Image: A Study of Yeats and Blake,* Routledge & Kegan Paul, 1953, Haskell House, 1970; *Organiz'd Innocence: The Story of Blake's Prophetic Books,* Routledge & Kegan Paul, 1956, Greenwood, 1973.

Poetry—under name Margaret Newlin: *The Fragile Immigrants,* Carcanet, 1971; *Day of Sirens,* Carcanet, 1973. Contributor to *Critical Quarterly*. Poetry editor of *Bryn Mawr Alumni Bulletin*.

WORK IN PROGRESS: The Snow Falls Upward, a collection of poems; *Maxim,* a book for children, illustrated with photographs; a study of chief women poets from the time of Sappho to the present.

SIDELIGHTS: "Most serious artists," Margaret Newlin wrote, "if they are honest, write in an effort to capture what they love before it dissipates, and to frame, distance, and explain to themselves that which is painful and difficult. . . .A gut response of gooseflesh, raised scalp, and tingling spine is, after all, the only possible criterion, a recognition. And yet it is the intellect that must affirm quality." *Avocational interests:* Children, animals, cooking, swimming, ice-skating, drawing, taking photographs, travel.

* * *

NEWLON, Clarke (Machael Clarke)

PERSONAL: Born in Griswold, Iowa; married Betty Sniffen, May 23, 1936; children: Michael, Richard. *Education:* Attended Grinnell College. *Politics:* Democrat. *Home and office:* 3714 Massachusetts Ave., Washington, D.C. 20016. *Agent:* Collins-Knowlton-Wing, Inc., 60 East 56th St., New York, N.Y. 10022.

CAREER: U.S. Air Force, career officer, 1942-58, retiring as colonel; has worked as newspaper reporter and editor, and magazine writer and editor; presently, writer. Former consultant to U.S. Intelligence Agency and National Aeronautics and Space Administration. *Member:* International Press Club, National Press Club.

WRITINGS—All published by Dodd, except as noted: *1001 Questions Answered about Space,* 1962, revised edition, 1964, revised edition also published as *1001 Answers to Questions about Space,* Grosset, 1966; *Famous Pioneers in Space,* 1963; *L.B.J.: The Man from Johnson City,* 1964, revised edition, 1966; *The Fighting Douglas MacArthur,* 1965; (compiler) *The Aerospace Age Dictionary,* F. Watts, 1965; *Famous Mexican-Americans,* 1972; *Men Who Made Mexico,* 1973; *Police Dogs in Action* (Junior Literary Guild selection), 1974. Contributor to magazines, sometimes under pseudonym Machael Clarke.

* * *

NEWTON, Brian 1928-

PERSONAL: Born July 24, 1928, in Wigan, England; son of Robert Drayton (a clerk) and Edith (Elliott) Newton; married Niki Papalou, June 29, 1955; children: Alexandra, Paul. *Education:* Queen's College, Oxford, M.A., 1953. *Politics:* Liberal. *Religion:* Agnostic. *Home:* 6465 Napier St., Burnaby, British Columbia, Canada. *Office:* Department of Linguistics, Simon Fraser University, Burnaby, British Columbia, Canada.

CAREER: Taught in Cyprus, 1952-55; Cape Town University, Cape Town, South Africa, lecturer in classics, 1957-64; University of Witwatersrand, Johannesburg, South Africa, senior lecturer in linguistics, 1964-65; Simon Fraser University, Burnaby, British Columbia, assistant professor, 1965-66, associate professor, 1966-71, professor of linguistics, 1971—. *Member:* Linguistic Society of America.

WRITINGS: Cypriot Greek: Its Phonology and Inflections, Mouton & Co., 1972; *The Generative Interpretation of Dialect,* Cambridge University Press, 1972. Contributor to *Lingua, Word, Language, Greece and Rome, Journal of Linguistics, Phoenix,* and *Canadian Journal of Linguistics.*

WORK IN PROGRESS: Research in the verb inflections of modern Greek dialects, and in verbal aspects in Greek and Macedonian dialects.

* * *

NGAGOYEANES, Nicholas 1939- (Nicholas Gage)

PERSONAL: Born July 23, 1939, in Greece; son of Christos (a chef) and Eleni (Haidis) Ngagoyeanes; married Joan Paulson (a writer); children: Christos. *Education:* Boston University, B.S., 1963; Columbia University, M.S., 1964. *Politics:* Democrat. *Religion:* Greek Orthodox. *Home:* 393 West End Ave., New York, N.Y. 10024. *Agent:* Stephen Kaufman, L. M. Rosenthal, Inc., 666 Fifth Ave., New York, N.Y. *Office: New York Times,* 229 West 43rd St., New York, N.Y. 10036.

CAREER: Associated Press, New York, N.Y., reporter, 1965-67; *Wall Street Journal,* New York, N.Y., investigative reporter, 1967-69; *New York Times,* New York, N.Y., investigative reporter, 1970—.

WRITINGS—All under pseudonym Nicholas Gage: *Portrait of Greece,* American Heritage Press, 1971; *The Mafia Is Not an Equal Opportunity Employer,* McGraw, 1972; *Mafia U.S.A.,* Playboy Press, 1973; *Bones of Contention* (novel), Putnam, 1974.

WORK IN PROGRESS: A novel about the world of Greek shipowners.

NICHOLAS, David M(ansfield) 1939-

PERSONAL: Born October 11, 1939, in Knoxville, Tenn.; son of David M. (an engineer) and Iris (Ward) Nicholas; married Karen Schroeder, July 2, 1967; children: Keith D., Jennifer M. *Education:* University of North Carolina, A.B., 1961; University of California, Berkeley, A.M., 1963; Brown University, Ph.D., 1967. *Home:* 3501 Mohawk St., Lincoln, Neb. 68510. *Office:* Department of History, University of Nebraska, Lincoln, Neb. 68508.

CAREER: University of Nebraska, Lincoln, assistant professor, 1967-71, associate professor of history, 1971—. *Member:* Mediaeval Academy of America, American Historical Association. *Awards, honors:* Social Science Research Council fellowship, 1966; American Council of Learned Societies grant-in-aid, 1969; National Endowment for the Humanities fellowship for younger scholars, 1969-70.

WRITINGS: Town and Countryside: Social, Economic, and Political Tensions in Fourteenth-Century Flanders, University of Ghent Press, 1971; *Stad en Platteland in de Middeleeuwen* (title means "Town and Countryside in the Middle Ages"), Fibula-Van Dishoeck, 1971; *The Medieval West: A Preindustrial Civilization,* Dorsey, 1973. Contributor to journals.

WORK IN PROGRESS: Ghent in the Age of the Arteveldes; Social Flanders in the Fourteenth Century.

* * *

NICOL, Eric (Patrick) 1919- (Jabez)

PERSONAL: Born December 28, 1919, in Kingston, Ontario, Canada; son of William (an accountant) and Amelia (Mannock) Nicol; married Myrl Mary Helen Heselton (a nurse), September 13, 1955; children: Catherine, Claire, Christopher. *Education:* University of British Columbia, B.A., 1941, M.A., 1948; attended Sorbonne, University of Paris, 1949-50. *Politics:* "Anarchist, in theory; liberal, in practice." *Religion:* No church affiliation. *Home and office:* 3993 West 36th Ave., Vancouver, British Columbia V6N 2S7, Canada.

CAREER: Free-lance writer for radio and television in London, England, 1949-51; *Province* (newspaper), Vancouver, British Columbia, syndicated columnist, 1951—. *Military service:* Royal Canadian Air Force, 1942-45. *Awards, honors:* Stephen Leacock Medal for Humour, for *The Roving I,* 1950, *Shall We Join the Ladies?,* 1955, and *Girdle Me a Globe,* 1957.

WRITINGS: (Under pseudonym Jabez) *Sense and Nonsense,* Ryerson, 1948; (under pseudonym Jabez) *The Roving I,* Ryerson, 1950; *Twice Over Lightly,* Ryerson, 1953; *Girdle Me a Globe,* Ryerson, 1957; *Shall We Join the Ladies?,* Ryerson, 1958; *In Darkest Domestica,* Ryerson, 1959; *An Uninhibited History of Canada,* D. Hackett, 1959, 5th edition, Musson, 1965; (with Peter Whalley) *Say Uncle: A Completely Uncalled-for History of the U.S.,* Harper, 1961; *A Herd of Yaks: The Best of Eric Nicol,* Ryerson, 1962; (with Whalley) *Russia, Anyone? A Completely Uncalled-for History of the USSR,* Harper, 1963; *Space Age, Go Home!,* Ryerson, 1964; (with Whalley) *100 Years of What?,* Ryerson, 1966; *A Scar Is Born,* Ryerson, 1968; *Vancouver,* Doubleday, 1970; *Don't Move! Renovate Your House & Make Social Contracts,* McClellan and Stewart, 1971; *Still a Nicol,* McGraw-Ryerson, 1972; *Letters to My Son,* Macmillan, 1974.

Plays: "Like Father, Like Fun" (three-act), first produced in Vancouver, B.C., at Playhouse Theatre, 1966, produced as "A Minor Adjustment" on Broadway at Brooks Atkinson Theatre, October 6, 1967; "Beware the Quickly Who" (for children; two-act), first produced in Vancouver, B.C., at Metro (now Holiday) Theatre, 1967; "The Clam Who Made a Face" (for children; one-act), first produced at Holiday Theatre, 1968; "The Fourth Monkey" (three-act), first produced at Playhouse Theatre, 1969; "Pillar of Sand" (two-act), first produced in Ottawa, Ont., at National Theatre, 1973. Also author of three-act play, "Regulus," first produced in Vancouver, B.C., at Peretz Theatre.

Television plays: "The Bathroom," 1963; "The Man from Inner Space," 1974.

Also author of several dozen radio plays and contributor to radio revue, "Inside from the Outside" (CBS), 1970—. Contributor to *Maclean's* and *Saturday Night*.

WORK IN PROGRESS: A stage play.

AVOCATIONAL INTERESTS: Tennis, badminton, and gardening.

* * *

NICOLAS, F. R. E.
See FREELING, Nicolas

* * *

NIEDZIELSKI, Henri 1931-

PERSONAL: Born March 30, 1931, in Troyes, France; naturalized U.S. citizen; son of Sigismond (a tailor) and Anna (Pelik) Niedzielski; married Doris Poscente, October 5, 1957; children: Henri, Jr., Daniel, Robert, Annapia. *Education:* University of Dijon, Ph.B., 1954; University of Connecticut, B.A., 1959, M.A., 1963, Ph.D., 1964. *Religion:* Roman Catholic. *Home:* 1890 East West Center Road, Honolulu, Hawaii 96822. *Office:* Department of European Languages, University of Hawaii, Honolulu, Hawaii 96822.

CAREER: Instructor in French at University of Connecticut, Storrs, 1962, and University of Massachusetts, Amherst, 1962-64; Laval University, Quebec City, Quebec, assistant professor of medieval French literature, 1964-65; University of Massachusetts, assistant professor of French, 1965-66; University of Hawaii, Honolulu, associate professor of French, 1966—. Fulbright lecturer in Poland, 1972-74. Free-lance translator, 1960—. President, Family Education Centers of Hawaii, 1968-72; family counselor in Adlerian psychology. *Military service:* French Army, 1951-53; became sergeant. *Member:* American Association of Teachers of French, American Council on the Teaching of Foreign Languages, American Society of Adlerian Psychology, Alliance Francaise (member of chapter board of directors, 1968-70), Hawaiian Association of Language Teachers (president, 1968-69).

WRITINGS: Le Roman de Helcanus, Droz, 1966; (with T. H. Mueller) *Basic French: A Programmed Course,* Appleton, 1968; (with Mueller and E. Mayer) *Handbook of French Structure: A Systematic Review,* Harcourt, 1968; *Intermediate French: Individualized Instruction,* Intermedia, 1972; *Handbook of French Composition,* Educational Research Associates, in press. Editor, *Language and Literature in Hawaii,* 1968—.

WORK IN PROGRESS: Getting Into the International Scene; developing audiovisual aids for the teaching of phonetics.

SIDELIGHTS: In addition to French, Niedzielski is competent in Italian, German, Polish, Russian, and Spanish.

* * *

NIMMER, Melville B(ernard) 1923-

PERSONAL: Born June 6, 1923, in Los Angeles, Calif.; son of Frank Edward and Mrs. Nimmer; married Gloria Dee Madoff (a teacher), 1946; children: Rebecca (Mrs. Paul Marcus), Laurence, David. *Education:* University of California, Berkeley, A.B., 1947; Harvard University, LL.B., 1950. *Home:* 715 Malcolm Ave., Los Angeles, Calif. 90024. *Office:* School of Law, University of California, Los Angeles, 405 Hilgard, Los Angeles, Calif. 90024.

CAREER: University of California, Los Angeles, lecturer, 1961-62, acting professor, 1962-63, professor of law, 1963—. Member of Library of Congress Panel of Experts, 1957—. *Military service:* U.S. Army, 1942-46; became sergeant. *Member:* American Bar Association, Copyright Society of the U.S. (trustee, 1962—). *Awards, honors:* Grants from Ford Foundation, 1964-65, and National Endowment for the Arts, 1967-68.

WRITINGS: Nimmer on Copyright, Matthew Bender, 1963; *Cases and Materials on Copyright and Other Aspects of Law Pertaining to Literary, Musical and Artistic Works,* West Publishing, 1971.

* * *

NIXON, George 1924-

PERSONAL: Born September 10, 1924, in Yugoslavia; son of Milos (a steelworker) and Milica (Trbovich) Nixon; married Joan Waddilove (a biologist), September 17, 1945; children: Jill, Rebecca. *Education:* University of Pittsburgh, B.S., 1949, M.S., 1951; George Washington University, Ed.D., 1970. *Politics:* "Liberal in human affairs; conservative fiscally." *Religion:* Episcopalian. *Home:* 8933 Cherbourg Dr., Potomac, Md. 20854. *Office:* Department of Health, Education, and Welfare, U.S. Public Health Service, Health Services Administration, 5600 Fishers Lane, Rockville, Md. 20852.

CAREER: Standard Register Co., Dayton, Ohio, director of organization development, 1951-64; Leadership Resources Inc., Washington, D.C., senior associate, 1960-64; Department of Health, Education, and Welfare, U.S. Public Health Service, Washington, D.C., chief training officer, 1964-73; George Washington University, Washington, D.C., associate professorial lecturer, 1964—; Department of Health, Education and Welfare, Health Services Administration, Rockville,Md., Chief of employee development, 1973—. *Military service:* U.S. Army, 1943-46; served in Europe; received four battle stars. *Member:* International Personnel Management Association, American Psychological Association, American Society for Training and Development, Division of Industrial and Organizational Psychology, Adult Education Association.

WRITINGS: People Evaluation and Achievement, Gulf Publishing, 1973.

* * *

NIXON, Marion 1930-

PERSONAL: Born August 11, 1930, in Croydon, England; daughter of Ernest Alfred (an insurance agent) and Ethel Annie (Bond) Putnam; married Dennis Andrew Nixon (a university senior lecturer in physiology), August 6, 1955 (died December 9, 1972); children: Ann Helen Sarah, Peter Mark Ian. *Education:* University of London, B.Sc., 1962, Ph.D., 1968. *Politics:* Liberal. *Religion:* Church of England. *Home:* 60 Norfolk Rd., New Barnet, Hertfordshire EN5 5LT, England. *Office:* Department of Anatomy, University College, Gower St., London WC1E 6BT, England.

CAREER: University College, University of London, London, England, research assistant working on octopi and other cephalopods, 1962—. *Member:* Zoological Society (London), Marine Biological Association, Society of Experimental Biologists.

WRITINGS: *The Oxford Book of Vertebrates,* Oxford University Press, 1972. Contributor to *Journal of Zoology* and other science publications.

AVOCATIONAL INTERESTS: Fossil hunting, reading, walking, and photography.

* * *

NOBLE, David Watson 1925-

PERSONAL: Born March 17, 1925, in Princeton, N.J.; son of Charles John (an attorney) and Agnes (Konow) Noble; married Lois Keller, August 2, 1944; children: David, Jr., Jeffrey, Douglas, Patricia. *Education:* Princeton University, B.A., 1948; University of Wisconsin, M.A., 1949, Ph.D., 1952. *Religion:* Episcopalian. *Home:* 2089 Commonwealth Ave., St. Paul, Minn. 55108. *Office:* 723 Social Science, University of Minnesota, Minneapolis, Minn. 55455.

CAREER: University of Minnesota, Minneapolis, instructor, 1952-55, assistant professor, 1955-58, associate professor, 1958-65, professor of American history, 1965—. *Military service:* U.S. Army, 1943-44. *Member:* American Studies Association.

WRITINGS: *The Paradox of Progressive Thought,* University of Minnesota Press, 1958; *Historians Against History,* University of Minnesota Press, 1965; *The Eternal Adam and the New World Garden,* Braziller, 1968; *The Progressive Mind,* Rand McNally, 1970; (with Peter Carroll) *The Restless Centuries: A History of the American People,* Burgess, 1973.

WORK IN PROGRESS: *Negative Revolution: The Failure of the American Political Imagination.*

* * *

NODDINGS, Thomas C. 1933-

PERSONAL: Born December 30, 1933, in Perth Amboy, N.J.; son of William C. and Sarah S. (Cox) Noddings; married Edna Francene Christoph, February 6, 1954; children: Douglas S., Thomas D., John G. *Education:* Purdue University, B.S., 1955; Rutgers University, M.B.A., 1958. *Home:* 4731 Grand Ave., Western Springs, Ill. 60558. *Office:* E. F. Hutton & Co., 141 West Jackson, Chicago, Ill. 60604.

CAREER: Trane Co., La Crosse, Wis., product manager, 1958-67; Crane Co., Chicago, Ill., director of engineering, 1967-71; E. F. Hutton & Co., Chicago, Ill., stock broker, 1971—.

WRITINGS: *The Dow-Jones-Irwin Guide to Convertible Securities,* Dow-Jones-Irwin, 1973.

WORK IN PROGRESS: Research on options traded on the Chicago Board Options Exchange.

NOON, Brian 1919- (Stephen Kurdsen)

PERSONAL: Born September 30, 1919; son of James Patrick and Elizabeth (McKee) Noon; married Tamar Anne Kindleysides, April 3, 1948; children: Anthony, Pamela, Elizabeth H. *Education:* Attended St. Anselm's College, Birkenhead, England. *Politics:* Liberal. *Home:* 18 Reddenhill Rd., Torquay, Devonshire, England.

CAREER: Artist and graphologist. *Military service:* British Army, 1939-45. *Member:* National Union of Journalists.

WRITINGS: (Under pseudonym Stephen Kurdsen) *Graphology: The New Science,* Acropolis Books, 1971. Contributor of poems and articles to periodicals.

WORK IN PROGRESS: Research in mental and psychological symptoms shown in handwriting.

* * *

NORDYKE, James W(alter) 1930-

PERSONAL: Born June 21, 1930, in Rock Springs, Wyo.; son of Raymond B. (in farm management) and G. Marie (Perry) Nordyke. *Education:* Stanford University, B.A., 1952; Princeton University, M.A., 1957, Ph.D., 1959. *Home:* 1810 East Missouri Ave., Las Cruces, N.M. 88001. *Office address:* Department of Economics, New Mexico State University, Box 3CQ, Las Cruces, N.M. 88001.

CAREER: Kenyon College, Gambier, Ohio, instructor, 1958-60, assistant professor of economics, 1960-64; New Mexico State University, Las Cruces, associate professor, 1964-69, professor of economics, 1969—. Consultant to *Choice.* *Military service:* U.S. Army, 1953-55. *Member:* American Economic Association, American Association of University Professors, Association for Evolutionary Economics, Association for Comparative Economics, Western Economic Association, Phi Beta Kappa, Phi Kappa Phi.

WRITINGS: (With Martin Schnitzer) *Comparative Economic Systems,* South-Western, 1971.

* * *

NORLAND, Howard Bernett 1932-

PERSONAL: Born March 1, 1932; son of Ludwig Herman and Gerda A. (Canton) Norland; married LuJean Ann Pierce, December 14, 1954; children: Genevieve Lynne, Timothy James. *Education:* St. Olaf College, B.A., 1954; University of Wisconsin, M.S., 1958, Ph.D., 1962. *Residence:* Lincoln, Neb. *Office:* Department of English, University of Nebraska, Lincoln, Neb. 68508.

CAREER: University of Kansas, Lawrence, instructor in English, 1961-63; University of Nebraska, Lincoln, assistant professor, 1963-67, associate professor, 1967-71, professor of English, 1971—. *Military service:* U.S. Air Force, 1954-56; became first lieutenant. *Member:* Renaissance Society of America, Modern Language Association of America. *Awards, honors:* Folger Shakespeare Library fellow, 1967.

WRITINGS: (Editor) Francis Beaumont and John Fletcher, *The Maid's Tragedy,* University of Nebraska Press, 1968; (editor) A. C. Swinburne, *A Study of Ben Jonson,* University of Nebraska Press, 1969. Member of advisory board of *Genre.*

* * *

NORMAN, Donald A(rthur) 1935-

PERSONAL: Born December 25, 1935, in New York,

N.Y.; son of Noah N. (with U.S. Public Health Service) and Miriam (Friedman) Norman; children: Cynthia, Michael. *Education:* Massachusetts Institute of Technology, B.S.E.E., 1957; University of Pennsylvania, M.S.E.E., 1959, Ph.D., 1962. *Office:* Department of Psychology, University of California at San Diego, La Jolla, Calif. 92037.

CAREER: Harvard University, Cambridge, Mass., lecturer in psychology, 1964-66; University of California at San Diego, La Jolla, associate professor, 1966-69, professor of psychology, 1969—. Fellow, Center for Advanced Study in the Behavioral Sciences, 1973-74. *Member:* American Psychological Association, Association for Computing Machinery, American Association for the Advancement of Science, Psychonomic Society. *Awards, honors:* National Science Foundation postdoctoral fellow at Harvard University, 1962-65.

WRITINGS: Memory and Attention: An Introduction to Human Information Processing, Wiley, 1968; (editor) *Models of Human Memory,* Academic Press, 1970; (with Peter Lindsay) *Human Information Processing,* Academic Press, 1972. Contributor to professional journals. Member of editorial board, *Cognitive Psychology.*

WORK IN PROGRESS: With D. E. Rumelhart, *Explorations in Cognition.*

* * *

NORMAN, Marc 1941-

PERSONAL: Born February 10, 1941, in Los Angeles, Calif.; son of Harry Fisher and Molly (Gillis) Norman; married Dale Moore (a psychotherapist), 1967; children: Zachary, Alexander (twins). *Education:* University of California, Berkeley, M.A., 1964. *Agent:* Robert Lescher, 155 East 71st St., New York, N.Y. 10021.

MEMBER: Phi Beta Kappa.

WRITINGS: Bike Riding in Los Angeles, Dutton, 1973; *Oklahoma Crude,* Dutton, 1973. Author of two screenplays, "Oklahoma Crude" and "Zandy's Bride."

SIDELIGHTS: Norman is an acrobatic pilot.

* * *

NORRIS, Donald F(ranklin) 1942-

PERSONAL: Born October 2, 1942, in Memphis, Tenn.; married; children: two. *Education:* Memphis State University, B.S., 1964; University of Virginia, M.A., 1968, Ph.D., 1971. *Home:* 905 Chippewa S.E., Grand Rapids, Mich. 49506. *Office:* Greater Grand Rapids Chamber of Commerce, 300 Federal Square Bldg., Grand Rapids, Mich. 49502.

CAREER: U.S. Public Health Service, St. Louis, Mo., member of staff of Venereal Disease Branch working with St. Louis City Health Department, 1964-65; Memphis Municipal Juvenile Court, Memphis, Tenn., probation and non-support officer, 1965-66; Aquinas College, Grand Rapids, Mich., assistant professor of political science and head of department, 1970-72; Greater Grand Rapids Chamber of Commerce, Grand Rapids, Mich., director of community development and governmental affairs, 1973—. Member of board of directors of Greater Grand Rapids Housing Corp., 1974—. *Military service:* U.S. Marine Corps Reserve, 1962-68; became sergeant. *Member:* American Political Science Association, Midwest Political Science Association, Southern Political Science Association, West Michigan Civil Liberties Union (member of board of directors, 1971-73; chairman of board, 1972).

WRITINGS: Police-Community Relations: A Program That Failed, Lexington Books, 1973. Writer of monographs on police-school liaison. Contributor to *Virginia Town and City* and *Grand Rapids.*

WORK IN PROGRESS: An Analysis of Local Governmental Reform in Michigan: The Case of County Home Rule; and *A Study of Criminal Victimization in a Grand Rapids Neighborhood.*

* * *

NORTH, Alvin J(ohn) 1917-

PERSONAL: Surname originally Kleinsasser; name legally changed in 1948; born June 21, 1917, in Chasely, N.D.; son of Jacob George and Anna (Wipf) Kleinsasser; married Dorothy Phillips, January 6, 1943; children: Linda Schmidt. *Education:* University of South Dakota, B.A., 1940; Yale University, M.A., 1942, Ph.D., 1948. *Home:* 6622 Lupton Dr., Dallas, Tex. 75225. *Office:* University of Texas Health Science Center at Dallas, 5323 Harry Hines Blvd., Dallas, Tex. 75235.

CAREER: Southern Methodist University, Dallas, Tex., assistant professor, 1948-51, associate professor, 1951-58, professor of psychology, 1958-68; University of Texas Health Science Center at Dallas, professor of psychology and neurology, 1968—. Member of Texas State Board of Examiners of Psychologists, 1969-74. *Military service:* U.S. Army Air Forces, 1941-46; became captain. U.S. Air Force Reserve, 1965—; current rank, lieutenant colonel. *Member:* American Psychological Association (fellow), Psychonomic Society, Phi Beta Kappa.

WRITINGS: (With A. Q. Sartain, J. R. Strange, and H. M. Chapman) *Psychology: Understanding Human Behavior,* McGraw, 1958, 4th edition, 1973.

WORK IN PROGRESS: Research on human learning and memory.

AVOCATIONAL INTERESTS: Painting, drawing, photography, playing violin.

* * *

NORTH, Eleanor B(eryl) 1898-

PERSONAL: Born July 6, 1898, in Mercer, Pa.; daughter of Jacob Z. (a businessman) and Lois (Caldwell) North. *Education:* Pennsylvania State University, B.A., 1923, M.A., 1925; graduate study at Cambridge University, 1929, 1930-32, Oxford University, 1934-36, and Harvard University, 1942-43; also attended University of London and Sorbonne, University of Paris. *Home and office:* 204 East Hamilton Ave., State College, Pa. 16801.

CAREER: Juniata College, Huntingdon, Pa., assistant professor of English, 1925-28; Youngstown College (now Youngstown State University), Youngstown, Ohio, professor of English, 1929-37; Maryland State College, St. Mary's City, professor of English, 1941-49; Berry College, Mt. Berry, Ga., associate professor of English, 1951-63. *Member:* World Poetry Society, American Association of University Professors, American Association of University Women, National Education Association, Young Women's Christian Association of America, American Poetry League, Royal Order of Bookfellows, Great Books Association, Shakespeare Foundation, Daughters of the American Revolution, Delta Kappa Gamma, Sigma Tau Delta.

Awards, honors: Medal from Accademia Internazionali, Rome, Italy, 1968.

WRITINGS—Poetry: *Star Dust,* Torch Press, 1930; *Fall of Dew,* Torch Press, 1936; *Grace Notes,* Torch Press, 1953; *My Heart Sings,* National Poetry Press, 1969. Contributor to *American Poet, Prairie Poet, Fleur, Filigree, Wings, Quaderni Di Poesia, Alpen, United Poets, Church Advocate, Church Window, Gem, Sea to Sea in Song, National Poetry Anthology,* and *Poetry.*

WORK IN PROGRESS: A book of poetry, *High Tide.*

* * *

NORTON, Mary Beth 1943-

PERSONAL: Born March 25, 1943, in Ann Arbor, Mich.; daughter of Clark Frederic (an employee of U.S. Senate) and Mary (a professor; maiden name, Lunny) Norton. *Education:* University of Michigan, A.B., 1964; Harvard University, A.M., 1965, Ph.D., 1969. *Residence:* Ithaca, N.Y. *Office:* Department of History, McGraw Hall, Cornell University, Ithaca, N.Y. 14850.

CAREER: University of Connecticut, Storrs, assistant professor of history, 1969-71; Cornell University, Ithaca, N.Y., assistant professor of American history, 1971—. *Member:* American Historical Association, Organization of American Historians, Society of American Historians, Berkshire Conference of Women Historians, Coordinating Committee of Women in the Historical Profession, Phi Beta Kappa, Mortar Board, Phi Kappa Phi. *Awards, honors:* Woodrow Wilson fellowship, 1964; Allan Nevins Prize of Society of American Historians, 1969, for best doctoral dissertation in American history.

WRITINGS: The British-Americans: The Loyalist Exiles in England, 1774-1789, Little, Brown, 1972. Contributor to *History Today, William and Mary Quarterly,* and other journals.

WORK IN PROGRESS: Research on revolutionary committees in America, 1774-1776, and on women in eighteenth-century America.

* * *

NORWICH, John Julius (Cooper) 1929-

PERSONAL: Born September 15, 1929, in London, England; son of Alfred Duff (a historian and statesman; named first Viscount Norwich) and Lady Diana (Manners) Cooper; married Anne Frances May Clifford (a painter), August 5, 1952; children: Artemis, Jason Charles Duff Bede Cooper. *Education:* Attended University of Strasbourg, and New College, Oxford. *Politics:* Liberal. *Home:* 24 Bloomfield Rd., London W.9, England. *Agent:* Curtis Brown Ltd., 1 Craven Hill, London W.2, England.

CAREER: Her Majesty's Foreign Service, 1952-64, served as third secretary of British Embassy in Belgrade, 1955-57, as second secretary of British Embassy in Beirut, 1957-60, and as first secretary of Foreign Office, London, 1961-64, member of British delegation to Disarmament Conference (Geneva), 1960-64; Serenissima Travel, London, England, chairman, 1972—. Lecturer on conservation, travel, history, and the fine arts; chairman of British Theatre Museum, 1966-71; member of executive committee of National Trust, 1969—; trustee of National Central Library, 1971—; chairman of Venice in Peril Fund. *Military service:* Royal Navy, writer, 1947-49. *Member:* Royal Society of Literature (fellow), Beefsteak Club.

WRITINGS: (With Reresby Sitwell) *Mount Athos,* Harper, 1966; *The Other Conquest,* Harper, 1967 (published in England as *The Normans in the South: 1016-1130,* Longmans, Green, 1967); *Sahara,* Weybright and Talley, 1968; *The Kingdom in the Sun: 1130-1194* (a sequel to *The Normans in the South*), Harper, 1970.

Historical documentary films for British Broadcasting Corp.-Television: "The Other Conquest," "The Fall of Constantinople," "The Hundred Days," "Cortes and Montezuma," "History of Persia," "The Gates of Asia" (six films on the history of Turkey), "Maximilian of Mexico." Contributor to *Sunday Times, Spectator,* and *History Today.*

WORK IN PROGRESS: A history of the republic of Venice.

SIDELIGHTS: Of *The Other Conquest* Sir Charles Petrie writes, "Lord Norwich. . .paints a very real picture of these roving Normans." Observes Joanna Richardson, "The story. . .is not merely. . .of battles, dynastic alliances and endless diplomatic machinations, it is. . .particularly that of the great flamboyant adventurer Robert Guiscard. This is a tautly argued survey. Lord Norwich has a nice eye for character and a lucid, comprehensive view of events."

Ambrose Agius says, "For here is the brilliant assemblage of complicated historical fact. . .set out. . .with a mastery of English that charms the ear and refreshes the mind." Guernsey Le Pelley feels "if [Lord Norwich] doesn't prove his pen to be mightier than the invaders' sword, he bids well for it being sharper. As far as the lay reader is concerned, he can present strong claim to being a proper historian, even though he does not suppress a certain unclassical proclivity for writing history with tongue in cheek."

Lord Norwich speaks French, German, Italian, Russian, and Serbo-Croat; he has traveled in Sicily and the Sahara. *Avocational interests:* Travel, theater, music, opera.

* * *

NOURSE, Edwin G(riswold) 1883-1974

May 20, 1883—April 7, 1974; American economist, government official, and author of books in his field. Obituaries: *New York Times,* April 10, 1974; *Current Biography,* June, 1974.

* * *

NOVACK, George (Edward) 1905- (William F. Warde)

PERSONAL: Born August 5, 1905, in Boston, Mass.; son of Israel and Ada (Marcus) Novack; married Evelyn Andreas, June 22, 1942. *Education:* Harvard University, student, 1922-27. *Politics:* Socialist. *Home:* 326 West 19th St., New York, N.Y. 10011.

CAREER: Writer and lecturer. Fund for the Republic, Santa Barbara, Calif., research associate, 1958; associate editor, *International Socialist Review,* 1965-74. Treasurer of national campaign committee, Socialist Workers Party, 1968, secretary, 1972.

WRITINGS: An Introduction to the Logic of Marxism, Merit Publishers, 1942, fifth edition, 1969; *The Irregular Movement of History* (essays; originally published in three issues of *Labour Review*), New Park Publications, 1957; (under pseudonym William F. Warde) *The Long View of History,* Merit Publishers, 1958, Pioneer Publishers, 1960.

Who Will Change the World?, YSF Publication (Toronto), 1961; *Moscow versus Peking,* Pioneer Publishers, 1963; (editor with Isaac Deutscher) Leon Trotsky, *The Age of Permanent Revolution,* Dell, 1964; *The Origins of Materialism,* Merit Publishers, 1965; (author under pseudonym William F. Warde of introduction with Joseph Hansen) Leon Trotsky, *In Defense of Marxism,* Merit Publishers, 1965; (with Robert Vernon) *Watts and Harlem: The Rising Revolt in the Black Ghettos,* Pioneer Publishers, 1965; (editor and author of introduction) *Existentialism versus Marxism: Conflicting Views on Humanism,* Dell, 1966; (with Lawrence Stuart and Derrick Morrison) *The Black Uprisings,* Merit Publishers, 1967; *The Understanding of History* (two essays), Merit Publishers, 1967, new edition, 1974; (with George Breitman) *Black Nationalism and Socialism,* Merit Publishers, 1968; (with Paul Boutelle and others) *Murder in Memphis: Martin Luther King and the Future of the Black Liberation Struggle,* Merit Publishers, 1968; *Black Slavery and Capitalism: The Rise and Fall of the Cotton Kingdom,* National Education Dept., Socialist Workers Party, 1968; *Empiricism and Its Evolution: A Marxist View,* Merit Publishers, 1968; *How Can the Jews Survive: A Socialist Answer to Zionism,* Merit Publishers, 1969; (with Ernest Mandel) *The Revolutionary Potential of the Working Class,* Merit Publishers, 1969, new edition, Pathfinder Press, 1974; (with Pierre Frank and Ernest Mandel) *Key Problems of the Transition from Capitalism to Socialism,* Merit Publishers, 1969.

Genocide against the Indians: Its Role in the Rise of U.S. Capitalism, Pathfinder Press, 1970; *Marxism versus Neo-Anarchist Terrorism,* Pathfinder Press, 1970; *Revolutionary Dynamics of Women's Liberation,* Pathfinder Press, 1970; (with Ernest Mandel) *The Marxist Theory of Alienation,* Pathfinder Press, 1970, second edition, 1973; *Democracy and Revolution,* Pathfinder Press, 1971; (compiler with Joseph Hansen) *The Transitional Program for Socialist Revolution,* Pathfinder Press, 1973; *Humanism and Socialism,* Pathfinder Press, 1973.

Contributor: Robert Himmel, editor, *Marxist Essays in American History,* Merit Publishers, 1966; (and author of introduction) *Their Morals and Ours,* Merit Publishers, 1966. Contributor to numerous periodicals.

SIDELIGHTS: Novack has been actively engaged in socialist causes since 1932. In 1937 he was a prime mover in organizing the International Commission of Inquiry into the Moscow Trials headed by philosopher John Dewey.

A reviewer noted that in *Democracy and Revolution,* "Novack deals with democracy from Athenian society to the present . . . [contending that] democracy has been the product of class and economic power—it will be achieved by the vast majority only with the arrival of the socialist revolution. . . . The author envisages social revolution in the U.S. . . . and popular revolution in the U.S.S.R." George Charney commented: "Novack's concept of socialism is far different from the Soviet model."

* * *

NOVAK, Michael Paul 1935-

PERSONAL: Born July 6, 1935, in Chicago, Ill.; son of Joseph Francis (a civil engineer) and Mae (Killian) Novak; married Julia Callanan (a teacher and journalist), July 12, 1958; children: Brian, Christina. *Education:* Catholic University of America, B.A., 1957; University of Iowa, M.F.A., 1962. *Politics:* Democrat. *Religion:* Roman Catholic. *Home:* 1816 Cherokee, Leavenworth, Kan. 66048. *Office:* Department of English, Saint Mary College, Leavenworth, Kan. 66048.

CAREER: Illinois State University, Normal, instructor in English, 1962-63; Saint Mary College, Leavenworth, Kan., assistant professor, 1963-69, associate professor of English, 1969—, head of department, 1972—. Has given readings at numerous workshops; participant in Poets in the Schools program of National Endowment for the Arts. *Military service:* U.S. Army, 1958-60. *Awards, honors: Kansas City Star* award, 1969, for "English 101—The State Prison," and 1970, for "Seeing Winter"; *Kansas Quarterly* award, 1973, for "Museo de Cataluna."

WRITINGS: The Leavenworth Poems, Bookmark Press, 1972. Contributor of poems and translations to over forty literary magazines. Book reviewer for *Kansas City Star,* 1973—, and *New Newspaper,* 1973.

WORK IN PROGRESS: Two books of poems, *The Year Away* and *A Story To Tell; The Selected Poems of Attila Jozsef,* translations from the Hungarian.

SIDELIGHTS: Novak told *CA* he believes "poetry and politics can merge, the way they do in certain Eastern European and South American poets. [I] want to write a poetry of speech, the sound of a person talking."

BIOGRAPHICAL/CRITICAL SOURCES: Seattle Times, March 4, 1973; *Midwest Quarterly,* summer, 1973.

* * *

NOYES, Peter R. 1930-

PERSONAL: Born July 23, 1930, in Los Angeles, Calif.; son of Philip (a pharmacist) and Amelia (a teacher; maiden name, Stikeleather) Noyes; married Grace Bohanon (a teacher), October 3, 1959; children: Jack. *Education:* Loyola University, Los Angeles, Calif., B.S., 1952; University of California, Los Angeles, M.S., 1957. *Politics:* Democratic. *Religion:* Roman Catholic. *Residence:* Rancho Palos Verdes, Calif. *Agent:* Don Shepherd, 16810 Vine St., Suite 1105, Hollywood, Calif. 90028. *Office:* ABC-TV, Los Angeles, Calif. 90027.

CAREER: Los Angeles City News Service, Los Angeles, Calif., city editor, 1956-61; CBS-TV, Los Angeles, Calif., writer and producer, 1961-65, executive producer, 1966-72; KX-TV, Sacramento, Calif., news director, 1965-66; ABC-TV, Los Angeles, Calif., senior producer, 1972—. Member of Big Brothers and of Committee to Investigate Assassinations. *Military service:* U.S. Navy; served in Korea and China. *Member:* National Academy of Television Arts and Sciences, Catholic Press Council of Southern California, Sigma Delta Chi, Kappa Tau Alpha. *Awards, honors:* Emmy awards, 1970, 1971; Greater Los Angeles Press Club award, 1972; also recipient of four Golden Mike awards for broadcasting excellence, six Associated Press awards, and a Sigma Delta Chi award.

WRITINGS: Legacy of Doubt, Pinnacle Books, 1973. Contributor to magazines and newspapers. Author of television documentaries. Assistant city editor of *Pacific Stars & Stripes,* 1953-54.

WORK IN PROGRESS: Life without Hope, the story of six G.I.'s sentenced to life imprisonment by President Eisenhower with the proviso they never be paroled.

AVOCATIONAL INTERESTS: Gardening, professional football.

BIOGRAPHICAL/CRITICAL SOURCES: Los Angeles Times, December 7, 1973; *Rolling Stone,* January 3, 1974.

NUGENT, Tom 1943-

PERSONAL: Born July 1, 1943, in St. Joseph, Mo.; son of Thomas Norman (a coach) and Margaret (Foley) Nugent; married Sara Mann, July 16, 1964 (divorced, 1971); children: Kerry Elizabeth. *Education:* Attended William and Mary College, 1961; University of Maryland, B.A., 1967. *Politics:* None. *Religion:* None. *Home and office:* 1304 Eliza St., Apt. 1, Key West, Fla. 33040.

CAREER: Liberty Mutual Insurance Co., Washington, D.C., salesman, 1967-68; *Charlotte Observer,* Charlotte, N.C., reporter, 1968-69; *Detroit Free Press,* Detroit, Mich., reporter, 1969-72. *Military service:* U.S. Marine Corps Reserve, 1962-68.

WRITINGS: Death at Buffalo Creek, Norton, 1973. Contributor to *Nation, Washington Post, Chicago Sun-Times,* and *Miami Herald.*

WORK IN PROGRESS: A novel, *Is Detroit Dying?,* other fiction.

SIDELIGHTS: Nugent told *CA:* "*Death at Buffalo Creek* was written after I covered the 1972 West Virginia flood disaster in depth for the *Detroit Free Press.* The book documents a typical case of industrial murder."

* * *

NUSSBAUM, Aaron 1910-

PERSONAL: Born July 9, 1910, in New York, N.Y.; son of Samuel Joshua and Dora (Biesenstock) Nussbaum; married Helen Lew, September 15, 1934; children: Carol (Mrs. Henry Peck), Robert Paul. *Education:* St. John's University, Brooklyn, N.Y., LL.B., 1932, LL.M., 1934. *Religion:* Jewish. *Home:* 2 West End Ave., Brooklyn, N.Y. 11235. *Agent:* Patricia Lewis, 390 Riverside Dr., New York, N.Y. *Office:* 150 Fifth Ave., New York, N.Y. 10011.

CAREER: Lawyer, admitted to Brooklyn, New York State, and bar of United States Supreme Court. Criminal Appeals Bureau of Kings County, New York, N.Y., assistant district attorney, 1947-1974. Associate chief counsel for State Hotel Association and American Hotel Association, both 1945-47; member of Governor's Commission on Law Enforcement, 1950-60.

MEMBER: American Correctional Association, National District Attorneys Association, National Council of Crime and Delinquency, Amnesty League of America (national chairman, 1974—), International Platform Association, Rehabilitation of Fighters for Freedom of Israel (national chairman, 1952-55).

WRITINGS: First Offenders: A Second Chance (pamphlet), Case Press, 1956; *Second Chance: Amnesty for the First Offender,* Hawthorn, 1974.

BIOGRAPHICAL/CRITICAL SOURCES: Sol Rubin, *Crime and Delinquency,* Oceana Publications, 1958; Harry Elmer Barnes, *New Horizons in Criminology,* Prentice-Hall, 1959.

* * *

O'BARR, William M(cAlston) 1942-

PERSONAL: Born December 1, 1942, in Sylvania, Ga.; son of William J. and Mary (Clark) O'Barr; married Jean Ellen Fox (director of continuing education and lecturer in political science at Duke University), September 4, 1965; children: Claire Anne. *Education:* Emory University, B.A., 1964; Northwestern University, M.A., 1966, Ph.D., 1969; also attended University of California at Los Angeles, Archaeological Field School, summer, 1963, and University of the Americas, Mexico City, summer, 1964. *Home:* 713 Anderson St., Durham, N.C. 27706. *Office:* Department of Anthropology, Duke University, Durham, N.C. 27706.

CAREER: U.S. Public Health Service, Atlanta, Ga., medical sociology researcher, 1964; University of Dar es Salaam, Dar es Salaam, Tanzania, research associate, 1967-68; Duke University, Durham, N.C., assistant professor, 1969-74, associate professor of anthropology, 1974—, director of graduate studies in anthropology, 1971-73. Visiting lecturer for American Anthropological Association, 1970—. *Member:* International African Institute (London, England), American Anthropological Association, American Ethnological Society. *Awards, honors:* Wenner-Gren Foundation grant, Netherlands, 1970; National Science Foundation grant, 1974-76.

WRITINGS: (With Johannes G. Mlela; wife, Jean F. O'Barr; and Alice Grant) *Shindano: Swahili Essays and Other Stories* (language textbook), Program of Eastern African Studies, Syracuse University, 1971; (editor with David H. Spain and Mark Tessler, and contributor) *Survey Research in Africa: Its Applications and Limits,* Northwestern University Press, 1973; (with Spain and Tessler) *Tradition and Identity in Changing Africa,* Harper, 1973; (with Gerald Hartwig) *The Student Africanist's Handbook,* Schenkman, 1974; (editor with Jean F. O'Barr, and contributor) *Language and Politics,* Mouton, in press. Contributor of articles and reviews to anthropology and social science journals, including *Anthropological Linguistics, Current Anthropology, Social Forces,* and *American Journal of Sociology.*

WORK IN PROGRESS: Language and Legal Processes; a book on Arusha, Meru, Chagga, Taveta, Pare, and Shambala, for "Ethnographic Survey of Africa," a series edited by John Middleton, for International African Institute (London); survey research in Africa from an anthropologist's point of view; research on national culture in the developing nation of Tanzania; research on language and legal processes in the United States.

* * *

OFFEN, Neil 1946-

PERSONAL: Born April 25, 1946, in New York, N.Y.; son of Herman N. (a lawyer) and Miriam (Kramer) Offen; married Carol DiFalco (an editor), June 5, 1970. *Education:* Attended City College of the City University of New York, 1963-67. *Home and office:* 222 East 31st St., New York, N.Y. 10016. *Agent:* Theron Raines, 244 Madison Ave., New York, N.Y. 10016.

CAREER: New York Post, New York, N.Y., reporter, 1968-71; writer, 1971—. *Member:* Common Cause.

WRITINGS: (With Jim Bouton) *I Managed Good, But Boy Did They Play Bad!,* Playboy Press, 1973; *God Save the Players,* Playboy Press, 1974.

WORK IN PROGRESS: The New Doctor, a look at urban medicine.

* * *

OKPEWHO, Isidore 1941-

PERSONAL: Born November 9, 1941, in Nigeria; son of David O. (a laboratory technician) and Regina (Attoh)

Okpewho. *Education:* Attended University of Ibadan, 1961-64, and University of Denver, 1972-74. *Religion:* Christian. *Home:* 3700 East Jewell, #214C, Denver, Colo. 80210.

CAREER: Longman Nigeria, Lagos, publisher and editor, 1965-72. *Awards, honors:* African Arts Prize from African Studies Center of University of California, Los Angeles, 1972, for "The Last Duty."

WRITINGS: The Victims (novel), Longman Nigeria, 1970, Doubleday, 1971. Also author of "The Last Duty" (novel). Contributor to magazines. Associate editor of *Okike.*

WORK IN PROGRESS: Research on comparative classical and American literature.

AVOCATIONAL INTERESTS: African art and music, jazz, cinema, swimming, tennis, billiards.

* * *

OLIEN, Michael D(avid) 1937-

PERSONAL: Born April 16, 1937, in Milwaukee, Wis.; son of Henry Conrad (a chemist) and Hazel (Serles) Olien; married Joan C. Etlinger (a secretary), July 15, 1959; children: Karen Joy. *Education:* Beloit College, B.A., 1959; University of North Carolina, M.A., 1962; University of Oregon, Ph.D., 1967. *Home address:* P.O. Box 6071, Athens, Ga. 30604. *Office:* Department of Anthropology, University of Georgia, Athens, Ga. 30602.

CAREER: Associated Colleges of the Midwest, member of anthropological staff, Central American Field Program, San Jose, Costa Rica, 1964-65; University of Oregon, Eugene, instructor in anthropology, 1965-66; American University, Washington, D.C., assistant professor of anthropology, 1966-67; University of Georgia, Athens, assistant professor, 1967-73, associate professor of anthropology, 1973—. Visiting summer professor at Portland State College, 1966. *Member:* American Anthropological Association (fellow), American Society for Ethnohistory, Latin American Studies Association, Southern Anthropological Society (secretary-treasurer, 1968-70), Latin American Anthropology Group, Royal Anthropological Institute of Great Britain and Ireland (fellow).

WRITINGS: The Negro in Costa Rica; The Role of an Ethnic Minority in a Developing Society (monograph), Overseas Research Center, Wake Forest University, 1970; *Latin Americans: Contemporary Peoples and Their Cultural Traditions,* Holt, 1973.

Compiler with Edwin M. Shook and Jorge A. Lines—all published by Tropical Science Center-Associated Colleges of the Midwest: *Anthropological Bibliography of Aboriginal Panama,* 1965; *Anthropological Bibliography of Aboriginal Nicaragua,* 1965; *Anthropological Bibliography of Aboriginal El Salvador,* 1965; *Anthropological Bibliography of Aboriginal Honduras,* 1966.

Contributor: Elizabeth M. Eddy, editor, *Urban Anthropology: Research Perspectives and Strategies,* Southern Anthropological Society, 1968; Fred W. Voget and Robert L. Stephenson, editors, *For the Chief: Essays in Honor of Luther S. Cressman,* University of Oregon Anthropological Papers, 1972; Ann Pescatello, editor, *The Afro-Latino After Independence,* University of Pittsburgh Press, in press.

WORK IN PROGRESS: Afro-Americans: Black and Part-Black Populations of the New World, completion expected in 1975; *Puerto Limon: Life in a Costa Rican Port,* 1977.

OLIVERA, Otto 1919-

PERSONAL: Born April 20, 1919, in Pedro Betancourt, Cuba; came to United States, 1946, naturalized citizen, 1957; son of Jose Francisco (a lawyer) and Matilde (Ibarra) Olivera; married Ruth Ritchey, December 27, 1950; children: Deborah Ann, Rebecca Ruth, Maria Elena. *Education:* University of Havana, Doctorado en Filosofia y Letras, 1945; Louisiana State University, M.A., 1947; Tulane University, Ph.D., 1953. *Politics:* Democrat. *Religion:* None. *Home:* 6 Trianon Plaza, New Orleans, La. 70125. *Office:* Department of Spanish, Tulane University, New Orleans, La. 70118.

CAREER: Tulane University, New Orleans, La., instructor in Spanish, 1950-54; Syracuse University, Syracuse, N.Y., assistant professor, 1954-58, associate professor, 1958-65, professor of Romance languages, 1965; Tulane University, professor of Spanish, 1965—. *Member:* Modern Language Association of America, American Association of Teachers of Spanish and Portuguese, Instituto Internacional de Literatura Iberoamericana, American Association of University Professors.

WRITINGS: Breve historia de la literatura antillana, Ediciones de Andrea (Mexico), 1957; *Cuba en su poesia,* Ediciones de Andrea, 1965; *La prosa modernista en Hispanoamerica,* Ediciones el Colibri (Mexico), 1971; (with A.M. Vazquez) *La Literatura en publicaciones periodicas de Guatemala (Siglo XIX),* Tulane Studies in Romance Languages and Literatures, 1974. Contributor to journals in his field.

WORK IN PROGRESS: La Literatura en periodicos y revistas de Puerto Rico, a study of writing in Puerto Rican newspapers and journals of the nineteenth century.

* * *

OLSEN, Ib Spang 1921- (Padre Detine, a joint pseudonym)

PERSONAL: Born June 11, 1921, in Denmark; son of Ole Christian (a gardener) and Soffu (Nielsen) Olsen; married Grete Geisler, May 3, 1947 (divorced, 1960); married Nulle Oeigaard (an artist), September 8, 1962; children: (first marriage) Tune, Martin, Lasse, Tine (daughter). *Education:* Blaagaards Seminarium, teacher training, 1939-43; Royal Danish Academy of Art, study of graphic art, 1945-49. *Politics:* Democratic Socialist. *Religion:* None. *Home:* Aldershvilevej 193, Bagsvaerd 2880, Denmark. *Agent:* International Children's Book Service, Kildeskovsvej 21, Gentofte 2820, Denmark.

CAREER: Began illustrating for Sunday magazine supplements of Danish newspapers, 1942; schoolteacher in Denmark, 1952-60; full-time illustrator and writer, 1960—. In addition to book illustrating he has done book covers, murals for schools, posters, and ceramic pieces. Began work in Danish television, 1964 and has done numerous programs for young people.

AWARDS, HONORS: Danish Ministry of Culture Award for best illustrated children's book of the year for *Drengen i maanen,* 1962, *Regnen* and *Blaesten,* 1963, *Boernerim,* 1964, and *Mosekonens bryg,* 1966; Danish Society of Bookcraft honor list of year's outstanding books included *Kiosken paa Torvet,* 1964, *Lars Peters cykel,* 1968, *Hokus Pokus og andre boernerim,* 1969, and *Roegen,* 1971; Hendrixen Medal for outstanding bookcraft for *Halfdans abc,* 1967; runner-up for Hans Christian Andersen Medal of International Board on Books for Young People, 1968, and

1970, and winner, 1972; Storm Petersen Legatet for whole body of work, 1971; other awards at Bratislava Biennial, from Organization for Friends of Books, 1966, and from Association of Authors of Juvenile Literature in Finland, 1971.

WRITINGS—Self-illustrated children's books; *Det lille lokomotiv* (title means "The Little Locomotive"), Gad, 1963; *Mosekonens bryg,* Kunst & Kultur, 1957, translation by Virginia Allen Jensen published as *The Marsh Crone's Brew,* Abingdon, 1960; *Boernene paa vejen,* Gjellerup, 1958; *Bedstemors vaegtaeppe,* Kunst & Kultur, 1958; *Drengen i maanen,* Gyldendal, 1962, translation by Virginia Allen Jensen published as *The Boy in the Moon,* Abingdon, 1963; *Regnen* (title means "Rain"), Gyldendal, 1963; *Blaesten* (title means "Wind"), Gyldendal, 1963; *Kiosken paa torvet* (title means "The Kiosk on the Square"), Gyldendal, 1964; *Kattehuset,* Gyldendal, 1968, translation by Virginia Allen Jensen published as *Cat Alley,* Coward, 1971; *Marie-hoenen,* Gyldendal, 1969; *Hvordan vi fik vores naboer,* Gyldendal, 1969; *Roegen,* Gyldendal, 1970, translation by Virginia Allen Jensen published as *Smoke,* Coward, 1972; *Pjer Brumme: Historier em en lille bjoern,* Gyldendal, 1971.

Other books: (With Erik E. Frederiksen, under joint pseudonym Padre Detine) *En Sydamerikaner i Nordsjaelland* (humorous tales), privately printed, 1960; (with Torben Brostroem) *Boern: Det Foerste aar i ord og tegninger,* Hasselbalch, 1962.

Illustrator: *Prinsessen paa glasbjerget,* circa, 1945; *Danish Folk Tales,* J. H. Schultz, 1946; *Danske folkeeventyr,* Kunst & Kultur, 1950; Frank Jaeger, *Hverdaghistorier,* Wivel, 1951; Frank Jaeger, *Tune, det foerste aar,* Branner, 1951; *Fem smaa troldeboern,* Danske Forlag, 1952; *Nissen flytter med,* Gyldendal, 1955; *Abrikosia,* Hoest & Soen, 1958; Virginia Allen Jensen, *Lars-Peter's Birthday,* Abingdon, 1959; Jakob J. B. Nygaard, *Tobias tryllemus,* Martins Forlag, 1961, translation by Edith Joan McCormick published as *Tobias, the Magic Mouse,* Harcourt, 1968; Halfdan W. Rasmussen, *Boernerim,* Schoenberg, 1964; Hans Christian Andersen, *Digte,* edited by Bo Groenbech, Dansk Arnkrone, 1966; *Morten poulsens urtehave,* Hoest & Soen, 1967; Rasmussen, *Halfdans abc,* Illustrationsforlaget, 1967; *Molbohistorier,* Schoenberg, 1967; Virginia Allen Jensen, *Lars Peters cykel,* Gyldendal, 1968, translation published as *Lars Peter's Bicycle,* Angus & Robertson, 1970; Lise Soerensen, *Da Lyset gik ud,* Gyldendal, 1968; Rasmussen, *Hokus Pokus og andre boernerim,* Schoenberg, 1969, translation published as *Hocus Pocus,* Angus & Robertson, in press; Ole Restrup, *Odin og Tor,* Gad, 1969; Rasmussen, *Den Lille fraekke Frederik og andre boernerlm,* Branner & Korch, 1971; *Folkene paa vejen,* Gyldendal, 1972.

Television films: "Hvad bliver det naeste?"; "Taarnuret"; "Vitaminerne"; "Den store krage"; "Nikolai"; "Stregen der loeb henad"; "Stregen der loeb opad."

WORK IN PROGRESS: Illustrations for a three-volume edition of Danish medieval folksongs.

SIDELIGHTS: Olsen writes: "Almost all of my picture books have been produced as original lithography in photo offset. The original art work is done directly on film, one separate film for each of the four colours to be used in a single picture. In other words, for each illustration I draw four films, and the colours are then mixed for the first time by the printer cooperating closely with me. The finished books are the originals, they are not reproductions. In this way we can produce original lithography of quality at reasonable prices."

Olsen's books have been published in Finland, Greenland, Netherlands, Australia, Sweden, Germany, Norway, South Africa, and England, in addition to United States. He has given original illustrations for four of the books to the Kerlan Collection at University of Minnesota. Besides the Scandinavian languages, he is competent in English and German.

* * *

OLSEN, James 1933-

PERSONAL: Born January 14, 1933, in New York, N.Y.; son of Anthony (a doorman) and Lucy Regina (McGettrick) Olsen; married Janet Marie Deskins, November 29, 1956 (divorced, 1973); children: James, Glen, Peter. *Education:* Columbia University, B.A., 1954, graduate study, 1955-56. *Politics:* Liberal Democrat. *Home and office:* 230 West 78th St., New York, N.Y. 10024.

CAREER: Longshoreman and truck driver in New York, N.Y., 1956-58; public school teacher in New York, N.Y., 1958-63; Scholastic Magazines, New York, N.Y., editor, 1963-64; McGraw Hill Book Co., New York, N.Y., editor-in-chief, 1964-67; Educreative Systems, New York, N.Y., president, 1967—. *Member:* National Council of Teachers of English.

WRITINGS: (With Elsa Jaffe) *Skyline Series,* Books A, B, and C, McGraw, 1965; *Your Job and Your Future,* Books 1 and 2, McGraw, 1965; *Scholastic Scope's Teacher's Guide for 1965,* Scholastic Publications, 1965; *Step Up Your Reading Power,* Books 1, 2, 3, 4, and 5, McGraw, 1966; *Sandy, the Lineman* (a "What Job for Me" booklet), McGraw, 1966; *Exiles from the American Dream,* (nonfiction) Walker, 1974; *Runaway,* Harper, in press. Author of booklets for New York Life Insurance Co.; author of teacher's film guide for "Harriet Tubman and the Underground Railroad." Contributor of about twenty articles to magazines, including *High Points, Journal of Reading, Phi Delta Kappan, Reading Teacher, National Elementary Principal,* and *Educational Forum.*

WORK IN PROGRESS: A novel.

* * *

OLSON, David F. 1938-

PERSONAL: Born January 15, 1938; son of Gilbert E. (a businessman) and Hedwig (Melander) Olson; married Gun Ingeborg Kemperyd, June 24, 1961; children: Johanna, Fredrika. *Education:* Augustana College, B.A.; Pacific Lutheran Theological Seminary, M.Div. *Home:* Tungelstavaegen 23C Vaesterhaninge, Sweden.

CAREER: Pastor, working in the Church of Sweden.

WRITINGS: *The Inner Revolution,* Lutherwood Press, 1973; *Grinding and Polishing Stones,* Sterling Press, 1973; *En bok foer folk som Smygtror,* Haekan Ohlssons, 1974.

* * *

OLSON, James R(obert) 1938-

PERSONAL: Born August 24, 1938, in Kewanee, Ill.; son of Robert Preston (a soldier) and Josephine (Shimek) Olson; married Carol Milauc (a registered nurse), April 24, 1965; children: Eric James, Andrew Jon (twins). *Education:* Student at University of Wisconsin, Manitowoc, 1959-60; Marquette University, 1960-62. *Politics:* Independent. *Reli-*

gion: Roman Catholic. *Home:* 711 Highway C, Crafton, Wis. 53024. *Agent:* Margot Johnson Agency, 405 East 54th St., New York, N.Y. 10022. *Office:* Uhlemann Custom Opticians, 1212 West Wisconsin Ave., Milwaukee, Wis. 53233.

CAREER: C. J. Radl, M.D., Manitowoc, Wis., dispensing optician, 1958-60; Herslof Opticians, Milwaukee, Wis., dispensing optician, 1960-68; Vista Contact Lenses, Inc., Milwaukee, contact lens technician, 1968-70, president and chairman of the board, 1968-70; Uhlemann Custom Opticians, Milwaukee, optical manager, 1970—. *Military service:* U.S. Marine Corps, 1956-58. *Member:* Contact Lens Society of America, Wisconsin Society of Opticianry (member of the board of directors, 1967-69).

WRITINGS: Ulzana, Houghton, 1973.

WORK IN PROGRESS: Continuing work on trilogy concerning the Chiricahua Apaches from 1539-1950 (*Ulzana* will be used as the second book), with the first book tentatively titled *A Whisper on the Wind,* and the third book still in the planning stage.

AVOCATIONAL INTERESTS: Oil painting, wood sculpting.

* * *

OLSON, Keith W(aldemar) 1931-

PERSONAL: Born August 4, 1931, in Poughkeepsie, N.Y.; son of Ernest Waldemar and Elin (Rehnstrom) Olson; married Marilyn Wittschen, September 10, 1955; children: Paula, Judy. *Education:* State University of New York, Albany, B.A., 1957, M.A., 1959; University of Wisconsin, Ph.D., 1964. *Religion:* Unitarian Universalist. *Home:* 10746 Kinloch Rd., Silver Springs, Md. 20903. *Office:* Department of History, University of Maryland, College Park, Md. 20746.

CAREER: Syracuse University, Syracuse, N.Y., historian, 1963-66; University of Maryland, College Park, historian, 1966—. *Military service:* U.S. Army, Finance Corps, 1952-54. *Member:* American Historical Association, Organization of American Historians, American-Scandinavian Foundation, State Historical Society of Wisconsin.

WRITINGS: The G. I. Bill, the Veterans, and the Colleges, University Press of Kentucky, 1974. Contributor to *Encyclopedia Americana,* and to *American Quarterly, Historian, Wisconsin Magazine of History,* and *Progressive.* Book reviewer for *Washington Star,* 1966-70.

WORK IN PROGRESS: Franklin K. Lane: A Biography (tentative title); a short interpretive biography of John F. Kennedy.

AVOCATIONAL INTERESTS: Swedish culture, camping.

* * *

OLSON, Ted
See OLSON, Theodore B.

* * *

OLSON, Theodore B. 1899-
(Ted Olson)

PERSONAL: Born April 18, 1899, in Laramie, Wyo.; son of Hans (a rancher) and Bertha (Johnson) Olson; married Louise Charlotte Silber, July 26, 1934. *Education:* University of Wyoming, B.A. (with honor), 1920. *Home:* 5021 Allan Rd., Washington, D.C. 20016.

CAREER: Newspaper man on *Oakland Enquirer, San Francisco Journal, New York Tribune, Laramie Republican-Boomerang, Casper* (Wyo.) *Herald, Denver Post, New York Herald Tribune,* and others, 1920-41; U.S. Office of War Information, member of staff in New York, N.Y., and London, England, 1941-45; U.S. State Department, member of staff in Oslo, Norway, 1945-50, and Washington, D.C., 1950-53; U.S. Information Agency, member of staff in Washington, D.C., 1953, and Athens, Greece, 1953-57; U.S. State Department, member of staff in Reykjavik, Iceland, 1957-59. *Member:* National Press Club, Phi Beta Kappa.

WRITINGS—Under name Ted Olson: *A Stranger and Afraid* (poetry), Yale University Press, 1928; *Hawk's Way* (poetry), League to Support Poetry, 1941; *Ranch on the Laramie,* Atlantic Monthly Press, 1973.

Represented in anthologies, including: *Rocky Mountain Reader,* edited by Ray B. West, Jr., Dutton, 1945; *Saturday Review Treasury,* edited by John Haverstick and others, Simon & Schuster, 1957; *Ideas and Backgrounds,* edited by Keith G. Huntress and others, American Book Co., 1957; *Starting with Poetry,* edited by Judith K. Moore, Harcourt, 1973.

Contributor of poems, articles, and stories to many magazines.

WORK IN PROGRESS: Revising his published and unpublished verse; annotating his wartime and foreign service journals.

SIDELIGHTS: Olson said he is interested in "saving a few scraps of wilderness, battling the strip-miners, the polluters, the eagle-and coyote-poisoners. Also battling polluters of the English language. Travel: extensive, both on my own (tramp steamer, Model T, afoot) and at government expense."

* * *

O'MALLEY, Lady
See BRIDGE, Ann

* * *

ONDAATJE, Christopher 1933-

PERSONAL: Born February 22, 1933, in Kandy, Ceylon. *Education:* Attended Blundell's School, Tiverton, England. *Religion:* Church of England. *Home:* 45 Highland Ave., Toronto, Ontario, Canada. *Office:* 335 Bay St., Toronto, Ontario, Canada.

CAREER: Writer, publisher, banker. Pagurian Press, Toronto, Ontario, president, 1968—; Loewen, Ondaatje, McCutcheon & Co., Toronto, vice-president, 1970—.

WRITINGS: The Prime Ministers of Canada: 1867-1967, Pagurian Press, 1967; *Olympic Victory,* Pagurian Press, 1968; *Fool's Gold: The First $1,000,000,* Scribner, 1974.

* * *

O'NEAL, Glenn (Franklin) 1919-

PERSONAL: Born February 11, 1919, in Sunnyside, Wash.; son of Fred W. (a farmer) and Nannie (Shockley) O'Neal; married W. Phoebe Schilperoort, June 1, 1940; children: Dale, Donna (Mrs. Jim Speer), Rebecca (Mrs. Tim Terry), Roanna (Mrs. Jim Brazeau), Phyllis. *Education:* University of California, Santa Barbara, B.A., 1951; Grace Theological Seminary, B.D., 1952; University of

Southern California, M.A., 1954, Ph.D., 1957. *Politics:* Republican. *Home:* 410 South Redwood Dr., Anaheim, Calif. 92806. *Office:* Talbot Seminary, 13800 Biola Ave., La Mirada, Calif. 90635.

CAREER: Pastoral posts in Brethren Church, 1941-61; Talbot Seminary, La Mirada, Calif., part-time instructor, 1952-61, professor of practical theology, 1961—. *Member:* Speech Association of America.

WRITINGS: Make the Bible Live, Brethren Missionary Herald, 1972.

* * *

OOSTERMAN, Gordon 1927- (G. Don Eastman)

PERSONAL: First syllable of surname is pronounced "oh"; born November 17, 1927, in Northbridge, Mass.; son of T. T. and Gertrude (Nydam) Oosterman; married Marilyn Ferguson, August 5, 1952; children: Tim, William, Mary Elizabeth, David Lee. *Education:* Calvin College, A.B., 1951; University of Pennsylvania, graduate study, 1951-52. *Religion:* Evangelical Protestant. *Home:* 2128 College Ave. S.E., Grand Rapids, Mich. 49507.

CAREER: Teacher of history and social studies in Evergreen Park, Ill., 1952-54, and Edgerton, Minn., 1954-58; school administrator in Pantego, N.C., 1958-62, and Oostburg, Wis., 1962-66; National Union of Christian Schools, consultant in social studies, 1966—. Instructor in geography, Calvin College, 1972—. *Military service:* U.S. Army, 1946-47. *Member:* National Council for Geographic Education, Michigan Council for Geographic Education (president, 1973-74). *Awards, honors:* U.S. Office of Education grant, spring, 1973, for study in India.

WRITINGS: Nigeria, National Union of Christian Schools, 1968; *The People: Three Indian Tribes of the Southwest,* Eerdmans, 1973; *Geneva to Geelong,* National Union of Christian Schools, 1974. Contributor to journals, sometimes under pseudonym, G. Don Eastman.

WORK IN PROGRESS: Dutch Immigration to North America.

SIDELIGHTS: Oosterman has travelled extensively in the United States and Canada. He writes that he is "deeply concerned about continuing injustices forced upon ethnic, religious, and educational minorities." He also feels that "much needs to be said and written to offset prevailing cruel and false myths concerning 'democracy,' the 'melting pot,' and the 'American way of life.'"

* * *

OPPENHEIM, A(dolph) Leo 1904-1974

June 7, 1904—July 21, 1974; Viennese-born American Assyriologist, editor, and author of books in his field. Obituaries: *New York Times,* July 24, 1974.

* * *

OPPER, Jacob 1935-

PERSONAL: Born November 4, 1935, in Lodz, Poland; naturalized U.S. citizen in 1954; son of Abram (a beautician) and Maria (Solovsky) Opper. *Education:* Attended City University of New York, 1953-55, and University of Miami, 1956-58; Florida State University, B.M., 1960, M.M., 1965, Ph.D., 1970. *Home:* 146 Wood St., Frostburg, Md. 21532. *Office:* Department of Music, Frostburg State College, Frostburg, Md. 21532.

CAREER: Frostburg State College, Frostburg, Md., assistant professor of music and humanities, 1970—. *Member:* American Society for Eighteenth Century Studies (treasurer of East Central Regional Conference, 1972-73).

WRITINGS: Science and the Arts: A Study in Relationships from 1600-1900, Fairleigh Dickinson University Press, 1973. Contributor of reviews to *Cumberland Evening Times.*

WORK IN PROGRESS: Root Metaphors of Hellenic, Medieval, and Renaissance Culture; The Cultural Implications of Natural Science in the Twentieth Century.

SIDELIGHTS: Opper told *CA* that his work has been guided "by the conviction that the dominant character of the great periods of Western culture is ultimately traceable to the implicit or explicit theory of nature which these periods hold. Once the root metaphors of a given theory of nature are discovered, their specific connection to the manifold products in the sciences and humanities should be demonstrated. This approach allows us to appreciate the 'wholeness' of these periods, while giving some insight into the causal agents of change in the evolution of Western culture from its beginnings to the present day."

* * *

ORIANS, George H(arrison) 1900-

PERSONAL: Surname is pronounced *Or*-yuns; born April 19, 1900, in Marion, Ohio; son of George J. and Nettie K. (Zachman) Orians; married Dorothy Ruth Schmidlin (a teacher), August 29, 1941; children: Daryl Phyllis (Mrs. George Alexander), Margaret Janelle (Mrs. Scott Willen), George Randall. *Education:* North Central College, Naperville, Ill., A.B., 1922; University of Illinois, M.A., 1923, Ph.D., 1926. *Politics:* Republican. *Religion:* Congregational. *Home:* 2240 Middlesex, Toledo, Ohio 43606. *Office:* Scott Hall, University of Toledo, Toledo, Ohio 43606.

CAREER: University of Illinois, Urbana, instructor in English, 1924-27; University of Idaho, Moscow, associate professor of English, 1928-29; University of Toledo, Toledo, Ohio, lecturer, 1929-32, professor of English, 1932-69, director of summer sessions, 1934-47, chairman of department of English, 1938-51. Visiting professor at University of Michigan, 1966-68; visiting summer professor at University of Washington, Seattle, Southern Methodist University, University of Colorado, and several colleges. Researcher at Yale University, Harvard University, and Library of Congress. Lecturer across America for National Audubon Society, 1946-64; photographer and narrator of nine nature films, including "Great Smoky Skyland," "By Erie's Changing Shores," and "Gay Wings." Trustee of Ohioana Library, 1948-72.

MEMBER: Modern Language Assocation of America, College English Association, Northwestern Ohio Wildlife Resources Council, Maumee Valley Historical Society Toledo Naturalist Association (president, 1946-47), Phi Beta Kappa, Phi Kappa Phi. *Awards, honors:* Named Ohio Water Conservationist of the Year, 1966.

WRITINGS: The Indian in the Metrical Romance, University of Illinois Press, 1929; *A Short History of American Literature,* Crofts, 1940; (editor with Harry Redcay Warfel) *American Local-Color Stories,* American Book Co., 1941, reprinted, Cooper Square, 1970; (editor with Lyon K. Richardson and Herbert Brown) *Heritage of American Literature,* two volumes, Ginn, 1951; (editor and author of introduction) Cotton Mather, *Days of Humiliation: Times of*

Affliction and Disaster, Scholars Facsimiles & Reprints, 1970; (editor and author of introduction) *Specimens of the American Poets,* Scholars Facsimiles & Reprints, 1972.

Contributor: Harry Redcay Warfel and E. W. Manwaring, editors, *Of the People,* Oxford University Press, 1942; C. W. Garrison, editor, *The United States, 1865-1900,* Hayes Foundation, 1944; Randolph C. Downs, editor, *Lake Port,* Lucas County Historical Scoeity, 1951; H. H. Clark, editor, *Transitions in American Literary History,* Duke University Press, 1953; Downs, editor, *Industrial Beginnings,* Lucas County Historical Society, 1954.

Author of series of studies in Americal literary motifs; a history of Toledo's Burt Theatre, published in three installments in *Northwest Ohio Quarterly;* and articles for yearbooks, professional journals, and *Toledo Blade Sunday Magazine.* Member of editorial board, Northwest Ohio Historical Society, 1946—.

WORK IN PROGRESS: Studies in Hawthorne's Methods; also writing on Sir Walter Scott and on natural history in literature.

AVOCATIONAL INTERESTS: Conservation, hiking, traveling by rail and car, collecting books (has a six-thousand volume library which he is cataloging and preparing to distribute).

BIOGRAPHICAL/CRITICAL SOURCES: Toledo Blade Sunday Magazine, December 5, 1965.

* * *

OSIPOW, Samuel H(erman) 1934-

PERSONAL: Born April 18, 1934, in Allentown, Pa.; son of Louis M. (a businessman) and Tillie (Wolfe) Osipow; married Sondra Feinstein, August 26, 1956; children: Randall, Jay, Reva, David. *Education:* Lafayette College, B.A., 1954; Columbia University, M.A., 1955; Syracuse University, Ph.D., 1959. *Home:* 575 Enfield Rd., Columbus, Ohio 43209. *Office:* Department of Psychology, Ohio State University, 1945 North High St., Columbus, Ohio 43210.

CAREER: University of Wisconsin, Madison, lecturer in education, 1961; Pennsylvania State University, University Park, assistant professor of psychology and counselor, 1961-67; Ohio State University, Columbus, associate professor, 1967-69, professor of psychology, 1969—. Research associate in education at Harvard University, 1965; visiting professor at Tel-Aviv University, 1972. *Military service:* U.S. Army Reserve, 1954-63, active duty, 1959-60; became captain. *Member:* American Psychological Association (fellow).

WRITINGS: Theories of Career Development, Appleton, 1968, 2nd edition, 1973; (with W. B. Walsh) *Strategies in Counseling for Behavior Change,* Appleton, 1970; (editor with Walsh) *Behavior Change in Counseling,* Appleton, 1970. Contributor to counseling, personnel, and psychology journals. Editor, *Journal of Vocational Behavior;* consulting editor, *Journal of Counseling Psychology.*

WORK IN PROGRESS: Further research on vocational counseling and on the empirical foundations of counseling.

* * *

OSTERHAVEN, M(aurice) Eugene 1915-

PERSONAL: Born December 8, 1915, in Grand Rapids, Mich.; son of John (a businessman) and Mattie L. (Van Zoeren) Osterhaven; married Margaret Nagy, 1942; children: David Earl, Ellen Jane, Calvin Eugene, Janice Elizabeth. *Education:* Hope College, A.B., 1937; Western Theological Seminary, B.D., 1941; Princeton Theological Seminary, Th.D., 1948. *Politics:* Republican. *Home:* 999 Morningside Dr., Holland, Mich. 49423. *Office:* Western Theological Seminary, Holland, Mich. 49423.

CAREER: Clergyman of Reformed Church in America; minister in Raritan, N.J., 1943-45; Hope College, Holland, Mich., professor of Bible, 1945-52; Western Theological Seminary, Holland, Mich., professor of systematic theology, 1952—. Honorary professor, Sarospatak Reformed Academy, Reformed Church of Hungary, 1948.

WRITINGS: What is Christian Baptism?, Society for Reformed Publications, 1952; *Our Confession of Faith,* Baker Book, 1962; *The Spirit of the Reformed Tradition,* Eerdmans, 1971. Departmental editor, *Church Herald,* 1946-61; editor, *Reformed Review,* 1965—.

* * *

OSTOW, Mortimer 1918-

PERSONAL: Born January 8, 1918, in New York, N.Y.; son of Kalman I. and Gertrude (Liebman) Ostow; married Miriam Furst, 1942; children: Robin Ostow Bodeman, Meir J., Abigail R., Rachel A. *Education:* Columbia University, B.A., 1937, M.A., 1938, Med.Sc.D., 1949; New York University, M.D., 1941; New York Psychoanalytic Institute, graduate study, 1946-50. *Home and office:* 5021 Iselin Ave., Riverdale, Bronx, N.Y. 10471.

CAREER: Diplomate in psychiatry and neurology, American Board of Psychiatry and Neurology, 1949. Beth Israel Hospital, New York, N.Y., intern, 1941-42; St. Elizabeth's Hospital, Washington, D.C., resident in psychiatry, 1942-44; George Washington University, School of Medicine, instructor in clinical neurology, 1942-44; Mount Sinai Hospital, New York, N.Y., resident in neurology, 1946-47, Isidor Abrahamson fellow for research in neurophysiology, 1948; Beth Israel Hospital, associate neuropsychiatrist, 1949-55; private practice in psychiatry in Bronx, N.Y., 1954—. Assistant attending neurologist, 1949—, and preceptor in psychiatry, 1969—, at Mount Sinai Hospital; associate attending psychiatrist at Montefiore Hospital, 1960-66. Jewish Theological Seminary, visiting assistant professor, 1953-65, visiting lecturer, 1954-63, Edward T. Sandrow visiting professor of pastoral psychiatry, 1965—, director of Bernstein Center for Pastoral Counseling, 1965—. Past president of Psychoanalytic Research and Development Fund. *Military service:* U.S. Public Health Service, active duty, 1944-46; became senior assistant surgeon. *Member:* American Psychiatric Association (fellow), American Psychoanalytic Association, American Electroencephalographic Society (charter member), Group for the Advancement of Psychiatry, American Arbitration Association, Federation of Jewish Philanthropies, New York Society for Clinical Psychiatry, New York Academy of Medicine, New York Psychoanalytic Society, Bronx County Medical Society, Phi Beta Kappa, Alpha Omega Alpha, Sigma Xi.

WRITINGS: (With H. Strauss and Louis Greenstein) *Diagnostic Electroencephalography,* Grune, 1952; (with Ben-Ami Scharfstein) *The Need to Believe: The Psychology of Religion,* International Universities Press, 1954; (contributor) Silvano Arieti, editor, *American Handbook of Psychiatry,* Basic Books, 1959; (contributor) N. S. Kline, editor, *Psychopharmacology Frontiers,* Little, Brown, 1959; (contributor) G. J. Sarwer-Foner, editor, *The Dy-*

namics of Psychiatric Drug Therapy, C.C Thomas, 1960; (contributor) John H. Nodine and John H. Mayer, editors, *Psychosomatic Medicine: The First Hahnemann Symposium,* Lea & Febiger, 1962; *Drugs in Psychoanalysis and Psychotherapy,* Basic Books, 1962; (contributor) Yale D. Keskoff and Robert J. Shoemaker, editors, *Vistas in Neuropsychiatry,* University of Pittsburgh Press, 1964; (contributor) Norman S. Greenfield and William C. Lewis, editors, *Psychoanalysis and Current Biological Thought,* University of Wisconsin Press, 1965; (contributor) Philip Solomon, editor, *Psychiatric Drugs,* Grune, 1966; (contributor) Charles Hanly and Morris Lazerowitz, editors, *Psychoanalysis and Philosophy,* International Universities Press, 1970; *The Psychology of Melancholy,* Harper, 1970; (contributor) Seymour C. Post, editor, *Moral Values and the Superego Concept in Psychoanalysis,* International Universities Press, 1972; (contributor) David Sidorsky, editor, *The Future of the Jewish Community in America,* Basic Books, 1973; (editor with H. Z. Winnik and R. Moses) *Psychological Bases of War,* Quadrangle, 1973; (editor) *Sexual Deviations,* Quadrangle, 1974.

* * *

OTT, Thomas O(liver) III 1938-

PERSONAL: Born August 4, 1938, in LaGrange, Ga.; son of Thomas Oliver (a mill engineer) and Marian (Swindell) Ott; married Margaret Franklin, November 25, 1961; children: John, Victoria. *Education:* Asbury College, B.A. (cum laude), 1961; Appalachian State University, M.A., 1963; University of Tennessee, Ph.D., 1970. *Home:* 330 Hermitage Dr., Florence, Ala. 35630. *Office address:* Box 503, University of North Alabama, Florence, Ala. 35630.

CAREER: High school teacher of Spanish in Arden, N.C., 1961-63, of history in Sorrento, Fla., 1963-65; University of North Alabama, Florence, assistant professor, 1967-71, associate professor of history, 1971-74. *Member:* Association of Alabama Historians.

WRITINGS: The Haitian Revolution, 1789-1804, University of Tennessee Press, 1973.

WORK IN PROGRESS: Revolutionaries from the North: Disciples of U.S. Democracy in the Latin American Struggle for Independence, 1808-1826.

* * *

OUELLETTE, Fernand 1930-

PERSONAL: Surname is pronounced wel-*let;* born September 24, 1930, in Montreal, Quebec, Canada; son of Cyrille (a carpenter) and Gilberte (Chalifour) Ouellette; married Lisette Corbeil, July 9, 1955; children: Sylvie, Andree, Jean. *Education:* Universite de Montreal, License es Sciences sociales, 1952. *Religion:* Catholic. *Home:* 37, Terrasse Paquin, Laval, Quebec H7G 3S2, Canada. *Office:* Societe Radio-Canada, 1400 boul Dorchester est, Montreal, Quebec, Canada.

CAREER: Societe Radio-Canada, Montreal, Quebec, producer, 1960—. Member of Commission d'enquete sur l'enseignement des arts du Quebec, 1966-68; co-founder of Rencontre internationale quebecoise des ecrivains, 1972. *Awards, honors:* Prix France-Quebec, 1967, for *Edgard Varese;* Prix du Gouverneur general, 1971, for *Les Actes retrouves* (refused); Prix France-Canada, 1972, for *Poesie: 1953-1971.*

WRITINGS: Ces Anges de sang (poems; title means "These Angels of Blood"), l'Hexagone (Montreal), 1955; *Sequences de l'aile* (poems; title means "Wing Sequences"), l'Hexagone, 1958; (editor and contributor) *Visages d'Edgard Varese* (title means "Aspects of Edgard Varese"), l'Hexagone, 1959; *Le Soleil sous la mort* (poems; title means "The Sun under Darkness"), l'Hexagone, 1965; *Edgard Varese* (biography), Seghers (Paris), 1966, translation by Derek Coltman published under same title, Orion Press, 1968; *Dans le sombre* (poems; title means "In the Dark"), l'Hexagone, 1967; *Les Actes retrouves: essais* (title means "Recovered Acts"), HMH, 1970; *Poesie: 1953-71,* l'Hexagone, 1972; *Depuis Novalis: essai* (title means "From Novalis"), HMH, 1973. Also author of text, "Psaume pour abri" (cantata; title means "Psalm for a Shelter") by Pierre Mercure, produced by Radio Canada, 1963; author of film commentaries for l'Office national du film, 1955-59.

Represented in more than a dozen anthologies, including *How Do I Love Thee: Sixty poets of Canada (and Quebec) Select and Introduce Their Favourite Poems from Their Own Work,* edited by John Robert Colombo, M. G. Hurtig, 1970. Contributor to numerous periodicals. Co-founder and editor, *Liberte,* 1958, member of editorial board, 1958—.

WORK IN PROGRESS: Journal denoue (title means "Unknotted Diary"), a book of autobiographical essays; a book of poems; other essays.

SIDELIGHTS: Ouellette told *CA* of his six-year-long correspondence with Henry Miller, who arranged for Ouellette to meet Edgard Varese, the French-American composer. Eric Salzman has called Ouellette's biography of Varese "a necessary first step . . . an important book. . . . It will 'place' Varese for most people—not in relation to the other artistic and musical trends of his day but simply with respect to his own inner ideas." *Avocational interests:* Music, travel.

BIOGRAPHICAL/CRITICAL SOURCES—Books: Gerard Tougas, *Histoire de la litterature canadienne-francaise,* Presses universitaires de France, 1960; Guy Robert, *Litterature du Quebec,* Volume I, Deom, 1964; Pierre de Grandpre, *Histoire de la litterature francaise du Quebec,* Beauchemin, 1969; Gilles Marcotte, *Le Temps des poetes,* HMH, 1969; *Voix et images du pays,* Volume III, Presses de l'Universite du Quebec, 1970; Serge Brindaud, *La Poesie francaise contemporaine depuis 1945,* Editions Saint-Germain-des-Pres, (Paris), 1973.

Periodicals: *Livres et auteurs quebecois,* 1969, 1970, 1972, 1973; *Europe,* February-March, 1969; *Ellipse,* number 10, 1972; *Esprit,* June, 1973; *La Barre du jour,* number 11, 1973.

* * *

OXTOBY, Willard Gurdon 1933-

PERSONAL: Surname is accented on first syllable; born July 29, 1933, in Kentfield, Calif. son of Gurdon Corning and Miriam Burrell (White) Oxtoby; married Layla Jurji, September 27, 1958; children: David Merrill, Susan Elizabeth. *Education:* Stanford University, B.A., 1955; American School of Oriental Research, Jerusalem, further study, 1958-60; Princeton University, M.A., 1961, Ph.D., 1962; Harvard University, postdoctoral study, 1964-66. *Religion:* United Presbyterian Church in the U.S.A. *Home:* 2 Gordon Rd., Willowdale, Toronto, Ontario M2P 1E1, Canada. *Office:* Trinity College, University of Toronto, Toronto, Ontario M5S 1H8, Canada.

CAREER: McGill University, Montreal, Quebec, lecturer, 1960-63, assistant professor of Old Testament, 1963-64; Harvard University, Cambridge, Mass., teaching fellow in world religions, 1965-66; Yale University, New Haven, Conn., associate professor of religious studies, 1966-71; University of Toronto, Toronto, Ontario, professor of religious studies and Near Eastern studies, 1971—. Visiting professor of Near Eastern languages at University of Michigan, 1964. *Member:* Canadian Society for the Study of Religion, American Society for the Study of Religion (secretary, 1969—), American Academy of Religion, American Oriental Society, Society for Religion in Higher Education.

WRITINGS: Some Inscriptions of the Safaitic Bedouin, American Oriental Society, 1968; *Ancient Iran and Zoroastrianism in Festschriften: An Index,* Council on the Study of Religion (Waterloo, Ontario), 1973. Editor, American Academy of Religion monograph series, "Studies in Religion," 1968-70; member of editorial board, *Soundings* (publication of Society for Religion in Higher Education), 1968-71.

* * *

OZAKI, Robert S(higeo) 1934-

PERSONAL: Born February 28, 1934, in Tokyo, Japan; son of Shigeru (a college professor) and Harumi (Hayashi) Ozaki; married Cecilia E. Levine, December, 1961; children: Rebecca N., Jennifer H. *Education:* Ohio Wesleyan University, B.A., 1956; Harvard University, M.A., 1958, Ph.D., 1960. *Home:* 633 San Luis Rd., Berkeley, Calif. 94707. *Office:* Department of Economics, California State University, Hayward, Calif. 94542.

CAREER: California State University at Hayward, assistant professor, 1960-64, associate professor, 1964-68, professor of economics, 1968w8. member of Japan Economic Research Center, Tokyo. *Member:* American Economic Association, Association for Asian Studies, Phi Beta Kappa, Omicron Chi Epsilon. *Awards, honors:* American Council of Learned Societies research fellow in Japan, 1968-69.

WRITINGS: (Translator) Ryutaro Komiya, editor *Postwar Economic Growth in Japan,* University of California Press, 1966; *Inflation, Recession. . .and All That,* Holt, 1972; *The Control of Imports and Foreign Capital in Japan,* Praeger, 1972. Contributor of technical and general articles to journals in United States, Japan, and Italy. Member of editorial advisory board, Association for Asian Studies, 1969-72.

* * *

PACE, Denny F. 1925-

PERSONAL: Born August 27, 1925, in Clemenceau, Ariz.; son of Leroy L. (a rancher) and Mauretta (Eager) Pace; married Eleanore Ruth Brown, May 19, 1946; children: Cynthia Ann (Mrs. Robert Stewart), Susan (Mrs. Victor Malvaiz), Taina (Mrs. Eric Nordbak). *Education:* University of Southern California, B.S., 1955, M.S., 1964. *Home:* 1301 Highway 30, Apt. 291, College Station, Tex. 77840.

CAREER: Police officer in Los Angeles, Calif., 1945-64; California State University at Long Beach, assistant professor of criminology, 1965-67; Tarrant County Junior College, Fort Worth, Tex., associate professor of criminology, 1967-68; Kent State University, Kent, Ohio, assistant professor of criminology, 1968-70; Texas Criminal Justice Council, Austin, police planner, 1970-71; U.S. Department of Justice, Law Enforcement Assistance Administration, Dallas, Tex., deputy regional administrator, 1971-73; Texas A & M University, College Station, instructor in highway safety, 1973—; private consultant in management and criminal justice, 1973—. *Military service:* U.S. Marine Corps, 1942-45. U.S. Army, 1950; became staff sergeant.

WRITINGS: Handbook on Vice Control, Prentice-Hall, 1971; (with Jimmie C. Styles) *Handbook on Narcotics Control,* Prentice-Hall, 1972.

WORK IN PROGRESS: With Jimmie C. Styles, *Organized Crime: Concepts and Control,* for Prentice-Hall; two fiction manuscripts.

* * *

PACHECO, Henry L(uis) 1947-

PERSONAL: Surname is pronounced Patch-*echo;* born July 27, 1947, in Holman, N.M.; son of Henry Benjamin Pacheco and Resauda (Martinez) Pacheco Cordova; married Lynda DeCroo (a high school guidance counselor), August 9, 1969; children: Joseph. *Education:* Highlands University, summer study, 1965-67; University of Wyoming, B.A., 1970, M.A., 1973. *Politics:* Democrat. *Religion:* Roman Catholic. *Home:* 2513 Ridge Rd., Cheyenne, Wyo. 82001. *Agent:* Priscilla Salazar, 4036 Morrisson Rd., Denver, Colo. 80201.

CAREER: Journalist, copywriter; Fleetwood Corp., Cheyenne, Wyo., manager of editorial services, 1973; free-lance writer. Director of University of Wyoming Ethnic Cultural Media Center, 1972. *Military service:* U.S. Marine Corps, 1970-72. *Member:* Marine Corps Combat Correspondents, Sigma Delta Chi. *Awards, honors:* Harcourt, Brace, & World poetry fellowship, 1968, to University of Colorado Writer's Conference.

WRITINGS: The Kindred/La Familia, Totinem, 1972. Contributor to "Chicano Renaissance," produced on KOA-TV, Denver, Colo.

WORK IN PROGRESS: The Mexican Relic, a book of poetry; *Testudo,* an anthology.

SIDELIGHTS: "In order for poetry to grow in America," Pacheco wrote, "it has had to draw from the spirits of all its peoples. The Chicano experience will be one of American poetry's most valuable works and unlike American Indian poetry, most writers will be native to the culture and experience—Chicanos and Hispanos."

BIOGRAPHICAL/CRITICAL SOURCES: Alurista, editor, *O Festival de flory canto: An Anthology of Chicano Literature,* Centro Chicano, University of Southern California, 1974.

* * *

PACKER, J(ames) I(nnell) 1926-

PERSONAL: Born July 22, 1926, in Twyning, Gloucestershire, England; son of James Percy (a clerk) and Dorothy (Harris) Packer; married Ethel Mullett; children: Ruth, Naomi, Martin. *Education:* Corpus Christi College, Oxford, B.A., 1948, M.A. and D.Phil., both 1954; also studied at Wycliffe Hall, Oxford, 1949-52. *Politics:* "Eclectic." *Religion:* Anglican. *Office:* Trinity College, Stoke Hill, Bristol BS9 1JP, England.

CAREER: Anglican clergyman; assistant curate in Birmingham, England, 1952-54; Tyndale Hall, Bristol, England, tutor, 1955-61; Latimer House, Oxford, England, librarian, 1961-64, warden, 1964-69; Tyndale Hall, principal, 1970-71; Trinity College, Bristol, England, associate principal, 1971—. Visiting professor at Westminster Theological Seminary, 1968, and Gordon-Conwell Seminary, 1975. *Member:* Society for the Study of Theology, Victoria Institute, Tyndale Fellowship for Biblical Research.

WRITINGS: "Fundamentalism" and the Word of God, Eerdmans, 1958, 2nd edition, in press; (translator and editor, with O. R. Johnston) *Luther's Bondage of the Will,* Revell, 1958; *Evangelism and the Sovereignty of God,* Inter-Varsity Press, 1961; *God Has Spoken,* Westminster, 1965; (with A. M. Stibbs) *The Spirit Within You,* Hodder & Stoughton, 1967; *Knowing God,* Inter-Varsity Press, 1973.

WORK IN PROGRESS: The Refining Fire, a history of the Puritans; *The Way of Salvation;* research on biblical, historical, and systematic theology.

AVOCATIONAL INTERESTS: Music (Western classical and early American jazz), cricket, railroads.

* * *

PADOVER, Saul K(ussiel) 1905-

PERSONAL: Born April 13, 1905, in Vienna, Austria; came to United States, 1920; son of Keva (a merchant; an American citizen) and Frumet (Goldmann) Padover; married Margaret Thompson Fenwick, April 13, 1957. *Education:* Wayne State University, B.A. (cum laude), 1928; Yale University, graduate student, 1928-29; University of Chicago, M.A., 1930, Ph.D., 1932. *Home:* 129 Amity St., Brooklyn, N.Y. 11201. *Agent:* Nannine Joseph, 200 West 54th St., New York, N.Y. 10019. *Office:* Department of Political Science, New School for Social Research, 66 West 12th St., New York, N.Y. 10011.

CAREER: University of California, Berkeley, research associate in history, 1933-36; U.S. Department of the Interior, Washington, D.C., assistant to Secretary of the Interior, 1938-43, director of research unit on territorial policy, 1942-44; *PM,* New York, N.Y., editorial writer, 1946-48; New School for Social Research, New York, N.Y., professor of political science, Graduate Faculty, 1948—, distinguished service professor, 1971—, dean of School of Politics, 1950-55. Visiting professor at Sorbonne, University of Paris, 1949, Columbia University, 1954-55, University of Tokyo, spring, 1960, University of Malaya, fall, 1960, and Wayne State University, 1971. Conductor of Friends Service Committee international seminars in Europe, 1949—; project director, Carnegie Endowment for International Peace, 1955-56. *Military service:* Office of Strategic Services, intelligence officer, 1944-45; received Bronze Star, Presidential Citation, and Legion of Honor (France).

AWARDS, HONORS: Commonwealth Silver Medal, 1935; Guggenheim fellow in Paris, 1936-37; Rockefeller Foundation fellow, 1945-46; Alumni Award, Wayne State University, 1965; Professional Achievement Award, University of Chicago, 1970.

WRITINGS: The Revolutionary Emperor, Joseph the Second, 1741-1790, Ballou, 1934, revised edition published as *The Revolutionary Emperor, Joseph II of Austria,* Archon, 1967; (with James Westfall Thompson) *Secret Diplomacy: A Record of Espionage and Double-Dealing,* Jarrolds, 1937, published as *Secret Diplomacy: Espionage and Cryptography, 1500-1815,* Ungar, 1963; *The Life and Death of Louis XVI,* Appleton, 1939, 2nd edition, Taplinger, 1963; (contributor) James Westfall Thompson, principal author, *The Medieval Library,* University of Chicago Press, 1939.

Jefferson, Harcourt, 1942, revised and abridged edition, New American Library, 1952; *Experiment in Germany: The Story of an American Intelligence Officer,* Duell, Sloan & Pearce, 1946 (published in England as *Psychologist in Germany,* Phoenix House, 1946); *La Vie politique des Etats-Unis,* Editions Domat-Montchrestien, 1949.

Psychological Warfare [and] The Strategy of Soviet Propaganda (latter study by Harold D. Lasswell), Foreign Policy Association, 1951; *Europe's Quest for Unity [and] The U.S. and European Union* (latter study by L. Larry Leonard), Foreign Policy Association, 1958; (with assistance of Francois Goguel, Louis Rosenstock-Franck, and Eric Weil) *French Institutions: Values and Politics,* Stanford University Press, 1954; *U.S. Foreign Policy and Public Opinion,* Foreign Policy Association, 1958.

The Genius of America: Men Whose Ideas Shaped Our Civilization, McGraw, 1960; *The Meaning of Democracy: An Appraisal of the American Experience,* Praeger, 1963; *Foreign Affairs* (high school text), Holt, 1964; *Thomas Jefferson and The Foundations of American Freedom,* Van Nostrand, 1965.

Editor, and author of introductions to most of the edited books: *Thomas Jefferson on Democracy,* New American Library, 1939.

Wilson's Ideals (selections from writings and speeches of President Woodrow Wilson), American Council on Public Affairs, 1942; *The Complete Jefferson: Containing His Major Writings, Published and Unpublished, Except His letters,* Duell, Sloan & Pearce, 1943, reprinted, Books for Libraries, 1969; *Thomas Jefferson and the National Capital,* Government Printing Office, 1943.

The Forging of American Federalism: Selected Writings of James Madison, Harper, 1953; (and author of historical notes) *The Living U.S. Constitution,* Praeger, 1953, revised and enlarged edition, New American Library, 1968; *The Complete Madison: His Basic Writings,* Harper, 1953, reprinted, Kraus Reprint Co., 1971; *The Washington Papers: Basic Selections from the Public and Private Writings of George Washington,* Harper, 1955; *A Jefferson Profile as Revealed in His Letters,* John Day, 1956; (and author of commentaries) *Confessions and Self-Portraits: 4600 Years of Autobiography,* John Day, 1957; *The Mind of Alexander Hamilton,* Harper, 1958.

Nehru on World History (condensed from Jawaharlal Nehru's *Glimpses of World History*), John Day, 1960; *The World of the Founding Fathers: Their Basic Ideas on Freedom and Self-Government,* Yoseloff, 1960; *To Secure These Blessings: The Great Debates of the Constitutional Convention of 1787,* Washington Square Press, 1962; *The Writings of Thomas Jefferson,* Heritage Press, 1967.

Sources of Democracy: Voices of Freedom, Hope and Justice, McGraw, 1973.

Translator, editor, and author of introduction: "Karl Marx Library" series, McGraw, Volume I: *Karl Marx on Revolution,* 1972; Volume II: *Karl Marx on America and the Civil War,* 1972; Volume III: *Karl Marx on the First International,* 1973; Volume IV: *Karl Marx on Freedom of the Press and Censorship,* 1974; Volume V: *Karl Marx on Religion,* 1974.

Writer of booklets and public affairs pamphlets. Contributor to journals and magazines.

WORK IN PROGRESS: Translating, arranging, and editing further material for the "Karl Marx Library" series, planned to run to twelve volumes; a biography of Karl Marx, for McGraw.

PAGNOL, Marcel 1895-1974

February 25, 1895—April 18, 1974; French playwright, producer, director, and writer of films, and author of memoirs and other works. Obituaries: *New York Times,* April 19, 1974; *Washington Post,* April 19, 1974; *Newsweek,* April 29, 1974; *Time,* April 29, 1974; *Current Biography,* June, 1974.

* * *

PALINCHAK, Robert S(tephen) 1942-

PERSONAL: Born December 25, 1942, in Coaldale, Pa.; son of Michael and Susan (Karas) Palinchak; married Patricia Secara, July 4, 1967. *Education:* East Stroudsburg State College, B.S., 1964; graduate study at Lehigh University, 1964, Temple University, 1964-66, Pennsylvania State University, 1964-65, University of Notre Dame, 1965, and Villanova University, 1965-66; Loyola College, Baltimore, Md., M.A., 1969; Syracuse University, Ph.D., 1972. *Office:* Department of Physics, Essex Community College, Baltimore County, Md. 21237.

CAREER: Teacher of physics and mathematics in the public schools of Johnsville, Pa., 1964, and Ambler, Pa., 1964-66; Essex Community College, Baltimore County, Md., assistant professor, 1966-69, associate professor of physics, 1970—, head of department of physical science, 1966-69, head of department of physics, engineering, and technology, 1970—. Visiting professor at Towson State College, summer, 1968, 1969, and Loyola College, summer, 1972. *Member:* World Future Society, American Association for Higher Education, American Association of University Administrators, American Association of University Professors, Maryland Association of Community and Junior Colleges.

WRITINGS: The Evolution of the Community College, Scarecrow, 1973. Contributor to publications of Educational Resources Information Center, and to *Improving College and University Teaching* and *Educational Forum.*

WORK IN PROGRESS: Research on the future of post-secondary education.

* * *

PANGLE, Thomas L(ee) 1944-

PERSONAL: Surname rhymes with "angle"; born November 29, 1944, in Gouverneur, N. Y.; son of James Lee (an attorney) and Helen (a teacher; maiden name, Carey) Pangle; married Diane Rennell (a teacher), December 30, 1970. *Education:* Attended Yale University, 1962-64; Cornell University, A.B., 1966; University of Chicago, Ph.D., 1972. *Religion:* Episcopalian. *Home:* 1805 Silliman College, Yale University, New Haven, Conn. 06520. *Office:* Department of Political Science, Yale University, New Haven, Conn. 06520.

CAREER: Yale University, New Haven, Conn., assistant professor of political philosophy, 1971—. *Member:* American Political Science Association, Northeastern Political Science Association, Boston Area Conference for the Study of Political Thought, Phi Beta Kappa. *Awards, honors:* Woodrow Wilson fellow, 1966-67; National Security Education Seminar fellow, 1973.

WRITINGS: Montesquieu's Philosophy of Liberalism: A Commentary on the Spirit of the Laws, University of Chicago Press, 1972; (with Klaus Knorr and others) *Historical Introduction to National Security Problems,* Praeger, in press. Contributor to *American Political Science Review, Essays in Arts and Sciences,* and *Yale Review.*

WORK IN PROGRESS: The Ethical Basis of Politics: A Study of Aristotle, Kant, and Plato.

* * *

PANTER, Carol 1936-

PERSONAL: Born January 19, 1936, in New York, N.Y.; daughter of Irving J. (an investment analyst) and Rosalie (Kluge) Yeckes; married Gideon G. Panter (a physician), February 2, 1956; children: Danielle, Ethan, Abigail. *Education:* Attended Juilliard School of Music, 1947-53, and Bennington College, 1953-54; New York University, A.B., 1957; City College of the City University of New York, M.S., 1961. *Home:* Ludlow Lane, Palisades, N.Y. 10964. *Agent:* Russell & Volkening, 551 Fifth Ave., New York, N.Y. 10017.

CAREER: Harpsichordist. Palisades Free Library, Palisades, N.Y., member of board of trustees, 1968-75, president of board, 1969-70; member of board of directors, Montessori Associates School, Englewood, N.J., 1972-77, and Juvenile Diabetes Association, 1973-75.

WRITINGS: (With Kathleen Lukens) *Thursday's Child Has Far to Go,* Prentice-Hall, 1969; *Beany and His New Recorder,* Four Winds, 1972; (with Ellen Liman) *Decorating Your Room,* F. Watts, 1974. Contributor of short stories to *Redbook* and of articles to medical magazines.

WORK IN PROGRESS: A book with Samuel Basch, *The Major* (tentative title), publication by Harper expected in 1975.

* * *

PARK, William John 1930-

PERSONAL: Born April 6, 1930, in Philadelphia, Pa.; son of William John, Jr. (a banker) and Darthea (Jordan) Park; married Marlene Shubert (a professor of art history), April 11, 1957; children: Jonathan, Geoffrey, Catharine, William. *Education:* Princeton University, A.B., 1951; Columbia University, M.A., 1954, Ph.D., 1962. *Politics:* Independent. *Religion:* Christian. *Address:* P.O. Box 16, Sarah Lawrence College, Bronxville, N.Y. 10708.

CAREER: Hamilton College, Clinton, N.Y., instructor in English, 1954-57; Columbia University, New York, N.Y., instructor in English, 1957-62; Sarah Lawrence College, Bronxville, N.Y., member of faculty of literature and film, 1962—, director of summer session in London, 1966-70. *Military service:* U.S. Marine Corps, 1951-53; became captain. *Member:* Modern Language Association of America. *Awards, honors:* American Council of Learned Societies grant-in-aid, 1968-69.

WRITINGS: (Editor with A. Kent Hieatt) *The College Anthology of British and American Poetry,* Allyn & Bacon, 1964, 2nd edition, 1971. Contributor to professional journals. Editor, *Sarah Lawrence Journal.*

WORK IN PROGRESS: Caesar or Nothing, a novel; *Hoorah for Hollywood,* nonfiction.

* * *

PARKER, Frank J(oseph) 1940-

PERSONAL: Born October 10, 1940, in New York, N.Y.; son of Frank J. (an attorney) and Louise (Lynch) Parker. *Education:* Holy Cross College, B.S., 1962; Fordham University, J.D., 1965; Institute of Theological Studies, Louvain, Belgium, M.Div., 1973. *Home:* Saint Mary's Hall, Boston College, Newton, Mass. 02167. *Office:* Fulton Hall, Room 403, Boston College, Newton, Mass. 02167.

CAREER: Ordained Roman Catholic priest of the Society of Jesus (Jesuit), 1973; admitted to the Bar of Massachusetts, 1967; Berkshire County Anti-Poverty Agencies, Berkshire County, Mass., legal counsel, 1967-68; Boston College, Newton, Mass., lecturer, 1969-74, associate professor of management, 1974—. Missionary priest in Diocese of Douala, Cameroun, 1973-74; visiting lecturer at School of Social Work, University of Rhodesia, 1974; legal counsel to Weston College, Cambridge, Mass., 1969-74. *Member:* American Bar Association, National District Attorney's Association, National Association of College and University Attorneys, Authors Guild of Authors League of America, Massachusetts Bar Association, Waltham Bar Association.

WRITINGS: Law and the Poor, Orbis Books, 1973; *Caryl Chessman: The Red Light Bandit,* Nelson-Hall, 1974. Contributor to law journals.

WORK IN PROGRESS: An American in Douala (tentative title), a book on everyday life in an urbanizing city (Douala, Cameroun) in French-speaking Equatorial Africa.

* * *

PARKER, Geoffrey 1933-

PERSONAL: Born January 13, 1933, in Aberdare, Wales; son of Henry James and Nora (Brunt) Parker; married Brenda Williams (an administrator), October 23, 1960; children: Martin, Julie. *Education:* University of Aix-Marseille, graduate study, 1957-58; University College of Wales, M.A., 1960. *Home:* 102 Birmingham Rd., Lichfield, Staffordshire, England. *Office:* Department of Extramural Studies, University of Birmingham, Birmingham, England.

CAREER: University of Birmingham, Birmingham, England, lecturer in extramural studies, 1969—. *Member:* Royal Geographical Society (fellow), Geographical Association, Universities Association for Contemporary European Studies.

WRITINGS: The Geography of Economies, Longmans, Green, 1965, 2nd edition, 1972; *The Logic of Unity,* Longmans, Green, 1968, published as *An Economic Geography of the Common Market,* Praeger, 1969. Contributor to *Geography, Geographical Magazine, Spectator,* and *Times Educational Supplement.*

WORK IN PROGRESS: A book, *The Community of Nine,* completion expected in 1975; research on the European Economic Community (Common Market).

* * *

PARKER, Nancy Winslow 1930-

PERSONAL: Born October 18, 1930, in Maplewood, N.J.; daughter of Winslow Aurelius (a textile executive) and Beatrice (Gaunt) Parker. *Education:* Mills College, B.A., 1952; also studied at Art Students League, 1956, 1957, and School of Visual Arts, New York, N.Y., 1966-67. *Home:* 51 East 74th St., New York, N.Y. 10021.

CAREER: NBC-Television, New York, N.Y., sales promoter, 1956-60; New York Soccer Club, New York, N.Y., sports promoter, 1961-63; Radio Corp. of America (RCA), New York, N.Y., sales promoter, 1964-67; Appleton, Century, Crofts, Inc. (publishers), New York, N.Y., art director, 1968-70; Holt, Rinehart & Winston, Inc. (publishers), New York, N.Y., graphic designer, 1970-72; free-lance writer and illustrator of children's books, 1972—. *Member:* Bichon Frise Club of America (past member of board of directors), Mills College Club of New York.

WRITINGS—Juvenile: *The Man with the Take-Apart Head,* Dodd, 1974.

Illustrator: John Langstaff, *Oh, A-Hunting We Will Go!,* Atheneum, 1974; Carter Houck, *Warm as Wool, Cool as Cotton,* Seabury, 1975.

WORK IN PROGRESS: Research for a children's book on American history; several fictional works for children; illustrating a children's book on natural fibers; making five wood constructions combining oils, wood carving, and construction.

SIDELIGHTS: Ms. Parker writes: "I cannot remember when I have not been interested in children's literature. As a writer, the field has limitless potential for fantasy and the joy of creation. As an illustrator, the opportunity to let yourself go in wild interpretation is an artist's dream come true.

"My background in American corporate business life was invaluable for the human experience it offered. However, the philosophy of the human condition as expressed by the surrealists and its protege Rene Magritte have been a profound influence on my thinking and creating. My life, my writing and my art are devoted to these expressions of time, space and reality."

AVOCATIONAL INTERESTS: Travel (Hawaii, West Indies, France), all things French (history, theater, literature, language, painting, architecture), carpentry, breeding and showing Bichon Frise, tennis, gardening.

* * *

PARKER, Robert B(rown) 1932-

PERSONAL: Born September 17, 1932, in Springfield, Mass.; son of Carroll Snow (a telephone company executive) and Mary Pauline (Murphy) Parker; married Joan Hall (a college teacher), August 26, 1956; children: David F., Daniel T. *Education:* Colby College, B.A., 1954; Boston University, M.A., 1957, Ph.D., 1970. *Politics:* None. *Religion:* None. *Residence:* Lynnfield, Mass. *Agent:* Paul R. Reynolds, Inc., 599 Fifth Ave., New York, N.Y. 10017. *Office:* Department of English, Northeastern University, Boston, Mass. 02115.

CAREER: Curtiss-Wright Co., Woodridge, N.J., management trainee, 1957; Raytheon Co., Andover, Mass., technical writer, 1957-59; Prudential Insurance Co., Boston, Mass., advertising writer, 1959-62; Boston University, Boston, Mass., lecturer in English, 1962-64; Massachusetts State College, Lowell, instructor in English, 1964-66; Massachusetts State College, Bridgewater, instructor in English, 1966-68; Northeastern University, Boston, Mass., assistant professor, 1968-74, associate professor of English, 1974—. Co-chairman for Parker-Farman Co. (advertising agency), 1960-62; lecturer at Suffolk University, 1965-66; film consultant to Arthur D. Little, 1962-64. *Military service:* U.S. Army, 1954-56. *Member:* Mystery Writers of America.

WRITINGS: (With others) *The Personal Response to Literature,* Houghton, 1970; (with Peter L. Sandberg) *Order and Diversity: The Craft of Prose,* Wiley, 1973; (with John R. Marsh) *Sports Illustrated Weight Training,* Lippincott, 1974; *The Godwulf Manuscript* (fiction), Houghton, 1974;

God Save the Child (fiction), Houghton, in press. Contributor to *Lock Haven Review* and *Revue des Langes Vivantes*. Member of editorial board of *Studies in American Fiction*.

WORK IN PROGRESS: Mortal Stakes, fiction.

* * *

PARKINSON, Ethelyn M(inerva) 1906-

PERSONAL: Born September 13, 1906, in Oconto County, Wis.; daughter of James Nelson (a salesman) and Ethel (a teacher; maiden name, Bigelow) Parkinson. *Education:* Oconto County Normal School, first grade teaching certificate, 1923; Bellin Memorial Hospital School of Nursing, R.N., 1928. *Religion:* Presbyterian. *Residence:* Green Bay, Wis.

CAREER: Has taught in elementary school and practiced private nursing; writer. *Awards, honors:* First place in playwriting from Wisconsin Dramatic Society, 1933, for "Shepherd's Queen"; first place for children's short fiction from Scholastic Book Services, 1957, for "A Man or a Mouse"; Abingdon Press Award, 1970, for *Never Go Anywhere with Digby;* award of merit from Wisconsin Historical Society, 1971.

WRITINGS—For children: *Double Trouble for Rupert*, Scholastic Book Services, 1958; *Triple Trouble for Rupert*, Scholastic Book Services, 1960; *The Terrible Troubles of Rupert Piper*, Abingdon, 1963; *The Operation that Happened to Rupert Piper*, Abingdon, 1966; *Today I am a Ham*, Abingdon, 1968; *Higgins of the Railroad Museum*, Abingdon, 1970; *Elf King Joe*, Abingdon, 1970; *Never Go Anywhere with Digby*, Abingdon, 1971; *Rupert Piper and Megan, the Valuable Girl*, Abingdon, 1972. Also author of play, "Shepherd's Queen," and of short juvenile fiction.

* * *

PARR, James A(llan) 1936-

PERSONAL: Born October 7, 1936, in Petroleum, W.Va.; son of James William (a farmer and Virginia (Bragg) Parr; married Franciszka Duda, May 4, 1957 (divorced, 1967); married Carmen Salazar (a college instructor), August 19, 1968; children: (first marriage) Jacqueline. *Education:* Ohio University, B.A., 1959, M.A., 1961; University of Pittsburgh, Ph.D., 1967. *Politics:* Libertarian. *Religion:* Humanist. *Home:* 634 Palisades Ave., Santa Monica, Calif. 90402. *Office:* Department of Spanish and Portuguese, University of Southern California, Los Angeles, Calif. 90007.

CAREER: Ohio University, Athens, instructor in Spanish, 1960-61; University of Toledo, Toledo, Ohio, instructor in Spanish, 1963-64; Murray State University, Murray, Ky., professor of Spanish and chairman of department of modern languages, 1964-70; University of Southern California, Los Angeles, associate professor of Spanish literature, 1970—. *Military service:* U.S. Army, 1954-57; became sergeant.

MEMBER: American Association of Teachers of Spanish and Portuguese (secretary-treasurer, Southern California chapter, 1971-72), Modern Language Association of America (chairman, Spanish 3, 1974—), American Association of University Professors, Philological Association of the Pacific Coast, Phi Beta Kappa, Sigma Delta Pi, Pi Delta Phi. *Awards, honors:* Southeastern Institute of Medieval and Renaissance Studies postdoctoral fellowship at Duke University, summer, 1968.

WRITINGS: (Editor) *Critical Essays on the Life and Work of Juan Ruiz de Alarcon*, Editorial Dos Continentes (Madrid), 1972. Contributor of articles and reviews to *Revista de estudios hispanicos, Hispanic Review, Modern Language Review*, and other journals.

WORK IN PROGRESS: Further research on Golden-Age drama; research on *Don Quixote* and on the generation of 1898.

* * *

PARSONS, Howard L(ee) 1918-

PERSONAL: Born July 9, 1918, in Jacksonville, Fla.; son of Howard Lee and Edna (Powell) Parsons; married Helen Brummall (a psychiatric social worker), March 31, 1946; children: Deborah, Margaret, Susan. *Education:* University of Missouri, student, 1936-39, 1940-41; University of Chicago, B.A., 1942, Ph.D., 1946. *Office:* Department of Philosophy, University of Bridgeport, Bridgeport, Conn. 06602.

CAREER: University of Southern California, Los Angeles, visiting assistant professor of philosophy of religion, 1946-47; University of Illinois, Galesburg Campus, instructor in philosophy, 1947-49; University of Tennessee, Knoxville, assistant professor of philosophy, 1949-57; Coe College, Cedar Rapids, Iowa, associate professor, 1957-60, professor of philosophy, 1960-65, chairman of department of philosophy and religion, 1959-65; University of Bridgeport, Bridgeport, Conn., Bernhard Professor of Philosophy and chairman of department, 1965—. Member of advisory board, Center for Creative Exchange.

MEMBER: American Philosophical Association, Society for Religion in Higher Education, Society for the Philosophical Study of Dialectical Materialism (president, 1962-63; vice-president, 1963), American Institute for Marxist Studies (founding sponsor; member of board, 1964—), Societe Europeenne de Culture, American Association of University Professors, Iowa Philosophical Society (president, 1964-65). *Awards, honors:* Research grants from Wenner-Gren Foundation, 1956, and Kavir Institute, 1963-64.

WRITINGS: Ethics in the Soviet Union Today, American Institute for Marxist Studies, 1967; *Humanistic Philosophy in Poland and Yugoslavia*, American Institute for Marxist Studies, 1968; *Humanism and Marx's Thought*, C.C Thomas, 1971; *Man East and West*, R. B. Gruener, 1973; (editor with John Somerville) *Dialogues on the Philosophy of Marxism*, Greenwood Press, 1974; (editor with Somerville) *Marxism, Revolution, and Peace*, R. B. Gruener, 1974. Contributor to *Praxis, Comprendre, Voprosy Filosofii*, and other philosophy journals.

WORK IN PROGRESS: Marxism and Christianity.

* * *

PASTON, Herbert S. 1928-

PERSONAL: Born April 6, 1928, in Philadelphia, Pa. *Education:* Philadelphia College of Art, B.F.A., 1952; Columbia University, M.A., 1956, Ed.D., 1970. *Home:* South Silver Lane, Sunderland, Mass. 01375. *Office:* Department of Art, Skinner Hall, University of Massachusetts, Amherst, Mass. 01002.

CAREER: Philadelphia College of Art, Philadelphia, Pa., assistant professor of art, 1959-61; Pratt Institute, New York, N.Y., instructor in art, 1963-64; Columbia University, New York, N.Y., instructor in art, 1964-65; Northern Illinois University, DeKalb, assistant professor of art, 1965-66; University of Massachusetts, Amherst, 1966—, currently associate professor of art. *Military service:* U.S. Army. *Member:* National Art Education Association (chairman, 1960), National Society of Interior Designers, American Institute of Decorators. *Awards, honors:* Educator's travel grant to Attingham College, England, 1971, from National Society of Interior Designers.

WRITINGS: Learning to Teach Art, Professional Educators Publications, 1973.

* * *

PATEMAN, Trevor 1947-

PERSONAL: Born July 19, 1947, in Dartford, Kent, England; son of Albert George (a shopkeeper) and Hilda (Stevens) Pateman. *Education:* St. Peter's College, Oxford, B.A., 1968; graduate study at University of London, 1968-70, and Ecole Pratique des Hautes Etudes, 1971-72. *Home:* 1 Church Green, Newton Poppleford, Sidmouth, Devon, England.

CAREER: University of Sussex, Brighton, England, temporary lecturer in philosophy, 1970-71; Exeter College, Devon, England, lecturer in liberal studies, 1972-73; Polytechnic of Central London, London, England, research fellow in television studies, 1973-74.

WRITINGS: (Editor) *Counter Course,* Penguin, 1972; *Language, Truth, and Politics,* Harvester, 1974; *Television and the 1974 General Election* (monograph), British Film Institute, in press. Contributor to journals, including *Philosophy and Phenomenological Research, Human Context, Radical Philosophy,* and *Women and Film.*

* * *

PATRICK, Alison (Mary Houston) 1921-

PERSONAL: Born March 21, 1921, in Melbourne, Victoria, Australia; daughter of Hubert Ralph (a lawyer) and Elizabeth (a nurse; maiden name, McLuckie) Hamer; married James Finlay Patrick (a company lawyer), April 5, 1945; children: Katharine Anne, James Finlay, Timothy David John, Margaret Laurie. *Education:* University of Melbourne, B.A. (honors), 1942, Ph.D., 1969. *Religion:* Anglican. *Home:* 10 Gwenda Ave., Canterbury 3126, Melbourne, Victoria, Australia. *Office:* Department of History, University of Melbourne, Parkville 3052, Victoria, Australia.

CAREER: University of Melbourne, Melbourne, Australia, lecturer, 1950-69, senior lecturer in history, 1969—. *Member:* Australian Society for European History, Australian Historical Association.

WRITINGS: The Men of the First French Republic, Johns Hopkins Press, 1972; (editor) *The Empire of Napoleon III* (documents), Edward Arnold, 1973. Contributor to *Journal of Modern History* and *Historical Studies.*

WORK IN PROGRESS: Research in departmental administration in France, 1790-1792, and the development of religious policy in France, 1790-1793.

* * *

PATROUCH, Joseph F(rancis), Jr. 1935-

PERSONAL: Born May 23, 1935, in Allentown, Pa.; son of Joseph F. (a businessman) and Ruth (May) Patrouch; married Ruth Sweitzer (a registered nurse), September 6, 1958; children: Joseph III, Katherine, Denise, Jean. *Education:* University of Cincinnati, B.A., 1958, M.A., 1960; University of Wisconsin, Ph.D., 1965. *Politics:* Democrat. *Religion:* Roman Catholic. *Home:* 3280 Southern Blvd., Kettering, Ohio 45409. *Office:* Department of English, University of Dayton, Dayton, Ohio 45469.

CAREER: University of Dayton, Dayton, Ohio, assistant professor, 1964-70, associate professor of English, 1970—. *Member:* Science Fiction Writers of America.

WRITINGS: Reginald Pecock, Twayne, 1970; *The Science Fiction of Isaac Asimov,* Doubleday, 1974. Contributor of short stories to magazines.

WORK IN PROGRESS: A study of time travel stories.

* * *

PAUL, Robert
See ROBERTS, John G(aither)

* * *

PAX, Clyde 1928-

PERSONAL: Born March 20, 1928, in New Weston, Ohio; son of Jacob G. and Antoinette (Nordenbrock) Pax; married Ann Hoeffer, April 11, 1953; children: Christopher, Benedict, Mary, Paul, Margaret, Anne. *Education:* University of Notre Dame, A.B., 1951, Ph.D., 1962; St. Louis University, M.A., 1956. *Religion:* Roman Catholic. *Home:* 11 Chesterfield Rd., Worcester, Mass. 01602. *Office:* Department of Philosophy, Holy Cross College, Worcester, Mass. 01610.

CAREER: Holy Cross College, Worcester, Mass., 1961—, currently associate professor of philosophy and chairman of department.

WRITINGS: An Existential Approach to God, Nijhoff, 1973.

WORK IN PROGRESS: The Logic of Human Relations.

* * *

PAYES, Rachel C(osgrove) 1922-
(Rachel Cosgrove, E. L. Arch)

PERSONAL: Born December 11, 1922, in Westernport, Md.; daughter of Jacob A. (a mine superintendent) and Martha (Brake) Cosgrove; married Norman M. Payes (a laboratory specialist with IBM), September 12, 1954; children: Robert, Ruth. *Education:* West Virginia Wesleyan College, B.Sc., 1943. *Politics:* Republican. *Religion:* United Methodist. *Home:* 3589 Frost Rd., Shrub Oak, N.Y. 10588.

CAREER: Registered medical technologist; American Cyanamid, Research Division, Pearl River, N.Y., research associate, 1945-57; novelist. *Member:* Science Fiction Writers of America.

WRITINGS—Mystery novels, except where noted otherwise; all published by Bouregy: *Forsythia Finds Murder,* 1960; *Death Sleeps Lightly,* 1960; *Shadow of Fear,* 1961; *Curiosity Killed Kitty,* 1962; *Memoirs of Murder,* 1964; *Mystery of Echo Caverns,* 1966; *Peace Corps Nurse* (romance), 1967.

Under name Rachel Cosgrove Payes: *O Charitable Death,* Doubleday Crime Club, 1968; *The Silent Place* (gothic novel), Ace Books, 1969; *Malverne Hall* (gothic novel), Ace Books, 1970.

Under name Rachel Payes: *Forbidden Island* (gothic novel), Berkley Publishing, 1973; *Devil's Court* (gothic novel), Berkley Publishing, 1974; *House of Tarot* (gothic novel), Berkley Publishing, in press.

Novels; under name Rachel Cosgrove; all published by Bouregy, except where noted otherwise: *Hidden Valley of Oz,* Reilly & Lee, 1951; *Marjory Thurman, Lab Technician,* 1960; *Long Journey Home,* 1962; *Not for Glory,* 1963; *The Candystripers,* 1964; *Ann Gordon of the Peace Corps,* 1965; *Linda's Gifts,* 1966; *Designs for Love,* 1966.

Science fiction; under pseudonym E. L. Arch; all published by Bouregy: *Bridge to Yesterday,* 1963; *Planet of Death,* 1964; *The Deathstones,* 1964; *The First Immortals,* 1965; *The Double-Minded Man,* 1966; *The Man with Three Eyes,* 1967.

Science fiction is represented in the following anthologies: *And Walk Now Gently through the Fire,* edited by Roger Elwood, Chilton, 1972, *Children of Infinity,* edited by Elwood, Watts, 1973, *Androids, Time Machines and Blue Giraffes,* edited by Elwood and Vic Ghidalia, Follett, 1973, *Alien Condition,* edited by Stephen Goldin, Ballantine, 1973.

Contributor of articles and stories to *Light and Life Evangel, Adult Bible Class, True Medic, Classmate, One, Hearthstone, Covenant, Walther League, Contact, Crossword Treat, Magazine of Horror, Writer, Straight, Worlds of If, Worlds of Tomorrow, Amazing,* and *Vertex;* contributor of fillers and puzzles to magazines and newspapers, including *Herald Tribune, Weekday,* and *New York Journal American.* Writer of verse for Buzzo Cardoza and Barker greeting cards.

WORK IN PROGRESS: A science fiction novel.

* * *

PAYSON, Dale 1943-

PERSONAL: Born June 3, 1943, in White Plains, N.Y.; daughter of Henry and Frances T. Payson. *Education:* Endicott Junior College, graduate, 1963; attended School of Visual Arts, summers, 1961 and 1962, and 1963-64. *Home and office:* 800 West End Ave., New York, N.Y. 10025. *Agent:* Florence Alexander, 50 East 42nd St., New York, N.Y.

CAREER: Sylvox Display Co., New York, N.Y., window display designer, 1965; Famous Artists, Westport, Conn., teacher of correspondence course, 1967; Encore Fashions, New York, N.Y., fabric designer, 1969-70; Fairfield Co., New York, N.Y., colorist, 1970-71.

WRITINGS: *Almost Twins* (for children), Prentice-Hall, 1974.

* * *

PEARL, Chaim 1919-

PERSONAL: Born November 25, 1919, in Liverpool, England; son of Alexander and Rebecca (Epstein) Pearl; married Anita Newman, October 16, 1941; children: David, Jonathan, Simon, Judith. *Education:* Graduate of Rabbinical College of Liverpool, and Jews' College, London; University of London, B.A., 1947, Ph.D., 1957; University of Birmingham, M.A., 1951. *Home:* 5360 Arlington Ave., New York, N.Y. 10471. *Office:* Conservative Synagogue, 250th St. and Henry Hudson Parkway, New York, N.Y. 10471.

CAREER: Ordained Jewish rabbi, 1945; rabbi in Birmingham, England, 1945-60, and London, England, 1960-64; Conservative Synagogue of Riverdale, New York, N.Y., rabbi, 1964—. Vice-president of British section, World Jewish Congress, 1955-62.

WRITINGS: *Guide to Jewish Knowledge,* Jewish Chronicle, 1957; *Guide to Shavuoth,* Jewish Chronicle, 1959; *Minor Jewish Festivals and Fasts,* Jewish Chronicle, 1962; *Rashi's Commentaries on Pentateuch,* Norton, 1970; *The Medieval Jewish Mind,* Jewish Chronicle, 1971. Editor of "Popular Jewish Library" of World Jewish Congress, 1950-60. Contributor to journals.

* * *

PEARMAN, Jean R(ichardson) 1915-

PERSONAL: Born July 15, 1915, in Cherry, Neb.; son of William Francis (a rancher) and Ruth G. (Richardson) Pearman; married A. Valier Stevenson, July 15, 1941; children: Allen Lee, Sandra Jean (Mrs. Paul Lillis), Marlene Ann, Patricia Valier. *Education:* Nebraska State College at Chadron, B.A., 1938; University of Nebraska, M.A., 1945; graduate study at University of Michigan, 1948-56, and University of Arkansas, summer, 1950; University of Minnesota, Ph.D., 1959; postdoctoral study at Florida State University, 1972-73. *Politics:* Democrat. *Home:* 1330 Sharon Rd., Tallahassee, Fla. 32303. *Office:* School of Social Work, Florida State University, Tallahassee, Fla. 32306.

CAREER: Nebraska Public Assistance, Lincoln, caseworker, 1939-41; Work Projects Administration, Omaha, Neb., senior social worker, 1941; U.S. Employment Service, Manpower Commission, Alliance, Neb., interviewer-superintendent, 1942-43; superintendent in the public schools of Ashby, Liberty, and Chester, Neb., public schools, 1943-46; Veterans Administration, Des Moines, Iowa, social worker, 1946-47; Northern Michigan University, Marquette, assistant professor, 1947-55, associate professor, 1955-59, professor of economics, sociology, and social work, 1959-64, head of department, 1961-64; Florida State University, Tallahassee, professor of social work, 1964—, head of department, 1964-69. Lecturer at Rackham School of Graduate Studies, University of Michigan, 1948-59; visiting professor at University of Wisconsin, Milwaukee, summer, 1962; president of Catholic Social Service Board, Marquette, Mich., 1962, and Marquette Council of Social Agencies, 1962-63; co-chairman of American Red Cross Board, Leon County, Fla., 1970; consultant for Public Welfare Policy and School of Social Work for the State of Florida, 1964—. *Member:* American Economic Association, National Association of Social Workers, American Federation of Teachers, American Academy of Political and Social Science, American Public Welfare Association, National Conference on Social Welfare, Association for Evolutionary Economics, Common Cause.

WRITINGS: (Contributor) Leland R. Robinson, John F. Adams, and Harry L. Dillin, editors, *Introduction to Modern Economics,* Dryden Press, 1952; (with Albert Burrows) *Social Services in the School,* Public Affairs Press, 1955; *Social Science and Social Work: Applications in Helping Professions,* Scarecrow, 1973. Contributor to journals in his field.

WORK IN PROGRESS: *Orientation to Helping Services and Professions.*

AVOCATIONAL INTERESTS: Agriculture, fishing, small real estate development.

PEARSON, John 1934-

PERSONAL: Born October 22, 1934, in Washington, D.C.; son of John Hale (a minister) and Eudora (Yerby) Pearson; married Josephine Strain, February 4, 1960 (divorced, 1965); children: Karen. *Education:* Duke University, A.B.; Union Theological Seminary, New York, N.Y., B.D. *Home:* 1343 Sacramento St., Berkeley, Calif. 94702.

CAREER: Served as Methodist minister in Windsor and Napa, Calif.; University of California, Berkeley, extension program coordinator of department of arts and humanities, 1966-74; writer and photographer.

WRITINGS: To Be Nobody Else, Jomeri Publications, 1968; *Kiss the Joy As It Flies,* Random House, 1970; *The Sun's Birthday,* Doubleday, 1973.

WORK IN PROGRESS: A book of nature photographs accompanied by children's writings.

SIDELIGHTS: Pearson told *CA* that he would be interested in receiving children's writing about nature, especially from very young children. His stream-of-consciousness autobiography sketches parts of his life: " . . . minister two years . . . think about nuclear war . . . poverty . . . What can I do? . . . Who am I? . . . quit . . . two degrees—no job . . . intense searching, boredom, despair . . . separation, divorce, depression, tranquilizers, analysis, shock therapy . . . thirty . . . forget the princess, embrace the dragons, feel the sun, taste the ocean, let go . . . miracle . . . re-birth . . . hack photographer . . . photograph what I love and feel in free time. . . .

"The future . . . 14,000 days left? . . . more music . . . more poetry . . . more dreams . . . more dragons . . . more art . . . more nature . . . more life. . . ."

* * *

PEASTON, Monroe 1914-

PERSONAL: Born September 5, 1914, in Liverpool, England; son of Arthur (a retailer) and Lydia (Green) Peaston; married Phyllis Gleave, June 12, 1940; children: Ann Christine (Mrs. Terrence Munro Staten). *Education:* Brasenose College, Oxford, B.A., 1936, M.A., 1943; University of London, B.D., 1948; Union Theological Seminary, New York, Th.D., 1964; University of Pennsylvania, further study, 1972-73. *Politics:* Liberal. *Home:* 239 Kensington Ave., 502 H, Montreal, Quebec, Canada. *Office:* 3520 University St., Montreal, Quebec, Canada.

CAREER: Ordained priest of Church of England, 1939; parochial and scholastic appointments in England, 1938-48; rector of Episcopal church in Wellington, New Zealand, 1948-52; Christchurch College, Christchurch, New Zealand, vice-principal, 1952-64; McGill University, Montreal, Quebec, professor of pastoral psychology, 1964—. Principal of Montreal Diocesan Theological College, 1965—; honorary canon of Christchurch Cathedral, Christchurch, New Zealand, and Christ Church Cathedral, Montreal. Member of board of directors, Mental Hygiene Institute, Montreal, 1969-71.

WRITINGS: A Time to Keep, Presbyterian Bookroom (Christchurch, New Zealand), 1963; *Personal Living: An Introduction to Paul Tournier,* Harper, 1972.

WORK IN PROGRESS: Studies in religion and personality, in religion and psychiatry, and in marriage counseling.

PECK, John 1941-

PERSONAL: Born January 13, 1941, in Pittsburgh, Pa.; son of Clarence Erwin (an engineer) and Louise (Sayenga) Peck; married Ellen McKee, September 2, 1963. *Education:* Allegheny College, A.B., 1962; Stanford University, Ph.D., 1973.

CAREER: Princeton University, Princeton, N.J., instructor in English, 1968-70, visiting lecturer, 1972-74.

WRITINGS: Shagbark (poems), Bobbs-Merrill, 1972.

BIOGRAPHICAL/CRITICAL SOURCES: Contemporary Literary Criticism, Volume III, Gale, 1974; Robert Boyers, editor, *Fifteen American Poets,* Schocken, in press.

* * *

PELL, Claiborne (de Borda) 1918-

PERSONAL: Born November 22, 1918, in New York, N.Y.; son of Herbert Claiborne (a public servant) and Matilda (Bigelow) Pell; married Nuala O'Donnell, December 16, 1944; children: Herbert Claiborne III, Christopher Thomas Hartford, Nuala Dallas, Julia Lorillard Pell Wampage. *Education:* Princeton University, A.B. (cum laude), 1940; Columbia University, M.A., 1946. *Religion:* Episcopalian. *Home address:* Ledge Rd., Newport, R.I. 02840. *Office:* U.S. Senate, Washington, D.C. 20510.

CAREER: Instructor at Navy School of Military Government and lecturer at Army Civil Affairs training schools, 1944-45; special assistant to U.S. State Department at San Francisco Conference, 1945; U.S. State Department, Washington, D.C., member of staff, 1945-46, foreign service officer, U.S. Embassy, Prague, Czechoslovakia, 1946-47, established consulate general at Bratislava, Czechoslovakia, 1947-48, vice-consul in Genoa, Italy, 1949-50, State Department Staff, 1950-52; consultant to Democratic National Committee, 1953-60; Democratic member of U.S. Senate from Rhode Island, 1960—. U.S. delegate to Inter-Governmental Maritime Consultative Organization, 1959. Director of International Investors, Inc., 1955-60; vice-president of North American Newspaper Alliance, Inc., 1955-60; U.S. delegate to General Assembly of United Nations, 1970. Vice-president of International Rescue Committee, American Immigration and Citizenship Conference, World Affairs Council, 1956-60; member of National Council of Refugees and National Historic Publications Commission; co-chairman of U.S. Flag Foundation. Trustee of St. George's School (Newport, R.I.). *Military service:* U.S. Coast Guard Reserve, 1941-74, active duty, 1941-45; served in North Atlantic, Africa, and Italy; became captain; decorated by principality of Liechtenstein, and received Knight Crown of Italy, Red Cross of Merit (Portugal), Legion of Honor (France), Order of Merit with Crown, and Knight of Malta.

MEMBER: Rhode Island Society of Cincinnati, Hope Club (Providence, R.I.), Knickerbocker Club, Racquet and Tennis Club, Brook Club (New York), Metropolitan Club (Washington, D.C.), Travellers Club (Paris), St. James Club (London). *Awards, honors:* Thirteen honorary degrees from colleges and universities in New England; Caritas Elizabeth Medal from Cardinal Franz Loenig, 1957.

WRITINGS: Megalopolis Unbound, Praeger, 1966; (with Hal Goodwin) *Challenge of the Seven Seas,* Morrow, 1966; *Power and Policy,* Norton, 1972. Contributor to proceedings of the Naval Institute. Contributor to *Dalhousie Review.*

SIDELIGHTS: Pell has supported easing of relations with Communist countries, and argued that each Communist nation be dealt with as a unit rather than as a member of the Soviet bloc. He visited Russia in 1968. In 1963, he urged a clampdown on aid to Southeast Asia and a reassessment of security needs there. He was the principal sponsor of the National Sea Grant College and Program Act of 1966, promoting expansion of oceanographic research and a clarification of legal jurisdiction over the ocean floor. He was also principal sponsor of the Arts and Humanities Foundation Act which established the National Council on the Arts. Pell comes from a family of statesmen: five of his forebears have been U.S. Senators or Representatives.

* * *

PELTON, Beverly Jo 1939- (Jo Jensen)

PERSONAL: Born January 17, 1939, in Eatonville, Wash.; daughter of Andrew (a construction engineer) and Alberta (Aitken) Jensen; married Robert W. Pelton (a marine engineer and writer), April 3, 1965; children: Mark Eugene, Kevin Scott. *Education:* Attended Long Beach State College (now California State University), 1967-68, University of California, Los Angeles, 1968-72, and Mount San Antonio College, 1970-72. *Politics:* "Uncommitted to any party." *Religion:* Protestant. *Home:* 5928 Firestone Rd., Apt. 224, Jacksonville, Fla. 32210. *Agent:* Lenniger Literary Agency, Inc., 437 Fifth Ave., New York, N.Y. 10016. *Office:* Cancer Education Program, American Cancer Society, St. Vincent's Medical Center, Barrs & St. John's Ave., Jacksonville, Fla. 32203.

CAREER: Free-lance writer, 1969—; American Cancer Society, Jacksonville, Fla., director of Cancer Education Program, 1973—. Has taught creative writing in high school and college adult education programs; has made public speaking and television appearances. *Member:* American Cancer Society.

WRITINGS: (With R. W. Notlep) *The Autograph Collector: A New Guide,* Crown, 1968; (with Kevin Martin) *What Your Handwriting Reveals,* Meredith, 1969; (with Mark Milton) *Free for Housewives,* Ace Books, 1970; *Beautiful Hair for Everyone,* Bantam, 1970; *College by Mail,* Arco, 1972. Contributor of over one hundred articles to magazines and trade journals.

WORK IN PROGRESS: Health Food Cookery; Beauty is Natural Food; Diet for Heart Problems; Natural Old-Time Baking.

SIDELIGHTS: The names of Mrs. Pelton's co-authors, R. W. Notlep, Kevin Martin, and Mark Milton are pseudonyms of her husband, Robert W. Pelton. *Avocational interests:* Travel, public speaking, camping.

* * *

PENNINGROTH, Paul W(illiam) 1901-

PERSONAL: Born May 27, 1901, in Tipton, Iowa; son of William and Elizabeth (Mensendick) Penningroth; married Persis Carney; children: Barbara (Mrs. James O'Brien), Emily (Mrs. James Olson), R. Paul. *Education:* University of Iowa, B.A., 1922; Columbia University, M.A., 1927, Ph.D., 1932. *Home:* 3242 West Roxboro Rd. N.E., Atlanta, Ga. 30324.

CAREER: American University of Beirut, Beirut, Lebanon, professor of psychology, 1928-29; St. Petersburg Junior College, St. Petersburg, Fla., head of psychology department, 1934-44; Child Guidance Clinic, St. Petersburg, Fla., director, 1944-54; Florida State Board of Health, Jacksonville, director of Mental Health Division, 1954-56; Southern Regional Education Board, Atlanta, Ga., assistant director of training and research in mental health, 1956-66. Former president, Community Welfare Council, St. Petersburg. *Member:* American Psychological Association. *Awards, honors:* Distinguished Service Award, State University of Iowa, 1965.

WRITINGS: Programs for Emotionally Disturbed Children, Foote & Davies, 1965; (contributor) Jacob Riess, editor, *New Directions in Mental Health,* Grune, 1968; (contributor) Henry P. David, editor, *Child Mental Health in International Perspective,* Harper, for Joint Commission on Mental Health of Children, 1972.

* * *

PENNINGTON, Howard (George) 1923-

PERSONAL: Born December 6, 1923, in Detroit, Mich.; son of Alfred Henkel (a wholesaler) and Esther (King) Pennington; married Lois Louise Burke, June 22, 1946; children: Alice (Mrs. David Michel), Laura (Mrs. Dennis Rogers), Alfred Henkel II. *Education:* University of Detroit, B.S., 1946. *Politics:* "Freedom oriented." *Home and office:* 2258 Noah, Honolulu, Hawaii 96816. *Agent:* Raines & Raines, 244 Madison Ave., New York, N.Y. 10016.

CAREER: A. H. Pennington & Son (wholesale outlet), Lincoln Park, Mich., co-owner, 1946-55; Grant Advertising Co., Detroit, Mich., copywriter, 1956; J. Walter Thompson Co., Detroit, Mich., creative group head and copywriter, 1956-67; free-lance writer and consultant in Honolulu, Hawaii, 1967—. Deputy Marine Affairs coordinator, Office of the Governor, Honolulu, Hawaii, 1972—; special consultant, Mayfield Smith Park Advertising, 1972—; member of board of directors, Pacific Maritime Academy, 1974—. *Member:* American Civil Liberties Union, Marine Technology Society (chairman of Hawaii section, 1974), Common Cause.

WRITINGS: The New Ocean Explorers: Into the Sea in the Space Age, Little, Brown, 1972. Contributor of over one hundred articles to special interest magazines and periodicals.

WORK IN PROGRESS: Writing on how to best utilize ocean resources and oceanic potential, such as manganese nodules, ocean energy, ocean space, and transportation.

* * *

PEREZ LOPEZ, Francisco 1916-

PERSONAL: Born July 23, 1916, in Almeria, Spain; son of Juan (a railwayman) and Maria (Couteriere) Perez; married wife, Marie Jeanne, February 24, 1962. *Education:* Attended schools in France. *Politics:* Republican. *Religion:* Catholic. *Home:* 3 Rue Baudanoni, Arles, France.

CAREER: Worked as a stoker in Arles, France, 1927-31, and as a baker in Sidi-bel-Abbes, Algeria, 1936. Fought in Spanish Civil War as officer in an International Brigade, was sentenced to thirty years at hard labor. Escaped in 1939, after serving two years; joined guerillas. Managing eventually to enter German-occupied France, he fought with Resistance, 1943-45, becoming a major. Was a farmworker, 1945-68; has been an artist, 1968—. *Member:* Association des Anciens Combattants de la resistance Francaise. *Awards, honors:* L'aigle d'or, Festival de Nice, for documentary book; Carte de la resistance Francaise; Medaille de bronze de la republique.

WRITINGS: (With Victor Guerrier) *El Mexicano: Journal de F. Perez Lopez,* R. Laffont, 1970, translation by Joseph D. Harris published as *Dark and Bloody Ground: A Guerrilla Diary of the Spanish Civil War,* Little, Brown, 1972.

WORK IN PROGRESS: Suite du Mexicano.

SIDELIGHTS: Scholar Victor Guerriere, who transcribed *El Mexicano,* met Perez Lopez and learned of his diary by chance. He knew of no other comparable, first-hand document out of the postwar guerilla movement; and he felt that the journal was a work of art. American reviewers agreed it was a "most unusual" find, "an exciting, often a shocking book," "infinitely detailed, infinitely precise, and as graphic as a documentary film."

* * *

PERKINS, Newton Stephens 1925- (Steve Perkins)

PERSONAL: Born June 21, 1925; son of David Newton (a theatrical artist) and Neva (Stephens) Perkins; married Aileen Schepp (a painter), September 29, 1960; children: Paula Ann, Harper, Gregory, Wayne, Ida. *Education:* Attended Tulane University, 1942-43; University of Texas, B.A., 1948. *Politics:* Democrat. *Religion:* Roman Catholic. *Home and office:* 4344 Harvest Hill, Dallas, Tex. 75234. *Agent:* Julian Bach, 3 East 48th St., New York, N.Y. 10017.

CAREER: Sportswriter on newspapers in New Orleans, La., Evansville, Ind., Houston, Tex., and Dallas, Tex.; writer with Mickey Herskowitz of Universal Press syndicated sports column, "Sports Hot Line," Dallas, Tex. *Military service:* U.S. Navy, aerial gunnery instructor, 1943-46. *Awards, honors:* Awards from New Orleans Press Club and Dallas Press Club.

WRITINGS—Under name Steve Perkins *Next Year's Champions,* World Publishing, 1969; *Winning the Big One: The Story of the Dallas Cowboys,* Grosset, 1972; *The Drive to Win,* Tempo, 1973; (with Bill Braucher) *The Miami Dolphins: Winning Them All,* Grosset, 1973. Also author of television play, "Narrative in Death," 1950. Contributor to *Sport,* and *Sports Illustrated.* Editor, *Sportscene.*

WORK IN PROGRESS: History of the Texas Rangers: 1823 to Present; two professional football books, one with Herskowitz; a Little League baseball book with Herskowitz.

AVOCATIONAL INTERESTS: Reading, travel.

* * *

PERKINS, Steve

See PERKINS, Newton Stephens

* * *

PERON, Juan (Domingo) 1895-1974

October 5, 1895—July 2, 1974; Argentinian ruler, soldier, and politician. Obituaries: *New York Times,* July 2, 1974, July 5, 1974; *Washington Post,* July 2, 1974.

* * *

PERRY, Huey 1936-

PERSONAL: Born January 19, 1936, in Baisden, W.Va.; son of Uley C. and Hallie (Cline) Perry; married Joan Hatfield, June 2, 1958 (divorced, 1969); married Shirley Ann Stewart, August 15, 1969; children: John, Jane, Matthew. *Education:* Berea College, A.B., 1957; Marshall University, M.A., 1958. *Politics:* Democratic. *Home:* 104 Stratford Pl., Charleston, W.Va. 25303. *Office:* Buffalo Housing, Inc., P.O. Box 183, Montgomery, W.Va. 25136.

CAREER: High school teacher in the public schools of Mingo County, W.Va., 1958-65; Mingo County Economic Opportunity Commission, Mingo County, W.Va., executive director, 1965-70; Mingo County Economic Development Corp., Mingo County, W.Va., executive director, 1970-71; Tech Foundation, Inc., West Virginia Institute of Technology, Montgomery, chairman of Division of Community Services, 1971-73; Buffalo Housing, Inc., Montgomery, W.Va., executive director, 1973—. Town of Gilbert, Gilbert, W.Va., recorder, 1964-66, mayor, 1966-68; consultant to Robert Weaver, secretary of the Department of Housing and Urban Development, 1967; member of board of directors of National Leadership Institute for Community Development, 1968-71. *Member:* National Education Association, West Virginia Education Association, Gilbert Lions Club.

WRITINGS: (Contributor) Wilma Dykeman, James Stokely, and the editors of *Time, Border States,* Time-Life, 1968; *They'll Cut Off Your Project: A Chronical of Mingo County,* Praeger, 1972; *Blaze Starr: Her Life as Told to Huey Perry,* Praeger, 1974.

* * *

PERRY, Peter John 1937-

PERSONAL: Born December 22, 1937, in Sherborne, Dorsetshire, England; son of Leslie John (a headmaster) and Marjorie F. (Baker) Perry; married Rachel-Mary Stewart Armitage (a nurse and midwife), December 1, 1973. *Education:* Clare College, Cambridge, B.A., 1959, M.A., 1963, Ph.D., 1963. *Politics:* Independent. *Religion:* Church of England. *Home:* 12 Dorset St., Christchurch 1, New Zealand. *Office:* Department of Geography, University of Canterbury, Christchurch 1 N2, New Zealand.

CAREER: University of Canterbury, Christchurch, New Zealand, 1966—, began as lecturer, now senior lecturer in geography. *Member:* Institute of British Geographers, New Zealand Geographical Society, British Agricultural History Society, Economic History Society.

WRITINGS: (Editor) *British Agriculture, 1875-1914,* Methuen, 1973; *British Farming in the Great Depression, 1870-1914: An Historical Geography,* David & Charles, 1974.

WORK IN PROGRESS: Historical geography of nineteenth-century Europe and New Zealand.

* * *

PETERS, Robert Anthony 1926-

PERSONAL: Born July 11, 1926, in Cleveland, Ohio; son of L. J. (a physician) and Helen Peters; married Ellen Rae, 1956; children: Audrey, Stuart, Elizabeth. *Education:* Ohio State University, B.A., 1948; Western Reserve University (now Case Western Reserve University), M.A., 1955; University of Pennsylvania, Ph.D., 1961. *Politics:* Republican. *Religion:* Episcopalian. *Home:* 404 Hillcrest Way, Bellingham, Wash. 98225. *Office: Journal of English Linguistics,* Western Washington State College, Bellingham, Wash. 98225.

CAREER: Trenton State College, Trenton, N.J., assistant professor of English, 1959-61; University of Idaho, Moscow, assistant professor of English, 1961-64; Western Washington State College, Bellingham, associate professor, 1964-68, professor of English and linguistics, 1968—. *Member:* Modern Language Association of America, Linguistic Society of America, American Dialect Society.

WRITINGS: A Linguistics History of English, Houghton, 1968; (with R. D. Brown) *Guide to Better Themes,* Scott, Foresman, 1970. Editor, *Journal of English Linguistics,* 1966—.

WORK IN PROGRESS: A book entitled *Chaucer's Language.*

* * *

PETERSON, Charles S. 1927-

PERSONAL: Born January 30, 1927, in Snowflake, Ariz.; married Betty Hayes, August 17, 1953; children: five. *Education:* Brigham Young University, B.A., 1952, M.A., 1958; University of Utah, Ph.D., 1967. *Office:* Man and His Bread Museum, Utah State University, Logan, Utah.

CAREER: Rancher, 1952-56; College of Eastern Utah, Price, instructor in history, 1958-66, dean of instruction, 1966-68; University of Utah, Salt Lake City, assistant professor of history, 1968-69; Utah State Historical Society, Salt Lake City, director, 1969-71; Utah State University, Logan, associate professor of history and director of Man and His Bread Museum, 1971—. Member of advisory committee of Pioneer Village State Park, 1970—; member of board of directors of Charles Redd Center for Western Studies, 1972—. *Member:* Organization of American Historians (assistant secretary-treasurer, 1968-69), Mormon History Association (member of council, 1971—), American Association of State and Local History, Living Historical Farms Association, Western History Association, Utah Academy.

WRITINGS: (With others) *Mormon Battalion Trail Guide,* Utah Historical Society, 1972; *Take Up Your Mission: Mormon Colonizing Along the Little Colorado, 1870-1900,* University of Arizona Press, 1973; (contributor) Thomas Alexander, editor, *Charles Redd Center Monograph on the American West,* Charles Redd Center for Western Studies, 1974. Contributor to *Western Historical Quarterly, Utah Historical Quarterly,* and *Forest History.* Editor of *Utah Historical Quarterly,* 1969-71; associate editor of *Western Historical Quarterly,* 1971—.

* * *

PETERSON, Fredrick Alvin 1920-

PERSONAL: Born June 23, 1920, in Sheboygan, Wis.; son of Oscar and Minnie (Sievers) Peterson; married Maria de los Angeles Cuesy Pola, November, 1959 (died November, 1973); children: Claudia Patricia, Fredrick Albert. *Education:* Attended University of Wisconsin, Sheboygan Center, 1946; Mexico City College, B.A. (magna cum laude), 1948; University of the Americas, M.A. (cum laude), 1949; Indiana University, Ph.D. candidate, 1973—. *Politics:* Independent. *Religion:* Non-sectarian. *Home:* 15 Elizabeth St., Buckhannon, W.Va. 26201. *Office:* Campus Box 48, West Virginia Wesleyan College, Buckhannon, W.Va. 26201.

CAREER: Government radio operator, then stock clerk in Madison, Wis., 1940-41; field assistant on expedition to Lacandon Jungle in Chiapas, Mexico, 1950; photographed Meso-American artifacts in private collections in Mexico under Wenner-Gren Foundation grant, 1951-52; field assistant on ethnographic study of Kickapoo Indians, Coahuila, Mexico, 1954; director of archaeology, Centro de Estudios Antropologicos de Mexico expedition to Lacandon Jungle, 1955; *Mexico/This Month* (magazine), Mexico City, Mexico, production and photo editor, 1957; New World Archaeological Foundation, Tuxtla Gutierrez, Chiapas, Mexico, field archaeologist, 1958-59, field director, 1960; Tehuacan Archaeological-Botanical project (sponsored by R. S. Peabody Foundation), Puebla, Mexico, assistant director, 1961-63; University of Texas, Austin, research scientist associate, 1963-64; West Virginia Wesleyan College, Buckhannon, assistant professor, 1964-67, associate professor of anthropology, 1967—. Visiting professor at University of the Americas, summers, 1964-69; visiting lecturer, West Virginia Academy of Arts and Sciences, 1966-67. *Military service:* U.S. Army, 1942-45; became master sergeant/sergeant major.

MEMBER: American Anthropological Association (fellow), Interamerican Institute (fellow), Sociedad Antropologico de Mexico, International Paleoanthropology Association, Omicron Delta Kappa, Pi Gamma Mu.

WRITINGS: Ancient Mexico, Putnam, 1959; *The Prehistory of the Tehuacan Valley,* University of Texas Press, Volume III: (with Richard S. MacNeish and Kent V. Flannery) *Ceramics,* 1970, Volume V: (with MacNeish and James Schoenwetter) *Excavations and Reconnaisance,* in press.

Monographs: (With Robert E. Ritzenthaler) *The Mexican Kickapoo Indians,* Milwaukee Museum Publications in Anthropology, 1956; (with Jose L. Franco) *Motivos Decorativos en la Ceramica Azteca,* National Museum of Mexico, 1957; (with Richard S. MacNeish) *The Santa Marta Rock Shelter, Ocozocoautla, Chiapas, Mexico,* New World Archaeological Foundation, 1962; *Some Ceramics from Mirador, Chiapas, Mexico,* New World Archaeological Foundation, 1963. Contributor of more than forty articles to journals, including *American Antiquity, Natural History,*and*Ethnos,* and several hundred articles and reviews to newspapers.

WORK IN PROGRESS: A History of Mexico; two other books.

AVOCATIONAL INTERESTS: Philately, amateur radio, photography.

* * *

PETERSON, Hans 1922-

PERSONAL: Born October 26, 1922, in Varing, Sweden; son of Emil G. (an electrician) and Hilda (Peterson) Peterson; married Anne Marie Nordstrand (a photographer), June 17, 1958; children: Lena, Jan. *Education:* Attended public schools in Sweden. *Home:* Marstrandsgatan 21, Gothenburg, Sweden 41724.

CAREER: Has worked at various jobs, including lift-boy, factory worker, and electrician; author, 1947—. *Awards, honors:* Nils Holgersson prize, 1958, for *Magnus and the Van Horse;* German young-books prize, 1959, for *Magnus and the Squirrel; Liselott and the Goloff* included in Hans Christian Andersen Honor List, 1964; several Swedish State and Gothenburg town prizes for collected work.

WRITINGS: Den uppdaemda ravinen: Roman (novel), Bonnier (Stockholm), 1949; *Flicken och sommaren* (title means "The Girl and the Summer"), Tidens forlag (Stockholm), 1950; *Laerkorna* (title means "The Larks"), Tidens forlag, 1952; *Hejda solnedgaangen* (title means "Stop the Sunset"), Tidens forlag, 1955; *Kvinnors Kaerlek: Noveller* (novel; title means "Women's Love"), Norstedt (Stockholm), 1956; *Skaadespelaren* (title means "The Actor"), Norstedt, 1957; *Aelskarinnan* (title means "The Mistress"), Norstedt, 1959; *Resebidrag* (title means "Traveling Letters"), Norstedt, 1961; *Kvinnorna: Tre beraettelser* (short stories; title means "The Women: Three Stories"), Norstedt, 1962; *Historien om en by: Roman* (novel; title means "A Story about a Village"), Norstedt, 1963.

Children's books; all Swedish editions published by Raben & Sjoegren (Stockholm), except as indicated: *Magnus och ekorrungen,* 1956, translation by Madeleine Hamilton published as *Magnus and the Squirrel,* Viking, 1959; *Magnus, Mattias och Mari,* 1958, translation by Marianne Turner published in England as *Magnus and the Van Horse,* Burke, 1961, published as *Magnus and the Wagon Horse,* Pantheon, 1966; *Magnus i hamn,* 1958, translation by Turner published as *Magnus in the Harbor,* Pantheon, 1966; *Naer vi snoeade inne,* 1959, translation by Irene Morris published as *The Day It Snowed,* Burke, 1969; *Magnus i fara,* 1959, translation by Turner published as *Magnus in Danger,* Pantheon, 1967; *Petter Joensson hade en gitarr,* 1959, adaptation by Kay Ware and Lucille Sutherland published as *Peter Johnson and His Guitar,* Webster, 1961, stage adaptation by Turner, Burke, 1965.

Naer vi regnade inne (title means "The Day It Rained"), 1960; *Gubben och Kanariefaageln,* 1960, adaptation by Ware and Sutherland published as *The Old Man and the Bird,* Webster, 1964, stage adaptation by Marianne Helweg, Burke, 1966; *Maens och mia,* 1960, translation published as *Tom and Tabby,* Lothrop, 1965; *Magnus och skeppshunden Jack,* 1961, translation by Turner published as *Magnus and the Ships Mascot,* Burke, 1964; *Lille-Olle och sommardagen,* 1962, adaptation by Ware and Sutherland published as *Benjamin Has a Birthday,* Webster, 1964; *Liselott och Garaffen,* 1962, translation by Annabelle Macmillan published as *Liselott and the Goloff,* Coward, 1964; *Det nya huset,* 1962, adaptation by Ware and Sutherland published as *The New House,* Webster, 1964, stage adaptation by Helweg, Burke, 1966; *Mick och Malin,* 1962, translation published as *Mickey and Molly,* Lothrop, 1964; *Boken om Magnus* (title means "A Book about Magnus"; includes *Magnus och ekorrungen, Magnus, Mattias och Mari, Magnus i hamn, Magnus i fara),* 1963; *Haer kommer Petter,* 1963, translation by Turner published as *Here Comes Peter,* Burke, 1965; *Hunden Buster,* 1963, translation published as *Brownie,* Lothrop, 1965; *Stina och Lars rymmer,* 1964, translation by Patricia Crampton published as *Stina and Lars in the Mountains,* Burke, 1970; *Petter kommer igen,* 1964, translation by Turner published as *Peter Comes Back,* Burke, 1966; *Naer hoensen blaaste bort,* 1964, translation by Morris published as *The Day the Chickens Blew Away,* Burke, 1970; *Liselott och de andra,* 1965, translation by Morris published as *Lisa Settles In,* Burke, 1967; *Den nya vaegen,* 1965, translation by Morris published as *The New Road,* Burke, 1967; *Petter klarar allt,* 1966, translation by Evelyn Ramsden published as *Peter Makes His Way,* Burke, 1968; *Bara Liselott,* 1967, translation by Morris published as *Just Lisa,* Burke, 1969; *Den nya bron,* 1967, translation by Morris published as *The New Bridge,* Burke, 1969; *Sara och sommerhuset,* 1967, translation by Morris published as *Sara in Summer-time,* Burke, 1973; *Expedition Snoestorm* (title means "Expedition Snowstorm"), 1968; *Jag vill inte, sa Sara,* 1968, translation by Morris published as *I Don't Want to, Said Sara,* Burke, 1969; *Lill-Anna, Johan och den vilda bjoernen* (title means "Lill-Anna, Johan and the Wild Bear"), Geber (Stockholm), 1968; *Magnus Lindberg och haesten Mari,* 1968, adaptation by Christine Hyatt published as *Eric and the Christmas Horse,* Burke, 1969, Lothrop, 1970; (with Harald Wiberg) *Naer Per gick vilse i skogen,* 1969, translation published as *When Peter Was Lost in the Forrest,* Coward, 1970.

Franssonsbarna i Faagelhult (title means "These Children in Bird-Cottage"), Geber, 1970; *Aake gaar till sjoess* (title means "Aake Goes on Board"), Geber, 1970; *Ett lejon i huset* (title means "A Lion in the House"), 1970; *Pelle Jansson, en kille med tur,* 1970, translation by Hanne Barnes published as *Pelle Jansson,* Burke, 1974; *Sara och Lillebror,* 1970, translation by Morris published as *Sara and Her Brother,* Burke, 1973.

Also author of novels, "Elise and Richard," 1971; "Elise Alone," 1972; "Elise and the Others," 1973; "The Tale about Elin," 1973; "Helge and Annie," 1974.

WORK IN PROGRESS: Novels, short stories, picture-books, children's books.

SIDELIGHTS: Peterson has written novels for adults with seeing and hearing difficulties and intends to write more. *Avocational interests:* Traveling, working at his summer house, meeting friends, living.

* * *

PFEIFER, Carl J(ames) 1929-

PERSONAL: Born June 22, 1929, in St. Louis, Mo.; son of Carl J. (a baker) and Emma (Heine) Pfeifer. *Education:* St. Louis University, A.B., 1953, M.A., 1954, Ph.L., 1954, S.T.L., 1963; graduate study at Laval University, 1956, Georgetown University, 1957, and Innsbruck University, 1957; Catholic University of America, doctoral candidate, 1963—. *Office:* U.S. Catholic Conference, 1312 Massachusetts Ave. N.W., Washington, D.C. 20005.

CAREER: Ordained Roman Catholic priest of the Society of Jesus (S.J.), 1961; high school teacher in St. Louis, Mo., 1954-57; counsellor-chaplain in Topeka, Kan., 1958-61; Catholic University of America, Washington, D.C., lecturer, 1962-64; U.S. Catholic Conference, Washington, D.C., consultant to National Center Confraternity of Christian Doctrine, 1965-66, assistant director of Division of Religious Education, 1966—. Instructor, St. Louis University, summer, 1956, and Catholic University of America, summers, 1965-69; television panelist, Bauman Bible Telecast, 1967—; delegate to International Catechetical Study Week, Colombia, 1968, International Catechetical Congress, Rome, 1971, and White House Conference on Children and Youth, 1971. *Member:* Religious Education Association, Camerabugs.

WRITINGS: (With Janaan Manternach) *Life, Love, Joy,* twenty-nine volumes, Silver Burdett, 1968, revised edition, 1974; *The Living Faith in a World of Change,* Ave Maria Press, 1973; *Other Religions in a World of Change,* Ave Maria Press, 1974. Author of *Know Your Faith,* a weekly column published by National Catholic News Service, 1970—. Contributor to *Living Light, Religious Education, Review for Religious, Catholic World, America, Homeletic and Pastoral Review,* and *Theology Digest.* Member of editorial board of *Theology Digest,* 1958-63; consultant to National Catholic Conference of Bishops *Religious Source Book,* 1967-69.

WORK IN PROGRESS: A revised edition of *Life, Love, Joy;* research on media, on audio-visual communication, on photography, and on religious education.

SIDELIGHTS: Pfeifer has traveled through Europe, Hawaii, Mexico, and South America.

* * *

PHARR, Robert D(eane) 1916- (C. Washington)

PERSONAL: Born July 5, 1916, in Richmond, Va.; son of John Benjamin (a minister) and Lucie (Deane) Pharr; married Nellie Ellis, February 14, 1937; children: Lorelle (Mrs. Donald Jones). *Education:* Attended St. Paul's College, Lawrenceville, Va., 1933, Lincoln University, Lincoln University, Pa., 1934; Virginia Union University, B.A., 1939; Fisk University, graduate study. *Politics:* Nonc. *Religion:* None. *Home:* 435 West 119th St., New York, N.Y. 10027.

CAREER: Employed chiefly as a waiter at exclusive resort hotels and private clubs, including a period at Columbia University's faculty club; novelist. *Member:* Omega Psi Psi.

WRITINGS—Novels: *The Book of Numbers,* Doubleday, 1969; *S.R.O.,* Doubleday, 1971.

WORK IN PROGRESS: The Welfare Bitch.

SIDELIGHTS: Although critics find some flaws in Pharr's first novel, *The Book of Numbers,* they overwhelmingly praise its unique style and its unambiguous and relentless portrayal of American Negro life. Christopher Lehmann-Haupt writes that Pharr "will not be credited with having advanced the frontiers of fiction by any degree, but he has written an unusually good book—a gnarled old oak tree of a book, rich and grainy in texture, sprawling and complex in configuration, a curiously friendly book to get lost in. He has made more than a few technical errors, but they are simply overwhelmed by his absolute belief in his characters and his total love for them."

The novel has been acquired by Raymond St. Jacques' production company for filming.

* * *

PHELPS, Arthur Warren 1909-

PERSONAL: Born June 14, 1909, in Westmoreland County, Va.; son of Richard Roscoe and Margaret Anderson (Petar) Phelps; married Grace Rowell, June 30, 1936 (died November 23, 1965); married Virginia Welton, December 27, 1967; children: (first marriage) Grace Rowell (Mrs. W. Donald Rhinesmith), Margaret (Mrs. Alan Vaugnan). *Education:* Washington and Lee University, A.B. (magna cum laude), 1932; Ohio State University, M.A., 1932; University of Cincinnati, LL.B., 1935 (converted to J.D., 1967); Columbia University, LL.M., 1940. *Politics:* Democrat. *Religion:* Episcopalian. *Home:* 313 Burns Lane, Williamsburg, Va. 23185. *Office:* Marshall-Wythe School of Law, College of William and Mary, Williamsburg, Va. 23185.

CAREER: Admitted to Ohio Bar, 1935, and Virginia Bar, 1946; Ohio Northern University, Ada, instructor, then assistant professor of law, 1935-42; Office of Price Administration, counsel in Cleveland, Ohio, and later Washington, D.C., 1942-45; College of William and Mary, Williamsburg, Va., professor of law, 1945—, dean of Marshall-Wythe School of Law, 1947—. Chief counsel, Petroleum Price Division, Office of Price Stabilization, 1950-52; exchange professor in England at University of Exeter, 1966-67. *Member:* American Bar Association, Virginia Bar Association, Phi Beta Kappa, Rotary International.

WRITINGS: Handbook of Virginia Procedure in Actions at Law, Michie Publishing, 1959, 3rd edition, 1974, *Supplement,* 1971; *Handbook of Virginia Rules of Equity Practice and Procedure,* Michie Publishing, 1961, *Supplement,* 1972; *Divorce and Alimony in Virginia and West Virginia,* Michie Publishing, 1963, *Supplement,* 1970; *Handbook of Virginia Rules of Appellate Procedure,* Michie Publishing, 1964, *Supplement,* 1971.

WORK IN PROGRESS: A revision of *Divorce and Alimony in Virginia and West Virginia.*

* * *

PHELPS, Roger P(aul) 1920-

PERSONAL: Born September 6, 1920, in Batavia, N.Y.; son of Harvey W. and Viola (Woolf) Phelps; married Mildred T. Wade (a teacher), August 20, 1947; children: Roger Paul, Jr., Homer. *Education:* University of Rochester, B.M., 1941; Northwestern University, M.M., 1947; University of Iowa, Ph.D., 1951. *Politics:* Republican. *Religion:* Baptist. *Home:* 718 Barnes Ave., Baldwin, N.Y. 11510. *Office:* Music Education Division, New York University, Room 777, Education Building, New York, N.Y. 10003.

CAREER: Supervisor of instrumental music in public schools of Mount Morris, N.Y., 1941-42; Bob Jones University, Greenville, S.C., instructor in woodwinds and music education and theory, 1947-48; University of Southern Mississippi, Hattiesburg, associate professor of woodwinds and music education and conductor of university-community symphony, 1951-59; New York University, School of Education, New York, N.Y., associate professor, 1959-69, professor of music education, 1969—, coordinator of doctoral research proposals committee, 1971—, chairman of doctoral appeals committee, 1973—. *Military service:* U.S. Army, Infantry, 1942-46; served in European theater; became staff sergeant.

MEMBER: Music Teachers National Association (first vice-president, Southern Division, 1958-60), National Association of College Wind and Percussion Instructors (vice-president, 1962-64), Music Education Research Council (national chairman, 1964-66), American Educational Research Association, Music Educators National Conference, American Musicological Association, Music Teachers Association, Music Library Association, American Association of University Professors (secretary, Mississippi state chapters, 1958-59), New York State Music Teachers Association (secretary, 1961-64), Rotary International (district governor, 1971-72). *Awards, honors:* U.S. Office of Education research grants, 1966-67, 1968.

WRITINGS: A Guide to Research in Music Education, W. C. Brown, 1969. Contributor to *Seventh Mental Measurements Yearbook,* 1972; contributor of about fifty articles and reviews to professional publications. Editor, *Mississippi Notes,* 1957-59; publications editor, *NACWPI Bulletin* (publication of National Association of College Wind and Percussion Instructors), 1958-62; member of editorial committee, *Journal of Research in Music Education,* 1962—.

PHILIP, Cynthia Owen 1928-

PERSONAL: Born November 29, 1928; daughter of James Collins Farish and Dorothy (Wheaton) Owen; married Nicholas Philip (a consulting engineer), March 28, 1953; children: Elizabeth, Maria, Nicholas. *Education:* Smith College, B.A., 1950; graduate study at Harvard School of Design, 1952-53, and Union Theological Seminary, New York, N.Y., 1967-69. *Office:* 507 East 84th St., New York, N.Y. 10028.

CAREER: Free-lance writer and editor in New York, N.Y.

WRITINGS: Imprisoned in America: Communications from Prison, 1776 to Attica, Harper, 1973.

* * *

PHILLIPS, Louis 1942-

PERSONAL: Born June 15, 1942, in Lowell, Mass.; son of Louis James and Dorothy (Perkins) Phillips; married Patricia Ranard (chairman of preparatory school English department), August 23, 1972. *Education:* Stetson University, B.A., 1964; University of North Carolina, M.A. (radio, television, and motion pictures), 1967; City University of New York, M.A. (English and comparative literature), 1968. *Home:* 324 East 34th St., Apt. E-2, New York, N.Y. 10016. *Agent:* Barbara Rhodes, Kahn, Lifflander & Rhodes Agency, 853 Seventh Ave., New York, N.Y. 10019. *Office:* State University of New York Maritime College, Bronx, N.Y. 10465.

CAREER: State University of New York Maritime College, Bronx, assistant professor of English, 1967—. *Member:* Dramatists' Guild, Society of American Magicians.

WRITINGS: The Man Who Stole the Atlantic Ocean, Prentice-Hall, 1972; *The Emancipation of the Encyclopedia Salesman,* Prologue Press, 1972; *Theodore Jonathan Wainwright Is Going to Bomb the Pentagon,* Prentice-Hall, 1973; *The Film Buff's Calendar,* Drake Publishers, 1973; *A Catalogue of Earthly Pleasures* (poems), Prologue Press, 1973; *The Animated Thumb-Tack Railroad Dollhouse and All Round Surprise Book* (juvenile), Lippincott, in press. Author of play "The Last of the Marx Brothers' Writers," first performed at Brandeis University, April, 1973. Contributor to *Dramatists' Guild Quarterly.*

WORK IN PROGRESS: Fist, a collection of poems.

SIDELIGHTS: Phillips has written: "As a playwright, my first desire is to write well, to write with feeling, thoughtful, well-crafted theatrically exciting plays. By craft I do not mean three-act structure, or five-act structure, or even necessarily 'the well-made play.' Screw the well-made play. By craft I mean the discovery of the best form, the only form the material can take."

* * *

PHILLIPS, Michael Joseph 1937-

PERSONAL: Born March 2, 1937, in Indianapolis, Ind.; son of Hayes A. (stepfather) and Bernice (Farmer) Phillips Hollibaugh. *Education:* Attended Purdue University, 1955-56, University of Edinburgh, 1957-58, 1959-60, University of Paris, 1958; Wabash College, B.A. (cum laude), 1959; graduate study at New York University, 1960-61; Indiana University, M.A., 1964, Ph.D., 1971; graduate study at Oxford University, 1969, 1971, and Harvard University, 1970. *Home:* Colony Apartments, 2012A, West 76th St., Indianapolis, Ind. 46260.

CAREER: Curry's Inc., Bloomington, Ind., bookstore manager, 1961-63; Bobbs-Merrill, Indianapolis, Ind., college traveler, 1964-65; University of Wisconsin-Milwaukee, lecturer in English, 1970, 1971; Free University of Indianapolis, Indianapolis, Ind., instructor in English, 1973; Indiana-Purdue University at Indianapolis, instructor in English, 1973—. *Member:* International Comparative Literature Association, Modern Language Association of America, American Comparative Literature Association, United Nations Association, American Association of University Professors, Midwest Modern Language Association, Phi Beta Kappa, Mensa.

WRITINGS: 9 Concrete Poems, Department of Fine Arts, Indiana University, 1967; *Girls, Girls, Girls* (poems), Bitterroot Press, 1967; *4 Poster Poems,* Department of Fine Arts, Indiana University, 1968; *4 Poems for a Chocolate Princess,* Phillips Publishing Corp., 1968; *7 Poems for Audrey Hepburn,* J. Mark Press, 1968; *Libretto for 23 Poems,* Satori Record Co., 1968; *Kinetics & Concretes,* Department of Fine Arts, Indiana University, 1971; *The Concrete Book,* Terrestial Press, 1971; *8 Page Poems,* Department of Fine Arts, Indiana University, 1971; *Love, Love, Love,* Print Center, 1973; *Concrete Sonnets,* Print Center, 1973. Contributor of poems to magazines, newspapers, and journals.

SIDELIGHTS: Phillips, who regards himself as one of the better hippie poets, has also been active in Concrete Poetry and related movements.

* * *

PHILLIPS, Rachel 1934-

PERSONAL: Born September 30, 1934, in Milford Haven, Pembrokeshire, Wales; daughter of Ivor Wilfrid James and Kathleen (Hall) Phillips; married Franklin Zimmerman, April 11, 1957 (divorced, 1969); children: Eve, Guy, Claire, Grace. *Education:* Oxford University, B.A., 1957, M.A., 1962; University of Kentucky, Ph.D., 1970. *Office:* Department of Spanish, Vassar College, Poughkeepsie, N.Y. 12601.

CAREER: Vassar College, Poughkeepsie, N.Y., assistant professor of Spanish, 1970—. *Member:* Modern Language Association of America, American Association of University Professors, American Association of Teachers of Spanish and Portuguese.

WRITINGS: The Poetic Modes of Octavio Paz, Clarendon Press, 1972; (translator from the Spanish) Octavio Paz, *Children of the Mire,* Harvard University Press, 1974; *Alfonsina Storni: Poetess to Poet,* Tamesis Books, 1975. Contributor to journals.

WORK IN PROGRESS: An anthology of Latin American literature in translation.

AVOCATIONAL INTERESTS: Playing cello,

* * *

PHILLIPS, Richard
See DICK, Philip K(indred)

* * *

PHIPPS, Joyce 1942-

PERSONAL: Born May 23, 1942, in Washington, D.C.; daughter of Heimo Ilmari (a linotypist) and Lucille (Jones) Antila; married Robert William Phipps, June 9, 1962 (died April 24, 1972); children: Keith Madison, Craig Eugene.

Education: University of Maryland, B.A., 1963; Southern Connecticut State College, M.L.S., 1973; Yale University, graduate study, 1973—. *Politics:* Democrat. *Religion:* United Church of Christ. *Home:* 52 Westerfield Rd., Hamden, Conn. 06514.

CAREER: U.S. Census Bureau, statistician in Suitland, Md., 1964-66, liaison work with local government officials in New Haven, Conn., 1967-69; Willoughby Wallace Memorial Library, Stony Creek, Conn., librarian, 1973. Member of Maryland Open Suburban Housing, 1961-66; secretary of Hamden Mayor's Anti-Pollution Task Force, 1971-73; active in Democratic party politics. *Member:* League of Women Voters (member of board of local chapter, 1967-73), Phi Alpha Theta.

WRITINGS: Death's Single Privacy: Grieving and Personal Growth, Seabury, 1974. Contributor to *Christian Century.*

WORK IN PROGRESS: Research on bereavement typology among certain groups of people; a children's series for use in elementary schools using a single-parent family as a model; short stories.

SIDELIGHTS: "Death is a subject normally avoided in our society," Mrs. Phipps wrote. "Discussing the grieving process. . .is not normally considered polite by those who have not 'experienced' death at close range. It is my feeling that we are all survivors, and have been since the moment of our births. . .The openness with which we are able to view our survival. . .often reflects the openness we have toward the future and its uncertainty. Part of the problem is that we who are survivors of death at close range appropriate the language of the world—'recover,' 'get over,' 'forget'—which even further confuses the issue. . . .we [should] learn to live with our own lives and deaths. . .and learn to live beyond. . .the ensuing grief. We use the totality of the experience of the person who has died and integrate it—internalize it—into the fabric of our being."

BIOGRAPHICAL/CRITICAL SOURCES: New Haven Register, December 5, 1972.

* * *

PICTON, Bernard
See KNIGHT, Bernard

* * *

PIERSON, Howard 1922-

PERSONAL: Born August 18, 1922, in Brooklyn, N.Y.; son of Jack H. and Minna (Berman) Pierson; married Sally Rochwarger, September 30, 1949; children: Linda, Robert. *Education:* Brooklyn College (now Brooklyn College of the City University of New York), B.A. (cum laude), 1943; New York University, M.A., 1948, Ph.D., 1967. *Address:* Box 2042, North Babylon, N.Y. 11703.

CAREER: Syosset Public Schools, Syosset, N.Y., high school principal, 1961—. Instructor at Nassau Community College, 1969—. *Military service:* U.S. Army Air Forces, 1943-46. *Member:* National Council of Teachers of English, National Association of Secondary School Principals, New York State Association for Supervision and Curriculum Development, Dickens Fellowship (London), New York State Congress of Parents and Teachers (honorary life member), Nature Conservancy, Nassau Hiking and Outdoor Club.

WRITINGS: Teaching Writing: Theories and Practices for College and Secondary Teachers of English, Prentice-Hall, 1972. Contributor to academic journals.

AVOCATIONAL INTERESTS: Theater, music (classical and folk), baroque art, nature, walking, handball, swimming.

* * *

PIHL, Marshall R(alph) 1933-

PERSONAL: Surname is pronounced "peel"; born October 12, 1933, in Boston, Mass.; son of Marshall R. (a lawyer) and Nelle (Allen) Pihl; married Natalie J. Fisher, July 5, 1969; children: Nathaniel, Sarah. *Education:* Harvard University, B.A., 1960, Ph.D., 1974; Seoul National University, M.A., 1965. *Home:* 50 Peacock Farm Rd., Lexington, Mass. 02173. *Office:* Council on East Asian Studies, Room 305, 1737 Cambridge St., Cambridge, Mass. 02138.

CAREER: Harvard University, Cambridge, Mass., instructor in Korean Language and literature and executive assistant for Council on East Asian Studies, 1972—. *Military service:* U.S. Army, 1956-58; received commendation ribbon with metal pendant. *Member:* Association of Asian Studies. *Awards, honors:* First annual translation award from *Korea Times,* 1970, for Oh Young-su's "Nami and the Taffyman."

WRITINGS: (Editor and translator from the Korean) *Listening to Korea: A Korean Anthology,* Praeger, 1973. Translator of numerous articles and short stories from Korean to English.

WORK IN PROGRESS: A critical anthology, *Modern Korean Fiction,* completion expected in 1975; *The Tale of Sim Ch'ong: A Korean Oral Narrative.*

SIDELIGHTS: Pihl was the first Westerner to receive a degree from Seoul National University in Korea.

* * *

PINCHERLE, Marc 1888-1974

June 13, 1888—June 20, 1974; French music historian and expert on the works of Vivaldi, educator, critic, and author. Obituaries: *New York Times,* June 21, 1974.

* * *

PINNA, Giovanni 1939-

PERSONAL: Born March 3, 1939, in Turin, Italy; son of Luigi (an army general) and Annamaria (DeLuca) Pinna; married Teresa Cremisi (a writer), September 30, 1967. *Education:* University of Parma, Ph.D., 1962. *Home:* Via Privata Letizia 5, Milan, Italy. *Office:* Museo Civico di Storia Naturale, Corso Venezia 55, Milan, Italy.

CAREER: University of Parma, Parma, Italy, professor of paleontology, 1969; Museo Civico di Storia Naturale (Civic Museum of Natural History), Milan, Italy, assistant director, 1969—. *Military service:* Italian Army, 1964-65; became lieutenant. *Member:* Societa Paleontologica Italiana, Palaeotographical Society of London, Schweizerische Naturforschende Gesellschaft, Paleontological Society (Washington).

WRITINGS: Fossili Invertebrati, De Agostini, 1968, translation published as *The Dawn of Life,* World Publishing, 1972; *Geologia,* Martello, 1971; *Fossili,* Mondadori, 1971; *Paleontologia ed Evoluzione,* Martello, 1973. Writer of scripts for cultural television programs. Contributor of about sixty papers on palaeontology to journals.

WORK IN PROGRESS: Introduzione alla Paleobiologia (title means "An Introduction to Palaeobiology").

* * *

PINTEL, Gerald 1922-

PERSONAL: Born June 21, 1922, in New York, N.Y.; son of Charles Jacob (a certified public accountant) and Eva (Billowitz) Pintel; married Zelda Kimmel; children: Kenneth L., Ellen J. *Education:* New York University, B.S., 1946, M.A., 1964, Ph.D., 1972. *Religion:* Jewish. *Home:* 68 Mitchell Ave., Plainview, N.Y. 11803. *Office:* Department of Business Administration, Nassau Community College, Stewart Ave., Garden City, N.Y. 11533.

CAREER: Pintel, Berliner & Pintel (certified public accountants), New York, N.Y., partner, 1946-62; Nassau Community College, Garden City, N.Y., 1962—, member of faculty in department of business administration. *Military service:* U.S. Army Air Forces, 1942-46; became sergeant first class. *Member:* American Institute of Certified Public Accountants, American Accounting Association.

WRITINGS: (With Jay Diamond) *Mathematics of Business,* Prentice-Hall, 1970; (with Diamond) *Principles of Retailing,* Prentice-Hall, 1971; (with Diamond) *Basic Business Mathematics,* Prentice-Hall, 1972; (with Diamond) *Principles of Marketing,* Prentice-Hall, 1972; (with Diamond) *Introduction to Business,* Prentice-Hall, in press.

* * *

PIRO, Richard 1934-

PERSONAL: Born July 18, 1934, in Somerville, Mass.; son of James (a printer) and Louise (Capone) Piro. *Education:* Boston University, B.Mus., 1956, M.Mus., 1962. *Politics:* Independent. *Religion:* None. *Home:* 2906 Forest Ave., Berkeley, Calif. 94705. *Office:* Vector Magazine, 83 Sixth St., San Francisco, Calif. 94103.

CAREER: Junior high school teacher of music and drama in New York, N.Y., 1963-73; *Vector,* San Francisco, Calif., editor, 1973—. Member of San Francisco Opera Co., San Francisco Symphony Chorus, and Oakland Symphony Chorus. *Military service:* U.S. Army, 1956-58. *Awards, honors: Black Fiddler* was an American Library Association Notable Book, 1972.

WRITINGS: Black Fiddler, Morrow, 1971. Regular contributor to journals of Music Educators National Conference and American Theatre Association.

WORK IN PROGRESS: A film script of *Black Fiddler.*

* * *

PIVEN, Frances Fox 1932-

PERSONAL: Born October 10, 1932, in Calgary, Alberta, Canada; daughter of Albert and Rachel (Paperny) Fox; children: Sarah. *Education:* University of Chicago, B.A., 1953, M.A., 1956, Ph.D., 1962. *Home:* 35 Claremont Ave., New York, N.Y. 10027. *Office:* Department of Political Science, Boston University, Boston, Mass. 02215.

CAREER: Free Press, Glencoe, Ill., assistant editor, 1953-54; Voorhees, Walker, Smith & Smith, New York, N.Y., assistant in preparation of rezoning proposal for New York City Planning Commission, 1956-58; Columbia University, New York, N.Y., research fellow, Metropolitan Region Program, 1958-60, research associate, School of Social Work, 1962-66, assistant professor, School of Social Work, 1966-68, associate professor, 1968-72; Boston University, Boston, Mass., professor of political science, 1972—. Lecturer at Hunter College of the City University of New York, 1966-67. Consultant to Mobilization for Youth, Inc., 1962-67, National Welfare Rights Organization, 1966-72, and other agencies; member of Metropolitan Council on Housing.

MEMBER: Society for the Study of Social Problems, American Political Science Association, Caucus for a New Political Science, Union of Radical Political Economists, Planners for Equal Opportunity (president, 1971-73), American Civil Liberties Union (member of board, 1973—). *Awards, honors:* Ford Foundation study grant, 1968-69; C. Wright Mills Award of Society for the Study of Social Problems, 1971, for *Regulating the Poor: The Functions of Public Welfare;* Metropolitan Applied Research Corp. fellowship, 1971; Guggenheim fellowship, 1973-74.

WRITINGS: (With Richard A. Cloward) *Regulating the Poor: The Functions of Public Welfare,* Pantheon, 1971; (with Cloward) *Politics of Turmoil: Race, Poverty, and the Urban Crisis,* Pantheon, 1974.

Contributor: Murray Silberman, editor, *The Role of Government in Promoting Social Change,* Columbia University Press, 1966; *Personnel in Anti-Poverty Programs: Implications for Social Work Education,* Council on Social Work Education (New York), 1967; George Brager and Francis Purcell, editors, *Community Action against Poverty,* College & University Press, 1967; Mathew Ahmanad and Margaret Roach, editors, *The Church and the Urban Crisis,* National Catholic Conference for Interracial Justice, 1967; R. H. Connery, editor, *Urban Riots: Violence and Social Change,* Random House, 1969; Robert Paul Wolff, editor, *1984 Revisited,* Random House, 1972; Wil J. Smith and Frederick A. Zeller, editors, *Public Welfare, Right or Privilege: A System under Attack,* West Virginia University Press, 1972; Herbert G. Gutman and Gregory S. Kealey, editors, *Many Pasts: Readings in American Social History, 1965 to the Present,* Prentice-Hall, 1973.

Contributor to *Nation, New Republic, Commonweal, Social Work, Transaction,* and other periodicals; a number of the articles have been reprinted in anthologies, readings, and other books. Member of editorial and publications committee, Society for the Study of Social Problems, 1973—; member of editorial board, *Civil Liberties Review, Social Policy,* and *Working Papers for a New Society.*

WORK IN PROGRESS: With Richard A. Cloward, *Poor Peoples' Movements and Why They Fail,* for Pantheon.

* * *

PIZZAT, Frank J(oseph) 1924- (Mark Venafro)

PERSONAL: Born August 27, 1924, in Creekside, Pa.; son of Paul (a baker) and Sarah (Gualtieri) Pizzat; married Annette Grimaldi, December 27, 1947; children: Margaret, Cynthia, Valerie. *Education:* University of Pittsburgh, B.S., 1948, M.S., 1949, Ph.D., 1952. *Politics:* Independent. *Religion:* Roman Catholic. *Home:* 3827 Sassafras St., Erie, Pa. 16508. *Office:* Gannon College, Perry Sq., Erie, Pa. 16501.

CAREER: Veterans Administration Hospital, Erie, Pa., chief clinical psychologist, 1952-54; Neuropsychiatric Hospital, Pittsburgh, Pa., staff psychologist, 1954-55; Gannon College, Erie, Pa., director of psychological services, 1955-60; Erie Guidance Center, Erie, Pa., executive director, 1960-66; Gannon College, director of psychological services, 1966—. Diplomate in clinical psychology, American Board of Examiners in Professional Psychology, 1960. Member of board of directors, Erie County mental health-mental retardation program, 1966-71, president, 1969. *Military service:* U.S. Army, 1943-45; served in European theater. *Member:* American Psychological Association, Association for Advancement of Behavior Therapy, Pennsylvania Psychological Association (fellow).

WRITINGS: (Under pseudonym Mark Venafro) *The Grand Chase,* Pageant, 1956; *Behavior Modification in a Residential Treatment for Children,* Behavioral Publications, 1973.

WORK IN PROGRESS: With C. T. Lundy, *Short-Term Career Counseling.*

* * *

PLATT, Eugene Robert 1939-

PERSONAL: Born February 20, 1939, in Charleston, S.C.; son of Paul Calhoun (a machinist) and Estell (Bell) Platt; married Troye Matthews, June 8, 1963 (divorced, 1965); married Kathleen Gemmell (a university administrator), October 26, 1968; children: Troye-Suzanne Kathleen, Paul Calhoun II. *Education:* University of South Carolina, A.B., 1964; Trinity College, Dublin, Diploma in Anglo-Irish Literature, 1970; Clarion State College, M.A., 1973. *Religion:* Episcopal. *Home:* 355-1 Pennell Circle, Tallahassee, Fla. 32304; and 840 Wood St., Clarion, Pa. 16214.

CAREER: Held various administrative posts with U.S. Civil Service in Charleston, S.C., Nashville, Tenn., and Washington, D.C., 1964-69; Clarion State College, Clarion, Pa., assistant to dean of student affairs, 1970—. Has been active in "Poetry in the Schools" program and has given public readings of his poetry at various colleges. *Military service:* U.S. Army, 1957-60. *Awards, honors:* Hart Crane and Alice Crane Williams Memorial Award, 1968, for poem, "Above and Beyond," and, 1969, for poem "Carolina Sands."

WRITINGS—Poetry: *coffee and solace,* privately printed, 1970; (with John Tomikel) *Six of One. Half Dozen of the Other,* Allegheny Press, 1971; *Allegheny Reveries,* privately printed, 1972; (editor) *A Patrick Kavanagh Anthology,* privately printed, 1973; *an original sin,* Briarpatch Press, 1974.

WORK IN PROGRESS: Editing *An Outer Banks Anthology* and *Don't Ask Me Why I Write These Things;* editing a projected literary magazine, *The Briar Patch.*

SIDELIGHTS: The 13th issue of *Tar River Poets* was designated "Eugene Robert Platt Issue."

* * *

PLAYER, Ian 1927-

PERSONAL: Born March 15, 1927, in Johannesburg, South Africa; son of Francis Harry (a mining official) and Muriel (Ferguson) Player; married Felicity Ann Farrer, May 16, 1957; children: Kenneth, Jessica, Amyas. *Education:* Attended St. John's College, Johannesburg, South Africa, 1936-43. *Politics:* "Apolitical." *Religion:* Church of England. *Home:* Phuzamoya Farm, P.O. Box 192, Howick, Natal, South Africa. *Office address:* International Wilderness Leadership Foundation, 150 East 42nd St., New York, N.Y. 10017; and Wilderness Leadership School, P.O. Box 36, Bellair, Natal, South Africa.

CAREER: Natal Parks Board, Natal, South Africa, 1952-74, holding posts as game ranger, senior game ranger, senior game warden, chief game conservator of Zululand, and chief nature conservator; International Wilderness Leadership Foundation, New York, N.Y., director, 1973—. *Military service:* South African Army, 1944-46; served in Italy. *Member:* Wild Life Society of South Africa, Wild Life Management Institute. *Awards, honors:* Gold medal from San Diego Zoo, 1966; Game Conservation International award, 1969; conservationist of the year awards from African Safari Clubs, Washington, D.C. and Philadelphia, Pa., 1974.

WRITINGS: Men, Rivers, and Canoes, Simondium, 1963; (with T. C. Robertson) *Big Game,* Caltey, 1972; *The White Rhino Saga,* Collins, 1972.

WORK IN PROGRESS: The story of the Wilderness Leadership School, nonfiction; a novel about northeastern Zululand; a novel on the Langalibeue Rebellion.

BIOGRAPHICAL/CRITICAL SOURCES: Sports Illustrated, March, 1972.

* * *

PLUMB, Charlie
See PLUMB, Joseph Charles, Jr.

* * *

PLUMB, Joseph Charles, Jr. 1942-
(Charlie Plumb)

PERSONAL: Born November 3, 1942, in Gary, Ind.; son of Joseph Charles (a carpenter) and Margery (a secretary; maiden name, Stanford) Plumb. *Education:* U.S. Naval Academy, B.S., 1964. *Religion:* Presbyterian. *Agent:* Robert P. Mills Ltd., 156 East 52nd St., New York, N.Y. 10022. *Office:* Inform, Inc., 6700 Squibb Rd., Mission, Kan. 66062.

CAREER: Inform, Inc., Mission, Kan., president, 1974—. Director of Empire State Bank, 1974—; lecturer. *Military service:* U.S. Navy, 1960-74; became lieutenant commander; received Air Medal, Navy Commendation Medal, Combat Action Medal, Vietnam Service Medal, Republic of Vietnam Campaign Medal, Purple Heart, and Silver Star.

WRITINGS: (Under name Charlie Plumb) *I'm No Hero,* Independence Press, 1973. Author, under name Charlie Plumb, of "Plumb Line," column appearing in *Squire* (magazine).

WORK IN PROGRESS: Communicate, a book about letters from prison and analyses by graphologists of those letters; *Response,* a book about letters and artwork received from children responding to Plumb's writing and lectures.

SIDELIGHTS: Plumb was a fighter pilot flying F4-B Phantom jets from the deck of the aircraft carrier *U.S.S. Kitty Hawk.* He flew seventy-five combat missions during the Vietnam war, his plane was shot down, and he spent more than two thousand days in captivity. During that time, he served as specialist in underground communications and as group chaplain. He was repatriated early in 1973, and has made more than three hundred public appearances before schools, churches, and professional groups, telling the POW story and secrets of endurance.

PODLECKI, Anthony J(oseph), 1936-

PERSONAL: Born January 25, 1936, in Buffalo, N.Y.; son of Anthony Joseph (a civil servant) and Eugenia (Jendrasiak) Podlecki; married Jennifer Grube, July 28, 1962; children: Christopher, Julia, Antonia. *Education:* College of the Holy Cross A.B., 1957; Oxford University, B.A., 1960, M.A., 1963; University of Toronto, M.A., 1961, Ph.D., 1963. *Politics:* Democrat. *Religion:* Roman Catholic. *Home:* 336 West Ridge Ave., State College, Pa. 16801. *Office:* Department of Classics, Carnegie Building, Pennsylvania State University, University Park, Pa. 16802.

CAREER: Northwestern University, Evanston, Ill., instructor, 1963-65, assistant professor of classics, 1965-66; Pennsylvania State University, University Park, associate professor, 1966-70, professor of classics, 1970—, head of department, 1966—. Visiting fellow at Wolfson College, Oxford University, 1970.

MEMBER: American Philological Association, Archaeological Institute of America, American Association of University Professors, Classical Association of Canada, Classical Association of Great Britain, Joint Association of Classical Teachers (Great Britain), Cambridge Philological Association (Great Britain), Classical Association of Atlantic States (member of executive committee), Pennsylvania Classical Association (member of executive committee, Phi Sigma Iota. *Awards, honors:* Woodrow Wilson fellowship and Fulbright scholarship, 1957.

WRITINGS: (Editor) Cecil Torr, *Ancient Ships,* Argonaut, 1964; *The Political Background of Aeschylean Tragedy,* University of Michigan Press, 1966; (translator and author of commentary) Aeschylus, *Persians,* Prentice-Hall, 1970; *The Life of Themistocles: A Critical Survey of the Literary and Archaeological Evidence,* McGill-Queen's University Press, 1974.

WORK IN PROGRESS: The Classical Age of Greece, for Macmillan's high school history series; *The Historical Background of Early Greek Poetry.*

* * *

PODULKA, Fran 1933-

PERSONAL: Surname is pronounced "pa-*dawl*-ka"; born May 7, 1933, in New Britain, Conn., daughter of Frank Charles (a theatre manager) and Frances (Frawley) Thomas; married Philip Podulka (a securities agent), August, 1957; children: Sue, Lisa, Karen, Jim. *Education:* Michigan State University, B.A., 1955; Northwestern University, M.A., 1957. *Residence:* Glenview, Ill.

CAREER: Speech therapist at Michigan State School for the Deaf, Flint, 1955-56, and New Trier East High School, Winnetka, Ill., 1958-59. *Awards, honors:* Indiana University Writer's Conference short story award, 1968, for "Wonder Jungle," and poetry award, 1970.

WRITINGS: The Wonder Jungle (novel), Putnam, 1974. Contributor of short stories to *American Girl,* and poetry to *Folio,* and *Mississippi Valley Review.*

WORK IN PROGRESS: A novel; a collection of poems; short stories.

SIDELIGHTS: In 1970, Mrs. Podulka began to expand her short story, "Wonder Jungle," into a novel, both works incorporating her interest in the region of the Everglades and in the survival of all life forms. Of her writing, she told *CA:* "I prefer a lean style, unpretentious use of language that leads to lucidity, an impressionistic style sometimes lyrical using the devices of poetry as well as prose form. I'm interested in people and the quiet unreported dramas that weave a life rather than the topical and sensational. I believe the question of religion, belief, control, control of behavior and environment must be taken apart and re-examined in human terms, and fiction is sometimes the best vehicle for moving these ideas."

* * *

POIRIER, Frank E(ugene) 1940-

PERSONAL: Born August 7, 1940, in Paterson, N.J.; son of Alice (Apelian) Poirier; married Darlene Macko, July 6, 1963; children: Alyson, Sevanne. *Education:* Paterson State College, B.A., 1962; University of Oregon, M.A., 1964, Ph.D., 1967. *Home:* 1534 Austin Dr., Columbus, Ohio 43220. *Office:* Department of Anthropology, Ohio State University, 65 South Oval, Columbus, Ohio 43210.

CAREER: University of Florida, Gainesville, assistant professor of psychiatry and anthropology, 1967-68; Ohio State University, Columbus, assistant professor, 1968-70, associate professor of anthropology, 1970—. *Member:* International Primatological Society, American Association of Physical Anthropologists, American Anthropological Association, American Association for the Advancement of Science, Current Anthropology, Sigma Xi.

WRITINGS: (Editor) *Primate Socialization,* Random House, 1972; *Fossil Man: An Evolutionary Journal,* Mosby, 1973; *In Search of Ourselves: Introduction to Physical Anthropology,* Burgess, 1974.

WORK IN PROGRESS: Research on the ecology and social behavior of the Nilgiri Langur.

* * *

POLAKOFF, Keith Ian 1941-

PERSONAL: Born December 12, 1941, in Queens, N.Y.; son of Irwin L. (a businessman) and Edna (Sopkin) Polakoff; married Carol Joyce Gershuny (a teacher), June 21, 1964; children: Amy. *Education:* Clark University, B.A., 1963; Northwestern University, M.A., 1966, Ph.D., 1968. *Politics:* Democrat. *Religion:* Jewish. *Home:* 2971 Druid Lane, Rossmoor, Calif. 90720. *Office:* Department of History, California State University, Long Beach, Calif. 90840.

CAREER: Herbert H. Lehman College of the City University of New York, Bronx, N.Y., lecturer in history, 1967-69; California State University, Long Beach, assistant professor, 1969-73, associate professor of history, 1973—. *Member:* American Historical Association, Organization of American Historians.

WRITINGS: The Politics of Inertia: The Election of 1876 and the End of Reconstruction, Louisiana State University Press, 1973. Editor of *History Teacher,* 1972—.

WORK IN PROGRESS: Studies of Reconstruction and the American political party system.

SIDELIGHTS: Polakoff wrote: "My principal field of research is the American political system, the purposes it has served, and the ways it has changed over the years; no doubt this is a substitute for direct political involvement, for which I do not have the stomach." *Avocational interests:* Photography, growing desert plants.

* * *

POLK, Dora (Beale) 1923-

PERSONAL: Born January 30, 1923, in Wales; daughter of

Arthur Edward Beale and Margaret (Jones) Beale Stockwell. *Education:* University of Wales, B.A., 1943, Education Diploma, 1944; University of Colorado, M.A. (political science), 1950; University of California, Irvine, M.A. (English), 1966, M.F.A., 1967, Ph.D., 1970. *Politics:* Democrat. *Religion:* Protestant. *Residence:* El Segundo, Calif. *Agent:* Larry Sternig, 2407 North 44th St., Milwaukee, Wis. 53210. *Office:* Department of English, California State University, 6101 East Seventh St., Long Beach, Calif. 90840.

CAREER: Aldershot County High School, Aldershot, England, teacher, 1945-48; Yankton College, Yankton, S.D., instructor in English, 1948-49; National Farmer's Union, Denver, Colo., staff writer, 1956-58; University of California, Irvine, 1966-68, began as teaching assistant, became teaching associate; California State University, Long Beach, associate professor of English, 1968—. *Member:* Modern Language Association of America, National Council of Teachers of English, Mystery Writers of America, Authors Guild.

WRITINGS: *The Farmer's Share,* National Farmer's Union, 1958; *The Linnet Estate* (novel), McKay, 1974; *Tower of the Crow* (novel), McKay, in press. Contributor of poems to *Centennial Review, College English, Anglo-Welsh Review, Poetry Wales,* and *Perspective.*

WORK IN PROGRESS: A novel, *Bird in the Crystal,* for McKay; research on a text in poetry for creative writing students; research on Welsh poet Vernon Watkins; a collection of poems; several novels.

BIOGRAPHICAL/CRITICAL SOURCES: *Long Beach Independent-Press Telegram,* February 26, 1974; *Daily Breeze* (Torrance, Calif.), March 6, 1974; *Los Angeles Times,* March 8, 1974, June 2, 1974.

* * *

POLLACK, (Wilburt) Erwin 1935-

PERSONAL: Born January 8, 1935, in Chicago, Ill.; son of Morris (a salesman) and Bluma (Lipson) Pollack; married Eunice Berger, July 3, 1969. *Education:* Roosevelt University, B.S.C., 1956; Loyola University, Chicago, Ill., M.Ed., 1963; University of Illinois, graduate study, 1963-66. *Politics:* Democrat. *Religion:* Jewish. *Home:* 5541 South Everett, Chicago, Ill. 60637. *Office:* Chicago Board of Education, 5631 South Kimbark, Chicago, Ill. 60637.

CAREER: Chicago Board of Education, Chicago, Ill., teacher of high school and elementary school, 1956-68, project director of Elementary and Secondary Education Act, 1968-71, design laboratory manager and director of district gifted program, 1971-74; Chicago Community Colleges, Chicago, Ill., training skills specialist, 1974—. Consultant, Education Development Corp.; director of Project Horizons of the Ethical Humanist Society of Chiago, 1966-72. *Member:* National Society for the Study of Education, National Association for Gifted Children, Alliance to End Repression, Phi Delta Kappa.

WRITINGS: (With Julius Menacker) *Spanish Speaking Students and Guidance,* Houghton, 1971; (contributor) D. U. Levine, editor, *Models for Integrated Education,* Charles Jones, 1971; (with Menacker) *Emerging Educational Issues: Conflicts and Contrasts,* Little, Brown, 1974. Contributor to *Humanist* and *Phi Delta Kappa.*

WORK IN PROGRESS: *A Photographic Study of an Urban School,* completion expected in 1976; *An Innovation in Education: The Ray Learning Center,* 1976; *Diary of an Urban School Teacher,* 1977.

SIDELIGHTS: Pollack has travelled in Japan, Hong Kong, Thailand, Greece, Israel, Costa Rica, and Canada to study schools.

* * *

POLLACK, Robert H(arvey) 1927-

PERSONAL: Born June 26, 1927, in New York, N.Y.; son of Solomon (a business executive) and Bertha (Levy) Pollack; married Martha Katz, August 20, 1948; children: Jonathan, Lance, Scott. *Education:* City College (now City College of the City University of New York), B.S., 1948; Clark University, M.A., 1950, Ph.D., 1953. *Home:* 190 Gatewood Pl., Athens, Ga. 30601. *Office:* Department of Psychology, University of Georgia, Athens, Ga. 30601.

CAREER: University of Sydney, Sydney, Australia, lecturer in psychology, 1953-61; Institute for Juvenile Research, Chicago, Ill., deputy director of research, 1961-69; University of Georgia, Athens, professor of psychology, 1969—. Visiting lecturer at Tennessee Wesleyan College, 1972. *Military service:* U.S. Army, 1945-46. *Member:* International Council of Psychologists (fellow), American Association for the Advancement of Science, American Psychological Association (fellow), Australian Psychological Society, Psychonomic Society, Society for Research in Child Development, Eastern Psychological Association, Southern Society for Philosophy and Psychology, Sigma Xi.

WRITINGS: (Contributor) R. N. Haber, editor, *Contemporary Theory and Research in Visual Perception,* Holt, 1968; (editor with Margaret Jean Brenner) *The Experimental Psychology of Alfred Binet,* Springer Publishing, 1969; (contributor) David Elkind and John Flavell, editors, *Essays in Cognitive Development: Studies in Honor of Jean Piaget,* Oxford University Press, 1969; (contributor) Sylvia Farnham-Diggory, editor, *Information Processing in Children,* Academic Press, 1972; (contributor) K. F. Riegel and J. A. Meacham, editors, *The Developing Individual in a Changing World,* Volume I: *Historical and Cultural Issues,* Mouton, in press. Contributor of about sixty articles and book reviews to psychology journals. Consulting editor, *Psychonomic Science,* 1972, and *Memory and Cognition,* 1973.

WORK IN PROGRESS: Contributing to *Advances in Child Development and Behavior;* research on perceptual development and its relation to intelligence.

AVOCATIONAL INTERESTS: Military history, opera, drama, sea travel.

* * *

POLLOCK, David H(arold) 1922-

PERSONAL: Born June 14, 1922, in Prince Albert, Saskatchewan, Canada; son of Norman and Bertha (Karner) Pollock; married Sheila Lepofsky (a teacher), November 5, 1951; children: Michael, Barry, Steven. *Education:* University of Saskatchewan, B.A., 1946; University of Chicago, M.A., 1949, completed all work for Ph.D. except thesis. *Home:* 1812 Kimberly Rd., Silver Spring, Md. 20903. *Office:* United Nations Economic Commission for Latin America, 1801 K St. N.W., Suite 1261, Washington, D.C. 20006.

CAREER: International Bank for Reconstruction and Development (World Bank), Washington, D.C., research trainee, 1950-51; United Nations Economic Commission for Latin America, staff member, 1951—, associate officer in Chile, 1953-55, second officer in Washington, D.C., 1955-58, and in Mexico, 1958-59, first officer in Washington, D.C., 1959-63, chief of studies and policies, and special assistant to Secretary General, United Nations Conference on Trade and Development, Geneva, Switzerland, 1963-67, director of Washington office, 1968—. Visiting professor at Carleton University, 1971-72; lecturer at Georgetown University and Canadian universities. *Military service:* Royal Canadian Air Force, 1941-46; became flying officer. *Member:* Society for International Development, American Economic Association.

WRITINGS: (Editor with Arch R. Ritter) *Latin American Prospects for the 1970's: What Kind of Revolutions?,* Praeger, 1973. Contributor to economic journals.

* * *

POLMAR, Norman 1938-

PERSONAL: Born May 14, 1938, in Washington, D.C.; son of David William and Ida (Wolf) Polmar; married Beverly Rosenfeld (a speech pathologist), November 17, 1962; children: Deborah Beth, Michael Louis. *Education:* American University, B.A., 1965. *Religion:* Jewish. *Residence:* Alexandria, Va. *Office:* Churchill Press, Inc., Skyline Center, Falls Church, Va. 22041.

CAREER: Washington Daily News, Washington, D.C., copy boy and reporter, 1958-60; *Navy Times,* Washington, D.C., associate editor, 1961-63; *Naval Institute Proceedings,* Annapolis, Md., assistant editor, 1963-67; Northrop Corp., Washington, D.C., technical support adviser, 1967-70; Lulejian & Associates, Falls Church, Va., assistant to the president, 1970—; also associated with Churchill Press, Inc., Falls Church, Va. *Member:* American Military Institute, American Aviation Historical Society, Naval Institute, National Press Club.

WRITINGS: Atomic Submarines, Van Nostrand, 1963; *Death of the Thresher,* Chilton, 1964; *Aircraft Carriers,* Doubleday, 1969; *Soviet Naval Power,* National Strategy Information Center, 1972; (with Ken W. Sayers) *Anchors and Atoms,* McKay, 1974. Contributor to journals on military aviation. United States editor of *Jane's Fighting Ships;* Washington editorial representative for *Air International* and *Ships of the World.*

WORK IN PROGRESS: Studies in the Soviet maritime-naval area.

* * *

POMPIDOU, Georges (Jean Raymond) 1911-1974

July 5, 1911—April 2, 1974; French leader and politician. Obituaries: *Washington Post,* April 3, 1974, April 5, 1974; *Time,* April 15, 1974; *Newsweek,* April 15, 1974; *Current Biography,* May, 1974.

* * *

PONCE de LEON, Jose Luis S. 1931-

PERSONAL: Born September 23, 1931, in Vigo, Spain; son of Vicente (a lawyer) and Amelia (Ponce de Leon) Sierra. *Education:* University of Santiago, Lic. en Derecho, 1953; further study at Harvard University, 1956-57, and University of Madrid, 1959-60; Stanford University, M.A., 1963, Ph.D., 1966. *Home:* 937 Church, San Francisco, Calif. 94114. *Office:* Department of Foreign Languages and Literatures, California State University, Hayward, Calif. 94542.

CAREER: Stanford University, Stanford, Calif., assistant professor of Spanish, 1966-72; California State University at Hayward, associate professor of Spanish language and literature, 1972—. *Military service:* Spanish Army, 1954; became second lieutenant. *Member:* Modern Language Association of America, American Association of University Professors, American Association of Teachers of Spanish and Portuguese.

WRITINGS: El Arte de la conversacion, Harper, 1967; *La Novela espanola de la guerra civil (1936-1939),* Insula, 1971; (editor with Isabel M. Schevill) Alfonso Sastre, *La Mordaza: Drama en seis Cuadros y un Epilogo,* Appleton, 1972. Contributor of articles to academic journals and short stories to *Transatlantic Review.*

WORK IN PROGRESS: Criticism on the contemporary Spanish novel; short stories.

* * *

POPE, Elizabeth Marie 1917-

PERSONAL: Born May 1, 1917, in Washington, D.C.; daughter of Christopher (a banker) and Florence (Thompson) Pope. *Education:* Bryn Mawr College, A.B., 1940; Johns Hopkins University, Ph.D., 1944. *Politics:* Democrat. *Religion:* Episcopalian. *Office:* Department of English, Mills College, Oakland, Calif. 94613.

CAREER: Mills College, Oakland, Calif., assistant professor, 1944-55, associate professor, 1955-62, professor of English, 1962—. *Member:* American Association of University Professors, Renaissance Society, Mediaeval Society of America, Society for Creative Anachronism.

WRITINGS: Paradise Regained: The Tradition and the Poem, Johns Hopkins Press, 1947; *The Sherwood Ring* (novel), Houghton, 1956; *The Perilous Gard* (novel), Houghton, 1974.

* * *

POPHAM, Melinda 1944-

PERSONAL: Born April 25, 1944, in Kansas City, Mo.; daughter of Arthur C. Popham (a lawyer) and Mary C. Hawn; married John H. Benton (chairman of board of Encyclopaedia Britannica Educational Corp.), January 9, 1971. *Education:* Attended Mills College, 1962-64; University of Chicago, B.A., 1966; Stanford University, M.A., 1967. *Residence:* Chicago, Ill. *Agent:* Ellen Levine, Curtis Brown Ltd., 60 East 56th St., New York, N.Y. 10022. *Office:* 920 North Michigan Ave., Room 806, Chicago, Ill. 60611.

CAREER: Crystal Springs School for Girls, Hillsborough, Calif., teacher, 1967-69; *Oui* magazine, Chicago, Ill., foreign correspondent, 1972-73. *Awards, honors:* Marjorie Fisher Winston Award for fiction, 1963; Paul Shorey short story prize, 1965; National Foundation for the Arts grant, 1966.

WRITINGS: A Blank Book, Bobbs-Merrill, 1974. Contributor to *Oui* and *Ms.*

WORK IN PROGRESS: A novel.

* * *

POST, Elizabeth L(indley) 1920-

PERSONAL: Born May 7, 1920, in Englewood, N.J.; daughter of Allen L. (a broker) and Elizabeth (Ellsworth) Lindley; married George E. Cookman, May 31, 1941 (died,

1943); married William G. Post (president of an equipment company), August 5, 1944; children: (first marriage) Allen; (second marriage) William G., Lucinda (Mrs. Edward C. Palmer), Peter. *Education:* Miss Masters School, student, 1935-38. *Religion:* Episcopalian. *Home:* Thistle Lane, Rye, N.Y. 10580. *Office:* Emily Post Institute, 6 East 45th St., New York, N.Y. 10017.

CAREER: Has been continuing the work of Emily Post, her husband's grandmother; director of Emily Post Institute, New York, N.Y., 1965—.

WRITINGS: (Reviser) Emily Post, *Emily Post's Etiquette,* 11th edition, Funk, 1965, 12th edition, 1969; (editor) *The Emily Post Book of Etiquette for Young People,* Funk, 1967; *The Wonderful World of Weddings,* Funk, 1970; *Please Say Please,* Little, Brown, 1972. Writer of syndicated newspaper column, "Doing the Right Thing," 1966—.

WORK IN PROGRESS: New revision of *Emily Post's Etiquette,* completion expected in 1975.

SIDELIGHTS: Elizabeth Post lived in Bogota, Colombia, for six years; she has made a photographic safari in East Africa, and has traveled extensively in other countries. *Avocational interests:* Deep-sea, lake, and stream fishing.

* * *

POTTER, Marian 1915-

PERSONAL: Born January 9, 1915, in Blackwell, Mo.; daughter of Samuel and Flora (Bookstaver) McKinstry; married David Potter (a radio station manager), October 18, 1943; children: Andrew, Pamela, Rebecca. *Education:* University of Missouri, B.J., 1939. *Politics:* Democrat. *Religion:* Presbyterian. *Home:* 124 Beaty St., Warren, Pa. 16365.

CAREER: University of Missouri, Columbia, editor, 1940-41; *St. Louis Globe-Democrat,* St. Louis, Mo., copyreader, 1942-43; United Nations Information Office, New York, N.Y., assistant press officer, 1944; WNAE and WRRN (radio stations), Warren, Pa., editorial writer, 1962—. Member of board of directors of Northern Allegheny Broadcasting Co., 1965—; Warren Library Association, member of board of control, 1970—, president, 1974—; president of Warren County Family Service and Children's Aid Society, 1973—. *Member:* Kappa Tau Alpha.

WRITINGS: *The Little Red Caboose,* Golden Press, 1953; *Milepost 67,* Follett, 1965; *Copperfield Summer,* Follett, 1967.

AVOCATIONAL INTERESTS: Archeology, Mayan Indian culture.

* * *

POTTERTON, Gerald 1931-

PERSONAL: Born March 8, 1931, in London, England; son of Albert James (a musician) and Rosa (Cudd) Potterton; married Judith Merrit (a film editor), May 8, 1958; children: Richard, Oliver. *Education:* Attended Hammersmith Art School, 1947. *Religion:* Protestant. *Home:* 17 Chesterfield Ave., Apt. 6, Westmount, Montreal, Quebec, Canada. *Office:* Potterton Productions, Place Bonaventure, Montreal, Quebec, Canada.

CAREER: National Film Board of Canada, Montreal, Quebec, film animator, writer, and director, 1954-67; Potterton Productions (film production company), Montreal, Quebec, president, writer, and director of feature and children's films for television, 1967—. Art director, Lars Calonius Productions, New York, N.Y., 1960-61. *Military service:* Royal Air Force, 1949-51. *Awards, honors:* Academy Award nomination, 1963, for "My Financial Career," and 1964, for "Christmas Cracker"; Belgian Prix Femina, 1965; award for "outstanding film of the year" from London Film Festival, 1965, for "The Railrodder"; Chicago Film Festival best film award, 1969, for "Pinter People"; Atlanta Film Festival Bronze Medal, 1973, for "The Rainbow Boys"; and numerous other film awards.

WRITINGS: (Self-illustrated) *The Star (and George),* Harper, 1968.

Screenplays: "The Ride," 1963, "The Railrodder," 1965, "The Quiet Racket," 1967, "The Rainbow Boys," 1973.

WORK IN PROGRESS: Adapting Oscar Wilde's short story, "The Remarkable Rocket," as animated film for television; "Summerlight," screenplay for a comedy feature.

SIDELIGHTS: Potterton told *CA:* "I am very interested in comedy and the apparent lack of it in a time when we need it most. Since I have known and worked with Buster Keaton and Harold Pinter I have come to appreciate more and more the importance of simplicity as an aim, no matter how complex one's efforts are to arrive at that end result—and they are usually very complex indeed."

* * *

POULTER, S(cott) L(arry) 1943-

PERSONAL: Born October 27, 1943, in Peoria, Ill.; son of Jesse H. (a salesman) and La Vonne (a tavern owner; maiden name, Timmerman) Poulter; married Elizabeth Ann Bouzek, September 29, 1963 (divorced May 24, 1973); children: Carrie, Jodi, Rhonda. *Education:* Studied at University of Wisconsin—Madison, 1969-72, Nicolet College, 1972, and University of Wisconsin—Milwaukee, 1972—. *Politics:* Democrat. *Religion:* Bahai. *Home:* 1527 West Mitchell St., Milwaukee, Wis. 53204. *Agent:* Paul Riechel, Wisconsin Arts Board, Madison, Wis. 53706. *Office:* Shelters Press, P.O. Box 5168, Milwaukee, Wis. 53204.

CAREER: Has worked as dental assistant, painter, salesman, baker, and boxer; publisher, Shelters Press and Peacock Press, both Milwaukee, Wis. Speaker at conferences, colleges, schools, clubs, prisons, and rehabilitation centers.

MEMBER: Poetry Society of America, Haiku Society of America, National Federation of State Poetry Societies, Academy of American Poets, Wisconsin Fellowship of Poets, Wisconsin Poetry Alliance, Wisconsin Regional Writers Association. *Awards, honors:* Jade Ring poetry award from Wisconsin Regional Writers Association, 1971, for "The Holy Trinity"; Wausau Festival of Arts award, 1971, for "To President Nixon—12/25/71"; award for best book of poetry by a Wisconsin poet, from Council for Wisconsin Writers, 1973, for *The Glass Partition;* awards from National Federation of State Poetry Societies, including Kentucky Award, 1973, for "Lesson," and Tennessee Award, 1974, for "In This Season."

WRITINGS—Poems: *The Glass Partition,* South & West, 1972; *Distant Thunder,* Shelters Press, 1974; (with Peter Morino) *Fables,* Shelters Press, in press. Work is represented in anthologies, including *Yearbook of Modern Poetry,* 1972, and *Contemporary American Love Scene,* 1972. Contributor of more than four hundred poems to literary magazines, including *Epos, Quartet, Second Coming, Choice, Modern Haiku,* and *Voices International.* Editor of *Wisconsin's Impact* and *Bird Two Review.*

WORK IN PROGRESS: A Collection of Time, poems.

SIDELIGHTS: Poulter spent five years in Wisconsin State Prison. Before that time he knew almost nothing about poetry; before his release he had been published in more than seventy-five literary magazines in the United States and abroad. He has recently begun a program which involves visits to prisons by himself and two other poets, in order to teach creative writing and conduct poetry workshops for prisoners.

BIOGRAPHICAL/CRITICAL SOURCES: Bachaet, December, 1970; *Wisconsin State Journal,* May, 1973; *Insight,* September 30, 1973.

* * *

POUND, Omar S(hakespear) 1926-

PERSONAL: Born September 10, 1926, in Paris, France; son of Ezra Loomis (the poet) and Dorothy (Shakespear) Pound; married Elizabeth Parkin, May 14, 1955; children: Katherine, Oriana. *Education:* Hamilton College, A.B., 1951; McGill University, M.A., 1958. *Politics:* "Nil." *Religion:* "Nil." *Home:* 12 Kinnaird Way, Cambridge CB1 4SN, England.

CAREER: Roxbury Latin School, Boston, Mass., member of faculty, 1957-62; American School of Tangier, Tangier, Morocco, headmaster, 1962-65; Cambridgeshire College of Arts and Technology, Cambridge, England, lecturer in Islamic studies, 1967—. *Military service:* U.S. Army, 1945-46; served in Germany.

WRITINGS: (Translator from the Arabic) *Arabic and Persian Poems,* New Directions, 1970; (translator from the Persian) Nizam al-Din 'Ubayd Zakani, *Gorby and the Rats,* New Directions, 1972.

AVOCATIONAL INTERESTS: Anything Islamic, choral music.

* * *

POWELL, Norman J(ohn) 1908-1974

September 28, 1908—May 23, 1974; American political scientist, educator, and author of books in his field. Obituaries: *New York Times,* May 25, 1974. (*CA*-21/22).

* * *

POYER, Joe
See POYER, Joseph John, Jr.

* * *

POYER, Joseph John, Jr. 1939-
(Joe Poyer)

PERSONAL: Born November 30, 1939, in Battle Creek, Mich.; son of Joseph John (a salesman) and Eileen (Powell) Poyer; married Susan Pilmore; children: Joseph III, Geoffrey. *Education:* Kellogg Community College, A.A., 1959; Michigan State University, B.A., 1961. *Politics:* Independent. *Religion:* None. *Home:* 546 Laurinda Lane, Orange, Calif. 92669. *Agent:* International Famous Agency, 1301 Avenue of the Americas, New York, N.Y. 10019; and Anthony Sheils, 52 Floral St., London, England.

CAREER: Michigan Tuberculosis and Respiratory Disease Association, Lansing, assistant director of public information, 1961-62; Pratt & Whitney Aircraft, East Hartford, Conn., proposals writer, 1963-65; Beckman Instruments, Fullerton, Calif., proposals writer, 1965-67; Bioscience Planning, Anaheim, Calif., manager of interdisciplinary communications, 1967-68; Allergan Pharmaceuticals, Irvine, Calif., senior project manager, 1968—. Teacher of writing course at Golden West College.

WRITINGS—All under name Joe Poyer; novels: *Operation Malacca,* Doubleday, 1968; *North Cape* (Book-of-the-Month Club selection in England), Doubleday, 1969; *The Balkan Assignment,* Doubleday, 1971; *The Chinese Agenda* (Junior Literary Guild selection; Book-of-the-Month Club selection in Sweden), Doubleday, 1972; *The Shooting of the Green,* Doubleday, 1973.

Editor: *Instrumentation Methods for Predictive Medicine,* Instrument Society of America, 1966; *Biomedical Sciences Instrumentation,* Plenum, 1967.

Contributor of about a dozen short stories and articles to magazines.

WORK IN PROGRESS: A novel on disarmament talks between the United States and the Soviet Union, a novel about a major European bank robbery; textbooks on writing action and adventure-oriented fiction.

AVOCATIONAL INTERESTS: Travel, photography, karate.

* * *

PRASSEL, Frank Richard 1937-

PERSONAL: Born October 5, 1937, in San Antonio, Tex.; son of Frank Gustav (a manufacturer) and Julie (Oge) Prassel; married Ann Hetherington (a librarian), July 30, 1966. *Education:* Trinity University, San Antonio, B.A., 1959, M.A., 1961; University of Texas, LL.B. (since converted to J.D.), 1965, Ph.D., 1970. *Religion:* Lutheran. *Address:* P.O. Box 957, San Antonio, Tex. 78294.

CAREER: Admitted to Texas Bar, 1965; San Antonio College, San Antonio, Tex., assistant professor and director of law enforcement, 1966-70; Sacramento State College (now California State University), Sacramento, Calif., associate professor of police science, 1970-71; Fulbright professor of law in Taiwan, 1971-72; Stephen F. Austin State University, Nacogdoches, Tex., associate professor and coordinator of criminal justice, 1972-74. *Military service:* U.S. Army Reserve, 1959-73; became captain. *Member:* Texas Bar Association.

WRITINGS: The Western Police Officer: The Legacy of Law and Order, University of Oklahoma Press, 1972; *Introduction to American Criminal Justice,* Harper, in press.

WORK IN PROGRESS: Writing on criminal justice, American and comparative.

* * *

PREGER, Paul D(aniel), Jr. 1926-

PERSONAL: Born May 16, 1926, in New York, N.Y.; son of Paul D. (a financial consultant) and Esther (Hyman) Preger; married Marjorie Koch (a plant store manager), June 25, 1955; children: Lisa, June, Mary. *Education:* Cornell University, B.A., 1947; Columbia University, M.A., 1949. *Politics:* "Variable." *Religion:* "Mixed." *Home:* 131 Allenwood Rd., Great Neck, N.Y. 11023. *Agent:* Theron Raines, 240 Madison Ave., New York, N.Y. 10016.

CAREER: Journalist, 1953—; *Medical World News,* New York, N.Y., columnist, 1963—. *Military service:* U.S. Navy, 1944-45.

WRITINGS: (With David A. Loehwing) *The Professional Man's Money,* Prentice-Hall, 1973. Contributor to *Barron's, New Yorker,* and *Emergency Medicine.*

WORK IN PROGRESS: A book on diabetes with Dr. B. E. Loewnstein; a book on psychic healing, completion expected in 1975.

* * *

PREIL, Gabriel 1911-

PERSONAL: Surname rhymes with "file"; born August 21, 1911, in Dorpat, Estonia; came to U.S. in 1922; naturalized citizen, 1928; son of Elias and Clara (Matzkel) Preil. *Education:* Attended Rabbi Isaac Elchanan Theological Seminary, 1923-24, Teachers' Institute (now part of Yeshivah University), 1924-26. *Religion:* Jewish. *Home and office:* 1011 Walton Ave., Bronx, N.Y. 10452.

CAREER: In early youth, did occasional work of great variety, manual as well as intellectual; free-lance writer, translator, and editor of Hebrew, Yiddish, and English prose and poetry, 1935—. Member of Israeli delegation to World P.E.N. Congress, New York, N.Y., 1966. *Awards, honors:* Louis La Med award for Hebrew literature, 1942; Kovner Memorial Hebrew Poetry prize, Jewish Book Council of America, 1955, 1961; Bitzaron award for Hebrew poetry, 1960; Congress of Jewish Culture grant, 1965; D.H.L., Hebrew Union College-Jewish Institute of Religion, 1972; Irving and Bertha Neuman Literary Award from New York University, 1974.

WRITINGS—Hebrew poetry, except as indicated: *Nor shemesh ukhfor* (title means "Landscape of Sun and Frost"), Ohel Publishing, 1944; *Ner mul kohavim* (title means "Candle against Stars"), Bialik Institute (Jerusalem), 1954; *Mapat erev* (title means "Map of Evening"), Dvir (Tel Aviv), 1961; *Gabriel Prail Mivhar Shirim Udevarim al Yezirato* (title means "Gabriel Preil: A Selection of Poems and a Study of His Poetry"), Mahbarot Lesifrut (Tel Aviv), 1965; *Lider* (poems in Yiddish), Yiddish P.E.N. Club (New York), 1966; *Haesh vehademama* (title means "Fire and Silence"), Israeli Writers' Association (Tel Aviv), 1968; *Mitoch zeman vanof* (title means "Of Time and Place"), Bialik Institute, 1973.

Essays: *Hebrew Poetry in Peace and War,* Herzl Press, 1959. Also translator of poems of Robert Frost, Carl Sandburg, and Robinson Jeffers.

Represented in anthologies, including *The Modern Hebrew Poem Itself: From the Beginnings to the Present,* edited by Ezra Spicehandler, Stanley Burnshaw, and others, Holt, 1965; *Anthology of Modern Hebrew Poetry,* volume I, edited by S. Y. Penueli and Azriel Ukhmani, Institute of Translation of Hebrew Literature (Tel Aviv), 1966; *Antologia Poesia Hebrea Moderna,* Aguilar (Madrid), 1971. Contributor to periodicals. Editor, *Niv* (magazine), 1937-39, *Bitzaron* (magazine), 1969—.

WORK IN PROGRESS: A new volume of poems.

SIDELIGHTS: Preil told *CA* he is an anomaly, "a Hebrew poet living in the U.S., considered among the better practitioners of the art, well-known in Israel. Invited by the City of Haifa in Israel to accept residence there for life (1953), guest of Jerusalem Municipality and of President Shazar (1968), I am yet unable to leave the U.S. Family reasons—yet they are more intricate than that. In any case, here I work in isolation, rooted in Israeli literature, affected by English and American influences." Other languages he knows are Russian and German. *Avocational interests:* Art, music.

BIOGRAPHICAL/CRITICAL SOURCES: Meyer Waxman, editor, *A History of Jewish Literature,* Yoseloff, 1960; *Judaism,* spring, 1966; Eisig Silberschlag, editor, *From Renaissance to Renaissance: Hebrew Literature 1492-1967,* Ktav, 1972.

* * *

PRESTBO, John A(ndrew) 1941-

PERSONAL: Born September 26, 1941, in Northwood, N.D.; son of Oscar B. (an educator) and Jeanne (Schol) Prestbo; married Darlene Parrish (a psychiatric social worker), August 14, 1965; children: Bradford Jonathan. *Education:* Northwestern University, B.S., 1963, M.S., 1964. *Religion:* Presbyterian. *Home:* 26 Parkview Ter., Summit, N.J. 07901. *Office: Wall Street Journal,* 22 Cortlandt St., New York, N.Y. 10007.

CAREER: Wall Street Journal, reporter in Chicago, Ill., 1964-73, editor and writer in New York, N.Y., 1974—. *Military service:* U.S. Air Force Reserve, 1965-74; became captain. *Awards, honors:* University of Missouri award for distinguished writing in business, 1967; G.M. Loeb achievement award, 1968, for material written for *Wall Street Journal.*

WRITINGS: (With Frederick C. Klein) *News and the Market,* Regnery, 1974; (editor) *This Abundant Land* (articles on agriculture and farming from *Wall Street Journal),* Dow Jones, 1974.

* * *

PRETO-RODAS, Richard (Anthony) 1936-

PERSONAL: Born May 30, 1936, in Yonkers, N.Y.; son of Manuel (a businessman) and Beatrice (Carvalho) Preto-Rodas. *Education:* Fairfield University, A.B., 1958; Boston College, M.A., 1960: University of Michigan, M.A., 1963, Ph.D., 1966. *Home:* 705 West Ohio St., Urbana, Ill. 61801. *Office:* Department of Foreign Languages, University of Illinois, Urbana, Ill. 61801.

CAREER: Fairfield University, Fairfield, Conn., instructor in English, 1960-61; University of Florida, Gainesville, assistant professor of Spanish and Portuguese, 1966-70; University of Illinois, Urbana, associate professor of Spanish and Portuguese, 1970—. *Member:* American Association of Teachers of Spanish and Portuguese, American Association of University Professors, Phi Beta Kappa.

WRITINGS: Negritude as a Theme in the Poetry of the Portuguese-Speaking World, University of Florida Press, 1970; *Francisco Rodrigues Lobo: Dialogue and Courtly Lore in Renaissance Portugal,* University of North Carolina Press, 1971; (editor with Alfred Hower) *Cronicas Brasileiras: A Portuguese Reader,* University of Florida Press, 1971.

WORK IN PROGRESS: Irony in Luso-Brazilian Literature.

* * *

PREUS, Anthony 1936-

PERSONAL: Surname rhymes with "voice"; born July 5, 1936, in Perth Amboy, N.J.; son of Christian K. (a Lutheran pastor) and Dorothy (a musician; maiden name, Bollum) Preus; married Nicole Lemoine (a librarian), April 14, 1962; children: Christian Marius. *Education:* Luther College, B.A., 1958; Trinity College, Oxford, B.A., 1962, M.A., 1966; Johns Hopkins University, Ph.D., 1968; Sorbonne, University of Paris, postdoctoral study, 1971-72. *Politics:* "Uninterestingly independent leftish." *Religion:* "Heretical Lutheran." *Home:* 28 Johnson Ave., Binghamton, N.Y. 13905. *Office:* Department of Philosophy, State University of New York at Binghamton, Binghamton, N.Y. 13903.

CAREER: While attending college worked for two construction companies out of Fergus Falls, Minn., and played jazz and classical bass viol; State University of New York at Binghamton, assistant professor, 1964-70, associate professor of philosophy, 1970—, resident director of Mediterranean studies program in Malta and Tunis, 1973-74. *Member:* American Philosophical Association, Society for Ancient Greek Philosophy, American Association of University Professors, Association of American Rhodes Scholars. *Awards, honors:* Woodrow Wilson fellow, 1958-59; Rhodes scholar, 1959-62; American Council of Learned Societies study fellowship in Paris, 1971-72.

WRITINGS: Science and Philosophy in Aristotle's Biological Works, Georg Olms (Hildesheim), 1974. Contributor to *Studi Internazionali di Filosofia, Classical Quarterly,* and other journals.

WORK IN PROGRESS: Aristotle and Michael of Ephesus on Animal Movement.

SIDELIGHTS: Preus is fluent in French, speaks some German, Spanish, and modern Greek, and reads ancient Greek and Latin. *Avocational interests:* Restoring old houses.

* * *

PRICE, Frances Brown 1895-

PERSONAL: Born February 21, 1895, in Columbus, Ohio; daughter of Frank Irwin (an attorney and court reporter) and Flora (a music teacher; maiden name, Herd) Brown; married Ralph A. Price (a teacher), November 23, 1955. *Education:* Oberlin College, B.A., 1918; Ohio State University, M.A., 1949; also studied at Sorbonne, University of Paris, 1927, Columbia University, University of Wisconsin, University of Minnesota, and Wittenburg University. *Religion:* Methodist. *Home:* 1070 West Jefferson St., Franklin, Ind. 46131.

CAREER: High school mathematics and science teacher in Connellsville, Pa., 1918-20; high school English and journalism teacher in Dayton, Ohio, 1920-34; Roosevelt High School, Dayton, Ohio, English teacher, 1934-50, director of guidance, 1947-63, assistant principal, 1950-63; writer, 1963—. Has taught in a rural one-room school house; has judged state and national poetry contests; has given poetry readings and lectures on poetry in public meetings and on radio and television.

MEMBER: World Poetry Society Intercontinental, International Poetry Society (fellow), Academy of American Poets, National Federation of State Poetry Societies, National League of American Pen Women, Avalon, Audubon Club, Ohio Poetry Society, Poetry Society of Texas, Indiana State Federation of Poetry Clubs, Dayton High School Women's Club, Dayton Council on World Affairs, Phi Beta Kappa. *Awards, honors:* Poet laureate of Indiana State Federation of Poetry Clubs, 1966—; distinguished service citation from World Poetry Society Intercontinental, 1973, for having served world poetry with special merit.

WRITINGS—Poems: *Blue Flame,* Naylor, 1967; *Miracle Windows,* Naylor, 1974. Poems are represented in anthologies, including: *The Quiet Time,* edited by Virginia Moran Evans, Dayton Poets' Round Table, 1967; *Indiana Sesquicentennial Poets,* edited by Thomas H. Wetmore, Ball State University, 1967; *Feline World,* edited by Helen Eckert, North Side Letter Shop (Columbus, Ohio), 1970; *Spring Anthology,* Mitre Press, 1970; *Noels for Now,* edited by Myriam Page, Dayton Poets' Round Table, 1971. Poetry is also included in *Prize Poems of the National Federation of State Poetry Societies, 1965, 1966, 1967,* edited by Joseph Cherwinski, published as one volume by Candor Press.

Contributor of poems and translations of Scandinavian poems to magazines, including *Poet Lore, Lyric, Laurel Leaves* (Philippines), *Iceland Review* (Reykjavik), *Poet* (India), *American Bard, Baptist Leader, Bitterroot, Pen Women, North American Mentor,* and *Green World.* Guest editor of *Poet* (of World Poetry Society Intercontinental), May, 1972.

SIDELIGHTS: Frances Brown Price introduced into the Dayton school system one of the first American high school journalism programs. She was encouraged to become a poet, after her retirement from school teaching, by one of her former students. She writes: "Evidence indicates that I am a late starter—I learned to fly an airplane at age fifty; I married at sixty; and I published my first book of poetry . . . at seventy." *Avocational interests:* National and international travel, sports fan (basketball; former women's tennis champion at Oberlin College), golf, swimming, riding, flying (holds private pilot's license).

BIOGRAPHICAL/CRITICAL SOURCES: Cyclo Flame, Volume 17, number 1, 1969.

* * *

PRICE, Richard 1949-

PERSONAL: Born October 12, 1949, in New York, N.Y. *Education:* Cornell University, B.S., 1971; Columbia University, graduate study, 1972-74; Stanford University, further graduate study, 1973. *Politics:* None. *Religion:* None. *Home and office:* 325 West End Ave., New York, N.Y. 10023. *Agent:* Carl Brandt, Brandt & Brandt, 101 Park Ave., New York, N.Y. 10017.

CAREER: Hostos Community College, Bronx, N.Y., lecturer in English as a second language, 1973; New York University, New York, N.Y., lecturer in urban affairs, 1973; State University of New York at Stony Brook, Long Island, N.Y., lecturer in creative writing, 1974—. *Awards, honors:* Edith Mirrilees grant in fiction from Stanford University, 1972; Mary Roberts Rinehart Foundation grant, 1973; MacDowell Colony grant, 1973.

WRITINGS: The Wanderers (novel), Houghton, 1974.

WORK IN PROGRESS: Nuns in Trouble, a novel.

* * *

PRICE, Steven D(avid) 1940-

PERSONAL: Born April 17, 1940, in Brooklyn, N.Y.; son of Martin and Rose (Myiofis) Price; married Jenene C. Levy, August 18, 1968 (divorced, 1972). *Education:* University of Rochester, B.A., 1962; Yale University, LL.B., 1965. *Home:* 510 East 85th St., New York, N.Y. 10028.

CAREER: Lawyer, subsidiary rights director, and editor in publishing field in New York, N.Y., 1965-71; free-lance writer, 1971—.

WRITINGS: Teaching Riding at Summer Camps,

Greene, 1971; *Panorama of American Horses,* Westover Publishing, 1972; *Get a Horse! Basics of Back-yard Horse-keeping,* Viking, 1974; *Take Me Home,* Praeger, 1974; (with William J. Goode) *The Second-Time-Single Man's Survival Handbook,* Praeger, 1974. Contributor to *American Horseman, Village Voice.*

WORK IN PROGRESS: Horseback Vacation Guide and *Old as the Hills,* a history of Bluegrass music, completion expected in 1975.

SIDELIGHTS: Price wrote to *CA:* "After a stint as lawyer and in publishing, I decided to try to write full-time on the subjects in which I am involved. So far, so good."

* * *

PRIME, C(ecil) T(homas) 1909-

PERSONAL: Born August 30, 1909, in Cambridge, England; son of Thomas Edgar (a company director) and Edith (Harvey) Prime; married Frances Welby, March 30, 1940; children: Edith Claire, Helen Frances, Catherine Mary. *Education:* Christ's College, Cambridge, B.A., 1931, M.A., 1934; Chelsea College, London, Ph.D., 1951. *Politics:* None. *Religion:* Church of England. *Home:* Thriplow, 7 Westview Rd., Warlingham, Surrey, England.

CAREER: Whitgift School, South Croydon, England, assistant master, 1931-62, head of science department, 1962-69. *Member:* Institute of Biology (fellow), Botanical Society of the British Isles (member of council), Linnean Society of London (fellow).

WRITINGS: (With R. J. Deacock) *How to Identify Trees and Shrubs from Leaves or Twigs in Summer or Winter,* Heffer, 1935, 6th edition, revised and enlarged, 1970; (with Deacock) *The Shorter British Flora,* Methuen, 1948, 2nd edition, 1953; *Lords and Ladies,* Collins, 1960; (with Maurice Burton) *Nature,* Grolier Society, 1963; *The Young Botanist,* Nelson, 1963; *Investigations in Woodland Ecology,* Heinemann, 1970; *Experiments for Young Botanists,* Bell, 1971; *Seedlings and Soil,* Doubleday, 1973; *Plant Life in Britain,* Collins, in press.

WORK IN PROGRESS: Translating, with A. H. Ewen, John Ray's *Catalogus plantarum circa cantabrigiam,* completion expected in 1975.

* * *

PROKASY, William F(rederick) 1930-

PERSONAL: Born November 27, 1930, in Cleveland, Ohio; son of William Frederick (an insurance salesman) and Margaret Lima (Chapman) Prokasy; married Barbara Alice Benditz (a bookkeeper), March 23, 1953; children: Kathi Lynn, Cheryl Anne. *Education:* Baldwin-Wallace College, B.A., 1952; Kent State University, M.A., 1954; University of Wisconsin, Ph.D., 1957; also studied at Piedmont College, 1950-51. *Politics:* Democrat. *Religion:* None. *Home:* 4287 South 2900 St., Salt Lake City, Utah 84117. *Office:* College of Social and Behavioral Science, University of Utah, 205 Spencer Hall, Salt Lake City, Utah 84112.

CAREER: Pennsylvania State University, State College, assistant professor, 1957-63, associate professor of psychology, 1963-66; University of Utah, Salt Lake City, professor of psychology, 1966—, distinguished research professor, 1971-72, chairman of department, 1966-69, dean of division of social and behavioral science, 1968-70, dean of College of Social and Behavioral Science, 1970—. Member of experimental psychology research review panel of National Institute of Mental Health, 1971-75, chairman, 1973-75. Delegate to Utah's Democratic state convention, 1968, 1972.

MEMBER: American Psychological Association (fellow), Psychonomic Society, Society for Psychophysiological Research, American Association for the Advancement of Science, Rocky Mountain Psychological Association, Utah Psychological Association (president, 1972-73), Sigma Xi, Phi Kappa Phi. *Awards, honors:* Senior postdoctoral fellowship from National Science Foundation, 1963-64.

WRITINGS: (Editor) *Classical Conditioning: A Symposium,* Appleton, 1965; (editor with A. H. Black) *Classical Conditioning Two,* Appleton, 1972; (editor with D. C. Raskin) *Electrodermal Activity in Psychological Research,* Academic Press, 1973. Contributor of more than fifty articles to psychology journals. Consulting editor of *Journal of Experimental Psychology,* 1968—; associate editor of *Learning and Motivation,* 1969—; editor of *Psychophysiology,* 1974—.

WORK IN PROGRESS: Research on Pavlovian conditioning, with emphases on the control processes required in order to demonstrate conditioning with autonomic nervous system measures and on mathematical models of conditioned skeletal responding.

SIDELIGHTS: Prokasy wrote to *CA* regarding "some of the major difficulties in academics," that "one of the major tasks which confront us is the reshaping of undergraduate education so that its major mission is to provide the beginnings of the kinds of inquiry which result in an educated citizenry. Similarly, the university must be seen as a place to which all persons of any age level or career can go simply because it is an academy, not because degrees are awarded."

* * *

PRONIN, Alexander 1927-

PERSONAL: Born September 30, 1927, in Luck (Lutsk), Poland (now Soviet territory); son of George F. and Zinaida (Uspenski) Pronin; married, wife's name, Barbara S. (an editor). *Education:* University of California, Berkeley, B.A., 1955; University of Geneva, graduate study, 1955-58; Georgetown University, Ph.D., 1965. *Residence:* Fresno, Calif. *Office:* Department of Foreign Languages, California State University, Fresno, Calif. 93710.

CAREER: U.S. Army Language School, Monterey, Calif., instructor in Russian, 1949-50; Johns Hopkins School of Advanced International Studies, Washington, D.C., instructor in Russian, 1959-63; University of Akron, Akron, Ohio, assistant professor of Russian, 1963-65; California State University at Fresno, 1965—, currently professor of Russian. Accredited interpreter for U.S. Department of State. *Member:* American Association of Teachers of Slavic and East European Languages (president of California chapter; chapter vice-president, 1971—).

WRITINGS: History of Old Russian Literature (series of lectures in English and Russian), Possev-Verlag (Frankfurt), 1969; *Byliny: Heroic Tales of Old Russia,* Possev-Verlag, 1971; *Russian Vocabulary Builder,* two books, Lawrence Publishing, 1971; (with wife, Barbara Pronin) *Russian Folk Arts,* A. S. Barnes, 1973. Editor, "Russian Emigre Archives" series, Faculty Press, Volume I, 1972.

WORK IN PROGRESS: Compiling further documents for "Russian Emigre Archives," a series with about one hundred volumes contemplated.

PRONZINI, Bill 1943-
(Jack Foxx, Alex Saxon)

PERSONAL: Born April 13, 1943, in Petaluma, Calif.; son of Joseph (a farm worker) and Helene (Guder) Pronzini; married Laura Patricia Adolphson, May 15, 1965 (divorced, 1967); married Brunhilde Schier, July 28, 1972. *Politics:* Liberal Democrat. *Home and office:* 40 San Jacinto Way, San Francisco, Calif. 94127. *Agent:* Henry Morrison, Inc., 311½ West 20th St., New York, N.Y. 10011.

CAREER: Petaluma Argus-Courier, Petaluma, Calif., reporter, 1957-60; writer, 1969—. *Member:* Authors Guild, Mystery Writers of America, Science Fiction Writers of America, Western Writers of America, Writers Guild of America, West.

WRITINGS—All novels: *The Stalker,* Random House, 1971; *The Snatch,* Random House, 1971; *Panic!,* Random House, 1972; (under pseudonym Jack Foxx) *The Jade Figurine,* Bobbs-Merrill, 1972; *The Vanished,* Random House, 1973; *Undercurrent,* Random House, 1973; (under pseudonym Alex Saxon) *A Run in Diamonds,* Pocket Books, 1973; *Snowbound,* Putnam, 1974; (under pseudonym Jack Foxx) *Dead Run,* Bobbs-Merrill, in press; (with Barry N. Malzberg) *Bloodstone,* Putnam, in press. Contributor of about one hundred-fifty short stories to *Cosmopolitan* and other magazines.

WORK IN PROGRESS: A screen version of *Snowbound* for Columbia Pictures; a novel, *The Guilty,* for Random House.

SIDELIGHTS: Pronzini told *CA* he has collected about 3000 copies of pulp magazines, dating from 1915 to 1955, as well as other old books and magazines. He lived in Europe for almost four years, and met his present wife while living on Majorca. *Avocational interests:* All types of sports, old movies, old radio shows.

* * *

PROPES, Steve 1942-

PERSONAL: Born July 21, 1942, in Berkeley, Calif.; son of Clarence Bernard (a writer) and Aileen (a writer; maiden name, Williams) Propes; married Sylvia Theresa Liebi (a free-lance artist), September 11, 1965; children: Heather, Shea. *Education:* California State University, Long Beach, B.A., 1965. *Politics:* Democratic. *Home:* 5338 Hanbury St., Long Beach, Calif. 90808.

CAREER: Rehabilitation counselor; social worker; free-lance writer.

WRITINGS: Those Oldies but Goodies: A Guide to 50's Record Collecting, Macmillan, 1973; *Golden Oldies: A Guide to 60's Record Collecting,* Chilton, 1974.

WORK IN PROGRESS: Further books on record-collecting; fiction.

* * *

PROUTY, Olive Higgins 1882(?)-1974

1882(?)—March 24, 1974; American novelist. Obituaries: *Washington Post,* March 28, 1974; *Newsweek,* April 8, 1974. (*CA*-11/12).

* * *

PUGH, Ellen (Tiffany) 1920-

PERSONAL: Born June 2, 1920, in Cleveland, Ohio; daughter of Clarence Romaine (a railroad man) and Margaret May (Williams) Tiffany; married David Benjamin Pugh (a university administrator), July 3, 1949. *Education:* Western Reserve University (now Case Western Reserve University), A.B., 1943, B.S.L.S., 1945; Northwestern University, M.A., 1947. *Politics:* "Democrat (usually)." *Religion:* Unitarian Universalist. *Home:* Southwest 600 Crestview, Apt. 15, Pullman, Wash. 99163. *Agent:* Ruth Cantor, Room 1005, 156 Fifth Ave., New York, N.Y. 10010. *Office:* Room 120, Holland Library, Washington State University, Pullman, Wash. 99163.

CAREER: Western Reserve University (now Case Western Reserve University), Cleveland, Ohio, cataloger, 1943-45; Northwestern University, Evanston, Ill., cataloger, 1945-47; Cincinnati Public Library, Cincinnati, Ohio, branch librarian, 1955-58; University of Nebraska, Lincoln, order librarian, 1958-63; University of Oregon, Eugene, cataloger, 1963-65; University of Rochester, Rochester, N.Y., cataloger, 1965-68; Washington State University, Pullman, serials librarian, 1969—. *Member:* American Library Association, American Folklore Society, American Society for Psychical Research, Spiritual Frontiers Fellowship, Ananda Marga Yoga, Spokane Writers Guild (vice-president, 1971—).

WRITINGS—Children's books: *Tales from the Welsh Hills,* Dodd, 1968; *Brave His Soul: The Story of Prince Madog of Wales and His Discovery of America in 1170,* Dodd, 1970; *More Tales From the Welsh Hills,* Dodd, 1971.

WORK IN PROGRESS: A book of Welsh castle legends, *There Was A Day;* an Indian legend of the Pacific Northwest; research for a book on Marie Dorion, an Indian woman.

BIOGRAPHICAL/CRITICAL SOURCES: Spokane Chronicle, October 8, 1970; *Pullman Herald,* October 21, 1970; *Spokesman Review,* Spokane, Wash., January 8, 1971.

* * *

PULEO, Nicole
See MILLER, Nicole (Puleo)

* * *

PULGRAM, Ernst 1915-

PERSONAL: Born September 18, 1915, in Vienna, Austria; naturalized U.S. citizen in 1943; son of Sigmund (a businessman) and Gisela (Bauer) Pulgram. *Education:* University of Vienna, Dr.phil., 1938; Harvard University, Ph.D., 1946. *Politics:* Liberal. *Religion:* None. *Home:* 1050 Wall St., Ann Arbor, Mich. 48105. *Office:* Department of Romance Languages, University of Michigan, Ann Arbor, Mich. 48104.

CAREER: Harvard University, Cambridge, Mass., instructor in French, 1944-46; Union College, Schenectady, N.Y., assistant professor of French and German, 1946-48; University of Michigan, Ann Arbor, assistant professor, 1948-51, associate professor, 1951-56, professor of Romance languages and classical linguistics, 1956—. Visiting professor at University of Florence, 1957, University of Cologne, 1970, and University of Heidelberg, 1972. *Military service:* U.S. Army, 1942-44. *Member:* International Linguistic Association, International Society of Phonetic Sciences, Linguistic Society of America. *Awards, honors:* Henry Russell Award from University of Michigan, 1951;

American Council of Learned Societies, fellowship, 1951-52, 1959-60; Guggenheim fellowship, 1954-55, 1962-63.

WRITINGS: *Theory of Names,* University of California Press, 1951; (editor) *Studies Presented to Joshua Whatmough,* Mouton & Co., 1957; *The Tongues of Italy: Prehistory and History,* Harvard University Press, 1958, reprinted, Greenwood Press, 1969; *Introduction to the Spectrography of Speech,* Mouton & Co., 1959; *Syllable, Word, Nexus, Cursus,* Mouton & Co., 1970; *Latin-Romance Phonology: Prosodics and Metrics,* Fink, 1974. Contributor of 90 articles and 60 reviews to journals in his field.

WORK IN PROGRESS: *Latin-Italian Texts and Commentary: 600 B.C. to 1300 A.D.*

* * *

PULITZER, Margaret Leech
See LEECH, Margaret

* * *

PUMROY, Donald K(eith) 1925-

PERSONAL: Born March 28, 1925, in Ottumwa, Iowa; son of Thomas Conrad and Hazel (Brown) Pumroy; married Shirley Spence (a psychologist), September 3, 1949; children: Keith Spence, Patricia Ruth, Nancy Elizabeth. *Education:* University of Iowa, B.A., 1949; University of Wisconsin, M.S., 1951; University of Washington, Seattle, Ph.D., 1954. *Home:* 4006 Oliver St., Hyattsville, Md. 20782. *Office:* School of Education, University of Maryland, College Park, Md. 20742.

CAREER: University of Maryland, College Park, instructor and counselor, 1955-57, assistant professor, 1957-61, associate professor of psychology, 1961-71, associate professor of education, 1967-68, 1969-71, professor of education and psychology, 1971—. Diplomate in clinical psychology, American Board of Examiners in Professional Psychology, 1963; member of Maryland Board of Examiners in Psychology, 1965-67, vice-chairman, 1966-67. Member of advisory council, Maryland Association for Children with Specific Learning Disabilities, 1971—; member of board of directors, Child Care Center, Inc., 1972—. *Military service:* U.S. Army Air Forces, 1943-46; became second lieutenant.

MEMBER: American Psychological Association, American Personnel and Guidance Association, International Council on Education for Teaching, Society for Research in Child Development, Association for the Advancement of Behavior Therapy, National Association of School Psychologists, Society of Behaviorists, Eastern Psychological Association, Maryland Psychological Association (president, 1962-63), Maryland Personnel and Guidance Association, Maryland School Psychology Association.

WRITINGS: (Contributor) Bernard Lubin and E. E. Levitt, *The Clinical Psychologist: Background, Roles, and Functions,* Aldine, 1967; (contributor) Paul McReynolds, editor, *Advances in Psychological Assessment,* Science & Behavior Books, 1971. Contributor of about twenty articles to professional journals.

WORK IN PROGRESS: *The Behavioral Approach for Nursery Preschool Teachers; Modern Childrearing: Behavioral Principles Applied to the Raising of Children,* with wife, Shirley S. Pumroy.

PURCELL, Sally 1944-

PERSONAL: Born December 1, 1944, in Stourport, England; daughter of Robert Joseph and Hilda May (Ingram) Purcell. *Education:* Lady Margaret Hall, Oxford, B.A., 1966, M.A., 1970. *Home:* 19 Crown St., Oxford, England.

CAREER: Has worked as a barmaid, typist, and fruit-picker; currently author, editor, translator.

WRITINGS: *The Devil's Dancing Hour,* Anvil, 1968; (translator) *Provencal Poems,* Carcanet, 1969; (editor with Libby Purves) *The Happy Unicorns,* Sidgwick & Jackson, 1969; (editor) *George Peele,* Carcanet, 1971; *The Holly Queen,* Anvil, 1972; (editor) *Monarchs and the Muse,* Carcanet, 1972; (translator) *The Exile of James Joyce,* David Lewis, 1972; (editor) *The Poems of Charles of Orleans,* Carcanet, 1973; (contributor of translations) Peter Jay, editor, *The Penguin Greek Anthology,* Allen Lane, 1973; *Dark of Day,* Anvil, 1974. Contributor to *New Measure, Carcanet, Isis, Minnesota Review,* and others.

WORK IN PROGRESS: A biography of Charles d'Orleans; research on Saint Robert Southwell and English Tudor Catholic poets generally; a bestiary; a work on alchemy.

SIDELIGHTS: Miss Purcell told *CA:* "Detest most of the 19th and more of the 20th centuries; happiest in the 12th or 16th." She is competent in French, German, Spanish, Italian, Latin, Greek, Mediaeval Provencal, Middle English, Anglo-Saxon, and reads Portuguese.

* * *

PURPEL, David E(dward) 1932-

PERSONAL: Born June 5, 1932, in Cambridge, Mass.; son of I. W. and Sybil (Bergelson) Purpel; married Elaine Ladd (a school secretary), August 28, 1958; children: Mark A., Rachel A., Nancy. *Education:* Tufts University, A.B., 1954; Harvard University, M.A., 1956, Ed.D., 1961. *Home:* 1615 South College Park, Greensboro, N.C. 27403. *Office:* Department of Education, University of North Carolina, Greensboro, N.C. 27412.

CAREER: Teacher of history in Newton, Mass., 1956-57; Harvard University, Boston, Mass., assistant professor, 1961-67, associate professor of education, 1967-72; University of North Carolina, Greensboro, professor of education, and coordinator of field experiences in teacher education, 1972—. Member of board of directors of New Garden Friends School, 1973—. *Member:* Association for Supervision and Curriculum Development.

WRITINGS: (With Ralph Mosher) *Supervision: The Reluctant Profession,* Houghton, 1972; (with Maurice Belanger) *Curriculum and the Cultural Revolution,* McCutchan, 1972. Series editor for McCutchan Publishing Co., 1972—. Contributor to *Journal of Teacher Education* and *Harvard Graduate School of Education Association Bulletin.*

WORK IN PROGRESS: A book on moral education.

* * *

QUINT, Jeanne
See BENOLIEL, Jeanne Quint

* * *

QUITSLUND, Sonya A(ntoinette) 1935-

PERSONAL: Born March 8, 1935, in Portland, Ore.;

daughter of Phelps Garney (a businessman and engineer) and Leona Agnes (Ederer) Quitslund. *Education:* Duchesne College, student, 1953-54; Seattle University, A.B. (magna cum laude), 1958; further study at University of Clermont-Ferrand, 1959-60, and Sorbonne, University of Paris, 1960-61; Catholic University of America, M.A., 1964, Ph.D., 1967. *Religion:* Roman Catholic. *Office:* Department of Religion, George Washington University, Washington, D.C. 20006.

CAREER: Teacher at private school in Seattle, Wash., 1956-57, and public schools in Edmonds, Wash., 1958-59, 1961-63; Catholic University of America, Washington, D.C., instructor in religion, 1964-67; George Washington University, Washington, D.C., assistant professor of religion, 1967—. Member of advisory board on religious education, Catholic Archdiocese of Washington, D.C., 1967-71; member of task force on the liturgy, National Council of Catholic Women, 1969—.

MEMBER: Catholic Biblical Association of America, American Academy of Religion, Catholic Theology Society of America (member of regional board of directors, 1973—; chairperson, 1974—), American Association of University Professors, Women for the Unborn. *Awards, honors:* Fulbright scholar in France, 1959-60; College Theology Society book of the year award, 1973, for *Beauduin: A Prophet Vindicated;* Underwood fellowship, Danforth Foundation, 1974-75.

WRITINGS: Beauduin: A Prophet Vindicated, Paulist-Newman, 1973. Contributor of articles and about forty reviews to Catholic and other periodicals.

WORK IN PROGRESS: Research on the biblical concept of woman and its relevance to emerging woman.

* * *

QUOIREZ, Francoise 1935- (Francoise Sagan)

PERSONAL: Born June 21, 1935, in Cajarc (Lot), France; daughter of Pierre (an industrialist) and Marie (Laubard) Quoirez; married Guy Schoeller, March 13, 1958 (divorced, 1960); married Robert James Westhoff, January 10, 1962 (divorced, 1963); children: Denis. *Education:* Attended Couvent des Oiseaux, Couvent du Sacre Coeur, and Sorbonne, University of Paris. *Residence:* Equemauville, Calvados, France. *Agent:* M. Rene Julliard, 30 rue de l'-Universite, Paris 7e, France.

CAREER: Full-time writer. *Awards, honors:* Prix des Critiques, 1954, for *Bonjour tristesse.*

WRITINGS—Under pseudonym Francoise Sagan; novels: *Bonjour tristesse,* Julliard, 1954, translation by Irene Ash, Dutton, 1955; *Un Certain Sourire,* Julliard, 1956, translation by Anne Green published as *A Certain Smile,* Dutton, 1956; *Dans un mois, dans un an*, Julliard, 1957, translation by Frances Frenaye published as *Those Without Shadows,* Dutton, 1957; *Aimez-vous Brahms?,* Julliard, 1959, translation by Peter Wiles, Dutton, 1960; *Les Merveilleux Nuages,* Julliard, 1961, translation by Anne Green published as *The Wonderful Clouds,* Murray, 1961, Dutton, 1962; *La Chamade,* Julliard, 1965, translation by Robert Westhoff, Dutton, 1966, reissued and edited by Kenneth I. Perry, Prentice-Hall, 1970; *Le Garde du coeur,* Julliard, 1968, translation by Robert Westhoff published as *The Heart Keeper,* Dutton, 1968; *Un peu de soleil dans l'eau froide,* Flammarion, 1969, translation by Terence Kilmartin published as *A Few Hours of Sunlight,* Harper, 1971 (translation by Joanna Kilmartin published in England as *Sunlight on Cold Water,* Weidenfeld & Nicolson, 1971).

Plays: *Chateau en Suede* (comedy; title means "Castle in Sweden"; first produced in Paris at Theatre d'Atelier, March, 1960), Julliard, 1960; *Les Violins parfois* (first produced in Paris at Theatre Gymnase, 1961), Julliard, 1962; *La Robe mauve de Valentine* (first produced at Theatre des Ambassadeurs, 1963), Julliard, 1963; *Bonheur, impair, et passe,* Julliard, 1964; *Le Cheval evanoui* [and] *L'Echarde* (title means "The Fainted Horse" [and] "The Splinter"; first produced together in Paris at Theatre Gymnase, September, 1966), Julliard, 1966; *Un Piano dans l'herbe* (two-act comedy; title means "A Piano in the Grass"; first produced in Paris at Theatre d'Atelier, October 15, 1970), Flammarion, 1970.

Other: *Toxique* (autobiographical fragments; illustrated by Bernard Buffet), Julliard, 1964, translation by Frances Frenaye, Dutton, 1964; (author of text with Federico Fellini) Wingate Paine, photographer, *Mirror of Venus,* Random House, 1966.

Filmscripts: "Dans un mois, dans un an" (based on her novel); (with Claude Chabrol) "Landru"; (with Alain Cavalier) "La Chamade" (based on her novel), co-produced by Les Films Ariane, Les Productions and Artistes Associes, and P.E.A. (Rome), 1969; (co-author, with Philippe Grumbach, of dialogue) "Le Bal du Comte d'Orgel" (based on the novel by Raymond Radiguet), produced by Les Films Marceau-Cocinor, 1970.

Co-author, with Michael Magne, of scenario for ballet "Le Rendez-vous manque" (title means "The Broken Date"), first produced in Monte Carlo, January, 1958; author of commentary for a volume of photographs of New York City; writer of lyrics for singer Juliette Greco.

SIDELIGHTS: Praising *La Chamade* as one of Sagan's best novels, a *Time* reviewer has called the author "a precise miniaturist" and "a Gallic Maugham who knows instinctively how deep to probe, what not to say, and when to quit. Her swift vignettes, like Maugham's, are the product of a far more complex and searching intelligence than cold type exposes, and her novels are like fragile sand dollars—elegant, delicate designs." Andre Maurois once described Sagan's style as sober, elliptical, and with a tone befitting our times. "If Sagan's tone—knowing, world-weary, unemotional—has remained constant over the years," writes a *Time* reviewer, "so has her devotion to the single theme of the interaction of youth and age." "The confrontation of young and old in my plays, just as in my books, is something more than a device," she says: "The older one is always the fixed element faced with someone who is still searching for himself. Besides, people who have aged well are often more interesting than younger ones. They know something about life the others still ignore."

Several critics have named Sagan spokesman for disillusioned French youth, whose mood, like the moods of many of her characters, is one of skepticism, boredom, and aimlessness. She is said to admire the writing of Proust and Stendhal. In an interview with Blair Fuller and Robert Silvers she described her own writing: "For me writing is a question of finding a certain rhythm. I compare it to the rhythms of jazz. Much of the time life is a sort of rhythmic progression of three characters. If one tells oneself that life is like that, one feels it less arbitrary. . . . I don't search for exactitude in portraying people. I try to give to imaginary people a kind of veracity. Art should not, it seems to me, pose the 'real' as preoccupation. Nothing is more unreal than certain so-called 'realist' novels—they're nightmares. It is possible to achieve in a novel a certain sensory truth—the true feeling of a character—that is all. Of course the illusion of art is to make one believe that great literature is very close to life, but exactly the opposite is true. Life is amorphous, literature is formal."

"Bonjour tristesse" was filmed by Columbia Pictures in 1958; "A Certain Smile" was filmed by Twentieth Century-Fox in 1958; *Aimez-vous Brahms?* was produced as "Goodbye Again" by United Artists, 1961. *Bonjour tristesse* has been translated into over twenty languages.

BIOGRAPHICAL/CRITICAL SOURCES: Malcolm Cowley, editor, *Writers at Work,* Viking, 1958; *Holiday,* January, 1969; *Contemporary Literary Criticism,* Volume III, Gale, 1974.

* * *

RABE, Berniece (Louise) 1928-

PERSONAL: Surname rhymes with "Abe"; born January 11, 1928, in Parma, Mo.; daughter of Grover Cleveland (a farmer) and Martha (Green) Bagby; married Walter Henry Rabe (vice-president of Precision Diamond Tool Co.), July 30, 1946; children: Alan Walter, Brian Cleve, Clay Victor, Dari Mari. *Education:* National College of Education, B.A., 1963; graduate study at Northern Illinois University and at Roosevelt University. *Religion:* Church of Jesus Christ of Latter-Day Saints (Mormon). *Home:* 860 Willow Lane, Sleepy Hollow, Ill. 60118. *Agent:* Patricia S. Myrer, McIntosh & Otis, Inc., 18 East 41st St., New York, N.Y. 10017.

CAREER: Model with Patricia Stevens Model Agency, Chicago, Ill., 1945-46; teacher and tutor in special education classes, Elgin, Ill., 1963-67. Teacher-trainer with Chicago Stake of Church of Jesus Christ of Latter-Day Saints. *Member:* Fox Valley Writers (member of executive board), Off-Campus Writers (member of executive board). *Awards, honors:* Novel awards at Indiana University Writers' Conference and Judson Writers' Conference for manuscript of *Rass;* a chapter of *Rass* received first prize for short story in Chicago Fine Arts competition.

WRITINGS: Rass (juvenile novel), Nelson, 1973. Contributor of stories to children's magazines.

WORK IN PROGRESS: Two picture books; three juvenile novels, *Secret Teacher, Secret of Strongbox,* and *Naomi.*

* * *

RABIN, Edward H(arold) 1937-

PERSONAL: Born March 6, 1937, in New York, N.Y.; son of George (in insurance business) and Flora (a teacher; maiden name, Guttman) Rabin; married Jane Hurwitz (a musician); children: Daniel, Rebecca. *Education:* Columbia University, A.B., 1956, LL.B., 1959. *Politics:* Democrat. *Religion:* Jewish. *Home:* 619 Barbera Pl., Davis, Calif. 95616. *Office:* School of Law, University of California, Davis, Calif. 95616.

CAREER: Lawyer in New York, N.Y., 1959-63; Rutgers University, Camden, N.J., assistant professor of law, 1963-66; University of California, Davis, acting professor, 1966-67, professor of law, 1967—. Visiting professor at University of Texas, University of North Carolina, and Duke University. Acting city attorney in Davis, Calif., 1973. *Member:* California Bar Association, New York Bar Association, Yolo County Bar Association.

WRITINGS: Problems in Real Property, with teacher's manual, Foundation Press, 1969; *Fundamentals of Modern Real Property Law,* with teacher's manual, Foundation Press, 1974; (editor with Mortimer Schwartz) *The Pollution Crisis,* Oceana, Volume I, 1972, Volume II, in press. Contributor to law reviews.

WORK IN PROGRESS: Research on land use planning and control.

SIDELIGHTS: Rabin writes: "I plan to spend part of 1975 and 1976 in Israel where I will be doing a comparative study of Israeli and American law pertaining to land use controls."

* * *

RABKIN, Eric S. 1946-

PERSONAL: Born March 8, 1946, in Queens, N.Y.; son of Joseph (a manufacturer) and Annette (Schwartz) Rabkin; married Elizabeth Jane Backer, July 1, 1967; children: David Ivan. *Education:* Cornell University, A.B., 1967; University of Iowa, Ph.D., 1970. *Home:* 1432 White St., Ann Arbor, Mich. 48104. *Office:* Department of English, University of Michigan, Ann Arbor, Mich. 48104.

CAREER: University of Michigan, Ann Arbor, assistant professor, 1970-74, associate professor of English, 1974—. *Member:* Modern Language Association of America, Popular Culture Association, Midwest Modern Language Association. *Awards, honors:* Fellowship from American Council of Learned Societies, 1973.

WRITINGS: Narrative Suspense: "When Slim turned sideways...", University of Michigan Press, 1973; (with David Hayman) *Form in Fiction,* St. Martin's, 1974.

WORK IN PROGRESS: Escapes from Victorianism (tentative title), an exploration of the importance of fantasy in art.

* * *

RADBILL, Samuel X. 1901-

PERSONAL: Born June 15, 1901, in Philadelphia, Pa.; son of Abraham and Fanny (Gordon) Radbill; married Frances Hoffman, December 26, 1925; children: Gloria Rae Radbill Hamilton, Estelle Kitty (Mrs. David Berley). *Education:* University of Pennsylvania, M.D., 1924. *Politics:* Republican. *Religion:* Jewish. *Home:* 224 Welsh Terr., Merion, Pa. 19066. *Office:* 7043 Elmwood Ave., Philadelphia, Pa. 19142.

CAREER: Private practice of pediatrics in Philadelphia, Pa., 1925—; University of Pennsylvania, Graduate School of Medicine, Philadelphia, lecturer in history of pediatrics, 1954-72. Staff member of Children's Hospital of Philadelphia, 1925—, and Philadelphia General Hospital, 1940—. *Military service:* U.S. Army, Medical Corps, 1942-46; became major. *Member:* International Association for the History of Medicine, American Association for the History of Medicine (secretary, 1953-56), American Academy of Pediatrics (fellow), American Medical Association, American Association of Bookplate Collectors and Designers, Pennsylvania Medical Society, Philadelphia County Medical Association (vice-president, 1967-68), College of Physicians of Philadelphia (honorary librarian, 1974).

WRITINGS: Twenty-five Years After: The Class of 1924, School of Medicine, University of Pennsylvania in 1949, University of Pennsylvania, 1949; *Bookplates of Philadelphia Physicians,* American Association of Bookplate

Collectors and Designers, 1950; *Bibliography of Medical Ex Libris Literature,* Hilprand Press, 1951; (editor and author of introduction) *The Autobiographical Ana of Robley Dunglison,* American Philosophical Society, 1963; (contributor) Ray E. Kelfer and C. Henry Kempe, editors, *The Battered Child,* University of Chicago Press, 1968. Contributor to *Dictionary of Scientific Biography;* contributor of about seventy articles to journals.

WORK IN PROGRESS: History of Pediatrics; articles on medical symbolism and pediatric folklore.

* * *

RADCLIFF, Alan L(awrence) 1920-

PERSONAL: Surname legally changed, 1959; born May 27, 1920, in New York, N.Y.; son of Benjamin (a builder) and Molly (Kirman) Rachleff; married Barbara B. Brown (an art museum conservator and chief of graphic research), August 29, 1959; children: Jonathan B., Bennett J. *Education:* Cornell University, B.A., 1941, M.A., 1942. *Home:* 3341 Poinciana, Coconut Grove, Fla. 33133.

CAREER: Duane Jones Co., New York, N.Y., marketing director, 1951-53; Alan Radcliff Co., New York, N.Y., president, 1953-55; Top Value Enterprises, Dayton, Ohio, regional director, 1955-57; Airguide Corp., Miami, Fla., founder, 1957, president, 1957-71; retired, 1971. Founder and president, Friends of the Theatre and Friends of the Playhouse, Miami; chairman of board of trustees, Players Civic repertory Theatre, Miami; member of board of directors, Lowe Art Museum, 1972—; vice president, Museum of Science, 1974—; chairman of Miami Bicentennial Celebration historical pageant and member of executive committee, Third Century; chairman of art review panel, annual fund-raising auction, Channel 2. *Military service:* U.S. Army Air Forces, 1942-46. *Member:* Antique Automobile Club of America, Rolls-Royce Owners' Club, A-C-D Club, Viscayas, Society of Founders (University of Miami), Alpha Psi Omega. *Awards, honors:* National first prize, Antique Automobile Club of America, 1972; named Outstanding Citizen of Dade County, 1973; Governor's Award for the Fine Arts, State of Florida, 1974.

WRITINGS: Adventures of a Vintage Car Collector, E. A. Seemann Publishing, 1972. Contributor to *Advertising Age, Printers' Ink,* and *Premium Practice.*

WORK IN PROGRESS: A novel, *A Time for Images,* first of a projected trilogy; an essay, "My Son, the Dog."

AVOCATIONAL INTERESTS: Sailing, painting in oils, photography, theater work, travel in Europe.

BIOGRAPHICAL/CRITICAL SOURCES: Miami Herald, November 19, 1972; *Miami Magazine,* February, 1973, May, 1974.

* * *

RADNER, Roy 1927-

PERSONAL: Born June 29, 1927, in Chicago, Ill.; son of Samuel and Ella (Kulansky) Radner; married Virginia Honoski, July 26, 1949; children: Hilary, Erica, Amy, Ephraim. *Education:* University of Chicago, Ph.B. (with honors), 1945, B.S., 1950, M.S., 1951, Ph.D., 1956. *Home:* 2275 Eunice St., Berkeley, Calif. 94709. *Office:* Department of Economics, University of California, Berkeley, Calif. 94720.

CAREER: University of Chicago, Chicago, Ill., assistant professor of economics, 1954-55; Yale University, New Haven, Conn., assistant professor of economics and member of staff of Cowles Foundation for Research in Economics, 1955-57; University of California, Berkeley, associate professor, 1957-61, professor of economics and statistics, 1961—, chairman of department of economics, 1965-69. Fellow of Center for Advanced Study in the Behavioral Sciences, 1955-56; member of economic advisory panel of National Science Foundation, 1963-65; member of technical advisory committee of Carnegie Commission on the Future of Higher Education, 1967-73; member of mathematical social science board of Social Science Research Council, 1970-74; member of Committee on Econometrics and Mathematical Economics of National Bureau of Economic Research, 1971—; member of advisory committee on economics of education of National Academy of Education, 1972-73; member of National Research Council, National Academy of Science, 1972—. Consultant to RAND Corp., National Academy of Science, Boeing Airplane Co., Systems Development Corp., Carnegie Commission, and Kaiser Foundation. *Military service:* U.S. Army, 1945-47.

MEMBER: American Economic Association, Econometric Society (fellow; vice-president, 1971-72; president, 1972-73), Institute of Mathematical Statistics, American Statistical Association, Institute of Management Sciences (vice-president, 1962-65), American Association for the Advancement of Science, American Academy of Arts and Sciences (fellow), American Association of University Professors, Phi Beta Kappa. *Awards, honors:* Guggenheim fellowships for study of mathematical theory of organization, 1961-62, and for research on resource allocation planning and decentralization, 1965-66; overseas fellow of Churchill College, Cambridge, 1969-70.

WRITINGS: Notes on the Theory of Economic Planning, Center for Economic Research (Athens, Greece), 1963; (with D. W. Jorgenson and J. J. McCall) *Optimal Replacement Policy,* Rand McNally, 1967; (with C. B. McGuire) *Decision and Organization,* North-Holland Publishing, 1972; (with Jacob Marshak) *Economic Theory of Teams,* Cowles Foundation and Yale University Press, 1972; (with L. S. Miller) *Demand and Supply in U.S. Higher Education,* Carnegie Commission on Higher Education and McGraw, in press.

Contributor: K. J. Arrow, S. Karlin, and H. Scarf, editors, *Studies in Applied Probability and Management Science,* Stanford University Press, 1963; M. O. L. Bacharach and E. Malinvaud, editors, *Activity Analysis in the Theory of Growth and Planning,* Macmillan (London), 1967; G. Bruckman and W. Weber, editors, *Contributions to the von Neumann Growth Model,* Springer-Verlag, 1971; A. V. Balakrishnan, editor, *Techniques of Optimization,* Academic Press, 1972; R. A. Day, editor, *Mathematical Topics in Economic Theory and Computation,* SIAM Publications, 1972; M. D. Intriligator and D. A. Kendrick, editors, *Frontiers of Quantitative Economics,* Volume II, North-Holland Publishing, in press; M. Bornstein, editor, *Economic Planning: East and West,* University of Michigan Press, in press.

Contributor of about thirty articles and reviews to mathematics and economics journals, including *Bell Journal of Economics and Management Science, Econometrica, Journal of Economic Theory, American Economic Review, Review of Economic Studies,* and *International Economic Review.* Associate editor of *Management Science,* 1959-70, *Econometrica,* 1961-68, and *Journal of Economic Theory,* 1968—; member of advisory board of *Journal of Mathemat-*

ical Economics, 1973—; consultant to *Mathematica*, 1956-66.

WORK IN PROGRESS: Research on capital accumulation under uncertainty, on organization theory, and on economics of higher education.

* * *

RAINEY, Patricia Ann 1937-

PERSONAL: Born October 14, 1937, in Dover, N.H.; daughter of Wilbur Robert and Helen Mary (Keddy) Rainey. *Education:* University of New Hampshire, B.A., 1960, M.Ed., 1967; graduate study at University of Maine, 1967, George Peabody College for Teachers, 1968, and University of New Hampshire, 1972—. *Politics:* Democrat. *Religion:* Baptist. *Home:* 173 Mt. Vernon St., Dover, N.H. 03820.

CAREER: Colebrook Academy, Colebrook, N.H., social studies teacher, 1961-65; high school counselor in Exeter, N.H., 1965-66 (part-time), and Newport, N.H., 1966-68; Cleveland State Community College, Cleveland, Tenn., assistant professor of psychology, 1968-72.

WRITINGS: *Illusions: A Journey into Perception* (partly self-illustrated), Linnet Books, 1973. Contributor to *Saturday Review, Creative Teacher,* and *Today's Education.*

WORK IN PROGRESS: Research in music therapy; a book, *Death: An Adventure in Eternity* (tentative title).

* * *

RAINSFORD, George Nichols 1928-

PERSONAL: Born June 27, 1928, in New York, N.Y.; son of W. Kerr and Christine (Nichols) Rainsford; married Jean Wedmore, September 23, 1953; children: Guy, Amy, Anne, Angela, Emily. *Education:* Williams College, student, 1946-47; University of Colorado, B.A. (cum laude), 1950; London School of Economics and Political Science, further study, 1950-51; Yale University, LL.B., 1954; University of Denver, M.A., 1963; Stanford University, Ph.D., 1967. *Office:* Kalamazoo College, Kalamazoo, Mich. 49001.

CAREER: Holme, Roberts, More & Owen (law firm), Denver, Colo., associate lawyer, 1954-56; University of Denver, Denver, Colo., director of development, 1956-63; University of Washington, Seattle, Ellis L. Phillips Foundation intern, serving as assistant to president, 1963-64; University of Denver, assistant professor of history and law and associate dean of College of Arts and Sciences, 1967-69, associate professor of history and assistant to president, 1969-71; Kalamazoo College, Kalamazoo, Mich., president and professor of history, 1972—. Trustee of Colorado Outward Bound School and Graduate Theological Union, Berkeley.

MEMBER: American Academy of Political and Social Science, American Historical Association, American Association for Higher Education, American Association of University Professors, Great Lakes Colleges Association (secretary-treasurer, 1972-74), Phi Gamma Mu, Phi Alpha Theta, Phi Delta Phi, Theta Delta Chi, Economic Club (Detroit).

WRITINGS: *Congress and Higher Education in the 19th Century,* University of Tennessee Press, 1972. Contributor to education, business, and historical periodicals.

* * *

RALBOVSKY, Martin Paul 1942-

PERSONAL: Surname is accented on second syllable; born December 21, 1942, in Schenectady, N.Y.; son of Anthony and Mary (Trela) Ralbovsky; married Susan Schermerhorn, April 7, 1967; children: Kevin, Andrea. *Education:* Attended public high school in Rotterdam, N.Y. *Politics:* "Marxist-Leninist, with no place to go." *Religion:* None. *Residence:* Closter, N.J.

CAREER: *Schenectady Union-Star,* Schenectady, N.Y., sports writer, 1959-61, assistant sports editor and columnist, 1961-68; Newspaper Enterprise Association, Cleveland, Ohio, syndicated writer in Cleveland, Ohio, 1968-69, and New York, N.Y., 1969-71; *New York Times,* New York, N.Y., sports writer, 1971-72; writer, 1972—. *Military service:* U.S. Army Reserve, 1964-70.

WRITINGS: *Super Bowl: The Illustrated History,* Hawthorn, 1971; *Destiny's Darlings: A World Championship Little League Team Twenty Years Later* (non-fiction), Hawthorn, 1974; *Lords of the Locker Room: The American Way of Coaching and Its Effect on Youth,* Peter H. Wyden, 1974. Work is anthologized in *Best Sports Stories: 1970,* edited by Edward Ehre and Irving Marsh, Dutton, 1970. Contributor to sports magazines and other periodicals, including *New York* (magazine), *TV Guide, Sport* (magazine), and *Atlantic Monthly.*

WORK IN PROGRESS: A biography of Robert (Evel) Knievel, the motorcycle daredevil; *The Nuclear Athlete,* non-fiction about the "robotization" process in American sports.

SIDELIGHTS: Ralbovsky writes: "I have seen the dark side of life, and the dark side of American sports particularly. With most of the established media people taking a Pollyanna view of the entire sports syndrome in America, I feel I have an obligation to write about the reverse side of things. My concerns are the fourteen-year-old kids who drop dead at high school football practices that are held in ninety-five-degree heat; the twelve-year-old kids who are turned into ugly little eunuchs while pursuing Little League world championships; the untold thousands of kids who are brainwashed annually by coaches into thinking that there is something very American chic about success in sports. Somebody, too, has to question whether or not the manufactured violence in sports contributes to this society's acceptance of real violence as being a commonplace thing. That's what I do, lonely voice in the night that I am."

* * *

RALSTON, James Kenneth 1896-

PERSONAL: Born March 31, 1896, in Choteau, Mont.; son of William R. and Ellen (Mathewson) Ralston; married Willo Arthaud, June, 1923; children: Willo Marjorie (Mrs. C. L. Walter), Lloyd Kenneth. *Education:* Studied at Art Institute of Chicago, 1918-21. *Politics:* Independent. *Religion:* Congregationalist. *Home and studio:* 2103 Alderson Ave., Billings, Mont. 59102.

CAREER: Cowboy in early years; professional artist and illustrator, specializing, since the 1920's, in the historical West. Paintings and murals are exhibited at Whitney Gallery of Western Art, Montana Historical Society Museum, Jefferson National Expansion Memorial in St. Louis, Custer Battlefield National Monument, and other museums and historical sites. *Military service:* U.S. Army, Infantry, 1918. *Member:* Montana Historical Society, Sons and Daughters of Montana Pioneers, Eastern Montana Pioneers, Veterans of World War I, Range Riders (Miles City, Mont.). *Awards, honors:* Member of National

Cowboy Hall of Fame; D.F.A., Rocky Mountain College, 1971.

WRITINGS: (Self-illustrated) *Rhymes of a Cowboy,* Rimrock, 1969.

BIOGRAPHICAL/CRITICAL SOURCES: Edward M. Ainsworth, *The Cowboy in Art,* World Publishing, 1968.

* * *

RALSTON, Melvin B. 1937-

PERSONAL: Born June 27, 1937, in Pueblo, Colo.; son of Melvin B. (a shoe store owner) and Mary Elizabeth (Sease) Ralston; married Judith Ann Ayers, January 13, 1962 (divorced, 1972); married Kathryn Ann Hobbs, August 5, 1973; children: Debra Kay, Darcy Danylle. *Education:* Ottawa University, B.A.; Kansas State Teachers College, M.A. *Home address:* R.R. #1, Box 16, Leon, Kan. 67074. *Office:* National Cash Register Co., 37th N. and Rock Rd., Wichita, Kan. 67226.

CAREER: Butler County Community Junior College, El Dorado, Kan., instructor in English, 1967-73; National Cash Register Co., Wichita, Kan., master scheduler, 1974—.

WRITINGS: Emblems of Reality, Glencoe Press, 1973.

* * *

RAMP, Eugene A(ugust) 1942-

PERSONAL: Born September 13, 1942, in Michigan; son of August V. and Irma V. Ramp. *Education:* Western Michigan University, B.A., 1966, M.A., 1968; University of Kansas, Ph.D., 1972. *Home:* 431 East 19th St., Lawrence, Kan. 66044. *Office:* Department of Human Development, University of Kansas, Lawrence, Kan. 66045.

CAREER: Veterans Administration Hospital, Battle Creek, Mich., clinical psychologist, 1967-69; University of Kansas, Lawrence, instructor, 1970, assistant professor of human development, 1972—, advisor for Behavior Analysis Model of Project Follow Through, 1969-74, co-director of Support and Development Center for Follow Through, 1974—. Adjunct adviser to University without Walls, 1972—. Member of board of directors of Foundation for Creative Education, 1973—; member of New York State Advisory Council for Follow Through Technical Assistant Program, 1973—. Technical director of films: "Teaching with Tokens"; "Behavior Analysis Classrooms." Director of workshops; consultant. *Member:* American Psychological Association, American Association for the Advancement of Science.

WRITINGS: (Editor with Bill L. Hopkins) *A New Direction for Education: Behavior Analysis, 1971,* University of Kansas, 1971; (editor with George Semb) *Behavior Analysis: Areas of Research and Application,* Prentice-Hall, in press.

Films: "Behavior Analysis Classrooms," Bureau of Visual Instruction, University of Kansas, 1970; "Teaching with Tokens," Bureau of Visual Instruction, University of Kansas, 1970; (with Drew Moniot) "Behavior Analysis Presents: A New Direction for Education, "Department of Human Development, University of Kansas, 1973; (with Charles Bemis) "Monitoring and Quality Control in Education," Department of Human Development, University of Kansas, 1973. Contributor to *Journal of Applied Behavioral Analysis.*

RAMSEY, John F(raser) 1907-

PERSONAL: Born December 17, 1907, in Lawrence, Kan.; son of Joseph Reeves and Della (Frazer) Ramsey. *Education:* University of California, Berkeley, A.B., 1931, M.A., 1932, Ph.D., 1935. *Home:* 20½ Audubon Pl., Tuscaloosa, Ala. 35401. *Office:* Department of History, University of Alabama, Tuscaloosa, Ala. 35486.

CAREER: University of Alabama, Tuscaloosa, instructor, 1935-37, assistant professor, 1937-45, associate professor, 1945-47, professor of European history, 1947—, head of department, 1971—. U.S. Government, coordinator of war training program at Washington State University, 1943-44, senior historian, Air Staff Intelligence, Department of War, 1944-45. *Member:* American Historical Association, American Association of University Professors, Alabama Council for the Social Studies (president, 1960-62; executive secretary, 1962-66), Phi Beta Kappa, Phi Alpha Theta, Phi Kappa Psi. *Awards, honors:* Algernon Sydney Sullivan Award, 1964; Carleton K. Butler Award of Alabama chapter of Theta Chi, 1973, for university service.

WRITINGS: Anglo-French Relations, 1763-1770: A Study of Choiseul's Foreign Policy, University of California Press, 1939; (editor with others and contributor) *Studies in Modern European History in Honor of Franklin Charles Palm,* Bookman Associates, 1956; *Spain: The Rise of the First World Power,* University of Alabama Press, 1973.

AVOCATIONAL INTERESTS: "Anything connected with classical music"; collecting records and books.

* * *

RAND, James S.
See ATTENBOROUGH, Bernard George

* * *

RANDOLPH, David James 1934-

PERSONAL: Born May 13, 1934, in Elkton, Md.; son of David James and Elsie (Lloyd) Randolph; married Juanita Fenby, June 16, 1957; children: David James III, Tracey Anne. *Education:* University of Delaware, B.A., 1956; Drew University, M.Div., 1959; Boston University, Ph.D., 1962. *Home:* 854 Rodney Dr., Nashville, Tenn. 37205. *Office:* Director, Worship and the Arts, Board of Discipleship, United Methodist Church, 1908 Grand Ave., Nashville, Tenn. 37203.

CAREER: Methodist minister in Wilmington, Del., 1957-60, Lowell, Mass., 1960-62, and Wilmington, Del., 1962-63; Drew University, School of Theology, Madison, N.J., assistant professor of homiletics and pastoral ministry, 1963-68; United Methodist Church, Nashville, Tenn., director of department of new life ministries, 1968-70, assistant general secretary, 1970-72, assistant general secretary, General Board of Discipleship, 1972—. Lecturer in theology at Vanderbilt University, 1973. U.S. director of Salvation Today study for National Council of Churches. *Member:* Academy of Homiletics (president, 1968-69), Theological Institute (Oxford, England).

WRITINGS: (Author of introduction) Gerhard Ebeling, *On Prayer,* Fortress, 1966; *Baptism: Historical, Theological and Practical Considerations,* Abingdon, 1968; *The Renewal of Preaching,* Fortress, 1969; *God's Parade,* Tidings, 1974; *God's Party: A Guide to New Forms of Worship,* Abingdon, in press.

Editor and contributor: *Faith Alive,* Tidings, 1969; *Ven-*

tures in Worship, Abingdon, Book I, 1969, Book II, 1970, Book III, 1973; (and author of accompanying film script) *The Swinging Church: Christian Mission in Leisure Revolution,* Tidings, 1971; (with Bill Garrett) *Ventures in Song,* Abingdon, 1972; *Peace Plus,* Tidings, 1974. Contributor to denominational and other periodicals.

WORK IN PROGRESS: The Search for Salvation and *Ventures in Faith.*

SIDELIGHTS: Randolph is "attempting to develop theology through images, or a theology of the imagination, which will crack the crust of custom and release the living springs of faith....Celebrations—secular and religious—are the nexus for these concerns, and I expect to be at work in this area for time to come. I believe deeply that the basic issue today is not religion, or politics, or education, but life. Can man survive with significance?"

* * *

RANKINE, John
See MASON, Douglas R(ankine)

* * *

RANSOM, John Crowe 1888-1974

April 30, 1888—July 3, 1974; American poet, educator, and founder and editor of the *Kenyon Review.* Obituaries: *New York Times,* July 4, 1974; *Washington Post,* July 5, 1974; *Time,* July 15, 1974; *Newsweek,* July 15, 1974; *Publishers Weekly,* July 29, 1974. (*CA*-7/8).

* * *

RAPHAEL, Phyllis 1938-

PERSONAL: Born May 22, 1938, in New York, N.Y.; daughter of Samuel and Rose (Beck) Raphael; married Robert Chartoff (a film producer), December 23, 1957 (divorced, 1970); children: Jenifer, Billy, Julie Raphael. *Education:* Barnard College, A.B., 1957. *Home:* 390 West End Ave., New York, N.Y. 10024. *Agent:* Helen Brann, 14 Sutton Place South, New York, N.Y. 10022.

CAREER: Actress; novelist, journalist.

WRITINGS: They Got What They Wanted (novel), Norton, 1972. Contributor to *Village Voice.*

WORK IN PROGRESS: A novel.

* * *

RAYGOR, Alton Lamon 1922-

PERSONAL: Born November 5, 1922, in Erie, Pa.; son of Elmer Ellsworth and Twila (London) Raygor; married Betty Ruth Muntz, July 8, 1944; children: Robin Douglas, Diana Jeanne, Richard Nelson. *Education:* University of Toledo, B.A., 1948; University of Michigan, M.A., 1951, Ph.D., 1957. *Office:* 101 Eddy Hall, University of Minnesota, Minneapolis, Minn. 55455.

CAREER: University of Michigan, Ann Arbor, resident house director of International House, 1951-53; University of Minnesota, Minneapolis, instructor, 1955-57, assistant professor, 1957-59, associate professor, 1959-64, professor of educational psychology, 1964—, coordinator of reading and study skills center, Student Counseling Bureau, 1959—. Visiting lecturer at University of Chicago, Rutgers University, University of Manitoba, University of Montana, and other institutions. Member of advisory board, U.S. Office of Education Clearinghouse for Information on Reading; director of consulting services, Reading Research Service, Inc. *Military service:* U.S. Army Air Forces, 1942-45.

MEMBER: International Reading Association, National Reading Conference (member of board of directors, 1961-63; vice-president, 1966-68; president, 1968-70), American Personnel and Guidance Association, American Psychological Association, American Educational Research Association, Psychonomic Society, North Central Reading Association (treasurer, 1963-64), Minnesota Reading Association (president, 1957-59; member of board, 1959-68), Minnesota Education Association, Minnesota Psychological Association, Psi Chi, Phi Alpha Theta, Phi Delta Kappa.

WRITINGS: (Contributor) *College-Adult Reading Instruction,* International Reading Association, 1964; (contributor) Harry Rivlin and others, editors, *Background for College Success,* Golenpaul, 1964; (contributor) Rivlin, editor, *The First Years of College,* Houghton, 1965; *Reading for the Main Idea,* McGraw, 1970; *Reading for Significant Facts,* McGraw, 1970; (with George B. Schick) *Reading at Efficient Rates,* McGraw, 1970; (with David M. Wark) *Systems for Study,* McGraw, 1970; *Study-Type Reading Kit,* McGraw, Book I: *Natural Sciences,* 1970, Book II: *Social Science and Humanities,* 1970.

Editor of seventeen texts in reading and other skills, and author or editor of various tests published by McGraw, 1970. Editor, *Yearbook* of North Central Reading Association, 1962-63, and contributor to numerous yearbooks and proceedings of reading conferences. Contributor to reading, counseling, and psychology journals. Formerly member of editorial advisory board, *Journal of Developmental Reading, Journal of Reading, Reading Research Quarterly,* and *Journal of Reading Improvement;* currently member of editorial advisory board, *Journal of Reading Behavior.*

* * *

RAYMOND, Steve 1940-

PERSONAL: Born July 7, 1940, in Bellingham, Wash.; son of Frederick R. (career officer in U.S. Army) and Grace A. (Reeder) Raymond; married Joan Zimmerman, August 17, 1963; children: Stephanie, Randy. *Education:* University of Washington, Seattle, B.A., 1962. *Home:* 4500 Beach Dr. S.W., Seattle, Wash. 98116. *Office: Seattle Times,* P.O. Box 70, Seattle, Wash. 98111.

CAREER: Seattle Times, Seattle, Wash., assistant city editor, 1967—. Trustee of Museum of American Fly Fishing, 1972—. *Military service:* U.S. Navy Reserve, 1962-70; became lieutenant commander. *Member:* Federation of Fly Fisherman (secretary, 1970-71; member of board of directors, 1970—), Outdoor Writers Association of America, Lambda Chi Alpha.

WRITINGS: Kamloops: An Angler's Study of the Kamloops Trout, Winchester Press, 1971; *The Year of the Angler,* Winchester Press, 1973. Contributor to *Seattle Times Sunday Magazine* and to outdoor magazines.

AVOCATIONAL INTERESTS: Conservation.

* * *

REAGAN, Michael D(aniel) 1927-

PERSONAL: Born March 12, 1927, in New York, N.Y.; son of Oliver Edward (an architect) and Katherine (Wagner) Reagan; married wife, Vera H., June 23, 1951 (divorced March 8, 1970); married Celeste Mellom Schleen, March 21, 1970; children: Deborah S., Kevin M., Timothy A. *Education:* College of the Holy Cross, A.B. (cum laude), 1948; Princeton University, M.A., 1956, Ph.D., 1959. *Home:* 2515 Horace St., Riverside, Calif. 92506. *Office:* College of Social and Behavioral Science, University of California, Riverside, Riverside, Calif. 92502.

CAREER: Various work with book publishing firms, 1948-53; Princeton University, Princeton, N.J., instructor in political science, 1955-56; Williams College, Williamstown, Mass., teaching intern, 1956-57, instructor in political science, 1956-59, lecturer, 1959-60; Princeton University, visiting assistant professor of politics, 1960-61; Syracuse University, Syracuse, N.Y., assistant professor, 1961-63, associate professor of political science, 1963-64; University of California, Riverside, professor of political science, 1964—, head of department, 1971-73, director of Center for Social and Behavioral Science Research, 1972—, dean of College of Social and Behavioral Science, 1973—. *Military service:* U.S. Marine Corps Reserve, active duty, 1945-46, 1950-61; became staff sergeant. *Member:* American Political Science Association, American Society for Public Administration. *Awards, honors:* Social Science Research Council and National Science Foundation research grants, 1967-68.

WRITINGS: *The Managed Economy,* Oxford University Press, 1963; (editor) *Politics, Economics and the General Welfare,* Scott, Foresman, 1965; (editor) *The Administration of Public Policy,* Scott, Foresman, 1969; *Science and the Federal Patron,* Oxford University Press, 1969; *The New Federalism,* Oxford University Press, 1972. Contributor to political science journals, and to *Harvard Business Review, Science, Nation, New Republic,* and *Challenge.*

WORK IN PROGRESS: Research on intergovernmental relations and revenue sharing.

* * *

REAGEN, Edward P(aul) 1924-

PERSONAL: Born November 4, 1924, in Girard, Ohio; son of Paul J. (a lawyer) and Regina (Cullen) Reagen; married Lillian Ann Hura (an assistant librarian); children: Margaret Ann. *Education:* Western Reserve University (now Case Western Reserve University), A.B., 1949, A.M., 1950; Indiana University, Ph.D., 1957. *Home:* R. D. 1, Nelson Ave., Saratoga Springs, N.Y. 12866. *Office:* Department of Economics, Skidmore College, Saratoga Springs, N.Y. 12866.

CAREER: Washington and Jefferson College, Washington, Pa., assistant professor of economics, 1956-60; Skidmore College, Saratoga Springs, N.Y., associate professor, 1960-69, professor of economics, 1969—. *Military service:* U.S. Army Air Forces, navigator, 1943-46; became first lieutenant. *Member:* American Economic Association, American Association of University Professors. *Awards, honors:* Ford Foundation faculty fellow at Princeton University, 1961; Fulbright fellow in Taiwan, 1962.

WRITINGS: *Fiscal Problems and Economic Growth,* University of Pittsburgh Press, 1960; *Comparative Economic Systems,* Pitman, 1970. Contributor to academic journals.

WORK IN PROGRESS: A study of water quality management in the Chesapeake Bay estuary.

REB, Paul 1924-

PERSONAL: Born November 3, 1924, near Artesia, N.M.; son of James Matthew (a clergyman) and Clara (Henderson) Reb; married Hertha A. M. Dobnikar (an actress), November, 1954. *Education:* Art Center School, Los Angeles, Calif., student, 1943. *Politics:* "Christian Humanist." *Religion:* "Human Christian." *Home and office:* 198 Hillcrest, Ashland, Ore. 97520.

CAREER: Photographer, prospector, free-lance writer, living in Alaska, 1937-70. *Military service:* U.S. Army Air Forces, 1944-46.

WRITINGS: *Confessions of a Future Scotsman* (novel), Braziller, 1973. Also author of one-act play, "A Sunday Etude for Fernandel," 1970. Contributor of poems to literary journals, and short stories to magazines, including *Playboy.*

WORK IN PROGRESS: A novel and several other fiction and nonfiction books.

SIDELIGHTS: "Heads and hearts must ripen before they can make the kind of literature *I* like to read, and am missing so much these days, and this twin process apparently takes a longer time in some centuries, some societies, than it does in others—for certain people, anyway. So be it. Sufficient unto the day are the hurdles, traps, and seductive but deadly gold-plated shortcuts thereof. But now it is beginning to look as though I were trying to write 'Confessions (or Excuses) of a Past Slowpoke,' and this is intolerable. Besides, 'Wisdom Day' is not until next week."

BIOGRAPHICAL/CRITICAL SOURCES: *Daily Tidings* (Ashland, Ore.), September 8, 1973, October 15, 1973; *Sunday Oregonian,* October 7, 1973; *Time,* October 15, 1973.

* * *

REDMAN, Eric 1948-

PERSONAL: Born June 3, 1948, in Palo Alto, Calif.; son of M. Chandler (a lawyer) and Marjorie (Sachs) Redman; married Anne Mygatt Mueller (a lawyer), June 19, 1971. *Education:* Harvard University, B.A. (magna cum laude), 1970, J.D., 1975; Magdalen College, Oxford, B.A. and M.A. (first class honors), 1972. *Politics:* Democrat. *Home:* 1402 38th Ave., Seattle, Wash. 98122.

CAREER: Harvard University, Cambridge, Mass., instructor in general education, 1973-74. Legislative assistant to U.S. Senator Warren G. Magnuson, 1968-71, campaign aide, 1968, 1974. *Member:* Authors Guild. *Awards, honors:* Rhodes scholar, 1970-72.

WRITINGS: *The Dance of Legislation,* Simon & Schuster, 1973. Book reviewer for *Rolling Stone,* 1973—.

* * *

REDSTONE, Louis G(ordon) 1903-

PERSONAL: Born March 16, 1903, in Grodno, Poland; son of Aaron and Anna Redstone; married Ruth Roslyn Rosenbaum, June, 1939; children: Daniel Aaron, Eliel Gordon. *Education:* University of Michigan, B.S.A., 1929; Cranbrook Academy of Art, M.A., 1948. *Home:* 19303 Appline, Detroit, Mich. 48235. *Office:* Louis G. Redstone Associates, Inc., 10811 Puritan, Detroit, Mich. 48238.

CAREER: Levant Fair, Tel Aviv, Israel, associate architect, 1933-34; self-employed architect in Tel Aviv, Israel, 1934-37; Louis G. Redstone Associates, Inc., Detroit,

Mich., president, 1937—. Former art chairman of Jewish Community Center. Has had one-man shows at Detroit galleries; work represented in exhibition at national show "Watercolor U.S.A."

MEMBER: Pan American Federation of Architects, American Institute of Architects (fellow; president, 1965), American Technion Society (president, 1950), Michigan Society of Architects (member of board of directors, 1959), Engineering Society of Detroit, Tau Sigma Delta. *Awards, honors:* Awards of merit for design of local businesses and shopping centers, 1958-60; Gold Medal from Detroit chapter of American Institute of Architects, 1969, for outstanding contribution to the profession; Architectural and Engineering Award of Distinction from Great Lakes Fabricators and Erectors Association, 1970; award of merit from Michigan chapter of National Society of Interior Designers, 1971.

WRITINGS: Art in Architecture, McGraw, 1968; *New Dimensions in Shopping Centers and Stores,* McGraw, 1973. Contributor of articles and travel sketches to professional journals, including *Architectural Record, Progressive Architecture, Domus, Vitrum,* and publications of American Institute of Architects and Michigan Society of Architects.

WORK IN PROGRESS: The Revival of the Central Business District in Action (tentative title).

* * *

REESE, Sammy
See REESE, Samuel Pharr

* * *

REESE, Samuel Pharr 1930-
(Sammy Reese)

PERSONAL: Born September 11, 1930, in Montgomery, Ala.; son of John Dudley (an employee of the State of Alabama) and Mary Scotland (a teacher in the home mission field; maiden name, Pharr) Reese. *Education:* Attended Southwestern College at Memphis, 1948-50, and Feagin Drama School, 1950-52. *Religion:* Presbyterian. *Residence:* Montgomery, Ala. *Agent:* Marcia Nasatir, Ziegler-Ross, 9255 Sunset Blvd., Los Angeles, Calif. 90069.

CAREER: Film and television actor. His feature films include "King Rat," "PT 109," "Captain Newman," and "The Traveling Executioner." He has appeared in more than twenty television series, including "Dr. Kildare," "Robert Taylor's Detectives," "Kentucky Jones," Alfred Hitchcock's series, "Gunsmoke," and "The Virginian," and in stock stage productions in Sea Cliff, N.Y., Atlantic City, N.J., and Dorset, Vt. *Member:* Actors Equity, Screen Actors Guild, American Federation of Television and Radio Artists, Writers Guild of America.

WRITINGS: I'm Waiting (novel), Doubleday, 1974.

SIDELIGHTS: Reese told *CA*: "I always knew that when I had time, I would write all of those books that I have always known I could write. Time was the only thing I needed. Then, Lord help me, my parents ran out of health, I came home to take care of them, and realized that sudnly time was one of the few things I had a lot of. I started a novel. It was rotten. I started four novels. They were all rotten. Then came number five . . . and Doubleday said yes."

REICH, Ilse Ollendorff 1909-

PERSONAL: Born March 13, 1909, in Breslau, Germany; daughter of Georg (a businessman) and Margarete (Muhr) Ollendorff; married Wilhelm Reich (a physician, psychoanalyst, and writer), December 24, 1939 (deceased); children: E. Peter. *Education:* University of Hartford, B.S. (summa cum laude), 1960; Columbia University, M.A., 1963, professional diploma for teaching foreign languages, 1964. *Home:* 13 Folwell Rd., Norwalk, Conn. 06851.

CAREER: New Canaan Board of Education, New Canaan, Conn., high school teacher of French and German, 1966—. *Member:* National Education Association, American Association of Teachers of German, Women's International League for Peace and Freedom, Connecticut Education Association, Connecticut Prison Association.

WRITINGS: Wilhelm Reich: A Personal Biography, St. Martin's, 1969.

WORK IN PROGRESS: Translating *Wilhelm Reich: A Personal Biography* into German.

* * *

REID, Inez Smith

PERSONAL: Born in New Orleans, La.; married Frantz F-J. Reid (an assistant professor). *Education:* Tufts University, B.A. (magna cum laude), 1959; Yale University, LL.B., 1962; University of California at Los Angeles, M.A., 1963; Columbia University, Ph.D., 1968. *Office:* Department of Political Science, Barnard College, Columbia University, New York, N.Y.

CAREER: Admitted to the Bar of New York State and the Bar of California; Ecole Nationale de Droit et d'Administration, Congo-Kinshasa, Zaire, member of faculty, 1963-64; State University of New York, College at New Paltz, assistant professor of African studies and political science, 1964-65; City University of New York, New York, N.Y., lecturer in political science at Hunter College, 1965-66, associate professor of political science at Brooklyn College, 1966—; Columbia University, Barnard College, New York, N.Y., associate professor of political science, 1972—. Executive director of Black Women's Community Development Foundation, 1971—; member of executive committee and board of trustees of Antioch College; consultant to Ford Foundation Fellowship Program for Afro-Americans interested in Africa and the Middle East. *Member:* African Law Association, African Heritage Studies Association, American Political Science Association, African-American Scholars Council, National Conference of Black Lawyers, National Conference of Black Political Scientists, American Council on Education (member of overseas liaison committee), California Bar Association, New York Bar Association.

WRITINGS: (Editor) *The Black Prism: Perspectives on the Black Experience,* Faculty Press, 1970; *"Together" Black Women,* Emerson Hall, 1972, 2nd edition, Third Press, 1974; (contributor) Christian Potholm and Richard Dale, editors, *Southern Africa in Perspective: Essays in Regional Politics,* Free Press, 1972. Contributor to *Negro Yearbook;* contributor to *Pan-African Journal, African Forum, Afro-American Studies, Essence,* and law journals.

* * *

REID, W(illiam) Stanford 1913-

PERSONAL: Born September 13, 1913, in Montreal,

Quebec, Canada; son of William Dunn (a Presbyterian clergyman) and Daisy (Stanford) Reid; married Priscilla Lee, August 24, 1940. *Education:* McGill University, B.A., 1934, M.A., 1935; Westminster Theological Seminary, Th.B. and Th.M., 1938; University of Pennsylvania, Ph.D., 1941. *Politics:* Independent liberal. *Residence:* Guelph, Ontario, Canada. *Office:* Department of History, University of Guelph, Guelph, Ontario, Canada.

CAREER: McGill University, Montreal, Quebec, lecturer, 1941-44, assistant professor, 1944-51, associate professor, 1951-63, professor of history, 1963-65, director of men's residences, 1951-65; University of Guelph, Guelph, Ontario, professor of history, 1965—, chairman of department, 1965-70. Presbyterian clergyman in Montreal, Quebec, 1941-51. Visiting lecturer at Oxford University, 1959, and University of West Indies, 1962. *Member:* Canadian Historical Association (member of council), American Historical Association, Conference on Scottish Studies (president), American Society of Church History (member of council), American Association for Reformation Research (member of council), Royal Historical Society (fellow), Economic History Society, Conference on British Studies, Conference on Faith and History, American Scientific Affiliation, P.E.N., Scottish Church History Society, The History Association (London), Society for Netherlandic Studies, Mediaeval Academy of America, Montreal Historical Society (president). *Awards, honors:* Research grants from American Philosophical Association, 1949, 1951, Nuffield Foundation, 1962, British Council, 1963, Canada Council, 1960-74, Government of France, 1971, Institute for Advanced Christian Studies, 1972-74.

WRITINGS: The Church of Scotland in Lower Canada: Its Struggle for Establishment, Thorn Press, 1936; *Economic History of Great Britain,* Ronald, 1954; *Skipper from Leith: The History of Robert Barton of Over Barnton,* University of Pennsylvania Press, 1962; *The Protestant Reformation: Revival or Revolution?,* Holt, 1970; *Trumpeter of God: A Biography of John Knox,* Scribner, 1974. Contributor to history and theology journals, including *Catholic Historical Review, Church History, Canadian Historical Review, Juridical Review, Mariner's Mirror, Scottish Historical Review,* and *Westminster Theological Journal.*

WORK IN PROGRESS: Editing *The Scottish Tradition in Canada;* editing a centennial collection of biographies of Canadian Presbyterians; research on the social and economic background of the Reformation, especially in Scotland, France, and the Netherlands.

* * *

REINA, Ruben E. 1924-

PERSONAL: Born December 5, 1924, in Cordoba, Argentina; naturalized U.S. citizen; son of Domingo and Margarita (Videla) Reina; married Betty Burton (a public health educator), September 1, 1951; children: Mark, Randall, Roger. *Education:* National College, Cordoba, A.B., 1945; University of Michigan, A.B., 1950; Michigan State University, M.A., 1951; University of North Carolina, Ph.D., 1957. *Home:* 213 Martroy Lane, Wallingford, Pa. 19086. *Office:* Department of Anthropology, University of Pennsylvania, 33rd and Spruce, Philadelphia, Pa. 19174.

CAREER: University of North Carolina, Greensboro, instructor in anthropology, 1954-55; University of Puerto Rico, Rio Piedras, assistant professor of anthropology, 1956-57; University of Pennsylvania, Philadelphia, assistant professor and assistant curator of Latin American ethnology, 1957-63, associate professor and associate curator, 1963-67, professor of anthropology and curator of Latin American ethnology, University Museum, 1967—, chairman of department of anthropology, 1971—. Member of advisory board, Fundacion Bariloche, Argentina, 1964-66; consultant to Ford Foundation, 1965-67. Member of Philadelphia Mayor's Science and Technology Advisory Council, 1972—. *Military service:* Argentine Army, 1944-45.

MEMBER: American Anthropological Association (fellow), Society for Applied Anthropology, American Ethnological Society, Latin American Studies Association, Philadelphia Anthropological Society (vice-president, 1959-60; president, 1961-62). *Awards, honors:* Grants from National Science Foundation, 1960-62, and American Philosophical Society, 1967-69.

WRITINGS: Chinautla, a Guatemalan Indian Community: A Study in the Relationship of Community Culture and National Change, Middle American Research Institute, Tulane University, 1960; (with Thomas Cochran) *Entrepreneurship in Argentine Culture,* University of Pennsylvania Press, 1962, reprinted under title *Capitalism in Argentine Culture,* 1970; *The Law of the Saints: A Pokomam Pueblo and Its Community Culture,* Bobbs-Merrill, 1967; *Parana: Social Boundaries in an Argentine City,* University of Texas Press, 1973. Contributor to journals in his field. Associate editor, *American Anthropologist,* 1966-70.

WORK IN PROGRESS: With Robert Sharer, *Ethnography of Guatemala Pottery,* completion expected in 1974; with Virginia Lathbury, *Ethnography of Guatemala Textiles,* 1975.

AVOCATIONAL INTERESTS: Music, especially piano; painting; Spanish literature.

* * *

REINHARDT, James Melvin 1894-1974

October 5, 1894—April 23, 1974; American criminologist and author. Obituaries: *New York Times,* April 25, 1974. (*CA*-2).

* * *

REISER, Oliver Leslie 1895-1974

November 15, 1895—June 6, 1974; American professor of philosophy and author. Obituaries: *New York Times,* June 7, 1974. (*CA*-3).

* * *

REITERMAN, Carl 1921-

PERSONAL: Born June 18, 1921, in Palo Alto, Calif.; son of Carl (an educator) and Marlene (Graham) Reiterman; married Ruth Wininger (a psychiatric social worker), March 28, 1964; children: Marc, June, Ellen. *Education:* University of California, Berkeley, B.A., 1950, M.A., 1965, Ph.D., 1968. *Home:* 2329 Eunice St., Berkeley, Calif. 94708. *Office:* Department of Sociology, University of San Francisco, San Francisco, Calif. 94117.

CAREER: University of San Francisco, San Francisco, Calif., instructor, 1966-68, assistant professor, 1968-72, associate professor of sociology, 1972—. Visiting lecturer at University of California, Berkeley, 1967-69, and School of Medicine, University of California, San Francisco, 1970.

Member: International Union for the Scientific Study of Population, American Sociological Association, Population Association of America, American Association of University Professors. *Awards, honors:* National Institute of Mental Health grant, 1971, to edit *Abortion and the Unwanted Child.*

WRITINGS: Birth-control Policies and Practices in Fifty-eight California County Welfare Departments, Planned Parenthood-World Population, 1966; *Readings in Population,* Simon & Schuster, 1969; *Sociology of Education,* Simon & Schuster, 1970; *Social Change,* Simon & Schuster, 1970; (editor) *Abortion and the Unwanted Child,* Springer Publishing, 1971.

WORK IN PROGRESS: Research on population policies concerning fertility, birth control, and abortion.

* * *

REITMEISTER, Louis Aaron 1903-

PERSONAL: Born February 2, 1903, in New York, N.Y.; son of Nathan and Jennie (Crane) Reitmeister; married Betty Richmond, January, 1931 (divorced, 1956). *Education:* "Prefer not to list." *Politics:* Non-partisan. *Religion:* None. *Home and office:* 100 Hicks Lane, Great Neck, N.Y. 11024.

CAREER: Writer, 1923—, lecturer, 1925—. Associate editor, Lewis Copeland Publishing Co., New York, N.Y., 1928-31; associate editor, *Esthete* magazine, Chicago, Ill., 1928-31; director, Childville (home for disturbed and retarded children), New York, N.Y., 1938—. Member of Founders Society, Einstein College of Medicine, 1959—; Keren Or Institute for the Blind, Jerusalem, 1967—, served as American director, now member of honorary committee; sponsors' council chairman, Kfar Zvi Sitrin of Israel, Inc., 1971—. Consultant to Indian National Congress, American Committee, 1928-31. *Military service:* U.S. Army Air Forces, 1943-45. *Member:* International Oceanographic Foundation, American Academy of Political and Social Sciences, Center for the Study of Democratic Institutions, American Humanist Association, Association on American Indian Affairs, National Geographic Society, National Audobon Society, Defenders of Wildlife, Committee for Humane Legislation, Bide-A-Wee Home Association, Friends of Animals, Oceanic Society, Project Jonah, Friends of the Sea Otters, Phi Beta Kappa, Long Key Fishing Club.

WRITINGS: Paradise Found, Grafton Press, 1926; *Ten Commandments of Friendship,* Copeland, 1927; *Philosophic Concepts in Crime Prevention,* privately printed, 1928; *Music and Philosophy,* Aesthete, 1930; *Philosophy of Love,* Copeland Publishing, 1930; *Ten Commandments of Love,* Copeland, 1930; *What Life Means to Great Philosophers,* Whitman Publishing, 1931; *If Tomorrow Comes,* Walden Press, 1934, reprinted, Arno, 1971; *Gist of Philosophy,* Barrows-Mussey, 1936; *When Tomorrow Comes,* privately printed, 1938; *An Appeal to Common Sense,* privately printed, 1938; *Nature of Power,* Walden Press, 1943; *Brief Essay about the Gods and My Friends,* Walden Press, 1948; *By the Way: Epigrams and Notes,* Exposition, 1953; *A Philosophy of Time,* Citadel, 1959; *A Philosophy of Freedom,* Poseidon, 1970; *My Credo,* privately printed, 1973. Also author of three-volume work, *Nature and Philosophy of Friendship,* 1948. Contributor of articles to numerous academic journals and popular periodicals.

WORK IN PROGRESS: Shayneh: The Life and Times of My Mother; Reality and Process: A Philosophy.

SIDELIGHTS: Reitmeister told *CA* that *If Tomorrow Comes* is the book he likes best of all his writings. *Avocational interests:* Travel, fishing, gardening, painting.

* * *

REITZE, Arnold W(infred), Jr. 1938-

PERSONAL: Born April 25, 1938, in Jersey City, N.J.; son of Arnold W. and Harriet (Logan) Reitze. *Education:* Fairleigh Dickinson University, B.A., 1960; Rutgers University, J.D., 1962. *Office:* George Washington University Law School, Washington, D.C. 20006.

CAREER: Indiana University, Bloomington, instructor, in law, 1963-64; University of Michigan, Ann Arbor, instructor in law, 1965; Case-Western Reserve University, Cleveland, Ohio, assistant professor, 1965-67, associate professor of law, 1967-70; George Washington University, Washington, D.C., professor of law, 1970—, director of environmental law program of the National Law Center, 1970—.

WRITINGS: Environmental Law, North American International, Volume I: *Pollution Control,* 1971, revised edition, 1972, Volume II: *Resource Planning,* 1973. Contributor to professional journals.

* * *

RENFREW, Jane Margaret 1942-

PERSONAL: Born October 31, 1942, in Windermere, Westmorland, England; daughter of Walter Frederick (an archdeacon) and Ida Margaret (Whitworth) Ewbank; married Andrew Colin Renfrew (a university professor), April 21, 1965; children: Helena Margaret, Alban Robert. *Education:* New Hall, Cambridge, B.A., 1964, M.A., 1968, Ph.D., 1969. *Home:* 17 Malcolm Close, Chandlers Ford, Eastleigh, Hampshire, England. *Agent:* Christopher Busby, 27 Southampton St. Strand, London WC2E 7JA, England. *Office:* Department of Archaeology, University of Southampton, Southampton, England.

CAREER: University of Sheffield, Sheffield, England, lecturer in European prehistory, 1967-72; University of Southampton, Southampton, England, visiting lecturer in archaeology, 1972—. *Member:* National Institute of Agricultural Botany (fellow), Cumberland and Westmorland Archaeological Society, Hampshire Field Club, Butses Hill Ancient Farm Project.

WRITINGS: Antiquary on Horseback, Titus Wilson, 1964; *Palaeoethnobotany,* Columbia University Press, 1973.

WORK IN PROGRESS: Research in the origins of agriculture in the Near East, especially Southwest Iran, the spread of agriculture to Europe and its development in prehistoric times, and the evolution of crop plants.

* * *

REUBER, Grant L(ouis) 1927-

PERSONAL: Surname is pronounced *Rye*-ber; born November 23, 1927, in Mildmay, Ontario, Canada; son of J. Daniel (a farmer) and Gertrude C. Reuber; married Margaret L. J. Summerhayes (a librarian), October 21, 1951; children: Rebecca, Barbara, Mary. *Education:* University of Western Ontario, B.A., 1950; Harvard University, A.M., 1954, Ph.D., 1957; also studied at Sidney Sussex College, Cambridge, 1954-55. *Religion:* Anglican. *Home:* 101 Wychwood Ct., London, Ontario, Canada. *Office:* Department of Economics, University of Western Ontario, London, Ontario, Canada.

CAREER: Bank of Canada, Ottawa, Ontario, economist, 1950-52; Canadian Department of Finance, Ottawa, Ontario, economist, 1955-57; University of Western Ontario, London, assistant professor, 1957-59, associate professor, 1959-62, professor of economics, 1962—, chairman of department, 1963-69, dean of social sciences, 1969—. Member of Royal Commission on Banking and Finance, 1962-63; member of Joint Committee on Economic Policy of the Province of Ontario, 1972—; chairman of Ontario Economic Council, 1973—; member of Task Force on International Monetary Reform of Trilateral Commission, 1973—. Consultant to National Council of Applied Economic Research (India), Canadian International Development Agency, and Economic Council of Canada.

MEMBER: Canadian Economic Association (chairman of founding committee; president, 1967-68), Royal Society of Canada (fellow), American Economic Association, Econometric Society, Economic Study Society, Royal Economic Society, University Club (Ottawa).

WRITINGS: Britain's Export Trade with Canada, University of Toronto Press, 1960; *Canada-United States Trade: Its Growth and Changing Composition,* Private Planning Association of Canada, 1960; (with R. J. Wonnacott) *The Cost of Capital in Canada,* Resources for the Future, 1961; *Canada's Interest in the Trade Problems of the Less-Developed Countries,* Private Planning Association of Canada, 1964; *The Objectives of Monetary Policy,* Queen's Printer, 1964; (with J. V. Graham, S. G. Peitchinis and others) *The Role of the Trust and Loan Companies in the Canadian Economy,* University of Western Ontario, 1965; (with R. G. Bodkin, E. P. Bond, and T. R. Robinson) *Price Stability and High Employment: The Options for Canadian Economic Policy,* Queen's Printer, 1967; (contributor) John H. G. Crispo, editor, *Wages, Prices, Profits, and Economic Policy,* University of Toronto Press, 1968; (with Frank Roseman) *The Take-Over of Canadian Firms, 1945-1961: An Empirical Analysis,* Queen's Printer, 1969; (with R. E. Caves) *Canadian Economic Policy and the Impact of International Capital Flows,* University of Toronto Press, 1969.

(With Caves) *Capital Transfers and Economic Policy: Canada, 1951-1962,* Harvard University Press, 1970; *Wage Determination in Canadian Manufacturing: 1953-1966,* Queen's Printer, 1971; (contributor) Paul Streeten and Hugh Corbet, editors, *Commonwealth Policy in a Global Context,* Frank Cass, 1971; (contributor) Fritz Machlup, W. S. Salant, and Lorie Tarshis, editors, *International Mobility and Movement of Capital,* National Bureau of Economic Research, 1972; (contributor) *Canadian-United States Financial Relationships,* Federal Reserve Bank of Boston, 1972; (contributor) H. H. Binhammer, J. P. Cairns, and R. W. Broadway, editors, *Canadian Banking and Monetary Policy,* McGraw (Canada), 1972; (contributor) J. F. Chant, editor, *Canadian Perspectives in Economics,* Collier (Canada), 1972; (contributor) D. A. L. Auld, editor, *Contemporary Economic Issues in Canada,* Holt, 1972; *Private Foreign Investment in Development,* Clarendon Press (of Oxford University), 1973; *The Riddle of International Monetary Reform,* Atlantic Council of Canada, 1973; (editor with T. N. Guinsburg) *Perspectives on the Social Sciences in Canada,* University of Toronto Press, 1974; (contributor) L. H. Officer and L. B. Smith, editors, *Issues in Canadian Economics,* McGraw, 1974.

Contributor of about thirty articles and reviews to economic and business journals.

WORK IN PROGRESS: Research on income distribution.

REVE, Karel van het
See van het REVE, Karel

* * *

ReVELLE, Penelope 1941-

PERSONAL: Surname is pronounced "ra-*vel*"; born September 17, 1941, in New York, N.Y.; daughter of Maximilian and Maude (Peltier) Rottmann; married Charles ReVelle (a professor), June 12, 1962; children: Cynthia. *Education:* Cornell University, B.S., 1962, Ph.D., 1968. *Home:* 826 Loyola Dr., Baltimore, Md. 21204. *Office:* Department of Biology, Essex Community College, Essex, Md. 21221.

CAREER: Ithaca College, Ithaca, N.Y., instructor, 1969-70, lecturer in cell physiology, 1970; Essex Community College, Essex, Md., instructor in biology, 1972—. *Member:* American Association for the Advancement of Science, Sierra Club, Phi Kappa Phi, Sigma Xi.

WRITINGS: (With husband, Charles ReVelle) *Sourcebook on the Environment: The Scientific Perspective,* Houghton, 1974.

WORK IN PROGRESS: Research on ecosystem contaminants.

* * *

REYBURN, Wallace (Macdonald) 1913-

PERSONAL: Born July 3, 1913, in Auckland, New Zealand; son of William Robert (a dentist) and Florence (Fisher) Reyburn; married Lucille Peart, February 7, 1941 (divorced, November 6, 1946); married Elizabeth Munro (a magazine editor), November 21, 1946; children: (second marriage) Ross Macdonald, Lorna Robin (Mrs. Steven Bicknell), William Scott. *Education:* Attended school in England. *Politics:* Conservative. *Religion:* Church of England. *Home and office:* 16 Harley Rd., London N.W.3, England. *Agent:* Collins-Knowlton-Wing, Inc., 60 East 56th St., New York, N.Y. 10022.

CAREER: Reporter and assistant editor for newspapers in New Zealand, 1931-34, and their correspondent in London, England, 1935-36; assistant editor, then editor, of Canadian magazines in Toronto and Montreal, 1937-40, 1946-50; assistant and features editor of magazines in London, England, 1950-53; *Toronto Telegram,* Toronto, Ontario, daily columnist in London, England, 1954-64; *Queen Magazine,* London, England, deputy editor, 1965-66; writer, 1966—. *Wartime service:* War correspondent for *Montreal Standard,* 1941-45. *Awards, honors:* Order of the British Empire.

WRITINGS: Rehearsal for Invasion, Harrap, 1943; *Glorious Chapter,* Oxford University Press, 1943; *Some of It Was Fun,* Nelson (Canada), 1948; *Follow a Shadow* (novel), Cassell, 1956; *Port of Call* (novel), Cassell, 1957; *The Street That Died* (novel), Cassell, 1958; *Three Women* (novel), Cassell, 1959.

Good and Evil (novel), Cassell, 1960; *Getting the Boy* (novel), Elek, 1965; *The World of Rugby,* Elek, 1966; *The Lions,* Stanley Paul, 1967; *The Unsmiling Giants,* Stanley Paul, 1968; *Frost: Anatomy of a Success,* Macdonald & Co., 1968; (editor) *Best Rugby Stories,* Faber, 1969; *The Rugby Companion,* Stanley Paul, 1969; *Flushed with Pride: The Story of Thomas Crapper,* Macdonald & Co., 1969, Prentice-Hall, 1970; *There Was Also Some Rugby,* Stanley Paul, 1970; *Bust Up: The Story of Otto Titzling,* Macdonald & Co., 1971, Prentice-Hall, 1972; *A History of Rugby,* Arthur Barker, 1972; *Bridge Across the Atlantic,* Harrap, 1973; *The Inferior Sex,* Prentice-Hall, 1973; *The Winter Men,* Stanley Paul, 1973.

Contributor to *New Yorker, Life, Reader's Digest,* and other magazines. Editor of *New Liberty* (a Canadian journal).

WORK IN PROGRESS: Call Me Madam: The Sociable History of the Brothel.

SIDELIGHTS: Reyburn commented to *CA:* "I have been writing since I was eight, because I have a nagging desire to do so. . . . I think self-discipline is the most important attribute for an author. . . . Not without reason has it been said that the longest trip in the world is from the armchair to the typewriter."

* * *

REYES, Carlos 1935-

PERSONAL: Born June 2, 1935, in Marshfield, Mo.; son of Herman Carrol and Alice (Day) King; married wife, Barbara, September 13, 1958 (divorced, 1973); children: Michael Hollingsworth, Amy Sofia, Nina Heloise, Rachel Kathleen. *Education:* University of Oregon, B.A., 1961; University of Arizona, M.A., 1965. *Home:* 2737 Southwest 2nd, Portland, Ore. 97201.

CAREER: University of Maine, Orono, instructor in foreign languages, 1965-66; Portland State University, Portland, Ore., assistant professor of Spanish and Italian, 1966-73; Portland Art Museum School, Portland, Ore., instructor in English, 1971-72; upholstery worker in Portland, Ore., 1973—. Member of Oregon Governor's Advisory Committee on the Arts, 1971-72. *Military service:* U.S. Army, 1953-56.

WRITINGS: The Windows (poems), Weed Flower Press, 1967; *Odes for Every Occasion* (poems), Runcible Spoon, 1971; *The Prisoner* (poems), Capra, 1973. Contributor to *Yes!,* an anthology. Contributor to *Chelsea.*

WORK IN PROGRESS: Translation of Neruda's last book of poems; two books of poetry.

SIDELIGHTS: Reyes told *CA:* "After a frustrating career in college teaching I was forced to realize that first and foremost I am a poet (everything else takes second place to that). Poetry writing to me is real and constant in an otherwise chaotic existence."

* * *

RHODE, John
See CARR, John Dickson

* * *

RICE, Edward E. 1918-

PERSONAL: Son of Edward and Elizabeth Rice; children: Edward III, Christopher. *Education:* Attended Columbia College. *Home address:* Box 381, New York, N.Y. 11962.

CAREER: Writer, artist, photographer.

WRITINGS: The Man in the Sycamore Tree: The Good Times and Hard Life of Thomas Merton, Doubleday, 1970; *Mother India's Children: Meeting Today's Generation in India,* Pantheon, 1971; (editor) Pagal Baba, *Temple of the Phallic King,* Simon & Schuster, 1973; *John Frum He Come: A Polemical Work about a Black Tragedy,* Doubleday, 1974; *The Ganges: A Personal Encounter,* Four Winds, 1974; *Journey to Upolu: Robert Louis Stevenson, Victorian Rebel,* Dodd, 1974; *Cities of the Unicorn,* Simon & Schuster, in press.

WORK IN PROGRESS: Eastern Definitions, publication by Doubleday expected in 1976.

* * *

RICHARDS, Cara E(lizabeth) 1927-

PERSONAL: Born January 13, 1927, in Bayonne, N.J.; daughter of Vere S. (a teacher of singing) and Virginia M. (Tyler) Richards; married Henry F. Dobyns, September 11, 1958 (divorced, 1968); children: York H. Dobyns. *Education:* Queens College (now Queens College of the City University of New York), A.B., 1952; Columbia University, graduate study, 1952-53; Cornell University, Ph.D., 1957. *Residence:* Lexington, Ky. *Office:* Department of Economics, Psychology and Sociology, Transylvania University, Lexington, Ky. 40508.

CAREER: Cornell University, Ithaca, N.Y., curatorial assistant in primitive art at White Art Museum, 1956-57, resident at Many Farms Navajo-Cornell Experimental Field Health Clinic in Arizona, 1958-59, field director of family life study in Peru, 1960-61; Escuela de Servicio Social del Peru, Lima, professor of anthropology, 1961, 1962; area studies coordinator for Peace Corps training programs for South America at University of Washington, Seattle, and Springfield College, Springfield, Mass., 1963; Cornell University, lecturer in anthropology, 1963-64, and summers, 1963, 1965-68; Ithaca College, Ithaca, N.Y., associate professor of anthropology, 1964-67; Transylvania College, Lexington, Ky., associate professor of sociology, 1967—, chairman of department of economics, psychology, and sociology.

MEMBER: American Anthropological Association (director of visiting lecturer program, 1963-69), Society for Applied Anthropology, American Association for the Advancement of Science, American Ethnological Society, American Society for Ethnohistory, American Association of University Professors, Central States Anthropological Association, Anthropologists and Sociologists of Kentucky (president, 1973-74), Phi Beta Kappa, Phi Alpha Theta. *Awards, honors:* American Association of University Women fellow, 1957-58; Russell Sage Foundation fellow, 1958-59.

WRITINGS: (Contributor) Elisabeth Tooker, editor, *Iroquois Culture, History and Prehistory,* New York State Museum and Science Service, 1967; *Man in Perspective: An Introduction to Cultural Anthropology,* Random House, 1971. Contributor to *Human Organization* and anthropology journals.

WORK IN PROGRESS: Research on the role of women and history of the Onondaga Indians.

AVOCATIONAL INTERESTS: Reading science fiction, swimming, playing baseball.

* * *

RICHARDSON, Beth
See GUTCHEON, Beth R(ichardson)

* * *

RICHARDSON, Bradley M. 1928-

PERSONAL: Born September 6, 1928, in Toledo, Ohio; son of Harold L. (a journalist) and Marjory Richardson;

married Barbara Fumiko Shiba, July 8, 1958; children: Paul Stephen, Stephanie Mari. *Education:* Harvard University, A.B. (cum laude), 1951; Columbia University, M.A., 1960; University of California, Berkeley, Ph.D., 1966. *Office:* Ohio State University, 154 North Oval Dr., Columbus, Ohio 43210.

CAREER: Ohio State University, Columbus, assistant professor, 1965-69, associate professor, 1969-74, professor of political science, 1974—. *Military service:* U.S. Navy, 1954-57; became lieutenant. *Member:* American Political Science Association. *Awards, honors:* Fulbright fellowship, 1962-65 and 1969-70; Social Science Research Council grant, 1974-75; Japan Foundation grant, 1974-75.

WRITINGS: *The Political Culture of Japan,* University of California Press, 1974.

WORK IN PROGRESS: Research on Japanese political behavior, for a research survey program.

* * *

RICHARDSON, Robert S(hirley) 1902- (Philip Latham)

PERSONAL: Born April 22, 1902, in Kokomo, Ind.; son of Joel Howard (a salesman) and Arlene (Moore) Richardson; married Delia Shull, August 19, 1929 (died January 2, 1940); married Marjorie Helen Engstead; children: (second marriage) Rae (daughter). *Education:* University of California at Los Angeles, B.A., 1926; University of California at Berkeley, Ph.D., 1931. *Religion:* None. *Home and office:* 1533 East Altadena Dr., Altadena, Calif. 91001. *Agent:* Scott Meredith, 580 Fifth Ave., New York, N.Y. 10036.

CAREER: Hale Observatory (formerly Mt. Wilson and Palomar Observatory), Pasedena, Calif., staff astronomer, 1931-58; Griffith Observatory, Los Angeles, Calif., associate director, 1958-64; writer, 1964—. *Member:* American Astronomical Society, Astronomical Society of the Pacific, Los Angeles Astronomical Society (life member), Excelsior Telescope Club (honorary life member), Pasadena Art Museum, Friends of Altadena Library. *Awards, honors:* New York Academy of Sciences Children's Science Book Award, 1971, for *The Stars & Serendipity.*

WRITINGS: (With William T. Skilling) *Astronomy,* Holt, 1947; *Man and the Planets,* Muller, 1954; (with Skilling) *A Brief Text in Astronomy,* Holt, 1954, revised edition, 1959; *Exploring Mars,* McGraw, 1954; *Second Satellite* (fiction), Whittlesey House, 1956; (with Skilling) *Sun, Moon and Stars,* McGraw, 1959, revised edition, 1964; *The Fascinating World of Astronomy,* McGraw, 1960; *Man and the Moon,* World Publishing, 1961; *Astronomy in Action,* McGraw, 1962; (with Chesley Bonestell) *Mars,* Harcourt, 1964; *Getting Acquainted with Comets,* McGraw, 1967; *The Star Lovers,* Macmillan, 1967; *The Stars & Serendipity* (juvenile), Pantheon, 1971.

Under pseudonym Philip Latham; novels: *Five Against Venus,* Winston, 1952; *Missing Men of Saturn,* Winston, 1953.

Contributor of articles and short stories to *Analog, Magazine of Fantasy and Science Fiction, Galaxy, Colliers.*

WORK IN PROGRESS: Short stories.

SIDELIGHTS: Richardson told *CA* that his major interest is science—tending toward the supernatural, but "because I write about the occult does not mean I believe it. (I DO NOT)."

RICHMOND, Lee 1943-

PERSONAL: Name legally changed in 1947; born July 14, 1943, in Portsmouth, Va.; son of Capel Weems (an inventor) and Virginia (Lee) McNash; married Martha Weiss (a psychotherapist), May 24, 1970. *Education:* Williams College, B.A., 1966. *Politics:* Anarchist. *Religion:* Pantheist. *Home:* 43 Greenville St., Somerville, Mass. 02143. *Agent:* Knox Burger, 39½ Washington Sq. S., New York, N.Y. 10012.

CAREER: Novelist. Has worked as taxi cab driver, 1966-69, and welder-mechanic, 1972—. *Member:* Phi Beta Kappa.

WRITINGS: *High on Gold* (novel), Charterhouse, 1972.

WORK IN PROGRESS: A historical novel about the Hoosac Tunnel in North Adams, Mass., 1848-1873; another novel, completion expected in 1974.

SIDELIGHTS: Richmond wrote: "I favor clarity, straightforwardness, and complex subjects, and haven't been able to get the three together yet. Find, in the eighth year of writing full-time, the motivation of confidence in my skill giving way to a kind of blind wilfulness. Burning all the other bridges is a good way to keep writing."

* * *

RICHTER, Maurice N(athaniel), Jr. 1930-

PERSONAL: Born May 21, 1930, in New York, N.Y.; son of Maurice Nathaniel (a physician) and Brina (Kessel) Richter. *Education:* Bard College, B.A., 1953; University of Chicago, M.A., 1954, Ph.D., 1962. *Office:* Department of Sociology, State University of New York, 1400 Washington Ave., Albany, N.Y. 12222.

CAREER: Syracuse University, Syracuse, N.Y., instructor in sociology, 1955-56; University of Toronto, Toronto, Ontario, lecturer in sociology, 1956-57; Antioch College, Yellow Springs, Ohio, assistant professor of sociology, 1957-58; University of Chicago, Chicago, Ill., research associate, 1958-60; University of New Hampshire, Durham, assistant professor of sociology, 1960-64; University of Southern California, Los Angeles, assistant professor of sociology, 1964-65; State University of New York at Albany, associate professor of sociology, 1966—. Visiting associate professor at University of Hawaii, 1972-73. *Member:* American Sociological Association.

WRITINGS: *Science as a Cultural Process,* Schenkman, 1972.

* * *

RIEFF, Philip 1922-

PERSONAL: Born December 15, 1922, in Chicago, Ill.; son of Joseph Gabriel and Ida (Hurrwitz) Rieff; married second wife, Alison Douglas Knox, December 31, 1963; children: (first marriage) David. *Education:* University of Chicago, B.A., 1946, M.A., 1947, Ph.D., 1954. *Office:* Department of Sociology, University of Pennsylvania, Philadelphia, Pa. 19104.

CAREER: University of Chicago, Chicago, Ill., instructor in sociology, 1947-52; Brandeis University, Waltham, Mass., assistant professor of sociology, 1952-58; University of California, Berkeley, associate professor of sociology, 1958-61; University of Pennsylvania, Philadelphia, professor, 1961-67, Benjamin Franklin Professor of Sociology, 1967—. Fellow of Center for Advanced Study in the Behavioral Sciences, 1957-58; visiting fellow at Center for the Study of Democratic Institutions, 1963-64, and at All Souls College, Oxford, 1970—. Fulbright professor at University of Munich, 1959-60; visiting associate professor at Harvard University, 1960. Chief consultant to planning department of National Council of Churches, 1961-64.

MEMBER: American Sociological Association, Society for the Scientific Study of Religion (member of council), Royal Society of Arts (fellow), Societe Europeene de Culture, Garrick Club. *Awards, honors:* Guggenheim fellowship, 1970.

WRITINGS: Freud: The Mind of the Moralist, Viking, 1959, revised edition, 1961; *The Triumph of the Therapeutic: Uses of Faith after Freud,* Harper, 1966; (editor) *The Collected Papers of Sigmund Freud,* ten volumes, Collier, 1961; *Fellow Teachers,* Harper, 1973. Associate editor of *American Sociological Review,* 1958-61; founding editor of *Journal of the American Academy of Arts and Sciences,* 1956-59, and *Daedalus;* contributing editor for Harper, 1969—; chief editorial consultant to Beacon Press, 1952-58.

* * *

RIESE, Walther 1890-

PERSONAL: Born June 30, 1890, in Berlin, Germany; son of Emil and Anna (Rosenthal) Riese; married Hertha R. I. Pataky (a physician), August 7, 1915; children: Renee (Mrs. Judd Hubert), Beatrice (Mrs. Willie Riese). *Education:* Attended University of Berlin, 1909-10, 1910-14, University of Greifswald, 1910; University of Koenigsberg, M.D., 1914; University of Lyon, B. of Phil., 1937. *Home and office address:* Box 397, Route 2, Francis Rd., Glen Allen, Va. 23235.

CAREER: University of Koenigsberg, Koenigsberg, Germany, assistant in neuropsychiatric clinic, 1914-15; Municipal Hospital, Wiesbaden, Germany, employed with neuropsychiatric and internal services, 1915-16; University of Frankfurt, Frankfurt-am-Main, Germany, assistant in neuropsychiatric clinic, 1917-19; Frankfurt Hospital for Brain-injured Soldiers, Frankfurt-am-Main, Germany, assistant, 1919-20; University of Frankfurt, Frankfurt-am-Main, assistant in Neurological Institute, 1920-26, chief of neuroanatomical laboratory of neuropsychiatric clinic, 1926-27, professor emeritus; University of Lyon, Lyon, France, assistant in neuropsychiatric clinic, 1933-37; National Center of Scientific Research, Paris, France, chief of research, 1937-40; Medical College of Virginia (now Virginia Commonwealth University), Richmond, Va., research associate with neuropsychiatric clinic, 1941-47, associate professor of neurology, psychiatry, and history of medicine, 1948-60, associate professor emeritus, 1960—. Member of faculty, Washington School of Psychiatry, 1951-54; consultant to Department of Mental Hygiene and Hospitals of Commonwealth of Virginia, 1942-60, U.S. Department of Health, Education, and Welfare and National Institute of Mental Health, 1960-62; visiting professor of psychology, Richmond Professional Institute, 1960-69.

MEMBER: Societe Internationale de Psychopathologie de l'Expression (honorary member; past vice-president), American Association for the Advancement of Science, American Association of Neuropathologists, American Association of the History of Medicine, American Association of University Professors, American Geriatric Society, American Society of Mammalogists, American Medical Association, Academy of Psychoanalysts, Societe Moreau de Tours, Onto-analytic Association, Medical Society of Virginia, Archeological Society of Virginia, Richmond Academy of Medicine. *Awards, honors:* Rockefeller fellowship, 1933-36, to University of Lyon, 1941-43, to Medical College of Virginia; Virginia State Hospital Board first prize, 1944, 1945, for medical research; Richmond Area University Center research grants, 1950, 1952.

WRITINGS: Vincent van Gogh in der Krankheit: Ein Betrag zum Problem der Beziehung zwischen Kunstwerk und Krankheit (title means "Vincent van Gogh as a Victim of Disease: A Contribution to the Problem of Interrelation of Disease and Art"), J. F. Bergmann (Munich), 1926; *Das Sinnesleben eines Dichters: Georg Trakl* (title means "The Life and the Senses of a Poet"), J. Puettmann (Stuttgart), 1928; (with others) *Die Unfallneurose als Problem der Gegenwartsmedizin* (title means "The Traumatic Neurosis as a Problem of Contemporary Medicine"), Hippokratesverlag, 1929; (with Otto Rothbarth) *Die Unfallneurose und das Reichsgericht* (title means "The Traumatic Neurosis and the Supreme Court"), Hippokratesverlag, 1930; *Das Triebverbrechen: Untersuchungen ueber die unmittelbaren Ursachen des Sexual-und Affektdelikts, sowie ihre Bedeutung fuer die Zurechnungsfaehigkeit des Taeters* (title means "The Impulsive Crime: Investigations on the Immediate Causes of the Sexual and Emotional Crime and Their Significance for the Responsibility of the Offender"), H. Huber (Bern), 1933; (Andre Requet) *L'Idee de l'homme dans la neurologie contemporaine* (title means "The Concept of Man in Contemporary Neurology"), Alcan (Paris), 1938.

Systeme nerveux cerebrospinal (title means "The Central Nervous System"), Hermann et Cie, 1940; *La pensee causale en medecine* (title means "Causal Thought in Medicine"), Presses Universitaires de France, 1950; *Principles of Neurology in the Light of History and Their Present Use,* Williams & Wilkins, 1950; *The Conception of Disease: Its History, Its Versions and Its Nature,* Philosophical Library, 1953; *La pensee morale en medecine, premiers principes d'une ethique medicale* (title means "Moral Thought in Medicine: First Principles of Medical Ethics"), Presses Universitaires de France, 1954; (contributor) F. N. L. Poynter, editor, *The History and Philosophy of Knowledge of the Brain and Its Functions,* Blackwell Scientific Publications, 1958; *A History of Neurology,* M. D. Publications, 1959.

(Author of introduction and commentary) *Galen on the Passions and Errors of the Soul,* Ohio State University Press, 1963; (with others) *Phyloanalysis,* S. Karger, 1963; *La theorie des passions a la lumiere de la pensee medicale du XVIIe siecle* (title means "The Theory of Passions in Light of Medical Thought of the XVII Century"), S. Karger, 1965; *The Legacy of Pinel: An Inquiry into Thought on Mental Alienation,* Springer Publishing, 1969. Contributor to *Encyclopaedia Britannica.* Contributor of 275 scientific articles and papers to journals in Europe and North America.

WORK IN PROGRESS: Doctrine of Metamorphosis.

SIDELIGHTS: Riese told *CA:* "For a number of years, I have been pursuing historical investigations concerning the structure and origin of contemporary psychiatry, investigations which are a sequel to the studies devoted to the structure and origin of contemporary neurology. Inevitably, these investigations led me to study carefully the work of Philippe Pinel, who is outstanding in the history of medicine as a compassionate and humane alienist and as the instigator of 'moral treatment.'"

RIESENBERG, Saul H(erbert) 1911-

PERSONAL: Born August 28, 1911, in Newark, N.J.; son of Jacob (a broker) and Leah (Rothman) Riesenberg; married Mildred Rose Rand (a teacher), December 19, 1942; children: Jared, Daniel, Thomas. *Education:* University of California, Los Angeles, A.B., 1932; University of California, Berkeley, Ph.D., 1950. *Home:* 10105 Kinross Ave., Silver Spring, Md. 20901. *Office:* Department of Anthropology, Smithsonian Institution, Washington, D.C. 20560.

CAREER: Worked in various capacities with U.S. Railway Mail Service in Los Angeles and San Francisco, Calif., 1936-42; University of Hawaii, Honolulu, assistant professor, 1949-53, associate professor of anthropology, 1954-57; Smithsonian Institution, Washington, D.C., curator of anthropology, 1957-73, senior ethnologist, 1973—, chairman of department of anthropology, 1967-70. Staff anthropologist, U.S. Trust Territory, Pacific Islands, 1953-54, and Government of American Samoa, 1955-56; visiting research fellow at Australian National University, 1970-71. Has done field work in Ponape, 1947-48, 1963, Samoa, 1955-56, Puluwat, 1967. *Military service:* U.S. Army Air Forces, 1942-45; became captain.

MEMBER: American Anthropological Association (fellow), American Ethnological Society, American Society for Ethnohistory, Polynesian Society, Current Anthropology, Association for Social Anthropology in Oceania, Association for Micronesian Anthropology, Anthropological Society of Hawaii (president, 1952-53), Anthropological Society of Washington, D.C. (president, 1959-60), Sigma Xi (president of Hawaii chapter, 1956-57). *Awards, honors:* Grants from Pacific Science Board of National Research Council, 1947, Wenner-Gren Foundation, 1949, 1970, Carnegie Corp., 1955, National Science Foundation, 1967, and National Geographic Society, 1973.

WRITINGS: The Native Polity of Ponape, Smithsonian Institution Press, 1968; (editor and author of introduction and notes) James F. O'Connell, *A Residence of Eleven Years in New Holland and the Caroline Islands* (originally published in 1836), University Press of Hawaii, 1972; (editor with John L. Fischer) *The Book of Luelen,* Australian National University Press, in press. Contributor of about forty articles to anthropology journals.

WORK IN PROGRESS: A book on the ruins of Nan Madol, an archeological site in Ponape, for Smithsonian Institution Press.

* * *

RILLA, Wolf 1925-

PERSONAL: Born March 16, 1925, in Berlin, Germany; son of Walter (an actor) and Theresia Rilla; married Valery Hanson, October 13, 1951 (divorced, December, 1967); married Shirley Graham Ellis (a public relations consultant), January 21, 1968; children: (first marriage) Madeleine Peta; (second marriage) Nicolas Walter Diego. *Education:* St. Catharine's College, Cambridge, M.A., 1945. *Politics:* "Vaguely Leftish Liberal." *Religion:* None. *Home:* 18 Lyndhurst Rd., London NW3 5NL, England. *Agent:* Roslyn Targ, 325 East 57th St., New York, N.Y. 10022.

CAREER: Free-lance film director, scriptwriter, and author. Producer, director, and writer for British Broadcasting Corp., 1945-51; managing director of Rilla Productions, 1959—; director of Cyclops Film Productions, 1962—. Course director for London Film School. *Member:* Writers Guild (England), Association of Cinematograph and Television Technicians. *Awards, honors:* Boston Film Festival award, 1963, for direction and original script of "Jessy."

WRITINGS: Greek Chorus (novel), Secker & Warburg, 1947; *The Commitment* (novel), Secker & Warburg, 1965; *A-Z of Movie Making,* Viking, 1969; *The Dispensable Man* (novel), John Day, 1974; *The Writer and the Screen,* Morrow, 1974.

Screenplays: "Roadhouse Girl," Rank, 1954; "The Scamp," Renown, 1958; "Jessy," Renown, 1959; (with Stirling Silliphant and George Barclay) "Village of the Damned," Metro-Goldwyn-Mayer, 1960; "The World Ten Times Over," ABPC, 1962; "The Domain of Power," Cyclops, 1963; "Pax?," Mexican Olympic Committee, 1967; "Quarry," Rilla Productions, 1969; "The Condemned," Rilla Productions, 1971; "The Wheelchair," Rank, 1974.

Television plays: "Cinema Verite," Associated Television Ltd., 1967; "The Greater Good," BBC, 1970; "A Family Affair," BBC, 1971; "Death Comes to Fasching," BBC, 1971; "I Never Promised You a Rosegarden," BBC, 1973.

WORK IN PROGRESS: The Illusionists, a novel.

SIDELIGHTS: Rilla writes: "I tend to combine the career of a writer with that of a film director: indeed, I find that both activities have the same creative source, but because they are logistically different (the one intensively private, the other very public) I regard each as a holiday from the other. In addition, film making gives me the opportunity of extensive travel to which I am passionately attached, and which has frequently provided me with creative source material."

The Wolf Rilla collection is in Mugar Memorial Library at Boston University.

* * *

RINZLER, Carol Eisen 1941- (Carol G. Eisen)

PERSONAL: Born September 12, 1941, in Newark, N.J.; daughter of Irving Y. (a professor) and Ruth (Katz) Eisen; married Carl Rinzler (a psychiatrist), July 21, 1962; children: Michael, Jane. *Education:* Goucher College, B.A., 1962. *Politics:* "Democrat/Liberal." *Religion:* Jewish. *Home:* 1215 Fifth Ave., New York, N.Y. 10029. *Agent:* Knox Burger Associates Ltd., 39 ½ Washington Sq. S., New York, N.Y. 10012. *Office:* Charterhouse Books, Inc., 750 Third Ave., New York, N.Y. 10017.

CAREER: Commentary, New York, N.Y., advertising manager, 1970-71; Charterhouse Books, Inc., New York, N.Y., associate publisher, 1972-73, publisher, 1973—.

WRITINGS: (Editor) *Frankly McCarthy,* Public Affairs Press, 1968; (under name Carol G. Eisen) *Nobody Said You Had to Eat Off the Floor,* McKay, 1971.

WORK IN PROGRESS: A novel.

* * *

RIPPERGER, Henrietta

See HAWLEY, Henrietta Ripperger

* * *

RIPPON, Marion E(dith) 1921-

PERSONAL: Born October 24, 1921, in Drumheller, Alberta, Canada; daughter of Arthur W. and Louise (Brownell) Simpson; married Clive Langley Rippon (a military judge in the Canadian Armed Forces), February 25, 1944; children: Michelle (Mrs. Ed Burleson), David, Thomas. *Education:* University of Alberta, B.S.C., 1940; Holy Cross Hospital School of Nursing, R.N., 1943. *Home:* 849 Pemberton Rd., Victoria, British Columbia V8S 3R5, Canada.

CAREER: Victoria General Hospital, Halifax, Nova Scotia, night supervisor, 1950; Rockcliffe Hospital, Ottawa, Ontario, night supervisor, 1951-54; Stadacona Hospital, Halifax, Nova Scotia, psychiatric nurse, 1961-63; Correspondence Branch of the Department of Education, Victoria, British Columbia, instructor in creative writing, 1971-74; University of Victoria, Victoria, British Columbia, lecturer in creative writing, 1974—. *Member:* Elizabeth Fry Society.

WRITINGS—Novels: *The Hand of Solange,* Doubleday, 1969; *Behold, the Druid Weeps,* Doubleday, 1970; *The Ninth Tentacle,* Doubleday, 1974. Contributor to *Writer.*

WORK IN PROGRESS: The House on Indigo Street, a novel.

SIDELIGHTS: Marion Rippon wrote: "I always have a new book churning around in my mind, and another begun on paper. As I didn't start writing until five years ago, I have a whole lifetime of ideas longing to be given life."

* * *

RISATTI, Howard A(nthony) 1943-

PERSONAL: Born October 8, 1943, in Blue Island, Ill.; son of James Bruno and Zoila (Munarin) Risatti; married Michaeline Mannino (a teacher), December 29, 1969. *Education:* Wilson Junior College, student, 1962-64; Roosevelt University, B.M., 1967, M.M., 1968; University of Illinois, D.Mus., 1970, M.A., 1970, Ph.D. candidate, 1973—. *Home:* 1003 West Clark St., Urbana, Ill. 61801. *Office:* Art and Design Department, Fine and Applied Arts Bldg., University of Illinois, Urbana, Ill. 61801.

CAREER: Risatti Construction Firm, Chicago, Ill., partner, 1969—. Composer. *Member:* International Society for Contemporary Music, Pullman (Ill.) Historical Society, Champaign-Urbana Art Historical Society.

WRITINGS: New Music Vocabulary: A Guide to Notational Signs for Contemporary Music, University of Illinois Press, 1974. Author of "The Pit and the Pendulum," a ballet in two scenes based on Edgar Allan Poe's short story.

WORK IN PROGRESS: Research on the cultural history of the early twentieth century, especially Mondrian and the Schoenberg School.

AVOCATIONAL INTERESTS: Pre-Columbian art.

* * *

RIST, Ray C(harles) 1944-

PERSONAL: Born December 7, 1944, in Carbondale, Ill.; son of Ray C. (a clergyman) and Mildred (Borman) Rist; married Marilee Carol Esala (a professor), 1966; children: Paul. *Education:* Valparaiso University, B.A., 1967; Washington University, St. Louis, Mo., M.A., 1968, Ph.D., 1970. *Home:* 720 Southwest Dolph St., Portland, Ore. 97219. *Office:* Department of Sociology, Portland State University, Portland, Ore. 97207.

CAREER: Portland State University, Portland, Ore., assistant professor, 1970-72, associate professor of sociology, 1972—. Consultant to U.S. Commission on Civil Rights and National Institute of Education. *Member:* American Sociological Association, Society for the Study of Social Problems, Pacific Sociological Association, Midwest Sociological Association, European Group for the Study of Deviance and Social Control. *Awards, honors: American School Board Journal* named *The Urban School* one of nine outstanding education books of 1973; National Science Foundation grant, 1974.

WRITINGS: (Editor) *Restructuring American Education,* Trans-Action, 1972; *The Quest for Autonomy,* Afro-American Center, University of California, Los Angeles, 1972; *The Urban School: A Factory for Failure,* M.I.T. Press, 1973; (editor) *The Pornography Controversy,* Trans-Action, 1974. Contributor of about thirty articles to journals, including *Harvard Educational Review, Phylon,* and *Social Problems.* Associate editor of *Northwest Journal of African and Black American Studies* and *Journal of Black Social Research.*

WORK IN PROGRESS: A book on American minority group relations and a book on the process of school desegregation, both for Trans-Action.

* * *

RITCHIE, Elisavietta (Yurievna Artamonoff)

PERSONAL: Born in Kansas City, Mo.; daughter of George Leonidovich (a businessman) and Jessie (in public relations and interior decorating; maiden name, Downing) Artamonoff; married Lyell Hale Ritchie (engaged in international economic development), July 11, 1953; children: Lyell Kirk, Elspeth Cameron, Alexander George. *Education:* Sorbonne, University of Paris, Degre Superieur, 1951; attended Cornell University, 1951-53; University of California, Berkeley, B.A., 1954; American University, graduate study, 1968—. *Home:* 3207 Macomb St. N.W., Washington, D.C. 20008.

CAREER: Author, poet, editor, translator; free-lance writer for U.S. Information Agency, San Francisco Area Council, World Trade Center, and other agencies and organizations, 1955—; contract translator of French and Russian for U.S. Department of State and other government agencies and private clients, 1960—. Has given poetry readings on radio and television and at schools, theatres, and poetry societies in and around Washington, D.C.; poet-in-residence, John Eaton School, 1973—. *Member:* Poetry Society of America. *Awards, honors:* Conrad Aiken Prize of Georgia Poetry Society, 1971; William Marion Reedy Memorial Prize of Poetry Society of America, 1973.

WRITINGS: (Translator) Aleksandr Blok, *The Twelve* (translations first published in *Ann Arbor Review,* 1968), Ann Arbor Books, 1969; *Timbot* (novella in verse), Lit Press, 1970; (contributor of translations) Abraham Brumberg, editor, *In Quest of Justice: Protest and Dissent in the Soviet Union Today,* Praeger, 1970; *Tightening the Circle Over Eel Country,* Acropolis Books, 1974. Co-author of *Readings from the French-Speaking World,* two volumes, for Department of Language and Foreign Studies, American University, 1969.

Contributor of more than 300 poems to general, literary, and little magazines, with poems anthologized in *The Diamond Anthology, Adam Among the Television Trees,*

Washington Poets, New Generation Poetry, and other collections. Articles, stories, translations, and reviews have been published in magazines and newspapers, including *New York Times, New York Quarterly, New Republic, Washington Post, Voyages, Chicago Tribune, Christian Science Monitor, New England Review,* and others.

WORK IN PROGRESS: Two novels; a play; a film script; short stories; translations of contemporary Russian stories.

SIDELIGHTS: Elisavietta Ritchie, who has made recordings of her poetry for the Library of Congress, has lived in France, Japan, Cyprus, Lebanon, and traveled in other countries of Europe, Middle East, South America, and Central America. *Avocational interests:* Marine biology.

BIOGRAPHICAL/CRITICAL SOURCES: Washington Star-News, July 10, 1973.

* * *

RITCHIE, John C(ollins) 1927-

PERSONAL: Born May 20, 1927, in Philadelphia, Pa.; son of John Collins and Martha (Taggart) Ritchie; married Shirley E. Seiverd, September 16, 1950; children: John K., Kathleen A. *Education:* Temple University, B.S. (with honors), 1950, M.B.A., 1954; University of Pennsylvania, Ph.D., 1963. *Home:* 14 Newington Dr., Hatboro, Pa. 19040. *Office:* Room 321, Speakman Hall, Temple University, Philadelphia, Pa. 19122.

CAREER: E. I. duPont de Nemours & Co., Wilmington, Del., accountant, 1950-51, credit man, 1951-54; Temple University, Philadelphia, Pa., instructor, 1954-61, assistant professor, 1961-66, associate professor, 1966-70, professor of finance, 1970—. Consultant to Provident National Bank, 1971—, and Parker Allen Co., 1971—. Member of board of examiners, Chartered Property and Casualty Underwriters, 1960-64. *Military service:* U.S. Navy, 1945-46. *Member:* American Economic Association, American Finance Association.

WRITINGS: (With Douglas H. Bellemore) *Investments: Principles, Practices and Analysis,* 3rd edition (Ritchie was not associated with earlier editions), South-Western Publishing, 1967, 4th edition, 1973. Contributor to *Magazine of Bank Administration* and other journals.

WORK IN PROGRESS: A short monograph on the president's role in financial planning, for American Management Association; a book tentatively titled *Long Range Planning for Banks.*

* * *

RIVERA, Tomas 1935-

PERSONAL: Born December 22, 1935, in Crystal City, Tex.; son of Florencio M. (a laborer and cook) and Josefa (Hernandez) Rivera; married Concepcion Garza, November 27, 1958; children: Ileana, Irasema, Florencio Javier. *Education:* Southwest Texas Junior College, A.A., 1956; Southwest Texas State College (now University), B.A., 1958, M.Ed., 1964; University of Oklahoma, M.A., 1969, Ph.D., 1969. *Home:* 5912 Trone Trail, San Antonio, Tex. 78238. *Office:* College of Multidisciplinary Studies, University of Texas, 4242 Piedras Dr., San Antonio, Tex. 78284.

CAREER: Teacher of English and Spanish in public schools of San Antonio, Tex., 1957-58, Crystal City, Tex., 1958-60, and League City, Tex., 1960-65; Southwest Texas Junior College, Uvalde, instructor in English, French, and Spanish, 1965-66; University of Oklahoma, Norman, instructor in Spanish, 1968-69; Sam Houston State University, Huntsville, Tex., associate professor of Spanish, 1969-71; University of Texas, San Antonio, professor of Spanish, 1971—, associate dean of College of Multidisciplinary Studies, 1973—. Visiting professor at Trinity University, San Antonio, Tex., 1973. *Member:* Phi Theta Kappa, Sigma Pi. *Awards, honors: Premio Quinto Sol* National Literary Award, 1970, for *Y no se lo trago la tierra/And the Earth Did Not Part.*

WRITINGS: Y no se lo trago la tierra/And the Earth Did Not Part (bilingual edition of short stories), Quinto Sol Publications, 1971; (contributor) Joseph Flores, editor, *Songs and Dreams,* Pendulum Press, 1972; (contributor) Octavio Romano and Herminio Rios, editors, *El espejo/The Mirror,* Quinto Sol Publications, revised edition, 1972; *Always and Other Poems,* Sisterdale Press, 1973. Also contributor to *Cafe Solo,* edited by Ernest Padilla, 1974. Work is represented in anthologies, including *Aztlan: An Anthology of La Raza Literature,* edited by Luis Valdez and Stan Steiner, Knopf, 1972; *Chicano Literature: An Anthology,* edited by Phillip Ortego, Simon & Schuster, 1973; *Anthology of Texas Poets,* edited by Dave Oliphant, Prickley Pear Press, 1974; *The Chicano Short Story,* edited by Luis Davila, University of Indiana Press, 1974. Contributor to professional journals. Member of editorial board of MICTLA Publications, 1971—, and *El Magazin,* 1972—; contributing editor, *El Grito,* 1971—, and *Revista Chicana-Riquena,* 1973—.

WORK IN PROGRESS: Contributing to *An Anthology of Mexican-American Literature;* a novel, *The Large House in Town;* a large volume of poetry.

SIDELIGHTS: Rivera wrote: "Up to the time I started teaching, I was part of the migrant labor stream that went from Texas to. . .the Midwest. I lived and worked in Iowa, Minnesota, Wisconsin, Michigan, and North Dakota."

BIOGRAPHICAL/CRITICAL SOURCES: Luis Davila, editor, *Chicano Literature and Tomas Rivera* (monograph), University of Indiana Press, 1974.

* * *

RIVERS, Caryl 1937-

PERSONAL: First name is pronounced Carol; born December 19, 1937; daughter of Hugh F. (a lawyer) and Helen (Huhn) Rivers; married Alan Lupo (executive editor of *Boston Magazine*), May 19, 1962; children: Steven, Alyssa. *Education:* Trinity College, Washington, D.C., A.B., 1959; Columbia University, M.S., 1960. *Religion:* Roman Catholic. *Home:* 54 Johnson Ave., Winthrop, Mass. 02152. *Agent:* Bertha Klausner International Literary Agency, Inc., 71 Park Ave., New York, N.Y. 10016. *Office:* School of Public Communications, Boston University, Boston, Mass. 02215.

CAREER: Middletown Record, Middletown, N.Y., family editor, 1960-62; *El Mundo,* San Juan, P.R., Washington correspondent, 1962-66; Boston University, Boston, Mass., lecturer in journalism, 1966—; free-lance writer. Public affairs commentator for WGBH-TV, Boston, 1968—. *Member:* Women in Communication. *Awards, honors:* J.C. Penney-University of Missouri Award, 1961, for editing one of the best newspaper women's sections in the United States.

WRITINGS: Aphrodite at Midcentury: Growing Up Female and Catholic in Postwar America, Doubleday, 1973.

Contributor to *World, Saturday Review, New York Times Magazine, Ms., Glamour, McCall's, Boston Magazine, Baltimore Sun,* and *Louisville Courier Journal.*

WORK IN PROGRESS: Stories of the Silent Generation, a collection of short stories; a novel.

* * *

ROBERTS, John G(aither) 1913- (Robert Paul)

PERSONAL: Born January 14, 1913, in New Britain, Conn.; son of Rankin Handley (a businessman) and Dorothy (Lamps) Roberts; married Elizabeth Kneipple (a writer; pseudonym, Edith Roberts), 1936; married Elinor Nowinski, 1941; married Jacqueline Paul, 1946; married Midori Yamakawa (a researcher and translator), September 3, 1965; children: Christopher, Molly Alice. *Education:* University of Chicago, B.Sc., 1936. *Politics and religion:* Unaffiliated. *Home and office:* 441-10, 1-chome, Suzuki-cho, Kodaira City, Tokyo, Japan 187. *Agent:* Barthold Fles, 507 Fifth Ave., New York, N.Y. 10017.

CAREER: Worked variously as translator, photography teacher, and assistant to painter, David Alfaro Siqueiros in Mexico, 1947-51, free-lance writer and photographer in San Francisco, Calif., 1951-59, business writer, ghost writer, and editor in Japan, 1959—; International Public Relations Co. Ltd., Tokyo, Japan, writer and editor, 1963—. President, Visual Arts International Ltd., 1962—. Translator. *Military service:* U.S. Army, 1942-46; became lieutenant; received Purple Heart. *Member:* International House of Japan, Foreign Correspondents Club of Japan.

WRITINGS: (Author of text) *Hiroshima-Nagasaki Document,* Japan Council Against A and H Bombs, 1961; (editor with Jacqueline Paul) *Japan Quest,* Tuttle, 1962; *Black Ships and Rising Sun: The Opening of Japan to the West,* Messner, 1971; *The Industrialization of Japan,* F. Watts, 1972; *Mitsui: Three Centuries of Japanese Business,* Weatherhill, 1973. Author of documentary filmscripts. Contributor, sometimes under pseudonyms Robert Paul and others, to *New York Times, Times* (London), *Wall Street Journal, Chicago Daily News, Guardian, Nation, Fortune, Time, Financial Times, Medical Tribune, Asahi Journal, Sekai, Chuo Koron,* and others. Correspondent, *Medical Tribune,* 1965-69, *Far East Trade and Development,* 1960-70, *Far Eastern Economic Review,* 1965—, *Burroughs Clearing House,* 1967—; editor, *Japan Banking Briefs,* 1964—.

WORK IN PROGRESS: The Colonial Conquest of Asia, for young people, completion expected in 1975; with wife, Midori Roberts, *Healing Arts of Asia,* 1976; a book on the political-economic power structure of Japan.

SIDELIGHTS: Roberts told *CA:* "Arriving in Japan in 1959, I was immediately swept up in the torrent of events from which "Japan Incorporated" was born. To understand the dynamics of the process I concentrated on studies of Japanese history and political economy while earning a livelihood as a business journalist, ghost writer and editor. One tangible result of these experiences was *Mitsui: Three Centuries of Japanese Business,* which may be regarded as a sampling of other works in progress. My ambition is to live until some of them are completed; and my avocation, shared by my wife Midori, is to ferret out the secrets of health and longevity as expounded by sages of the orient."

ROBERTS, Walter R(onald) 1916-

PERSONAL: Born August 26, 1916, in Waltendorf, Austria; came to United States, 1939; naturalized citizen, 1944; son of Ignatius R. (an editor and writer) and Elisabeth (Diamant) Roberts; married Gisela K. Schmarak, August 22, 1939; children: William M., Charles E., Lawrence H. *Education:* Cambridge University, M.Litt., 1940. *Home:* 4449 Sedgwick St., N.W., Washington, D.C. 20016. *Office:* Center for Strategic and International Studies, Georgetown University, 1800 K St. N.W., Washington, D.C. 20006.

CAREER: Harvard University, Law School, Cambridge, Mass., research assistant, 1940-42; U.S. Office of War Information, Voice of America, New York, N.Y., writer and editor, 1942-49; U.S. Department of State, Washington, D.C., foreign affairs officer, 1950-53; U.S. Information Agency, Washington, D.C. deputy assistant director, 1954-60; counselor for public affairs at U.S. Embassy in Belgrade, Yugoslavia, 1960-66; counselor to U.S. Mission to International Organizations, Geneva, Switzerland, 1967-69; U.S. Information Agency, deputy associate directory, 1969-71, associate director, 1971-74; Georgetown University, Washington, D.C., director of diplomatic studies at the Center for Strategic and International Studies, 1974—. Press officer, U.S. Delegation to Austrian Treaty Talks, 1949, 1955. Diplomat in residence, Brown University, 1966-67.

WRITINGS: Tito, Mihailovic and the Allies, 1941-1945, Rutgers University Press, 1973.

* * *

ROBERTS, Willo Davis 1928-

PERSONAL: Born May 29, 1928, in Grand Rapids, Mich.; daughter of Clayton R. and Lealah (Gleason) Davis; married David W. Roberts (a building supply salesman), May 20, 1949; children: Kathleen, David M., Larrilyn (Mrs. Eric Lindquist), Christopher. *Education:* Graduated from high school in Pontiac, Mich., 1946. *Religion:* Lutheran. *Home:* 220 Hillsdale St., Eureka, Calif. 95501. *Agent:* Curtis Brown Ltd., 60 East 56th St., New York, N.Y. 10022.

CAREER: Writer of suspense novels. Has worked in hospitals and doctors' offices in a paramedical capacity. *Member:* Mystery Writers of America, Science Fiction Writers of America, Authors Guild of Authors League of America, National League of American Penwomen.

WRITINGS: Murder at Grand Bay, Arcadia House, 1955; *The Girl Who Wasn't There,* Arcadia House, 1957.

Murder Is So Easy, Vega Books, 1961; *The Suspected Four,* Vega Books, 1962; *Nurse Kay's Conquest,* Ace Books, 1966; *Once a Nurse,* Ace Books, 1966; *Nurse at Mystery Villa,* Ace Books, 1967; *Return to Darkness,* Lancer Books, 1969.

Shroud of Fog, Ace Books, 1970; *Devil Boy,* New American Library, 1970; *The Waiting Darkness,* Lancer Books, 1970; *Shadow of a Past Love,* Lancer Books, 1970; *The House at Fern Canyon,* Lancer Books, 1970; *The Tarot Spell,* Lancer Books, 1970; *Invitation to Evil,* Lancer Books, 1970; *The Terror Trap,* Lancer Books, 1971; *King's Pawn,* Lancer Books, 1971; *The Gates of Montrain,* Lancer Books, 1971; *The Watchers,* Lancer Books, 1971; *The Ghosts of Harrel,* Lancer Books, 1971; *Inherit the Darkness,* Lancer Books, 1972; *Nurse in Danger,* Ace Books, 1972; *Becca's Child,* Lancer Books, 1972; *Sing a Dark Song,* Lancer Books, 1972; *The Nurses,* Ace Books,

1972; *The Face of Danger,* Lancer Books, 1972; *Dangerous Legacy,* Lancer Books, 1972; *Sinister Gardens,* Lancer Books, 1972; *The M.D.,* Lancer Books, 1972; *The Evil Children,* Lancer Books, 1973; *The Gods in Green,* Lancer Books, 1973; *Nurse Robin,* Lennox Hill, 1973; *Didn't Anybody Know My Wife?,* Putnam, 1974; *White Jade,* Doubleday, in press.

WORK IN PROGRESS: The Imposters; Cape of Black Sands; revising a suspense novel, for Putnam.

* * *

ROBERTSON, Elizabeth Chant 1899-

PERSONAL: Born April 17, 1899, in Toronto, Ontario, Canada; daughter of Clarence Augustus (a professor) and Jean (Laidlaw) Chant; married H. Grant Robertson, June 30, 1926; children: Mary (Mrs. Lincoln James), Helen (Mrs. William Currie). *Education:* University of Toronto, B.A. (honors), 1921, M.D., 1924, M.A., 1928, Ph.D., 1937. *Politics:* Liberal. *Religion:* United Church of Canada. *Home:* 503 Davenport Rd., Toronto M4V 1B8, Ontario, Canada. *Office:* Hospital for Sick Children, 555 University Ave., Toronto M5G 1X8, Ontario, Canada.

CAREER: Certified specialist in pediatrics and nutrition; Hospital for Sick Children, Toronto, Ontario, research assistant, 1927-45, research associate, 1945—; University of Toronto, Toronto, Ontario, junior clinician, 1943-47, senior clinician, 1947-60, associate in pediatrics, 1960-61. Nutrition adviser to Canadian Broadcasting Corp., 1946-65. *Member:* American Institute of Nutrition, Canadian Pediatric Society, Nutrition Society of Canada, Alpha Omega Alpha.

WRITINGS: (With Alan G. Brown) *The Normal Child,* Century, 1923, 4th edition, McClelland & Stewart, 1948; *Low Mineral Diets and Intestinal Stasis,* University of Toronto Press, 1938; *Fundamentals of Health,* Copp Clark, 1943, 2nd edition (with Grover W. Mueller) published as *Fundamentals of Health and Safety,* Van Nostrand, 1952; *Nutrition for Today,* McClelland & Stewart, 1951, 3rd edition, 1968; (with others) *Food and Textiles I,* W. J. Gage, 1964; (with others) *Food and Textiles II,* W. J. Gage, 1965, (with others) "Health, Science and You" series, six books, Holt, 1967-69; (with Margaret I. Wood) *Today's Child: A Modern Guide to Baby Care and Child Training,* Pagurian Press, 1971, Scribner, 1972; (with others) *Tomorrow is Now,* Holt, 1971.

WORK IN PROGRESS: Food, a text for junior high school.

* * *

ROBINSON, Charles 1931-

PERSONAL: Born June 25, 1931, in Morristown, N.J.; son of Powell (an investment banker) and Ruth (Wyllis) Taylor; married Cynthia Margetts (a sixth-grade teacher), August 17, 1967; children: Mimi, Charles, Edward. *Education:* Harvard University, A.B., 1953; University of Virginia, LL.B., 1958. *Home and studio:* Millbrook Rd., New Vernon, N.J. 07976.

CAREER: Fiduciary Trust Co. of New York, New York, N.Y., assistant securities analyst, 1954; McCarter & English (law firm), Newark, N.J., associate, 1958-60; Mutual Benefit Life Insurance Co., Newark, N.J., attorney, 1960-68; switched from corporation law to full-time illustrating, 1968. *Military service:* U.S. Army, Signal Corps, 1953-54. *Member:* New Jersey Watercolor Society. *Awards, honors:* Society of Illustrators Gold Medal for cover of *Audubon: The Man Who Painted Birds,* 1971; *The Dead Tree* was nominated for Caldecott Medal of American Library Association, 1972; *The Mountain of Truth* was an Honor Book in *Book World's* Children's Spring Book Festival, 1972.

WRITINGS—Self-illustrated: *Yuri and the Mooneygoats,* Simon & Schuster, 1969.

Illustrator: M. Caporale Schector and Harriet May Savitz, *The Moon Is Mine,* John Day, 1968; Gunilla B. Norris, *The Good Morrow,* Atheneum, 1969; Ruth Philpott Collins, *Mystery of the Giant Giraffe,* Walck, 1969; Betty Horvath, *Will the Real Tommy Wilson Please Stand Up?,* F. Watts, 1969; Anne Norris Baldwin, *The Sometimes Island,* Norton, 1969; Jean Bothwell, *The Mystery Tunnel,* Dial, 1969.

Jane Louise Curry, *Mindy's Mysterious Miniature,* Harcourt, 1970; Helen Chetin, *Tales of an African Drum,* Harcourt, 1970; Jane Louise Curry, *Daybreakers,* Harcourt, 1970; Barbara Corcoran, *The Long Journey,* Atheneum, 1970; Sonia Levitan, *Journey to America* (Junior Literary Guild selection), Atheneum, 1970; Nathan Kraveta and Muriel Farrell, *Is There a Lion in the House?,* Walck, 1970; Florence Parry Heide, *Giants Are Very Brave People,* Parents' Magazine Press, 1970; Norah Smaridge, *Audubon: The Man Who Painted Birds,* World Publishing, 1970; Mattie Lamb Curtis, *Blizzard,* Dutton, 1970; Bronson Potter, *Chibia, the Dhow Boy,* Atheneum, 1971; Gunilla B. Norris, *Green and Something Else,* Simon & Schuster, 1971; Mildred Wilds Willard, *The Luck of Harry Weaver,* F. Watts, 1971; Winston M. Estes, *Another Part of the House,* Reader's Digest Condensed Books, 1971; Leonore Klein, *Only One Ant,* Hastings House, 1971; Ruth Whitehead, *The Mother Tree,* Seabury, 1971; Arthur Durham Divine, under pseudonym David Divine, *The Stolen Seasons,* Crowell, 1971; Elizabeth Coatsworth, *The Snow Parlour,* Grosset, 1971; Marion Renick, *Take a Long Jump,* Scribner, 1971; Francis Kalnay, *It Happened in Chichipica,* Harcourt, 1971; Jane Louise Curry, *Over the Sea's Edge,* Harcourt, 1971; Adelaide Leitch, *The Blue Roan,* Walck, 1971; Anatolii Aleksin, *A Late Born Child,* World Publishing, 1971.

Jack Finney, *Time and Again,* Reader's Digest Condensed Books, 1972; Dale Carlson, *The Mountain of Truth,* Atheneum, 1972; Babbis Friis, *Wanted! A Horse!,* Harcourt, 1972; Maggie Duff, *Jonny and His Drum,* Walck, 1972; Mary Francis Shura, *Topcat of Tam,* Holiday House, 1972; Alvin Tresselt, *The Dead Tree,* Parents' Magazine Press, 1972; Emmy West and Christine Govan, *Danger Downriver,* Viking, 1972; William Corbin, *The Pup With the Up and Down Tail,* Coward, 1972; Mabel Esther Allen, *Island in a Green Sea,* Atheneum, 1972; Evelyn Sibley Lampman, *Go Up the Road,* Atheneum, 1972; Marden Dahlstedt, *The Terrible Wave* (Junior Literary Guild selection), Coward, 1972; Lew Bennett Hopkins, *Charlie's World,* Bobbs-Merrill, 1972; Betty Dinneen, *A Lurk of Leopards,* Walck, 1972; Patricia McKillup, *The House on Parchment Street,* Atheneum, 1973; Miriam Young, *A Witches Garden,* Atheneum, 1973; Jean Robinson, *The Secret Life of T. K. Dearing,* Seabury, 1973; Marion Renick, *Five Points for Hockey,* Scribner, 1973; Doris Buchanan Smith, *A Taste of Blackberries,* Crowell, in press; Barbara Corcoran, *All the Summer Voices,* Atheneum, in press; Carol Beach York, *The Midnight Ghost,* Coward, in press.

SIDELIGHTS: Robinson wrote: "Until I made the switch

in mid-career from law to illustrating, my major area of avocational interest was being a 'Sunday painter.' Now that I paint all week I find other pursuits for weekends, i.e., woodworking, gardening. Wish I had made this move 15 years earlier. Enjoy working in a fairly realistic style—favor watercolors to oils, generally. I have plans for doing a far-out fanciful kind of book one of these days."

* * *

ROBINSON, Eric 1924-

PERSONAL: Born March 8, 1924, in Calne, Wiltshire, England; son of Percival (an organ builder) and Dorothy (Smith) Robinson; married Rosemary Melville, August 6, 1949 (divorced, 1972); married Joan Cahalin, July 17, 1973; children: (first marriage) Shelley (Mrs. Peter Heath), Sara. *Education:* Jesus College, Cambridge, B.A. (first class honors, with distinction), 1948, M.A., 1950. *Home:* 181 Moss Hill Rd., Boston, Mass. 02130. *Agent:* Curtis Brown Ltd., 1 Craven Sq., London, England. *Office:* Department of History, University of Massachusetts—Boston, Boston, Mass. 02125.

CAREER: University of London, King's College, London, England, assistant lecturer in English language and literature, 1948-50; University of Ibadan, Ibadan, Nigeria, lecturer in English, 1950-53; Bristol Grammar School, Bristol, England, English master, 1954-57; University of Manchester, Manchester, England, Simon research fellow, 1957-58; Coventry College of Education, Coventry, England, principal lecturer in English and head of department, 1958-60; University of Manchester, lecturer, 1960-66, senior lecturer in economic history, 1966-69; University of Pittsburgh, Pittsburgh, Pa., visiting Carroll Amundson Professor of British History, 1969-70; University of Massachusetts—Boston, professor of modern history and director of graduate studies in history, 1970—. Research fellow at University of Bristol, 1953-54. *Military service:* Royal Naval Volunteer Reserve, 1943-46; became lieutenant.

MEMBER: Economic History Society, Society for the History of Technology, Newcomen Society, Royal Society of the Arts. *Awards, honors:* Guggenheim fellowship, 1972-73.

WRITINGS: (With Leila Brown) *Rhyme and Reason* (poems, with teacher's book), University of London Press, 1956; (editor with Geoffrey Summerfield) *Later Poems of John Clare,* Manchester University Press, 1964; (editor with Summerfield) Frederick Martin, *The Life of John Clare,* Frank Cass, 1964; (editor with Summerfield) John Clare, *The Shepherd's Calendar,* Oxford University Press, 1964; (contributor) Brian Jackson, editor, *English versus Examinations,* Chatto & Windus, 1965; *The Lunar Society Bicentenary Exhibition Catalogue,* privately printed, 1966; (editor with Summerfield) Clare, *Selected Poems and Prose,* Clarendon Press (of Oxford University), 1966; (editor with Summerfield) *Selected Poems and Prose of John Clare,* Oxford University Press, 1967; (editor with Douglas McKie) *Partners in Science: The Scientific Correspondence of James Watt and Joseph Black,* Harvard University Press, 1969; (with A. E. Musson) *Science and Technology in the Industrial Revolution,* Manchester University Press, 1969; (with Musson) *James Watt and the Steam Revolution,* Evelyn, Adams & Mackay, 1969; (contributor) Arthur Pollard, editor, *Companion to Western Literature,* London International Press, 1969.

(Contributor) F. M. Jevons and other editors, *University Perspectives,* Manchester University Press, 1971; (contributor) R. H. Donaldson, editor, *Bicentenary of the James Watt Patent,* Glasgow University Publications, 1971; (contributor) Ian M. G. Quimby and Polly Anne Earl, editors, *Technological Innovation and the Decorative Arts,* University Press of Virginia, 1974. Contributor to *Lexicon der Literature der Gegenwart* (title means "Encyclopedia of Contemporary Literature"). Contributor of more than fifty articles and reviews to science, history, and literature journals, including *Review of English Studies, Use of English, Cambridge Review, Annals of Science, Journal of Economic History,* and *Journal for the History and Philosophy of Science.*

WORK IN PROGRESS: Books about Boulton and Watt, marriage in the eighteenth century, and history of English patent law; editing poetry of John Clare, for Clarendon Press (of Oxford University); a critical monograph on Clare; research on comparative history of technology, relating it to social and literary history; research to help further the education of society about death and dying.

* * *

ROBINSON, Frank M(alcolm) 1926- (Thomas Benji, Robert Courtney, James Walsh)

PERSONAL: Born August 9, 1926, in Chicago, Ill.; son of Raymond (an artist and photographer) and Leona (White) Robinson. *Education:* Beloit College, B.S., 1950; Northwestern University, M.S. Journalism, 1955. *Politics:* Liberal. *Religion:* Protestant. *Residence:* San Francisco, Calif. *Agent:* Curtis Brown Ltd., 60 East 56th St., New York, N.Y. 10022.

CAREER: Family Weekly, Chicago, Ill., assistant editor, 1955-56; *Science Digest,* Chicago, Ill., assistant editor, 1956-59; *Rogue* (magazine), Chicago, Ill., editor, 1959-65; *Cavalier* (magazine), Los Angeles, Calif., managing editor, 1965-66; *Censorship Today,* Los Angeles, Calif., editor, 1967; *Playboy,* Chicago, Ill., staff writer, 1969-73; freelance writer, 1973—. *Military service:* U.S. Navy, radar technician, 1944-45, 1950-51. *Member:* Phi Beta Kappa, Sigma Delta Chi.

WRITINGS: The Power (fiction), Lippincott, 1956; (editor with Nat Lehrman) *Sex, American Style,* Playboy Press, 1972; (with Thomas N. Scortia) *The Glass Inferno* (fiction), Doubleday, 1974. Contributor to popular magazines and newspapers, sometimes under pseudonyms Thomas Benji, Robert Courtney, and James Walsh.

WORK IN PROGRESS: The Prometheus Crisis, fiction, with Thomas N. Scortia.

SIDELIGHTS: The Power was adapted and filmed by MGM in 1968.

* * *

ROBINSON, John W(esley) 1929-

PERSONAL: Born July 8, 1929, in Long Beach, Calif.; son of John Wesley (a minister) and Loreen (Buffum) Robinson; divorced, June, 1972; children: Robyn, Cathleen, Jeanne. *Education:* University of Southern California, A.B., 1951; California State University, Long Beach, M.A., 1966. *Politics:* Democratic. *Home:* 2700 Peterson Way, 12-F, Costa Mesa, Calif. 92626.

CAREER: Elementary and junior high school teacher of history in public schools of Redondo Beach, Calif., 1953-56, Newport Beach, Calif., 1956-67, and Costa Mesa,

Calif., 1967—. *Military service:* U.S. Army, 1953-55. *Member:* Sierra Club, California Historical Society, Southern California Historical Society.

WRITINGS: (Editor) *Jose Joaquin Arrillaga: Diary of His Surveys of the Frontier,* Dawson's Book Shop, 1969; *Trails of the Angeles,* Wilderness Press, 1971; *San Bernardino Mountain Trails,* Wilderness Press, 1972; *Mines of the San Gabriels,* La Siesta Press, 1973; *Mount Wilson Story,* La Siesta Press, 1973. Contributor to *Pomona Valley Historian.*

WORK IN PROGRESS: Research on *Mines of the San Bernardino Mountains; Pictorial History of the San Gabriel Mountains; Biblio-History of the Sierra Nevada.*

AVOCATIONAL INTERESTS: Conservation, mountain climbing, hiking (has led more than fifty Sierra Club trips).

* * *

ROBINSON, Marguerite S. 1935-

PERSONAL: Born October 11, 1935, in New York, N.Y.; daughter of Philip Van Doren (an author) and Lillian (Diamond) Stern; married Allan R. Robinson (a professor), June 12, 1955; children: Sarah Penelope, Perrine, Laura Ondine. *Education:* Radcliffe College, B.A., 1956; Newnham College, Cambridge, graduate study, 1959-60; Harvard University, Ph.D., 1965. *Home:* 24 Warwick Rd., Brookline, Mass. 02146. *Office:* Dean of the College, Brandeis University, Waltham, Mass. 02154.

CAREER: Brandeis University, Waltham, Mass., lecturer, 1964-65, assistant professor, 1965-72, associate professor of anthropology, 1972—, dean of the college, 1973—. National Science Foundation fellow, Centre of South Asian Studies, Newnham College, Cambridge University, 1966-67; research fellow in ethnology of India, Peabody Museum, Harvard University, 1969—. Field work in Ceylon, 1963, 1967; Medak District, Andhra Pradesh, India, field work, summers, 1969, 1970; project officer for National Institutes of Health project, 1971-72. *Member:* American Anthropological Association (fellow), Society of Radcliffe Institute Fellows. *Awards, honors:* National Institute of Mental Health postdoctoral fellowship, 1964-65; National Science Foundation research grants, 1966-68, 1968-70; biomedical sciences support grant from Brandeis University, 1969; National Institutes of Health travel grants, summers, 1969, 1970, and winter, 1973, for research in India, and research grant, 1970-72; Ford Foundation grant, 1972.

WRITINGS: (Contributor) *Cambridge Papers in Social Anthropology,* Cambridge University Press, Volume III, edited by Meyer Fortes, 1962, Volume V, edited by E. R. Leach, 1968; (contributor) Mark Lane, editor, *Structuralism: A Reader,* J. Cape, 1970; *Political Structure in a Changing Sinhalese Village,* Cambridge University Press, 1974. Contributor to professional journals.

* * *

ROCA-PONS, Josep 1914-

PERSONAL: Born December 12, 1914, in Barcelona, Spain.; son of Jaume Miquel and Anna Soca (Pons) Roca; married Teresa Boix Gubert, July 1, 1964. *Education:* University of Barcelona, M.Law, 1935, M.Phil., 1941; University of Madrid, Ph.D., 1953. *Home:* 612 Knightridge Rd., Apt. 25C, Bloomington, Ind. 47401. *Office:* Department of Spanish, Indiana University, Bloomington, Ind. 47401.

CAREER: University of Barcelona, Barcelona, Spain, adjunct professor of Romance philology, 1947-55; University of Santiago, Santiago, Cuba, professor of Spanish linguistics, 1955-56; Indiana University, Bloomington, associate professor, 1957-62, professor of Spanish, 1963—. Visiting professor at Georgetown University, 1962-63, and University of Barcelona, 1970-71. *Member:* Societat Catalana d'-Estudis Historics, Linguistic Society of America, Modern Language Association of America, American Association Teachers of Spanish and Portuguese.

WRITINGS: Estudios sobre las perifrasis verbales del espanol, Consejo Superior de Investigaciones Cientificas (Madrid), 1958; (translator with A. Badia Margarit) Joseph Vendryes, *El lenguaje,* Montaner & Simon (Mexico), 1958; *Introduccion a la gramatica,* two volumes, Vergara (Barcelona), 1960, 2nd revised edition, Teide (Barcelona), 1970; *Introduccio a l'estudi de la llengua catalana,* Vergara, 1971; *El lenguage,* Teide, in press. Contributor to several festschrift volumes and to journals.

WORK IN PROGRESS: Brief History of Catalan Literature; new editions of *Introduccion a la gramatica* and *Estudios sobre las perifrasis verbales del espanol.*

* * *

ROCHLIN, Gregory 1912-

PERSONAL: Born October 19, 1912, in Baltimore, Md.; son of Howard and Marie (Ross) Rochlin; married Helen Buker, December 17, 1938; children: Martha (Mrs. Stephen Kopec), Gregory M. *Education:* University of Maryland, M.D., 1936. *Home and office:* 200 Brattle St., Cambridge, Mass. 02138.

CAREER: Child psychiatrist, certified by American Board of Psychiatry and Neurology, 1960. Sinai Hospital, Baltimore, Md., medical intern, 1936-37; Worcester State Hospital, Worcester, Mass., resident in psychiatry, 1937-38; New Haven Hospital and Dispensary, Psychiatric Service, New Haven, Conn., junior assistant resident, 1938-39, senior resident in psychiatry, 1939-40; Yale University School of Medicine, New Haven, Conn., assistant in department of psychiatry, 1938-40; Fairfield State Hospital, Newtown, Conn., senior psychiatrist, 1940-42; Massachusetts General Hospital, Boston, assistant in psychiatry, 1942-43; psychiatrist, Judge Baker Guidance Clinic, 1943-44, James Jackson Putnam Children's Center, 1943-50; Boston Psychoanalytic Society and Institute, Boston, Mass., psychiatrist, 1944-48, graduate, 1945, seminar leader, 1948-50, 1959—, training analyst, 1950—, president, 1960-63; Peter Bent Brigham Hospital, Boston, Mass., senior associate physician in psychiatry, 1949-51; Harvard University Medical School, Boston, Mass., assistant, 1949-51, instructor, 1951-52, clinical associate, 1952-56, assistant clinical professor, 1956-63, associate clinical professor of psychiatry, 1963—; Massachusetts Mental Health Center, Boston, chief child psychiatrist and director of Child Psychiatry Services, 1950—.

MEMBER: American Academy of Child Psychiatry (charter member; member of council, 1960-62), American Psychiatric Association, American Psychoanalytic Association, International Psychoanalytic Association, American Medical Association, Massachusetts Medical Association.

WRITINGS: Griefs and Discontents: The Forces of Change, Little, Brown, 1965; (contributor) Earl A. Grollman, editor, *Explaining Death to Children,* Beacon Press, 1967; *Man's Aggression: The Defense of the Self,* Gambit,

1973. Contributor to *Encyclopaedia Britannica* and to journals in his field.

WORK IN PROGRESS: A book, *Psychology of Masculinity* (tentative title).

* * *

ROCK, Milton L(ee) 1921-

PERSONAL: Born February 25, 1921, in Philadelphia, Pa.; son of Maurice and Mary (Lee) Rock; married Shirley Cylinder, August 3, 1943; children: Susan (Mrs. Richard Herzog), Robert Henry. *Education:* Temple University, B.A., 1946, M.A., 1947; University of Rochester, Ph.D., 1949. *Office:* Hay Associates, 1845 Walnut St., Philadelphia, Pa. 19103.

CAREER: Hay Associates (management consultants), Philadelphia, Pa., managing partner, 1949—, also member of board of directors of Hay Associates Canada Ltd., 1960—, Hay-MSL Ltd., England, 1963—, Hay y Asociados, Mexico, 1968—. Chairman of Mid-Atlantic Regional Manpower Advisory Committee of U.S. Department of Labor, 1972-73. *Military service:* U.S. Army Air Forces, 1942-45. *Member:* American Psychological Association, Association of Consulting Management Engineers (member of board of directors, 1969—; president, 1971-73), Institute of Management Consultants.

WRITINGS: (With Zygmunt Z. Piotrowski) *The Perceptanalytic Executive Scale,* Grune, 1963; (with D. M. Glasner) *Development of Bank Management Personnel,* American Bankers Association, 1969; (editor) *Handbook of Wage and Salary Administration,* McGraw, 1972.

* * *

ROCKWELL, F(rederick) F(rye) 1884-

PERSONAL: Born April 2, 1884, in Brooklyn, N.Y.; son of Francis Warren (a surgeon) and Elizabeth Trowbridge (Hammill) Rockwell; married Marjorie Hughan, 1910 (divorced, 1939); married Esther C. Grayson (a writer), September 21, 1939; children: (first marriage) Hugh Wallace, Frederick F., Donald West, Margaret (Mrs. H. Leroy Finch). *Education:* Attended Wesleyan University, 1903-06. *Politics:* Liberal independent. *Religion:* Protestant. *Home address:* Box 66, Orleans, Mass. 02653.

CAREER: Author, editor, photographer, and lecturer on gardening; *New York Times,* New York, N.Y., editor of Sunday garden section, 1933-43; *Home Garden* (became *Flower Grower-Home Garden,* 1953), New York, N.Y., editor, 1943-63, senior editor, 1963—. Organizer of many garden clubs and judge of numerous flower shows; organized first municipal war garden in New York City during WWI. *Member:* Men's Garden Clubs of America (president, 1940-45), Horticultural Society of New York, Massachusetts Horticultural Society, Orleans Men's Garden Club (founder and president, 1957), Men's Garden Club of New York (founder and president, 1949). *Awards, honors:* Men's Garden Clubs of America large gold medal, 1954; Massachusetts Horticultural Society citation, 1954, and large gold medal, 1961; Dutch Bulb Association citation, 1955; American Horticultural Society citation, 1959; Men's Garden Club of New York Sterling Revere Silver Bowl, 1959.

WRITINGS: Home Vegetable Gardening: A Complete and Practical Guide to the Planting and Care of All Vegetables, Fruits and Berries Worth Growing for Home Use, McBride, Winston & Co., 1911; *Gardening Indoors and Under Glass: A Practical Guide to the Planting Care and Propagation of House Plants, and to the Construction and Management of Hotbed, Cold-frame and Small Greenhouse,* McBride, Nast & Co., 1912; *The Gardener's Pocket Manual,* McBride, Nast & Co., 1914; *Making a Garden of Small Fruits,* McBride, Nast & Co., 1914; *The Key to the Land: What a City Man Did with a Small Farm,* Harper, 1915; *The Little Pruning Book: An Intimate Guide to the Surer Growing of Better Fruits and Flowers,* Peck, Stow & Wilcox Co., 1917; *Around the Year in the Garden: A Seasonable Guide and Reminder for Work with Vegetables, Fruits, and Flowers, and Under Glass,* with photographs by author and E. R. Rollins, Macmillan, 1917, new edition, 1926; *Practical Gardening* (pamphlet), McCall's Magazine, 1918; *Save It for Winter: Modern Methods of Canning, Dehydrating, Preserving and Storing Vegetables and Fruit for Winter Use, with Comments on the Best Things to Grow for Saving, and When and How to Grow Them,* Frederick A. Stokes Co., 1918.

Gardening Under Glass: A Little Book of Helpful Hints Written Particularly for Those Who Would Extend Their Gardening Joys Around the Twelvemonth, Doubleday, 1923, 2nd edition, A. T. De La Mare Co., 1928; *The Book of Bulbs: A Guide to the Selection, Planting, and Cultivating of Bulbs for Spring, Summer, and Autumn Flowering–and to Winter-long Beauty from Bulbs Indoors,* Macmillan, 1927; *Gladiolus,* Macmillan, 1927; *Shrubs,* Macmillan, 1927; *Evergreens for the Small Place,* Macmillan, 1928; (with William G. Breitenbucher) *Gardening with Peat Moss: A Guide to Easier Methods in Growing More Beautiful Flowers, Shrubs and Trees amd Making More Permanent Lawns,* Atkins & Durbrow, 1928; *Irises,* with drawings by author and George L. Hollrock, Macmillan, 1928; *Rock Gardens,* with drawings by author and Hollrock, Macmillan, 1928; *Perennial Gardening* (pamphlet), Ladies' Home Journal, 1928; *Annual Gardening* (pamphlet) Ladies' Home Journal, 1929; *Dahlias,* with drawings by author and Hollrock, Macmillan, 1929; *Landscaping the Rural Home: How to Make Your Grounds More Beautiful,* Macmillan, 1929; *Lawns,* with photographs by author and drawings by author and Hollrock, Macmillan, 1929; *Your Home Garden and Grounds,* Macfadden, 1929.

Roses, with photographs by author and drawings by author and Hollrock, Macmillan, 1930; *Peonies,* with drawings by author and Hollrock, Macmillan, 1933; (with wife, Esther C. Grayson Rockwell) *Flower Arrangement,* Macmillan, 1935; (with Esther C. Grayson Rockwell) *Gardening Indoors: The Enjoyment of Living Flowers and Plants the Year Round, and New Opportunities for Home Decoration,* Macmillan, 1938.

(With Esther C. Grayson Rockwell) *Flower Arrangement in Color,* Wise & Co., 1940; (editor) *10,000 Garden Questions Answered by 15 Experts,* American Garden Guild, Doubleday, 1944, revised eidtion, 1959, new revised edition, 1974; (with Esther C. Grayson Rockwell) *The Complete Book of Flower Arrangement, for Home Decoration, for Show Competition,* American Garden Guild, Doubleday, 1947.

(Editor with Montague Free) *House Plants: Everyday Questions Answered by Experts,* Garden City Books, 1953; (with Esther C. Grayson Rockwell) *The Complete Book of Bulbs: A Practical Manual on the Uses, Cultivation, and Propagation of More Than 100 Species, Hardy and Tender, Which the Amateur Gardener Can Enjoy Outdoors and in the Home,* American Garden Guild, Doubleday, 1953; (with Esther C. Grayson Rockwell) *The Complete*

Book of Annuals: How to Use Annuals and Plants Grown as Annuals to Best Effect, Out-of-doors and in, with Cultural Information and Other Pointers on More than 500 Species and Varieties, with photographs by F. F. Rockwell, American Garden Guild, Doubleday, 1955; (with Esther C. Grayson Rockwell) *The Complete Book of Lawns: How to Determine What Kind of Lawn You Should Have, and Sure-fire Methods for Constructing and Maintaining It, Lawn Grasses (and Grass Substitutes) for All Sections of the United States, and Their Particular Requirements,* American Garden Guild, 1956; (editor with James Marston Fitch) *Treasury of American Gardens,* Harper, 1956; (with Esther C. Grayson Rockwell) *The Rockwells' Complete Book of Roses: A Practical Guide to the Uses, Selections, Planting, Care, Exhibition, and Propagation of Roses of All Types,* American Garden Guild, Doubleday, 1958, revised edition, 1966.

(With Esther C. Grayson Rockwell) *New Complete Book of Flower Arrangement,* American Garden Guild, Doubleday, 1960; (with Esther C. Grayson Rockwell and Jan de Graaff) *The Complete Book of Lilies: How to Select, Plant, Care for, Exhibit, and Propagate Lilies of All Types,* Doubleday, 1961; (with Esther C. Grayson Rockwell) *The Rockwells' Complete Guide to Successful Gardening,* Doubleday, 1965.

* * *

RODGERS, Mary 1931-

PERSONAL: Born January 11, 1931, in New York, N.Y.; daughter of Richard (composer) and Dorothy (Feiner) Rodgers; married Julian B. Beaty, Jr., December 7, 1951 (divorced, 1957); married Henry Guettel (a vice-president of a motion picture company), October 14, 1961; children: (first marriage) Richard R., Linda M., Constance P.; (second marriage) Adam, Alexander. *Education:* Attended Wellesley College, 1948-51. *Politics:* Liberal. *Religion:* Jewish. *Home:* 115 Central Park West, New York, N.Y. 10023. *Agent:* Shirley Bernstein, Paramuse Artists, Inc., 1414 6th Ave., New York, N.Y. 10019.

CAREER: Composer and lyric writer. Assistant producer of New York Philharmonic's Young People's Concerts, 1957-71. Member of board of trustees, Brearley School, 1973—. *Member:* Dramatists Guild (member of council), American Federation of Television and Radio Artists (AFTRA), Screen Actors Guild, Cosmopolitan Club. *Awards, honors: Book World* Spring Book Festival Award, 1972, and Christopher Award, 1973, both for *Freaky Friday.*

WRITINGS: The Rotten Book, Harper, 1969; (with mother, Dorothy Rodgers) *A Word to the Wives,* Knopf, 1970; *Freaky Friday,* Harper, 1972; *A Billion for Boris,* Harper, 1974.

Musical plays: (Composer of music and author of book and lyrics) "Three to Make Music," first produced in New York, N.Y., at Hunter College of the City University of New York, 1959; (composer of music) "Once Upon a Mattress," first produced on Broadway at Phoenix Theatre, 1959; (composer of music) "Hot Spot," first produced on Broadway at Majestic Theatre, 1963; (composer of music) "Mad Show," first produced Off-Broadway at New Theatre, 1966.

Also composer of numerous children's musicals, including "Davy Jones' Locker," performed with Bill Baird Marionettes, 1959; "Young Mark Twain," 1964; "Pinocchio," performed with Baird Marionettes, 1973.

Co-author, with mother Dorothy Rodgers, of monthly column, "Of Two Minds," *McCall's,* 1971—.

* * *

ROEBUCK, Janet 1943-

PERSONAL: Born September 1, 1943, in Rotherham, Yorkshire, England; daughter of Ernest and Olive (Dean) Roebuck. *Education:* University of Wales, B.A., 1964; University College, London, Ph.D., 1968. *Home address:* Box 79, Sandia Park, N.M. 87047. *Office:* Department of History, University of New Mexico, Albuquerque, N.M. 89131.

CAREER: University of New Mexico, Albuquerque, assistant professor, 1968-72, associate professor of history, 1972—. *Member:* American Historical Association, Anglo-American Associates, American Association of University Women.

WRITINGS: The Making of Modern English Society from 1850, Scribner, 1973; *The Shaping of Urban Society: A History of City Forms and Functions,* Scribner, 1974.

WORK IN PROGRESS: Southwest London, 1838-1888: A Study of Local Government and the Expanding Urban Community, for Phillimore; research on aging in England from 1801 to the present.

* * *

ROGERS, Michael 1950-

PERSONAL: Born November 29, 1950, in Santa Monica, Calif.; son of Don Easterday (an engineer) and Mary (Gilbertson) Rogers. *Education:* Stanford University, B.A., 1972. *Agent:* Elizabeth McKee, Harold Matson Co., 22 East 40th St., New York, N.Y. 10016. *Office: Rolling Stone,* 625 Third St., San Francisco, Calif. 94107.

CAREER: Rolling Stone, San Francisco, Calif., contributing editor, 1973—. *Member:* Authors Guild, Amateur Astronomers.

WRITINGS: Mindfogger, Knopf, 1973. Books columnist, *Rolling Stone,* 1973-74. Contributor of short fiction to *Playboy, Esquire,* and *Rolling Stone.*

WORK IN PROGRESS: A short story collection; a book on the Alaskan pipeline.

SIDELIGHTS: Rogers told *CA:* "I write journalism to support my fiction habit. If I wasn't a writer I'd like to be a forest ranger, a doctor, a rural mailman, or a photographer." *Avocational interests:* Fly-fishing, skiing, travel.

* * *

ROGERS, Pamela 1927-

PERSONAL: Born October 8, 1927, in Horsham, Sussex, England; daughter of Rex Owen (a banker) and Doris (Haygarth) Folkard; married Clifford Rogers (a teacher), August 15, 1951; children: Gabrielle, Andrew, Matthew, Imogen. *Education:* Bedford College, London, B.A. (with honors), 1949; Institute of Education, London, diploma in teaching, 1950. *Home:* 32 Yew Tree Rd., Tunbridge Wells, Kent, England.

CAREER: Teacher; writer of children's books.

WRITINGS—All juveniles; all published by Lutterworth: *The Runaway Pony,* 1961; *The Rag and Bone Pony,* 1962; *Dan and His Donkey,* 1964; *Secret in the Forest,* 1964; *Thomasina,* 1966; *The Lucky Bag,* 1969; *The Magic Egg,* 1971.

Juveniles published by Hamish Hamilton: *Fish and Chips,* 1970; *The Big Show,* 1971; *The Tractor,* 1971; *The Rainy Picnic,* 1972; *Sport's Day,* 1972; *The Weekend,* 1972, Nelson, 1973; *The Visitor,* 1973; *The Rare One,* 1973; *The Jinx,* 1973; *All Change,* 1974; *To Market,* 1974; *Anne and Her Mother,* 1974.

WORK IN PROGRESS: Science fiction ("Asimov style") for children; books for children aged eleven and twelve; television plays for children.

SIDELIGHTS: Mrs. Rogers wrote to *CA:* "I think that a writer for children must hook them on to reading at an early age; therefore, I believe that more emphasis should be placed on writing and the importance of it for the earlier age group, six to twelve. After that it is too late. More awards, financial and otherwise, are given to books for older children, to my mind not so essential."

* * *

ROGERS, Rosemary 1932-
(Marina Mayson)

PERSONAL: Born December 7, 1932, in Panadura, Ceylon; daughter of Cyril Allan (an owner and manager of a private school) and Barbara Jansze; divorced; children: Rosanne, Sharon, Michael, Adam. *Education:* University of Ceylon, B.A. *Politics:* Democrat. *Religion:* Episcopalian. *Home:* 1126 Dove Way, Fairfield, Calif. 94533. *Office:* Solano County Parks Department, Courthouse Annex, Fairfield, Calif. 94533.

CAREER: Associated Newspapers of Ceylon, Colombo, writer of features and public affairs information, 1959-62; Travis Air Force Base, Calif., secretary in billeting office, 1964-69; Solano County Parks Department, Fairfield, Calif., secretary, 1969—. Part-time reporter for *Fairfield Daily Republic. Member:* Authors Guild of Authors League of America.

WRITINGS: (Under pseudonym Marina Mayson) *Magnificent Animals,* Olympia, 1971; *Sweet Savage Love,* Avon, 1974; *Dangerfield Devil,* Avon, 1974; *Dark Fires* (a sequel to *Sweet Savage Love*), Avon, in press.

WORK IN PROGRESS: A historical novel, based in Ceylon.

SIDELIGHTS: Mrs. Rogers wrote her first short story at the age of eight, and as a teen-ager wrote novels for her own enjoyment. She writes: "I wrote the kind of book I enjoyed reading myself (at various stages I have been an addict of crime, mystery, western, and sloppy love stories!). Right now I want to concentrate on writing historical novels. I enjoy the research, the colorful backgrounds, the period flavor. I have travelled in Europe and parts of the east (India, Thailand, Singapore, Hongkong)—have lived in London—have an uncle who is a Knight (Sir Eric Jansz), and a family scattered all over the world." *Avocational interests:* Reading, music, watching some sports.

* * *

ROLERSON, Darrell A(llen) 1946-

PERSONAL: Born February 21, 1946, in Camden, Me.; son of Clyde Andros (a farmer) and Lydia M. (a nurse; maiden name, Coombs) Rolerson. *Education:* Graduated from high school in Maine, 1964. *Politics:* "Free thinker." *Religion:* "Unorthodox Buddhist and Baba Lover." *Home address:* Rebel Hill Rd., Islesboro, Me. 04848. *Agent:* Rosemary Casey, 79 Madison Ave., New York, N.Y. 10016.

CAREER: Farmer and herbalist.

WRITINGS—For children: *A Boy and a Deer,* Dodd, 1970; *Mr. Big Britches,* Dodd, 1971; *In Sheep's Clothing,* Dodd, 1972; *A Boy Called Plum,* Dodd, 1974. Contributor to *Down East, Yankee, Organic Gardening, Mother Earth News,* and *Boy's Life.*

WORK IN PROGRESS: The River Song, a study of life and death in a folk culture; *On My Way to the Renaissance,* an autobiography; *Why the Eagle Soars,* a nature study of life in the Maine wilderness.

AVOCATIONAL INTERESTS: World travel.

* * *

ROLL, Winifred 1909-

PERSONAL: Born March 9, 1909, in Harwood, Lancashire, England; daughter of Elliott and Sophia (Hepworth) Taylor; married Sir Eric Roll (a director of Bank of England), September 22, 1934; children: Joanna (Mrs. Stuart Holland), Elizabeth (Mrs. Robin Greenhill). *Education:* University of Hull, B.A. (honors in English), 1932, Cambridge Diploma in Education, 1933. *Religion:* Church of England. *Home:* D2 Albany, Piccadilly, London W1V 9RG, England.

CAREER: Taught English and Latin in earlier years; worked in Ministry of Economic Welfare in Washington during World War II.

WRITINGS: Pomegranate and the Rose: The Story of Katherine of Aragon, Prentice-Hall, 1970.

WORK IN PROGRESS: A book on Mary Tudor.

SIDELIGHTS: Lady Roll resided for several years in Washington, D.C., and Paris, and has traveled extensively in the United States as well as in Europe.

* * *

ROLLINS, Bryant 1937-

PERSONAL: Born December 13, 1937, in Boston, Mass.; son of Edward Bryant (a plumber) and Edith (Wade) Rollins; married; wife's name Judith (separated); children: Malikkah Kenyatta, Khari Camara. *Education:* Northeastern University, B.A., 1961; University of Massachusetts, graduate study, 1962. *Politics:* Black Nationalism. *Religion:* None. *Home:* 138 Manhattan Ave., New York, N.Y. 10025. *Agent:* Anita Diamant, 51 East 42nd St., New York, N.Y. 10017. *Office:* Graduate School of Journalism, Columbia University, 116th St. and Broadway, New York, N.Y. 10025.

CAREER: Boston Globe, Boston, Mass., reporter, 1961-65; *Bay State Banner* (Black community newspaper), Boston, Mass., founder, 1965, editor, 1965-66; Educational Development Centers, Cambridge, Mass., coordinator of Afro-American history curriculum working party, 1966-67; Urban League of Greater Boston, Boston, Mass., director of community development, 1967-69, director of Boston College-Urban League Joint Center for Inner City Change, 1968-69, director of Small Business Development Center, 1968; H. Carl McCall and Associates (urban affairs consultants), New York, N.Y., vice-president, 1969-71; *New York Amsterdam News,* New York, N.Y., executive editor, 1971-72; Columbia University, New York, N.Y., administrator of Michele Clark fellowship program at Graduate School of Journalism, 1973-74; *New York Times,* New York, N.Y., editor and writer, 1974—. Part-time writer, *Time* and *Newsweek,* 1963-66; associate member of National Training Laboratories Institute for Applied Behavioral Science, 1971—; lecturer in New England area. Former chairman of board of directors, Operations Exodus; former vice-president of Circle Associates; former director of Roxbury Freedom House and Grove Hall Community Development Corp.; former member of board of directors, Committee for Community Educational Development. *Awards, honors:* Obie Award, 1969, for "Riot."

WRITINGS: Danger Song (fiction), Doubleday, 1967; *Blues and Greens and All the Rhythms in Between* (poems), privately printed, 1973; *The Cocoon Dream* (fiction), Doubleday, in press.

Plays: "Riot," first performed in Boston, Mass., at Arlington St. Church by OM Theatre Workshop, May, 1968.

Work is represented in *American Anthology of College Poetry,* 1959.

WORK IN PROGRESS: The Cab Calloway Story (tentative title), with Cab Calloway, for Crowell; *Goin Down Slow,* a novel, for Doubleday.

SIDELIGHTS: A "Bryant Rollins Collection" is currently being established at Boston University in the special collection section of the Mugar Memorial Library.

* * *

ROLOFF, Leland Harold 1927-

PERSONAL: Born August 15, 1927, in San Diego, Calif.; children: Peter Jared, Kent Durham. *Education:* San Diego State University, B.A., 1950; Northwestern University, M.A., 1951; University of Southern California, Ph.D., 1967. *Home:* 1410 Chicago, #702, Evanston, Ill. 60201. *Office:* Northwestern University, Evanston, Ill. 60201.

CAREER: University of Vermont, Burlington, instructor in English, 1951-52; high school teacher of English in Grossmont, Calif., 1952-57, and Glendale, Calif., 1957-62; Occidental College, Los Angeles, Calif., assistant professor of communications, 1962-66; Southern Methodist University, Dallas, Tex., assistant professor of communications, 1966-68; Northwestern University, Evanston, Ill., associate professor of interpretation, 1968—. *Military service:* U.S. Navy, 1945-46. *Member:* Speech Communication Association of America, Analytical Psychology Club of Chicago (president and member of board of directors). *Awards, honors:* Midland author's award from Illinois Arts Council, and Institute of Graphic Arts award, both 1973, for *Perception and Evocation of Literature.*

WRITINGS: Perception and Evocation of Literature, Scott, Foresman, 1973.

WORK IN PROGRESS: Biopoetics: Approaches to Body Thinking; The Presence of Madness: Man and His Media.

* * *

ROOS, Hans
See MEISSNER, Hans-Otto

* * *

ROSCOE, A(drian) A(lan) 1939-

PERSONAL: Born June 5, 1939, in Ellesmere Port, England; son of Alan and Mary (Dickinson) Roscoe; married Janice Dean, July 22, 1961; children: Julian Francis, Wilma Anne, Claire Louise. *Education:* University of Sheffield, B.A. (honors), 1960, Dip.Ed., 1961; McMaster University, M.A., 1965; Queen's University, Kingston, Ontario, Ph.D., 1968. *Religion:* Roman Catholic. *Home:* 38 Park Dr., Ellesmere Port, Cheshire, England. *Office:* Department of English, University of Malawi, Zomba, Malawi, Africa.

CAREER: University of Nairobi, Nairobi, Kenya, lecturer in English, 1968-70; University of Malawi, Zomba, Malawi, senior lecturer in English, 1972—. Visiting associate professor at State University of New York at Oswego, 1968-70. Part-time musician.

WRITINGS: Mother Is Gold: A Study in West African Literature, Cambridge University Press, 1971; (with Onyango Ogutu) *Keep My Words,* East African Publishing House, 1974. Contributor to journals. Editorial overseer of *Busara,* 1968-70; assistant editor of *Pan-African Journal,* 1971—.

WORK IN PROGRESS: A sequel to *Mother Is Gold,* for Cambridge University Press; a novel, *Sutton's Way; Stanmere: Portrait of a Northern Town; Tales of Old Malawi,* a collection of tales and myths.

AVOCATIONAL INTERESTS: Squash, tennis, music, and swimming.

* * *

ROSE, Anne

PERSONAL: Born in Antwerp, Belgium; naturalized U.S. citizen; daughter of Chaim A. (a diamond dealer) and Tyla (Kolber) Kaufman; married Gilbert J. Rose (a physician); children: Renee (Mrs. Paul Hield), Dan, Cecily, Ron. *Education:* Hunter College (now Hunter College of the City University of New York), B.A. *Politics:* Democrat. *Office:* Gallery Imago, Becket, Mass.

CAREER: Five Mile River Gallery, Rowayton, Conn., director, 1961-62; Gallery Imago, Becket, Mass., director, 1973—. *Member:* American Field Service (chapter chairman, 1969-70), Planned Parenthood.

WRITINGS: Samson and Delilah, Lothrop, 1968; *How Does a Czar Eat Potatoes?,* Lothrop, 1973; *Sand and Dreams,* Harcourt, in press. Contributor to *Cricket.*

WORK IN PROGRESS: A collection of original tales, and one of African stories; stories for adults and children.

SIDELIGHTS: Anne Rose is interested in anthropology, myths, and folktales of primitive peoples. She has travelled extensively in Central America, Europe, the Near East, Ethiopia, Russia, Japan, and India. She has also been on a dugout canoe trip in Surinam and a whaling trip in Iceland. The languages she speaks include French, Flemish, German, Yiddish, and Spanish.

* * *

ROSEN, Martin Meyer
See ROSEN, Moishe

* * *

ROSEN, Moishe 1932-
(Martin Meyer Rosen)

PERSONAL: Born April 12, 1932, in Kansas City, Mo.; son of Ben (a junk dealer) and Rose (Baker) Rosen; married Ceil Starr, August 28, 1950; children: Ruth, Lyn (Mrs. Alan Bond). *Education:* Attended Colorado University, 1947-51; Northeastern Bible Institute, diploma, 1957. *Home:* 455 Holly Dr., San Rafael, Calif. 94903. *Office:* Jews for Jesus, P.O. Box 309, Corte Madera, Calif. 94925.

CAREER: Ordained Baptist minister; Minister of Hebrew-Christian fellowships in Los Angeles, Calif., 1957-67, New York, N.Y., 1967-70, and San Francisco, Calif., 1970—. Consultant on communications, fund raising, and religious subjects, especially Jewish-Christian relations and evangelism.

WRITINGS: (Under name Martin Meyer Rosen) *How to Witness Simply and Effectively,* American Board of Missions to the Jews, 1968; *Revolutionary for Our Time,* Moody, 1969; (under name Martin Meyer Rosen) *Jews for Jesus,* Revell, 1974; *Sayings of Chairman Moishe,* Creation House, 1974. Author of pamphlets. Contributor to religious journals, including *Christianity Today, Eternity,* and *Christian Life.*

WORK IN PROGRESS: First Century Jewish Christians; Jewish Christian Relations; History of Jewish Missions.

SIDELIGHTS: Rosen writes: "You can take from me everything but my Jewishness and my belief in God. You can say I'm a nuisance, a Christian, out of step with the Jewish community, but you can't say I'm not a Jew.

Rosen ministers to college students and young people, the street people of the San Francisco area. He teaches them (or reteaches them) a new regard for their Jewish heritage, but his goal, admittedly a near-impossible one, is to make it possible for every Jew and Gentile to "experience the person of Christ with an open-minded attitude." He hopes for an atmosphere of individual liberty for spiritual inquiry. *Avocational interests:* Collecting and publishing aphorisms.

BIOGRAPHICAL/CRITICAL SOURCES: Church Herald, August 10, 1973; James Hefley, *The New Jews,* Tyndale, 1974.

* * *

ROSENBAUM, Veryl 1936-

PERSONAL: Born October 6, 1936, in Windsor, Ontario, Canada; daughter of Archibald Henry (a bookkeeper) and Edith (Bernard) Ellis; married Jean Rosenbaum (a physician, psychoanalyst, writer, and composer), February 14, 1962; children: Ronnie, Marc. *Education:* Attended University of Michigan; Wayne State University, B.A., 1960; attended New Mexico Psychoanalytic Institute, 1969. *Politics:* None. *Religion:* None. *Home and office address:* Durango, Colo.

CAREER: Catholic Maternity Institute, Sante Fe, N.M., family counselor, 1964-67; psychoanalyst in private practice, 1965—. *Member:* National Association for Accreditation in Psychoanalysis, Southwest Association for Psychoanalysis (president, 1973—), New Mexico Association for Psychoanalysis (secretary, 1971-73).

WRITINGS: Long Way From Home (poems), American Poet Press, 1965; (with husband, Jean Rosenbaum) *The Psychiatrists' Cookbook,* Sunstone Press, 1972; (with Jean Rosenbaum) *Conquering Loneliness,* Hawthorn, 1973; *Being Female: Understanding and Enjoying Your Physical, Sexual, and Emotional Nature,* Prentice-Hall, 1973; (with Jean Rosenbaum) *Successful Retirement: Planning Ahead for Leisure Years,* Syracuse University Press, in press. Author of column, "Emotionally Speaking," for *Coronet,* 1972-73. Contributor to *Prism, Parents' Magazine, New Ingenue, Dental Economics,* and *Dynamic Maturity,* and other popular magazines.

WORK IN PROGRESS: Research for a book on step-parenting, with husband, Jean Rosenbaum.

SIDELIGHTS: Veryl Rosenbaum told *CA:* "As a psychoanalytic writer I feel a responsibility to translate for the general public the confused jargon concerning psychological matters that affect their daily living." *Avocational interests:* Hiking, fishing, writing songs.

* * *

ROSENBERG, Israel 1909-

PERSONAL: Born February 28, 1909, Munkacs, Czechoslovakia; son of Moses Wolf (a rabbi) and Bertha (Gross) Rosenberg; married Esther Bloch, June 23, 1931 (died, 1971); children: Rochelle (Mrs. Saul Isserow), Herbert. *Education:* Studied at Yeshiva academies and rabbinical institute in Czechoslovakia, 1920-30. *Politics:* Zionist. *Home:* 219 Hollis, Wharton, Tex. 77488. *Office:* Congregation Shearith Israel, P.O. Box 127, Wharton, Tex. 77488.

CAREER: Rabbi in Czechoslovakia, 1927-39, then in Buffalo, N.Y. 1939-55; Congregation Shearith Israel, Wharton, Tex., rabbi, 1955—. *Member:* Zionist Organization of America, Kallah of Texas Rabbis (president, 1964-65).

WRITINGS: Zevach Pessach (on the Passover Hagadah), [Czechoslovakia], 1937; *The Righteous Perished* (eulogy on President Kennedy), privately printed, 1964; *Agnon Umaase Merkavto,* Union of Israeli Writers, 1972; *The Word of Words,* Philosophical Library, 1973. Contributor to journals and newspapers.

WORK IN PROGRESS: The Message of Genesis; and *Agnon as an Apocalyptist,* in English and Hebrew.

* * *

ROSENBLATT, Louise M(ichelle) 1904-

PERSONAL: Born August 23, 1904, in Atlantic City, N.J.; daughter of Samuel (a businessman) and Jennie (Berman) Rosenblatt; married Sidney Ratner (a professor of history), June 16, 1932; children: Jonathan. *Education:* Barnard College, B.A. (honors), 1925; University of Grenoble, Certificat d'etudes, 1926; Sorbonne, University of Paris, graduate study, 1927-30, D.Comp.Lit., 1931; Columbia University, graduate study, 1927-28. *Home:* 11 Cleveland Lane, Princeton, N.J. 08540.

CAREER: Barnard College, New York, N.Y., instructor in English, 1929-38; Brooklyn College (now Brooklyn College of the City University of New York), Brooklyn, N.Y., assistant professor of English, 1938-48; New York University, New York, N.Y., professor of English education, 1948-72; Rutgers University, New Brunswick, N.J., visiting professor, 1972—. Consultant on English curriculum to New York and Connecticut State Departments of Education, College Entrance Examination Board, Educational Testing Service, U.S. Office of Education, and Cooperative Research Agency. Member of Foreign Broadcast Intelligence Service of Federal Communications Commission, 1943-44; Bureau of Overseas Intelligence, Office of War Information, associate chief of Western European Section, 1944, chief of Central Reports Section, 1944-45.

MEMBER: Modern Language Association of America, National Council of Teachers of English, National Conference on Research in English, American Association of University Professors, Comparative Literature Association, New York Council of Teachers of English, Phi Beta Kappa. *Awards, honors:* Franco-American Exchange fellow, 1925-26; Guggenheim fellow, 1942-43; U.S. Office of Education grants, 1963, 1971; California State Department of Education Committee on the English Program choice as one of Ten Indispensable Books on Literature, 1967, for *Literature as Exploration;* National Council of Teachers of English, Distinguished Lecturer, 1970, Distinguished Service award, 1973; New Jersey Association of Teachers of English nonfiction award, 1972.

WRITINGS: L'Idee de l'art pour l'art (title means "The Idea of 'Art for Art's Sake'"), Champion, 1931; *Literature as Exploration,* Appleton, 1938, revised edition, Noble, 1968; (with W. S. Gray and others) *Reading in an Age of Mass Communication,* Appleton, 1950; *Programs for International Understanding,* American Association of Colleges for Teacher Education, 1956; *The English Language Arts in the Secondary School,* Appleton, 1956; *Research Development in English Teaching,* U.S. Office of Education, 1963; (contributor) Alfred Grommon, editor, *The Education of Teachers of English,* Appleton, 1963; (contributor) Frank L. Steeves, editor, *The Subjects in the Curriculum,* Odyssey, 1968; (with James E. Miller and others) *The Promise of English,* National Council of Teachers of English, 1970. Contributor to journals.

WORK IN PROGRESS: A book on proponents of the idea of "art for art's sake" and its contemporary impact, with the tentative title, *Art For Art's Sake?;* a book on critical theory with the tentative title, *The Journey Itself: Criticism and the Literary Experience,* completion expected in 1975.

SIDELIGHTS: Louise Rosenblatt has traveled in Western Europe, Greece, Taiwan, Mexico, Japan, and the Union of Soviet Socialist Republics.

BIOGRAPHICAL/CRITICAL SOURCES: New York University Alumni News, April, 1972; *Princeton Packet,* May 3, 1972.

* * *

ROSENDALL, Betty 1916-

PERSONAL: Born June 6, 1916, in East Grand Rapids, Mich.; daughter of Leo Jay (a pioneer in broadcasting) and Hazel M. (Beemer) Robinson; married Theodore H. Rosendall (a traffic manager at Fisher Body), March 2, 1940; children: Jo-Ellen (Mrs. Perry Mellema). *Education:* Western Michigan University, B.Sc., 1937, graduate study (currently). *Religion:* Methodist. *Home:* 1314 Breton Rd., East Grand Rapids, Mich. 49506. *Office:* Woodcliff Elementary School, East Grand Rapids, Mich. 49506.

CAREER: Elementary teacher, 1937—, presently at Woodcliff Elementary School, East Grand Rapids, Mich. *Member:* National Education Association, Michigan Education Association, American Humane Association, Welfare of Animals in Research and Drugs, Animal Protection Institute of California.

WRITINGS: Number Ten Duckling, Childrens Press, 1972. Regular contributor to *Wee Wisdom;* occasional contributor to *Jack and Jill* and Scholastic Magazines publications.

* * *

ROSENFELD, Alvin H(irsch) 1938-

PERSONAL: Born April 28, 1938, in Philadelphia, Pa.; son of Max and Bertha (Cohen) Rosenfeld; married Erna Baber, August 2, 1966; children: Gavriel (son), Dalia. *Education:* Temple University, B.A., 1960; Brown University, M.A., 1962, Ph.D., 1967. *Religion:* Jewish. *Home:* 1026 East Wylie St., Bloomington, Ind. 47401. *Office:* Department of English, Indiana University, Bloomington, Ind. 47405.

CAREER: Brown University, Providence, R.I., instructor in English, 1967-68; Indiana University, Bloomington, assistant professor, 1968-72, associate professor of English, 1972—. Lecturer in American literature at University of Kiel, 1964-65. *Member:* Modern Language Association of America, Association of American Professors for Peace in the Middle East.

WRITINGS: (Editor) *William Blake: Essays,* Brown University Press, 1969; (editor) *Collected Poems of John Wheelwright,* New Directions, 1972. Contributing editor, *American Poetry Review,* 1973—.

WORK IN PROGRESS: Research in American poetry, Jewish-American literature, and literature of the Holocaust.

* * *

ROSENFIELD, James A(lexander) 1943-

PERSONAL: Born January 27, 1943, in Spokane, Wash.; son of Joseph J. (a motion picture exhibitor) and Rosina (Miller) Rosenfield; married June 1, 1970. *Education:* University of Washington, Seattle, B.A., 1961; University of California, Los Angeles, graduate study, 1962-64; University of Oklahoma, M.A., 1968. *Politics:* "Disillusioned Liberal." *Religion:* "Humanist (still)." *Home and office:* 334A Angier Ave., Raleigh, N.C. 27610.

CAREER: Lou Lily Productions, Hollywood, Calif., publicist, 1964-65; Favorite Theatres, Spokane, Wash., publicist, 1965-67; reporter, *Daily Phoenix* and *Times-Democrat,* Muskogee, Okla., 1967-68; University of Colorado, Boulder, Shubert playwright in residence, 1968-69; *Quarterly Journal of Speech,* Boulder, Colo., editorial assistant, 1969-70; Midland Lutheran College, Fremont, Neb., assistant professor of communication arts, 1970-72; *Raleigh News & Observer,* Raleigh, N.C., music and dance critic, 1972—; Meredith College, Raleigh, N.C., lecturer in film history, 1974—.

WRITINGS: The Lion and the Lily (young adult novel), Dodd, 1972.

Plays: "Geoffrey" (three-act), reading performance given at University of Colorado, Boulder, May, 1969; "Stoned" (three-act), first produced in Boulder, Colo., at New Playwrights' Theatre, December, 1969; "Reality: An Absurdist Entertainment" (one-act), first produced in Boulder, Colo, at Spare Change Theatre, April, 1970; "A Night in the Mind of" (three-act), first produced in Denver, Colo., at Changing Scene Theatre, August, 1970; "Petya Prince of Pennsylvania" (three-act), first produced at Changing Scene Theatre, August, 1971; "A Strange Kind of Morning" (three-act), reading performance given in Omaha, Neb., January, 1972.

WORK IN PROGRESS: Edward and Isabella; an adaptation of "A Strange Kind of Morning"; a mystery, *King Bitch.*

SIDELIGHTS: "Being a very private person," Rosenfield writes, "my chief fascination in life as in art (enjoyed or practical) are the facets of intimacy, in the best sense of the word. I have a passion for privacy, botany, history, travel and most of my conflicts occur when a private desire or standard is attacked by the rude brutality of most of life. . . .The question is how to survive intact, rather than corrupted."

ROSENGART, Oliver A. 1941-

PERSONAL: Born December 23, 1941, in Englewood, N.J.; son of Lutz S. (a lawyer) and Irma (Kent) Rosengart; formerly married to Cheryl Pelavin (a writer and illustrator of children's books). *Education:* City College (now City College of the City University of New York), New York, N.Y., B.Eng., 1964; New York University, J.D., 1967; University without Walls, candidate for Ph.D. *Politics:* "Radical left." *Religion:* None. *Home:* 110 Bleecker St., New York, N.Y. 10012.

CAREER: Berger, Kramer & Levenson, New York, N.Y., attorney, 1967-68; Mobilization for Youth Legal Services, New York, N.Y., staff attorney, 1968-70; New York University, New York, N.Y., clinical instructor in criminal law at School of Law, 1970-73, assistant professor at Washington Square College, 1973—. Member of Metropolitan Council on Housing. *Member:* National Lawyers Guild.

WRITINGS: Busted! A Handbook for Lawyers and Their Clients, St. Martin's, 1972; *A Brief Introduction to Cross Examination,* National Lawyers Guild, 1973; *The Rights of Suspects,* Avon, 1974.

AVOCATIONAL INTERESTS: Carpentry and woodworking.

* * *

ROSS, Donald K. 1943-

PERSONAL: Born June 29, 1943, in New York, N.Y.; son of Hugh J. (a worker) and Helen (Kemp) Ross; married wife, Susan C. (a lawyer and author), February 1, 1969. *Education:* Fordham University, B.A., 1965; New York University, J.D., 1970. *Office:* New York Public Interest Research Group, 5 Beekman St., New York, N.Y. 10038.

CAREER: Member of U.S. Peace Corps, 1965-67; attorney for Ralph Nader in Washington, D.C., 1970-73; New York Public Interest Research Group, New York, N.Y., lawyer, 1973—.

WRITINGS: (With Ralph Nader) *Action for a Change,* Grossman, 1972, revised edition, 1973; *A Public Citizens Action Manual,* Grossman, 1973.

* * *

ROSS, James Davidson 1924-

PERSONAL: Born March 23, 1924, in London, England; son of Kenneth Duncan (a business executive) and Marguerite Frances (Roberts) Ross; married Clare Josephine Carwithen, May 11, 1946 (died June 5, 1963); married Johanna Anne McCarthy, December 5, 1965; children: (second marriage) Jonathan Mark, Rebecca Clare. *Education:* Educated in England. *Politics:* Liberal. *Religion:* Anglican. *Home and office:* 21 Wimbledon Rd., Westbury Park, Bristol, England.

CAREER: Qualified member of Institute of Dispensing Opticians, 1946—. Worked as government factory inspector, 1942-43; dispensing optician, 1943-51; heraldic artist, 1951-56; author and journalist, 1956-62; Coventry Diocesan Retreat and Conference House, Coventry, England, warden, 1962-65; *Shire and Spire* (newspaper), Coventry, England, editor, 1965-68; author and free-lance journalist, 1968—. Broadcaster and writer for British Broadcasting Co. (BBC). *Military service:* Royal Air Force, 1939-42. *Member:* Society of Authors, Institute of Advanced Motorists, Spare Parts Club, British Heart Association.

WRITINGS: Margaret, Hodder & Stoughton, 1957, Dutton, 1958; *Dorothy: A Portrait,* Hodder & Stoughton, 1958; *The Race Before Us,* Hodder & Stoughton, 1961; *Clare,* Hodder & Stoughton, 1965; *The Heart Machine,* Mowbray, 1973; *Children of the Ashes,* Lutterworth, 1974. Contributor to magazines and newspapers.

WORK IN PROGRESS: A book on raising children, for Lutterworth; research on sociological, spiritual, and mental problems faced by parents and children in the modern world.

SIDELIGHTS: Ross writes that he carries two U.S.—made metal valves in his heart, in place of the ones he was born with. Without them he would not be alive. His books have been published in France, Germany, Denmark, Netherlands, Norway, and Switzerland. *Avocational interests:* Travel, reading, classical music.

* * *

ROSS, Joseph
See WRZOS, Joseph Henry

* * *

ROSSMANN, Jack E(ugene) 1936-

PERSONAL: Born December 4, 1936, in Walnut, Iowa; son of Wilbert C. (a farmer) and Claire (Mickel) Rossmann; married Marilyn Martin, June 14, 1958; children: Ann, Charles, Sarah. *Education:* Iowa State University, B.S., 1958, M.S., 1960; University of Minnesota, Ph.D., 1963. *Office:* Office of Research and Planning, Macalester College, St. Paul, Minn. 55105.

CAREER: University of Minnesota, Minneapolis, research fellow, 1962-64, instructor in education, 1963-64; Macalester College, St. Paul, Minn., assistant professor, 1964-67, associate professor, 1968-70, 1972-73, professor of psychology, 1973—, director of educational research, 1968-70, 1972-73, director of research and planning, 1973—. Director of research, Counseling Center, University of California, Berkeley, 1967-68; research associate, American Council on Education, 1972-72; visiting lecturer at University of Minnesota, 1972—. Certified consulting psychologist in State of Minnesota, 1970—. *Military service:* U.S. Army, 1959; became second lieutenant. *Member:* American Psychological Association, American Educational Research Association, Association for Institutional Research, American Association for the Advancement of Science, Phi Kappa Phi.

WRITINGS: (Contributor) David P. Campbell, editor, *The Results of Counseling: Twenty-five Years Later,* Saunders, 1965; (with Helen S. Astin, Alexander W. Astin, and Elaine H. El-Khawas) *Open Admissions at the City University of New York,* Appleton, 1974. Contributor of articles and book reviews to journals in his field. Member of editorial board of *Journal of College Student Personnel,* 1972—, and *Journal of Research in Higher Education,* 1972—.

* * *

ROSSOMANDO, Frederic William 1924-

PERSONAL: Born July 25, 1924, in Philadelphia, Pa.; son of Paul and Jean (Viola) Rossomando; married Elisa Bartolucci (a teacher), July 3, 1954; children: Donna, Marisa. *Education:* Boston University, B.A., 1949; Columbia University, M.A., 1950; New York University, Sixth Year

Professional Diploma, 1962. *Religion:* Roman Catholic. *Home:* 144 Huntington Rd., New Haven, Conn. 06512. *Office:* New Haven Public Schools, One State St., New Haven, Conn. 06510.

CAREER: University of Hartford, Hartford, Conn., instructor in business, 1950-52; East Haven Public Schools, East Haven, Conn., associate superintendent, 1967-68; Quinnipiac College, Hamden, Conn., comptroller, 1968-71; New Haven Public Schools, New Haven, Conn., teacher of business, 1952-63, coordinator of economic education, 1957-63, city supervisor of business education, 1963-66, director of facilities, 1966-67, director of Office of Special Projects and Program Planning, 1971-73, assistant superintendent of schools for instruction, 1973—. Evening principal at Riverside Business College, 1949-50; visiting professor at Mankato State College, Mankato, Minn., summer, 1950, and at Pennsylvania State College, summer, 1951; adjunct instructor at Central Connecticut State College, 1952-54, and at University of Connecticut, 1960-66; member of State Advisory Board on Business Education, 1957-71; director of Workshop in Economic Education, Southern Connecticut State College, 1960-63; member of Joint Council on Economic Education, 1967—; executive secretary of Greater New Haven Council on Economic Education, 1968-72; City of New Haven, member of board of aldermen, 1969-71, member of board of finance, 1971-72. *Military service:* U.S. Army, 1943-46; became technical sergeant. *Member:* American Association of School Administrators, Association of School Business Officials, American Vocational Association, Eastern Business Education Association, Connecticut Business Education Association.

WRITINGS: (With Florence Leventhal) *Earning Money,* F. Watts, 1968; (with Leventhal) *Spending Money,* F. Watts, 1968. Contributor to *Balance Sheet, Journal of New Haven Teachers League,* and *Eastern Business Teachers Association Yearbook.*

WORK IN PROGRESS: Four textbooks, *Producing Goods, Distributing Goods, Consuming Goods,* and *Producing Services.*

* * *

ROTH, Samuel 1894-1974 (Norman Lockridge)

November 17, 1894—July 3, 1974; Austrian-born American poet, editor, and publisher. Obituaries: *New York Times,* July 4, 1974; *Washington Post,* July 6, 1974; *Publishers Weekly,* July 22, 1974.

* * *

ROTHERY, Brian 1934-

PERSONAL: Born January 23, 1934, in Dublin, Ireland; son of Thomas (an entrepreneur) and Mary (Gaffney) Rothery; married Mary Cullen, June 29, 1957; children: Sean-Paul; Grainne (an adopted daughter). *Education:* Completed secondary school in Dublin, Ireland; additional study in correspondence accounting courses. *Home:* 33 Avondale Lawn, Dublin, Ireland. *Agent:* Laurence Pollinger, 18 Maddox, London W. 1, England. *Office:* Irish Transport Co., Abbey St., Dublin, Ireland.

CAREER: Bell Telephone Co., Montreal, Quebec, analyst, 1957-63; International Business Machines Corp., Dublin, Ireland, computer systems engineer, 1963-66; Irish Transport, Co., Dublin, Ireland, manager, 1966—. Visiting lecturer at Dublin University. *Member:* Author's Guild (United States), Irish Computer Society, University College of Dublin Computer Society (patron).

WRITINGS: Installing and Managing a Computer, Business Books, 1968, Brandon/Systems, 1969; (editor, and author with Alan Mullally and Brendan Byrne) *The Art of Systems Analysis,* Business Books, 1969, Prentice-Hall, 1971; (with Mullally) *The Practice of Systems Analysis,* Business Books, 1970; *The Crossing* (novel), Constable, 1970, Lippincott, 1971; *The Myth of the Computer,* three volumes, Business Books, 1971; (editor) *A Computel-Constable Course,* Constable, 1971; *The Storm* (novel), Constable, 1972; *Survival by Competence,* Business Books, 1972, Petrocelli Books, 1973; *How to Organize Your Time and Resources,* Business Books, 1972; *The Celtic Queen* (novel), Mason & Libscomb, 1974.

WORK IN PROGRESS: Research in future society, in power-politics, and in frustration and achievement; historical research.

AVOCATIONAL INTERESTS: Mountain exploring (Arctic, Rockies, Alps), collecting and restoring late-nineteenth century landscape oil paintings.

* * *

ROUECHE, John E(dward) 1938-

PERSONAL: Surname is pronounced "roosh"; born September 3, 1938, in Statesville, N.C.; son of John E. (a furniture worker) and Mary (Harris) Roueche; married Nelda Watts (a writer of textbooks), August 28, 1960; children: Michelle Renee, John E. III. *Education:* Lenoir Rhyne College, B.A., 1960; Appalachian State Teachers College (now Appalachian State University), M.A., 1961; Florida State University, Ph.D., 1964. *Religion:* Methodist. *Home:* 4213 Far West Blvd., Austin, Tex. 78731. *Office:* College of Education, University of Texas, Austin, Tex. 78712.

CAREER: Gaston College, Gastonia, N.C., dean, 1964-67; University of California, Los Angeles, associate research educator, 1967-69; National Laboratory for Higher Education, Durham, N.C., director of community college division, 1969-71; University of Texas, Austin, director and professor of community college education, 1971—. Consultant to U.S. Office of Education. *Member:* Phi Delta Kappa.

WRITINGS: Salvage, Redirection, or Custody, American Association of Junior Colleges, 1968; *Accountability and Community Colleges,* American Association of Junior Colleges, 1972; (with John Pitman) *A Modest Proposal: Students Can Learn,* Jossey-Bass, 1972; (with B. R. Herrscher) *Toward Instructional Accountability,* Westinghouse, 1973; (with Wade Kirk) *Catching Up: Remedial Education,* Jossey-Bass, 1973. Contributor of more than one hundred articles to journals.

WORK IN PROGRESS: A book on personalizing instruction; research on student self-concept development.

* * *

ROUTSONG, Alma 1924- (Isabel Miller)

PERSONAL: Born November 26, 1924, in Traverse City, Mich.; daughter of Carl John (a policeman) and Esther (a nurse; maiden name, Miller) Routsong; married Bruce Brodie, June 14, 1947 (divorced, 1962); children: Natalie,

Joyce, Charlotte, Louise. *Education:* Attended Western Michigan University, 1942-44; Michigan State University, B.A., 1949. *Residence:* New York, N.Y. *Agent:* Charlotte Sheedy, 145 West 86th St., New York, N.Y.

CAREER: Columbia University, New York, N.Y., editor, 1968-71. *Military service:* U.S. Navy, Hospital Apprentice, 1945-46. *Awards, honors:* Friends of American Writers award, 1954, for *A Gradual Joy;* American Library Association Gay Book Award, 1971, for *Patience and Sarah.*

WRITINGS: A Gradual Joy, Houghton, 1953; *Round Shape,* Houghton, 1959; (under pseudonym Isabel Miller) *A Place for Us,* Bleecker Street Press, 1969, published as *Patience and Sarah,* McGraw, 1972.

SIDELIGHTS: Alma Routsong has been active in the gay liberation movement since 1970.

* * *

ROVERE, Richard H(alworth) 1915-

PERSONAL: Surname is pronounced Row-VEER; born May 5, 1915, in Jersey City, N.J.; son of Lewis Halworth (an engineer) and Ethel (Roberts) Rovere; married Eleanor Burgess, December 20, 1941; children: Ann Megan, Richard Mark, Elizabeth. *Education:* Columbia University, A.B., 1937. *Politics:* Independent. *Home:* 108 Montgomery St. Rhinebeck, N.Y. 12572. *Office: New Yorker,* 25 West 43rd St., New York, N.Y., 10036.

CAREER: New Masses, New York, N.Y., associate editor, 1938-39; *Nation,* New York, N.Y., assistant editor, 1940-43; *Common Sense,* New York, N.Y., editor, 1943-44; *New Yorker,* New York, N.Y., staff writer, 1944—. Lecturer at Yale University, 1972-73; associate in American civilization at Columbia University, 1957-59. Trustee of Bard College, 1956-61. *Member:* P.E.N., American Academy of Arts and Sciences (fellow), National Press Club, (Washington, D.C.), Century Association (New York, N.Y.). *Awards, honors:* Chubb fellow at Yale University, 1951; D.Litt., Bard College, 1962; L.H.D., Grinnell College, 1967.

WRITINGS: Howe and Hummel: Their True and Scandalous History, Farrar, Straus, 1947; (with A. M. Schlesinger, Jr.) *The General and the President,* Farrar, Straus, 1951; *Affairs of State: The Eisenhower Years,* Farrar, Straus, 1956; *Senator Joe McCarthy,* Harcourt, 1959; *The American Establishment,* Harcourt, 1962; *The Goldwater Caper,* Harcourt, 1965; *Waist Deep in the Big Muddy: Personal Reflections on 1968,* Little, Brown, 1968 (published in England as *Waist Deep in the Big Muddy: Reflections on United States Policy,* Bodley Head, 1968). Contributing editor, *Harper's,* 1949-54, book critic, 1949-50; American correspondent for *Spectator,* 1954-62; member of board of editors of *American Scholar,* 1958-67; chairman of editorial advisory board, *Washington Monthly,* 1969—.

WORK IN PROGRESS: Continuing research on American Politics, American life, international affairs, and eighteenth century English literature.

* * *

ROY, Reginald H(erbert) 1922-

PERSONAL: Born December 11, 1922, in New Glasgow, Nova Scotia, Canada; son of Charles H. and Joan (Potkin) Roy; married Ardith J. Christie, November 14, 1945; children: Franklyn Ann. *Education:* Attended University of Victoria, 1946-48; University of British Columbia, B.A., 1950, M.A., 1951; University of Washington, Ph.D., 1963. *Religion:* United Church of Canada. *Home:* 2841 Tudor Ave., Victoria, British Columbia, Canada. *Office:* Department of History, University of Victoria, Victoria, British Columbia, Canada.

CAREER: University of Victoria, Victoria, British Columbia, assistant professor, 1961-65, associate professor, 1965-70, professor of history, 1970—. *Military service:* Canadian Army, 1939-45; became major. *Member:* Royal Historical Association (fellow), Canadian Historical Association, Canadian Institute of International Affairs, American Military Institute, International Institute for Strategic Studies.

WRITINGS: Ready for the Fray, Evergreen Press, 1958; *Sinews of Steel,* Charters, 1965; *The Seaforth Highlanders of Canada, 1919-1965,* Evergreen Press, 1969; *Telegrams of North West Campaign, 1885,* Chaplain Society, 1973.

WORK IN PROGRESS: A Biography of Major-General G. R. Pearkes.

* * *

RUBIN, Leona G(reenstone) 1920-

PERSONAL: Born January 1, 1920, in Tacoma, Wash.; daughter of Joseph L. and Anna (Aronson) Greenstone; married Simon Rubin (a social worker and businessman), July 2, 1939; children: Richard, Suzanne (deceased), Andrew. *Education:* Studied at Northwestern University, 1936-39, and University of Florence, 1960. *Home:* 279 Brownell Ave., New Bedford, Mass. 02740.

CAREER: Professional painter, whose work has been exhibited in Boston and New York shows. Art critic and travel writer, *New Bedford Standard Times.*

WRITINGS: How to Defend Yourself at Auctions, Westover, 1972. Contributor to *Esquire, House and Garden, Continental,* and *Christian Science Monitor.*

* * *

RUBIN, Zick 1944-

PERSONAL: Born April 29, 1944, in New York, N.Y.; son of Eli H. (a physician) and Adena (a teacher; maiden name, Lipschitz) Rubin; married Carol Moses (a psychiatric social worker), June 21, 1969. *Education:* Yale University, B.A., 1965; University of Michigan, Ph.D., 1969. *Office:* Department of Psychology and Social Relations, Harvard University, Cambridge, Mass. 02138.

CAREER: Harvard University, Cambridge, Mass., assistant professor, 1969-73, lecturer in social psychology, 1973—. *Member:* American Psychological Association, American Sociological Association, Society for the Psychological Study of Social Issues, Phi Beta Kappa, Sigma Xi. *Awards, honors:* Socio-Psychological prize from American Association for the Advancement of Science, 1969, for research on social psychology of romantic love.

WRITINGS: Liking and Loving: An Invitation to Social Psychology, Holt, 1973; (editor) *Doing unto Others: Joining, Molding, Conforming, Helping, Loving,* Prentice-Hall, 1974. Editor of "Patterns of Social Behavior," a series published by Prentice-Hall.

WORK IN PROGRESS: Becoming Intimate: The Development of Dating Relationships, with Anne Peplau and Charles T. Hill.

RUDD, Margaret
See NEWLIN, Margaret Rudd

* * *

RUKSENAS, Algis 1942-

PERSONAL: Born May 7, 1942, in Kaunas, Lithuania; son of Anthony and Elena (Maciokas) Ruksenas. *Education:* Western Reserve University (now Case Western Reserve University), B.A., 1965; Illinois State University, M.A., 1971. *Religion:* Roman Catholic. *Residence:* Mentor, Ohio. *Agent:* Julian Bach Literary Agency, 3 East 48th St., New York, N.Y. 10014. *Office:* City of Cleveland, 1201 Lakeside Ave., Cleveland, Ohio 44114.

CAREER: Public school teacher in Willoughby, Ohio, 1967-68; United Press International (UPI), Cleveland, Ohio, reporter, 1968-71; City of Cleveland, Ohio, projects director, 1972—. Reporter for *Painesville Telegraph* and writer for Educational Research Council of America, both in 1968.

WRITINGS: Day of Shame, McKay, 1973. Contributor to Lithuanian journals and newspapers.

WORK IN PROGRESS: Social commentary based on experience as reporter; research on the partisan movement in the Baltic, 1940-52; general research on Soviet affairs and U.S.-Soviet relations.

* * *

RUMBELOW, Donald 1940-

PERSONAL: Born March 16, 1940, in Cambridge, England; son of William Hart and Dorothy (Summerfield) Rumbelow; married Polly Stephens (a private secretary), October 22, 1960; children: Laurence, Sally. *Education:* Attended grammar school in Cambridge, England. *Politics:* Tory (Conservative Party). *Religion:* Church of England. *Home:* 49 Polsted Rd., Catford, London S.E.6., England. *Agent:* Shaw Maclean, 11 Rumbold Rd., London S.W.6., England. *Office:* City of London Police, 26 Old Jewry, London E.C.2., England.

CAREER: Cambridge University Press, Cambridge, England, journals clerk, 1957-63; City of London Police, London, England, policeman, 1963—. *Member:* Crime Writer's Association.

WRITINGS: I Spy Blue, Macmillan, 1971; *The Houndsditch Murders,* Macmillan, 1973. Author and narrator of television series on London history for BBC, 1973. Contributor to *Crime* and *Liveryman.* Editor of *City* (magazine), 1972—.

WORK IN PROGRESS: The Complete Jack the Ripper for W. H. Allen; four-part television series on *The Houndsditch Murders;* a play, "Lobsters and Bowmen"; a thriller novel.

SIDELIGHTS: Rumbelow told *CA:* "I collect information which is worthless to anyone else but me and write whatever appeals to my junk yard mind." *Avocational interests:* Book collecting, London history, and theatre.

BIOGRAPHICAL/CRITICAL SOURCES: Observer, June 13, 1971, October 31, 1971; *People,* November 7, 1971; *Mercury,* January 20, 1972; *City Press* (London), February 24, 1972; *Sunday Times,* March 12, 1972; *Smith's Trade News,* June 23, 1973, September 15, 1973; *Cambridge Evening News,* August 27, 1973.

RUSHING, Jane Gilmore 1925-

PERSONAL: Born November 15, 1925, in Pyron, Tex.; daughter of Clyde Preston (a farmer) and Mabel (Adams) Gilmore; married James Arthur Rushing (a teacher), November 29, 1956; children: James Arthur, Jr. *Education:* Texas Tech University, B.A., 1944, M.A., 1945, Ph.D., 1957. *Politics:* Independent. *Religion:* Protestant. *Home:* 3809 39th St., Lubbock, Tex. 79413.

CAREER: Abilene Reporter-News, Abilene, Tex., reporter, 1946-47; high school teacher of English in the public schools of Ira, Tex., 1947-48, Snyder, Tex., 1948-52, and Levelland, Tex., 1953-54; University of Tennessee, Knoxville, instructor in English, 1957-59. Reporter, *Snyder Daily News,* Snyder, Tex., summers, 1951-53; part-time instructor, Texas Tech University, 1959—. *Member:* Authors League, Authors Guild, Texas Institute of Letters. *Awards, honors:* American Association of University Women fellowship, 1956-57; Emily Clark Balch Award from *Virginia Quarterly Review,* 1961, for *Against the Moon;* fiction fellowship to Breadloaf Writers' Conference, 1964.

WRITINGS—All novels: *Walnut Grove,* Doubleday, 1964; *Against the Moon,* Doubleday, 1968; *Tamzen,* Doubleday, 1972; *Mary Dove,* Doubleday, 1974.

WORK IN PROGRESS: History of Texas Tech University; research on the history of the Massachusetts Bay Colony.

BIOGRAPHICAL/CRITICAL SOURCES: Writer, September, 1969.

* * *

RUSSELL, Annie V(est) 1880(?)-1974

1880(?)—May 6, 1974; American educator and lawyer. Obituaries: *Washington Post,* May 8, 1974.

* * *

RUSSELL, Norman H(udson), Jr. 1921-

PERSONAL: Born November 28, 1921, in Big Stone Gap, Va.; son of Norman H., Sr. (a bookkeeper) and Lois (a teacher; maiden name Katherine); married Arline Borgquist (a teacher), June 26, 1963; children: Beverly, Nancy, Katherine. *Education:* Slippery Rock State Teachers College (now part of Pennsylvania State University), B.S., 1946; University of Tennessee, graduate study, 1946-47; University of Minnesota, Ph.D., 1951. *Residence:* Edmond, Okla. *Office:* Office of the Dean, School of Science, Central State University, Edmond, Okla. 73034.

CAREER: Grinnell College, Grinnell, Iowa, instructor, 1951-54, assistant professor, 1954-55, associate professor, 1955-56, professor of biology, 1957-59; Arizona State University, Tempe, professor of botany and chairman of department, 1959-63; Rutgers University, Newark, N.J., visiting professor of botany, 1963-65; Central State University, Edmond, Okla., associate professor, 1966-68, professor of biology, 1970-73, dean, School of Science, 1973—. Visiting professor, Buena Vista College, 1968-70. *Military service:* U.S. Army Air Forces, 1942-46; served two years in India; became staff sergeant. *Awards, honors:* National Science Foundation grants, 1954-70.

WRITINGS—Scientific: *An Introduction to the Plant Kingdom,* Mosby, 1958; (with Paul C. Lemon) *The Plant Kingdom: A Laboratory Manual,* Mosby, 1959, 3rd edition published as *General Botany Manual: Exercises on the*

Life Histories, Structures, Physiology, and Ecology of the Plant Kingdom, 1970; *Violets of Central and Eastern United States,* Sida Press, 1965; *Ecological Botany,* West Publishing, in press.

Poems: *At the Zoo,* JRD Publishing, 1969; *Indian Thoughts: The Small Songs of God,* Northeast/Juniper Books, 1972; *Open the Flower,* Perishable Press, 1974; *Collected Poems,* Northwoods Press, 1974; *The Ways of the World,* Inca Press, 1974; *I Am Old,* San Marcos Press, 1974.

Represented in anthologies: *American Literary Anthology/3,* edited by George Plimpton and Peter Ardery, Viking, 1970; *Voices of Man/The Blue Guitar,* edited by Bethel Bodine, Addison-Wesley, 1970; *Voices of Man/Like It Is,* edited by Bethel Bodine, Addison-Wesley, 1970; *Poems and Perspectives,* edited by Robert H. Ross and William E. Stafford, Scott, Foresman, 1971; *The Turquoise Horse,* edited by Flora Hood, Putnam, 1972; *From the Belly of the Shark,* edited by Walter Lowenfels, Vintage Press, 1973; *Literature of the American Indian,* edited by Thomas E. Sanders and Walter W. Peek, Glencoe Press, 1973; *Messages,* edited by X. J. Kennedy, Little, Brown, 1973; *Outlooks through Literature,* edited by Leo B. Kneer, Scott, Foresman, 1973; *Come to Power,* edited by Dick Lourie, Crossing Press, 1974; *Voices from Wah' Koh-Tah,* edited by Robert K. Dodge and Joseph B. McCullough, International Publishers, 1974.

Contributor of scientific articles to *Encyclopaedia Britannica, Reinhold Scientific Encyclopedia,* and numerous journals; contributor of poems and stories to *Virginia Quarterly Review, Educational Forum, Poetry Northwest,* and more than two hundred twenty other magazines.

SIDELIGHTS: Russell told *CA:* "I write separately in Science and in Poetry, and sometimes combine them. But my Science is not Poetry, and my Poetry is not Science."

* * *

RUTT, M. E.
See SHAH, Amina

* * *

RYAN, Bob 1946-

PERSONAL: Born February 21, 1946, in Trenton, N.J.; son of William P. and Mary (Halloran) Ryan; married Elaine Murray, May 17, 1969; children: Keith Charles. *Education:* Boston College, A.B., 1968. *Politics:* Independent. *Religion:* Roman Catholic. *Home:* 13 Sycamore Lane, Hingham, Mass. 02043. *Office: Boston Globe,* 135 Morrissey Blvd., Boston, Mass. 02107.

CAREER: Boston Globe, Boston, Mass., sports writer, 1968—. *Military service:* U.S. Army Reserve, 1968-74. *Member:* Professional Basketball Writers of America (chairman of Atlantic Division).

WRITINGS: Wait Till I Make the Show, Little, Brown, 1974; *Seven O'Clock in the Lobby: The Boston Celtics Rebuild,* Little, Brown, in press. Author of "NBA East," a column in *Sporting News,* 1974—. Contributor to *Street and Smith's College and Pro Basketball Yearbook.*

WORK IN PROGRESS: A book on professional basketball, for Rutledge Books.

SIDELIGHTS: Ryan writes: "I basically feel that people are what make sports interesting, that owners are guilty (if anything) until proven otherwise, that front office people and coaches think writers and fans are stupid, that many writers are stupid, that, despite this, the influx of young writers has made sportswriting better than ever, and that writers should always remember that sports should be fun!"

* * *

RYAN, John (Gerald Christopher) 1921-

PERSONAL: Born March 4, 1921, in Edinburgh, Scotland; son of Andrew and Ruth (van Millingon) Ryan; married Priscilla Ann Blomfield, January 1, 1950; children: Marianne, Christopher, Isabel. *Education:* Attended school in England. *Home and office:* 12 Airlie Gardens, London W8, England.

CAREER: Artist, illustrator, and maker of films for children. *Military service:* British Army, 1941-45; became captain.

WRITINGS—All self-illustrated; all for children; all published by Bodley Head: *Captain Pugwash,* 1955; *Pugwash Aloft,* 1957; *Pugwash and the Ghostship,* 1962; *Pugwash in the Pacific,* 1973. Author and producer of films for BBC-Television: "Captain Pugwash" series, 1958-68; "Mary Mungo and Midge," 1969; "Sir Prancelot," 1972.

* * *

RYAN, Michael 1946-

PERSONAL: Born February 24, 1946, in St. Louis, Mo.; son of Paul Henderson (an accountant) and Elvera (a teacher; maiden name, Krings) Ryan; married Patricia Hackett (a teacher), May 25, 1974. *Education:* University of Notre Dame, A.B., 1968; Claremont Graduate School, M.A., 1970; University of Iowa, M.F.A., 1972, Ph.D., 1974. *Home address:* c/o 1630 Whitehall St., Allentown, Pa. 18102. *Office:* Department of English, Southern Methodist University, Dallas, Tex. 75275.

CAREER: Iowa Review, Iowa City, associate editor, 1972-73, poetry editor, 1973-74; Southern Methodist University, Dallas, Tex., assistant professor of English, 1974—. Translator for international writing program and visiting lecturer at University of Iowa, 1973-74. *Awards, honors:* Prize from Academy of American Poets, 1972; Yale Series of Younger Poets award, 1973.

WRITINGS: Threats Instead of Trees (poems), Yale University Press, 1974. Contributor of poems to literary journals, including *American Poetry Review, New Yorker, Poetry, Nation,* and *Poetry Northwest.*

WORK IN PROGRESS: Poems for a second book.

SIDELIGHTS: A poetry recording, "Michael Ryan Reading His Poems," has been made by Library of Congress, 1974. One of Ryan's poetry readings has been videotaped by the Poetry Center at San Francisco State University, 1974.

* * *

RYMER, Alta (May) 1925-

PERSONAL: Born June 20, 1925, in San Diego, Calif.; daughter of Rendal H. and Rachel Marie (Worden) Bickford; married Keith C. Rymer (a former employee of North Island), May 27, 1943; children: Sharon (deceased), Timothy, Rebecca, Tracy. *Education:* Grossmont Community College, student, 1971. *Home and office address:* P.O. Box 104, Tollhouse, Calif. 93667.

CAREER: Standard Parachute Co., San Diego, Calif., trimmer and thread supplier, 1943-44; Ryan Aeronautical Co., San Diego, Calif., cadmium plater, 1944-45; free-lance writer. Speaker in schools.

WRITINGS—Self-illustrated: *Beep-Bap-Zap-Jack* (children's book), Bordeaux Press, 1972.

WORK IN PROGRESS—Twelve children's books, all self-illustrated: *Princess Sugarfoot, Rosiepola Tickletoes, Hoibonki Tomoty, Hobart and Humbert Gruzzy, Oopletrump's Odyssey, Exony's Excursion, Captain Zomo, Chambo Returns, Up from Uzam, Visit to Voltassia, Ippy from Tron,* and *Doctor UU's Success Story.*

AVOCATIONAL INTERESTS: Painting, lettering, photography, clothes designing, rock collecting, ecology.

* * *

SADUN, Elvio H. 1918(?)-1974

1918(?)—April 24, 1974; Italian-born American zoologist and author. Obituaries: *New York Times,* April 26, 1974.

* * *

SAGAN, Francoise
See QUOIREZ, Francoise

* * *

SAGAN, Leonard A. 1928-

PERSONAL: Born February 18, 1928, in San Francisco, Calif.; married; children: three. *Education:* Stanford University, A.B., 1950; University of Chicago, M.D., 1955; Harvard University, M.P.H., 1965. *Office:* Department of Environmental Medicine, Palo Alto Medical Clinic, Palo Alto, Calif.

CAREER: Licensed to practice medicine in California; certified by American Board of Internal Medicine, 1963. University of California Hospital, San Francisco, intern, 1955-56, fellow with Metabolic Unit, 1956-57, resident in internal medicine, 1959-61; Atomic Bomb Casualty Commission, Nagasaki, Japan, chief of department of medicine, 1961-64; U.S. Atomic Energy Commission, Washington, D.C., physician in nuclear medicine, associated with Medical Research Branch of Division of Biology and Medicine, 1965-68; Palo Alto Medical Clinic, Palo Alto, Calif., associate director of department of environmental medicine, 1968—. Visiting lecturer at Howard University, 1966-68; associate in ambulatory and community medicine at University of California, San Francisco, 1968-71. *Military service:* U.S. Army, Medical Corps, 1957-59; became captain. *Member:* American College of Physicians (fellow), Santa Clara County Medical Society.

WRITINGS: (Editor) *Human and Ecologic Effects of Nuclear Power Plants,* C. C Thomas, 1974. Author of technical reports. Contributor to *General Electric Source Book,* 1972. Also contributor of about twenty articles to science journals, including *Nature, Science, Journal of the American Medical Association, Health Physics, Archives of Environmental Health,* and *New Scientist.*

* * *

SAGHIR, Marcel T(awfic) 1937-

PERSONAL: Born August 6, 1937, in Beirut, Lebanon; married Jane Stocker, May 5, 1968; children: Jason, Peter. *Education:* American University of Beirut, B.Sc., 1959, M.D., 1963. *Home:* 6 Ridgetop, Richmond Heights, Mo. 63117. *Office:* 4511 Forest Park Blvd., St. Louis, Mo. 63108.

CAREER: Physician in St. Louis, Mo., 1965—. Assistant professor at Washington University, St. Louis, Mo., 1971—. *Member:* American Medical Association, American Psychiatric Association, American Association for the Advancement of Science, Royal Medico-Psychological Association, Eastern Psychiatric Association, Missouri State Medical Society, St. Louis Medical Society, Sigma Xi.

WRITINGS: (With Eli Robins) *Male and Female Homosexuality: A Developmental, Psychiatric, and Sociologic Investigation,* Williams & Wilkins, 1973.

WORK IN PROGRESS: Research on gender problems and on transvestitic and transsexual phenomena.

* * *

SAINER, Arthur 1924-

PERSONAL: Born September 12, 1924, in New York, N.Y.; son of Louis and Sadie (Roth) Sainer; married Stefanie Janis, December 23, 1956 (divorced, 1961). *Education:* New York University, B.A., 1946; Columbia University, M.A., 1948. *Religion:* Jewish. *Home:* 79 Sullivan St., New York, N.Y. 10012. *Agent:* Ellen Levine, Curtis Brown Ltd., 60 East 56th St., New York, N.Y. 10022.

CAREER: *Village Voice,* New York, N.Y., drama and literary critic, and book editor, 1961-65; C. W. Post College, Brookline, Long Island, N.Y., instructor in English, 1963-67; Bennington College, Bennington, Vt., member of drama division, 1967-69; *Village Voice,* drama critic, 1969—. Lecturer at Sarah Lawrence College, spring, 1964, and Nathaniel Hawthorne College, spring, 1969; associate professor of fiction writing at Staten Island Community College, spring, 1974. Instructor at numerous workshops, including Living Theatre playwriting workshop, 1962, and Chautauqua Writers' Workshop, 1969. Conductor of series of radio broadcasts on contemporary theatre, WBAI-FM, 1971-72. Member of academic council, Campus-Free College, Boston, 1971—. *Member:* Playwrights Group (president, 1971—). *Awards, honors:* John Golden playwriting award, 1946, for "Grab Your Hat"; Rockefeller grant, 1967.

WRITINGS: *The Sleepwalker and the Assassin,* Bridgehead Books, 1964; *The Radical Theatre Notebook,* Avon, in press.

Plays: "The Bitch of Waverly Place," first produced Off-Off-Broadway at Judson Poets' Theatre, March, 1964; "The Game of the Eye," first produced in Bronxville, N.Y., at Sarah Lawrence College, May, 1964; "The Day Speaks but Cannot Weep," first produced Off-Off-Broadway at Cafe La Mama, January, 1965; "The Blind Angel," first produced in New York, N.Y., at Bridge Theatre, February, 1965; "Untitled Chase," first produced in New York, N.Y., at Washington Square Park, September, 1965, produced Off-Broadway at Astor Place Playhouse, November, 1965; "God Wants What Men Want," first produced at Bridge Theatre, May, 1966; "The Bomb Flower," first produced at Bridge Theatre, November, 1966; "The Children's Army Is Late," first produced on Long Island, N.Y., at C. W. Post College, May, 1967, produced in New York, N.Y., at Theater for the New City, March, 1974; "The Thing Itself" (first produced in Minneapolis, Minn., at Firehouse Theatre, July, 1967, produced at Theater for the New City, November, 1972), published in *Playwrights for Tomorrow,* Volume VI, edited by Arthur H. Ballet, University of Minnesota Press, 1969; "Noses," first produced in New York, N.Y., at St. Mark's Church in the Bouwerie, November, 1967; "Boat Sun Cavern," first produced in Bennington, Vt., at Bennington College, May, 1969.

"Van Gogh," first produced Off-Off-Broadway at La Mama Experimental Theatre Club, February, 1970; "I Hear It Kissing Me, Ladies," first produced in New York, N.Y., at Unit Theatre, November, 1970; "Images of the Coming Dead," first produced in New York, N.Y., at Open Space, April, 1971; "The Celebration: Jooz/Guns/Movies/The Abyss," first produced in New York, N.Y., at Theater for the New City, February, 1972; "Go Children Slowly," first produced Off-Off-Broadway at The Cubiculo, May, 1973; "The Spring Offensive," first produced in New York, N.Y., at Super Nova, June, 1973.

Television plays: "A New Year for Margaret," CBS, 1951; "The Dark Side of the Moon," NBC, 1957; "1 Piece Smash," WGBH (Boston), 1972, published in *The Scene,* Volume II, edited by Stanley Nelson, Smith, 1974; "A Man Loses His Dog More or Less," WGBH, 1972.

Author of experimental church service produced by OM-Theatre Workshop in Boston, Mass. at Arlington Street Church, May, 1968. Short fiction is anthologized in *American Judaism Reader,* edited by Paul Kresh, Abelard, 1967. Contributor to *Contemporary Dramatists,* and to periodicals, including *Bennington Review, Cavalier, Cimaise* (Paris), *yale/theatre,* and *Vogue.* Film critic, *Show Business Illustrated,* 1961; founder and contributing editor, *Ikon,* 1967.

WORK IN PROGRESS: A novel, *Survivals.*

* * *

ST. CLAIR, Margaret 1911-

PERSONAL: Born February 17, 1911, in Hutchinson, Kan.; daughter of George A. (an attorney) and Eva (Hostetler) Neeley; married Eric St. Clair, May 25, 1932. *Education:* University of California, M.A., 1933. *Residence:* Manchester, Calif. *Agent:* McIntosh & Otis, Inc., 18 East 41st St., New York, N.Y. 10017.

CAREER: St. Clair Rare Bulb Gardens, El Sobrante, Calif., horticulturist, 1938-41; novelist. *Member:* Science Fiction Writers of America, Dramatists Guild, Society for Hellenic Studies, American Civil Liberties Union.

WRITINGS—All novels, except as indicated: *Agent of the Unknown,* Ace Books, 1956; *The Green Queen* (first published in *Universe* as "Mistress of Viridis," 1955), Ace Books, 1956; *The Games of Neith,* Ace Books, 1960; *Sign of the Labrys,* Bantam, 1963; *Message from the Eocene* [and] *Three Worlds of Futurity,* Ace Books, 1964; *The Dolphins of Altair,* Dell, 1967; *The Shadow People,* Dell, 1969; *The Dancers of Noyo,* Ace Books, 1973; *Change the Sky* (short stories), Ace Books, 1974.

WORK IN PROGRESS: A novella about choice of identity.

SIDELIGHTS: Mrs. St. Clair told *CA:* "The most important influences on me, as a writer and adult, have probably been Homer, Aeschylus, Herodotus, Boccaccio, and Dante. The books that affected me most when I was a child were George MacDonald's Curdie books, the Oz books, and the *Book of Knowledge.* Currently I read a good many French novels, and a little Greek." *Avocational interests:* Gardening and cooking.

ST. JOHN-STEVAS, Norman Anthony Francis 1929-

PERSONAL: Born May 18, 1929, in London, England; son of Stephen S. (a civil engineer and company director) and Kitty (St. John O'Connor) Stevas. *Education:* Attended Ratcliffe College, Leicester, England; Fitzwilliam College, Cambridge, B.A. (first class honors in law), 1950, M.A., 1954; Christ Church, Oxford, M.A., 1952, B.C.L., 1954; University of London, Ph.D., 1957. *Home:* 1 Hampstead Sq., London N.W.3, England.

CAREER: Admitted as Barrister of Middle Temple, 1952; Southampton University, Southampton, England, lecturer in law, 1952-53; King's College, University of London, London, England, lecturer in law, 1953-56; Oxford University, Oxford, England, tutor in jurisprudence at Christ Church, 1953-55, and Merton College, 1955-57; *Economist,* London, England, beginning 1959, holding positions as editor of collected works of Walter Bagehot, and legal, ecclesiastical, and political correspondent. Regents' professor at University of California, Santa Barbara, 1969. Conservative candidate for Parliament from Dagenham, 1951; founder member of Institute of Higher European Studies, Bolzano, Italy, 1955; lecturer in the United States, 1958-68. Secretary of Home Affairs Committee of Conservative Party, 1969—. Legal adviser to Sir Alan Herbert's committee on book censorship, 1954-59; member of Fulbright Commission, 1961; delegate to Council of Europe and Western European Union of North Atlantic Treaty Organization, 1967-71.

MEMBER: Royal Society of Literature (fellow), Christian-Social Institute of Culture (Rome; founding member), Garrick Club. *Awards, honors:* Yale Law School fellow, 1957; Fulbright award, 1957; honorary Doctor of Science and Law degree from Yale University, 1960; Knight of St. Lazarus of Jerusalem, 1963; Order of Merit from the Italian Republic, 1965.

WRITINGS: Obscenity and the Law, Macmillan, 1956; *Walter Bagehot,* Longmans, Green, 1963; *Life, Death, and the Law,* World Publishing, 1961; *The Right to Life,* Hodder & Stoughton, 1963, Holt, 1964; *Law and Morals,* Hawthorn, 1964; (editor) *Bagehot's Historical Essays,* Anchor Books, 1965; (editor) *The Collected Works of Walter Bagehot,* Harvard University Press, 1965—; *The Agonising Choice: Birth Control, Religion, and the Law,* Indiana University Press, 1971. Contributor to periodicals in England and abroad, including *Critical Quarterly, Modern Law Review, Criminal Law Review,* and *Law and Contemporary Problems.* Editor of *Dublin Review,* 1961.

AVOCATIONAL INTERESTS: Reading, talking, listening to music, travelling, walking, appearing on television.

* * *

SALEM, Elie Adib 1930-

PERSONAL: Born March 5, 1930, in Lebanon; son of Adib (a notary public) and Lamya (Malik) Salem; married Phyllis Sell (a teacher), June 23, 1954; children: Elise, Nina, Adib, Paul. *Education:* American University of Beirut, B.A., 1950; Johns Hopkins University, Ph.D., 1953. *Religion:* Christian. *Office:* Faculty of Arts and Sciences, American University of Beirut, Beirut, Lebanon.

CAREER: Johns Hopkins University, Baltimore, Md., assistant professor of Middle East politics, 1956-62; American University of Beirut, Beirut, Lebanon, associate professor,

1962-68, professor of politics, 1968-74, dean of Faculty of Arts and Sciences, 1974—. Consultant on administrative reform to the Lebanese Council of Ministers, 1973.

WRITINGS: The Political Theory and Institutions of the Khawarij, Johns Hopkins Press, 1956; *Modernization without Revolution: Lebanon's Experience,* Indiana University Press, 1973. Contributor to *Middle East Journal, Muslim World, Orbis, International Journal,* and *Al-Abhath.*

WORK IN PROGRESS: Research on rural politics in the Middle East.

SIDELIGHTS: Salem wrote: "I am a Christian Lebanese Arab, specialized in Islamics and also greatly interested in American culture and its relations with the Arab World. Traveled extensively in these two civilizations."

* * *

SALES, Jane M(agorian) 1931-

PERSONAL: Born March 9, 1931, in Cincinnati, Ohio; daughter of Irving M. (a businessman) and Annie Laurie (Robertson) Magorian; married Richard W. Sales (a missionary), June 30, 1956; children: Mark, Anne, James. *Education:* College of Wooster, B.A., 1953; University of Chicago, B.D., 1956, M.A., 1971, Ph.D., 1972; Hartford Seminary Foundation, theological studies, 1956-57. *Home address:* P. O. Box 6, Selebi-Pikwe, Botswana. *Office:* United Church Board for World Ministries, 475 Riverside Dr., New York, N.Y. 10027.

CAREER: United Church of Christ missionary, with her husband, in Southern Africa, 1957-71, 1972—; teacher of history at Inanda Seminary, Durban, Natal, South Africa, 1963-68; lecturer in church history at Federal Theological Seminary, Alice, Cape Province, South Africa, 1969-71; general church work and theological education in Botswana, 1972—.

WRITINGS: Planting of the Churches in South Africa, Eerdmans, 1971. Editor of Zulu edition, "All-Africa Sunday School Curriculum," eleven books, Lovedale Press, 1962-68.

WORK IN PROGRESS: A study of the colored community in the Eastern Cape, South Africa, in the first half of the nineteenth century, for A. A. Balkema (Cape Town); research on independent churches in Botswana; materials for theological education.

SIDELIGHTS: Jane Sales and her husband were refused re-entry to South Africa in 1971, at the time of the church purge connected to the French-Beytagh trial. They were later reassigned to Botswana. Mrs. Sales speaks Zulu and Tswana.

* * *

SALK, Jonas Edward 1914-

PERSONAL: Born October 28, 1914, in New York, N.Y.; son of Daniel Bonn (a fashion designer) and Dora (Press) Salk; married Donna Lindsay, June 8, 1939 (divorced, 1968); married Francoise Gilot (an artist and writer), June 29, 1970; children: (first marriage) Peter Lindsay, Darrell John, Jonathan Daniel. *Education:* City College (now City College of the City University of New York), B.S., 1934; New York University, M.D., 1939. *Home:* 2444 Ellentown Rd., La Jolla, Calif. 92037. *Office:* Salk Institute for Biological Studies, 10010 North Torrey Pines Rd., La Jolla, Calif. 92037.

CAREER: Developer of vaccine for prevention of poliomyelitis, 1954. New York University, College of Medicine, New York, N.Y., fellow in bacteriology, 1939-40; Mount Sinai Hospital, New York, N.Y., intern, 1940-42; University of Michigan, School of Public Health, Ann Arbor, National Research Council fellow in medical sciences, 1942-43, research fellow in epidemiology, 1943-44, research associate in epidemiology, 1944-46, assistant professor of epidemiology, 1946-47 (research work, 1942-47, was focused on influenza vaccine experiments); University of Pittsburgh, School of Medicine, Pittsburgh, Pa., associate research professor, 1947-49, research professor of bacteriology, 1949-55, Commonwealth Professor of Preventive Medicine, 1955-57, Commonwealth Professor of Experimental Medicine, 1957-63, director of Virus Research Laboratory, 1947-63; Salk Institute for Biological Studies, La Jolla, Calif., fellow and director, 1963—. Adjunct professor of health sciences, University of California, San Diego, 1970—. Consultant in epidemic diseases to Secretary of War, 1944-46, and Secretary of the Army, 1946-54; member of expert panel on virus diseases, World Health Organization, 1951—.

MEMBER: Association of American Physicians, American Society for Clinical Investigation, American Epidemiological Society, American Academy of Pediatrics (honorary fellow), American Association for the Advancement of Science (fellow), American Public Health Association (fellow), American Academy of Arts and Sciences (fellow), American College of Preventive Medicine, Society for Experimental Biology and Medicine, Society of American Bacteriologists, Royal Society of Health (honorary fellow), Phi Beta Kappa, Sigma Xi, Alpha Omega Alpha, Delta Omega.

AWARDS, HONORS: Presidential Citation, Congressional Gold Medal, French Legion of Honor, Orden del Quetzal (Guatemala), and Criss Award, all 1955; Albert Lasker Award, 1956; Howard Taylor Ricketts Award and Albert Gallatin Award, 1957; Gold Medal Award of National Institute of Social Sciences, 1959; Truman Commendation Award, 1966; Mellon Institute Award, 1969. Honorary degrees from universities in the United States, England, Israel, Italy, and the Philippines, including University of Michigan and University of Pittsburgh, 1955, University of Turin, 1957, and University of Leeds, 1959.

WRITINGS: Man Unfolding, Harper, 1972; *The Survival of the Wisest,* Harper, 1973.

Contributor: B. H. Top and others, *Handbook of Communicable Diseases,* 2nd edition (Salk's section on influenza did not appear in earlier edition), Mosby, 1947; Frank W. Hartman and others, editors, *The Dynamics of Virus and Rickettsial Infections,* Blakiston, 1954; Thomas Milton Rivers, editor, *Viral and Rickettsial Infections of Man,* 3rd edition (Salk's section on poliomyelitis control did not appear in earlier editions), Lippincott, 1959. Contributor of about a hundred articles, largely on influenza and poliomyelitis control, to medical and other scientific journals.

WORK IN PROGRESS: His autobiography.

BIOGRAPHICAL/CRITICAL SOURCES: Richard Carter, *Breakthrough: The Saga of Jonas Salk,* Trident, 1966.

* * *

SALLS, Betty Ruth 1926-

PERSONAL: Born August 22, 1926, in Homestead, Fla.; daughter of Ernest E. and Edith (Imler) Bailey; married

Lawrence Salls, March 12, 1944 (deceased); married Ellison Wilkins (U.S. Air Force Ret.), July 15, 1973; children: (first marriage) Bonnie, Barbara (Mrs. Verne Benson), Linda (Mrs. Wayne Benson), Jeannie (Mrs. Lawrence Benson), Ruth (Mrs. Ken Wires). *Education:* Educated in Florida schools. *Religion:* Presbyterian. *Home:* 27802 Southwest 140th Ave., Naranja, Fla. 33030.

CAREER: Dade County (Fla.) Schools, secretary, 1965-69, 1970-73. *Member:* National League of American Pen Women.

WRITINGS: Death Is No Dead End, Moody, 1972; *The Greatest of These Is Love,* Grace Publishing, 1973. Contributor of articles to *Camping Guide, Progressive Farmer, Guideposts,* and other church magazines.

WORK IN PROGRESS: A children's book set in a south Florida hurricane, *Jeannie in the Eye of a 'Cane;* a book dealing with divorce in Christian families, *Now We See through a Glass Darkly.*

* * *

SALMON, Charles Gerald 1930-

PERSONAL: Born October 28, 1930, in Detroit, Mich.; son of Harold Gerald (a structural engineer) and Gwendolen (Charles) Salmon; married Elizabeth Ellen Corbett (an elected county official), September 12, 1953; children: Margaret Elizabeth, David Charles, Martha Anne. *Education:* University of Michigan, B.S.C.E., 1952, M.S.C.E., 1954; University of Wisconsin—Madison, Ph.D., 1961. *Home:* 614 South Segoe Rd., Madison, Wis. 53711. *Office:* University of Wisconsin, 2214 Engineering Bldg., Madison, Wis. 53706.

CAREER: Registered professional engineer in State of Wisconsin. University of Wisconsin—Madison, instructor, 1956-61, assistant professor, 1961-64, associate professor, 1964-67, professor of civil engineering, 1967—. Engineer for Bridge Section of State Highway Commission of Wisconsin, summers, 1957-62. *Military service:* U.S. Army, Quartermaster Research and Development, Field Evaluation Agency, 1954-56. *Member:* International Association for Bridge and Structural Engineering, American Society of Civil Engineers (president of Madison branch, 1968), American Society for Engineering Education, National Society of Professional Engineers, American Concrete Institute, American Welding Society, American Association of University Professors, Wisconsin Society of Professional Engineers, Technical Club of Madison, Sigma Xi, Chi Epsilon, Tau Beta Pi.

WRITINGS: (With Leo Schenker and Bruce G. Johnson) *Structural Steel Connections,* Engineering Research Institute, University of Michigan, 1954; (with C. K. Wang) *Reinforced Concrete Design,* International Textbook Co., 1965, 2nd edition, 1973; (with J. E. Johnson) *Steel Structures: Behavior and Design,* Intext Educational Publishers, 1971. Contributor to *Transactions of the American Society of Civil Engineers, Journal of the Engineering Mechanics Division* of the American Society of Civil Engineers, *Journal of the Structural Division* of the American Society of Civil Engineers, *Civil Engineering,* and *American Concrete Institute Journal.* Manuscript reviewer for American Society of Civil Engineers, 1965—, and for International Textbook Co., 1964, and McGraw, 1967.

* * *

SALVENDY, Gavriel 1938-

PERSONAL: Born September 30, 1938, in Budapest, Hungary; son of Paul (a professor) and Katherine (Brown) Salvendy; married Catherine V. Dees, April 1, 1966; children: Laura, Dorin. *Education:* University of Birmingham, M.Sc., 1966, Ph.D., 1968. *Religion:* Jewish. *Home:* 2845 Ashland St., West Lafayette, Ind. 47906. *Office:* School of Industrial Engineering, Purdue University, West Lafayette, Ind. 47907.

CAREER: State University of New York, Buffalo, assistant professor of industrial engineering, 1968-71; Purdue University, West Lafayette, Ind., associate professor of industrial engineering, 1971—. *Member:* American Institute of Industrial Engineers, American Psychological Association, Ergonomics Research Society, American Society of Engineering Education, Human Factors Society, British Institute of Work Study (fellow), Sigma Xi. *Awards, honors:* Gold medal award from Japanese Industrial Management Association, 1972; Phil Carroll award from American Institute of Industrial Engineers, 1973, for outstanding achievement in work measurement and methods engineering.

WRITINGS: (With W. D. Seymour) *Prediction and Development of Industrial Work Performance,* Wiley, 1973. Contributor to transactions and proceedings; contributor of about two dozen articles to psychology and engineering journals.

WORK IN PROGRESS: Research in the nature and acquisition of psychomotor skills and the application of them for increased satisfaction and productivity in dentistry, surgery, and industry.

* * *

SAMUELS, Charles Thomas 1936-1974

February 20, 1936—March 13, 1974;American professor of English and film critic. Obituaries: *Washington Post,* March 17, 1974. (*CA*-41/44).

* * *

SANDBERG, John H(ilmer) 1930-

PERSONAL: Born June 21, 1930, in Ashland, Wis.; son of Hilmer S. and Florence (Brown) Sandberg; married Ann Holland (an artist), May 1, 1954; children: Emily, Eric. *Education:* University of Wisconsin, B.S., 1952; University of Virginia, M.A., 1957, Ed.D., 1962. *Office:* Carnegie-Mellon University, Pittsburgh, Pa. 15213.

CAREER: Pennsylvania Department of Public Instruction, Harrisburg, curriculum specialist, 1962-63; Carnegie-Mellon University, Pittsburgh, Pa., assistant professor, 1963-65, associate professor, 1965-70, professor of education and psychology, 1970—. *Military service:* U.S. Naval Reserve, active duty, 1952-55; became lieutenant junior grade.

WRITINGS: Introduction to the Behavioral Sciences, Holt, 1969, revised edition, in press.

WORK IN PROGRESS: A book on informal education for the young, tentatively titled *What I Learned in the Second Grade.*

* * *

SANDBERG, Karl C. 1931-

PERSONAL: Born March 7, 1931, in Salt Lake City, Utah; married 1954, wife's name, Dawn; children: David, Stephanie, Mark, Shireen. *Education:* Brigham Young University, B.A., 1954, M.A., 1957; University of Wisconsin, Ph.D., 1960. *Home:* 2983 North Chatsworth, St. Paul, Minn. 55113. *Office:* Department of French, Macalester College, 1600 Grand Ave., St. Paul, Minn. 55105.

CAREER: Duke University, Durham, N.C., instructor in French, 1954-61; University of Arizona, Tucson, assistant professor, 1961-66, associate professor of French, 1966-68; Macalester College, St. Paul, Minn., professor of French and humanities, 1968—, chairman of department of French, 1968—. Visiting professor of English and humanities at University of Colorado, summers, 1958, 1960-61, 1965-69, 1972. *Member:* American Association of Teachers of French, Modern Language Association of America, American Council on the Teaching of Foreign Languages.

WRITINGS: *A Study of the Modern Foreign Language Programs in Utah Public Schools,* Brigham Young University Press, 1957; (editor and translator) *The Great Contest of Faith and Reason: Selections from the Writings of Pierre Bayle,* Ungar, 1963; *At the Crossroads of Faith and Reason: An Essay on Pierre Bayle,* University of Arizona Press, 1967; (with Eddison C. Tatham) *French for Reading: A Programmed Approach,* Appleton, 1968; (with Thomas Brown) *Conversational English,* Blaisdell, 1969; *Lectures et Conversations,* Appleton, 1970; (with John R. Wende) *German for Reading: A Programmed Approach,* Appleton, 1973.

* * *

SANDERS, Mary Dolling
See BRIDGE, Ann

* * *

SANDERS, Sol (Witner) 1926-

PERSONAL: Born July 10, 1926, in Atlanta, Ga.; son of Jack (a merchant) and Anna (Witner) Sanders. *Education:* University of Missouri, B.J., 1946; graduate study at Columbia University, 1954, 1957-58, and at Sorbonne, University of Paris, 1948. *Religion:* Jewish. *Home:* 908 Massachusetts Ave. N.E., Washington, D.C. 20002. *Agent:* Julian Bach, Jr., 3 East 48th St., New York, N.Y. *Office:* Research Institute of America, Inc., 852 National Press Bldg., Washington, D.C. 20045.

CAREER: United Press International, New York, N.Y., and Hanoi, North Vietnam, reporter, 1946-48, 1950-51; *Business Week,* New York, N.Y., deputy foreign editor in the Far East, 1953-57, correspondent in Tokyo, Japan, 1957-61; *U.S. News and World Report,* New Delhi and Bangkok, South Asia editor, 1961-70; World Bank (International Bank for Reconstruction and Development), Washington, D.C., deputy chief of mission in Tokyo, 1970-72; Chinese University of Hong Kong, professor of journalism, 1972-73; now with Research Institute of America, Washington, D.C. *Wartime service:* American Field Service, served in Italy and India, 1945. *Member:* National Press Club, Tokyo Foreign Correspondents' Club. *Awards, honors:* Edward R. Murrow fellowship from Council on Foreign Relations, 1967-68.

WRITINGS: *A Sense of Asia,* Scribner, 1968. Contributor to periodicals. Member of board of editors of *Asian Affairs,* 1974—.

WORK IN PROGRESS: A book on Soichiro Honda, the Japanese automotive manufacturer and designer.

* * *

SANDY, Stephen
See SANDYS, Stephen

* * *

SANDYS, Stephen 1935-
(Stephen Sandy)

PERSONAL: Born August, 1935; son of Alan F. Sandys. *Home:* Pine Rd., Bennington, Vt.

CAREER: University of Tokyo, Fulbright lecturer, 1967-68. Visiting assistant professor, Brown University, 1968-69. *Awards, honors:* Dexter fellowship, 1961; Yaddo fellowships, 1964-68; Vermont Council on the Arts grant, 1974; Ossabaw fellowship, 1974.

WRITINGS—Under pseudonym Stephen Sandy; poems: *Mary Baldwin,* Dolmen Press, 1962; *The Destruction of Bulfinch's House,* Identity Press, 1964; *Stresses in the Peaceable Kingdom,* Houghton, 1967; *Japanese Room,* Hellcoal Press, 1969; *Roofs,* Houghton, 1971.

Author of text of "Vita de Sancto Hieronymo," an antiphonal cantata with music by Henry Brant, MCA Music, 1973.

* * *

SARGENT, Wyn

PERSONAL: Born in California; children: Jmy (son). *Education:* Occidental College, B.A., 1950; further study in Mexico and France. *Agent:* Lola Wilson Celebrities, 139 South Beverly Dr., Beverly Hills, Calif. 90212.

CAREER: Writer and photographer. Has worked as school teacher. *Awards, honors:* Named humanitarian of the year by Orange County (Calif.) Press Club, 1969; first woman to receive member's flag from Adventurer's Club of Los Angeles, Calif., 1974.

WRITINGS: *My Life with the Headhunters,* Doubleday, 1974; *People of the Valley,* Random House, 1974.

SIDELIGHTS: During the summer of 1968, Wyn Sargent, accompanied by her young son, spearheaded an expedition to explore the headhunters' jungle of Central Borneo. Deeply touched by the overwhelming poverty and disease in the area, she incorporated the Sargent-Dyak Fund, Inc., in an effort to save these rapidly vanishing tribes from extinction.

In 1972, at the urging of the Indonesian President, Suharto, Ms. Sargent journeyed to West New Guinea to see what could be done for the tribes in that region. There she again made headlines when she married a tribal chief in a symbolic wedding ritual intended to halt hostilities between warring tribes. Inadvertently, the native ceremony made world news when the Indonesian Government, miffed by her harsh accusations of Government brutality and exploitation of the tribes, asked her to leave the country. She is presently waiting for the time when she will be permitted to return to West New Guinea to build a hospital for the natives she was trying to protect. *Avocational interests:* Flying (first American woman to fly a Russian TU-104 turbo-jet).

* * *

SATTLER, Jerome M(urray) 1931-

PERSONAL: Born March 3, 1931, in New York, N.Y.; son of Nathan (a furrier) and Pearl (Diener) Sattler; married Virginia R. Lewis, December 27, 1957; children: Heidi, David. *Education:* City College (now City College of the City University of New York), B.A., 1952; University of Kansas, M.A., 1953, Ph.D., 1959. *Politics:* Democrat. *Religion:* Jewish. *Home:* 5260 Stone Ct., San Diego, Calif. 92115. *Office:* Department of Psychology, San Diego State University, San Diego, Calif. 92115.

CAREER: Osawatomie State Hospital, Osawatomie, Kan., clinical psychologist, 1959; Kansas State College, Fort Hays, assistant professor of psychology, 1959-61; University of North Dakota, Grand Forks, assistant professor of psychology, 1961-65; San Diego State University, San Diego, Calif., assistant professor, 1965-67, associate professor, 1967-71, professor of psychology, 1971—. Visiting associate professor at Miami University, 1969-70; Fulbright lecturer at Kebangsaan National University of Malaysia, 1972-73. *Military service:* U.S. Army, 1953-54. *Member:* American Psychological Association, Western Psychological Association, North Dakota Psychological Association (president, 1965), Sigma Xi, Psi Chi. *Awards, honors:* Research grants from Department of Health, Education, and Welfare, U.S. Office of Education, 1965, 1966; research grants from Department of Health, Education, and Welfare, Social and Rehabilitation Service, 1969-71.

WRITINGS: (Contributor) K. S. Miller and R. M. Dreger, editors, *Comparative Studies of Blacks and Whites in the United States,* Seminar Press, 1973; (contributor) Lester Mann and David Sabatino, editors, *The First Review of Special Education,* Volume II, Journal of Special Education Press, 1973; *Assessment of Children's Intelligence,* with instructor's manual, Saunders, 1974. Contributor of about fifty articles to abstracts and professional journals.

WORK IN PROGRESS: Editing *The Black Client in Psychotherapy, Counseling, and Casework.*

* * *

SAUNDERS, Beatrice

PERSONAL: Daughter of Arthur John and Isabella (Orton) Surgey; married Archibald Saunders (a captain in the Royal Navy; deceased); children: three sons, two daughters. *Home:* 8 Albany Court, Oatlands Dr., Weybridge, Surrey, England.

CAREER: Writer. *Member:* Authors Society (London).

WRITINGS: The Age of Candlelight: The English Social Scene in the Seventeenth Century, Centaur Press, 1959, Dufour, 1961; *Portraits of Genius,* J. Murray, 1959; *Tchehov: The Man,* Centaur Press, 1960, Dufour, 1961; *Henry the Eighth,* Redman, 1963; *John Evelyn and His Times,* Pergamon, 1970.

WORK IN PROGRESS: Three books, *Our Scottish Ancestors of the Eighteenth Century; Sarah, Duchess of Marlborough;* and *Memoirs of an Author,* an autobiography.

SIDELIGHTS: The film "The Wives of Henry VIII" was made from her book *Henry the Eighth.*

* * *

SAUNDERS, Rubie (Agnes) 1929-

PERSONAL: Born January 31, 1929, in New York, N.Y.; daughter of Walter St. Clair and Rubie (Ford) Saunders. *Education:* Hunter College (now Hunter College of City University of New York), B.A., 1950. *Home:* 26 Glenwood Ave., New Rochelle, N.Y. 10801. *Office:* Parents' Magazine Enterprises, Inc., 52 Vanderbilt Ave., New York, N.Y. 10017.

CAREER: Parents' Magazine Enterprises, Inc., New York, N.Y., member of editorial staff, 1950-54, managing editor, 1955-60, editor of *Young Miss,* 1960-67, editorial director of *Humpty Dumpty* and *Children's Digest,* 1967—. *Awards, honors:* Outstanding Graduate award, Hunter College, 1960.

WRITINGS—For young people: *Calling All Girls Party Book,* Parents' Magazine Press, 1966; *Marilyn Morgan, R.N.,* New American Library, 1970; *Marilyn Morgan, Cruise Nurse,* New American Library, 1971; *Nurse Morgan Sees It Through,* New American Library, 1971; *The Franklin Watts Concise Guide to Baby Sitting,* F. Watts, 1972, published as *Baby Sitting: A Concise Guide,* Pocket Books, 1974; *The Franklin Watts Concise Guide to Good Grooming for Boys,* F. Watts, 1973; *The Franklin Watts Concise Guide to Smart Shopping and Consumerism,* F. Watts, 1973.

WORK IN PROGRESS: Concise Guide to the Caribbean; and a novel, *City Summer.*

* * *

SAVAGE, Thomas Gerard 1926-

PERSONAL: Born July 27, 1926, in Oak Park, Ill.; son of William Joseph (a salesman) and Agnes (Bohan) Savage. *Education:* Loyola University, Chicago, A.B., 1949, A.M., 1953; Oxford University, M.A., 1962; Bellarmine School of Theology, S.T.L., 1958. *Politics:* Democrat. *Home and office:* Xavier University, Cincinnati, Ohio 45207.

CAREER: Roman Catholic priest of Society of Jesus (Jesuits); Xavier High School, Cincinnati, Ohio, instructor in English and speech, 1951-54; Xavier University, Cincinnati, Ohio, instructor, 1962-64, assistant professor, 1964-66, associate professor, 1966-71, professor of English, 1971—, chairman of department, 1965—. *Member:* Modern Language Association of America, National Council of Teachers of English, Christian Preaching Conference. *Awards, honors:* Outstanding Service Award, Xavier University, 1973.

WRITINGS: And Now a Word from Our Creator, Loyola University Press (Chicago), 1972.

* * *

SAXE, Richard W(arren) 1923-

PERSONAL: Born August 8, 1923, in Homewood, Ill.; son of Edmund Albert (a grocer) and Edith (Humphries) Saxe; married June Hoffman, June 15, 1947. *Education:* George Williams College, B.S., 1949; University of Chicago, A.M., 1953, Ph.D., 1964. *Politics:* Democrat. *Religion:* Methodist. *Home:* 3232 Raleigh Dr., Toledo, Ohio 43606. *Office:* Department of Educational Administration and Supervision, University of Toledo, Toledo, Ohio 43606.

CAREER: Public schools of Chicago, Ill., elementary school teacher, 1949-55, principal 1955-63; Chicago Teachers College, Chicago, Ill., instructor in education, 1957-62 (part time); University of Chicago, Midwest Administration Center, Chicago, Ill., staff associate, 1963-64; Chicago State College, Chicago, Ill., associate professor of education, 1964-65, director of student teaching, administrative coordinator, and acting dean of teacher education, 1965-66; University of Toledo, Toledo, Ohio, associate professor, 1966-68, professor of educational administration and supervision, 1968—, head of department, 1969—, assistant dean for research and development, 1968-72, associate dean, 1972—. *Military service:* U.S. Army, Infantry, 1942-46, 1950-52; became captain; received Combat Infantry Badge, eight campaign medals, and six battle stars. *Member:* American Association of School Administrators, American Educational Research Association, Department of Elementary School Principals, Future Scientists of America, Illinois Association for Higher Education (chapter president, 1965-66), Chicago Principals Auxiliary (president, 1962-63), Chicago Teachers Union, Phi Delta Kappa.

WRITINGS: (Editor with John Beck) *Teaching the Culturally Disadvantaged Pupil,* C. C Thomas, 1965; *Schools Don't Change,* Philosophical Library, 1967; (editor) *Perspectives on the Changing Role of the Principal,* C. C Thomas, 1968; (editor) *Contexts for Teacher Education,* University of Toledo, 1969; *Mayors and Schools: A Report,* University of Toledo, 1969; (editor) *Source Materials for Educational Administration: Critiques* (monograph), University of Toledo, 1969; (with David Rosenberger) *The Ohio Legislature and Educational Issues* (monograph), University of Toledo, 1969; (with Ronald Flora) *Research Studies in Education* (monograph), University of Toledo, 1970; *Perceptions of the Changing Role of the Urban Elementary Principal: Report of a Survey,* University of Toledo, 1970; (with G. E. Dickson) *Partners for Educational Reform and Renewal,* McCutchan, 1973; *Changing School-Community Relations,* McCutchan, in press. Contributor of about eighty articles and more than fifty reviews to education journals. Assistant editor of *Administrators' Notebook,* 1963-64; editor of *Memos for the School Executive,* 1966—.

* * *

SAXON, Alex
See PRONZINI, Bill

* * *

SCAGNETTI, Jack 1924-

PERSONAL: Born December 24, 1924, in Piney Fork, Ohio; son of Quinto and Albina (Tardella) Scagnetti; married, 1950 (divorced); children: Kimberly, Craig. *Education:* Attended schools in Detroit, Mich. *Home and office:* 4641 Fulton, Sherman Oaks, Calif. 91403.

CAREER: Reporter and editor for weekly newspapers in Detroit, Mich., and concurrently public relations director for private athletic club in Detroit, 1948-57; copywriter and editorial director for automotive advertising agency, Detroit, 1953-54; publicity director and promotion manager for chain of seventeen bowling centers, Norwalk, Calif., 1958-65; *Popular Hot Rodding* (magazine), Los Angeles, Calif., chief editor, 1966-68; free-lance magazine and publicity writer and photographer, Sherman Oaks, Calif., 1968—. *Military service:* U.S. Army, 1943-46.

WRITINGS: (With George Barris) *Famous Custom and Show Cars* (Junior Literary Guild selection), Dutton, 1973; (with Mac Hunter) *Golf for Beginners,* Grosset, 1973; (with Count Yogi) *Five Simple Steps to Perfect Golf,* Nash Publishing, 1973; (with Barris) *Cars of the Stars,* Jonathan David, 1974. Contributor of more than six hundred articles to *Hi-Performance Cars, Inside Golf, Cars, Golf Guide,* and other magazines; also writer and editor of twenty-four special single-appearance magazines in auto and golf field. Contributing editor, *Motor Life,* 1958-61.

WORK IN PROGRESS: Books on a famous golfer, on golf instruction, on Rudolph Valentino, and nostalgia photo books of movie stars.

* * *

SCALZO, Joe 1941-

PERSONAL: Born June 16, 1941, in Pasadena, Calif.; son of J. R. and Dorothy (Bains) Scalzo; married Annie in't Groen. *Education:* Attended public school in Glendora, Calif. *Address:* Box 8, Sierra Madre, Calif. 91024.

CAREER: Writer and professional motorcycle racer, 1959-69; feature editor, Bond Publishing Co., 1969-71; free-lance writer, 1971—. *Awards, honors:* Winner of American Auto Racing Writers and Broadcasters Association writing contest, 1971, runner-up, 1972.

WRITINGS: Racer: The Story of Gary Nixon, Parkhurst, 1970; *The Unbelievable Unsers,* Regnery, 1971; *The Bart Markel Story,* Bond & Parkhurst, 1972; (with Dick Mann) *Motorcycle Ace: The Dick Mann Story,* Regnery, 1972; *Evel Knievel and Other Daredevils,* Grosset, 1974; *Stand on the Gas!,* Prentice-Hall, 1974. Contributor to *Sport, Saga, National Observer, West,* and other periodicals and newspapers.

* * *

SCHACHTEL, Hyman Judah 1907-

PERSONAL: Born May 24, 1907, in London, England; came to United States, 1914; naturalized citizen, 1921; son of Bernard (a cantor) and Janie (Spector) Schachtel; married Barbara H. Levin (a psychologist), October 15, 1941; children: Bernard, Ann Mollie. *Education:* University of Cincinnati, B.A., 1928; Hebrew Union College, Rabbi, 1931, B.H., 1931; attended Columbia University, 1933-37; University of Houston, Ed.D., 1948. *Politics:* Democrat. *Home:* 2527 Glenhaven, Houston, Tex. 77025. *Office:* 5600 North Braeswood, Houston, Tex. 77035.

CAREER: West End Synagogue, New York, N.Y., rabbi, 1931-43; Temple Beth Israel, Houston, Tex., rabbi, 1943-75. Lecturer at University of Houston, 1950-55, 1974—, University of St. Thomas, 1970—, and St. Mary's Seminary, 1970—. Lecturer and guest on numerous television programs. President of Mental Health of Houston, 1960-62, Kallah of Texas Rabbis, 1962, and Southwest Central Conference of American Rabbis, 1968-70; member of Commission on Human Relations of Texas, 1968-70. *Wartime service:* Civilian chaplain, 1943-45. *Member:* United Nations Association, Central Conference of American Rabbis, Foreign Policy Association, Texas Philosophical Society, Houston Rabbinical Association (president, 1970-73), Kiwanis, Phi Delta Kappa, Phi Epsilon Pi. *Awards, honors:* D.H.L., Southwestern University, 1955; D.D., Hebrew Union College, 1958; Coronat Medal of St. Edwards University, 1963.

WRITINGS: The Eternal People, Behrman, 1940; *Real Enjoyment of Living,* Dutton, 1954; *Life You Want to Live,* Dutton, 1956; *The Shadowed Valley,* Knopf, 1964; *How to Meet the Challenge of Life and Death,* Gulf Publishing, 1974. Author of syndicated column, "Enjoyment of Life," 1949—.

SIDELIGHTS: Schachtel's musical abilities include piano and the composition of hymns, songs, and liturgical music. He also enjoys reading and golf.

SCHAEFER, Leah Cahan 1920-

PERSONAL: Born February 27, 1920, in Milwaukee, Wis.; daughter of Boas (a rabbi) and Miriam (Harris) Cahan; married Hal Schaefer (a pianist), August 29, 1955; children: Katherine Rebecca. *Education:* Roosevelt College (now Roosevelt University), B.M.Ed., 1940; Columbia University, M.A., 1956, Ed.D., 1964. *Religion:* Jewish. *Home:* 285 Riverside Dr., New York, N.Y. *Agent:* Georges Borchardt, Inc., 145 East 52nd St., New York, N.Y. 10022.

CAREER: Professional singer prior to 1957, recording with the Barries, Capitol Records, 1941-45, the Wayfarers (folk-singing triozn RCAdVictor, 1952-55, and as soloist for United Artists records, 1957, 1959; Community Guidance Services, New York, N.Y., staff member, 1956—; private practice of psychotherapy, New York, N.Y., 1957—. *Member:* Society for the Scientific Study of Sex (fellow), American Psychological Association, American Association of Marriage and Family Counselors, American Association of Sex Education Counselors, Society for the Psychological Study of Social Issues, National Council on Family Relations, International Council of Psychologists, American Group Psychotherapy Association, New York Society of Clinical Psychologists, Kappa Delta Pi, Pi Lambda Nu.

WRITINGS: (Contributor) George Goldman and Donald S. Milman, editors, *Modern Woman: Her Psychology and Sexuality,* C. C Thomas, 1969; *Women and Sex: Sexual Experiences of Thirty Women as Told to a Female Psychotherapist,* Pantheon, 1973. Co-editor of questions and answer section, *Sexology,* 1974—.

* * *

SCHAEFFER, Susan Fromberg 1941-

PERSONAL: Born March 25, 1941, in Brooklyn, N.Y.; daughter of Irving (a clothing manufacturer) and Edith (Levine) Fromberg; married Neil J. Schaeffer (a college professor), October 11, 1970; one child. *Education:* University of Chicago, B.A., 1961, M.A. (with honors), 1963, Ph.D. (with honors), 1966. *Religion:* Jewish. *Agent:* Harriet Wasserman, Russell & Volkening, 551 Fifth Ave., New York, N.Y. 10017. *Office:* Department of English, Brooklyn College of the City University of New York, Brooklyn, N.Y. 11210.

CAREER: Wright Junior College, Chicago, Ill., instructor in English, 1963-64; Illinois Institute of Technology, Chicago, assistant professor of English, 1964-66; Brooklyn College of the City University of New York, Brooklyn, N.Y., associate professor of English, 1966—. *Member:* Modern Language Association of America.

WRITINGS: The Witch and the Weather Report (poems), Seven Woods Press, 1972; *Falling* (novel), Macmillan, 1973; *Anya* (novel), Macmillan, 1974; *Granite Lady* (poems), Macmillan, 1974. Contributor to *Modern Fiction Studies, University of Windsor Review,* and *Centennial Review.*

WORK IN PROGRESS: The Major Fiction of Vladimir Nabokov.

SIDELIGHTS: Mrs. Schaeffer told CA: "I am married, teach full time, have one child, and have a full time writing career. I hate writing about my life and am something of a hermit."

SCHAFER, William J. 1937-

PERSONAL: Born September 18, 1937, in Richmond, Ind.; son of Robert Adam (an engineer) and Gladys (Brotherton) Schafer; married Martha Quick, September 5, 1958; children: Richard Ransom, Amelia Anne. *Education:* Attended Purdue University, 1955-56; Earlham College, A.B., 1959; University of Minnesota, M.A., 1964, Ph.D., 1967. *Religion:* Society of Friends. *Home:* 221 Jackson St., Berea, Ky. 40403. *Office:* Department of English, Berea College, Berea, Ky. 40403.

CAREER: Berea College, Berea, Ky., instructor, 1964-66, assistant professor, 1966-70, associate professor, 1970-74, professor of English, 1974—. *Member:* American Association of University Professors. *Awards, honors:* Younger Humanist fellowship from National Endowment for the Humanities, 1971-72.

WRITINGS: Rock Music, Augsburg, 1972; (with Johannes Riedel) *The Art of Ragtime,* Louisiana State University Press, 1973. Editor and designer of publications.

WORK IN PROGRESS: A study of brass band jazz in New Orleans, *New Orleans Parade,* completion expected in 1975.

SIDELIGHTS: Schafer told *CA:* "I am working on studies of the impact of black music on white popular culture in America, especially the extensive covert influences of black esthetics and sensibility on the course of popular art."

* * *

SCHALDENBRAND, Mary 1922- (Sister Mary Aloysius)

PERSONAL: Born August 24, 1922, in Detroit, Mich.; daughter of Louis G. and Mary (Brichetto) Schaldenbrand. *Education:* Nazareth College, A.B., 1951; University of Notre Dame, M.A., 1955; Catholic University of America, Ph.D., 1960. *Home:* 1000 West Loyola, Chicago, Ill. 60626. *Office:* Department of Philosophy, Loyola University, 6525 North Sheridan Rd., Chicago, Ill. 60626.

CAREER: Roman Catholic nun with religious name of Sister Mary Aloysius; Nazareth College, Kalamazoo, Mich., instructor, 1957-67, assistant professor of philosophy, 1967-69; Loyola University, Chicago, Ill., associate professor of philosophy, 1969—. *Member:* American Philosophical Association, Society for Phenomenology and Existential Philosophy. *Awards, honors:* Fulbright grant for research at Catholic University of Louvain and in Paris, 1962-63.

WRITINGS: (Contributor) John K. Ryan, editor, *Twentieth-Century Thinkers,* Alba, 1965; (under name Sister Mary Aloysius; with others) *Primacy of the Person in the Church,* Fides, 1968; (contributor) Maryellen Muckenhirn, editor, *The Future as the Presence of Shared Hope,* Sheed, 1968. Contributor to journals.

WORK IN PROGRESS: Imagination of Freedom: A Study in the Thought of Paul Ricoeur.

* * *

SCHAPPES, Morris U(rman) 1907-

PERSONAL: Surname is pronounced *Shapp*-iss; name originally Moise ben Haim Shapshilevich, changed upon enrollment in school in 1914; born May 3, 1907, in Kamenets-Podolsk, Ukraine; came to United States in

1914; son of Hyman (a wood-turner) and Ida (Urman) Shapshilevitch; married Sonya Laffer, April 6, 1930. *Education:* City College (now City College of the City University of New York), B.A., 1928; Columbia University, M.A., 1930, further graduate study 1930-34. *Politics:* Radical. *Religion:* "Jewish atheist." *Home:* 700 Columbus Ave., #8-E, New York, N.Y. 10025. *Office: Jewish Currents,* 22 East 17th St., New York, N.Y. 10003.

CAREER: City College (now City College of the City University of New York), New York, N.Y., tutor in English department, 1928-41; Jefferson School of Social Sciences, New York, N.Y., instructor in Jewish studies, 1948-57; School of Jewish Knowledge, New York, N.Y., instructor in Jewish studies, 1958-69; Queens College of the City University of New York, Flushing, N.Y., adjunct professor of American Jewish history, 1972—. *Member:* American Historical Association, American Jewish Historical Society, Immigration History Society, Association for the Study of Afro-American Life and History, Yiddisher Kultur Farband (member of presidium). *Awards, honors:* Tercentenary award from Emma Lazarus Federation of Jewish Women's Clubs, 1954; Zhitlovsky Award from Zhitlovsky Foundation for Jewish Culture, 1969.

WRITINGS: Letters from the Tombs, introduction by Richard Wright), Schappes Defense Committee, 1941; (editor) *Selections of Prose and Poetry of Emma Lazarus,* Jewish Book League, 1944; (editor) *The Letters of Emma Lazarus,* New York Public Library, 1950; (editor) *A Documentary History of the Jews in the U.S.A.: 1654-1875,* Citadel, 1950, 3rd edition, Schocken, 1971; *The Jews in the United States, 1654-1954: A Pictorial History,* Citadel, 1958, revised edition, Munsell, 1965. Contributor to journals, including *Saturday Review, Mainstream, Publications of the American Jewish Historical Society, Publications of the Modern Language Association, Journal of Ethnic Studies,* and *Poetry.* Member of editorial board of *Jewish Currents,* 1946-58, editor-in-chief, 1958—.

WORK IN PROGRESS: Revising *The Jews in the U.S.A.: 1654-1954,* to include the period, to 1965, completion expected about 1976.

SIDELIGHTS: Operations of the Rapp-Coudert New York State Investigating Committee, delving into "subversive" activities on municipal college campuses, led to Schappes' suspension from City College in 1941, then imprisonment and academic black-listing. These experiences led him away from study of English and American literature and toward the study of Jewish literature and history.

* * *

SCHEER, Julian (Weisel) 1926-

PERSONAL: Born February 20, 1926, in Richmond, Va.; son of George Fabian and Hilda (Knopf) Scheer; married Mary Virginia Williams, 1947 (divorced, 1963); married Suzanne Huggan, October 9, 1965; children: (first marriage) Susan, Scott, Grey; (second marriage) Hilary. *Education:* Attended Richmond Professional Institute, 1946; University of North Carolina at Chapel Hill, A.B., 1950. *Politics:* Democrat. *Religion:* Jewish. *Home address:* R. D. 2 Box 24, Catlett, Va. 22019. *Agent:* G. F. Scheer, P. O. Box 807, Chapel Hill, N.C. *Office:* Sullivan, Murray & Scheer, 1120 Connecticut Ave. Washington, D.C.

CAREER: Mid-Virginia Publications, Richmond, reporter, 1939-43; free-lance writer, 1945-62; Scheer Syndicate, Chapel Hill, N.C., president, 1947-53; University of North Carolina, Chapel Hill, sports publicist, 1949-53; *Charlotte News,* Charlotte, N.C., columnist-reporter, 1953-62; National Aeronautics and Space Administration (NASA), Washington, D.C., assistant administrator of public affairs, 1962-71; Sullivan, Murray & Scheer (communications firm), Washington, D.C., 1971—. *Wartime and military service:* U.S. Merchant Marine, 1943-46. U.S. Naval Reserve, 1946-53. *Member:* Algonquin Society, Sigma Delta Chi, Pi Lambda Phi, Cedar Run Club. *Awards, honors:* Caldecott Award runner-up, 1965, for *Rain Makes Applesauce.*

WRITINGS: (With Robert Quincy) *Choo Choo: Charlie Justice Story,* Colonial Press, 1958; (with Elizabeth Black) *Tweetsie: The Blue Ridge Stemwinder,* Heritage House, 1958; (with Theodore J. Gordon) *First into Outer Space,* St. Martin's, 1959; *Rain Makes Applesauce,* Holiday House, 1964; *Upside Down Day,* Holiday House, 1968.

SIDELIGHTS: Of *Upside Down Day,* Jerome Beatty, Jr. has written in the *New York Times Book Review:* "'Water won't trickle. Feathers won't tickle. Rain won't drop. Balloons won't pop.' That's Mr. Scheer's plot. . . . As most youngsters are fond of the notion of things not happening the way adults insist they do, they should be pleased with "Upside Down Day" and its whimsy."

* * *

SCHEICK, William J(oseph) 1941-

PERSONAL: Born July 15, 1941, in Newark, N.J.; son of Joseph Edward (an engineer) and Irene (Corvi) Scheick; married Marion Ruth Voorhees, August 3, 1963. *Education:* Montclair State College, B.A., 1963; University of Illinois, M.A., 1965, Ph.D., 1969. *Home:* 7306 Marywood Circle, Austin, Tex. 78723. *Office:* Parlin Hall, University of Texas, Austin, Tex. 78712.

CAREER: University of Texas, Austin, assistant professor, 1969-74, associate professor of English, 1974—.

WRITINGS: The Will and the Word: The Poetry of Edward Taylor, University of Georgia Press, 1974; (editor and author of introduction) Increase Mather, *The Life and Death of That Reverend Man of God, Mr. Richard Mather,* York Mail-Print, 1974; *H. G. Wells: An Annotated Bibliography of Writings about Him,* Northern Illinois University Press, in press; (contributor) J. A. Leo Lemay, editor, *Essays on Early Virginia Literature Honoring Richard Beale Davis,* University Press of Virginia, in press. Contributor of about thirty articles and book reviews to academic and literary journals. Member of editorial board of *Texas Studies in Literature and Language,* 1970—, and *English Literature in Transition,* 1970—.

WORK IN PROGRESS: A study of Jonathan Edwards.

* * *

SCHER, Steven Paul 1936-

PERSONAL: Born March 2, 1936, in Budapest, Hungary; married Helene Lenz (an assistant professor of German), June 21, 1962. *Education:* Yale University, B.A., 1960, M.A., 1963, Ph.D., 1966. *Home:* 143 Linden St., New Haven, Conn. 06511. *Office:* 5 W.L. Harkness Hall, Yale University, New Haven, Conn. 06520.

CAREER: Columbia University, New York, N.Y., instructor in German, 1965-67; Yale University, New Haven, Conn., assistant professor, 1967-70, associate professor of German, 1970—. *Member:* Modern Language Association of America, American Comparative Literature Association, American Association of Teachers of German, Thomas Mann Gesellschaft (Zurich), E.T.A. Hoffman Gesellschaft (Bamberg).

WRITINGS: Verbal Music in German Literature, Yale University Press, 1968. Contributor to literary journals.

WORK IN PROGRESS: Postwar German Culture, an anthology, for Dutton; *Literatur und Musik,* an anthology, for Erich Schmidt Verlag; *E.T.A. Hoffmann: A Biography,* for University of Chicago Press.

* * *

SCHICK, Eleanor 1942-

PERSONAL: Born April 15, 1942, in New York, N.Y.; daughter of William (a psychiatrist) and Bessie (a social worker; maiden name, Grossman) Schick; children: Laura, David. *Education:* Attended high school in New York, N.Y. Studied modern dance with Martha Graham, Alvin Ailey, and others. *Religion:* Jewish. *Home:* 41 West 96th St., New York, N.Y. 10025. *Office:* Behrman House Publishers, 1261 Broadway, New York, N.Y. 10001.

CAREER: Author and illustrator of children's books; professional dancer, giving solo performances with Tamaris-Nagrin Dance Company and the American Dance Festival, and member of Juilliard Dance Theatre; lectured and taught dance at Hofstra University, Bryn Mawr College, and Connecticut College. Parent chairman of St. Matthew and St. Timothy Day Care Center, 1972-73.

WRITINGS—All self-illustrated children's books; all published by Macmillan, except as indicated: *Surprise in the Forest,* Harper, 1964; *The Little School in Cottonwood Corners,* Harper, 1965; *The Dancing School,* Harper, 1966; *I'm Going to the Ocean,* 1966; *5A and 7B,* 1967; *Katie Goes to Camp,* 1968; *Jeanie Goes Riding,* 1968; *City in the Summer,* 1969; *Making Friends,* 1969; *Peggy's New Brother,* 1970, *City in the Winter,* 1970; *Andy,* 1971; *Peter and Mr. Brandon,* illustrated by Donald Carrick, 1973; *Student's Encounter Book for When a Jew Celebrates,* Behrman House, 1973; *City Green,* 1974; *City Sun,* 1974.

Illustrator: Jan Wahl, *Christmas in the Forest,* Macmillan, 1967.

SIDELIGHTS: City in the Winter and *City in the Summer* have been made into filmstrips.

* * *

SCHICKEL, Julia Whedon 1936-
(Julia Whedon)

PERSONAL: Born June 30, 1936, in New York, N.Y.; daughter of John Ogden (a writer) and Carroll (a writer; maiden name, Angell) Whedon; married Richard Schickel (a writer, director, producer, and critic), March 11, 1961; children: Erika Tracy, Jessica Avery. *Education:* Sarah Lawrence College, B.A., 1958; Harvard University, graduate study, 1958-60. *Agent:* Sterling Lord, 660 Madison Ave., New York, N.Y. 10021.

CAREER: Columbia Broadcasting System, New York, N.Y., researcher, 1960-61.

WRITINGS—Under name Julia Whedon: *Girl of the Golden West,* Charter House, 1973. Contributor of short stories and criticism to *Harper's, Ladies' Home Journal, Redbook, Seventeen, New York Times,* and *Washington Post.*

WORK IN PROGRESS: A novel about sports.

SIDELIGHTS: "Raising a family and trying to write are difficult to integrate in one life," Julia Whedon Schickel told *CA.* "The one requires noise—the other silence. So much for circumstances. Motivation: Developing thought and seeing it through is vital to me. Otherwise all of life is distraction—and, finally, rather trivial when you look back on it." She also noted, "My father, mother, brother, husband, uncle, and cousin are writers—something in my blood must keep me at it!"

* * *

SCHIFF, Ken(neth Roy) 1942-

PERSONAL: Born August 3, 1942, in New York, N.Y.; son of Louis (a banker) and Alice (Neubauer) Schiff. *Education:* Grinnell College, B.A., 1964; Columbia University, M.A.T., 1966. *Home:* 12 Summer St., Somerville, Mass. 02143. *Office:* Massachusetts Institute of Technology, Cambridge, Mass. 02139.

CAREER: Westport News, Westport, Conn., sports editor, 1964-65; Globe Book Co., New York, N.Y., editor, 1966-73; permanent substitute social studies teacher in junior high school in Newton, Mass., 1973; Massachusetts Institute of Technology, Cambridge, instructor in humanities, 1974—. Instructor in American popular culture, and in fiction workshop, Boston Center for Adult Education, 1972—; associate managing editor for Robert Bentley, Inc., 1973-74. *Member:* Sigma Delta Chi (past president of Grinnell College chapter), Friars. *Awards, honors: Passing Go* was nominated for a National Book Award, 1973, and was an ALA Notable Book.

WRITINGS: Passing Go (novel), Dodd, 1972; *American Popular Culture* (text), Learning Trends, 1974. Editor-in-chief of *Grinnell Review,* 1962-63; feature editor for *Scarlet and Black,* 1962-63.

* * *

SCHIFFMAN, Jack 1921-

PERSONAL: Born September 6, 1921, in New York, N.Y.; son of Frank (a theatre owner) and Lee Schiffman; married wife, Frances, October, 1943 (divorced, 1967); children: Amy Jane. *Education:* University of Wisconsin, B.D., 1943. *Religion:* Jewish. *Home:* 700 Melrose Dr., Winter Park, Fla. 32789. *Agent:* Richard Curtis, 1265 Fifth Ave., New York, N.Y.

CAREER: Has worked as real estate broker, citrus grower, and caretaker. *Member:* Friends of Orlando Public Library (president, 1962-64). *Military service:* U.S. Naval Reserve during World War II; became lieutenant junior grade; served in European and Mediterranean theatres; received three battle stars.

WRITINGS: Uptown: The Story of Harlem's Apollo Theatre, Cowles, 1971.

WORK IN PROGRESS: A protean collection of essays on observed aspects of human behavior; short stories.

* * *

SCHILLER, Rose Leiman
See GOLDEMBERG, Rose Leiman

* * *

SCHMIDT, Frederick G. 1924-

PERSONAL: Born April 19, 1924, in Milwaukee, Wis.;

son of E. F. (a printer) and Helen C. (Thomsen) Schmidt; married Joan Christopherson (a teacher), February 4, 1961; children: Erik F., Kristin H. M. *Education:* Dartmouth College, A.B., 1948; Yale University, LL.D., 1951. *Home:* 2416 East Edgewood Ave., Milwaukee, Wis. 53211. *Office address:* P. O. Box 14, Milwaukee, Wis. 53201.

CAREER: Farmer; Blackhawk Manufacturing Co., Milwaukee, Wis., personnel director, 1952-55; Schmidt Publications, Inc., Milwaukee, Wis., publisher and editor, 1955-72; Schmidt/Anderson Associates (publishers), Milwaukee, Wis., editor and writer, 1972—. *Military service:* U.S. Army, 10th Mountain Division, 1943-46; became lieutenant. *Member:* Izaak Walton League of America, Sierra Club, Milwaukee Press Club, Milwaukee Farmers, Society of Tympanuchus Cupido Pinnatus, Esker Society of Riveredge Nature Center.

WRITINGS: *How to Introduce a New Employee* (pamphlet), American Management Association, 1952; (editor with Muriel F. Anderson) *Trees of America,* Country Beautiful Foundation, 1973; (with Anderson) *The Complete Buyer's Guide to Photographic Equipment,* Service Communications, 1973.

WORK IN PROGRESS: *The Complete Buyer's Guide to Photographic Equipment* (a new book); *The Complete Buyer's Guide to Used Cars.*

* * *

SCHMIDT, Michael Norton 1947-

PERSONAL: Born March 2, 1947, in Mexico City, Mexico; son of Carl Bernhardt (an aviator) and Elizabeth (a horticulturalist; maiden name, Hill) Schmidt. *Education:* Attended Harvard University, 1966-67; Wadham College, Oxford, B.A., 1970. *Home and office:* 266 Councillor Lane, Cheadle Hulme, Cheadle, Cheshire SK8 5PN, England. *Agent:* A. D. Peters & Co., 10 Buckingham St., London W.C.2, England.

CAREER: Carcanet Press Ltd., Cheadle Hulme, Cheshire, England, managing director, 1971—; Carcanet New Press, Cheadle Hulme, Cheshire, England, director, 1974—. Director of Puckle Press Ltd., 1974—. *Awards, honors:* Gulbenkian fellow in poetry at University of Manchester, 1972-75.

WRITINGS—Poems, except as indicated: *Black Buildings,* Carcanet, 1969; *Bedlam and the Oakwood,* Carcanet, 1970; *Desert of the Lions,* Carcanet, 1972; (editor) *British Poetry since 1960,* Carcanet, 1972; *It Was My Tree,* Anvil, 1973. Editor of *Poetry Nation,* 1973—.

WORK IN PROGRESS: *My Brother Gloucester,* completion expected in 1976; *Fifty Modern British Poets: A Critical Study,* for Pan Books, 1977.

* * *

SCHMITTROTH, John 1924-

PERSONAL: Born June 29, 1924; son of William L. and Helen (Sexton) Schmittroth; married; children: John, Susan, James, Steven, Teresa. *Education:* Creighton University, B.A., 1949; University of Detroit, M.A., 1951. *Home:* 18112 Greenlawn, Detroit, Mich. 48221.

CAREER: University of Detroit, Detroit, Mich., instructor, 1951-55, assistant professor, 1956-60, associate professor, 1961-65, professor of English, 1966—.

WRITINGS—Editor with John Mahoney: *The Insistent Present,* Houghton, 1968; *New Poets, New Music,* Winthrop, 1970; *New Fiction, Non-Fiction,* Winthrop, 1971.

WORK IN PROGRESS: *New Poets, New Music II.*

SIDELIGHTS: Schmittroth told *CA:* "An interest in the poetry and music of Jacques Brel led me to produce "Jacques Brel Is Alive and Well and Living in Paris" [a musical revue]. The production, directed by Phil Marcus Esser, bowed in October 11, 1973, and has been taking bows ever since. It is a Detroit phenomenon—and wildly exciting."

* * *

SCHNEIDER, Kenneth Ray 1927-

PERSONAL: Born February 18, 1927, in Oasis, Utah; son of Bert L. and Mandy (Kelly) Schneider; married Blanche M. Duvivier (a music teacher), March 22, 1959; children: Leslie, Lowell, Mari, Loren, Matthew. *Education:* Brigham Young University, student, 1947-48; University of California, Berkeley, A.B., 1952, graduate study, 1952-54. *Home:* 5790 East Park Circle Dr., Fresno, Calif. 93727.

CAREER: Teacher on Hopi Indian reservation in northern Arizona, 1954-55; Stanislaus County Planning Commission, Modesto, Calif., associate planner, 1955-56; Fresno-Clovis Area Planning Commission, Fresno, Calif., transportation planner, 1956-57; Kern County Planning Commission, Bakersfield, Calif., principal planner, 1958-59; associated with Albert Mayer (an architect, planner, and community developer), New York, N.Y., 1959-60; CARE, special overseas representative in the Philippines, 1961, chief of mission in Sierra Leone and Jordan, 1962-64; writer, 1964—. Instructor at California State University, Fresno, autumn, 1972. Consultant to United Nations, 1966-71. *Member:* American Institute of Planners, Society for International Development.

WRITINGS: (Editor) *Planning of Metropolitan Areas and New Towns,* United Nations, 1967; *Destiny of Change: How Relevant Is Man in the Age of Development?,* Holt, 1968; *Autokind versus Mankind: An Analysis of Tyranny, A Proposal for Rebellion, A Plan for Reconstruction,* Norton, 1971. Contributor to conference reports. Contributor to *Traffic Quarterly, Journal of the American Institute of Planners, International Review of Community Development, Ekistics, Architectural Forum, Cry California,* and other periodicals.

* * *

SCHOENBRUN, David (Franz) 1915-

PERSONAL: Born March 15, 1915, in New York, N.Y.; son of Max (a jeweler) and Lucy (Cassirer) Schoenbrun; married Dorothy Scher (a painter), September 23, 1938; children: Lucy (Mrs. Robert Szekely). *Education:* City College (now City College of the City University of New York), B.A., 1934; Columbia University, graduate study, 1965-66. *Politics:* Independent. *Religion:* Jewish. *Agent:* N. S. Bienstock, Inc., 850 Seventh Ave., New York, N.Y. 10019.

CAREER: High school teacher of French and Spanish in New York, N.Y., 1934-36; Dress Manufacturers Association, New York, N.Y., labor relations adjustor, 1936-40, editor of trade newspaper, 1937-40; free-lance writer for newspapers and magazines, 1940-41; U.S. Office of War Information, chief of European propaganda desk, 1942-43; Overseas News Agency, chief of Paris (France) Bureau, 1945-47; Columbia Broadcasting System (CBS), Inc., chief of Paris Bureau, 1945-60, chief correspondent, and chief of Washington, D.C., bureau, 1960-63; Metromedia, New

York, N.Y., news commentator and chief correspondent, 1964, 1965—. Guest commentator, ABC News, 1967-70; senior lecturer at Columbia University, 1968-70, and New School for Social Research, 1970—. *Military service:* U.S. Army, Intelligence, 1943-45; chief of Allied Forces newsroom and commentator for United Nations radio in Algiers, 1943; U.S. intelligence liaison officer with French Army, 1944-45; combat correspondent with U.S. Seventh Army, 1945; received Croix de Guerre.

MEMBER: Overseas Press Club, American Federation of Radio and Television Artists, Association of Radio-Television News Analysts, Anglo-American Press Club (Paris; past president), Common Cause, Friars Club. *Awards, honors:* Named Chevalier of Legion of Honor, Government of France, 1952; Emmy Award from Academy of Television Arts and Sciences, 1958, for reporting from overseas; Overseas Press Club award, 1958, for *As France Goes,* and in other years for distinguished reporting and writing; Alfred I. duPont Best Commentator of the Year Award, 1959.

WRITINGS: As France Goes, Harper, 1957; *The Three Lives of Charles de Gaulle,* Atheneum, 1965; *Viet Nam: How We Got In, How to Get Out,* Atheneum, 1968; *The New Israelis,* Atheneum, 1973. Contributor to numerous magazines and newspapers in the United States and Europe.

WORK IN PROGRESS: A biography of Jean Monnet; a book on the year 1947, *The Watershed Year.*

AVOCATIONAL INTERESTS: Reading, travel.

* * *

SCHOETTLE, Lynn

PERSONAL: Surname sounds like "shuttle"; daughter of Herbert A. (a supervisor for Ford Motor Co.) Calkins and Gloria (a postal clerk; maiden name, Sexton) Calkins Kerwin; married John D. Schoettle (a research instrument technician), November 18, 1961; children: Susan Elizabeth, James Joseph. *Education:* Oakland Community College, student, 1970-73, 1974—. *Home:* 412 North Connecticut, Royal Oak, Mich. 48067. *Agent:* Patricia Myrer, McIntosh & Otis, Inc., 18 East 41st St., New York, N.Y. 10017.

CAREER: Writer. Renwell Electronics, Granby, Mass., stock clerk, 1965; Gale Research Co., Detroit, Mich., assistant editor, 1974; Oakland Community College, Oakland County, Mich., creator and teacher of juvenile picture book course, 1974. Volunteer in Head Start program, 1969. Speaker at annual writer's conference at Oakland University, 1973, 1974. *Member:* Detroit Women Writers.

WRITINGS: Grandpa's Long Red Underwear (juvenile), Lothrop, 1972. Author and illustrator of how-to-decorate column, *Detroit News,* 1967-68. Contributor to *American Home, Woman's Day,* and local newspapers.

WORK IN PROGRESS: Two adult novels, *Just Like Him* and *M.S.Mom.*

SIDELIGHTS: Lynn Schoettle's early employment was brief because, she told *CA:* "my young children and husband needed [me] full time." She wrote eight hours a day in a rented office during 1972-73, then worked briefly on *Contemporary Authors* "to support a full-time writing habit," but left to return to "that habit" and to resume her schooling. She is "concerned with Human Rights, and women's lives in contemporary society (I *am* a Women's Libber—I've included my mother's vocation, she's worked nearly as long as my father)."

AVOCATIONAL INTERESTS: Painting (completed first commissioned portrait in 1974), embroidery, gardening, and sculpting ("I've been beating my flustrations out on a walnut tree stump for five years. Its title will be 'The Origin of My Fat Red Thumb.'").

* * *

SCHOTT, Webster 1927-

PERSONAL: Born September 8, 1927, in Belleville, Ill. *Education:* University of Missouri, B.J., 1948. *Politics:* Independent. *Religion:* Unitarian. *Home address:* Lake Quivira, Kan. 66106. *Office:* April House, Inc., 11847 West 83rd Ter., Lenexa, Kan. 66215.

CAREER: Potts-Woodbury Advertising, Inc., Kansas City, Mo., group copy chief, 1951-59; Hallmark Cards, Inc., Kansas City, Mo., editor, 1959-65, vice-president and editor-in-chief, 1965-71; April House, Inc., Lenexa, Kan., vice-president and partner, 1971—. Lecturer at University of Kansas, 1973. *Member:* National Endowment for the Arts (member of literary panel), American Civil Liberties Union (member of board of directors of western Missouri unit, 1961-71).

WRITINGS: (Editor) *Poetry for Pleasure,* Doubleday, 1960; (editor with Robert J. Meyers) *American Christmas* (poems), Hallmark-Doubleday, 1965, 2nd edition, 1967; (editor and author of introduction) William Carlos Williams, *Imaginations,* New Directions, 1970. Contributor to *Time, Life, New Republic, Nation, Saturday Review, Washington Post,* and *New York Times.* Literary editor, *Focus/Midwest,* 1963-68.

* * *

SCHRAFF, Anne E(laine) 1939-

PERSONAL: Born September 21, 1939, in Cleveland, Ohio; daughter of Frank C. and Helen (Benninger) Schraff. *Education:* Pierce Junior College, A.A., 1964; San Fernando Valley State College (now California State University, Northridge), B.A., 1966, M.A., 1967. *Politics:* Republican. *Religion:* Roman Catholic. *Address:* P.O. Box 1345, Spring Valley, Calif. 92077.

CAREER: Academy of Our Lady of Peace, San Diego, Calif., teacher of social studies, 1967—. *Member:* California Social Studies Council.

WRITINGS: (With brother, Francis N. Schraff) *Jesus Our Brother* (children's book), Liguorian Books, 1968; *Black Courage* (nonfiction), Macrae, 1969; *North Star* (novel), Macrae, 1972; *The Day the World Went Away* (novel), Doubleday, 1973. Contributor of reviews to *Scholastic Teacher.*

WORK IN PROGRESS: Please Don't Ask Me to Love You, completion expected in 1974; *Oath on A Blood Red Moon,* 1974.

AVOCATIONAL INTERESTS: Music, hiking.

* * *

SCHRAG, Oswald O. 1916-

PERSONAL: Born June 4, 1916, in Marion, S.D.; son of John J. (a farmer and minister) and Katherine (Miller) Schrag; married wife, Orpha V., September 5, 1945. *Education:* Bethel College, North Newton, Kan., A.B., 1942; Hartford Theological Seminary, M.Div., 1945, S.T.M., 1948; Boston University, Ph.D., 1952. *Home:* 960 Davidson Dr., Nashville, Tenn. 37205. *Office:* Department of Religion, Fisk University, Nashville, Tenn. 37203.

CAREER: Ordained Congregational minister serving in Bolton, Conn., 1945-48, and Chicopee Falls, Mass., 1951-52; Fisk University, Nashville, Tenn., associate professor, 1952-58, professor of religion and philosophy, 1958—, chairman of department, 1957-73. *Member:* American Philosophical Society, Metaphysical Society of America, American Theological Society, Society for Phenomenology and Existential Philosophy, American Academy of Religion, Society for Philosophy of Religion (president, 1972-73), Tennessee Council of Churches.

WRITINGS: Existence, Existenz, and Transcendence: An Introduction to the Philosophy of Karl Jaspers, Duquesne University Press, 1971.

WORK IN PROGRESS: Existentialism and Religion: Philosophy of Essence and Philosophy of Existence.

AVOCATIONAL INTERESTS: Fishing, golfing.

* * *

SCHRIER, Arnold 1925-

PERSONAL: Born May 30, 1925, in Bronx, N.Y. *Education:* Attended Bethany College, 1943-44, and Ohio Wesleyan University, 1944-45; Northwestern University, B.S., 1949, M.A., 1950, Ph.D., 1956; postdoctoral study at Indiana University and in the Soviet Union, 1963-64. *Office:* Department of History, McMicken College of Arts and Sciences, University of Cincinnati, Cincinnati, Ohio 45221.

CAREER: University of Cincinnati, Cincinnati, Ohio, assistant professor, 1956-61, associate professor, 1961-66, professor of history, 1966-72, Walter C. Langsam Professor of Modern European History, 1972—, director of graduate studies in history, 1969—. Visiting summer professor at Northwestern University, 1960; visiting associate professor at Indiana University, 1965-66; visiting lecturer at Duke University, summer, 1966. *Military service:* U.S. Naval Reserve, active duty, 1943-46, 1952-54; became lieutenant senior grade.

MEMBER: American Association for the Advancement of Slavic Studies, American Historical Association, Historians Film Committee, Immigration History Society (member of executive council, 1970-72), American Association of University Professors (president of local chapter, 1970-71), Midwest Conference on Slavic Studies, Southern Conference on Slavic Studies, Ohio Academy of History (vice-president, 1972-73; president, 1973-74), Phi Alpha Theta. *Awards, honors:* Foreign area fellowship from Social Science Research Council and American Council of Learned Societies, 1963-64.

WRITINGS: Ireland and the American Emigration: 1850-1900, University of Minnesota Press, 1958; (editor with H. J. Carroll, Jr. and others) *The Development of Civilization: A Documentary History of Politics, Society, and Thought,* two volumes, Scott, Foresman, 1961-62, revised edition, 1969; (editor with Carroll and others) *Modern European Civilization: A Documentary History of Politics, Society, and Thought from the Renaissance to the Present,* Scott, Foresman, 1963; (with T. W. Wallbank) *Living World History,* Scott, Foresman, 1964, 3rd edition, 1973; (contributor) Franklin D. Scott, editor, *World Migration in Modern Times,* Prentice-Hall, 1968; (with Wallbank) *Twentieth Century World,* Scott, Foresman, 1974.

Contributor of about fifteen articles and reviews to history journals, including *Cincinnati Historical Society Bulletin, Publications of the Ohio Academy of History, American Historical Review,* and *Historian.*

WORK IN PROGRESS: Translating from Russian a two-volume account of the United States, originally written in 1857 by a traveler to this country.

* * *

SCHROEDER, John H(erman) 1943-

PERSONAL: Born September 13, 1943, in Twin Falls, Idaho; son of Herman J. (a physician) and Azalia (Kimes) Schroeder; married Sandra Ann Barrow (a college teacher), June 16, 1965; children: John Kimes, Andrew Barrow. *Education:* Lewis and Clark College, B.A., 1965; University of Virginia, M.A., 1967, Ph.D., 1971. *Religion:* Episcopalian. *Home:* 2738 North Summit Ave., Milwaukee, Wis. 53211. *Office:* Department of History, Bolton Hall, University of Wisconsin, Milwaukee, Wis. 53211.

CAREER: University of Wisconsin, Milwaukee, assistant professor of history, 1970—, assistant chairman of department, 1972—. *Member:* Organization of American Historians, Southern Historical Association, Phi Alpha Theta. *Awards, honors:* University of Wisconsin Edward and Rosa Uhrig Award for distinguished teaching, 1973-74.

WRITINGS: Mr. Polk's War: American Opposition and Dissent, 1846-1848, University of Wisconsin Press, 1973.

WORK IN PROGRESS: Research on the Whig Party, expansion, and slavery in the United States during the 1840's.

* * *

SCHUG, Willis E(rvin) 1924-

PERSONAL: Born June 20, 1924, in Easton, Pa.; son of Willis E. and Ruth A. (Williams) Schug; married June Curtis, June 8, 1946; children: Susan, Judy Schug Winslow, Wendy, Terry. *Education:* U.S. Military Academy, B.Sc., 1946; Ohio State University, M.Sc., 1948; Columbia University, LL.B., 1954. *Home:* 76 Canaan Pl., Allendale, N.J. 07401. *Office:* School of Law, Columbia University, New York, N.Y. 10027.

CAREER: U.S. Army, Quartermaster Corps, Judge Advocate General's Corps, 1955-68, retiring with rank of lieutenant colonel; legal work in Army included trial or defense counsel in more than seventy-five general courts-martial, 1955-59, assistant professor of law at U.S. Military Academy, West Point, N.Y., 1957-60, and supervisory or administrative assignments in criminal and international law and military justice, 1961-68; Columbia University, School of Law, New York, N.Y., lecturer in military law, 1969-73, assistant dean, 1968-71, associate dean, 1971-73; Jack, Kookogey and Schug, Meadville and Titusville, Pa., partner, 1973—. Lecturer in law, University of Pittsburgh, Titusville. *Member:* American Bar Association, Phi Delta Phi, Sigma Alpha Epsilon. *Awards, honors*—Military: Legion of Honor and Army Commendation Medal with oak-leaf cluster.

WRITINGS: (Editor) *United States Law and the Armed Forces: Cases and Materials on Constitutional Law, Courts-Martial, and the Rights of Servicemen,* Praeger, 1972.

AVOCATIONAL INTERESTS: Sports in general, including golf and coaching baseball.

* * *

SCHULTZ, Pearle Henriksen 1918-

PERSONAL: Born September 10, 1918, in Havre, Mont.;

daughter of Louis G. (an architect) and Anne (Jacobson) Henriksen; married Harry Pershing Schultz (a professor of chemistry), September 25, 1943; children: Stephanie, Tor and Alison (twins). *Education:* University of Wisconsin, B.S., 1939; University of Miami, Coral Gables, Fla., M.Ed., 1951. *Politics:* Republican. *Religion:* Methodist. *Home:* 5835 Southwest 81st St., South Miami, Fla. 33143. *Agent:* Bertha Klausner International Literary Agency, 71 Park Ave., New York, N.Y. 10016.

CAREER: Teacher of English and history and guidance counselor in Racine, Wis., Middleton, Wis., Rahway, N.J., and Dade County, Fla., 1940-51; Cutler Cove Preparatory School, Miami, Fla., principal, 1956-63; Dade County Public Schools, Miami, Fla., supervisor of curriculum publications, 1963-72; full-time writer in South Miami, Fla., 1972—. Florida Independent School Council, director, 1961-63.

WRITINGS: Sir Walter Scott: Wizard of the North, Vanguard, 1968; (with husband, Harry P. Schultz) *Isaac Newton: Scientific Genius,* Garrard, 1972; *The Generous Strangers,* Vanguard, 1974; *Paul Laurence Dunbar,* Garrard, 1974.

WORK IN PROGRESS: The story of the brilliant Black woman who was an early advocate of woman's suffrage, *Mary Church Terrell: Fighter for Justice,* publication expected in 1975; a fiction portrayal of large public school systems, tentatively entitled, *System!,* 1976.

BIOGRAPHICAL/CRITICAL SOURCES: Science Books, September, 1972.

* * *

SCHWARTZ, Howard 1945-

PERSONAL: Born April 21, 1945, in St. Louis, Mo.; son of Nathan (a dealer in jewelry and antiques) and Bluma (Rubin) Schwartz. *Education:* Washington University, St. Louis, Mo., B.A., 1967, M.A., 1969. *Politics:* "Pro-human." *Religion:* Jewish. *Home:* 7011 Tulane, University City, Mo. 63130. *Office:* University of Missouri, 8001 Natural Bridge Rd., St. Louis, Mo. 63121.

CAREER: Forest Park Community College, St. Louis, Mo., instructor in English, 1969-70; University of Missouri, St. Louis, instructor in English, 1970—. Teacher of poetry writing at Metropolitan Educational Center in the Arts; has been a camp counselor and folk dance teacher.

WRITINGS: A Blessing Over Ashes, Tree Books, 1974. Poems anthologized in *Doctor Generosity's Almanac: Seventeen Poets,* edited by Ray Freed, Doctor Generosity Press, 1970, and *The Missouri Poets,* edited by Robert Killoren and Joseph Clark, Eads Bridge Press, 1971. Contributor of more than fifty articles and poems to literary journals, including *Granite, New Laurel Review, Small Pond, Cardinal Poetry Quarterly, White Elephant,* and *Illuminations.* Former co-editor of *Reflections* and *Tambourine.*

WORK IN PROGRESS: Braille Landscape, a book of poems; *Dreaming Back,* selections from his dream journals; editing *Imperial Messages,* an anthology of twentieth-century parables.

* * *

SCOTT, Ellis L(averne) 1915-

PERSONAL: Born June 11, 1915, in Casey, Iowa; son of Alexander C. (a land agent) and Cora (Tilman) Scott; married Fern Garner, February 22, 1943 (died, 1948); married Florence Louise Green, September 7, 1950. children: Susan (Mrs. George Sergent), Katherine, Robert Tilman. *Education:* Ohio State University, B.S. (summa cum laude), 1947, Ph.D., 1953. *Home:* 124 Colonial Dr., Athens, Ga. 30601. *Office:* Department of Management, University of Georgia, Athens, Ga. 30601.

CAREER: Ohio State University, Columbus, research associate, 1948-53; University of New Mexico, Albuquerque, assistant professor of sociology, 1953-57; RAND Corp., Santa Monica, Calif., human factors scientist, 1957-64; University of Georgia, Athens, professor of management, 1964—. Consultant to U.S. Atomic Energy Commission, 1954-56, and to industry. *Military service:* U.S. Army Air Forces, 1942-46; became first lieutenant. *Member:* American Sociological Association, Academy of Management (chairman, 1970-72), Commission on Social Implications of Automation, American Automatic Control Council, International Federation of Automatic Control.

WRITINGS: (Editor) *Electronic Data Processing Systems for Public Management,* Rand McNally, 1967; (editor) *Automation and Society,* Center for the Study of Automation and Society, University of Georgia, 1969; (editor) *Automation Management,* Center for the Study of Automation and Society, University of Georgia, 1970. Other publications include monographs and articles.

WORK IN PROGRESS: Investigations of the social implications of technology, especially automation.

* * *

SCOTT, W(illiam) E(dgar), Jr. 1929-

PERSONAL: Born January 26, 1929, in Newtown, Ind.; son of William E. and Inez Irene (Roger) Scott; married Jean Wooster, May 19, 1956; children: Kimberly, Cynthia. *Education:* Indiana University, A.B., 1955; Purdue University, M.S., 1957, Ph.D., 1963. *Home:* Route 12, 900 Pleasant Ridge Rd., Bloomington, Ind. 47401. *Office:* Graduate School of Business, Indiana University, Bloomington, Ind. 47401.

CAREER: Certified by State of Indiana as consulting psychologist, 1969; private practice as consulting psychologist, 1962—. Purdue University, Lafayette, Ind., assistant personnel director, 1957-62; Indiana University, Graduate School of Business, Bloomington, assistant professor, 1962-66, associate professor, 1966-71, professor of organizational behavior, 1971—. Member of board of directors of Monon Trailer and Body Manufacturing Co., 1957-62. *Military service:* U.S. Navy, 1949-53; carrier pilot; became lieutenant, junior grade. *Member:* Academy of Management, American Psychological Association, Industrial Psychologists' Roundtable, Midwest Psychological Association, Indiana Psychological Association, Psi Chi, Sigma Xi, Beta Gamma Sigma.

WRITINGS: (Editor with L. L. Cummings, and contributor) *Readings in Organizational Behavior and Human Performance,* Homewood, 1969, revised edition, 1973. Contributor of about twenty articles to management and psychology journals.

* * *

SEABORG, Glenn T(heodore) 1912-

PERSONAL: Born April 19, 1912, in Ishpeming, Mich.; son of Herman Theodore and Selma (Erickson) Seaborg; married Helen Lucille Griggs, June 6, 1942; children: Peter, Lynne (Mrs. William Cobb), David, Stephen, John Eric, Dianne. *Education:* University of California, Los Angeles, A.B., 1934; University of California, Berkeley, Ph.D., 1937. *Religion:* Protestant. *Home:* 1154 Glen Rd., Lafayette, Calif. 94549. *Office:* Lawrence Berkeley Laboratory, University of California, Berkeley, Calif. 94720.

CAREER: Co-discoverer of numerous radioactive isotopes since 1937 and of plutonium and seven other new elements (atomic numbers 94-102), 1940-58; co-winner of Nobel Prize in chemistry, 1951; first scientist to head U.S. Atomic Energy Commission. Associated with University of California, Berkeley, 1937—, as research associate, 1937-39, instructor in chemistry, 1939-41, assistant professor, 1941-45 (on leave, 1942-46), professor, 1945-71 (on leave, 1961-71), university professor, 1971—, head of Nuclear Chemistry Division, Lawrence Radiation Laboratory (renamed Lawrence Berkeley Laboratory), 1946-58, 1971—, associate director of laboratory, 1954-61, 1971—, chancellor of university, 1958-61. Director of plutonium work for Manhattan Project at University of Chicago Metallurgical Laboratory, 1942-46; chairman of U.S. Atomic Energy Commission, 1961-71. Member of scientific and governmental bodies, including: joint commission on radioactivity, International Council of Scientific Unions, 1946-56; first general advisory committee, Atomic Energy Commission, 1946-50, and historical advisory committee, 1958-61; national science board, National Science Foundation, 1960-61; Federal Radiation Council, 1961-69; Federal Council for Science and Technology, 1961-70; National Aeronautics and Space Council, 1961-71. U.S. representative at annual conferences of International Atomic Energy Agency in Vienna, 1961-64, 1966-71, and Tokyo, 1965; chairman of U.S. delegation and president, United Nations International Conference on the Peaceful Uses of Atomic Energy, Geneva, 1971. Identified as trustee, officer, or consultant with Educational Television, American-Scandinavian Foundation, and a variety of coeducational and scientific services. Distinguished lecturer in United States and abroad, 1946—, including Royal Swedish Academy lecturer, 1949, Centenary lecturer of British Chemical Society, 1956, Silliman lecturer at Yale University, 1957, Edgar Fahs Smith memorial lecturer of American Chemical Society, 1960, and Harrelson lecturer at University of North Carolina, 1964.

MEMBER: American Association for the Advancement of Science (fellow; president, 1972; chairman of board, 1973), American Chemical Society (division chairman and councilor, 1951-52), National Academy of Sciences, American Academy of Arts and Sciences (fellow), American Physical Society (fellow), Royal Society of Arts (England; fellow), American Nuclear Society (honorary fellow), Chemical Society (England; honorary fellow), American Swedish Historical Foundation (life member), International Platform Association (president, 1968-69), World Future Society (member of board of directors, 1969—), Bavarian Academy of Sciences (corresponding member), Royal Swedish Academy of Sciences (foreign member), U.S.S.R. Academy of Sciences (foreign member), California Academy of Sciences (fellow), Washington Academy of Sciences (fellow), New York Academy of Sciences (honorary fellow); honorary member of other American and foreign societies and academies; Authors Guild, Phi Beta Kappa, Sigma Xi; Cosmos Club, Metropolitan Club, and Chevy Chase Club (all Washington, D.C.), Bohemian Club and Commonwealth Club (San Francisco).

AWARDS, HONORS: Named one of America's ten outstanding young men by U.S. Junior Chamber of Commerce, 1947; American Chemical Society Award in Pure Chemistry, 1947; John Ericsson Gold Medal, American Society of Swedish Engineers, 1948; Nobel Prize in chemistry (shared with Edwin M. McMillan), 1951; Perkin Medal, American Section of Societe de Chemie Industrielle, 1957; Thomas Alva Edison Foundation Award for best science book for youth, 1958, for *Elements of the Universe;* Enrico Fermi Award ($50,000) of U.S. Atomic Energy Commission, 1959; Charles Lathrop Parsons Award of American Chemical Society, 1964; Leif Erickson Award, Leif Erickson Foundation, 1964; Chemical Pioneer Award, American Institute of Chemists, 1968; Mugunghwa Medal, Order of Civil Merit (Korea), 1970; Nuclear Pioneer Award, Society of Nuclear Medicine, 1971; Golden Plate Award, American Academy of Achievement, 1972; Gold Medal Award, American Institute of Chemists, 1973; decorated Officier, French Legion of Honor, 1973; and numerous other scientific, academic, and public service awards. More than forty honorary degrees, 1951—, including D.Sc., Sc.D., LL.D., D.P.S., D.P.A., D.Eng., Litt.D., and L.H.D.

WRITINGS: (With Joseph J. Katz) *The Chemistry of the Actinide Elements,* Wiley, 1957; (contributor with Earl K. Hyde) *Handbuch der Physik,* Volume LXII, Springer-Verlag, 1957; (with Evans G. Valens) *Elements of the Universe* (youth book), Dutton, 1958; *The Transuranium Elements* (Silliman lectures at Yale University, 1957), Yale University Press, 1958; *Man-Made Transuranium Elements,* Prentice-Hall, 1963; (with Daniel M. Wilkes) *Education and the Atom,* McGraw, 1964; (with Hyde and Isadore Perlman) *The Nuclear Properties of the Heavy Elements,* two volumes, Prentice-Hall, 1964, Volume I: *Systematics of Nuclear Structure and Radioactivity,* Volume II: *Detailed Radioactivity Properties;* (with others) *Oppenheimer,* Scribner, 1969; (with William R. Corliss) *Man and Atom: Shaping a New World Through Nuclear Technology,* Dutton, 1971; *Nuclear Milestones* (expansion of collection of speeches published under that title by Division of Technical Information, U.S. Atomic Energy Commission, 1971), W. H. Freeman, 1972.

Editor: (With Joseph J. Katz and Winston M. Manning) *The Transuranium Elements* (Plutonium Project record), McGraw, 1949; (with Leonard I. Katzin) *Production and Separation of U-233* (Plutonium Project record), Technical Information Service Extension, U.S. Atomic Energy Commission, 1951; (with W. N. Lipscomb, P. R. O'-Connor, M. Cannon Sneed, J. Lewis Maynard, and Robert C. Brasted) *Comprehensive Inorganic Chemistry,* Volume I, Van Nostrand, 1953; (with Katz) *The Actinide Elements* (Plutonium Project record), McGraw, 1954.

Collections of speeches published by Technical Information Service, U.S. Atomic Energy Commission: *Science and Society* (ten speeches), 1966; *Science, Man and Change* (nine speeches), 1968; *Peaceful Uses of Nuclear Energy* (ten speeches), 1970.

Contributor of more than two hundred scientific articles and papers to journals in United States, Netherlands, and Soviet Union. Associate editor, *Journal of Chemical Physics,* 1948-50; member of editorial board, *Journal of the American Chemical Society,* 1950-59; member of editorial advisory board, *Journal of Inorganic and Nuclear Chemistry,* 1954—, and *Chemical and Engineering News,* 1957-59; member of panel, *Golden Picture Encyclopedia for Children,* 1957-61, and *American Heritage Dictionary,* 1964—. Consultant on *Funk and Wagnall's Universal Standard Encyclopedia* and other publications.

WORK IN PROGRESS: *Travels in the New World,* about his visits to sixty countries while chairman of the Atomic Energy Commission; *Notes on the Nuclear Age,* a historical commentary; a history of the C-1 (Plutonium Project) section of the University of Chicago Metallurgical Laboratory; a revision of *The Chemistry of the Actinide Elements.*

SIDELIGHTS: Seaborg is the author of the "actinide concept" of heavy element electronic structure—demonstrating that the heaviest naturally occurring elements and the first eleven synthetic transuranium elements form a transition series of actinide elements in a manner analogous to the rare earth series of lanthanide elements. In addition to research, his major interests are focused on public understanding of science, science education, the peaceful uses of atomic energy, and international cooperation in science and technology.

Five of his books—*The Actinide Elements, The Chemistry of the Actinide Elements, Elements of the Universe, Man and Atom,* and *Man-Made Transuranium Elements*—have been translated into Russian. *Elements of the Universe* also has been published in Persian, Slovak, and Japanese, *The Chemistry of the Actinide Elements* into Japanese, and *Man-Made Transuranium Elements,* a textbook for senior high schools and up, into Japanese, German, Polish, French, and Portuguese.

BIOGRAPHICAL/CRITICAL SOURCES: *Saturday Review,* March 5, 1960; *Fortune,* April 1961; *Newsweek,* October 16, 1961; *The Way of the Scientist,* Simon & Schuster, 1966; Irving Stone, editor, *There Was Light,* Doubleday, 1970; *Science,* February 19, 1971.

* * *

SECUNDA, Sholom 1894-1974

August 23, 1894—June 13, 1974; Russian-born American songwriter. Obituaries: *New York Times,* June 14, 1974; *Washington Post,* June 15, 1974; *Time,* June 24, 1974.

* * *

SEGAL, Mendel 1914-

PERSONAL: Born June 8, 1914, in Chattanooga, Tenn.; son of Samuel George and Beckie (Lewis) Segal; married Mynette Kahn, January 22, 1939; children: Joseph Nathan. *Education:* Attended Emory University, 1931-33. *Religion:* Jewish. *Home:* 475 Hillside Dr. N.W., Atlanta, Ga. 30342. *Office:* 2161 Monroe Dr. N.E., Atlanta, Ga. 30324.

CAREER: Stein Printing Co., Atlanta, Ga., managing partner, 1935—; Segal Services, Inc., Atlanta, Ga., president, 1946—; Oak Realty Co., Atlanta, Ga., president, 1959—. President of Gate City Lodge B'nai B'rith, 1969, Metro Atlanta Mental Health Association, 1970, and Community Friendship, Inc., 1970—; chairman of Fulton County Mental Health Advisory Committee, 1969; treasurer of Georgia Mental Health Association, 1974; member of board of Better Business Bureau, 1972, and Atlanta Jewish Home, 1974; chairman of Northside Community Mental Health Center Advisory Committee, 1970. *Member:* National Conference of Christians and Jews (member of board, 1969), Printing Industries of America (chairman of board, 1964), Union Employers Section of Printing Industry of America (president, 1962-63), Printing Industry of Atlanta (president, 1954-55). *Awards, honors:* Man of year from Atlanta Club Printing House Craftsmen, 1959; Silver Award from Atlanta Advertising Club/*Printers' Ink,* 1961.

WRITINGS: *How to Sell Printing Creatively,* Segal Services, 1955; *How to Develop Your Personal Selling Power,* Dartnell, 1965, 2nd edition, 1971; *Sales Management for Small and Medium-sized Businesses,* Prentice-Hall, 1969; *How to Sell More Profitable Printing,* North American Publishing Co., 1972. Contributor to *Printing Impressions* and *Printing.*

WORK IN PROGRESS: A layman's overview of psychology, *How To Understand Yourself and Others,* completion expected in 1975.

* * *

SENNA, Carl 1944-

PERSONAL: Born April 13, 1944, in Jennings, La.; son of Francisco Jose (a boxer) and Anna Maria Franklyn (Pierce) Senna; married Fanny Quincy Howe (a writer), October 27, 1968; children: Ann Lucien Quincy, Danzy Maria, Maceo Carl. *Education:* Boston University, student, 1962-67; Columbia University, student, 1968-70. *Home:* 1 Robeson St., Jamaica Plain, Mass. 02130. *Office:* 755 Boylston St., Suite 801, Boston, Mass. 02116.

CAREER: Tufts University, Medford, Mass., lecturer in English, 1968-69; Beacon Press, Boston, Mass., editor, 1968-69; University of Massachusetts, Boston, lecturer in English, 1969-73; Northeastern University, Boston, writer-in-residence, 1970—. Writer-in-residence at Xavier University, New Orleans, La., 1972, and Allen University, Columbia, S.C., 1973. *Member:* American Society of Aesthetics, National Rifle Association, Pan-American Society of New England.

WRITINGS: (Editor) *Parachute Shop Blues and Other Poems,* Diensthul, 1972; (editor) *The Fallacy of I. Q.,* Third Press, 1973. Contributor to *Commonweal, National Catholic Reporter, Fire-Exit, Hibernia,* and *Africa.*

* * *

SEUREN, Pieter A. M. 1934-

PERSONAL: Born July 9, 1934, in Haarlem, Netherlands; son of John Theodore (a businessman) and Catherine (Schavemaker) Seuren. *Education:* Attended University of Amsterdam, 1951-58. *Religion:* None. *Home and office:* Magdalen College, Oxford University, Oxford, England.

CAREER: University of Amsterdam, Amsterdam, Netherlands, assistant in linguistics, 1955-59; Classic School, Amsterdam, teacher of Latin and Greek, 1959-63; University of Amsterdam, assistant in logic, 1963-64; University of Groningen, Groningen, Netherlands, assistant in linguistics, 1964-66; Cambridge University, Cambridge, England, linguistics research for Dutch Ministry of Education for development of Dutch language course, 1966-67, lecturer in linguistics, 1967-70; Oxford University, Oxford, England, lecturer in linguistics, 1971—. *Member:* Linguistic Society of America, Linguistics Association of Great Britain, Societa Linguistica Italiana, Algemene Vereniging voor Taalwetenschap.

WRITINGS: *L'Italiano per gli Olandesi,* H. Stam, 1966; *Operators and Nucleus: A Contribution to the Theory of Grammar,* Cambridge University Press, 1969.

WORK IN PROGRESS: Writing on the theory of grammar; semantics.

SIDELIGHTS: Besides Dutch and English, Seuren is competent in French, German, Italian, Latin, and ancient and modern Greek.

SEWELL, (Margaret) Elizabeth 1919-

PERSONAL: Born March 9, 1919, in Coonoor, India; daughter of Robert Beresford Seymour (a marine biologist) and Dorothy (Dean) Sewell; married Anthony C. Sirignano (a university lecturer in classics), January 2, 1971. *Education:* Newnham College, Cambridge, B.A., 1942, M.A., 1945, Ph.D., 1949. *Residence:* Greensboro, N.C. *Agent:* Ober Associates, Inc., 40 East 49th St., New York, N.Y. 10017. *Office:* Department of Religious Studies, University of North Carolina, Greensboro, N.C. 27412.

CAREER: Fordham University, New York, N.Y., professor of English, 1954-55, 1958-59; Tougaloo College, Tougaloo, Miss., professor of English, 1963-64; Fordham University, professor of English, 1967-69; Hunter College of the City University of New York, New York, N.Y., professor of English, 1971-74; University of North Carolina, Greensboro, member of faculty in department of religious studies, 1974—. *Member:* P.E.N. International, American Association of University Professors, Lewis Carroll Society. *Awards, honors:* Litt.D. from St. Peter's College, 1963, and Fordham University, 1968.

WRITINGS: *The Structure of Poetry,* Routledge & Kegan Paul, 1951; *The Dividing of Time* (novel), Doubleday, 1951; *Paul Valery: The Mind in the Mirror,* Yale University Press, 1952; *The Field of Nonsense,* Chatto & Windus, 1952; *The Singular Hope* (novel), Chatto & Windus, 1955; *The Orphic Voice: Poetry and Natural History,* Yale University Press, 1960; *Now Bless Thyself* (novel), Doubleday, 1963; *Poems: 1947-1961,* University of North Carolina Press, 1963; *The Human Metaphor,* University of Notre Dame Press, 1964; *Signs and Cities* (poems), University of North Carolina Press, 1968.

* * *

SEYMOUR, W(illiam) Douglas 1910-

PERSONAL: Born September 21, 1910, in Newark, England; son of William Willock and Maud (Harmston) Seymour; married Marjorie Hilda Gill, 1937; children: John Anthony. *Education:* University of Nottingham, B.A. (honors), 1931; University College, London, graduate study, 1938-40. *Home:* Hackmans Gate, Clent, Worchester DY9 OEP, England.

CAREER: Industrial consultant in England; University of Birmingham, Birmingham, England, honorary research fellow in engineering production, 1960—. Member of Central Training Council, Ministry of Labour, 1964-67. *Member:* British Psychological Society (fellow), Institute of Personnel Management (fellow).

WRITINGS: *The Heating, Ventilation, and Lighting of School Buildings,* Oxford University Press, 1939; *A Guide to Heating, Ventilation, and Lighting,* Oxford University Press, 1944; *Industrial Training for Manual Operations,* Pitman, 1954, reprinted, 1966; *Industrial Skills,* Pitman, 1966; *Skills Analysis Training,* Pitman, 1968; (with Gavriel Salvendy) *Prediction and Development of Industrial Work Performance,* Wiley, 1973.

WORK IN PROGRESS: Revised edition of *Industrial Skills,* completion expected in 1976.

BIOGRAPHICAL/ CRITICAL SOURCES: *Industrial Training International,* February 20, 1967.

SHAH, Amina 1918-
(M. E. Rutt)

PERSONAL: Born October 31, 1918, in Edinburgh, Scotland; daughter of Ikbal Ali (The Sirdar) and Sairah (Khanum) Shah. *Education:* Educated privately and in a girls' school. *Residence:* London, England.

CAREER: Writer.

WRITINGS: *Tiger of the Frontier,* Sampson Low, 1937; *Caravanserai,* Doorway, 1944; (editor) *Arabian Fairy Tales,* Muller, 1969; (editor) *Folk Tales of Central Asia,* Octagon, 1970; (editor) *Short Story Collection,* Odhams Press, 1973; (editor) *Folk Tales of Persia,* Octagon, in press. Contributor of short stories under pseudonym M. E. Rutt to various publications.

SIDELIGHTS: Amina Shah has resided and traveled in many countries of the Middle East, carrying out broadcasting and social welfare interests there. She told *CA*: "Descended from the Prophet Mohammed through Musa el-Kazim, ancestry documented to seventh century." *Avocational interests:* Cookery, shooting.

* * *

SHAHN, Bernarda Bryson
See BRYSON, Bernarda

* * *

SHAPELL, Nathan 1922-

PERSONAL: Original name, Natan Schapelski; name legally changed; born March 6, 1922, in Sosnowitz, Poland; naturalized U.S. citizen; son of Benjamin and Hela Schapelski; married Lilly Szenes, July 17, 1946; children: Vera (Mrs. Paul Guerin), Benjamin. *Education:* Attended primary school in Poland. *Religion:* Jewish. *Office:* Shapell Industries, 8383 Wilshire Blvd., Beverly Hills, Calif. 90211.

CAREER: Shapell Industries, Inc. (builders and community developers), Beverly Hills, Calif., co-founder, chairman of board of directors, and chief executive officer, 1955—. Member of California Commission on Government Reorganization and Economy; member of Los Angeles County District Attorney's advisory council; member of board of governors of Claremont Men's College; member of advisory board of Beverly Hills Union Bank; member of board of trustees of City of Hope; past member of board of Vista Del Mar Child Care Center, Project Hope, Cedars-Sinai Medical Center, and Jewish Federation Council of Los Angeles. *Member:* Authors Guild of Authors League of America, American Friends of Tel Aviv University (member of Los Angeles board of directors), Hillcrest Country Club, Georgetown Club, Beverly Hills Stock Exchange Club. *Awards, honors:* Awards from National Conference of Christians and Jews and American Academy of Achievement, both 1974.

WRITINGS: *Witness to the Truth,* McKay, 1974.

SIDELIGHTS: Shapell spent the years 1939-1945 in Nazi concentration camps, where at least nineteen members of his family died. At the end of the war, Shapell, then twenty-three, led a small group, including his only surviving sister, out of the Russian-occupied zone of Germany. With the help of an American occupation officer, he organized a community of thousands in the Bavarian village of Munchberg, preparing displaced persons for immigration to permanent homes around the world. In 1951, after the last of the refugees had been resettled, Shapell emigrated to the United States with his wife, also a survivor of the camps.

Witness to the Truth recounts Shapell's experiences during and after the war. Proceeds from the book, as well as any future movie or television sales, are being donated to a foundation to aid the needy children of all nations.

AVOCATIONAL INTERESTS: Horseback riding, public speaking.

* * *

SHAPIRO, Harry L(ionel) 1902-

PERSONAL: Born March 19, 1902, in Boston, Mass.; son of Jacob and Rose (Clemens) Shapiro; married Janice Sandler (an artist), June 26, 1938 (deceased); children: Thomas Clemens, Harriet Rose, James Earnest. *Education:* Harvard University, A.B. (magna cum laude), 1923, A.M., 1925, Ph.D., 1926. *Religion:* Jewish. *Home:* 26 East 91st St., New York, N.Y. 10028. *Office:* American Museum of Natural History, Central Park West at 79th St., New York, N.Y. 10024.

CAREER: American Museum of Natural History, New York, N.Y., assistant curator, 1926-31, associate curator of anthropology, 1931-41, curator of physical anthropology and chairman of department of anthropology, 1942-70, curator and chairman emeritus, 1970—. Research professor at University of Hawaii, 1930-35; professor at Columbia University, 1939-74; visiting professor, University of Pittsburgh, 1970. Has done field work in Central and South Pacific, West Indies, Hawaii, Alaska, Japan, China, India and Europe. Associate of Bernice P. Bishop Museum, Honolulu; member of board, Field Foundation, 1966-71. *Wartime service:* Civilian consultant to quartermaster general's office of American Graves Registration Command, 1945—.

MEMBER: American Anthropological Association (president, 1948), American Ethnological Society (president, 1942-43), American Eugenics Society (president, 1955-62), American Association of Physical Anthropology (secretary, 1935-39; vice-president, 1941-42), National Academy of Sciences (member of council, 1957-60), National Research Council (chairman of anthropology and psychology division, 1953-57), American Academy of Arts and Sciences, Association of American Indian Affairs (member of board of directors, 1947-55), Die Anthropologische Wien (honorary fellow). *Awards, honors:* Theodore Roosevelt Distinguished Service Medal, 1964.

WRITINGS: *Heritage of the Bounty,* Simon & Schuster, 1936, revised edition published as *The Pitcairn Islanders,* 1968; *Migration and Environment,* Oxford University Press for University of Hawaii, 1939; (editor) *Man, Culture, and Society,* Oxford University Press, 1956, revised edition, 1971; *Aspects of Culture,* Rutgers University Press, 1957, reissued, Books for Libraries, 1970; (contributor) *The Race Question in Modern Science: Race and Science,* Columbia University Press for UNESCO, 1961; *Peking Man,* Simon & Schuster, 1974. Contributor of about one hundred fifty articles and over two hundred reviews to scientific journals.

SIDELIGHTS: Shapiro's interests and expertise have led to a variety of experiences, some controversial and some international in implication. For example, it was his responsibility, in 1952, to deny Communist press charges that missing Peking Man bones had been stolen by Americans and placed in the American Museum of Natural History. He has disproved several widely held theories about race and population, perhaps his best-known study being of Pitcairn Island inhabitants, all descendants of six mutinous sailors from HMS *Bounty;* he concluded that, contrary to common expectation, the closely inbred islanders were robust and healthy. Shapiro's resulting book, *Heritage of the Bounty,* was pronounced not only of significant scientific value and scholarly merit, but also fascinating reading, humane and insightful.

Scientists were also impressed with *Migration and Environment.* In this study, he had discovered that immigrants to Hawaii come to differ physically from their relatives still in China and Japan, indicating that racial characteristics may be altered by environment.

In 1946, following a law that all war dead must be brought back to the United States, Shapiro went to Europe, where he set up the present system of anatomical identification for difficult cases where no other means was available. He still assists with particularly difficult cases.

* * *

SHARP, Daniel A(sher) 1932-

PERSONAL: Born March 29, 1932, in San Francisco, Calif.; son of Joseph C. and Miriam (Asher) Sharp; married Jacqueline Borda, February 24, 1967; children: Benjamin Daniel. *Education:* University of California, Berkeley, B.A. (with honors), 1954; Harvard University, J.D., 1959. *Politics:* Democrat. *Religion:* Jewish. *Home:* 50 Glenbrook Rd., Stamford, Conn. 06902. *Office address:* Xerox Latinamerican Group, P.O. Box 890, Stamford, Conn. 06904.

CAREER: U.S. Department of Justice, San Francisco, Calif., deputy attorney general, 1959-61; U.S. Peace Corps, director of staff training in Washington, D.C., Peru, and Bolivia, 1961-68; University of Chicago, Chicago, Ill., director of education and Latin American programs at Adlai Stevenson Institute, 1968-70; International Telephone & Telegraph Co., New York, N.Y., director of training and manager of management development, 1970-73; Xerox Latinamerican Group, Stamford, Conn., manager of human resources development, 1973—. Trustee of Latin American Scholarship Program of American Universities and Chicago Council on Foreign Relations. *Military service:* U.S. Army, Judge Advocate Generals Corps, 1954-55; served in Korea.

MEMBER: American Society for Training and Development, Society for International Development, World Affairs Council, Bar Association of California, Harvard Club (New York). *Awards, honors:* Gold Medal and Diploma of Honor from Peruvian Government.

WRITINGS: (Editor) *U.S. Foreign Policy and Peru,* University of Texas Press, 1972.

* * *

SHARPE, Lawrence A(lbright) 1920-

PERSONAL: Born July 22, 1920, in Burlington, N.C.; son of Luther Armenius (a building contractor) and Myrtie (Lawrence) Sharpe; married Virginia Pacofsky, October 10, 1944; children: Virginia Ann (Mrs. Robert W. Wright), Lawrence A., Jr., Alice Cecilia, James Philip, Donald Charles, Judith Patricia. *Education:* Attended Elon College, 1936-38; University of North Carolina, A.B., 1940, Ph.D., 1956; University of Havana, graduate study, 1940-41. *Religion:* Roman Catholic. *Home:* 101 Virginia Dr., Chapel Hill, N.C. 27514. *Office:* 334 Dey Hall, University of North Carolina, Chapel Hill, N.C. 27514.

CAREER: Federal Bureau of Investigation, Washington, D.C., interpreter-translator, 1942-44; Instituto Brasil-Estados Unidos no Ceara, Fortaleza, Brazil, director, 1951-53; University of North Carolina, Chapel Hill, lecturer, 1953-56, assistant professor, 1956-60, associate professor of Portuguese and Spanish, 1960—. *Military service:* U.S. Army, 1944-46; became technical sergeant. *Member:* Modern Language Association of America, American Association of Teachers of Spanish and Portuguese, Instituto de Literatura Iberoamericana, Sociedade de Lingua Portuguesa, South Atlantic Modern Language Association, Southeastern Conference on Latin American Studies. *Awards, honors:* Grant from Fundacao Calouste Gulbenkian (Lisbon), summer, 1968.

WRITINGS: (Editor) *The Old Portuguese: Vida de Sam Bernardo,* University of North Carolina Press, 1971. Coeditor, *Bibliography of Contemporary Spanish Literature,* Spanish Section V, Modern Language Association of America, 1956-58. Contributor to articles on such auxiliary languages as Esperanto, Interlingue, and Ido, and on other topics to professional journals.

WORK IN PROGRESS: Studies on the twentieth-century novel and on the life and works of Camilo Castelo Branco.

* * *

SHAW, Bob 1931-

PERSONAL: Born December 31, 1931, in Belfast, Northern Ireland; son of Robert William (a policeman) and Elizabeth (Megaw) Shaw; married Sarah Gourley, July 3, 1954; children: Alisa Claire, Robert Ian, Elizabeth Denise. *Education:* Attended a technical high school in Belfast. *Politics:* None. *Religion:* None. *Home:* 31 Birchwood Dr., Ulverton, Cumbria, England. *Agent:* Scott Meredith Literary Agency, 580 Fifth Ave., New York, N.Y. 10036.

CAREER: Short Brothers & Harland Ltd. (aircraft manufacturers), Belfast, Northern Ireland, public relations officer, 1960-66; Belfast Telegraph Newspapers Ltd., Belfast, Northern Ireland, journalist, 1966-69; free-lance writer in Belfast, Northern Ireland, 1969-70; Short Brothers & Harland Ltd., public relations officer, 1970-73; Vickers Shipbuilding Group, Barrow-in-Furness, England, public relations officer, 1973—.

WRITINGS—All novels, except as indicated: *Night Walk,* Avon, 1967; *The Two-Timers,* Ace Books, 1968; *The Palace of Eternity,* Ace Books, 1969; *The Shadow of Heaven,* Avon, 1969; *One Million Tomorrows,* Ace Books, 1971; *The Ground Zero Man,* Avon, 1971; *Other Days, Other Eyes,* Ace Books, 1972; *Tomorrow Lies in Ambush* (short stories), Ace Books, 1973. Contributor of about forty short stories to American and British science fiction magazines.

WORK IN PROGRESS: Several novels, as yet untitled.

* * *

SHAW, David 1943-

PERSONAL: Born January 4, 1943, in Dayton, Ohio; son of Harry (a photoengraver) and Lillian (Walton) Shaw. *Education:* University of California at Los Angeles, B.A., 1965. *Religion:* Jewish. *Home:* 330 South Berendo St., Apt. 305, Los Angeles, Calif. 90020. *Agent:* Mitchell Hamilburg, 1105 Glendon Ave., Los Angeles, Calif. 90024. *Office:* Los Angeles Times, 202 West First St., Los Angeles, Calif. 90053.

CAREER: Huntington Park Daily Signal, Huntington Park, Calif., reporter, 1963-66; *Long Beach Independent,* Long Beach, Calif., feature writer, 1966-68; *Los Angeles Times,* Los Angeles, Calif., feature writer, 1968—. *Awards, honors:* More than twenty-five major journalism awards including awards from American Political Science Association, 1969, Education Writers Association, 1969, Los Angeles Press Club, 1969, 1971-74, and American Bar Association, 1973.

WRITINGS: (With Wilt Chamberlain) *Wilt: Just Like Any Other 7-Foot Black Millionaire Who Lives Next Door,* Macmillan, 1973; *The Levy Caper,* Macmillan, 1974. Contributor to *Oui, Penthouse, Esquire, Smithsonian,* and *Today's Health.*

* * *

SHAYON, Robert Lewis

PERSONAL: Born in New York, N.Y.; married Sheila Russell; children: Diana Russell, Sheila Russell. *Education:* Educated in public schools of New York City. *Home:* 135 South 18th St., Philadelphia, Pa. 19103. *Office:* 3620 Walnut St., Philadelphia, Pa. 19174.

CAREER: Free-lance writer, producer, and director for radio, television, and films; Mutual Broadcasting System, New York, N.Y., producer and director, 1938-42; Columbia Broadcasting System (CBS), New York, N.Y., executive producer, 1942-49; National Broadcasting System (NBC), New York, N.Y., producer of television series, "The Big Story," 1955-57; Westinghouse Broadcasting Company, New York, N.Y., producer of television series, "You've Got a Right," 1965-67; University of Pennsylvania, Philadelphia, professor of communications at Annenberg School of Communications, 1965—. Producer and narrator of American Heritage Sound Archives of World War II; member of board of directors, National Citizens Committee for Better Broadcasting and WHYY-TV (Philadelphia); member of founding board of directors, International University of Communications; member of national advisory board, National Commission for the Assessment of Technology; consultant to White House Conference on Children and Youth, 1970, and U.S. Department of Health, Education, and Welfare, 1972—.

MEMBER: International Communications Association, National Association for Better Broadcasting (member of board of directors), American Institute of Public Opinion. *Awards, honors:* Ohio State University award, 1943, for "American School of the Air"; Peabody Award, 1947, for "You Are There" and "The Eagle's Brood" television series; New York Radio Critics Circle award, 1948, for "The Eagle's Brood"; Sylvania television award for creative programming, 1956, for "The Whole Town's Talking"; School Bell Award from National Education Association, 1960; Directors Guild of America outstanding critic of the year award, 1963; M.A., University of Pennsylvania, 1971.

WRITINGS: Television and Our Children, McKay, 1951; *Television: The Dream and the Reality,* Marquette University Press, 1957; (author of introduction) *The Eighth Art,* Holt, 1962; *Open to Criticism,* Beacon Press, 1969; *The Crowd-Catchers: Introducing Television,* Dutton, 1973.

Also author of television series, including "Operation Crossroads," "The Eagle's Brood," "You Are There," "You've Got a Right." Author of radio series, "Everybody's Mountain," 1959, and American Heritage record albums, including "Historic Words and Music of World

War One," "Historic Music of the Great West," "Historic Voices and Music of World War Two," and "The Invention of the Presidency."

Author of documentary film on Soviet schools for American Broadcasting Corp. Television. Contributor to *Childcraft Encyclopedia* and to magazines, including *New Republic, Image,* and *Show.* Radio and television critic, *Christian Science Monitor,* 1950-51; radio and television critic and contributing editor, *Saturday Review,* 1950-70.

WORK IN PROGRESS: A Curriculum Guide for Instructors Training; a training program of communications recruitment for young black people and Hispanic-Americans in broadcasting management careers.

* * *

SHEEHAN, Valerie Harms
See HARMS, Valerie

* * *

SHEEHY, Gail

PERSONAL: Daughter of Harold Merritt and Lillian (Rainey) Henion; married Albert Sheehy (an internist), August 20, 1960 (divorced, 1968); children: Maura. *Education:* University of Vermont, B.S., 1958; Columbia University, graduate study, 1970. *Residence:* New York, N.Y. *Agent:* Creative Management Associates, 600 Madison Ave., New York, N.Y. 10022. *Office: New York Magazine,* 207 East 32nd St., New York, N.Y. 10016.

CAREER: Traveling home economist; *Democrat and Chronicle,* Rochester, N.Y., fashion editor, 1961-63; *New York Herald Tribune,* New York, N.Y., feature writer, 1963-66; *New York Magazine,* New York, N.Y., contributing editor, 1968—; free-lance writer. *Member:* Author's Guild, Common Cause, National Organization for Women, Newswomen's Club of New York, Executive Woman (member of advisory board, 1973-74). *Awards, honors:* Front Page award from Newswomen's Club of New York, 1964, for most distinguished feature of interest to women, and 1973, for best magazine feature; National Magazine award, 1972, for reporting excellence; Alicia Patterson Foundation fellowship, 1974.

WRITINGS: Lovesounds, Random House, 1970; *Panthermania: The Clash of Black against Black in One American City,* Harper, 1971; *Speed Is of the Essence,* Pocket Books, 1971; *Hustling: Prostitution in Our Wide Open Society,* Delacorte, 1973. Contributor to *Cosmopolitan, McCall's, Glamour, Good Housekeeping, London Sunday Telegraph, Paris Match,* and *New York Times Magazine.*

WORK IN PROGRESS: A book concerning the ages and stages of adult life, for Dutton.

* * *

SHELDRICK, Daphne 1934-

PERSONAL: Born June 4, 1934, in Nakuru, Kenya; daughter of Brian (a farmer) and Marjorie (Webb) Jenkins; married Frank William Woodley, June 26, 1953 (divorced, 1959); married David Leslie William Sheldrick (a park warden), October 25, 1960; children: (first marriage) Gillian Sala Ellen; (second marriage) Angela Mara. *Education:* Attended schools in Kenya. *Politics:* Conservative. *Religion:* Protestant. *Home and office:* Tsavo East National Park, Box 14, Voi, Kenya.

CAREER: Naturalist (raises orphaned wild animals and rehabilitates them to live in their wild state). *Awards, honors:* Grand Prix Verite from *Le Parisien,* 1967, for *The Orphans of Tsavo.*

WRITINGS: The Orphans of Tsavo, Collins, 1966; *The Tsavo Story,* Collins, 1973. Contributor to *Collier's Yearbook* and to magazines, including *Saturday Review* and *Africana.*

WORK IN PROGRESS: The Tsavo Sequel, completion expected in 1976; *More Orphans of Tsavo,* for children.

SIDELIGHTS: "Living in the vast Tsavo Park as wife of the warden," Daphne Sheldrick wrote, "it has been my lot to nurture and care for very varied species of wild animal ophans, ranging from elephant and rhino calves to the minute dikdik. These orphans are never penned, but are free to roam where they wish and finally the objective is to rehabilitate them to their wild environment.

"Some when fully grown sever their tics with their foster parents completely, while others opt to remain in the vicinity of the Park Headquarters and enjoy the best of both worlds. By so doing they can be studied closely, and contribute toward a better understanding of their wild counterparts. Many former orphans have bred and raised families near the headquarters. . . ."

* * *

SHEPARD, Jean H(eck) 1930-

PERSONAL: Born February 2, 1930, in New York, N.Y.; daughter of Chester Reed (a publisher) and Anna S. (Charig) Heck; married Lawrence V. Hastings (a lawyer and doctor), March 29, 1950 (divorced 1953); married Daniel A. Shepard (a business executive and writer), July 26, 1954; children: (first marriage) Lance Hastings; (second marriage) Bradley Reed. *Education:* Barnard College, A.B., 1950. *Politics:* Independent. *Religion:* Methodist. *Home address:* Middle Rd., Sudbury, Mass. 01776.

CAREER: Viking Press, New York, N.Y., member of school and library services staff, 1956-57; E. P. Dutton & Co., New York, N.Y., assistant director of library promotion, 1957-58; Thomas Y. Crowell Co., New York, N.Y., director of publicity, advertising, and promotion, 1958-62; Charles Scribner's Sons, New York, N.Y., director of advertising, 1962-67; writer, 1967—. Consultant to Stephen Greene Press, 1970-72. *Member:* Authors' Guild, Authors' League of America, American Library Association, Publishers Advertising Club, Women's National Book Association.

WRITINGS: Simple Family Favorites (Doubleday Book Club selection), Stein & Day, 1971; *Herb and Spice Cooking,* Greene, 1971; *Cook with Wine!* Greene, 1972; (with husband, Daniel A. Shepard) *Earth Watch: Notes on a Restless Planet,* Doubleday, 1973; *The Harvest Home Steak Cookbook,* Greene, 1973; *The Vegetable Kingdom,* Little, Brown, in press. Contributor to magazines.

WORK IN PROGRESS: A book about women in today's economic society, for Little, Brown.

* * *

SHERRY, Norman 1925-

PERSONAL: Born in 1925, in Newcastle-upon-Tyne, England; married Sylvia Brunt (a novelist). *Education:* University of Durham, B.A. (with honors), 1955, Ph.D., 1965. *Home:* 6 Gillison Close, Melling, near Carnforth, Lancashire, England. *Office:* Department of English, University of Lancaster, Lancaster, Lancashire, England.

CAREER: University of Singapore, Singapore, lecturer in English, 1960-66; University of Liverpool, Liverpool, England, lecturer, 1966-68, senior lecturer in English, 1968-70; University of Lancaster, Lancaster, England, professor of English, 1970—. Chairman of organizing committee, Conrad Conference, 1974. *Military service:* Served in British Army, in Burma. *Member:* Society of Authors, Joseph Conrad Society (president).

WRITINGS: Conrad's Eastern World, Cambridge University Press, 1966; *Jane Austen,* Evans Brothers, 1966, Arco, 1969; *Charlotte and Emily Bronte,* Evans Brothers, 1969, Arco, 1970; *Conrad's Western World* (sequel to *Conrad's Eastern World*), Cambridge University Press, 1971; *Conrad and His World* (biography), Thames & Hudson, 1973; *Thomas Hardy: A Reassessment,* Bell, in press; *Edwardian Literature and Its Background,* Thames & Hudson, in press.

Editor: (With Thomas Moser) *Lord Jim,* Norton, 1967; (and author of introduction) *Conrad: The Critical Heritage,* Routledge & Kegan Paul, 1973; *Critical Essays on Joseph Conrad,* Routledge & Kegan Paul, in press.

Author of introduction and notes; all by Joseph Conrad, except as indicated; all published by Dent: *Nostromo,* Everyman Edition, 1972, Collected Conrad Edition, 1974; *"An Outpost of Progress" and "Heart of Darkness": Two African Stories,* 1973; *The Nigger of the "Narcissus," Typhoon, Falk, and Other Stories,* 1974; *Lord Jim,* 1974; *Youth,* 1974; *The Secret Agent,* 1974; *Under Western Eyes,* 1974; Robert Browning, *Men and Women,* 1974.

Contributor of articles and reviews to periodicals and journals, including *Guardian, Language Review, Times Literary Supplement, Notes & Queries, Daily Telegraph,* and *Philological Quarterly*. Editor, *Conradiana;* special editor of Conrad issue, *English* magazine, 1974.

WORK IN PROGRESS: A biography of Conrad for BBC's Omnibus program.

SIDELIGHTS: Having taken full advantage of his strategic location in Singapore while teaching there, Sherry researched *Conrad's Eastern World* in numerous sources, including old newspapers and shipping documents, to produce, in one critic's words, "remarkable contributions to an understanding of five of the Eastern novels [using] careful analytic focus and professional scholarship." Sherry's prodigious efforts have, at the same time, turned up much new information and put an end to speculation on numerous points. With the publication of *Conrad's Western World,* writes T. W. Schultheiss, "once again, Sherry has provided a number of striking examples of literary detective work [in a] unique and stimulating scholarly contribution." "Professor Sherry has greatly enlarged our knowledge," adds a *Times Literary Supplement* reviewer. "His industry compels admiration; a footnote tells us that in his search for source material for *Nostromo* he read 'about 200 books.'" J. I. M. Stewart estimates that *Conrad's Eastern World* and *Conrad's Western World* "are perhaps the most exciting books of the source-hunting kind (commonly so dreary) to have appeared since John Livingston Lowes published *The Road to Xanadu* in 1937."

* * *

SHERRY, (Dulcie) Sylvia

PERSONAL: Born in Newcastle-upon-Tyne, England; married Norman Sherry (a professor and author). *Education:* University of Durham, B.A. *Home:* 6 Gillison Close, Melling, near Carnforth, Lancashire, England.

CAREER: College of Education, Newcastle-upon-Tyne, England, teacher and lecturer, 1955-60; editor in Singapore, 1960-64; full-time writer, 1964—. *Awards, honors: The Liverpool Cats* was listed as an "honor book" by the Chicago Tribune's Book World Festival, 1969; *A Snake in the Old Hut* was a selection of the Foyles Children's Book Club, 1974.

WRITINGS—Juvenile fiction: *Street of the Small Night Market,* Cape, 1966, published as *Secret of the Jade Pavilion,* Lippincott, 1967; *Frog in a Coconut Shell,* Lippincott, 1968; *The Liverpool Cats,* Lippincott, 1969 (published in England as *A Pair of Jesus Boots,* Cape, 1969); *The Haven-Screamers,* Lippincott, 1970 (published in England as *The Loss of the Night Wind,* Cape, 1970); *A Snake in the Old Hut,* Cape, 1972, Nelson, 1974; *Dark River, Dark Mountain,* Cape, 1974.

Contributor: *Miscellany Five,* Oxford University Press, 1968; *In Love, Out of Love,* Macmillan, 1974.

WORK IN PROGRESS: A book for children, aged seven to nine, for "Grasshopper" series; a book for Macmillan; an adult novel set in the Far East.

SIDELIGHTS: Mrs. Sherry told *CA* that she began writing at age nine, writing her first novel *(Secret of the Jade Pavillion)* some time later as a result of being inspired by the atmosphere of the Far East—particularly that of Singapore where she lived for six years. She feels that setting continues to be important to her novels, and when necessary, she travels to other countries to research her books. This interest in setting is reflected in a *Young Readers' Review* writer's comment that "Besides a good plot, interesting people, and lots of excitement the author gives us a bonus. The setting is as well-realized as the people. She makes [Singapore] as understandable and familiar as our own neighborhoods."

BIOGRAPHICAL/CRITICAL SOURCES: Sheila G. Ray, *Children's Fiction,* Brockhampton, 1972.

* * *

SHOCKLEY, Ann Allen 1927-

PERSONAL: Born June 21, 1927, in Louisville, Ky.; daughter of Henry (a social worker) and Bessie (a social worker; maiden name, Lucas) Allen; divorced; children: William Leslie Shockley, Jr., Tamara Ann Shockley. *Education:* Fisk University, B.A., 1948; Western Reserve University (now Case Western Reserve University), M.S.L.S., 1959. *Politics:* Independent. *Home:* 1809 Morena St., Apt. G-4, Nashville, Tenn. 37208. *Office:* Fisk University Library, Nashville, Tenn. 37203.

CAREER: Delaware State College, Dover, Del., assistant librarian, 1959-60; University of Maryland, Princess Anne, assistant librarian, 1960-66, associate librarian, 1966-69; Fisk University, Nashville, Tenn., associate librarian and head of special collections, 1969—, associate professor of library science; free-lance writer. *Member:* Association for Study of Afro-American Life and History, American Library Association, Oral History Association, American Association of University Professors, Society of American Archivists, National Organization of Women, Tennessee Library Association. *Awards, honors:* American Association of University Women short story award, 1962.

WRITINGS: (Editor with Sue P. Chandler) *Living Black American Authors: A Biographical Directory,* Bowker, 1973; *Loving Her* (novel), Bobbs-Merrill, 1974. Contributor of short stories and articles to magazines, newspapers, and professional journals.

WORK IN PROGRESS: A collection of short stories; a book on Black oral history, consisting of interviews with prominent Black Americans.

* * *

SHOESMITH, Kathleen A(nne) 1938-

PERSONAL: Born July 17, 1938, in Keighley, Yorkshire, England; daughter of Roy and Lilian Shoesmith. *Education:* Avery Hill Teachers' Training College, Diploma, 1956. *Home:* 351 Fell Lane, Keighley BD22 6DB, Yorkshire, England.

CAREER: Teacher in Keighley, Yorkshire, England, 1958—, at Lees County Primary School, 1973—.

WRITINGS—Historical romances: *Jack O'Lantern,* R. Hale, 1969, Ace Books, 1973; *Cloud Over Calderwood,* R. Hale, 1969, Ace Books, 1973; *The Tides of Tremannion,* R. Hale, 1970, Ace Books, 1973; *Mallory's Luck,* R. Hale, 1971, Ace Books, 1974; *Return of the Royalist,* R. Hale, 1971; *The Reluctant Puritan,* R. Hale, 1972, Ace Books, 1973; *The Highwayman's Daughter,* R. Hale, 1972; *Belltower,* R. Hale, 1973, Ace Books, 1974.

Juvenile series: "Playtime Stories," six books, E. J. Arnold, 1966; "Judy Stories," four books, Charles & Son, 1968; "Easy to Read," six books, Charles & Son, 1968; "How Do They Grow?," four books, Charles & Son, 1969; "Do You Know About?," twelve books, Burke Publishing, 1970-74; "Use Your Senses," five books, Burke Publishing, 1973.

WORK IN PROGRESS: The Black Domino, a historical romance set in Sussex England in 1812; four new books for "Do You Know About?" series.

SIDELIGHTS: Most of Kathleen Shoesmith's historical romances have been published in paperback in France, Italy, and the Netherlands, as well as in America. *Avocational interests:* Sewing, reading, and touring by car in the Yorkshire countryside.

* * *

SHOUKSMITH, George A. 1931-

PERSONAL: Surname is pronounced *Shook*-smith; born November 2, 1931, in York, England; son of Albert (a business manager) and Elsie (Wheeler) Shouksmith; married Audrey Elizabeth Budge, July 16, 1954; children: Andrew, Patricia. *Education:* University of Edinburgh, M.A. (summa cum laude), 1954; Queen's University, Belfast, Ph.D., 1967. *Religion:* Church of England. *Home:* 76 Clifton Ter., Palmerston North, New Zealand. *Office:* Department of Psychology and Sociology, Massey University, Palmerston North, New Zealand.

CAREER: British European Airways, London, England, psychologist, 1954-56; University of Edinburgh, Edinburgh, Scotland, assistant lecturer in applied psychology, 1956-57; University of Canterbury, Christ Church, New Zealand, lecturer in psychology, 1957-64; Queen's University of Belfast, Belfast, Northern Ireland, senior lecturer in psychology, 1964-70; Massey University, Palmerston North, New Zealand, professor of psychology and head of department of psychology and sociology, 1970—. Visiting professor at University of New Brunswick, 1968, and Mount Allison University, 1970. Member of executive board of National Association of Youth Clubs (London), 1967-70; chairman of social environment subcommittee of Palmerston North (New Zealand) City Council, 1972—. *Member:* International Association of Applied Psychology, British Psychological Society.

WRITINGS: A First Year Manual of Experimental Psychology, Queen's University Press, 1967; *Assessment through Interviewing: A Handbook for Individual Interviewing and Group Selection Techniques,* Pergamon, 1968; *Intelligence, Creativity, and Cognitive Style,* Interscience, 1970. Also author of a vocational guidance handbook. Contributor of forty articles to learned journals.

WORK IN PROGRESS: Research in driving behavior and human factors in driving safety.

* * *

SHOUP, Carl S(umner) 1902-

PERSONAL: Born October 26, 1902, in San Jose, Calif.; son of Paul and Rose (Wilson) Shoup; married Ruth Snedden, September 27, 1924; children: Dale (Mrs. John Mayer), Paul Snedden, Donald Sumner. *Education:* Stanford University, A.B., 1924; Columbia University, Ph.D., 1930. *Residence:* Sandwich, N.H. *Office:* Dalhousie University, Halifax, Nova Scotia, Canada.

CAREER: Columbia University, New York, N.Y., instructor, 1928-31, assistant professor, 1931-38, associate professor, 1938-45, professor of economics, 1945-71, director of International Economic Integration Program and Capital Tax Projects, 1962-64; United Nations, New York, N.Y., inter-regional adviser on tax reform planning, 1971-74; Dalhousie University, Halifax, Nova Scotia, visiting research professor of economics, 1974-75. Staff member of New York State Special Tax Commissions, 1930-35; conducted tax study for U.S. Department of the Treasury, 1934, 1937; director of Twentieth Century Fund survey of taxation in the United States, 1935-37; assistant to U.S. Secretary of the Treasury, 1937-38, research consultant, 1938-46, 1962-71; member of staff of Council of Economic Advisers, 1946-49; director of Shoup Tax Mission to Japan, 1949-50; co-director of New York City finance study, 1950-52; director of fiscal survey of Venezuela, 1958; director of tax mission to Liberia, 1969.

MEMBER: International Institute of Public Finance (president, 1950-53), National Tax Association (president, 1948-49), American Economic Association (fellow). *Awards, honors:* Honorary degree from University of Strasbourg, 1967; named to Order of the Sacred Treasure, second class, by Emperor of Japan, 1968.

WRITINGS: The Sales Tax in France, Columbia University Press, 1930; (with E. R. A. Seligman) *A Report on the Revenue System of Cuba,* Government of Cuba, 1932; (with Robert M. Haig) *The Sales Tax in the American States,* Columbia University Press, 1934; (with Roy Blough and Mabel Newcomer) *Facing the Tax Problem,* Twentieth Century Fund, 1937; (with Roswell Magill) *The Fiscal System of Cuba,* Government of Cuba, 1939; *Federal Finances in the Coming Decade,* Columbia University Press, 1941; (with Milton Friedman and Ruth Mack) *Taxing to Prevent Inflation,* Columbia University Press, 1943; *Principles of National Income Analysis,* Houghton, 1947; (with others) *Report of the Shoup Tax Mission to Japan,* Supreme Commander of the Allied Powers in Tokyo, 1949.

(With others) *The Fiscal System of Venezuela,* Johns Hopkins Press, 1959; *Ricardo on Taxation,* Columbia University Press, 1960; (with C. Lowell Harriss and William Vickrey) *The Fiscal System of the Federal District of Venezuela,* Johns Hopkins Press, 1961; *The Tax System of*

Brazil, Vargas Institute, 1964; *Federal Estate and Gift Taxes,* Brookings Institution, 1966; (editor) *Fiscal Harmonization in Common Markets,* Columbia University Press, 1966; *Public Finance,* Aldine, 1969.

(With others) *The Tax System of Liberia,* Columbia University Press, 1970; (with Carolyn S. Scott) *Test Your Bible Knowledge,* Revell, 1971. Contributor to economics and finance journals, including *American Economic Review, Economic Journal, National Tax Journal,* and *Public Finance.* Editor of *Bulletin of the National Tax Association,* 1931-35.

WORK IN PROGRESS: Research on international tax problems and on tax problems in developing countries.

SIDELIGHTS: Shoup's books have been published in Japanese, German, and Chinese.

BIOGRAPHICAL/CRITICAL SOURCES: R. M. Bird and J. G. Head, editors, *Modern Fiscal Issues: Essays in Honor of Carl S. Shoup,* University of Toronto Press, 1972.

* * *

SHRADY, Maria 1924-

PERSONAL: Born March 9, 1924, in Austria; daughter of Theodor and Louise (von Peter) Likar-Waltersdorff; married Frederick Charles Shrady (a sculptor), July 9, 1946; children: Alexander, Maria Theresia, Marie-Antoinette, Marie-Louise, Maria Christina, Nicholas. *Education:* Educated at public and private schools in Vienna. *Politics:* Independent. *Religion:* Roman Catholic. *Home:* Easterfields, Monroe, Conn. 06468.

AWARDS, HONORS: Christopher Book Award, 1961, for *In the Spirit of Wonder.*

WRITINGS: Come, Southwind, Pantheon, 1957; *In the Spirit of Wonder,* Pantheon, 1961; (editor and author of commentaries) *Moments of Insight* (anthology), Harper, 1972. Contributor to *Thought.*

WORK IN PROGRESS: The History of the Holy Year, completion expected in 1975.

* * *

SHREVE, Susan Richards 1939-

PERSONAL: Born May 2, 1939, in Toledo, Ohio; daughter of Robert Kenneth (a broadcaster-writer) and Helen Elizabeth (Greene) Richards; married Porter Gaylord Shreve (a school head), May 26, 1962; children: Porter Gaylord, Elizabeth Steward, Caleb Richards, Katharine Taylor. *Education:* University of Pennsylvania, B.A. (magna cum laude), 1961; University of Virginia, M.A., 1969. *Home:* 515 Auburn Ave., Philadelphia, Pa. 19118. *Agent:* Timothy Seldes, Russell & Volkening, Inc., 551 Fifth Ave., New York, N.Y. 10017. *Office:* Community Learning Center, 1 West Springfield, Philadelphia, Pa. 19118.

CAREER: Teacher of English in private schools in Cheshire, England, 1962-63, Rosemont, Pa., 1963-66, Washington, D.C., 1967-68, and Philadelphia, Pa., 1970-72; Community Learning Center (alternative school), Philadelphia, Pa., co-founder, 1972—. *Member:* Phi Beta Kappa.

WRITINGS: A Fortunate Madness (novel), Houghton, 1974.

WORK IN PROGRESS: A second novel, *Kate and Tommy Sittin' in a Tree.*

SHULMAN, Albert M(aimon) 1902-

PERSONAL: Born March 21, 1902, in Russia; came to the United States in 1904; son of Morris and Rachel (Nemirov) Shulman; married Rose Rosenberg, June 15, 1924; children: Jeremy, Naomi (Mrs. Allan Eckhaus). *Education:* University of Southern California, A.B., 1926, M.A. and certificate in social work, 1927; Hebrew Union College, Rabbi and M.H.L., 1932. *Politics:* Liberal Democrat. *Home and office:* 305 West Madison St., South Bend, Ind. 46601.

CAREER: Ordained rabbi in 1932; Temple Beth-El, South Bend, Ind., rabbi, 1934-67, rabbi emeritus, 1967—. Former president of B'nai B'rith and of National Association for the Prevention of Blindness; member of Governor's Advisory Committee on Mental Health, beginning 1960; national chaplain of the American Legion, 1962-63; member of board of governors, Jewish Institute of Religion of Hebrew Union College, beginning 1963; former chairman and board member of South Bend Housing Authority. *Military service:* U.S. Naval Reserve, chaplain, 1943-46; became lieutenant commander. *Member:* Alpha Kappa Delta, Masons, Elks, Urban Coalition, South Bend Round Table. *Awards, honors:* Indiana State Citation for meritorious service, 1956; Brotherhood Award, Annual Conference of Christians and Jews, 1957; D.D., Hebrew Union College, Jewish Institute of Religion, 1961; Chapel of Four Chaplains Award, 1963.

WRITINGS: Gateway to Judaism: An Encyclopedic Guide to the Doctrines, Ceremonies, Customs, Languages, and Community Life of the Jews, two volumes, Yoseloff, 1971; *Manual on Judaism,* Ktav, 1974. Also author of pamphlet, *The Welfare of Man,* 1939.

SIDELIGHTS: Since his retirement, Shulman has been offering his services to small congregations in remote communities that cannot afford full-time rabbinical leadership.

* * *

SHULTZ, Gladys Denny 1895- (Anne Gardner)

PERSONAL: Born August 13, 1895, in Des Moines, Iowa; daughter of Charles Oscar (a professor) and Lily (Wisner) Denny; married Victor Harold Shultz, May 2, 1918 (died, 1931); children: Eleanor Margaret (Mrs. William Dale), Peter Denny. *Education:* Drake University, B.A., 1918; graduate study at University of Iowa and City College (now City College of the City University of New York). *Politics:* Democrat. *Religion:* Christian Church. *Home:* 6054 Kantor St., San Diego, Calif. 92122. *Agent:* James Oliver Brown, 22 East 60th St., New York, N.Y. 10022.

CAREER: Des Moines Register, Des Moines, Iowa, state and later Sunday editor, 1918-23; *Better Homes and Gardens,* Des Moines, Iowa, writer in department of child care, 1927-45; *Ladies Home Journal,* Philadelphia, Pa., writer and corresponding editor, 1946-61; free-lance writer, 1961—. *Member:* Authors' Guild. *Awards, honors:* Ben Franklin Award for best scientific article printed in a magazine, 1957, for "The Insulted Child."

WRITINGS: (With Beulah Schenk) *The House That Runs Itself,* John Day, 1929; *Baby Book: A Handbook for Mothers,* Volume I, Better Homes and Gardens, 1943; (with Lee Forrest Hill) *Your Baby: The Complete Baby Book for Mothers and Fathers,* Doubleday, 1948; *Letters to Jane,* Lippincott, 1948, revised edition, 1960; *Widows, Wise and Otherwise: A Practical Guide for the Woman Who Has Lost Her Husband,* Lippincott, 1949; *It's Time You Knew,*

Lippincott, 1955; (with Daisy Gordon Lawrence) *Lady from Savannah: The Life of Juliette Low,* Lippincott, 1958; *Jenny Lind: The Swedish Nightingale,* Lippincott, 1962; *How Many More Victims? Society and the Sex Criminal,* Lippincott, 1965; *The Successful Teen-Age Girl,* Lippincott, 1968; *Letters to a New Generation: For Today's Inquiring Teen-Age Girl,* Lippincott, 1971.

Under pseudonym Anne Gardner: *Reputation: A Story of April Low, Known as "the Wickedest Woman in Hollywood",* A. L. Burt & Co., 1929; *The Love Coward,* E. J. Clode, 1930; *Working Wives,* Grosset, 1931; *Masquerade,* Grosset, 1931; *The Husband Campaign,* Grosset, 1932; *All That Glitters,* J. H. Hopkins & Sons, 1935; *Along Came Romance,* J. H. Hopkins & Sons, 1936.

Contributor to *Reader's Digest* and others.

WORK IN PROGRESS: A book dealing with the American Revolution.

SIDELIGHTS: Mrs. Shultz told *CA:* "I am glad to have a chance to express myself here, having been a liberated woman ever since I went to work on the *Des Moines Register* the day after I graduated from college in June, 1918. I grew up in the period of the Votes for Women agitation and was an ardent feminist, determined to make use of the career opportunities opened to my sex. I had worked on the college paper from my freshman year onward and was elected editor my senior year, the first girl editor of the Drake *Delphic* since Susan Glaspell had held the post in 1898, over three male contenders whose chief argument against me, since I had had more experience than they had, was that I was a girl, would get married, and all that valuable experience would be wasted.... I am just a professional writer, having been compelled to make money from the time I have spent at the typewriter, but there is a pleasure in using professional skills beyond the financial reward. At the age of 78, I don't have to make money any more but I become restive after a while away from the typewriter and would not trade lives with the richest woman in America, if her wealth has prevented her from mastering a skill which gives her pleasure."

* * *

SIDNEY, Jonathan
See COOPER, Emmanuel

* * *

SIEGLER, Frederick Adrian 1932-

PERSONAL: Born March 14, 1932, in Cleveland, Ohio. *Education:* Oxford University, B.A., 1955, M.A., 1964; University of Paris, graduate study, 1955-56; Stanford University, Ph.D., 1960. *Politics:* None. *Home:* 1542 Grand Ave., Seattle, Wash. *Office:* Department of Philosophy, University of Washington, Seattle, Wash.

CAREER: University of Chicago, Chicago, Ill., instructor, 1959-61, assistant professor, 1961-65, associate professor of philosophy, 1966-67; University of Washington, Seattle, associate professor of philosophy, 1967—. Guest professor, University of Michigan, 1964, Oxford University, 1964, 1968, University of Oregon, 1967, University of Calgary, 1968, University of Minnesota, 1970. *Awards, honors:* Quantrell Prize from University of Chicago, 1962, for excellence in teaching; Harvard Law School fellowship, 1968-69.

WRITINGS: Hustling: A Study of Illegal Incomes in Three Major Cities, U.S. Dept. of Labor, 1972. Contributor of numerous articles to journals.

AVOCATIONAL INTERESTS: Playing the flute.

* * *

SIKULA, Andrew F(rank) 1944-

PERSONAL: Born October 7, 1944, in Akron, Ohio; son of John and Anna Marie (Shimko) Sikula; married Celeste Marie Casey (a social worker), June 12, 1971. *Education:* Hiram College, B.A., 1966; Michigan State University, M.B.A., 1967, Ph.D., 1970. *Home:* 1S200 Forest Trail Dr., Timber Trails, Oak Brook, Ill. 60521. *Office:* Department of Management, College of Business, University of Illinois, Box 4348, Chicago, Ill. 60680.

CAREER: Michigan State University, East Lansing, assistant professor of personnel management, 1966-70; University of Illinois at Chicago Circle, College of Business, assistant professor, 1970-73, associate professor of management, 1973—. Instructor at Elmhurst College, 1971—, George Williams College, 1972—, and Roosevelt University, 1972-73. Member of Chicago Leadership Council for Open Metropolitan Communities, Elmhurst Civic Association of Butterfield Heights, and Timber Trails Homeowners Association. Investigator, Human Relations Commission of Evanston, 1972-73. *Member:* American Management Association, American Society for Training and Development, Society for the Advancement of Management, National Academy of Management, Midwest Academy of Management, Beta Gamma Sigma, Alpha Kappa Psi, Pi Gamma Mu, Omicron Delta Kappa, Kappa Delta Phi, Sigma Iota Epsilon.

WRITINGS: Conflict Via Values and Value Systems, Stipes, 1971; (editor and contributor) *Values, Motivation and Management,* Stipes, 1972; *Management and Administration,* C. E. Merrill, 1973; (editor and contributor) *Essays in Management and Administration,* C. E. Merrill, 1973; *Personnel Administration,* Wiley, in press. Contributor to business, education, and psychology journals. Member of editorial review board, *Business Ideas and Facts,* 1973—.

WORK IN PROGRESS: Readings in Personnel Administration, completion expected in 1975.

* * *

SILBERSTANG, Edwin 1930-

PERSONAL: Born January 11, 1930, in New York, N.Y.; son of Louis (a lawyer) and Fay (Berkowitz) Silberstang; children: Julian, Joyce, Allan. *Education:* University of Michigan, B.A., 1950; Brooklyn Law School, J.D., 1957. *Religion:* Jewish. *Home:* 10 Capra Way, San Francisco, Calif. 94123. *Agent:* Mary Yost, 141 East 55th St., New York, N.Y. 10022.

CAREER: Private practice of law in Brooklyn, N.Y., 1958-67; writer, 1967—. *Military service:* U.S. Army, special agent for Counter-Intelligence Corps, 1951-53. *Member:* Authors Guild.

WRITINGS: Rapt in Glory (novel), Pocket Books, 1964; *Nightmare of the Dark* (novel), Knopf, 1967; (editor) Eric Offner, *Worldwide Trademark Protection,* Fieldston, 1968; *Sweet Land of Liberty* (novel), Putnam, 1972; *Playboy's Book of Games,* Playboy Press, 1972; *Insider's Guide to Las Vegas,* John Mechigian, 1973; (editor) Robert Tsay, *Encyclopedia of Chinese Acupuncture,* New Chinese Medicine Association, 1974.

WORK IN PROGRESS—Novels: *Losers Weepers,* for Doubleday; *The Vegas Nerve.*

* * *

SILVERMAN, William B. 1913-

PERSONAL: Born June 4, 1913, in Altoona, Pa.; son of Simon and Rae (Friedland) Silverman; married Pearl Biales, June 23, 1940; children: Joel J., Eldon E. *Education:* Western Reserve University (now Case Western Reserve University), B.A., 1935; Hebrew Union College, B.H.L., 1937, M.H.L. and Rabbi, 1941, D.D., 1949. *Home:* 8401 Briar Lane, Shawnee Mission, Kan. 66207. *Office:* Temple B'nai Jehudah, 712 East 69th, Kansas City, Mo. 64131.

CAREER: Temple Bethel, Battle Creek, Mich., rabbi, 1941-43; Temple Emanuel, Gastonia, N.C., senior rabbi, 1943-46; Temple Emanuel, Duluth, Minn., senior rabbi, 1946-50; Temple Ohabai Shalom, Nashville, Tenn., senior rabbi, 1950-60; Temple B'nai Jehudah, Kansas City, Mo., senior rabbi, 1960—. Visiting lecturer, St. Paul School of Theology, 1969; professor of modern Jewish history, University of Missouri, Kansas City, 1970. Member of Minnesota Governor's Commission of Parents and Family, 1949; has held positions, at various times, as member of national program committee of B'nai B'rith, member of Kansas City Council on Alcoholism, member of Kansas City Health Society, chaplain, Kansas City, Mo. Fire Department, and member of board of directors of Kansas City Cancer Society, Florence Crittenton Home, Jackson County Medical Society, Big Brothers of America, and Seventh Step Foundation of Kansas City; president of Greater Kansas City Council on Religion and Race, 1963-64. *Wartime service:* Civilian chaplain at Fort Custer, Mich., 1941-43.

MEMBER: American Association of Marriage Counselors (clinical member), Central Conference of American Rabbis (former financial secretary, member of executive board, and member of regional conciliation commission), Planned Parenthood Association, Rabbinical Association of Greater Kansas City (past president), Rotary Club, Wranglers' Club (past president). *Awards, honors:* D.D., Northland College, 1950; Rockne Club of America Clergyman of the Year Award, 1964; D.H.L., Hebrew Union College, 1966; Greater Kansas City Council on Religion and Race "God and Man in Community Award," 1971.

WRITINGS: The Still Small Voice: The Story of Jewish Ethics, Behrman, 1955; *The Still Small Voice Today: Jewish Ethical Living,* Behrman, 1957; *Rabbinic Stories for Christian Ministers and Teachers,* Abingdon, 1958, revised edition published as *Rabbinic Wisdom and Jewish Values,* Union of American Hebrew Congregations, 1971; *God Help Me!: From Kindergarten Religion to the Radical Faith,* Macmillan, 1961, published as *Religion for Skeptics,* Jonathan David, 1967; *Judaism and Christianity: What We Believe,* Behrman, 1968; *Basic Reform Judaism,* Philosophical Library, 1969. Also author of *High Cost of Jewish Living,* 1948; *Judaism and Christianity Compare Notes,* 1949, and *Strength of Faith,* 1954.

WORK IN PROGRESS: Co-editing *Kivie Kaplan: A Legend in His Time.*

* * *

SILVERSTEIN, Alvin 1933- ("Dr. A")

PERSONAL: Born December 30, 1933, in New York, N.Y.; son of Edward (a carpenter) and Fannie (Wittlin) Silverstein; married Virginia B. Opshelor (a translator and writer), August 29, 1958; children: Robert Alan, Glenn Evan, Carrie Lee, Sharon Leslie, Laura Donna, Kevin Andrew. *Education:* Brooklyn College (now Brooklyn College of the City University of New York), B.A., 1955; University of Pennsylvania, M.S., 1959; New York University, Ph.D., 1962. *Home address:* R. D. 2, Lebanon, N.J. 08833. *Office:* Staten Island Community College of the City University of New York, 715 Ocean Ter., Staten Island, N.Y. 10301.

CAREER: Staten Island Community College of the City University of New York, Staten Island, N.Y., instructor, 1959-63, assistant professor, 1963-66, associate professor, 1966-70, professor of biology, 1970—. *Member:* Authors Guild, American Association for the Advancement of Science, American Chemical Society, American Institute of Biological Sciences, National Collegiate Association for the Conquest of Cancer (national chairman, 1968-70).

WRITINGS: The Biological Sciences (textbook), Holt, 1974.

Juvenile books, with wife, Virginia B. Silverstein: *Life in the Universe,* Van Nostrand, 1967; *Rats and Mice: Friends and Foes of Mankind,* Lothrop, 1968; *Unusual Partners,* McGraw, 1968; *The Origin of Life,* Van Nostrand, 1968; *The Respiratory System,* Prentice-Hall, 1969; *A Star in the Sea,* Warne, 1969; *A World in a Drop of Water,* Atheneum, 1969; *Cells: Building Blocks of Life,* Prentice-Hall, 1969; *Carl Linnaeus,* John Day, 1969; *Frederick Sanger,* John Day, 1969.

Germfree Life: A New Field in Biological Research, Lothrop, 1970; *Living Lights,* Golden Gate, 1970; *Circulatory Systems,* Prentice-Hall, 1970; *The Digestive System,* Prentice-Hall, 1970; *Bionics,* McCall Publishing, 1970; *Harold Urey,* John Day, 1971; *Metamorphosis: The Magic Change,* Atheneum, 1971; *Mammals of the Sea,* Golden Gate, 1971; *The Nervous System,* Prentice-Hall, 1971; *The Sense Organs,* Prentice-Hall, 1971; *The Endocrine System,* Prentice-Hall, 1971; *The Reproductive System,* Prentice-Hall, 1971; *The Code of Life,* Atheneum, 1972; *Guinea Pigs,* Lothrop, 1972; *The Long Voyage,* Warne, 1972; *The Muscular System,* Prentice-Hall, 1972; *The Skeletal System,* Prentice-Hall, 1972; *Cancer,* John Day, 1972; *The Skin,* Prentice-Hall, 1972; *The Excretory System,* Prentice-Hall, 1972; *Exploring the Brain,* Prentice-Hall, 1973; *The Chemicals We Eat and Drink,* Follett, 1973; *Rabbits,* Lothrop, 1973; *Sleep and Dreams,* Lippincott, 1974; *Animal Invaders,* Atheneum, 1974; *Hamsters,* Lothrop, 1974.

Author, under pseudonym, of syndicated juvenile fiction column, "Tales from Dr. A," appearing in about 250 American and Canadian newspapers, 1972-74.

SIDELIGHTS: Various of the Silversteins' juvenile books have been described as "stimulating," "cogent," "a concise, accurate treatment." In *A Star in the Sea,* notes *Christian Education Findings,* "the life cycle of the starfish is told simply but in an interesting way, with superb illustrations. This is science as it should be presented." A number of the books are of a more technical nature, however; Zena Sutherland notes that in *Germfree Life,* which treats a relatively new research approach called gnotobiology, "the straightforward, brisk writing is lucid, the material neatly organized, the subject one of the most intriguing on the biological frontier." *Avocational interests:* Reading nonfiction, vegetable gardening, sports.

SILVERSTEIN, Norman 1922-1974

March 15, 1922—July 29, 1974; American professor of English and film critic. Obituaries: *New York Times,* August 1, 1974. (*CA*-37/40).

* * *

SILVERSTEIN, Virginia B(arbara Opshelor) 1937-

PERSONAL: Born April 3, 1937, in Philadelphia, Pa.; daughter of Samuel W. (an insurance agent) and Gertrude (Bresch) Opshelor; married Alvin Silverstein (a professor of biology and writer), August 29, 1958; children: Robert Alan, Glenn Evan, Carrie Lee, Sharon Leslie, Laura Donna, Kevin Andrew. *Education:* University of Pennsylvania, A.B., 1958; also studied at McGill University, summer, 1955. *Home address:* R.D. 2, Lebanon, N.J. 08833.

CAREER: American Sugar Co., Brooklyn, N.Y., chemist, 1958-59; free-lance translator of scientific Russian, 1960—. *Member:* Authors Guild.

WRITINGS—Juvenile books, with husband, Alvin Silverstein: *Life in the Universe,* Van Nostrand, 1967; *Rats and Mice: Friends and Foes of Mankind,* Lothrop, 1968; *Unusual Partners,* McGraw, 1968; *The Origins of Life,* Van Nostrand, 1968; *The Respiratory System,* Prentice-Hall, 1969; *A Star in the Sea,* Warne, 1969; *A World in a Drop of Water,* Atheneum, 1969; *Cells: Building Blocks of Life,* Prentice-Hall, 1969; *Carl Linnaeus,* John Day, 1969; *Frederick Sanger,* John Day, 1969.

Germfree Life: A New Field in Biological Research, Lothrop, 1970; *Living Lights,* Golden Gate, 1970; *Circulatory Systems,* Prentice-Hall, 1970; *The Digestive System,* Prentice-Hall, 1970; *Bionics,* McCall Publishing, 1970; *Harold Urey,* John Day, 1971; *Metamorphosis: The Magic Change,* Atheneum, 1971; *Mammals of the Sea,* Golden Gate, 1971; *The Nervous System,* Prentice-Hall, 1971; *The Sense Organs,* Prentice-Hall, 1971; *The Endocrine System,* Prentice-Hall, 1971; *The Reproductive System,* Prentice-Hall, 1971; *The Code of Life,* Atheneum, 1972; *Guinea Pigs,* Lothrop, 1972; *The Long Voyage,* Warne, 1972; *The Muscular System,* Prentice-Hall, 1972; *The Skeletal System,* Prentice-Hall, 1972; *Cancer,* John Day, 1972; *The Skin,* Prentice-Hall, 1972; *The Excretory System,* Prentice-Hall, 1972; *Exploring the Brain,* Prentice-Hall, 1973; *The Chemicals We Eat and Drink* Follett, 1973; *Rabbits,* Lothrop, 1973; *Sleep and Dreams,* Lippincott, 1974; *Animal Invaders,* Atheneum, 1974; *Hamsters,* Lothrop, 1974.

Translator from Russian of numerous books, including: V. N. Kondratev, *Kinetics of Chemical Gas Reactions,* Atomic Energy Commission, 1960; M. A. Elyashevich, *Spectra of the Rare Earths,* Atomic Energy Commission, 1960; L. K. Blinov, *Hydrochemistry of the Aral Sea,* Office of Technical Services, 1961; R. A. Belyaev, *Beryllium Oxide,* Atomic Energy Commission, 1963; G. V. Samsonov, *High-Temperature Compounds of Rare Earth Metals with Nonmetals,* Plenum, 1965; M. B. Neiman, *Aging and Stabilization of Polymers,* Plenum, 1965. Regular contributor of translations to about twenty scientific journals; translator of bi-monthly journal, *Radiobiologiya.*

SIDELIGHTS: Mrs. Silverstein told *CA:* "I slipped into both my professions (translating and writing) somewhat accidentally, but was ideally prepared for both by my strong school background in both sciences (chemistry major) and languages (formal studies in French, Latin, and German, plus Spanish and Russian self-taught). Writing is done in collaboration with my husband, with whom I (nearly always) have an almost perfect meshing of minds. So far we've averaged one major shift of career emphasis every three years or so; if the past is any guide, the future should be interesting—and probably unexpected." Mrs. Silverstein adds that "two professions, six children, and a seventeen-acre farm don't leave much time for either travel or avocations, but I do read voraciously, and enjoy listening to classical music and doing various handcrafts."

* * *

SIMMONS, S. H.
See SIMMONS, Sylvia

* * *

SIMMONS, Sylvia (S. H. Simmons)

PERSONAL: Born in New York, N.Y.; married Hans H. Neumann (a public health physician), 1963. *Education:* Brooklyn College (now Brooklyn College of the City University of New York), B.A. (cum laude), 1940; Columbia University, M.A., 1941. *Home and office:* 74 Old Belden Hill Rd., Wilton, Conn. 06897. *Agent:* Stephen F. Rohde, 6922 Hollywood Blvd., Hollywood, Calif. 90028.

CAREER: American Red Cross, Italy, staff assistant, 1942-45; Crey Advertising Agency, New York, N.Y., copywriter, 1950-52, promotion copy chief, 1952-54; Amos Parrish Co. Advertising Agency, New York, N.Y., creative director, 1955; McCann-Erickson, Inc. (advertising agency), New York, N.Y., director of sales promotion section, 1955-60; Young & Rubicam, Inc. (advertising agency), New York, N.Y., special project work, 1960-62, vice-president, 1962-71. Speech writer and coach.

MEMBER: Sales Promotion Executives Association, Direct Mail Advertising Association, Authors Guild, Sales Promotion Executives Club, Advertising Women, and Copy Club (all New York), Sigma Tau Delta, Propylaea. *Awards, honors:* Purple Heart, 1944, and Medal of Freedom, 1945 (in connection with war service with Red Cross); Sales Promotion Executives Association Award, 1958, for contribution to the advancement of sales promotion in the direct mail area.

WRITINGS: (Under name S. H. Simmons) *New Speakers Handbook: How to be the Life of the Podium,* Dial, 1972; (with husband, Hans H. Neumann) *The Straight Story on V.D.,* Paperback Library, 1973.

* * *

SIMONELLI, Maria Picchio 1921-

PERSONAL: Born May 16, 1921, in Florence, Italy; daughter of Gino (a professor of physiology) and Assunta (Cerroti) Simonelli; married Riccardo Picchio (a professor at Yale University), September 8, 1969. *Education:* University of Florence, Doctor of Humanities, 1946; University of Rome, Libera Docenza, 1965. *Politics:* Giustizia e Liberta (underground in World War II). *Religion:* Roman Catholic. *Home:* 168 Westwood Rd., New Haven, Conn. 06515. *Office:* Carney Hall, Boston College, Chestnut Hill, Mass. 02167.

CAREER: University of Florence, Florence, Italy, assistant professor of Romance philology, 1948-54, professor in Fulbright postdoctoral program, 1950-61; University of Rome, Rome, Italy, lecturer in Old Italian, Old Provencal, and Old French literatures, 1963-68; Boston College, Boston, Mass., professor of Romance literature, 1968—. Visiting professor at Harvard University, 1966, Cornell University, 1967, and Yale University, 1968-69. *Member:* Dante Society of America (member of council).

WRITINGS: (Editor) Dante, *Convivio* (critical edition), Patron (Bologna), 1966; *Materiali per un'edizione critica del Convivio di Dante,* Ateneo (Rome), 1970; *Poesia moralistica nell'occitania del 12 secolo,* Mucchi (Modena), 1974. Contributor of articles in Italian and English to journals. Associate editor, *Studi Danteschi,* 1952-56; co-editor, *Studia Historica e Philologica.*

WORK IN PROGRESS: A history of Old Provencal poetry.

* * *

SIMONSON, Conrad 1931-

PERSONAL: Born December 5, 1931, in Tacoma, Wash.; son of Gustav (a commercial fisherman) and Jennie (Jacobson) Simonson; married Margaret Minke, August 28, 1955; children: Paul, Kathryn, Gail, Heidi. *Education:* Pacific Lutheran University, B.A., 1954, B.D., 1958; University of Chicago, Ph.D., 1970. *Home:* 307 West Broadway, Decorah, Iowa 52101. *Office:* Luther College, Decorah, Iowa 52101.

CAREER: Ordained Lutheran minister, 1958; pastor in Fremont, Calif., 1958-64, and part-time minister for other parishes; Luther College, Decorah, Iowa, assistant professor of religion, 1969—. *Member:* American Academy of Religion, American Association of University Professors.

WRITINGS: (Contributor) Edmund Steinle, editor, *Renewal in the Pulpit,* Fortress, 1966; *The Christology of the Faith and Order Movement,* E. J. Brill, 1972; (contributor) George Devine, editor, *A World More Human, a Church More Christian,* Alba, 1973; *In Search of God,* Pilgrim Press, 1974. Contributor to journals.

WORK IN PROGRESS: A book on the meaning of being religious.

* * *

SIMPSON, Robert 1924-

PERSONAL: Born January 8, 1924, in London, England; son of Barnett (a mantle manufacturer) and Sonia (Daggers) Simpson; married Margaret Legman, February 11, 1951; children: Nancy. *Agent:* Freida Fishbein, 337 West 57th St., New York, N.Y.

CAREER: Playwright, novelist. Resident playwright, East End Jewish Theatre, eighteen months. Has also held jobs as reporter, editor, salesman, and management consultant. *Military service:* British Army, General Service Corps.

WRITINGS: April's There (novel), Harper, 1973. Author of musical librettos, motion picture scenarios, comedy routines, sketches, and other material.

SIDELIGHTS; Simpson wrote: "*April's There,* my first novel, has been submitted for Pulitzer and National Book Awards prizes in fiction category. This indicates, I believe, confirmation of the standard I set myself, merely to at all times have my reach exceed my grasp."

* * *

SINCLAIR, Bennie Lee 1939-

PERSONAL: Born April 15, 1939, in Greenville, S.C.; daughter of Waldo Graham (an engraver) and Bennie Lee (Ward) Sinclair; married Don Lewis (a potter), August 1, 1958. *Education:* Furman University, B.A., 1961. *Address:* P.O. Box 278, Campobello, S.C. 29322.

CAREER: Poet. Poet-in-the-schools for South Carolina, 1972-73, 1973-74, under program sponsored by National Endowment for the Arts and South Carolina Arts Commission; also gives poetry readings in colleges and universities. *Awards, honors:* Stephen Vincent Benet Award for narrative poem from *Poet Lore,* 1970, for "David, the Grit Salesman"; *South Carolina Review* Poetry Award, 1972; awards for individual poems from state poetry societies of Pennsylvania, South Carolina, and Kentucky, and from Poets Club of Chicago.

WRITINGS: Little Chicago Suite (poems), Drummer Press, 1971. Poem, "The Conditions," has been printed in limited editions with block print by Fannie Mennen. Contributor of poems and short stories to literary magazines, including *Foxfire, South Carolina Review, and Human Voice;* one short story and poems have been included in anthologies. Advisory and contributing editor, *Appalachian Heritage,* 1973—.

WORK IN PROGRESS: A second collection of poems, *The Arrowhead Scholar;* a collection of short stories, *For Those Outside.*

SIDELIGHTS: Bennie Lee Sinclair writes: "I earn my living as a poet through readings and workshops—and while many of these are at colleges and universities, I also do community programs in small and out-of-the-way places. I have found audiences of farm and mill families to be just as sensitive to poetry as academia-oriented people. And I love the challenge of breaking through the old prejudices against poetry: I want my poems to reach all sorts of people—not just those educated to it.

"My husband and I live in a rural area of upstate South Carolina. We built our home and studios ourselves, and have raised most of our food since we moved here in 1959. We find his pottery and my poetry compatible for a continuing exchange of ideas on form and subject matter."

BIOGRAPHICAL/CRITICAL SOURCES: Furman Magazine (publication of Furman University), Volume 20, number 3, summer, 1973.

* * *

SINGER, Kurt D(eutsch) 1911-

PERSONAL: Adopted mother's maiden name as his surname; born August 10, 1911, in Vienna, Austria; came to United States, 1940, naturalized citizen, 1951; son of Ignatz (an importer-exporter) and Irene (Singer) Deutsch; married Hilda Tradelius, December 24, 1932; married second wife, Jane Sherrod (an author and columnist), April 4, 1955; children: (first marriage) Marianne Alice Birgit, Kenneth Walt. *Education:* Received primary and secondary education in Berlin; studied at University of Zurich and Labor College, Stockholm; Divinity College of Metaphysics, Indianapolis, Ind., Ph.D., 1951. *Office:* BP Singer Features, Inc., 3164 West Tyler Ave., Anaheim, Calif. 92801.

CAREER: Worked in his teens as apprentice in German factory making railroad cars; editor of *Mitteilungsblaetter* (underground weekly), Berlin, Germany, 1933; fled to Sweden, 1934, and founded committee to free Nobel laureate Carl von Ossietzky from Nazi concentration camp; correspondent and journalist in Sweden, 1935-40; correspondent in America for Swedish newspapers, 1940; author and lecturer, principally on spies and espionage, 1940—; president of BP Singer Features, Inc., Anaheim, Calif., 1955—. Member of speaker's research committee and editor of *UN Calendar,* United Nations, 1948-52; editor-in-chief, Oceanic Press Service, North Hollywood, 1955—. *Member:* International Platform Association (vice-president, 1948-52), Western Writers of America.

WRITINGS: Det Kommandet Kriget (title means "The Coming War"), Federatif Foerlag (Stockholm), 1934; *Europas diktatorer: 24 diktatorer fraan Hitler till Stalin,* Holmstroem, 1936; *Martin Niemoeller, praesten i koncentrationslaegret,* Fredens Foerlag, 1939.

Goering: German's Most Dangerous Man, Hutchinson, 1940; *Duel for the Northland: The War of Enemy Agents in Scandinavia,* McBride, 1943; *Spies and Traitors of World War II,* Prentice-Hall, 1945; (editor) *Three Thousand Years of Espionage: An Anthology of the World's Greatest Spy Stories,* Prentice-Hall, 1948; (with Franz J. Polgar) *Polgar: Story of a Hypnotist,* Thomas Nelson, 1948.

The World's 30 Greatest Women Spies, Funk, 1951; *Gentlemen Spies,* W. H. Allen, 1952; *Spies and Traitors: A Short History of Espionage,* W. H. Allen, 1953; *The Men in the Trojan Horse,* Beacon Press, 1953; (editor) *The World's Best Spy Stories: Fact and Fiction,* Funk, 1954 (published in England as *The World's Greatest Spy Stories: Fact and Fiction,* W. H. Allen, 1954); *The Laughton Story: An Intimate Story of Charles Laughton,* Winston, 1954; *More Spy Stories,* W. H. Allen, 1955; *Spy Stories from Asia,* Funk, 1955 (published in England as *Spies Over Asia,* W. H. Allen, 1956); (editor) *My Greatest Crime Story, by Police Chiefs of the World,* Hill & Wang, 1956; *The Danny Kaye Saga,* R. Hale, 1957, Thomas Nelson, 1958; (editor) *My Strangest Case, by Police Chiefs of the World,* W. H. Allen, 1957, Doubleday, 1958; *Spy Omnibus,* W. H. Allen, 1959, Denison, 1960.

(Editor and author of introduction) *Spies Who Changed History,* Ace Books, 1960; (editor) *Eight Tales Complete from the World's Greatest Spy Stories,* Belmont Books, 1961; *Crime Omnibus,* W. H. Allen, 1961; *Hemingway: Life and Death of a Giant,* Holloway House, 1961; *The Unearthly: The World's Greatest Stories of the Occult,* Panther House, 1962; *Horror Omnibus,* W. H. Allen, 1965; (editor) *I Can't Sleep at Night: 13 Weird Tales,* Whiting & Wheaton, 1966; (editor) *Weird Tales of the Supernatural,* W. H. Allen, 1966; *Mata Hari,* Award Books, 1967; (editor) *Tales of Terror,* W. H. Allen, 1967; (editor) *The Gothic Reader,* Ace Books, 1968; *Tales of the Uncanny,* W. H. Allen, 1968; (editor) *Famous Short Stories,* two volumes, Denison, 1968; (editor) *Tales of the Macabre,* New English Library, 1969; (editor) *Bloch and Bradbury,* Belmont Books, 1969.

(Editor) *The House in the Valley, and Other Tales of Terror,* Sphere Books, 1970; *Plague of the Living Dead,* Sphere Books, 1970; (editor) *Tales from the Unknown,* W. H. Allen, 1970, published in America as *Tales of the Unknown,* Pinnacle Books, 1971.

With wife, Jane Sherrod: *Spies for Democracy,* Denison, 1960; *Great Adventures of the Sea,* Denison, 1962; (editors) *Great Adventures in Crime,* Denison, 1962; *Dr. Albert Schweitzer: Medical Missionary* (juvenile), Denison, 1962; *Ernest Hemingway: Man of Courage* (juvenile), Denison, 1963; (editors) *Ghost Book: The World's Greatest Stories of the Known Unknown,* W. H. Allen, 1963; *Lyndon Baines Johnson: Man of Reason* (juvenile), Denison, 1964, revised edition, 1966.

Other juveniles: (Translator) Esther Gretor, *Kippie the Cow,* Messner, 1951; *Tales from the South Pacific,* Denison, 1969; *Folktales from Mexico,* Denison, 1970.

Writer of "News Background Reports" during World War II. Contributor to *This Month, Dalhousie Review, Saturday Evening Post, Christian Science Monitor, National Star, American Weekly,* and other magazines and newspapers. His column, "Hollywood Interviews," has been published in twenty countries, 1955—.

WORK IN PROGRESS: "Usually write or edit two books a year."

SIDELIGHTS: Singer's *Spies and Traitors of World War II* was adapted for a film and for television, and his books on espionage have appeared in multiple translations, including Norwegian, Portuguese, Japanese, German, Italian, Hebrew, Swedish, Spanish, and French. He speaks eight languages.

* * *

SINGER, (Dennis) Robert 1931-

PERSONAL: Born September 8, 1931, in Budapest, Hungary; son of Eugene (an accountant) and Pearl (Kaufman) Singer; married Anne Stauffer (a psychologist), March 24, 1961; children: Elizabeth, Susan. *Education:* University of Pennsylvania, B.A., 1953, M.A., 1955, Ph.D., 1960. *Politics:* Democrat. *Religion:* None. *Home:* 2127 Brentwood Dr., Palm Springs, Calif. 92262. *Office:* Department of Psychology, University of California at Riverside, Riverside, Calif. 92502.

CAREER: University of California at Riverside, 1969—, currently professor of psychology. *Member:* American Psychological Association, American Academy of Political and Social Sciences, Interamerican Society of Psychology, New York Academy of Sciences. *Awards, honors:* Center for Advanced Study in the Behavioral Sciences fellowship, 1966-67.

WRITINGS: (With wife, Anne Singer) *Psychological Development in Children,* Saunders, 1969; (with Seymour Feshbach) *Television and Aggression,* Jossey-Bass, 1971. Contributor to *Journal of the American Medical Association, Archives of General Psychiatry, Journal of Personality,* and *Journal of Social and Abnormal Psychology.*

WORK IN PROGRESS: Psychology of Human Adaptation; research on the effects of psychotherapy training.

* * *

SINGH, Arjan 1917-

PERSONAL: Born August 15, 1917, in Gorakhpur, India; son of Kanwar Jasbir and Mabel (Golaknath) Singh. *Education:* Allahabad University, B.A., 1938. *Religion:* Christian. *Home:* Tigerhaven, Pallia, District Kheri, Uttar Pradesh, India.

CAREER: Farmer and conservationist. Member of Indian national and state wildlife boards. *Military service:* Indian Army, 1940-45. *Member:* International Union for Conservation of Nature and Natural Resources (member of cat specialist group and Deer Group), Wild Life Preservation Society of India (member of executive committee).

WRITINGS: Tiger Haven, Harper, 1973.

WORK IN PROGRESS: The Prince of Cats, a book on the rehabilitation of the leopard, for Collins.

SIDELIGHTS: Singh told *CA* his writing is "motivated by adverse impact on Indian wild life, especially the cats, by human acquisitiveness and pressure of exploding population in India."

* * *

SINGH, Surender 1932-

PERSONAL: Born September 12, 1932, in Hardoi, Utter Pradesh, India; son of Rockwell (a landlord) and Rukmani Singh; married wife, Virginia (a school principal), June 21, 1957. *Education:* Lucknow Christian College, Diploma, 1954; Macalester College, B.A., 1956; University of Minnesota, M.A., 1957, Ph.D., 1960. *Office:* Department of Political Science, University of Wisconsin, La Crosse, Wis. 54601.

CAREER: Administrative positions with educational institutions in Utter Pradesh, India, 1960-62; Carthage College, Carthage, Ill., professor of political science, 1962-64; University of Wisconsin—La Crosse, associate professor of political science, 1964—, chairman of department, 1966-69, 1974—. *Member:* Hardoi Educational Society of India (president, 1968—), Wisconsin Political Science Association (secretary, 1970-71; president, 1971-72), Rotary International.

WRITINGS: American National Government: George Washington to Johnson, Curtiss Books, 1965; *Twin Democracies: India and United States,* Upper India Publishing House, 1970. Contributor to *Asian Productivity Journal* and other journals and newspapers.

WORK IN PROGRESS: Writing on women prime ministers and on American government.

* * *

SINGHAL, D(amodar) P(rasad) 1925-

PERSONAL: Born September 24, 1925, in India; son of Bishan Gopal and Kailashi Devi (Garg) Singhal; married Devahuti Maniktala (a university teacher), May 18, 1950. *Education:* University of Punjab, B.A., 1946; University of Panjab, M.A., 1949; University of London, Ph.D., 1955. *Home:* 193 Carmody Rd., St. Lucia, Brisbane, Queensland 4067, Australia. *Office:* Department of History, University of Queensland, St. Lucia, Brisbane, Australia 4067.

CAREER: University of Malaya, Singapore, lecturer in history, 1956-61; University of Queensland, Brisbane, Australia, senior lecturer, 1961-69, reader and professor of history, 1969—. *Member:* Royal Historical Society (fellow), Royal Asiatic Society (fellow), American Association for Asian Studies, American Academy of Political Science (fellow). *Awards, honors:* Ph.D., 1972, and D.Litt., 1974, from University of Queensland.

WRITINGS: The Annexation of Upper Burma, Eastern Universities Press (Singapore), 1960; *India and Afghanistan, 1876-1907: A Study in Diplomatic Relations,* University of Queensland Press, 1963; *Nationalism in India and other Historical Essays,* Munshiram Manoharlal (Delhi), 1967; *India and World Civilization,* two volumes, Michigan State University Press, 1969; *Pakistan,* Prentice-Hall, 1972. General editor of "Library on Modern Asia" series for Sidgwick & Jackson, 1969-72; and "Modern Asia" series for Cheshire Publishing Co., 1973-74.

WORK IN PROGRESS: A book, *Modern India;* research on transfer of power in India.

SISK, Henry L(ybran) 1914-

PERSONAL: Born June 22, 1914, in Los Angeles, Calif.; son of Joseph L. and Henrietta (Berry) Sisk; married Hazel Halladay, April 6, 1946; children: Duncan. *Education:* Arizona State University, A.B., 1935; University of Arizona, M.A., 1937; Cornell University, Ph.D., 1939. *Home:* 2803 Foxcroft Circle, Denton, Tex. 76201. *Office address:* P.O. Box 5114 North Texas Station, Denton, Tex. 76203.

CAREER: Diplomate, American Board of Examiners in Professional Psychology (Industrial). State University of New York at Albany, instructor in psychology, 1939-42; Veterans Administration Guidance Center, Tempe, Ariz., director, 1946-47; Stevenson, Jordan, & Harrison, Inc. (management consultants), Chicago, Ill., staff psychologist, 1947-49; Milprint, Inc., Milwaukee, Wis., director of industrial relations, 1949-52; Continental Can Co., Chicago, Ill., supervisor of organization development, 1952-56; Dresser Industries, Dallas, Tex., assistant to vice-president for industrial relations, 1956-59; North Texas State University, Denton, professor of business administration, 1960—. Member of labor arbitration panels of American Arbitration Association, Federal Mediation and Conciliation Service, and National Mediation Board. *Military service:* U.S. Army, 1942-46; became captain. *Member:* American Psychological Association (fellow), Academy of Management, Industrial Relations Research Association.

WRITINGS: Principles of Management: A Systems Approach to the Management Process, South-Western, 1969, 2nd edition published as *Management and Organization,* 1973. Contributor to psychology and business journals.

* * *

SKELTON, Geoffrey (David) 1916-

PERSONAL: Born May 11, 1916, in Springs, South Africa; son of Richard Hugh (a mining engineer) and Saizy (Watson) Skelton; married Gertrude Klebac, September 4, 1947; children: Stephen, Robert Piers. *Education:* Attended schools in England and Hong Kong. *Home:* 49 Downside, Shoreham, Sussex BN4 6HF, England.

CAREER: Reporter and sub-editor for various newspapers and periodicals, 1935-38; free-lance writer and journalist, 1938-40; sub-editor, *Sussex Daily News,* 1946-48; Press Association, London, England, sub-editor, 1948-49; British Information Services, Foreign Office in Germany, controller on *Die Welt,* Hamburg, 1949, information officer in Dortmund and Hamburg, 1950-56; British Broadcasting Corp., London, sub-editor in External Services News Department, 1956-58, program assistant in BBC German Service, 1958-66, program organizer, 1966-67; full-time writer and translator, 1967—. *Wartime service:* Conscientious objector; served in British Army Medical Corps, 1940-46. *Member:* Radiowriters Association (member of executive committee, 1969-72), Translators Association (member of executive committee, 1972—, chairman, 1974). *Awards, honors:* American P.E.N. Club translation award, 1965, for *The Persecution and Assassination of Jean-Paul Marat as Performed by the Inmates of the Asylum of Charenton under the Direction of the Marquis de Sade.*

WRITINGS: Wagner at Bayreuth: Experiment and Tradition, Barrie & Rockliff, 1965, Braziller, 1966; *Wieland Wagner: The Positive Sceptic* (biography), St. Martin's, 1971; (editor with Robert L. Jacobs) *Wagner Writes from Paris,* John Day, 1973.

Plays; all one-act: *Flowers for the Leader,* Samuel French,

1939; "Summer Night," published in *Twelve One-Acts,* edited by Elizabeth Everard, Allen & Unwin, 1939; *Have You Seen My Lady?,* Muller, 1948; "Memories for Sale," published in *Twenty Minute Theatre,* J. Garnet Miller, 1955.

Translations from the German: Theodor Storm, *The White Horseman* (short stories), New English Library, 1962; Guenter Herburger, *A Monotonous Landscape* (short stories), Harcourt, 1968; Friedrich Heer, *God's First Love: Christians and Jews Over 2000 Years,* Weidenfeld & Nicolson, 1970, Weybright and Talley, 1971; Robert Lucas, *Frieda Lawrence: The Story of Frieda von Richtofen and D. H. Lawrence,* Viking, 1973; Max Frisch, *Sketchbook, 1966-1971,* Harcourt, 1974.

Plays translated from the German: (With Adrian Mitchell) Peter Weiss, *The Persecution and Assassination of Marat as Performed by the Inmates of the Asylum of Charenton under the Direction of the Marquis de Sade* (English version by Skelton, verse adaptation by Mitchell; first produced by Royal Shakespeare Company in London, England, at Aldwych Theatre, August 20, 1964; produced on Broadway at Martin Beck Theatre, 1966), Calder & Boyars, 1965, 4th edition, 1969, published in America as *The Persecution and Assassination of Jean-Paul Marat. . .,* Atheneum, 1966; Erich Fried, *Arden Must Die* (opera; music by Alexander Goehr; first produced in London at Sadler's Wells Theatre, April 17, 1974), Schott, 1967; Bertolt Brecht, *Lesson on Consent* (cantata; music by Paul Hindemith; first produced in Brighton, England at Brighton Festival, May 5, 1968), Schott, 1968; Weiss, *Discourse on the Progress of the Prolonged War of Liberation in Viet Nam,* published with *Song of the Lusitanian Bogey* as *Two Plays,* Atheneum, 1970 (published in England as *Discourse on Vietnam,* Calder & Boyars, 1970); Weiss, *Trotsky in Exile* (broadcast by BBC Radio Three, November 1970), Methuen, 1971, Atheneum, 1972. Also author of unpublished translation of "The Mountain King," by Ferdinand Raimund, first produced in Nottingham, England at Nottingham Theatre, 1968.

Radio scripts, all produced by BBC: (With Christopher Sykes) "Return to the Shrine," 1961; (with Sykes) "Bayreuth Backstage I," 1962, ". . . II," 1963, ". . . III," 1965; "Pleasant Are the Tears which Music Weeps," 1965; "Wagner's Comic Masterpiece: *Die Meistersinger,*" 1968; "Music from the Dead Composers," 1969; "Rossini and Wagner," 1970; "Wagner's Problem Child: *Tannhaeuser,*" 1972; "The Art of Wagnerian Singing," 1974.

Contributor of short stories to periodicals, including *New Writing, Penguin Parade, English Story, Bugle Blast, Adelphi, London Magazine,* and of articles on music and theatre to *World Review, Musical Times, Musical Opinion, Music & Musicians, Plays & Players,* and other publications.

WORK IN PROGRESS: Translating Max Frisch's *Diaries, 1946-49,* for Harcourt; a biography of Paul Hindemith.

AVOCATIONAL INTERESTS: "Enthusiastic piano player for own private amusement (serious music only)."

* * *

SKINNER, G(eorge) William 1925-

PERSONAL: Born February 14, 1925, in Oakland, Calif.; son of John James (a pharmacist) and Eunice (Engle) Skinner; married Carol Bagger, March 25, 1951 (divorced, January, 1970); children: Geoffrey Crane, James Lauriston, Mark Williamson, Jeremy Burr. *Education:* Student at Deep Springs College, 1942-43, Missouri Valley College, 1943-44, and University of Colorado, 1944-46; Cornell University, B.A. (with distinction), 1947, Ph.D., 1954. *Home:* 1700 Willow Rd., Apt. 408, Palo Alto, Calif. 94304. *Office:* Department of Anthropology, Stanford University, Stanford, Calif. 94305.

CAREER: Cornell University, Ithaca, N.Y., instructor in sociology, 1949, field director of Southeast Asia Program in Bangkok, 1951-55, research associate in Far Eastern studies in Indonesia, 1956-58; Columbia University, New York, N.Y., assistant professor of sociology, 1958-60; Cornell University, associate professor, 1960-62, professor of anthropology, 1962-65; Stanford University, Stanford, Calif., professor of anthropology, 1965—. Senior specialist in residence at East-West Center's Institute of Advanced Projects, 1965-66; fellow of Center for Advanced Study in the Behavioral Sciences, 1969-70. Field research includes studies and surveys in Cundiyo, N.M., 1948, Chengtu, Szechwan, China, 1949-50, Southeast Asia, 1950-51, Bangkok, Thailand, 1951-53, 1954-55, and in Indonesia in general, 1956-58. Member of joint committee of American Council of Learned Societies and Social Science Research Council on contemporary China, 1961-65; director of Social Science Research Council's Chinese Society bibliography project, 1964-73; member of committee of American Council of Learned Societies, Social Science Research Council, and National Academy of Sciences on scholarly communication with the People's Republic of China, 1966-70; member of Education and World Affairs' International Committee on Chinese Studies, 1964-65. *Military service:* U.S. Naval Reserve, active duty, 1943-46.

MEMBER: American Anthropological Association (fellow), American Sociological Association (fellow), Society for Applied Anthropology, American Ethnological Society, American Association for the Advancement of Science (fellow), American Association of University Professors, Asia Society, Association for Asian Studies (member of board of directors, 1962-65), Siam Society, Society for Ch'ing Studies, American Academy of Political and Social Science, Royal Anthropological Institute (fellow), Phi Beta Kappa, Sigma Xi. *Awards, honors:* Travel grants from Social Science Research Council for research in China, 1949-50, in Thailand, 1951-53, and grant for research on political socialization, 1966; fellowship from Cornell Modern Indonesia Project for research in Java, 1956-58; National Science Foundation research grant, 1963-64; Guggenheim fellowship, 1969; National Institute of Mental Health special fellowship, 1970; National Science Foundation grant for research on the dynamics of organizational process in China, 1972-73.

WRITINGS: Report on the Chinese in Southeast Asia, Southeast Asia Program, Cornell University, 1951; (editor) *The Social Sciences and Thailand,* Cornell Research Center, Cornell University, 1956; *Chinese Society in Thailand: An Analytical History,* Cornell University Press, 1957; *Leadership and Power in the Chinese Community of Thailand* (monograph), Cornell University Press, 1958; (editor and contributor) *Local, Ethnic, and National Loyalties in Village Indonesia: A Symposium,* Southeast Asia Studies, Yale University, 1959; (editor) *Modern Chinese Society: An Analytical Bibliography,* Stanford University Press, Volume I: *Publications in Western Languages, 1644-1972,* 1973, Volume II (with Winston Hsieh): *Publications in Chinese, 1644-1969,* 1973, Volume III (with Shigeaki Tomita): *Publications in Japanese, 1644-1971,* 1973; (editor with Mark Elvin) *The Chinese City Between Two Worlds,*

Stanford University Press, in press; (editor) *The City in Late Imperial China,* Stanford University Press, in press; (editor with A. Thomas Kirsch) *Change and Persistence in Thai Society,* Cornell University Press, in press.

Contributor: Morton H. Fried, editor, *Colloquium on Overseas Chinese,* Institute of Pacific Relations, 1958; Ruth T. McVey, editor, *Indonesia,* Human Relations Area File Press, 1963; Immanuel M. Wallerstein, editor, *Social Change: The Colonial Situation,* Wiley, 1966; Donald J. Tugby, editor, *Readings in South-east Asian Anthropology,* University of Queensland Press, 1967; Gehan Wijeyewardene, editor, *Leadership and Authority,* University of Malaya Press, 1968; Amitai Etzioni, editor, *A Sociological Reader on Complex Organizations,* Holt, 2nd edition (Skinner was not included in earlier edition), 1969; Paul Ward English and Robert C. Mayfield, editors, *Man, Space, and Environment: Concepts in Contemporary Human Geography,* Oxford University Press, 1972; John T. McAlister, Jr., editor, *Southeast Asia: The Politics of National Integration,* Random House, 1973.

Contributor to annals. Contributor of about forty articles and reviews to social and political science journals, including *Comparative Studies in Society and History, Journal of Asian Studies, Asia, Journal of the South Seas Society, Population Studies, Far Eastern Quarterly,* and *Pacific Affairs.*

SIDELIGHTS: Skinner's books have been published in Japanese and Thai.

* * *

SKRIVANEK, John M(arion) 1913-

PERSONAL: Born June 6, 1913, in Caldwell, Tex.; son of Joseph John (a farmer-rancher) and Mary (Drgac) Skrivanek; married Lil M. Marek, May 15, 1938; children: John D., Deann (Mrs. D. L. Jones), Sharon L. *Education:* University of Texas, B.A., 1938, M.A., 1946; Charles University (Prague), Ph.D., 1948. *Home:* 1212 Merry Oaks Dr., College Station, Tex. 77840. *Office:* Department of Modern Languages, Texas A&M University, College Station, Tex. 77843.

CAREER: High school teacher in Texas, 1938-41; University of Texas, Austin, instructor in Slavonic languages, 1941-46; University of Houston, Houston, Tex., assistant professor of Slavonic languages and chairman of department, 1948-51; South Texas College, Houston, chairman of department of languages, 1951-52; Texas A&M University, College Station, professor of modern languages, 1952—. *Member:* American Association of Teachers of Slavic and East European Languages, Czechoslovak Society of Arts and Sciences in America, Slavonic Benevolent Order of the State of Texas, Czech Educational Foundation of Texas, Phi Eta Sigma, Phi Delta Kappa.

WRITINGS: Education of the Czechs in Texas, Department of Modern Languages, Texas A&M University, 1946; *Russian Conversation and Reading,* Exchange Store, Texas A&M University, 1966; *Modern Conversational Czech,* Department of Modern Languages, Texas A&M University, Book I, 1966, Book II, 1969; *Czech Area Reader,* Department of Modern Languages, Texas A&M University, 1970.

WORK IN PROGRESS: Scientific Czech Reader.

SIDELIGHTS: Skrivanek has spent more than three years in Czechoslovakia, two years studying at Charles University, then 1968-69, and the summer of 1972. He has traveled in England, Germany, Belgium, France, Russia, and Mexico.

* * *

SLATE, Sam J(ordan) 1909-

PERSONAL: Born September 27, 1909, in Columbus, Ga.; son of Sam J. (a lawyer) and Sarah (Yonge) Slate; married Ella Phillips, February 27, 1939; children: Sallie N. *Education:* University of Georgia, A.B., 1929. *Politics:* Democrat. *Religion:* Protestant. *Residence:* Sherman, Conn. 06784. *Agent:* Florence Crowther, 200 West 57th St., New York, N.Y. 10019.

CAREER: Employed by United Press in Atlanta, Ga., and Montgomery, Ala., 1929-32; Columbia Broadcasting System (CBS), New York, N.Y., publicity department, 1933-36; free-lance writer for radio, 1936-41, vice-president in radio division, 1950-64; RKO-General Broadcasting Co., New York, N.Y., vice-president, 1964-70; now full-time writer. *Member:* New York State Broadcasters (president, 1964), New York City Radio and Television Society (vice-president, 1961-64), Sigma Delta Chi, Players Club, Dutch Treat Club. *Awards, honors:* Peabody Award, 1964, for "This is New York."

WRITINGS: (With Joe Cook) *It Sounds Impossible,* Macmillan, 1963; *As Long as the Rivers Run* (novel), Doubleday, 1972; *Satan's Backyard* (novel), Doubleday, 1974. Also author of numerous scripts for radio programs, including "The Gangbusters," "Mr. District Attorney," and "This Nation at War."

WORK IN PROGRESS: An historical novel based on Georgia's Galdin Isles, publication expected in 1975.

* * *

SLOCHOWER, Harry 1900-

PERSONAL: Born September 1, 1900, in Bukowina, Austria; came to United States in 1913; son of Mayer (a merchant) and Frieda (Schnapp) Zloczower; married Reggie Schattner; married second wife, Muriel Zimmerman; children: Joyce Anne. *Education:* City College (now of the City University of New York), B.S.S., 1923; Columbia University, M.A., 1924, Ph.D., 1928. *Religion:* Jewish. *Home:* 221 East 18th St., Brooklyn, N.Y. *Office:* 46 East 73rd St., New York, N.Y. 10021.

CAREER: Certified psychologist. Brooklyn College of the City University of New York, Brooklyn, N.Y., member of faculty, 1930—, became professor of German and humanities, serving as visiting professor, 1973—. Teacher of German and comparative literature at City College (now City College of the City University of New York) and at Columbia University, at various times, 1924-52; lecturer at New School for Social Research, 1947—, and at William Alanson White Institute for Psychiatry, 1948-52. Visiting lecturer at Humboldt Academy, University of Berlin, 1929, Brooklyn Academy of Arts and Sciences, 1967, and University of Rochester, 1967; adjunct professor at Syracuse University, 1969; visiting professor at Sir George William University, summer, 1973, and at Drew University. *Member:* Association for Applied Psychoanalysis (president, 1960—). *Awards, honors:* Guggenheim fellowship, 1929; Bollingen Foundation fellowship, 1952.

WRITINGS: Richard Dehmel: Der Mensch und der Denker (title means "Richard Dehmel: The Man and the Thinker"), Carl Reissner, 1928; *Three Ways of Modern Man,* International Publishers, 1937; *Thomas Mann's Jo-*

seph Story: An Interpretation, Knopf, 1938; (contributor) Dorothy Norman, editor, *Franz Kafka: A Miscellany,* Twice a Year Press, 1940; *No Voice Is Wholly Lost,* Creative Age Press, 1945; (contributor) Paul A. Schlipp, editor, *Ernst Cassirer,* Library of Living Philosophers, 1949; *Mythopoesis: Mythic Patterns in the Literary Classics,* Wayne State University Press, 1970. Contributor to symposia, and to *Encyclopedia of the Social Sciences* and *Nelson's People's Encyclopedia.* Contributor of over two hundred articles, essays, and reviews to general periodicals and professional journals. Contributing editor of *Philosophic Abstracts,* Volume V; editor of *Guide to Psychological and Psychiatric Literature,* 1955-57, and *American Imago,* 1963—.

WORK IN PROGRESS: Contributing to *Philosophical Principles in Freudian Psychoanalysis: Festschrift for Dr. Richard Sterba.*

BIOGRAPHICAL/CRITICAL SOURCES: Maynard Solomon, *Marxism and Art,* Knopf, 1973.

* * *

SMERUD, Warren D(ouglas) 1928-

PERSONAL: Surname is pronounced *Smear*-rood; born December 5, 1928, in Fargo, N.D.; son of Melvin R. (a retailer) and Ella T. (Edlund) Smerud; married Audrey J. Miller (a theatre manager), January 9, 1958; children: Peter, Carl. *Education:* Concordia College, Moorhead, Minn., B.A., 1951; University of Washington, Seattle, M.A., 1958, Ph.D., 1967. *Home:* 915 South 11th St., Moorhead, Minn. 56560. *Office:* Department of Philosophy, Concordia College, Moorhead, Minn. 56560.

CAREER: Seattle Department of Buildings, Seattle, Wash., housing code inspector, 1961-65, technical staff assistant, 1965-66; Concordia College, Moorhead, Minn., assistant professor, 1967-70, associate professor of philosophy, 1970—. *Military service:* U.S. Air Force, 1951-55; became staff sergeant. *Member:* American Philosophical Association, American Society of Dowsers, British Society of Dowsers, American Foundation for Homeopathy, Academy of Parapsychology and Medicine, Northwest Magnetics Research Society.

WRITINGS: Can There Be a Private Language? An Examination of Some Principal Arguments, Mouton & Co., 1970; (author of introduction) Henry Turkel, *New Hope for the Mentally Retarded: Stymied by the FDA,* Vantage, 1972.

WORK IN PROGRESS: Investigating various aspects of radiesthesia and radionics.

* * *

SMITH, Dana Prom 1927-

PERSONAL: Born April 7, 1927, in Glendale, Calif.; son of Tom Nelson Miles (a dentist) and Hazel (Prom) Smith; married Grace Marie Rinck (an organist), August 11, 1951; children: Paul, Timothy, Elizabeth. *Education:* Princeton University, A.B., 1951; Louisville Presbyterian Theological Seminary, B.D., 1954, Th.M., 1955; University of Arizona, M.A., 1958; further study at University of Chicago, 1958-63, and San Francisco Theological Seminary, 1963-68. *Politics:* Republican. *Home:* 6425 Parklynn Dr., Palos Verdes Peninsula, Calif. 90274. *Agent:* Roland Tapp, 1051 Niel's Lane, West Chester, Pa. 19380. *Office:* 26825 Rolling Hills Rd., Rolling Hills Estates, Calif. 90274.

CAREER: Presbyterian clergyman; pastor of Presbyterian churches in Tucson, Ariz., 1955-58, and Geneva, Ill., 1960-68; St. Luke's Presbyterian Church, Rolling Hills, Calif., pastor, 1968—. *Military service:* U.S. Army, 1945-47; became sergeant major.

WRITINGS: Educated Servant, Board of Christian Education, Presbyterian Church, 1967; *Debonair Disciple: A New Piety for a Disordered World,* Fortress, 1973.

WORK IN PROGRESS: A Questionable Faith.

* * *

SMITH, Dave
See SMITH, David (Jeddie)

* * *

SMITH, David (Jeddie) 1942-
(Smith Cornwell, Dave Smith)

PERSONAL: Born December 19, 1942, in Portsmouth, Va.; son of Ralph Gerald (a naval engineer) and Catherine (Cornwell) Smith; married second wife, Deloras Mae Weaver, March 31, 1966; children: (second marriage) David Jeddie, Jr., Lael Cornwell. *Education:* University of Virginia, B.A. (with highest distinction), 1965; College of William and Mary, graduate study, 1966; Southern Illinois University, M.A., 1969; Ohio University, further graduate study, 1972-73. *Home:* 2308 Abbott Court, Kalamazoo, Mich. 49001. *Office:* Western Michigan University, Kalamazoo, Mich. 49001.

CAREER: High school teacher of French, English, and football coach in Poquoson, Va., 1965-67; instructor in Night School Divisions of College of William and Mary, Williamsburg, Va., Christopher Newport College, Newport News, Va., and Thomas Nelson Community College, Hampton, Va., all 1969-72; Western Michigan University, Kalamazoo, instructor in English, 1973—. Has given poetry readings at colleges and universities. *Military service:* U.S. Air Force, 1969-72; became staff sergeant. *Member:* American Association of University Professors, Escondidos, Phi Delta Theta. *Awards, honors:* Fiction prize from *Miscellany,* 1972; scholarship to attend Breadloaf Writer's Conference, summer, 1973; poetry prize from *Sou'wester,* 1973.

WRITINGS—Poems: *Bull Island,* Back Door Press, 1970; *Mean Rufus Throw Down,* Basilisk Press, 1973; (under name Dave Smith) *The Fisherman's Whore,* Ohio University Press, 1974.

Poems are represented in anthologies, including *I Love You All Day: It Is That Simple,* edited by Philip Dacey and Gerald Knoll, Abbey Press, 1970; *Yearbook of Modern Poetry,* edited by Jeanne Hollyfield, Young Publications, 1971; *New Voices in American Poetry,* edited by Dave Allen Evans, Winthrop, 1973; *Heartland II,* edited by Lucien Stryk, Northern Illinois University Press, in press.

Contributor, sometimes under pseudonym Smith Cornwell, of short stories, poems, articles, and reviews to popular magazines and poetry magazines, including *Nation, Southern Review, Shenandoah, Poetry Northwest, Prairie Schooner,* and *Open Places.* Editor, founder, and publisher of *Back Door;* editor of *Sou'wester,* 1967-68.

WORK IN PROGRESS: All the Early Letters (tentative title), a book of poems; *Onliness* (tentative title), a novel; compiling an anthology of sports poems, with David Allen Evans.

SIDELIGHTS: Smith told *CA:* "Any comment about one's art is apt to be suspect and fickle. In general, however, I wish to write poems and fiction which give ballast to the world as it really is, which enhance the heart's desires, which speculate in the market of small defeats and great beauties. Or, to paraphrase foolish Eisenhower, things are more like they are today than they ever were. My writing is influenced by being a Virginian and a native of the Atlantic seacoast, and by having that perspective mitigated by a number of years of residence in the Mid-West. My interests are eclectic. As an ex-athlete and coach, I have a respect for both physical and intellectual discipline. I speak French awkwardly. I believe in the engendering condition of joy any art form makes possible."

BIOGRAPHICAL/CRITICAL SOURCES: Sou'wester, spring, 1974.

* * *

SMITH, David C(layton) 1929-

PERSONAL: Born November 14, 1929, in Lewiston, Me.; son of William G. (a housepainter) and Ella (Churchill) Smith; married Sylvia White (a teacher), August 9, 1953; children: Clayton, Katherine. *Education:* Farmington State Teachers College (now University of Maine at Farmington), B.S., 1955; University of Maine, M.Ed., 1956, M.A., 1958; Cornell University, Ph.D., 1960. *Politics:* Democratic. *Home:* 5 Dunning Blvd., Bangor, Me. 04473. *Office:* Department of History, 207 East Annex, University of Maine, Orono, Me. 04473.

CAREER: Hobart and William Smith Colleges, Geneva, N.Y., instructor in history, 1960-63, historian, 1963-65; University of Maine, Orono, assistant professor, 1965-68, associate professor, 1968-73, professor of history, 1973—. Chairman of Maine Historical Preservation Commission, 1972—; president of board of trustees, Penobscot Heritage Museum of Living History, 1972—. *Military service:* U.S. Navy, 1948-52. *Member:* Agricultural History Society, Agricultural History Association, Economic History Association, Forest History Society, Maine Historical Society.

WRITINGS: (Editor with E. L. Ives) *Fleetwood Pride: A Bibliography,* Northeast Folklore Society, 1969; *A History of United States Papermaking, 1690-1970,* Lockwood Publishing, 1971; *Lumbering and the Maine Woods: A Bibliography* (monograph), Maine Historical Society, 1971; *A History of Maine Lumbering 1860-1960,* University of Maine Press, 1972. Contributor to *Business History, Forest History,* and other journals. Regular review columnist, *Maine Sunday Telegram.*

WORK IN PROGRESS: A history of the University of Maine; a literary/historical biography of H. G. Wells, completion expected in 1976.

AVOCATIONAL INTERESTS: Camping, travel, hiking.

* * *

SMITH, Don(ald Taylor) 1909-

PERSONAL: Born August 2, 1909, in Port Colborne, Ontario, Canada; son of David Russell and Rebecca (Taylor) Smith. *Education:* Attended Ridley College, St. Catharines, Ontario. *Politics:* Liberal. *Religion:* Protestant. *Home:* 33 avenue Franklin Roosevelt, Paris 75008, France. *Agent:* Blanche Gregory, 2 Tudor City Pl., New York, N.Y. 10017.

CAREER: Toronto Daily Star, Toronto, Ontario, foreign correspondent in China, 1934-39; professional yachtsman in Tangier, Morocco, 1946-52; free trader in Majorca, 1953-63; full-time writer, 1964—. *Military service:* Royal Air Force, fighter pilot, 1939-45; received Distinguished Flying Cross.

WRITINGS: Out of the Sea, Fawcett, 1952; *China Coaster,* Henry Holt, 1953; *Perilous Holiday,* Henry Holt, 1953; *Red Curtain,* Award Books, 1966; *The Man Who Played Thief,* Fawcett, 1969; *The Padrone,* Fawcett, 1971; *The Payoff,* Fawcett, 1973; *The Corsican Takeover,* Fawcett, 1974.

"Secret Mission" series, published by Universal Publishing & Distributing: *Secret Mission: Peking,* 1968; ... *Prague,* 1968; ... *Corsica,* 1968; ... *Morocco,* 1968; ... *Istanbul,* 1969; ... *Tibet,* 1969; ... *Cairo,* 1970; ... *North Korea,* 1970; ... *Angola,* 1970; ... *Munich,* 1970; ... *Athens,* 1971; ... *The Kremlin Plot,* 1971; *Death Stalk in Spain,* 1972; *The Marseilles Enforcer,* 1972; *Night of the Assassin,* 1972; *Haitian Vendetta,* 1973.

WORK IN PROGRESS: "Tim Parnell" series for Fawcett, and "Phil Sherman" series for Universal Publishing & Distributing.

* * *

SMITH, Geoffrey Sutton 1941-

PERSONAL: Born March 16, 1941, in San Francisco, Calif.; son of Harry Bell (a business executive) and Dorothy (Tuck) Smith; married Bonnie Louise Seevers, May 4, 1963; children: David Geoffrey, Brian William, Kristin Bell. *Education:* University of California, Santa Barbara, B.A., 1963, Ph.D., 1969; University of California, Berkeley, M.A., 1965. *Politics:* Independent. *Religion:* Roman Catholic. *Home:* 4231 Bath Rd., Kingston, Ontario, Canada. *Office:* Department of History, Queen's University, Kingston, Ontario, Canada.

CAREER: Chabot College, Hayward, Calif., instructor in history, 1965; Macalester College, St. Paul, Minn., instructor, 1967-69, assistant professor of history, 1969; Queen's University, Kingston, Ontario, assistant professor, 1969-73, associate professor of history, 1973—. Member, Ontario Co-operative Programme in Latin American and Caribbean Studies, 1969—. *Member:* Canadian Historical Association, American Historical Association, Organization of American Historians, Society for Historians of American Foreign Relations. *Awards, honors:* Canada Council grant, 1970, for research on American naval diplomat, Charles Wilkes, 1798-1877.

WRITINGS: To Save a Nation: American Countersubversives, the New Deal, and the Coming of World War II, Basic Books, 1973; (contributor) Arch Ritter and David Pollock, editors, *Latin American Prospects for the 1970s: What Kinds of Revolutions?,* Praeger, 1973; (contributor) Frank Merli and Theodore Wilson, editors, *Makers of American Diplomacy,* two volumes, Scribner, 1973. Contributor to *Encyclopedia Americana, Hispanic American Historical Review, Macalester College Bulletin, Pacific Historical Review,* and *Queen's Quarterly.*

WORK IN PROGRESS: Research on naval history, on domestic revisionism; a book tentatively entitled *The Bifocal Vision in American Foreign Relations: American Images of Europe and Asia,* completion expected in 1978.

AVOCATIONAL INTERESTS: Photography, film, athletics.

SMITH, George Harmon 1920-

PERSONAL: Born January 12, 1920, in Spearsville, La.; son of Harmon (a farmer) and Eva (Rogers) Smith; married Willa Horne, December 22, 1943; children: George W., Donna, Bette, James, Angela. *Education:* University of Arkansas, M.S., 1954; University of Mississippi, Advanced M.A., 1962. *Politics:* Democrat. *Religion:* Baptist. *Home address:* Box 125, Marion, La. 71260. *Agent:* Alex Jackinson, 55 West 42nd St., New York, N.Y. 10036. *Office:* Union Parish Media Center, Box 338, Farmerville, La. 71241.

CAREER: High school coach in Junction City, Ark., 1954-64; Union Parish School Board, Union Parish, La., supervisor of guidance, 1964-68; high school principal in Marion, La., 1968-72; Union Parish School Board, director of federal programs, 1972—. Mayor of Junction City, Ark., 1964-68. *Military service:* U.S. Navy, 1942-43. *Member:* Union Parish Principal's Association (president), Sigma Tau Delta. *Awards, honors: Bayou Boy* was runner-up for Sequoya Children's Book Award of Oklahoma, 1966, and received other awards.

WRITINGS—Juvenile: *Bayou Boy,* Follett, 1965; *Wanderers of the Field,* John Day, 1966; *Bayou Belle,* John Day, 1967; *Bayou Boy and the Wolf Dog,* Quality Books, 1974; *Old Crip,* Quality Books, 1974.

Also author of about fifty adult adventure and suspense novels, occasionally under pseudonyms Peter McCurtin and Frank Scarpetta, for Belmont-Tower and other publishers.

WORK IN PROGRESS: The Voice of Turtle Ann; Delta Boy; Ring Out Sweet Bell of Freedom, a bicentennial novel.

SIDELIGHTS: Smith told *CA* he believes his experience in writing suspense novels has accounted for the success of *Bayou Boy,* which was adapted for a Walt Disney film.

* * *

SMITH, Harris (Gordon) 1921-

PERSONAL: Born October 26, 1921, in Mt. Pulaski, Ill.; son of Frank D. and Mary (Anderson) Smith; married Donna Preston (an editor), August 31, 1952; children: Erik P. *Education:* University of Illinois, B.S., 1950, M.S., 1952. *Politics:* Democrat. *Religion:* Unaffiliated. *Home:* 21 Upper River Rd., Ipswich, Mass. 01938. *Office:* Division of Journalism, Boston University, 640 Commonwealth Ave., Boston, Mass. 02215.

CAREER: Chicago Sun-Times, Chicago, Ill., assistant picture editor, 1953-55; Boston University, Boston, Mass., instructor, 1955-57, assistant professor, 1957-65, associate professor of journalism, 1965—. Free-lance writer and photographer, 1955—; publisher, *Ipswich Today,* Ipswich, Mass., 1970—. *Military service:* U.S. Marine Corps, 1941-46; became major; received Distinguished Flying Cross and four air medals.

WRITINGS: Erik Visits Old Ironsides, Howard Doyle, 1971. Contributor to *National Observer* and *Ipswich Today.* New England correspondent, *National Observer,* 1965—.

* * *

SMITH, Irving H(arold) 1932-

PERSONAL: Born January 27, 1932, in Montreal, Quebec, Canada; son of Nick and Betty (Baronoff) Smith; married Estelle Horowitz, 1953; children: Lawrence, Erica, Tania. *Education:* Sir George Williams University, B.A., 1953; McGill University, M.A., 1955, Ph.D., 1963. *Office:* Department of History, Sir George Williams University, Montreal 107, Quebec, Canada.

CAREER: Texas College of Arts and Industries, Kingsville, associate professor of history, 1960-65; Michigan State University, East Lansing, assistant professor of humanities, 1965-66; Sir George Williams University, Montreal, Quebec, associate professor of history, 1966—. *Member:* American Association for the Advancement of Slavic Studies.

WRITINGS: Trotsky, Prentice-Hall, 1973. Associate editor, *Canadian-American Slavic Studies,* 1968-74.

WORK IN PROGRESS: The Modern Political Witch Hunt: A Study in Social Pathology, completion expected in 1975.

* * *

SMITH, J(ohn) Malcolm 1921-

PERSONAL: Born January 24, 1921, in Vancouver, British Columbia, Canada; son of George John (with U.S. Coast Guard) and Henrietta Smith; married Connie Grace Shaw (a school personnel employee), June 7, 1943; children: Sheila Smith Swiadon, Nancy L., Patricia L. *Education:* University of Washington, Seattle, B.A., 1946, M.A., 1948; Stanford University, Ph.D., 1951. *Home:* 1054 Avondale Lane, Hayward, Calif. 94545. *Office:* Department of Political Science, California State University, Hayward, Calif. 94542.

CAREER: Columbia University, New York, N.Y., 1950-52, member of political science faculty; University of California, 1954-57, member of political science faculty; U.S. Commission on Civil Rights, Office of U.S. Senator Kuchel, Washington, D.C., 1957-61; California State University, Hayward, professor of political science, 1965—. *Military service:* U.S. Army; became first lieutenant. *Member:* American Political Science Association, American Society of Public Administration, American Society for International Law.

WRITINGS: (With Cornelius P. Cotter) *Powers of the President during Crises,* Public Affairs Press, 1960; (co-author) *The President and National Security,* Kendall/Hunt, 1972. Contributor to *Journal of Politics, Western Political Quarterly,* and *Stanford Law Review.*

WORK IN PROGRESS: Second volume of *The President as Commander-in-Chief,* covering Kennedy through Nixon; a textbook on the presidency; research on President Eisenhower and on Horace Gray of the Supreme Court.

* * *

SMITH, Jessica 1895-

PERSONAL: Born November 29, 1895; daughter of Walter (an artist) and Jessie May (Stout) Granville-Smith; married Harold Ware, January, 1925 (died, 1935); married John Abt (a lawyer), March, 1937; children: (first marriage) David. *Education:* Swarthmore College, A.B., 1915. *Home:* 444 Central Park West, New York, N.Y. 10025. *Office: New World Review,* 156 Fifth Ave., New York, N.Y. 10010.

CAREER: New World Review, New York, N.Y., editor, 1936—. Vice-chairman, National Council of American-Soviet Friendship.

WRITINGS: Women in Soviet Russia, Vanguard, 1928; (translator from the Russian) George Baidukov, *Over the North Pole,* Harrap, 1938; (with Bayer and Brody) *War and Peace In Finland,* SRT Publications, 1940; *People Come First,* International Publishers, 1948; (editor) *The U.S.S.R. and World Peace,* International Publishers, 1949, 2nd edition, Books for Libraries, 1969; *Soviet Democracy and How It Works,* New World Review Publications, 1969; (editor with Daniel Mason) *Lenin's Impact on the United States,* New World Review Publications, 1971; (editor) *Voices of Tomorrow,* New World Review Publications, 1971. Author of pamphlets. Contributor to journals.

SIDELIGHTS: Jessica Smith has long been interested in the study and interpretation of the Soviet Union, where she has lived for five years. She has made nine trips there, the latest being in 1971, and she is competent in the Russian language.

* * *

SMITH, Larry 1940-

PERSONAL: Born October 5, 1940, in Central Lake, Mich.; son of William Lysle and Mary (Baumbach) Smith; married Dorothea Steudle (an artist), November 13, 1961; children: Stacey Louise, Jennifer Lee, Stephen Alexander. *Education:* University of Michigan, B.A., 1962. *Home:* 12 South Ferris St., Irvington, N.Y. 10533.

CAREER: Hayward Daily Review, Hayward, Calif., reporter, 1964-65; *Reporter Dispatch,* White Plains, N.Y., night editor and assistant city editor, 1965-68; *Tarrytown Daily News,* Tarrytown, N.Y., editor, 1968-69; *New York Daily News,* New York, N.Y., copy editor, 1969—.

WRITINGS: The Original (novel), Herder & Herder, 1972. Contributor of a short story to *Redbook.* Contributing editor, *Columbia Journalism Review.*

WORK IN PROGRESS: A novel for McGraw.

* * *

SMITH, T(ed) C. 1915-

PERSONAL: Born June 5, 1915, in Pineville, La.; son of Isaac Denon (an engineer) and Lillian Lee (Corley) Smith; married Ellen Bernice Stewart (a librarian), June 27, 1943; children: Taylor C., Jr., Stewart Lynn, Jeffrey Leon. *Education:* Louisiana College, A.B., 1938; Southern Baptist Theological Seminary, Th.M., 1941, Th.D., 1944; University of Edinburgh, Ph.D., 1949; Hebrew Union College, postdoctoral study, 1955-56. *Politics:* Republican. *Home:* Route 3, Tulane Ave., Greenville, S.C. 29609. *Office:* Department of Religion, Furman University, Greenville, S.C. 29613.

CAREER: Southern Baptist Theological Seminary, Louisville, Ky., 1947-58, became professor of Greek and New Testament; University of Chicago, Divinity School, Chicago, Ill., professor of New Testament, 1958-59; First Baptist Church, Mooresville, N.C., pastor, 1959-62; Berkeley Baptist Divinity School, Berkeley, Calif., professor of New Testament, 1962-66; Furman University, Greenville, S.C., professor of religion, 1966—. *Military service:* U.S. Navy, chaplain, 1945-46. U.S. Naval Reserve, chaplain; now captain. *Member:* International New Testament Congress, Association of Baptist Professors of Religion, Studiorum Novi Testamenti Societas, Society of Biblical Literature (vice-president of Western region, 1965-66), American Schools of International Research, American Academy of Religion, Kiwanis Club.

WRITINGS: Jesus in the Gospel of John, Broadman, 1959; *Commentary on Acts,* Broadman, 1970. Contributor to *Review and Expositor, Chaplain, Foundation,* and *Furman Studies.*

WORK IN PROGRESS: New Testament Theology; *The Sermon on the Mount.*

SIDELIGHTS: Smith has competence in Greek, Hebrew, Syriac, Aramaic, Latin, French, and German.

* * *

SMITH, Virginia Carlson 1944-

PERSONAL: Born June 30, 1944, in Pasadena, Calif.; daughter of Kenneth William (an administrator) and Dorothy (Stapleton) Carlson; married Clark Cornwell Smith (a contractor), January 24, 1970. *Education:* University of California, Santa Barbara, B.A. (honors), 1966; University of California, Berkeley, M.L.S., 1969. *Home:* 2509-A Bath St., Santa Barbara, Calif. 93105. *Office:* Arts Library, University of California, Santa Barbara, Calif. 93106.

CAREER: University of California, Arts Library, Santa Barbara, assistant art librarian, 1969—. *Member:* Art Libraries Society of North America.

WRITINGS: Juan de Borgona and His School: A Bibliography, Hennessey & Ingalls, 1973. Contributor to *Art Libraries Society of North America Newsletter* and *Library Trends.*

* * *

SMITH, Wilford E(mery) 1916-

PERSONAL: Born May 16, 1916, in Holladay, Utah; son of George Carlos and Lillian (Emery) Smith; married Ruth Christensen, August 31, 1940; children: Charlotte Elaine (Mrs. Kent Knudsen), Wilford Emery, Jr., Sherman Christensen, Ronald Tye, Jeffery Randall. *Education:* University of Utah, B.A. (with high honors), 1943; Brigham Young University, M.A., 1948; University of Washington, Seattle, Ph.D., 1952; postdoctoral study at Claremont Men's College, 1955, and University of Wisconsin, 1962. *Politics:* Republican. *Religion:* Church of Jesus Christ of Latter-Day Saints. *Home:* 1177 Ash Ave., Provo, Utah 84601. *Office:* Department of Sociology, 154 FOB, Brigham Young University, Provo, Utah 84601.

CAREER: Panguitch Latter-Day Saints Seminary, Panguitch, Utah, administrator, 1943-44; Brigham Young University, Provo, Utah, 1948—, now professor of sociology, tour director and teacher in residence programs in France and Austria; visiting professor at four universities. Custodial officer at Utah State Prison, 1958. Vice-president of Provo City School Board. *Military service:* U.S. Army, chaplain, 1944-46; became captain. U.S. Army Reserve, 1946—; present rank, colonel. *Member:* American Sociological Association (fellow), Academy of Political Science, American Association of University Professors, Utah Academy of Sciences, Arts, and Letters.

WRITINGS: (With others) *Introductory Sociology,* W. C. Brown, 1964; *His Work and His Glory: A Treatise on Human Free Agency,* Brigham Young University Press, 1966; *Reflections and Sentiment* (poems), Utah Printing Co., 1966; *Social Organization and Deviant Behavior,* Brigham Young University Press, 1968, revised edition, 1971.

WORK IN PROGRESS: A continuing study of the moral behavior and moral judgements of college students toward

Mormon standards which are intended to maintain certain patterns of conduct.

SIDELIGHTS: Smith states his work at the Utah State Prison, in 1958, was undertaken "to improve my understanding of penology in action."

* * *

SMITH, William Dale 1929- (David Anthony)

PERSONAL: Born July 25, 1929, in Hollidays Cove, W. Va.; son of James Harold (an open-hearth steel mill worker) and Irma (Ankrom) Smith; married Jacqueline Feldenkreis (a television executive), December 26, 1954; children: David, Elinor. *Education:* Antioch College, B.A., 1955; Stanford University, graduate study, 1956-57. *Residence:* Encino, Calif. 91396.

CAREER: Antioch Press, Yellow Springs, Ohio, editorial work and office duties, 1955-56; *San Francisco News,* San Francisco, Calif., editorial assistant and feature writer, 1957-58; free-lance writer, 1958-59; Appleton-Century-Crofts (publishers), New York, N.Y., advertising manager for trade books, 1960-61; Sussman & Sugar (advertising agency), New York, N.Y., accounting executive, 1961-67; free-lance writer, 1967—. *Military service:* U.S. Marine Corps, 1947-50, 1950-51; became staff sergeant. *Member:* Authors Guild of Authors League of America.

WRITINGS: A Multitude of Men, Simon & Schuster, 1960; *Naked in December* (novel), Bobbs-Merrill, 1968.

Under pseudonym David Anthony, mystery novels: *The Midnight Lady and the Mourning Man,* Bobbs-Merrill, 1969; *The Organization,* Coward, 1970; *Gift from a Stranger,* Pocket Books, 1972; *Blood on a Harvest Moon,* Coward, 1972.

WORK IN PROGRESS: A novelette, *Farewell, My Darling Husband;* two novels; screenplay for a television film based on *Gift from a Stranger.*

SIDELIGHTS: Smith observes, "The more novels I write and publish, the less am I able to write *about* them. Let me say simply that *Naked in December* is my most ambitious—and, in my opinion—my best novel. In it I explored . . . the discrepancy and conflict between the tenderness and toughness in the American character, between the civilized man and the savage, the man of peace at odds with the man of war—within one individual. In my suspense fiction, I have dealt with the same theme on a different level—in the vernacular, so to speak." Smith's novels have been optioned to motion pictures, issued in British, French, and Danish editions, and serialized in Australia, Norway, Spain, and South Africa.

* * *

SNAVELY, Guy Everett 1881-1974

October 26, 1881—March 12, 1974; American educator and author. Obituaries: *Washington Post,* March 25, 1974. (*CA*-5/6).

* * *

SNEED, Joseph Donald 1938-

PERSONAL: Born September 23, 1938, in Durant, Okla.; son of Dabney W. (a civil service employee) and Sallybelle (Atkinson) Sneed; married Ruta Medenis, September 5, 1962 (divorced, April 7, 1969); married Constance Gierla, October 11, 1970; children: (second marriage) Ian M. *Education:* Rice University, B.A. (summa cum laude), 1960; University of Illinois, M.S., 1962; Stanford University, Ph.D., 1964. *Home:* 121 Stanford Ave., Menlo Park, Calif. *Office:* Department of Philosophy, Stanford University, Stanford, Calif. 94305.

CAREER: Oak Ridge National Laboratory, Oak Ridge, Tenn., student trainee and research associate, summers, 1957-61; University of Michigan, Ann Arbor, assistant professor of philosophy, 1964-66; Stanford University, Stanford, Calif., assistant professor, 1966-68, associate professor of philosophy, 1968—. Visiting professor of theoretical philosophy at University of Uppsala, spring, 1969. *Member:* Phi Beta Kappa, Sigma Xi. *Awards, honors:* National Science Foundation research grants, 1966-68, 1968-70.

WRITINGS: The Logical Structure of Mathematical Physics, Reidel, 1971. Contributor of articles and reviews to professional journals.

WORK IN PROGRESS: Urban Syndrome, with others.

* * *

SNEVE, Virginia Driving Hawk 1933- (Virginia Driving Hawk)

PERSONAL: Surname rhymes with "navy"; born February 21, 1933, in Rosebud, S.D.; daughter of James H. (an Episcopal priest) and Rose (Ross) Driving Hawk; married Vance M. Sneve (a teacher of industrial arts), July 14, 1955; children: Shirley Kay, Paul Marshall, Alan Edward. *Education:* South Dakota State University, B.S., 1954, M.Ed., 1969. *Politics:* Republican. *Religion:* Episcopal. *Residence:* Flandreau, S.D.

CAREER: Teacher of English in the public schools of White, S.D., 1954-55, and Pierre, S.D., 1955-56; Flandreau Indian School, Flandreau, S.D., teacher of English and speech, 1965-66, guidance counselor, 1966-70; Brevet Press, Sioux Falls, S.D., editor, 1972—. Member of Rosebud Sioux Tribe; member of board of directors of United Sioux Tribes Cultural Arts, 1972-73. *Member:* National League of American Pen Women, South Dakota Press Women. *Awards, honors:* Manuscript award in American Indian category from Interracial Council for Minority Books for Children, 1971, for *Jimmy Yellow Hawk.*

WRITINGS: Jimmy Yellow Hawk (juvenile), Holiday House, 1972; *High Elk's Treasure* (juvenile), Holiday House, 1972; (editor) *South Dakota Geographic Names,* Brevet Press, 1973; *The Dakota's Heritage,* Brevet Press, 1973; *When Thunders Spoke* (juvenile), Holiday House, 1974; *Betrayed* (juvenile), Holiday House, 1974. Contributor to educational units on American Indians, and to journals.

WORK IN PROGRESS: Fool Soldier Society of Teton Sioux; editing a history of the Episcopal Church in South Dakota.

SIDELIGHTS: Virginia Sneve told *CA:* "In my writing, both fiction and nonfiction, I try to present an accurate portrayal of American Indian life as I have known it. I also attempt to interpret history from the viewpoint of the American Indian and in so doing I hope to correct the many misconceptions and untruths which have been too long perpetrated by non-Indian authors who have written about us."

BIOGRAPHICAL/CRITICAL SOURCES: Sioux Falls Argus-Leader, August 5, 1973.

SNOEK, J(aap) Diedrick 1931-

PERSONAL: Born January 31, 1931, in Netherlands; naturalized U.S. citizen; son of Jacob Louis (a physicist) and Atie (Loogen) Snoek; married Barbara Buchman (a weaver), July 31, 1955; children: Eric Jan, Martha Ellen. *Education:* University of Amsterdam, student, 1949-50; Western Reserve University (now Case Western Reserve University), B.A. (cum laude), 1954; University of Michigan, Ph.D., 1960. *Politics:* Liberal Democrat. *Religion:* Society of Friends (Quakers). *Home:* 38 Paradise Rd., Northampton, Mass. 01060. *Office:* Department of Psychology, Smith College, Northampton, Mass. 01060.

CAREER: University of Michigan, Ann Arbor, study director at Institute for Social Research, 1959-62; Smith College, Northampton, Mass., assistant professor, 1962-68, associate professor of psychology, 1968—. Visiting assistant professor at Carnegie-Mellon University, 1966-67. Member of board of managers, Pendle Hill, Wallingford, Pa. *Member:* American Psychological Association, Friends Conference on Religion and Psychology, Association for Humanistic Psychology, New England Psychological Association.

WRITINGS: (With Robert L. Kahn, Donald M. Wolfe, and Robert P. Quinn) *Organizational Stress,* Wiley, 1964; (with George Levinger) *Attraction in Relationship,* General Learning Press, 1972. Contributor to psychology and sociology journals. Special editor, *Journal of Social Issues,* 1969-71.

WORK IN PROGRESS: A study of women's lives through a life-history method.

AVOCATIONAL INTERESTS: Music, sailing.

* * *

SNYDER, Charles M. 1909-

PERSONAL: Born February 13, 1909, in Glen Iron, Pa.; son of Charles M. (a coal and lumber merchant) and Flora (Fessenden) Snyder; married Mary Burrowes, February 12, 1932; children: Sara Snyder Smith, Daniel M., Elizabeth (Mrs. Thomas Marston). *Education:* Bucknell University, A.B., 1930, A.M., 1933; University of Pennsylvania, Ph.D., 1949. *Politics:* Democrat. *Religion:* Lutheran. *Home:* 55 Maple St., Mifflinburg, Pa. 17844.

CAREER: State University of New York College at Oswego, assistant professor, 1946-49, associate professor, 1949-50, professor of history, 1950-73, professor emeritus, 1973—. Member of Union County (Pa.) Government Study Commission, 1974. *Military service:* U.S. Navy, 1943-45; became lieutenant. *Member:* American Historical Association, New York State Historical Association, Oswego County Historical Society (president, 1953-64), Union County Historical Society (president, 1974).

WRITINGS: The Jacksonian Heritage in Pennsylvania, Pennsylvania Historical Commission, 1958; *Dr. Mary Walker: The Little Lady in Pants,* Vantage, 1962, reprinted, Arno, 1974; *Oswego: From Buckskins to Bustles,* Kennikat, 1968; (contributor) Harry J. Sievers, editor, *New York State's Six Presidents,* Sleepy Hollow Restorations, 1974. Contributor to *Vermont History, New York History, Maryland Historical Magazine.*

WORK IN PROGRESS: Joint biographies of Dorothea Dix and Millard Fillmore, based in part upon discovery of Fillmore papers in an Oswego County farmhouse, completion expected in 1975.

SNYDER, Eldon E. 1930-

PERSONAL: Born September 6, 1930, in Anthony, Kan.; son of Murrel K. (a professor) and Frances (Roderick) Snyder; married Margaret Miller, March 20, 1951; children: Connie Lynn, Susan Linda. *Education:* Southwestern College, A.B. (magna cum laude), 1952; University of Kansas, M.S., 1956, Ed.D., 1962; University of Southern California, graduate study, 1957; Colorado University, postdoctoral study, 1962. *Religion:* Protestant. *Home:* 1102 Clark, Bowling Green, Ohio 43402. *Office:* Department of Sociology, Bowling Green State University, Bowling Green, Ohio 43403.

CAREER: Public school teacher of social studies, 1952-53, 1956-59; Kansas State Teachers College, Emporia, 1960-64, began as instructor, became associate professor of social sciences; Washburn University, Evening College, Topeka, Kan., lecturer in sociology, 1964; Bowling Green State University, Bowling Green, Ohio, assistant professor, 1964-67, associate professor, 1967-71, professor of sociology, 1971—, coordinator of Sociology Block of Summer Institute for Teachers of Disadvantaged Youth, 1965, 1966. Visiting lecturer at Western Michigan University, 1965 (summer). *Military service:* U.S. Army, 1953-55; became sergeant first class. *Member:* International Committee of Sport Sociology, American Sociological Association, American Association of University Professors, Ohio Valley Sociological Association, Pi Gamma Mu, Pi Kappa Delta, Phi Delta Kappa, Alpha Kappa Delta. *Awards, honors:* National Science Foundation institutional research grant; U.S. Office of Education research grant; Danforth Foundation summer fellow, 1961.

WRITINGS: (Contributor) Joseph S. Roucek, editor, *Programmed Teaching,* Philosophical Library, 1965; (contributor) Dorothy Rogers, editor, *Issues in Adolescent Psychology,* Appleton, 1969; (contributor) Lawrence W. Drabick, editor, *Interpreting Education: A Sociological Approach,* Appleton, 1971; (editor with Joseph E. Kivlin) *Studies in Sociology,* Kendall-Hunt, 1971; (contributor) Robert V. Guthrie and Edward J. Barnes, editors, *Man and Society,* James Freel, 1972; (contributor) R. Serge Denisoff, editor, *The Sociology of Radical Dissent,* Harcourt, 1972; (contributor) James H. Humphrey and Anne Gayle Ingram, editors, *Sociological Aspects of Sport: A Contemporary Anthology,* Appleton, in press. Contributor of articles and book reviews to *Adolescence, International Review of Sport Sociology, Pacific Sociological Review, Sociological Quarterly,* and other journals in his field.

WORK IN PROGRESS: Sociology of Sport and Leisure; Sex Roles of Women Athletes.

* * *

SOKOL, David M(artin) 1942-

PERSONAL: Born November 3, 1942, in New York, N.Y.; son of Harry (a businessman) and Ruth (Waldman) Sokol; married Sandra Schorr, June 15, 1963; children: Adam, Andrew. *Education:* Hunter College of the City University of New York, A.B., 1963; New York University, A.M., 1966, Ph.D., 1971. *Politics:* Independent. *Religion:* Jewish. *Home:* 330 South Taylor Ave., Oak Park, Ill. 60302. *Office:* History of Architecture and Art Department, University of Illinois at Chicago Circle, Chicago, Ill. 60680.

CAREER: City University of New York, New York, N.Y., lecturer in art at Bronx Community College, 1965-

66, instructor in art at Kingsborough Community College, 1966-68; Western Illinois University, Macomb, assistant professor of art, 1968-71; University of Illinois at Chicago Circle, associate professor of art history, 1971—. *Member:* American Association of University Professors, College Art Association, American Society for Aesthetics.

WRITINGS: John Quidor: Painter of American Legend, Wichita Art Museum, 1973. Contributor of articles and book reviews to *American Art Journal, Journal of Aesthetics and Art Criticism, Antiques, Art Journal,* and *American Art Review.*

WORK IN PROGRESS: A bibliographical volume on American art and architecture for the Gale "Information Guide" Series, publication expected in 1975; a series of articles for *American Art Review.*

* * *

SOLOMON, Kenneth Ira 1942-

PERSONAL: Born February 1, 1942, in Chicago, Ill.; son of Morris (an attorney) and Frieda (Krupka) Solomon; married Ellen F. Lewis, January 31, 1965; children: David, Michael, Todd. *Education:* University of Illinois, B.S. (with highest honors), 1963, M.S., 1964; University of Chicago, J.D., 1967. *Home:* 7840 Church, Morton Grove, Ill. 60053. *Office:* Laventhol Krekstein Horwath & Horwath, 111 East Wacker, Chicago, Ill. 60601.

CAREER: Certified public accountant in Illinois; admitted to Bar of State of Illinois, 1967; Chicago City College, Chicago, Ill., assistant professor of accounting, 1964-67; Case Western Reserve University, Cleveland, Ohio, professor of law, 1967-68; Laventhol Krekstein Horwath & Horwath (certified public accountants), Chicago, Ill., partner, 1968—. Curriculum consultant to Walton School of Commerce. *Member:* American Institute of Certified Public Accountants, Decalogue Society of Lawyers, Young Men's Jewish Council (member of board of directors, 1972—), Illinois Society of Certified Public Accountants, Chicago Bar Association.

WRITINGS: Lawyer's Handbook of Accounting Theory and Practice, Commerce Clearing House, 1971; (with Norman Katz) *Profitable Restaurant Management,* Prentice-Hall, 1974. Contributor to journals in his field.

* * *

SOLOT, Mary Lynn 1939-

PERSONAL: Born May 7, 1939, in New York, N.Y.; daughter of Leonard M. and Virginia (Wise) Marx; married Edwin Lee Solot (a lawyer), June 24, 1962; children: Edwin Lee, Jr., Claire. *Education:* Sarah Lawrence College, B.A., 1962. *Home:* Havemeyer Rd., Ardsley-on-Hudson, N.Y. 10503.

CAREER: Free-lance writer; composer of music for children's theatre, and song writer.

WRITINGS—Juvenile: *100 Hamburgers,* Lothrop, 1972.

WORK IN PROGRESS: Several juvenile books.

* * *

SOLTIS, Andrew 1947-

PERSONAL: Born May 28, 1947, in Hazleton, Pa.; son of Andrew Edward (an engineer) and Bette K. (Eden) Soltis. *Education:* City College of the City University of New York, B.A. (cum laude), 1969. *Politics:* Republican. *Religion:* Methodist. *Home:* 117 West 13th St., New York, N.Y. 10011. *Office: New York Post,* 210 South St., New York, N.Y. 10002.

CAREER: New York Post, New York, N.Y., reporter, 1969—. *Member:* International Association of Chess Reporters, Marshall Chess Club (member of the board of governors, 1970—). *Awards, honors:* Senior Master, one of twenty highest rated players in the United States, by U.S. Chess Federation, 1971—.

WRITINGS: Best Games of Boris Spassky, McKay, 1973; (with Fred Reinfeld) *Morphy Masterpieces,* Macmillan, 1974.

WORK IN PROGRESS: With Arthur Bisguier, *American Chess Champions from Morphy to Fischer; Great Chess Tournaments and Their Stories.*

* * *

SOMMER, Elyse 1929-

PERSONAL: Born January 26, 1929; daughter of Julius (a businessman) and Meta (Bluethenthal) Vorchheimer; married Mike Sommer (a salesman), May 24, 1952; children: Paul, Joellen. *Education:* New York University, B.Sc., 1949. *Address:* P.O. Box E, Woodmere, N.Y. 11598.

CAREER: Elyse Sommer, Inc. (literary agency), Woodmere, N.Y., owner and president, 1952—. Teacher of crafts in high school and adult education classes; also teacher of adult illiterates. *Member:* American Crafts Council, Long Island Craftsmen's Guild.

WRITINGS: Decoupage Old and New, Watson-Guptill, 1971; *The Bread Dough Craft Book,* Lothrop, 1972; (with daughter, Joellen Sommer) *Sew Your Own Accessories,* Lothrop, 1972; *Designing without Outs,* Lothrop, 1973; *Rock and Stone Craft,* Crown, 1973; *Make It with Burlap,* Lothrop, 1973; *Contemporary Costume Jewelry: A Multimedia Approach,* Crown, in press. Contributor to *Writer's Digest* and *Creative Crafts.* Formerly wrote monthly newsletter for writers.

WORK IN PROGRESS: Creating with Driftwood and Weathered Wood, for Crown.

* * *

SOMMERFELDT, John R(obert) 1933-

PERSONAL: Born February 4, 1933, in Detroit, Mich.; son of Melvin J. (an engineer) and Virginia (Gruenheck) Sommerfeldt; married Patricia N. Levinske, August 25, 1956; children: Ann, James, John, Elizabeth. *Education:* University of Michigan, A.B., 1954, A.M., 1956, Ph.D., 1960; graduate study at University of Freiburg, 1954-55, and University of Notre Dame, 1955-56; Western Michigan University, postdoctoral study, 1973—. *Politics:* Republican. *Religion:* Roman Catholic. *Home:* 1709 Greenbriar Dr., Kalamazoo, Mich. 49008. *Office:* Medieval Institute, Western Michigan University, Kalamazoo, Mich. 49001.

CAREER: Stanford University, Stanford, Calif., instructor in history, 1958-59; Western Michigan University, Kalamazoo, instructor, 1959-60, assistant professor, 1960-63, associate professor, 1963-65, professor of history, 1965—, director of Medieval Institute, 1961—, executive director of Institute of Cistercian Studies, 1973—. President of Cistercian Publications.

WRITINGS: (Editor) *Studies in Medieval Culture,* Western Michigan University Press, Volume I, 1964, Volume II, 1966, Volume III, 1970, Volume IV, Part 1,

1973, Volume IV, Part 2, and Volume IV, Part 3, 1974; (editor) *Studies in Medieval Cistercian History,* two volumes, Cistercian Publications, in press.

WORK IN PROGRESS: An Intellectual History of the Cistercian Order in the Twelfth and Thirteenth Centuries.

* * *

SONDERMANN, Fred A. 1923-

PERSONAL: Born December 20, 1923; son of Walter S. and Hedwig (Eltzbacher) Sondermann; married Marion Obermeyer (a school counselor), January 29, 1950; children: Eric Warren, Gary Frank, Judy Ellen. *Education:* Butler University, A.B., 1949; Indiana University, M.A., 1950; Yale University, Ph.D., 1953. *Politics:* Democratic. *Religion:* Jewish. *Home:* 1809 North Tejon St., Colorado Springs, Colo. 80907. *Office:* Department of Political Science, Colorado College, Colorado Springs, Colo. 80903.

CAREER: Colorado College, Colorado Springs, instructor, 1953-55, assistant professor, 1955-58, associate professor, 1958-64, professor of political science, 1964—. Associate of Graduate School of International Studies, University of Denver, 1970—. Member of Colorado Springs Planning Commission, 1960-64; member of county executive committee of Democratic Party, 1970-72; president of Citizens Lobby for Sensible Growth, 1971-72; chairman of Colorado Springs Public Housing Authority, 1972-73. *Military service:* U.S. Army, 1943-46; served in South Pacific. *Member:* International Studies Association, American Political Science Association, Association of American University Professors, Western Political Science Association.

WRITINGS: (Editor with David S. Maclellan and William C. Olson) *Theory and Practice of International Relations,* Prentice-Hall, 1960, 4th edition, 1974. Editor of *International Studies Quarterly,* 1967-71. Contributor to journals.

* * *

SONNEBORN, Ruth (Cantor) 1899-1974

October 14, 1899—February 24, 1974; American author of children's books. Obituaries: *New York Times,* February 27, 1974. (*CA*-21/22).

* * *

SONSTEGARD, Manford Aldrich 1911-

PERSONAL: Born February 23, 1911, in Kandiyohi County, Minn.; son of Peter Olaf (a farmer) and Selma (Stenerson) Sonstegard; married Ruth Dorthea Porisch, August 27, 1939 (died, 1967); children: Karen, Kirsten, Tamar (Mrs. Terry Williams), Valerie. *Education:* St. Cloud State College, B.E., 1937; University of Minnesota, M.A., 1941; Northwestern University, Ph.D., 1952. *Home:* 329 Wagner Rd., Morgantown, W.Va. 26505. *Office:* School of Medicine, West Virginia University, Morgantown, W.Va. 26506.

CAREER: Teacher in Minnesota, 1930-42, in rural schools, 1930-34, as elementary principal, 1935-36, and junior high school principal, 1937-42; Chadron State College, Chadron, Neb., associate professor of social science, 1945; Iowa State Teachers College (now University of Northern Iowa), Cedar Falls, assistant professor, 1945-49, associate professor of education, 1950-55; U.S. Operations Mission/Ethiopia, adviser on teacher education, 1955-57; Iowa State Teachers College, director of guidance and counseling, Malcolm Price Laboratory School, 1957-63, professor of teaching, 1959-63; Southern Illinois University, Edwardsville Campus, professor of guidance and educational psychology, 1963-67; West Virginia University, Morgantown, professor of guidance and counseling, 1967—. *Military service:* U.S. Navy, 1943-45.

MEMBER: American Society of Adlerian Psychology (president, 1963-65), National Society for the Study of Education, National Education Association, American Personnel and Guidance Association, American Society of Group Psychotherapy and Psychodrama, American Psychological Association, National Society of College Teachers of Education, Association for Higher Education, West Virginia Education Association, New York Academy of Sciences, Phi Delta Kappa. *Awards, honors:* Distinguished Alumni Award, St. Cloud State College, 1971.

WRITINGS: (With Rudolph Dreikurs, R. J. Corsini, and Ray Lowe) *Adlerian Family Counseling: A Manual for Counselors,* University of Oregon Press, 1959; (contributor) Corsini and D. D. Howard, editors, *Critical Incidents in Teaching,* Prentice-Hall, 1964; (contributor) G. N. Gazda, editor, *Basic Approaches to Group Psychotherapy and Counseling,* C. C Thomas, 1968; *The Basic Principles and Rationale of Group Counseling* (pamphlet), Chronicle Guidance Publications, 1968; (contributor) D. C. Dinkmeyer, editor, *Guidance and Counseling in the Elementary School,* Holt, 1968. Contributor to professional journals. Editor, *Individual Psychologist,* 1967-74, and *ASAP Calendar Newsletter,* 1967-73.

WORK IN PROGRESS: Two books, *Perhaps You Are Not a Failure* and *Oh! Those Kids;* research on the effectiveness of the para-professional counselor, on change of parent self-concept as a result of group counseling, and on family education center programs.

* * *

SORRENTINO, Joseph N. 193(?)-

PERSONAL: Born in Brooklyn, N.Y.; son of Nicholas (a street sweeper) and Angelina Sorrentino. *Education:* University of California, Santa Barbara, B.A. (magna cum laude), 1963, M.A., 1969; Harvard University, J.D. (and valedictorian of Law School), 1967; Oxford University, further study, 1969. *Religion:* Christianity. *Home:* 12131 Mayfield, Brentwood, Calif. 90291. *Agent:* (Lectures) American Program Bureau. *Office:* 1901 Avenue of Stars, Los Angeles, Calif. 90067.

CAREER: Went to work at fourteen after flunking out of high school four times; failed at about thirty factory and laboring jobs before enlisting in U.S. Marines, 1955; booted out of Marines with a general discharge (as an incorrigible), he attended Erasmus Hall High School nights while working days in a supermarket, graduating with highest honors in the night school's history; after graduating with honors from University of California, reenlisted in Marines, 1963-66, to wipe out the general discharge, and became a platoon leader; admitted to California Bar, 1967; practiced law as partner in Olsen & Sorrentino, Los Angeles, Calif., 1967-72; University of California, Santa Barbara, professor of law, 1970—. Public lecturer, traveling in forty-five states; guest on network television programs, including "Tonight" and "Mike Douglas Show." Active in Sugar Ray Robinson Youth Foundation. *Awards, honors:* Golden Glove finalist, 1954; *Up from Never* was an American Library Association Notable Book, 1971; National University Extension Association Award for outstanding creative program, 1971.

WRITINGS: Up from Never (autobiographical), Prentice-Hall, 1971; *The Moral Revolution,* Nash Publishing, 1972.

WORK IN PROGRESS: New Man for a Better World.

* * *

SOUZA, Steven M. 1953-

PERSONAL: Born November 3, 1953, in New Bedford, Mass.; son of Arthur A. (a machinist) and Helen (Macedo) Souza. *Education:* Stonehill College, student, 1971—. *Politics:* Independent. *Religion:* Catholic. *Home:* 7 North Anthony Dr., Acushnet, Mass. 02743.

MEMBER: American Chemical Society.

WRITINGS: The Espers (fiction), Lenox Hill Press, 1972.

* * *

SPAATZ, Carl A(ndrew) 1891-1974

June 28, 1891—July 14, 1974; American Army officer, aviator, and first Air Force Chief of Staff. Obituaries: *New York Times,* July 15, 1974; *Washington Post,* July 15, 1974; *Time,* July 29, 1974; *Newsweek,* July 29, 1974.

* * *

SPALATIN, Christopher 1909-

PERSONAL: Born October 15, 1909, in Ston, Croatia, Yugoslavia; son of Simon (an internal revenue official) and Frances (Carevic) Spalatin; married Helen Barabas (a professor of languages), February 15, 1937; children: Mario, Christopher, Ivo. *Education:* University of Zagreb, M.A., 1931, Ph.D., 1934; University of Paris, graduate study, 1931-32. *Religion:* Roman Catholic. *Home:* 3909 West Oklahoma Ave., Milwaukee, Wis. 53215. *Office:* Department of French, Marquette University, 526 North 14th St., Milwaukee, Wis. 53233.

CAREER: University of Zagreb, Zagreb, Croatia, lector in French, 1935-41; University of Rome, Rome, Italy, lector in Croatian, 1941-48; Iowa Wesleyan College, Mount Pleasant, professor of languages, 1948-52; Marquette University, Milwaukee, Wis., professor of French, 1952—. *Member:* Modern Language Association of America, Croatian Academy of America, Croatian Civic Club.

WRITINGS: Saint Evremond (in French), Azinger (Zagreb), 1934; (editor) *Croatia: Land, People, Culture,* University of Toronto Press, Volume I, 1964, Volume II, 1970. Translator from French to Croation, Daniel-Rops' *Communisme et les chretiens,* [Zagreb], 1937.

WORK IN PROGRESS: Editing the third volume of *Croatia: Land, People, Culture;* research in false cognates in the Croatian language.

* * *

SPARROW, (John Walter) Gerald 1903-

PERSONAL: Born in 1903, in Buxton, Derbyshire, England; married, wife's name Chaluey. *Education:* Cambridge University, B.A., 1925, LL.B., 1925. *Home:* 31 Sussex Sq., Brighton 67754, England. *Agent:* Robert Stepwood Organization, 67 Brook St., London W.1, England.

CAREER: Barrister-at-law of Inner Temple; International Court, Bangkok, Thailand, judge, 1930-45; writer, 1953—. *Member:* Authors Club. *Awards, honors:* Knight commander of Order of the Crown of Thailand.

WRITINGS: Land of the Moonflower (memoirs of Siam), Elek, 1955; *The Sphinx Awakes,* R. Hale, 1956; *Opium Venture,* R. Hale, 1957; *Murder Parade,* R. Hale, 1957, Roy, 1967 *Return Ticket,* R. Hale, 1958; *The Star Sapphires* (memoirs of Siam), Jarrolds, 1958; *The Great Swindlers,* John Long, 1959; *How to Become an M.P.,* Anthony Blond, 1959.

How to Become a Millionaire, Anthony Blond, 1960; *Hussein of Jordan,* Harrap, 1960; *Lawyer at Large,* John Long, 1960; *Modern Jordan,* Allen & Unwin, 1961; *Not Wisely But Too Well,* Harrap, 1961; *No Other Elephant,* Jarrolds, 1961; *Gordon: Mandarin and Pasha,* Jarrolds, 1962; *The Great Imposters,* John Long, 1962; *The Golden Orchid,* Jarrolds, 1963; *The Great Forgers,* John Long, 1963; *The Great Abductors,* John Long, 1964; *Visiting Egypt,* Jarrolds, 1964; *Churchill: Man of the Century, 1874-1965,* Odhams, 1965; *Confessions of an Eccentric,* Jarrolds, 1965; *The Great Traitors,* John Long, 1965; *"R.A.B.": Study of a Statesman, The Career of Baron Butler of Saffron Walden, C.H.,* Odhams, 1965; *Rhodesia: An Independent Presentation of the Facts,* Knightly Vernon, 1966; *Satan's Children,* Odhams, 1966; *The Great Deceivers,* John Long, 1967, Roy, 1968; *Rhodesia in "Rebellion",* Knightly Vernon, 1967; *The Great Assassins,* John Long, 1968, Arco, 1969; *The Great Defenders,* John Long, 1968; *Gang Warfare: A Probe into the Changing Pattern of British Crime,* Feature Books, 1968; *The Great Spies,* John Long, 1969; *The Great Conspirators,* John Long, 1969; *Sanctions,* British Commonwealth Union, 1969.

Women Who Murder, Arthur Barker, 1970; *The Great Defamers,* John Long, 1970; *Vintage Victorian Murder,* Arthur Barker, 1971, Hart Publishing, 1972; *Vintage Edwardian Murder,* Arthur Barker, 1971; *Vintage Murder of the Twenties,* Arthur Barker, 1972.

Also author of a television play, "The Great Bullion Robbery," and radio plays, including "The Bank Clerk."

SIDELIGHTS: The rights to *Opium Venture, Java Weed,* and *The Golden Orchid* have been sold to film production companies.

* * *

SPEARING, Judith (Mary Harlow) 1922-

PERSONAL: Born November 29, 1922, in Boston, Mass.; daughter of Ralph Volney (a historian and writer) and Judith (Moss) Harlow; married Edward A. Spearing (a chemical engineer), September 21, 1942; children: Peter, Sara, Diana, Janet. *Education:* Attended Syracuse University, 1940-42. *Politics:* Independent. *Religion:* Episcopalian. *Home:* 241 High St., Chagrin Falls, Ohio 44022. *Agent:* Carolyn Willyoung Stagg, Lester Lewis Associates, 156 East 52nd St., New York, N.Y. 10022.

CAREER: Free Public Library, Elizabeth, N.J., reference assistant, 1946-51; Chagrin Falls Branch, Cuyahoga County Library, Chagrin Falls, Ohio, adult and children's services assistant, 1961—.

WRITINGS—Children's books: *Ghosts Who Went to School,* Atheneum, 1966; *Museum House Ghosts,* Atheneum, 1969. Contributor of short stories to *Episcopalian, New Ingenue,* and *American Girl.*

WORK IN PROGRESS: A mystery for children.

AVOCATIONAL INTERESTS: Gardening, sewing.

* * *

SPENCE, Eleanor (Rachel) 1928-

PERSONAL: Born October 21, 1928, in Sydney, New

South Wales, Australia; daughter of William Charles (a farmer) and Eleanor (Henderson) Kelly; married John A. Spence (a management consultant), June 17, 1952; children: Alister Martin, Nigel Henderson, Lisette Eleanor. *Education:* University of Sydney, B.A., 1949. *Religion:* Church of England. *Home:* 11 Handley Ave., Turramurra, New South Wales 2074, Australia.

CAREER: Author of children's books. Commonwealth Public Service Board, Canberra, Australia, librarian, 1950-52; Coventry City Libraries, Coventry, England, children's librarian, 1952-54; Autistic Children's Association of New South Wales, Sydney, Australia, teaching assistant, 1974—. *Member:* Autistic Children's Association of New South Wales, Australian Society of Authors, Royal Australian Historical Society. *Awards, honors:* Australian Children's Book of the Year award, 1964, for *The Green Laurel.*

WRITINGS—Children's books; all published by Oxford University Press, except as noted: *Patterson's Track,* 1958; *Summer in Between,* 1959; *Lillipilly Hill,* 1961, Roy, 1963; *The Green Laurel,* 1963, Roy, 1965; *The Year of the Currawong,* Roy, 1965; *The Switherby Pilgrims,* Roy, 1967; *Jamberoo Road,* Roy, 1969; *The Nothing Place,* 1972, Harper, 1973; *Time to Go Home,* 1973; *The Travels of Hermann,* Collins, 1973.

SIDELIGHTS: Mrs. Spence told *CA* that she became interested in writing Australian fiction for children as a result of her work as a librarian in Coventry, where there was a lack of reading matter for children of families intending to move to Australia. She is keeping journals of her work with autistic and handicapped children for possible literary use in the future.

* * *

SPENCER, Charles 1920-

PERSONAL: Born August 26, 1920, in London, England; son of Samuel (a merchant) and Henrietta (Cohen) Spencer. *Education:* Attended Courtauld Institute of Art of University of London; studied privately in Italy. *Politics:* None. *Religion:* Jewish. *Home:* 44 Grove End Rd., #11, London NW8 9NE, England. *Agent:* Mrs. C. Bernard, 7 Well Rd., London NW3, England.

CAREER: Anglo-Jewish Association, London, England, director, 1956-66; Grosvenor Gallery, London, England, consultant, 1966-71; *Art and Artists,* London, England, 1968-71; Editions Alecto, London, England, editor, 1971—. Lecturer in British art colleges, and for British Council abroad. Trustee for Camden Arts Centre. *Member:* International Association of Art Critics (honorary secretary for British section).

WRITINGS: Erte, C. N. Potter, 1970; *The Aesthetic Movement,* St. Martin's, 1973; *A Decade of Print Making,* St. Martin's, 1973; *Alecto Monographs,* Editions Alecto, 1973; *Leon Bakst,* St. Martin's, 1974. Art critic for European edition of *New York Times* (Paris) and *London Daily Mail.* Contributor to yearbooks and annuals; contributor to art journals all over the world.

WORK IN PROGRESS: Editing a series of books on famous theatrical figures of the last hundred years; books on Sir Lawrence Alma Tadema, painter, and Sir Cecil Beaton, stage designer.

* * *

SPERKA, Joshua S. 1905-

PERSONAL: Born November 15, 1905, in Poland; came to United States, 1921; son of Shlomo (a clergyman) and Leeba (Friedman) Sperka; married Yetta Peiman, May 31, 1931; children: Shlomo, Joel J., Judith (Mrs. Matthew Clark), Ahava R. (Mrs. Leon Ehrenpreis). *Education:* Hebrew Theological College, Rabbi, 1930; Lewis Institute of Chicago, B.S., 1931; University of Michigan, M.A., 1933; graduate study at Columbia University, and University of Chicago. *Home:* 14281 Wales Ave., Oak Park, Mich. 48237. *Office:* Young Israel, 15140 East Ten Mile Rd., Oak Park, Mich. 48237.

CAREER: Rabbi in Mt. Clemens, Mich., in Ann Arbor, Mich., and Detroit, Mich., before 1961; Congregation Young Israel of Greenfield, Oak Park, Mich., rabbi, 1961—. Chaplain of Michigan State Prisons, 1937-55. Regional president of Jewish National Fund, American Jewish Congress, and Hapoel Hamizrachi; vice-president of Religious Zionists of Detroit; member of board of governors of Jewish Welfare Federation, Jewish Community Center, Yeshiva Beth Yedudah, and Akiva. *Member:* American Prison Chaplains Association (secretary), Council of Orthodox Rabbis.

WRITINGS: Eternal Life, Bloch, 1939, 2nd edition, 1945; *Proverbs to Live By,* Bloch, 1967; *Ecclesiastes: Stories to Live By,* Bloch, 1971.

WORK IN PROGRESS: A manuscript on *The Book of Job.*

SIDELIGHTS: Sperka has travelled widely in Israel and Europe.

* * *

SPERLING, John G(len) 1921-

PERSONAL: Born January 9, 1921, in Willow Springs, Mo.; son of Leon (a farmer) and Lena (McNama) Sperling; married Virginia Vandegrift, 1951 (divorced, 1965); children: Peter Vandegrift. *Education:* Reed College, B.A., 1948; University of California, Berkeley, M.A., 1950; King's College, Cambridge, Ph.D., 1955. *Home:* 580 East William St., San Jose, Calif. 95112. *Office:* Department of Humanities, California State University, San Jose, Calif. 95192.

CAREER: California State University, San Jose, Calif., professor of humanities, 1960—. *Military service:* U.S. Army Air Forces, 1941-44. *Member:* American Federation of Teachers. *Awards, honors:* Ehrman Fellow at King's College, Cambridge University, 1953-55.

WRITINGS: The South Sea Company, Baker Library, Harvard University, 1962; (with Suzanne Helburn) *Economic Concepts and Institutions,* Addison-Wesley, 1974; *Industry Performance,* Addison-Wesley, 1974; *National Economic Policies,* Addison-Wesley, 1974; *Social and Economic Priorities,* Addison-Wesley, in press; *Communist Economies,* Addison-Wesley, in press; *Third World Economies,* Addison-Wesley, in press.

WORK IN PROGRESS: A volume on the impact of collective bargaining on governance in higher education.

* * *

SPERRY, (Sally) Baxter 1914- (S.S.E.)

PERSONAL: Born July 10, 1914, in Wurzburg, Germany; daughter of John Augustus (a physician) and Lillian (Mason) Sperry; married Sterling Robert Newman, March 16, 1934 (divorced, 1941). *Education:* Attended California

School of Fine Arts, 1928-30; Saline-Johnstone Business College, 1931-32; University of California, Berkeley, 1943; San Francisco College for Women (now Lone Mountain College), B.A., 1956; San Francisco State College (now University), M.A., 1958; Washington State University, additional graduate study, 1960-62. *Residence:* Galt, Calif. *Office address:* Laurel Hill Press, P. O. Box 202, Galt, Calif. 95632.

CAREER: Utah Magazine, Salt Lake City, women's editor, 1937-38; U.S. Army, Okinawa, teacher, 1951, writer, 1952-53; U.S. Navy, Philippine Islands, teacher, 1956; teacher in Sacramento County, Calif., 1958-59; California Redwood Association, San Francisco, editorial writer and assistant director of public relations, 1963; California Department of Rehabilitation, Los Angeles, counselor, 1966-67; Laurel Hill Press and Covenant Press, Galt, Calif., publisher, 1968—. Currently director of Galt Bicentennial Commission. *Member:* California Teachers Association, American Security Council, San Joaquin County Historical Association, Dry Creek Antiquarian Association (secretary, 1968—), Sacramento County Property Owners Association (chairman of Galt chapter, 1969—), Psi Chi. *Awards, honors:* Third prize from San Francisco Browning Society, 1968, for dramatic monologue, *Nikita, Prophet.*

WRITINGS—All under name Baxter Sperry, except as noted: (Under initials S. S. E.) *Mad Dog Daze,* privately printed, 1951; *Long Remember,* privately printed, 1957.

Cruachan, Peach Pit Press, 1966; *Ne Obliviscaris,* privately printed, 1967; *Nikita, Prophet,* Covenant Press, 1968; *Senator Joe McCarthy, Martyr,* Covenant Press, 1968; *This King, No Crown in Heaven,* Covenant Press, 1968; *Spring* (first volume in "Star Storm" Sonnet series), Covenant Press, 1968; *For Our Long Future's Sake,* Covenant Press, 1969; *Death is a Moment's Wonder,* Covenant Press, 1969; *Dramatic Monologues,* Laurel Hill Press, 1969.

Old Buildings, Sacramento, etc., Laurel Hill Press, 1970; *The City of Galt,* Laurel Hill Press, 1970; *Recollections of Joe Woodard,* Laurel Hill Press, 1971; *Recollections of Maude Quiggle Proctor,* Laurel Hill Press, 1971; *Summer* (second volume, "Star Storm" series), Laurel Hill Press, 1971; *Recollections of Jim Sawyer,* Laurel Hill Press, 1972; Reincarnation, *Laurel Hill Press, 1974;* Recollections of Eloisa Del Castillo Sifers, *Laurel Hill Press, 1974;* Engravings of Galt, *Laurel Hill Press, 1974.*

WORK IN PROGRESS: Other recollections of aged local people in Sacramento County, usually of Gold Rush era, for a book, *Recollections: Autumn, Winter, Second Spring,* and other books, all for "Star Storm" series, which will eventually include 855 poems.

BIOGRAPHICAL/CRITICAL SOURCES: California Librarian, April, 1972; *American Book Collector,* May-June, 1973.

* * *

SPERRY, Stuart M(ajor) 1929-

PERSONAL: Born February 22, 1929, in New York, N.Y.; son of Stuart Major (a businessman) and Doris (Laidlaw) Sperry; married Sophie Zeytoon, June 11, 1966. *Education:* Princeton University, A.B., 1951; Harvard University, M.A., 1955, Ph.D., 1959. *Politics:* Independent. *Home:* 908 South Hill St., Bloomington, Ind. 47401. *Office:* Department of English, Indiana University, Bloomington, Ind. 47405.

CAREER: Indiana University, Bloomington, lecturer, 1958-59, instructor, 1959-62, assistant professor, 1962-65, associate professor of English, beginning 1965. Visiting associate professor at University of California, Riverside, 1968-69. *Military service:* U.S. Army, Artillery, 1951-53; became first lieutenant; received Bronze Star and Purple Heart. *Member:* Modern Language Association of America. *Awards, honors:* Essay prize, Wordsworth Bicentenary Colloquium at Temple University, 1970.

WRITINGS: Keats the Poet, Princeton University Press, 1973.

* * *

SPILKA, Arnold 1917-

PERSONAL: Born November 13, 1917, in New York, N.Y.; son of Charles (a designer) and Celia (Altner) Spilka. *Education:* Studied evenings at Art Students' League, New York. *Residence:* New York, N.Y.

CAREER: Sculptor, painter, and writer and illustrator of children's books.

WRITINGS—Self-illustrated: *Whom Shall I Marry?,* Holiday House, 1960; *Aloha from Bobby,* Walck, 1962; *Paint All Kinds of Pictures,* Walck, 1963; *A Lion I Can Do Without* (nonsense poems), Walck, 1964; *Little Birds Don't Cry,* Viking, 1965; *Once Upon a Horse* (nonsense poems), Walck, 1966; *A Rumbudgin of Nonsense* (nonsense poems), Scribner, 1970; *The Frog Went "BLAH"* (nonsense poems), Scribner, 1972.

Illustrator: Beman Lord, *The Trouble With Francis,* Walck, 1958; Michael Sage, *If You Talk to a Boar,* Lippincott, 1960; Lord, *Quarterback's Aim,* Walck, 1960; Sage, *Words Inside Words,* Lippincott, 1961; Lord, *Guards for Matt,* Walck, 1961; Lord, *Bats and Balls,* Walck, 1962; Don Lang and Sage, *New Star in a Big Cage,* Lippincott, 1963; Lord, *Rough Ice,* Walck, 1963; Lord, *Mystery Guard at Left End,* Walck, 1964; Adele and Cateau De Leeuw, *The Salty Skinners,* Little, Brown, 1964; Robert Froman, *Faster and Faster* (Junior Literary Guild selection), Viking, 1965; Solveig Paulson Russell, *Lines and Shapes,* Walck, 1965; John Lawson, *You Better Come Home With Me,* Crowell, 1966; Aileen Fisher, *Best Little House,* Crowell, 1966; Sage, *Deep in a Haystack,* Viking, 1966; Sage, *Careful Carlos,* Holiday House, 1967; Sage, *Dippy Dos and Don'ts,* Viking, 1967; Ann McGovern, reteller, *Robin Hood of Sherwood Forest,* Crowell, 1968; Sage, *The Tree and Me,* Walck, 1970; Lee Bennett Hopkins, compiler, *Poems to Remember,* Scholastic Book Services, 1973.

* * *

SPINDLER, Louise Schaubel 1917-

PERSONAL: Born March 4, 1917, in Chicago, Ill.; daughter of Louis A. (a lawyer) and Cora (Field) Schaubel; married George Spindler (a professor, author, and editor), May 29, 1942; children: Sue (Mrs. Harry Lloyd Walker). *Education:* Carroll College, Waukesha, Wis., B.A., 1938; graduate study, University of Wisconsin, 1947-49, and University of California, Los Angeles, 1949-50; Stanford University, M.A., 1952, Ph.D., 1956. *Home:* 4750 Alpine Rd., Portola Valley, Calif. 94025. *Office:* Department of Anthropology, Stanford University, Stanford, Calif. 94305.

CAREER: Park Falls High School, Park Falls, Wis., teacher of English and dramatics, 1940-42; University of Wisconsin, Madison, research assistant in anthropology,

1947-49; University of California, Los Angeles, research assistant in anthropology, 1949-50; Stanford University, Stanford, Calif., teaching assistant in anthropology, 1950-54, assistant coordinator of culture change program, 1954-57, research associate, 1957-70, lecturer in anthropology, 1957—. *Member:* American Anthropological Association, American Sociological Association, Sigma Tau Delta. *Awards, honors:* Wenner-Gren Foundation grant, 1952; National Institute of Mental Health grant, 1958.

WRITINGS: Menomini Women and Culture Change, American Anthropological Association, 1962; (with A. R. Beals and with husband, George Spindler) *Culture in Process,* Holt, 1967, revised edition, 1973; (with George Spindler) *Dreamers without Power,* Holt, 1971; (contributor) *Handbook of American Indians,* Smithsonian Press, 1973; *Review of Psychological Anthropology,* Mouton, 1973; *Culture Change,* Holt, in press. Editor with George Spindler of series, "Case Studies in Cultural Anthropology," Holt, 1960—. Contributor to journals. Assistant editor of *American Anthropologist,* 1962-67.

AVOCATIONAL INTERESTS: Camping, traveling, vacationing at summer cottage in Wisconsin and at house on coast of Spain.

* * *

SPIVACK, Kathleen (Romola Drucker) 1938-

PERSONAL: Born September 22, 1938, in Bronxville, N.Y.; daughter of Peter F. (a writer and economist) and Doris (a patent agent; maiden name, Schmitz) Drucker; married Mayer Spivack (an inventor and designer), December 23, 1959; children: Nova Timothy, Marin Tobiah. *Education:* Oberlin College, B.A., 1959; Boston University, M.A., 1963. *Home and office:* 53 Spruce St., Watertown, Mass. 02172. *Agent:* John Cushman Associates, Inc. 25 West 43rd St., New York, N.Y. 10036.

CAREER: Poets in the Schools, Massachusetts, instructor, 1972-74; Advanced Poetry Workshop, Cambridge, Mass., instructor, 1973-74. *Awards, honors:* Fellowship in poetry writing from Radcliffe Institute for Independent Study, Radcliffe College, 1969-72.

WRITINGS: Flying Inland (poems), Doubleday, 1973; *The Jane Poems,* Doubleday, 1974. Contributor to anthologies, magazines, and newspapers.

WORK IN PROGRESS: A third collection of poems.

* * *

SPIVAKOVSKY, Erika 1909-

PERSONAL: Surname is accented on next to last syllable; born November 4, 1909, in Hamburg-Altona, Germany; naturalized U.S. citizen in 1945; daughter of Joseph (a businessman) and Rosi (Wohlauer) Lipsker; married Tossy Spivakovsky (a concert violinist), November 21, 1934; children: Ruth (Mrs. Paul H. Voorhis). *Education:* University of Buenos Aires, B.A., 1928; University of Berlin, Ph.D., 1933. *Home:* 29 Burnham Hill, Box 188, Westport, Conn. 06880.

CAREER: Freelance writer in Westport, Conn., 1959—. *Member:* American Historical Association, Society for Spanish and Portuguese Historical Studies, Renaissance Society of America, American Association of Teachers of Spanish and Portuguese, Society of Radcliffe Institute Fellows. *Awards, honors:* Radcliffe Institute fellowships, 1962-63, 1963-64.

WRITINGS: Son of the Alhambra: Diego Hurtado de Mendoza, 1504-1575, University of Texas Press, 1970; *Cartas ineditas de Felipe II* (title means "Unpublished Letters of Philip II"), Espasa-Calpe S.A. (Madrid), in press. Contributor of articles and reviews to *Chronica Nova, American Historical Review, Renaissance Quarterly, Hispania, Symposium, Journal of the History of Ideas, Archivum, Renaissance News, Chicago Jewish Forum,* and *Hispanofila.*

WORK IN PROGRESS: A biography of Philip II of Spain, for Twayne's "Rulers and Statesmen of the World" series.

* * *

SPRING, Joel Henry 1940-

PERSONAL: Born September 24, 1940, in San Diego, Calif.; son of William C. (a naval officer) and Hazel I. (Meachem) Spring; married Deanna D. Demiduk; children: Dawn Persephone. *Education:* Roosevelt University, B.A., 1964; University of Wisconsin, M.A., 1965, Ph.D., 1969. *Politics:* Anarchist. *Home:* 11429 Glenwood Ave., Cleveland, Ohio 44106. *Office:* Department of Education, Case Western Reserve University, Cleveland, Ohio 44106.

CAREER: University of Wisconsin, Madison, instructor in education, 1968-69; Case Western Reserve University, Cleveland, Ohio, associate professor of education, 1969—.

WRITINGS: (Editor with Jordan Bishop) *Formative Undercurrents in Compulsory Education,* Centro Intercultural de Documentacion, 1970; *Education and the Rise of the Corporate State,* Beacon Press, 1972; (with Clarence Karier and Paul Violas) *Roots of Crisis,* Rand McNally, 1973. Contributor to education journals, *Socialist Revolution,* and *Libertarian Analysis.*

WORK IN PROGRESS: Anarchism, Marxism and Neo-Freudianism: A Study of Radical Forms of Education.

* * *

S.S.E.
See SPERRY, (Sally) Baxter

* * *

STADTFELD, Curtis K(arl) 1935-

PERSONAL: Born April 9, 1935, in Remus, Mich.; son of Lawrence Robert (a farmer) and Dorothy (Merritt) Stadtfeld; divorced; children: Peter, Christopher. *Education:* Michigan State University, B.A., 1957, graduate study, 1958-59; Eastern Michigan University, M.A., 1969. *Agent:* Paul R. Reynolds, 599 Fifth Ave., New York, N.Y. 10017. *Office:* Department of English, Eastern Michigan University, Ypsilanti, Mich. 48197.

CAREER: Jackson Citizen-Patriot, Jackson, Mich., reporter, 1959-61; *St. Louis Post Dispatch,* St. Louis, Mo., reporter, 1962-64; Lemoine Skinner, Jr. (public relations), St. Louis, Mo., account executive, 1964-65; Eastern Michigan University, Ypsilanti, director of information services, 1966-71, assistant professor of English and journalism, 1971—.

WRITINGS: From the Land and Back, Scribner, 1972. Contributor to *Yankee, Family Circle, Ms.,* and *Audubon Magazine.*

WORK IN PROGRESS: Year of the Deer, for Dial.

STALLARD, John (Richard) 1935-

PERSONAL: Born March 28, 1935, in Weeksbury, Ky.; son of John and Adeline (Newman) Stallard; married Sandra K. Lee, August 27, 1960; children: Elizabeth L., John D., Amy H. *Education:* Ohio University, B.S., 1961. *Home address:* Route 1, Fox Coulee, Nelson, Wis. 54756. *Agent:* Harold Matson Co., Inc., 22 East 40th St., New York, N.Y. 10016. *Office: Capital Times,* Madison, Wis. 53701.

CAREER: Associated Press, Charleston, W.Va., reporter, 1961; *Middletown Journal,* Middletown, Ohio, state editor, 1961-62; *Akron Beacon-Journal,* Akron, Ohio, reporter, 1962-64; *Milwaukee Journal,* Milwaukee, Wis., writer and Vietnam war correspondent, 1964-71; *Wabasha Herald,* Wabasha, Minn., editor, 1972; *Capital Times,* Madison, Wis., nature and environmental writer, 1973—. *Military service:* U.S. Army, 1953-56; became sergeant. *Awards, honors:* Scripps Howard award for municipal reporting, 1965; Richard S. Davis Award from *Milwaukee Journal,* 1968, for reporting on Vietnam war; awards from Milwaukee Press Club.

WRITINGS: Four in a Wild Place (family adventure novel), Norton, 1972. Contributor to magazines.

WORK IN PROGRESS: A nature book; writing about pioneer homesteading.

SIDELIGHTS: Stallard writes: "Having been a status conscious, success oriented, urban dwelling ladder climbing bright bastard, I am now a drop out from all such nonsense in the pursuit of a meaningful life that is not so damn bogged down with hangups and I intend to write about my convictions and some of these discoveries. I crusade to protect the environment, nature, and wildlife and in 1974 I was credited with getting a bill passed by the Wisconsin Legislature to keep idiots from hunting black bear in this state by both baiting methods and chasing them with dogs."

* * *

STAM, James H(enry) 1937-

PERSONAL: Born December 29, 1937, in Paterson, N.J.; son of Jacob (a lawyer) and Deana (Bowman) Stam; married Liga Ziemelis (a librarian), May 27, 1961; children: Andra Lisa, Ronald Karlis, Maira Vlasta, Deana Elvira, Silvia Valda Consuelo. *Education:* Upsala College, B.A., 1958; graduate study at University of Vienna; Brandeis University, M.A., 1961, Ph.D., 1964. *Home:* 60 Midland Ave., East Orange, N.J. 07017. *Office:* Department of Philosophy and Religion, Upsala College, East Orange, N.J. 07019.

CAREER: Upsala College, East Orange, N.J., instructor, 1962-65, assistant professor, 1965-69, associate professor of philosophy, 1969—. *Member:* American Philosophical Association, American Association of University Professors, Hegel Society of America. *Awards, honors:* Fellow of Newberry Library, summer, 1968; fellow of National Endowment for the Humanities, 1969, and summer, 1974; Lindback Foundation award for distinguished teaching, 1970.

WRITINGS: (Translator) Walter Leibrecht, *God and Man in the Thought of Hamann,* Fortress, 1966; (editor) J. D. Michaelis, *Influence of Opinions on Language and of Language on Opinions,* AMS Press, 1973; (editor) Etienne Bonnot de Condillac, *An Essay on the Origin of Human Knowledge,* AMS Press, 1974. Contributor to *Journal of Psycholinguistics.* Member of editorial board of "Language, Man, and Society" series published by AMS Press.

WORK IN PROGRESS: Inquiries into the Origin of Language (tentative title), for publication by Harper; *Classic German Essays,* a translation of German essays, 1770-1820; *Language True and Flase; The Workings of the Spirit,* on the philosophy of language in German idealism.

SIDELIGHTS: Stam is competent in Greek, Latin, German, Spanish, and French. *Avocational interests:* Pianist (chamber music).

* * *

STANWOOD, P(aul) G(rant) 1933-

PERSONAL: Born April 25, 1933, in Des Moines, Iowa; son of Harry Glen and Florence (Sprague) Stanwood; married Dorothy McNeill (a social worker), January 25, 1964; children: Christopher, Mary. *Education:* Iowa State Teachers College (now University of Northern Iowa), B.A., 1954; University of Michigan, M.A., 1956, Ph.D., 1961; University of Mainz, graduate study, 1958-59. *Religion:* Episcopalian. *Home:* 5592 Trafalgar St., Vancouver 13, British Columbia, Canada. *Office:* Department of English, University of British Columbia, Vancouver 8, British Columbia, Canada.

CAREER: Tufts University, Medford, Mass., instructor, 1961-63, assistant professor of English, 1963-65; University of British Columbia, Vancouver, assistant professor, 1965-67, associate professor, 1967-75, professor of English literature, 1975—. *Member:* Modern Language Association of America, Milton Society of America, Renaissance Society of America, Canadian Association of University Teachers, Association of Canadian University Teachers of English, Friends of Little Gidding. *Awards, honors:* Fulbright scholar in Germany, 1958-59; Frank L. Weil Institute grant, 1963, and Canada Council fellowships, 1968-69, and 1974-75, for study at Peterhouse, Cambridge University; senior fellow, Folger Shakespeare Library, 1972.

WRITINGS: (Editor with Daniel O'Connor) John Cosin, *A Collection of Private Devotions,* Oxford University Press, 1967; (editor) Henry More, *Democritus Platonissans,* Augustan Reprint Society, 1968; (editor) Richard Hooker, *Laws of Ecclesiastical Polity,* Books VII-VIII, Folger Shakespeare Library, in press. Contributor to *New Cambridge Bibliography of English Literature, Texas Studies in Literature and Language,* and to journals.

WORK IN PROGRESS: The Sempiternal Season: Essays on Eliot, Donne and the Seventeenth Century; editing Jeremy Taylor's *Holy Living and Holy Dying,* for Clarendon Press, completion expected in 1976.

* * *

STAPLES, Robert (Eugene) 1942-

PERSONAL: Born June 28, 1942, in Roanoke, Va.; son of John Ambrose (a cook) and Anna (Anthony) Staples. *Education:* Los Angeles Valley College, A.A., 1958; San Fernando Valley State College (now California State University) B.A., 1964; San Jose State College (now California State University) M.A., 1965; University of Minnesota, Ph.D., 1970. *Office:* Department of Sociology, Howard University, Washington, D.C. 20001; and Department of Sociology, University of California, San Francisco, Calif. 94122 (temporary).

CAREER: St. Paul Urban League, St. Paul, Minn., director of research, 1966; Bethune-Cookman College, Daytona Beach, Fla., associate professor of sociology, 1967-68; California State College (now University), Hayward, assistant professor of sociology, 1968-70; Howard University, Washington, D.C., associate professor of sociology, 1970-72; University of California, San Francisco, associate professor of sociology, 1973-74; Howard University, professor of sociology, 1974—. Visiting professor at Fisk University, 1969-70, and at University of California, San Francisco, 1974—. Lecturer at University of California, Irvine, 1970-71; adjunct professor at University of Maryland, 1970-72.

MEMBER: American Academy of Political and Social Science, National Council of Family Relations (member of executive committee, 1970-72), Society for the Scientific Study of Sex (fellow), American Association of University Professors, Caucus of Black Sociologists, African Heritage Studies Association, Sex Information and Education Council of the United States (member of board of directors), Pacific Sociological Association, Groves Conference on Marriage and the Family.

WRITINGS: The Lower-Income Negro Family in Saint Paul, St. Paul Urban League, 1967; (editor and contributor) *The Black Family: Essays and Studies,* Wadsworth, 1971; *The Black Woman in America,* Nelson-Hall, 1973; *The Sociology of Black People: An Introduction to the Study of Black Culture,* McGraw, in press.

Contributor: Carlfred Broderick, editor, *A Decade of Family Research and Action,* National Council on Family Relations, 1971; Mildred Weil, editor, *Sociological Perspectives in Marriage and the Family,* Interstate, 1972; Joyce Ladner, editor, *The Death of White Sociology,* Random House, 1973; Edgar Epps, editor, *Race Relations,* Winthrop, 1973; Carlene Young, editor, *The Black Experience,* Learning Press, 1973; Elanor Morrison and Vera Borasaze, editors, *Human Sexuality: Contemporary Perspectives,* National Press Books, 1973; Arlene Skolneck and Jerome Skolneck, editors, *Intimacy, the Family, and Society,* Little, Brown, 1974; Hare and Robert Chrisman, editors, *Contemporary Black Thought,* Bobbs-Merrill, 1974; Mary Calderone, editor, *Sexuality and Human Values,* Association Press, 1974; Rose Eshelman, editor, *Perspectives in Marriage and the Family,* Rand McNally, in press.

Contributor of about fifty articles and reviews to sociology journals, including *Sexual Behavior, CORElator, Essence, Ebony, Family Coordinator,* and *Journal of Sex Research.* Associate editor of *Journal of Marriage and the Family* and *Journal of Social and Behavioral Sciences;* advisory editor of *Black Scholar: Journal of Black Studies and Research.*

* * *

STARK, Bradford 1948-

PERSONAL: Born May 27, 1948, in New York, N.Y.; son of Bernard (a milliner) and Judith (Glasgow) Stark; married Meryl Payenson, February 4, 1968; children: Kio (daughter). *Education:* City College of the City University of New York, B.A., 1969; Columbia University, M.Sc., 1972. *Home:* 57 Kneeland Ave., Binghamton, N.Y. 13905. *Office:* Crandell Associates, 1901 Vestal Pkwy. E., Vestal, N.Y. 13850.

CAREER: Westermann-Miller Associates, New York, N.Y., urban planner, 1969-70; Crandell Associates, Vestal, N.Y., senior urban planner, 1970—. Editor, Loose Change Press, 1970—; instructor in writing workshop at Off Campus College, State University of New York at Binghamton, 1973—.

WRITINGS: An Unlikely but Noble Kingdom (poems), Rainbow Press, 1974. Poems have appeared in *Caterpillar, For Now, Gnosis, Endymion, Mulch, World, Mysterious Barricades, Choice,* and other little magazines. Editor, *Promethean,* 1968-69.

WORK IN PROGRESS: A new collection of poems, *Friends & Neighbors.*

* * *

STARK, Jack
See STARK, John H.

* * *

STARK, John H. 1914-
(Jack Stark)

PERSONAL: Born April 26, 1914, in New York, N.Y.; son of John H. (a businessman) and Elizabeth (Erb) Stark; married Lucienne Kucker; children: Jack, Charles, Lucienne Rita (Mrs. Ken Cassidy). *Education:* Attended University of Miami, Coral Gables. *Politics:* Democrat *Religion:* Protestant. *Home and office:* 515 Loretto Ave., Coral Gables, Fla. 33146.

CAREER: Feature writer for *Miami Herald* in the 1930's; Curtiss-Wright Corp., worked in public relations in New York, N.Y., and Indianapolis, Ind., 1941-45; Trans World Airlines, Inc., Kansas City, Mo., worked in public relations, 1945-46; J.C. Nichols Co. (real estate developers), Kansas City, Mo., worked in public relations, 1945-53; Dade County Parks Department, Miami, Fla., worked in public relations, 1959-73; *Miami News,* Miami, Fla., outdoor editor, 1973-74; free-lance writer and author, 1974—.

WRITINGS—Under name Jack Stark: *Successful Publicity and Public Relations for Real Estate,* Prentice-Hall, 1958; *Loggerhead* (juvenile fiction), Seeman, 1972; *Sponge Pirates* (juvenile fiction), Seeman, 1972. Contributor to sports and outdoor magazines.

WORK IN PROGRESS: An adult novel, *The Gulf Stream.*

AVOCATIONAL INTERESTS: Fishing, boating, photography.

* * *

START, Clarissa 1917-
(Clarissa Start Davidson)

PERSONAL: Born March 28, 1917, in St. Louis, Mo.; daughter of George Michael (a civil engineer) and Ada A. (Huebel) Start; married E. Gary Davidson (a state senator), May 14, 1938 (died, March 5, 1967); married Raymond J. Lippert (a businessman), December 21, 1972; children: (first marriage) Bruce Benton. *Education:* University of Missouri, B.J., 1936. *Politics:* Republican. *Religion:* United Church of Christ. *Address:* Box 196, Route 4, High Ridge, Mo. 63049.

CAREER: St. Louis Post-Dispatch, St. Louis, Mo., feature writer, 1938-72. Moderator of "Youth Speaks Up" on KSD-TV, 1960-61; member of Missouri Commission on Status of Women, 1963-73, Salvation Army Tree of Lights, 1971. *Member:* American Newspaper Guild, Daughters of the American Revolution, Women's Advertising Club (president, 1949-50), Missouri Press Women (president, 1963-65), Missouri Writers Guild, Theta Sigma Phi (president of St. Louis chapter, 1955). *Awards, honors:* National

Headliner award from Theta Sigma Phi, 1958; Missouri Writer's Guild award, 1970, for *Never Underestimate the Little Woman;* Top Ten award from National Federation of Press Women, 1971; Missouri Press Women first place award, 1973, for *Look Here, Lord.*

WRITINGS: (Under name Clarissa Start Davidson) *God's Man: The Story of Pastor Niemoeller,* Washburn, 1959; *When You're a Widow,* Concordia, 1968, published as *On Becoming a Widow,* Pyramid Publications, 1973; *Never Underestimate the Little Woman,* Concordia, 1969; *Look Here, Lord,* Augsburg, 1972. Author of weekly column, "The Happy Gardener," *St. Louis Post Dispatch.* Contributor to *Missouri State Manual.*

WORK IN PROGRESS: A book on second marriage; a book on flower preservation, with Muriel Lane.

SIDELIGHTS: Clarissa Start told *CA:* "I am an example of the age-old advice to writers: write about what you know. For many years I wrote a column about my home, family, hobbies, philosophy, later about my widowhood and religious beliefs, and now I still write: about my garden and my very happy second marriage and retirement years."

* * *

STAVIS, Barrie 1906-

PERSONAL: Surname, legally adopted in 1934; born June 16, 1906, in New York, N.Y.; son of Abraham Max (in textile business) and Fanny (Garfinkle) Stavisky; married Leona Heyert, 1925 (divorced, 1939); married Bernice Coe (president of Coe Film Associates, Inc.), May 17, 1950; children: (second marriage) Alexander Mark, Jane Devon. *Education:* Columbia University, night school student, 1924-27. *Residence:* New York, N.Y. *Agent:* Jill Dargeon Literary Agency, 160 East 84th St., New York, N.Y. 10028.

CAREER: Playwright and author. Worked days in a New York textile house while attending Columbia University at night, and wrote his first play during this period; free-lance foreign correspondent in Europe, 1937-38; free-lance magazine writer in New York, 1945-47; co-founder of New Stages (cooperative Off-Broadway theater venture), New York, 1947, and subsequently member of board of directors and treasurer. Visiting fellow at Institute for the Arts and Humanistic Studies, Pennsylvania State University, 1971; lecturer or conductor of playwriting seminars at University of Minnesota, University of Wisconsin, University of Oregon, Columbia University, and other universities across the country. *Military service:* U.S. Army, Signal Corps, 1942-45; became technical sergeant; medically discharged because of spinal injury.

MEMBER: U.S. Institute for Theatre Technology (member of board of directors, 1961-64, 1969—), American Theatre Association, American National Theatre and Academy (ANTA), Dramatists Guild and Authors Guild of Authors League of America, American Society of Composers Authors and Publishers (ASCAP), P.E.N. *Awards, honors:* Yaddo fellowship, 1939; National Theatre Conference grants to work on play about Joe Hill, 1948, 1949.

WRITINGS—Published and produced plays: *Refuge* (one-act; first produced in London at Unity Theatre, fall, 1938), Samuel French, 1939; *Lamp at Midnight: A Play about Galileo* (first produced Off-Broadway at New Stages Theatre, December 21, 1947; produced in England at Bristol Old Vic, November 11, 1956), acting edition with introduction by John Mathews, Dramatists Play Service, 1948, acting edition with introduction by Linus Pauling, Dramatists Play Service, 1955, revised general edition with illustrations and introduction by Tyrone Guthrie, A. S. Barnes, 1966, revised acting edition, with introduction by Herb Shore, Dramatic Publishing Co., 1974, abridged acting edition, with introduction by Glenn Loney, Dramatic Publishing Co., 1974; *The Man Who Never Died: A Play about Joe Hill* (first produced in St. Paul at Hamline University, November, 1955; produced Off-Broadway at Jan Hus Playhouse, November 21, 1958), published with illustrations and "Notes on Joe Hill and His Times," historical material by the playwright, Haven Press, 1954, acting edition, including illustrations and the "Notes," Dramatists Play Service, 1959, revised general edition with illustrations and a preface by the playwright and introduction by Pete Seeger, A. S. Barnes, 1972; *Harpers Ferry: A Play about John Brown* (first produced as "Banners of Steel" in Carbondale at Southern Illinois University, May 18, 1962; revised version first produced as "Harpers Ferry" in Minneapolis at Tyrone Guthrie Theatre, June 3, 1967), published with introduction by Tyrone Guthrie, A. S. Barnes, 1967; *Coat of Many Colors: A Play about Joseph in Egypt* (first produced in Provo at the Pardoe Theatre of Brigham Young University, April 20, 1966), published with introduction by John Lewin, A. S. Barnes, 1968.

Other books: *The Chain of Command* (novella; foreword by Marion Hargrove), Ackerman, 1945; *Home, Sweet Home!* (novel), Sheridan, 1949; (editor with Frank Harmon) *The Songs of Joe Hill,* People's Artists, 1955, new edition, Oak Press, 1960; *John Brown: The Sword and the Word* (historical nonfiction), A. S. Barnes, 1970.

Plays produced only: "In These Times," first produced in New York at a community theatre, in February, 1933; "The Sun and I," first produced in New York at Columbia University, March, 1933; revised for production on Broadway at Adelphi Theatre, February 26, 1937, under sponsorship of Federal Theatre Project.

During Army days wrote fourteen training manuals and collaborated on film scripts. Contributor of short stories, articles, and essays to magazines, including *Collier's, Saturday Evening Post, Folk Music, Reader's Digest, Ladies' Home Journal, Tomorrow, Drama Survey,* and *This Week.*

WORK IN PROGRESS: Joe Hill: The Man and the Myth, for publication by A. S. Barnes; an oratorio based on *Lamp at Midnight,* with Lee Hoiby, to be premiered March, 1975, at the opening of the Arts Complex, Huntsville, Alabama; a trilogy of plays, each play separate and independent but linked to the others by a binding theme.

SIDELIGHTS: Stavis wrote about a dozen plays (all later destroyed) while he was striving for a new theatrical form that resulted in the quartet of dramas about Galileo, Joe Hill, John Brown, and Joseph. He had outlined *Lamp at Midnight* some years before, during a period of free-lance writing in Europe which gave him the opportunity to do research about Galileo in Rome, Florence, Milan, and Venice. Returning to New York he completed the play before entering military service; five more years elapsed before New Stages opened its doors with *Lamp at Midnight.*

"Historically," Stavis says, "New Stages was the theatre organization which began the revival of the Off-Broadway movement. During the days of the old Provincetown Playhouse—Eugene O'Neill, Robert Edmund Jones, Susan Glaspell, Edna St. Vincent Millay, John Reed, etc.—the

Off-Broadway theatre had great life and vitality. After this period there was a severe fading off, and meretricious plays, shoddily produced, were the order of the day. Critics refused to attend these productions, considering them a waste of time. However, *Lamp at Midnight* had a substantial reputation even before opening and the critics came to review the play. . . . Encouraged by the experience of New Stages, many other groups, including Circle-in-the-Square, soon began to function Off-Broadway."

Peter O'Toole was in the British production of *Lamp at Midnight* at the Bristol Old Vic. On April 27, 1966, Hallmark Hall of Fame televised the play with a cast headed by Melvyn Douglas and David Wayne; it had an estimated audience of twenty-million viewers. In 1969 Tyrone Guthrie directed a touring cast starring Morris Carnovsky that opened on the East Coast and played in more than fifty cities across the country. The play was chosen to inaugurate the Pardoe Theatre at Brigham Young University in 1964, and the new theatre at Hardin-Simmons University, 1967. Excerpts from the play were included in *50 Great Scenes for Student Actors,* published by Bantam, 1970.

Stavis wrote to *CA* about the abridgement of *Lamp at Midnight*—"The abridged edition came into being when the Goodman Theatre, in conjunction with the Museum of Science and Industry, both in Chicago, received a grant from the National Science Foundation to produce four hour-long plays dealing with various aspects of science, to be presented free of charge for high school students. I was asked if I would be interested in doing an abridgement of *Lamp at Midnight* to open the series. The idea attracted me greatly. I have always been interested in the presentation of plays outside of conventional theatre structures, and the ambiance of the Museum seemed fortuitous. I was stirred by the idea of young students walking through the rooms and corridors of the scientific exhibits on the way to see a play about Galileo. [Later] St. Peter's Church in New York City invited me to do a fifty-minute abridgement for their Epiphany service. It was, in fact, the sermon for the day. Again, the idea appealed to me greatly—doubly so, the idea of doing a play about Galileo and the Church *in* a church. The production was gratifying. Although over the years I had seen many and different productions of the play, there were lines, which, because they were being spoken in a church, had resonances and overtones I had never before encountered. The final abridgement which has just been published is the combination of the two productions mentioned above."

The basic research and writing of *The Man Who Never Died,* about the folk poet and union organizer Joe Hill, who was imprisoned on a murder charge, covered about five years. That play has been translated into nineteen languages, produced on radio or on television in Berlin, Toronto, Moscow, Stockholm, Prague and other cities. It also was made into an opera, "Joe Hill," with libretto by Stavis and music by Alan Bush which opened at the Staatsoper in Berlin, September 29, 1970. The historical material, "Notes on Joe Hill and His Times," has been translated and published in Russia, and in several other countries. Stavis' collection and compilation of further historical material was published in *Folk Music,* in two parts, under the title "Joe Hill: Poet/Organizer."

Harpers Ferry was the first *new* play ever produced by the Tyrone Guthrie Theatre in Minneapolis. Up to that time the theater had staged only classics or semi-classics. The play received a Title III grant from the Federal Government which made it possible for tens of thousands of children to be bussed in from a seven-county area to see the play free of charge. During 1968 *Harpers Ferry* was chosen as the inaugural play for the new theater at the University of Wisconsin-Milwaukee. Stavis' prose history dealing with John Brown, *The Sword and the Word,* is a work separate and apart from "Harper's Ferry," but the play and prose, Stavis points out, complement and reinforce each other.

Stavis' manuscripts are in the theater collection of the New York Public Library and Pennsylvania State University.

AVOCATIONAL INTERESTS: Sailing, fishing, and swimming.

BIOGRAPHICAL/CRITICAL SOURCES: Educational Theatre Journal, December, 1973.

* * *

STEBBINS, Robert C(yril) 1915-

PERSONAL: Born March 31, 1915, in Chico, Calif.; son of Cyril Adelbert (a teacher) and Louise (Beck) Stebbins; married Anna-rose Cooper, June 8, 1941; children: Robert John, Melinda Louise (Mrs. Normand Broadhurst), Mary Anna-rose. *Education:* University of California, Los Angeles, A.B., 1940, M.A., 1942, Ph.D., 1943. *Home:* 601 Plateau Dr., Kensington, Calif. 94708. *Office:* Department of Zoology, University of California, Berkeley, Calif. 94720.

CAREER: National Park Service, ranger, summers, 1941, 1942; University of California, Berkeley, instructor, 1944-46, assistant professor, 1946-51, associate professor, 1951-58, professor of zoology, 1958—, curator in herpetology, Museum of Vertebrate Zoology, 1948—. Represented National Academy of Sciences in tour of South and Southeast Asia in interest of improving biological science teaching, 1963.

MEMBER: American Society of Ichthyologists and Herpetologists, Society of Systematic Zoology (past president), Herpetologists' League, Friends of the Earth, Zero Population Growth, California Academy of Sciences (fellow), Sierra Club. *Awards, honors:* Guggenheim fellowship, 1949; National Science Foundation senior postdoctoral fellowship, 1958-59.

WRITINGS: Amphibians of Western North America, University of California Press, 1951; (with father, Cyril A. Stebbins) *Birds of Yosemite,* Yosemite Natural History Association, 1954; *Reptiles and Amphibians of Western North America,* McGraw, 1954; *Reptiles and Amphibians of the San Francisco Bay Area,* University of California Press, 1958; (with Alden H. Miller) *The Lives of Desert Animals in Joshua Tree National Monument,* University of California Press, 1964; *A Field Guide to the Western Reptiles and Amphibians,* Houghton, 1966; (contributor) Martin Brown, editor, *The Social Responsibility of the Scientist,* Free Press, 1971; (with T. I. Storer, R. L. Usinger, and J. W. Nybakken) *General Zoology,* 5th edition, McGraw, 1972; *Amphibians and Reptiles of California,* University of California Press, 1972.

Writer of script and producer of "Nature Next Door," 1962, and "No Room for Wilderness," 1967, both for Sierra Club. Contributor of articles on herpatology and vertebrate pineal to scientific journals.

WORK IN PROGRESS: A book on biological science teaching at the secondary level.

SIDELIGHTS: Stebbins has done field studies in zoology in Africa, Australia, South America, Europe, Galapagos, and eastern Mediterranean, in addition to Asia. *Avocational interests:* Landscape and wildlife painting.

STEEGMUELLER, Francis
See STEEGMULLER, Francis

* * *

STEEGMULLER, Francis 1906-
(David Keith, Byron Steel)

PERSONAL: Born July 3, 1906, in New Haven, Conn.; son of Joseph F. and Bertha R. (Tierney) Steegmuller; married Beatrice Stein, July 1, 1935 (died June, 1961); married Shirley Hazzard, December 22, 1963. *Education:* Attended Dartmouth College, 1923-24; Columbia University, B.A., 1927, M.A., 1928. *Home:* 200 East 66th St., New York, N.Y. 10021.

CAREER: Author and novelist. *Member:* National Institute of Arts and Letters, Phi Beta Kappa, Century Club (New York), Coffee House (New York), Athenaeum (London). *Awards, honors:* Red Badge Mystery Prize, 1940, for *A Matter of Iodine*; National Book Award, 1971, for *Cocteau: A Biography*; Chevalier of French Legion of Honor.

WRITINGS: The Musicale, J. Cape, 1930; (with Marie Dresden Lane) *America on Relief,* Harcourt, 1938; *Flaubert and Madame Bovary: A Double Portrait,* Viking, 1939, 2nd revised edition, Farrar, Strauss, 1950; *States of Grace* (novel), Reynal, 1946; *French Follies & Other Follies: 20 Stories from The New Yorker,* Reynal, 1946; *Maupassant: A Lion in the Path,* Random House, 1949, reprinted, Books for Libraries, 1972 (published in England as *Maupassant,* Collins, 1950); *The Two Lives of James Jackson Jarves,* Yale University Press, 1951; (editor and translator) Gustave Flaubert, *Selected Letters,* Farrar, Straus, 1954, reprinted, Books for Libraries, 1971; *The Grand Mademoiselle,* Farrar, Straus, 1956; (translator) Flaubert, *Madame Bovary,* Random House, 1957; *The Christening Party,* Farrar, Straus, 1960; (translator into French) Edmund Lear, *Le hibou et la poussiquette* (title means "The Owl and the Pussycat"), Little, Brown, 1961; *Apollinaire: Poet Among Painters,* Farrar, Straus, 1963, reprinted, Books for Libraries, 1971; (editor) Charles Augustin Sainte-Beuve, *Selected Essays,* Doubleday, 1964; (author of introduction) *Jacques Villon, Master Printmaker,* High Grade Press, 1964; (translator with Norbert Guterman) Eugene Field, *Papillot, Clignot et Dodo,* Farrar, Straus, 1964; (editor) Flaubert, *November,* Serendipity Press, 1967; (author of introduction and notes and translator) Flaubert, *Intimate Notebook, 1840-1841,* Doubleday, 1967; *Cocteau: A Biography,* Little, Brown, 1970; *Stories and True Stories,* Little, Brown, 1972; (editor and translator) Flaubert, *Flaubert in Egypt: A Sensibility on Tour,* Little, Brown, 1973; (editor) *Love Letters: Isadora Duncan to Gordon Craig,* Random House, in press.

Crime novels; under pseudonym David Keith: *A Matter of Iodine,* Dodd, 1940; *A Matter of Accent,* Dodd, 1943; *Blue Harpsichord,* Dodd, 1949, paperback edition published under name Francis Steegmuller.

Under pseudonym Byron Steel: *O Rare Ben Jonson,* Knopf, 1927; *Java-Java,* Knopf, 1928; *Sir Francis Bacon: The First Modern Mind,* Doubleday, 1930.

Contributor to *New Yorker, New York Times Book Review,* and others.

SIDELIGHTS: Of *Cocteau: A Biography,* Mark Schorer has written: "[Mr. Steegmuller] had the problem of obtaining documentary materials and confidences not previously available, and these he . . . uses skillfully and tactfully. . . . [For the] ambiguous relationships with men like Gide, Stravinsky, Diaghilev, Apollinaire, as with certain powerful fugures in the salons . . . Cocteau's own memoirs are of little use. Mr. Steegmuller straightens out the record with precision and clarity in this book that is surely a model of the biographer's art."

* * *

STEEL, Byron
See STEEGMULLER, Francis

* * *

STEELE, Robert (Scott) 1917-

PERSONAL: Born November 7, 1917, in Butler, Pa. *Education:* Ohio Wesleyan University, B.A., 1940; Hartford Seminary Foundation, B.D., 1944; University of London, further study, 1956-58; Ohio State University, Ph.D., 1959. *Home:* 452 Park Ave., No. 14, Boston, Mass. 02215. *Agent:* Bertha Klausner International Literary Agency, Inc., 71 Park Ave., New York, N.Y. 10016; (lectures) Margaret Kelley, University Speakers' Bureau, 14 Pond View Rd., Canton, Mass. 02021. *Office:* Boston University, 640 Commonwealth Ave., Boston, Mass. 02215.

CAREER: Radio writer and producer in Tennessee, 1944-45; *Motive* (religious magazine), Nashville, Tenn., assistant editor, 1945-46, managing editor, 1946-49; Ohio State University, Columbus, research associate in community education and cinema, 1950-52; film writer and director in India, 1953-56; British Broadcasting Corp., London, England, radio writer in Far East Division, 1956-58; Boston University, Boston, Mass., associate professor of cinema and communications, 1958—. Lecturer at universities and colleges throughout America, and in Europe, India, Japan, and Turkey; instructor and co-director, Institute of Advanced Cinema Studies, Vence-St. Paul, France, and Tufts University workshops in cinema and religion. Director of film programs for Boston Arts Festival, Boston Museum of Fine Arts, Cambridge Center for Adult Education, and Syracuse Museum of Fine Arts; juror at film festivals; voting member of National Screen Council; founder and first chairman of Boston Film Council.

MEMBER: Society for Cinema Studies (president, 1964-66; senior member of council, 1966-70), American Federation of Film Societies, University Film Association, Society for Film and Television Education (London), Union International de la Critique de Cinema (Paris), Asia Society, American Society for Aesthetics, Cinema Critics Guild, Society of Film History and Research (London), Phi Delta Kappa, Theta Alpha Phi, Delta Sigma Rho. *Awards, honors:* Grants from Lilly Foundation, 1963-64, Louis E. Taubman Foundation, 1965, and Glide Foundation, 1968.

WRITINGS: The Cataloging and Classification of Cinema Literature, Scarecrow, 1967; *La Strada: The Mirror of Fellini,* Ballantine, 1968; (editor) Federico Fellini, *8½,* Ballantine, 1968.

Contributor: David M. White and Richard Averson, editors, *Sight, Sound and Society,* Beacon Press, 1968; Bernard Rosenberg and David M. White, editors, *Mass Culture Revisited,* Van Nostrand, 1971; G. Ramchandran and T. K. Mahadevan, editors, *Quest for Gandhi,* Gandhi Peace Foundation, 1970; Howard Hunter, editor, *Humanities, Religion, and the Arts Tomorrow,* Holt, 1972.

Script writer, photographer, and director of four films,

"Kaleidoscope Orissa," "Mahatma Gandhi," "Silent Revolution," and "Vinoba Bhave: Walking Revolutionist," all distributed in America by International Film Bureau.

Contributor of more than four hundred articles and film and book reviews to more than forty journals and newspapers, including film periodicals, *Kenyon Review, Christian Century, Current Anthropology, Arts and Society,* and *Adult Leadership*. Associate editor, *Film Heritage,* 1965-68; film critic, *Friends Journal*.

WORK IN PROGRESS: Books on Maya Deren and Satyajit Ray.

* * *

STEFANSSON, Evelyn
See NEF, Evelyn Stefansson

* * *

STEGER, Shelby 1906-
(Rae Loomis)

PERSONAL: Born May 29, 1906, in Berkeley, Calif.; daughter of Olin Shelby (an architect and manufacturer) and Minnie (Guy) Grove; married Athol Bruce Steger, November 3, 1943. *Education:* Attended public schools in Oakland, Calif. *Residence:* Tampa, Fla.

CAREER: Novelist, short story writer. Assistant to syndicated feature columnist Ted Cook in Beverly Hills, Calif., in the 1930's; free-lance writer in St. Louis and Van Buren, Mo., 1945-55; Florida Grower Press, Inc., Tampa, acting editor of *Florida Purchaser,* and advertising production manager of *Purchaser* and *Florida Grower and Rancher,* 1956-58; secretary at Tampa General Hospital, 1958-60, Johns-Eastern (insurance claims adjusters), 1960-65, and Kemper Insurance Co., 1965-66; medical secretary, 1966-68. Free-lance editor, Ace Books, 1954.

WRITINGS—All novels: *Desire in the Ozarks,* Ace Books, 1957.

Under pseudonym Rae Loomis: *The Marina Street Girls,* Ace Books, 1953; *Luisita,* Ace Books, 1954, reissued as *Massage Parlor,* Macfadden, 1970; *House of Deceit,* Ace Books, 1955, reprinted, Macfadden, 1970.

Contributor of about two hundred stories to magazines.

WORK IN PROGRESS: A novel, *The Last Three Virgins in Town;* a collection of "humorous, rather bawdy verse."

SIDELIGHTS: Mrs. Steger told *CA* she had never thought in terms of a career, but "simply did a variety of things for a living. As a writer, thought of self as a story-teller, not an 'author.' I simply wrote stories because I had a knack for it, and needed the money." At a friend's suggestion, she began to write short stories, and between 1945 and 1955 turned out some two hundred "above-the-chin shorts, plus some confessions" for pulp love magazines. After her work began to sell, she and her husband moved from St. Louis to the Missouri Ozarks, living on a forty-acre plot in a dwelling "somewhat larger than the outhouse. Swell—not much housework. Until an REA line eventually came in, no electricity—gasoline lanterns. Water pumped to the kitchen sink from our own well. Summers, bathe in the river; winters, in a washtub on the kitchen floor. . . . Elections, pie suppers, ice cream socials, square dances, covered dish dinners, graveyard cleanings, showers, weddings, shivarees . . . We loved it all," Mrs. Steger summarizes, and much of the experience is reflected in *Desire in the Ozarks*. She estimates that she worked about six hours a day—"not nearly so regularly as I should have . . . am slow at book-lengths, because am not always certain where my people are going till I know where they've been so far."

* * *

STEIN, Maurice Robert 1926-

PERSONAL: Born September 19, 1926, in Buffalo, N.Y.; son of Edward (a teacher) and Rebecca (Joffe) Stein; married Bernice Ortenberg, June, 1949 (divorced, 1963); married Phyllis Rosenstein (a teacher), August 29, 1964; children: (second marriage) Paul Radin. *Education:* University of Buffalo, B.A., 1949; Columbia University, Ph.D., 1959. *Home:* 59 Parker St., Cambridge, Mass. 02138. *Office:* Department of Sociology, Brandeis University, Waltham, Mass. 02154.

CAREER: Dartmouth College, Hanover, N.H., instructor in sociology and anthropology, 1952-53; Oberlin College, Oberlin, Ohio, instructor in sociology and anthropology, 1953-55; Brandeis University, Waltham, Mass., assistant professor, 1955-59, associate professor, 1959-67, professor of sociology, 1967—. *Military service:* U.S. Army, 1944-46. *Member:* American Association of University Professors, American Sociological Association.

WRITINGS: *Eclipse of Community: An Interpretation of American Studies,* Princeton University Press, 1960, expanded edition, 1971; (editor with Arthur Vidich and David M. White) *Identity and Anxiety: Survival of the Person in Mass Society,* Free Press, 1960; (editor with Vidich) *Sociology on Trial,* Prentice-Hall, 1963; (editor with Vidich and Joseph Bensman) *Reflections on Community Studies,* Wiley, 1964; (contributor) Eleanor Pavenstedt, editor, *The Drifters: Children of Disorganized Lower-Class Families,* Little, Brown, 1967; (with Larry H. Miller) *Blueprint for Counter Education,* Doubleday, 1970.

WORK IN PROGRESS: *The Emergence of Community.*

* * *

STEIN, Robert 1924-

PERSONAL: Born March 4, 1924, in New York, N.Y.; son of Isidor and Gertrude (Bohrer) Stein; married Dorothy Price Weichel, March 31, 1956; children: Gregory, Keith, Clifford. *Education:* City College (now City College of the City University of New York), B.A., 1947; Columbia University, graduate study, 1948-49. *Agent:* Robert Lescher, 155 East 71st St., New York, N.Y. 10021. *Office:* *McCall's,* 230 Park Ave., New York, N.Y. 10017.

CAREER: Interrupted college in 1943 to work briefly as copy boy for *New York Daily News,* New York, N.Y., before going into the Army; City College (now City College of the City University of New York), New York, N.Y., associate director of public relations and later executive editor of alumni magazine, 1947-51; *Argosy,* New York, N.Y., articles editor, 1951-53; *Redbook,* New York, N.Y., associate editor, later managing editor, 1953-58, editor-in-chief, 1958-65; McCall Publishing Co., New York, N.Y., editor-in-chief of *McCall's,* 1965-67, 1972—, executive assistant to president of firm, 1967-70, director of Book Division, 1969-71, senior vice-president, 1970—. *Military service:* U.S. Army, 1943-46; served in Europe with 80th Infantry Division; received Purple Heart and Combat Infantryman's Badge. *Member:* American Society of Magazine Editors (chairman, 1965-67). *Awards, honors:* Neuberger Award of Society of Magazine Writers.

WRITINGS: Media Power: Who Is Shaping Your Picture of the World?, Houghton, 1972. Contributor to *This Week, Saturday Review, Popular Science, Coronet, New York Magazine, Reader's Digest,* and other magazines.

BIOGRAPHICAL/CRITICAL SOURCES: Roy Newquist, *Conversations,* Rand McNally, 1967.

* * *

STEIN, Sol 1926-

PERSONAL: Born October 13, 1926, in Chicago, Ill.; son of Louis (a jeweler) and Zelda (Zam) Stein; married, 1947; married second wife, Patricia Day (a book publisher), March 31, 1962; children: Kevin David, Jeffrey Lewelyn, Leland Dana, Robert Bruce, Andrew Charles, David Day, Elizabeth Day. *Education:* City College (now City College of the City University of New York), B.S.S., 1948; Columbia University, M.A., 1949, Ph.D. candidate, 1949-51. *Residence:* Scarborough-on-Hudson, N.Y. *Office:* Stein & Day, Scarborough House, Briarcliff Manor, N.Y. 10510.

CAREER: City College (now City College of the City University of New York), New York, N.Y., lecturer in social studies, 1948-51; Voice of America, New York, N.Y., editor of ideological advisory staff, 1951-53; Beacon Press, Boston, Mass., general editor and originator of Beacon Press paperbacks, 1954—; Stein & Day (publishers), New York, N.Y., president, 1962—. Executive director of American Committee for Cultural Freedom, 1953-56; lecturer in dramatic arts, Columbia University, 1958-60; executive vice-president, Mid-Century Book Society, 1959-62; member of executive committee of American Friends of the Captive Nations. *Military service:* U.S. Army, 1945-47; became first lieutenant. *Member:* International Brotherhood of Magicians (honorary life member), New Dramatists Committee (member of council), Playwrights Group, Actors Studio. *Awards, honors:* Yaddo fellowship, 1952; MacDowell Colony fellowship, 1952, 1953, 1954; first prize in Dramatists Alliance competition for "The Illegitimist," 1953.

WRITINGS—Novels: *The Husband,* Coward, 1969; *The Magician,* Delacorte, 1971; *Living Room,* Arbor House, 1974.

Plays: "The Illegitimist," first produced on Broadway at ANTA Theatre, 1953; "A Shadow of My Enemy," first produced at ANTA Theatre, 1957.

Contributor of poetry, articles, and reviews to literary journals.

WORK IN PROGRESS: Courtesy, a nonfiction book.

* * *

STEINBERG, Charles S. 1913-

PERSONAL: Born October 23, 1913, in New York, N.Y.; son of Herman (a builder) and Henrietta (Side) Steinberg; married Hortense Rosenson, December 14, 1952; children: Harriet. *Education:* New York University, B.A., 1937, M.A., 1939, Ph.D., 1954. *Politics:* Independent. *Religion:* Jewish. *Address:* Belle Harbor, New York. *Office:* Department of Education, Hunter College, City University of New York, 695 Park Ave., New York, N.Y. 10021.

CAREER: Warner Brothers Pictures, New York, N.Y., director of education, 1944-57; CBS-TV, New York, N.Y., vice-president, 1957-72; Hunter College, City University of New York, New York, N.Y., professor of education, 1972—. Member of board of trustees of Council on Religion and International Affairs. *Member:* International Radio and Television Society. *Awards, honors:* Silver medal from Venice Biennial, 1966, for *Mass Media and Communication;* Broadcast Preceptor award.

WRITINGS: The Mass Communicators, Harper, 1954; *Mass Media and Communication,* Hastings House, 1966; *The Communicative Arts,* Hastings House, 1970; *Broadcasting: The Critical Challenges,* Hastings House, 1974. Contributor to more than twenty journals.

WORK IN PROGRESS: Public Relations and Mass Media, completion expected in 1975.

* * *

STEPHENS, M(ichael) G(regory) 1946-

PERSONAL: Born March 4, 1946; son of James Stewart (a U.S. customs employee) and Rose (Drew) Stephens. *Education:* Yale University, drama student, 1971-72. *Home and office:* 141 Sullivan St., Apt. 6, New York, N.Y. 10012. *Agent:* Georges Borchardt, Inc., 145 East 52nd St., New York, N.Y. 10022.

CAREER: Writer; has worked as cashier in bookshop at various times, 1968—. *Awards, honors:* MacDowell Colony fellowship, 1968; Fletcher Pratt prose fellowship at Breadloaf Writers Conference, 1972.

WRITINGS: Season at Coole (novel), Dutton, 1972; *Alcohol Poems,* Loose Change Press, 1973; *Paragraphs* (short stories), Mulch Press, 1974. "A Splendid Occasion in Spring," a play, first performed in New York at West End Bar, February 9, 1974. Contributor of articles, stories, poems, and reviews to literary magazines and newspapers, including *Tri-Quarterly, Rolling Stone, Evergreen Review, Boston Phoenix, Strange Faces,* and *Galley Sail Review.*

WORK IN PROGRESS: Gulfweed Voices, a novel; "Still Life," a short story; poems.

* * *

STEPTOE, John (Lewis) 1950-

PERSONAL: Born September 14, 1950, in Brooklyn, N.Y.; son of John Oliver (a transit worker) and Elesteen (Hill) Steptoe; children: Bweela (daughter), Javaka (son). *Education:* Attended New York School of Art and Design, 1964-67. *Home and office:* 66 Grove St., Peterborough, N.H. 03458. *Agent:* Alice Bach, 222 East 75th St., New York, N.Y.

CAREER: Painter and writer of children's books. Teacher at Brooklyn Music School, summer, 1970. *Member:* Amnesty International. *Awards, honors:* Gold Medal from Society of Illustrators, 1970, for *Stevie.*

WRITINGS—For children; all self-illustrated: *Stevie,* Harper, 1969; *Uptown,* Harper, 1970; *Train Ride,* Harper, 1971; *Birthday,* Holt, 1972.

Illustrator: Lucille B. Clifton, *All Us Come cross the Water,* Holt, 1972; Eloise Greenfield, *She Come Bringing Me That Little Baby Girl,* Lippincott, in press.

WORK IN PROGRESS: My Special Best Words, for Viking, and *Marcia,* both books for children.

SIDELIGHTS: Steptoe told *CA:* "One of my incentives for getting into writing children's books was the great and disastrous need for books that black children could honestly relate to. I ignorantly created precedents by writing such a book. I was amazed to find that no one had successfully written a book in the dialogue which black children speak." *Stevie* was written when Steptoe was sixteen.

STERCHO, Peter George 1919-

PERSONAL: Born April 14, 1919, in Kuzmyno, Ukraine; son of Yurko and Olena (Molnar) Stercho; married Irena Julia Urban (a medical technologist), November 6, 1954; children: Olena Wanda, Yuriy Petro, Maria Irena. *Education:* Ukrainian School of Economics, Munich, Germany, Ph.D., 1949; University of Notre Dame, Ph.D., 1959. *Home:* 340 Meeting House Lane, Narberth, Pa. 19072. *Office:* Department of Economics, Drexel University, Philadelphia, Pa. 19104.

CAREER: University of Notre Dame, Notre Dame, Ind., research fellow, 1953-55; St. Vincent College, Latrobe, Pa., assistant professor, 1955-60, associate professor of economics and political science, 1960-63; Drexel University, Philadelphia, Pa., associate professor, 1963-69, professor of economics, 1969—. President of Bishop Ortyns'kyy Scholarship and Publishing Foundation, Philadelphia, 1969—; vice-president of Carpathian Research Center, New York, 1957—; member of executive board, United Ukrainian American Relief Committee, Philadelphia, 1968—, Ukrainian Congress Committee of America, 1966—, and The World Congress of Free Ukrainians, 1973—.

MEMBER: American Economic Association, American Political Science Association, American Association for the Advancement of Slavic Studies, American Academy of Political and Social Science, American Association of University Professors, Ukrainian American Association of University Professors (president, 1967-71), Shevchenko Scientific Society (vice-president, 1968—), Phi Sigma Alpha, Beta Gamma Sigma, Delta Tau Kappa.

WRITINGS: *Karpato-Ukrayins'ka Derzhava* (title means "The Carpatho-Ukrainian Republic"), Shevchenko Scientific Society, 1965; *Diplomacy of Double Morality: Europe's Crossroads in Carpatho-Ukraine, 1919-1939,* Carpathian Research Center, 1971; (with Matthew Stachiw and Nicholas Chirovsky) *Ukraine and the European Turmoil, 1917-1919,* Shevchenko Scientific Society, 1973. Also author of monograph, *Soviet Concept of National Self-Determination: Theory and Reality from Lenin to Brezhnev.* Contributor of articles to *Ukrainian Quarterly* and other periodicals. Member of editorial advisory board, *Ukrainian Quarterly,* 1969—.

WORK IN PROGRESS: *Ukrainians in America.*

SIDELIGHTS: Besides his native tongue, Stercho is competent in German, Russian, Czech, Polish, and Slovak.

* * *

STERLING, Philip 1907-

PERSONAL: Surname originally Shatz; legally changed to Sterling, 1936; born July 12, 1907, in New Rochelle, N.Y.; son of William (a house painter) and Helen (Levine) Shatz; married Dorothy Dannenberg (a writer under name Dorothy Sterling), May 14, 1937; children: Peter, Anne (Mrs. Nelson Fausto). *Education:* Attended public schools in Cleveland, Ohio. *Residence:* Wellfleet, Mass. *Address:* Box 626, South Wellfleet, Mass. 02663.

CAREER: Reporter, writer, or copy editor for *Cleveland Press, Omaha World Herald,* and then for suburban New York newspapers, 1926-31; New York Emergency Home Relief Bureau, New York, N.Y., clerk, later caseworker, 1933-35; Federal Writers Project (under Works Progress Administration), New York, N.Y., associate editor of *Film Index,* 1936-39; Columbia Broadcasting System, New York, N.Y., writer with radio and television press information departments, 1945-65, assistant director of radio press information, 1959-63. *Awards, honors:* Christopher Book Award, 1971, for *Sea and Earth: The Life of Rachel Carson.*

WRITINGS—For young readers, except as noted: (With wife, Dorothy Sterling) *Polio Pioneers,* Doubleday, 1955; (with Bella Rodman) *Fiorello LaGuardia,* Hill & Wang, 1962; (editor) *Laughing on the Outside* (anthology of Negro humor for adults), Grosset, 1965; (with Rayford W. Logan) *Four Took Freedom: The Lives of Harriet Tubman, Frederick Douglass, Robert Smalls and Blanche K. Bruce,* Doubleday, 1967; (with Maria Brau) *The Quiet Rebels: Four Puerto Rican Leaders,* Doubleday, 1968; *Sea and Earth: The Life of Rachel Carson,* Crowell, 1970; *The Real Teachers: Conversations After the Bell* (adult nonfiction), Random House, 1972; *The Question of Color: Marcus Garvey and Malcolm X* (biography), Scholastic Book Services, 1973.

* * *

STEVENSON, (William) Bruce 1906-

PERSONAL: Born February 26, 1906, in Glasgow, Scotland; son of John Gilchrist and Jeanette (Bramston) Stevenson; married Eva Timme, September 8, 1934; children: Helen Corinna. *Education:* Library Association (England), fellow by examination, 1937. *Home:* 20 Collingwood Ave., London, N10 3ED, England.

CAREER: Wallasey Public Libraries, Wallasey, Cheshire, England, assistant, 1925-29; Hendon Public Libraries, London, England, senior assistant, 1929-33, branch librarian, 1933-37, Hornsey Public Libraries, Hornsey, Middlesex, England, 1937-64, began as deputy librarian, became borough librarian; Haringey Libraries, London, England, director of libraries, museum, and arts, 1965-66; retired, 1966; writer, indexer, and library consultant, 1966—. *Member:* Association of Assistant Librarians (councillor), Library Association (councillor), National Book League (member of executive committee, 1957-70; chairman of Carnegie Medal committee, 1946-66), Society of Bookmen. *Awards, honors:* Coronation Medal, 1953.

WRITINGS: *Detective Fiction: A Reader's Guide,* Cambridge University Press, 1949, 2nd edition, 1958; *Middlesex,* Hastings House, 1972. Contributor to *Collier's Encyclopedia* and library journals. Editor, *Library Assistant,* 1939-46, and *Library Association Record,* 1946-52.

WORK IN PROGRESS: *A Check-List of Foreign Fiction Translated into English* (tentative title); *Italy: A Select Bibliography.*

AVOCATIONAL INTERESTS: Renaissance art, recorded music, theater, wine, collecting the works of W. H. Auden, reading poetry aloud, "*not* looking at television."

* * *

STEVENSON, Dorothy E(mily) 1892-1973

1892—December 30, 1973; Scottish novelist. Obituaries: *Publishers Weekly,* February 4, 1974. (*CA*-15/16).

* * *

STEWART, Elizabeth Laing 1907-

PERSONAL: Born September 1, 1907, in Colorado Springs, Colo.; daughter of Herbert Greysen and Della (Mann) Laing; married Donald M. Stewart (an editor and writer), 1938 (divorced, 1947); married Charles Sweetland (an editor and writer), 1958 (divorced, 1960); children: (first marriage) Robert Laing Stewart. *Education:* Barnard College, A.B., 1929. *Politics:* Democrat or independent. *Religion:* "Attend Quaker meetings (not member)." *Home:* 238 Lee St., Evanston, Ill. 60202. *Agent:* Max Siegel & Associates, 154 East Erie St., Chicago, Ill. 60611.

CAREER: Columbia University, New York, N.Y., secretary in Spanish department, 1933-34; Bobbs-Merrill Co., Inc., Indianapolis, Ind., associate editor, 1934-38; Reilly & Lee Co., Chicago, Ill., editor, 1938-41, 1946-49; Scott, Foresman & Co., Glenview, Ill., editor, 1950-72, editorial consultant in driver education, 1972—. *Member:* Children's Reading Round Table.

WRITINGS—Picture books with vocabulary for beginning readers; all published by Reilly & Lee except as shown: *Billy Buys a Dog,* 1950; *Funny Squirrel,* 1952; *Patch, You Just Be You,* 1953; *Little Dog Tim,* 1959; *See Our Pony Farm,* 1960; *Kim the Kitten,* 1961; *Mogul Finds a Friend,* 1962; *The Lion Twins,* Atheneum, 1964.

Directing editor, Maxwell Halsey and Richard Kaywood, *Let's Drive Right,* 3rd edition (she was not associated with earlier editions), Scott, Foresman, 1964, 5th edition (with Richard Meyerhoff as additional author), 1972.

WORK IN PROGRESS: Keeping up with driver education field to prepare for any changes in next edition of *Let's Drive Right.*

SIDELIGHTS: Mrs. Stewart wrote: "For many years, my chief avocational interest has been in organizations that promote peace in world affairs. Currently I do volunteer work for the Peace Center of Evanston. Though I'm sure it isn't obvious, the point I wanted to get across to children in *Little Dog Tim,* the favorite of my own books, was to help children live at peace with their fellow-beings and promote peace in the world."

* * *

STEWART, Horace Floyd, Jr. 1928-

PERSONAL: Born April 20, 1928, in Daytona Beach, Fla.; son of Horace Floyd and Ruth (Dawson) Stewart; married E. Joyce Dunn (a teacher), September 16, 1954; children: Dona E., Bonnie C., Pamela A., Terence E. *Education:* Pennsylvania State University, B.S., 1953; Florida State University, M.S., 1954; University of Florida, Ph.D., 1962. *Home address:* Route 7, Box 134, Carrollton, Ga. 30117. *Office:* Department of Psychology, West Georgia College, Carrollton, Ga. 30117.

CAREER: Spring Grove State Hospital, Spring Grove, Pa., intern, 1954-55; Raleigh State Hospital, Raleigh, N.C., staff psychologist, 1955-56; Chattahoochee State Hospital, Chattahoochee, Fla., staff psychologist, 1956-58; Central State Hospital, Milledgeville, Ga., staff psychologist, 1958-65; Augusta College, Augusta, Ga., assistant professor of psychology, 1965-67; West Georgia College, Carrollton, professor of psychology, 1967—. Consultant, Georgia Public Health Service, 1968-72, and Anneewakee Residential Treatment Center, 1968—. Visiting assistant professor, Mercer College, 1964-65. *Military service:* U.S. Army, 1946-49. *Member:* American Psychological Association, National Rehabilitation Association, Southeastern Psychological Association.

WRITINGS: (Editor with James Thomas) *Introductory Experimental Psychology,* Kendall/Hunt, 1970. Contributor of more than a dozen articles to professional journals.

WORK IN PROGRESS: A revised edition of *Introductory Experimental Psychology.*

* * *

STEWART, Kaye
See HOWE, Doris Kathleen

* * *

STEWART, Robert Wilson 1935-

PERSONAL: Born July 14, 1935, in London, England; son of John Archibald (a bank clerk) and Elizabeth (Wilson) Stewart. *Education:* Attended Eltham College, 1949-54; Brasenose College, Oxford, B.A., 1957. *Home:* 47 Park Hill Rd., Sidcup, Kent, England. *Office:* College of St. Mark and St. John, Derriford Rd., Plymouth, England.

CAREER: College of St. Mark and St. John, Plymouth, England, librarian, 1961—.

WRITINGS: (Editor) *Benjamin Disraeli: A List of Writings by Him and Writings about Him,* Scarecrow, 1972.

WORK IN PROGRESS: Editing an anthology of literary criticism of Disraeli.

* * *

STILLMAN, Irwin M(axwell) 1895-

PERSONAL: Born September 11, 1895, in New York, N.Y.; son of Louis (a manufacturer) and Anne (Mankoff) Stillman; married Ruth Silverhart (a technician), August 18, 1919; children: Paul, Edmund, Barbara Bookbinder. *Education:* New York Medical College, Flower and Fifth Ave. Hospitals, M.D., 1918. *Politics:* Republican. *Religion:* Jewish. *Home:* 10275 Collins Ave., Bal Harbour, Fla. 33154. *Agent:* Collins-Knowlton & Wing, 60 East 56th St., New York, N.Y. *Office:* 470 Ocean Ave., Brooklyn, N.Y. 11226.

CAREER: Physician, in private practice, 1919-1974; diplomate in internal medicine. Coney Island Hospital, Brooklyn, N.Y., attending physician in medicine, 1919-65, consultant, 1965—. Attending physician, Harbor Hospital, 1919-30; instructor, Long Island College, 1930-36; member of staff, Maimonides Hospital, 1935-50; executive director, of outpatient department, King's County Hospital, 1965-66. *Military service:* U.S. Army, 1917-18. *Member:* American Heart Association (fellow), American Geriatric Society (fellow), American College of Angiology. *Awards, honors:* Gold diploma from New York Medical College, 1968.

WRITINGS—All with Samm Sinclair Baker: *The Doctor's Quick Weight Loss Diet,* Prentice-Hall, 1967; *The Doctor's Quick Inches-Off Diet,* Prentice-Hall, 1969; *The Doctor's Quick Teenage Diet,* McKay, 1971; *The Doctor's Quick Weight Loss Diet Cookbook,* McKay, 1972; *The Dr. Stillman's Shape Up Program,* Delacorte, 1974.

SIDELIGHTS: Dr. Stillman has appeared on 400 television programs in the United States and Canada; he has given about 300 press interviews; he also lectures at spas and women's organizations. His books have sold millions of copies in hardcover and paperback, and have appeared in translation in seventeen countries.

* * *

STIPE, Robert Edwin 1928-

PERSONAL: Born July 28, 1928, in Easton, Pa.; son of John Norwood and Ethel M. (Rockafellow) Stipe; married

Josephine Davis Weedon, 1952; children: two sons. *Education:* Duke University, A.B., 1950, LL.B., 1953 (converted to J.D., 1969); University of North Carolina, M.R.P., 1959. *Home:* 100 Pine Lane, Chapel Hill, N.C. 27514. *Office:* Institute of Government, University of North Carolina, P.O. Box 990, Chapel Hill, N.C. 27514.

CAREER: Private practice as a city planning consultant in North Carolina and Virginia, 1956-57; University of North Carolina, Chapel Hill, instructor, 1957-61, assistant professor, 1961-63, associate professor, 1963-69, professor of public law and government, 1969—, assistant director of the Institute of Government, 1957—. Visiting lecturer at North Carolina State University and Cornell University. Member of North Carolina Governor's Advisory Committee on Beautification, 1966—. *Member:* International Council of Monuments and Sites, International Federation for Housing and Planning (member of board of trustees), National Trust for Historic Preservation, American Association for State and Local History, Association for Preservation Technology, National Trust (Great Britain), Council for the Protection of Rural England, American Institute of Planners (member of national committee on historic preservation, 1964—), American Society of Planning Officials, Town and Country Planning Association, North Carolina Preservation Society, Chapel Hill Historical Society (founder, 1966), Chapel Hill Preservation Society (member of board of directors, 1974—). *Awards, honors:* Fulbright research fellow at University College, University of London, 1968-69; Cannon Cup Award for Distinguished Service in Historic Preservation, 1973.

WRITINGS: (Editor) *Perception and Environment: Foundations of Urban Design,* University of North Carolina Press, 1965; (with H. G. Jones and others) *North Carolina State Plan for Historic Preservation,* Department of Archives and History and Institute of Government, University of North Carolina, 1970. Author of films issued by University of North Carolina, Institute of Government. "The Piedmont Crescent," 1968, and "Has Anyone Seen North Carolina Lately?" 1970. Also author of numerous monographs on planning, historic preservation, and urban design. Member of editorial advisory committee, *Environment and Behavior,* 1967-70; columnist, *Preservation News,* 1969-72.

WORK IN PROGRESS: Layman's Guide to Historic Preservation Law, and *Lectures on Historic Preservation,* for Institute of Government, University of North Carolina.

* * *

STODDARD, Hope 1900-

PERSONAL: Born March 31, 1900; daughter of Bode Moseley and Rosa Lee Stoddard; married Hermann Johns (separated). *Education:* Studied violin at Juilliard School of Music in earlier years; University of Michigan, B.A., 1923. *Home:* 4 Peter Cooper Rd., New York, N.Y. 10010.

CAREER: Etude, Philadelphia, Pa., editorial staff, 1924-32; then went to Europe and taught for two years at Berlitz schools in Copenhagen, Denmark, and Hamburg, Germany; on her return her joint interest in music and writing led to her becoming an editor of *International Musician,* Newark, N.J., 1940-65.

WRITINGS: From These Comes Music: Instruments of the Band and Orchestra (young adult book), Crowell, 1952; *Symphony Conductors of the U.S.A.* (young adult book), Crowell, 1957; *Subsidy Makes Sense,* International Press (Newark), 1960; *The Noon Answer* (poems), Humphries, 1965; *Famous American Women* (young adult book), Crowell, 1970.

SIDELIGHTS: Ms. Stoddard said: "I wrote *Famous American Women* because I felt there was an imbalance in the man-woman relationship—an imbalance not caused by any particular unfairness exercised by either sex, but one built up by customs and attitudes over the years. Dorothea Dix revolutionized the treatment of the mentally ill. Clara Barton founded the Red Cross in America. Lillian Gilbreth pioneered in the field of motion study. Susanne Langer has broadened the field of philosophy, as has Dr. Margaret Mead that of anthropology. It seemed only sensible to me that the contributions of women to the development of our country be set down. So I wrote the book."

* * *

STOLL, John E(dward) 1933-

PERSONAL: Born March 3, 1933, in Chicago, Ill.; son of Herman E. and Mary (Fobes) Stoll; married Alice M. Bertilson, October 1, 1955; children: John Durham, Alice Ingeborg. *Education:* Northwestern University, B.A., 1954, M.A., 1966; Wayne State University, Ph.D., 1966. *Home:* 125 Devonshire Dr., Athens, Ga. 30601. *Office:* Department of English, University of Georgia, Athens, Ga. 30601.

CAREER: University of Notre Dame, South Bend, Ind., instructor in English, 1958-60; Michigan State University Extension, instructor in English, 1960-61; Southeast Missouri State College, Cape Girardeau, assistant professor of English, 1961-63; Grove City College, Grove City, Pa., assistant professor of English, 1964-65; Wayne State University, Detroit, Mich., instructor in English, 1965-66; Ball State University, Muncie, Ind., assistant professor of English, 1966-70; Belmont College, Nashville, Tenn., professor of English, 1970-71; University of Georgia, Athens, assistant professor of English, 1971—. *Member:* Modern Language Association of America.

WRITINGS: D. H. Lawrence's "Sons and Lovers": Self-Encounter and the Unknown Self (monograph), Ball State University, 1968; *W. H. Auden: A Reading* (monograph), Ball State University, 1970; *The Great Deluge: A Yeats Bibliography,* Whitson, 1971; *The Novels of D. H. Lawrence: A Search for Integration,* University of Missouri Press, 1971; *D. H. Lawrence, 1911-1972: An International Bibliography,* Whitson, 1973. Contributor to literature journals.

* * *

STONE, Gregory P(rentice) 1921-

PERSONAL: Born October 28, 1921, in Olean, N.Y.; son of Horace P. (a commercial artist) and Grace (Emerson) Stone; married Margaret Renee Cuthbertson, July, 1944 (deceased); married Gladys Ishida (a sociologist), June, 1962; children: (first marriage) Mead Meredith, Susan Lea. *Education:* Hobart College, B.A., 1942; Princeton University, certificate in Turkish studies, 1944; University of Chicago, M.A., 1952, Ph.D., 1959. *Politics:* Democratic Liberal. *Religion:* "Atheist Episcopalian." *Home:* St. Croix Cove, Route 3, Hudson, Wis. 54016. *Office:* Department of Sociology, University of Minnesota, Minneapolis, Minn. 55455.

CAREER: University of Minnesota, Minneapolis, instructor, 1955-59, associate professor, 1961-64, professor of sociology, 1964—, professor of American studies, 1964—, member of board of trustees of University Episcopal Center, 1971—. *Military service:* U.S. Army, Infantry, 1943-45; received three battle stars and presidential citation. *Member:* International Sociological Association, International Committee for the Sociology of Sport, International Platform Association, American Sociological Association, Society for the Study of Social Problems, American Association for the Advancement of Science, American Civil Liberties Union, World Future Society, Midwest Sociological Association, Society for the Study of Symbolic Interaction (founder and co-chairman).

WRITINGS: (With William H. Form and others) *Community in Disaster,* Harper, 1958; (editor with Harvey A. Farberman) *Social Psychology Through Symbolic Interaction,* Xerox College Publishing, 1970; (editor) *Games, Sport, and Power,* Transaction Books, 1972.

Monographs: (With Form) *The Social Significance of Clothing in Occupational Life,* Michigan Agricultural Experiment Station, 1955; (with Form) *Clothing Inventories and Preferences among Rural and Urban Families,* Michigan Agricultural Experiment Station, 1955; (with Form) *The Local Community Clothing Market: A Study of the Social and Social Psychological Contexts of Shopping,* Michigan Agricultural Experiment Station, 1957.

Contributor: Eric Larrabee and Rolf Meyerson, editors, *Mass Leisure,* Free Press, 1958; Talcott Parsons and other editors, *Theories of Society,* Volume I, Free Press, 1961; Jack P. Gibbs, editor, *Urban Research Methods,* Van Nostrand, 1961; Charles R. Snyder and David Pittman, editors, *Society, Culture, and Drinking Patterns,* Wiley, 1962; Arnold M. Rose, editor, *Human Behavior and Social Processes,* Houghton, 1962; Alvin W. Gouldner and other editors, *Modern Sociology,* Harcourt, 1963; Richard L. Simpson and Ida Harper, editors, *Social Organization and Behavior,* Wiley, 1964; Ralph Slovenko and James A. Knight, editors, *Motivations in Play, Games, and Sport,* C.C Thomas, 1967; Gerald S. Kenyon, editor, *Sociology of Sport,* Athletic Institute, 1969; Robert Gutman and David Popenoe, editors, *Neighborhood, City, and Metropolis,* Random House, 1970; David J. Rachman, editor, *Retail Management Strategy,* Prentice-Hall, 1970; Eric Dunning, editor, *Sport and Society,* Cass, 1971.

Contributor to *Encyclopedia International.* Contributor of about twenty articles to professional journals. Member of board of editors of *International Review of Sport Sociology;* consultant to *Sports Illustrated.*

WORK IN PROGRESS: Sport, Play, and Leisure; Theoretical Contributions of Herman Schmalenbach; Symbolic Interaction as Social Psychology; Being Urban: A Social Psychological View of City Life; research on honesty in social circles, "the philosophy of the act," hustling as a way of life, the professionalization of sport, play among the Sanema Indians of Venezuela, and interpersonal relations and social structure.

SIDELIGHTS: Stone describes his viewpoint: "The strange and confused manner in which we are 'meeting' the energy crisis has little to do with the intrinsic nature of our resources (in particular the sun), but very much to do with the meanings we attach to fossil fuels; or the meaning we attach to work in our society seems to blind us to the importance of planning for our society in which distribution, rather than production, is the most fundamental socio-political-economic problem. Nor do we seem ever to grasp the meaning of our activities in the larger context of socio-economic history." *Avocational interests:* Symphonic music (especially contemporary), paintings, sculpture.

* * *

STONE, Nancy (Young) 1925-

PERSONAL: Born December 15, 1925, in Crawfordsville, Ind.; daughter of William Foster (a newspaperman) and Mary Emma (Engle) Young; married William Royal Stone (a graphic designer), July 28, 1947; children: John Conrad, Emily Foster. *Education:* Antioch College, B.A., 1948; Western Michigan University, M.A., 1970. *Politics:* Democrat. *Religion:* Unitarian Universalist. *Home:* 2219 Sycamore Lane, Kalamazoo, Mich. 49008.

CAREER: Cleveland Press, Cleveland, Ohio, reporter, writer, and copy girl, 1944-46; *Washington Court House Record Herald,* Washington Court House, Ohio, reporter and writer, 1946-47; Sequoia Press, Kalamazoo, Mich., office worker and copywriter, 1950-52, 1954-55; Upjohn Co. (pharmaceuticals), Kalamazoo, Mich., office worker, 1953-54; Western Michigan University, Kalamazoo, instructor in English, 1970—. *Member:* Modern Language Association of America, League of Women Voters (vice-president of local chapter, 1972-73).

WRITINGS: Whistle Up the Bay (juvenile), Eerdmans, 1966; *The Wooden River* (juvenile), Eerdmans, 1973. Contributor to *Dimensions.* Author of filmstrip script for Michigan Children's Aid Society, 1968.

WORK IN PROGRESS: A Michigan historical novel for children, completion expected in 1975.

* * *

STONEHOUSE, Bernard 1926-

PERSONAL: Born May 1, 1926, in Hull, England; married Sally Clacey, September 17, 1954; children: Caroline, Ann Felicity, Paul. *Education:* Student at University College, Hull, 1943-44; University College, London, B.Sc. (special honors), 1953; Merton College, Oxford, D.Phil., 1957, M.A., 1959. *Home:* 12 Heaton Grove, Bradford, Yorkshire, England. *Office:* Postgraduate School of Environmental Science, University of Bradford, Bradford 7, Yorks., England.

CAREER: University of Canterbury, Christchurch, New Zealand, senior lecturer, 1960-64, reader in zoology, 1964-69; Yale University, New Haven, Conn., visiting associate professor of biology, 1969; University of British Columbia, Vancouver, Commonwealth research fellow in zoology, 1969-70; writer, 1970-72; University of Bradford, Bradford, Yorkshire, England, senior lecturer in ecology and chairman of Postgraduate School of Environmental Science, 1972—. *Military service:* Royal Navy, 1944-45. Royal Air Force Volunteer Reserve, 1950-53; became pilot officer. *Member:* Society of Authors. *Awards, honors:* Polar Medal for services in Antarctica, 1953; Union Medal from British Ornithologists Union, 1971.

WRITINGS: The Emperor Penguin: Aptenodytes Forsteri Gray, H.M.S.O., 1953; *The Brown Skua: Chataracta Skua Loennbergi (Mathews), of South Georgia* (illustrated), H.M.S.O., 1956; *Het Bevroren Continent* (title means "The Frozen Continent"), C.de Boer, Jr., 1958.

The King Penguin: Aptenodytes Patagonica, of South Georgia, H.M.S.O., 1960; *Wideawake Island: The Story of the B.O.U. Centenary Expedition to Ascension,* Hutchinson, 1960; *Whales* (juvenile), A.H. & A.W. Reed, 1964;

Gulls and Terns (juvenile), A.H. & A.W. Reed, 1965; *Penguins,* Golden Press, 1968; *Birds of the New Zealand Shore,* A.H. & A.W. Reed, 1968.

Animals of the Arctic: The Ecology of the Far North, Holt, 1971; *Animals of the Antarctic: The Ecology of the Far South,* 1972; *Young Animals,* Viking, 1973; (editor) *Biology of Penguins* (symposium), Macmillan, in press. Contributor of about fifty articles to scientific journals in the United States and England.

* * *

STOREY, Anthony 1928-

PERSONAL: Born November 10, 1928, in Wakefield, Yorkshire, England; son of Frank Richmond (a miner) and Lily (Cartwright) Storey; married June Bridgewater (a nurse), June 26, 1954; married Anne-Marie Guludec (a teacher), March 22, 1970; children: (first marriage) Christopher, Jane, John. *Education:* University of Leeds, B.A., 1956; Cambridge University, graduate study, 1966—. *Politics:* "Of the left." *Home:* 35 Westley Rd., Bury St. Edmunds, Suffolk, England. *Office:* King's College, Cambridge University, Cambridge, England.

CAREER: British Army, 1949-66, serving in Malaya and Northern Ireland, leaving service as major; King's College, Cambridge University, Cambridge, England, tutor in psychology, 1966—. *Member:* Illiterary Society, Bury St. Edmund Squash Club.

WRITINGS—Novels: *Jesus Iscariot,* Calder, 1967; *Graceless Go I,* Calder, 1969; *The Rector* (Volume I of a trilogy), Calder, 1970; *Platinum Jag,* Calder, 1972; *The Centre Holds* (Volume II of trilogy), Calder, 1973; *Platinum Ass,* W.H. Allen, 1974. Also author of screenplays, "Graceless Go I," "The Plumed Serpent," and "Islandhwana."

WORK IN PROGRESS: Ceremony of Innocence, third volume of trilogy, completion expected in 1975.

SIDELIGHTS: "Jesus Iscariot," wrote one critic, "is a regional novel, exploiting the masculine vigor of the Northern working-classes." Piers Brendon commented that "the title is . . . particularly apposite. It fits Alistair, the paranoic hero, like a made-to-measure crown of thorns. . . .the novel itself is extremely enjoyable. . . .clever, violent, uneven, and funny." B. A. Young noted: "Funny thing: near the end, the author slips in a description of Alistair, his anti-hero—long, untidy hair, spotty face, stubby upturned nose. . . . And there's Anthony Storey on the jacket—long untidy hair, spotty face . . . More. Alistair has a younger brother Donald who writes a novel; Anthony has a younger brother David who writes novels."

Storey told *CA:* "Each of my novels is about (gruesome) individuals who want to be whole. The themes are grievously profane with robust, sacred under-themes."

* * *

STOREY, (Elizabeth) Margaret (Carlton) 1926-

PERSONAL: Born June 27, 1926, in London, England; daughter of Harold (an editor) and Lyn (a chemist; maiden name, Bramwell) Storey. *Education:* Girton College, Cambridge, B.A., 1948, M.A., 1953.

CAREER: Teacher of English language and literature in London, England, 1957—. Has also done secretarial and publicity work. *Member:* Institute for Comparative Study of History, Philosophy, and the Sciences.

WRITINGS—All for children; all published by Faber, except as indicated: *Kate and the Family Tree,* Bodley Head, 1965, published as *The Family Tree,* Nelson, 1973; *Pauline,* 1965, Doubleday, 1967; *Timothy and Two Witches,* 1966, Dell, 1974; *The Smallest Doll,* 1966; *The Smallest Bridesmaid,* 1966; *The Stone Sorcerer,* 1967; *The Dragon's Sister, and, Timothy Travels,* 1967; *A Quarrel of Witches,* 1970; *The Sleeping Witch,* 1971; *The Mollyday Holiday,* 1971; *Wrong Gear,* 1973; *Keep Running,* 1974.

WORK IN PROGRESS: More books for children.

SIDELIGHTS: Ms. Storey told *CA:* "I like writing for children because they are nice people. For the same reason I enjoy teaching. I'm not interesting otherwise. . . . it's hard to take myself seriously as an Author."

* * *

STOTTS, Jack L. 1932-

PERSONAL: Born November 5, 1932, in Dallas, Tex.; son of L. E. and Nancy (Moseley) Stotts; married Virginia Grafa (a secretary), June 12, 1954; children: Stuart, Nancy, Anna. *Education:* Trinity University, San Antonio, B.A. (cum laude), 1954; McCormick Theological Seminary, M.Div. (cum laude), 1957; Yale University, M.A., 1960, Ph.D., 1965; Oxford University, postdoctoral study, 1971-72. *Home:* 850 West Belden Ave., Chicago, Ill. 60614. *Office:* McCormick Theological Seminary, 800 West Belden Ave., Chicago, Ill. 60614.

CAREER: Assistant minister of Congregational church in Wallingford, Conn., 1957-59; University of Tulsa, Tulsa, Okla., assistant professor of religion and chaplain, 1959-60; pastor of United Presbyterian church in San Angelo, Tex., 1960-63; McCormick Theological Seminary, Chicago, Ill., instructor, 1963-66, assistant professor, 1966-69, associate professor, 1969-72, professor of Christian ethics, 1972—. Member of Council on Church and Society, United Presbyterian Church in the U.S.A. *Member:* American Society for Christian Ethics, Society for the Scientific Study of Religion. *Awards, honors:* American Association of Theological Schools faculty fellowship at Oxford University, 1971-72.

WRITINGS: Believing, Deciding, Acting, Geneva Press, 1968; *Shalom: The Search for a Peaceable City,* Abingdon, 1973. Contributor to *Christian Century, Enquiry,* and other journals.

WORK IN PROGRESS: Studies on the impact of technology upon culture change, particularly with reference to the religious component of the culture, and on the logic of moral discourse.

* * *

STOUDT, John Joseph 1911-

PERSONAL: Born March 11, 1911, in Northampton, Pa.; son of John Baer (an historian) and Elizabeth (de Long) Stoudt; married Nancy Feather Yost (a decorator), July 28, 1944; children: John Yost. *Education:* Haverford College, B.S., 1933; Yale University, B.D., 1936; graduate study at University of Heidelberg, 1938, and University of Marburg, 1939; University of Edinburgh, Ph.D., 1943. *Politics:* Republican. *Home:* Stauderhof, Box 3, Route 1, Fleetwood, Pa. 19522.

CAREER: Ordained minister of United Church of Christ,

1936; pastor of churches at various times, 1936-67. Has taught at Talladega College, 1947-50, University of Delaware, 1950-51, University of Pennsylvania, 1955-56, and Kutztown State College, 1965-71. Lecturer at historical and folklore societies, and at University of Bristol, Haverford College, University of Marburg, University of Waterloo (Canada), and other schools. *Military service:* U.S. Army, chaplain, 1942-44. *Member:* American Philosophical Association (emeritus member), Pennsylvania German Society, East Berks Association of the Southeast Pennsylvania Conference of the United Church of Christ, Phi Beta Kappa. *Awards, honors:* First prize, George Washington Bi-Centennial Commission essay contest, 1932; Doctor of Theology, University of Marburg, 1956.

WRITINGS: Consider the Lilies How They Grow: An Interpretation of the Symbolism of Pennsylvania German Art, Pennsylvania German Folklore Society, 1938; (translator) Jacob Boehme, *The Way to Christ,* Harper & Bros., 1947; *Pennsylvania Folk Art: An Interpretation,* Schlechter's, 1948, published as *Pennsylvania German Folk Art: An Interpretation,* 1966; (editor) *Pennsylvania German Poetry: 1685-1830* (anthology), Pennsylvania German Folklore Society, 1956; (editor and translator) *Private Devotions for Home and Church,* Christian Education Press, 1956; *Sunrise to Eternity: A Study in Jacob Boehme's Life and Thought,* preface by Paul Tillich, University of Pennsylvania Press, 1957, published as *Jacob Boehme: His Life and Thought,* Seabury Press, 1968; (editor and translator) Johann Arndt, *Devotions and Prayers,* Baker Book, 1958; *Montgomery County: A Cultural Picture,* Livingston, 1959.

(Translator) Caspar Schwenckfeld, *Passional and Prayerbook in Modern Translation,* Schwenckfelder Library (Pennsburg, Pa.), 1961; (with James Ernst) *Ephrata: A History,* Pennsylvania German Folklore Society, 1963; *Ordeal at Valley Forge,* University of Pennsylvania Press, 1963; *Early Pennsylvania Arts and Crafts,* A. S. Barnes, 1964; *Sunbonnets and Shoofly Pies: A Pennsylvania Dutch Cultural History,* A. S. Barnes, 1973; (editor and translator) L. A. Wollenweber, *Mountain Mary: An Historical Tale of Early Pennsylvania,* Shumway, 1973.

Contributor to *Encyclopaedia Britannica, Collier's Encyclopedia,* and *Schaff Herzog.* Contributor of over 250 articles, poems, and book reviews to periodicals, including *Ministers Quarterly* and *Pennsylvania Magazine of History and Biography.*

WORK IN PROGRESS: Friends and Brethren in the Holy Experiment: A Book of Documents.

* * *

STOVER, Leon E(ugene) 1929-

PERSONAL: Born April 9, 1929, in Lewistown, Pa.; son of George Franklin (a university professor) and Helen (Haines) Stover; married Takeko Kawaii (a college lecturer in Far Eastern history), October 12, 1956. *Education:* Western Maryland College, B.A., 1950; graduate study at University of New Mexico, 1950, and Harvard University, 1951; Columbia University, M.A., 1952, Ph.D., 1962. *Home:* 602 Cunningham Hall, 3100 South Michigan Ave., Chicago, Ill. 60616. *Agent:* Robert P. Mills Ltd., 156 East 52nd St., New York, N.Y. 10022; and Hilary Rubenstein, A. P. Watt & Son, 26/28 Bedford Row, London WC1R 4HL, England. *Office:* Department of Sociology, Illinois Institute of Technology, Chicago, Ill. 60616.

CAREER: American Museum of Natural History, New York, N.Y., instructor, 1955-57; Hobart and William Smith Colleges, Geneva, N.Y., instructor, 1957-63, assistant professor of anthropology, 1963-65; Illinois Institute of Technology, Chicago, associate professor, 1966-74, professor of anthropology, 1974—. Visiting assistant professor of cultural anthropology at University of Tokyo, 1963-65, 1965-66. Chairman of awards committee, John W. Campbell Memorial Award, 1972—. *Member:* Association for Asian Studies, International Society for Technology Assessment, Current Anthropology (associate), Science Fiction Writers of America. *Awards, honors:* Human Ecology Fund fellow in Japan, 1963-64; National Institutes of Health fellow in Japan, 1964-65; Chris Award and Cine Award, both 1973, for "Power and Wheels" (filmscript).

WRITINGS: (Contributor) *U.S. Area Army Handbook on Communist China,* U.S. Government Printing Office, 1967; (editor with Harry Harrison) *Apeman, Spaceman: Anthropological Science Fiction,* Doubleday, 1968; (editor with Willis E. McNelly) *Above the Human Landscape: An Anthology of Social Science Fiction,* Goodyear Publishing, 1972; (with Harrison) *Stonehenge* (historical novel), Scribner, 1972; *La Science-Fiction americaine: Essai d'anthropologie culturelle* (title means "American Science-Fiction: An Essay in Cultural Anthropology"), Aubier Montaigne (Paris), 1972; *The Cultural Ecology of Chinese Civilization: Peasants and Elites in the Last of the Agrarian States,* Universe Books, 1973; (with wife, Takeko Kawaii Stover) *China: An Anthropological Perspective* (textbook), Goodyear Publishing, 1974.

Author of "Power and Wheels" (filmscript) and other scripts for Encyclopaedia Britannica Films. Contributor of occasional short stories to magazines and a number of professional articles to journals. Science editor, *Amazing Stories,* 1967-69.

WORK IN PROGRESS: The Anthropology of Stonehenge, an explanation of how he came to the conclusion in *Stonehenge* (the novel) that Stonehenge was a tribal assembly of the Wessex warriors; another historical novel, *The Bamboo Annals of Confucius: Games Chinese Play; The Yin/Yang Handbook of Human Culture,* under a Chinese pseudonym; and an English-language version of *La Science Fiction Americaine.*

SIDELIGHTS: Stover's course in science fiction at Illinois Institute of Technology was among the first to be taught at the university level in the country. He writes: "SF may also be treated as a symptom of its cultural background, as in the anthropological study of any body of oral literature or mythology from a tribal culture, which is what I have done in *La Science Fiction Americaine.* Harry Harrison and I have made use of the rhetorical technique of SF, in which background is hero or subject, to write a new kind of historical novel, the novel *about* history and shall do the same for my novel about Confucius." Stover's nonfiction book about China is based on his lectures at Tokyo University, where he was the first non-Japanese ever to teach in the graduate school.

* * *

STRANGE, Susan 1923-

PERSONAL: Born June 9, 1923, in Dorset, England; daughter of Louis Arbon (a colonel in Royal Flying Corps) and Marjorie (Beath) Strange; married Denis Marritt (a physician), September 5, 1942; married Clifford Selly (a farmer and writer), December 14, 1955; children: (first marriage) Giles, Jane Franklin; (second marriage) Mark,

Roger, Kate, Adam. *Education:* Attended Universite de Caen, 1940, and London School of Economics and Political Science, 1940-43. *Politics:* "Radical non-Communist." *Religion:* None. *Home:* Pendley Farm, Tring, Hertfordshire, England. *Office:* Royal Institute of International Affairs, 10 St. James Sq., London S.W.1, England.

CAREER: Economist, London, England, editorial writer, 1944-46; *Observer,* London, England, correspondent from United Nations and Washington, D.C., 1946-48, economic correspondent, 1951-57; University College, University of London, London, England, lecturer in international relations, 1949-64; Royal Institute of International Affairs, London, England, research fellow, 1964-74. Visiting lecturer, London School of Economics and Political Science, 1964-74.

WRITINGS: The Soviet Trade Weapon, Phoenix House, 1959; *The Sterling Problem and the Six,* Chatham House, 1967; (with Geoffrey Goodwin) *Research on International Organization,* Heinemann, 1968; (contributor) Robert Cox, editor, *International Organization and World Politics,* Macmillan, 1970; *Sterling and British Policy: A Political Study of an International Currency in Decline,* Oxford University Press, 1971; (contributor) Kenneth Twitchett, editor, *The Evolving United Nations: A Prospect for Peace,* Europa Publications, 1971; (contributor) Cox and Harold Jacobson, editors, *The Anatomy of Influence,* Yale University Press, 1972; (contributor) Roger Morgan, *International Studies Today,* Oxford University Press, 1972.

* * *

STRASSOVA, Helena 1924-

PERSONAL: Born March 20, 1924, in Prague, Czechoslovakia; daughter of Jacob and Camilla (Gruenbaum) Strass. *Education:* Studied at Conservatory of Music, Vienna, Austria. *Religion:* Jewish. *Home:* 3 rue St. Louis en l'Isle, Paris 4e, France. *Office:* 4 rue Git-de-Couer, Paris 6e, France.

CAREER: Owner of literary agency in Paris, France.

WRITINGS: Le Chemin, translation by Peter Freixa published as *The Path,* Orion Press, 1970.

* * *

STRATHERN, Andrew (Jamieson) 1939-

PERSONAL: Born January 19, 1939, in Colchester, England; son of Robert and Mary (Sharp) Strathern; married Ann Marilyn Evans (a researcher); children: Barbara Helen Mary. *Education:* Trinity College, Cambridge, B.A. (first class honors), 1962, M.A., 1965, Ph.D., 1968. *Home:* Section C, Lot 5, Fourth St., Waigani University Housing, Port Moresby, Papua New Guinea. *Office:* University Post Office, Box 4820, University of Papua New Guinea, Port Moresby, Papua New Guinea.

CAREER: Cambridge University, Cambridge, England, research fellow at Trinity College, 1965-68; Australian National University, Canberra, research fellow and fellow of Research School of Pacific Studies, 1969-72; University of Papua New Guinea, Port Moresby, professor of anthropology and sociology and head of department, 1973—. *Member:* Royal Anthropological Institute (fellow). *Awards, honors:* Carl Bequest Prize from Royal Anthropological Institute, 1968, for essay.

WRITINGS: (With wife, Marilyn Strathern) *Self-decoration in Mount Hagen,* Duckworth, 1971; *The Rope of Moka: Big-men and Ceremonial Exchange in Mount Hagen,* Cambridge University Press, 1972; *One Father, One Blood: Descent and Group Structure among the Melpa People,* Australian National University Press, 1972. Contributor to anthropological journals, including *Man, Journal of the Polynesian Society, Mankind, Ethnology,* and *Oceania.*

WORK IN PROGRESS: Continuing research on social change in the Western and Southern highlands district of Papua New Guinea; general research on culture, including courting songs in the Melpa language of Mount Hagen.

* * *

STRATHERN, Ann Marilyn 1941-

PERSONAL: Born March 6, 1941, in England; married Andrew J. Strathern. *Education:* Cambridge University, B.A. (honors), 1963, M.A., 1967, Ph.D., 1968. *Office:* New Guinea Research Unit, Australian National University, Box 1238, Boroko, Papua, New Guinea.

CAREER: Cambridge University, Cambridge, England, assistant curator, Museum of Archaeology and Anthropology, 1966-68, director of studies at Girton College, 1968; Australian National University, New Guinea Research Unit, Papua, research fellow, 1970-72, 1974—. *Member:* Royal Anthropological Society (fellow), Association of Social Anthropologists (England), Association of Social Anthropologists (Australia).

WRITINGS: (With husband, Andrew J. Strathern) *Self-Decoration in Mount Hagen,* Duckworth, 1971; *Women In Between: Female Roles in a Male World, Mount Hagen, New Guinea,* Seminar Press, 1972. Contributor to *New Guinea Research Bulletin.*

WORK IN PROGRESS: A book, for Penguin; further contributions to *New Guinea Research Bulletin.*

* * *

STRAUGHAN, Robert P(aul) L(ouis) 1924-

PERSONAL: Surname is pronounced Strawn; born December 6, 1924, in Lowell, Mass.; son of Jesse Bird and Aurore Straughan; married Rosemary Thomas (a bookkeeper), September 23, 1951; children: Robert Paul, Julie Marie. *Education:* Attended University of New Hampshire and University of Miami, Coral Gables, Fla. *Politics:* Independent. *Religion:* Roman Catholic. *Home and office address:* P.O. Box 1000, Belleview, Fla. 32620.

CAREER: Coral Reef Exhibits, Belleview, Fla., president, 1954—. Has spent more than thirty thousand hours under water as a scientific marine collector; found a sunken galleon loaded with treasure ("but didn't get any"). Has also worked as a forester, lithographer, gold prospector, private photographer for a millionaire, and has owned and operated seven pet and aquarium stores. *Military service:* U.S. Navy, photographer, 1943-46. *Member:* International Oceanographic Foundation, National Geographic Society, Fauna Preservation Society, East African Wildlife Society, Florida Zoological Society, Museum of Natural History, Audubon Society.

WRITINGS: Keeping the Dwarf Sea Horse, All-Pets Books, 1956; *Keeping Sea Horses,* T.F.H. Publications, 1961; *The Salt Water Aquarium in the Home,* A. S. Barnes, 1954, 4th edition, 1974; *Sharks, Morays, and Treasure,* A. S. Barnes, 1965; *Exploring the Reef,* A. S. Barnes, 1968, revised edition, 1974; *The Marine Collector's*

Guide, A. S. Barnes, 1973; *Jet Safari to Africa,* A. S. Barnes, 1973; *Build a Jungle Zoo,* A. S. Barnes, 1973; *Adventures in Marine Collecting,* A. S. Barnes, 1973; *Adventure in Belize,* A. S. Barnes, 1974.

Illustrator with others of *Poisonous and Venomous Marine Animals,* by Bruce Halstead, 1965, 1970, and *Salt Water Aquarium Fish,* by Herbert Axelrod, 1973.

Author of column in *All Pets,* 1956-66, and *Aquarium Journal,* 1957-65. Contributor of several hundred articles to magazines, including *National Geographic.* Publisher and editor of *Salt Water Aquarium,* 1965-73.

WORK IN PROGRESS: Books on open air zoos, jungles, rain forests, deep sea fauna, automobile safety, safe highways, and giant ships six miles in diameter.

SIDELIGHTS: Straughan writes: "I tell things as they are, not how they are supposed to be, and I feel great sadness over the despoliation of our wild areas and wildlife. I am distressed with so-called conservation agencies both public and private who conserve little more than their jobs. The destruction of the vast Amazon hurts me for I can see the Amazon eventually as foul as the Detroit River. If I could protect the rainforests and jungles I would realize a great dream."

* * *

STRAUSS, Richard L(ehman) 1933-

PERSONAL: Born May 4, 1933, in Philadelphia, Pa.; son of Lehman (a clergyman) and Elsie (Hannah) Strauss; married Mary Getz, June 19, 1954; children: Stephen, Michael, Mark, Timothy. *Education:* Wheaton College, Wheaton, Ill., A.B., 1954; Dallas Theological Seminary, Th.M., 1958, Th.D., 1962. *Home:* 410 Mira Loma La., Escondido, Calif. 92025. *Office:* Emmanuel Faith Community Church, 639 East Felicita, Escondido, Calif. 92025.

CAREER: Ordained Baptist minister, 1958; minister in Fort Worth, Tex., 1958-64, Huntsville, Ala., 1964-72; Emmanuel Faith Community Church, Escondido, Calif., clergyman, 1972—.

WRITINGS: Marriage Is for Love, Tyndale, 1973.

* * *

STREIKER, Lowell D(ean) 1939-

PERSONAL: Born March 14, 1939, in Chicago, Ill.; son of Frederic Burton (a podiatrist) and Alice (Peller) Streiker; married Lois Susanne Leff (a medical records administrator), March 14, 1957; children: Stephen Dean, Susan Lynn. *Education:* Temple University, B.A., 1962; Princeton University, M.A., 1966, Ph.D., 1968. *Home:* 1214 Heather Lane, Carrcroft Crest, Wilmington, Del. 19803. *Agent:* Curtis Brown Ltd., 60 East 56th St., New York, N.Y. 10022. *Office:* Mental Health Association of Delaware, 1813 North Franklin St., Wilmington, Del. 19802.

CAREER: Temple University, Philadelphia, Pa., assistant professor, 1964-72; Mental Health Association of Delaware, Wilmington, executive director, 1973—. Producer and moderator of television series, "Counterpoint," broadcast by WCAU-TV, Philadelphia, 1970-71.

WRITINGS: (With Thomas E. Bird and others) *Modern Theologians: Christians and Jews,* University of Notre Dame Press, 1967; *Promise of Buber,* Lippincott, 1969; *The Gospel of Irreligious Religion,* Sheed, 1969; (editor) *Who Am I?: Second Thoughts on Man, His Loves, His Gods,* Sheed, 1970; *The Jesus Trip: Advent of the Jesus Freaks,* Abingdon, 1971; (with Gerald S. Strober) *Religion and the New Majority: Billy Graham, Middle America, and the Politics of the Seventies,* Association Press, 1972.

WORK IN PROGRESS: The Study of Religion, a college textbook.

* * *

STROH, Guy W(eston) 1931-

PERSONAL: Born March 28, 1931, in Elizabeth, N.J.; son of G. A. (a newspaperman) and Hannah (Weston) Stroh; married Marion Kopec, August 13, 1966. *Education:* Princeton University, A.B., 1953, M.A., 1955, Ph.D., 1957. *Home:* 501 Parkway Ave., Trenton, N.J. 08618. *Office:* Department of Philosophy, Rider College, Lawrenceville, N.J. 08602.

CAREER: Rider College, Lawrenceville, N.J., assistant professor, 1956-63, associate professor, 1963-66, professor of philosophy, 1966—, chairman of department, 1963—. *Member:* American Philosophical Association, American Association of University Professors (state president, New Jersey, 1969-71), New Jersey Regional Philosophical Association. *Awards, honors:* Lindback Foundation Award for distinguished teaching, 1966.

WRITINGS: Plato and Aristotle: An Introduction, Rider College, 1964, revised edition, Boyd & Fraser, 1970; *American Philosophy from Edwards to Dewey,* Van Nostrand, 1968.

WORK IN PROGRESS: A study of the development of moral philosophy in the United States; inquiry into some problems of ethical naturalism.

* * *

STRONG, Roy (Colin) 1935-

PERSONAL: Born August 23, 1935, in London, England; son of George Edward Clement (a businessman) and Mabel Ada (Smart) Strong; married Julia Trevelyan Oman (a designer), October 9, 1971. *Education:* Queen Mary College, London, B.A. (with honors), 1956; Warburg Institute, London, Ph.D., 1959. *Home:* 2E Morpeth Ter., London SW1 P1EW, England. *Office:* Victoria and Albert Museum, South Kensington, London S.W.7, England.

CAREER: National Portrait Gallery, London, England, assistant keeper, 1959-67, director, 1967-73; Victoria and Albert Museum, London, director, 1974—. *Member:* Society of Antiquaries, Athenaeum, Beefsteak, Garrick, Grillions.

WRITINGS: Portraits of Queen Elizabeth I, Clarendon Press, Oxford, 1963; (with J. A. van Dorsten) *Leicester's Triumph,* Sir Thomas Browne Institute, University of Leiden, 1964; *Holbein and Henry VIII,* Pantheon, 1967; *The House of Tudor,* Pendragon, 1967; (editor) *Festival Designs by Inigo Jones* (exhibition catalog), University Press of Virginia, 1967; *The Elizabethan Image: Painting in England, 1540-1620* (exhibition catalog), Arno, 1969; *The English Icon: Elizabethan and Jacobean Portraiture,* Routledge & Kegan Paul, for Paul Mellon Foundation for British Art, 1969, Yale University Press, 1970; *Tudor and Jacobean Portraits,* two volumes, Pendragon, 1969.

(With wife, Julia Trevelyan Oman) *Elizabeth R,* Secker & Warburg, 1971, Stein & Day, 1972; (with Oman) *Mary Queen of Scots,* Secker & Warburg, 1972, Stein & Day, 1973; *Van Dyck: Charles I on Horseback,* Viking, 1972; *Splendour at Court: Renaissance Spectacle and the*

Theatre of Power, Houghton, 1973; (with Stephen Orgel) *Inigo Jones: The Theatre of the Stuart Court,* two volumes, University of California Press, 1973; (with Colin Ford) *A Victorian Album: The Hill-Adamson Collection,* J. Cape, 1974.

Author of numerous exhibition catalogs; writer of television scripts. Contributor of articles and reviews to scholarly journals and popular periodicals.

SIDELIGHTS: Of *Tudor and Jacobean Portraits,* a *Spectator* reviewer wrote: "For students of the period, it is as though a new gold mine had been thrown open, not only without restrictions, but with the addition of the most comprehensive system of signposts, and notices . . . Dr. Strong says of his own work that 'it is intended primarily as a working tool for students of the period regardless of the field in which they are active.' He has certainly provided an instrument which will cut the corners of many a future historian's task."

* * *

STRONGIN, Lynn 1939- (Lynn Michaels)

PERSONAL: Born February 27, 1939, in New York, N.Y.; daughter of Edward Israel (a psychologist) and Marguerite (an artist; maiden name, Rosenblum) Strongin. *Education:* Manhattan School of Music, student, 1956-59; Hunter College of the City University of New York, B.A. (cum laude), 1963; Stanford University, M.A., 1965; University of New Mexico, graduate study, 1971—. *Home:* 1177 Cardenas S.E., #135, Albuquerque, N.M. 87108.

CAREER: Long Island University, Long Island, N.Y., instructor in English at C. W. Post College, 1965-66; Merritt College, Oakland, Calif., instructor in English, 1967-68; Mills College, Oakland, Calif., instructor in English, 1968-69; Anna Head School, Oakland, Calif., instructor in English, 1970; University of New Mexico, Albuquerque, teaching assistant, 1971-75. *Member:* American Association of University Professors, Alumnae Association of Hunter College. *Awards, honors:* Woodrow Wilson fellow, 1963-64; P.E.N. research grant, 1971; creative writing fellowship from National Endowment for the Arts, 1972-73.

WRITINGS: The Dwarf Cycle (poems), Thorp Springs Press, 1972.

Poetry is represented in the following anthologies: *Thirty-one New American Poets,* edited by Ron Schrieber, Hill & Wang, 1969; *Green Flag,* edited by Schreiber, City Lights, 1969; *Sisterhood Is Powerful,* edited by Robin Morgan, Random House, 1970; *American Literary Anthology 3,* edited by George Plimpton, Viking, 1970; *Mark in Time: Portraits and Poets of San Francisco,* edited by Nick Harvey, Glide, 1971; *The San Francisco Bark,* edited by Christa Fleischman and Harvey, Thorp Springs Press, 1972; *Probes: An Introduction to Poetry,* edited by William K. Harlan, Macmillan, 1973; *Rising Tides: Contemporary American Women Poets,* edited by Laura Chester and Sharon Barba, Simon & Schuster, 1973; *"No More Masks!,"* edited by Ellen Bass, Doubleday, 1973; *The Touch of the Poet,* edited by Paul Holmes, Harper, 1974.

Author of a verse play, "Nocturne," produced by KPFA, Berkeley, Calif., 1969. Author of two poems set to music and performed in *Premiere Concert,* Studio 58, New York, N.Y., 1972. Author of *Homestretch,* five poems set to dance performed in "Four Premieres: Four Women Choreographers" at Barnard College, Dance Uptown Concert Series, 1973.

Contributor of short stories, under pseudonym Lynn Michaels, to *Ladder;* contributor of poetry to *Poetry, English Journal, New York Quarterly, Aphra, Chicago Sunday Tribune, Cafe Solo, Hiram Poetry Review, Human Voice, Sumac, Trace, Hyperion, Motive, Man-Root, Occident, Everywoman, Woodrow Wilson Newsletter, Echo, Bay Podium, Goliards, Confrontation, Illuminations-Gar, Stooge, Galley Sail Review, Buttons, West End, Thunderbird, New Mexico Magazine, Sunstone Review, Southern Poetry Review, Wisconsin Review, Ark River Review, Mosaic, Ladder, Bartleby's Review, Granite,* and *Empty Elevator Shaft.*

WORK IN PROGRESS: A book of poems; a novella, *Lee & Sarne.*

AVOCATIONAL INTERESTS: Chamber music, photography, translations from French to English.

BIOGRAPHICAL/CRITICAL SOURCES: Bartleby's Review, winter, 1974; *Shocks,* summer, 1973; *Man-Root,* spring, 1974.

* * *

STROUSSE, Flora G. 1897(?)-1974

1897(?)—March 9, 1974; American author of books for children. Obituaries: *Publishers Weekly,* April 22, 1974.

* * *

STRUVE, Walter 1935-

PERSONAL: Born May 6, 1935, in Somers Point, N.J.; son of Louis W. and Mary (Russell) Struve; married Cynthia R. Rivers, February 21, 1959; children: Adam, Derick. *Education:* Lafayette College, A.B., 1955; University of Kiel, graduate study, 1955-56; Yale University, M.A., 1957, Ph.D., 1963; Free University of Berlin, graduate study, 1960-61. *Residence:* New York, N.Y. *Office:* Department of History, City College of the City University of New York, 138th St. and Convent Ave., New York, N.Y. 10031.

CAREER: Princeton University, Princeton, N.J., instructor in history, 1961-64; City College of the City University of New York, New York, N.Y., instructor, 1964-65, assistant professor, 1965-73, professor of history, 1974—. *Member:* American Historical Association, Conference Group on Central European History.

WRITINGS: Elites Against Democracy: Leadership Ideals in Bourgeois Political Thought in Germany, 1890-1933, Princeton University Press, 1973. Contributor of articles and reviews to historical journals.

WORK IN PROGRESS: History of a German White-Collar Union.

* * *

STRYJKOWSKI, Julian 1905-

PERSONAL: Born April 27, 1905, in Stryj, Union of Soviet Socialist Republics (formerly in Poland). *Education:* University of Lwow, D.Ph., 1932. *Home:* Wyzwolenia 2/47, Warsaw, Poland.

CAREER: Tworczesc (literary monthly), Warsaw, Poland, editor, 1954.

WRITINGS: Bieg do Fragala (short stories; title means "Course to Fragala"), Czytelnik, 1951; *Pozegnanie z Italia* (title means "Farewell to Italy"), Czytelnik, 1954; *Glosy w ciemnosci* (novel; title means "Voices in the Dark"), Czytelnik, 1956; *Imie wlasne: Opowiadania* (short stories), Czytelnik, 1961; *Czarna roza* (short stories; title means "The Black Rose"), Czytelnik, 1962; *Austeria,* Czytelnik, 1966, translation by Celina Wieniewska published as *The Inn,* Harcourt, 1971.

Plays: "Dziedzictwo" (title means "Heir"), first produced in 1955; "Sodoma" (title means "Sodom"), first produced in 1963.

SIDELIGHTS: Stryjkowski's books have been translated into fourteen languages.

* * *

SUELTZ, Arthur Fay 1928-

PERSONAL: Surname rhymes with "Schultz"; born August 19, 1928, in Aberdeen, S.D.; son of Arthur Frederick (an insurance agent) and Persis (Taylor) Sueltz; married Mildred Hovland (a medical laboratory assistant), August 19, 1950; children: Stephen, Fay, Garret. *Education:* University of California, Berkeley, B.A., 1950; Princeton Theological Seminary, M.Div., 1953. *Home:* 3146 Arlotte Ave., Long Beach, Calif. 90808. *Office:* 3955 Studebaker St., Long Beach, Calif. 90808.

CAREER: Assistant pastor of Presbyterian church in Concord, Calif., 1953-57; pastor of Presbyterian church in Hanford, Calif., 1957-64; Lakewood First Presbyterian Church, Long Beach, Calif., pastor, 1964—. Vice-president of program agency of general assembly of United Presbyterian Church, 1973—.

WRITINGS: When the Wood Is Green, Harper, 1973. Contributor to *Faith at Work.*

WORK IN PROGRESS: If I Should Die Before I Live, for Harper.

SIDELIGHTS: Sueltz was coach of the Princeton University lightweight rowing crews, 1951-53.

* * *

SUHL, Benjamin

EDUCATION: Columbia University, Ph.D., 1968. *Home:* 89 Wadsworth Ter., New York, N.Y. 10040.

CAREER: Fairleigh Dickinson University, Teaneck, N.J., currently professor of French.

WRITINGS: Jean-Paul Sartre: The Philosopher as a Literary Critic, Columbia University Press, 1970.

* * *

SUNG, P. M.
See CHUN, Jinsie K(yung) S(hien)

* * *

SURET-CANALE, Jean 1921-

PERSONAL: Born April 27, 1921, in Paris, France. *Education:* French Ministry of Education, Professeur Agrege de l'Universite, 1946; Institute of Africa, Academy of Sciences of the U.S.S.R., Docteur es sciences historiques, 1963; University of Paris, Docteur de 3e cycle, 1969. *Home:* 3 Rue des Arts, 92100 Boulogne, Brittancourt, France. *Office:* Institute of Geography, University of Oran, Oran, Algeria.

CAREER: Professor at lycees in France and Senegal, 1946-59; Lycee de Conakry, Conakry, Guinea, principal, 1959-61; Institut National de Recherches, Conakry, Guinea, director, 1960-62; Ecole Normale Superieure, Kindia, Guinea, director, 1962-63; Centre d'Etudes et de Recherches Marxistes, Paris, France, deputy director, 1963—; Centre National de la Recherche Scientifique, Section de Geographie, Paris, France, attache de recherches, 1966-68, charge de recherches, 1968-74; University of Oran, Institute of Geography, Oran, Algeria, maitre-assistant, 1974—. *Wartime service:* French Resistance, 1940-44.

WRITINGS: Afrique noire, occidentale et centrale, Editions Sociales (Paris), Volume I, 1958, 3rd revised and updated edition, 1968, Volume II, 1964, Volume III, 1972, translation by Till Gottheiner of Volume II published as *French Colonialism in Tropical Africa, 1900-1945,* Pica Press, 1971; (with Djibril T. Niane) *Histoire de l'Afrique occidentale,* Presence Africaine, 1961; *La Naissance des dieux,* Editions de l'Union Rationaliste, 1966; *La Republique de Guinee,* Editions Sociales, 1970; (with Emma Maquet and Ibrahima Baba Kake) *Histoire de l'Afrique centrale,* Presence Africaine, 1972; (with Jean-Emil Vidal) *La Coree Populaire,* Editions Sociales, 1973. Author of other historical and economic studies.

* * *

SUSAC, Andrew 1929-

PERSONAL: Born July 4, 1929, in Provident, Ohio; son of Nikola and Janja (Mustapic) Susac; married Nan Selle (a puppeteer and actress), June, 1954; children: Jenny, Paul, Marc. *Education:* University of Missouri, A.B., 1948; University of Colorado, M.A., 1949; Tulane University, graduate study, 1950-54. *Politics:* Independent. *Religion:* Yogi. *Home:* 405 Arguello Blvd., San Francisco, Calif. 94118. *Agent:* Barthold Fles Agency, 507 Fifth Ave., New York, N.Y. 10017.

CAREER: Teacher of drama and science in private schools in San Francisco and vicinity, 1960—. Actor in summer and winter stock; writer, director, and actor with little theatre groups; teacher of drama at Walt Baptiste Yoga Center; spent 1971-72, teaching and writing in Guadalajara, Mexico. *Member:* National Collegiate Players.

WRITINGS: Paracelsus: Monarch of Medicine (juvenile), Doubleday, 1968; *The Clock, the Balance and the Guillotine* (juvenile), Doubleday, 1970; *God's Fool* (adult), Doubleday, 1972. Also author of 18 plays, two of which were produced Off-Broadway. Poems have been published in magazines in United States and Canada. Editor, *California Nurse,* 1963-66, and *New Ways in Education and Art,* 1970.

WORK IN PROGRESS: A history of classical and medieval medicine; a beginner's guide to yoga; two novels, one on a Mexican theme titled *Wind Devil.*

* * *

SUTHERLAND, Earl Wilbur 1915-1974

November 19, 1915—March 9, 1974; American biochemist and Nobel laureate. Obituaries: *New York Times,* March 10, 1974; *Washington Post,* March 10, 1974; *Time,* March 18, 1974; *Newsweek,* March 18, 1974.

* * *

SUTHERLAND, James (Edward) 1948-

PERSONAL: Born August 25, 1948, in Greenwich, Conn.; son of Hector H. (a college instructor) and Martha (Scofield) Sutherland. *Education:* Rochester Institute of Technology, A.A.S., 1968, B.S., 1970; State University of New York College of Environmental Science and Forestry, graduate study, 1974—. *Home:* 95 Williamsburg Rd., Pittsford, N.Y. 14534.

CAREER: Peace Corps, Washington, D.C., volunteer trainee in South Korea, 1971. *Awards, honors:* First prize for best editorial in a high school newspaper from American Newspaper Publishers Association, 1966; Ford Foundation grant.

WRITINGS: Stormtrack, Pyramid Publications, 1974. Work is represented in anthologies, including *Generation,* edited by David Gerrold, Dell, 1972; *Clarion II,* edited by Robin Scott Wilson, New American Library, 1972; *Omega,* edited by Roger Elwood, Walker & Co., 1974. Contributor of short stories, and science and travel articles to national magazines.

WORK IN PROGRESS: A novel about psychical research; a book about wilderness survival.

SIDELIGHTS: Sutherland writes: "In most of my writing I have been exploring the impact of science and technology on ordinary persons, and vice versa, both in and out of fiction. I fully expect to be occupied by this theme for the rest of my life."

* * *

SUTHERLAND, N(icola) M(ary) 1925-

PERSONAL: Born October 15, 1925, in Hythe, Kent, England; daughter of Herbert Orr (a soldier) and Eileen (Watney) Sutherland. *Education:* Newnham College, Cambridge, B.A. (honors), 1947, M.A., 1954; University of London, Ph.D., 1958; University of Paris, Diplome de civilisation francaise, 1953. *Home:* 13 Escuan Lodge, Aberdeen Park, London N5 2AP, England. *Agent:* Shaw Maclean, St. John's Chambers, 2-10 St. John's Rd., London S.W. 11, England. *Office:* Bedford College, University of London, Regent's Park, London NW1 4NS, England.

CAREER: Assistant to chief, World Health Organization Mission to Italy, 1947-49; *Time and Tide,* London, England, editorial assistant, 1949-52; research assistant to C. Veronica Wedgwood (now Dame Veronica Wedgwood), 1950-52, and to the History of Parliament Turst, 1959-61; University of London, Bedford College, London, England, assistant lecturer, 1962-64, lecturer in history, 1964—. *Member:* Royal Historical Society (fellow).

WRITINGS: The French Secretaries of State in the Age of Catherine de Medici, Athlone Press, 1962; *Catherine de Medici and the Ancien Regime* (pamphlet), Historical Association (London), 1966; (contributor) John H.M. Salmon, editor, *The French Wars of Religion,* Heath, 1967; (contributor) Werner L. Gundersheimer, editor, *French Humanism, 1470-1600,* Macmillan, 1969, Harper, 1970; *The Massacre of St. Bartholomew and the European Conflict 1559-1572,* Barnes & Noble, 1973; (contributor) J. F. Bosher, editor, *French Government and Society 1500-1850: Essays in Memory of Alfred Cobban,* Athlone Press, 1973. Contributor to *History Today, English Historical Review, Annali* (Milan), and other historical journals.

WORK IN PROGRESS: The Huguenot Struggle for Survival 1555-1598 and *The Origins of the First French Civil War* (tentative title).

AVOCATIONAL INTERESTS: Music, architecture.

SVENSSON, Arne 1929-

PERSONAL: Born February 12, 1929, in Karlskrona, Sweden; son of Sven Peter and Olivia (Fornander) Svensson; married Barbro Cronbladh (a teacher), 1965. *Education:* University of Lund, Fil.Mag., 1953; University of Stockholm, further study as film researcher. *Religion:* None. *Address:* P.O. Box 6002, 381 06 Kalmar 6, Sweden.

CAREER: Teacher of English and Swedish in secondary schools of Sweden, 1954-63; film censor, Stockholm, Sweden, 1964-65; Kalmar Nautical College, Kalmar, Sweden, teacher of English and Swedish, 1965-72. *Military service:* Swedish Coastal Artillery, 1948-49. *Member:* Federation of Swedish Film Societies (chairman, 1968-71).

WRITINGS: (Collaborator on Volume I, with Peter Cowie) *Sweden,* two volumes, A. S. Barnes, 1970; *Japan,* A. S. Barnes, 1971. Regular contributor to *Filmrutan* (quarterly publication of Federation of Swedish Film Societies), 1960—.

SIDELIGHTS: Svensson has attended film festivals in Berlin, London, Moscow, Leipzig, Oberhausen, and other cities of Europe.

* * *

SWAMY, Subramanian 1939-

PERSONAL: Born September 16, 1939, in Madras, India; son of Sitarama (a government official) and Padma (Iyer) Swamy; married wife, Roxna (a research associate), June 10, 1966; children: Gitanjali, Suhasini. *Education:* Delhi University, B.A. (honors), 1960; Indian Statistical Institute, M.A., 1962; Harvard University, Ph.D., 1965. *Politics:* Member of Chief Executive of Bharatiya Jana Sangh. *Religion:* Hindu. *Home:* 16 Nepean Sea Rd., Bombay, India 400036. *Office:* Department of Economics, Littauer 210, Harvard University, Cambridge, Mass. 02138.

CAREER: Indian Institute of Technology, Delhi, professor of economics, 1969-72; Harvard University, Cambridge, Mass., professor of economics, 1972—. Member of board of directors of Krishnaram Baldeo Bank, Gwalior, India. *Member:* Econometric Society, American Economic Society.

WRITINGS: Indian Economic Planning, Vikas, 1971; *Economic Growth of China and India, 1952-70,* University of Chicago Press, 1973. Contributor to *Los Angeles Times* and *Motherland* (New Delhi).

WORK IN PROGRESS: Economic Policy in China; Mathematics for Economists.

SIDELIGHTS: Swamy speaks, reads, and writes Chinese.

* * *

SWANGER, David 1940-

PERSONAL: Born August 1, 1940, in Newark, N.J.; son of Saul S. (a schoolteacher) and Pearl (Ginevsky) Swanger; married Lynn Lundstrom, April 5, 1970; children: Ana Lauren, Elissa Molly. *Education:* Swarthmore College, B.A., 1962; Harvard University, M.A.T., 1963, Ed.D., 1970. *Office:* College Five, University of California, Santa Cruz, Calif. 95064.

CAREER: University of California at Santa Cruz, assistant professor of education, 1970-72, associate academic preceptor, 1972—. Consultant to New Careers for the Poor and to Artists Returning to Schools. *Member:* Common Cause, Phi Delta Kappa. *Awards, honors:* Woodrow Wilson fellowship, 1970.

WRITINGS: (Contributor) Donald N. Bigelow, editor, *The Liberal Arts and Teacher Education,* University of Nebraska Press, 1971; *The Poem as Process,* Harcourt, 1974. Contributor of articles, poems and short stories to *College English, Free Lance, Stone Soup, Educational Forum, Cutbank, New: American and Canadian Poetry, Poetry Northwest, Sundaze, Quarry, Minnesota Review, Idea Exchange, Boston Sunday Globe,* and *Cum Grano.* Staff writer for "Public Issues Series: Harvard Project Social Studies," 1966.

WORK IN PROGRESS: A book of poetry; research on moral reasoning in literature.

* * *

SWANSEN, Vern 1916-

PERSONAL: Born August 9, 1916, in Klamath Falls, Ore.; son of James Edward (a businessman) and Alice (Halverson) Swansen; married Marie Elizabeth Pierce (an artist-painter), August 12, 1958. *Education:* Pasadena City College, A.A., 1936; University of Southern California, B.Arch., 1939; graduate study at Centre Universitaire Mediterraneen, 1951, and Institut d'Etudes Litteraires of the University of Aix-Marseilles, 1957. *Politics:* Republican. *Religion:* Episcopalian. *Home:* 1140 Montalban St., San Luis Obispo, Calif. 93401. *Agent:* Lachlan P. MacDonald, 2719 El Cerrito, San Luis Obispo, Calif. 93401. *Office:* School of Architecture, California Polytechnic State University, San Luis Obispo, Calif. 93407.

CAREER: Architectural design and presentation work in southern California and southern Oregon, 1939-42, 1946-48, 1956-61; Santa Barbara City College, Santa Barbara, Calif., instructor in continuing education division, 1960—; Santa Barbara Museum of Art, Santa Barbara, Calif., curator of education, 1961-71; California Polytechnic State University, San Luis Obispo, assistant professor of architecture, 1971—. Special Services, Fifth Army Headquarters, Chicago, arts and crafts director, 1955-56. *Military service:* U.S. Navy, 1942-46. *Member:* Santa Barbara Art Association (president, 1964-66), Santa Barbara Museum of Art.

WRITINGS: Epsilon: A Journey Along the Epsilon River from the Eastern Mountains to the Sea, Padre Productions, 1974.

WORK IN PROGRESS: Theta: A Journey on the Sea of Theta.

SIDELIGHTS: Swansen has had numerous one-man shows of paintings in Paris, on the Riviera, and in the United States. He has also executed murals and stained glass window designs for churches in Los Angeles and Santa Barbara.

* * *

SWINDEN, Patrick 1941-

PERSONAL: Born January 10, 1941, in Huddersfield, Yorkshire, England, son of Jack (a chemist) and Mary (Saunders) Swinden; married Serena Helen Sugar; children: Edward James. *Education:* University of Hull, B.A. (honors), 1963; Cambridge University, Ph.D., 1967. *Politics:* Social Democrat. *Religion:* "Humanist." *Home:* 75 Station Rd., Cheadle Hulme, Cheshire, England. *Office:* Department of English, University of Manchester, Manchester, England.

CAREER: University of Manchester, Manchester, England, lecturer in English language and literature, 1967—.

WRITINGS: (Editor) *George Eliot: A Casebook,* Macmillan, 1972; *Unofficial Selves: Character in the Novel from Dickens to the Present Day,* Macmillan, 1973; *An Introduction to Shakespeare's Comedies,* Macmillan, 1973. Contributor to *Twentieth Century Mind, Critical Survey,* and *Critical Quarterly.*

WORK IN PROGRESS: Research on social history of the middle and late nineteenth century; preparation for a book on Shelley.

* * *

SWORTZELL, Lowell (Stanley) 1930-

PERSONAL: Born August 5, 1930, in Washington, D.C.; son of Stanley and Ora (Van Pelt) Swortzell; married Nancy Ellen Foell (an associate professor of educational theater at New York University), September 14, 1959. *Education:* George Washington University, B.A., 1952, M.A., 1953; New York University, Ph.D., 1963. *Home:* 22 Riverside Dr., Princeton, N.J. 08540. *Office:* Program in Educational Theatre, Press Annex, 54, New York University, Washington Sq., New York, N.Y. 10003.

CAREER: Yale University, New Haven, Conn., assistant in playwriting and theater history, 1958-59; Tufts University, Medford, Mass., assistant professor of speech and drama, 1959-60; New York University, New York, assistant professor of dramatic art, 1960-65; University of Wisconsin, Madison, associate professor of speech and education, 1965-66; New York University, associate professor of educational theater, 1966—. Trustee of Children's Museum, Washington, D.C., 1960—. *Military service:* U.S. Army, 1954-56. *Member:* American Theatre Association, Children's Theatre Association, American Society for Theatre Research, Speech Communication Association.

WRITINGS: (Editor) *All the World's a Stage: Modern Plays for Young People,* Delacorte, 1972.

Plays: *A Partridge in a Pear Tree* (one-act), Samuel French, 1967. Also author of three one-act plays, "Praises to the Peacock," "London Bridge," and "The Fisherman and His Wife," published in *Plays Magazine.* Contributor to *Reader's Encyclopedia of World Drama,* Crowell, 1969.

WORK IN PROGRESS: The Art of Children's Theatre, with wife, Nancy Ellen Swortzell, for Houghton; *Here Come the Clowns,* for Holt.

* * *

SYMONS, Julian (Gustave) 1912-

PERSONAL: Born May 30, 1912, in London, England; son of Morris Albert (an auctioneer) and Minnie Louise (Bull) Symons; married Kathleen Clark, October 25, 1941; children: Sarah Louise, Marcus Richard Julian. *Education:* Educated in state schools in England. *Politics:* "Left wing, with no specific party allegiance." *Religion:* None. *Home:* 37 Albert Bridge Rd., London S.W.11, England. *Agent:* Curtis Brown, Ltd., 1 Craven Hill, London W2 3EW, England.

CAREER: Company secretary in London, England, 1929-41; copywriter in London, 1944-47; author and novelist. Member of council, Westfield College, University of London, 1972—. *Military service:* British Army, Royal Armoured Corps, 1942-44. *Member:* Crime Writers Association (chairman, 1958-59), Society of Authors (chairman of committee of management, 1970-71), Mystery Writers of America, P.E.N., Garrick Club. *Awards, honors:* Crime

Writers Association award for best crime story of the year, 1957, for *The Colour of Murder,* and special award for *Crime and Detection,* 1966; Mystery Writers of America award for best crime story of the year, 1960, for *The Progress of a Crime,* and special award, 1973, for *Bloody Murder.*

WRITINGS: Confusions About X (poems), Fortune Press, 1939; (editor) *An Anthology of War Poetry,* Penguin, 1942; *The Second Man* (poems), Routledge, 1943; (editor and author of introduction) Samuel Johnson, *Selected Writings,* Grey Walls, 1949, British Book Centre, 1950; *A.J.A. Symons: His Life and Speculations,* Eyre & Spottiswoode, 1950; *Charles Dickens,* Roy, 1951, 2nd edition, Barker, 1969; *Thomas Carlyle: The Life and Ideas of a Prophet,* Oxford University Press, 1952, reprinted, Books for Libraries, 1970; *Horatio Bottomley: A Biography,* Cresset Press, 1955; (editor) Thomas Carlyle, *Selected Works, Reminiscences and Letters,* Clarke, Irwin, 1956; *The General Strike: A Historical Portrait,* Cresset Press, 1957; *The Hundred Best Crime Stories,* The Sunday Times, 1959.

A Reasonable Doubt: Some Criminal Cases Re-examined, Cresset Press, 1960; *The Thirties: A Dream Revolved,* Cresset Press, 1960, reprinted, Greenwood, 1973; *The Detective Story in Britain,* British Council, 1962; *Buller's Campaign,* Cresset Press, 1963; *England's Pride: The Story of the Gordon Relief Expedition,* Hamish Hamilton, 1965; *Critical Occasions,* Hamish Hamilton, 1966; *A Pictorial History of Crime,* Crown, 1966 (published in England as *Crime and Detection: An Illustrated History from 1840,* Studio Vista, 1966); (editor) *Essays and Biographies by A.J.A. Symons,* Cassell, 1969; *Mortal Consequences: A History–from the Detective Story to the Crime Novel,* Harper, 1972 (published in England as *Bloody Murder: From the Detective Story to the Crime Novel: A History,* Faber, 1972); (editor and author of introduction) *Between the Wars: Britain in Photo,* Batsford, 1972.

Novels: *The Immaterial Murder Case,* Gollancz, 1945, Macmillan, 1957; *A Man Called Jones,* Gollancz, 1947, reprinted, Collins, 1963; *Bland Beginning,* Harper, 1949 (published in England as *Bland Beginning: A Detective Story,* Gollancz, 1949); *The 31st of February* (also see below), Harper, 1950 (published in England as *The Thirtyfirst of February: A Mystery Novel,* Gollancz, 1950); *The Broken Penny,* Harper, 1953; *The Narrowing Circle,* Harper, 1954 (published in England as *The Narrowing Circle: A Crime Novel,* Gollancz, 1954, reprinted, Collins, 1956); *The Paper Chase,* Crime Club, 1956, published as *Bogue's Fortune,* Harper, 1957; *The Color of Murder,* Harper, 1957; *The Gigantic Shadow,* Crime Club, 1958, published as *The Pipe Dream,* Harper, 1959; *The Progress of a Crime* (also see below), Harper, 1960; *Murder! Murder!,* Collins, 1961; *The Plain Man,* Harper, 1962 (published in England as *The Killing of Francie Lake,* Crime Club, 1962); *The End of Solomon Grundy* (also see below), Harper, 1964; *The Belting Inheritance,* Harper, 1965; *The Julian Symons Omnibus* (includes *The 31st of February, The Progress of a Crime, The End of Solomon Grundy),* Crime Club, 1966; *The Man Who Killed Himself,* Harper, 1967; *The Man Whose Dreams Came True,* Harper, 1968; *The Man Who Lost His Wife,* Harper, 1970; *The Players and the Game,* Harper, 1972; *The Plot Against Roger Rider,* Harper, 1973.

Also author of radio play, "Affection Unlimited," and of television plays. Contributor to *Times Literary Supplement, Washington Post,* and others. Editor, *Twentieth Century Verse,* 1937-39; reviewer, *Sunday Times* (London), 1958—.

WORK IN PROGRESS: A new crime story and an anthology of crime short stories.

SIDELIGHTS: Of *A Man Whose Dreams Came True,* Clifford Ridley writes in the *National Observer:* "An absolutely brilliant piece of work, lacking nothing in the way of plotting, characterization, or style, yet keeping all these things under the strictest control. The convolutions of the exquisitely conceived, slyly cynical tale make it a genuine can't-put-down item; and the cast includes a wonderfully dogged aging detective and an absolute bounder whom you can't help liking through it all. A marvelous book." Of another novel, Anthony Boucher has written in the *New York Times Book Review:* "The latest Symons novel, *The Man Who Killed Himself. . . .,* is very nearly his best. It offers a delightful picture of an oppressed Walter Mitty who manages to achieve some of his dreams by creating an alternative self; it goes on to utilize this situation in plotting a nobly ingenious 'perfect crime'; and it even manages to shift successfully to a more serious tone in the aftermath of murder. Only the author's resort to a rather conventional and facile ending, more suited to a short-short than to a novel, keeps this highly enjoyable book from classic status."

AVOCATIONAL INTERESTS: Watching cricket and football.

BIOGRAPHICAL/CRITICAL SOURCES: Francis Scarfe, *Auden and After: The Liberation of Poetry 1930-1941,* Routledge, 1942.

* * *

SYNGE, (Phyllis) Ursula 1930-

PERSONAL: Surname rhymes with "bring"; born April 8, 1930, in Minehead, Somerset, England; daughter of Walter John Reginald (a chartered accountant) and Kathleen Phyllis (Vowles) Synge; married Bernard Perrin (an artist), 1951; children: Jonathan, Abigail. *Education:* Attended West of England College of Art, 1944-46. *Politics:* "Totally a-political." *Religion:* "I subscribe to all religious beliefs without preference for any particular one." *Home:* 10 Highbury Villas, St. Michael's Hill, Bristol, England.

CAREER: Writer. Has worked as bookseller's assistant, photographer's assistant, manager of a village shop in rural England, and accounts clerk. *Member:* Booksellers Association.

WRITINGS: Weland: Smith of the Gods, Bodley Head, 1972, S. G. Phillips, 1973; *The People and the Promise,* Bodley Head, 1974. Editor of quarterly news-sheet for Bristol branch of Society for Mentally Handicapped Children, 1958-61.

WORK IN PROGRESS: A novel-length fairy tale; a prehistorical story set in the Canary Islands; research on medieval and ancient history, on folk-lore and legends, and on mythology.

AVOCATIONAL INTERESTS: Walking, "unspoiled" country, English villages and small country towns.

* * *

SZERLIP, Barbara 1949-

PERSONAL: Born November 28, 1949, in New Jersey; daughter of Stewart S. (an insurance broker) and Ziril (Weinstein) Szerlip. *Education:* Attended University of

Miami, 1967-69, and University of California, Santa Barbara, 1969-71. *Home:* 1900 Eddy, #18, San Francisco, Calif. 94115; and 508 Twin Oaks Rd., Union, N.J. 07083.

CAREER: Sivananda Yoga Ashram, Val Morin, Quebec, instructor in Hatha Yoga and Kirtan Mantras, cook, and baker, 1969; leather craftsman in Montreal, Quebec, 1969; *Tractor* (literary magazine), San Francisco, Calif., founder and editor, 1971—; professional masseuse in San Francisco, 1973; assistant technical director, actress, dancer, and singer with summer stock theaters in White Lake, N.Y., and East Monticello, N.Y., various years. *Member:* Coordinating Council of Literary Magazines, Cooperative of Small Magazine Editors and Publishers. *Awards, honors:* Coordinating Council of Literary Magazines grant, 1973, for continued publication of *Tractor.*

WRITINGS: Teopantiahuac, Water Table Press, 1971; *Bear Dancing,* Doggerel Press, 1974; *Sympathetic Alphabet,* Mother's Hen Press, 1974. Work included in *Four Young Women: Poems,* edited by Kenneth Rexroth, McGraw, 1973.

WORK IN PROGRESS: More poetry; translations from contemporary Mexican and French poets.

* * *

SZUMIGALSKI, Anne 1926-

PERSONAL: Born January 3, 1926, in London, England; daughter of Herbert E. (an army officer and chartered accountant) and Mary (Winder-Allen) Davis; married Jan Szumigalski (a land surveyor), March, 1945; children: Katharine Szumigalski Bitney, Elizabeth Szumigalski Carrier, Anthony, Mark. *Education:* Privately educated. *Home:* 9 Connaught Pl., Saskatoon, Saskatchewan, Canada.

CAREER: Teacher of creative writing (poetry) in Saskatoon, Saskatchewan, elementary and secondary schools, 1971—. Instructor in poetry at Saskatchewan Summer School of the Arts, 1971—; founder and coordinator of Saskatoon Poets, a cooperative group of working poets. *Wartime service:* British Red Cross and Friends Ambulance Unit, civilian relief worker, 1943-46.

WRITINGS: Woman Reading in Bath, Doubleday, 1974. Author of radio script, "The Eyes of the Fishes," with Terrence Heath, for Canadian Broadcasting Corp., 1973. Contributor of poetry and line drawings to literary magazines. Associate editor of *Grain.*

WORK IN PROGRESS: A collection of short stories.

SIDELIGHTS: Mrs. Szumigalski speaks French, Dutch, German, and Polish. *Avocational interests:* Wild plants and their uses as food and medicine; crafts, children's recreational theatre.

* * *

TABORI, George 1914-

PERSONAL: Born May 24, 1914, in Budapest, Hungary; son of Kornel (a journalist) and Elsa (Ziffer) Tabori; married Hanna Freund (divorced, 1954); married Viveca Lindfors (an actress), July 4, 1954; children: (second marriage) John, Lena (Mrs. Martin Fried), Kristoffer (stepson). *Education:* Attended high school in Hungary, 1928-32. *Politics:* "Left." *Religion:* "A Jew, but not Jewish." *Home:* 172 East 95th St., New York, N.Y. 10028. *Agent:* Bertha Case, 42 West 53rd St., New York, N.Y. 10019.

CAREER: Playwright, novelist, and screenwriter. *Military service:* British Army, 1941-43; became lieutenant. *Member:* Dramatists Guild, Authors League of America, Screenwriters Guild. *Awards, honors:* British Academy Award, 1953, for "Young Lovers."

WRITINGS—Novels: *Beneath the Stone,* Houghton, 1945 (published in England as *Beneath the Stone the Scorpion,* Boardman, 1945); *Companions of the Left Hand,* Houghton, 1946; *Original Sin,* Houghton, 1947 (abridged version published in *Cosmopolitan* Magazine); *The Caravan Passes,* Appleton, 1951; *The Journey: A Confession* (based on the screenplay), Bantam, 1958; *The Good One,* Pocket Books, 1960.

Plays: *Flight into Egypt* (three-act; first produced on Broadway at Music Box Theatre, March 18, 1952), acting edition, Dramatists Play Service, 1953; "The Emperor's Clothes," first produced on Broadway at Ethel Barrymore Theatre, February 9, 1953; (adapter) August Strindberg "Miss Julie," first produced Off-Broadway at Phoenix Theatre, February 21, 1956; "Brouhaha," first produced in London at Aldwych Theatre, August 27, 1958, produced on Broadway at 175 East Broadway Playhouse, April 26, 1960; (adapter) Bertholt Brecht, *Brecht on Brecht: Am Improvisation* (first produced Off-Broadway at Theatre de Lys, January 3, 1962, produced in London at Royal Court Theatre, 1962), Samuel French, 1968; (adapter) Max Frisch, "Andorra," first produced on Broadway at Biltmore Theatre, February 9, 1963; (adapter) Brecht, *The Resistable Rise of Arturo Ui* (two-act; with music by Hans-Dieter Hosalla; first produced on Broadway at Lunt-Fontanne Theatre, November 11, 1963, produced in London at Saville Theatre, 1969), Samuel French, 1972; "The Niggerlovers" (two one-acts, "The Demonstration" and "Man and Dog"; with music by Richard Peaslee), first produced Off-Broadway at Orpheum Theatre, October 1, 1967; "The Cannibals," first produced Off-Broadway at American Place Theatre, November, 1967; (translator and adapter) Brecht, "The Guns of Carrar" (one-act), first produced at Theatre de Lys, December 9, 1968; "Pinksville" (one-act), with music by Stanley Walden, first produced in Stockbridge, Mass., at Berkshire Theatre Festival, August, 1970, produced at American Place Theatre, March 17, 1971.

Also author of plays, "Clowns" and "The Prince"; adapter of Bertholt Brecht's "Mother Courage."

Screenplays: "Young Lovers," 1952; "I Confess," 1953; "The Journey," 1959; "No Exit," 1962; "Secret Ceremony," 1968.

SIDELIGHTS: "The Prince" was adapted and filmed by United Artists in 1970 as "Leo the Last." *Avocational interests:* Chess.

* * *

TAKAYAMA, Akira 1932-

PERSONAL: Born June 28, 1932, in Yokohama, Japan; son of Tsunaki (a lawyer) and Shoko (Takeuchi) Takayama; married Machiko Onabe, January 31, 1970. *Education:* International Christian University, B.A., 1957; University of Rochester, M.A., 1960, Ph.D., 1962; Hitotsubashi University, Ph.D., 1964. *Religion:* Protestant. *Home:* 400 North River Dr., Apt. 811, West Lafayette, Ind. 47906. *Office:* Department of Economics, Purdue University, West Lafayette, Ind. 47907.

CAREER: International Christian University, Tokyo, Japan, 1962-64, began as instructor, became assistant professor of economics; University of Manchester, Manchester, England, fellow in economic statistics, 1964-65;

University of Minnesota, Minneapolis, visiting associate professor of economics, 1965-66; Purdue University, West Lafayette, Ind., associate professor, 1967-68, professor of economics, 1968—. Visiting professor at Australian National University, 1966, University of Rochester, 1969-70, and University of Hawaii, 1971-72. *Member:* American Economic Association, Econometric Society.

WRITINGS: International Trade: An Approach to the Theory, Holt, 1972; *Mathematical Economics,* Holt, in press. Contributor to economic reviews.

* * *

TANK, Ronald W(arren) 1929-

PERSONAL: Born June 14, 1929, in Milwaukee, Wis.; son of Rudolph L. and Mabel (Does) Tank; married Barbara Lieberum (a teacher), May 28, 1955; children: Alice, Kristen. *Education:* University of Wisconsin, B.S., 1951, M.S., 1955; University of Copenhagen, diploma, 1959-60; Indiana University, Ph.D., 1962. *Religion:* Lutheran. *Home:* 214 North Union St., Appleton, Wis. 54911. *Office:* Department of Geology, Lawrence University, Appleton, Wis. 54911.

CAREER: Exploration geologist at Standard Oil Company of California, Bakersfield, 1955-56, and Salt Lake City, Utah, 1956-59; Milwaukee-Downer College, Milwaukee, Wis., assistant professor of geology, 1962-64; Lawrence University, Appleton, Wis., associate professor of geology, 1964—, director of German Study Center, 1972-73. Assistant curator of Milwaukee Public Museum, 1962. Geological consultant. *Military service:* U.S. Army, 1951-53; became first lieutenant. *Member:* Society of Economic Paleontologists and Mineralogists, National Association of Geology Teachers, Wisconsin Academy of Science, Arts and Letters. *Awards, honors:* Fulbright fellowship, Denmark, 1959-60.

WRITINGS: (Editor) *Focus on Environmental Geology,* Oxford University Press, 1973. Contributor to proceedings and to professional journals.

WORK IN PROGRESS: Research on environmental geology and on clay mineralogy of oil shales.

* * *

TANNAHILL, Reay 1929-

PERSONAL: Born December 9, 1929, in Glasgow, Scotland; daughter of Hamish Cowan (a marine engineer) and Olive (Reay) Tannahill; married Michael Edwardes (an author), August 8, 1958. *Education:* University of Glasgow, M.A., 1951. *Residence:* London, England. *Agent:* Campbell Thomson & McLaughlin, 80 Chancery Lane, London WC2A 1DD, England.

CAREER: Times, London, England, reporter for educational supplement, 1952-56; Thames & Hudson, London, England, advertising manager, 1956-58; Folio Society, London, England, advertising consultant, 1958-62; writer, 1962—.

WRITINGS: Regency England, Folio Society, 1964; *Paris in the Revolution,* Folio Society, 1966; *The Fine Art of Food,* Folio Society, 1968; *Food in History* (Book-of-the-Month Club selection), Stein & Day, 1973; *Flesh and Blood: A History of the Cannibal Complex,* Stein & Day, in press.

WORK IN PROGRESS: Sex in History: How Relationships Between Man and Woman Have Shaped History.

BIOGRAPHICAL/CRITICAL SOURCES: Washington Post, August 11, 1973; *Los Angeles Times,* August 23, 1973.

* * *

TAPP, Jack Thomas 1934-

PERSONAL: Born August 23, 1934, in Clinton, Ill.; son of Charles Carroll (a spectrographer) and Edna Mae (Collins) Tapp; married Dona June Wooldridge, July 16, 1954 (divorced, April, 1972); married Marilyn Campbell (a psychologist), June 23, 1972; children: (first marriage) Jon Thomas, David Lee, Charles R., Julie, Steven Miller; Jeanel Arterbery and Lynelle Arterbery (stepchildren). *Education:* University of Illinois, B.S., 1956, M.A., 1958, Ph.D., 1961. *Politics:* Liberal Democrat. *Religion:* None. *Home:* 310 Washington Hwy., Snyder, N.Y. 14226. *Office:* Mental Health Manpower and Training, Inc., 260 Elmwood Ave., Buffalo, N.Y. 14222.

CAREER: Certified psychologist by State of New York. Vanderbilt University, Nashville, Tenn., assistant professor, 1962-66, associate professor, 1966-70, professor of psychology, 1970-71; Suicide Prevention and Crisis Service, Buffalo, N.Y., senior research therapist, 1971-73; Mental Health Manpower and Training, Inc., Buffalo, N.Y., program evaluation coordinator, 1973—. Clinical associate in psychology at State University of New York at Buffalo, 1971—; chairman of program and planning committee of Amherst Youth Board, 1972—.

MEMBER: American Psychological Association, Psychonomic Society, American Association of Suicidology, American Federation of State, County, and Municipal Employees, American Association for the Advancement of Science. *Awards, honors:* U.S. Public Health Service grants, 1962-63, 1963-66, 1967-68, 1969-71, 1970-71, 1972-74; National Science Foundation grant to study rhinencephalon and olfaction, 1968-70.

WRITINGS: (Contributor) H. C. Haywood, editor, *Brain Damage in the School Age Child,* Council for Exceptional Children, 1966; (editor and contributor) *Reinforcement and Behavior,* Academic Press, 1969. Author of handbooks and technical reports. Contributor of more than thirty articles to science and social science journals, including *Journal of Research on Crime and Delinquency, Crisis Intervention, American Journal of Community Psychology, Journal of Consulting Clinical Psychology, Psychological Bulletin,* and *Personnel and Guidance Journal.* Editorial consultant to *American Journal of Community Psychology* and *Crisis Intervention.*

WORK IN PROGRESS: Training the Crisis Counselor, with Robert Fink and John Russell; a review of the adjustment problems of second families, with wife, Marilyn Tapp; a novel about mental health work; research includes a follow-up study of suicide center volunteers, the prediction of shows and no shows to a crisis center, changes in clinical and technical effectiveness as a function of work experience in volunteer telephone counselors, the development of a task analysis scale of telephone counseling, a comparison of Red Cross and suicide center volunteers on several measures of personality, and a study of criteria for appropriate and inappropriate referrals to a crisis center.

SIDELIGHTS: Tapp writes: "As a professional psychologist much of my work has been in research on the belief that knowledge is the source of change in the world. In the past three years I have been working in a world of political reality and have come to appreciate the futility of idealism without a basis in the political structure. My idealism has been severely challenged by the 'other truth' only partially based in knowledge. For myself. . . .this has been a significant though rude awakening."

* * *

TASKER, James 1908-

PERSONAL: Born December 5, 1908, in Kimberley, South Africa; son of James (a company director) and Edith Elizabeth (Lark) Tasker; married Elaine English (a novelist), October 3, 1946. *Education:* Attended high school in Port Elizabeth, South Africa. *Home:* Peartree Cottage, Park St., Greyton, Cape 7233, South Africa. *Agent:* Evelyn Singer Agency, P.O. Box 163, Briarcliff Manor, N.Y. 10510.

CAREER: J. Walter Thompson Co. (advertising agency), New York, N.Y., manager of branches in Port Elizabeth, South Africa, 1946-50, and Frankfurt-am-Main, Germany, 1951, account executive in New York, N.Y., 1951-52, associate director of branch in London, England, 1952-62; artist and writer, 1962—. Has lectured at Principia College, Elsah, Ill., and University of California, Riverside. *Military service:* South African Army, intelligence officer, 1940-46, served in Abyssinia, Egypt, Libya, and Italy. *Member:* Botanic Society of South Africa.

WRITINGS: African Treehouse (for children), Harvey House, 1974. Contributor to local newspapers.

WORK IN PROGRESS: A children's book in verse on Australian animals.

* * *

TATE, Joan 1922-

PERSONAL: Born in 1922; married; three children. *Home:* 32 Kennedy Rd., Shrewsbury SY3 7AB, England.

CAREER: Writer. *Member:* Society of Authors, PEN International, Translators Association, Amnesty International.

WRITINGS—All children's fiction, except as noted; all published by Heinemann except as noted: *Jenny,* 1964; *The Crane,* 1964; *The Rabbit Boy,* 1964; *Coal Hoppy,* 1964; *The Silver Grill,* 1965; *The Next Doors,* 1965; *Picture Charlie,* 1965; *Lucy,* 1965.

The Tree, 1966, published as *Tina and David,* Nelson, 1973; *The Holiday,* 1966; *Tad,* 1966; *Bill,* 1966; *Mrs. Jenny,* 1966; *The Lollipop Man,* Almqvist & Wiksell, (Stockholm), 1967, Macmillan, 1969; *The Wild Boy,* Almqvist & Wiksell, 1967, Harper, 1973, published as *Wild Martin,* Heinemann, 1968; *The Train,* Almqvist & Wiksell, 1967.

Bits and Pieces, 1968; *The Circus and Other Stories,* 1968; *Letters to Chris,* 1968; *The Crow,* 1968; *Luke's Garden,* 1968; *The New House,* Almqvist & Wiksell, 1968; *The Soap Box Car,* Almqvist & Wiksell, 1968; *Jenny and Mrs. Jenny,* 1968, (published as *Out of the Sun,* 1968;) *Sam and Me,* Macmillan, 1968, Coward, McCann, 1969; *Polly,* Almqvist & Wiksell, 1969; *The Great Birds,* Almqvist & Wiksell, 1969; *Whizz Kid,* Macmillan, 1969, published as *An Unusual Kind of Girl,* Scholastic Book Services; *Clipper,* 1969, published as *Ring on My Finger,* 1971; *The Old Car,* Almqvist & Wiksell, 1969; *The Nest,* Macmillan, 1969; *The Cheapjack Man,* Macmillan, 1969; *The Gobbleydock,* Macmillan, 1969; *The Tree House,* Macmillan, 1969; *The Ball,* Macmillan, 1969; (with Sven Johansson and Bengt Astrom) *Going Up One* (nonfiction; language text) with *Workbook and Key,* Almqvist & Wiksell, 1969; *The Letter and Other Stories,* Almqvist & Wiksell, 1969; *Puddle's Tiger,* Almqvist & Wiksell, 1969; *The Caravan,* Almqvist & Wiksell, 1969; *Edward and the Uncles,* Almqvist & Wiksell, 1969; *The Secret,* Almqvist & Wiksell, 1969; *The Runners,* Almqvist & Wiksell, 1969.

(With Johansson and Astrom) *Going Up Two* (nonfiction) with *Workbook and Key,* Almqvist & Wiksell, 1970; *Night Out and Other Stories,* Almqvist & Wiksell, 1970; *The Match and Other Stories,* Almqvist & Wiksell, 1970; *Dinah,* Almqvist & Wiksell, 1970; *The Man Who Rang the Bell,* Almqvist & Wiksell, 1970; *Ginger Mick,* Almqvist & Wiksell, 1970; *Luke's Garden,* Almqvist & Wiksell, 1970; *Journal for One,* Almqvist & Wiksell, 1970; *Gramp,* Chatto & Windus, 1971; *The Long Road Home,* 1971.

Your Town (nonfiction), David & Charles, 1972; *Wump Day,* 1972; *Dad's Camel,* 1972; *Ben and Annie,* Doubleday, 1972; *Jack and the Rock Cakes,* Brockhampton, 1972; *Grandpa and My Little Sister,* Brockhampton, 1972; *Taxi!,* Schoeningh, 1973; *How Do You Do* (nonfiction), Schoeningh, 1974; *The World of the River* (nonfiction), Dent, 1974; (with Johansson and Astrom) *Going Up III* with *Workbook and Key,* Almqvist & Wiksell, in press.

Translator: John Einar Aberg, *Do You Believe in Angels,* Hutchinson, 1963; Dagmar Edqvist, *Black Sister,* Doubleday, 1963; Maertha Buren, *A Need to Love,* Dodd, 1964; Berndt Olsson, *Noah,* Hutchinson, 1964; Buren, *Camilla,* Dodd, 1965; Per Wahloo, *The Assignment,* Knopf, 1965; Ralph Herrmanns, *River Boy: Adventures on the Amazon,* Harcourt, 1965; Mika Waltari, *The Roman,* Putnam, 1966; Folke Henschen, *History of Diseases,* Longmans, 1966, published as *The History and Geography of Diseases,* Dial, 1967; Nan Inger, *Katrin,* Hamish Hamilton, 1966; Maria Lang, *Wreath for the Bride,* Hodder & Stoughton, 1966; Lang, *No More Murders,* Hodder & Stoughton, 1967; Lang, *Death Awaits Thee,* Hodder & Stoughton, 1967; Sven Gillsaeter, *From Island to Island,* Allen & Unwin, 1968; Per Wahloo, *A Necessary Action,* Pantheon, 1968 (published in England as *The Lorry,* M. Joseph); Margit Fjellman, *Queen Louise of Sweden,* Allen & Unwin, 1968; Wahloo and Maj Sjoewall, *The Man Who Went Up in Smoke,* Pantheon, 1969; Carl Nylander, *The Deep Well,* Allen & Unwin, 1969; Hans Heiberg, *Ibsen,* Allen & Unwin, 1969.

Wahloo, *The Steel Spring,* Knopf, 1970; Goeran Bergman, *Why Does Your Dog Do That?,* Hutchinson, 1970; Anders Bodelsen, *Freezing Point,* Knopf, 1970; Wahloo and Sjoewall, *The Fire-Engine That Vanished,* Pantheon, 1970; Gunnel Beckman, *Admission to the Feast,* Macmillan, 1971; Doris Dahlin, *The Sit-In Game,* Viking, 1972; Beckman, *A Room of His Own,* Viking, 1972; Wahloo, *The Generals,* Pantheon, 1973; Beckman, *Mia,* Bodley Head, 1974, Viking, in press; Astrid Lindgren, *That Emil,* Brockhampton, 1974; Barbro Lindgren, *Alban,* A. & C. Black, 1974; Olle Hoegstrand, *The Debt,* Pantheon, 1974; Astrid Lindgren, *The Lionheart Brothers,* Brockhampton, 1974; Lennart Frick, *The Threat,* Brockhampton, 1974.

WORK IN PROGRESS: Stories for adult non-readers, publication by Cassell expected in 1975; two nonfiction books, *Waste* and *Kites;* numerous other fiction books for various publishers.

TAYLOR, John W(illiam) R(ansom) 1922-

PERSONAL: Born June 8, 1922, in Ely, England; son of Victor Charles (a police inspector) and Florence Hilda (Ransom) Taylor; married Doris Haddrick, September 7, 1946; children: Susan H. H. (Mrs. G. Rodney Young), Michael J. H. *Education:* Attended primary and grammar school in England. *Politics:* None. *Religion:* Church of England. *Home and office:* 36 Alexandra Dr., Surbiton, Surrey KT5 9AF, England.

CAREER: Hawker Aircraft Ltd., Kingston-upon-Thames, England, member of design staff, 1941-47; Fairey Aviation Group, London, England, editorial publicity officer, 1947-54; Jane's Yearbooks, London, England, assistant to editor of *Jane's All the World's Aircraft,* 1955-59, editor, 1959—. Aviation book adviser, Ian Allan, 1967—; district commissioner for Surbiton, England, boy scouts, 1964-69. *Member:* Royal Historical Society (fellow), Royal Aeronautical Society (associate fellow), Society of Licensed Aircraft Engineers and Technologists (fellow), United Service Club, Royal Aero Club, Fenland Motor Club. *Awards, honors:* Ministry of Defence Robertson Trophy, 1959, for *C.F.S., Birthplace of Air Power;* Kingstown Award, 1965, and De La Rue Award, 1971, both for work on *Air BP* magazine.

WRITINGS: (With Maurice Allward) *Spitfire,* Harborough, 1946; (with Allward) *Wings for Tomorrow,* Ian Allan, 1951; *Eagle Book of Aircraft,* Hulton Press, 1953, 4th edition, 1958; *Picture History of Flight,* Hulton Press, 1955, 4th edition, 1960; *Passengers, Parcels, and Panthers,* Dobson, 1955; (editor) *Scientific Wonders of the Atomic Age,* Ariel Productions/Macdonald & Co., 1956; *Know Your Airliners,* Shell Petroleum, 1956; *Great Moments in Flying,* Roy, 1956; (editor) *Best Flying Stories,* Faber, 1956; (with Basil Arkell) *Helicopters Work Like This,* Roy, 1957, 4th edition published as *Helicopters and VTOL Aircraft Work Like This,* 1972; *Jet Planes Work Like This,* Phoenix House, 1958, Roy, 1962, 3rd edition, 1968; *C.F.S., Birthplace of Air Power,* Putnam (London), 1958; *Rockets and Satellites Work Like This,* Roy, 1959, 5th edition published as *Rockets and Spacecraft Work Like This,* 1970.

Warplanes of the World, Simmons-Boardman, 1960, 2nd edition, Ian Allan, 1968; (with Maurice Allward) *Eagle New Book of Aircraft,* Longacre Press, 1960; (with Allward) *Eagle Book of Rockets & Space Travel,* Longacre Press, 1961; *Rockets and Missiles,* Ian Allan, 1962, Grosset, 1970; *Royal Air Force,* Oxford University Press, 1965; (with Allward) *Westland 50,* Ian Allan, 1965; *Encyclopedia of World Aircraft,* Odhams, 1966; *Aircraft, Aircraft,* Hamlyn, 1967, 4th edition, 1974; *Civil Aircraft of the World,* Ian Allan, 1967, Scribners, 1972, 3rd edition, Ian Allan, 1974; *The Book of Aircraft,* Time-Life, 1968; *V.T.O.L. Aircraft and Helicopters,* Ian Allan, 1967, published in America as *Helicopters and VTOL Aircraft,* Doubleday, 1968; (editor and compiler) *Combat Aircraft of the World: From 1909 to the Present,* Putnam, 1969; *Pictorial History of the Royal Air Force,* three volumes, Ian Allan, 1968-69; *Into the 70's with the Royal Air Force,* Ministry of Defence, 1970; *The Lore of Flight,* Time-Life, 1972; (with David Mondey) *Spies in the Sky,* Ian Allan, 1972; (editor with Michael J. H. Taylor and David Mondey) *Guinness Book of Air Facts & Feats,* 2nd edition, Guinness Superlatives, 1973; *History of Aerial Warfare,* Hamlyn, 1974.

Author of annual series, *Aircraft Today,* 1949—, name subsequently changed and published as *Aircraft Annual,* and in 1974 as *Aircraft '74;* co-author, with Gordon Swanborough, of bi-annual series, *Military Aircraft of the World,* Scribners, 1959—; also author of several handbook series for aircraft observers. Contributor to *Encyclopaedia Britannica* and to *Defence Attache, Air Force Magazine.* Air correspondent, *Meccano Magazine,* 1943-72; editor, *Air BP,* a publication of British Petroleum Co., 1956-73.

* * *

TEE-VAN, Helen Damrosch 1893-

PERSONAL: Born May 26, 1893, in New York, N.Y.; daughter of Frank (a musician) and Hetty (Mosenthal) Damrosch; married John Tee-Van (an ichthyologist and zoological park director), July 17, 1923 (died, 1967). *Education:* Attended New York School of Display and Veltin School, New York, N.Y.; studied art under George de Forest Brush and Jonas Lie; also studied anatomy at Columbia University Medical School. *Home:* 120 East 75th St., New York, N.Y. 10021; and Route 1, Box 275, Sherman, Conn. 06784 (summer).

CAREER: Artist and illustrator; writer. New York Zoological Society, New York, N.Y., scientific artist participating in expeditions to South America and the Caribbean, at various times, 1922-63, designer of New York World's Fair exhibits, 1939-40, designer of zoo aquarium murals, 1941, and of murals for Children's Zoo, 1949. Work is in permanent collections at Berkshire Museum, Pittsfield, Mass., where commissioned, 1938-39, and at Bronx Zoo. Landscape and undersea paintings, and silk designs have been exhibited in numerous galleries and museums, including National Academy of Design and American Museum of Natural History (both New York, N.Y.), Buffalo Museum of Science, Pennsylvania Academy of Fine Arts, and Los Angeles Museum of Art. Occupational therapist, U.S. Army, 1918-19. *Member:* Society of Animal Artists, Society of Woman Geographers (vice-president and chairman of New York chapter, 1945-48), New York Zoological Society (life member), China Institute of America, Cosmopolitan Club.

WRITINGS—Juveniles, except as noted; all self-illustrated: *Red Howling Monkey,* Macmillan, 1926; (adapter) *The Trees Around Us* (adult), Dial, 1960; *Insects Are Where You Find Them,* Knopf, 1963; *Small Mammals Are Where You Find Them,* Knopf, 1966.

Illustrator: Emily Niles Huyk and Frank Damrosch, *Birthday Greetings and Other Songs,* G. Schirmer, 1918; Satis Coleman, *Creative Music in the Home,* Lewis E. Myers & Co., 1927; Elswyth Thane, *Reluctant Farmer* (adult), Duell, Sloan & Pearce, 1950; Roger Burlingame, *Mosquitoes in the Big Ditch: The Story of the Panama Canal,* Winston, 1952; Clifford Pope, *Reptiles Round the World,* Knopf, 1957; William Knowlton, *Sea Monsters,* Knopf, 1959; Alfred Milotte, *The Story of the Platypus,* Knopf, 1959; Naomi Talley, *Imported Insects* (adult), Dial, 1961; Alfred Milotte, *The Story of the Hippopotamus,* Knopf, 1964; Alfred Milotte and Elma Milotte, *The Story of an Alaskan Grizzly,* Knopf, 1969.

Contributor of illustrations to *Encyclopaedia Britannica, Collier's Encyclopedia,* New York Zoological Society publications, and to scientific journals and popular periodicals.

SIDELIGHTS: Mrs. Tee-Van has traveled in Canada, South America, Europe, Australia, and the Caribbean and Pacific Islands. Her work is collected at the research library, University of Oregon, Eugene. *Avocational interests:* Ecology, particularly conservation of land resources and animal preservation; color photography.

TELEKI, Geza 1943-

PERSONAL: Born December 7, 1943, in Kolozsvar, Hungary; naturalized U.S. citizen; son of Geza (a politician and scientist) and Hanna (Mikes) Teleki; married Lori Ann Baldwin (an ethologist), June 21, 1971. *Education:* George Washington University, B.A., 1967; Pennsylvania State University, M.A., 1970, doctoral candidate, 1973—; graduate study at University of Georgia, 1971-73. *Politics:* None. *Religion:* None. *Home address:* P.O. Box 467, Lemont, Pa. 16851. *Office:* Department of Anthropology, Pennsylvania State University, University Park, Pa. 16802.

CAREER: University of New Mexico, Albuquerque, field assistant in archaeology at Sapawe, a Pueblo Indian site, 1966; Smithsonian Institution, Washington, D.C., laboratory assistant in physical anthropology, 1967; Gombe Stream Research Centre, Gombe National Park, Tanzania, field research assistant, 1968-69, senior field researcher in primatology, 1970-71; Hall's Island Gibbon Colony, Hall's Island, Bermuda, senior research assistant in primatology, 1971. Field assistant in ethology at Ngorongoro Crater, Tanzania, 1968, and Serengeti National Park, 1970; research consultant on gibbon behavior. *Member:* American Museum of Natural History.

WRITINGS: The Predatory Behavior of Wild Chimpanzees, Bucknell University Press, 1973; (contributor) D. M. Rumbaugh, editor, *Gibbon and Siamang,* S. Karger, 1974.

Contributor of photographs: Pierre Rossion, *Science et Vie* (title means "Science and Life"), Excelsior (Paris), 1973; R. S. Lazarus, *The Riddle of Man,* Prentice-Hall, 1974; *Animals in Action,* Reader's Digest Books, 1974; *East African Wildlife,* Time-Life, 1974; *Our Vanishing Wildlife,* Reader's Digest Books, 1974; John Alcock, *An Evolutionary Approach to Animal Behavior,* Sinauer, 1974; Helena Curtis, *Biology,* Worth Publishers, 1974; S. I. Rosen, *Introduction to Physical Anthropology,* McGraw, 1974. Has also made films of his field research on gibbons.

Author of research reports. Contributor of photographs to *Il Libro Del Anno* and *Encyclopaedia Britannica Yearbook.* Contributor of articles to journals, including *Scientific American, Primates, Journal of Human Evolution,* and *Folia Primatologica.* Editor of *Matrix* (interscience journal of George Washington University), 1965-67.

WORK IN PROGRESS: Editing a book on predatory behavior in human evolution, with R. S. O. Harding.

* * *

TEMKO, Florence

PERSONAL: married second husband, Henry Petzal (a silversmith); children: (first marriage) Joan Temko, Ronald Temko, Stephen Temko. *Education:* Attended Wycombe Abbey, London School of Economics and Political Science, New School for Social Research. *Home and office:* 2 Plunkett St., Lenox, Mass. 01240.

MEMBER: American Craftsman, Artist-Craftsmen of New York.

WRITINGS: Paperfolding to Begin With, Bobbs-Merrill, 1968; *Papercutting,* Doubleday, 1973; *Feltcraft,* Doubleday, 1974; *Paper: Folded, Cut, Sculpted,* Macmillan, 1974; *Paper Fun,* Arrow Book Club, 1974. Author of weekly column, "Things to Make," in *Berkshire Eagle* and other newspapers.

WORK IN PROGRESS: Self-Stick Craft, Decoupage, Make Something, all for Doubleday.

AVOCATIONAL INTERESTS: Travel.

TENENBAUM, Shea 1910-

PERSONAL: Born April 14, 1910, in Ireno, Poland; came to United States, 1934; son of Abraham Motek (a watchmaker) and Rachel Leah (Grossman) Tenenbaum. *Education:* Privately educated. *Religion:* Jewish. *Home:* 45-35 44th St., Long Island City, N.Y. 11104.

CAREER: Author, novelist, printer. *Member:* Yiddish P.E.N., Jewish National Workers Alliance. *Awards, honors:* American Committee for Emigree Scholars, Writers, and Artists fellowship, 1947, for *The Writing on the Horizon;* Zvi Kessel Prize for Jewish Literature, 1951, for *In the Image of God;* Congress for Jewish Culture and Yiddish P.E.N. Karl Rotman Stipendium, 1967, for *Job of Lemberg.*

WRITINGS: Euphorion, [Antwerp], 1931; *Bei der welt zugast* (title means "A Visitor to the World"), [Warsaw], 1937; *Der sfinks* (title means "The Sphinx"), Chicago Courier, 1938; *Kinder fun der zun* (title means "Children of the Sun"), Voice (Mexico), 1942; *Gold un zhaver* (novel; title means "Gold and Rust"), Voice, 1943; *Di schrift oifn horizont* (title means "The Writing on the Horizon"), [New York], 1947; *Shnit fun mayn feld* (title means "Harvest"), [New York], 1949; *In Got's geshtalt* (title means "In the Image of God"), [New York], 1951; *A hant farshraybt* (title means "A Hand Is Writing"), [New York], 1953; *Dikhter un doyres* (title means "Poets and Generations"), [New York], 1955; *Un di erd bashteyt oyf eybik* (title means "And the Earth Remains Forever"), [New York], 1957; *Ana Frank, du vos host getrunken fun gots hant* (title means "Anna Frank Who Hast Drunk from the Hand of God"), [New York], 1958; *Der emes zol zayn dayn shtern* (autobiography; title means "The Truth Should Be Your Star"), [New York], 1960; *Der sar fun lebn* (title means "The Angle of Life"), [New York], 1963; *Ayzik Ashmeday* (title means "Isaac Ashmedai"), Central Yiddish Culture Organization, 1965; *Iyev fun Lemberg* (title means "Job of Lemberg"), Central Yiddish Culture Organization, 1967; *Geshtaltn baym shrayb'tish* (title means "Personalities by My Desk"), Central Yiddish Culture Organization, 1969; *Hunger tsum vort* (title means "Hunger for the Word"), Central Yiddish Culture Organization, 1972; *Der letzter eides* (title means "The Last Witness"), Central Yiddish Culture Organization, 1972; *In der keiserlicher Weinshenk* (title means "In the Royal Tavern"), Central Yiddish Culture Organization, 1973.

Work represented in anthology, *Yisroel, 1st Jewish Omnibus,* edited by Joseph Leftwich, Yoseloff, 1963. Contributor to *Memorial Book of Korif* and to periodicals, including *Chicago Courier, Dorem Afrike, Forois, Haint, Israel-Stimme.*

WORK IN PROGRESS: Evenings with Writers; a new edition of *The Truth Should Be Your Star.*

SIDELIGHTS: Tenenbaum told *CA:* "In addition to having had twenty books published I have had published in the Jewish press of the world more than 10,000 stories and essays. In recent years it has been my special purpose to put down my remembrances of the Jewish writers and painters I have known, also of my family, and of the Jewish life in Eastern Europe which is no more."

BIOGRAPHICAL/CRITICAL SOURCES: Isaac Liebman, *Builders and Creators of My Generation,* [New York], 1953; Mordecai Yardeini, *Interviews with Jewish Writers,* [New York], 1955; Joseph Hillel Levy, *Collected Writings,* [London], Volume 2, 1958; Benjamin Skuditsky,

Of A Whole Life, [Buenos Aires], 1958; Yeheskel Brownstein, *People Whom I Have Known,* [Los Angeles], 1962; Yossel Cohen, *At the Edge of the Beginning,* [New York], 1963; Schloime Bickel, *Writers of My Generation,* [Tel Aviv], Volume 3, 1970; Rebecca Kope, *Authors, Books, Opinions,* [Paris], 1973.

* * *

TERCHEK, Ronald John 1936-

PERSONAL: Born July 29, 1936, in Cleveland, Ohio; son of John Anthony and Ann (Race) Terchek; married Mary Ellen Joseph, March 23, 1968; children: Kristin, Daniel. *Education:* University of Chicago, B.A., 1958, M.A., 1960; University of Maryland, Ph.D., 1965. *Politics:* Democrat. *Religion:* Catholic. *Home:* 919 Sligo Creek Pkwy., Takoma Park, Md. 20012. *Office:* Department of Government and Politics, University of Maryland, College Park, Md. 20740.

CAREER: University of Maryland, College Park, instructor, 1964-65, assistant professor, 1965-70, associate professor of government and politics, 1970—. *Member:* American Political Science Association, American Society for Political and Legal Philosophy. *Awards, honors:* Outstanding Teacher award, University of Maryland, 1968.

WRITINGS: The Making of the Test Ban Treaty, Nijhoff, 1970, International Publications Service, 1971. Contributor of articles and reviews to journals in his field.

WORK IN PROGRESS: A study of protest with emphasis on its role in the democratic community.

* * *

TEUNE, Henry 1936-

PERSONAL: Born March 19, 1936, in Chicago, Ill.; son of Julius (a printer) and Grace (Vander Veen) Teune; married Elaine Meltz (a teacher), February 10, 1962; children: Elana. *Education:* Central University of Iowa, B.A., 1957; University of Illinois, M.A., 1958; Indiana University, Ph.D., 1961. *Home:* 8201 Henry Ave., G-11, Philadelphia, Pa. 19118. *Office:* Department of Political Science, University of Pennsylvania, Philadelphia, Pa. 19174.

CAREER: University of Pennsylvania, Philadelphia, assistant professor, 1961-65, associate professor, 1965-72, professor of political science, 1972—, vice-dean of Graduate School of Arts and Sciences, 1967-69, acting chairman of department of political science, 1970-71. Visiting associate professor and fellow at Cornell University, Center for International Studies, 1969; Fulbright research grant at University of Ljubljana, 1972. *Member:* International Studies Association, American Political Science Association, American Sociological Association. *Awards, honors:* American Council of Learned Societies grant, Yugoslavia, 1969-70.

WRITINGS: (Contributor) P. E. Jacobs and J. V. Toscano, editors, *The Integration of Political Communities,* Lippincott, 1964; (with A. Przeworski) *The Logic of Comparative Social Inquiry,* Wiley, 1970; (contributor) *Values and the Active Community,* Free Press, 1971; (contributor) Robert H. Lauer, editor, *Perspectives on Social Change,* Wiley, 1973. Contributor to *Comparative Political Studies.*

WORK IN PROGRESS: The Dynamics of Developmental Change, completion expected in 1975; research on methodology, on comparative politics, or political development, on political systems, and on local politics.

SIDELIGHTS: Teune has travelled and done research in several countries in Asia and Europe, especially Poland and Yugoslavia.

* * *

THACKRAY, Arnold 1939-

PERSONAL: Born July 30, 1939, in England; son of Wilfrid (a company secretary) and Mary (Clarke) Thackray; married Barbara Mary Hughes, July 25, 1964; children: Helen Mary, Gillian Winifrid. *Education:* University of Bristol, B.Sc. (first class honors), 1960; University of Leeds, graduate study, 1962-63; Cambridge University, M.A., 1965, Ph.D., 1966; University of Pennsylvania, M.A., 1971. *Residence:* Wayne, Pa. *Office:* Department of History and Sociology of Science, University of Pennsylvania, Philadelphia, Pa. 19174.

CAREER: Cambridge University, Cambridge, England, research fellow and member of governing body of Churchill College, 1965-68; University of Pennsylvania, Philadelphia, assistant professor of the history of science, 1968-69, associate professor of history and of the history of science, 1969-73, professor of history and of the history and sociology of science, 1973—, curator of Edgar Fahs Smith Collection in the History of Chemistry, 1969—, chairman of department of history and sociology of science, 1970—, faculty assistant to the president, 1972-74. Lecturer at Whipple Science Museum, 1965-67, internal examiner in the history and philosophy of science, 1966-67; visiting lecturer at Harvard University, 1967-68, and Bryn Mawr College, 1968—; visiting professor at London School of Economics and Political Science of University of London, 1971-72. Fellow of Center for Advanced Study in the Behavioral Sciences, Palo Alto, Calif., 1974, 1975. Member of history and philosophy of science panel of National Science Foundation, 1972-74; member of history and medicine fellowship panel of Josiah Macy, Jr. Foundation, 1973—; member of history of science panel of John Simon Guggenheim Memorial Foundation, 1974—. Co-director of Van Leer Jerusalem Foundation project on science and values, 1970-72; co-director of American Bicentennial Celebration Conference on the Eighteenth Century Revolution in Science, to be held in 1976.

MEMBER: History of Science Society, Society for the History of Technology (member of advisory council, 1972—; member of executive council, 1974—), American Association for the Advancement of Science, Manchester Literary and Philosophical Society (corresponding member). *Awards, honors:* National Science Foundation grants, 1968-70, 1970-72, 1972-75; Guggenheim fellowship, 1971-72.

WRITINGS: Atoms and Powers: An Essay on Newtonian Matter-Theory and the Development of Chemistry, Harvard University Press, 1970; *John Dalton: Critical Assessments of His Life and Science,* Harvard University Press, 1972; (editor with Everett J. Mendelsohn, and contributor) *Science and Values: Patterns of Tradition and Change: Proceedings of the August 1970 Van Leer Jerusalem Conference,* Humanities Press, 1974; (editor with Yehuda Elkana, R. K. Merton, and Harriet Zuckerman) *Classcis, Staples, and Precursors in the History, Philosophy, and Sociology of Science,* Arno, in press; *A Guide to the History of Science,* American Historical Association, in press.

Contributor: D. S. L. Cardwell, editor, *John Dalton and the Progress of Science,* University of Manchester Press, 1968; H. E. Roscoe and Arthur Harden, editors, *New View of Dalton's Atomic Theory,* Johnson Reprint, 1970; Roger

M. Steuwer, editor, *Historical Perspectives of Philosophy and Science,* University of Minnesota Press, 1970. Contributor of about fifty articles and reviews to scholarly journals, including *American Historical Review, Minerva, Science, Isis, Annals of Science, American Political Science Quarterly,* and *Journal of the History of Philosophy.* Member of editorial boards of *Historical Studies in the Physical Sciences,* 1968—, *History of Science,* 1972—, and *Social Studies of Science,* 1975—; member of editorial committee of *Isis,* 1970-73, chairman of committee, 1972-73; advisory editor of *Science History Publications,* 1971—.

* * *

THAYER, Lee (Osborn) 1927-

PERSONAL: Born December 18, 1927, in Greenfield, Kan.; son of Garrett O. (an oil operator) and Ruth (Ray) Thayer; married Nancy Lee Wright (an author), August 14, 1964; children: Cassandra Lee, Stephanie Lynn, Joshua Lee. *Education:* University of Wichita (now Wichita State University), B.A. (cum laude), 1953, M.A., 1956; University of Oklahoma, Ph.D., 1963. *Home:* 530 Newdale Pl., West Vancouver, B.C., Canada. *Office:* Department of Communication Studies, Simon Fraser University, Burnaby 2, B.C., Canada.

CAREER: University of Oklahoma, Norman, instructor in College of Business Administration, 1956-58; University of Wichita (now Wichita State University), Wichita, Kan., assistant professor, 1958-61, associate professor of administration and psychology, 1961-64; University of Missouri at Kansas City, professor of administration and director of research, 1964-68; University of Iowa, Iowa City, Gallup Professor of Communication and director of Center for the Advanced Study of Communication, 1968-73; Simon Fraser University, Burnaby, B.C., professor of communication studies, 1973—. Visiting professor at Harvard University, 1961, Institut de l'Environment, Paris, 1970, and University of Amsterdam, 1972. Member of board, Institute of General Semantics and Instituto de Comunicacion Social (Mexico). Consultant to U.S. Government and to industry. *Military service:* U.S. Naval Reserve, 1953-56; became lieutenant.

MEMBER: Academy of Management, American Association for the Advancement of Science, Creative Education Foundation, Society for General Systems Research, American Society for Information Sciences, National Society for the Study of Communication (president, 1968-69), International Association for Cybernetics, International Society for General Semantics, New York Academy of Sciences, Alpha Kappa Psi, Psi Chi. *Awards, honors:* Fellow of Foundation for Economic Education, 1964, 1966; research grants from National Science Foundation, National Aeronautics and Space Administration, Ford Foundation, Marketing Science Institute, U.S. Office of Education, and others.

WRITINGS—Sometimes under name Lee O. Thayer: (With George E. Harris) *Sales and Engineering Representation,* McGraw, 1958; *Administrative Communication,* Irwin, 1961; *Communication and Communication Systems in Organization, Management, and Interpersonal Relations,* Irwin, 1968.

Editor: *Communication: Theory and Research,* C.C Thomas, 1967; *Communication: Concepts and Perspectives,* Spartan, 1967; *Communication-Spectrum '7: Proceedings of the 15th Annual Conference of the National Society for the Study of Communication,* Allen Press, 1968; *Communication: General Semantics Perspectives,* Spartan, 1969; (and contributor) *Communication: Ethical and Moral Issues,* Gordon & Breach, 1973; *Ethical Issues in Mass Communication,* Gordon & Breach, 1974.

Contributor: F.W. Wilson, editor, *Numerical Control in Manufacturing,* McGraw, 1963; J.G. Longenecker, editor, *Principles of Management and Organizational Behavior,* C.E. Merrill, 1964; *Occasional Papers in Advertising,* University of Illinois Press, 1966; F.E.X. Dance, editor, *Human Communication Theory: Original Essays,* Holt, 1967; Frank Greenwood, editor, *Casebook for Management and Business Policy: A Systems Approach,* International Textbook Co., 1968; D.L. Arm, editor, *Vistas in Science,* University of New Mexico Press, 1968.

Johnnye Akin and others editors, *Language Behavior: A Book of Readings in Communication,* Mouton, 1970; D.E. Costello, editor, *Communication: On Being Human,* Simon & Schuster, 1971; Rubin Gotesky and Ervin Laszlo, editors, *Evolution–Revolution: Patterns of Development in Nature, Society, Man, and Knowledge,* Gordon & Breach, 1971; Laszlo, editor, *The Relevance of General Systems Theory,* Braziller, 1972; Laszlo and J.B. Wilbur, editors, *Values and the Man-Made Man,* Gordon & Breach, 1972; Costello, editor, *Learning and Communication Education,* Simon & Schuster, 1972; Laszlo and Emily B. Sellon, editors, *Festschrift for Henry Margenau,* Gordon & Breach, in press.

Author of numerous invited papers and published reports. Contributor to journals. Editor, *Communication.*

WORK IN PROGRESS: A book, *Towards a Philosophy for the Social Sciences;* articles and research projects on communication and social change, managerial competence, and other aspects of communications and education.

* * *

THEBAUD, Jo 1914-

PERSONAL: Surname is pronounced *Tay*-bo; born February 27, 1914, in Vineland, N.J.; daughter of Jules Stephen (a postmaster) and Ethel (Bliss) Thebaud; married Nicholas A. Torrell, June 13, 1934 (died, May 16, 1958); children: Noelita M., Mary Alice (Mrs. Richard J. Hartman), Josephine M. (Mrs. Thomas Armstrong), Marie L. (Mrs. Frank L. Baglio), Michael T., John Patrick, Jerome Stephen, Paul Christopher, Mary Ethel (Mrs. John Bonner), Peter Francis. *Education:* Attended high school in Camden, N.J.; additional study privately and by correspondence courses. *Politics:* Democrat. *Religion:* Roman Catholic. *Home and office:* 250 North St., Calais, Me. 04619. *Agent:* Bertha Klausner, 71 Park Ave., New York, N.Y. 10021.

CAREER: Substitute teacher, boarding house owner, house-mother, free-lance writer; Torrell-Hilton Studios, Cedar Run, N.J. and Calais, Me., partner, 1973—.

WRITINGS: Today and Other Days, St. Mary's College Press, 1971; *Less Than Angels,* St. Mary's College Press, 1972. Contributor to magazines, newspapers, and radio. Regular columnist, "Taken at Random," for *Courier-Post* newspapers in the 1940's, "Faithfully Yours," *Catholic Star Herald,* 1950's, and "Friendship Corner," *Calais Advertiser,* 1960's—.

WORK IN PROGRESS: Several books of poetry and prose.

THOENE, Alma E(vans) 1903-

PERSONAL: Surname is pronounced Thone; born November 7, 1903, in Akron, Ohio; daughter of James O. (a barber) and Sarah (Dandridge) Evans; married William Lewis Arthur Thoene, Sr. (a printer), October 1, 1921; children: William Arthur Lewis, Jr., Bernice Goldberg (deceased). *Education:* Attended Territorial Normal School, Honolulu, Hawaii; University of Hawaii, B.Ed., 1935, M.Ed., 1938. *Religion:* Roman Catholic. *Home:* 2837 Puuhonua St., Honolulu, Hawaii. *Mailing address:* P. O. Box 2552, Honolulu, Hawaii 96804.

CAREER: Elementary school teacher in public schools of Kipahula, Maui, 1918-19, Pauwela, Maui, 1919-20, and Honolulu, Hawaii, 1920-24, 1925-38; intermediate school English teacher in Honolulu, Hawaii, 1938-45; Central Intermediate School, Honolulu, Hawaii, vice-principal and boys' advisor, 1945-46; principal in public schools of Honolulu, Hawaii, 1946-66. *Member:* American Museum of Natural History, National Education Association, National Retired Teachers Association, Smithsonian Association, Hawaii Association of Elementary School Principals, Hawaii Elementary School Administrators Association, Hawaii State Retired Teachers' Association, Hawaii Congress of Parents and Teachers, Daughters of Hawaii, Hawaii Historical Society, Hawaii Opera Theater, Friends of the Library of Hawaii, Hawaii Foundation for History and the Humanities, Oahu Retired Teachers Association, Oahu Elementary School Principals Association, Honolulu Academy of Arts, Pilot Club of Honolulu, Bishop Museum Society, University of Hawaii Alumni Association (life member), Oceanic Society.

WRITINGS: A Critical Evaluation of the Parent-Teacher Association in Hawaii Based on a Survey of the Movement, University Press of Hawaii, 1938; *Hawaii* (textbook), F. Watts, 1968. Contributor to *Hawaii Education Review.* Editor of *Hawaii Parent-Teacher,* 1941.

WORK IN PROGRESS: Research on education in Hawaii for a book on the changes in education in Hawaii from 1918-1960, as compared with the 1970's.

AVOCATIONAL INTERESTS: Symphony concerts, community activities, traveling.

BIOGRAPHICAL/CRITICAL SOURCES: Men and Women of Hawaii, Honolulu Star-Bulletin, 1966, 1972; *honolulu Advertiser,* June 9, 1966.

* * *

THOMAS, Arline 1913-

PERSONAL: Born November 12, 1913, in Bayshore, N.Y.; daughter of Charles Edgar (an engineer) and Mary (Frost) Abrams; married George Paul Thomas, November 2, 1940 (died, 1959). *Education:* Attended New York University, 1956-58. *Home:* 188-05 Soho Dr., Hollis, N.Y. 11423.

CAREER: J. H. Thorp and Co. (importers), New York, N.Y., bi-lingual secretary, 1930-41. *Member:* National Audubon Society, New York Zoological Society, Queens County Bird Club.

WRITINGS: Bird Ambulance, Scribner, 1971; *Mockingbird Trio,* Scribner, 1973. Contributor to *American Heritage, McCall's, Harper's,* and *Saturday Evening Post.*

WORK IN PROGRESS: Research on mute swans for a proposed children's book.

SIDELIGHTS: Arline Thomas holds a bird salvage permit from the New York Conservation Department and Fish and Wildlife Service which enables her to take care of injured wild birds. She has appeared on television programs, including the Mike Douglas Show, and lectures as the Bird Lady at schools and garden clubs.

BIOGRAPHICAL/CRITICAL SOURCES: New York Times, May 23, 1971; *Long Island Press,* August 22, 1972; *New York Daily News,* March 18, 1974; *Miami Herald,* March 24, 1974.

* * *

THOMAS, Donald 1926-

PERSONAL: Born April 21, 1926, in Pittsburgh, Pa.; son of Louis (a machinist) and Rose (Manna) Thomas; married Frances Gaylord, December 21, 1948; children: Marc, Marcia, David. *Education:* University of Dubuque, B.A., 1948; University of Illinois, M.A., 1951, Ed.D., 1965. *Home:* 860 18th Ave., Salt Lake City, Utah 84103. *Office:* Salt Lake City School District, 440 East First St. S., Salt Lake City, Utah 84111.

CAREER: High school teacher of English, speech, and remedial reading in Mason City, Iowa, 1950-52, and in Chicago Heights, Ill., 1952-57; counselor, director of testing and evaluation, assistant principal, and principal in Mount Prospect, Ill., 1959-65; superintendent in Elk Grove, Ill., 1965-68, Amsterdam, N.Y., 1968-71, Newark, Calif., 1971-73; Salt Lake City School District, Salt Lake City, Utah, superintendent, 1973—. Lecturer at International Graduate School of Education, Denver, Colo., University of Illinois, Bradley University, St. Mary's College, University of California, Berkeley and Haywood, and Chapman College; negotiations trainer in Illinois, New York, and California, 1964-67; chairman of steering committee for North Cook County Office of Economic Opportunity, 1965-67; member of advisory committee to Cook County Superintendent of Schools, 1966-68; member of Aspen Conference on Education and the Human Potential, 1967, 1968, 1969; director of Aspen Center for the Study of Education, 1967-71. Consultant to Tri-County Division of Illinois Association of School Boards, New York Department of Education, California Department of Education, U.S. Office of Education, and Alameda County Schools Department.

MEMBER: International Education Association (president of Calumet Valley Division, 1956-57, and Northwest Suburban Division, 1959-60), Toastmasters International (parliamentarian of Calumet Valley Division, 1956-59), National Association of Teachers of English, National Education Association (director, 1968-70), Illinois Education Association (parliamentarian of Calumet Valley Division, 1956-57), Rotary. *Awards, honors:* Toastmaster International district speech winner, 1956; Institute for Development of Educational Activities summer fellow, 1967, 1968; Council for the Advancement of Education best magazine article winner, 1972-73; D.Litt., Westminster College, Salt Lake City, Utah, 1974.

WRITINGS: (Contributor) Joseph A. Johnston, editor, *Selected Readings on Helping Relationships,* Simon & Schuster, 1970; (contributor) James E. Heald, editor, *Selected Readings on General Supervision,* Macmillan, 1971; *Directory of Educational Consultants,* School Management Study Group, Ralka Press, Volume I: *1971,* 1971, Volume II: *1972,* 1972, Volume III: *1973,* 1973; (contributor) Warren Seifert, editor, *Theory into Practice,* Ohio State University Press, 1972; *Winters Are Unfair,* Ralka Press, 1973. Author of monographs, workbooks, and teachers' guides. Contributor of more than fifty articles to journals.

WORK IN PROGRESS: A career booklet, *The School Superintendent; Helping Children to Learn at Home; Teaching Values.*

AVOCATIONAL INTERESTS: Travel, collecting antiques, especially historical items related to the colonial period, reading biographies, hiking.

* * *

THOMAS, Jack W(illiam) 1931-

PERSONAL: Born October 24, 1931, in Seattle, Wash.; son of Edward Moore (a photographer) and Margaret (Walker) Thomas; married Cathleen F. Cagney, February 17, 1962; children: Verney Lee, Christina May. *Education:* University of Arizona, B.A., 1957. *Home and office:* 1961 Lookout Dr., Agoura, Calif. 91301. *Agent:* James Fox, 2195 Roberto Dr., Palm Springs, Calif. 92262.

CAREER: Free-lance writer for motion pictures, 1959-62; Los Angeles County Probation Department, Los Angeles, Calif., probation officer, 1964-70; writer, 1970—. *Military service:* U.S. Navy, 1950-54. *Member:* Writers Guild of America West.

WRITINGS—All published by Bantam: *Turn Me On,* 1969; *Reds,* 1971; *Bikers,* 1972; *Girls Farm,* 1974; *Redeemers,* in press.

Screenplays: "Lone Texan," Fox, 1959; "Thirteen Fighting Men," Fox, 1960; "20,000 Eyes," Fox, 1961; "Francis of Assisi," Fox, 1961; "We'll Bury You," Columbia, 1962.

Also author of script for documentary, "Nine Bows to Conquer," 1964.

WORK IN PROGRESS: *Shannon,* a novel, completion expected in 1974.

SIDELIGHTS: Thomas told *CA:* "My experience as a probation officer made me aware of the abuse of drugs in many young people's lives. I try to inject anti-drug themes in my books without making it propaganda that kids will not buy."

Thomas spent 1958 travelling in Europe and Mexico, and lived in Egypt for nine months in 1964.

* * *

THOMAS, John 1890-

PERSONAL: Born May 27, 1890, in Aberdare, Glamorganshire, South Wales; son of Thomas (a coal miner) and Eleanor Thomas; married Annie Longton, August 12, 1918. *Education:* University College, Cardiff, B.A. (honors), 1911; University of Wales, M.A., 1922; University of London, Ph.D., 1936. *Religion:* "Nonconformist Protestant." *Home:* 2 Priory Gardens, Clothorn Rd., Didsbury, Manchester M2O OBG, England.

CAREER: Elementary teacher in Aberdare, Wales, 1906-08; general secretary of Workers' Educational Association for Wales, Aberdare, 1911-14; national war service on farms in Wales, 1914-18; trade union leader with anthracite miners at Diamond Colliery, Swansea, Wales, 1918-20, then miner's agent for South Wales Anthracite Coalfield, 1920-25; resident tutor for Oxford University in Staffordshire potteries, 1925-39; Cooperative College, Manchester, England, principal, 1939-43; British Broadcasting Corp., Manchester, England, director of talks for North Region, 1943-46; Ministry of Fuel, Manchester, England, director of personnel recruitment, 1946; Ministry of Works and Public Buildings, assistant director for North Region, Manchester, England, 1946-54; Leonard Fairclough Ltd. (engineers and contractors), London, England, industrial adviser and writer of company magazine, 1954-62; industrial consultant and writer, 1962—. Extramural lecturer at University College, Cardiff, and University College of Aberystwyth, 1911-25, and Oxford University, 1925-39; lecturer at summer schools in Denmark and United States. Member of National Pottery Industrial Council, 1925-40. *Member:* Royal Statistical Society (fellow), Royal Economic Society (fellow), Royal Society of Arts (fellow), Royal Society of Teachers.

WRITINGS: *The Miner's Conflict with the Mineowners,* International Bookshops, 1921; (with G.D.H. Cole) *British Trade Unionism Today,* Gollancz, 1939; *Pottery and Its Making,* Penguin, 1950; (author of introduction) Henry Allen Wedgwood, *People of the Potteries* (originally published in the 1870's), Augustus M. Kelley, 1970; *The Rise of the Staffordshire Potteries,* Augustus M. Kelley, 1971. Writer of booklets and pamphlets on cooperative education, adult education, and economics of coal. Contributor to *Lleufer* (Welsh monthly), 1951-56, and to *Nature, Welsh Outlook, Wedgwood Magazine, Apollo, Connoisseur,* and other publications.

WORK IN PROGRESS: A history of the South Wales Anthracite Coalfield, in English and Welsh; also writing on the future industrial development of mid-Wales and on Robert Owen and his American descendents; his memoirs of pioneering adult education in Wales and England.

BIOGRAPHICAL/CRITICAL SOURCES: Mary Stocks, *The Workers' Educational Association: The First 50 Years,* Allen & Unwin, 1953.

* * *

THOMAS, Virginia Castleton
See CASTLETON, Virginia

* * *

THOMPSON, Charles Lowell 1937-

PERSONAL: Born February 25, 1937, in Columbus, Ohio; son of Charles Hollington (a physician) and Naomi (Jones) Thompson; married Harriet Wolstenholme, June 21, 1957; children: Charles, Cynthia, Marcia. *Education:* Attended Ohio Wesleyan University, 1955-58; University of Tennessee, B.S., 1959, M.A., 1961; Ohio State University, Ph.D., 1967. *Politics:* Conservative. *Religion:* Methodist. *Home:* 7817 Luxmore Dr., Knoxville, Tenn. 37919. *Office:* Department of Educational Psychology and Guidance, University of Tennessee, 108 CEB, Knoxville, Tenn. 37916.

CAREER: University of Tennessee, Knoxville, assistant professor, 1967-70, associate professor, 1970-73, professor of educational psychology and guidance, 1973—. *Member:* American Psychological Association, American Personnel and Guidance Association, East Tennessee Personnel and Guidance Association (president, 1971-72), Phi Delta Theta, Phi Delta Kappa. *Awards, honors:* East Tennessee Personnel and Guidance Association publications award, 1973.

WRITINGS: (Contributor) Herman J. Peters, Richard S. Dunlop, Roger F. Aubrey, editors, *The Practice of Guidance,* Love, 1972; (with William A. Poppen) *For Those Who Care: Ways of Relating to Youth,* C. E. Merrill, 1972; (with Poppen) *School Counseling: Theories and Concepts,* Professional Educators Publications, 1974. Contributor to guidance and education journals. Member of editorial board of *Elementary School Guidance and Counseling,* 1972.

WORK IN PROGRESS: Research on career education materials for use in the public schools.

* * *

THOMPSON, Donald L(ambert) 1930-

PERSONAL: Born March 31, 1930, in New York, N.Y.; son of Rexford Leslie (an accountant) and Olga Annie (Lambert) Thompson; married Mary Green, January 11, 1955 (divorced, 1965); married Sally Tollerton, June 15, 1967; children: (first marriage) Jillian, David. *Education:* University of Pennsylvania, B.S., 1951; San Francisco State College, M.S., 1958; University of California, Berkeley, Ph.D., 1963. *Home:* 201 North Main St., Slippery Rock, Pa. 16057. *Office:* Slippery Rock State College, Slippery Rock, Pa. 16057.

CAREER: U.S. Army, 1951-56, with final assignment as first lieutenant with National Security Agency; Standard Oil Co. of California, San Francisco, organization specialist, 1956-58; University of California, Berkeley, instructor in marketing, 1960-63; University of Oregon, Eugene, assistant professor, 1963-65, associate professor of marketing and assistant dean of Graduate School of Management and Business, 1965-69; Slippery Rock State College, Slippery Rock, Pa., professor of economics and vice-president for administrative affairs, 1969—. *Member:* American Marketing Association, Alpha Kappa Psi, Delta Upsilon, Rotary International.

WRITINGS: (Contributor) *Real Estate Office Administration,* California State Real Estate Association, 1963; *Analysis of Retailing Potential in Metropolitan Areas,* Bureau of Business and Economic Research, University of California, 1964; (editor with Douglas J. Dalrymple) *Retail Management Cases,* Free Press, 1969; (with Dalrymple) *Retailing: An Economic View,* Free Press, 1969; (contributor) Harper Boyd and Robert T. Davis, editor, *Readings in Sales Management,* Irwin, 1970; (with Leslie P. Anderson and Vergil P. Miller) *The Finance Function,* International Textbook Co., 1971; (contributor) Robert Ferber, editor, *Marketing Research Handbook,* McGraw, 1974. Contributor of about twenty articles to business and economic journals.

WORK IN PROGRESS: *Higher Education Administration: Text and Cases.*

* * *

THOMPSON, Ewa M(ajewska) 1937-

PERSONAL: Born August 23, 1937, in Kaunas, Lithuania; naturalized U.S. citizen in 1971; married James R. Thompson (a university professor), 1967. *Education:* University of Warsaw, B.A., 1963; Sopot Conservatory of Music, M.F.A., 1963; Vanderbilt University, Ph.D., 1967. *Office:* Department of Russian, Rice University, Houston, Tex. 77001.

CAREER: University of Virginia, Charlottesville, associate professor of Slavic languages, 1973-74; Rice University, Houston, Tex., associate professor of Russian, 1974—. *Member:* Modern Language Association of America, American Comparative Literature Association, American Association for the Advancement of Slavic Studies, American Association of Slavic and East European Languages.

WRITINGS: *Russian Formalism and Anglo-American New Criticism,* Mouton & Co., 1971. Contributor to Slavic and English professional journals.

SIDELIGHTS: Ewa Thompson wrote that she is very much interested in changing the shape of literary education at American universities, and in developing social awareness of sex inequality in contemporary culture.

* * *

THOMPSON, Julius Eric 1946-

PERSONAL: Born July 15, 1946, in Vicksburg, Miss.; son of Josie Thompson. *Education:* Summer study at Columbia University, 1967, and Yale University, 1968; Alcorn State University, B.S. (cum laude), 1969; Princeton University, M.A., 1971. Ph.D., 1973. *Home:* 508 Bluebird Dr., Natchez, Miss. 39120. *Office:* Department of History, Jackson State University, Jackson, Miss. 39217.

CAREER: Jackson State University, Jackson, Miss., assistant professor of history, 1973—. *Member:* American Historical Association, Association for the Study of Afro-American Life and History, Alpha Kappa Mu, Alpha Phi Alpha. *Awards, honors:* Danforth Foundation fellow and Princeton fellow, 1969-73; Ford Foundation fellow, 1972-73.

WRITINGS: *Hopes Tied Up in Promises,* Dorrance, 1970.

WORK IN PROGRESS: *Blues Said: Walk On,* a volume of poetry; *Hiram R. Revels: A Biography, 1827-1901.*

* * *

THOMPSON, Kent 1936-

PERSONAL: Born February 3, 1936, in Waukegan, Ill.; naturalized Canadian citizen, 1971; son of Maurice Madison (a teacher and draftsman) and Clarice (Graves) Thompson; married Hildred Michaele Fowler (a laboratory technician), August 1, 1960; children: Kevin, G. David. *Education:* University of Exeter, student, 1954-55; Hanover College, B.A. (magna cum laude), 1957; State University of Iowa, M.A., 1962; University of Wales, Ph.D., 1965. *Politics:* Conservative. *Religion:* "No formal religion." *Residence:* Fredericton, New Brunswick, Canada. *Office:* Department of English, University of New Brunswick, Fredericton, New Brunswick, Canada.

CAREER: Ripon College, Ripon, Wis., instructor in English, 1961-63; Colorado Woman's College, Denver, assistant professor of English, 1965-66; University of New Brunswick, Fredericton, assistant professor, 1966-68, associate professor, 1968-74, professor of English, 1974—. *Military service:* U.S. Army, Intelligence Corps, 1958-61; became sergeant. *Member:* Writers Union of Canada (member of national council). *Awards, honors:* Woodrow Wilson fellowship, 1957-58; Fulbright fellowship, 1963-65; holder of Canada Council arts bursary, 1972-73.

WRITINGS: *Hard Explanations* (poems), New Brunswick Chapbooks, 1968; *The Tenants Were Corrie and Tennie,* St. Martin's, 1973; (editor and contributor) *Stories from Atlantic Canada,* Macmillan (Canada), 1973; *Across from the Floral Park,* St. Martin's, 1974.

Radio plays, for Canadian Broadcasting Corp.: "I Am the Greengrocer's Daughter," 1969; "Deadburn's Ditch," 1970; "Parting," 1972; "Understanding in a Meat Market," 1973.

Work is anthologized in *Best Little Magazine Fiction, 1971,* edited by Curt Johnson and Alvin Greenberg, New York University Press, 1971; *Fourteen Stories High,* edited by David Helwig and Tom Marshall, Oberon Press, 1971; *Kaleidoscope,* edited by John Metcalf, Van Nostrand, 1972; *The Narrative Voice,* edited by John Metcalf, McGraw, 1972; *Ninety Seasons,* edited by Robert Cockburn and Robert Gibbs, McClelland & Stewart, 1974.

Contributor to Canadian literary periodicals. Editor of *Fiddlehead,* 1966-70, 1973—.

WORK IN PROGRESS: A Band of My Ancestors, a cycle of poems; a novel; a television play.

SIDELIGHTS: Thompson told *CA:* "I became a writer because, first, I could not hit a curve ball, and second, because I obtained a job teaching creative writing and wanted to keep it, and third, because the activity of writing excites me. I am fascinated by technique, and consider myself the best punctuator in North America. I tend to write about both sides of a joke. I like to challenge the reader, but I'm not avant-garde. I speak little French and understand less."

* * *

THOMPSON, Robert (Grainger Ker) 1916-

PERSONAL: Born April 12, 1916, in Stanmore, England; son of William Grainger (a canon) and Margaret (Ker) Thompson; married Merryn Newboult, October 10, 1950; children: Isabel, Hugh. *Education:* Sidney Sussex College, Cambridge, B.A., 1937, M.A., 1945. *Religion:* Church of England. *Home:* Winsford, Minehead, Somerset, England. *Agent:* John Cushman, John Cushman Associates, Inc., 25 West 43rd St., New York, N.Y. 10036.

CAREER: Malayan Civil Service, Malaya, cadet, 1938-45, assistant commissioner of labor in Perak, 1946, joint services staff college, 1948-49, civil staff officer to director of operations, 1950-52, coordinating officer, security, 1955-57, deputy secretary for defense of Federation of Malaya, 1957-59, permanent secretary for defense, 1959-61; head of British Advisory Mission to Vietnam, 1961-65. Consultant to United States and other governments, and to National Security Council, RAND Corp., and Battelle Memorial Institute. *Military service:* Royal Air Force, wing commander, 1941-46; received Distinguished Service Order and Military Cross. *Member:* Institute for the Study of Conflict. *Awards, honors:* Created Knight of the British Empire, 1965, and Companion of the Order of St. Michael and St. George, 1961.

WRITINGS: Defeating Communist Insurgency, Praeger, 1966; *Royal Flying Corps,* Leo Cooper, 1968; *No Exit from Vietnam* (with maps), McKay, 1969; *Revolutionary War in World Strategy,* Taplinger, 1970; *Peace Is Not at Hand,* McKay, 1974. Contributor to magazines, including *Foreign Affairs, Spectator, Statist,* and *Reader's Digest.*

SIDELIGHTS: "Thompson has written a speculative and theoretical analysis of the war in Vietnam," said Robert T. Redden, of *No Exit from Vietnam.* "He applies to that situation concepts and perspectives gained from long experience.... His is a worthwhile analysis somewhat prejudiced by background and experience." *Avocational interests:* Country pursuits, traveling.

* * *

THORWALD, Juergen 1916- (Heinz Bongartz)

PERSONAL: Original name, Heinz Bongartz, pseudonym, Juergen Thorwald, adopted as name, 1949; born October 28, 1916, in Solingen, Germany; son of Jacob (a schoolteacher) and Auguste (Hartmann) Bongartz; married Hanna Seen, April 12, 1942 (divorced, 1948); married Inge Wetzel (a physical therapist), October 4, 1955; children: (second marriage) Robert Kim. *Education:* Attended University of Cologne, 1935-40. *Politics:* None. *Religion:* Protestant. *Home:* Villa California, Via Bellavista 8, Lugano, Switzerland; and 1341 Las Canoas Rd., Pacific Palisades, Calif. 90272. *Agent:* Felix Guggenheim, 725 North Roxbury Dr., Beverly Hills, Calif. 90210.

CAREER: Christ und Welt (a weekly newspaper), Stuttgart, Germany, editor, 1947-52; author, 1952—. *Military service:* German Navy, 1940. *Awards, honors:* Edgar Allan Poe special award, 1966.

WRITINGS: Es begann an der Weichsel (also see below), Steingrueben, 1950, and *Das Ende an der Elbe* (also see below), Steingrueben, 1950, condensation and translation by Fred Wieck published as *Flight in the Winter: Russia Conquers,* Pantheon, 1951, reissued as *Defeat in the East: Russia Conquers, January to May 1945,* Ballantine, 1959; *Die ungeklaerten Faelle,* Steingrueben, 1950; *Wen sie verderben wollen: Bericht des grossen Verrats,* Steingrueben, 1952; *Hoch ueber Kaprun* (novel), Suedverlag, 1954; *Das Jahrhundert der Chirurgen: Nach den Papieren meines Grossvaters, des Chirurgen H. St. Hartmann* (also see below), Steingrueben, 1956, translation published as *The Century of the Surgeon,* Pantheon, 1957; *Das Weltreich der Chirurgen. Nach den Papieren meines Grossvaters, des Chirurgen H. St. Hartmann* (also see below), Steingrueben, 1958, translation by Richard and Clara Winston published as *The Triumph of Surgery,* Pantheon, 1960.

Die Entlassung: Das Ende des Chirurgen Ferdinand Sauerbruch, Droemer, 1960, translation by Richard and Clara Winston published as *The Dismissed: The Last Days of Ferdinand Sauerbruch, Surgeon,* Thames & Hudson, 1961, published as *The Dismissed: The Last Days of Ferdinand Sauerbruch,* Pantheon, 1962; *Die grosse Flucht: Es begann an der Weichsel. Das Ende an der Elbe,* Steingrueben, 1962; *Macht und Geheimnis der fruehen Aerzte: Aegypten, Babylonien, Indien, China, Mexiko, Peru,* Droemer, 1962, translation by Richard and Clara Winston published as *Science and Secrets of Early Medicine: Egypt, Mesopotamia, India, China, Mexico, Peru,* Harcourt, 1963; *Das Jahrhundert der Detektive: Weg und Abenteuer der Kriminalistik,* Droemer, 1964, translation by Richard and Clara Winston published as *The Century of the Detective,* Harcourt, 1965 (translation of first section of *Das Jahrhundert der Detektive* published in England as *The Marks of Cain,* Thames & Hudson, 1965, second section as *Dead Men Tell Tales,* Thames & Hudson, 1966, and third section as *Proof of Poison,* Thames & Hudson, 1966); *Die Geschichte der Chirurgie: Das Jahrhundert der Chirurgen. Das Weltreich des Chirurgen. Nach den Papieren meines Grossvaters, des Chirurgen H. St. Hartmann,* Steingrueben, 1965; *Die Stunde der Detektive: Werden und Welten der Kriminalistik,* Droemer, 1966, translation by Richard and Clara Winston published as *Crime and Science: The New Frontier in Criminology,* Harcourt, 1967; *Die Traum Oase (Beverly Hills),* Droemer, 1968.

Die Patienten, Droemer, 1971, translation by Richard and Clara Winston published as *The Patients,* Harcourt, 1972; *The Illusion,* Harcourt, 1974.

Under name Heinz Bongartz: *Luftkrieg im Westen: Fluege, Kaempfe, Siege deutscher Flieger,* W. Kohler, 1940; *Luft-*

macht Deutschland, aufstieg, kampf und sieg, Essener verlaganstalt, 1941; *Seemacht Deutschland, Wiederaufstieg. Kampf und Sieg,* Essener verlaganstalt, 1941.

Contributor to *Speigel, Stern, Zeit, Weltwoche,* and *Reader's Digest.*

WORK IN PROGRESS: A book, *The Gynecologist,* a history of gynecology; research for *Generation 16,* a personal history of the author's generation in Europe.

SIDELIGHTS: Thorwald adopted his pseudonym in order to avoid harassment while doing research in Soviet occupied Germany. The popularity of the books written under that pseudonym led him to use it as a legal name. *Avocational interests:* Architecture, boating, and aviation.

* * *

THURMAN, Judith 1946-

PERSONAL: Born October 28, 1946, in New York, N.Y.; daughter of William A. (a lawyer) and Alice (a teacher; maiden name, Meisner) Thurman. *Education:* Brandeis University, A.B., 1967. *Residence:* New York, N.Y.

CAREER: Writer and poet in New York, N.Y., 1972—. Adjunct lecturer at Brooklyn College of the City University of New York, 1973—.

WRITINGS: Putting My Coat On (poems), Covent Garden Press (London), 1972; (editor with Lilian Moore) *To See the World Afresh,* Atheneum, 1974; *I Became Alone* (essays), Atheneum, in press. Poems represented in anthologies, including *The New York Times Book of Poems,* edited by Thomas Lask, Macmillan, 1970; *The Logic of Poetry,* edited by Briggs and Monaco, McGraw, 1974. Contributor to *Ms, New York Times,* and *Shenandoah.*

WORK IN PROGRESS: Translating poems for *Penguin Book of Women Poets;* a book of original poems for young children; an anthology of mid-century poetry; a biography of Isak Dinesen.

SIDELIGHTS: Judith Thurman speaks four languages and can translate from three of them: French, Italian, and Spanish. She has lived in Italy and England. Of her work she writes: "My energy as a writer is 'feminist,' but my poetry has no consistent bias. Poems are occasions—I think they exist as much outside as inside a poet."

* * *

THURMAN, Wayne L(averne) 1923-

PERSONAL: Born June 11, 1923, in Detroit, Mich.; son of Lewis J. and Gladys (Stroup) Thurman. *Education:* Southeast Missouri State College, B.S.Ed. and B.A., 1947; Iowa State University, M.A., 1949; Purdue University, Ph.D., 1953. *Home:* 877 First St., Charleston, Ill. 61920. *Office:* Department of Speech, Eastern Illinois University, Charleston, Ill. 61920.

CAREER: Eastern Illinois University, Charleston, assistant professor, 1953-58, associate professor, 1959-62, professor of speech pathology and audiology, 1963—. *Military service:* U.S. Army, 1943-46; became staff sergeant; served in European Theater; received Combat Infantry Badge and Bronze Star. *Member:* Illinois Speech and Hearing Association (president, 1967-68), Sigma Alpha Eta (national president, 1957-58).

WRITINGS: (With T. D. Hanley) *Developing Vocal Skills,* Holt, 1963, revised edition, 1970; (with Hanley) *Projects Book,* Holt, 1963; (contributor) Morton Cooper, editor, *Approaches to Vocal Rehabilitation,* C.C Thomas, in press.

* * *

TIEN, H. Yuan 1926-

PERSONAL: Born June 20, 1926; married; children: two. *Education:* Haverford College, B.A., 1953; University of Pennsylvania, M.A., 1955; Australian National University, Ph.D., 1959. *Office:* Department of Sociology, Ohio State University, Columbus, Ohio 43210.

CAREER: Redevelopment Authority of City of Philadelphia, Pa., planning analyst, summer, 1954, 1955; University of Wisconsin, Milwaukee, 1959-65, began as assistant professor, became associate professor of sociology; University of Illinois, Urbana, associate professor of sociology, 1965-69; Ohio State University, Columbus, professor of sociology, 1969—, director of Institute for Comparative Sociology, 1969-72. Visiting associate professor at University of Illinois, 1964-65, and Indiana University, summer, 1967; visiting Fulbright professor at University of Hong Kong, 1972-73. Consultant to Ford and Rockefeller Foundations Program in Support of Social Science and Legal Research on Population Policy, 1970—. Instructor in Peace Corps training programs. *Member:* International Union for the Scientific Study of Population, American Sociological Association, American Council of Learned Societies (fellow), Population Association of America, Association for Asian Studies. *Awards, honors:* Research grants from Social Science Research Council, 1961-62, 1963-64; senior Fulbright-Hays lectureship, 1972-73; research grant from Population Council, 1973; research grant from American Philosophical Society, 1973.

WRITINGS: Social Mobility and Controlled Fertility, College & University Press, 1965; (contributor) Charles Nam, editor, *Population and Society,* Houghton, 1968; (contributor) Marvin Sussman and Betty Cogswell, editors, *Cross-Cultural Family Research,* E. J. Brill, 1972; *China's Population Struggle: Demographic Decisions of the People's Republic, 1949-1969,* Ohio State University Press, 1973; (contributor) Sussman, editor, *Sourcebook on Marriage and the Family,* 4th edition (Tien was not represented in earlier editions), Houghton, 1974; (editor with Frank Bean) *Comparative Family and Fertility Research,* E. J. Brill, 1974. Contributor to proceedings and to *Encyclopaedia Hebraica;* contributor of about forty articles and reviews to journals in his field. Editor of *Comparative Events,* 1969-72.

WORK IN PROGRESS: Inside China's Population Pyramid: Impressions and Issues; Planned Reproduction and Family Formation.

* * *

TIETZE, Andreas 1914-

PERSONAL: Born April 26, 1914, in Vienna, Austria; son of Hans (an art historian) and Erica (an art historian; maiden name, Conrat) Tietze; married Sue Uyar, June 28, 1952; children: Phyllis, Denise, Noor, Ben. *Education:* University of Vienna, Ph.D., 1937. *Home:* 10577 Eastborne Ave., Los Angeles, Calif. 90024. *Office:* Department of Near Eastern Languages, University of California, Los Angeles, Calif. 90024.

CAREER: Istanbul University, Istanbul, Turkey, lecturer in German, 1938-52; University of Illinois, Urbana, research assistant professor of Spanish, 1952-53; Istanbul University, lecturer in English, 1953-58; University of California, Los Angeles, associate professor of Turkish and Persian, 1958-60, professor of Turkish, 1960—. Director of dictionary project, American Board Publication Office, Istanbul, 1946-58; member of committee on Uralic and Altaic studies, American Council of Learned Societies, 1961—.

MEMBER: International Society for Oriental Research (founding member), American Oriental Society (president of Western branch, 1970-71), Middle East Studies Association, American Name Society, Middle East Institute, Philological Association of the Pacific Coast. *Awards, honors:* Distinguished Teaching Award, University of California, Los Angeles, 1971.

WRITINGS: (With others) *Revised Redhouse Dictionary, English-Turkish,* American Board Publication Office, 1950; (with Henry Kahane and Rene Kahane) *The Lingua Franca in the Levant,* University of Illinois Press, 1958; (editor) *The Turkish Literary Reader,* Research Center for the Language Sciences, Indiana University, 1963, revised edition, 1968; *Die Oelweide: Moderne tuerkische Erzaehler,* Gute Schriften (Basel), 1964; *The Koman Riddles and Turkic Folklore,* University of California Press, 1966; (with others) *New Redhouse Turkish-English Dictionary,* Redhouse Press (Istanbul), 1968; (with Ilhan Basgoez) *A Corpus of Turkish Riddles,* University of California Press, 1973; (editor) *Advanced Turkish Reader: Texts in the Social Sciences and Related Fields,* Research Center for the Language Sciences, Indiana University, 1973; *Mustafa Ali's Description of Cairo in 1599,* Austrian Academy of Science, in press. Translator of modern fiction—Turkish into German, German into Turkish, and Azerbaijani into Turkish.

SIDELIGHTS: "I started as a historian with a special interest in the Balkan area and the Near East," Tietze writes. "When Turkey became my basic field of operation my interests spread, first to the language and gradually to folklore and literature."

* * *

TIFFT, Ellen 1916-

PERSONAL: Born June 28, 1916, in Elmira, N.Y.; daughter of Halsey and Julia (Day) Sayles; married Bela Tifft (a lawyer), July 16, 1938; children: Wilton, John, Nicol. *Education:* Elmira College, student, 1936-38. *Politics:* Democrat. *Religion:* Society of Friends (Quakers). *Home address:* Crane Rd., East Hill, Elmira, N.Y. 14901.

CAREER: Poet and writer. Has made a television film, reading from her own work. *Member:* Poetry Society of America.

WRITINGS—Poems: *A Door in a Wall,* Hors Commerce Press, 1966; *The Kissed Cold Kite,* Hors Commerce Press, 1968; *The Live-Long Day,* Charas Press, 1972. Work is included in anthologies, including *The Best Poems of 1941,* edited by Thomas Moult, Harcourt, 1942, and *Abraxas 5 Anthology,* edited by James Bertolino, 1973. Contributor of poems and short stories to literature journals, including *Plume and Sword, Western Review, Transatlantic Review, Saturday Evening Post, Today's Poets,* and *New Yorker.*

WORK IN PROGRESS: Good Night, Irene, a novel.

SIDELIGHTS: Ellen Tifft writes: "I think I write mostly to persuade people to listen to their own inner selves rather than to books. I am shocked at all the mirror-living there is in the world, people doing things simply for the effect. I think I write to help the existence of innocence and joy. I like certain aspects of people who have existed alone or nearly alone for a long time; back country people. I like lakes and cottages on them and certain areas like small islands between railroad tracks and rivers—most small towns have areas like this and some large towns do and they have been enchanted places, often, in people's childhoods. I think I write also for the survival of honesty and courage. I like lovers of all ages."

* * *

TILL, Barry 1923-

PERSONAL: Born January 6, 1923, in Thames, England; son of John Johnson and Hilda (Dorn) Till; married Antonia Clapham, July 6, 1966; children: Nicholas, Jeremy, Lucy, Emily. *Education:* Jesus College, Cambridge, B.A., 1947, M.A., 1949. *Home:* 44 Canonbury Sq., London N1 2AW, England.

CAREER: Ordained priest of Church of England, 1950; Parish Church, Bury, Lancashire, England, curate, 1950-53; Cambridge University, Jesus College, Cambridge, England, fellow, 1953-60, dean, 1956-60, tutor, 1957-60; St. John's Cathedral, Hong Kong, China, dean, 1960-64; Morley College, London, principal, 1965—. Governor and vice-chairman of British Institute of Recorded Sound, 1967-73. *Military service:* Coldstream Guards, 1942-46; served in Italian campaign; became lieutenant.

WRITINGS: (Contributor) K. M. Carey, editor, *The Historic Episcopate,* Dacre, 1954; *Change and Exchange,* Church Information Office, 1964; *Changing Frontiers,* S.P.C.K., 1965; (contributor) C. P. M. Jones, editor, *Holy Week Manual,* S.P.C.K., 1967; *The Churches Search For Unity,* Penguin, 1972. Contributor of articles and reviews to journals.

WORK IN PROGRESS: Research on the decline of the ecclesiastical courts in England after 1660.

* * *

TINNIN, David B(ruce) 1930-

PERSONAL: Born October 22, 1930, in Fort Worth, Tex.; son of John Vaughn and Grace Elizabeth (Hall) Tinnin; married Helga Ruth Sommer, December 26, 1952; children: Claudia Ruth and Mark Stefan (twins). *Education:* Washington and Lee University, student, 1948-49; University of Heidelberg, certificates in Hebrew, 1952, and German, 1953; Cambridge University, B.A., 1956, M.A., 1966. *Politics:* Independent. *Religion:* Presbyterian. *Home:* 18 rue Jean Goujon, Paris 8, France. *Agent:* James Oliver Brown, James Brown Associates, Inc., 22 East 60th St., New York, N.Y. 10022. *Office: Time,* 17 Avenue Matignon, Paris 8, France.

CAREER: University of Maryland, Overseas Program, Mildenhall, England, instructor in German, 1953-55; special correspondent from Cambridge, England, for *Time* and *Life* (magazines), 1956; U.S. Air Force, London, England, assistant to chief of education branch, 1957; *Sports Illustrated,* New York, N.Y., reporter, 1958; Time Inc., correspondent in Chicago, Ill., 1958-60, then in New York, N.Y. as contributing editor for business, 1960-64, for Latin American affairs, 1964-66, and for foreign affairs, 1966-68, associate editor for foreign affairs, 1968-71, deputy foreign editor, 1970-71, European correspondent based in Paris, 1971—.

WRITINGS: Just About Everybody versus Howard Hughes, Doubleday, 1973.

* * *

TOBEY, George B., Jr. 1917-

PERSONAL: Born May 28, 1917, in Kingston, Mass.; son of George B. Tobey; married Mary Elizabeth Smith, February 7, 1942; children: Gayle Burton Tobey Flanagan, Christopher George. *Education:* Massachusetts State College, B.S., 1940; Harvard University, M.L.A., 1950. *Home:* 1645 Merrick Rd., Columbus, Ohio 43212. *Office:* Department of Architecture, Ohio State University, 190 West 17th Ave., Columbus, Ohio 43210.

CAREER: Ohio State University, Columbus, 1950—, now professor of landscape architecture. *Military service:* U.S. Army, 1940-45. U.S. Army Reserve, 1945-64. *Member:* Masons.

WRITINGS: A History of Landscape Architecture: Relationship of People to Environment, American Elsevier, 1973.

WORK IN PROGRESS: Research on watercourses as corridors or edges.

* * *

TODD, Janet M(argaret) 1942-

PERSONAL: Born September 10, 1942, in Wales; daughter of George and Elizabeth (Jones) Dakin; married Aaron R. Todd (a professor of mathematics), December 21, 1966; children: Julian, Clara. *Education:* Cambridge University, B.A., 1964; University of Leeds, diploma, 1968; University of Florida, Ph.D., 1971. *Office:* Department of English, Douglass College, Rutgers University, New Brunswick, N.J. 08903.

CAREER: School teacher in Cape Coast, Ghana, 1964-65; University College of Cape Coast, Cape Coast, Ghana, lecturer in English, 1965-66; English teacher in Bawku, Ghana, 1966-67; University of Puerto Rico, Mayaguez, assistant professor of English, 1972-74; Rutgers University, Douglass College, New Brunswick, N.J., assistant professor of English, 1974—. *Member:* Modern Language Association of America, Woman's Caucus of Modern Languages.

WRITINGS: In Adam's Garden: A Study of John Clare's Pre-Asylum Poetry, University of Florida Press, 1973. Contributor to *Mary Wollstonecraft Newsletter, Philological Quarterly, Phylon, Atenea,* and *British Studies Monitor.* Editor of *Mary Wollstonecraft Journal.*

WORK IN PROGRESS: A critical study of Mary Wollstonecraft; a biographical study of Helen Maria Williams; editing material by Wollstonecraft and Williams.

SIDELIGHTS: Dr. Todd writes: "In my critical writing I am . . . concerned primarily with the scholarly treatment of women writers. . . . I hope to do further work on them and on other authors not usually regarded as belonging to the mainstream of English literature. These include peasant, dialect, and early Commonwealth writers." Dr. Todd has lived in Bermuda and Ceylon.

* * *

TOLLER, Kate Caffrey
See CAFFREY, Kate

TOLLES, Martha 1921-

PERSONAL: Born September 7, 1921, in Oklahoma City, Okla.; daughter of Willis and Mary Natalie (Dunbar) Gregory; married Edwin Leroy Tolles (an attorney), June 21, 1944; children: Stephen, Henry, Cynthia, Roy, James, Thomas. *Education:* Smith College, B.A., 1943. *Religion:* Presbyterian. *Home:* 860 Oxford Rd., San Marino, Calif. 91108.

CAREER: Port Chester Daily Item, Port Chester, N.Y., reporter, 1943-44; *Publishers Weekly,* New York, N.Y., member of editorial staff, 1945. *Member:* California Writers Guild, Southern California Council on Literature for Children and Young People.

WRITINGS: Too Many Boys, Thomas Nelson, 1965, published as *Katie and Those Boys,* Scholastic Arrow Book Club, 1974. Contributor to children's magazines.

WORK IN PROGRESS: A sequel to *Too Many Boys.*

* * *

TOLZMANN, Don Heinrich 1945-

PERSONAL: Born August 12, 1945, in Granite Falls, Minn.; son of Eckhart Heinrich and Pearl (Lundeberg) Tolzmann; married Patricia Ann Himebaugh (a newspaper editor), March 20, 1971. *Education:* University of Minnesota, B.A., 1968; Northwestern Lutheran Theological Seminary, graduate study, 1968-71; United Theological Seminary, M.Div., 1972; University of Kentucky, M.A., 1973. *Religion:* Christian. *Home:* 2545 Harrison Ave., Cincinnati, Ohio 45211. *Office:* University of Cincinnati Library, Cincinnati, Ohio 45221.

CAREER: University of Cincinnati Library, Cincinnati, Ohio, reference librarian and bibliographer, 1974—. *Member:* Society for German-American Studies, National Association of German-American Authors, Swedish Pioneer Historical Society, Minnesota German Radio Committee, Society for the History of the Germans in Maryland. *Awards, honors:* Certificate of merit from Society for German-American Studies, 1973, for *Handbuch eines Deutschamerikaners: Gedichte.*

WRITINGS: Handbuch eines Deutschamerikaners: Gedichte (title means "Handbook of a German-American"; poems), Andrew S. Kinsinger, 1973; *Bibliography of German-Americana,* Scarecrow, in press. Contributor to *Der Milwaukee Herold.* Co-editor, *German-American Studies,* 1973—.

WORK IN PROGRESS: Aus Deutschamerika: Geschichte, Lyrik, und Prosa; German-American History.

SIDELIGHTS: Tolzmann told *CA* he is attempting to organize the one hundred German language poets in America into a German-American school of poetry. He has competence in Greek, Hebrew, Dutch, Swedish, and Aramaic.

* * *

TOOKER, Elisabeth (Jane) 1927-

PERSONAL: Born August 2, 1927, in Brooklyn, N.Y.; daughter of Clyde (a lawyer) and Amy (Luce) Tooker. *Education:* Radcliffe College, B.A., 1949, Ph.D., 1958; University of Arizona, M.A., 1953. *Office:* Department of Anthropology, Temple University, Philadelphia, Pa. 19122.

CAREER: University of Buffalo, Buffalo, N.Y., instructor in anthropology, 1957-60; Mount Holyoke College, South Hadley, Mass., assistant professor of anthropology, 1961-

65; Temple University, Philadelphia, Pa., assistant professor, 1965-67, associate professor of anthropology, 1967—. *Member:* American Anthropological Association (fellow), American Association for the Advancement of Science (fellow).

WRITINGS: An Ethnography of the Huron Indians, 1615-1649, Bureau of American Ethnology, 1964; (editor) *Iroquois Culture, History, and Prehistory* (proceedings of Conference on Iroquois Research, 1965), New York State Museum and Science Service, 1967; *The Iroquois Ceremony of Midwinter,* Syracuse University Press, 1970.

* * *

TOPKINS, Katharine 1927-

PERSONAL: Born July 22, 1927, in Seattle, Wash.; daughter of Paul Joseph (an accountant) and Katherine (Crane) Theda; married Richard Marvin Topkins (an advertising man), July 18, 1952; children: Rick, Joan, Deborah. *Education:* Attended Maryville College, Maryville, Tenn., 1945-47; Columbia University, B.S., 1949; Claremont Graduate School, M.A., 1951. *Address:* Box 198, Ross, Calif. 94957. *Agent:* Curtis Brown Ltd., 60 East 56th St., New York, N.Y. 10022.

AWARDS, HONORS: Rockefeller grant, 1967.

WRITINGS—All novels: *All the Tea in China,* Macmillan, 1962; *Kotch,* McGraw, 1965; (with husband, Richard Topkins) *Passing Go,* Little, Brown, 1968; (with Richard Topkins) *Il Boom,* Random House, 1974. Contributor of short stories to journals.

* * *

TOPPING, Seymour 1921-

PERSONAL: Born December 11, 1921, in New York, N.Y.; son of Joseph and Anna (Seidman) Topping; married Audrey Elaine Ronning (a photo-journalist), November 19, 1949; children: Susan, Karen, Lesley, Rebecca, Joanna. *Education:* University of Missouri, B.J., 1943; also attended College of Chinese Studies, Peking, China. *Home:* 5 Heathcote Rd., Scarsdale, N.Y. 10583. *Office: New York Times,* 229 West 43rd St., New York, N.Y. 10036.

CAREER: International News Service, 1946-48, correspondent in North China covering civil war there, 1946-47, later chief of bureau based in Nanking; Associated Press (AP), correspondent in Nanking, 1948-49, head of Indochina war staff in Saigon, 1950-51, London correspondent, 1952, diplomatic correspondent for London and the Continent, 1952-56, chief of Berlin Bureau, 1956-59; *New York Times,* New York, N.Y., member of metropolitan staff, 1959, chief correspondent from Moscow, 1960-63, and Southeast Asia, 1963-66, foreign editor, 1966-69, assistant managing editor, 1969—. Corporate member of Institute of Current World Affairs. *Military service:* U.S. Army, infantry, 1943-46; served in Philippines; became captain. *Member:* Council on Foreign Relations, Asia Society, National Committee for United States-China Relations, Century Association. *Awards, honors:* Distinguished service award from University of Missouri School of Journalism, 1968.

WRITINGS: Journey Between Two Chinas, Harper, 1972. Member of board of directors of *New York Quarterly.*

TOROK, Lou 1927- ("The Convict Writer")

PERSONAL: Born August 7, 1927, in Toledo, Ohio; married Priscilla Marie Hansen, August, 1956 (divorced August, 1963); children: Hans Anthony. *Education:* Attended evening classes at University of California, San Francisco, San Francisco State College (now University), Marin Junior College, and Montana State University. *Home address:* P.O. Box 1217, Cincinnati, Ohio 45202.

CAREER: San Francisco Examiner, San Francisco, Calif., book reviewer and member of promotion department, 1950-53; *Harper's Bazaar,* New York, N.Y., member of promotion department, 1954; KBTK-Radio, Missoula, Mont., sales manager, 1955-57; KCAP-Radio, Helena, Mont., manager and co-owner, 1958-60; KCHY-Radio, Cheyenne, Wyo., founder and manager, 1960-62; KLYQ-Radio, Hamilton, Mont., founder, 1961; Plus Schools of Business, Me., public relations director, 1965-66; Woodmar Farm (home for boys), Cincinnati, Ohio, social worker, 1966-68; Federation for Boys (private social work agency; now defunct), Toledo, Ohio, founder and director, 1968. Has been at various times, free-lance writer, editor, and broadcast consultant. Founded literacy program for inmates at Chillicothe (Ohio) Correctional Institute, 1971. Guest speaker at numerous civic and business functions in Ohio through "Cons-In-Service to Society" program, 1971-72. *Military service:* U.S. Navy, 1944-46; served in Pacific theatre. *Member:* International Platform Association.

WRITINGS: The Strange World of Prison, Bobbs-Merrill, 1973; *Straight Talk from Prison,* Behavioral Publications, 1974; *A Child's Guide to Prison,* Bantam, in press. Author of "A New World Prayer," first published in *Christian Science Monitor;* published in pamphlet form by Christian Science Publishing Society, 1971. Also author of unpublished books, *Life in a Prison Zoo, A Convict Writes to Teen Agers, Cops and Robbers, The Inferno,* and *Behind Bars.* Author of two-act play, "The Inferno," first produced at Ohio State University, Columbus, 1972. Author of syndicated newspaper columns, "Life in a Prison Zoo," King Features, 1971-72, and "Behind Bars," Chicago Tribune-New York News Syndicate, 1971-72. Writer for nationally syndicated radio program, "John Doremus Show," 1970-72.

Contributor of numerous articles, formerly using, at times, the pseudonym "The Convict Writer," to forty magazines and newspapers, including *Harper's, Saturday Review, National Observer, Popular Mechanics, New York Times, Christian Science Monitor, Chicago Tribune, Los Angeles Times, National Enquirer, Cleveland Plain Dealer,* and *Toledo Blade;* contributor of reviews to *Chicago Sun-Times, National Observer, Christian Science Monitor,* and other newspapers.

WORK IN PROGRESS: Beware–The Crooks Are Coming, for Association Press; writing free-lance articles for magazines and newspapers; planning speaking engagements.

SIDELIGHTS: Torok began writing professionally while a convict in an Ohio prison; most of his writings since have been related to his experiences in prison and with crime. Although he had previously held jobs that required writing, he has said that "all those jobs required a detached kind of writing. This time I was writing about personal experiences, and had to admit I was a convict. I was never able to do that before, and perhaps that was the root of my trouble. . . . [Writing is] the most I can do for others now, and it also helps keep me sane. I've learned the hard way to become involved with others to find any meaning in life." While in prison in Chillicothe, Torok wrote "A New World Prayer" as "a positive reaction by a convict to the bloody tragedy at Attica State Prison in New York." He describes it as a "statement of a philosophy of life," and told *CA* that it has been reprinted throughout the world, including the U.S.S.R. and People's Republic of China.

Torok is presently a free citizen. He was released on parole from Chillicothe Correctional Institute in November, 1972, after serving two years of a 1-10 year sentence for assault, and was released from parole one year later. He previously served nine months in Maine for breaking and entering, and two years in California for grand theft.

* * *

TORRES-BODET, Jaime 1902-1974

April 17, 1902—May 13, 1974; Mexican author, educator, and diplomat. Obituaries: *New York Times,* May 14, 1974; *Time,* May 27, 1974; *Current Biography,* July, 1974.

* * *

TOSTI, Donald Thomas 1935-

PERSONAL: Surname is pronounced *Toast*-ee; born December 6, 1935, in Kansas City, Mo.; son of Thomas Joseph (a chemist) and Mary (Parsons) Tosti; married Carol Curless, January 31, 1957; children: Renee, Alicia, Roxanna, Brett, Tabitha, Todd. *Education:* University of New Mexico, B.S., 1958, M.S., 1962, Ph.D., 1967. *Politics:* Democrat. *Religion:* None. *Home:* 41 Marinita, San Rafael, Calif. 94901. *Office:* Independent Learning Institute, Inc., P.O. 602, Corte Madera, Calif. 94925.

CAREER: Teaching Machines, Inc., Albuquerque, N.M., chief program editor, 1960-64; Westinghouse Learning Corp., Albuquerque, N.M., general manager, 1965-69; Individual Learning Systems, Inc., San Rafael, Calif., senior vice-president, 1970-74; Independent Learning Institute, Inc., Corte Madera, Calif., president, 1974—. Visiting assistant professor at University of New Mexico, 1964-66. *Member:* American Psychological Association, National Society for Performance and Instruction, Sigma Xi.

WRITINGS: Behavior Technology, Individual Learning Systems, 1971; *Learning Is Getting Easier,* Individual Learning Systems, 1972; *Introductory Psychology,* Individual Learning Systems, 1973. Contributor to *AV Communication Review.*

WORK IN PROGRESS: Development of materials in the field of individualized instruction.

* * *

TOURNIER, Michel 1924-

PERSONAL: Born December 19, 1924, in Paris, France; son of Alphonse and Marie-Madeleine (Fournier) Tournier. *Education:* Studied law and philosophy in Paris, France, and Tuebingen, Germany. *Residence:* 78460 Choisel, France. *Office:* Editions Plon, 8 rue Garanciere, Parie 6e, France.

CAREER: Novelist. Has been literary director for Editions Plon, Paris, France, and has also worked in radio and television, and for newspapers. *Member:* Academie Goncourt (1972—). *Awards, honors:* Grand Prix du Roman from Academie Francaise, 1967, for *Vendredi, ou les Limbes du Pacifique;* Prix Goncourt, 1970, for *Le Roi des Aulnes.*

WRITINGS—Novels: *Vendredi, ou les Limbes du Pacifique,* Gallimard, 1967, revised edition, 1972, translation by Norman Denny published in America as *Friday,* Doubleday, 1969 (translation by Denny published in England as *Friday, or The Other Island,* Collins, 1969), French edition reissued as *Vendredi, ou la vie sauvage,* Flammarion, 1971, translation by Ralph Manheim published as *Friday and Robinson: Life on Esperanza Island,* Knopf, 1972; *Le Roi des Aulnes,* Gallimard, 1970, translation by Barbara Bray published as *The Ogre,* Doubleday, 1972.

WORK IN PROGRESS: A novel, *Les Meteores.*

SIDELIGHTS: In *Friday* (once described as the story of Robinson Crusoe "seen through the eyes of Freud, Jung, and Claude Levi-Strauss"), Tournier "has attempted nothing less than an exploration of the soul of modern man." Thomas Fleming continues: "Again and again, he finds fresh and original ways of viewing primary experiences such as time and work and religious faith, the relationship of men to animals and trees and their own shadowy selves, to civilization and the essential earth. The telling is intensely French. The focus is on thinking, and thinking about feeling. There is little or no attempt to build up massive amounts of believable detail or anecdote." With a similar, predominantly interior emphasis, Tournier's second novel, *The Ogre,* is a blend of myth and mythic symbols with reality. The author, writes R. Z. Sheppard, "proves a clever exploiter of the current enthusiasm for mysticism and mythology." He calls Tournier "a good Hegelian," but also "a good Jungian. Signs, symbols and archetypes are pried from every incident and lifted chaotically into the mythological vacuum of the modern world. . . . [His synthesis] has much to do with his notion that symbols have lives of their own and possess a diabolical potential."

* * *

TOWNSEND, James B(arclay) J(ermain) 1910- (Peter Van Rensselaer Livingston)

PERSONAL: Born June 12, 1910, in Buffalo, N.Y.; son of Frederic de Peyster and Katharine Jermain (Savage) Townsend; married Vera C. Chenoweth, May 3, 1944; children: Victoria Selden Townsend Sauer. *Education:* Attended Williams College, 1928-29. *Politics:* Republican. *Religion:* Episcopalian. *Home:* 712 11th St., McKees Rocks, Pa. 15136.

CAREER: U.S. Army Air Forces, 1940-51; served as assistant chief of staff of XII Tactical Air Command in Europe, 1946-47, chief of materiel analysis and plans in Washington, D.C., 1948-49, Air Force representative on foreign aid to Joint Chiefs of Staff, 1950-51; U.S. Department of Defense, civilian consultant to secretary general of North Atlantic Treaty Organization in Paris, 1951-53; Chronic Disease Research Institute, Buffalo, N.Y., deputy director and administrator, 1954-57; Westfield Memorial Hospital, Westfield, N.Y., administrator, 1957—. Member of board of directors of Chautauqua County Chapter of American Red Cross, 1959-64. *Awards, honors*—Military: Bronze Star, 1944; Army Commendation Medal, 1945; Croix de Guerre (France), 1945.

WRITINGS: (Under pseudonym Peter Van Rensselaer Livingston) *How to Cook a Rogue Elephant: The Recollections and Recipes of Peter Van Rensselaer Livingston,* Little, Brown, 1971.

WORK IN PROGRESS: Be My Guest, a novel.

TRAVEN, Beatrice
See GOLDEMBERG, Rose Leiman

* * *

TRAVERS, Robert J. 1911(?)-1974

1911(?)—June 14, 1974; American novelist and public-relations consultant. Obituaries: *New York Times,* June 16, 1974.

* * *

TREAT, Lawrence 1903-
(Lawrence A. Goldstone)

PERSONAL: Original name Lawrence Arthur Goldstone, changed legally in 1940; born December 21, 1903, in New York, N.Y.; son of Henry and Daisy (Stein) Goldstone; married Margery Dallet, June, 1930 (divorced, 1939); married Rose Ehrenfreund, May, 1943. *Education:* Dartmouth College, B.A., 1924; Columbia University, L.L.B., 1927. *Residence:* Gay Head, Mass. *Agent:* Robert P. Mills, 156 East 52nd St., New York, N.Y. 10022.

CAREER: Author of mystery novels. Member of Gay Head Zoning Board of Appeals. *Member:* Authors Guild, Mystery Writers of America (past director), Boston Mycological Club. *Awards, honors:* Edgar Allen Poe Award for best mystery short story from Mystery Writers of America, 1965.

WRITINGS—All under name Lawrence Treat, except as noted; all mystery novels: (Under name Lawrence A. Goldstone) *Run Far, Run Fast,* Greystone, 1937.

B As in Banshee, Duell, Sloan & Pearce, 1940; *D As in Dead,* Duell, Sloan & Pearce, 1941; *H As in Hangman,* Duell, Sloan & Pearce, 1942; *O As in Omen,* Duell, Sloan & Pearce, 1943; *The Leather Man,* Duell, Sloan & Pearce, 1944; *V As in Victim,* Duell, Sloan & Pearce, 1945; *H As in Hunted,* Duell, Sloan & Pearce, 1946; *Q As in Quicksand,* Duell, Sloan & Pearce, 1947; *T As in Trapped,* Morrow, 1947; *F As in Flight,* Morrow, 1948; *Over the Edge,* Morrow, 1948; *Trial and Terror,* Morrow, 1949.

Big Shot, Harper, 1951; *Weep for a Wanton,* Ace Books, 1956.

Lady, Drop Dead, Abelard, 1960; *Venus Unarmed,* Doubleday, 1961; (editor) *Murder in Mind: An Anthology of Mystery Stories by the Mystery Writers of America,* Dutton, 1967.

P As in Police, Davis Publications (Worcester, Mass.), 1970. Contributor of several hundred short stories to numerous magazines; also published early poetry under name Lawrence Goldstone.

WORK IN PROGRESS: A new edition of *The Mystery Writer's Handbook.*

* * *

TREJOS, Carlota 1920-

PERSONAL: Surname is pronounced *Tray*-hose; born July 5, 1920, in Trout Lake, Mich., daughter of Charles (a minister) and Lula (Force) Draper; married Jose Mario Trejos (a dispatcher), January 8, 1961; children: Jose Mario, Jr. *Education:* Has studied at El Camino College, 1958-60, Harbor College, 1970, and University of California, Los Angeles, 1973. *Politics:* Democrat. *Religion:* Baptist. *Home and office:* 22503 Meyler St., #33, Torrance, Calif. 90502.

CAREER: Northrop Aircraft, Hawthorne, Calif., engineering analyst, 1955-62; El Colegio Anglo-Americano, Cochabamba, Bolivia, teacher, 1964-65; teacher in Hawthorne Christian Schools, Hawthorne, Calif., 1967-71; Harbor City Christian School, Harbor City, Calif., remedial teacher, 1972—. *Member:* International Platform Association, Federation of Chaparral Poets (president of Apollo chapter, 1973—). *Awards, honors:* Certificate of merit from American Poets Fellowship Society, 1973.

WRITINGS: Variegated Verse, Prairie Poets Books, 1973. Work is represented in anthologies, including *Poetry Parade,* Young Publications, 1963; *The Soul and the Singer,* edited by Jean Hollyfield and G. Yvonne Jones, Young Publications, 1968; *Lyrics of Love,* Young Publications, 1972. Contributor to magazines and newspapers, including *Los Angeles Herald-Examiner, Fate, Foreign Car Guide, Gospel Herald,* and poetry magazines.

WORK IN PROGRESS: Santiago, Save Me, a novel about witchcraft and folklore in South America; *Ballads of Bolivia.*

AVOCATIONAL INTERESTS: Travel, especially in Mexico, and Central and South America.

BIOGRAPHICAL/CRITICAL SOURCES: Talent, November, 1971.

* * *

TREKELL, Harold E(verett) 1910-

PERSONAL: First syllable of surname is pronounced "tree"; born January 20, 1910, in Wellington, Kan.; son of Harry Esle and Polly Pearl (Wood) Trekell; married Mabel Roepke, March 3, 1934; children: Barbara Joan (Mrs. Melvin Ashley), David Allan. *Education:* Kansas State University, B.S.E.E., 1931; General Electric Corp., study in advanced engineering, 1932-34. *Home and office:* 1744 East Alvarado, Fallbrook, Calif. 92028.

CAREER: General Electric Corp., Schenectady, N.Y., engineer, 1932-34, engineer in Lynn, Mass., 1934-70. President of East Middlesex Association for Retarded Children, 1957-59; Massachusetts Retardate Trust, founder, 1963, chairman, 1963-70. *Member:* American Institute of Electrical and Electronics Engineers. *Awards, honors:* Coffin awards from General Electric Corp., 1937, 1948.

WRITINGS: (Contributor) I. F. Kinnard, editor, *Applied Electrical Measurements,* Wiley, 1956; *Borrowing Money,* Aero, 1972. Contributor to journals.

WORK IN PROGRESS: Research on a new product.

SIDELIGHTS: Trekell has nine patents in products for measurement and instrumentation and control. His hobbies are gardening and hi-fi.

* * *

TREMAYNE, Jonathan
See FORREST-WEBB, Robert

* * *

TRENT, Jimmie Douglas 1933-

PERSONAL: Born November 17, 1933, in Lima, Okla.; son of George Calvin (a petroleum engineer) and Floy (Smith) Trent; married second wife, Judith Swanlund (a professor), December 19, 1969; children: (first marriage) Terri Lynn, Douglas Bryan. *Education:* Kansas State Teachers College, B.S., 1955, M.S., 1959; Purdue University, Ph.D., 1966. *Politics:* Democrat. *Religion:* Unitarian-Universalist. *Home:* 101 Country Club Lane, Oxford, Ohio 45056. *Office:* Department of Communication and Theatre, Miami University, Oxford, Ohio 45056.

CAREER: Kansas State Teachers College, Emporia, director of forensics, 1957-60; Purdue University, West Lafayette, Ind., instructor in speech, 1960-62; Eastern Illinois University, Charleston, assistant professor of speech communication, 1962-64; Wayne State University, Detroit, Mich., associate professor of speech communication, 1964-71; Miami University, Oxford, Ohio, professor of speech communication, 1971—, chairman of department of communication and theatre. *Member:* International Communication Association, Speech Communication Association, Central States Speech Association, Ohio Speech Association.

WRITINGS: (With W. Charles Redding) *A Survey of Communication Opinions of Executives in Large Corporations* (monograph), Communication Research Center, Purdue University, 1964; (contributor) Ronald F. Reid, editor, *Introduction to the Field of Speech,* Scott, Foresman, 1966; (with wife, Judith S. Trent, and Daniel O'Neill) *Concepts in Communication,* with teacher's manual, Allyn & Bacon, 1973; (with Judith S. Trent) *The National Women's Political Caucus: A Rhetorical Biography* (monograph), Educational Resources Information Center, 1973; (with Judith S. Trent) *Communication Strategies of George Stanley McGovern in the 1972 Presidential Campaign* (monograph), Educational Resources Information Center, 1973. Contributor of articles and reviews to speech journals.

* * *

TRESSELT, Alvin 1916-

PERSONAL: Surname is pronounced *Treh*-selt; born September 30, 1916, in Passaic, N.J.; son of Alvin and Elizabeth Ellen (Thaller) Tresselt; married Blossom Budney (a writer of children's books), April 9, 1949; children: Ellen Victoria, India Rachel. *Education:* Graduate of high school in Passaic. *Politics:* Democrat. *Home:* R.D. 3, West Redding, Conn. 06896. *Office:* Parents' Magazine Press, 52 Vanderbilt Ave., New York, N.Y. 10017.

CAREER: Held a variety of jobs, including work in a defense plant in Connecticut, 1934-46; B. Altman & Co., New York, N.Y., 1946-52, began as interior display designer, became advertising copywriter; *Humpty Dumpty's Magazine,* New York, N.Y., editor, 1952-65; Parents' Magazine Press, New York, N.Y., editor, 1966-67, executive editor and vice-president, 1967-74; free-lance writer and editor, 1974—. *Awards, honors:* Caldecott Medal from the American Library Association, 1948, for *White Snow, Bright Snow,* illustrated by Roger Duvoisin; Caldecott honor book citation (runner-up), 1946, for *Rain Drop Splash,* illustrated by Leonard Weisgard, and 1965, for *Hide and Seek Fog,* illustrated by Duvoisin; first prize in picture-book division of *New York Herald Tribune's* Children's Spring Book Festival, 1949, for *Bonnie Bess, the Weathervane Horse,* illustrated by Marylin Hafner; *The Dead Tree* won the Irma Simonton Black Award given by the Bank Street College of Education and was named an American Library Association Notable Book, both 1973.

WRITINGS—All for children: *Rain Drop Splash,* Lothrop, 1946; *Johnny Maple Leaf,* Lothrop, 1948; *The Wind and Peter,* Oxford University Press, 1948; *White Snow, Bright Snow,* Lothrop, 1948; *Bonnie Bess, the Weathervane Horse,* Lothrop, 1949, reissued with new illustrations done by Eric Blegvad, Parents' Magazine Press, 1970; *Sun Up,* Lothrop, 1949; *Little Lost Squirrel,* Grosset, 1950; *Follow the Wind,* Lothrop, 1950; *Hi Mister Robin,* Lothrop, 1950; *Autumn Harvest,* Lothrop, 1951; *The Rabbit Story,* Lothrop, 1952; *Follow the Road,* Lothrop, 1953; *I Saw the Sea Come In,* Lothrop, 1954; *Wake Up, Farm,* Lothrop, 1955; *Wake Up, City,* Lothrop, 1956; *Frog in the Well,* Lothrop, 1958; *Smallest Elephant in the World,* Knopf, 1959.

Timothy Robbins Climbs the Mountain, Lothrop, 1960; *Under the Trees and through the Grass,* Lothrop, 1962; *Elephant Is Not a Cat,* Parents' Magazine Press, 1962; *How Far is Far?,* Parents' Magazine Press, 1964; *The Mitten,* Lothrop, 1964; *Hide and Seek Fog,* Lothrop, 1965; *A Thousand Lights and Fireflies,* Parents' Magazine Press, 1965; *The World in the Candy Egg,* Lothrop, 1967; *Old Man and the Tiger,* Grosset, 1967; *Fox Who Traveled,* Grosset, 1968; (with Nancy Cleaver) *The Legend of the Willow Plate,* Parents' Magazine Press, 1968; *It's Time Now!,* Lothrop, 1969; *The Beaver Pond,* Lothrop, 1970; *Stories from the Bible,* Coward, 1971; *The Dead Tree,* Parents' Magazine Press, 1972.

Author of English adaptations from original Japanese stories—All published by Parents' Magazine Press: *Tears of the Dragon,* 1967; *Crane Maiden,* 1968; *Witch's Magic Cloth,* 1969; *Rolling Rice Ball,* 1969; *Fisherman under the Sea,* 1969; *Eleven Hungry Cats,* 1970; *A Sparrow's Magic,* 1970; *Gengorah and the Thunder God,* 1970; *Land of Lost Buttons,* 1970; *Ogre and His Bride,* 1971; *Lim Fu and the Golden Mountain,* 1971; *Little Mouse Who Tarried,* 1971. Also author of English adaptation from an original German story, *Wonder Fish from the Sea,* 1971.

BIOGRAPHICAL/CRITICAL SOURCES: Lee Bennett Hopkins, *Books Are by People,* Citation, 1969.

* * *

TRIGG, Roger (Hugh) 1941-

PERSONAL: Born August 14, 1941, in Pontypridd, Wales; son of Ivor (a Methodist minister) and Grace (Collins) Trigg; married Julia Gibbs (a music teacher), July 12, 1972; children: Nicholas Mark. *Education:* New College, Oxford, B.A., 1964, M.A., 1967, D.Phil., 1968. *Home:* 36 Rushbrook Rd., Stratford-upon-Avon, Warwickshire, England. *Office:* Department of Philosophy, University of Warwick, Coventry, England.

CAREER: University of Warwick, Coventry, England, lecturer, 1966-74, senior lecturer in philosophy, 1974—.

WRITINGS: *Pain and Emotion,* Oxford University Press, 1970; *Reason and Commitment,* Cambridge University Press, 1973.

WORK IN PROGRESS: Research on epistemology, moral philosophy, and philosophy of the social sciences.

* * *

TRIMBLE, Vance H(enry) 1913-

PERSONAL: Born July 6, 1913, in Harrison, Ark.; son of Guy Lee (a lawyer) and Josephine (Crump) Trimble; married Elzene Miller, January 9, 1932; children: Carol Ann Trimble Weisenfeld. *Education:* Educated in public schools in Wewoka, Okla. *Politics:* Independent. *Religion:* Southern Baptist. *Home:* 1013 Sunset Ave., Kenton Hills, Covington, Ky. 41011. *Office: Kentucky Post and Times-Star,* 421 Madison Ave., Covington, Ky. 41011.

CAREER: Okemah Daily Leader, Okemah, Okla., cub reporter, 1927; *Wewoka Times-Democrat,* Wewoka, Okla., cub reporter, 1928-31, reporter, 1931; *Maud Daily Enterprise,* Maud, Okla., news editor, 1931-32; reporter for *Seminole Morning News, Seminole Producer, Seminole Reporter* (all in Seminole, Okla.), *Wewoka Morning News,* Wewoka, Okla., *Shawnee Morning News,* Shawnee, Okla., and *Muskogee Times-Democrat and Phoenix,* Muskogee, Okla., 1932-35; *Okmulgee Times,* Okmulgee, Okla., news editor, 1936; *Tulsa Tribune,* Tulsa, Okla., desk man and financial writer, 1937; *Beaumont Daily Enterprise,* Beaumont, Tex., reporter, fall, 1937; *Port Arthur Daily News,* Port Arthur, Tex., telegraph editor, 1938-39; *Houston Press,* Houston, Tex., copy editor, 1939, city editor, 1939-50, managing editor, 1950-55, also founded promotion department; Scripps-Howard Newspaper Alliance, Washington, D.C., news editor, 1955-63; *Kentucky Post and Times-Star,* Covington, editor, 1963—. *Military service:* U.S. Army, Signal Corps, editor of camp newspaper, 1944-45; became staff sergeant.

MEMBER: American Society of Newspaper Editors, Authors Guild, National Press Club, Sigma Delta Chi, Cincinnati Club. *Awards, honors:* Pulitzer Prize for national reporting, Sigma Delta Chi award for national reporting, and Raymond Clapper award for distinguished Washington correspondence, all 1960, all for series of articles exposing widespread payroll nepotism and secrecy in Congress.

WRITINGS: The Uncertain Miracle, Doubleday, 1974.

WORK IN PROGRESS: The Newspaper Press of Kentucky, for University Press of Kentucky; research for a book on digestive diseases.

SIDELIGHTS: In 1958, Trimble began to investigate rumors of widespread nepotism in Congress by combing through Congressional payroll records and conducting personal interviews. His research resulted in a series of articles, the first of which appeared early in 1959. Trimble's continued pursuit of the issue revealed further examples of abuse, public awareness was aroused, and his articles were inserted into the *Congressional Record.* Trimble then filed suit to compel Congress to fully disclose payroll and expense records, and although the suit was dismissed, within a matter of months the Senate had adopted measures providing for the disclosure of these records. *Avocational interests:* Photography, architecture.

* * *

TROCME, Etienne 1924-

PERSONAL: Born November 8, 1924, in Paris, France; son of Pierre Edouard (a physician) and Aline (de Saint-Affrique) Trocme; married Ann Bowden (a teacher), August 19, 1950; children: Suzanne, Claire, Jean-Pierre, Marie. *Education:* University of Paris, Archiviste-paleographe, 1946, Baccalaureat en Theologie et Licence es Lettres, 1950; graduate study at University of Southern California, 1946-47, and University of Basel, 1950-51; University of Strasbourg, Licencie en Theologie, 1955, Docteur en Theologie, 1960. *Politics:* Socialist. *Religion:* Protestant. *Home:* 9 rue Berlioz, 67000 Strasbourg, France. *Office:* Palais Universitaire, 9 place de l'Universite, 67000 Strasbourg, France.

CAREER: University of Strasbourg, Strasbourg, France, reader, 1951-56, associate professor, 1956-65, professor of New Testament, 1965-70; Universite des Sciences Humaines, Strasbourg, France, professor of New Testament, 1970—, dean of the Faculty of Protestant Theology, 1971-73, president of the University, 1973—. *Member:* Studiorum Novi Testamenti Societas, Societe Ernest-Renan (Paris), Rotary Club (Strasbourg). *Awards, honors:* Named Officier of l'Ordre des Palmes Academiques, 1966, by French Ministry of Education; D.D. from University of Glasgow, 1974.

WRITINGS: (With Marcel Delafosse) *Le Commerce Rochelais de la fin du 15e au debut du 17e siecle* (title means "The Trade of La Rochelle from the End of the 15th to the Beginning of the 17th Century"), Armand Colin, 1952; *Le Livre des Actes et l'histoire* (title means "The Book of Acts and History"), Presses Universitaires de France, 1957; *La Formation de l'Evangile selon Marc* (title means "The Formation of the Gospel of Mark"), Presses Universitaires de France, 1963, English translation by M. Gaughan, S.P.C.K., in press; *Jesus de Nazareth vu par les temoins de sa vie,* Delachaux-Niestle, 1972, translation by R. A. Wilson published as *Jesus as Seen by His Contemporaries,* Westminster, 1973.

Contributor: J. J. von Allmen, editor, *Vocabulaire biblique* (title means "Wordbook of the Bible"), Delachaux-Niestle, 1954, revised edition, 1956; A. Vernet, editor, *Recueil de travaux offerts a M. Clovis Brunel* (title means "Clovis Brunel Festschrift"), two volumes, Societe de l'Ecole des Chartes, 1955; B. Reicke and L. Rost, editors, *Biblisch-historisches Handwoerterbuch* (title means "Historical Lexicon to the Bible"), three volumes, Vandenhoeck-Ruprecht, 1962-66; F. L. Cross, editor, *Studia Evangelica* (title means "Studies in the Gospels"), Berlin Akademie-Verlag, 1964; F. Christ, editor, *Oikonomia, Heilsgeschichte als Thema der Theologie* (title means "Oikonomia: Salvation-History as a Theological Theme"), H. Reich, 1967; *L'Evangile hier et aujourd'hui* (title means "The Gospel Yesterday and Today"), Labor et Fides, 1968; S. Dockx, editor, *L'Esprit saint et l'eglise* (title means "The Holy Spirit and the Church"), A. Fayard, 1969; *I Protagonisti della storia universale* (title means "The Main Figures in the History of Mankind"), Volume III, Compagnia Edizioni Internazionali, 1970; H. Ch. Peuch, editor, *Histoire des religions* (title means "History of Religions"), Volume II, Gallimard, 1972; *Traduction oecumenique de la Bible: Nouveau Testament* (title means "Ecumenical Translation of the Bible: New Testament"), Cerf-Les Bergers et les Mages, 1972; B. Lindars and S. Smalley, editors, *Christ and Spirit in the New Testament,* Cambridge University Press, 1973.

Contributor of articles and reviews to academic journals. Editor of *Revue du christianisme social,* 1953-65, and *Revue d'historie et de philosophie religieuses,* 1967-74.

WORK IN PROGRESS: A commentary to the Gospel of Mark; articles on various New Testament themes.

* * *

TROJANOWICZ, John M.
See TROYANOVICH, John M(ichael)

* * *

TROYANOVICH, John M(ichael) 1936-
(John M. Trojanowicz)

PERSONAL: Surname is pronounced Troy-a-*no*-vich; original surname, Trojanowicz: legally changed in 1966; born August 22, 1936, in Bay City, Mich.; son of Chester R. (a detective) and Loretta (Duffy) Trojanowicz; married Kathleen Gallagher (a bookkeeper), September 1, 1956; children: John L., Stephan J., Mark M., Rita M., Josef G. *Education:* University of Michigan, B.A., 1960; University of Illinois, M.A., 1961; Michigan State University, Ph.D., 1964. *Home:* 1405 North Clinton Blvd., Bloomington, Ill. 61701. *Office:* Department of Foreign Languages, Illinois Wesleyan University, Bloomington, Ill. 61701.

CAREER: Michigan State University, East Lansing, instructor, 1962-64, assistant professor of German, 1964-68; University of Kansas, Lawrence, associate professor of German and education, 1968-71; Illinois Wesleyan University, Bloomington, professor of modern languages and education, 1971—, chairman of department of foreign languages, 1971—. Member of board of directors of McLean County Mental Health Center. *Military service:* U.S. Army, Security Agency, interpreter and translator in German and Rumanian, 1955-58.

MEMBER: American Council on the Teaching of Foreign Languages, American Association of Professors of German, Association of Departments of Foreign Languages, American Translators Association, Illinois Foreign Language Association. *Awards, honors:* Woodrow Wilson fellowship, 1960; study grant from Germanistic Society of America, 1964, to University of Tuebingen; travel grant from Republics of Germany and Austria, 1973.

WRITINGS: (With Kurt W. Schild) *German Conversational Reader,* American Book Co., 1969; *German: From Language to Literature,* Van Nostrand, 1972; (under name John M. Trojanowicz, with brother, Robert C. Trojanowicz and Forrest M. Moss) *Community Based Crime Prevention,* Goodyear Publishing, in press. Contributor to foreign language periodicals, including *American Foreign Language Teacher, Foreign Language Annals,* and *Die Unterrichtspraxis.*

WORK IN PROGRESS: Research in German-American cross-cultural contrasts especially in the area of law enforcement and on innovations in foreign language teaching methodology.

* * *

TRUUMAA, Aare 1926-

PERSONAL: Born August 6, 1926, in Tartu, Estonia; son of Peeter (a civil engineer) and Anna Helen (Lohmus) Truumaa; married Frances Louise Halbing, October 17, 1959; children: Karen Louise. *Education:* Studied medicine at United Nations Relief and Rehabilitation University in Munich, 1946-47, economics at University of Erlangen, 1947, and medicine at University of Heidelberg, 1947-48; Occidental College, B.A., 1951, M.A., 1952; Purdue University, Ph.D., 1957. *Home:* 8330 North Park Ave., Indianapolis, Ind. 46240. *Office:* School of Medicine, Indiana University, Indianapolis, Ind. 46207.

CAREER: Trainee at Veterans Administration hospitals in Indiana, 1955-57; Beatty Memorial Hospital, Westville, Ind., supervisor of psychological services, Continued Treatment Center, 1957-58; Indiana University, Indianapolis Campus, staff pyschologist, 1958-60, then chief clinical psychologist, Children's Outpatient and Consultation Services at Medical center, 1960-70, director of training in clinical psychology at Medical Center, 1970—, instructor in clinical psychology at School of Medicine, 1958-61, assistant professor, 1961-66, associate professor, 1966-73, professor, 1973—. Psychological consultant to hospitals and school systems. Diplomate in clinical psychology, American Board of Professional Psychology.

MEMBER: American Psychological Association, American Orthopsychiatric Association (fellow), National Association of School Psychologists, Midwestern Psychological Association, Indiana Psychological Association, Central Indiana Psychological Association, Sigma Xi, Psi Chi.

WRITINGS: (With Eugene E. Levitt) *The Rorschach Technique with Children and Adolescents,* Grune, 1972. Contributor to scientific journals.

* * *

TUCHMAN, Maurice 1936-

PERSONAL: Born November 30, 1936, in Jacksonville, Fla. *Education:* City College (now City College of the City University of New York), B.A., 1957; Columbia University, M.A., 1959, Ph.D. candidate. *Home:* 2210 Astral Dr., Los Angeles, Calif. 90046. *Office:* Los Angeles County Museum of Art, 5905 Wilshire Blvd., Los Angeles, Calif. 90036.

CAREER: Guggenheim Museum, New York, N.Y., curatorial and lecture staff member, 1962-64; Los Angeles County Museum of Art, Los Angeles, Calif., senior curator of modern art, 1964—. Director of new art for U.S. Pavilion at world exposition, Osaka, Japan, 1970. *Awards, honors:* Fulbright scholarship to Berlin, Germany, 1960-61.

WRITINGS: *American Sculpture of the Sixties,* New York Graphic Society, 1967; *Chaim Soutine: 1893-1940,* Los Angeles County Museum of Art, 1968; (editor) *Art and Technology: Report on the Art and Technology Program of the Los Angeles County Museum of Art,* Viking, 1971; (editor) *New York School: The First Generation,* New York Graphic Society, 1971; (with Jane Livingston) *The Billy Wilder Collection,* Los Angeles County Museum of Art, 1972; *Bruce Nauman,* Los Angeles County Museum of Art, 1972.

Exhibition catalogs; all published by Los Angeles County Museum of Art, except as indicated: *Peter Voulkos,* 1965; *New York School: The First Generation,* 1965; *R. B. Kitaj,* 1965; *David Smith,* 1965; *Five Younger California Artists,* 1965; *Edward Kienholz,* 1966; *Robert Irwin–Kenneth Price,* 1966; *John Mason,* 1966; *American Sculpture of the Sixties,* 1967; *Chaim Soutine, 1893-1940,* 1968; *Fifty Tantric Mystical Diagrams,* 1970; *Scott Grieger,* 1971; *Art and Technology,* 1971; *11 Los Angeles Artists,* Hayward Gallery (London), 1971; *24 Young Los Angeles Artists,* 1971; *Los Angeles 72,* Sidney Janis Gallery (New York, N.Y.), 1972.

Art editor of modern art sections of *Columbia Encyclopedia,* 3rd edition, 1962.

* * *

TUFTE, Edward R(olf) 1942-

PERSONAL: Born March 14, 1942, in Kansas City, Mo.; son of Edward E. and Virginia (James) Tufte. *Education:* Stanford University, B.S., 1963, M.S., 1964; Yale University, Ph.D., 1968. *Office:* Woodrow Wilson School, Princeton University, Princeton, N.J. 08540.

CAREER: Princeton University, Princeton, N.J., assistant professor, 1968-71, associate professor, 1971-74, professor of politics and public affairs, 1974—. Fellow, Center for Advanced Study in the Behavioral Sciences, 1973-74.

WRITINGS: (Editor) *The Quantitative Analysis of Social Problems,* Addison-Wesley, 1970; (with Robert A. Dahl) *Size and Democracy,* Stanford University Press, 1973; *Data Analysis for Politics and Policy,* Prentice-Hall, 1974.

WORK IN PROGRESS: A book on voting and elections in the United States; a book on applications of statistics to politics and policy analysis.

* * *

TURNER, Alberta Tucker 1919-

PERSONAL: Born October 22, 1919, in New York, N.Y.; daughter of Albert Chester (a financier) and Marion (Fellows) Tucker; married William Arthur Turner (a college professor), April 9, 1943; children: Prudence Mab (Mrs. Sidney D. Comings), Arthur Brenton. *Education:* Hunter College (now Hunter College of the City University of New York), B.A., 1940; Wellesley College, M.A., 1941; Ohio State University, Ph.D., 1946. *Politics:* None. *Religion:* Protestant. *Home:* 482 Caskey Ct., Oberlin, Ohio 44074. *Office:* Department of English, Cleveland State University, Euclid at 24th St., Cleveland, Ohio 44115.

CAREER: Oberlin College, Oberlin, Ohio, lecturer in English literature, 1947-50, 1951-69; Cleveland State University, Cleveland, Ohio, lecturer, 1964-69, assistant professor, 1969-73, associate professor of English literature, 1973—, director of Poetry Center, 1964—. *Member:* Academy of American Poets, Milton Society of America, Midwest Modern Language Association, Ohio Poets Association.

WRITINGS: *North* (poems), Triskelion Press, 1970; *Need* (poems), Ashland Poetry Press, 1971; *Learning to Count,* University of Pittsburgh Press, 1974. Associate editor of *Field,* 1969—, *Contemporary Poetry and Poetics,* 1969—.

WORK IN PROGRESS: Research in Oxford and Cambridge poetical miscellanies, 1600-1660, Milton's use of slant rhyme, and criticism of contemporary poetry and poetics; poems.

AVOCATIONAL INTERESTS: Collecting islands.

* * *

TURNER, Henry Ashby, Jr. 1932-

PERSONAL: Born April 4, 1932, in Atlanta, Ga.; son of Henry Ashby and Katherine (Bradley) Turner; married Jane Swanger, June 14, 1958; children: Bradley, Sarah, Matthew. *Education:* Washington and Lee University, B.A., 1954; University of Munich, graduate study, 1954-55; Free University of Berlin, graduate study, 1955; Princeton University, M.A., 1957, Ph.D., 1960. *Home:* 215 Livingston St., New Haven, Conn. 06511. *Office:* Department of History, Yale University, New Haven, Conn. 06520.

CAREER: Yale University, New Haven, Conn., instructor, 1958-60, assistant professor, 1961-64, associate professor, 1964-70, professor of history, 1970—.

WRITINGS: *Stresemann and the Politics of the Weimar Republic,* Princeton University Press, 1963; (editor, author of introduction, and contributor) *Nazism and the Third Reich,* Quadrangle, 1972; *Faschismus und Kapitalismus in Deutschland* (title means "Fascism and Capitalism in Germany"; collected essays), Vandenhoeck & Ruprecht, 1972. Contributor to professional journals.

WORK IN PROGRESS: Studies of fascism and modern German history.

* * *

TWARK, Allan J(oseph) 1931-

PERSONAL: Born July 21, 1931, in Ravenna, Ohio; son of Peter J. (an upholsterer) and Mary (Kuhar) Twark; married Charlene Stessman, July 3, 1965; children: Jill, Lisa. *Education:* Kent State University, B.S., 1953, M.B.A., 1954; University of Illinois, Ph.D., 1959. *Religion:* Roman Catholic. *Home:* 404 Valley View Dr., Kent, Ohio 44240. *Office:* Department of Finance, Kent State University, Kent, Ohio 44240.

CAREER: Pennsylvania State University, University Park, assistant professor of statistics, 1960-62; Arizona State University, Phoenix, associate professor of finance, 1962-64; Creighton University, Omaha, Neb., associate professor of finance, 1964-66; Kent State University, Kent, Ohio, associate professor of finance, 1966—. *Member:* American Finance Association, Financial Management Association.

WRITINGS: (With W. P. Duker and O. D. Bowlin) *Security Analysis and Portfolio Management,* Holden-Day, 1973.

WORK IN PROGRESS: Research papers, *Mutual Fund Performance;* a textbook, *Modern Portfolio Management,* completion expected in 1975.

* * *

TWERSKY, Jacob 1920-

PERSONAL: Born November 19, 1920, in Lublin, Poland; came to the United States in 1928; son of Israel (a rabbi) and Gertrude (Levinson) Twersky; married Esther Bachrach, August 26, 1951; children: Laura. *Education:* City College (now City College of the City University of New York), B.S.S., 1943; Columbia University, M.A., 1944; New York University, Ph.D., 1947. *Residence:* Bronx, N.Y.

CAREER: Veterans Administration, New York, N.Y., counselor, 1946-48, educational therapist, 1956-66; City College (now City College of the City University of New York), New York, N.Y., instructor in history, 1948-56; Bronx Community College of the City University of New York, Bronx, N.Y., assistant professor, 1966-69, associate professor, 1969-70, professor of history, 1970—.

WRITINGS: *The Face of the Deep* (novel), World Publishing, 1953; *The Sound of the Walls* (autobiography), Doubleday, 1959; *A Marked House* (novel), A. S. Barnes, 1968.

SIDELIGHTS: Twersky has been totally blind since the age of thirteen.

* * *

TYLER, Parker 1907-1974

March 6, 1907—July 24, 1974; American author and film critic. Obituaries: *New York Times,* July 26, 1974. (*CA*-5/6).

* * *

TYRMAND, Leopold 1920-

PERSONAL: Born May 16, 1920, in Warsaw, Poland; came to United States in 1966; son of Mieczyslaw and Maria Tyrmand; married Mary Ellen Fox, August, 1971. *Education:* Attended Academie des Beaux-Arts, Paris, 1937-39. *Home:* 110 Millport Ave., New Canaan, Conn. 06840. *Agent:* Russell & Volkening, Inc., 551 Fifth Ave., New York, N.Y. 10017.

CAREER: Between 1941 and 1946, Tyrmand served part of

a twenty-five year Russian-imposed sentence for anti-Stalinist activities, became active in the Polish underground and, as its agent, held jobs with the German railroads and German Merchant Marine, and was later interned by the Germans at Grini concentration camp in Norway; he returned to Poland in 1946; writer for *Tygodnik Powszechny* (title means "Universal Weekly"), a Catholic liberal newspaper, 1950-53, at which time the paper was closed for refusing to print a Stalin eulogy; full-time writer, 1953—. Instructor in Polish literature at Columbia University, 1968-69; lecturer at various schools, including Harvard University, Yale University, University of Pennsylvania, and University of California, Los Angeles. Former president, Polish Jazz Federation. *Member:* P.E.N. International. *Awards, honors:* U.S. State Department travel grant, 1966; Ford Foundation grant, 1966.

WRITINGS: Hotel Ansgar: Opowiadania (short stories; title means "Hotel Ansgar"), Poznaniu, 1947; *Zly* (novel), Czytelnik, 1956, translation by David J. Welsh published in England under same title, M. Joseph, 1958, published as *The Man with the White Eyes,* Knopf, 1959; *Gorzki smak czekolady Lucullus* (short stories; title means "Bitter Taste of Lucullus Chocolate"), Czytelnik, 1957; *U brzegow jazzu* (nonfiction; title means "On the Border of Jazz"), Polskie Wydawnictwo Muzyczne, 1957; *The Seven Long Voyages* (novel), translated by Welsh, M. Joseph, 1959; *Filip* (novel; title means "Philip"), Wydawnictwo Literackie, 1961; *Zycie towarzyskie i uczuciowe* (fiction; title means "High Society and Sentimental Life"), Institut Litteraire (Paris), 1968.

Notebooks of a Dilettante (collected essays, in English; sections first published in *New Yorker,* 1967), Macmillan, 1970; (editor) *Explorations in Freedom: Prose, Narrative and Poetry from Kultura* [and] *Kultura Essays* (two-volume anthology of works previously published in *Kultura*), Free Press, in cooperation with State University of New York at Albany, 1970; *The Rosa Luxemburg Contraceptives Cooperative: A Primer on Communist Civilization,* Macmillan, 1972.

Contributor of articles and literary and theatre criticism to Polish periodicals, prior to 1966; contributor to *New Yorker, Reporter, Atlantic, New Leader,* and other periodicals, since 1966.

WORK IN PROGRESS: A book-length essay, *Notes on Sex as Jumble.*

SIDELIGHTS: "No foreign visitor's notebooks since those of our 1830s French aristocrat are more worth reading than Polish Mr. Tyrmand's," writes David Brudnoy of *Notebooks of a Dilettante,* Tyrmand's first book written in English. Tyrmand "looks with the innocent eyes of a wise man," notes S. K. Oberbeck: "His feeling for his adopted country is balanced by his knowledge of communism, and his insights are often edged with a subtle bitterness. . . ." Tyrmand's short aphoristic paragraphs, adds Anthony Hartley, "have in them the bite of the great tradition of moralists, which is the backbone of French literature, providing perhaps the most genuinely European view of man and his place in the universe. His is the disillusioned wisdom which has left enthusiasm far behind and gone beyond cynicism: an assurance which has lost its power to hurt and its astonishment at being wounded."

Tyrmand's first novel, *Zly,* was published in Poland during the 1950's cultural thaw; it became an underground best-seller and was translated into seventeen languages. "It was the first novel in a Socialist country that was totally devoid of politics," says Tyrmand. "'Party' was not mentioned a single time." Now writing in English, Tyrmand finds that he likes "this endless browsing through dictionaries and thesauruses—this look for words which in a native language come osmotically. . . .Although it's an exhausting and painful process, it gives me pleasures which are unknown to someone who does not have my problems with the language."

BIOGRAPHICAL/CRITICAL SOURCES: New York Times, April 7, 1970.

* * *

UENO, Noriko
See NAKAE, Noriko

* * *

UHLIN, Donald M(acbeth) 1930-

PERSONAL: Born September 16, 1930, in Minneapolis, Minn.; son of Bernard W. (a foreman) and Mildren D. (a floral designer; maiden name, Wilson) Uhlin; married Phyllis R. Michel, August 7, 1954; children: Deborah, Sara. *Education:* University of Minnesota, B.Sc., 1952, M.Ed., 1954; Pennsylvania State University, Ph.D., 1959. *Residence:* Sacramento, Calif. *Office:* California State University, 6000 J St., Sacramento, Calif. 95819.

CAREER: Art teacher in public schools in Prince George's County, Md., 1954-58; California State University, Sacramento, instructor, 1959-60, assistant professor, 1960-64, associate professor, 1964-68, professor of art, 1968—. Has presented workshops and directed art programs; has participated in more than fifty group art exhibits; has had about a dozen one-man shows of prints and printmaking in Sacramento, Houston, and Oregon.

MEMBER: International Society of Psychopathology of Expression, American Society of Psychopathology of Expression (fellow; secretary general), National Art Education Association, American Association of University Professors, California Art Education Association, California Teachers Association. *Awards, honors:* Purchase award at Third Biennial Prints and Drawings Exhibition, Minneapolis, Minn., 1954.

WRITINGS: Recognition and Therapy of Neurologically Handicapped Children through Art (monograph), California Association for Neurologically Handicapped Children, 1966; (contributor) Irene Jakab, editor, *Art Interpretation and Art Therapy,* Volume II: *Psychiatry and Art,* S. Karger, 1968; (contributor) Jakab, editor, *Conscious and Unconscious Expressive Art,* Volume III: *Psychiatry and Art,* S. Karger, 1971; *Art for Exceptional Children,* W. C. Brown, 1972. Contributor to *Christian Educator's Journal, Journal of Clinical Psychology, Ars Gratis Hominis, Studies in Art Education,* and *Canvas.*

WORK IN PROGRESS: The Psychology of Art.

* * *

ULANOV, Ann Belford 1938-

PERSONAL: Born January 1, 1938, in Princeton, N.J.; daughter of Ralph Jones (a surgeon) and Ruth (Pine) Belford; married Barry Ulanov (a professor and writer), August 21, 1968; children: Alexander; (stepchildren) Anne Pietrasanta, Nicholas, Katherine. *Education:* Radcliffe College, B.A., 1959; Union Theological Seminary, New York, N.Y., M.Div., 1962, Ph.D., 1967; graduate of Institutes of Religion and Mental Health, 1965, and C. G. Jung Institute of Analytical Psychology, 1967. *Religion:* Episcopalian. *Home:* 606 West 122nd St., #7E, New York, N.Y. 10027. *Office:* 185 East 85th St., #35J, New York, N.Y. 10028.

CAREER: Psychotherapist in private practice in New York, N.Y. Union Theological Seminary, New York, N.Y., professor of psychiatry and religion, 1966—. Member of board of directors of C. G. Jung Institute for Analytical Psychology; adviser to department of religion of Princeton University. *Member:* International Association of Analytical Psychology, American Association of Pastoral Counselors, American Association of University Professors, New York Association for Analytical Psychologists, Joint Council for Mental Health.

WRITINGS: The Feminine in Jungian Psychology and Christian Theology, Northwestern University Press, 1971; (with husband, Barry Ulanov) *Religion and the Unconscious,* Westminster, in press. Contributor of articles and reviews to religion and psychology journals, including *Journal of Religion and Mental Health, Religion in Life, International Journal of Analytical Psychology, American Journal of Psychiatry,* and *Union Seminary Quarterly Review.*

* * *

UMPHLETT, Wiley Lee 1931-

PERSONAL: Born October 25, 1931, in Norfolk, Va.; son of James Vernon (a plumber) and Dollie Virginia (Woolard) Umphlett; married Joyce Estelle Campbell (a travel agent), April 23, 1966; children: Reginald, Donald, Edward (stepsons). *Education:* Southwestern at Memphis, B.A., 1954; Columbia University, M.A., 1960; Florida State University, Ph.D., 1967. *Home:* 3172 Runnymede Rd., Pensacola, Fla. 32504. *Office:* University of West Florida, Pensacola, Fla. 32504.

CAREER: English teacher in public school in Norfolk, Va., 1958-61; Longwood College, Farmville, Va., instructor in English, 1962-64; Florida State University, Tallahassee, director of off-campus program, 1967-68; University of West Florida, Pensacola, director of continuing education, 1969—. *Military service:* U.S. Army, 1954-57; served in Germany. *Member:* National University Extension Association, Benevolent and Protective Order of Elks.

WRITINGS: The Sporting Myth and the American Experience, Bucknell University Press, 1974. Contributor to literary journals, including *Laurel Review.*

WORK IN PROGRESS: Beach People (tentative title), a novel; research on contemporary literature and on nostalgic subjects.

* * *

UPDIKE, L(e Roy) Wayne 1916-

PERSONAL: Born September 17, 1916, in Des Moines, Iowa; son of Lewis S. (a farmer) and Hazel (Babcock) Updike; married Mary Elizabeth Brown, October 27, 1944; children: Lee W., Vivika Rae (Mrs. Thomas Morain). *Education:* Graceland College, A.A., 1939; University of Wisconsin, Ph.B., 1942. *Politics:* Independent. *Home:* 4706 South Wabash St., Denver, Colo. 80237. *Office:* RLDS Denver Stake Office, 480 Marion, Denver, Colo. 80218.

CAREER: Ordained minister of the Reorganized Church of Jesus Christ of Latter Day Saints, 1942; minister in Illinois, 1942, Kansas City, Mo., 1943-50, Detroit, Mich., 1950-54, Independence, Mo., 1954-60, 1962-67, and London, Ontario, 1960-62; RLDS Denver Stake Office, Denver, Colo., Stake president, 1968—.

WRITINGS: Whosoever Repenteth, Herald House, 1958; *Ministry of the Bereaved,* Herald House, 1973. Contributor to *Herald* and *Restoration Witness.*

* * *

UTGARD, Russell O(liver) 1933-

PERSONAL: Born July 30, 1933, in Polk County, Wis.; son of Bert O. (a farmer) and Mildred (Hansen) Utgard; married Doris Schaffer (a teacher), February 11, 1956; children: Louise, Thomas, Jane. *Education:* Wisconsin State College—River Falls, B.S., 1957; University of Wisconsin, M.S., 1958; Indiana University, M.A., 1966, Ed.D., 1969. *Home:* 3487 Colchester Rd., Columbus, Ohio 43221. *Office:* Department of Geology and Mineralogy, Ohio State University, 125 South Oval Dr., Columbus, Ohio 43210.

CAREER: Joliet Junior College, Joliet, Ill., instructor in geology and earth science, 1958-67; Ohio State University, Columbus, assistant professor, 1969-72, associate professor of geology and mineralogy, 1972—. Field geologist for Minerva Oil Co., 1966. *Military service:* U.S. Navy, 1952-54. *Member:* National Science Teachers Association, National Association of Geology Teachers, Ohio Academy of Science.

WRITINGS: (With G. T. Ladd and H. O. Andersen) *Sourcebook for Earth Sciences and Astronomy,* Macmillan, 1972; (with G. D. McKenzie) *Man and His Physical Environment,* Burgess, 1972; (with R. L. Bates and W. C. Sweet) *Geology: An Introduction,* Heath, 1973; (with McKenzie) *Man's Finite Earth,* Burgess, 1974.

WORK IN PROGRESS: Research on geoscience education and environmental education.

* * *

UTLEY, Francis Lee 1907-1974

May 25, 1907—March 8, 1974; American professor of English and author. Obituaries: *New York Times,* March 10, 1974. (*CA*-3).

* * *

VACCA, Roberto 1927-

PERSONAL: Born May 31, 1927, in Rome, Italy; son of Giovanni (a mathematician and sinologist) and Virginia (an Arabic scholar and fiction writer; maiden name, De Bosis) Vacca; married Stefania Piscini (a psychotherapist), February 25, 1954; children: Giovanni. *Education:* University of Rome, doctorate in electrical engineering, 1951, libera docenza, 1960. *Religion:* None. *Home:* 3 Via Oddone di Cluny, Rome, Italy. *Office:* Compagnia Generale Automazione, 3 Via Fumaroli, Rome, Italy.

CAREER: Engineer in Italy, designing and building electric power transmission lines, 1951-55; National Research Council of Italy, Rome, researcher in digital computers, 1955-62; University of Rome, Rome, Italy, professor of digital computers, 1960-66; Compagnia Generale Automazione, Rome, Italy, technical manager, 1962-64, general manager, 1964—. UNESCO visiting fellow at Cambridge University and Harvard University, both 1961. *Member:* Institute of Electrical and Electronics Engineers, Institute of Traffic Engineers.

WRITINGS: Il robot e il minotauro (stories and essays in science fiction; title means "The Robot and the Minotaur"), Rizzoli, 1963; *Esempi de avvenire* (stories and essays in science fiction; title means "Examples of the Future"), Rizzoli, 1965; *Il medioevo prossimo venturo,* Mondadori, 1971, translation by J.S. Whale published as *The Coming Dark Age,* Doubleday, 1973; *La morte di megalopoli* (novel; title means "The Death of Megalopolis"), Mondadori, 1974; *Handbook for an Improbable Salvation,* Mondadori, in press.

Contributor to *Traffic Quarterly, Mathematics of Computation, Playmen, Playboy, Il Mondo, L'Espresso,* and *Il Messaggero.*

SIDELIGHTS: Vacca speaks French, German, Spanish, Portuguese, Russian, and reads Latin and ancient Greek. *Avocational interests:* Psychology, theory of numbers, sociology, music (has composed songs and ballads in English and Pisan dialect), writing limericks.

* * *

VALDES, Joan 1931-

PERSONAL: Born July 1, 1931, in San Francisco, Calif.; daughter of Merrill Robert (a carpenter) and Dianne (Christman) Burns; married Luis F. Valdes (a teacher), January 19, 1958 (divorced, 1972); children: Alexander, Jason. *Education:* San Jose State College (now California State University, San Jose), A.B., 1952; San Francisco State College (now University), graduate study, 1957-58. *Home:* 184 Spruce St., Menlo Park, Calif. 94025. *Office:* San Carlos High School, San Carlos, Calif.

CAREER: San Carlos High School, San Carlos, Calif., teacher of English, 1960—.

WRITINGS: (With Jeanne Crow) *The Media Works,* Pflaum, 1973; (editor with Crow) *The Media Works Anthology,* Pflaum, 1974.

WORK IN PROGRESS: A television production textbook for Pflaum.

* * *

VALE, C(orwyn) P(hilip) 1921-

PERSONAL: Born April 26, 1921, in Darlaston, England; son of John and Olive Louisa (Hill) Vale; married Muriel Craven, September 1, 1945; children: Heather Catharine, Philip Andrew. *Education:* St. Catharine's College, Cambridge, B.A., 1942, M.A., 1946. *Religion:* Church of England. *Home:* Brynawelon, Bromley Lane, Kingswinford, Staffordshire, England. *Office:* Chemicals Division, British Industrial Plastics Ltd., Warley, England.

CAREER: Assistant master at grammar school in Walsall, England, 1946; British Industrial Plastics Ltd. (B.I.P.), Chemicals Division, Warley, England, research chemist, 1942-46, 1947-52, senior research chemist, 1952-60, assistant research manager, 1960-62, group research manager, 1962-68, research manager (new products), 1968—. Examiner in plastics technology for Plastics Institute, 1964—. Co-holder of four British patents in plastics. *Member:* Royal Institute of Chemistry (fellow), Plastics Institute (fellow), Society of Chemical Industry.

WRITINGS: Aminoplastics, Interscience, 1950; (with Alfred Brookes) *Resins from Urea, Melamine and Related Compounds* (monograph), Plastics Institute, 1953; (contributor) Phillip Morgan, editor, *Glass-reinforced Plastics,* Iliffe & Sons, 1954, 3rd edition, 1961; (with W. G. K. Taylor) *Aminoplastics,* Iliffe & Sons, for Plastics Institute, 1964; *Plastics* (juvenile), Hart-Davis, 1971, John Day, 1972. Contributor to industrial and other journals.

AVOCATIONAL INTERESTS: Music (plays the piano), reading (mainly prose), English heraldry, chess and chess problems, American history, philately, cultivation and use of herbs, wine-making.

* * *

VAN BRUNT, H(owell) L(loyd) 1936-

PERSONAL: Born July 18, 1936, in Tulsa, Okla.; son of Howell Harold and Elva (Johnson) Van Brunt. *Education:* Allan Hancock College, A.A., 1956. *Politics:* None. *Religion:* None. *Home:* 53 Leroy St., New York, N.Y. 10014.

CAREER: Reporter for *Medical Tribune,* 1966, and *Home Furnishings Daily,* 1967; The Smith (publishers), New York, N.Y., editor, 1967-70; *Saturday Review,* New York, N.Y., assistant book review editor, 1971. Poet.

WRITINGS: Uncertainties (poems), Smith, 1968; *Indian Territory and Other Poems,* Smith, 1974.

Represented in anthologies, including the *Living Underground: Contemporary American Poetry,* edited by High Fox, Whitston Publishing, 1973. Contributor of more than two hundred poems to *American Poetry Review, Poetry NOW, Arts in Ireland, Southwest Review, South Dakota Review,* and other publications.

WORK IN PROGRESS: A long poem on the settling of the West; a novel about everything.

* * *

VANCE, Lawrence L(ee) 1911-

PERSONAL: Born January 16, 1911, in St. Louis, Mo.; son of Archie Clifton (a certified public accountant) and Myrtle (Lee) Vance; married Mary McLaury Gardner, September 29, 1934; children: Lawrence Lee, Jr., Virginia McLaury (Mrs. Peter Hindes). *Education:* University of Minnesota, B.B.A., 1932, M.A., 1933, Ph.D., 1947. *Home:* 1465 Rancho View Dr., Lafayette, Calif. 94549. *Office:* Graduate School of Business Administration, University of California, Berkeley, Calif. 94720.

CAREER: Peat, Marwick, Mitchell & Co. (certified public accountants), Minneapolis, Minn., accountant, 1933-39; University of Kansas, Lawrence, instructor in business administration, 1939-41; University of California, Berkeley, lecturer, 1941-47, associate professor, 1947-52, professor of business administration, 1952—, associate dean of Graduate School of Business Administration, 1965-69. *Member:* American Accounting Association (president, 1966-67), American Institute of Certified Public Accountants, American Orchid Society (president, 1972-74), California Society of Certified Public Accountants, Phi Beta Kappa, Beta Gamma Sigma, Beta Alpha Psi, Delta Sigma Rho, Theta Chi.

WRITINGS: Scientific Method for Auditing, University of California Press, 1950; *Theory and Technique of Cost Accounting,* Foundation Press, 1952, 2nd edition, Holt, 1958; (with John Neter) *Statistical Sampling for Auditors and Accountants,* Wiley, 1956; *Accounting Principles and Control,* Holt, 1960, 3rd edition (with Russell Tausig), 1972; (with R. Gene Brown) *Sampling Tables for Error Rates or Other Proportions,* Institute of Business and Economic Research, University of California, Berkeley, 1961; (with Wayne Boutell) *Auditing,* Dryden, in press. Contributor to professional journals. Editor of *Accounting Review,* 1962-64.

WORK IN PROGRESS: Cost Analysis for Management, with T. N. Jain.

* * *

VANDERBILT, Cornelius, Jr. 1898-1974

April 30, 1898—July 7, 1974; American author and journalist. Obituaries: *New York Times,* July 8, 1974; *Washington Post,* July 10, 1974; *Time,* July 22, 1974; *Newsweek,* July 22, 1974. (*CA*-9/10).

* * *

van de WETERING, Janwillem 1931-

PERSONAL: Born February 12, 1931, in Rotterdam, Netherlands; son of Jan Cornelius (a businessman) and Catharina van de Wetering; married Juanita Levy, December, 1960; children: Thera. *Education:* Attended Delft University, 1948, College for Service Abroad, 1949-51, Cambridge University, 1951, University of London, 1958. *Home:* Van Neijenrodeweg 483, Amsterdam, Netherlands.

CAREER: Salesman in Dutch companies located in Johannesburg and Capetown, South Africa, 1952-58; layman in Buddhist monastery in Kyoto, Japan, 1958-59; director of companies in Bogota, Colombia, 1959-62, and Lima, Peru, 1963; land salesman in Brisbane, Australia, 1964-65; director of textile company in Amsterdam, Netherlands, 1965—. Apprentice non-commissioned officer in Special Constabulary.

WRITINGS: De Lege Spiegel, Driehoek, 1971, translation published as *The Empty Mirror: Experiences in a Japanese Zen Monastery,* Houghton, 1974; *Het Dagende Niets,* Driehoek, 1973, translation to be published as *The Crack of the Door,* Houghton, in press.

WORK IN PROGRESS—Mystery thrillers: *A Papua in Amsterdam; Tumbleweed; The Dishwasher.*

SIDELIGHTS: Van de Wetering told *CA* that *The Empty Mirror* was motivated by his "desire to try and express what really goes on in a Buddhist monastery, stressing the 'negative' aspects of human endeavour which always seem to be deleted by other writers who mention the hazy top level of 'enlightenment' and 'insight' and 'holiness' only." His books on the police and crime, he continues, "are motivated by sharing my experiences, and trying to analyse the behaviour of the offenders while underlining the serving duty of the police. . . . At the same time these books give me an opportunity to satisfy my sense of adventure." Van de Wetering sees elements of surrealism in his writing, "whatever that may be and whatever I may think it is." His favorite authors include Poe, Rimbaud, Tolkien, Castaneda, Gurdjeff, Simenon, and Queneau.

* * *

VAN DYKE, Henry 1928-

PERSONAL: Born October 3, 1928, in Allegan, Mich.; son of Henry Lewis (a professor) and Bessie (Chandler) Van Dyke. *Education:* University of Michigan, A.B., 1953, M.A., 1955. *Home:* 64 St. Mark's Pl., New York, N.Y. 10003. *Agent:* Curtis Brown Ltd., 60 East 56th St., New York, N.Y. 10022.

CAREER: University of Michigan, Ann Arbor, associate editor, University Engineering Research Institute, 1956-58; Crowell Collier & Macmillan, Inc., New York, N.Y., correspondent for book clubs, 1959-67; full-time writer, 1967—. Writer-in-residence, Kent State University, fall terms, 1969—. *Military service:* U.S. Army, 1948-50. *Awards, honors:* Jule and Avery Hopwood Award for fiction, 1954; Guggenheim fellowship, 1971; American Academy of Arts and Letters award, 1974.

WRITINGS—All novels: *Ladies of the Rachmaninoff Eyes,* Farrar, Straus, 1965; *Blood of Strawberries,* Farrar, Straus, 1969; *Dead Piano,* Farrar, Straus, 1971.

WORK IN PROGRESS: Another novel.

SIDELIGHTS: Van Dyke's first novel, *Ladies of the Rachmaninoff Eyes,* was described in the *Times Literary Supplement* as "pithily and wittily written. It has the extraordinary virtue of dealing with race relations as if they were ordinary human relations, and thus makes an efficiently quiet and humorous contribution to this raucous dialogue." The *National Observer* notes that Van Dyke is "adept at tricky plotting, hybrid characterization, and madcap pace" in *Blood of Strawberries;* "he is a good man at clown shows, showing us both surfaces of the clown's visage—the front view, designed to produce a boffola, and the oblique surface, seen in a different light, which reveals what is small and human and pathetic in us all. He reaches for an offbeat mixture of comedy and suspense." Alfred Kazin has called Van Dyke "one of the most brilliant and unpredictable of the younger black novelists. . . .His mind is too independent, ironic, and even humorous for messages. He is essentially a novelist of individual character, of the hidden idiosyncrasies."

BIOGRAPHICAL/CRITICAL SOURCES: Pembroke, spring, 1973.

* * *

van het REVE, Karel 1921-

PERSONAL: Born May 19, 1921, in Amsterdam, Netherlands; son of Gerardus Johannes Marinus and Jeanetta (Doornbusch) van het Reve; married Jozina Israeel, 1945; children: Jozina Jeanetta (Mrs. Evert Johannes Driessen), David. *Education:* University of Amsterdam, Ph.D., 1954. *Home address:* Amstel 268, Amsterdam, Netherlands. *Office:* Faculty of Arts, University of Leiden, Leiden, Netherlands.

CAREER: University of Amsterdam, Amsterdam, Netherlands, staff member of Russian Institute, 1948-57; University of Leiden, Leiden, Netherlands, professor of Slavic literature, 1957—. Moscow correspondent for *Het Parool* (Netherlands daily newspaper), 1967-68; founder and secretary of Alexander Herzen Foundation, 1969—. *Awards, honors:* Rockefeller Foundation grant, 1954-55; Wyenand Francken Prize, 1973.

WRITINGS: Goed en schoon in de Sovjetcritiek: Beschouwingen over de aesthetica van het Sovjetrussische Marxisme (title means "Good and Beautiful in Soviet Criticism: Essays on the Aesthetics of Soviet Marxism"), van Oorschot, 1954; *De "Øuderwetse roman" in Rusland* (title means "The Old-fashioned Novel in Russia"), van Oorschot, 1957; *Twee minuten stilte* (novel; title means "Two Minute Silence"), van Oorschot, 1959.

Nacht op de kale berg (novel; title means "Night on the Bald Mountain"), van Oorschot, 1961; *Rusland voor beginners: Tien opstellen over literatuur* (title means "Russia for Beginners"; includes *De "ouderwetse roman" in Rusland*), van Oorschot, 1962; *De literator en de holbewoner* (title means "The Man of Letters and the Troglodyte"), van

Oorschot, 1964; *Siberisch dagboek* (title means "Siberian Diary"), van Oorschot, 1966; (editor and author of notes) *Dear Comrade: Pavel Litvinov and the Voices of Soviet Citizens in Dissent,* Pitman, 1969, published as *Letters and Telegrams to Pavel Litvinov, December 1967-May 1968* (text in Russian and English), Reidel, 1969; (author of preface) Pavel M. Litvinov, *The Demonstration in Pushkin Square,* Gambit, 1969.

Het Geloof der kameraden: Kort overzicht van de communistiche wereldbeschouwing (title means "The Faith of the Comrades: A Short Summary of Communist Philosophy"), van Oorschot, 1970; *Marius wil niet in Joegoslaviee wonen en andere stukken over cultuur, recreatie en maatschappelijk werk* (title means "Marius Does Not Want to Live in Yugoslavia"), van Oorschot, 1970; *Met twee potten pindakaas naar Moskou* (title means "To Moscow with Two Jars of Peanut Butter"), van Oorschot, 1970; *Lenin heeft echt bestaan* (title means "Lenin Was a Real Person"), van Oorschot, 1972.

Contributor to other collections and to *Britannica Book of the Year.*

SIDELIGHTS: Van het Reve spent 1954-55 in the United States under a Rockefeller grant and returned in 1971 with his wife under the Department of State international visitor program. In addition to his one-year stay in the Soviet Union, he visited there in 1948, 1958, 1961, 1965, and 1966.

AVOCATIONAL INTERESTS: Sailing, classical music.

* * *

van VUUREN, Nancy 1938-

PERSONAL: Born December 16, 1938, in Boston, Mass. *Education:* University of New Hampshire, B.A., 1960; Duquesne University, M.A., 1965; University of Pittsburgh, Ph.D. candidate, 1970—. *Home and office address:* P.O. Box 8150, Pittsburgh, Pa. 15217.

CAREER: Elementary and secondary school teacher in Washington, D.C., 1962-63, and Pittsburgh, Pa., 1963-67; Carnegie-Mellon University, Pittsburgh, Pa., instructor in history, 1967-68; University of Pittsburgh, Pittsburgh, Pa., assistant professor of history, 1968-70; Pennsylvania Human Relations Commission, Harrisburg, Pa., director of planning and research, 1970-72; Allegheny Regional Planning Council, Governor's Justice Commission, Pittsburgh, Pa., planning director, 1973—. Coordinator of Joint Task Force on Sexism in Education of Pennsylvania Human Relations Commission, Department of Education, and Pennsylvanians for Women's Rights, 1970-72; co-chairperson of Pennsylvania Governor's Equal Rights Task Force Contract Compliance Committee, 1971. *Member:* Pennsylvanians for Women's Rights (president, 1972-74).

WRITINGS: The Subversion of Women as Practiced by Churches, Witch-Hunters, and Other Sexists, Westminster Press, 1973.

WORK IN PROGRESS: Testing the thesis in *The Subversion of Women* by looking at women in the trade unions, communist parties, and Anglican and Methodist Churches in England and South Africa, 1914-1968, completion expected in 1975.

* * *

VAUGHAN, James A(gnew) 1936-

PERSONAL: Born February 21, 1936, in Shannon, Miss.; son of James Agnew and Merle (Hill) Vaughan; married Peggy Barnett, May 29, 1955; children: Vicki, Andrew. *Education:* Millsaps College, B.A., 1958; Wesleyan University, Middletown, Conn., M.A., 1960; Louisiana State University, Ph.D., 1963. *Home and office address:* Institute for Training and Development Ltd., P.O. Box 5626, Hilton Head Island, S.C. 29928.

CAREER: University of Pittsburgh, Graduate School of Business, Pittsburgh, Pa., assistant professor, 1962-65, associate professor of business administration, 1966-68, University of Rochester, Rochester, N.Y., associate professor of business administration and psychology and associate director, Management Research Center, 1968-70; Institute for Training and Development Ltd. (INSTAD), Hilton Head Island, S.C., president, 1970—. Consultant to National Training Laboratories, American Management Association, U.D. Department of Commerce, and other industries, organizations, and government agencies. *Member:* American Psychological Association, American Society for Training and Development, Sigma Xi. *Awards, honors:* Ford Foundation faculty fellowship, 1965-66.

WRITINGS: (With B.M. Bass) *Training in Industry: The Management of Learning,* Wadsworth, 1966; (with Avner M. Porat) *Banking Computer Style: The Impact of Computers on Small and Medium-Sized Banks,* Prentice-Hall, 1969. Contributor to *Banking* and other journals.

* * *

VEGA, Janine Pommy 1942-

PERSONAL: Born February 5, 1942, in Jersey City, N.J.; daughter of Joseph P. (a businessman) and Irene H. (Telkowski) Pommy; married Max Fernando Braun Vega (a painter), July, 1962 (died November 22, 1965). *Politics:* "Not affiliated/liberal." *Religion:* "All religions pass by many roads to the Same Place; I worship the One." *Home and office address:* Bearsville Post Office, Bearsville, N.Y. 12409.

CAREER: Poet and lecturer; has worked as dancer, barmaid, office-worker, teacher, translator, and as story-teller in homes for the aged, reform schools, and for Headstart Projects. Has taught English in Europe and South America.

WRITINGS—Poems: *Poems to Fernando,* City Lights, 1968; *Visions, Tales and Lovesongs,* Cranium Press, in press. Contributor of poems to more than twenty-five literary journals in the United states and abroad, including *Extensions, Interim Pad, Mademoiselle, Caterpillar, Journal of the Arts, Woodstock Oracle, Residu #2, Great Society, Floating Bear, Good Soup, Niagara Frontier Review,* and *Grist.*

WORK IN PROGRESS: Journal of a Hermit, completion expected about 1974.

SIDELIGHTS: Mrs. Vega told *CA:* "Fortunately or unfortunately, there has never been a question nor a choice with me: I HAVE to write. My work has been influenced by the years I spent with the Beat Poets in New York City; by my drug experiences; by the death of my husband; by my travels; by the work of certain visionary poets (Tagore, Yeats, Corso); and, most recently (the last three years), by what I believe is the most important WORK of every soul on the earth: The Journey Within. A catalyst of this journey, I believe, is all the external traveling I have done: to Israel, through Europe, back to America, to Hawaii, to Puerto Rico, and lastly to South America. . . . My journey is really to the Home within, and my work but a record of the visions along the way." As a result of her travels, Mrs. Vega has learned Hebrew, French, and Spanish.

VEILLON, Lee 1942-

PERSONAL: Surname is pronounced *vay*-yon; born October 2, 1942, in Church Point, La.; daughter of LeRoy (a store owner) and Dorothy (Sylvester) Veillon. *Education:* Our Lady of the Lake College, B.A., 1966; University of Southwestern Louisiana, M.A., 1970. *Address:* P.O. Box 616, Castroville, Tex. 78009. *Agent:* Joan Daves, 515 Madison Ave., New York, N.Y. 10022.

CAREER: Roman Catholic nun of Sisters of Divine Providence Order, 1958-65; elementary teacher in San Antonio, Tex., 1964-65; elementary and junior high teacher in Lafayette, La., 1967-68; Southwest Missouri State University, Springfield, instructor in English, 1970-73; writer. *Member:* American Civil Liberties Union. *Awards, honors:* Deep South Writers Conference first drama award, 1970, for *The Sidelong Glances of a Pillow Kicker;* Arts and Humanities Award from Our Lady of the Lake College, 1974.

WRITINGS: Hart (novel), Harper, 1974.

Plays: *The Sidelong Glances of a Pillow Kicker* (one-act), Edgemoor Publishing, 1970; *There Are No Bunions in the Presence of a Lady* (one-act), Edgemoor Publishing, 1971; *Italians and Army Surplus Toilet Seats* (one-act), Edgemoor Publishing, 1971.

WORK IN PROGRESS: A comic novel; a southern regional novel set on a crawfish farm in Louisiana, tentatively entitled *Going Home the Long Way*.

SIDELIGHTS: Lee Veillon told *CA:* "As a Creole, my southern novels are set in the southern half of Louisiana and embody Cajun-Creole cultures. I am a 'stylist' and have definite ideas about quality writing or competence. . . . I also believe in objectivity on the part of the writer as opposed to exposes of dirty laundry. My aim is to explore truth about humanity or people as I know it, truth about the practice of justice, the effects of religion, the search for happiness, the constructs of personality embodied, of course, in a good story. My interests include photography, travel, Mayan art and 'primitive' cultures as well as social philosophy."

* * *

VELER, Richard P(aul) 1936-

PERSONAL: Surname rhymes with "sealer"; born October 29, 1936, in Lorain, Ohio; son of Herbert W. (a minister) and Mildred (Bitter) Veler. *Education:* Wittenberg University, A.B., 1958; Harvard University, M.A., 1959; Ohio State University, Ph.D., 1964. *Religion:* Lutheran. *Home:* 505½ North Fountain Ave., Springfield, Ohio 45504. *Office:* Department of English, Wittenberg University, Springfield, Ohio 45501.

CAREER: Ohio State University, Columbus, instructor in English, 1964-65; Wittenberg University, Springfield, Ohio, assistant professor, 1965-69, associate professor of English, 1969—, head of department, 1971—, associate dean of the college, 1969-71. *Member:* Modern Language Association of America, College English Association, National Council of Teachers of English, Association of Departments of English, Midwest Modern Language Association, College English Association of Ohio.

WRITINGS: (Editor) *Papers on Poe: Essays in Honor of John Ward Ostrom,* Chantry, 1972. Co-editor of *CEAO English Notes,* 1966-72.

WORK IN PROGRESS: Research on Mark Twain's plays, the periodical reception of *Sister Carrie,* James Joyce, and Walter Tittle.

VENAFRO, Mark
See PIZZAT, Frank J(oseph)

* * *

VENNING, Corey 1924-
(Tracy Elliot Hyde)

PERSONAL: Born July 4, 1924, in Spanish Fork, Utah; daughter of Robert Aloysius and Blanche Elizabeth (Rockhill) Brown; divorced; children: Robert, Ruth, Alan. *Education:* Attended University of Idaho, 1941-42, University of California, Berkeley, 1942, and Boise Junior College, 1943-45; University of Chicago, M.A., 1948, Ph.D., 1968; University of Oregon, graduate study, 1962-63. *Politics:* "Common sense: I value the American federal-constitutional system." *Religion:* Nonsectarian. *Home:* 1015 Easy Hyde Park Blvd., Chicago, Ill. 60615. *Agent:* Roy E. Porter, Max Siegel & Associates, 145 East Erie St., Chicago, Ill. 60611. *Office:* Department of Political Science, Loyola University, Chicago, Ill.

CAREER: U.S. Department of State, research analyst in Indonesia and Korea, 1948-49; U.S. Foreign Service, American vice-consul in Bombay, India, 1949-52, second secretary of U.S. Embassy in Athens, Greece, 1952-55; Goodbody & Co., Charlotte, N.C., broker, 1955-56; Internal Revenue Service (IRS), Boise, Idaho, stenographer, then auditor, 1961-62; University of Oregon, Eugene, associate director of Nepal III Peace Corps training program, 1963; University of Chicago, Center for Continuing Education, Chicago, Ill., conference coordinator, 1964-65; Loyola University, Chicago, Ill., instructor, 1965-68, assistant professor of political science, 1968—. Secretary, South Side Condominium/Coop Owners' Association, Chicago, 1972-73. *Member:* International Studies Association, American Political Science Association, Conference for the Study of Political Thought, Women's Caucus for Political Science, National Organization of Women, National Women's Political Caucus, Midwest Political Science Association, University and College Women of Illinois (treasurer, 1974-75), Pi Sigma Alpha, Hyde Park-Kenwood Community Conference and Cook County Hospital Auxiliary (both Chicago).

WRITINGS: (Under pseudonym Tracy Elliot Hyde) *The Single Grandmother,* Nelson-Hall, 1974; (contributor) Peter Merkl and Ruth Ross, editors, *Social and Political Change: The Role of Women,* American Bibliographical Center—CLIO Press, in press. Contributor to *University of Michigan Papers in Women's Studies,* and to *Journal of the History of Ideas*.

WORK IN PROGRESS: Grandma Goes to College, under pseudonym Tracy Elliot Hyde; *National Greatness and the Imperial Imperative, The Silent Presence: Women in Political Philosophy,* and *The Diotima Complex,* all under name Corey Venning.

BIOGRAPHICAL/CRITICAL SOURCES: Lifestyles, fall, 1974.

* * *

VERNON, Glenn M(orley) 1920-

PERSONAL: Born April 6, 1920, in Vernal, Utah; son of William Morley (a teacher) and Roseltha (Bingham) Vernon; married June A. Andersen, December 24, 1942; children: Gregory G., Rebecca, Paul B. *Education:* Brigham Young University, B.S., 1947, M.S., 1950; Washington State University, Ph.D., 1953. *Religion:* Church of

Jesus Christ of Latter-Day Saints. *Home:* 3646 East 3580 S., Salt Lake City, Utah 84109. *Office:* Department of Sociology, University of Utah, Salt Lake City, Utah 84112.

CAREER: Auburn University, Auburn, Ala., assistant professor of sociology, 1953-54; Central Michigan University, Mount Pleasant, assistant professor, 1954-57, associate professor of sociology, 1957-59; Brigham Young University, Provo, Utah, associate professor of sociology, 1959-63; University of Maine, Orono, professor of sociology and head of department, 1963-68; University of Utah, Salt Lake City, professor of sociology, 1968—, head of department, 1970-73. *Military service:* U.S. Army Air Forces, 1942-45; became first lieutenant.

MEMBER: International Conference on Sociology of Religion, International Congress of Sociology, American Sociological Association, Society for the Scientific Study of Religion (member of board of directors, 1971-74), Academy of Religion and Mental Health, Religious Research Association, American Association of University Professors, Eastern Sociological Society, Pacific Sociological Association (vice-president, 1972-73), Sigma Xi.

WRITINGS: The Sociology of Religion, McGraw, 1962; *Human Interaction: An Introduction to Sociology,* Ronald, 1965, 2nd edition, 1972; *Sociology of Death: An Analyses of Death-Related Behavior,* Ronald, 1970; (author of foreword) J. D. Cardwell, *Social Psychology,* F. A. Davis, 1971; (contributor) Erwin O. Smigel, editor, *Handbook on the Study of Social Problems,* Rand McNally, 1971; (editor and contributor) *Social-Symbolic Dimensions of Religion,* Association for the Study of Religion, 1971; *Interactions and Symbols,* Association for the Study of Religion, 1972; (editor and contributor) *Research on Mormonism,* Association for the Study of Religion, 1974. Contributor to *International Yearbook on the Sociology of Religion;* contributor of about twenty-five articles to journals, some of them reprinted in books.

WORK IN PROGRESS: A revision of *The Sociology of Religion.*

* * *

VESEY, Paul
See ALLEN, Samuel

* * *

VETOE, Miklos 1936-

PERSONAL: Surname is pronounced "vay-*toe*"; born August 22, 1936, in Budapest, Hungary; son of Miklos M. and Anna (Sabel) Vetoe; married Odile Wattre (a professor of Italian), July 3, 1962; children: Etienne, Nicolas, Marie-Elisabeth. *Education:* Attended University of Szeged, 1954-56; Sorbonne, University of Paris, Licence de Philosophie, 1959, D.E.S., 1960, Doct. 3. cycle, 1971, Doct. es Lett., 1974; Oxford University, Ph.D., 1964. *Religion:* Roman Catholic. *Home:* 71 Ingram, Hamden, Conn. 06517. *Office:* Department of Philosophy, Yale University, New Haven, Conn. 06520.

CAREER: Marquette University, Milwaukee, Wis., instructor in philosophy, 1963-65; Yale University, New Haven, Conn., instructor, 1965-66, assistant professor, 1966-71, associate professor, 1971-73, lecturer in philosophy, 1973—, fellow of Jonathan Edwards College, 1966—. *Military service:* Hungarian People's Army, 1955. *Member:* Internationale Hegel Gesellschaft, International Scientific Advisory Council, Societe des Professeurs Francais en Amerique, Metaphysical Society of America, Society for Phenomenology and Existential Philosophy, Catholic Commission on Intellectual and Cultural Affairs. *Awards, honors:* American Philosophical Society research grant, summer, 1965; Morse fellowship from Yale University, 1969-70.

WRITINGS: La metaphysique religieuse de Simone Weil (title means "The Religious Metaphysics of Simone Weil"), Vrin, 1971; (editor) *Friedrich J. W. Schelling: Stuttgarter Privatvorlesungen* (title means "Friedrich J. W. Schelling: The Private Lectures of Stuttgart"), Bottega d'Erasmo, 1973; *Le Fondemont selon Schelling* (title means "The Ground According to Schelling"), Vrin, in press. Consulting editor of *Journal of Value Inquiry,* 1967—.

WORK IN PROGRESS: Histoire des theories philosophiques et theologiques du mal, completion expected in 1975; *Theologie de la conservation.*

AVOCATIONAL INTERESTS: Study of medieval and Mayan architecture.

* * *

VICKERY, Robert L. (Jr.) 1932-

PERSONAL: Born December 19, 1932, in Missouri; son of Robert L. (a publisher) and Margaret (Ray) Vickery; married Mary Knudstad; children: Clare M., Kevin L. *Education:* University of Missouri, B.Journalism, 1954; Washington University, St. Louis, Mo., B.Arch. (with honors), 1960; University of Madrid, graduate study, 1960-61. *Home:* 521 North First St., Charlottesville, Va. 22901. *Office:* School of Architecture, University of Virginia, Charlottesville, Va. 22903.

CAREER: Washington University, St. Louis, Mo., associate professor of architecture, 1963-70, assistant dean of School of Architecture, director of campus planning; University of Virginia, Charlottesville, professor of architecture, 1970—, co-chairman of Division of Architecture. Architect for Performing Arts Center of Washington University.

WRITINGS: Anthrophysical Form, University Press of Virginia, 1973. Contributor to *St. Louis Post-Dispatch.*

WORK IN PROGRESS: On Sharing Architecture, a textbook for beginning students.

* * *

VILAR, Esther 1935-

PERSONAL: Born September 16, 1935, in Buenos Aires, Argentina; daughter of Federico (a farmer) and Anna (Schindler) Vilar; married Klaus Wagn (a philosopher), 1961 (divorced, 1963); children: Martin. *Education:* University of Buenos Aires, M.D., 1958. *Religion:* None. *Office:* Caann Verlag, Diefenbachstrasse nr. 1A, Munich 8000, Germany.

CAREER: Physician in Munich, Germany, 1960-61; presently free-lance writer.

WRITINGS: Der Dressierte Mann, Caann Verlag (Munich), 1971, published as *The Manipulated Man,* Farrar, Straus, 1973.

* * *

VIORST, Judith

PERSONAL: Born in Newark, N.J.; daughter of Martin (an accountant) and Ruth (Ehrenkranz) Stahl; married

Milton Viorst (a writer); children: Anthony, Nicholas, Alexander. *Education:* Rutgers University, B.A. (with honors). *Religion:* Jewish. *Home:* 3432 Ashley Ter. N.W., Washington, D.C. 20008. *Agent:* Robert Lescher, 155 East 71st St., New York, N.Y. 10027.

CAREER: Poet, journalist, author of children's books. Contributing editor, *Redbook* magazine. *Member:* Phi Beta Kappa. *Awards, honors:* Emmy Award, 1970, for poetic monologs written for CBS special, "Annie, The Women in the Life of a Man."

WRITINGS: *The Village Square* (poems), Coward, 1965; *It's Hard to Be Hip Over Thirty, and Other Tragedies of Married Life* (poems), World Publishing, 1968; (with husband, Milton Viorst) *The Washington, D.C. Underground Gourmet,* Simon & Schuster, 1970; *People and Other Aggravations* (poems), World Publishing, 1971; *Yes, Married: A Saga of Love and Complaint* (collected prose pieces), Saturday Review Press, 1972.

Juvenile fiction: *Sunday Morning,* Harper, 1968; *I'll Fix Anthony,* Harper, 1969; *Try It Again, Sam: Safety When You Walk,* Lothrop, 1970; *The Tenth Good Thing About Barney,* Atheneum, 1971; *Alexander and the Terrible, Horrible, No Good, Very Bad Day,* Atheneum, 1972; *My Mama Says There Aren't Any Zombies, Ghosts, Vampires, Creatures, Demons, Monsters, Fiends, Goblins, or Things,* Atheneum, 1973; *Rosie and Michael,* Atheneum, in press.

Juvenile nonfiction: (Editor with Shirley Moore) *Wonderful World of Science,* Science Service, 1961; *Projects: Space,* Washington Square Press, 1962; *One Hundred and Fifty Science Experiments, Step-by-Step,* Bantam, 1963; *Natural World,* Bantam, 1965; *The Changing Earth,* Bantam, 1967.

Author of syndicated column for Washington Star Syndicate, 1970-72, and of regular column for *Redbook,* 1972—. Author of poetic monologs for television. Contributor of poems and articles to *New York, New York Times, Holiday, Venture, Washingtonian,* and other periodicals.

SIDELIGHTS: Judith Viorst has been described as a "sort of rhymeless latter-day Dorothy Parker," her poems as "wry and amusing," and "more aptly termed metered reflection." She is called "a poet of the ordinary, the everyday . . . with more reason than rhyme in her work and more humor than either."

One reviewer felt that *How to be Hip* . . . "may help her less articulate sisters bear their fates." Arline Youngman says "she has learned to laugh both at herself and the threat of disaster—to be content with the life-style she has." Viorst herself estimates her light, humorous verse to be "reasonably real, more or less based on the family life of the Viorsts. I also steal from all my friends' lives."

* * *

VIVIAN, Cordy Tindell 1924-

PERSONAL: Born July 30, 1924, in Booneville, Mo.; son of Cordy Robert (a union worker) and Euzetta (Tindell) Vivian; married W. Octavia Geans (a writer), February 22, 1953; children: Jo Anna, Denise, Cordy, Jr., Kira, Mark, Charisse, Albert. *Education:* Western Illinois University, A.B.; American Baptist Theological Seminary, B.D., 1959. *Office:* Seminary Without Walls, Shaw University, Raleigh, N.C. 27602.

CAREER: Ordained Baptist minister; pastor of community churches in Nashville, 1955-61, and Chattanooga, Tenn., 1961-63; member of executive staff of Southern Christian Leadership Conference (under Martin Luther King, Jr.), 1963-67; Urban Training Center for Christian Mission, Chicago, Ill., director of black ministry development, 1967-69; Shaw University, Raleigh, N.C., university minister and dean of chapel, 1969—, also national director of Seminary Without Walls. Organized National Black Training Center; member of board of directors of Joint Action for Community Service; developed Interracial Resources, Inc. (consultants) and Edu-Plex Systems, Inc.; director for Asia and community relations for Inter-Church Center of National Council of Churches; member of executive committee of National Foundation for Cooperative Housing; member of National Advisory Council for Black Economic Development of the Small Business Administration; member of Black Caucus of Urban Coalition; consultant to institutions, organizations, and business boards; lecturer at Africana Study Center of Cornell University and at sixty-six other colleges in the United States; has participated in lecture tours through Japan, the Netherlands, Hong Kong, and Manila. *Member:* National Council of Industrial Missions (member of board of directors), National Council of Community Churches (member of executive committee).

WRITINGS: *Black Power and the American Myth* (Ebony Book Club selection), Fortress, 1970. Founder of *Baptist Layman* and *Nashville News Star.*

WORK IN PROGRESS: *Joseph: The Blackening of America; Messages to Black Youth,* for Fortress; *Interdependence: Means of Black Survival,* completion expected in 1976; *Date and Fact Book of Black America.*

SIDELIGHTS: Vivian has participated in non-violent civil rights action in Albany, Ga., Danville, Va., Birmingham and Selma, Ala., and St. Augustine, Fla., often in executive positions associated with the Southern Christian Leadership Conference. He was a close associate of Martin Luther King, Jr.; his wife, Octavia Vivian, is author of a biography of Mrs. Coretta King.

BIOGRAPHICAL/CRITICAL SOURCES: Earl and Mariam Selby, *Odyssey: A Journey Through Black America,* Putnam, 1971; J. Alan Winter and others, *Clergy in Action Training,* IODC Press, 1971.

* * *

VODOLA, Thomas M(ichael) 1925-

PERSONAL: Born July 11, 1925, in New York, N.Y.; son of Thomas (a musician) and Mae (Grindstaff) Vodola; married Theresa H. Volponi, December 22, 1946; children: Thomas A., Anthony F., Lilimaria, Theresa. *Education:* New York University, B.S., 1950, M.A., 1958; Temple University, Ed.D., 1970. *Politics:* Independent. *Religion:* Roman Catholic. *Home:* 32 Fourth Ave., Neptune City, N.J. 07753. *Office:* Township of Ocean School District, Dow Ave., Oakhurst, N.J. 07755.

CAREER: Elementary and high school teacher of health and physical education in Wall Township, N.J., 1955-65; Township of Ocean School District, Oakhurst, N.J., high school teacher of health, physical education, and driver education, 1965-71, district director of health, physical education, and program for the handicapped, 1971—. Part-time instructor at Montclair State College; adjunct professor, Monmouth College. Chairman of New Jersey Youth Fitness Committee, 1964—; co-chairman of subcommittee on the handicapped, New Jersey Governor's Committee on Children and Youth, 1970—; games director, New Jersey Special Olympics, 1971-72, and New Jersey Office of

Champion Games, 1972—. *Military service:* U.S. Army Air Forces, 1943-46.

MEMBER: American Association for Health, Physical Education and Recreation, National Education Association, American Educational Research Association, National Council on Measurement, New Jersey Association for Health, Physical Education and Recreation (president, 1969-71), New Jersey Education Association, New Jersey Association for Retarded Children, Phi Delta Kappa.

WRITINGS: Individualized Physical Education Program for the Handicapped Child, Prentice-Hall, 1973; *Statistics Made Easy for the Classroom Teacher,* C.F. Wood, 1974; (contributor) Robert E. Weber, editor, *New Perspectives in Developmental Disabilities,* Prentice-Hall for New Jersey Association for Children with Learning Disabilities, in press. Contributor to publications of American Association for Health, Physical Education and Recreation.

WORK IN PROGRESS: Additional research in his field.

* * *

VOGEL, Lucy E(laine)

EDUCATION: Brooklyn College of the City University of New York, B.A. (cum laude), 1960; Fordham University, M.A., 1963; New York University, Ph.D., 1968. *Home:* 20 University Dr., Setauket, N.Y. 11733. *Office:* Department of Germanic and Slavic Languages, State University of New York at Stony Brook, Stony Brook, N.Y. 11790.

CAREER: Queens College of the City University of New York, Flushing, N.Y., instructor in Russian and Italian, 1961-67; State University of New York at Stony Brook, assistant professor, 1967-72, associate professor of Russian, 1973—, director of Slavic studies, 1974—. Instructor, Adelphi University, summers, 1961, 1962. *Member:* American Association of Teachers of Slavic and East European Languages, American Association of University Women.

WRITINGS: Alexander Blok: A Journey to Italy, Cornell University Press, 1973. Contributor to *Slavic and East European Journal* and *Russian Review.*

WORK IN PROGRESS: Blok in the Critical Works of His Contemporaries.

SIDELIGHTS: Dr. Vogel grew up in Milan, Italy and completed her secondary education there.

* * *

VOGELSANG, Arthur 1942-

PERSONAL: Born January 31, 1942, in Baltimore, Md.; son of Leo and Muriel (Valke) Vogelsang; married Judith Ayers, June 14, 1966. *Education:* University of Maryland, B.A., 1965; Johns Hopkins University, M.A., 1966; University of Iowa, M.F.A., 1970. *Home:* 519 Montgomery Ave., Haverford, Pa. 19041. *Office:* 401 South Broad St., Philadelphia, Pa. 19147.

CAREER: McGraw-Hill Book Co., New York, N.Y., editing supervisor, 1966-68; Wichita State University, Wichita, Kan., instructor in English, 1970-71; *American Poetry Review,* Philadelphia, Pa., co-editor, 1974—. Has also been free-lance editor for publishers and television station; director and visiting writer of Kansas Poetry and Fiction Workshops, 1973. Advisor, Kansas Arts Commission, 1971-73.

WRITINGS: Stanzas Done for Alberta Coke (a chapbook of poems), goodly company press, 1969. Contributor of more than one hundred poems and short stories to journals. Co-editor and founder of *Ark River Review,* 1971—.

* * *

VROMAN, Leo 1915-

PERSONAL: Born April 10, 1915, in Gouda, Netherlands; came to United States, 1945, naturalized citizen; son of Samuel Jacob (a physicist) and Anna (a mathematician) Vroman; married Georgine Marie Sanders (an anthropologist), September 10, 1947; children: Geraldine E. (Mrs. David Griffin), Peggy Ann. *Education:* Rijkuniversiteit Utrecht, candidaat (biology), 1937, Ph.D. (comparative physiology), 1958; Jakarta Medical College, doctorandus (comparative physiology), 1941. *Politics:* "Love, honesty, equality, etc." *Religion:* "Many." *Home:* 2365 East 13th St., Brooklyn, N.Y. 11229. *Office:* Veterans Administration Hospital, Interface Laboratory, Brooklyn, N.Y. 11209.

CAREER: Escaped to England when Netherlands surrendered to Germany, 1940, then traveled to Jakarta, Indonesia, where he worked as a free-lance illustrator and writer, 1940-41; joining the Netherlands Indies Army in 1941, he was taken prisoner of war and interned in Java and Japan, 1942-45; arrived in the United States, 1945, and worked as free-lance illustrator and writer, 1946-47; St. Peter's General Hospital, New Brunswick, N.J., research associate, 1947-55; Rutgers University, New Brunswick, N.J., researcher in department of parasitology, 1955; Mt. Sinai Hospital, New York, N.Y., 1955-58, began as research assistant, became research associate in hematology department; American Museum of Natural History, New York, N.Y., researcher in department of animal behavior, 1958-61; Veterans Administration Hospital, Brooklyn, N.Y., research physiologist, 1961—; writer and artist. Chairman of planning committee, Columbia University Seminar on Biomaterials, 1970-71. *Military service:* Netherlands Indies Army, 1941-46. *Member:* American Institute of Chemists (fellow), American Association for the Advancement of Science, New York Academy of Sciences (member of planning committee, 1973), New York Society for the Study of Blood, P.E.N. *Awards, honors:* Wayne State University Individual's Science Lecture Award, 1970; numerous poetry and literature awards from organizations in the Netherlands.

WRITINGS—All published by Querido (Amsterdam), except as indicated: *Tineke,* 1948; *De adem van Mars* (title means "The Breath of Mars"; also see below), 1956; *Snippers* (also see below), 1958; *Tineke, De adem van Mars, Snippers: Proza,* 1960; *Het Grauwse Diep* (three-act play; title means "Rabble's Deep"; first produced in Utrecht, Netherlands, at City Theatre, 1966), 1966; *Blood,* Natural History Press for American Museum of Natural History, 1967; *Agenda uit het jaar 2000* (title means "Diary Left in 2000"), Rap, 1968; *Voorgrond, achtergrond* (three-act play; title means "Foreground, Background"; first produced in The Hague, at City Theatre, 1969), 1969; *Het Carnarium* (novel; title means "The Carnarium"), 1973.

Poetry—All published by Querido: *Gedichten* (title means "Poems"), 1946; *Gedichten: Vroegere en latere* (title means "Poems: Earlier and Later Ones"), 1949; *Poems in English* (also see below), 1953; *Inleiding tot een leegte* (title means "Introduction to a Void"), 1955; *Uit slaapwandelen* (title means "Out Sleepwalking"), 1957; *De ontvachting, en andere gedichten,* 1960; *Twee gedichten* (title means "Two Poems"), 1961; *Fabels,* 1962; *Manke vliegen* (title means "Limping Flies"; also see below), 1963; *126 gedichten,* 1964; *Almanak* (also see below), 1965; *God en Godin* (title means "God and Goddess"; also see below), 1967; *114 gedichten* (includes *Manke vliegen, Almanak, God en Godin,* "Verpreide gedichten," *Poems in English*), 1969.

Editor, *Thrombosis Research,* 1972—.

WORK IN PROGRESS: Laboratory research, leading to publication; a science fiction work combining microscope photographs and poems.

SIDELIGHTS: Vroman told *CA:* "I presume I am like most who are actively involved in literature, arts and sciences: aware that the work in all has much in common, and in love with the complexities of life as it expresses itself on a molecular scale as well as globally, all we ask from life is the gift to understand so that we can love it even more."

Vroman also said: "I write in Dutch and in English, read German and French when I must, but in general I rather make my own things than admire those of others."

* * *

WACHTEL, Howard M(artin) 1938-

PERSONAL: Born December 31, 1938, in Philadelphia, Pa; son of Leo and Betty (Babbitt) Wachtel; married Dawn Day, 1963. *Education:* Temple University, B.S., 1960; University of Connecticut, M.A., 1962; University of Michigan, Ph.D., 1969. *Office:* Department of Economics, American University, Massachusetts and Nebraska Aves. N.W., Washington, D.C. 20016.

CAREER: U.S. Department of Commerce, Washington, D.C., research assistant, 1962-64; University of Michigan, Ann Arbor, instructor in labor and industrial relations, 1965-66, consultant on low-wage project, Institute of Labor and Industrial Relations, 1969-70; American University, Washington, D.C., assistant professor, 1969-73, associate professor of economics, 1973—. *Member:* American Economic Association, Industrial Relations Research Association, American Association of University Professors, Union for Radical Political Economics. *Awards, honors:* Rackham travel grant, University of Michigan, for research in Yugoslavia, 1967-68; American Council of Learned Societies travel grant to Hungary, 1973.

WRITINGS: (With Louis Ferman, William Murphy, and John Parker) *The Hard-Core Unemployed of Detroit: An Economic and Social Portrait,* Institute of Labor and Industrial Relations, University of Michigan-Wayne State University, 1971; *Workers' Management and Workers' Wages in Yugoslavia: The Theory and Practice of Participatory Socialism,* Cornell University Press, 1973; *Theory of Radical Political Economy: A Book of Readings,* Praeger, in press.

Contributor: James H. Weaver, editor, *Modern Political Economy: Radical and Orthodox Views on Crucial Issues,* new edition (Wachtel did not contribute to earlier edition), Allyn & Bacon, 1973; Harold Wolozin and Raymond G. Torto, editors, *Domestic Economic Problems: A Reader,* Holbrook, 1973; Pamela Roby, editor, *The Poverty Establishment,* Prentice-Hall, 1974; Bertram Silverman and Murray Yanowitch, editors, *The Worker in "Post-Industrial" Capitalism: Liberal and Radical Responses,* Free Press, 1974; Richard Edwards, David Gordon, and Michael Reich, editors, *Labor Market Segmentation,* Heath, in press. Contributor of articles and reviews to journals in his field. Member and coordinator of editorial board, *Review of Radical Political Economics,* 1969-73; referee, *Journal of Political Economy,* 1972.

WORK IN PROGRESS: Research with Charles Betsey, on low wage workers and the dual labor market.

SIDELIGHTS: Wachtel visited the People's Republic of China in 1972.

* * *

WAGNER, Jack Russell 1916-

PERSONAL: Born May 18, 1916, in San Jose, Calif.; son of John Andrew (a builder and rancher) and Carrie H. (Fowler) Wagner; married LaVerne Ann DeSerio, 1947 (divorced, 1951). *Education:* San Jose State College (now California State University), student, 1934-36. *Religion:* Protestant. *Home:* 350 Sausalito Blvd., Sausalito, Calif. 94965. *Office:* Radio Station KCBS, One Embarcadero Center, San Francisco, Calif. 94111.

CAREER: U.S. Army, Signal Corps, civilian radio engineer, 1942-45; Siskiyou County Broadcasting Co., Yreka, Calif., planner, then station manager of KSYC, 1947-50; KDB, Santa Barbara, Calif., manager, 1951; KVON, Vallejo-Napa, Calif., co-manager, 1952; KNBR, San Francisco, Calif., program manager, 1953-66, operations manager, 1966-67; Radio Station KCBS, San Francisco, Calif., director of broadcast operations, 1968—. Holds Federal Communications Commission radio telephone operator's license, first class. Instructor at Radio-Television Institute, Stanford, University, 1958-64. President of Sausalito Foundation, 1965-68, trustee, 1968—. *Member:* Press Club of San Francisco, Masons, Kiwanis Club.

WRITINGS: *Short Line Junction,* Academy Guild Press, 1956, 2nd edition, Valley Publishers, 1971; *Gold Mines of California,* Howell-North Brooks, 1970. Contributor of articles on travel, transportation, and historical subjects to *Westways, True, American Forests,* and other magazines.

* * *

WAGNER, Karl Edward 1945-

PERSONAL: Born December 12, 1945, in Knoxville, Tenn.; son of Aubrey Joseph (chairman of board of directors of Tennessee Valley Authority) and Dorothea (Huber) Wagner. *Education:* Kenyon College, A.B., 1967; University of North Carolina, M.D., 1974. *Politics:* Independent. *Residence:* Chapel Hill, N.C. *Agent:* Kirby McCauley, 220 East 26th St., New York, N.Y. 10010.

CAREER: Carcosa (publishing house), Chapel Hill, N.C., founder and editor, 1972—; John Umstead Hospital, Butner, N.C., resident in psychiatry, 1974—. *Member:* Science Fiction Writers of America, North Carolina Writers Conference.

WRITINGS: *Darkness Weaves with Many Shades...,* Powell Publications, 1970; *Death Angel's Shadow,* Warner Paperback Library, 1973; *Midnight Sun* (collection), Gary Hoppenstand, 1974; *Bloodstone,* Warner Paperback Library, in press.

WORK IN PROGRESS: Three novels, *In the Wake of Night, Satan's Gun,* and *Blue Lady, Come Back.*

SIDELIGHTS: Wagner considers himself a writer first, a psychiatrist second.

* * *

WAHL, Jean 1888-1974

May 22, 1888—June 19, 1974; French existentialist philosopher. Obituaries: *New York Times,* June 22, 1974; *Washington Post,* June 24, 1974; *Time,* July 1, 1974.

* * *

WAHL, Robert (Charles) 1948-

PERSONAL: Born May 24, 1948, in Toledo, Ohio; son of Russell Rothenberger (a physician) and Nina Marie (Boyer) Wahl. *Education:* Attended Ohio State University, 1966-67, and University of Toledo, 1967-73. *Politics:* Independent. *Home:* 2116 Potomac Dr., Toledo, Ohio 43607. *Agent:* Elaine Markson, 44 Greenwich Ave., New York, N.Y. 10011.

CAREER: Parks developer in Toledo, Ohio, 1966-67; Lasalle, Inc., Toledo, Ohio, clothing salesman, 1969; Augusta National Golf Club, Augusta, Ga., assistant maintenance supervisor, 1973.

WRITINGS: What Will You Do Today, Little Russell?, Putnam, 1972.

WORK IN PROGRESS: Ride the Giant Wolf; Old Swayback; Scarleaf.

AVOCATIONAL INTERESTS: Target shooting (named professional rifle marksman at National Target Shoot, 1959-60); early American life styles, especially Indian.

* * *

WAKEMAN, Frederic (Evans), Jr. 1937-

PERSONAL: Born December 12, 1937, in Kansas City, Kan.; son of Frederic Evans (an author) and Margaret (Keyes) Wakeman; married Nancy Schuster, December 28, 1957 (divorced January, 1974); children: Frederic Evans III. *Education:* Harvard University, A.B., 1959; Institut d'etudes politiques, graduate study, 1959-60; University of California, Berkeley, M.A., 1962, Ph.D., 1965. *Home:* 922 Ventura, Albany, Calif. 94707. *Office:* Center for Chinese Studies, University of California, Berkeley, Calif. 94720.

CAREER: University of California, Berkeley, assistant professor of Chinese history, 1965-67; Inter-University Program for Chinese Language Studies, Taipei, Taiwan, director, 1967-68; University of California, Berkeley, associate professor, 1968-70, professor of Chinese history, 1971—, chairman of Center for Chinese Studies. *Member:* American Historical Association, Association for Asian Studies, Society for Ch'ing Studies. *Awards, honors:* Guggenheim fellowship, 1973-74; nominated for National Book Award, 1974, for *History and Will: Philosophical Perspectives of the Thought of Mao Tse-tung.*

WRITINGS: Seventeen Royal Palms Drive (novel), New American Library, 1962; *Strangers at the Gate: Social Disorder in South China, 1839-1861,* University of California Press, 1966; *Nothing Concealed: Essays in Honor of Liu Yu-yun,* Chinese Materials and Research Aids Service Center, 1970; (with Thomas Metcalf and Edward Tannenbaum) *A World History,* Wiley, 1973; *History and Will: Philosophical Perspectives of the Thought of Mao Tse-tung,* University of California Press, 1973; (editor) *Conflict and Control in Late Imperial China,* University of California Press, in press; *The Fall of Imperial China,* Free Press, in press. Contributor of articles and reviews to scholarly journals.

WORK IN PROGRESS: A book on the Manchu conquest of China in the seventeenth century.

WALKER, Diana 1925-

PERSONAL: Born April 24, 1925, in Stoke Poges, Buckinghamshire, England; daughter of George Frederick (a civil servant) and Lillian (Loring) Taylor; married Barrie Neil Walker (a technical engineer), June 4, 1960. *Education:* Attended Blackpool Art College, Blackpool, England, 1944-46. *Address:* R.R. 1, Bolton LOP IAO, Ontario, Canada. *Agent:* Paul R. Reynolds, Inc., 599 Fifth Ave., New York, N.Y. 10017.

CAREER: Secretary, at various times, 1945-65.

WRITINGS—Juvenile: *Caterpillar Capers,* Thomas Nelson, 1947; *Singing Schooners,* Abelard, 1965; *An Eagle for Courage,* Abelard, 1967; *Mystery of Black Gut,* Abelard, 1968; *Skiers of Ste. Celeste* (Junior Literary Guild selection), Abelard, 1970; *Never Step on an Indian's Shadow,* Abelard, 1973.

WORK IN PROGRESS: The Year of the Horse, for Abelard; a story set on Prince Edward Island.

* * *

WALKER, (Addison) Mort 1923-

PERSONAL: Born September 3, 1923, in El Dorado, Kan.; son of Robin A. (an architect) and Carolyn (a designer and illustrator; maiden name, Richards) Walker; married Jean Suffill, March 12, 1949; children: Greg, Brian, Polly, Morgan, Marjorie, Neal, Roger. *Education:* University of Missouri, B.A., 1948. *Residence:* Greenwich, Conn.

CAREER: Hallmark Greeting Cards, Kansas City, Mo., designer, 1942-43; Dell Publishing Co., New York, N.Y., editor, 1948-50; King Features Syndicate, New York, creator of comic strips "Beetle Bailey," 1950—, "Hi and Lois," 1954—, "Sam's Strip," 1961-63, and "Boner's Ark," 1969—. Former member of President's Committee for Employing the Handicapped; has given public lectures. *Military service:* U.S. Army, 1943-46; served in Europe; became first lieutenant. *Member:* National Cartoonists Society (past president), Artists and Writers Association, Newspaper Comic Council. *Awards, honors:* National Cartoonists Society Reuben Award for best cartoonist, 1954; Banshee Award, 1955; National Cartoonists Society plaque for best comic strip, 1966, 1969; Il Secolo XIX, 1972.

WRITINGS—Cartoon books: *Beetle Bailey and Sarge,* Dell, 1958; (with Dik Browne) *Trixie,* Avon, 1960; *Beetle Bailey,* Grosset, 1968; *Fall Out Laughing, Beetle Bailey,* Grosset, 1969; *At Ease, Beetle Bailey,* Grosset, 1970; (with Browne) *Hi and Lois,* Grosset, 1970; *I Don't Want to Be Out Here Any More than You Do, Beetle Bailey,* Grosset, 1970; *Sam's Strip Lives,* Carriage House, 1970; *What Is It Now, Beetle Bailey?,* Grosset, 1971; (with Browne) *Hi and Lois in Darkest Suburbia,* Grosset, 1971; *Beetle Bailey on Parade,* Grosset, 1972; *I'll Throw the Book at You, Beetle Bailey,* Grosset, 1973; *We're All in the Same Boat, Beetle Bailey,* Grosset, 1973; *Shape Up or Ship Out, Beetle Bailey,* Grosset, 1974.

Juvenile fiction; illustrated by Dik Browne: *Most,* Windmill Books, 1971; *Land of Lost Things,* Windmill Books, 1972.

Work is widely anthologized in the United States and abroad. Contributor of cartoons to popular magazines, including *New Yorker* and *Saturday Evening Post.* Former editor of *National Cartoonists Society Album.*

SIDELIGHTS: Walker has said: "I try to make people laugh, and keep my own views out of it. People don't want ideas pressed on them. They get plenty of that on the editorial page. I wouldn't want a clown in a circus to deliver an ecology speech. I wouldn't want to find anti-war messages on my golf balls. The papers are full enough of tragedy. The comic pages should be a relief from that other stuff.'' Walker began selling his cartoons at the age of twelve. "Beetle Bailey" now appears in some twelve hundred publications, including those of thirty-seven foreign countries.

BIOGRAPHICAL/CRITICAL SOURCES: Greenwich Review, October 12, 1972.

* * *

WALL, Wendy Somerville 1942-

PERSONAL: Born November 4, 1942, in New York, N.Y.; daughter of John Alden (an accountant) and Joan (an advertising executive; maiden name, Grant) Somerville; married John T. Wall (in finance), April 16, 1966; children: Jonathan Alden, Clinton David. *Education:* Rosemont College, B.A., 1964. *Politics:* Independent. *Religion:* Roman Catholic. *Home:* 6309 Massachusetts Ave., Washington, D.C. 20016.

CAREER: Ladies' Home Journal, New York, N.Y., editor, 1964-68; *Reader's Digest,* New York, N.Y., reporter-researcher, 1968-70. *Member:* New York Association of Laity (president, 1971-72).

WRITINGS: The Creative Wedding Handbook, Newman, 1973.

WORK IN PROGRESS: Research on biographies of famous women and on women's current role conflicts and accomplishments; children's material.

* * *

WALLACE, William A(lan) 1935-

PERSONAL: Born October 21, 1935, in Albany, N.Y.; son of William E. (an oil company employee) and Claire Mae (Chamberlain) Wallace; married Emma Jean Horton, July 28, 1958; children: Jack Norris, William Edward, Robert Kyle, Roland Frederick. *Education:* Illinois Institute of Technology, B.Ch.E., 1956; Rensselaer Polytechnic Institute, M.S., 1961, Ph.D., 1965. *Home:* Hillcrest Circle, Averill Park, N.Y. 12018. *Office:* Rensselaer Polytechnic Institute, Troy, N.Y. 12181.

CAREER: Armour Research Foundation, Chicago, Ill., research engineer, 1956-57; Rensselaer Polytechnic Institute, Troy, N.Y., instructor and research assistant, 1960-65, director of urban-environmental studies, 1968-71, director of program in public management, 1971—. *Military service:* U.S. Navy, communications officer, 1957-60. *Member:* Institute of Management Sciences, Operations Research Society of America, American Association of University Professors, Epsilon Delta Sigma, Sigma Xi.

WRITINGS: (Contributor) R. M. Haas, editor, *Science Technology and Marketing,* American Marketing Association, 1966; (contributor) S. A. Yefsky, editor, *Law Enforcement Science and Technology,* Thompson Book Co., 1967; (contributor) W. J. Bursnall, G. K. Chacko, and G. W. Morgenthaler, editors, *Planning Challenges of the Seventies in the Public Domain,* American Astronautical Society, 1970; (editor with Ernest Uhr) *Brands: A Selected Annotated Bibliography,* American Marketing Association, 1972; (with Richard Heroux) *Financial Analysis and the New Community Development Process,* Praeger, 1973; (with Edward Risse and William Shuster) *Educational Resources in New York State in Environmental Design, Engineering, and Management,* Office of Sciences and Technology, New York State Office of Education, in press. Contributor to journals in his field.

WORK IN PROGRESS: Planning in Higher Education: An Operations Research Approach, completion expected in 1974; research in cost-effectiveness in public systems and capital budgeting for municipalities.

* * *

WALSH, Donald Devenish 1903-

PERSONAL: Born October 31, 1903, in Providence, R.I.; son of John Francis and Catherine (Devenish) Walsh; married Donna Rowell (an editor), May 22, 1954. *Education:* Harvard University, S.B. (magna cum laude), 1925. *Politics:* Democrat. *Religion:* None. *Home:* Bushnell Lane, Madison, Conn. 06443.

CAREER: Choate School, Wallingford, Conn., teacher of French and Spanish, 1928-53, 1955-59, director of studies, 1952-53, 1955-59; Modern Language Association of America, New York, N.Y., assistant secretary, 1953-55, director of foreign language program, 1959-65; Northeast Conference on the Teaching of Foreign Languages, Madison, Conn., secretary-treasurer, 1964-73. Trustee of Hammonasset School and The Country School, both in Madison. *Member:* American Association of Teachers of Spanish and Portuguese (president, 1959), Modern Language Association of America, American Association of Teachers of French (honorary member), American Translators Association, P.E.N. American Center. *Awards, honors:* L.H.D., Middlebury College, 1968; Northeast Conference Award, 1974.

WRITINGS: Introductory Spanish: Reading, Writing, Speaking, privately printed, 1944, Norton, 1946, revised edition published as *A Brief Introduction to Spanish,* Norton, 1950; (with Harlan Sturm) *Repaso: Lectura, explicacion, practica,* Norton, 1948, revised edition, 1971; *What's What: A List of Useful Terms for the Teacher of Modern Languages* (booklet), Modern Language Association of America, 1963, 3rd edition, 1965; (with Oscar Cargill and William Charvat) *The Publication of Academic Writing* (booklet), Modern Language Association of America, 1966; *A Handbook for Teachers of Spanish and Portuguese,* Heath, 1969.

Editor: *Seis relatos americanos,* Norton, 1943; *Cuentos y versos americanos,* Norton, 1942, revised edition published as *Cuentos americanos con algunos versos,* 1948, 3rd edition (with Lawrence Bayard Kiddle), 1970; (and author of introduction and notes) Arturo Uslar Pietri, *Las Lanzas coloradas,* Norton, 1944; (and author of introduction and notes) Jesus Goytortua Santos, *Pensativa,* Crofts, 1947; Goytortua Santos, *Lluvia roja,* Appleton, 1949; Gregorio Martinez Sierra, *Sueno de una noche de agosto,* Norton, 1952.

Translator: Pablo Neruda, *The Captain's Verses,* New Directions, 1972; Neruda, *Residence on Earth,* New Directions, 1973; Julio Alvarez Del Vayo, *Give Me Combat,* Little, Brown, 1973; Ernesto Cardenal, *In Cuba,* New Directions, 1974. Former editor, *Hispania.*

WORK IN PROGRESS: Translating Ernesto Cardenal's poetry and his "The Bible in Solentiname," and the poetry of Angel Gonzalez.

WALSH, James
See ROBINSON, Frank M(alcolm)

* * *

WALSH, William B(ertalan) 1920-

PERSONAL: Born April 26, 1920, in Brooklyn, N.Y.; son of Joseph W. and Irene Walsh; married Helen Rundvold, December 19, 1943; children: William, Jr., John Thomas, Thomas Stephen. *Education:* St. John's University, Jamaica, N.Y., B.S., 1940; Georgetown University, M.D., 1943. *Home:* 5101 Westpath Way, Washington, D.C. 20016. *Office:* Project HOPE, 2233 Wisconsin Ave. N.W., Washington, D.C. 20007.

CAREER: Served internship at Long Island College Hospital, Brooklyn, N.Y.; resident at Georgetown University Hospital, Washington, D.C.; heart specialist in private practice, 1946-58; People-to-People Health Foundation, Inc., Washington, D.C., founder, president, and medical director of Health Opportunity for People Everywhere (Project HOPE; a volunteer-staffed overseas health operation conducted from *S.S. Hope*), 1958—. Clinical professor and member of board of regents at Georgetown University. Vice-chairman of President's Advisory Committee for Selection of Doctors, Dentists, and Allied Specialists for the Selective Service System; co-chairman of President's Committee on Medicine and Health Professions; member of President's Committee on Employment of the Handicapped; vice-chairman of health resources advisory committee of Office of Civil and Defense Mobilization; member of President's Advisory Committee on the Physical Fitness of Youth; chairman of President's Project Vietnam (a pilot program to send volunteer American physicians to help with the medical needs of South Vietnamese civilians). Vice-chairman of People-to-People Programs, Inc. Consultant to Surgeon General of U.S. Air Force. *Military service:* U.S. Navy, during World War II; served as medical officer aboard a destroyer in the South Pacific.

MEMBER: American Medical Association, National Medical Veterans Society (past president), District of Columbia Medical Society, Alpha Omega Alpha. *Awards, honors:* Awards from colleges and universities include D.Sc., Georgetown University, 1962; Povarello Medal from College of Steubenville, 1966; D.H.L. from Beaver College, 1967; D.Health Sciences from University of Cartagena, 1967; D.Sc. from St. John's University, 1968; LL.D. from Trinity College, 1969; D.Sc. from Howard University, 1969; D.H.L. from Carthage College, 1970; Laetare Medal from University of Notre Dame, 1970. Awards from professional organizations include Health U.S.A. Award, 1961; special service award from American Association of Industrial Nurses, 1963; certificate of meritorious service from Medical Society of the District of Columbia, 1964; citation for outstanding contribution to international goodwill from Committee for the Handicapped of People-to-People Programs, Inc., 1967, distinguished service award, 1967; fellowship from International College of Dentists, 1967; distinguished service award from American Medical Authors, 1967; Stritch Medal from Loyola University Medical Center, 1970; distinguished service award from American College of Cardiology, 1971. Awards from governmental bodies include distinguished service award from U.S. Information Agency, 1961; named Knight of the Magisterial Palms and Knight of the Daniel A. Carrion Order by Government of Peru, both 1962; gold medal from City of Trujillo, Peru, 1963; Star of October from City of Guayaquil, Ecuador, 1964; Medal of Merit from Government of Ecuador, 1964; named Grand Official Grade of Order of Ruben Dario by Government of Nicaragua, 1966; Order of San Carlos of Government of Colombia, 1967; decoration de la Republique de Tunisie from Government of Tunisia, 1970; officer of Order of the Tunisian Republic, 1971; named honorary citizen of State of Rio Grande do Norte, Brazil, 1972, City of Natal, Brazil, 1972, and State of Alagoas, Brazil, 1973; named commander of Order of the Southern Cross by Government of Brazil, 1974. Other awards include Silver Anvil Award of American Public Relations Association, 1960; International Freedom Festival Award from City of Detroit, 1961; volunteer of the year award from American Society of Association Executives, 1961; humanitarian of the year award from Lions International, 1961; service to mankind award from Sertoma International, 1961; national citizenship award from Military Chaplains Association of the United States of America, 1963; Thomas Wildey Award from Independent Order of Odd Fellows, 1965; Order of Magellan Medal from Circumnavigators Club, 1965; distinguished service award from Institute of International Education and Reader's Digest Foundation, 1967; distinguished service medal from Theodore Roosevelt Association, 1967; Americas Award from Americas Foundation, 1967; Freedom Leadership Medal from Freedoms Foundation at Valley Forge, 1968; Lawrence C. Kline World Peace Award, 1968.

WRITINGS: A Ship Called Hope, Dutton, 1964; *Yanqui, Come Back!,* Dutton, 1966; *HOPE in the East,* Dutton, 1970.

WORK IN PROGRESS: Research on the history of Project HOPE.

SIDELIGHTS: The idea for Project HOPE originated during Walsh's period of military service in the South Pacific. He decided that one way of improving substandard medical conditions and lack of facilities abroad was by using a floating medical center to visit, help, teach, and leave behind trained local personnel. The *S.S. Hope* has, since 1960, visited Brazil, Ceylon, Colombia, Ecuador, Guinea, Indonesia, Nicaragua, Peru, Vietnam, Tunisia, and the West Indies. It goes only at the invitation of the country it visits, bringing a fully-staffed hospital ship equipped for teaching and practice. More recently Project HOPE has established fourteen land-based programs, including two in the United States (in a Navajo Indian community in Arizona and in Laredo, Tex.), all supported by donations from American industry, foundations, and individuals.

BIOGRAPHICAL/CRITICAL SOURCES: Monsanto Magazine, December, 1965; *Medical World News,* April 21, 1967; *U.S. Congressional Record,* March 21, 1968; *Lab World,* May, 1969; *Norwegian Medical Journal,* August 15, 1970; *Finance,* November, 1972; *World,* April 10, 1973.

* * *

WALTERS, Janet Lane 1936-

PERSONAL: Born July 17, 1936, in Wilkensburg, Pa.; daughter of Norman Martin (a steelworker) and Nettie Agnes Lane; married Denny W. Walters (a physician), August 14, 1959; children: Keith, Scott, Sharon, Veronica (adopted). *Education:* Western Pennsylvania Hospital School of Nursing, R.N. *Politics:* Independent. *Religion:* Presbyterian. *Home:* 325 Old Plank Rd., Butler, Pa. 16001.

CAREER: Registered nurse in Pittsburgh, Pa., 1958-60,

and in Akron, Ohio, 1960. *Member:* Pennsylvania Poetry Society, Butler Poetry Society, Butler Writers Guild (vice-president, 1973-74).

WRITINGS: New Nurse in Town, Lennox Hill, 1973; *Pediatric Nurse,* Lennox Hill, 1973; *New Head Nurse,* Lennox Hill, 1974. Contributor of short stories to journals.

WORK IN PROGRESS: The Reluctant Student Nurse; poetry; short stories.

AVOCATIONAL INTERESTS: Studying music composition, gourmet cooking, reading, and being with people.

* * *

WALVIN, James 1942-

PERSONAL: Born February 1, 1942, in Manchester, England; son of James (an engineer) and Emma (Wood) Walvin. *Education:* University of Keele, B.A. (first class honors), 1964; McMaster University, M.A. (first class honors), 1965; University of York, Ph.D., 1970. *Home:* 24 Holgate Rd., York, England. *Agent:* Busby and Rose, John St., York, England. *Office:* Department of History, University of York, York, England.

CAREER: University of York, York, England, currently member of faculty in department of history.

WRITINGS: (With M. J. Craton) *A Jamaican Plantation,* University of Toronto Press, 1970; *The Black Presence,* Orbach & Chambers, 1971, Schocken, 1972; *Black and White: The Negro and English Society, 1555-1945,* Allen Lane, 1972.

* * *

WALZ, Jay 1907-

PERSONAL: Born October 26, 1907, in South Bend, Ind., son of George H. and Nellie (Rupel) Walz; married Audrey Boyers (a writer), March 6, 1934; children: Christopher, Terry. *Education:* University of Notre Dame, B.A., 1929. *Home:* 103 MacLaren St., Ottawa, Ontario, Canada. *Office: New York Times,* 150 Wellington St., Ottawa, Ontario, Canada.

CAREER: South Bend News-Times, South Bend, Ind., reporter, 1929-35; *Washington Post,* Washington, D.C., reporter, 1935-41; Office of Price Administration, Washington, D.C., information officer, 1941-43; *New York Times,* New York, N.Y., member of Washington Bureau, 1943-58, correspondent in Middle East, 1958-64, in Canada, 1964—. President of South Bend Symphony Orchestra, 1933-35. *Member:* National Press Club (Ottawa), Rideau Club (Ottawa).

WRITINGS: The Middle East, Atheneum, 1965.

With wife, Audrey Walz: *The Bizarre Sisters,* Duell, 1950; *The Undiscovered Country* (novel), Duell, 1958; *Portrait of Canada,* American Heritage Press, 1970.

SIDELIGHTS: The Undiscovered Country, wrote the *New York Times,* is "based on what was, in its day, a sensational, hinted-at-but-never-proved scandal—the affair between the famous Arctic explorer, Elisha Kane and Maggie Fox, the pretty and notorious spiritualist." Jeanette Mursky pronounced the novel "extremely good reading," and added, "From material gathered by searching through books . . . newspaper files . . . diaries, letters and memoirs, [the authors] have revealed a touching love story. . . ."

WAMSLEY, Gary L(ee) 1935-

PERSONAL: Born August 18, 1935, in Falls City, Neb.; son of William Charles (a plant engineer) and Jacqueline (Callahand) Wamsley; married Diane M. Stevenson, September 28, 1956; married Susan B. Gauthier, March 5, 1971; children: (first marriage) Christina Marie, Carrie Lynn, Maria Alissa, Alissa Ann, David Bradley; (second marriage) Jonathan Asbury. *Education:* Attended El Camino College, 1953-54; University of California, Los Angeles, B.A., 1958, M.A., 1961; University of Pittsburgh, Ph.D., 1968. *Home:* 1500 Haskell Rd., Lawrence, Kan. 66044. *Office:* Institute of Public Affairs and Community Development, Annex C, University of Kansas, Lawrence, Kan. 66045.

CAREER: State of California, Department of Finance, Sacramento, assistant budget analyst, 1963-64, research assistant, 1964-65; San Diego State College (now University), San Diego, Calif., assistant professor of political science, 1966-67; Vanderbilt University, Nashville, Tenn., assistant professor of political science, 1967-72, co-director of Robert A. Taft Seminars on Politics and Government, 1967-70; University of Kansas, Lawrence, associate professor of political science, and director of Institute of Public Affairs and Community Development, 1972—. Member of Inter-University Seminar on the Armed Forces and Society, 1968—, Participant, National Science Foundation Institute on Mass Political Communications, Ohio University, 1971. *Military service:* U.S. Air Force, 1959-63; became captain. *Member:* International Studies Association, American Society for Public Administration, American Political Science Association.

WRITINGS: Selective Service and a Changing America, C. E. Merrill, 1969; (contributor) Roger Little, editor, *Selective Service and American Society,* Russell Sage, 1969; (contributor) Mayer N. Zald, editor, *Power in Organizations,* Vanderbilt University Press, 1970; (with Zald) *The Political Economy of Public Organizations,* Lexington Books, 1973; (contributor) LeRoy Rieselbach, editor, *Responsiveness of American Political Institutions,* Indiana University Press, in press; (contributor) *Southern Metropolis: Aspects of Development in Nashville,* Vanderbilt University, in press.

Contributor to publications of Division of Field Surveys and Research, George Peabody College for Teachers: *Pickens County South Carolina Public Schools, Webster Parish Louisiana Public Schools,* and *Calcasieu Parish Louisiana Public Schools,* all published in 1968.

Contributor to *Americana Annual,* and to journals, including *American Journal of Sociology, Journalism Quarterly, Business and Government Review,* and *Social Science Quarterly.* Member of editorial board, *Administrative Science Quarterly,* 1972-73, and *Administration and Society,* 1974—.

WORK IN PROGRESS: Research on the politics and administration of ground water conservation.

* * *

WARD, James A(rthur) 1941-

PERSONAL: Born June 9, 1941, in Buffalo, N.Y.; son of James A. (an electrical engineer) and Rose (an English teacher; maiden name, Pfendler) Ward; married Roberta Shannon, August 28, 1965; children: Anne Elizabeth. *Education:* Purdue University, B.A., 1964, M.A., 1965; Louisiana State University, Ph.D., 1969. *Politics:* Democrat.

Religion: Roman Catholic. *Home:* 3109 East Court Dr., Chattanooga, Tenn. 37404. *Office:* Department of History, University of Tennessee, Chattanooga, Tenn. 37401.

CAREER: University of Tennessee, Chattanooga, assistant professor, 1969-74, associate professor of history, 1974—. *Member:* Organization of American Historians, Economic History Association, Railway and Locomotive Historical Society. *Awards, honors:* American Philosophical Society grant, 1972.

WRITINGS: That Man Haupt: A Biography of Herman Haupt. Louisiana State University Press, 1973. Contributor to *Pennsylvania Magazine of History and Biography, Journal of Southern History,* and *Business History Review.*

WORK IN PROGRESS: John Edgar Thomson: A Biography, completion expected in 1975; *The Philadelphia Parties: A Study of Regional Impact on the National Economy,* 1976.

AVOCATIONAL INTERESTS: Bridge, travel, architecture, reading, summers on a private lake in the Adirondacks.

* * *

WARD, Ralph T(homas) 1927-

PERSONAL: Born July 18, 1927, in New York, N.Y.; son of Royce Clifford (a railroad engineer) and Madeline (Smith) Ward.

CAREER: Illustrator.

WRITINGS: Steamboats: A History of the Early Adventure, Bobbs-Merrill, 1973; *Ships through History,* Bobbs-Merrill, 1973; *Pirates in History,* York Press, 1974.

* * *

WARD, Robert E(rnest) 1927-

PERSONAL: Born April 17, 1927, in Utica, N.Y.; son of Ernest R. (an electrician) and Maud (Schelhorn) Ward; married Catherine Coogan (a university instructor), April 7, 1969. *Education:* Syracuse University, A.B., 1953; State University of New York at Albany, M.A., 1954; University of Iowa, Ph.D., 1969. *Politics:* Democrat. *Religion:* Roman Catholic. *Home:* 842 Ironwood Dr., Bowling Green, Ky. 42101. *Office:* Department of English, Western Kentucky University, Bowling Green, Ky. 42101.

CAREER: Worked as a high school English teacher in New York, 1954-65; Western Kentucky University, Bowling Green, assistant professor, 1969-73, associate professor of English, 1973—. *Military service:* U.S. Army, Engineers, 1946-47, 1950-51; served in Korea. *Member:* Modern Language Association of America, Modern Humanities Research Association, American Society for Eighteenth Century Studies, American Committee on Irish Studies, Irish-American Cultural Institute, Southern Atlantic Modern Language Association, Phi Delta Kappa.

WRITINGS: (Editor) *Prince of Dublin Printers: The Letters of George Faulkner,* University Press of Kentucky, 1972; (with wife, Catherine Coogan Ward) *Checklist and Census of 400 Imprints of George Faulkner from 1725-1775* (monograph), Ragnarok Press, 1973. Contributor to *Eire-Ireland.*

WORK IN PROGRESS: Collection and transcription of Irish imprints of George Faulkner; *Five Minor Irish Dramatists of the Eighteenth Century,* for Twayne.

AVOCATIONAL INTERESTS: Folklore, folk music, colonial history, western art, baroque and classical music.

WARD, Robert Elmer 1937-

PERSONAL: Born March 7, 1937, in Cleveland, Ohio; son of Elmer Frank and Elsa Marie (Leyerle) Ward; married Darlene Kay Buschow; children: Robert E., Jr., Heidi Darlene, Kurt R. *Education:* Attended Inter-Agency Bank Examiner's School and Fenn College; Baldwin-Wallace College, B.A., 1961; Indiana University, M.A., 1963; Western Reserve University (now Case Western Reserve University), further graduate study, 1963-65; Vanderbilt University, Ph.D., 1967; University of Akron, postdoctoral study, 1971—. *Home:* 7204 Langerford Dr., Parma, Ohio 44129. *Office:* Society for German-American Studies, 7204 Langerford Dr., Parma, Ohio 44129.

CAREER: Employed by Cleveland Trust Co., 1955-56, National City Bank, 1956-57, and U.S. Treasury Department, National Bank Examiners Division, 1957-58, all in Cleveland, Ohio; high school teacher of German, business mathematics, and English in Cleveland, 1962-64; University of Toledo, Toledo, Ohio, instructor in German, 1965-66; Tennessee Technological University, Cookeville, assistant professor of German, 1966-67; Youngstown State University, Youngstown, Ohio, associate professor of German, 1967-73, chairman of department of foreign languages and literatures, 1967-73; City of Cleveland, director of project for Department of Human Resources and Economic Development, 1973-74; currently with Society for German-American Studies, Parma, Ohio. Instructor at Cleveland College, 1963-64, and at Pennsylvania State University, 1971. German language announcer for WXEN-FM Radio, 1963-64. Accountant and bookkeeper for Curiale Meats, 1956-73; accountant and tax consultant for Badura Builders, 1963-73; West German representative for Lang & Lang, Inc., summer, 1966; translator for Wean Industries, 1966. Public speaker.

MEMBER: Society for German-American Studies (chairman, 1968—), American Association of Teachers of German, American Historical Society of Germans from Russia, American Judicature Society, Verband deutschsprachiger Schriftsteller in Amerika (honorary president, 1974—), Danube Swabians of America, Pennsylvania German Society, Western Reserve Historical Society, Cleveland Gaelic Society, Greater Cleveland German Cultural Gardens Association (first vice-president and member of board of trustees, 1974-75), German Central Organization (Cleveland), Phi Kappa Phi, Delta Phi Alpha. *Awards, honors:* Hilbert T. Ficken Memorial Citation for excellence in the teaching of foreign languages, from Baldwin-Wallace College, 1969; certificate of merit from American Judicature Society, 1973.

WRITINGS: Progress and Problems in the Teaching of Modern Foreign Languages, Waechter und Anzeiger Publishing, 1964; *Key to Translation Techniques for German,* privately printed, 1964; *Deutsche Lyrik aus Amerika: Eine Auswahl* (title means "German Lyric Poetry from America: A Selection"), Literary Society Foundation, 1969; *An Exercise Manual for Reading Fraktur,* Department of Foreign Languages and Literatures, Youngstown State University, 1970.

Other writings: *Unser Geist: Die Geschichte der Familien Ward, Leyerle, und Hohenstatt* (title means "Our Spirit: The History of the Families Ward, Leyerle and Hohenstatt"), 1971; *Handbook of German-American Creative Literature: 1675-1975,* in press; (contributor) Gerhard Friesen, editor, *Festschrift in Honor of Dr. Karl J. R. Arnst,* in press.

Co-editor of "Bibliography Americana Germanica," a column in *German Quarterly,* 1970-72. Contributor of about thirty-five articles and reviews to German language publications and to *Michigan Heritage* and *Grand Prairie Historical Bulletin.* Editor-in-chief of *German-American Studies: A Journal of History and Literature,* 1969—.

WORK IN PROGRESS: The German-Speaking Element of Greater Cleveland, with John R. Sinnema, publication by German-American Cultural Society of Cleveland expected in 1976; "Die deutsche Sprache in Ohio seit 1920," an article for inclusion in *Handbuch der deutschen Sprache in Nordamerika,* edited by Heinz Kloss, publication by Institut fuer deutsche Sprache expected in 1976.

* * *

WARDE, William F.
See NOVACK, George (Edward)

* * *

WARNER, Val 1946-

PERSONAL: Born January 15, 1946, in Harrow, England; daughter of Alister Alfred (a schoolmaster) and Ivy Miriam (a teacher; maiden name, Robins) Warner. *Education:* Somerville College, Oxford, B.A. (honors), 1968. *Politics:* Socialist. *Religion:* Atheist. *Residence:* England.

CAREER: Teacher and librarian in London, England, 1969-72; free-lance Writer in London, England, 1972—. *Awards, honors:* Translators' grant from Arts Council of Great Britain, 1972, for Corbire translations.

WRITINGS: These Yellow Photos (poems), Carcanet, 1971; *Under the Penthouse* (poems), Carcanet, 1973; (translator) Tristan Corbire, *The Centenary Corbire,* Carcanet, 1974. Contributor of poems to magazines, including *Scotsman, Poetry Nation, Antaeus, Tribune, Poetry Review, Dublin Magazine,* and *Critical Quarterly.*

WORK IN PROGRESS: Before Lunch, a sequence of about a hundred and fifty sonnets, for Carcanet; editing *The Background to Modernism,* the essential texts of Modernism in England, for Carcanet; a novel.

* * *

WARNER, Wayne E(arl) 1933-

PERSONAL: Born June 4, 1933, in Wendling, Ore.; son of Harry E. (a mill worker) and Ethel (Bowers) Warner; married Evangeline Joy Mitchell, May 3, 1958 (died, August 28, 1973); children: Lori Lee, Avonna Marie, Lolisa Joy. *Education:* Eugene Technical School, student, 1956-58; Eugene Bible College, ministerial diploma, 1961; Drury College, graduate study, 1969, 1970. *Politics:* Republican. *Home:* 3055 South Ferguson, Springfield, Mo. 65807. *Office:* Gospel Publishing House, 1445 Boonville, Springfield, Mo. 65802.

CAREER: Ordained minister of the Assemblies of God, 1963; pastor in Yacolt, Wash., 1962, 1963, Perryton, Tex., 1963, 1964, and Hopedale, Ill., 1964-68; *Mackinaw Valley News,* Minier, Ill., editor, 1964-68; Gospel Publishing House, Springfield, Mo., book editor, 1968—. *Military service:* U.S. Army, 1953-55; became sergeant. *Member:* Missouri Writer's Guild.

WRITINGS: Good Morning, Lord: Devotions for Servicemen, Baker Book, 1971; *1000 Stories and Quotations of Famous People,* Baker Book, 1972.

WORK IN PROGRESS: Two books, *Letters to Tony* and *Faith, Hope, and Love.*

* * *

WARREN, Earl 1891-1974

March 19, 1891—July 9, 1974; former chief justice of the United States Supreme Court. Obituaries: *New York Times,* July 10, 1974, July 13, 1974; *Time,* July 22, 1974; *Newsweek,* July 22, 1974.

* * *

WARREN, (Francis) Eugene 1941-

PERSONAL: Born October 3, 1941, in Craig, Colo.; son of George William (a farmer) and Elizabeth (Wilson) Warren; married Rosalee Cecelia Bazil, January 19, 1963; children: Cynthia, Matthew, Timothy, Jennifer. *Education:* Attended College of Emporia, 1959-62; Kansas State Teachers College, B.A., 1966, M.A., 1967. *Politics:* "Radical Christian." *Religion:* Christian. *Home:* 107 South Rolla, Rolla, Mo. 65401. *Office:* Department of English, University of Missouri, Rolla, Mo. 65401.

CAREER: Has worked as farmhand, grocery clerk, orderly, truck driver, cable television lineman, janitor; University of Missouri, Rolla, instructor, 1967-73, assistant professor of English, 1973—. *Member:* Conference on Christianity and Literature, New York C. S. Lewis Society, Fine Arts Fellowship.

WRITINGS: Christographia (poems), Ktaadn Poetry Press, 1973; *The Fifth Season* (poems), Cranium Press, 1974; *Rumors of Light* (poems), Grafiktrakts, 1974. Contributor of poems and articles to professional journals. Editor, Grafiktrakts, a series of pamphlets, 1974—. Contributing editor, *Post-American,* 1973—.

WORK IN PROGRESS: Two books of verse, *Bareback in Kansas* and *Songs of the End-Time.*

SIDELIGHTS: Warren told *CA:* "Raised on a farm, S.W. of Topeka, Kan., the rhythms and creatures of that area are a part of who I am, how I sound. Organic view of verse, life, kosmos. More or less deliberate Christian since 1963—theology Anabaptist—Mennonite heritage. Large interest in apocalypse, visionary image. Happily married 11 years, 4 children. Ideas of poetry influenced by Pound, William Carlos Williams, Gerard Manley Hopkins, David the king [psalms]."

* * *

WASHBURN, (Henry) Bradford (Jr.) 1910-

PERSONAL: Born June 7, 1910, in Cambridge, Mass.; son of Henry Bradford and Edith (Hall) Washburn; married Barbara T. Polk, April 27, 1940; children: Dorothy Polk, Edward Hall, Elizabeth Bradford. *Education:* Groton School, graduate, 1929; Harvard University, A.B., 1933, graduate work at Institute of Geographical Exploration, 1934-35, A.M., 1960. *Home:* 76 Sparks St., Cambridge, Mass. 02138. *Office:* Museum of Science, Science Park, Boston, Mass. 02114.

CAREER: Museum director, mountaineer, and explorer, who began Alpine ascents at age sixteen and Alaska climbs in 1930; Harvard University, Cambridge, Mass., instructor at Institute of Geographical Explorations, 1935-42; Museum of Science, Boston, Mass., director, 1939—. Leader of National Geographic Society expeditions in Yukon, 1935, and over Mount McKinley (photographic flights),

1936-38; consultant on cold climate equipment to U.S. Army Air Forces and director of Alaskan test projects, 1942-45; leader or co-leader of other Alaskan expeditions, mainly on Mount McKinley, 1947, 1949, 1951, 1955, 1965; his first ascents of Alaska peaks include Mount Lucania, 1937, Mount Sanford and Mount Marcus, 1938, Mount Bertha, 1940, Mount Hayes, 1941, west ridge of Mount McKinley, 1951. Director or trustee of John Hancock Mutual Life Insurance Co., New England Telephone & Telegraph Co., National Rowing Foundation, Inc., and WGBH Educational Foundation, Inc. Member of advisory bodies to National Armed Forces Museum, 1964-68, U.S. Commissioner of Education, 1965-66, and Secretary of the Interior (on national parks), 1966—. Member of board of overseers, Harvard College, 1955-61; member of Massachusetts Rhodes Scholars Committee, 1959-64; trustee of Smith College, 1962-68. Consultant to American Heritage Press.

MEMBER: American Academy of Arts and Sciences (fellow), Arctic Institute of North America (fellow), Royal Geographical Society (London; fellow), American Geographical Society (honorary fellow), California Academy of Sciences (honorary fellow), American Association for the Advancement of Science (fellow), Groupe de Haute Montagne (France), Explorers Club (New York), Harvard Travellers Club (honorary fellow), Tavern Club (Boston); honorary member of other mountaineering, naturalist, and camera clubs in United States, England, and Canada.

AWARDS, HONORS: Cuthbert Peek Award of Royal Geographical Society, 1938, for Alaskan exploration and glacier studies; Franklin L. Burr Prize of National Geographic Society for Alaskan exploration, 1940, and Yukon exploration, 1965; Exceptional Civilian Service Award from Secretary of War, 1946; Ph.D., University of Alaska, 1951; Sc.D. from Tufts University and Colby College, 1957, and Northeastern University, 1958; Gold Medal of Harvard Travellers Club, 1959; Bradford Washburn Gold Medal and Award was established in his honor by trustees of Museum of Science, 1964; Ph.D., University of Suffolk, 1965; Richard Hopper Day Medal of Philadelphia Academy of Arts and Sciences, 1966; Julius Adams Stratton Prize of Friends of Switzerland, 1970; Certificate of Honor, National Conference on the Humanities, 1971; Sc.D., University of Massachusetts, 1972.

WRITINGS: The Trails and Peaks of the Presidential Range of the White Mountains (guide book), Davis Press, 1926; *Mount McKinley and the Alaska Range in Literature* (descriptive bibliography), Museum of Science (Boston), 1951; (with Caroline Harrison) *Allan and Trisha Visit Science Park* (juvenile), Little, Brown, 1953; *A Tourist Guide to Mount McKinley,* Northwest Publishing, 1971. Editor, "Mount McKinley, Alaska: A Reconnaissance Map," published under auspices of Museum of Science, Swiss Foundation for Alpine Research, and American Academy of Arts and Sciences, 1960. Contributor of features to *National Geographic, Life, Mountain World,* and articles or photographs to *Look, Sports Illustrated, Illustrated London News, Scientific American, Polar Record, New England Journal of Medicine,* and other periodicals in United States, England, Japan, and Germany.

SIDELIGHTS: Before he was out of school Washburn had climbed the Matterhorn and Mount Rosa as well as most of the major peaks in the Mont Blanc chain, and had photographed the ascent of Mont Blanc and the Grepon for Burton Holmes. Aerial photography work outside of Alaska includes Bermuda in 1938, and ten flights in Switzerland to photograph the Mont Blanc, Matterhorn, and Bernese Oberland areas in 1958. His photographs have been exhibited at Museum of Modern Art and in "The World from the Air" show at Kodak Pavilion, New York World's Fair. In 1971 Washburn did field work preliminary to a mapping project covering eighty square miles in the heart of the Grand Canyon, work financed by a grant from the National Geographic Society.

* * *

WASHINGTON, C.
See PHARR, Robert D(eane)

* * *

WASSERMAN, Dale 1917-

PERSONAL: Born November 2, 1917, in Rhinelander, Wis.; son of Samuel and Hilda (Paykel) Wasserman; married Ramsay Ames (an actress), 1966. *Residence:* Palm Springs, Calif., and Malaga, Spain. *Office:* c/o Carro, Spanbock & Londin, 10 East 40th St., New York, N.Y. 10016.

CAREER: Lighting designer, director, producer; writer for theatre, motion pictures, and television, 1954—. *Member:* Dramatists Guild, Authors League of America, Writers Guild of America, East (member of national council, 1960-64), French Society of Authors and Composers, Spanish Society of Authors. *Awards, honors:* "Top TV Play of the Year" award from Publishers' Guild, 1954, for "Elisha and the Long Knives"; Writers Guild of America awards for television plays, "The Fog," 1957, "The Citadel," 1959, "I, Don Quixote," 1960, and "The Lincoln Murder Case," 1961; Outer Circle Award, 1965-66, Tony Award for best musical, 1965-66, New York Drama Critics Circle award for best musical, 1966, Variety Award, 1966, Spanish Pavillion Award, 1966, and awards from France, Spain, and Czechoslovakia, all for "Man of La Mancha"; and other awards for writing.

WRITINGS—Plays: (With Bruce Geller) "Living the Life," first produced Off-Broadway at Phoenix Theatre, 1955; "The Pencil of God," first produced in Cleveland, Ohio, at Karamu Theatre, 1961; "998," first produced in Hollywood, Calif., at Professional Workshop Theatre, 1966; *One Flew over the Cuckoo's Nest* (adapted from the novel by Ken Kesey; first produced on Broadway at Cort Theatre, November 13, 1963), Samuel French, 1970; *Man of La Mancha* (musical based on Cervantes' *Don Quixote;* music by Mitch Leigh, lyrics by Joe Darion; first produced Off-Broadway at ANTA Washington Square Theatre, November 22, 1965; run continued on Broadway at Martin Beck Theatre, March 19, 1968), Random House, 1966.

Screenplays: "World of Strangers," 1954; "The Vikings," United Artists, 1955; "Two Faces to Go," 1959; "Aboard the Flying Swan," 1962; "Jangadeiro," 1962; "Cleopatra," Twentieth Century-Fox, 1963; "Quick, Before It Melts," MGM, 1964; "Mister Buddwing," MGM, 1965; "A Walk with Love and Death," Twentieth Century-Fox, 1969; "Man of La Mancha," United Artists, 1972.

Television plays: "Elisha and the Long Knives," 1954; "The Fog," 1957; "Eichmann," 1958; "Engineer of Death," 1959; "I, Don Quixote," Dupont Show of the Month, 1959; "The Citadel," ABC, 1959; "The Power and the Glory," 1960; "The Lincoln Murder Case," 1961; "Stranger," 1962; and about twenty-five additional plays, 1955-65.

Contributor to *Redbook, True, Argosy, Variety, New York Times,* and other periodicals.

SIDELIGHTS: "Man of La Mancha" is the third-longest running musical in the history of New York theatre. It has been taken into the repertory of the Komische Oper in East Berlin. The screen rights to "One Flew over the Cuckoo's Nest" were acquired by Kirk Douglas for filming by Bryna Productions in 1974.

* * *

WATERFIELD, Robin (Everard) 1914-

PERSONAL: Born August 27, 1914, in Beccles, Suffolk, England; son of Noel Everard (a surgeon) and Ellen Mabel (Crowfoot) Waterfield; married Sophie Harper, September 17, 1945. *Education:* Attended University of London. *Religion:* Christian. *Home:* 31 Stanley Rd., Oxford, England.

CAREER: David Low (booksellers), London, England, director, 1939-50; Berkshire County Council, Berkshire County, England, child care worker, 1951-56; Church Missionary Society, London, missionary, 1957-73. Managing director of Julian & Everard (booksellers).

WRITINGS: Christians in Persia, Barnes & Noble, 1972. Contributor to religious publications.

WORK IN PROGRESS: Comprehensive Bibliography of Persia, for Garland; a book on the British in Persia.

* * *

WATERMAN, Charles F(rederick) 1913-

PERSONAL: Born December 6, 1913, in Girard, Kan.; son of Edgar Charles (a farmer) and Fannie (Price) Waterman; married Clara DeBie, 1951. *Education:* Kansas State College, A.B., 1933. *Politics:* Republican. *Home and office:* 123 North High, DeLand, Fla. 32720. *Agent:* Lurton Blassingame, 60 East 42nd St., New York, N.Y. 10017.

CAREER: Worked as a newspaper photographer, reporter, and editor in Pittsburg, Kan., Fort Scott, Kan., and San Mateo, Calif., 1934-51; Stetson University, DeLand, Fla., instructor in English, 1953; Florida Game and Fresh Water Fish Commission, DeLand, Fla., worked in public relations, 1959-60. *Military service:* U.S. Navy, during WW II; became lieutenant; received Bronze Star. *Member:* Outdoor Writers Association of America. *Awards, honors:* Florida Governor's conservation award, 1964, for articles devoted to conservation.

WRITINGS: The Hunter's World (Outdoor Life Book Club choice), Random House, 1971; *The Fisherman's World (Outdoor Life* Book Club choice), Random House, 1972; *Modern Fresh and Salt Water Fly Fishing (Outdoor Life* Book Club choice), with photographs by the author, Winchester Press, 1972; *Hunting Upland Birds (Field & Stream* Book Club selection), with photographs by the author, Winchester Press, 1972; *Hunting in America (Outdoor Life* Book Club choice), Holt, 1973; *The Part I Remember,* Winchester Press, 1974. Columnist for *Florida Times Union, Salt Water Sportsman, Fishing World,* and *Florida Wildlife.*

* * *

WATER RAT, The
See JONES, Stephen (Phillip)

* * *

WATERS, William R(oland) 1920-

PERSONAL: Born February 5, 1920, in Baltimore, Md.; son of William L. (in meat business) and Loretta (Moylan) Waters; married Regina F. Trimp, August 19, 1950; children: Gerard, Karen, Patricia, Marc. *Education:* Loyola College, Baltimore, A.B., 1942; Yale University, further study, 1943-44; Georgetown University, Ph.D., 1953; Northwestern University, postdoctoral study, 1954-55. *Religion:* Roman Catholic. *Home:* 2222 North Dayton St., Chicago, Ill. 60614. *Office:* Department of Economics, DePaul University, 2323 North Seminary Ave., Chicago, Ill. 60614.

CAREER: Loyola College, Baltimore, Md., part-time lecturer in economics, 1948-50; DePaul University, Chicago, Ill., instructor, 1950-53, assistant professor, 1953-57, associate professor, 1957-62, professor of economics, 1962—, head of Behavioral and Social Sciences Division, 1966—. Treasurer of Lincoln Park Renewal Corp., 1963—; secretary of Lincoln Park Conservation Community Council, 1967-73. *Military service:* U.S. Army Air Forces, 1942-46; served on Okinawa.

MEMBER: American Economic Association, Association for Social Economics, Economic History Association, American Association of University Professors, American Real Estate and Urban Economics Association, Gold Key Society, Pi Gamma Mu, Delta Epsilon Sigma.

WRITINGS: (Editor and contributor) *Man Among Men: An Introduction to the Behavioral and Social Sciences,* Division of Behavioral and Social Sciences, DePaul University, 1967, revised edition published as *Man and Men: An Introduction to the Study of Man in Society,* Selected Academic Readings, 1969. Contributor to *Modern Society, World Justice,* and other journals. Editor-in-chief and business editor, *Review of Social Economy,* 1965—; member of editorial advisory board, *International Journal of Social Economics,* 1973—.

WORK IN PROGRESS: Continuing research on social economics in America and on U.S. and Chicago economic development.

* * *

WATSON, Clyde 1947-

PERSONAL: Born July 25, 1947, in New York, N.Y.; daughter of Aldren Auld (an art editor, writer, and illustrator) and Nancy (an author; maiden name, Dingman) Watson. *Education:* Smith College, B.A., 1968; University of Massachusetts, Ed.D. candidate. *Home:* Vinegar Lane, Putney, Vt. 05346. *Office:* 191 Sycamore St., Watertown, Mass. 02172.

CAREER: Teacher at elementary schools in Amherst, Mass., 1968-70, and Indian Township, Me., 1970-72. *Awards, honors: Father Fox's Pennyrhymes* was named one of the best children's books of 1971 by American Library Association, *New York Times,* and Child Study Association of America, and runner-up in the Children's Division of National Book Awards, 1972.

WRITINGS—Children's books; all illustrated by her sister, Wendy Watson: (Writer of music) *Fisherman Lullabies,* World Publishing, 1968; (writer of music) Nancy Dingman Watson, *Carol to a Child,* World Publishing, 1969; *Father Fox's Pennyrhymes,* Crowell, 1971; *Tom Fox and the Apple Pie,* Crowell, 1972.

WORK IN PROGRESS: Further writing ("bad luck to talk about").

SIDELIGHTS: "I love children and I write not specifically for children but to communicate in a certain way which children understand—adults are beginning to understand the language of 'children's books' too. Lived one year in Switzerland at age eleven. I speak German and Spanish."

* * *

WATSON, Nancy Dingman

PERSONAL: Born in Paterson, N.J.; daughter of Norman McLeod and Ann (Bauer) Dingman; married Aldren A. Watson (an author and artist); children: Wendy, Peter, Clyde (daughter), Linda, Ann, Cameron, Caitlin, Thomas. *Education:* Attended Wheaton College, Norton, Mass.; Smith College, B.A., 1965. *Home:* Sugar Farm, R.D. 2, Putney, Vt. 05346. *Agent:* Marilyn Marlowe, Curtis Brown Ltd., 60 East 56th St., New York, N.Y. 10022.

CAREER: Writer. Field Worker of the American Friends Service Committee. *Member:* Authors League (New York).

WRITINGS—Juvenile books: *What Is One?*, Knopf, 1954; *Whose Birthday Is It?*, Knopf, 1954; *Toby and Doll*, Bobbs-Merrill, 1955; *When Is Tomorrow?*, Knopf, 1955; *What Does A Begin With?*, Knopf, 1956; *Annie's Spending Spree*, Viking, 1957; *Picture Book of Fairy Tales*, Garden City Books, 1957; *The Arabian Nights Picture Book*, Garden City Books, 1959; *Sugar On Snow*, Viking, 1964; *Katie's Chickens*, Knopf, 1965; *Carol to a Child*, World Publishing, 1969; *New Under the Stars*, Little, Brown, 1970; *Tommy's Mommy's Fish*, Viking, 1971; *The Birthday Goat*, Crowell, in press; *Muncus Agruncus, a Bad Little Mouse*, Western Publishing, in press; *Atlas of the American Revolution*, Western Publishing, in press.

Author of column, "One Woman's View," in *Brattleboro Daily Reformer*, 1960—.

* * *

WATSON, Wendy (McLeod) 1942-

PERSONAL: Born July 7, 1942, in Patterson, N.J.; daughter of Aldren Auld (an art editor, illustrator, and writer) and Nancy (an author; maiden name, Dingman) Watson; married Michael Donald Harrah (an actor and singer), December 20, 1970; children: one. *Education:* Bryn Mawr College, B.A. (magna cum laude with honors in Latin literature), 1964; studied painting with Jerry Farnsworth, Cape Cod, summers, 1961, 1962, and drawing and painting at National Academy of Design, 1966, 1967. *Religion:* Society of Friends (Quaker). *Residence:* New York, N.Y. *Agent:* Curtis Brown Ltd., 60 East 56th St., New York, N.Y. 10022.

CAREER: Hanover Press, Hanover, N.H., compositor and designer, 1965-66; free-lance illustrator of books, 1966—. *Member:* Authors Guild. *Awards, honors: Father Fox's Pennyrhymes* was named one of the best children's books of 1971 by American Library Association, *New York Times*, and Child Study Association of America, and was runner-up in the Children's Division of National Book Awards, 1972.

WRITINGS—Self-illustrated children's books: *Very Important Cat*, Dodd, 1958; (editor) *Fisherman Lullabies*, World Publishing, 1968; (adapter) Grimm Brothers, *The Hedgehog and the Hare*, World Publishing, 1969.

Illustrator: Yetta Speevach, *The Spider Plant*, Atheneum, 1965; *A Comic Primer*, Peter Pauper, 1966; *Love Is a Laugh*, Peter Pauper, 1967; Alice E. Christgau, *Rosabel's Secret*, W.R. Scott, 1967; Paul Tripp, *The Strawman Who Smiled by Mistake*, Doubleday, 1967; *The Poems of Longfellow*, Peter Pauper, 1967; Edna Boutwell, *Daughter of Liberty*, World Publishing, 1967; Ogden Nash, *The Cruise of the Aardvark*, M. Evans, 1967; Miska Miles, *Uncle Fonzo's Ford*, Atlantic-Little, Brown, 1968; *The Best in Offbeat Humor*, Peter Pauper, 1968; Kathryn Hitte, *When Noodlehead Went to the Fair*, Parents' Magazine Press, 1968; Nancy Dingman Watson and Clyde Watson, *Carol to a Child*, World Publishing, 1969; Louise Bachelder, compiler, *God Bless Us Everyone*, Peter Pauper, 1969; *The Jack Book*, Macmillan, for Bank Street School of Education, 1969.

Helen Keller, Scholastic Book Services, 1970; Ogden Nash, *The Animal Garden*, Deutsch, 1970; Mary H. Calhoun, *Magic in the Alley*, Atheneum, 1970; Mabel Harmer, *Lizzie, the Lost Toys Witch*, Macrae Smith, 1970; *How Dear to My Heart*, Peter Pauper, 1970; Bachelder, compiler, *Happy Thoughts*, Peter Pauper, 1970; Clyde Watson, *Father Fox's Pennyrhymes*, Crowell, 1971; *Life's Wondrous Ways*, Peter Pauper, 1971; *America! America!*, Peter Pauper, 1971; *A Gift of Mistletoe*, Peter Pauper, 1971; Charles Linn, *Probability*, Crowell, 1972; Clyde Watson, *Tom Fox and the Apple Pie*, Crowell, 1972; Clyde R. Bulla, *Open the Door and See All the People*, Crowell, 1972.

WORK IN PROGRESS: Several books ("as always").

SIDELIGHTS: "I like *very* much: Opera, theater, classical music. I make my own bread, jelly, etc., my clothes, and some of my husband's (jackets). I read all the time. I love to garden. My parents provided, indirectly, a great deal of my basic training in drawing and books in general. About my work—I just work very hard and make everything as good as possible!"

* * *

WAYNE, Jane Ellen 1938-

PERSONAL: Born April 6, 1938, in Philadelphia, Pa.; daughter of Jesse Allen and Eleanor (Brundle) Stump; married Ronald Wayne, May 26, 1957 (divorced, May 26, 1967); children: Elizabeth Jo. *Education:* Attended Grove City College, 1955-57, American Academy of Dramatic Arts, 1957, and New York University, 1957. *Politics:* Republican. *Religion:* Protestant. *Home and office:* 97-20 57th Ave., Elmhurst, N.Y. 11368. *Agent:* Gerald Pollinger, 18 Maddox St., London W.1, England.

CAREER: National Broadcasting Co., New York, N.Y., in public relations and promotion, 1957-65; Prestige Club, World's Fair, New York, N.Y., in customer relations, 1965-66; free-lance writer.

WRITINGS: The Life of Robert Taylor, Warner Paperback Library, 1973.

WORK IN PROGRESS: Kings of Tragedy, composite biographies of thirteen "doomed" male celebrities, including Clark Gable, Spencer Tracy, Montgomery Clift, Ernest Hemingway, and John Garfield.

AVOCATIONAL INTERESTS: Travel; Ms. Wayne has been all over the world, and found Alaska "the most fascinating."

WEBB, Forrest
See FORREST-WEBB, Robert

* * *

WEBB, Robert Forrest
See FORREST-WEBB, Robert

* * *

WEBER, Marc 1950-

PERSONAL: Born November 26, 1950; son of Frank John and Pauline Weber; married, September 21, 1973. *Education:* University of Colorado, B.A. and M.A., 1971.

CAREER: Poet.

WRITINGS: Forty-Eight Small Poems, University of Pittsburgh Press, 1973.

WORK IN PROGRESS: A cyclic story of frontier versus entropy, poetry.

* * *

WEBSTER, C(onstance) Muriel 1906-

PERSONAL: Born November 25, 1906, in Glasgow, Scotland; daughter of William (secretary of Scottish Liberal Association) and Mary (Hughes) Webster. *Education:* Anstey College of Physical Education, diploma, 1928; Chartered Society of Physiotherapy, diploma, 1928. *Politics:* Liberal. *Religion:* Church of Scotland. *Home:* 3 Clarendon Crescent, Edinburgh EH4 1PT, Scotland.

CAREER: Anstey College of Physical Education, Sutton, Coldfield, Scotland, lecturer in dance, 1939-55, principal, 1955-69. Examiner in physical education of University Institutes of London, Sussex, Craigie College of Education, and Dumfermline College of Physical Education. *Member:* International Association of Sports and Physical Education for Girls and Women (vice-president, 1958-74), British Association of Organisers and Lecturers in Physical Education, Physical Education Association of Great Britain and Northern Ireland, American Academy of Physical Education, Royal Scottish Country Dance Society, English Folk Dance Society.

WRITINGS: (Technical editor) Violet Alford, editor, *Handbook of European Folk Dance,* Max Parrish, 1948; (with Audrey Bambra) *Teaching Folk Dance,* Batsford, 1972.

* * *

WEBSTER, Graham 1915-

PERSONAL: Born May 31, 1915, in Stamford, Lincolnshire, England; son of Henry Alexander and Esther (Terry) Webster; married Margaret Kathleen Baxendale, November 12, 1938 (divorced, 1972); children: Anthony Graham, John Terry. *Education:* University of Manchester, M.A., 1952; University of Birmingham, Ph.D., 1959. *Politics:* Liberal-Socialist. *Religion:* Humanist. *Home:* Old School House, Chesterton, Harbury, Warwickshire CV33 9LF, England. *Office:* Extramural Department, University of Birmingham, Birmingham, England.

CAREER: Practicing civil engineer in England prior to 1948; Grosvenor Museum, Chester, England, curator, 1948-54; University of Birmingham, Birmingham, England, Edward Cadbury research fellow, 1954-57, staff tutor in archaeology, extramural department, 1957-71, reader in Romano-British archaeology, extramural department, 1971—. *Member:* Society of Antiquaries (London; fellow), Museums Association (associate member); national, regional, and local archaeological societies.

WRITINGS: The Roman Army: An Illustrated Study, Grosvenor Museum, 1956, revised edition, 1973; (with Donald Reynolds Dudley) *The Rebellion of Boudicca,* Barnes & Noble, 1962; *Practical Archaeology: An Introduction to Archaeological Field-Work and Excavation,* A. & C. Black, 1963; (with Dudley) *The Roman Conquest of Britain, A.D. 43-57,* Dufour, 1965; *Exploring Roman Britain* (juvenile), Encyclopaedia Britannica, 1967; (editor) *Romano-British Coarse Pottery* (guide booklet for students), Council for British Archaeology, 1967; *The Roman Imperial Army of the First and Second Centuries A.D.,* A. & C. Black, 1969, Funk, 1970; *The Cornovii,* Duckworth, in press. Author of several official guides for Ministry of Public Buildings and Works and of museum exhibition guides. Contributor of articles and reviews to archaeological periodicals.

WORK IN PROGRESS: Gazetteer of Roman Britain, for Batsford.

AVOCATIONAL INTERESTS: Food, claret, music (Mozart and earlier), art (painting), good conversation, and "quiet life no one is ever likely to write about."

* * *

WECKSTEIN, Richard (Selig) 1924-

PERSONAL: Born February 11, 1924, in New York, N.Y.; son of Isidore (a banker) and Flo (Litwin) Weckstein; married Muriel Watenmaker (a psychologist), 1947; children: Beth Alison, Leslie Ellen. *Education:* University of Wisconsin, Ph.B., 1947; Yale University, M.A., 1948, Ph.D., 1953. *Home:* Stonehedge, Lincoln, Mass. 01773. *Office:* Department of Economics, Brandeis University, Waltham, Mass. 02154.

CAREER: Yale University, New Haven, Conn., instructor in economics, 1948-50; New York University, New York, N.Y., instructor in economics, 1950-53; University of Buffalo, Buffalo, N.Y., assistant professor of economics, 1953-57; Gadjah Mada University, Jogjakarta, Indonesia, professor of economics, 1957-58; University of Rochester, Rochester, N.Y., visiting associate professor of economics, 1958-59; Williams College, Williamstown, Mass., assistant professor of economics, 1959-62; Brandeis University, Waltham, Mass., associate professor, 1962-68, Carl Marks Professor of Economics, 1968—. Member of Consumers Council, Commonwealth of Massachusetts, 1964—. Consultant on Indonesian development to Ford Foundation. *Military service:* U.S. Army Air Forces, 1942-46; became first lieutenant. *Member:* American Economic Association, Association of Appraisers of Earning Capacity. *Awards, honors:* Research grants from Social Science Research Council, 1962, and Agricultural Development Council, 1966.

WRITINGS: (Contributor) G.F. Papanek, editor, *Development Policy: Theory and Practice,* Harvard University Press, 1968; *The Expansion of World Trade and the Growth of National Economies,* Harper Torchbooks, 1968; (contributor) *Transport Planning and Transport Evaluation,* British Commonwealth Secretariat, 1969. Contributor to conference volumes of World Congress of Engineers and Architects, to *Encyclopedia Americana,* and to economic and other journals.

WORK IN PROGRESS: Investigations of unemployment

in poor countries and of irrigation as a fragile social-economic system.

SIDELIGHTS: Weckstein studied land reform in Mexico, 1962, 1964, visited Liberia as consultant to Harvard Mission to that country, 1963, 1965, and did research in Indonesia, 1972.

* * *

WEEKS, Grace E(zell) 1923-

PERSONAL: Born March 3, 1923, in Clanton, Ala.; daughter of Samuel Jones (a minister) and Grace (Hicks) Ezell; married Arthur A. Weeks, March 22, 1943 (divorced, 1970); married Francisco Marquez, May 26, 1974; children: (first marriage) John David, Carol Christine, Grace Nancy Anna. *Education:* Samford University, A.B., 1942; University of North Carolina, M.A., 1945; Inter-American University, Ph.D., 1964. *Politics:* Independent. *Religion:* Baptist. *Address:* Apartado Postal 98, Cordoba, Veracruz, Mexico. *Office:* Department of English, Colegio Gonzalez Pena, Cordoba, Veracruz, Mexico.

CAREER: Samford University, Birmingham, Ala., instructor in English, 1945-47; Cumberland University, Lebanon, Tenn., instructor in English and Spanish, 1947-51; Belmont College, Nashville, Tenn., assistant professor of Spanish, 1953-54; Samford University, instructor in English and Spanish, 1955-58, assistant professor, 1958-64. associate professor, 1964-66, professor of Spanish, 1966-70; Colegio Gonzalez Pena, Cordoba, Veracruz, Mexico, advisor for English program, 1972—. *Member:* American Association of Teachers of Spanish and Portuguese, Teachers of English to Speakers of Other Languages. *Awards, honors:* Fulbright fellowship, Columbia, South America, 1958.

WRITINGS: Manuel Maria Flores: El Artista y el hombre (title means "Manuel Maria Flores: The Artist and the Man"), B. Costa-Amic, 1969.

WORK IN PROGRESS: Mexican Literature; research on methods of teaching English as a second language.

* * *

WEERTS, Richard Kenneth 1928-

PERSONAL: Born October 7, 1928, in Peoria, Ill.; son of Gerhard Nicholas (a salesman) and Ellen Marie (Lindeburg) Weerts; married Joan Elizabeth Metzger (a bacteriologist), December 26, 1956; children: Lawrence Richard, Lynn Marie, Andrew Edward, Christie Ann. *Education:* University of Illinois, B.Sc., 1951; Columbia University, M.A. (music education), 1956, Ed.D., 1960; Northeast Missouri State University, M.A. (counseling and guidance), 1973. *Home:* 1 Grim Ct. N., Kirksville, Mo. 63501. *Office:* Room 218, Baldwin Hall, Northeast Missouri State University, Kirksville, Mo. 63501.

CAREER: U.S. Army, member of U.S. Military Academy Band, West Point, N.Y., 1951-55; teacher of instrumental music in public schools of Lyndhurst, N.J., 1956-57; director of instrumental music in public schools of Scotch Plains-Fanwood, N.J., 1957-61; Northeast Missouri State University, Kirksville, assistant professor, 1961-62, associate professor, 1962-65, professor of music, 1965—, chairman of music education faculty, 1970—. Clarinet recitalist; director of music at First United Methodist Church, Kirksville, 1970—. *Member:* Music Educators National Conference, National Association of College Wind and Percussion Instructors (executive secretary, 1971—), Phi Mu Alpha, Phi Delta Kappa.

WRITINGS: (Compiler) *Original Manuscript Music for Wind and Percussion Instruments,* Music Educators National Conference, 1964, revised edition, 1973; *Handbook for Woodwinds,* Simpson Printing and Publishing, 1966; *Developing Individual Skills for the High School Band,* Parker Publishing, 1969; *How to Develop and Maintain a Successful Woodwind Section,* Parker Publishing, 1972. Contributor of more than seventy articles and monographs to music and education journals. Associate editor, *Woodwind World,* 1965-69, contributing editor, 1971—; editor, *National Association of College Wind and Percussion Instruments Journal,* 1968—.

WORK IN PROGRESS: Handbook of Rehearsal Techniques for the High School Band.

* * *

WEI, Yung 1937-

PERSONAL: Born May 5, 1937, in Wuhan, China; son of Shao-cheng (a journalist) and Pei-chi (a cartographer; maiden name, Shin) Wei; married Serena N. Sun (a librarian), December 31, 1964; children: Yuan, Lynn (daughters). *Education:* National Chengchi University, LL.B., 1959; University of Oregon, M.A., 1963, Ph.D., 1967. *Home:* 3646 Barron Rd., Apt. 1, Memphis, Tenn. 38111. *Office:* Department of Political Science, Memphis State University, Southern Ave., Memphis, Tenn. 38152.

CAREER: University of Nevada, Las Vegas, instructor, 1966-67, assistant professor of political science, 1967-68; Memphis State University, Memphis, Tenn., assistant professor, 1968-69, associate professor, 1969-74, professor of political science, 1974—. National fellow, Hoover Institution, Stanford University, 1974-75; visiting scholar at Survey Research Center, University of Michigan, summer, 1969; visiting associate professor at National Chengchi University and senior research fellow at Institute of International Relations, Taiwan, 1970-71; visiting scholar at Bureau of Applied Social Research, Columbia University, 1972. *Military service:* Republic of China Army, 1959-61; became second lieutenant. *Member:* American Political Science Association, International Studies Association, Association for Asian Studies, American Association of University Professors, Pi Sigma Alpha.

WRITINGS: She Hui k'o Hsueh Ti shing-chih chi Fa chan ch'u shih (title means "The Nature and Methods of Social Sciences"), Commercial Press (Taipei), 1971; (editor and contributor) *Communist China: A System-Functional Reader,* C. E. Merrill, 1972; (contributor) Paul K. T. Sih, editor, *Taiwan in Modern Times,* St. John's University Press, 1972; (contributor) Hungdah Chiu, editor, *China and the Question of Taiwan: Documents and Analysis,* Praeger, 1973; *The Modernization of a Chinese Society: Taiwan's Path to Development,* Praeger, 1974; (contributor) Yung-Huan Jo, editor, *The Future of Taiwan,* Union Research Institute, 1974. Contributor to *Encyclopedia of Social Sciences* and to *Comparative Communism, Polity, Oriental,* and other journals, and to *Central Daily News* (Taipei). Executive editor, *Annals* of Chinese Political Science Association, 1971—; chairman of board of directors, *Jen Yu She Hui* (Man and Society), 1973—.

WORK IN PROGRESS: Research on electoral behavior in Memphis, inter-nation intellectual migration, and comparative modernization process.

WEIL, Lisl 1910-

PERSONAL: Lisl rhymes with "easel," and Weil rhymes with "style"; born 1910, in Vienna, Austria; came to United States, 1939; naturalized U.S. citizen, 1944; married Julius Marx (deceased). *Education:* Educated in Vienna. *Home:* 25 Central Park W., New York, N.Y. 10023.

CAREER: Author and illustrator. Has performed with Little Orchestra Society of New York at young people's concerts in Carnegie Hall and Philharmonic Hall since the late 1940's, illustrating the story of the music being played; also has appeared with Boston Pops Orchestra, the Chicago, Detroit, Indianapolis, Baltimore, New Haven, Hartford, Davenport, and Grand Rapids symphony orchestras, and on network television specials; had weekly television show, "Children's Sketch Book," produced by National Broadcasting Co., 1963-64.

WRITINGS—Self-illustrated: (Reteller) *Jacoble Tells the Truth,* Houghton, 1946; *The Happy ABC,* World Publishing, 1946; *Bill the Brave,* Houghton, 1948; *Pudding's Wonderful Bone,* Crowell, 1956; *I Wish, I Wish,* Houghton, 1957; *The Busiest Boy in Holland,* Houghton, 1959.

Bitzli and the Big Bad Wolf, Houghton, 1960; *Mimi,* Houghton, 1961; *The Lionhearted One,* Houghton, 1962; (reteller) *The Sorcerer's Apprentice: A Musical Picture Story* (based on music by Paul Dukas with transcriptions for piano by David Shapiro), Little, Brown, 1962; *The Happy Ski ABC,* Putnam, 1964; *Eyes So-Big,* Houghton, 1964; *Happy Birthday in Barcelona,* Houghton, 1965; (reteller) *The Fantastic Toy Shop* (musical story-ballet; music adapted by David Shapiro), Abelard, 1966; *Melissa,* Macmillan, 1966; *Melissa's Friend Fabrizzio,* Macmillan, 1967; *The Story of Smetana's "The Bartered Bride,"* Putnam, 1967; *Shivers and the Case of the Secret Hamburgers,* Houghton, 1967; *Alphabet of Puppy Care,* Abelard, 1968; (reteller) *The Golden Spinning Wheel: An Old Bohemian Folk Tale* (music of Antonin Dvorak adapted by David Shapiro), Macmillan, 1969; *King Midas' Secret and Other Follies,* McGraw, 1969; *Things That Go Bang,* McGraw, 1969; *In and Out,* Scholastic Book Services, 1969.

The Hopping Knapsack, Macmillan, 1970; *The Wiggler,* Houghton, 1971; *Monkey Trouble,* Scholastic Book Services, 1972; *Fat Ernest,* Parents' Magazine Press, 1973; *The Little Chestnut Tree Story,* Scholastic Book Services, 1973; *The Funny Old Bag,* Parents' Magazine Press, 1974; *Walt and Pepper,* Parents' Magazine Press, 1974.

Illustrator: Marion Moss, *Doll House,* World Publishing, 1946; Dori Furth, *Back in Time for Supper,* McKay, 1947; Ruth Langland Holberg, *Catnip Man,* Crowell, 1951; Henry Steele Commager, *Chestnut Squirrel,* Houghton, 1952; Christine N. Govan, *The Super-Duper Car,* Houghton, 1952; Ruth Corabel Simon, *Mat and Mandy and the Little Old Car,* Crowell, 1952; Holberg, *Three Birthday Wishes,* Crowell, 1953; Simon, *Mat and Mandy and the Big Dog, Bigger,* Crowell, 1954; Elizabeth Duryea, *The Long Christmas Eve,* Houghton, 1954; Dorris W. Hendrickson, *Breakneck Hill,* Follett, 1954; Pamela Brown, *Windmill Family,* Crowell, 1955; Marion Flood French, *Mr. Bear Goes to Boston,* Follett, 1955; Emilie Warren McLeod, *Clancy's Witch,* Little, Brown, 1959.

Mary Elting, *Miss Polly's Animal School,* Grosset, 1961; Helen Diehl Olds, *What Will I Wear?,* Knopf, 1961; Alice Low, *A Day of Your Own: Your Birthday,* Random House, 1964; Lucretia Peabody Hale, *Stories from the Peterkin Papers,* Scholastic Book Services, 1964; Margaret V. D. Bevans, *"I Wonder Why?" Thought the Owl,* Putnam, 1965; Aileen Lucia Fisher, *Human Rights Day,* Crowell, 1966.

Sesyle Joslin, *Doctor George Owl,* Houghton, 1970; Marjorie W. Sharmat, *51 Sycamore Lane,* Macmillan, 1971; Eda J. Le Shan, *What Makes Me Feel This Way?: Growing Up with Human Emotions,* Macmillan, 1972.

Also illustrator of "What Is?" series, written by Lee P. McGrath and Joan Scobey, published by Essandess: *What Is a Grandmother?,* 1970; *What Is a Brother?,* 1970; *What Is a Grandfather?,* 1970; *What Is a Friend?,* 1971: *What Is a Pet?,* 1971.

SIDELIGHTS: Lisl Weil writes: "Upon invitations I have given countless chalk-talks for children and their elders at schools and library meetings around the country. [For concerts] my life-sized drawings with colored chalks are done in perfect rhythm. It all is choreographed with movements and so becomes a real picture-ballet. It is my very own way of making my audiences listen with their eyes as well as their ears.

"One of my books, *The Sorcerer's Apprentice,* has been made into a sound movie by the Weston Woods Studios, in which I am drawing the pictures to the music, just as I do on the concert stages."

* * *

WEINER, Hyman J(oseph) 1926-

PERSONAL: Born August 22, 1926, in New York, N.Y.; son of Ben (a tailor) and Sadie (Lindy) Weiner; married Shirley Beckerman (a teacher), October 31, 1948; children: Robert, Susan, Daniel. *Education:* Brooklyn College (now Brooklyn College of the City University of New York), B.S., 1949; Columbia University, M.S.W., 1951, Ph.D., 1964. *Religion:* Jewish. *Home:* 353 Old Mamaroneck Rd., White Plains, N.Y. 10605. *Office:* School of Social Work, Columbia University, New York, N.Y. 10025.

CAREER: Sidney Hillman Health Center, New York, N.Y., director of Mental Health Clinic, 1961-68; Columbia University, New York, N.Y., associate professor, 1968-72, professor of social work, 1972—. Member of President's Commission on the Mentally Handicapped.

WRITINGS: (With Sheila Akabas and John Sommer) *Mental Health Care in the World of Work,* Association Press, 1973. Contributor to journals.

WORK IN PROGRESS: A book on industrial social welfare.

* * *

WEINER, Sandra 1922-

PERSONAL: Born September 14, 1922, in Poland; naturalized U.S. citizen in 1937; daughter of Oscar and Leah Smith; married Daniel Weiner, March 12, 1942 (died, 1959); children: Dore. *Education:* Attended public schools in New York, N.Y. *Home and office:* 30 West 60th St., New York, N.Y. 10023.

CAREER: Free-lance photo-journalist, 1946-59; photographer for *Sports Illustrated,* 1959-64; New York University, New York, N.Y., instructor in photography, 1967-72; free-lance photographer in New York, N.Y., 1968—.

WRITINGS—Children's books illustrated with photographs by the author: *It's Wings That Make Birds Fly: The Story of a Boy,* Pantheon, 1968; *Small Hands, Big Hands,* Pantheon, 1970; *They Call Me Jack,* Pantheon, 1973.

WEINGARTNER, Charles 1922-

PERSONAL: Born May 30, 1922, in New York, N.Y.; married Mary Babcock, December 25, 1946; children: Jan (daughter). *Education:* Syracuse University, B.S., 1950, M.A., 1951; Columbia University, Ed.D., 1958. *Home address:* P. O. Box 16000 D, Temple Terrace, Fla. 33617. *Office:* College of Education, University of South Florida, Tampa, Fla. 33620.

CAREER: Daytona Beach Junior College, Daytona Beach, Fla., chairman of department of English, 1958-59; Jersey City State College, Jersey City, N.J., professor of English and chairman of department, 1959-61; Committee on Institutional Cooperation, Chicago, Ill., staff associate, 1961-62; State University of New York College at New Paltz, professor of English and education, 1962-64; New York University, New York, N.Y., associate director of Linguistics Demonstration Center, 1964-65; Queens College of the City University of New York, Flushing, N.Y., coordinator of secondary education, 1965-70; University of South Florida, Tampa, professor of education, 1970—. *Military service:* U.S. Army Air Forces, 1941-45. *Member:* National Council of Teachers of English (chairman of semantics committee, 1966). *Awards, honors: Teaching as a Subversive Activity* appeared on the *New York Times* list of best books of 1969; *The Soft Revolution* was listed by American Library Association as one of the best books for adolescents, 1971.

WRITINGS—All with Neil Postman: *Linguistics: A Revolution in Teaching,* Dell, 1966; *Teaching as a Subversive Activity,* Delacorte, 1969; *Language in America,* Pegasus, 1970; *The Soft Revolution,* Dell, 1971; *The School Book,* Delacorte, 1973.

* * *

WEISGERBER, Robert A(rthur) 1929-

PERSONAL: Born June 2, 1929, in Havertown, Pa.; son of Gustavus Adolphus (an insurance agent) and Ada (Loux) Weisgerber; married Adrienne Peterman (a home economist), October 13, 1956; children: Laraine Alison, Scott Austin. *Education:* West Chester State College, B.S., 1950; Indiana University, M.S., 1958, Ed.D., 1960. *Home:* 2917 Adeline Dr., Burlingame, Calif. 94010. *Office:* American Institutes for Research, P.O. Box 1113, Palo Alto, Calif. 94302.

CAREER: Junior high school teacher in Philadelphia, Pa., 1954-57; Indiana University, Bloomington, production supervisor and assistant professor of education, 1958-62; San Francisco State College (now University), San Francisco, Calif., associate professor of education and director of media center, 1962-67; American Institutes for Research, Palo Alto, Calif., senior research scientist, 1967-73, principal research scientist, 1974—. *Military service:* U.S. Air Force, 1950-54. *Member:* Council for Exceptional Children, Association for Educational Communications and Technology, American Educational Research Association, Society of Motion Picture and Television Engineers.

WRITINGS: (Editor) *Instructional Process and Media Innovation,* Rand McNally, 1968; (editor) *Perspectives in Individualized Learning,* F. E. Peacock, 1971; (editor) *Developmental Efforts in Individualized Learning,* F. E. Peacock, 1971. Writer of scripts for educational films, "Adaptation in Plants," "Food for Plants," "The Fish That Turned Gold," and "Earthworm Anatomy." Contributor to professional journals.

WORK IN PROGRESS: Adult fiction; a children's book; and a 16mm film.

* * *

WEISS, Jess E(dward) 1926-

PERSONAL: Born March 12, 1926, in New York, N.Y.; son of Jerome (a salesman) and Martha (Levy) Weiss; married Shirley Levy, January 17, 1943; married second wife, Joyce Greco, December 11, 1973; children: (first marriage) Gary Lynn, Gail Susan. *Education:* American University, Veterans Representative Degree, 1947. *Religion:* Christian Science. *Home:* Split Rock Rd., East Norwich, N.Y. 11732. *Agent:* Anita Reisner, 160 Broadway, New York, N.Y. 10038. *Office:* 2161 Milburn Ave., Baldwin, N.Y. 11510.

CAREER: American Veterans Committee, Veterans Claims Service, Washington, D.C., director, 1946-52; Aetna Life Insurance Co., New York, N.Y., claims supervisor, 1952-63; Self Insured Insurance Agency, Baldwin, N.Y., owner, 1963—. *Military service:* U.S. Army, 1941-46; served in Africa and Europe; received Purple Heart and Bronze Star. *Member:* American Veterans Committee.

WRITINGS: The Vestibule (nonfiction), Ashley Books, 1972, 3rd edition, 1973.

* * *

WELCH, Jean-Louise
See KEMPTON, Jean Welch

* * *

WELLS, John Warren 1938-

PERSONAL: Born June 25, 1938, in Rhinebeck, N.Y.; son of James Francis (an attorney) and Rebecca (Warren) Wells; married Lesley Evans, March 12, 1962 (divorced, 1965); married Jill Emerson (a writer), August 29, 1971. *Education:* Fordham University, B.A., 1958; Columbia University, M.A., 1960; Trinity College, Dublin, D.Phil., 1963. *Politics:* "Sinn Fein." *Religion:* "Lapsed Catholic." *Home:* 21 West 35th St., New York, N.Y. 10001. *Agent:* Henry Morrison, Inc., 311½ West 20th St., New York, N.Y. 10011. *Office: Swank,* 1560 Broadway, New York, N.Y. 10036.

CAREER: Free-lance writer, 1963-65; researcher on human sexual behavior, 1965-71; *Swank* (magazine), New York, N.Y., columnist and contributing editor, 1971—. *Member:* Author's League, American Academy of Political and Social Sciences, Irish Republican Brotherhood.

WRITINGS: Eros and Capricorn, Lancer Books, 1967; *The Taboo Breakers,* Lancer Books, 1968; *The New Sexual Underground,* Lancer Books, 1969; *The Mrs. Robinson Syndrome,* Lancer Books, 1969; *Sex and the Stewardess,* Lancer Books, 1969; *The Wifeswap Report,* Dell, 1970; *Tricks of the Trade,* New American Library, 1970; *Three Is Not a Crowd,* Dell, 1970; *The Male Hustler,* Lancer Books, 1971; *Versatile Ladies,* Lancer Books, 1971; *Their Own Thing,* Dell, 1972.

Motion picture scripts: "Little Miss Beaver," 1969; "Girl from Beaver Falls," 1970.

WORK IN PROGRESS: New Styles in Marriage (tentative title).

WELLS, Robert W(ayne) 1918-

PERSONAL: Born June 16, 1918, in Greene, Ohio; son of Anthony W. (a salesman) and Maude (Dennison) Wells; married Edith V. Jersin (a speech clinician), February 9, 1945; children: Richard, Nancy (Mrs. Jeff Byers), John, Robert G. *Education:* Ohio State University, B.S., 1940. *Home:* W 32902 Government Hill, Delafield, Wis. 53018. *Agent:* Larry Sternig, 2407 North 44th St., Milwaukee, Wis. 53201. *Office: Milwaukee Journal,* Milwaukee, Wis. 53201.

CAREER: Canton Repository, Canton, Ohio, copyreader, 1940; *Warren Tribune-Chronicle,* Warren, Ohio, reporter, 1940-41; *Columbus Dispatch,* Columbus, Ohio, reporter, 1941-43, assistant city editor, 1943-44; *Milwaukee Journal,* Milwaukee, Wis., columnist and feature writer, 1946—. Lecturer at University of Wisconsin, Milwaukee, 1972-73. *Military service:* U.S. Navy, 1944-46. *Member:* Council for Wisconsin Writers, Milwaukee Press Club. *Awards, honors:* Gold medal from Boys Clubs of America, 1968, for *Five-Yard Fuller of the New York Gnats;* Wisconsin Historical Society award, 1969, for *Fire at Peshtigo;* Council for Wisconsin Writers book award, 1972, for *Vince Lombardi.*

WRITINGS—Nonfiction: *Fire at Peshtigo,* Prentice-Hall, 1968; *This Is Milwaukee,* Doubleday, 1970; *Vince Lombardi: His Life and Times,* Wisconsin House, 1971; (with Ray Nitschke) *Mean on Sunday,* Doubleday, 1973.

Juvenile fiction; all published by Putnam, except as indicated: *Five-Yard Fuller,* 1964; *Five-Yard Fuller of the New York Gnats,* 1967; *Five-Yard Fuller and the Unlikely Knights,* 1967; *Saga of Shorty Gone,* 1969; *Mad Anthony Wayne,* 1970; *Five-Yard Fuller's Mighty Model,* 1970; *Horse on the Roof,* Lippincott, 1970.

* * *

WERKMAN, Sidney L(ee) 1927-

PERSONAL: Born May 3, 1927, in Washington, D.C.; children: Russell. *Education:* Williams College, B.A., 1948; Cornell University, M.D., 1952. *Home:* 277 South Dexter St., Denver, Colo. *Office:* School of Medicine, University of Colorado, 4200 East 9th Ave., Denver, Colo. 80220.

CAREER: Certified in psychiatry and neurology, 1959, and in child psychiatry, 1961; University of Virginia Hospital, Charlottesville, intern, 1952-53; resident in psychiatry at Yale University, New Haven, Conn., 1953-55, and St. Elizabeth's Hospital, Washington, D.C., 1955-56; Children's Hospital, Washington, D.C., fellow in child psychiatry, 1956-58, Commonwealth Fund fellow, 1963-64, associate director of department of psychiatry; George Washington University, Washington, D.C., associate clinical professor of psychiatry, 1961-69; University of Colorado, School of Medicine, Denver, associate professor, 1969-73, professor of psychiatry, 1973—. *Military service:* United States Army, 1944-46.

WRITINGS: The Role of Psychiatry in Medical Education, Harvard University Press, 1966; *Only a Little Time* (nonfiction), Little, Brown, 1972. Contributor of twelve chapters to books and twenty-three articles to journals.

* * *

WESCHE, Percival A. 1912-

PERSONAL: Born June 14, 1912, in Ashland, Wis.; son of Wilmer Edgar (a land manager) and Emma (Plank) Wesche; married Marjorie MacKellar (a home economics teacher), June 25, 1939; children: Joy Dell (Mrs. Ronald Russell), Jody Kay. *Education:* Taylor University, A.B., 1934; Asbury Theological Seminary, B.D., 1938; Winona Lake School of Theology, M.A., 1941; University of Chicago, M.A., 1945; University of Oklahoma, Ph.D., 1954; Hamline University, postdoctoral study, 1966; University of Manchester, postdoctoral study, 1971. *Politics:* Republican. *Home:* 323 19th Ave. S., Nampa, Idaho 83651. *Office:* Department of History, Northwest Nazarene College, Nampa, Idaho 83651.

CAREER: Ordained minister of Church of the Nazarene; Northwest Nazarene College, Nampa, Idaho, 1954—, currently professor of history and political science. President of International Publishing Co.; representative in Idaho State Legislature, 1972—. *Member:* American Historical Association, Association of American Historians, American Society of Church History, Christian Historians, Southern Historical Society.

WRITINGS: Crusader Saint: The Life of Henry Clay Morrison, Asbury Theological Seminary Press, 1963; (with Kenneth Sadler) *Complete Chinchilla Training Manual,* International Publishing, 1965; *Outline of Church History,* International Publishing, 1968; *Outline of United States History to 1877,* International Publishing, 1969; *Outline of United States History since 1865,* International Publishing, 1969.

AVOCATIONAL INTERESTS: Raising chinchillas.

* * *

WESLEY, Mary 1912-

PERSONAL: Born June 24, 1912, in Englefield Green, England; daughter of Mynors (a colonel) and Violet (Dalby) Farmar; married Lord Swinfen, January, 1937 (divorced, 1944); married Eric Siepmann (a writer), April 22, 1951; children: (first marriage) Roger Eady, Toby Eady; (second marriage) William. *Education:* Attended Queens College, London, 1928-30, and London School of Economics and Political Science, 1931-32. *Politics:* "Left-wing/Catholic." *Religion:* Roman Catholic. *Home:* Cullaford, Buckfastleigh, Devon, England. *Agent:* John Farquarson, 15 Red Lion Sq., London W.C.1, England.

CAREER: War Office, England, member of staff, 1939-41. *Member:* London Library.

WRITINGS: The Sixth Seal, MacDonald, 1969, Stein & Day, 1971; *Speaking Terms,* Faber, 1969, Gambit, 1971.

WORK IN PROGRESS: A children's book, *Father's Staircase.*

* * *

WESTON, Glen E(arl) 1922-

PERSONAL: Born July 21, 1922, in Shawnee, Okla.; son of Earl P. (a soil conservationist) and Sue (Petty) Weston; married Elizabeth Gruver (self-employed), May 30, 1943; children: Nancy Lynn, Sherry Sue. *Education:* University of Maryland, B.S., 1943; George Washington University, J.D., 1948; Yale University, graduate fellow, 1951-52. *Politics:* Independent. *Religion:* Methodist. *Home:* 6005 Dinwiddie St., Springfield, Va. 22150. *Office:* George Washington University Law School, Washington, D.C. 20006.

CAREER: Admitted to the Bar of the District of Columbia, 1948, and the Bar of the State of Virginia, 1955; McFarland & Sellers (law firm), Washington, D.C., associate,

1948-50; George Washington University, Washington, D.C., assistant professor, 1949-54, associate professor, 1954-58, professor of law, 1958—. Visiting professor at University of Michigan, summer, 1963, Northwestern University, 1963-64, and University of Illinois, summer, 1972. *Military service:* U.S. Army, 1943-46; became captain; received Silver Star. *Member:* American Bar Association, Federal Bar Association, American Association of University Professors, District of Columbia Bar Association, Virginia State Bar Association.

WRITINGS: (With S. C. Oppenheim) *Federal Antitrust Laws: Cases and Comments,* West Publishing, 1968; (with Oppenheim) *The Lawyer's Robinson-Patman Act Source Book,* four volumes, Little, Brown, 1971; (with Oppenheim) *Unfair Trade Practices and Consumer Protection: Cases and Comments,* West Publishing, 1974. Antitrust law editor of *Antitrust Bulletin.*

* * *

WEVERKA, Robert 1926- (Robert McMahon)

PERSONAL: Surname is accented on second syllable; born November 17, 1926, in Los Angeles, Calif.; son of Lloyd J. (an executive) and Blanche (McPhee) Weverka; married Ethel Gough, July 7, 1956; children: Peter, Thomas, Anne, Robert Philip. *Education:* University of Southern California, B.A., 1950. *Home and office address:* P.O. Box 976, Idyllwild, Calif. 92349.

CAREER: Salesman for Gough Industries, Inc., 1950-55; advertising director for Huddle Restaurants, Inc., 1956-57; Weverka & Associates, Inc. (advertising agency), Beverly Hills, Calif., president, 1957-68. *Member:* Writers Guild of America (Western section).

WRITINGS—All novels: (Under pseudonym Robert McMahon, with Leo Bergson) *The Widowmaster,* Gold Medal, 1968; *One Minute to Eternity,* Morrow, 1968; *I Love My Wife,* Bantam, 1970; *Search,* Bantam, 1971; *Moonrock,* Bantam, 1972; *Griff,* Bantam, 1974; *The Sting,* Bantam, 1974; *The Waltons,* Bantam, 1974.

* * *

WHEDON, Julia See SCHICKEL, Julia Whedon

* * *

WHITE, Terence de Vere 1912-

PERSONAL: Born April 29, 1912, in Dublin, Ireland; son of Frederick S.D. de Vere (a doctor of laws) and Ethel (Perry) White; married Mary O'Farrell (a potter), 1941; children: Deborah White Singmaster, Ralph, John. *Education:* Trinity College, Dublin, B.A. (honors), 1931, LL.B., 1931. *Politics:* None. *Religion:* Roman Catholic. *Home:* 5 Wellington Place, Dublin 4, Ireland. *Agent:* R.S. Simon, 36 Wellington St., London W.C., England. *Office: Irish Times,* Dublin, Ireland.

CAREER: Solicitor; called to Bar, 1933; Incorporated Law Society, Dublin, Ireland, member of council, 1954-61; *Irish Times,* Dublin, Ireland, literary editor, 1961—; author and novelist. Vice-chairman of board, National Gallery of Ireland, 1967—; member of board of trustees, National Library of Ireland, 1949—, and Chester Beatty Library, 1968—; member of board of directors, Gate Theatre, 1970—; professor of literature, Royal Hibernian Academy, 1973—. *Member:* Irish Academy of Letters, Royal Hibernian Academy (honorary member), Kildare Street Club.

WRITINGS: The Road of Excess (biography), Brown and Nolan, 1946; *Kevin O'Higgins,* Methuen, 1948; *The Story of the Royal Dublin Society,* Kerryman, 1955; *A Fretful Midge,* Routledge & Kegan Paul, 1957; (editor) George Egerton, pseud., *A Leaf from the Yellow Book,* Richards Press, 1958; *An Affair with the Moon* (novel), Gollancz, 1959; *Prenez Garde* (novel), Gollancz, 1966; *The Remainderman,* Gollancz, 1963; *Lucifer Falling* (novel), Gollancz, 1966, World Publishing Co., 1967; *The Parents of Oscar Wilde: Sir William and Lady Wilde,* Hodder & Stoughton, 1967; *Tara,* Gollancz, 1967; *Ireland,* Walker & Co., 1968; *Leinster,* Faber, 1968; *The Lambert Mile* (novel), Gollancz, 1969, published as *The Lambert Revels,* Little, Brown, 1970; *The March Hare,* Gollancz, 1970; *The Minister for Justice,* Gambit, 1971 (published in England as *Mr. Stephen,* Gollancz, 1971); *The Anglo-Irish,* Gollancz, 1972; *The Distance & the Dark,* Gambit, 1973.

Contributor to *Horizon, Cambridge Review, Sunday Times* (London), *Observer* (London).

SIDELIGHTS: Of *Lucifer Falling,* N.J. Loprete in *Best Sellers* has written: "It is rare that a reviewer agrees with the incantatory prose of dust-jacket blurbs, but, in [this] case, I am compelled to give my vigorous assent to what is described as a 'witty and explosive journey into the world of the academe.'" In the *Listener,* Edwin Morgan has written of *The March Hare:* "[It] is a very readable comic novel set in Dublin at the beginning of the present century. The action, as the author cannot help inserting during a chaotic country-house weekend, is 'like an Irish comic novel,' but some shrewd thrusts are made at Irish society, manners and politics."

* * *

WHITFIELD, Shelby 1935-

PERSONAL: Born April 13, 1935, in Dallas, Tex.; son of Isaac Louis and Mary (Hill) Whitfield; married Lora Napierski, January 18, 1958; children: Drew Stanley, Shauna Louise, Tina Marie, Sharon Heather. *Education:* University of Texas, B.A., 1956. *Religion:* Protestant. *Home:* 8303 Eugenia St., Oxon Hill, Md. 20022. *Office:* Associated Press Radio, 1825 K St. N.W., Washington, D.C. 20006.

CAREER: Armed Forces Radio-Television, Washington, D.C., sports director, 1960-68; radio and television broadcaster for Washington Senators (baseball team), 1969-71; WWDC-Radio and WTOP-TV, Washington, D.C., reporter, talkmaster, and producer, 1971-73; Associated Press Radio, Washington, D.C., national sports director, 1973—. Free-lance sportscaster for Columbia Broadcasting System, American Broadcasting Corp., British Broadcasting Corp., and Canadian Broadcasting Corp.; producer and host of "The Ted Williams Show." *Military service:* U.S. Army, 1957-60. *Member:* American Federation of Television and Radio Artists, National Association of Sportscasters and Sportswriters.

WRITINGS: Kiss It Goodbye, Abelard, 1973; (with Moses and Mary Malone) *Courtship of Moses Malone,* Dell, in press. Author of columns in *Washington Football Weekly* and *Washington Sports Scene.*

WORK IN PROGRESS: A keepsake book about Vince Lombardi.

SIDELIGHTS: Whitfield wrote that *Kiss It Goodbye* dealt

with the Bob Short-Ted Williams baseball era, and exposed pressures placed on broadcasters by clubs, which led to investigation and corrective action by the Federal Communications Commission.

* * *

WHITNEY, J(ohn) D(enison) 1940-

PERSONAL: Born September 23, 1940, in Pasadena, Calif.; son of John K. and Nathalie A. (Crane) Whitney; married Judy A. Weyenberg, January 30, 1971; children: Barbara, Joanne, David, Roger, Douglas. *Education:* University of Michigan, B.A., 1962, M.A., 1966. *Home:* 614 Adams, Wausau, Wis. 54401. *Office:* Department of English, University of Wisconsin, Marathon Center, Wausau, Wis. 54401.

CAREER: Teacher of English in the public schools of Allen Park, Mich., 1962-66; University of Wisconsin, Platteville, instructor in English, 1966-69; University of Wisconsin, Marathon Center, Wausau, assistant professor of English, 1969—.

WRITINGS—Poems: *Hello,* Artists Workshop Press, 1965, 2nd edition, 1967; *Tracks,* Elizabeth Press, 1969; *The Nabisco Warehouse,* Elizabeth Press, 1971; *sd,* Elizabeth Press, 1973. Editor and publisher of *It,* 1965-72.

WORK IN PROGRESS: Tongues, for Elizabeth Press, publication expected in 1976.

* * *

WIESE, Kurt 1887-1974

April 22, 1887—May 27, 1974; German-born American author and illustrator of children's books. Obituaries: *New York Times,* May 29, 1974. (*CA*-11/12).

* * *

WILCOX, Wayne Ayres 1932-1974

July 13, 1932—March 3, 1974; American educator, author, and diplomat. Obituaries: *Washington Post,* March 7, 1974. (*CA*-7/8).

* * *

WILFORD, Walton T. 1937-

PERSONAL: Born September 27, 1937, in Murray, Ky.; son of Jasper D., Sr. and Rebecca (Sykes) Wilford. *Education:* Southern Methodist University, B.B.A., 1958, Ph.D., 1964. *Religion:* Methodist. *Home:* 4874 Charmes Ct., New Orleans, La., 70129. *Office:* Department of Economics and Finance, Louisiana State University, New Orleans, La. 70122.

CAREER: University of Georgia, Athens, assistant professor of economics, 1962-63; University of Idaho, Moscow, assistant professor of economics, 1963-65; U.S. Department of State, Agency for International Development, Washington, D.C., economic adviser to Bolivia, 1965-67, monetary-fiscal adviser in Guatemala City, Guatemala, 1968; Louisiana State University at New Orleans, associate professor, 1968-70, professor of economics, 1970—, chairman of department of economics and finance, 1973—. Visiting professor California State University, San Jose, 1972. Adviser to Bolivian Tax Reform Commission, 1966. *Member:* American Economic Association, Southern Economic Association, Southwestern Economic Association, Western Economic Association, Smithsonian Association, Omicron Delta Epsilon.

WRITINGS: (With Raul Moncarz) *Essays in Latin American Economic Issues,* Division of Business and Economic Research, Louisiana State University at New Orleans, 1970.

Contributor to annals and proceedings. Contributor of articles and reviews to economics and finance journals, including *National Tax Journal, Social Science Quarterly, Journal of Economic Issues, Journal of InterAmerican Studies and World Affairs, Economic Development and Cultural Change,* and *Indian Economic Journal.* Member of board of editors of *Mississippi Valley Journal of Business and Economics.*

WORK IN PROGRESS: Tax Reform in Latin America; Trade in the Central American Common Market; Labor Intensive Industrialization in the Emerging World.

* * *

WILKINSON, Ernest Leroy 1899-

PERSONAL: Born May 4, 1899, in Ogden, Utah; son of Robert Brown and Annie Cecilia (Anderson) Wilkinson; married Alice Valera Ludlow, August 15, 1923; children: Ernest Ludlow, Marian (Mrs. Gordon Jensen), Alice Ann (Mrs. John K. Mangum), David Lawrence, Douglas Dwight. *Education:* Weber College, student, 1917-18; Brigham Young University, A.B., 1921; George Washington University, J.D., 1926; Harvard University, S.J.D., 1927. *Politics:* "Jeffersonian Republican." *Religion:* Church of Jesus Christ of Latter-Day Saints. *Home:* 2745 North University Ave., Provo, Utah 84601. *Office:* Brigham Young University, Provo, Utah 84601.

CAREER: Admitted to Washington State Bar, 1926, Utah Bar, 1927, and New York State Bar, 1928; New Jersey Law School, Newark, professor of law, 1927-33; Hughes, Schurman & Dwight, New York, N.Y., associate, 1928-35; Moyle & Wilkinson, Washington, D.C., partner, 1935-40; head of Ernest L. Wilkinson, Washington, D.C., 1940-51, and Wilkinson, Cragun & Barker, Washington, D.C., 1951—; Brigham Young University, Provo, Utah, president, 1950-64, 1965-71, director and editor of *Centennial History,* 1971—. Member of board of directors of Deseret News Publishing Co., 1954—, Beneficial Life Insurance Co., 1957-60, KSL, Radio Service Corp. of Utah, 1960—, Rolling Hills Orchard, 1961-71, and Ellison Ranching Co., 1962—. Member of National Committee of Army and Navy Chaplains, 1947-50; chancellor of Unified School System of Church of Jesus Christ of Latter-Day Saints, 1953-64; president of National Right to Work Legal Defense and Education Foundation, 1969-73. Trustee of Utah Foundation, 1960—, and Foundation for Economic Freedom, 1960-71. *Military service:* U.S. Army, 1918.

MEMBER: International Platform Association, Provo Chamber of Commerce, Salt Lake City Chamber of Commerce, Order of the Coif, Phi Kappa Phi. *Awards, honors:* LL.D., Brigham Young University, 1957; George Washington Medal of Freedoms Foundation of America for speech on free enterprise, 1961, and for speech on student riots, 1971; American Coalition of Patriotic Societies Award, 1963; Business Man of the Year in Education Award of Religious Heritage of America, Inc., 1971.

WRITINGS: Earnestly Yours (collected speeches), Deseret, 1971. Contributor to *American Bar Association Journal.*

WILKINSON, Rosemary Challoner 1924-

PERSONAL: Born February 21, 1924, in New Orleans, La.; daughter of William Lindsay (a wholesale jewelry materials salesman) and Julia (Sellen) Challoner; married Henry Bertram Wilkinson, 1949; children: Denis, Marian, Paul, Richard. *Education:* College of San Mateo, student, 1964-65, and 1966; University of Minnesota, student by correspondence, 1967. *Politics:* Democrat. *Religion:* Catholic. *Home:* 1239 Bernal Ave., Burlingame, Calif. 94010.

CAREER: Bookkeeper at hospitals in Lafayette and New Albany, Ind., 1939-44; St. James Hospital, Chicago Heights, Ill., administrative supervisor, 1944-47; St. Joseph Hospital, Phoenix, Ariz., administrative supervisor, 1947-48; West Disinfecting Co., San Francisco, Calif., bookkeeper, 1948-51; Peninsula Hospital, Burlingame, Calif., billing officer, 1961-62; full-time writer, 1964—. Coordinator of California's second chapter of Hospital Audiences, Inc., 1972; advisor to Third World Congress of Poets, 1976. *Member:* Poetry Society of England, United Poets Laureate International (Philippines), Cosmosynthesis League (honorary life member), California Federation of Chaparral Poets (president of Toyon chapter, 1972-74). *Awards, honors:* Certificate of merit from American Poets Fellowship Society, Charleston, Ill., 1973.

WRITINGS: A Girl's Will (poems), Prairie Press, 1973. Also author of unpublished volumes of poetry, *Earth's Compromise* and *It Happened to Me,* a novel, *The Captain Artist,* and *An Historical Epic.*

SIDELIGHTS: A Girl's Will is being translated for publication in Taiwan.

* * *

WILL, Frederic 1928-

PERSONAL: Born December 4, 1928, in New Haven, Conn.; son of Samuel (a professor) and Constance (Bicknell) Will; married Elizabeth Lyding (a professor), July, 1952; children: Alex, Barbara. *Education:* Indiana University, A.B., 1949; Yale University, Ph.D., 1954. *Religion:* Roman Catholic. *Home:* 84 High Point Dr., Amherst, Mass. 01002. *Office:* 826 Thompson Hall, University of Massachusetts, Amherst, Mass. 01002.

CAREER: Dartmouth College, Hanover, N.H., instructor in classics, 1952-54; Pennsylvania State University, University Park, assistant professor of classics, 1954-59; University of Texas at Austin, assistant professor of classics, 1960-65; University of Iowa, Iowa City, associate professor of comparative literature, 1965-70; University of Massachusetts, Amherst, professor of comparative literature, 1970—. *Awards, honors:* Fulbright grant, 1954; American Council of Learned Societies grant, 1958; Bollingen grant, 1958.

WRITINGS: Intelligible Beauty in Aesthetic Thought, from Winckelmann to Victor Cousin, M. Niemeyer, 1958; *Mosaic, and Other Poems,* Pennsylvania State University Press, 1959.

A Wedge of Words (poems), University of Texas at Austin, 1962; (translator and author of introduction) Kostes Palamas, *The Twelve Words of the Gypsy,* University of Nebraska Press, 1964; (editor) *Hereditas: Seven Essays on the Modern Experience of the Classical,* University of Texas Press, 1964; (editor and author of introduction) *Metaphrasis: An Anthology from the University of Iowa Translation Workshop, 1964-65,* Verb, 1965; *Flumen historicum: Victor Cousin's Aesthetic and Its Sources,* University of North Carolina Press, 1965; *Literature Inside Out: Ten Speculative Essays,* Press of Western Reserve University, 1966; *Planets* (poems), Golden Quill, 1966; (translator and author of introduction) Kostes, *The King's Flute,* University of Nebraska Press, 1967; *From a Year in Greece,* University of Texas Press, 1967; *Archilochos,* Twayne, 1969.

Herondas, Twayne, 1972; *Brandy in the Snow* (poetry), New Rivers Press, 1973; (translator with Knut Tarnowski) Theodor Adorno, *The Jargon of Authenticity,* Northwestern University Press, 1973; *The Knife in the Stone,* Mouton, 1974; *The Fact of Literature,* Rodopi, 1974.

WORK IN PROGRESS: Travel books on the unity of Canada, Latin America, and the United States; a book on the possibility of imaginative freedom in a technocracy; a volume of poems.

SIDELIGHTS: Will told *CA:* "I see writing as an obsolescent rear-guard action against a new oral culture. The writer's obligation is to defend the values of the classical tradition without failing to see that they are no longer his. Hope and the future are intimately linked to the whole process of writing."

* * *

WILLCOX, Donald J. 1933-

PERSONAL: Born July 23, 1933, in Minneapolis, Minn.; son of Herbert Henry (a judge and lawyer) and S. Barbara (Johnstone) Willcox; married Sandra Alice Belden (an artist and book illustrator), May 7, 1955 (divorced, September, 1971); children: Kristin, Jody, Kimberly. *Education:* Attended Augsburg College, 1951-53, University of Minnesota, 1953-54, and William Mitchell College of Law, 1956-57; Goddard College, B.F.A., 1967. *Agent:* Irene Friedman, 225 West 12th St., New York, N.Y. 10011.

CAREER: Sculptor in Peacham, Vt., 1961-68; free-lance lecturer and teacher of design, contemporary crafts, and marketing for Australian Arts Council, Danish Institute, Canadian government, and Association of Independent Art Colleges in the U.S.A. Staff member at Breadloaf Writers Conference, 1965, 1966, 1967; teacher at Aspen Poetry Workshop, 1968. *Military service:* U.S. Army, 1954-56. *Member:* Vermont Council on the Arts, Vermont League of Writers (director, 1965-67).

WRITINGS—Poems: *The First Time Out,* Vermont Stoneside Press, 1967; *Hard edge/Soft-center,* Salt Creek Press, 1969; *Not Quite Rodney Height,* Hemorrhoid Books, 1972.

Design Criticism: *Suomalaisen muotoilun kuviot,* Werner Soderstrom, 1973; *Finnish Design: Facts and Fancy,* Van Nostrand, 1973. Craft and Design: *Wood Design,* Watson-Guptill, 1967; *Modern Leather Design,* Watson-Guptill, 1969; *Techniques of Rya Knotting,* Van Nostrand, 1970; *Laeder,* Gyldendal, 1972; *Leather,* Regnery, 1973; *Body Jewelry: International Perspectives,* Regnery, 1973.

Scandinavian Design: "New Design" series, published by Van Nostrand: *New Design In Jewelry,* 1970; *. . .In Ceramic,* 1970; . . .In Weaving, *1970; . . .In Stitchery,* 1970; *. . .In Wood,* 1970.

Contributor of articles, poems, and short stories to *Encyclopedia Americana,* and to *Saturday Review of Literature, Goddard Journal, Quixiote,* and others. Editor, *Vermonter,* 1964-66.

WORK IN PROGRESS: Forms of Social Conscience, completion expected in 1975; a children's book, 1975.

SIDELIGHTS: Willcox told *CA:* "Am a halfwit sculptor and poet. Have had shows in Vermont, North Carolina, Florida, and Colorado. . . .never in New York City. Primarily work in wood, and in leather. After a couple more books I hope to find myself a teaching position in a small college. My biggest problem in life is that I'm into too many areas, and do not have my 'thing,' which seems to be the license for greatness these days. Poetry is perhaps the closest thing to my gut; it forces me to suck life from language."

Willcox is fluent in Danish with competence in Swedish and Norwegian. He has lived for two years in Finland and four years in Denmark, since 1967.

* * *

WILLIAMS, Alan F. 1933-

PERSONAL: Born February 23, 1933, in Gloucestershire, England; married Sally G. Stanhope. *Education:* University of Bristol, B.A. (special honors), 1955, Ph.D., 1961. *Home:* 10 Prince William Pl., St. Johns, Newfoundland, Canada. *Office:* Department of Geography, Memorial University of Newfoundland, St. Johns, Newfoundland, Canada.

CAREER: University of Glasgow, Glasgow, Scotland, assistant lecturer in geography, 1959-62; Memorial University of Newfoundland, St. Johns, assistant professor of geography, 1962-65; University of Birmingham, Birmingham, England, lecturer in geography, 1965-71; Memorial University of Newfoundland, professor of geography, 1971—, acting head of department, 1971-72. Member of executive, Community Planning Association of Canada. 1971-72. *Member:* Institute of British Geographers, Geographical Association.

WRITINGS: (With Brian Fullerton) *Scandinavia,* Praeger, 1972.

WORK IN PROGRESS: Research on human and economic geography, with special reference to the Atlantic realm.

* * *

WILLIAMS, Barbara 1925-

PERSONAL: Born January 1, 1925, in Salt Lake City, Utah; daughter of Walter (a lawyer) and Emily (Jeremy) Wright; married J. D. Williams (a professor of political science), July 5, 1946; children: Kirk, Gil, Taylor, Kimberly. *Education:* Banff School of Fine Arts, student, 1945; University of Utah, B.A., 1946, M.A., 1972; Boston University, graduate study, 1949-50. *Politics:* Democrat. *Home:* 3399 East Loren Von Dr., Salt Lake City, Utah 84117.

CAREER: Deseret News, Salt Lake City, Utah, occasional society reporter and columnist, 1944-50; Library of Congress, Washington, D.C., secretary, 1946-48, 1951; University of Utah, Salt Lake City, remedial English teacher, 1960-71; *Marriage,* St. Meinrad, Ind., children's book reviewer, 1972—. *Awards, honors:* First place winner in Utah Fine Arts Writing Contest, 1965, for *William H. McGuffey: Boy Reading Genius,* and 1971, for *The Secret Name.*

WRITINGS—Juvenile, except as indicated: *Let's Go to an Indian Cliff Dwelling,* Putnam, 1965; *I Know a Policeman,* Putnam, 1966; *I Know a Fireman,* Putnam, 1967; *I Know a Mayor,* Putnam, 1967; *I Know a Garageman,* Putnam, 1968; *William H. McGuffey: Boy Reading Genius,* Bobbs-Merrill, 1968; *I Know a Bank Teller,* Putnam, 1968; *Twelve Steps to Better Exposition* (textbook), C. E. Merrill, 1968; *Boston: Seat of American History,* McGraw, 1969; *I Know a Weatherman,* Putnam, 1970; *The Well-Structured Paragraph* (textbook), C. E. Merrill, 1970; *The Secret Name,* Harcourt, 1972; *Gary and the Very Terrible Monster,* Childrens Press, 1973; *We Can Jump,* Childrens Press, 1973; *Albert's Toothache* (Junior Literary Guild selection), Dutton, 1974; *Kevin's Grandma,* Dutton, in press.

Plays: *Eternally Peggy* (three-act), Deseret News Press, 1957; *The Ghost of Black Jack* (one-act), Samuel French, 1961; *Just the Two of Us* (one-act), Utah Printing, 1965.

WORK IN PROGRESS: A picture book, *Someday I Will Take Care of You,* publication by Dutton expected in 1976.

* * *

WILLIAMS, Hosea L(orenzo) 1926-

PERSONAL: Born January 5, 1926, in Attapulgis, Ga.; married Juanita Terry; children: Barbara Jean, Elizabeth LaCenia, Hosea Lorenzo II, Andre Jerome, Yolanda Felicia. *Education:* Morris Brown College, B.A.; also attended Atlanta University.

CAREER: Ordained clergyman; high school science teacher in Georgia, 1951-52; research chemist, U.S. Department of Agriculture, 1952-63; Southern Christian Leadership Conference, special projects director, 1963-70, regional vice-president, 1970, national program director, 1971, president of metropolitan Atlanta chapter, 1972; organizer of Poor People's Union of America, 1973. Publisher of *Chatham County Crusader,* 1961-63. Speaker, lecturer, and civil rights leader. *Military service:* U.S. Army, 1944-46; served in European theater; became staff sergeant.

MEMBER: National Black Coalition, National Committee of Black Churchmen, New Party, National Association for the Advancement of Colored People, American Legion, Disabled American Veterans, Veterans of Foreign Wars, Natural Science Club, Young Men's Christian Association, Southern Christian Leadership Conference, Black Image Theatre, Metro Summit, Georgia Voters League, Phi Beta Sigma, Elks, Masons. *Awards, honors:* U.S. Department of Agriculture award for civil achievement, 1956; award from Savanna branch of National Association for the Advancement of Colored People, 1960-61, for courageous leadership in the freedom movement; award from Coastal Empire Emancipation Association, 1962, for unselfish public service in the field of race relations; community service award from Savannah chapter of Delta Sigma Theta, 1963; award from Georgia State-Wide Registration Committee and Southern Christian Leadership Conference, 1963, for the cause of freedom in the tradition of true democracy; national chapter award from Southern Christian Leadership Conference, 1973.

WRITINGS: The Situation of the Blacks, Atheneum, 1973.

WORK IN PROGRESS: An autobiography.

SIDELIGHTS: Hosea Williams represented the Southern Christian Leadership Conference in 1971 on a "World-Wide Brotherhood Tour," visiting ten countries of Africa, and India, South Viet Nam, Hong Kong, and the People's Republic of China.

WILLIAMS, Jerome 1926-

PERSONAL: Born July 15, 1926, in Toronto, Ontario, Canada; son of Maurice Edward (in social services) and Bertha (Bronstein) Williams; married Lelia Holden (a proofreader), March 1, 1953; children: Pamela Jean, Robert Stuart. *Education:* University of Maryland, B.S., 1950; Johns Hopkins University, M.A., 1952. *Politics:* Liberal. *Religion:* Unitarian Universalist. *Home:* 2804 Pine Dr., Annapolis, Md. 21401. *Office:* Environmental Sciences Department, United States Naval Academy, Annapolis, Md. 21402.

CAREER: Chesapeake Bay Institute, Annapolis, Md., research associate, 1951-69; United States Naval Academy, Annapolis, Md., assistant professor, 1957-65, associate professor, 1965-74, professor of oceanography, 1974—. *Military service:* U.S. Navy, 1944-46; served in Pacific theater. *Member:* American Geophysical Union, American Society of Limnology and Oceanography, American Association for the Advancement of Science, Marine Technology Society, Instrument Society of America, American Association of Physics Teachers, Estuarine Research Federation (vice-president, 1971-73; secretary, 1973-75), Atlantic Estuarine Research Society (president, 1967). *Awards, honors:* First prize in poetry reading from Anne Arundel Poetry Association, 1971.

WRITINGS: Oceanography: An Introduction to the Marine Sciences, Little, Brown, 1962; (with John J. Higginson and John D. Rohrbough) *Sea and Air,* U.S. Naval Institute, 1968, revised edition, 1973; *Optical Properties of the Sea,* U.S. Naval Institute, 1970; *Oceanography: A First Book,* F. Watts, 1972; *Oceanographic Instrumentation,* U.S. Naval Institute, 1973. Contributor to transactions and to *Journal of Marine Technology.*

WORK IN PROGRESS: Research in marine optics and pollution; ocean engineering text, completion expected in 1975; reports on progress in physics.

* * *

WILLIAMS, Martin 1924-

PERSONAL: Born August 9, 1924, in Richmond, Va.; son of John Bell and Rebecca (Yancey) Williams; married Martha Coker, October 15, 1960; children: Charles, Frederick, Frank. *Education:* University of Virginia, B.A., 1948; University of Pennsylvania, M.A., 1950; Columbia University, graduate study, 1950-53. *Home:* 1946 Martha's Rd., Alexandria, Va. 22307. *Office:* Smithsonian Institution, Washington, D.C. 20560.

CAREER: Columbia University, New York, N.Y., lecturer, 1951-53, instructor in English, 1952; Macmillan Co., New York, N.Y., editor, 1953; *Encyclopedia Americana,* New York, N.Y., editor, 1959; Smithsonian Institution, Washington, D.C., director of jazz program, Division of Performing Arts, 1972—. *Military service:* U.S. Naval Reserve, 1942-52; became lieutenant junior grade. *Member:* Phi Delta Epsilon. *Awards, honors:* Award from American Society of Composers, Authors and Publishers, 1973, for *The Jazz Tradition.*

WRITINGS: (Editor) *The Art of Jazz,* Oxford University Press, 1959; *King Oliver,* A. S. Barnes, 1961; *Jelly Roll Morton,* A. S. Barnes, 1962; (editor) *Jazz Panorama,* Collier Books, 1964; *Where's the Melody?: A Listener's Introduction to Jazz,* Pantheon, 1966, revised edition, 1969; *Jazz Masters of New Orleans,* Macmillan, 1967; *The Jazz Tradition,* Oxford University Press, 1970; *Jazz Masters in Transition, 1957-1969,* Macmillan, 1970. Contributor of articles on popular arts to *Saturday Review, Harper's, New York Times, Washington Post,* and other publications.

WORK IN PROGRESS: A historical-critical book on television; a young people's biography of film director D.W. Griffith.

* * *

WILLIAMS, Selma R(uth) 1925-

PERSONAL: Born October 26, 1925, in Malden, Mass.; married Burton L. Williams (a lawyer), June 26, 1949; children: Pamela, Wendy. *Education:* Radcliffe College, A.B. (cum laude), 1946; Tufts University, Ed.M., 1964. *Politics:* "Independent-liberal." *Home:* 17 Dane Rd., Lexington, Mass. 02173.

CAREER: Harvard Law Record, Cambridge, Mass., executive director, 1946-50; Diamond Junior High School, Lexington, Mass., history teacher, 1964-67; Concord-Carlisle Senior High School, Concord, Mass., history teacher, 1967-68; Middlesex Community College, Bedford, Mass., lecturer in history, 1973—. *Member:* Authors League, National Organization for Women (member of educational task force committee), League of Women Voters (member of local executive board, 1955-60), New England Association of Women Historians.

WRITINGS: Fifty-Five Fathers: The Story of the Constitutional Convention, Dodd, 1970; *Kings, Commoners, and Colonists: Puritan Politics in Old and New England, 1603-1660,* Atheneum, 1974.

WORK IN PROGRESS: Women in United States History, completion expected in 1976.

* * *

WILLIAMS, Thomas (Andrew) 1931- (Thomas Andreas)

PERSONAL: Born September 22, 1931, in Dover, Ga.; son of Thomas A. and Neva (Freeman) Williams; married Christina Dunaway (a dancer and choreographer), September 27, 1959; children: Andrea, Lisa. *Education:* University of Georgia, A.B., 1954, M.A., 1957; University of Grenoble, graduate study, 1955-56; University of North Carolina, Ph.D., 1965. *Home:* 807 East Third St., Greenville, N.C. 27834. *Office:* Department of Romance Languages, East Carolina University, Greenville, N.C. 27834.

CAREER: University of Georgia, Athens, instructor in English, 1957-58; Troy State College (now University), Troy, Ala., instructor in English, French, and Spanish, 1959-60; High Point College, High Point, N.C., assistant professor of French, 1961-62; University of South Carolina, Columbia, assistant professor of French, 1963-64; Davidson College, Davidson, N.C., associate professor of French, 1964-71; East Carolina University, Greenville, N.C., professor of Romance languages, 1971—, member of permanent graduate faculty. President of Editorial Research Associates (formerly Heritage Foundation, Inc.), Greenville, 1973—. *Military service:* U.S. Air Force, 1951-52. *Member:* American Association of Teachers of French, South Atlantic Modern Language Association, Phi Beta Kappa, Rotary International. *Awards, honors:* Fulbright fellow at University of Grenoble, 1955-56; Alumni Foundation fellowship, University of Georgia, 1965-67; summer research grants, Davidson College, 1965, 1967; Martin Luther Cannon Family Foundation grant for travel and research, 1966; Ford Foundation grant for travel and research, 1970-71; award from East Carolina University, 1972, for excellence in teaching.

WRITINGS: *Mallarme and the Language of Mysticism,* University of Georgia Press, 1970; (contributor) Harold Taussig, editor, *Shoestring Sabbatical,* Westminster Press, 1971; *Eliphas Levi: Master of Occultism,* University of Alabama Press, in press; *Tales of the Tobacco Country,* Editorial Research Associates, in press. Author of column, "Strange but True," under pseudonym Thomas Andreas, in *Advocate,* Greenville, N.C., 1972-73. Contributor to festschrift and to journals.

WORK IN PROGRESS: *The Literature of Occultism,* an anthology of writings from the Cabala and the Hermetic texts to Ouspensky and Gurdjieff; *An Introduction to the Study of Literature;* articles and reviews.

SIDELIGHTS: Williams told *CA:* "Thus far my work has been mostly in the field of mysticism and occultism and related areas . . . of folktale and folklore. This has gotten me into local history, and [Editorial Research Associates] has been formed to . . . work more on an oral history basis than on mere name-and-date approach (who begat who, and who settled where and when). I hope to capture the essence of the personalities involved." Williams adds that he is especially interested in the influence on modern literature of occult and mystical traditions.

* * *

WILLIAMSON, Audrey (May) 1913-

PERSONAL: Born May 29, 1913, in Thornton Heath, Surrey, England; daughter of Herbert and May (Tester) Williamson. *Education:* Attended English schools. *Home:* 14 Cygnet House, Belsize Rd., London N.W.6., England. *Agent:* John Cushman Associates Ltd., 25 West 43rd St., New York, N.Y. 10036.

CAREER: Author, journalist, television actress, and lecturer to historical and literary societies; ballet critic, *Tribune,* 1951-53; London theatre correspondent, *Age,* 1952-66; assistant drama critic, *Times,* 1956-64; New York theatre correspondent, *Scotsman,* 1963-64; New York opera and ballet correspondent, *Guardian,* 1963-64; book reviewer, *Tribune,* 1973—. *Member:* Society of the Study of Labour History, Thomas Paine Society, Richard III Society, Crime Writers Association.

WRITINGS: *Contemporary Ballet,* Rockliff, 1946, Macmillan, 1950; *Ballet Renaissance,* Golden Galley Press (London), 1948; *Old Vic Drama: A Twelve Years' Study of Plays and Players,* Rockliff, 1948, Macmillan, 1949.

The Art of Ballet, Macmillan, 1950, revised edition, 1953; *Theatre of Two Decades,* Rockliff, 1951, Macmillan, 1952; *Gilbert and Sullivan Opera: A New Assessment,* Macmillan, 1953, second edition, Rockliff, 1955; *Contemporary Theatre, 1953-56,* Macmillan, 1956; *Paul Rogers,* Rockliff, 1956; *Old Vic Drama 2: 1947-1957* (sequel to *Old Vic Drama*), Macmillan, 1957; (with Charles Landstone) *The Bristol Old Vic: The First Ten Years,* Miller, 1957; (illustrator) Carla Greene, *I Want to be a Coal Miner,* Childrens Press, 1957; *Ballet of Three Decades,* Macmillan, 1958.

Wagner Opera, J. Calder, 1962; *Bernard Shaw: Man & Writer,* Crowell-Collier, 1963.

Funeral March for Siegfried (detective novel), Frewin, 1970; *Thomas Paine: His Life, Work, and Times,* St. Martin's, 1973; *Wilkes: A Friend to Liberty,* Reader's Digest Services, 1974. Contributor to *Enciclopedia Della Spettacolo* and to *Theatre Arts, Opera News, Musical America,* and other periodicals.

WORK IN PROGRESS: Research on Thomas Paine in England and on Pre-Raphaelite and Aesthetic movements.

* * *

WILLMINGTON, Harold L. 1932-

PERSONAL: Born April 7, 1932, in Patterson, Ill. son of Paul L. (a bookstore owner) and Valma (Brown) Willmington; married wife, Marjorie Sue, April 15, 1961; children: Matthew. *Education:* Moody Bible Institute, diploma, 1955; Culver-Stockton College, B.A.; graduate study at Dallas Seminary and Ashland Seminary. *Home:* 126 Londonberry Rd., Forest, Va. 24551. *Office:* Thomas Road Baptist Church, Lynchburg, Va.

CAREER: Ordained Baptist minister; currently pastor of Thomas Road Baptist Church, Lynchburg, Va.

WRITINGS: *The King Is Coming,* Tyndale, 1973.

* * *

WILLSON, Meredith 1902-

PERSONAL: Born May 18, 1902, in Mason City, Iowa; son of John David (a lawyer) and Rosalie (Reiniger) Willson; married Elizabeth Wilson, August 29, 1920 (divorced March 5, 1948); married Ralina Zarova, March 13, 1948 (died December 6, 1966); married Rosemary Sullivan, February 14, 1968. *Education:* Attended Damrosch Institute (now Juilliard School of Music), 1919-22. Studied privately with Henry Hadley, Julius Gold, Bernard Wagenaar, and Georges Barrere. *Religion:* Congregationalist. *Home:* 1750 Westridge Rd., Los Angeles, Calif. 90049. *Office:* c/o Julius Lefkowitz & Co., 9171 Wishire Blvd., Beverly Hills, Calif. 90210.

CAREER: Composer, lecturer, author. Began as professional musician with John Philip Sousa Band, 1921-23, New York Philharmonic Symphony Orchestra, 1924-29, and New York Chamber Music Society, 1925-29; American Broadcasting System, Seattle, Wash., music director of northwest division, 1929-30; KFRC-Radio, San Francisco, Calif., music director, 1930-33; National Broadcasting Co. (NBC), music director of western division, 1933-37, music director of Maxwell House Radio Program, 1937-42, master of ceremonies of "The Meredith Willson Show," 1949, music director and personality for "The Big Show," 1950-52, master of ceremonies of "Music Room," 1959. Guest conductor, Cleveland, Detroit, Chicago, Minneapolis, American, and other symphony orchestras. Member of Council on Arts and Humanities, 1966-68. *Military service:* U.S. Army, 1942-45; head of music division of Armed Forces Radio Service; became major. *Member:* International Academy of Arts and Letters (fellow), American Society of Composers, Authors, and Publishers, Dramatists Guild, Friars Club, Big Brothers of Greater Los Angeles (president, 1956-61).

AWARDS, HONORS: In 1958, *The Music Man* received the Drama Critic's Circle Award for best musical, best music, and best lyrics, Outer Circle Award, Thespian Award, five Antoinette Perry (Tony) awards, best musical award from *Variety* and *Sign* magazines; also, Academy Award (Oscar) for best musical score, 1962, and numerous other awards. *Honorary degrees:* Mus.D., Parsons College, 1956, Coe College, 1960; Litt.D., Indiana Institute of Technology, 1963. National Big Brothers Award, 1962.

WRITINGS: What Every Musician Should Know (booklet), Robbins, 1938; *And There I Stood with My Piccolo* (autobiographical), Doubleday, 1948; *Who Did What to Fedalia?* (novel), Doubleday, 1952; *Eggs I Have Laid* (autobiographical), Holt, 1955; *"But He Doesn't Know the Territory"* (autobiographical), Putnam, 1959; *The Music Man* (novel based on musical), Pyramid, 1962.

Musicals: (Author of book, music, and lyrics) *The Music Man* (two-act; first produced on Broadway at Majestic Theatre, December 19, 1957), Putnam, 1958; (author of music and lyrics) *The Unsinkable Molly Brown* (two-act; first produced on Broadway at Winter Garden Theatre, November 3, 1960), Putnam, 1961; (author of book, music, and lyrics) "Here's Love" (two-act; based on novel, *Miracle on 34th Street* by Valentine Davies), first produced on Broadway at Shubert Theatre, October 3, 1963; (author of book, music, and lyrics) "1491" (two-act), first produced in Los Angeles at Dorothy Chandler Pavilion, September 2, 1969.

Musical compositions: "Symphony No. 1 in F Minor," 1936; "Symphony No. 2 in E Minor," 1940; (composer of score) "The Great Dictator," 1940; (composer of score) "The Little Foxes," 1941; "The Jervis Bay," 1943; "Radio Suite," 1946; "Symphonic Variations on American Themes," 1948; "Prelude to America," 1961. Songs: "May the Good Lord Bless and Keep You"; "I See the Moon"; "You and I"; "It's Beginning to Look Like Christmas."

WORK IN PROGRESS: More Eggs—As Laid by Meredith Willson (tentative title).

SIDELIGHTS: Willson's musicals, *The Music Man*—which was Broadway's fifth longest running play—and *The Unsinkable Molly Brown,* were made into motion pictures. Another play, "Here's Love," had the most successful opening week in the 50 year history of Broadway's Shubert Theatre.

* * *

WILMA, Dana
See FARALLA, Dana

* * *

WILSON, Beth P(ierre)

PERSONAL: Born in Tacoma, Wash.; daughter of Samuel Deal (a tailor) and Mae (Conna) Pierre; married William Douglas Wilson (a dentist); children: Diane M. Wilson Thomas. *Education:* University of Puget Sound, B.A.; graduate study at University of California, Los Angeles. *Residence:* Berkeley, Calif. 94707.

CAREER: Oakland Public Schools, Oakland, Calif., elementary teacher, 1936-44, elementary assistant, 1945-60. Member of Links, Inc., and Jack and Jill of America, Inc. *Member:* National Association for the Advancement of Colored People, Alpha Kappa Alpha. *Awards, honors:* Senior citizens award, 1971, and Cate award from California Association of Teachers of English, 1972, both for *Martin Luther King, Jr.*

WRITINGS: Martin Luther King, Jr., Putnam, 1971; *Muhammed Ali,* Putnam, 1974; *The Great Minu,* Follett, 1974.

SIDELIGHTS: Beth Wilson has travelled throughout Europe, Canada, Hawaii, Mexico, Scandinavia, and western Africa.

WILSON, Ellen (Janet Cameron)

PERSONAL: Born in Pittsburgh, Pa.; daughter of Henry Nesmith (a clergyman) and Belle (Morgan) Cameron; married William E. Wilson (a writer), June 29, 1929; children: William E. III, Cameron and Douglas (twins). *Education:* Ohio Wesleyan University, A.B., 1924; Radcliffe College, A.M., 1927; Universite Aix-Marseille, School for Foreign Students, graduate study, 1956-57. *Politics:* Democrat. *Religion:* Protestant. *Home:* 1326 Pickwick Pl., Bloomington, Ind. 47401.

CAREER: Rhode Island School of Design, Providence, teacher of English, 1931-33; Katherine Gibbs School, Providence, R.I., teacher of English, 1933-37; Indiana University, Bloomington, teacher of independent study courses in history of children's literature, 1953—. Leader of children's literature workshop, University of Colorado Writers Conference, 1967. *Member:* National Society of Arts and Letters, Kappa Alpha Theta, Theta Sigma Phi. *Awards, honors:* Indiana Authors' Day Award for best biography for young people, 1972, for *American Painter in Paris: A Life of Mary Cassatt.*

WRITINGS—Juvenile fiction; with Nan Agle, "Three Boys" series, published by Scribner: *Three Boys and a Lighthouse,* 1951; *...and the Remarkable Cow,* 1952; *...and a Tugboat,* 1953; *...and a Mine,* 1954; *...and a Train,* 1956; *...and a Helicopter,* 1958; *...and Space,* 1962; *...and H2O,* 1968.

Biographies for children, except where otherwise noted: *Ernie Pyle: Boy from Back Home,* Bobbs-Merrill, 1955; *Annie Oakley: Little Sure Shot,* Bobbs-Merrill, 1958; *Robert Frost: Boy with Promises to Keep,* Bobbs-Merrill, 1967; *American Painter in Paris: A Life of Mary Cassatt* (for young adults), Farrar, Straus, 1971; *They Named Me Gertrude Stein* (for young adults), Farrar, Straus, 1973.

Contributor of stories and articles to *Cricket, American Heritage,* and *Horn Book.* Book reviewer, *Providence Journal,* 1951—, Louisville *Courier Journal,* 1963—.

WORK IN PROGRESS: A biography of Margaret Fuller, focusing on her part in literature and in women's liberation, for Farrar, Straus.

SIDELIGHTS: Mrs. Wilson began writing fiction books for children some time after her own three boys were in school. "It was an artist friend and neighbor in Baltimore who gave me the initial push," she writes. "Nan Agle and I wrote our first book together—*Three Boys and a Lighthouse.* By the time that Scribner's told us that we should make our manuscript longer, we Wilsons had moved to Boulder, Colorado. Nan and I finished the *Lighthouse* book by correspondence, and have since written seven more 'Three Boys' books by mail between Bloomington and Baltimore. For all of those children's books we developed a workable theory and procedure: give children both facts and adventure. Whether we wrote of the three boys and a train, a tugboat, or a helicopter, we separately not only did thorough library research, but rode in diesel engines, tugboats, and in helicopters so that we would know what it felt like to have the adventures our three boys had."

Now concentrating on biographies for young adult readers, Mrs. Wilson continues to do extensive research for each book. She told *CA* that "when people say 'You put all that work and research in writing just for children?,' I resent it. I resent the implication that young people deserve less than adults. I feel strongly that they deserve an author's best work both in research and in writing." In the process of writing her biography of Mary Cassatt, for example, Mrs. Wilson not only read books about her life and work, but interviewed relatives, borrowed letters she had written home from France, studied her paintings, and visited her chateau in France. She followed the same procedure in writing her biography of Gertrude Stein, using libraries in American and Europe, as well as visiting Stein's various homes in France.

* * *

WILSON, Eugene E. 1887(?)-1974

1887(?)—July 10, 1974; American corporation president and author. Obituaries: *New York Times,* July 12, 1974.

* * *

WILSON, Jacques M(arcel) P(atrick) 1920-

PERSONAL: Born August 4, 1920, in New York, N.Y.; son of James F. D. (a civil servant) and Simone (Micheau) Wilson; married Clotilde Tavares de Lima, December 25, 1943; children: Jacqueline (Mrs. Stephen Martin), James, Alfred, John Patrick, Gregory, Guy. *Education:* University of Miami, Coral Gables, Fla., A.B., 1941, M.Ed., 1960; graduate study at University of Havana, summer, 1941, Sophia University, 1951-52, and Purdue University, summer, 1961; University of Texas, Ph.D., 1966. *Politics:* Democrat. *Religion:* Roman Catholic. *Home:* 601 West Mallory St., Pensacola, Fla. 32501. *Office:* Omega College, University of West Florida, Pensacola, Fla. 32504.

CAREER: Teacher of French and Spanish at private school in Coral Gables, Fla., 1940-41; Ministry of Foreign Affairs, Rio de Janeiro, Brazil, interpreter and translator, 1941-42; U.S. Air Force, personnel and management analyst, 1942-57, leaving service as captain; teacher of French, Spanish, and social studies in public schools of Dade County, Fla., 1958-62; Appalachian State Teachers College (now Appalachian State University), Boone, N.C., visiting professor of linguistics, summer, 1964; Fulbright lecturer in linguistics at Universidad Central de Quito and Catholic University of Guayaquil (both in Ecuador), both 1964-65; Our Lady of the Lake College, San Antonio, Tex., assistant professor of Romance languages, 1965-67, chairman of department of foreign languages, 1966-67; University of Miami, Coral Gables, Fla., associate professor of comparative education and associate director of Institute of Inter-American Studies, 1967-70; University of West Florida, Omega College, Pensacola, professor of foreign languages and chairman of department, 1970-73, chairman of Latin-American Interdisciplinary Studies Program, 1971—, assistant to provost for international programs, 1973—. English language program coordinator for Fulbright Commission in Ecuador, 1964-65; language coordinator of Peace Corps training project at Antioch College, summer, 1966; Fulbright lecturer and academic director of seminars in Ecuador, 1970. Has testified as expert witness before U.S. House of Representatives; consultant to President of Ecuador. Member of board of directors of Pensacola People-to-People Program.

MEMBER: Modern Language Association of America, American Association of Teachers of Spanish and Portuguese, Teachers of English to Speakers of Other Languages, National Education Association, Latin American Studies Association, American Council for the Teaching of Foreign Languages, Asociacion de Profesores de Ingles del Ecuador, Southern Conference on Language Teaching, Florida Education Association, Florida Foreign Language Association, Phi Delta Kappa, Iron Arrow. *Awards, honors:* Ford Foundation research grant for analysis of development of education in Cuba, 1967-69; U.S. Department of Defense research grant to study the role of the military in non-military activities in Brazil, 1969.

WRITINGS: Metodologia Para la Ensenanza de Idiomas Extranjeros (title means "Methodology for the Teaching of Foreign Languages"), Our Lady of the Lake College Press, 1967; *The Development of Education in Ecuador,* University of Miami Press, 1971; (translator and editor) Paulo de Carvalho Neto, *The Concept of Folklore,* University of Miami Press, 1971; (translator and editor) Neto, *Folklore and Psychoanalysis,* University of Miami Press, 1972; (translator and editor) Neto, *Folklore in South America,* University of Miami Press, 1974. Contributor of about thirty-five articles and reviews to journals and newspapers, including *Journal of Inter-American Studies, Florida Educator, Hispania, Florida Foreign Language Reporter,* and *Florida Adult Educator.* Editor of *Latin American Studies: Interdisciplinary Occasional Papers,* University of West Florida, 1973; associate editor of *Florida Foreign Language Reporter,* spring, 1969.

WORK IN PROGRESS: The History of Jamaican Education.

AVOCATIONAL INTERESTS: Swimming, fishing, hunting, philately.

* * *

WILSON, Robert M. 1944-

PERSONAL: Born October 4, 1944, in New York, N.Y.; son of D. M. (a lawyer) and Loree (Hamilton) Wilson. *Education:* Attended University of Texas, 1959-62; Pratt Institute, M.F.A., 1965. *Agent:* Ninon Karlweis, 250 East 65th St., New York, N.Y. 10021. *Office:* Byrd Hoffman Foundation, Inc., 147 Spring St., New York, N.Y. 10012.

CAREER: Teacher, painter, architect. Byrd Hoffman Foundation, Inc., artistic director. Has conducted seminars or workshops at institutions including University of California, Berkeley, Newark State College, and Centre de Development du Potential Humain, Paris; lecturer at University of Iowa Center for New Performing Arts, Ohio State University, International School (Paris), UNESCO International Theater Institute (Durdan, France), and at European theatre festivals. Designed set for original production of van Itallie's "America Hurrah," 1963; has made 16-mm films, including "Slant," for NET-TV, 1963, and adaptation of own play "Overture for a Deafman," 1971. Art work has been exhibited at Willard Gallery, New York, and Musee Galliera, Paris. *Member:* Societe des Auteurs et Compositeurs Dramatiques (Paris). *Awards, honors:* Award for best foreign play from Syndicat de la Critique Dramatique et Musicale (Paris), 1970, for "Deafman Glance"; Vernon Rice Drama Desk Award, 1971, for direction of "Deafman Glance"; Guggenheim fellowship, 1971.

WRITINGS—Plays: "Theater Activity" (one-act), first produced in New York, N.Y. at Bleecker Street Cinema, 1967; "ByrdwoMAN" (two-act), first produced in New York at Byrd Hoffman Studio, 1968; "The King of Spain" (one-act; first produced Off-Broadway at Anderson Theater, 1969), published in *New American Plays,* Volume III, edited by William Hoffman, Hill & Wang, 1970; "The Life and Times of Sigmund Freud" (three-act), first produced Off-Broadway at Brooklyn Academy of Music Opera House, 1969.

"Deafman Glance" (one-act), first produced in Iowa City, Iowa at University Theater, 1970; produced Off-Broadway at Brooklyn Academy of Music Opera House, 1971; first produced as a four-act play in Nancy, France at Grand Theatre de la Nancy, 1971; "Program Prologue Now, Overture for a Deafman" (three-act), first produced in Paris at Espace Pierre Cardin, 1971; "Overture" (two-act), first produced at Byrd Hoffman Studio, 1972, produced as one-act in Shiraz, Iran at Khaneh-e Zinatolmolk, 1972, produced as a "twenty-four hour continuous one-act" in Paris at Musee Galliera and Opera Comique, 1972; "KA MOUNTAIN AND GUARDenia TERRACE" ("seven-day continuous one-act"), produced in Shiraz at Haft Tan Mountain, 1972; "king lyre and lady in the wasteland" (one-act), first produced at Byrd Hoffman Studio, 1973; "The Life and Times of Joseph Stalin" (seven-act), first produced in Copenhagen at Det Ny Teater, 1973, produced at Brooklyn Academy of Music Opera House, 1973; "A Letter for Queen Victoria," produced in Italy at Spoleto Festival, June, 1974.

SIDELIGHTS: "Robert Wilson is a genius," writes D. Keith Mano in the *National Review*. He describes "The Life and Times of Joseph Stalin" as having less to do with Stalin than with theatrical life and times, and calls it "the most significant theatrical act since Cro-Magnon men first mimed their kills. I am stunned and excited. . . . Wilson's characters are planetary, cometary; they have separate orbits, they seldom touch. But they do form mad conjunctions and a terrific gravitational pull-push occurs onstage. It drags your eyes; it drags your viscera. It makes you breathless and tense. . . . There are numberless series [of events that] build and build with infuriating determination . . . to no effect. Yet amazing things happen constantly without previous notice. . . . Normal perception, the mind's bread-crumb trail, gets tricked." The twelve hours needed to present "The Life and Times of Joseph Stalin" are essential, Mano estimates, as is the fatigue one experiences: "Time allows Wilson to break your peevish habits of logic. *Stalin* is a spectacular, terrorizing tour de force: the force emphasized. Everyone could profit from an extended session with Robert Wilson."

Wilson studied painting privately in Paris in 1962, and was apprenticed to Paolo Soleri in Phoenix, Arix., in 1966.

BIOGRAPHICAL/CRITICAL SOURCES: Fernando Arrabal, editor, *Le Teatre 1972,* Volume I, C. Bourgois, 1972.

* * *

WINDSOR, Patricia 1938-

PERSONAL: Born September 21, 1938, in New York, N.Y. *Education:* Attended Bennington College. *Agent:* International Famous Agency, 1301 Avenue of the Americas, New York, N.Y. 10019.

CAREER: Novelist. *Awards, honors: The Summer Before* named *Chicago Tribune* honor book at *Book World*'s spring book festival, 1973, and chosen by *Library Journal* as one of Best Books for Young Adults, 1973.

WRITINGS: The Summer Before (novel), Harper, 1973; *Something's Waiting for You, Baker D* (novel), Harper, 1974; *Old Coat's Cat* (short story), Macmillan, 1974. Also lyricist for popular songs composed by Yseult Freilicher.

SIDELIGHTS: Patricia Windsor divides her time between London and New York.

WING, Cliff W(aldron), Jr. 1922-

PERSONAL: Born December 28, 1922, in Reed City, Mich.; son of Cliff Waldron and Edna (Vail) Wing; married Lucie Lee, 1949; children: Steven B., Scott L. *Education:* University of Grand Rapids, B.A., 1943; University of Denver, M.A., 1948; Tulane University, Ph.D., 1951. *Residence:* Durham, N.C. *Office:* Department of Psychology, Duke University, Durham, N.C. 27706.

CAREER: Tulane University of Louisiana, New Orleans, staff associate, Urban Life Research Institute, 1950-56, assistant professor of psychology, 1951-56, director of admissions, 1956-65; Duke University, Durham, N.C., associate professor of psychology and director of student resources, 1965—. Harvard University, Phillips Foundation intern in academic administration as assistant dean of Harvard College, 1962-63. Trustee of College Entrance Examination board, 1961-64; member of National Merit Scholarship Selection Committee, 1964-67. *Military service:* U.S. Naval Reserve, active duty, 1943-46; served in European and Pacific theaters; became lieutenant.

MEMBER: American Psychological Association, American Association for the Advancement of Science, Association of College Admissions Counselors (president, 1963-64). *Awards, honors:* Richardson Foundation research grant, 1966-68.

WRITINGS: (With Leonard Reissman and K. H. Silvert) *The New Orleans Voter: A Handbook of Political Description,* Tulane Bookstore, Tulane University, Volume II, 1955, also contributor to Volume III, 1955; (with M. A. Wallach) *The Talented Student: A Validation of the Creativity-Intelligence Distinction,* Holt, 1969; (with Wallach) *College Admissions and the Psychology of Talent,* Holt, 1971.

Contributor: John H. Rohrer and Leonard Reissman, editors, *Change and Dilemma in the Nursing Profession,* Putnam, 1956; Jerome Kagan, editor, *Creativity and Learning,* Houghton, 1967; D. K. Whitlan, editor, *Handbook of Measurement and Assessment in Behavioral Sciences,* Addison-Wesley, 1967. Contributor to *American Universities and Colleges,* 9th edition, and to research reports and journals.

* * *

WINN, Wilkins B(owdre) 1928-

PERSONAL: Born January 19, 1928, in Fort Worth, Tex.; son of Raymond and Joanna (Bowdre) Winn; married Barbara Evelyn Weaver (a medical technologist), May 11, 1950; children: Barbara Anne, John Bowdre, Albert Payne. *Education:* Samford University, A.B., 1952; University of Alabama, M.A., 1959, Ph.D., 1964; Dallas Theological Seminary, Th.M. (with honors), 1959. *Home address:* P.O. Box 2354, 207 Churchill Dr., Greenville, N.C. 27834. *Office:* Department of History, East Carolina University, Box 2744, Greenville, N.C. 27834.

CAREER: Ordained minister of Baptist Church; Mobile College, Mobile, Ala., assistant professor of history, 1963-66; East Carolina University, Greenville, N.C., associate professor of Latin American history, 1966—, coordinator of Latin American Studies Program, 1968-70. Presently guest minister at Baptist churches. *Member:* American Historical Association, Conference of Latin American Historians, Latin American Studies Association, Conference on Faith and History, Southern Historical Association, Southeastern Conference on Latin American Studies, Phi Alpha

Theta, Alpha Kappa Delta, Greenville Tennis Club (member of board of directors).

WRITINGS: (Contributor) Eugene R. Huck and Edward H. Moseley, editors, *Militarists, Merchants, and Missionaries: United States Expansion in Middle America,* University of Alabama Press, 1970; *Pioneer Protestant Missionaries in Honduras: A. E. Bishop and J. G. Cassel and the Establishment of the Central American Mission in Western Honduras, 1896-1901,* Centro Intercultural de Documentacion (Cuernavaca), 1973. Contributor to *Americas* and other journals.

WORK IN PROGRESS: United States Diplomacy for Religious Liberty in Latin America, 1817-1870; A. E. Bishop and the Protestant Struggle in Guatemala, 1899-1946; The Origins of Protestantism in Guatemala, 1846-1940, completion expected in 1975.

AVOCATIONAL INTERESTS: Tennis (playing in tournaments and giving free lessons to juniors and adults), boating, fishing.

* * *

WINSTON, R(obert) A(lexander) 1907-1974 (Col. Victor J. Fox)

October 25, 1907—June 3, 1974; American aviator and author. Obituaries: *New York Times,* June 4, 1974; *Washington Post,* June 7, 1974. (*CA*-25/28).

* * *

WINTER, Gibson 1916-

PERSONAL: Born October 6, 1916, in Boston, Mass.; son of Howard and Cecelia (Gibson) Winter; married Sara Blair Ballard, April 11, 1942; children: Marcus Cole, Sara Winter Lake, Anne Winter Forsyth, Jacqueline Winter de Terrazas. *Education:* Harvard University, A.B., 1938, Ph.D., 1952; Cambridge Episcopal Theological School, B.D., 1941. *Home:* 5805 South Dorchester, Chicago, Ill. 60637. *Office:* Divinity School, University of Chicago, Chicago, Ill. 60637.

CAREER: Ordained priest of the Protestant Episcopal Church, 1941; curate in Waterbury, Conn., 1941-43; rector in Belmont, Mass., 1943-44, and Foxboro, Mass., 1946-49; member of Parishfield Community (a lay training center), Brighton, Mich., 1949-56; University of Chicago, Chicago, Ill., assistant professor, 1956-61, associate professor, 1961-64, professor of social ethics, 1964—. *Military service:* U.S. Navy, Chaplains Corps, 1944-46; became lieutenant junior grade. *Member:* American Society for Christian Ethics, Society for the Scientific Study of Religion. *Awards, honors:* S.T.D. from Cambridge Episcopal Theological School, 1967.

WRITINGS: Love and Conflict: New Patterns in Family Life, Doubleday, 1958; *The Suburban Captivity of the Churches,* Doubleday, 1961; *The New Creation as Metropolis,* Macmillan, 1963; *Elements for a Social Ethic: Scientific and Ethical Perspectives on Social Process,* Macmillan, 1966; *Being Free: Reflections on America's Cultural Revolution,* Macmillan, 1970.

WORK IN PROGRESS: Religious Foundations of Urban Form; Religion in the Social Scientific Tradition.

SIDELIGHTS: Reviewing *Elements for a Social Ethic,* Joseph Dabney Bettis observed in the *Christian Century,* "This book will alter radically the debate on social ethics. Through a major restructuring of the ethical problematic, Winter reorders the field and develops new potentials for interrelating social ethics, social science and social policy."

* * *

WINTER, William O(rville) 1918-

PERSONAL: Born October 1, 1918, in Richmond, Mo.; son of William Emmett and Deborah (Hauser) Winter; married Mary Crossland, February 9, 1939 (divorced, 1953); married Alice Beardslee, September 12, 1955; children: (first marriage) William Steven, Sharon Marie (Mrs. John C. Burdick, Jr.); (second marriage) Susan Ann, Lucy Emily. *Education:* University of Missouri, A.B., 1942, M.A., 1947, Ph.D., 1950. *Politics:* Democrat. *Religion:* Protestant. *Home:* 505 Pine, Boulder, Colo. 80302. *Office:* Department of Political Science, University of Colorado, Boulder, Colo. 80302.

CAREER: University of Michigan, Ann Arbor, research associate, Bureau of Government, 1949-50; Southern Illinois University, Carbondale, assistant professor, 1950-56, associate professor of political science, 1957-63; University of Colorado, Boulder, professor of political science, 1963—, chairman of department, 1965-69. Fulbright professor at University of Vienna, 1956-57. Consultant on municipal finance. *Military service:* U.S. Naval Reserve, active duty, 1943-46; became lieutenant junior grade; received Presidential Unit Citation; inactive duty, 1947-64. *Member:* International City Management Association, American Political Science Association, American Society for Public Administration, National Municipal League, Sierra Club.

WRITINGS: The Special Assessment Today, University of Michigan Press, 1952; *The Urban Polity,* Dodd, 1969. Contributor to public administration and economics journals.

WORK IN PROGRESS: The Urban Republic, an introductory work on American government and politics, written from an urban perspective; *The City's Money,* a model of a consumer-based urban revenue system.

* * *

WISE, John E. 1905-1974

May 21, 1905—June 21, 1974; American educator, author, and Roman Catholic priest. Obituaries: *Washington Post,* June 22, 1974. (*CA*-15/16).

* * *

WITTICH, Walter A(rno) 1910-

PERSONAL: Born June 14, 1910, in Sheboygan, Wis.; son of Walter Julius and Freida (Mayer) Wittich; married Florence Lucille Evenson, July 18, 1935; children: Rita Louise, Lois Ann, Walter C., Wendy. *Education:* University of Wisconsin, B.A., 1932, M.A., 1934, Ph.D., 1944. *Religion:* Presbyterian. *Home:* 5119 Palaole Pl., Honolulu, Hawaii. *Office:* Department of Educational Communications, University of Hawaii, 1776 University Ave., Honolulu, Hawaii 96822.

CAREER: University of Wisconsin, Madison, instructor in education, 1932-40 (in LaCrosse, 1935-36, and Milwaukee, 1936-40), supervising principal, 1941-44, professor of education, 1944-61; University of Hawaii, Honolulu, professor of education and chairman of department of educational communications, 1961—, program director, 1970-73. *Member:* National Education Association, Association for Educational Communications and Technology, Phi Delta Kappa. *Awards, honors:* Distinguished Service Award, Association for Educational Communications and Technology, 1972.

WRITINGS: (With J. G. Fowlkes) *Audio-Visual Paths to Learning,* Harper, 1946; (editor with Charles F. Schuller) *Audio-Visual Materials: Their Nature and Use,* Harper, 1953, 5th edition published as *Instructional Technology: Its Nature and Use,* 1973; (compiler with G. L. Hanson) *Educators Guide to Free Tapes, Scripts and Transcriptions,* Educators Progress Service, 1953, 20th edition (compiled by Wittich and Raymond H. Suttles), 1973.

* * *

WITTLIN, Jozef 1896-

PERSONAL: Born August 17, 1896, in Dmytrow, Poland; emigrated to United States in 1941; became citizen, 1949; son of Karol and Eliza (Rosenfeld) Wittlin; married Halina Anna Handelsman (a librarian), July 6, 1924; children: Elizabeth (Mrs. Michel Lipton). *Education:* University of Vienna, student, 1915-1916; University of Lwow, student, 1918-1919. *Home:* 5400 Fieldston Rd., New York, N.Y. 10471.

CAREER: High school and college teacher of Polish language and literature in Lwow, Poland, 1919-21; Municipal Theater, Lodz, Poland, literary director, 1922-23; School of Drama, Lodz, founder and professor, 1922-23; writer, 1923—; left Warsaw for Paris, France, first days of July, 1939; fled from France to Portugal via Spain in 1940, and then came to United States; Radio Free Europe, New York, N.Y., scriptwriter and broadcaster, 1952-72. *Military service:* Polish Eastern Legion, 1914-15; Austro-Hungarian Army, 1916-18.

MEMBER: P.E.N. American Center, P.E.N.-in-exile (chairman of American branch, 1960-63; honorary member of executive board), Polish Institute of Arts and Sciences in America, Deutsche Akademie fuer Dichtung und Sprache (German Academy of Poetry and Language; corresponding member). *Awards, honors:* Polish P.E.N. Club award, 1935, for translation of Homer's *Odyssey* from Greek into Polish hexameter; awards from "Academy of the Independents" and from readers of *Wiadomosci Literackie* (literary magazine; Warsaw), 1936, for *Sol ziemi;* Golden Laurel from Polish Academy of Literature, 1937; awards from American Academy of Arts and Letters and National Institute of Arts and Letters, 1943, for *Salt of the Earth;* Alfred Jurzykowski Foundation prize, 1965, for entire literary work.

WRITINGS: Hymny (poems; title means "Hymns"), [Poznan, Poland], 1920; (translator) Homer, *Odyseja,* [Lwow], 1924, 3rd edition, Veritas (London), 1957; *Wojna, pokoj, i dusza poety* (essays; title means "War, Peace, and a Poet's Soul"), Z. Pomaranski [Zamosc, Poland], 1925; *Sol ziemi* (novel), Roj (Warsaw), 1935, translation by Pauline de Chary published as *The Salt of the Earth,* Methuen, 1939, Sheridan, 1941, new edition with postscript, Stackpole, 1970; (editor with Manfred Kridl and Wladyslaw Malinowski) *For Your Freedom and Ours: Polish Progressive Spirit through the Centuries* (anthology), translated by Ludwik Krzyzanowski and revised by Sidney and Edith Sulkin, Ungar, 1943 (published in England as *The Democratic Heritage of Poland: "For Your Freedom and Ours,"* Allen & Unwin, 1944); *Moj Lwow* (title means "My Lwow"), Biblioteka Polska, [New York], 1947; *Etapy* (title means "Stages"), Roj, 1952; *Orfeusz w piekle XX wieku* (essays; title means "Orpheus in the Hell of the Twentieth Century"), Instytut Literacki (Paris), 1963.

Contributor: Emil Ludwig and Henry B. Kranz, editors, *The Torch of Freedom: Twenty Exiles of History,* Farrar-Rinehart, 1943; Manfred Kridl, editor, *Adam Mickiewicz, Poet of Poland,* Columbia University Press, 1951; Leopold Tyrmand, editor, *Explorations in Freedom: Prose, Narrative and Poetry from Kultura,* Free Press, 1970.

Also translator into Polish from original language: Herman Hesse, *Steppenwolf;* John Hersey, *Hiroshima;* Carlo Collodi, *Pinocchio;* five novels by Joseph Roth; works by Wilfred Owen, W. H. Auden, Robinson Jeffers, William Carlos Williams, e.e. cummings, Langston Hughes, Stephen Vincent Benet, Richard Dehmel, R. M. Rilke, Hermann Kesten, Salvatore Quasimodo, Umberto Saba, Alphonso Gatto, Miguel Hernandez, Jose Hierro, and Francisco Brines.

Represented in numerous anthologies in United States and abroad, including: *Heart of Europe,* edited by Klaus Mann and Hermann Kesten, L. B. Fischer, 1943; *Poetry of Freedom,* edited by William Rose Benet and Norman Cousins, Random House, 1945; *A World of Great Stories,* edited by Hiram Haydn and John Curnos, Crown, 1947; *An Anthology of Polish Literature,* edited by Manfred Kridl, Columbia University Press, 1947; *Poeti polacchi contemporanei,* translated and edited by Carlo Verdiani, Silva Editore (Genoa), 1961; *Introduction to Modern Polish Literature: An Anthology,* edited by Adam Gillon and Ludwik Krzyzanowski, Twayne, 1964; *Polnische Poesie des 20. Jahrhunderts,* translated and edited by Karl Dedecius, Carl Hanser Verlag, 1964; *Neue Polische Lyrik,* edited and translated by Karl Dedecius, Moderner Buchclub, 1965; *Anthologie de la poesie polonaise,* edited by Constantin Jelenski, Editions du Seuil, 1965.

WORK IN PROGRESS: Two sequels to *The Salt of the Earth;* a collection of poems, original and translated.

SIDELIGHTS: A saga of the unknown soldier, *Sol ziemi* was inspired by the author's own infantry experiences. Here, as in his other writing, he contrasts nobility of the human spirit with the degradation and brutality of war and contemporary life; the style has been compared with biblical prose. *Sol ziemi* has been translated into thirteen languages. A product of ten years efforts, it was intended to be the first volume of a trilogy. Wittlin assured *CA* he still plans to complete the trilogy.

BIOGRAPHICAL/CRITICAL SOURCES: Zoya Yurieff, *Joseph Wittlin,* Twayne, 1973.

Saturday Review of Literature, August 2, 1941; *New York Herald Tribune,* October 25, 1941; *New Republic,* October 27, 1941; *Polish Review IX,* Number 1, 1964.

* * *

WITTROCK, M(erlin) C(arl) 1931-

PERSONAL: Born January 3, 1931, in Twin Falls, Idaho; son of Herman C. (a businessman) and Eleanor (Baumann) Wittrock; married Nancy McNulty, April 3, 1953; children: Steven, Catherine, Rebecca. *Education:* University of Missouri, B.S., 1953, M.Ed., 1956; University of Illinois, Ph.D., 1960. *Politics:* Democrat. *Religion:* Lutheran. *Home:* 2310 Banyan Dr., Los Angeles, Calif. 90049. *Office:* 321 Moore Hall, University of California, Los Angeles, Calif. 90024.

CAREER: University of California, Los Angeles, assistant professor, 1960-64, associate professor, 1964-67, professor of education, 1967—, director of Laboratory of Instructional Research, 1963-66, director of Center for the Study of Evaluation of Instructional Programs, 1966—. Fellow, Center for Advanced Study in the Behavioral Sciences, 1967-68. Director of Ford Foundation research project on improving instruction, 1964—; member of board of reviewers, Division of Special Education, U.S. Office of Education, 1965—. *Military service:* U.S. Air Force, 1953-55; became captain. U.S. Air Force Reserve, 1955-61.

MEMBER: American Psychological Association (fellow), Educational Data Processing Association, American Association for the Advancement of Science, American Educational Research Association, Western Psychological Association, California Educational Research Association, Phi Delta Kappa. *Awards, honors:* Award for excellent teaching from Associated Students of University of California, Los Angeles, 1961; Social Science Research Council fellowship, 1964.

WRITINGS: (Editor with David Wiley) *The Evaluation of Instruction,* Holt, 1970; (editor) *Research Based Alternatives in Education,* Prentice-Hall, in press. Editor in chief of series and editor of volume IV, "Readings in Educational Research," Wiley, Volume I-II, 1971, Volume III-IV, in press. Editor, *Evaluation Comment,* 1966—; consulting editor, *American Educational Research Journal,* 1966—; contributing editor, *Educational Psychologist,* 1966—.

* * *

WOLF, Leonard 1923-

PERSONAL: Born March 1, 1923, in Vulcan, Romania; son of Joseph and Rose (Engel) Wolf; married Patricia Evans, December 2, 1944; Deborah Goleman (a cultural anthropologist), April 10, 1960; children: Sarah, Aaron, Naomi. *Education:* Attended Ohio State University, 1941-43; University of California, Berkeley, A.B., 1945, M.A., 1950; University of Iowa, Ph.D., 1954. *Religion:* Jewish. *Home:* 36 Farnsworth Lane, San Francisco, Calif. 84117. *Agent:* Julian Bach, Jr., 3 East 48th St., New York, N.Y. 10017. *Office:* San Francisco State University, San Francisco, Calif. 94132.

CAREER: Instructor in English at Coe College, Cedar Rapids, Iowa, and University of Iowa, Iowa City, both 1952-54; University of Minnesota, Duluth, lecturer in English, 1954-55; St. Mary's College, Moraga, Calif., assistant professor of English, 1955-57; San Francisco State University, San Francisco, Calif., 1957—, currently professor of English. Visiting professor at Columbia University, New York University, University of Shiraz, Ben Gurion University, and University of Hawaii. *Military service:* U.S. Army. *Awards, honors:* Recipient of James Phelan Poetry Award from University of California and O. Henry fiction award.

WRITINGS: *Hamadryad Hunted* (poems), Bern Porter, 1945; (translator) Itzik Manger, *The Book of Paradise,* Hill & Wang, 1964; (editor with wife, Deborah Wolf) *Voices from the Love Generation,* Little, Brown, 1968; (editor) *The Uses of the Present,* McGraw, 1969; *The Passion of Israel,* Little, Brown, 1970; *A Dream of Dracula,* Little, Brown, 1972; *The Annotated Dracula,* C. N. Potter, 1974; *Monsters,* Straight Arrow, 1974. Contributor of poems and short fiction to magazines.

WORK IN PROGRESS: *Shabbatai: Messiah of Fire and Clay,* a novel, for Little, Brown.

SIDELIGHTS: Wolf writes: "My interests seem to be polymorphous. They are saved from being perverse by my admiration of the power of history on the present. I admire Hellenism with a Hebrew passion."

* * *

WOLFF, Anthony 1938-

PERSONAL: Born October 17, 1938, in Brookline, Mass.; son of Harold Arnold (a management consultant) and Selma (Strauss) Wolff; married Pamela Perry, 1965; children: Nicolas Perry, Rebecca Meredith. *Education:* University of North Carolina, B.A., 1960. *Politics:* "Usually Democrat." *Religion:* None. *Home and office:* 223 West 21st St., New York, N.Y. 10011. *Agent:* Marie Rodell, 141 East 55th St., New York, N.Y.

CAREER: *Look,* New York, N.Y., senior editor, 1967-70; *American Heritage,* New York, N.Y., conservation editor, 1970. Consultant to Ford Foundation, 1972, and Rockefeller Foundation, 1973—.

WRITINGS: (Editor) *The Sand Country of Aldo Leopold,* Sierra Club, 1973; *Unreal Estate,* Sierra Club, 1974.

* * *

WOLFF, Cynthia Griffin 1936-

PERSONAL: Born August 20, 1936, in St. Louis, Mo.; daughter of James T. (a businessman) and Eunice (Heyn) Griffin; married Robert Paul Wolff (a professor of philosophy), June 9, 1962; children: Patrick Gideon, Tobias Barrington. *Education:* Radcliffe College, B.A., 1958; Harvard University, Ph.D., 1965. *Home:* 26 Barrett Pl., Northampton, Mass. 01060.

Office: Department of English, University of Massachusetts, Amherst, Mass. 01002.

CAREER: Part-time instructor at Boston University, 1961-62, and Illinois Institute of Technology, 1962-63; Boston University, Boston, Mass., instructor, 1963-64; Queens College of the City University of New York, instructor, 1965-68; Manhattanville College, Purchase, N.Y., assistant professor, 1968-71; University of Massachusetts, Amherst, assistant professor, 1971-73, associate professor of English, 1973—, director of university honors program.

WRITINGS: *Samuel Richardson and the Eighteenth-Century Puritan Character,* Archon, 1972; (editor) *Other Lives,* Goodyear Publishing, 1973. Contributor to *American Quarterly, Massachusetts Review,* and other journals.

WORK IN PROGRESS: Research for an extensive analysis of the novels of Edith Wharton.

* * *

WOLFF, Kurt H(einrich) 1912-

PERSONAL: Born May 20, 1912, in Darmstadt, Germany; came to United States, 1939; naturalized citizen, 1945; son of Oscar Louis and Ida Bertha (Kohn) Wolff; married Carla Elisabeth Bruck, June 11, 1936; children: Carlo Thomas. *Education:* Attended University of Frankfurt, 1930-31, 1932-33, University of Munich, 1931-32; University of Florence, laurea (doctorate), 1935; postdoctoral study, University of Chicago, 1943-44, Harvard University, 1955-56. *Home:* 58 Lombard St., Newton, Mass. 02158. *Office:* Department of Sociology, Brandeis University, Waltham, Mass. 02154.

CAREER: Schule am Mittelmeer, Recco, Italy, high school teacher, 1934-36; Istituti Mare-Monte, Ruta, Italy, high school teacher, 1936-38; Southern Methodist University, Dallas, Tex., research assistant in sociology, 1939-43; Earlham College, Richmond, Ind., assistant professor of sociology, 1944-45; Ohio State University, Columbus, assistant professor, 1945-52, associate professor of sociology, 1952-59; Brandeis University, Waltham, Mass., professor of sociology, 1959-69, Yellen Professor of Social Relations, 1969—, chairman of department of sociology, 1959-62. Member, Social Science Research Council summer seminar, Northwestern University, 1952; specialist, U.S. Department of State at Frankfurt Institute of Social Research, 1952, 1953; faculty fellow, Fund for Advancement of Education, Harvard University, 1955-56; senior Fulbright lecturer, University of Rome, 1963-64. Visiting professor, College of the Pacific, summer, 1948, New School for Social Research, summer, 1950, Institute of Social Research (Oslo, Norway), 1959, Sir George Williams University, 1965, University of Freiburg, summer, 1966, University of Frankfurt, 1966-67, University of Paris-Nanterre, spring, 1967, York University, 1971. *Member:* International Sociological Association (chairman of research committee on the sociology of knowledge, 1966-72), International Society for the Sociology of Knowledge (president, 1972—), American Sociological Association (fellow), American Association of University Professors, American Civil Liberties Union. *Awards, honors:* Social Science Research Council fellowship, 1943-44, grant, 1966-67; Viking Fund (now Wenner-Gren Foundation for Anthropological Research) grant, 1947, 1949.

WRITINGS: (Editor and translator) Georg Simmel, *The Sociology of Georg Simmel,* Free Press, 1950; (translator with Reinhold Bendix) Simmel, *Conflict & The Web of Group Affiliations,* Free Press, 1955; (editor, contributor, and translator) *Georg Simmel, 1858-1918,* Ohio State University Press, 1959, also published as *Essays on Sociology, Philosophy and Aesthetics,* Harper, 1965; (editor, contributor, and translator) *Emile Durkheim, 1858-1917,* Ohio State University Press, 1960, also published as *Essays on Sociology and Philosophy,* Harper, 1964; (editor and contributor) *Transactions of the 4th World Congress of Sociology,* Volume 4, International Sociological Association, 1961; (editor and author of introduction) Karl Mannheim, *Wissenssoziologie,* Luchterhand, 1964; (editor with Barrington Moore, Jr., and contributor) *The Critical Spirit: Essays in Honor of Herbert Marcuse,* Beacon Press, 1967; *The Sociology of Knowledge in the United States of America,* Mouton & Co., 1967; *Versuch zu einer Wissenssoziologie,* Luchterhand, 1968; *Hingeburg und Begriff,* Luchterhand, 1968; (editor, translator, and author of introduction) Mannheim, *From Karl Mannheim,* Oxford University Press, 1971; *Trying Sociology,* Wiley, 1974. Contributor to journals in his field. Member of board of directors, *Sociological Abstracts,* 1963—; member of advisory editorial board, *Praxis,* 1966, and *International Journal of Contemporary Sociology,* 1971—; member of editorial board, *Sociological Focus,* 1972—.

WORK IN PROGRESS: Surrender and Catch, a book on "Loma."

AVOCATIONAL INTERESTS: Drawing and painting.

* * *

WOLFLE, Dael (Lee) 1906-

PERSONAL: Surname is pronounced Wolf-lee; born March 5, 1906, in Puyallup, Wash.; son of David H. (a school administrator) and Elizabeth (Pauly) Wolfle; married Helen Morrill, December 28, 1929; children: Janet Helen (Mrs. W. D. Chapman), Lee Morrill, John Morrill. *Education:* University of Washington, Seattle, B.S., 1927, M.S., 1928; Ohio State University, Ph.D., 1931. *Home:* 4545 Sand Point Way N.E., Seattle, Wash. 98105. *Office:* Graduate School of Public Affairs, DP-30, University of Washington, Seattle, Wash. 98195.

CAREER: Ohio State University, Columbus, instructor in psychology, 1929-32; University of Mississippi, University, professor of psychology, 1932-36; University of Chicago, Chicago, Ill., examiner in biological sciences, 1936-39, assistant professor, 1938-43, associate professor of psychology, 1943-45; American Psychological Association, Washington, D.C., executive secretary, 1946-50; Commission on Human Resources and Advanced Training, Washington, D.C., director, 1950-54; American Association for the Advancement of Science, Washington, D.C., executive officer and publisher of *Science,* 1954-70; University of Washington, Seattle, professor of public affairs, Graduate School of Public Affairs, 1970—, acting dean of College of Architecture and Urban Planning, 1972-73. During World War II was civilian training adminstrator for electronics, U.S. Army Signal Corps, 1941-43, and technical aide, Office of Scientific Research and Development, 1944-46. Montgomery lecturer at University of Nebraska, 1959; Walter V. D. Bingham lecturer at Columbia University, 1960; Herbert S. Langfeld lecturer at Princeton University, 1969. Member of research advisory committee, American Council on Education, 1968-73; member of board on human resources, National Academy of Sciences-National Research Council, 1970—; chairman of revision committee for science resources studies, National Science Foundation, 1972-73. Trustee of Russell Sage Foundation, 1961—, James McKeen Cattell Fund, 1962—, Pacific Science Center Foundation, 1962—.

MEMBER: American Psychological Association, American Council on Education (secretary, 1966-67), American Association for the Advancement of Science, American Academy of Arts and Sciences, National Association of Science Writers (honorary member).

AWARDS, HONORS: Presidential Certificate of Merit, 1948; D.Sc. from Drexel Institute of Technology, 1956, and Ohio State University, 1957; Exceptional Service Medal, U.S. Air Force, 1957; D.Sc., Western Michigan University, 1960.

WRITINGS: The Relation Between Linguistic Structure and Associative Interference in Artificial Linguistic Material, Linguistic Society of America, 1932; *Factor Analysis to 1940,* University of Chicago Press, 1941; (editor) *Human Factors in Military Efficiency,* Office of Scientific Research and Development, 1946; (with others) *Improving Undergraduate Instruction in Psychology,* Macmillan, 1952; *America's Resources of Specialized Talent,* Harper, 1954; (editor) *Symposium on Basic Research,* American Association for the Advancement of Science, 1959; *Science and Public Policy,* University of Nebraska Press, 1959; (editor) *The Discovery of Talent* (Walter Van Dyke Bingham lectures), Harvard University Press, 1969; (editor with others) *The International Migration of High-Level Manpower,* Praeger, 1970; *The Uses of Talent,* Princeton University Press, 1971; *The Home of Science: The Role of the University,* McGraw, 1972. Contributor to scientific and academic journals. Editor, *Science,* 1955; member of editorial advisory board, *Science Yearbook,* 1967—.

WORK IN PROGRESS: Research on the social management of technology.

WOODWARD, James B(rian) 1935-

PERSONAL: Born October 10, 1935, in Stoke on Trent, England; son of James and Nora (Scarratt) Woodward; married Patricia Anne Scott, April 9, 1959; children: Kirsten Patricia, Natalie Helen. *Education:* Oriel College, Oxford, B.A. (first class honors), 1959, M.A., 1963, D. Phil., 1965. *Home:* 493 Hendrefoilan Rd., Killay, Swansea, Glamorganshire, Wales. *Office:* Department of German, University College of Swansea, Swansea, Glamorganshire, Wales.

CAREER: University of British Columbia, Vancouver, instructor in Russian, 1962-65; University of Wales, University College of Swansea, Swansea, lecturer, 1965-67, lecturer in charge of Russian, 1967-70, senior lecturer in Russian, 1970—. *Military service:* Royal Air Force, 1954-56. *Member:* British Universities Association of Slavists, Association of Teachers of Russian, Oriel Society.

WRITINGS: (Editor) *Selected poems of Aleksandr Blok,* Clarendon Press, 1968; *Leonid Andreyev: A Study,* Clarendon Press, 1969. Contributor to Slavic and drama journals.

WORK IN PROGRESS: Research in the development of the Russian short story, the art of Ivan Bunin, and aspects of form and structure in Russian prose and poetry.

* * *

WOOLLEY, (Lowell) Bryan 1937-

PERSONAL: Born August 22, 1937, in Gorman, Tex.; son of G. L., Jr. (a farmer) and Beatrice (a politician; maiden name, Gibson) Woolley; married Julianne Nelson, August 31, 1958 (divorced, 1968); married Margaret Ray Hilpert, July 13, 1968; children: (second marriage) Bryan Edward, John Patrick. *Education:* University of Texas at El Paso, A.B., 1958; Texas Christian University, B.D., 1963; Harvard University, Th.M., 1966. *Politics:* Democrat. *Home:* 1226 Everett Ave., Louisville, Ky. 40204. *Agent:* Gloria Safier, 667 Madison Ave., New York, N.Y. 10021. *Office: Louisville Courier-Journal and Times,* Louisville, Ky. 40202.

CAREER: High school English teacher in El Paso, Tex., 1958-59; minister of Christian Church (Disciples of Christ), 1963-67; Christian Board of Publication, St. Louis, Mo., magazine editor, 1966-67; Associated Press, Tulsa, Okla., night editor, 1967-68; *Anniston Star,* Anniston, Ala., city editor, 1968-69; *Louisville Courier-Journal and Times,* Louisville, Ky., magazine writer, 1969—.

WRITINGS: Some Sweet Day (novel), Random House, 1974. Contributor of poems to literary journals, including *Christian Century, Descant,* and *Approaches.*

WORK IN PROGRESS: A novel, publication expected by Random House; research for a historical-psychological novel about the nineteenth-century religious group known as the Shakers; a documentary book on the life of a coal miner's family in Harlan County, Kentucky, to be published by the *Louisville Courier-Journal and Times.*

SIDELIGHTS: Woolley wrote: "As a novelist and a journalist, I am fascinated with the dynamics of human relationships—individual to family; family to community; the present generation to past generations. My work is set in the South and Southwest, because this is where I have experienced these relationships, and they are expressed more openly and honestly here than in other regions."

WOON, Basil 1894(?)-1974

1894(?)—June 4, 1974; English-born American author and journalist. Obituaries: *New York Times,* June 5, 1974.

* * *

WRIGHT, D(onald) I(an) 1934-

PERSONAL: Born October 22, 1934, in Aldgate, South Australia; son of Cyril Noel (a farmer) and Florence (Lemaitre) Wright; married Janice Gambling (a tutor), January 9, 1960; children: David Arthur, Alan Michael, Ian Mark. *Education:* University of Adelaide, B.A., 1956; Australian National University, Ph.D., 1968. *Politics:* Labour. *Religion:* Methodist. *Home:* 66 E.K. Ave., Charlestown 2290, New South Wales, Australia. *Office:* Department of History, University of Newcastle, Newcastle 2308, New South Wales, Australia.

CAREER: University of Newcastle, Newcastle, New South Wales, Australia, lecturer, 1968-70, senior lecturer in history, 1970—. *Military service:* Australian Army, 1953. *Member:* Australian Society for the Study of European History, Australian Historical Association, Asian Studies Association of Australia (Newcastle correspondent), Societe des Etudes Robespierristes, Australian Society for the Study of Labour History, Specific Learning Difficulties Association of New South Wales (president).

WRITINGS: Shadow of Dispute: Aspects of Commonwealth-State Relations, 1901-1910, Australian National University Press, 1970. Contributor to Australian history journals, including *Journal of the Royal Australian Historical Society, South Australiana, Queensland Heritage, Historical Studies of Australia and New Zealand, Tasmanian Historical Research Association Journal,* and *Australian National University Historical Journal.*

WORK IN PROGRESS: Editing a book comparing the early years of the federation in Canada and in Australia, with B. W. Hodgins; a series of articles on the political history of the River Murray; translating and editing a book of documents for undergraduates on the French Revolution.

* * *

WRIGHT, James (Arlington) 1927-

PERSONAL: Born December 13, 1927, in Martins Ferry, Ohio; married second wife, Edith Anne Runk; children: Two sons. *Education:* Kenyon College, B.A., 1952; University of Washington, M.A., 1954, Ph.D., 1959. Studied with John Crowe Ransom and Theodore Roethke. *Home:* 466 Lexington Ave., 13th Floor, New York, N.Y. 10017. *Office:* Department of English, Hunter College of the City University of New York, New York, N.Y. 10021.

CAREER: Poet. University of Minnesota, Minneapolis, formerly instructor in English; Macalester College, St. Paul, Minn., formerly instructor in English; Hunter College of the City University of New York, New York, N.Y., currently professor of English. Visiting lecturer, State University of New York at Buffalo, 1974. *Military service:* U.S. Army. *Member:* Academy of American Poets (fellow). *Awards, honors:* Fulbright fellow in Austria, 1952-53; Eunice Tietjens Memorial Prize, 1955; *Kenyon Review* fellowship in poetry, 1958; National Institute of Arts and Letters grant in literature, 1959; Ohiona Book Award, 1960, for *Saint Judas;* Oscar Blumenthal Award from *Poetry* magazine, 1968; Guggenheim fellowship; Pulitzer Prize in poetry, 1972.

WRITINGS—Poems: *The Green Wall,* Yale University Press, 1957; *Saint Judas,* Wesleyan University Press, 1959; (with William Duffy and Robert Bly) *The Lion's Tail and Eyes,* Sixties Press, 1962; *The Branch Will Not Break,* Wesleyan University Press, 1963; (translator with Bly) *Twenty Poems of Georg Trakl,* Sixties Press, 1963; (translator) Theodor Storm, *The Rider on the White Horse,* New American Library, 1964; (translator) *Twenty Poems of Cesar Vallejo,* Sixties Press, 1964; *Shall We Gather at the River,* Wesleyan University Press, 1968; (translator with Bly) *Twenty Poems of Pablo Neruda,* Sixties Press, 1968; (editor and translator) Hermann Hesse, *Poems,* Farrar, Straus, 1970; *Collected Poems,* Wesleyan University Press, 1971; *Two Citizens,* Farrar, Straus, 1973.

Represented in anthologies including *Poems on Poetry,* edited by Robert Wallace and J. G. Taaffe, Dutton, 1965; *An Introduction to Poetry,* edited by Louis Simpson, St. Martin's, 1967; *Heartland,* edited by Lucien Stryk, Northern Illinois University Press, 1967; *Poems of Our Moment,* edited by John Hollander, Pegasus, 1968. Contributor to *Hudson Review, Kenyon Review, Sewanee Review, Western Review, Yale Review, Harper's, Poetry, Frescoe, New Poets of England and America, Paris Review, London Magazine, Botteghe Obscure, New Yorker, Minnesota Review, Big Table, Audience, Nation,* and others.

SIDELIGHTS: "James Wright is one of the two or three finest young poets of the present generation," writes John Logan. "His third book, *The Branch Will Not Break,* is his best. One of the marks of superb talentiis its capacity for change in expression and form as the artist himself grows. The new book shows the fruits of Wright's encounter with the rich contemporary poetry of Latin America."

Stephen Stepanchev considers Wright to be one of the ablest poets among those who "put emphasis on the 'subjective image,' that is, the image that arises from the unconscious of the poet and generates powerful emotions beyond the reach of logic or analysis."

BIOGRAPHICAL/CRITICAL SOURCES: Stephen Stepanchev, *American Poetry Since 1945,* Harper, 1965; *The Sixties,* Spring, 1966; *Chicago Review,* Volume 19, number 2, 1967; Paul Carroll, *The Poem in Its Skin,* Follett, 1968; *Contemporary Literary Criticism,* Volume III, Gale, 1974.

* * *

WRIGHT, James C(laud), Jr. 1922-
(Jim Wright)

PERSONAL: Born December 22, 1922, in Fort Worth, Tex.; son of James C. and Marie (Lyster) Wright; married Mary Ethelyn Lemons; married second wife, Betty Hay, 1972; children: (first marriage) Jimmy, Virginia Sue, Patricia, Alicia Marie. *Education:* Studied at Weatherford College and University of Texas. *Religion:* Presbyterian. *Office:* 2459 Rayburn House Office Building, Washington, D.C. 20515.

CAREER: Member of Texas Legislature, 1947-49; mayor of Weatherford, Tex., 1950-54; U.S. House of Representatives, Washington, D.C., congressman from 12th District of Texas, 1954—. Has served as chairman of House Public Works Subcommittee on Investigations and Review, chairman of Commission on Highway Beautification, and member of House delegation to U.S.-Mexico Interparliamentary Conference, 1963-72; deputy Democratic whip of House, 1973—. *Military service:* U.S. Army Air Forces, pilot, 1941-46; flew combat missions in South Pacific; received Distinguished Flying Cross. U.S. Air Force Reserve; received Legion of Merit. *Member:* Texas League of Municipalities (president, 1953).

WRITINGS: You and Your Congressman, Coward, 1965; *The Coming Water Famine,* Coward, 1966; *Of Swords and Plowshares,* Stafford-Lowdon, 1968; (contributor) J. B. Anderson, editor, *Congress and Conscience,* Lippincott, 1970. Contributor to *Saturday Evening Post, Harper's, This Week, Coronet,* and other publications.

* * *

WRIGHT, Jim
See WRIGHT, James C(laud)

* * *

WRIGHT, Stephen 1922-

PERSONAL: Born November 30, 1922, in New York, N.Y.; son of Martin (a painter) and Yolanda K. Wright; married Sylvia Halpert, May, 1954 (divorced, 1960). *Education:* Long Island University, B.A., 1949; New York University, M.A., 1950. *Residence:* New York, N.Y. *Office:* P.O. Box 1341, F.D.R. Postal Station, New York, N.Y. 10022.

CAREER: Writer. Has held "a long line of jobs, too numerous to mention." *Military service:* U.S. Navy, pharmacist's mate, 1943-46. *Member:* Authors Guild of Authors League of America.

WRITINGS: (With Sylvia Wright) *Crime in the Schools* (novel), Contemporary Research Library, 1959; (editor and author of introduction) *Different: An Anthology of Homosexual Short Stories,* Bantam, 1974.

WORK IN PROGRESS: The Paradise Road, a novel of an American writer who does not fulfill his purpose; a nonfiction book on homosexuality.

SIDELIGHTS: Wright told *CA:* "In addition to my having had many diverse jobs, I also at one time in my life tried to start my own business. It seemed to me that if I could offer amateur writers an honest, cheap, and comprehensive subsidiary plan, they would be interested in letting me publish their books. So I set up my own imprint and advertised in the writers' journals. I did manage to publish some books, but I'm afraid I was not a very good businessman and much too honest to succeed in this highly competitive, sharp field. Later I became a literary consultant, which was even less successful than the press operation. I once ran a writers' club, and in that capacity I published a little pamphlet called *The Literary Jungle,* which enjoyed quite a vogue around the early 1960's. My aim in writing this booklet was to warn authors to be wary of certain types of agents, 'cooperative' publishers, and correspondence schools of writing who really did not help the beginning writer. The only literary enterprise I care to be in nowadays is as writer or editor of a book."

AVOCATIONAL INTERESTS: Early silent and sound films, ragtime music, old records (particularly those of Ruth Etting), collecting books (has first editions of Somerset Maugham's work).

* * *

WRZOS, Joseph Henry 1929-
(Joseph Ross)

PERSONAL: Surname is pronounced Vi-*zhus;* born September 9, 1929, in Newark, N.J.; son of Joseph and Aniela (Szugan) Wrzos; married Anita Laufer, June 13, 1952; children: Michael Geoffrey, Kenneth Stephen. *Education:* Rutgers University, B.A. (cum laude), 1952; Columbia University, graduate study, 1952-53. *Home:* 70 St. Charles Ave., West Caldwell, N.J. 07006. *Office:* Millburn Senior High School, Millburn, N.J. 07041.

CAREER: Gnome Press, Inc., New York, N.Y., assistant editor, 1953-54; high school librarian in Roselle Park, N.J., 1956-57; Millburn Senior High School, Millburn, N.J., English teacher, 1957—, chairman of department, 1969—. *Member:* National Education Association, Eastern Science Fiction Association, Association of Secondary School Supervisors and Department Heads of New Jersey, New Jersey Association of Teachers of English, Millburn Education Association, Phi Beta Kappa.

WRITINGS: (Editor, under pseudonym Joseph Ross) *The Best of Amazing* (science fiction anthology), Doubleday, 1967; (author of introduction) Garrett Putnam Serviss, *The Second Deluge: Serviss' Masterwork* (science fiction novel first published in 1912), Hyperion, 1974. Contributor of poems to *Hawk and Whippoorwill: Poems of Man and Nature* and *Inside-Riverside Quarterly*. Managing editor of *Amazing Stories* and *Fantastic Stories* (science fiction magazines), both 1965-67.

AVOCATIONAL INTERESTS: Reading.

* * *

WULFF, Robert M. 1926-

PERSONAL: Born August 28, 1926, in Albert Lea, Minn.; son of Jacob B. (a postal employee) and Kathleen (Meinhard) Wulff; married Ajana Watana, May 31, 1960; children: Timothy R., Daniel R. *Education:* St. Olaf College, B.A., 1951. *Religion:* Lutheran. *Office:* U.S. Agency for International Development, Vientiane, Laos.

CAREER: Was involved in leprosy rehabilitation in Chiengmai, Thailand, 1952-65; U.S. Agency for International Development, Washington, D.C., refugee relief officer in Saigon, South Vietnam, 1967-69, and Vientiane, Laos, 1969—. *Military service:* U.S. Army, 1945-47; served in China.

WRITINGS: *Village of the Outcasts,* Doubleday, 1967; *A Comparative Study of Refugee and Non-Refugee Villages,* U.S. Agency for International Development, Part I, 1973, Part II, 1974.

* * *

YARBER, Robert Earl 1929-

PERSONAL: Born September 28, 1929, in East St. Louis, Ill.; son of Earl (an accountant) and Dorothy (O'Dwyer) Yarber; married Mary Winzerling (a teacher), November 27, 1952; children: Robert, Charles, Mary. *Education:* McKendree College, A.B., 1951; St. Louis University, A.M., 1953; Exeter College, Oxford, further graduate study, 1969. *Politics:* Liberal Democrat. *Religion:* Roman Catholic. *Home:* 4125 Rochester Rd., San Diego, Calif. 92116. *Office:* San Diego Mesa College, San Diego, Calif.

CAREER: Supervisor of schools in East St. Louis, Ill., 1953-63; San Diego Mesa College, San Diego, Calif., professor of English, 1963—. *Member:* Modern Language Association of America, National Council of Teachers of English, Conference on College Composition and Communication.

WRITINGS: (With James Burl Hogins) *Reading, Writing, and Rhetoric,* Science Research Associates, 1967, revised edition, edited by Jim Budd and Sara Boyd, 1972; (with Hogins) *College Reading and Writing,* Macmillan, 1968; (editor with Hogins) *Language: An Introductory Reader,* Harper, 1969; (compiler) *Breakthrough: Contemporary Reading and Writing,* Cummings, 1969, second edition, with Barbara Heywood, 1973; *Phase Blue,* Science Research Associates, 1970; (editor with Emil Hurtik) *An Introduction to Poetry and Criticism,* Xerox College Publishing, 1970; (editor with Hurtik) *An Introduction to Short Fiction and Criticism,* Xerox College Publishing, 1971; (editor with Hurtik) *An Introduction to Drama and Criticism,* Xerox College Publishing, 1971; (compiler with Hogins) *Cycle Seven,* Science Research Associates, 1973; (with Lionel Ruby) *The Art of Making Sense,* Lippincott, 1973. Series editor of English textbooks for Lippincott.

WORK IN PROGRESS: A novel; short stories.

* * *

YATES, W(illiam) E(dgar) 1938-

PERSONAL: Born April 30, 1938, in Hove, Sussex, England; son of Douglas (a university professor) and Doris (Goode) Yates; married Barbara Fellowes, April 6, 1963; children: Thomas Henry Benedick. *Education:* Emmanuel College, Cambridge, B.A., 1961, M.A., 1965, Ph.D., 1965. *Home:* 7 Clifton Hill, Exeter EX1 2DL, England. *Office:* Department of German, University of Exeter, Exeter EX4 4QH, England.

CAREER: University of Durham, Durham, England, lecturer in German, 1963-72; University of Exeter, Exeter, England, professor of German, 1972—. *Military service:* British Army, 1956-58; became second lieutenant.

WRITINGS: (Editor) Hugo von Hofmannsthal, *Der Schwierige,* Cambridge University Press, 1966; (editor) Franz Grillparzer, *Der Traum ein Leben,* Cambridge University Press, 1968; *Grillparzer: A Critical Introduction,* Cambridge University Press, 1972; *Nestroy: Satire and Parody in Viennese Popular Comedy,* Cambridge University Press, 1972; (contributor) Heinz Kindermann, editor, *Das Grillparzer-Bild des 20. Jahrhunderts,* Bochlau, 1972; *Humanity in Weimar and Vienna: The Continuity of an Ideal,* University of Exeter, 1973; (contributor) Juergen Hein, editor, *Theater und Gesellschaft,* Bertelsmann, 1973. Contributor to language journals.

WORK IN PROGRESS: *Josef Schreyvogel as Critic and Translator,* and *Literary Life in Biedermeier Vienna.*

AVOCATIONAL INTERESTS: Theater, books, gardening, and travel.

* * *

YEE, Albert H(oy) 1929-

PERSONAL: Born June 14, 1929, in Santa Barbara, Calif.; son of George H. (a merchant) and Bertha (Lee) Yee; married Irene Tang (a home management teacher), August 24, 1958; children: Lisa D., Hoyt B., Cynthia R. *Education:* Lingnan University, student, 1947-48; Santa Rosa Junior College, A.A., 1950; University of California, Berkeley, B.A., 1952; San Francisco State College (now University), M.A., 1959; Stanford University, Ed.D., 1965; University of Oregon, postdoctoral study, 1966-67. *Home:* 16591 Melville Circle, Huntington Beach, Calif. 92649. *Office:* Graduate Studies and Research Center, California State University, Long Beach, Calif. 90840.

CAREER: Elementary school teacher in Sonoma County, Calif., 1955-59; San Francisco State College (now University), San Francisco, Calif., instructor, 1959-63, assistant professor of education, 1963-64; University of Texas, Austin, lecturer, 1964-65, assistant professor of curriculum and instruction, 1965-67; University of Wisconsin, Madison, associate professor, 1967-70, professor of curriculum and instruction, 1970-73; California State University, Long Beach, professor of educational psychology and dean of graduate studies and research, 1973—. Founder and chairman-secretary of Committee for Sino-American Educational Exchange and Relations, jointly sponsored by American Educational Research Association and Society for the Psychological Study of Social Issues. Consultant to Macmillan Co. and Holt, Rinehart & Winston, Inc. *Military service:* U.S. Army, Signal Corps, 1952-55; served in Korea and Japan; became staff sergeant.

MEMBER: American Association for the Advancement of Science (fellow), American Educational Research Association, American Psychological Association, National Conference on Research in English (fellow), Society for the Psychological Study of Social Issues, Western Psychological Association. *Awards, honors:* U.S. Office of Education research grants, 1965-66, 1970-73; Fulbright lecturer in Japan, 1972; first Fulbright scholar to People's Republic of China, 1972.

WRITINGS: (Editor) *Social Interaction in Educational Settings,* Prentice-Hall, 1971; (with Carl Personke) *Comprehensive Spelling Instruction: Theory, Research and Application,* International Publishing Co., 1971; (editor) *Perspectives on Management Systems Approaches in Education: A Symposium,* Educational Technology Publications, 1973; (contributor) Dwight Allen and Jeffrey Hecht, editors, *Controversies in Education,* Saunders, 1974. Contributor of more than sixty articles to education and psychology journals. Consultant to *Review of Educational Research, Journal of Educational Research,* and *American Educational Research Journal.*

* * *

YEP, Laurence Michael 1948-

PERSONAL: Born June 14, 1948, in San Francisco, Calif.; son of Thomas Gim (a postal clerk) and Franche (Lee) Yep. *Education:* Marquette University, student, 1966-68; University of California, Santa Cruz, B.A., 1970; State University of New York at Buffalo, Ph.D. candidate, 1974—. *Home:* 921 Populus Pl., Sunnyvale, Calif. 94086. *Agent:* Lurton Blassingame, 60 East 42nd St., New York, N.Y. 10017.

CAREER: Writer. *Member:* Modern Language Association of America, Science Fiction Writers of America.

WRITINGS: *Sweetwater* (novel for young people), Harper, 1973. Work is represented in anthologies, including *World's Best Science Fiction of 1969,* edited by Donald A. Wollheim and Terry Carr, Gollancz, 1969; *Quark Number Two,* edited by Samuel Delaney and Marilyn Hacker, Paperback Library, 1971; *Protostars,* edited by David Gerrold, Ballantine, 1971; *Strange Bedfellows: Sex and Science Fiction,* edited by Thomas N. Scortia, Random House, 1973; also represented in *The Demon Children,* published by Avon, 1973. Contributor to science fiction magazines, including *Galaxy.*

WORK IN PROGRESS: A science fiction novel; research on William Faulkner's early novels.

YIN, Robert K(uo-zuir) 1941-

PERSONAL: Born March 31, 1941, in New York, N.Y. *Education:* Harvard University, B.A., 1962; Massachusetts Institute of Technology, Ph.D., 1970. *Office:* Rand Corporation, 2100 M St. N.W., Washington, D.C. 20037; and Massachusetts Institute of Technology, Building 9, Room 635, Cambridge, Mass. 02139.

CAREER: Rand Corporation, Washington, D.C., research psychologist, 1970—; Massachusetts Institute of Technology, Cambridge, assistant professor of urban studies and planning, 1972—.

WRITINGS: (Editor) *The City in the Seventies,* F. E. Peacock, 1972; (editor) *Race, Creed, Color, or National Origin,* F. E. Peacock, 1973.

WORK IN PROGRESS: Urban policy research.

* * *

YOHE, W(illiam) Frederick 1943-

PERSONAL: Born June 4, 1943, in Canton, Ohio; son of W. Edward (a tool designer) and A. Lorraine (Graening) Yohe; married Charyl L. Shiltz (a registered nurse), September 17, 1965. *Education:* Attended Akron Art Institute School of Design and University of Akron, 1963-65. *Politics:* None. *Address:* P.O. Box 804, Warren, Ohio 44482. *Office:* Graphique, Inc., 8256 East Market, Warren, Ohio 44484.

CAREER: Graphique, Inc., Warren, Ohio, chairman, 1969—.

WRITINGS: *Someone Is About to Happen to You* (poems), Little, Brown, 1973; *You/Pianissimo, Pianissimo, Pianissimo* (poems), Little, Brown, 1973; *Five Seasons with You* (poems), Graphique Publications, 1973; *You've Had a Walk through My Mind* (poems), Graphique Publications, 1973.

WORK IN PROGRESS: Some volumes of poetry; a novel; humor.

SIDELIGHTS: Yohe told *CA:* "During the third quarter of 1973 I was introduced to transcendental meditation which has had drastic effects on my writing, its clarity, flow, communication."

* * *

YORKE, Henry Vincent
See GREEN, Henry

* * *

YOUNG, Edith

PERSONAL: Born in Dublin, Ireland; daughter of Daniel (a publicity manager) and Eleanor (FitzPatrick) Dunlop; married Gibson Young (a musician), November 8, 1916; children: Michael. *Education:* Attended Primary Girls School Teachers Training College, Royal Academy of Dramatic Art, Martins School of Art, and Stanhope Institute. *Office:* 18 Victoria Park Square, Bethnal Green, London E2 9PF, England.

CAREER: Artist and lecturer. Has exhibited paintings in various British galleries, including Whitechapel Upper Gallery and Library.

WRITINGS: *Lisa* (novel), Dent, 1930, Morrow, 1931; *Inside Out* (autobiography), Routledge & Kegan Paul, 1971.

WORK IN PROGRESS: Second volume of autobiography.

SIDELIGHTS: Of Mrs. Young's autobiography, James Delehanty writes: "Her compulsively readable book ends with the death of her father, a half-way point in her life, we are told. The account of the other half has still to come, and given her strongly unconventional personality and lively pen, should make equally compulsive reading."

BIOGRAPHICAL/CRITICAL SOURCES: Manchester Evening News, May 25, 1971; *Sunday Press* (Dublin), May 30, 1971; *New Society,* June 3, 1971; *Observer* (London), June 6, 1971; *Sunday Times* (London), June 6, 1971; *Guardian,* July 8, 1971; *Tribune* (London), September 10, 1971.

* * *

YOUNG, James O(wen) 1943-

PERSONAL: Born October 19, 1943, in Los Angeles, Calif.; son of James Oscar (a locksmith) and Jeanie Margaret (an animator; maiden name, Christie) Young; married Angela Merle Wingfield, September 5, 1964; children: Timothy Howard, Andrew James. *Education:* University of Southern California, B.A., 1966, M.A., 1968, Ph.D., 1971. *Home:* 2222 Clark, Burbank, Calif. 91506. *Office:* University of Southern California, Los Angeles, Calif. 90007; and Riverside City College, Riverside, Calif. 92506.

CAREER: California State University, Los Angeles, instructor in history and American studies, 1971-74; University of Southern California, Los Angeles, instructor in history, 1974—. Instructor at Riverside City College, 1974—. *Member:* American Historical Association, Organization of American Historians.

WRITINGS: Black Writers of the Thirties, Louisiana State University Press, 1973.

WORK IN PROGRESS: Studying the social-cultural, political, and intellectual influence of the black history movement in the twentieth century.

SIDELIGHTS: "I think it relevant to mention," Young wrote, "that as a *young* teacher-scholar I, like so many others, have had to moonlight to survive. In my case, I have had to work as a teamster at a dairy (twenty to fifty hours a week) these past five years."

* * *

YOUREE, Gary 1931-

PERSONAL: Born May 19, 1931, in Arkansas City, Ark.; son of Donovan Allen (an abstractor) and Mary (Turnage) Youree; married Barbara Harris (divorced); married Florence Korsin (divorced); married Margaret Kinnicutt (an actress), September, 1970; children: (first marriage) Gary Don, Renee; (second marriage) Rachel; (third marriage) Daphne, Luke. *Education:* Ouachita Baptist University, B.A., 1954; graduate study at New Orleans Baptist Theological Seminary, 1955-57, and Tulane University, 1958. *Politics:* Independent. *Religion:* Christian. *Home address:* R.F.D. 172A, Boney Lane, St. James, N.Y. 11780. *Agent:* Max Gartenberg, 331 Madison Ave., New York, N.Y. 10017.

CAREER: Writer; has worked as teacher, preacher, social worker, automobile salesman, farm laborer, housepainter, caretaker, carpenter, plumber, typist, driving instructor, truck driver, and real estate speculator.

WRITINGS: Birds You Should Know (poems), Theo Publications, 1967; (editor with Lynne Banker) *Poets for Peace Anthology,* privately printed, 1967; *Big Cy* (satire), Bobbs-Merrill, 1974. Poetry is anthologized in *Inside Outer Space,* edited by Robert Vas Dias, Doubleday, 1970. Contributing editor of *Family Bible Encyclopedia.* Contributor of short stories and articles to *Avant Garde.*

WORK IN PROGRESS: The Gospel According to the Iceman, a mystery surrounding the identity of a first century Gallilean corpse thawed out of an iceberg and placed in the hands of a cryonics expert who attempts resuscitation; *Prayer,* non-fiction which examines some historical and current attitudes toward prayer, including some prayer experiments.

SIDELIGHTS: Youree's main interest is theology. He writes: "What I could not accomplish as a minister, due to personal inadequacies and to inadequacies of the established church, I hope to accomplish as a writer. Future projects include a novel dramatizing the evolutionary thought of Teilhard de Chardin, an autobiographical novel, and a novel centered on the life of Jesus, which will require a trip to Israel."

* * *

ZALBEN, Jane Breskin 1950-

PERSONAL: Born April 21, 1950, in New York, N.Y.; daughter of Murry (a certified public accountant) and Mae (a librarian; maiden name, Kirshbloom) Breskin; married Steven Zalben (a teacher and architecture student), December 25, 1969. *Education:* Queens College of City University of New York, B.A., 1971; Pratt Graphic Center, graduate study in lithography, 1971-72. *Politics:* "Honest politics, if it exists." *Religion:* Jewish. *Home:* Top Floor Loft, 44 West 36th St., New York, N.Y. 10018. *Office:* Holt, Rinehart & Winston, Inc., 383 Madison Ave., New York, N.Y. 10017.

CAREER: Painter, etcher, lithographer, and illustrator, designer, and author of children's books. Dial Press, New York, N.Y., assistant to art director of children's book department, 1971-72; Thomas Y. Crowell Co., New York, N.Y., free-lance book designer, 1972; Holt, Rinehart & Winston, Inc., New York, N.Y., free-lance book designer.

WRITINGS—Self-illustrated books for children: *Cecilia's Older Brother,* Macmillan, 1973; *Lyle and Humus,* Macmillan, 1974; *Basil and Hillary,* Macmillan, in press.

Illustrator: Jan Wahl, *Jeremiah Knucklebones,* Holt, 1974.

WORK IN PROGRESS: Illustrating *Invitation to the Butterfly Ball* (tentative title), by Jane Yolen, for Parents' Magazine Press.

AVOCATIONAL INTERESTS: Travel, gardening, gourmet cooking, pets.

* * *

ZAPPLER, Lisbeth 1930-

PERSONAL: Born September 30, 1930, in Geneva, N.Y.; daughter of Maxmillian (a physician) and Anne (Bolton) Moses; married Peter Cohen, November 22, 1953; married Georg Zappler (a zoo director), January 15, 1961; children: (first marriage) Daniel, Joshua; (second marriage) Leopold, Amanda, Konrad. *Education:* University of Miami, Coral Gables, Fla., B.A., 1952. *Home:* 7 Laurel Ave., Kingston, N.J. 08528.

CAREER: Singer, journalist.

WRITINGS—Children's books: *The World after the Dinosaurs: The Evolution of Mammals,* Natural History

Press, 1970; *The Natural History of the Tail,* Doubleday, 1972; *Amphibians as Pets,* Doubleday, 1973; *Science in Summer and Fall,* Doubleday, 1974; *Science in Winter and Spring,* Doubleday, 1974.

WORK IN PROGRESS: Mammals in the Suburbs; The Natural History of the Nose.

* * *

ZARISKI, Raphael 1925-

PERSONAL: Born July 18, 1925, in Rome, Italy; son of Oscar (a professor) and Yole (Cagli) Zariski; married Birdine Adelstein, August 15, 1954; children: Daniel Alfred, Adrienne Muriel. *Education:* University of Illinois, student, 1946; Harvard University, B.A., 1948, M.A., 1949, Ph.D., 1952. *Politics:* Democrat. *Religion:* Jewish. *Home:* 2312 Calumet Ct., Lincoln, Neb. 68502. *Office:* 505 Oldfather Hall, University of Nebraska, Lincoln, Neb. 68508.

CAREER: Massachusetts Institute of Technology, Cambridge, research associate of Center for International Studies, 1952-54; University of Vermont, Burlington, instructor in political science, spring, 1955; Bennington College, Bennington, Vt., assistant professor of political science, 1955-57; University of Nebraska, Lincoln, assistant professor, 1957-62, associate professor, 1962-71, professor of political science, 1971—. Fulbright lecturer at University of Florence, 1960-61. *Military service:* U.S. Army, 1943-45; received Purple Heart, Bronze Star, and Combat Medical Badge.

MEMBER: International Political Science Association, American Political Science Association, Society for Italian Historical Studies, Southern Political Science Association, Midwest Conference of Political Scientists, Nebraska Political Science Association. *Awards, honors:* Fulbright fellow in Italy, 1950-51; Woods Foundation fellowship from Woods Foundation, 1966-67.

WRITINGS: Italy: The Politics of Uneven Development, Dryden, 1972. Contributor to political science journals in United States and to *Mulino.*

WORK IN PROGRESS: Research on intra-party politics in Italy.

* * *

ZASLAVSKY, Claudia 1917-

PERSONAL: Born January 12, 1917, in New York, N.Y.; daughter of Morris N. (a businessman) and Olga (Reisman) Cogan; married Sam Zaslavsky (a college mathematics teacher), July 19, 1941; children: Thomas, Alan. *Education:* Hunter College (of the City University of New York), B.A., 1937; University of Michigan, M.A., 1938; graduate study at Wesleyan University, 1962-64, New York University, 1969-70; currently Ph.D. candidate at Columbia University. *Home:* 45 Fairview Ave., New York, N.Y. 10040. *Office:* Woodlands High School, 475 West Hartsdale Ave., Hartsdale, N.Y. 10530.

CAREER: Block Drug Co., Jersey City, N.J., cost accountant, 1938-42; Remington Arms Co., Ilion, N.Y., engineer, 1942-43; high school teacher of mathematics and department chairman in New Rochelle, N.Y., 1959-65; Woodlands High School, Hartsdale, N.Y., teacher of mathematics, 1965—. Consultant to Education Development Center, Newton, Mass., 1973—; lecturer at various colleges on "mathematics in African culture," 1970—. *Member:* Historica Mathematica, National Council of Teachers of Mathematics, American Federation of Teachers, League of Women Voters, Phi Beta Kappa. *Awards, honors:* Delta Kappa Gamma Society honorable mention award, 1974, for *Africa Counts.*

WRITINGS: (Contributor) Stanley Brown, editor, *Realm of Science,* Volume IV, Touchstone, 1972; (contributor) Dan Matthews, editor, *A Current Bibliography On African Affairs,* African Bibliographic Center, 1972; *Africa Counts: Number and Pattern in African Culture,* Prindle, 1973. Contributor to *Mathematics Teacher, Journal of Cameroon Affairs, Summation,* and *Arithmetic Teacher.*

WORK IN PROGRESS: A textbook for in-service courses for teachers.

AVOCATIONAL INTERESTS: Playing chamber music on the violin, singing a capella music, peace movement and community activities, prison reform.

* * *

ZASSENHAUS, Hiltgunt 1916-

PERSONAL: Born July 10, 1916, in Hamburg, Germany; came to United States in 1952, naturalized in 1957; daughter of Julius (an historian) and Margret Zassenhaus. *Education:* University of Hamburg, diploma in Scandinavian languages, 1938, premedical studies, 1941-43; University of Copenhagen, M.D., 1952. *Home and office:* 7028 Bellona Ave., Baltimore, Md. 21212.

CAREER: Private practice, specializing in internal medicine, Baltimore, Md., 1954—. Affiliated with Greater Baltimore Medical Center, 1960—. *Member:* American Medical Association, Baltimore County Medical Association. *Awards, honors:* Medal of Danish Red Cross and of Norwegian Red Cross, both 1948; Order of St. Olaf (Norway; first class), 1963; Order of the Dannenbro (Denmark; first class), 1964; Verdienstkreuz Irst (Germany; first class), 1969; nominated by Norway for Nobel Peace Prize, 1974.

WRITINGS: Halt Wacht in Dunkel (title means "On Guard in the Dark"), Otto Braun, 1948; *Walls: Resisting the Third Reich—One Woman's Story,* Beacon Press, 1974.

SIDELIGHTS: Because of her knowledge of Scandinavian languages, Miss Zassenhaus was appointed to censor the mail of Danish and Norwegian prisoners held by the Germans during World War II. Soon she began to smuggle drugs, vitamins, food, clothing, and mail in to these prisoners, thus becoming one of a minority of German anti-Nazi activists. *Walls* is an autobiographical account of these years of undercover work—an "admirable memoir," notes the *New Yorker,* "set down in cool reflection but charged with inescapable emotion . . . Her book is not an account of heroics (though there are plenty of them at hand) but an attempt to depict, to recover, perhaps to exorcise that time. . . ." Miss Zassenhaus told *CA* that she wrote *Walls* because she felt her experiences had some bearing on the problems of today: "I wanted to demonstrate that the most dangerous wall in human relationships is the wall of indifference. We must get involved even if our own interests are not at stake. We must recognize that history is not made by governments but by our own daily actions."

* * *

ZAVATSKY, Bill

See ZAVATSKY, William Alexander

ZAVATSKY, William Alexander 1943-
(Bill Zavatsky)

PERSONAL: Surname is pronounced Zuh-*vot*-ski; born June 1, 1943, in Bridgeport, Conn.; son of Alexander (an auto mechanic) and Jane (Henderson) Zavatsky; married Phyllis Geffen (employed in a college administrative post), June 29, 1968. *Education:* Attended Columbia University, 1965-72. *Politics:* "Leftist, nonaligned." *Religion:* "No formal religion." *Home:* 456 Riverside Dr., Apt. 2C, New York, N.Y. 10027.

CAREER: Former professional musician (jazz pianist), factory worker, bookstore clerk, and newspaperman; teacher of writing for Teachers' and Writers' Collaborative and Poets and Writers, Inc., both New York, N.Y., 1971—, and at Bedford Lincoln Neighborhood Museum, Brooklyn, N.Y., 1971-73.

WRITINGS—Under name Bill Zavatsky: *Theories of Rain and Other Poems,* Sun, 1972. Poems have been published in little literary magazines and reviews in *New York Times Book Review.* Editor, *Sun,* 1971—, and *Roy Rogers,* 1971—.

WORK IN PROGRESS: Translating, with Rod Padgett, *The Poems of A. O. Barnabooth,* by Valery Larbaud; translating French surrealist poetry, particularly that of Robert Desnos.

SIDELIGHTS: Zavatsky told *CA:* "I strive to expand those footholds that dream, fantasy, and the event or chance occurrence supply. I believe, with Robert Desnos, in 'inspiration, language, and imagination,' and, with Paul Valery, that frequency and depth of revision is an index of literary integrity. I believe deeply in humor, and absurdly in seriousness of purpose. Working with children and their writing takes up a good deal of my time, as does my own poetry, and translating."

* * *

ZEITLIN, Joseph 1906-

PERSONAL: Born May 18, 1906, in Brooklyn, N.Y.; son of Isaac (a manufacturer) and Esther Mathilde (Levinson) Zeitlin; married Josephine Cohen Gershman (a teacher and executive); children: Judith. *Education:* City College (now City College of the City University of New York), B.A., 1926; Jewish Theological Seminary of America, M.H.L., rabbi, 1930; Columbia University, M.A., 1942, Ph.D., 1945. *Home:* 25 East 86th St., New York, N.Y. 10028. *Office:* 7 East 86th St., New York, N.Y. 10028.

CAREER: Ordained rabbi, 1930; served in Temple Ansche Chesed, 1932-50, and Riverside Synagogue, 1950—, both in New York, N.Y.; University of Bridgeport, Bridgeport, Conn., 1965—, began as adjunct associate professor, now visiting professor of speech. Grand chaplain, Free Sons of Israel, 1945—; chairman of committee on church and state, New York Board of Rabbis, 1943—; chairman of speakers bureau, United Synagogues of America, 1945—; member of executive committee, Rabbinical Assembly of America, United Jewish Appeal, Zionist Organization of America, and Federation of Jewish Philanthropies; advisor to president, American College in Jerusalem, 1971—. *Member:* Town Club (New York; chaplain). *Awards, honors:* National Association of Authors and Journalists citation for outstanding contribution to contemporary literature, 1945; La Fundacion Internacional Eloy Alfaro Grand Medal of Honor, 1967; New York City Police Department medal of honor, 1969; and numerous other awards.

WRITINGS: Disciples of the Wise: The Religious and Social Opinions of American Rabbis, Teachers College, Columbia University, 1945, reprinted, Books for Libraries, 1970; (with Shushannah Spector) *Hebrew Made Easy,* Liveright, 1948; *Speech Power: How to Convince People,* American Press, 1969; *Speech Power (Through Listening),* Vantage, 1974.

SIDELIGHTS: Of his book *Speech Power (Through Listening),* Zeitlin told *CA:* "[It] is more than a book on oratory. It is an attempt to show that communication is the key to understanding and happiness as it relates to human beings and to the nations of the world." *Avocational interests:* Tennis, table tennis, swimming.

* * *

ZELDIN, Jesse 1923-

PERSONAL: Born April 8, 1923, in New York, N.Y.; son of Isidor and Dorothy (Kaufman) Zeldin; married Mary-Barbara Kauffman (a professor), June 19, 1948; children: Xenia Valerie. *Education:* New York University, A.B., 1947; Columbia University, M.A., 1948, Ph.D., 1953. *Home:* 6836 Fair Oaks Rd., Hollins, Va. 24019. *Office:* Department of Literature, Hollins College, Hollins College, Va. 24020.

CAREER: Hollins College, Hollins College, Va., instructor, 1953-55, assistant professor, 1955-62, associate professor, 1962-70, professor of comparative literature, 1970—. Fulbright lecturer at Chinese University of Hong Kong, 1965-66. *Military service:* U.S. Army Air Forces, 1943-46; served in Pacific theater; became sergeant. *Member:* American Association for the Advancement of Slavic Studies, American Association of University Professors, Southern Conference on Slavic Studies (president, 1972-73).

WRITINGS: (Editor, translator, and author of introduction and notes) Nikolai Gogol, *Selected Passages from Correspondence with Friends,* Vanderbilt University Press, 1969; (editor and translator with Paul Debreczeny) *Literature and National Identity: Nineteenth-Century Russian Critical Essays,* University of Nebraska Press, 1970; (editor, translator, and author of introduction and notes) *Poems and Political Letters of F. I. Tyutchev,* University of Tennessee Press, 1974. Contributor to journals, including *Russian Review* and *South Atlantic Quarterly.*

WORK IN PROGRESS: A translation with introduction and notes, *Essays and Articles of N. I. Gogol;* a critical monograph on Gogol.

SIDELIGHTS: Besides Russian, Zeldin is competent in French, German, Latin, Italian, and Mandarin. He has lived at intervals in France, Italy, Austria, Switzerland, India, as well as in Hong Kong.

* * *

ZELLMANN-FINKBEINER, Peter 1942

PERSONAL: Original surname Zellmann; born July 16, 1942, in Mannheim, Germany; adopted son of Hans (a professor of gynecology) Finkbeiner. *Education:* University of Heidelberg, diploma in languages; Oxford University, P.P.E., 1962; University of Munich, further study, 1965. *Politics:* "Totally unpolitical." *Religion:* "Totally unreligious." *Home and office:* 8-Munich 22, 50 Widenmayerstrasse, Germany.

CAREER: Journalist and photographer.

WRITINGS—Self-illustrated with photographs: *South*

Seas Inside, IN Publishing Est., 1972; *IN World Guide,* Doubleday, 1973. Author of filmscripts. Contributor to guidebooks and magazines.

WORK IN PROGRESS: Guidebooks; travel books.

* * *

ZERBY, Lewis Kenneth 1916-

PERSONAL: Born December 24, 1916, in Donavan, Ill.; son of Guy Lewis (a minister) and Nettie (Anderson) Zerby; married Margaret Schiller (a teacher), August 11, 1943; children: Thelma Ruth Rebecca Zerby Byrne, Ruth Elizabeth, James Lewis Robert. *Education:* University of Illinois, B.A., 1939, M.A., 1941; Iowa State University, Ph.D., 1945. *Politics:* Democrat. *Home:* 4534 Hawthorn, Okemos, Mich. 48864. *Office:* Department of Philosophy, Michigan State University, East Lansing, Mich. 48823.

CAREER: Michigan State University, East Lansing, assistant professor, 1946-52, associate professor, 1952-58, professor of philosophy, 1958-62; University of Nigeria, Nsukka, professor of philosophy and head of department, 1962-66; Michigan State University, professor of philosophy, 1966—, head of justice, morality, and constitutional democracy program at James Madison College, 1967-72. *Member:* American Philosophical Association, Philosophy of Science Association, Torch Club.

WRITINGS: (With wife, Margaret Zerby) *If I Should Die Before I Wake: The Nsukka Dream* (history of University of Nigeria), Institute for International Studies in Education, Michigan State University, 1971; (with Glenn Johnson) *What Economists Do About Values,* Center for Rural Manpower and Public Affairs, Michigan State University, 1973. Contributor of thirty articles to professional journals. Managing editor, *Philosophy of Science,* 1952-61.

WORK IN PROGRESS: Revolution, Radicalism, and Reason.

AVOCATIONAL INTERESTS: Music (received B.A. degree in music and has continued his interest).

* * *

ZIEGLER, Alan 1947-

PERSONAL: Born August 21, 1947, in Brooklyn, N.Y.; son of Matthew and Pearl (Popowsky) Ziegler. *Education:* Union College, Schenectady, N.Y., B.S., 1970; City College of the City University of New York, M.A., 1974. *Home:* 311 West 91st St., New York, N.Y. 10024. *Office:* Environment Information Center, New York, N.Y.

CAREER: Press-Enterprise (daily newspaper), Riverside, Calif., reporter, 1969; *Evening Press* (daily newspaper), Binghamton, N.Y., reporter, 1970; Consolidated Computer Corp., New York, N.Y., machine operator, 1971-72; Environment Information Center (publisher), New York, N.Y., associate editor, 1972—. *Member:* Committee of Small Magazine Editors and Publishers, Coordinating Council of Literary Magazines. *Awards, honors:* Newspaper Fund award, 1969.

WRITINGS: Planning Escape (poems), Release Press, 1973. Contributor of poems, fiction, and articles to literary magazines and other periodicals. Editor of *Paper Highway,* 1968-69; associate editor of *Environment Information Access,* 1972—; co-editor of *Some,* 1972—.

WORK IN PROGRESS: Handball against the Great Wall, a book of poems; *The Collect Phone Call and Other Long Distance Connections,* collaborative poems with Larry Zirlin and Harry Greenberg; a novel.

SIDELIGHTS: Of his beginnings as a poet, Ziegler told *CA:* "I had written mostly journalism and only several poems when, a year out of college, I was accepted into a poetry workshop with David Ignatow in 1971. Ignatow showed me that poetry could both be grounded in society and transcend it; he's a major influence. In the workshop, I met Harry Greenberg and Larry Zirlin, who became my co-editors of *Some.* Another big help has been Joel Oppenheimer, who has been trying to 'separate the poet from the tumuller' in me. . . . I've been influenced by my work doing poetry with children (allowing, not teaching). They travel so freely in their imaginations, while most adults have to struggle for visas. I'd like to find more of a place for politics in my writing, without forcing it. . . . the poetry scene is still too insular and separate from communities." He adds, "My recent work has included many 'prose poems,' an important literary trend."

* * *

ZIEGLER, Philip (Sandeman) 1929-

PERSONAL: Born December 24, 1929, in Ringwood, Hampshire, England; son of Colin Louis (a soldier) and Dora (Barnwell) Ziegler; married Sarah Collins, August 8, 1960 (died, 1966); married Clare Charrington, January 7, 1970; children: (first marriage) Sophia Anne, Colin Christian; (second marriage) Tobias Mark. *Education:* New College, Oxford, graduate (first class honors in jurisprudence), 1951. *Religion:* Church of England. *Home:* 22 Cottesmore Gardens, London W.8, England. *Office:* William Collins Sons & Co. Ltd., 14 St. James Pl., London S.W.1, England.

CAREER: British Diplomatic Service, agent in Vientiane, Pretoria, Paris, and Bogota, 1952-66; William Collins Sons & Co. Ltd. (publishers), London, England, member of staff, 1966—. *Military service:* British Army, 1946-48; became second lieutenant. *Member:* Royal Society of Literature (fellow).

WRITINGS: The Duchess of Dino (biography), John Day, 1962; *Addington* (biography), John Day, 1965; *The Black Death* (history), John Day, 1968; *William IV* (biography), Harper, 1971; *Omdurman,* Knopf, 1974. Contributor to *Spectator, History Today,* and to British and American newspapers.

WORK IN PROGRESS: A biography of William Lamb, second Viscount Melbourne, publication expected about 1977.

SIDELIGHTS: Of *The Black Death,* a *New Statesman* reviewer wrote: "Anyone who hopes that history is not just for mandarins should be glad when a layman puts his oar in. Philip Ziegler is an amateur, as he confesses, though he has a reputation as a 19th-century biographer. . . . it is some time since medieval historians rescued this agonising visitation of 14th-century Europe from the calendar of picturesque disasters and set it in place as a structural condition of a whole phase of European history." Other reviewers have commented on Ziegler's scholarly thoroughness, while at the same time recognizing, in one reviewer's words, that *The Black Death,* "as [Ziegler] explains himself, is not a scholar's book; he has come to his task 'in a happy spirit of untrained enterprise.' He has done virtually no original research. But here, between two covers, is a vivid and illuminating survey which should fascinate the general reader."

ZIONTS, Stanley 1937-

PERSONAL: Surname rhymes with "science"; born January 18, 1937, in Pittsburgh, Pa.; son of Samuel E. (an architect) and Henrietta (Steinberg) Zionts; married Harriette Abrams, June 5, 1960; children: David, Michael, Rebecca Jo, Andrew. *Education:* Carnegie Institute of Technology, B.S., 1958, M.S., 1960, Ph.D., 1966; University of Pittsburgh, graduate study, 1961-63. *Home:* Avenue de Boetentael 35, 1180 Brussels, Belgium. *Office:* European Institute for Advanced Studies in Management, Place Stephanie 20, 1050 Brussels, Belgium.

CAREER: U.S. Steel Corp., Monroeville, Pa., operations research technologist in Applied Research Laboratory, 1960-65; Ford Foundation program specialist to Indian Ministry of Steel and Mines, Calcutta, 1965-67; State University of New York at Buffalo, associate professor, 1967-70, professor of management science, 1970—, on leave, 1974—. *Military service:* U.S. Army, 1960-61; became second lieutenant. *Member:* Operations Research Society of America, Institute of Management Sciences, Mathematical Programming Society, Operational Research Society of India. *Awards, honors:* Ford Foundation research grant, 1970-72.

WRITINGS: (Contributor) H. B. Maynard, editor, *Handbook of Business Administration,* McGraw, 1967; (contributor) Edwin J. Elton and M. J. Gruber, editors, *Security Evaluation and Portfolio Analysis,* Prentice-Hall, 1972; *Linear and Integer Programming,* Prentice-Hall, 1974. Contributor of about twenty articles to business and management journals. Associate editor, *OPSEARCH* (publication of Operational Research Society of India), 1969-74.

WORK IN PROGRESS: Studies on financial portfolio analysis, mathematical programming, and the application of mathematical methods to poverty reduction.

* * *

ZURCHER, Arnold John 1903(?)-1974

1903(?)—July 9, 1974; American educator and political scientist. Obituaries: *New York Times,* July 10, 1974.

* * *

ZWICKY, Fritz 1898-1974

February 14, 1898—February 8, 1974; American astronomer and physicist. Obituaries: *New York Times,* February 11, 1974; *Current Biography,* April, 1974.